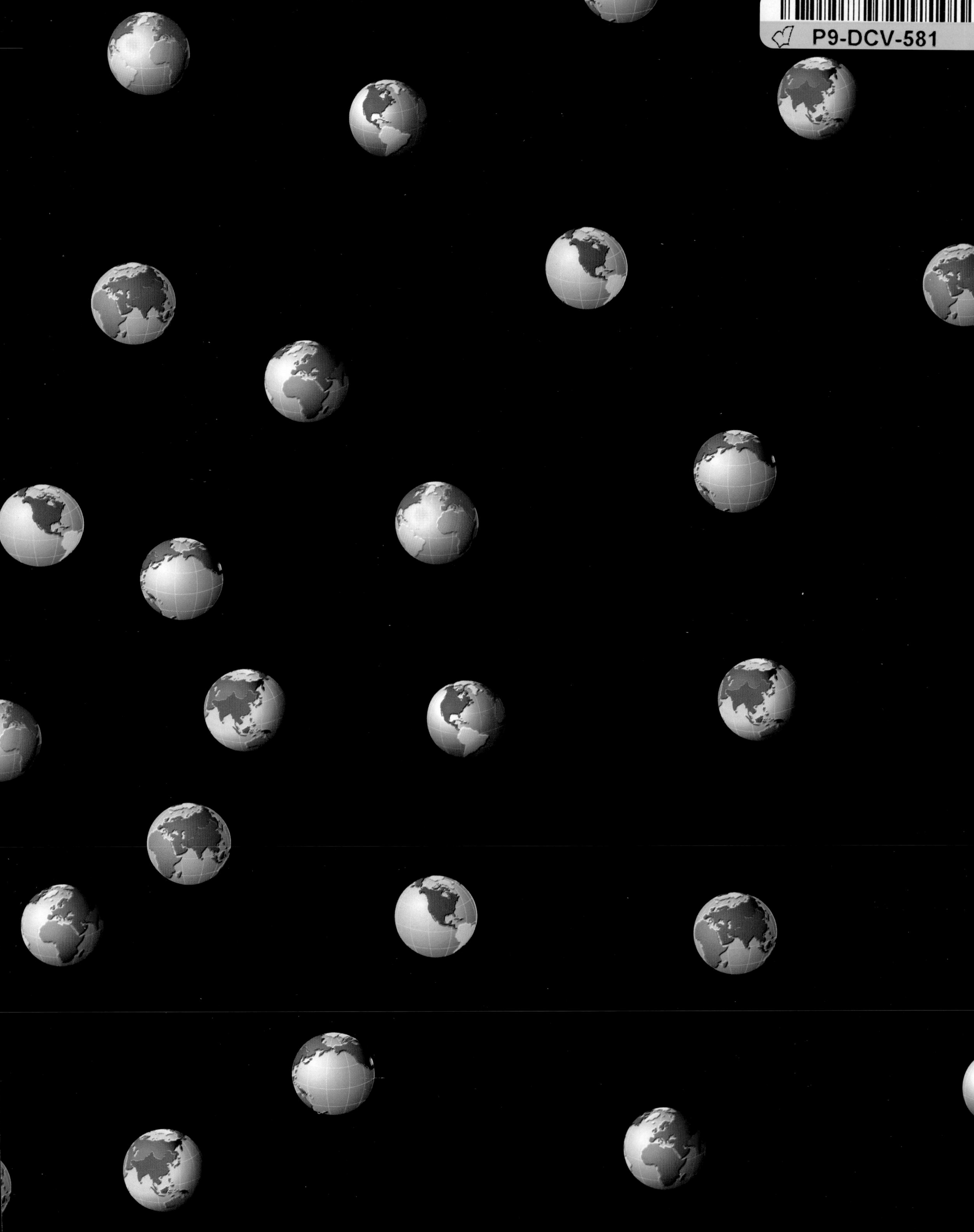

P9-DCV-581

OUR TIMES

The Illustrated History of the 20th Century

The Illustrated History of the 20th Century

OUR TIMES

Editor in Chief
LORRAINE GLENNON

Chairman, Editorial Advisory Board
JOHN A. GARRATY

Creative Directors
WALTER BERNARD MILTON GLASER DANIEL OKRENT

Turner Publishing, Inc.
ATLANTA

Our Times

Editor in Chief: Lorraine Glennon

Managing Editor: Susan Roediger

Art Director: Linda Root

Senior Writers: Kenneth Miller, Kevin Markey, Harold Itzkowitz

---

Writers: Stacey Bernstein, Jonathan Danziger, Rana Dogar, David Fischer, Edward Glennon, Rebecca Hughes, Sydney Johnson, Toni L. Kamins, Brad Kessler, Daniel Lazare, Nancy Ramsay, Gregory Root, Elizabeth Royte, Stephen Williams, Christopher Zurawsky

Contributing Editors: Mark Baker, Alice Gordon, Killian Jordan, Robert Nylen, Helen Rogan

Research: Josephine Ballenger, Peter Balogh, Kathleen Berry, Staci Bonner, Toby Chiu, Liza Featherstone, Deborah Flood, Kate Gordy, Liza Hamm, Arlene Hellerman, Denis Herbstein, Anthony Kaye, Nathaniel Knight, Jeff Kunken, Michelle Maryk, Joe McGowan, Jill McManus, Andrew Milner, Susan Murray, Laurie Ouellette, Lisa Reed, Marc Romano, Andrea Rosenthal, Annys Shin, Susan Skipper, Sara Solberg, Robin Sparkman, Cynthia Stewart, Carol Volk

Copy Editors: Jill Jaroff, Nancy Nasworthy, Jeff Reid, John Shostrom, Celestine Ware

---

Picture Editors: Laurie Platt Winfrey, Marla Kittler

Picture Research: Carousel Research: Fay Torres-yap, Van Bucher, Beth Krumholz (New York), Denise Dorrance (London), Barbara Nagelsmith (Paris)

Design Staff: Frank Baseman, Chalkley Calderwood, Christopher Lione, Sharon Okamoto, Nancy Stamatopoulos

Production/Technology Coordinator: Sharon Schanzer

The World in 1900–1990
Illustrations: Mirko Ilić
Charts and Diagrams: Nigel Holmes

Maps, Chronolog Charts and Diagrams: Laurie Grace, Joshua Simons, Jim Sullivan Design

Interns: Jennifer Falkove, Amy Forester, Kevin Hamblin, Lee Noriega, Jana Rohloff, Howard Sun, Lisa Velez

---

CREATED AND PRODUCED BY CENTURY BOOKS, INC.
207 East 32nd Street, New York, NY 10016

Walter Bernard, Milton Glaser, Lorraine Glennon, Daniel Okrent

Consultants: Duncan Baird, Anthony M. Schulte

Published by Turner Publishing, Inc.
A Subsidiary of Turner Broadcasting System, Inc.
1050 Techwood Drive, NW, Atlanta, Georgia 30318

Distributed by Andrews and McMeel
A Universal Press Syndicate Company
4900 Main Street, Kansas City, Missouri 64112

Editorial Advisory Board

Chairman: John A. Garraty,
Columbia University

Philip D. Curtin,
Johns Hopkins University

Robert Gildea,
Oxford University

David A. Hollinger,
University of California, Berkeley

Barbara G. Rosenkrantz,
Harvard University

Copyright ©1995 by Turner Publishing, Inc., and Century Books, Inc. All rights reserved under international copyright conventions. No part of the contents of this book may be reproduced or utilized in any form or by any means, electronic or mechanical, including photocopying, recording, or by any information storage and retrieval system, without the written consent of the publisher.

Library of Congress Cataloging-in-Publication Data

Our Times: The Illustrated History of the
20th Century / editor in chief, Lorraine
Glennon.
p. cm
Includes index.
ISBN 1-878685-58-9
1. History, Modern–20th century–Chronology.
2. History, Modern–20th century–Pictorial works. I.
Glennon, Lorraine.
D422.089 1995
909.82–dc20

94-43900
CIP

First edition 10 9 8 7 6 5 4 3 2 1

Printed in the U.S.A.

Contents

A Note to Readers

U.S. President Theodore Roosevelt, ca. 1904.

Confronted with a subject as monumental and sprawling as the twentieth century, the editors of *Our Times* realized that the best way to approach it was from several different angles at once.

The heart of the book is the "Chronolog." *(See diagram on opposite page.)* This year-by-year breakdown aims not only to pinpoint the salient events of each year from 1900 to 1994 and to provide a succinct account of what happened, but also to impart a sense of *why* those particular events matter. The advantage of this format is that it gives readers at least three options: They can proceed chronologically from the beginning of the book to the end; they can spot-read, moving around the pages somewhat randomly, guided only by where their eyes are drawn; or they can create a selective chronology within an area of interest by using the system of cross-referencing that directs them to other stories on a related subject or theme. Readers may thus follow the development of a large, overarching story—that of the conception, birth, and slow death of the Soviet Union, say—from the early 1900s right up to the present.

U.S. astronaut John Glenn, photographed by Ralph Morse, 1962.

Just as the individual Chronolog stories let readers examine at close range the warp and woof of the extraordinary tapestry that is the twentieth century, the material that opens each decade—each "chapter"—encourages the reader to stand back and view the whole. Each decade begins with a two-page graphic summation, a kind of visual census, of the state of the world in the year at hand. Synthesizing the broad changes that have taken place over the previous decade (and including a selective summary of "What We Knew," or rather, *thought* we knew, at that moment in time), this feature provides a context for understanding the century's long-range trends. It is followed by an essay—one in a series of ten—in which a distinguished writer explores in depth one of the major "Ideas that Shaped the Century."

Detail, *Les Demoiselles d'Avignon*, by Pablo Picasso, 1907.

Above all, this "Illustrated History of the Twentieth Century" is just that. No previous time period has granted its historians such a wealth of visual documentation as this one—and the editors have sought to take full advantage of that bounty. In its wide-ranging illustrations, as well as in its text, *Our Times* has a single mandate: to bring the drama of this tumultuous century to life.

Detail, *Marilyn Diptych*, by Andy Warhol, 1962.

A Key to the Chronolog

STORY OF THE YEAR:
The single event or development that stands out as the year's most significant.

QUOTATIONS:
Direct quotations pertaining to one of the stories found on that page.

MARGINALIA:
Three elements, including:
1) on the second page of each Chronolog, a listing of the important births and deaths that occurred during the year;
2) on the third and fourth pages, a list of what's "New In" the year, followed by "In the United States," a series of capsulized stories of specifically American interest;
3) on the fifth page, "Around the World," a column containing capsulized stories of international interest.

12

"With The Interpretation of Dreams *I had completed my life work ... there was nothing more for me to do ... I might just as well lie down and die."*—Sigmund Freud, in a letter to Carl Jung

1900

STORY OF THE YEAR

Freud Unlocks the Unconscious

1 Epochal, iconoclastic, the book arrived with the dawn of the century and shaped its intellectual course, dispatching mankind's timeworn assumptions about itself and erecting in their place a new, often frightening, always penetrating, theory of human nature. The book was *The Interpretation of Dreams*; its author, Dr. Sigmund Freud.

Released in 1899 (but dated 1900 by a publisher cannily aware of the book's significance), *The Interpretation of Dreams* was Freud's most important psychoanalytic study. In it he elaborated his ground-breaking ideas about dreams, the "royal road to a knowledge of the unconscious"—where they come from, why they occur, how they work. Distinguishing between the remembered facts of a dream, which he called manifest content, and the hidden meaning, or latent content, Freud argued that, properly decoded, dreams opened a window on a person's unconscious mind. The view was disturbing: forbidden desire, childhood sexuality, castration terror, the Oedipus complex.

Sigmund Freud, spiritual father to a new age of neurosis.

The Interpretation of Dreams sold only a few hundred copies in its first half-dozen years in print. Its limited audience recoiled with almost unanimous disgust. Freud himself recognized that his ideas were "odious" and "bound to put people off." Even so, he constantly revised and clarified the book throughout the rest of his long career, defending dream work as "the securest foundation of psychoanalysis and the field in which every worker must acquire his convictions and seek his training." Freud argued that because all people dream, interpretation works with healthy minds as well as pathological ones. Psychiatrists, heretofore limited to the study of mental illness, were thus able to begin exploring general psychology. But the method's chief asset, its universal applicability, was also the source of popular resistance to it. In 1900, the vast majority of Europeans and Americans—Victorian, optimistic, self-assured—were not ready to hear that the aggressive, sex-obsessed machinations of the Id were normal. The coming bloodbath of World War I helped put to rest their doubts, and their optimism, about mankind's true nature. ►1909.3

POPULAR CULTURE

Newspapers Reach a Million

2 When news happened in 1900, more people read about it than ever before. Literacy had soared in the nineteenth century, bringing with it a huge appetite for popular journalism. Paris's daily *Petit Journal* boasted hundreds of thousands of readers. New York had its "yellow press" (named for a comic strip character, the Yellow Kid, who appeared in rival versions in Joseph Pulitzer's *World* and William Randolph Hearst's *Journal*, then involved in a sensationalistic battle for readers). In London, the news hunger became spectacularly apparent when the *Daily Mail* became the first British daily to achieve a circulation of one million. C. Arthur Pearson promptly launched the *Daily Express* as the paper's main competitor. (The two papers remained archrivals into the 1990s.

Founded four years earlier, when the nation's dailies were highbrow journals usually associated with the Conservatives or Liberals, the *Daily Mail* offered something different: news and gossip in easy-to-read snippets, illustrated with photographs instead of line drawings—all for a halfpenny. Headlines were big and eye-catching, and the stories targeted female, as well as male, readers. The first issue sold 250,000 copies. (The respected London *Times* and *Manchester Guardian* each sold about 50,000.) The founder, Alfred Harmsworth, "does not concern himself greatly about the formation of public opinion," said one magazine. "But he does claim to give his readers more news at a glance than any of his contemporaries." ►1913.12

Daily Express
WHEN SHALL THEIR GLORY FADE?
THE BOERS' LAST GRIP LOOSENED.

The launch of the *Daily Express* in 1900 set off a competition with the *Daily Mail* that would endure throughout the century.

TECHNOLOGY

A Camera for the People

3 "You press the button, we do the rest," boasted the ad for the Eastman Kodak Company's remarkable new box camera, the Brownie. Introduced in 1900, it was the final step in the democratization of photography. The process itself had been around for more than half a century but had been practiced only by a select few until the 1880s, when Eastman had developed the Kodak fixed-focus box camera. The Brownie (the popular sprite image was used by Kodak to emphasize the camera's small size and to enhance its appeal to young people) took Eastman's revolution to a new level, making it possible for even children to make a picture.

"Les 'Brownie' Kodaks"—both the camera and the sprite—appeared in a French advertisement.

A point-and-shoot camera, the hand-held Brownie cost a mere dollar and produced reliably good pictures, without the fuss of focusing the lens or timing the exposure. Better still, Kodak took care of developing the film, liberating amateurs from having to master the mysteries of the darkroom. The era of the snapshot was born. Birthday parties would never be the same.

A quarter of a million were sold in the first year, breaking all records. The Brownie remained on the market in various forms for the next 80 years, an early manifestation of the great twentieth-century trend to take technological innovations, simplify them and lower their cost, and put them squarely in the hands of the middle class. ►1902.13

13

"It is true and undeniable that, from their Majesties on the Throne down to the very lowest of our people, all have suffered from the constant aggression of foreigners and their unceasing insults."—Jung Lu, an adviser to the Empress of China

1900

MUSIC

Sibelius's Gift to Finland

4 In 1900 Finland received the rare gift of a national anthem—albeit an unofficial one—written by one of the world's great composers. Jean Sibelius's tone poem *Finlandia*, like much of his other early work, blended folk themes with influences from the German Romantics and Tchaikovsky.

In the 1890s, as Finland struggled against Russian rule, Sibelius had become a nationalist hero—and in the century's first decade his fame spread well beyond his country's borders. Sibelius's seven symphonies have been ranked with Beethoven's for their emotional grandeur, their architectural elegance, and their sense of organic unity. But his finest works—the last three symphonies and the tone poem *Tapiola*—were written after World War I, when he abandoned the expressly patriotic mode. Although his music became increasingly austere and abstract, it never ceased to evoke the ancient Nordic sagas and the brooding Scandinavian landscape. Then in 1925, at the height of his success, Sibelius stopped composing. He died at 92, after three decades in seclusion. ►1903.7

CHINA

Boxers Target the Enemy

5 In 1900, the anti-foreign uprising of the Chinese society called Yi He Tuan—"the Righteous, Harmonious Fists," or Boxers, as they were called in English—culminated in unmitigated disaster for China, eroding her precarious sovereignty and spelling the beginning of the end of the Qing Dynasty.

China was in the throes of a deep-seated xenophobia, the understandable result of a long history of foreign intervention in its affairs and, more recently, an attendant decline in social and economic conditions. The secretive Boxer society stepped up its campaigns, vowing to kill all foreigners ("Primary Hairy Men" in Boxer terminology), along with their Chinese sympathizers (the "Secondary Hairy Men"). The crusade was abetted by Ci Xi, the Empress Dowager who had seized power in 1898. Following the lead of the Empress, various provincial governors began sanctioning the Boxers' violent resistance in their jurisdictions.

Thus encouraged, the Boxers pillaged the country, destroying railway stations and telegraph lines, ultimately killing 231 foreigners and thousands of Chinese Christians. On June 21, 1900, the Empress was moved by their patriotism to declare war on all foreign powers pursuing self-interested aims within China. The Boxers then began a two-month assault on the legations in Beijing. The nations under attack, including Japan, Russia, Germany, Britain, the United States, Austria-Hungary, and Italy, quickly assembled an international force, which arrived in Beijing on August 14 and easily overcame the sword-wielding Boxers.

The terms of the Boxer Protocol, the peace agreement ending the rebellion, were extremely harsh: China was assessed a $333 million indemnity; foreign troops were garrisoned from Beijing to the sea; civil service exams were suspended for five years; and three officials with Boxer sympathies were executed, and another compelled to commit suicide. Gloated Kaiser Wilhelm II, one of whose ministers had been assassinated by the Boxers: "No Chinese will ever again even dare to look askance at a German."

Internationally, Chinese prestige was brought to an all-time low. The indemnity consumed half the national product, enfeebling the Qing Dynasty. Another unexpected outcome was the occupation of Manchuria by Russia, which moved thousands of troops into the region during the rebellion. After the Boxer Protocol was signed in 1901, the troops remained there in the guise of "railway guards." Within three years, their presence provoked the Russo-Japanese War. ►1904.1

This propaganda print depicts the siege by the Boxers of foreign settlements at Tianjin.

BIRTHS

George Antheil, U.S. composer.
Louis Armstrong, U.S. musician.
Humphrey Bogart, U.S. actor.
Luis Buñuel, Spanish filmmaker.
Herbert Butterfield, U.K. historian.
Aaron Copland, U.S. composer.
Erich Fromm, German-U.S. psychoanalyst.
Heinrich Himmler, German Nazi official.
Ruhollah Khomeini, Iranian religious and political leader.
Ernst Krenek, U.S composer.
John Willard Marriott, U.S. hotelier.
Margaret Mitchell, U.S. novelist.
Louis Mountbatten U.K. statesman.
Joseph Needham, U.K. science historian.
Louise Nevelson, U.S. sculptor.
Sean O'Faolain, Irish writer.
V.S. Pritchett, U.K. writer.
Antoine de Saint Exupéry, French writer and aviator.
Spencer Tracy, U.S. actor.
Kurt Weill, German-U.S. composer.
Thomas Wolfe, U.S. novelist.

DEATHS

Stephen Crane, U.S. novelist.
Gottlieb Daimler, German automaker.
Marcus Daly, U.S. industrialist.
Collis P. Huntington, U.S. railroad tycoon.
John "Casey" Jones, U.S. railroad engineer.
Wilhelm Liebknecht, German socialist leader.
Friedrich Nietzsche, German philosopher.
John Ruskin, U.K. art critic.
Arthur Sullivan, U.K. composer.
Oscar Wilde, Irish writer.

ART & CULTURE: Books: *Lord Jim* (Joseph Conrad); *Sister Carrie* (Theodore Dreiser); *To Have and To Hold* (Mary Johnston); *The Wonderful Wizard of Oz* (Frank Baum); *Little Black Sambo* (Helen Bannerman) ... Music: "A Bird in a Gilded Cage" (Von Tilzer and Lamb); *Tosca* (Giacomo Puccini); "The Flight of the Bumble Bee," from *The Tale of Czar Saltan* (Nicolai Rimsky-Korsakov) ... Painting & Sculpture: *La Modiste* (Henri de Toulouse-Lautrec); *Le Moulin de la Galette* (Pablo Picasso) ... Films: *Searching Ruins on Broadway, Galveston, For Dead Bodies* (Albert Smith); *Cinderella* (Georges Méliès); *The Downward Path* (Marvin and McCutcheon); *Grandma's Reading Glass* (G.A. Smith) ... Theater: *You Never Can Tell* (G.B. Shaw); *When We Dead Awaken* (Henrik Ibsen).

DATALINE:
A listing of the year's important achievements in the categories of Art & Culture—including Books, Music, Painting & Sculpture, Films (beginning in 1929, the first film listed each year is the Academy Award winner for "Best Picture"), Theater, Radio (from 1930 to 1946), and Television (from 1947); Sports; Politics and Business (including the Gross National Product for that year); and Nobel Prizes.

CHRONOLOG ENTRIES:
Stories detailing internationally significant events or developments.

INTERACTIVE INDEX:
Every Chronolog entry concludes with at least one reference forward or backward to a specific year and entry on a related subject or theme.

VOICES:
The last element in each year's Chronolog is a text artifact—a piece of "found" copy—that illuminates one of the year's events or an aspect of the culture pertinent to the year.

Predictions for a New Century
By John Elfreth Watkins, Jr., from *Ladies' Home Journal*, December 1900

The dawn of the twentieth century found humanity still ensconced in the nineteenth. The verities of God and country had not yet been tested by global war, communist revolution—or the world's inexorable shrinkage by air travel and mass communications.

1900 1909

Paris's Champs Elysées was as green in 1900 as it had been when a newly ascendant Napoleon commissioned his Arc de Triomphe nearly a century earlier. But across town at the Exposition Universelle were displayed the sorts of high-tech gadgets that would quickly transform the city and the world. Cars replaced horses on boulevards around the planet, skyscrapers replaced trees—and the clamor of an increasingly industrialized, commercialized society made urban calm an ever-scarcer commodity.

THE WORLD IN 1900

World Population

Britannia Rules

In 1900, Queen Victoria presided over the largest empire in history. Her "Majesty's dominions, on which the sun never sets" (as Christopher North wrote in *Noctes Ambrosianae* in 1829), included possessions on every continent—11 million square miles (nearly one fifth the earth's surface) and 400 million people (a quarter of the world's population) in all. Yet the Empire's power—both economic and military—had begun to wane. The United States was outproducing Britain in coal, steel, and pig iron; Germany (intent on its own "place in the sun") was outarming it; and its colonies were growing increasingly restless. Some 90 years later, Britain's possessions had dwindled to 15 "dependent territories," including the Falkland Islands, Hong Kong, and Gibraltar.

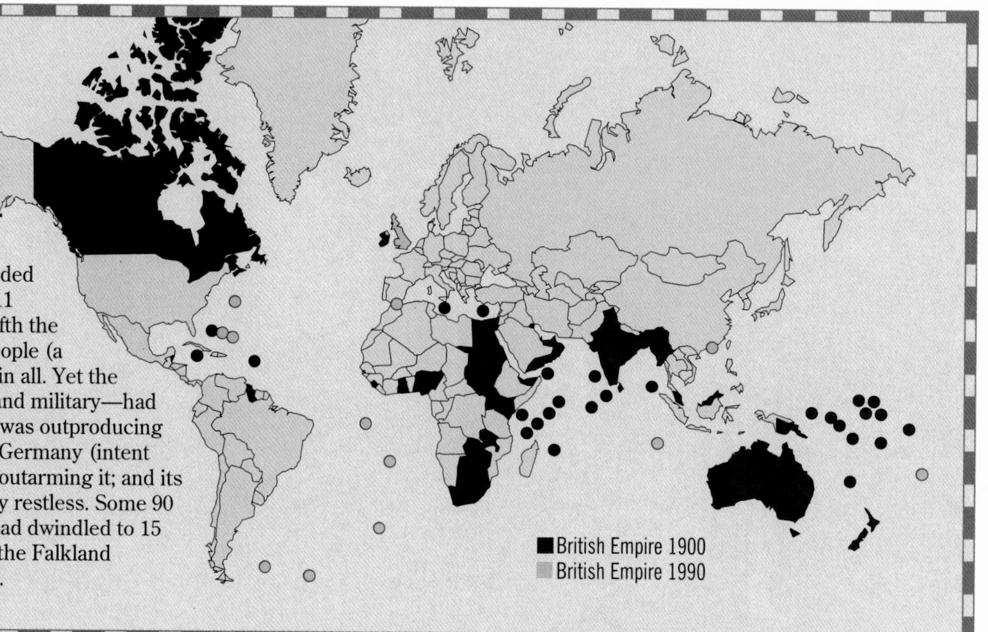

Fashion Essential

A lady did not venture out of her house without donning the finishing touch to her ensemble—a **hat** such as this elaborately plumed and beribboned model from the early part of the century.

STATE OF THE ART

The **phonograph** was, by 1900, the most popular home entertainment device. Early wax cylinders, perhaps one minute in length, were eventually replaced by 78 rpm flat discs. They, in turn, were rendered obsolete by later technologies.

	Year introduced	# sold in 1993 in the U.S.
LP Record	1948	1,200,000
Audiocassette	1964	339,500,000
Compact Disc	1983	495,400,000

Life Span, in years (men ■ women ■)

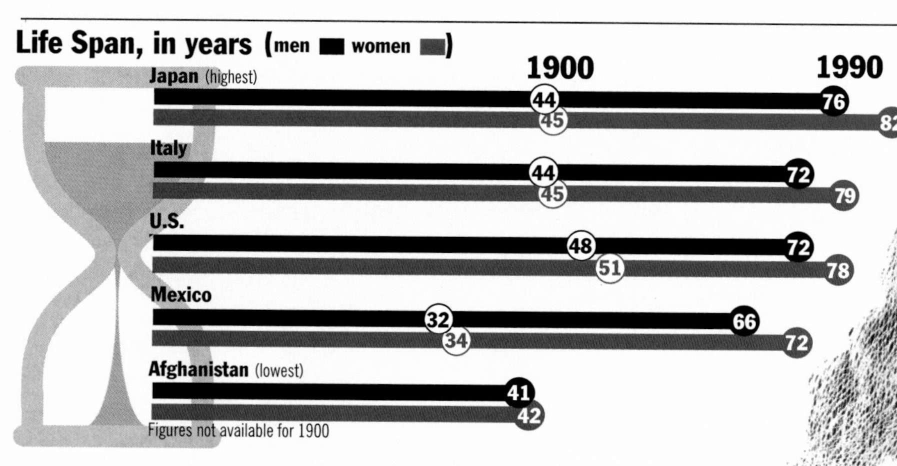

Average Working Hours

Per week, industrial occupations

1900		1990
51.7	Denmark	35.3
51.7	France	40.3
51.6	Germany	39.9
51.7	Japan	46.8
52.0	Netherlands	34.3
52.4	U.K.	37.2
52.0	U.S.	38.9

Percent of Workforce in Farming

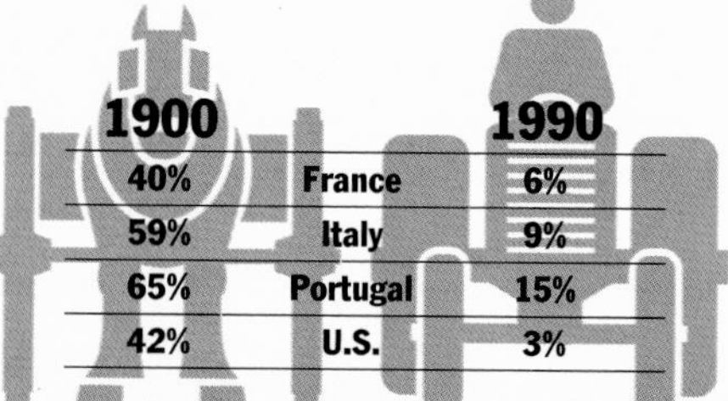

1900		1990
40%	France	6%
59%	Italy	9%
65%	Portugal	15%
42%	U.S.	3%

Reign of the Railroad As the century dawned, railroads were in their Golden Age; they dominated land travel until World War I. In the car-oriented, highway-building post-World War II era, only a few countries (Russia and India, for example) continued to expand rail capacity. The advent of high speed intercity passenger lines in Japan and Europe in the late 1970s helped revive train travel.

Operating Miles of Railway

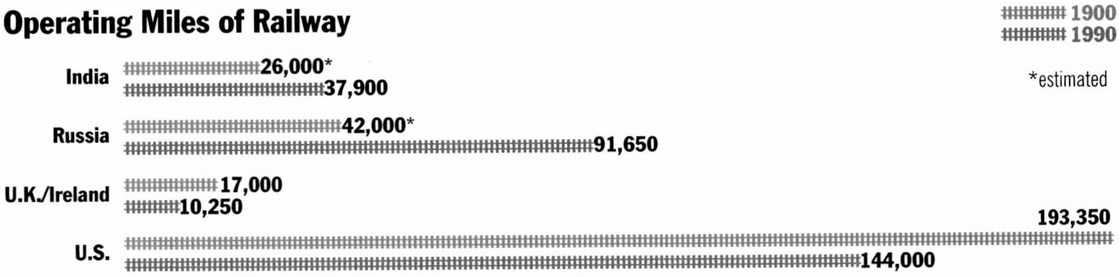

	1900	1990
India	26,000*	37,900
Russia	42,000*	91,650
U.K./Ireland	17,000	10,250
U.S.	193,350	144,000

*estimated

1900 Average speed, French express train **54mph**

1990 Average speed, French Train à Grande Vitesse (TGV) **160mph**

1990 Share of the World's 800,000 Miles of Railroad

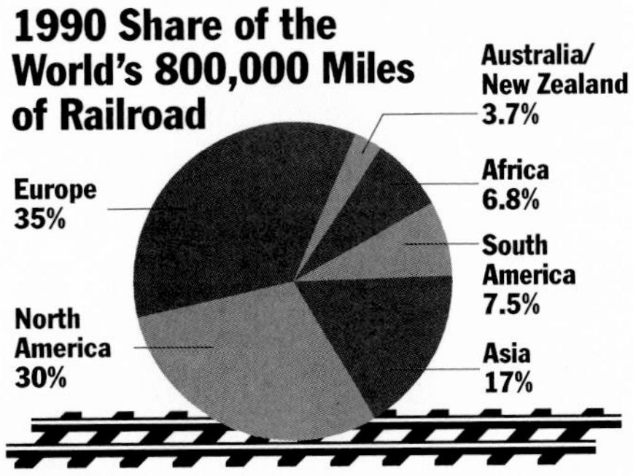

Europe	35%
North America	30%
Asia	17%
South America	7.5%
Africa	6.8%
Australia/New Zealand	3.7%

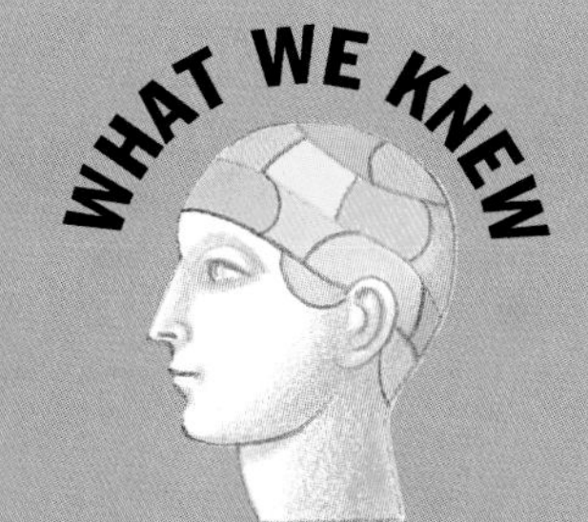

Air travel is assumed to be decades away. Two years before flying the first successful airplane, Wilbur Wright states that "man will not fly for 50 years."

Automobiles are widely considered impractical, dangerous, and faddish. "The horse is here to stay, but the automobile is only a novelty," a bank president tells Henry Ford's lawyer, advising him not to invest in the Ford Motor Company.

Synthesized in Germany in 1898 and available in many over-the-counter medicines, heroin (a term coined by the Bayer Company, manufacturer of aspirin) is touted as a cure for morphine addiction as well as an excellent cough syrup. "It is not hypnotic," declares *The Boston Medical and Surgical Journal*, and "there is no danger of acquiring the habit."

Most scientists have not yet conceived of the subatomic world and believe atoms to be solid bodies of matter. British physicist J.J. Thomson has discovered the electron, but the theory that an atom consists mostly of space, with its mass concentrated in a tiny nucleus, will not be proposed until 1913.

Nicaragua has been selected by the U.S. Congress's Isthmian Canal Commission as the site of a United States-built canal through Central America. French engineer (and activist for Panamanian independence from Colombia) Philippe Bunau-Varilla lobbies heavily for a route through Panama, on the grounds that heavy volcanic activity renders Nicaragua unsuitable.

A tropical plague for over 300 years, yellow fever is thought to result from unsanitary living conditions. Doctors believe that airborne bacteria enter the body via the respiratory system and then lodge in the lungs. Cuban doctor Carlos Finlay's theories (advanced since the 1880s) that the disease is carried by mosquitoes are largely dismissed by the medical community.

D.M. Thomas

Mysteries of the Unconscious

Freudianism Arrives

1900
1909

IN 1900 A BOOK APPEARED that had as its epigraph a quotation from Vergil's *Aeneid*: *"Flectere si nequeo superos, Acheronta movebo"* ("If I cannot bend the gods on high, I will move the infernal powers"). The book was *The Interpretation of Dreams*; its author, Sigmund Freud.

Both the book and its brilliantly chosen epigraph mark a turning point between the centuries. The nineteenth century had tried to emulate the gods on high with its seemingly unstoppable march of progress—in science, industry, medicine, ideology; the twentieth, while pursuing the same aims of secular happiness, has seen the future and realized that, in many ways, it does not work. Marx produced misery; industrialization—alienation and pollution; science—miracles but also the Nazi doctors in the death camps. One reason Freud has stood the test of time infinitely better than Marx is his realism, his skepticism, and his humanity. "Don't try to make people happy," he urged an idealistic young socialist patient. "They don't want it."

Delving into the human mind like Aeneas into the Underworld, Freud should have prepared humanity for its twentieth-century anxieties and nightmares (including the living nightmares, like the Holocaust). He discovered the unconscious forces, over which we have little control unless we have the courage to confront them. For a century or more the unconscious had been hinted at, and Freud—a brilliant writer himself and a man of discriminating literary taste—always acknowledged that the great artists had preceded him. They had touched the unconscious uncertainly, as Leif or Brendan touched the American coast; but Freud was the Columbus who proved the unconscious was really there, who opened up its riches and its terrors.

He liked to think of himself as a *conquistador*, an explorer. He didn't mind if he found enemies to fight, and sometimes made enemies of his friends. When his disciples, such as Adler, Rank, and Jung, departed from his views, he consigned them to darkness. Only one revisionist was allowed—the ceaselessly speculative Sigmund Freud.

He began as a research scientist, turning to medicine only because he needed to earn enough money to marry his fiancée, Martha Bernays. Curiously, therefore, love and desire propelled him to a career in which his great study was love and desire—as well as hate and aggression, since the unconscious, he found, was profoundly ambivalent. And, for all his noted aloofness and reserve, he would describe the therapy of psychoanalysis as a "cure through love."

He stumbled upon psychoanalysis through his colleague and mentor Josef Breuer, an outstanding Viennese physician. Treating a young woman called Bertha Pappenheim for a variety of hysterical symptoms, Breuer found that if, under hypnosis, she talked about the first moment a symptom had appeared, and the emotions she had felt, the symptom disappeared. "Hysterics," Breuer and Freud concluded, "suffer mainly from reminiscences." Breuer was fearful of the strongly sexual material uncovered and fled altogether when his patient ("Anna O." in the jointly written *Studies in Hysteria* of 1893) went into a phantom pregnancy, proclaiming that she was bearing Breuer's child.

Though of chaste habits personally, Freud was in no way frightened of the sexuality that poured out of Bertha and his own patients. Hypnosis gave way to the technique of pressing his hand on a patient's brow, then, permanently, to the method of free association, in which he mostly listened

The pioneer of psychoanalysis, Sigmund Freud, in his study at 19 Berggasse, Vienna in 1905. Beside him is a plaster reproduction of Michelangelo's *Dying Slave*. Above, a 15-inch, terra-cotta *Eros* from Greece, circa 150-100 BC—one of at least six in Freud's extensive collection of antiquities. For Freud, Eros represented the life instinct, which, he wrote, is locked in constant struggle with Thanatos, the instinct of destruction.

and the patient wandered at will, through memory, through dream, creating her own "talking cure." Her relationship to the analyst (the "transference") also became of paramount importance in helping him to understand her primary childhood relationships, to her mother, her father. Freud did not claim he achieved miracles. If he helped turn people's "hysterical misery into ordinary human unhappiness," it was perhaps through their gain in self-knowledge and the awareness that someone cared, listened to them, day after day, month after month. His famous patient, the "Wolf-Man," observed late in his long life, "If you look at everything critically, there isn't much in psychoanalysis that will stand up. Yet it helped me. He was a genius."

1900
1909

ONE ELEMENT THAT OCCURRED repeatedly in the reminiscences of his patients was childhood seduction. At first he believed their stories, and even thought his own father might have been guilty of it with his siblings; then during an exhaustive, tormented, courageous self-analysis leading up to *The Interpretation of Dreams*, he came to the momentous conclusion that for the most part his patients were fantasizing—that sons desired their mothers and were jealous of their fathers; similarly, daughters fantasized sexually about their fathers. Not for the only time, a great writer had intuitively shown prior knowledge: Sophocles in his *Oedipus Rex*. The Oedipus Complex became the linchpin of Freudian belief.

In the incest-conscious 1980s and '90s, Freud has been accused of deliberately covering up the reality of childhood seduction for fear of offending his contemporaries. Actual seduction may well have occurred in genteel Viennese families more often than Freud would credit, but it would have been totally against his character, which valued truth above all else, to have suppressed knowledge—quite apart from the fact that bourgeois gentlemen were not likely to find the idea of having wanted to sleep with their mothers any less offensive than actually having done it!

Freud's own history was fertile ground for such a discovery. His father, Jakob, a wool merchant, was a Galician Jew who moved to Moravia with his two grown sons and a mysterious second wife called Rebecca who instantly vanished from record. Jakob Freud married for the third time, Amalie, a girl of 19. Sigmund, born in 1856, was their first child. His playmates were his infant nephew and niece, offspring of his half-brother Emanuel. Sigmund's attractive, vivacious mother was of an age with her unmarried stepson Philipp; it must have seemed that Philipp was a much more fitting sharer of the mother's bed than the grandfatherly, bookish father. It was as if God—in whom Freud never believed—gave him the perfect family for falling in love with his mother.

When Freud was three the family split up, the half-brothers moving to England and the rest of the clan to Vienna. Freud lived there for the next 79 years, always looking back at his Moravian infancy as a lost paradise. After his marriage to Martha Bernays, they moved into the now famous address of 19 Berggasse. Martha looked after the apartment and, eventually, six children with perfect equanimity, making sure her husband did not even need to put toothpaste on his brush. Youthful passion ebbed gradually into "not a bad solution to the marriage problem"; he increasingly turned for intellectual and emotional closeness to his youngest daughter, Anna. He also had a close intellectual relationship with Martha's sister, Minna, who came to live with them.

Drawn to women of powerful intelligence and equally strong emotion, he had lifelong friendships with Lou Andreas-Salomé and Princess Marie Bonaparte. Psychoanalysis was the first profession that gifted women could take up on equal terms with men. Anna, analyzed by her father, also became an outstanding analyst, specializing in children. (She never married: Perhaps the Oedipus Complex was too strong to permit it.)

Repressed childhood desires, Freud believed, turned into neurotic symptoms, like a hidden boil that has nowhere to shed its poison. Adults could become "trapped" at various infantile stages: oral (the breast), anal, or phallic. A male infant's powerful desire for his mother was normally tamed by the fear of castration. A constant struggle goes on between the three components of personality:

Psychoanalysis's most enduring symbol: the couch. Patients who lay on this one in Freud's last home in London (to which he fled from Nazi-dominated Austria in 1938), could gaze upon their therapist's massive collection of Oriental, Roman, Etruscan, and Egyptian antiquities. It has been said that Freud furnished the room for rebirth, like the tomb of a pharaoh.

the id (the unconscious, the instincts), the ego (the conscious mind), and the superego (parental lessons and prohibitions). Few modern analysts believe the psyche can be schematized so rigidly, or that problems in relationships are necessarily sexual. A man of his time, Freud did not, until near the end of his life, give sufficient attention to the vital importance of the mother; he confessed that woman remained "a dark continent" to him.

And yet—partly because of his own quite feminine nature and his conviction that everyone is bisexual—one cannot read Freud on women without feeling enlarged in knowledge and sympathy. His belief that women suffer from "penis envy" is highly dubious; nor did it occur to him that men might suffer from uterus envy. Nevertheless, in the words of an eminent British analyst, Hanna Segal, "Freud was the first to treat women as human beings in the sense that he gave a proper place to female sexuality. He didn't consider them asexual beings." His female case studies of "Dora" and "Elisabeth von R." present them as having the power and sexuality of Hedda Gabler or Tess of the d'Urbervilles. Freud is fertile ground for feminism to grow from—and not wholly in antagonism.

EVEN WHEN HE IS WRONG, there is usually something intuitive that stimulates thought and counterargument. His case histories are beautiful semifictions, telling truth "aslant," to use Emily Dickinson's adverb, and he wrote, in *Delusions and Dreams in Jensen's "Gradiva,"* a far more beautiful "story" than the original fiction (the work of a Nobel laureate). Freud won the Goethe Prize for Literature in 1930. He was, in all his work, an artist who believed mistakenly he was a pure scientist.

His influence on our century can scarcely be exaggerated. He defines the way we study human personality. Though he can be seen as part of a reductive tendency—Darwin showing us we are one with the animals, Freud that we are determined by our animal instincts—the effect of his explorations of the "infernal powers" is to enlarge our sense of the psyche's life. Before Freud, dreams were the jetsam of a day's events; today, many scientists would see dreams as no more than "programming." Not all dreams are sexual, as Freud tended to think; not all are wish fulfillment, as he believed. His interpretations often seem over-elaborate. But no intelligent person, after reading *The Interpretation of Dreams*, can fail to be dazzled by the creative power of the unconscious mind. Freud showed that we are all, in our sleep, poets—creators of meaningful, imaginative myths about ourselves. It is surely also not reductive of our human spirit to realize that beneath our humdrum daily lives mythic battles worthy of Greek tragedy are occurring.

After the First World War, Freud's own theater darkened. *Beyond the Pleasure Principle* (1920) sets up Thanatos, the death wish, to oppose Eros. Man has a compulsion to repeat, Freud argued, and this must ultimately be a yearning for the primal state, before life. Our self-destructiveness becomes aggression toward others. *Civilization and Its Discontents*, published in 1930, takes a pessimistic look at human destructiveness, though in its original form it ends with the cautious hope that Eros will prevail over "his equally immortal adversary." Hitler then became powerful in Germany, and Freud added, "But who can foresee with what success and with what result?"

The result, in Freud's lifetime, was the Anschluss, persecution of Jews, and forced exile from Austria. He spent the last year and a half of his life in Hampstead, London. He died on September 23, 1939. "Is this the last war?" asked his doctor. "For me, at any rate," Freud dryly replied. Four of his sisters perished in the Nazi death camps.

It is indicative of Freud's range of vision that one well-regarded study of him, by Frank J. Sulloway, is called *Freud: Biologist of the Mind*, and another, by Diana Hume George, *Blake and Freud*. To Sulloway, he is a deterministic scientist; to George, he has a fraternity with the mystical Romantic poet. Few Freudians today accept his theories blindly, or swallow them whole. His views have been grotesquely trivialized. But few in our century have written so much that is wise, sane, revolutionary; no one has more illuminated our human condition. Many have tried to kill him, but he remains, toward the end of the century, stubbornly alive. □

Freudian theory and themes have cropped up in popular media throughout the century. In Alfred Hitchcock's *Spellbound* (1945), psychoanalysis provided the backdrop as psychiatrist Ingrid Bergman grappled with the thorny problem of whether Gregory Peck was merely a neurotic colleague or a murderous amnesiac. The movie's most memorable sequence was an elaborate dream murder adapted from paintings specially commissioned from Salvador Dali. The surrealist was heavily influenced by Freud, and during the 1930s set out to produce what he called "hand-colored photographs of the subconscious."

"With The Interpretation of Dreams *I had completed my life work … there was nothing more for me to do … I might just as well lie down and die."*—**Sigmund Freud, in a letter to Carl Jung**

STORY OF THE YEAR

Freud Unlocks the Unconscious

1 Epochal, iconoclastic, the book arrived with the dawn of the century and shaped its intellectual course, dispatching mankind's timeworn assumptions about itself and erecting in their place a new, often frightening, always penetrating, theory of human nature. The book was *The Interpretation of Dreams*; its author, Dr. Sigmund Freud.

Released in 1899 (but dated 1900 by a publisher cannily aware of the book's significance), *The Interpretation of Dreams* was Freud's most important psychoanalytic study. In it he elaborated his ground-breaking ideas about dreams, the "royal road to a knowledge of the unconscious"—where they come from, why they occur, how they work. Distinguishing between the remembered facts of a dream, which he called manifest content, and the hidden meaning, or latent content, Freud argued that, properly decoded, dreams opened a window on a person's unconscious mind. The view was disturbing: forbidden desire, childhood sexuality, castration terror, the Oedipus complex.

Sigmund Freud, spiritual father to a new age of neurosis.

The Interpretation of Dreams sold only a few hundred copies in its first half-dozen years in print. Its limited audience recoiled with almost unanimous disgust. Freud himself recognized that his ideas were "odious" and "bound to put people off." Even so, he constantly revised and clarified the book throughout the rest of his long career, defending dream work as "the securest foundation of psychoanalysis and the field in which every worker must acquire his convictions and seek his training." Freud argued that because all people dream, interpretation works with healthy minds as well as pathological ones. Psychiatrists, heretofore limited to the study of mental illness, were thus able to begin exploring general psychology. But the method's chief asset, its universal applicability, was also the source of popular resistance to it. In 1900, the vast majority of Europeans and Americans—Victorian, optimistic, self-assured—were not ready to hear that the aggressive, sex-obsessed machinations of the Id were normal. The coming bloodbath of World War I helped put to rest their doubts, and their optimism, about mankind's true nature. ►1909.3

POPULAR CULTURE

Newspapers Reach a Million

2 When news happened in 1900, more people read about it than ever before. Literacy had soared in the nineteenth century, bringing with it a huge appetite for popular journalism. Paris's daily *Petit Journal* boasted hundreds of thousands of readers. New York had its "yellow press" (named for a comic strip character, the Yellow Kid, who appeared in rival versions in Joseph Pulitzer's *World* and William Randolph Hearst's *Journal*, then involved in a sensationalistic battle for readers). In London, the news hunger became spectacularly apparent when the *Daily Mail* became the first British daily to achieve a circulation of one million. C. Arthur Pearson promptly launched the *Daily Express* as the paper's main competitor. The two papers remained archrivals into the 1990s.

Founded four years earlier, when the nation's dailies were highbrow journals usually associated with the Conservatives or Liberals, the *Daily Mail* offered something different: news and gossip in easy-to-read snippets, illustrated with photographs instead of line drawings—all for a halfpenny. Headlines were big and eye-catching, and the stories targeted female, as well as male, readers. The first issue sold 250,000 copies. (The respected London *Times* and *Manchester Guardian* each sold about 50,000.) The founder, Alfred Harmsworth, "does not concern himself greatly about the formation of public opinion," said one magazine. "But he does claim to give his readers more news at a glance than any of his contemporaries." ►1913.12

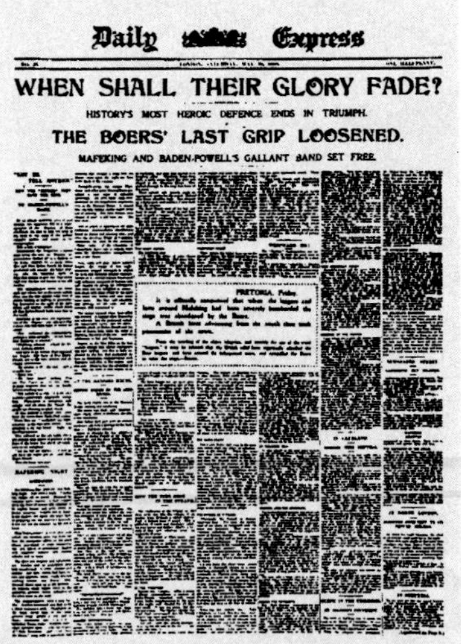

Daily Express

WHEN SHALL THEIR GLORY FADE?

HISTORY'S MOST HEROIC DEFENCE ENDS IN TRIUMPH.

THE BOERS' LAST GRIP LOOSENED.

MAFEKING AND BADEN-POWELL'S GALLANT BAND SET FREE.

The launch of the *Daily Express* in 1900 set off a competition with the *Daily Mail* that would endure throughout the century.

TECHNOLOGY

A Camera for the People

3 "You press the button, we do the rest," boasted the ad for the Eastman Kodak Company's remarkable new box camera, the Brownie. Introduced in 1900, it was the final step in the democratization of photography. The

"Les 'Brownie' Kodaks"—both the camera and the sprite—appeared in a French advertisement.

process itself had been around for more than half a century but had been practiced only by a select few until the 1880s, when Eastman had developed the Kodak fixed-focus box camera. The Brownie (the popular sprite image was used by Kodak to emphasize the camera's small size and to enhance its appeal to young people) took Eastman's revolution to a new level, making it possible for even children to make a picture.

A point-and-shoot camera, the hand-held Brownie cost a mere dollar and produced reliably good pictures, without the fuss of focusing the lens or timing the exposure. Better still, Kodak took care of developing the film, liberating amateurs from having to master the mysteries of the darkroom. The era of the snapshot was born. Birthday parties would never be the same.

A quarter of a million were sold in the first year, breaking all records. The Brownie remained on the market in various forms for the next 80 years, an early manifestation of the great twentieth-century trend to take technological innovations, simplify them and lower their cost, and put them squarely in the hands of the middle class. ►1902.13

ART & CULTURE: Books: ***Lord Jim*** **(Joseph Conrad);** ***Sister Carrie*** **(Theodore Dreiser);** ***To Have and To Hold*** **(Mary Johnston);** ***The Wonderful Wizard of Oz*** **(Frank Baum);** ***Little Black Sambo*** **(Helen Bannerman) … Music: "A Bird in a Gilded Cage" (Von Tilzer and Lamb);** ***Tosca*** **(Giacomo Puccini); "The Flight of the Bumble Bee," from** ***The Tale of Czar Saltan*** **(Nicolai Rimsky-Korsakov) … Painting & Sculpture:**

"It is true and undeniable that, from their Majesties on the Throne down to the very lowest of our people, all have suffered from the constant aggression of foreigners and their unceasing insults."—**Jung Lu, an adviser to the Empress of China**

MUSIC

Sibelius's Gift to Finland

4 In 1900 Finland received the rare gift of a national anthem—albeit an unofficial one—written by one of the world's great composers. Jean Sibelius's tone poem *Finlandia*, like much of his other early work, blended folk themes with influences from the German Romantics and Tchaikovsky.

In the 1890s, as Finland struggled against Russian rule, Sibelius had become a nationalist hero—and in the century's first decade his fame spread well beyond his country's borders. Sibelius's seven symphonies have been ranked with Beethoven's for their emotional grandeur, their architectural elegance, and their sense of organic unity. But his finest works—the last three symphonies and the tone poem *Tapiola*—were written after World War I, when he abandoned the expressly patriotic mode. Although his music became increasingly austere and abstract, it never ceased to evoke the ancient Nordic sagas and the brooding Scandinavian landscape. Then in 1925, at the height of his success, Sibelius stopped composing. He died at 92, after three decades in seclusion. ►**1903.7**

CHINA

Boxers Target the Enemy

5 In 1900, the anti-foreign uprising of the Chinese society called Yi He Tuan—"the Righteous, Harmonious Fists," or Boxers, as they were called in English—culminated in unmitigated disaster for China, eroding her precarious sovereignty and spelling the beginning of the end of the Qing Dynasty.

China was in the throes of a deep-seated xenophobia, the understandable result of a long history of foreign intervention in its affairs and, more recently, an attendant decline in social and economic conditions. The secretive Boxer society stepped up its campaigns, vowing to kill all foreigners ("Primary Hairy Men" in Boxer terminology), along with their Chinese sympathizers (the "Secondary Hairy Men"). The crusade was abetted by Ci Xi, the Empress Dowager who had seized power in 1898. Following the lead of the Empress, various provincial governors began sanctioning the Boxers' violent resistance in their jurisdictions.

Thus encouraged, the Boxers pillaged the country, destroying railway stations and telegraph lines, ultimately killing 231 foreigners and thousands of Chinese Christians. On June 21, 1900, the Empress was moved by their patriotism to declare war on all foreign powers pursuing self-interested aims within China. The Boxers then began a two-month assault on the legations in Beijing. The nations under attack, including Japan, Russia, Germany, Britain, the United States, Austria-Hungary, and Italy, quickly assembled an international force, which arrived in Beijing on August 14 and easily overcame the sword-wielding Boxers.

The terms of the Boxer Protocol, the peace agreement ending the rebellion, were extremely harsh: China was assessed a $333 million indemnity; foreign troops were garrisoned from Beijing to the sea; civil service exams were suspended for five years; and three officials with Boxer sympathies were executed, and another compelled to commit suicide. Gloated Kaiser Wilhelm II, one of whose ministers had been assassinated by the Boxers: "No Chinese will ever again even dare to look askance at a German."

Internationally, Chinese prestige was brought to an all-time low. The indemnity consumed half the national product, enfeebling the Qing Dynasty. Another unexpected outcome was the occupation of Manchuria by Russia, which moved thousands of troops into the region during the rebellion. After the Boxer Protocol was signed in 1901, the troops remained there in the guise of "railway guards." Within three years, their presence provoked the Russo-Japanese War. ►**1904.1**

This propaganda print depicts the siege by the Boxers of foreign settlements at Tianjin.

BIRTHS

George Antheil, U.S. composer.

Louis Armstrong, U.S. musician.

Humphrey Bogart, U.S. actor.

Luis Buñuel, Spanish filmmaker.

Herbert Butterfield, U.K. historian.

Aaron Copland, U.S. composer.

Erich Fromm, German-U.S. psychoanalyst.

Heinrich Himmler, German Nazi official.

Ruhollah Khomeini, Iranian religious and political leader.

Ernst Křenek, U.S composer.

John Willard Marriott, U.S. hotelier.

Margaret Mitchell, U.S. novelist.

Louis Mountbatten U.K. statesman.

Joseph Needham, U.K. science historian.

Louise Nevelson, U.S. sculptor.

Sean O'Faolain, Irish writer.

V.S. Pritchett, U.K. writer.

Antoine de Saint-Exupéry, French writer and aviator.

Spencer Tracy, U.S. actor.

Kurt Weill, German-U.S. composer.

Thomas Wolfe, U.S. novelist.

DEATHS

Stephen Crane, U.S. novelist.

Gottlieb Daimler, German automaker.

Marcus Daly, U.S. industrialist.

Collis P. Huntington, U.S. railroad tycoon.

John "Casey" Jones, U.S. railroad engineer.

Wilhelm Liebknecht, German socialist leader.

Friedrich Nietzsche, German philosopher.

John Ruskin, U.K. art critic.

Arthur Sullivan, U.K. composer.

Oscar Wilde, Irish writer.

La Modiste **(Henri de Toulouse-Lautrec);** ***Le Moulin de la Galette*** **(Pablo Picasso) ... Films:** ***Searching Ruins on Broadway, Galveston, For Dead Bodies*** **(Albert Smith);** ***Cinderella*** **(Georges Méliès);** ***The Downward Path*** **(Marvin and McCutcheon);** ***Grandma's Reading Glass*** **(G.A. Smith) ... Theater:** ***You Never Can Tell*** **(G.B. Shaw);** ***When We Dead Awaken*** **(Henrik Ibsen).**

"For years I had a mass of notes in my diary, but I never would have dared to think them readable."—**Sidonie-Gabrielle Colette**

NEW IN 1900

Guide Michelin **(first systematic European restaurant survey).**

Firestone Tire & Rubber.

Paris Métro.

U.S. College Entrance Examination Board (Scholastic Aptitude Tests).

Daisy Air Rifles (BB guns).

Wesson Oil.

National Automobile Show (Madison Square Garden, New York City).

Davis Cup (officially, the International Lawn Tennis Challenge Trophy).

IN THE UNITED STATES

►RAILROAD HERO—John Luther "Casey" Jones became immortal by dying at the throttle of the *Cannonball Express* on April 29. The 36-year-old engineer was speeding

through Mississippi at 3:52 AM, when a stalled train appeared around a bend. Jones shouted for the fireman to jump and managed to slow the train enough to save his passengers' lives before the collision took his own.

►ISLAND POSSESSIONS—Congress officially made Hawaii a territory in 1900, two years after it was annexed by the U.S. government. President McKinley saw the string of islands as a gateway to Asian trade and an ideal site for military bases (midway to America's new holdings in the Philippines). The first governor of the

ARCHAEOLOGY

Kingdom at Knossos

6 At Knossos, on the Mediterranean island of Crete, in 1900, British archaeologist Sir Arthur Evans unearthed the ruins of an astonishingly advanced Bronze Age civilization. Citing the legend of King Minos, storied Cretan lawgiver and keeper of the terrible Minotaur, the half-man, half-bull creature of Greek myth, Evans called the culture Minoan. The discovery thrilled the world.

Described by a colleague as a "small, dreadfully nearsighted man who always carried a small cane in order to feel his way along," Evans was a tenacious archaeologist. Independently wealthy, he bought the excavation site and spent 25 years uncovering and restoring the extensive ruins, which included a mazelike, five-and-a-half acre palace that suggested the fabled labyrinth of King Minos. The palace yielded colorful murals, ornate pottery, jewelry, and thousands of tablets in the famous Linear A and Linear B systems of writing (which Evans was never able to decipher). It became clear that Minoan civilization, which reached its golden age between 2200 and 1500 BC, had been the center of European culture a thousand years before the rise of the Ancient Greeks. Obsessed with his sophisticated Minoans, who built three-story houses, dressed elegantly, produced superb art, played sports, and traded with the Egyptians, Evans employed a hundred workers at a time and developed excavational techniques that have since become standard. Evans may have thwarted science by hoarding his findings (linguist Michael Ventris didn't crack Linear B until 1952, a decade after Evans's death), but his discovery was one of history's greatest archaeological achievements. ►**1904.M**

LITERATURE

Colette Makes Her Debut

7 The literary sensation of Paris in 1900 was a naive but salacious 15-year-old country girl, the narrator and protagonist of *Claudine à l'école*. Critics praised the "purity" of her creator's prose, and called Claudine a new type of heroine. Her "joyous and melancholy immorality," wrote one, "is neither perverse nor licentious, but springs from the ... high spirits of the graceful and intelligent animal that she is." The novelist credited with the success of this rustically racy book was a top-hatted roué whose nom de plume was Willy. But the real author was his young wife, Sidonie-Gabrielle Colette.

The book was credited to "Willy," but Colette's face appeared on the poster for *Claudine*.

Colette herself had been an ingenue from Burgundy when she married "Willy" (Henri Gauthier-Villars), a music critic and occasional publisher of soft pornography. Although she wrote four Claudine books, Colette was famous at first only for inspiring Willy (whose chief contribution to her work was to press for more sex scenes). After the couple divorced in 1906, she quit writing to become a music-hall performer. But the stories resumed the following year—under her own name.

Colette's two dozen novels include *Chéri*, *Gigi*, and *La Chatte*. Largely centered on the delights and distresses of love, they were hailed for their sympathetic but unsparing portrayals of women, and for their precise, poetic evocation of the sensual world. By the time Colette died in 1954, her compatriots considered her a national treasure. ►**1921.4**

LITERATURE

Wilde's Ignominious Exit

8 Bankrupted and disgraced by his notorious sodomy conviction and his two years in prison, Oscar Wilde, champion aesthete and playwright of consummate wit, lived out his final years in Paris, sustained by what George Bernard Shaw called "an unconquerable gaiety of soul." On November 30, 1900, Wilde, only 46, died of encephalitis brought on by an ear infection. The press, often hostile to the flamboyant writer, reveled in his demise,

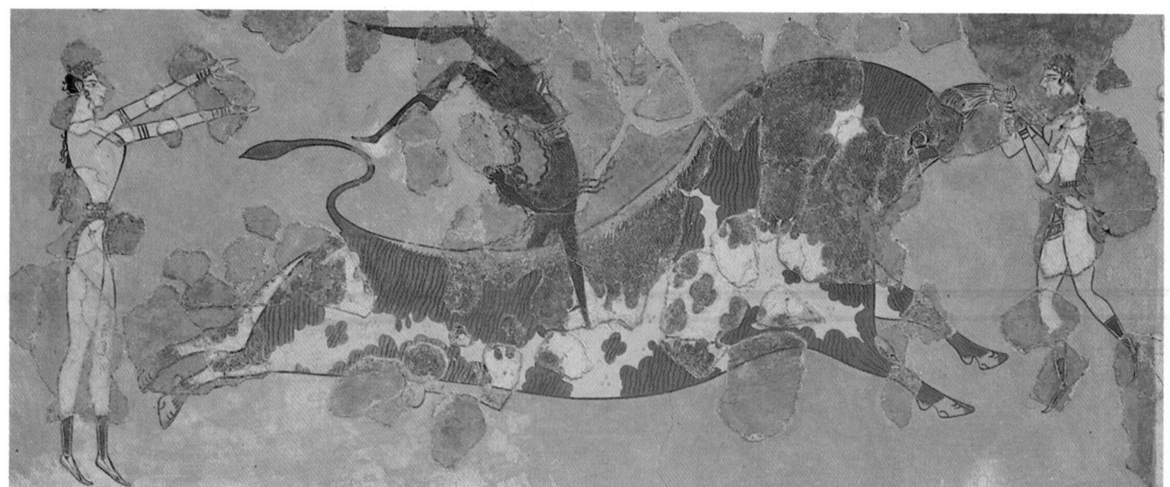
This depiction of athletes jumping over a bull was one of the Bronze Age frescoes unearthed by Arthur Evans at Knossos.

SPORTS: Baseball: Five-sided home plate becomes standard; American League formed in Chicago ... Olympics held in Paris (competitions include fishing, croquet, checkers, and tug-of-war) ... Basketball: Dribbling introduced ... Boxing: James J. Jeffries beats Jack Finnegan in 15 sec. (shortest World Heavyweight Championship fight ever) ... Golf: "Par" becomes criterion in calculating handicaps.

"The two great turning points of my life were when my father sent me to Oxford, and when society sent me to prison."
—Oscar Wilde

gloating over his poverty and insinuating suicide.

Wilde often said that it is not art that imitates life but the reverse. In his case the epigram turned out to be painfully prophetic. His plots often revolve around the exposure of a character's secrets; in 1895 the Marquess of Queensberry (who codified boxing), upset about Wilde's affair with his 20-year-old son, Lord Alfred Douglas, accused Wilde of being a sodomite, which was illegal in Britain. Wilde, at the height of his fame, had just come out with his comic masterpieces, *Lady Windermere's Fan* and *The Importance of Being Earnest*, and his novel *The Picture of Dorian Gray*. Rashly, he sued for libel. At the hearing the affair was exposed. Wilde was tried, convicted, and sentenced to two years' hard labor (an experience that inspired his poem "The Ballad of Reading Gaol" and the brilliant *De Profundis*). The public pillorying that

Wilde, an eccentric who often carried a sunflower, was immortalized on this song-sheet cover.

accompanied his conviction, as vitriolic as it was voyeuristic, became an international pastime. Upon his release from prison, the ruined playwright fled to Paris, where he lived in forced isolation in a series of hotels, writing no more plays.

Distracted by his dandyism, his flouting of Victorian morality, and his wit, most turn-of-the-century critics failed to accord Wilde's writing the esteem it deserves. The art, like the author, was ahead of its time. Although Wilde has affinities with the two great titans of twentieth-century drama (both, like him, Irish-born), his belief that verbal wit provides the only semblance of salvation in a chaotic world is closer in spirit to Samuel Beckett, the magnificent absurdist, than to George Bernard Shaw, the great Victorian. ▸1904.7

POPULAR CULTURE

Exposition Universelle

9 **Tribal villages, exotic belly dancers, and magical contraptions like Valdemar Poulsen's magnetic recording tape machine wowed the 40 million visitors to the 1900 Exposition Universelle. Such modern-day Parisian landmarks as the Grand Palais, the Petit Palais, and the Gare d'Orsay (now the Musée d'Orsay) were among the Beaux-Arts pavilions built for the occasion, transforming the banks of the Seine into an architectural wonderland. The syncopated rhythms of American ragtime music, introduced at the exposition by John Philip Sousa, filled the air and quickly became the rage all over Europe. The public flocked to see the scandalous statue of Balzac by Auguste Rodin. Heralded as the greatest sculptor since Michelangelo, Rodin was the only artist at the expo to receive his own pavilion.** ▸1904.M

SCIENCE

Mendel's Theory Surfaces

10 One of the most astute deductions in the history of science was belatedly recognized in 1900: Gregor Mendel's deciphering of how inherited traits are passed from one generation to the next. Mendel's findings—radical, remarkably prescient—were published in an obscure journal in 1866, where they languished for the next 34 years. Then, in 1900, three botanists separately published plant-breeding experiments that cited and confirmed Mendel's work.

An Austrian farm boy turned Augustinian monk, Mendel conducted his experiments in the small garden of the monastery in Moravia (later part of Czechoslovakia), where he lived and cultivated peas. When Mendel crossed two strains of different-shaped peas—one round, the other wrinkled—the first generation of hybrid offspring produced only round peas. Self-pollinated, these peas yielded three round peas to each wrinkled one. Mendel concluded that the round trait was "dominant," and the wrinkled one "recessive."

Crossing strains that differed in color as well as shape, Mendel found that the parental hereditary units determining these two characteristics were not necessarily passed on to the next generation together. Instead, these units were assorted independently, or reshuffled, in all possible combinations. Since then, geneticists have identified various exceptions to the mathematical patterns of heredity that Mendel described, but his initial discovery of particulate heredity by units (genes) remains a fundamental tenet of biology. ▸1902.M

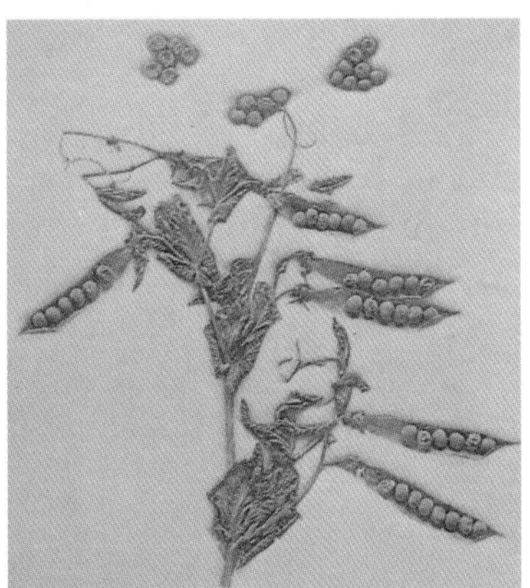

Botanical plate illustrating "the result of crossing a yellow wrinkled with a green round pea."

IN THE UNITED STATES

Territory of Hawaii was the former republic's president, plantation owner Sanford B. Dole. ▸1902.M

▸DRESSMAKERS UNITE—The International Ladies' Garment Workers Union was founded in 1900 to protect workers in the women's clothing industry, who typically toiled 70 hours a week for 30 cents a day. Most early members were Jewish immigrants employed in sweatshops—small factories with extreme temperatures, poor ventilation, and tyrannical overseers. Successful ILGWU strikes in New York in 1909 and 1910 led to better working conditions and higher wages. ▸1911.M

▸PREMIER PROGRESSIVE—Robert La Follette, a maverick Republican set on making his state a "laboratory of democracy," was elected governor of Wisconsin in 1900. During his five years in office, the fiery populist pioneered tax and electoral reform, shorter working hours for women and children, safer factories, and conservation. He resigned in 1906 and was elected a U.S. senator (he served for two decades, running in 1924 as a

Progressive candidate for president), and founded an influential magazine, *La Follette's Weekly* (later called *The Progressive*).

▸BOOMTOWN BUSTED—Built on a mile-wide sandbar and standing only nine feet above sea level, Galveston, Texas, was the fastest-growing port in the U.S. when, on the morning of September 8, a hurricane hit with little warning. More than 6,000 people died, and 3,000 homes were destroyed. The next day the city was underwater. But the remaining residents stayed put, rebuilding their city from the ground up, raising all city sidewalks, streets, and even phone poles to 17 feet above high-tide level. ▸1902.10

POLITICS & BUSINESS: GNP: $18.7 billion ... Republican William McKinley reelected President, defeating William Jennings Bryan ... U.S. population: 76,094,000 (New York state, the most populous at 7,268,894; Nevada, the least at 42,335) ... Currency Act sets gold as standard for currency ($150 million gold reserve backs legal tender).

"Man is a rope stretched between the animal and the Superman—a rope over an abyss."—**Friedrich Nietzsche, *Thus Spake Zarathustra***

AROUND THE WORLD

▶**MURDERED MONARCH**—In July, Italy's King Umberto I was assassinated by an anarchist seeking revenge for the bloody suppression of a labor uprising. Umberto's 22-year reign was characterized by a blustering, often unsuccessful foreign policy. His son, Vittorio Emanuele III, ushered in a period of liberalization—but after siding with Germany's foes in World War I, he surrendered Italy to fascism. ▶1911.12

▶**GREAT RACE**—Five entrants from four countries competed in the first international championship automobile race on June 14, from

Paris to Lyons. All the cars finished, but the winner was a French Panhard that averaged 38.5 mph. ▶1910.2

▶**RADON DISCOVERED**—Studying radium in 1900, German chemist Friedrich Dorn observed that, in addition to radiation, it gave off a colorless, odorless gas that was also radioactive. Later research showed this "radium emanation" (renamed radon in 1923) was a distinct element, deriving from radium's radioactive decay just as radium derives from decaying uranium. In the 1980s it was found that naturally occurring radon could seep through basements, posing a serious lung-cancer threat. ▶1903.6

▶**A TRAGIC POLICY**—Despite the territorial gains of the British forces in South Africa, the Boers' guerrilla tactics threatened Britain's position. After becoming Britain's Commander in Chief in late November, Lord Horatio Kitchener decided to weaken guerrilla strongholds by systematically stripping the countryside of people and livestock, a strategy that included rounding up women and children into "refugee" camps. By the end of the war, 20,000 of the 120,000 Boers interned in Kitchener's concentration camps had died of disease and neglect. ▶1902.1

A brooding Nietzsche, painted by brooding Norwegian Edvard Munch.

IDEAS

Master Moralist

11 Friedrich Wilhelm Nietzsche was dead. And so was God, though it would take years for the rest of the world to appreciate the importance of that insight. Deranged from what was probably advanced syphilis, the German philosopher died misunderstood and underappreciated in August 1900, after two decades of worsening insanity and lonely wandering.

He once wrote that some men are born posthumously, and that would have been a fitting epitaph for this thinker who, said Sigmund Freud, possessed more self-understanding than any other man who ever lived. Although Nietzsche wrote in the nineteenth century, his ideas about the nature of man and morality in a changing world are resolutely modern. In his 1886 work, *Beyond Good and Evil*, Nietzsche rejected not only Christianity but all moral absolutes as artificial and culturally determined, arguing instead—in a famous phrase—for a "transvaluation of values." *Thus Spake Zarathustra*, a narrative fable in which an ancient Persian philosopher functions as the author's stand-in, developed Nietzsche's theory of the *Übermensch*, or superman—a heroic, life-affirming figure who, embodying the best of "feminine" and "masculine" virtues, aspires to greatness rather than conventional Christian goodness. The "death of God," Nietzsche realized, created a vacuum, a lack of purpose and meaning in the world, and he saw the creeping nationalism around him as a futile, and dangerous, attempt to fill that void.

Complex and at times nearly impenetrable, his books were commonly found in German field packs during World War I, and the Nazis who followed had no trouble distorting his theories in support of their own notions of a superior German race. ▶**1927.4**

MEDICINE

Blood Groups Discovered

12 Nearly three centuries after William Harvey explained the circulation of blood, the Austrian immunologist Karl Landsteiner found that all blood is not the same. Landsteiner, who learned about pathology by performing almost 4,000 autopsies during a ten-year stint at the Vienna Pathological Institute, discovered in 1900 that blood serum drawn from one person often agglutinated, or clumped, when mixed with the blood cells of another. The following year he showed that the clumping was caused by different antigens contained in blood. The antigens were characteristic of different blood types, which Landsteiner called A, B, and O (he later added a fourth, AB). His discovery rescued surgery from the barbarism of bloodletting and random, often lethal, transfusions. Surgeons had had to transfuse blood indiscriminately (animal blood and milk were commonly used), not knowing whether their operations would cure or kill the patient.

Nearly four decades later, Landsteiner identified the Rhesus factor in human blood (first discovered in the Rhesus monkey), a breakthrough that allowed modern medicine to seek ways to prevent unborn children from being adversely affected by their mothers' lack of the RH factor.

Landsteiner's pioneering achievement received little notice until World War I, when the wholesale carnage visited upon Europe created a desperate need for blood. The massive blood drives of the war years were mounted according to his blood-typing schemata, laying the groundwork for the modern blood bank. ▶**1994.M**

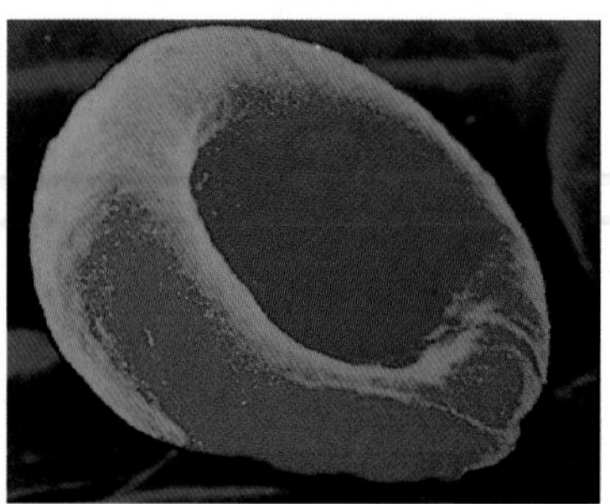

Color-enhanced photo of a red blood cell.

SCIENCE

The Birth of Quantum Physics

13 In one of history's rare instances of conformity to chronology, the launch of the new century marked the definitive dividing line between classical and modern physics. Before 1900, when German physicist Max Planck discovered that at their fundamental level atoms emit and absorb radiant energy in invisible packetlike bursts, or quanta, it was always assumed that atoms radiated energy continuously and smoothly. Planck's quantum theory revolutionized the field, providing the basis for, among other developments, Einstein's 1905 explanation of the photoelectric effect and Bohr's 1913 theory of atomic structure.

Planck's development of quantum theory earned him the 1918 Nobel Prize—and a stamp in his honor in Ivory Coast.

Building on the unsuccessful attempts of earlier physicists, Planck managed to devise a way to measure the distribution of thermal radiation from a perfect absorber (a so-called "black body") by calculating the discontinuous emission or absorption of light and establishing its relationship to a constant figure. That figure—6.63×10^{34} joule-second (represented by the letter "h")—is one of the most famous in physics: Planck's constant. Thus, energy was defined in terms of its relationship to the atom—in other words, energy to matter.

Planck earned the Nobel Prize in 1918. He spent nearly his entire life in Berlin, which, thanks to his collaboration with Einstein, became the world center for theoretical physics in the era directly before and after World War I. ▶**1905.1**

NOBEL PRIZES: First awarded in 1901.

A VOICE FROM 1900

Predictions for a New Century

By John Elfreth Watkins, Jr., from *Ladies' Home Journal*, December 1900

Founded in 1883 by Cyrus H.K. Curtis, the Ladies' Home Journal *became, under the 30-year stewardship of Edward W. Bok (editor from 1889 to 1919), an important agent for reform—campaigning for women's suffrage, clean cities and towns, wildlife conservation, better maternal health care, and truth in advertising. Packed with worldly information and common sense advice, the* Journal *was the prototype for the responsible, highly successful women's magazines of the twentieth century.*

These predictions, in 1900, for the 100 years stretching before America are sometimes quaint, but more often remarkably prescient—especially in view of the fact that the author was still living in the age of steam and cast iron.

Five Hundred Million People. There will probably be from 350,000,000 to 500,000,000 people in America and its possessions by the lapse of another century. Nicaragua will ask for admission to our Union after the completion of the great canal. Mexico will be next. Europe, seeking more territory to the south of us, will cause many of the South and Central American republics to be voted into the Union by their own people.

There will be No C, X, or Q in our every-day alphabet. They will be abandoned because unnecessary. Spelling by sound will have been adopted, first by the newspapers. English will be a language of condensed words expressing condensed ideas, and will be more extensively spoken than any other. Russian will rank second.

Hot and Cold Air from Spigots. Hot and cold air will be turned on from spigots to regulate the temperature of a house as we now turn on hot or cold water from spigots to regulate the temperature of the bath.

Automobiles will be Cheaper than Horses are to-day. Farmers will own automobile hay-wagons, automobile truck-wagons, plows, harrows and hay-rakes. A one-pound motor in one of these vehicles will do the work of a pair of horses or more. Children will ride in automobile sleighs in winter. Automobiles will have been substituted for every horse vehicle now known. There will be as already exist to-day, automobile hearses, automobile police patrols, automobile ambulances, automobile street sweepers. The horse in harness will be as scarce, if, indeed, not even scarcer, then as the yoked ox is to-day.

Everybody will Walk Ten Miles. Gymnastics will begin in the nursery, where toys and games will be designed to strengthen the muscles. Exercise will be compulsory in the schools.... A man or woman unable to walk ten miles at a stretch will be regarded as a weakling.

Aerial War-Ships and Forts on Wheels. Giant guns will shoot twenty-five miles or more, and will hurl anywhere within such a radius shells exploding and destroying whole cities.... Fleets of air-ships, hiding themselves with dense, smoky mists, thrown off by themselves as they move, will float over cities, fortifications, camps or fleets. They will surprise foes below by hurling upon them deadly thunderbolts.... Huge forts on wheels will dash across open spaces at the speed of express trains of to-day. They will make what are now known as cavalry charges. Great automobile plows will dig deep intrenchments as fast as soldiers can occupy them. Rifles will use silent cartridges. Submarine boats submerged for days will be capable of wiping a whole navy off the face of the deep. Balloons and flying machines will carry telescopes of one-hundred-mile vision with camera attachments, photographing an enemy within that radius. These photographs, as distinct and large as if taken from across the street, will be lowered to the commanding officer in charge of troops below.

Man will See Around the World. Persons and things of all kinds will be brought within focus of cameras connected electrically with screens at opposite ends of circuits, thousands of miles at a span. American audiences in their theatres will view upon huge curtains before them the coronations of kings in Europe or the progress of battles in the Orient. The instrument bringing these distant scenes to the very doors of people will be connected with a giant telephone apparatus transmitting each incidental sound in its appropriate place. Thus the guns of a distant battle will be heard to boom when seen to blaze, and thus the lips of a remote actor or singer will be heard to utter words or music when seen to move.

Strawberries as Large as Apples will be eaten by our great-great-grandchildren for their Christmas dinners a hundred years hence. Raspberries and blackberries will be as large. One will suffice for the fruit course of each person.

In its Christmas issue of 1900 the *Ladies' Home Journal* offered up a host of predictions—some prescient, some merely quaint—for the coming century, touching on everything from eating habits to wildlife extinction.

"Radio has no future."—**Lord Kelvin, British mathematician and physicist**

STORY OF THE YEAR

First Long-Distance Radio Transmission

1 Seated in a power station on the Cornish coast of England, electrical engineer John Ambrose Fleming, using a transmitter of his own design, tapped out the letter "s" in Morse code. It was noon, Greenwich time, December 12, 1901. Almost instantaneously, 1,800 miles away in a receiving station at St. John's, Newfoundland, the physicist and inventor Guglielmo Marconi heard three short clicks through the crude radio speaker he held to his ear. The signal Marconi picked up was the first ever transmitted across the Atlantic Ocean. The era of radiotelegraphy ("radio" for short) had begun. Within a few years Marconi opened the first commercial transatlantic wireless telegraph service, with stations in Ireland and Nova Scotia.

By 1901, radio waves per se were old news. But until Marconi began conducting his experiments in 1894, no one had successfully transmitted a signal at a distance greater than a few yards.

Marconi at his Newfoundland receiving station, December 12, 1901.

Just out of school, Marconi set out to perfect wireless telegraphy. Working at his family's estate in Pontecchio, Italy, he hit upon his great innovation: the grounded antenna. By fitting both his transmitter and receiver with wires that extended vertically from the ground into the air, Marconi discovered he could increase the range of the instruments. He added Morse telegraph apparatus to his system and started transmitting without any connecting wires, eventually flashing signals across the estate to a receiver a mile away. After moving to England, he continued to experiment, gradually extending the distances he was able to span until, on that historic day, he and Fleming completed the first transatlantic transmission.

The power station in Cornwall and the receiving station in Newfoundland were essentially larger versions of Marconi's backyard equipment. His receiving aerial at St. John's consisted of long wires suspended from kites flying high overhead. Marconi had found that the distance traveled by a radio wave corresponded to its length: The longest waves could be picked up the farthest away. (Shortwave transmissions were not perfected until the 1920s.) For the transatlantic signal he used equipment that could handle mile-long waves. Thus, Marconi needed no special technology to radiate the waves over great distances—just more of it. ▸**1904.8**

A heroic figure: Giuseppe Verdi, painted by Boldini.

MUSIC

A Beloved Maestro Dies

2 For five days, all of Italy kept vigil, waiting as a country for news. Silent crowds gathered outside the Grand Hotel in Milan, where the streets were blanketed with straw so the rattle of horse-drawn carriages would not disturb Giuseppe Verdi. Inside the hotel, Verdi lay unconscious, the victim of a stroke. The dreaded announcement came on January 27, 1901: The maestro was dead.

A national hero, Verdi was the last remaining towering figure of the Risorgimento, the movement that in 1861 achieved nationhood for Italy. Patriots had shouted his name, an acronym for *Vittorio Emanuele, Re D'Italia*. *"Viva VERDI"* —Long live Victor Emmanuel, King of Italy.

During his long life, Verdi absorbed the spirit of the movement and distilled it into music, writing operas—*Rigoletto*, *Il trovatore*, *La traviata*, *Aida*, *Otello*, and *Falstaff* —that inspired his countrymen and secured his reputation as one of the three (along with Mozart and Wagner) transcendent masters of the form. In his music, Italians heard the sound of their nation—its aspirations, its pain, and, especially, its glory. For that Verdi was revered as far more than merely a musical genius. When he died, wrote his friend the poet Arrigo Boito, who was present at the deathbed, "he carried away with him a great quantity of light and vital warmth." ▸**1904.4**

BUSINESS AND INDUSTRY

World's Richest Company

3 "Mr. Carnegie," said J.P. Morgan, "I want to congratulate you on becoming the richest man in the world." The occasion: the 1901 sale of Carnegie's massive Carnegie Steel Corporation to a team of Morgan-backed industrialists. The price: $492 million. After the sale, Andrew Carnegie, 66 years removed from his humble Scottish origins, retired from business and spent the remaining years of his life creating charities to distribute his money. Morgan went on to make the Carnegie company the centerpiece of a new trust—U.S. Steel, the world's first billion-dollar corporation.

To complete the formation of U.S. Steel, Morgan and his partners acquired several other huge metal concerns. Capitalized at $1.4 billion, U.S. Steel controlled mines, mills, and plants, and could produce eight million tons of steel annually—better than half the U.S. total, more than that of most countries. Directed by Judge Elbert Gary, who later lent his name to the Indiana city laid out by his corporation, U.S. Steel cleared $90 million in its first year. (Gary, who ran U.S. Steel for 26 years, supervised the rapid expansion of the American steel industry, successfully eluding antitrust prosecution from the government while openly negotiating with lesser barons to eliminate "unreasonable" competition.)

"I should have asked you for another hundred million," Carnegie wistfully told Morgan when they met on a transatlantic liner years later.

"If you had, I should have paid it," Morgan responded. ▸**1913.8**

Notoriously abrupt, J.P. Morgan brandished his cane at a news photographer.

ART & CULTURE: Books: ***The Life of the Bee*** **(Maurice Maeterlinck);** ***Erewhon Revisited*** **(Samuel Butler);** ***Jerusalem*** **(Selma Lagerlöf);** ***The Octopus*** **(Frank Norris);** ***Francesca da Rimini*** **(Gabriele D'Annunzio) ... Music: "High Society" (Porter Steele); "I Love You Truly" (Carrie Jacobs-Bond);** ***Piano Concerto in C Minor*** **(Sergei Rachmaninoff) ... Painting & Sculpture:** ***Girls on the Bridge*** **(Edvard Munch);**

"Words seem to express less than facts … black mourning London; black mourning England; black mourning Empire. The sensation of universal change haunted me."—**Lady Battersea on the death of Victoria**

Queen Victoria's coffin, followed by the royal funeral cortege, as it was conveyed through the streets of Windsor.

GREAT BRITAIN

Victoria Is Buried

4 When she died, on January 22, 1901, Victoria had been queen for almost 64 years, reigning longer than any other British monarch in history. Victoria's thoroughly exemplary life was emblematic of her time and place. She was a paragon of stuffy decorum and ardent imperialism; under her, Britain expanded its empire, simultaneously becoming ever more stolidly British. When Victoria died, wrote the poet Robert Bridges, "It seemed as though the keystone had fallen out of the arch of heaven." Among British subjects grief was nearly universal. Even London prostitutes walked the streets in black mourning.

With the accession of Edward VII, the fusty Victorian age officially ended. In its place came a new spirit of liberation, the spirit of the twentieth century. The portly, balding, gray-bearded Edward was 59 years old when he took over and had a reputation as something of a rake. "We cannot pretend there is nothing in his long career," conceded *The Times*, "which those of us who respect and admire him could wish otherwise." They were alluding to Edward's history of womanizing and high living, which he conducted in the public eye.

Edward may have been a roué, but he was a thoroughly modern one. For that he was ultimately loved by the British people. Casting off 64 years of dowdy propriety, he infused the Crown with vitality and a refreshing sense of fun. He dressed nattily and spoke off the cuff, and when his horse won the Derby, the crowd cheered wildly. "The monarch to make things hum," people sang, "the King, the runabout King." Unlike his mother, who actively shaped public policy, Edward was content with a largely ceremonial role. That, more than his levity, was his enduring contribution. The Edwardian era lasted a mere nine years, ending with Edward's death in 1910, but during that time—which only a few years later the war-weary English would look back on as a golden age of prosperity and good cheer—he laid the groundwork for the modern constitutional monarchy. ►**1910.M**

PHILANTHROPY

First Nobels Given

5 Alfred Nobel was a successful industrialist but an unsuccessful novelist and playwright, the inventor of dynamite but a committed pacifist. After a newspaper mistakenly printed the Swedish tycoon's obituary, calling him a "merchant of death," the very much alive Nobel grew obsessed with leaving a legacy of peace. When he did die, in 1896, his relatives were flabbergasted at the provisions of his will: 94 percent of his vast fortune was to be used to bestow an annual award on a handful of people around the globe whose work—in physics, chemistry, medicine, literature, and peacemaking (the economics category was added in 1969)—had "conferred the greatest benefit on mankind." The will's wording was so vague, however, that its executors spent five years wrangling over rules and finances. The first Nobel Prizes were finally bestowed by the King of Sweden on December 10, 1901, the fifth anniversary of Nobel's death.

Each winner, known as a "laureate" (for the laurel crowns awarded ancient athletes), received about $42,000, a sum dozens of times greater than any comparable prize (or the average professor's salary). While the monetary award (now close to $1 million) may be less princely than some lottery prizes, the Nobel is still regarded as the ultimate professional honor. ►**1913.8**

The Nobel medal for peace, front and back. Peace is the only prize that can be bestowed on institutions as well as individuals.

BIRTHS

- **Fulgencio Batista, Cuban president.**
- **Gary Cooper, U.S. actor.**
- **Marlene Dietrich, German-U.S. actress.**
- **Walt Disney, U.S. film animator.**
- **Jean Dubuffet, French artist.**
- **Enrico Fermi, Italian-U.S. physicist.**
- **Clark Gable, U.S. actor.**
- **George Gallup, U.S. pollster.**
- **Alberto Giacometti, Swiss sculptor.**
- **Jascha Heifetz, Russian-U.S. violinist.**
- **Werner Heisenberg, German physicist.**
- **Hirohito, Japanese emperor.**
- **Leopold III, Belgian king.**
- **André Malraux, French writer.**
- **Margaret Mead, U.S. anthropologist.**
- **William S. Paley, U.S. businessman.**
- **Linus Pauling, U.S. chemist.**
- **Salvatore Quasimodo, Italian poet.**
- **Lee Strasberg, U.S. director and educator.**
- **Sukarno, Indonesian president.**
- **Stefan Wyszynski, Polish Roman Catholic prelate.**

DEATHS

- **Benjamin Harrison, U.S. president.**
- **William McKinley, U.S. president.**
- **Milan I, Serbian king.**
- **Henri de Toulouse-Lautrec, French painter.**
- **Giuseppe Verdi, Italian composer.**
- **Victoria, U.K. queen.**

Golden Bodies **(Paul Gauguin);** ***Seated Nude*** **(Aristide Maillol) … Film:** ***Blue Beard*** **(Georges Méliès);** ***Fire!*** **(James Williamson);** ***Street Scene, Tokyo, Japan*** **(Robert K. Bonine);** ***Execution of Czolgosz with Panorama of Auburn Prison*** **(Edwin S. Porter) … Theater:** ***The Three Sisters*** **(Anton Chekhov);** ***Dance of Death*** **(August Strindberg);** ***Monsieur Beaucaire*** **(Booth Tarkington).**

"Settle in Kenya, Britain's youngest and most attractive colony. Low prices at present for fertile areas.... Secure the advantage of native labor to supplement your own effort."—**Newspaper advertisement, circa 1900**

NEW IN 1901

Instant coffee.

First illusion ride (Trip to the Moon Adventure Ride at Pan-American Expo in Buffalo).

Electric hearing aid (Acousticon).

Safety razor (Gillette).

Electric typewriter.

Driving school (Liver Motor Car Depot and School of Automobilism, Birkenhead, England).

IN THE UNITED STATES

▶CUBAN PROTECTORATE—With the Platt Amendment, Congress made Cuba a de facto U.S. colony in 1901. Under its terms, American troops (who'd occupied the island since helping to oust Spain in 1898) would pull out only if Havana granted Washington the right to intervene in its affairs, and to establish a naval base on Guantánamo Bay. The hard-pressed Cubans complied, writing those concessions into their new constitution. The troops went home—temporarily—in 1902. ▸1903.2

▶DRAMA DYNASTY—Critics proclaimed Ethel Barrymore America's outstanding young actress for her performance in the 1901 play *Captain Jinks of the Horse Marines.* It was the first starring role on Broadway for Barrymore, whose wit and imperious style enthralled audiences for the

next five decades. When her brothers John and Lionel took to the stage in succeeding years, the Barrymores—whose parents had also been actors—became the "royal family" of acting. ▸1922.V

Jung speculated that Picasso's use of blue—as in this 1901 self-portrait—was a manifestation of schizophrenia.

ART

Picasso's Blues

6 Although many theories have been offered to explain Pablo Picasso's "Blue Period," which began in 1901, no single theory is adequate. The 20-year-old artist had made his first trip to Paris from his native Spain the previous year. He was already a fully trained painter, and he enjoyed modest commercial success in Paris with his scenes of urban life. Inspired by Toulouse-Lautrec, Picasso became enthralled with Paris's colorful nightlife, painting the cabarets and cafes, the prostitutes, musicians, and blind beggars of urban society, high and low. That much is known and understood. What no one can fully explain is why Picasso, from late 1901 until spring 1904, relied almost exclusively on the color blue. Art historians have cited reasons ranging from the young painter's inability to afford any other colors to his infatuation with fin de siècle melancholy, but none suffices.

More significant than motivation is the fact that during the Blue Period, Picasso embarked in earnest on the career that came to dominate twentieth-century art. Enduring abject poverty (at one point, he tried unsuccessfully to sell the contents of his studio for the price of a ticket to Spain), Picasso willfully abandoned the styles, subjects, and colors that were beginning to bring him recognition. Instead he concentrated on blazing a unique artistic path—a pattern that would become characteristic of his long career. For this reason, Picasso's friend, the poet Jaime Sabartés, called the Blue Period—out of which came such great works as the *Absinthe Drinker* and *La Vie*—"a testimony of conscience." **▸1907.1**

CENTRAL AFRICA

Britain's "Lunatic Express"

7 On December 20, 1901, an engineer's wife hammered in the last spike of the Uganda Railway, at the lakeside town of Port Florence, Uganda (now Kisumu, Kenya). Her act marked the fulfillment of a dream long cherished among officials of the Imperial British East Africa Company.

Officials had been lobbying for a railroad since the 1880s. Railroads, they argued, spread commerce and Christianity; besides, the other empires were all building them. Parliament balked until 1895, when Tory leaders raised a terrifying specter: What if an enemy were to seize Uganda (then a remote corner of British territory) and dam the headwaters of the Nile? Egypt might dry up, and Britain would have to withdraw from the devastated country, losing control of the Suez Canal and, ultimately, India. Granted, such a dam was not technologically feasible—but it was best to take no chances. A railway might be needed to speed troops from Mombasa, Kenya (on the Indian Ocean), westward to Lake Victoria, the source of the Nile.

Thus was born the Uganda Railway, dubbed the "lunatic express" by those who questioned its tremendous costs. The British paid more than £5 million for the 582-mile road, more than double the projected outlay. Of the 32,000 Indian laborers brought in for the job, 2,500 died and 6,000 more were permanently disabled. Lions ate 28 Indians, more than 100 Africans, and a European supervisor. Smaller creatures caused even more misery: Amoebic dysentery and mosquito-borne malaria were rampant; chiggers burrowed into workers' toes, often necessitating amputation. Work was delayed by flood and drought, and by the problems of hauling food, water, and construction supplies over deserts and 9,000-foot mountains.

By 1899, the rails reached the village of Nairobi, nearly halfway to their destination. It would be four more years before they were fully operational. The Indians' contracts allowed them to stay on, and journalists speculated that the area would become an "African Punjab." But, in fact, colonial authorities made it difficult for Indians to purchase land, and all but 7,000 left. The railroad opened Kenya's highlands—largely vacant due to the decimation of the Kikuyu population by natural disasters and a plague of European smallpox—to whites from Britain and South Africa. These settlers came to dominate the colony's economy and politics; by 1912, income from exports of coffee and sisal (grown with cheap local labor) had

The Uganda Railway: vast expense in a questionable cause.

SPORTS: Baseball: Chicago White Sox win first American League championship; foul ball becomes strike in National League; Connie Mack named manager of Philadelphia Athletics ... Basketball: Amateur Athletic Union (AAU) established to oversee sport.

"This great disturber of our quietude reposes in his coffin."—**Le Galois, a French opposition newspaper, on the assassination of U.S. president McKinley**

recouped the money spent in laying track.

As for the Ugandan dam, it was finally built in 1954—by the British. Egypt was not seriously affected. ▸**1904.12**

LITERATURE

Mann's Literary Debut

8 "The latest news is that I am making preparations for a novel, a big novel," wrote Thomas Mann to a friend in 1897. "What do you think of that?" Four years later, in 1901, the 26-year-old Mann published *Buddenbrooks*. With this novel, his first, he introduced the trademark descriptive prose style that established him as the century's preeminent German writer.

Buddenbrooks chronicles, through four generations, the decline of a bourgeois German family from social and financial prominence into artistic decadence and oblivion. Mann used the Buddenbrook family, based largely on his own, to symbolize the clash between life and art, a theme that he continued to explore throughout his long career.

The book was immediately acclaimed in Germany, but outside his native country its reception was cooler. The chief critical objection to *Buddenbrooks* was its conventional realistic style, which many avant-garde writers and critics saw as old-fashioned and incompatible with the changing social and political landscape of the new century.

Mann, however, was anything but reactionary. He imbued his prose with a distinctively modern tone of ironic detachment, which, combined with his themes of decline and alienation, made *Buddenbrooks* a kind of literary steppingstone from the traditions of the nineteenth century to the experiments of the twentieth.

Mann's achievement did not go unrecognized for long. It was emphatically acknowledged in 1929, when the Nobel committee awarded him the literature prize for a body of work that by then included *Death in Venice* (1912) and *The Magic Mountain* (1924), which is almost universally regarded as his masterpiece. ▸**1902.3**

THE UNITED STATES

McKinley Assassinated

9 The President of the United States, William McKinley, had just finished patting a little girl's head at the 1901 Pan-American Exposition, in Buffalo, New York, when suddenly a man lurched toward him. McKinley extended his hand to the man's right hand, which was wrapped in a handkerchief. Two shots rang out and McKinley slumped forward. Guards and bystanders tackled the gunman, Leon Czolgosz, 28, an anarchist and unemployed steelworker from Cleveland.

The President was carried to a friend's home, where he lay for eight days clinging to life. In the hysterical aftermath of the shooting, dozens of anarchists nationwide were arrested, although most disavowed Czolgosz's act (including Emma Goldman, the colorful revolutionary leader Czolgosz claimed as his inspiration). Others who dared to criticize the fallen President—from ministers to policemen—were dismissed from their jobs, beaten, even tarred and feathered.

Crowds gathered on city street corners to read newspaper bulletin boards: The wounded statesman was reported to be strengthening daily on a diet of whiskey, water, and raw eggs ("administered by injection"). But on Friday the 13th of September, doctors tried feeding him solid food, and McKinley took a turn for the worse. By two o'clock the next morning, just six months into his second term, he was dead—the third American president to be assassinated in less than 50 years.

Vice President Theodore Roosevelt had to be located in the Adirondack Mountains, where he was hunting, and rushed back to Buffalo. At his inauguration a few hours later, Roosevelt vowed to "continue absolutely unbroken" the policies of his predecessor, which included a foreign policy that supporters and detractors alike termed "imperialistic." Under McKinley, the Spanish-American War had made the United States a world power. Cuba, Guam, Hawaii, the Philippines, Puerto Rico, and two islands in what later became American Samoa had all come under U.S. control. In this area, Roosevelt was true to his word. But McKinley's economic policy, which had brought both unprecedented prosperity and the wild growth of monopolies (or trusts), was reined in under the new administration, earning Roosevelt the sobriquet, the Trust Buster.

As for Czolgosz, he received his constitutionally guaranteed "speedy and public" trial—with a vengeance. He was convicted within two weeks of the shooting, and one month after that, he was electrocuted in front of 26 spectators (admitted out of a total applicant pool of 1,000) at New York's Auburn Prison. ▸**1903.2**

McKinley's assassin—here in an artist's re-creation—was Catholic, but Pope Leo XIII used the death to warn against "the perils of Freemasonry and Judaism."

IN THE UNITED STATES

▸HATCHET WOMAN—Carry Nation took her anti-saloon campaign to Topeka, Kansas, in 1901. Selling liquor there was already illegal, but booze halls flourished. The grandmotherly Nation had begun with peaceful protests but quickly changed her tactics. Leading several hundred troops of a mostly female "Home Defenders' Army," she smashed saloons across Kansas—and convinced lawmakers to tighten prohibition. With her famous hatchet in hand, Nation traveled the U.S., wrecking taverns, getting arrested, lecturing at carnivals, and telling women, "You don't know how much joy you will have until you begin to smash, smash, smash." **▸1919.V**

▸NEW OLDS—The first commercially successful car in America was the Oldsmobile, unveiled this year by 36-year-old Ransom P. Olds. The car's curved dashboard and simple, carriage-style construction gave it a jaunty look—and inspired a hit song, "In My Merry Oldsmobile." Despite a fairly steep price tag of $650, the Lansing, Michigan–based Olds sold 600 cars in 1901; by 1904, that number had grown almost tenfold. **▸1903.8**

▸FATAL FEVER—A U.S. commission sent to Cuba in 1901 to find the cause of yellow fever confirmed that the tropical plague was spread by mosquitoes. A Cuban doctor, Carlos Finlay, had championed that theory for 20 years, only to be ridiculed by the medical establishment. But the American team, headed by Dr. Walter Reed, arrived at the truth through hard science and cruel experience—one member died after being bitten. Mosquito control soon eliminated the disease in areas where epidemics once raged. **▸1905.9**

POLITICS & BUSINESS: GNP: $20.7 billion ... President McKinley assassinated, succeeded by Vice President Theodore Roosevelt ... U.S. Army War College opens in Washington, D.C. ... U.S. surpasses Great Britain in export of steel, iron, and coal ... The Texas Co. (later Texaco) founded ... The Guggenheim family takes over ASARCO copper trust, extending interests into Chile, Alaska, and Belgian Congo.

"I worshipped Kipling at 13, loathed him at 17, enjoyed him at 20, despised him at 25, and now again rather admire him. The one thing that was never possible ... was to forget him."—**George Orwell in 1936**

AROUND THE WORLD

▶DIRT BUSTER—An English bridge engineer named Hubert Booth patented the first practical electric vacuum cleaner in 1901. His door-to-door vacuuming service—which involved running hoses through windows from a van equipped with a vacuum pump—soon boasted Buckingham Palace as a client (a fact that helped his invention win acceptance among the fashionable set). A portable, upright version of Booth's device was marketed in 1908 by an American harness maker, W.H. Hoover.

▶FAMOUS MARCH—Edward Elgar is known as the century's greatest English composer for such works as the *Enigma Variations* (a piece based on the countermelody to a popular song whose identity has never been guessed). But in 1901 he penned the eminently hummable *Pomp and Circumstance* (No. 1). The march—the first of five with that title—is used to establish a mood of dignity at events ranging from royal coronations to high-school graduations.

▶RUSSIAN REBELS—"To put an end to czardom" was the stated goal of the new Socialist-Revolutionary Party, whose tactics included bombing and assassination. Formed in 1901 from several leftist groups, the SRP's primary aim was to unite the peasants against not only the monarch but also the bureaucrats and landowners. Although the head of its terrorist wing was revealed in 1909 to be a police agent, by 1917 the party was the largest non-Marxist radical organization in Russia. ▶1903.11

AUSTRALIA

Commonwealth Proclaimed

10 Although Queen Victoria had assented to Australian independence the previous July, the official transformation of six colonies into a nation of federated states took place on New Year's Day 1901 in a ceremony in Sydney's Centennial Park. "The newest nation on the earth," gushed a Sydney newspaper, "was imbued with the breath of constitutional life."

The constitution of the rugged, sparsely populated country was modeled after that of another former group of British colonies, the United States. There was one important difference: Instead of an elected president, Australia was to have a prime minister, appointed by a governor-general representing the English Crown. That the man tapped for the job was Edmund Barton *(above)*, a longtime leader of the independence movement, was a measure of the remarkable lack of acrimony between Britain and its former wards. Indeed, little changed with independence—or federation, as it was tactfully called. While the 3.8 million Australians gained greater control over their internal affairs and a stronger cultural identity, the imperial ties of trade and mutual defense (Australia provided 16,000 volunteers for the Boer War) remained strong. Australian membership in the British Empire simply went from compulsory to voluntary, and Britain—bogged down militarily in China as well as South Africa—had six fewer governments to administer. ▶**1902.1**

LITERATURE

Kipling's Ode to India

11 The 1901 publication of *Kim*, a tale of an Irish orphan in India receiving life lessons from an aged Tibetan lama, confirmed Rudyard Kipling's niche in English letters as the poet and novelist of Empire. Both an entertaining children's story and a brilliant evocation of the vestiges of imperial glory, *Kim*—like all of Kipling's best work—is informed by his years in colonial India and his love for that land and its people.

Born in Bombay of English parents, Kipling was sent to England at the age of six and endured a miserable eleven years there, living as a near orphan, first in a foster home and later at a second-rate boarding school. He returned to India when he was 17 and established himself as a journalist. His stories about life in India under the British Raj proved so spectacularly popular in England that when he returned there seven years later, in 1889, he rapidly assumed a kind of unofficial poet laureate status.

In 1907, Kipling, just 41, became the first Englishman to win the Nobel Prize in literature. But not long thereafter his reputation began to decline—at least partly because the personal and political prejudices so fundamental to his vision put him at odds with the leading critics and writers of the day. In all his writing—even *Kim*, with its sympathetic portrayal of Indian mysticism—Kipling maintained an unswerving belief in "The White Man's Burden," the title of a poem he wrote in 1899. (This justification of colonialism held that Englishmen had a moral obligation to spread their superior European culture to the uncivilized "heathen" world.)

British caricaturist Max Beerbohm takes aim at Kipling, arm in arm with "Britannia, 'is gurl."

Still, when he died in 1936 few questioned his burial in the Poets' Corner of Westminster Abbey. Among his eulogists was George Orwell, who condemned Kipling's late-Victorian imperialism as "sentimental and ignorant and dangerous," but also praised "the storyteller who was so important in my youth." ▶**1902.5**

BUSINESS AND INDUSTRY

Birth of the Boom

12 **Early in 1901, just after being rejected by Standard Oil as a drilling ground, Spindletop, a hill outside the town of Beaumont on the East Texas plains, became the most desirable piece of real estate in the world. There was oil underneath Spindletop, oil that gushed 200 feet into the air when drillers struck it. The well blew out 110,000 barrels of Texas crude a day for nine days before workers could cap it.**

Wildcatters, roughnecks, roustabouts, and fortune-seekers descended on Beaumont, swelling its population from 10,000 to 50,000. More oil was discovered outside of Tulsa, Oklahoma, to the north, more still in Louisiana. But by summer the limited market (oil's main use in 1901 was to light lamps) was saturated, and the price dropped to three cents a barrel. While speculators all around them went bust, a few prescient capitalists began to explore the use of oil as heating fuel and to power ships and locomotives. Their companies—Gulf, Sunoco, Texaco—grew rich. The boom was back on. **▶1909.5**

ANNUAL WORLDWIDE OIL PRODUCTION

Over a 60-year period, production increased sevenfold. By 1990, it reached 21.7 billion gallons.

NOBEL PRIZES: Peace: Jean Henri Dunant (Swiss; Geneva Convention and International Red Cross) and Frédéric Passy (French; French peace society) ... Literature: Sully Prudhomme (French; poet) ... Chemistry: Jacobus van't Hoff (Dutch; chemical dynamics and osmotic pressure) ... Medicine: Emil von Behring (German; tetanus and diphtheria immunization) ... Physics: Wilhelm Röntgen (German; X-rays).

A VOICE FROM 1901

A Slave Child's Lonely Road

From *Up from Slavery,* by Booker T. Washington, 1901

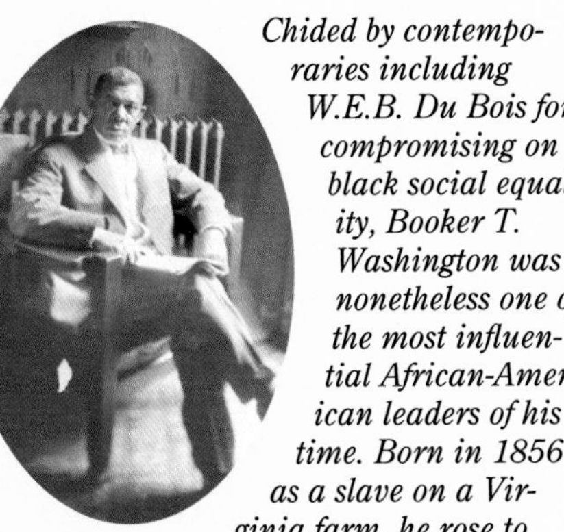

Chided by contemporaries including W.E.B. Du Bois for compromising on black social equality, Booker T. Washington was nonetheless one of the most influential African-American leaders of his time. Born in 1856 as a slave on a Virginia farm, he rose to become the founder of the Tuskegee Institute, an industrial and agricultural college for blacks. Washington believed that in order for blacks to achieve full social and economic equality, they first had to become a productive workforce. His nonthreatening approach to black equality was well received by whites, and allowed him to collect millions of dollars in funding for Tuskegee from wealthy northerners. His autobiography, Up from Slavery, *was published in 1901. In the following passage, he remembers a childhood deprived of play or schooling.* ►**1903.V**

I was asked not long ago to tell something about the sports and pastimes that I engaged in during my youth. Until that question was asked it had never occurred to me that there was no period of my life that was devoted to play. From the time that I can remember anything, almost every day of my life has been occupied in some kind of labour; though I think I would now be a more useful man if I had had time for sports. During the period that I spent in slavery I was not large enough to be of much service, still I was occupied most of the time in cleaning the yards, carrying water to the men in the fields, or going to the mill to which I used to take the corn, once a week, to be ground. The mill was about three miles from the plantation. This work I always dreaded. The heavy bag of corn would be thrown across the back of the horse, and the corn divided about evenly on each side; but in some way, almost without exception, on these trips, the corn would so shift as to become unbalanced and would fall off the horse, and often I would fall with it. As I was not strong enough to reload the corn upon the horse, I would have to wait, sometimes for many hours, till a chance passer-by came along who would help me out of my trouble. The hours while waiting for someone were usually spent in crying. The time consumed in this way made me late in reaching the mill, and by the time I got my corn ground and reached home it would be far into the night. The road was a lonely one, and often led through dense forests. I was always frightened. The woods were said to be full of soldiers who had deserted from the army, and I had been told that the first thing a deserter did to a Negro boy when he found him alone was to cut off his ears. Besides, when I was late getting home I knew I would always get a severe scolding or a flogging.

I had no schooling whatever while I was a slave though I remember on several occasions I went as far as the schoolhouse door with one of my young mistresses to carry her books. The picture of several dozen boys and girls in a schoolroom engaged in study made a deep impression upon me, and I had the feeling that to get into a schoolhouse and study in this way would be about the same as getting into paradise.

So far as I can now recall, the first knowledge that I got of the fact that we were slaves, and that freedom of the slaves was being discussed, was early one morning before day, when I was awakened by my mother kneeling over her children and fervently praying that Lincoln and his armies might be successful, and that one day she and her children might be free. In this connection I have never been able to understand how the slaves throughout the South, completely ignorant as were the masses so far as books or newspapers were concerned, were able to keep themselves so accurately and completely informed about the great National questions that were agitating the country.

From the time that Garrison, Lovejoy, and others began to agitate for freedom, the slaves throughout the South kept in close touch with the progress of the movement. Though I was a mere child during the preparation for the Civil War and during the war itself, I now recall the many late-at-night whispered discussions that I heard my mother and the other slaves on the plantation indulge in. These discussions showed that they understood the situation, and that they kept themselves informed of events by what was termed the "grape-vine" telegraph.

Born into slavery and emancipated into bitter poverty, Booker T. Washington rose to become the most prominent black leader and educator of his time.

"Starving, ragged men, clad in skins and sacking, their bodies covered with sores from lack of salt and food."
—Marthinus Theunis Steyn, President of the Orange Free State, describing Lord Kitchener's concentration camps

STORY OF THE YEAR

The Boer War Ends

1 The British won the Boer War, but the treaty that ended it—signed at the South African town of Vereeniging in 1902—granted such favorable terms to the enemy that Britain might well have asked, "With victory like this, who needs defeat?"

When the war began, in 1899, Britain had been the undisputed leader of the world for over 80 years. When it ended three years (and tens of thousands of deaths) later, Britain was spiritually and economically drained. Moreover, the rest of Europe, especially Germany, had had ample opportunity to draw its own conclusions about Britain's much-vaunted military might. Indeed, the Boer War—which has been likened to America's Vietnam—marked the beginning of the end of the empire.

Britain's mobilization for the Boer War was its largest until World War I.

The conflict erupted after the Boer states of the South African Republic (now Transvaal), seeking to protect their rich goldfields from British exploitation, refused to grant political rights to *uitlanders*, resident foreigners. (British *uitlanders* actually outnumbered the ruling Afrikaners, themselves descendants of seventeenth-century Dutch settlers.) Tensions ran high, and when Britain increased troop strength in the Cape Colony (its southernmost territory), the Boers attacked.

On paper, the South African Republic and its ally, the Orange Free State, were a weak enemy, with no navy, no real army, no massive industrial base, no far-flung empire. Against a British mobilization of 450,000 troops (the empire's largest until World War I), the Boers mustered about 87,000 men. But despite Britain's presumed superiority, the war dragged on for almost three years. After a few early victories, the Boer army dissolved into guerrilla groups, raiding the British garrisons and the railroad. The mighty British army was like Gulliver among the Lilliputians, stung on all sides. It finally prevailed only after Commander in Chief Horatio Kitchener resorted to a scorched-earth policy that starved out the Boers and cut them off from their land.

The treaty of Vereeniging stipulated that in return for laying down their arms and recognizing King Edward VII as their sovereign, the Afrikaners would retain their property; pay no special taxes to compensate for the war; and teach both English and Dutch in the schools. Britain would contribute £3 million toward reconstruction. The treaty's most fateful clause postponed settling the issue of nonwhite suffrage until after the Afrikaners had been granted self-government. When it came—ending forever British hopes of dominion in South Africa—blacks were excluded. ◂**1900.M** ▸**1908.9**

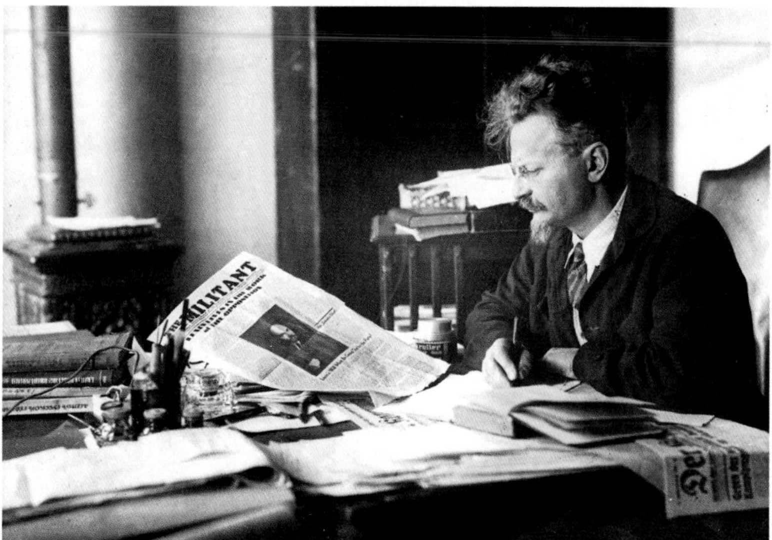

In prison, Trotsky wrote, he longed for "the smell of the printing ink of a fresh newspaper."

RUSSIA

Trotsky Escapes to London

2 In the autumn of 1902, a 23-year-old exile at the Siberian settlement of Verkholensk told police that he was sick. Duly, they checked in every day on the exile, whose name was Lev Davidovich Bronstein, finding him always in the same position: lying on his side, face toward the wall. One day they took a closer look and discovered the bedridden man was actually a dummy. By then Bronstein was well on his way to Irkutsk, concealed under the hay in a peasant's cart.

Bronstein's friends in Irkutsk provided him with a conspicuously bourgeois suit of traveling clothes and a blank passport. On the line where his name belonged, he wrote *Trotsky*, probably from the German word for defiance. Henceforth he would be known as Leon Trotsky, nicknamed "the Pen" for his facility with the written word.

During his four years of prison and Siberian exile, Trotsky had remained active in the revolutionary movement, producing a steady stream of essays for various underground newspapers. He kept abreast of developments through radical literature smuggled into Verkholensk from London and Geneva. One pamphlet in particular, "What Is to Be Done?", piqued his interest and strengthened his resolve to escape from Siberia. The pamphlet's author, a relatively unknown ideologue named V.I. Lenin, argued that an elite cadre of professionals must assume control of the proletarian revolution, relegating the workers to a subservient position. Trotsky wasn't sure he agreed, but he recognized in Lenin the pragmatic leadership the revolution needed.

Crossing international borders with his new identity, Trotsky made it to London, where, equipped with a street address provided by radical associates, he turned up at Lenin's doorstep. Lenin's wife, Nadezhda, answered the door, took one look at the young man outside, and exclaimed, "The Pen has come!" Within two years Trotsky was attacking Lenin in print, but on that October morning in 1902 he was welcomed by the future chairman as a protégé and comrade. ▸**1903.11**

LITERATURE

Conrad's Dark Tale

3 At the height of the Western powers' scramble for colonial territory, tales of exotic adventure were often bestsellers. But it took an inward-looking expatriate from a conquered land to turn such a story into a profound study of evil and self-deception. Polish-born Joseph Conrad was one of the century's most powerful writers, and *Heart of Darkness,* published in 1902, was one of his greatest achievements: a gripping yarn, a stylistic tour de force, and a penetrating work of philosophy and psychology.

The novella centers on a perilous journey by riverboat, captained by an Englishman named Marlow, into the remote interior of the Belgian Congo, where a mysterious white trader named Mr. Kurtz dwells in a jungle outpost. When Marlow and his companions reach

ART & CULTURE: Books: *The Immoralist* (André Gide); *Salt-Water Ballads* (John Masefield); *Just So Stories* (Rudyard Kipling); *The Virginian* (Owen Wister); *The Wings of the Dove* (Henry James); *The Path to Rome* (Hilaire Belloc) ... Music: "Bill Bailey, Won't You Please Come Home?" (Hughie Cannon); "In the Good Old Summertime" (Evans and Shields); *Le Jongleur de Notre Dame* (Jules Massenet) ...

"There is no theory. You have merely to listen. Fantasy is the law."—**Claude Debussy**

Kurtz—a brilliant idealist who has supposedly been "educating" the natives while sending back record shipments of ivory—they discover that he has become a tyrannical chieftain, his hut decorated with the skulls of his victims. Ailing and insane, but in despair over his own corruption, Kurtz dies on his way downriver, gasping, "The horror! The horror!"

In an era when Europeans boasted of taking civilization to savages, Conrad demonstrated how extremes of power and isolation—common aspects of the imperialist experience—could bring out the savagery that lurks in every human heart.

The author himself had suffered at the hands of empire. Born Jozef Konrad Korzeniowski in 1857, he spent part of his childhood in a frigid Russian town, to which his father, a poet prominent in the Polish independence movement, had been banished. Conrad's mother died in exile when he was eight. At 17 he became a merchant seaman, and for the next two decades, on French and British ships, he lived the stories he later fictionalized in masterpieces like *Lord Jim* (1900) and *Nostromo* (1904).

Working in English, a language he'd taught himself at home and later at sea, he developed a dense, poetic style admired by authors ranging from Thomas Mann to William Faulkner. But Conrad sometimes bemoaned the fact that critics—many of whom were unequipped to cope with his originality—treated him as "a sort of freak, an amazing bloody foreigner writing in English." ◄**1901.8** ►**1929.3**

Portrait of Conrad by English artist Walter Tittle.

A set from Debussy's opera (with libretto by Maeterlinck): Mélisande, with her lover, Pelléas, loses her wedding ring at the moment her husband, Goland, suffers an accident.

MUSIC

Impressionist of Sound

4 "This music overwhelms you, drives deep into your heart with a power of inspiration that I admire but cannot fully understand," wrote a leading Paris critic after the 1902 premiere of Claude Debussy's opera, *Pelléas et Mélisande.* Others were less impressed with Debussy's radical innovations, which included the elimination of traditional arias and sung dialogue in favor of blocks of sound. The director of the Conservatoire de Paris, where Debussy had studied, ordered students to stay away from the opera. It could only have, he insisted, a corrupting influence. Music lovers who did attend disrupted performances with catcalls, jeering, "Why don't they give us some music!"

A consummate intellectual snob, Debussy shrugged off the public's hostility, attributing it to the philistinism of the masses. "The present state of affairs," he once said, "is due to the motto inscribed on all public monuments, 'Liberty, Equality, Fraternity'—words which, at best, are fit only for cabdrivers." Supremely confident of his rarefied taste, Debussy composed for himself, seeking to widen the vocabulary of Western music and to liberate it from ancient conventions. With *Pelléas et Mélisande* (his only completed opera), as well as with such orchestral works as the 1905 *La Mer (The Sea)* and his celebrated 1894 "tone poem," *Prelude à l'après-midi d'un faune (Prelude to the Afternoon of a Faun)*, Debussy invented a fluid, dreamlike style of music that is the musical equivalent of impressionism in painting. The great Russian composer Igor Stravinsky called Debussy the "century's first musician," and to many critics, he remains the most original. ►**1909.6**

BIRTHS

Ansel Adams, U.S. photographer.

Marian Anderson, U.S. singer.

Alfred H. Barr, Jr., U.S. art historian.

Marcel Breuer, Hungarian-U.S. architect.

Paul A.M. Dirac, U.K. physicist.

Erik Erikson, German-U.S. psychoanalyst.

Edward Evans-Pritchard, U.K. anthropologist.

Langston Hughes, U.S. writer.

Bobby Jones, U.S. golfer.

Ray A. Kroc, U.S. franchiser.

Juscelino Kubitschek, Brazilian president.

Carlo Levi, Italian novelist.

Charles Lindbergh, U.S. aviator.

Georgi Malenkov, U.S.S.R. political leader.

Odgen Nash, U.S. writer.

Karl Popper, Austrian-U.K. philosopher.

Leni Riefenstahl, German filmmaker.

Richard Rodgers, U.S. composer.

Saud, Saudi Arabian king.

John Steinbeck, U.S. novelist.

William Walton, U.K. composer.

William Wyler, German-U.S. filmmaker.

DEATHS

John Acton, U.K. historian.

Samuel Butler, U.K. writer.

Bret Harte, U.S. writer.

Thomas Nast, U.S. cartoonist.

Frank Norris, U.S. novelist.

Walter Reed, U.S. surgeon.

Cecil Rhodes, U.K. colonialist.

Elizabeth Cady Stanton, U.S. suffragist.

Emile Zola, French novelist.

Painting & Sculpture: ***Lord Ribblesdale*** **(John Singer Sargent);** ***Comin' Through the Rye*** **(Frederic Remington) ... Film:** ***A Trip to the Moon*** **(Georges Méliès);** ***Uncle Josh at the Moving-Picture Show*** **and** ***Jack and the Beanstalk*** **(Edwin S. Porter) ... Theater:** ***Soldiers of Fortune*** **(Thomas and Davis);** ***The Girl with the Green Eyes*** **(Clyde Fitch);** ***The Lower Depths*** **(Maxim Gorky).**

"Religion, in short, is a monumental chapter in the history of human egotism."—**William James, *The Varieties of Religious Experience***

NEW IN 1902

Fan club (for English actor Lewis Waller).

Gas-powered lawn mower.

Automat (Philadelphia).

Teddy bear (named for Teddy Roosevelt, after he declined to shoot a bear while on a hunting expedition).

Crayola-brand crayons.

Times Literary Supplement.

Pepsi-Cola Company.

Nabisco's Barnum's Animal Crackers.

The Ritz hotel in London.

Tournament of Roses football game (later called the Rose Bowl).

IN THE UNITED STATES

▶GENETIC KEY—Columbia medical student Walter Sutton announced in 1902 that all the cells of grasshoppers contain dissimilar pairs of matching chromosomes—a finding that on the microscopic level recalled Mendel's theory that each inheritable trait is controlled by a pair of genetic factors. Sutton hypothesized that chromosomes contain these factors (later called genes), and that their behavior during sex-cell division (meiosis) lends a randomness to heredity. His work formed the basis for modern genetics. ◀1900.10 ▶1909.12

▶U.S. TAKES CONTROL OF THE PHILIPPINES—An exceptionally brutal three-year war waged by the U.S. Army against independence-minded Filipino revolutionists—angry at being handed over to the U.S. as spoils of the Spanish-American War—ended in 1902, with the U.S. in possession of the archipelago of 7,100 islands (and, not incidentally, a strategic military base in the Pacific). Directed by General Arthur MacArthur (father of Douglas), the Philippine War was

SOUTHERN AFRICA

An Agent of Empire

5 In 1980, a crowd of newly independent citizens of the republic of Zimbabwe gathered in the capital city of Harare (formerly Salisbury) to take revenge on a man who had died in 1902. Employing a crane, authorities toppled the enormous bronze statue of Cecil Rhodes that stood over the center of the city, and then the people set upon it with steel bars and rocks.

Rhodes was an unlikely embodiment of imperialism. A sickly, not terribly bright child who was first sent off to Africa at 17 to improve his health, he ended up becoming a kind of self-appointed agent of empire on the continent. Between repeated trips back to England during the 1870s, Rhodes began building mining claims, eventually consolidating his holdings by creating the De Beers Mining Company. By 1891, Rhodes controlled 90 percent of world diamond production.

He used his personal fortune and power to implement his grand scheme, which was to found a secret society, "the true aim and object whereof shall be the extension of British rule throughout the world." (His vision included "the ultimate recovery of the United States"; the society evolved into the prestigious Rhodes Scholarships to Oxford University.) Accordingly, he drove Africans from their land, bought off any opposition, plotted war against the Boers in South Africa, and underwrote pioneering sorties to the north. In 1895, the territory he had amassed—three times the size of England and Wales, together—was named Rhodesia, cementing the legacy that, 85 years later, the people of Zimbabwe would so memorably dismantle. **◀1901.11 ▶1908.2**

Enormously wealthy, Cecil Rhodes regarded money as a means for fulfilling his imperialist vision.

A pro-Dreyfus politician leads the charge to enshrine Zola's ashes in the Panthéon.

LITERATURE

Death of a National Antihero

6 Emile Zola inspired so much hatred, it was easy to imagine him dying violently. But the 62-year-old French novelist's death in September 1902 was by asphyxiation from fumes caused by a blocked chimney.

As the most prominent defender of Alfred Dreyfus (a Jewish captain in the French army who was framed for treason in 1894), Zola was attacked by rightist mobs, convicted of libel against French military authorities, and forced to flee to England. His novels—such shockingly frank works as *Nana* and *La Terre*—were denounced by most critics as "filth" and "pornography" and censored at home and abroad. Newspaper cartoons showed him dipping his pen into chamber pots. Yet he was France's most popular writer, and his books were a major export.

Zola's leadership of the new literary movement called naturalism was shaped by his experience as a journalist, as well as his readings in philosophy and science (especially Charles Darwin's work). Going a step beyond the "realistic" fiction of the nineteenth century, the naturalists sought in an almost scientific way to expose the underlying laws of human behavior. In Zola's two dozen hefty and well-researched novels—with settings ranging from coal mines to mansions, gin mills to stock markets, farmhouses to the houses of Parliament—he described greed, envy, sloth, even lust in clinically graphic terms that enraged the guardians of public taste.

The public itself, however, couldn't get enough. His funeral attracted 50,000 mourners, with the cavalry on hand in case of riot. The writer Anatole France, who had once written that Zola should never have been born, now eulogized him as "the conscience of mankind." Soon afterward, Zola's picture began appearing in ads for a safety device for chimneys. **▶1906.12**

IDEAS

William James's Pragmatism

7 Just after his treatise on faith, *The Varieties of Religious Experience*, was published in 1902, William James ran into his fellow philosopher George Santayana. "You have done the religious slumming for all time," Santayana said.

James's book presented a broad range of religious experience, culled from firsthand accounts. Santayana objected to James's reliance on believers outside the realm of conventional faith. Their extremism, he felt, discredited their views. James countered that vivid personal experiences of individual believers were more revealing than the gray abstractions of theologians.

The son of theologian Henry

SPORTS: Baseball: John "Little Napoleon" McGraw becomes manager of New York Giants ... Boxing: 167-lb. Bob Fitzsimmons challenges 206-lb. heavyweight champion James J. Jeffries (coins phrase "The bigger they come, the harder they fall," but loses nonetheless).

"For one brief moment I saw the city of St. Pierre before me. Then it was blotted out by the overwhelming flood."
—Ellery S. Scott, officer on the steamship *Roraima*, witness to the Mount Pelée eruption

James (and brother of the novelist of the same name), James was trained as a physician but made extended forays into other disciplines, including zoology (accompanying the naturalist Louis Agassiz to Brazil), experimental psychology, and physiology.

James's chief contribution to philosophy was the theory of pragmatism, which holds that in a pluralistic universe, a belief is true if it is useful and consistent with experience. Since experience varies greatly from person to person, any given situation can contain more than one truth. Applying this thinking to religion, James concluded that an individual's belief in a god, regardless of its origins, is in some sense true if it imparts something useful, such as emotional comfort. There is, James maintained, no absolute truth; rather, "truth happens to an idea. It becomes true, is made true, by events." ▶**1903.12**

DIPLOMACY

Britain and Japan as Allies

8 With the signing of the Anglo-Japanese Alliance in 1902, Britain and Japan forged a diplomatic union that remained the anchor of Japanese foreign policy for two decades. The treaty's primary aim was the strategic protection of the two countries' interests in China and Korea, which were being threatened by Russia. Japan believed that control of Korea was vital to its national security; Britain had significant investments in China. By putting the Japanese navy at Britain's service in the Far East, the treaty also left Britain free to concentrate on the threat of the German navy in home waters.

Japan in 1902 was still a fledgling modern nation, having emerged only 33 years earlier from 700 years of feudal rule. The alliance signaled that Japan had fully arrived on the world scene. (The *Japan Times* likened the nation to a youth who has awakened to find himself "a grown-up person of high position, great reputation, and with a consequential burden of onerous responsibilities.") Japan had learned the hard way about the importance of having allies: In 1895 it had won the Sino-Japanese War but, because of its diplomatic isolation, was soon compelled by the triple intervention of Russia, Germany, and France to relinquish its goal of annexing Korea and return the Liaotung Peninsula to vanquished China.

When the Russo-Japanese War broke out in 1904, the Anglo-Japanese Alliance ensured that Russia

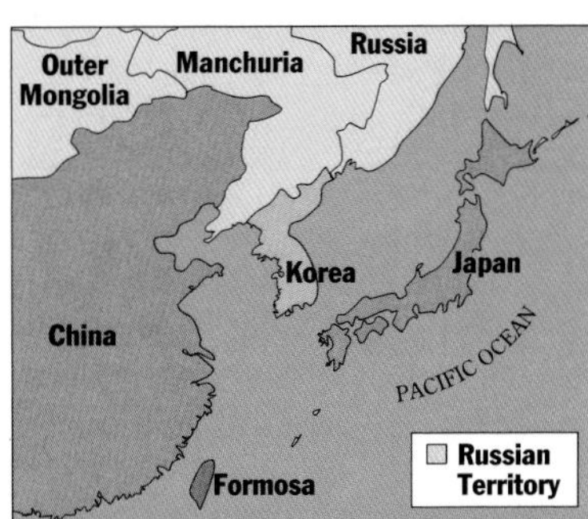

Fear of Russian encroachment in China and Korea motivated the Anglo-Japanese Alliance.

would receive no help from its ally France, because France would not risk retribution from Britain. Japan won the war, and this time no other European powers intervened in the peace negotiations. ▶**1904.1**

EGYPT

Aswan Dam Completed

9 The jewel of the British plan to develop Egypt was the damming of the Nile River at the city of Aswan, in upper Egypt. When the Aswan Dam was completed in 1902, it stood as the major engineering feat of its day, measuring more than a mile in length and rising to a height of 176 feet. For the first time in history, most of the Nile floodwater could be stored. The whole of lower Egypt and most of middle Egypt were converted to perennial irrigation, a system that supported two or three crops each year instead of only one. Within a short time, cultivated land was increased by more than a million acres and Egyptian cotton production went up by 40 percent.

The Aswan Dam shepherded Egypt into the modern era, recovering for it some of its past glory and positioning it for regional dominance in the twentieth century. The dam remained Egypt's primary system of irrigation until 1970, when the Aswan High Dam increased the system's storage capacity by 30 times. ▶**1910.11**

In just 10 years, the Aswan Dam increased Egypt's annual exports by 33 percent.

DISASTERS

Caribbean Catastrophe

10 On the morning of May 8, 1902, the residents of St. Pierre, Martinique—the largest town in the French West Indies—were headed for church when the mountain that loomed above their heads exploded. "A great mass of flames," wrote an eyewitness, "with twisting giant wreaths of smoke, rolled thousands of feet into the air, and then overbalanced and came rolling down." Within minutes, this seventeenth-century colonial capital lay burned and buried in lava. A tidal wave slammed into the harbor, ablaze with flammable rum from ruined distilleries. Few on shipboard lived, and of St. Pierre's 30,000 inhabitants, only a drunk in a jail cell survived Mount Pelée's eruption.

Pillars of smoke seven miles high marked the grave of St. Pierre, Martinique.

Several smaller towns were also destroyed. And hours later, a volcano on St. Vincent, touched off by Mount Pelée, killed hundreds. Ash fell as far away as Jamaica—two million tons on Barbados alone. Despite U.S. and European aid, St. Pierre never recovered: By 1970, it had recouped just a fifth of its former population. ◀**1900.M** ▶**1906.5**

IN THE UNITED STATES

America's first guerrilla engagement in Southeast Asia. Assessments of total Filipino casualties vary wildly—low estimates put them at 50,000, high at two million—but whatever the number, it was a slaughter. After declaring the war over, Roosevelt commended the Army for its "successful conclusion of hostilities." Many prominent citizens, however, were outraged. Inveighed William James, "God damn the U.S. for its vile conduct in the Philippine Isles." **◀1900.M ▶1903.2**

▶RAGTIME KING—Seven decades after the great ragtime composer Scott Joplin wrote The *Entertainer* (1902),

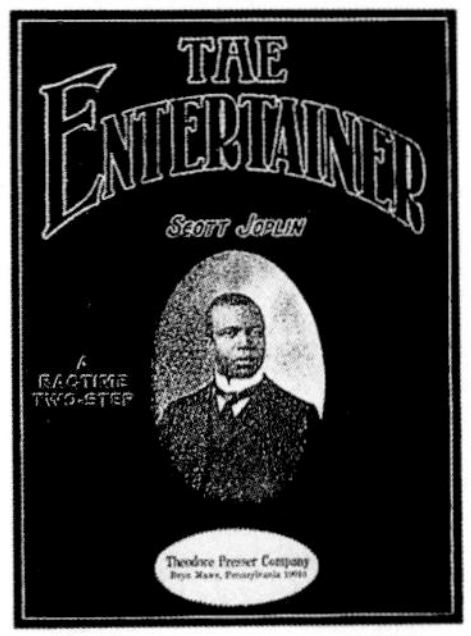

it became the theme song of a hit film, *The Sting*—sparking a vogue for Joplin's music that surpassed anything he'd known in his lifetime. His *Maple Leaf Rag* (1899) had made the syncopated rhythms of ragtime, a precursor to jazz, a national craze, but his attempts to win acceptance for his ragtime opera, *Treemonisha*, as a "serious" work flopped. Chronically frustrated, he died in 1917 in a New York mental hospital. **▶1917.5**

▶COMIC DUO—Buster Brown and his dog, Tige, hit *The New York Herald* in 1902. Cartoon-

ist R.F. Outcault (whose earlier comic strip, "The Yellow Kid," gave rise to the phrase "yellow journalism") created a winning combination of harmless mischief and sugarcoated moralizing that proved irresistible to millions of young readers across the country. **▶1907.13**

POLITICS & BUSINESS: GNP: $21.6 billion ... Newlands Reclamation Act authorizes large-scale federal irrigation in the West ... United Mine Workers begin 5-month strike (coal climbs from $5 to $30 a ton) ... Oliver Wendell Holmes appointed to Supreme Court ... Dow Jones begins publishing of daily closing prices of selected stocks ... Pepsi-Cola Co. founded ... J.C. Penney opens first store, in Wyoming.

"Steel True/Blade Straight/Arthur Conan Doyle/Knight/Patriot, Physician, & Man of Letters"—**Inscription on grave marker of Sir Arthur Conan Doyle**

AROUND THE WORLD

▶ART NOUVEAU—The decorative style called art nouveau was at its peak in 1902 when it was the subject of a major exhibition at Paris's Société Nationale des Beaux-Arts. The style's sinuous, undulating lines, evoking garden and forest, appeared in the buildings of Louis Sullivan, Victor Horta,

and Antonio Gaudí; the Paris Métro stations of Hector Guimard; the lamps of Louis Comfort Tiffany *(above)*; the jewelry of René Lalique; and the posters of Alphonse Mucha. ▶1925.M

▶HORMONES DISCOVERED—Studying how the stomach works, William Bayliss and Ernest Starling discovered a class of chemicals that act as messengers within the body. Disproving Ivan Pavlov's widely accepted theory that the nervous system alone rules digestion, the British researchers found that, even when stomach nerves were severed, the intestines' orders still reached the pancreas—through the bloodstream. They called the messenger molecule secretin, and coined the term "hormone" (from the Greek for "to excite") to denote such substances. ▶1904.9

▶VENEZUELA BLOCKADED—High-handed Venezuelan dictator General Cipriano Castro ignited the wrath of Britain, Germany, and Italy by refusing to pay Venezuela's debts and for the cost of property damages from the 1899 coup that placed him in power. The three countries moved boldly into the Western Hemisphere and seized the Venezuelan navy, blockaded the coast, and shelled the Fort of San Carlos for two months. Castro eventually capitulated, agreeing to a settlement of the allies' claims. ▶1903.2

MUSIC

Caruso on Disk

11 By 1902, Enrico Caruso had been popular in his native Italy for four years, but with his triumph earlier in the year at Monte Carlo, the tenor was faced for the first time with the prospect of an international career. Now he had contracts for appearances in London and New York—and he was apprehensive.

To the rescue came Fred Gaisberg, a British talent scout for one of the pioneering manufacturers of records and record players. "I lost my head," Gaisberg wrote after hearing Caruso perform in the premiere of Alberto Franchetti's *Germania* at Milan's La Scala. Backstage after the show he urged Caruso to record a few arias on gramophone disks. The singer's advisers cautioned him not to waste his talents on a mechanical toy, but Caruso liked the Briton's face. The following day, he was won over completely when Gaisberg assured him that the records could go on sale in London before his debut—an unprecedented publicity coup that gave the jittery virtuoso the opportunity to win over his listeners before facing them from the stage.

Gaisberg cabled his superiors that he had guaranteed Caruso £100; they wired back: FEE EXORBITANT. FORBID YOU TO RECORD. Ignoring the message, he set up a makeshift studio in a hotel room. Caruso breezed through ten arias in two hours, accompanied by a pianist perched on a packing crate. Gaisberg's gamble paid off: The records were a hit in London, making a profit of £15,000. The first top-quality, commercially successful gramophone disks ever cut, they helped speed the obsolescence of wax-cylinder records (based on Thomas Edison's invention). They also launched Caruso's 18-year run as a recording star and the most adulated, highly paid singer of his time. **▶1904.4**

A case of nerves brought about Caruso's first recording contract and gave the nascent recording industry a big boost.

LITERATURE

Doyle's Dodge

12 *The Hound of the Baskervilles,* published in 1902, was Arthur Conan Doyle's answer to a problem the author had brought on himself nine years earlier. As every Sherlock Holmes devotee knows, the inimitable detective met his maker—or appeared to—in a plunge over Switzerland's Reichenbach Falls in 1893's "The Adventure of the Final Problem." But by decade's end, Doyle had begun to believe he'd been too hasty in dispatching his hero. *The Hound of the Baskervilles* was his way of resurrecting him.

It was less a resolution, however, than a crafty dodge—Doyle set the story in the period preceding Holmes's death. The tale, which was spectacularly successful (when it was serialized in *The Strand* magazine, fans formed long lines to purchase the latest installment), concerned a ghostly hound who, according to legend, haunted the Baskerville moors. In the end, Doyle supplied a rational explanation: The creature was an ordinary dog whose mouth had been painted with phosphorus to give it an unearthly glow. (Later, after his son died in World War I, Doyle the good Victorian rationalist became a devoted spiritualist, forging an unusual friendship with Harry Houdini.)

In his next story, Doyle faced the dilemma of the dead detective more squarely. "The Adventure of the Empty House" explained that Holmes, after throwing archfiend Moriarty into the abyss, had only *appeared* to plunge over the falls. Rather than face retribution from Moriarty's men, he'd let the world believe he was dead. Far-fetched, yes, but fans were too delighted by their hero's return to care. **▶1926.11**

PHOTOGRAPHY

Shaking Up the Art Scene

13 "Photography is a fad well-nigh on its last legs, thanks largely to the bicycle craze," wrote Alfred Stieglitz in 1897. His pronouncement was a celebration, not a eulogy. He believed that, with its eclipse as a fad, photography could at last become an art. At the time, many painters scorned photography as mechanistic; many practitioners thought it involved nothing more than pointing the camera and shooting. Five years later, in 1902, Stieglitz, already an internationally recognized photographer, put his theory to the test, curating a show called "An Exhibition of American Photography arranged by the Photo-Secession."

Under the banner of the Photo-Secession—a somewhat mysterious term suggesting alternatives to conventional photography—a new class of photographers set out to shake up the staid American art scene. Aligning themselves with the painting vanguard in Europe, they crusaded on behalf of the new, in whatever medium. In order to show photographs alongside paintings—virtual apostasy at the time—the secessionists opened their own New York gallery in 1905 at 291 Fifth Avenue.

Alfred Stieglitz photographed New York's Flatiron Building in 1902, the year it was completed.

Over the years "291" introduced Europe's top painters to America's art-viewing public. Among the young artists who came, saw, and were influenced were Georgia O'Keeffe (who married Stieglitz in 1924) and Paul Strand, whose work helped validate photography as an art form. **◀1900.3 ▶1913.2**

NOBEL PRIZES: Peace: Elie Ducommun (Swiss; International Peace Bureau) and Charles A. Gobat (Swiss; Inter-Parliamentary Union) ... Literature: Theodor Mommsen (German; historian) ... Chemistry: Emil Fischer (German; sugar and purine synthesis) ... Medicine: Ronald Ross (U.K.; transmission of malaria) ... Physics: Hendrik Lorentz and Pieter Zeeman (Dutch; influence of magnetism on radiation).

A VOICE FROM 1902

A Story of Four Little Rabbits

From *The Tale of Peter Rabbit,* by Beatrix Potter, 1902

It started out as a letter to the young son of a former governess: "Dear Noel," the letter began, "I don't know what to write to you, so I shall tell you a story about four little rabbits, whose names were Flopsy, Mopsy, Cotton-tail, and Peter." It ended up becoming the bestselling children's book of all time. When Frederick Warne & Co. published The Tale of Peter Rabbit *in 1902, Beatrix Potter was 36 years old and still living under her parents' roof. The book was an instant commercial success, eventually enabling Potter, who aspired to be a scientist but was thwarted because of her sex, to establish a measure of independence.* Peter Rabbit *was quickly followed by such other classics as* Jemima Puddle-duck, The Tale of Tom Kitten, *and* The Roly-Poly Pudding. ▸**1926.6**

THE TALE OF
PETER RABBIT

BY

BEATRIX POTTER

FREDERICK WARNE

ONCE upon a time there were four little Rabbits, and their names were—
Flopsy,
Mopsy,
Cotton-tail,
and Peter.
They lived with their Mother in a sand-bank, underneath the root of a very big fir-tree.

8

9

'NOW, my dears,' said old Mrs. Rabbit one morning, 'you may go into the fields or down the lane, but don't go into Mr. McGregor's garden: your Father had an accident there; he was put in a pie by Mrs. McGregor.'

10

11

Potter, who exercised tight control over the marketing of her books, insisted that they have illustrations on every other page and that they be small enough for children to hold easily.

"Success. Four flights Thursday morning.... Inform press. Home Christmas."—**The Wrights' telegram to their father after the first flight at Kitty Hawk**

STORY OF THE YEAR

Wright Brothers Take to the Sky

1 On the morning of December 17, 1903, in the dunes near the village of Kitty Hawk, North Carolina, Orville and Wilbur Wright shook hands, said a witness, "like two folks parting who weren't sure they'd ever see each other again." Cold gusts blew as Orville strapped himself face down into a latticework of wood struts, wire, and cotton cloth. Beside him sputtered a tiny homemade engine. This fragile vessel, he hoped, would take him on a world-changing journey: the first controlled flight by a human in a motorized, heavier-than-air craft.

The Kitty Hawk craft, complete with a homemade engine, was the Wrights' third model.

Orville's outing, however, was brief and clumsy, a lunge into the sand. Each brother made another abortive try. And then, at noon, Wilbur managed to hold an altitude of 15 feet, skimming above the beach for over a tenth of a mile before crash-landing. The trip lasted 59 breathtaking seconds.

The Wright brothers had begun their quest in 1896 after reading of the death of German scientist Otto Lilienthal in a glider he'd designed. The brothers, who made their living manufacturing custom bicycles in Dayton, Ohio, found that as their engineering skills flourished, so did their long-held interest in human flight. After Lilienthal's crash, interest became obsession. The Wrights read every available aeronautical study, made experimental kites, corresponded with top scientists, watched birds. In 1900, they asked the U.S. Weather Bureau to recommend a site with moderate winds and enough space to test large gliders—and so began their yearly trip to Kitty Hawk. For three stormy autumns they risked death in unstable, motorless aircraft; back in Dayton, they refined their designs with the help of improvised wind tunnels and original physics formulas.

When the Wright brothers finally achieved powered flight, only a handful of newspapers carried the story. But as they repeated the miracle, they became celebrities. They made deals with governments and industrialists around the globe—as did competitors who pirated their technology. Within a dozen years, the air battles of World War I were raging; by 1939, airliners plied the Atlantic skies. Orville was still alive when an airplane dropped an atomic bomb. And within his nieces' and nephews' lifetimes (neither brother ever married), the first fliers reached the moon. ►**1909.V**

THE UNITED STATES

Roosevelt Secures Canal Zone

2 "A greater engineering feat than has yet been accomplished during the history of mankind" was how, in a 1903 speech, President Theodore Roosevelt described the canal he wanted built through the Isthmus of Panama. Roosevelt's grandiloquence aside, the canal was to be more than a monument to American ingenuity: It offered huge commercial and (especially) military benefits. The government had been convinced of the need for such a canal since the Spanish-American War of 1898, when a U.S. battleship bound for Cuba from the Philippines had taken 69 days to get around Cape Horn and up to its destination.

The Panama Canal was the centerpiece of Roosevelt's foreign policy. Accordingly, in 1904 he proposed an extension of the Monroe Doctrine of the United States' manifest destiny. The Roosevelt Corollary not only reiterated the Monroe Doctrine's prohibition of European intervention in Latin America, but it also proclaimed that the United States had "police power" over its Latin American neighbors and would therefore guarantee that they met their international obligations. Roosevelt's strategy—symbolized by the phrase "Speak softly and carry a big stick" (which he'd introduced in a foreign policy speech at the 1901 Minnesota State Fair)—made the United States into a major naval power.

In 1903, the Panamanian isthmus was an unhappy province of Colombia. Anti-Colombian sentiments had been brewing for 70 years, with Panamanian secessionists repeatedly rebelling and repeatedly being quashed. The United States had always willingly supported Colombia, but in 1903 Colombia refused to grant the United States the right to build a canal across Panama. "You could no more make an agreement with the Colombian rulers," Roosevelt decided, "than you could nail currant jelly to a wall." Instead of renegotiating, he sent warships to Panama, where the secessionists had already received tacit American approval to rebel. The uprising occurred on November 2; the next day, American sailors went ashore and prevented the Colombian army from suppressing the revolt. Panama had achieved autonomy, and the United States had gained a "vest pocket" republic in which to build its canal.

Roosevelt claimed a moral, and therefore legal, imperative for his unprecedented military action. It was undertaken, he said, not merely for the United States or the Panamanians, but "for the good of the entire civilized world." Attorney General Philander C. Knox acerbically replied, "Oh, Mr. President, do not let so great an achievement suffer from any taint of legality."

The new Republic of Panama's independence was predicated on American support—Panamanians understood that if the United States withdrew, Colombia would quickly reassert its domination. As a result, the Panama Canal treaty (called the Hay Bunau-Varilla Treaty), signed on November 18, 1903, granted the United States the power of a sovereign nation within the Canal Zone. ◄**1901.M** ►**1904.6**

Warships at his feet, a giant, cartoon Roosevelt dumps a shovelful of Panamanian soil on the capital of Colombia.

ART & CULTURE: Books: ***Lady Rose's Daughter*** **(Mrs. Humphry Ward);** ***Rebecca of Sunnybrook Farm*** **(Kate Douglas Wiggin);** ***The Riddle of the Sands*** **(Robert Erskine Childers) ... Music: "Sweet Adeline" (Armstrong and Gerard); "Gold and Silver" (Franz Lehár);** ***Sea Drift*** **(Frederick Delius);** ***Kindertotenlieder*** **(Gustav Mahler);** ***Hiawatha*** **(Samuel Coleridge Taylor);** ***Kossuth Symphony*** **(Béla Bartók) ...**

"Suffragettes believe that the horrible evils which are ravaging our civilization will never be removed until women get the vote."—**Emmeline Pankhurst**

Emmeline Pankhurst, restrained by police during a 1914 demonstration.

SOCIAL REFORM

Battle for Suffrage

3 In 1890, 13 years before Emmeline Pankhurst formed the often-violent organization that propelled her to worldwide notoriety, her husband, Richard, asked her a question she would remember the rest of her life: "Why don't you *force* us to give you the vote? Why don't you *scratch our eyes out*?" Although Pankhurst, a full-time mother of four small children, was already known in London feminist circles as the founder (with Richard) of a women's suffrage league and the hostess of a radical salon, it wasn't until 1903, 111 years after the publication of Mary Wollstonecraft's *Vindication of the Rights of Woman*, that she formed the Women's Social and Political Union—if not the most important suffragist organization in Britain, certainly the most notorious.

The WSPU grew out of Pankhurst's impatience with the male-dominated labor movement. Running on a left-wing ticket, she'd been elected a poor-law guardian in her native Manchester in 1894; after Richard died in 1898, she became a city registrar of births and deaths. These experiences deepened her sympathy for working-class women—and convinced her, and her eldest daughter, Christabel (like Emmeline an eloquent orator for socialism and feminism), that "working men are as unjust to women as are those of the other classes." With Christabel, Emmeline founded the WSPU to pressure trade unions and the Independent Labour Party (ILP) to back the vote for women.

That strategy soon changed drastically. Emmeline and Christabel came to believe that since voting rights in Britain were based on property ownership—40 percent of men were thus disenfranchised—women's suffrage most urgently concerned the moneyed classes. So the WSPU dropped its proletarian trappings and began recruiting society matrons to heckle Liberal candidates who failed to support women's rights—resulting in the spectacle of well-bred ladies being thrown screaming out of public halls. Once the Liberals took power, the Pankhursts (another daughter, Sylvia, had come aboard) escalated the attack: Their wealthy followers took to slashing telegraph wires and valuable paintings, burning empty houses and cricket grandstands. "Every man with a vote was considered to be a foe," wrote Christabel, "unless prepared actively to be a friend." ▸**1920.11**

FILM

The Great Western

4 With his 1903 film, *The Great Train Robbery*, Edwin S. Porter, a cameraman for Thomas Edison's production company, ushered in the age of the motion picture. In a single twelve-minute movie, Porter effectively launched three film traditions: editing, the chase scene, and the Western. Heretofore, most movies proceeded in real time, with one long shot recording an actual event. Porter's great innovation was to cut and splice footage in a way that removed the action from linear time, enhancing a story by creating drama and suspense.

The Great Train Robbery's running time was almost unprecedented. A cast of 40 acted out a simple, partially scripted plot: In a series of 14 scenes, some bandits break into a railway office, tie up the hapless operator, rob a train, then flee into the woods. Meanwhile, the operator's daughter shows up at the office and liberates her father. He organizes a posse that overtakes the villains in the woods. A gun battle ensues and justice is served when all the robbers are killed. In the film's most famous—and most unrelated—shot, a gun-toting outlaw looks directly into the camera and fires, seemingly right at the audience.

What was revolutionary about Porter's technique was the way he shifted scenes from the telegraph operator to the bandits, so that parallel stories developed simultaneously. Other directors, most notably Georges Méliès of France, had presented multiple scenes sequentially before. But their movies played like condensed versions of stage shows. *The Great Train Robbery* played like a movie. ▸**1915.1**

This scene from *The Great Train Robbery* caused viewers, who packed the theaters, to shriek in fear.

BIRTHS

Theodor Adorno, German philosopher.

Bruno Bettelheim, Austrian-U.S. psychologist.

Erskine Caldwell, U.S. novelist.

Countee Cullen, U.S. poet.

John Dillinger, U.S. bank robber.

Walker Evans, U.S. photographer.

Red Grange, U.S. football player.

Bob Hope, U.S. actor and comedian.

Konrad Lorenz, Austrian zoologist.

Clare Boothe Luce, U.S. writer and diplomat.

Vincente Minnelli, U.S. film director.

Anaïs Nin, French-U.S. writer.

Olaf V, Norwegian king.

George Orwell, U.K. writer.

Alan Paton, South African writer.

Mark Rothko, U.S. painter.

Georges Simenon, Belgian-French novelist.

Benjamin Spock, U.S. writer and pediatrician.

John Von Neumann, Hungarian-U.S. mathematician.

Evelyn Waugh, U.K. novelist.

Nathanael West, U.S. novelist.

DEATHS

Cassius M. Clay, U.S. abolitionist.

Richard Jordan Gatling, U.S. inventor.

Robert Gascoyne-Cecil, U.K. prime minister.

Paul Gauguin, French painter.

Josiah Gibbs, U.S. physicist.

Leo XIII, Roman Catholic pope.

Camille Pissarro, French painter.

Herbert Spencer, U.K. philosopher.

James Abbott McNeill Whistler, U.S. painter.

Hugo Wolf, Austrian composer.

Painting & Sculpture: ***Judith and Holofernes*** **(Gustav Klimt) ... Film:** ***Life of an American Fireman, Uncle Tom's Cabin,*** **and** ***The Gay Shoe Clerk*** **(Edwin S. Porter);** ***A Daring Daylight Burglary*** **... Theater:** ***Babes in Toyland*** **(Victor Herbert);** ***Man and Superman*** **(G.B. Shaw);** ***Glad of It*** **(Clyde Fitch);** ***Rose Bernd*** **(Gerhart Hauptmann).**

"Dust, the air of the room, and one's clothes, all become radioactive.... In the laboratory where we work the evil has reached an acute stage."—Marie Curie on the effects of radium in her laboratory

NEW IN 1903

Postage-franking meter.

License plate (first issued in Massachusetts).

Sanka decaffeinated coffee.

Complete opera recording (Leoncavallo's *Pagliacci*).

Tour de France bicycle race.

Ford Motor Company.

Steuben Glass Works.

Prix Goncourt (French literary prize).

New York Stock Exchange building.

IN THE UNITED STATES

▶**FIRST WORLD SERIES**—To the roar of record crowds, a squad of upstart American Leaguers from Boston defeated the established Pirates of Pittsburgh in baseball's first World Series. Still struggling in 1903 to break the older National League's stranglehold on organized baseball, the fledgling American League earned legitimacy with the Red Sox victory. Thereafter, baseball became the national pastime, and an October showdown between the two circuits an annual pageant. ▶1920.6

▶**IROQUOIS THEATER FIRE**—A performance by comedian Eddie Foy at Chicago's lavish Iroquois Theater ended in horror on December 30 when fire swept through the building. Some 600 patrons died in the worst single-building blaze in American history, most crushed to death rushing for the exits as Foy pleaded for calm. In the tragedy's aftermath, many U.S. cities adopted new public fire codes. ▶1911.M

ART

A Postimpressionist Master Dies in Polynesia

5 Twelve years before he died in 1903—decrepit at 55, half-mad, alone—Paul Gauguin had fled "rotten and corrupt Europe" for Polynesia, seeking "barbarism, which is to me rejuvenation." While the sensuous, dreamlike paintings he shipped back to France helped liberate a generation of artists, Gauguin found misery as well as freedom in paradise. But even as syphilis reduced him to a crippled, raving paranoiac, he continued to paint, and some of his finest works, like the magnificent *Where Do We Come From? What Are We? Where Are We Going? (above)*, date from this final, painful period. ▶1906.6

SCIENCE

A Nobel for the Curies

6 The 1903 Nobel Prize in physics was awarded to Marie and Pierre Curie and Antoine-Henri Becquerel. The research they'd begun six years earlier laid the groundwork for the nuclear age.

When X-rays were discovered in 1895, they came from an electric vacuum tube; nothing like them had been observed in nature. Then Becquerel found that uranium compounds produced the same kind of radiation—but the how and why remained a mystery. To Marie Curie, a student in Paris at the Sorbonne, those questions posed an irresistible challenge. In December 1897, she decided to write her doctoral thesis on "uranic rays." Her husband, Pierre (an accomplished but underpaid young scientist), found her free lab space: a chilly storeroom at the School of Physics and Industrial Chemistry, where he taught. Leaving her infant daughter with a nurse, she went to work.

The Curies in their lab; Pierre abandoned his study of crystals to aid in Marie's research.

Marie had started by measuring uranium's potency, using devices of Pierre and his brother Jacques's design. But her focus soon came to seem too narrow: other substances, she suspected, might emit similar rays. After testing every known element, she discovered that thorium behaved much like uranium. She coined the term "radioactivity" for the properties both elements shared. Next she began to analyze radioactive ores for their uranium and thorium content. To her surprise, some specimens turned out to be far "hotter" than her findings could explain. The difference could come only from a tiny quantity of some unknown, fabulously radioactive element.

Now Pierre joined his wife in the laboratory. Together they broke down tons of pitchblende, a uranium ore, until they'd isolated thimblefuls of two powerful new elements: polonium (named after Marie's native Poland, then under military occupation) and radium. Between 1899 and 1904, the Curies published 32 papers on both the physics of radioactivity and its physiological effects. They grew painfully intimate with the latter, through burns and radiation sickness, but their clinical self-observations formed the basis of nuclear medicine. "I love this radium," Becquerel once said to the couple after suffering a radiation burn himself, "but I've got a grudge against it!" **◂1900.M ▸1908.M**

MUSIC

Janáček Completes *Jenůfa*

7 Czech composer Leoš Janáček was a late bloomer. He was 49 in 1903 when he finished his first mature work, the opera *Jenůfa*. A powerful drama of jealousy and infanticide among the Moravian peasantry, its jagged rhythms and soaring melodies grew out of folk tradition as well as modernist daring.

The opera premiered in 1904 in the provincial capital of Brno, but Janáček remained an obscure music professor until 1916, when *Jenůfa* finally played in Prague, to wild success (his ardent nationalism dovetailed with the growing movement for Czechoslovakian independence). Two years later, in 1918—the year of independence—it was performed in Vienna, launching Janáček on an international career and, happily, a ten-year burst of creativity that ended only with his death. **◂1900.4 ▸1939.16**

SPORTS: Baseball: New York Giant Christy Mathewson wins 30 games with 267 strikeouts (record for 50 years) ... Boxing: Bob Fitzsimmons defeats George Gardner for light-heavyweight title (first fighter to win championship in three divisions) ... Horse Racing: Jamaica Race Track on Long Island, N.Y., opens.

"Future generations in all civilized countries will laugh at the cumbrous and illogical efforts their forefathers made to restrict the use of the automobile."—**The Honourable John Scott Montagu, M.P.**

POPULAR CULTURE

The Age of the Automobile

8 Although the automobile had its enthusiasts, to most people in 1903, it was a toy for the rich—and a noisy, vulgar, dangerous toy at that. Editorialists railed against the "terror-creating machine" that struck down children and sent horses bolting. Indeed, animals set speed limits in cities like Antwerp, Belgium, which prohibited motorcars from outrunning horse-drawn carriages. Cars were banned from whole cantons in Switzerland. In Austria, women drivers were verboten. But elsewhere, certain quiet events were paving the way for the Age of the Automobile.

In Britain, Parliament raised the speed limit from twelve to 20 miles per hour in 1903, balancing the demands of motoring enthusiasts (who opposed any limit) with those of farmers (who wanted autos outlawed). It was also the year the Express Motor Service Company of London rolled out the world's first gas-powered taxi: one among 11,400 horse-drawn cabs. By 1914, however, the number of equine-powered cabs on London's streets had dwindled to 1,400, and were outnumbered by their automotive counterparts five to one.

In America, 1903 was the year that Dr. H. Nelson Jackson and his chauffeur, Sewall K. Crocker, made the first transcontinental car trip. The pair drove from San Francisco to New York City in 63 days in their Winton tourer, undaunted by dirt trails and trackless deserts. That same summer, in Michigan, a farmer's son named Henry Ford founded a company that revolutionized not only the fledgling auto industry but *all* industry.

Ford, 40, had abandoned two earlier car-making ventures. This time, however, the self-taught engineer had an example to follow. Fellow Detroiter Ransom P. Olds was setting world production records (3,000 cars in 1903) with his small, low-priced Oldsmobile, which his workers assembled out of parts from nearby machine shops. With $28,000 backing from a local coal dealer, Ford began by emulating Olds; by 1907 his cars had outsold all others on the planet. The next year Ford introduced the simple, durable, inexpensive Model T, the first full-size car designed for the masses. And in 1913, to meet soaring demand, he implemented the first assembly line, unleashing productive forces only dreamed of in past centuries. **◂1901.M ▸1904.10**

Even the most technologically advanced early autos were helpless in the face of unpaved roads after a heavy rain.

LITERATURE

The Allure of the Primitive

9 Jack London's *The Call of the Wild*, set in the Klondike during the gold rush of 1897, follows the adventures of a sled dog named Buck, who, after his beloved master is killed, flees into the wild and ends up leading a pack of wolves. Synopsized, the book sounds like a boys' adventure novel. But when it was first published in 1903 it was judged a literary masterpiece. And though London's work has since passed in and out of critical fashion, the book remains a perennial bestseller, read by adults in more than 50 languages.

One of *Call*'s illustrations showed Buck, the canine protagonist, unleashing "his 140 pounds of fury."

When *Call* appeared, London, 27, had already published two novels, as well as dozens of short stories. Drawing on his own colorful life—from the age of 14, he held jobs as various as waterfront pirate, Alaskan gold miner, and socialist orator—London wrote terse, forceful outdoor tales that a reading public sated with sentimental romances found irresistible. But in *Call*, London was aiming for something more profound.

With near-mystical intensity and lyricism, *The Call of the Wild* expressed the often terrifying allure of the "primitive" in a supposedly civilized world. Readers were electrified, and London was immediately thrust into an unaccustomed position of celebrity. He died only 13 years later of an overdose of morphine prescribed to counter kidney pain brought on by alcoholism, but by then this indefatigable writer (he wrote 15 hours a day) had composed 200 short stories, 400 articles, and 50-odd books of fiction and nonfiction. **▸1926.2**

IN THE UNITED STATES

▶HARLEY HITS THE ROAD—In Milwaukee, Wisconsin, draftsman William Harley and the brothers Arthur, Walter, and William Davidson joined forces to build a new kind of motorbike. Low, loud, and gasoline-powered, the first Harley-Davidson rolled off the

line in 1903. Quickly becoming the country's most popular motorcycle, the Harley "hog" provided a lasting symbol of the wide-open American road.

▶POWER OF THE PEN—*McClure's* magazine began in 1903 to publish a series of articles that exposed corruption and greed in big business and politics, and the powerlessness of the common people—jolting the consciences of middle-class citizens in the process. Dubbed the "muckrakers" by President Theodore Roosevelt (after a character in *Pilgrim's Progress* who was so busy raking filth that he forgot to look at the stars), such journalists as Lincoln Steffens, Ida Tarbell, Ray Stannard Baker, and Upton Sinclair redefined the mission of the press and planted the seeds of modern investigative journalism. **▸1906.11**

▶A CHOCOLATE FACTORY—Promising chocolate for the masses, confectioner Milton Snavely Hershey laid the cornerstone of a new factory at

Derry Church, Pennsylvania, in 1903. Soon redubbed Hershey, the company town quickly came to dominate world production of milk chocolate—a sweet that Hershey, by making it inexpensive, helped popularize around the globe.

POLITICS & BUSINESS: GNP: $22.9 billion ... Elkins Act makes rebates on railroad freight rates illegal ... Departments of Commerce and Labor created ... U.S. Supreme Court *(Champion v. Ames)* upholds the right of Congress to prohibit interstate mailing of lottery tickets, expanding federal police powers ... Pelican Island off Florida is first federal wildlife refuge.

"Religious persecution is more sinful and more fatuous even than war. War is sometimes necessary, honorable, and just; religious persecution is never defensible."—**U.S. Secretary of State John Hay in a letter to Czar Nicholas II**

AROUND THE WORLD

▶BUTLER'S LAST LAUGH—Published posthumously in 1903, Samuel Butler's satirical novel *The Way of All Flesh* heralded an eruption of anti-Victorian sentiment in the arts and literature. A ruthless dissection of middle-class British family life, Christianity, and general prissiness of spirit, the book provoked a maelstrom of debate. Butler, in death, was recognized as a bellwether of his times. ▸1918.4

▶SPACE MAN—Inspired by the science fiction of Jules Verne, Russian aeronautic theorist Konstantin Tsiolkovsky applied his wide-ranging mind to space travel, publishing in 1903 *The Exploration of Cosmic Space by Means of Reaction Devices.* Stunningly insightful, the work posited liquid fuel as the only means to power rockets in

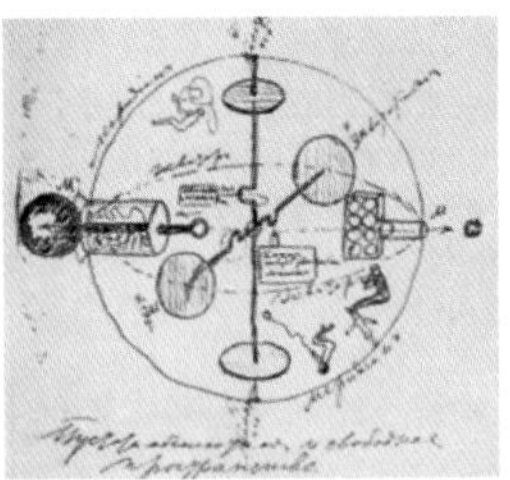

space and foresaw the necessity of multistage rocket design. Tsiolkovsky's prescient theories were borne out by modern developments in rocketry. ▸1914.3

▶MEASURING HEARTBEATS—Invented in 1903 by Dutch physiologist Willem Einthoven, the electrocardiogram unlocked the secrets of the human heart. By measuring and recording the natural electrical pulse of heartbeats, Einthoven's clinical instrument allowed physicians to observe cardiac irregularity and diagnose heart disease. Now a basic tool in cardiac care, the EKG won Einthoven the 1924 Nobel Prize for physiology and medicine. ▸1910.M

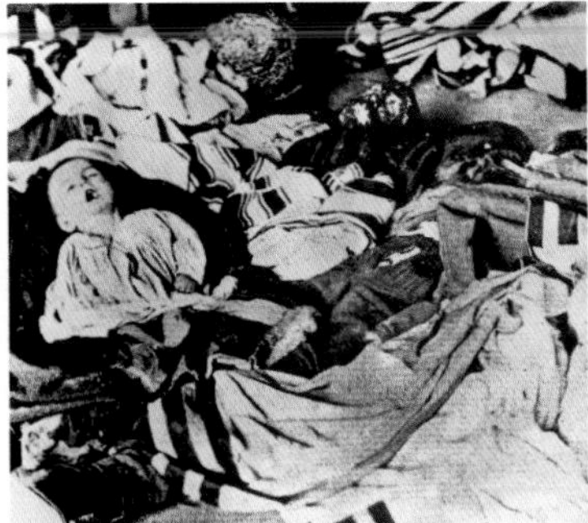

The corpse of a baby lies amid the smashed skulls of adult victims of the 1903 Kishinev pogrom.

RUSSIA

Pogrom in Kishinev

10 Beginning on Easter Sunday 1903, a barbarous mob in the Moldavian city of Kishinev ran amok for two days, murdering Jewish residents and plundering their homes and businesses. The pogrom was incited by the government-supported, anti-Semitic screed sheet *Bessarabetz*, which, in a classic instance of "blood libel," had recently published a series of articles that accused Jews of practicing ritual murder. Police and militia stood by as rioters killed 45 Jews, injured some 600 more, and ransacked 1,500 Jewish homes.

Anti-Semitism had been on the rise in Russia long before the slaughter. Using blatantly discriminatory policies (which, among other things, prevented Jews from owning land), the government brutally attempted to divert workers' frustration by insinuating that Jews were somehow responsible for social inequities. Indeed, many Jews in Kishinev were convinced the violence was organized by the state—a belief that the government's inaction during the attacks did nothing to controvert.

When news of the Kishinev atrocity reached the rest of the world, the international community uniformly denounced Russia. Nevertheless, Russian pogroms occurred regularly from 1903 to 1906, inducing an early twentieth-century wave of Jewish emigration to the United States and Palestine. **▸1904.M**

RUSSIA

Russian Socialists Split

11 The second party congress of the Russian Social Democratic Labor Party, held in Brussels and London in 1903, gave V.I. Lenin a chance to reiterate the position he had asserted relentlessly in *Iskra* (*The Spark*), the journal in which RSDLP activists formulated the ideology that would culminate in the Russian Revolution. Aiming to silence the moderates within the party, Lenin wanted to use the conference to consolidate his power.

Mere wage and hour reforms simply would not suffice, he announced. Anything less than revolution was an unconscionable acquiescence to the czarists. Therefore, the Socialists would have to work alone, isolated from other political parties. Party organization should be centralized, with membership limited to those versed in Marxist doctrine. Lenin also proposed that he be given editorial control of *Iskra.*

Unexpectedly, Lenin was opposed on all three points by L. Martov, his ally, friend, and fellow editor. Martov wanted a less rigidly centralized party, open to organized labor as a whole. He believed Socialists could cooperate with the Liberals to improve conditions in Russia, and he strongly disapproved of Lenin's designs on *Iskra*.

Lenin's views prevailed by a narrow margin. His side dubbed themselves the Bolsheviks, "the majority," reserving the deprecatory name Mensheviks, "the minority," for Martov and his supporters. The party was irreparably split, setting the stage for all that followed. Also destroyed was the friendship of Lenin and Martov, who remained ideologically unreconciled to the end. Still, Lenin retained some personal affection for his former partner, who continued to work against him after the Bolsheviks took power. In 1924, when Lenin suffered a mortal stroke, one of his last remarks was, "They say Martov is dying, too." **◂1902.2 ▸1905.2**

Lenin and Martov together in St. Petersburg before their ideological rift.

LITERATURE

Henry James's Gem

12 Henry James called *The Ambassadors* "frankly, quite the best, 'all round,' of my productions." When the novel came out in 1903, James was at the height of his narrative powers, an internationally recognized master of English prose style. While his detractors point out that his dauntingly verbose novels contain little real action, James nonetheless achieved in his work a near perfection of formal structure. This, along with his unrivaled skill at psychological portraits, makes him one of the most emulated of all modern novelists.

Portrait of a gentleman: Henry James by John Singer Sargent.

The Ambassadors represents the apotheosis of the Jamesian subject matter: the clash of Old and New World values, of liberty and morality, decadence and industry. James dramatized these themes through the story of Lambert Strether, a pragmatic, middle-aged New Englander who travels to Paris and finds himself succumbing to the city's gaiety and sensuality. Forced to reconsider all his comfortable moral convictions, Strether advises his fiancée's errant son to "live all you can; it's a mistake not to."

James understood the struggle. Born to one of America's most prominent families, he spent virtually his entire adult life abroad. He found American culture stultifying, but Continental Europe just as unpalatable. "I saw that I should be an eternal outsider," he said after an abortive attempt to live in France. In England, James found a happy compromise, residing there more or less permanently after 1876, and finally becoming a British subject in 1915. **◂1902.7 ▸1920.9**

NOBEL PRIZES: Peace: William Cremer (U.K.; International Arbitration League) ... Literature: Björnstjerne Björnson (Norwegian; poet) ... Chemistry: Svante Arrhenius (Swedish; electrolytic dissociation) ... Medicine: Niels Finsen (Danish; light therapy for skin disease) ... Physics: Henri Becquerel and Pierre and Marie Curie (French; radioactivity).

A VOICE FROM 1903

Within and Without the Veil of Color

From *The Souls of Black Folk*, by W.E.B. Du Bois, 1903

William Edward Burghardt Du Bois was the most influential African-American leader of the first half of the twentieth century. A sociologist and the first African-American to receive a doctorate from Harvard University, Du Bois believed that knowledge had to be combined with activism if black people were to be truly equal in American culture. He led the dissent against Booker T. Washington's policy of accommodation and was instrumental in the formation of the National Association for the Advancement of Colored People (NAACP). In The Souls of Black Folk, *Du Bois described the personal and public conflict of being both black and American: "One ever feels his twoness—an American, a Negro; two souls, two thoughts, two unreconciled strivings; two warring ideals in one dark body, whose dogged strength alone keeps it from being torn asunder." In 1961, just two years before his death (at age 95), Du Bois joined the Communist Party and moved to Ghana. Soon thereafter he renounced his American citizenship.* ◂**1901.V** ▸**1905.M**

From the double life every Negro must live, as a Negro and as an American, as swept on by the current of the nineteenth while yet struggling in the eddies of the fifteenth century—from this must arise a painful self-consciousness, an almost morbid sense of personality and a moral hesitancy which is fatal to self-confidence. The worlds within and without the Veil of Color are changing, and changing rapidly, but not at the same rate, not in the same way; and this must produce a peculiar wrenching of the soul, a peculiar sense of doubt and bewilderment. Such a double life, with double thoughts, double duties, and double social classes, must give rise to double words and double ideals, and tempt the mind to pretense or to revolt, to hypocrisy or to radicalism....

To-day the young Negro of the South who would succeed cannot be frank and outspoken, honest and self-assertive, but rather he is daily tempted to be silent and wary, politic and sly; he must flatter and be pleasant, endure petty insults with a smile, shut his eyes to wrong; in too many cases he sees positive personal advantage in deception and lying. His real thoughts, his real aspirations, must be guarded in whispers; he must not criticise, he must not complain. Patience, humility, and adroitness must, in these growing black youth, replace impulse, manliness, and courage. With this sacrifice there is an economic opening, and perhaps peace and some prosperity. Without this there is riot, migration, or crime. Nor is this situation peculiar to the Southern United States—is it not rather the only method by which undeveloped races have gained the right to share modern culture? The price of culture is a Lie.

On the other hand, in the North the tendency is to emphasize the radicalism of the Negro. Driven from his birthright in the South by a situation at which every fibre of his more outspoken and assertive nature revolts, he finds himself in a land where he can scarcely earn a decent living amid the harsh competition and the color discrimination. At the same time, through schools and periodicals, discussions and lectures, he is intellectually quickened and awakened. The soul, long pent up and dwarfed, suddenly expands in new-found freedom. What wonder that every tendency is to excess—radical complaint, radical remedies, bitter denunciation, or angry silence....

Between the two extreme types of ethical attitude which I have thus sought to make clear wavers the mass of the millions of Negroes, North and South; and their religious life and activity partake of this social conflict within their ranks. Their churches are differentiating—now into groups of cold, fashionable devotees, in no way distinguishable from similar white groups save in color of skin; now into large social and business institutions catering to the desire for information and amusement of their members, warily avoiding unpleasant questions both within and without the black world, and preaching in effect if not in word: *Dum vivimus, vivamus.*

But back of this still broods silently the deep religious feeling of the real Negro heart, the stirring, unguided might of powerful human souls who have lost the guiding star of the past and are seeking in the great night a new religious ideal. Some day the Awakening will come, when the pent-up vigor of ten million souls shall sweep irresistibly toward the Goal, out of the Valley of the Shadow of Death, where all that makes life worth living—Liberty, Justice, and Right—is marked "For White People Only."

Throughout a long life of activism, W.E.B. Du Bois became more and more radical in championing the cause of black people worldwide.

"Victory or defeat depend on this battle. You will do your utmost."—**Message flashed by signal flag to Japanese fleet before it attacked Port Arthur**

STORY OF THE YEAR

Russo-Japanese War Begins

1 Czar Nicholas II "did not wish it"—"it" being war between Russia and Japan; therefore, "it" would not happen. Nicholas clung to this conviction despite the hostile Japanese response to Russia's military occupation of China's eastern province of Manchuria, and despite the Japanese fear that Russia was poised to move into Korea, a country Japan considered vital to its own national security. In February 1904 Nicholas suffered a rude awakening. Japanese forces attacked the strategic, Russian-controlled city of Port Arthur, at the tip of the Liaotung Peninsula, west of Korea in southern Manchuria, and the Russo-Japanese War was launched. Introducing the first large-scale use of automatic weapons, the war was one of the largest armed conflicts the world had ever seen.

The report of the capture of Port Arthur, as depicted in a Japanese print.

Russia had expanded eastward throughout the nineteenth century, opening a window on the Pacific. This expansion offended and threatened Japan, an emerging nation that felt its own imperial designs were being trampled by the czar and his army. The world watched the hostilities escalate and speculated as to which side was bluffing. Japan was a small country, relatively unknown to the West. Russia was a great European power. When war erupted, as everyone save the Czar fully anticipated it would, Russia was expected to rout the Island Kingdom. "Japan is not a country that can give an ultimatum to Russia," wrote one Russian military official, expressing a common sentiment.

Once the fighting began, however, Japan emerged as the more effective combatant. It staged a surprise attack on the Russian naval fleet in the Pacific, then laid siege to Port Arthur. (Nicholas promptly dispatched the Baltic fleet as a replacement, with disastrous consequences.) The Japanese army invaded Korea and crossed the Yalu River into Manchuria, its soldiers singing as they advanced: "Now is the hour—for we are marching. Down with Russia! On, Japan!" Despite being overmatched and losing on all fronts, Czar Nicholas refused to back down. At stake were the glory and honor of Russia, which Nicholas knew God would defend. Battles might be lost, but the war was Russia's to win. Consequently, he reacted slowly to Japanese advances. "A soft haze of mysticism refracts everything he beholds and magnifies his own functions and person," explained a Russian minister to a colleague baffled by the Czar's inadequate response. By the end of the year, when Nicholas finally awoke to martial realities, Japan had already all but won the war. **◂1902.8 ▸1905.3**

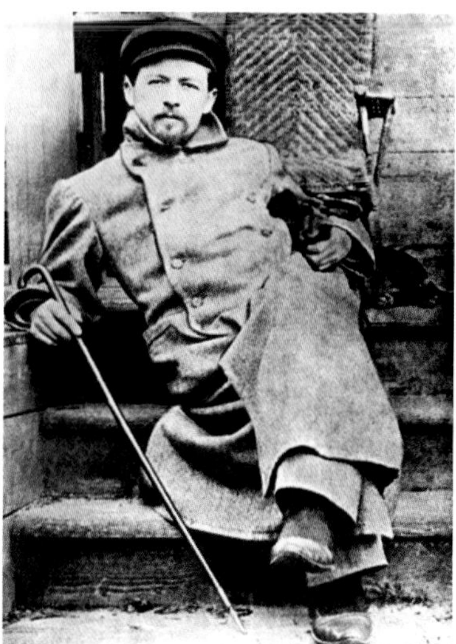
Playwright and humanist Anton Chekhov.

LITERATURE

Shakespeare's Second

2 Shortly after midnight on July 2, 1904, Anton Chekhov awakened his wife, the actress Olga Knipper, and asked her to summon a doctor. The Russian playwright and short-story writer was at a spa in Germany's Black Forest, where he was seeking relief for his worsening tuberculosis. When Chekhov failed to respond to a camphor injection, the doctor prepared to send for oxygen. "Everything's useless now," said the playwright, remaining calm. "I'll be a corpse before it gets here." The doctor ordered champagne instead. Accepting a glass, Chekhov smiled at Olga and said, "It's a long time since I've had champagne." They were among his last words. He was 44 years old and at the height of a career as a dramatist generally conceded to be second only to Shakespeare in the pantheon of world literature.

Trained as a doctor, Chekhov began writing humorous magazine sketches while still in medical school in Moscow, using his earnings to support his bankrupt family back home in Taganrog, a provincial village in Crimea. After receiving his degree, Chekhov continued to write, but considered medicine his primary vocation. His first play, *The Seagull* (1876), was a failure. Two years later the director Konstantin Stanislavsky revived it at his fledgling Moscow Art Theatre, this time to critical and popular acclaim. The company went on to produce Chekhov's masterpieces, *Uncle Vanya*, *The Three Sisters*, and *The Cherry Orchard*, replacing the conventions and artifices of the nineteenth-century stage with simple, lyrical but unflinching realism.

In his writing, Chekhov valued honesty above all else. "The good thing about art," he said, "is that it does not allow you to lie." Empathetic, profoundly humane studies of common human suffering and boredom, his plays and stories present characters who, caught up in a web of failure, dream of a brighter future. Chekhov's spare, balanced prose and themes of frustration and battered dignity exerted a far-reaching influence on later writers as diverse as Ernest Hemingway and Luigi Pirandello. The deeply humble Chekhov would have been astonished at his impact. "I'll be read for seven years, possibly seven and a half," he once told a friend, "then I'll be forgotten." **▸1926.10**

SOCIAL REFORM

A Landmark Graduation

3 "I had a joyous certainty that deafness and blindness were not an essential part of my existence, since they were not in any way a part of my immortal mind," wrote Helen Keller after her graduation from Radcliffe College in 1904. The event was a watershed in the life of a woman who, through her writing on behalf of women's suffrage, socialism, and the rights of the handicapped, became an international symbol of what anarchist Emma Goldman appreciatively called "the almost illimitable power of the human will."

Even before graduation, Sullivan *(right)* and Keller had collaborated on Keller's 1902 autobiography.

Even so, the logistics of college were almost impossibly difficult for Keller, who had lost her hearing and sight after a childhood bout with scarlet fever. Annie Sullivan, the teacher who had broken through Keller's childhood isolation

ART & CULTURE: **Books:** ***Cabbages and Kings*** **(O. Henry);** ***The Golden Bowl*** **(Henry James);** ***The Psychopathology of Everyday Life*** **(Sigmund Freud);** ***Nostromo*** **(Joseph Conrad);** ***The Late Mattia Pascal*** **(Luigi Pirandello);** ***The History of the Standard Oil Company*** **(Ida M.Tarbell) ... Music: "Meet Me in St. Louis, Louis" (Mills and Sterling);** ***Domestic Symphony*** **(Richard Strauss) ... Painting & Sculpture:**

"In the wonderland of Mind I should be free as another."—**Helen Keller**

by showing her that the water she felt on her hand had a name, accompanied Keller to every class. She spelled out the lectures into Keller's hand, and helped her with reading. If a text had not been translated into Braille, as was often the case, Sullivan read it to Keller by touch. In this painstaking way Keller mastered not only English literature, history, and math, but also French, Latin, and Greek, languages unfamiliar to Sullivan.

The process was exhausting, but at the age of 24, 17 years after learning her first word—indeed, learning that there was such a thing as a word—Helen Keller graduated *cum laude*. Her only disappointment was that Annie Sullivan's central role went largely unappreciated—a wrong righted, at least in part, by William Gibson's 1960 play *The Miracle Worker*. ►**1931.M**

MUSIC

Madama Butterfly Flops

4 By 1904, his compatriots already regarded Giacomo Puccini as the successor to the revered Giuseppe Verdi. Puccini's *Manon Lescaut*, *La Bohème*, and *Tosca* had won him public adulation and made him rich. But success could mean trouble in the cutthroat world of Italian opera—as Puccini discovered the night his *Madama Butterfly* premiered at Milan's famed La Scala theater.

The disruptions began with the opening curtain. Each time a passage recalled Puccini's earlier work, occupants of the cheap seats cried, "*Bohème*! Again *Bohème*!" The first act was drowned out by a rising chorus of jeers, and when the composer, who was recovering from an auto accident, limped onstage at intermission, the hisses only grew louder. The onslaught escalated right up to the opera's tragic climax, when loud laughter punctuated the onstage suicide that ends this drama of a Japanese maiden and her faithless American lover. The next day, the critics were merciless: "A diabetic opera," pronounced one, mocking both the sweetness of the music and the gourmandizing maestro's struggle with the disease. "It bored," declared another.

Some Puccini partisans have claimed the heckling was organized by three rival composers, and indeed Milan was seething with professional antagonism. Yet the work *was* flawed: Act Two, for instance, was an interminable 80 minutes long. The composer (usually a great worrier) had ignored warnings, convinced that this was "the best opera I have ever written." But after the La Scala show closed, he began furiously rewriting, to good effect: His revised, much-improved *Madama Butterfly* is now one of the best-loved operas in the world, a standard in the repertoire of companies from Omaha to Osaka. ◄**1901.2** ►**1913.5**

In this scene from *Madama Butterfly*, the naval officer Pinkerton—Butterfly's lover—brings his American wife to Japan.

DIPLOMACY

The Entente Cordiale

5 Months of wary bargaining between those ancient adversaries France and Britain finally bore fruit in 1904 with the signing of the Entente Cordiale (literally, "cordial understanding")—not quite an alliance, but enough to shift significantly the global balance of power. The two countries had compelling reasons to come together. Britain, the world's top power, was losing ground. The grinding Boer War had strained the empire's resources and confidence; meanwhile, Russia, Japan, the United States, France, and especially Germany were building navies that challenged Britannia as ruler of the waves. The French, in turn, hoped to dissuade the British from blocking their colonial ambitions in Africa. They also wanted to avoid being drawn into hostilities between their ally Russia and British-backed Japan.

The entente covered matters as prosaic as fishing rights off Newfoundland, but its most important clauses addressed long-standing disputes over two North African countries. France's policy of "peaceful penetration" of Morocco (amounting to a gradual takeover) distressed Britain, whose ships had to pass through the Strait of Gibraltar to reach the Mediterranean. Britain's occupation of Egypt (once a part of Napoleon's empire) galled the French. The entente declared those issues closed: Thereafter, neither nation would obstruct the action of the other in those regions.

Besides ironing out certain matters of policy, the agreement had another, more subtle virtue—it demonstrated that the two countries could work together after all. Egypt and Morocco had no say-so in determining their fates. Neither did expansion-minded Germany, which viewed the newfound coziness between France and Britain with alarm.

Kaiser Wilhelm II soon tried to test the entente by presenting himself as the protector of Moroccan independence. The result, ironically, was Germany's further isolation and a deepening of Anglo-French understanding. The sides were already forming for World War I. ◄**1902.8** ►**1906.9**

France and Britain decided to split up the continent that had come between them.

BIRTHS

George Balanchine, Russian-U.S. choreographer.

William "Count" Basie, U.S. musician.

Cecil Beaton, U.K. photographer.

Ralph Bunche, U.S. diplomat.

Bing Crosby, U.S. singer.

Salvador Dali, Spanish artist.

Willem de Kooning, Dutch-U.S. painter.

Deng Xiaoping, Chinese revolutionary and political leader.

Arshile Gorky, U.S. painter.

Cary Grant, U.K.-U.S. actor.

Graham Greene, U.K. writer.

Moss Hart, U.S. playwright.

Coleman Hawkins, U.S. musician.

Reinhard Heydrich, German Nazi official.

Vladimir Horowitz, Russian-U.S. pianist.

Christopher Isherwood, U.K. writer.

George F. Kennan, U.S. diplomat.

Alexei N. Kosygin, U.S.S.R. statesman.

Peter Lorre, Hungarian-U.S. actor.

Glenn Miller, U.S. bandleader.

Pablo Neruda, Chilean poet.

J. Robert Oppenheimer, U.S. physicist.

S.J. Perelman, U.S. humorist.

Lal Bahadur Shastri, Indian prime minister.

Isaac Bashevis Singer, Polish-U.S. writer.

B.F. Skinner, U.S. psychologist.

Johnny Weissmuller, U.S. swimmer and actor.

DEATHS

Anton Chekhov, Russian writer.

Kate Chopin, U.S. writer.

Antonín Dvořák, Czech composer.

Henri Fantin-Latour, French painter.

Theodor Herzl, Austrian founder of Zionism.

Isabella II, Spanish queen.

Paul Kruger, South African statesman.

Henry Morton Stanley, U.K.-U.S. explorer.

Mont-Ste-Victoire **(Paul Cézanne);** ***General Sherman Memorial*** **(Augustus Saint-Gaudens) ... Film:** ***The Escaped Lunatic*** **(Wallace McCutcheon and Frank Marion);** ***Personal*** **(Wallace McCutcheon);** ***The Ex-Convict*** **(Edwin S. Porter)... Theater:** ***The Cherry Orchard*** **(Anton Chekhov);** ***The Daughter of Jorio*** **(Gabriele D'Annunzio);** ***Riders to the Sea*** **(J.M. Synge).**

"I felt his clothes might not contain him ... He was so steamed up, so ready to go, to attack anything, anywhere."
—Muckraking journalist Ida Tarbell on Theodore Roosevelt

NEW IN 1904

Times Square (had been Long Acre Square until *The New York Times* moved to Broadway and 42nd Street).

Double-sided gramophone disks.

Metal-encased vacuum flask (Thermos).

Novocain (procaine).

Campbell's Pork and Beans.

Tea bags.

National Ski Association (Ishpeming, Michigan).

IN THE UNITED STATES

▶NYC SUBWAY—Clean and bright, with gleaming new cars, the first section of New York City's subway opened in

1904. Running from the Brooklyn Bridge uptown to Broadway at 145th Street, the line attracted more than a half million curious riders in its first days of operation. The world's first electric underground railway had opened in London in 1890; the New York system became the world's largest.

▶INNOVATION ON BROADWAY —George M. Cohan's *Little Johnny Jones* burst onto Broadway in 1904, brimming with a rambunctious, peculiarly American energy that immediately distinguished it from the delicate British imports that dominated the musical stage of the day. Featuring the hit tunes "Give My Regards to Broadway" and "The Yankee Doodle Boy," Cohan's musical strove to integrate songs, dances, and story line—an endeavor that would reach full maturity 39 years later with Rodgers and Hammerstein's *Oklahoma!* **▶1917.V**

THE UNITED STATES

The Rise of Roosevelt

6 The agrarian radical William Jennings Bryan had twice failed to lead the Democrats to victory, so in 1904 the party chose a bland centrist, Judge Alton Parker, as its presidential candidate. The strategy flopped: Parker's opponent won by the biggest landslide in three decades. Elected at last to the office he'd inherited three years earlier, Theodore Roosevelt could tell his wife, "I am no longer a political accident."

But Roosevelt's rise to leadership owed little to accident and almost everything to wiliness, will, and nerve—the same qualities that had allowed this once-sickly heir of rich Manhattanites to mold himself into a celebrated outdoorsman and soldier. His decision to enter politics, a profession held in contempt by most members of his class, showed this same boldness of character. At only 23, he became a progressive New York State legislator with a skill for courting the press. In 1884 his first wife died, and he retreated briefly to his Dakota ranch, but he was soon back in the fray, bursting onto the Washington scene as a brash, reform-minded civil service administrator. After an interlude as New York City's police commissioner, during which he publicly toured the slums to spotlight crime, corruption, and his own politics, he was back in Washington as McKinley's assistant secretary of the Navy. A noisy advocate of the Spanish-American War, Roosevelt quit his post to lead a cavalry unit called the Rough Riders. "I don't want to be in office during war," he explained. "I want to be at the front." His swashbuckling deeds in Cuba made him a national hero and led to his election as New York's governor in 1898.

Roosevelt's ambition and charisma irritated the Republican Party bosses, who viewed him as an untamed cowboy. They gladly sent him off to what they assumed would be near oblivion as McKinley's running mate in 1900. But an assassin's bullet soon delivered Roosevelt from political limbo. He seized the reins of the presidency with characteristic gusto, but his predecessor's shadow lingered. It wasn't until he was elected in his own right that the larger-than-life Roosevelt finally made the office his own. **◂1903.2 ▸1905.3**

Roosevelt in 1904: a confident heavyweight ready to take on any challenger.

THEATER

Shaw Triumphs in London

7 George Bernard Shaw didn't finish a presentable play until he was 35, and he labored for another dozen years before scoring his first theatrical hit in 1904 with *John Bull's Other Island*. By that time the self-educated Irishman was already famous as a tireless socialist stump speaker and an awesomely prolific writer, and he continued to churn out plays, criticism, and essays on topics ranging from feminism and vegetarianism, which he supported, to war and vivisection, which he opposed, until his death at age 94. But his early plays were seldom produced. Shaw's ingeniously iconoclastic scripts made producers skittish and censors censorious.

John Bull grew out of W.B. Yeats's request that the London-based Shaw write something for Dublin's Abbey Theatre. But when the Abbey's directors backed out, objecting to the play's irreverent view of Ireland, the prestigious Royal Court Theatre in London—run by two Shaw protégés—came to the rescue. And to the surprise of detractors who'd called Shaw's work overly cerebral, *John Bull* was a box-office triumph—even King Edward attended a performance. Over the next three years, the Court staged eleven plays by Shaw, including several neglected works from the 1890s. All proved wildly popular.

What made Shavian drama revolutionary—especially such masterpieces as *Man and Superman* (1903) and *Major Barbara* (1905)—was its mix of intellectual rigor, high moral seriousness, social relevance, formal experimentation, and biting humor.

As a critic, Shaw derided the glib farces and sentimental melodramas of the day, championing Henrik Ibsen's "theater of ideas." But Ibsen was dark, heavy, and growing dated. Shaw, with his operatic sense of drama (his mother was a singing teacher) and his orator's gift for the spoken word, created a theater of ideas for the new century—and he made it funny. **◂1900.8 ▸1905.6**

SPORTS: Baseball: World Series called off by John McGraw; Cy Young pitches perfect game; height of pitcher's mound limited to 15" above the plate ... Olympics held in St. Louis (basketball is a demonstration sport) ... Hockey: International Pro Hockey League established; six-man teams introduced ... Soccer: Federation of International Football Associations founded (establishes universal rules).

"When I dissect and destroy a living animal, I hear within myself a bitter reproach that with rough and blundering hand I am crushing an incomparable artistic mechanism."—Ivan Pavlov

TECHNOLOGY

Triumphant Tubes

8 When John Ambrose Fleming fashioned the Fleming thermionic valve (or diode) in 1904, Morse code was regularly beamed across the Atlantic, but radio transmission of sound remained impossible. The Briton's invention—the first radio vacuum tube—proved essential in shattering that barrier. His breakthrough stemmed from Thomas Edison's discovery that current in a light bulb would jump a gap between a hot, negatively charged filament and a cold, positively charged electrode called a "plate." Fleming found that when the plate took the form of a metal cylinder surrounding the filament, alternating current could be "rectified" (converted into unidirectional current) and picked up by a telephone receiver.

The diode enabled U.S. physicist Reginald A. Fessenden to make the first sound broadcast on December 24, 1906, transmitting music from the Massachusetts coast. Instead of the short bursts required for Morse transmission, he generated a continuous signal whose amplitude (the height of the radio waves) varied with the irregularities of sound waves. This type of signal, characterized by amplitude modulation, came to be known as AM.

Also in 1906, another American, Lee De Forest, invented the triode—a more advanced tube—containing a third electrode that could boost or decrease the intensity of the signal, an effect known as "amplification." Among their many uses (including in television and public-address systems), triode vacuum tubes made long-range sound broadcasts possible, allowing radio to become a worldwide source of news and entertainment within two decades. **◂1901.1 ▸1907.M**

The diode broke radio's "sound barrier."

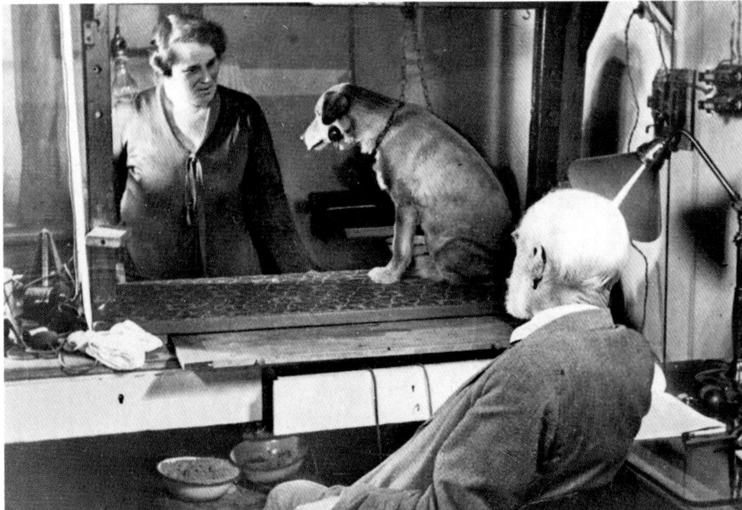

Pavlov, here in 1934, never missed his appointments with his laboratory dogs.

SCIENCE

Pavlov Wins Nobel

9 When he won the 1904 Nobel, Ivan Pavlov had barely begun the behavioral experiments that made "Pavlovian" a household word. (Dogs taught to associate food with, say, a ringing bell would then salivate whenever they heard the bell—a learned response that the Russian physiologist called a "conditional reflex.") Rather, the Nobel committee was recognizing his years of research on digestive glands, which he'd begun in 1890.

Others exploring that field had experimented on live dogs, making a surgical pouch to observe the stomach—an operation that required the severing of nerves. Since Pavlov believed the nervous system regulated digestion, such crude (and ultimately deadly) cutting would compromise his experiments. He set up the world's first specialized operating theater for animals, and devised the "Pavlov pouch," which allowed observation but left the nerves—and the dogs' physical health—intact. He also found ways to gather saliva and siphon it through the jaw, and to make anything swallowed fall out through a hole in the neck. These methods, still in use, enabled Pavlov to monitor the digestive "chemical factory" from mouth to belly. He found that the *taste* of food triggered the production of stomach and pancreatic juices, and that the composition of saliva varied according to the substance ingested. His discoveries proved that the nervous system does, indeed, largely control digestion—and, until 1902, it looked as if ruled alone. Then William Bayliss and Ernest Starling discovered that hormones set off some digestive functions without the nerves' involvement. Pavlov's attachment to his doctrine of "nervism" was so strong that he feuded with Bayliss and Starling for years. Eventually, each side accepted the partial correctness of the other's view. In the meantime, Pavlov discovered another use for his saliva-measuring device: the study of animal—and by extension, human—behavior. **◂1902.M ▸1948.7**

BUSINESS AND INDUSTRY

Luxury On Wheels

10 While most of the world's automakers in 1904 were concentrating on ways to make cars available to the masses, there was also a small countermovement afoot to create the ultimate luxury vehicle. That year, the high-spirited British motorist and aviator Charles S. Rolls—the first pilot to make a nonstop round-trip across the English Channel—met Henry Royce, an electrical engineer and experimental carmaker, and began collaborating on a high-quality car. Within two years they had founded Rolls-Royce Ltd. and introduced the Silver Ghost model, which quickly acquired the reputation of "the best car in the world." American automobile makers were likewise tapping into this new market, unveiling in 1904 the elegant Pierce Arrow. **◂1903.8 ▸1908.1**

"Spirit of Ecstasy"—the Rolls-Royce hood ornament, designed by Charles Sykes.

IN THE UNITED STATES

▸ST. LOUIS EXPO—Opening a year behind schedule (it was supposed to commemorate the centennial of the 1803 Louisiana Purchase), the 1904 St. Louis World's Fair became a de facto celebration of life in a new era. Apart from some egregious lapses (like the so-called Anthropology Days of the Olympic Games, which featured an African pygmy, an American Indian, and an Ainu from Japan competing in unlikely athletic events), on the whole the fair did justice to its themes of education and know-how. Among the highlights: a motorcar display and the popular debut of hamburgers, iced tea, and ice-cream cones. ◂1900.9 ▸1915.M

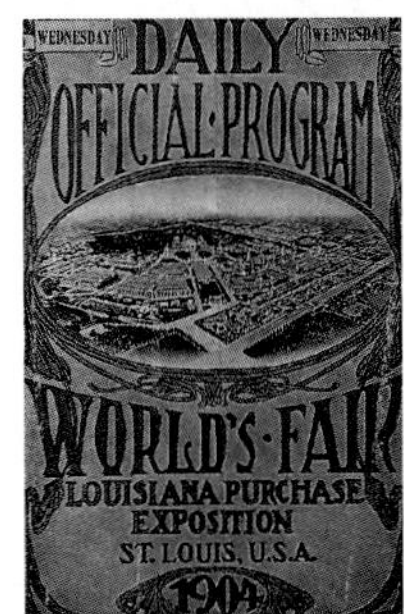

▸CHILD LABOR LOBBY—Railing against the worst excesses of the Industrial Revolution, reformers in 1904 founded the National Child Labor Committee. The first national organization of its kind in the U.S., the NCLC lobbied to get children out of coal mines, factories, and sweatshops, where, unprotected by legislation, they routinely worked more than 60 hours a week. ▸1905.V

▸TRUST-BUSTING—Promising a "square deal" for the workingman, Teddy Roosevelt took on American big business. His first target, J.P. Morgan's mammoth Northern Securities railroad holding company, was ordered broken up by the Supreme Court in 1904. Greeted with wild applause in the street and much consternation in the boardroom, the decision sealed Roosevelt's reputation as a trustbuster. ◂1904.6

POLITICS & BUSINESS: GNP: $22.9 billion ... President Roosevelt is elected to a full term, defeating Judge Alton B. Parker ... Supreme Court rules in favor of the antitrust dissolution of Northern Securities ... Jersey Standard controls 85% of domestic oil trade, 90% of oil exports ... Andrew Carnegie establishes a $5,000,000 hero fund for rescuers.

"I made Peter by rubbing the five of you violently together, as savages with two sticks produce a flame. That is all he is, the spark I got from you."—J.M. Barrie, author of *Peter Pan*, to the Davies family

AROUND THE WORLD

▶SECRETS OF THE SACRED—Abandoned to the jungle, the wells and pyramids and ball court of the ancient Mayan city of Chichén Itzá remained largely undisturbed for half a millennium. Although excavations had begun in the late-nineteenth century, an expedition led by amateur archaeologist and U.S. consul to Mexico Edward Thompson, in 1904, uncovered the most remarkable finds to date. His search, which centered on the Sacred Well, a prominent Mayan religious site, turned up the tools, jewelry, and golden ornaments (many illegally spirited back to the U.S.) of an advanced civilization. ◂1900.6 ▸1911.4

▶REFORM-MINDED STUDY—Britain's Interdepartmental Committee on Physical Deterioration issued a 1904 report detailing the abhorrent conditions in the country's slums. Besides decrying the high rate of infant mortality and the decline in breast-feeding (not only did poor mothers have to work, but many could not lactate because of poor nutrition or chronic illness), the report revealed that a third of the children studied were hungry—a statistic that induced the Liberal government to pass a bill two years later providing meals for poor children. ▸1905.V

▶ZIONIST PIONEER—Theodor Herzl died in 1904 at 44, seven years after founding the World Zionist Organization. Covering the Dreyfus affair in the 1890s, the Austrian journalist had lost his faith that his fellow Jews could eliminate anti-Semitism through cultural assimilation. Herzl went on to convert millions to his vision of a resurrected Jewish nation, and to negotiate with Turkey and Britain for a suitable site. His writings spurred emigration to Palestine—but, unlike most of his followers, he was willing to accept Britain's offer of a piece of Uganda. ▸1917.10

THEATER

A Fantasy of Eternal Youth

11 "I have written a play for children," wrote J.M. Barrie to the American actress Maude Adams in 1904. "I should like you to be the boy and the girl and most of the children and the pirate captain." The play was *Peter Pan*, the ultimate fantasy of eternal youth. A year later, Adams opened in the title role in New York and thoroughly appropriated the character. For the next 20 years the sprightly, vivacious actress made *Peter Pan* a career, starring in countless revivals before a cumulative audience of more than two million.

Adams inspired the stage role, but Barrie's inspiration for the story itself was five little boys in London: George, Jack, Peter, Nicholas, and Michael Davies. *Peter Pan* grew out of stories Barrie concocted to amuse the children. He turned the group's private daydreams into a play, he once wrote to the adult brothers, only when he felt he was losing his grip on them as children. Against his desires, the boys were growing up—though in some ways *Peter Pan* stunted their development. They became celebrities, the progress of their lives recorded in the British tabloids: "PETER PAN MARRIES," "PETER PAN JOINS THE ARMY." Peter Davies, who became a highly regarded publisher, called the play "that terrible masterpiece." In a tragic footnote to the story, in 1960, at the age of 63, Davies leaped in front of a London Underground train. "THE BOY WHO NEVER GREW UP IS DEAD," screamed the headlines. **◂1902.V ▸1926.6**

"It seemed made for her and she for it," said a critic of Adams's role in *Peter Pan.*

Working on the railroad—the Trans-Siberian was 13 years in the making.

RUSSIA

The Trans-Siberian Finished

12 It took 13 years and $250 million, but the far-flung Russian Empire was finally spanned by rail in 1904. Sergei Witte, the Russian minister of finance who had directed the construction of the 5,500-mile-long Trans-Siberian Railroad, called it "one of the greatest enterprises of the century in the entire world." The line stretched from the Ural Mountains in European Russia, across desolate Siberia, and through Manchuria to Vladivostok, on the Sea of Japan. "I devoted myself body and soul to the task," said a proud Witte. Critics said he had done a first-class job building a third-class railroad.

The tracks were poorly designed, built on the cheap with inferior materials, and prone to collapse. "After a spring rain," one traveler reported, "the trains run off the tracks like squirrels." In fact, in September, when the final leg of the Trans-Siberian, around the treacherous southern end of Lake Baikal, was at last in place, the test train derailed ten times.

Even so, the Ministry of Finance declared the line a success. Russia could wait no longer: It desperately needed the railroad to shunt soldiers and supplies across the continent to Manchuria, where the Russo-Japanese War was in full swing.

Ironically, the railroad itself was a major cause of the war. Because of the difficulty of the terrain in eastern Siberia, the builders of the Trans-Siberian, with the permission of the Chinese government, had taken a shortcut to the coast through Manchuria. When the Boxer rebellion erupted, Russia deployed thousands of troops to Manchuria to protect its property. Japan, which had designs of its own on the region, strenuously objected. Seven months before the last stake was driven, war broke out. **◂1904.1 ▸1905.3**

IDEAS

Ethics and Capitalism

13 With the 1904 publication of "The Protestant Ethic and the Spirit of Capitalism," Max Weber launched a debate that has continued to divide some of the century's greatest thinkers. The central focus of Weber's essay was the relationship between religious values and other social behavior, especially economic. Pitting himself against the prevalent Marxism of the day, Weber rejected the idea that economics alone—or, indeed, any single factor—determines social conduct. Instead, he argued, ideas, especially religion, often shape economic institutions. Comparing Europe, China, and India, he attempted to identify the "degree of favorableness" for capitalism in each country. He concluded that Calvinism, by conferring moral value and dignity on hard work, was a driving force behind the growth of capitalism.

Weber, who was trained as a lawyer and economist, refined many of the ideas in "The Protestant Ethic" in his later studies of modern bureaucracy. Recognized as one of the most influential social thinkers of the century and as a founder of sociology (with Emile Durkheim), he strove to develop a cross-cultural, value-free methodology of abstract models, or "ideal types," for analyzing social institutions. **◂1902.7 ▸1928.12**

NOBEL PRIZES: Peace: Institute of International Law (France) ... Literature: Frédéric Mistral (French; poet) and José Echegaray (Spanish; playwright) ... Chemistry: William Ramsay (U.K.; inert gases) ... Medicine: Ivan Pavlov (Russian; physiology of digestion) ... Physics: John Strutt and Lord Rayleigh (U.K.; gas density and argon).

A VOICE FROM 1904

Wishing Upon a Book

From the Montgomery Ward Catalogue, 1904

Montgomery Ward's motto, "Suppliers for Every Trade and Calling on Earth," was not so immodest, considering that in 1904, the world's first mail-order house distributed over three million of its four-pound catalogues for free (previously they sold for 15 cents each). Founded in 1872 by Aaron Montgomery Ward, the Chicago-based company freed pre-mall, rural Americans from their dependence on the local general store and provided them with a full Saturday night's entertainment. The catalogue showcased furnishings and fashion, farm equipment and guns, toys and pets—all sold with a money-back guarantee. A few years later, the catalogue of Sears, Roebuck, & Co. (founded in 1893) surpassed Montgomery Ward's as the number-one "Wish Book" in the United States. ▸**1905.M**

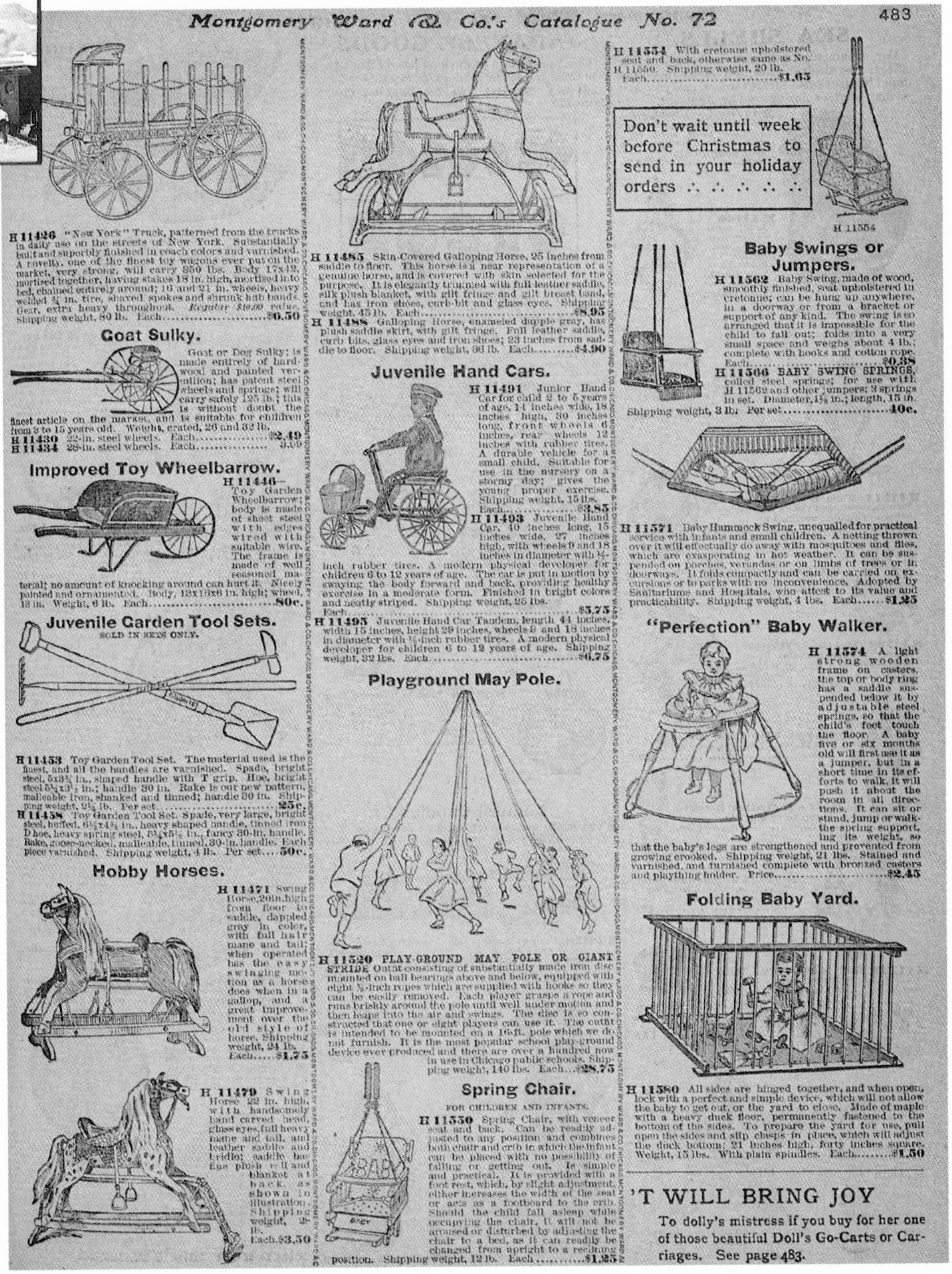

Montgomery Ward & Co.'s Catalogue No. 72 483

H 11426 "New York" Truck, patterned from the trucks in daily use on the streets of New York. Substantially built and superbly finished in coach colors and varnished. A novelty, one of the finest toy wagons ever put on the market, very strong, will carry 850 lbs. Body 17x42, mortised together, having stakes 18 in. high, mortised into bed, chained entirely around; 16 and 21 in. wheels, heavy welded ¼ in. tire, shaved spokes and shrunk hub bands. Gear, extra heavy throughout. *Regular $10.00 value.* Shipping weight, 80 lb. Each........**$6.50**

Goat Sulky.

Goat or Dog Sulky; is made entirely of hard-wood and painted vermilion; has patent steel wheels and springs; will carry safely 125 lb.; this is without doubt the finest article on the market, and is suitable for children from 3 to 15 years old. Weight, crated, 26 and 32 lb.

H 11430 22-in. steel wheels. Each........**$2.49**
H 11434 28-in. steel wheels. Each........3.99

Improved Toy Wheelbarrow.

H 11446—Toy Garden Wheelbarrow; body is made of sheet steel with edges wired with suitable wire. The frame is made of well seasoned material; no amount of knocking around can hurt it. Nicely painted and ornamented. Body, 13x16x6 in. high; wheel, 13 in. Weight, 6 lb. Each........**80c.**

Juvenile Garden Tool Sets.

SOLD IN SETS ONLY.

H 11453 Toy Garden Tool Set. The material used is the finest, and all the handles are varnished. Spade, bright steel, 5x3¾ in., shaped handle with T grip. Hoe, bright steel 5½x3½ in.; handle 30 in. Rake is our new pattern, malleable iron, shanked and tinned; handle 30 in. Shipping weight, 2½ lb. Per set........**25c.**

H 11458 Toy Garden Tool Set. Spade, very large, bright steel, buffed, 6½x4½ in., heavy shaped handle, tinned iron D hoe, heavy spring steel, 5¼x5½ in., fancy 30-in. handle. Rake, goose-necked, malleable, tinned, 30-in. handle. Each piece varnished. Shipping weight, 4 lb. Per set....**50c.**

Hobby Horses.

H 11471 Swing Horse, 20 in. high from floor to saddle, dappled gray in color, with full hair mane and tail; when operated has the easy swinging motion as a horse does when in a gallop, and a great improvement over the old style of horse. Shipping weight, 24 lb. Each.....**$1.75**

H 11479 Swing Horse 22 in. high, with handsomely hand carved head, glass eyes, full heavy mane and tail, and leather saddle and bridle; saddle has fine plush [illegible] and blanket at back, as shown in illustration. Shipping weight, [illegible] lb. Each.$3.50

H 11485 Skin-Covered Galloping Horse, 25 inches from saddle to floor. This horse is a near representation of a genuine horse, and is covered with skin selected for the purpose. It is elegantly trimmed with full leather saddle, silk plush blanket, with gilt fringe and gilt breast band, and has iron shoes, curb-bit and glass eyes. Shipping weight, 45 lb. Each........**$8.95**

H 11488 Galloping Horse, enameled dapple gray, has plush saddle skirt, with gilt fringe. Full leather saddle, curb bits, glass eyes and iron shoes; 23 inches from saddle to floor. Shipping weight, 36 lb. Each........**$4.90**

Juvenile Hand Cars.

H 11491 Junior Hand Car for child 2 to 5 years of age, 14 inches wide, 18 inches high, 30 inches long, front wheels 6 inches, rear wheels 12 inches with rubber tires. A durable vehicle for a small child. Suitable for use in the nursery on a stormy day; gives the young proper exercise. Shipping weight, 15 lbs. Each........**$3.85**

H 11493 Juvenile Hand Car, 40 inches long, 15 inches wide, 27 inches high, with wheels 9 and 18 inches in diameter with ½-inch rubber tires. A modern physical developer for children 6 to 12 years of age. The car is put in motion by swaying the body forward and back, providing healthy exercise in a moderate form. Finished in bright colors and neatly striped. Shipping weight, 25 lbs. Each........**$5.75**

H 11495 Juvenile Hand Car Tandem, length 44 inches, width 15 inches, height 29 inches, wheels 9 and 18 inches in diameter with ½-inch rubber tires. A modern physical developer for children 6 to 12 years of age. Shipping weight, 32 lbs. Each........**$6.75**

Playground May Pole.

H 11520 PLAY-GROUND MAY POLE OR GIANT STRIDE Outfit consisting of substantially made iron disc mounted on ball bearings above and below, equipped with eight ½-inch ropes which are supplied with hooks so they can be easily removed. Each player grasps a rope and runs briskly around the pole until well under motion and then leaps into the air and swings. The disc is so constructed that one or eight players can use it. The outfit is intended to be mounted on a 16-ft. pole which we do not furnish. It is the most popular school play-ground device ever produced and there are over a hundred now in use in Chicago public schools. Shipping weight, 140 lbs. Each...**$28.75**

Spring Chair.

FOR CHILDREN AND INFANTS.

H 11550 Spring Chair, with veneer seat and back. Can be readily adjusted to any position and combines both chair and crib in which the infant can be placed with no possibility of falling or getting out. Is simple and practical. It is provided with a foot rest, which, by slight adjustment, either increases the width of the seat or acts as a footboard to the crib. Should the child fall asleep while occupying the chair, it will not be aroused or disturbed by adjusting the chair to a bed, as it can readily be changed from upright to a reclining position. Shipping weight, 12 lb. Each........**$1.25**

H 11554 With cretonne upholstered seat and back, otherwise same as No. H 11550. Shipping weight, 20 lb. Each........**$1.65**

Don't wait until week before Christmas to send in your holiday orders ∴ ∴ ∴ ∴ ∴

H 11554

Baby Swings or Jumpers.

H 11562 Baby Swing, made of wood, smoothly finished, seat upholstered in cretonne; can be hung up anywhere, in a doorway or from a bracket or support of any kind. The swing is so arranged that it is impossible for the child to fall out; folds into a very small space and weighs about 4 lb.; complete with hooks and cotton rope. Each........**$0.38**

H 11566 BABY SWING SPRINGS, coiled steel springs; for use with H 11562 and other jumpers; 3 springs in set. Diameter, 1⅛ in.; length, 15 in. Shipping weight, 3 lb. Per set........**40c.**

H 11571 Baby Hammock Swing, unequalled for practical service with infants and small children. A netting thrown over it will effectually do away with mosquitoes and flies, which are exasperating in hot weather. It can be suspended on porches, verandas or on limbs of trees or in doorways. It folds compactly and can be carried on excursions or to parks with no inconvenience. Adopted by Sanitariums and Hospitals, who attest to its value and practicability. Shipping weight, 4 lbs. Each......**$1.25**

"Perfection" Baby Walker.

H 11574 A light strong wooden frame on casters, the top or body ring has a saddle suspended below it by adjustable steel springs, so that the child's feet touch the floor. A baby five or six months old will first use it as a jumper, but in a short time in its efforts to walk, it will push it about the room in all directions. It can sit or stand, jump or walk—the spring supporting its weight, so that the baby's legs are strengthened and prevented from growing crooked. Shipping weight, 21 lbs. Stained and varnished, and furnished complete with bronzed casters and plaything holder. Price........**$2.45**

Folding Baby Yard.

H 11580 All sides are hinged together, and when open, lock with a perfect and simple device, which will not allow the baby to get out, or the yard to close. Made of maple with a heavy duck floor, permanently fastened to the bottom of the sides. To prepare the yard for use, pull open the sides and slip clasps in place, which will adjust the duck bottom; 21 inches high, forty inches square. Weight, 15 lbs. With plain spindles. Each........**$1.50**

'T WILL BRING JOY

To dolly's mistress if you buy for her one of those beautiful Doll's Go-Carts or Carriages. See page 483.

Montgomery Ward's giant Chicago headquarters was pictured on the cover of the company's 1904 catalogue. Inside, the merchandise for children ranged from a garden-tool set (25¢) to a "goat sulky" (large size, $3.99) to a playground Maypole ($28.75).

"The most incomprehensible thing about the world is that it is comprehensible."—**Albert Einstein**

STORY OF THE YEAR

Einstein's Special Theory of Relativity

1 In a flurry of activity unlike any seen before or since in the history of science, an unknown, 26-year-old German-born patent examiner in the national patent office in Bern, Switzerland, published three papers in the German scientific journal *Annalen der Physik* that are among the world's most important achievements in theoretical physics—more than enough to secure their author's greatness if he had never written another word. Within a few years, the brightest scientific thinkers of the age were hailing him as a new Copernicus. During his lifetime he became universally recognized as the foremost thinker of the century. His very name, Albert Einstein, became synonymous with genius.

Einstein's special theory led to history's most famous equation: $E = mc^2$.

The 1905 papers were written in an unusual, highly literate style, containing little mathematics and few references to scientific precedents. The logic was natural and complete. It was as if the author had been shown the inner workings of the universe and recorded what he had seen.

In one of the three papers, Einstein explained Brownian motion—the random movement of particles suspended in fluid. He correctly attributed the movements to the collisions between the component molecules of the particles and the fluid. Before this explanation, many scientists still doubted the atomic structure of the universe; afterward, no one could.

A second paper, which earned Einstein the 1921 Nobel for physics, dealt with the photoelectric effect—how light is radiated. Confirming a hypothesis advanced five years earlier by Max Planck, Einstein demonstrated that light is emitted and absorbed in "quanta," small bursts, rather than continuous waves. This work became the basis for modern quantum theory.

The third paper introduced the special theory of relativity. Einstein showed that space and time, formerly believed to be absolutes, are relative; only the speed of light is constant, independent of the observer. Einstein postulated that as an object's velocity approaches the speed of light, its length shortens, its mass increases, and time slows. At the speed of light an object would have a length of zero, an infinite mass, and time would cease to exist. This impossibility led Einstein to conclude that, therefore, nothing can move equal to or faster than the speed of light. The special theory of relativity toppled the assumptions of two centuries of Newtonian physics. With it, Einstein integrated space and time and created a new, four-dimensional geometry of the universe. **◂1900.13 ▸1911.3**

RUSSIA

The First Revolution

2 Bloody Sunday, January 9, 1905, marked the beginning of the end for a man who'd never wanted to rule Russia in the first place. Under the leadership of Georgy Gapon, a radical priest, 300,000 workers marched on the Winter Palace in St. Petersburg to deliver a petition to Czar Nicholas II. The workers demanded wage increases, an eight-hour day, universal suffrage, and a constituent assembly. "If you do not order and do not respond to our pleas," the petition concluded, "we shall die on this square before your palace."

For Nicholas, the confrontation was a living nightmare. "What am I going to do?" he had written in his diary on the occasion of his father's death in 1894. "I am not prepared to be a czar." Once on the throne, however, he vowed to "maintain the basis of autocracy with the same firmness as did my unforgettable father." Rejecting the petition, Nicholas deployed his troops to intercept the marchers, who carried portraits of the Czar and placards pleading, "Soldiers! Do Not Shoot at the People." The troops ordered the marchers to disperse. Neither side gave ground, and the soldiers opened fire. By the end of the day more than 100 protesters were dead and hundreds more wounded. With this act, the "Little Father," Czar Nicholas, forfeited the loyalty of his people.

Immortalized here in painting and later on film: mutiny on the battleship *Potemkin*.

The events of Bloody Sunday stunned Russia and the world. Lenin and other revolutionaries seized upon the event, using it to rally workers. Cities all over Russia were crippled by massive strikes. Universities erupted in dissent. The peasants rioted and burned estates, acts they ironically called "illuminations." In June, sailors on the battleship *Potemkin,* in a mutiny immortalized 20 years later by the great Russian filmmaker Sergei Eisenstein, killed their captain and ran up the red flag of revolution. The citizens of the port city of Odessa showed their solidarity by staging a general strike. On October 8, as Russia reeled from its disastrous loss in the Russo-Japanese War, the railway workers' party paralyzed the country with a strike, which soon became general. Nicholas was forced to make concessions.

On October 17, he agreed to convene a parliamentary body, the Duma, with legislative and advisory powers. He also granted freedom of speech, assembly, and association to the Russian people, and guaranteed the enfranchisement of every class. With this "October Manifesto" Nicholas II, the reluctant but steadfast Czar, sealed the fate of his Romanov dynasty. **◂1903.11 ▸1906.4**

DIPLOMACY

Russia Loses to Japan

3 "They are all heroes, and have done more than could be expected of them," Czar Nicholas wrote in his diary in January 1905 after the Russian-controlled Manchurian city of Port Arthur fell to the Japanese. "Therefore it must be God's will." The defeat spelled the end for Russia, but Nicholas remained blindly optimistic. As late as August, when ministers of the two warring nations convened in Portsmouth, New Hampshire, to work out a peace, the Czar had not fully accepted the fact that Japan had supplanted Russia as the dominant power in the Far East.

Contrary to Nicholas's belief, the fall of Port Arthur represented neither Russian heroism nor divine intercession. When the city surrendered, after an eleven-month siege, some 30,000 well-armed Russian soldiers were still inside the garri-

ART & CULTURE: Books: ***The House of Mirth*** **(Edith Wharton);** ***Where Angels Fear to Tread*** **(E.M. Forster);** ***The Clansman*** **(Thomas Dixon);** ***Songs of Life and Hope*** **(Rubén Darío);** ***The Book of Hours*** **(Rainer Maria Rilke) ... Music: "Wait till the Sun Shines, Nellie" (Von Tilzer and Sterling); "In My Merry Oldsmobile" (Edwards and Bryan);** ***Salomé*** **(Richard Strauss);** ***La Mer*** **(Claude Debussy) ...**

"To witness the spectacle was to receive the impression that one had actually been present at the metamorphosis of a serpent taking a woman's form."—**A spectator commenting on Mata Hari's performance**

Peace broker Teddy Roosevelt hoped to balance the power in the East between Russia and Japan. Roosevelt's diplomacy won him the 1906 Nobel Peace Prize.

son. *The Times* of London reported that "no more discreditable surrender has been recorded in history."

More humiliating still was the defeat of the Baltic fleet, the most vaunted branch of the Russian navy. It had arrived in the Far East in early 1905, bearing the hopes of the empire, only to be annihilated by the Japanese, led by Vice Admiral Togo, in May. It achieved a single victory—against an armada of British fishing trawlers that it mistook for Japanese torpedo boats.

The sinking of the Baltic fleet so far from home finally turned public sentiment in Russia against the war. A crushing defeat, it came after Russia had already lost its Pacific fleet, the vital city of Port Arthur, and, in the Battle of Mukden just two months earlier, the largest land engagement of the war. There, in southern Manchuria, some 300,000 Russian troops confronted a like-sized Japanese army across a 90-mile-long front. After two weeks of intense fighting, the Japanese took Mukden in March. The victory exhausted the Japanese army, but Russia, overextended on land and soon to be deprived of its navy, was too weak to capitalize on the opportunity. Peace was now possible.

The Treaty of Portsmouth, which ended the Russo-Japanese War, was brokered by Teddy Roosevelt. Signed in September 1905, the treaty granted Japan its three principal demands: lease of the Manchurian city of Port Arthur on the same terms enjoyed by Russia before the war; cession back to China of the Manchurian territory not covered by the lease, with Japan gaining valuable railway concessions; and total influence, amounting to a protectorate, over Korea. Russian expansion was thwarted; Japan was ascendant. "In the palace there began a festival prayer on the occasion of the conclusion of the peace," Nicholas confided to his diary. "I must confess that I did not feel in a joyful mood." ◂1904.1 ▸1910.1

ESPIONAGE

Mata Hari Debuts in Paris

4 The library of the Musée Guimet, a respected repository of Asiatic art, was fixed up as an Indian temple for Mata Hari's 1905 debut. Clad in a diaphanous sarong, jeweled breast cups, and several filmy shawls, the "Hindu dancer" (as she was billed) swayed from the shadows and began to writhe before a statue of Shiva, Hindu god of destruction. As her sacred passion mounted, her shawls floated off one by one. Then someone snuffed out the candles. It took a moment for the audience—lords and ladies, industrialists, lions of art and literature—to see that she was naked. When the lights came back on, she was draped in a sari and bowing to wild applause. Jaded Parisians had seen nothing like her; even the scholars in the crowd were too dazzled to cry fraud.

Fraud she was, but an extremely successful one—profiting from a vogue for everything "Oriental" that was sweeping the Continent. Soon Mata Hari was playing the foremost music halls of the European capitals. She ended her solo shows with her life story: She was born, she said, on the Malabar coast to a temple dancer who died in childbirth, and raised by priests of Shiva to follow in her mother's footsteps. Her name meant "eye of the day"—Malay for dawn.

This last was true, but little else. Her real name was Margaretha Zelle MacLeod. The daughter of an Amsterdam milliner who'd gone broke, she spent five years in Java, where she enjoyed mimicking Javanese dancers. After her Scottish-born husband left her (taking their daughter), she went to Paris and worked as an artist's model. With the help of an aristocratic lover, she soon discovered a more lucrative livelihood. Few knew her true identity—not even her scores of socially prominent paramours—until a dozen years later, when she was executed as a German spy. Mata Hari, French authorities claimed, bore responsibility for 50,000 deaths. ▸1917.M

Mata Hari (née Margaretha Zelle), exotic dancer and German spy.

BIRTHS

Elias Canetti, Bulgarian-U.K. writer.

Christian Dior, French fashion designer.

Dorothy Fields, U.S. lyricist.

Henry Fonda, U.S. actor.

Greta Garbo, Swedish-U.S. actress.

Wladyslaw Gomulka, Polish communist leader.

Dag Hammarskjöld, Swedish diplomat.

Lillian Hellman, U.S. playwright.

Earl "Fatha" Hines, U.S. musician.

Felix Houphouët-Boigny, Ivory Coast president.

Howard Hughes, U.S. aviator and industrialist.

Kathleen Kenyon, U.K. archaeologist.

Arthur Koestler, Hungarian-U.S. writer.

René Lacoste, French tennis player.

Serge Lifar, Russian-French choreographer.

John O'Hara, U.S. writer.

Jean-Paul Sartre, French writer and philosopher.

Max Schmeling, German boxer.

Mikhail A. Sholokhov, Russian novelist.

C.P. Snow, U.K. writer and physicist.

Albert Speer, German architect and Nazi official.

Michael Tippett, U.K. composer.

Lionel Trilling, U.S. critic.

Robert Penn Warren, U.S. writer.

DEATHS

Meyer Guggenheim, U.S. industrialist.

John Hay, U.S. statesman.

Henry Irving, U.K. actor.

Constantin Meunier, Belgian sculptor.

Jules Verne, French writer.

Lewis Wallace, U.S. soldier and writer.

Painting & Sculpture: ***Saltimbanques*** **(Pablo Picasso);** ***The Bathers*** **(Paul Cézanne);** ***The Marlborough Family*** **(John Singer Sargent) ... Film:** ***The Kleptomaniac*** **(Edwin S. Porter);** ***The Life of Charles Peace; Slippery Jim*** **(Ferdinand Zecca);** ***A Policeman's Love Affair*** **(Sigmund Lubin) ... Theater:** ***Mrs. Warren's Profession*** **(G.B. Shaw);** ***Mlle. Modiste*** **(Victor Herbert);** ***Girl of the Golden West*** **(David Belasco).**

"Let us ... save ... this noble animal, which up to date has been repaid chiefly with brutality and with persecution to the very brink of extermination."—**Ernest Harold Baynes, first secretary of the American Bison Society**

NEW IN 1905

Norway (independence gained from Sweden after 91 years of union).

Self-measuring gas pump (Fort Wayne, Indiana).

Rotary Club.

Electromagnetic seismograph.

Chemical fire extinguisher.

Vicks VapoRub (marketed as Vick's Magic Croup Salve).

Palmolive soap.

***Variety*.**

Spiegel mail-order catalogue.

National Audubon Society.

IN THE UNITED STATES

▶REASON'S ADVOCATE—Calling it "a presumptive biography of the human intellect," George Santayana in 1905 published the first installment of his early masterwork, *The Life of Reason*. Comprising five volumes, the Spanish-born

American philosopher's brilliant inquiry into the nature of reason famously warned, "Those who cannot remember the past are condemned to repeat it."

▶PATENT MEDICINES—Before Congress passed the Pure Food and Drug Act, exotic patent "medicines" like La Dore's Bust Food ("unsurpassed for developing the bust, arms and neck") flourished in the U.S., especially in rural areas, where doctors were scarce. Usually, the most medicinal ingredient in these concoctions—which were sold largely through mail-order catalogues—was alcohol. But in 1905, Edward Bok, editor of the *Ladies'*

ENVIRONMENTALISM

Protecting a Noble Beast

5 With loggers, miners, and farmers aswarm in the Wild West's shrinking wilderness, Americans began to realize that their natural resources were not infinite. The early twentieth century saw the rise of "conservationism," a protoenvironmentalism whose proponents—most notably Theodore Roosevelt—were more often hunters seeking to preserve the unspoiled beauty of their playgrounds than believers in animal rights. In 1905, a group of 14 prominent conservationists formed the American Bison Society, dedicated to the "permanent preservation and increase" of the noble American bison, or buffalo.

As late as 1868, bison roamed the plains by the tens of millions. Travelers encountered herds that sprawled to the horizons; when the shaggy, 2,000-pound beasts stampeded, they derailed trains. Then the slaughter began—for meat to feed tracklayers and bones to make charcoal, for buffalo robes, for bloodthirsty sport. By 1889, when naturalist William Hornaday made a census of free-ranging bison in the United States, he counted only 85. "There is no reason to hope," he wrote, "that a single wild and unprotected individual will remain alive ten years hence." When the ABS was formed, there were only 20 wild bison, and the fate of the 1,100 in captivity was precarious.

The ABS was one of the world's first groups to lobby for protection of an endangered species. It offered to provide a nucleus herd if the U.S. government would fence off part of a federal game preserve and maintain the animals there. Congress agreed, and in 1907 the New York Zoological Park sent 15 of its finest specimens to Oklahoma's Wichita Mountain Wildlife Refuge. By touting the bison's potential as a source of meat, wool, and farm labor (none of which proved practical), the ABS won public sympathy and donations. A decade later, bison thrived at four new federal preserves, and their numbers had tripled. By 1970 there were 30,000 buffalo in North America, and hunting them was back in fashion. The ABS, however, was extinct; its mission accomplished, it disbanded in 1930. **▸1907.10**

On the early American frontier, bison were shot from train windows by the thousands and their carcasses left to rot.

IRELAND

Gaelic Spirit Awakens

6 By 1905, England had ruled Ireland for more than 700 years—yet no one had quite conquered the Irish. A cultural revival was sweeping the captive country. The Gaelic League championed the use of the Irish language (officially suppressed by the British) in speech, song, and writing; the Gaelic Athletic Association boosted such native sports as hurling, and expelled any member caught playing English football. A literary renaissance in Dublin revolved around the Abbey Theatre, which opened in 1904 and achieved worldwide eminence for plays—most notably by John Millington Synge and W.B. Yeats—that were distinctively Irish yet universally significant.

Less conspicuous amid this tumult was the birth in 1905 of a political society that would eventually lead to the Irish Free State. Called Sinn Féin (Gaelic for "ourselves alone"), the society was established to unite a loose association of nationalist discussion clubs. It was the brainchild of Arthur Griffith, editor of the pro-independence newspaper *The United Irishman*. The group's original goal was to restore the Irish monarchy, out of power since the eighteenth century. It preached passive resistance to British rule, if for no other reason than practicality. "The four-and-a-quarter millions of unarmed people in Ireland would be no match in the field for the British Empire," wrote Griffith. "If we did not believe so ... our proper residence would be a padded cell."

The legendary Queen Maeve, symbol of the Abbey Theatre.

Sinn Féin spent nearly a dozen years in relative obscurity. When it suddenly emerged after the Easter Rising of 1916 to spearhead the movement for a modern, monarchless Irish republic, guns had become part of its strategy.
◂1904.7 ▸1907.4

SOCIAL REFORM

Wobblies Make Their Mark

7 Before the Bolshevik revolution gave American capitalists something greater to fear, their number-one bête noire was an organization nicknamed the Wobblies—the Industrial Workers of the World. Founded in 1905 at a meeting of 200 radical labor activists in Chicago, the IWW aimed to gather the country's poorest and most exploited workers into "one big union" that would ultimately challenge capitalism itself. In an era when near-starvation wages and brutal working conditions were standard, leftist unions sprang up around the globe. But few had to deal with a workforce as multicultural, polyglot, and racially divided as America's. The Wobblies never had more than

SPORTS: Baseball: World Series, New York Giants (Christy Mathewson, 3 shutouts) defeat Philadelphia Athletics, 4–1; Ty Cobb begins career ... Football: Intercollegiate Athletic Association Football League founded due to 18 deaths and 159 injuries in the previous college season ... Golf: Dimple-covered golf ball patented in U.K ... Tennis: May Sutton is first U.S. player to win singles title at Wimbledon.

"There can be no peace so long as hunger and want are found among millions of working people and the few, who make up the employing class, have all the good things of life."—**Industrial Workers of the World constitution**

In posters and stickers, the IWW exhorted workers everywhere to "Join the One Big Union."

100,000 dues-paying members, and their failures outnumbered their successes, but they nevertheless left an indelible mark on the labor movement.

In the United States, that movement had long been dominated by the American Federation of Labor. Run by a London-born cigarmaker named Samuel Gompers, the AFL represented only skilled white male workers, mostly of northern-European heritage. Avoiding politics, it relied on strikes and negotiations to win its limited goals of higher pay and shorter hours. That approach, however, was irrelevant to the millions excluded from membership, as well as to those who favored sharper tactics.

The IWW mixed the European ideologies of socialism, anarchism, and anarcho-syndicalism with a uniquely American spirit. Its founders included William "Big Bill" Haywood, head of the Western Federation of Miners (and a former cowboy), whose militancy later got him kicked off the executive board of the Socialist Party; septuagenarian Mary "Mother" Jones, a coal-mine organizer and avowed "hell-raiser"; and Eugene Debs, the charismatic Socialist Party leader and perennial presidential candidate. (Debs polled 900,000 votes in 1912, socialism's high-water mark in the United States.)

In 1907, after Haywood was acquitted of the bombing murder of an ex-governor of Idaho, the IWW began to be dominated by his syndicalist faction, which envisioned unions as the fundamental units of a new, transnational society. Advocates of syndicalism—prominent among them anarchists who later fought in the Spanish Civil War—saw strikes as rehearsals for a massive *general* strike in which workers would seize power. But the IWW—in spite of winning some major (and often bloody) strikes—never came close to realizing its utopian vision. What made it important was its trailblazing attitude.

Traveling in boxcars, organizers hoboed from Oregon lumber camps to Pennsylvania steel mills—uniting black and white, immigrant and native, as no one had before. Wobbly songwriters like Joe Hill spread their gospel with humorous folk songs. Practicing civil disobedience, the Wobblies got arrested in "free speech fights" for the right to organize.

Following the IWW's lead, the AFL gradually grew more inclusive and more political. And the IWW's concept of a union organized by industry rather than craft became central to the later Congress of Industrial Organizations, which in 1955 merged with the AFL to form the AFL-CIO—the leading force in American trade unionism during the second half of the century. **◂1900.M ▸1911.M**

ARCHITECTURE

Glasgow Masterpiece

8 In 1905, when the governors of the Glasgow School of Art decided to expand their building, they turned to Charles Rennie Mackintosh, the hometown architect and designer who some eight years earlier had designed the school's main structure. It was a propitious choice: The west wing of the Glasgow School of Art is a masterpiece. With it, Mackintosh sloughed off like a worn skin the listless fin de siècle sensibilities of his earlier work and forged an austere style that in its simple forms and full integration of interior and exterior design anticipated architecture's future. The building has been compared to the Parthenon and the cathedral at Chartres, not in form but in spirit: It is as emblematically modern as they are ancient and Gothic. **▸1909.4**

An emblem of modernity: Mackintosh's west wing of the Glasgow School of Art.

MEDICINE

Conquering Consumption

9 German physician Robert Koch won the 1905 Nobel Prize for his research into a disease that had long been the world's leading cause of death—killing, in Koch's own estimate, as much as one third of the adult population. Tuberculosis, which primarily affects the lungs, was known by chillingly evocative names: consumption, white plague, phthisis (Greek for "to melt away"). Some scientists thought a tumor caused the wasting symptoms; others blamed heredity. But Koch suspected germs.

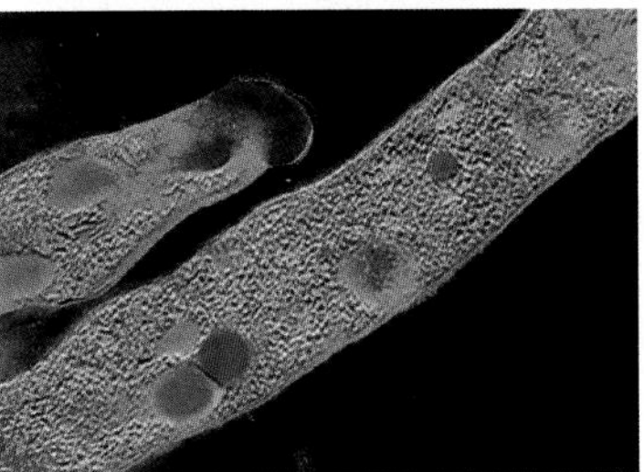

***Mycobacterium tuberculosis*—the main cause of TB in humans.**

When he began his tuberculosis research, Koch was already revered as the father of bacteriology, having isolated the anthrax bacillus in 1876 and proven that microbes cause disease. Citing an "urgent duty," Koch then set out to isolate a tuberculosis bacillus. He finally succeeded after 272 attempts. He cultured the tiny organism and administered it to animals; when they became ill, Koch released his findings to jubilant headlines.

From there, Koch developed a serum called tuberculin, which he mistakenly believed cured tuberculosis. To his embarrassment, further tests showed it didn't work. But the serum later proved useful in diagnosing symptomless carriers, a crucial step toward controlling the spread of the disease. **◂1901.M ▸1909.2**

IN THE UNITED STATES

***Home Journal*, ran a series of exposés on patent medicines, including Mrs. Winslow's Soothing Syrup, a morphine-laden teething medication that was labeled poisonous in Britain. By the end of the next year, these feel-good remedies were illegal. ◂1904.V ▸1906.11**

▶NICKEL PLEASURES—The advent of the nickelodeon in 1905 gave America—especially its working class—a way to satisfy a newfound lust for "the flickers." Small theaters converted from storefronts, nickelodeons charged five cents (hence the name) for a 20-30-minute showing of a series of short-subject films. They proved so popular that within three years more than 10,000 were in operation across the country. ▸1908.8

▶WRITING PIONEER—Abandoning a career in dentistry, Zane Grey turned to pioneers as the subject of his first novel, *The Spirit of the Border*, published in 1905. Based on an ancestor's journal, the bestselling book turned its author into a pioneer of a brand-new literary genre called the Western. Grey went on to perfect the form in over 80 novels, all of them set in the American West.

▶NIAGARA MOVEMENT—Meeting on the Canadian side of Niagara Falls in 1905, a group of prominent black intellectuals issued a manifesto demanding full political, civil, and economic rights for all Americans. A forerunner of the NAACP, the Niagara Movement was led by W.E.B. Du Bois and provided an activist alternative to Booker T. Washington's principles of accommodation. ◂1903.V ▸1910.7

POLITICS & BUSINESS: GNP: $25.1 billion ... President Roosevelt mediates the Treaty of Portsmouth, ending the Russo-Japanese war ... Supreme Court rules limits on length of working day unconstitutional ... Population density in parts of New York City slums reaches 1,000 persons per acre (exceeding density in Bombay) ... Long Island Rail Road is the first to completely abandon steam locomotion.

"It was like proof that the dance could and should satisfy not only the eye but through the medium of the eye should penetrate the soul."—**Choreographer Michel Fokine on Anna Pavlova's performance in *The Dying Swan***

AROUND THE WORLD

▶CHINA ABOLISHES CIVIL SERVICE EXAM—For 2,000 years the civil service exam was the chief source of social mobility and imperial stability in China. In 1905, citing the need to modernize, Qing Dynasty reformers abolished it. A manneristic relic, the test had long rewarded mastery of arcane style over any ability to think or govern. ◀1900.5 ▶1906.13

▶STATE DIVORCES CHURCH—Inspired by widespread anger over the Church's role in the Dreyfus affair, French legislators undid Napoleon's century-old *concordat* that made Catholicism France's state religion. The Pope balked, and in the ensuing chaos the Church lost much of its property. ▶1906.12

▶BINET'S IQ TEST—Seeking a way to distinguish retarded children from those of normal intelligence, French psychologist Alfred Binet *(below, with young subject)*, along with Théodore Simon, concocted a series of diagnostic tests. Expanded and published in

Binet's journal, *L'Année Psychologique*, in 1905, the Binet IQ tests gave the world its first standardized means of measuring human intelligence.

▶*RESCUED BY ROVER*—In this six-minute film, British director Cecil Hepworth not only transcended a plot cliché (family dog rescues baby kidnapped by Gypsies), but also demonstrated that a fresh approach to editing (cutting from one shot to another as the dog ran) could speed up the film's pace, creating suspense and fluidity. This landmark film was one of the most successful of its era. ◀1903.4

Henri Matisse's 1905 *View of Collioure.*

ART

Wild Beasts in Paris

10 His fellow art critics dismissed the artists exhibiting at the 1905 Salon d'Automne in Paris as "the incoherents" or "the invertebrates," but Louis Vauxcelles saw "a luxuriant generation of young painters, daring to the point of excess." In his review of the artists' first major show, Vauxcelles praised them as *les fauves*—"the wild beasts."

Fauvism possessed no unifying creed; what really defined the movement was its central figure, Henri Matisse, who, besides being one of the great masters of the century, was a catalyst for the experiments of other artists. Fauvism was passé a scant two years later, but it was a turning point that enabled other artists to skip impressionism and postimpressionism, and proceed directly to abstraction—the first art movement belonging wholly to the twentieth century. **▶1907.1**

MUSIC

Merriment Goes Worldwide

11 The brief period directly preceding the first World War—remembered fondly as the Edwardian Age in England and La Belle Epoque in France—was a heady time, full of merriment and prosperity not only for the high society of every country, but for the middle classes as well. The music halls were filled every night, and musical comedies like *A Country Girl* or *The Arcadians* packed the theaters in England. Throughout Europe, ragtime was the rage. But nothing in this new age of mass entertainment matched the popularity of Franz Lehár's *The Merry Widow,* which opened in Vienna in 1905.

***The Merry Widow* featured an unforgettable second-act waltz.**

Lehár's operetta, said one critic, "set all Europe humming and strumming his tunes." In New York, several Broadway revivals succeeded its initial run of 422 performances. On one gaudy night in Buenos Aires, Argentina, *The Merry Widow* was performed in five different theaters in five different languages.

The key to *The Merry Widow*'s success was its lively mix of diverse music and dances, ranging from waltzes to Parisian cancans. Theatergoers found the confection irresistible, but most critics were dismissive, especially of the show's thin plot, about the efforts of an ambassador from Marsovia (located, as one writer put it, in "comic-opera land east of the sun and west of the moon") to get one of his country's noblemen to woo a wealthy young widow and thus secure her fortunes for his impoverished country. Even so, one such curmudgeon admitted, "[T]he music has this, at least, in its favor, that we should like to hear it again." **▶1911.11**

DANCE

Ballet's Popularizer

12 Just before Christmas 1905, the ballet dancer Anna Pavlova asked the choreographer Michel Fokine, her classmate from the Imperial School of Ballet in St. Petersburg, Russia, to create a dance for her. Fokine had been studying *Carnival of the Animals* by the French composer Camille Saint-Saëns and decided a dance set to *The Swan* would suit the delicate Pavlova. Working for less than half an hour, the two ascendant stars of twentieth-century ballet came up with *The Dying Swan*, destined to become Pavlova's signature.

For the next 25 years, until her death in 1931, Pavlova almost single-handedly popularized the art of ballet. She commanded a vast repertoire, but it was *The Dying Swan*, a technically simple but extremely dramatic and expressive dance, that audiences craved. In the solo, Pavlova interpreted the movements of a weak, ancient swan as it glided across water. She used her arms to simulate the beating of wings as the swan struggled helplessly to fly, while the quivering movements of her body and head suggested the animal's death throes. At the end, Pavlova's fluttering movements quieted, and she sank upon the stage. **▶1909.6**

Created for the great Pavlova, *The Dying Swan* became the most famous ballet solo of the century.

NOBEL PRIZES: Peace: Bertha von Suttner (Austrian; Austrian Society of Friends of Peace) ... Literature: Henryk Sienkiewicz (Polish novelist) ... Chemistry: Adolf von Baeyer (German; organic dyes and aromatic compounds) ... Medicine: Robert Koch (German; tuberculosis) ... Physics: Philipp Lenard (German; cathode rays).

A VOICE FROM 1905

Brutality in Birmingham

From *The Child-Slaves of Britain,* by Robert Harborough Sherard, 1905

In 1905, nearly one million school-age children were working outside of school hours in Britain, and the numbers were just as grim on the other side of the Atlantic, in the United States. Robert Sherard's groundbreaking book, The Child-Slaves of Britain—*"a fair and impartial account of the deplorable conditions under which a large number of English and Scotch children live and labour," he wrote in his preface—made many would-be reformers sit up and take notice. (Actual reform, however, was slower in coming.)*

Sherard spent six months living among and extensively interviewing the children whose lives he chronicled. In this selection from his chapter entitled "On Child-Slavery in Birmingham," Sherard describes children who work carding hooks and eyes. ◄**1904.M** ►**1906.1**

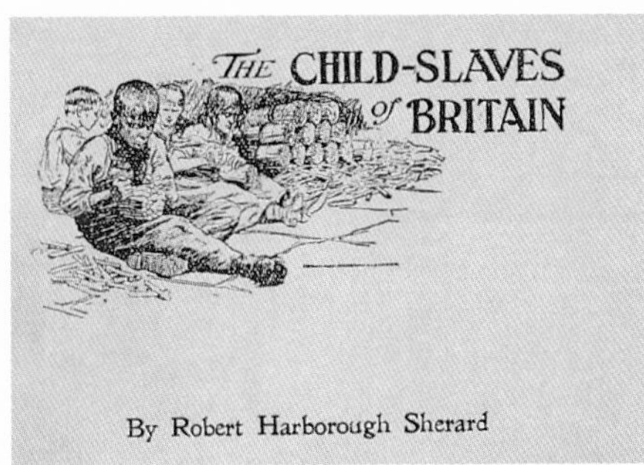

Back of Richard Street I found a woman and a little girl, who were both as white of face as is the paper upon which I trace their painful records, who were dying of starvation in the hook-and-eye trade. "Starting," she said, "the two of us early on Saturday morning and working hard all day Saturday, and beginning again on Monday morning and on till dinner-time, we earned 1s. 6d. You get 10d. for a pack, and you find your own cotton and needles. Me and my little girl—she is the only one of my five children who can help as yet—worked yesterday from 4:30 p.m. till past 11, and we earned 4d. between us." None of these people had eaten anything all that day. There was only a little tea and sugar in the house. The babies were crying.

A miserable woman living in a "furnished" room in Hospital Street, for which she pays 5s. 3d. a week, can earn, with child-help, 8d. a day at this same trade.

I heard of a woman—a handless woman doubtless—in Coleshill Street who, working with two girls, got 2s. a week for herself and 2s. a week for the fogger. This woman's husband was earning 18s. a week, but needed most of it for himself.

There was deep pathos in all these scenes, but the spectacle which, when I think back upon these heavy hours, will always haunt me with greatest sorrow is one I saw in a kitchen, in a house off Jennens Row, in a courtyard under the lee of a common lodging. Here, late one evening, I found three little children, busy at work at a table on which were heaped up piles of cards, and a vast mass of tangled hooks and eyes. The eldest girl was eleven, the next was nine, and a little boy of five completed the companionship. They were all working as fast as their little fingers could work. The girls sewed, the baby hooked. They were too busy to raise their eyes from their tasks—the clear eyes of youth under the flare of the lamp! Here were the energy, the interest, which in our youth we all bring to our several tasks in the happy ignorance of the weight and stress of the years and years of drudgery to come.

I looked at these bright eyes, these quick and flexible fingers, and I thought of the old woman of ninety whom I had seen in the morning in Unit Street. I remembered her eyes which had the glaze of approaching dissolution upon them; I remembered the knotted, labour-gnarled hands. Her eyes had been bright once. She, too, had brought interest and energy to the miserable tasks in which her life began. Years had followed years, decade had added itself to decade. There had been no change brought by chance or time.

The drudgery is eternal. There is no hope of relief. One treads, firmly at first, and then with faltering steps, the mill-round of one's allotted task, until the end, which is the nameless grave. And it was because I read in the clear eyes of those children the ignorance of this cruel but indisputable postulate of the lives of the very poor, that their very brightness, their cheerfulness filled me with more poignant sorrow than any I had felt till then. *Quous Tandem.* How long? How long? All your life and till the grave.

London Match-makers at Work.

Sherard characterized the "small lieges of His Majesty King Edward VII" as "generally courageous, these little lads and lasses, willing to work, and, in most cases, glad to take the coppers home to mother." His book *(original illustrations, above and at left)* singled out for special condemnation the children's substandard nutrition.

"Socialism marks the growth of society, not the uprising of a class."—**Future Labour prime minister James Ramsay MacDonald in 1905**

1906

STORY OF THE YEAR

A Political Hybrid Forms in Britain

1 The British Labour Party, founded in 1906, was part of a worldwide movement for political and social reform that had been mounting for two decades. As industrialism expanded the middle class and brought unprecedented wealth and power to a few, it also delivered to the masses new forms of misery—crowded tenements, murderous factories, ceaseless toil. With increasing insistence, the disempowered demanded their fair share. Feminism, unionism, anti-clericalism, and socialism (whether parliamentary or revolutionary) all attracted thousands of adherents.

In most European nations, the primary vehicles of political opposition were socialist parties (such as the Social Democrats in Germany). But in Britain, that role fell to a unique political hybrid that put workers first and ideology second—the British Labour Party.

For decades, Britain's Parliament had been dominated by the Conservatives and the Liberals. The Liberals were the party of reform, but they allowed only the well-to-do on their ticket. After the Liberals rejected his candidacy, a Scottish coal miner named Keir Hardie established the Scottish Labour Party. His idea spread to other areas. After Hardie and two other candidates from regional labor parties were elected to Parliament, they formed a coalition party called the Independent Labour Party (ILP).

"From the Workshop to St. Stephen's" —an illustration to a contemporary account of the growth of the Labour Party.

For the elections of 1900, ILP leaders joined forces with those of the trade unions, the Social Democratic Federation (a Marxist Party), and the high-profile Fabian Society (a liberal socialist group led by George Bernard Shaw and Beatrice and Sidney Webb). The resulting Labour Representation Committee (LRC) set one goal—getting friends of labor elected, regardless of their ideology. Only two laborites won the 1900 elections, but for the 1906 race, the LRC made a secret deal with the Liberals: The latter would let LRC candidates run unopposed for 23 seats, in exchange for labor's support in other districts.

The Liberals wound up trouncing the Conservatives—and a stunning 29 LRC candidates won seats in Parliament. The LRC declared itself the Labour Party. Within two decades, Labour had its first prime minister. The Liberals, meanwhile, all but withered away. **►1924.4**

An Edvard Munch painting of a set from a 1906 production of Ibsen's *Ghosts*.

THEATER

Norway's Dramatist of Ideas

2 "I hold that that man is in the right," said Henrik Ibsen, "who is most closely in league with the future." For most of his life, the Norwegian playwright, who died at 78 in 1906, followed his own dictum, enduring poverty, rejection, and self-imposed exile in Germany and Italy in order to pursue his "drama of ideas"—a conscious rejection of the nineteenth-century model of the "well-made play" (a plotty, sentimental creation in which social issues were either avoided or couched in melodrama, and conventional morality ruled).

Ibsen's work was at once shockingly frank and subtly symbolic; his central theme was always the protagonist's struggle to be true to him- or herself, whatever the consequences. Works like *A Doll's House*, whose heroine boldly leaves her respectable husband, and *Ghosts*, in which a deceived wife's loyalty lands her with a syphilitic baby, were too closely "aligned with the future" for most Victorian playgoers. Conservative critics called his plays "revoltingly suggestive and blasphemous." But to his reverential successors he was the father of modern theater.
◄1904.7 ►1926.10

INDIA

A Minority Organizes

3 The nationalist movement in India considered domestic unity a prerequisite to liberation from British rule. But for India's Muslim minority, unity bespoke subjection to the Hindu majority. In 1906, the Aga Khan III, acting on behalf of some 36 Indian Muslim leaders, founded the All-India Muslim League to defend Muslim interests against the Indian National Congress, the Hindu-dominated organ of Indian nationalism.

Formed in 1895, the Indian National Congress initially sought to increase native participation in the British colonial government; independence became an aim only after World War I. From the Aga Khan's perspective, native participation as defined by the congress looked like Hindu participation, with Muslims consigned to permanent impotence. He formed the Muslim League to lobby for "communal representation," a system whereby each of India's religious and ethnic groups would receive a certain number of political offices. (The provision was one of the so-called Minto-Morley reforms of 1909.)

The Hindu-Muslim schism had been fostered by the British when they partitioned Bengal into two administrative units in 1905, creating a Muslim majority in the new East Bengal. Hindus protested

His Highness the Aga Khan III in full regalia.

ART & CULTURE: Books: ***The City of the Yellow Devil*** (Maxim Gorky); ***White Fang*** (Jack London); ***Poems*** (Siegfried Sassoon); ***The Devil's Dictionary*** (Ambrose Bierce); ***Psychology of Dementia Praecox*** (Carl Jung); ***The Man of Property*** (John Galsworthy) ... Music: "Anchors Aweigh"

"The low brick buildings built in the pioneer days had nearly all thrown their fronts into the narrow streets, and their interiors were shown cross-sectioned like the doll houses you see in toy stores."—James Hopper, San Francisco journalist, in *Everybody's Magazine*

vehemently, prompting the founders of the Muslim League to embrace the British presence as an antidote to strident Hindu nationalism. During India's long struggle for independence, relations between the Muslim League and the Indian National Congress constantly shifted, sometimes achieving rapprochement, sometimes disintegrating into open hostility, but always marked by deep, mutual suspicion. To this day, India remains beleaguered by the often bloody enmity of its Hindu and Muslim citizens. ►**1911.7**

RUSSIA

A Legislative Experiment

4 When modern Russia's first truly representative legislative body convened in 1906, most of its 513 deputies—representing a gamut of political parties—opposed Czar Nicholas II. Among those with seats in the Imperial Duma (from the Russian word for "thought") were the Russian Social Democratic Workers' Party with its Menshevik and Bolshevik factions, and the more moderate Party of People's Freedom. More remarkable than the factions' diversity was that they existed at all. Before the 1905 revolution, political parties of any kind had been illegal in Russia.

The Duma, which ushered in a period of constitutional monarchy, was created by Nicholas's October Manifesto of 1905 (which also reserved his right to disband it). Nicholas had acted only out of necessity, to beat back the chaos that gripped his country. He hoped nothing more would come of it, but Duma members had other plans. They quickly drew up a series of demands, including the seizure and reapportionment of large estates. When Nicholas balked, a Duma deputy proclaimed, "Let the executive authority submit to the legislative."

Deeply offended, the Czar and his ministers issued a statement saying that expropriation of private land was beyond consideration. The Duma fired back that it would "reject all suggestions not in accord with this principle." Nicholas then decided to exercise his option: The first Duma was dissolved just two months after it had assembled. Russia's first experiment with representative government had ended abruptly, but as Nicholas was beginning to learn, the organized opposition was not about to go away. ◄**1905.2** ►**1912.12**

Members of the Duma assembled clandestinely in a forest in Finland.

DISASTERS

San Francisco Gets Shaken

5 On the Richter scale of one to ten, the San Francisco earthquake was a nine. One survivor likened it to a bulldog, with the city "a rat, shaken in the grinding teeth." The shaking began at 5:16 AM on April 18, 1906, and ended 47 seconds later. Most of the city's buildings still stood at that moment; in an area that probably averaged 15 minor quakes a year, flexible wood was the construction material of choice. But the new, $6 million city hall was made of stone and brick, and it collapsed like a giant house of cards. Hotels set on landfill slid down hillsides. The cupola of the California Hotel crashed through the roof of the firehouse where San Francisco's fire chief slept, burying him in rubble.

But when the fires started—leaping from broken gas pipes, fallen lanterns, crossed electric wires—wood became the enemy. Firemen raced from blaze to blaze, only to find all water mains severed. The flames spread unimpeded, spanning 3,400 acres, burning for three full days. In the end, more than 28,000 buildings were destroyed. Over half of San Francisco's 450,000 people lost their homes. Some 670 were known to be dead, another 350 were missing.

San Francisco was a notoriously bawdy frontier city—full of bordellos, saloons, and music halls—and there were those who applauded its apparent demise. In Michigan, a group of fundamentalists even celebrated with a parade. But one San Franciscan, noting the survival of an infamous distillery, responded with this poetic question:

If, as some say, God spanked
the town
for being over-frisky
Why did he burn the churches
down
and save Hotaling's Whisky?

With a similar insouciance, the citizens began rebuilding. By 1909, they'd raised 20,500 new structures, most far sturdier than the originals. And by 1915, when San Francisco held the Panama-Pacific International Exposition to mark the opening of the Panama Canal, not a trace of the catastrophe remained. ►**1914.9**

A fire surpassing even the Chicago blaze of 1871 caused most of the significant damage.

BIRTHS

Hannah Arendt, German-U.S. philosopher.

Frederick Ashton, U.K. choreographer.

Josephine Baker, U.S.-French entertainer.

Samuel Beckett, Irish-French writer.

Hans Albrecht Bethe, German-U.S. physicist.

John Betjeman, U.K. poet.

Dietrich Bonhoeffer, German theologian.

Leonid Brezhnev, U.S.S.R. political leader.

Ernst Chain, U.K. biochemist.

Adolf Eichmann, German Nazi official.

John Huston, U.S. filmmaker.

Clifford Odets, U.S. playwright.

Aristotle Onassis, Greek shipping magnate.

Otto Preminger, Austrian-U.S. filmmaker.

Roberto Rossellini, Italian filmmaker.

Léopold Senghor, Senegalese poet and statesman.

Dmitri Shostakovich, Russian composer.

David Smith, U.S sculptor.

A.J.P. Taylor, U.K. historian.

Luchino Visconti, Italian filmmaker.

T.H. White, U.K. writer.

Billy Wilder, Austrian-U.S. filmmaker.

DEATHS

Susan B. Anthony, U.S. suffragist.

James A. Bailey, U.S. circus owner.

Paul Cézanne, French painter.

Christian IX, Danish king.

Pierre Curie, French chemist.

Paul Laurence Dunbar, U.S. poet.

Henrik Ibsen, Norwegian playwright.

Carl Schurz, German-U.S. political leader.

(Zimmerman and Miles) ... Painting & Sculpture: *The Joy of Life* (Henri Matisse); *Portrait of Gertrude Stein* (Pablo Picasso) ... Film: *The Story of the Kelly Gang* (Charles Tait); *Dream of a Rarebit Fiend* (Edwin S. Porter) ... Theater: *Caesar and Cleopatra* (G.B. Shaw); *George Washington, Jr.* (George M. Cohan); *Brewster's Millions* (Smith and Ongley).

"I can do one of two things. I can be president of the United States, or I can control Alice. I cannot possibly do both."
—Theodore Roosevelt, when asked why he was not more strict with his daughter

NEW IN 1906

Lifeguards (Sydney, Australia).

Electric washing machine.

The Victrola.

Milk cartons (introduced by G.W. Maxwell in San Francisco).

The name "hot dog" (from a cartoon showing a dachshund inside a frankfurter bun).

Permanent waves (introduced in England at a cost of $1,000, taking eight to twelve hours).

Fuller Brush Company (Hartford, Conn.).

Wassermann test for syphilis.

S.O.S. distress signal (replaced C.Q.D. call adopted two years earlier).

Mack truck.

Le Mans Grand Prix auto race.

IN THE UNITED STATES

▶**GORKY VISITS U.S.**—Internationally acclaimed Russian writer Maxim Gorky toured the United States in 1906 but failed in his mission

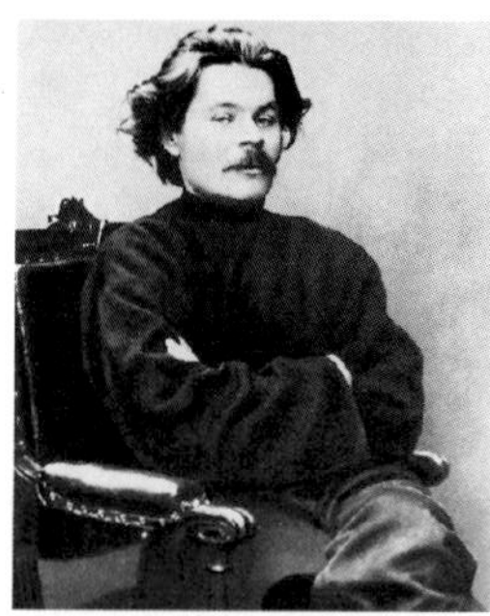

to raise support for the Russian revolution of 1905. A fiery champion of the Russian working class, Gorky penned *Mother,* the novel later deemed the first work of socialist realism, during his U.S. interlude. ◀1905.2 ▶1932.8

ART

The Father of Modern Art

6 Paul Cézanne, the painter Pablo Picasso called "the father of us all," died in 1906 in his boyhood home of Aix-en-Provence. He had gone there eleven years earlier, after leaving Paris and severing his relationship with the impressionists, with whom he was invariably identified. In a solitude of his own choosing, the artist (who'd spent most of his career scorned by critics and ignored by the public) realized his full creative powers. The landscapes from this period (including *Le Château Noir,* above) use color and form in a wholly original way that transcends the conventions of nineteenth-century representational painting and points the way toward modern abstract art. "The landscape," Cézanne once said, explaining his inspiration, "becomes human, becomes a thinking, living being within me. I become one with my picture." ◀**1905.10** ▶**1907.1**

FILM

Cartoons Are Animated

7 It had long been known that pictures shown in rapid succession give the impression of continuous movement. When a vaudeville caricaturist named J. Stuart Blackton applied that technique to a series of photographed drawings in 1906, he came up with the first example of what some film scholars maintain is the only form of "pure" cinema—the motion picture cartoon.

After quitting vaudeville and becoming a founder of the Vitagraph Company, one of the giant studios of the early silent era, the British-born Blackton had become interested in stop-frame animation, a form of trick photography in which only a few frames of film are exposed at a time. Between exposures, objects in the scene may be added, removed, or altered. When the entire stop-frame film is shown, the objects appear, disappear, or change form and position as if by magic. Blackton realized that this technique could bring a set of drawings to life.

His experiment, *Humorous Phases of Funny Faces,* is a crude elaboration of his vaudeville chalkboard routine. The caricatured face of a man blows cigar smoke at the face of a woman, making her disappear; a man in a bowler seems to draw himself, then tips his hat; the words "coon" and "Cohen" transform themselves into nasty portraits of a black and a Jew. Blackton himself appears occasionally, adding or erasing details.

Today, *Humorous Phases* fails to amaze, or even to amuse. But Blackton pointed the way for such finer and subtler animators as France's Emile Cohl and America's Winsor McCay. ▶**1908.V**

The first animated cartoon: crude in both technique and content.

THE UNITED STATES

Princess Alice Gets Married

8 A "wild animal," said her stepmother's friend, "put into good clothes." Her own father pronounced her fiancé "insane" when he heard of the couple's plans to marry. But Alice Roosevelt—First Daughter and, in the eyes of the world, the embodiment of that Gay '90s ideal of feminine perfection, the Gibson Girl—married the man of her dreams, Congressman Nicholas Longworth, at the White House in February 1906.

The fame of Theodore Roosevelt's eldest child stretched from Japan, where a postcard bearing her portrait and the inscription "An American Princess" was issued in honor of her 1905 visit, to Europe, where she was routinely paired with the Continent's most eligible dukes and princes. "Princess Alice" was such a favorite of Kaiser Wilhelm II that, during World War I, when the monarch's personal yacht was pressed into service by the German navy, he had it rechristened the *Alice Roosevelt.* Back home, she smoked in public, drank whiskey, bet on horses, and played poker. American women dressed in "Alice blue" and hummed the popular song "Alice, Where Art Thou?"

Alice Roosevelt's marriage did nothing to lower her high profile around the capital.

But Alice's private life was never as lucky as her social one. Overshadowed by his glamorous wife and famous father-in-law, Longworth drank and womanized up until his death in 1931. Alice never remarried but, sharp-tongued and witty as ever, continued to reign as the grande dame of Washington, D.C., for another 50 years. ◀**1904.6**

SPORTS: Baseball: World Series, Chicago White Sox defeat Chicago Cubs, 4–2 ... Football: Hazardous tactics forbidden, forward pass introduced ... Boxing: Tommy Burns (shortest heavyweight champion ever at 5 feet 7 inches) dethrones Marvin Hart ... Billiards: 18-year-old Willie Hoppe, "Boy Wonder of Billiards," defeats 60-year-old Maurice Vignaux 500–283 at world championship.

"They have said I spread a disease that I've never had. I've never been a full day in bed in my life."—"Typhoid Mary" Mallon

DIPLOMACY

A Pie in the Face for Germany

9 Germany was the fastest-growing economic and military dynamo in Europe, but in 1906 it was a relative newcomer to the scramble for colonies. Chancellor Bernhard von Bülow vowed to win his nation "a place in the sun," but the established powers made the Germans feel shut out. Bülow and Kaiser Wilhelm II were skeptical of the waltz between once-bitter rivals Britain and France (as exemplified by 1904's Entente Cordiale). They decided to see what a little pressure could accomplish in Morocco, which the Entente Cordiale had declared to be under French influence. The result was the 1906 Algeciras Conference—a pie in the face for Germany, and an important step toward forging the alliances of World War I.

The previous year, the Kaiser had sailed to Tangiers, where—appropriating Britain's old stance—he proclaimed his support of Moroccan independence. The Kaiser demanded that the Moroccan question be referred to Morocco's young sultan, Abd al-Aziz. The Sultan called an international conference to be held in the Spanish town of Algeciras, just across the Gibraltar strait. The Kaiser's agenda included the promotion of free (i.e., German) trade and the elimination of French advantages in Morocco. He also hoped to reopen the rift between France and Britain. The delegations that were invited reinforced German confidence. Italy and Austria-Hungary would surely support their partner in the Triple Alliance. America and the smaller European states would doubtless be moved by free-market rhetoric. Spain would go with the majority. And Britain would hardly stick its neck out for France.

But the German delegates, alternating inconsistent arguments with threats of war, alienated almost everyone, while the French were charming. Additionally, France had already bribed the Spaniards with a sphere of influence in Morocco, and the Italians with a secret promise not to meddle in Libya. The Americans, nominally neutral, were under orders from President Roosevelt to do nothing to imperil Anglo-French good feeling. And Britain did stick its neck out, defiantly.

In the end, the Germans won little more than a pact mandating equal customs duties. The French and Spaniards got to *collect* those duties and police the ports. After the conference, the Entente Cordiale grew more cordial, and Germany more alone. ◂**1904.5** ▸**1911.1**

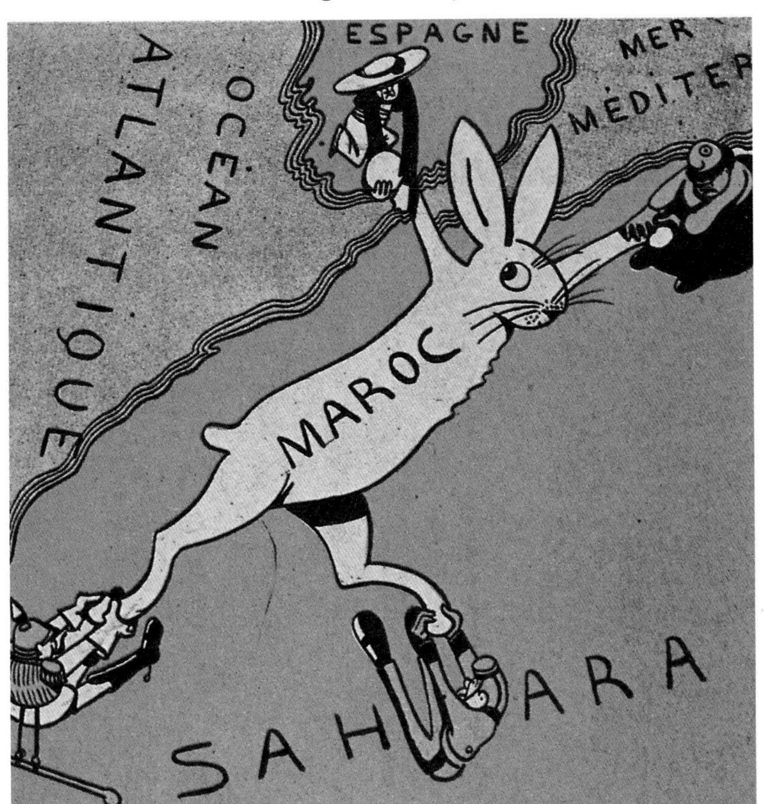

Morocco in a French cartoon: a scared rabbit tugged in every direction by European powers.

MEDICINE

Typhoid Mary

10 No one did more to raise the public's awareness that a healthy person can spread a deadly disease than Typhoid Mary, the first carrier of typhoid bacilli to be identified—and horribly vilified—by the press. Ignorant of microbes, knowing only that some kind of "hoodoo" dogged her heels, the robust-looking Mary Mallon worked in kitchens across the northeastern United States. Wherever she went, typhoid followed. Only Mallon herself noticed this trail of illness—until 1906, when a New York City health official named Dr. George Soper went to investigate an outbreak of typhoid in a wealthy home.

Mary Mallon lunged at a health official with a fork when she was apprehended.

Soper questioned the cook—who promptly vanished. Familiar with recent research on contagion by German Nobel laureate Robert Koch, Soper did some sleuthing and discovered that typhoid had appeared in all but one of the eight households in which Mallon had previously worked. By March 1907, when she was captured, Soper had linked her to 25 cases, including one death.

Typhoid Mary, as the newspapers called her, was placed in virtual solitary confinement in an island hospital off Manhattan. She went free in 1910, after pledging to stay away from other people's food. But four years later, typhoid outbreaks took two more lives at health-care institutions where she had cooked. Nabbed in 1915, the incorrigible carrier went back to her island quarantine, where she became a laboratory aide and moved into her own cottage. She died there in 1938, at around age 68. ◂**1905.9** ▸**1928.11**

IN THE UNITED STATES

▸REOCCUPATION OF CUBA—The provisional U.S. military government of Cuba, declared Secretary of War William Howard Taft in 1906, would be maintained "only long enough to restore order, peace, and public confidence." Translation: until the safety of $160 million in American tobacco, sugar, and other investments was assured. The U.S. had withdrawn its troops, there since the end of the Spanish-American War, from Cuba in 1902. But when the local government collapsed a few years later, Taft called in the Marines. They stayed two years, furthering the entanglement of U.S. business and U.S. militarism in the Caribbean. **◂1903.2 ▸1916.2**

▸NAZIMOVA'S AMERICAN DEBUT—After emigrating to the United States and undertaking a six-month crash course in English, acclaimed

Russian actress Alla Nazimova made her American debut in Henrik Ibsen's *Hedda Gabler* in 1906. Passionate, intense, exotic, Nazimova quickly became Ibsen's leading interpreter. Her success continued in Hollywood, where, from 1915 to '25, she vamped through 17 movies. **◂1906.2**

▸BROWNSVILLE AFFAIR—On August 13, rifle shots interrupted the midnight calm in Brownsville, in southern Texas. One white man died, another was wounded. In a town already twisted by racial tension, the mayor quickly blamed black infantrymen garrisoned at nearby Fort Brown. Despite their pleas of innocence (supported by the testimony of white commanding officers), 167 black soldiers were dishonorably discharged. They were not vindicated until 1972. **▸1931.9**

POLITICS & BUSINESS: GNP: $28.7 billion ... President Roosevelt travels to Panama, first sitting president to leave U.S. territory ... A.P. Giannini makes fortune providing loans to rebuild San Francisco after earthquake ... William Randolph Hearst founds International News Service (INS) ... U.S. corn crop exceeds 3 billion bushels ... Haloid Co. (later Xerox) and Standard Oil of California (Chevron Corp.) founded.

"I was not much better dressed than the workers, and found that by the simple device of carrying a dinner-pail I could go anywhere."—**Upton Sinclair on his infiltration of the Chicago stockyards**

AROUND THE WORLD

▶THE BIG CHILL—By 1906, in the heated race to reach absolute zero—the temperature at which all matter is devoid of thermic capacity—temperatures as low as 14°C above zero had been achieved. German scientist Walther Hermann Nernst cast a chill on these efforts with his third law of thermodynamics, stating that, although absolute zero can be approached, it can never be reached by any scientific procedure. ▶1911.2

▶DOMINION OF THE HIGH SEAS—As military tensions intensified in Europe, Britain struck first in 1906, launching the fearsome and fast H.M.S. *Dreadnought*, a battleship whose ten twelve-inch guns immediately rendered all other warships obsolete. Not to be outdone, in Berlin the Kaiser commissioned a new German fleet and ordered the widening of the Kiel Canal, between the Baltic and North seas, to allow passage of larger craft. ◀1906.9 ▶1907.2

▶BRIDGE TO THE FUTURE—Calling their movement *Die Brücke* ("the Bridge"), four German architectural students exhibiting at a lamp factory in Dresden displayed a bold new form of expressionist painting. Drawing inspiration from the visceral power of African and

Oceanic art, the artists—Ernst Ludwig Kirchner, Karl Schmidt-Rottluff, Fritz Bleyl, and Erich Heckel *(woodcut, above)*—declared their work a bridge to the future. ▶1910.6

Sinclair exposed American meatpackers' disregard for consumers and animals alike.

THE UNITED STATES

The Jungle Prompts Reform

11 "I aimed at the public's heart," Upton Sinclair commented some years after the publication of *The Jungle*, "and by accident I hit it in the stomach." Sinclair had meant for his novel to document the plight of workers in Chicago's stockyards. But its exposure of horrific sanitary abuses in the meatpacking industry made it a sensation and led directly to the passage of the Pure Food Bill of 1906, the U.S. government's first comprehensive law regulating the production of processed foods and a powerful blow to the freewheeling, laissez-faire capitalism that dominated American industry.

Sinclair, on assignment for a socialist weekly, spent two months in slaughterhouses posing as a laborer. He saw tubercular cattle and cholera-ridden hogs ground into sausage. Rotten meat was doctored with dangerous chemicals; rats and filth were rampant. Tainted products were killing consumers. Sinclair wove his exposé around the fictional tale of a Slavic immigrant named Jurgis Rudkus. Serialized, the story was a hit—Jack London called it "the *Uncle Tom's Cabin* of wage-slavery"—but five publishers turned the book down before Doubleday, Page and Co. took it on. It quickly became a best-seller, and outraged readers began to deluge President Roosevelt with angry mail.

The Pure Food Bill was passed six months after *The Jungle*'s publication. It regulated food processing of every kind, as well as the manufacture of drugs—the latter a victory for Sinclair's fellow muckrakers, who'd long denounced the alcohol- and opium-based "medicines" that filled pharmacy shelves. **◀1905.M**

FRANCE

The End of the Affair

12 The greatest scandal in French history ended in 1906 when civil judges, overruling their military counterparts, rendered a final verdict: Alfred Dreyfus was not guilty of treason.

The twelve-year juggernaut known as the Dreyfus Affair began in 1894 when a Parisian cleaning woman in the German embassy found French military data in a wastebasket. Army investigators concluded that the spy must have been an artillery officer, and the young Captain Dreyfus was the perfect culprit: a Jew, and Alsatian to boot. (Alsace shuttled between French and German control, and Alsatians were often suspected of pro-German sympathies.) Anti-Semitism was rampant in France; by accusing an "outsider," the army avoided casting doubt on itself.

With the press, the government, and the Vatican calling for his blood, Dreyfus was court-martialed and sentenced to life imprisonment. Two years later, evidence implicating another officer was unearthed by a new head of French intelligence, who was then fired. The implicated officer was court-martialed, but his acquittal was preordained.

After the bogus court-martial, novelist Emile Zola—foremost among a small group of defenders who rallied behind Dreyfus—wrote one of history's most celebrated pieces of newspaper journalism, *J'Accuse*, an open letter to France's president detailing all that was false in the Dreyfus case. Zola was convicted of libel and fled to England.

When one of Dreyfus's original accusers committed suicide (after confessing to forgery), the government finally reopened the case. Incredibly, Dreyfus was again found guilty. The government pardoned him, but Dreyfus continued to fight for full exoneration, which he won seven years later in a civil court.

The case brought lasting change in France. Popular revulsion against Dreyfus's persecution led to the separation of church and state in 1905 and the rise to power of France's left wing. **◀1902.6 ▶1921.1**

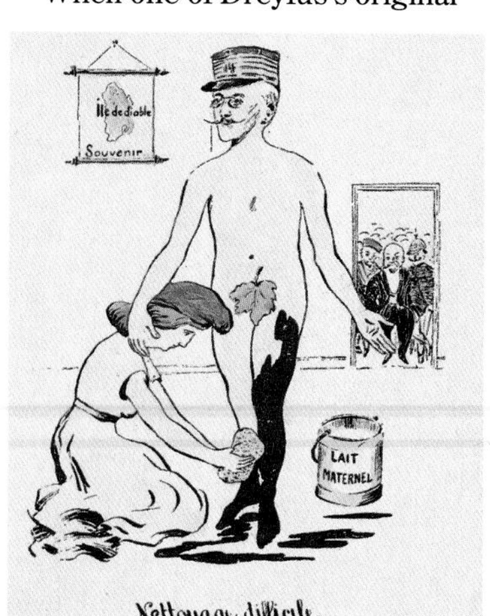

"A difficult cleaning": Dreyfus getting washed down with mother's milk.

CHINA

A War on Drugs

13 Amid public demands for action, the Chinese government in 1906 issued a set of laws that laid out a long-term plan for loosening opium's grip on the estimated 100 million Chinese addicts.

According to one estimate, 100 million Chinese were addicted to opium.

The devastating epidemic was relatively recent. Opium was rare in China until the 1700s, when Britain recognized a vast market for a product of its Indian colonies. The Chinese emperor's opposition to the mounting drug trade precipitated the Opium War of 1839-42. The British easily won the war, and the trickle became a flood.

The 1906 regulations gave users, sellers, and poppy farmers up to ten years to stop. Anti-addiction medicine was distributed free or at cost. Anyone still using opium after ten years would be publicly disgraced—a severe penalty in China. Meanwhile, negotiations began with Britain and other opium-dealing countries to phase out their profitable China trade.

The New York Times predicted that a newly sober China, "having found herself, [would] reorganize her own Government" in defiance of foreign powers. Indeed, while there were other factors at work, the Chinese revolution began within five years. **◀1905.M ▶1911.9**

NOBEL PRIZES: Peace: Theodore Roosevelt (U.S.; mediation of Russo-Japanese War) ... Literature: Giosuè Carducci (Italian; poet) ... Chemistry: Henri Moissan (French; fluorine and electric arc furnace) ... Medicine: Camillo Golgi and Santiago Ramón y Cajal (Italian, Spanish; nervous system) ... Physics: Joseph Thomson (U.K; electrical conduction by gases).

A VOICE FROM 1906

Where the Elite Meet to Eat

Special menu from Delmonico's restaurant, 1906

Abraham Lincoln, a frequent patron of Delmonico's restaurant in New York, once said to owner Lorenzo Delmonico, "In Washington, there are many mansions but, alas, we have no cooks like yours." He was not alone in his sentiment; from a small wine shop opened in 1825, Delmonico's grew into the nation's preeminent dining establishment, serving such notables as Charles Dickens, Jenny Lind, and Ulysses S. Grant. By the turn of the century, members of a new American aristocracy—industrial tycoons like the Vanderbilts, the Rockefellers, and the Morgans—were gathering at the restaurant to sip turtle soup and admire one another. In the restaurant's heyday—which ended with Prohibition—dining at Delmonico's, along with summering in Newport, wintering in Palm Beach, and sailing via yacht to London, became de rigueur for anyone with social aspirations. ►**1908.10**

MENU

HUÎTRES

POTAGE

TORTUE VERTE, AMONTILLADO

HORS D'OEUVRE

JAMBON DE VIRGINIE

HARICOTS VERTS, NOUVEAUX

POISSON

ALOSE SUR PLANCHE À LA MANHATTAN

CONCOMBRES POMMES PERSILLADE

RELÉVE

SELLE D'AGNEAU, COLBERT

CÉLERI BRAISE

ENTRÉE

TERRAPÈNE, MARYLAND

SORBET CALIFORNIENNE

RÔTI

CANARD À TÊTE-ROUGE

TOMATES FARCIES AU CÉLERI MAYONNAISE

ENTREMETS DE DOUCEUR

GLACES DE FANTAISIE

PETITS FOURS

FROMAGE

CAFÉ

GRAVES

SHERRY

MONOPOLE, ENGLISH IMPORTATION

APOLLINARIS

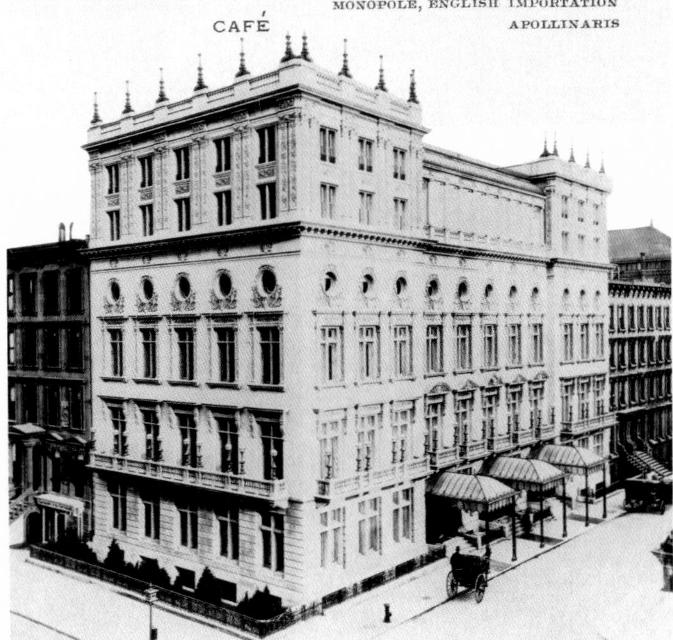

After moving from locations farther downtown to Fifth Avenue and 44th Street (the lower tip of New York City's "Gold Coast"), Delmonico's vied with another restaurant, Sherry's, as the favored dining spot of the very rich. At an honorary dinner held for Mr. Patrick Francis Murphy, the Tiffany-designed, all-French menu included oysters, turtle soup, Virginia ham, rack of lamb, and redheaded duck.

"A man like Picasso studies an object as a surgeon dissects a cadaver."—**French critic Guillaume Apollinaire**

STORY OF THE YEAR

Picasso and Braque Invent Cubism

1 In 1907 a group of prostitutes from a brothel on Barcelona's Carrer d'Avinyó (Avignon Street) became the subject of a painting that heralded an artistic revolution so sweeping that, in art historian Herschel Chipp's words, "the means by which images could be formalized in a painting changed more during the years from 1907 to 1914 than they had since the Renaissance." With his masterful *Les Demoiselles d'Avignon*, arguably the most important painting of the century, Pablo Picasso ushered in cubism, though that name would not be widely used for four more years.

Finding inspiration in nearly equal parts from earlier works by Cézanne and from African sculpture (a vogue at the time among French artists and intellectuals), Picasso used violently fragmented forms to create an image of unsettling power. For an art-viewing public accustomed to seeing the female figure treated with a respectful awe bordering on reverence, the picture was strong medicine.

Les Demoiselles d'Avignon **changed the course of twentieth-century art.**

The following year, painter Georges Braque took his friend Picasso's breakdown of conventional imagery even further, exhibiting a series of paintings that prompted Henri Matisse to observe that they resembled "little cubes." Picasso and Braque were attempting to discover the "truth" of an object through its deconstruction. Instead of using such traditional techniques as light and shadow, perspective, and two-dimensional representation, they analyzed their subjects by taking them apart, then representing an object's every angle and detail with geometric shapes. By 1912, they were working the other way around—building images from geometric shapes.

The movement exploded across the Paris art world, its liberating aesthetic embraced by artists as diverse as Juan Gris, Marie Laurencin, Fernand Léger, Robert and Sonia Delaunay, and Marcel Duchamp. Cubism not only played a key role in the development of artistic movements abroad, but its spirit pervaded all the arts of the century—sculpture, architecture, theater design, even literature and music. At the 1911 Salon des Indépendents, the reigning cultural king, Guillaume Apollinaire, enthusiastically embraced the controversial new style—as well as its once-derisive name, cubism. His blessing signified that such shocking pictorial innovations as two eyes on the same side of a head and a piece of newspaper glued to a painted canvas were here to stay. **◂1906.6 ▸1913.2**

The massive *Lusitania*'s total area was double that of the U.S. Capitol building.

BUSINESS AND INDUSTRY

Great Ships on the High Seas

2 The waterfront in Liverpool, England, was crowded with 200,000 cheering people as the *Lusitania*, set off on its maiden Atlantic crossing in September 1907. With the launching of this grand ocean liner and its sister ship, the *Mauretania*, two months later, Britain's Cunard Steam Ship Company Limited hoped to usher in a new era of transatlantic travel. The vessels were the biggest, fastest, most lavishly appointed ships ever built. With 68,000 horsepower, they were designed to maintain a speed of 24.5 knots in moderate seas. The *Lusitania*, using only 75 percent of its power, crossed from Ireland to New York in five days, 54 minutes—six hours faster than any before. On a similar voyage, the *Mauretania* averaged nearly a knot faster.

Cunard built the vessels—financed by a $13 million low-interest government loan—with a nervous eye on Germany. The ships could beat that country's speed record, and they were constructed to match the military capabilities of German merchant liners that could be converted to armed cruisers. Built to Admiralty specifications, the *Lusitania* and the *Mauretania* could each carry twelve six-inch guns; in order to facilitate their conversion into warships, they were manned in part by members of the naval reserve. The Admiralty also retained the right to commandeer the vessels.

In the end, however, Germany did prevail over the *Lusitania*. Eight years later, the great ship, still nominally a commercial vessel, sank within 20 minutes of being torpedoed by a German U-boat, taking 1,200 passengers (including 128 Americans) down with it. Outrage over the incident became a rallying cry for Americans who favored U.S. entry into World War I. **◂1906.M ▸1915.3**

INDIA

Plague Sweeps the Country

3 The pandemic bubonic plague, which originated in China in 1894, peaked in 1907, having spread to every continent and

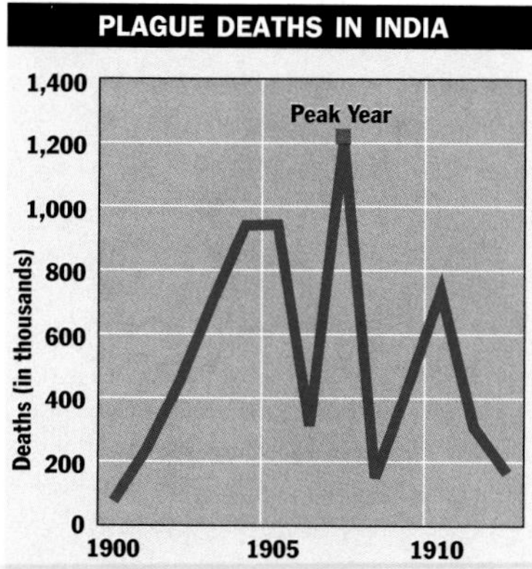

From 1894 to 1916 total deaths from the plague surpassed 6.5 million.

infected 52 countries. Nowhere was the toll higher than in India. More than 1.2 million Indians succumbed to the disease in 1907, better than three in every 1,000 people. As with the plagues of the sixth and

ART & CULTURE: Books: ***Three Weeks*** **(Elinor Glyn);** ***The Secret Agent*** **(Joseph Conrad);** ***Mother*** **(Maxim Gorky);** ***Cautionary Tales*** **(Hilaire Belloc);** ***The Wonderful Adventures of Nils*** **(Selma Lagerlöf);** ***Pragmatism*** **(William James) ... Music: "The Glow Worm" (Lincke and Robinson); "School Days" (Edwards and Cobb); "On the Road to Mandalay" (Speaks and Kipling);** ***Spanish Rhapsody*** **(Maurice Ravel) ...**

"In a good play every speech should be as fully flavoured as a nut or apple, and such speeches cannot be written by any one who works among people who have shut their lips on poetry."—**John Millington Synge, in the preface to *The Playboy of the Western World***

fourteenth centuries, the 1894-1912 pandemic all but wiped out entire villages, leaving a trail of devastation in its dreadful wake: "The only sounds which occasionally broke the silence were the noise and clang of the funeral processions," wrote a British journalist of Poona, India, "and the wails and cries of the mourners at houses in which a death had recently occurred." (The British themselves mostly managed to avoid being stricken, thanks mainly to their isolation from the "natives" and better rat control. As one British woman in India wrote in a letter home, "We white people are not afraid of plague and dance at the Club every evening as gayly as ever.")

Contributing to India's high death rate was the refusal of many Muslims to evacuate contaminated villages. It was widely believed that to flee the plague was to flee the wrath of Allah, which the Koran expressly forbids. Eventually the government issued a proclamation stating that Allah wanted his faithful to protect themselves from the disease. **◄1901.M ►1918.7**

THEATER

Playboy at the Abbey

4 Theatergoers attending the world premiere of John Millington Synge's *The Playboy of the Western World* in January 1907 may not have known the term "antihero," but that's exactly what they saw when a character named Christy Mahon burst onstage and announced that he had killed his father. The play's action—and much of the ensuing controversy—centers on the other characters' lionization of Christy (who is quickly de-lionized when his father turns up alive). But its enduring power derives from the pure, lilting Irish poetry that its peasant characters speak. (Synge always claimed that the dialogue in his plays was merely a transcription of the spirited vernacular of his Anglo-Irish compatriots.)

In both form and content, *The Playboy* was a shocking and irreverent departure from dramatic conventions of the day. It was not easily classified as comedy or tragedy, and its concerns with violence, love, community, and the nature of heroism were distinctly modern. Reviewers branded it decadent and obscene (one called it a "protracted libel upon Irish peasant men and worse still, upon Irish peasant girlhood"), but the play weathered the criticism. Appealing, as Synge put it, to the "popular imagination that is fiery, and magnificent, and tender," *The Playboy* is a pivotal work of the Irish Literary Renaissance. **◄1905.6 ►1923.3**

***Playboy*'s treatment of the working class and use of the vernacular broke taboos.**

DIPLOMACY

Slowing the Buildup

5 An international arms race was in high gear by 1907, with the Great Powers spending up to 6 percent of national income on military costs—levels never before seen in peacetime. Each country blamed its competitors for the buildup; all claimed to want only peace. On June 15, 1907, representatives of 44 nations, pledging to halt what an American journalist called "this insensate rivalry," convened in The Hague, the Netherlands, for a four-month conference aimed at starting the process of global disarmament.

The Second Hague Conference was a follow-up to a like-minded convention of 1899, called by Czar Nicholas II, which had established the first court of international law, agreed on legal codes for settling disputes between nations, and set guidelines for the conduct of warfare. The 1907 conference went further—but no further toward world peace. It expanded the powers of the Hague court (which still exists, although it has been superseded by the World Court and the United Nations) and established conventions on the rights and duties of neutral powers, the laying of underwater mines, the status of enemy merchant ships, and the proprieties of naval bombardment. The First Hague Conference's ban on balloon warfare was maintained, though combat airplanes would soon make it irrelevant. Previous bans on dumdum bullets and asphyxiating gas were allowed to lapse.

As in 1899, the issue of disarmament was barely addressed. Instead, the conference's main (if unwitting) accomplishment was to lay down the rules by which World War I would be fought seven years later. **►1914.1**

The Second Hague Conference. A third, scheduled for 1915, was scrapped because the war was in full swing.

BIRTHS

W.H. Auden, U.K.-U.S. poet.

Rachel Carson, U.S. biologist and writer.

Daphne du Maurier, U.K. writer.

François "Papa Doc" Duvalier, Haitian president.

Charles Eames, U.S. furniture designer.

Christopher Fry, U.K. playwright.

Katharine Hepburn, U.S. actress.

William J. Levitt, U.S. builder.

Pierre Mendès-France, French writer and political leader.

James Michener, U.S. novelist.

Alberto Moravia, Italian writer.

Laurence Olivier, U.K. actor.

Barbara Stanwyck, U.S. actress.

Alexander Todd, U.K. biochemist.

John Wayne, U.S. actor.

Robert Weaver, U.S. economist.

DEATHS

Edvard Grieg, Norwegian composer.

J.K. Huysmans, French novelist.

Dmitri Mendeleyev, Russian chemist.

Sully Prudhomme, French poet.

Augustus Saint-Gaudens, U.S. sculptor.

William Thomson, Lord Kelvin, U.K. physicist.

Painting & Sculpture: *The Snake Charmer* (Henri Rousseau); *Stag at Sharkey's* (George Bellows); *Cavalry Charge on the Southern Plains* (Frederic Remington) ... **Film:** *Ben Hur* (Sidney Olcott); *Rescued from an Eagle's Nest* (Edwin S. Porter) ... **Theater:** *Follies of 1907* (Florenz Ziegfeld); *The Talk of the Town* (George M. Cohan); *A Flea in the Ear* (Georges Feydeau); *The Ghost Sonata* (August Strindberg).

"These people expect to be treated with oil, soap, and embraces. But what they need—and what they will get—is a good fist."
—Pope Pius X

NEW IN 1907

Movie titles instead of commentators.

Canned tuna fish (San Pedro, California).

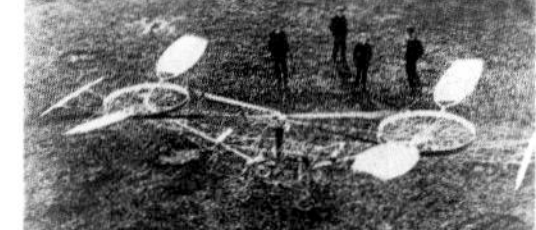

Helicopter (designed by Frenchman Paul Cornu).

Household detergent (Persil).

Ski school (St. Anton in the Austrian Alps).

Armstrong Linoleum.

Canada Dry Pale Dry Ginger Ale.

L'Oréal perfume and beauty products (France).

United Methodist Church.

Oklahoma (46th state).

Bullock's (Los Angeles) and Neiman-Marcus (Dallas) department stores.

IN THE UNITED STATES

▶**EUROPEAN WOMEN COME TO AMERICA**—The steamship *Baltic* arrived in New York on September 27 with 1,002 unmarried "Old World beauties" on board. A band played "Cupid's Garden" as a throng of bachelors welcomed America's newest immigrants. "They tell me," said one maiden, "that there are no men but millionaires in Pittsburgh. I'm going there." ▸1907.6

▶**CURTIS'S NATIVE AMERICANS**—The first volume of Edward S. Curtis's remarkable photographic record of Native American life, *The North American Indian*, was published in 1907. The project—which eventually ran to 20

volumes, each costing up to $3,500—was backed by J.P. Morgan, who wanted the set to be "the handsomest ever published." ▸1955.M

▶**PLAZA HOTEL**—American architect Henry Janeway Hardenbergh's latest shrine to opulence, the Plaza Hotel, opened on October 1. Built at Grand Army Plaza on Central Park

Immigrants aboard the *Lafayette*: Once docked, they might wait several days before being ferried to Ellis Island.

THE UNITED STATES

Immigrant Flow Peaks

6 They came from the whole of Europe, from rural villages and urban ghettos, subsisting as much on their faith in a brighter future on the "gold-paved" streets of America as on the diet of salt herring and coarse bread served on the nauseating ten-day Atlantic crossing. More than 13 million immigrants arrived in the United States between 1900 and 1914, when World War I stanched the flow. In 1907 alone, when the great migration of the early twentieth century peaked, more than 1.2 million came.

The "new" immigrants (so called to distinguish them from their nineteenth-century predecessors) came largely from central and eastern Europe, a trend that brought out American society's worst nativist tendencies—which included a healthy dose of anti-Semitism and anti-Catholicism. Reactionaries, citing the 1890 U.S. census, which had acknowledged the end of the frontier, worried that the republic could no longer accommodate new citizens. Most anti-immigration arguments were couched in racial terms; an eminent historian went so far as to state that the blood of Anglo-Saxon people contained special democratic properties. The dual expansion of cities and the urban working class, which most immigrants naturally entered, began to alarm parts of the public.

In 1907 the United States Immigration Commission began a study of the issue. Its report, published four years later, recommended that immigration be restricted, planting the seeds for future anti-immigration legislation, including quotas and literacy requirements. The war and attendant fears of anarchy further fueled the growing anxiety. The gateways to America slowly and inexorably narrowed, and the flood of immigrants never returned to its prewar peak. ▸**1917.2**

RELIGION

Church Purges Modernists

7 "These people," Pope Pius X fumed, "expect to be treated with ... embraces. But what they need—and what they will get—is a good fist." In July 1907, the Pope came out punching, with a purge that rocked the Church and two European governments.

"These people" were the Modernists, Catholics who were part of a movement to adapt their faith (as one leader put it) "to the intellectual, moral and social needs of the times." Citing new scientific and historical discoveries, Modernists—including many respected theologians—began to challenge Church dogma. An Austrian professor of canonical law questioned the immaculate conception. French prelates interpreted the six-day story of creation as meaning "six periods of years." A religious novelist tried to reconcile Catholicism with Darwinism. Others exhorted Rome to side with workers against their oppressors.

The Pontiff counterattacked, authorizing the removal of all dissenting personnel from Catholic universities and seminaries, the appointment of a censor for Catholic publications, and the installation of a vigilance committee in every diocese. He ordered bishops to report on their subordinates, and to "tear from the hands of the faithful all bad books and writings." Priests were to sign an anti-Modernist oath. Spies drew clerics into incriminating conversations, and even secretly photographed theologians' correspondence. An anonymous denunciation could be enough to get a Modernist author excommunicated or a priest stripped of office.

The clampdown only strengthened the Church's external foes—particularly in Germany and the Netherlands. There, the mostly Protestant populations reacted angrily to a papal encyclical that called the founders of their denominations "anti-Christian" and "materialistic." Both countries were governed by coalitions that depended on a Catholic party to keep the socialists out of power; those coalitions barely survived the furor. Throughout Europe, the liberal press and secular governments deplored the Vatican's actions. The purge, however, persisted

SPORTS: Baseball: World Series, Chicago Cubs (fielding trio Joe Tinker, Johnny Evers, and Frank Chance) defeat Detroit Tigers, 4–1 (1 tie) ... Football: All-America Jim Thorpe stars for Carlisle Indian School ... Hockey: Canadian Owen McCort of Cornwall beaten to death by former Ottawa Victorias teammates during March 6 match ... Auto Racing: First Beijing to Paris long rally (Prince Scipione Borghese wins).

"For the lure of gold the trust magnates have put the lives of the people in jeopardy."—**Arena magazine, July 1907, shortly before the panic of '07**

until 1914—when a new pope, Benedict XV, began to reverse its edicts and restore some Modernist priests to their parishes. ►**1929.10**

IDEAS

The Life Force

8 The doctrine of élan vital swept the world like a tidal wave in 1907. Introduced by French philosopher Henri Bergson in his seminal work, *Creative Evolution*, élan vital, or "life force," was the principle by which the spiritual and the physical are synthesized. Bergson argued that life does not develop mechanistically, but is driven by the élan vital, which infuses all matter, allowing the generation of an almost infinite variety of life-forms. In other words, evolution is creative.

Bergson's theory not only influenced other great twentieth-century thinkers, including George Santayana and Alfred North Whitehead, but also seized the public imagination. Titillated admirers, many of whom erroneously believed élan vital was some sort of essence of sex that pulsed through their veins, besieged Bergson with letters and invitations to tryst. Bergson sought to escape by constantly changing his Paris address, a tactic for which he became known as the Wandering Jew.

He published a study of religious faith, *The Two Sources of Morality and Religion*, in 1932. "My reflections have led me closer and closer to Catholicism," he confided a few years later, "which I see in the complete fulfillment of Judaism." He would have converted to Catholicism, he said, but wanted "to remain among those who tomorrow were to be persecuted."

When the Vichy government imposed racial laws during World War II, Bergson, old and near death, refused the exemption he had been offered and registered as a Jew. ►**1923.M**

Bergson's book garnered him as many "groupies" as a modern-day rock star.

Worried investors on Wall Street waited out the panic of 1907.

BUSINESS AND INDUSTRY

The Panic of '07

9 It started with a precipitous drop in copper prices, which eroded the market for copper mining stocks, in turn undermining banks with heavy interests in the copper industry. Certain banks, it was whispered, would collapse. Mentioned most often was Manhattan's venerable Knickerbocker Trust Company, and on October 22, 1907, its depositors began a wholesale withdrawal of their money. Within a day, the bank's cash supply was depleted and the directors suspended payments. The panic of 1907 was on. From the Knickerbocker, the run on the banks spread to other New York institutions; within days the panic engulfed the country.

The sight of a desperate mob besieging a bank became common in the following weeks. Meanwhile, a coterie of New York financiers, led by the estimable J.P. Morgan, ponied up enough cash to import $100 million in European gold to finance the stricken banks. In Washington, Teddy Roosevelt assured the nation that its financial institutions were secure. Just to make sure, he authorized Secretary of the Treasury George Cortelyou to transfer massive sums directly to struggling New York banks, and also to issue $150 million in low-interest government bonds. The cash infusion reassured skittish depositors, and they stopped their runs.

The panic forced the nation to focus on the inadequacy of its banking and monetary systems. Congress opened hearings that culminated, in 1913, in the creation of the Federal Reserve System. ◄**1901.3** ►**1908.M**

POPULAR CULTURE

The First Modern Zoo

10 Decades before animal rights and environmentalism would loom large in the popular consciousness, a German animal trainer named Carl Hagenbeck opened, in 1907, an ambitious, radically new type of zoo that redefined the relationship between captive animals and the homo sapiens who come to view them. At that time most zoos exhibited animals in improbably small, rigorously armored and barred cages. Hagenbeck, who had campaigned against the use of needlessly cruel techniques in training wild animals, came up with a way to display animals in close approximations of their natural habitats.

Hagenbeck had purchased the 67-acre site in the outskirts of Hamburg in 1902 and spent five years developing it. Through careful study and frequent experimentation, he found the optimum balance between spectators' safety and their immediacy to the animals. Great unseen pits separated the animals from one another and from their observers, making the facility safe but giving it an illusion of natural continuity.

The polar bears were still in cages, but Hagenbeck's zoo was more natural than its predecessors.

But Hagenbeck's re-creation of the animals' environments was an enormously expensive proposition. For that reason, Hagenbeck's techniques, though hailed as innovative, were not immediately adopted by other zoos. With time, however, their superiority became evident: The London Zoo (in 1913) and the St. Louis Zoo (1919) were two of the first to incorporate Hagenbeck's ideas. Today the architecture of nearly every zoo in the world owes a debt to Hagenbeck's efforts toward environmental naturalism. ◄**1905.5**

IN THE UNITED STATES

South (site of the old Vanderbilt Mansion), the 1,000-room Plaza was the last word in ornate Beaux-Arts elegance, outdoing even Hardenbergh's other lavish hostelries—the Waldorf, the Willard, and the Astor.

►"THE GREATEST SHOW ON EARTH"—For sheer gaudy entertainment, there was no spectacle like the circus. Of

the dozens touring the country, two stood out: the Barnum & Bailey and the Ringling Brothers. In 1907 the Ringlings bought out their chief rival, assembling under one big top the most extravagant show-biz sensation ever seen.

►GREAT WHITE FLEET—Recent territorial acquisitions in the Pacific—Hawaii, the Philippines, Guam—had given the United States a fresh appreciation of naval preparedness. In December, 16 battleships—the Great White Fleet—steamed out of Hampton Roads, Virginia, on an around-the-world voyage. The yearlong parade of might vanquished any international doubt that the U.S. was now a bona fide two-ocean power. ◄1906.M ►1911.1

►EMPEROR OF AIR—An eccentric American physicist named Lee De Forest greatly hastened the arrival of widespread radio broadcasting when he patented, in 1907, his invention of a triode vacuum tube that amplified weak radio signals. Simple and inexpensive, the Audion, as the tube was named, soon became the standard in all radio sets. Said its inventor, "I discovered an Invisible Empire of the Air." ◄1904.8 ►1920.3

POLITICS & BUSINESS: GNP: $30.4 billion ... U.S. Division of Forestry coins term "conservation" ... Congress outlaws corporate contributions to political campaigns for national office ... Coal-mine explosions in West Virginia and Pennsylvania kill total of 600 miners ... United Press (later UPI) founded by E.W. Scripps.

AROUND THE WORLD

▶ALLIANCES CLARIFIED—The sometimes inscrutable web of European geopolitics assumed new dimensions in 1907, when England and Russia formed an alliance known as the Triple Entente. A natural extension of earlier rapprochements between France and Russia, and England and France, the Triple Entente survived as the core of the Allied Powers in World War I. Meanwhile, Germany, Austria-Hungary, and Italy would renew the Triple Alliance, their secret military pact, several times before World War I. ◀1906.9 ▶1911.1

▶OIL MERGER—Dutch oil giant Royal Dutch Oil and its British counterpart, Shell, merged in 1907. Royal Dutch chairman Hendrik W.A. Deterding became director and Shell's Marcus Samuel chairman of the new, truly massive

international corporation, which maintained a presence anywhere on the globe that oil could be found. ◀1901.12 ▶1909.5

▶HOME RULE—New Zealand was granted dominion status by Britain in 1907. Britain, however, continued to direct its foreign policy for the next 40 years. ▶1926.9

▶SURPRISE ACCORD—In a development that raised eyebrows around the globe, France and Japan signed an agreement to recognize and respect each other's interests in China, and to abide by the "open door" policy of equal international commercial opportunity there. The surprise Franco-Japanese Accord, formalized on June 10, 1907, established a rapprochement between the two dissimilar and occasionally antagonistic countries, whose relations had recently reached their nadir over Japan's defeat of Russia—France's longtime ally—in the Russo-Japanese War. ◀1905.3 ▶1914.2

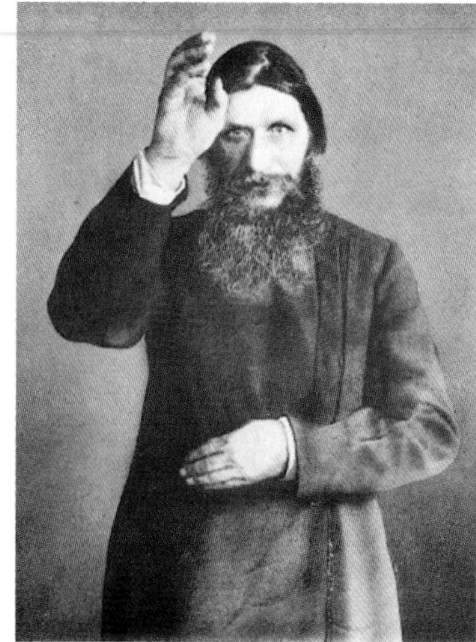

Many people found Rasputin's searing gaze impossible to withstand for more than a few seconds.

RUSSIA

Mad Monk in Czar's Court

11 The two-year-old hemophiliac heir to the Russian throne lay in his crib hemorrhaging, and the imperial physicians lacked, in 1907, the medical knowledge to help him. The empress Alexandra was beside herself with anguish and guilt. Four of her immediate male relatives had died from hemophilia, and her only son, Alexis, had inherited the condition. Desperate to save him, the deeply spiritual empress sent for Grigory Yefimovich Rasputin, a dissolute Siberian peasant and self-proclaimed holy man who had recently shown up in St. Petersburg and become a pet of the aristocracy. Rasputin arrived in the sickroom, uttered some prayers, and the bleeding stopped.

Alexandra and the Czar, Nicholas II, had previously met and been impressed with Rasputin; now they accepted him into their inner circle. Alexandra adored Rasputin as a saint, and through her he gained enormous political influence. By 1915, after apparently saving Alexis from multiple attacks of hemorrhaging, the "mad monk" was the most powerful man in Russia, filling the court with his unscrupulous appointees.

His license, however, was his undoing. His female congregation spoke in awe of his searing gaze. He encouraged their feelings, preaching that physical contact with him cleansed sinners of their sins. Stories of his debauchery circulated everywhere. The clergy spoke out against Rasputin, and political leaders, worried about his influence, implored the Czar to banish him. When newspapers castigated Rasputin, Alexandra persuaded her husband to outlaw negative reports. But public sentiment against the "holy man" continued to swell. In 1916, when a group of conservative political leaders began to fear that he and the Czarina were plotting to make peace with Germany, they resolved to murder him. As legend has it, they lured Rasputin to a private house and served him poisoned wine and cake. When the "monk" did not succumb, Prince Felix Yusupov opened fire with a revolver. Struck several times, Rasputin still did not die. The conspirators finally finished him off by throwing him into the icy Neva River, where he drowned. **▶1917.1**

CHINA

Sun's Revolutionary Platform

12 In 1907, four years before the Chinese Revolution, Dr. Sun Yat-sen, often called the father of modern China, outlined his program for democracy to a meeting of 5,000 pro-revolution students in Tokyo. Sun's Three People's Principles included *min-zu*, the doctrine of nationalism, whereby all Chinese citizens would be accorded freedom and equality; *min-quan*, the doctrine of popular sovereignty, whereby the Chinese people would gain the right of self-government; and *min-sheng*, the doctrine of livelihood, whereby land and capital would be equitably distributed among the masses.

Sun's platform garnered qualified support from China's revolutionary elite. But students by the thousands rushed to join the Tung Meng Hui, or Revolutionary Alliance. A historic manifesto established the tenor of the upheaval that was in the making. "The revolutions of earlier history were hero-revolutions wrought by a few brave men," it declared. "The present revolution is of the people as a whole. This means that all should possess the spirit of liberty, equality, and fraternity, and that all should share the responsibility of the revolution." **◀1905.M ▶1911.9**

POPULAR CULTURE

Comics Hit the Dailies

13 The criticism was scathing. "It is not quite clear what these comics are. We cannot call them caricatures, for a caricature is based or aimed at something that exists," wrote a disgruntled reader. "But these effigies ... have no actual relationship with anything that is to be seen upon our earth." The naysayers were outnumbered, however, and in 1907 the comic strip *Mr. A. Mutt,* about the misadventures of a tall, hapless racetrack junkie, settled in at the San Francisco *Chronicle*, running six days a week in its racing pages. Cartoonist Bud Fisher later introduced a short, top-hatted, bewhiskered character named Jeffries to the strip (he and Mutt met in an insane asylum), and the enduring tandem of Mutt and Jeff was born. Their huge popularity ensured the permanence of daily comic strips and added an idiom to American English.

Before *Mutt and Jeff,* comics were confined to supplements to the Sunday papers. One of the earliest Sunday cartoons—launched in 1896 as part of the newspaper circulation wars of the day—chronicled the life of the Yellow Kid, a street urchin in a yellow shirt who appeared in Joseph Pulitzer's tabloid, *The New York World.* The Yellow Kid gave rise to the phrase "yellow journalism" to describe the kind of sensationalism Pulitzer and his chief rival, William Randolph Hearst, liked to print. To compete with the Yellow Kid, Hearst launched his own colored Sunday comic supplement, calling it "eight pages of iridescent polychromous effulgence that makes the rainbow look like a piece of lead pipe." From then on, the funnies became a Sunday institution. It was only a matter of time before they jumped to the daily editorial pages. **◀1902.M ▶1908.V**

With Bud Fisher's introduction of Jeff *(left)*, Mutt got a pint-sized companion.

NOBEL PRIZES: Peace: Ernesto Moneta (Italian; Lombard League of Peace) and Louis Renault (French; jurist at Hague Peace conferences) ... Literature: Rudyard Kipling (U.K.; novelist and poet) ... Chemistry: Eduard Buchner (German; cell-free fermentation) ... Medicine: Charles Laveran (French; protozoa as disease agents) ... Physics: Albert Michelson (U.S.; spectroscopy and metrology).

A VOICE FROM 1907

The Gibson Girl Goes to Court

Testimony by Evelyn Nesbit in the murder trial of Harry K. Thaw, January 1907

Evelyn Nesbit was a 16-year-old chorus-line dancer when she met Stanford White, a prominent New York architect famous for his lavish entertainments and philandering. White was nearly 50 when he began his affair with the hauntingly beautiful Nesbit. She went on to have a brief dalliance with actor John Barrymore, and then took a new lover—the extravagantly rich and mentally unstable sadomasochist Harry Kendall Thaw of Pittsburgh. Thaw married Nesbit in 1903, knowing of her earlier affair but tormented by jealousy. On the night of June 25, 1906, in the outdoor restaurant atop the Madison Square Garden building White had designed, Thaw pulled a pistol from his evening clothes, walked up to White's table, and fired three shots at point-blank range into his rival's head.

At her husband's trial for murder early the next year (he pleaded insanity), Nesbit was the star defense witness, repeating to the court the story she'd told Thaw about White's drugging and raping her. The trial ended in a hung jury, and in a second trial Thaw was acquitted. Within three weeks of the verdict, the two were negotiating a divorce. Nesbit pursued a steadily declining acting career, until her death in 1967 at age 82. Thaw, who died in 1947 at age 76, spent the rest of his life in and out of trouble and insane asylums.

Evelyn Nesbit: Mr. White asked me to come to see the back room, and he went through some curtains, and the back room was a bedroom, and I sat down at the table, a tiny little table. There was a bottle of champagne, a small bottle, and one glass. Mr. White picked up the bottle and poured the glass full of champagne. I paid no attention to him, because I was looking at a picture over the mantel, a very beautiful one that attracted my attention. Then he told me he had decorated this room himself, and showed me all the different things about it. It was very small. Then he came to me and told me to finish my champagne, which I did, and I don't know whether it was a minute after or two minutes after, but a pounding began in my ears, a something and pounding, then the whole room seemed to go around. Everything got very flat. [The witness weeps.]

Defense Attorney Delmas: I do not desire to distress you any more than is necessary in this matter, but it is absolutely essential that you should go on with your testimony.

A: Then when I woke up, all my clothes were pulled off of me, and I was in bed. I sat up in the bed and started to scream. Mr. White was there and got up and put on one of the kimonos. The kimono was lying on a chair, and then I moved up and pulled some covers over me and sat up, and there were mirrors all around the bed. There were mirrors on the side of the wall and on top. Then I screamed, and he came over and asked me to please keep quiet, that I must not make so much noise. He said, "It is all over, it is all over." Then I screamed, "Oh, no!" And then he brought a kimono over to me and he went out of the room. Then as I got out of bed I began to scream more than ever. Then he came back into the room and tried to quiet me. I don't remember how I got my clothes on or how I went home, but he took me home. Then he went away and left me, and I sat up all night.

Q: Where was Mr. White, madam, at the time you regained your consciousness? You say you found that you had been stripped. Did you describe to Mr. Thaw where White was?

A: Yes. He was right there beside me.

Q: Where?

A: In the bed.

Q: Dressed or undressed?

A: Completely undressed.

Q: What was the effect of this statement of yours upon Mr. Thaw?

A: He became very excited.

Q: Will you kindly describe it?

A: He would get up and walk up and down the room a minute and then come and sit down and say, "Oh, God! Oh, God!" and bite his nails like that, and keep sobbing.

Q: Sobbing?

A: Yes, it was not like crying. It was a deep sob. He kept saying, "Go on, go on, tell me the whole thing about it."

Evelyn Nesbit's beauty captured by the camera *(right)* and by artist Charles Dana Gibson *(above, left)* for one of his idealized portraits of the "Gibson Girl." A more staid-looking Nesbit *(top)* took the witness stand at her husband's trial.

"That the automobile has practically reached the limit of its development is suggested by the fact that during the past year no improvements of a radical nature have been introduced."—**Scientific American, January 1909**

STORY OF THE YEAR

Ford Introduces the Model T

1 "I will build a car for the great multitude," vowed Henry Ford in 1908, as he unveiled the Model T, the car that sold the world on automobiles and spawned assembly-line production, thereby launching a second industrial revolution. By the end of the century, the tinkering former farm boy's early vision of individual car ownership for the masses had not only been realized beyond his wildest dreams, but had affected almost every area of life—from the way cities look, to the role of oil in international politics, to the very air earthlings breathe.

Durable, lightweight, extraordinarily flexible, the Model T stood up to rough country roads, creating a market for cars among rural working people—a vast share of all Americans in 1908. More important, at $850, Ford's car was affordable, no longer a plaything of the rich. (Over the years, as production was streamlined, the price actually came down, bringing Ford, who founded his Detroit company in 1903, ever nearer his then-revolutionary goal of building a car "that no man making a good salary will be unable to afford.") Within a year of its introduction, 10,000 Model T's were putt-putting across America. By the time production stopped in 1927, more than 15 million had been sold worldwide.

With its four-cylinder engine, semiautomatic "planetary" transmission (forward and reverse pedals enabled quick, rocking changes of direction), rugged spring suspension, and a magneto-powered electrical system that replaced heavy, dry-storage batteries, the innovative Model T was far and away the sturdiest car of its time. It could go just about anywhere a horse and cart could go, and get there faster. "Your car lifted us out of the mud," an American farm woman wrote to the tycoon in 1918—sweet praise indeed to the populist prophet of technology and its everyday applications.

Ford got 1,000 inquiries about the Model T *(1910 model, above)* after his first public ad.

What made the Model T truly radical, and a gold mine for Ford, was the interchangeability of its parts. From 1913, every component, from axles to gear boxes, was tooled to precise tolerances, so that each Model T was like every other one—allowing the car to be mass-produced at a time when other automobiles had to be painstakingly handcrafted. (Component parts also made for cheaper repairs.) In 1909, faced with a seemingly insatiable demand, Ford opened his massive plant at Highland Park, Michigan. A few years later, still trying to reduce production time, he introduced the moving assembly line, creating at a turn the modern automobile industry—all to serve the humble Model T. **◂1903.8 ▸1913.6**

H. M. Leopold, King of the Congo, in his national dress.

King Leopold II in a British cartoon, getting as good as he gave.

CENTRAL AFRICA

Leopold Loses the Congo

2 In just over two decades, King Leopold II of Belgium had turned a piece of central Africa 80 times the size of his native country into his own private estate. Revenues from the lucrative rubber and ivory industries were funneled directly into his own pocket. By 1908, his imperial excesses and his brutal treatment of the Africans had created such an uproar that the Belgian parliament, in an effort to preserve the constitution and rein in the King's powers, voted to annex the Congo Free State and make it a formal colony.

Leopold had begun taking possession of the land in the late 1870s when explorer Henry Morton Stanley navigated the Congo River and offered the treaties he'd negotiated with African chiefs first to an uninterested Britain, then to an eager Leopold. By 1884, 450 chiefs had granted their rights of sovereignty to Leopold (who by then was employing Stanley to negotiate on his behalf). After the King built a road through the interior, the "scramble for Africa" escalated. The Berlin Act of 1885 established borders and rules of free trade for colonial Africa and called for the moral improvement of the African native. Leopold ignored the act's every provision, ruling the Congo with a bloody fist.

For him the Congo was "the great African cake." The King imposed exorbitant taxes, which virtually abolished international trade and foreign investment. The Congolese were stripped of all rights and forced into harvesting rubber without pay. "Here is a basket," regional commissioners were instructed to tell their subjects. "Go to the forest at once, and if in a week you have not returned with ten pounds of rubber, I shall set fire to your hut and you will burn." Some 15 million people were thus enslaved, tens of thousands more killed. Groups like the Congo Reform Association in England sprang up in protest.

After first buying yachts, Mediterranean villas, and mistresses, Leopold plowed money into Belgium. He built lavish public works —roads, parks, museums—all calculated to keep the Belgian people on his side even as the rest of the world rose up to condemn him. When Leopold realized that public opinion had turned irrevocably against him and that the annexation movement was unstoppable, he quietly and cagily transferred the Free State's wealth into secret trusts and mining concessions beyond the Belgian government's grasp. The Congo he ceded to Belgium, though rich in natural resources, was bankrupt. **◂1902.5 ▸1909.M**

GREAT BRITAIN

Boys into Fighting Men

3 If Britain had won the Boer War more handily, the Boy Scouts, founded in 1908, might never have existed. But it had taken 450,000 troops three years to subdue 40,000 Dutch farmers. Many in the Empire were worried about the quality of the British fighting man—especially since three out of five recruits had been rejected as physically deficient. Back home, industrialization was

ART & CULTURE: Books: *A Room with a View* (E.M. Forster); *The Wind in the Willows* (Kenneth Grahame); *Anne of Green Gables* (Lucy Maud Montgomery); *Penguin Island* (Anatole France); *The Man Who Was Thursday* (G.K. Chesterton); *The Old Wives' Tale* (Arnold Bennett) ... Music: "Take Me Out to the Ball Game" (Von Tilzer and Norworth); "Shine on, Harvest Moon" (Bayes and Norworth);

A VOICE FROM 1909

Monsieur Blériot Flies Across the Channel

By Louis Blériot, from the London *Daily Mail*, July 26, 1909

Louis Blériot made the first successful overseas flight in a heavier-than-air aircraft when he piloted an airplane of his own design from Calais, France, across the English Channel to Dover, winning international fame and the prize of £1,000 offered by the London Daily Mail, *which published this account of his flight. The aircraft, which looked like an elegant insect, was a monoplane constructed of steel tubing, ash, and bamboo, with a fabric covering and bicycle-type wire landing wheels. It was powered by a 25 horse-power, three-cylinder engine, and had a top speed of about 40 mph. The airplane had no flaps or ailerons and was maneuvered by warping the entire wing. Blériot's flight only lasted 37 minutes, but it focused world attention on the economic and military potential of the airplane.* **◂1903.1 ▸1927.1**

At 4:30 we could see all around. Daylight had come. M. Le Blanc endeavored to see the coast of England, but could not. A light breeze from the south-west was blowing. The air was clear. Everything was prepared. I was dressed as I am at this moment, a khaki jacket lined with wool for warmth over my tweed clothes and beneath my engineer's suit of blue cotton overalls. My close-fitting cap was fastened over my head and ears. I had neither eaten nor drunk anything since I rose. My thoughts were only upon the flight, and my determination to accomplish it this morning. 4:35! Tout est prêt! Le Blanc gives the signal and in an instant I am in the air, my engine making 1,200 revolutions—almost its highest speed—in order that I might get quickly over the telegraph wires along the edge of the cliff. As soon as I am over the cliff, I reduce my speed. There is now no need to force my engine.

I begin my flight, steady and sure, towards the coast of England. I have no apprehension, no sensations, pas du tout. The Escopette has seen me. She is driving ahead at full speed. She makes perhaps 42 kilomètres (about 26 miles) an hour. What matters? I am making at least 68 kilomètres … Rapidly, I overtake her, travelling at a height of 80 mètres … The moment is supreme, yet I surprise myself by feeling no exultation. Below me is the sea, the surface disturbed by the wind, which is now freshening. The motion of the waves beneath me is not pleasant. I drive on. Ten minutes have gone. I have passed the destroyer, and I turn my head to see whether I am proceeding in the right direction. I am amazed. There is nothing to be seen, neither the torpedo-destroyer, nor France, nor England. I am alone. I can see nothing at all—*rien du tout!* For ten minutes I am lost. It is a strange position to be alone, unguided, without compass, in the air over the middle of the Channel. I touch nothing. My hands and feet rest lightly on the levers. I let the aeroplane take its own course. I care not whither it goes. For ten minutes I continue, neither rising nor falling nor turning. And then, 20 minutes after I have left the French coast, I see the green cliffs of Dover, the Castle, and away to the west the spot where I had intended to land.… The flight could easily be done again. Shall I do it? I think not. I have promised my wife that after a race for which I have entered I will fly no more.

Above, Blériot just before takeoff. At left, Blériot's plane as it approached Dover, as illustrated in a supplement to Paris's *Le Petit Journal.* On the ground, a binational team of "traffic controllers" greets him and guides him to his landing.

It was a decade seared by the most horrible war the world had ever known. When the fighting stopped, Victorian innocence had expired and the modern world begun.

1910 1919

World War I brought new diabolism to the age-old art of mass killing, as chemical warfare took a prominent place alongside old-fashioned, mechanical weaponry. Gas—chlorine and tear, followed by the more lethal mustard and phosgene—was tried by the French (in the form of rifle grenades) in 1914, but the Germans were the first to use it extensively, beginning with the Battle of Ypres in 1915. It was then taken up by the Allies as well. These British soldiers, blinded by a German gas attack during the Lys offensive near Béthune, France, in April 1918, form a human chain as they shuffle off for medical treatment.

THE WORLD IN 1910

World Population

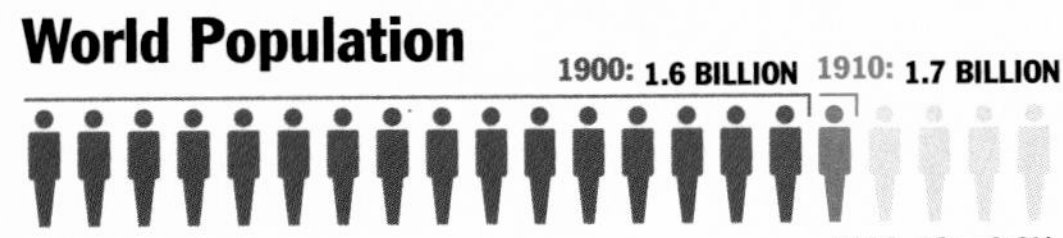

European Immigration to the United States

Total for 1907
1,199,566
(the peak year)

Denmark, Iceland, Norway, Sweden	49,965
Baltics, Finland, Russia	258,943
Ireland	34,530
U.K.	79,037
Germany	37,807
Belgium, France, Luxembourg, Netherlands, Switzerland	26,512
Austria-Hungary	338,452
Greece, Spain, Portugal	52,079
Bulgaria, Romania, Turkey	36,510
Italy	285,731

Total Immigrants to the U.S.

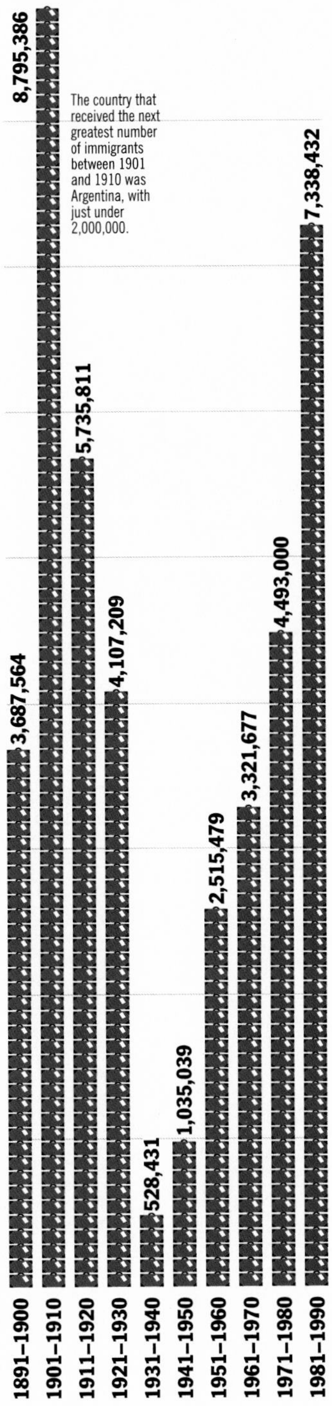

Decade	Immigrants
1891–1900	3,687,564
1901–1910	8,795,386
1911–1920	5,735,811
1921–1930	4,107,209
1931–1940	528,431
1941–1950	1,035,039
1951–1960	2,515,479
1961–1970	3,321,677
1971–1980	4,493,000
1981–1990	7,338,432

The country that received the next greatest number of immigrants between 1901 and 1910 was Argentina, with just under 2,000,000.

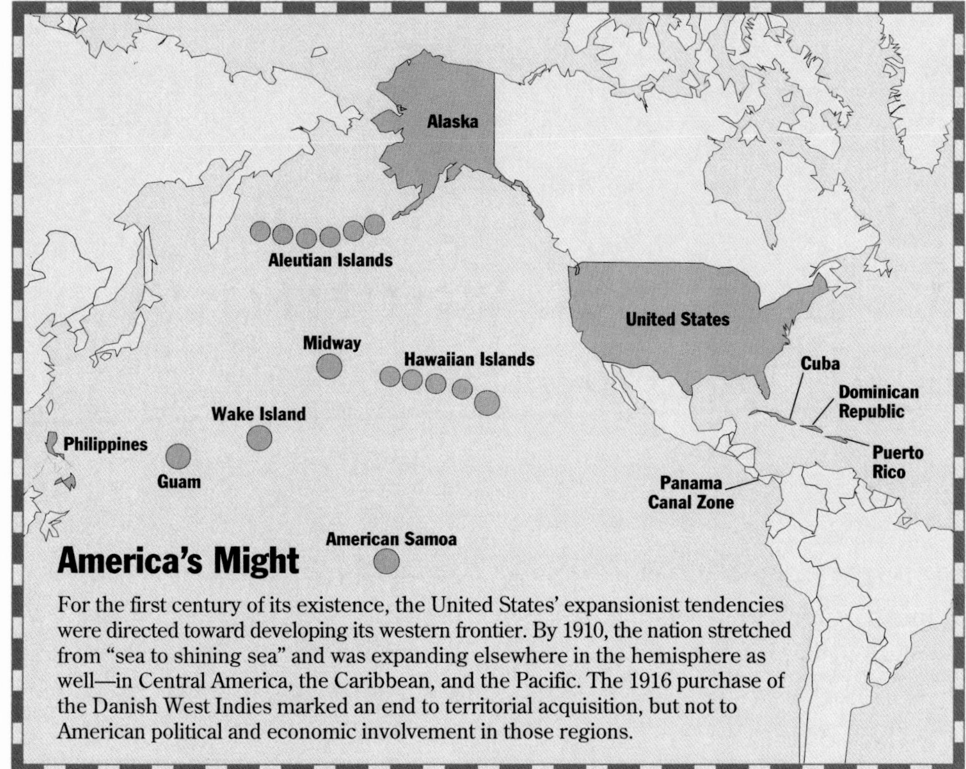

America's Might

For the first century of its existence, the United States' expansionist tendencies were directed toward developing its western frontier. By 1910, the nation stretched from "sea to shining sea" and was expanding elsewhere in the hemisphere as well—in Central America, the Caribbean, and the Pacific. The 1916 purchase of the Danish West Indies marked an end to territorial acquisition, but not to American political and economic involvement in those regions.

Daily Newspapers

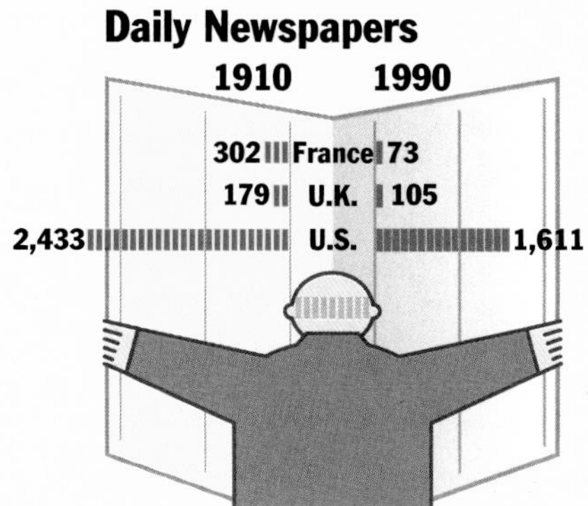

Summer Olympic Games

London 1908		Barcelona 1992
22	Nations	171
2,035	Athletes	10,563
323	Medals	815

Sports competition was becoming increasingly sophisticated. The Olympic Summer Games of 1908, attended by 22 nations, though modest compared to today's games, were the first to be organized and controlled by an international athletic committee, rather than private promoters.

By 1910, a decade after Eastman Kodak's introduction of the **Brownie**—the first camera to allow nonprofessionals to take pictures—amateur photography enjoyed wild popularity. From 1889 to 1909, sales of cameras and other photography equipment grew by an average 11 percent per year.

Fashion Essential

The **wristwatch** was becoming a standard accessory for both men and women. It had been invented just six years earlier when a Brazilian aviator complained to French watchmaker Louis-François Cartier about the difficulty of pulling out a pocket watch while flying a plane. Cartier presented him with a small watch designed to be fastened to the wrist by a leather strap. Cartier designed this platinum bracelet model in 1910.

The Great Wave The first decade of the century saw a dramatic mass movement of Europeans to other continents. While many countries received large influxes of foreigners seeking better lives (the population of Argentina, for example, was nearly one third European-born in 1910), no nation's identity has been more shaped—politically, economically, and culturally—by the presence of a large immigrant population than that of the United States.

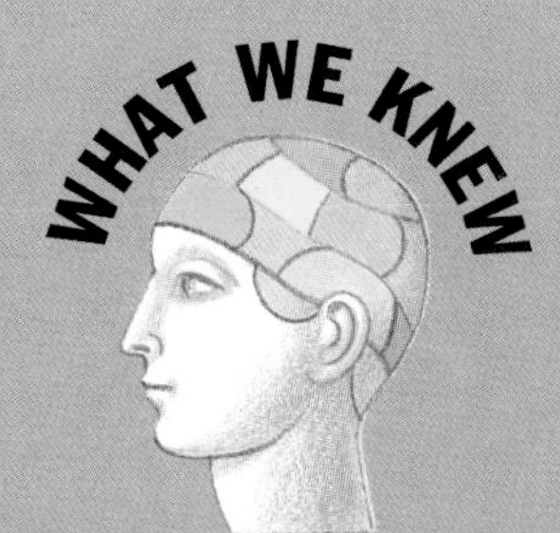

Military strategists believe the airplane to be of only limited use in battle. French Marshal Ferdinand Foch declares that airplanes "are interesting toys, but of no military value."

■

General Alfred von Schlieffen, chief of Germany's general staff, devises a plan that will allow Germany to win a war on two fronts. A quick, heavily fortified advance through Belgium and Holland into France will force the French into Switzerland or up against the German frontier. Weaker forces will hold back the French in the South and the Russians in the East.

■

In all but three countries of the world (New Zealand, Australia, and Finland), women are still considered unworthy of the vote. "Sensible and responsible women do not want to vote," former U.S. President Grover Cleveland has said, expressing a common sentiment. "The relative positions to be assumed by man and woman in … our civilization were assigned long ago by a higher intelligence than ours."

■

Inventor Thomas Edison predicts that gasoline engines will soon be rendered obsolete by the stored energy of nickel-iron batteries.

■

Although movies are attended by some 26 million Americans every week, *The Independent*, a weekly magazine, asserts that "the fad will die out in the next few years."

■

Although citrus fruits are known to prevent scurvy (and to alleviate its worst symptoms), the presence of vitamins in foods will not be discovered until 1912.

■

In France, fashion designer Paul Poiret's new, free-flowing sheath has encouraged women to begin abandoning the corset, but elsewhere steel-reinforced supports are an essential part of a respectable woman's underpinnings. (When the United States enters World War I in 1917, corset donations yield enough steel for two battleships.)

WITOLD RYBCZYNSKI

The Ceaseless Machine

The Coming of Mass Production

1910
1919

THE YEAR 1913 WAS A WATERSHED IN THE HISTORY of the twentieth century, for it was then that Henry Ford organized the first assembly line. It happened in Highland Park, Michigan, where Ford was starting to manufacture the Model T automobile. The first line did not involve the entire car, only the magneto, and although it was a small enough improvement it was a historic moment nonetheless. It was one of those rare instances that define an era, like Johann Gutenberg's first printing of a book using movable type in the middle of the fifteenth century, or James Watt's development of a practicable high-pressure condensing steam engine, which he patented in 1769. Just as these events were followed by what people came to refer to as the Age of Print and the Age of Steam, after 1913 one can speak of the Age of Mass Production.

In fact, Henry Ford was not the first manufacturer to use an assembly line. One hundred and thirty years earlier, Oliver Evans, a Delaware mechanic, built a flour mill in Philadelphia that used a variety of waterwheel-powered devices to mechanically convey grain from one milling process to another. In 1804, the British Navy built a factory for producing ship's biscuits in which five bakers, each performing one step of the operation, worked in a line. The Swiss inventor Johann Georg Bodmer built a number of textile factories in England in the 1830s in which fixed work stations were connected to one another by mechanical conveyance systems. Even the overhead rails that transported car chassis from one assembly to another in Ford's factory were not original but based on a device used to convey animal carcasses in Cincinnati packing houses. Nor did Ford (who had no formal training in either science or engineering) contribute any crucial technological refinements to the car itself. In that regard he was different from Gottlieb Daimler, say, or Karl Benz, who both pioneered crucial advances in automobile technology; unlike the diesel engine, named after its inventor, Rudolf Diesel, no automobile component bears Ford's name.

Even after Henry Ford *(above)* introduced the assembly line, in many industries individual workers continued to take a single item through every phase of the production process. In the wheel-making department of the Nash Motor Company in Kenosha, Wisconsin *(right)*, a complex set of machine tools was assigned to each worker. Ford himself was a visionary who nonetheless despised many of the changes his mass-produced Model T helped bring about, including America's transition from a rural to an increasingly urban society. In later life, Ford devoted himself to pursuits aimed at preserving the "plain-folk," agrarian values of his Michigan childhood.

Though Ford did not invent the assembly line or the automobile, he was a visionary nonetheless: He can be said to have thought up the idea of the car as a form of popular transportation. "It will be so low in price that no man making a good salary will be unable to own one—and enjoy with his family the blessing of hours of pleasure in God's great open spaces," Ford grandly proclaimed. Previously, in both Europe and America, automobiles had been luxury products, used exclusively by the rich and chiefly for pleasure. Ford brought cars to a larger market. But he was not simply selling cheaper cars so that more people could go on Sunday drives. Almost overnight, the Model T, which Ford called the "universal car," put inexpensive, individual, rapid transportation in the hands of thousands, and then millions, of ordinary people, people who lived in a country of large distances.

To understand Ford's accomplishment it is necessary to know that nineteenth-century America was replete with examples of standardized, mass-produced items for individual use: shovels turned out by the Ames company of Massachusetts; John Landis Mason's famous jars; domestic clocks made in huge numbers by Eli Terry of Plymouth, Connecticut, in the early 1800s; sewing machines from Isaac Singer. The Model T was different from any of these products, however. After all, cheaper shovels were no better than the old-fashioned handcrafted kind, Mason jars did not really change the traditional practice of home canning, cheap clocks were still

clocks, and although the sewing machine made complicated stitching both easier and faster, it was still cheaper to sew with a needle and thread. But an inexpensive car was unprecedented.

It's obvious that the automobile was faster than the horse and carriage. What is less obvious is that a car like the Model T was much *cheaper* than a horse and carriage. A car consumes fuel only when it is moving; horses must be fed year-round. Moreover, since travel on horseback or by carriage requires a constant supply of fresh animals provided at pre-arranged stops, the unflagging car also represents an opportunity for unplanned, spontaneous travel. Mobility and freedom, and at a lower cost: This was a product that sold itself.

A brief history of the production of the Model T summarizes its spectacular achievement. Although the first car rolled out of the Highland Park factory in 1908, it was only after Ford started using assembly lines, five years later, that the effect of mass production on lowering costs became visible. Over the years, the number of man-hours necessary to assemble a car dropped from 12.5 to an amazing 1.5, and the price fell accordingly—from an original sales tag of $850 to as low as $310, which made the Model T 40 percent cheaper than its nearest competitor.

The reduction in price was not merely the result of manufacturing large numbers. Unlike previous examples of mass production, which were merely conventional products made in large quantities, the Model T was specifically designed to be mass produced. Simplicity was the watchword. There were no doors, for example, and no side windows; there was no speedometer or windshield wipers, and no choice of body colors (for the first twelve years, all Model Ts were black). Such wholesale simplification sounds commercially ruthless, and it was, but Ford's car was designed with the owner's needs in mind. The first buyers of Model Ts were chiefly farmers and small-town folk (city people could travel on streetcars and omnibuses) and the 20-horsepower engine and the rugged mechanics were intended to cope with bad country roads, just as the simple mechanical systems could be easily repaired by the driver himself without recourse to expert assistance. The sales of this revolutionary car skyrocketed: In 1914, only six years after it was introduced, a quarter of a million Model Ts were sold; when production was finally halted in 1927, 15 million had rolled off the assembly line.

BUT FORD'S GENIUS WAS NOT MERELY to find a way to bring more cars to more people. His entire industrial endeavor was based on a simple but crucial insight: Mass production is only one side of the supply-and-demand coin; the other is mass consumption. Earlier manufacturers of mass products like shovels or sewing machines understood that to realize the advantages of mass production, there had to be mass demand. Where Ford went one step further—and it was a giant step—was in recognizing that mass production could *fuel* demand. The assembly line could be used simultaneously to increase production and to lower costs—everybody knew that—but Ford was the first to realize that higher profits allowed for higher wages. Raise wages and you increase consumption, he reasoned; raise consumption and you increase production.

Ford proceeded to put his chicken-and-egg theory into practice. In 1914, when the industry was paying $2.40 a day, Ford paid $5.00; by 1929 the average wage at Ford had risen to $7.00 a day. Increasing consumption meant not only increasing wages, but also increasing free time. In 1914, Ford reduced the workday in his plants from nine hours to eight. Now his workers had not only more money, but also more free time during which to spend it. Ford didn't stop there: In 1926, while almost all American industry operated a six-day week, he announced that his factories would be closed all day Saturday as well as Sunday. This made the Ford Motor Company one of the first large industries in the world to observe the two-day weekend.

Over time there came a major consequence that not even the farsighted industrialist could have anticipated: Mass production changed not merely the process of manufacturing consumer goods, it changed the consumers themselves. Car buyers grew bored with the limited choice that early mass

By the mid-1930s, the assembly-line process had been apotheosized in the popular imagination. In Detroit, Edsel Ford, who succeeded his father as president of the Ford Motor Company, commissioned Mexican muralist Diego Rivera to paint a series of frescoes for the courtyard of the Detroit Institute of Arts. The resulting 27 panels managed both to celebrate the efficiency and underscore the brutality of the modern factory. In answer to critics on the religious right who accused the artist of creating a "communist manifesto" and of being "cold and hard," Rivera responded, "I paint what I see.... [the murals'] subject is steel, and steel is both cold and hard."

production offered, and demanded more variety. Ford sternly resisted this tendency, but his competitors' success meant that eventually he, too, had to bend. The Model T's successor, the Model A, came in as many as 17 body styles and four different colors. Ford had come face-to-face with a fundamental paradox of mass production: While it begins by producing standardized commodities for the masses, it ends by offering a wide variety of products geared to the demands of the individual. This ability to provide choices, whether in cars or running shoes, is the keystone of consumer society, and the chief reason for consumerism's ever-expanding appeal throughout the world.

But it wasn't only consumers who wanted variety. Workers, while appreciating their increased pay, also became bored—with the repetitive nature of assembly-line work. It may have been ungrateful of them (pre-industrial work was, if anything, more debilitating), but such is the nature of human progress. In 1949, two years after Ford died, Yale University issued its landmark study of the automobile industry, *Man on the Assembly Line*. Of the workers surveyed, 90 percent said the only thing they liked about their assembly-line jobs was the high pay; the great majority hated the mechanical pacing and repetitive nature of their work, and many were frustrated by the lack of skill required by the simplified operations. Industrial management has been plagued with these problems ever since. Dissatisfaction with assembly-line work has been at the core of many labor disturbances, and is only today being addressed by the introduction of work teams, industrial democracy, and quality management. The ultimate solution to boredom on the assembly line is probably robotics, which substitutes machines for humans doing the most dulling, repetitive tasks.

HISTORY IS MORE OR LESS BUNK," Ford famously remarked, but it is history that reveals the real effects of the mass-produced automobile. A look back at the twentieth century shows these effects to be breathtakingly broad. Cars changed how cities are planned, for example, by speeding up suburban growth (although the first suburbs were the result of streetcars and railroads, not cars). The automobile altered shopping habits by enabling the introduction of regional shopping centers and malls which, in turn, contributed to the decay of the traditional downtown. The pursuit of leisure, which had been part of Ford's vision, was furthered by the happy union of cars and weekends, and gave rise to weekend cottages, campgrounds, and a variety of highway-related activities. The car also reconfigured family life by taking many recreations out of the home, and by giving unprecedented mobility to two groups: teenagers and women. The unexpected relationship between cars and feminism is apparent in the restrictions on women drivers enforced by some fundamentalist Islamic countries.

Ford, adopting the visionary tone that he favored in later life, maintained that "the automobile is the product of peace." On the contrary, the gasoline engine contributed to the destructive power of the military, making possible the blitzkrieg of World War II. Indeed, America's dependence on the car, and hence petroleum, can even be said to have caused at least one war: the Persian Gulf conflict of 1991. Perhaps the least anticipated—but arguably most deleterious—result of the widespread use of the automobile is its effect on the physical environment, since car engines produce carbon dioxide emissions that create local atmospheric pollution and also damage the ozone layer.

Technologies always have unintended consequences, of course: Just think how the invention of type finally altered religious belief in northern Europe, or how artillery changed the shape of medieval cities, or how steam power opened up the American West. But mass production vastly accelerates and enlarges those consequences; it is the *scale* of technology's impact on human life that sets the Age of Mass Production apart. The effect of the personal computer on individual work, of the television on political power, or of the videocassette recorder on public entertainment are all examples of how mass production has changed human life. Ultimately, the chief legacy of Henry Ford and the era he launched is not the material products that roll off the assembly line, but the transformations in our lives that those products have wrought. □

With the advent of computers, the traditional, human-driven assembly line has been largely supplanted by such superior forms of automation as robotics. In many automobile factories, highly sophisticated, electronically programmed machines have entirely replaced human workers. Here, at a General Motors factory in West Germany in 1989, robots weld the bodies of cars that move automatically down the line from robot to robot. The machines are so self-regulating that, aside from technicians to service them, no humans are needed.

"It is the wish and command of the Japanese Emperor that every effort shall be made to make the Koreans feel that there is no humiliation but rather a relief in annexation." **—Official statement of the Imperial Japanese Majesty's resident general in Korea after the annexation**

STORY OF THE YEAR

Japan Crushes Korea

1 Emboldened by its decisive military victory over the Russians in Manchuria, imperial Japan turned a hungry eye on Korea, the strategically important, underdeveloped kingdom to its west. On August 22, 1910, the implicit reality of Japan's relationship with Korea was made explicit: Japan formally annexed its powerless protectorate.

Japan's intentions had been increasingly clear since 1905, when Korean ministers were coerced into signing the convention that made Korea a Japanese protectorate: Nothing short of total domination was the goal.

Korean justice, as depicted in Japanese propaganda: "old style" police interrogation in a "primitive" office before annexation *(top)* contrasted with orderly rectitude in a modern, "hygienic" office afterward *(bottom)*.

Under the terms of the protectorate, Japan assumed control of Korea's internal administration and foreign policy. Two years later, Korean Emperor Kojong was forced to abdicate in favor of his more pliant son, Sunjong. The judiciary fell under Japanese dominion in 1909, followed quickly by police powers. The Korean-Japanese Treaty of 1910, by which Korean rights of sovereignty were ceded to Japan, was negotiated in strict secrecy. By the time it was announced, annexation was a fait accompli.

Japan loosed a crushing reign of terror to ensure that the violent protests and suicidal revolts of 1905 and 1907 would not be repeated: Troops patrolled Seoul, the capital, barring protest; censors eliminated negative stories from Korean newspapers; police cracked down on nationalist organizations.

Other countries stood by and watched. The United States had already tacitly approved the annexation with the Portsmouth Treaty of 1905, which formally recognized Japanese supremacy in Korea. Other foreign powers, particularly Great Britain, were only concerned that annexation might jeopardize the rights and financial interests of their subjects.

Japan had become the strongest power in Asia, and this event marked the succession to power of ultranationalists within Japan. Meanwhile, the people of Korea, primitively armed and politically compromised, read the posted official announcements, saw Japanese sentries everywhere they looked, and suffered the furious resignation of the powerless. **◂1905.3 ▸1921.5**

Oldfield posted ever higher speeds, but spent his final years preaching safety.

SPORTS

Two Miles a Minute

2 After spending the decade setting new records, race-car driver Barney Oldfield posted his most impressive speed yet in 1910, when he drove a "Blitzen" Benz a phenomenal 131.724 miles per hour in Daytona Beach, Florida. In just seven years Oldfield had more than doubled the world record he set in 1903 when he piloted his Ford-Cooper 999 a mile a minute during an automobile test in Indianapolis. (Carmakers like Henry Ford often tried out their new models by racing them on speedways the year before they were introduced.)

The Indianapolis 500 was instituted a year after Oldfield set his 1910 record, but his remarkable speed was not surpassed on that speedway until 1937. The 500-mile Indy, held every Memorial Day weekend, now ranks as one of the top racing events in the world, along with Le Mans, established in 1906, and the Monte Carlo, first run in 1911.

Oldfield raced just twice at Indy, finishing fifth in both 1914 and 1916. But he grew to disdain his sport's disregard for safety, referring to it as a "Roman circus." He retired in 1918, and spent the rest of his life promoting safe driving. **◂1908.1 ▸1957.11**

PORTUGAL

A Conservative Revolution

3 Portugal's doomed constitutional monarchy, the last incarnation of the 270-year-old royal House of Bragança, ended ingloriously in 1910 with the overthrow of 20-year-old King Manuel II by Republican revolutionaries. The hapless King, who had been thrust upon the throne two years earlier following the assassination of his father and brother, fled to England, where he quietly collected books until his death in 1932.

The new Portuguese republic was one of the most curiously conservative of all revolutionary governments. Established in reaction to a monarchy that had been slowly failing for a century, the new regime looked backward rather than forward for inspiration. The patriotic hymn of the republic said it all:

Heroes of the sea, noble people,
Nation valiant and immortal,
Raise today once again,
The splendor of Portugal.

Manuel II, the 20-year-old Portuguese monarch, bids adieu to his country as he escapes to England.

The Republicans had been united only in their opposition to the monarchy. Once the King was deposed, unity quickly dissolved. Beyond a desire to return Portugal to her former glory (which meant restoring the colonial empire, which had

ART & CULTURE: Books: ***Howards End*** **(E.M. Forster);** ***Clayhanger*** **(Arnold Bennett);** ***The Vagabond*** **(Colette);** ***The Town Down the River*** **(Edwin Arlington Robinson) ... Music: "Let Me Call You Sweetheart" (Friedman and Whitson);** ***The Girl of the Golden West*** **(Giacomo Puccini);** ***String Quartet, Op. 3*** **(Alban Berg);** ***Fantasia on a Theme by Thomas Tallis*** **(Ralph Vaughan Williams) ... Painting & Sculpture:**

"I like mathematics because it is not *human & has nothing particular to do with this planet or with the whole accidental universe—because, like Spinoza's God, it won't love us in return."*—**Bertrand Russell**

eroded precipitously under the constitutional monarchy), the Republicans had few specific goals. Consequently, the First Republic was marked by political squabbling and deepening economic turmoil. It survived only until 1926, when the dictatorial New State was established and Portugal, under the long reign of António de Oliveira Salazar, effectively withdrew from world affairs. **►1933.9**

IDEAS

Mathematics and Logic

4 With the appearance in 1910 of the first volume of *Principia Mathematica* (published in three volumes, 1910-1913), an attempt to reduce mathematics to pure logic, Bertrand Russell *(top)* and Alfred North Whitehead *(bottom)* established a foundation for future forays into theoretical mathematics, analytic philosophy, and symbolic logic. Few other works have exerted as profound or enduring an influence on modern thought.

Brilliant, iconoclastic, and deeply humane, Russell, the orphaned scion of an aristocratic family, matriculated at Trinity College, Cambridge University, in 1890, ten years behind Whitehead, the son of an Episcopal clergyman, who was already established as a lecturer in mathematics. Under the influence of his teacher G.E. Moore, whose *Principia Ethica* (1903) was a cornerstone of modern analytic philosophy, Russell began looking to mathematics as a philosophic model of exactness and absolute knowledge. His first book, *The Principles of Mathematics* (1903), led to the collaboration with Whitehead. Russell became well-known to the general public for his pacifism and his progressive social ideas, but it was mathematics that sustained him—literally. Late in his long life (he died in 1970 at 98), Russell remembered his early years as a daily struggle against suicide, from which he was "restrained by the desire to know more mathematics."

Among the theoreticians inspired by the *Principia* was Ludwig Wittgenstein, who, after reading the treatise, went to Cambridge to study under Russell. Wittgenstein's elegantly precise *Tractatus Logico-Philosophicus*, a work that he initially claimed solved all the problems of philosophy, developed out of the inquiries into the nature of logic the two men made together at Cambridge. **►1918.4**

SCIENCE

Halley's Comet Returns

5 As dusk settled over Constantinople on the evening of May 18, 1910, 100,000 people took to their roofs. Some huddled together for comfort; others prayed for salvation. The scene was repeated around the world. Many people believed the end of the world was at hand. The source of this widespread terror? Halley's Comet, which had recently returned from its 75-year odyssey through space.

For years scientists, excited by the opportunity to increase their astronomical knowledge, had been gearing up for Halley's reappearance. By late 1909 many of the world's most important observatories were engaged in an active search for the comet. Professor Max Wolf, at Heidelberg, Germany, detected it in September 1909. As enthusiasm spread, the public eagerly awaited the moment when the comet would become visible to the naked eye. Scientists produced a number of calculations, including one predicting that Halley's tail would pass very close to earth—perhaps even sweep right across it—between May 18 and 19. With this revelation, the public grew uncertain. Whipped up by the tabloids, which discussed in gruesome detail the deleterious effect the gaseous comet could have on the earth's atmosphere, people panicked. In the United States some coal miners refused to enter the shafts, preferring to die on the surface with their families. Across North America a few souls, fearing Armageddon, attempted suicide. A rancher in California crucified himself, nailing both his feet and one hand to a rough-hewn cross.

The coming of Halley's Comet generated a wealth of comet paraphernalia around the world.

In fact, the tail of Halley's Comet never came any closer to the earth's surface than 400,000 kilometers, and it would have been harmless at any distance. Said the *Seattle Post-Intelligencer:* "The comet came, the comet went and this old earth is no worse and no better and thus far no wiser." **►1929.9**

Halley's Comet photographed in Honolulu on May 12, 1910, by a camera with a telescopic lens.

BIRTHS

Joseph Alsop Jr., U.S. journalist.

Jean Anouilh, French playwright.

Samuel Barber, U.S. composer.

Jacques Cousteau, French oceanographer.

Jean Genet, French playwright.

Akira Kurosawa, Japanese filmmaker.

Eero Saarinen, Finnish-U.S. architect.

William Schuman, U.S. composer.

William Shockley, U.S. physicist.

Art Tatum, U.S. musician.

Mother Teresa, Albanian Roman Catholic nun.

Wilfred Thesiger, U.K. explorer and writer.

DEATHS

Björnstjerne Björnson, Norwegian writer.

Jean Henri Dunant, Swiss philanthropist.

Samuel Clemens (Mark Twain), U.S. writer.

Mary Baker Eddy, U.S. religious leader.

Winslow Homer, U.S. painter.

Julia Ward Howe, U.S. abolitionist and suffragist.

Holman Hunt, U.K. painter.

William James, U.S. philosopher.

Robert Koch, German bacteriologist.

Florence Nightingale, U.K. nurse.

William S. Porter (O. Henry), U.S. writer.

Henri Rousseau, French painter.

Leo Tolstoy, Russian novelist.

***Enigma of an Autumn Afternoon* (Giorgio de Chirico); *Sleeping Muse* (Constantin Brancusi) ... Film: *The Unchanging Sea, Ramona, The House with Closed Shutters* (D.W. Griffith); *The Abyss, Uncle Tom's Cabin* (Urban Gad) ... Theater: *Misalliance* (G.B. Shaw); *The Guardsman* (Ferenč Molnár); *Naughty Marietta* (Victor Herbert).**

"The art critic is the worst enemy of art."—**Wassily Kandinsky**

NEW IN 1910

Father's Day.

Policewoman (Los Angeles).

Good Housekeeping Seal of Approval.

Neon lights.

Hallmark, Inc. (Kansas City, Missouri).

Food mixer (Hamilton Beach).

Women's Wear Daily.

Safety glass.

Girl Guides (founded in England by Robert and Agnes Baden-Powell).

Trench coat (Burberry's Tielocken coat).

Boy Scouts of America.

IN THE UNITED STATES

►GIFTED DIAGNOSTICIAN—Chicago doctor James Byran Herrick identified a hitherto unknown disease. In 1910, after examining a West Indian student, Herrick diagnosed a painful blood condition: sickle-cell anemia. Potentially lethal, it was found to affect up to 3 percent of American blacks. ◄1903.M

►RED DOOR OPENS—New York secretary Florence Nightingale Graham, moved by Tennyson's poem *Enoch Arden*, changed her name to Elizabeth Arden and in 1910 opened a beauty salon on Fifth Avenue. The shop was so successful that she opened in other locations and launched a line of cosmetics that soon numbered more than 300 items. She always emphasized the "ladylike" nature of her cosmetics. By the time she died in 1966, her trademark red door opened into more than 100 salons.

ART

The Visual Music of Abstraction

6 **Wassily Kandinsky, an artist who had an almost mystical relationship with color, completed what is generally conceded to be the first purely abstract painting in modern art, *Improvisation XIV (above)*, in 1910. Kandinsky, who had turned to art at the age of 30 after earning degrees in law and economics in his native Russia, used colors and shapes to invent a pictorial equivalent of music. He described his *Improvisations* as "largely unconscious, spontaneous expressions of inner character, non-material in nature."**

But Kandinsky's work was not abstract for abstraction's sake: He wished to free painting from the depiction of objects so that it could better express ideas and evoke deep emotion. In fact, he warned that pure abstraction ran the risk of degenerating into mere decoration, "like a necktie or a carpet." (*Improvisation XIV*, for instance, clearly retains some figurative tendencies.) Kandinsky led the Russian avant-garde after the 1917 revolution, but this descendant of Mongolian royalty fell from favor and left for Berlin in 1921. ◄1907.1 ►1913.2

SOCIAL REFORM

NAACP Leads the Fight

7 After antiblack riots swept the United States, a group of 60 black intellectuals and sympathetic whites met on Lincoln's 100th birthday in New York City and formed a committee that, in 1910, became the National Association for the Advancement of Colored People (NAACP). Cofounder Mary White Ovington dedicated the organization to toppling "the walls of intolerance, prejudice, injustice, and arrogance" that divided the world's largest democracy. The NAACP spawned a new mass movement that eventually inspired human-rights advocates around the world.

The Civil War freed African-Americans from slavery, but it hardly won them full citizenship. Southern states enacted Jim Crow laws (named after a minstrel-show stereotype of a doltish Negro), which disenfranchised blacks and relegated them to separate (and usually inferior) schools, housing, hospitals, hotels, transportation, restrooms, theaters, even cemeteries. Scores of blacks were lynched yearly by vigilantes. The situation in the North was only marginally better.

The interracial NAACP grew out of the Niagara Movement, a black group founded in 1905 to oppose the accommodationism of Booker T. Washington, the head of Alabama's Tuskegee Institute, who urged blacks to drop demands for social equality in exchange for jobs and business opportunity. The Niagara activists, led by the brilliant historian W.E.B. Du Bois (*left*), held that blacks could never compete economically until they'd won their political rights. Although the NAACP's early officers were white—except for Du Bois, who ran the publicity and research departments—its policies, thanks to the efforts of its black cofounders, kept the Niagara spirit alive.

The NAACP fought racial prejudice on two fronts: education and litigation. It bombarded white America with pamphlets, press releases, and speeches on both the sufferings and the achievements of blacks. Du Bois ran groundbreaking sociological studies in the NAACP publication, *Crisis,* alongside the work of black authors and artists.

The NAACP struck back at Jim Crow with lawsuits. In 1915, the U.S. Supreme Court voided "grandfather clauses," which gave the right to vote only to those men whose grandfathers had voted, a de facto exclusion of blacks, most of whose grandparents had been slaves. Other successes followed, culminating in the 1954 *Brown v. Board of Education of Topeka* decision, which declared segregation in public schools unconstitutional. By then, the NAACP, at half a million members strong, was the foremost civil rights organization in the world. **◄1905.M ►1915.1**

SPORTS: Baseball: World Series, Philadelphia Athletics (the "$100,000 infield") defeat Chicago Cubs, 4–1 ... Football: Intercollegiate Athletic Association changes name to National Collegiate Athletic Association (NCAA) ... Basketball: Personal foul limit reduced from five to four ... Boxing: Jack Johnson retains heavyweight title against James J. Jeffries.

"The party is the nation and the nation is the party."—**An Afrikaner National Party slogan**

SOUTHERN AFRICA

Botha's Fragile Federation

8 The Union of South Africa, a federation of Great Britain's four southern African colonies, emerged in 1910 from the ruins of the Boer War as a self-governing dominion of the British Empire. As first prime minister of the new Afrikaner-dominated colony, Louis Botha, commander of the vanquished Boer army, had the unenviable and ultimately impossible task of forging an alliance among divided Afrikaner political factions and between the Afrikaner factions and their British counterparts. British unionists, among whom Botha now counted himself, believed full expression of Afrikaner nationalism could be achieved from within the empire. Afrikaner separatists, led by J.B.M. Hertzog, would accept nothing less than independence. British South Africans found suspect anything Afrikaner. Excluded entirely from the rancorous debate were the first South Africans, the disenfranchised blacks relegated to the base of the colonial pyramid.

Asked by British Governor-General Lord Gladstone to form a cabinet, Botha appointed a coalition administration reflecting the spectrum of Afrikaner opinion. Included were representatives of the Cape's South African party, the Transvaal's Het Volk, and the Free State's Orangia-Unie. Hertzog was minister of justice. Aiming to appease both English-speakers and Afrikaner separatists, Botha succeeded only in alienating both. The English felt betrayed by the inclusion of separatists in the government, while the separatists reviled his overtures to the unionists. In parliamentary elections later that year, the three Afrikaner parties won a handy majority over the two largest English parties. The following year, the Afrikaner parties merged into the South African party.

Botha's coalition, badly stitched from the beginning, soon began to tear. Hertzog's incessant advocacy of separatism gravely embarrassed the government and alarmed the English constituency. In a speech at De Wildt rail station in 1912, Hertzog declared that the "time has come when South Africa can no longer be ruled by non-Afrikaners." (The phrase is regarded as the spiritual birth of the strident National Party, which was officially founded two years later.) Outraged, Botha first resigned, dissolving the cabinet, then returned and reformed it without Hertzog. But the lines had been drawn, and although the Union survived another 20 years, it was doomed from that moment on. **◂1908.9 ▸1912.10**

First prime minister Louis Botha *(above)* was attacked by his nemesis, J.B.M. Hertzog, as a "protagonist of imperialism."

THEATER

Ziegfeld's Top Talents

9 Its publicity proclaimed it "A National Institution Glorifying the American Girl." In truth, it was a Broadway vaudeville revue, but with European taste and American pizzazz: stupendous sets and costumes, soon-to-be legendary comics and singers, and a bevy of seminude chorines, who simultaneously scandalized and entranced the public. The Ziegfeld Follies, produced by Florenz Ziegfeld Jr., had been bringing opulence and sophistication to the American musical theater for three years when, in 1910, Ziegfeld introduced to Broadway three of the Follies' best-loved stars: Fanny Brice, Irving Berlin, and Bert Williams.

Fanny Brice was a far cry from the ideal Ziegfeld Girl. Eighteen years old, Jewish, with a large nose, big eyes, and a broad, tight-lipped grin, she sang comic numbers with a daffy Yiddish accent; later, she belted out heartbreaking torch songs. As her Follies debut, Brice performed Irving Berlin's dialect novelty "Goodbye, Becky Cohen." Berlin, still a year away from his first smash song, "Alexander's Ragtime Band," worked on and off for the Follies for years, and in 1919 supplied its best-remembered theme song, "A Pretty Girl Is Like a Melody."

In daring to put a black performer on a "white" Broadway stage, Ziegfeld defied convention with Bert Williams. But the impresario loved clowns and hired only the best: W.C. Fields, Will Rogers, Eddie Cantor, Ed Wynn. Williams was the best; therefore Ziegfeld wanted him. (He did insist that the light-skinned comic perform in black face, however.) Not only was Williams a master of comic timing, but he was also a touching dramatic actor. W.C. Fields called him "the funniest man I ever saw and the saddest man I ever knew."

Ziegfeld staged his extravaganza for 24 years. And though he produced other musicals, including the immortal *Show Boat*, there is nothing else in American show-business memory quite equal to the glitzy grandeur and pure talent of the Ziegfeld Follies. **◂1905.11 ▸1911.6**

"Ziegfeld thought I was funny," said Fanny Brice, "but positively not good-looking."

IN THE UNITED STATES

▸MANN PROTECTS WOMEN—Riled by unconfirmed stories about international prostitution rings, the U.S. Congress in 1910 passed the Mann Act forbidding the transport of women across state lines for "immoral purposes." Popularly known as the "white slave traffic act," the law reflected an American fixation on supposedly loose European morals. ▸1922.11

▸AN AMERICAN ORIGINAL—Winslow Homer once remarked to a friend, "If a man wants to be an artist, he should never look at pictures." Indeed,

Homer's oeuvre *(including the engraving above)* at the time of his death in 1910 reflects his rejection of European constraints and his establishment of an indigenous style with an authority and elegance heretofore unseen in American art. ▸1942.17

▸FUNDAMENTALS OF FUNDAMENTALISM—A booklet entitled *The Fundamentals: A Testimony to the Truth*, published in 1910, asserted the literal truth of five basic tenets of Christianity, including the Virgin birth and the physical resurrection of Christ. The booklet inspired the modern fundamentalist movement in the U.S. ▸1950.12

▸BROWNING'S SEMIAUTOMATIC—Firearms designer John Moses Browning patented his new semiautomatic, .45-caliber handgun, the Browning Model 1910. Marketed as the Colt .45, it was adopted by the U.S. Army and remained a standard sidearm through World War II. By 1935, one million had been made.

POLITICS & BUSINESS: GNP: $35.3 billion ... U.S.: population 91,972,266 ... Washington state adopts female suffrage ... Arthur J. Morris of Fidelity Loan and Trust in Norfolk, Va., pioneers personal bank loans to local citizens ... "Taylorization" heralds beginning of scientific labor and machinery management in industry ... U.S. cigarette sales reach 8.6 billion (62% is controlled by American Tobacco Trust).

"All modern American literature comes from one book by Mark Twain called Huckleberry Finn. *There was nothing before. There has been nothing good since."*—**Ernest Hemingway, 1935**

AROUND THE WORLD

▶EDWARD VII DIES—After nine years of shaking off the stuffy traditions of Victorian England, popular King Edward VII of Britain died on May 6, 1910, at the age of 68. His second (and eldest surviving) son, George V, took the throne and guided the empire through World War I and up to the eve of World War II. ◂1901.4 ▸1936.V

▶POSTIMPRESSIONISM—Works by Cézanne, Van Gogh, Gauguin, Matisse, Picasso, and other pioneering artists were shown together for the first time outside of France in 1910. Called "Manet and the Post-Impressionists," the show, at London's Grafton Galleries, raised hackles in

England, causing what the exhibition's organizer, Roger Fry, called "an outbreak of militant philistinism." But the new art caught on, and Fry's term, postimpressionism, entered the art-history lexicon. ▸1916.4

▶CRETAN LEADS GREECE—In January, after staging a coup, the Greek military made master politician Eleuthérios Venizélos their adviser in creating a reform government; by year's end he'd been elected prime minister. Venizélos, a Cretan with dual citizenship, was the leader of his island's movement to unite with Greece. His new role angered Turkey (Crete's nominal master), whose rulers rightly feared he would forge powerful alliances against their shaky empire. ▸1924.12

***The Revolution Against the Porfirio Díaz Dictatorship*, by one of Mexico's great muralists, David Alfaro Siqueiros.**

MEXICO

Madero Leads Revolution

10 Mexican dictator Porfirio Díaz had ruled his country with an iron fist for 33 years when revolutionary leader Francisco Madero—aristocratic, reform-minded, politically shrewd—openly challenged him in the presidential campaign of 1910. During his long reign, Díaz had earned the admiration of the developed world for his efforts to transform Mexico into a modern industrial nation. Unfortunately, his economic advances came at the expense of the country's agricultural workers, who had fallen into a condition alarmingly close to serfdom, working for subsistence wages to enrich a minuscule class of elite landowners. Díaz ruthlessly quashed any resistance to his economic programs, jailing or executing dissidents.

The dictator stole the presidential election and had Madero arrested. But Madero was released on bond and escaped to Texas, where he raised a call to arms. Aided in the south by Indian revolutionary Emiliano Zapata and in the north by bandit-rebel Francisco "Pancho" Villa, Madero orchestrated a popular uprising against Díaz. The rebels burned plantations and dynamited mines and railroads, plunging the country into chaos. Díaz promised reforms, but it was too late. The insurrectionists would not be appeased until he resigned. He did so in May 1911, saying, "Madero has unleashed a tiger! Let us see if he can control it!"

Díaz went into exile in Paris, and after a short-term interim government, Madero became president. His precarious coalition of radicals proved unstable. Within two years he lay murdered, and the country was once again engulfed in treachery and bloodshed. **▸1913.M**

EGYPT

Death on the Nile

11 Boutros Pasha Ghali was the first Egyptian to be appointed prime minister by the British in their 27 years of occupation of Egypt. In 1910, a radical Egyptian nationalist, calling Boutros Pasha a collaborator, gunned him down. His chief crime: support of the Suez Canal Convention, a British proposal that would have extended Britain's concession to the canal through the year 2008. For many Egyptians, the canal concession represented all that was wrong with Britain's custodial treatment of their country.

National pride in the 1908 appointment of Boutros Pasha had been dampened by the fact that he was a Copt, an Egyptian Christian, who was cozy with the foreign occupiers. The Muslim-dominated Nationalist Party saw his appointment as an attempt to further disenfranchise Muslims. When debate over the Suez Canal heated up, nationalistic rage focused on Boutros Pasha.

Following the assassination, Britain clamped down, quieting Egypt's nationalists. In 1914, Britain declared war on the Ottoman Empire, a German ally, and made Egypt a protectorate, a condition that lasted until the country received "modified" independence in 1922. **◂1902.9 ▸1922.5**

LITERATURE

The Novel Loses Two Masters

12 Although Leo Tolstoy *(top)* and Mark Twain *(bottom)* seem rooted in different eras, these towering figures of world literature had roughly identical life spans. Both died in 1910, leaving behind sublime, yet enormously divergent, examples of an art form each helped to define.

With his two masterpieces, *War and Peace* and *Anna Karenina*, Tolstoy, the great chronicler of nineteenth-century Russian life, helped elevate the realistic novel into the ranks of great art, proving that in its social and metaphysical reach the novel could stand on equal footing with the drama of Sophocles, the poetry of Shakespeare.

As for Twain (the pen name of Samuel Langhorne Clemens), it seems little more than a technicality that a man who has been called the most important American writer of the twentieth century actually lived and wrote largely in the nineteenth. His *The Adventures of Huckleberry Finn* (1884) liberated American writers from the constraints of European tradition and offered readers a wholly original creation: a hilarious, deeply satirical mock-epic of childhood along the Mississippi River narrated in colloquial American English (itself a revolutionary act for a writer of "serious" fiction) by an irreverent, footloose, motherless boy named Huck Finn. **▸1926.2**

NOBEL PRIZES: Peace: Permanent International Peace Bureau (Switzerland) ... Literature: Paul Heyse (German; novelist) ... Chemistry: Otto Wallach (German; camphors and perfumes) ... Medicine: Albrecht Kossel (German; structure of proteins and nucleic acids) ... Physics: Johannes van der Waals (Dutch; modification of the Joule-Thomson law of gases).

A VOICE FROM 1910

Boys' Book Bravery

From "Frank Merriwell in Diamond Land," by Burt L. Standish, for *Tip Top Weekly,* March 5, 1910

Every boy's daydream champion and ultimate pal, Frank Merriwell was the most popular literary hero of his era. As created by George Patten, known to his readers by the nom de plume Burt L. Standish, Merriwell was impossibly strong, smart, handsome, patriotic, and downright good. *For a fee of never more than $150 an issue, Patten wrote some 20,000 words a week for* Tip Top Weekly, *pumping out far-flung adventures to thrill his multitude of young fans.*

Frank Merriwell suddenly drew rein, bringing his horse to a full stop. He had heard hoarse, broken cries like the excited shouting of one or more men, and now, as he drew rein to listen, he heard still further cries, and this time the voice was that of a female. There was mingled terror and pleading in that voice, although Merry could not understand the words.

Apparently, the sounds came out of a thicket which lay between Frank and a steep, almost perpendicular bluff which rose not ten rods distant at the base of a high, ledgy, barren hill.

A leap carried Merry from the saddle to the ground. He paused in order to fling the bridle rein of the horse over a bush, hoping that would prevent the animal from straying. This done, he plunged into the thicket, and tore his way through, regardless of thorns or branches which slashed and scraped him as he passed.

As if his approach had been heard, the cries of the female rose shriller and more distinct. This sort of an appeal for help seemed to spur Merriwell to still greater exertions. He fought his way through that tangled growth, and burst forth suddenly into a small open space at the base of the bluff.

At a single glance he took in the main feature of the somewhat exciting scene which was being enacted in that open space. Two men, one aged and seemingly feeble, whose hair and beard were almost snowy white; the other young, pantherish, dark-skinned and evil eyed, were engaged in a hand to hand struggle. The younger man had fastened his sinewy hands upon the throat of the elder, whom he had forced to his knees. Evidently that choking grip, which was rapidly causing the old man's face to turn purple, had checked the shouts which had first attracted Merry's attention.

On the ground, with her hands and feet securely bound, which rendered her helpless to interfere, lay a slender girl not over twenty years of age. She was still calling for help as Frank burst forth from the thicket. Seeing him, she pantingly implored:

"Oh, señor, señor, save my father—save him from Carrejas!"

Merry needed no urging. With two immense leaps, he had reached the men, and fastened his hands on the neck of the younger.

"Let go, you dog!" he shouted.

And then, as the astonished man obeyed, releasing his hold on the other, Merry actually picked him up bodily and flung him aside with a tremendous sidelong surge.

Wheezing hoarsely, the aged man toppled over exhausted.

Frank bent over him.

Again the girl screamed:

"Beware, señor! Beware of Carrejas!"

Every nerve tense, every muscle ready for action, the young man from North America turned to see the one called Carrejas coming at him like a mad wolf. The fellow's eyes were red with passion and his lips drawn back, exposing his teeth in a snarl like that of an infuriated wolf.

FRANK MERRIWELL IN DIAMOND LAND
TIP TOP WEEKLY
An Ideal Publication for the American Youth
No.725
MARCH 5,1910
5 CENTS
STREET & SMITH, PUBLISHERS, NEW YORK.
As he swung from the swaying rope, pistol ready for instant use, Merry uttered a loud shout which caused the beast to lift its hideous head, snarling ferociously.

Patten wrote of his hero, "His handsome proportions, his graceful, muscular figure, his fine, kingly head and that look of clean manliness ... stamped him as a fellow of lofty thoughts and ambitions."

"The imperial government has decided to send a warship to the port of Agadir ... to protect the important German interests in the territory in question."—Germany's announcement of the *Panther*'s arrival in Agadir

STORY OF THE YEAR

Crisis at Agadir

1 The *Panther* was an unimpressive battleship, with only "two or three little popguns on board," as Kaiser Wilhelm put it. But when it sailed into the shallow harbor of Agadir in southern Morocco in 1911, it set off a crisis that made headlines as far away as Mexico. Soon the armed forces of three countries were on alert, and the world was swept with rumors of war. The so-called Second Moroccan Crisis lasted 151 harrowing days.

The First Moroccan Crisis had occurred in 1905, when the Kaiser himself arrived in a gunboat to contest French claims on the still-independent country. The result was the Algeciras Conference of 1906, which only strengthened France's hold. Yet German strategists, striving to amass territory in a world already divided among the older imperial powers, still hoped to use Morocco as leverage. When tribal unrest swept Morocco in 1911—and the French responded by occupying Fez—the Germans made their move.

The ramparts at Agadir: When the Germans sailed into the harbor, they nearly provoked a war.

Claiming (falsely) that German interests near Agadir were threatened, they sent the *Panther* to "protect lives and property." The real motive was to throw France off balance—and, as in 1905, to try to undermine their uneasy alliance with the British. Calculating that Britain would back off if France was threatened with force, the Germans let the world assume that they were planning further naval action. Historians remain puzzled as to exactly what Germany wanted: One day, it was a piece of Morocco; the next, some other property—say, the whole French Congo—as compensation. While such deals were common practice among imperial rivals, the German request was obviously outrageous. Negotiations dragged on for months.

The thought of Germany succeeding in this sort of brinkmanship while engaged in a naval-arms race with Britain alarmed Foreign Minister David Lloyd George. He delivered a bellicose speech (without, however, mentioning Germany by name), and the British navy geared for battle. The German stock market plummeted. And within a few weeks the crisis was over: Germany accepted a mere 100,000 square miles of Congo hinterland and relinquished any ambitions in Morocco.

Britain and France began to formalize arrangements for their mutual defense, while German officials complained more bitterly than ever of their nation's "encirclement" by hostile powers. The long fuse leading to World War I was burning fast. ◂1906.9 ▸1912.8

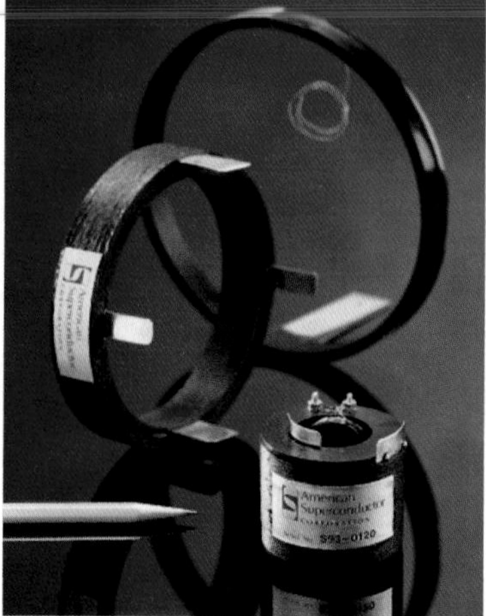

Modern superconductors operate at much higher temperatures than the near-absolute zero Kamerlingh Onnes worked with.

SCIENCE

Path of No Resistance

2 Dutch physicist Heike Kamerlingh Onnes dramatically expanded the body of scientific knowledge in 1911 with his discovery that at extremely low temperatures certain metals and alloys acquire a new physical property, which he called superconductivity. In the superconductive state—which occurs at temperatures approaching absolute zero (–273.15°C)—a substance manifests no resistance to electrical conduction. To demonstrate this absence, Kamerlingh Onnes rigged up the world's first superconducting circuit. He applied an electrical charge to the circuit, then removed the battery. The electric current continued to flow. In fact, as long as the superconductor's low temperature is maintained, the current should flow virtually forever.

Kamerlingh Onnes, whose motto was "Knowledge through measurement," conducted his experiments at the Cryogenic Laboratory he founded at the University of Leiden, in the Netherlands. He achieved his first major breakthrough in 1908, when he liquefied helium, coming within about five degrees of absolute zero. (Gases become liquids at very low temperatures, and most had been liquefied by the end of the nineteenth century. Before Kamerlingh Onnes, however, no one had been able to cool helium sufficiently.) This accomplishment, which allowed him to cool substances to much lower temperatures than previously possible, led directly to his discovery of superconductivity and provided the first steps toward the development of superconducting magnets and powerful particle accelerators much later in the century. ◂1906.M ▸1986.M

SCIENCE

Atom as Solar System

3 British physicist Ernest Rutherford has been called "the father of nuclear energy," a title he secured in 1911, when he theorized that an atom is composed of a central nucleus surrounded by orbiting electrons. Rutherford also became aware of the enormous amount of energy stored in an atom's nucleus, thus accounting for the existence of radioactivity.

Three years earlier, the New Zealand–born Rutherford had won the Nobel Prize in chemistry for first discovering and naming the particles expelled from radium, and then identifying the alpha particle as a helium atom. Rutherford used this particle in his further investigations into atomic structure. He proved that atoms were not solid, as most physicists thought, when he shot a stream of alpha particles—positively charged helium atoms—at a sheet of gold foil (a barrier 2,000 atoms thick) and found that most particles penetrated easily. This demonstrated that most of the space occupied by an atom is empty. Yet some particles *were* deflected, indicating that at least a small part of the atom was a mass.

Rutherford hypothesized that the atom's positive charges were concentrated in a nucleus some 10,000 times smaller than the entire atom. To put that in perspective, if the nucleus were the size of a basketball, the electrons' orbits would be 1.5 miles away—a pretty wide-open space for something previously believed to be nearly solid. To account for an entire atom's neutral electrical charge, Rutherford theorized that the positive charge on the nucleus must be balanced by an equal negative charge from orbiting electrons. If there were no such charge to hold them in their orbits, the electrons would fly in all directions.

In later experiments on a variety of other elements, Rutherford discovered that sending a stream of alpha particles through a nitrogen atom caused it to transmute into an oxygen atom. This experiment,

ART & CULTURE: Books: *Ethan Frome* (Edith Wharton); *Zuleika Dobson* (Max Beerbohm); *The White Peacock* (D.H. Lawrence); *In a German Pension* (Katherine Mansfield); *Mr. Perrin and Mr. Traill* (Hugh Walpole); *The New Machiavelli* (H.G. Wells); *The Secret Garden* (Frances Hodgson Burnett) ... Music: "I Want a Girl, Just Like the Girl That Married Dear Old Dad" (Von Tilzer and Dillon); "Oh, You Beautiful Doll"

"I am thrice homeless, as a native of Bohemia in Austria, as an Austrian amongst Germans, as a Jew throughout the world. Always an intruder, never welcomed."—**Gustav Mahler**

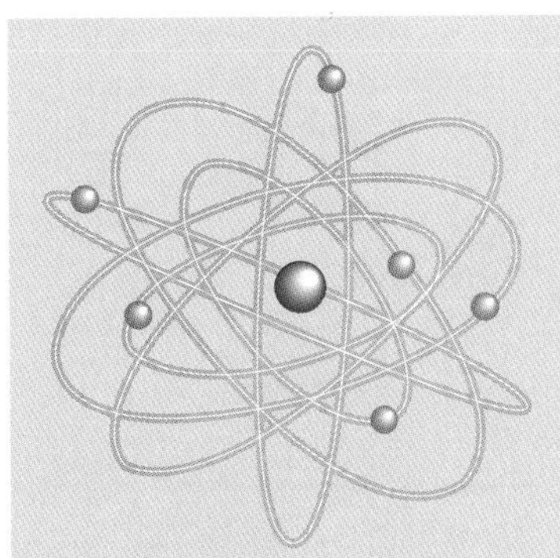

Rutherford was the first to visualize the atom as a dense, positively charged nucleus around which negatively charged electrons orbit.

the first artificial nuclear reaction, helped pave the way for the development of nuclear energy. **◄1905.1 ►1913.1**

EXPLORATION

Ancient City of the Incas

4 Hiram Bingham was searching for the last capital of Peru's ancient Inca civilization in 1911 when he stumbled across the ruins of Machu Picchu—one of the best-preserved urban centers of pre-Columbian civilization. A Yale University professor of Latin American history, Bingham was also an accomplished mountaineer. Less agile expedition members stayed in camp while their leader (accompanied by an armed escort and an Indian guide) struggled up jungly slopes and sheer rock faces to find a ghost city perched between two sharp Andean peaks. Marvels of masonry, its houses, garden terraces (linked by some 3,000 steps), and temples were expertly constructed without mortar.

The age and identity of Machu Picchu remain a mystery, but its awesome splendor is unequivocal. Bingham went on to become a U.S. senator; in the 1950s, he chaired the Civil Service Loyalty Review Board, ruling on cases of alleged Communist infiltration of the government. **◄1904.M ►1927.M**

MUSIC

Mahler the Modernist

5 He was a musical genius more celebrated during his brief life for his greatness as a conductor than for his visionary compositions. A full appreciation of Gustav Mahler's sprawling, unorthodox symphonies (and of later composers' indebtedness to them) didn't arrive until years after his death, at 50, on May 18, 1911.

Alienation haunted Mahler's career. The Austrian's services as a conductor were sought throughout Europe, but wherever he went—Prague, Budapest, Hamburg—there was controversy. Musicians dreaded his merciless demands for perfection; profit-minded producers loathed his uncompromising artistry. Against the odds, Mahler progressed through the most famous opera houses of Europe, eventually reaching the apex of his profession with an appointment as director of the Vienna Opera. There he shone, only to be hounded out after ten years by an anti-Semitic press.

Despite his enormous success on the podium, Mahler viewed conducting as a sideline, a way to earn a living while he pursued his true vocation, composing. His music was highly original—a full, unwieldy expression of human experience. A most prolific composer, Mahler tried to squeeze everything into his nine completed symphonies (he died while working on his tenth), presenting life's vulgarity and banality along with its rarer moments of transcendence. He infused his work with the sounds of ordinary life—snatches of popular tunes, bugle alarms, military marches, birdcalls. Although his creations are often unconventionally orchestrated and idiosyncratically structured, the music is always passionately expressive. To nineteenth-century critics weaned on Romantic idealism, Mahler's work sounded half mad. But, the composer maintained, "My time will come." Indeed, Mahler was, in the words of his biographer Kurt Blaukopf, the "future's contemporary." **◄1900.4 ►1911.11**

Treasure in the Andes: Long known to Peruvians, Machu Picchu was claimed as a "discovery" by Hiram Bingham.

BIRTHS

Lucille Ball, U.S. actress.

William Bernbach, U.S. advertising executive.

Elizabeth Bishop, U.S. poet.

Konstantin Chernenko, U.S.S.R. political leader.

Hume Cronyn, Canadian-U.S. actor.

Juan Manuel Fangio, Argentine automobile racer.

Max Frisch, Swiss writer.

Klaus Fuchs, German-U.K. physicist and spy.

William Golding, U.K. novelist.

Chet Huntley, U.S. newscaster.

Bruno Kreisky, Austrian socialist leader.

Gian Carlo Menotti, Italian-U.S. composer.

Erwin Mueller, German-U.S. physicist.

Georges Pompidou, French president.

Ronald Reagan, U.S. president.

Tennessee Williams, U.S. playwright.

DEATHS

William S. Gilbert, U.K. librettist.

Gustav Mahler, Austrian composer.

Carry Nation, U.S. temperance crusader.

Joseph Pulitzer, U.S. publisher.

Pyotr Stolypin, Russian prime minister.

(Ayer and Brown) ... Painting & Sculpture: *Man with a Guitar* (Georges Braque); *The Geranium* (Max Weber); *The City Rises* (Umberto Boccioni); *The Red Studio* (Henri Matisse); Oscar Wilde Memorial (Jacob Epstein) ... Film: *A Tale of Two Cities, Enoch Arden,* and *The Lonedale Operator* (D.W. Griffith); *Little Nemo* (Winsor McCay) ... Theater: *Fanny's First Play* (G.B. Shaw); *Kismet* (Edward Knoblock).

"Irving Berlin has no place in American music. He is *American music."*—Songwriter Jerome Kern

NEW IN 1911

Airplane with an enclosed passenger cabin (the *Berline,* built by Louis Blériot).

Transcontinental airplane flight (flown by Calbraith P. Rodgers from Sheepshead Bay, New York, to Long Beach, Calif.).

Crisco hydrogenated vegetable shortening.

Domino-brand sugar.

Indianapolis 500.

Salaries for members of Britain's House of Commons (£400 annually).

Seaplane.

IN THE UNITED STATES

▶AMERICA'S FIRST FEMALE PILOT—Before Amelia Earhart there was Harriet Quimby, a magazine writer who in 1911 became the first U.S. woman to become a licensed pilot, the second woman in the world. (The first was Baroness Raymonde de la Roche of

France.) The following year Quimby was the first woman to fly across the English Channel, using a monoplane loaned to her by Louis Blériot. The glamorous Quimby died later that year in an accident at an aviation meet in Boston. ◂1909.V ▸1927.1

▶STANDARD OIL BROKEN UP—If it was oil, it came from John D. Rockefeller—until 1911, when the Supreme Court decided that Rockefeller's gargantuan Standard Oil holding company, with near-absolute monopolies over the drilling, transportation, refinement, and sale of petroleum, constituted a restraint

MUSIC

Berlin's American Tune

6 As a boy, Israel Baline sang for pennies on the streets of New York's Lower East Side. By the time he was 22 his name was Irving Berlin and he had written a song that redefined popular music. "Alexander's Ragtime Band" was not a true rag, and its author was not the inventor of syncopated rhythm by a long stretch, but the song elevated Berlin to international renown as the "Ragtime King." People couldn't get enough of the jazzy, modern, audacious tune. The sheet music sold a million copies within seven months of being issued in the spring of 1911, and by the end of the year Berlin was rich. He went into songwriting, he always maintained, to make money.

During a career that spanned seven decades, Berlin published more than 1,000 songs, including such standards as "There's No Business Like Show Business," and "White Christmas." But "Alexander's Ragtime Band" remains the cornerstone of his legacy, the breakthrough that popularized an American vernacular sound. "The reason American composers have done nothing highly significant is because they won't write American music," Berlin told a critic. "They're as ashamed of it as if it were a country relative. So they write imitation European music which doesn't mean anything. Ignorant as I am, from their standpoints, I'm doing something they all refuse to do: I'm writing American music." **◂1910.9 ▸1917.5**

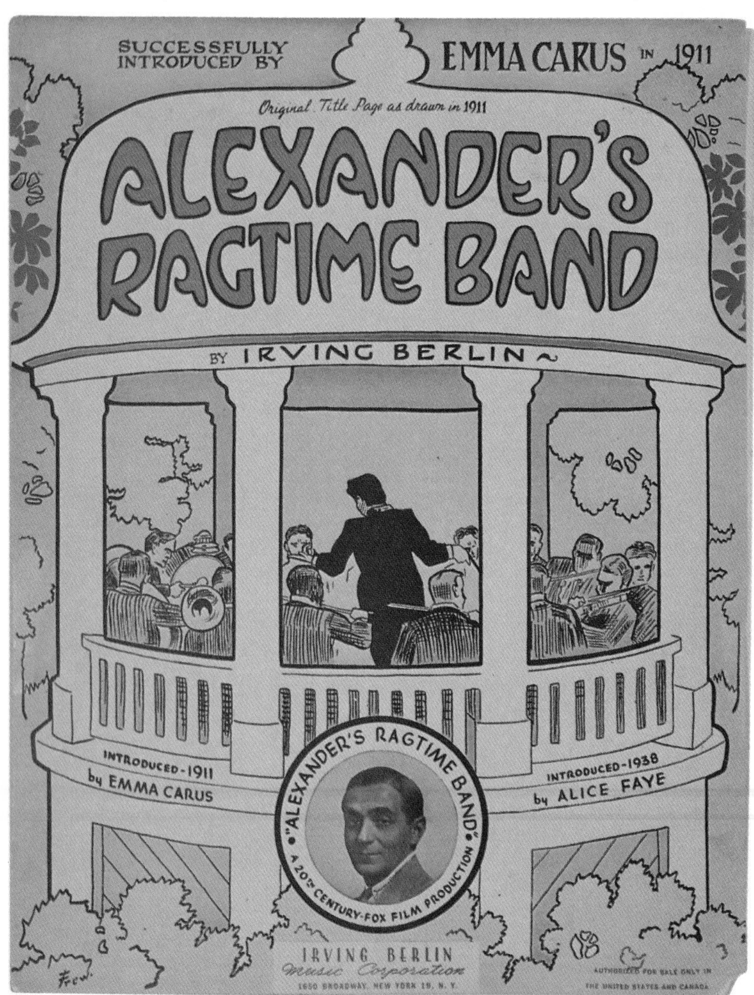

Irving Berlin called syncopation the "soul of every American."

INDIA

George V Crowned Emperor

7 Wearing a sparkling £60,000 crown created for the occasion and paid for by the Indian people, King George V of England stood before thousands of his Indian subjects and formally assumed the emperorship of India. The 1911 durbar marked the first time a reigning British monarch had ever visited the vast subcontinental colony, "the chief jewel in the British Crown." George V's magisterial display was designed to awe the native population and to shore up its wavering support for the Crown. (By 1911, the Indian independence movement was well under way.)

Dressed to impress: George V and Queen Mary at the Delhi durbar.

George V, who had visited India as Prince of Wales, had long dreamed of a triumphant return as king. Mindful of the trip's political mission, he wrote of his hope that his visit "would tend to allay unrest and, I am sorry to say, seditious spirit which unfortunately exists in some parts of India." And indeed, the dazzling pageant, replete with a 101-gun salute and a parade of 50,000 soldiers, did drum up some local enthusiasm for the Crown. But spectacle alone could not contain nationalist longings, and the drive toward independence continued unchecked.

King George wrapped up his official business by announcing two new raj policies that were generally received favorably by the Hindu majority—the ending of the 1905 partition of Bengal, and the transfer of the capital from Calcutta to New Delhi. Afterward, he embarked on what some cynics said was the real purpose of his visit: a two-week big-game hunting trip in Nepal. He bagged 21 tigers, eight rhinoceroses, and one bear. "A record," he proudly reported, "and one I think will be hard to beat." **◂1906.3 ▸1914.4**

SPORTS: Baseball: World Series, Philadelphia Athletics (Frank "Home Run" Baker) defeat New York Giants, 4–2 ... Hockey: National Hockey League formed with all Canadian teams ... Golf: Bobby Jones wins his first golf title, the Junior Championship of Atlanta, at age 9 ... Auto Racing: First Indianapolis 500 won by Ray Harroun (74.59 mph).

"We should all be concerned about the future because we will have to spend the rest of our lives there."—**Charles Kettering**

TECHNOLOGY

Electrifying the Automobile

8 It is arguably the single most important invention in the history of the automobile. The electric self-starter, developed by Charles Franklin Kettering in 1911, revolutionized driving, making it safer and more convenient. Kettering's golden invention replaced the troublesome hand crank, an unreliable and often dangerous apparatus.

The corporate impetus for a self-starter came after a friend of Henry Martyn Leland, the president of Cadillac, died when the crank of a car he was attempting to start sprang from its housing and crushed his face. By that time, Kettering, headquartered in the hayloft of a barn in Dayton, Ohio, was already hard at work on a design. Skeptics maintained that an electric self-starter was a practical impossibility. The problem was the size of the motor needed to turn over an automobile engine: Such a motor, and its batteries, everyone agreed, would weigh so much the car would not be able to carry passengers. Kettering, however, recognized that the motor that started the car did not have to run it.

He devised a small motor-and-generator unit. The motor, activated by a storage battery, had just enough power to start the engine. The engine, once it was running, powered the generator, which in turn charged the battery. "This man has profaned every fundamental law of electrical engineering" is what one member of the American Institute of Electrical Engineers had to say shortly after Kettering introduced his device. Nevertheless, the system worked. Within a year Cadillac was producing the world's first self-starting cars. **◂1908.1 ▸1913.6**

Kettering, here with a new Buick, took the terror out of starting a car.

Out with the old: Chinese revolutionary soldiers cut off a countryman's pigtail—a symbol of the old imperial regime.

CHINA

Dynasty at an End

9 The Chinese Revolution introduced republican government to China and closed the book on 2,000 years of imperial rule. It began on October 10, 1911, when dissident army soldiers in the city of Wuhan, in central China, seized the Wuhan arsenal and forcibly persuaded a brigade commander, Li Yuanhong, to lead them in rebellion. General Li adroitly switched allegiances from the Qing Emperor to the side of the rebels—a shift that was instrumental in spreading the mutiny.

The corrupt Qing Dynasty, reeling from successive defeats in the Sino-Japanese War (1895) and the disastrous Boxer Rebellion (1900), had attempted to save itself by belatedly implementing constitutional reforms. However, Chinese radicals (most notably Revolutionary Alliance leader-in-exile Sun Yat-sen) were determined to bring it down. Anti-Qing sentiments were further compounded because many Chinese considered the dynasty a foreign imposition. It was founded in 1644 by warriors who swept down from Manchuria and conquered China. After 250 years, the Manchus had still not assimilated into Chinese society. This put the royal court at a disadvantage when it attempted to raise an army to put down the mutineers.

The dynasty enlisted the support of retired general Yuan Shikai, who retained the loyalty of many army officers in the northern part of the country. Meanwhile, Sun Yat-sen had returned to China from his 16-year exile and taken command of the revolution. In December, a republican convention was convened at Nanking and the delegates elected Sun Yat-sen president of a newly declared republic in southern China. Recognizing Yuan's strength in the north, and aware of the frailty of a divided nation, Sun offered the presidency to the general on the condition that the dynasty be dissolved. Yuan quickly assented and, rattling his saber, advised Pu Yi, the defenseless boy emperor, to abdicate.

On February 12, 1912, Pu Yi formally resigned. The next day, Sun Yat-sen stepped aside and Yuan Shikai became president of the whole of China. **◂1908.M ▸1916.8**

IN THE UNITED STATES

of trade and ordered Standard Oil broken up. (Two weeks later, the Court ordered a similar breakup of James B. Duke's American Tobacco Co. trust.) Rockefeller retired to enormous wealth and grand acts of philanthropy; his combine was dissolved into some 30 nominally independent companies. **◂1904.M ▸1914.5**

▸TRIANGLE SHIRTWAIST FIRE—A devastating fire ripped through the Triangle Shirtwaist factory in New York City on March 25, killing 146 people, mostly immigrant seamstresses. Trapped by locked doors, many workers leaped to their deaths from upper-story windows; others died when an overloaded, poorly maintained fire escape collapsed. The tragic conflagration focused public attention on sweatshop conditions and produced an outcry for better fire-safety and labor laws. **◂1900.M ▸1917.7**

▸DIME-STORE KING—F.W. Woolworth in 1911 closed the deal that made his name the most recognizable in American retailing: a $65 million buyout of his four biggest rivals. That same year, he hired architect Cass Gilbert to erect a lasting monument to his success in New York City. The 60-story Woolworth building *(above)*—complete with such embellishments as a Dutch Gothic trim, green copper roof, and gilded finials—opened in 1913, standing for the next 17 years as the tallest building in the world. **▸1930.7**

POLITICS & BUSINESS: GNP: $35.8 billion ... Appalachian Forest Reserve Act is passed ... Yale economist Irving Fisher's *The Purchasing Power of Money* influences economic thought ... U.S. Supreme Court orders American Tobacco to dissolve ... First SAE handbook on standardization of auto parts is published by the Society of Automotive Engineers.

"Every honest socialist must disapprove of this Libyan adventure. It means only useless and stupid bloodshed."
—Benito Mussolini, before becoming a Fascist

AROUND THE WORLD

▶REFORMER AND TYRANT—Attending an opera with Nicholas II in September 1911, Pyotr Arkadyevich Stolypin, the Czar's conservative prime minister, was assassinated by a revolutionary who'd used his police connections to gain admittance to the theater. Stolypin had alienated Russia's far right by instituting peasant reforms that included the right of former serfs to leave communes and acquire private lands. And he had earned the enmity of Russia's left wing by dissolving both the first and second dumas and ordering the hanging without trial (the dreaded "Stolypin's necktie") of thousands of suspected "rebels and terrorists." ◀1906.4 ▶1917.1

▶WILSON'S CLOUD CHAMBER—Attempting to reproduce clouds in the laboratory, Scottish physicist Charles Thomson Rees Wilson observed that, in a dust-free atmosphere, clouds form by condensing on charged atomic particles. Wilson used this information to perfect a device, the cloud chamber, in which the trail of condensation produced by ions could be used to trace their trajectories. An indispensable tool in nuclear research, the cloud chamber won Wilson a 1927 Nobel. ◀1911.3 ▶1913.1

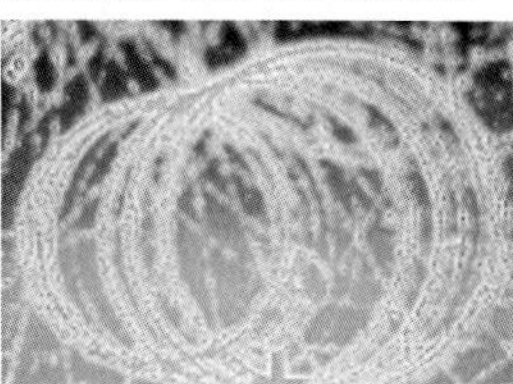

▶ENGLAND'S REFORMS—Never before had a nation embraced such a broad piece of social legislation. In 1911, Britain's Liberal government adopted the National Insurance Act, providing some 14 million people, virtually the entire working class, with health and disability insurance and limited unemployment insurance. Designed by future prime minister David Lloyd George (with help from young Winston Churchill), the legislation laid the groundwork for the British welfare state. ◀1906.1 ▶1948.13

EXPLORATION

Amundsen at the South Pole

10 Roald Amundsen's successful expedition to the South Pole in 1911 was a testament less to the Norwegian's extraordinary navigational and survival skills than to preparation and foresight. Not only did his five-man team complete its 1,860-mile trek from the Bay of Whales, its Antarctic mooring point, to the South Pole without incident, it returned exactly on schedule. The men were so well equipped that they actually gained weight during their four-month journey over treacherous glaciers and mountains in temperatures as low as –76°F.

For Amundsen, reaching the South Pole carried a personal irony. He had been obsessed with the North Pole since childhood, and had navigated the Northwest Passage by 1906. But Robert Peary had beaten him to the North Pole, so in August 1910 Amundsen loaded his ship with 19 men, 97 robust sled dogs, four pigs, and six pigeons and set off for the earth's other end.

Amundsen's departure provoked a fierce competition with British explorer Robert Falcon Scott, who was already en route to the South Pole. Scott's expedition ended in tragedy: His party arrived at the Pole 36 days after Amundsen (who had left a message behind), and then died of exposure and starvation on the return trip.

Amundsen and his four companions reached the South Pole on December 14, 1911. They established the pole's location, then placed their fists around a staff bearing a Norwegian flag and planted it in triumph. **◀1909.1 ▶1912.V**

First picture of the South Pole: Amundsen's shot of his lieutenant, the Norwegian flag, and "some of the dogs which helped to plant it."

Strauss *(above, with his son)* called himself "a first-class second-rate composer."

MUSIC

Strauss's Biggest Hit

11 From the time he was 25, Richard Strauss had been celebrated as the most important German composer since Brahms, and his early works, consciously styled after Wagner, exude Romantic bombast. But in 1911 the 47-year-old composer took the musical world by surprise with an exquisitely Viennese opera, *Der Rosenkavalier*, that was triumphantly received in Dresden.

Strauss had begun the work two years earlier when, seeking new expression, he wrote to his librettist, the Austrian poet and dramatist Hugo von Hofmannsthal, and requested something like "a Mozart opera." Von Hofmannsthal obliged with the sweet, playful plot and words of *Der Rosenkavalier*. Thrilled, Strauss filled the opera with tender, airy waltzes and gentle love duets. The result proved wildly popular with audiences, and within months of its Dresden premiere, *Der Rosenkavalier* had been staged at Europe's grandest opera houses—Munich, Hamburg, Vienna, Milan, Berlin.

Strauss's later operatic work never equaled *Der Rosenkavalier*, and he failed to adjust to the innovations in serious music made after World War I. Just before World War II, the aging composer—politically naive, isolated in his music—was easy prey for the Nazis, who made him director of the state music bureau. After the war, he was cleared by the denazification tribunal and went into exile in Switzerland. **◀1905.11**

ITALY

A Grab for Libya

12 Italy had coveted Libya since 1881, when France took Tunisia from the Ottoman Empire. Now, in 1911, with France also controlling Morocco—and with the Ottoman Turks busy battling a revolt in Yemen—the Italians decided to grab the last non-European-owned slice of North Africa. First, they reiterated their longstanding gripes about "disorder and neglect" in Tripoli (which supposedly imperiled Italians living there). The Ottoman Sultan, smelling trouble, sent guns to Libyan chieftains. Italy, pronouncing the act "manifestly hostile," invaded in September.

Italy won several key coastal towns in the war's opening weeks. (One tactic, the first use of aerial bombing, caused a worldwide stir: Italian pilots tossed grenades from open cockpits.) But the invaders underestimated the Libyans' loyalty to their fellow Muslims. Farther inland, desert fighters with ancient rifles blocked Italian advances. A settlement in October 1912 broke the stalemate: The Turks, preoccupied with a war in the Balkans, ceded political control of Libya to Italy; Italy pledged to honor the Sultan's spiritual authority (analogous to the Pope's). But, supplied with Turkish, Austrian, and German arms, Libyan guerrillas fought on, driving the Italians back to the coast by 1915.

Even after a settlement was reached, Libyan guerrillas continued their resistance to the Italian presence into the 1930s.

In Italy, the Libyan war raised right-wing militarism to a frenzy, split the Socialists (lifting antiwar hard-liner Benito Mussolini to power), and toppled the Liberal government. For the Ottoman Empire, the loss of Libya hastened a decline that soon helped ignite World War I. **◀1909.10 ▶1912.8**

NOBEL PRIZES: Peace: Tobias Asser (Dutch; Institute of International Law) and Alfred H. Fried (Austrian; peace publications) ... Literature: Maurice Maeterlinck (Belgian; poet and playwright) ... Chemistry: Marie Curie (French; radium and polonium) ... Medicine: Allvar Gullstrand (Swedish; dioptrics) ... Physics: Wilhelm Wien (German; heat and radiation).

A VOICE FROM 1911

A Fallen Woman of Uncommon Virtue

From *Jennie Gerhardt,* by Theodore Dreiser, 1911

A great literary naturalist and political crusader in the tradition of Emile Zola, Theodore Dreiser wrote of American life with unparalleled power and pungency, despite an undeniably heavy-handed style. His first novel, Sister Carrie *(1900)—the story of a midwestern girl who rises to fame and fortune on the New York stage at the expense of her once-wealthy paramour—should have secured his reputation. But the book was suppressed after the wife of its publisher pronounced it "morally reprehensible."* Jennie Gerhardt *(1911), Dreiser's "comeback," gave readers a more palatable heroine. Unlike her predecessor, Jennie, a woman of almost saintly goodness, suffers mightily at the hands of a cold, unjust society that fails to measure up to her virtue. A young unwed mother, she is driven out of the house by her stern father and later abandoned by her rich lover, Lester, for whom she has sacrificed everything. In the following passage, Jennie watches Lester dance with the woman he will eventually marry.* ◂**1902.6** ▸**1920.8**

Lester and Letty strolled away. They made a striking pair—Mrs. Gerald in dark wine-coloured silk, covered with glistening black beads, her shapely arms and neck bare, and a flashing diamond of great size set just above her forehead in her dark hair. Her lips were red, and she had an engaging smile, showing an even row of white teeth between wide, full, friendly lips. Lester's strong, vigorous figure was well set off by his evening clothes, he looked distinguished.

"That is the woman he should have married," said Jennie to herself as he disappeared. She fell into a reverie, going over the steps of her past life. Sometimes it seemed to her now as if she had been living in a dream. At other times she felt as though she were in that dream yet. Life sounded in her ears much as this night did. She heard its cries. She knew its large-mass features. But back of it were subtleties that shaded and changed one into the other like the shifting of dreams. Why had she been so attractive to men? Why had Lester been so eager to follow her? Could she have prevented him? She thought of her life in Columbus, when she carried coal; to-night she was in Egypt, at this great hotel, the chatelaine of a suite of rooms, surrounded by every luxury, Lester still devoted to her. He had endured so many things for her! Why? Was she so wonderful? Brander had said so. Lester had told her so. Still she felt humble, out of place, holding handfuls of jewels that did not belong to her. Again she experienced that peculiar feeling which had come over her the first time she went to New York with Lester—namely, that this fairy existence could not endure. Her life was fated. Something would happen. She would go back to simple things, to a side street, a poor cottage, to old clothes.

And then as she thought of her home in Chicago, and the attitude of his friends, she knew it must be so. She would never be received, even if he married her. And she could understand why. She could look into the charming, smiling face of this woman who was now with Lester, and see that she considered her very nice, perhaps, but not of Lester's class. She was saying to herself now no doubt as she danced with Lester that he needed some one like her. He needed some one who had been raised in the atmosphere of the things to which he had been accustomed. He couldn't very well expect to find in her, Jennie, the familiarity with, the appreciation of the niceties to which he had always been accustomed. She understood what they were. Her mind had awakened rapidly to details of furniture, clothing, arrangement, decorations, manner, forms, customs, but—she was not to the manner born.

If she went away Lester would return to his old world, the world of the attractive, well-bred, clever woman who now hung upon his arm. The tears came into Jennie's eyes; she wished, for the moment, that she might die. It would be better so. Meanwhile Lester was dancing with Mrs. Gerald, or sitting out between the waltzes talking over old times, old places, and old friends. As he looked at Letty he marvelled at her youth and beauty. She was more developed than formerly, but still as slender and shapely as Diana. She had strength, too, in this smooth body of hers, and her black eyes were liquid and lusterful....

They strolled into the garden as the music ceased, and he squeezed her arm softly. He couldn't help it; she made him feel as if he owned her.

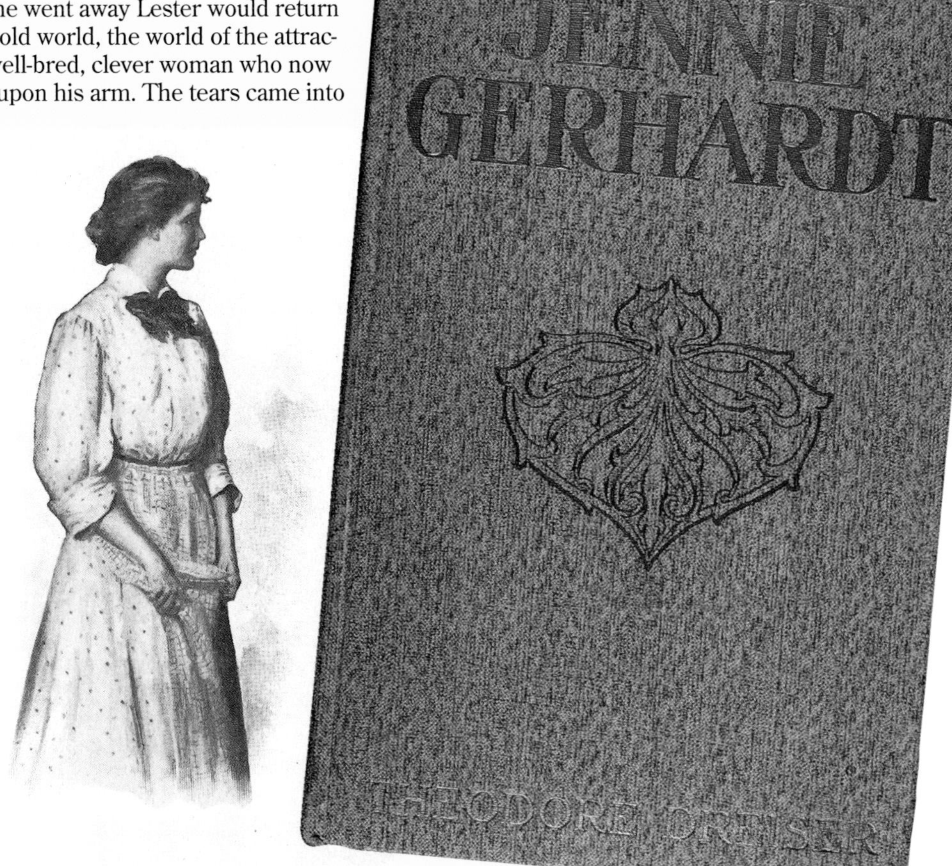

Theodore Dreiser *(left)* chronicled a harsh American society. The success of *Jennie Gerhardt* *(frontispiece and cover, above)* prompted the reissue of his suppressed 1900 novel, *Sister Carrie*.

"God himself could not sink this ship."—***Titanic* deckhand in response to a passenger's question about the ship's safety**

STORY OF THE YEAR

Titanic Sinks on Maiden Voyage

1 The *Titanic* was one of the marvels of its age. Stood on end, the 892-foot vessel would have towered above the tallest skyscraper yet built. The world's biggest ship was also the most luxurious—a "floating palace," as reporters called it, whose staterooms, restaurants, parlors, swimming pools, and indoor gardens rivaled the swankiest hotels'. The *Titanic* was also considered unsinkable, thanks to a double-bottomed hull divided into 16 watertight compartments. Yet the liner's maiden voyage (from Southampton, England, bound for New York) proved to be its last. Shortly before midnight on April 14, 1912, its fifth day at sea, the *Titanic* was steaming at a reckless speed through an ice field off Newfoundland when the great ship collided with an iceberg on the starboard side. Most passengers were in bed and felt only a slight tremor. The *Titanic* went down within three hours.

Of the 2,224 people aboard, 1,513 died. The survivors, rescued at about 4:00 AM by the liner *Carpathia*, described a scene of courage and chaos. Since the *Titanic* had lifeboat space for only half its occupants, the ship's officers ordered women and children to be loaded first. Many passengers and crew members voluntarily sacrificed their seats for others. But the evacuation was so disorganized that many boats were sent off before they were full. And the poorest passengers, immigrants packed in steerage far below, were never told of the accident; most found out too late, as the vessel slid underwater. They died along with aristocrats and tycoons—and with the band from the first-class lounge, which played on stoically to the end.

"She slowly tilted straight on end," read the caption on this newspaper illustration of the shipwreck.

The disaster, one of the worst in maritime history, prompted important reforms. The first International Convention for Safety of Life at Sea, held in 1913, passed requirements that ships provide enough lifeboats for all passengers; hold safety drills during voyages; and, because a nearby liner hadn't heard the *Titanic*'s distress calls, keep a 24-hour radio watch. And the International Ice Patrol was established to warn ships of ice in the treacherous North Atlantic. **◂1907.2 ▸1915.3**

IDEAS

Jung in His Own Right

2 Until 1912, when he presented his revolutionary theories of the unconscious in *Wandlungen und Symbole der Libido* (translated as *Psychology of the Unconscious*), Swiss psychiatrist Carl Gustav Jung was best known as a protégé of Sigmund Freud. The book marked a departure from Freudian concepts and established Jung's own school of analytic psychology. For Freud, it meant the revolt of his handpicked heir, a brazen and unforgivable affront. Onetime friends and collaborators, psychology's two brightest luminaries never spoke again.

Besides extending the definition of libido to include nonsexual, as well as sexual, energy, Jung expanded Freud's concept of the personal unconscious—an individual's collection of repressed memories and experience—to include a second, universally shared dimension: the collective unconscious, the inborn reservoir of symbols and images from which all humans construct their myths, fantasies, and dreams. In psychoanalysis, the unconscious is paramount, manifesting itself in dreams and fantasies, whose interpretation is the key to treatment. Jung said some images are archetypal, drawn from the collective unconscious and beyond the individual's experience. Hence Freud's rejection: Jung's ideas threatened his life's work.

Erudite, methodical, and tirelessly curious, Jung went on to develop the theories of introversion and extroversion and of animus and anima—the male and female components of the unconscious. Over time, he redefined therapy's mission as less a treatment of neurosis than an attempt to bring into wholeness and harmony the unconscious and conscious elements of human behavior. **◂1909.3 ▸1913.3**

ARCHAEOLOGY

Darwin's Missing Link

3 At last, Britain had an ancient ancestor to call its own. Charles Dawson, a British lawyer and amateur geologist, announced in 1912 his discovery of pieces of a human skull and an apelike jaw in a gravel pit near the town of Piltdown, England. Up until then, it had seemed that early man was everywhere—Java, Croatia, Gibraltar, Germany—everywhere, that is, except England. Fueled by Charles Darwin's positing of a "missing link," in *On the Origin of Species* (1859), fossil fever had gripped the world, and Britain's glaring lack of an archaeological history invited worldwide scorn, especially from the French, who called British paleontologists "*chaissons de caillous*" ("pebble hunters"). Dawson's announcement stopped the scorn cold. Experts instantly declared *Eoanthropus dawsoni*, a.k.a. Piltdown Man (estimated to be 300,000 to one million years old), the evolutionary find of the century. Darwin's missing link had been identified.

Or so it seemed for the next 40 or so years. Then, in the early fifties, safely removed from fossil fever and blessed with new testing methods, scientists began to suspect misattribution. (The gravels where the bones were found had already been proved to be much less ancient than formerly assumed.)

In 1953 that suspicion gave way to a full-blown scandal: Piltdown Man was a hoax. Radiocarbon tests

THE ILLUSTRATED LONDON NEWS

A British newspaper's "reconstruction" of Piltdown Man in December 1912.

proved that its skull belonged to a 600-year-old woman and its jaw to a 500-year-old orangutan from the East Indies. The culprit's identity remains a mystery (though several theories hold that it was Dawson himself), but the prank managed to confuse evolutionary research for nearly half a century. **▸1925.3**

ART & CULTURE: Books: ***The Elementary Forms of Religious Life*** **(Emile Durkheim);** ***The Financier*** **(Theodore Dreiser);** ***Riders of the Purple Sage*** **(Zane Grey);** ***A Dome of Many-Coloured Glass*** **(Amy Lowell) ... Music: "When the Midnight Choo-Choo Leaves for Alabam' " (Irving Berlin); "The Sweetheart of Sigma Chi" (Vernor and Stokes); "Moonlight Bay" (Wenrich and Madden);** ***On Hearing the First Cuckoo in Spring***

"A pie in the face represents a fine, wish-fulfilling, universal idea, especially in the face of authority, as in cop or mother-in-law."—**Producer-director Mack Sennett**

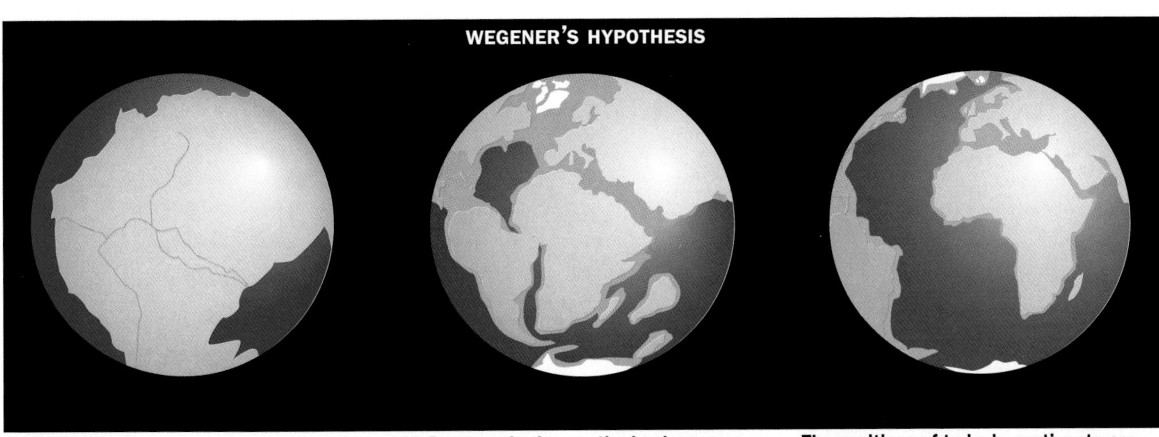

Some 200 million years ago, there was one "supercontinent," Pangaea.

As Pangaea broke up, the land masses resembled present-day continents.

The positions of today's continents are still slowly shifting.

SCIENCE

A Drifting Continent

4 On a map of the earth, the Atlantic coastlines of each hemisphere seem to fit together like pieces of a puzzle. Yet until 1912, when German meteorologist and explorer Alfred Wegener presented his theory of continental drift, no one could explain this phenomenon. Wegener hypothesized that at one time the planet's seven continents formed a giant supercontinent, which he called Pangaea (from the Greek for "all lands"), and that they gradually drifted apart. As empirical evidence, he cited fossils and ancient rocks that appeared exclusively in Brazil and South Africa, and he matched up truncated mountain ranges by schematically returning the continents to their original positions.

Unhappily for Wegener, the first quarter of the twentieth century, when many scientists believed geophysics finally rested on sound principles, was an inauspicious time to introduce a radical new model. "The delirious ravings of people with bad cases of moving crust disease and wandering pole plague," sneered one paleoclimatologist. Wegener's critics clung to the idea of fixed land masses, and mysterious sunken continents like Atlantis.

With little encouragement, Wegener refined his theory over the next decade. Unfortunately, he lacked a plausible explanation for why the continents drift. He suggested that forces related to the earth's rotation somehow propelled them, but he died (in 1930) before he could find confirmation.

Wegener was vindicated in the sixties, when scientific discoveries proved his thinking fundamentally sound. His ideas opened the door to the new study of plate tectonics, the unifying principle of geology today. **►1963.4**

FILM

Sennett Founds Keystone

5 For some movie buffs, the silent era was the golden age of screen comedy. Never would comedy be kinetically faster, visually richer, or breathtakingly funnier than in the 1910s and '20s. And the Pericles of this period was producer and director Mack Sennett (1880-1960), a former burlesque clown and D.W. Griffith protégé who, in 1912, joined two former bookmakers to establish the Keystone studio, Hollywood's greatest comedy factory.

Sennett gave American film comedy its distinctive brashness and verve. In short subjects that parodied everything from domestic life—tyrannical wives were frequent targets—to popular movie melodrama, the satire was broad and vulgar, the pace frenetic. Audiences loved the low-down vitality, and laughed in agreement at the caricatures. Sennett's work even entered the language: His crazy, careening coterie of incompetents, the Keystone Kops, who raced to disasters and then made them worse, are invoked to cover all manner of mishaps.

Sennett was the mentor of an astonishing array of influential talent, most notably an English music-hall comic named Charles Spencer Chaplin, who made 35 comedies at Keystone.

Sennett's best players, weary of his artistic dictatorship and resistance to high salaries, left him for other studios. Gradually, to accommodate an increasingly sophisticated audience, Keystone de-emphasized slam-bang and produced "cheesecake" pictures (with the Mack Sennett Bathing Beauties), some romantic comedies with Gloria Swanson, and a series of "Kid Komedies," that prefigured the *Our Gang* shorts.

As the twenties wore on and the sound era kicked in, audiences began to prefer the subtler work of former Sennett disciples like Chaplin, and the story- and character-centered films of Laurel and Hardy (produced by Sennett's rival, Hal Roach). Sennett's career declined, and he spent his final years in poverty in a nursing home. But his legacy lives wherever there is a laugh in the dark. **◄1908.8 ►1913.10**

The Keystone Kops, in a shot from *Keystone Hotel.*

BIRTHS

Charles Addams, U.S. cartoonist.

Michelangelo Antonioni, Italian filmmaker.

John Cage, U.S. composer.

John Cheever, U.S. writer.

Lawrence Durrell, U.K. writer.

Milton Friedman, U.S. economist.

Eugène Ionesco, Romanian-French playwright.

Gene Kelly, U.S. dancer and actor.

Kim Il-Sung, North Korean political leader.

Mary McCarthy, U.S. writer.

Kim Philby, U.K. double agent.

Jackson Pollock, U.S. painter.

Glenn Seaborg, U.S. chemist.

Sam Snead, U.S. golfer.

Georg Solti, Hungarian-U.S. conductor.

Studs Terkel, U.S. writer.

Alan Turing, U.K. mathematician.

Wernher von Braun, German-U.S. aerospace engineer.

Raoul Wallenberg, Swedish diplomat.

DEATHS

Clara Barton, U.S. nurse.

Samuel Coleridge-Taylor, U.K. composer.

Joseph Lister, U.K. surgeon.

Jules Henri Poincaré, French mathematician.

Harriet Quimby, U.S. aviator.

Robert F. Scott, U.K. explorer.

Bram Stoker, U.K. writer.

August Strindberg, Swedish playwright.

Wilbur Wright, U.S. aviator.

(Frederick Delius) ... Painting & Sculpture: *Doubting Thomas* (Emil Nolde); *Ma Jolie* (Pablo Picasso); *Fruit Dish and Glass* (Georges Braque) ... Film: *Queen Elizabeth* (Louis Mercanton, with Sarah Bernhardt); *An Unseen Enemy* (D.W. Griffith, with Lillian and Dorothy Gish); *Quo Vadis?* (Enrico Guazzoni) ... Theater: *The Firefly* (Rudolf Friml); *Death and Damnation* (Frank Wedekind).

"Rules are like steam rollers. There is nothing they won't do to flatten the man who stands in their way."
—Jim Thorpe, on the International Olympic Committee's decision to strip him of his medals

NEW IN 1912

Universal Pictures.

Self-service grocery stores (Ward's Groceteria and Alpha Beta Food Market, California).

Oreo and Lorna Doone cookies (Nabisco).

Prizes in Cracker Jack boxes.

New Mexico and Arizona (47th and 48th states).

Parachuting from an airplane.

Hellmann's Mayonnaise.

Girl Scouts of America.

L.L. Bean (Freeport, Maine).

IN THE UNITED STATES

▶**POETRY MAGAZINE**—One of the first and greatest of the little magazines, *Poetry: A Magazine of Verse,* debuted in 1912. Published in Chicago by Harriet Monroe and dedicated to originality, the journal remained for years at the center of modern American letters. Among the writers *Poetry* launched: Hart Crane, Carl Sandburg, Marianne Moore, Wallace Stevens, and William Carlos Williams. ▶1930.V

▶**BULL MOOSE AIDS WILSON**—Theodore Roosevelt liked to boast of having the vigor of a bull moose. So when dissident Republicans formed a progressive third party to back his 1912 presidential bid against his handpicked successor, President William Howard

Taft, that's the nickname that stuck. Roosevelt finished second in November—better than any third-party candidate since—but, by splitting the vote, the Bull Moose Party put a Democrat, Woodrow Wilson, in the White House. ◀1904.6 ▶1915.9

The crystalline structure of vitamin B_1 viewed under polarized light through a modern microscope.

MEDICINE

Funk Identifies Vitamins

6 Scurvy plagued the high seas. Beriberi was endemic throughout Southeast Asia. Pellagra was a worldwide menace. Except for the British Navy's famous scurvy antidote (large quantities of limes—hence the nickname "limey" for a British sailor), there existed no known protection from these feared diseases until 1912, when Casimir Funk published his groundbreaking paper, "The Etiology of the Deficiency Diseases." In the paper, Funk, a brilliant young Polish biochemist—he received his doctorate at 20 and was only 28 at the time of his breakthrough—theorized that the diseases were caused by dietary deficiencies. "The deficiency substances," he wrote, "we will call vitamines." Over the course of his research Funk postulated four such substances (later identified as vitamins B_1, B_2, C, and D) that were vital to good health.

As others had before him, Funk observed that deficiency diseases occurred in places where people subsisted on monochromatic diets. Working at the Lister Institute in London, Funk experimented with feeding birds a diet consisting exclusively of polished rice. They came down with a disease very much like beriberi, which was common among people who ate a similarly restricted diet. Funk restored the parts of the rice kernel that had been polished away, and the birds recovered. But where others had attributed the illness to toxins in the rice introduced by polishing (for which the restored "polishings" were an antidote), Funk correctly posited that what mattered was not what was in the rice but what was missing.

After further study, Funk was able to link certain organic substances, his "vitamines," to the prevention of specific diseases. He spoke of a beriberi vitamin and a scurvy vitamin. "All the deficiency diseases," he concluded, "can be prevented by a complete diet." His words changed the way the world eats. **◀1906.11 ▶1928.9**

SPORTS

Thorpe's Olympic Triumph

7 When King Gustav V of Sweden told Jim Thorpe, "Sir, you are the greatest athlete in the world," Thorpe groped for the right words. "Thanks, King," he replied. The moment was a pinnacle for Thorpe, a Native American born in 1888 in the Oklahoma Territory. A few moments earlier, he had won the 1912 Olympic decathlon in Stockholm (a grueling three-day, ten-event competition) with a world-record score of 8,412.955 points—a performance so remarkable that a generation later, it still would have merited a silver medal in the 1948 London Olympic Games.

Upon his return to the United States, the gold-medal winner was hailed as the nation's first great Olympic hero, but the adulation was short-lived. Six months later, a newspaper revealed that Thorpe had earned $25 a week playing minor-league baseball in North Carolina during his college vacations in 1909 and 1910. His standing as an amateur was challenged and his appeal to the Amateur Athletic Union (AAU) to "not be too hard in judging me" was rebuffed. The AAU stripped Thorpe of his records and the International Olympic Committee (IOC) asked for its medals and trophies back (Thorpe had also won the pentathlon). But Thorpe's colleagues stood by him; the runners-up in both events declined his medals.

In 1950 an Associated Press poll of sportswriters voted Thorpe the greatest athlete of the first half of the century. He died three years later at age 64 and was buried in a Pennsylvania town that immediately changed its name to Jim Thorpe. His full vindication did not come until 1982, when the IOC finally

A dazzling athlete, Thorpe excelled in all sports; as a college halfback, he made the All-America football team.

SPORTS: Baseball: World Series, Boston Red Sox (Smokey Joe Wood, Tris Speaker) defeat New York Giants, 4–3 ... Olympic Games held in Stockholm ... Football: Fourth down added; touchdown valued at 6 points (formerly 5); field standardized at 360 × 160 feet ... Basketball: Nets opened at bottom to let ball go through.

"One sees many wounded soldiers with broken noses, the result of having held their guns improperly while firing."
—German ambassador Wangenheim on the inexperienced Turkish army

restored his name to the record books and the following January, presented Thorpe's Olympic medals to his children. **◄1908.6 ►1920.6**

THE OTTOMAN EMPIRE

Balkans Unite

8 By 1912, the Ottoman Turks were so obviously vulnerable—nearly bankrupt, shaken by their 1908 revolution, and busy fending off the Italians in Libya—that the Balkan states finally decided to shelve, if only temporarily, their own enmities and unite against the Ottoman Empire. It was a move that Russia, using the ploy of Slavic solidarity (and hoping to gain hegemony in the region), had been urging for years, without success. But now, clearly, the time to strike had come.

First, Serbia and Bulgaria signed a secret treaty in March, followed by Bulgaria and Greece in May. By autumn Montenegro was on board. The countries in the newborn Balkan League had widely differing agendas, but they shared common grievances. All wanted to stop the political and cultural "Ottomanization" that the Turks had forced on enclaves of Greeks, Serbs, Bulgarians, and Montenegrins in parts of Macedonia and Albania. Ignoring a warning from the European powers (including a disingenuous Russia) that no change in the area's borders would be tolerated, Montenegro attacked the Turks in Macedonia on October 8. The rest of the Balkan League entered the war ten days later.

The Turks crumbled almost instantly. Their 400,000 soldiers were outnumbered three to one, and even worse, were mostly unseasoned recruits—the newly elected Liberal government had purged the army of its rightist troops. Within a month, the allies had overrun nearly all of the empire's European holdings. Peace talks commenced in December, and a truce was called. But hawks within the Turkish heartland staged a coup the following January, and the fighting was soon in full swing again.

When it ended, in May, the Ottoman Empire was a fraction of its former size. Most of the Balkan League's wishes had come true—as had those of Crete, whose union with Greece was consummated at last, and Albania, which got its independence at the insistence of Austria and Italy.

But Bulgaria was discontented; its hoped-for piece of Macedonia had been claimed by Greece and Serbia. In June, it launched the second Balkan War against its erstwhile allies. When the smoke cleared, the geopolitical landscape was radically altered. And the embers that sparked the inferno in the Balkans were still smoldering and ready to ignite. **◄1911.12 ►1913.11**

Macedonia and Albania, the battlegrounds of the first Balkan War.

MEDICINE

Cushing's Syndrome

9 Harvey Cushing, a pioneer of modern neurosurgery, oversaw the treatment of more than 2,000 patients, developing lifesaving techniques—most notably a means to decrease spinal fluid pressure and to stop hemorrhaging of the brain during surgery—that reduced the mortality rate from 40 to less than 5 percent. But it was the Cleveland-born surgeon's 1912 research on the pituitary gland system that secured his international reputation. Cushing correlated pituitary functions to growth and to a form of obesity of the face and trunk that is still known as Cushing's syndrome. Examining cells of the pituitary glands under a microscope, Cushing discovered that the cells secreted growth hormones, and that oversecretion led to gigantism and undersecretion to dwarfism.

One summer, as he sought to learn more about the pituitary system, Cushing befriended giants and dwarfs, visiting them at circuses and sideshows, and compiling their medical histories. One troupe of dwarfs kept hoping that someday Cushing would solve their plight. But a growth hormone that one of Cushing's colleagues had isolated had no effect on the several dwarfs who received injections, and to this day any abnormalities in growth can only be controlled (if caught early in childhood) and not reversed after maturation. **◄1902.M ►1922.2**

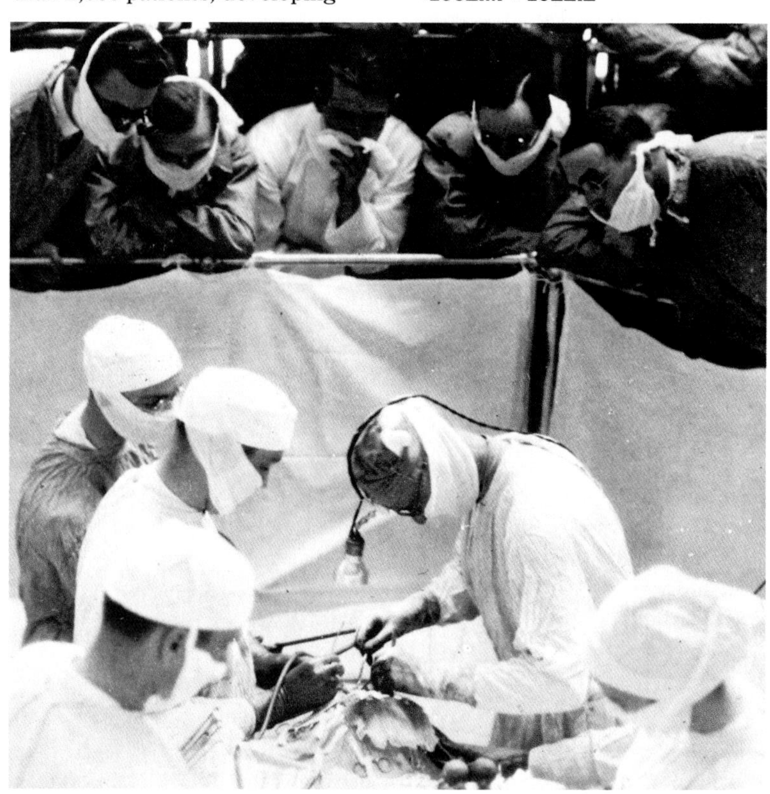

Harvey Cushing *(wearing headlamp)* was the dominant figure in modern neurosurgery.

IN THE UNITED STATES

►STOKOWSKI TAKES PHILADELPHIA—After 30-year-old Leopold Stokowski became conductor in 1912, the mediocre Philadelphia Orchestra began to metamorphose into a world-class institution. With his mane of fair hair, his long, expressive fingers (he disdained the baton), his avant-garde tastes, and his scandalous private life, the London-born conductor fit the public's image of a brilliant artiste. Yet for all his hauteur, he was one of music's great popularizers. ◄1911.5 ►1937.M

►MARINES IN CENTRAL AMERICA—Uncle Sam flexed his considerable military muscle in Central America in 1912, sending marines to Honduras, Nicaragua, and Cuba. The crack assault troops landed in Honduras in February to protect Yankee banana investments during a popular uprising. Marines also landed in Cuba after thousands of Afro-Cubans, fed up with racial discrimination, took to the streets in May. Then, in August, a detachment arrived in Nicaragua to quash a revolt against U.S.-installed President Adolfo Díaz. Washington maintained an almost unbroken military presence in Nicaragua until 1933. ◄1906.M ►1913.4

►ONE STRIKE, TWO VICTORIES— In January, when the textile-mill workers of Lawrence, Massachusetts, had their hours cut without warning, 10,000 of them spontaneously walked out. The radical Industrial Workers of the World organized the two-month strike, which provoked one of the era's bloodiest anti-union crackdowns. But the workers eventually prevailed, winning raises of up to 25 percent. And Massachusetts passed the nation's first minimum-wage law soon after. ◄1905.7 ►1917.7

POLITICS & BUSINESS: GNP: $39.4 billion ... Woodrow Wilson becomes president, defeating William H. Taft ... Congress extends 8-hour day to all federal contract employees ... Massachusetts textile workers, led by the "Wobblies," strike successfully ... National Cash Register officers indicted for conspiracy in restraint of trade ... U.S. postal regulation requires all advertising in the media to be labeled as such.

"We have discovered that in the land of their birth, Africans are treated as hewers of wood and drawers of water."
—Pixley ka Izaka Seme, a founder of the African National Congress

AROUND THE WORLD

▶RAILROAD FOR RUBBER—The 255-mile-long Madeira-Mamoro Railway, completed in 1912 (some six years and 6,000 lives after construction began), was intended to rescue the Brazilian rubber industry, but it proved to be too much, too late. Financed by Brazil's rubber barons, the railway cost the equivalent of three tons of gold, bypassed 19 major waterfalls, and stretched into the wilds of the Amazon basin where laborers gathered "tappings" of wild rubber and sold them to dealers. This haphazard system was being outpaced by rubber plantations in Southeast Asia. The railroad failed to stem the tide: Within six years, Brazil was no longer a major player in the world rubber market. ◂1904.12 ▸1920.10

▶SOCIAL DEMOCRATS WIN BIG—Parliamentary elections in Germany gave the Social Democrats an unprecedented triumph in January 1912: They were now the largest party in the Reichstag. But their antimilitarist stance (as socialists, they urged solidarity among workers around the world) could not prevent their country's drift toward war. ▸1914.1

▶UNTRADITIONAL SCHOOLS—*The Montessori Method*, Italian psychiatrist Maria Montessori's 1912 account of her successful efforts to teach Roman slum children to read, helped spawn a long-term, worldwide rejection of traditional schools (where, said Montessori, "children, like butterflies mounted on pins, are fastened each to his place"). The book became an international bestseller, paving the way for the Montessori system, which emphasizes self-education and individual initiative. The first Montessori School in North America opened in 1912 in Tarrytown, New York. ▸1916.3

Pixley ka Izaka Seme, in his graduation photo, Columbia University, Class of '06.

SOUTHERN AFRICA

A Congress for Change

10 After graduating from New York City's Columbia University and receiving a law degree from Oxford, Pixley ka Izaka Seme, a Zulu, returned to his native South Africa hoping to establish a law practice and to help rebuild the Zulu nation. When he arrived in Johannesburg, he found that he wasn't allowed to use sidewalks, leave his home without carrying as many as twelve official passes, venture out after 9:00 PM, or vote.

Appalled and outraged, Seme organized a conference to unite all the black South African ethnic factions as a single political force. Under Seme's guidance, the various leaders met in the city of Bloemfontein on January 8, 1912, and set up the South African Native National Congress, later the African National Congress, the first unified political body in colonial Africa composed of black Africans.

Standing in the way of Seme's dream were centuries of ethnic rivalries and hostilities. "We are one people," Seme pleaded. "These divisions, these jealousies, are the cause of all our woes." Recognizing their common plight, the delegates passed a motion to form a congress whose goal would be to force the South African government to end racial discrimination. Its tools would be trade unions, "peaceful propaganda," and Gandhian passive resistance. The mood in Bloemfontein was euphoric. "We felt wonderfully optimistic," said a delegate. "To us freedom was just around the corner." **◂1910.8 ▸1926.7**

MUSIC

A Strange New Language

11 "If this is music," wrote a critic of the 1912 world premiere of Arnold Schoenberg's *Pierrot lunaire*, "then I pray my Creator not to let me hear it again." The critic was at least partially right: This was not music in the conventional sense. When the Austrian-born composer introduced atonality, the signature concept of modern music, he was aspiring to nothing less than the total reinvention of the art. A cycle of 21 poems set to music and scored for eight instruments, *Pierrot lunaire* was one of Schoenberg's early formal experiments, in which he moved boldly away from the Romantic tradition toward a strange, altogether new musical language.

Critical and popular reaction was violent, often literally so. Disturbances were routine at Schoenberg concerts. After the tumultuous premiere of *Pierrot lunaire*, a member of the audience injured in the fracas sued his attacker for assault. At the trial, a doctor testified that Schoenberg's haunting music was to blame: It induced neurotic fits in its listeners.

Schoenberg, however, remained steadfastly devoted to atonality (or, as he preferred to call it, pantonality), refining his invention over several years and eventually introducing, in 1923, the rigorous twelve-tone system. The system's chief deviation from three centuries of Western music was that it was not organized around a tonal center: Twelve tones of the chromatic scale create a melodic line in which no one tone is more important than any other, and no tone is repeated until all the other eleven have been used.

A composer more respected than loved: Schoenberg, painted by Richard Gerstl.

The most influential figure in twentieth-century composition, Schoenberg dispensed with melodic symmetry, putting dissonance on an equal footing with consonance. **◂1902.4 ▸1913.5**

RUSSIA

Bolsheviks Launch *Pravda*

12 In 1912, V.I. Lenin was directing the Bolsheviks from exile in Austria. He wanted a means to disseminate his views—a cheap, daily paper, published in Russia (where czarist press restrictions had recently been loosened) and written in a style that the workers could understand. *Pravda (Truth)* was his answer. Lenin vowed to make the workers' daily the "chief means for Marxist agitation among the masses."

V.I. Lenin *(left)* installed Joseph Stalin as editor but couldn't control what he wrote.

But factionalism within the Party proved too much for his style of directing-at-a-distance. When the first issue of *Pravda*, published on April 22, 1912, reached Lenin in Austria, he was enraged to discover not the pure blast of Bolshevik ideology he expected but a paper that discussed Party differences openly.

After struggling for two years, Lenin eventually succeeded in putting his stamp on *Pravda*, and within six years, he had assumed full control of the paper. By World War I it had evolved into the voice of Bolshevism. Until 1991, when the Soviet Union collapsed, *Pravda* was not only the official organ of the Central Committee of the Communist Party, it was one of the most widely distributed newspapers in the world. **◂1911.M ▸1917.1**

NOBEL PRIZES: Peace: Elihu Root (U.S.; arbitration treaties) ... Literature: Gerhart Hauptmann (German; playwright) ... Chemistry: Victor Grignard (French; Grignard reagent) and Paul Sabatier (French; hydrogenating organic compounds) ... Medicine: Alexis Carrel (French; blood vessel and organ transplants) ... Physics: Nils Dalén (Swedish; gaslight regulation).

A VOICE FROM 1912

The Last Days of a Gentleman Explorer

By Robert Falcon Scott, from his diary, March 1912

Eighty-one days after setting off into the Antarctic wasteland from their base camp, British Royal Navy Captain Robert Falcon Scott and his four remaining companions reached the South Pole on January 18, 1912. But their dreams of being the first to reach the pole and winning glory for Britain were dashed when they realized that Roald Amundsen had beaten them to it by 36 days. (The Norwegian had left a letter for them.) The team's 800-mile trek back to the camp turned into a slow death march, as their supplies dwindled and temperatures routinely dipped to –40°F. In November a search party discovered their bodies, frozen in a tent eleven miles from their destination. With Scott was the diary he kept almost up to his final moments, when he scribbled his "Last entry." ◂1911.10 ▸1928.M

Captain Robert Scott writing in his diary inside his hut at Cape Evans, Ross Island, Antarctica, before setting off for the pole. Below, the hut's exterior, photographed in 1992.

Friday, March 16 or Saturday 17
Lost track of dates, but think the last correct. Tragedy all along the line. At lunch, the day before yesterday, poor Titus Oates said he couldn't go on; he proposed we should leave him in his sleeping-bag. That we could not do, and we induced him to come on, on the afternoon march. In spite of its awful nature for him he struggled on and we made a few miles. At night he was worse and we knew the end had come.

Should this be found I want these facts recorded. Oates' last thoughts were of his mother, but immediately before he took pride in thinking that his regiment would be pleased with the bold way in which he met his death. We can testify to his bravery. He has borne intense suffering for weeks without complaint, and to the very last was able and willing to discuss outside subjects. He did not—and would not—give up hope till the very end. He was a brave soul. This was the end. He slept through the night before last, hoping not to wake; but he woke in the morning—yesterday. It was blowing a blizzard. He said, "I am just going outside and may be some time." He went out into the blizzard and we have not seen him since.

I take this opportunity of saying that we have stuck to our sick companions to the last. In case of Edgar Evans, when absolutely out of food and he lay insensible, the safety of the remainder seemed to demand his abandonment, but Providence mercifully removed him at this critical moment. He died a natural death, and we did not leave him till two hours after his death. We knew that poor Oates was walking to his death, but though we tried to dissuade him, we knew it was the act of a brave man and an English gentleman. We all hope to meet the end with a similar spirit, and assuredly the end is not far.

Sunday, March 18
My right foot has gone, nearly all the toes—two days ago I was proud possessor of best feet. These are the steps of my downfall. Like an ass I mixed a small spoonful of curry powder with my melted pemmican—it gave me violent indigestion. I lay awake and in pain all night; woke and felt done on the march; foot went and I didn't know it. A very small measure of neglect and have a foot which is not pleasant to contemplate. Bowers takes first place in condition, but there is not much to choose after all. The others are still confident of getting through—or pretend to be—I don't know!

Monday, March 19
Lunch. We camped with difficulty last night, and were dreadfully cold till after our supper of cold pemmican and biscuit and a half a pannikin of cocoa cooked over the spirit. Then, contrary to expectation, we got warm and all slept well. Today we started in the usual dragging manner. Sledge dreadfully heavy. We are 15½ miles from the depot and ought to get there in three days. What progress! We have two days' food but barely a day's fuel.

Thursday, March 22 and 23
Blizzard bad as ever—Wilson and Bowers unable to start—tomorrow last chance—no fuel and only one or two of food left—must be near the end. Have decided it shall be natural—we shall march for the depot with or without our effects and die in our tracks.

Thursday, March 29
Since the 21st we have had a continuous gale from W.S.W. and S.W. We had fuel to make two cups of tea apiece and bare food for two days on the 20th.
Every day we have been ready to start for our depot eleven miles away, but outside the door of the tent it remains a scene of whirling drift. I do not think we can hope for any better things now. We shall stick it out to the end, but we are getting weaker, of course, and the end cannot be far.

It seems a pity, but I do not think I can write more.

—R. Scott

Last entry
For God's sake look after our people.

"It could be that perhaps I have solved a little something ... which perhaps is ... a small piece of reality."—**Niels Bohr in a letter to his wife, 14 days before he began his paper on the structure of the atom**

STORY OF THE YEAR

The Atom Demystified

1 Niels Bohr's quantum theory of the structure of atoms, published in 1913, radically changed the way scientists conceive of the invisible world of atomic particles. Before Bohr's breakthrough proposal, his mentor, Ernest Rutherford, had theorized that the atom's structure consisted of a positively charged nucleus surrounded by a cloud of smaller, negatively charged electrons that orbit the nucleus like planets circling a star. But if the laws of classical physics were applied to this model, the atom would become unstable and collapse. Expanding on the ideas of Max Planck and Albert Einstein, Bohr proposed that an atom in its stable state does not emit energy (in the form of photons, small units of light); only when an electron jumps abruptly from one orbit to another is energy emitted—or absorbed—in bundles called "quanta." Additionally, any specific atom has a limited number of electron orbits; this number precisely determines the atom's potential for combining with other atoms. By employing Planck's Constant—the invariable number that Planck discovered to quantify the relationship between energy and matter—Bohr produced a purely mathematical description of how electrons behave. He defined the very nature of the atom itself.

Niels Bohr *(above)* was a scientist's scientist. "Ask Bohr," Ernest Rutherford used to say when confronted with a difficult theoretical question.

As they confirmed Bohr's theory through spectroscopic measurements, other scientists, including Einstein, quickly recognized it as an enormous achievement. Bohr's discovery earned him the Nobel Prize in 1922, and throughout the twenties his Institute of Theoretical Physics in Copenhagen served as the hub of international research in the field. "It was a heroic time," remembered J. Robert Oppenheimer, who became famous in the forties as leader of the team that produced the first atomic bomb. "It involved the collaboration of scores of scientists from many different lands, though from first to last, the deeply creative and subtle and critical spirit of Niels Bohr guided, restrained, deepened, and finally transmuted the enterprise." Bohr, a remarkably modest man, and as much a philosopher as a scientist, went on to develop his principle of correspondence, which seamlessly linked the concepts of classical physics (which applied to the visible world) with those of the abstract world of quantum theory. **◂1911.3 ▸1917.M**

ART

The Avant-Garde Hits America

2 A "shabby French vagabond, a half-insane Flemish recluse and suicide, and a disreputable world wanderer." Such was one visitor's summary dismissal of Paul Cézanne, Vincent van Gogh, and Paul Gauguin upon seeing their work at the first International Exhibition of Modern Art, which opened in February 1913 at New York City's 69th Regiment Armory. But the work of those painters was among the tamest stuff at the show, which gave Americans their first taste of the avant-garde of Europe.

The Armory Show was the brainchild of Arthur B. Davies, president of the Association of American Painters and Sculptors, a group of 25 of the country's most progressive artists (including those from the Ashcan school and Alfred Stieglitz's "291" gallery). Touring the Salon d'Automne the previous summer, Davies and his friend artist Walter Kuhn had been so stunned by the artistic developments taking place that they'd vowed to mount an exhibition even Europeans would concede was "greater than any ever held anywhere on earth."

More than 300,000 people paid to see the show's 1,300 paintings and sculptures by such artists as Picasso, Braque, Duchamp, Matisse, and Brancusi. The American public was almost completely unprepared for nonrepresentational works of art that, to them, displayed a shocking irreverence for the lessons of Raphael, Rembrandt, and Titian.

Duchamp's *Nude Descending a Staircase*—compared to "an explosion in a shingle factory"—came to emblemize the Armory Show.

But for artists, the Armory Show was a turning point, destroying their complacency and demanding that they look at and think about art in a new way. Although exposure to the European avant-garde created an exodus to Paris, which became the center of modernism in the decades that followed, America was no longer culturally isolated. Indeed, European works in the show outsold American four to one. **◂1908.4 ▸1920.4**

LITERATURE

Fiction Echoes Freud

3 Just as Sigmund Freud's theories began to circulate in the English-speaking world, an English novel appeared that powerfully illustrated a central Freudian doctrine: the Oedipus complex. Yet novelist D.H. Lawrence had arrived at his theme intuitively. Published in 1913, *Sons and Lovers*, the autobiographical tale of obsessive love between a mother and son, was Lawrence's third novel, but the first to identify him as one of the century's major writers.

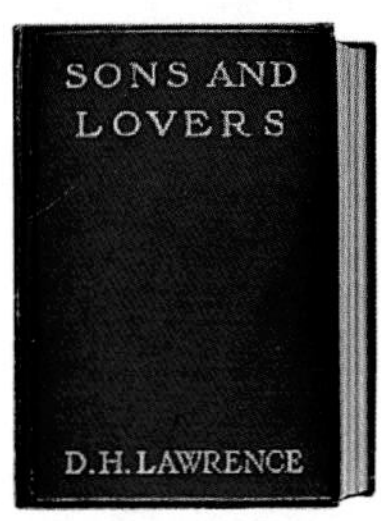

Sons and Lovers tells the story of Paul Morel, whose refined, educated mother—married to a violent, alcoholic coal miner—overwhelms him with her unswerving devotion. When Paul falls in love with two compelling women, his bond with his mother keeps him from making an emotional commitment to either. Paul realizes that to free himself, he must break with her—even though it may kill her.

Critics rhapsodized over Lawrence's poetic evocation of landscape and character. The novel's sexuality was less mystical, its indictment of industrial civilization less polemical, than those found in such later Lawrence novels as *The Rainbow* and *Lady Chatterley's Lover* (both of which were banned as obscene). But like those books, *Sons and Lovers* revealed a yearning for escape. Starting with his 1912 elopement—with Frieda von Richthofen, sister of the World War I flying ace—Lawrence lived throughout Europe, and in Ceylon, Australia,

ART & CULTURE: Books: *Totem and Taboo* (Sigmund Freud); *O, Pioneers* (Willa Cather); *General William Booth Enters Heaven* (Vachel Lindsay); *Pollyanna* (Eleanor H. Porter); *Virginia* (Ellen Glasgow); *Death in Venice* (Thomas Mann); *The Custom of the Country* (Edith Wharton) ... Music: "Peg O' My Heart" (Fisher and Bryan); "Ballin' the Jack" (Smith and Burris); "Danny Boy" (adapted by F. Weatherly);

Tahiti, Mexico, and New Mexico.

He was searching not only for a climate that would cure his tuberculosis, but also for a truly vital culture. With Carl Jung and others, Lawrence preached that Western society must tap "primitive" instincts, myths, and symbols to renew its vigor. These ideas led him to toy with fascism, but he died in 1930, at 44, before the fascists' experiments had borne their fatal fruit. **◂1912.2 ▸1922.1**

CENTRAL AMERICA

The Republic of United Fruit

4 Guatemalans called the American-owned United Fruit Company "the octopus," and in 1913 United Fruit demonstrated once more the aptness of that nickname: It established the Tropical Radio and Telegraph Company. With this virtual monopoly of Guatemala's communications industry, United Fruit's stranglehold on the country's infrastructure—and its politics—was complete. Guatemala had become a so-called "banana republic" (though in fact its major export was coffee).

United Fruit was the United States' number-one ambassador of "dollar diplomacy": good old-fashioned imperialism with a convenient new twist. In the name of free trade and capitalism, the United States could promote its interests —and be spared the task of setting up a colonial government—through gigantic export companies doing business in Central America and the Caribbean.

In exchange for helping to build a railroad, United Fruit (formed in the 1899 merger of the Boston Fruit Company and the Tropical Trading and Transport Company) was granted tax exemption, vast acreage, and ownership of Guatemala's main port. Seduced by the possibility of further American investment, Guatemala's ruling elite turned over control of all the nation's railways to United Fruit; meanwhile, the company's merchant navy dominated shipping.

As it had in other Central American countries, United Fruit functioned as a shadow government. On its lands (as well as those of other big fruit companies like Standard Fruit and Steamship in Honduras), employee commissaries drove peasants into unredeemable debt. The company imported black workers from Jamaica and the West Indies, and imposed U.S.-style racial segregation. It built hospitals, but few schools, and literacy rates stayed low. Peasants owned tiny plots, while United Fruit kept hundreds of thousands of acres uncultivated. By 1930, when it absorbed 20 rivals, United Fruit was Central America's biggest employer. And because the primacy of agriculture prevented industrialization, Guatemala remained hostage to shifting world demand for its two cash crops, coffee and bananas—a predicament whose repercussions are still being felt throughout Central America. **◂1912.M ▸1954.9**

Throughout Central America and the Caribbean *(above, in Cuba)*, exploitation of agricultural workers was rampant.

MUSIC

The Stravinsky Riot

5 One of the most important compositions of the century, Igor Stravinsky's *The Rite of Spring,* premiered on May 29, 1913, at the Théâtre des Champs-Elysées in Paris. The critics' descriptions of the sprawling, polyrhythmic score apply equally to the audience's reaction: brutal, aggressive, savage. The music, played fortissimo, was often drowned out by an incessant thunder of boos and whistles. Stravinsky himself, seated near the front of the theater, was forced to retreat backstage.

Stravinsky *(above)* and Nijinsky *(his sketches, below)* disturbed audiences with their emphasis on the savagery and upheaval of springtime.

Parisian audiences had greeted the Russian composer's previous, more conventionally romantic collaborations with ballet impresario Sergei Diaghilev—*The Firebird* (1910) and *Petrushka* (1911)—with acclaim. But the audience at *The Rite* was unprepared for the barbaric, pagan images evoked by Vaslav Nijinsky's vigorous choreography, and for the way Stravinsky's score pushed the boundaries of traditional tonality. European music (as well as literature and art) had always characterized the onset of spring in soft, dewy tones. Stravinsky sought to make the listener feel spring's fecund emergence from the earth. "What I was trying to convey," the composer said later, "was the magnificent upsurge of nature reborn."

Audiences and critics proved surprisingly adaptable; within a year, Monteux again conducting, *The Rite* was performed as a symphonic piece at the Casino de Paris. This time, the composer was carried triumphantly from the hall on the shoulders of his admirers. It was a tableau that signified the end of the Romantic Era, and the arrival of the Modern. **◂1909.6 ▸1918.9**

BIRTHS

Bao Dai, Vietnamese emperor.

Menachem Begin, Israeli prime minister.

Willy Brandt, West German chancellor.

Benjamin Britten, U.K. composer.

Albert Camus, French writer.

Gerald R. Ford, U.S. president.

Edward Gierek, Polish communist leader.

Lionel Hampton, U.S. musician.

William Inge, U.S. playwright.

Danny Kaye, U.S. actor.

Burt Lancaster, U.S. actor.

Lon Nol, Cambodian prime minister.

Makarios III, Cypriot archbishop.

Richard M. Nixon, U.S. president.

Jesse Owens, U.S. runner.

Rosa Parks, U.S. civil-rights activist.

Tyrone Power, U.S. actor.

Ad Reinhardt, U.S. painter.

Loretta Young, U.S. actress.

DEATHS

Adolphus Busch, German-U.S. brewer and philanthropist.

Rudolf Diesel, German mechanical engineer.

Francisco Madero, Mexican president.

John Pierpont Morgan, U.S. financier.

Alfred von Schlieffen, German military tactician.

Harriet Tubman, U.S. abolitionist.

Aaron Montgomery Ward, U.S. retailer.

***Second String Quartet* (Charles Ives) ... Painting and Sculpture: *The Little Mermaid* (Edvard Eriksen); *Woman in a Chemise* (Pablo Picasso) ... Film: *The Student of Prague* (Stellan Rye); *Traffic in Souls* (George Lone); *The Battle at Elderbrush Gulch, Judith of Bethulia* (D.W. Griffith) ... Theater: *Androcles and the Lion* (G.B. Shaw); *The Passion Flower* (Jacinto Benavente); *Sweethearts* (Victor Herbert).**

"The idea came in a general way from the overhead trolley that the Chicago packers use in dressing beef."
—Henry Ford on the source of his inspiration for the assembly line

NEW IN 1913

American Cancer Society.

B'nai B'rith Anti-Defamation League.

Camel cigarettes.

Duesenberg automobile.

Quaker's Puffed Rice and Puffed Wheat.

Consumer Price Index (compiled by U.S. Bureau of Labor Statistics).

U.S. Parcel Post service.

Peppermint Life Savers.

Actors' Equity Association.

IN THE UNITED STATES

▶**A GRAND STATION**—The world's largest railway station opened in New York City in February 1913. A giant, neoclassical structure, Grand

Central Terminal dwarfed Penn Station and had a total of 48 tracks. ▸1966.M

▶**WATER COMES TO L.A.**—With the words "There it is; take it!" Los Angeles city engineer William Mulholland opened the Owens River Aqueduct. Built in five years, the 234-mile delivery system brought 260 million gallons of water daily to the small city, enabling it to grow into a major metropolis within a few decades—and allowing Mulholland's associates who knew of the plan's development to become vastly wealthy through real estate speculation. ▸1974.12

▶**THE MODERN BRA**—Tired of whalebone bodices and long corsets, New York debutante Mary Phelps Jacob in 1913 stitched together a new kind of undergarment: a prototype brassiere. With the help of her French maid, Jacob (later famous as Caresse Crosby) fashioned the device from two handkerchiefs and a

After the assembly line was introduced, Ford's Highland Park plant could turn out as many as 1,000 cars a day.

BUSINESS AND INDUSTRY

Assembly Line Rolls

6 By 1913, automobile production at Henry Ford's immense plant in Highland Park, Michigan, had reached a plateau. Using conventional methods—bringing the car's components, painstakingly assembled by individual workers, to the stationary chassis—the Ford Motor Company could turn out nearly 160,000 cars per year, an average of eleven cars per worker.

Then Henry Ford introduced the assembly line. Modeled on the so-called "process lines" pioneered by Singer (sewing machines) and Colt (firearms), Ford's line contained one critical innovation: While a process line brought the item being manufactured to a specific work station, where it would halt for a process to be completed, the assembly line *never* stopped. Its conveyor belts moved continuously as workers repeated specific, small tasks hundreds of times each day, racing to keep up with the belt's pace.

Ford first tried the assembly line in the magneto department. A skilled worker took 20 minutes to build a single magneto wheel. On the assembly line, 29 unskilled men turned out a magneto wheel every 13 minutes. Further refinements brought the time down to five minutes. The engine department was mechanized next. Finally, the chassis itself was placed on the line. The time needed to build and equip each one plunged from 12.5 hours to 93 minutes. In terms of man-hours, one worker now accomplished what used to require four. After repeated adjustments, the time required to build a Model T at Highland Park was ultimately reduced to the point where a car was being produced every 24 *seconds*, enabling Ford to vastly increase production—and simultaneously cut prices. The price of a Model T dropped from $850 in 1908 to $440 six years later. By 1915, Ford had become the unrivaled king of the road, producing nearly half of all the world's cars.

Ford's workers had to endure the numbing boredom of the repetition inherent in their jobs and the occasional line speedups ordained by factory bosses, but the assembly line also helped bring about the eight-hour shift, and the five-dollar day, double the average wage of the pre-assembly-line worker. **◂1908.1 ▸1915.M**

WESTERN AFRICA

Schweitzer Goes to Lambaréné

7 Although the particular form of noblesse oblige embraced by Albert Schweitzer is out of sync with modern values, the German doctor in his own lifetime was an international symbol of humanitarian goodness. In 1913, Schweitzer, keeping a vow he'd made as a young man to dedicate his life after age 30 to helping his fellow man, sailed from Europe to French Equatorial Africa (now Gabon) and founded a hospital at the village of Lambaréné. There, in a clearing in the jungle, Schweitzer spent the rest of his life battling leprosy, malaria,

"I feel for them like a brother, but like an older brother," said Schweitzer of the Africans he treated.

and syphilis. His work earned him the 1952 Nobel Peace Prize.

By the time Schweitzer established his hospital at Lambaréné he was already a well-known scholar and musician. He had earned a doctorate in philosophy from the University of Strasbourg (where he also studied theology) and was among the finest concert organists of his time. In 1905, he published a definitive biography of the composer Johann Sebastian Bach. The following year he published his influential theological work, *The Quest of the Historical Jesus*. Its thesis that Jesus was "an immeasurably great man" created the framework of secular humanism. Upon reaching his self-appointed deadline, he enrolled in medical school, using book royalties and concert earnings to pay for his education.

"We must all carry our share of the misery which lies upon the world," he wrote later, explaining why he gave up his music and academic pursuits. By the end of his life, however, Schweitzer's paternalistic tendencies made him seem hopelessly out of touch. He was also criticized for refusing to modernize his primitive hospital, even after he became famous and increased funding was available. He argued that "simple people need simple healing methods." Schweitzer died in Lambaréné in 1965. **▸1979.11**

PHILANTHROPY

Foundations for Giving

8 "Pity the poor millionaire," Andrew Carnegie once wrote, "for the way of the philanthropist is hard." Fellow tycoon John D. Rockefeller learned that lesson firsthand as he struggled to establish the biggest charitable trust the world had ever seen. The $50 million Rockefeller Foundation was born in 1913, but only after three years of wrangling with a suspicious Congress.

Rockefeller wanted to create a newfangled institution, like the one Carnegie endowed in 1911. (Both men had been involved in more traditional philanthropy for years.) Instead of sticking to a single cause (like building libraries or leprosariums) or to simply helping the needy, his foundation would fund a variety of experts working to better

SPORTS: Baseball: World Series, Philadelphia Athletics (Chief Bender, Eddie Plank) defeat New York Giants, 4–1; Walter Johnson of Washington Senators sets record for most consecutive shutout innings (56); Ebbets Field opens in Brooklyn, N.Y. ... Shuffleboard: First U.S. deck-shuffleboard game played on a hotel court in Daytona, Florida.

the human condition. Convinced that such a foundation should be overseen by public officials, Rockefeller applied for a federal charter. But shortly afterward, his Standard Oil Company was judged an illegal monopoly by the Supreme Court. Progressives denounced his proposed nonprofit corporation as a scheme to buy both a good name and influence over the government. The rapacious magnate's money, they insisted, was "tainted." In the end, Rockefeller gave up on Congress and chartered his foundation with New York State. By 1990, its assets had reached nearly $2 billion. Though no longer the richest fund of its kind, it is still one of the world's top ten.

After another brush with controversy (his foundation sponsored a 1914 labor-relations study while one of his companies brutally suppressed a miners' strike), Rockefeller steered the institution mainly toward medical matters. Rockefeller dollars paid for hookworm- and malaria-control programs, and new or improved medical schools, in 62 countries. Outside of public-health issues, politics were avoided.

It was the foundation set up by the Scottish-born steel baron that gained a deeper influence in Washington—and in a way the Progressives would have applauded. The Carnegie Corporation concentrated on educational development and social research throughout the English-speaking world; over the decades, it funded reports on U.S. schools and race relations that led to major reforms. But while Carnegie had envisioned his brand of "scientific philanthropy" as a model for moguls everywhere, it remained mostly an American phenomenon. Today, whether because of the nation's tax laws or its civic values, 95 percent of all foundations with assets over $10 million are based in the United States. ◂**1911.M** ▸**1982.M**

The Scottish-born Carnegie showered his wealth on libraries and other educational institutions across the country.

LITERATURE

Proust's Landmark

9 Marcel Proust completed *Swann's Way*—the first volume of his sprawling hymn to memory, *Remembrance of Things Past*—in the quiet of a cork-lined room in his Paris apartment nearly a year before it reached the public in 1913. In complex, meandering sentences, the 41-year-old Proust transformed his own bourgeois past into the stuff of a philosophical quest—for the meaning of time, character, and social caste; for the keys to the basic secrets of human existence. Proust ended up financing the book's publication himself because every publisher he showed it to rejected it. One wondered why "anyone should take 30 pages to describe how he tossed about in bed because he couldn't get to sleep."

Proust's notebooks, containing some original passages from *Remembrance*.

Yet it was just this intensity that gave Proust's 520-page work its power. Chronic illness had turned Proust from a socialite into a recluse, and convalescence gave him an opportunity to ponder all that had happened in his life. His memories stirred by the taste of a madeleine, the narrator of *Swann's Way* (named Marcel, like the author) tells the love story of his parents' neighbor, Charles Swann, and the courtesan Odette de Crécy—and in doing so, reconstructs his childhood almost moment by moment. At the dawn of the psychoanalytic age, here was the most relentlessly introspective novel yet written. As the old world stood on the brink of a war that would sweep it from existence, here was the most keenly observed record imaginable of one intimate corner.

Jean Cocteau and other avant-gardists hailed the book as a work of genius. Conservative critics balked at Proust's syntax ("damned awkward") and his obsessively detailed descriptions. "We cannot help wondering," wrote one, "how many libraries he would fill if he narrated his whole life." The answer came in 1927, five years after the writer's death, when the last of *Remembrance*'s seven volumes (totaling some 3,000 pages) was published. By then—abetted by C.K. Scott-Moncrieff's masterful English translation—it had become one of the century's most influential works of literature. ▸**1922.1**

IN THE UNITED STATES

bit of pink ribbon. Soft, supportive, separating, the brassiere was a boon to modern, active middle-class women. ▸1921.V

▶HIT OF THE CHRISTMAS SEASON—Inspired by heady construction in New York City, Connecticut toy maker A.C. Gilbert—a two-time Olympic pole-vault champion, magician, and Yale M.D.—invented the Erector Set. Gilbert publicized his collection of nuts, bolts, and miniature, multi-holed girders in a national ad campaign, the first ever for a toy. American boys responded with unprecedented enthusiasm, and the Erector Set became a perennial favorite.

▶NOTRE DAME AND THE FORWARD PASS—Working in the obscurity of their small Catholic college in South Bend, Indiana, undergraduate

football players Knute Rockne *(above)* and Gus Dorais perfected a new technique to compensate for their team's lack of size. Unveiled in a game against powerful Army, the forward pass led not only to a 35-13 upset that put Notre Dame on the football map but to a revolution in the game itself. ◂1912.7 ▸1920.6

▶FEDERAL RESERVE FORMED—Enacted by Congress in December, the Federal Reserve Act established twelve regional banks, which in turn were joined by 213 commercial banks. The system enabled the boards of the regional Federal Reserve Banks to control the amount of currency in circulation and thereby regulate the availability of cash and credit. ◂1908.M ▸1929.1

POLITICS & BUSINESS: GNP: $39.6 billion ... U.S. Department of Labor created ... Alice Paul leads march in Washington, D.C., for women's suffrage, founds National Woman's Party ... House Committee on Banking and Currency report exposes the interests controlling U.S. economic power ... Underwood Act reduces tariffs ... 16th Amendment allows federal government to levy direct income tax.

"Have proceeded to California. Want authority to rent barn in place called Hollywood for $75 a month. Regards to Sam."
—Telegram sent by Cecil B. DeMille to Jesse Lasky

AROUND THE WORLD

▶VON STÜRGKH TAKES CONTROL—Invoking his country's constitution, Austrian prime minister Count Karl von Stürgkh in 1913 seized unilateral control of the government. The reason: a paroxysm of nationalism among the member states of Austria-Hungary —Hungary, Bohemia, Slovakia, Moravia, Austria—was about to rip apart the empire. Not even absolutism could save the federation, however, when Archduke Ferdinand was assassinated a year later. The same fate awaited von Stürgkh in 1916. ▶1914.1

▶MADERO MURDERED—Capitalizing on the turmoil of civil war, right-wing army officer Victoriano Huerta seized power in Mexico during the Decena Trágica—Ten Tragic Days—in February 1913. Huerta had popularly elected president Francisco Madero executed, dissolved the congress, and unleashed a wave

of violence on the land. Within a year, Huerta himself fell before the combined opposition of Mexican revolutionists Emiliano Zapata and Pancho Villa and the U.S. government. ◀1910.10 ▶1916.6

▶HERTZSPRUNG-RUSSELL DIAGRAM—Working independently, Dutch astronomer Ejnar Hertzsprung and American astronomer Henry Norris Russell devised a means to plot the magnitudes of stars against their temperatures. The Hertzsprung-Russell diagram, named in 1913, revealed patterns of stellar organization and evolution. It became a basic tool of modern astronomy. ▶1914.10

▶SUFFRAGIST SACRIFICES—On June 4, 1913, at the Derby, English suffragist Emily Davison sacrificed herself to the cause of women's suffrage when she ran in front of King George's horse and was trampled to death. Elsewhere, Emmeline Pankhurst was sentenced to three years in jail for attempting to firebomb the house of Chancellor of the Exchequer David Lloyd George. ◀1903.3 ▶1920.11

FILM

Features Go True West

10 Although ten-minute films still flourished, by 1913 moviegoers (who numbered five million daily in the United States alone) were clamoring for longer feature films. That year, the alliance of a movie-struck glove seller, his brother-in-law, and a debt-ridden writer created a spicy Western that put Hollywood, California, on the map as the feature-film capital of the world.

After attending his first movie, an ambitious New York glove merchant named Sam Goldfish—agog with possibilities—hectored his reluctant brother-in-law, vaudeville impresario Jesse L. Lasky, into forming a company to produce feature-length films. Lasky enlisted a mediocre playwright named Cecil B. DeMille to provide artistic vision.

As its first project, the Jesse L. Lasky Feature Play Company chose *The Squaw Man*, a 1905 stage melodrama about a British aristocrat in the wild American West who marries the Indian woman who saved his life. Most Westerns at the time were shot in New Jersey. But DeMille wanted the "true West," so he set out for Flagstaff, Arizona. After taking one look at the dull landscape, he ordered his crew to reboard the train and head for the end of the line: Los Angeles.

Short films had been shot in Los Angeles since 1907, but *The Squaw Man* was its first feature. The production, operating out of a barn on Vine Street, was beset with problems. Soon after filming began, a saboteur (probably from the Motion Picture Patents trust) broke into the barn and ruined DeMille's footage. (Fortunately, he had a duplicate negative.) On two occasions, a sniper's bullet whizzed by.

At six reels long, *The Squaw Man* was Hollywood's first feature.

All grievances were redressed, however, when *The Squaw Man* became a huge hit, advancing the fortunes of feature films in general and the Lasky Company in particular. DeMille moved on to sex comedies and biblical epics and became a titan and a tyrant. Hollywood became Hollywood. And the glove merchant Sam Goldfish? He changed his name to Goldwyn, and left gloves forever. **◀1908.8 ▶1919.3**

OTTOMAN EMPIRE

Prologue to the Great War

11 At the end of the First Balkan War in May 1913, the members of the Balkan League had taken everything they wanted from

These irregular troops were rounded up and armed by the Ottoman Turks to oppose Bulgarian forces.

the Ottoman Empire—almost. The Bulgarians craved a piece of Macedonia, but strategic necessities had confined their battles to Thrace. Macedonia was instead divided between Greece and Serbia, neither of which wished to cede territory. Russia, which had helped forge the Balkan alliance, failed to arbitrate a solution. So on June 29, Bulgaria, prompted by Austria (Russia's rival), attacked its two former comrades-in-arms.

The Second Balkan War was a brief, bloody free-for-all. Romania, having skipped the first war, joined in against Bulgaria. The Turks mustered the strength to win back Adrianople from Bulgarian occupiers. As battles became massacres, the outgunned Bulgarians turned and ran. It was over by August.

The Balkan wars rearranged the map of southeastern Europe. The Ottoman Empire lost two thirds of its European population. Greece, Serbia, and Montenegro roughly doubled in size; even Bulgaria got 20 percent bigger. Nationalism grew more intense than ever. With the gutting of the empire, the balance of power became dangerously fragile. Bulgaria had fallen into the Austrian camp; Romania had fallen out. Serbia, hungry for Austrian-held Bosnia, Hercegovina, and Croatia, aligned itself with Russia, as did Greece and Montenegro. Just one slip would propel Russia and Austria into direct conflict and sweep all the variously allied European powers into a great war. That slip would come less than a year later. **◀1912.8 ▶1914.1**

POPULAR CULTURE

Crossword Puzzle Debuts

12 The "Word Cross" puzzle that appeared in the New York *World*'s Sunday supplement on December 21, 1913, was shaped like a diamond, not a square. Some of its clues were duplicated, and the workers who typeset it were flummoxed by its exasperating complications. Still, the puzzle proved so immediately popular that, when it was briefly replaced by military maps at the outbreak of World War I, reader protest was immense.

Within a decade, crosswords appeared in most American newspapers, and by 1924 they had migrated from the Sunday "fun" pages to the daily papers. Trains

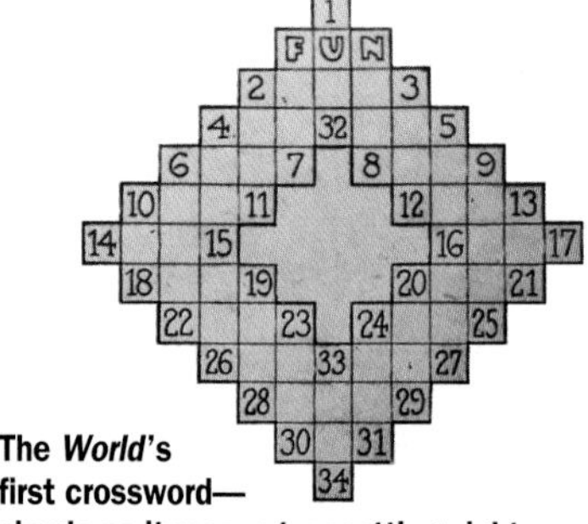

The *World*'s first crossword—simple as it was, a typesetting nightmare.

stocked puzzles for travelers, and tournaments blossomed on college campuses. Pickpockets stalked their prey in hotel lobbies while pretending to be engaged in crosswords.

The crossword reached London in 1930, in *The Times*, and by 1942 had finally penetrated the Sunday edition of *The New York Times*. By century's end, crossword puzzles appeared in 99 percent of the world's daily newspapers. **◀1900.2**

NOBEL PRIZES: Peace: Henri Lafontaine (Belgian; president of International Peace Bureau) ... Literature: Rabindranath Tagore (Indian; poet) ... Chemistry: Alfred Werner (Swiss; structure of inorganic elements) ... Medicine: Charles Richet (French; anaphylactic shock) ... Physics: Heike Kamerlingh Onnes (Dutch; superconductivity).

A VOICE FROM 1913

Optimism and White Paint

From *The House in Good Taste,* by Elsie de Wolfe, 1913

"I believe in plenty of optimism and white paint," Elsie de Wolfe proclaimed, "comfortable chairs with lights beside them, open fires on the hearth, and flowers where they 'belong,' mirrors and sunshine in all rooms." Such surroundings may be commonplace today, but in 1913, when de Wolfe published The House in Good Taste *(she popularized the term "good taste"), she changed the way Americans lived. Establishing home decoration as a branch of fashion and becoming the nation's first professional interior decorator, de Wolfe replaced dark, plush, knickknack-strewn Victorian rooms with a combination of French antiques, modern colors, and the latest conveniences. Although rich patrons like Henry Clay Frick (for whom de Wolfe created an American counterpart of London's Wallace Collection) paid her extravagant fees to redecorate their homes, she counseled women with limited budgets on the creative art of making do. Wildly energetic and egocentric ("It's beige," she exclaimed, beholding the Parthenon, "my color!"), the former actress also was active in the art world, business, and women's rights.* ◂**1908.10** ▸**1921.4**

When I am asked to decorate a new house, my first thought is suitability. My next thought is proportion. Always I keep in mind the importance of simplicity.... We are sure to judge a woman in whose house we find ourselves for the first time, by her surroundings. We judge her temperament, her habits, her inclinations, by the interior of her home. We may talk of the weather, but we are looking at the furniture. We attribute vulgar qualities to those who are content to live in ugly surroundings. We endow with refinement and charm the person who welcomes us in a delightful room, where the colors blend and the proportions are as perfect as in a picture. After all, what surer guarantee can there be of a woman's character, natural and cultivated, inherent and inherited, than taste? It is a compass that never errs. If a woman has taste she may have faults, follies, fads, she may err, she may be as human and feminine as she pleases, but she will never cause a scandal!...

A woman's environment will speak for her life, whether she likes it or not. How can we believe that a woman of sincerity of purpose will hang fake "works of art" on her walls, or satisfy herself with imitation velvets or silks? How can we attribute taste to a woman who permits paper floors and iron ceilings in her house? We are too afraid of the restful commonplaces, and yet if we live simple lives, why shouldn't we be glad our houses are comfortably commonplace? How much better to have plain furniture that is comfortable, simple chintzes printed from old blocks, a few good prints, than all the sham things in the world? A house is a dead-give-away, anyhow, so you should arrange it so that the person who sees your personality in it will be reassured, not disconcerted.

Elsie de Wolfe *(top, with her dogs Tai Chu and Ting-a-ling)* has been credited with the "introduction of new American money to old French furniture." Once called the "best-dressed actress off Broadway," de Wolfe dressed her rooms just as stylishly. Photographs in her book included a dressing room done in black chintz and "Miss Anne Morgan's Louis XVI boudoir."

"The lamps are going out all over Europe; we shall not see them lit again in our lifetime."—**Sir Edward Grey, British foreign minister**

STORY OF THE YEAR

Assassination in Sarajevo

The archduke and his wife; their assassinations were the catalyst for the war, not its cause.

1 Archduke Franz Ferdinand knew his first official visit to Sarajevo would be dangerous. The capital of Bosnia and Hercegovina—twin provinces once part of Serbia, later conquered by Turkey, then occupied and finally annexed by Austria-Hungary—had become a hotbed of pan-Serbian nationalism. Although he supported greater autonomy for the region, the archduke was heir to the Austro-Hungarian throne, and therefore was widely hated. On June 28, 1914, as he rode into town in an open car, a would-be assassin threw a bomb at him. The archduke knocked it away, and it exploded near another vehicle. His luck, however, didn't hold. After attending a reception at city hall, the archduke set off to visit those wounded in the bomb attack. A Bosnian student named Gavrilo Princip lunged at his car, firing three shots and killing the nobleman and his wife, Sophie. This act set in motion the interlocking cogwheels of national alliances, driven by imperialism and fear, that would start World War I.

Events unfolded quickly. By mid-July, an Austrian investigator linked the attackers to the Serbia-based Black Hand terrorist group. (Later it was discovered that they'd been aided by Serbian officials, who hoped to make Bosnia-Hercegovina part of a "greater Serbia.") The imperial government issued an ultimatum on July 23, insisting that Serbia put a stop—within 48 hours—to "the intrigues which form a perpetual menace to the tranquillity of the monarchy." Among Vienna's demands were that Belgrade censor anti-Austrian publications and arrest anti-Austrian activists. Serbia refused these stipulations, accepted others, and suggested international arbitration. Austrian authorities, determined to break the unruly Serbs, rejected outside interference.

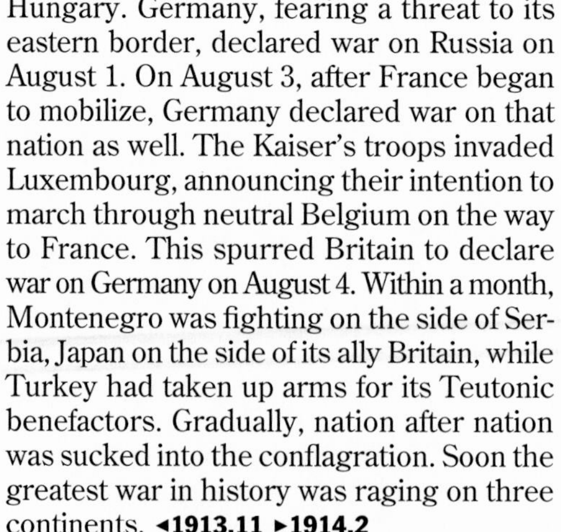

The blood-splattered tunic of the murdered archduke.

Serbia was backed by Russia—and by France and Britain, Russia's partners in the Triple Entente. Germany (with reservations) backed its Austrian ally. A flurry of diplomacy failed to break the deadlock. Austria-Hungary declared war on Serbia on July 28.

Russia mobilized its troops the next day, ostensibly to defend Serbia and itself from Austria-Hungary. Germany, fearing a threat to its eastern border, declared war on Russia on August 1. On August 3, after France began to mobilize, Germany declared war on that nation as well. The Kaiser's troops invaded Luxembourg, announcing their intention to march through neutral Belgium on the way to France. This spurred Britain to declare war on Germany on August 4. Within a month, Montenegro was fighting on the side of Serbia, Japan on the side of its ally Britain, while Turkey had taken up arms for its Teutonic benefactors. Gradually, nation after nation was sucked into the conflagration. Soon the greatest war in history was raging on three continents. ◄1913.11 ►1914.2

WORLD WAR I

Major Powers Mobilize

2 Within two months of the incident at Sarajevo, 17 million soldiers were mobilized from eight nations and their far-flung colonies. At the outset, strategists for both the Allies (the countries grouped around France, Britain, and Russia) and the Central Powers (those siding with Germany and Austria-Hungary) predicted a brief war. French recruits, leaving Paris, shouted, "To Berlin!" The Kaiser promised his troops, "You will be home before the leaves have fallen." But by Christmas 1914, about 1.5 million on each side had been killed, wounded, or captured—and the end was nowhere in sight.

German hopes for a quick victory centered on the Schlieffen Plan. While divisions to the east kept Russia pinned down, others would attack France with lightning speed at its weakest frontier, via the neutral Low Countries. Once France had collapsed, Russia's hordes of peasant troops could be vanquished by Germany's better-trained and better-armed men. It almost worked. Belgium was trampled by mid-August, despite tough resistance by its army and a British force, and the Germans quickly reached the Marne River near Paris. But the French, in a battle called the "Miracle of the Marne," drove them back to the Aisne River, where both sides dug in—literally.

Hundreds of thousands of men were lost in a matter of weeks because of the efficiency of modern weaponry. Generals realized that fighting on open ground was suicidal, so each army built lines of trenches, which soon zigzagged hundreds of miles from the English Channel to Switzerland. There the front would remain for four years, barely moving, as incessant

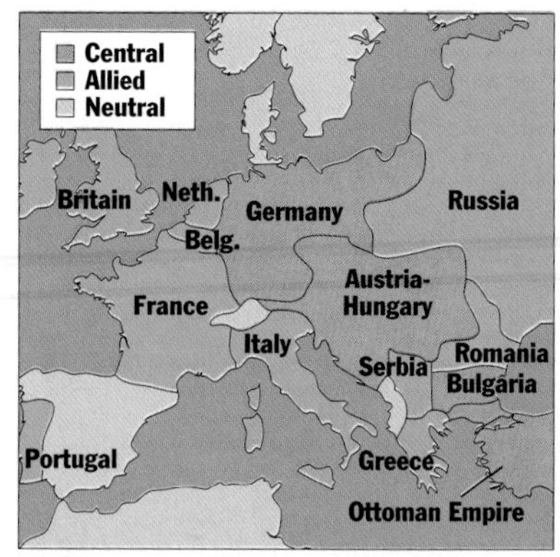

The European alliances of World War I.

ART & CULTURE: Books: ***Dubliners*** (James Joyce); ***The Congo*** (Vachel Lindsay); ***Trees*** (Joyce Kilmer); ***North of Boston*** (Robert Frost); ***The Titan*** (Theodore Dreiser); ***Penrod*** (Booth Tarkington); George Jean Nathan and H.L. Mencken become coeditors of ***The Smart Set*** ... Music: "Castle House Rag" (Irving Berlin); "St. Louis Blues" (W.C. Handy); ***A London Symphony*** (Ralph Vaughan Williams) ...

"Wounded; wounded everywhere, maimed men at every junction; hospitals crowded with blind and dying and moaning men."—**Philip Gibbs, British war correspondent, on the first six months of World War I**

shelling obliterated everything around it, turning the land into a desolate moonscape.

On the Eastern Front, the Russians attacked far more swiftly than expected. German troops under General Paul von Hindenburg (hero of the Franco-Prussian War of 1870) halted the enemy offensive against East Prussia, but were driven from the key city of Lodz, Poland. The Austrians wrested Belgrade from the Serbs, then lost it. In the Balkans, too, stalemate set in with winter.

Shooting erupted wherever the European powers had interests. Indian troops took Basra, Mesopotamia (now Iraq), for their British rulers. South Africa's pro-German Boers staged an insurrection. In the German territory of Kiaochow (now Jiaoxian, China), Japanese forces (which had joined the Allies on August 23) overran the port city of Qingdao. A German cruiser bombed Penang, British Malaysia.

On the open seas, gunboats constructed at great cost during a fevered arms race sank one another in scattered skirmishes, but Britain's superior navy soon had Germany locked in a stifling blockade. Germany's answer—a submarine war against British commercial shipping—was about to begin.
◂1914.1 ▸1915.3

SCIENCE

Stage One of Rocketry

3 Since the age of 17, Robert H. Goddard had been consumed by a desire (as the young man had written in his new diary) "to make some device which had even the *possibility* of ascending to Mars." In 1914 he made perceptible progress toward realizing that fantasy. Fresh from graduate school, Goddard filed two patents containing the fundamental concepts of modern rocketry, including liquid-fuel propulsion and the multistage rocket. Within 12 years, Goddard would launch his invention, ushering in the rocket age.

During his years of experimentation, Goddard shunned publicity. In grant proposals, he spoke only of developing a means to collect atmospheric data. When a local newspaper got wind of his vision of space travel, it dubbed the reclusive Clark University professor "Moony." Periodic explosions lighting up the farm in Massachusetts

Misunderstood genius: Goddard on his Massachusetts farm with his liquid-propellant rocket in 1926.

where he conducted his tests seemed only to confirm his nuttiness. He was vindicated (personally, if not publicly) in 1926, about a quarter century after the Wright brothers' first flight. Goddard's breakthrough rocket measured ten feet in length, weighed under five pounds when empty, and was powered by liquid oxygen and gasoline. It achieved a height of 41 feet and traveled 184 feet. The flight lasted 2.5 seconds. Goddard wrote in his diary the next day: "It looked almost magical as it rose, without any appreciably greater noise or flame, as if it said: 'I've been here long enough; I think I'll be going somewhere else if you don't mind.'"
◂1903.M ▸1944.2

INDIA

Gandhi Returns Home

4 "The saint has left our shores," wrote South African political leader Jan Smuts in 1914. "I hope forever." The saint was Mohandas K. Gandhi, who had come to Natal to practice law in 1893, expecting to stay just a year. Instead, confronted by racism and political injustice, he remained for 20 years, and organized the Indian immigrant community's stand against persecution. It was in South Africa that the father of Indian independence developed *satyāgraha,* "firmness in truth," his program of enlightened passive resistance.

Gandhi's moment of truth came during a train ride he took from Durban to Pretoria shortly after arriving in Africa. He was thrown out of a first-class compartment by the white conductor; farther down the line, a coach driver beat him for refusing to vacate his seat for a European traveler. "I cannot conceive a greater loss to a man," Gandhi later wrote, "than the loss of his self-respect." When, in 1907, the Transvaal government passed a racist resolution mandating the registration of all Indians, Gandhi led the resistance, vowing to defy the law and peaceably accept the consequences. Hundreds, then thousands of Indians embraced his example. The movement entered a new, broader stage in 1913, after the Cape Colony Supreme Court decided non-Christian marriages were invalid. Indian wives, said the court, were concubines without legal rights, their children illegitimate. Women now rushed to join Gandhi's "non-violent war."

Gandhi was repeatedly arrested and jailed (during one incarceration he made a pair of sandals for his rival Smuts), but he had succeeded in focusing the world's attention on his cause. Impelled by

After studying law in London, Mohandas Gandhi *(center)* worked as an attorney in South Africa.

the British government to negotiate with Gandhi, the South African parliament enacted the Indian Relief Bill in 1914, abolishing, among other things, the marriage provision. "He is a dangerous and uncomfortable enemy," observed an British commentator, "because his body, which you can always conquer, gives you so little purchase upon his soul." The South African years steeled Gandhi's resolve, and taught him the lessons he would employ with such monumental success in his homeland.
◂1911.7 ▸1916.12

BIRTHS

Yuri Andropov, U.S.S.R. political leader.

Pierre Balmain, French fashion designer.

John Berryman, U.S. poet.

William S. Burroughs, U.S. novelist.

Joe DiMaggio, U.S. baseball player.

Ralph Ellison, U.S. novelist.

Alec Guinness, U.K. actor.

John Hersey, U.S. writer.

Thor Heyerdahl, Norwegian anthropologist and explorer.

Alan Hodgkin, U.K. neurologist.

Joe Louis, U.S. boxer.

Bernard Malamud, U.S. writer.

Octavio Paz, Mexican writer.

Sviatoslav Richter, Russian musician.

Dylan Thomas, Welsh poet.

William C. Westmoreland, U.S. general.

Babe Didrikson Zaharias, U.S. athlete.

DEATHS

Ambrose Bierce, U.S. writer.

Franz Ferdinand, Austrian archduke.

August Macke, German painter.

Frédéric Mistral, French poet.

John Muir, U.S. naturalist.

Pius X, Roman Catholic pope.

Richard W. Sears, U.S. retailer.

John Tenniel, U.K. illustrator.

George Westinghouse, U.S. inventor and industrialist.

Painting & Sculpture: ***The Betrothed of the Wind*** **(Oskar Kokoschka);** ***Horse*** **(Raymond Duchamp-Villon);** ***Project for the New City*** **(Antonio Sant 'Elia) ... Film:** ***Tillie's Punctured Romance*** **(Mack Sennett);** ***The Avenging Conscience*** **(D.W. Griffith);** ***The Perils of Pauline*** **(with Pearl White) ... Theater:** ***Pygmalion*** **(G.B. Shaw);** ***Watch Your Step!*** **(Irving Berlin);** ***Twin Beds*** **(Fields and Mayo).**

"We are doing everything we can to threaten and demoralize trade, to hold the penitentiary over men who invest capital, and to put men in fear."—**Representative James R. Mann, urging Congress to reject the Clayton Antitrust bill**

NEW IN 1914

Automobile maps, by Gulf Oil.

National 4-H Club.

***The New Republic* magazine.**

Wrigley's Doublemint chewing gum.

Teletype machine.

Grossinger's resort (in New York's Catskill Mountains).

Feature-length film comedy (Mack Sennett's *Tillie's Punctured Romance*).

IN THE UNITED STATES

▶LABOR UNDER FIRE—In a politically charged trial, Swedish-born IWW leader (and peerless songwriter) Joe Hill *(below)* was convicted in June 1914 of murdering a Salt Lake City shopkeeper. Despite contradictory evidence, lack of motive, and appeals by Woodrow Wilson and the Swedish government, Utah executed Hill in 1915. His last statement: "Don't waste time mourning. Organize." Meanwhile, in April 1914 the Colorado state militia opened fire on miners striking for recognition of their United Mine Workers union. The Ludlow massacre claimed 21 lives, including those of 11 children. ◀1905.7 ▶1917.7

▶PEANUT PROMOTER—Devastated by the boll weevil and cotton overplanting, southern agriculture found a savior in George Washington Carver, a botanist whose mother had been a slave. In 1914, Carver, working at Alabama's Tuskegee Institute, announced the results of his experiments with two alternative crops, peanuts and sweet potatoes. In addition to replenishing soil, they yielded hundreds of byproducts—including flour, cheese, synthetic rubber, and soap. By 1940, peanuts trailed only cotton as a cash crop in the South. ◀1901.V

BUSINESS AND INDUSTRY

Freedom and Free Enterprise

5 "The laws of this country," declared American president Woodrow Wilson, "do not prevent the strong from crushing the weak." Keeping his campaign promise of reform, Wilson signed the Clayton Antitrust Act into law in 1914 to shore up the woefully inadequate Sherman Antitrust Act, on the books since 1890. Designed to check the growth of protean corporations whose many arms controlled every aspect of a business, from production to distribution, Clayton prohibited intercorporate stock holdings, unfair price-slashing, and sales contracts that bound dealers exclusively to one manufacturer.

During 20 years of unprecedented growth in American big business, almost every branch of industry—tobacco, railroads, public utilities, farm equipment—came to be dominated by a single diversified corporation. John D. Rockefeller and his Standard Oil controlled 85 percent of the domestic oil trade, 90 percent of American exports; James Duke grabbed 80 percent of the tobacco market with his American Tobacco Company; George Pullman's company produced 85 percent of the country's railcars. The concentration of wealth alarmed many Americans. It seemed undemocratic. Small businessmen and labor leaders complained they couldn't get a fair deal. Wall Street financiers argued that the function of business is to grow. The Clayton Act marked the early culmination of the United States' continuing struggle to achieve an equitable balance between free enterprise and equal opportunity. **◀1911.M ▶1982.M**

WESTERN AFRICA

Britain's Patchwork Colony

6 In a supreme act of imperialistic vanity, the British government in 1914 stitched its two west African colonies, Northern and Southern Nigeria, into a single territory to simplify colonial administration. The new Colony and Protectorate of Nigeria subsumed various African kingdoms, city-states, ethnic groups, and trade blocs, without regard to their wildly divergent linguistic, religious, and social traditions. Unified Nigeria remained under British control until 1960, when it gained independence and erupted in civil war.

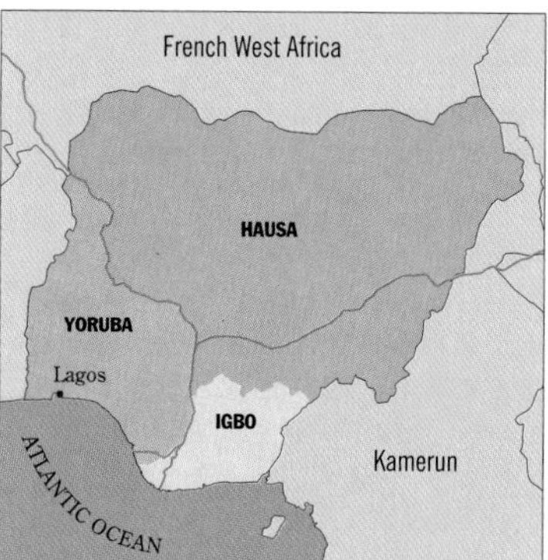

The new, amalgamated Nigeria had a polyglot population of over 17 million.

The 1914 amalgamation joined two large territories that were themselves contentious colonial amalgams. The northern territory was controlled by Islamic Fulani emirates; in the west were the urban kingdoms of the Yoruba and the Benin; the east was dominated by the Igbo-speaking peoples. More than 100 different languages and dialects were spoken within the territories. Britain relied on preexisting social structures to hold its patchwork colony together. Traditional chiefs controlled their localities but answered directly to the Crown. King George V, for one, was pleased with the arrangement. "On the occasion of the amalgamation of the two Nigerias," he wrote to his governor-general, "I wish you to convey to the emirs, chiefs, and all the inhabitants of the new Protectorate and the Colony my best wishes for their future happiness." **▶1967.6**

POPULAR CULTURE

The Dance Craze

7 The century's second decade was a prosperous period in the United States, and people celebrated by kicking up their heels. The ballroom aesthetic glorified by the wildly popular *Merry Widow* spawned a

Standard Oil, seen as an octopus wrapping its tentacles around the institutions of the U.S. government.

SPORTS: Baseball: World Series, Boston Braves ("Miracle Braves," managed by George Stallings) defeat Philadelphia Athletics, 4–0; Federal League begins play ... Football: Yale Bowl opens, seats 60,000 (will be enlarged to hold 75,000) ... Boxing: Jack Dempsey debuts as "Kid Blackie" ... Golf: Walter Hagen begins career, wins U.S. Open at 21.

"Objections to dancing have been made on the ground that it is wrong, immoral, and vulgar. This it certainly is not—when the dancers regard propriety."—**Irene and Vernon Castle, in *Modern Dancing***

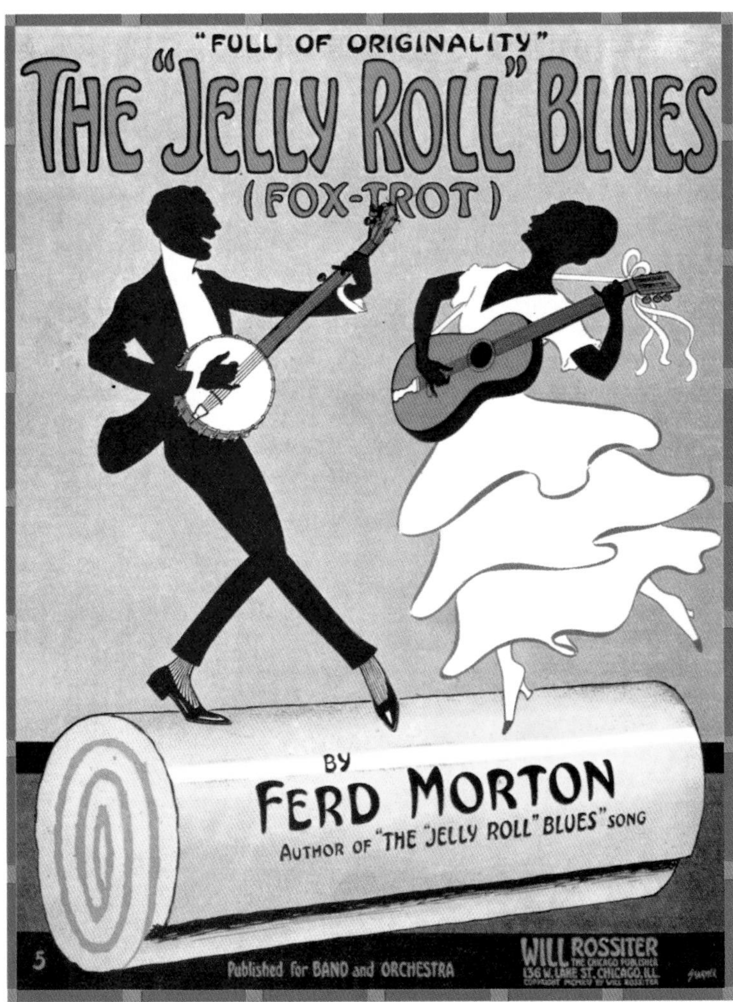

Fancy footwork: The fox-trot *(steps in diagram, below)* took America by storm.

"dance craze" that peaked in 1914 with the fox-trot rage. Combining ragtime ebullience with high-society smoothness, the fox-trot flawlessly reflected the image of the up-to-date American. It became a favorite in Europe, too, its insouciance appealing to a people at war.

The dance got its name from a vaudeville entertainer named Harry Fox, who incorporated a trotting step into his Ziegfeld Follies routine. In its ballroom incarnation, it usually involved two walking steps, a sidestep, and a quarter turn, executed by a man and a woman holding each other in traditional ballroom positions and moving to a four-four time, syncopated melody.

Among the dance's endless variations was the one-step, popularized by Irene and Vernon Castle. According to legend, the two unemployed Broadway actors, in Paris on their honeymoon, had gotten up to dance at a posh café and, because Irene's dress restricted her movements, had accidentally created a slightly speeded-up, more understated version of the fox-trot. Returning to New York, the newlyweds performed their "Castle walk" (as well as other dance steps of the day) in a triumphant round of Broadway musicals, cabaret shows, and ballroom demonstrations. The couple, thanks to their incredible popularity, also wielded a powerful cultural influence. Early and avid jazz fans, they helped make black music and dance an integral part of white culture. And Irene struck a blow for women's emancipation: Imitating her style, millions of women bobbed their hair and discarded their stifling corsets. **◀1905.11 ▶1915.8**

SOCIAL REFORM

Garvey Founds UNIA

8 Marcus Garvey's Universal Negro Improvement Association (UNIA), founded in Jamaica in 1914, was the first international mass movement of black people. The organization, which began as a blend of a chamber of commerce, missionary league (UNIA hoped to Christianize "backward" Africans), mutual-aid society, and educational foundation, was Garvey's vision of what blacks could achieve if they stopped being victims of empire, and established corporations, nations, even empires of their own. Economic independence was its top priority. "The Negro is living on borrowed goods," said Garvey, a newspaper publisher who had conceived the UNIA after studying African history in England. "Let Edison turn off his electric light and we are in darkness." In 1916, Garvey moved his crusade from Jamaica to the United States, where his fiery oratory attracted thousands. Soon he'd set up several businesses, notably a steamship company called the Black Star Line.

As the UNIA grew (in 1925 it claimed six million members), it focused on sending blacks "back to Africa" to build a utopian state. The Black Star Line became central to this scheme—and led to Garvey's downfall, when U.S. authorities charged the company with mail fraud. Often appearing in a Napoleonic uniform, the corpulent, self-educated Jamaican was an easy target for ridicule. To black intellectuals like W.E.B. Du Bois, he was a demagogue. To the United States government, he was a swindler. But to millions of people of African heritage, he was a prophet, and his ideas influenced later visionaries like Malcolm X and Jamaican reggae singer Bob Marley. **◀1910.7 ▶1928.13**

Marcus Garvey's "back to Africa" movement seized the imaginations of later generations of blacks.

IN THE UNITED STATES

▶A MODERN MYTH—Paul Bunyan and his big blue ox, Babe, made their first appearance this year in a promotional pamphlet created for Minnesota's Red River Lumber Company. Drawing on north-woods folktales, the Bunyan mythology—such as the legend that the towering lumberjack had created the Grand Canyon with his pick—caught on instantly.

▶MOTHER'S DAY—Anna May Jarvis's six-year campaign to create a national holiday to honor mothers paid off this year when President Wilson officially designated the second Sunday in May as Mother's Day. Convinced that she had somehow neglected her mother in life, Jarvis, a Philadelphia suffragist, temperance worker, and schoolteacher, had begun her campaign with a memorial service for her mother at which she presented a carnation to all mothers present. From there, her idea spread throughout the country.

▶HANDY MAN—With his now-classic 1914 tune "St. Louis Blues," black composer W.C. Handy elevated the blues from little-known Southern folk music to a form commanding international attention. The song, a blend of ragtime and a budding new genre called blues, introduced traditional orchestral arrangements into the rich, nostalgic melodies of black folklore. (Though blind, Handy conducted his own orchestra.) His technique depended on the use of "blue" notes—slightly slurred or flattened tones that fall between the major and minor scales. Providing a framework for harmonic improvisation, Handy's music was a crucial link in the transition from ragtime to jazz. **◀1902.M ▶1917.5**

POLITICS & BUSINESS: GNP: $38.6 billion ... Houston and Cape Cod ship canals open ... Henry Ford offers workers an unprecedented $5 for an 8-hour day ... Federal Trade Commission established ... Clayton Antitrust Act passed ... Van Camp Seafood and National Dairy Corp. founded.

"Space is not a lot of points close together; it is a lot of distances interlocked."—**Sir Arthur Stanley Eddington**

WORLD WAR I

▶THE WAR BEGINS—The Battle of the Frontiers, August 14-25, which opened the Western Front in World War I, cost 250,000 French lives. (These numbers were censored until after the war.) Not only did the Germans retake the Lorraine, but they defeated the French at Charleroi and the British at Mons in Belgium, and, led by General Alexander von Kluck, advanced to within sight of Paris.

▶BATTLE OF FLANDERS—Allied troops retreated beyond the Marne River and dug in. The Battle of the Marne, September 5-12, stopped the German advance on Paris. The

French counterattacked at the Aisne River, at the Somme, and in the First Battle of Arras, but could not dislodge the Germans. A race to the North Sea ensued. Called the Battle of Flanders, this series of engagements was the last open-field battle on the Western Front.

▶RUSSIAN ADVANCE STOPPED—The Battle of Tannenberg, August 26-30, ended Russia's string of victories across East Prussia and Galicia. The German army under General Paul von Hindenburg surrounded the Russians, capturing 100,000 men.

▶TRENCH WARFARE—The First Battle of Ypres, October 30-November 24, marked the advent of trench warfare, as outnumbered French, British, and Belgians resisted the Germans' drive for Calais and Dunkirk for 34 days.

▶BATTLE OF THE FALKLANDS—On December 8, after inflicting severe damage on French and British ports in the South Pacific, Admiral Graf Maximilian von Spee returned to the Atlantic and lost four of five cruisers to a British squadron led by Rear Admiral Sir Frederick Charles Doveton Sturdee.

THE UNITED STATES

Panama Canal Opens

9 Teddy Roosevelt grandly called his pet project in the malarial jungles of Panama "the most important and ... formidable" engineering feat in history. Successfully completed in 1914, the new Panama Canal connected the Atlantic and Pacific oceans, providing Western freighters with a shortcut to the markets of Asia, and gave the United States unprecedented naval communication between its coasts. The 51-mile-long canal was hailed by a British statesman as "the greatest liberty Man has ever taken with nature."

Although Roosevelt was the prime mover behind the canal, Woodrow Wilson was in office by the time it opened, a quirk of fate that galled the rambunctious former president beyond measure. When Wilson proposed that the United States compensate Colombia with a $25 million indemnity for having seized the Canal Zone, Roosevelt, aquiver with righteous indignation, attacked the plan as a "crime against the United States." Cowed by his rantings, the U.S. Senate rejected Wilson's treaty. (In 1921, after Roosevelt was dead, the United States gave Colombia $25 million.) Between them, Roosevelt and Wilson embraced the emotional spectrum that defined the United States' relationship with the valuable canal throughout the century: proprietary and proud at one end, slightly embarrassed and guilty at the other. **◂1903.2 ▸1921.M**

SCIENCE

Eddington's Stellar Career

10 With his appointment in 1914 as director of the Cambridge Observatory, in England, Sir Arthur Stanley Eddington, the founder of modern theoretical astrophysics, embarked in earnest on a 30-year career that changed the way human beings looked at the stars. After publishing his first book, *Stellar Movements and the Structure of the Universe*, a compendium of everything known about the motion of stars, Eddington delved further and unlocked some of the deepest mysteries of the universe: how stars radiate energy, what they are made of, and the way their luminosity is related to their mass.

Always fascinated by large numbers, Eddington had tried as a boy to count all the words in the Bible. With characteristic assurance, he later predicted the number of protons in the universe. Expressed as 136×2^{256}, the figure became known as "Eddington's number."

In 1919, Eddington headed the experimental expedition that tested Einstein's general theory of relativity. Although Eddington's view of a solar eclipse was hampered at first by rain and cloud cover on the island of Príncipe, off the west coast of Africa, his team observed that the light rays emitted by stars were deflected as they neared the sun, just as Einstein predicted. A few months later, measurements made by his team in Brazil confirmed these observations. "You must be one of three persons in the world who understand general relativity," a fellow scientist remarked to him afterward. Eddington brushed off the compliment. "Don't be modest, Eddington," the other scientist chided. "On the contrary," Eddington replied, "I'm trying to think who the third person is." **◂1913.1 ▸1916.9**

MEDICINE

Opening Up the Heart

11 American colleagues of Dr. Alexis Carrel received as a revelation his announcement at the 1914 convention of the American

A French caricaturist took a skeptical view of Dr. Carrel's transplant experiments.

Surgical Association that he had successfully performed experimental heart surgery on a dog. Working at the Rockefeller Institute for Medical Research in New York, the French-born Carrel had clamped the blood vessels leading to and from the lab animal's heart and safely stopped blood circulation for as long as two-and-a-half minutes, giving him enough time to perform several minor heart-valve operations.

The purpose, explained the surgeon, was to demonstrate that heart surgery on humans was a medical possibility. "It is hoped," said Carrel, who'd won a 1912 Nobel Prize for his pioneering method of suturing blood vessels and his early efforts to transplant organs, "that this technique may, by degrees, be applied to human surgery." **◂1912.9 ▸1952.12**

Gates to the east chamber of the Panama Canal's lower locks, under construction in 1913.

NOBEL PRIZES: Peace: No award ... Literature: No award ... Chemistry: Theodore Richards (U.S.; atomic weights of elements) ... Medicine: Robert Bárány (Austrian; balancing apparatus of the inner ear) ... Physics: Max von Laue (German; X-ray diffraction).

A VOICE FROM 1914

An International Folk Hero

From *Tarzan of the Apes,* by Edgar Rice Burroughs, 1914

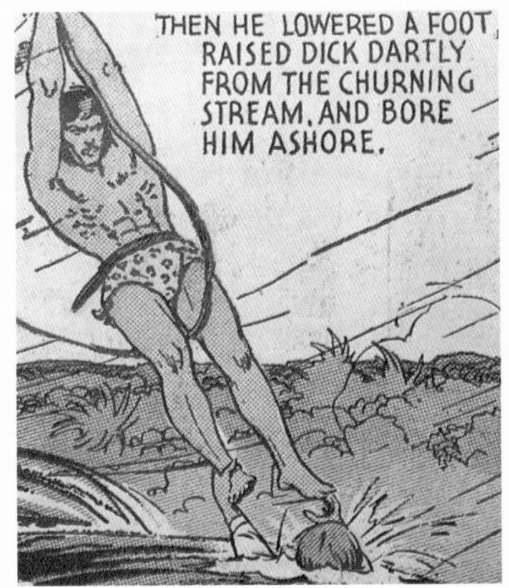

THEN HE LOWERED A FOOT, RAISED DICK DARTLY FROM THE CHURNING STREAM, AND BORE HIM ASHORE.

The son of a wealthy American businessman, novelist Edgar Rice Burroughs turned to writing fiction only after 14 years of unsuccessful business ventures. With the 1914 publication of Tarzan of the Apes, *Burroughs not only contrived an exotic adventure story, he created an international folk hero: Tarzan, son of a British nobleman, orphaned in the African jungle and raised by a tribe of great apes. The novel and its many sequels were translated into 56 languages and have sold over 25 million copies worldwide. The scene below tells of Tarzan's first meeting with Jane, the intelligent, headstrong daughter of an American scientist. She has been kidnapped and dragged into the impenetrable forest by Terkoz, a huge, rogue ape and the archenemy of Tarzan.* ►**1924.10**

Jane—her lithe, young form flattened against the trunk of a great tree, her hands tight pressed against her rising and falling bosom, and her eyes wide with mingled horror, fascination, fear, and admiration—watched the primordial ape battle with the primeval man for possession of a woman—for her.

As the great muscles of the man's back and shoulders knotted beneath the tension of his efforts, and the huge biceps and forearm held at bay those mighty tusks, the veil of centuries of civilization and culture was swept from the blurred vision of the Baltimore girl.

When the long knife drank deep a dozen times of Terkoz' heart's blood, and the great carcass rolled lifeless upon the ground, it was a primeval woman who sprang forward with outstretched arms toward the primeval man who had fought for her and won her.

And Tarzan?

He did what no red-blooded man needs lessons in doing. He took his woman in his arms and smothered her upturned, panting lips with kisses.

For a moment Jane lay there with half-closed eyes. For a moment—the first in her young life—she knew the meaning of love.

But as suddenly as the veil had been withdrawn it dropped again, and an outraged conscience suffused her face with its scarlet mantle, and a mortified woman thrust Tarzan of the Apes from her and buried her face in her hands.

Tarzan had been surprised when he had found the girl he had learned to love after a vague and abstract manner a willing prisoner in his arms. Now he was surprised that she repulsed him.

He came close to her once more and took hold of her arm. She turned upon him like a tigress, striking his great breast with her tiny hands.

Tarzan could not understand it.

A moment ago and it had been his intention to hasten Jane back to her people, but that little moment was lost now in the dim and distant past of things which were but can never be again, and with it the good intention had gone to join the impossible.

Since then Tarzan of the Apes had felt a warm, lithe form close pressed to his. Hot, sweet breath against his cheek and mouth had fanned a new flame to life within his breast, and perfect lips had clung to his in burning kisses that had seared a deep brand into his soul—a brand which marked a new Tarzan.

Again he laid his hand upon her arm. Again she repulsed him. And then Tarzan of the Apes did just what his first ancestor would have done.

He took his woman in his arms and carried her into the jungle.

Burroughs's ape-man hero has had dozens of incarnations—in movies, radio, television, and comic books *(top left)*. The first celluloid Tarzan was Elmo Lincoln *(top, right)*, in 1918. The most famous was former Olympic star Johnny Weissmuller *(above,* in 1934's *Tarzan and His Mate,* with Maureen O'Sullivan, as Jane). Miles O'Keeffe *(inset)* played the title role in the forgettable *Tarzan, the Ape Man* (1981).

"Remember how small the world was before I came along. I brought it all to life: I moved the whole world onto a 20-foot screen."—**D.W. Griffith, director of *The Birth of a Nation***

STORY OF THE YEAR

The Birth of a Medium

1 David Wark Griffith's *The Birth of a Nation* aroused controversy from the moment it premiered in New York on March 3, 1915. On one hand, it announced itself immediately as the first wholly realized piece of "art" that the nascent discipline of cinema had yet produced. With this ambitious, sweeping epic, Griffith perfected many of cinema's most vital techniques: the close-up (which demanded a new, subtler acting style, tailored to the screen rather than the stage); the panoramic long shot; the fade-in and fade-out; and crosscutting to suggest simultaneous action in different locations. As one of the film's stars, Lillian Gish, later explained, Griffith "gave us the grammar of filmmaking." On the other hand, the movie's retelling of history was overtly and unapologetically white-supremacist. The NAACP, mounting the most meaningful protest since its formation five and a half years earlier, tried to prevent the film from being screened in cities across the country.

Between 1908 and 1913, Griffith, the son of a Confederate colonel, had made over 400 one- and two-reelers for the Biograph Company, eleven of them on the Civil War. But with *The Birth,* Griffith was working on a grander scale. The film cost an unheard of $110,000 to make (and an equally unheard-of $2 to see), and ran three hours. The story focused on two families: the Stonemans from the North and the Camerons from the South. Family histories were interwoven with such actual events as Lincoln's freeing of the slaves, Sherman's march on Atlanta, Civil War battles (staged with astonishing accuracy), and, most infamously, a sympathetic account of the formation of the Ku Klux Klan.

THE FIERY CROSS OF THE KU KLUX KLAN
D.W. GRIFFITH'S MIGHTY SPECTACLE
THE BIRTH OF A NATION
FOUNDED ON THOMAS DIXON'S THE CLANSMAN

The promotion for *The Birth* forthrightly presented a Klansman as hero.

Thus was born the film's double legacy: It was at once an overpowering cinematic achievement and an apologia for the most lamentable aspects of the American character. The film and its creator soon found themselves out of favor, as both the nation's political climate and the technology of filmmaking passed them by. Still, some 30 years later, critic James Agee praised *The Birth* as "equal with Brady's photographs, Lincoln's speeches, Whitman's war poems ... the one great epic, tragic film." ◂1910.7 ▸1919.3

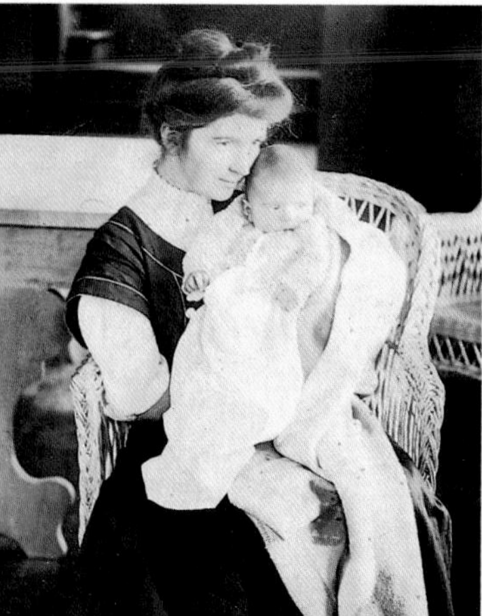

Birth-control pioneer Margaret Sanger with son Grant, one of her three children.

SOCIAL REFORM

Sanger and Birth Control

2 After running from the law for a year, Margaret Sanger returned to New York in September 1915, determined to face trial. Sanger was accused of disseminating obscenity through the mail, in violation of the Comstock Act of 1873. A nurse and a radical, she'd begun publishing a political magazine called *Woman Rebel* the previous year. Included among articles on women's suffrage and workers' rights was a call to prevent conception in order to frighten the "capitalist class." The references to contraception—Sanger was the first to call it birth control—caused the trouble, even though the article contained no specific advice. New York's postmaster determined that the magazine should not be mailed, but Sanger mailed it anyway. In August, Sanger was charged. While awaiting trial, she published the pamphlet "Family Limitation," which was unmistakably specific.

A novice at political causes, Sanger had prepared no defense. When her case was called, she panicked and fled to safety in London. There she met the sex researcher Havelock Ellis, who became her lover and mentor. During the next year, Sanger, under Ellis's tutelage, narrowed her rather broad, unfocused leftist agenda to concentrate strictly on the issue of birth control. She studied everything available on the subject, and took to heart Ellis's advice that changing the law "needs *skill* even more than it needs strength."

She returned to New York hoping to force the courts to rule on whether or not contraceptive advice was obscene. She was disappointed when—after months of legal sparring—the district attorney dropped her case. A few months later, in October 1916, Sanger opened America's first birth-control clinic, in Brooklyn.

The clinic saw 464 people in its first nine days of operation. On day ten, Sanger was arrested again. The judge offered clemency in exchange for a promise not to disseminate contraceptive information again. Sanger refused, and was sentenced to 30 days in the workhouse. She continued to lecture for the next decade, and founded the American Birth Control League in 1921 and helped to organize the first World Population Conference in 1927. ▸1960.1

WORLD WAR I

Central Powers Advance

3 World War I grew more horrific in 1915, as the conflict widened and intensified. Germany's peerless military organization gave the Central Powers the

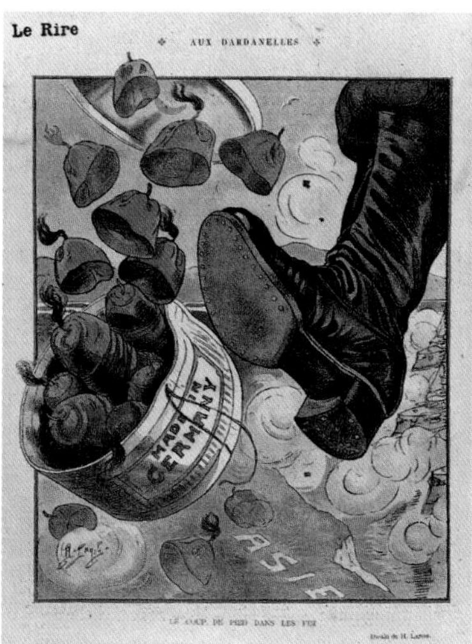

The French and British aimed to give the Central Powers a big kick, but met with calamity in the Dardanelles.

advantage on almost every front. Despite greater numbers and naval superiority, the Allies endured countless setbacks.

The year began well for the Allies, but soured quickly. In January, British cruisers sank one German warship and crippled two others in a battle off England's east coast. Soon afterward, a French and British fleet set off to break Turkey's grip on the Dardanelles, the strait linking the Mediterranean to the Black Sea. After they

ART & CULTURE: Books: *America's Coming of Age* (Van Wyck Brooks); *A Spoon River Anthology* (Edgar Lee Masters); *The Rainbow* (D.H. Lawrence); *The Good Soldier* (Ford Madox Ford); *The "Genius"* (Theodore Dreiser); *Corona* (Paul Claudel); *Cathay* (Ezra Pound) ... Music: "I Didn't Raise My Boy to Be a Soldier" (Piantadosi and Bryan); "Keep the Home Fires Burning" (Novello and Ford);

"They fought with terror, running blindly in the gas cloud.... Hundreds of them fell and died; others lay helpless, froth upon their agonized lips and their racked bodies powerfully sick.... "—**A British officer describing troops attacked with chlorine gas**

shelled the forts guarding the passage into apparent submission, the attackers closed in, only to come under withering fire. Several ships and 2,000 men were lost before a retreat was called. In August, a land assault on Gallipoli—the peninsula commanding the strait—was even more calamitous, with 70,000 Allied casualties. Another 40,000 were killed, wounded, or captured by December, when the effort was abandoned.

The Russians, too, suffered humbling reversals. From January to April they swept through Galicia, an Austrian crown land later held by Poland. But by autumn, German and Austro-Hungarian forces had taken back most of the region, including the key city of Warsaw—and had cut wide swaths through Russia's own western provinces. Russian casualties numbered 1.5 million. In September, Czar Nicholas II took personal command of the Russian army. Although he had no combat experience, the Czar hoped his royal presence would boost morale among the troops, a third of whom lacked weapons.

On the Western Front, the Allies attempted a spring offensive in Belgium and France. Leaping from their trenches, soldiers were mowed down by the thousands; the Allied line advanced a mile at most. Anglo-Indian troops pushed 500 miles into the interior of Turkish Mesopotamia. Before reaching Baghdad, however, the 19,000-man expedition met overwhelming resistance. Driven back to the town of Kut-el-Amara, the British force was surrounded and besieged.

New combatants joined the fray. In May, Italy, reviving its old rivalry with Austria-Hungary, abandoned neutrality and began a series of attacks along the Isonzo River. The Italians gained little ground and lost over 200,000 men. Bulgaria took up arms against the Allies in October, and with Austro-Hungarian and German troops, subjugated Serbia.

In February, Germany escalated its assaults on British shipping, declaring any ship in the waters around Britain and Ireland open to submarine attack. Dozens of commercial vessels, from many nations, were sunk, most infamously the British passenger liner *Lusitania*, on May 7. Among the 1,198 people killed were 128 Americans, a fact that began to turn U.S. public opinion in favor of intervention.

◄1914.2 ►1916.1

World War I fronts: Except in the east, they barely moved over the course of the war.

WORLD WAR I

New Ways to Kill

4 New weapons technology added to the war's horrors. Each innovation bred countermeasures, which in turn bred further innovation in an unending spiral of violence. Submarines had been used for coastal defense since the 1880s. But Germany's reliance on U-boats for offense, spurred by Britain's blockade, was unprecedented. In 1915 the hydrophone was developed, an underwater microphone designed to warn of a U-boat's approach. (The U-boat could then be sunk using the newly invented depth charge.) The Allies' increasing ability to interdict submarines prompted the Germans to strike more hastily, increasing the risk of sinking unarmed vessels.

Aerial bombs—dropped sporadically by the Italians in their 1911 campaign against the Ottoman Turks in North Africa—were first used extensively in February, when German zeppelins began bombing Britain. Although the Kaiser had ordered that only military targets be hit, accuracy was not technically possible. By year's end, 700 people—mostly London civilians—had been killed or wounded in 55 attacks. In March, British airplane squadrons began bombing trains carrying German troops. Bombs, attached to a rack on the fuselage, were released when the pilot pulled a string. By 1918, both sides were launching giant four-engine planes loaded with tons of explosives. The bombers were guarded by agile little fighter planes, some piloted by aces like Germany's Baron Manfred von Richthofen, France's René Fonck, Britain's Edward Mannock, and (starting in 1918) America's Eddie Rickenbacker. Aerial dogfights provided a rare showcase for individual valor in a vast, impersonal war.

Arms merchant Gustav Krupp and son, in caricature: The Krupps spearheaded Germany's development of new weapons.

Another new weapon, poison gas, could not have been less individual. The Germans used gas for the first time on the Russian Front in January 1915, and began regular gas attacks in April at Ypres, Belgium. The Allies soon responded in kind. Both sides began wearing protective masks, so new varieties of gas were devised that penetrated the skin. Trapped in the trenches, men and rats alike died in slow agony. **◄1911.12 ►1916.10**

BIRTHS

Roland Barthes, French critic.

Saul Bellow, Canadian-U.S. novelist.

Ingrid Bergman, Swedish-U.S. actress.

Don Budge, U.S. tennis player.

Moshe Dayan, Israeli military and political leader.

Fred Hoyle, U.K. astronomer.

Billie Holiday, U.S. singer.

Arthur Miller, U.S. playwright.

Beyers Naudé, South African anti-apartheid activist.

Les Paul, U.S. musician and inventor.

Edith Piaf, French singer.

Augusto Pinochet, Chilean president.

David Rockefeller, U.S. banker.

R. Sargent Shriver, U.S. political leader.

Frank Sinatra, U.S. singer.

Muddy Waters, U.S. musician.

Orson Welles, U.S. actor and filmmaker.

DEATHS

Nelson Aldrich, U.S. senator.

Rupert Brooke, U.K. poet.

Porfirio Díaz, Mexican president.

Paul Ehrlich, German bacteriologist.

Keir Hardie, U.K. labor and political leader.

Alexander Scriabin, Russian composer.

Booker T. Washington, U.S. writer and educator.

Anne Whitney, U.S. sculptor.

"The Jelly Roll Blues" (Jelly Roll Morton); *Mozart Variations, Op. 32* (Max Reger); *Alpine Symphony* (Richard Strauss); *Symphony No. 5 in E-flat Major* (Jean Sibelius) ... Painting & Sculpture: *The Chessboard* (Juan Gris); *Compiègne Barracks* (Maurice Utrillo) ... Film: *The Cheat* (Cecil B. DeMille); *The Tramp* (Charles Chaplin) ... Theater: *He Who Gets Slapped* (Leonid Andreyev); *Very Good Eddie* (Kern and Greene).

"Who remembers a million Armenians?"—**Adolf Hitler before the invasion of Poland in 1939**

NEW IN 1915

Aspirin in tablet form (introduced by Bayer).

Chlorine gas.

Gas masks.

Pyrex (heat- and shock-resistant borosilicate glass).

Kraft processed cheese.

IN THE UNITED STATES

▶PAN-PACIFIC FESTIVAL—Nearly 19 million tourists flocked to newly rebuilt San Francisco, the "City Loved 'Round the World," for the Panama-Pacific International Exposition of 1915. Ostensibly a celebration of the completion of the Panama Canal, the

fair was an excuse for San Francisco to revel in its post-earthquake modernity. Attractions included John Philip Sousa's band and the country's first air show (marred by the fatal crash of the lead stunt pilot). ◀1904.M

▶FRANK LYNCHING—On August 17, in Marietta, Georgia, a racist mob—inflamed by the governor's commutation of factory superintendent Leo Frank's death sentence to life in prison—dragged Frank, a Jew, from his jail cell and beat and hanged him. Frank's wrongful conviction for the murder of 14-year-old Mary Phagan at the National Pencil Company in Atlanta was overturned by the state of Georgia 70 years after his lynching.

▶BRYAN RESIGNS—After the sinking of the *Lusitania* on May 7, pacifist Secretary of State William Jennings Bryan saw President Wilson drifting toward compromise with the hawks and resigned in protest. Once America entered the hostilities, however, he staunchly supported the war effort. ▶1917.9

WORLD WAR I

The United States Prepares

5 At the outbreak of World War I, the U.S. Army consisted of only 92,710 men. Of these, nearly half were stationed in the Philippines, the Panama Canal Zone, and other American possessions. Some 25,000 (backed by 120,000 ill-trained militiamen) were assigned to defend the continental United States. That left a "mobile army" of just 24,602—the smallest since before the Civil War. Those numbers suited President Woodrow Wilson fine; he had pledged neutrality and discounted the danger of attack from overseas. But they outraged many influential citizens, who saw American involvement in the Great War as inevitable, desirable, or both. Led by ex-president Theodore Roosevelt, they mounted a campaign for military "preparedness." By late 1915, it had become a national movement.

Roosevelt, a Spanish-American war hero now anxious to revive his political career, reviled Wilson as a friend of "the professional pacifists, the flubdubs and the mollycoddles." He was seconded by the blustery General Leonard Wood, who lent his prestige to such preparedness groups as the National Security League, the American Defense Society, and the American Legion. A group of well-known cartoonists and writers, calling themselves the Vigilantes, churned out propaganda for the cause. A scholarly 700-page book called *The Military Unpreparedness of the United States* created a sensation. Films like *The Battle Cry of Peace* terrified audiences with scenarios of Germany invading the United States.

Antiwar advocates noted that the preparedness push was led largely by industrialists, army officers, right-wing politicians, and others who stood to profit by militarization. But the campaign's mix of flag-waving, fear-mongering, and machismo proved effective. Private military training camps sprang up nationwide, attracting thousands, and preparedness parades filled the main streets of major cities.

Wilson was soon leading such parades himself. He remained opposed to intervention but said, "I would be ashamed if I had not learned something in 14 months." In December he called for a 50 percent increase in the regular army, 300 percent in the reserves. By the time the United States entered the war in 1917, troop strength was 208,000—still not nearly enough to be effective. With the help of a draft, the country eventually committed over four million soldiers to the fight. **◀1915.3 ▶1916.1**

Boston women collected peach pits to be made into gas-mask filters for the troops.

THE OTTOMAN EMPIRE

Turks Slaughter Armenians

6 Starting in April 1915 and continuing throughout the war years, the Ottoman Empire's Armenian subjects became the victims of a systematic slaughter unmatched before the Nazis' extermination of the Jews. The Armenians—who'd suffered Turkish violence in the 1890s, when the Sultan suspected that a Russian plot lurked behind their separatist stirrings—had rejoiced when the Young Turks seized power in 1908, promising freedom and equality for all. But the new regime cruelly broke its promise, forcing non-Turkish ethnic groups to assimilate. The Christian Armenians were targeted by the Muslim rulers for especially harsh treatment. After the Ottoman Turks joined the German side in World War I (Armenians outside the empire sided with the Russians), repression turned to genocide.

The killing began inconspicuously. Armenians in the army were disarmed and assigned to labor crews. Denied food, shelter, and rest, they

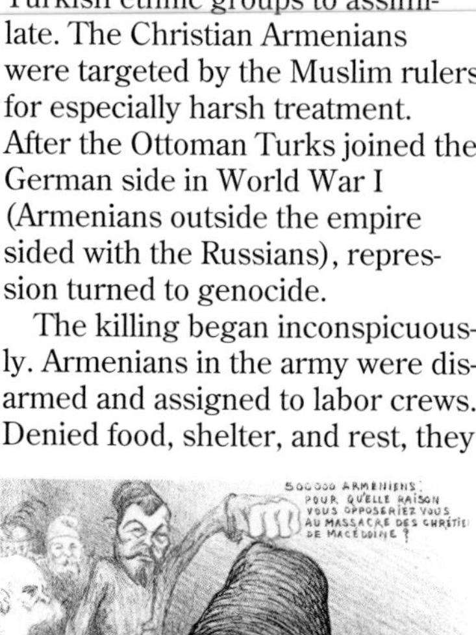

Turkish sultan Abd al-Hamid II butchered Armenian Christians. But they suffered even more cruelly at the hands of the Young Turks.

were worked to death or else murdered outright. After being ordered to assemble and turn in their weapons, men in the countryside were marched off and shot or bayoneted. Intellectuals and suspected subversives were tortured before being executed. Women, children, and the elderly were forced to march hundreds of miles through mountains, swamps, and deserts to concentration camps in Syria and Mesopotamia. Raped and robbed along the way by their military escorts and local civilians, they died of hunger, thirst, and exposure—or were killed for sport. "We had seen massacres," wrote an Armenian pastor, "but we had never seen this before. A massacre at least ends quickly, but this prolonged anguish of soul is almost beyond endurance." A few Armenian enclaves offered fierce, but futile, resistance. In the end, between 600,000 and 1.5 million died, out of a population of 2.5 million. **◀1909.10 ▶1915.M**

SPORTS: Baseball: World Series, Boston Red Sox (Babe Ruth leads team in home runs; wins 18 as pitcher) defeat Philadelphia Phillies, 4–1; Federal League plays last season ... Boxing: Jack Johnson loses heavyweight crown (after 7 years) to Jess Willard ... Tennis: Wimbledon suspended for duration of the war; Men's U.S. Lawn Tennis Championships moved to Forest Hills, N.Y.

"She adored sex, she served art with passion, she worshipped God, and she kept doing penance to one or the other for faithlessness."—**Dance critic Walter Terry, on Ruth St. Denis**

Officers of the Chicago Telephone Company demonstrate the transcontinental telephone line, which reached their city in June.

TECHNOLOGY

Telephones Reach Out

7 New York City officials, prominent businessmen, and the directors of the American Telephone and Telegraph Company (AT&T) all surrounded Alexander Graham Bell on January 25, 1915, as Bell sat by his invention, the telephone, on the 15th floor of New York's Telephone Building. Across the continent in San Francisco, Thomas A. Watson also waited, similarly flanked by business executives and politicians. At 4:30 PM Eastern Time, Dr. Bell picked up the telephone receiver in front of him and said, "Mr. Watson, are you there?" Watson pressed the receiver to his ear, assured his erstwhile boss that, yes, he had heard the question clearly. Bell then repeated the words he had spoken in 1876, when he and Watson had conducted the world's first telephone conversation, between two floors of a Boston boardinghouse. "Mr. Watson," he said, "come here. I want you." From 2,572 miles away came Watson's response: "It would take me a week to get to you this time." Thus was transcontinental telephone communication established.

The telephone line that allowed Watson and Bell to speak across the continent weighed nearly 3,000 tons and was suspended from 130,000 telephone poles. The main line had spurs running to Jekyll Island, Georgia, and Washington, D.C., and operated as one large party line, allowing hundreds of people to listen in on a conversation between two principals in any of the four cities. As Bell and Watson conversed, Theodore Vail, president of AT&T, interrupted from Jekyll Island to offer his congratulations. Later, President Woodrow Wilson broke in from Washington, declaring, "It appeals to the imagination to speak across the continent."

By March, commercial operation of the transcontinental line had begun. A New York-to-San Francisco call cost $20.70 for the first three minutes and $6.75 for each additional minute. **◂1901.1 ▸1927.M**

DANCE

Denishawn School Opens

8 By the time Ruth St. Denis and Ted Shawn opened their first dance school in 1915, they had already made a mark on twentieth-century dance. Like her contemporary Isadora Duncan, St. Denis had invented a disciplined, highly personal style that drew on ancient traditions but eschewed ballet's conventions. Unlike the more classical Duncan, St. Denis was shaped by pop culture: She'd started as a vaudeville hoofer, and her inspiration to explore Asian dance was an "Egyptian goddess" on a cigarette poster. St. Denis had also triumphed in Europe before being accepted at home, and, again like Duncan, she'd established no system to pass on to the next generation. It was Shawn who found the method in St. Denis's divine madness, and with her established the first real school devoted to modern dance.

An athlete who'd turned to ballet for physical therapy, Shawn had idolized St. Denis since seeing her perform in 1911. Other dancers, like Little Egypt in America and Mata Hari in Europe, were exploiting the fad for Orientalism, but most were glorified striptease artists. St. Denis was a serious student of non-Western dance—which she blended with a homegrown vocabulary of movement, spectacular stage sets, and evocative lighting. Watching her dance, Shawn had wept.

He followed his idol to New York, hoping to become her student. She, hoping to find the next Vernon Castle to her Irene, hired him as a partner. On tour, as she later wrote, their "idyll began to bloom," and they were married, though he was 14 years her junior.

Shawn developed the plan for a dance institute as they traveled. The Denishawn School was born in Los Angeles in 1915, and branches later opened nationwide. In the 1920s, the Denishawn performing companies brought unprecedented popularity to serious dance in America. Among their earliest alumni were Martha Graham, Doris Humphrey, and Charles Weidman—the leading lights of modern dance between the wars. **◂1914.7 ▸1931.12**

Ted Shawn in eclectically "Oriental" garb. After he and St. Denis separated in 1931, he founded an all-male dance company at Jacob's Pillow in Massachusetts.

IN THE UNITED STATES

▶PEACE SHIP—Automobile tycoon and political isolationist Henry Ford in 1915 chartered a "Peace Ship" and sailed for Europe. With the slogan "Out of the trenches and back to their homes by Christmas," Ford hoped to

WE ARE ALL FOR PEACE.
1ST DAY OUT.

persuade world leaders to end the war. The heavily publicized, futile expedition became a rallying point for pacifists. ◂1913.6

▶THE ORIGINAL VAMP—Theda Bara shocked and titillated moviegoers with her star turn as a femme fatale in the 1915 film *A Fool There Was.* "Kiss me, my fool," she de-

manded, in the come-on of the decade. For the next five years, as moralizers agonized over Bara's effect on public values, moviegoers flocked to her dozens of pictures. ▸1921.10

▶THEATER GROUPS—The Neighborhood Playhouse and the Washington Square Players in New York City, and the Provincetown Players in Massachusetts, all founded in 1915 as showcases for serious, experimental drama, helped legitimize American theater. The Provincetown Players staged Eugene O'Neill's first play in 1916. ▸1926.10

POLITICS & BUSINESS: GNP: $40 billion ... Delaware starts liberalizing its laws to attract corporations; the "Mother of Trusts" will become the charter state for the largest corporations in the U.S. ... Ford produces its 1 millionth Model T ... U.S. wheat crop reaches 1 billion bushels for first time.

"The death of Rupert Brooke fills me more and more with the sense of the fatuity of it all. He was slain by bright Phoebus' shaft —it was in keeping with his general sunniness—it was the real climax of his pose."—**D.H. Lawrence in a letter to Lady Ottoline Morrell**

WORLD WAR I

▶GORLICE ATTACK—Austro-German forces attacked the Eastern Front near the Polish town of Gorlice on May 2, and unexpectedly smashed the center of the Russian

defense, bisecting its armies. By May 14, the Central Powers had advanced 80 miles. Although the Central Powers took 750,000 prisoners in four months, they failed to execute a bold pincer movement that would have destroyed the Russian army's ability to pursue the war. Instead, the Russians retreated out of the trap.

▶TURKS DEFEATED IN ARMENIA—The Turkish campaign against Russia's Kars-Ardahan positions in the Caucasus ended in defeat in January. Harsh cold and poor supplies killed more Turks through exhaustion and exposure than died in battle (12,400 men survived of the 190,000-strong Third Army; 30,000 were killed in the fighting). Armenians behind Turkish lines had disrupted supply and communications, and on June 11, the Turkish government decided to deport the Armenians, using the war as an excuse for atrocities on a large scale.

▶UPROAR OVER EXECUTION—On October 12, 1915, German officials shot Edith Cavell, an English nurse living in German-occupied Belgium, for aiding in the underground transport of Allied soldiers into occupied Holland. Cavell provided shelter and money at the hospital where she worked and arranged for the soldiers to be guided into the Netherlands. By the time she was arrested in August, 200 British, French, and Belgian men had been spirited to safety. Despite an international outcry and pleas for leniency from then-neutral Spain and the U.S., she was executed by a firing squad. Her death became a rallying force for Allied soldiers for the remainder of the war.

THE UNITED STATES

A Visionary's Blind Spots

9 In its absurd way, the flap over President Wilson's courtship of Edith Bolling Galt—the great American scandal of 1915—pointed up the character flaws that made one of the century's foremost visionaries a frustrated man. The story began the previous year, when the death of his wife sent Wilson into a paralyzing depression. Hoping to cheer him up, friends introduced him to Galt, a beautiful widow. Even Wilson's opponents had sympathized with his grief, but public opinion soured when he began courting Mrs. Galt just six months after his bereavement.

As it so often did in his presidency, Wilson's puritanical image worked against him. Eager to brand him a hypocrite, critics made him the butt of off-color jokes; they spread rumors that the romance had started during his wife's illness—even that he'd murdered her. Another supposed affair was also dredged up. The son of a Presbyterian minister, Wilson reacted to the gossip with stiff hauteur. He refused to defend himself, and ignored advisers' warnings to postpone his marriage until after the 1916 election. The citizenry put his record in office ahead of his alleged sins: Wilson, running on the slogan "He kept us out of war," won reelection.

Wilson was less lucky with U.S. congressmen. In the heyday of nationalism, his internationalism struck many of them as a righteous pose. (He fared no better among European leaders, many of whom viewed him as a New World naïf.) His grandest project, the League of Nations, was ridiculed in 1919 as the invention of an idealist too noble for the "real world." Instead of cajoling the doubters, Wilson assailed them with grim stubbornness. Just before Congress, predictably, rejected the League, Wilson suffered a stroke from which he never wholly recovered. For three months his wife assumed the role of acting president. By this time her popularity had outpaced his. ◂**1912.M** ▸**1920.1**

Wilson and wife, Edith Galt Wilson, at the 1916 World Series.

LITERATURE

Bards of War

10 The death of British soldier-poet Rupert Brooke *(below)* in 1915 came to symbolize the disillusionment that swept the combatant nations soon after World War I began.

Young, handsome, and wellborn, the 27-year-old Brooke gained instant fame for his sonnet cycle, *1914*, which portrayed the war in gorgeously idealistic terms; his countrymen idealized Brooke himself as personifying the virtues for which the Allies fought. But he perished unheroically of blood poisoning, on a troopship headed for the disastrous Battle of the Dardanelles.

"If I should die," Brooke had written, "think only this of me:/ That there's some corner of a foreign field/That is forever England." Such lines attained an antique quality as the grinding, anonymous realities of trench warfare ate away at notions of glory. The great British soldier-poet of that phase of the war—which Brooke never lived to see—was Wilfred Owen, the bitter elegist of "those who die as cattle."

Technically experimental, favoring alliterative assonance for rhyme, Owen's oeuvre would be a major influence on postwar poets. Unknown during his lifetime, Owen was encouraged by Siegfried Sassoon, whose own verse portraits of the "doomed, conscripted, unvictorious ones" had been coldly received by a public still thirsting for patriotic rhapsodies. The two men met in 1917, in a hospital where they'd been sent for shell shock. (Sassoon, already decorated for bravery, was actually suffering from acute pacifism.) After Owen was killed—a week before the armistice—Sassoon shepherded his work into print. By then, the innocent world Brooke represented was gone forever. ▸**1916.V**

LITERATURE

Maugham's Tale of Torment

11 The publication in 1915 of William Somerset Maugham's *Of Human Bondage* transformed a second-rate British author of light dramas into a figure of international stature. The book broke new ground for Maugham, but its exploration of individual morality and psychological development placed it firmly in the tradition of such contemporary authors as Forster, Lawrence, and Joyce.

For Maugham, the book was a way to make peace with his past—the death of his mother, the breakup of his home, his lonely and alienated youth. Partially autobiographical, the novel tells the story of Philip Carey, an orphan tormented by his sexuality and isolation who rebels against the values of family and church.

In *Of Human Bondage*, Maugham wrote of his feelings of enslavement by a manipulative lover.

Of Human Bondage's late-nineteenth-century naturalistic style had little in common with the popular hothouse prose of the day, and its woebegone protagonist was hardly a heroic figure to a nation preoccupied by war. In America, the novel got a better reception. Theodore Dreiser called it "the perfect thing which we love and cannot understand, but which we are compelled to confess a work of art." ◂**1913.3** ▸**1922.1**

NOBEL PRIZES: Peace: No award ... Literature: Romain Rolland (French; novelist) ... Chemistry: Richard Willstätter (German; plant pigments, including chlorophyll) ... Medicine: No award ... Physics: William Henry Bragg and William Lawrence Bragg (U.K.; crystal structure analysis).

The Power and Pitfalls of Propaganda

From the Report of the Committee on Alleged German Outrages, appointed by His Britannic Majesty's Government and presided over by the Right Hon. Viscount Bryce, 1915

SOUVENEZ-VOUS DE LA BELGIQUE
ET DU NORD DE LA FRANCE
N'ACHETEZ RIEN AUX BOCHES

While not unknown as a tool for rallying people to a cause, propaganda—aided and abetted by the advent of mass communication—reached new levels of sophistication in World War I. The British were the first to tap this newfound power, and they exploited it ruthlessly. Atrocity stories abounded in the British dailies, but the most galvanizing piece of contemporary propaganda was the official Bryce Report on German atrocities in Belgium. Commissioned by the King and issued in 1915, just five days after the Lusitania*'s sinking, the 300-page report was bulging with "eyewitness" accounts (from Belgian refugees living in England) of rape, murder, mutilation—all presented in graphic yet official-sounding detail. That much of the material was completely unsubstantiated and unverified mattered little to a population eager to believe the worst of its enemy.*

The Bryce Report cast a long shadow: Indeed, many historians cite its distortions as one of the reasons so many people ignored or dismissed (as simply more propaganda) the early accounts of atrocities in Nazi Germany. Meanwhile, Hitler—having clearly absorbed Britain's methods—was producing Nazi propaganda that made Bryce seem a rank amateur. ►**1935.14**

THE HUN AND THE HOME
A BIT OF ENGLAND
OUR Homes are secure.
OUR Mothers & Wives safe.
OUR Children still play and fear no harm.
A BIT OF BELGIUM
THEIR Homes are destroyed.
THEIR Women are murdered & worse.
THEIR Children are dead or slaves.
BACK UP THE MEN WHO HAVE SAVED YOU

Witness: Immediately my mistress came in, one of the officers who was sitting on the floor got up, and, putting a revolver to my mistress' temple, shot her dead. The officer was obviously drunk. The other officers continued to drink and sing, and they did not pay great attention to the killing of my mistress. The officer who shot my mistress then told my master to dig a grave and bury my mistress. My master and the officer went into the garden, the officer threatening my master with a pistol. My master was then forced to dig the grave, and to bury the body of my mistress in it. I cannot say for what reason they killed my mistress. The officer who did it was singing all the time.

Witness: One day when the Germans were not actually bombarding the town I left my house to go to my mother's house in High Street. My husband was with me. I saw eight German soldiers, and they were drunk. They were singing and making a lot of noise and dancing about. As the German soldiers came along the street, I saw a small child, whether boy or girl I could not see, come out of a house. The child was about two years of age. The child came into the middle of the street so as to be in the way of the soldiers. The soldiers were walking in twos. The first line of two passed the child; one of the second line, the man on the left stepped aside and drove his bayonet with both hands into the child's stomach lifting the child into the air on his bayonet and carrying it away on his bayonet, he and his comrades still singing. The child screamed when the soldier struck it with his bayonet, but not afterwards.

Witness: About September the 20th our regiment took part in an engagement with the Germans. After we had retired into our trenches a few minutes after we got back into them the Germans retired into their trenches. The distance between the trenches of the opposing forces was about 400 yards. I should say about 50 or 60 of our men had been left lying on the field from our trenches. After we got back to them I distinctly saw German soldiers come out of their trenches, go over the spots where our men were lying, and bayonet them. Some of our men were lying nearly halfway between the trenches.

Propaganda in words and pictures flourished on both sides. Ultimately, however, the Bryce Report and such anti-German propaganda as the political cartoons of Dutch artist Louis Raemaekers *(above)* served to instill skepticism in the citizenry.

"Humanity ... must be mad to do what it is doing."—**A French lieutenant, writing in his diary on May 23, 1916, at Verdun**

STORY OF THE YEAR

The War's Bloodiest Battles

1 The third year of the war saw two battles of such horror, devastation, and sheer futility that their names remain synonymous with twentieth-century warfare's descent into hell—a descent that was almost literal, as soldiers hunkered down for months in trenches. Of the first, at the strategic Meuse River town of Verdun, France, a German soldier wrote, "Whoever floundered through this morass full of the shrieking and dying ... had passed the last frontier of life." The second, along France's Somme River, was bloodier yet.

The Battle of Verdun, in February 1916, came after a year and a half of deadlock. The Allies, counting on Britain's vast new armies (augmented by the start of conscription in January) and massive munitions production, had been planning a general offensive along the Western and Eastern fronts. But the Germans—after dismissing any threat from Italy or Russia—struck first. Their Verdun offensive aimed to bog France down in an unwinnable battle, leaving Britain hopelessly isolated.

Bloody Somme: Over 4 months, some 3 million men clashed along 23 miles of front, which moved only 5 miles in all.

The battle for the town and its nearby hills raged for six months without interruption. But General Henri Philippe Pétain mounted a stubborn defense—and before the Germans could seize Verdun's fortresses, the Allies launched a huge offensive along the Somme River. The First Battle of the Somme, the war's deadliest, diverted Germany's forces, allowing Allied troops at Verdun to regain some ground. French forces were so depleted, however, that the Somme offensive petered out when November rains turned the battlefield into a swamp.

Outside France, even major battles accomplished little. Russia's grandest offensive, its summer assault on Bukovina and Galicia, began gloriously but stalled in the Carpathian Mountains; by September, one million Russians had been lost, largely through capture or desertion—further eroding that nation's morale. Italy's costly battles on the Isonzo River, while diverting enemy forces from the Somme, netted few gains and forced it to stand by while Montenegro and Albania were invaded. Romania joined the Allies and invaded Transylvania, but was itself overrun in December. In Mesopotamia, a besieged and starving British expedition surrendered. The Russians lost much of Persia. An Allied attempt to "liberate" Serbia faltered.

A year that had begun with both sides expecting imminent victory ended in the same, awful stalemate. **◂1915.3 ▸1916.M**

After Uncle Sam landed in Haiti, the country became a virtual protectorate.

THE CARIBBEAN

Gunboat Diplomacy

2 After decades of meddling in the affairs of the Dominican Republic, and impatient with an unstable government crippled by successive revolutions, the United States resorted to force in May 1916, sending Marines to restore order and protect American political and economic interests in that country. (The United States was the republic's only foreign creditor and since 1905 had run its customs operations.) After troops landed in the south to secure Santo Domingo, the capital, president Juan Isidro Jiménez—the nominal beneficiary of the U.S. intervention—resigned in protest. This put the United States in the awkward position of having invaded a friendly state and deposed its leader. The invasion widened into occupation; the occupation settled into a state of semipermanence, buoyed along by World War I, which diverted Washington's attention to Europe. Although it was apparent the United States had no coherent plan for governing the country, constitutional rule was not restored until 1924.

To the west of the Dominican Republic on the same island of Hispaniola was Haiti, where the situation was perhaps worse. (Haiti was labeled a "public nuisance" by one U.S. State Department official.) The United States, fearing that Haiti's continual instability would provoke its European creditors, had decided to intervene. It hoped to take the country's customs into receivership—as it had done across the mountains in the Dominican Republic—and establish political and financial order. The U.S.S. *Washington* had steamed into Port au Prince on July 27, 1915, in time to witness the bloody ouster of President Vilbrun Guillaume Sam, who was dismembered by an angry mob. The Marines landed, and Sam's successor, Phillippe Sudre Dartiguenave, was forced to accept a treaty relegating Haiti to virtual protectorate status. The occupation lasted for two decades, but failed to establish a political infrastructure.

The disastrous realities awaiting the United States' attempts to impose order on Latin America were fully illustrated on the island of Hispaniola. The advantages gained by U.S. intervention in the Dominican Republic, wrote State Department official Sumner Welles, "have been of infinitesimal importance when compared to the suspicions, fears, and hatred to which the Occupation gave rise throughout the American continent." **◂1913.4 ▸1926.8**

IDEAS

Dewey's Teachings

3 *Democracy and Education*, philosopher John Dewey's seminal work of educational theory, took the teaching world by storm when it was released in 1916.

Dewey's rejection of old-fashioned, autocratic teaching methods in favor of curricula that fostered independent thinking and problem solving helped change the direction of American education.

One of the most influential and controversial thinkers of his generation, Dewey developed a theory of philosophy called instrumentalism, which was closely related to the pragmatism of William James. According to the precepts of instrumentalism, philosophy is simply a tool used by people to solve practical problems. It follows, Dewey said, that truth is not absolute, but

ART & CULTURE: Books: ***A Portrait of the Artist as a Young Man*** **(James Joyce);** ***The Chicago Poems*** **(Carl Sandburg);** ***The Four Horsemen of the Apocalypse*** **(Vicente Blasco Ibañez);** ***Seventeen*** **(Booth Tarkington);** ***You Know Me Al*** **(Ring Lardner) ... Music: "Ireland Must Be Heaven for My Mother Came from There" (Fred Fisher); "I Ain't Got Nobody" (Williams and Graham);** ***Violanta*** **(E. W. Korngold);**

"MacDonagh and MacBride/And Connolly and Pearse/Now and in time to be,/Wherever green is worn/Are changed, changed utterly:/A terrible beauty is born."—**William Butler Yeats, "Easter 1916"**

rather a measure of an idea's usefulness. Applying instrumentalism to educational theory, Dewey concluded that what is taught in school must be relevant to the experience of the pupil. Instead of merely memorizing discrete facts and figures, a child should "stop and think," incorporating lessons into his understanding of life and culture. Such learning is critical, Dewey argued, for full participation in a fluid, democratic society.

An ardent believer in democracy, Dewey wrote prolifically on the need to use rational thought to improve society. Just as natural science has been advanced through observation and experimentation, he argued, so must public policy be advanced. Active in civil-rights causes throughout his life, Dewey contributed to the formation of the American Civil Liberties Union. **◂1902.7 ▸1920.M**

ART

Monet's Masterpiece

4 In 1916 Claude Monet began work on the murals that artist André Masson later praised as "The Sistine Chapel of Impressionism." The *Waterlilies (Nymphéas)* is a series of monumental oil paintings of Monet's lily pond at Giverny. Monet's lifelong struggle as an artist was to record on canvas, with color, first impressions of nature and light. (His 1873 painting *Impression, Sunrise* provided the impressionist movement with its name.) As he explained it, recalling the first time he painted out-of-doors, "My eyes were finally opened and I understood nature; I learned at the same time to love it."

Painting the same subject again and again at different times of the day, Monet went beyond scientific examination to imbue his studies with poetry and emotion. He continued to paint water lilies—despite poor health and near blindness—until his death in 1926. **◂1906.6**

IRELAND

The Easter Uprising

5 On the quiet Easter Monday holiday of 1916, when much of Dublin was away at the races, a handful of Irish nationalists stormed the largely deserted General Post Office and declared Irish independence from Great Britain. As a few curious passersby looked on in amazement, rebel leader and poet Patrick Pearse stood on the front steps of the building and read a proclamation: "Irishmen and Irishwomen: In the name of God and of the dead generations from which she receives her old tradition of nationhood, Ireland, through us, summons her children to her flag and strikes for her freedom."

The Easter Uprising lasted less than a week. By Thursday the British Army had established strong positions within Dublin and was shelling the post office; by Saturday, Pearse had surrendered. More than 450 were dead and 2,614 wounded. Initially, there was very little popular support for the doomed revolt (Dubliners jeered as the rebels were led off in chains). But, having quashed the rebellion, General Sir John Maxwell, the British commander in chief, badly blundered. He ordered the peremptory execution of 15 insurrectionists, and proceeded to ferret out and intern members of Sinn Féin, the nationalist organization he assumed was behind the uprising. (In fact, elements of the Irish Republican Brotherhood and the Irish Volunteers were responsible.) Maxwell's harshness inspired a

Irish Life **published a special issue on the Irish rebellion of 1916.**

newfound patriotism in the populace. Irish citizens joined Sinn Féin in droves, transforming it into Ireland's most powerful political organization.

"It is absolutely impossible to slaughter a man [Pearse] in this position without making him a martyr and a hero even though the day before the rising he may have been only a minor poet," wrote George Bernard Shaw, a supporter of independence. "The shot Irish men will now take their places beside Emmet and the Manchester Martyrs in Ireland ... and nothing in heaven or earth can prevent it." **◂1905.6 ▸1920.7**

A detail from *Waterlilies: The Morning.* Monet painted his lily pond for 10 years before he began his enormous murals.

BIRTHS

Eddie Arcaro, U.S. jockey.

Milton Babbitt, U.S. composer.

Pieter Willem Botha, South African president.

Walter Cronkite, U.S. newscaster.

Francis Crick, U.K. biologist.

Roald Dahl, U.K. writer.

Kirk Douglas, U.S. actor.

Edward Heath. U.K. prime minister.

Yehudi Menuhin, U.S. musician.

François Mitterrand, French president.

Irving Wallace, U.S. writer.

Harold Wilson, U.K. prime minister.

DEATHS

William Merritt Chase, U.S. painter.

Rubén Darío, Nicaraguan poet.

Thomas Eakins, U.S. painter.

Hetty Green, U.S. financier.

Victoriano Huerta, Mexican president.

Henry James, U.S. novelist.

H.H. Kitchener, U.K. military leader.

Jack London, U.S. writer.

Percival Lowell, U.S. astronomer.

Franz Marc, German painter.

Grigory Rasputin, Russian mystic.

Antonio Sant'Elia, Italian architect.

Alan Seeger, U.S. poet.

Henryk Sienkiewicz, Polish novelist.

Yuan Shikai, Chinese warlord.

Fountains of Rome **(Ottorino Respighi) ... Painting & Sculpture:** ***Evangelical Still Life*** **(Giorgio de Chirico);** ***Demon Above the Ships*** **(Paul Klee) ... Film:** ***Intolerance*** **(D.W. Griffith);** ***Civilization*** **(Thomas H. Ince);** ***Hell's Hinges*** **(with William S. Hart) ... Theater:** ***Our Mrs. McChesney*** **(Edna Ferber);** ***Magical City*** **(Zoë Akins);** ***See America First*** **(Cole Porter);** ***Robinson Crusoe, Jr.*** **(Atteridge and Smith).**

"Madame, I shall die on the stage; it is my battlefield!"—**Sarah Bernhardt, when asked by Queen Mary of England why she continued to perform**

NEW IN 1916

Guide dogs for the blind (Germany).

Windshield wipers.

Lipstick in metal cartridges.

Professional Golfers Association.

Open-air public-address system.

Radio tuning device.

Keds sneakers.

Lucky Strike cigarettes.

Lincoln Logs.

National Park Service (U.S. Department of the Interior).

IN THE UNITED STATES

▶**OWEN-KEATING LAW ADDRESSES CHILD LABOR**—With some 13 percent of the textile workforce under age 16, Congress in 1916 out-

lawed the interstate trade of goods produced in factories where children under age 14 worked, or where children between ages 14 and 16 worked more than eight hours a day. The law was struck down in 1918 by the Supreme Court, which said Congress had exceeded its power to regulate interstate commerce. ◀1905.V

▶**EIGHT-HOUR DAY**—Hours before the railway brotherhoods, representing 400,000 employees, were to walk out on strike, Woodrow Wilson signed into law an eight-hour day for rail workers. In forcing railroad owners to adopt labor's demand, Wilson narrowly averted a national catastrophe: In 1916 interstate

MEXICO

Villa Crosses the Border

6 Mexican revolutionary Francisco "Pancho" Villa led his ragtag band of guerrillas across the border to raid the U.S. Army garrison town of Columbus, New Mexico, in the predawn hours of March 9, 1916. Militarily, the attack ended in defeat for the Villistas, who lost more than 100 men, but it enhanced Villa's folk-hero legend and secured him enough popular support to continue his campaign against Mexican leader Venustiano Carranza. Villa's specific goals for the raid were unclear, but two possibilities suggest themselves: to revenge himself on an American arms dealer headquartered in the town who had taken his money and failed to deliver weapons, and to draw the United States into the Mexican Civil War, which he hoped would demonstrate the weakness of the Carranza regime.

General John J. "Black Jack" Pershing, in command of 12,000 troops, pursued Villa. As Pershing's Punitive Expedition wandered ever deeper into Mexican territory, Mexican resentment increased, pressuring Carranza to resist the Americans. The elusive Villa gained political stature as the defender of national sovereignty. Rural villagers rallied around him, abetting his escape and misleading the expedition as to his whereabouts.

After a fruitless year, President Wilson's secretary of war admitted it was "foolish to chase a single bandit all over Mexico." Wilson withdrew the troops, a concession to both Carranza, who became president in 1917, and Villa, who was now celebrated as the cunning rascal who had made a fool of the mighty U.S. Army. ◀**1913.M** ▶**1917.11**

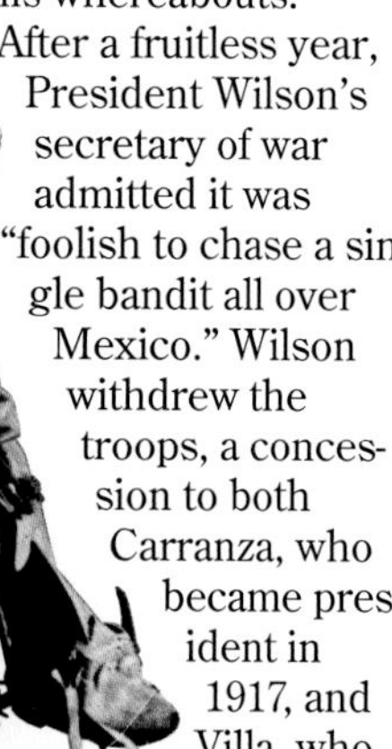

The battle cry of *"Viva Villa!"* resounded through Columbus, New Mexico, as several hundred Villistas raided the town.

This Mucha poster for a "last visit" predated the actual final tour by 6 years.

THEATER

Divine Sarah's Final U.S. Tour

7 Broke and in failing health, the celebrated 71-year-old French actress Sarah Bernhardt set off in 1916 for her eighth and final U.S. tour. She had weathered the years well, considering her adventures: lead actress with the Comédie-Française in Paris; mistress of Henri, Prince de Ligne; victim of the anti-Semitism of the French aristocracy, who scorned her as *"nouvelle."* Worse still, she'd lost her right leg to gangrene in 1915—an encumbrance that did not stop her from visiting soldiers at the front during World War I. This, after all, was the woman who first played Hamlet at the age of 54.

The Divine Sarah wasn't well enough to perform an entire play; instead, her performances in America consisted mostly of familiar scenes, echoes of past triumphs—the title role of Racine's *Phèdre*, the death scene from *Camille,* and parts written for her in the late nineteenth century by French melodramatist Victorien Sardou. In a new piece, *Au Champs d'Honneur,* written by a young French soldier, Bernhardt played a youthful standard-bearer who, even in death, will not give up his battalion's flag to the enemy. This work helped rally American audiences to the cause of the war in Europe and won over the critics, who hailed the actress as "the greatest missionary whom France or any other country has sent abroad."

Bernhardt herself was skeptical. "I have donned my mask, my fool's cap and bells, and taken up my wanderings across America once again," she wrote to her son, Maurice. "How many cities there are, ugly and unknown. Some are fine, some ghastly." A few critics suggested that her tour was more curiosity than theater. "To contend that Madame Sarah Bernhardt is still a great actress is to permit chivalry to obscure criticism," wrote one detractor. "The public goes to the theatre less to venerate Sarah Bernhardt the actress than to see Sarah Bernhardt the freak."

The strain of the tour proved to be too much for Bernhardt. She'd battled uremia for years, and in New York was rushed to the hospital for an emergency kidney operation. Taking her illness in stride, she said, "They can cut out everything as long as they leave me my head." After a lengthy convalescence, she resumed her tour on the vaudeville circuit until the fall of 1918, when she returned to France. She died in Paris in 1923 without seeing America again. ▶**1922.V**

CHINA

Power Passes to Warlords

8 Yuan Shikai, the first president of the Republic of China, died in 1916 after four turbulent years in power. His demise left China without a clear political leader, and plunged the fledgling republic into the chaos of rule by feuding warlords.

Yuan had commanded China's most powerful army before the Chinese Revolution. He became president in 1912 in return for his military support of revolutionary leader Sun Yat-sen, which ensured the end of the Qing Dynasty. Once in office, however, Yuan double-crossed his republican sponsors. When Sun's Nationalist Party (Guomindang) won a resounding majority in China's parliamentary elections, Yuan balked

SPORTS: Baseball: World Series, Boston Red Sox defeat Brooklyn Dodgers (Zack Wheat, Jake Daubert), 4–1 ... Football: Rose Bowl resumes as annual event (suspended after 1902 debut), Washington State defeats Brown, 14–0 ... Golf: First U.S. PGA tournament held at Siwanoy Country Club in Bronxville, N.Y.

"This last month I have lived through the most exciting and the most exacting period of my life: and it would be true to say that it has also been the most fruitful."—**Albert Einstein, November 1915**

and attempted to seize unilateral control of the government. Within a year he outlawed the Nationalist Party—forcing Sun into Japanese exile—and dissolved parliament.

By early 1916, Sun, aided by the Japanese government, mounted an armed revolt against the dictator, and encouraged restive warlords to declare the independence of the provinces under their control. For Yuan, the final blow came in March 1916, when two of his own generals refused to back him. Two months later, the dictator succumbed to illness. The Chinese Revolution had been won, but republicanism remained elusive. In the absence of stable constitutional rule, military strength would decide succession. **◂1911.9 ▸1921.6**

SCIENCE

Time, Space, and Matter

9 The publication in 1916 of Albert Einstein's general theory of relativity completed the modification of Newtonian physics that he'd begun eleven years earlier. To his continuum of space and time, described in his special theory of relativity, Einstein now added matter, which he said accounted for the curvature of space and time, otherwise known as gravitation or acceleration. Matter, Einstein postulated, was also a property of space, inseparable from time. With this baffling pronouncement he created a new geometry of the universe. Rightly or wrongly, this abstract physical theory became a metaphor for the human condition in the twentieth century, a state marked by uncertainty, isolation, and the search for meaning.

Smuggled out of wartime Berlin, where Einstein was a professor of physics and a vocal opponent of German militarism, the general theory was disseminated by Sir Arthur Eddington, the British astronomer, and immediately created a stir in the world scientific community. The wonder of Einstein's work is that he was operating in the realm of pure theory, supported by little else than his own immense intellectual power. His postulates did not derive from observations, but predicted them. Einstein stated that if his theory was correct, a ray of light passing across the surface of the sun would bend twice as much as could be accounted for

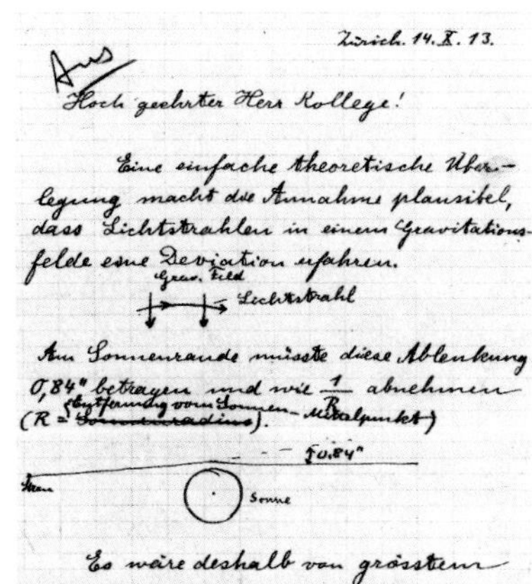

Zürich. 14. X. 13.

Hoch geehrter Herr Kollege!

Eine einfache theoretische Überlegung macht die Annahme plausibel, dass Lichtstrahlen in einem Gravitationsfelde eine Deviation erfahren.

Am Sonnenrande müsste diese Ablenkung 0,84" betragen und wie 1/R abnehmen (R = Abstand vom Sonnen-Mittelpunkt).

Es wäre deshalb von grösstem

In a letter to American astronomer George Ellery Hale, Einstein described how a light ray is bent in a gravitational field and how the sun deflects light from a star.

by the Newtonian system. In 1919, during a solar eclipse, this prediction was confirmed, proving relativity. **◂1905.1 ▸1924.2**

WORLD WAR I

The Emotional Toll

10 In some respects, World War I was the last nineteenth-century war. Officers still carried swords. Cavalrymen regularly rode horseback. Kings and nobles played a major role in military affairs. But technologically, it was a decidedly twentieth-century conflict. Walled forts no longer provided security against gargantuan howitzers. Infantry charges were suicidal against machine guns. Combat now consisted largely of sitting in a narrow, muddy hole while explosives rained from the sky. Trench warfare combined terror with helplessness—and led, with unprecedented frequency, to a disorder known as shell shock. With symptoms ranging from paralyzing anxiety to hallucinations, shell shock was initially thought to be a form of brain damage caused by the force of a blast. By late 1916, doctors agreed that the problem was emotional.

The French kept shell-shocked casualties near the front under the command of officers recovering from physical wounds. The British generally sent victims back to England. Most, strangely, deteriorated; many became permanently disabled. The French soldiers recovered quickly and returned to the fight. A U.S. commission sent to Europe to study shell shock in case America entered the war endorsed the French technique, and soon all the Allies had adopted it.

This war was the first in which psychiatrists served as integral members of army medical staffs. What they learned about shell shock, however, was forgotten by the next world war. In the 1940s, Allied psychiatrists tried to prevent an outbreak of the syndrome by screening potential soldiers for lack of "moral fiber." Although psychiatric rejections were much more common than during World War I, so-called "war neuroses" were two to three times as frequent, aggravated by the stresses of an even more violent conflict. And the practice of having soldiers recover at the front had to be learned again. **◂1916.1 ▸1918.1**

Huddled in trenches and further confined by gas masks, these German soldiers were ripe for a new disorder called shell shock.

IN THE UNITED STATES

transportation of food and fuel depended utterly on the railroads. The radical eight-hour workday became a standard industrial measure. ◂1913.6 ▸1917.7

▸AMERICA'S WEALTHIEST WOMAN—Eccentric financier Hetty Green, the "Witch of Wall Street," died in 1916 at 80. After inheriting a fortune as a young woman, Green

exponentially expanded it, becoming the wealthiest woman in America. Frugal to a fault, she once denied her son medical treatment, costing him a leg. She lived sparingly in a Hoboken apartment and died worth a cool $100 million.

▸HARRISON DRUG ACT—An early salvo in the war on drugs was fired in 1916 when Woodrow Wilson signed into law the Harrison Drug Act. Named for Congressman Francis Burton Harrison, the act attempted to control the availability of opiates by requiring pharmacists to register their stocks of narcotics with the IRS. ◂1906.11

▸GERMAN SABOTAGE IN AMERICA—An explosion of ammunition at the loading docks in Toms River Island, New Jersey, in July killed seven and wounded 35, and wreaked $40 million worth of damage. The suspected cause was German sabotage.

▸FLYERS IN THE WAR—Seven American volunteer pilots made combat flights for the French in the Escadrille Américaine. On May 18, Kiffin

Rockwell scored the unit's first victory, but the German ambassador in Washington complained that the flyers violated U.S. neutrality. ◂1916.1 ▸1917.9

POLITICS & BUSINESS: GNP: $48.3 billion ... Woodrow Wilson reelected president, barely defeating Charles Evans Hughes ... Jeanette Rankin of Montana is the first elected U.S. congresswoman ... Over 2,000 strikes by U.S. workers from January to July ... Congress passes Workmen's Compensation Act for federal employees ... U.S. National Park Service created ... New York City passes first zoning law in the U.S.

"Like Shelley and like Baudelaire, it may be said of him that he suffered, in his own person, the neurotic ills of an entire generation."—**Christopher Isherwood, on T.E. Lawrence**

WORLD WAR I

▶BATTLE OF JUTLAND—For years, the Germans had been gearing up for a naval confrontation with the British. They finally had it on May 31, when the German High Seas Fleet, attempting to break the Allied blockade of Germany's coast, attacked the British Grand Fleet. The battleships and cruisers skirmished through the late evening and early morning, when both sides evidently retreated. Victory was claimed by both sides, but the British suffered more, with the Germans wiping out 117,025 tons of U.K. warships. (The Germans lost just over half that amount.) When the battle was over, the blockade remained in place.

▶DEATH OF A MILITARY GIANT—As minister of war, Lord Horatio Herbert Kitchener, the embodiment of Britain's military might, publicly upheld the belief that democratic societies should, and could, organize effective volunteer armies. His face appeared with that message on British recruitment posters *(below)*, but privately Kitchener—who was gradually being stripped of his power—voiced doubts that victory could be achieved without conscription. He was killed on June 5, 1916, on his way to visit Czar

Nicholas of Russia, when his ship struck a German mine off the Orkney Islands. (It went down in 15 minutes.) Kitchener's successor, David Lloyd George, enacted conscription upon becoming prime minister in December.

▶CASUALTIES TO DATE—A contemporary estimate put the number of the war's victims by year's end at 4.75 million killed, 19 million wounded or interned.

THE MIDDLE EAST

Arabian Knight

11 Soldier and writer Thomas Edward (T.E.) Lawrence went by several names—but history remembers him as Lawrence of Arabia. His legendary career began

T.E Lawrence in the Arab garb he preferred to wear.

in 1916, when, in exchange for British guarantees of an expanded kingdom, Husayn ibn Ali, emir of Mecca, proclaimed an Arab revolt against the Ottoman Empire. A 28-year-old British intelligence officer, Lawrence became the liaison between the British Army—then engaged in its own fight against the Ottoman Turks—and Husayn's son Faisal, who led a rebel force.

Lawrence had learned Arabic, and conceived a romantic admiration for the Arabs, during archaeological expeditions he made while still a student at Oxford. Slight and boyish-looking, he was an unlikely hero. But after he donned Bedouin robes, the rebels accepted him as one of them—and soon, as he related in his bestselling *Seven Pillars of Wisdom* (1926), he'd transformed a motley gang of tribesmen into an effective guerrilla force. He became the chief strategist for the whole rebel army, temporarily converting its self-interested leaders to his vision of a unified Arab nation—and persuading British commanders to back it. Lawrence inspired his men with his willingness to share their extreme hardships; he fought on even after being gang-raped by Turkish troops.

Or so he said. The reliability of Lawrence's memoir—a strange, poetic mixture of self-inflation and self-abasement—remains in doubt. Beyond question was his crucial role in driving the Turks from Syria and western Arabia. Yet Lawrence refused a medal from King George V. He served briefly as adviser on Arab affairs to Winston Churchill (then colonial minister), but in the 1920s, after lobbying unsuccessfully for Arab independence, he enlisted as a common soldier—under pseudonyms—in the RAF and the tank corps. He died in a motorcycle crash in 1935.

Husayn, too, died in obscurity. He reigned over the Hejaz until 1924, when Saud conquered the region and exiled him to Cyprus. Husayn's sons Faisal and Abdullah, however, became kings—Faisal in Iraq and Abdullah in what is now Jordan, where Husayn's dynasty still ruled some 80 years later. **▸1920.2**

INDIA

Nehru the Nationalist

12 Mohandas Gandhi and Jawaharlal Nehru, the two great movers for Indian independence, met each other for the first time in 1916 at the annual meeting of the Gandhi-led Indian National Congress. Nehru, a young Brahman and lawyer educated at Harrow and Cambridge, had long been interested in politics and approved philosophically of independence. But it was Gandhi, 20 years Nehru's elder, who awakened him to the plight of his less-privileged countrymen and inspired him to action. After the massacre at Amritsar in 1919, when English soldiers opened fire on a political rally, Nehru became a member of the Indian National Congress and devoted himself totally to the nationalist cause. His leadership role culminated in 1947 with his election as independent India's first prime minister.

Thoroughly modern in outlook, Nehru eventually rejected Gandhi's vision of an India restored to her pristine glory, dismissing as impractical and quaint a "deliberately simple peasant life." He advocated industrial development as India's salvation. Later, the two men also differed over the technicalities of independence. While Gandhi was willing to accept dominion status, Nehru drafted a 1930 resolution demanding unequivocal independence (a stance he later modified, out of pragmatism, as prime minister). The Indian National Congress unanimously adopted Nehru's motion, tacitly endorsing him as India's leading political activist. Gandhi remained the movement's spiritual leader, but it was Nehru who shouldered the traditional political burden. **◂1914.4 ▸1919.10**

THE UNITED STATES

The Caribbean Gibraltar

13 The political affairs journal *Current Opinion* called the islands of St. Thomas, St. John, and St. Croix "three little flyspecks," but in 1916 the U.S. State Department considered them a Gibraltar in the Caribbean. The United States, in its most expensive territorial acquisition, agreed to pay Denmark $25 million for the Danish West Indies. (The Gadsden Purchase, containing large parts of New Mexico and Arizona, cost $10 million; Alaska cost a mere $7.2 million.)

The U.S. Virgin Islands, as they became known after the sale, offered little other than beaches and bay rum. The purchase was designed to prevent the islands from falling under German control during World War I. If Germany absorbed Denmark, these islands could provide the Germans with a base for naval operations perilously close to the Panama Canal. "The United States would be under the necessity of seizing and annexing them," Secretary of State Robert Lansing warned Denmark, "though it would be done with the greatest reluctance." Both sides preferred a sale. **◂1914.9 ▸1921.M**

Uncle Sam (with Woodrow Wilson's face) leads his new charges, St. Thomas, St. Croix, and St. John, in a Danish cartoon.

A VOICE FROM 1916

A Poet's Dispatches from the Abyss

By John Masefield, from letters to his wife, 1916

John Masefield was 38 when he accompanied the U.S. volunteer ambulance service to France in 1916, on a research mission for the British Army. A future English poet laureate (from 1930 to his death in 1967), Masefield was already known for works like those in Salt-Water Ballads, *based on his boyhood naval apprenticeship. His long narrative poem* The Everlasting Mercy *had scandalized critics with its vernacular coarseness. But nothing Masefield had written, or seen in his seafaring days, was as shocking as the scenes he witnessed on the Western Front. His keen wartime observations were published in such books as* The Old Front Line *(1917). The excerpts below are from letters to his wife, recording some of the appalling results of the First Battle of the Somme.* ◄1916.1 ►1929.11

[At a Military Dental Clinic in Neuilly], "Where the Face-Making Begins," September 4, 1916:

They get hold of the man, and clean the infection of the wound first, and then lay the sort of foundation of his future face by moulding new jaws for him; the jaws they make out of his spare ribs or out of bits of his leg, and when they have got the framework laid the surgeons set to work to put on a new covering of flesh, which they cut from the patients [sic] cheeks or elsewhere.... [T]hey have a good many cases to see, some of them very terrible to look at. Some of them were done by rifle bullets at 15 metres, evidently with dum dum bullets, and these are frightful in the early stages.... I saw men with new noses, just setting, so to speak, but not yet in a condition to stand a blow. Then there were men with no mouths, and men with mouths between the ear and the throat somewhere, and men with nothing but mouth between the throat and the chest and men with little round orifices instead of mouths, and other men with already one lip set and a second beginning to grow, and all as perky as could be. Then there was one man who had been "finished" by certain surgeons in a condition of such awful ugliness as would have wrecked the poor fellow's life; but he was being taken in hand, and they were going to make him a nose, and straighten out his eyes, and give him a mouth; and they thought he would finish as a beau.

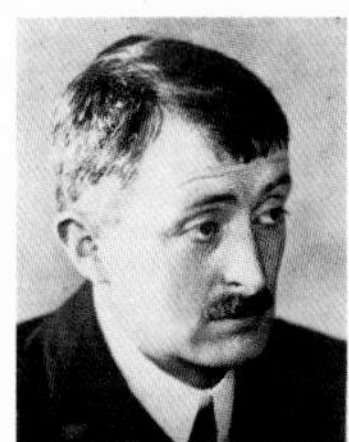

With horrifying, yet poetic, imagery, Masefield *(inset)* rendered scenes of wounded men and shattered cities. Top: Two weary soldiers carry a wounded comrade away from the trenches along the La Boisselle-Amiens Road. Middle: Battered British naval fighters return from the frontline in Belgium. Bottom: A shattered church in Neuilly becomes a makeshift hospital.

[In the Graveyard of a Ruined Village], September 21, 1916:

The ruins near me were mostly whitish oolite stone, almost the colour of the moon, & all the crosses of the graves were casting shadows. Someone said something that made me look down, & there, just at my feet, lying on stretchers on the graves, where they had been laid but a minute before, were two dead French soldiers, whose flesh was still warm. One lay on his back, one on his side, as though asleep, & their dignity in death broke my heart. One had been shot through the heart, one through the head, & both must have died at once. I think the one on his back was a city dweller but the other was a countryman, very big and strong and grave, older than the other, & a finer character.... [V]ery likely they had seen me passing only a few hours before & had stood aside with their comrades to let me pass.

[On the Battlefield], October 4, 1916:

If you will imagine any 13 miles × 9 miles known to you, say from Goring to Abingdon ... you will get a hint of its extent. Then imagine in all that expanse no single tree left intact, but either dismembered or cut off short, & burnt quite black. Then imagine that in all that expanse no single house is left, nor any large part of a house, except one iron gate & half a little red chapel, & that all the other building is literally blasted into little bits, so that no man can tell where villages were, nor how they ran, nor what they were like.... To say that the ground is "ploughed up" with shells is to talk like a child. It is gouged & blasted & bedeviled with the pox of war, & at every step you are on the wreck of war, & up at the top of the ridge there is no ground, there is nothing but a waste of big graceless holes ten feet deep & ten feet broad, with defilement & corpses & hands & feet & old burnt uniforms & tattered leather all flung about & dug in & dug out again, like nothing else on God's earth.

"I cannot protest too energetically against the slanderous statements spread by capitalists ... that we are in favor of a separate peace with Germany."—**Vladimir Ilyich Lenin, November 1917, four months before his government signed the Brest-Litovsk Treaty**

STORY OF THE YEAR

Lenin Leads the Russian Revolution

1 In April 1917, Vladimir Ilyich Ulyanov, better known by his revolutionary name, V.I. Lenin, arrived in Russia secretly via a boxcar from Finland. (His safe passage across Europe had been facilitated by the Germans, who had a vested interest in increasing Russia's internal turmoil.) The Bolshevik leader carried with him three demands: "End the war! All land to the peasants! All power to the Soviets!" The Czar had abandoned his throne, a victim of his own terminally bad judgment. The badly damaged ship of state now listed under the leadership of onetime revolutionist Aleksandr Kerensky, whose provisional government was tottering. Lenin, whose hopes for revolution had been receding during the seemingly endless world war, saw that now was the time to seize power.

Decades of czarist incompetence had already wreaked economic havoc on Russia; World War I broke it entirely. By 1917, food shortages were endemic, and wartime inflation was devouring the incomes of militant urban workers—200,000 of whom spilled into the streets of Petrograd in February to protest. A freezing, hungry militia offered only halfhearted resistance. As strikes and rioting engulfed the city, Nicholas abdicated, ending the three-century-old Romanov dynasty.

Kerensky's provisional government—which instituted universal suffrage, equal rights for women, and basic civil liberties—barely managed to fill the void until the night of October 25, when Lenin delivered his death blow. Armed Bolshevik workers, soldiers, and sailors stormed Petrograd and seized the Winter Palace and all government operations. The next morning, Lenin introduced a new Soviet government, the dictatorship of the proletariat; its leaders were Lenin and his second-in-command, Leon Trotsky. The new state quickly confiscated estates and nationalized land, banks, transport, and industry, and, in March 1918, withdrew from World War I by signing the humiliating separate peace of Brest-Litovsk, which Trotsky negotiated with the Germans.

Lenin had spent 30 years building a party that could effect revolution; now, at age 47, he had succeeded.

But there was to be no peace for the masses. Civil war swept the country. The anti-Bolshevik White Army, led by former czarist admirals and generals (and abundantly provisioned by the Allies, who refused to recognize the Soviet government), fought desperately to overthrow the Red regime. Both sides trampled the peasants. The carnage during the next two years cost Russia millions of lives and untold destruction, compounding the deprivation already inflicted by czarist misadventure and the world war. **◂1916.1 ▸1918.5**

THE UNITED STATES

Slowing Down Immigration

2 After 20 years of debate and three presidential vetoes, the U.S. Congress enacted a law in 1917 that required immigrants over the age of 16 to pass a literacy test

2674

Class No. 5 Serial Number Armeno-Turkish

Վէ եէտի պին գօյուն վէ իւչ պին տէվէ վէ պէշ եիւզ չիֆթ էօքիւզ վէ պէշ եիւզ տիշի մէրքէպէ մալիք օլուպ՝ փէք չօգ պէնտէլէրի տախի վար իտի. վէ պու ատէմ՝ շարգ էհալիսինին քեաֆֆէսին-տէն պէօյլիւք իտի։

His substance also was seven thousand sheep, and three thousand camels, and five hundred yoke of oxen, and five hundred she asses, and a very great household; so that this man was the greatest of all the men of the east.

(Job 1:3)

Under the new law, any immigrant who was not literate in some language was deported.

proving they could read and write a language or dialect before entering the country. The bill's proponents were concerned mainly with excluding those who, either as anarchists or as public charges, would menace U.S. institutions.

The literacy requirement would also, as the ensuing debate revealed, selectively curtail immigration from southern and eastern Europe, Asia, Africa, and Latin America, but not from northern and western Europe. Over the years, Congress endlessly debated the connection between literacy and anarchism. "Was there ever a menace of harm to the government of the United States ... that did not come from conspirators who were educated men?" asked a congressman in 1902. "The more illiterate of the aliens, once here, quickly absorb the teachings [of industrial sabotage]," countered another.

The test's opponents, unmoved by its racist overtones, argued instead that it would put a serious dent in the pool of cheap labor—a pressing concern in times of industrial expansion. Such a law, one legislator noted, would exclude those who do "the drudgery that this country requires." Thus it fell to the Immigration Commission to devise a policy that would selectively filter out "undesirables" (which already included the insane, physically unfit, and "degenerate") without substantially reducing the pool of new labor.

President Wilson's final veto was overridden in February. There was no mistaking Congress's xenophobic mood, for the bill also contained provisions to exclude people from the "Asiatic Barred Zone," to expand the definition of "undesirables," and to raise the head tax on immigrants from $4 to $8. In accordance with its framers' intentions, the new law effectively reduced the number of immigrants. Those allowed into the country were primarily white and culturally familiar to the majority of Americans. **◂1908.M ▸1921.8**

MUSIC

Tango Argentino

3 Argentina's most famous export, the tango, got a new twist and a new wave of popularity in 1917, when Carlos Gardel released his first recording, *"Mi noche triste."* The tango *song*—with

A huge bronze monument to Gardel stands in the cemetery where he is buried.

its passionate vocals, accordion, and violin swirling over a haughtily deliberate beat—was on the road to worldwide popularity.

ART & CULTURE: Books: *Parnassus on Wheels* (Christopher Morley); *Prufrock and Other Observations* (T.S. Eliot); *King Coal* (Upton Sinclair); *Abel Sánchez* (Miguel de Unamuno) ... Music: "For Me and My Gal" (Meyer and Goetz); "Goodbye Broadway, Hello France" (Baskette, Reisner, and Davis); *Parade* (Erik Satie); *Classical Symphony* (Sergei Prokofiev); *Le Tombeau de Couperin* (Maurice Ravel) ...

"I threw the bottlerack and the urinal in their faces and now they admire them for their aesthetic beauty."—**Marcel Duchamp in 1962, on the elevation of his ready-mades to the status of high art**

In the *guardia vieja* ("old guard") tango, vocals had always been secondary to movement. As a dance form, the tango had originated in the slums of Buenos Aires; it incorporated the motions of knife fights and sex acts into a drama of machismo and swooning femininity. A diluted version was the favorite step of bourgeois New Yorkers, Londoners, Parisians, and—eventually—Argentines throughout the 1910s and '20s.

The Argentine incarnation was usually set to traditional Cuban-style dance tunes played without vocals or matched with lyrics about faithless women, booze, brothels, and the cruelty of society. (The genre had much in common with such folk forms as Mexican *canciones* and American blues.) But by World War I, a newer, more lyrical and aurally refined tango music had emerged. *"Mi noche triste"* was a prime example, and Gardel's rendition was an unprecedented hit.

Gardel became a star abroad (Bing Crosby said he'd "never heard a voice so beautiful"), but at home his celebrity took on an almost mythic stature. For Argentines, Gardel, like the tango itself, was an expression of the soul of their largely immigrant nation. His movie lines are still quoted and an exceptional person is referred to as a "Gardel." Transforming himself from a poor, illegitimate immigrant into a wealthy, glamorous sophisticate, the singer embodied the aspirations of millions of other Argentines. When he died in a plane crash in 1935, his funeral drew record crowds. ►**1935.7**

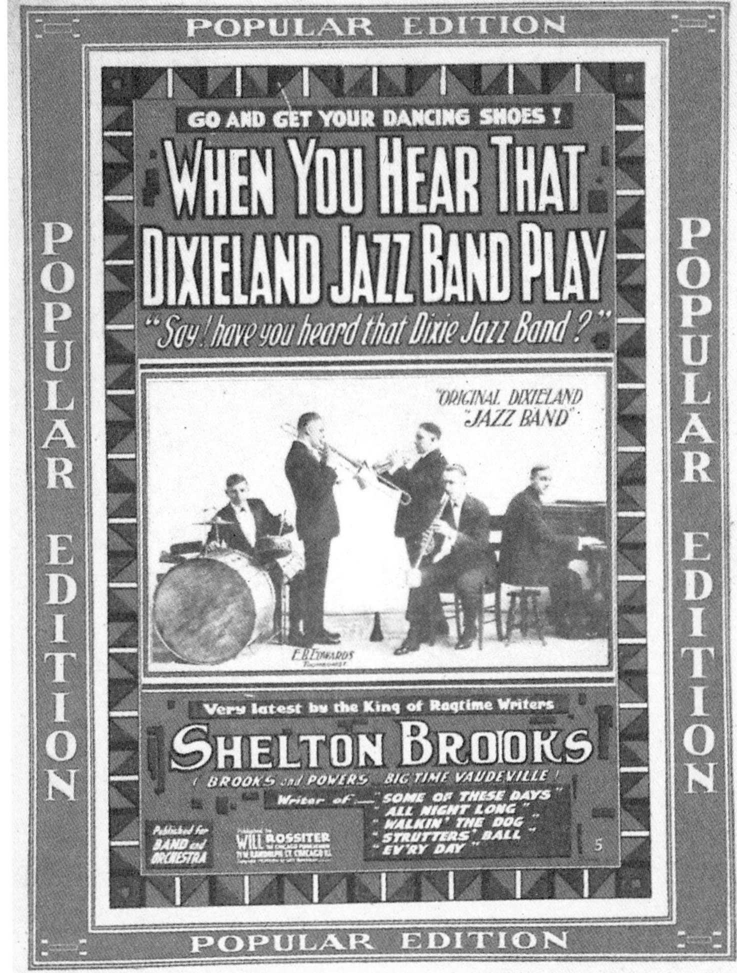

The first jazz recording: ODJB's music was mediocre but popular.

MUSIC

Jazz Goes on Record

5 The first jazz recording ever—"The Darktown Strutters' Ball," by the Original Dixieland Jazz Band—was cut in New York City in 1917. The band, appropriately, was from New Orleans, where jazz itself (a newborn hybrid of such African-American and European forms as ragtime, blues, marches, and opera) had gestated over the past two decades. Less appropriate was the choice of this *particular* New Orleans band: a second-rate group of white musicians, led by a Canadian-born cornet player named Nick LaRocca.

Jazz had been conceived and nurtured by black musicians like Buddy Bolden and Jelly Roll Morton. Legend has it, however, that some of those great artists had turned down offers to record out of fear that others would steal their improvisations if they were put down on wax. The ODJB, though, jumped at the chance, and LaRocca never stopped trying to get credit as a key player in jazz's invention. In fact, his music was rhythmically stilted and mediocre at improvisation. Still, it had an infectious vigor and dancers loved the music. By year's end, thanks in large part to the ODJB's record, jazz was a nationwide phenomenon. ►**1925.6**

ART

Duchamp's Ready-mades

4 **He stopped painting at the age of 25 and spent his final years studying chess, but Marcel Duchamp remains the most revolutionary artist of the twentieth century. (His *Nude Descending a Staircase*, the sensation of 1913's Armory Show, virtually defined the term avant-garde.) In 1917, he signed a common urinal "R. Mutt," titled it *Fountain*, and included it in an exhibition in New York City. With this gesture, Duchamp decreed that art was no longer a matter of technique or training; it was whatever the artist deemed it to be.**

Duchamp had been producing his "ready-mades" since 1913, but by placing *Fountain* in a museumlike setting, he erased the distinction between high and low culture. All the definition-extending art movements—dada and surrealism in the twenties, pop art in the sixties, and performance art in the eighties—that came after Duchamp were almost anticlimactic. **◄1913.2 ►1920.4**

BIRTHS

Anthony Burgess, U.K. novelist.

Arthur C. Clarke, U.K. writer.

Indira Gandhi, Indian prime minister.

Dizzy Gillespie, U.S. musician.

Katharine Graham, U.S. publisher.

Lena Horne, U.S. singer.

Andrew Huxley, U.K. physiologist.

John F. Kennedy, U.S. president.

Robert Lowell, U.S. poet.

Carson McCullers, U.S. writer.

Ferdinand Marcos, Filipino president.

Robert Mitchum, U.S. actor.

Thelonius Monk, U.S. musician.

Conor Cruise O'Brien, Irish writer and diplomat.

Irving Penn, U.S. photographer.

Arthur Schlesinger, Jr., U.S. historian.

Byron R. White, U.S. jurist.

Andrew Wyeth, U.S. painter.

DEATHS

"Diamond Jim" Brady, U.S. financier.

Mother Cabrini, Italian-U.S. Roman Catholic nun.

"Buffalo Bill" Cody, U.S. showman.

Edgar Degas, French painter.

George Dewey, U.S. admiral.

Emile Durkheim, French sociologist.

Scott Joplin, U.S. musician and composer.

Auguste Rodin, French sculptor.

Ferdinand von Zeppelin, German aeronautical designer.

Painting & Sculpture: *Portrait of a Girl* (Amedeo Modigliani); *Parade amoureuse* (Francis Picabia) ... Film: *The Immigrant* (Charlie Chaplin); *The Poor Little Rich Girl* (with Mary Pickford); *Terje Vigen* (Victor Sjöström) ... Theater: *Right You Are, If You Think You Are* (Luigi Pirandello); *Dear Brutus* (J.M. Barrie); *Our Betters* (W. Somerset Maugham); *Maytime* (Sigmund Romberg).

"This war is a businessman's war, and we don't see why we should go out and get shot in order to save the lovely state of affairs that we now enjoy."—**A defendant at the IWW trial**

NEW IN 1917

Bayerische Motoren Werke (BMW).

Baseball games on Sunday (Cincinnati Reds vs. New York Giants at the Polo Grounds in New York).

Bobbed hair.

Pulitzer prizes (awarded for biography, history, journalism).

The *World Book* encyclopedia.

IN THE UNITED STATES

▶POET OF UNCONVENTIONALITY—No one embodied the life of the bohemian better than the poet, dramatist, and occasional actress Edna St. Vincent Millay. Her move to Greenwich Village in 1917 coincided with the publication of her first book, *Renascence and Other Poems.* Influenced by John Keats and Gerard Manley Hopkins, Millay, the most famous poet of her day, used a conventional style to celebrate the unconventional. When in her second book she

wrote, "My candle burns at both ends," she captured the sentiment of her literary generation, who had shed the Victorian mores of their parents in favor of a new freedom of love and expression.

▶*THE MASSES*—The journalistic counterpart to Edna Millay's poetic sensibility was the Greenwich Village weekly *The Masses.* Under editor Max Eastman, the newspaper was the leading organ of left-wing intellectuals. In 1917,

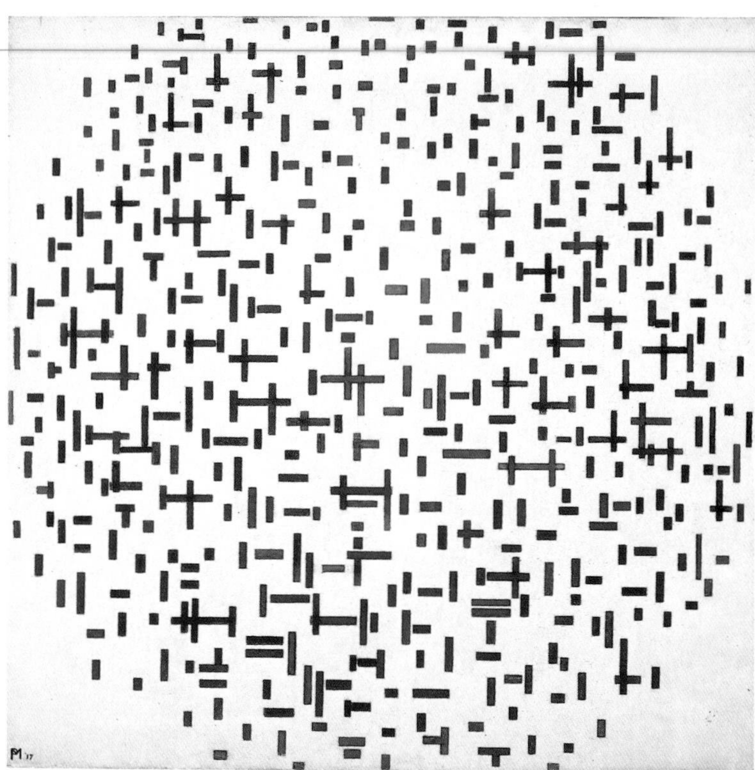

Piet Mondrian's *Composition in Black and White* from 1917. De Stijl, the art movement he led, was the forerunner of Bauhaus and International Style architecture.

ART

Mondrian and De Stijl

6 With the humble proposal "to make modern man receptive to what is new in the visual arts," a group of avant-garde Dutch artists got together in the summer of 1917 to publish *De Stijl (The Style)*. This small art magazine, which never sold more than 300 copies, was the germination of one of modern art and architecture's most influential movements. Artist-provocateur Theo van Doesburg edited the journal, and the painters Bart van der Leck and Vilmos Huszár contributed. But the prime mover was the radically abstract painter Piet Mondrian. His artistic theories, expounded in the magazine, became De Stijl the movement.

Opinionated, ascetic, evangelical, Mondrian was a holy man of modern art. His signature paintings—the famous geometric grids in which rectangles of pure red, blue, and yellow are delineated by strong black lines—expressed his quasi-religious belief in harmony: individual elements stripped to essentials, perfectly integrated into a collective whole. In the future, Mondrian said, universal harmony would evolve into a social utopia on earth (an appealing idea in the war-torn world of 1917). Until that time, the job of the artist was to interpret and reveal a natural order. Belief in harmony created by the artist, faith in the redemptive power of technology, and commitment to the social role of art became the central tenets of De Stijl.

Characterized by total abstraction, exclusive use of primary colors on a neutral background, and strict angularity of vertical and horizontal lines, Mondrian's "neoplasticist" paintings garnered much attention after the war, helping to spread the gospel of De Stijl and contributing to such quintessentially modern artistic developments as Bauhaus and International Style architecture. **◂1910.6 ▸1919.9**

SOCIAL REFORM

Wobblies Are Disabled

7 The war heightened political repression in almost every country, from the autocratic to the democratic. In the United States, draconian laws against sedition and hindrance of the war effort were passed in 1917. Thousands of individuals were prosecuted for preaching peace, and one important organization was virtually destroyed: the Industrial Workers of the World.

The radical labor union had been flourishing with the wartime production boom, reaching a peak membership of some 100,000. Despite having suffered lynchings, massacres, beatings, and arrests, the Wobblies (as they were nicknamed) had continued to stage walkouts and slowdowns—and to advocate revolution. Although the union took no official position on the war (its members in the high-paying armaments industry quietly did their jobs), newspapers spread rumors that the IWW was financed by Germany, and that it planned destructive sabotage. Even President Wilson told his attorney general that the Wobblies "certainly are worthy of being suppressed."

On September 5, Justice Department officials raided 48 IWW meeting halls, seizing five tons of written material (much of it undeniably antiwar). Later that month, 165 of the union's leaders were arrested for conspiring to obstruct the draft, encourage desertion, and intimidate others in labor disputes. The following April, 101 of them went on trial—a five-month ordeal that was America's longest criminal trial to date.

The jury found all the defendants guilty, including IWW founder William "Big Bill" Haywood, who, with 14 others, was sentenced to 20 years in prison. Haywood jumped bail and fled to the Soviet Union, where he died ten years later.

The IWW had been decapitated; it continued with feeble, sporadic activities, but it was effectively dead. Ironically, many embittered former members were driven into the arms of America's nascent Communist Party (formed in 1919)—an organi-

The IWW's initials, said detractors, stood for "Imperial Wilhelm's Warriors."

SPORTS: Baseball: World Series, Chicago White Sox (Eddie Cicotte, Red Faber) defeat New York Giants, 4–2 ... Hockey: Toronto Arenas are the first team to use man-made ice ... Horse Racing: Thoroughbred Man O'War is foaled in Kentucky.

zation far less democratic and with far deeper "foreign" ties than the anarchic, homegrown Wobblies. **◂1912.M ▸1919.6**

LITERATURE
Valéry's Comeback

8 Having abandoned poetry 25 years earlier (out of artistic frustration exacerbated by an unhappy love affair), Paul Valéry re-emerged in 1917 at age 46 as the major "new" poet of the year with a 512-line, introspective monologue titled "La Jeune Parque" ("The Young Fate"). The poem, which Valéry had begun at the urging of his friend André Gide, lacked a conventional narrative; instead, Valéry evoked a series of psychological states in the mind of a young woman—nominally the youngest of the three ancient Fates—as she sits by the sea at dawn and considers the pains and pleasures of human life. Valéry claimed that he had little interest in poetry, that he used literary composition the same way a scientist uses mathematics, as a shorthand for the workings of his mind. Poetry, Valéry said, was his way of expressing "that thing … which is obscurely attempted by cries, tears, caresses, kisses, sighs."

When asked once why he was a writer, Valéry replied, "Through weakness."

"La Jeune Parque" cemented Valéry's position in the French literary canon. His later work linked the Symbolists of the nineteenth century with the Modernists of the twentieth. **▸1918.9**

WORLD WAR I
America Declares War

9 Woodrow Wilson had tried hard to keep America out of World War I. Not only was he reluctant to send his countrymen to die in a war whose moral basis was unclear, but peace was better business. While the European powers destroyed one another, the United States grew rich off exports and international banking. But by early 1917, after making repeated efforts to bring the warring countries to the bargaining table, Wilson felt he had no other choice.

Two factors forced his hand. The first was Germany's war on commercial shipping. For two years, in response to the Allied blockade of German waters, the Germans had attacked unarmed ships in British waters. In January they announced that, as of February 1, they would sink any ship near any Allied country. By mid-March, German submarines had torpedoed three U.S. nonbelligerent vessels, as well as some 1.3 million tons of Allied ships. Dozens of Americans were among the casualties. Then U.S. agents intercepted the so-called "Zimmermann telegram"—a secret message (in all likelihood a setup) from the German foreign minister ordering his ambassador in Mexico to offer Mexico aid in retaking New Mexico, Texas, and Arizona from the United States. In April, proclaiming that "the world must be made safe for democracy," Wilson asked Congress to declare war.

U.S. troops arrived in France in June, and went into combat in October—just in time to fill the vacuum created by the Russian Revolution. The Russian army was in chaos; by fall it had lost more territory than it had won the previous year. Mutiny was spreading, and soon the Bolsheviks were suing for peace. This left the Central Powers free to focus on Italy, their weakest enemy. An Austro-German offensive drove Italian forces out of the Isonzo River region almost to Venice. France and Britain had to detach two armies from the Western Front to help protect Italy's heartland.

These setbacks far outweighed the Allies' successes, which included pushing the Central Powers back several miles around the Somme and the Aisne, and at Verdun, Arras, Cambrai, and Flanders. (Even so, Allied casualties were enormous, and the retreating German troops laid waste to towns and fields.) The British rallied in Mesopotamia, driving back the Turks, and in December they took Jerusalem. Aided by T.E. Lawrence, the British engineered an uprising in Arabia. Most of these gains, however, were more symbolic than strategic. China, Siam, and several Latin American nations, emulating the United States, declared war on Germany. Greece followed suit in late June. But none of these countries could provide a decisive edge. It was up to the Americans to determine the fate of the Allies in the following year. **◂1916.1 ▸1918.1**

American doughboys, the *poilus* (literally, "hairy ones") in Paris—a welcome sight to their French counterparts.

IN THE UNITED STATES

19-year-old Dorothy Day, a socialist, suffragist, and future founder of the *Catholic Worker*, joined a staff that also included such noted artists as John Sloan, George Bellows, and Boardman Robinson, who

all created acerbic political cartoons *(above)*. The following year, *The Masses* was suppressed by the government for its antiwar stance. ▸1917.7

▶"I WANT YOU"—James Montgomery Flagg, a New York illustrator, used his own face to depict Uncle Sam for

recruitment posters. The U.S. Army distributed four million copies of his image.

▶MILLIKAN AND ELECTRON—University of Chicago physicist Robert Andrews Millikan published *The Electron* in 1917, describing his experiments with atomic particles. A onetime student of Max Planck, Millikan first determined the precise charge of an electron in 1912. Four years later he confirmed Einstein's equation for photoelectric effect. ◂1916.9 ▸1919.5

▶WIRELESS IN A BOX—David Sarnoff (familiar to American newspaper readers as the wireless operator who accidentally picked up the message that the *Titanic* was sinking) in 1917 suggested to the American Marconi Company that it sell a simple "radio music box" that, he predicted, would eventually become a fixture in every household. ◂1912.1 ▸1920.3

POLITICS & BUSINESS: GNP: $60.4 billion … U.S. declares war on Germany … General "Black Jack" Pershing recalled from pursuit of Pancho Villa to head U.S. war forces … U.S. has more than 40,000 millionaires … Suffragists picket White House, 10 arrested, 4 sentenced to 6 months … Camel cigarettes have over 30% of the U.S. market … Union Carbide and Carbon, and Phillips Petroleum founded.

"There are those of us who came here with no illusions. We have none because we know that the government, the Church, and the capitalists are the born enemies of the worker."—**Nicolás Cano, a delegate to the 1917 Mexican Constitutional Convention**

WORLD WAR I

▶ALLIED OFFENSIVE—On March 16, Austro-German troops—anticipating a renewed Allied offensive along the Western Front—threw the Allies off-balance by falling back to the previously prepared defenses *(the Hindenburg line, below)* along the

Aisne River. The offensive included the Battle of Arras (April 9-May 4), in which Canadian troops overran the heavily fortified Vimy Ridge. The British gained four miles of German-held territory, but could not keep it. Reckless French losses on the Aisne and at Champagne, combined with news of a March revolt of Russian troops, led to a paralyzing mutiny among French troops.

▶THIRD BATTLE OF YPRES—The British opened the third major offensive around the small village of Ypres (July 31-November 10) by successfully gaining the high ground at Messines. But the advance was ultimately halted after heavy rainfall and Allied bombardment turned the battlefield into a swamp.

▶FATAL FEMALE—Exotic dancer and convicted spy Mata Hari faced the firing squad on October 15. While French officials had long known of her German contacts, they lacked conclusive evidence until they intercepted a damning telegram. At least 50,000 Allied casualties were attributed to her treachery. ◂1905.4

▶BATTLE OF CAMBRAI—The British began their attack on November 20, with 324 tanks in a mass assault. The battle marked the first use of tanks—introduced as a weapon in 1916—in a mass assault, and established a new form of warfare.

THE MIDDLE EAST

Hopes for a Homeland

10 On the surface, the November 2, 1917, Balfour Declaration was merely a letter from Lord Arthur Balfour, the British foreign secretary, to Baron Lionel Walter Rothschild, a British Jewish leader, declaring British support for a Jewish national home in Palestine. But the document's outward simplicity belied the international political machinations behind it. The letter would become the hope of a long-persecuted Jewish people, the bane of a budding Arab nationalism, and a bloody tether binding Great Britain to its shrinking empire in ways it could never have anticipated.

By 1917, the Allies were making plans for the postwar Middle East, with the British and the French jockeying for hegemony. At the same time, efforts by the young World Zionist Organization and Zionist leaders Chaim Weizmann and Nahum Sokolow to secure support for Jewish historical claims to a national home in Palestine were also reaching a climax.

The British had a political interest in placating both Jews and Arabs. A Palestinian Jewish community, made up of Jews from Poland and postrevolutionary Russia with sentimental attachments to Britain, would, the British believed, safeguard British Middle Eastern commerce, the Suez Canal, and their route to India. The cooperation of Arab leaders was equally crucial.

Consequently, the Balfour Declaration viewed "with favour the establishment in Palestine of a national home for the Jewish people," but stopped short of granting outright statehood. It specifically stated that, although Britain supported Jewish aspirations, nothing could be done to abrogate the rights of other indigenous groups.

The World Zionist Organization was nonetheless enthusiastic. And the increasingly nationalistic Arabs, with whom Jewish settlers had lived in relative peace since the end of the last century, became anxious at the prospect of massive Jewish immigration to Palestine.

Lord Arthur Balfour: attempting to appease all parties.

By July 1922, the Balfour Declaration had become part of the British mandate over Palestine approved by the League of Nations. **◂1904.M ▸1920.2**

MEXICO

A Surprise for Carranza

11 In the first election after the revolution, Venustiano Carranza became president of Mexico on May 1, 1917. Unlike Pancho Villa and Emiliano Zapata, who led

Emiliano Zapata, in a mural by Diego Rivera: Carranza kept the revolutionary leader at arm's length.

peasant campaigns in the revolt, Carranza was a moderate from the middle class. When he'd called a constituent assembly the previous year to draw up a new constitution, Carranza had handpicked the delegates in an effort to consolidate his power. The peasants and their leaders were kept at arm's length.

The delegates—lawyers, engineers, schoolteachers, generals, journalists, doctors, store clerks, and businessmen—surprised Carranza by writing an unexpectedly radical constitution. Article 27 dismantled the notorious hacienda system, which had kept the peasantry in virtual serfdom, and created the legal mechanism for redistribution of land. Article 123, called the Magna Carta of Mexican labor, established some of the most liberal labor regulations in the world: an eight-hour workday, a minimum wage, legalization of unions, and child work restrictions. Anticlerical articles divested the Catholic Church of extensive property and restricted its participation in education and politics.

Carranza accepted the new constitution only under pressure. During his presidency, he flatly refused to implement the provisions for land reform and labor regulation. The followers of Villa and Zapata continued to agitate, and Mexico's fragile stability soon collapsed. By 1920 Carranza had been murdered, and the internal battle for control of the country was once again in full cry. **◂1916.6 ▸1919.M**

TECHNOLOGY

Fresh from the Freezer

12 Clarence Birdseye returned to his native New York in 1917 from several years of fur trading in Labrador determined to perfect the methods of freezing fresh foods he had witnessed among the Eskimos. He discovered that rapid freezing, which the Eskimos practiced in their subzero-temperature environment, sealed in food's freshness much more effectively than slow freezing, which took up to 18 hours. With the latter method, ice crystals would form and break down the cell walls, destroying the tissues and fibers of the food and robbing it of freshness. By freezing the food in a mist of brine at –57°C, Birdseye found that the taste and texture could be preserved for months. He spent $7 for a fan, ice, and salt to test his method. Later, a friend gave Birdseye a corner in his icehouse to continue his experiments.

Clarence Birdseye sold his company in 1929, but his name became synonymous with frozen food.

In 1924, he and three partners formed General Seafoods Company in Gloucester, Massachusetts, to quick-freeze and market fish fillets, giving birth to a multibillion-dollar industry that revolutionized the way food is marketed and how the world eats. In 1929, the Postum Company, later General Foods, paid Birdseye $22 million for his company and the rights to use the patented Birdseye process. **▸1923.11**

NOBEL PRIZES: Peace: International Red Cross (1863) ... Literature: Karl Gjellerup (Danish; poet) and Henrik Pontopiddan (Danish; novelist) ... Chemistry: No award ... Medicine: No award ... Physics: Charles Barkla (U.K.; X-ray analysis of elements).

A VOICE FROM 1917

A Song for the Yankee Soldiers

"Over There," by George M. Cohan, 1917

On the morning of April 6, 1917, banner headlines proclaimed America's declaration of war on Germany. Actor, musical producer, and popular songwriter George M. Cohan was at his home in Great Neck, New York, getting ready to go to work. "I read those war headlines," he later recalled, "and I got to thinking and humming to myself—and for a minute I thought I was going to dance. I was all finished with the chorus and the verse by the time I got to town, and I also had a title." The song, "Over There," *was a major success and became inextricably tied to the memory of World War I.*

Within three months of publication, 400,000 copies of the sheet music had been sold; sales topped the two-million mark by the end of the war. It was recorded by many singers of the day, including opera star Enrico Caruso, and sold over a million records. President Woodrow Wilson described the song as "a genuine inspiration to all American manhood," and its message of hope and defiance was soon on the lips of the Tommies, poilus, and doughboys in the trenches all along the Western Front. The song won Cohan a belated Congressional Medal of Honor in 1940. **◄1904.M ►1918.1**

Song-and-dance man George M. Cohan *(left)* was the original Yankee Doodle Boy on Broadway in *Little Johnny Jones* (1904). "Over There" tapped into the same patriotic spirit.

Johnnie get your gun, get your gun, get your gun
Take it on the run, on the run, on the run
Hear them calling you and me
Ev'ry son of liberty

Hurry right away, no delay, go today
Make your daddy glad to have had such a lad
Tell your sweetheart not to pine
To be proud her boy's in line.

Over there, over there
Send the word, send the word over there
That the Yanks are coming, the Yanks are coming
The drums rum-tumming ev'rywhere

So prepare, say a pray'r
Send the word, send the word to beware
We'll be over, we're coming over
And we won't come back till it's over over there.
Over there.

Johnnie get your gun, get your gun, get your gun
Johnnie show the Hun you're a son of a gun
Hoist the flag and let her fly
Yankee Doodle do or die

Pack your little kit, show your grit, do your bit
Yankees to the ranks from the towns and the tanks
Make your mother proud of you
And the old Red White and Blue.

Over there, over there
Send the word, send the word over there
That the Yanks are coming, the Yanks are coming
The drums rum-tumming ev'rywhere

So prepare, say a pray'r
Send the word, send the word to beware
We'll be over, we're coming over
And we won't come back till it's over over there.
Over there.

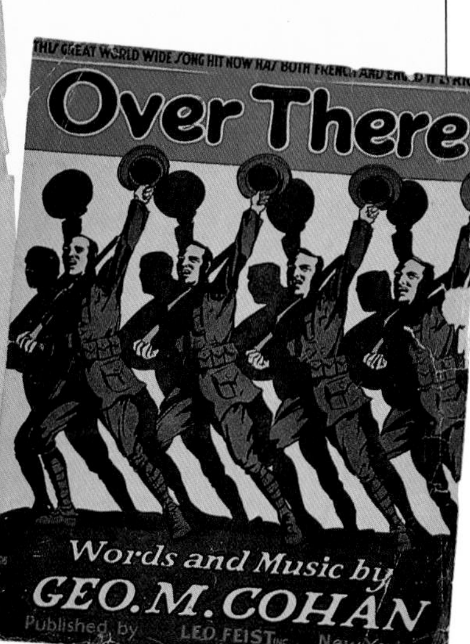

"Better a terrible end than terror without end."—**German socialist Philipp Scheidemann, commenting on Germany's surrender in World War I**

STORY OF THE YEAR

Allies Victorious

1 "The culminating and final war for human liberty," as Woodrow Wilson optimistically called World War I, ended officially on November 11, 1918, when the Germans signed an armistice near Compiègne, France. The Allied victory came after some of the conflict's bloodiest fighting, but it resulted as much from politics as from military strategy.

The Allies had suffered major setbacks between March and July, when Germany launched five massive offensives on the Western Front, hoping to crush its opponents before the Americans reached full fighting strength. Breaking through battle lines that had been nearly stationary for four years, the attacks cost each side hundreds of thousands of men. The defenders hung on doggedly until the Germans extended themselves as far as they could. Then, with American soldiers arriving at a rate of 10,000 a day, the Allies counterattacked. Soon the invaders were retreating all along the front.

American troops (from New York) in Cambrai, France, celebrate the armistice with a makeshift Liberty Bell.

Meanwhile, the Bulgarians were driven from Serbia and the Austrians from Italy. Bulgaria, threatened with an Allied invasion, surrendered on September 30. This left the Ottoman Turks vulnerable at home, while their territories in the Near East were overrun by British and Arab troops. The Turks capitulated on October 30, and Austria-Hungary sued for peace on November 3. Germany could not go on alone for long.

The arrival of four million fresh American troops was not the only factor in the collapse of the Central Powers. By summer, both sides in the war zone faced exhaustion and severe shortages. Yet among the Allied nations (excluding breakaway Russia, which had signed a separate peace with its former enemies in March), hardship bred unity. Their armies finally agreed to follow a supreme commander, France's Marshal Ferdinand Foch, and political dissent at home was reduced to a whisper. Among the Allies' foes, however, dissension was rampant. In Germany and Austria-Hungary, peace movements flourished. German officials wrangled publicly over the conduct of the war. German and Austro-Hungarian troops grew mutinous. All four Central Powers bickered over how they would carve up the spoils of their expected victory. In October, revolution broke out in Germany and throughout the Austro-Hungarian Empire. The people could tolerate the slaughter no more. **◂1917.9 ▸1918.6**

The Fordson changed farming, but a rival company, International Harvester, eventually drove Ford out of the tractor business.

TECHNOLOGY

Tractors Revolutionize Farming

2 One machine helped win World War I without ever seeing combat. By March 1918, only a year after its invention, the world's first mass-produced tractor was being turned out at a rate of 80 a day. Henry Ford's lightweight, cheap Fordson allowed American farmers to meet soaring wartime demand as draught horses and manpower were shipped off to the fight. Just three years earlier, tractors had been so expensive and cumbersome that less than 1 percent of U.S. farms had used them.

The tractor revolution came to Europe (outside the Soviet Union) only after World War II, and was controlled by government policies. But in America, it began with the first Fordson and continued to accelerate through the 1920s. At first the changes all seemed good. Land once reserved for feed could now grow crops. For the first time in history, crop surpluses became the norm.

But with surpluses came low crop prices. Farmers couldn't cut back: They needed to produce as much as possible to pay off loans for equipment. As they expanded and specialized, they grew dependent on costly chemical fertilizers and pesticides. More and more family farms went bankrupt; as banks foreclosed on them, corporate "agribusiness" moved in. During the Depression, the federal government began granting subsidies to farmers, but the biggest beneficiaries were large landowners. Meanwhile, cities continued to swell with displaced farmers—and farmhands rendered obsolete by mechanization. In 1910, 32.5 percent of American workers were engaged in agriculture. By 1920, the figure was 25.6 percent, and by 1990, it had shrunk to a minuscule 2.4 percent. **◂1913.6 ▸1944.M**

LITERATURE

Adams's Autobiography

3 Henry Brooks Adams, scholar, biographer, and historian, died in March 1918, prompting the general publication of his brooding autobiography, *The Education of Henry Adams*, the apex of his dark and profoundly pessimistic intellectual journey.

Adams had every advantage that nineteenth-century America could offer: His grandfather (John Quincy Adams) and great-grandfather (John Adams) were U.S. presidents; his father, Charles Francis Adams, was a diplomat and congressman; and his mother, Abigail Brown Brooks, was a descendant of one of Boston's oldest families. Adams himself graduated from prestigious Harvard University and eventually returned there as a professor of medieval history.

But where his contemporaries saw latitude and privilege, Adams saw only acute disappointment and intellectual torpor. His countrymen, he wrote, "had no time for thought; they saw, and could see, nothing beyond their day's work; their attitude to the universe outside them was that of the deep-sea fish."

With its understated tone, *The Education of Henry Adams* (which had been published privately twelve years earlier) repudiated the writer's Brahmin upbringing and his elitist education. Adopting the symbol of "the dynamo" as a

ART & CULTURE: Books: ***My Antonia*** **(Willa Cather);** ***Cornhuskers*** **(Carl Sandburg);** ***Tarr*** **(Wyndham Lewis);** ***Valmouth*** **(Ronald Firbank)... Music: "K-K-K-Katy" (Geoffrey O'Hara); "Oh, How I Hate to Get Up in the Morning" (Irving Berlin);** ***Bluebeard's Castle*** **(Béla Bartók);** ***The Soldier's Story*** **(Igor Stravinsky) ... Painting & Sculpture:** ***White on White*** **(Kasimir Malevich);** ***The Crucifixion*** **(Georges Rouault);**

"The world will never know what we did with them."—**Boast attributed to a Bolshevik commissar at the time of the Romanovs' execution**

metaphor for the new, godless world of technology, Adams described his quest for enlightenment as a notorious failure, his education as hopelessly defective. Such extended self-examination (albeit intellectual, not emotional: He never mentions his wife's 1885 suicide, for example) was without precedent in American letters. *The Education* broke new literary ground, redefining the genre of American autobiography. **◂1902.7**

LITERATURE

Strachey in Bloomsbury

4 Queen Victoria had been dead for years, but the Victorian era lingered on until World War I dealt it a fatal blow. But it was the 1918 publication of Lytton Strachey's *Eminent Victorians*—a collection of irreverent biographical sketches of such idols as Florence Nightingale and General Charles "Chinese" Gordon —that buried the corpse. Others had lampooned Victorian pomp, prudery, and imperial pretensions, but no one had done it with Strachey's verve, erudition, and malicious wit. A hit with postwar youth, the book transformed biographical writing. Traditional life-and-letters tomes tended to be adoring and tedious. *Eminent Victorians* was a masterpiece of concision, more concerned with probing character and personal relationships than with cataloguing accomplishments.

Strachey's refined iconoclasm was characteristic of the Bloomsbury group—a circle of left-leaning intellectuals who from 1907 to 1930 met at the houses of painter Vanessa Bell and her sister, author Virginia Woolf, in London's Bloomsbury section. Devoted to the analytic philosophy of Cambridge don G.E. Moore, mostly educated at Cambridge, and mostly ex-Apostles (the university's elite discussion club), the "Bloomsberries" were among the most influential English-language thinkers of their time. In addition to Woolf, Bell, and Strachey, their ranks included economist John Maynard Keynes, novelist E.M. Forster, critics Roger Fry and Clive Bell (Vanessa's husband), and essayist Leonard Woolf (Virginia's). **▸1929.V**

THE SOVIET UNION

Romanovs Executed

5 The fledgling regime in Russia had planned a grandiose public trial for the deposed czar. Leon Trotsky, darling of the revolutionary intelligentsia, was to prosecute. But in the summer of 1918, civil war forced the new leaders to make a rash decision. As the anti-Bolshevik White Army neared Ekaterinburg, the Ural Mountain city where Czar Nicholas II and his family were being detained, the Soviet government authorized their immediate execution.

On the evening of July 16, Nicholas, his wife, Alexandra, and their five children—four daughters and Alexis, the 14-year-old heir apparent—were ordered to the cellar of their detention house. Gunfire nearby made the upper floors unsafe, the guards told them. The family complied, suspecting nothing. In the cellar, a hastily assembled firing squad met the Romanovs with a hail of bullets at close range. Four servants died with the family. The shooting continued until the air was thick with smoke. The Czar and Czarina died instantly. Some of the children were less lucky. An official memorandum of the murder notes Alexis's "strange vitality." His sisters may have been partially shielded by the jewelry hidden in their corsets. The executioners finished their grisly work with bayonets.

To prevent enemies of the new Soviet state from displaying the Romanovs' bodies as relics of martyrdom, the ravaged corpses were thrown down a mine shaft. Later, they were moved to a shallow grave in the forest and drenched with acid to prevent recognition. The government said nothing, and the whereabouts of the bodies became the most notorious mystery of the revolution. Rumors circulated that either Alexis or his sister Anastasia had somehow escaped. Throughout the century dozens of women claimed to be Anastasia, most notably Anna Anderson, who materialized in Berlin in 1920, speaking Russian and bearing scars from a brutal assault. She died in 1984, her assertions widely dismissed. Then, in 1991, an unmarked grave in Ekaterinburg was officially identified as that of the Romanovs. Authorities recovered the remains of nine bodies, two short of the expected total. Although DNA tests performed in 1994 on a tissue sample from Anderson's intestine and compared with a blood sample donated by Britain's Prince Philip (related through his mother to Alexandra) showed that Anderson was *not* Anastasia, the full story surrounding the Romanovs' deaths remains hazy. **◂1917.1 ▸1919.8**

An artist's depiction of the sloppy, ill-conceived execution of Nicholas II and his family.

BIRTHS

Ingmar Bergman, Swedish director.

Leonard Bernstein, U.S. composer and conductor.

Nicolae Ceaușescu, Romanian president.

Richard Feynman, U.S. physicist.

Ella Fitzgerald, U.S. singer.

Billy Graham, U.S. evangelist.

Nelson Mandela, South African president.

Gamal Abdal Nasser, Egyptian president.

Jerome Robbins, U.S. choreographer.

Anwar al-Sadat, Egyptian president.

Aleksandr Solzhenitsyn, Russian novelist.

Muriel Spark, U.K. writer.

Mickey Spillane, U.S. novelist.

Jacqueline Susann, U.S. writer.

Kurt Waldheim, Austrian president.

Mike Wallace, U.S. broadcast journalist.

Ted Williams, U.S. baseball player.

DEATHS

Henry Adams, U.S. historian.

Guillaume Apollinaire, French poet.

Vernon Castle, U.K. dancer.

Claude Debussy, French composer.

Raymond Duchamp-Villon, French sculptor.

Gustav Klimt, Austrian painter.

Nicholas II, Russian czar.

Wilfred Owen, U.K. poet.

Georgi Plekhanov, Russian socialist theorist.

Edmond Rostand, French playwright.

Egon Schiele, Austrian painter.

Seated Youth **(Wilhelm Lehmbruck) ... Film: *Shoulder Arms* (Charlie Chaplin); *Hearts of the World* (D.W. Griffith); *The Whispering Chorus* (Cecil B. DeMille); *Father Sergius* (Yakov Protazanov, with Ivan Mozhukhin) ... Theater: *Mystery-Bouffe* (Vladimir Mayakovsky); *Yip Yip Yaphank* (Irving Berlin); *Oh, Lady! Lady!* (Kern, Bolton, and Wodehouse).**

"Make your dirt by yourselves."—**King Frederick of Saxony's farewell message to Germany after the collapse of the Austro-Hungarian Empire**

NEW IN 1918

Airmail service.

United Lutheran Church.

Three-color traffic light (New York City).

Daylight Savings Time.

***Stars & Stripes* magazine.**

Granulated laundry soap (Rinso, from Lever Brothers).

Raggedy Ann doll.

Ripley's "Believe It or Not!"

Pop-up toaster (patented by U.S. inventor Charles Strite).

Kotex sanitary napkins.

Suffrage for women over 30 and all men over 21 in Britain.

IN THE UNITED STATES

▶LIBERTY BONDS—In spite of a low interest rate, more than $18 billion in Liberty Bonds were sold to support the war effort, with sales peaking in 1918. Their appeal

was enhanced by pitches from such Hollywood superstars as Charlie Chaplin, Mary Pickford, and Douglas Fairbanks.

▶A MODERN COPERNICUS—While working at California's Mount Wilson Observatory in 1918, astronomer Harlow Shapely made the discovery that earned him the nickname "a modern Copernicus." By measuring the distances between globular clusters—closely aligned groups of up to one million stars—Shapely noticed that the majority of known clusters formed a

During the Berlin riots, German troops used a recently captured British tank to patrol the city and protect police headquarters.

WORLD WAR I

Empires Crumble

6 The Austro-Hungarian and German empires fell in 1918 within days of each other, but in markedly different ways. Austria-Hungary, always an uneasy amalgam of peoples, simply dissolved into its component parts. Emperor Charles started the process in mid-October: Amid strikes and demonstrations, he decreed his realm a federation of semi-independent states. Within a month his subjects had taken matters further. The southern Slavs joined Serbia to form the Kingdom of the Serbs, Croats, and Slovenes (later Yugoslavia); the Czechs, Slovaks, and Ruthenians proclaimed the republic of Czechoslovakia; and Austria, Hungary, and Poland split into separate republics. Charles went into exile.

The German empire, by contrast, had already been reduced to Germany itself. Territories in Africa, China, and the South Pacific had been stripped away during the war. (Only in East Africa did colonial troops continue fighting until the end.) By late October, most Germans knew total defeat was imminent. A series of hasty reforms, clearly undertaken in hopes that the Allies would offer lenient surrender terms, exposed the imperial government's weakness.

When the German navy was ordered to make a last-ditch attack on the British fleet, its sailors rebelled. After they seized the main naval base, at Kiel, on November 3, the revolt was taken up by soldiers and civilians nationwide. Organizing themselves in councils modeled on Russia's soviets, they met little resistance—and soon the rebels had invaded the imperial palace in Berlin. On November 9, Kaiser Wilhelm's chancellor, Prince Max of Baden, summoned Social Democratic Party chairman Friedrich Ebert, leader of the largest faction in the parliament. "I commend the German Reich to your loving care," Max said. The next morning, Kaiser Wilhelm fled to Holland.

The center-left Social Democrats joined with the more radical Independents to form a government they called the Council of People's Commissars. Its rhetoric and other trappings resembled those of the Bolsheviks to the east. But power took these socialists by surprise; they weren't prepared to try to remake society. Their actions in the next few months saved Germany from the ravages of a Russian-style revolution, but set the stage for ravages of quite another kind. **◂1917.1 ▸1919.2**

MEDICINE

Flu Pandemic

7 A mysterious, exceedingly virulent strain of influenza appeared without warning in spring 1918 and swept the globe in three terrible waves over the next year. Then, just as suddenly, it vanished.

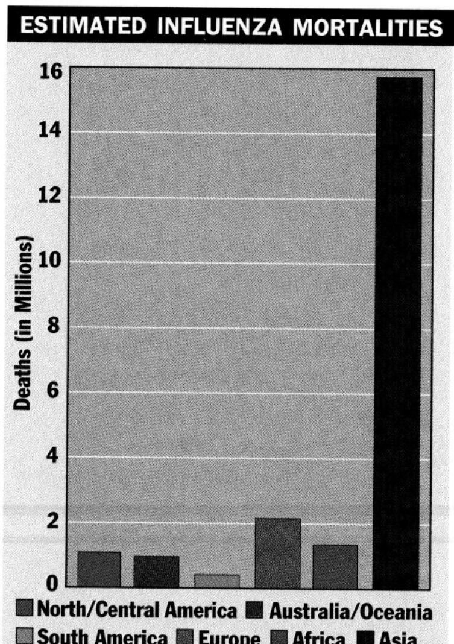

The flu pandemic claimed more victims in a year—an astounding 21,642,274—than had been wounded in four years of World War I.

The war was instrumental in the spread of the disease, which was known as the Spanish flu for the rapacity of its attack in Spain. From three distant military ports—Freetown, Sierra Leone; Brest, France; and Boston, Massachusetts—the flu radiated in all directions, communicated by sailors and soldiers to the civilian population. Before long, six continents were infected, and the number of sick troops hampered the war effort.

In the United States, San Francisco passed ordinances mandating the wearing of surgical masks, and Chicago movie theaters, in cooperation with the Department of Health, refused to admit coughing patrons. Despite those and similar efforts elsewhere, it is estimated that half the world's population was touched by the pandemic of 1918. **◂1907.3 ▸1955.1**

CZECHOSLOVAKIA

Masaryk Declares a Republic

8 The son of a Slovak father and Czech mother, Tomáš Masaryk was a philosophy professor and member of Austria-Hungary's parliament before he fled to London at the beginning of the war. There, the man who became known to his admirers as *Taticek* (Little Father), founded the Czech National Council, which lobbied the Allied governments and raised an exile army to fight the Central Powers. Masaryk was in America in 1918, when Hapsburg emperor Charles decreed the Austro-Hungarian Empire a federation of semiautonomous states. On October 14, at Philadelphia's Independence Hall, Masaryk declared Czechoslovakia a republic. The National Council became the provisional government, and elected him president. Two weeks later, a peaceful revolution swept the Bohemian capital of Prague, and a jubilant crowd pulled down the column the Hapsburgs had erected 300 years earlier to mark their victory over the Czechs.

Masaryk returned in December to face a nation of 13.5 million people. Cobbled together from Bohemia, Moravia, Slovakia, and some smaller territories, it was an unlikely household: Czech urbanites, Slovak and Ruthenian peasants, and a host of minorities whose loyalties lay elsewhere. The country, moreover, was surrounded

SPORTS: Baseball: World Series, Boston Red Sox (Babe Ruth now primarily an outfielder) defeat Chicago Cubs, 4–2 ... Football: Knute Rockne named head coach at Notre Dame (will have 105–12–5 record over next 13 years) ... Boxing: Jack Dempsey, now the "Manassa Mauler," knocks out Carl Morris in 14 sec. ... Horse Racing: Exterminator, a 30-to-1 shot, wins Kentucky Derby.

by ambitious neighbors. Nonetheless, with the help of Foreign Minister Eduard Beneš, Masaryk intended to create "a fortress of liberty in the heart of Europe and the advance guard of democracy towards the east."

Philosopher, statesman, and humanist Tomáš Masaryk.

For two decades, Czechoslovakia thrived. But after Masaryk's retirement in 1935, the nation began to crumble under pressure from Germany. Its fall would be part of the chain reaction that exploded into World War II. **◂1918.6 ▸1936.8**

LITERATURE

Poetry's New Spirit

9 Guillaume Apollinaire spent his short life shaking up the literary establishment with his radical ideas about the role of art and the supremacy of truth over beauty. When he died in 1918, at 38, Apollinaire was the acknowledged master of the modern aesthetic—a "new spirit" that asked poetry to scrutinize *all* aspects of life and to render them in contemporary language, unfettered. He believed that poetry must exploit new ideas to keep pace with the modern world.

Apollinaire's early work was influenced by the nineteenth-century French symbolists—Verlaine, Rimbaud, Mallarmé—but around 1903 he fell in with artists who became the Parisian avant-garde, including Picasso, Braque, and the early absurdist playwright Alfred Jarry. Apollinaire's flamboyant personality and eccentric habits attracted many followers who, together, comprised a whole prewar generation that looked outward into a world overflowing with raw material—thanks to such innovations as the automobile, the airplane, motion pictures, and radio. Believing such new experiences demanded a new mode of expression, Apollinaire constructed a system he called "simultaneity." A sort of literary counterpart to cubist painting, it abruptly juxtaposed perceptions and ideas, forcing the reader to synthesize them along with the poet.

Best known for his short stories, verse, and drama (his play *Les Mamelles de Tirésias* is regarded as the first surrealist literary work), Apollinaire also wrote countless articles, translations, book introductions, newspaper columns, and critical reviews. Indeed, he wrote almost constantly, even in the trenches during the war, where he suffered a serious head wound. He was slowly recovering when he contracted the Spanish influenza that killed him. **◂1907.1 ▸1924.3**

Marie Laurencin's 1908 painting of herself and her companion Apollinaire *(center)*, their friends Pablo Picasso and his wife, Fernande Olivier, and Fricka the dog.

IDEAS

Civilization's Obituary

10 The first volume of the magnum opus of an iconoclastic schoolteacher-turned-philosopher appeared in German bookstores in the summer of 1918 and ignited a bitter literary controversy that lasted for the next decade. Oswald Spengler's *Decline of the West*, an immediate commercial—if not critical—success, proposed that civilizations have a distinct organic form that grows, matures, and decays according to a predetermined historical cycle. The West, Spengler believed, had passed from its creative stage into one of reflection and material comfort. What remained was irreversible decline, marked by imperialism and warfare. Spengler, a man of no small ego, was convinced that his philosophy was the worldview to which all nineteenth-century thought had been leading. Critics accused the author of factual errors, shallowness, and incompetence. He countered that they saw only his pessimism and ignored his "ethical" ideas.

The German public, however, embraced the book. Spengler's gloomy predictions provided a kind of comfort to a country seeking to rationalize its postwar despair, as did his conviction that all the nations of the world—even Germany's former foes—were equally doomed. (Later, despite Spengler's personal aversion to Nazism, propaganda minister Joseph Goebbels latched onto him as a kind of prophet.) Spengler died in isolation in 1936, but his view of civilization as a cyclical rather than linear process was later adopted by such scholars as Arnold Toynbee, Pitirim Sorokin, and Alfred Kroeber. **◂1900.11 ▸1934.M**

IN THE UNITED STATES

spherical arrangement around the constellation Sagittarius. Studying this special pattern, Shapely deduced that the sun is not at the center of our galaxy, the Milky Way, but rather is located some 50,000 light-years (later revised to 30,000 light-years) from the center. His investigations into the size and shape of the Milky Way provided the first realistic measurement of our galaxy. ◂1914.10 ▸1929.9

▶DOUGHBOY HERO—Alvin Cullum York's Tennessee draft board had denied his petition to be exempted from service as a conscientious objector. In the Meuse-Argonne offensive, Private York led a successful attack on a German machine gun emplacement that killed 25 Germans. Then, almost single-handedly, York

captured 132 prisoners and 35 machine guns. Awarded the Congressional Medal of Honor and the French Croix de Guerre, he was promoted to Sergeant York on November 1. The war hero later ran for vice president on the Prohibition Party ticket in 1936.

▶DOGFIGHTERS—Clinching his title as America's number-one ace, Eddie Rickenbacker *(below)* outwitted seven German planes in a dogfight on September 25. Frank Luke was less lucky. In combat for only 16 days (and having downed 16 enemy planes), he defied orders and flew to meet ten German Fokkers searching the skies for his Spad. He destroyed two before antiair-

craft shrapnel sent him down behind enemy lines. Before dying, Luke emptied his handgun at approaching enemy troops. ▸1927.V

POLITICS & BUSINESS: GNP: $76.4 ... President Wilson sets out his "Fourteen Points" for peace ... Owen-Keating Child Labor Law is ruled unconstitutional by the Supreme Court ... U.S. Post Office begins regular air mail service ... U.S. begins sugar rationing (8 oz. per week per citizen); Food Administration suggests "wheatless" Mondays and Wednesdays and meatless Tuesdays ... Sauerkraut is now "liberty cabbage."

"Those who are unable to understand are requested by me to maintain an attitude of complete submission and inferiority."
—From Erik Satie's program notes at the first public performance of *Socrate*

WORLD WAR I

▶AMERICAN TROOPS ENTER WAR—From March 21 to July 15, the Germans launched a major offensive against British and French forces on the Western Front in an attempt to defeat them before American reinforcements arrived. The German thrust took Messines Ridge from the British. A surprise attack against the French on the Aisne brought German forces once again within 40 miles of Paris. American troops helped stop the German advance at Château-Thierry, and U.S. Marines captured Belleau Wood June 6, and held it 19 days against continual German assault.

▶RED BARON DIES—Baron Manfred von Richthofen, who led the German air force's "Flying Circus," was shot down on April 21. Credited with 80 "kills," he was buried with full military honors by the Allies.

▶PERSHING'S MAJOR PUSH—The Battle of Amiens had forced the Germans back to the Hindenburg Line in August. American General John J. "Black Jack" Pershing led American troops in their first independent action, September 12-13, at Saint-Mihiel, taking 15,000 prisoners and forcing the Germans to turn over terrain they had held since 1914. In the Battle of the Meuse-Argonne, the Americans drove the Germans from the Argonne forest but suffered enormous losses as the fighting dragged on for more than six weeks.

▶AUSTRIANS SHATTERED—The Austrian army was decimated in the Battle of Vittorio Veneto in Italy, October 24-November 3. Allied forces took several hundred thousand prisoners; the rest of the army fled into Austria.

Communist groups flourished amid the postwar wreckage. Here, a German Red-Guard unit enters Berlin through the Brandenburg Gate.

WORLD WAR I

The Aftermath of War

11 The lasting impact of the war went beyond its cost to those who were killed, disabled, widowed, orphaned, or rendered homeless—and beyond its transformation of the map of Europe and the balance of power. It altered the very way people saw themselves and their place in the world.

The returning soldiers were deeply changed: Millions of unseasoned young men had been exposed to mind-numbing brutality, to the desperate pleasures of military life, and to corners of the planet they might never have visited. An American song of the period asked, "How you gonna keep 'em down on the farm after they've seen Paree?"

But the change in attitude was not limited to those who'd worn a uniform. The civilization that both sides in the war claimed to defend had plunged into an orgy of slaughter. For the next decade, poets, novelists, and painters would produce an art of disorientation and disillusionment. Others would express a similar attitude through extreme lifestyles. The wild hedonism of the 1920s reflected a collective loss of innocence, as did the era's violence—the parade of storm troopers, fascist *squadri*, and leftist street brawlers in Europe, and gangsters in the United States.

The mobilization of whole populations for war had required the systematic use of propaganda on an unprecedented scale. Posters, pamphlets, news reports, and "scientific" studies depicted the enemy as subhuman savages given to vile atrocities. To the Allies, the Germans were Huns, racial and spiritual kin to the ancient barbarians. The Germans sang a "Hymn of Hate" for England. The effects of mass indoctrination lingered, preparing the emotional ground for World War II.

Bureaucracy and industry had expanded enormously in all the combatant nations. Labor shortages had led to new roles for women—and for American blacks, thousands of whom left the rural South for northern factories. But the rise of the downtrodden was matched by heightened social divisions. The war had whipped Americans into a xenophobic frenzy, which later expressed itself in political witch-hunts and a burgeoning Ku Klux Klan. Black soldiers who'd gone off to fight in Europe returned home to discover that the democracy they'd been making the world safe for did not exist for them. In Europe, the polarization of left and right grew sharper than ever, honed by economic dislocations and the specter of the revolution in Russia. A few in every nation called for a return to the old order. But in the postwar era, struggles among the supporters of radically new orders would be the deadliest contests.

◂1918.1 ▸1919.1

MUSIC

Surrealism's Composer

12 With the completion in 1918 of *Socrate,* a vanguard rendering of Plato's *Dialogues* for chamber orchestra and voice, Erik Satie transcended his reputation as a composer of whimsical, incidental music. Lean, focused, stripped of all lingering traces of nineteenth-century Romanticism, the intensely modern *Socrate* marked Satie's emergence from the shadow of his brilliant, domineering friend and rival Claude Debussy, and cemented the "rediscovery" of his music that had been engineered three years earlier by Jean Cocteau. (Satie, Cocteau, Picasso, and Diaghilev collaborated on the 1917 ballet *Parade*, which was scored for typewriters, telegraph tape, airplane propellers, and sirens; its program notes, written by Guillaume Apollinaire, mark the first use of the word "surrealism.")

In ill health, Satie deteriorated quickly after *Socrate*, but his musical ideas outlived him, influencing composers like Maurice Ravel and John Cage. Satie spent the last months before his death in 1925 sitting mutely in a Paris hotel rooms, staring at his reflection in the mirror, and playing with a string contraption he had rigged to operate the lights and doors.

◂1918.9 ▸1924.3

Picasso's drawing of his friend and colleague Erik Satie.

NOBEL PRIZES: Peace: No award ... Literature: No award ... Chemistry: Fritz Haber (German; synthesis of ammonia) ... Medicine: No award ... Physics: Max Planck (German; quantum theory).

A VOICE FROM 1918

The Pride Before the Fall

From *The Magnificent Ambersons,* by Booth Tarkington, 1918

Booth Tarkington was one of the most widely read novelists of his age; between 1902 and 1932, his books appeared on annual bestseller lists nine times. He is remembered today largely for his young people's classics, especially Penrod, *but two of his most important novels for adults,* The Magnificent Ambersons *and* Alice Adams, *won Pulitzer prizes.* The Magnificent Ambersons, *published in 1918, chronicled, in wry, conversational prose, three generations of the wealthy, influential Amberson family of Indiana—their grandeur and their greed, their beauty and their narcissism, their overweening confidence and ultimate failure. In this excerpt, the spoiled and headstrong George Minafer, Major Amberson's only grandchild, receives guests at a party given in honor of his return home from college.* ►1942.M

George, white-gloved, with a gardenia in his buttonhole, stood with his mother and the Major, embowered in the big red and gold drawing room downstairs, to "receive" the guests; and, standing thus together, the trio offered a picturesque example of good looks persistent through three generations. The Major, his daughter, and his grandson were of a type all Amberson: tall, straight, and regular, with dark eyes, short noses, good chins; and the grandfather's expression, no less than the grandson's, was one of faintly amused condescension....

Isabel, standing between her father and her son, caused a vague amazement in the mind of the latter.... The woman ... was a stranger to her son; as completely a stranger as if he had never in his life seen her or heard her voice. And it was tonight, while he stood with her, "receiving," that he caught a disquieting glimpse of this stranger whom he thus fleetingly encountered for the first time.... George was disturbed by a sudden impression, coming upon him out of nowhere, so far as he could detect, that her eyes were brilliant, that she was graceful and youthful—in a word, that she was romantically lovely....

The fantastic moment passed, and even while it lasted, he was doing his duty, greeting two pretty girls with whom he had grown up, as people say, and warmly assuring them that he remembered them very well—an assurance which might have surprised them "in anybody but Georgie Minafer!" It seemed unnecessary, since he had spent many hours with them no longer ago than the preceding August. They had with them their parents and an uncle from out of town; and George negligently gave the parents the same assurance he had given the daughters, but murmured another form of greeting to the out-of-town uncle, whom he had never seen before. This person George absently took note of as a "queer-looking duck." ...

The Sharon girls passed on, taking the queer-looking duck with them, and George became pink with mortification as his mother called his attention to a white-bearded guest waiting to shake his hand. This was George's great-uncle, old John Minafer: it was old John's boast that in spite of his connection by marriage with the Ambersons, he never had worn and never would wear a swaller-tail coat.... George's purpose had been to ignore the man, but he had to take his hand for a moment; whereupon old John began to tell George that he was looking well, though there had been a time, during his fourth month, when he was so puny that nobody thought he would live. The great-nephew, in a fury of blushes, dropped old John's hand with some vigour, and seized that of the next person in the line. "Member you v'ry well 'ndeed!" he said fiercely....

George began to recover from the degradation into which this relic of early settler days dragged him. What restored him completely was a dark-eyed little beauty of nineteen, very knowing in lustrous blue and jet; at sight of this dashing advent in the line of guests before him, George was fully an Amberson again.

"Remember you very well *indeed!* " he said, his graciousness more earnest than any he had heretofore displayed. Isabel heard him and laughed.

"But you don't, George!" she said. "You don't remember her yet, though of course you *will*! Miss Morgan is from out of town, and I'm afraid this is the first time you've ever seen her. You might take her up to the dancing; I think you've pretty well done your duty here."

Like most of Tarkington's novels, *The Magnificent Ambersons* is set in his home state of Indiana. In Orson Welles's ill-fated 1942 movie version, the character of George Amberson Minafer was played by Tim Holt *(above, left);* Lucy Morgan, the woman George meets for the first time in the excerpt here, was played by Anne Baxter *(above, right).*

"This solemn moment of triumph, one of the greatest moments in the history of the world ... is going to lift up humanity to a higher plane of existence for all the ages of the future."—**British prime minister David Lloyd George, in his armistice speech, November 11, 1918**

STORY OF THE YEAR

Treaty of Versailles Ends the War

1 On June 28, 1919, exactly five years after an assassination in Sarajevo sparked World War I, the belligerents signed an agreement to end hostilities. The Treaty of Versailles, named for the French palace where it was unveiled, was the culmination of the Paris Peace Conference. It was meant to usher in what U.S. President Woodrow Wilson called a "new international order" based, he hoped, on his "Fourteen Points"—a list of postwar aims that envisioned a nonpunitive "peace without victory" secured by popular votes and open discussion. But the six months of talks were conducted largely in secret by the victorious "Big Four"—France, Italy, Britain, and the United States. The three European countries wanted to see Germany crippled, and Wilson was forced to acquiesce.

The treaty established a worldwide League of Nations (Wilson's all-important 14th point), but Germany was excluded from membership. Additionally, Germany was to forfeit more than 25,000 square miles, with six million inhabitants and half its coal and iron resources, to its neighbors. East Prussia would be cut off from the rest of Germany by the "Polish Corridor." The Allies would occupy the Rhine Valley, and, under the League's mandate, Germany's former colonies. The German army was limited to 100,000 men, the navy to a handful of small ships; the air force was abolished. War criminals—including Kaiser Wilhelm II—were to be tried by an international tribunal.

The Signing of Peace in the Hall of Mirrors, Versailles, June 28, 1919, **by Sir William Orpen.**

Most damaging were the reparations Germany was required to pay the Allies. No precise sum was named, but British economist John Maynard Keynes put Allied claims at $40 billion. Keynes warned that payment of more than $10 billion would mean "the destruction of the economic life of Germany"—something the German people would never put up with.

German chancellor Philipp Scheidemann and his cabinet resigned rather than sign the treaty, but the National Assembly meekly accepted it. The French found the terms too merciful—and voted out Premier Georges Clemenceau in protest. Wilson championed the document, despite its divergence from his ideals, but could not persuade Congress to accept it. (His attempts to ensure world peace were recognized with the 1919 Nobel Peace Prize.) The stage was being set for another world war. **◂1918.1 ▸1920.1**

GERMANY

The Spartacist Revolt

2 By the start of 1919, Germany looked like a Leninist state. Kaiser Wilhelm had abdicated and the country was governed by a six-man Council of People's Deputies; *Räte* ("soviets") of workers occupied factories. But this was not Russia. Elections for a National Assembly were set for January 19. There had been no seizures of property, no purges of the old regime's bureaucrats or military officers (who by rights should have been discredited by the imperial army's recent defeat in World War I). Indeed, to Friedrich Ebert, the moderate Social Democrat who dominated the ruling council, those officers seemed the best defense against a Bolshevik-style coup. Days before the elections, with such a coup apparently under way, Ebert enlisted their aid. The alliance brought bloodshed and paved the way for the rise of the Nazis.

The trouble began in December 1918, when the People's Marine Division (a thousand sailors and an equal number of supporters) moved into Berlin to "protect" the government—and to buttress the three radical Independent Socialist council members against their more centrist colleagues. Ebert asked the sailors to leave; when they mutinied, he called in loyal troops. But thousands of demonstrators forced the soldiers to withdraw, and the council's Independents resigned in protest. Then Berlin's Independent police chief was fired. On January 5, as radicals filled the streets and took over newspapers, the week-old Communist Party—formerly the tiny, far-left Spartacus League—declared the council deposed. The uprising became known as the Spartacist Revolt.

The Communists were less unified than it appeared. They were divided over whether Germany was ready for a complete revolution, and many—including one of Europe's most eloquent leftist leaders, Spartacus League founder Rosa Luxemburg—opposed Bolshevik tactics. But Luxemburg's faction was overridden by the pro-putsch faction, led by fellow Spartacist Karl Liebknecht (whose pen name, Spartacus, gave the league its name). Ebert panicked, authorizing Defense Minister Gustav Noske to call in his newly formed Freikorps, mercenaries commanded by the Kaiser's officers. "I guess someone has to be the pig," Noske said, assuming responsibility. Among those summarily executed were Luxemburg *(top)* and Liebknecht *(bottom)*. The Freikorps killed another 1,200 Berliners over the next two months, then crushed a rebellion in Bavaria.

The elections proceeded, and Ebert became president. The new republic's capital was Weimar, hometown of the poet Goethe; its constitution was one of the world's most liberal. But the military was in the hands of men who despised liberalism, socialism, communism, and democracy—the same men who would help boost Hitler to power. **◂1912.M ▸1921.7**

FILM

Talent Takes Control

3 Three of Hollywood's biggest stars—Charlie Chaplin, Douglas Fairbanks, and Mary Pickford—and its most prestigious director, D.W. Griffith, joined forces in 1919 to form United Artists, the first studio owned and run by the creative talents.

At the time, the four reigned supreme in the business. Theaters had merely to post a cutout of Chaplin's tramp with the words "I'm Here," and lines formed. Griffith was revered for creating *The Birth of a Nation*. Matinee-idol Fairbanks starred in a string of carefree satires that were smash hits. And his soon-to-be wife, Mary Pickford (the two married the following year), was "America's Sweetheart," the biggest box-office power in the industry as well as its shrewdest businesswoman. In contrast to her screen image of sugar-sweet child-woman, Pickford stood up to Hollywood's strongest men, pioneering actors' fights for more money and artistic control.

Because the principals had to fulfill contractual obligations with other studios, United Artists got off to a shaky start, losing money during

ART & CULTURE: Books: *Economic Consequences of the Peace* (John Maynard Keynes); *Winesburg, Ohio* (Sherwood Anderson); *The Pastoral Symphony* (André Gide); *Behaviorism* (J.D. Watson) ... Music: "How Ya Gonna Keep 'Em Down on the Farm (After They've Seen Paree)" (Lewis, Young, and Donaldson); "Alice Blue Gown" (Tierney and McCarthy); "Swanee" (Gershwin and Caesar); *The Three-Cornered Hat*

"So the lunatics have taken charge of the asylum."—**Movie mogul Richard Rowland, on hearing of the formation of United Artists**

Hollywood's Big Four *(left to right)*: Fairbanks, Pickford, Chaplin, and Griffith.

the twenties. Griffith soon left. But Fairbanks's swashbucklers and Chaplin's comedies were successful, and, thanks to good management, the company stayed afloat. In the fifties, the two surviving partners, Pickford and Chaplin, sold UA to a group of businessmen. **◂1915.1 ▸1924.M**

AFGHANISTAN

Independence and Identity

4 Afghanistan, under Habibullah Khan, maintained strict neutrality during World War I, a position designed to curry favor with Britain and Russia, which, along with Persia, were historical rivals for control of Afghanistan. (Two major wars had been fought among those countries for hegemony in the strategic buffer state, which had no coherent political identity as it was continually torn by ethnic rivalries.) At the close of World War I, Habibullah Khan sent a letter to the British viceroy in India demanding that his country's independence be recognized by the Paris Peace Conference. But Habibullah Khan was assassinated in February 1919 by radical members of an anti-British movement.

Amanullah Khan, the third son of Habibullah, seized power, ordained himself king, and declared Afghan independence. British India refused recognition, and the Third Afghan War broke out on May 3. It ended less than a month later with no clear military victory for either side, but Afghans did gain the conduct of their own foreign affairs. Two years later, the treaty ending the war was amended and Britain recognized Afghanistan as an independent nation.

Before signing the final treaty with Britain, Afghanistan concluded a friendship treaty with the newly emerging Bolshevik regime in Russia, becoming one of the first nations in the world to recognize the Soviet Union. A special relationship between the two nations lasted until 1979, when they faced each other in yet another Afghan war. **◂1917.1 ▸1978.7**

SCIENCE

Theory of Isotopy Confirmed

5 Returning to Cambridge in 1919 after World War I, Francis Aston, a brewery chemist turned physicist, invented the mass spectrograph—an instrument that allowed him to solve a fundamental problem of nuclear physics.

Until 1905, it had been assumed that if atoms had different weights, they differed chemically and hence were different elements. Then scientists discovered radiothorium, produced by the radioactive decay of the element thorium. Radiothorium atoms weighed less than those of regular thorium but behaved the same way chemically. Further experiments proved that a similar phenomenon occurred with other radioactive elements. In 1913, physicist Frederick Soddy introduced the term "isotope" (from the Greek for "same place") to describe chemicals whose atoms apparently contained the same number of electrons but possessed a different atomic weight (or "mass"). A crucial question remained, however: Did stable (that is, nonradioactive) elements have isotopes as well?

Cambridge University physicist Sir J. J. Thomson (who'd discovered the electron in 1897, and whose "plum pudding" model was the first theoretical description of atomic structure) nearly solved the mystery in 1912. Shooting atoms of the stable element neon through a magnetic field, he discovered that 90 percent were deflected at an angle indicating an atomic weight of 20. But the rest seemed to possess an atomic weight of 22. Hesitant to conclude that he'd discovered variations of the same element, Thomson speculated that the second substance might be an unknown compound.

Seven years later, Aston, Thomson's student, perfected a device that separated particles far more accurately than his teacher's had, and deflected them onto a photographic plate. The mass spectrograph confirmed not only that neon consisted mainly of two "isotopic species," but that the theory of isotopy in general was sound. Aston went on to show that many elements are mixtures of isotopes: Of the 287 naturally occurring isotopes, he discovered 212. His research eventually led to the possibility of human control of nuclear fission through the discovery and enrichment of the uranium-235 isotope. **◂1913.1 ▸1930.14**

Aston's mass spectrograph separated isotopes—and thus maintained the periodic table.

The Third Afghan War: The British countered the Afghan rebellion with a force of more than 250,000 men.

BIRTHS

Nat "King" Cole, U.S. musician.

Merce Cunningham, U.S. choreographer.

Margot Fonteyn, U.K. ballet dancer.

Malcolm Forbes, U.S. publisher.

Edmund Hillary, New Zealand mountaineer.

Mikhail Kalashnikov, U.S.S.R. gun designer.

Doris Lessing, U.K. writer.

Liberace, U.S. musician.

Primo Levi, Italian writer.

Iris Murdoch, Irish-U.K. novelist and philosopher.

Muhammad Reza Shah Pahlevi, Iranian ruler.

J.D. Salinger, U.S. writer.

Pete Seeger, U.S. folksinger.

Ian Smith, Rhodesian prime minister.

Pierre Trudeau, Canadian prime minister.

George C. Wallace, U.S. governor.

DEATHS

William Waldorf Astor, U.S.-U.K. publisher.

L. Frank Baum, U.S. writer.

Andrew Carnegie, Scottish-U.S. industrialist and philanthropist.

Henry Clay Frick, U.S. industrialist.

Augustus D. Juilliard, U.S. music patron.

Alexander Kolchak, Russian admiral.

Ruggiero Leoncavallo, Italian composer.

Pierre Auguste Renoir, French painter.

Theodore Roosevelt, U.S. president.

Frank W. Woolworth, U.S. retailer.

Emiliano Zapata, Mexican revolutionary.

(Manuel de Falla) ... Painting & Sculpture: *The City* (Paul Klee) ... Film: *Male and Female* (Cecil B. DeMille); *Broken Blossoms, True Heart Susie* (D.W. Griffith); *Blind Husbands* (Erich von Stroheim); *His Majesty the American* (with Douglas Fairbanks); *Madame du Barry* (Ernst Lubitsch) ... Theater: *Clarence* (Booth Tarkington); *Déclassée* (Zoë Akins); *Irene* (Tierney and McCarthy).

"Verily, poor as we are in democracy how can we give of it to the world?"—**American anarchist Emma Goldman**

NEW IN 1919

Pogo stick.

Grand Canyon, Zion, and Lafayette (later Acadia) national parks.

Gasoline tax (imposed in Oregon).

American Legion.

Nonstop airborne crossing of the Atlantic (Newfoundland to Ireland by Alcock and Brown).

Greyhound racing with mechanical rabbits.

Commercial airline service (Deutsche Luftreederie).

Dial telephones.

Bentley and Citroën cars.

Pulp magazines *(True Story)*.

IN THE UNITED STATES

▶BASEBALL SCANDAL—Amid a swirl of rumors, the favored Chicago White Sox lost the 1919 World Series to the Cincinnati Reds. An investigation of the intrusion of professional gambling into baseball resulted in the indictment of eight Chicago players the following year. The players—dubbed the "Black Sox"—were acquitted of throwing the Series, but subsequently banned for life from the American pastime. Among those

punished: "Shoeless" Joe Jackson *(above)*, whose stellar play in the Series belied participation in a fix. "Say it ain't so, Joe," pleaded his fans. **▶1920.6**

▶REED THE RED—After covering World War I, radical American journalist John Reed traveled to Russia, became enamored of the Bolsheviks,

THE UNITED STATES

The Red Year

6 In the United States, 1919 has been called the Red Year because of bloody race riots and a "red scare" that led to the deportation of thousands of alleged subversives. Despite severe discrimination in the armed forces, black soldiers had fought heroically in World War I, and black labor had been essential to the war effort. But in the postwar recession, competition for jobs and housing heightened racial tension. Sensationalist newspapers printed lurid stories depicting blacks as rapists and bandits. Black homes in white neighborhoods were burned, and lynchings went from 38 in 1917 to 83 in 1919.

The riots began in April, erupting in 25 cities. In Chicago, whites stoned black youths swimming on the wrong side of a segregated beach, drowning one. Soon white mobs were assaulting blacks around the city. In Washington, D.C., following the alleged rape of a white woman in July, police announced they would search every black man found on the streets after dark. White soldiers took this as license to shoot at blacks; police invaded homes without warrants. But there was a new aspect to these disturbances: Blacks fought—and shot—back. Across the country, dozens from both races were killed before troops restored order. Black leaders warned of a race war; white politicians cried, "Bolshevism!"

Bolshevism was the accusation hurled at the labor movement as well. A wave of strikes in steel, coal, and textiles swept the country. In February, most of Seattle's residents joined in a five-day general strike. During the summer, leftist intellectuals and union activists in Chicago founded the American Communist Party. In Washington, a terrorist bomb damaged the homes of several top officials. Attorney General A. Mitchell Palmer retaliated in December by rounding up 249 Russian-born immigrants and shipping them to the Soviet Union. The famous anarchist Emma Goldman *(left)* was among them. As one federal judge noted, so were many "quiet and harmless working people." In January 1920, thousands of "red aliens" were rounded up, and some tried for sedition in secret hearings. Caught up in the prevalent postwar xenophobia, most Americans supported the so-called Palmer raids. Ironically, the left was divided over the Bolshevik revolution; labor was divided over the issue of race; and blacks were divided over the question of integration versus separatism. In America, revolution made a muddled retreat. **◀1917.7 ▶1920.1**

The Palmer raids and other crackdowns sent American Bolsheviks running for cover.

ITALY

Foundations of Fascism

7 Benito Mussolini founded the Fascist movement on March 23, 1919, at a meeting in Milan of 120 nationalists, futurists, action-starved war veterans, syndicalists, and former socialists. This motley group of extremists and adventurers declared itself the first *fascio di combattimento*—literally, "combat bundle." (The name is derived from the ancient Roman symbol of authority called the *fasces*, a bundle of sticks tied around an ax.) Soon there were *fasci* all over Italy, engaged in a campaign of arson, beatings, and intensive propaganda against socialists and communists.

The young socialist turned Fascist Mussolini. The *fasci* believed that only they, the "dynamic minority," were revolutionaries.

Mussolini, a prominent socialist journalist until the outbreak of World War I, initially opposed the war. But he'd always seen violence as the surest road to radical change, and counted on a elite vanguard to spark the revolution. He quickly came to see the war as a crucible for making revolutionary leaders, and became a strident advocate of Italian intervention. Ejected from the Socialist Party, Mussolini began his shift toward a new brand of politics.

The first Fascist program, proclaimed in August 1919, had much in common with socialism: It called for universal suffrage, abolition of the monarchy, and a partially centralized economy. But these policies took a backseat to romanticized nationalism, an exaltation of war, a cult of the strong leader, and the

SPORTS: Baseball: World Series, Cincinnati Reds defeat Chicago White Sox, 5–3 (from 1919 to 1921 Series requires best of nine games to win); Babe Ruth hits 587-foot home run for Boston against New York Yankees; Jim Thorpe concludes 7-year major-league career and begins 7-year professional-football career ... Boxing: Jack Dempsey defeats Jess Willard for World Heavyweight title.

"History will never forgive me if I surrender what Peter the Great won."—**A.V. Kolchak, leader of the White Russian forces, refusing to acknowledge Finnish independence, which had been recognized by the Bolsheviks**

"dynamic minority." (Inspired by Mussolini, poet and fighter pilot Gabriele D'Annunzio in September led 300 black-shirted followers—"Blackshirts"—to seize the disputed Dalmation port of Fiume. D'Annunzio's dictatorial "republic" lasted more than a year.)

As Fascist attacks on leftists began attracting support from industrialists, landowners, police, and army officers, the movement grew increasingly vague about its goals—except that of taking power. The Fascists formed a political party in 1921, sending members to Parliament. **◂1911.12 ▸1922.4**

THE SOVIET UNION

Civil War Seizes Country

8 Throughout the winter of 1919, Alexander Kolchak, self-appointed "supreme ruler" of the anti-Bolshevik "All-Russian Government," pushed his White Army across the Ural Mountains. Aided by the Western Allies, who helped train and supply his troops, Kolchak laid siege to city after city. Concurrently with Kolchak's campaigns in the east, Anton Denikin led the White advances on the southern front. After taking the cities of Kharkov, Poltava, Odessa, Kiev, and Kursk, Denikin's troops reached the city of Orel, only 250 miles from Moscow, in October 1919. But by then, his troops were dispirited, undersupplied, and overextended. The countryside lay in ruins. At Orel, the Reds dug in. Heavy fighting drove the Whites back. Denikin resigned in the spring, transferring control of his wasted army to Pyotr Wrangel, like him, a former Imperial Army officer. The front by now had been contained within the war-torn Crimean Peninsula, where severe food shortages and peasant uprisings hampered military efforts. The civil war was all but over by April, but the Red and White Armies continued to fight limited battles throughout the summer and into the fall, when Wrangel evacuated the Crimea and fled to Constantinople.

The rural population were driven from the savaged land; cities were reduced to rubble. Refugees clogged the roads; disease and famine raged. In the years immediately following the war, as the Bolsheviks consolidated their power, millions of Russians died of starvation, one of the new state's most potent enemies. **◂1918.5 ▸1919.11**

As the Red and White Armies clashed, rural Russians suffered in the terrible famine.

Meanwhile, Leon Trotsky, Soviet minister of war, was lying low, waiting for the snows to melt and stealing time to muster the Red Army. In April, as the White forces advanced on the Volga River cities of Kazan and Samara, Trotsky counterattacked. Spread too thin, the Whites were forced to retreat. The tide had turned in Russia's civil war, and the Allies withdrew their support from Kolchak. In November, he lost Omsk, capital of his counterrevolutionary government, and fled eastward to Irkutsk. There, his army decimated by desertion and defeat, he was turned over to the Red Guards and imprisoned. In February, he was quietly executed.

ARCHITECTURE

Bauhaus Opens

9 The most important movement in twentieth-century architecture and design began in 1919 when architect Walter Gropius, convinced that "the designer must breathe a soul into the dead product of the machine," established the Bauhaus school (literally, "house of building") in Weimar, Germany.

Bauhaus Stairway **(1932) by Oskar Schlemmer, an instructor at the school.**

Gropius's "new" approach to design education resembled a medieval guild. Teachers were called "masters" and students "apprentices." Paul Klee offered a stained-glass workshop; Wassily Kandinsky taught wall painting; Marcel Breuer, interiors. Students were required to attain technical proficiency in practical crafts to acquaint themselves with materials and processes. Gropius sought to integrate fine craftsmanship with assembly-line mass production, arguing that aesthetically pleasing design should be a part of everyday life, not restricted to expensive goods produced for an elite.

But the idea of squandering artistic sensibility on "mere" crafts aroused the ire of traditionalists, and the internal chaos and rampant inflation in postwar Germany made it difficult for students to find affordable room and board. After it moved to Berlin, the Bauhaus was closed by the Nazis in 1933.

Its spirit and influence lived on, however. Designer László Moholy-Nagy founded the New Bauhaus (later called the Institute of Design) in Chicago; Ludwig Mies van der Rohe, who briefly headed the Bauhaus, established an architecture department at the Illinois Institute of Technology. Gropius became chairman of the Harvard School of Architecture. The stylistic legacy of the Bauhaus—functional, unornamented design; simple, geometric forms; smooth surfaces; and the use of primary colors and modern materials—permeates twentieth-century life. **◂1909.4 ▸1923.8**

IN THE UNITED STATES

and in 1919 published his eyewitness account of the October revolution, *Ten Days That Shook the World.* Back in the States, Reed, a Harvard graduate born to wealth, became leader of the U.S. Communist Labor Party. Indicted for sedition, he fled back to Russia, where he died in 1920, becoming the only American to be buried in the Kremlin wall. ◂1919.6

▶WIT IN THE ROUND—It began in 1919, when a group of writers, including George S. Kaufman, Robert Benchley, Alexander Woollcott, Dorothy Parker, Franklin P. Adams, and Robert Sherwood, began to meet for lunch every day around a table at the Algonquin Hotel in New York City; it became one of the most celebrated literary and theatrical

circles of the century. Noted for its sparkling wit and caustic sarcasm—such famous sayings as Kaufman's "Satire is what closes on Saturday night" were coined there—the Algonquin Round Table survived (albeit without most of its major players) until 1943. ▶1920.V

▶FIRST AMENDMENT LIMIT—In a landmark 1919 decision, Supreme Court Justice Oliver Wendell Holmes enunciated the limits of the First Amendment's protection of free speech: when it represented a "clear and present danger that [it] will bring about the substantive evils that Congress has a right to prevent." Holmes's example: "falsely shouting fire in a theatre." Instigated by a challenge to wartime security measures, the decision set a lasting First Amendment precedent.

▶TRIPLE CROWN—Chestnut colt Sir Barton in 1919 pulled off an unheard-of sweep, winning horse racing's Triple Crown: the Kentucky Derby, the Preakness, and the Belmont Stakes. This first of the great American thoroughbreds remained the lone Triple Crown winner until 1930. ▶1920.M

POLITICS & BUSINESS: GNP: $84 billion ... World War I costs the U.S. over $20 billion ... Oregon enacts first gasoline tax ... Asa G. Candler sells Coca-Cola to Robert W. Woodruff for $25 million ... Hilton Hotel Corp. founded ... New York City's cost of living 79% higher than in 1914 ... U.S. ice-cream sales reach 150 million gallons, up 500% in 10 years.

"For me the battlefield of France or Amritsar is the same.... Obey my orders and open shops, and speak up if you want war."
—Brigadier General Reginald Dyer, defending his order to open fire at Amritsar

AROUND THE WORLD

▸DEATH OF ZAPATA—Emiliano Zapata's quixotic and bloody crusade for agrarian reform ended on April 10 in a hail of bullets at the Chinameca hacienda in Morelos, where the revolutionary leader was ambushed by agents of Mexican president Venustiano Carranza. At the height of his power, Zapata, who with his huge sombrero, heavy mustache, and crossed bandoliers gave the world the popular image of a Mexican revolutionary, controlled much of southern Mexico. Within his sphere of influence, Zapata expropriated huge tracts of private land and distributed them among the peasantry, and established Mexico's first agricultural credit organization. ◂1910.10

▸CINEMATIC EXPRESSIONISM—Moody, intense, and visually stunning in its depiction of the fantasy life of a deranged person, *The Cabinet of Dr. Caligari*, released in 1919, is a classic of German

expressionism. Despite its greatness, however, the film has been called a cinematic dead end, exerting no lasting influence on the course of the art form. ▸1926.5

▸KUN'S COUP—Released from prison March 20, 1919, Hungarian communist Béla Kun wasted no time in gathering an army, overthrowing the government, recapturing Hungarian territory annexed by Romania and Czechoslovakia, and establishing an orthodox communist regime. But his radicalism alienated the peasants and the army. Ousted on August 1, Kun fled to Vienna, leaving his failed utopia behind. ▸1944.11

INDIA

Massacre at Amritsar

10 Few among the 15,000 demonstrators gathered in the Punjabi city of Amritsar on April 13, 1919, seemed surprised when troops appeared to disperse their protest of the Rowlatt Acts. Indians had been protesting these new laws—which authorized the British to jail without trial anyone suspected of revolutionary activity—for weeks, and in some cities the demonstrations had turned to riots. But the April 13 protest in Amritsar, in a large walled park, was peaceful. It was a Sunday, and some of those gathered were peasants from neighboring villages celebrating a Hindu festival.

Public floggings followed the massacre, which the British officially condemned. But the House of Lords praised its leader.

When the soldiers arrived, many in the crowd began to chant: *"Agaye. agaye."* ("They have come. They have come.") Without warning, the British regional commander, Brigadier General Reginald Dyer, gave the order to fire. Protesters scrambled madly over garden walls or tried to squeeze through narrow exits already blocked by troops or piles of bodies. After ten minutes of steady rifle fire, the troops withdrew, leaving nearly 500 dead and 1,500 wounded.

For war-weary Indians—who'd made tremendous sacrifices on behalf of Britain and the Allies—the Amritsar massacre added unbearable insult to the injury of the Rowlatt Acts. In the violent days that followed, General Dyer proclaimed martial law and ordered public floggings. Indians were forced to crawl down the street where a British "lady doctor" had been beaten during the riots.

The Government of India Act, calling for greater Indian representation in government, was finally passed in late 1919. By then, however, such concessions were insufficient to placate Indian nationalists. They believed self-rule was their right, not a favor to be granted by even the most enlightened despot. **◂1916.12 ▸1921.12**

THE SOVIET UNION

First Comintern Convenes

11 Seeking to consolidate their control over the world's communist parties, the leaders of the Moscow Bolshevik Party—Lenin, Nikolai Bukharin, Grigori Zinoviev—convened the Third Socialist International in Moscow in 1919. Attracting 60 delegates from 19 nations, the organization—called the Comintern—succeeded the Second International, which dissolved during World War I when various member parties disagreed about whether to support their countries' war efforts.

From the beginning, Comintern congresses were dominated by the Bolsheviks. Their policies were militant, their goals grandiose. The Moscow leaders shaped the Comintern into a body designed to foment worldwide proletarian revolution—which, as worker unrest spread across a war-scarred Europe, seemed not only reasonable but imminent. Member parties were pressured to conform to the Russian model and call themselves Communist; those who balked at violent revolution were excluded. Members also pledged their commitment to the Soviet state and promised to agitate at home on its behalf. The Comintern lasted until 1943, when it was disbanded by Stalin. **◂1919.8 ▸1921.2**

LITERATURE

Hesse's Breakthrough

12 Hermann Hesse had already written several conventional bestsellers when, in 1919, *Demian*—the product of a nervous breakdown and a subsequent "rebirth"—established him as one of the century's major authors. A few years earlier, the German-born Hesse had grown restless with his bourgeois life in Switzerland; travel (including an Asian trip that inspired his later *Siddhartha*) hadn't helped. Then, with World War I came a series of crises: His pacifist essays drew fierce hostility, his father died, his wife went mad. Despondent, he consulted a Jungian psychoanalyst. The result was the first of Hesse's novels to systematically explore his trademark theme: An alienated hero's attempt to resolve within himself such archetypal dualities as spirit and flesh, emotion and intellect, action and contemplation.

Demian was embraced by the war-shattered generation it described. Its protagonist, unable to accept his elders' ethos of rationality and order, seeks "a god who also encompasses within himself the devil"—a god of lust *and* reason. Hesse's own search, played out in such works as *The Glass Bead Game*, won him the 1946 Nobel Prize, as well as a devoted following among the disaffected youth of the sixties. **◂1901.8**

LONG LIVE THE THIRD COMMUNIST INTERNATIONAL!
VIVE LA TROISIÈME INTERNATIONALE COMMUNISTE!
EVVIVA IL TERZA INTERNAZIONALE COMMUNISTA!
ES LEBE DIE DRITTE KOMMUNISTISCHE INTERNATIONALE!

The Comintern urged workers everywhere to rise up against their oppressors.

NOBEL PRIZES: Peace: Woodrow Wilson (U.S.; League of Nations) ... Literature: Carl Spitteler (Swiss; poet and novelist) ... Chemistry: No award ... Medicine: Jules Bordet (Belgian; immunology and serology) ... Physics: Johannes Stark (German; splitting spectrum lines in electric fields).

A VOICE FROM 1919

Saving for a Dry Day

Advertisement from *The New York Times*, May 4, 1919

In 1919, Congress ratified the 18th Amendment, prohibiting the "manufacture, sale, or transportation of intoxicating liquors." The new law had wide public endorsement: Sobriety had been touted during the war as essential to victory; moreover, drunkenness was considered to be the root cause of violence, poverty, and the breakdown of the family. By the time Prohibition went into effect, 33 states governing 63 percent of the U.S. population had already banned alcohol. Prohibition worked—sort of. While the country was hardly "dry" (bootleggers and speakeasies abounded), alcohol consumption did *decline. (Pre-Amendment levels of consumption were not reached again until 1975.) But Prohibition also has been blamed for a variety of social ills—the rise of organized crime, government corruption, and widespread contempt for the law. Before Prohibition went into effect in January 1920, liquor-store advertisements, like the one below from* The New York Times, *urged people to stock up while supplies lasted.* ◂**1901.M** ▸**1930.M**

UNCLE SAM WILL ENFORCE
PROHIBITION
BUY NOW!
This is the time to acquire your Wines and Liquors. Prices are advancing daily and will continue to advance whether Prohibition becomes effective July 1, 1919, or January 20, 1920. No Wines or Liquors may now be manufactured or imported—and existing stocks of good merchandise are almost extinct. Even if the ban on manufacture were lifted it would require years to mature the new product.
Specials This Week
Per Case. Per Bottle.
Imperial Gin $24.50 $2.15
Dove Gin 27.00 2.30
Gordon Gin 29.00 2.45
Cocktail Rum (H. H. Dove Brand) 32.00 2.75
Bacardi Rum 37.00 3.20
Allash Kummel 30.00 2.60
Old Bridgeport Whiskey 36.00 3.10
(Six years old; bottled in bond)
Green Creme de Menthe 34.00 3.00
(Imported in glass from Mouchotte Freres)
Special inducements given to those buying Ports, Sherries, Clarets, Rhine and Moselle Wines in quantity.
HENRY HOLLANDER
Importers of Wines and Whiskies for the Connoisseur
ESTABLISHED 1877.
Telephone: Greeley 3218-3219
149-151 West 36th St.
(Just West of B'way.)

The wake of the Great War brought disillusionment, then prosperity, then reckless indulgence. While artists and writers proclaimed the death of a discredited culture, flappers and their beaus danced frantically to a Jazz Age beat—until the party ended in 1929 with the crash heard 'round the world.

1920 1929

The artistic ferment of the twenties was centered in American cities, where jazz was changing the face of popular culture—and in France's capital, where an extraordinary collection of expatriates was revolutionizing art and literature. The Paris café, where such talents as Hemingway, Joyce, Stein, and Fitzgerald went to drink, think, write, and socialize, became a symbol of the era. The Café du Dôme on Boulevard Montparnasse *(right)*, is captured by André Kertész, a Hungarian émigré whose groundbreaking photography helped publicize Paris's scene.

DU DOME
GLACES

THE WORLD IN 1920

World Population

1910: 1.7 BILLION 1920: 1.9 BILLION

1910–20: +11.8%

Europe Redrawn

The First World War changed the face of Europe. The 636-year-old Austro-Hungarian Empire—a fractious mélange of Germans, Hungarians, Poles, Czechs, Serbians, Croatians, Italians, and Romanians—collapsed just four years after helping to ignite the war. (Emperor Franz Josef fatally ignored the Hapsburgs' centuries-old motto, "Let others wage war; thou, happy Austria, marry.") Peacemakers at Versailles reassembled Central Europe and the Balkans, outlining new borders for Germany, Austria, Hungary, and Romania, carving out the nations of Poland, Czechoslovakia, and the Kingdom of Serbs, Croats, and Slovenes (later Yugoslavia). The artificiality of these borders helped lay the groundwork for the renewed nationalism and violent irredentism that would surface 70 years later.

Divorces per 100 married couples

1920		1990
0.6	Austria	34
0*	Italy	7
9.8	Japan	22
2.1	U.K.	43
13.6	U.S.	48

*Divorce not legal until 1970

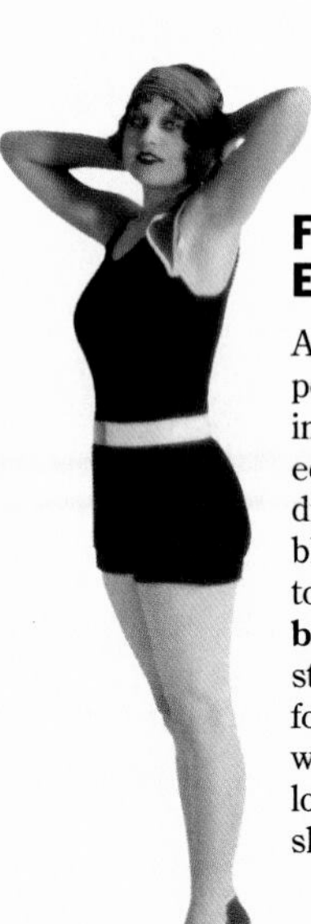

Fashion Essential

As women in the postwar era became increasingly liberated, elaborate swim dresses worn with bloomers gave way to the **modern bathing suit.** Early styles featured a formfitting knitted wool tunic pulled low and belted over short wool shorts.

The **telephone**, by 1920, was nearly half a century old and becoming ever more capable of drawing people closer together. (The first transcontinental telephone line was established in 1915.) In the United States, there were approximately 12 phones for every 100 people. Today, phones are nearly universal and a caller can reach any place on the planet from almost any other place—all while walking down the street.

Number of Telephones per 100 people

	Germany	Spain	U.K.	U.S.
1910	1.7	0.1	0.3	8.2
1920	2.9 (1925)	0.3	2.2	12.3
1990	67.1/11.5 (West/East Germany)	32.3	43.4	50.9

Most Populous Metropolitan Areas (population in millions)

1920	New York 5.6	London 4.5	Berlin 3.8	Paris 2.9	Chicago 2.7
1991	Tokyo 27.2	Mexico City 20.9	São Paulo 18.7	Seoul 16.8	New York 14.6

Illiteracy Rates

	1920	1990*
Cuba	28%	3.8%*
Hungary	13%	1.1%
India	92%	52%
Somalia		88% (1920 figure not available)
U.S.	6%	2.7%

*or closest available year

The twentieth century's sophisticated media and its emphasis on public education have brought the lowest rates of illiteracy in history. Although the meaning of the term varies widely from country to country (some define illiteracy as the inability to read and write a simple sentence, others as the lack of more than five years' schooling), its elimination is everywhere a matter of national pride and an important indicator of development.

Women and the Vote The call for female suffrage was first answered by New Zealand in 1893, but it wasn't until after the First World War that European and American women began gaining the vote. The war gave many women (who went off to work as men went off to fight) their first taste of economic independence; more importantly, its senseless brutality undermined many of the age-old assumptions about the male's innate superiority in matters of politics and foreign affairs. By 1994, women in every country in the world except Kuwait had the right to vote.

Women's Right to Vote

Extension of suffrage, by year

- 1901 Australia
- 1906 Finland
- 1913 Norway
- 1915 Denmark, Iceland
- 1917 Russia
- 1918 U.K., Austria, Canada, Ireland
- 1919 Netherlands, Luxembourg, Germany
- 1920 U.S.

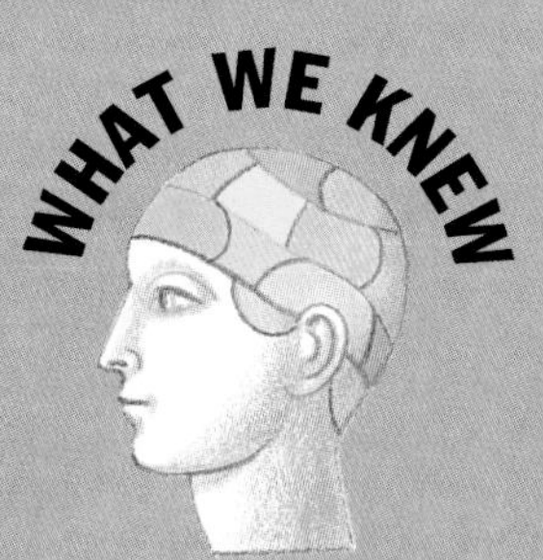

The signing of the Treaty of Versailles in 1919 and the establishment of the League of Nations (minus U.S. participation) have convinced European leaders that a new, and lasting, international order has been created that will, in the words of British Prime Minister David Lloyd George, "lift up humanity to a higher plane of existence for all the ages of the future."

Three years into the Russian Revolution, pundits are predicting its imminent demise. Former U.S. Secretary of State Elihu Root cites "abundant evidence that the Bolshevik terror is drawing steadily toward its downfall."

There are only eight known planets in the Solar System. The ninth, Pluto, will not be discovered until 1930.

Tuberculosis, the second most deadly ailment in the United States (after heart disease), kills 150,000 a year. The only known treatments consist of long periods (sometimes years) of bed rest, and the occasional surgical removal of destroyed lung tissue; neither is predictably effective. The only known prevention is quarantine.

"This radio or wireless telephony or what-you-may-call-it isn't even worthy of discussion," writes a newspaper critic of the first broadcasts of Westinghouse's KDKA radio station in Pittsburgh. And despite further predictions that, as one trade journal proclaims, "any attempt to make radio an advertising medium would … prove positively offensive to great numbers of people," New York City's WEAF carries the first paid commercial ($50 for 10 minutes) in 1922.

The manufacture and sale of alcoholic beverages has just been outlawed in the United States, prompting the anti-Saloon League of New York to declare the beginning of "an era of clear thinking and clean living!"

GERALD EARLY

Mixed Messages

The Birth of Mass Culture

1920
1929

The gaudy, grandiose movie palaces of the twenties, capable of seating thousands of fans, embodied not only the allure of the movies, but also the heterogenous spirit that was the hallmark of the emerging mass culture. Seattle's 5th Avenue Theatre *(right)*, built in 1926, was typical: It offered dazzling art (produced by major corporations) and "authentic" exoticism (the ceiling was a twice-life-sized replica of the one in Beijing's Imperial Throne Room). Tycoon and tramp alike could sit here absorbing the magic, and feel like emperors.

INEVITABLY, WHEN WE THINK of the twenties, we conjure up scenes of Victorian cultural barriers beginning to crumble. I am not speaking primarily of "high" culture (painting, literature, "serious" music and theater), though the European capitals were ablaze with writers and artists struggling to dissolve the distinctions between high and low, sacred and profane. It's true that in a single evening at Gertrude Stein's Paris salon, one could have found Joyce, Hemingway, Pound, and Picasso all arguing over the meaning of modernism; what's more remarkable is the fact that for millions of ordinary people, the experience of culture increasingly involved crossing old lines of class and color. (That the *material* boundaries between black and white, worker and employer, remained largely impassible did not affect this trend.)

This was the decade when movies began truly to come into their own (began, even, to talk), and rich and poor lined up outside ornate picture palaces for a chance to gawk at former factory hands playing millionaires and actual millionaires playing factory hands. It was the age of the uncorseted flapper, with her dress above her knees, a cigarette in one hand and a flask of bootleg whiskey in the other. And above all, it was the Jazz Age—when white millionaires, factory hands, gangsters, professors, and debutantes crammed into nightclubs in New York, Chicago, and Kansas City to witness the genius of black performers like Duke Ellington and Louis Armstrong. From San Francisco to Berlin, Caucasians were dancing the funky Charleston and the Black Bottom.

What made the twenties different from any previous decade in human history was the arrival in force of mass culture—popular culture shaped by mass production, mass consumption, and mass media. In its hunger for novelty, mass culture tends toward inclusion, drawing raw material from the margins of society into the mainstream; it seeks, as well, an ever broader audience (or market) for its products. And its vast power inexorably changes not only popular culture but fringe culture and high culture. Something so revolutionary could hardly have taken hold without a major social cataclysm—and indeed, the event that shaped twenties culture was World War I.

In many ways, the first perfect example of a mass-culture hero was a figure from that war—T.E. Lawrence, known as Lawrence of Arabia. The illegitimate son of a delinquent Irish lord, Lawrence rose from obscurity to lead a force of Bedouin warriors in guerrilla warfare against the Turks. He became a household name in both Great Britain and the United States largely through the writings and lecture tours of the sensationalistic American journalist Lowell Thomas—who found the idea of a white man dressed as an Arab prince, leading dark, "savage" tribesmen against a far stronger enemy, to have an irresistibly romantic appeal. But what really made Lawrence a star were the motion pictures of Thomas's cameraman, Henry Chase. For the story of Lawrence was visual, and would not have succeeded nearly so well with mass audiences if they could not actually have seen him riding camels through the desert sands and blowing up Turkish trains. Lawrence of Arabia became the first multi-media hero of a shrinking world. Lawrence remained a celebrity throughout the twenties. An ambivalent hero in an ambivalent age, he was a man of action who felt defiled by his actions; a soldier painfully conscious of being as much an agent of British imperialism as of Arab liberation; a writer eager for fame (his remarkable 1926 memoir, *Seven Pillars of Wisdom*, helped cement his legend), yet sufficiently repelled by it to seek

5TH AVE
THEATRE

anonymity under an assumed name as an ordinary enlisted man. Like Hemingway's Jake Barnes in *The Sun Also Rises*—the fictional embodiment of Lost Generation disillusionment—Lawrence was psychically devastated by the war's horrors and its betrayal of his ideals. Above all, Lawrence personified the dissolution of Victorian social hierarchies in the crucible of the war.

Film's power to transform a vision of history into the most compelling kind of mass mythology had already been proved by D.W. Griffith's 1915 *Birth of a Nation*. But Griffith's movie, however much it did to transform the medium from primitive entertainment to sophisticated art, glorified the nineteenth-century Ku Klux Klan; it clung to a Victorian mode of thinking about racial purity. Lawrence, conversely—with his own socially ambiguous origins, his intimate association with the Arabs, his enlistment as a common soldier after the war—symbolized the commonality of all blood. He was a self-created, unabashedly *impure* hero: a new kind of man for the mass-culture age.

LAWRENCE'S UNEASY ASCENT REFLECTS the function of the Great War as a great leveler, which allowed men from "tainted" backgrounds to rise to prominence. The war exercised an egalitarian influence in other ways as well, as many young men left provincial homes for the first time to see (and be seen in) other parts of the world. No nation was more deeply affected by this process than the United States—and no nation's culture, in turn, influenced the world's more deeply.

Although scholars often speak of the mood of discontent and despair that induced, paradoxically, both the hedonism and the widespread reactionism of the era (the Chicago speakeasies and the Berlin cabarets; the resurgence of the Klan and the rise of Mussolini), the 1920s also marked the climax, in America, of a leveling trend that began during the previous decade. Between 1913 and 1920, four major amendments to the Constitution resulted from that democratizing tendency: the federal income tax and direct election of senators in 1913; Prohibition (meant to free the lower classes from demon rum) in 1919; and women's right to vote in 1920.

For African-Americans, however, those measures (aside from Prohibition) were virtually meaningless, except as a gauge of their own exclusion from the benefits of civil society. What galvanized blacks was the war. Most black American soldiers had never been outside the South or an urban ghetto. Segregated even in the trenches, fighting for a country that denied them the most basic rights, many returned home determined to change their own status and that of their fellows. The black community broadly became interested in international affairs for the first time, and took a more international view of their own predicament. Thousands rallied to the black nationalism of the fiery, Jamaican-born Marcus Garvey, or to the rival Pan-Africanism of the NAACP's urbane W.E.B. Du Bois. Suddenly, the average black was no longer a cipher in a degraded caste, with no history and no future: He was a member of a grand, glorious nation spanning the globe. If every white with a bit of disposable income was playing the wildly climbing stock market, growing numbers of African-Americans were investing in their race.

Meanwhile, white Americans—their sense of cultural boundaries loosened by the war, and their hunger for novelty fed by the new mass media of the phonograph and radio—were gyrating (with far more abandon than during the ragtime fad of the early 1900s) to African-American music. Blacks became a subject of fascination and romanticization for white intellectuals. (Some, like Gertrude Stein and Carl Van Vechten, even made them the protagonists of novels.) And the gifted African-Americans of the Harlem Renaissance—the poets Langston Hughes and Countee Cullen, the novelists Zora Neale Hurston and Jean Toomer, among many others—brought black American literature and art to true maturity for the first time.

African-Americans made their biggest impact on the world through their music, which has been one of the prime shapers of mass culture. Even before the war, avant-garde practitioners of *high* culture, sensing that the Western world's old moral and aesthetic verities were nearing exhaustion, had turned to various new sources of inspiration. Marcel Duchamp displayed

Nearly all the avant-gardists of the twenties experimented with the mixing of forms and themes—high and low, sacred and profane—but the "miscegenated" art form that has had the most far-reaching and lasting influence is jazz. Here, in a 1974 collage entitled *Wrapping It Up at the Lafayette* (from his *Of the Blues* series), African-American artist Romare Bearden recaptures the exhilaration of the early 1930s, when New York City was alive with the sounds of jazz bands, led by the likes of Count Basie and Chick Webb and featuring such soloists as tenor saxophonist Lester Young and vocalist Ella Fitzgerald.

industrial objects and called them sculpture; Picasso poached African sculpture. This artistic mingling of high and low (to the West, artifacts produced by blacks were low culture by definition) intensified after the madness of World War I cast the sanctity of "civilized" values into serious doubt. The dadaists celebrated chaos; the futurists glorified gasoline-powered speed; T.S. Eliot and James Joyce exploded syntax and sense, mixed the esoteric language of the sacred with the vernacular of the roughest street. But only jazz—the supremely impure art form, invented by a radically marginalized people—wound up making a truly broad impact on society at large.

This was the case, in part, because the African-American was seen as a charismatic being—possessed of a "natural" poetry and sense of rhythm, a spontaneous sensuality lacking in the culture that had recently launched history's most destructive war. But jazz's popularity also owed much to the fact that it was created not to express some theory about art, but to entertain audiences and appeal to them on an immediate emotional level. Jazz was about pleasure and all-too-common forms of pain. Its aesthetic principles were simple enough: syncopation and a blues "feeling"; freedom within the structure of a group; improvisation within the confines and around the edges of a blues, march, hymn, or pop song. Jazz, in short, was built on egalitarian, democratic precepts. And it influenced all sorts of high-culture art—beginning with the music of Stravinsky and Gershwin, and continuing through the painting of the surrealists, through the dance of Martha Graham and her followers, on to the poetry of the Beats, and beyond.

Some intellectuals were appalled by the jazz craze; they saw it as *anti*-intellectual, as nihilistic, as a degradation of culture by the crowd. But their attempts at counterrevolution were crushed not just by the trends in both high and popular culture, but by the emergence of a middlebrow compromise. This was represented in the 1920s by the strange phenomenon of symphonic jazz, a hybrid of jazz and classical music. Its chief exponent, the white bandleader Paul Whiteman, wanted to make jazz respectable for white, middle-class adults who felt uneasy about what their children danced to—and about the licentious, "Africanized" way their children danced. Mass culture was increasingly revealing its tendency to miscegenate. (Indeed, the word "jazz" originally meant copulation, and many conservatives feared the music would bring blacks and whites together sexually as well as culturally.) The change, moreover, was happening at a giddy pace. Even critics—formerly the guardians of elevated taste—had to jump aboard or be left behind.

IRONICALLY, THE MAN WHO NAMED the Jazz Age, the novelist F. Scott Fitzgerald, neither knew much about nor liked jazz: He had in mind the decade's mood of egalitarianism, immediacy, freedom, and speed; its pursuit of empty thrills to stave off boredom, the scourge of a prosperous and disillusioned era.

Developed in bordellos (where a good deal of literal miscegenation went on), jazz was, from its origins, a commercial music—though one in revolt against traditional bourgeois commercial music. It was created by young men on the make, both black and white—men who resembled, in that respect, T.E. Lawrence, Fitzgerald himself (to his discomfort), and the protagonist of Fitzgerald's masterpiece, *The Great Gatsby.* Jay Gatsby, too, is a self-created hero, a tycoon from a mysterious, possibly shady background, who seduces a crowd of bluebloods with his charm, his jazz parties, and his flashy cars (another potent symbol of twenties mass culture).

Yet however ambivalent Fitzgerald felt about the changes Gatsby represented, even he recognized that they would only accelerate in the decades to come. Indeed, mass culture has increasingly become *global* culture, subsuming local cultures from Buenos Aires to Beijing. It should come as no surprise, then, that the most pervasive, and most influential, cultural artifact of our own time is the music video. With its breakneck editing, its high-tech gloss, and its mélange of miscegenated musical genres (rock, rap, soul, and, yes, jazz), the music video is a logical outgrowth of the cultural revolution launched in the twenties. Neither Fitzgerald nor Lawrence could have envisioned such a phenomenon, but each, in his own way, predicted it. □

The mass culture of the twentieth century has not only spawned hybrid, quintessentially modern art forms like the music video, it has produced worldwide superstars of a magnitude that would have been unimaginable in previous centuries. Probably the most widely recognized celebrity in history (and certainly one whose public persona has revolved around the breaking down of traditional boundaries—especially those of race and gender), Michael Jackson brought the music video form to its apogee in 1982, with his 14-minute *Thriller* video *(right),* an overt homage to Hollywood horror films.

"Sometimes people call me an idealist. Well, that is the way I know I am an American. America is the only idealistic nation in the world."—**U.S. president Woodrow Wilson**

STORY OF THE YEAR

League of Nations Convenes in Geneva

1 The first general meeting of the League of Nations was held in Geneva on November 19, 1920—without an envoy from the nation whose leader was the organization's architect and most passionate advocate.

The League (a precursor to the United Nations) was Woodrow Wilson's fondest dream—an international body that would work toward global disarmament, self-determination for subject peoples, and better relations between labor and capital. Its members would pledge to honor one another's territory and independence, and to submit to discussion, arbitration, and a cooling-off period if war with another member seemed imminent. Unlike the old alliances and ententes, it would admit virtually every country in the world. But the U.S. Senate failed three times to ratify the Treaty of Versailles, which contained the League's covenant.

Ironically, Wilson himself had urged the "no" votes, because of amendments to the treaty bill added by his bitter enemy, the conservative Republican senator Henry Cabot Lodge. During the summer of 1919, Lodge had proposed a set of "reservations" to be tacked onto the section of the treaty dealing with the League; they underscored the fact that the covenant was not legally binding and that the President could not make war without consulting Congress. Wilson embarked on a grueling tour of the Western states to drum up public support for unconditional ratification. Already exhausted from his months leading the U.S. negotiating team in France, he suffered a physical breakdown in September, soon followed by a stroke.

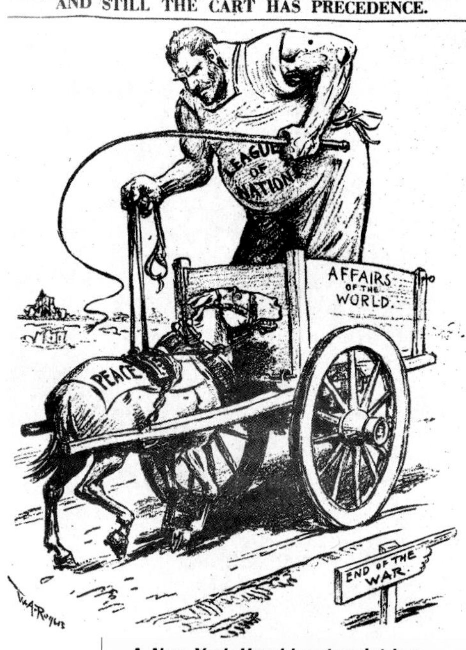

A *New York Herald* cartoonist lampooned the League of Nations.

Incapacitated for months, Wilson was not nominated to run in the 1920 presidential election. (He died in 1924, never having fully recovered.) The Democratic candidate, James Cox, championed League membership, but the voters preferred his Republican opponent, Warren Harding, who evaded the issue. In his inaugural address the following year, Harding announced that the United States would no longer concern itself with European affairs. Later that year, he concluded a separate peace with Germany. America was retreating into isolationism, as the world once again began to spin toward war. **◂1919.1 ▸1921.7**

THE MIDDLE EAST

League Creates Mandates

2 The defeat of Germany and Ottoman Turkey in World War I meant that the vast and diverse colonies of those former empires were up for grabs. In 1920, the short-lived League of Nations carried out one of colonialism's last gasps—and made one of its own few lasting marks on the modern world—when it carved up Ottoman holdings in the Middle East and awarded them to Britain and France as mandates. The mandate system—which gave the Allied powers administrative control of the territories (including those in Africa as well)—was devised by the League as a compromise that allowed the victors to gain "spoils of war" while technically upholding their wartime statements opposing territorial annexation.

Great Britain's dubious prizes were Iraq and Palestine; it divided the latter into Transjordan (present-day Jordan) and Palestine (present-day Israel, including the West Bank of the Jordan River, and the Gaza Strip). Because Britain, in order to secure support for her war aims, had made commitments to both Arabs and Jews, dominion here proved more complicated than anticipated. In 1932, Britain granted independence to Iraq and then had only to wait for Palestine to explode. The conflicting nationalism of Jews and Arabs, coupled with the impending holocaust in Europe, meant the wait would not be long.

France was given control over Lebanon and Syria—no less ambiguous an award, considering the region's volatility. France held on to both countries until World War II, letting go only under the duress of its own occupation by the Germans. Both Syria and

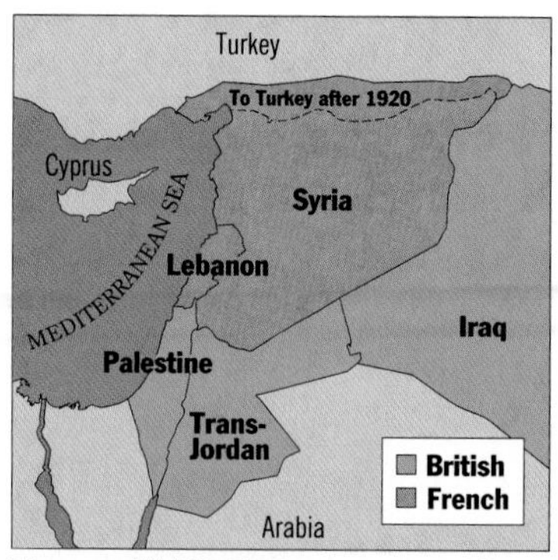

The new Middle East as re-created by the League of Nations in 1920.

Lebanon gained independence in the mid-forties with the support of the United States and the Soviet Union. By the time World War II began, colonialism was so worn down by the politics of the interwar years that it never recovered. **◂1920.1 ▸1921.M**

POPULAR CULTURE

Voices over the Wireless

3 On the evening of November 2, 1920, a few hundred amateur radio enthusiasts tuned their home-rigged receivers to KDKA out of Pittsburgh and heard the first live broadcast of American presidential election returns. By midnight the small audience knew what most Americans would have to wait to read in their morning newspapers: Warren G. Harding had defeated James M. Cox. Westinghouse, which operated the 100-watt KDKA from the roof of its Pittsburgh plant, became the most talked-about company in the United States. Suddenly, radio receivers were in great demand.

Listeners needed earphones to hear commercial radio's first broadcasts.

Radio, which had begun attracting hobbyists before the war, caught on in earnest with the lifting of military restrictions after the Peace of Versailles. Amateurs in Europe and the United States took to the air over homemade transmitters, whose signals were picked up by other enthusiasts on primitive equipment. In England, the Marconi Company launched a twice-daily half-hour broadcast from its new 15,000-watt transmitter at Chelmsford, in February 1920. The broadcasts reached their zenith on June 15 with a live concert by opera diva Dame Nellie Melba (for whom peach melba and melba toast are named) and ended in November, when the government suspended experimental broadcasting. But the hobbyists would not be denied, and in 1922 the government oversaw the

ART & CULTURE: Books: ***Outline of History*** **(H.G. Wells);** ***Chéri*** **(Colette);** ***This Side of Paradise*** **(F. Scott Fitzgerald);** ***A Few Figs from Thistles*** **(Edna St. Vincent Millay);** ***Women in Love*** **(D.H. Lawrence);** ***Bliss*** **(Katherine Mansfield) ... Music: "Look for the Silver Lining" (Kern and DeSylva); "Avalon" (DeSylva, Rose, and Jolson); "I'll Be with You in Apple Blossom Time" (Von Tilzer and Fleason);** ***Amériques***

"Art is dead. This is the new machine art."—**A sign carried by artist George Grosz at the first International Dada Fair**

creation of the British Broadcasting Company. Reorganized five years later as a government-controlled public corporation, the BBC monopolized British radio until 1973, when commercial radio was introduced.

In the United States, radio developed along strictly commercial lines. Spurred by the success of the 1920 election coverage, Westinghouse quickly erected stations at its other plants, generating a market for the receivers it was soon manufacturing. A year later, hundreds of thousands of baseball fans listened to Westinghouse's play-by-play coverage of the World Series. Radio was big business. **◂1917.M ▸1928.3**

ART

Dumbstruck by Dada

4 Visitors entered the gallery through a public toilet and were met by a girl in a first-communion dress reciting obscene poetry. A model of a pig dressed in a German officer's uniform hung from the ceiling. Elsewhere a banner proclaimed, DADA FIGHTS ON THE SIDE OF THE REVOLUTIONARY PROLETARIAT. It was the first International Dada Fair, held in Berlin in 1920—the largest anti-art art exhibition ever mounted. No one was surprised when Berlin authorities arrested several artists and temporarily closed the show.

Dada had been founded four years earlier by a circle of dissident artists and writers from all over Europe—playwright Hugo Ball, poet Tristan Tzara, and artists George Grosz and Jean Arp, among others—who'd flocked to neutral Zurich, Switzerland, during World War I. (Tzara chose the name *dada*, colloquial French for "hobbyhorse," at random.) The dadaists staged anarchic performances combining song, dance, recitation, sculpture, and sheer noise, with audience participation encouraged. They made artwork out of junk, and poems out of words cut from newspapers and haphazardly assembled. The point, as Grosz later put it, was "organized use of insanity to express contempt for a bankrupt world."

After the movement spread to Berlin—where the war and its aftermath made artmaking, except in explicit protest, seem obscenely self-indulgent—it became expressly political. Grosz drew ugly portraits of the greedy bourgeoisie; John Heartfield developed the technique of photomontage, using it to devastating satiric effect. Elsewhere in Germany, dada attracted the talents of collagists Max Ernst and Kurt Schwitters. In Paris its chief exponents were writers André Breton and Paul Eluard; in New York, artists Francis Picabia and Man Ray.

John Heartfield and George Grosz created the catalogue for the International Dada Fair.

After 1920, most of these pioneers abandoned dada's shock tactics for the psychological explorations of surrealism. Dada was dead, but its spirit rose again and again: in hippie "happenings," punk-rock album covers, 1980s performance art—wherever artists wanted, above all else, to shake up the status quo. **◂1917.4 ▸1924.3**

LITERATURE

Christie Introduces Poirot

5 Taking as a challenge her sister's pronouncement that she had never read a mystery where she didn't know straightaway "whodunit," Agatha Christie wrote her first novel, *The Mysterious Affair at Styles*, while working as a nurse during World War I. The manuscript bounced from publisher to publisher before it was accepted by The Bodley Head (which later bilked the author out of a good portion of her royalties). When the book finally appeared in 1920, readers met one of the most famous detectives in fiction—the short, fussy, and egotistical Belgian with the grand name, Hercule Poirot. "His head was exactly the shape of an egg, and he always perched it a little on one side," wrote Christie. "The neatness of his attire was almost incredible; I believe a speck of dust would have caused him more pain than a bullet wound."

Ten years and many hugely popular books later, Christie introduced her other principal detective, Miss Jane Marple, an elderly spinster with a shrewd mind for homicide. Together, in some 80-odd novels over the next half century, these two characters came to symbolize the Christie-style murder story: an intricate, ingeniously plotted puzzle set among England's cozy leisure classes. Christie specialized in domestic crime—and never has crime been more domesticated than in her novels, which typically contain little real violence or grisly detail.

Her enduring appeal was perhaps best summarized by critic Edmund Crispin: "You know, relaxing with a Christie, that for an hour or two you can forget the authentic nastiness of life and submerge yourself in a world where, no matter how many murders take place, you are essentially in never-never land." **◂1902.12 ▸1930.11**

BIRTHS

Bella Abzug, U.S. political leader.

Isaac Asimov, Russian-U.S. scientist and writer.

Ray Bradbury, U.S. writer.

David Brinkley, U.S. newscaster.

Dave Brubeck, U.S. musician.

Federico Fellini, Italian filmmaker.

Rosalind Franklin, U.K. biochemist.

John Paul II, Roman Catholic pope.

Sun Myung Moon, Korean religious leader.

Peggy Lee, U.S. singer.

Charlie "Bird" Parker, U.S. musician.

Sugar Ray Robinson, U.S. boxer.

Ravi Shankar, Indian musician.

DEATHS

Alexander, Greek king.

Max Brüch, German composer.

William C. Gorgas, U.S. Army physician.

William Dean Howells, U.S. writer and editor.

Amedeo Modigliani, Italian artist.

Robert Peary, U.S. explorer.

John Reed, U.S. journalist.

Jacob Schiff, German-U.S. financier.

Max Weber, German sociologist.

(Edgard Varèse) ... Painting & Sculpture: *Landscape at Céret* (Chaim Soutine); *Reclining Nude* (Amedeo Modigliani) ... Film: *Way Down East* (D.W. Griffith); *The Toll Gate* (with William S. Hart); *One Week* (with Buster Keaton); *Why Change Your Wife?* (Cecil B. DeMille) ... Theater: *The Emperor Jones* and *Beyond the Horizon* (Eugene O'Neill); *Heartbreak House* (G.B. Shaw).

"I had a better year."—**Babe Ruth, in 1930, when asked if he realized that he earned more than the president of the United States**

NEW IN 1920

Trojan condoms.

The Tommy gun (patented by John T. Thompson).

Legalized abortion (U.S.S.R.).

Canonization of Joan of Arc by the Catholic Church.

Baby Ruth candy bar.

Boysenberries (hybrid of black-, logan-, and raspberries, developed by Rudolph Boysen).

International Telephone and Telegraph (ITT).

Qantas Airways Ltd. (Queensland and Northern Territory Aerial Services Ltd.).

IN THE UNITED STATES

▶**MAN O' WAR RETIRES**—Man O' War needed just two seasons to become the greatest American racehorse of the

first half of the century. Before retiring in 1920, the chestnut colt won 20 of his 21 races (his defeat by a horse named Upset gave rise to the term "upset victory"), acing the Preakness and the Belmont Stakes and establishing five speed records. He went on to sire 64 stakes horses—among them the spectacular War Admiral, winner of the 1937 Triple Crown. ◂1919.M ▸1973.9

▶**GARMENT STRIKE**—In December, the 100,000-member Amalgamated Clothing Workers of America began a strike against the sweatshop bosses of New York, Boston, and Baltimore. When the strike ended six months later, management had lost $10 million, while workers had accepted a 15 percent pay cut and promised to raise productivity by the same figure. But labor did make some gains: Clothing manufacturers agreed to a union shop and dropped demands for a return to piecework pay. ◂1919.6 ▸1936.M

SPORTS

A Golden Age Commences

6 His name is part of the American vernacular, and his reputation extends far beyond national boundaries: In Japan, for example, a "Babu Rusu Day" was once declared in his honor. Indeed, George Herman "Babe" Ruth is probably the most famous athlete of all time. And when the New York Yankees paid $125,000 for his contract in 1920, they launched a golden age of sports that has had no equal before or since.

There were heroes and heroines on every conceivable playing field throughout the twenties—Red Grange and Knute Rockne and the Four Horsemen of Notre Dame, who became football's first superstars; swimmer (and, later, Hollywood Tarzan) Johnny Weissmuller and distance runner Paavo Nurmi, who made Olympic history; Bill Tilden, Suzanne Lenglen, and Helen Wills, whose exploits thrust tennis into the international spotlight; Bobby Jones, who retired from golf in 1930, with 13 major championships under his belt; and Jack Dempsey and Gene Tunney, whose 1927 "long count" boxing match remains one of that sport's most controversial.

But towering above them all is the legendary Ruth. In 1921 he hit an astonishing 59 home runs, so boosting his already immense popularity that, in 1923, New York opened Yankee Stadium and dubbed it "The House That Ruth Built." The Yankees were the marvel of the twenties, winning world championships in 1923, 1927, and 1928. The '27 team is still talked about as the greatest of all time. That was the year Ruth hit 60 home runs, which remains the record for a 154-game season. His career mark of 714, reached in 1935, stood until 1974, when Hank Aaron slugged his 715th. Ruth's well-chronicled flamboyance—his womanizing and carousing; his enormous (by twenties' standards) salary—only fueled his fans' insatiable appetite for news about their hero.

As the 1930s approached, the golden age began to wane. But the passion for sports that gripped the Roaring Twenties has never subsided. **◂1919.M ▸1920.M**

The Babe propelled sports to unprecedented heights.

IRELAND

Sunday, Bloody Sunday

7 In a bungled attempt to resolve the chronic Irish Question, the British Parliament passed the ill-fated Government of Ireland Act, partitioning its island colony into two administrative regions, each with limited domestic autonomy. This measure in 1920 effectively laid the groundwork for a future of sectarian violence.

Britain's decision was designed largely to appease an increasingly censorious international community, but within Ireland it managed to satisfy none of the various constituencies. The result was bloodshed and chaos. The IRA, outraged at the way the north had been divided so as to create Protestant majorities, stepped up its guerrilla campaign against British forces; Britain retaliated by imposing martial law and creating a special police unit—the notorious Black and Tans, so nicknamed for their mixed khaki-and-blackish-green uniforms—to enforce it. The situation rapidly degenerated into a terrorist competition, with the IRA and the Black and Tans trading brutal attacks.

On Bloody Sunday, November 21, 1920, the violence reached a gruesome peak. In the morning, IRA operatives in Dublin assassinated 11 suspected British intelligence agents; that afternoon, the Black and Tans retaliated by opening fire on the crowd watching a football match in a Dublin park. The fusillade lasted for several minutes; when it ended, 12 spectators were dead, 60 others injured. Throughout Ireland, hostility toward British rule intensified exponentially. As the guerrilla warfare continued, British prime minister Lloyd George was forced to readdress the Irish Question. His answer, in 1922, was to grant the 26 counties of southern Ireland dominion status within the commonwealth. But the partition between those counties and the six Protestant counties in the north stood fast. **◂1916.5 ▸1922.12**

British troops look down on Dublin.

LITERATURE

Exile on Main Street

8 In the years before the publication of *Main Street*, Sinclair Lewis's controversial 1920 novel, rural American villages represented all that big cities were not: cleanliness, virtue, and a population of caring individuals. Lewis's novel shattered this image, probably forever. Carol Milford, the young bride who comes to Gopher Prairie, Minnesota (which bears a strong resemblance to Lewis's hometown of Sauk Centre, Minnesota), with her kindly but dull doctor husband, quickly discovers that the seemingly idyllic town is stultifying, complacent, intolerant of diversity, and uninterested in cultural enrichment. *Main Street* was a work of unblinking realism, and though leavened by overtones of optimism, and even humor, it was an indictment of the middle class and its verities.

Main Street established Lewis as

SPORTS: Baseball: World Series, Cleveland Indians defeat Brooklyn Dodgers, 5–2; Brooklyn Dodgers and Boston Braves play longest game ever (26 innings, tie 1–1) ... Olympics held in Antwerp ... Football: American Professional Football Association (later the NFL) founded.

"'I have never made love to you ... and I never shall. But you are the woman I would have married if it had been possible for both of us.' "—**Edith Wharton, *The Age of Innocence***

a major writer and indefatigable social critic. A former newspaperman, Lewis had a keen eye for physical detail and would immerse himself in exhaustive research, spending weeks among the people his characters were modeled on, writing down their jargon, mannerisms, and peculiarities of dress and habit. In subsequent novels, like *Babbitt* (1922), *Arrowsmith* (1925), and *Elmer Gantry* (1927), he railed against the average American businessman, condemned the materialism of scientists, and exposed racial prejudice and religious hypocrisy. Some readers denounced Lewis as a traitor, but many more loved his books. Of all the so-called "debunking" authors working between the wars, he was the most popular.

Lewis turned down the 1926 Pulitzer Prize for *Arrowsmith*, but accepted when the 1930 Nobel committee selected him as the first American to win the literature prize. Many of his contemporaries left America for Europe, but Lewis never strayed for long from the Midwest. He died in 1951 on an excursion to Rome. **◂1911.V**

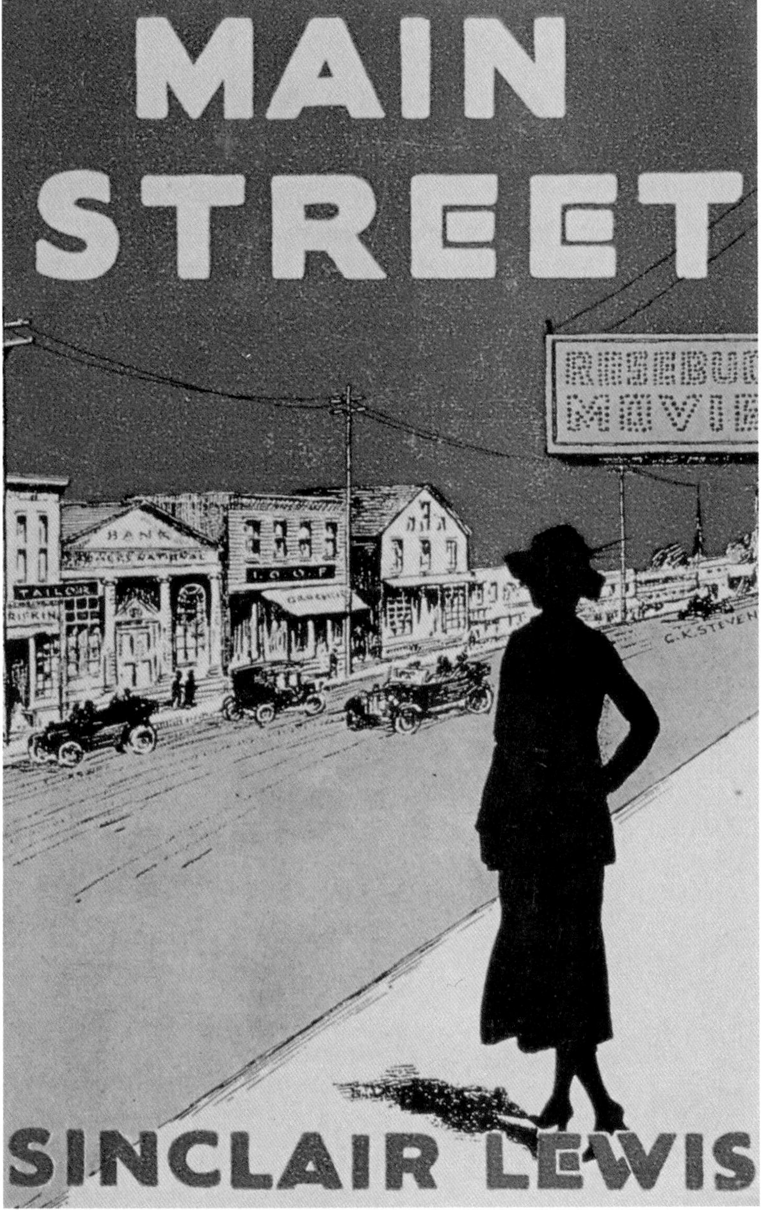

Small-town America: Lewis exploded the myth of its wholesome virtues.

LITERATURE

A Tale of Thwarted Love

9 While Sinclair Lewis lampooned Gopher Prairie, Edith Wharton offered a tragicomic critique of a very different side of American life: the New York high society of her youth. *The Age of Innocence*, a tale of thwarted love, made Wharton, in 1920, the first woman to win a Pulitzer Prize.

Edith Wharton saw through the glitter on both sides of the Atlantic.

The novel explored a recent past transformed into ancient history by the Great War, and measured the moral gulf between America's elite and that of Europe—two "tribes" whose territories intersected, but whose values remained deeply alien. Wharton's New Yorkers worship European culture but shudder at European mores: Despite their distance from Lewis's Main Streeters, despite their polish, they are provincials—and innocents. Asked by the woman he loves (his wife's European-bred cousin) if he means to make her his mistress, the novel's protagonist, Newland Archer, stammers, "I want somehow to get away with you into a world where words like that—categories like that—won't exist." Her reply: "Oh, my dear—where is that country? Have you ever been there?"

Wharton's chosen country was France, where she lived from 1907 until her death in 1937. (Her relief work during the war, when she took in 600 Belgian orphans, earned her the Cross of the Legion of Honor.) But the books that made her one of the era's most penetrating writers, among them *The House of Mirth* and *Ethan Frome*, were set in her native land. Like her friend, mentor, and fellow expatriate, Henry James, she was a detached, cosmopolitan observer of the American character.

Also like James, she had a deep conservative streak (despite her exasperation with "polite" society). At the end of *The Age of Innocence*, Archer is 57 and baffled by the ways of his grown children. "The new generation," he muses, "had swept away all the old landmarks, and with them the signposts and the danger-signal." **◂1903.12**

IN THE UNITED STATES

▶ACLU FOUNDED—Appalled at seeing the Bill of Rights trampled to suppress "reds," lawyer Roger Baldwin recruited prominent citizens (among them Helen Keller, Clarence Darrow, Upton Sinclair, and future Supreme Court justice Felix Frankfurter) to form the American Civil Liberties Union. In a host of famous cases—from the Scopes "Monkey Trial" of 1925 to the Nazi march in Skokie in 1978—the ACLU would defend the constitutional rights of leftists, rightists, and everyone in between. ◂1919.6 ▸1924.V

▶TILDEN'S TRIUMPH—"Big Bill" Tilden in 1920 became the first American to win Britain's Wimbledon championship, and went on to dominate world tennis for a decade. The flamboyant six-footer transformed the sport from country-club pastime to

popular spectacle, but he died in poverty in 1953, ostracized for his homosexuality. ◂1920.6 ▸1926.M

▶WALL STREET BOMB—Blood and broken glass rained over Manhattan's financial district on September 16, when a bomb planted near the headquarters of J.P. Morgan & Co. killed 30 and wounded 200. Authorities suspected an anarchist plot—and several publicity-seekers claimed responsibility for the blast—but no conclusive proof was ever found. ▸1993.M

▶PONZI'S CON—"Financial wizard" Charles Ponzi provided Boston investors with colossal returns on an odd commodity: foreign postal coupons. But in August, investigators found the coupons were a sham; Ponzi—whose name became a synonym for fraudulent pyramid schemes—was paying some clients part of what he took from others, and keeping the difference. Thousands lost their savings and six banks failed when the pyramid crumbled. ▸1989.10

POLITICS & BUSINESS: GNP: $91.5 billion ... U.S. population: 105,710,620 ... Warren G. Harding elected president, defeating James M. Cox ... U.S. wells supply 65% of world's oil ... U.S. railroad-track miles peak at 253,000 ... National League of Women Voters, the American Civil Liberties Union, and the American Farm Bureau Federation are organized ... 18th Amendment (Prohibition) goes into effect.

"There is no sphere which we regard as so peculiarly women's sphere as that of love. Yet there is no sphere which in civilisation women have so far had so small a part in regulating."—Havelock Ellis, ***On Life and Sex***

AROUND THE WORLD

▶CARRANZA ASSASSINATED—Though a revolution had put him in power, Mexican president Venustiano Carranza was never much of a revolutionary. Dragging his feet on social reform, he'd faced armed opposition led by radicals like

Emiliano Zapata. But when he tried to force the election of a handpicked successor, even his confederates revolted. Carranza was murdered by one of his own guards in May, as he fled a rebellion led by General Alvaro Obregón—who became the second president of the Mexican republic. ◀1917.11 ▶1926.M

▶KAPP PUTSCH—The German government's attempt to disband the Freikorps backfired in March, when the rightist mercenaries—swastikas painted on their helmets—revolted in Berlin. Supported by World War I commander Erich Ludendorff, they seized key buildings and installed American-born royalist Wolfgang Kapp as head of state. After the army refused to oppose the insurrection, the government fled to Stuttgart and called a general strike. The strike paralyzed the capital; the putsch collapsed, and Kapp fled to Sweden. A similar revolt succeeded in Bavaria, however, where rightists overthrew the state government. ◀1919.2 ▶1921.7

▶TREATY OF TRIANON—Having seized power from Hungary's communists, Admiral Miklós Nagybányai Horthy signed a pact at the Trianon Palace in Versailles ceding three quarters of Hungary to its neighbors. The treaty, which fulfilled Allied terms for officially ending World War I, made Austria, Czechoslovakia, and Yugoslavia bigger. ◀1919.M

SCIENCE

The Puzzle of Polymers

10 Chemists had been fabricating synthetic alternatives to rubber, a naturally occurring polymer, since the 1860s. But the results were unsatisfactory—largely because the chemists were working from an imperfect perception of a polymer's molecular structure. Then, in 1920, German chemist Hermann Staudinger unveiled a radical new theory that proved to be a crucial breakthrough in the development of plastics. In a paper entitled *"Uber Polymerisation,"* Staudinger proposed that natural polymers are composed not of individual molecules joined one to another, as previously believed, but of chains of giant "macromolecules" that result from chemical reactions among thousands of simpler substances. To scientists accustomed to thinking of molecules as infinitely tiny specks of matter, Staudinger initially appeared to be a crank. The scales began to tip in his favor during a series of scientific symposia held between 1925 and 1930. After one meeting, a chemist brought grudgingly around to Staudinger's view confessed, "Such enormous organic molecules are not to my personal liking, but it appears that we all shall have to become acquainted [with] them."

By establishing a sound theoretical basis for polymer chemistry, Staudinger's breakthrough eventually enabled scientists to fabricate artificial macromolecules in the laboratory. In the United States, Wallace Carothers, an early convert to Staudinger's theory (and later well known as the inventor of nylon), built on Staudinger's work, studying the formation of polyesters, polyanhydrides, polyamides, and other polymers. It wasn't until 1953 that Staudinger's work was recognized with a Nobel Prize. **◀1909.7 ▶1934.9**

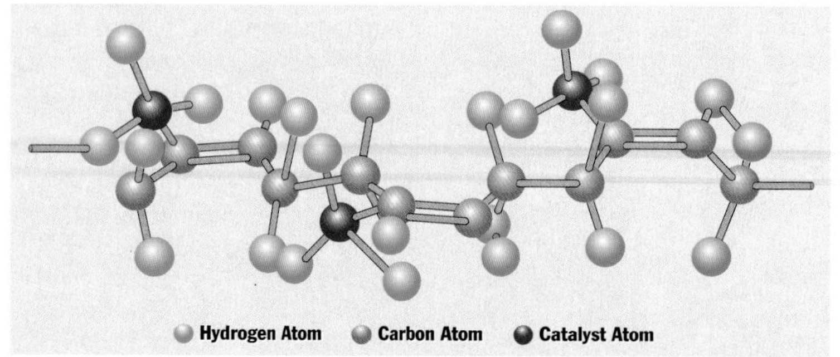

Thousands of molecules join together to create a single "macromolecule" of rubber.

After eight decades: breaking the male voting monopoly at last.

SOCIAL REFORM

Women Get the Vote

11 Although women in some nations—New Zealand, Finland, Norway—were granted the vote early in the century, World War I quickened the pace, with women's suffrage coming, in widely varying degrees, to the Soviet Union in 1917, to Canada and the United Kingdom in 1918, and to Austria, Poland, Germany, and Czechoslovakia in 1919. The United States was part of this postwar tide, and in August 1920, it became the first country to grant all its female citizens over the age of 21 the same voting rights as their male counterparts. The culmination of an 80-year struggle by American suffragists, universal female enfranchisement was established by the 19th Amendment to the U.S. Constitution.

The amendment's road to ratification had been bumpy, with rancorous debate in Congress. Opponents argued that the vote would upset the social order, coarsening women and eroding their femininity. The House approved a suffrage-amendment resolution in early 1918, but the measure got stalled in the Senate, largely because southern legislators feared white control of the South would collapse if both black men and women could vote. Twice rejected, the resolution was adopted in June 1919; the amendment was ratified by the required two thirds of the states just in time for the 1920 presidential election.

Many other countries followed in the path of the United States, especially just after World War II. But as late as the 1970s, women in some countries, including Switzerland and Syria, had only begun to obtain what the great nineteenth-century suffragist Susan B. Anthony called "the pivotal right, the one that underlies all other rights." **◀1903.3 ▶1959.M**

IDEAS

Havelock Ellis, Sexologist

12 If Sigmund Freud provided the theoretical framework for the revolution in sexual attitudes that took place after World War I, much of the basic research was done by a bookish British physician named Havelock Ellis. Ellis anticipated Freud in exploring preadolescent sexuality, and coined the terms "narcissistic" and "autoerotic," later used by Freud and others. Most important, perhaps, was Ellis's pioneering support of sex education and feminism—including what he called "the love-rights of women," a phrase he coined in his 1920 book, *On Life and Sex.*

The book was one of seven volumes that make up Ellis's major work, *Studies in the Psychology of Sex* (1897-1928), which explored such topics as homosexuality, masturbation, and sexual physiology. However scholarly, the books were hot stuff for their era: A British judge banned the first one as a "filthy publication."

Unlike earlier sexologists, who catalogued "perversions" in order to condemn them, Ellis regarded any sexual practice as healthy so long as no one was hurt. Ellis's views were informed by his own quirks. He was a virgin until his marriage at age 32. His wife preferred women, and the couple—who were extremely devoted to each other—became one of the first to maintain an "open relationship." **◀1915.2 ▶1948.10**

NOBEL PRIZES: Peace: Léon Victor Bourgeois (French; Covenant of the League of Nations) ... Literature: Knut Hamsun (Norwegian; novelist) ... Chemistry: Walther Nernst (German; third law of thermodynamics) ... Medicine: August Krogh (Danish; capillary motion) ... Physics: Charles E. Guillaume (Swiss; precision measurements).

A VOICE FROM 1920

Our Great American Sport

By Dorothy Parker, from *Vanity Fair*, January 1920

"Three things shall I have till I die," wrote Dorothy Parker: "Laughter and hope and a sock in the eye." Few humorists have parried life's blows—or delivered epigrammatic punches—with more wit than Parker, whose acerbic reviews, verse, and essays graced America's best magazines in the 1920s. With fellow wag Robert Benchley and playwright Robert Sherwood, she founded the Round Table at New York City's Algonquin Hotel, an informal luncheon club whose verbal swordplay made the papers nationwide. Parker went on to more serious business—tragicomic short stories, dramatic screenplays (A Star Is Born)*, Spanish Civil War reportage, and left-wing politics. The excerpts that follow (with illustrations "by Fish") were sparked by news that the nation's divorce rate had reached unprecedented heights in the wake of World War I.* ◄**1919.M** ►**1922.V**

Old Home Week

It is so nice for the new bridegroom to meet his wife's collection of former husbands. It is something for him to look forward to, all through the honeymoon. These little family gatherings are so delightfully homey—it is always reassuring to feel that you are all members of the same club. Men who thoughtlessly marry a hitherto unmarried girl do miss so much in life; they never have the chance to meet their brother heroes, and to while away an hour exchanging experiences.

The Dawn of a New Life

Perhaps the sweetest time in a young girl's life is that roseate moment when she gets her first divorce. It is a time that comes but once to a girl. When at last her final decree is her very own, she stands, in innocent wonder, on the threshold of a new life. What pretty, girlish dreams are hers as she goes out into the great world with her new hope, in search of the nearest minister, so that she can start things up all over again. No, there's nothing like the thrill of an initial divorce—from the second on, they are about as exciting as shampoo.

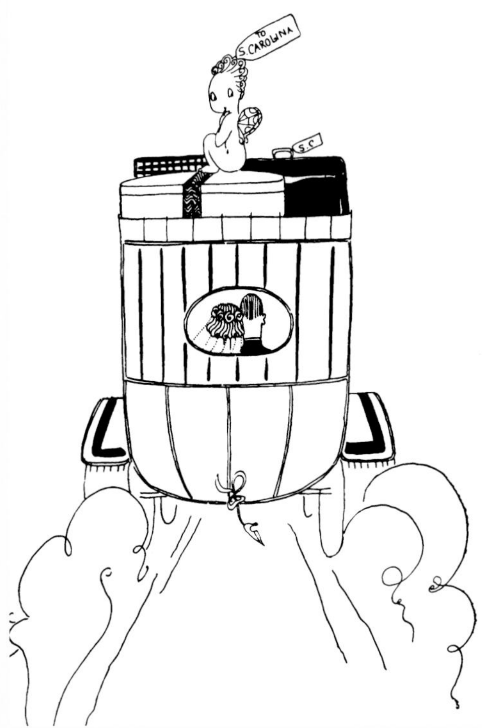

Back to the Start

This little scene is the sort of thing that divorce leads to—hope springs eternal, and all that. A divorce simply gets one into the right frame of mind for a fresh start in matrimony. After all, Nature will have its own way; there's nothing like love—it is what the divorce lawyers and Reno hotel keepers attribute all their success to.

"Everybody that knows these two arms knows very well that I did not need to ... kill a man to take the money. I can live with my two arms and live well."—**Bartolomeo Vanzetti, in 1927, before being sentenced to death**

STORY OF THE YEAR

Sacco and Vanzetti

1 It was an ordinary, if brutal, crime: In April 1920, bandits stole $16,000 from a shoe factory in South Braintree, Massachusetts, killing the paymaster and a guard. But the alleged criminals were extraordinary: a pair of committed anarchists, Nicola Sacco and Bartolomeo Vanzetti. Their 1921 trial created an international furor not seen since the Dreyfus case.

Times were tough for radicals in the United States. With revolutions erupting overseas, many Americans lumped anarchists, socialists, and communists into one "red menace" to be crushed at any cost. Immigrant leftists were especially suspect (thousands were deported after World War I). In this atmosphere, only a supremely impartial judge could ensure a fair trial for two Italian-born revolutionaries—and Webster Thayer clearly was not that judge. Out of court, he derided "those anarchistic bastards"; in court, he made no allowances for the defendants' poor English and permitted the prosecutor, whose weak case was based on circumstantial evidence (some witnesses said they saw two men resembling the accused among the bandits), to harp on their subversive ideology.

Sacco *(right)* and Vanzetti: murderers or political scapegoats?

Neither defendant had a solid alibi, both had been armed when arrested, and both had lied to police during questioning. But the stolen money was never traced to them, and neither man had a criminal record. Both were employed: Sacco as a skilled shoe-factory laborer, Vanzetti as a fishmonger. Still, an all-native jury convicted them of robbery and murder—a capital offense. *"Siamo innocente!"* cried Sacco.

Over the next six years, the pair fought to have their case reopened. But even after a convicted killer confessed to the crime, authorities held fast. In April 1927, Judge Thayer sentenced them to the electric chair.

As demonstrations erupted and letters of protest—from leading intellectuals like Albert Einstein and Marie Curie as well as from thousands of ordinary people—poured in from around the world, the governor of Massachusetts pondered a clemency appeal. Despite the outcry—and an official report chiding Judge Thayer for his prejudicial remarks during the trial—the governor upheld the sentence. The U.S. Supreme Court refused to hear a last-minute appeal.

On August 23, 1927, Sacco and Vanzetti were executed at Boston's Charlestown State Prison. After thanking the warden for his kindness, Vanzetti said, "I wish to forgive some people for what they are now doing to me." **◂1919.6**

THE SOVIET UNION

Lenin Relaxes the Revolution

2 Vladimir Lenin's New Economic Policy for Soviet recovery, announced in 1921, was a sharp retreat from the Communist leader's oft-repeated revolutionary doctrines. But NEP was, in Lenin's view, a necessary corrective to the famine, ruined infrastructure, and persistent backwardness that afflicted his country. "When you live with wolves," Lenin conceded, "you must howl as they do."

NEP was nothing more radical than modified capitalism; it established a mixed economy—communism, private agriculture, limited private trade, and manufacturing. The policy slowed the total nationalization of industry begun after the revolution and gave the government's blessing to small-scale private enterprises. Some socialized businesses were returned to their former owners. Most significant, NEP replaced *prodrazverstka*, the state's policy of confiscating agricultural surpluses from the peasantry, with *prodnalog*, a fixed agricultural tax. The move tacitly recognized private property: Farmers, not the state, owned what they grew.

The reforms were necessitated by famine, which, compounded by a poor transportation system and a disorganized relief system, caused widespread starvation. Hard-liners attacked Lenin, and he answered them candidly. "It happens that Russia, economically one of the most backward capitalist countries," wrote Lenin, "has not succeeded in its 'storm attack,' and finds itself forced to resort to slow and gradual 'siege' operations." The perfect communist state would have to wait. **◂1919.11 ▸1924.1**

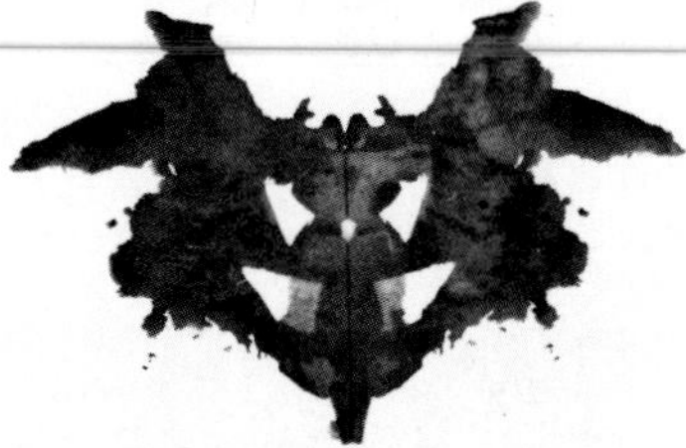

Rorschach test: Shapes on a blotter reveal the shape of the mind.

IDEAS

Images in Inkblots

3 "The subject," wrote Swiss psychiatrist Hermann Rorschach of his novel diagnostic test, introduced in his 1921 book, *Psychodiagnostik*, "is given one plate after another and asked, 'What might this be?' "

"This" was a symmetrical inkblot, shaded black and gray with occasional color highlights. The key to the test lies in the ambiguity of each blot's shape, which might be interpreted as a butterfly or a bat, a dancer, a clown, or a human face. The patient provides the content: What he sees and how he presents his vision, Rorschach (a student of Carl Jung) maintained, is indicative of his psychological state. "The experiment," he explained, "consists in the interpretation of accidental forms."

Though now almost a pop-culture cliché, the Rorschach test is still a widely used diagnostic tool. Perhaps its most memorable application was in 1946, when it was administered to Nazi war criminals at Nuremberg. The results were telling: Where others might see furry animals and exotic flowers, Hermann Goering, the man who created the Gestapo and the first concentration camps, found fish eyes and violent trolls. **◂1912.2 ▸1946.V**

With millions waiting for bread, Lenin decided that communism had to wait as well.

ART & CULTURE: Books: *Crome Yellow* (Aldous Huxley); *Alice Adams* (Booth Tarkington); *The Sheik* (Edith Hull); *Three Soldiers* (John Dos Passos); *Héloïse and Abelard* (George Moore); *The Triumph of the Egg* (Sherwood Anderson); *Poems 1918–1921* (Ezra Pound); *Queen Victoria* (Lytton Strachey) ... Music: "I'm Just Wild About Harry" and "Shuffle Along" (Sissle and Blake); "Second Hand Rose"

"Good taste ruins certain true spiritual values: such as taste itself."—Coco Chanel

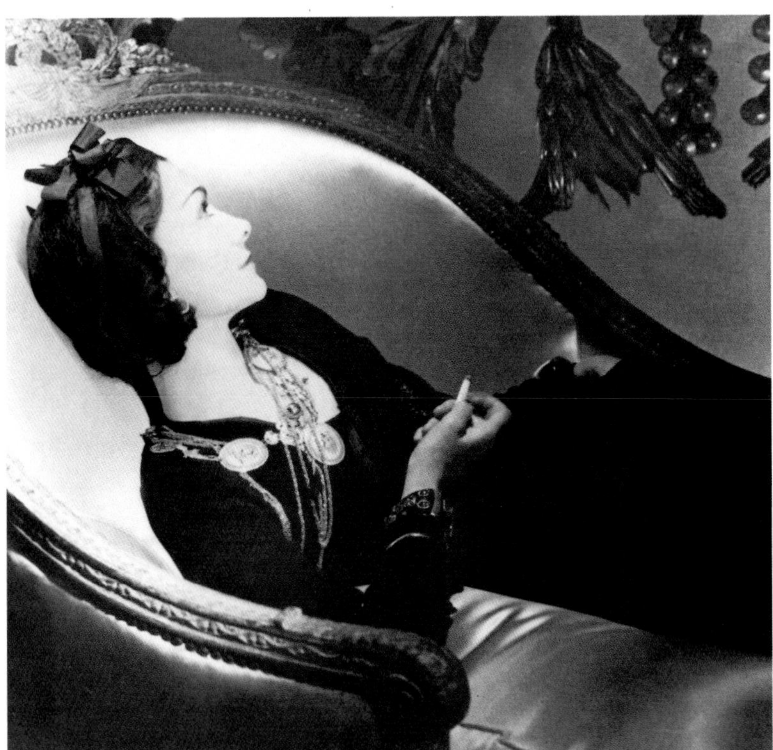

Coco Chanel's seemingly effortless chic is captured by photographer Horst.

FASHION

Chanel No. 5 Appears

4 Designer Gabrielle "Coco" Chanel was already a near legend in the world of haute couture when, in 1921, she introduced what became the most successful perfume ever marketed.

Together with chemist Ernest Beaux, Chanel had concocted a fragrance that contained some 80 ingredients, including jasmine. (Informed of jasmine's high cost, Chanel replied, "In that case, put even more jasmine in it.") When the perfume appeared on the market, it was notable for its simple packaging and its bold name: Chanel No. 5. Simplicity and boldness were characteristic of the woman who had led high fashion into the twentieth century.

Discarding the "fussy bits and pieces" that bedeviled most clothes of the day, Chanel introduced an uncomplicated elegance, coupled with unprecedented comfort, into the wardrobes of wealthy women: tweed suits, beige jersey blouses, trench coats, turtleneck sweaters, and the "little black dress." With her approbation, fake jewelry, especially strings of faux pearls, became acceptable. The Chanel suit—a skirt topped by a collarless cardigan jacket trimmed in braid—is probably the single-most-copied design in fashion. At its height, Chanel Industries employed 3,500 people, but the empire's financial success was based above all on Chanel No. 5. Chanel's example inspired scores of later designers, who recognized that lending their names to a successful fragrance line could often earn them more than several seasons' worth of clothing lines.

Chanel, who grew up orphaned and poor in the French countryside, was as smart and stylish about her social life as she was about her business. She traveled in circles that included Picasso, Churchill, Cocteau, and Stravinsky. As a teenager she ran off with a young cavalry officer, in the first of many celebrated affairs. Her most famous liaison was with Hugh Richard Arthur Grosvenor, the Duke of Westminster and one of Europe's wealthiest men. But Chanel, who never married, had no interest in becoming his wife. "There are a lot of duchesses," she pointed out, "but only one Coco Chanel." **◂1900.7 ▸1947.12**

JAPAN

Murder and Madness

5 In the span of a single, dramatic month in 1921, Japan lost its leading liberal reformer to murder and its conservative emperor to madness. On November 4, Takashi Hara, the country's first nonroyal prime minister and a symbol of Japanese modernism, was stabbed to death by a right-wing assassin. Days later, mental illness forced out the emblematically traditional Emperor Taisho; his son, the westward-looking Crown Prince Hirohito, became imperial regent.

After becoming prime minister in 1918, Hara, the dominant Japanese civilian politician of his day, solidified his popular support by dispensing patronage through Seiyukai (the political party he built into an American-style machine), easing property requirements for voting, and opposing the military's untrammeled power. His assassination stunned the world, spreading fear that Japan might slip back into shogunism. In fact, his Seiyukai Party remained in control for the next 10 years—and the military, without Hara's restraining hand, grew increasingly, ominously, powerful.

Hirohito, 20, shattered precedent and raised eyebrows when he became the first Japanese crown prince to leave his native shores. Returning home from a six-month European tour—three weeks spent with Edward VIII, the Prince of Wales—and displaying a newfound taste for golf and bacon-and-egg breakfasts, Hirohito took control of the imperial government from his mentally unstable father. Upon his coronation as emperor five years later, Hirohito embarked on a 63-year reign that witnessed his country's transformation from insular island kingdom to modern world power. **◂1910.1 ▸1928.5**

Crown Prince Hirohito, scion of the world's oldest imperial family, 124th descendant of Japan's first emperor.

BIRTHS

Karel Appel, Dutch painter.

Joseph Beuys, German artist.

Roy Campanella, U.S. baseball player.

Alexander Dubček, Czechoslovak political leader.

Friedrich Dürrenmatt, Swiss playwright.

Betty Friedan, U.S. writer and feminist leader.

John Glenn, U.S. astronaut and senator.

Alex Haley, U.S. writer.

Sergio Leone, Italian filmmaker.

Yves Montand, French actor and singer.

Brian Moore, Irish-Canadian novelist.

Joseph Papp, U.S. theater producer.

Philip Mountbatten, Duke of Edinburgh, U.K. prince consort.

Satyajit Ray, Indian filmmaker.

Maurice Richard, Canadian hockey player.

Andrei Sakharov, U.S.S.R. physicist and rights activist.

DEATHS

John Burroughs, U.S. naturalist.

Enrico Caruso, Italian singer.

José Miguel Gómez, Cuban president.

Engelbert Humperdinck, German composer.

Pyotr Kropotkin, Russian geographer and revolutionary.

Bat Masterson, U.S. sheriff and sportswriter.

Nicholas I, Montenegrin king.

Camille Saint-Saëns, French composer.

(Hanley and Clarke); "Ain't We Got Fun" (Whiting, Egan, and Kahn) ... Painting & Sculpture: *Composition with Red, Yellow and Blue* (Piet Mondrian); *Variegated Circle* (Wassily Kandinsky); *Three Musicians* (Pablo Picasso) ... Film: *The Kid* (Charles Chaplin); *The Four Horsemen of the Apocalypse* (Rex Ingram, with Rudolph Valentino) ... Theater: *Dulcy* (Kaufman and Connelly); *R.U.R.* (Karel Capek).

"Either you receive your emancipation at the hands of the proletariat, in cooperation with it, under its guidance, or you are doomed to remain the slaves of English, American, and Japanese camarilla."—**Grigory Zinoviev, addressing CCP delegates in Moscow**

NEW IN 1921

Wise potato chips.

Betty Crocker (created to promote Gold Medal Flour).

Polygraph (lie detector) test.

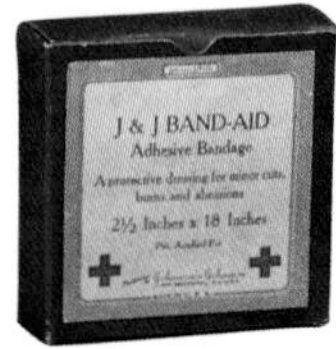

Band-Aid-brand adhesive bandages (Johnson & Johnson).

Peter Paul's Mounds Bar.

Van Heusen's starchless stiff collars.

IN THE UNITED STATES

▶UNKNOWN SOLDIER—Like so many others killed in World War I, he lay unidentified on a muddy French battlefield. But three years after the armistice, one of America's anonymous dead came home to accept his country's homage on behalf of all the rest. In a plain black coffin, the Unknown Soldier was laid to rest first in the Capitol rotunda, where only murdered presidents had lain before. After the crowds paid their respects, he was buried among heroes in Arlington National Cemetery on November 11. His tomb became a memorial to the dead of all U.S. wars. ◀1918.11

▶THERE SHE IS ...—The first Miss America pageant in September was an obscure publicity stunt aimed at extending Atlantic City's tourist season past Labor Day. Only eight contestants participated, representing

towns, not states; hosted by arms-industry heir Hudson Maxim, the contest featured a "bathing revue" (even the all-male orchestra donned swimsuits) but no talent

A young Mao *(right)* and his future second-in-command, Lin Biao.

CHINA

Communist Party Founded

❻ The long journey toward a communist state in China began humbly, with a series of clandestine meetings in and around Shanghai during the summer of 1921. The First Party Congress, as the sessions came to be called, was convened aboard a boat moored on a lake outside the city—the only place the delegates felt safe from police surveillance. From this shaky beginning grew what would, by century's end, be the most powerful communist party in the world.

The bitter fall of the Chinese Republic to warlords in 1916 and the country's subsequent reversion to feudalism produced a passion for revolution in China. Students, especially, had enjoyed a taste of enlightenment, and refused to let the state's fragile advances slip away. The void left by the warlords was filled with radical talk, and many young activists, inspired by the success of the Bolsheviks, held up the Soviet model for emulation. Recognizing an opportunity, the Comintern, the Bolshevik vehicle for world revolution, sent envoys to China to help organize the country's socialist groups into a coherent communist party. The Comintern's liaison in China was Chen Duxiu, a cofounder of the Chinese Communist Party (CCP), who led the efforts to recruit new members and send them to the Soviet Union to train as revolutionary organizers. (The Chinese communists returned the favor later in 1921 when their Red Army helped the Soviets defeat the White Russians who had been occupying Mongolia since the previous year.)

The new generation of Chinese radicals emerged rapidly. Mao Zedong, a 27-year-old teacher, started a communist cell in his home province of Hunan; Deng Xiaoping, 16, and Zhou Enlai, 23, both students in Paris, joined the French Communist Party. The players were in position. At Shanghai they came together and focused their goals. **◀1916.8 ▶1924.M**

GERMANY

War Reparations Set

❼ Germany's finances and territory came under growing pressure from the victorious Allies in 1921, and its already fractured social order began to disintegrate under the strain.

The nation finally received the bill for World War I in January. After long and bitter wrangling between the British and the French over the proper sum (French estimates were higher), the European Allies demanded of their vanquished enemy $63 billion (i.e., gold dollars) in cash and goods, payable over 42 years. Germany countered with an offer of $7 billion. As talks proceeded, Allied troops occupied parts of the country to show that its creditors meant business. In March, German officials reluctantly agreed to a revised figure of $32 billion. While the amount still seemed overwhelming—no nation had ever shouldered such a debt—the government decided on a policy of "fulfillment": It would make the payments until even the Allies could see the burden was intolerable, then renegotiate.

But the policy depended on the cooperation of the German people, a scarce commodity. Besides continued assaults from the left—a communist uprising in Prussia was violently suppressed in March—the government also faced mounting opposition from right-wing nationalists, who considered *any* war reparations unacceptable.

Meanwhile, Germany was still losing territory. After a popular vote in the southeastern province of Upper Silesia (required by the Treaty of Versailles) endorsed unification with Germany, the region's large Polish minority staged a revolt; although German Freikorps mercenaries scored major victories, the Allies decided in October that the Germans should cede the most industrially developed part of the province to the Poles—further outraging the nationalists and depriving the nation of a major resource for payment of its staggering debt. Inflation accelerated as government coffers dwindled.

Hitler's officers (here at a 1923 Nazi rally in Munich) were little more than street fighters—for the moment.

The radical right began a campaign of assassinations against politicians and journalists. And in Munich, the Storm Detachment (SA), a paramilitary group attached to the infant National Socialist German Workers' Party—the Nazis—began its reign of terror. The storm troopers were ex-soldiers and Freikorps men who protected the

SPORTS: Baseball: World Series, New York Giants defeat New York Yankees, 5–3 (last best-of-nine series); Judge Kenesaw Mountain Landis becomes first commissioner of baseball ... Boxing: Jack Dempsey defends heavyweight title against Georges Carpentier (first fight gate of $1 million) ... Golf: Walter Hagen wins first of five PGA titles ... Chess: Cuban José Capablanca wins World Championship.

"I've known rivers:/I've known rivers ancient as the world and/older than the flow of human blood in/human veins./ My soul has grown deep like the rivers."—**Langston Hughes, "The Negro Speaks of Rivers"**

Nazis and harassed their opponents. They invaded political meetings, beat up the speakers, and intimidated the crowd while the Nazi leader Adolf Hitler seized the podium. Hitler would then rant against the Jews and other enemies of the German "race" until the police arrived and sent everyone home.

Most Germans did not yet know Hitler's name. In two years, however, he would make his first attempt to take over the country by force. **◂1920.M ▸1922.7**

THE UNITED STATES

Closing America's Doors

8 Spurred by a phobia of anarchy and communism, and abetted by organized labor, the United States Congress in 1921 enacted a temporary quota bill, the first law limiting the number of immigrants allowed into the United States. Avowedly racial, it was designed to curtail rising immigration from southern and eastern Europe, whose peoples were perceived as a dual threat to the American political system and to the job security of American workers.

The new policy restricted total annual Asian and European immigration to 150,000 people; furthermore, the number of aliens of any nationality who could emigrate to the U.S. each year was limited to 3 percent of the number of that nationality already in residence. At the time, better than 70 percent of foreign-born United States residents hailed from Germany, Great Britain, and Ireland. Thus, the quotas were stacked in favor of those immigrants at the expense of so-called "new" immigrants, mostly Italians, Jews, and Slavs, whose countries' leaders were characterized in Congress as waiting to unload these dangerously radical "undesirables" on the United States.

In 1924, a new law made the European quotas permanent (they were abolished by the Immigration and Nationality Act of 1965), banned immigration altogether from east Asia, and established the Western Hemisphere as a "nonquota" area. **◂1917.2 ▸1946.12**

IMMIGRATION INTO THE U.S., BEFORE AND AFTER LEGISLATION

The new quota law turned a torrent of unwanted aliens into a trickle.

LITERATURE

The Harlem Renaissance

9 Once a fashionable neighborhood of New York City, the "great, dark city" (in poet Langston Hughes's phrase) of Harlem was one of the most impoverished urban areas in North America when, in the 1920s, it served as the backdrop to a remarkable artistic efflorescence known as the Harlem Renaissance.

In the boom years following World War I, clubs and cabarets blossomed as skylarking young whites flocked uptown in search of music, drink, and a hedonism that they viewed as distinctively African-American. At the same time, a sophisticated literary aesthetic—one that celebrated black experience (especially urban)—was emerging among writers like Countee Cullen, James Weldon Johnson, Claude McKay, Zora Neale Hurston, Jean Toomer, and W.E.B. Du Bois. While McKay's *Home to Harlem*, about a black soldier returning from World War I, tended toward traditional characterizations, Rudolph Fisher's *Walls of Jericho*, published the same year, explored Harlem's complicated class structure, in which proletarian blacks raged against well-dressed, middle-class "dicty" types.

But the most original and important literary voice to emerge out of this milieu was that of Langston Hughes, whose first published poem, "The Negro Speaks of Rivers," appeared in *Crisis* magazine in 1921, the summer after he graduated from high school. Four years later, he was "discovered" by the American poet Vachel Lindsay when Hughes, who was working in a Washington, D.C., hotel dining room, shyly placed three of his poems beside

"I am a Negro," wrote Langston Hughes, premier poet of the Harlem Renaissance, "and beautiful!"

Lindsay's plate. The next day, newspapers trumpeted Lindsay's amazing find, a "Negro busboy" who wrote poetry.

Adopting the rhythms of the blues and jazz he loved, and using direct, often idiomatic language, Hughes documented the experience of urban American blacks in such collections as *The Weary Blues* (1926) and *The Dream Keeper* (1932). Adept in every literary genre, he continued to pour out a stream of poetry, essays, translations, plays, journalism, and short stories until his death in 1967. Perhaps his most beloved literary creation was the near-legendary Jesse B. Semple, nicknamed Simple, an uneducated Harlem street philosopher who appeared as a character in humorous sketches that Hughes wrote for a black newspaper.

The Harlem Renaissance, like much of twenties culture, flickered and died with the 1929 stock-market crash. Hughes later dismissed the movement as lightweight and faddish, but it unquestionably laid the foundation for Richard Wright, James Baldwin, and other important African-American writers to come. **◂1910.7 ▸1927.9**

IN THE UNITED STATES

show. The winner: skinny 16-year-old Margaret Gorman. Though *The New York Times* condemned the event, it appealed to Jazz Age tastes—and the following year, 57 cities sent their young beauties to be judged.

▶TOP KILLER—After ten years in the number-two slot (behind tuberculosis), coronary disease became the nation's leading cause of death in 1921. Heart ailments accounted for 14 percent of U.S. deaths; in five decades the figure would reach 39 percent. ◂1914.11

▶U.S. PAYS FOR PANAMA—In 1921, 18 years after Panama's U.S.-backed secession from Colombia, Washington paid in full for the country it had bought. For $25 million, Colombia acknowledged the autonomy of its former province, which had revolted in 1903, when Colombia's senate refused to let the U.S. complete and operate the Panama Canal. Panama had gotten rent from Uncle Sam ever since—and now Colombia was remunerated as well. ◂1914.9 ▸1926.8

▶HARDING TAKES OFFICE—Promising a "return to normalcy" after the violent upheavals wrought by World War I, Republican presidential candidate Warren Gamaliel Harding had swept into office with an unprecedented 60.3 percent

of the popular vote in 1920. A mediocre but affable man who was nominated as a compromise candidate, Harding was singularly unfit for the job, which he assumed on March 4. He died in office in 1923, just as the Teapot Dome Scandal was breaking. ▸1923.9

POLITICS & BUSINESS: GNP: $69.6 billion ... Almost 20,000 businesses fail in the U.S. ... Unemployment reaches 11.7% (highest since war; Secretary of Commerce Herbert Hoover recommends price cuts and public-works programs) ... U.S. negotiates separate peace agreements with Germany, Austria, and Hungary ... Federal Highway Act enacted to standardize road building.

"The gigolo of every woman's dreams."—John Dos Passos, on Rudolph Valentino

AROUND THE WORLD

▶TWICE A KING—The French drove King Faisal I from Syria when they invaded in 1920, but he quickly found another throne: In 1921, the British chose him to rule the new kingdom of Iraq—and 96 percent of Iraqi voters agreed. Faisal's anti-Ottoman exploits during World War I made him a national hero and also endeared him to the British, who had inherited Iraq as a postwar mandate. Faisal guided the country to independence in 1932. ◂1920.2 ▸1922.5

▶DEATH OF CARUSO—Enrico Caruso, history's most celebrated opera singer, died in August at age 48. Beloved as much for his humor and zest as for the strength, lyricism, and warmth of his peerless voice, the flamboyant tenor had sung some 50 roles since his debut at Milan's La Scala in 1900. He was the longtime main attraction of the New York Metropolitan Opera; his recordings and relentless touring spread his fame world-

wide. A son of the Naples slums, he died there of a lung infection, and his funeral was held in the city's Royal Basilica, an honor usually reserved for monarchs. ◂1902.11

▶PIRANDELLO'S PERSONAGGI—The 1921 premiere of Italian playwright Luigi Pirandello's *Six Characters in Search of an Author* confirmed its author as one of the century's most innovative dramatic imaginations. In the play, six characters from a discarded play appear on a bare stage where actors appear to be preparing to rehearse; they insist that their untold stories be told. The technique allowed Pirandello to explore one of his favorite themes: the many layers and facets of what is assumed to be "real." Pirandello's plays were a powerful influence on the later Theater of the Absurd. ▸1950.7

Women swooned when Valentino appeared on-screen.

FILM

Valentino as *The Sheik*

10 Today, his overripe sensuality—the flashing eyes, the flaring nostrils—seems coarse and ridiculous. But to millions of women in the early twenties, Rudolph Valentino was sweet carnality incarnate. "For lover," gushed one female reporter, "the thesaurus gives us Lothario, Romeo, Casanova, Don Juan; most people, I discover, give you Valentino." In 1921 he made the movie that cemented his fame and created a new breed of screen hero: suave, dashing, and menacingly hot. He was *The Sheik*.

Previous screen heroes had been clean-cut Joes who respectfully courted the girls. But the Sheik wanted more than a date, and women said yes.

The film tells the story of a proper Englishwoman in Arabia who is abducted by a smoldering sheik, with whom she eventually falls in love. In the title role was a 26-year-old Italian immigrant and former taxi driver who had shortened his name from Rodolfo Alfonzo Raffaele Philibert Guglielmi to Rudolph Valentino. Valentino had been kicking around in Hollywood since 1918, scoring big in 1920 with *The Four Horsemen of the Apocalypse*, in which he danced an unforgettably steamy tango.

But not everyone was seduced. The trade newspaper *Variety* branded Valentino "a player without resource" and called *The Sheik* "inept." A few years later, when Valentino appeared powdered and rouged in fey costume dramas, a *Chicago Tribune* columnist blamed him for the decline of American manliness: This ideal lover, the writer fumed, was "a painted pansy." (The star, outraged, challenged him to a duel.)

When Valentino died of a perforated ulcer in 1926, 30,000 women stormed the funeral home. For decades, a mysterious Lady in Black faithfully visited his tomb in Hollywood on the anniversary of his death. Today Valentino fan clubs still flourish, and there are always fresh flowers next to his crypt. ◂1919.3 ▸1922.11

MEDICINE

Tuberculosis Vaccine

11 A vaccine that increased children's resistance to tuberculosis, one of the world's most deadly (and, until midcentury, most incurable) diseases, was first made available to European schoolchildren in 1921. The result of nearly 15 years of experimentation by French scientists Albert Léon Calmette and Camille Guérin, the bacillus Calmette-Guérin (BCG) vaccine consisted of a weakened strain of live tuberculosis bacteria introduced into the body by injection.

Calmette *(above)* and Guérin: Their vaccine built resistance but did not immunize.

Quickly accepted in Europe, the BCG vaccine was not administered in the United States and Britain until 1940. One obstacle to its use was the 1930 Lübeck, Germany, disaster in which 73 of 249 vaccinated infants died within a year. (The batch was later found to have been accidentally contaminated.)

By the time of Guérin's death in 1961, more than 200 million people worldwide had received the vaccine. Its use today is rare in Western Europe and the United States, where tuberculosis—before its apparently AIDS-related comeback in the late eighties—was once considered all but extinct. ◂1905.9 ▸1944.17

INDIA

Noncooperation Begins

12 For keepers of the empire, political change in India represented a grand concession. For most independence-minded Indians, however, the 1921 restructuring of the colonial government, authorized by the 1919 Montagu-Chelmsford Reforms, amounted to too little too late: a national bicameral legislature, only some of whose members were elected, and with limited power, and provincial governments subject to British authority.

Anathema to India's colonial rulers, Gandhi later shared stamp space with the Queen.

Led by Mohandas K. Gandhi, the Indian National Congress (the political organization dedicated to home rule) refused to participate in the legislative elections and implemented a policy of noncooperation with the British regime. Gandhi also urged his countrymen to boycott British goods, withdraw from government schools, renounce British titles, and, eventually, withhold taxes. British institutions, he warned, "are like the fabled snake with a brilliant jewel on its head, but which has fangs full of poison." With this program of noncooperation, Gandhi became the undisputed leader of the independence movement. ◂1919.10 ▸1924.5

NOBEL PRIZES: Peace: Karl H. Branting (Swedish; peace activist) and Christian L. Lange (Norwegian; Inter-Parliamentary Union) ... Literature: Anatole France (French; novelist) ... Chemistry: Frederick Soddy (U.K.; radioactive substances and isotopes) ... Medicine: No award ... Physics: Albert Einstein (German; photoelectric effect).

A VOICE FROM 1921

The Trouble with American Women

By Elinor Glyn, from *Cosmopolitan*, November 1921

English novelist Elinor Glyn's daring, passion-filled novels were mildly shocking in their day. Her depiction of an adulterous love affair between an Englishman and a Balkan queen in Three Weeks *(1907) created a sensation, and her novel* It *(which she adapted for the Hollywood movie starring Clara Bow) turned the pronoun into a synonym for sex appeal. But when the flappers of the twenties first appeared on the scene, it was Glyn's turn to be scandalized. She shared her views on the dire state of American womanhood with the readers of* Cosmopolitan *magazine in 1921.* ▸**1923.5**

The flapper's persona was a paradox: at once defiantly independent and desperately seductive; wholesomely high-spirited and devil-may-care decadent.

What strikes a sympathetic stranger, revisiting America after ten years, is the great spirit of dissatisfaction and unrest which appears to be abroad among the young women of all classes.... There is a feverish chase after some unknown desired thing which eludes them....

A famous sculptor said to me the other day:

"This is the age of the body, all interests are centered round the body, its wants, its feelings, its preservation, its covering, its emotions. No one is interested in the spirit at all."

Between the sexes there is an antagonism. The bond is frequently merely a physical one, which would express itself by free love did the law permit—and only evades it in name, while indulging in change of husbands and wives under the aegis of the divorce principle.

Amusements to kill time, not to give recreation, are the goal of each day. Drugs, under various forms, have to be resorted to, to produce new sensations. Superfluous energy, in short, has to be got rid of in a wasteful way—energy which is the God-given endowment of this splendid young race, and should be used for constructive purposes, not destructive ones.

Think of the modern young American girl seen in every town and every city of this great country. She is the loveliest physical creature since the age of the Greeks, and has the brightest mentality—if it were only used....

Do they ever think, these beautiful young girls? Do they ever ask whence they have come, whither they are going? It would seem not. Their aim appears to be to allure men, and to secure money....

What can a man with a mind find to hold him in one of these lovely, brainless, unbalanced, cigarette-smoking morsels of undisciplined sex whom he meets continually?...

Has the American girl no innate modesty—no subconscious self-respect, no reserve, no dignity? I know what I think of them.

"Wall, Mr. Joice, I recon' your a damn fine writer, that's what I recon'. An' I recon' this here work o' yourn is some concarn'd litershure. You can take it from me, an' I'm a jedge."—**Ezra Pound, in a letter to James Joyce**

STORY OF THE YEAR

Joyce's Modernist Masterpiece

1 "Stately, plump Buck Mulligan came from the stairhead, bearing a bowl of lather on which a mirror and a razor lay crossed." So begins what is almost universally acknowledged as the century's most important work of English-language fiction, James Joyce's *Ulysses*. Brought out in a limited edition in Paris in 1922, the linguistically virtuosic, richly human, boisterously frank novel was acclaimed immediately as a work of genius. It was also deemed obscene in America and Britain and its author branded a pervert.

The book's narrative, insofar as it can be said to have one, focuses on a single, average day—June 16, 1904—in the life of its Jewish-Irish hero, Leopold Bloom, a newspaper ad agent; his wife, Molly; and Stephen Dedalus, the protagonist of Joyce's 1916 *A Portrait of the Artist as a Young Man*. The book's structure is meant to parallel that of *The Odyssey* (with Odysseus's 19 years of wandering compressed into a single day of Bloom's roaming Dublin), although Joyce also throws in a host of other, even more obscure allusions to everything from Roman Catholic theology to Gypsy slang. Bloom's mental journey, complete with meditations on sex, defecation, flatulence, and other earthy matters, is rendered in a rich idiom—detailed, textured, intensely immediate—that becomes a celebration of language itself. This "stream of consciousness" style reaches its apotheosis in the book's famous final chapter, a long, punctuation-free soliloquy by Molly Bloom, ending with the words "And yes I said yes I will Yes."

James Joyce with his friend and patron, Sylvia Beach, at her Paris bookstore, Shakespeare and Company.

Ulysses had been generating controversy since 1918, when it was serialized in *The Little Review*, an avant-garde American journal. The following year the U.S. Post Office confiscated an issue, the first of four such seizures, and in 1921 the courts declared the material obscene, even though two of the three ruling judges admitted they could not understand Joyce's abstruse style. *The Little Review* was fined for printing pornography; Joyce, in Paris, despaired, because now American (and, assuredly, British) publication would be impossible.

To the rescue came Sylvia Beach, the American owner of Shakespeare and Company bookstore, the hub of Paris's expatriate art scene. Beach offered to publish the book under the bookstore's imprint, and Joyce gratefully accepted. The first copies reached him on February 2, 1922, his 40th birthday. It was not until 1934 in the United States and 1936 in Britain that the ban on *Ulysses* was finally lifted. ►**1922.9**

MEDICINE

Diabetics Receive Insulin

2 Until Canadian physician Frederick Banting and his assistant Charles H. Best isolated insulin, people with diabetes, a disorder marked by abnormally high glucose levels in the blood, were condemned to a slow but inevitable death. First administered to humans in 1922, insulin extended diabetics' lives and enabled them to lead relatively normal existences.

Diabetes research had long focused on the pancreas, since removing the gland in laboratory animals triggered a diabetes-like disease. Patches of cells within the pancreas—known as "islets of Langerhans," after their discoverer—were believed to secrete a hormone called "insulin" (from the Latin for "island"). Insulin was evidently responsible for controlling the body's metabolizing of glucose molecules. Yet efforts to isolate the hormone via the traditional method of mashing up the pancreas had failed because the gland also contained digestive enzymes that destroyed the protein-based insulin molecules.

Banting suddenly conceived of an alternative after reading an article that described how tying up the duct that delivered digestive enzymes to the intestines in dogs caused the pancreas to degenerate. Since the islets of Langerhans were not involved in digestion, Banting suspected that such a procedure might leave them intact within the shriveled, enzyme-depleted pancreas. After obtaining laboratory space and an assistant (Best, still an undergraduate) from John J.R. Macleod, a physiology professor at the University of Toronto, Banting repeated the canine experiment and waited seven weeks to see if his hypothesis would be verified. It was: The islets of Langerhans remained in good shape, and the solution extracted from them relieved the dogs' diabetes symptoms. Insulin had been isolated; within a year it was being administered to humans. (It would not be synthesized in the laboratory for 43 more years.)

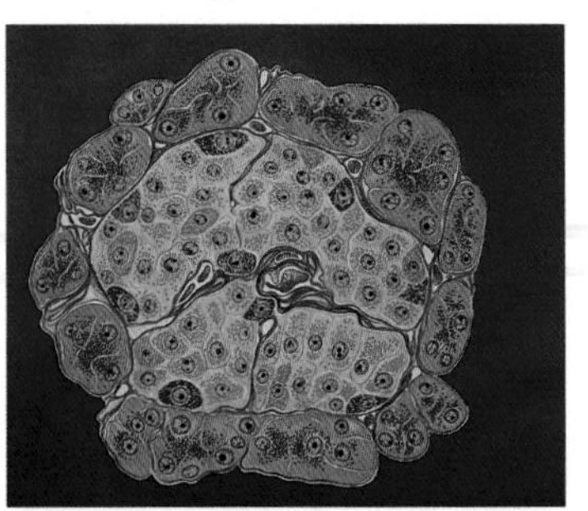
Pancreatic tissue: The yellow cells are the insulin-producing islets of Langerhans.

Banting and Macleod were awarded a 1923 Nobel Prize. Banting balked at accepting—he resented sharing the award with someone whose only contribution, he felt, had been to grant lab space—then insisted on splitting his prize money with Best. ◄**1912.9** ►**1982.M**

ARCHAEOLOGY

King Tut's Tomb Opened

3 Candle in hand, inhaling 3,000-year-old air, British Egyptologist Howard Carter peered through a hole at the bottom of an ancient underground staircase.

Howard Carter *(kneeling)*, just before entering the burial chamber.

"Can you see anything?" asked his financial backer and partner, the Earl of Carnarvon. "Yes," a stunned Carter managed to reply, "wonderful things."

On November 26, 1922, after more than two years of dead ends, Carter was finally peering into the antechamber of the tomb of King Tutankhamen, the boy king who ruled ancient Egypt from 1333 BC until his death nine years later. The antechamber held incredible riches—gold amulets, statues, weapons, ceremonial beds—lying in untidy heaps. (Eventually, Carter deduced that it had been pillaged in the years after Tut's death.) But the tomb's most important treasure would not be uncovered for several more months: the never-before-opened burial chamber

ART & CULTURE: Books: ***The Beautiful and Damned*** **(F. Scott Fitzgerald);** ***La Maison de Claudine*** **(Colette);** ***Siddhartha*** **(Hermann Hesse);** ***Babbitt*** **(Sinclair Lewis);** ***The Garden Party*** **(Katherine Mansfield);** ***The Enormous Room*** **(e.e. cummings) ... Music: "Way Down Yonder in New Orleans" (Layton and Creamer); "Chicago" (Fred Fisher); "Carolina in the Morning" (Donaldson and Kahn) ...**

"Rome, ancient mistress of the world, in the name of our glorious dead who died to render this wonderful day possible, we salute thee."—**Benito Mussolini, just after marching into Rome**

holding Tut's massive stone sarcophagus. When its lid was pried open, there lay the king, untouched for over three thousand years, in a nest of three anthropoid coffins, the innermost made of solid gold. For the first time in modern history, Egyptologists were able to see exactly how an ancient pharaoh had been buried.

Tutankhamen's tomb had escaped earlier detection because his name had been stricken from royal lists by his successors. Furthermore, the tomb had been buried in rubble when that of Ramses VI, who reigned from 1156 to 1148 BC, was built immediately above it by workers ignorant of the earlier tomb's existence. Carnarvon had become fascinated with the legend of King Tut in 1903, while convalescing in Egypt's Valley of the Kings. He later met Carter there, and the two became obsessed with discovering Tut's tomb. But World War I postponed work until 1917.

By 1922, Carter's team had found nothing but frustration. Carter was growing desperate; Carnarvon was wearying of the financial drain. Finally, on November 2, as he explored the only area of the entire Valley of the Kings that remained unexamined, Carter discovered a staircase underneath some laborers' huts. Squelching his urge to keep digging, he ordered the work stopped until Carnarvon could be summoned from London.

Gold wasn't all the archaeologists uncovered. Many believed that opening the tomb unleashed an ancient curse that condemned to death anyone who disturbed the king. Just one year later, Carnarvon died from an infected mosquito bite, and others connected with the excavation met untimely deaths. The gods must have forgiven Carter, however, for he lived another 17 years, to age 65.
◄1912.3 ►1922.M

This gold-leafed, richly inlaid coffin was the second in a nest of three within King Tut's sarcophagus.

Alfredo Ambrosi's rendering of Benito Mussolini's face superimposed on Rome.

ITALY

Blackshirts March on Rome

4 Unlike the other Allies, Italy, which had received very little in the Versailles Treaty's division of spoils, was left impoverished and in chaos by World War I. Its inflation rate was second only to Germany's. Its parliament was corrupt and deadlocked, its public works decaying. Left-wing violence raised the specter of bolshevism. Hungry for drastic change but fearful of Russian-style revolution, many Italians turned to Fascism—a quasimystical nationalist movement calling for a state united behind one "superior" man. Even after sending 35 representatives to Parliament, the Fascists used terror tactics against leftists.

One such legislator was Benito Mussolini, the movement's charismatic leader. In 1922, Mussolini decided the time was ripe for a Fascist takeover. On October 28, some 40,000 of his black-shirted followers marched on Rome, seizing prefectures, post offices, and train stations as they went—and meeting little resistance from a largely sympathetic army.

Camped outside the city in pouring rain, the marchers were ill-equipped, ill-fed, and disorganized; Rome's military garrison might easily have chased them away. But King Vittorio Emanuele III panicked and refused to sign a decree of martial law. His aide called Mussolini in Milan, offering partial control of a new cabinet—but Il Duce hung up the phone. The next day, he was asked to form a new government. Mussolini took a train to Rome, but the tracks outside the city had been torn up by defending troops. The King sent a car for the Fascist leader, who entered the city at the head of his legions.

"From this moment," read the new regime's first declaration, "Mussolini is the Government of Italy." Yet while the government did make changes—bringing the police, bureaucracy, banks, and trade unions under Fascist control and establishing a new militia—for the moment, much continued as before. The full extent of Mussolini's plans for Italy would remain unclear for two more years.
◄1919.7 ►1924.8

BIRTHS

Kingsley Amis, U.K. writer.

Jack Anderson, U.S. journalist.

Christiaan Barnard, South African heart surgeon.

Enrico Berlinguer, Italian political leader.

Helen Gurley Brown, U.S. writer and editor.

Pierre Cardin, French fashion designer.

Richard Diebenkorn, Jr., U.S. painter.

Judy Garland, U.S. actress and singer.

Jack Kerouac, U.S. novelist.

Philip Larkin, U.K. poet.

Norodom Sihanouk, Cambodian king.

Yitzhak Rabin, Israeli prime minister.

Charles Schulz, U.S. cartoonist.

Kurt Vonnegut, Jr., U.S. writer.

DEATHS

Alexander Graham Bell, Scottish-U.S. inventor.

Nellie Bly, U.S. journalist.

Jacob Gimbel, U.S. retailer.

Arthur Griffith, Irish nationalist.

Alfred Harmsworth, U.K. newspaper publisher.

Marcel Proust, French novelist.

Walther Rathenau, German diplomat.

Lillian Russell, U.S. singer and actress.

Ernest Shackleton, U.K. explorer.

Georges Sorel, French socialist.

Wolfgang Kapp, German political leader.

Painting & Sculpture: ***Dance, Monster, to My Soft Song!*** **(Paul Klee) ... Film:** ***Foolish Wives*** **(Erich von Stroheim);** ***Manslaughter*** **(Cecil B. DeMille);** ***Nosferatu, A Symphony of Horror*** **(F.W. Murnau);** ***Robin Hood*** **(Douglas Fairbanks) ... Theater:** ***Back to Methuseleh*** **(G.B. Shaw);** ***Anna Christie*** **(Eugene O'Neill);** ***Antigone*** **(Jean Cocteau);** ***Abie's Irish Rose*** **(Anne Nichols).**

"Why worry about the rind, if we can obtain the fruit?"—**British foreign secretary Lord Curzon, on Britain's decision to grant Egypt independence "with reservations"**

NEW IN 1922

3-D movies (Perfect Pictures' *The Power of Love*).

Vitamin D.

Union of Soviet Socialist Republics (formerly Russia).

Skywriting.

IN THE UNITED STATES

▶SPEAKEASY QUEEN—The Prohibition era's premier nightclub hostess, salty-tongued Texas Guinan, began her career in 1922 at New York's Café des Beaux Arts. The strapping former movie cowgirl, 38, was hired as a singer, but her real talent was for inciting crowds to frantic

merrymaking. Undaunted by raids, she presided over a string of speakeasies, where celebrities and unknowns alike paid outrageous prices for bootleg hooch—and for the privilege of hearing Guinan blow her police whistle and holler her famous greeting: "Hello, sucker!" ◂1919.V ▸1923.5

▶MRS. MANNERS—Emily Post began her long career as America's foremost social authority with the 1922 publication of her 619-page *Etiquette in Society, in Business, in Politics and at Home.* Unlike previous manners mavens, who wrote for the affluent and polished, Post offered common-sense advice to anyone who wished to behave well.

▶*READER'S DIGEST* PUBLISHED—The first edition of *Reader's Digest* went out to 1,500 subscribers in February. Founded by young marrieds De Witt and Lila Acheson Wallace (a former Minneapolis

EGYPT

Modified Independence

5 Egypt achieved nominal independence in 1922 after centuries of foreign rule. Except for a brief period of occupation by Napoleon's army, the once-powerful land of the pharaohs had been a nominally self-governing province of the Ottoman Empire until 1882, when the British invaded and began occupying the country. In 1914, Britain deposed the Ottoman-installed khedive (viceroy) and declared Egypt a protectorate. Bestowing the new title of sultan on the khedive's uncle Husayn Kamil, the British imposed martial law on the strategically vital territory for the duration of World War I.

When Husayn Kamil died in 1917, he was succeeded by his more ambitious brother, Ahmad Fuad. By then, wartime repression and deprivations had raised Egyptian nationalism to a fever pitch. Almost immediately after the war ended—and the Ottoman Empire dissolved—Egyptian politicians petitioned the British for autonomy. Not only did Britain refuse to receive the nationalists' proposed delegation to London, but it had their charismatic leader, Zaghlul Pasha, arrested—an event that provoked strikes and attacks on British personnel.

Lord Allenby, who'd led the British victory over the Ottomans in Palestine, negotiated with the nationalists. In February 1922, the British declared Egypt independent "with reservations" (which included protection of foreign interests and continued British supervision of defense). Sultan Fuad was crowned King Fuad I, and Egypt became a constitutional monarchy. But with British troops still in the country—and both the autocratic Fuad and opportunistic nationalists vying for British favor—constitutionality and independence existed mainly on paper. **◂1910.11 ▸1936.M**

NAVAL LIMITATION TREATY'S QUOTAS FOR WARSHIPS OVER 10,000 TONS

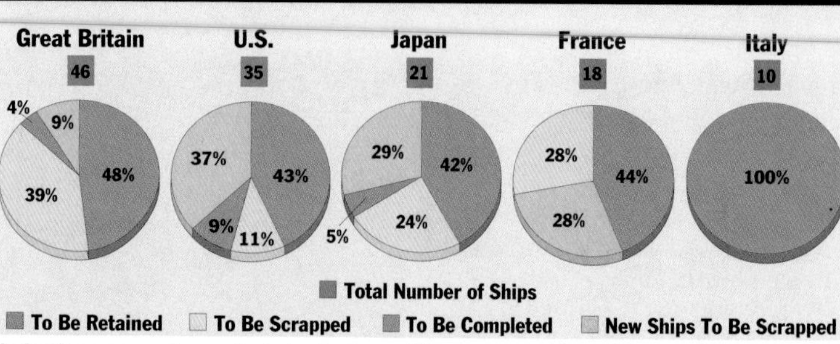

Limitations on each country's largest warships were an attempt to equalize naval power.

DIPLOMACY

Demilitarizing the Seas

6 War demolished the old-world balance of power, setting off an arms race between the nations left in control of the globe. Each craved naval superiority above all else: Britain, traditional ruler of the seas; Japan, new master of the Pacific; the United States, economic dynamo with far-flung business interests. With tensions escalating, these and lesser powers convened at the Washington Conference, which ended in 1922, having produced four major pacts designed to stabilize relations and slow the financially draining naval competition.

Most important was the Naval Limitation Treaty, covering warships weighing more than 10,000 tons. *(See chart, above.)* Britain, the United States, Japan, and France also signed the Four Power Pact, promising to respect one another's Pacific possessions and to resolve differences through diplomacy.

Within a few years, however, the major powers were busily constructing ships in classes not restricted by the Naval Limitation Treaty. So in 1930, the London Naval Conference was convened, with much fanfare, to take another stab at disarmament. (King George V opened the proceedings with the first worldwide live radio address.) Britain, Japan, and the United States hammered out a weak agreement, but France and Italy refused to sign anything that would hold them to equality with each other. Soon all pretenses of arms control were abandoned and the frenzied buildup to World War II began. **◂1906.M ▸1936.11**

GERMANY

Germany Slides Further

7 To his admirers, the industrialist and social theorist Walther Rathenau *(below)* was an independent-minded German patriot. During World War I, he had overseen distribution of raw materials; as postwar minister of reconstruction, responsible for making

reparations (decried by rightists) to the victors, he staunchly resisted many harsh Allied demands. After becoming foreign minister in January 1922, he signed a treaty with the Soviet Union, defying the Allies (none of which recognized the communist government) and gaining cancellation of war debts owed to Russia. Scion of a distinguished family—his father had founded the giant electric company AEG—Rathenau was outspoken in his love of the blond, blue-eyed German *Volk*. Yet to Germany's growing right-wing nationalist movement, Rathenau was a treacherous "alien"—a Jew—and his position as Germany's spokesman, therefore, a travesty.

Royal opening of Parliament in Cairo. The government inside still had to answer to the British.

SPORTS: Baseball: World Series, New York Giants defeat New York Yankees, 4–0, 1 tie ... Boxing: Harry Greb unseats Gene Tunney as light-heavyweight champion (only loss in Tunney's career) ... Golf: 21-year-old caddy Gene Sarazen wins his first PGA and first U.S. Open titles ... Track & Field: Clarence H. DeMar wins first of three straight Boston Marathons, with record time of 2:18.10.

"He wrote a new, a really new poetry, which set up connections with the old, the really old."—**Stephen Spender, on T.S. Eliot**

Rathenau was murdered by machine-gun fire and a grenade on June 20 as he rode to work. His death—one in a string of rightist assassinations—set off nationwide strikes and demonstrations. The Reichstag immediately passed a law for "the protection of the republic," imposing severe penalties for conspiracy to murder and providing a means to outlaw extremist groups. Speaking for the measure, centrist chancellor Joseph Wirth proclaimed, "The enemy is on the right!" (Since most judges were left over from the Kaiser's regime, however, the law would be used most often against the left.) Months later, Wirth's government fell victim to the Reichstag's endless shifting of political coalitions and was replaced by a moderate rightist government headed by shipping magnate Wilhelm Cuno.

Immediately after the assassination, as investor confidence plummeted, Germany's already declining currency began a nosedive. The government canceled Rathenau's "policy of fulfillment," declaring a moratorium on reparations. Confrontation with France, the nation's most relentless creditor, was imminent. **◂1921.7 ▸1923.1**

FILM

Technicolor Introduced

8 The silver screen blazed with new hues in 1922 as Hollywood produced its first Technicolor feature, a version of *Madama Butterfly* entitled *Toll of the Sea*. But despite the lavish praise the film received, Technicolor was so expensive that it was many years before it would become a staple of feature filmmaking.

Color, via hand-painted film or single tints, had been part of cinema since its inception. By the 1910s, British and French companies had tried to produce a full range of colors by combining two or three primary colors, but their processes involved cumbersome machinery—and the pictures caused eyestrain. Two scientists from the Massachusetts Institute of Technology, Herbert T. Kalmus and Daniel F. Comstock, set out to lick the problem in 1915, when they founded the Technicolor Motion Picture Company (named for their academic affiliation). In 1917 they released a film that was an improvement on the early attempts at color but still unsatisfactory. Then, seeking ways to combine two primary colors, red and green, with pleasing, natural results, they hit upon the idea of a camera containing two strips of film—one for red, one for green—and a prism to split the incoming light into the primary colors. The two strips were combined when the film was developed and printed, which meant that no special projectors were required. By 1922, the process was nearly perfected, and Hollywood came calling. **▸1927.5**

Toll of the Sea: **Technicolor was still too costly to catch on.**

LITERATURE

Poet of Desolation

9 A watershed year for modern literature, 1922 saw the publication of Hermann Hesse's *Siddhartha*, Eugene O'Neill's *Anna Christie* and *The Hairy Ape*, John Galsworthy's *The Forsyte Saga*, and, most importantly, James Joyce's *Ulysses*. And in poetry, T.S. Eliot *(left)*, a 34-year-old American working as a banker in London, produced a radical, convention-defying, 433-line epic that is the equivalent in its genre of Joyce's masterpiece. *The Waste Land* solidified Eliot's reputation, forged with his earlier "The Love Song of J. Alfred Prufrock" (1917), as the premier modernist poet.

The Waste Land links personal symbols to an erudite vocabulary of cultural references. Reflecting the fragmentation of the age, it presents a collage of images and voices—that jump from proletarian slang to bourgeois politesse, from churchly oratory to Homeric declamation. Its rhythms range from iambic pentameter to ragtime, its tone from slapstick to apocalyptic. What it's *about* is a difficult question. Indeed, Eliot introduced difficulty into modern poetry, demanding serious commitment from his readers. In published notes, he cited sources for his cryptic phrases; they include the Grail legends, the Hindu Vedas, Dante's *Divine Comedy*, and popular songs. But despite its obscurities, *The Waste Land* (which, on Ezra Pound's advice, Eliot cut to just over half its original length) brilliantly evokes the ugliness and impersonality of urban life—and Eliot's despair that civilization had passed from glory to mediocrity.

Conservative commentators labeled the poem unintelligible, which only heightened the avant-garde's devotion. But his own brand of conservatism—poet William Carlos Williams called him "a subtle conformist"—made Eliot enemies, especially after 1927, when he became a devout Christian. By 1948, when he won a Nobel Prize, many in the younger generation had, mistakenly, pronounced him passé. **◂1922.1 ▸1925.8**

IN THE UNITED STATES

book salesman, and an heiress), the monthly began as a collection of articles condensed from books and other journals. By the 1950s it was the world's bestselling magazine.

▸ANNIE GOT HER GUN—In one of her least flamboyant displays of skill, legendary markswoman Annie Oakley broke the world's record for women's trapshooting, smashing 98 out of 100 clay pigeons at a North Carolina gun club. Born in an Ohio log cabin in 1860, the cowboy-hatted Oakley starred for 17 years in Buffalo Bill Cody's Wild West show. She could hit the thin edge of a playing card at 30 paces, or an airborne dime; in Berlin, she once shot a cigarette from the mouth of future Kaiser Wilhelm II.

▸A MEMORIAL FOR LINCOLN—After seven years of work, the $2.94 million Lincoln Memorial was dedicated in Washington, in 1922. Architect Henry Bacon modeled the structure on the Parthenon in Athens, but incorporated American symbolism: The 36 pillars represent the 36 states in the Civil War–era Union. The monument's 19-foot statue of Lincoln was designed by Daniel Chester French and built with marble from the old Confederate state of Georgia. ◂1909.M

▸A PERFECT SPECIMEN—*Physical Culture* magazine, in 1922, pronounced 28-year-old Charles Atlas (né Angelo Siciliano) the "World's Most Perfectly Developed Man." A former 97-pound weakling, Atlas achieved his impressive physique through "dynamic tension," or isometrics—a technique based on tensing one group of muscles in opposition to another group or an immovable object. By 1927, his big build was big business—a mail-order campaign brought in $1,000 a day. ▸1978.13

POLITICS & BUSINESS: GNP: $74.1 billion ... Rebecca Latimer Felton appointed the first female U.S. senator (succeeded by elected senator, Walter F. George, after serving two days) ... Fordney-McCumber Tariff Act raises rates to protectionist levels ... Grain Futures Act helps curb speculation responsible for extreme fluctuations in grain prices ... Federal Narcotics Control Board established.

"Fatty Arbuckle, the comedian, exists no more.... He is Mr. Roscoe Arbuckle, the most serious visaged personality existent. His conduct and appearance ... made Hamlet and Macbeth and Jean Valjean look like circus clowns."—**Los Angeles Times**

AROUND THE WORLD

▶VENEZUELAN OIL—International oil prospectors hit pay dirt near Lake Maracaibo in eastern Venezuela in 1922. The opening of a Dutch well that gushed for nine days was soon followed by British and American strikes. By the end of the decade Venezuela was the world's leading exporter of petroleum, a position it maintained until the 1970s. ◂1909.5 ▸1935.M

▶ESKIMO MOVIE—The genre of documentary film was redefined in 1922 with Briton Robert J. Flaherty's *Nanook of the North.* Previous documentaries had presented unconnected vignettes; *Nanook* had a central theme, an Eskimo family's struggle to survive in the Arctic wilderness. And Flaherty was the first filmmaker to use the techniques of fiction films in a documentary: Hunting scenes were suspenseful, domestic scenes heartwarming. Though anthropologists deplored Flaherty's practice of staging incidents, audiences cheered when Nanook harpooned the mighty polar bear.

▶UR EXCAVATED—The world's earliest civilization was little more than a legend until English archaeologist Charles Leonard Woolley began digging it up in 1922. Woolley spent 12 years unearthing the 6,000-year-old Sumerian capital of Ur (first discovered by his colleague H.R. Hall, after World War I) in the Iraqi desert. *(At left, a statue unearthed in the dig.)* The biblical birthplace of Abraham also turned out to be the home of the city-state, codified laws, the written word, and wheeled transportation. ◂1922.3

▶KOALA CARE—Faced with the possibility of the koala bear's extinction, Australia enacted legislation in 1922 to protect the indigenous marsupial. Eight million koalas had been slaughtered for their thick, soft fur—marketed in North America as wombat fur—since 1918. ◂1905.5 ▸1987.9

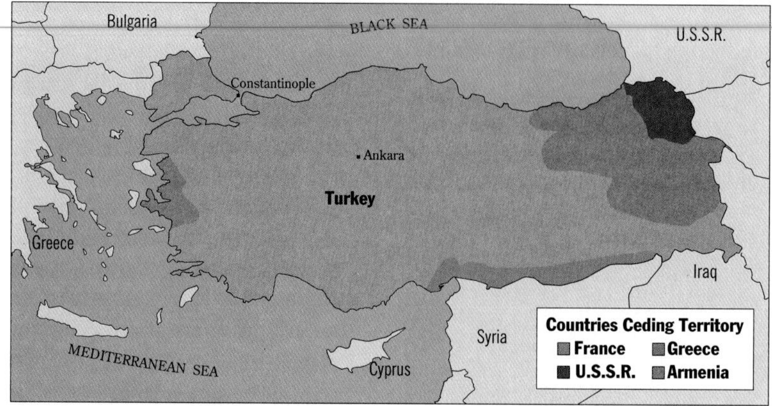

Hard-won treaties returned ethnically Turkish lands to Turkey.

TURKEY

Fight for Self-Determination

10 As a World War I commander, Mustafa Kemal (who would later be known as Atatürk) had been an Ottoman hero, defeating the British twice at Gallipoli. But when the 600-year-old empire crumbled, along with Germany's, the former Young Turk led the fight to abolish it entirely. Instead he gave birth, in 1922, to modern Turkey.

While others advocated making the empire a British or American protectorate after the world war, Kemal was determined to make the Turkish heartland a sovereign state. The army followed him in revolt; after traveling the country to growing popular acclaim, he set up a provisional government in Ankara to rival the Sultan's regime in Constantinople (now Istanbul).

The Chamber of Deputies in Constantinople endorsed Kemal's independence plan in 1920, prompting the British to occupy the city and dissolve the chamber. Undaunted, Kemal held elections for a new Grand National Assembly, which gave the name Turkey to the state Kemal aimed to govern. The army crushed rebellions in areas loyal to the Sultan.

Kemal was willing to cede lands that weren't ethnically Turkish, but many territories he claimed were occupied by other nations. His forces regained long-lost eastern territory from the Armenians and Georgians, and drove the French from the south. The British, however, refused to budge. The result for the nationalists was a year-long war with the British-supplied Greeks, who coveted large portions of the country.

Finally, after suffering a bloody rout in Anatolia, Greece also agreed to withdraw. In a series of treaties culminating in the 1923 Treaty of Lausanne, the Allies granted the Turks virtually everything they wanted. Kemal abolished the sultanate, and the last Ottoman supreme ruler fled to Malta. **◂1920.2 ▸1923.12**

FILM

Hollywood Censors Itself

11 On screen and off, sex and scandal infested the movies. First, there was beloved slapstick comedian Roscoe "Fatty" Arbuckle's acquittal in August 1922 of the rape and manslaughter of a Hollywood starlet at a wild party the previous year. Then there was the unsolved murder of director William Desmond Taylor, who was shot and killed in his Los Angeles apartment under mysterious circumstances involving drugs and two high-profile female stars. Films themselves were almost as racy.

Across America, moralists mobilized, but Hollywood struck preemptively: Amid cries for federal censorship and a Senate probe of the industry, fearful producers formed the Motion Picture Producers and Distributors of America, a self-regulating body headed by ex-Postmaster General Will Hays.

Arbuckle's trial prompted Hollywood to start tightening its standards.

Hays introduced morals clauses into movie contracts, and set standards—albeit voluntary ones—for permissible picture content. But producers ignored them, and films stayed sexy. Finally, in 1934, with the Catholic Church, Wall Street banks, and other conservative pressure groups rattling righteous sabers, Hays got tough and began enforcing a newer set of strictures. Henceforth, film content had to conform to the "Hays Code"; unapproved films could not be exhibited. The producers acquiesced, and for the next three decades Hollywood films forbade sex outside of marriage (and ignored it within), worshiped church and state, and insisted that crime never pays. **◂1910.M ▸1947.5**

IRELAND

Free State Established

12 The establishment of the Irish Free State, in 1922, wreaked havoc on a nation struggling for identity. The treaty ending the Anglo-Irish guerrilla war gave dominion status to the 26 counties of southern Ireland (today's Republic). Free Staters accepted dominion as a step toward complete independence, while radical republicans viewed it as an insult. When former IRA mastermind Michael Collins *(above)* signed the treaty and helped set up a provisional government, he got caught in the crossfire.

Collins, who would inspire such latter-day insurrectionists as Mao Zedong and Yitzhak Shamir, was a larger-than-life figure who used to bicycle undisguised around Dublin as his squad of hit men openly ambushed British operatives. "They won't shoot me in my own land," he once proclaimed.

Yet his own former allies did just that. Before the year's end, Collins, 31, was ambushed and killed in his native County Cork. The IRA, refusing to accept a separate Northern Ireland, split from the provisional government and vowed not to stop fighting until the entire island was free and united. **◂1920.7 ▸1949.9**

NOBEL PRIZES: Peace: Fridtjof Nansen (Norwegian; refugee relief) ... Literature: Jacinto Benavente (Spanish; playwright) ... Chemistry: Francis Aston (U.K; isotopes of nonradioactive elements) ... Medicine: Archibald Hill (U.K.; heat-production in muscles) and Otto Meyerhof (German; lactic acid production in muscle) ... Physics: Niels Bohr (Danish; atomic structure and radiation).

A VOICE FROM 1922

The First Freudian Hamlet

By Alexander Woollcott, et al., on John Barrymore's *Hamlet*, November 1922

Shakespeare was reinvented in 1922, when the younger son of America's reigning theater dynasty, John Barrymore, brought two decades' worth of Freudianism to his portrayal of the bard's famously confused hero. Previous renditions of Hamlet *had stressed either Shakespeare's poetry or the actor's headline appeal; Barrymore and his producer cut 1,250 lines and created a Hamlet whose tragedy lay, as Heywood Broun observed, "in the fact that he did not have the courage of his complexes." To put it simply, Barrymore's Hamlet was in love with his mother.*

Predictably, some critics squawked at the play's modernism (and its minimalism: Robert Edmond Jones's spare stage sets were just as controversial as Barrymore's carefully modulated performance). Most, however, grasped immediately that they were witnessing theater history. Below, excerpts from the reviews that appeared in three New York dailies. ◄**1901.M** ►**1944.18**

Alexander Woollcott, The New York Herald, *November 19, 1922:* John Barrymore's *Hamlet* was given Thursday night before an audience that cheered with a heartfelt satisfaction—a satisfaction in finding this most richly endowed of our players back on the road again, a satisfaction in the truest, realest *Hamlet* which the New York of this day has seen. Barrymore's Dane is masculine, princely, whimsical and when he lies there at Horatio's feet, little and slim and dead, you wince at the pang of a good fellow forfeited, a gay, charming, immensely likable person thwarted by a most cursed spite. It is the pang you must feel if *Hamlet* has been allowed to say its say again in the theater. It has this time, and under Hopkins' direction it emerges clearer and fresher and more a-tingle with its own endless and abundant life than we have ever had the good fortune to find it.

Heywood Broun in The New York World, *November 17, 1922:* John Barrymore is far and away the finest Hamlet we have ever seen. He excels all others we have known in grace, fire, wit and clarity.... Barrymore's performance clears up all doubtful points in the play to an extent which quite outdoes the most profound study of the footnotes and all the doodads in the back of the books. When he does it everything seems simple and straightforward. There are many strands in the man, to be sure, but the spectator need do nothing but keep his ears and his eyes open to get them all....

Barrymore's most original contribution to the role probably lies in his amplification of the unconscious motives of the Prince. He plays the closet episode with the Queen exactly as if it were a love scene. Nor did this seem fantastic to us. Shakespeare was a better Freudian than almost any of the moderns because he did not know the lingo. He merely set down the facts. After seeing Barrymore's interpretation we are convinced that he added nothing but merely grasped suggestions which were already there.

John Corbin, The New York Times, *November 16, 1922:* The atmosphere of historic happening surrounded John Barrymore's appearance last night as the Prince of Denmark; it was unmistakable as it was indefinable. It sprang from the quality and intensity of the applause, from the hushed murmurs that swept the audience at the most unexpected moments, from the silent crowds that all evening long swarmed about the theatre entrance. In all likelihood we have a new and lasting Hamlet.... [November 23, 1922] If John Barrymore fails to establish himself as the Hamlet of his generation, fit successor to Forbes-Robertson and Edwin Booth, it will not be for the lack of endowment in physique and in inward genius, nor yet for the lack of faithful and intelligent study. His is a performance to which the lover of acting must return again and again.

With his 1922 *Hamlet*, John Barrymore (a.k.a. The Great Profile) shifted the emphasis of the play from Shakespeare's poetry to the prince's psyche. Above, with Constance Collier, who played Gertrude, in the London production.

"Hitler called out: 'No one leaves the room alive without my permission.' "—**From the Bavarian police account of the Beer Hall Putsch**

STORY OF THE YEAR

The Beer Hall Putsch

1 Adolf Hitler's first attempt to conquer Germany could only have been launched from Bavaria. The monarchists who ran the state sympathized with his cause, and he had good army contacts there, thanks to his position as coordinator of Bavaria's right-wing paramilitary organizations. (Such groups were banned in most other states, as was Hitler's Munich-based, 55,000-member Nazi Party.) In September 1923, at Hitler's urging, the Bavarian government declared a state of emergency, giving state commissioner Ritter von Kahr dictatorial powers. The move was to be the first step toward a dreamed-of "march on Berlin"—modeled on Mussolini's march on Rome—to establish Nazi rule. Kahr and the Bavarian Army commander, Otto von Lossow, were willing to join such a march, but they distrusted Hitler and felt the timing was wrong.

On November 8 he forced their hand. Kahr was holding a "patriotic" rally in the Bürgerbräu, a Munich beer hall. Hitler surrounded it with 600 storm troopers, then burst in with armed escorts, declaring the Bavarian and national governments deposed. He forced Kahr, Lossow, and state police chief Hans von Seisser into a side room, where he persuaded them—at gunpoint—to join him in a coup. Back in the hall, Hitler jumped on a chair, fired a pistol at the ceiling, and won over the crowd with a rousing speech: Berlin must be taken immediately. He himself would head the new regime. Hitler's coauthor in the scheme, World War I hero General Erich Ludendorff, arrived, and the three hostages emerged to pledge their support. Then the putschists retired for the night to the local army headquarters (held by their henchmen).

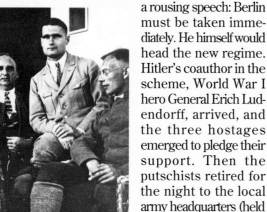

Hitler *(left)* said he "had the best of luck in prison." Rudolf Hess, to whom he dictated *Mein Kampf*, is second from right.

In the morning, Kahr, Lossow, and Seisser announced they'd changed their minds. The would-be coup leaders marched through town anyway, with 3,000 armed followers. A brief shootout with police ensued, and the rebels (except for the courtly Ludendorff) fled. Hitler, who'd injured his shoulder escaping, was arrested the next day—in his pajamas—at a nearby villa.

The so-called Beer Hall Putsch had failed, but Hitler's eloquence at his trial made him a celebrity. The plotters were acquitted or given light sentences by right-wing jurists. Hitler served just eight months. At the prison-fortress of Landsberg, he was treated like a visiting dignitary; it was there that he wrote the first volume of the Nazi bible, *Mein Kampf*. **◄1922.7 ►1923.2**

GERMANY

France Invades the Ruhr Valley

2 The Beer Hall Putsch occurred as Germany began to recover from months of chaos. The trouble started the previous autumn, when Berlin suspended war-reparation payments. In January 1923, France retaliated by sending 100,000 troops into the industrial Ruhr Valley. German authorities urged Ruhr residents to resist the invasion peacefully. Responding to strikes, slowdowns, and sabotage, the French arrested industrialists and labor leaders; 150,000 inhabitants were expelled and some resisters killed.

German children constructing a pyramid of worthless mark notes.

The burdens of the Ruhr occupation spurred the worst inflation yet: When it peaked, the German mark—worth a quarter of a dollar in 1914—was valued at 4.2 trillion to the dollar. The price of bread soared from 20,000 marks to five million in one day. People carried money in wheelbarrows. As the nation plunged into poverty, French-backed separatist groups in the Rhineland and Palatinate regions staged violent revolts. Although popular opposition prevented them from being successful, they added to Berlin's woes. In Saxony and Thuringia, where leftist state governments allowed "red" militias to form, another uprising loomed. And in Bavaria, the rightist state regime was a constant headache.

A despairing Chancellor Wilhelm Cuno quit in September. His successor, center-rightist Gustav Stresemann, ordered an end to resistance in the Ruhr, resumed reparation payments, and asked the Allies' Reparations Commission to investigate Germany's plight. He established a new, sounder currency. Then he declared martial law. The Saxon and Thuringian governments were deposed, a rightist coup in Küstrin crushed, and a minor communist revolt smashed with terrifying force. Indignant Socialist legislators forced Stresemann to resign in favor of a centrist, Wilhelm Marx. But the major crises seemed over—until the beer-hall conspirators used the "surrender" to France as a pretext for their putsch. **◄1923.1 ►1924.11**

LITERATURE

A Nobel for Yeats

3 Awarding the 1923 Nobel Prize for literature to its first Irish recipient, the Swedish Academy commended poet and dramatist William Butler Yeats "for his consistently emotional poetry, which in the strictest artistic form expresses a people's spirit." Such praise only hints at the full contribution made by this giant of twentieth-century literature. Brimming with powerful imagery and a profound moodiness, Yeats's poems—the apocalyptic "The Second Coming" (1919), the elegiac "Sailing to Byzantium" (1927)—illustrate his commanding vision, mystic bent, and ever-maturing musicality of language. To his poems of old age, Yeats brought the jaded sensibility of a true sage.

A nationalist who harbored an unrequited passion for the fiery Irish patriot Maud Gonne, Yeats considered his creative and his political lives to be intertwined. Together with J.M. Synge and Lady Gregory, Yeats played a pivotal role in the founding of Dublin's Abbey Theatre. Their struggle to forge a distinctive Irish "Unity of Culture" was the subject of his Nobel lecture—delivered the year after he became a senator of the Irish Free State.

Ireland's brooding bard W.B. Yeats.

ART & CULTURE: Books: *The Good Soldier Schweik* (Jaroslav Hašek); *The Theme of Our Time* (José Ortega y Gasset); *The Ego and the Id* (Sigmund Freud); *The Marsden Case* (Ford Madox Ford) ... Music: "Yes, We Have No Bananas" (Cohn and Silver); "Charleston" (Johnson and Mack); "Who's Sorry Now?" (Snyder, Kalmar, and Ruby); "Mexicali Rose" (Tenny and Stone); *Black Maskers* (Roger Sessions) ...

"A new generation, dedicated more than the last to the fear of poverty and the worship of success; grown up to find all Gods dead, all wars fought, all faiths in man shaken."—**F. Scott Fitzgerald, *This Side of Paradise***

Yeats was also fascinated with the occult and embraced many of the doctrines of theosophy. He said that much of his prose work *A Vision* (1925) was dictated to him by spirits through the "automatic writing" of his wife, Georgie Hyde Lees, a spiritualist medium. **◂1905.6 ▸1930.9**

IDEAS

How Children Learn

4 With the publication in 1923 of his first book, *The Language and Thought of the Child,* Swiss psychologist Jean Piaget presented a revolutionary vision of the way children learn. The work—which Piaget modestly discounted as "merely a collection of preliminary studies"—became the cornerstone of the century's most influential theory of human development.

Piaget, 27, had earned a doctorate in zoology before studying psychology under such pioneers as Carl Jung, but his deepest obsession was epistemology—the philosophy of knowledge. To find the universal principles that govern children's thinking, he observed and interviewed his own and others' offspring. Learning, Piaget theorized, takes place in four stages, from sensorimotor skills to abstract reasoning, whose timing (the last stage begins about age twelve) is genetically programmed.

Piaget's ideas had profound implications for education. Children, he argued, could learn only what they were ready to learn—and teachers, rather than force-feeding knowledge, should seek to enhance their pupils' process of discovery. **◂1912.M ▸1943.12**

POPULAR CULTURE

The Twenties Begin to Roar

5 America's "Roaring Twenties" were a decade that became a worldwide symbol of prosperity and good times. In 1923, the postwar recession was over, and the new president, Calvin Coolidge (who had succeeded to the office upon the death of Warren Harding), declared "the business of America is business." Stock-market values soared, the gross national product rose 14 percent from the previous year, and unemployment declined to 2.4 percent. New technologies increased manufacturing productivity while shortening the workweek, and the growth was accompanied by a loosening of credit.

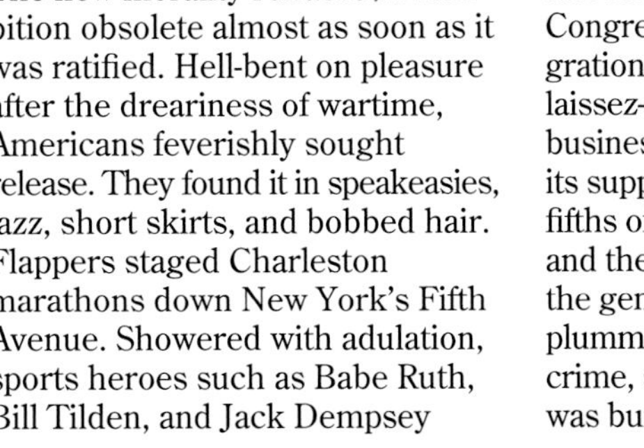

Old Victorian notions of propriety, already weakened by the brutal war, were all but demolished by a business climate that encouraged consumers to pursue bliss through mass-produced cars, clothes, cigarettes, and cosmetics. The new morality rendered Prohibition obsolete almost as soon as it was ratified. Hell-bent on pleasure after the dreariness of wartime, Americans feverishly sought release. They found it in speakeasies, jazz, short skirts, and bobbed hair. Flappers staged Charleston marathons down New York's Fifth Avenue. Showered with adulation, sports heroes such as Babe Ruth, Bill Tilden, and Jack Dempsey became demigods.

But the revolution ran deeper than raccoon coats and hip flasks. In the battle for equality, women made significant gains, only superficially reflected in the flappers' shorn hair, flattened breasts, and liberal use of profanity, tobacco, and alcohol. With manpower shortages during the war, women had gained a niche in the labor force; with the 19th Amendment, they had gained the vote.

But the Jazz Age was not all glamour and emancipation. The country turned inward after the war, falling back on isolationism and suspicion of all things foreign. Congress enacted restrictive immigration laws. President Coolidge's laissez-faire policies abetted big business's exploitation of labor and its suppression of trade unions. Two fifths of the population, farmers and their families, were cut off from the general affluence as farm prices plummeted. Meanwhile, organized crime, spurred by Prohibition, was burgeoning. **◂1919.V ▸1923.9**

Flapper as icon, by premier Jazz Age illustrator John Held.

BIRTHS

Diane Arbus, U.S. photographer.

Richard Avedon, U.S. photographer.

Brendan Behan, Irish playwright.

Maria Callas, U.S. singer.

Italo Calvino, Italian writer.

James Dickey, U.S. writer.

Nadine Gordimer, South African writer.

Joseph Heller, U.S. novelist.

Charlton Heston, U.S. actor.

Wojciech Jaruzelski, Polish president.

Henry Kissinger, German-U.S. statesman.

Roy Lichtenstein, U.S. artist.

Norman Mailer, U.S. writer.

Marcel Marceau, French mime.

Rocky Marciano, U.S. boxer.

Marcello Mastroianni, Italian actor.

Robert Maxwell, Czech-U.K. publisher.

Jean Nidetch, U.S. entrepreneur.

Shimon Peres, Israeli prime minister.

Alan Shepard, U.S. astronaut.

Hank Williams, U.S. singer.

Lee Kuan Yew, Singaporean prime minister.

Franco Zeffirelli, Italian film and stage director.

DEATHS

Sarah Bernhardt, French actress.

Alexandre Gustave Eiffel, French engineer.

Warren G. Harding, U.S. president.

Katherine Mansfield, U.K. writer.

L. Martov, Russian revolutionary.

Wilhelm Röntgen, German physicist.

Pancho Villa, Mexican revolutionary.

Painting & Sculpture: *The Farmer's Wife* (Joan Miró); *Woman and Dog* (Pierre Bonnard) ... Film: *The Covered Wagon* (James Cruze); *The Ten Commandments* (Cecil B. DeMille); *The Hunchback of Notre Dame* (with Lon Chaney); *The Street* (Karl Grune) ... Theater: *The Young Idea* (Noël Coward); *The Adding Machine* (Elmer Rice); *Saint Joan* (G.B. Shaw); *Icebound* (Owen Davis).

"Architecture is the masterly, correct, and magnificent play of forms brought together in light."—**Le Corbusier**

NEW IN 1923

Milky Way and Butterfinger candy bars.

Zenith Radio (Chicago).

Pan American Airways.

Rubber diaphragms (contraceptive device).

Hertz Drive-Ur-Self car rentals.

Maidenform brassieres.

Warner Bros. Pictures, Inc.

Autogiro (invented by Spanish aeronaut Juan de la Cierva).

IN THE UNITED STATES

▶MAH-JONGG MANIA—Perhaps the first California craze to conquer the U.S., mah-jongg was brought to the Golden State from Shanghai after World War I by an American missionary who adapted (and copyrighted) the old Mandarin gambling game. At the fad's peak, in 1923, some 10 million women were meeting regularly for mah-jongg parties. Played with tiles made of calves' shinbones and engraved with Chinese characters, the pastime provided an escape from household routine—and spurred huge sales of accessories like silk kimonos and paper fans.

▶CHARLESTON—An African-American folk dance adapted for Broadway in 1923, the Charleston set off a dance frenzy, giving Jazz Age swells a favorite ballroom recreation and earning harsh censure from offended moralists.

Masked Klansmen in New Jersey: a "Southern problem" comes north.

THE UNITED STATES

Ku Klux Klan on the Rise

6 On July 4, 1923, as Americans celebrated their nation's 147th birthday, a small town in Indiana played host to an ominous event: the largest Ku Klux Klan rally ever held in a northern state. Between 10,000 and 200,000 men, women, and children (estimates vary wildly), many dressed in white robes and pointed hoods, enjoyed picnics, speeches, a parade with floats depicting menacing blacks and "papists," and the burning of a giant cross.

The KKK, founded after the Civil War to safeguard southern white supremacy by terrorizing blacks, had been dormant for nearly 50 years when it resumed organizing nationwide after World War I. At its peak, in 1925, it boasted four million members. The group's primary target remained African-Americans, but now Jews, Catholics, immigrants, bootleggers, and indulgers in illicit sex were added to its list.

For all its xenophobia, the Klan mirrored Europe's right-wing nationalist movements. Its leaders admired Mussolini and understood the power of myth, ceremony—and a little bloodshed. Like Mussolini, they offered only a vague political program, but excelled at gaining political leverage. In states where Klan membership was high, they "owned" officials at all levels of government.

But after several highly publicized scandals (like the 1925 conviction of Indiana's Klan chief on second-degree murder charges), Americans finally soured on the Klan. By 1930 membership had dwindled to 100,000—mostly, as before, in the South. **◂1919.6 ▸1931.9**

LITERATURE

Elegiac Rilke

7 The ten poems of *The Duino Elegies*, completed in 1923, constitute the transcendent achievement of the German-born writer Rainer Maria Rilke, the quintessential wandering poet. The Austrian writer and humanist Stefan Zweig said of Rilke, "It was only in him that the mere word was already perfect music." The poems came to Rilke over a long, tortuous stretch of years, during which he traversed Europe and North Africa in search of inspiration and enlightenment.

The first two poems of the *Elegies* were written in 1912, when he was a guest at the castle Duino, near Trieste, Italy. The following year he finished the "Third Elegy" in Paris; the fourth was written in 1915 in Munich. It was only in February 1922 that, in a final burst of creativity, Rilke poured out his other great masterpiece, *The Sonnets to Orpheus*, and brought the *Elegies* to completion. The luminous language of these two works, which display the poet at the height of his creative powers, sheds light on fundamental questions of time, identity, life, and death. **▸1925.8**

ARCHITECTURE

Corbu's Constructions

8 "A house," declared the Swiss-French architect Le Corbusier in his 1923 book, *Toward a (New) Architecture*, "is a machine for living in." A prophet of the International Style, Le Corbusier (born Charles Edouard Jeanneret) championed an austere, rigorously modern aesthetic. To some critics, his early buildings—clinical, right-angled, severe—looked like enlarged cardboard boxes with cutout holes for windows. Others found a distinctly modern beauty in their ascetic geometry.

Le Corbusier was able to implement his ideas on a large scale in 1924 when he was hired to build a housing development for workers in the French town of Pessac, near Bordeaux. Without regard for the local vernacular style, Le Corbusier erected a series of cubic concrete houses with standardized banded windows and roof gardens. Each side of the various houses was painted a different strong color. The workers for whom they were intended hated the houses, and the affronted local government refused for years to supply water, but eventually Pessac was accepted as an important architectural experiment.

An urban planner as well as an architect and painter, Le Corbusier advocated vertically organized cities. Each age produces its own form, he argued, and the modern form was the skyscraper. He designed futuristic utopias of clustered towers surrounded by untrammeled parks, with traffic restricted to freeways whose axes

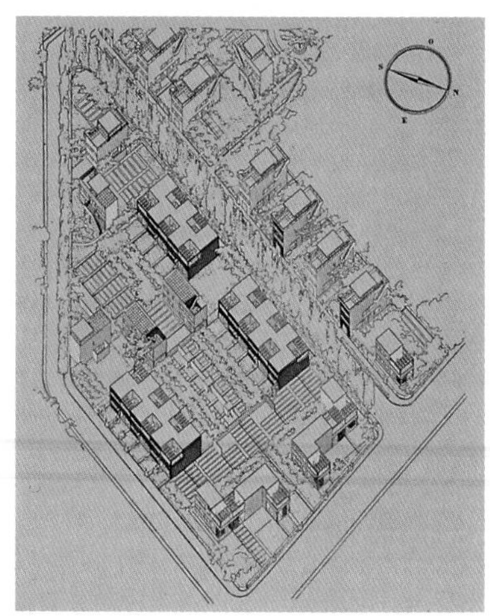

A Le Corbusier drawing of Pessac. His design pleased aesthetes more than occupants.

SPORTS: Baseball: World Series, New York Yankees defeat New York Giants, 4–2; Yankee Stadium opens ... Boxing: Heavyweight champion Jack Dempsey defeats Argentine Luis "Wild Bull of the Pampas" Firpo after being knocked out of the ring ... Golf: Bobby Jones wins his first U.S. Open ... Swimming: Johnny Weissmuller sets his 50th world record in the 100-meter freestyle (58.6 sec.).

ran between the buildings.

Although he never fully realized his urban concepts (or, ironically, built a skyscraper), his designs, especially the later ones, were widely imitated and accurately predicted the modern-age city of office parks, plazas, and access roads. **◂1919.9 ▸1930.7**

THE UNITED STATES

Scandal Rocks Washington

9 Until it was supplanted by Watergate in the early seventies, Teapot Dome was the most spectacular scandal in American political history—involving, ultimately, the mysterious death of the President and the suicide of two of his advisers. It erupted full bore in 1923, when a Senate investigation revealed that Albert B. Fall, President Warren Harding's secretary of the interior, had, at huge profit to himself, illegally leased Navy oil reserves at Teapot Dome, Wyoming, and Elk Hills and Buena Vista, California, to private oil concerns.

The corrupt deal was cut early in Harding's term, after Fall persuaded the President and Secretary of the Navy Edwin Denby to transfer control of the government's precious oil reserves to his department. Having secured the transfer, Fall quickly peddled drilling rights to the protected lands to two oil magnates in exchange for $400,000 in cash and government bonds. The Senate began to suspect something was amiss when Fall, who'd come into office deeply in debt, suddenly added acreage and cattle to his New Mexico ranch.

Fall resigned in the midst of the probe, but the investigation continued for years. "Teapot Dome" became the shorthand term for the wide-ranging corruption of Harding's administration. The President himself—widely considered a decent man wholly out of his depth in the office—was largely ignorant of the dishonorable activities of his unsupervised cabinet. Just as the sordid details of the scandals were coming to light, two of his advisers, Jess Smith of the Justice Department and Charles Cramer of Veterans Affairs, put bullets in their brains. Deeply distraught, Harding took mysteriously ill on a trip from Alaska to San Francisco (food poisoning and exhaustion were cited, but some suspected foul play) and died in San Francisco on August 2, 1923.

Eventually, Fall, Veterans Affairs bureau director Charles Forbes, and alien-property custodian Thomas Miller all drew prison terms for their schemes to bilk the government from within. Extensive litigation kept the cases in public view for almost a decade. But, oddly, the scandals did not hurt the Republican Party; the GOP ticket, headed by Calvin Coolidge, who became president upon Harding's death, prevailed in the 1924 election. **◂1923.5 ▸1972.10**

"Bargain day in Washington." Cabinet members sold out the government—cheap.

POPULAR CULTURE

Time Magazine Appears

10 "People in America are, for the most part, poorly informed," announced the prospectus for a new weekly magazine, "because no publication has adapted itself to the time which busy men are able to spend on simply keeping informed."

Stepping in to fill this vacuum were two young Yale graduates, Henry Luce and Briton Hadden. Their magazine, *Time*, appeared on newsstands for the first time in 1923, with a date of March 3 and a cover price of 15 cents. The Brooklyn-born Hadden died of a strep infection in 1929; Luce, the son of a Presbyterian missionary in China, went on to oversee a publishing empire that grew to include *Life*, *Fortune*, and *Sports Illustrated*.

***Time*'s first cover story was about Illinois congressman Joseph Cannon's retirement.**

Initially, the magazine summarized the news from big bundles of daily papers, emphasizing world events and cultural happenings. But within a decade, Time Inc. had established a far-reaching news-gathering organization of its own. *Time*'s success spawned a host of imitators: in America, *Business Week* (1929), *United States News*, and *Newsweek* (both 1933); in Germany, *Der Spiegel* (1947); in France, *L'Express* (1953); in Italy, *Panorama* (1962).

Time was concise, its tone omniscient, and its style peculiar unto itself. "Backward ran sentences until reeled the mind," wrote Wolcott Gibbs in a famous parody. Luce's political leanings invariably found their way into the magazine, frequently in its cover stories. A vehement anticommunist, Luce (who died in 1967) supported Chiang Kai-shek and Ngo Dinh Diem, as well as Mussolini and Franco. The great American journalist Theodore H. White lost his job at *Time* when he disagreed with Luce over China. Even so, said White, "it was exhilarating to be working for a man who could discuss, all at the same time, the Bible, Confucius, and the itchy gossip and color which sells readers on a magazine." **◂1900.2**

IN THE UNITED STATES

Showcased in the musical *Runnin' Wild*, the knee-slapping, hip-swaying, leg-swinging dance swept the country. Ministers condemned it. ◂1914.7 ▸1960.13

▶THE FUNNIEST FOUR-EYES—Chaplin was "The Little Tramp," and Keaton was "The Stone Face," but Hollywood's highest-paid comedian in the twenties—and its most popular—was Harold Lloyd, an Everyman with oversized black horn-rim glasses. His 1923 film, *Safety Last*, was one of his best. The scene in which he dangles from a clock tower showcases the surprising athletic prowess—he

never used doubles—that kept audiences screaming with laughter and fear. ◂1912.5 ▸1936.9

▶QUEEN OF THE BLUES—Bessie Smith, widely regarded as the greatest female blues singer of all time, scored a hit with 1923's "Down Hearted Blues" and "Gulf Coast Blues." For nearly a decade, the stately, deep-voiced Smith was the nation's top black performer. But by the time of her death in a car crash in 1937, her alcoholism and the

public's changing tastes had reduced her to making a humbling southern tour. ◂1914.M ▸1925.6

POLITICS & BUSINESS: GNP: $85.1 billion ... President W.G. Harding dies and is succeeded by Vice President Calvin Coolidge ... U.S. Steel reduces workday from 12 to 8 hours ... Alice Paul drafts Equal Rights Amendment at National Woman's Party meeting in Seneca Falls, N.Y. ... Federal tax-disclosure law passed ... Supreme Court rules D.C. minimum wage for women and children unconstitutional.

"Let us not be puffed up with military victories. Let us rather prepare for new victories in science and economics."
—Mustafa Kemal, on his plans to modernize Turkey

AROUND THE WORLD

▶SELF-HELP GURU—Before Dale Carnegie and Norman Vincent Peale, there was Emile Coué. In 1923, the French pharmacist published *Self-Mastery Through Conscious Auto-Suggestion*, in which he declared, "Every day, in every way, I'm growing better and better." Through hypnosis and the constant repetition of an optimistic phrase, Coué maintained, patients learned to help themselves. ◂1907.8 ▸1936.M

▶*BAMBI*, THE BOOK—Austrian writer Felix Salten won worldwide fame with *Bambi*, the tale of a deer's life in the forest and its dignified struggle against its nemesis: man. The 1923 novel became a classic of children's literature—and, in 1942, a landmark movie by Walt Disney. By then the Nazis had forced Salten, a Jew, to flee to Switzerland. ▸1928.10

▶BULGARIAN COUP—Bulgarian rightists murdered Premier Alexander Stamboliyski and installed an authoritarian regime in 1923. Stamboliyski had become a hero to his country's peasant majority—and angered the army and Czar Boris's court—by implementing land redistribution, universal suffrage, and other reforms. His allies staged an electoral comeback in 1931, but another coup in 1934 returned Bulgaria to a royalist-military dictatorship that took Germany's side in World War II. ◂1911.12 ▸1944.11

▶JAPAN EARTHQUAKE—On September 1, 143,000 people died and 600,000 homes were destroyed in Tokyo and Yokohama, when an earthquake in Sagami Bay devastated the coastal region of southern Honshu. The quake created one of the largest land displacements ever recorded (a shift of 15 feet horizontally and 6 feet vertically). A 36-foot tsunami and three days of raging fires laid waste to both cities. ◂1906.5 ▸1985.4

The Frigidaire: cool, clean, and admirably self-contained.

TECHNOLOGY

The Iceman Goeth

11 Before 1923, when Frigidaire, then a division of General Motors, introduced its new mechanical refrigeration unit, the iceman was a national institution in America and a national joke. He was apt to be a big, uncouth fellow who left muddy footprints on the floor as he delivered huge blocks of ice. Not only was the ice—harvested from northern lakes and stored in insulated warehouses—filled with impurities, but complaints about short-weighting were rife.

Then the revolution: In 1902, an engineer named Willis H. Carrier had designed a system to control humidity and temperature in a lithography plant in Brooklyn, New York. Mechanical refrigeration technology was developed further by fur-vault owners and dairies. Smaller, domestic refrigeration units—noisy, leaky contraptions with electric motors and belts installed in old-fashioned iceboxes—made a tentative appearance around World War I. But the Frigidaire of 1923 was designed with a special cabinet to enclose both the "icebox" for storing perishables and the machinery that made it cool. The device was neat, convenient, and compact. A style and a ubiquitous brand name were born.

Thereafter, prices plunged and numbers proliferated. By 1944 almost 85 percent of American homes were equipped with mechanical refrigerators. The icebox lingered only as a figure of speech. **◂1917.12**

TURKEY

Kemal's Reforms

12 Certified by the Treaty of Lausanne, Turkey became a sovereign state in the eyes of the world in July 1923. (Among the treaty's provisions: expulsion of a million Greeks from Turkey and 350,000 Turks from Greece.) The Turkish National Assembly proclaimed the country a republic, the first in the Islamic world. But for President Mustafa Kemal, the biggest task lay ahead. Envisioning a liberal democracy, Kemal used dictatorial powers to drag Turkey into the modern age.

First, he separated government from clergy. Since 1517, the Turkish sultan had also been caliph, or spiritual leader, of most of the world's Muslims. Now Kemal sponsored measures abolishing the caliphate and the religious courts, and introducing a European-style legal system. The state took over education.

Kemal granted women the vote. He banned polygamy and discouraged veil-wearing. And he fought to lift the veils dividing Turkey from the West. Turkish was to be written in Roman characters instead of Arabic script. (Kemal made impromptu visits to provincial capitals to encourage, instruct, and insist on the benefits of a simplified alphabet.) The Gregorian calendar was adopted, as were hats with brims. The fez was outlawed, on pain of death.

In 1933 a law was passed requiring the use of family names; the Assembly gave Kemal the surname Atatürk, meaning "Father of the Turks." When he died in 1938, full democracy had yet to come. Still, his reforms inspired the leaders of many developing nations, from India's Jawaharlal Nehru to Egypt's Anwar al-Sadat. **◂1922.10 ▸1925.10**

An admirer composed this photomontage of Kemal among his works. But his often bloody methods drew world criticism.

RELIGION

Buber's *I and Thou*

13 Martin Buber's *I and Thou*, published in 1923, became one of the world's most widely read philosophical treatises. The work, rooted in Judaism, posits two basic ways in which humans relate to the universe. The "I-It" is functional, one-sided, impersonal: people's everyday relationship with organisms (including other people) and objects as *things*. The "I-Thou" is a spontaneous, reciprocal, deeply intimate communion with creation: the state in which people sense the presence of God. Life is impossible without the I-It, but only the I-Thou makes a good life—and a good society—possible. "In our age," Buber wrote, "the I-It relation, gigantically swollen, has usurped ... the mastery and the rule."

After Hitler came to power, Buber became head of Germany's national center for Jewish adult education. But the authorities, stung by his critique of Nazism as the I-It's apotheosis, eventually silenced him. In 1938, when he was 60 years old, Buber received permission to travel to Palestine. The Gestapo agent sent to supervise his packing read one of his books—a study of Hasidism—and was so impressed that he asked Buber to sign it. Indeed, Buber's writings are so broadly appealing that they have influenced philosophers and theologians of all creeds.

Buber's philosophy led him to advocate a socialist, binational Arab-Jewish state in Palestine. It also allowed him to return to Germany to accept a peace prize in 1953, a conciliatory act denounced by many Jews. Buber refused to condemn the German people for supporting genocide. Instead, he left the matter of guilt up to each individual's conscience—the faculty that Hitler had derided as a "Jewish invention." **▸1932.7**

NOBEL PRIZES: Peace: No award ... Literature: William Butler Yeats (Irish; poet) ... Chemistry: Fritz Pregl (Austrian; microanalysis of organic compounds) ... Medicine: Frederick Banting and John MacLeod (Canadian; insulin) ... Physics: Robert A. Millikan (U.S.; electron's electric charge and photoelectric effect).

A VOICE FROM 1923

On Love

From *The Prophet,* by Kahlil Gibran, 1923

A mystic for the masses, Lebanese-American poet, essayist, and artist Kahlil Gibran became an international icon with the publication of his 1923 romantic effusion, The Prophet. *A celebration of love and spiritualism, the prose poem fused elements of Eastern and Western faith into a lyrical message of rapture that appealed just as much to twenties seekers-after-meaning as it did to the flower children who embraced it four decades later. A perennial bestseller,* The Prophet *has been translated into 13 languages.* ►**1968.11**

Then said Almitra, Speak to us of Love.
And he raised his head and looked upon the people, and there fell a stillness upon them. And with a great voice he said:
When love beckons to you, follow him,
Though his ways are hard and steep.
And when his wings enfold you yield to him,
Though the sword hidden among his pinions may wound you.
And when he speaks to you believe in him,
Though his voice may shatter your dreams as the north wind lays waste the garden.

For even as love crowns you so shall he crucify you. Even as he is for your growth so is he for your pruning.
Even as he ascends to your height and caresses your tenderest branches that quiver in the sun,
So shall he descend to your roots and shake them in their clinging to the earth.

Like sheaves of corn he gathers you unto himself.
He threshes you to make you naked.
He sifts you to free you from your husks.
He grinds you to whiteness.
He kneads you until you are pliant;
And then he assigns you to his sacred fire, that you may become sacred bread for God's sacred feast.

All these things shall love do unto you that you may know the secrets of your heart, and in that knowledge become a fragment of Life's heart.

But if in your fear you would seek only love's peace and love's pleasure,
Then it is better for you that you cover your nakedness and pass out of love's threshing-floor,
Into the seasonless world where you shall laugh, but not all of your laughter, and weep, but not all of your tears.

Love gives naught but itself and takes naught but from itself.
Love possesses not nor would it be possessed;
For love is sufficient unto love.

Gibran's self-portrait *(top)* and one of his illustrations for *The Prophet*. Words were not the only medium for his passionate vision.

"You cannot make a revolution with silk gloves."—**Joseph Stalin**

STORY OF THE YEAR

Stalin Succeeds Lenin

1 Like wanton children, the Communist leaders of the recently formed Union of Soviet Socialist Republics squabbled, jockeying to inherit the mantle of their Party's dying father. By 1924, when Vladimir Lenin succumbed to his final stroke, distinct lines had been drawn. On one side was the triumvirate of high Party officials: Joseph Stalin, Lev Kamenev, and Grigory Zinoviev. Against them stood Leon Trotsky, commissar of war, widely regarded as Lenin's true philosophical heir. In the balance hung the future of the Party, the Soviet state, and the 145 million Russian people.

It was barely a contest. Against the firmly entrenched infighters of the triumvirate, Trotsky, hamstrung by his intellectual idealism, stood no chance. The insiders, especially Stalin, ably positioned themselves at the head of the cult of Lenin that sprang up after the leader's death. (Never mind that in his last writings, subsequently suppressed by Stalin, Lenin warned against monomaniacal ambitions.) At the funeral, Stalin was everywhere, delivering eulogies, vowing loyalty. Trotsky, meanwhile, was miles away, receiving medical treatment. (He later claimed Stalin had lied to him about the dates.) Whatever the reason, the point was clear: Trotsky was out of the loop. His early anti-Bolshevik writings, dating from when he had sided with the Menshevik faction, were now used to portray him as an anti-Lenin heretic.

Trotsky was removed as commissar of war in 1925; soon afterward, it became clear to Kamenev and Zinoviev that Stalin's secret plans didn't include them—bitter medicine, since they considered Stalin their intellectual and doctrinal inferior. Having already dispensed with Trotsky, Stalin's only viable opponent, they were powerless to resist the dictator's machinations. Both were ousted from the politburo, the Party's governing body. Reluctantly, and somewhat desperately, they joined Trotsky; operating within the Party, Stalin had no trouble discrediting the alliance, making it look like a union of disappointed, unpatriotic malcontents. Trotsky, still dreaming of worldwide revolution, was permanently exiled in 1929. Kamenev and Zinoviev were allowed to languish inside the state but outside Stalin's ever-tightening circle of power until 1936, when both were tried for treason and executed. The Party belonged to Stalin. His cult began to supplant Lenin's. **◂1921.2 ▸1929.4**

The death of Lenin *(center)* divided Stalin *(left)* and Trotsky *(right)*.

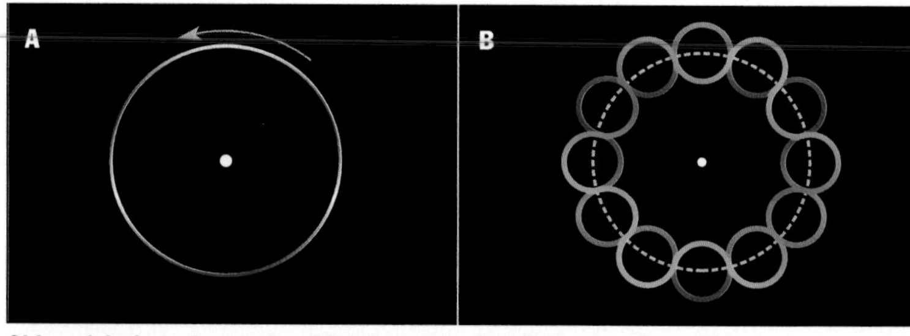

Old model of an electron's orbit (A), and de Broglie's new wave (B).

SCIENCE

De Broglie's Wave Mechanics

2 A basic principle of classical physics, first articulated by Isaac Newton in the seventeenth century, was that matter and energy are separate and distinct. But in the early twentieth century Einstein concluded that matter and energy are interchangeable ($E = mc^2$) and that light is composed of subatomic particles called photons. Then, in 1924, a young French aristocrat named Louis-Victor de Broglie theorized that just as waves could become particles, particles such as electrons and protons could behave as waves. His formulas laid the foundation for the new field of wave mechanics, which held, paradoxically, that matter and energy are simply different states of the same subatomic particle.

De Broglie was one of the revolutionary new field's leading thinkers. Yet in the forties he switched sides, arguing that even though an electron shows wavelike characteristics, it is not necessarily energy. He joined with Einstein in attacking the new science for undue emphasis on mathematics as an end in itself. Algebraic formulas had proved indispensable in predicting the behavior of subatomic particles but had done little to shed light on their underlying nature. Countering physicists who claimed that the formulas were all scientists could or needed to know, de Broglie and Einstein argued that the important thing was to penetrate the reality behind the formulas. **◂1916.9 ▸1925.7**

ART

First Surrealist Manifesto

3 "The imagination is perhaps on the point of reclaiming its rights," wrote André Breton in his *Manifeste du Surréalisme*, published in October 1924. Inspired by Freudian theory, the surrealist artists and writers of Paris hoped to stage an aesthetic revolution equal to the political revolutions that were taking place in Moscow and Rome—one that would cure Western culture's ills by liberating the unconscious. By juxtaposing words or images according to psychological—rather then logical—criteria, they aimed to destroy the boundaries between dream and reality. The result, for both creator and viewer, would be a plunge into "super-reality," a mental realm of freedom and self-knowledge.

***Two Children Are Threatened by a Nightingale* (1924), by surrealist artist Max Ernst.**

Surrealism—more so in the visual arts than in literature—became the dominant artistic movement of the interwar years, delighting millions with works of anarchic whimsy and haunting weirdness. Like most revolutions, however, surrealism did not stay revolutionary. Though Breton—nicknamed the "Pope of surrealism" for his orthodoxy—denounced comrades who pandered to the cultural establishment, surrealist art appealed to mainstream tastes: Museums snapped it up; René Magritte designed store catalogues; Salvador Dali designed "shoe hats" and "lobster dresses" for couturier Elsa Schiaparelli.

The surrealists were the century's last great creative avant-garde: Mass culture simply became too powerful, too capable of transform-

ART & CULTURE: Books: ***With Lawrence in Arabia*** **(Lowell Thomas);** ***The Magic Mountain*** **(Thomas Mann);** ***The Green Hat*** **(Michael Arlen) ... Music: "California, Here I Come" (Meyer, DeSylva, and Jolson); "Indian Love Call" (Friml, Harbach, and Hammerstein); "It Had to Be You" (Jones and Kahn); "Tea for Two" (Youmans and Caesar) ... Painting & Sculpture:** ***Dempsey and Firpo*** **(George Bellows);**

"It seems as if God has been dethroned. Let us reinstate Him in our hearts."—**Gandhi, announcing his 21-day fast**

ing such revolts into fashion. While surrealist tendencies resurface periodically in the art world, the movement's influence is clearest today in advertisements and music videos. **◂1920.4 ▸1928.6**

GREAT BRITAIN

First Labour Government

4 The British Labour Party, 18 years after its founding, was more than ready to have a crack at governing the nation—and with it, the world's vastest empire. The nation, however, was not ready for Labour, and Britain's first experiment in democratic socialism, in 1924, lasted less than ten months.

The party was propelled to power in October 1923, when Conservative prime minister Stanley Baldwin, over the objections of colleagues, called for new parliamentary elections after introducing a protectionist trade policy. (Baldwin was honoring his promise to clear any such fiscal changes with voters.) The Conservatives lost 90 seats while Labour solidified its place as the second-largest party in Parliament. For the first time, Labour and the Liberals together outnumbered the Conservatives. The Liberals agreed to back Ramsay MacDonald, a Labour Party founder, for prime minister.

MacDonald, a self-educated Scotsman and the son of an unmarried maidservant, began cautiously. He refrained from nationalizing industries and deftly averted an explosion in the Irish Free State, canceling its debt in exchange for its surrender of claims to six northern counties. But his downfall began in August 1924, when he agreed to recognize the Soviet government and to give it a loan and most-favored-nation trade status.

The treaties with the "reds" provoked an uproar; both Liberal and Conservative legislators refused to ratify them. Meanwhile, Conservatives accused the Prime Minister of secretly intervening to stop the prosecution of a communist journalist accused of inciting mutiny. MacDonald denied the charge but blocked an inquiry. Instead, he called for a parliamentary vote of confidence, which Labour lost. Baldwin returned as prime minister, with free-trader Winston Churchill as finance minister.

MacDonald did get another chance to govern (1929-35), but by then the Depression was in full swing. Forced to cut wages and social services, the pioneer Labourite faced riots by angry workers. **◂1906.1 ▸1926.4**

First Labour prime minister Ramsay MacDonald, before the fall.

INDIA

Gandhi Fasts for Unity

5 As he did repeatedly throughout his life when confronted with violence, in 1924 Mohandas Gandhi embarked on a 21-day fast for peace. He had recently been discharged from jail, having served two years of a six-year sentence for sedition.

Conditions in India had declined precipitously during his incarceration. His policy of nonviolent noncooperation with the British government had been abandoned by leaders of the independence movement; factionalism had ripped through the Indian National Congress, curtailing its effectiveness; and his political influence was at an all-time low. Most disturbing of all, a resurgence of religious intolerance between Muslims and Hindus had turned Indian against Indian.

Back in March 1922, Gandhi had called off his national civil-disobedience program after zealots in the remote village of Chauri Chaura rioted and killed a number of British civil servants. The move cost him political stature: His strict adherence to nonviolence (the first article of his faith, as he put it, and the last article of his creed) frustrated many colleagues in the Congress who craved action and immediate results. Recognizing Gandhi's political decline, British authorities then took him to trial, something they had been afraid to do when his influence was at its peak. Charged with sedition for writing newspaper articles inimical to the British Raj, Gandhi pleaded guilty: "In my opinion," he'd stated, "noncooperation with evil is as much a duty as is cooperation with good."

The trial was a remarkable affair, with both Gandhi and the sentencing judge displaying extreme courtesy and mutual respect. After serving two years in prison, Gandhi fell ill with acute appendicitis, and the government, dreading the disastrous publicity that would result should Gandhi die in its custody, provided him with medical attention and an unconditional release.

But if the Raj had correctly assessed the decline of Gandhi's political clout, it had failed to recognize his unflagging popularity with the masses. Released from prison, Gandhi quickly regained his political strength and, with his fast for Indian unity and religious tolerance, he again became the cynosure of the independence movement. **◂1921.12 ▸1930.4**

Gandhi—now called Mahatma (Sanskrit for "Great-Souled") by his followers—found strength in fasting.

BIRTHS

Lauren Bacall, U.S. actress.

James Baldwin, U.S. writer.

Marlon Brando, U.S. actor.

George Bush, U.S. president.

Truman Capote, U.S. writer.

Jimmy Carter, U.S. president.

Shirley Chisholm, U.S. congresswoman.

Janet Frame, New Zealand writer.

Kenneth Kaunda, Zambian president.

Robert Mugabe, Zimbabwean president.

Milton Obote, Ugandan president.

George Segal, U.S. artist.

DEATHS

Frances Hodgson Burnett, U.K.-U.S. writer.

Ferruccio Busoni, Italian musician and composer.

Joseph Conrad, Polish-U.K. novelist.

Eleonora Duse, Italian actress.

Gabriel Fauré, French composer.

Anatole France, French writer.

Samuel Gompers, U.K.-U.S. labor leader.

Victor Herbert, U.S. composer.

Franz Kafka, Czech writer.

V.I. Lenin, Russian revolutionary and Soviet ruler.

Henry Cabot Lodge, U.S. diplomat.

Gene Stratton Porter, U.S. novelist.

Maurice Prendergast, U.S. painter.

Giacomo Puccini, Italian composer.

Louis Sullivan, U.S. architect.

Woodrow Wilson, U.S. president.

Odalisque with Magnolias **(Henri Matisse) ... Film: *The Iron Horse* (John Ford); *Sherlock, Jr.* (Buster Keaton); *The Thief of Bagdad* (with Douglas Fairbanks) ... Theater: *What Price Glory?* (Anderson and Stallings); *Each in His Own Way* (Luigi Pirandello); *Desire Under the Elms* (Eugene O'Neill); *Juno and the Paycock* (Sean O'Casey); *Lady Be Good* (George and Ira Gershwin and Guy Bolton).**

"You can punch a hole in a card ... and you'll never have to write it down again. Machines can do the routine work. People shouldn't have to do that kind of work."—**Thomas Watson, founder of IBM**

NEW IN 1924

Italian autostrada from Milan to Varese (first motorway).

Wheaties cereal.

Kleenex tissues (Kimberly-Clark).

Self-winding wristwatch.

Macy's Thanksgiving Day Parade (New York City).

IN THE UNITED STATES

▸FOOTBALL HEROES—Sportswriter Grantland Rice in 1924 coined the nickname "Galloping Ghost" to describe the phenomenal gridiron exploits of University of Illinois halfback Red Grange, who scored a total of 31 touchdowns in 20 Illinois games. (When he joined the Chicago Bears, his presence doubled attendance figures.)

Another of Rice's coinages that year, "Four Horsemen of the Apocalypse," described the starting backfield at Notre Dame *(posing on horses, above)*, where legendary coach Knute Rockne was reinventing the game—and making his Fighting Irish all but unbeatable. ◂1913.M

▸TOP G-MAN—J. Edgar Hoover became director of the Bureau of Investigation in 1924, and started whipping the inefficient, scandal-plagued agency into shape. Among his innovations: a training academy, a fingerprint file (which grew into the world's largest), and a scientific crime lab. By 1935, when the word "Federal" was added to the Bureau's name, Hoover and his agents were national heroes. One of the most powerful men in the U.S., Hoover pursued criminals, radicals,

Composer at the keyboard: self-portrait of a musical rhapsodist.

MUSIC

Gershwin's *Rhapsody*

6 With *Rhapsody in Blue*—first performed at New York City's Aeolian Hall in 1924—American composer George Gershwin attained his lifelong goal of transcending the world of "popular" music and entering the ethereal realm of "serious" music. Billed as an "Experiment in Modern Music," *Rhapsody* was performed by the Paul Whiteman Orchestra; though some critics were upset that "popular" music was being played in a concert hall, the composition brought Gershwin fame, fortune, and, most important, respect.

Born Jacob Gershvin in Brooklyn, New York, in 1898, the composer demonstrated a prodigious gift for the piano from age 12 and honed his technique by playing the tunes of other songwriters for prospective clients in Tin Pan Alley. Soon, however, he was writing his own music. His first Broadway show, *La La Lucille,* opened in 1919. One year later Gershwin had his first smash-hit song, "Swanee." Sung by Al Jolson, it sold two million records and one million copies of sheet music.

An early appreciator of jazz (he'd been hooked since the day he heard it wafting through the door of a nightclub in Harlem, where his family briefly lived), Gershwin achieved in *Rhapsody in Blue* a unique melding of the harmonies, rhythms, and colorations of jazz with those of nineteenth-century Romantic symphonic music. While Jelly Roll Morton, King Oliver, and other musicians were enjoying considerable success at the time, jazz was considered a distinctly separate genre. By integrating jazz into the larger world of music, Gershwin gave it a new level of exposure.

In the years following *Rhapsody in Blue*, Gershwin collaborated with his brother, Ira, on a number of unforgettable shows, including their opera *Porgy and Bess* (1935). Only moderately successful at the time, it has endured as a classic of American music. **◂1917.5 ▸1926.M**

BUSINESS AND INDUSTRY

IBM Named

7 One of the first decisions new CEO Thomas Watson made when he took over the Computing-Tabulating-Recording Company in

Watson and watchword. His son made thinking machines IBM's specialty.

1924 was to rename it. The company's new name, International Business Machines, reflected the sweeping, aggressive optimism of its new leader. And as it turned out, Watson's optimism was more than justified: IBM grew into a corporate powerhouse, the world's largest manufacturer of accounting equipment and, later, computers.

CTR had been around since two struggling business-machine makers had merged into one struggling conglomerate in 1910. Watson joined the company as general manager in 1914, having already made his reputation as a salesman for National Cash Register, the industrial giant. When Watson took over, CTR had annual sales of $4 million. Concentrating on the company's best product, a tabulator that encoded statistical information on punched cards (invented by Herman Hollerith for the U.S. Census Bureau), he doubled revenue in three years.

The technology was not Watson's, but the marketing approach was. Promising lifetime employment and introducing the revolutionary practice of awarding performance bonuses, he mustered an army of salesmen, uniformed them in blue suits and white shirts, drilled them in corporate fight songs ("We can't fail for all can see/That to serve humanity has been our aim"), and sent them out to convert skeptical executives to mechanized record keeping. By the mid-twenties, IBM controlled 85 percent of the booming tabulator market, and 85 percent of the punch-card market.

Upon his death in 1956, Watson was succeeded by his son, Thomas Watson, Jr. Heeding his father's famous "Think" motto, the younger Watson moved "Big Blue" into the computer market. It achieved staggering success and, until its eclipse by the newer microcomputer companies in the 1980s, market domination. **▸1930.1**

ITALY

Mussolini Cracks Down

8 In April 1924, Italy held its first election since the Fascist takeover two years earlier. Momentarily, it appeared that Mussolini's totalitarian ambitions might somehow be compatible with democracy. But then a murder revealed the

SPORTS: Baseball: World Series, Washington Senators (managed by 24-year-old "boy wonder" Bucky Harris) defeat New York Giants, 4–3 ... Hockey: Boston Bruins are first U.S. team to join the NHL ... Tennis: Forest Hills tennis stadium opens in New York ... Horse Racing: Exterminator retires with 50–win record.

“ 'If it's fifty-five hundred years we shall get rid of you, yes, we shall drive every blasted Englishman into the sea, and then ... you and I shall be friends.' ”—**E.M. Forster, *A Passage to India***

Fascist's true nature in the harshest possible light.

That the voting occurred at all was remarkable. Il Duce had often derided the electoral process, saying it was sheerly by whim that he had not made the Parliament building "a bivouac for my platoons." Yet the results of the vote, which gave the Fascists a 65 percent victory, were generally accepted, even by the opposition.

More entrenched than ever, Mussolini said he hoped for a rapprochement with his former comrades, the Socialists. But when a leftist legislator, Giacomo Matteotti, called the elections a fraud—and threatened to expose corruption among the Fascist leadership—the mercurial dictator shouted in Parliament that such traitors should be killed. Soon afterward, Matteotti was murdered. Quickly tracked down, the assassins claimed to be following Mussolini's orders.

Most opposition legislators quit Parliament in protest. Though Mussolini denounced the murder and swore his innocence, he was assailed by the press, domestic and foreign. Demonstrators demanded his ouster. He swung between repression—imposing censorship for the first time—and attempts at conciliation. His popularity plummeted, but no one made a move to topple him. The following January, when a delegation of militia officers warned their leader that his vacillation was risking their support, Mussolini responded with a speech that marked a turning point in his rule. From now on, he announced, subversion would not be tolerated. In the following months he gutted Parliament and established a police state. Dissidents henceforth suffered exile or prison. Matteotti's killers fared better: Two were acquitted, and three released under an amnesty. **◂1922.4 ▸1926.1**

Fascism promises only "duty and battle," boasted Mussolini.

LITERATURE

Forster's Humanist Opus

9 After a hiatus of 14 years, the British novelist Edward Morgan Forster produced in 1924 his last and greatest novel, *A Passage to India*.

Based on visits to India in 1912 and 1921, the novel vividly portrays Muslim, Hindu, and Christian cultures in British-ruled India, and the nearly unbridgeable gaps among them. Of all Forster's work, *Passage* gives the fullest expression to his liberal humanism—a doctrine that values not merely tolerance but also open-mindedness and empathy toward people unlike oneself.

When *A Passage to India* appeared, Forster was already a respected and popular writer, having published four novels, as well as many short stories and essays. (A sixth novel, *Maurice*, written in 1913, did not appear until 1971; because it dealt with the subject of homosexuality, Forster insisted that it be suppressed until after his death.) But while *A Passage to India* was ultimately hailed as a triumph, Forster was at first accused of harboring anti-British sentiments. Yet the theme of sterility and repression among the English upper classes occurs, if somewhat less overtly, throughout his work. He set two novels, *Where Angels Fear to Tread* and *A Room with a View*, in Italy, which for him represented all the warmth and passion his own countrymen lacked. Forster had nothing against British pragmatism, but he had far more respect for spontaneity, creativity, compassion, and a sensitivity to nature—all qualities possessed by Mrs. Moore, the elderly Englishwoman who emerges as the true heroine of *A Passage to India*.

Scornful of convention and traditional Christianity, Forster was a romantic who believed in the sanctity of personal relationships; in both his Italian novels, salvation is achieved only through love. Perhaps the best summation of Forster's worldview is the frequently invoked epigraph from his novel *Howards End*: "Only connect." **◂1901.11 ▸1929.V**

IN THE UNITED STATES

and personal vendettas until his death in 1972.

▶MGM AND *GREED*—Hollywood's biggest studio, Metro-Goldwyn-Mayer, was formed in 1924 when the struggling Goldwyn and Mayer movie companies merged with the formidable Loew's theater chain, owners of Metro Pictures. The company promptly

released a landmark of cinematic realism: *Greed (above)*, Erich von Stroheim's drama of human degradation (cut from an endurance-defying 10 hours). MGM's roster would eventually include Garbo, Gable, Astaire, Crawford, Garland, Tracy, Hepburn, Taylor, the Marx Brothers—even Lassie. **◂1919.3 ▸1929.2**

▶GAS CHAMBER DEBUT—The first prisoner ever executed in a gas chamber was a Chinese immigrant, Gee Jon, convicted of killing a rival tong (gang) member. Gee's death sentence was carried out on February 8 at the state prison in Carson City, Nevada. Nevada had adopted gas as a more humane alternative to electrocution, hanging, or other methods.

▶MASTER BUILDER—Appointed as a state parks commissioner in 1924, Robert Moses began transforming New York City's landscape—and influencing urban planners across the country. Holding dozens of public-works posts over the next 44 years (and wielding more power than the elected officials he worked under), Moses built a host of monumental projects, including 75 parks, 11 bridges, 481 miles of highway, various public-housing complexes, Shea Stadium, and the 1964 World's Fair grounds. **▸1956.M**

POLITICS & BUSINESS: GNP: $84.7 billion ... President Coolidge elected to full term, defeating John W. Davis ... Johnson-Reed Immigration Act greatly restricts immigration, and its no-Japanese policy spawns "Hate America" rallies in Japan ... Congress grants native-born Indians citizenship ... Ford turns out 10 millionth automobile; over half the cars in the world are Model T Fords.

"He was as severe as the Finnish winter, as bleak as an icicle, as gloomy as the second act of an Ibsen play."
—Jim Murray of the *Los Angeles Times*, on Paavo Nurmi

AROUND THE WORLD

▶PERUVIAN REBELS–With Peru's government mortgaging itself to U.S. banks and oil companies, and reneging on promises to protect the country's indigenous peoples, in 1924 exiled dissidents formed the American Popular Revolutionary Alliance (APRA) in Mexico City. Led by Victor Raúl Haya de la Torre, the "Apristas" preached Indian unity and a non-Soviet brand of Marxism. Over the decades, as Peru seesawed between democracy and dictatorship, APRA was sometimes the country's strongest party, more often, illegal. ▶1968.7

▶ALBANIAN STRIFE—The power struggles that had racked Albania since it regained independence in 1920 climaxed violently in 1924. A popular revolt forced conservative Muslim leader Ahmed Zogu *(below)* to flee to Yugoslavia, and liberal Greek Orthodox bishop Fan S. Noli became premier. But six months later, Zogu (aided by Belgrade) overthrew Noli. Son of

a tribal chieftain, the dictatorial Zogu ruled for 14 years—four as president, the rest as King Zog I.

▶MONGOLIAN PEOPLE'S REPUBLIC—Four centuries of subjugation to China did not blunt Mongolia's desire for independence. In 1924, having survived the Manchu Dynasty and a White Russian invasion, and having expelled (with the aid of the Russian Red Army) the last Chinese, Mongolia declared independence. The new Mongolian People's Republic turned away from China and established close political and cultural ties with the Soviet Union. ◀1921.6 ▶1927.2

SPORTS

Scandinavian Success

10 The Finns and the Norwegians—led by the incomparable figure skater Sonja Henie—dominated the first Winter Olympiad, held in 1924 in the French Alpine town of Chamonix. Come summer, Finland again took center stage, in Paris, thanks to Paavo Nurmi—the greatest distance runner the world had ever seen.

Nicknamed the "Flying Finn," Nurmi *(left)* had dazzled spectators four years earlier, but in the Paris Games he shone even brighter. He set an Olympic record for 5,000 meters (14 minutes, 31.2 seconds). He won the 10,000-meter cross-country race by two minutes, on a day so hot that 24 out of the 39 starters collapsed before reaching the finish line. He was essential to the Finns' victories in the 3,000-meter relay and the 10,000-meter cross-country relay. A mechanic by trade, the dour, solitary Nurmi reputedly drew his strength from a diet of black bread and dried fish—though, when asked about it by a reporter, he snapped, "Why should I eat things like that?"

The only other performance in Paris that approached Nurmi's was that of American swimmer Johnny Weissmuller, who set an Olympic record in the 100-meter freestyle and a world record in the 400-meter. (He went on to further fame as Tarzan the Ape Man in movies.) Outbreaks of militant nationalism added to the drama. In one instance, a U.S. rugby victory over France sparked fistfights in the stands. And when an Italian fencer lost a dispute with judges, his teammates marched out singing the Fascist anthem. **◀1920.6 ▶1936.1**

DIPLOMACY

A Break for Germany

11 In August 1924, Germany got a reprieve from its postwar economic turmoil, which had been worsened by partial French occupation and the need to pay reparations to the victors. At a London conference, the Allied powers heard a report on the nation's plight from a Reparations Commission investigative panel—and agreed to a compromise proposed by the panel's head, U.S. financial official (and future vice president) Charles G. Dawes.

The Dawes Plan owed its acceptance to the electoral defeat of French premier Raymond Poincaré's hard-line government and its replacement by a leftist coalition under Edouard Herriot. Pressured by the United States and Britain, Herriot agreed to end French occupation of the Ruhr within a year, to lift sanctions on the Rhineland, and to refrain from imposing further sanctions on Germany without approval from the Reparations Commission. France was to finance its own rebuilding, instead of depending on the money from Germany.

Germany's debt remained the same, but its payments were reduced to between one and 2.5 million marks yearly—until 1929, when the terms would be renegotiated. The United States (not one of Germany's war creditors) would lend Germany $200 million to "prime the pump." That seemed like good business: Payments from Germany to France and Britain would end up largely in U.S. coffers as its allies repaid their war loans.

In the end, Germany received more money than it paid in reparations. But the Dawes Plan helped stabilize the currencies of Europe and the Americas; a brief international boom followed, financed mainly by American credit. Germany's Weimar democracy prospered too—until the Great Depression threw the world economy into chaos. **◀1923.2 ▶1929.12**

GREECE

An Uneasy Republic

12 The land where the republic was invented two millennia earlier *became* one, in 1924—and for most of the next eleven dizzying years, it remained one.

In March, Parliament once again abolished the monarchy, which had been in and out of exile since 1917. Elections had brought the forces of former premier Eleuthérios Venizélos *(above)* back into power. Yet oddly enough, Venizélos—unlike his supporters—favored the King's return, fearing that the country wasn't ready to be without one. Venizélos resigned the premiership after just two months; a year later, a coup by General Theodore Pangalos replaced the republic with a brutal dictatorship.

In 1926, Pangalos was overthrown by another general, George Kondylis. Kondylis reinstated the republic, and in 1928 Venizélos became premier again.

Venizélos had long personified Greek antipathy toward the Turks. But now he effected a rapprochement with Turkey's new leader, Atatürk, which impressed the international community and brought Greece much-needed foreign aid. But Venizélos's economic reforms were undermined by the Depression, and he lost his last election, in 1932. Two years later, the republic fell once more, and the exiled King, George II, returned to rule. **◀1923.12 ▶1935.2**

A British cartoonist depicted the Dawes Plan concessions to Germany on reparations as casting Britain in shadow and Germany in sunshine.

NOBEL PRIZES: Peace: No award ... Literature: Wladyslaw Reymont (Polish; novelist) ... Chemistry: No award ... Medicine: Willem Einthoven (Dutch; electrocardiogram) ... Physics: Karl Siegbahn (Swedish; X-ray spectroscopy).

A VOICE FROM 1924

A Plea for Mercy

By Clarence Darrow, from the Leopold-Loeb trial, August 23, 1924

Leopold *(left)*, Loeb *(right)*, and the man who saved their lives—the most famous lawyer of his time, Clarence Darrow.

Nathan Leopold, 19, and Richard Loeb, 18, were emblems of gilded 1920s youth: rich, handsome, brilliant, and frivolous. So when the two Chicago men confessed to the 1924 "thrill-killing" of 14-year-old Bobby Franks, the case made sensational headlines. The pair's lawyer, Clarence Darrow, knew an insanity defense was hopeless. But he invented a novel argument to save them from almost certain execution: though sane, he said, they were mentally ill, damaged by heredity and environment. The judge's sentence was life plus 99 years—an outcome regarded as a triumph for Darrow, who also managed during the trial to suppress possibly prejudicial information about the pair's Judaism and homosexuality. ▸**1925.3**

There are causes for this terrible crime. There are causes, as I have said, for everything that happens in the world. War is a part of it; education is a part of it; birth is a part of it; money is a part of it—all these conspired to compass the destruction of these two poor boys.

Has the court any rights to consider anything but these two boys? The State says that your Honor has a right to consider the welfare of the community, as you have. If the welfare of the community would be benefited by taking these lives, well and good. I think it would work evil that no one could measure. Has your Honor a right to consider the families of these two defendants? I have been sorry, and I am sorry for the bereavement of Mr. and Mrs. Frank, for those broken ties that cannot be healed. All I can hope and wish is that some good may come from it all. But as compared with the families of Leopold and Loeb, the Franks are to be envied—and everyone knows it.

I do not know how much salvage there is in these two boys. I hate to say it in their presence, but what is there to look forward to? I do not know but what your Honor would be merciful if you tied a rope around their necks and let them die; merciful to them, but not merciful to civilization, and not merciful to those who would be left behind. To spend the balance of their days in prison is mighty little to look forward to, if anything.... I know that these boys are not fit to be at large. I believe they will not be until they pass through the next stage of life, at forty-five or fifty. Whether they will then, I cannot tell. I am sure of this; that I will not be here to help them. So far as I am concerned, it is over....

I am pleading for life, understanding, charity, kindness, and the infinite mercy that considers all. I am pleading that we overcome cruelty with kindness and hatred with love. I know the future is on my side. Your Honor stands between the past and the future. You may hang these boys; you may hang them by the neck until they are dead. But in doing it you will turn your face toward the past. In doing it you are making it harder for every other boy who in ignorance and darkness must grope his way through the mazes which only childhood knows. In doing it you will make it harder for unborn children. You may save them and make it easier for every child that sometime may stand where these boys stand. You will make it easier for every human being with an aspiration and a vision and a hope and a fate. I am pleading for the future; I am pleading for a time when hatred and cruelty will not control the hearts of men. When we can learn by reason and judgment and understanding and faith that all life is worth saving, and that mercy is the highest attribute of man.

"For God's sake go down to reception and get rid of a lunatic who's down there. He says he's got a machine for seeing by wireless! Watch him—he may have a razor on him."—**Editor of London's *Daily Express*, on John Logie Baird**

STORY OF THE YEAR

Baird Televises Human Face

1 In 1925—the year that Scottish inventor John Logie Baird became the first person to transmit live moving images to a remote receiver—only a handful of engineers and a few farsighted businessmen had even heard of the radical new technology that was about to give birth to modern culture.

But among those early visionaries the race to develop television was already heating up. Working out of his makeshift lab in a London attic, the obscure and chronically underfunded Baird built a camera that scanned an object with a concentrated beam of light. He used a photoelectric cell to convert the light and shade of the scanned object into electricity, and built a receiver that reversed the process. On October 2, he scanned a doll's head and watched with elation as its face was flickeringly reproduced on the screen he set up in the next room. Running to a building across the street, he hired an office boy to sit in front of his camera. Young William Taynton became the first person ever televised.

Baird's system was a crude mechanical affair that used spinning disks with holes punched in them to scan the object, break the light into lines, and convert the lines into a projectable image of the original object. It worked, but the flickering pictures brought on nausea-inducing headaches in the viewer.

While Baird tinkered with his mechanical model, other pioneers pursued electronic systems. Electronic television had been theorized by British physicist A.A. Campbell Swinton in 1908. "Should something suitable be discovered," Swinton wrote, "distant electric vision will, I think, come within the region of possibility." The discoveries he hinted at were realized by Vladimir Kosma Zworykin and Philo T. Farnsworth. The Russian-born American physicist and the Utah student both developed early picture tubes. In 1927 Farnsworth unveiled a system free of the clunky Nipkow disks that Baird had relied on. With Farnsworth's invention, the region of possibility had become a probability. **◂1904.8 ▸1941.14**

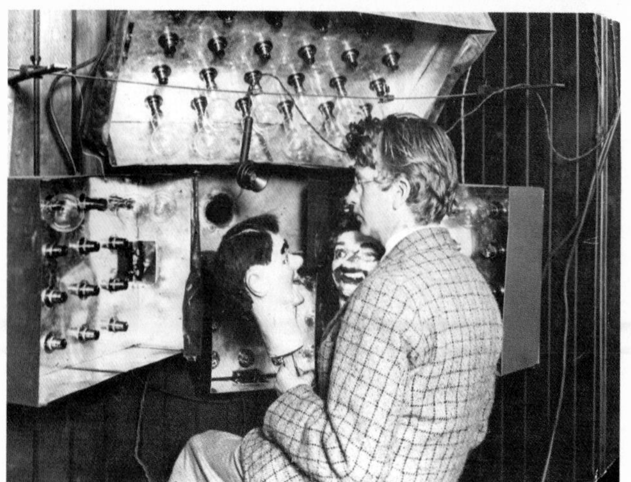

Baird, holding dolls' heads, demonstrates his invention.

NORTHERN AFRICA

Morocco's Fierce Resistance

2 That a group of "primitive" warriors could prevail over a modern European army was remarkable enough. But Muhammad Abd el-Krim's achievement went deeper. He not only led the tribes of Morocco's mountainous Rif country in their 1921 uprising against Spanish rule, but also succeeded in binding the fractious tribesmen into a nation, the Republic of the Rif, which had a legal system based on Berber custom and Islamic law. To other colonial-era revolutionaries, Abd el-Krim was a hero. But the French, who ruled Morocco below the small Spanish zone, feared he would be an inspiration—and in the spring of 1925 he found himself battling a new foe.

Rifian rebels, rendered by a German cartoonist.

To provoke a fight, French troops built several forts near the rebel republic's southern boundary, refusing all requests for talks. But when the Rifians attacked, France was stunned: The ferocity and prowess of Abd el-Krim's troops were genuine, not merely a function (as the French had assumed) of Spanish ineptitude. Their outposts fell swiftly; within days Rifian guerrillas were camped 20 miles from the city of Fez. Humiliated, the French met with the Spanish to arrange a joint defense—and a joint peace plan offering the Rifians independence in all but name. Abd el-Krim, however, insisted on absolute self-rule. The war raged on.

The tide began to turn in August, thanks to a new commander—Marshal Henri Pétain—and 100,000 fresh French troops. In September the Spanish entered Alhucemas Bay with 99 ships, backed by 100 planes. (Spain's future dictator, Colonel Francisco Franco, led the amphibious assault.) The Rifians lost the month-long battle; it was their last major stand. Abd el-Krim surrendered in May 1926, and was exiled to the island of Réunion. He moved to Cairo in 1947, where he remained until his death in 1963. Even after Morocco won full independence in 1958, he refused to return to his homeland as long as French soldiers remained in North Africa. **◂1911.1 ▸1931.13**

THE UNITED STATES

Darwin on Trial

3 By the mid-1920s, the rural Protestant values that had shaped the United States were in crisis. Immigration, urbanization (for the first time, more Americans lived in cities than on farms), and postwar hedonism were deeply unsettling to many country-bred Americans, a large number of whom sought refuge in Christian fundamentalism. To these believers in the literal truth of the biblical story of creation, the theory of evolution—proposed by Charles Darwin in 1859—was blasphemy, and its widespread acceptance only confirmed society's decadence. Southern states, where fundamentalism was strongest, passed laws banning the teaching of evolution. When a Tennessee teacher named John T. Scopes broke the law in 1925, his trial became an international symbol of the battle between old and new.

Creationist William Jennings Bryan was lampooned on a magazine cover.

The ten-day "Monkey Trial," as

ART & CULTURE: Books: ***In the American Grain*** **(William Carlos Williams);** ***Mrs. Dalloway*** **(Virginia Woolf);** ***An American Tragedy*** **(Theodore Dreiser);** ***Manhattan Transfer*** **(John Dos Passos);** ***Arrowsmith*** **(Sinclair Lewis);** ***The American Mercury*** **begins publication ... Music: "If You Knew Susie" (Meyer and DeSylva); "Yes, Sir, That's My Baby" (Donaldson and Kahn); "Sweet Georgia Brown"**

"Paris is marvelous. And your dressmakers are divine."—**Josephine Baker, upon moving to Paris**

reporters dubbed it, pitted Clarence Darrow, whose dazzling defense of Leopold and Loeb the previous year had restored his reputation as the nation's top defense lawyer, against fundamentalist William Jennings Bryan, a three-time presidential candidate and former secretary of state who'd offered his services to the prosecution. The judge forbade Darrow to discuss the validity of evolutionary theory. So Darrow put Bryan on the stand. Forced to defend his belief in the Bible's literal truth, Bryan was evasive and illogical. His testimony, which was not helped by the 100-degree heat, made creationists look ridiculous—though some reporters (including the political commentator Walter Lippmann) took the hot-tempered Darrow to task for his merciless "heckling" of Bryan, who died of a heart attack just five days after the trial ended.

Because he proudly admitted teaching evolution, Scopes was found guilty and fined $100 (later reduced to $1) but there was no doubt that the evolutionists had prevailed. Tennessee's law survived —but was not enforced—until 1967. **◂1924.V ▸1943.V**

POPULAR CULTURE

The Passion of Paris

4 Josephine Baker arrived in France in 1925, a shy but spirited 19-year-old. Within three months, she was the most-loved woman in Paris.

The black American dancer was part of a troupe recruited from Broadway to stage Paris's first black song-and-dance revue. Baker's erotic, ebullient tour de force in *La Revue Nègre* enchanted the city. Male Parisians desired her; their wives and mistresses emulated her, slicking down their hair, soaking themselves in walnut oil to darken their skin. For Baker, the most gratifying aspect of being in Paris was that for the first time in her life she could do what was impossible in her native country: sit wherever she wanted in a restaurant, a train, or a theater.

The daughter of a laundress, Baker grew up in the slums of East St. Louis, Illinois. At 13, already an accomplished dancer, she left home to join a traveling vaudeville group. She wound up in New York, landing comic roles in the black Broadway shows of Eubie Blake and Noble Sissle. Next stop: Paris.

Baker loved France. During World War II, she aided the Resistance.

A combination of prurient colonial fantasy and liberated American jazz, *La Revue Nègre* created a cultural sensation. At its center was Baker and her seminude, wildly energetic dance. "There seemed to emanate from her violently shuddering body, her bold dislocations, her springing movements, a gushing stream of rhythm," gushed one critic. She was the "black Venus."

After a three-month run, *La Revue Nègre* closed, and Baker moved to the Folies-Bergère, where she debuted her famous banana dance. Naked except for a skirt of swaying bananas, Baker brought down the house night after night. **◂1905.4**

LITERATURE

A Tragic Tycoon

5 Twenty-nine-year-old F. Scott Fitzgerald already had four books (including a spectacularly successful first novel, *This Side of Paradise)* and a play under his belt when, in 1925, he published *The Great Gatsby*, one of the century's acknowledged masterpieces of fiction. The novel, like most of Fitzgerald's work, concerns itself with the glamorous creatures of what he termed the "Jazz Age": rich, brash, and cynical young men and women who move between parties and romances with breathless ease. In *Gatsby*, the story of a mysterious, lowborn millionaire named Jay Gatsby and his doomed, idealistic love for the wild, beautiful (and married) Daisy Buchanan, Fitzgerald explored the spiritual ruin of the American dream.

The prototype for Daisy was the brilliant, high-spirited Zelda Sayre, whom Fitzgerald married in 1920 (the year that *Paradise* was published). Moving between resorts on the Riviera and homes in New York City, Long Island, and Paris, the peripatetic Fitzgeralds lived the kind of life his fiction so brutally dissects.

In France the Fitzgeralds circulated freely among the crowd of artistic expatriates that included Ernest Hemingway and Gertrude Stein. But by the thirties the seemingly golden couple's life had begun a slow decline—into near financial collapse, mental illness (in Zelda's case, incurable; she ended up in an asylum), and alcoholism. After a nervous breakdown of his own, Fitzgerald tried his hand at screenwriting. He was nearly finished with his novel about Hollywood, *The Last Tycoon* (which many critics feel would have been his finest), when he died of a heart attack, in 1940, at age 44. **◂1923.5 ▸1926.2**

Smiles or no, Scott and Zelda (with daughter Scottie) were as tortured as the characters in *Gatsby*.

BIRTHS

Robert Altman, U.S. filmmaker.

Idi Amin, Ugandan ruler.

William F. Buckley, Jr., U.S. writer.

Seymour Cray, U.S. computer designer.

Robert Kennedy, U.S. senator.

B.B. King, U.S. singer.

Malcolm X, U.S. activist.

Yukio Mishima, Japanese writer.

Paul Newman, U.S. actor.

Flannery O'Connor, U.S. writer.

Robert Rauschenberg, U.S. artist.

Peter Sellers, U.K. actor.

Rod Steiger, U.S. actor.

William Styron, U.S. novelist.

Maria Tallchief, U.S. ballet dancer.

Margaret Thatcher, U.K. prime minister.

Jean Tinguely, Swiss sculptor.

Robert Venturi, U.S. architect.

Gore Vidal, U.S. writer.

DEATHS

George Bellows, U.S. painter.

William Jennings Bryan, U.S. political leader.

George Curzon, U.K. political leader.

James B. Duke, U.S. tobacco magnate.

Robert M. La Follette, U.S. political leader.

Amy Lowell, U.S. poet.

John Singer Sargent, U.S. painter.

Erik Satie, French composer.

Rudolph Steiner, Austrian educator.

Sun Yat-sen, Chinese premier.

(Bernie, Pinkard, and Casey) ... Painting & Sculpture: *Three Dancers* (Pablo Picasso) ... Film: *The Big Parade* (King Vidor); *The Gold Rush* (Charlie Chaplin); *The Phantom of the Opera* (Lon Chaney); *The Freshman* (Harold Lloyd); *Body and Soul* (Oscar Micheaux, with Paul Robeson) ... Theater: *Dearest Enemy* (Rodgers, Hart, and H. Fields); *Hay Fever* (Noël Coward); *Sunny* (Kern, Harbach, and Hammerstein).

"*Man, if you gotta ask, you'll never know.*"—**Louis Armstrong, when asked to define jazz**

NEW IN 1925

Cinemascope (wide-screen cinema).

National Spelling Bee.

THE
NEW YORKER

The New Yorker.

Dry ice (sold commercially).

Belinographe Telephoto Machine (precursor to the fax).

IN THE UNITED STATES

▶FLORIDA BOOM—The Florida land rush recalled those of "Wild West" times—and reflected the national climate of prosperity, optimism, and speculative frenzy. Tens of thousands flocked to buy

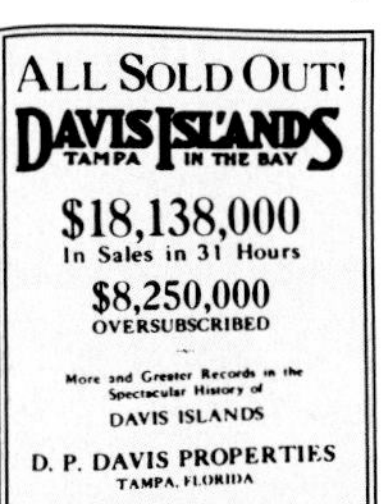
ALL SOLD OUT!
DAVIS ISLANDS
TAMPA IN THE BAY
$18,138,000
In Sales in 31 Hours
$8,250,000
OVERSUBSCRIBED
More and Greater Records in the Spectacular History of DAVIS ISLANDS
D. P. DAVIS PROPERTIES
TAMPA, FLORIDA

pieces of a state touted by developers as a Mediterranean-style paradise. Some wanted to settle down, others merely to buy cheap and sell dear; many purchased real estate sight unseen, and wound up with swampland. The boom peaked in 1925, and was finished off by a hurricane in 1926.

▶JESUS CHRIST, ADMAN—Nobody expressed the cockiness of Roaring Twenties capitalists better than advertising genius Bruce Barton, whose biography of Jesus Christ, *The Man Nobody Knows*, was a bestseller in 1925 and '26. The inventor of Betty Crocker for General Mills and a founder of one of the world's largest ad agencies (Batten, Barton, Durstine and Osborne, now BBDO/Needham), Barton claimed that Christ himself was the father of modern business—and the greatest pitchman of his day. The "advertisements

MUSIC

Satchmo Improvises

6 Louis Armstrong was born at about the same time and place as jazz itself: 1900, New Orleans. He grew up playing the cornet in marching bands and on riverboats, and jumped from being a child prodigy to playing with the hottest bands in Chicago. When bandleader Fletcher Henderson called him to New York, and Satchmo—short for "satchel mouth"—began leading his own bands in 1925, he helped change the face of jazz music. Soon, all the sophisticated people in Harlem were imitating the musical and sartorial styles of this charismatic young trumpeter from the hinterlands.

In their performances and recordings, Armstrong's bands, the Hot Five and the Hot Seven, challenged all accepted notions of range and tone. Before Armstrong, most jazz bands were fronted by a clarinet, trumpet, and trombone working to create a wall of sound. Satchmo blew those conventions wide open with innovative solos. He was harmonically gifted, and drew people into the long, melodic improvisations that poured from his horn. Singing meaningless syllables, he pioneered a technique that showed up later in the scat singing of Ella Fitzgerald and others. He was, in short, the first true revolutionary of jazz. ◂**1923.M** ▸**1927.9**

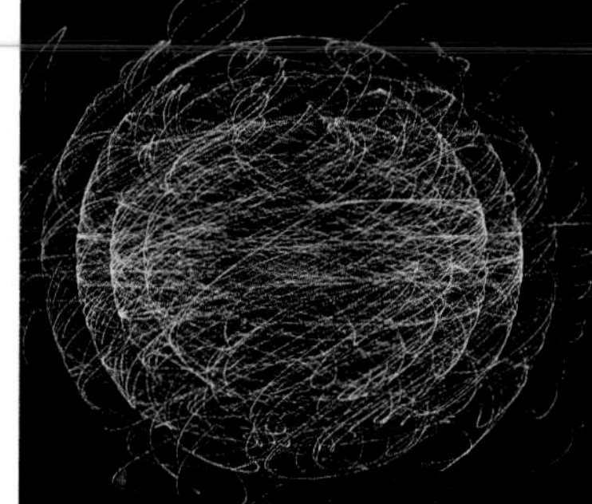

The subatomic world of quantum physics: a modern model of a uranium-235 atom.

SCIENCE

Physics' Quantum Leap

7 In 1925, a year after de Broglie advanced his bold theory that subatomic particles of matter could also act as waves of energy, Werner Heisenberg showed that quantum physics need not be bound up with trying to visualize such events. Heisenberg, 24, offered the first system of quantum mechanics—a term used to describe theoretical formulas explaining and predicting such phenomena as the shifts of energy known as quantum jumps. An assistant to Max Born at the University of Göttingen, Germany, Heisenberg had based his own search for such a system solely on observable changes in frequency and intensity of light, sidestepping the debate about light's nature that preoccupied others.

Heisenberg's system, which he called matrix mechanics, relied on an arcane, "homegrown" form of calculus. But other physicists were devising other forms of quantum mechanics. Erwin Schrödinger, building on de Broglie's ideas and working independently of Heisenberg (with whom he waged a professional feud), came up with wave mechanics—a system that turned out to be mathematically equivalent to Heisenberg's. A Briton, Paul Dirac, arrived at another, even more useful, wave-based formula. Yet strangely, though each of these theories functioned well, none worked with perfect consistency—and no one really understood why they worked at all.

Born took a brave step forward by publishing a paper suggesting that since events at a subatomic level (where a wave could be a particle and vice versa) didn't follow ordinary rules of causality, all quantum mechanics could really offer was an estimate of the *probability* of a given outcome. That idea flew in the face of scientific doctrine, which since the time of Newton had insisted that no phenomenon was inherently unknowable. But it formed the basis for Heisenberg's revolutionary "uncertainty principle," unveiled in Copenhagen in 1927. ◂**1924.2** ▸**1927.6**

Louis Armstrong's Hot Five,
Exclusive Okeh Record Artists

With his Hot Five, Armstrong *(center)* recorded such tunes as "Cornet Chop Suey."

LITERATURE

Modernism's Motivator

8 It is hard to overstate the literary importance of Ezra Pound: Through his own writing and through the writers he championed, he shaped the course of modern literature. He shepherded James Joyce, T.S. Eliot, William Carlos Williams, Wyndham Lewis, Marianne Moore, and Ernest Hemingway into print; discovered Robert Frost and D.H. Lawrence; and persuaded W.B. Yeats to adopt a leaner style. Despite the daunting obscurity of his work—and despite his political obsessions that led to his fall from grace—his poems have influenced poets everywhere. Pound's best-known, never-finished poem, *The Cantos*, is a 23,000-line epic crammed with cryptic historical references, bizarre economics lectures, and anti-Semitic ravings. Its first volume appeared in 1925, its last in 1968.

Having emigrated to London from Indiana in 1908, Pound

SPORTS: Baseball: World Series, Pittsburgh Pirates defeat Washington Senators, 4–3; Lou Gehrig joins New York Yankees ... Tennis: Bill Tilden wins sixth straight U.S. title; René Lacoste wins his first Wimbledon and French Open championships ... Philadelphia Soldiers Field opens (Army–Navy football games).

"A village explainer, excellent if you were a village, but if you were not, not."—**Gertrude Stein, on Ezra Pound**

became a critic, editor, and founder of a movement called "imagism," which advocated a poetry of strong images, stripped of conventional structure and sentiment. After World War I his work began to assail a "botched civilization." In gracefully bitter poems like *Hugh Selwyn Mauberley*, he denounced war, commercialism, and money-lending. In 1921, at age 36, he moved to Paris, where he became the patriarch of the expatriates, and then, in 1924, to Rapallo, Italy.

Pound had begun *The Cantos* a decade earlier, as a way of gathering his thoughts on the social order. (After 1920, he wrote almost no other poetry.) True to his intentions, the poem is a jumble of ideas, whose links can be seen only by a reader willing to make an effort. Its language jumps wildly from colloquial to biblical to Homeric, with moments of great beauty and humor; its meditations on the ideal society range from Confucian China to Jeffersonian America. But

Pound and his circle, painted by onetime protégé, artist and writer Wyndham Lewis.

his poetry increasingly reflected his fascist sympathies, which he also expressed, infamously, in 300 rambling, largely incoherent propaganda broadcasts on Italian radio.

Confined to a prison camp by U.S. forces in 1945, Pound wrote *The Pisan Cantos*, considered by many his most brilliant work. He was judged mentally unfit to stand trial for treason, however, and spent twelve years in a Washington, D.C. asylum. After his release in 1958, he returned to Italy, where he wrote two more volumes of the *Cantos* before his death in 1972. **◂1922.1 ▸1926.2**

***Potemkin*'s "Odessa Steps" sequence—the most influential 10 minutes in cinema.**

FILM

Eisenstein's *Potemkin*

9 Charles Chaplin called Sergei Eisenstein's *Battleship Potemkin* "the best film ever made." Douglas Fairbanks raved that seeing it was "the most intense and profoundest experience of my life." The storytelling techniques introduced in this 1925 Soviet-made paean to revolution changed the fundamental nature of cinema.

Eisenstein, a theater director with only one feature film to his credit, was commissioned to make the film by the Soviet government to mark the 20th anniversary of the failed 1905 revolution. Eisenstein used a fact-based story of the 1905 mutiny aboard the Czar's battleship *Potemkin*, docked at Odessa, as a symbol for the entire revolution. The townspeople rallied to support the ill-treated sailors, but imperial soldiers slaughtered the citizens on the harborside steps as the Imperial Navy gathered offshore. In the film, the men of the *Potemkin* decide to confront the flotilla; the crews in the threatening ships lower their guns, refusing to fire on their brother sailors while the mutineers sail away. (In real life, the mutineers quarreled and finally surrendered; some escaped, others were executed.)

Eisenstein's technique turned this agitprop into art. He pounded home the propagandistic power of montage, which until now had striven to be unobtrusive. Eisenstein devised a method—brilliantly displayed in the film's famous "Odessa Steps" sequence—in which quick shots are juxtaposed to create a strong visceral or intellectual effect. Also, by showing the same scene repeatedly from different angles, Eisenstein was able to expand and dramatically highlight a pivotal scene.

Eisensteinian montage, tamed and stripped of its Marxism, has been wholly incorporated into mainstream film grammar. (Witness music videos.) A revolutionary achievement, *Potemkin* seldom fails to claim a spot on critics' lists of all-time best films. **◂1915.1 ▸1926.5**

IRAN

Reza Khan Modernizes Iran

10 Reza Khan was elected in 1925 to ascend to the throne of Iran (then known as Persia). Establishing the Pahlevi dynasty, he vowed to lead his country into the twentieth century—and for a good part of it, he succeeded.

Iran—long a locus of the imperial aspirations of Britain, Germany, and Russia—was ripe for upheaval. By the end of World War I, German and British interests within Iran had struggled for control of the Majles (the parliament set up in 1906). When the British quit Iran in 1919, the road was cleared for Reza Khan, an officer of the Persian Cossack Brigade, to seize power. In 1921 he staged a coup d'état. And in 1925, despite strong opposition from Islamic clergymen, he overturned the Qajar Dynasty and established his own, taking the name Pahlevi.

Like Mustafa Kemal Atatürk, whom he emulated, Reza Khan Shah Pahlevi attempted to modernize his country. He modified ancient Islamic divorce laws to be more favorable to women and did away with veil requirements, decreeing European dress for both sexes. His reign brought the country's first railroad, as well as improvements in education and public sanitation. By negotiating more equitable oil agreements, he loosened the foreign grip on Iran. But his methods were ruthless, and he had a habit of seizing large areas of land for himself. Though nominally neutral, he backed Germany during World War II, prompting Britain and the U.S.S.R.—anxious to have a clear route to the Soviet front—to move in and force his abdication. **◂1923.12 ▸1941.15**

IN THE UNITED STATES

of Jesus," Barton wrote, "have survived for 20 centuries."

▶CONTRACT BRIDGE—The most challenging of all card games became incalculably more so when New York railroad heir Harold S. Vanderbilt invented contract bridge in 1925. A variant of auction bridge (which had evolved from whist at the turn of the century), the new game introduced a complex system of scoring based on achieving an exact contract, which opened up dazzling new possibilities for creative players in one of the best-loved games in history.

▶IZZY AND MOE—America lost its two most effective—and flamboyant—Prohibition agents in 1925. In five years on the job, New York–based partners Isadore Einstein and Moe Smith had made almost 4,400 arrests and seized $15 million worth of liquor. Moe and Izzy infiltrated speakeasies disguised as fishermen, football players, frostbite victims, and corrupt lawmen. But their high-profile antics led to their firing. "Izzy and Moe," huffed one official, "belong on the vaudeville stage." They went into insurance instead. ◂1919.V

▶A FLIER'S CRUSADE—The U.S. Army sought to remove a thorn in its side in 1925 by court-martialing Brigadier General Billy Mitchell. An Allied air-force commander in World War I, Mitchell believed that control of the skies was the key to victory—but an entrenched military establishment rejected his calls for an independent air force. After one of the U.S.'s state-of-the-art dirigibles was destroyed by a storm, Mitchell accused his detractors of "incompetency,

criminal negligence, and almost treasonable administration of the national defense." Convicted of insubordination and suspended from the Army for five years, Mitchell died before World War II brutally proved his point. The U.S. Department of the Air Force was created in 1947. ▸1941.1

POLITICS & BUSINESS: GNP: $93.1 billion ... President Coolidge slashes White House budget ... Nellie Ross of Wyoming inaugurated as first woman governor in U.S. (Texas's Miriam "Ma" Ferguson is second, by 16 days). ... Corrupt Practices Act prohibits direct corporate campaign contributions ... Scripps-Howard newspaper empire established ... American Medical Association endorses birth control.

"There is a bit of me in [Wozzeck's character], since I have been spending these war years just as dependent on people I hate ... in chains, sick, captive, resigned, humiliated."—**Alban Berg, in a letter to his wife**

AROUND THE WORLD

▶BRITAIN RETURNS TO GOLD STANDARD—Desperate to shake Great Britain from its postwar slump, Chancellor of the Exchequer Winston Churchill in 1925 returned the U.K. to the gold standard at inflated prewar rates. With the pound now overvalued at $4.87, British export prices rose a full 10 percent above world prices. The result: trade imbalance and staggering unemployment and wage cuts that culminated in the cataclysmic general strike of 1926. ▶1926.4

▶ART DECO—The design style that graced some of the most remarkable structures of the 1930s—from New York's Empire State Building to the interior of the French ocean liner *Normandie* (chairs from *its first-class dining room, above*)—was born in 1925 at the Exposition Internationale des Arts Décoratifs et Industriels Modernes in Paris. At first associated with luxury items handcrafted from expensive materials, during the Depression, art deco spread its elegance to everything from kitchen appliances to railway stations. ▶1930.7

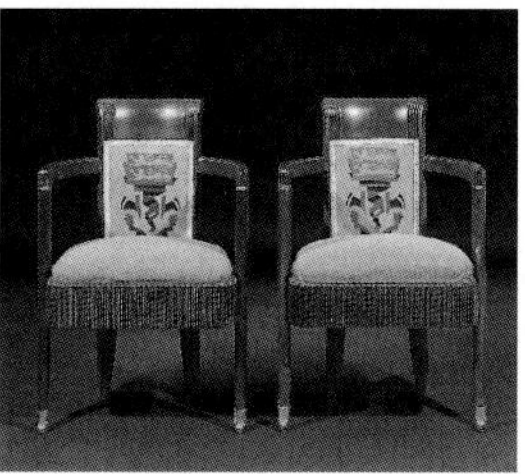

▶LOCARNO PACTS—In October, the European powers negotiated five agreements in Locarno, Switzerland, designed to bury the old enmities of World War I. France, Germany, and Belgium pledged to respect one another's borders, and Britain and Italy vowed to fight any country that violated the demilitarized Rhineland. Germany and its neighbors agreed to submit future disputes to arbitration. At the talks' conclusion, the British foreign minister wept with joy; newspaper headlines declared, "France and Germany Bar War Forever." But *forever* lasted only 13 years. ◀1920.1 ▶1928.1

1925

LITERATURE

Master of Angst

11 In 1925, Max Brod published his friend Franz Kafka's novel *The Trial*, the tale of a man (known only as "K") who finds himself charged with a crime he is helpless to defend himself against. Brod was acting against the express wishes of his friend—who, on his deathbed the previous year, had instructed him to burn his manuscripts. Brod's decision catapulted Kafka to international literary fame.

Kafka himself never tried to publish his work. He led a double life, toiling unhappily at an accident-insurance company during the day and writing strange tales of alienation and despair at night. He didn't get along with his father; he despised his job, was unsuccessful in romance, and suffered from ill health. Throughout his life, he considered himself an outcast: a Jew in a Christian society, a speaker of German in Prague.

As Brod (himself a novelist) began publishing more of his friend's work, Kafka's name became synonymous with paradox and absurdity, with the fruitless pursuit of meaning in a world where nothing—personal relationships, community, existence itself—made sense. His characters, suffering from nearly constant, but inexplicable, anxiety, find themselves trapped in nightmarish situations. The first sentence of the short story "The Metamorphosis"—"As Gregor Samsa awoke one morning from uneasy dreams he found himself transformed in his bed into a gigantic insect"—depicts the archetypal "Kafka-esque" situation.

Widely hailed in the late twenties, Kafka's work was suppressed by the Nazis, who condemned him as a "decadent" Jew. After the war, he was quickly rediscovered by other writers, particularly the French surrealists, who saw in his keen sense of the absurd the mark of a kindred spirit.

Critics have always reveled in Kafka's ambiguity and to this day enjoy debating whether his works are profound existential allegories or simply straightforward stories about what Kafka once called his "dreamlike inner life." Their sheer power makes the question irrelevant. **▶1942.13**

MUSIC

Alban Berg's *Wozzeck*

12 An excited buzz preceded the December 14, 1925, premiere of Austrian composer Alban Berg's *Wozzeck*. Excerpts from the opera had been well received, and no less a personage than Gustav Mahler's widow, Alma, had financed the printing of the score. Still, speculation about the quality of the entire work mounted as Berlin State Opera director Erich Kleiber, whose dedication to the work actually jeopardized his own career, led his company though a seemingly endless series of rehearsals. When the first notes were finally sounded and the curtain raised, the audience confronted a masterful fusion of atonality, dissonance, and lyricism that cemented Berg's reputation as one of modern music's leading innovators.

Inspired by Georg Büchner's nineteenth-century drama *Woyzeck*, Berg's story of a downtrodden soldier's plunge into homicide and suicide vividly captured the mood of the composer and his German expressionist counterparts in the years following World War I.

Response to the opera was not universally positive. "I had the sensation of having been not in a public theater but an insane asylum," snapped one critic. "All these mass attacks and instrumental assaults have nothing to do with European music and musical evolution."

Nonetheless, *Wozzeck* proved to be the first popular success of the works emanating from the circle of Arnold Schoenberg, Berg's friend and mentor. Berg enjoyed a brief period of prosperity that was cut short by Nazi condemnation of his art. But he continued to compose until his death at age 50, in 1935. By then he had all but completed his second opera, *Lulu*, written entirely in Schoenberg's twelve-tone system. **◀1912.11 ▶1961.M**

An English National Opera production of *Wozzeck*: difficult music and scenes of mayhem.

SCIENCE

A Modern-Day Alchemy

13 The need to find a coal-based substitute for petroleum as a source of gasoline propelled much of the chemistry research going on in interwar Germany. In 1925 two different methods were unveiled.

German chemist Friedrich Bergius had derived gasoline directly from coal as early as 1912, by treating the coal with hydrogen. But it took him a dozen years to adapt his hydrogenation method for industrial application. By then, two other German chemists, Franz Fischer and Hans Tropsch, had hit upon another, somewhat less direct, method for synthesizing liquid fuel from carbon monoxide and hydrogen.

Friedrich Bergius made synthetic gasoline—and won a Nobel Prize in 1931.

The novel technology quickly spread around the world; within years Japan, France, and England opened large synthesizing facilities. Germany, however, retained the edge, and by the early 1940s was operating a dozen fuel plants (mostly using the Fischer-Tropsch process) to meet its war demands.

Ultimately, the Bergius process proved better for producing gasoline, while the Fischer-Tropsch approach was more efficient at synthesizing methane and other chemicals. The Second World War galvanized international interest in synthetic fuel, especially in Europe, which lacked America's vast oil reserves. But by the 1950s, with the opening of the Middle East as a rich source of cheap crude, the need for alternatives began to seem less urgent. **▶1960.M**

NOBEL PRIZES: Peace: Austen Chamberlain (U.K.; Locarno Pact) and Charles Dawes (U.S.; German reparations) ... Literature: George Bernard Shaw (U.K.; playwright) ... Chemistry: Richard Zsigmondy (German; colloid solutions) ... Medicine: No award ... Physics: James Franck and Gustav Hertz (German; effect of electron collisions upon atoms).

A VOICE FROM 1925

Coining a Phrase

Advertisement for Listerine, by Milton Feasley, 1925

"Often a bridesmaid but never a bride." Like many "timeless" expressions, this one first appeared in an advertisement. Created by copywriter Milton Feasley for Listerine Antiseptic (a product that three years earlier had provided another coinage: halitosis), the advertising campaign was so successful it ran for more than ten years. **►1960.V**

1925

"I intend absolutely to stop periodic attempts against my life. I say this not on account of myself, because I truly love to live in danger, but on account of the Italian people."—**Benito Mussolini, after the third assassination attempt**

STORY OF THE YEAR

Year One of Mussolini's Revolution

1 Benito Mussolini's transformation of Italy into a totalitarian state was hastened by a string of fortuitous events: four assassination attempts between April and October 1926.

The first attempt, by a deranged Irishwoman, wounded him in the nose; blaming the incident on an international conspiracy, the government shut down several opposition journals. The second, by a socialist deputy and a leftist Freemason, led to the banning of the moderate Unitary Socialist Party and any association (such as the Masons) not approved by the regime; several independent newspapers, including the renowned *Corriere della Sera*, were taken over by the Fascist Party. The third attempt, by an anarchist who'd lived in France, fueled a propaganda campaign against that country—whose leadership, unlike Britain's, disdained Il Duce.

After the fourth attempt, allegedly by a 16-year-old boy (who was lynched on the spot, and his body parts paraded about Bologna), Mussolini decided to complete his seizure of absolute power. He had already declared 1926 Year One of his revolution. With the opposition boycotting Parliament, he had easily passed laws abridging freedom of expression and allowing him to rule without consulting the legislature. He had replaced elected local governments with his own handpicked officials. Now he abolished Parliament itself, replacing it with a body whose members were chosen by Fascist organizations; the public was allowed only to vote their approval or disapproval of the nominees. He established a special police force for political offenses, and "revolutionary tribunals" to judge such crimes—swiftly, secretly, and without possibility of appeal.

Mussolini, a bandage on his wounded nose, risks a public appearance.

Finally, he instituted capital punishment: for treason, insurrection, incitement to civil war, and, of course, attempted assassination of the dictator or royal persons. Executions, Mussolini told the Fascist Grand Council, would "make Italians more virile, [and] habituate them to the sight of blood and the idea of death."

Many Italians applauded Il Duce's firmness; many disliked the repression but saw it as the only alternative to chaos. From now on, those with other ideas had to keep silent—or risk their lives. **◂1922.4 ▸1929.10**

Ernest Hemingway, photographed by his friend Man Ray.

LITERATURE

A Perfected Prose Style

2 Almost immediately after it was published in 1926, Ernest Hemingway's *The Sun Also Rises* became the bible of America's "lost generation"—a term the 27-year-old author, quoting Gertrude Stein, introduced in the novel's preface to describe those coming of age in a moral landscape shattered by World War I. University students began talking in the terse, world-weary cadences of Hemingway dialogue. Other young writers aped his tough-but-sensitive narrative style. And Hemingway himself—genius, sportsman, war correspondent—was soon an international literary star.

The Sun Also Rises centers on a group of Paris-based expatriates, modeled after the author's own circle of writers, artists, and thrill-seeking socialites. The senior members of this loose clique were Stein and Ezra Pound, both of whose literary theories helped Hemingway develop a prose of concrete images and hypnotic repetition; its affiliates included Pablo Picasso and F. Scott Fitzgerald. The novel's characters, however, are based on less eminent figures.

The American narrator, Jake Barnes (like Hemingway, a journalist), loves the reckless Lady Brett Ashley, but a war wound has left him impotent (though that word never appears in the book). Lady Brett is also loved by another American, the hopelessly idealistic novelist Robert Cohn, but she's engaged to Mike Campbell, a ruined Scottish businessman. These unhappy souls haunt the city's cafés and nightclubs; later they travel to Pamplona for the bullfights, where Brett runs off with a young matador. Yet the end of the novel finds her in a Madrid taxicab with Jake. "We could have had such a damned good time together," she says, lamenting the impossibility of their love. "Yes," he replies. "Isn't it pretty to think so?"

Hemingway's exiles are all, in their own ways, wounded and sterile. Unable to connect to any great cause, they look for meaning in brave, beautiful, and sometimes cruel gestures—like those of the bullfighters they admire. *The Sun Also Rises* caught the mood of its time with exquisite precision. And today's readers still respond to its bleak power. **◂1925.8 ▸1933.10**

LITERATURE

Gide's Moral Diagnosis

3 Late in his life, André Gide was asked what had given him the most enjoyment. The iconoclastic French novelist replied, "*The Arabian Nights*, the Bible, the pleasures of the flesh, and the Kingdom of God." His answer reflects the same difficult contradictions inherent in his alternately reviled and celebrated works.

In his best-known book, the 1926 novel, *Les Faux-Monnayeurs (The Counterfeiters)*, Gide examined the human capacity for hypocrisy and self-deception, attributes of a spiritually ill society. Defiantly honest, intellectually curious, Gide offended many critics by rejecting traditional religious taboos, including the condemnation of homosexuality. (His 1902 novel, *The Immoralist*, was banned by the Vatican.) Ultimately, Gide was an intensely moral writer whose great struggle was to try to resolve the conflict between body and spirit. Both, he maintained, must be satisfied. Author of more than 80 works that are experimental in style and theme, Gide—who received the 1947 Nobel—helped guide the course of twentieth-century French literature. His contribution was summed up by his compatriot Jean-Paul Sartre: "He taught or retaught us that everything could be said—this is his audacity—but that it must be said

ART & CULTURE: Books: *History of England* (G.M. Trevelyan); *Seven Pillars of Wisdom* (T.E. Lawrence); *Debits and Credits* (Rudyard Kipling); *The Castle* (Franz Kafka); *Soldier's Pay* (William Faulkner); *My Mortal Enemy* (Willa Cather) ... Music: "Bye Bye Blackbird" (Henderson and Dixon); "Someone to Watch Over Me" (George and Ira Gershwin); "Baby Face" (Akst and Davis); *The Lyric Suite* (Alban Berg) ...

"Not a minute on the day, not a penny off the pay."—**British coal miners' slogan during the general strike of 1926**

according to specific rules of good expression—that is his prudence." That duality is perhaps best expressed by the author's own habit of carrying a Bible under the voluptuous cape he liked to wear. **◂1913.9 ▸1943.10**

GREAT BRITAIN

Strike Delivers a Blow

4 Prosperity was not among the fruits of Britain's victory in World War I. After 1920 (except for a brief upturn in 1924), the economy slumped and unemployment remained above 10 percent. A prime victim of the stagnation was the British labor movement, once among the strongest in the world. Trade-union membership had peaked at eight million in 1920, comprising nearly half the country's workforce. Now union ranks dwindled, and employers in many industries began reversing labor's gains. In 1926, when coal-mine owners demanded that miners toil longer hours for lower wages, the national Trades Union Council (TUC) called for the biggest work stoppage in British history.

The general strike idled some four million workers. As a counterattack, the government set up an Organization for the Maintenance of Supplies; OMS volunteers, along with soldiers, kept food supplies moving and provided some passenger transport. Finance minister Winston Churchill commandeered the *Morning Post*'s presses to print an anti-union newspaper, publishing false reports of labor leaders' intransigence and of strikers returning to work.

While the strike failed in its intention to paralyze the country, the inconveniences it did create alienated the public. Meanwhile, government officials insinuated that the action was unconstitutional, and might lead to forfeiture of union funds. TUC leaders, growing nervous, suggested a settlement based on a royal-commission report advocating partial nationalization of the coal industry. But since the report also proposed a pay cut, the miners rejected it.

Judging the situation hopeless, the TUC called off the strike nine days after it began. A million miners, however, stayed out for seven more months—when, near starvation, they too surrendered. The foreign press praised the restraint with which both sides had waged the struggle. But one side had clearly lost. The unions lay low for the next five years, their numbers bottoming out at 4.4 million in 1933. British organized labor would not fully recover until World War II. **◂1924.4 ▸1945.M**

Soldiers in London celebrate the end of the nation's biggest strike.

FILM

Lang's Expressionist Epic

5 An epic fantasy about a workers' revolt in a city of the future, Fritz Lang's *Metropolis*, completed in 1926, is the high point of the influential Golden Age of German filmmaking, the 1920s.

Expressionism held sway over the arts of postwar Germany. The style's high-contrast light and shadow and distorted, weirdly angled space, expressive of the artist's emotions, found their way into German movies with Robert Wiene's *The Cabinet of Dr. Caligari*, a 1919 horror film in which the nightmarish, fractured decor represents the mind of a madman. Tamed and made more realistic, expressionism appears hypnotically strange and gorgeous in the decade's best German films: F.W. Murnau's *Nosferatu* (the first Dracula film), E.A. Dupont's *Variety*, Lang's *Dr. Mabuse the Gambler*.

Lang began working on *Metropolis* in 1924, after returning from the United States. He'd been struck by New York City's "crossroads of multiple and confused human forces [exploiting] each other and thus living in perpetual anxiety." In the movie's futuristic city, demoralized workers labor in the bowels of the earth while their merciless bosses dwell in skyscraper luxury. (The class warfare is resolved by a disastrous flood.) *Metropolis*'s soaring, superbly imaginative set design, rich in expressionist light and lines, and the bravura sequence in which the evil capitalist plots to create a villainous robot double of a beloved female workers' leader, have inspired a generation of filmmakers. **◂1919.M ▸1933.M**

Metropolis is set in a futuristic city fraught with class warfare.

1926

BIRTHS

Ralph Abernathy, U.S. civil-rights activist.

Chuck Berry, U.S. musician.

Fidel Castro, Cuban president.

John Coltrane, U.S. musician.

Miles Davis, U.S. musician.

Elizabeth II, U.K. queen.

Michel Foucault, French philosopher.

John Fowles, U.K. novelist.

Allen Ginsberg, U.S. poet.

Valéry Giscard d'Estaing, French president.

Hugh Hefner, U.S. publisher.

Ivan Illich, Austrian-U.S. educator.

Marilyn Monroe, U.S. actress.

Joan Sutherland, Australian singer.

DEATHS

John Moses Browning, U.S. inventor.

Luther Burbank, U.S. horticulturist.

Mary Cassatt, U.S. painter.

Emile Coué, French psychotherapist.

Eugene V. Debs, U.S. labor leader.

Felix Dzerzhinsky, U.S.S.R. official.

Ronald Firbank, U.K. writer.

Antonio Gaudí, Spanish architect.

Harry Houdini, U.S. magician.

Claude Monet, French painter.

Annie Oakley, U.S. entertainer.

Rainer Maria Rilke, German poet.

Edward Scripps, U.S. publisher.

Rudolph Valentino, Italian-U.S. actor.

Painting & Sculpture: ***Black Iris*** **(Georgia O'Keeffe);** ***Draped Reclining Figure*** **(Henry Moore) ... Film:** ***Don Juan*** **(with John Barrymore);** ***What Price Glory?*** **(Raoul Walsh);** ***Ben-Hur*** **(Fred Niblo, with Ramon Novarro);** ***The Lodger*** **(Alfred Hitchcock);** ***Mother*** **(V.I. Pudovkin) ... Theater:** ***The Great God Brown*** **(Eugene O'Neill);** ***The Silver Cord*** **(Sidney Howard);** ***The Plough and the Stars*** **(Sean O'Casey).**

"I am a Bear of Very Little Brain, and long words Bother me."—Winnie-the-Pooh

NEW IN 1926

Greyhound Corporation.

Prestone antifreeze.

National Broadcasting Company.

Good Humor Corporation.

Miniature golf (Fairyland Inn, resort in Tennessee).

IN THE UNITED STATES

▶JELLY'S JAZZ—Jelly Roll Morton made musical history in 1926 when he assembled the first of several small bands he called the Red Hot Peppers. The rambunctious pianist and composer was the first bandleader to blend the formal arrangements of ragtime with the loose, improvisational, brass-band style of his native New Orleans—creating a hybrid that was crucial to the evolution of jazz. Morton and company had a string of hits in the '20s; via recordings, their brilliant musicianship still delights fans today. ◀1925.6 ▶1927.9

▶MELLON CUTS TAXES—Arguing that low taxes fueled economic growth, Treasury Secretary Andrew W. Mellon, one of the wealthiest men in America, successfully lobbied Congress for massive corporate- and income-tax cuts. A boon to the rich, the 1926 Revenue Act did not have the precise trickle-down effect Mellon had envisioned, although it helped reduce the national deficit after World War I. Affluent tax-cut beneficiaries pumped the windfall into the stock market, helping to create the heady boom that ended with the Crash of '29. ▶1929.1

LITERATURE

Milne's Classic Bear

6 One of the most famous characters in children's literature came into the world on Christmas Eve 1925, when the *Evening News* of London published a short story by the playwright, detective novelist, and light versifier A.A. Milne. Its chief character was a teddy bear miraculously endowed with the ability to walk, talk, and engage in adventure with his owner, Christopher Robin (the name of Milne's real-life son). Winnie-the-Pooh reappeared in a full-length book in 1926, surrounded by other creatures from Christopher Robin's nursery: Piglet, Tigger, Eeyore, Kanga, and Roo. *Winnie-the-Pooh* was witty, affectionate, briskly plotted, and therefore a publishing triumph in both Britain and the United States. In 1928, Milne brought Pooh and his companions back for a second time in the no less successful *The House at Pooh Corner.*

Although *Winnie-the-Pooh* was quickly established as a children's classic, its neo-Victorian sweetness and light sometimes strike modern sensibilities as cloying. In a famous 1963 parody of lit-crit jargon, *The Pooh Perplex*, Frederick Crews took aim at both Milne and modern academic criticism with his "inquiries" into such profundities as "The Hierarchy of Heroism in *Winnie-the-Pooh*" and "*A la recherche du Pooh perdu*." Yet critics like novelist and children's-book writer Alison Lurie could not resist their own analyses of the book's enduring power: Milne, said Lurie, "created out of a few acres of Sussex countryside a world that has the qualities both of the Golden Age of history and legend, and the lost paradise of childhood—two eras which, according to psychologists, are often one in the unconscious mind." ◀1902.V ▶1957.V

Pooh and Piglet amble into childhood's paradise.

Oppenheimer and the architects of apartheid kept black miners out of the skilled trades.

BUSINESS AND INDUSTRY

Market Manipulator

7 For ten years the German-born industrialist Ernest Oppenheimer had been trying to join the board of De Beers Consolidated Mines, the South African diamond empire begun by Cecil Rhodes in the 1870s. Finally, in July 1926, Oppenheimer was elected a director; three years later, he became chairman. Eventually, under his command, De Beers controlled 95 percent of the world's diamonds. At his death in 1957, Oppenheimer was one of the world's wealthiest men.

Oppenheimer was a shrewd manipulator of the market. Although diamonds had been mined since 1867, two new sources of alluvial diamonds were discovered in South Africa in 1926 and 1927. Unrestricted overproduction sent prices plummeting. When the Depression hit, anyone still buying diamonds was aware of the newfound sources and held off. The market threatened to collapse completely.

Oppenheimer responded on two fronts: He cornered the diamonds for £13 million, later selling them for £40 million and using the capital to build up his copper, zinc, and lead holdings. He also restricted production, then closed the De Beers mines in the early thirties, and reopened them on a limited scale in the mid-thirties. (Such tight control over the market ensured that prices remained high.)

Oppenheimer was not alone in consolidating power in 1926. The entire white South African population did likewise, passing The Mines and Works Amendment Act, which shut black Africans out of the skilled mining trades. ◀1902.5 ▶1948.1

SPORTS: World Series: St. Louis Cardinals (Grover Cleveland Alexander) defeat New York Yankees, 4–3; Satchel Paige begins pitching career in the Negro leagues ... Boxing: Gene Tunney defeats Jack Dempsey to become the new world heavyweight champion.

"In the creative process there is the father, the author of the play; the mother, the actor pregnant with the part; and the child, the role to be born."—**Konstantin Stanislavsky, *An Actor Prepares***

NICARAGUA

Sandino's Revolt

8 In a diplomatic blunder of the first order, the United States in 1926 escalated its military meddling in Nicaragua to an undeclared guerrilla war. The move clouded U.S.-Latin American relations for decades, creating the climate that led inexorably to the Iran-Contra imbroglio of the Reagan years.

By the 1920s, Nicaragua had become the paradigmatic banana republic: Its monetary system, customs, and railway were run by New York bankers for the benefit of U.S. business interests. Comfortable as the arrangement was for North American oil magnates, mine operators, and plantation owners, in Nicaragua there was widespread popular opposition to puppet president Adolfo Díaz, protected since 1912 by a U.S. military detachment. In 1924, Díaz's Conservative Party was voted out of office. Two years later, when the U.S. State Department restored Díaz to nominal power, Nicaragua's Liberal Party rose in armed revolt. Citing a communist threat to American "investments and business interests," the United States sent in the Marines.

From his base in Cuba, an imperial-size Calvin Coolidge listens for gunfire in nearby Nicaragua.

Within a year, the United States had brokered a status-quo-preserving peace between Liberals and Conservatives. A young Liberal general named Augusto César Sandino, however, calling the Liberal and Conservative leaders alike a "bunch of scoundrels, cowards, and traitors, incapable of leading a valiant and patriotic people," refused to give up. Comparing himself to George Washington, Sandino marched a ragtag band of rebels into Nicaragua's northern mountains and launched a guerrilla campaign to end U.S. intervention. A game of cat and mouse ensued, with the wily Sandino leading 6,000 U.S. Marines on a wild chase across the countryside. He won no major battles, but he did gain the support and admiration of a large segment of the Nicaraguan population. In February 1933, a month after the U.S. occupation forces finally withdrew, Sandino signed a peace treaty with Díaz's popularly elected successor. One year later, Sandino was abducted and executed by Nicaragua's Civil Guard. But his fight was carried on by his followers, the Sandinistas. **◂1913.4 ▸1934.M**

GREAT BRITAIN

Dominions Defined

9 Seeking to determine the function of its empire in a world ineradicably changed by global war, the British government in 1926 convened the Imperial Conference in London. The old conception of the British Empire, a system of docile satellite states encircling England and its monarch, had lost its Victorian luster. Mutual defense of the motherland and her fledglings was a pressing concern, but the sticking point was how to reconcile the domestic autonomy of the dominions—Australia, Canada, Ireland, South Africa, New Zealand, Newfoundland—with their subservience in foreign affairs.

As of 1926, dominions were defined as follows: "autonomous communities within the British Empire, equal in status, in no way subordinate one to another in any aspect of their domestic or external affairs, though united by a common allegiance to the Crown and freely associated as members of the British Commonwealth of Nations." **▸1949.9**

THEATER

Father of "the Method"

10 With his 1926 book, *An Actor Prepares,* the great Russian theater director and theorist Konstantin Stanislavsky explained in

writing for the first time the technique that transformed twentieth-century acting. The "Stanislavsky Method," as the technique came to be called ("the Method" for short), was first introduced in 1898 when the Moscow Art Theater, which Stanislavsky had founded that same year, staged a production of Anton Chekhov's *The Seagull.* Instead of the histrionic, declamatory style of acting then in vogue, theatergoers saw stripped-down psychological realism. (The playwright himself was so pleased that he reversed his earlier decision to give up writing.)

The actor's ultimate goal, Stanislavsky always said, was to be convincing as a living person on stage, with a complex psychological and emotional life. His most dreaded admonition to students was "I don't believe you."

The Stanislavsky Method caught on in the rest of the world, especially in the United States during the Moscow Art Theater's 1922–24 European and American tour. Three members of the troupe stayed behind in New York to teach; their students went on to found the Group Theatre (1931) and, later, the famous Actors Studio (1947). Under the directorship of Lee Strasberg, the Actors Studio turned out some of the finest stage and screen actors of the second half of the century. **◂1904.2 ▸1947.13**

The Imperial Conference hammered out a solution that reflected the postwar world.

IN THE UNITED STATES

▶OLD-TIME RELIGION—"The World's Most Pulchritudinous Evangelist," Aimee Semple McPherson, set off a nationwide furor in May when she was abducted in Los Angeles. McPherson commanded a huge following at her $1.5 million, 5,000-seat Angelus Temple in Los Angeles, built with the donations of her faithful followers. Her "Foursquare Gospel," delivered in costume and backed by Broadway-style revues, suffered a serious blow when it turned out that the "kidnapping" was a tryst with a married lover. ▸1950.12

▶THE GREAT STONE FACE—Buster Keaton secured his legend in 1926 with *The General,* the comedy commonly considered his masterpiece. The son of vaudevillians, Keaton, having mastered slapstick by the age of six, grew up on-stage.

(Fellow medicine-show traveler Harry Houdini dubbed him "Buster" after six-month-old Keaton survived a fall down a flight of stairs.) With his outrageous stunts, impassive demeanor, and impeccable timing, Keaton rivaled Chaplin as the silent era's biggest draw and one of cinema's rare comic geniuses. ◂1923.M ▸1936.9

▶TRUDY'S TRIUMPH—In a golden age of sports, she was among the biggest heroes: Gertrude "Trudy" Ederle, in 1926, became the first woman to swim across the English

Channel. The American Olympian completed the 35-mile trip in 14 hours and 31 minutes, shaving two hours off the previous record, held, of course, by a man. Strong, fast, determined, Ederle at one time owned 29 national and world swimming records. ◂1920.6

POLITICS & BUSINESS: GNP: $97 billion ... The U.S. celebrates its 150th year of independence ... Bootlegging nets $3.5 billion a year ... U.S. Supreme Court rules presidents can remove executive appointees without Senate consent ... U.S. Forest Service designates 55 million acres as wilderness area ... Air Commerce Act provides federal aid for airlines and airports.

"Dear Heart, do not grieve. I shall be at rest by the side of my beloved parents, and wait for you."—**Harry Houdini, in a letter to his wife several days before his death**

AROUND THE WORLD

▶CRISTEROS REBELLION—A religious insurrection erupted in Mexico in 1926 when President Plutarco Elias Calles implemented the anticlerical provisions of the revolutionary constitution of 1917. Calles closed Catholic schools, seminaries, and convents, forced the registration of priests, and nationalized church property. Outraged believers, called the *cristeros,* took up arms. By 1928, government soldiers had crushed the bloody rebellion. ◂1920.M ▸1934.2

▶MATCH OF THE CENTURY—At Cannes, six-time French Wimbledon winner Suzanne Lenglen *(below)* took on young American singles champ Helen Wills in tennis's "Match of the Century." At the peak of her form, Lenglen won the 1926 contest and later turned pro.

(She was the first tennis player to do so.) Wills, called "Little Miss Poker Face" for her seriousness, went on to become the greatest champion of the era. ◂1920.M ▸1938.M

▶LAISSEZ-FAIRE—Cambridge don John Maynard Keynes in 1926 published *The End of Laissez-Faire.* Developed more fully later (especially in his 1936 *The General Theory of Employment, Interest, and Money*), Keynes's advocacy of government intervention in the marketplace became an international model for recovery during the Great Depression. ◂1919.1 ▸1946.4

▶A SUPREME CREATOR—In his 1926 treatise *The Non-Objective World,* Russian avant-garde painter Kasimir Malevich described the theoretical basis of suprematism—the movement he invented in 1913. Like Kandinsky, and unlike fellow Russian Vladimir Tatlin (founder of constructivism), Malevich, whose paintings consist of precise, elegant straight lines and geometric shapes, was a mystic who believed in "the supremacy of pure feeling" in art. ◂1910.6 ▸1950.4

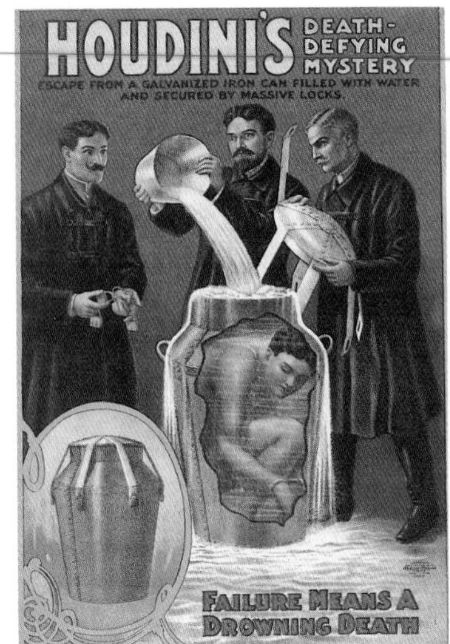

Budapest-born Houdini could wriggle out of anything—but death.

POPULAR CULTURE

The Great Escapist

11 Although he campaigned against charlatans among mind readers, mediums, and other spiritualists, Harry Houdini promised his wife he would try to stay in touch after he died. Upon her husband's death on Halloween night 1926, Bess Houdini posted a reward of $10,000 for the first medium who could tell her the secret phrase they had agreed to use. The money went unclaimed.

Houdini was an escape artist, a conjurer, a magician, and most of all an entertainer who never professed supernatural powers—just great strength, agility, and an amazing ability to penetrate the logic behind locks and the secrets of the great magicians. Countless audiences were enthralled by his death-defying escapes from shackles, jail cells, and coffins bound with chains and tossed into deep water. He extricated himself from straitjackets while suspended upside down, 75 feet in the air. Houdini appeared unstoppable until one day a young man took a few sucker punches at his rock-hard stomach without giving him time to flex his muscles. The unprotected blows led to a ruptured appendix, which he left untreated for days.

Houdini's final trick was to orchestrate his own funeral. He'd left an envelope in a New York Elks' Club safe, to be opened only after his death. Inside were instructions to bury him next to his mother, Cecilia, with her letters to him resting under his head. **◂1902.12**

POLAND

Pilsudski Rules Again

12 When Józef Pilsudski staged a coup in May 1926, many Poles welcomed him back gratefully. After all, Pilsudski—who'd fought for Polish independence in the 1890s and had led Polish troops in World War I—was his nation's founding father, having become president of the new Polish state after Germany's defeat in the war. Since retiring in 1923, Pilsudski, a non-Marxist socialist, had watched his country vacillate between right- and left-wing governments every time the economy took a nosedive.

Sick of the instability (14 cabinets in just four years), frustrated by the current regime's conservatism, sure of his own support, Pilsudski assembled sympathetic troops and marched on Warsaw. After a few days of street fighting, he established an unorthodox dictatorship that would last a decade.

Refusing the post of president, Pilsudski ruled from behind the scenes as minister of defense. Instead of imposing one-party rule, he organized the Non-Party Bloc for Cooperation with the government—which, in coalition with leftist parties, generally ensured a majority in Parliament. At first there was little repression, and Poland prospered as technocrats revamped industries and the infrastructure. But in 1930, when the Depression spurred political unrest, authorities arrested thousands of opposition party members.

Still, the parties were not dissolved; unlike Hitler and Stalin, Pilsudski was not a thoroughgoing totalitarian. In 1934, he signed non-aggression pacts with those leaders, hoping to preserve the independence he'd fought so long for. But he died the following year, and in 1939 Poland again fell under an invader's boot. **▸1939.1**

Soviet anti-Pilsudski poster from 1920, when Poles fought the Red Army.

DIPLOMACY

An Exile's Return

13 In September 1926, exactly twelve years after its advance on Paris was halted at the Marne, Germany was readmitted to the world diplomatic community. The process by which the onetime pariah nation joined the League of

French premier and foreign minister Aristide Briand addresses the League.

Nations had begun the previous autumn, at Locarno, Switzerland, with the signing of pacts with other European nations pledging mutual protection. But for the treaties to take effect, Germany had to join the League, which meant it had to be admitted by the other members.

As one of the world's great powers, Germany requested a permanent seat on the League's governing body, the Council. Only four such seats existed, and they were occupied by Britain, France, Italy, and Japan. A place was being held for the United States, in case it joined (it never did), and one for the U.S.S.R. (which joined in 1934). But Spain, Poland, and Brazil each insisted any newly established permanent seat should be theirs.

Brazil quit the League entirely when its claim was denied; Spain later followed (rejoining soon afterward). Poland backed down. In the end, Germany was admitted by a unanimous vote of the General Assembly. Germany and Japan left in protest seven years later, as the League tried to restrain their growing militarism. **◂1920.1 ▸1929.12**

NOBEL PRIZES: Peace: Aristide Briand and Gustav Stresemann (French, German; Locarno Pact) ... Literature: Grazia Deledda (Italian; novelist) ... Chemistry: Theodor Svedberg (Swedish; ultracentrifuge) ... Medicine: Johannes Fibiger (Danish; Spiroptera carcinoma) ... Physics: Jean Perrin (French; discontinuous structure of matter and sedimentation equilibrium).

A VOICE FROM 1926

Move Over, Madonna

From *Sex*, by Mae West, 1926

Sixty-six years before a book called Sex *created a stir for its author, a play called* Sex *was doing the same for Mae West. Despite 25 years in burlesque and vaudeville, West had not yet achieved full-blown stage and screen stardom when the 1926 comedy (written under the pseudonym Jane Mast) made her famous as a pornographer. The adventures of a saucy, streetwise Montreal prostitute named Margy Lamont (played by West herself in her signature self-mocking, tough-talking style),* Sex *was filled with sexual innuendo and graphic gestures. Police closed the New York City production on morals charges after 375 performances, landing West, her manager, and her producer in prison for ten days.*

In the scene below, one of the play's most notorious, Margy exchanges double entendres with Lieutenant Gregg, a British naval officer who wants to marry her. After uttering the line, "You've got to be very careful not to bend it," the actor playing Gregg made what one critic called "a Rabelaisian gesture to indicate a certain anatomical virtuosity" just before reaching into his pocket and pulling out an ostrich feather. ►**1982.8**

Gregg: Oh, I've got something for you, wait until you see this, wait until you see this.

Margy: Well, come on and let's see it.

Gregg: You'll get it, you'll get it. I don't mind telling you I had an awful time saving it for you. Why, all the women were fighting for it.

Margy: It better be good.

Gregg: It's good, all right. It's the best you could get, but you've got to be very careful not to bend it.

Margy: What a bird, what a bird. How did you know I wanted one?

Gregg: Oh, I know your little weaknesses.

Margy: You know too much. Where did you get it, honey?

Gregg: Away down south.

Margy: Won't I burn the janes up when I wear this....

Gregg: Now you're happy, suppose you spill the trouble....

Margy: I'm sick of this town and everything that goes with it. Damn him.

Gregg: Oh, the gentleman friend, eh?

Margy: Gentleman, hell. You're the first one to ever call him that.

Gregg: Well, of course, I never met him. Why don't you chuck the bugger. Leave him and travel around a bit. You'd soon forget him. Good lord, gal, I've forgotten a hell of a lot in the same way....

Margy: The way I feel now I'd take a trip to hell if I could get a return ticket.

With her lush, overblown figure, Mae West *(left, and above, with codefendant Barry O'Neil)* was the antithesis of the chic, boyish flapper of the twenties. Her humorous, iconoclastic celebration of sexuality was ahead of its time.

1926

"I saw a fleet of fishing boats ... I flew down almost touching the craft and yelled at them, asking if I was on the right road to Ireland.... An hour later I saw land."—**Charles Lindbergh, after flying solo from New York to Paris**

STORY OF THE YEAR

Lindbergh Crosses the Atlantic

1 Charles A. Lindbergh was not the first person to cross the Atlantic by airplane, nor the first to make a nonstop flight. (Both feats were accomplished in 1919.) But he was the first to cross nonstop *alone*. His audacious endeavor grabbed the world's attention as no event had done since the signing of the armistice.

Lindbergh took off from Roosevelt Field in Long Island, New York, at 7:54 AM on May 20, 1927. When he landed 33½ hours later at Bourget Aerodrome in Paris, a cheering crowd of 100,000 awaited; souvenir-seekers nearly tore his plane, the *Spirit of St. Louis,* to bits. In June, four million New Yorkers welcomed him back with a ticker-tape parade. The press treated the 26-year-old midwesterner like a new Columbus—an image commensurate with his ambition. For Lindbergh aimed to thrust humanity into a new era: the age of transoceanic flight.

They called him "Lucky" Lindbergh, but skill and will were his talismans.

He'd hatched the idea while flying airmail runs between St. Louis and Chicago. "Think of being able to leap over the earth at will," he later wrote, "landing on this hemisphere or that!" When he read that a French-born New York hotelier was offering a $25,000 prize for a nonstop flight between his adopted city and Paris, Lindbergh decided to try for it. After securing financing from St. Louis businessmen, he went looking for a manufacturer to build a plane to his specifications. Several turned him down, thinking him foolhardy. A California company called Ryan Airlines finally agreed.

The *Spirit* was built in a hurry: Several other pilots, including the Arctic explorer Richard E. Byrd, were also seeking the prize in May. But only Lindbergh planned a solo flight, so the press focused on him. The night before his historic voyage, he couldn't sleep; already exhausted when he started the 3,614-mile trip, he fought to stay conscious as the hours wore on. Storms, fog, and the plane's instability (caused by modifications to save on weight and space) made his task more harrowing.

Afterward, Lindbergh became an international hero-at-large, promoting the concept of commercial overseas air travel to kings, financiers, anyone who'd listen. With his wife, Anne Morrow, he conducted survey flights, establishing routes still in use. In 1935, when Pan Am inaugurated passenger service across the Pacific, Lindbergh's dream became a reality. **◂1909.V ▸1929.6**

In Shanghai, these soldiers were ready to fire, but the gun stayed silent.

CHINA

Chiang Kai-shek Takes Over

2 General Chiang Kai-shek and his revolutionary army swept into Shanghai, the country's industrial and commercial hub, in March 1927. Paralyzed by strikes organized by the Chinese Communist Party (CCP), the city offered no resistance; not a single shot was fired. Chiang's forces, an unorthodox alliance of the CCP and the Guomindang, China's bourgeois revolutionary party, now controlled most of the country. The civil war appeared to be over, and the Communists wore the laurels. Only Manchuria, ruled by the warlord Zhang Zuolin, remained outside Chiang's sphere of influence.

From Moscow, Stalin, locked in bitter combat with Trotsky for command of the Bolsheviks, exulted. A Communist victory in China's civil war was widely interpreted as a victory for Stalin. The world's most populous country was about to become his oyster. But Chiang had other plans. In a stunning development, after taking Shanghai he quickly moved his troops against the trade unions, purged the Guomindang of Communists, outlawed the CCP, established the Nationalist government, and named himself president. The Communists were out. Chiang alone was in.

Thus jilted, Moscow broke off diplomatic relations with Chiang's anti-Communist regime. As Comintern agents in China fled back to Russia and Stalin indulged in desperate revisionism (Communism, he said, was stronger for knowing Chiang's true colors), the general renewed his campaign against Zhang Zuolin, the final obstacle to his dream of a unified China. By 1928, the warlord had been assassinated and his son and successor had made peace with Chiang. Unification of China under the nationalists was complete. **◂1921.6 ▸1929.14**

SCIENCE

Lemaître's Universe

3 Georges Lemaître's ideas transformed modern cosmology, but until 1927 this Belgian Catholic cleric and physics teacher was almost completely unknown in the scientific community. That year Lemaître approached Einstein at a physics conference, only to be told, "Your calculations are correct, but your physics is abominable." Yet within three years, enough had changed in the world of physics that at another conference, at California's Mount Wilson Observatory, Einstein, after listening to Lemaître lecture, jumped to his feet and declared, "This is the most beautiful and satisfactory explanation of creation to which I have ever listened."

The breakthrough in question was Lemaître's theory of an expanding universe—later popularized as the "Big Bang." Earlier, a Russian mathematician named Alexander A. Friedmann had come up with a dynamic model of the universe that was at odds with the static model used by Einstein and others, but his work was almost entirely mathematical. Working independently, Lemaître incorporated the latest discoveries in physics and astronomy into his theory. Since, he proposed, evidence indicated that galaxies were flying apart from one another, there was a time when they were all concentrated at a single point, which he called "the primeval atom." This hyperconcentration of matter and energy may have triggered an immense explosion, scattering debris and setting the universe on its expanding course.

The Big Bang theory, however,

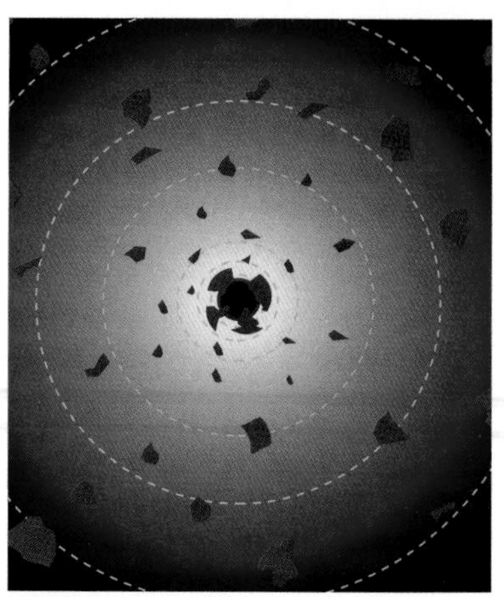
The birth of the universe, according to Lemaître's speculations.

ART & CULTURE: Books: *The Bridge of San Luis Rey* (Thornton Wilder); *Steppenwolf* (Hermann Hesse); *To the Lighthouse* (Virginia Woolf); *Death Comes for the Archbishop* (Willa Cather); *Amerika* (Franz Kafka); *Elmer Gantry* (Sinclair Lewis); *The Treasure of the Sierra Madre* (B. Traven) ... Music: "Me and My Shadow" (Jolson, Dreyer, and Rose); "I'm Looking Over a Four Leaf Clover" (Woods and Dixon);

"Nothing can be proven in the realm of thought; but thinking can point to many things."—**Martin Heidegger**

left one question unanswered: Would the day come when the universe would begin to collapse again, setting the stage for yet another colossal explosion? Lemaître was unsure. It was possible, he wrote years later, that the universe might someday reverse direction and begin to contract. But, he added, "it is quite possible that the expansion has already passed the equilibrium radius and will not be followed by a contraction"—in which case, "the suns will become colder, the nebulae will recede, the cinders and smoke of the original fireworks will cool off and disperse." ►1929.9

IDEAS

The Thinker

4 In *Being and Time*, Martin Heidegger, a onetime Jesuit novitiate, posited a new method of inquiry into the nature of being, with a capital B. Systematic and creative, the book, published in 1927, dismissed the traditional dichotomy between rational man and the insensate universe he inhabits, and recast man as an active participant in the world of things. Despite its near-unreadability, Heidegger's opus was hailed as a major contribution to philosophy, and his methodology (less a system than a challenge to think) became a cornerstone of the quintessential atheistic philosophy of the twentieth century—the existentialism of Jean-Paul Sartre.

Heidegger was influenced by Kierkegaard and Nietzsche, but his abstruse style, peppered with Greek and German neologisms and fanciful etymologies, was uniquely his own. Heidegger was a professor at the University of Freiburg when he wrote *Being and Time*; later, he joined the Nazi Party and was rector of Freiburg during Hitler's rise to power. He resigned in 1934 and after the war repudiated Nazism. Some scholars, however, maintained that his political failings discredited his philosophy. In later work, Heidegger explored industrial society and the dehumanization of modern life. ◄1910.4 ►1943.10

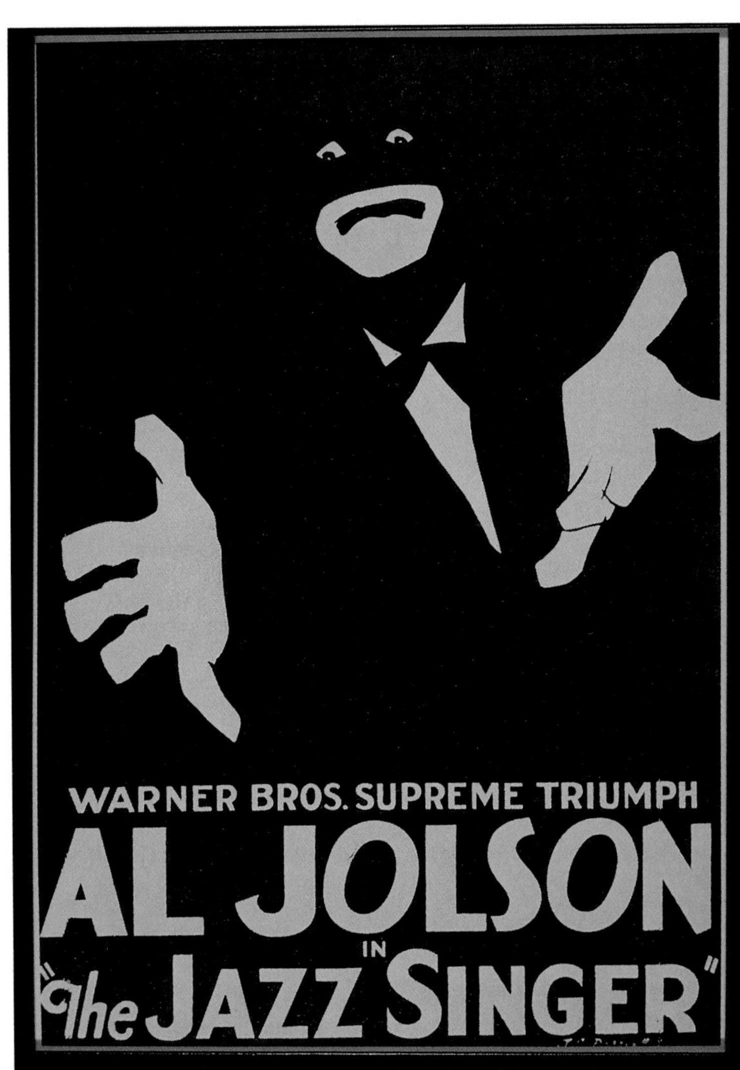

The stark expressionist poster for *The Jazz Singer* makes no mention of dialogue.

FILM

The End of Silence

5 "Wait a minute! Wait a minute! You ain't heard nothin' yet!" With these prophetic words, audibly uttered by Al Jolson in the 1927 film *The Jazz Singer*, movies changed forever. Silent films became history and the sound era began. *The Jazz Singer* was almost instantly designated "the first talkie"—but that description was neither completely accurate nor intentionally sought out.

Purists, of course, like to point out that film was never silent. In theaters, live music had long accompanied the screening of silent films. Furthermore, various systems for linking sight and recorded sound had been tried—with some success in short films—since the 1890s. By the 1920s most of the technical problems had been solved: Bell Labs perfected a sound-on-disk system, linking the movie apparatus with phonograph records; private inventors developed various sound-on-film systems in which sound waves were transcribed on the filmstrip itself. Warner Bros., then a fledgling Hollywood studio, invested in the Bell device. The system—christened Vitaphone—was introduced with 1926's *Don Juan*, which had a music track by the New York Philharmonic. But dialogue in features was still not part of the plan.

When the Warners decided to make a Vitaphone film of the hit play *The Jazz Singer*, about a Jewish cantor's son who must choose between singing in the synagogue and singing on Broadway, they intended to use silent sequences to tell the story and sound for the songs only. But the entertainer playing the title role, Al Jolson (then the biggest star in America), ad-libbed dialogue in two scenes. When *The Jazz Singer* premiered in New York on October 6, the audience went wild. Sound was here to stay. ◄1922.8 ►1927.M

BIRTHS

John Ashbery, U.S. poet.

Maurice Béjart, French choreographer.

Cesar Chavez, U.S. labor leader.

Bob Fosse, U.S. choreographer and filmmaker.

Stan Getz, U.S. musician.

Hubert de Givenchy, French fashion designer.

Günter Grass, German writer.

R.D. Laing, U.K. psychiatrist.

Gina Lollobrigida, Italian actress.

César Milstein, Argentine-U.K. biologist.

Daniel Patrick Moynihan, U.S. political leader.

Marshall Nirenberg, U.S. immunologist.

Marcel Ophüls, German-French filmmaker.

Olof Palme, Swedish prime minister.

Mstislav Rostropovich, Russian cellist and conductor.

Neil Simon, U.S. playwright.

DEATHS

Brooks Adams, U.S. historian.

Lizzie Borden, U.S. accused murderer.

Georg Brandes, Danish critic and historian.

John Dillon, Irish nationalist.

John Drew, U.S. actor.

Isadora Duncan, U.S. dancer.

Willem Einthoven, Dutch physiologist.

Elbert Gary, U.S. steel magnate.

Juan Gris, Spanish artist.

Jerome K. Jerome, U.K. humorist.

Gaston Leroux, French writer.

Juliette Low, U.S. Girl Scout founder.

Sam Warner, U.S. film executive.

Leonard Wood, U.S. general and physician.

"My Blue Heaven" (Donaldson and Whiting); *Arcana* (Edgard Varèse) ... Painting & Sculpture: *The Villagers* (André Masson); *Radiator Building, New York* (Georgia O'Keeffe) ... Film: *Napoléon* (Abel Gance); *Wings* (William Wellman); *Flesh and the Devil* (with Greta Garbo and John Gilbert) ... Theater: *Funny Face* (George and Ira Gershwin); *The Royal Family* (Kaufman and Hart); *Mahagonny Songspiel* (Weill and Brecht).

"God is subtle, but he is not malicious."—**Albert Einstein, on the implications of Heisenberg's uncertainty principle**

NEW IN 1927

Hostess Cakes.

All-electric jukeboxes.

Wonder Bread.

Borden's homogenized milk.

Gerber Baby Foods.

Automatic traffic lights (in London).

Volvo motorcars.

IN THE UNITED STATES

▶**THE IT GIRL**—Clara Bow, called the "It" girl after the 1927 movie smash of the same name, embodied the flapper ideal: bobbed and tousled hair, slim hips, bee-stung mouth, long, beaded necklaces, and a voracious appetite for scandal. The bubbly Bow gave women a glimpse of emancipation's possibilities, men, a glimpse of her legs. Among the biggest Jazz Age silent stars,

Bow fared poorly in the talkies (her Brooklyn accent didn't help), and by 1933 had retired from the screen. ◂1921.V

▶**A PHONE FIRST**—Transatlantic telephone service began in January, when (after a brief exchange between the officials supervising the hookup) the publisher of *The New York Times* and the editor of the London *Times* held a conversation across 3,000 miles of water. Three minutes of talk cost $75. ◂1915.7

▶**FORD'S MODEL A**—By 1927, even Henry Ford had to admit that his strictly utilitarian Model T—an unparalleled success for 19 years—was outdated. To compete with more innovative carmakers, he closed his plants for five

SCIENCE

Heisenberg's Principle

6 One of the most famous ideas in physics was unveiled in 1927 by Werner Heisenberg, a brilliant young German physicist who had recently come to Denmark to study with Niels Bohr. The theory was formulated on a cold January night as Heisenberg strolled through a Copenhagen park, wrestling with what might be called the chicken-and-egg problem of modern theoretical physics: If a mathematical formula correctly predicted the behavior of certain subatomic particles, was the formula valid in and of itself or merely a successful attempt to describe a natural phenomenon? Suddenly, Heisenberg remembered a remark made by Albert Einstein: "It is the theory which decides what can be observed."

Later that year, Heisenberg published a paper entitled "About the Quantum-Theoretical Reinterpretation of Kinetic and Mechanical Relationships," which became known more simply as the uncertainty principle. In the paper, Heisenberg articulated a formal means for physicists to come to terms with the fundamental unknowability of the subatomic world—a world that Newton's classical physics (still adequate for the visible world) could not account for. Heisenberg used the uncertainty principle to show why it was impossible for a scientist to determine the position of a subatomic particle without his intrusion affecting the particle's velocity. In other words, it was impossible to measure position and velocity simultaneously.

It quickly became apparent that the principle had large philosophical implications both within physics and without. If the observer was always part of the process under observation, then objectivity as it had long been understood was no longer a valid concept. Any observer—a field anthropologist studying another culture, for instance, or a celebrity journalist covering a fire—had to be aware that his very presence became part of the story.

If old-fashioned notions of objectivity were called into question by Heisenberg's theory, so were old-fashioned notions of truth. Heisenberg felt that physics henceforth should confine itself to "a formal description of the relation between perceptions" and abandon the search for the truth underlying the perceptions. Although the uncertainty principle deeply troubled Einstein (who spent many years attempting to prove Heisenberg wrong), most physicists hailed it as a major theoretical breakthrough. **◂1925.7 ▸1930.14**

MEDICINE

Mutations from X-Rays

7 With the publication in 1927 of Hermann Joseph Muller's discovery that X-rays and ultraviolet light can cause hereditary changes, known as mutations, scientists were able to create mutations themselves, instead of waiting for nature to produce them spontaneously. Muller and other geneticists used artificially induced mutations to tease out how genes are arranged linearly on chromosomes—and how they "cross over" (or reshuffle) in sexual reproduction.

Muller made the prescient argument that genes must ultimately produce all other components of living cells. His reasoning rested on the fact that genes, unlike all other cellular components, can reproduce the changes that arise in them. He also suggested that life began with the appearance of self-replicating molecules, or "naked genes," which he thought similar to viruses.

An American socialist, Muller moved to the U.S.S.R. in 1933, hoping to pursue his research there. But up until the death of Stalin, Soviet genetics was dominated by the politically powerful agronomist Trofim Denisovich Lysenko, who rejected Mendelian genetics. Muller was stymied by Lysenko's conviction that offspring inherit characteristics that their parents acquire by use, disease, and environmental influences.

Eager to get out of the U.S.S.R., Muller volunteered for the Spanish Civil War in 1937. Increasingly concerned that mutations were accumulating in people's genes and threatening future generations, he began, on his return to the United States, to promote public awareness of the dangers of radiation and industrial processes. Muller was also enthusiastic about the potential

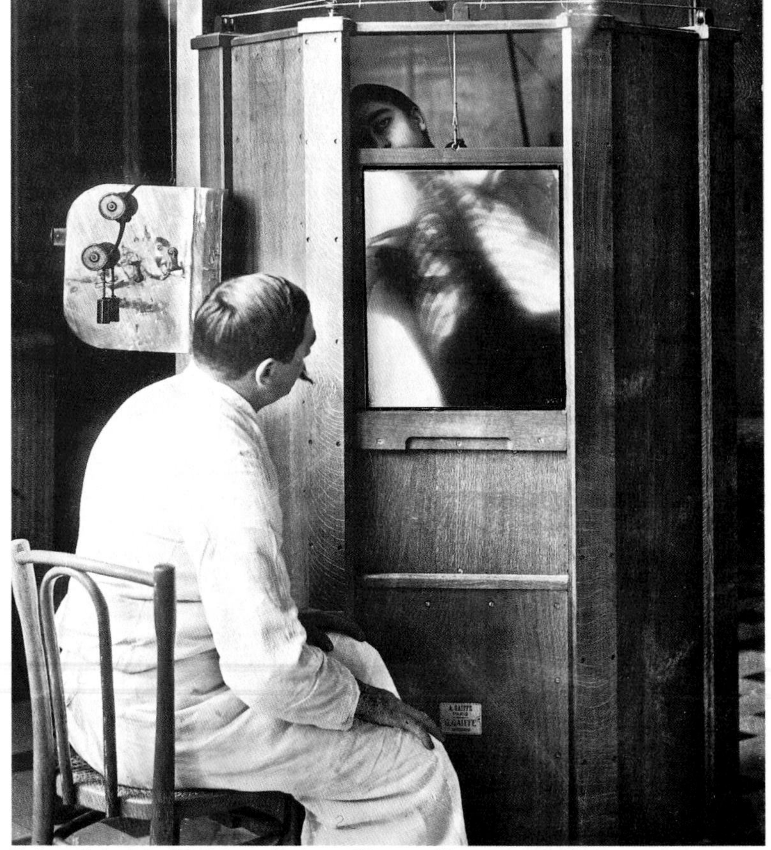

Early radiologists didn't know their machines could cause mutations.

SPORTS: Baseball: World Series, New York Yankees defeat Pittsburgh Pirates, 4–0; Babe Ruth hits 60 home runs in one season (record for 34 years) ... Football: NFL is organized into 12 teams ... Golf: Walter Hagen wins fourth consecutive PGA title ... Swimming: Johnny Weissmuller sets new record, 100 yd. in 51 sec ... Chess: Alexander Alekhine defeats José Capablanca for World Championship.

"One of those epochal works about which garrulous old men gabble for 25 years after the scenery has rattled off to the storehouse."—**New York Times critic J. Brooks Atkinson, on *Show Boat***

of eugenics, or "hereditary improvement," which would get a bad name as one of the Nazis' pet projects. Muller's goal was to guide human evolution consciously; toward that end, he made the controversial suggestion that the sperm of unusually healthy and gifted men be frozen and preserved as a resource for later generations. **◂1909.12 ▸1943.18**

THEATER

Musical on the Mississippi

8 "The history of the American musical theatre," stage scholar Miles Kreuger has observed, "is divided into two eras: everything before *Show Boat*, and everything after *Show Boat*." Until Jerome Kern and Oscar Hammerstein's lyric version of Edna Ferber's novel debuted on December 27, 1927, Broadway musicals were lighthearted, light-headed affairs of the boy-meets-girl sort, with high-society plots and enjoyable, irrelevant dances and songs. It was immediately obvious that *Show Boat* was different.

After an unusually ominous overture, the opening scene replaced the traditional line of high-kicking chorus girls with a chorale of black riverbank stevedores angrily declaiming, "Niggers all work on de Mississippi, /Niggers all work while de white folks play." Chronicling life aboard a floating theater on the Mississippi River from the late 1880s through 1927, *Show Boat* dealt squarely with racism, miscegenation, failed marriages, alcoholism, gambling, and white America's cultural debt to African-American music. Kern and Hammerstein's deft blend of melodrama, high drama, comedy, jazz, black spirituals, blues, and operetta created an epic panorama of American society and show business. Every word of Hammerstein's dialogue and lyrics, every note of Kern's music, advanced the drama or revealed character.

For once, innovation was rewarded: *Show Boat* was a tremendous hit. The score produced a staggering number of "standards": "Can't Help Lovin' Dat Man" and "Bill" (both performed by the great torch singer Helen Morgan), "Make Believe," "Life upon the Wicked Stage," "You Are Love," and a song that remains a high point of theater music, "Ol' Man River" (sung by Jules Bledsoe in New York and, legendarily, by Paul Robeson in the 1928 London production).

With *Show Boat*, the American musical came of age.

For all its success, *Show Boat* was something of an anomaly. It would be years before its lessons were absorbed and reflected in such later "adult" musicals as the Gershwins' *Porgy and Bess*; Rodgers and Hart's *Pal Joey*; and *Oklahoma!*, *Carousel*, *South Pacific*, and *The King and I*, all by Rodgers and Hammerstein. **◂1904.M ▸1943.11**

MUSIC

Nightspot Number One

9 Bandleader, composer, and pianist Duke Ellington transformed the Cotton Club into the capital of jazz—and in the Jazz Age, that was tantamount to the center of the universe. The premier innovator in African-American music began a three-year run at the Harlem nightspot in December 1927, fronting his first large ensemble. Ellington built complex compositions around a stable of virtuoso improvisers, creating lush textures and rich colors with unusual blends of instruments (including such seldom-used instruments as the bass clarinet and the wordless human voice). Although he boasted of a "jungle sound," he juggled notions of the primitive with as much wit as Picasso.

Like Ellington's music, the Cotton Club offered sophistication spiced with a dash of low-down exotica. Run by gangsters (who freed the artist from a prior engagement by warning the rival club owner, "Be big—or you'll be dead"), the tropically decorated boîte featured steak, lobster, and occasional armed confrontations. Its chorus line of light-skinned beauties was so famous that white women tried to pass as black to join. But though it employed blacks to entertain and serve, and though it sat in the middle of America's largest black neighborhood, the club's clientele—like its management—was strictly white.

Bandleader and singer Cab Calloway followed Duke Ellington as a star at Harlem's famous Cotton Club.

Whites were seeking amusement in black neighborhoods across the country, lured by lax enforcement of Prohibition laws and a vogue for African-American culture. (The literary Harlem Renaissance was a contributing factor.) Some ghetto nightclubs had mixed clienteles, but an increasing number catered exclusively to the white trade. For adventurous Caucasians—whether hoodlums, intellectuals, farm-belt tourists, or European royalty—a trip uptown to the Cotton Club was an unforgettable pilgrimage. For those with darker skin, less prestigious venues had to suffice. **◂1921.9 ▸1934.10**

IN THE UNITED STATES

months of retooling and came out with the Model A. Just slightly spiffier than the old "Tin Lizzie," the new model sold only moderately well. Ford's leadership of the auto industry was on the wane. ◂1908.1

▶"LONG COUNT" BOUT—A record 150,000 raucous fans packed Chicago's Soldier Field on September 22 for the heavyweight grudge match between world champ Gene Tunney *(below)* and the man he displaced, Jack Dempsey. Flattened by a vicious Dempsey barrage in the seventh of ten rounds, Tunney was granted a reprieve when

Dempsey failed to retreat to a neutral corner. Three to five seconds elapsed before the referee began the customary count of ten. Tunney got to his feet at nine, and went on to victory in the notorious "Battle of the Long Count." ◂1920.6 ▸1937.9

▶A COMIC DUO—British-born Stan Laurel (né Arthur Stanley Jefferson), a one-time understudy to Charlie Chaplin, teamed up with American vaudevillean Oliver Norvell Hardy, Jr., in 1927 in *Putting Pants on Philip* (*below*), the first of nearly 90 hit comedies they made as a team. "Mr. Laurel" was meek and thin, "Mr. Hardy" bumptious and fat. Through sheer stupidity the characters escalated the simplest workaday situations into unmitigated catastrophes (Laurel devised most of the duo's knockdown routines), creating comedy of universal and timeless appeal. 1945.V.

POLITICS & BUSINESS: GNP: $94.9 billion ... President Coolidge announces "I do not choose to run for president in 1928" ... U.S. and Canada establish independent diplomatic relations ... Supreme Court rules illegal income is taxable (Al Capone's yearly income is $105 million, largest gross private income to date for a U.S. citizen) ... Massachusetts becomes the first state to require automobile insurance.

"Odessa is a miserable town. Everyone knows what they do to the Russian language there ... but all the same, quand même et malgré tout, *[the place] is extraordinarily, quite extraordinarily, interesting."*—**Isaac Babel, from *Odessa Tales***

AROUND THE WORLD

▶KIRKUK OIL—Oil gushed uncontrollably for ten straight days in October after drillers made a strike in the desert near Kirkuk, Iraq. Baba Gurgur No. 1, a joint French, British, American, and Iraqi project, spewed 140 feet in the air, disgorging oil at the rate of 80,000 barrels a day. One of the richest fields ever drilled, Kirkuk became a center of the Middle East oil trade. ◂1909.5 ▸1960.M

▶PRE-COLUMBIAN MYSTERY—While flying over arid southern Peru in 1927, a Peruvian pilot discovered strange figures cut into the highland

desert. The mysterious Nazca lines, depicting animals, reptiles, and geometric shapes, were hundreds of feet long and predated the Incas. Exactly when, why, and by whom the lines were drawn is unknown. ◂1911.4

▶BRITAIN SPLITS WITH U.S.S.R.—Calling its diplomatic relations with the Soviet government "a hollow sham," in 1927 Great Britain severed ties with Moscow. "We have pushed patience to the point at which further persistence in it would become weakness or dupery," said Sir Austen Chamberlain, British secretary of foreign affairs, explaining the expulsion of Soviet officials from his country. Britain's move presaged the Cold War. ▸1939.3

▶AUSTRIAN UPRISING–Vienna exploded in July, when a jury acquitted three rightists of killing an old man and a child in a clash between socialist and quasifascist militias. A mass demonstration turned into a riot in which leftists occupied the University of Vienna (a hotbed of Nazi activity) and burned down the ministry of justice; nearly 100 people were killed by police. Quiet returned after a four-day general strike, but the stage for dictatorship was being set. ▸1931.1

These fuzzy-looking gray snappers were a photojournalistic first—and proof of a magazine's preeminence.

TECHNOLOGY

Photography Goes Under

10 The 1927 publication of the world's first underwater color picture confirmed *National Geographic*'s hold on state-of-the-art photographic journalism. Led by editor Gilbert H. Grosvenor, the magazine had gone from being a dry, scientific journal to a publication dedicated to "carrying the living, breathing, human-interest truth about this great world of ours." Using clear, concise narratives and groundbreaking photography, Grosvenor brought the gauchos of the Argentine pampas and the giant polar bears of the Arctic Circle into readers' living rooms. He shocked the public with a 1903 photo of a halfclad Filipino laborer, and in 1906, 74 nighttime photographs of wild animals prompted the resignation of two board members outraged at the magazine's "picture book" quality. Grosvenor understood readers' desire to see the exotic and unknown, and used photography to satisfy it.

The underwater pictures were his greatest coup yet. Staff photographer Charles Martin and scientist W.H. Longley designed underwater equipment and used magnesium flash powder for this extraordinary feat—made more so by the fact that neither the Leica camera, which freed photographers from bulky cameras and awkward tripods, nor 35mm Kodachrome color film was yet available.

Later on, *National Geographic* published the first photograph to show the earth's curvature and the first natural-color underground picture (2,400 flashbulbs were used to illuminate New Mexico's Carlsbad Caverns). **◂1900.3**

LITERATURE

A Celebration of Chaos

11 The hurricane of change sweeping the old Russian empire found a powerful expression in the writings of Isaac Babel, whose *Odessa Tales* appeared in 1927. Babel's greatness had been certified the previous year with the publication of *Red Cavalry*, a series of fragmented, supercharged sketches of a society gripped by revolutionary turmoil. Now, in the four interrelated stories of *Odessa Tales*, Babel returned to the swarming Jewish quarter of his youth—terrain that Yiddish writers like Sholem Aleichem had bathed in a golden glow of nostalgia. But Babel (who, unlike Aleichem, wrote in Russian) came not to perpetuate that tradition but to bury it. The ghetto might be colorful, he suggested, but it was also backward and confining.

Abandoning the well-worn Jewish themes of moral and intellectual struggle, Babel celebrated instead the anarchic vitality of the gangster Benya Krik. His tone—sardonic, unsentimental—presaged Brecht's in *The Threepenny Opera*, which explored similar themes; the knife-edge spareness of his language was as modern as Hemingway's.

Babel and baby: He welcomed the future but harbored few illusions.

Babel had fought for the Bolshevik cause, joining the Cheka (the Soviet political police) in 1918 and taking part in raids to seize food for starving workers. During the civil war, he'd seen action as a propagandist with Budenny's First Calvary (a group of Cossacks led by revolutionary Semyon Mikhailovich Budenny to fight anti-Bolsheviks). But his relish for upheaval was laced with ambivalence, and he was guardedly skeptical about Communist orthodoxy.

Like the bespectacled narrator of the *Red Cavalry* stories, Babel "tried to anticipate the mysterious curve in Lenin's straight line." The curve hit him broadside when Stalin began his cultural clampdown. Increasingly at odds with the authorities, Babel was arrested in 1939 and died in a labor camp, in March 1941. His works remained unavailable to Soviet readers until his "rehabilitation" in the 1960s. **◂1926.2 ▸1928.4**

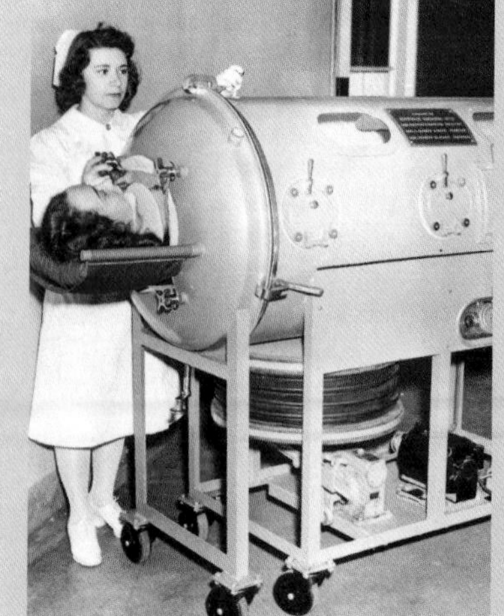

MEDICINE

Iron Lung Invented

12 Until the development of the iron lung—as the artificial breathing device designed in 1927 by Harvard physician Philip Drinker was instantly dubbed—doctors stood helpless while patients slowly suffocated as polio paralyzed their lungs. Using old vacuum-cleaner parts, Drinker built a respirator that, through the use of a vacuum pump, rhythmically moved air in and out of the tanklike apparatus in which patients were enclosed. Forced to inhale, patients could thus be kept alive until they recovered.

For 20 years the iron lung remained polio victims' only hope. Then, in the early fifties, came the miraculous vaccine that all but obliterated the disease. ▸1955.1

NOBEL PRIZES: Peace: Ferdinand Buisson (French; human rights activist) and Ludwig Quidde (German; peace activist) ... Literature: Henri Bergson (French; philosopher) ... Chemistry: Heinrich Wieland (German; bile acids) ... Medicine: Julius Wagner von Jauregg (Austrian; inoculation for general paresis) ... Physics: Arthur Compton (U.S.; wavelengths in X-rays) and Charles Wilson (U.K.; ionizing radiation).

A VOICE FROM 1927

Germany's Great War Bird

From *The Red Knight of Germany*, by Floyd Gibbons, 1927

Clayton Knight's illustration of a German aerial attack appeared in Gibbons's book with the caption "Where the machine was smashed against a block of houses." Below, Baron Manfred von Richthofen.

The aviation-mad 1920s spawned new genres of popular literature, as American boys exhibited a seemingly insatiable appetite for adventure stories about the legendary flying aces of World War I. Titles like Bill Bruce and His Battle Aces *fed the fantasies of the generation that would grow up to be fighter pilots in the next world war.* The Red Knight of Germany*, published in 1927, was a favorite of older readers as well. A biography of Baron Manfred von Richthofen, who downed an unparalleled 80 planes before being blasted from the sky, it was written—breathlessly—by former war correspondent Floyd Gibbons. A hero even to his foes, the dashing Red Baron (nicknamed for his scarlet triplane) was buried by the British with full military honors. Cartoonist Charles Schulz resurrected him decades later as the imaginary nemesis of a dog named Snoopy.* **◂1918.M ▸1929.11**

Into the grisly story of World War there came a refreshing gleam of the chivalry of old, when the pick of the flower of youth on both sides carried the conflict into the skies. Into that Knighthood of the Blue, Richthofen has been given a place of highest merit by those he fought with and against.

His life and death, his victories and his defeat, his loves, his hopes, his fears bring a new record to the halls of that same Valhalla in which rest the spirits of Guynemer, Hawker, Ball, McCudden, Immelmann, Lufberry, Quentin Roosevelt, and many others who fought aloft and died below with hearts that held emotions other than hate.

Young blood, hot and daring, raced through their veins, even as the winged steeds they rode raced on the wind to conquest or disaster. With keen young eyes, glinting along the barrels of their jibbering machine guns, they looked at close range into one another's souls as they pressed the triggers that sent one another tumbling down to death.

Some went down like flaming comets, burned beyond recognition before the charred remains struck the earth thousands of feet below. Some plunged earthward through the blue in drunken staggers as their bullet-riddled bodies slumped forward lifelessly on the controls. Some fell free from shattered planes at fearsome heights, poured out like the contents of a burst paper bag, and some, hurtling down in formless wrecks, buried themselves in the ground.

This was the death that Richthofen dealt out to his adversaries in the air—it was the same death they dealt to him. As he had given to many, so he received. As he fought, he died.

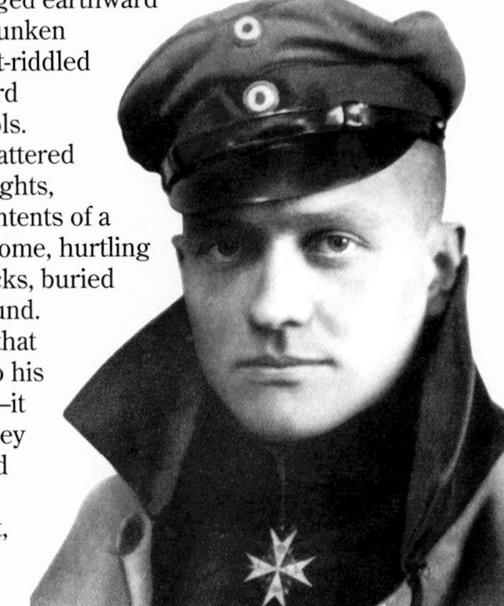

"The time has come when a frank renunciation of war as an instrument of national policy should be made to the end that the peaceful and friendly relations now existing between their peoples may be perpetuated."—**The Kellogg-Briand Pact**

STORY OF THE YEAR

Nations Declare: No More War

1 In the annals of quixotic gestures, the Kellogg-Briand Pact ranks high. On August 27, 1928, a decade past what H.G. Wells had called "the war that will end war," and less than a dozen years away from the global conflagration that would make the Great War look like a trial run, 15 nations signed an agreement in Paris that officially abolished war.

Recalling the Locarno pacts of 1925, Kellogg-Briand grew out of French foreign minister Aristide Briand's request that the United States make a nonaggression pact with France, aimed at protecting that nation from any revival of German expansionism. U.S. secretary of state Frank B. Kellogg was loath to see his country (which would not join the League of Nations) drawn back into international power struggles. But under pressure from a burgeoning "outlawry of war" movement, Kellogg decided to parlay the French overture into a grand gesture: a multilateral pact that would ban war under international law.

"If I can only get that treaty through," Kellogg wrote his wife during the negotiations, "I think quite likely that I would get [the Nobel] prize." (He did, the following year.) After the initial signing—the first such ceremony to be recorded on film—nearly every country on earth endorsed the pact. There were two problems, however, which were little noted at the time. One was that the treaty contained no provisions for its own enforcement. The other was that the signatories were allowed all sorts of qualifications and interpretations: The pact would not prohibit wars of self-defense, for instance, or the meeting of military obligations under the Monroe Doctrine, the League of Nations Covenant, or postwar treaties of alliance.

In the first article of the pact, the signatories agreed to "renounce [war] as an instrument of national policy." Eleven years later, those same countries would once again take up arms. **◂1925.M ▸1938.2**

"Married again," read this cartoon's caption. But peace wouldn't last.

LITERATURE

The Last Victorian

2 When Thomas Hardy died in 1928, at the age of 87, England lost one of its great writers, and with him a link to simpler, more rustic times. In his novels and poetry, the author of *Tess of the D'Urbervilles, The Return of the Native,* and *The Mayor of Casterbridge* immortalized the stalwart peasants and pristine villages, heaths, and woodlands of his native Dorsetshire, a place that, even at the time of his birth in 1840, was already inexorably passing into the Industrial Age. As a youth Hardy had listened to older neighbors talking firsthand about the Napoleonic wars; at his death, the horrors of World War II were fast approaching.

Hardy's Wessex County, his fictional world in southwestern England, was fixed in time and custom—a place where vivid individuals, having acquired modern man's signature self-awareness, struggle to assert themselves against nature and society and are invariably crushed. The philosophy is nineteenth-century scientific determinism, with an elegiac touch of classical notions of fate: Man is subject to universal forces, a plaything of the gods.

Wistful and pessimistic, Hardy was also deeply empathetic, a quality that lifted his work above melodrama and made him a national hero. **◂1910.12**

POPULAR CULTURE

America's Court Jester

3 "It gives me great pleasure to report on the state of the nation," intoned a presidential voice on NBC radio on January 4, 1928. "The nation is prosperous as a whole, but how much prosperity is there in a hole?" The voice delivering this "state of the union" message, which was being transmitted over a transcontinental hookup of 45 stations, may have sounded just like that of Calvin Coolidge, but it belonged to a man infinitely more popular: Will Rogers.

From the 1910s to his death (with aviator Wiley Post) in an Alaska plane crash in 1935, Rogers was the era's reigning political satirist. And radio, the newest entertainment medium, offered him the largest forum yet for dispensing his unique blend of folk wisdom, cracker-barrel populism, and good-natured skepticism about government. His fans loved it when one of his jokes was read into the *Congressional Record,* and Rogers quipped that "with Congress, every time they make a joke, it's a law. And every time they make a law, it's a joke."

An Oklahoman of Cherokee Indian descent, Rogers began in show business as a vaudeville cowboy and rope trickster, eventually incorporating wry topical comedy into his act. He was a surprise sensation in the chic Ziegfeld Follies; *The New York Times* compared him to Aristophanes. In addition to his radio work in the twenties, he wrote a syndicated newspaper column and frequently appeared in silent films. By the early thirties, with a new, top-rated weekly radio show and a string of talking-picture successes, he was Hollywood's number-one box-office attraction. **◂1910.9 ▸1943.V**

Will Rogers was dubbed the U.S. "poet lariat" —his words roped in audiences by wrangling the elite.

ART & CULTURE: Books: ***Lady Chatterley's Lover*** **(D.H. Lawrence);** ***Orlando*** **(Virginia Woolf);** ***John Brown's Body*** **(Stephen Vincent Benét);** ***Point Counter Point*** **(Aldous Huxley) ... Music: "Makin' Whoopee" (Donaldson and Kahn); "I Wanna Be Loved By You" (Stothard, Kalmar, and Ruby);** ***An American in Paris***

"What keeps a man alive? He lives on others. He likes to beat them, cheat them, eat them whole if he can."—From "What Keeps a Man Alive?" *The Threepenny Opera*

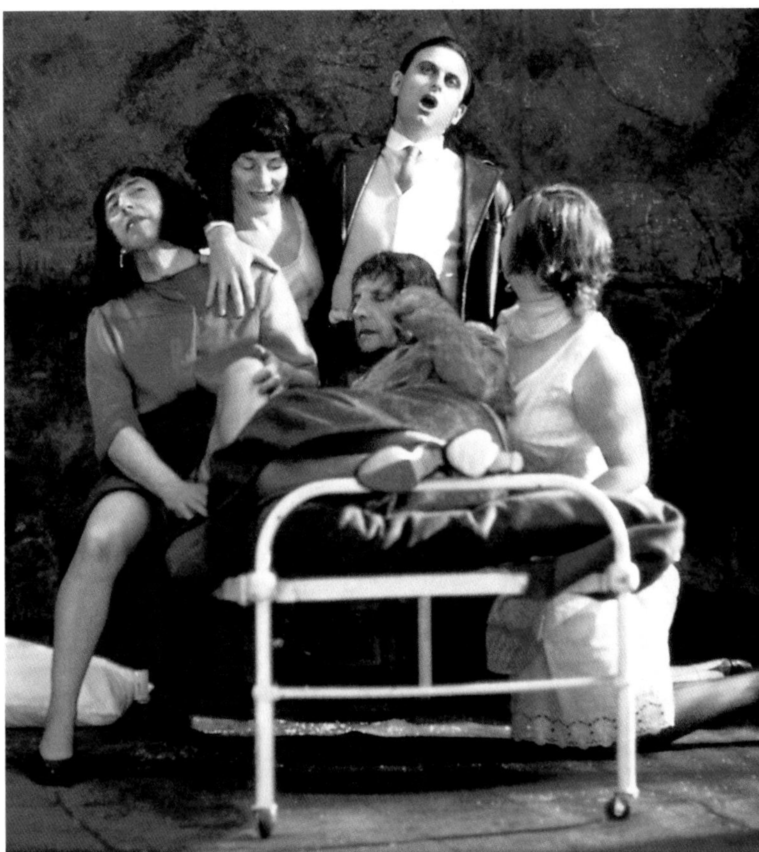

***The Threepenny Opera*: a satire so entertaining even its targets adored it.**

THEATER

A Beggar's Banquet

4 The rehearsals were disastrous. Peter Lorre, who was to have played the Beggar King, fell ill and had to be replaced. The actress cast as his wife refused to sing the "Ballad of Sexual Slavery"; she was replaced as well. The dress rehearsal ended in a shouting match. But on opening night, August 31, 1928, during the antimilitarist "Cannon Song," the audience began to stomp in rhythm. From that moment on, *The Threepenny Opera* was a hit—the biggest stage success of Germany's theater-mad Weimar era, and still one of the world's most popular productions. Its abrasively catchy, jazz-tinged songs, from "Mack the Knife" to "Pirate Jenny," have been covered by lounge singers, folksingers, and rock stars.

The show grew out of the brief collaboration between Bertolt Brecht, a leather-jacketed, guitar-slinging playwright-poet, and Kurt Weill, a shy, bespectacled composer known for his experimental orchestral pieces. Both men were Marxists who aspired to a new kind of opera: shorn of sentiment and naturalist pretensions, aggressively modern, politically didactic, and aimed at the working class. Their joint efforts captured perfectly the mood of postwar Germany, with its inflation-driven crime and corruption, its freedom and cynicism, gaiety and despair.

The Threepenny Opera transformed the London underworld of John Gay's 1728 satire, *Beggar's Opera*, into the Berlin underworld of 1928. It concerned the attempt of a gangster, Macheath, to wed the daughter of a beggar chief, and his betrayal by a prostitute (who was played in the Berlin production by Weill's wife, Lotte Lenya). For Brecht, Macheath represented the decadent bourgeoisie—a detail that did not stop bourgeois theatergoers from flocking to the show.
◂1927.11 ▸1966.8

JAPAN

Raids Shut Down Left

5 The contradictions inherent in prewar Japanese society emerged dramatically in 1928, when the first general election after the introduction of universal male suffrage, in 1925, was followed by a severe government crackdown on the country's nascent dissident movement. Citing the notorious 1925 Peace Preservation Law, which banned attempts to overthrow the Japanese state as well as all "dangerous thoughts," the government raided the offices of a gamut of leftist groups and arrested more than 1,000 individuals. Collectively, the feared left-wing groups had polled fewer than half a million votes in the elections. Later in the year, an imperial ordinance increased the stiffest penalty for political subversion from ten years' imprisonment to death. Japan had begun its slide into fascism.

Japan's increasingly reactionary political climate of the twenties and thirties was the product of a period of intense industrialization, when a few large business combines, the *zaibatsu*, came to dominate. Spurred by victories in wars against China (1895) and Russia (1905), which opened new export markets, Japan began to shift from an agricultural to an industrial economy. After 1920, the economic revolution was abetted by falling farm prices, which drove more and more workers into the cities in search of a steady income. As the industrial workforce burgeoned, so did trade unions, along with socialist and communist political parties. The liberalization of the vote, in 1925, was a direct concession to these new political voices. By then, however, real political power was concentrated in the hands of the *zaibatsu*, which controlled some 60 percent of all Japanese capital—and in the alarmingly independent military, without whose consent no politician could form a cabinet. The Peace Preservation Law, following quickly on the heels of male suffrage, dispensed with notions of democracy. Industry and the military were the state. **◂1921.5 ▸1931.4**

Party members toast a victory in the first elections under universal male suffrage. But democracy soon suffered a defeat.

BIRTHS

Edward Albee, U.S. playwright.

Maya Angelou, U.S. writer.

Shirley Temple Black, U.S. actress and diplomat.

Noam Chomsky, U.S. linguist and political activist.

Gabriel García Márquez, Colombian writer.

Ernesto "Che" Guevara, Argentine revolutionary.

Gustavo Gutiérrez, Peruvian theologian.

Grace Kelly, U.S. actress and princess of Monaco.

Stanley Kubrick, U.S. filmmaker.

Hans Küng, Swiss theologian.

Pol Pot, Cambodian dictator.

Maurice Sendak, U.S. illustrator and writer.

Anne Sexton, U.S. poet.

Eduard Shevardnadze, U.S.S.R. political leader.

Aaron Spelling, U.S. television producer.

Karlheinz Stockhausen, German composer.

Andy Warhol, U.S. artist.

James Watson, U.S. biochemist.

Elie Wiesel, Romanian-U.S. writer

DEATHS

Roald Amundsen, Norwegian explorer.

Vicente Blasco Ibáñez, Spanish writer.

Thomas Hardy, U.K. writer.

Leoš Janáček, Czech composer.

Charles Rennie Mackintosh, U.K. architect.

James Packard, U.S. engineer and automaker.

Emmeline Pankhurst, U.K. suffragist.

(George Gershwin) ... Painting & Sculpture: *Sixth Avenue Elevated at Third Street* (John Sloan); *Men of Opinion* (George Grosz) ... Film: *The Crowd* (King Vidor); *The Wedding March* (Erich von Stroheim) ... Theater: *Strange Interlude* (Eugene O'Neill); *Rosalie* (George and Ira Gershwin, Romberg, and Wodehouse); *Present Arms* (Rodgers and Hart, H. Fields); *The Front Page* (Hecht and MacArthur).

"In fact, Evelyn's abiding complex and the source of much of his misery was that he was not a six-foot-tall, extremely handsome and rich duke."—Photographer Cecil Beaton on Evelyn Waugh

NEW IN 1928

Cloverleaf highway intersection (Woodbridge, New Jersey).

Hydrogenated, homogenized peanut butter (Peter Pan).

Breuer chair.

Broccoli (introduced into the U.S. from Italy).

Bubble gum (Fleer's Dubble Bubble).

Columbia Broadcasting System (CBS; founded by 27-year-old cigar company executive William S. Paley).

IN THE UNITED STATES

▶TY COBB RETIRES—One of baseball's greatest offensive players ended his career in 1928 with a pop fly to shortstop. In 22 seasons with the Detroit Tigers and two—his last—with the Philadelphia Athletics, Cobb's lifetime batting average was a still unsurpassed .367. His records for hits (4,191), runs (2,244), and stolen bases (892) remained unbroken for decades. Unfortunately, Cobb is remembered as much for his nastiness as for his prowess. ◂1920.6 ▸1939.V

▶CHRYSLER JOINS THE MAJORS—A new megacompany appeared on the automaking scene in 1928, when Walter Chrysler bought out Dodge. The beefed-up Chrysler Corporation promptly introduced new low- and mid-priced lines—the Plymouth and the DeSoto—to compete with Ford and General Motors.

▶HOOVER CAMPAIGN—A consummate twentieth-century man, Herbert Hoover, engineer

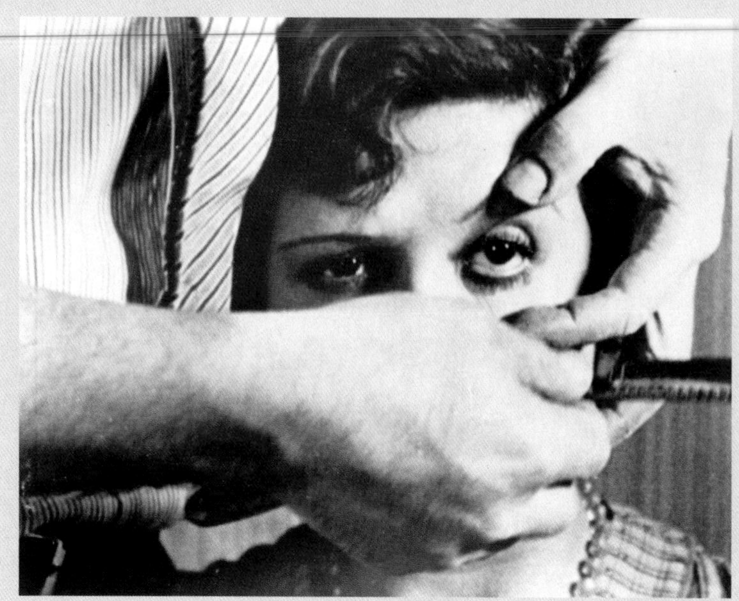

FILM

Celluloid Surrealism

6 **Director Luis Buñuel and painter Salvador Dali rocketed to notoriety in 1928 with *Un Chien Andalou (An Andalusian Dog)*. One of the first surrealist movies—and the start of Buñuel's 50-year career as one of the world's great filmmakers—it grew out of a three-day exchange of fantasies and dreams between the two Spaniards, then living in Paris. A 17-minute stream of disturbing, hallucinatory images—a hand crawling with ants, a young woman's eyeball being slashed by a razor *(above)*—the film shocked most viewers, but won its creators a place in the vanguard of their generation's most important artistic movement. ◂1924.3 ▸1930.10**

MUSIC

Ravel's Crowd-Pleaser

7 A serious composer who believed that music came from the deepest pockets of the soul, Joseph Maurice Ravel became most famous for *Boléro*, a popular composition that he himself didn't respect. Ravel described *Boléro*, which premiered in Paris in November 1928, as having no contrasts, no invention—just a simple theme borrowed from a Spanish folk tune and stretched into an orchestration.

Ravel: most popular for a crescendo.

Audiences, however, loved it from the first drumbeat. The drums were joined by flutes, then clarinets, followed by bassoons, trumpets, and saxophones. Each arrived in turn to reinforce the repetitive drums. The music built to an emotional climax, and the audience erupted in frenzied applause. The work became famous around the world; Hollywood even based a movie on it.

Ravel was a scrupulous craftsman and a perfectionist, and his somewhat mechanical compositions led Igor Stravinsky to call him a "Swiss watchmaker." Ravel's musical accomplishments (none of which gained the incredibly widespread popularity of *Boléro)*, paved the way for Stravinsky and the anti-Romantic school of the late twenties and thirties. **◂1913.5 ▸1934.5**

LITERATURE

A Master Satirist

8 Witty, mordant, sophisticated, *Decline and Fall* announced the arrival in 1928 of a major new literary talent, Evelyn Waugh. The novel, Waugh's first, provoked an immediate sensation in London's smart set, a number of whose members were recognizable as characters. Regarded by many critics as the best of Waugh's early satirical works, *Decline and Fall* launched the author's career as a sardonic observer of the "Bright Young Things," his phrase for the milieu from which he sprang—the dandified upper-crust world of Oxford and Cambridge in the 1920s.

After Oxford, Waugh had turned to fiction primarily as a distraction from the biography of Pre-Raphaelite poet and painter Dante Gabriel Rossetti that he was writing. *Decline and Fall*, a trenchant black comedy with references to homosexuality, pederasty, and incest, was rejected as obscene by the first publisher he tried. A second accepted it after Waugh substantially revised the manuscript—a circumstance that became literary legend when Waugh's subsequent novels began to generate huge profits. Both *Decline and Fall* and the critically acclaimed *Rossetti* appeared in 1928—the same year Waugh married his first wife, also named Evelyn.

Waugh, captured by another Bright Young Thing: photographer Cecil Beaton.

After serving in World War II, Waugh retreated from the satire that had made his early reputation and began to explore religious issues in his fiction, including what is probably his best-known work, *Brideshead Revisited.* (Waugh had converted to Catholicism in 1930.) He withdrew to a country estate in the west of England, drank copious amounts of alcohol, and became alarmingly peevish, conservative, and misanthropic. He died in 1966. **▸1956.12**

SPORTS: World Series, New York Yankees defeat St. Louis Cardinals, 4–0; Jimmy Foxx begins career with Philadelphia Athletics ... Olympics held in Amsterdam and St. Moritz ... Boxing: Gene Tunney retires (76 wins, 1 defeat) ... Swimming: Johnny Weissmuller retires with 67 world records and 5 Olympic gold medals.

"I love Mickey Mouse more than any woman I've ever known."—**Walt Disney**

MEDICINE

Vitamin C Isolated

9 The isolation of vitamin C in 1928 was a crucial step in the transformation of the science of nutrition. The change was galvanized by Polish-American biochemist Casimir Funk's 1914 discovery of vitamin B_1, a substance whose absence appeared to be responsible for the devastating disease beriberi.

Funk's discovery had given a big boost to deficiency-theory advocates, and by the early twenties, research into scurvy, another of Funk's "deficiency diseases," was focused on an unknown factor dubbed vitamin C. But until the vitamin could be isolated and crystallized, scientists could not study it or even determine if it was one substance or a group of several compounds.

It was a Hungarian biochemist working in England, Albert Szent-Györgyi, who, in the course of research unrelated to scurvy or vitamins, made the 1928 breakthrough. Taking a sugarlike substance from the adrenal gland of an ox, he isolated crystals of what he called hexuronic acid, which exhibited vitamin C–like characteristics. A few years later, after resettling in Hungary, Szent-Györgyi was able to demonstrate that hexuronic acid and ascorbic acid (the other name for vitamin C) were in fact the same. In 1932, vitamin C became the first vitamin to be synthesized in a laboratory.

For the first time, scientists understood not only that human life depends on the ingestion of certain substances, but also that those substances can be replaced artificially. The isolation of other vitamins quickly followed—vitamin A in 1933, vitamins E, G, H, and K, from the late '30s through the '40s, and vitamin B_{12}, the anti-pernicious anemia vitamin, in 1948–49. With the exception of a few isolated outbreaks, scurvy became a disease of the past. ◂**1912.6**

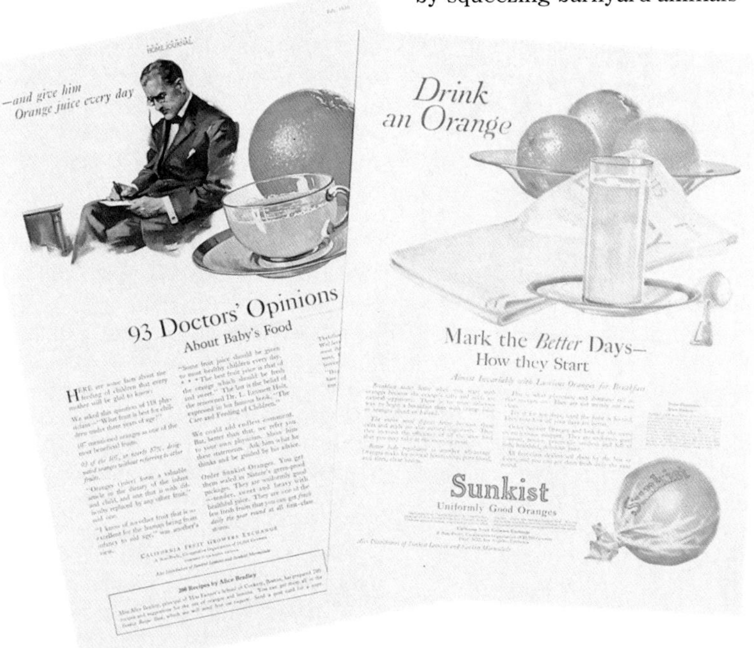

Szent-Györgyi isolated what made oranges a scurvy fighter.

Walt Disney liked mice so much that he kept live ones in his desk drawer to sketch.

FILM

Mickey Mouse Debuts

10 Audiences in New York's Colony Theater on September 19, 1928, watched in fascination as, on the screen, a film hero piloted a riverboat, made some music by squeezing barnyard animals until they mooed, brayed, or squawked, and rescued his girlfriend from a towering brute. The film was the landmark sound cartoon, *Steamboat Willie*. The versatile protagonist was a rodent named Mickey. The genius behind it all was Walt Disney.

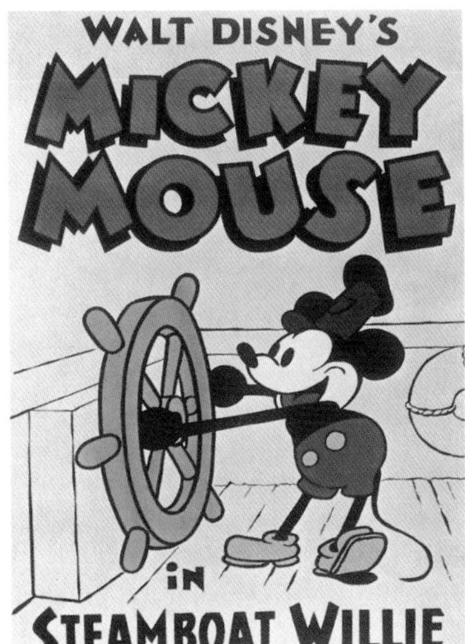

Over the years, Mickey Mouse grew cuter, younger-looking, and altogether less rodentlike.

Sound was the key to Disney's success with Mickey Mouse. The character—the joint creation of Disney and his fellow cartoonist Ub Iwerks—had appeared in two previous silent films, but no exhibitor would buy them. By making music and sound effects integral parts of the humor, the inventive Disney distinguished himself from his competitors. Comically crude (but technologically daring) gags like the mouse's use of the farm animals as musical instruments abound in early Disney cartoons and should be required viewing for those who associate his name with the sugary sentimentality and respectably realistic animation of the later pictures.

Within ten years, Mickey Mouse was among the best-known, best-loved figures in the world. For Depression-scarred audiences, plucky Mickey became an Everymouse. Theaters billed his short subjects over the feature pictures. Franklin Roosevelt and Britain's George V were big fans, as was Mussolini. The *Encyclopædia Britannica* gave Mickey his own entry. A magazine cartoon of the period showed a dejected moviegoer leaving the theater and sobbing, "No Mickey Mouse!" ◂**1906.7** ▸**1940.10**

IN THE UNITED STATES

and self-made millionaire, took full advantage of new technology during the 1928 presidential campaign against Democrat Al Smith. Using the airwaves to broadcast his speeches, Hoover got out his message on film and radio. When the votes were counted, Hoover had defeated Smith (whose Catholicism was no help) by one of the largest popular-vote margins ever. ▸**1930.6**

▸GIANNINI'S BANK OF ITALY —In an age of dizzying economic expansion, Amadeo Peter Giannini, stepson of an immigrant produce man, built the largest bank chain in the world. Starting with the single San Francisco–based Bank of Italy, in 1904, Giannini created the first statewide branch-banking system in the U.S. by catering to workers, small farmers, and the fledgling motion-picture industry. In 1928, having added the Bank of America chain to his ever-expanding network, Giannini

formed Transamerica Corporation *(San Francisco headquarters, above)* as a holding company for his two chains. By 1929, the financial giant's assets exceeded $1 billion.

▸BOULDER DAM—The power needs of a nation on the go were in the thoughts of Congress in 1928, when it passed the Boulder Dam Project Act. The legislation was the beginning of federal government involvement in the production of hydroelectric power. The damming of the Colorado River in Black Canyon, at the Arizona-Nevada border, begun in 1930, was completed six years later. In 1947 the massive structure was renamed Hoover Dam after the former president. ◂**1913.M** ▸**1933.M**

POLITICS & BUSINESS: GNP: $97 billion ... Herbert Hoover elected president, defeating Alfred E. Smith ... Flood Control Act earmarks $325 million for levees on the lower Mississippi ... Commercial Cable-Postal Telegraph joins International Telephone and Telegraph, forming world's first combined radio, cable, and telegraph service.

"Princes come out of Egypt; Ethiopia shall soon stretch out her hands unto God."—**From *Psalms* 68:31, quoted by Rastafarians who hailed Haile Selassie's coronation as Emperor of Ethiopia**

AROUND THE WORLD

▶IT'S A BIRD!—U.S. customs agents created a stir in the international art world when they accused sculptor Constantin Brancusi of trying to smuggle an unidentified piece of bronze industrial equipment into the U.S. The apparatus was in fact *Bird in Space*, one of a series of sculptures Brancusi had begun making in 1912. The Romanian-born French artist won his case against the Feds in 1928, and *Bird in Space*, hailed as a perfect representation of flight, is now recognized as a modern masterpiece. ▸1932.13

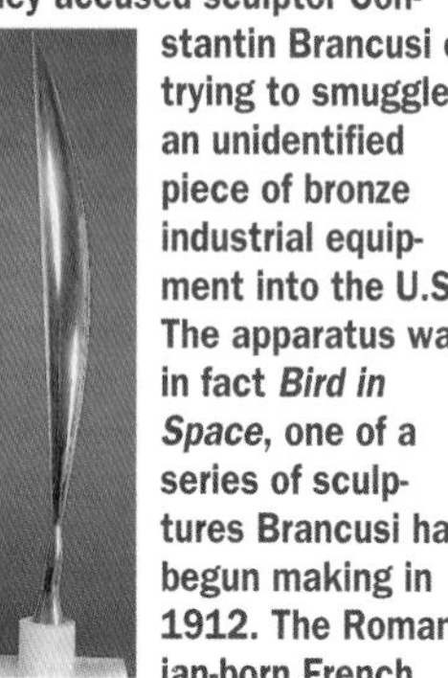

▶DREYER'S PASSION—*The Passion of Joan of Arc*, the first of Danish auteur Carl Dreyer's cinematic masterpieces, earned critical raves, if not a popular audience, in 1928. A powerful depiction of the last days of the French mystic, the silent feature established Dreyer as a serious, spiritual filmmaker. French actress Renée Falconetti earned accolades for a performance that many consider to be the best ever recorded on film.

▶AMUNDSEN DIES—Roald Amundsen suffered his last Arctic defeat in June, when he died trying to rescue Italian explorer Umberto Nobile. The Norwegian's goal of discovering the North Pole was frustrated in 1909, when Robert Peary got there first. (Amundsen then discovered the South Pole.) In 1926, Floyd Bennett and Richard Byrd piloted the first craft to fly over the North Pole, beating Amundsen by two days. Nobile, who'd flown with Amundsen and U.S. explorer Lincoln Ellsworth on that trip, crashed on an Arctic ice floe in 1928. Amundsen left Norway in a plane to find his former colleague—and, with a companion, disappeared at sea. Nobile, saved by others, lived into his 90s. ◂1912.V ▸1929.6

MEDICINE

Fleming Discovers Penicillin

11 Dr. Alexander Fleming arrived at his lifesaving discovery of penicillin partly through luck, partly through superior training and skill. In 1928, Fleming, a medical bacteriologist at St. Mary's Hospital Medical School in London, noticed that a staphylococcus culture he was cultivating had been contaminated by a mold and that, in the area around the mold, the bacteria were dissolving. An airborne spore had serendipitously alit on his slide. After isolating the mold for testing, he found that its active substances—which he named "penicillin" (the mold was from the *Penicillium* genus)—inhibited the growth of bacteria. With caution befitting the son of lowland Scottish farmers, Fleming reported in 1929 that penicillin "appears to have some advantages over the well-known chemical antiseptics."

Having served in the Royal Army Medical Corps during World War I, Fleming was painfully aware of the limitations of those antiseptics. Besides being useless for sterilizing complicated wounds, they were more likely to destroy white blood cells than bacteria. The ideal antibacterial agent would wipe out bacteria without harming the infected tissue. Fleming's penicillin appeared to do that.

Fleming published his findings without fanfare and in very conservative terms. Small notice was taken, and though he continued to experiment with penicillin, the substance's unstable chemistry prevented him from purifying it. It was not until 1940, when Oxford medical researchers Ernst Chain and Howard Florey stabilized penicillin, that Fleming received his due. As penicillin became the wonder antibiotic of World War II, he was hailed as a conquering hero. A knighthood in 1944 was followed, in 1945, by the Nobel Prize for medicine, which he shared with Chain and Florey. **▸1941.16**

Bacteria dissolved when a petri dish was swabbed with penicillin.

IDEAS

Mead Comes of Age

12 What role does culture play in determining human behavior? Anthropologists like Franz Boas and Ruth Benedict had been debating the issue for years, but few outside academia paid much heed until 1928, when Margaret Mead published *Coming of Age in Samoa*, her groundbreaking study of adolescent girls in the American Samoan village of Ta'u.

Mead's focus on sexual permissiveness as an index of a society's overall health created a stir, bringing the little-known discipline of social anthropology to the attention of a much wider audience.

Unlike Western girls, Mead wrote, the girls of Ta'u experienced the biological condition of adolescence not as a "period of crisis or stress, but … an orderly development of a set of slowly maturing interests and activities." Their "uniform and satisfying ambitions" were "to live as a girl with many lovers as long as possible and then to marry in one's own village, near one's own relatives and to have many children." This absence of Western-style neuroses resulted, Mead said, in a happy, noncompetitive society where "the capacity for intercourse only once in a night is counted as senility" and there is "no frigidity, no impotence, except as the temporary result of severe illness."

Mead was a 24-year-old graduate student when she went to Samoa.

Some anthropologists, then as now, challenged her rosy view of Ta'u, suggesting that her data-gathering was selective and her analysis oversimplified. Others see her as too strict a cultural determinist. But few would dispute her impact. An expert in fieldwork, she was instrumental in the maturation of a discipline that, as her biographer Jane Howard has noted, had largely been a matter of males studying males, or males measuring bones and artifacts. Mead was a woman who studied women. **◂1904.13 ▸1929.M**

NORTHERN AFRICA

Ethiopia's Royal Modernizer

13 Ras ("prince") Tafari Makonnen claimed descent from the biblical Solomon and the Queen of Sheba. As regent to Ethiopia's Empress Zauditu, he was the power behind an ancient throne. But Tafari, a cosmopolitan man, wanted to modernize his realm, and Zauditu refused. In September 1928 he staged a palace coup. After his troops trapped a pro-Zauditu commander in the royal mausoleum, a second commander's forces surrounded them. But another ring of soldiers—this time Tafari's—encircled the whole palace. The empress abdicated, crowning her 30-year-old cousin at an Old Testament–style ceremony that dazzled European diplomats.

King Tafari began his reign by using aerial bombs to quell a rash of rural insurrections—a clear victory for modern methods. Zauditu's death in 1930 freed him from all constraints except a chronic lack of funds. As Emperor Haile Selassie I, he stepped up construction of roads, schools, and hospitals; tried to update the army; and brought in foreign advisers on everything from phone systems to an antislavery campaign. He pushed through a new constitution and established a parliament (appointed, for the time being).

But Haile Selassie's efforts were interrupted when Italy invaded in 1935. After resisting the powerful aggressor for several months, he fled to Geneva. (He returned in 1941 with Britain's help.)

The century's first great African statesman, Haile Selassie is much more than that to the Rastafarians—a religious movement founded in Jamaica and inspired by Marcus Garvey and biblical prophecy—who worship him as a messiah. Long after his overthrow in 1974 (and his death a year later), his name lived on in the reggae hits of "Rastas" like Bob Marley. **◂1914.8 ▸1935.4**

NOBEL PRIZES: Peace: No award … Literature: Sigrid Undset (Norwegian; novelist) … Chemistry: Adolf Windaus (German; sterols, notably cholesterol) … Medicine: Charles Nicolle (French; typhus) … Physics: Owen Richardson (U.K.; electron emission from hot metals).

A VOICE FROM 1928

Laughing Over Spilled Milk

From *Amos 'n Andy*, WMAQ Radio, March 19, 1928

Blackface comedians Freeman Gosden *(left)* and Charles Correll contemplate their white alter egos. Below, the pair in 1935, in one of the first photographs allowed of them impersonating the characters of Kingfish and Andy.

The phenomenal success of Amos 'n Andy, *a program performed by two blackface clowns five nights a week on radio during the late twenties and thirties, defies easy analysis. The show's popularity among whites, in a segregated America, is less difficult to fathom than its popularity with many blacks. Amos, Andy, Kingfish, Sapphire, et al., were gross racial stereotypes, but they* were *lovable—and, by the unenlightened standards of the day, they were also funny. The show debuted on Chicago's WMAQ in 1928 and soon reached 40 million listeners over the NBC network. The pair's comic personae—Amos was eager and industrious, Andy a buffoonish shirker—were fixed in the first moments of the first episode* (below). *The show lingered (on television as well as radio) until 1958 amid growing protests over its racism.*

Announcer: Amos and Andy, two lifelong buddies, from Dixie, have spent most of their life on a farm just outside of Atlanta, Ga. Amos is a hard-working little fellow who tries to do everything he can to help others and to make himself progress, while his friend Andy is not especially fond of hard work and often has Amos to assist him in his own duties. As the curtain goes up we find the boys returning to the farmhouse with a bucket of milk—both are enthusiastic about going to Chicago where they have heard good high-salaried jobs are available. Here they are:

Amos: I was sittin' dere dreamin' 'bout Chicago an' 'stead o' putting de milk in de bucket, I put half of it on de ground.

Andy: Dat's what yo' git fo' not tendin' to yo' bizness. If I'd been milkin' dat cow, son, I wouldn't-a wasted a drop o' milk.

Amos: When I tell Mr. Hopkins dat I lost half de milk, he goin' git mad wid me.

Andy: Let him git mad wid yo'. You ain't got no bizness shootin' de milk on de ground.

Amos: I gotta tell him though 'cause he knows I ought to have mo' milk dan dis.

Andy: Instead o' payin' 'tention to whut yo' was doin', you was sittin' der dreamin'.

Amos: Yeh—if I hadn't been thinkin' 'bout goin' to Chicago den, I'd-a got de milk in de bucket a'right.

Andy: Well, it's yo' own fault—dat's all I gotta say.

Amos: You know, YOU was de one he told to milk de cow.

Andy: Dat IS right, ain't it?

Amos: So 'tis. He tol' you to milk de cow—he didn't tell me to do it. You is de one dat's gotta take de milk in to him.

Andy: On second thought heah, we betteh not tell him nuthin' 'bout losin' part o' de milk 'cause I don' want him jumpin' all oveh me.

"The industrial condition of the United States is perfectly sound."—**Charles E. Mitchell, chairman of the National City Bank, a week before the crash**

STORY OF THE YEAR

The Crash

1 By noon on Thursday, October 24, 1929, the financial boom of the 1920s lay shattered on the floor of the New York Stock Exchange. Thousands of Americans, from poor widows to tycoons, had lost their life savings; by day's end eleven financiers had committed suicide.

In retrospect, the signs leading to "Black Thursday" were written on the wall. Stock prices had more than doubled since 1925, and in September the Dow Jones Industrial Index (a gauge of the value of major stocks) had reached a record high of 381 in frenzied trading. Yet hints of a worldwide economic slowdown—and warnings from experts that stocks were grossly overpriced—prompted some major investors to begin pulling out of the market. On October 19, the impulse to sell reached epidemic proportions, and prices began to tumble. The momentum grew until five days later the market was gripped by the worst panic in its history.

Amid a blizzard of ticker tape, the world plunged into depression, as depicted on the cover of this magazine.

The slide continued long after the initial crash, setting off global chain reactions. As investment capital dried up, companies cut back on production or failed altogether, putting millions out of work. Wages and prices spiraled downward, as did consumption. Banks called in loans and foreclosed mortgages; many failed anyway, wreaking financial ruin on their depositors. European nations whose economies depended heavily on American credit felt the crash almost as keenly as the United States. World trade suffered, and the imposition of protective tariffs only worsened matters.

Conventional wisdom held that capitalism was a self-correcting system, and that intervention would be harmful—so governments did little. By 1933, unemployment in the industrialized nations was estimated at 30 million, more than five times the 1929 level. In the United States, where social welfare programs provided little more than soup kitchens, "Hoovervilles"—shantytowns named for the President, who stubbornly insisted that prosperity was "just around the corner"—sprang up in major cities. Far from being self-correcting, capitalism appeared moribund. Revolutionary movements of the left and right began to flourish in countries where, until recently, their appeal had been waning.

The reckless optimism of the Jazz Age—epitomized by easy credit and wild stock-market speculation—had proved its own undoing. The Great Depression settled in, grim and intractable, until the greatest war in history came along to pry it loose. **◂1923.5 ▸1930.3**

Best actress Janet Gaynor, surrounded by Hollywood's most powerful men.

FILM

First Academy Awards

2 When the two-year-old Academy of Motion Picture Arts and Sciences presented its first "Awards of Merit" in 1929 (for work done in 1927-28), the ceremony—unlike today's conspicuously long, overblown extravaganza—was a simple, five-minute affair. Yet even then, as now, the event's overriding agenda was public relations, not merit. The Academy was the anti-labor brainchild of MGM mogul Louis B. Mayer—a producer-controlled, pan-industry company union that virtually guaranteed that workers' grievances would be resolved to the studios' benefit. The awards were conceived as a sop to the very people Mayer sought to disempower—as well as a reminder to the general public of the young art form's legitimacy.

Among the winners were actress Janet Gaynor for her performances in *Seventh Heaven*, *Street Angel*, and *Sunrise*, and actor Emil Jannings for his hamming in *The Last Command* and *The Way of All Flesh*. The best-picture award was split into two categories: best production (for big commercial movies) and artistic quality of production (for specialized highbrow films). *Wings* won the former, F.W. Murnau's *Sunrise* the latter. Thereafter, the two categories were combined, with art usually getting short shrift.

The gold-plated statuette earned the sobriquet "Oscar" in 1931, after an Academy secretary cracked that it looked "just like my Uncle Oscar!" Notoriously blind—no best director award *ever* for Alfred Hitchcock or Orson Welles; no best actor for Richard Burton or Cary Grant—Oscar nevertheless has made some good calls. Katharine Hepburn received four awards, as did director John Ford, and each of the first two *Godfather* films was named best picture. **◂1924.M ▸1939.8**

LITERATURE

A Quartet of Voices

3 To most of his neighbors in Oxford, Mississippi, the eccentric "Mr. Bill" remained an enigma even as the 1,789-copy initial printing of his fourth, and arguably finest, novel was quietly securing his lasting literary eminence. Published in 1929, William Faulkner's *The Sound and the Fury* repelled some readers with its bleakness and seeming impenetrability. Others instantly appreciated its tragic, dusky beauty.

Set in the imaginary Mississippi county of Yoknapatawpha (modeled on Faulkner's real-life Lafayette County), *The Sound and the Fury* conveyed the unraveling of a local family, the Compsons, through the pained and poignant voices of three brothers—the retarded Benjy (who is alluded to in the book's title, from *Macbeth*: "A tale told by an idiot, full of sound and fury"), the introverted Quentin, and the misanthropic Jason—as well as that of a fourth, third-person narrator with the perspective of Dilsey, the family's black cook. Into this form, Faulkner incorporated the innovative stream-of-consciousness technique recently pioneered by Joyce.

Published just weeks before the stock-market crash heralded the Great Depression, *The Sound and the Fury*, and its themes of uncer-

ART & CULTURE: ***Goodbye to All That*** **(Robert Graves);** ***Dodsworth*** **(Sinclair Lewis);** ***The Holy Terror*** **(Jean Cocteau);** ***A Farewell to Arms*** **(Ernest Hemingway) ... Music: "Ain't Misbehavin'" and "Honeysuckle Rose" (Waller and Razaf); "Happy Days Are Here Again" (Ager and Yellen); "Am I Blue?" (Akst and Clarke); "Singin' in the Rain" (Brown and Freed);** ***The Prodigal Son*** **(Sergei Prokofiev) ...**

"I'm gonna send Moran a Valentine he'll never forget."—**Al "Scarface" Capone**

tainty, decay, and doom, resonated far beyond the Deep South. Faulkner's favorite among his works, it also represented the flowering of his genius. Over the following years, he created a monumental body of fiction, much of it set in Yoknapatawpha, most of it exploring what he called "the tragic fable of southern history." Faulkner received the Nobel Prize in 1949. **◂1922.1 ▸1950.V**

THE SOVIET UNION

Brutality as Policy

4 The first Five-Year Plan, Stalin's frenzied drive to industrialize his embattled, backward nation, actually ended in four. Implemented in 1929, the "revolution from above" engendered a significant increase in Soviet industrial productivity—at the cost of murder, famine, and mass migration. For Stalin, the high price of progress was immaterial: "We are 50 or 100 years behind the advanced countries," he said. "Either we do it, or we shall go under."

Replacing Lenin's liberal New Economic Program of the early twenties, the plan set impossibly ambitious goals—the doubling of coal production, a trebling of pig-iron production—and constantly revised them upward. Enormous steel mills and tractor plants were built and displayed to the world as palaces of Soviet ingenuity. Manned by unskilled laborers, crippled by chronic fuel shortages, the factories in fact produced little at this stage. Behind imposing facades, workers ignored the gleaming new conveyor belts, installed to out-Ford the great American capitalist, and slowly assembled tractors by hand.

To supply the new Soviet industrial state, Stalin embarked on a wholesale collectivization of agriculture. He confiscated grain and organized independent peasant-owned farms (which accounted for 97 percent of Soviet agriculture) into state-run collectives.

The penalty for resisting collectivization was execution or a labor camp. Propelled again into a condition of serfdom, many peasants slaughtered their cattle and burned their crops; millions more left the land to seek industrial jobs in the cities, further taxing the short supply of food, housing, power, and water. The collectives produced less than the independent farms had, and more of the output was seized by the state. By 1932, half of Soviet farms had been collectivized. Unable to meet the quotas and forced to deliver their crops to the regime, countless peasants—even those in Ukraine, the Soviet breadbasket—starved to death on what had been their own land.

Proclaiming collectivization and the Five-Year Plan an unmitigated triumph, Stalin tried to conceal the disaster from the world. Meanwhile, disaster struck his own home. In 1932, at the peak of the crisis, his young wife, Nadia Alliluyeva, committed suicide. **◂1924.1 ▸1931.3**

An allegorical poster celebrated the first Five-Year Plan.

CRIME

St. Valentine's Day Massacre

5 By 1929, the twenties' gang wars in Chicago had left Al "Scarface" Capone, who ruled a $50 million crime empire, at the top of the heap. Only one organization still challenged his control of the city's underworld: George "Bugs" Moran's North Side gang. Capone chose St. Valentine's Day to put a bloody end to the rivalry.

The biggest gangland killing to date backfired on Capone.

The scheme relied on killers masquerading as cops. Although most policemen took mob payoffs, they routinely raided the gangs for appearance's sake. On February 14, a Cadillac disguised as a police car pulled up in front of the garage that served as Moran's headquarters. Four men got out—two dressed as patrolmen, two as plainclothes detectives. Inside the garage, the phony plainclothesmen lined up six gangsters (and a visitor, local optometrist Reinhardt Schwimmer) against a wall. Suddenly, they opened fire with submachine guns; the other two assassins used shotguns to finish off anyone still twitching.

One of Moran's men miraculously survived for a few hours. When a real policeman asked who had shot him, he followed gangster code. "No one," he said. But Moran, who'd escaped by chance (arriving late, he'd seen the "police raid" in progress and decided to wait it out at a coffee shop), was less prudent. Pressed for a comment by a reporter, he shouted, "Only Capone kills like that!" His prestige as a mobster ruined, Moran soon left the rackets.

Public outrage against Capone was enormous, and President Hoover gave orders to have him jailed at any cost. Two and a half years later, Scarface was a federal prisoner, convicted, improbably, of the quiet crime of tax evasion. **◂1923.5 ▸1931.M**

BIRTHS

Yasir Arafat, Palestinian political leader.

Roger Bannister, U.K. physician and runner.

Jacques Brel, Belgian-French singer and composer.

Brigid Brophy, U.K. writer.

Anne Frank, Dutch diarist.

Murray Gell-Mann, U.S. physicist.

Jürgen Habermas, German philosopher.

Robert Hawke, Australian prime minister.

Audrey Hepburn, Belgian-U.S. actress.

Milan Kundera, Czech writer.

Martin Luther King, Jr., U.S. civil-rights leader.

Claes Oldenburg, Swedish-U.S. artist.

Jacqueline Kennedy Onassis, U.S. first lady.

John Osborne, U.K. playwright.

Arnold Palmer, U.S. golfer.

Adrienne Rich, U.S. poet.

Beverly Sills, U.S. singer.

DEATHS

David D. Buick, U.S. auto manufacturer.

Georges Clemenceau, French premier.

Sergei Diaghilev, Russian impresario.

Benjamin Duke, U.S. tobacco manufacturer.

Wyatt Earp, U.S. lawman.

Ferdinand Foch, French military leader.

Robert Henri, U.S. painter.

Hugo von Hofmannsthal, Austrian playwright.

Lillie Langtry, U.K. actress.

Gustav Stresemann, German statesman.

Oscar W. Underwood, U.S. senator.

Thorstein Veblen, U.S. economist.

Painting & Sculpture: *Georgia Cotton Pickers* (Thomas Hart Benton) ... Film: *Broadway Melody* (Harry Beaumont); *Diary of a Lost Girl* (G.W. Pabst, with Louise Brooks); *Blackmail* (Alfred Hitchcock) ... Theater: *Street Scene* (Elmer Rice); *The Bedbug* (Vladimir Mayakovsky); *Gypsy* (Maxwell Anderson); *June Moon* (Kaufman and Lardner); *Fifty Million Frenchmen* (Fields and Porter).

"Each color almost regains the fun it must have had within itself, on forming the first rainbow."—**American artist Charles Demuth, on the paintings of Georgia O'Keeffe**

NEW IN 1929

Front-wheel drive.

Popeye the Sailor Man.

Nudist colony in the U.S. (N.J.).

Home-applied hair coloring (Nestlé Colorinse).

Mobile homes.

Tin Tin.

Lithiated Lemon (later 7-Up).

IN THE UNITED STATES

▶LINDBERGH'S AIRLINE—Three companies introduced coast-to-coast passenger flights in 1929, using trains for portions of the trip. Transcontinental Air Transport—dubbed the "Lindbergh Line" (the aviator was its technical adviser)—offered the fastest, fanciest service, charging from $337 to $403 one-way between New York and Los Angeles. The journey often took longer than the

advertised 48 hours and involved considerable discomfort and risk, so TAT stressed glamour: Movie stars christened planes; stewards served meals on golden plates. But travelers still suffered aboard the era's unpressurized, unheated planes. Mergers turned the company into Trans World Airlines (TWA), which eccentric billionaire Howard Hughes turned into one of the world's biggest businesses. ◂1927.1 ▸1938.5

▶LOOKING HOMEWARD—One of America's great autobiographical novels appeared in 1929: Thomas Wolfe's *Look Homeward Angel*, an acerbic and sometimes brutal account of life in the town of Altamont—a fictionalized version of Wolfe's hometown of Asheville, North Carolina.

Birds of a feather: explorer Richard Byrd and flightless Antarctic friends.

EXPLORATION

Byrd Flies over Antarctica

6 Richard Byrd's historic mission to Antarctica in 1929 closed the last polar frontier and fulfilled the U.S. Navy commander's long-standing ambition to be the first navigator to survey both poles by air.

Byrd's 15½-hour flight over the North Pole in 1926, piloted by the legendary Floyd Bennett, had made him famous. Now, as he prepared to journey across the Antarctic continent, he easily attracted backing from tycoons like Edsel Ford and John D. Rockefeller, as well as from the public, which chipped in some $400,000. His 80-man team was so well equipped that critics scorned the venture as a cushy "million-dollar expedition." But despite the relative comforts of Little America (Byrd's base camp on the Ross Ice Shelf) and the brevity of the flight, the trip had hair-raising perils.

Unreliable under ordinary conditions, airplanes were murderously risky in the extreme Antarctic cold. Byrd and his team spent months testing their customized Ford monoplane, growing expert at dousing engine fires and making repairs in temperatures that froze motor oil. Adding to their anxiety was the presence of a rival aviator who might attempt the Pole at any moment.

Byrd's flight began on November 28, Thanksgiving Day in the United States. When the plane reached the mountains bounding the polar plateau, the engines balked; Byrd had to throw two 125-pound bags of emergency food overboard—putting him and his three-man crew at risk of starvation in case of a crash landing. The machine shot upward between two peaks, and the explorers dropped an American flag on the snowfield half a mile below. They were back at Little America nine hours later. **◂1927.1 ▸1931.10**

THE MIDDLE EAST

Ancient Quarrel Resurfaces

7 In August 1929, the century's first large-scale attack on Jews by Arabs rocked Jerusalem. The riots, in which Palestinians killed 133 Jews—and suffered 116 deaths, mostly inflicted by British troops—were sparked by a dispute over use of the Wailing Wall. (A remnant of the Jewish Second Temple and part of the wall surrounding two Islamic shrines, the site is sacred to both Jews and Muslims.) But the roots of the violence lay deeper—in Arab fears of the burgeoning Zionist movement, which aimed to make at least part of British-administered Palestine a Jewish state.

The British had made promises to both Arabs and Zionists. The 1917 Balfour Declaration supported the establishment of a "national home" for the Jews, while pledging that nothing would be done to "prejudice the civil and religious rights" of the Arabs. But the very presence of a Jewish homeland would, Arabs insisted, infringe on those rights. After trying to make the mandate territory independent (the Palestinians rejected a proposed constitution as pro-Zionist), the British set up advisory "agencies" to represent the two groups. The Arabs abstained in protest; the Jews used their agency as a shadow government. Meanwhile, they bought up more and more Arab land.

After the riot, Arabs on the streets of Jerusalem were searched for forbidden weapons.

British commissions investigating the August uprising warned of a growing class of "landless and discontented" Palestinians, and recommended a moratorium on Jewish expansion. But Zionist pressure—and Arab refusal to discuss a new constitution with Jewish leaders—prevented mandate authorities from enforcing a ban. In the 1930s, when Hitler's persecutions increased the flow of Jewish immigrants, Palestine erupted in all-out war. **◂1920.2 ▸1930.M**

ART

An Austere Sensualist

8 Monumentally intimate, austerely sensual, Georgia O'Keeffe's paintings could transform a flower into an object of overwhelming (and, said many critics, distinctly sexual) power, or old cow bones into an icon of vigor and grace. O'Keeffe found beauty in unexpected places, most notably the desert landscape of the American Southwest, to which she relocated in May 1929, feeling she had "used up" the subject matter that had brought her New York success.

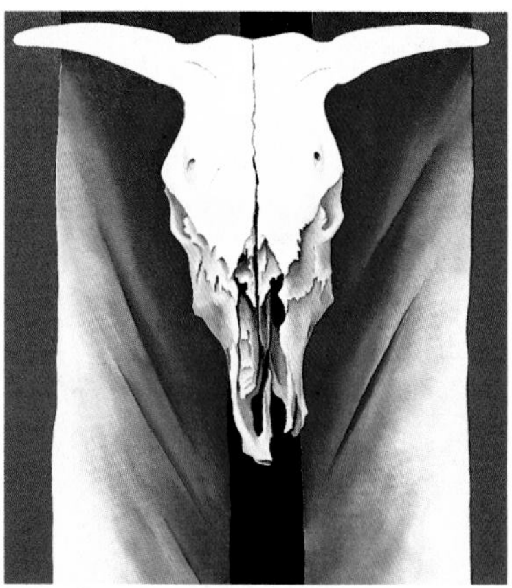

O'Keeffe painted *Cow's Skull: Red, White, and Blue* two years after moving to Taos.

O'Keeffe's husband, the great photographer Alfred Stieglitz, had been exhibiting her work since 1916 at his "291" gallery, where her shows of flowers and city views were enthusiastically received by the public and critics alike. O'Keeffe was also the subject of hundreds of

SPORTS: Baseball: World Series, Philadelphia Athletics defeat Chicago Cubs, 4–1; Babe Ruth hits 500th home run ... Football: 101,000 attend Rose Bowl ... Tennis: Helen Wills wins U.S. and Wimbledon championships for third consecutive year (wins 8 Wimbledons and 6 Opens in entire career) ... Horse Racing: U.K. bookmakers introduce pari-mutuel betting.

"Against literary betrayal of the soldiers of the World War, for education of the nation in the spirit of truthfulness, I consign to the flames the works of Erich Maria Remarque."—**Speech accompanying a public burning of Remarque's books in Berlin, May 11, 1933**

Stieglitz's portraits. But her own vision was never subsumed by his—or, for that matter, any other artist's. Defiantly independent, O'Keeffe discovered, in her new home near Taos, New Mexico, the unsettling imagery that would dominate, nourish, and define her work for the remainder of her long career, which ended with her death in 1986, at age 98. **◂1902.13 ▸1942.17**

SCIENCE

The Expanding Universe

9 Edwin Hubble changed humanity's concept of the cosmos more profoundly than any other astronomer since Galileo. First, he offered a radical new view of Earth's role in the universe by proving that there were other galaxies besides the Milky Way. Then five years later, in 1929, Hubble sparked another revolution when he published a paper confirming what had been a fringe theory: that the universe is expanding.

As director of California's Mount Wilson Observatory, Hubble had the advantage of a new 100-inch telescope, then the world's largest. (Appropriately, the Hubble Space Telescope, launched in 1990 from the space shuttle *Atlantis*, was named for him.) Using measurements of red shift—a result of the Doppler effect (the variations in a sound's pitch, for example, according to whether the sound's source is moving closer or farther away) in which the light of distant stars shifts toward the red end of the spectrum—he concluded that the apparent speed of a galaxy's retreat is directly proportional to its remoteness from the observer. This formula *(illustrated below)* became known as Hubble's Law—a pillar of the "Big Bang" theory of cosmic origins, and a basic tool for determining the universe's age, size, and future. Hubble's calculations of speeds and distances have been radically revised over the years. But his basic discoveries, and his ironclad law, stand unshaken. **◂1927.3 ▸1930.M**

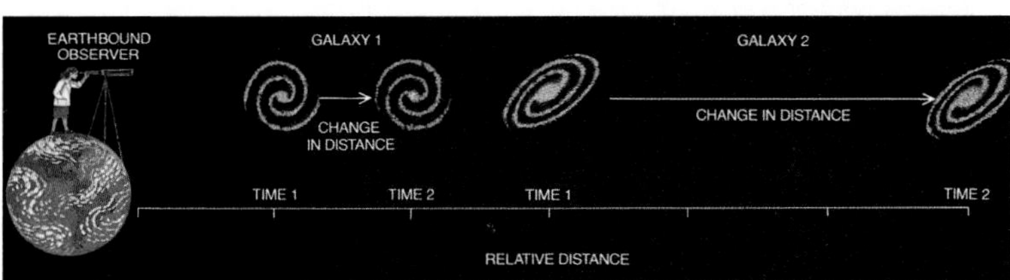

Hubble's law: The farther away the galaxy, the faster it recedes.

ITALY

A Union of Church and State

10 Breaking a 59-year stalemate between the Catholic Church and the Italian state, the Lateran Pacts, signed in 1929, made Catholicism Italy's state religion—and Vatican City an independent country.

Church and state had been feuding since 1870, when the forces of King Vittorio Emanuele II captured Rome and the papally held areas around it and declared them part of the new Kingdom of Italy. Refusing to recognize such a kingdom's existence, Pope Pius IX declared himself a "prisoner of the Vatican," and never again set foot outside its walls. His successors did likewise.

As Mussolini—a fierce anticlericist early in his career—began establishing his dictatorship, he realized he needed the Church's stamp of legitimacy. Pope Pius XI, in turn, was eager to end the Church's isolation, and to gain protection against more totalitarian Fascists who saw no room in Italy for any institutions but their own.

Mussolini and papal secretary of state Monsignor Pietro Gaspari at the signing.

The pacts, signed in the Lateran Palace (the papal residence in the Middle Ages), were a victory for both sides. Central to the agreement was papal recognition of the state of Italy—and the state's recognition of papal sovereignty over the 10.9-acre Vatican City. The union of church and state wobbled throughout the Fascist years, but it remained in place until 1985—nearly half a century after Mussolini's fall. **◂1926.1 ▸1933.3**

Illustration from Remarque's novel. Death was the only peace his soldiers knew.

LITERATURE

A War Stripped of Heroism

11 *All Quiet on the Western Front*, published in Germany in 1929, struck a deep chord in a generation still reeling from the displacements of the First World War. The novel sold a phenomenal 1.5 million copies in its first year; the film version, made in Hollywood, won the Academy Award for best picture of 1930. For a brief spell, the young author of this epic novel of World War I, Erich Maria Remarque, was one of Germany's top celebrities. But in 1932, Remarque went into exile; the following year, both book and film were banned, targeted as symbols of the antimilitarist sentiment that had weakened the fatherland. The turnabout was a grim sign of the swiftness with which the Nazis were transforming German culture.

As an 18-year-old draftee, Remarque had been wounded by shrapnel on the Western Front. Haunted by the carnage he'd witnessed, he decided to write a book about "a generation of men who, even though they may have escaped its shells, were destroyed by the war." In prose shockingly stark for its time, Remarque depicted the conflict as a mechanized bloodbath in which the instinct for survival replaced heroism or patriotism.

Outside Germany, Remarque not only survived but prospered. He moved first to Switzerland, then to the United States, where he dated Marlene Dietrich and married her fellow screen star Paulette Goddard. **◂1915.10 ▸1948.11**

IN THE UNITED STATES

Maxwell Perkins, the great editor at Charles Scribner and Sons whose other authors included Hemingway and Fitzgerald, played a major role in shaping *Look Homeward Angel*, originally a manuscript of gigantic proportions. ◂1926.2

▶MAIN STREET, U.S.A.—In 1929, sociologists Robert S. and Helen Lynd published their groundbreaking examination of an American city, *Middletowne—A Study in Contemporary American Culture.* Applying to American culture the anthropological techniques pioneered by Franz Boas and developed further by Margaret Mead, the Lynds analyzed the midwestern city of Middletowne, a.k.a. Muncie, Indiana. They discovered that two of America's greatest ideals, the egalitarian society and the primacy of individual freedom, had fallen victim to class structure and a bland uniformity dictated by the demands of industrialization and an integrated economy. ◂1928.12

▶MOMA OPENS—A museum dedicated to the painting and sculpture of the late-nineteenth and twentieth centuries opened in New York City in 1929 with an exhibition of works by Cézanne, Gauguin, Seurat, and Van Gogh. The Museum of Modern Art was founded by Abby Aldrich (Mrs. John D.) Rockefeller, Jr., Mary Quinn (Mrs. Cornelius J.) Sullivan, and Lillie P. Bliss (whose personal collection became

the museum's first bequest). Its first exhibition *(above)*, in an office building at 730 Fifth Avenue, was curated by 27-year-old Alfred Barr, Jr. Under Barr's stewardship, MOMA acquired what is arguably the world's finest collection of modern art. ▸1959.M

POLITICS & BUSINESS: GNP: $103.9 billion ... Former secretary of the interior Albert B. Fall found guilty in the Teapot Dome scandal ... Supreme Court upholds "pocket" veto ... Agricultural Marketing Act helps stabilize farm prices ... Blue Cross Health Insurance and Continental Oil Corp. (CONOCO) founded ... Coca-Cola sales reach $39 million.

"We Croats and Serbs are one people, especially we Croats and Serbs who live together ... and we as one people should have one free state."—**Stjepan Radic, leader of the Croatian Peasant Party, on the need for democracy in Yugoslavia**

AROUND THE WORLD

▶ZEPPELIN ODYSSEY—Carrying 16 passengers and a crew of 37, the *Graf Zeppelin* completed the first round-the-world flight, traveling 19,000 miles in 21 days and seven hours. ◀1927.1 ▶1937.V

▶UNIFIED FIELD THEORY—While other physicists immersed themselves in the newly developing field of quantum theory, Albert Einstein struck out on his own to try to frame a single elegant formula to explain the behavior of everything in the universe, from electron to galaxy. In 1929, the Prussian Academy published his first attempt at a unified field theory. An immediate sensation, the theory was soon dismissed by ranking physicists, who urged Einstein to rejoin them in their less lofty pursuits. He persisted on his lonely, intriguing, and ultimately unsuccessful course for the rest of his life. ◀1927.6 ▶1967.10

▶THE AUSTRALIAN MIRACLE—Only a year after going professional, Australian cricketer Donald Bradman became famous, setting a world record in 1929 with his score of 452 not out. Statistically the greatest batsman in cricket history—he never lost a test series—Bradman was also a brilliant fielder and inspiring captain. Thanks in large part to his star power, cricket became a beloved sport throughout the British Empire. In 1948, Bradman led the Australian team to victory over England, 4–0. The following year, the man who learned to play by hitting a soft ball against a water tank retired with a knighthood, the first ever granted to an Australian cricket player. ◀1920.6

Leaving Paris, Young shook hands with German delegate Hjalmar Schacht.

GERMANY

Young Plan Eases Debt

12 After years of patchwork solutions to the emotionally charged problem of German war reparations, the Allied Reparations Commission in 1929 assembled an international team of financial experts to fix a schedule of payments through 1988. The panel, headed by American industrialist Owen Young—and including, for the first time, German representatives—devised a plan designed not only to lighten the defeated nation's burden of debt, but to stabilize its fractured society and its relations with the rest of the world.

The Young Plan, released in Paris in June, contained the deepest concessions yet made to the Germans. They would no longer be required to cover the whole cost of postwar reconstruction. Annual payments would be reduced by one third, to about $407 million. Allied supervision of the German economy would be abolished along with the Reparations Commission itself. The debt would be paid to a new international bank, of which Germany would be a member. During economic downturns, the Germans could declare a partial moratorium on payments.

The plan was endorsed by the Allied and German governments. "All the dregs of mistrust and enmity that had been eddying about since the days of the Armistice," wrote an American envoy, "were finally drained off." But three years later, the payments were suspended for good. **◀1924.11 ▶1930.12**

YUGOSLAVIA

Binding a Loose Union

13 In January 1929, a parliamentary crisis that had been brewing for months came to a full boil in the loosely bound Kingdom of the Serbs, Croats, and Slovenes. Determined to unify his unruly realm into a South Slav state, King Alexander I suspended the constitution, declared himself absolute ruler, and renamed his country the Kingdom of Yugoslavia.

It had always been an unlikely nation. Created by the Allies after World War I by combining Serbia and Montenegro with pieces of the fallen Austro-Hungarian Empire, the kingdom tied together a handful of mutually mistrustful Slavic peoples. Only the Serbs had any experience with self-government; many Croats and Macedonians, however, resented them and wanted independence. Parliamentary sessions often erupted in brawls, and in 1928, a Montenegrin legislator shot several of his Croat colleagues. Alexander's move to consolidate in January came amid threats of secession by the Croats.

Promising that the dictatorship would last only as long as necessary to "study and implement measures" leading to democracy, the government instituted censorship and political tribunals. There were relatively few arrests and little bloodshed, and for a time the various opposition groups—relieved at being spared a civil war—accepted the crackdown. Alexander and his advisers set about reorganizing the country into districts based on natural boundaries rather than ethnicity; they implemented long-overdue reforms. But the worldwide Depression undermined many of their efforts—and soon both ethnic nationalists and defenders of democracy were agitating again.

King Alexander I, ruler of the new Kingdom of Yugoslavia.

Alexander began restoring civil rights in 1931 but never regained his popularity; he was assassinated in 1934. The badly divided nationalists failed, however, to fulfill their agendas before the communists took over in 1943. **◀1918.6 ▶1943.9**

CHINA

Showdown in Manchuria

14 Sino-Soviet relations took a turn for the worse in July 1929, threatening the region's delicate balance of power, and dragging Europe and Asia to the brink of war. At issue was the portion of the Trans-Siberian Railroad that cut across Manchuria to the Soviet port of Vladivostok. The rail line—built at staggering expense by czarist Russia on land ceded by China—was theoretically a joint enterprise, but in reality the Soviets asserted sovereignty over both the railroad and the land. Weakened by internal disorder and the hegemony of warlords, China seethed and put up with the situation.

The Trans-Siberian Railroad was the focus of the Sino-Soviet dispute.

But resentment became open hostility after Zhang Zuolin, the warlord ruler of Manchuria (who'd maintained a separate army and conducted his own foreign policy with the Soviets) was assassinated, and his son and successor made tentative peace with Chiang Kai-shek's Nationalist government. In May, the Manchurians moved to retake the railroad. The Soviets immediately marshaled troops along the Manchurian border.

Playing to the international community, especially Japan and the United States, Manchuria claimed the Soviets had been using the railway as a cover for communist activities. Japan, with valuable holdings of its own in Manchuria, sided with the Soviets and warned the United States to steer clear.

As the world watched nervously, the dispute raged for six months, frequently erupting into military skirmishes. Then, in January 1930, the crisis was defused as rapidly as it had escalated: The estranged parties agreed to resume joint administration of the railway. But lasting peace was elusive. The following year Japan began deploying troops in Manchuria. **◀1927.2 ▶1931.4**

NOBEL PRIZES: Peace: Frank B. Kellogg (U.S.; Kellogg-Briand Pact) ... Literature: Thomas Mann (German; novelist) ... Chemistry: Arthur Harden and Hans von Euler-Chelpin (U.K., Swedish; sugar fermentation and its enzymes) ... Medicine: Christiaan Eijkman and Frederick Hopkins (Dutch, U.K.; vitamins) ... Physics: Louis-Victor de Broglie (French; wavelike nature of electrons).

A VOICE FROM 1929

Poetic Common Sense

From *A Room of One's Own,* by Virginia Woolf, 1929

Renowned for such experimental novels as To the Lighthouse *and* Orlando, *Virginia Woolf published a nonfiction work of stunning common sense in 1929:* A Room of One's Own. *Based on the premise that "a woman must have money and a room of her own if she is to write fiction," the book-length essay (adapted from lectures delivered the previous year) offered a feminist answer to the question "Why have so few women been great artists?"*

Woolf was both a great artist and an intellectual impresario. With her husband, Leonard, she founded the Hogarth Press, printing T.S. Eliot's early works and the first English edition of Freud. And with her sister, the painter Vanessa Bell, she hosted the Bloomsbury Group, a London circle of defiantly highbrow leftist thinkers. **◀1918.4 ▶1949.13**

Intellectual freedom depends upon material things. Poetry depends upon intellectual freedom. And women have always been poor, not for two hundred years merely, but from the beginning of time. Women have had less intellectual freedom than the sons of Athenian slaves. Women, then, have not had a dog's chance of writing poetry. That is why I have laid so much stress on money and a room of one's own. However, thanks to the toils of those obscure women in the past, of whom I wish we knew more, thanks, curiously enough, to two wars, the Crimean which let Florence Nightingale out of her drawing-room, and the European War which opened the doors to the average woman some sixty years later, these evils are in the way to be bettered. Otherwise you would not be here tonight, and your chance of earning five hundred pounds a year, precarious as I am afraid that it still is, would be minute in the extreme.

Still, you may object, why do you attach so much importance to this writing of books by women when, according to you, it requires so much effort, leads perhaps to the murder of one's aunts, will make one almost certainly late for luncheon, and may bring one into very grave disputes with certain very good fellows? My motives, let me admit, are partly selfish. Like most uneducated Englishwomen, I like reading—I like reading books in bulk. Lately my diet has become a trifle monotonous; history is too much about wars; biography too much about great men; poetry has shown, I think, a tendency to sterility, and fiction—but I have sufficiently exposed my disabilities as a critic of modern fiction and will say no more about it. Therefore I would ask you to write all kinds of books, hesitating at no subject however trivial or however vast. By hook or by crook, I hope that you will possess yourselves of money enough to travel and to idle, to contemplate the future or the past of the world, to dream over books and loiter at street corners and let the line of thought dip deep into the stream. For I am by no means confining you to fiction. If you would please me—and there are thousands like me—you would write books of travel and adventure, and research and scholarship, and history and biography, and criticism and philosophy, and science. By so doing you will certainly profit the art of fiction. For books have a way of influencing each other. Fiction will be much better for standing cheek by jowl with poetry and philosophy. Moreover, if you consider any great figure of the past, like Sappho, like the Lady Murasaki, like Emily Brontë, you will find that she is an inheritor as well as an originator, and has come into existence because women have come to have the habit of writing naturally; so that even as a prelude to poetry such activity on your part would be invaluable.

Although war may have liberated some women, as Woolf noted above, she herself was thrown into a black depression by World War II. In 1941, she committed suicide by drowning.

The growing interdependence of the world's nations had a grim side, which showed itself as the Great Depression spread from America around the globe. In the economic chaos that ensued, fascism found fertile ground—and as the decade ended, history's greatest conflict began.

1930
1939

The Depression hit hard in the land where it began: By 1932, up to 30 percent of the U.S. workforce was unemployed. When Franklin D. Roosevelt became president the following year, he instituted a host of programs aimed at putting Americans back to work. In a 1937 image by Dorothea Lange, a jobless man waits for better times in San Francisco *(right)*. One of the century's most influential documentary photographers, Lange participated in a federal project that commissioned artists to record the conditions of America's poor.

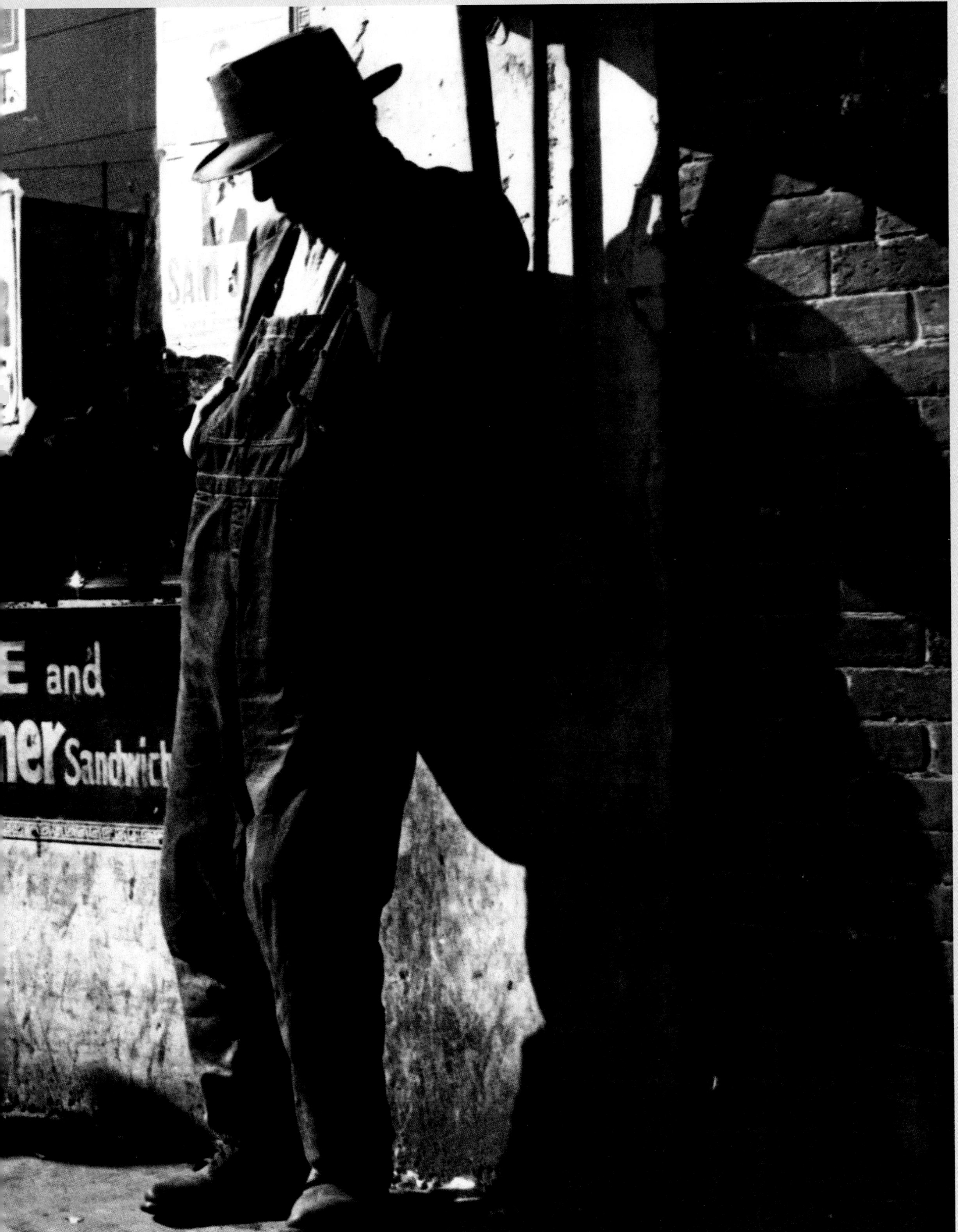
E and
ner Sandwich

THE WORLD IN 1930

World Population

1920: 1.9 BILLION 1930: 2.1 BILLION

1920–30: +10.5%

China Struggles to Unify

By 1930, General Chiang Kai-shek of the Guomindang army had succeeded in unifying eastern and northern China. The warlords, who had kept China in a state of continual chaos for more than a decade, were subdued.

Starting in 1926, the Guomindang worked its way up from the south and by 1927 had captured Hankou, Nanjing, and Shanghai. Beijing fell the following year, as did Manchuria (though in name only). After setting up a government, Chiang consolidated his power by purging many Communists. But his efforts were thwarted when the Japanese invaded Manchuria in 1931.

STATE OF THE ART

The **radio** brought the world into one's living room at the turn of a knob, providing free entertainment for Depression-era families, and later, during the Second World War, carrying news of fighting men in Europe and the Pacific back to the homefront. Superseded by television, the radio was, by century's end, so prevalent it went almost unnoticed.

Percentage of Households with Radios

	U.K.	U.S.
1930	30%	46%
1940*	71%	82%
1990	90%	99%

*or nearest available year

Aviation Firsts

1921 In a demonstration, naval vessels were sunk by aircraft for the first time

1923 First nonstop transcontinental flight (New York to California)

1924 First round-the-world flight (175 days)

1926 First flight over the North Pole

1927 First solo nonstop transatlantic flight (3,600 miles in under 34 hours)

1928 First east-west transatlantic crossing (Dublin to New York)

1929 Endurance record (150 hours and 40 minutes in the air)

1929 First blind flight (takeoff and landing entirely on instruments)

The World Cup

Attendance at championship matches of the world's most poular sport

1930
434,500 spectators

1994
3,500,000 spectators
32,000,000,000 television audience

Aircraft Speeds

1904	32.6 mph	Wright Brothers' plane
1919	118.5 mph	Curtiss NC-4
1927	150 mph	Lockheed Vega
1940	200 mph	Boeing Stratoliner
1953	300 mph	Douglas DC-7
1990		

Dream Factories The introduction of "talkies" (crude as the early ones were) only deepened the world's infatuation with Hollywood movies. As early as 1920, more than 90 percent of the films shown in Europe, Africa, Asia, and South America came out of Hollywood; by 1930, the American film industry was the largest in the world. By 1990, American movies remained the most influential worldwide, but both the United States and Japan (also home to a large film industry) were being outproduced by the world's most prolific filmmaking nation: India.

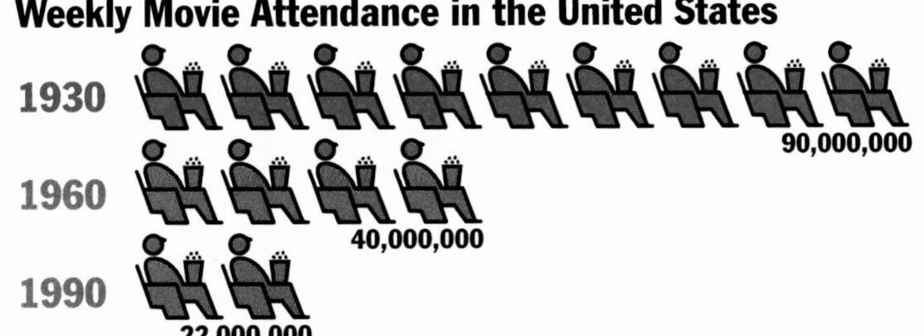

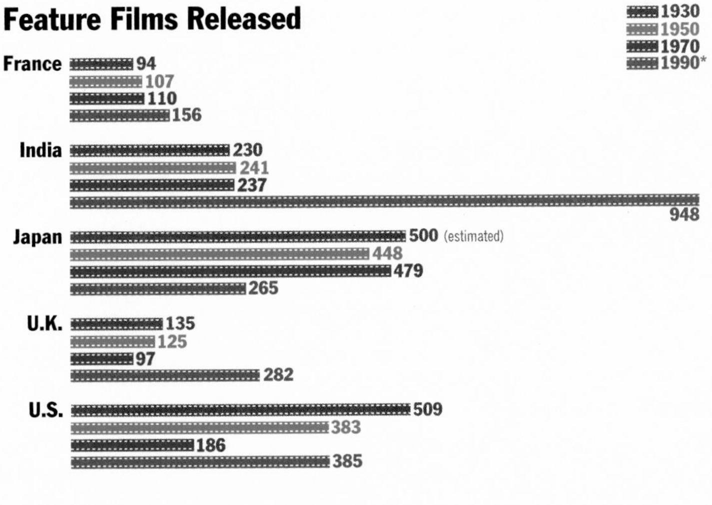

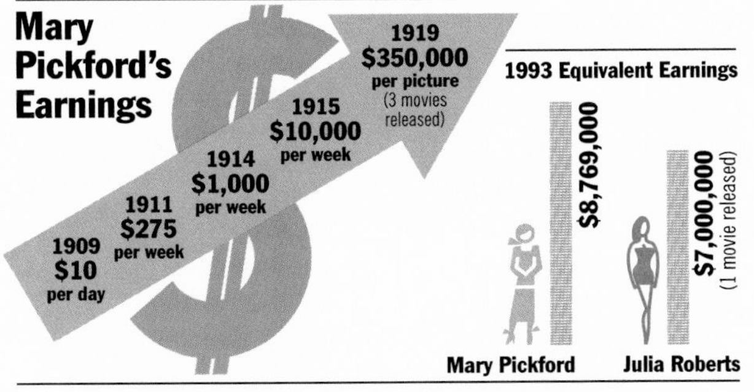

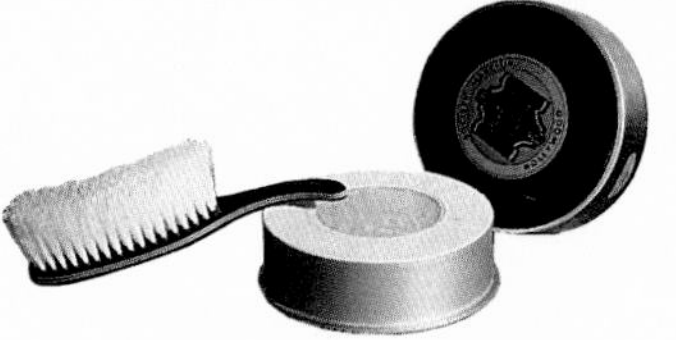

Fashion Essential

Formerly taboo, or at least associated with women "of a certain type," **cosmetics** were widely accepted by 1930. "Even the most conservative," noted *Vogue* magazine "must now concede that a woman exquisitely made up yet may be … a faithful wife and devoted mother." By the 1990s, cosmetics had become a worldwide $80-billion-a-year business.

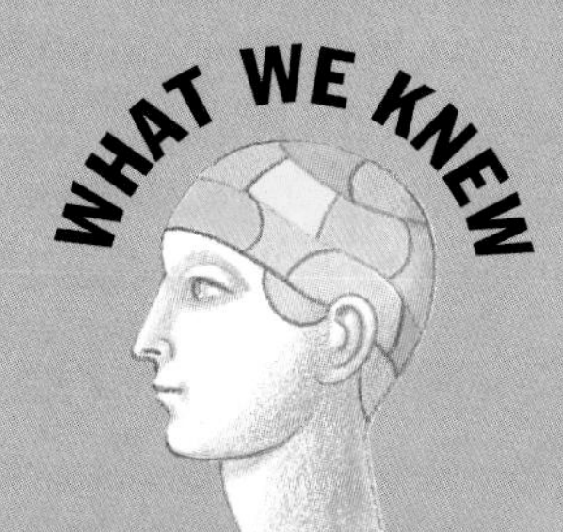

Six months after the Crash of 1929, President Hoover assures the American public that "the Depression is over." His optimism has been bolstered by Harvard economists, one of whom writes, "With the underlying conditions sound, we believe that the recession … will be checked shortly and that improvement will set in during the spring months."

■

Despite the fact that the 18th amendment to the U.S. Constitution, Prohibition, is widely regarded as a failure, few believe that it can successfully be repealed. "There is as much chance of repeal," says Texas senator Morris Sheppard, "as there is for a hummingbird to fly to the planet Mars with the Washington Monument tied to its tail."

■

Movie critics bemoan the poor quality of "talkies" (especially their lighting and camera work) compared with silent films. "Talking films are a very interesting invention," says Louis-Jean Lumière, coinventor of the first film projector, "but I do not believe that they will remain long in fashion."

■

Airplanes continue to be the domain solely of adventurous explorers and daredevil record-breakers. Passenger airships however, are the quickest, safest (not a single passenger fatality to date), and most luxurious means of crossing the Atlantic.

■

Despite the German Nazi Party's strong showing in the 1930 national election, Adolf Hitler's influence is thought to be on the wane. Hitler himself is dismissed by German President Paul von Hindenburg as "a queer fellow who [will] never become Chancellor; the best he [can] hope for [is] to head the Postal Department."

■

"There is not the slightest indication that [nuclear] energy will ever be obtainable," physicist Albert Einstein declares. "It would mean that the atom would have to be shattered at will."

STEPHEN SPENDER

Nations in Goose Step

The Age of Totalitarianism

1930
1939

LOOKING UP "TOTALITARIANISM" in the *Oxford English Dictionary*, I was astonished to find that the word entered that comprehensive reference work only in 1926. (My O.E.D. cites an early definition from the London *Times*: "a reaction against parliamentarianism in favor of a 'totalitarian' or unitary state, whether Fascism or Communism.") By then, Mussolini had ruled Italy for four years, yet Fascism was just proving itself a new kind of dictatorship. When he first marched on Rome with his legions, Il Duce simply looked like an updated *condottiere*—one of the mercenary chieftains who'd swept into power during the Renaissance. Not until 1926, when a string of assassination attempts prompted him to impose his full, repressive program, did the true nature of the right-wing totalitarian state emerge. And not until the 1930s, when Mussolini, Hitler, and Stalin all ruled—and fascism and communism were the poles between which the currents of politics arced with ever greater force—could the world be said to have entered an Age of Totalitarianism.

If totalitarian ideologies were rooted in the nineteenth century, in the writings of Darwin, Marx, and Nietzsche, their practical realization became possible only in the twentieth, when the advent of mass communications and mass production allowed whole societies and economies to be mobilized for a single goal. The key to totalitarianism, right or left, is its ambition to *totalize*—to bring all aspects of life under the supervision of a central authority. In Italy, the Fascists began totalizing in earnest four years after seizing Rome. In the Soviet Union, the Communist Party had started the process upon winning the revolution in 1917 (but suffered setbacks in the early years). In Germany, by contrast, the Nazis exhibited their totalizing intentions long before coming to power in 1933. As early as 1928, Nazi propaganda chief Joseph Goebbels was using party publications and matters to shape Germans' views not merely on political issues, but in realms hitherto considered nonpolitical—child rearing, music, sports, literature. When the party became one with the state, the government became the arbiter of all these realms and more.

Both Fascism and Nazism promised eternal, or near-eternal, national glory: a resurrected Roman Empire, a Thousand-Year Reich. The people of each nation—whether Italians or German "Aryans"—were Supermen, entitled by destiny to rule over others. At the same time, they were mere clay for a truly transcendental being: the Leader. In Italy and Germany, all policies issued from a man who was regarded as a virtual god, and were passed down through a hierarchy of individuals and institutions explicitly charged with transmitting his will.

The Soviet Union's dictator was quite as ruthless as Hitler and the object of as much adulation. Yet there were important differences between the right- and left-wing police states. Stalin was not considered the embodiment of an eternal principle (Hitler's *Führerprinzip*), but merely of a transitional phase in the development of world communism: the dictatorship of the proletariat. This dictatorship, communists insisted, was a defensive measure forced upon the Soviet Union by capitalist enemies. It would last, according to Marxist theory, only until all nations were firmly in the hands of the working class, whereupon the state (and national borders) would wither away.

Communism's avowed egalitarianism and internationalism were poles apart from the Nazi-Fascist obsession with authority and nationalism (which eventually unleashed the Second World War),

For totalitarians of all stripes, ritual pomp has been an essential way of affirming the myth of a people united behind an infallible leader. In 1933, at an elaborately staged Nazi rally in Nuremberg, a newly appointed chancellor Adolf Hitler addressed 250,000 Germans *(right)*. An even bigger rally the following year was chillingly immortalized by Leni Riefenstahl in her documentary *Triumph of the Will*.

LA GARRA DEL INVASOR ITALIANO PRETENDE ESCLAVIZARNOS

and the Nazi obsession with race (which led to the murder of six million Jews). This distinction helps to explain why, in the 1930s, so many intellectuals—from poets, like me, to physicists—flocked to their nations' communist parties. It also helps to explain why some avowedly anti-egalitarian (and incidentally anti-Semitic) intellectuals, most notably Ezra Pound, declared for fascism. Indeed, even leftists could feel fascism's dark allure—the temptation to claim the Superman's murderous privileges. We felt all the more righteous for resisting it.

The Great Depression engendered a sense that the capitalist system was doomed. In my homeland, England, as in other Western countries, spreading poverty and unemployment gave rise to talk of revolution; there were marches and riots. But in Germany, where I spent much of the early thirties, the chaos that culminated in Hitler's ascension was truly overwhelming. There, the economy had barely recovered from the nation's defeat in World War I (and the punitive reparations payments that followed) when the Depression hit. The hopelessly unpopular Weimar government stumbled from crisis to crisis, while the representatives of 29 parties howled at one another in the Reichstag. In the name of democracy, Chancellor Brüning governed undemocratically, by decree—yet he could not decree an end to the street battles between militants of the two fastest-growing parties, the Nazis and Communists. Formerly middle-class young women sold themselves on street corners, in front of restaurants where the rich dined in splendor. Virtually everyone saw him- or herself as a member of a political interest group. Hatreds among those groups flourished. For young writers like me and Christopher Isherwood (soon to be famous for his *Berlin Stories*), Germany's atmosphere was extraordinarily stimulating, and—with its vibrant avant-gardism in art, architecture, music, theater, even social relations—incomparably freer than that of our native country. But it was ominous, too. To many Western intellectuals Germany was a harbinger. Humanity, it seemed, faced two choices: the hell of fascism or the potential paradise of communism.

My own decision to embrace the latter hinged on several factors. I had read much of the Nazi literature and found it both brutal and cynical: Along with racism, anti-Semitism, and expansionist militarism, Nazi leaders openly embraced the Big Lie (as Goebbels called it) as an indispensible organizing tool. Meanwhile, I'd become entranced by the new Soviet films that were shown almost nightly in Berlin. Masterpieces like *Potemkin* spoke to my hunger for hope, beauty, and heroism, as well as to my modernist sensibilities. I attended political meetings and engaged in endless disputations in bars and cafés. And when a friend of Isherwood's returned from the Soviet Union burning with enthusiasm for Stalin's achievements, I began a process of conversion.

I HAD LONG HELD VAGUELY LEFTIST views, based on pity for the poor, sympathy with the oppressed, a desire for peace; if socialism "happened," I should accept it willingly. Now, however, a more analytical and active approach seemed in order. The world, my German experience had convinced me, was indeed divided into Marx's opposing camps of bourgeoisie and proletariat. Fascism, even if it called itself National Socialism, proposed to leave the means of production in the hands of the bourgeoisie, and to obliterate the proletariat's power as a class. The Nazis clearly hoped to attack the Soviet Union with backing from capitalist Britain and America. To prevent apocalyptic war—and the worldwide fascist tyranny that would likely follow—one must stand with the workers.

I became a Communist Party member in 1936, at the invitation of Harry Pollitt, head of the British chapter. He had read my book *Forward from Liberalism*, in which I'd argued (quite ineffectively, I later concluded) for a reconciliation between liberal notions of freedom and communist notions of social justice. Pollitt took issue with many points—he defended the Moscow show trials, for instance—but asked me to lend my voice to the antifascist struggle in Spain, where the civil war had just begun. It was during my travels in Spain, however, that my lingering reservations about communism (particularly communist morality) began to sharpen into opposition.

Spain was where fascism first met concerted armed resistance. In July 1936, when Franco's

The Spanish Civil War of 1936–39 was the century's first struggle that pitted a democratic republic against military forces backed by fascist Germany and Italy. (This Republican poster urges Spaniards to fight the "Italian invader who aims to enslave us.") Paradoxically, defense of that republic against Franco's Nationalist rebels was largely organized by fascism's hated enemy, the Soviet Union—itself a totalitarian power.

Nationalist forces attacked from Morocco, it was widely assumed that the Spanish Republic would surrender, as Italy had done, to the rightist rebels. People everywhere were astonished and inspired when the Spanish navy, portions of the army, and thousands of civilians rose to defend the democratic state. Italy and Germany sent arms, troops, and money to the Nationalists; the Soviet Union sent the Republicans arms and money, and (through the Comintern) organized an army of largely noncommunist volunteers from many lands, the International Brigades.

1930
1939

THE ROLE OF THE SOVIET UNION raises the question of whether the Spanish Civil War was not ultimately a conflict between two forms of totalitarianism. Yet to most of the Republic's supporters, the war symbolized nothing less than democracy heroically fighting for its life. And to many Marxists, Spain represented the hope for a more democratic, less totalitarian communism.

Republican ranks included anarchists, ethnic separatists, liberals, and independent intellectuals like André Malraux and George Orwell; the Communists presented themselves as unifiers. Too often, however, they enforced unity through bloodshed.

In July 1937, I attended the Communist-organized Writers' Congress in Madrid. The great dividing issue at the international gathering turned out to be André Gide's just-published *Retour de L'URSS,* an account of his recent, government-sponsored visit to the Soviet Union. Gide had found much to praise, but was also critical, particularly of the idolatry of Stalin. And he put on record the terror of persecution of those who, meeting with him in secret, dared to criticize the regime.

The Congress split between those who supported Gide in freely expressing his views, and those who denounced him as a "fascist monster" for supplying moral ammunition to Fascists who that very moment were shelling Madrid. The fight to build an equitable society in Russia, some argued, justified Stalin's iron-fisted measures, just as anti-fascism justified the Communists' fascistic tactics (against anarchists and other far-leftists) in Spain. I found myself drawn to the opposite argument—that tainted means would inevitably lead to polluted ends. And I was appalled by the obdurate refusal of more doctrinaire communists to acknowledge that "our side" (and not just Franco's) had committed atrocities. Returning to England, I let my Party ties lapse.

The idealism that led intellectuals to support the Soviet version of socialism became ever more difficult to sustain after 1939, when the Spanish Republic fell—at least partly because of the failure of communist strategy—and Moscow and Berlin signed their infamous nonaggression pact. Five months later, when Hitler invaded Poland, only capitalist Britain and France intervened. After that, the struggle against fascism was a matter not for individuals but for armies.

By 1945, Europe's expansionist fascist states had been defeated in a terrible world war, though less belligerent varieties of fascism persisted for decades in Spain and Portugal (and continue to thrive on other continents). Left-wing totalitarianism survived in Eastern Europe and the Soviet Union almost to the end of the century; it was vanquished there not by force of arms but by popular discontent with a system that never outgrew the "necessary" cruelty and deception of its creation. Far from withering away, the dictatorial state had evolved into a repressive monstrosity. When the clamp was loosened, under Gorbachev, communist society's pent-up pressures simply exploded.

One of the most curious political phenomena of recent years has been the convergence of the two types of totalitarianism. In the 1970s in Argentina, for example, Juan Perón, a disciple of Mussolini, inspired violent (and mutually opposed) left- *and* right-wing movements. And in post-Soviet Russia, former apparatchiks have flocked to a conservative, ultranationalist movement scarcely distinguishable from fascism. Perhaps the totalitarian impulse, the craving for absolute order in times of frightening chaos, transcends the philosophical differences—over who should own the means of production, over whether nation or class is paramount—that once made fascism and communism seem so fundamentally opposed. No immunization against political chaos has yet been found, and so nations return again and again to a drastic, and terribly destructive, cure. □

Totalitarianism thrived well past the 1930s. Here, in Christmas 1961, West Germans peer across the Berlin Wall—a barrier that had been raised a few months earlier by East Germany to keep its citizens in and the ideas of a pluralistic democracy out. Until 1989, when the wall fell (bringing down the East German regime with it), it was widely seen as an emblem of the world's division into communist and capitalist camps. The picture was complicated, however, by the persistence of right-wing totalitarian regimes—many of them propped up by the democratic powers as bulwarks against communism.

SACHS

"It was a long hard road from the adding machine of Pascal to the perforated card accounting machines of today."
—Vannevar Bush

STORY OF THE YEAR

The First Modern Computer

1 Led by electrical engineer Vannevar Bush, a team of scientists at the Massachusetts Institute of Technology began work on a "differential analyzer" in 1930. Put into use a year later, Bush's device—an incremental, yet crucial, step above mechanical adding machines and a precursor to electronic calculators—was the first modern analog computer.

Like the automobile or airplane, the computer is a device that scientists and mathematicians had pondered for years before gaining the technological means to put their ideas in motion. In the seventeenth century, French philosopher and scientist Blaise Pascal had envisioned an ingenious mechanical adding machine. Gottfried Wilhelm Baron von Leibniz, an eighteenth-century German philosopher and mathematician, designed a machine for solving algebraic equations. In the mid-nineteenth century, the British mathematician and inventor Charles Babbage (widely considered the father of the modern computer) came up with several machines that performed complicated mathematical calculations. And in the late-nineteenth century, Babbage's compatriot Lord Kelvin actually set out to build a steam-driven computing machine. Kelvin did make an analog device that predicted the tides, but his dream of a "differential analyzer" never materialized because of the insurmountable limitations of his Victorian hardware. Yet Bush, 50 years later, used the same basic design (first solving a torque problem) and built a computer that worked.

Bush's machine was a far cry from today's swift, silent, ultracompact computers; it covered several hundred square feet of floor space at MIT and consisted of hundreds of rotating steel rods that simulated numerical operations. Instead of a modern keyboard, programmers used screwdrivers and hammers to set it up for each new run. Although primitive, the device proved immediately useful; the machine could solve lengthy sets of differential equations and handle up to 18 independent variables at a time.

Bush *(left)* with his "mechanical mind." Its programmers worked "with a wrench in one hand and a gear in the other."

The next generation of computers, developed during World War II, used electronic technology rather than Bush's electro-mechanical methods. For instance, Colossus, a computer built in Bletchley Park, England, in the 1940s, used more than a thousand vacuum tubes to decipher German military codes. Eventually, the development of transistors, solid circuitry, and the microchip led to ever smaller, faster, and more powerful machines. **►1937.11**

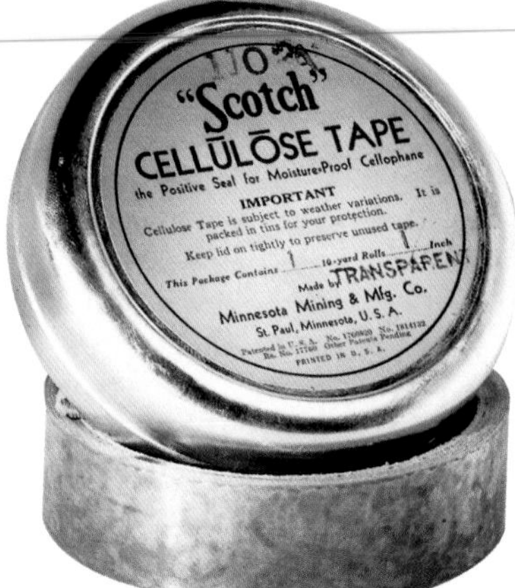

The earliest Scotch tape was packed in moisture-resistant tins.

TECHNOLOGY

A Tape for the Thrifty

2 Like most historical catastrophes, the Depression had its beneficiaries. The owners of the Minnesota Mining and Manufacturing Company (3M), for example, found a surprisingly broad market for a specialized new product it introduced in 1930—a transparent, adhesive cellulose tape. It was intended for sealing cellophane-wrapped goods but was soon rendered obsolete for that purpose when Du Pont perfected heat-sealing. By then, however, financially strapped Americans had discovered the usefulness of Scotch tape (the brand name referred to the Scots' reputed thriftiness) for mending torn clothes and curtains, fixing broken toys, holding decaying plaster to ceilings, and mending ripped currency. By 1935, when a dispenser was added, the product was an institution.

Demand for transparent tape spread and 3M soon faced competition from other manufacturers. But no matter who made the tape, the name Scotch was forever attached to it. **◄1908.M ►1938.6**

ECONOMICS

The Deepening Depression

3 Within a year of the Crash of '29, unemployment throughout the industrialized world had quadrupled to an estimated 21 million. Wages were plummeting, banks and businesses failing. For millions, the struggle for food, clothing, and shelter grew desperate. Shantytowns appeared in urban areas from Australia to Argentina. Homesteaders in Arkansas moved into caves, in California into sewer pipes. Once-affluent Britons patched their shoes with cardboard and gathered coal from railroad sidings for heat. Breadlines in major cities stretched for blocks. While relatively few actually starved to death (New York City counted 110 in 1934), malnutrition was rampant.

Social patterns reflected the spreading poverty. Marriage, divorce, and childbearing, being expensive, all declined—but suicide and desertion rates soared. Family and class roles were turned upside down: Jobless men stayed home while their wives and children worked (when they could) as domestics; bankers sold apples on the street. Small towns emptied as their populations took to the road in search of work. To ease competition for jobs, the United States expelled 400,000 citizens (both naturalized and American-born) of Mexican descent, and France deported as many Polish, Spanish, and Italian immigrants. Brazil relocated 40,000 unemployed urbanites to the countryside.

Those who lived through the Depression were transformed by it. Workers awoke from the torpor of the 1920s and staged militant

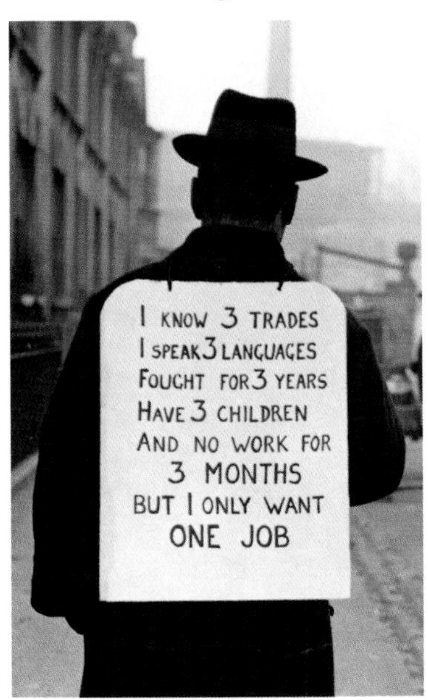

A jobless Briton mounts a one-man demonstration against the Depression.

strikes. Some of the jobless marched or rioted; others sank into apathy. Novelists became crusading journalists. Liberals, impressed by the apparent prosperity of the Soviet Union, became Marxists. And conservatives, fearing Bolshevism above all else, turned increasingly to fascism. **◄1929.1 ►1932.1**

ART & CULTURE: Books: ***As I Lay Dying*** **(William Faulkner);** ***The 42nd Parallel*** **(John Dos Passos);** ***The Revolt of the Masses*** **(José Ortega y Gasset);** ***Cimarron*** **(Edna Ferber) ... Music: "Georgia on My Mind" (Carmichael and Gorrell); "Body and Soul" (Green, Heyman, Sour, and Eyton); "On the Sunny Side of the Street" (McHugh and Fields);** ***Marosszék Dances*** **(Zoltán Kodály) ... Painting & Sculpture:**

"Let not my companions or the people at large be disturbed by my arrest, for it is not I but God who is guiding the movement."—**Mahatma Gandhi**

INDIA

Gandhi Marches for Salt

4 Completing a 200-mile march to the sea, Mahatma Gandhi arrived at Dandi, on the western coast of India, on April 6, 1930, and illegally harvested salt from the ocean. His richly symbolic act was a latter-day version of the Boston Tea Party, as the Raj maintained a monopoly on salt production and levied a hated tax on it. In defying the British government, Gandhi created an example of self-sufficiency.

Gandhi and fellow reformer Sarojini Naidu (the first woman president of the Indian National Congress) at the Gulf of Gambay.

His dramatic gesture—a response to the formation in 1927 of the Simon Commission, dictated by the Montagu-Chelmsford Act of 1919—launched a second nationwide civil disobedience campaign. In theory, the commission, an investigative body charged with evaluating British reforms in India, demonstrated Britain's goodwill toward India. But after the British Parliament failed to appoint a single Indian member to the commission, outraged leaders of the Indian National Congress rejected it, demanding for the first time full independence. (After independence, the date of that resolution, January 26, became Republic Day.)

The British tried to ignore Gandhi's salt protest, but they could not escape the groundswell of defiance it unleashed: picketing, marches, salt raids, boycotts of British goods, work stoppages, and, to Gandhi's dismay, riots. The government responded by imprisoning more than 60,000 Indians, including Gandhi, Nehru, and every other nationalist leader. Predictably, Gandhi's arrest intensified the wave of civil disobedience, and jail terms and beatings became badges of honor. Its authority severely tested, the government cracked down further in June. **◂1924.5 ▸1931.M**

THEATER

A Talent to Amuse

5 Playwright Noël Coward's best works are acid chronicles of British high life between the wars. The best of the best, *Private Lives*, opened in London on September 24, 1930, with Coward himself playing the male lead.

The play, which Coward wrote in a Shanghai hotel during a four-day bout with the flu, is a quicksilver series of nasty, witty duologues between a formerly married couple, Elyot and Amanda, who just happen to be honeymooning with new spouses at the same French hotel. (Amanda was played by Gertrude Lawrence and Victor, her twit-husband, by a young Laurence Olivier.) There is little plot and less depth, but such lines as "Strange how potent cheap music is" and "Certain women should be struck regularly, like gongs" do resonate with a kind of timeless quotability. And, as one critic observed, Elyot and Amanda's exhilarating and dangerous compatibility evokes a certain sadness.

Despite lukewarm reviews, *Private Lives* was such a hit that Coward, Lawrence, and Olivier brought it to Broadway the following year. It is constantly revived. **▸1934.V**

THE UNITED STATES

Smoot-Hawley: No Protection

6 Instead of cushioning the American economy against the Depression, 1930's Smoot-Hawley Tariff intensified the catastrophe at home and helped spread it worldwide. Tariffs on imported goods were raised from an (already high) average of 33 percent to an all-time high of 40 percent. More than a thousand economists, fearing a disastrous decline in international commerce, urged President Hoover *(caricatured above)* to veto the bill. But Hoover insisted that American industry—reeling from the stock-market crash of 1929—needed protection from "unfair" foreign competition.

The economists were right. The volume of world trade dropped from $2.9 billion a month in 1929 to less than $1 billion by 1933. The loss of exports helped depress production practically everywhere but the Soviet Union, exacerbating unemployment. Between 1930 and 1932, U.S. unemployment rose from three million to 13 million; by 1932, there were 30 million unemployed throughout the industrialized world. Far from a solution, protectionist tariffs were a big part of a devastating problem. **◂1929.1 ▸1932.1**

Noël Coward and Gertrude Lawrence in a performance of *Private Lives*.

BIRTHS

Chinua Achebe, Nigerian writer.

Edwin "Buzz" Aldrin, U.S. astronaut.

Neil Armstrong, U.S. astronaut.

Baudouin I, Belgian king.

Ornette Coleman, U.S. musician.

Sean Connery, U.K. actor.

Clint Eastwood, U.S. actor and filmmaker.

Jean-Luc Godard, French filmmaker.

Ted Hughes, U.K. poet.

Jasper Johns, U.S. painter.

Helmut Kohl, German chancellor.

Sandra Day O'Connor, U.S. jurist.

H. Ross Perot, U.S. business and political leader.

Harold Pinter, U.K. playwright.

Mobutu Sese Seko, Zairian president.

Stephen Sondheim, U.S. composer and lyricist.

Jean-Louis Trintignant, French actor.

Derek Walcott, West Indian poet.

Joanne Woodward, U.S. actress.

Ahmed Zaki Yamani, Saudi oil minister.

DEATHS

Edward Bok, U.S. editor.

Lon Chaney, U.S. actor.

Glenn H. Curtiss, U.S. aviator and inventor.

Herbert Dow, U.S. industrialist.

Arthur Conan Doyle, U.K. writer.

D.H. Lawrence, U.K. writer.

Vladimir Mayakovsky, Russian poet.

Mabel Normand, U.S. actress.

Miguel Primo de Rivera, Spanish fascist leader.

William Howard Taft, U.S. president.

Early Sunday Morning **(Edward Hopper);** ***Standing Woman*** **(Gaston Lachaise) ... Film:** ***All Quiet on the Western Front*** **(Lewis Milestone);** ***Morocco*** **(Josef von Sternberg);** ***Little Caesar*** **(Mervyn LeRoy);** ***Animal Crackers*** **(Victor Heerman, with the Marx Brothers);** ***The Golden Age*** **(Luis Buñuel) ... Theater:** ***Penny Arcade*** **(Marie Baumer);** ***As You Desire Me*** **(Luigi Pirandello) ... Radio:** ***Believe It or Not*** **(Robert L. Ripley).**

"What when drunk one sees in other women, one sees in Garbo sober."—**Critic Kenneth Tynan, on Greta Garbo**

NEW IN 1930

Plexiglas.

Pinball machine (Baffle Ball, created by David Gottlieb).

Blondie (by Chic Young).

Airline stewardess (United Airlines' Ellen Church).

Snickers candy bar.

Hostess Twinkies.

Sliced bread (Wonder Bread).

Flashbulbs.

IN THE UNITED STATES

▶AMERICAN GOTHIC—Grant Wood's austere painting, depicting a farm couple standing board straight and without expression in front of their Gothic-style farmhouse, created a sensation when it was exhibited in 1930 at the Art Institute of Chicago. Wood's models for this study of sturdy American rural stock were actually his sister and his dentist. Along with fellow midwesterner Thomas Hart Benton, Wood became part of the American Regionalist movement. ◂1908.4 ▸1942.17

▶WHERE IS JUDGE CRATER?—One of the great unsolved mysteries of New York politics began in August, when Joseph Crater, a Tammany Hall lawyer who'd been appointed in April to the New York State Supreme Court, abruptly disappeared without a trace. The judge, a well-known ladies' man, had interrupted a Maine vacation with his wife to go to New York City, where he gathered up some documents from his office, withdrew $5,000 from his bank account, and cashed in $16,000 worth of stocks. After dining with

The apotheosis of Art Deco architecture: New York's Chrysler Building. "It is the fulfillment in metal and masonry of a one-man dream," said a contemporary critic.

ARCHITECTURE

Aesthetics for Industry

7 Completed in 1930, William van Alen's 1,048-foot Chrysler Building was, for a brief moment, the tallest structure in the world. The building's Art Deco ornamentation—nickel-plated steel radiator caps and eagle-faced gargoyles—and its sky-piercing tower unabashedly promoted its owner, Walter P. Chrysler, along with the glories of capitalism. Indeed, the Art Deco style allowed American architects to dress up their skyscrapers like modern-day Parthenons, complete with pediments and friezes devoted to industry and progress. (A 1916 New York City zoning law enhanced the templelike effect by insisting that "skyscrapers," at a certain height, retreat from the street to allow the penetration of air and light. The result was the curious ziggurat shape of many of the buildings.)

At a height of 1,250 feet, the Empire State Building, completed in 1931, surpassed the Chrysler and was lauded for its lack of ornamentation and its maximization of profitable rental space. Eventually, the Great Depression brought an end to grandiose projects like Rockefeller Center, which was built in the thirties. Smaller Art Deco buildings, however, continued to flourish as a "knockout for pessimism" in places like Miami Beach and Hollywood. But the style petered out as business demands and World War II rendered it frivolous, outmoded, and too expensive. Architects like John M. Howells and Raymond Hood faded into obscurity as the rigid purity of the International Style, exemplified by the work of Le Corbusier, Mies van der Rohe, and Philip Johnson, shaped skylines from Frankfurt to Los Angeles for the next half-century. ◂1919.9 ▸1931.M

FILM

Garbo Talks

8 "The most eagerly and fearfully awaited cinema event" since the birth of the talkies was the way a critic characterized the New York opening of the sound screen version of Eugene O'Neill's hit play *Anna Christie* on March 14, 1930. On that day, Garbo talked.

For over two years, Metro-Goldwyn-Mayer had protected its greatest star, Greta Garbo, from the microphone. Early audio recording was low-fidelity and tricky; romantic idols with light voices or heavy accents could sound comical or incomprehensible. The Swedish-born Garbo, with her divine face and smoldering soul, was the world's favorite silent love goddess, steaming up theaters with *The Temptress, Flesh and the Devil,* and *Love.* But how would the former Stockholm shopgirl *sound?*

Garbo *(above, with Marie Dressler in* Anna Christie*)* successfully made the transition from silents to sound pictures.

In choosing O'Neill's drama about a Swedish-born, American-bred prostitute who falls for a sailor, MGM played it safe. Garbo enters a half hour into the picture, standing for an endless moment in the door of a waterfront saloon, her face an emblem of exhaustion and disgust. She shuffles to a table, collapses into a chair, and, in a husky, world-weary, Scandinavian voice says, "Gimme a visky. Ginger ale on the side. And don' be stingy, babee." One film historian quipped, "The world breathed again."

Garbo has been called the screen's greatest star and (more arguably) its greatest actress. Still, despite success with *Grand Hotel* (in which she pined, "I want to be alone") and *Camille*, Garbo proved too exotic for the down-to-earth Depression, and by the mid-1930s she had lost her American audience. She retired from the screen in 1941 and divided her time between New York and Switzerland until her death in 1990. ◂1921.10 ▸1941.M

LITERATURE

Eliot's Worthy Successor

9 The dominant figure in English-language poetry in the disillusioned, decadent 1920s was T.S. Eliot, chronicler of *The Waste Land.* But as the Depression deepened and the international mood changed, alienation and angst increasingly gave way to radical politics. Eliot withdrew into religion and conservatism, but a new poetic heir became apparent in 1930 when W.H. Auden's first book, *Poems*, was published by Faber & Faber (where it was edited by Eliot).

Witty, moving, philosophically profound, Auden's poems, like Eliot's, drew on a dazzling array of sources—Anglo-Saxon verse, Restoration court lyrics, music-hall ballads, Byron, Yeats, Rilke, even Eliot himself. But Auden was also a Marxist—albeit a somewhat equivocal one (Freud and Nietzsche were equally important in shaping his analysis of social ills). A member of a circle of leftist poets—most notably his former Oxford classmates Cecil Day Lewis and Stephen Spender—Auden packed the ten volumes of verse he published over the next decade with references to the era's pressing issues. "In the nightmare of the dark," he wrote, "All the dogs of Europe bark/And

SPORTS: Baseball: World Series, Philadelphia Athletics defeat St. Louis Cardinals, 4–2 ... Boxing: Max Schmeling defeats Jack Sharkey on a foul in the world heavyweight championship ... Horse Racing: Gallant Fox wins Triple Crown.

"There are no schools, only individuals."—**Jean Cocteau**

the living nations wait/Each sequestered in its hate."

A stint as an ambulance driver during the Spanish Civil War led to Auden's own disillusionment, and by the early forties his career had begun to mirror Eliot's in odd ways. Eliot, an American, had moved to England and converted to Anglicanism; Auden, an Englishman, moved to the United States and became engrossed in Protestant theology. Like Eliot, Auden lost many followers after finding religion. But he, too, became a grand old man of letters, molding America's taste in poetry as a critic and as editor of the Yale Younger Poets series. From the time of Eliot's death in 1965, until his own, in 1973, Auden was regarded by many as the greatest living poet in the language. **◂1922.9 ▸1946.11**

FILM

Jean of All Trades

10 Master avant-gardist in a host of media, Jean Cocteau turned to film—the art form for which he's best remembered—in 1930. Like much of his work, *The Blood of a Poet* dispenses with narrative logic, weaving dreamlike images into a meditation on the creative process. The "poet" of the film's title (really a painter) draws a portrait whose mouth begins to move; when he wipes it off in a panic, the mouth clings to his hand and speaks. Transferred to a statue, it commands him to walk through a mirror. The poet's adventures behind the looking glass include two suicides and a resurrection.

Although Cocteau's films (particularly *Beauty and the Beast* and *Orpheus*), novels *(Les Enfants terribles)*, plays *(La Voix humaine)*, and paintings are often considered masterpieces of surrealism, he disdained the surrealists as political dogmatists and rejected all artistic labels. A self-taught genius who barely finished high school, Cocteau had his first triumph with the ballet *Parade* (1917), for which he enlisted an extraordinary group of collaborators: Sergei Diaghilev as producer, Léonide Massine as choreographer, Erik Satie as composer, and Pablo Picasso as designer. It was Diaghilev who dared the young librettist to "astonish me!"—a phrase that remained Cocteau's motto up until his death in 1963. **◂1918.12 ▸1959.7**

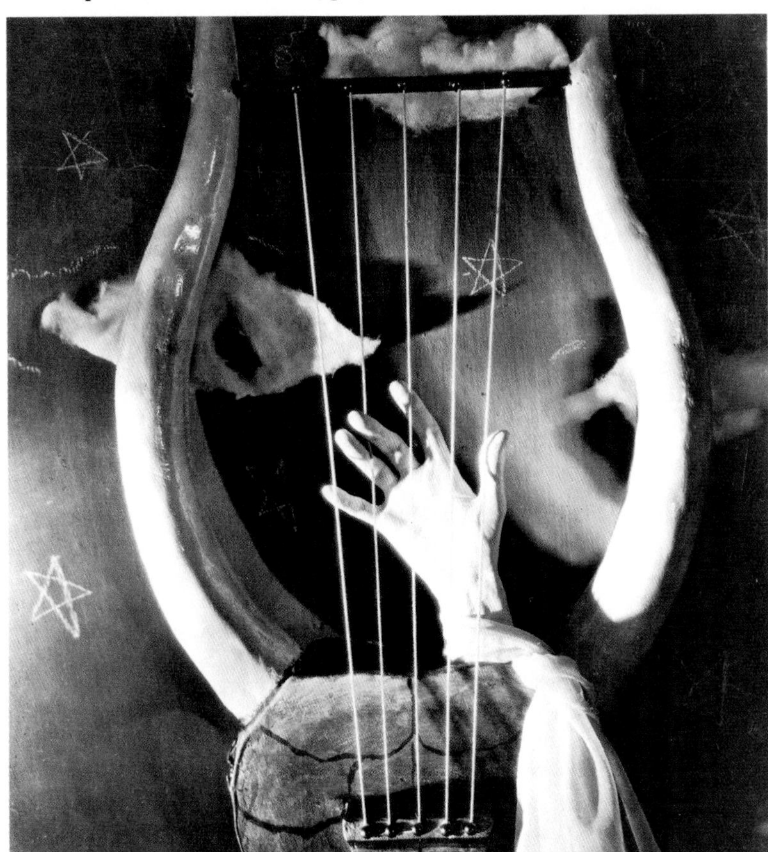

In this still from *The Blood of a Poet*, a cinematic depiction of Cocteau's inner life, a disembodied hand plays an orphic lyre.

LITERATURE

Sam Spade, Private Eye

11 As pioneered by Agatha Christie and Arthur Conan Doyle, the classic British detective story was fundamentally optimistic: once the mystery was solved, everything returned to normal. That genre was turned on its head by the American writer Dashiell Hammett, whose coldly cynical novels evoke a gritty, pitiless world where normalcy doesn't exist and no mystery is ever truly solved. In 1930, with *The Maltese Falcon*, Hammett introduced his most famous character, a laconic, world-weary "private eye" named Sam Spade.

The book's title refers to a statuette that is stolen and restolen. The double crosses multiply until the only honest person left is the proto-existentialist hero. Explaining to beautiful Brigid O'Shaughnessy why he must turn her in for murder, Spade cites professional honor, against which, he says, "All we've got is the fact that maybe you love me and maybe I love you." The operative word is *maybe*. The only certainty in a world awash in deceit is one's personal code.

The Maltese Falcon, as well as his 1932 novel *The Thin Man* made Hammett, in the words of playwright Lillian Hellman (his companion of many years), "the hottest thing in Hollywood and New York." *The Maltese Falcon* was made into a movie three times, the last and most famous version starring Humphrey Bogart. *The Thin Man* sparked a five-movie series starring William Powell and Myrna Loy as Nick and Nora Charles, a couple of witty, martini-imbibing sophisticates who also solve crimes.

A passionate leftist during the thirties and forties, Hammett went to prison for six months in 1951 for refusing to testify before the House Un-American Activities Committee—an experience that, along with his habitual heavy drinking and smoking, left him frail and haggard until his death in 1961. **◂1920.5 ▸1951.V**

IN THE UNITED STATES

friends, he stepped into a taxicab and was never seen again. Some newspapers linked his disappearance to an investigation of corruption in city government.

▶BOOTLEGGERS—The term "bootlegger" may have originated in the American frontier custom of hiding bottles of illegal liquor in boot tops. The hiding place and name were also popular during the Civil War. But the practice itself hit a new high in 1930. On February 10, 158 people from 31 crime organizations were arrested in Chicago as part of a major bootlegging operation that sold more than seven million gallons of whiskey to speakeasies all over the country, with a gross value of $50 million. But in May, the Supreme Court made Prohibition harder to enforce by ruling that buying liquor did not violate the Constitution. **◂1923.5**

▶JONES'S GRAND SLAM—On the last hole of the 1930 U.S. Amateur championship, Atlanta lawyer and amateur golfer Robert Tyre "Bobby" Jones took out his favorite putter, "Calamity Jane," and made golfing history by becoming the first player ever to win the Grand Slam—the Open and Amateur in the U.S.

and Britain. Afterward, Jones retired from tournament play without ever going professional. **◂1920.6 ▸1964.M**

▶THEN THERE WERE NINE—A 24-year-old amateur astronomer, Clyde Tombaugh, hired by the Lowell Observatory in Flagstaff, Arizona, to search for a ninth planet that astronomers had postulated to exist beyond Neptune, got lucky on February 18. After only a year of checking the photos taken by an astronomical camera attached to the telescope at Lowell, Tombaugh detected the "dim star" that was Pluto, moving across the constellation Gemini on its 248-year orbit around the sun. **◂1929.9 ▸1963.11**

POLITICS & BUSINESS: GNP: $91.1 billion ... U.S. population: 123,202,624 ... U.S. emigration exceeds immigration for the first time ... Over 1,300 banks close ... Federal unemployment census reports 4.5 million out of work; government creates a Committee for Unemployment Relief ... United Airlines, Transcontinental and Western Air (later TWA), and American Airways (later Airlines) founded.

"His words go like an arrow to their target; he touches each private wound ... liberating the mass unconscious, expressing its innermost aspirations, telling it what it most wants to hear."—**Otto Strasser, an exiled German journalist, on his former associate Adolf Hitler**

AROUND THE WORLD

▶ALLIES QUIT RHINELAND—In June, the last Allied forces (by then only French) left the Rhineland—five years ahead of the Versailles Treaty's schedule. The early withdrawal was a milestone in the short-lived normalization of German-Allied relations after World War I. ◀1919.1

▶VON STERNBERG'S ANGEL—One of film's most famous collaborations began in 1930, when Josef von Sternberg directed Marlene Dietrich in

Der blaue Engel. **So convincing was Dietrich's portrayal of the amoral cabaret singer Lola Lola that the character came to exemplify Dietrich herself. When the Berlin-born actress arrived in Hollywood later in the year, Paramount (which released an English version of *The Blue Angel*) undertook to make her a star equal to MGM's Garbo. ◀1930.8**

▶PASSFIELD WHITE PAPER—Arab riots against the Palestinian Jews prompted Palestine, a British mandate, to launch two successive inquiries in 1930. Both revealed Arabs' fears of losing their land if Jewish immigration continued, and both recommended imposing restrictions on Jewish immigration and land acquisition. The British government's Passfield White Paper then urged this policy, but Britain was forced to back down after an outcry by Palestinian Jews and world Zionist leaders. ◀1929.7 ▶1937.12

▶CATHOLIC CONTRACEPTION—On December 30, Pope Pius XI issued his encyclical concerning Christian marriage. Birth control was declared "an offense against the law of God and of nature, incurring the guilt of a grave sin." Catholics wishing to avoid conception were restricted to total abstinence or periodic abstinence (i.e., refraining from intercourse when the woman is known to be ovulating). ▶1968.M

GERMANY

Nazis Win Big

12 Just two years after gaining only twelve seats in the Reichstag (parliament), the Nazis polled a whopping 6.5 million votes in Germany's 1930 national elections, taking 107 out of 577 seats and becoming the nation's second-largest party. The change in Nazi fortunes can be attributed to the Great Depression.

Hitler had been trying since his release from prison in 1924 to take over Germany by legal means. But the nation's growing prosperity had made extremes of both right *and* left less alluring to voters. The Nazis won a majority in the Bavarian legislature in 1928, but remained a minor party nationwide.

Then prosperity (built largely on U.S. credit) vanished. And with the Depression came an epidemic of rage unseen since the days of hyperinflation. The Communist Party enjoyed a resurgence, but the Nazis—appealing not to a single class, but to *national* pride, resentments, and fears—had a far broader appeal. The German *Volk* (people) were said to be the highest expression of the superior "Aryan race." The will of the *Volk* was embodied in the *Führer* (leader); the state should be a machine for carrying out his orders. Democracy was a sham—but Marxism, with its promotion of internationalism and class conflict, was downright diabolical. Like the world financial system that had ruined Germany, said the Nazis, all leftist movements were created by the Jews, the incarnation of evil. The *Volk* must rid itself of Jews and other "aliens," and gather its brethren in neighboring lands into a "greater Germany."

Except for its avowed anti-Semitism (a widespread prejudice, exploited by Nazi leaders), Nazism resembled Italy's Fascism. Like the Fascists, the Nazis exalted militarism and used uniformed strong-arm squads to suppress opponents. Both promised social justice (for the majority), an end to parliamentary paralysis, a return to national greatness—and a savior. To more and more Germans, the hypnotic, fiery-tongued Hitler seemed to fit the bill. **◀1929.11 ▶1932.2**

Hitler and his principal lieutenants in a rare early photo (discovered after the war in the photo album of a follower).

SPORTS

World Cup Soccer

13 What is probably the most coveted trophy in modern sports, the World Cup in soccer, was introduced inauspiciously in July 1930 with a small tournament in Montevideo, Uruguay, involving only 13 nations. For the host Uruguayans, however, the championship game was a matter of high consequence: A crowd of 90,000 (many of whom arrived six hours early) jammed Montevideo's yet-unfinished Centenary Stadium to watch their country's 1924 and '28 Olympic champions rally from behind to triumph 4–2 over their Argentine rivals. The Uruguayan government proclaimed a national holiday in honor of the victory; in Buenos Aires, the Uruguayan consulate was stoned.

The World Cup competition had been created two years earlier by the Fédération Internationale de Football Association (FIFA) as a way for amateurs and professionals alike to compete internationally. (The only other international soccer competition was in the Olympics, off-limits to pro players.) Initially, just five countries outside of South America participated in World Cup play: the United States, France, Yugoslavia, Romania, and Belgium. Two tournaments later, in 1938 (the competition is held every four years), the roster of participating countries had grown to 36.

Interrupted by World War II, the tournament was not played again until 1950. The modern World Cup involves qualifying tournaments that cut the field to 22 teams, plus the host nation and the reigning champion. **▶1958.11**

SCIENCE

A Smashing Invention

14 Ernest Lawrence, a physicist at the University of California, Berkeley, was only 29 when, in 1930, he unveiled a solution to one of his discipline's thorniest technical problems: how to accelerate a subatomic particle to a speed sufficient to penetrate a tightly bound atomic nucleus and break it apart, so scientists could study its structure and better understand the nature of radioactivity. Previous experiments had used a linear accelerator, developed by British physicist John Douglas Cockcroft and his Irish colleague Ernest T.S. Walton, in which a particle was hurled along with the aid of one or more explosive bursts of energy. The biggest problem with the device was that it had to be tremendously long to achieve enough power to cause a particle to approach the speed of light.

Lawrence's idea was simple. Instead of sending a particle along a linear track, the new accelerator would spin it in circles. Energy would be applied in smaller, incremental doses in a magnetic field set up between two electrodes, rather than in short, powerful bursts; each magnetic-field push would cause the particle to whirl about faster and faster.

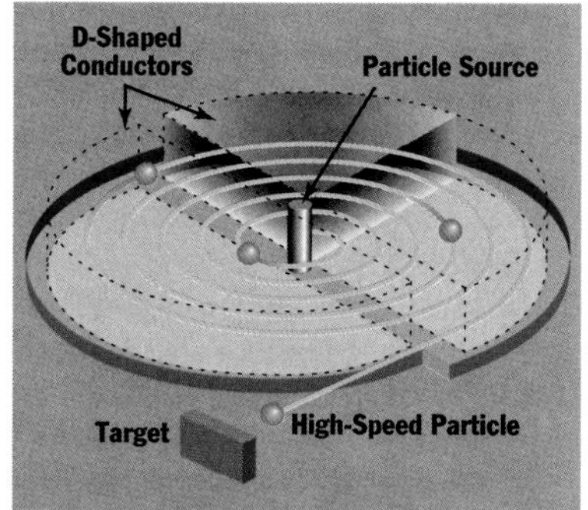

Lawrence dubbed his atom smasher the cyclotron because the particles moved in a circular path—a crucial innovation.

In September 1930, the cyclotron, as the device was called, succeeded in accelerating a proton to the speed of 37,000 miles per second, one-fifth the speed of light. Quickly dubbed the "atom smasher," it became as essential to the burgeoning field of subatomic physics as the microscope to microbiology or the telescope to astronomy. Lawrence later played a leading role in the development of the atomic bomb. **◀1919.5 ▶1932.10**

NOBEL PRIZES: Peace: Nathan Söderblom (Swedish; ecumenical movement) ... Literature: Sinclair Lewis (U.S.; novelist) ... Chemistry: Hans Fischer (German; synthesis of hemin) ... Medicine: Karl Landsteiner (U.S.; blood types) ... Physics: Chandrasekhara Raman (Indian; diffusion of light).

A VOICE FROM 1930

An Ode to Engineering

From *The Bridge*, by Hart Crane, 1930

If American expatriate T.S. Eliot was the first major poet to link the imagery of the modern, industrialized world to the myths, philosophies, and passions of the past, Hart Crane was the first to do so with the optimistic pioneer spirit for which America is famous. The Bridge, *published in 1930, is Crane's magnum opus—and one of the century's greatest poems in any language. Some 75 pages long, it uses the Brooklyn Bridge as a symbol of the way human creativity connects the present to antiquity. (The excerpt at right, an ode to the mighty span, is from the "Proem," or preface.) Characters in* The Bridge *include Columbus, Walt Whitman (whose poetry also expresses a uniquely American exuberance), Emily Dickinson, burlesque dancers, office workers, hoboes, and Native Americans. But Crane's enthusiasm for modernity did not save him from despair: In 1932, the 32-year-old poet jumped to his death from a ship in the Caribbean.* **◄1922.9 ►1936.M**

Proem: To Brooklyn Bridge

How many dawns, chill from his rippling rest
The seagull's wings shall dip and pivot him,
Shedding white rings of tumult, building high
Over the chained bay waters Liberty—

Then, with inviolate curve, forsake our eyes
As apparitional as sails that cross
Some page of figures to be filed away;
—Till elevators drop us from our day …

I think of cinemas, panoramic sleights
With multitudes bent toward some flashing scene
Never disclosed, but hastened to again,
Foretold to other eyes on the same screen;—

And Thee, across the harbor, silver-paced
As though the sun took step of thee, yet left
Some motion ever unspent in thy stride,—
Implicitly thy freedom staying thee!

Out of some subway scuttle, cell or loft
A bedlamite speeds to thy parapets,
Tilting there momently, shrill shirt ballooning,
A jest falls from the speechless caravan.

Down Wall, from girder into street noon leaks,
A rip-tooth of the sky's acetylene;
All afternoon the cloud-flown derricks turn …
Thy cables breathe the North Atlantic still.

And obscure as that heaven of the Jews,
Thy guerdon … Accolade thou dost bestow
Of anonymity time cannot raise:
Vibrant reprieve and pardon thou dost show.

O harp and altar, of the fury fused,
(How could mere toil align thy choiring strings)
Terrific threshold of the prophet's pledge,
Prayer of pariah, and the lover's cry,—

Again the traffic lights that skim thy swift
Unfractioned idiom, immaculate sigh of stars,
Beading thy path—condense eternity:
And we have seen night lifted in thine arms.

Under thy shadow by the piers I waited;
Only in darkness is thy shadow clear.
The City's fiery parcels all undone,
Already snow submerges an iron year …

O Sleepless as the river under thee,
Vaulting the sea, the prairies' dreaming sod,
Unto us lowliest sometime sweep, descend
And of the curveship lend a myth to God.

Crane wanted his poem to be illustrated with *The Bridge* *(above)*, an oil painting by Naples-born American modernist Joseph Stella. Unable to obtain reproduction rights, Crane's publisher opted instead for photographs by Walker Evans.

"We know that if the Credit Anstalt ... were driven into liquidation an unprecedented catastrophe would sweep over the Austrian workers and salaried employees."—**Social Democratic Party leader Otto Bauer**

STORY OF THE YEAR

Credit Anstalt Collapses

1 Austria had lost its empire in World War I, but Vienna remained the financial capital of Central Europe. So when the Credit Anstalt, the nation's biggest bank, failed in the spring of 1931, the impact rocked Germany as well. The result for both countries was an ominous strengthening of the antidemocratic right.

Austria's banking system had been shaky even before the Crash of 1929, thanks mostly to bad management. When banks fell, they were simply absorbed by richer institutions. But after the Credit Anstalt swallowed a debt-ridden rival, it found that the Depression had made digestion impossible. Facing insolvency, it sought government help. With 70 percent of Austrian trade and industry dependent on the bank, the situation was desperate. But the government itself was broke.

While federal officials scrambled in search of aid from abroad, nervous depositors in the Credit Anstalt and other Austrian banks rushed to withdraw their funds. Fear spread to Germany, sparking a run on the banks there. In July, the giant Danat-Bank went under; other bank closings followed before the German government belatedly declared a two-day bank holiday. (In fact, most of the institutions remained shuttered for weeks.) Millions lost their life savings. Meanwhile, the Austrians had obtained some international loans and a debt moratorium from foreign creditors. But in exchange for French cooperation, Austria had to cancel its planned customs union with Germany—dashing both countries' best hope for economic recovery.

The collapse of Credit Anstalt in Austria and the Danat-Bank at home had Berliners rushing to withdraw their funds.

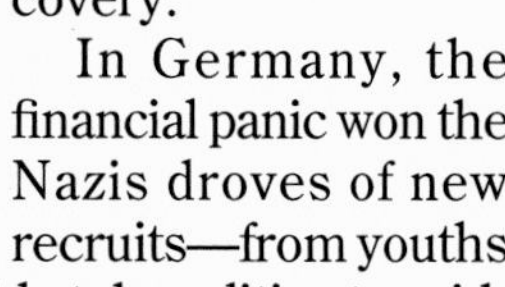

In Germany, the financial panic won the Nazis droves of new recruits—from youths embittered by the failures of old-style politics to middle-class conservatives fearful that those failures would usher in a communist revolution. In Austria, although the crisis united Parliament behind austerity measures, it emboldened a regional Heimatbloc (fascist) leader, Dr. Walter Pfrimer, to stage a putsch. In September, his paramilitary troops marched on Graz, but the rising was too poorly organized to succeed. Yet the active or passive support of many civil and police officials—and the army's lackadaisical response—revealed just how vulnerable Austria's democracy would be to a more determined drive. The putschists went unpunished, and were allowed to take their weapons home. Less than two years later, a dictator was running the country, having accomplished legally what Pfrimer failed to do by force. ◄1930.12 ►1932.2

CHINA

Marxism Goes Rural

2 Late in 1931, 80,000 students rioted in Nanjing, capital of Chiang Kai-shek's Nationalist government, to protest the general's policy of nonresistance to Japan's seizure of Manchuria. Capitalizing on Chiang's problems, the leaders of a separatist regime in Canton, Wang Jingwei and Sun Fo, endorsed resistance (while actually making overtures to Tokyo). In December, Chiang *(above)* abdicated to Sun Fo.

Chiang's move was an elaborate ruse. In retirement, he still commanded the support of his army (China's largest), several provincial governments, and the minister of finance (T.V. Soong, Chiang's brother-in-law), who deliberately left the treasury in a shambles. Hamstrung from the beginning, Sun Fo's government was doomed. A month after leaving, Chiang, his indispensability affirmed, returned to unprecedented power.

Meanwhile, Mao Zedong, the man who would become Chiang's archrival in the epic struggle to shape modern China, had strengthened his own hand. Operating in the inland Jiangxi province, Mao repulsed a series of anti-Communist offensives by Chiang's Nationalists in the winter and spring of 1931. The victories lent credibility to "Marxism in the mountains," Mao's homegrown rural communism. Mao's system was a near-heretical deviation from the urban proletarian ideology of Marx and Lenin, but its inarguable success impelled the traditional, Shanghai-based Central Committee of the Chinese Communist Party to reconsider its policies.

In November, on the 14th anniversary of Lenin's revolution, the CCP elected Mao Chairman of the first Soviet Republic of China. The wishful "Republic" described only a few dozen minuscule Communist bastions in south central China; of real significance was Mao's ascendancy. Slowly, and with profound difficulty, the balance of Chinese Communist power was shifting from the city to the mountains, from Moscow-trained theoreticians to a native activist. ◄1927.2 ►1931.4

THE SOVIET UNION

Silencing the Intelligentsia

3 As Stalin solidified his command of the Communist Party, he imposed ever-stiffer penalties on dissent. By 1931 the revolution had entered a period of conservative retreat. The state was now to be revered, traditional values embraced. To ensure conformity, the dictator employed a new trick: He loosed his secret police, once used primarily against the opposition, on the entire society, including the Party itself. In this totalitarian crackdown, an inclination to formulate opinions became a deadly liability. Artists and intellectuals were silenced. "There isn't a single thinking adult in this country," observed the novelist Boris Pilnyak, "who hasn't thought he might get shot." (Pilnyak was shot in 1938.)

During the early, promise-filled years of the revolution, there occurred a brilliant artistic flowering in Russia. Poets like Anna Akhmatova, Osip Mandelstam, and Vladimir Mayakovsky experimented with new forms and voices; novelists like Pilnyak and Isaac Babel wrote strong, honest books; film director Sergei Eisenstein explored the possibilities of his young medium. Some of these artists, notably Akhmatova, were suspicious of Communism, but willing to give it a chance. Others, including Mayakovsky, Mandelstam, and Eisenstein,

One of Stalin's targets: poet Anna Akhmatova, in a portrait by N.I. Altman.

ART & CULTURE: Books: ***Hatter's Castle*** **(A.J. Cronin);** ***Sanctuary*** **(William Faulkner);** ***The Brown Decades*** **(Lewis Mumford) ... Music: "All of Me" (Marks and Simons); "Lady of Spain" (Tilsley, Damerell, Evans, and Hargreaves); "Mood Indigo" (Ellington and Bigard);** ***Ionization*** **(Edgard Varèse) ... Painting & Sculpture:** ***The Persistence of Memory*** **(Salvador Dali);** ***Portrait of Frida and Diego*** **(Frida Kahlo) ...**

"The nucleus of the deuterium atom is at present one of the most delightful playthings for scientists."
—Harold Urey, in the *Columbia University Quarterly*

were unabashedly enthusiastic. By the late 1920s Stalin had pressed art into the service of the state, aborting the renaissance. Flat, sentimental, officially sanctioned "Soviet realism" became the only acceptable style. Artists who resisted, like Mandelstam, often disappeared. Others, including Mayakovsky and Sergei Yesenin, Russia's "last village poet," were terrorized by secret police and driven to suicide.

Those who escaped death did so by adopting views not naturally their own, or remaining silent. Akhmatova, one of Russia's greatest poets, was denounced as a "harlot nun," and "alien to the Soviet people," and forbidden to publish for nearly 20 years. Secretly, she kept writing, memorializing the despairing Russian people in *Requiem*, her masterpiece.
◂1929.4 ▸1932.8

This U.S. cartoon lambasted Japan for its failure to abide by international treaties.

JAPAN
Invasion of Manchuria

4 With the occupation of Manchuria in 1931, Japan initiated a chain of events that culminated in world war. The fateful invasion of China's northeast territory was launched in retaliation for the bombing, allegedly by Chinese troops, of a piece of Japan's South Manchuria Railway. (Japan had gained treaty rights to the railroad and its defense in 1905, spoils of the Russo-Japanese War.) The railroad bombing, however, was merely a pretext: Japan had long eyed the relatively underpopulated and resource-rich Manchuria as a source of raw materials and an outpost for the steadily growing Japanese population.

Immediately after the September bombing of the railroad at Mukden, in southern Manchuria, the Japanese Kwantung Army, charged with policing the line, marched on Mukden. It captured the Chinese barracks and commandeered the city. The invasion was undertaken without the official consent of either the military authorities in Tokyo or the Japanese civilian government. Facing only nominal resistance from Zhang Xueliang, the Chinese marshal responsible for defending Manchuria, the Kwantung forces rapidly advanced northward. Within days Japan had seized most of the cities in the Manchurian provinces of Liaoning and Kirin, situated to the north and west of Korea (then a Japanese colony).

Zhang, it was revealed, had been ordered by Chiang Kai-shek, leader of the Chinese Nationalist government, to concede his territory to the Japanese aggressors. Advised Chiang, "At this time we ought to observe strict discipline, absolute procedures, in order not to give the Japanese a pretext." The general apparently believed passivity would strengthen his appeal to the League of Nations. (Also, he did not command enough military strength to win against Tokyo.) Indeed, the commission sent to China by the League to investigate Chiang's complaint denounced the Japanese invasion. But if Chiang expected stronger medicine, he was disappointed. The League, demonstrating its inherent weakness, failed to adopt any sanctions whatsoever. The Japanese territorial gains, though roundly excoriated, were allowed to stand. **◂1929.14 ▸1932.5**

SCIENCE
The Heaviness of Hydrogen

5 In the century's first decades, scientists watched as one truism after another concerning atomic structure was toppled. One of physics' most cherished pieces of dogma—that a hydrogen atom consists of a single electron whirling about a nucleus that contains a single proton—gave way in 1931 when Harold C. Urey, a Columbia University chemist, demonstrated that approximately one hydrogen atom in 5,000 also contains a neutron that effectively doubles its weight.

Since regular hydrogen boils at 13.9° Kelvin (–259° C), while the heavier variety boils at 18.6° K, Urey was able to dissipate (through evaporation) the lighter hydrogen by maintaining a temperature just below the higher boiling point. What remained was a concentrated sample of the new substance, dubbed deuterium.

While deuterium was hardly the first isotope (an isotope has the same number of protons as its corresponding atom, but a different number of neutrons) to be discovered, the fact that it involved the most elementary, common atom in existence was extraordinary. Deuterium led to the discovery of an even rarer hydrogen isotope called tritium, which occurs in about one hydrogen atom per 10 billion and consists of a proton, an electron, and two neutrons. The two substances subsequently emerged as the basic ingredients of the hydrogen, or fusion, bomb. The isotopes fuse to form a helium atom consisting of two protons, two electrons, and two neutrons; the mass lost in the process is converted to the energy that gives the H-bomb its devastating force.
◂1919.5 ▸1932.10

Combined with oxygen, deuterium yields "heavy water."

BIRTHS

Alvin Ailey, Jr., U.S. choreographer.

Carlos Castaneda, Brazilian-U.S. anthropologist.

James Dean, U.S. actor.

E.L. Doctorow, U.S. novelist.

Mikhail Gorbachev, U.S.S.R. political leader.

John Le Carré, U.K. novelist.

Mickey Mantle, U.S. baseball player.

Willie Mays, U.S. baseball player.

Toni Morrison, U.S. writer.

Rupert Murdoch, Australian-U.S. publisher.

Mike Nichols, U.S. filmmaker.

Dan Rather, U.S. broadcast journalist.

Bhagwan Shree Rajneesh, Indian religious leader.

Willie Shoemaker, U.S. jockey.

Desmond Tutu, South African religious and political leader.

Barbara Walters, U.S. broadcast journalist.

Tom Wolfe, U.S. writer.

Boris Yeltsin, Russian president.

DEATHS

Bix Beiderbecke, U.S. musician.

Arnold Bennett, U.K. writer.

Thomas Alva Edison, U.S. inventor.

Daniel Chester French, U.S. sculptor.

Kahlil Gibran, Lebanese-U.S. writer.

Frank Harris, Irish-U.S. writer.

Vachel Lindsay, U.S. poet.

Thomas Lipton, U.K. tea merchant.

Nellie Melba, Australian singer.

Anna Pavlova, Russian ballet dancer.

Knute Rockne, U.S. football coach.

Film: *Cimarron* (Wesley Ruggles); *City Lights* (Charles Chaplin); *Dracula* (Tod Browning, with Bela Lugosi); *M* (Fritz Lang); *The Champ* (King Vidor); *Tabu* (Murnau and Flaherty) ... Theater: *Mourning Becomes Electra* (Eugene O'Neill); *The Barretts of Wimpole Street* (Rudolf Besier); *Of Thee I Sing* (George and Ira Gershwin, Kaufman and Ryskind) ... Radio: *The Eddie Cantor Show*.

"I'm glad we didn't use the omelet."—**James Cagney, on his pushing a grapefruit into costar Mae Clarke's face in *The Public Enemy***

NEW IN 1931

George Washington Bridge in New York City (world's longest suspension bridge to date).

Alka-Seltzer.

Jehovah's Witnesses (formerly the International Bible Students' Association).

Bisquick biscuit mix.

Dick Tracy ("Plainclothes Tracy" in the *Chicago Tribune*).

Clairol hair dye.

Electric razor (Schick).

New Delhi, India.

IN THE UNITED STATES

▶**THE SOCIAL WORKER**—Jane Addams was awarded the 1931 Nobel Peace Prize in recognition of a lifetime of social service, as well as her efforts to bring about international peace. Hull House, the settlement house Addams established in 1889 in an impoverished section of Chicago, was considered the best educational and social service organization in America.

▶**TALLEST BUILDING**—President Hoover pressed a button in Washington on April 30, and the lights went on in Manhattan's Empire State Building—at a Depression-defying 1,250 feet high (including a mooring mast for dirigibles). Aided by some extra altitude from a TV broadcasting antenna, the Art

Deco structure retained its place as the world's tallest building until 1972. ◂1930.7

▶**NAUGHTY NEVADA**—In an effort to raise revenue, the Nevada legislature legalized gambling and passed the nation's most liberal residency requirement (which facilitated "quickie" divorces). The state began to prosper from a steady stream of transients—

1931

LITERATURE

Buck's Chinese Epic

6 Although China produced brilliant indigenous writers like Lu Xun, that land became known to the rest of the world largely through the novels of a woman from West Virginia. Raised in China by missionary parents, Pearl S. Buck derived the engrossing style of *The Good Earth*, published in 1931, from the King James version of the Bible and from Chinese sagas she enjoyed in her youth.

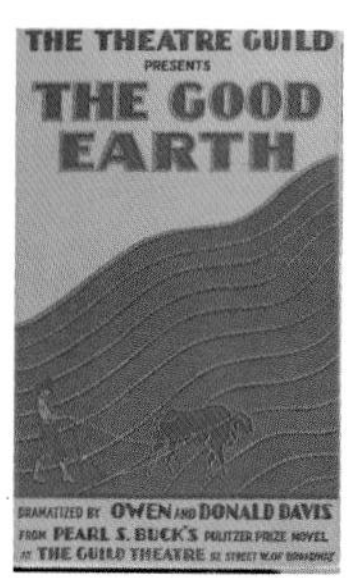

The epic, first in a trilogy tracing the lives of the industrious peasant Wang Lung and his descendants, was immensely popular, but some critics claimed Buck's work misrepresented Chinese culture. She refuted such charges in print and, indirectly, in her Nobel lecture on the Chinese novel, delivered after she received the 1938 prize for literature.

Her receipt of the Nobel—she was the first American woman to get it—was controversial, with detractors arguing that no female (except, maybe, Willa Cather) deserved it and that Buck, still in her 40s, was neither old enough nor prolific enough to have earned it. But at a time of Japanese aggression against China—and mounting discord throughout the world—her championing of humanitarian causes put her squarely in line with the intentions Alfred Nobel had when he endowed the award. Buck founded two international child-welfare organizations and wrote more than 85 books. **◂1901.5**

TECHNOLOGY

First Electron Microscope

8 The basic technology of the microscope had remained essentially unchanged for nearly 500 years when, in 1931, German scientists Max Knoll and Ernst Ruska introduced the most important innovation in the device since sixteenth-century Dutchmen had added a second lens: They built an electron microscope. Capable of magnifying an object 17 times, the microscope worked by focusing a beam of electrons through an electromagnetic or electrostatic field in a vacuum chamber. Within a decade, there was an improved version that could magnify objects 100,000 times.

Two discoveries laid the groundwork for Knoll and Ruska's breakthrough. In 1924, French physicist Louis de Broglie showed that beams of electrons move in waves but with a much shorter wavelength than light. De Broglie's discovery meant that, if a way could be found to focus the electron beam, it could be used to magnify an image. Two years later, German physicist Hans Busch demonstrated the focusing effects that a magnetic or electrostatic field has on electrons. The field, in effect, becomes a lens; electrons become light. Because the electron wavelength is shorter than that of light, electrons are capable of spectacular feats of magnification.

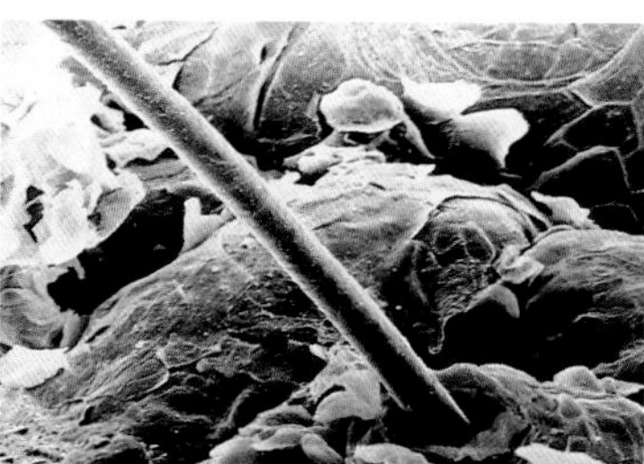

A shaft of hair magnified 380 times under a modern-day electron microscope.

The basic principles of electron optics were refined in the 1930s by such technology giants as Siemens in Germany, Metropolitan-Vickers in England, and RCA in the United States. **◂1924.2**

FILM

An In-Your-Face Movie Star

7 **"I ain't so tough," gasped a bullet-riddled James Cagney near the end of *The Public Enemy*, released in 1931. On the contrary, Cagney's vicious mob enforcer is one of the toughest, truest, and most electrifying gangsters ever seen on screen. In an era ablaze with real and celluloid criminals, Cagney's authenticity and energetic amorality gave even the most jaded viewers a jolt. In this, his fifth movie, he robbed, he threatened, he assaulted, he killed with evil wit and (until the end) without regret. In the movie's most memorable—and shocking—moment, he smashed a breakfast grapefruit into his nagging girlfriend's face. With a twist of a citrus fruit, James Cagney became a star.**

THE UNITED STATES

Scottsboro Boys Railroaded

9 During the Depression, thousands of Americans illegally hopped freight trains in search of work. In March 1931, on a train crossing Alabama, a group of white youths brawled with a group of blacks. Forced off, the whites filed a complaint at the next station. Sheriff's deputies searched the train, rounding up nine black youths, aged 13 to 20—and two young white women. Possibly fearing prosecution for vagrancy or prostitution, the women claimed the blacks had raped them. Accusers and accused were taken to Scottsboro, the county seat. The ensuing case was one of the century's most controversial.

The "Scottsboro Boys" went to trial the following month. Despite contradictions between the alleged victims' stories—and doctors' testimony that no rape had occurred—the all-white jury convicted a pair of the defendants on the first day. (Outside the courthouse, 10,000 spectators cheered the

SPORTS: Baseball: World Series, St. Louis Cardinals defeat Philadelphia Athletics, 4–3 ... Football: Chicago, Green Bay, and Portsmouth receive $1,000 fines for using college players ... Boxing: Max Schmeling loses heavyweight title for refusing to fight Jack Sharkey ... Horse Racing: Twenty Grand, ridden by Charles Kurtsinger, sets new Kentucky Derby time of 2:01 ⅘ (record until 1941).

"We had a great time."—**Wiley Post to correspondent Floyd Gibbons, when asked to describe his record flight**

The nine defendants and their lawyer, Sam Leibowitz, in the Scottsboro jail.

verdict while a brass band played.) The rest were judged guilty soon afterward, and all but the 13-year-old sentenced to the electric chair. He was too young to be executed, but seven jurors insisted he be given the chair anyway. The judge then declared his case a mistrial.

Amid a storm of international protest, the case was appealed, and in 1932 the U.S. Supreme Court, citing the defendants' inadequate legal counsel, overturned the convictions. One of the nine was then convicted again, in a trial marred by the prosecution's blatant anti-Semitic attacks on the defense attorney. A 1935 Supreme Court decision overturned the new conviction, ruling that the state had systematically excluded blacks from juries.

Despite the landmark rulings—and a recantation from one of the accusers—the Scottsboro Boys were tried again and again, while the NAACP and the Communist Party battled publicly over who would represent them. Under rising political pressure, the state dropped charges against the five youngest defendants in 1937, and later paroled all but one. The last, Clarence Norris, was paroled in 1946 and pardoned by Alabama's governor in 1976. **◂1923.6 ▸1941.M**

AVIATION

Around the World in 8½ Days

10 The last time anyone had flown around the world in an airplane, in 1924, it had taken six months. Now, in the wake of Charles Lindbergh's transatlantic flight and the subsequent explosion of aviation firsts (including an around-the-world trip by the *Graf Zeppelin* that took 21½ days), a one-eyed Oklahoman named Wiley Post announced in 1931 that he could make the trip in just ten days. It took him less than nine.

A former stunt pilot, Lockheed test pilot, and oil-field roughneck, Post was working as an aerial chauffeur when his employer, an oil tycoon, let Post borrow his plane—a single-engine Lockheed Vega called the *Winnie Mae*—to pursue his dream. The flier hired Australian-born navigator Harold Gatty and began modifying the *Winnie Mae* for long-distance flight.

Post and Gatty flew from New York to Newfoundland on June 23, and then to Liverpool. Thousands greeted them in Berlin, but after flying through a storm, they were snubbed in Moscow. In Siberia, horses hauled the *Winnie Mae* out of mud. After landing on an Alaskan beach, Post fixed a bent propeller with a hammer and a stone. The aviators crossed the Canadian Rockies to Edmonton, where a street doubled as a runway. In the final stretch, the pair returned to New York—8 days, 15 hours, and 51 minutes after they left—where a wild mob of 10,000 watched them land. The adventure proved, Post wrote, that "a good airplane with average equipment and careful flying" could outdo any dirigible. **◂1929.M ▸1938.5**

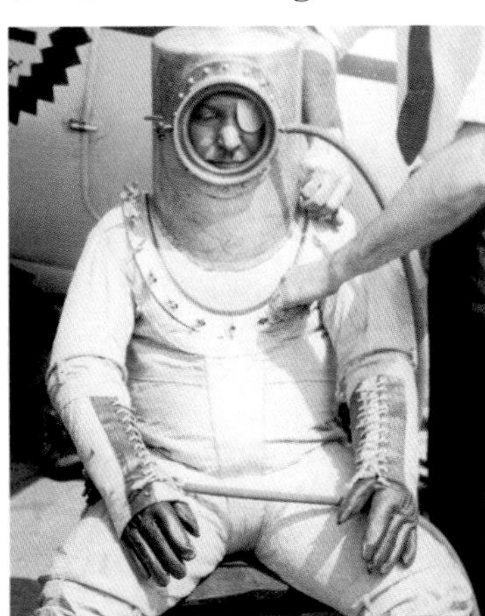

Post, here in his flight suit, bested the *Graf Zeppelin*'s 1929 record by 12 days.

LITERATURE

Of Critical Importance

11 "My single aim has been literature," wrote Edmund Wilson when he was just 22. Rarely has singularity been so broadly defined.

Poet, novelist, playwright, journalist, editor, historian, and, above all, social and literary critic, Wilson was America's foremost intellectual tastemaker from the mid-1920s through the 1950s, and one of the world's leading men of letters until his death in 1972. His first book of criticism, *Axel's Castle*, published in 1931, traced the influence of symbolism on Yeats, Valéry, Eliot, Proust, Joyce, Rimbaud, and Gertrude Stein. Like much of Wilson's work, it helped shape the thought of a generation.

As an editor at *The New Republic* and *Vanity Fair*, Wilson had already helped establish Hemingway, Faulkner, and Fitzgerald. In *To the Finland Station* (1940), he made a history of communism as enthralling as a detective novel, helping to popularize the ideology among America's intelligentsia. He switched from Marx to Freud in *The Wound and the Bow* (1941), a groundbreaking exploration of the links between art and neurosis.

Also in the forties, Wilson, as chief reviewer for *The New Yorker*, curated the literary canon, publishing a collection of his own short stories along the way. In the fifties, he learned Hebrew to write a book on the Dead Sea Scrolls. By then, despite his radicalism, he'd become a national institution: He received the Presidential Medal of Freedom in 1953. **◂1925.5**

IN THE UNITED STATES

those who came to shed their money at the casinos, and those who came to shed unwanted mates. Later, lax nuptial laws led to a proliferation of marriage mills as well.

▶YOUNG MAN WITH A HORN—The legendary cornetist Bix Beiderbecke died of pneumonia (triggered by severe alcoholism) in Queens, New York, on August 6 at age 28. Perhaps the first great lyrical jazz soloist, the German-American horn player—who was fascinated by symphonic music that he could barely read—perfected an exquisitely controlled, introverted style that was poles apart from the intense New Orleans sound of Louis Armstrong and his followers.

▶ANNIE ON THE AIR—Little Orphan Annie was already a popular comic-strip character when, on March 6, NBC began broadcasting a radio show featuring the "little chatterbox ... with pretty auburn locks," her wealthy benefactor, Oliver "Daddy" Warbucks, and her faithful dog, Sandy. The show, like the comic strip, was a bastion of political conservatism. It aired until 1943. ◂1928.V ▸1932.M

▶MEMORABLE MONSTER—Boris Karloff launched his career as horror-film icon, delivering a surprisingly sensi-

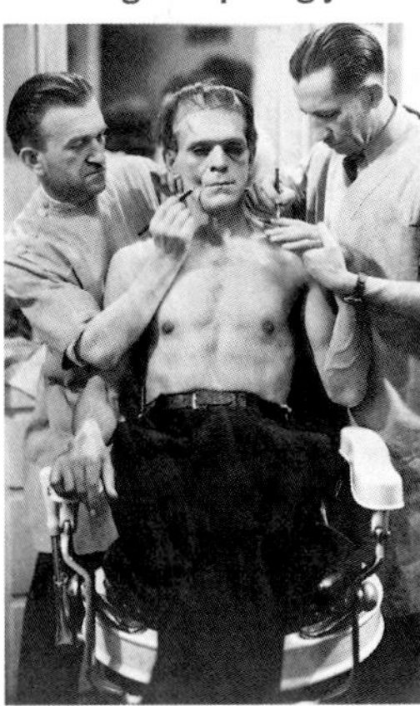

tive portrayal of the monster in 1931's *Frankenstein* (a part turned down by Bela "Dracula" Lugosi). ▸1974.V

▶PUBLIC ENEMY—Compared with his other crimes, the one that sent Al Capone to prison was tame indeed. Thanks to a 28-year-old Justice Department agent named Eliot Ness, in October America's foremost gangster received an eleven-year sentence for income tax evasion. ◂1929.5

POLITICS & BUSINESS: GNP: $76.3 billion ... National income down 33% from 1929 ... Unemployment nears 16% ... Canada raises tariffs, expects a 60% drop in U.S. imports ... Hattie T. Caraway of Arkansas is the first woman elected to the U.S. Senate ... U.S. wheat crops at an all-time high, some Kansas counties forgo taxes to prevent foreclosures ... "Star-Spangled Banner" becomes the U.S. national anthem.

"Her jumps are jolts; her walks, limps and staggers; her runs, heavy blind impulsive gallops; her bends, sways. Her idiom of motion has little of the aerial in it, but there's a lot of rolling on the floor."—**Dance patron Lincoln Kirstein, on Martha Graham**

AROUND THE WORLD

▶SKY'S THE LIMIT—On May 27, Swiss physicist Auguste Piccard and his associate Paul Kipfer became the first men to pilot a large balloon into the Earth's stratosphere, reaching an altitude of 51,762 feet. Previous flights had demonstrated that the low pressure of extreme altitude could be fatal to passengers, so Piccard designed an airtight aluminum sphere that became a model for future pressurized cabins. ▶1958.6

▶BRITISH FASCIST—Sir Oswald Mosley was defeated in his 1931 campaign for Parliament under the banner of a socialist party of his own formation. His next political creation was the British Union of Fascists, whose members distributed anti-Semitic propaganda, demonstrated in Jewish sections of East London, and took far-right-wing political stances. An accomplished orator, Mosley was an apologist for Hitler; he was interned soon after the outbreak of World War II. In 1948, he established the Union Movement, which continued his right-wing policies.

▶SYMBOL OF A CITY—*Christ the Redeemer*, a monumental concrete statue built atop the 2,310-foot Corcovado (Hunchback Mountain) on the south side of Rio de Janeiro, Brazil,

was dedicated in 1931. The giant figure, standing some 125 feet tall with outstretched arms that span 92 feet, was the work of French sculptor Paul Maximilian Landowski.

▶GANDHI-IRWIN PACT—Lord Irwin, the conciliatory viceroy of India, and Mahatma Gandhi (on special release from prison) concluded lengthy negotiations on March 5, signing the Gandhi-Irwin Pact. Though Gandhi made more concessions (opponents decried his acceptance of certain restrictions on Indian autonomy), his very presence at the bargaining table symbolized a new order wherein an Indian might be treated as the equal of an Englishman. ◀1930.4 ▶1932.4

DANCE

Transcending Prettiness

12 Since leaving the celebrated Denishawn dance troupe in 1923, dancer and choreographer Martha Graham had been searching for her own niche. She finally found it in 1931, when she made her creative and professional breakthrough with a work called *Primitive Mysteries*.

A Denishawn star, Graham had grown weary of its folk-dance-based exoticism. On her own, she developed stark, angular movements—complete with shockingly sexual contractions—that contrasted sharply with the flowing prettiness of even the most avant-garde dance of the time. In a tubular jersey dress and dead-white makeup ("my period of long woolens," she later quipped), she performed to dissonant modern music. Audiences and critics alike tended to jeer.

But Graham's explorations paralleled those of the abstract artists, who were slowly gaining widespread acceptance. And after the stock-market crash of 1929, her seriousness and her social consciousness (one piece was called *Revolt*) began to attract a cult of admirers. Her all-woman troupe moved like an army, eschewing softness and romance for a harsh vitality—an appropriate aesthetic for a world moving away from individualism toward collectivism.

Primitive Mysteries was inspired by a sojourn in New Mexico among a group of Native American mystics. But its images of ritual initiation weren't taken from any particular tradition; rather, they were a strikingly successful attempt to create a universal mythic language. The work, along with four companion pieces, earned glowing reviews. Graham had found her basic subject matter.

For the rest of her long career (she died in 1991 at age 96), Graham mined similar spiritual veins, whether evoking the myths of ancient Greece or the American frontier. But she soon left long woolens behind for some of the richest costumes and staging in modern dance history. **◀1915.8 ▶1944.14**

SPAIN

Republicans Buck a Trend

13 With Nazism rising in Germany, Stalinism gripping the Soviet Union, and Fascism deepening its hold on Italy, Spain bucked the trend in 1931: After seven years of authoritarian rule, the nation deposed its king and declared itself a republic.

King Alfonso XIII had almost lost his throne in 1923 amid military and political crises, but was saved by General Miguel Primo de Rivera, who'd suspended the constitution and declared himself dictator. The left bridled under the general's repressive policies, the right despised his attempts (modest though they were) at social reform, and everyone condemned his incompetence, which doubled the country's deficit in five years.

Primo de Rivera resigned in January 1930 (and died a few weeks later), but Alfonso's troubles worsened. Spain was already one of Europe's poorest nations, and the Great Depression squeezed it hard. By December, the country was in revolt. Forced to make a few concessions to democracy, the king held municipal elections in April 1931. To his astonishment—his chief minister exclaimed, "A country we believed to be monarchist turned republican in 24 hours"—the voters overwhelmingly picked antimonarchist candidates. When the Army refused to guarantee Alfonso's continued rule, he fled to France.

In June's elections, the Socialist Workers' Party (PSOE) was the biggest winner, and Manuel Azaña,

The new republic's centrist president, Niceto Alcalá Zamora *(center)*.

a liberal, became prime minister, with centrist Niceto Alcalá Zamora as president. The new leaders built schools, legalized divorce, separated church and state, and pledged autonomy to the province of Catalonia. But internal schisms and lack of funds kept the government from fulfilling promises of land redistribution—a failure that angered the left. Meanwhile the right was outraged by perceived attacks on clergy, royalty, and the wealthy—and the government's willingness to "dismember" Spain. Most Spaniards welcomed the return of democratic rule. But five years after its creation, Spain would erupt in civil war. **◀1925.2 ▶1933.7**

IDEAS

The Incomplete Theorist

14 "All Cretans are liars; thus saith Epimenides the Cretan. This statement is false."

Everyone is familiar with the logical conundrum known as a self-conflicting statement, a proposition that is simultaneously true and untrue—or, as a mathematician might put it, "undecidable" because it exists outside the laws of any known system of math or logic. In 1931, Kurt Gödel, a mathematician at the University of Vienna (and, later, Princeton University), came up with a theorem proving that no mathematical system is immune to such paradoxes. Rather, each one has "holes" and is in some respect "incomplete."

Abstract, yes, but Gödel's incompleteness theorem revolutionized mathematics. Previously, mathematicians (notably, Russell and Whitehead, in their *Principia Mathematica*) had invested enormous energy in trying to resolve paradoxes, contradictions, and ambiguity through the creation of an airtight mathematical system; the incompleteness theorem persuaded them that such loose ends were not only inevitable but fruitful, allowing unexpected truths to be revealed. Gödel's theory proved highly fertile in opening up new fields of study, especially in the areas of linguistics and artificial intelligence. **◀1927.6 ▶1957.13**

NOBEL PRIZES: Peace: Jane Addams (U.S.; Woman's International League for Peace and Freedom) and Nicholas Murray Butler (U.S.; Carnegie Endowment for International Peace) ... Literature: Erik A. Karlfeldt (Swedish; poet) ... Chemistry: Carl Bosch and Friedrich Bergius (German; high-pressure processes) ... Medicine: Otto H. Warburg (German; respiratory enzyme) ... Physics: No award.

A VOICE FROM 1931

A Princely Pachyderm

From *The Story of Babar*, by Jean de Brunhoff, 1931

Cécile de Brunhoff's bedtime story for her sons Laurent and Mathieu might have remained just that if her husband, Jean, had not been a painter—and if Jean's family hadn't been in the publishing business. In 1931, his illustrated version of the tale became The Story of Babar*—an instant best-seller and a classic of children's literature. Babar is a young elephant whose mother is killed by a hunter; he escapes to a city much like the de Brunhoffs' Paris, where he learns civilized ways before returning to rule over his brethren. Perhaps inevitably, this and later Babar books have been criticized as colonialist and racist. But the series' simple yet sophisticated artwork and its light-handed lessons about growing up have made it a worldwide favorite.* ◂1926.6 ▸1957.V

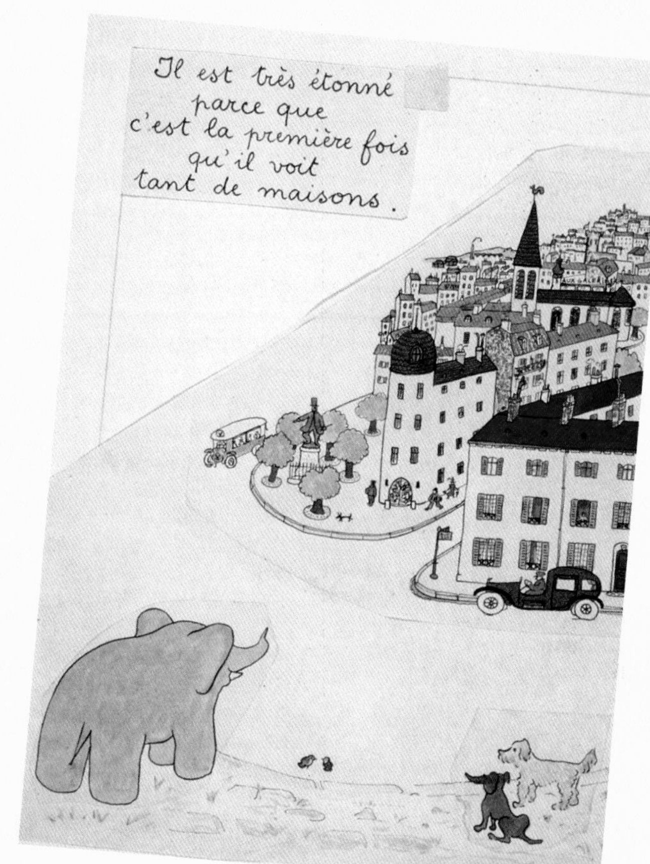

The pages reproduced here are Jean de Brunhoff's original watercolors for the book, with his handwritten text. Babar marvels at the city *(right)*. "This is the first time," the text reads, "that he has seen so many houses." On his return to the jungle *(below)*—with Céleste and her cousin Arthur, who joined him in town—the elephants exclaim over his car and the trio's clothes. Babar and Céleste soon marry and become king and queen.

1931

"These unhappy times call for ... plans ... that put their faith once more in the forgotten man at the bottom of the pyramid."
—Franklin Delano Roosevelt

STORY OF THE YEAR

FDR Beats Hoover

1 The Depression turned politics topsy-turvy in the countries it hit hardest. In Britain, it put a founder of the Labour Party, Ramsay MacDonald, at the head of a Parliament dominated by the largest Conservative majority ever. In Germany, it aligned businessmen behind the avowedly (if insincerely) anticapitalist Adolf Hitler. And in the United States, it enabled patrician Franklin D. Roosevelt to run for president as the champion of the working class. Roosevelt's opponent, Herbert Hoover, had once been known as a progressive and a humanitarian. (He'd directed U.S. relief operations in Europe during World War I.) But in 1932, after three years in office, he was widely seen as a reactionary who'd done nothing for his nation's impoverished masses—an image that still lingers.

In fact, Hoover intervened in the economy more extensively than any previous president. His program's centerpiece was the Reconstruction Finance Corporation, established in January 1932. The RFC was endowed with $1.5 billion (later $3.5 billion) to lend to various savings institutions and the railroads. The idea was to provide businesses with capital to start hiring again. Soon, despite Hoover's reluctance, the RFC was funding public works as well. And though he'd long opposed direct aid to the unemployed—America as yet had no federal social-welfare system—Hoover eventually authorized the Federal Farm Board to distribute surplus wheat to the needy.

But even these unprecedented efforts were too little, too late. Banks still failed by the dozens. Unemployment continued to soar. Critics denounced the RFC as a "breadline for business," as many Americans starved. Meanwhile, Hoover claimed that things were not so bad.

Roosevelt's campaign platform was hardly radical (he criticized Hoover for overspending), but he struck a nerve by promising a "new deal" for the "forgotten man." Ebullient despite the polio that had put him in a wheelchair, the New York governor made a bright contrast to the dour incumbent. In the November election, Roosevelt won by a landslide: 22.8 million votes to Hoover's 15.8 million. Over the next dozen years, FDR, as he was nicknamed, would transform his country—and with it, the world. **◂1930.3 ▸1932.12**

Campaigning in Los Angeles: FDR *(far left)* being introduced by humorist Will Rogers *(far right)*. Above, a car reflector beams the message.

1932

German family values: A campaign poster implored women to elect Hitler.

GERMANY

Hitler Reaches the Threshold

2 Germany's elections in 1932 marked the beginning of the end of democracy there. The Depression had wrecked the old coalition between socialists and middle-class parties in the Reichstag. Centrist chancellor Heinrich Brüning (who alone might have saved the Weimar Republic) was immensely unpopular, undone by heavy-handed austerity measures; only the Nazi Party flourished. In April, it won control of four state governments, and its leader, Adolf Hitler, came in second (with 37 percent of the vote) after conservative president Paul von Hindenburg, who was narrowly reelected. Then Brüning resigned, and his successor, Franz von Papen, called for Reichstag elections in July.

The elections doubled the Nazi delegation to 230 seats, making the party the Reichstag's biggest. Its rowdy, brown-uniformed delegates turned debates into near-riots—while all across Germany, street battles between Nazi storm troopers and communist paramilitary fighters became nightly events. Still, Papen needed Nazi support to govern. Grudgingly, he offered Hitler the post of vice-chancellor. But Hitler demanded the chancellorship.

A desperate Papen dissolved the Reichstag and called for new elections, in November. The Nazis lost 61 seats—but remained the largest party. Papen nearly persuaded Hindenburg to declare his own dictatorship to keep Hitler out, but the army was judged too weak to suppress both the communists and half a million storm troopers. Besides, too many officers supported Hitler. Hindenburg dismissed Papen and appointed Defense Minister Kurt von Schleicher chancellor. Schleicher offered the vice-chancellorship to the leader of the Nazis' left wing, but the gesture only united party members behind their Führer.

After trying without success to form a government with the socialists or the conservative nationalists, Schleicher resigned on January 28, 1933. By then, he and Papen (both still powerful in the Reichstag) had convinced themselves that Hitler could be "controlled" if he were surrounded by moderate cabinet ministers.

After feverish negotiations, Hitler became chancellor on January 30. Papen became vice-chancellor; the cabinet included only two Nazis—Hermann Goering and Wilhelm Frick. Clearly, however, Hitler was not about to be controlled. **◂1930.12 ▸1933.5**

LITERATURE

Huxley's Future

3 Aldous Huxley's anti-utopian novel, *Brave New World*, published in early 1932, combined technological optimism and spiritual pessimism in a single gripping package. In Huxley's nightmarish vision of the year 632 AF (After Ford), people move about in a clean, orderly world of material abundance from which war, sickness, and squalor have been eliminated, and in which, thanks to eugenics, everyone has been perfectly bred to his or her station in life. Loneliness, insecurity, questioning have been banished, history and art eliminated, and anxiety and depression muffled by drugs. As political and economic freedom have decreased, state-sanctioned sexual promiscuity has expanded to fill the void.

The novel sold well in Huxley's native Britain, but in the United States, a jeremiad against soul-destroying material abundance seemed incongruous. Later, however, amid the mass conformity and political hysteria of America's post–World War II boom, the

ART & CULTURE: Books: *1919* (John Dos Passos); *Light in August* (William Faulkner); *Young Lonigan* (James T. Farrell); *The International Style: Architecture Since 1922* (Henry-Russell Hitchcock and Philip Johnson); *Conquistador* (Archibald MacLeish) ... Music: "Brother, Can You Spare a Dime" (Gorney and Harburg); "Night and Day" (Cole Porter); *Concerto for Two Solo Pianos* (Igor Stravinsky)...

"We can do without the goodwill of [the Indian National] Congress, and in fact I do not believe for a moment that we shall ever have it."—**a British minister, to Lord Willingdon**

book's warnings about a pleasure-surfeited society that's been lulled into slavery took on a new resonance, and Huxley was hailed as a latter-day prophet. His 1954 book, *The Doors of Perception,* about Huxley's experiences with mescaline, provided the name for the rock group The Doors. ►**1949.4**

INDIA

Crackdown on Resistance

4 Frustrated by perceived British foot-dragging on the question of Indian sovereignty, the Indian National Congress early in 1932 resumed its nationwide civil-disobedience campaign. The uneasy truce hammered out just a year earlier by Lord Irwin and Mahatma Gandhi was over, replaced by mutual acrimony. Eager to prevent a repeat of 1930's vitiating strike and boycott campaign, hard-liner Lord Willingdon, Irwin's successor as viceroy of India, wasted no time in cracking down on the Indian resistance. Within months Gandhi, Jawaharlal Nehru, and 34,000 other dissidents were back behind bars, and the Congress had been declared an outlaw body, its property confiscated.

The impetus for the campaign was the failure of the second session of the Round Table conference, which had convened in London in September 1931, to create a framework for eventual Indian sovereignty. The conference accomplished nothing. Britain, preoccupied with the international Depression, had little time or sympathy for Indian claims to independence. For Gandhi, the Congress's lone representative at the conference, the failed negotiations were a major personal defeat. He returned home to a restless constituency and a Congress determined to forge ahead with civil disobedience—with or without his blessing.

Unlike Irwin, Willingdon refused to use Gandhi as a liaison between the British and an increasingly radical Congress. From jail in Poona, Gandhi refocused the freedom movement, announcing "a perpetual fast unto death" to win electoral reform for the Hindu Depressed Classes, the so-called untouchables, or Harijans (Children of God), as he now began calling them. Bewildered nationalist leaders felt Gandhi had lost sight of his priorities. Nevertheless, five days into his fast the British government agreed to expand representation for lower-class Hindus and—Gandhi's ultimate objective—to provide for a later electoral stage at which voting would not be segregated into high- and low-caste electorates. ◄**1931.M** ►**1935.13**

A procession of untouchables—Gandhi's Harijans—defies the caste system.

DIPLOMACY

Perils of Japanese Expansion

5 In Manchuria—as in the rest of the world during the hell-bent buildup to World War II—diplomacy proved no match for belligerence. Acting independently, U.S. secretary of state Henry Stimson warned Tokyo in 1932 that the United States would not recognize the Japanese conquest of Manchuria. It was a bold but fruitless move. The other major powers with conspicuous commercial interests in China—Britain, France, the Soviet Union—failed to support the United States in challenging Japanese aggression. The implication: As long as nothing impinged on Western trade, Japan was free to do as it pleased.

Young Communists from northern China captured by the Japanese.

Emboldened by Western inaction, the Japanese army undertook, on January 28, a shocking attack on Shanghai, one of China's most important trade centers (and far removed from Manchuria). A Chinese boycott of Japanese goods there had seriously damaged Japan's economy. Aiming to end the boycott, Japan repeatedly bombed the city, killing thousands of civilians. The Shanghai Incident awoke Europe to the dangers of Japanese expansionism. Britain (which had enormous holdings in the area), France, and Italy now joined the U.S. protest. The Japanese, meanwhile, were meeting unexpected resistance from the Chinese. On May 5, the Chinese and Japanese, having entered a truce mediated by the Western powers, removed their forces from a newly created Shanghai Demilitarized Zone.

Thwarted in Shanghai, the Japanese army remained adamant about Manchuria, where it had established a Japanese puppet state called Manchukuo. The legitimate Japanese government in Tokyo was cautious, reluctant to incite international wrath. Ten days after the truce at Shanghai, Japanese premier Tsuyoshi Inukai, an opponent of the Manchurian campaign, was assassinated. From then on, the Japanese government was effectively run by the military. Within a month the cowed Diet formally recognized Manchukuo. ◄**1931.4** ►**1933.8**

BIRTHS

Jacques Chirac, French president.

Mario Cuomo, U.S. governor.

Milos Forman, Czech-U.S. filmmaker.

Dick Gregory, U.S. comedian and political activist.

Edward Kennedy, U.S. senator.

Luc Montagnier, French virologist.

V.S. Naipaul, Trinidadian–U.K. writer.

Sylvia Plath, U.S. poet.

Gay Talese, U.S. journalist.

Elizabeth Taylor, U.K.-U.S. actress.

François Truffaut, French filmmaker.

John Updike, U.S. writer.

DEATHS

Aristide Briand, French statesman.

Hart Crane, U.S. poet.

George Eastman, U.S. inventor.

Kenneth Grahame, U.K. writer.

Lady (Isabella) Gregory, Irish playwright.

William H. Hoover, U.S. manufacturer.

André Maginot, French political leader.

John Philip Sousa, U.S. composer.

Lytton Strachey, U.K. biographer.

William Wrigley, Jr., U.S. manufacturer.

Florenz Ziegfeld, U.S. theater producer.

Painting & Sculpture: ***The Passion of Sacco and Vanzetti*** **(Ben Shahn) ... Film:** ***Grand Hotel*** **(Edmund Goulding);** ***Dr. Jekyll and Mr. Hyde*** **(Rouben Mamoulian);** ***Tarzan, the Ape Man*** **(W.S. Van Dyke, with Johnny Weissmuller) ... Theater:** ***Dinner at Eight*** **(Kaufman and Ferber);** ***The Ermine*** **(Jean Anouilh);** ***Face the Music*** **(Berlin and Hart) ... Radio:** ***The George Burns and Gracie Allen Show; Walter Winchell.***

"The basic hero of our books should be labor; that is, man organized by the processes of labor."
—Maxim Gorky, at the 1934 Congress of Soviet Writers

NEW IN 1932

Zippo lighter.

Frito corn chips.

Skippy peanut butter.

Three Musketeers candy bar.

Radio City Music Hall.

The Family Circle (first magazine to be distributed solely through grocery stores).

Revlon.

Gasoline tax.

IN THE UNITED STATES

▶**THE OTHER BABE**—Mildred "Babe" Didrikson—widely considered the greatest female athletes of all time—dominated the 1932 National Amateur Athletic Union track and field championships and the Olympic trials. At the Los Angeles Olympic Games two weeks later, the 18-year-old won two gold medals and set new world records for the javelin throw and the 80-meter hurdles. She would have won the high jump, too, but she used an unauthorized technique, the "Western roll," and was relegated to a silver medal. By 1950, she had won every women's golf championship at least once;

she also excelled at basketball, swimming, and baseball (once striking out Joe DiMaggio in an exhibition game). ◂1920.6

▶**A STRIKE FOR LABOR**—Republican senator George W. Norris of Nebraska was known for voting his conscience because he would "rather be right than regular." With New York senator Fiorello LaGuardia, he sponsored the Norris-LaGuardia Act, which passed into law March 23. The

Charles Lindbergh, Jr. ("Baby Lindy"), in a snapshot taken at his first birthday party.

CRIME

Lindberghs' Baby Kidnapped

6 The dark side of celebrity became brutally evident to the world on the night of March 1, 1932, when the 20-month-old son of Charles and Anne Morrow Lindbergh was kidnapped from the couple's grand, just-completed house in rural New Jersey. The case became one of the most famous of its era, launching a wave of "copycat" abductions and spreading fear among parents.

The kidnapper left a homemade ladder beneath the child's bedroom window and a ransom note in broken English on the sill—but no detailed instructions. Letters from strangers claiming to have inside information (ranging from the imprisoned Al Capone to an ex-FBI agent who bilked the Lindberghs out of $100,000) poured in. Then a man with a German accent called, with knowledge available only to the abductor. Meeting with a go-between in a cemetery, the German, in exchange for $50,000, handed over a note saying the baby was on the island of Martha's Vineyard, 300 miles away. But a search turned up nothing.

In May, while Lindbergh was away on another fruitless search (for a schooner on which he'd been told his son was being held), a truck driver found the child's corpse by a road near the Lindbergh mansion.

Police failed to break the case until 1934, when a German-born carpenter named Bruno Richard Hauptmann spent a ten-dollar bill from the cemetery transaction at a New York gas station. Some $30,000 more turned up at his home, along with lumber matching that used in the ladder. Although he protested his innocence to the end (a belief many still hold to this day), Hauptmann was convicted of murder and executed in 1936. **◂1927.1**

RELIGION

A Theological Revolution

7 Karl Barth's *Church Dogmatics*—the first of whose four volumes appeared in 1932—had an impact on Protestant theology

comparable to that of Einstein's theories on physics. Just as Einstein revolutionized scientists' notions of space and time, Barth overturned Christians' ideas about God and creation. Like Einstein, who based his colossally complex work on a single constant, the velocity of light, Barth founded his philosophical system on one concept: Jesus Christ. And like Einstein's formulas, the Swiss pastor's writings, though impenetrable to laypeople, indirectly influenced the beliefs of millions.

Since the nineteenth century, theologians had portrayed God as an ethical being essentially resembling humans; they'd sought to understand God through the workings of history, nature, and psychology. In his *The Epistle to the Romans* (1919), Barth had called for the recognition of God as "wholly other"—a deity knowable only as he chose to reveal himself in Jesus. Barth's erudite, eloquent, yet *anti*-theological theology won him an instant following. In *Church Dogmatics*, Barth extended his "Christocentric" ideology to almost every aspect of Christian doctrine. (He died in 1968 before tackling a volume on redemption.)

The theologian's arguments were central to Germans who were resisting the Nazis' "German Christian" movement, which took over the mainstream German Evangelical Church. Barth, a professor in Germany, co-wrote the charter of the Confessing Church, whose members rejected Hitler's messianic pretensions. Deported to Switzerland (where he joined the army), Barth continued to encourage the Confessors' activities in the anti-Nazi underground. **◂1923.13 ▸1943.M**

THE SOVIET UNION

The New Artistic Orthodoxy

8 As Stalin's autocracy expanded from politics and economics into the arts, he forced a new orthodoxy upon his young nation. In 1932 the freshly created Congress of Soviet Writers elaborated the official doctrine of socialist realism: "It demands of the artist a truthful, historically concrete depiction of reality in its revolutionary development."

Seldom had a state so emphatically circumscribed the liberty of its artists.

Diversity of opinion and expression was banished. The glorification of Stalin, of the Red Army, of collective farms, tractors, and factories was ordained as art's proper role. In literature, the New Soviet Man was authorized as the only suitable hero. Abstraction and experimentation were unacceptable.

Gorky's return from exile to serve the revolution through art was depicted on the cover of a newsmagazine.

SPORTS: Baseball: World Series, New York Yankees (Babe Ruth's "called shot") defeat Chicago Cubs, 4–0 ... Olympics held in Lake Placid, N.Y., and Los Angeles ... Basketball: College rules establish a 10-second limit for the ball to cross the midcourt line ... Boxing: Jack Sharkey defeats Max Schmeling in a 15-round decision, regains heavyweight title.

"I think we shall have to make a real search for the neutron. I believe I have a scheme which may just work."
—James Chadwick, in a letter to Ernest Rutherford in 1924

At its first meeting, the congress condemned the works of Proust, Joyce, and Pirandello.

Leading the crusade for artistic monotony was Maxim Gorky, the writer who had risen from abject poverty under the czars to become the greatest witness for Russia's lower classes. Angry, passionate, anarchic, Gorky (a pen name meaning "the bitter one") had befriended Lenin and committed himself to the revolution; his 1907 novel, *Mother,* is less fiction than Marxist tract. In 1921, disillusioned with the revolution's negative effects on Russia's cultural traditions, he went into voluntary exile in Europe, returning in 1927 in a show of patriotism. The revered Gorky lent credibility to socialist realism. When he said, "As for the subjects of their paintings, I'd like to see more children's faces, more smiles, more spontaneous joy," painters, fearing Stalinist reprisals, obliged. **◂1931.3 ▸1934.14**

DIPLOMACY

Stalin Courts the West

9 In 1932, after years of self-imposed isolation, Stalin began courting allies in the West, signing nonaggression treaties with France, Poland, Finland, Estonia, and Latvia. The sudden about-face was easy to explain: The Soviet Union, thwarted in its long romance with Germany, which was clearly not going communist, needed to erect a buffer between itself and the emerging fascists. In the past, the Soviet Union had scarcely made a secret of its dreams of conquering the Baltic states and Poland. Now, suddenly, it needed them to remain independent.

Economic conditions within the Soviet Union made war unthinkable. Famine-stricken peasants, forced out of their homes and onto collective farms, could scarcely be counted on to defend the government with their lives. The nonaggression pacts gave Stalin domestic breathing room and also alleviated some international tensions. (Polish-Soviet relations temporarily improved.)

In 1933, noting the Bolshevik state's new willingness to conduct business, the United States—having withheld recognition for 16 years (longer than any other major power)—opened diplomatic relations. The Soviet Union covered too large a portion of the earth's surface to be ignored. The capitalists and the communists, whose relations would delimit global security for much of the century, entered a wary rapprochement. **◂1931.3 ▸1934.14**

Economic conditions at home gave Stalin no choice but to reach out diplomatically.

SCIENCE

Banner Year in Physics

10 The Cavendish Laboratory, located amid Cambridge University's medieval spires and courtyards, emerged as a major center for pioneering physicists throughout the 1920s and '30s. But the banner year for the lab, which was headed by Ernest Rutherford, was 1932, when one member of the Rutherford team, James Chadwick, confirmed the existence of the neutron, and two others, Ernest Walton and John Cockroft, became the first scientists to break down an atomic nucleus.

The presence of a component other than protons in the nuclei of all atoms (except ordinary hydrogen, whose nucleus consists of just one proton) had been hypothesized by Rutherford in 1920 as a way to explain isotopes (heavier or lighter versions of an element), but because the neutron carries no electrical charge and thus was undetectable, it had resisted verification. Chadwick isolated the long-rumored particle by bombarding the nuclei of the light metal beryllium with massive alpha particles from the naturally radioactive element polonium; in the interaction, a stream of particles was ejected that was free of electrical charge. When Chadwick passed the particles through hydrogen-rich paraffin wax, they were massive enough to knock out readily identifiable protons.

Meanwhile, Walton and Cockroft, experimenting with an early subatomic-particle accelerator, aimed a speeded-up proton beam at a lithium atom consisting of three protons, three electrons, and four neutrons. The lithium atom and the proton combined briefly, then split into two fragments, each consisting of the nucleus of a helium atom containing two protons and two neutrons. This nuclear reaction—history's first man-made one—was accompanied by a large burst of energy, posing the possibility of a remarkable new energy source.

Another member of the Cambridge faculty, Paul Dirac, who had earlier predicted the existence of a positively charged electron called a positron (to much skepticism), was vindicated in 1932. His calculations were confirmed when Carl David Anderson, an American physicist at the California Institute of Technology, detected the presence of such a particle in a cloud chamber. The positron was the first confirmed example of antimatter, a particle identical in every respect to another particle, except that it is oppositely charged. **◂1931.5 ▸1938.1**

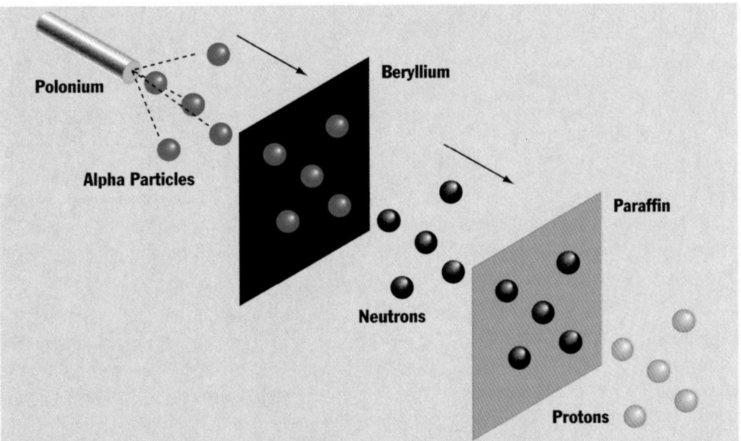

The neutron, large enough to knock protons out of paraffin, proved useful for bombarding nuclei—and hence vital both to war efforts and to the development of nuclear energy.

IN THE UNITED STATES

new law prohibited management from demanding that employees sign "yellow dog" contracts not to join labor unions. Norris-LaGuardia also restricted the use of injunctions in labor disputes, establishing workers' right to strike. **◂1919.6 ▸1936.M**

▶RADIO DAYS—Thanks to the prevalence of home radio sets, Americans—even during the depths of the Depression—kept themselves informed and entertained in record numbers. Two of radio's biggest stars began broadcasting their comedy programs in 1932. On NBC, *The Jack Benny Show* featured the 38-year-old Benny in the persona he soon honed to perfection: a violin-playing, perpetually 39-year-old miser. CBS had Fred Allen *(below right, with Benny)*, a former vaudeville juggler whose wry, laconic style and impeccable timing made him the consummate "comic's comic." Also that year, on NBC's western stations, *One Man's Family* began its long run as one of radio's most addictive "soap operas"—so called because the sponsors of these immensely popular serials (which numbered over 40 by decade's end) were soap companies. And in December, newspaper columnist Walter Winchell took his popular show-biz news and gossip column to the airwaves with the words "Good evening, Mr. and Mrs. America, and all the ships at sea." **◂1931.M ▸1938.M**

▶SHARECROPPERS' SORROWS—*Tobacco Road,* Erskine Caldwell's 1932 novel about white sharecroppers in Georgia, detailed the sordid (and occasionally near-comical) misadventures of Jeeter Lester, a sharecropper who lives on Tobacco Road with his reckless, calamity-prone family. The out-of-luck Lesters became so well-known (especially after the book was turned into a successful stage play in 1933) that the phrase "tobacco road" became a virtual synonym for rural squalor.

POLITICS & BUSINESS: GNP: $58.3 billion ... Franklin Delano Roosevelt elected president, defeating Herbert Hoover ... Unemployment reaches 24% ... Wages down 60% from 1929 ... Congress passes Reconstruction Finance Corporation law, the Emergency Relief Reconstruction Act, and the Home Loan Act.

"The first hole made through a piece of stone is a revelation."—Henry Moore, "The Sculptor Speaks," in *The Listener,* 1937

AROUND THE WORLD

▶DARK JOURNEY—Misanthropic and relentlessly pessimistic, Louis-Ferdinand Céline's 1932 novel, *Voyage au bout de la nuit (Journey to the End of Night)*, depicted—in rough, proletarian language

that was immediately condemned as vulgar—the purposeless wandering of its supremely alienated protagonist through a vile, war-torn landscape. A leftist as a young man, Céline (the pseudonym of Parisian physician Louis Ferdinand Destouches) was later drawn to fascism by his virulent anti-Semitism. He was accused (and later exonerated) of collaborating with the Nazis during World War II.

▶GRAN CHACO WAR—The Chaco Boreal, 100,000 square miles of mostly uninhabited, densely forested wasteland between Bolivia and Paraguay, was the site of a brutal 1932 war. Landlocked Bolivia needed a port on the Rio de la Plata in order to ship recently discovered oil to the Atlantic. But Paraguay's possessions in the Chaco stood in the way. Bolivia—with three times the population of Paraguay and a U.S.-supplied army—seemed poised to conquer. But many of its soldiers, Indian conscripts with low morale, died from disease and snakebite in the malaria-ridden lowlands. When the conflict ended in 1935, 100,000 men had died.

▶END TO REPARATIONS—In June, a conference in Lausanne, Switzerland, virtually wiped the slate clean on German reparations. The Lausanne Conference proposed reducing Germany's total bill from $26 billion (hammered out by the Young Plan of 1929) to a mere $714 million, payable after a three-year moratorium. The Lausanne Protocol was never ratified. German payments stopped anyway, and after Hitler rose to power, it became clear they'd never be resumed. ◂1929.12 ▸1935.M

1932

HUNGARY

A Failed Führer

11 Months before Hitler came to power in Germany, Hungary's prime minister attempted to transform his own nation along Nazi lines. General Gyula Gömbös was appointed premier in September 1932 by the regency of Admiral Miklós Horthy de Nagybányai after the collapse of the Austrian banking system led Gömbös's more moderate predecessor to resign.

Already an authoritarian state, Hungary had in Horthy—nominally the stand-in for the exiled Hapsburg emperor—a ruler for life. Gömbös, who'd helped overthrow communist dictator Béla Kun in 1919, wanted to go further. Like Hitler, he sought to become an all-powerful leader,

Aspiring fascist Gömbös *(left)* of Hungary meets with Mussolini in Venice.

uniting all classes in "racial" unity against common enemies: Jews, labor unions, leftists, and any country opposing Hungary's claims to lands lost in World War I.

As prime minister, Gömbös strengthened existing strictures against the Jews. He tightened diplomatic bonds with Fascist Italy, and after the Nazi takeover tried to convince Germany to make Hungary part of a "Rome-Berlin Axis" —coining the phrase that later became official.

But Hungarians were not desperate enough to want the uncharismatic Gömbös as their führer. A rigged election in 1935 gave parliamentary dominance to his right-wing faction of the National Unity Party, but he never gained grass-root support. And neither Germany nor Italy was willing to make Hungary an equal partner—or to help it recover its territories. Horthy was ready to replace Gömbös with a more tractable premier, when in 1936 Gömbös took sick and died. When Hungary finally joined the Axis several prime ministers later, it was entirely on Hitler's terms. **◂1931.1 ▸1938.3**

Troops led by Douglas MacArthur set fire to the Bonus Army's riverside shantytown.

THE UNITED STATES

Bonus Army Demolished

12 If one incident finished Herbert Hoover politically, it was his use of federal troops against an encampment of jobless war veterans in Washington, D.C. Led by Walter W. Waters, an unemployed cannery worker from Oregon, the 15,000-strong Bonus Expeditionary Force began arriving in Washington from around the country in late May 1932. Erecting shanties by the Anacostia River and occupying abandoned buildings near the Capitol, the BEF vowed to stay until Congress authorized immediate distribution of bonuses for World War I military service (a few hundred dollars apiece), scheduled for 1945.

Initially, the police were tolerant, even sympathetic. But after the Senate rejected the bonus bill in June, Waters, under pressure from critics within the BEF, became more militant. After he called a mass meeting and assumed dictatorial powers, the BEF's encounters with police grew hostile. The Bonus Army soon dwindled to half its original size.

On July 28, a crowd attacked officers evicting BEF members from a former armory; the police chief was injured, and two veterans were fatally wounded. That evening, Hoover called in the troops. Led by Army chief of staff Douglas MacArthur (who ignored Hoover's orders to stop after the infantry had driven protesters from the contested buildings) and backed by tanks and machine guns, cavalrymen surged through the BEF's riverside camp—swinging sabers, beating and teargassing scores of veterans and spectators. By midnight, the shantytown was in flames, and the Bonus Army had been routed.

Hoover defended MacArthur, claiming the BEF was riddled with criminals and revolutionaries. But the public agreed with the injured police chief, who correctly insisted that most of the protesters were middle-class family men. Three months later, Hoover was voted out of office. **◂1932.1 ▸1933.1**

ART

Henry Moore's Holes

13 Henry Moore is often credited with making modernism acceptable in British art. Part of a circle that included sculptor Barbara Hepworth and her husband, painter Ben Nicholson, Moore already had a modest following by 1932, the year he began systematically incorporating his trademark holes into his sculptures.

Moore's carved women—with their tiny heads and imposing, distorted torsos—were reminiscent of paleolithic earth goddesses; their curves suggested hills or stones. By adding seemingly eroded openings, Moore established a central theme in his work: the link between landscape and body, between nature and humanity. This son of a coal miner eventually became Britain's most popular modern artist.

Moore's hollowed-out sculptures provided fodder for generations of satirical cartoonists, who found in them all that was ugly, obscure, and elitist in abstract art. But the figures—and their air of heroic endurance—secured his lasting reputation. **◂1928.M ▸1944.16**

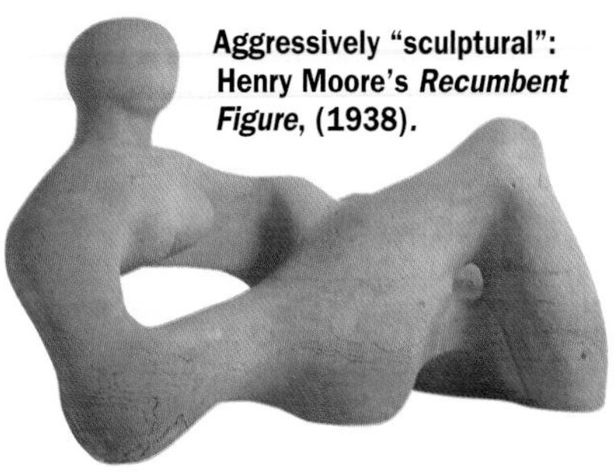

Aggressively "sculptural": Henry Moore's *Recumbent Figure*, (1938).

NOBEL PRIZES: Peace: No award ... Literature: John Galsworthy (U.K.; novelist) ... Chemistry: Irving Langmuir (U.S.; surface chemistry) ... Medicine: Charles Sherrington and Edgar D. Adrian (U.K.; neurons) ... Physics: Werner Heisenberg (German; uncertainty principle).

A VOICE FROM 1932

A South Side Boy After Sunset

From *Young Lonigan,* by James T. Farrell, 1932

In an era of spreading poverty and social breakdown, the "proletarian novel"—a direct descendant of the muckraking fiction of Upton Sinclair and Frank Norris—was cutting-edge literature. A master of the form was James T. Farrell, whose Young Lonigan, *an installment of the* Studs Lonigan *trilogy, appeared in 1932. Drawing on Farrell's own upbringing in the Irish-Catholic slums of Chicago's South Side, the grimly realistic novel shocked many readers with its unvarnished treatment of sex, but won critical praise for its sociological acuity and tragic power. William "Studs" Lonigan became an icon of the Depression years—"a normal American boy of Irish-Catholic extraction," Farrell wrote, for whom the institutions of church, school, and family "broke down and did not serve their desired function." In the excerpt below, an adolescent Studs is granted access to what he sees as the worldly paradise of the neighborhood pool hall.* **◂1906.11**

The July night leaked heat all over Fifty-eighth Street, and the fitful death of the sun shed softening colors that spread gauze-like and glamorous over the street, stilling those harshnesses and commercial uglinesses that were emphasized by the brighter revelations of the day. About the street there seemed to be a supervening beauty of reflected life. The dust, the scraps of paper, the piled-up store windows, the first electric lights sizzling into brightness. Sammie Schmaltz, the paper man, yelling his final box-score editions, a boy's broken hoop left forgotten against the elevated girder, the people hurrying out of the elevated station and others walking lazily about, all bespoke the life of a community, the tang and sorrow and joy of a people that lived, worked, suffered, procreated, aspired, filled out their little days, and died.

And the flower of this community, its young men, were grouped about the pool room, choking the few squares of sidewalk outside it....

Old toothless Nate shuffled along home from his day's work....

"How're the house maids?" asked young Studs Lonigan, who stood with the big guys, proud of knowing them, ashamed of his size, age, and short breeches. The older guys all laughed at Young Lonigan's wise-crack....

Percentage told Nate he had a swell new tobacco which he was going to let him try. Nate asked the name and price. Percentage said it was a secret he couldn't reveal, because it was not on the market yet, but he was going to give him a pipeful. He asked Nate for his pipe ... and started to thumb through his pockets. He winked at Swan, who poked the other guys. They crowded around Nate so he couldn't see, and got him interested in telling about all the chickens he made while he delivered groceries. Percentage slipped the pipe to Studs, and pointed to the street. Studs caught on, and quickly filled the pipe with dry manure.

Percentage made a long funny spiel, and gave the pipe to Nate. The guys had a hell of a time not laughing, and nearly all of them pulled out handkerchiefs. Studs felt good, because he'd been let in on a practical joke they played on someone else; it sort of stamped him as an equal.

Nate fumbled about, wasting six matches trying to light the pipe. He cursed. Percentage said it was swell tobacco, but a little difficult to light, and again their faces went a-chewing into their handkerchiefs....

Nate shuffled on, trying to light his pipe and talking to himself.

Percentage took Studs through the barber shop and back into the pool room to wash his hands. Studs said hello, casually, to Frank who always cut his hair; Frank was cutting the hair of some new guy in the neighborhood, who was reading the *Police Gazette* while Frank worked. The pool room was long and narrow; it was like a furnace, and its air was weighted with smoke. Three of the six tables were in use, and in the rear a group of lads sat around a card table, playing poker. The scene thrilled Studs, and he thought of the time he could come in and play pool and call Charley Bathcellar by his first name. He was elated as he washed his hands in the filthy lavatory....

Studs noticed the people passing. Some of them were fat guys and they had the same sleepy look his old man always had when he went for a walk.... Those old dopey-looking guys must envy the gang here, young and free like they were ... and they were the real stuff; and it wouldn't be long before he'd be one of them, and then he'd be the real stuff.

Chicago in the early part of the century. Like his Irish-Catholic creator, Studs Lonigan frequented such South Side locales as the elevated at 63rd and Halsted *(above)* and the Maxwell Street market *(top right).*

1932

"This may be the last presidential election America will have. The New Deal is to America what the early phase of Nazism was to Germany and the early phase of fascism to Italy."—**Reporter Mark Sullivan, in the *Buffalo Evening News***

STORY OF THE YEAR

FDR's First 100 Days

1 For Americans 1933 began in despair. A quarter of all heads of households were unemployed. Despite farm overproduction, famine loomed. A new financial crisis was eroding the already weakened banking system. But when Franklin D. Roosevelt became president in March, he delivered an inaugural address that heartened millions. "The only thing we have to fear," he intoned, "is fear itself." Proclaiming that the "money changers have fled from their high seats in the temple of our civilization," he warned Congress that, if it failed to approve his requests for resources, he would ask for power "as great as the power that would be given me if we were ... invaded by a foreign foe." He promised "action—and action now!"

Roosevelt fulfilled his vow in the opening months of his first term—the Hundred Days, as they came to be known—with an unprecedented barrage of new laws and executive orders. First, he called a weeklong "bank holiday" to prevent further panic withdrawals and gold hoarding. When still-solvent banks reopened, deposits soared: Confidence had been restored. Meanwhile, the President used a special session of Congress to push through a package of social legislation and financial reforms.

During the Hundred Days, the prohibition of alcoholic beverages was ended, boosting both morale and the economy. Washington relieved local governments of the task of feeding and clothing the neediest. And the foundation was laid for regulatory and public-works agencies—many designed by Roosevelt's team of unofficial advisers (called the "brain trust" for its plethora of professors). The National Recovery Administration would enforce new rules mandating minimum wages, maximum hours, and labor's right to organize. The Civilian Conservation Corps would hire inexperienced young men for environmental projects. The Agricultural Adjustment Administration would aid farmers. The Tennessee Valley Authority would build dams and hydroelectric plants.

A cartoon in *Vanity Fair* depicted Uncle Sam as Gulliver being attacked by Lilliputians and bound with the "alphabet soup" agencies of FDR's New Deal.

Journalists wryly referred to the CCC, AAA, TVA, and similar programs as "alphabet soup"; critics warned of creeping fascism or communism; and the Supreme Court eventually ruled the NRA unconstitutional. But the principle of an activist federal government, long established in Europe, had come to the United States—and despite the efforts of later presidents, it was there to stay. **◂1932.1 ▸1933.M**

FILM

Marxist Anarchy, Movie-Style

2 The scenario: It's 1933, and a garrulous little man with a mustache seizes absolute power in a bankrupt European country and provokes a war with its neighbor. The location: the fictional Freedonia, ruled by Rufus T. Firefly. The movie: the Marx Brothers' *Duck Soup*. This disreputable antiwar satire was so potent—"All God's chillun got guns," chorused the Marxes in a dark-humored "patriotic" production number—that it was actually banned in Fascist Italy.

From left: Chico, Zeppo, Groucho, and Harpo Marx.

The brothers were vaudeville and Broadway veterans who had made their talking-picture debut with *The Cocoanuts* (1929). There was no mistaking them: Groucho had the mustache, the eyebrows, and the cigar; Harpo, the harp, the hair, and no voice. Chico was the phony immigrant; Zeppo, the pleasant straight man. In *Duck Soup* and other classic movies (*Horse Feathers*, *A Night at the Opera*, *A Day at the Races*), the anarchic Marx Brothers merrily deflated the grand rituals of the time. **◂1926.M ▸1936.9**

GERMANY

Hitler Courts the Church

3 Although Germany's new dictator rejected his childhood Catholicism (he preached an entirely new faith, a neopagan amalgam of ancient Norse mythology and racialist ideology), he knew that in order to burnish his statesman image and keep the Church at bay politically, he must reach an understanding with the Vatican. The Church, for its part, sought legal security under a potentially hostile regime. In July 1933 Hitler signed a concordat with the Pope's envoy to Berlin, Cardinal Eugenio Pacelli, which guaranteed free operation for Catholic schools and institutions, and a continuation of religious education in public schools. But the government soon broke its word and began a propaganda war against any faith not committed to fatherland and Führer. By 1936, scores of priests, nuns, and Catholic leaders had been arrested.

At first, Pope Pius XI *(below)* and other Church officials suppressed their ire, but in 1937 a papal encyclical called *With Burning Anxiety* was smuggled into Germany. Assailing Nazism as a sacrilege, Pius fumed that Hitler's followers placed their Führer above God himself—but "He who dwelleth in the heavens laugheth at them." The government responded with new arrests, many for treason.

When Pius died in 1938, the far more pliant Cardinal Pacelli became Pius XII. He has been castigated for his wartime neutrality and his failure to condemn Nazi atrocities. His defenders claim that any protest would only have fanned the flames. **◂1929.10 ▸1962.1**

THE UNITED STATES

"Good Neighbor" Policy

4 Since the introduction of the Monroe Doctrine in 1823, U.S. troops had often been sent to Latin America and the Caribbean to install or rescue regimes obedient to Washington. But in his inaugural address in March 1933, Franklin Roosevelt hinted at a major change, promising a foreign policy "of the good neighbor." Later that year, at a conference in Montevideo, Uruguay, Secretary of State Cordell Hull made it official: The good neighbor policy meant no more U.S. intervention in the Western Hemisphere.

The new approach was tested in August, when civil war erupted in Cuba following President Gerardo Machado y Morales's clumsy attempt to free the island from U.S. economic domination. He was ousted by a popular revolt, and replaced, briefly, by Carlos Manuel de Céspedes. Over the four succeeding months of coups, countercoups, and upheaval, U.S. policy vacillated. The ambassador to Cuba, Sumner Welles, backed the coup against Machado—and then supported the pro-Machado officers who tried to

ART & CULTURE: Books: *Anthony Adverse* (Hervey Allen); *God's Little Acre* (Erskine Caldwell); *Miss Lonelyhearts* (Nathanael West) ... Music: "It's Only a Paper Moon" (Arlen, Harburg, and Rose); "Smoke Gets in Your Eyes" (Kern and Harbach); "Sophisticated Lady" (Ellington and Parish); "Stormy Weather" (Arlen and Koehler); *Arabella* (Richard Strauss); *Short Symphony* (Aaron Copland) ... Painting & Sculpture:

"When the Communist danger is eliminated, the normal order of things will return."
—Hitler, after the emergency decree of February 28, 1933

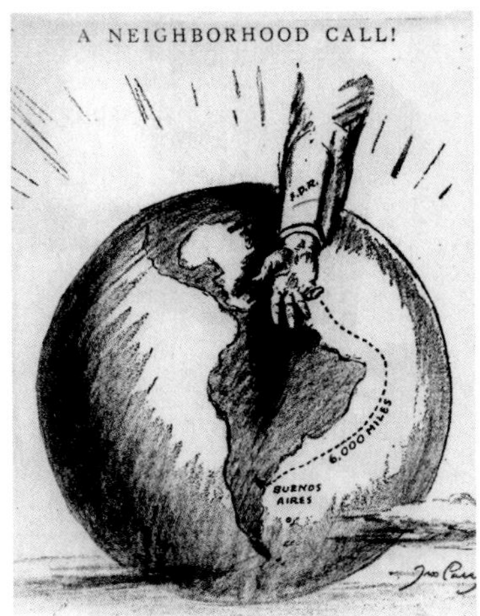

New policy: lending a neighborly hand.

overthrow one of his successors. U.S. warships sailed into Havana harbor, but no military action followed. Instead, after the crisis ended, Washington annulled the Platt Amendment of 1901, which had given it the right to invade. Three years later, the government formally renounced not only armed intervention but intervention of any kind in Latin America and the Caribbean. For the next two decades, Cuba's real ruler would be army chief of staff Fulgencio Batista y Zaldívar, who had led the coup against Céspedes. **◂1903.2 ▸1952.7**

GERMANY

Reichstag Burned

5 Appointed chancellor in January 1933, Adolf Hitler immediately set about acquiring absolute power, so that he could "purify" Germany, both politically and ethnically. First he ordered new elections, confident of gaining a Nazi majority in the Reichstag (parliament). The vote was set for March 5. As the date approached, state-run radio aired Nazi propaganda nonstop, and, as the police stood by, storm troopers harassed opponents. Then, on the night of February 27, the Reichstag building in Berlin burned to the ground. The fire—believed by many historians to have been set by the Nazis themselves—provided the necessary pretext for repression. A young Dutchman was arrested and linked with a supposed Communist plot. The government suspended civil rights, shut down the opposition press, and jailed 4,000 people.

Yet the expected landslide didn't happen: The Nazis won only 44 percent of the vote. But the right-wing Nationalist Party agreed to form a coalition with the Nazis, and the combined parties commanded a slim majority. Days later, after arranging the arrest or exclusion of all 81 Communist deputies and the co-optation of the centrists, Hitler pushed the Enabling Act through the Reichstag, which gave him a legal basis for dictatorship.

All political parties save the Nazis were dissolved. State governments were abolished, police and universities purged. Civil servants were required to prove political loyalty and lack of Jewish blood. Trade unions were reorganized into the puppet German Labor Front. Laws for the "perfection of the Aryan race" authorized sterilization of "defective" people. The government led a boycott of Jewish businesses and encouraged book burnings. Concentration camps appeared (Dachau was the first); by August they housed some 45,000 political prisoners under horrific conditions.

Finally, in October, Germany withdrew from the League of Nations, announcing its intention to rearm. The world, Hitler proclaimed, could no longer treat Germany like a "second-class citizen." Just how it *should* be treated soon became the world's most pressing problem. **◂1932.2 ▸1934.1**

As the Reichstag burned, so did any lingering hopes of salvaging the Weimar Republic.

ECONOMICS

Gold Standard Abandoned

6 In April 1933, in response to widespread bank failures and an increasingly nervous public, President Roosevelt made the decision to take the United States off the gold standard. The move was in part a reaction to Great Britain's break with gold in 1931, which was intended to push Britain toward economic recovery but resulted in a major depreciation of foreign investments.

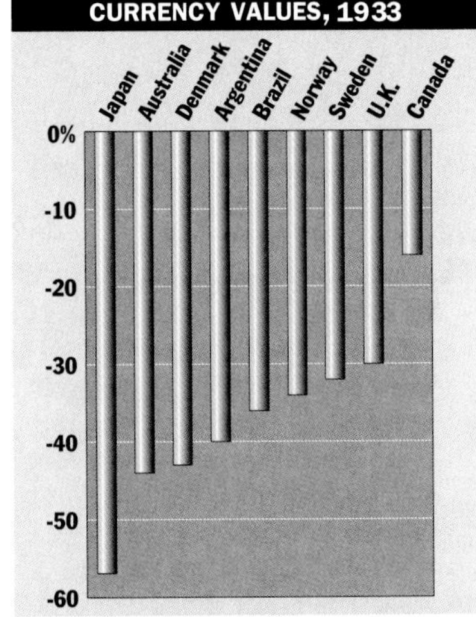

Roosevelt's decision to take the U.S. off the gold standard coincided with a dramatic devaluing of foreign currencies relative to their 1929 value in gold.

In the months preceding Roosevelt's inauguration in March, there was widespread speculation that he would follow Britain's example. Worried investors rushed to the banks for their currency while it was still convertible. Gold flowed out of the Federal Reserve at such an alarming rate that Roosevelt imposed a weeklong "bank holiday" that effectively froze gold's availability. A month later, he permanently ended the dollar's convertibility into gold; before year's end, gold was stabilized at $35 an ounce (remaining there until 1951).

Over the next few years, the European nations, beset by currency and balance-of-payment problems, one by one abandoned the collapsing international gold standard. By 1937 it no longer existed. **◂1931.1 ▸1944.12**

BIRTHS

Corazon Aquino, Filipino politician.

F. Lee Bailey, U.S. lawyer.

Jean-Paul Belmondo, French actor.

James Brown, U.S. singer.

Costa-Gavras, Greek-French filmmaker.

Jerry Falwell, U.S. evangelist.

Jerzy Grotowski, Polish stage director.

Quincy Jones, U.S. musician.

Jerzy Kosinski, Polish-U.S. novelist.

James Meredith, U.S. civil rights activist.

Stanley Milgram, U.S. psychologist.

Willie Nelson, U.S. singer.

Roman Polanski, Polish-French filmmaker.

James Rosenquist, U.S. artist.

Philip Roth, U.S. writer.

Susan Sontag, U.S. writer.

DEATHS

Roscoe "Fatty" Arbuckle, U.S. actor.

Irving Babbitt, U.S. scholar and educator.

Albert Calmette, French bacteriologist.

Calvin Coolidge, U.S. president.

Faisal I, Iraqi king.

John Galsworthy, U.K. writer.

Stefan George, German poet.

Mary Louise "Texas" Guinan, U.S. actress and hostess.

Hipólito Irigoyen, Argentine president.

Ring Lardner, U.S. writer.

George Moore, Irish writer.

F. Henry Royce, U.K. auto manufacturer.

Thubbstan rgyamtsho, 13th Dalai Lama, Tibetan religious leader.

Louis Comfort Tiffany, U.S. artist and designer.

***Departure* (Max Beckmann) ... Film: *Cavalcade* (Frank Lloyd); *42nd Street* (Lloyd Bacon); *Dinner at Eight* and *Little Women* (George Cukor); *Flying Down to Rio* (Thornton Freeland) ... Theater: *Ah, Wilderness!* (Eugene O'Neill); *Design for Living* (Noël Coward); *Blood Wedding* (Federico García Lorca); *Roberta* (Kern and Harbach) ... Radio: *The Jimmy Durante Show*; *Jack Armstrong, All-American Boy*; *The Lone Ranger*.**

"Democracy for us is not an end, but a means to conquest."—**Spanish Confederation of the Autonomous Right (CEDA) leader José Gil Robles**

NEW IN 1933

Ritz crackers (Nabisco).

News-Week magazine (later *Newsweek*).

Monopoly.

Men's magazine (*Esquire*).

The Catholic Worker.

Ernest & Julio Gallo winery.

Air France.

Windex glass cleaner.

Drive-in movie theater (Camden, New Jersey).

IN THE UNITED STATES

▶**BLONDE BOMBSHELL**—Art imitated life when platinum-blonde movie sex symbol Jean Harlow played a platinum-blonde movie sex symbol in 1933's lightning-fast satire of stardom, *Bombshell.* The glamorous superstar had an insouciant comic style, but her personal life was tortured: Her brief marriage to film

executive Paul Bern ended with his suicide, and she died of uremic poisoning in 1937 at age 26.

▶**PERRY MASON APPEARS**—With the success of two 1933 novels, *The Case of the Velvet Claws* and *The Case of the Sulky Girl*—both featuring a trial-lawyer-cum-detective named Perry Mason—a California-trial-lawyer-cum-pulp-magazine-writer named Earle Stanley Gardner retired from law to devote himself full-time to writing. Gardner eventually churned out 80 more books centered on his flamboyant courtroom sleuth.

SPAIN

Prelude to Civil War

7 Like Germany and Austria, Spain learned in 1933 that democracy could be exploited by antidemocratic forces. In November the Spanish Confederation of Autonomous Rights (CEDA) prevailed in parliamentary elections. A coalition of monarchists, Falangists (fascists), and other rightists, CEDA echoed the Nazis in its pledge to save Spain from "Marxists, Masons, Separatists, and Jews."

The new republic's harsh treatment of the Catholic Church had united the right. The Spanish people, while nominally Catholic, mostly disdained the Church for its staunch defense of property owners and the monarchy. But restrictions on religion by leftist local governments gave pious peasants a common cause with wealthy landlords. The bond was sealed when, in May 1932, the Cortes (parliament) banned parochial schools, dissolved the Jesuits, and nationalized Church property.

Meanwhile, the Cortes's ruling coalition of socialists and liberals was splintered by the slow pace of land reform. Anarchist revolts proliferated and were violently suppressed. The anarchists—now as numerous as the socialists—boycotted the fall elections, which played a major role in CEDA's strong performance.

After the elections, and despite CEDA's plurality, leftist legislators barred its members from the cabinet. But a non-CEDA rightist, Alejandro Lerroux García, became president. His government reversed its predecessors' reforms, sending the army's Civil Guard to uproot crops on redistributed land and arrest starving peasants for collecting acorns. In 1934, after Lerroux invited CEDA ministers to join the cabinet, the left rose against the regime. In Madrid, once-moderate socialists took up arms; they fell within a day. In Barcelona, a rebellion by Catalan nationalists was crushed with equal swiftness. In Asturias province, however, 50,000 anarchists and socialists revolted together, joined by the small Communist Party. Mostly miners (hence skilled in the use of dynamite), the rebels captured the city of Oviedo. But General Francisco Franco, commanding Moroccan and Spanish foreign legion troops, fought them with stunning brutality. Fallen insurgents were castrated. Captives were shot or tortured, women raped and mutilated. The Asturias revolt collapsed after two weeks.

In 1933, Catalan peasants celebrated the second anniversary of the Spanish Republic.

By 1935, Spain had 30,000 political prisoners. But the left and center would have one more chance to govern before all-out civil war engulfed them. ◂1931.13 ▸1936.2

JAPAN

A Brazen Move Forward

8 While the League of Nations deliberated over its proper role in the Sino-Japanese conflict, Japan extended its East Asian conquest to the northern edge of China proper. Asserting that the Chinese army posed a threat to so-called independent Manchukuo, the puppet state established by Japan in occupied Manchuria, the Japanese army in February 1933 invaded Jehol province. Despite its close association with the three Manchurian provinces, which had fallen to Japan in 1931–32, Jehol—just a 100-mile march from Beijing—had always been considered part of China.

Brazenly defending its usurpation

Cartoonist H.M. Talburt won a Pulitzer Prize for this cartoon condemning Japan's flouting of international treaties.

of the province, Japan declared that the presence in Jehol of "anti-Manchukuo forces is incompatible not only with the sovereignty of Manchukuo, but also with the restoration of peace and order in Jehol." The League, following the lead of the United States, had finally refused to recognize Manchukuo; now it directly attributed any loss of "peace and order in Jehol" to the Japanese invasion. Clinging to its fiction, Japan took grave offense. On March 27, the Emperor, citing Manchukuo's need for independence in Japan's quest to eradicate "sources of evil in the Far East," announced Japan's withdrawal from the League. ◂1932.5 ▸1936.11

PORTUGAL

A Diffident Dictator

9 A new constitution, passed by plebiscite in March 1933, made Portugal a corporative state, its single-party government controlled by modern Europe's most incongruous and longest-reigning dictator, António de Oliveira Salazar.

The Corporative Constitution established the Estado Nôvo (New State), in which the National Assembly contained only members of the ruling party, all government ministries were subject to Salazar's approval, and the government—effectively Salazar—had the right to suspend individual civil liberties "for the common good." This airtight formula for authoritarian rule

SPORTS: Baseball: World Series, New York Giants defeat Washington Senators, 4–2; baseball's first All-Star game (American League wins) ... Football: Chicago Bears defeat New York Giants, 23–21, in first NFL championship game ... Boxing: Primo Carnera, "Wild Bull of the Pampas," knocks out Jack Sharkey for heavyweight title ... Tennis: Helen Hull Jacobs is first woman to wear shorts in competition.

"Reading Gertrude Stein at length is not unlike making one's way through an interminable and badly printed game book."
—Richard Bridgeman, *Gertrude Stein in Pieces*

enabled Salazar to govern unchallenged until 1968.

A conservative, socially awkward professor of economics, Salazar had turned down the job of finance minister in 1926 after an Army coup toppled the corrupt parliamentary government. Two years later, President António Oscar de Fragoso Carmona again offered Salazar the post, this time with carte blanche. Salazar accepted, and proceeded to balance Portugal's chronically overdrawn budget, putting the country in the black for the first time in a century. In 1932, Carmona made Salazar prime minister, and the workaholic bachelor set up a state in his own likeness: conservative, cautious, withdrawn.

For the next 36 years, Salazar obsessively produced annual budget surpluses, ignoring the need for reinvestment. Economic growth ceased; illiteracy and rural poverty remained high. As political apathy took hold (only a small fraction of Portuguese were eligible to vote; women did not receive suffrage until the late sixties), quasifascist Portugal became Western Europe's oddest backwater. An understated tyrant, Salazar remained curiously hidden, never resorting to a cult of personality. He suffered a stroke in 1968 and was replaced by Marcello Caetano. Salazar lived for two more years, but his cowed ministers never told him he was no longer in charge. **◂1910.3 ▸1974.2**

LITERATURE

Stein's Shadow Autobiography

10 Gertrude Stein wrote her autobiography as if it were her lover's—a device that gave free rein to her considerable ego. *The Autobiography of Alice B. Toklas*, published in 1933, is full of witty, often malicious portraits of the artists, writers, intellectuals, and socialites who frequented Stein's Paris salon. Its most engaging portrait is of the author herself. "Only three times in my life have I met a genius," the narrator declares, "and each time a bell within me rang." The first bell ringer: Gertrude Stein. The runners-up: Pablo Picasso and philosopher Alfred North Whitehead.

Perhaps the century's most famous patron of the arts, Stein supported and promoted Picasso, Matisse, Braque, and Gris when they were unknown, and took such expatriate writers as Hemingway, Fitzgerald, and Pound under her wing. (Stein coined the phrase "the Lost Generation" to describe these writers and their contemporaries.) *The Autobiography* made her a literary star in her own right, as her earlier, more experimental (and much less accessible) books had not. **◂1926.2**

Gertrude Stein *(left)* with her companion and literary alter ego, Alice B. Toklas, upon their arrival in New York in 1934.

FILM

Berkeley's Beauties

11 Chorus girls revolving in kaleidoscopic patterns. Ginger Rogers dressed in huge gold coins, singing "We're in the Money" in pig Latin. Ruby Keeler tap-dancing atop a Times Square taxi. Such are the glories of Busby Berkeley, the dance director whose showstopping production numbers dominated three of Warner Bros.' hit movies in 1933: *Gold Diggers of 1933*, *42nd Street*, and *Footlight Parade*.

Berkeley never trained as a dancer or choreographer; in fact, his numbers featured very little dancing. Instead, Berkeley's camera danced as the performers swirled, surged, circled, marched, and floated to or from, past, above, or below it. It could swoop 60 feet in seconds or travel between the legs of a row of chorines. Later, through editing, he manipulated distance and scale to create spatial relationships unique to cinema.

Berkeley moved on from production numbers to whole movies, directing *Gold Diggers of 1935* and, most notably, the loony 1944 Technicolor blockbuster *The Gang's All Here*. One critic described the last moments of that movie's finale, "The Polka Dot Polka," as "the tiny disembodied heads of the entire cast [bobbing] about the screen in full-throated song." Beset by personal problems, including a drunk-driving and manslaughter charge (he was acquitted) and a nervous breakdown, Berkeley faded as Hollywood economized and musical tastes changed. But his idiosyncratic inventions still delight. **▸1934.6**

Berkeley's elaborate production numbers *(as in* Gold Diggers of 1933, *above)* liberated the movie musical from visual sluggishness.

IN THE UNITED STATES

▶RIVER REMADE—The Tennessee Valley Authority (TVA), created by Congress on May 18, oversaw the development of dams, hydroelectric plants, and waterways on the Tennessee River and its tributaries. The TVA eventually brought electricity, new agricultural practices, and much needed industry to Appalachian residents. **◂1933.1**

▶MOVIE GOES APE—"It was beauty killed the beast," proclaimed the white hunter who watched the ape he'd brought to New York get machine-gunned off the Empire State Building in the final sequence of 1933's *King Kong*. Robert Armstrong played the producer-promoter who captures Kong, Fay Wray the unwilling object of Kong's desire.

▶OBSCENITY RULINGS—In December, federal justice John M. Woolsey lifted the ban on James Joyce's 1922 novel, *Ulysses*, declaring "I do not detect anywhere the leer of a sensualist." And a city magistrate similarly determined that Erskine Caldwell's *God's Little Acre*, considered as a whole, was not obscene. **◂1922.1 ▸1934.M**

▶FANS OF FANS—Much of the success of the 1933 Chicago World's Fair, attended by 22 million people, can be credited to the fan dancer Sally Rand, who appeared in the "Streets of Paris" attraction. Carrying a giant opaque balloon, Rand sashayed across the stage to Claude Debussy's *Claire de Lune* and created a sensation without ever showing more than her face, arms, and legs. **▸1939.7**

POLITICS & BUSINESS: GNP: $55.9 billion ... 20th Amendment to U.S. Constitution ratified (moves presidential and vice-presidential inauguration date from March 4 to Jan. 20 and Congress's opening to Jan. 3) ... 21st Amendment ratified, repealing Prohibition (18th Amendment) ... U.S. grants diplomatic recognition to the U.S.S.R. ... Frances Perkins appointed secretary of labor (first female cabinet member).

"If man is not ready to risk his life, where is his dignity?"—**André Malraux, *Man's Fate***

AROUND THE WORLD

▶DESERT KINGDOM—In 1933, a year after proclaiming the Kingdom of Saudi Arabia, Ibn Saud, Sultan of Najd and King of Hejaz, granted a 60-year concession to Standard Oil of California—which soon formed the Arabian American Oil Co. (ARAMCO)—for exclusive rights to explore the Saudi Arabian desert for oil. The deal made Saudi Arabia one of the world's richest countries. But Saud, a puritanical Muslim, came to feel he'd made a pact with the devil: He saw a new religion of oil and wealth replacing ancient Islamic values. ◂1909.5

▶ASSYRIAN MASSACRE—Dissension began to spread in the summer of 1933 among the various factions of the newly united Iraq. King Faisal had negotiated an end to the British mandate over Iraq in 1932 on the condition that minority rights would be protected. But Faisal's efforts at domestic peace and unity were shattered when, while he was away in Europe, a former rival ordered Iraqi troops to massacre several hundred Assyrian Christians living in a northern region called Mosul. Faisal died in September with his carefully wrought coalition in chaos. ◂1920.2 ▸1941.3

▶LANG FLEES GERMANY—Fritz Lang's 1933 film, *Das Testament des Dr. Mabuse* expressed the German director's disdain for Nazism—the film's most villainous characters (including the decadent title character) spout Nazi slogans. The movie was banned, but Joseph Goebbels, minister of propaganda, called Lang into his office, apologized, then asked the director to head the Nazi film industry—ostensibly at the request of Hitler himself, who had greatly admired Lang's *Metropolis* (1926). Lang, whose mother was Jewish, smelled a trap. He fled by train to Paris the same night, leaving behind all his possessions as well as his wife, who later made propaganda films for the Nazis. ◂1926.5 ▸1935.14

1933

TECHNOLOGY

Armstrong Invents FM

12 From the birth of radio broadcasting early in the century, telecommunications giants such as RCA and AT&T had employed teams of engineers to find a cure for static interference. What distinguished American inventor Edwin Armstrong, who in 1933 took out four patents on FM broadcasting circuitry, was a willingness to buck tradition. While the experts tinkered with the existing system of transmission by amplitude modulation (AM), Armstrong devised a system (FM) that modulated the frequency, rather than the size, of radio waves. Practically immune to static and amenable to a wide range of sounds, Armstrong's system improved the clarity of radio beyond imagination.

Many engineers had experimented with FM before, only to dismiss it for the sound distortions it produced. Armstrong discovered that when the FM frequency band was widened, distortion disappeared, as did static. Most broadcasters believed that a narrower band meant less static; Armstrong demonstrated that static was a natural function of amplitude and that principles of AM static reduction therefore did not apply to FM.

Faced with change, the radio industry stonewalled. Radio was big business, and the commercial networks had invested heavily in AM; Armstrong's system threatened to make standard transmitters and receivers obsolete. Finally, in 1939, Armstrong established his own FM station (previous inventions had made him wealthy) and used it to nurture the system's growth. It slowly began to catch on, but in 1954 an ailing Armstrong, his fortune depleted by legal battles over the control of FM, committed suicide. **◂1920.3 ▸1941.14**

A few months before his assassination by Nazis, Chancellor Dollfuss addressed a gathering at an Austrian racetrack.

AUSTRIA

Dollfuss's Dilemmas

13 Although Adolf Hitler had begun his rise to power modeling himself after Benito Mussolini, the Fascist leader regarded Hitler as a dangerous upstart. By 1933 the two leaders (and future allies) were open rivals, and dire consequences awaited anyone who stood between them—as Austrian chancellor Engelbert Dollfuss quickly learned.

Dollfuss, hoping to protect his country from Hitler's lust for *Anschluss* (union), aligned his nation with Italy and cracked down on Austria's own increasingly powerful Nazis. As leader of the *Heimatbloc*—a coalition of conservatives and anti-Anschluss fascists—Dollfuss was despised by both the Austrian Nazis and the Social Democrats. When the German Nazis came to power in March 1933, Dollfuss feared that their Austrian counterparts would do as well in upcoming elections. Unwilling to join forces with socialists, he staged a preemptive strike. Two days after the German voting, he suspended parliament and invoked a wartime statute allowing him to govern by decree. Public meetings were banned (only the Heimatbloc's continued), as was the wearing of paramilitary uniforms (except those of the fascist *Heimwehr* storm troopers). Censorship was imposed, and Nazis were purged from the army.

The Austrian Nazis responded with terrorist bombings. Germany began a damaging boycott and sent a barrage of propaganda across the border, urging Austrians to overthrow their government. In June, Dollfuss outlawed the Nazi Party, deporting its leaders and sending thousands of members to detention camps. But the violence continued.

Prodded by Mussolini, Dollfuss set about restructuring his nation along fascist lines. Early in 1934, he established a new constitution that replaced Austria's political parties with a monolithic Fatherland Front and granted him absolute power. But in July, a detachment of Viennese Nazis stormed his office and murdered him. The ensuing Nazi putsch was defeated by loyal Heimwehr units, and Italian troops mobilized at the border to prevent a German invasion. Justice Minister Kurt von Schuschnigg succeeded Dollfuss as chancellor. The Anschluss was forestalled until 1938—when Hitler and Mussolini set aside their differences. **◂1933.5 ▸1934.1**

LITERATURE

Malraux's Fatalistic Tale

14 An intellectual and adventurer who caused an international scandal when he was arrested for stealing bas-reliefs from an ancient Cambodian temple, André Malraux emerged as a spokesman for an embattled generation with his 1933 novel, *La Condition humaine (Man's Fate)*.

The tale is set in Shanghai in 1927, when General Chiang Kai-shek did an about-face and massacred his former Communist allies. *Man's Fate* follows a group of international revolutionaries as they struggle to come to grips with a situation in which friends are now enemies and death is imminent. Suffused with a tragic fatalism, the novel presaged the political struggles leading to World War II, as well as the left-leaning, morally committed existentialism of the postwar years. In Malraux's view, the human condition is relentlessly grim, yet humanity has no choice but to engage in political struggle. **▸1942.13**

RADIO'S GREATEST THRILL
FM
TUNE IN
W65H
CONNECTICUT'S PIONEER FM BROADCASTER
ASK YOUR DEALER FOR AN FM DEMONSTRATION

A billboard advertising a Connecticut FM station in 1935.

NOBEL PRIZES: Peace: Norman Angell (U.K; writer) ... Literature: Ivan Bunin (Russian; poet and novelist) ... Chemistry: No award ... Medicine: Thomas Hunt Morgan (U.S.; heredity) ... Physics: Erwin Schrödinger and Paul A.M. Dirac (German, U.K.; quantum mechanics).

A VOICE FROM 1933

Clash of the Titans

Correspondence between Nelson Rockefeller and Diego Rivera, from *The New York Times,* May 1933

New York City's lavish Rockefeller Center was the most ambitious monument to capitalism yet undertaken. So perhaps conflict was inevitable when Nelson Rockefeller, the director of the complex, commissioned Mexican muralist and self-proclaimed revolutionary Diego Rivera to paint a 63′ × 17′ mural entitled Man at the Crossroads *in the great hall of the 70-story RCA Building. The two clashed over Rivera's inclusion of a portrait of V.I. Lenin. After they exchanged letters in* The New York Times (below), *Rockefeller canceled the project and shrouded the almost-finished work with canvas. Less than a year later, he ordered it smashed from the wall.* ◄**1930.7** ►**1954.11**

Nelson Rockefeller to Diego Rivera, May 4, 1933

Dear Mr. Rivera:

While I was in the No. 1 building at Rockefeller Center yesterday viewing the progress of your thrilling mural, I noticed that in the most recent portion of the painting you had included a portrait of Lenin. The piece is beautifully painted, but it seems to me that his portrait, appearing in this mural, might very easily seriously offend a great many people. If it were in a private house it would be one thing, but this mural is in a public building and the situation is therefore quite different. As much as I dislike to do so, I am afraid we must ask you to substitute the face of some unknown man where Lenin's face now appears.

You know how enthusiastic I am about the work which you have been doing and that to date we have in no way restricted you in either subject or treatment. I am sure you will understand our feeling in this situation and we will greatly appreciate your making the suggested substitution.

Diego Rivera to Nelson Rockefeller, May 6, 1933

Dear Mr. Rockefeller:

In reply to your kind letter of May 4, 1933, I wish to tell you my actual feelings on the matters you raise, after I have given considerable reflection to them.

The head of Lenin was included in the original sketch ... and in the drawings in line made on the wall at the beginning of my work.... I understand quite thoroughly the point of view concerning the business affairs of a commercial public building, although I am sure that that class of person who is capable of being offended by the portrait of a deceased great man would feel offended, given such a mentality, by the entire conception of my painting. Therefore, rather than mutilate the conception, I should prefer the physical destruction of the conception in its entirety, but conserving, at least, its integrity....

I should like, as far as possible, to find an acceptable solution to the problem you raise, and suggest that I could change the sector which shows society people playing bridge and dancing and put in its place, in perfect balance with the Lenin portion, a figure of some great American historical leader, such as Lincoln, who symbolizes the unification of the country and the abolition of slavery, surrounded by John Brown, Nat Turner, William Lloyd Garrison or Wendell Phillips and Harriet Beecher Stowe, and perhaps some scientific figure like McCormick, inventor of the McCormick reaper, which aided in the victory of the anti-slavery forces by providing sufficient wheat to sustain the Northern armies.

I am sure that the solution I propose will entirely clarify the historical meaning of the figure of a leader as represented by Lincoln, and no one will be able to object to them without objecting to the most fundamental feelings of human love and solidarity and the constructive social force represented by such men.

Rivera *(top, at work on the Lenin portrait)* painted this replica of the Rockefeller Center mural at the Palacio de Bellas Artes in Mexico City, making only minor changes to emphasize Mexican culture and history. He also included a scathing portrait of John D. Rockefeller, Jr., Nelson Rockefeller's father.

"I am not flattered to think that Adolf Hitler made a revolution after the pattern of my own. The Germans will end up by ruining our idea."—**Benito Mussolini, 1934**

STORY OF THE YEAR

Hitler Tightens His Grip

1 Adolf Hitler spent 1934 laying the groundwork for Germany's conquest of Europe. At home, he needed army support for his plan to seize absolute control when ailing President Paul von Hindenburg died. But the generals insisted that he first curb the SA—the storm troops who'd long intimidated the Nazis' opponents and who now demanded leadership of the military. On June 29, the "night of the long knives," Hitler used the pretext of a coup plot to launch a purge. Hermann Goering, Hitler's right-hand man, and Heinrich Himmler, head of the SS (the Nazis' elite guard organization, which henceforth became the government's police agency), directed the roundup and execution of SA chief Ernst Röhm and 400 others, including left-leaning Nazis and prominent monarchists. The SA was disarmed; most of its duties, such as concentration-camp administration, went to the SS.

The generals were satisfied, as were industrialists who had feared that the Nazi revolution might prove too revolutionary. When Hindenburg died in August, Hitler—already chancellor—became president as well, under a law he'd issued the day before. He thus became supreme commander of the armed forces. Officers and soldiers had to swear allegiance to the Führer. In a plebiscite, 90 percent of the electorate voted in favor of the new arrangement.

In foreign affairs, Hitler scored two clear successes. In January, he signed a ten-year nonaggression pact with Poland, whose army of 250,000 outnumbered his own by 2.5 to 1. The treaty lulled the Poles into a complacency that would cost them dearly five years later, and allowed Hitler to pose as a peacemaker while he secretly rearmed Germany. In June, he declared that Germany would never resume war-debt payments to the Allies—and got off scot-free. (The default of 13 other Depression-ridden nations helped blunt any reaction.)

Elsewhere, Hitler appeared to stumble. A first visit with his idol Mussolini (who privately called him a "buffoon") was fruitless. Soon afterward, an attempt to install a puppet regime in Austria—after Viennese Nazis murdered dictator Engelbert Dollfuss, Mussolini's ally—was foiled by local resistance and an Italian troop buildup. But Hitler shrewdly disowned Dollfuss's killing (though in fact he'd instigated it). His steady courtship of Il Duce would pay off two years later, with the forming of the Rome-Berlin Axis. Its first casualty: independent Austria. **◄1933.5 ►1935.3**

Eliminating his enemies, consolidating his power: Hitler in 1934.

MEXICO

Rescuer of the Revolution

2 The Mexican Revolution produced its last great hero in 1934, when Lázaro Cárdenas became president and finally implemented the radical reforms promised by the constitution of 1917. He succeeded a series of leaders who had done little to achieve the revolution's aims of land reform and workers' rights. During his six years in office, Cárdenas transferred 44 million acres from *haciendados,* Mexico's wealthy land-owners, into *ejidos,* agricultural cooperatives. The land was then parceled out, through the *ejidos,* to some 800,000 peasants. "The revolution was in the gutter," Cárdenas said. "It is necessary to raise it up."

For an encore, in 1938 he nationalized foreign-owned oil companies. That stunning act was precipitated by a long-standing wage dispute between the oil industry's Mexican workers and their foreign employers, mostly American and British. In 1937, the Mexican Supreme Court settled the dispute in favor of the workers. When the foreign companies ignored the ruling, refusing to increase wages or improve conditions, Cárdenas expropriated them. American firms implored FDR to intervene, but the President, not wanting to drive another Latin American government toward Germany (which had courted Mexico during the First World War with promises of the American Southwest), cited his "Good Neighbor" policy and declined. Mexican oil nationalization was a fait accompli—a fact that would have drastic economic consequences during the price boom of the seventies. **◄1933.4 ►1982.5**

FRANCE

Scandal Topples Government

3 When a bullet killed Serge Alexandre Stavisky in January 1934, the police called it suicide—but many Frenchmen believed he'd been murdered to protect his influential friends. Stavisky had been arrested in 1925 for defrauding investors of seven million francs, and served 18 months in jail awaiting trial. But somehow that trial had always been postponed. Meanwhile, he'd bilked investors out of another 200 million francs, using the money to buy newspapers and politicians. The scandal (which was just breaking in January, when he was found dead in an Alpine villa) nearly brought down the republic.

The Stavisky Affair touched several figures associated with Camille Chautemps's center-left government. As members of Action Française (an anti-Semitic royalist group) rioted, rightist legislators demanded that Chautemps resign. He soon complied. The new premier, Edouard Daladier, broadened the cabinet, appointing several right-wingers. But on February 6, after he disciplined a police prefect who'd been too lenient with the rioters, 5,000 rightists and fascists marched on Parliament, burning buildings and showering police with bricks along the way. At least 15 people were killed. Similar disturbances erupted nationwide, and Daladier resigned the next day.

Fearing a putsch, the socialists called a 24-hour general strike in support of parliamentary democracy; their old rivals the communists joined in. (Their alliance marked the birth of the Front Commun—a precursor of the myriad popular fronts of the mid-thirties.) Another coalition government was formed, and the threat from within receded. But after Pierre Laval's appointment as premier in 1935, France embarked on a path that would end in fascism imposed by German troops. **◄1906.12 ►1936.5**

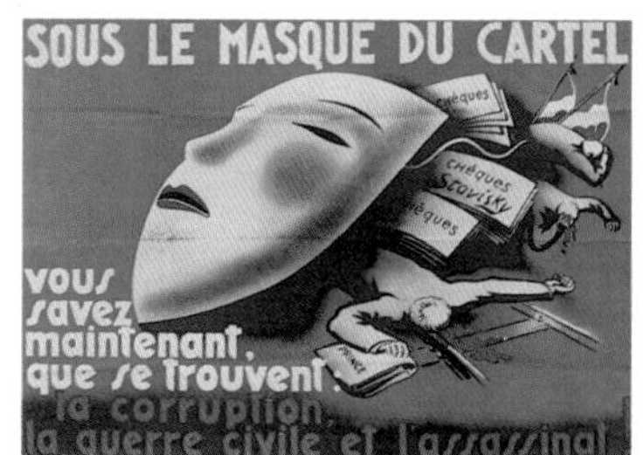

Right-wing propaganda poster accusing leftists of complicity in Stavisky's scams and the assassination of a key witness.

THE UNITED STATES

The Dust Bowl

4 By 1934, a 150,000-square-mile stretch of America's midwestern farmland was turning to desert, its topsoil blowing off in

ART & CULTURE: Books: *Tender Is the Night* (F. Scott Fitzgerald); *Appointment in Samarra* (John O'Hara); *Call It Sleep* (Henry Roth); *Good Bye, Mr. Chips* (James Hilton); *I, Claudius* (Robert Graves); *Patterns of Culture* (Ruth Benedict) ... Music: "Blue Moon" (Rodgers and Hart); "I Only Have Eyes for You"

"Can't act. Can't sing. Balding. Can dance a little."—**Report on the 1928 screen test of Broadway star Fred Astaire**

A "black roller" dust storm in Clayton, New Mexico, snapped by an amateur photographer who immediately fled indoors. The thick dust blocked the light from across the street.

mammoth dust storms. The phenomenon was triggered by a drought, but its roots lay in the economic excesses of the 1920s. Spurred by soaring postwar grain prices, farmers had plowed up vast tracts of earth that had been held down by native grasses. When the rains stopped, there was nothing to keep the prairie wind from stripping away the land.

The Dust Bowl, as it was called, covered parts of Kansas, Colorado, Oklahoma, Texas, and New Mexico. Farming in this zone became almost impossible. As farms failed, so did local businesses. Along with poverty, the dust brought peculiar hazards and discomforts. It sifted into buildings, ruining food, furniture, and medical instruments. Deadly respiratory diseases flourished. During the "black blizzards," train engineers missed their stations. Children playing outdoors were sometimes smothered.

Most Dust Bowl residents stayed put. They also cultivated a stoical sense of humor, joking about the man who fainted when a raindrop fell on his head and was revived by being doused with a bucketful of sand. But thousands of penniless families fled the region, an exodus captured in John Steinbeck's novel *The Grapes of Wrath.*

By 1935, migrating dust often darkened the skies of Washington, D.C., more than a thousand miles away. Urged on by President Roosevelt, Congress established the Soil Conservation Service, which helped farmers restore and safeguard their precious topsoil. Another agency, the Civilian Conservation Corps, planted millions of trees for windbreaks. Within two years the area of devastation had shrunk dramatically. The rains returned in 1940, and the Dust Bowl again became part of the nation's breadbasket. **◂1930.3 ▸1939.15**

MUSIC

A Russian Romantic

5 Convalescing after surgery in June 1934, Sergei Rachmaninoff, the leading piano virtuoso of his time and the last of the great Russian Romantic composers,

Rachmaninoff's music, a critic said, could have been composed "only by a man who in his inmost soul is a Russian."

vowed, "After returning home I shall begin to work seriously." Home, for the moment, meant Switzerland, not Rachmaninoff's beloved Russia. Since the 1917 revolution, he had lived in painful exile in Europe and the United States, and had produced no work of significance. Most critics considered him to be dried up as a composer. Then, later that year, Rachmaninoff finally recovered his powers and wrote one of his most lastingly popular compositions, *Rhapsody on a Theme of Paganini.*

Rachmaninoff, whose music remained firmly rooted in the nineteenth century, was a melodist in the Romantic tradition of Tchaikovsky. He had left his homeland to play in Sweden in 1917 just before the revolution, and had never returned. Later exile in the United States proved especially lonely; he never mastered English, and he traveled constantly, giving up to 65 performances a year for adoring audiences. In 1931, after he publicly criticized the Soviet regime, Rachmaninoff's music was branded decadent. For two years, it received no play in the land it celebrated. **◂1931.3 ▸1936.13**

FILM

Fred and Ginger on the Rise

6 One of the silver screen's most enchanting partnerships began in earnest in 1934, when Fred Astaire and Ginger Rogers got top billing for the first time in *The Gay Divorcée.* (The pair first appeared together the previous year in *Flying Down to Rio.*) *The Gay Divorcée* and its featured dance, the Continental (which was too complicated to really catch on), introduced a genre that would be honed to perfection over the course of eight more movies.

With Astaire and Hermes Pan choreographing, gargantuan, stagebound production numbers were minimized. Instead, dances were placed in nontheatrical settings and integrated into the story. The dancers were shown full figure in long, seamless takes; solos and pas de deux dominated. Astaire and Rogers brought cohesion, intimacy, and, especially, romance to the movie musical. (Indeed, in their pictures—produced during the days of strict Hays Code enforcement—the songs and dances function as an elaborate mating ritual; after one number in *The Gay Divorcée*, Cole Porter's "Night and Day," Astaire even flips open a cigarette case and offers an enervated Rogers a smoke.)

Rogers was never Astaire's dance equal, but she was his best partner. He was coolly experimental; she was warmly craftsmanlike. He was elegant, ethereal; she was streamlined and street-smart. As Katharine Hepburn allegedly said, "He gave her class, and she gave him sex." **◂1933.11 ▸1935.M**

Astaire and Rogers dance the Continental.

BIRTHS

Henry Aaron, U.S. baseball player.

Le Roi Jones (Amiri Baraka), U.S. writer.

Brigitte Bardot, French actress.

Pat Boone, U.S. singer.

Roberto Clemente, U.S. baseball player.

Van Cliburn, U.S. musician.

Bettino Craxi, Italian prime minister.

Joan Didion, U.S. writer.

Yuri Gagarin, Soviet cosmonaut.

Jane Goodall, U.K. zoologist.

Marilyn Horne, U.S. singer.

Larry King, U.S. talk show host.

Sophia Loren, Italian actress.

Kate Millett, U.S. writer.

Ralph Nader, U.S. consumer advocate.

Mary Quant, U.K. fashion designer.

Carl Sagan, U.S. astronomer.

Norman Schwarzkopf, U.S. general.

Wole Soyinka, Nigerian writer.

Bart Starr, U.S. football player and coach.

Gloria Steinem, U.S. writer and feminist leader.

DEATHS

Albert I, Belgian king.

Alexander I, Yugoslav king.

Clyde Barrow, U.S. criminal.

Marie Curie, Polish-French chemist.

John Dillinger, U.S. criminal.

Edward Elgar, U.K. composer.

Fritz Haber, German chemist.

Bonnie Parker, U.S. criminal.

Raymond Poincaré, French president.

(Warren and Dubin); *Lieutenant Kije Suite* (Sergei Prokofiev) ... Painting & Sculpture: *Prometheus* (Paul Manship) ... Film: *It Happened One Night* (Frank Capra); *The Thin Man* (W.S. Van Dyke); *Twentieth Century* (Howard Hawks); *Of Human Bondage* (John Cromwell, with Bette Davis) ... Theater: *The Children's Hour* (Lillian Hellman); *The Infernal Machine* (Jean Cocteau) ... Radio: *The Bob Hope Show.*

"Dillinger did not rob poor people. He robbed those who became rich by robbing the poor. I am for Johnny."
—Letter to an Indiana newspaper

NEW IN 1934

Flash Gordon, Li'l Abner, Donald Duck.

U.S. federal prison at Alcatraz Island (San Francisco, Calif.).

Seagram's Seven Crown whiskey.

Laundromat (The Washeteria, Fort Worth, Texas).

Pipeless organ (Hammond).

Secret Swiss bank accounts (Bank Secrecy Law).

IN THE UNITED STATES

▶BONNIE AND CLYDE—Far less glamorous than their film counterparts, Bonnie Parker and Clyde Barrow were hard-scrabble thieves and killers who robbed gas stations,

small-town banks, and luncheonettes from Missouri down through Oklahoma and Texas. They were responsible for 12 murders but never managed to steal more than $1,500 in a single heist. Their 21-month spree ended on May 23, near Gibsland, Louisiana. Betrayed by the father of another "Barrow Gang" member, the pair were ambushed and shot to death by five sheriff's deputies and a Texas Ranger. ▸1934.8

▶LOW-LIFE LUST—Immediately after Henry Miller's *Tropic of Cancer* was published in Paris in 1934, U.S. customs officials banned the book as obscene. Based on Miller's own wild days and nights of alternately starving, mooching, and partying as an American expatriate in Paris during the Depression, the novel mixed unabashed carnality with a comic acceptance of

CHINA

The Long March

7 Outnumbered and surrounded by Chiang Kai-shek's Nationalist forces, the Communists of China's Jiangxi province abandoned their beleaguered encampment in 1934. On October 16, under the cover of darkness, some 80,000 men broke out of Jiangxi, near the cities of Ganžhou and Huićhang, piercing Chiang's cordon. They left behind their wives and children and a rear guard of 28,000 troops, 20,000 of whom were sick and wounded. But from this abject defeat arose the defining event of Chinese communism: the Long March.

Dogged by Nationalist troops and hostile warlords, the retreating Communists marched for 6,000 miles, traversing 18 mountain ranges and crossing 24 rivers before reaching safety in Yan'an, in the northern province of Shaanxi. More than half the original contingent was lost during the yearlong ordeal, but the epic Long March was a powerful symbolic victory for the Communists. They preached China's socialist future as they traveled through territory inhabited by 200 million people. They also solidified their own revolutionary identity, creating the legend on which Chinese communism was founded. The march "has proclaimed to the world that the Red Army is an army of heroes," wrote Mao Zedong, the journey's chief architect, "while the imperialists and their running dogs, Chiang Kai-shek and his like, are impotent."

For Mao, it was also a personal triumph. Midway through, he had transformed the flight into a "mobile war," carrying out lethal guerrilla raids on Chiang's pursuing armies. Mao's rivals for military and political control of the Chinese Communist Party, Zhou Enlai and Bo Gu, conceded his superiority. By the march's end, Mao could claim equality with his great enemy, Chiang. **◂1931.2 ▸1936.10**

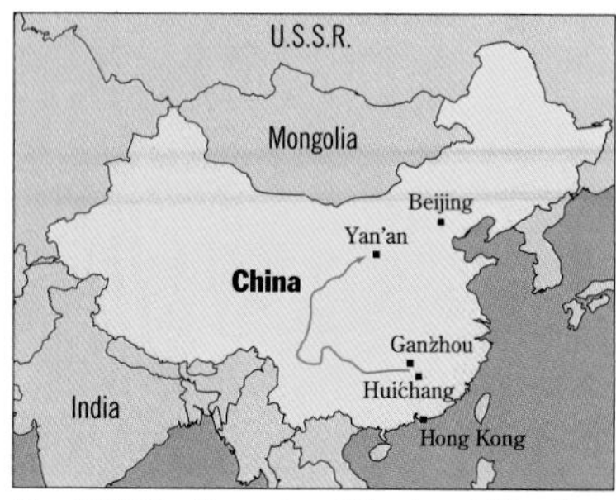

The 6,000-mile route of the Long March.

WANTED
JOHN HERBERT DILLINGER
$10,000.00
$5,000.00

For 13 months, Dillinger reigned as the most notorious and most wanted bank robber in the United States.

CRIME

A Dashing Desperado

8 The Depression brought back an old-fashioned American folk hero: the desperado. Bank robbers like Pretty Boy Floyd, Bonnie Parker, and Clyde Barrow (all killed in 1934) blasted their way across the country, stealing from the rich and sometimes giving to the poor—many of whom idolized them as heroes. The most celebrated of all was John Dillinger, whose brief, spectacular crime spree ended bloodily in July.

Dillinger had served nine years in prison for trying to rob an Indiana grocery store. Paroled in May 1933, he promptly robbed five banks, cutting a dashing profile with his natty clothes, his jaunty humor, and his agile leaps over turnstiles. Caught in September, Gentleman Johnny (as he was nicknamed) was sprung by some former prisonmates whose escapes he'd earlier engineered. Dillinger's gang staged holdups and raided police arsenals from Florida to Arizona—where he was caught again. This time, he threatened jail guards with a wooden pistol, then drove off in the sheriff's car.

After Dillinger repeatedly eluded the Federal Bureau of Investigation—once escaping from a Wisconsin hideout (with new gang member Baby Face Nelson) while panicky FBI agents fired on bystanders—Bureau director J. Edgar Hoover asked Congress for a broader mandate. (Theretofore, agents had been authorized only to *investigate*, not to make arrests; they'd used weapons at the risk of punishment.) Two months later, a Romanian-born brothel madam named Anna Sage, facing deportation, offered to deliver the bandit. A dozen FBI agents ambushed him as he and the "lady in red" left Chicago's Biograph Theatre. Decades later, evidence emerged that the victim was not Dillinger at all, but a decoy. (The FBI has held fast to its version of the events.) Hoover emerged from the operation a national hero. Over the next year, G-men, as his agents were popularly known, would kill or capture all the famous fugitives. Over the next 30 years, Hoover would amass personal power sometimes exceeding that of the presidents he served. Dillinger thus helped create the modern FBI. **◂1934.M. ▸1950.M**

TECHNOLOGY

Du Pont's Wonder Fiber

9 Severe shortages during World War I had alerted the world's scientists to the need for a synthetic alternative to costly, difficult-to-harvest natural rubber.

Wallace H. Carothers with a piece of neoprene, the first successful synthetic rubber.

Having unlocked some of the mysteries of natural polymers in the 1920s, chemists launched an all-out hunt for a synthetic polymer. A research team headed by Wallace H. Carothers at Du Pont Company in Wilmington, Delaware, developed neoprene, the first commercial synthetic rubber. Then, three years later, in 1934, the team came up with the first synthetic fiber—a superpolymer made from coal, air, and water; it was stronger than silk and could be spun into hair-thin fibers. Polyhexamethyleneadipamide, called nylon for short, would dramatically influence the course of world events.

Nylon's first use was for fashion. Following a feverish development and marketing effort, Du Pont put

SPORTS: Baseball: World Series, St. Louis Cardinals (Gashouse Gang) defeat Detroit Tigers, 4–3 ... Football: NFL, New York Giants defeat Chicago Bears, 30–13 ... Boxing: Max Baer knocks Primo Carnera down 12 times in 11 rounds (fight stopped, Baer awarded title) ... Golf: First Masters tournament ... Hockey: NHL introduces penalty shot ... Soccer: World Cup, Italy defeats Czechoslovakia, 2–1.

"One night, scuffling around Harlem, I fell in the Savoy. After dancing a couple of rounds, I heard a voice that sent chills up my spine."—**Pianist-arranger Mary Lou Williams, on first hearing Ella Fitzgerald sing**

ladies' sheer nylon hosiery on sale in Wilmington in 1939. Demand was overwhelming. But during World War II, stockings almost disappeared from sight, since nylon was of inestimable use to the military. Without nylon—used in everything from parachutes and sutures to rope, machine parts, and insulating material—the Allies might not have won the war.

Carothers was less fortunate. Severely depressed, he checked into a Philadelphia hotel room on April 29, 1937—two days after his 41st birthday and two years before nylons appeared in stores—and committed suicide by taking cyanide. **◂1920.10 ▸1940.M**

MUSIC

The Incomparable Ella

10 It was Amateur Night at the Harlem Opera House, and a tall, skinny 16-year-old took the stage, intending to dance. Her legs shaking with terror, she decided that dancing was out of the question and proceeded instead to sing the only two songs she knew, "The Object of My Affection" and "Judy." The Opera House audience, notorious for its merciless put-downs, was mesmerized. Ella Fitzgerald later remembered that night in 1934: "Three encores later," she said, "I had the $25 first prize."

Admired for her wide range, tonal clarity, and impeccable diction, Fitzgerald breathed life into even banal music. Her recording of "A-Tisket, A-Tasket," a nursery-rhyme novelty tune, became one of the most popular records of 1938. Later, Fitzgerald became a master of scat, using her flexible voice to improvise nonsense syllables to jazz songs. She reached her apotheosis as an interpreter of American popular songs during her long association, beginning in 1956, with entrepreneur Norman Granz. For his Verve label she made her beloved "Songbook" albums, recording definitive renditions of Gershwin, Ellington, Arlen, and Kern, among others. Music schools still use her vintage records to teach singing, but she's inimitable. "Ella Fitzgerald," said a fan after her landmark 1957 Hollywood Bowl concert, "could sing the Van Nuys telephone directory with a broken jaw and make it sound good." **▸1937.5**

Ella Fitzgerald, the "First Lady of Song."

POPULAR CULTURE

Comic Books Arrive

11 Although comic strips had been running in newspapers since the turn of the century (the first, in 1896, appeared in the *New York World*), it wasn't until the 1930s that comics were successfully published in non-newspaper form. George Delacorte of Dell Publishing Company tried two such variations. The first, a newspaper-style Sunday section containing only comics and sold separately on newsstands, was a flop; the second, a 68-page publication introduced in 1934, succeeded. Delacorte's "Famous Funnies" used the new eight-by-eleven-inch format and was offered to the public directly, for 10 cents, in big department stores. The initial press run of 35,000 was a sellout. The modern comic book was born.

Titles and characters proliferated as other companies followed suit. In 1936, the McKay Company of Philadelphia lifted Flash Gordon and Popeye out of the Sunday funnies and into books. Then, in June 1938, came the biggest breakthrough of all: Action Comics introduced a character created by a pair of frustrated comic-book artists named Jerry Siegel and Joe Shuster. Superman turned the comic-book world upside down, spawning radio and television shows, movies, and a host of other superheroes, including Batman, Wonder Woman, and other icons of modern mythology. **◂1907.13 ▸1939.M**

In addition to comic-strip characters, the first comic book offered "games, puzzles, magic."

IN THE UNITED STATES

squalor. *Tropic of Cancer* was not published in America until 1961; it was the focus of a series of obscenity trials that ended with a 1964 Supreme Court decision in the book's favor. ◂1933.M

▶EPIC UNMADE BY HOLLYWOOD—Muckraking author Upton Sinclair won the 1934 Democratic primary for governor, running on a platform called End Poverty in California (EPIC). That a declared socialist could be a political success so alarmed Louis B. Mayer that the movie mogul launched what was arguably the first instance of mass-media manipulation of a political campaign. Staged "newsreels" of poor migrants rushing off to California to benefit from EPIC programs paraded as hard news. Faked man-on-the-street interviews showed minority and poor interviewees planning to vote for Sinclair, while "upstanding" citizens declared loyalty to his Republican opponent. Sinclair lost the election. ◂1906.11

▶GABLE AND COLBERT—The role was meant as a way for MGM to put Clark Gable in his place. The star was getting uppity about the parts the studio was assigning him, so he was farmed out to relatively unprestigious Columbia to star as a reporter on the road in *It Happened One Night*. Directed by Frank Capra and costarring Claudette Colbert as a runaway heiress, the 1934 movie—the prototype for the era's "screwball" comedies—ended up being a critical and commercial smash, sweeping all five of the top Oscars. In one of the film's famous "walls of Jericho" sequences (the wall was a blanket strung on a rope to separate the unmarried couple in a shared motel room), Gable removed his shirt and revealed a bare chest. In the wake of the movie's popularity, undershirt sales plummeted. ▸1938.11

POLITICS & BUSINESS: GNP: $65.4 billion ... Federal Communications Commission (FCC) and Securities and Exchange Commission (SEC) are established (more than 30 new government agencies with 25,000 new employees established since 1933) ... Reciprocal Trade Agreement allows president to negotiate tariffs without Senate approval.

"I stopped believing in Santa Claus at an early age. Mother took me to see him at a department store and he asked for my autograph."—Shirley Temple

AROUND THE WORLD

▶TOYNBEE'S HISTORY—One of the century's most influential historians, Arnold Toynbee, published in 1934 the first book in his 12-volume magnum opus, *A Study of History.* The Oxford-educated Briton's thesis: Civilizations rise and fall in cycles. They gain strength from enlightened leadership, only to collapse when leaders abandon creativity for nationalism, militarism, and tyranny. ◂1928.12 ▸1962.12

▶MAGICAL NANNY—Australian-born Shakespearean actress Pamela "P.L." Travers was 28 when her first book, *Mary Poppins*—the story of a nanny with magical powers—became a runaway favorite of British children in 1934. The book and its sequels formed the basis for Disney's 1964 hit movie.

▶DIONNE QUINTS—On May 28, Oliva and Elzire Dionne became the parents of the first quintuplets ever to survive for more than a few days. The impoverished Ontario couple, who already had nine children, unwittingly signed the babies away to an unscrupulous promoter, and Emilie, Yvonne, Cécile, Marie, and Annette Dionne became international celebrities, endorsing everything from oatmeal to automobiles. To rescue them from exploitation, the Canadian government took custody, installing the year-old quints in a makeshift hospital across the street from their parents' home. Finally, after eight years, the Dionnes regained control of their offspring.

▶SANDINO ASSASSINATED—In 1934, one year after calling off guerrilla operations to end the seven-year-long U.S. occupation of Nicaragua, rebel leader Augusto César Sandino was assassinated by a death squad on the orders of national-guard commander Anastasio Somoza García. The murder paved the way for the 40-year dictatorship of Somoza and his sons. ◂1926.8 ▸1936.7

DANCE

Mr. B. Founds a Ballet

12 Until 1934, when George Balanchine was invited by the wealthy American dance enthusiast Lincoln Kirstein to establish the School of American Ballet in New York City, America was a wasteland for classical ballet, visited occasionally by touring companies but completely lacking its own tradition. The Russian-born Balanchine, who had defected to Paris in 1925 to work with Sergei Diaghilev, made American ballet matter.

Rooted in Russia's great traditions, Balanchine's dances were utterly modern. He emphasized movement and music rather than plot, and made the entire corps de ballet the star. In the process, he changed the vocabulary of dance. Every subsequent choreographer has been influenced by him.

The American Ballet became the New York City Ballet in 1948, after it performed the debut of Igor Stravinsky's *Orpheus* and moved to larger quarters. The following years, until 1964, are considered Balanchine's golden age. During that time, the chronically underfunded company developed its signature look: a spare, propless stage, with the dancers wearing practice leotards instead of costumes. Balanchine's work became more theatrical after the company moved to Lincoln Center in 1964, but it always retained a cool, neoclassical mood.

Mr. B., as he was known, died at 79 in 1983, a twentieth-century master often ranked with Picasso and Stravinsky. **◂1931.12 ▸1943.11**

Balanchine teaching class at the American Ballet School, photographed in 1959 by Henri Cartier-Bresson.

In 1934's *Bright Eyes*, Temple, here with costar James Dunn *(right)* and an unidentified extra, sashayed down an airplane aisle chirping "On the Good Ship Lollipop."

FILM

Bantam at the Box Office

13 For millions of moviegoers it was love at first sight. All dimples and ringlets, six-year-old Shirley Temple became a star in 1934 after she danced and sang through her first big hit, *Stand Up and Cheer.* Over the next three years, Temple was the world's top box-office star, grossing $5 million a year for her studio in an era when a ticket cost 15 cents. Toymakers sold six million dolls bearing her cutie-pie features.

By the end of 1934, Temple had been signed by Fox and had made nine more pictures, including her first star vehicle, *Bright Eyes.* Her "outstanding contribution" that year was recognized with a special Academy Award in 1935. Over the next four years, she perfected her screen persona—that of a Little Miss Fix-it for trouble-struck adults—in such hits as *The Little Colonel, Heidi,* and *Rebecca of Sunnybrook Farm.* Depression-scarred audiences couldn't get enough, but serious critics found her charms elusive, even disturbing. Graham Greene, then a film critic, implied that Temple's character was a wily mini-coquette who manipulated old men. Fox sued Greene's magazine for libel—and won.

In 1950 Temple married businessman Charles Black and gave up movies; as Shirley Temple Black she became active in Republican politics. **▸1938.M**

THE SOVIET UNION

Eliminating the Opposition

14 On the afternoon of December 1, 1934, Leonid Nikolayev, one of Joseph Stalin's henchmen, slipped into the Communist Party headquarters in Leningrad and waited outside the office of Sergei Kirov, a leading light of the party who had recently disagreed with aspects of Stalin's leadership. When Kirov appeared at his office door, Nikolayev emerged from the shadows and shot him dead. The assassination of Kirov, ostensibly Stalin's close friend, has been called the crime of the century. With it, Stalin achieved absolute power.

Stalin *(in center behind wheel)* showed no sign of guilt at Kirov's funeral.

Grieving conspicuously, Stalin gave Kirov a hero's burial and acted quickly to implicate his rivals in the crime. Working with the secret police, whom he controlled, Stalin accused a core group of opposition leaders of plotting the murder. Until then, the opposition had been the sole curb to Stalin's excesses. The assassination enabled him to persuade many comrades that his rivals were dangerous counterrevolutionaries.

After an initial round of show trials, forced confessions, and executions, the imaginary conspiracy took on a life of its own. It gave Stalin the rationale he needed for his Great Purge of the Communist Party, one of the most vicious bloodlettings ever visited on a nation by its ruler. **◂1932.9 ▸1936.6**

NOBEL PRIZES: Peace: Arthur Henderson (U.K.; international disarmament) ... Literature: Luigi Pirandello (Italian; novelist and playwright) ... Chemistry: Harold Urey (U.S.; heavy hydrogen) ... Medicine: George Minot, William Murphy, and George Whipple (U.S.; liver treatment for anemia) ... Physics: No award.

A VOICE FROM 1934

A Catalogue of Culture, Circa 1934

"You're the Top," from *Anything Goes,* by Cole Porter, 1934

Charming, witty, urbane, Cole Porter was a maestro of American popular song. Whatever the theme—Jazz Age glamour, collegiate earnestness (a Yale graduate, he wrote the Eli fight song), sophisticated love—Porter's sparkling lyrics and irresistible melodies brought high style to Broadway. His single greatest contribution to the pop genre may well be the playfully allusive catalogue song, exemplified by "You're the Top," from 1934's Anything Goes.

Verse 1
At words poetic, I'm so pathetic
That I always have found it best,
Instead of getting 'em off my chest,
To let 'em rest unexpressed.
I hate parading
My serenading,
As I'll probably miss a bar,
But if this ditty
Is not so pretty,
At least it'll tell you
How great you are.

Refrain 1
You're the top!
You're the Colosseum.
You're the top!
You're the Louvre Museum.
You're a melody from a
symphony by Strauss,
You're a Bendel bonnet,
A Shakespeare sonnet,
You're Mickey Mouse.
You're the Nile,
You're the Tow'r of Pisa,
You're the smile
On the Mona Lisa.
I'm a worthless check, a total wreck, a flop.
But if, baby, I'm the bottom
You're the top!

Refrain 2
You're the top!
You're Mahatma Gandhi.
You're the top!
You're Napoleon brandy.
You're the purple light of a summer night in Spain,
You're the National Gall'ry,
You're Garbo's sal'ry,
You're cellophane.
You're sublime,
You're a turkey dinner,
You're the time
Of the Derby winner.
I'm a toy balloon that is fated soon to pop,
But if, baby, I'm the bottom
You're the top!

Refrain 3
You're the top!
You're a Ritz hot toddy.
You're the top!
You're a Brewster body.
You're the boats that glide on the sleepy Zuider Zee,
You're a Nathan panning,
You're a Bishop Manning,
You're broccoli.
You're a prize,
You're a night at Coney,
You're the eyes
Of Irene Bordoni.
I'm a broken doll, a fol-de-rol, a blop,
But if, baby, I'm the bottom
You're the top!

Refrain 4
You're the top!
You're an Arrow collar.
You're the top!
You're a Coolidge dollar.
You're the nimble tread of the feet of Fred Astaire,
You're an O'Neill drama,
You're Whistler's mama,
You're Camembert.
You're a rose,
You're Inferno's Dante,
You're the nose
On the great Durante.
I'm just in the way, as the French would say "De trop,"
But if, baby, I'm the bottom
You're the top.

Refrain 5
You're the top!
You're a Waldorf salad.
You're the top!
You're a Berlin ballad.
You're a baby grand of a lady and a gent,
You're an old Dutch master,
You're Mrs. Astor,
You're Pepsodent.
You're romance,
You're the steppes of Russia,
You're the pants on a Roxy usher.

On Broadway, William Gaxton and the Great White Way's best belter, Ethel Merman, sang Porter's catalogue of current culture.

I'm a lazy lout that's just about to stop,
But if, baby, I'm the bottom
You're the top.

Refrain 6
You're the top!
You're a dance in Bali.
You're the top!
You're a hot tamale.
You're an angel, you, simply too, too, too diveen,
You're a Botticelli,
You're Keats,
You're Shelley,
You're Ovaltine.
You're a boon,
You're the dam at Boulder,
You're the moon over Mae West's shoulder.
I'm a nominee of the G.O.P. or GOP,
But if, baby, I'm the bottom
You're the top.

Refrain 7
You're the top!
You're the Tower of Babel
You're the top!
You're the Whitney Stable.
By the river Rhine,
You're a sturdy stein of beer,
You're a dress from Saks's,
You're next year's taxes,
You're stratosphere.
You're my thoist,
You're a Drumstick Lipstick,
You're da foist
In da Irish Svipstick.
I'm a frightened frog
That can find no log
To hop,
But if, baby, I'm the bottom
You're the top!

1934

"Imbued with the insight that the purity of German blood is prerequisite for the continued existence of the German people ... the Reichstag has unanimously adopted the following law."—**From the 1935 Law for the Protection of German Blood and German Honor**

STORY OF THE YEAR

The Nuremberg Laws

1 "Nothing like the complete disinheritance and segregation of Jewish citizens, now announced, has been heard since medieval times," wrote a British columnist, describing the Nuremberg Laws. Indeed, these decrees, signed by Hitler on September 15, 1935, were only the beginning of the nightmare for European Jews, priming the German citizenry to accept the much more chilling events that were to follow.

The Nuremberg Laws, which rescinded the civil rights of Germany's 600,000 Jews (and later the millions of Jews in countries occupied by Germany), represented the first stage of Hitler's "final solution," to rid Europe of all its Jews. The original two measures were called the Law of the Reich Citizen and the Law for the Protection of German Blood and German Honor. Under these and supplementary decrees, Jews were stripped of German citizenship (forbidden to vote, hold public office, or even fly the German flag), barred from practicing a profession, and prohibited from marrying, having sex with, or engaging in any other social relations with non-Jews. The laws extended to those who were partly Jewish (the definition of which included having one Jewish grandparent). Existing marriages between Jews and non-Jews were rendered illegal; couples who would not divorce were subject to imprisonment. This attempt at "racial purification" did not stop German soldiers from raping thousands of Jewish women, girls, and boys.

The Nuremberg Laws prompted many Jews to leave Germany. Here, a mural by Ben Shahn depicts prominent German Jews arriving in New York.

The Nuremberg Laws deprived Jews of their livelihoods and made them social outcasts. Supported by constant anti-Semitic propaganda via radio, newspapers, textbooks, and speeches, this legal degradation fatally reinforced long-established anti-Jewish sentiment. "It will be years before the Germans can find their way back to an ethical code of life," wrote German journalist Bella Fromm. "The evil Nazi doctrine ... is deeply planted in the minds of adults, youths and children." In the dark time ahead, few Germans would object when Jews were forced to sell their homes, businesses, and other property at unfair prices. Fewer still would speak up when entire Jewish families disappeared in the middle of the day or night, never to be heard from again. ◂1934.1 ▸1938.10

GREECE

Monarchy Restored

2 After a dozen years in English exile, Greece's King George II *(below)* returned in November 1935 to reign over a restored monarchy.

George had ruled briefly after his father, King Constantine I, disgraced himself by losing the war with Turkey, but had left the throne when antiroyalist forces won national elections. Greece had become a republic in 1924, and, except for a time of bloody dictatorship in 1926 under General Theodore Pangalos, had remained one. But the 1932 electoral defeat of former premier Eleutherios Venizélos's Liberal Party had left the government in the hands of a right-wing coalition. Three years later, with Parliament bitterly divided over the rightists' intention to bring back the king, Venizélos supporters staged a coup. Its failure made George's reinstatement inevitable.

Ironically, the man who presided over the monarchy's return was War Minister Giorgios Kondylis, who had overthrown the tyrannical Pangalos and restored democracy. This time, Kondylis (who'd moved to the right) put down the pro-Venizélos rising; after a general election in June, he became first deputy premier and then premier. He arranged a plebiscite, which approved the abolition of the republic and the restoration of the king.

The abolition of democracy was next. After new elections in 1936, the parliamentary power struggle between liberals and rightists reached a fever pitch. Meanwhile, the communists were planning a general strike. To forestall chaos, the King named former army chief of staff Ioannis Metaxas premier; soon, with the King's consent, Metaxas declared himself dictator.

The new regime, which mixed suppression of dissent with social and economic reforms, was widely labeled fascist—and when World War II arrived, many expected Metaxas (who'd been pro-German during World War I) to side with the Axis. Instead, he joined the Allies in 1940, and led Greek resistance to Italian invaders until his death the following year. ◂1924.12 ▸1941.4

GERMANY

Hitler Meets Conciliation

3 Resurgent Germans trampled the Treaty of Versailles—designed to prevent another world war (largely by permanently weakening Germany)—into oblivion in 1935. In January, in a plebiscite mandated by the treaty, residents of the coal-rich Saar region (between present-day France and Germany) voted nine to one to return to German rule after 15 years of French occupation. Two months later, Hitler's troops marched into the industrial city of Saarbrücken. The Führer promptly announced that he had begun rearming Germany (long an open secret) and that he would now reinstate conscription to expand its army. Both actions were flagrant breaches of the treaty. "End of Versailles!" crowed the headlines in Berlin.

Nuremberg 1934: Hitler Youth spell out the region Germany would acquire in 1935.

The League of Nations lodged a protest, but European leaders—reluctant to rile Hitler—responded mildly. British, French, and Italian statesmen met in Stresa, Italy, and agreed vaguely to oppose further treaty violations that might "endanger the peace of Europe." Britain was satisfied with a treaty limiting Germany's naval strength. Mutual-defense treaties were signed by France and the Soviet Union, and by the Soviet Union and Czechoslovakia, but both were noncommittal.

No major-power leader was more conciliatory toward Hitler than French premier Pierre Laval (who eventually ruled France under German occupation). An independent former socialist, now leaning rightward, Laval reversed the anti-German policies of foreign minister Louis Barthou, who was killed when right-wing Croat nationalists assassinated Yugoslavia's King Alexander in October 1934. Laval accepted Hitler's assurance that he wanted no French territory besides the Saar. Laval strove tirelessly for a "direct, honorable, and effective

ART & CULTURE: Books: ***Tortilla Flat*** **(John Steinbeck);** ***Judgment Day*** **(James T. Farrell);** ***Reason and Existence*** **(Karl Jaspers);** ***Theory of Flight*** **(Muriel Rukeyser);** ***Selected Poems*** **(Marianne Moore) ... Music: "I'm in the Mood for Love" (McHugh and Fields); "Summertime" (Gershwin and Heyward);** ***Violin Concerto*** **(Roger Sessions) ... Painting & Sculpture:** ***The Yellow Tablecloth*** **(Georges Braque);**

"It is us today, it will be you tomorrow. God and history will remember your judgment."—**Emperor Haile Selassie of Ethiopia**

rapprochement with Germany"; ultimately, his weak foreign policy helped boost enormously the strength of both Hitler and Mussolini. **◄1934.1 ►1936.4**

ITALY

Mussolini Invades Ethiopia

4 Benito Mussolini dismissed Ethiopia as "a country without a trace of civilization." Nonetheless, by 1935 he wanted it—mostly for reasons of revenge and pride. The Italian army had been badly defeated there in 1896. And for Italy to take its place among the great powers, it needed more colonies. Germany's rearmament made haste essential: Not only did Italy want to beat Hitler to the expansionist punch, but soon it might need to concentrate on defense at home.

Mussolini's decision to go ahead with the invasion was based on two misunderstandings. At a January meeting in Rome, French premier Laval secretly promised the dictator that France would disavow all interest in Ethiopia in exchange for Italy's help in restraining Germany. And at the Stresa Conference in April, British negotiators—though aware of Mussolini's tentative plans—did not mention Ethiopia, let alone oppose an attack.

Laval later claimed to have been referring only to economic questions; the British silence implied not consent but indecision. But over the next few months Mussolini shipped thousands of troops to neighboring Eritrea (already in Italy's possession). In October, despite belated British protests, the invasion began.

Militarily, the Italian campaign met with success: The underequipped defenders fought bravely but hopelessly against tanks and poison gas. Italians united behind their leader as never before. But diplomatically the war was a disaster for all concerned except Hitler, who finally gained a long-sought ally.

The League of Nations imposed trade sanctions on Italy. (Ethiopia was a member state.) But several members refused to comply, and several (including nonmembers Germany and the United States) complied only partially. Britain wanted to add an oil embargo, to which France would agree only if negotiations failed. The two governments worked out a deal that would allow Italy to control even more territory than it had already conquered, as long as Ethiopia remained nominally independent. But the scheme outraged the British public, and Ethiopian emperor Haile Selassie—who hadn't been consulted—rejected it. The plan, to the League's humiliation, was withdrawn.

Six months before Italy invaded, Ethiopian cavalry lined up for Emperor Haile Selassie.

In May 1936, Italy triumphed over the ancient African kingdom. But its relations with France and Britain lay in ruins, impervious to reconciliation. Mussolini had little choice but to embrace his upstart rival, Adolf Hitler. **◄1926.1 ►1936.4**

THE UNITED STATES

Weaving a Safety Net

5 The Depression spurred the United States to implement social-welfare programs of the kind that Western European nations had adopted in the nineteenth century. In 1935, Congress passed the Social Security Act—which President Franklin D. Roosevelt later called the "supreme achievement" of his administration—finally giving Americans a measure of federal protection against income loss from death, old age, unemployment, and blindness. (Coverage was later extended to those permanently disabled by illness or injury.)

A woodblock poster designed for the Works Progress Administration.

Meanwhile, millions of the able-bodied still faced financial and social doom. Direct relief had been paid since 1933, but Roosevelt distrusted it as "a narcotic, a subtle destroyer of the human spirit." In May he presented his alternative, an executive order establishing the Works Progress Administration, the largest public-works program ever attempted by any government.

Under the innovative leadership of Harry L. Hopkins, the WPA soon superseded and absorbed the Public Works Administration (PWA), which oversaw "heavy" projects. Modeled partly on the huge construction programs of Stalin and Mussolini (but, unlike theirs, entirely voluntary), the WPA built 8,000 parks, 1,600 schools, 800 airports, 3,300 storage dams, 78,000 bridges, and 650,000 miles of roads.

Professionals—from taxidermists to nurses—were put back to work, in their own fields when possible. The Depression was particularly hard on artists, musicians, and writers, so the WPA initiated cultural programs. The Federal Theatre Project performed modern and classic plays for some 30 million people. The Federal Arts Project hired artists to decorate public buildings. The Federal Writers Project produced tourist guides, regional studies, and history books.

Although highly popular, the WPA never reached its full potential. The highest number of people ever employed in any month was 3.2 million (out of a total jobless pool of eight to 14 million). In 1943, war production boosted the economy to near-full employment, and the WPA was shut down. **◄1933.1 ►1937.M**

BIRTHS

Woody Allen, U.S. filmmaker.

Bstandzin rgyamtsho, 14th Dalai Lama, Tibetan religious leader.

Eldridge Cleaver, U.S. writer and political activist.

Jim Dine, U.S. artist.

Phil Donahue, U.S. talk show host.

Geraldine Ferraro, U.S. political leader.

A.J. Foyt, U.S. auto racer.

Hussein, Jordanian king.

Christo (Javacheff), Bulgarian-U.S. artist.

Ken Kesey, U.S. novelist.

Loretta Lynn, U.S. singer.

Luciano Pavarotti, Italian singer.

Elvis Presley, U.S. singer.

Terry Riley, U.S. composer.

DEATHS

Jane Addams, U.S. political reformer.

Alban Berg, Austrian composer.

André Citroën, French auto manufacturer.

Alfred Dreyfus, French soldier.

Auguste Escoffier, French chef.

Carlos Gardel, Argentine singer.

Juan Vicente Gómez, Venezuelan president.

Childe Hassam, U.S. painter.

Oliver Wendell Holmes, U.S. jurist.

Gaston Lachaise, French-U.S. sculptor.

T.E. Lawrence, U.K. writer and military leader.

Huey Long, U.S. political leader.

Kasimir Malevich, Russian painter.

Józef Pilsudski, Polish military and political leader.

Wiley Post, U.S. aviator.

Edwin Arlington Robinson, U.S. poet.

Will Rogers, U.S. humorist.

Konstantin Tsiolkovsky, Russian rocket scientist.

Ecce Homo (Jacob Epstein) ... Film: *Mutiny on the Bounty* (Frank Lloyd); *Top Hat* (Mark Sandrich, with Astaire and Rogers); *The 39 Steps* (Alfred Hitchcock) ... Theater: *The Petrified Forest* (Robert Sherwood); *Awake and Sing* and *Waiting for Lefty* (Clifford Odets); *Jubilee* (Cole Porter); *Tiger at the Gates* (Jean Giraudoux) ... Radio: *Your Hit Parade*; *Fibber McGee and Molly.*

"Honestly, I think I've stretched a talent which is so thin it's almost transparent over a quite unbelievable term of years."
—Bing Crosby

NEW IN 1935

Fluorescent lights (General Electric Company).

Gallup poll.

Kodachrome film for 16-mm movie cameras.

Beer in cans (Krueger Beer, Newton, New Jersey).

Bra cup sizes (A-D).

Toyota automobiles.

Iran (new name for Persia).

Parking meter (Oklahoma City, Oklahoma).

Roller derby.

Richter scale (to measure magnitude of earthquakes).

IN THE UNITED STATES

►FIRST ACTIVIST–On December 30, Eleanor Roosevelt, continuing her transformation of the role of American First Lady into an activist office, began publishing "My Day," a six-day-a-week syndicated newspaper column, in which she shared her thoughts and daily activities with readers across the country. During her

12 years as First Lady, Roosevelt became on of the century's most admired figures by working tirelessly for humanitarian causes, notably urban renewal, child and family support, and equal rights—for minorities and for women. After her husband's death, Roosevelt served as chairman of the UN Commission on Human Rights from 1946-51 and remained active in international affairs until her death in 1962.

►"I LOVE YOU, PORGY"—The music was by George. The libretto was by brother Ira

Allen Lane chose these titles as "the first ten Penguins."

LITERATURE

Classics Go Mass-Market

6 In 1935, a London publisher named Allen Lane came up with the idea of issuing high-quality books by well-known authors in paperback—a form theretofore limited largely to detective and adventure stories, or shoddy reprints. As Lane later told it, the idea came to him in a train station on his way home from a weekend with Agatha Christie and her husband in Devon. Scouring the bookstalls for something to read, he could find nothing suitable amid the glossy magazines, expensive new editions, and shabby reprints. Sensing an opportunity, he and his two brothers, Richard and John, set about obtaining limited rights to hardcover works by such respected authors as Compton MacKenzie, Ernest Hemingway, and Dorothy L. Sayers.

The first ten titles of the new paperback line—which the brothers christened Penguin—were issued the same year, and by the end of the following year, the list had grown to 70 titles. The new format, like the huge spurt in literacy itself, democratized the act of reading: A book that might once have cost a half-day's wages now could be had for 20 minutes' pay. Immediately recognizable by their simply drawn Antarctic-waterfowl imprint, Penguins were sold in tobacconists' shops and big department stores rather than bookstores, which many Britons found snooty and intimidating. Cleanly and colorfully designed, the covers had none of the usual fussiness of the book-jacket designs of the times. The ranks of the book-buying public underwent one of the greatest expansions since Gutenberg. ◄1920.5

MUSIC

The Consummate Crooner

7 It seemed effortless, it seemed divine, the way this affable lad from Tacoma, Washington, delivered a tune, casually burbling out notes in his rich, relaxed baritone. Bing Crosby did not just sing, he *crooned*; indeed Crosby was the master of that intimate vocal sound (which had been created by Rudy Vallee in the late 1920s). In December 1935, he began work on the most popular of his many radio programs, NBC's *Kraft Music Hall*, a weekly hour-long variety show. Already an established star, Crosby hosted the show for almost ten straight years, propelling his career to sensational new heights.

Amplification and radio, unnegotiable challenges for many of his contemporaries (microphones made Jolson-style theatrics seem ludicrous), were well suited to the natural resonance of Crosby's voice. His "aw-shucks" persona and talent for light comedy completed a winning package on air and screen. (His behavior in private, by contrast, was often callous, even cruel.) The seven *Road* pictures he made with Bob Hope set new box-office records, and his portrayal of a Catholic priest in *Going My Way* won him an Oscar. But it is for his singing that "Der Bingle" (as he was called by the Germans who intercepted American Armed Forces Radio during World War II) is best remembered. In the 1942 movie musical *Holiday Inn*, Crosby, already the brightest star of the era, crooned what was to become the most popular song ever recorded, Irving Berlin's "White Christmas." He died in 1977, leaving an estate worth hundreds of millions of dollars. ►1943.16

MEDICINE

The First Sulfa Drug

8 The development of chemical agents to combat bacterial infection had lagged after Paul Ehrlich's dramatic 1909 discovery of a "magic bullet" to treat syphilis. By the late 1920s, however, the German bacteriologist Gerhard Domagk, conducting research for the giant chemical corporation I.G. Farben, began screening new dyes for medical applications. In 1935, Domagk made public his experiments with a low-toxicity, red leather dye called Prontosil, which effectively combated streptococcal bacterial infection in mice.

One of the first human tests of Prontosil was done on Domagk's daughter Hildegard, who had developed a serious streptococcal infection from pricking herself with a needle. After all other treatments had failed, Domagk injected the young girl—who was near death—with large quantities of Prontosil. She rapidly recovered. The efficacy of Prontosil (which was later found to have as its active principle an antimicrobial agent called sulfanilamide) led rapidly to the development of an enormous array of "sulfa"

Domagk in 1947, receiving the 1939 Nobel that Hitler had forced him to decline.

drugs for the treatment of such bacterial killers as cerebrospinal meningitis, pneumonia, and gonorrhea. Although the advent of penicillin (which is generally as effective but

SPORTS: Baseball: World Series, Detroit Tigers (Hank Greenberg) defeat Chicago Cubs, 4–2 ... Football: NFL, Detroit Lions defeat New York Giants, 26–7; first Heisman Memorial Trophy awarded, to Jay Berwanger ... Tennis: Helen Jacobs wins fourth consecutive U.S. singles title ... Auto Racing: Malcolm Campbell sets speed record of 301 mph ... Horse Racing: Omaha wins Triple Crown.

"You must be like a monk. You must sacrifice yourself to your work."—**Wallace Stevens, on what it takes to be a successful poet**

much less toxic) brought a decline in the use of sulfa drugs, their discovery was unquestionably one of the most important therapeutic breakthroughs in the history of medicine. **◂1928.11 ▸1941.16**

THE SOVIET UNION

Comintern Changes Course

9 The rise of fascism in Europe forced the Communist International, founded by Lenin in 1919 to consolidate and spread world communism, to reconsider its aims. At the Seventh Congress of the

English-language version of the Comintern's official publication, August 1935.

Third Comintern, convened in Moscow in July 1935, the body shelved its oft-repeated goal of fomenting worldwide proletarian revolution and vowed instead to "sweep fascism, and with it capitalism, from the face of the earth." The change in purpose was telling; threatened by fascism's hold in Germany, where Comintern leaders had hoped communism would take root, the organization became defensive, as anxious to prevent war as any of its capitalist adversaries.

To combat fascism, which they saw as a "counterrevolutionary coup d'état," the leaders of the Seventh Congress adopted their own counterrevolutionary strategy: joining forces with bourgeois parties in popular fronts, which (as in Spain and France) would steer their countries into military alliances with Moscow. Although heretical by old-line Comintern thought, popular fronts represented communism's best defense against fascism. Delegates even voiced support for capitalist, antifascist governments as the lesser of two evils. Attempting to put a positive spin on the perilous situation, the Comintern declared, "We stand today united in closed ranks as never before."

Trotsky, cleaving to his faith in world revolution, predicted that the 1935 meeting would "pass into history as the liquidation congress" of the Comintern. He was not far wrong: The Comintern never recovered its revolutionary ardor and was dissolved in 1943. **◂1919.11 ▸1943.M**

MUSIC

The King of Swing

10 Jazz music—which grew up in the bordellos of New Orleans and the speakeasies of Prohibition America—had always had a racy, faintly illicit image. But with the repeal of Prohibition, jazz was cast adrift, in search of a new style and a new mass audience. It found them in Benny Goodman, a clarinetist who had learned to play as a boy at Hull House, the Chicago settlement founded by Jane Addams. In 1935, Goodman, whose orchestra played uninspired dance music on the NBC radio series *Let's Dance*, decided to take his band on the road and give heartland Americans a taste of real jazz. Audience reaction was indifferent until the musicians reached Los Angeles, where they were greeted with hysterical enthusiasm. Swing was soon a full-fledged, nationwide rage.

Swing bands tended to be bigger than the old jazz combos, and their arrangements—Goodman's were mostly by Fletcher Henderson, a key developer (with Duke Ellington) of the "big band" sound—tended to be more formalized. Instead of emphasizing soloists, swing featured whole sections of brass, woodwind, or rhythm playing off one another, sometimes in counterpoint, sometimes in musical dialogue. In contrast to the cerebral bebop style that would predominate after the war, swing was finger-snapping music. It made people—particularly teenagers—want to get up and move.

The bespectacled "King of Swing," Benny Goodman *(left)*, with drummer Gene Krupa.

The Swing Era's apotheosis came in 1938 when Goodman played that bastion of classicism, Carnegie Hall. (*The New York Times* dismissed the concert as "a bore," but noted that the audience "was almost off its head with joy.") Goodman reigned as the "King of Swing" until the more commercial sound of Glenn Miller unseated him in 1941. **◂1927.9 ▸1941.18**

LITERATURE

The Flowering of Stevens

11 "One of the most difficult things in writing poetry," the American poet Wallace Stevens once confided to a friend, "is to know what one's subject is." With his breakthrough 1935 volume of poems, *Ideas of Order*, he found his: aesthetics as the pursuit of order. Passionately concerned with making sense of experience, Stevens used poetry to penetrate the welter of facts and perceptions that make up reality. Imagination, he said, was "the power that enables us to perceive the normal in the abnormal, the opposite of chaos in chaos." For him, the daily grind of the Hartford Accident and Indemnity Company, where he was an executive for nearly 40 years, complemented artistic creation, helping satisfy what he called his "reality-imagination complex."

Stevens, who was 56 when *Ideas of Order*—hailed as the first flowering of his mature poetic voice—came out, was one of a handful of modern writers who produced their best work in middle age. He started late, he said, because as a young man, although he loved poetry, he "didn't for a moment like the idea of poverty, so I went to work like anybody else and kept at it for a good many years." On evenings, weekends, and off-hours, Stevens wrote some of the finest modern poems in the English language. He remained the dean of American poetry until his death in 1955. **◂1922.9 ▸1946.11**

IN THE UNITED STATES

(along with DuBose Heyward). The Gershwins' masterly "folk opera" *Porgy and Bess*—based on Heyward's story about the inhabitants of Catfish Row, a black tenement street in Charleston, South Carolina—brought together such disparate musical idioms as jazz, gospel, blues, popular music, and opera. The result: a whole new category-defying form of musical theater. After opening on October 10, *Porgy and Bess* ran a scant 16 weeks but it has since come to be regarded as George Gershwin's masterpiece. ◂1927.8

▶KINGFISH KILLED—Huey "the Kingfish" Long was virtual dictator of Louisiana, strong-arming the legislature and seducing the general populace with a massive patronage system. Even after becoming a U.S. senator, the former governor still ran the state—from Washington. Long was preparing to mount a third-party run for president when, on September 8 at the Louisiana State House, he was shot in the stomach by the son-in-law of one of his political casualties. ▶1946.M

▶SINGING SWEETHEARTS—Former church choirboy Nelson Eddy and former chorus girl Jeannette MacDonald teamed up for the first time in 1935's *Naughty Marietta*. The pair, the most successful singing duo in movie musical history, appeared together in eight films that are now almost universally regarded as syrupy monuments to high camp.

▶JAZZ ROYALTY—In 1935, William Basie finally came into his own, acquiring a new title ("Count," courtesy of a Kansas City disc jockey) and a new band. After bandleader Bennie Moten died, Basie formed his own nine-piece orchestra, the Barons of Rhythm (soon called the Count Basie Band). The group was touted for its impeccable chording, its tonal balance—and its swing. Basie's stride-style piano playing won legions of fans, first in Chicago, then in New York City.

POLITICS & BUSINESS: GNP: $72.7 billion ... New Deal's National Industrial Recovery Act declared unconstitutional ... Senate refuses to ratify U.S. participation in the World Court ... Soil Conservation Service, Rural Electrification Administration, and National Labor Relations Board established ... John L. Lewis founds CIO.

"We are convinced that films constitute one of the most modern and scientific means of influencing the masses. Therefore a government must not neglect them."—**Joseph Goebbels, propaganda minister for Nazi Germany**

AROUND THE WORLD

►ART OF THE DEAL—In 1935, at age 65, Joseph Duveen, the most influential art dealer of the century, published his consummately self-serving memoir, *Art Treasures and Intrigue*. Duveen's career as an international tastemaker was built on brilliant salesmanship and his association with American art historian Bernard Berenson, who authenticated—some say fraudulently—the old-master paintings Duveen acquired and sold to new American millionaires, such as Henry Clay Frick, John D. Rockefeller, and Andrew Mellon. Their acquisitions formed the core collections of many American museums. ◄1908.10

►TYRANT OF THE ANDES—After ruling Venezuela as absolute dictator for 27 years, President Juan Vicente Gómez died on December 17. Gómez, a nearly full-blooded Andean Indian, terrorized the nation into submission through his efficient network of spies and the army's unrestricted use of force. He died one of the wealthiest men in South America, thanks to the discovery of oil in Venezuela in

1918. (His shrewd negotiations with foreign companies over drilling rights also helped him pay off all his country's debt.) ◄1922.M ►1945.M

►PREFRONTAL LOBOTOMY—After reading about chimpanzees who became less agitated when their frontal lobes were removed, Portuguese neurologist Antonio Egas Moniz theorized that a similar operation could help chronically distressed mental patients. In 1935, Moniz began performing prefrontal lobotomies, which involved drilling holes through the skull and severing the nerve pathways between the two frontal lobes of the brain. The operation did make patients more manageable, but it also reduced many of them to near-vegetative states.

TECHNOLOGY

The Waves of War

12 In the coming world war, few technological innovations would have as much impact as radar. In December 1935, the first stations using the invisible beams for tracking airplanes were authorized for construction in England (to guard the North Sea approaches to London). By 1938, Germany had a similar network.

In World War II, the Allies converted B-18A bombers into anti-submarine planes by installing radar devices in the planes' noses.

The idea itself wasn't new: In the 1880s Heinrich Hertz had found that radio waves could be bounced against objects to determine their position, and in 1904 a German engineer had patented a crude navigation device based on that principle. With the development in the 1930s of long-range bombers equipped to carry large payloads, U.S., European, and Japanese scientists all began seeking practical ways to use radar to track ships and airplanes.

Radar (short for "radio detecting and ranging") allowed combatants to locate targets despite such hindrances as fog or darkness. But the development of technical expertise took time. In 1940, England's array of antennae helped stave off disaster during the Battle of Britain. But a year later, Pearl Harbor commanders misinterpreted the radar warning of a massive Japanese attack.

Airborne radar—which eliminated the need for lofty transmission and reception towers—was a crucial improvement that began in 1940, when a beleaguered Britain sent its top scientists, along with a cavity magnetron, a transmitting device they'd developed, to work with American colleagues at the Massachusetts Institute of Technology. The resulting microwave radar was much more powerful and precise than anything that had come before. Microwave devices could be made small enough to fit into an airplane's nose; most Allied planes carried them by 1943. The Germans also developed airborne radar, but they didn't hit on microwaves until 1945, giving Allied fliers a significant edge. **►1940.11**

INDIA

Quietly Progressive

13 Despite recent setbacks in Anglo-Indian relations, Parliament in 1935 passed the Government of India Act, a sweeping piece of constitutional reform far bolder than anything before attempted. To England, the act signified goodwill; to India, it was a long overdue, tentative step toward independence.

The act created two new Indian provinces, for a total of eleven, and bestowed on all of them autonomy over internal affairs—except, of course, in an emergency, in which case all authority reverted to the British governor. It also separated Burma from India and guaranteed Muslims and other Indian minorities communal representation in the federal legislature. India's central government was practically unaffected by the act, since the British retained control of all defense, foreign affairs, and financial responsibility.

Critics in the Indian National Congress felt that the quietly progressive piece of legislation did not go far enough. Critics in Parliament—notably Winston Churchill, who called it "a monstrous monument to sham built by pygmies"—felt it went too far. Divergent opinions aside, the act served as an important constitutional foundation for both India and Pakistan in their early days as sovereign nations; the adopted reforms remained largely in place until India was formally declared a republic in 1950. **◄1932.4 ►1937.3**

Government of India Act: In a *Punch* cartoon, a mother hen worried whether "her" little ducklings could swim on their own.

Leni Riefenstahl on location in Nuremberg with cameraman Sepp Allgeier.

FILM

Hitler's Auteur

14 Aware that to be truly effective propaganda must be beautifully packaged, film buff and former art student Adolf Hitler turned to 32-year-old Leni Riefenstahl for a record of the 1934 annual Nazi convention at Nuremberg. Riefenstahl's film, which premiered in 1935 in Germany, is the most controversial documentary ever made: *Triumph of the Will*, an innovative, electrifying, and evil ode to Hitler and the power of his party.

Faced with a potentially mind-numbing string of hot-air oratory from the Reich's ringleaders, static mass audiences, and infinite parades, Riefenstahl—a former dancer and actress whose 1931 directorial debut, *The Blue Light*, had been an artistic and commercial success—used brilliant editing, constant camera movement, stunning visual composition, and a stirring pseudo-Wagnerian score to create a film that rarely flags. Riefenstahl's Hitler is a god—descending ethereally in his airplane in the beginning of the film, looming large in low-angle shots throughout the rest, his every word and gesture ecstatically received by the crowd. Morally repugnant as it is, *Triumph of the Will* is a stylistic masterpiece, a textbook for propagandists.

Riefenstahl was never a member of the Nazi Party and claimed to have been apolitical and ignorant of the atrocities around her. Her sole interest, she said, was in art. Yet an art born of such willful moral blindness is necessarily compromised by its lack of responsibility to the truth. **◄1933.M ►1936.1**

NOBEL PRIZES: Peace: Carl von Ossietzky (German; journalist) ... Literature: No award ... Chemistry: Frédéric and Irène Joliot-Curie (French; synthesis of radioactive elements) ... Medicine: Hans Spemann (German; embryonic development) ... Physics: James Chadwick (U.K.; discovery of the neutron).

A VOICE FROM 1935

Defeating Demon Rum

The Twelve Steps, by William Griffith Wilson and Dr. Robert Holbrook Smith, founders of Alcoholics Anonymous, 1935

Perhaps the most successful self-help program of all time was born in 1935, when a New York stockbroker and alcoholic named William Griffith Wilson, desperate to keep from falling off the wagon while on a business trip to Akron, Ohio, asked a local member of the Oxford Group, an evangelical Christian society, to introduce him to another struggling alcoholic. His fellow sufferer, Akron surgeon Robert Holbrook Smith, was so impressed with Wilson's premise that alcoholics could best help themselves by helping other alcoholics that he joined Wilson in devising a booze-beating regimen based on twelve steps (below). *By 1945, their organization, Alcoholics Anonymous, had enrolled 15,000 members (all technically anonymous); by 1992, there were an estimated two million. AA's principles—which conform to a Christian pattern of confession, absolution, and redemption, but also bear the mark of Carl Jung and William James—have become a model for a whole range of programs to cure addictions ranging from drugs to overeating to sexual obsessions.* ►**1961.14**

1. We admitted we were powerless over alcohol—that our lives had become unmanageable.

2. Came to believe that a Power greater than ourselves could restore us to sanity.

3. Made a decision to turn our will and our lives over to the care of God as we understood Him.

4. Made a searching and fearless moral inventory of ourselves.

5. Admitted to God, to ourselves and to another human being the exact nature of our wrongs.

6. Were entirely ready to have God remove all these defects of character.

7. Humbly asked Him to remove our shortcomings.

8. Made a list of all persons we had harmed, and became willing to make amends to them all.

9. Made direct amends to such people wherever possible, except when to do so would injure them or others.

10. Continued to take personal inventory and when we were wrong promptly admitted it.

11. Sought through prayer and meditation to improve our conscious contact with God as we understood Him, praying only for knowledge of His will for us and the power to carry that out.

12. Having had a spiritual awakening as the result of these steps, we tried to carry this message to alcoholics and to practice these principles in all our affairs.

At left, the coffee pot from which "Bill and Dr. Bob" (the privacy-preserving names by which AA literature refers to the founders) drank endless cups of coffee during their first, all-night session in Akron. The pot has come to symbolize both an alternative to liquor and the fellowship that the organization fosters.

"I hold my breath during the last stretch. I stick with the field, breathing naturally until 30 yards from the finish. Then I take one big breath, tense all my abdominal muscles, and set sail."—**Jesse Owens, on his sprint technique**

STORY OF THE YEAR

Owens Triumphs at the 1936 Olympics

1 They never competed against each other in a footrace. They never shook hands. Yet, when Jesse Owens, a black American athlete and the son of an Alabama sharecropper, won four gold medals at the 1936 Olympic Games in Berlin, it was Adolf Hitler who went away the loser, his claim of Aryan supremacy shattered. (Indeed, so sure had Hitler been that the Games would showcase the superiority of the German athletes, he had enlisted the Reich's filmmaker Leni Riefenstahl to make a documentary about them.)

The track star from Ohio State won the 100 meters (10.3 seconds), 200 meters (20.7 seconds), and the running broad jump (26' 5½"), and was a member of the American world-record-setting 400-meter-relay team (39.8 seconds). He'd already set the long-jump record (26' 8¼") the previous year in Ann Arbor, Michigan. It stood until 1960, when it was beaten by Ralph Boston.

Hitler was conspicuous in his refusal to offer congratulations. He left the stadium in fury while Owens accepted his laurel wreath and medals. "That's a grand feeling, standing up there," Owens told reporters. "I never felt like that before." Those close to Owens said later that the athlete was relieved that Hitler shunned him: He was spared the awkwardness of having to suppress his personal feelings while cordially accepting congratulations from someone he abhorred. Meanwhile the Nazi propagandists, headed by Joseph Goebbels, went to work. "The Yankees have been the great disappointment of the Games," they commented in their broadsheet *Der Angriff (The Offensive)*. "Without these members of the black race—these auxiliary helpers—a German would have won the broad jump." The "auxiliary helpers" had in fact dominated the Games: In all, ten African-Americans had won 13 medals, including eight golds.

In spite of all the fanfare, Owens's triumphs in Berlin did not translate into riches back home. To support himself, he ran exhibitions against horses and dogs, barnstormed with the Harlem Globetrotters, and worked as a playground janitor. Later, Owens served as a director of Negro personnel for Ford Motor Company and worked for the Illinois State Athletic Commission. He died in 1980 at age 66. **◂1935.14 ▸1937.9**

Owens's spectacular performance in Berlin earned him four gold medals and the title "Athlete of the Games."

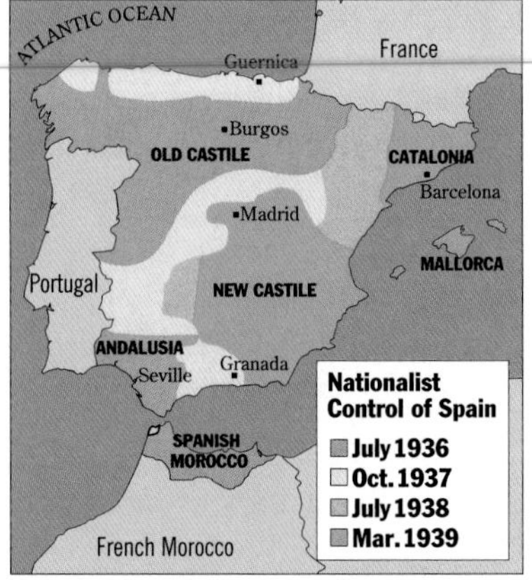

From its conception in the Canary Islands, Franco's Nationalist revolt worked its way from North Africa to Madrid by 1939.

SPAIN

Civil War Begins

2 For the totalitarian powers, the Spanish Civil War was a proxy war, and a rehearsal for World War II. For intellectuals throughout the world, it appeared to be the first stage of the struggle between fascism and communism over the dying body of world capitalism. For the Spaniards, the war meant three years of heroism and horror, followed by 35 years of dictatorship. The conflict began in July 1936, but the stage had been set much earlier.

After winning the elections of 1933 and quashing leftist rebellions in 1934, Spain's rightists had established a Catholic, conservative republic, although monarchists and Falangists (fascists) wanted to abolish the republic altogether. Meanwhile, communists worldwide—once a divisive force on the left—had been ordered by Moscow to join with other parties against the right. In February 1936, new elections gave a plurality to the Popular Front, a coalition of leftists and liberals.

Once in power, the coalition began to fray. In the Cortes (parliament), the formerly tame socialists tried to deprive rightist deputies of their seats on technical grounds. The socialist and communist youth organizations merged, and street fights with Falangist students followed. Churches were burned, peasants took over estates, and anarchists occupied factories, while authorities watched. In July, after a monarchist party leader was assassinated by government security forces, conservative generals decided they'd had enough.

The revolt began when one of them, General Francisco Franco, led his troops in from Morocco. Soon the right-wing insurgents—the Nationalists—controlled Spain's south and west, aided by Germany and Italy, which began providing them with troops, ammunition, and aircraft. The Soviets, in turn, sent arms and advisers to the republic's defenders. Other governments held back, despite Republican appeals. (France contributed 300 planes, then declared neutrality at Britain's urging.) But the Republican ranks were bolstered by the International Brigade, a 50-nation corps of volunteers ranging from industrial workers to celebrated writers like George Orwell and André Malraux. Spain was soon engulfed in all-out war. **◂1933.7 ▸1937.7**

SPAIN

A Poet's Martyrdom

3 The violence of the Spanish Civil War went far beyond the battlefield, as social animosities that had smoldered for decades burst into flame. Republicans murdered priests, nuns, and Falangists; Nationalist troops (among them many priests) killed leftists and intellectuals. By the war's end, civilian casualties on each side numbered some 50,000. The most famous victim was poet and dramatist Federico García Lorca, 38, who was slain in August 1936, a month after the fighting began.

One of Spain's most important twentieth-century authors, Lorca was already internationally known for works that combined folk, classical, and realist elements with an often harsh expressionism. Poems such as *Gypsy Ballads* (1928), and plays such as *Blood Wedding* (1933)—along with his personal magnetism—had won him a huge following. But many conservatives denounced him as decadent, especially after he declared himself a socialist.

Lorca had arrived for a rest at his family's summer home in Granada a few hours before Franco's uprising began. (He'd just completed his play *The House of Bernarda Alba*, in which five sisters become prisoners of their dictatorial mother.) When the Nationalists seized the

ART & CULTURE: Books: *Absalom, Absalom!* (William Faulkner); *Eyeless in Gaza* (Aldous Huxley); *The General Theory of Employment, Interest and Money* (J.M. Keynes); *Life with Father* (Clarence Day) ... Music: "I've Got You Under My Skin" (Cole Porter); "Pennies from Heaven" (Johnston and Burke); "The Way You Look Tonight" (Kern and Fields); *El Salón México* (Aaron Copland); *Adagio for Strings*

"Unity against a possible assault by fascism, and an effort to govern ... in such a way as to relieve the miseries and injustices in which fascism finds its breeding ground."—**French prime minister Léon Blum, stating the purpose of the Popular Front**

town, rounding up the mayor and scores of others for execution, Lorca went into hiding at the house of a conservative family friend, whose brother handed the writer over to the Falangist who eventually knocked at the door. Lorca was shot on the night of August 18, after two days of imprisonment in Granada's government headquarters. (Many readers see in Lorca's death a tragic culmination of the violence and foreboding that pervade his work.) His corpse was apparently thrown into a mass grave. The remains have never been found. **◂1936.2 ▸1937.7**

DIPLOMACY

Rome-Berlin Axis Formed

4 Adolf Hitler admired Benito Mussolini deeply. He'd modeled much of his persona and political approach on Il Duce's, even copying the Fascist salute. But Mussolini disliked Hitler, whom he privately called "an aggressive little man ... probably a liar, and certainly mad." Nazism, he complained, was "against everything and everyone." He didn't share the Nazis' anti-Semitism (Jews had been among the founders of Italian Fascism) or, despite his imperialism, their ambition to destroy "inferior" peoples. But in 1936 Mussolini cast his lot with Hitler's.

It was a purely pragmatic decision. Italy's Ethiopian adventure (the country was conquered in May) had alienated France and Britain. Not that Mussolini could have counted on them anyway: In March, when Germany broke the Versailles and Locarno treaties by occupying the demilitarized Rhineland, the two powers had done nothing. Nor had they punished Hitler for his treaty-breaking rearmament campaign. Hitler got what he wanted—and he wanted Austria, Italy's only buffer against the Germans. If, despite Italian protection, the Germans invaded Austria, Italy would have to choose between war and a forced alliance. Better to reach an understanding first. (Besides, Hitler had backed Mussolini on Ethiopia.)

In July, Hitler recognized Austrian sovereignty (and Austria agreed to be a "German state"). Four months later, Italy and Germany hammered out an entente that extended Ethiopian trade concessions to Germany and affirmed common policies toward Spain, the Danubian countries, the Soviet Union, and the League of Nations. Mussolini called the new alignment the "Rome-Berlin Axis."

On November 25, Germany concluded the Anti-Comintern Pact with Japan, pledging mutual support against the Soviets. Mussolini would add his signature in November 1937, extending the Axis from Rome to Tokyo—and forming the team that would battle the Allies in World War II. **◂1935.4 ▸1937.14**

WIR BEGRÜSSEN DIE
DEUTSCHEN ARBEITER
ES LEBE DIE AXE
ROM - BERLIN

Pragmatism guided Mussolini's alignment with Hitler, but Neapolitans celebrated it.

FRANCE

A Socialist at the Helm

5 After Pierre Laval's right-leaning government toppled in January 1936, France was briefly led by liberal premier Albert Sarraut. But spring elections brought a profound change: the nation's first Socialist prime minister. Léon Blum took office in June, heading the Popular Front's broad coalition of left-of-center parties. The left had long held a majority in Parliament, yet since 1920 only the Radical-Socialist Party (a middle-class, liberal group, despite its name) had formed a government. The Socialists and Communists refused to share power with them or each other. Now, however, the fascist threat made all of them bedfellows.

A fragile coalition: Socialist Léon Blum *(right)* and one of the Popular Front's pro-Communist radicals, Jean Zyromski.

Blum's cabinet included all the Front's major and minor parties except the Communists, who supported the government without entering it. They opted out in fear that the right would see them as harbingers of revolution, which they currently opposed because further disorder in France—a wave of postelection strikes had all but paralyzed industry—would play into the fascists' hands.

A master negotiator, Blum walked a tightrope between the strikers, whose cause he supported, and their employers, whom he dared not antagonize. He ignored the rightists, who were calling for the use of troops (and who baited the Jewish premier—another first for France—with anti-Semitic slurs), and the extreme leftists, who urged him to nationalize the factories. Within six weeks, he'd pushed through substantial raises and the biggest package of social legislation France had seen: The state would henceforth guarantee such rights as collective bargaining, a 40-hour week, and paid vacations. Only the Bank of France and arms factories were nationalized. Labor peace returned.

Blum enraged many of his comrades by refusing to intervene in the Spanish Civil War. And as the Depression continued to undermine the economy, his government grew increasingly unpopular. He resigned in June 1937, came back in March 1938, then was forced to resign again in April. By then, the Popular Front had disintegrated. **◂1934.3 ▸1940.7**

BIRTHS

Ursula Andress, Swiss actress.

Silvio Berlusconi, Italian business and political leader.

Herbert Boyer, U.S. biochemist.

Carol Burnett, U.S. comedian.

Wilt Chamberlain, U.S. basketball player.

F.W. De Klerk, South African president.

Vaclav Havel, Czech writer and political leader.

Jim Henson, U.S. puppeteer.

Anthony Kennedy, U.S. jurist.

Winnie Mandela, South African activist.

Zubin Mehta, Indian-U.S. conductor.

Mary Tyler Moore, U.S. actress.

Burt Reynolds, U.S. actor.

Yves Saint Laurent, French fashion designer.

Antonin Scalia, U.S. jurist.

Frank Stella, U.S. artist.

Mario Vargas Llosa, Peruvian novelist and political leader.

Bill Wyman, U.K. musician.

Charlie Watts, U.K. musician.

DEATHS

Louis Blériot, French aviator.

G.K. Chesterton, U.K. writer.

Federico García Lorca, Spanish writer.

John Gilbert, U.S. actor.

Maxim Gorky, Russian writer.

A.E. Housman, U.K. poet.

Rudyard Kipling, U.K. writer.

Ivan Pavlov, Russian physiologist.

Luigi Pirandello, Italian writer.

Ottorino Respighi, Italian composer.

Oswald Spengler, German philosopher.

Miguel de Unamuno, Spanish philosopher and writer.

Eleuthérios Venizélos, Greek statesman.

(Samuel Barber) ... Painting & Sculpture: *Twenty Cent Movie* (Reginald Marsh); *Dances and Sphere* (Alexander Calder) ... Film: *The Great Ziegfeld* (Robert Z. Leonard); *Camille* (George Cukor, with Greta Garbo); *Swing Time* (George Stevens, with Astaire and Rogers) ... Theater: *You Can't Take It with You* (Kaufman and Hart); *Idiot's Delight* (Robert Sherwood); *The Women* (Clare Boothe Luce) ... Radio: *The Kate Smith Show.*

"What I have done is a duty that any Nicaraguan who truly loves his country should have done a long time ago."
—Note found in the pocket of the gunman who assassinated Nicaraguan dictator Anastasio Somoza in 1956

NEW IN 1936

Polaroid sunglasses.

Photo-finish camera at horse races.

Waring blender.

Baseball Hall of Fame.

Tampons (Tampax, Inc.).

Trampolines.

IN THE UNITED STATES

▶POETIC JUSTICE—Illinois-born Carl Sandburg—the best-known of the so-called Prairie Poets—published in 1936 *The People, Yes,* his epic, free-verse celebration of democracy and the resiliency of ordinary

Americans. "The people will live on," Sandburg wrote in the depths of the Depression. "The people so peculiar in renewal and comeback." Sandburg was also the author of a Pulitzer Prize-winning six-volume biography of Abraham Lincoln. ◀1930.V ▶1949.8

▶OLD SOUTH REBORN—Published in June, Margaret Mitchell's *Gone with the Wind* was a ten-year labor of love that the former *Atlanta Journal* reporter had begun while laid up with an ankle injury. Beautiful, headstrong Scarlett O'Hara, rakish Rhett Butler, and the host of other characters who enliven the pages of *GWTW* (which sold a record-breaking 1.4 million copies the first year) were all inspired by the stories of the Old South and the Civil War that Mitchell had heard from her father. ▶1939.8

THE SOVIET UNION

Stalin's Great Purge

6 Beginning in 1936, Stalin systematically destroyed the old Bolshevik Party in order to ensure a Communist Party of sycophants loyal only to him. In a three-year period that lasted through 1938, Stalin and his secret police arrested five million citizens. Millions of these were executed; in Moscow alone, there were days when the rate of execution reached 1,000. Those left alive were banished to the gulag, a massive, country-wide system of labor camps built by Stalin when existing facilities (themselves grim vestiges of czarist rule) proved insufficient to accommodate the unprecedented number of prisoners. The number of Russians who perished during the Great Purge exceeds the number of American troops killed in all wars, from the American Revolution to Vietnam.

The purge followed an official pattern of accusation, arrest, conviction. A new round of recrimination was often accompanied by a lurid show trial in which the verdict was guilty. Stalin staged the first of these in August 1936, sending to the block Lev Kamenev and Grigori Zinoviev, his partners in the triumvirate that ruled after Lenin's death, and 14 other leading old Communists. All were charged with membership in a secret Trotsky-instigated cabal that, it was claimed, planned to assassinate the Soviet Union's top ministers, having already succeeded with Sergei Kirov (the Communist official whose 1934 death Stalin had orchestrated to look like a plot). All confessed and were sentenced to death. What the foreign correspondents who were allowed into the trials did not know was that the accused had been threatened and abused during pretrial imprisonment and that their confessions were fabricated. But the West, desperate for an ally against rising fascism, was anxious to believe Stalin.

Meanwhile, in July, the Central Committee circulated a new set of rules to the local cells: "The inalienable quality of every Bolshevik under present conditions should be the ability to recognize an enemy of the Party, no matter how well he may be masked." Failure to recognize an enemy was henceforth a criminal offense. Paranoia gripped the Party. Protected by his secret police, Stalin alone was safe. **◀1934.14 ▶1938.M**

Moscow factory workers vote in favor of capital punishment for Kirov's supposed killers.

NICARAGUA

Somoza Assumes Power

7 Drawing political strength from military might, General Anastasio Somoza García, leader of the Nicaraguan National Guard, staged an election in 1936 that he could not lose. No legitimate politician, no voting citizen, could resist Somoza's guns in the presidential contest. The general won by a landslide, deposing the freely elected Juan Sacasa, his uncle.

Born in San Marcos, Nicaragua, to a landed family, Somoza studied business in the United States before launching his political career. In 1933, the United States put him in charge of the Nicaraguan National Guard, an army it had created to make war on Nicaraguan revolutionist Augusto César Sandino. When American troops withdrew from Nicaragua in 1933, Sandino took himself off to a government-subsidized farm. Peace returned to the country, with power balanced between the heavily armed Somoza and the enormously popular Sandino. Within twelve months of the truce, Somoza had the ex-rebel killed. For two years Somoza groomed the army, securing the men's loyalty by making them rich—off extortion, prostitution, and gambling. Then, having outgrown government, Somoza made himself president.

The dictator remained in power until 1956 (during which time he amassed a personal fortune of some $50 million), alternating himself in the presidency with handpicked yes-men. He safeguarded his position by currying favor with the United States, first welcoming its military bases, later aping its anticommunist stance. A young poet finally gunned him down (and was immediately shot by Somoza's guards). But Somoza had ensured his own succession: One of his U.S.-educated sons commanded the National Guard, the other was president of the Congress. Through them and others, the Somoza dynasty continued to rule Nicaragua for the next quarter century. **◀1934.M ▶1979.8**

CZECHOSLOVAKIA

Hitler Eyes Sudetenland

8 In *Mein Kampf,* the Nazi bible, Hitler had called for the creation of a "greater Germany" whose borders would contain all the ethnically German areas controlled by other nations. He'd also stressed Germany's need for *Lebensraum* (living space), designating the countries of Central and Eastern Europe as targets for conquest. Both doctrines applied to Czechoslovakia, whose industrial Sudeten region was inhabited mostly by German speakers. In 1936 the Czechs began building fortifications along the Sudetenland's border with Germany; the fortifications were modeled on France's supposedly impregnable Maginot Line, which safeguarded the French-German border. But tank traps would prove futile against the forces that threatened Czechoslovakia's existence.

The Sudetenlanders had balked at joining the Czechoslovak republic when it was founded in 1919, and were often discriminated against by the Slav majority. Furthermore, the Depression had hit their region particularly hard. Conditions were ripe for the spread of separatist ideology. In the 1935 elections, the Sudeten German Party—secretly

SPORTS: Baseball: World Series, New York Yankees defeat New York Giants, 4–2; Joe DiMaggio signs with the Yankees; first players elected to the Hall of Fame (Ty Cobb, Walter Johnson, Christy Mathewson, Babe Ruth, Honus Wagner) ... Summer Olympics held in Berlin ... Football: NFL, Green Bay Packers defeat Boston Redskins, 21–6 ... Boxing: Max Schmeling knocks out Joe Louis.

"The son of a bitch is a ballet dancer.... He's the best ballet dancer that ever lived, and if I get a good chance I'll kill him with my bare hands."—**W.C. Fields, on Charlie Chaplin**

financed by Hitler—won two thirds of the local vote, becoming the country's second-largest party. Its leaders demanded regional autonomy, while Czech authorities sought compromise.

In the international arena, the Nazis seized the opportunity to trumpet the real and invented grievances of their Sudeten brethren. The propaganda campaign only intensified Czechoslovakia's precarious position. The Soviet Union had signed a treaty pledging to defend the country, but only if France intervened first—unlikely, since Germany lay between France and Czechoslovakia. Finally, rather than risk a major war, France and Britain forced Czechoslovakia to

Czech soldiers at target practice at the Czech version of the Maginot Line.

cede the Sudetenland to Germany at 1938's Munich Conference. It was a self-defeating move for the French: Upon inspecting the imitation Maginot Line, German generals learned the secrets of France's own defenses, which fell two years later. ▸**1937.2**

FILM

Chaplin's Machine-Age Satire

9 Nine years after the talking-picture revolution, Charlie Chaplin produced, wrote, scored, directed, and starred in the last of the great silent films. In 1936's *Modern Times*, which contains some spoken dialogue as well as music and sound effects, Chaplin bade farewell to a genre and to a comedy icon—the Little Tramp.

Chaplin had created the feisty, graceful hobo with a bowler, toothbrush mustache, ill-fitting suit, oversized shoes, and rattan cane for the 1914 Keystone studio short *Kid Auto Races at Venice*. By the following year, Chaplin's Little Tramp was the biggest box-office draw in the world.

Like Chaplin's other films—60-odd shorts and such features as

Chaplin's Depression-era fable about the evils of technology features some of his best gags.

The Kid (1921), *The Gold Rush* (1925), and *City Lights* (1931)—*Modern Times* mingled pathos, comedy, and social criticism. The film, a satire of the Machine Age, featured the Tramp as a demoralized assembly-line worker who runs amok in the factory, eventually landing in jail. At the end, the Tramp and his slum-waif girlfriend, the Gamine, turn their backs on a cruel society and head down a highway.

The film was a financial success, but its socialist bent disturbed right-wingers. Later, even Chaplin's fans were troubled by aspects of his personal life—several failed marriages, a celebrated paternity suit, and a fourth marriage at age 54 to the 18-year-old daughter of playwright Eugene O'Neill. In 1952, the London-born Chaplin, still a British subject, was refused reentry to the United States by a federal government in hot pursuit of perceived communists. Twenty years later, in cooler times, he returned to receive a special Academy Award; in 1975, two years before his death at age 88, he was knighted by Queen Elizabeth. ◂**1919.3**

CHINA

Chiang Is Kidnapped

10 The tumultuous situation in China—internal strife between the Nationalists and the Communists, external aggression by the Japanese—boiled over in 1936: Twelve units of the National Army kidnapped President Chiang Kai-shek *(left)* and attempted to force him into war against the Japanese. Chiang had

sent the Northeastern Army, commanded by young Marshal Zhang Xueliang, to Shanxi province to battle the Communists. Instead, the Army succumbed to their blandishments and began urging Chiang to unite with them in a full-scale war against the Japanese. The general refused. On Chiang's next visit to Shanxi, Zhang (son of Manchuria's former warlord) placed him under house arrest.

Chiang's policy of avoiding war while Japan encroached had grown deeply unpopular. In Beijing, Shanghai, and other major cities, students regularly rallied to demonstrate their displeasure. But Chiang refused to budge. In his opinion, China was no match for Japan's military machine. "The Communists," he insisted, "are our greatest traitors." They had to be eradicated before China could confront Japan. Zhang and his collaborators (who included Zhang's Communist mentor Zhou Enlai) demanded that Chiang stop battling the Communists and reorganize his government to admit "all parties and cliques to share the responsibility of national salvation." Chiang stood fast.

On December 25, as Chiang's Nanjing-based government prepared to move against the insurrectionists, the crisis was suddenly resolved. Zhang and his fellow captors (persuaded, some said, by an unspecified ransom put up by T.V. Soong, the "J.P. Morgan of China") let Chiang go on the promise that he would reexamine his policies. Hundreds of thousands of well-wishers turned out to welcome him back to Nanjing. China had discovered a reverence for him in his absence; and Chiang had realized he needed to stand up to the Japanese. ◂**1934.7** ▸**1937.1**

IN THE UNITED STATES

▸GM WORKERS TRIUMPH—In December, General Motors workers began a 44-day sit-down strike (a new twist in striking, which had previously favored walkouts), which ended with a forced acknowledgement by the country's third-largest corporation of its workers' right to organize. The galvanizing force in this heady era for American labor was a coal miner with a seventh-grade education and a penchant for the classics, John L. Lewis. Under Lewis's fiery leadership, the Congress of Industrial Organizations (CIO) organized automobile, steel, rubber, and other manufacturing workers. ◂1919.6 ▸1955.M

▸*LIFE* LIVES—Recognizing photography's potential for capturing news events and human-interest stories with

immediacy and candor, Henry Luce followed his successful *Time* and *Fortune* magazines with the photo magazine *Life* in 1936. For the first issue, Luce sent photojournalist Margaret Bourke-White, an industrial specialist, to photograph a dam-construction project in Montana. On the cover *(above)* was Bourke-White's photograph of Fort Peck Dam; inside, her nine pages of pictures of workers and their families launched a new narrative form in American journalism. ◂1923.10 ▸1941.V

ALWAYS A SMILE—Missouri-born Dale Carnegie fought his way out of rural childhood poverty to become a successful author, a syndicated newspaper columnist, a radio star, and a lecture-circuit fixture. In 1936, he revealed his recipe for success in his book *How to Win Friends and Influence People*. Among his bits of advice: Turn a handicap into an advantage. The book became the bestselling (after the Bible) nonfiction work of the century. ◂1923.M ▸1952.M

POLITICS & BUSINESS: GNP: $83.0 billion ... FDR wins second term by a landslide ... Supreme Court overturns Agricultural Adjustment Act, and Bituminous Coal Conservation Act, upholds Tennessee Valley Authority ... U.S. declares nonintervention policy for Spain ... Douglas Aircraft begins production of DC-3.

"Any government that lets me write my music in peace, publishes everything I compose before the ink is dry, and performs every note that comes from my pen is all right with me."—**Sergei Prokofiev**

AROUND THE WORLD

▶THE LAST PHARAOH—The last king of Egypt ascended the throne in 1936, a mere adolescent of 16. Throughout his reign King Farouk I was caught between the nationalist demands of the WAFD political party and the colonial demands of the British, who despite ending their protectorate retained a firm grip on the country up through World War II. Farouk attempted to institute land reform and other social programs, but corruption eroded his popularity over the years. The King became notorious for his gambling, nightclub romps, and uninhibited pursuit of pleasure. He was overthrown in 1952, in a military coup led by Gamal Abdal Nasser. ◂1922.5 ▸1945.M

▶MARKHAM'S MOMENT—In September, Beryl Markham became the first person to fly solo across the Atlantic Ocean from east to west. The daring, British-born aviatrix—who grew up in Kenya—learned to fly in her 20s, so she could scout elephants and other wild game from the air. Her historic 1936 flight began in Abingdon, England, and ended 21 hours later, when she landed in a bog on Cape Breton Island, Nova Scotia, many miles short of New York City, her goal. She received a ticker-tape parade there anyway. ◂1911.M ▸1937.M

▶GERMANY'S MODEL T—The *Volkswagen* ("people's car"), introduced in February and built from a design by Ferdinand Porsche, was Hitler's answer to Henry Ford's simple, inexpensive Model T. The following year, the German government began mass-producing the bubble-shaped, rear-engine vehicle (named the Beetle for its resemblance to the insect). The Volkswagen factory was destroyed during the war but was revitalized in West Germany afterward. By 1960 the

Beetle—whose design remained unchanged from year to year—was one of the most popular cars in the world. The model was discontinued in 1978. ◂1908.1 ▸1960.V

An *Evening Standard* cartoonist took a swipe at Japanese notions of naval parity.

DIPLOMACY

Japan Quits Naval Conference

11 The Second London Naval Conference of 1936, the third and final major interwar disarmament attempt, took a precipitous turn when Japan unceremoniously withdrew, thereby ending any hope of international disarmament. Yet the summit's other participants—Britain, France, Italy, and the United States—vaingloriously forged ahead. When Italy walked out, only the three friendly democracies were left to sign the new treaty.

A successor to the Washington Treaty of 1922 and the London Treaty of 1930, the Second London Treaty was instantly obsolete, since the signatories' potential enemies had already committed acts that made disarmament untenable. Japan, poised to invade China, had begun work on the world's two largest battleships—70,000 tons apiece, twice the treaty-permitted size. Mussolini had invaded Ethiopia. And Hitler had denounced the terms of Versailles and marched his ever-expanding army into the Rhineland.

Heeding the treaty's stipulations, Britain soon notified France and the United States of its ambitious program to build 38 new warships, the biggest naval project since the post-World War I arms race. All bets for peace were officially off. **◂1922.6 ▸1937.1**

JAPAN

Military Gains Upper Hand

12 The growing militarization of Japan reached a deadly pitch in February 1936 as a group of ultranationalistic army officers, hungry to shape national policy, carried out an assassination plot against key members of the moderate cabinet of Premier Keisuke Okada. Although they killed four officials and wounded one more, the insurgents failed to seize the government, and 13 of them were executed. In the period of martial law that followed the coup attempt, Okada and his gutted cabinet fell from power. Koki Hirota became premier, but real authority now belonged to the army, which blocked Hirota's cabinet appointments and maneuvered its own men into key positions. Hamstrung, Hirota adopted the army's vague, jingoistic platform: a defense of nationalism, increased military spending, foreign policy reform, and economic stability.

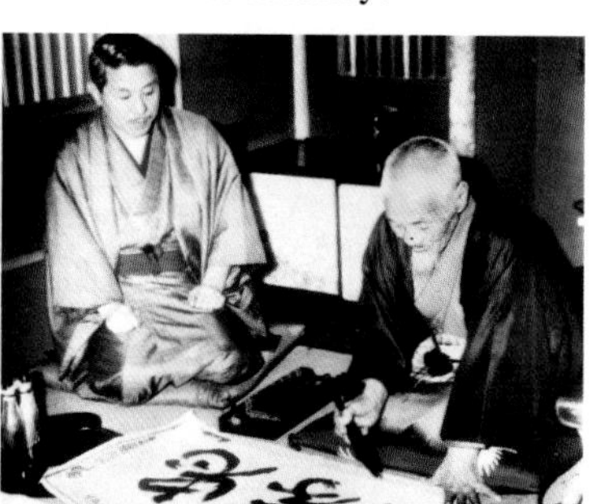

Hirota and his father write New Year's resolutions for 1937—a traditional ceremony.

Under Hirota, whose government lasted less than a year, and the series of weak premiers succeeding him, Japan allotted an ever-greater portion of its budget to the military. By 1937, defense consumed more than half of Japan's total budget. The country also embarked on a course of unprecedented industrial development, the overwhelming bulk of which was concentrated in the heavy war industries. "The tide has turned against the liberalism and democracy that once swept over the nation," observed one government official. In place of democracy, an alliance of military and industrial interests had erected a fascist dictatorship. **◂1936.11 ▸1937.1**

MUSIC

Prokofiev's Classic for Kids

13 "The most important thing is to find a common language with the young," said Sergei Prokofiev in 1936 while conceiving *Peter and the Wolf, a Symphonic Tale for Children.* It took the prolific composer a week to achieve his goal. Innumerable young audiences over the years have learned the basics of musical interpretation by linking Prokofiev's cleverly crafted motifs with the action his narrator describes: Forbidden to leave the property of his grandfather (represented by a cantankerous bassoon), Peter (a jaunty string quartet) nevertheless ventures forth to capture a wolf (ominous horns) that threatens Sasha the bird (flute), Ivan the cat (clarinet), and Sonya the duck (oboe). With its cheerful, folk-song-based musical language, this tale of an independent spirit somehow managed not to provoke the enforcers of Stalin's dogma of socialist realism, which had already cowed as great a composer as Dmitri Shostakovich.

A prodigal Russian son who—for reasons of art, not politics—had left his homeland soon after the 1917 revolution, Prokofiev wrote operas, symphonies, concerti, ballets (he collaborated with Sergei Diaghilev in Paris), and film scores. During his expatriate period, the composer-pianist (sketched above by artist and Ballets Russes designer Natalya Goncharova) dazzled audiences in Asia, North America, and Europe before returning in 1934 to settle in Moscow. Despite some initial suspicions that his work had been corrupted by the West, it was soon viewed as the musical embodiment of the revolution. In 1948, even Prokofiev became a target of Soviet censure. He wasn't rehabilitated until his last finished work, *Symphony No. 7* in 1952. **◂1934.5 ▸1941.12**

NOBEL PRIZES: Peace: Carlos Saavedra Lamas (Argentine; mediation of the Chaco War) ... Literature: Eugene O'Neill (U.S.; playwright) ... Chemistry: Peter J.W. Debye (Dutch; molecular structure of gases) ... Medicine: Henry Dale and Otto Loewi (U.K., German; chemical transmission of nerve impulses) ... Physics: Victor F. Hess (Austrian; cosmic radiation) and Carl D. Anderson (U.S.; positron).

A VOICE FROM 1936

A Role Model for Romantics

Radio Speech by Edward VIII, Prince of Wales and King of the United Kingdom of Great Britain and Ireland and of the British Dominions, and Emperor of India, December 11, 1936

"You must have no regrets—I have none," proclaimed the Duke of Windsor to Wallis Warfield Simpson after hearing a broadcast of his brother's coronation as King George VI. "This much I know: What I know of happiness is forever associated with you." The former king's decision to give up the throne of the British Empire, though wrenching, was in many ways characteristic of a nature that was both irresponsible and somewhat uncomfortable with power. During his eleven-month tenure as king, Edward VIII struggled to bring the British monarchy more in line with the modern world. He abolished old-fashioned court customs and was generally less rigid than his father, King George V. Yet, despite its widespread support among his subjects, the King's intention to marry Simpson, a twice-divorced American, brought anger, dismay, and censure from Church and Parliament—and the royal family. Forced to choose between the monarchy and personal happiness, Edward opted for the latter, provoking a constitutional crisis at a time when war threatened Europe. His abdication speech, delivered on December 11, 1936, rocked Great Britain, but romantics around the world were mesmerized. ◄1901.4 ►1952.1

At long last I am able to say a few words of my own. I have never wanted to withhold anything, but until now it has been not constitutionally possible for me to speak.

A few hours ago I discharged my last duty as King and Emperor, and now that I have been succeeded by my brother, the Duke of York, my first words must be to declare my allegiance to him. This I do with all my heart.

You all know the reasons which have impelled me to renounce the Throne. But I want you to understand that in making up my mind I did not forget the country or the Empire which as Prince of Wales, and lately as King, I have for 25 years tried to serve. But you must believe me when I tell you that I have found it impossible to carry the heavy burden of responsibility and to discharge my duties as King as I would wish to do without the help and support of the woman I love.

And I want you to know that the decision I have made has been mine and mine alone. This was a thing I had to judge entirely for myself. The other person most nearly concerned has tried up to the last to persuade me to take a different course. I have made this, the most serious decision of my life, upon a single thought of what would in the end be best for all.

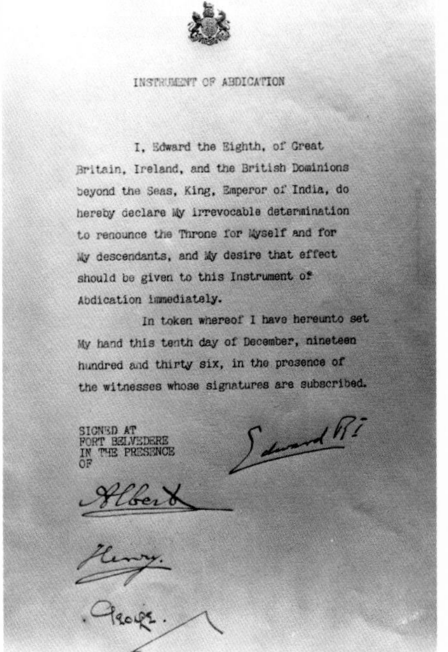

INSTRUMENT OF ABDICATION

I, Edward the Eighth, of Great Britain, Ireland, and the British Dominions beyond the Seas, King, Emperor of India, do hereby declare My irrevocable determination to renounce the Throne for Myself and for My descendants, and My desire that effect should be given to this Instrument of Abdication immediately.

In token whereof I have hereunto set My hand this tenth day of December, nineteen hundred and thirty six, in the presence of the witnesses whose signatures are subscribed.

SIGNED AT FORT BELVEDERE IN THE PRESENCE OF

Edward RI

Albert

Henry.

George.

Edward VIII formally renounced the throne in a letter to Parliament *(top)* a day before his BBC speech. Above, Edward (the new Duke of Windsor) and his duchess in France on their wedding day, June 3, 1937.

This decision has been made less difficult to me by the sure knowledge that my brother, with his long training in the public affairs of this country and with his fine qualities, will be able to take my place forthwith, without interruption to the life and progress of the Empire. And he has one matchless blessing, enjoyed by so many of you and not bestowed on me—a happy home with his wife and children.

During these hard days I have been comforted by my mother and by my family. The Ministers of the Crown, and in particular Mr. Baldwin, the Prime Minister, have always treated me with full consideration. There has never been any constitutional difference between me and them and between me and Parliament. Bred in the constitutional tradition by my father, I should never have allowed any such issue to arise.

Ever since I was Prince of Wales, and later on when I occupied the Throne, I have been treated with the greatest kindness by all classes, wherever I have lived or journeyed throughout the Empire. For that I am very grateful.

I now quit altogether public affairs, and I lay down my burden. It may be some time before I return to my native land, but I shall always follow the fortunes of the British race and Empire with profound interest, and if at any time in the future I can be found of service to His Majesty in a private section, I shall not fail.

And now we all have a new King. I wish him, and you, his people, happiness and prosperity with all my heart. God bless you all. God save the King.

"The outcome of this war will not be decided at Nanjing or in any other big city; it will be decided in the countryside of our vast country and by the inflexible will of our people."—**Chiang Kai-shek, after the invasion of China by Japan**

STORY OF THE YEAR

Japan Invades China

1 "I have no faith in pugnacious foreign policy," declared Japan's new premier, General Hayashi Senjuro, upon taking office in February 1937. Unfortunately for him and the rest of the world, other Japanese military leaders did. In a matter of a few months, Hayashi was replaced by Prince Konoe Fumimaro, whose cabinet was much more sympathetic to the military. Unchecked by the central government, the Japanese army quickly moved ahead with its long-brewing plan to conquer China.

On July 7, the Japanese instigated the skirmish that has been called the first battle of World War II. The Japanese army was running maneuvers near Lugouqiao, at a bridge spanning the Yongding River about ten miles west of Beijing, when a soldier disappeared. The Japanese accused the Chinese army across the river of abduction. The soldier soon turned up, but not before the Japanese commander had ordered an attack.

Fighting escalated; within weeks the Japanese controlled the east-west corridor from Beijing to Tianjin, on the Gulf of Chihli. "If we allow one more inch of our territory to be lost," declared Chiang Kai-shek, retreating from the policy of appeasement that had cost China Manchuria, "we shall be guilty of an unpardonable crime against our race." The Second Sino-Japanese War, prelude to World War II, had begun.

From Beijing, the Japanese swept southward toward Nanjing, seat of Chiang's Nationalist government, the Guomindang. The Chinese put up a heroic resistance at Shanghai, battling nearly to the last man (a quarter-million soldiers were lost) before falling to the invaders in October.

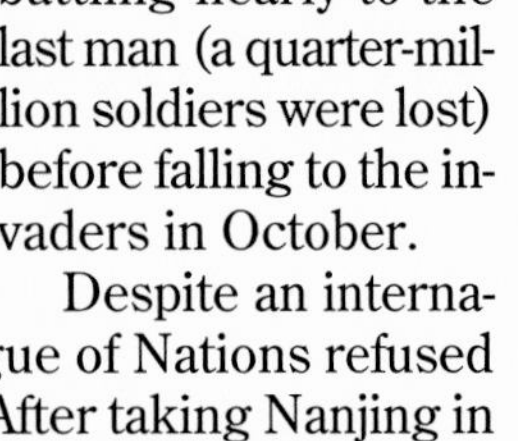

"Piece by piece" ran the caption for this American cartoon about Japan's intended takeover of China.

Despite an international outcry, the impotent League of Nations refused to mediate the undeclared war. After taking Nanjing in December (which forced Chiang to remove his government to the remote Sichuan city of Chongqing), the Japanese implemented one of the most horrific terrorist campaigns in modern warfare. For two months, soldiers ran amok, raping an estimated 7,000 women, killing hundreds of thousands of disarmed troops and civilians, and burning a third of the houses in Nanjing. In 1946, a lone Japanese general was executed for the Nanjing atrocities. **◂1936.10 ▸1938.4**

GREAT BRITAIN

A Policy of Appeasement

2 In three terms as prime minister, Stanley Baldwin had guided Britain through the general strike of 1926 and the abdication crisis a decade later. The popular Conservative had implemented major social reforms, but he was notoriously weak on foreign affairs. His vacillating response to Italy's invasion of Ethiopia appalled even his supporters. In May 1937, as the situation abroad grew ever more ominous, Baldwin retired, passing the reins to his decisive, detail-oriented chancellor of the exchequer, Neville Chamberlain. Yet it was Chamberlain's policy of appeasement that removed the last barriers to Hitler's dreams of conquest.

Before his appointment, Chamberlain had strongly supported his country's rearmament, and had urged sanctions against Italy over Ethiopia. But he'd also been the first British statesman to call for the lifting of sanctions, believing that Hitler and Mussolini could be pacified by careful concessions. As prime minister, he was conciliatory toward both dictators, sending personal notes to Il Duce and a stream of attentive envoys to the Führer.

In February 1938, he refused to join France in protesting German interference in Austrian politics; in March, when Hitler invaded Austria, Chamberlain immediately recognized the new regime (whereupon Foreign Secretary Anthony Eden resigned in disgust); weeks later, he recognized Italian sovereignty in Ethiopia in exchange for Mussolini's promise to withdraw from Spain after the civil war. Finally, in September, came the quintessential gesture of Chamberlain's appeasement of Hitler: He signed the Munich Pact, ceding Czechoslovakia's Sudetenland to Germany. Only when Hitler seized the rest of Czechoslovakia (less than a year later) did Chamberlain reverse his policy. **◂1936.8 ▸1938.2**

The Great Appeaser: After Munich, Chamberlain declared "peace for our time."

INDIA

Provincial Period Begins

3 India's long-awaited political reform began in earnest in 1937, after elections were held to fill the eleven new provincial legislatures created under the Government of India Act. These legislatures were locally autonomous, subject to the approval of a British governor. For that reason Indian nationalists were skeptical of the new arrangement (Jawaharlal Nehru went so far as to call it "a new charter of slavery"), fearing that it would distract participants from their true objective: complete independence.

In the elections, the Hindu-dominated Indian National Congress Party won decisively, and quickly established party governments in eight provinces, where they excluded nonmembers from the ministries—thus confirming the worst fears of many Muslims. In response, Muslim politicians threw all their support behind Muhammad Ali Jinnah *(above)*, head of the minority Muslim League. "Muslims," Jinnah declared, "can expect neither justice nor fair play under Congress government."

Despite the tensions, provincial legislatures amassed a strong record during their two years in power. By 1939, when World War II ended the provincial period, the legislatures had raised issues of education, health, and land reform. Hindu-Muslim relations continued to deteriorate, however, as it became increasingly clear that the Congress Party under Nehru would run post-British India. **◂1935.13 ▸1942.M**

BRAZIL

A Corporate Dictator

4 A new political system emerged in the 1930s: the bureaucratic-authoritarian state. Such nations could lean left (Pilsudski's Poland) or right (Salazar's

ART & CULTURE: Books: *Their Eyes Were Watching God* (Zora Neale Hurston); *Of Mice and Men* (John Steinbeck); *The Flowering of New England* (Van Wyck Brooks); *To Have and Have Not* (Ernest Hemingway); *Bread and Wine* (Ignazio Silone); *The Man with the Blue Guitar* (Wallace Stevens) ... Music: "The Lady Is a Tramp" and "My Funny Valentine" (Rodgers and Hart); *Lulu* (Alban Berg); *Carmina Burana*

"The whole basis of my singing is feeling. Unless I feel something, I can't sing."—**Billie Holiday, in her autobiography, *Lady Sings the Blues***

Portugal) or teeter both ways—as Brazil did in 1937, when President Getúlio Vargas, a rightist capable of feinting left, declared his country the Estado Nôvo (New State).

South America's largest country had been a republic since 1889—but a sluggish one, run by coffee growers and entrenched politicians. Within Brazil, the urban middle class and young military officers had long agitated for social reform—even if it meant suspending the constitution. In 1930, with the Depression wreaking havoc on coffee prices, the army revolted and named Vargas, governor of the state of Rio Grande do Sul, president.

At first, Vargas left Brazil's political structure virtually untouched. But in 1935, as Integralists (quasi-fascists known as "Greenshirts") battled leftists in the streets, he cracked down, jailing thousands of leftists. When he made himself dictator in 1937, the Integralists were

Brought to power by quasifascists, Vargas soon dispensed with ideology altogether.

ecstatic. But Vargas soon turned on them as well. After attempting a putsch, the Integralists faded away.

Under Vargas's Estado Nôvo, labor unions, the press, and the economy came under government control. Censorship, summary arrest, and torture became routine. But instead of erecting a one-party system, Vargas banned *all* parties. He established no ideology or personality cult, nor did he encourage expansionism. He supported the United States during World War II, in exchange for development aid. In 1945 he freed leftist political prisoners and moved against foreign investors. When grateful communists declared their support, his furious officers deposed him and restored democracy.

Vargas won the presidency again in 1950, but inflation and corruption undermined his popularity. In 1954, after he was implicated in the shooting of an opponent, the Army forced him to resign. He killed himself hours later. **▸1960.9**

MUSIC

Lady Day and Pres

5 One of the great collaborations in jazz history began in January 1937, when vocalist Billie Holiday and tenor saxophonist Lester Young, backed by the Teddy Wilson Ensemble, recorded "This Year's Kisses" in New York City. The understated drama of Holiday's haunting, bittersweet voice perfectly complemented Young's airy, laconic solos (which departed dramatically from the full-bodied, vibrato-laden sound of Coleman Hawkins, until then the era's dominant tenor player). Together, "Lady Day" and "Pres"—their nicknames for each other—established a new style that was the precursor of what came to be called "cool" jazz.

After a childhood of servitude and a stint as a prostitute, Holiday had begun her recording career in 1933 with clarinetist and bandleader Benny Goodman. Two years later, she joined Count Basie's band. Her seven-year partnership—personal as well as professional—with Young began when he rejoined Basie after a long absence. The records the pair made during that period are full of dazzling interplay between their respective instruments.

Both died in 1959. Young, an alcoholic who spent his last years alone in a New York hotel room, died at 49, hours after returning from a gig in Paris. Holiday, hounded by an on-again, off-again addiction to heroin, died in police custody at 44. To jazz fans everywhere, they rank among the immortals. **◂1935.10 ▸1945.15**

SCIENCE

Darwin Meets Mendel

6 With his 1937 book, *Genetics and the Origin of Species,* Ukrainian-American geneticist Theodosius Dobzhansky integrated Mendelian genetics and Darwinian evolution, pioneering the field of evolutionary genetics. Until Dobzhansky, the mechanics of evolution had eluded scientists, who generally believed that Darwin's natural selection occurred slowly over time, producing ideally adapted species. Dobzhansky demonstrated otherwise: Working with vinegar flies, he observed wide genetic diversity within the species. Yet this genetic variability, Dobzhansky argued, actually increased a species' odds for survival, making it more adaptable to environmental changes.

Dobzhansky, an avid writer, researcher, and traveler (he conducted fieldwork on every continent except Antarctica), had come to Columbia University in 1927 to work with Thomas Hunt Morgan, the discoverer of chromosomes. Dobzhansky's theory of "synthetic evolution" was supported by the independent findings of mathematical geneticists G.B.S. Haldane and R.A. Fisher in Great Britain and Sewall Wright in the United States, and by biologists Ernst Mayr and Julian Huxley. **◂1909.12 ▸1943.18**

Every female jazz vocalist since Holiday (here in 1945) has had to contend with her ghost.

BIRTHS

Bill Cosby, U.S. comedian.

Jane Fonda, U.S. actress.

Robert Gallo, U.S. virologist.

Philip Glass, U.S. composer.

David Hockney, U.K. painter.

Dustin Hoffman, U.S. actor.

Saddam Hussein, Iraqi president.

Peter Max, German-U.S. artist.

Mengistu Haile Mariam, Ethiopian president.

Jack Nicholson, U.S. actor.

Colin Powell, U.S. general.

Thomas Pynchon, U.S. novelist.

Robert Redford, U.S. actor.

Vanessa Redgrave, U.K. actress.

Bobby Seale, U.S. political activist.

Boris Spassky, U.S.S.R. chess player.

Tom Stoppard, Czech-U.K. playwright.

Lanford Wilson, U.S. playwright.

DEATHS

J.M. Barrie, U.K. playwright.

Wallace Carothers, U.S. chemist.

George Gershwin, U.S. composer.

Jean Harlow, U.S. actress.

Erich Ludendorff, German soldier and political leader.

Ramsay MacDonald, U.K. prime minister.

Guglielmo Marconi, Italian inventor.

Thomas Masaryk, Czech philosopher and president.

Andrew Mellon, U.S. financier.

Maurice Ravel, French composer.

John D. Rockefeller, U.S. industrialist.

Elihu Root, U.S. diplomat.

Ernest Rutherford, U.K. physicist.

Bessie Smith, U.S. singer.

Edith Wharton, U.S. writer.

(Carl Orff) ... Painting & Sculpture: *The Flame* (Jackson Pollock); *The Leg of Mutton Nude* (Stanley Spencer) ... Film: *The Life of Emile Zola* (William Dieterle); *A Star Is Born* (William Wellman); *Captains Courageous* (Victor Fleming); *Stella Dallas* (King Vidor) ... Theater: *I'd Rather Be Right* (Rodgers, Kaufman, and Hart); *Pins and Needles* (Harold Rome); *Electra* (Jean Giraudoux) ... Radio: *The Guiding Light.*

"I never hated any man, not even in the ring. You don't hate that easy."—Joe Louis

NEW IN 1937

Supermarket shopping cart (Oklahoma).

Drive-in bank (Los Angeles).

Spam (George A. Hormel Co.).

Franchise restaurants (Howard Johnson).

U.S. blood bank (Cook County Hospital, Chicago).

Antihistamines (discovered by French chemist Daniel Bovet).

Golden Gate Bridge (4,200 feet; the world's longest suspension bridge until 1964).

IN THE UNITED STATES

▶NATURAL BEAUTY—Frank Lloyd Wright completed one of American architecture's most stunning feats in 1937: a residence for Edgar Kaufmann in Pennsylvania's Allegheny Mountains. With its beige concrete terraces and stone masonry, the cantilevered house —called "Fallingwater" for its

perch above a waterfall—embodies Wright's belief in "organic architecture" that integrates seamlessly into its natural surroundings. ▶1959.M

▶DUMMY RULES RADIO—Dressed in white tie, wearing a monocle, Charlie McCarthy was the most obnoxious personality on radio. Luckily, he was just a dummy. With ventriloquist Edgar Bergen feeding him his lines, McCarthy debuted on NBC in May in *The Chase and Sanborn Hour.* McCarthy's outrageous repartee with such guests as W.C. Fields and Mae West appealed to listeners' licentious sides, keeping the show number one until 1940.

▶THE FAIREST OF THEM ALL —Walt Disney's 1937 *Snow White and the Seven Dwarfs* was not only the first full-

SPAIN

Hitler Practices on Guernica

7 When Nationalist leader Francisco Franco asked for aid at the start of the Spanish Civil War, the rulers of Fascist Italy and Nazi Germany immediately agreed. They expected a quick victory that would gain them an ally at very little cost; in the meantime, they'd have a chance to try out their own new war machinery. In April 1937, Germany's state-of-the-art Condor Legion bombed the provincial capital of Guernica for nearly four hours, destroying 70 percent of the town's buildings, strafing peasants at the marketplace and in their fields. More than 1,000 of Guernica's 7,000 people were killed, many gunned down as they fled.

While both sides in the war had hit civilian targets before, the Guernica bombing was the most savage and sustained attack in the short history of aerial warfare. And Guernica was special—a holy city to the fiercely independent Basque people.

The atrocity outraged Pablo Picasso, a Spaniard. Asked to create a painting for the Spanish Pavilion at the Paris World's Fair, the artist produced *Guernica,* an emotionally devastating mural memorializing the bombing. The painting caused an enormous stir in Paris, and again when it was shipped to the United States after the civil war's end. It stayed at New York's Museum of Modern Art for 43 years before moving back to Madrid's Prado in 1981—in accordance with Picasso's stated wish that the painting be returned to his homeland once democracy was restored there. ◀1936.2 ▶1939.9

Lacking a common language, Renoir's wartime prisoners communicated with pennywhistles.

FILM

Renoir's Pacifist Masterpiece

8 "I made *Grand Illusion* because I am a pacifist," said Jean Renoir upon the release, in 1937, of what is perhaps the richest and sharpest indictment of war ever captured on film. In this World War I tale of French prisoners of war and their German captors, Renoir (the son of French impressionist Pierre Auguste Renoir) created a subtle and moving meditation on the boundaries—between nations, classes, and religions—that make brotherhood an infinitely more difficult condition to sustain than warfare.

Of *Grand Illusion*—which starred Erich von Stroheim, Pierre Fresnay, and Jean Gabin—Franklin Roosevelt said, "Every democratic person should see this film." Joseph Goebbels called it "public cinematographic enemy number one," and banned it in Germany and Austria. Italy also banned it, as did the Belgian foreign affairs minister, Paul Henri Spaak, whose brother Charles was a writer on the film.

Yet Renoir himself was more modest in assessing the film's political power. "I made a picture in which I tried to express all my deep feelings for the cause of peace," he said years later. "The film was very successful. Three years later the war broke out. That is the only answer I can find." ▶1939.8

SPORTS

The Brown Bomber

9 For twelve tumultuous years, beginning with an eight-round knockout of James Braddock in 1937, fighter Joe Louis—a.k.a. the "Brown Bomber"—reigned as the heavyweight champion of the world. Scoring the championship knockout over Braddock in Chicago was a sweet victory for the African-American boxer, who had suffered his first professional defeat the previous year in a twelve-round decision with German Max Schmeling. Sweeter yet was the rematch with Schmeling in 1938 at New York's Yankee Stadium.

That bout was almost anticlimactic: Louis knocked out Schmeling, a

Picasso's *Guernica*: The painting's imagery of agonized humans and animals is still used to protest military brutality.

SPORTS: Baseball: World Series, New York Yankees defeat New York Giants, 4–1 ... Football: NFL, Washington Redskins defeat Chicago Bears, 28–21 ... Tennis: Don Budge takes all three titles at Wimbledon (singles, doubles, and mixed doubles) ... Boxing: Joe Louis begins 11-year reign as heavyweight champion, knocking out James J. Braddock ... Horse Racing: War Admiral wins Triple Crown.

"I have a feeling there is just about one more good flight left in my system, and I hope this trip is it."
—Amelia Earhart, before taking off on her last flight

presumed exemplar of Aryan superiority, delivering more than 50 blows in the first 124 seconds. Schmeling's loss was so intolerable to the Germans that they cut off the radio broadcast of the fight before it ended and later doctored the film version by inserting footage from the first Schmeling-Louis match.

Although Louis was not the first black to hold the heavyweight title—Jack Johnson had become champ in 1908—he was the first to give sociological significance to the fact. The press reveled in the image of Louis: a penniless pugilist who'd worked his way up from the streets of Detroit. But Louis never lost sight of his commitment to civil

Louis's unassuming disposition outside the ring contrasted with his ferocity within it.

rights. He refused to sit in "black only" sections, and after joining the Army in 1942, helped desegregate military baseball and football.

Louis continued to box until 1949, when he retired undefeated. Two years later he was forced back into the ring to pay off delinquent taxes. His career ended for good on October 26, 1951, courtesy of an eighth-round knockout by Rocky Marciano. **◂1936.1 ▸1956.M**

AVIATION

Earhart Disappears

10 By 1937, flying around the world was almost routine. Pan American Airways had just launched its San Francisco–Hong Kong service, the final link in a chain of Pacific routes. But no one had yet circled the planet the long way: around the equator. Amelia Earhart decided she would be the first pilot to make the journey.

She knew the risks. In 1932, on the journey that made her the first woman to fly the Atlantic alone, Earhart had had to make an emergency landing in Ireland after an electrical storm damaged her plane. (Undaunted, she simply climbed out of the cockpit and asked where she was.) With the same spirit and determination, the 39-year-old aviator and her veteran navigator, Fred Noonan, climbed into their twin-engine Lockheed Electra in Los Angeles on June 1, 1937, and took off for their flight around the world.

After a stop in Puerto Rico, they skimmed the northern coast of South America, crossed Africa and India, and hopped through Southeast Asia. They reached Australia on June 28, and New Guinea the following day. On July 2, they began a 2,556-mile haul over empty ocean to Howland Island, a tiny coral dot colonized in 1935 by the United States, which had built an airstrip for Earhart's landing.

She never reached that destination, and the exact fate of Earhart and her plane, which disappeared without a trace, remains a mystery. Historians have speculated that the sun's glare obscured the island, or that the plane ran out of gas. More recently, evidence was unearthed strongly suggesting that Earhart was on a spy mission for the United States and was captured by the Japanese and imprisoned at a Japanese base on Saipan, in the Mariana Islands. Her plane was said to have been equipped with the latest military navigation equipment, and her flight to have been carefully supervised by naval intelligence. Other researchers claim to have found, on a desert island 350 miles from Howland Island, a shoe heel resembling hers and a sheet of aluminum that might have come from her plane. But nothing is certain, and officials have declared the case unsolved. **◂1936.M ▸1938.5**

Amelia Earhart atop the Lockheed Electra in which she set out on her final flight.

TECHNOLOGY

Envisioning the Computer

11 Alan Turing was a graduate student at Cambridge in 1937 when he published the paper that established the theoretical basis for the digital computer—a machine whose efficiency and versatility would eventually make the analog computer (pioneered by Vannevar Bush earlier in the decade) obsolete for most purposes. Turing's "On Computable Numbers, with an Application to the *Entscheidungsproblem*" tackled a question posed by the great German mathematician David Hilbert at the turn of the century: Can all mathematical problems be solved by a fixed, definite set of procedures?

Turing answered no with a tour de force of arcane algebra. For concrete illustration, he sketched the idea of an automatic problem-solving machine. Such a device, he wrote, would contain an endless tape divided into squares, each printed with the numbers "0" or "1" —representing the "yes" or "no" units into which all information can ultimately be broken down. Moving the tape back and forth, the machine would scan the squares, erasing or inscribing those digits to provide coded solutions to an operator's coded queries.

Turing went on to lead the team that, during World War II, designed the world's first electronic digital computer. In 1954, after undergoing court-ordered estrogen "treatment" for homosexuality, he committed suicide. **◂1930.1 ▸1941.6**

IN THE UNITED STATES

length animated feature (82-minutes), but its subject matter (loosely adapted from the Grimms' fairy tales) represent-

ed a departure for Disney—instead of chatty animals, the protagonists were people (if not exactly ordinary mortals). ◂1928.10

▸CALDER'S MOBILES—Standing apart from the other avant-garde creations at the 1937 Paris World's Fair was Alexander Calder's *Mercury Fountain*, one of the Pennsylvania-born sculptor's moving sculptures. Calder had originated his motor-driven "mobiles" (Marcel Duchamp's coinage) in the

early '30s; after 1932, the sculptures—typically a group of abstract tin shapes suspended by thin wires—were driven by air currents. ◂1917.4

▸SYMPHONIC SUPERSTAR—Arturo Toscanini was already the most famous conductor in the world in 1937, when NBC president David Sarnoff created a symphony orchestra for him at the network. Winning his widest audience yet over the radio, the maestro served as principal conductor at NBC for 17 years. ◂1912.M ▸1957.9

▸CONSTITUTIONAL CRISIS—Worried that the Supreme Court would rule against pending Social Security legislation and the Wagner Act (guaranteeing collective bargaining for workers), the recently re-elected FDR proposed adding as many as six new justices to the country's highest court. Even diehard FDR supporters were aghast at the court-packing scheme, and Congress killed the proposal within months. Meanwhile, the Court upheld both legislative measures. ◂1935.5

POLITICS & BUSINESS: GNP: $91.2 billion ... Congress passes 1937 Neutrality Act (an attempt to maintain U.S. isolationism) ... U.S. Steel agrees to recognize United Mine Workers (CIO) without a strike ... Pierce Arrow goes out of business ... FDR inaugurated on January 20 (date moved from March 4 under terms of 20th Amendment).

"My God! Chaps, I must be going around the bend—it hadn't got a propeller!"—**RAF officer, on viewing the test flight of the Gloster E.28/39, Britain's first jet aircraft, in 1941**

AROUND THE WORLD

▶POWERS APPEASE JAPAN—In December, Japanese warplanes bombed British ships in the Chinese port of Wuhan. The U.S. gunboat *Panay* was sunk by the Japanese on the Yangzi River the same month. Yet the two Western powers refused to interfere with Japan's conquest of China. Britain's failure to retaliate stemmed from fear that its vast Chinese holdings might be harmed. The U.S.—though it had finally condemned Japan's invasion of China—accepted apologies and an offer of indemnification, but clung steadfastly to its nonintervention policy. ◂1937.1 ▸1938.4

▶DEGENERATE ART—A special commission appointed by Hitler seized over 5,000 works of "degenerate" modern art

from public and private collections in 1937. (Economics minister Hermann Goering was careful to earmark 14 paintings for himself, including four Van Goghs.) On July 19, in Munich, the "Exhibition of Degenerate Art"*(poster for Hamburg venue above)* opened in conjunction with the Nazi-approved "Great German Art Exhibition." More than two million visitors came to look at prime examples of dadaism, cubism, and German expressionism, while only 60,000 attended the state-sanctioned show. ◂1920.4

▶A MEMOIR OF AFRICA—Danish-born writer Karen Blixen lived on a coffee plantation in Kenya from 1914 to 1931. In 1937, her moving memoir of those years, *Out of Africa* (published under the pseudonym Isak Dinesen), appeared simultaneously in English and Danish versions. Dinesen's book mourns the loss of all that had mattered to her in Kenya—her farm, her husband (from whom she was long divorced), her lover (the big-game hunter Denys Finch-Hatton, who died), the simple way of life, and the people that she loved.

THE MIDDLE EAST

Abandoning All Hope

12 Since the Balfour Declaration of 1917 (which endorsed the idea of a Jewish state within Palestine), the British government had been struggling to reconcile the conflicting aspirations of Jews and Arabs in Palestine, which Britain administered under a League of Nations mandate. Those who still believed in the possibility of peaceful coexistence between the two groups got a grim comeuppance in July 1937, when the Peel Commission, headed by Lord Robert Peel, issued its report. Basically, the commission concluded, the mandate in Palestine was unworkable: There was no hope of any cooperative national entity there that included both Arabs and Jews.

The impetus for the commission's formation had been the most recent spate of Palestinian violence. Riots and Arab protests against the Jews in Palestine had been escalating throughout the 1920s and '30s. In the mid-1930s, in response to the thousands of Jews who'd arrived from Europe, Palestinian Arabs formed the Arab High Committee to defend themselves against what they perceived as a Jewish takeover. A general strike exploded into a revolt. Desperate for a solution, the British appointed Lord Peel to study the situation. The Arab leadership boycotted the study.

Palestinian Arabs carrying protest banners proclaim their hegemony in Palestine.

After dismissing the possibility of Arab-Jewish amity, the commission went on to recommend the partition of Palestine into a Jewish state, an Arab state, and a neutral "sacred-site" state to be administered by Britain. Within two years, Britain found itself in a no-win situation, and on the eve of World War II issued the infamous "White Paper" severely curtailing Jewish immigration into Palestine. **◂1930.M ▸1939.M**

R. Lovesey's oil painting of Frank Whittle and the "Whittle Unit," his first test engine.

AVIATION

Jet Aircraft Engine Tested

13 As Hitler conspicuously rearmed, the other powers responded by upgrading their own weapons systems—especially in aviation, which most strategists saw as key to victory in the next world war. New types of aircraft were developed, from dive-bombers to quick little low-winged fighters. Then, in 1937, the seeds of an air-power revolution were planted by two young engineers in Germany and Britain who independently tested the world's first jet aircraft engines—on the ground.

The Briton, former test pilot Frank Whittle, had patented his design in 1930, when he was just 23. The German, Hans von Ohain, had taken out a patent in 1935, at age 24. Ohain's engine made its first test flight in 1939, powering an He 178 fighter plane. Whittle's became airborne in 1941 in a custom-built Gloster E.28/39 fighter.

The revolutionary advantages of jet engines—vastly increased power, light weight, freedom from vibration, and excellent reliability—were evident from the start. But development of a combat-ready jet plane was slow: Only in 1944 did a few squadrons of British Gloster Meteors and German Messerschmitt Me 262s go into service. In the meantime, the Germans were perfecting another type of jet-powered craft: the V-1 guided missile, which would rain terror and destruction on London for months. **◂1903.1 ▸1944.2**

ITALY

A Mutual Admiration Society

14 Benito Mussolini officially acknowledged Italy's divorce from its World War I allies and its new marriage to Nazi Germany with two journeys in 1937. In March, he visited the Italian colony of Libya, where he declared himself protector of the Muslim world and opened a strategic coastal highway to the border of British Egypt. In September, he made a five-day trip to Germany that transformed him from Hitler's disdainful associate into his willing pawn.

Hitler treated his guest to a lavish parade in Munich and military maneuvers in Mecklenberg. Il Duce toured the ultramodern Krupp arms works in Essen, and was rushed by special train to address a rally in Berlin. Everywhere the two dictators went, they were greeted by huge, disciplined, apparently adoring crowds. Mussolini was thoroughly won over.

Back in Italy, he announced that the Italian army would adopt the German goose step. Three weeks later, German envoy Joachim von Ribbentrop arrived in Rome and persuaded Mussolini to make Italy a third party to the Anti-Comintern Pact, the year-old entente between Germany and Japan. Mussolini then confided to Ribbentrop that he was no longer interested in safeguarding the independence of an ungrateful Austria. In December, Italy withdrew from the League of Nations, as Germany had done four years earlier. Over the following year, after a long opposition to Nazi anti-Semitism, Mussolini imposed harsh laws against Italian Jews. Hitler—more driven, more ruthless, and a better strategist—was now calling the shots for the man who'd been his model. **◂1936.4 ▸1939.5**

Mussolini touring Libya before his conciliatory trip to Germany.

NOBEL PRIZES: Peace: Viscount Cecil of Chelwood (U.K.; League of Nations) ... Literature: Roger Martin du Gard (French; novelist) ... Chemistry: Walter Haworth and Paul Karrer (U.K., Swiss; vitamins) ... Medicine: Albert Szent-Györgyi (Hungarian; nutrient oxidation) ... Physics: Clinton Davisson and George Thomson (U.S., U.K.; electron diffraction).

A VOICE FROM 1937

Disaster in the Sky

Radio Broadcast of the *Hindenburg* landing, by Herbert Morrison, May 6, 1937

It looked to be an unremarkable event—the routine docking of the German airship Hindenburg *at the U.S. naval base in Lakehurst, New Jersey. (The luxurious* Hindenburg, *the largest zeppelin ever built and a crowning achievement of the rising Third Reich, had already made ten transatlantic round-trips since being launched the previous year.) There to cover the story for WLS radio station in Chicago was reporter Herb Morrison, who was recording his impressions into a recording phonograph for broadcast later that evening. (Live broadcasts were possible only for news events identified in advance as important.) As Morrison and his recording engineer, Charles Nehlson, stood watching the "great floating palace" prepare to dock, the airship suddenly exploded. Within minutes, 36 of the 97 passengers aboard were dead. Morrison's electrifying account* (right) *became famous because in his on-the-spot reaction to the catastrophe—which included a momentary breakdown, during which he vomited—he broke through the "voice-of-God" objectivity that radio news coverage had theretofore prided itself on.* ◄**1929.M**

Investigators concluded that the explosion in the rear of the *Hindenburg (top)* was caused by atmospheric electricity igniting a gas leak (the airship's fuel was highly flammable hydrogen). Others believed that the swastika-emblazoned ship was destroyed by anti-Nazi saboteurs. In a photo taken three hours and 20 minutes later *(above)*, the dirigible's charred skeleton lies collapsed on the ground.

Here it comes, ladies and gentlemen, and what a sight it is, a thrilling one, a marvelous sight. It is coming down out of the sky pointed toward us, and toward the mooring mast. The mighty diesel motors roar, the propellers biting into the air and throwing it back into galelike whirlpools. Now and then the propellers are caught in the rays of sun, their highly polished surfaces reflect.... No one wonders that this great floating palace can travel through the air at such a speed with these powerful motors behind it. The sun is striking the windows of the observation deck on the eastward side and sparkling like glittering jewels on the background of black velvet....

She is practically standing still now. The ropes have been dropped, and they have been taken hold of by a number of men on the field. It is starting to rain again. The rain has slacked up a bit. The back motors of the ship are holding her just enough to keep her from—

[Explosion occurs and there is a break in the recording, as the blast has blown apart the tone arm of the recorder, which Nehlson repaired.]

Get out of the way! Get this, Charley! Get out of the way, please. She's bursting into flames! This is terrible! This is one of the worst catastrophes in the world. The flames are shooting 500 feet up in the sky. It is a terrific crash, ladies and gentlemen. It is in smoke and flames now. Oh, the humanity! Those passengers! I can't talk, ladies and gentlemen. Honest, it's a mass of smoking wreckage. Lady, I am sorry. Honestly, I can hardly—I am going to step inside where I can see it. Charley, that is terrible! Listen, folks, I am going to have to stop for a minute because I have lost my voice.

[Background noises]

Coming back again, I have sort of recovered from the terrific explosion and the terrific crash that occurred just before it was pulled down to the mooring mast. I don't know how many of the ground crew were under it when it fell. There is not a possible chance for anyone to be saved! The relatives of the people who were here ready to welcome their loved ones as they came off the ships are broken up. They are carrying them, to give them first aid and to restore them. Some of them have fainted. The people are rushing down to the burning ship with fire extinguishers to see if they can extinguish any of the blaze. The blaze is terrific because of the terrible amount of hydrogen gas in it.

"Oh, what idiots we all have been! But this is wonderful! This is just as it must be!"—**Niels Bohr upon hearing of Otto Hahn, Fritz Strassmann, and Lise Meitner's discovery of nuclear fission**

STORY OF THE YEAR

The Discovery of Fission

1 Beginning in the mid-1930s, leading physicists from France, Germany, and Italy vied with one another to be the first to split the heavier atoms. French physicist Frédéric Joliot-Curie had signaled the beginning of the race when, upon being awarded (with his wife, Irène Joliot-Curie) the 1935 Nobel for the discovery of artificial radioactivity, he declared that "explosive nuclear

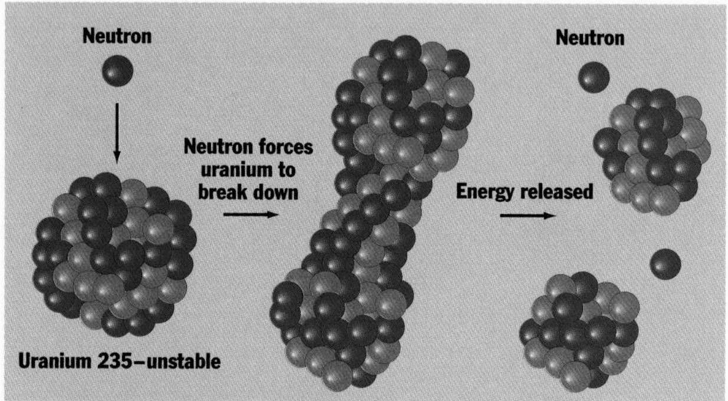

The splitting of a uranium nucleus, identified by Lise Meitner as fission.

chain reactions" would lead to "the liberation of enormous quantities of usable energy." In Berlin, a research team consisting of Otto Hahn, Fritz Strassmann, and Lise Meitner began bombarding uranium atoms with neutrons. The scientists expected the process to yield heavier radioactive elements similar to uranium—the results posited by Enrico Fermi in a similar experiment. Instead, in late 1938, Hahn and Strassmann (Meitner, an Austrian Jew, had fled to Sweden after Hitler's March invasion of Austria) were surprised to discover that their bombardment of uranium had produced a radioactive form of a much lighter element called barium.

Hahn and Strassmann forwarded their results to Meitner in Stockholm, where she and her nephew, the physicist Otto Frisch, pondered the mystery. They concluded that rather than emitting a particle or small bundle of particles as expected, the uranium nucleus had become elongated, developed a "waist," and then broken apart into two lighter, nearly equal fragments whose combined mass was less than that of the original uranium nucleus. The weight difference was converted into energy.

Meitner gave the name "fission" to the process. Joliot-Curie made the further discovery that uranium fission resulted in the release of additional neutrons that could in turn be used to split other uranium atoms. The groundwork had been laid for the sort of explosive chain reaction that would form the basis of the atomic bomb.

Hahn and Strassmann remained in Germany during the war. Hahn was captured by Allied troops in Spring 1945; while interned in England, he learned that he'd won the 1944 Nobel for chemistry. By the time he accepted the prize, his sense of scientific accomplishment had been tempered by the deeply distressing knowledge that a fission device was responsible for the destruction of Hiroshima and Nagasaki. After the war, Hahn became a leading exponent of nuclear-weapons controls. ◂1932.10 ▸1939.M

GERMANY

Hitler Absorbs Austria

2 Now that Italy was his ally, Adolf Hitler could complete the first stage of his plan for world domination: *Anschluss*—union—with Austria. To placate Mussolini, Austria's protector, Hitler had signed a 1936 agreement recognizing the country's sovereignty. But in return he'd forced Austrian chancellor Kurt von Schuschnigg (an independence-minded but weak-willed rightist) to declare his nation a "German state," and to promise to share power with the "national opposition." These provisions legitimized Austria's pro-*Anschluss* Nazis—and provided the pretext for the takeover Hitler launched two years later, in 1938.

The chain of events began in February, when Schuschnigg went to Germany to complain about a Nazi coup being plotted against him. Hitler browbeat him into signing a pledge to "give moral, diplomatic, and press support" to Germany, to stop prosecuting Nazi agitators,

Hitler in Vienna. His first conquest was accomplished without a blitzkrieg.

and to appoint a Nazi-affiliated lawyer, Arthur Seyss-Inquart, as interior minister. Once back home, Schuschnigg recovered himself and called a plebiscite on Austrian independence, with voting restricted to people over 24—thus excluding most Nazi sympathizers.

Hitler's second-in-command, Hermann Goering, demanded that the plebiscite be postponed. When Schuschnigg agreed, Goering demanded Schuschnigg's resignation. Schuschnigg complied. Then Goering demanded that Seyss-Inquart be made chancellor. At this point, Austrian president Wilhelm Miklas drew the line. German troops marched in on March 12. Schuschnigg urged the army not to resist—a move that failed to save him from spending the next seven years in prison.

The troops, followed by Austrian-born Hitler himself, were greeted by ecstatic crowds. (Swayed by Hitler's spellbinding speeches, many Austrians saw unification as a way to reclaim their lost Teutonic greatness.) Soon anti-Nazi dissidents were being forced to scrub Vienna's sidewalks. Jews were on their way to exile, like Sigmund Freud—or to concentration camps.

London and Washington quickly accepted the conquest; Rome sent congratulations. "Tell Mussolini I will never forget him for this," a grateful Hitler implored Il Duce's emissary. "Never, never, never, whatever happens." In a Nazi-run April plebiscite, 99.75 percent of Austrians approved the *Anschluss*. ◂1937.2 ▸1938.3

GERMANY

A Betrayal in Munich

3 With Austria firmly in Hitler's grasp, its northern neighbor Czechoslovakia was more vulnerable than ever. After three years of fomenting discontent among the Germans of the Sudetenland, Hitler was ready to attack. But in May 1938, rumors of German military preparations led France and Britain to warn Germany that they would defend the beleaguered country. Rather than call their bluff, Hitler set about weakening and isolating Czechoslovakia. The result, months later, was the Munich Pact, an act of appeasement that convinced Hitler he could get away with anything.

The Führer's strategy hinged on a coincidence: All Czechoslovakia's fortifications were in the German-speaking Sudetenland, which included most of the nation's 3.25 million ethnic Germans. Hitler instructed the Nazi-backed Sudeten

ART & CULTURE: Books: ***Uncle Tom's Children*** **(Richard Wright);** ***Rebecca*** **(Daphne du Maurier);** ***Nausea*** **(Jean-Paul Sartre);** ***Homage to Catalonia*** **(George Orwell);** ***Invitation to a Beheading*** **(Vladimir Nabokov);** ***U.S.A.*** **(John Dos Passos) ... Music: "Thanks for the Memory" (Rainger and Robin); "You Must Have Been a Beautiful Baby" (Warren and Mercer); "Jeepers Creepers" (Warren and Mercer);**

"It is intolerable at this moment to think of a large portion of our people exposed to the democratic hordes who threaten our people. I refer to Czechoslovakia!"—Adolf Hitler

Pro-Nazi terrorists in Czechoslovakia's Sudetenland. The Munich Pact delivered their country into Hitler's hands.

German Party to stir up demands for the region's independence. In the meantime, he escalated his propaganda campaign against the Czechs, accusing them of bloody atrocities against the Teutonic minority. He insisted that the Sudetenland was the last European territory he wanted. He made bellicose speeches, meant to frighten France and Britain away from intervention. The strategy worked: The barrage of words made a blitzkrieg unnecessary.

In September, British prime minister Neville Chamberlain and French premier Edouard Daladier met with Hitler in Munich. Mussolini acted as mediator. The two powers agreed to give Germany not only the Sudetenland but all of Czechoslovakia's predominantly German areas. (Czech president Eduard Beneš, who hadn't been consulted, resigned in protest.) Chamberlain announced that "peace with honor" had been won; he and Daladier went home to cheering crowds.

German troops arrived in the Sudetenland on October 1. Poland and Hungary, supported by Germany, annexed other regions of Czechoslovakia soon afterward. Finally, in 1939, Hitler threatened Slovakia into seceding and the Czech government into surrender.

Czechoslovakia was no more; its armaments and powerful industries were now in German hands. Too late, the French and British realized that they'd been hoodwinked. Poland, it was clear, would be Hitler's next target—but this time, victory would not come so easily. ◂1937.2 ▸1939.1

JAPAN

China Fights Back

4 The Japanese drive to conquer China culminated with the capture of Wuhan, the industrial hub of central China, late in 1938. After months of bitter fighting, the Japanese now controlled most of eastern China. With puppet regimes installed in occupied China, Chiang Kai-shek's Nationalist government was forced to retrench at Chongqing to the west, completely cut off from its normal communications. Japan's goal, to head a "new order in East Asia," seemed within reach.

The only obstacle to total occupation was China's vastness. By the end of 1938, Japan had already committed more troops to China than it wanted to, but guerrilla resistance was still active in the eastern countryside. North-central China was in the hands of the Chinese Communists under Mao Zedong, while the southeast was controlled by Chiang's Nationalists. In what Chiang called "a triumph of national sentiment over every other consideration," the two parties had suspended their civil war to present a unified front against the foreign invaders. An astute military strategist, Chiang recognized that his country's size was its greatest asset. Knowing the Japanese could not occupy the entire country, he decided to protract the hostilities.

His tactic resulted in the most stunning act of the long, gruesome war: In June 1938, the Chinese dynamited the dikes holding back the Yellow River in Henan province. The ensuing flood claimed the lives of many thousands of villagers, and swept away the homes of millions more, but it succeeded in bogging down the Japanese penetration into southern China. Meanwhile, isolated on the western side of the flood plain, the Nationalists embarked on a project to open a supply link with the rest of the world: the fabled Burma Road. Working by hand, hundreds of thousands of Chinese laborers carved a 715-mile route through a mountain wilderness from Kunming in China to Mandalay, Burma, in less than a year. The first supplies reached Kunming in December 1938. ◂1937.1 ▸1940.15

Despite the penetration of Japan's military, Chinese troops still controlled much of the countryside. Here, members of the Red Army guard the Great Wall in northwestern China.

BIRTHS

Leonardo Boff, Brazilian theologian.

Jerry Brown, U.S. political leader.

Juan Carlos I, Spanish king.

Giogetto Giugiaro, Italian industrial designer.

Peter Jennings, Canadian-U.S. newscaster.

Rod Laver, Australian tennis player.

Issey Miyake, Japanese fashion designer.

Rudolf Nureyev, U.S.S.R. dancer.

Joyce Carol Oates, U.S. writer.

Arthur Scargill, U.K. labor leader.

Romy Schneider, Austrian actress.

Ted Turner, U.S. entrepreneur.

Jerry West, U.S. basketball player.

DEATHS

Kemal Atatürk, Turkish president.

Karel Capek, Czech writer.

Benjamin Cardozo, U.S. jurist.

Fyodor Chaliapin, Russian singer.

Gabriele D'Annunzio, Italian writer and political leader.

Clarence Darrow, U.S. lawyer.

Harvey Firestone, U.S. industrialist.

William Glackens, U.S. painter.

Ernst Kirchner, German painter.

Suzanne Lenglen, French tennis player.

Mary Mallon, U.S. typhoid carrier.

King Oliver, U.S. musician.

Konstantin Stanislavsky, Russian actor and director.

Thomas Wolfe, U.S. novelist.

Billy the Kid (Aaron Copland); *Kol Nidre* (Arnold Schoenberg) ... Painting & Sculpture: *Dawn* (Lyonel Feininger); *Rich Harbor* (Paul Klee) ... Film: *You Can't Take It with You* (Frank Capra); *Alexander Nevsky* (Sergei Eisenstein) ... Theater: *Abe Lincoln in Illinois* (Robert Sherwood); *The Corn Is Green* (Emlyn Williams); *I Married an Angel* (Rodgers and Hart) ... Radio: *The Green Hornet*.

"Coming from Texas peculiarly fits a person for flying around the world.... After you've flown across Texas two or three times, the distance around the world doesn't seem so great."—**Aviator Howard Hughes**

NEW IN 1938

Domestic steam iron.

Superman (Action Comics).

Pressurized cabins in passenger airliners.

Instant coffee (Nestlé's Nescafé).

Electroconvulsive "shock" therapy.

Jefferson-head nickel.

March of Dimes.

Medical tests for marriage licenses (New York).

Fiberglas (Owens-Corning).

Hewlett-Packard.

IN THE UNITED STATES

▶A GRAND GRAND SLAM—Don Budge, an amateur tennis player from California, became the first person to gain the most coveted title in tennis, the Grand Slam, winning the Australian, French, British (Wimbledon), and U.S. Opens in 1938. At Wimbledon he took all three titles—singles, doubles, and mixed doubles. The first player to use the backhand as an offensive weapon, Budge won with tactical savvy and a deadly serve. In 1939, he turned professional; he dominated the game for the next two decades. ◂1926.M ▸1969.M

▶ALL-AMERICAN ROMANCE—In 1938's *Love Finds Andy Hardy*, the wholesome American hero—played by 18-year-old Hollywood veteran Mickey

Rooney—enjoys the attention of two new girlfriends, played by Lana Turner and Judy Garland *(above, with Rooney)*.

AVIATION

Hughes Closes Out an Era

5 Howard Hughes had always been larger than life. The handsome young film producer (*Hell's Angels*, *The Outlaw*), aircraft manufacturer, and multimillionaire was also a record-breaking pilot. Yet Hughes brought the era of the heroic aviator to a close when, on July 14, 1938, he landed his twin-engine Lockheed at New York's Floyd Bennett Field after circling the planet in three days, 19 hours, and 17 minutes—half the time it had taken Wiley Post on his 1933 solo trip. "Any one of the airline pilots of this nation," Hughes said afterward, "could have done the same thing."

No trailblazer, Hughes enjoyed the benefit of his predecessors' experience as well as unlimited funds. His Lockheed 14 was stuffed with state-of-the-art navigational instruments; radio-equipped ships and ground stations were deployed all along his route. Spare parts waited at six scheduled stops and at emergency sites in between.

The plane left for Paris on July 10. The only trouble it encountered was in Siberia, where a poorly charted mountain range loomed up unexpectedly. After stops in Fairbanks, Alaska, and Minneapolis, Minnesota, the plane landed back in New York—where 25,000 screaming fans waited. For the painfully shy Hughes, facing the crowd was the most traumatic portion of the trip. He mumbled a few words, then slipped into a limousine. It was the last time an airplane flight would create such a tumult. **◂1938.M ▸1958.6**

TECHNOLOGY

Carlson's First Copier

6 In a modest workshop in Queens, New York, a former patents administrator named Chester Carlson and his assistant coated a metal plate with sulfur and printed the date and place, "10-22-38 Astoria," in India ink on a glass slide. They rubbed the sulfur-coated plate with a cotton cloth to give it an electrical charge, placed the slide against it, and exposed both to a powerful light. After a few seconds, they removed the slide and sprinkled black powder on the plate's surface. A near-perfect image of the inscription appeared. They pressed a sheet of waxed paper to the plate and peeled it away, transferring the powder images. When the paper was heated, the wax melted and the result was the first xerographic (Latin for "dry writing") copy.

Carlson had begun his research by cooking up chemicals on his kitchen stove; he carried on for five years until, exhausted and out of money, he contacted the Battelle Memorial Institute, a private research foundation in Ohio, which purchased a 75 percent share of the invention for $3,000. In 1946, the Haloid Company, a small photographic paper manufacturer in Rochester, New York, signed on as well, and in 1949 the company made the first xerographic copier—an awkward, fragile machine (actually, three machines) that was dauntingly complicated to use.

Over the next decade of research and development, Carlson's lonely quest turned into a corporate crusade, as Haloid unleashed a bevy of engineers, designers, and marketers to work on the project. By 1959, a more practical copier, the Xerox 914, was ready for market. Although far bigger than the desktop machine Carlson had visualized, it was simple enough for a child to operate. Indeed, a television commercial showed a little girl copying a letter with the machine. (When her father asked which was the original and which was the copy, the child scratched her head and exclaimed, "I forget!") Despite skepticism about its practicality, sales took off: A $10,000 investment in Haloid (soon to become Xerox Corporation) stock in 1960 was worth more than $1 million by 1972. **▸1988.11**

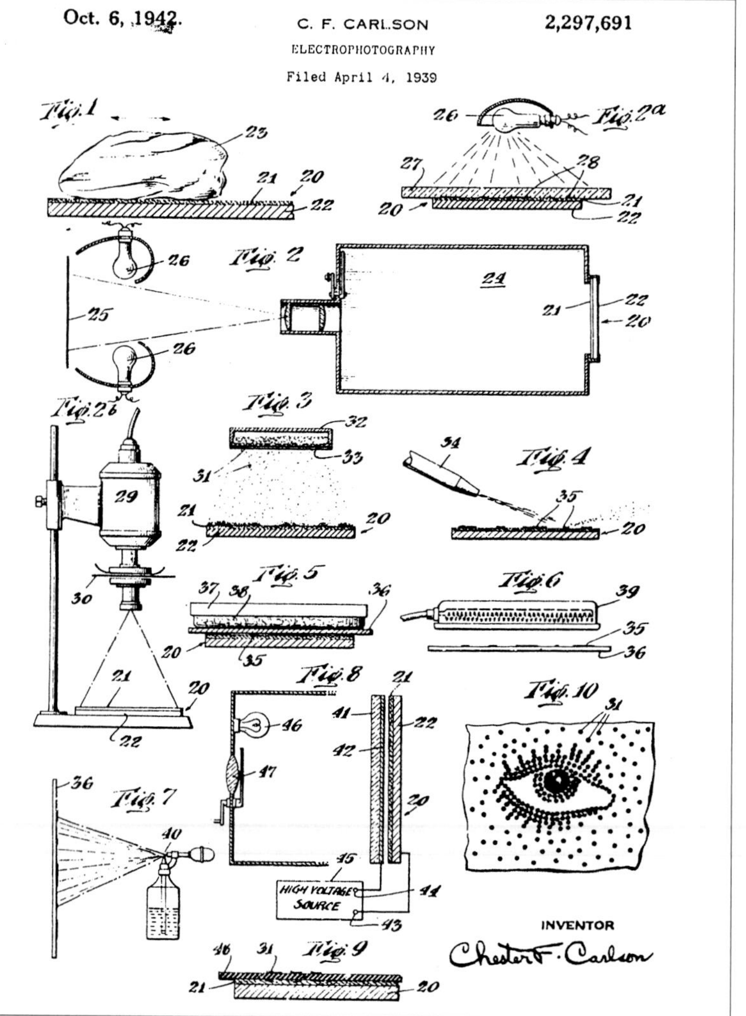

Carlson's drawings for the patent he took out on his "electrophotography" process.

SPORTS: Baseball: World Series, New York Yankees (Lombardi's "snooze") defeat Chicago Cubs, 4–0; Bob Feller (Cleveland Indians) strikes out a record 18 in one game ... Football: NFL, New York Giants defeat Green Bay Packers, 23–17 ... Boxing: Joe Louis knocks out Max Schmeling in first round ... Tennis: Helen Wills Moody wins eighth Wimbledon ... Soccer: World Cup, Italy defeats Hungary, 4–2.

"I am not interested in the ephemeral—such subjects as the adulteries of dentists. I am interested in those things that repeat and repeat and repeat in the lives of millions."—Thornton Wilder

***Jezebel*, costarring Henry Fonda, gave Davis a role tailor-made to her image as a rebel.**

FILM

The Redoubtable Bette

7 Like every other movie actor of the thirties and forties, Bette Davis was a slave to the studio system. She had made her screen debut in *Bad Sister* (1931), become a star with *Of Human Bondage* (1934), and won an Oscar for *Dangerous* (1935). But in 1936, disgusted with the pictures her contract obliged her to make, Davis left Hollywood for London. Warner Bros. sued for breach of contract, and won. But so did Davis: Upon her return to Hollywood, she was given better pictures. The first of them was *Jezebel*, released in 1938. Directed by William Wyler and co-written by John Huston, *Jezebel*, as its title suggests, gave the rebellious star a role she was born for—that of a strong-willed, magnetic, ambitious Southern belle. The performance earned her a second Oscar.

Over a six-decade career, Davis created dozens of other unforgettable portraits of strong women in love, in lust, or in extremis. Her huge headlight eyes, precise diction, and extravagant way with a cigarette made her a riveting screen presence, even when her material was weak. (She was equally formidable offscreen: Jack Warner affectionately called her "an explosive little broad with a straight left.") Davis could play a chilling mankiller *(The Little Foxes)*, a dying socialite (*Dark Victory*), or a Cinderella spinster *(Now, Voyager)* with equal aplomb. And at least three of her roles have become icons of camp: the frustrated harridan ("What a dump!") in *Beyond the Forest*; the Broadway diva Margo Channing, scared stiff of middle age, in *All About Eve*; and the demented ex-child star in *What Ever Happened to Baby Jane?* **▸1961.11**

THEATER

An American Innovator

8 Embraced by the public as a Rockwellesque portrait of American village life in the early 1900s, Thornton Wilder's innovative

Thornton Wilder at a rehearsal for a 1959 production of *Our Town* in Williamstown, Massachusetts.

1938 play, *Our Town,* was actually an expression of the author's peculiarly American existentialism. Dispensing with such theatrical conventions as stage sets, props, and a clear-cut story line, Wilder created an allegory of individual life and death measured out against the vast indifference of the universe. The innovative play, which won a Pulitzer Prize, became a classic of American drama.

On a bare stage, with running commentary provided by a Stage Manager sitting off to one side, *Our Town* examined an obdurately ordinary town—Grover's Corners, New Hampshire—from its "Daily Life" (Act I) to "Love and Marriage" (Act II) to "Death" (Act III). The play's unusual combination of quaintness and desolation—"She dies, we die, they die," Wilder said of his heroine's untimely death—confused critics, who dismissed it as either naively optimistic or grossly pessimistic. The play *is* easy to sentimentalize: In its hundreds of productions over the years, it has often been transformed into what Wilder complained was a portrait of "Quaint Hayseed Family Life." His own sympathies lay with Proust and Joyce, and with Japanese theater (whose spare stagings influenced *Our Town*). Actually, as his admirer Edmund Wilson observed, Wilder "occupies a unique position between the Great Books and Parisian sophistication one way, and the entertainment industry the other way." **◂1931.11 ▸1949.V**

TECHNOLOGY

One-Step Writing

9 "Among the things that are wanted by everybody," wrote a reporter for *Scientific American* in 1851, "is a substitute for pen and ink. It seems that a single instrument ought to perform the function." A modest wish, but it wasn't fulfilled until 1938, 87 years later, when two brothers from Hungary, Ladislao and Georg Biro, invented the ballpoint pen.

The Biros' pen contained a steel ball at the end of a narrow tube filled with ink. Capillary action within the tube moistened the ball, allowing it to spread the ink evenly. Fran Seech, an Austrian chemist living in California, later perfected the ink so that it dried immediately upon hitting the paper.

The Biro, introduced in the United States after World War II, was billed as "the only pen that writes underwater." (In New York City, demonstrators sat in front of Gimbels department store, writing in tanks of water.) The Biros set up a company to manufacture the pens; eventually it was taken over by the French company Bic, which developed an even cheaper, throwaway ballpoint pen. **◂1938.6**

Ladislao Biro's patent drawing for the original ballpoint pen.

IN THE UNITED STATES

The wildly popular series of 15 movies was recognized in 1942 with a special Oscar to MGM for "achievement in representing the American way of life."

▸URBAN PROPHET—*The Culture of Cities,* the second book in Lewis Mumford's *Renewal of Life* series, was published in 1938 to critical acclaim. Outlining the histories of modern cities, Mumford expressed his fear that technology might rob civilization of its culture, and warned against poorly planned, large-scale, impersonal public works that disfigure the urban landscape. ▸1960.9

▸CORRIGAN'S BROKEN COMPASS—Denied permission to make a transatlantic flight (his plane, said authorities, was "not airworthy"), Douglas Corrigan instead filed a flight plan for a return home from New York to Los Angeles. But after he took off, Corrigan turned his plane in the opposite direction and landed in Ireland 28 hours and 13 minutes later. The stunt earned him the nickname "Wrong Way" Corrigan. ◂1938.5

▸A SIGNATURE SONG—Through her popular radio show on Thursday nights on CBS, Kate Smith became known as the "First Lady of Radio." On Armistice Day, the Virginia-born singer—famous

for her rotund figure and her jovial manner—introduced her listeners to the song that would become an American institution and Smith's signature for the rest of her life—Irving Berlin's "God Bless America." Indeed, Smith's identification with the tune was so thorough that, for a time, she and she alone had Berlin's permission to sing it. ◂1911.6

POLITICS & BUSINESS: GNP: $85.3 billion ... FDR asks for buildup of Army and Navy; Naval Expansion Act is passed, $1 billion granted ... House Committee to Investigate Un-American Activities is formed ... Second Agricultural Adjustment Act, Fair Labor Standards Act passed ... Ludlow Resolution, proposing referendum before Congress can declare war, is defeated ... McDonnell Aircraft and Eastern Airlines founded.

"What seemed like hundreds of men, swinging great truncheons, jumped from lorries and began to smash up the shops all around us."—**Peter Oestereicher, a young Jewish boy who was window-shopping with his mother on *Kristallnacht***

AROUND THE WORLD

▶THE LAST ENEMY—Nikolai Bukharin, Stalin's last remaining opponent for political power still living in the Soviet Union, was found guilty of treason and executed in 1938 after a gruesome show trial. A member of the Bolshevik old guard, Bukharin had allied himself, after Lenin's death, with Stalin in supporting Lenin's moderate NEP over the more radical programs favored by Trotsky, Zinoviev, and Kamenev. But in 1929, having got his left-wing rivals out of the way, Stalin expelled Bukharin from the Comintern and the Politburo, and in 1937 had him secretly arrested for being a "Trotskyite." Bukharin's execution was the basis for Arthur Koestler's novel *Darkness at Noon*. ◀1936.6 ▶1941.M

▶LIVING FOSSIL—A fisherman off the coast of South Africa made the most extraordinary catch of the last 70 million years in December 1938, when he reeled in a *Latimeria chalumnae*, also known as a coelacanth. (The 350-million-year-old species has remained virtually unchanged from its original form.) Thought by scientists to have become extinct 70 million years earlier, the

lobe-finned fish had been eaten for years by the people of the Comoro Islands.

▶HINDEMITH'S HOORAH—German composer Paul Hindemith had been condemned as a "cultural Bolshevist" and a "spiritual non-Aryan" by Nazi propaganda minister Joseph Goebbels when the orchestral version of his opera *Mathis der Maler (Mathis the Painter)* debuted with the Berlin Philharmonic in 1934. When, in 1938, the opera was finally presented in its entirety in Zurich, Hindemith received the accolades he deserved. Though a modernist, Hindemith went against the avant-garde tide by upholding the primacy of tonality—a concept considered obsolete by other modernist composers like Arnold Schoenberg. ◀1912.11

Berliners survey the damage to a ladies' wear shop on the morning after *Kristallnacht*.

GERMANY

A Night of Broken Glass

10 Ernst vom Rath was a minor German diplomat, Herschel Grynszpan a Polish Jewish student whose parents had lived in Germany since 1914. Both lived in Paris. On the night of November 9, 1938, their disparate lives converged to ignite the rampage known as *Kristallnacht*, or "Night of Crystal" (a reference to all the glass that was shattered during the pogrom). The resulting carnage would escalate and continue unabated for the next seven years.

The pretext for the first truly explosive incident of Nazi violence against the Jews was the shooting of vom Rath (who'd been suspected of disloyalty himself) by Grynszpan. Pawns in a game being played by Poland and Germany over which country was responsible for the Polish Jews residing in Germany, Grynszpan's parents had been deported by the Nazis to the Polish border in October. Anguished over his parents' plight, Grynszpan charged into the German embassy, picked out vom Rath at random, and shot him. Vom Rath died two days later, on November 9.

As soon as news of vom Rath's death reached Munich (where Hitler and his cronies were celebrating the 15th anniversary of the Beer Hall Putsch), Joseph Goebbels, head of Nazi propaganda, called for the countrywide destruction of Jewish businesses, homes, and synagogues. Nazi storm troopers, SS men, and Hitler Youth took to the streets, burning nearly 200 synagogues to the ground, violating graves, breaking store windows, and attacking any Jew they encountered. In just 24 hours, 91 Jews were murdered, 36 severely injured, and 30,000 arrested and sent to Buchenwald, Dachau, and Sachsenhausen concentration camps.

Many of the Jews who were spared deportation and death were rounded up and marched to the charred synagogues, where they were beaten and forced to recite passages from *Mein Kampf*. Those sent to the camps were subject to even uglier treatment: On arrival at Sachsenhausen, 62 men were forced to run a gauntlet of spades, clubs, and whips. Twelve died. The stage was set for *die Endlösung der Judenfrage* ("the final solution to the Jewish question"). Within a year, Hitler had turned his attention to the Jews of Eastern Europe. **◀1935.1 ▶1939.18**

FILM

Screwball Sexiness

11 Thanks to such movies as *It Happened One Night* and such divinely daffy stars as Carole Lombard, moviegoers of the 1930s were introduced to the radical proposition that funniness could be sexy. Director Howard Hawks's 1938 *Bringing Up Baby* is the archetype of the film comedy genre known as "screwball." Starring Cary Grant as a straitlaced zoologist, Katharine Hepburn (playing against type) as the madcap heiress who loosens him up, and a leopard as the title character, the fast and furious film performed unspectacularly at the box office. But generations of filmgoers have since accorded it the status of a classic. ◀1934.M ▶1949.M

TECHNOLOGY

A Stick-Free Substance

12 Roy J. Plunkett, a young chemist for Du Pont Company just two years out of graduate school, was opening a canister of tetrafluoroethylene gas in April 1938 when, instead of a whoosh of escaping vapors, he heard no sound at all. Curious, Plunkett cut the canister with a hacksaw and found that the gas, known by the initials TFE, had turned into a greasy white powder. In technical terms, it had spontaneously polymerized; that is, the molecules had somehow rearranged themselves into long chains. Plunkett ordered some tests. The results proved the polymer to be chemically inert and absolutely stable. It was unaffected by electricity, acids, and solvents; it was corrosion proof; and it was the slipperiest substance ever discovered.

Dubbed Teflon by Du Pont, the polymer eventually emerged as an all-purpose industrial material. It was used secretly during World War II for gaskets capable of withstanding uranium hexafluoride, the highly corrosive material used in making uranium 235, the prime ingredient in the atom bomb. First available commercially in 1948, Teflon found its way into wire insulation and electrical components. By the 1950s, bakers had discovered its wonders, and in 1956, the first Teflon-coated frying pans went on sale (in Nice, France). Enthusiasm waned when Teflon was too easily dislodged from the metal it coated. But when Du Pont found a way to bond the substance more securely to the metal, the pans won a place in kitchens the world over. Since then, Teflon has penetrated even further into everyday life; it is found in everything from Gore-tex (a material that protects against extreme temperatures and wetness) to artificial arteries and ligaments. **◀1934.9 ▶1941.M**

NOBEL PRIZES: Peace: Nansen International Office for Refugees (Switzerland) ... Literature: Pearl Buck (U.S.; novelist) ... Chemistry: Richard Kuhn (German; carotenoids and vitamins; declined by order of German government) ... Medicine: Corneille Heymans (Belgian; respiratory regulation) ... Physics: Enrico Fermi (Italian; neutron-induced nuclear reactions).

A VOICE FROM 1938

The Martians Are Coming

From "The War of the Worlds," *Mercury Theatre on the Air*, CBS Radio, October 30, 1938

On Sunday, October 30, 1938, the 23-year-old actor-director-producer Orson Welles and his Mercury Theatre pulled a Halloween prank that incited one of the oddest mass panics in history. That evening, Welles and his troupe performed Howard Koch's adaptation of H.G. Wells's novel The War of the Worlds, *about a Martian invasion of Earth. The radio play simulated a news broadcast, with breaking bulletins and on-the-spot coverage of extraterrestrials landing in New Jersey and then vanquishing America. Despite prebroadcast announcements that the program was fiction, at least one million listeners were terrified. Across the country, families took flight, thousands prayed, and some readied themselves for battle. Welles never expected such a severe reaction, and he apologized. But the power of broadcasting had become chillingly obvious. In the following excerpt, "commentator Carl Phillips" reports "live" from the Wilmuth Farm at Grovers Mill, New Jersey.*
◂1932.M ▸1941.11

PHILLIPS: Just a minute! Something's happening! Ladies and gentlemen, this is terrific! This end of the thing is beginning to flake off! The top is beginning to rotate like a screw! The thing must be hollow!

VOICES: She's a movin'!
Look, the darn thing's unscrewing!
Keep back there! Keep back, I tell you.
Maybe there's men in it trying to escape!
It's red hot, they'll burn to a cinder!
Keep back there! Keep those idiots back!

(Suddenly the clanking sound of a huge piece of falling metal)

VOICES: She's off! The top's loose!
Look out there! Stand back!

PHILLIPS: Ladies and gentlemen, this is the most terrifying thing I have ever witnessed. ... Wait a minute! Someone's crawling out of the hollow top. Someone or ... something. I can see peering out of that black hole two luminous disks ... are they eyes? It might be a face. It might be....

(Shout of awe from the crowd)

Good heavens, something's wriggling out of the shadow like a gray snake. Now it's another one, and another. They look like tentacles to me. There. I can see the thing's body. It's large as a bear and it glistens like wet leather. But that face. It ... it's indescribable. I can hardly force myself to keep looking at it. The eyes are black and gleam like a serpent. The mouth is V-shaped with saliva dripping from its rimless lips that seem to quiver and pulsate. The monster or whatever it is can hardly move. It seems weighed down by ... possibly gravity or something. The thing's raising up. The crowd falls back. They've seen enough. This is the most extraordinary experience. I can't find words.... Wait! Something's happening!

(Hissing sound followed by a humming that increases in intensity)

A humped shape is rising out of the pit. I can make out a small beam of light against a mirror. What's that? There's a jet of flame springing from that mirror, and it leaps right at the advancing men. It strikes them head on! Good Lord, they're turning into flame!

(Screams and unearthly shrieks)

Now the whole field's caught fire. *(Explosion)* The woods ... the barns ... the gas tanks of automobiles ... it's spreading everywhere. It's coming this way. About twenty yards to my right....

(Crash of microphone ... Dead silence ...)

Welles went on the air opposite radio's number-one hit, *The Charlie McCarthy Show.* ("This only goes to prove my beamish boy," critic Alexander Woollcott wired to Welles after the broadcast, "the intelligent people were all listening to a dummy, and all the dummies were listening to you.") In the aftermath, Welles apologized *(top)* for the furor he had unleashed.

"I am only afraid that at the last moment some swine or other will yet submit to me a plan for mediation."
—Adolf Hitler, before the German invasion of Poland

STORY OF THE YEAR

Hitler Invades Poland, Igniting World War II

1 On August 22, 1939, Adolf Hitler made a fateful speech to the German High Command. One witness jotted down the gist of it: "Annihilation of Poland in foreground.... Close heart to pity. Proceed brutally." A few days of diplomatic wrangling passed as Hitler attempted to overcome British opposition to his plans, and Mussolini tried—with equal futility—to persuade him to keep negotiating with Poland. But on August 31, the Führer ordered his troops into action. (He also ordered the murder of all terminally ill patients in German hospitals, to make room for the wounded.) That night, to provide what Hitler called "the propagandistic pretext," SS men staged a sham Polish raid on a German radio station near the border. The invasion got under way at dawn. World War II began on September 3, when Britain and France declared war on the Reich.

By that time, Hitler's forces had reached the Vistula River deep in Poland's interior. Though the British bombed ships in the northern German port city of Kiel, while the French raided Germany's fortified western border, political and military unreadiness kept both Allied powers from helping Poland more substantially. The nation was doomed. Its troops were poorly positioned, its grand cavalry helpless against Germany's state-of-the-art panzers (tanks). German bombers destroyed Poland's transport system, smashed its tiny air force on the ground, and terrorized its cities. Krakow fell on September 6. By September 9, the remnants of the defending forces were encircled. When the fighting was almost done, Soviet troops marched from the east. They met their German counterparts in Brest-Litovsk on September 18, as the Polish government escaped into exile. Warsaw capitulated ten days later.

Of Poland's million soldiers, 700,000 had been taken prisoner, and another 80,000 had fled the country. (Total casualties are unknown.) Germany's expeditionary force of 1.5 million suffered only 45,000 dead, wounded, or missing. True to the pact he'd made a month earlier, Hitler presented Stalin with two thirds of Poland, and conceded the Baltic states and Finland to the Soviet sphere of influence. The next time he struck, it would be against the West. ◂1938.3 ▸1939.2

Germany's victorious 8th Army marches through the streets of Warsaw on October 5, 1939.

WORLD WAR II

The Fall of Prague

2 The stage for Hitler's invasion of Poland was set early in 1939 with the dissection of Czechoslovakia and the bloodless neutralization of one of Europe's strongest

In Brno, a German soldier hangs a sign in the newly designated Adolf Hitler Platz.

armies. The previous year's Munich Conference had transformed the nation into a federation of three republics. Then, in mid-March, Hungary seized Carpathian Ruthenia, and Slovakia seceded, becoming an independent (but German-dominated) state.

The Czech Republic was the last to go. Its president, Emil Hácha, tried to appease the Germans by enacting anti-Semitic and anticommunist laws. Nonetheless, the Wehrmacht began massing troops on the border. On March 14, the day Slovakia declared independence, Hácha traveled to Berlin to plead for his republic's life. He and his aides were summoned to meet with Hitler at 1:15 AM. The Führer announced that an invasion would begin at 6:00—then stalked off.

Remaining in the room were cabinet ministers Hermann Goering and Joachim von Ribbentrop, who told the Czechs that Prague would be bombed unless they signed surrender documents. Suddenly Hácha, who suffered from a heart condition, fainted. Hitler's physician gave him an injection that revived him long enough to sign the papers.

Afterward, Hitler hugged his henchmen. "Children!" he shouted. "This is the greatest day of my life!" That evening he rode with his troops into the Czech capital. Hácha remained as puppet president of the new German protectorate of Bohemia and Moravia. In the battle ahead, the former Czechoslovakia would provide Hitler's war machine with crucial resources. ◂1939.1 ▸1939.3

1939

ART & CULTURE: Books: ***Finnegans Wake*** **(James Joyce);** ***Pale Horse, Pale Rider*** **(Katherine Anne Porter);** ***Old Possum's Book of Practical Cats*** **(T.S. Eliot);** ***The Day of the Locust*** **(Nathanael West);** ***The Big Sleep*** **(Raymond Chandler) ... Music: "All the Things You Are" (Kern and Hammerstein); "The Beer Barrel Polka" (Vejvoda and Brown) ... Painting & Sculpture:** ***Portrait of the Bourgeoisie*** **(David Alfaro Siqueiros);**

"I cannot forecast to you the action of Russia. It is a riddle wrapped in a mystery inside an enigma."—**First Lord of the Admiralty Winston Churchill, after Stalin signed the nonaggression pact with Germany**

WORLD WAR II

Stalin Embraces Hitler

3 Hitler invaded Poland to clear a path to Russia—but only after trying to neutralize the Poles through negotiations. In March 1939, he offered to *protect* them from the Russians, in exchange for the return of Danzig (now Gdánsk), separated from Germany at the end of World War I. Mistrusting both of its mighty neighbors, Poland instead accepted an offer of defense from Britain.

Hitler was furious. He'd always counted on London's acquiescence in his plans against the Soviets. When the British instituted military conscription, he realized they, too, might have to be beaten before he could conquer Russia. But first he would use Russia against Poland. After revoking his 1935 treaties with Poland and Britain, he sent Foreign Minister Joachim von Ribbentrop to Moscow.

Unsure of Western aid in case of German attack, Soviet leader Joseph Stalin craved an understanding, however temporary, with Hitler. To show his eagerness, Stalin even fired his Jewish foreign minister. On August 23, the new minister, Vyacheslav Molotov, met with von Ribbentrop and signed a nonaggression pact—stunning a world that had seen fascism and communism as eternal enemies. A greater shock followed when the treaty's secret protocol took effect: In the event of a "territorial and political transformation" in the region, the Germans and Soviets were to divvy up Eastern Europe.

Joseph Stalin *(left)* shakes hands with enemy-to-be Joachim von Ribbentrop.

Hitler began that transformation days later. When it was over, Russia had its promised two thirds of Poland as a buffer zone against invasion. Germany, meanwhile, had a launching pad for that very purpose. **◂1939.1 ▸1939.6**

Indian troops in Egypt, captured by pioneering photojournalist Margaret Bourke-White.

WORLD WAR II

Empire at War

4 World War II went global soon after the Polish invasion, as the nations of the British Empire and Commonwealth took up arms. Lord Linlithgow, viceroy of India, declared war in September 1939—despite the opposition of the Indian National Congress, which controlled six out of 11 provinces. Canada's Parliament voted overwhelmingly to join the Allies, even though its army had only 4,000 fully trained men. Australian prime minister Robert Menzies didn't bother to consult his Parliament; he simply made a radio announcement: "Britain is at war, therefore Australia is at war." New Zealand, too, rallied to the cause.

In December, troops of the First Canadian Division landed in England, while Indian soldiers joined British forces in France. India eventually contributed two million troops, as many as the rest of Britain's colonies and dominions combined. Canada's navy expanded into the world's third-largest. Australia supplied half a million soldiers and would serve as the base for American operations in the southwest Pacific. And New Zealand (whose soldiers suffered the Commonwealth's highest casualty rate) provided Britain with much of the food that kept its people fit to fight. **◂1937.3 ▸1940.1**

WORLD WAR II

The Pact of Steel

5 Benito Mussolini was humiliated by Hitler's bloodless victory over the Czechs. Without firing a shot, his student had surpassed him as a conqueror. Scrambling to catch up, Il Duce decided to annex little Albania (over which Italy had exercised de facto control since 1934). But the far-from-glorious campaign led Mussolini to bind himself more slavishly than ever to Hitler, in a 1939 treaty he called (with unwitting irony) the Pact of Steel.

Bound by the pact, German and Italian soldiers converse in Tiranë, Albania's capital.

The invasion got off to a chaotic start on April 7. Instead of marching promptly on the capital, Tiranë, the Italian commanders paused to confer with envoys dispatched by Albania's King Zog. Meanwhile, Zog fled to Greece, Tiranë's prisons were opened, and mobs looted the city. The Italian consulate sent an SOS to Rome, to no avail. (Albanian volunteers finally restored order.) But the invaders' incompetence and equipment shortages met no organized resistance. On April 16, Albanian representatives in Rome turned over Zog's crown, and the country became a province of Italy.

Britain protested, but Germany sent congratulations. Convinced that the Führer was unstoppable, Mussolini accepted his long-standing offer of a formal alliance. (The 1937 Anti-Comintern Pact was merely an entente.) The pact, signed in May, bound Italy to Germany under practically any circumstances. **◂1937.14 ▸1940.2**

BIRTHS

Margaret Atwood, Canadian novelist.

Alan Ayckbourn, U.K. playwright.

John Cleese, U.K. actor.

Margaret Drabble, U.K. writer.

Germaine Greer, Australian-U.K. writer.

Seamus Heaney, Irish poet.

Bobby Hull, Canadian hockey player.

Ted Koppel, U.K.-U.S. broadcast journalist.

Ralph Lauren, U.S. fashion designer.

Ian McKellen, U.K. actor.

Brian Mulroney, Canadian prime minister.

Lee Harvey Oswald, U.S. assassin.

Amos Oz, Israeli writer.

Jackie Stewart, U.K. race car driver.

David Souter, U.S. jurist.

Lily Tomlin, U.S. actress.

DEATHS

Heywood Broun, U.S. writer.

Harvey Cushing, U.S. neurosurgeon.

Joseph Duveen, Dutch-U.K. art dealer.

Havelock Ellis, U.K. sexologist.

Douglas Fairbanks, Sr., U.S. actor.

Anton Fokker, German-U.S. aircraft designer.

Ford Madox Ford, U.K. novelist and editor.

Sigmund Freud, Austrian psychoanalyst and writer.

Zane Grey, U.S. novelist.

James A. Naismith, Canadian-U.S. inventor of basketball.

William Butler Yeats, Irish writer.

Man **(Willem de Kooning) ... Film: *Gone with the Wind* (Victor Fleming); *Mr. Smith Goes to Washington* (Frank Capra); *Wuthering Heights* (William Wyler); *The Rules of the Game* (Jean Renoir) ... Theater: *The Time of Your Life* (William Saroyan); *Life with Father* (Lindsay and Crouse); *The Philadelphia Story* (Philip Barry); *The Little Foxes* (Lillian Hellman) ... Radio: *The Dinah Shore Show.***

"One Finn is equal to ten Russians."—Popular Finnish saying

NEW IN 1939

Microfilm camera.

Food Stamps (Rochester, New York).

Tokyo Shibaura Electric Co. (Toshiba).

Automatic dishwasher.

Air-conditioned automobile (Packard).

Transatlantic airmail service.

Pressure cooker (National Presto Industries).

IN THE UNITED STATES

▶ROYAL VISIT—Traveling by train from Canada, King George VI and Queen Elizabeth arrived in Washington, D.C., on June 9. The visit, the first by a reigning British monarch to the United States, was designed to demonstrate Anglo-American unity in anticipation of war with Germany.

From sweltering Washington, the royals moved north to FDR's beloved Hyde Park, New York, home, where the King sampled his first hot dogs, and urged Roosevelt to increase aid to Europe. ▶1939.12

▶HOLY COMICS!—Created by graphic artist Bob Kane, age 18, the mysterious figure of "the Bat-Man" swooped into the pages of Detective Comics in 1939. Soon joined by Robin, the Boy Wonder, Batman crusaded against a motley array of archfiends. His popularity as comic-book hero was surpassed only by Superman's. ◀1934.11

▶KAUFMAN'S WICKED WIT—Two-time Pulitzer Prize–winning playwright George S. Kaufman had another resounding success in 1939 with *The Man Who Came to Dinner.* Written with longtime collaborator Moss Hart, the comedy—whose central character, Sheridan Whiteside, was based on Kaufman's Algonquin Round Table cohort Alexander

Finland ceded one tenth of its territory to the U.S.S.R. but kept its independence.

WORLD WAR II

Russo-Finnish War

6 Despite his nonaggression pact with Hitler, Joseph Stalin intended to take no chances. To prevent Germany from staging a blitzkrieg through Finland and into Leningrad, he hoped to station Soviet troops within the borders of Russia's little neighbor. In December 1939, he petitioned the Finnish government for land grants (mostly in the southeast) for that purpose—and when the Finns refused, he retaliated with an air raid on Helsinki that devastated the capital city and drove thousands of civilians from their homes. The Russo-Finnish War had begun.

The defenders dug in along the Mannerheim Line (named for their commander, Baron Carl Gustav Mannerheim, who'd defeated the Bolsheviks in Finland's 1918 civil war) on the Karelian Isthmus. About 125,000 Finns repelled the initial Soviet advance of half a million troops and a thousand tanks. North of the isthmus, from Lake Ladoga to the Arctic Ocean, the Finns relied on ten-man cross-country ski brigades to defend the 700-mile Finnish-Soviet border. The ski patrols harried the lumbering Red Army, swooping out of the night to claim heavy casualties. As temperatures plunged to –50°F, many Soviet soldiers simply froze to death in the desolate northern woods. Outnumbered five to one, Finnish troops held the invaders at bay for three months. "They are so many, and our country is so small," the Finns grimly joked, "where shall we find space to bury them all?"

In February 1940, Stalin launched a second massive assault. The Finns sought outside aid, but the Western powers delayed, fearing an aggressive German response to any Allied encroachment in Scandinavia. By the time the British and French agreed to move troops through Norway and a reluctant Sweden, it was too late. On March 12, Finland, which had suffered 25,000 fatalities to the U.S.S.R.'s 250,000, signed a peace treaty ceding a tenth of its land to the Soviet Union. In what remained of the country, independence was salvaged. ◀1939.3 ▶1940.12

POPULAR CULTURE

The World of Tomorrow

7 **Just five months before the start of history's most devastating war, the 1939 World's Fair opened in Queens, New York, with the theme "Building the World of Tomorrow." Millions flocked to see the biggest international exhibition ever, with its displays of technology (including television), art, and culture from 60 nations and 1,300 businesses. Mementos of the fair ranged from pins and buttons to table scarves *(above)*, most printed with images of the fair's distinctive structures—the Trylon (a 700-foot-tall obelisk) and the Perisphere (a 200-foot globe). President Roosevelt gave the kickoff speech, declaring the event "open to all mankind." In fact, Germany was notably absent, and many of the technological marvels on view would be employed in battle before they were applied to building a better planet. ◀1933.M**

FILM

The Miracle Year

8 It was a miracle year for movies. Worldwide, 2,012 feature films were released in 1939—483 of them produced in the United States—and an astonishing number were among the finest in cinematic history. Seldom has the list of nominees

GWTW's Vivien Leigh and Clark Gable as Scarlett O'Hara and Rhett Butler.

for the Best Picture Academy Award been so impressive: *Dark Victory*; *Goodbye, Mr. Chips*; *Love Affair* (remade as *An Affair to Remember*); *Mr. Smith Goes to Washington*; *Ninotchka*; *Of Mice and Men*; *Stagecoach*; *The Wizard of Oz*; *Wuthering Heights*; and, of course, the winner, *Gone with the Wind.* But many superb films didn't even make the roster: *Only Angels Have Wings*, *Young Mr. Lincoln*, *The Women*, *Intermezzo*, *Gunga Din*, *The Old Maid*, and *The Roaring Twenties.* The year's magic touched Europe as well: England produced such classics as *The Four Feathers* and *The Stars Look Down*, while in France, Jean Renoir directed another masterpiece, *The Rules of the Game.*

But in the popular imagination, *Gone with the Wind* clearly reigns as 1939's most significant film. (*The Wizard of Oz* runs a close second.) For three years, Americans had impatiently anticipated the screen version of Margaret Mitchell's smashingly successful novel. The casting of the role of Civil War heroine Scarlett O'Hara became a front-page debate. In December, when the film premiered in Atlanta, the city proclaimed

SPORTS: Baseball: World Series, New York Yankees defeat Cincinnati Reds, 4–0; Ted Williams joins Boston Red Sox; Little League begins, in Williamsport, Pa ... Football: NFL, Green Bay Packers defeat New York Giants, 27–0; new college rule requires helmets ... Auto Racing: Floyd Roberts, 1938 winner, dies in crash at Indianapolis 500 ... Tennis: Bobby Riggs wins U.S. Open and Wimbledon singles titles.

"Like all novices, we began with the helicopter ... but soon saw that it had no future and dropped it."
—Wilbur Wright, in a 1909 article that Orville Wright showed to Igor Sikorsky in 1942

a holiday, and producer David O. Selznick and stars Clark Gable, Vivien Leigh, and Olivia de Havilland paraded down boulevards lined with hordes of whooping fans.

Audiences adored the film's narrative energy, sweeping score, star performances, and romantic gallantry—and largely overlooked its unfortunate depiction of slaves as happy and childlike. Its box-office success was unmatched for a quarter of a century. *Gone with the Wind* won eight Oscars, and, thanks to frequent re-releases in theaters and on videotape, it is the "most-seen" movie in history. **◂1936.M ▸1941.11**

SPAIN

The Civil War Ends

9 Francisco Franco led his Nationalist troops into Madrid in March 1939, ending the Spanish Civil War after nearly three years of slaughter. The previous summer, a last-ditch Republican offensive along the Ebro River had failed to break the Nationalist stranglehold on Catalonia. That defeat prompted the Soviet government, the exhausted Republic's only ally, to cut off aid. In January, Franco's forces took the anarchist stronghold of Barcelona—with its libertarian tradition, the most potent symbol of Republican resistance. The rest was fairly easy.

Since most of the army had joined the rightist rebellion, the Republic's defense had initially been consigned to ragtag, often defiantly antiauthoritarian militias, and to the largely ill-trained International Brigades. Despite their Soviet weaponry, these fighters were no match for seasoned Nationalist troops backed by 60,000 German and Italian soldiers. The Spanish Communist Party, which had gained ascendacy via its moderate policies and ties to the Soviets, had insisted on transforming the militias into an orderly regular army—and on gaining behind-the-scenes control over the government. It succeeded in both goals only after bloody infighting, and the price was lowered morale. Growing shortages and the Nationalists' air superiority weakened the Republicans by late 1937. Their final hope died in September 1938, when Britain and France signed the Munich Pact with Germany: There would be no last-minute intervention by the democracies.

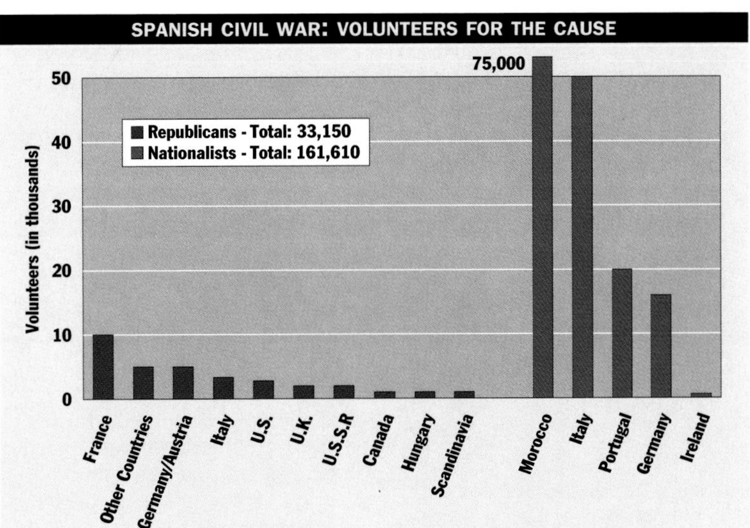

The Nationalists received volunteer manpower from fewer countries than did the Republicans, but the number was far higher. Moreover, contributions to the Nationalists of money, weapons, and other supplies far exceeded those to the Republicans.

The final toll was 90,000 Nationalists and 110,000 Republicans killed in action, and a million permanently disabled. Tens of thousands of civilians had starved to death or died in bombing raids. Some 500,000 Spaniards were in exile, half never to return.

For Republicans, the war had been a struggle to keep Spain out of the Nazi-Fascist orbit. Curiously, though Hitler and Mussolini gloated over Franco's victory—and thousands of Republicans were promptly shot or jailed—the Generalissimo did not transform Spain into a strictly fascist state. His Falange, the only legal party, was not an all-controlling totalitarian machine. The Catholic Church regained its old predominance. Franco remained friendly with the Axis powers, but he kept Spain neutral during World War II. "Spaniards," he said, "are tired of politics." He ruled until 1975, not as another führer or duce, but as a caudillo—a military strongman of the type Spain had known for generations. **◂1937.7 ▸1945.M**

AVIATION

Two Aerial Milestones

10 Americans made aviation history twice in 1939. On June 28, Pan American Airways' fleet of three Boeing Clipper seaplanes began the first transatlantic passenger service. Carrying 22 customers (for a steep $675 round trip), the *Dixie Clipper* flew from Port Washington, New York, to Lisbon, Portugal—with a layover in the Azores—in 22 hours. Pan Am had plied the Pacific skies for three years, but the new route marked what *The New York Times* called "man's aerial conquest of the last, and commercially most important, of the earth's oceans."

In September, near Stratford, Connecticut, Russian-born aeronautical engineer Igor Sikorsky pulled a lever in the cockpit of his skeletal VS-300 prototype and rose vertically a few yards into the air. Helicopters had flown before—the first success was Germany's twin-rotor Focke-Achgelis Fa-61, tested in 1936—but Sikorsky's incorporated the features that would characterize most such craft in the future: a main horizontal rotor, with a second small vertical rotor in the tail. This configuration provided the best balance of control, hovering ability, and horizontal speed. For Sikorsky, this early flight (his first production helicopter didn't appear until 1942) realized a dream from his boyhood, when Leonardo da Vinci's fanciful sketches for a muscle-powered helicopter had inspired him to try to build a motorized version. **◂1937.V ▸1958.6**

Pan Am's Clipper service introduced the lost luxury of zeppelins to airplane travel.

IN THE UNITED STATES

Woollcott—featured the snappy wit and pointed satire that made Kaufman an Algonquin terror, as well as one of Broadway's towering figures. ◂1919.M

NUCLEAR CHAIN LETTER—A letter to "F.D. Roosevelt," dated August 2, 1939, advised that German scientists had already achieved a nuclear chain reaction. "In view of this situation," the letter said, "you may think it desirable to have some permanent contact maintained between the Administration and the group of physicists working on chain reactions in America." It was signed by Albert Einstein, Edward Teller, and Alexander Sacks. ◂1938.1 ▸1940.8

▸AN AMERICAN ORIGINAL—After spotting Anna Mary Robertson Moses's naive paintings of rural scenes in an

upstate drugstore in 1939, a New York art collector bought all 15, exhibited several at the Museum of Modern Art, and turned the self-taught "Grandma" Moses (she was 78 when she began to paint) into an overnight success. ▸1942.17

▸HAWK'S HONK—Coleman Hawkins reinvented the tenor saxophone, transforming what had been a raucous musical joke into an essential jazz instrument. His brilliant chord harmonics, rich, lyrical tone, and technical virtuosity—nowhere displayed better than on his 1939 recording of "Body and Soul"—set the standard for mainstream jazz sax. ◂1937.5 ▸1945.15

▸SOUNDS OF IVES—Begun some 30 years earlier, Charles Ives's *Second Piano Sonata* (the *Concord*) was finally performed in 1939. Its four movements—"Emerson," "Hawthorne," "The Alcotts," and "Thoreau"—range from passionate dissonance to idyllic harmony; they reflect the New England–born composer's belief that all sound can become music. ▸1952.13

POLITICS & BUSINESS: GNP: $90.5 billion ... FDR asks Congress for $535 million for defense, orders U.S. to close ports and waters to all submarines from warring nations ... U.S. recalls ambassador to Germany ... Hatch Act prohibits government employees from politicking ... Congress repeals 1937 Neutrality Act and passes new one ... 9.5 million are still unemployed ... Ford Motor Co. introduces the Lincoln Mercury.

"I have seen war and ... I hate war. I say that again and again. I hope the United States will keep out of this war."
—Franklin D. Roosevelt, in his 1939 address reaffirming U.S. neutrality.

WORLD WAR II

▶HITLER'S PRETEXT—The Führer wanted Poland, so SS chief Heinrich Himmler concocted an excuse for him to take it. After dark on August 31, SS troops wearing Polish army uniforms "seized" a German transmitter at the border town of Gleiwitz (now Gliwice) and announced over the air, in Polish, that Poland had invaded Germany. Later that night, SS thugs dressed up a dozen German criminals like Polish soldiers and killed them. They arranged the corpses near the border, making it look like the "soldiers" had been shot invading. The Wehrmacht rolled into Poland the next day.

▶FIRST SHOT—By the time the German army streamed into Poland on September 1, the battleship *Schleswig Holstein* was in place near the harbor of Danzig (Gdánsk) and blazing away at Polish naval installations on the Westerplatte peninsula. At 4:45 AM, it boomed the start of what, within two days, would be world war.

▶CAVALRY DIES—A telling battle in the invasion of Poland: General Heinz Guderian's tank division against the Polish Pomorske Cavalry Brigade. The mounted, white-gloved Poles had style and spirit; the German invaders, a mighty war machine. Brandishing sabers, the cavalry charged. Guderian's panzers mowed down man and beast. Germany's advance continued unimpeded.

▶WARSAW RESISTS—For weeks, the Luftwaffe bombed Warsaw, smashing it to ruin, preparing it for occupation. Still the city resisted, soldiers

and civilians digging in, fighting the German ground advance street by street. *(Above, German troops disarm Polish soldiers.)* To show that the heroic cause was not yet lost,

Nominally on the other side of the fence, Turkey was not averse to German wooing.

WORLD WAR II
An Unsteady Ally

11 When strategically crucial Turkey (bordering the Soviet Union and the Middle East) joined the Allies in October 1939, *Time* magazine called it the "biggest victory" yet in the war against Hitler. The victory, however, was smaller than advertised.

Turkish officials had opened talks with Britain in May, after Italy invaded Albania. But when the Soviets and Germans signed their nonaggression pact in August, the Turks —despite their sizable army—began to worry about alienating Moscow. Dragging their feet in the treaty talks with the Allies, they made extravagant financial and economic demands. In the end, Turkey was not required to fight unless its own lands were threatened.

As the Nazis conquered their neighbors, the Turks retreated further into neutrality—even signing a friendship treaty with Germany. Only in 1945, when the Axis was nearly beaten, did they declare war. **◂1939.5 ▸1941.9**

WORLD WAR II
America's Neutrality Act

12 One casualty of the Polish invasion was America's policy of strict neutrality. Over the past four years, Congress had passed laws to prevent the kind of entanglements that had pulled the nation into World War I. But when World War II erupted, the public mood began to change. While still opposed to direct intervention, most Americans favored aid to the Allies. In November, Congress passed the Neutrality Act of 1939. The new law resembled its predecessors except for one important detail: It no longer included an arms embargo against all belligerent nations. Britain and France would be allowed to buy American weapons—as long as they took them home on their own ships.

This tentative move away from isolationism was largely President Roosevelt's doing. For two years, he'd gently prodded his nation to turn outward—while remaining careful not to let domestic foes accuse him of meddling in foreign disputes. When the shooting started in Poland, and a reporter asked him whether America could avoid becoming embroiled, he replied, "I not only sincerely hope so, but I believe we can." Soon, however, he called a special session of Congress to consider repeal of the arms embargo.

A powerful group of legislators opposed repeal, as did such popular figures as aviator Charles Lindbergh and Father Charles Coughlin (a radical right-wing Catholic priest whose radio show had a huge nationwide following). Pro-embargo mail deluged congressional offices. But through skilled politicking, Roosevelt managed to win over some of his staunchest adversaries, and after six weeks of debate, a solid majority voted to lift the ban on weapons.

Supplying the Allies with what ever they needed to combat aggression, Roosevelt argued, was a policy "better calculated than any other means to keep us out of war." In fact, while America increasingly threw its resources behind the Allies, U.S. forces *did* stay out of the fighting—until the Japanese attack on Pearl Harbor made it impossible to stand aside. **▸1940.M**

WORLD WAR II
Germany's Might

13 By 1939, Germany was better prepared—both psychologically and militarily—to fight a war than any other country in the world. Hitler's five-year rearmament program had strengthened the German home front: By gearing up weapons production and defense-related public works, he'd replaced the massive unemployment of 1932

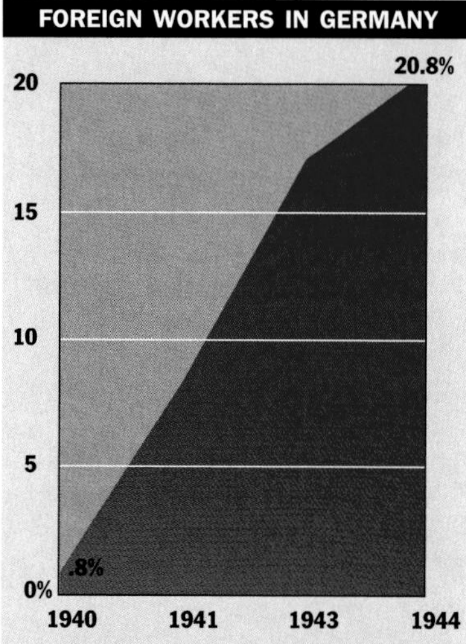

The percentage of foreign workers in Germany's total workforce—imported to work in factories to fuel the German war machine—rose radically in four years.

Over a nationwide radio hookup, Roosevelt spoke to Americans about the Neutrality Act.

WORLD WAR II: January: Chamberlain meets with Mussolini; Roosevelt asks for $552 million defense program; Barcelona falls ... February: Japan occupies Hainan; Britain and France recognize Franco's government in Spain, which remains neutral ... March: Germany invades and annexes Czechoslovakia; Britain and France support Poland ... April: Italy annexes Albania; Hitler denounces Allied pact with

"What a wonderful woman she is! She not only knows what is right, but she also does the right thing."
—Marian Anderson, on hearing of Eleanor Roosevelt's resignation from the DAR

with a labor shortage—earning his people's fervent gratitude.

In military terms, Germany's new offensive techniques reflected lessons German generals had learned through defeat in World War I. The invasion of Poland was something revolutionary: a blitzkrieg ("lightning war"). Hitler's fast-moving tanks and motorized artillery punched holes in the opposing line, isolating groups of the enemy to be surrounded and captured by infantrymen; meanwhile, dive-bombers sowed panic, disrupting supply operations and communications. The strategy showed Allied commanders (who mistakenly continued to see their victory in World War I—which had come about largely by their digging in and outlasting the Central Powers—as a vindication of static, defensive warfare) how formidable a foe they faced.

Together, Britain, France, and Poland overshadowed Germany in troops, population, and industrial resources. They had more airplanes and big warships, and almost as many tanks. But in important respects, German forces had the clear advantage. The training and discipline of Hitler's troops—and, thanks to the Nazi glorification of soldiery, their fighting spirit—were unequaled anywhere. Each German infantry division far exceeded its Allied counterpart in firepower. The Wehrmacht (army) organized its tanks into divisions, an arrangement that made them much more effective. And the planes in Germany's state-of-the-art Luftwaffe, equipped with standardized (and thus easily reparable) engines and airframes, could outperform most of the Allies' motley collection. **◂1939.1 ▸1940.16**

After being turned down by the DAR, Anderson performed at the Lincoln Memorial.

THE UNITED STATES

A Diva Denied

14 Marian Anderson was one of the finest contraltos of her era. She'd sung before the crowned heads of Europe; Jean Sibelius had written a piece ("Solitude") just for her. But when she tried to rent Constitution Hall in 1939 for her Washington, D.C., debut, she was rebuffed. The building's owner was the all-white Daughters of the American Revolution, a society of women descended from the nation's founding soldiers—and Anderson was black, a descendant of slaves.

The incident aroused widespread protest—most notably from Eleanor Roosevelt, the President's wife (and one of the world's leading human-rights activists), who announced her resignation from the DAR in her syndicated newspaper column. A group of prominent citizens, including Interior Secretary Harold L. Ickes, arranged an outdoor performance at the Lincoln Memorial. Some 75,000 people attended, enough to fill many Constitution Halls.

Anderson went on (in 1955) to become the first black to perform at New York's Metropolitan Opera. She also shared an honor with Mrs. Roosevelt: Both women were appointed delegates to the United Nations, Roosevelt in 1945 and Anderson in 1958. **▸1949.11**

LITERATURE

Steinbeck's Dust Bowl Saga

15 No literary work has better captured the plight of refugees—in this case, the midwesterners fleeing America's drought-ridden Dust Bowl—than John Steinbeck's epic *The Grapes of Wrath*, published in 1939. One of the greatest examples of the decade's characteristic genre, the proletarian novel, the book follows a family of Okies (the nickname for uprooted Oklahomans, as well as other Dust Bowlers) to rural California. Farmers reduced to seeking migrant work, the Joads encounter hunger, police brutality, and ruthless exploitation. But Steinbeck's realism—and his leftist preaching—was tempered with a deep sense of the sacred. His Okies have an almost biblical dignity; his landscapes are as holy as Canaan's. And his depiction of migrant-worker society is both anthropologically sharp and poetically moving.

Steinbeck feared the public would turn away from a story so unrelentingly grim. Viking Press, his publisher, worried that the language and imagery were too strong, particularly the ending: A young Joad woman, deserted by her husband, her new baby dead, suckles a dying old man. Their misgivings proved unfounded. The novel awakened social indignation as few have done since. It stayed on the bestseller lists well into the following year, when 20th Century Fox released the film version, directed by John Ford and starring Henry Fonda. **◂1934.4 ▸1940.18**

On film, Tom Joad was played by Henry Fonda *(left, with Russell Simpson as Pa Joad).*

WORLD WAR II

Radio Warsaw broadcast Chopin's "Polonaise in A-Flat" around the clock. On September 25, Hitler redoubled his blanket bombing. Three days later, the rousing "Polonaise" stopped playing. Heard in its place: Chopin's "Death March." Warsaw, bloody as a slaughterhouse, had finally fallen.

▶BATTLE OF THE ATLANTIC—The opening round of the Battle of the Atlantic, the war's longest campaign, went to Germany: On September 3, a U-boat torpedoed the British liner *Athenia*, killing 112 passengers. Under the command of Admiral Karl Dönitz, the German submarine fleet terrorized Allied shipping from Iceland to South Africa, nearly strangling import-reliant England.

▶EVACUATION—Anticipating a blitz from Hitler, London parents shipped their children to the countryside for safekeeping. Some 650,000 children, bearing name tags and return addresses around their necks, left the world's most populous city during the first days of war in 1939. By the New Year, after the anticipated raid failed to occur, about half the 1.5 million total evacuees had returned to London—briefly, as it turned out. The Battle of Britain began that summer, and the young people's pilgrimage to rural England began anew.

▶BATTLE OF THE RIVER PLATE—Determined to stand up to Germany's campaign against British shipping in the South Atlantic, a trio of British cruisers hunted down the German pocket battleship *Admiral Graf Spee* in December 1939. In the Battle of the River Plate, off Uruguay, the lighter British vessels inflicted serious damage. The German warship limped into Montevideo harbor, and was scuttled on Hitler's order. British morale soared.

"Ever since I found myself as a composer, I have been fully conscious of the brotherhood of peoples ... and I try to serve this idea in my music."—**Béla Bartók**

AROUND THE WORLD

►JOYCEAN EXPERIMENT—Seventeen years after starting it, James Joyce finished his long-standing "work in progress," *Finnegans Wake*—almost certainly the most cerebral, confounding, and revolutionary work in twentieth-century fiction. In it, Joyce unfolds the entire story of mankind in a wholly original language fabricated from sources as disparate as arcane Irish history and popular songs. ◄1922.1

►DDT INTRODUCED—The search for a cheap, quick, and long-lasting insecticide was completed in 1939, when a Swiss chemist, Paul Müller, confirmed the bug-killing properties of Dichlorodiphenyltrichloroethane (DDT). Used on everything from the potato beetle to disease-bearing lice and fleas (as well as in World War II to fumigate troops' bedding and clothing), DDT was heralded as a huge success for twentieth-century agriculture. But within 20 years, many insects developed strains resistant to the poison. Meanwhile, it wreaked havoc on the food chain by killing off beneficial insects and predators. ►1962.11

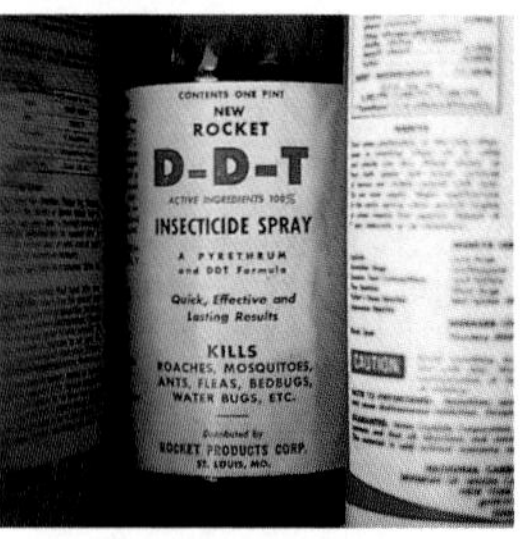

►WHITE PAPER—Attempting to set a British policy for Jewish settlement in Palestine, the MacDonald White Paper announced that a binational Arab-Jewish state (albeit with an Arab majority) would be established within a decade. It also imposed immigration quotas: For the next five years, a total of only 75,000 Jews would be allowed to settle in Palestine; thereafter, the numbers would in effect be determined by the Arab majority, with the British controlling Jewish land purchases. For Europe's imperiled Jews, the British "solution"—denounced by both sides—could not have come at a worse time. ◄1937.12 ►1945.14

MUSIC

Bartók's Sixth Quartet

16 Like his friend, fellow Hungarian and sometime collaborator Zoltán Kodály, Béla Bartók was as influential an ethnomusicologist as he was a composer. An internationally celebrated pianist as well, Bartók spent more than three decades studying Eastern European folk music. Finding inspiration and underlying unity in the traditions of different ethnic and national groups, he applied his discoveries to dozens of works for orchestra, chamber ensemble, voice, and solo piano that are still widely performed. In 1939, he wrote his sixth string quartet—completing a series the American composer and conductor Virgil Thomson called "the cream of Bartók's repertory, the essence of his deepest thought and feeling, his most powerful and humane communication."

Heartsick over the death of his mother and the growth of Nazism, Bartók imbued his final quartet with a deep melancholy. Each movement begins with the instruction *mesto*, meaning "mournful." Yet the composition's complex beauty—its handsome sonorities and rugged, percussive textures—transforms the sadness into something transcendent. After finishing the piece, Bartók left Budapest for self-imposed exile in the United States. Already frail when he arrived, he succumbed to leukemia in 1945. His remains were not returned to Hungary until 1988. **◄1936.13 ►1941.12**

A Swiss soldier guards Switzerland's border with Germany.

WORLD WAR II

Alpine Fortress

17 In the worldwide conflagration that began in 1939, one small country, landlocked between three of the principal belligerents, would prove fireproof. Neutral since 1648, Switzerland remained so throughout the war, surviving as Central Europe's only democracy.

To keep war at bay, Swiss officials avoided offending the Axis or the Allies, censoring press criticism of either side; Swiss enterprises (profitably) provided supplies to both. But the more important factors were the nation's formidable army, air force, and topography. Out of a population of four million, 850,000 soldiers were mobilized. A remote Alpine stronghold was supplied with arms, food, medical supplies, hydroelectric plants, and factories so that the Swiss could resist invaders even if their cities were overrun. Potential enemies knew that Swiss natives would take to the mountains in case of attack—and that they'd destroy roads and railways, making the country virtually impassable.

During the war, 400,000 refugees would move to or through Switzerland. The welcome was often chilly: Through much of the period, refugees were required to have visas, forbidden to work, and sent to internment camps. But when the Axis leaders themselves became fugitives, one rule remained firm: "Undeserving persons" were not entitled to asylum. **►1940.M**

WORLD WAR II

Jews Confined to Ghettos

18 In 1939, the Nazis reintroduced to Europe a form of social control abolished in the nineteenth century: the ghetto. Though the term is frequently used to describe an impoverished, segregated urban area, it originally meant the walled-in area of European cities to which Jews were legally restricted. After the Germans conquered Poland, they reestablished Jewish ghettos, first in the city of Lódź. Soon another was decreed in Warsaw, and eventually ghettos could be found in every Nazi-controlled city with a significant Jewish population.

The ghetto was typically surrounded by a wall topped with barbed wire. Entrances were guarded around the clock. Any movement in or out was strictly controlled. Living conditions were vile: Average density per dilapidated room was 13 people. Plumbing and sewage facilities were overburdened, and the stench fouled the air. Slow starvation was common: While a German in Warsaw consumed about 2,310 calories a day, the average for Jews was 184. Mothers often hid children for days after their deaths in order to get their food rations. In his diary,

The ghetto in Lublin—one of the many established in Poland to restrict Jews.

Warsaw ghetto leader Adam Czerniakow wrote about "endless complaints that there isn't anything to bury the dead in. They are laid in the ground naked, without even a piece of paper in place of cloth."

Before long, those who had not already perished of disease or starvation were carted off to death camps like Auschwitz, Bergen-Belsen, Treblinka, and Majdanek. **◄1938.10 ►1942.6**

NOBEL PRIZES: Peace: No award ... Literature: Frans Eemil Sillanpää (Finnish; novelist) ... Chemistry: Adolf Butenandt and Leopold Ruzicka (German, Swiss; sex hormones; Butenandt declines by order of German government) ... Medicine: Gerhard Domagk (German; sulfa drug therapy; declines by order of German government) ... Physics: Ernest Lawrence (American; cyclotron).

A VOICE FROM 1939

Gehrig Says Goodbye

Farewell Address, by Lou Gehrig, July 4, 1939

Henry Louis Gehrig never missed a game in 15-plus seasons as first baseman for the New York Yankees, although near the end of that record string of 2,130 games he didn't always finish. The Iron Horse, as he was called for his endurance, faltered so badly in the spring of 1939, that he went to the Mayo Clinic for diagnosis. He was suffering from amyotrophic lateral sclerosis, a degenerative nervous-system disorder (now known as Lou Gehrig's disease), and he withdrew from baseball. Between games of a holiday double-header on July 4, 1939, dubbed Lou Gehrig Appreciation Day, his Yankee teammates, past and present, and 61,808 fans gathered at Yankee Stadium to shower Gehrig with gifts and praise. He was so overcome with emotion that some observers doubted he would be able to speak. But Gehrig pulled himself together, stepped to the microphone, and delivered one of the sports world's most touching farewells. Then, as the crowd roared, he threw his arm around the neck of his old teammate Babe Ruth, and smiled into the photographers' bright flashes. He died two years later. **◄1920.6 ►1941.M**

Lou Gehrig Appreciation Day at New York's Yankee Stadium: Gehrig, led the Yankees to six World Series victories, accepts his teammates' tribute. The first baseman retired with a .340 lifetime batting average. Above, his pin *(front and back)* from the 1939 American League All-Star Game.

Fans, for the past two weeks, you have been reading about a bad break I got. Yet, today I consider myself the luckiest man on the face of the earth. I have been in ballparks for 17 years, and I have never received anything but kindness and encouragement from you fans.

Look at these grand men. Which of you wouldn't consider it the highlight of his career just to associate with them for even one day? Sure, I'm lucky. Who wouldn't consider it an honor to have known Jacob Ruppert? Also, the builder of baseball's greatest empire, Ed Barrow? To have spent six years with that wonderful little fellow Miller Huggins? Then to have spent the next nine years with that outstanding leader, that smart student of psychology, the best manager in baseball today, Joe McCarthy? Sure, I'm lucky. When the New York Giants, a team you would give your right arm to beat, and vice versa, sends you a gift, that's something. When everybody down to the groundskeepers and those boys in white coats remember you with trophies, that's something. When you have a father and mother who work all their lives so that you can have an education and build your body, it's a blessing. When you have a wife who has been a tower of strength and shown more courage than you dreamed existed, that's the finest I know. So I close in saying that I might have had a bad break, but I have an awful lot to live for.

Thank you.

The war that swept the globe made the one that ended two decades earlier seem a mere warm-up. Old codes of battle were permanently retired; civilians were as likely to die as soldiers. And a doomsday weapon was unveiled that colored everything that came after it: For the first time, humans held the means to annihilate themselves at the push of a button.

1940 1949

As men went off to fight, more and more women began working in traditionally male-dominated industries—including defense. At the Renton, Washington, plant of the Boeing Aircraft Company, a female worker takes inventory amid the glistening symmetry of stacks of vertical stabilizers for B-29 Superfortresses (used by the U.S. Army Air Force against the Japanese).

THE WORLD IN 1940

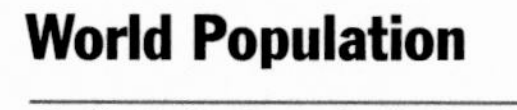

World Population

Pre-War Balance of Power, 1939

	POPULATION	PER CAPITA INCOME (1938)	COMBAT AIRCRAFT	MAJOR SHIPS*
ALLIES				
France	41,600,000	$248	735	155
Poland	34,662,000	$92	390	9
U.K.	47,692,000	$498	1,144	315
AXIS				
Germany	68,424,000	$487	2,765	74
Italy	43,779,000	$157	1,500	241
Japan	70,590,000	$81	1,980	212
NEUTRAL				
U.S.	129,825,000	$520	800	366
U.S.S.R.	167,300,000	$188	5,000	215

*battleships, carriers, cruisers, destroyers, submarines

Armed Forces

Standing Army, 1939 — Peak Strength of Forces During WWII

	Standing Army, 1939	Peak Strength of Forces During WWII
U.S.S.R.	1,700,000	12,500,000
U.S.	190,000	12,364,000
Germany	800,000	10,000,000

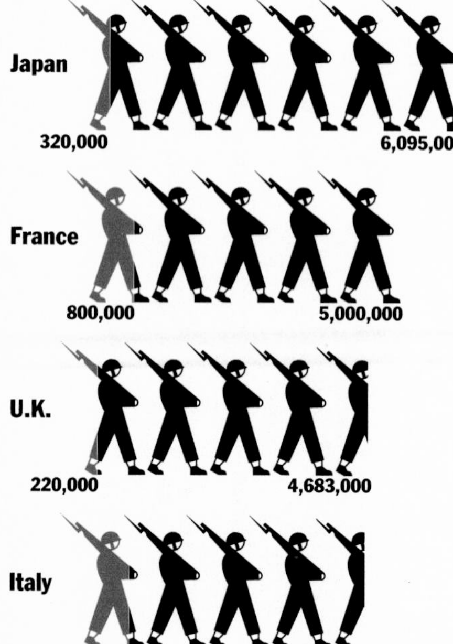

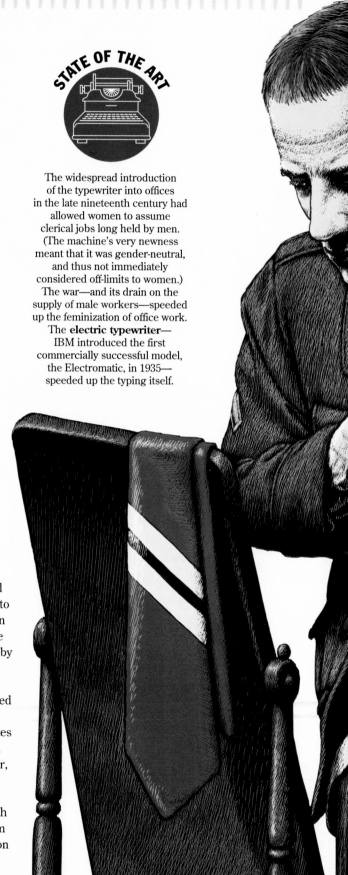

The widespread introduction of the typewriter into offices in the late nineteenth century had allowed women to assume clerical jobs long held by men. (The machine's very newness meant that it was gender-neutral, and thus not immediately considered off-limits to women.) The war—and its drain on the supply of male workers—speeded up the feminization of office work. The **electric typewriter**—IBM introduced the first commercially successful model, the Electromatic, in 1935—speeded up the typing itself.

A Truly Global War The Second World War was the first fully to live up to that appellation: Nearly every country in the world was eventually drawn into the conflict, and no country was unaffected by it. At the height of their expansionism, the Axis powers—Germany, Italy, and (after September 1940) Japan—controlled most of Europe and much of northern Africa, China, and Asia. The United States stayed out of the war until December 7, 1941, when Japan attacked Pearl Harbor, and the United States joined the Allies in fighting not only Japan but the other Axis powers as well. The war ended with the defeat of German and Italian fascism and Japanese militarism—and the creation of a new kind of ideologically driven global conflict: the Cold War.

Empire of the Third Reich

Germany's march across Europe began in 1936, when Hitler decided to remilitarize the Rhineland (in direct defiance of the 1919 Treaty of Versailles). Two years later, Germany annexed Austria and, with the acquiescence of Britain and France, the Czechoslovakian Sudetenland. Then, in 1939, Hitler swept through the remainder of Czechoslovakia and divided up Poland with the Soviet Union. Hitler's invasion of Poland prompted Britain and France finally to declare war: World War II had officially begun. By the end of May 1940, after a series of stunning military victories, Germany ruled Europe from the English Channel to the Balkans and the Soviet Ukraine. At its peak, two summers later, the Third Reich's European empire was larger than any since the days of ancient Rome.

- Germany 1930
- Demilitarized Rhineland
- Germany 1940
- German-occupied Territory

Fashion Essential

A scientific breakthrough quickly gave birth to a fashion breakthrough. Having synthesized nylon in 1934, DuPont began producing **nylon stockings** in 1939–1940. Some 64 million pairs (like the one worn above by actress and pinup model Betty Grable) sold in the first year. Military uses for nylon took precedence over stocking production during the war, but afterward, nylons made a huge—and sustained—comeback. By 1990, American women were buying 1.5 billion pairs of stockings or pantyhose a year.

Opening Nights

Broadway		West End
1,384	1910–19	3,278
2,194	1920–29	3,980
1,421	1930–39	4,256
425	1980–89	1,115*

*estimate

The Depression did not appreciably hurt the theater industry. More shows opened in London's West End in the 1930s than in any decade before or since. (The war, however, took a toll: London theaters were forced to close in 1939.) Broadway openings peaked in the 1920s and steadily declined thereafter.

What We Knew

England and France have declared war on Germany, but the likelihood of American involvement is perceived as small. "The United States is at present so demoralized and so corrupted," German Cabinet Minister Richard-Walther Darre assures Nazi party officials, that "it need not be taken into consideration as a military adversary." U.S. President Franklin D. Roosevelt reinforces that view when he tells a Boston audience, "I say it again and again and again: Your boys are not going to be sent into any foreign wars."

■

The Royal Air Force in England, which will soon be under bombardment by Germany, is widely considered to be no match for Hitler's Luftwaffe. "In three weeks," predicts French General Maxime Weygand in June 1940, "England will have her neck wrung like a chicken."

■

"Japan will never join the Axis," asserts General Douglas MacArthur in September 1940. Others in the American military establishment express their confidence that, in the words of a former chief of Naval Intelligence, "the Hawaiian Islands are over-protected; the entire Japanese fleet and air force could not seriously threaten Oahu."

■

Radiologists have misgivings, but U.S. consumers consider fluoroscopes (X-ray machines)—ubiquitous in shoe stores throughout the country—to be harmless, useful devices for determining whether a potential purchase fits properly.

■

With the widespread introduction of fluoride into public water supplies five years away (and into toothpastes a decade away), tooth decay plagues American youth. Each six-month trip to the dentist turns up four to five cavities, and dental defects are the most common health reason for a candidate to be rejected for military service.

ROBERT STONE

Total War

Global Conflict as a Way of Life

1940
1949

IN SHEER QUANTITY OF BLOOD SPILLED, THE SECOND WORLD WAR was certainly the most horrendous war in history. As in the First, more civilians died than soldiers—some 50 million of the former to 15 million of the latter. But even more than its predecessor, this world war was a *total* war, in which whole populations were mobilized for combat or military production, and whole peoples became military targets. At the outbreak of World War I in 1914, Lord Edward Grey, the British foreign secretary, had a vision of "the lamps ... going out all over Europe." The hatreds and rivalries that consumed much of the globe was deeper than anything Grey could have imagined.

Total war was made possible, above all, by modern technology—in weapons, communications, industrial production. Victory, however, hinged on many other factors, both material and intangible. Germany, the chief aggressor, initially had the edge, with a finely coordinated manufacturing sector geared entirely for warfare, an arsenal of advanced aircraft and weaponry, and a group of generals whose tactical ideas (learned the hard way, through defeat) were far more sophisticated than those of their adversaries. Animating the Nazi war machine—and the German people—was a man of fanatical determination, extraordinary political acumen, and unparalleled personal magnetism.

Adolf Hitler did not single-handedly cause World War II, but its strategic contours and moral dimensions were shaped by his obsessions. He was the embodiment of Yeats's line "the worst are full of passionate intensity." A marginal man cast up from the chaos of the old ruined empires, he was the demonic second coming of Napoleon, a conscienceless worshipper of possibility. To a militarily humiliated and economically depressed nation, Hitler offered a cheap elitism based on crank notions of race (an exaggeration of theories that were, in fact, widely held even among academics), and a vision of life itself as war: a Darwinian struggle between the superior "Aryans" and their genetic inferiors (particularly Jews and Slavs). Invoking a pseudo-historical image of the Germans as Nordic berserkers, the Führer transformed his orderly, sober countrymen into dedicated agents of genocide. At first, his recklessness served him well, as Germany's Blitzkrieg attacks confused and demoralized a world desperately unwilling to risk another Great War.

By December 1935, when this photomontage by Berlin-born artist John Heartfield (who'd anglicized his name from Helmut Herzfeld in protest against his native country's role in World War I) appeared in *AIZ*, a left-wing German newspaper, many observers were asking not whether war would come, but when. The caption (satirizing Nazi leader Hermann Goering's declaration that "Iron has always made a people strong; butter and lard only make a people fat") reads, "Hurrah, the butter is gone!" But in spite of his calls to sacrifice butter for guns, Hitler shrewdly did his best to keep his people comfortable during rearmament and the war that followed.

Yet Hitler—mindful that the revolt that toppled the Kaiser at the end of World War I was precipitated largely by shortages—tried to conquer Europe while creating the least possible disruption at home. Food rationing came late to Germany. The wealthy kept their servants. The Reich, unlike the other European combatants, made little use of women in the war effort. The German High Command compensated by looting occupied Europe, squeezing it to the point of famine. Yet the Nazi regime—for all its worship of efficiency—was far better at organizing death camps than supplying its armed forces. The Luftwaffe lacked long-range heavy bombers; the Wehrmacht failed to provide warm uniforms for its soldiers in frigid Russia. Moreover, Nazi leaders were ignorant and arrogant. When an assistant told Luftwaffe chief Hermann Goering that the Americans could make 40,000 aircraft a year, Goering told the man to see a psychiatrist. "They can make cars and refrigerators," Goering said, "not aircraft."

Hitler misjudged his own and his enemies' comparative strength to the point of what one historian has called "absurd complacency." The irrationalism at the core of Nazi ideology was

Hurrah, die Butter ist alle!

Goering in seiner Hamburger Rede: „Erz hat stets ein Reich stark gemacht, Butter und Schmalz haben höchstens ein Volk fett gemacht".

Fotomontage: John Heartfield

nowhere so manifest as in his personality, in which manic optimism mingled with debilitating paranoia. Insisting on directing military operations personally, he squandered his initial advantages at terrible cost in men and materiel.

But if Germany suffered from the Führer's complacency, each of the Axis nations was burdened by its leaders' needs, ambitions, and weaknesses. In following Hitler's lead in 1940, Mussolini offered his people the prospect of war against Poland and France—hardly Italy's traditional enemies. However much they idolized Il Duce, the situation pleased very few Italians. When the Soviet Union and then the United States were added to the list of enemies, their enthusiasm did not increase. The country shortly lost control of its own fortunes and became a battleground upon which the Germans and the Allies fought each other into the war's last days.

Japan's leadership, and most of its people, possessed a sense of national destiny as fierce and mystical as Germany's—but one deeply touched with fatalism. During the thirties military cliques forced the country ever further into adventure and imperialism, overcoming civilian opposition through assassination and terror. But while Imperial forces succeeded in subduing much of Asia and the Pacific, many Japanese leaders were privately pessimistic about their military chances against the United States. The island nation was dangerously dependent on seaborne supply lines; its productive capacity was one-tenth America's. Some senior officers, particularly in the Navy, expressed polite reservations about the war. Not one, however, seriously argued against it.

It was largely rigid notions of good manners and duty—Japanese tradition consecrated consensus and revered the warrior ethic—that kept the Empire of the Rising Sun advancing stoically toward disaster. To question the war would have been an unforgivable lapse of taste, if not of character. And later on, when all was manifestly lost, no one seemed to have the authority to effect disengagement.

An incident reported by George Feifer, in *Tennozan: The Battle of Okinawa and the Atomic Bomb*, is illuminating. In March 1945, U.S. forces were closing in on the island of Okinawa, just 300 miles from southern Japan. A war council convened at the Imperial Palace, where the chief of naval staff, Admiral Oikawa, briefed Emperor Hirohito. The defense would rely on a kamikaze force—3,500 planes that would become manned ballistic missiles as their pilots slammed them suicidally into the American ships. (Kamikaze attacks were common by then, as were suicide attacks—and simple suicides—by Japanese soldiers and civilians throughout the Pacific islands.) "But where is the Navy?" Hirohito demanded. "Are there no more ships?" Though the tiny remnant of the Imperial Navy could do little to resist the invasion, the fleet's commanders were suddenly seized with a horror of losing face. They decided to send a half-dozen vessels into the fray—including the world's biggest battleship, the *Yamoto*. All were sunk, and 4,000 sailors died.

As the war's stakes rose, so did the ferocity and sophistication of the weaponry, and the frequency of massive assaults on civilians. On August 9, 1945, the United States dropped history's second atomic bomb—on the Japanese city of Nagasaki *(left)*. The bombing followed just three days after the first nuclear attack, on Hiroshima. Soon, the Soviet Union also boasted such weapons *(above, the key to the first Soviet A-bomb)*. Their very existence, and their horrifying effects, lent an altogether new dimension to the term "total war."

THE SOVIET UNION, THE MOST DESPISED of Hitler's enemies, was the country that suffered most in the war. Overcoming early setbacks, Stalin used his dictatorial powers to rally his nation. After halting the German advance at Stalingrad in February 1943, the Soviets began what was essentially a prolonged counterattack, sometimes interrupted, but destined to finish in the ruins of Berlin. As Napoleon had discovered in the previous century, the Russian empire could be overrun, but its vast territory, enormous population, and murderous winters made it a hard piece of property to hold. Yet these natural advantages were not the only keys to the Soviet victory. Stalin's longtime boosting of heavy industry enabled the country to outproduce Germany. (Many factories were shipped eastward piece by piece, to continue operating out of German reach.) A quasi-religious love of the Russian motherland spurred its inhabitants to heroic feats of resistance. And Soviet Communism, long considered the weakest of the totalitarian systems, turned out to be highly resilient: Many of Stalin's subjects were willing to die in defense of the Revolution.

The Soviet way of war consisted principally of frontal advances in force, repeated over and over by progressive waves of infantry. The crudity and costliness of these attacks moved the Germans, of all people, to profess outrage at the Russians' indifference to the value of human life. But there is no doubt as to their ultimate effectiveness. According to historian John Ellis, the Red Army, from June 1941 to March 1945, accounted for between 80 and 90 percent of German casualties worldwide.

The English lost their hold on their Empire during World War II, but spectacularly saved their honor. For centuries, their disciplined, homogenous society had proved adept at conquest (quite as adept as the Germans); now it prevailed defensively as well. Fighting virtually alone for months, enduring bombs, missiles, and desperate shortages of the sort Hitler was wasting Europe to avoid, Britons experienced the war years as a moral golden age, full of grief and sacrifice but touched with heroism. (The images of that time—blackouts, ration books, Victory Gardens, bomb shelters in the Underground—remain potent national symbols to this day.) The wartime loosening of the Kingdom's traditional class boundaries, and the working class's sense that it had saved the country, helped bring a socialist government to power in the 1945 election, when Britain astonished the world by turning Winston Churchill—a great war chief but an unrepentant aristocrat—out of office.

HITLER'S ATTITUDE TOWARD THE UNITED STATES was similar to that of many Europeans then and now. He saw it as the philistine, buck-worshipping fatherland of mediocrity—without authenticity, unhistorical, incapable of ideals or greatness. Its promiscuous origins mocked his racial theories. Maybe the frustrated artist in him loathed the country's stubborn pragmatism. (All totalitarian ideologies were grounded in aestheticism—and in mythic notions of purification through struggle.) In any case, his ill-considered defiance of American power was the most significant factor in his downfall. The United States—protected by two oceans from the full ravages of the war, gifted with tremendous resources in manpower, industry, and agriculture, and technologically second to no country (especially after refugee scientists from Axis lands began arriving)—gave the Allies the edge they needed to vanquish their foe utterly.

But while both sides in the war focused their wrath on noncombatants, America's reputation became inextricably tied to the conflict's single most spectacular act of violence against civilians: the atomic bombing of Hiroshima and Nagasaki. The Big Bang that ended the war established the United States as the deadliest power on the planet.

Victory also made it the liveliest. By the late forties the U.S. economy, galvanized by war, represented half the world's industrial production, and its aid dollars were rebuilding Western Europe and Japan. Previously the United States had stood apart from the councils of the world; now it assumed leadership of what came to be called the "free world." Indeed, the country emerged from the war so well that most Americans felt justified in imposing their values—a unique mix of classical liberalism, Protestant rectitude, technocratic rationalism, and self-interested individualism—on the world. But the Soviets also believed their ideology had been vindicated, and both mighty nations were determined to protect their gains and extend their power. In a sense, the standoff known as the Cold War represented the *institutionalization* of total war—the military, economic, and psychological mobilization of whole nations in a global struggle against an alien, intolerable foe.

But America's introduction of the atomic bomb had irrevocably changed the nature of warfare. As Washington and Moscow embarked on a nuclear arms race, it became clear that World War III would likely mean the destruction of all human life. Over the following decades, though they sometimes came within inches of a catastrophic confrontation, the superpowers always managed to turn aside in time. Instead, as colonial systems fell in Africa and Asia, the Americans and the Soviets vied for the future in a series of proxy wars—limited conflicts in which the local population did most of the dying, and the "pro-Western" forces were generally no more democratic than the "pro-Soviet." In the end, the competition helped bankrupt the Soviets, leading in the 1990s to geopolitical realignments every bit as radical as those following World War II. □

For nearly half a century after World War II, the two superpowers, the Soviet Union and the United States, remained poised for a reprise of total war—their economies geared to weapons production, their propaganda machines working at full throttle, their armies ready for Armageddon. In the aftermath of the Cold War (which drove both nations into near-insuperable debt), both sides dismantled hundreds of bombs and planes—like these U.S. B-52s being chopped up in the "Bone Yards" at a U.S. Air Force base in Arizona. The B-52s originally cost $64 million apiece; as scrap metal, they sold for about 16¢ per pound.

"Situation desperate ... Personally I think we cannot extricate the BEF."—**British chief of staff William Edmund Ironside's diary entry, May 21, 1940, on the retreat of the British Expeditionary Forces from Dunkirk**

STORY OF THE YEAR

Deliverance at Dunkirk

1 The Nazi invasion of France and the Low Countries in 1940 might have finished the Allies, if not for the miraculous rescue, engineered by the British, of a third of a million troops from the French port of Dunkirk. The German advance had cornered some 200,000 Britons and 140,000 Frenchmen and Belgians in this city near the Belgian border. To save them, the British Admiralty rounded up every vessel available, from warships and passenger ferries to fishing smacks and pleasure boats. On May 26, the first vessels sailed across the English Channel, guarded by Royal Air Force planes—and the trapped soldiers thronged Dunkirk's beaches and piers to meet them.

The Allied rescue at Dunkirk, re-created on canvas by Charles Cundall.

The evacuation, code-named Operation Dynamo, lasted ten harrowing days. British (and a few French) destroyers raced in, crammed their decks full of soldiers, and—their guns firing constantly—raced back to Dover. Smaller vessels carried troops to ships lying outside the ruined harbor. German bombers were a persistent menace, showering land and sea with explosives; the RAF brought down 159. Adding to the tension was the approach of the invaders: Three days into the exodus, the nearby port of Calais fell, and the next day Belgium surrendered. The rescuers were aided by Hitler's ill-advised decision, on two occasions, to suspend his drive toward Dunkirk and concentrate on other objectives.

Although 243 ships and boats and untold tons of military equipment were lost in the sea lift, only 2,000 men died. The rest were greeted by cheering crowds when they landed in England, and soon marched off to fight again. "Wars are not won by evacuations," observed Prime Minister Winston Churchill, who'd overseen the operation, "but there was a victory inside this deliverance." Greater triumphs would follow, he promised Parliament. "We shall not flag or fail.... We shall fight on the seas and oceans, we shall fight with growing confidence and growing strength in the air, we shall defend our island, whatever the cost may be.... We shall fight in the fields and in the streets, we shall fight in the hills; we shall never surrender." **◂1939.1 ▸1940.6**

WORLD WAR II

Italy Declares War

2 For the first months of World War II, Benito Mussolini agonized over if and when to strike. Eager for glory, fearful that Germany might win the war before he'd seized any territory, the war-worshipping dictator itched to join the fray. Yet several factors restrained him. His people were in a pacifist mood, his army unprepared. He was angered by Hitler's pact with Stalin and his brutal treatment of the Poles. He also worried that Germany might *not* win, leaving Italy in the lurch. But gradually his thirst for action—and the Führer's urging—overcame his reservations. In March 1940, when the two dictators met at the Brenner Pass to formalize their alliance, Mussolini promised to commit his troops the moment Germany's attack on France appeared successful. On June 10, as the French wilted under Nazi fire, he declared war on the Allies.

Despite his own doubts, Mussolini had convinced Hitler of his country's might. But the truth quickly emerged. Italy's first assault, on southern France, netted a paltry few acres. An August invasion of British Somaliland by 40,000 Italian troops, while successful, was unimpressive: They outnumbered the defenders four to one, yet lost 2,000 men to Britain's 260, and the operation dragged on for two weeks. In September, 80,000 Italians marched out of Libya into Egypt, heading for the Suez Canal. Not only were they driven back by 30,000 Britons, but much of eastern Libya was lost as well. In October, without Hitler's consent (Hitler, after all, had just occupied Romania's oil district without consulting *him*), Il Duce sent 155,000 troops into Greece from Albania. Again they failed to conquer; moreover, one third of Albania fell to the Greeks, while the British took the strategic island of Crete.

In theory, Italy was waging a "parallel war" in the Mediterranean, while Germany concentrated on the northern theater. But over the following year, Hitler would have his hands full cleaning up Mussolini's messes—and Mussolini's independence would shrink accordingly. **◂1939.5 ▸1941.2**

WORLD WAR II

The War at Sea

3 For seven months after the invasion of Poland, Hitler bided his time—planning his next moves while waiting out a harsh winter. So little happened militarily that the English spoke derisively of a "phony war"; the French called it *la drôle de guerre*, while the Germans used the term *Sitzkrieg*. At sea, however, there was plenty of action.

Responding to a British naval blockade, German bombers and U-boats had sunk scores of commercial craft by January 1940—including the British liner *Athenia* (at a cost of 112 passengers) and many vessels from neutral countries. Battleships had clashed not only in European waters, but as far away as Uruguay, where a month earlier the crew of Germany's *Admiral Graf Spee* had scuttled their ship in the face of defeat by British cruisers.

In February, sailors from the British destroyer *Cossack* swarmed over a German prison ship, killed four crewmen in hand-to-hand combat, and freed 299 prisoners of war. (The half-starved captives came from ships sunk by the *Admiral Graf Spee* before its demise.) On the same day, the British government declared that all merchantmen and

Hitler and Mussolini review an Italian honor guard at the Brenner Pass, on Italy's border.

ART & CULTURE: Books: *The Man Who Loved Children* (Christina Stead); *For Whom the Bell Tolls* (Ernest Hemingway); *The Heart Is a Lonely Hunter* (Carson McCullers); *The Ox-Bow Incident* (Arthur van Tilburg Clark); *50 Poems* (e.e. cummings) ... Music: "When You Wish upon a Star" (Harline and Washington); "You Are My Sunshine" (Davis and Mitchell); *Xochipilli Macuilxochitl* (Carlos Chávez) ...

"I have nothing to offer but blood, toil, tears, and sweat."—**Winston Churchill, in his first speech as British prime minister, May 13, 1940**

Aircraft carriers added a new dimension to naval battles in World War II.

fishing boats in the North Sea must arm themselves. Germany promptly announced that it would treat such craft as warships, formalizing a policy it had been following all along. Soon British trawlers were shooting it out with German planes—and occasionally winning. **◂1939.M ▸1941.1**

WORLD WAR II

Norway and Denmark Invaded

4 To conquer the west, Hitler had first to secure the north. Germany got much of its iron ore from Sweden, mainly via the Norwegian port of Narvik. (Both Sweden and Norway had declared their neutrality.) Eager to cut off the supply, the Allies planned to invade Norway. But on April 9, 1940, 24 hours after British ships laid their first mines in a Norwegian harbor, the Germans beat them to it. Shielded by fog, German gunboats appeared in Norway's major ports, disgorging thousands of infantrymen. Meanwhile, paratroopers—the first ever used in warfare—seized important airfields. It took two months to subdue Norway; little Denmark, which Germany attacked simultaneously to provide a clear path northward, collapsed in just four hours.

Although the invaders encountered pockets of fierce opposition as they entered Norway, most of their objectives fell quickly. Oslo, the capital, surrendered within a day as hundreds of low-flying planes underscored German threats to bomb the population. The Nazis installed Vidkun Quisling, head of the country's small Fascist Party, as dictator. (His surname entered the English language as a synonym for traitor.) But King Haakon VII and his ministers refused to admit defeat. They fled to the snowbound mountains, hiding in caves, while Norway's tiny, ill-equipped army—joined by a hastily organized militia—waged guerrilla war against the occupiers.

As the invasion began, Norway had declared its allegiance to the Allied cause. But British and French troops took nearly a week to arrive. Even at Narvik, where they outnumbered the enemy five to one, they were unable to oust the Germans until May 27. By then, France was under fire, and Allied soldiers were needed there. They withdrew days later, and Haakon and the government escaped to London. Hitler had won not merely an uninterrupted supply of ore (Sweden, now isolated, could not refuse him), but bases from which to attack Britain. Yet victory

A French patrol guards a railway near Narvik in Norway.

had its downside: 300,000 troops had to be stationed in Norway, far from any battle front—and despite their presence, the country remained, like Denmark, a hotbed of resistance. **◂1939.6 ▸1940.6**

WORLD WAR II

The Allies' New Leaders

5 As the time approached when the Allies would have to defend themselves against invasion, the men who governed France and Britain began to look alarmingly inadequate. For years, Edouard Daladier and Neville Chamberlain had tried to appease Hitler—and though each had belatedly put his foot down, neither had grown into an inspiring leader. In both countries, cries went up for change. Daladier fell on March 21, 1940, and finance minister Paul Reynaud formed a new government. On May 10, as the rape of the Low Countries began, Chamberlain was succeeded by Winston Churchill. (Chamberlain died eight months later.)

Reynaud hoped to replace Daladier's passive military stance—based on the supposed invincibility of France's Maginot Line, a 200-mile chain of fortifications—with a more aggressive strategy. But the demands of French parliamentary politics forced him to keep Daladier on as minister of war, and to seat far-rightists in his cabinet. When the Germans invaded, France was stuck with outmoded defenses and with a government divided over whether or not to continue the fight. After the defeat, Reynaud and several colleagues (including Daladier, who'd joined the Resistance in North Africa) wound up in Nazi concentration camps.

Churchill, by contrast, received virtual carte blanche when he rose to lead Parliament. Since his election to that body in 1900, his political fortunes had swung wildly. But he had first won fame as a Boer War soldier-correspondent, and he'd never lost his martial spirit. On the first day of the Second World War, Chamberlain had given him back his World War I post as Admiralty chief, and Churchill soon became Britain's top advocate of intransigence against Hitler. As prime minister, he assembled a War Cabinet that included every faction *except* the extreme right and left.

To his people and the world, Churchill became the very symbol of British determination. With his bulldog face, his blunt cigar, his V-for-victory sign, and his unparalleled eloquence, he traveled the beleaguered country, urging Britons to make the war "their finest hour." They did not disappoint him. **◂1940.1 ▸1940.7**

The defiant new prime minister standing on the coast of England with his troops.

BIRTHS

Mario Andretti, Italian-U.S. race car driver.

Bernardo Bertolucci, Italian filmmaker.

Julian Bond, U.S. civil rights leader.

Tom Brokaw, U.S. newscaster.

Joseph Brodsky, Russian-U.S. poet.

J.M. Coetzee, South African novelist.

Herbie Hancock, U.S. musician.

John Lennon, U.K. musician.

Jack Nicklaus, U.S. golfer.

Pelé, Brazilian soccer player.

Richard Pryor, U.S. comedian.

David Rabe, U.S. playwright.

Wilma Rudolph, U.S. sprinter.

Ringo Starr, U.K. musician.

Fran Tarkenton, U.S. football player.

Tina Turner, U.S. singer.

Frank Zappa, U.S. musician.

DEATHS

Walter Benjamin, German literary critic.

Peter Behrens, German architect.

Neville Chamberlain, U.K. prime minister.

Walter Chrysler, U.S. industrialist.

F. Scott Fitzgerald, U.S. novelist.

Marcus Garvey, Jamaican-U.S. activist.

Emma Goldman, Lithuanian-U.S. political activist.

Paul Klee, Swiss artist.

Selma Lagerlöf, Swedish novelist.

Joseph J. Thomson, U.K. physicist.

Leon Trotsky, Russian revolutionary.

Edouard Vuillard, French painter.

Nathanael West, U.S. novelist.

Painting & Sculpture: ***Report from Rockport*** **(Stuart Davis) ... Film:** ***Rebecca*** **(Alfred Hitchcock);** ***The Philadelphia Story*** **(George Cukor);** ***The Great Dictator*** **(Charles Chaplin);** ***Fantasia*** **(Walt Disney) ... Theater:** ***The Male Animal*** **(Thurber and Nugent);** ***George Washington Slept Here*** **(Kaufman and Hart);** ***Pal Joey*** **(Rodgers and Hart);** ***Panama Hattie*** **(Cole Porter) ... Radio:** ***Truth or Consequences.***

"Has the last word been spoken? Must hope disappear? Is the defeat definitive? No!... Whatever happens, the flame of French resistance must not die and will not die."—**General Charles de Gaulle, broadcasting to Frenchmen over the radio from England, June 18, 1940**

NEW IN 1940

Automatic gearbox (General Motors).

Jeep (designed by Karl Pabst).

Color television (first experimental broadcast by CBS from the Chrysler Building in New York City).

M&Ms candy.

British Overseas Airways (BOAC).

IN THE UNITED STATES

▶**THE TIPPLER AND THE TEMPTRESS**—Two of the screen's most idiosyncratic comics, bulbous-nosed W.C. Fields and buxom Mae West, teamed up to write and star in *My Little Chickadee.* Erstwhile vaudevillians both, the stars reprised favorite roles in

the 1940 comedy: he a tippling misanthrope; she a mistress of risqué innuendo. ◀1926.V

▶**CHECK'S IN THE MAIL**—Ida May Fuller, a 35-year-old widow in Vermont, was the first recipient of a U.S. Social Security check. Mailed on January 30, the sum total of the first payout to eligible American pensioners equaled $75,844, of which $22.54 was Ida May Fuller's. By the time of her death in 1975, she had received over $20,000, and the government had delivered billions more. ◀1935.5

▶**NYLON RIOTS**—Nylon stockings went on sale nationwide in 1940—the peak of the nylon hysteria that was generated the previous year when Du Pont announced that the first sales of stockings would be limited to Wilmington, Delaware, residents.

WORLD WAR II

Blitzkrieg to the West

6 On May 10, 1940, Hitler blitzed the Netherlands, Belgium, and Luxembourg—the neutral lowland states that stood between him and his sworn enemy, France. "The fight beginning today," the Führer declared, "decides the fate of the German nation for the next thousand years!" The war in the west had finally begun.

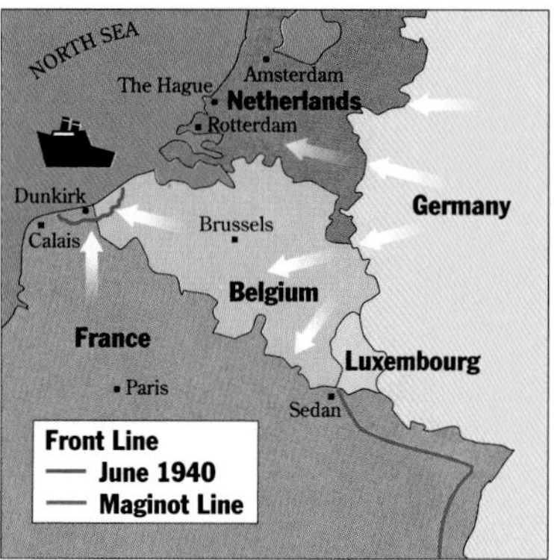

By invading the Low Countries and northern France, Germany skirted France's "impenetrable" Maginot Line and cornered the Allies at Dunkirk.

Before dawn, the Luftwaffe bombed military targets throughout the Low Countries, as well as several air bases in France. (Amsterdam and Rotterdam were later bombed as well, though the latter had already surrendered.) Then paratroopers—some disguised in Dutch uniforms—dropped out of the sky, while gliders deposited infantrymen on the Belgian side of the Albert Canal. Troops poured across the borders so quickly that defenders had no time to blow up key bridges. The Dutch opened the sluices on their dikes, flooding the countryside, but the Wehrmacht was ready with rubber boats. Stuka dive-bombers, their sirens screaming, strafed soldiers and civilians alike. Panzer divisions thundered through villages, leveling everything in their paths.

The Germans were helped by sympathizers who sabotaged power plants and air-raid warning systems. The defenders' weaknesses took a toll as well. Luxembourg was simply too tiny to resist. Belgium's King Leopold, clinging to neutrality, refused to integrate his army's actions with those of the Netherlands or France. The Dutch army lacked armored vehicles and tactical expertise. The French and British rushed in, only to be outgunned and outmaneuvered.

Luxembourg fell the first day, the Netherlands four days later. Belgium held out until May 28. By then, Hitler's forces had swarmed into northern France. ◀1940.1 ▶1940.7

WORLD WAR II

The Fall of France

7 Two days after the invasion of the Low Countries began, on May 12, 1940, German tanks roared into France from Belgium through the Ardennes Forest. French commanders, confident that these densely wooded hills were impassable, provided their guardians with few anti-tank or antiaircraft guns. Soon German troops were crossing the Meuse River at Sedan, as dive-bombers pounded the defenders. The vaunted Maginot Line proved irrelevant: The invaders had simply gone around it to the north. The French army was all but paralyzed with shock. With France's tank forces poorly organized and its planes hugely outnumbered, the end was inevitable.

On June 3, 200 planes bombed Paris—and eleven days later, the Nazis entered the capital unopposed, goose-stepping down the Champs-Elysées. (By then, the government had fled to Bordeaux.) On June 16, Premier Paul Reynaud resigned rather than surrender.

Reynaud was replaced by the octogenarian vice-premier, Marshal Henri Pétain (still revered as a World War I hero, though he'd fathered the defense policies that lost the current fight). Pétain signed an armistice on June 22, in the same railway car at Compiègne where the Germans had agreed to end the previous war. France's northern and western three fifths became an occupied zone, the rest nominally sovereign.

Pétain moved the capital south to Vichy. In July—after the British attacked French ships off of Algeria to keep them out of German hands —he severed relations with his erstwhile ally, and transformed unoccupied France into a fascist-style dictatorship.

Meanwhile, the former undersecretary of war, General Charles de Gaulle, began broadcasting appeals to his compatriots to continue the struggle. De Gaulle, who'd fled to London, founded the Free French movement—whose armed forces, culled from loyalists in exile or in France's colonies, aided the Allies for the duration. ◀1940.6 ▶1940.11

SCIENCE

Plutonium Discovered

8 The element that would fuel the first successful nuclear weapon was discovered by American scientists in 1940—a breakthrough made possible, ironically, by the work of Germans. In 1938, Otto Hahn and Fritz Strassmann had bombarded uranium with neutrons, trying to prove Italian physicist Enrico Fermi's theory that the process would produce new, ultraheavy elements. Instead, they'd stumbled across nuclear fission (identified by their colleague-in-exile Lise Meitner), in which uranium atoms split in two.

Two years later, at the University

In one of the war's most stirring images, a Frenchman weeps as he watches a parade in Marseilles of the flags of his country's defeated regiments.

SPORTS: Baseball: World Series, Cincinnati Reds defeat Detroit Tigers, 4–3 ... Football: NFL, Chicago Bears defeat Washington Redskins, 73–0 ... Wimbledon, the Olympics, and Davis Cup canceled due to war in Europe ... Auto Racing: Wilbur Shaw wins third Indy 500 ... Horse Racing: Seabiscuit retires as leading money winner (total earnings, $437,730) ... Track & Field: Cornelius Warmerdam is first to pole-vault 15'.

of California, Berkeley, a group of young scientists showed that, instead of splitting, some uranium atoms thus bombarded *absorbed* neutrons—and subsequently decayed into just the sorts of substances Fermi had predicted.

In experiments designed by Berkeley researchers Edwin McMillan and Philip Abelson, an element turned up that had one more proton than uranium, and hence an atomic number of 93. It was dubbed neptunium, after the planet Neptune, just beyond Uranus. Then a team led by their colleague Glenn Seaborg found that neptunium atoms decayed further into an element with an atomic number of 94.

This element was named plutonium, after the planet Pluto. The first isotope discovered was plutonium 238 *(left)*. A second isotope, plutonium 239, proved to be three times as fissionable as uranium 235 (the material later used in the Hiroshima bomb). Just 300 grams, in theory, could generate a blast equivalent to 20,000 tons of TNT. As the physicist Ernest Lawrence noted a few weeks after its discovery, plutonium had the potential to fuel a "superbomb." Lawrence's ominous prophecy was fulfilled in 1945, when such a bomb was exploded in the New Mexico desert—and weeks later another shattered Nagasaki, Japan. **◂1938.1 ▸1942.15**

ARCHAEOLOGY

A Prehistoric Treasure Trove

9 Four French schoolboys were hunting rabbits near the village of Montignac in the province of Dordogne in September 1940 when their dog disappeared down a hole. Climbing down to retrieve him, they found themselves in a grotto festooned with precise, graceful paintings of animals—many extinct or vanished from the area. One fresco showed a man fallen between a bison and a wounded rhinoceros; others depicted boars, horses, wolves, wild oxen, reindeer, and an unidentifiable (and perhaps mythical) unicornlike creature. When archaeologists examined the Lascaux Grotto—a magnificently decorated main cavern, dubbed the Great Hall of Bulls, connected by passageways to side galleries—they dated the pictures to about 18,000 BC, and declared the cave one of the richest troves of Paleolithic art ever discovered.

Horses, deer, and four bulls (one of them 11 feet long) circle the main cavern of Lascaux.

The experts speculated that squares painted in front of some animals represented pitfalls covered with sheets of skins; comblike patterns superimposed on some animals, they surmised, were fenced enclosures. But the purpose of the paintings—mostly rendered in black, brown, red, and yellow ocher mixed with animal fat—remained (and remains) unknown. They may have served a religious or magical function related to the hunt; they may have been purely decorative.

The cave quickly became a tourist attraction. But in 1963, when the colors had begun to fade and green fungus spots marred some of the frescoes, it was closed to the public. A simulated cave that tourists can visit has since been built nearby. **◂1900.6 ▸1947.6**

POPULAR CULTURE

An Antidote to Disney

10 On-screen, a hunter with a huge bald head turned to the audience and lisped, "Be vewy, vewy quiet—I'm hunting wabbits." Spotting his prey leaning against a tree, he aimed his rifle. And the rabbit, with wise-guy cool, asked, "Eh, what's up, Doc?" With that question, the animated idol Bugs Bunny made his debut in the 1940 Warner Bros. cartoon *A Wild Hare*. At last, there was a threat to Mickey Mouse.

Bugs's brash character was the creation of animation genius Tex Avery, one of Warners' unparalleled gang of artists and writers, which included Chuck Jones, Friz Freleng, Bob McKimson, Bob Clampett, and Mike Maltese. Bugs's Brooklyn accent belonged to versatile "voice man" Mel Blanc. Together, these unsung talents turned out six-minute snippets of high-octane pop art that challenged the hegemony of Hollywood's reigning cartoon maestro, Walt Disney.

Bugs Bunny and Daffy Duck rally for the war effort. Mel Blanc provided the voices for both characters.

Disney's characters were warm and adorable; Bugs and his colleagues—Daffy Duck, Sylvester, the Road Runner—were hip, snide, neurotic (only Porky Pig approached Disney niceness). Disney's animators strove for "the illusion of life"; Warners' preferred lunatic speed, wild perspectives, shocking transformations. Bugs and friends disrupted the opening credits or rudely addressed the viewer; they metamorphosed into Carmen Miranda or twirled their ears and became airplanes. And the Disney humor was cozily Middle American; Warners' had the edgy brio of New York vaudeville. **◂1928.10 ▸1950.6**

IN THE UNITED STATES

Out-of-towners converged on the city, renting hotel rooms and apartments. By 1941, most nylon was reserved for military use. ◂1934.9

▶PUTTING AMERICA FIRST—In a last-ditch effort to preserve U.S. isolationism, a group of prominent businessmen and politicians formed the America First Committee in fall 1940. Backed by the Hearst newspaper chain (and, indirectly, the Republican Party), the committee warned against involvement in another European war and became an unlikely ally of pacifist organizations, including *The Catholic Worker* and the Women's International League for Peace and Freedom. ◂1939.12 ▸1941.1

▶A LONELY HUNTER—Georgia-born Carson McCullers wrote her first, and some say best, novel, *The Heart Is a Lonely Hunter*, when she was only 23. The book, which appeared in 1940, tells the story of small-town southern life as seen through the eyes of a deaf-mute who is befriended by a young girl (based on McCullers herself). It expresses the author's characteristic themes of loneliness and yearning for human contact and love. ◂1929.3 ▸1953.V

▶THE L.A. LABYRINTH BEGINS—What has become the quintessential modern urban nightmare began innocently enough with the dedication of the Arroyo Seco Parkway in Los Angeles in December 1940. A six-mile span connecting Pasadena and Los Angeles, the first freeway in California spawned a byzantine maze of disparate neighborhoods, clogged highways, and vast parking lots. ◂1908.1 ▸1956.M

POLITICS & BUSINESS: GNP: $99.7 billion ... U.S. population: 132,164,569 ... Office of Emergency Management and National Defense Advisory Commission established ... Congress passes Selective Service Act (first U.S. peacetime draft) ... John L. Lewis votes Republican and resigns as head of CIO upon Roosevelt's reelection ... B.F. Goodrich introduces first synthetic tire (Ameripol) for commercial use.

"Never in the field of human conflict was so much owed by so many to so few."—**Winston Churchill, on the heroic performance of the RAF, outnumbered 30 to 1 by Hitler's Luftwaffe, August 20, 1940**

WORLD WAR II

▸MAGINOT LINE—Dreamed up by War Minister André Maginot as an antidote to France's massive World War I casualties, the Maginot Line

was the most expensive (half a billion dollars), most heavily fortified defensive installation ever built. Behind this "invincible" complex of underground forts and mounted guns running between Belgium and Switzerland, France from 1929 onward was secure from German attack—or so many strategists believed. When Hitler's Wehrmacht blitzed in 1940, it simply outflanked the Maginot Line, penetrating France through Ardennes and the Low Countries. Shielded for so long, the French army was wholly unprepared to resist the invaders.

▸A NEW UNDERGROUND RAILROAD—After Hitler's spring invasions, more than 20,000 Jews living in France, Belgium, and Holland escaped into Switzerland, Spain, and Portugal with the help of sympathetic citizens who provided false documents and safe passage to neutral countries. Many Danish Jews were smuggled to Sweden. In France, many Jews went underground and joined the Resistance.

▸FRENCH FLEET DESTROYED—The conquest of France gave Germany a potential new weapon: the formidable French navy. On July 3, Britain seized as many French ships as it could. Most went quietly, but at the Algerian port of Mers-el-Kebir, a major French fleet refused to surrender. British warships opened fire, killing 1,200 French sailors, who only a fortnight earlier had been allies.

▸RAF DEFENDS BRITAIN—In July, preparing for Operation Sea Lion—Hitler's proposed invasion of Britain—the Luftwaffe began bombing England. Ready and waiting were the daring young pilots of the Royal Air Force (23 years old,

WORLD WAR II

Battle of Britain

11 With France beneath the jackboot, Britain was Europe's last bastion against Nazi aggression. The unrivaled British navy and the natural barrier of the English Channel protected Britain from blitzkrieg. Before Hitler could launch Operation Sea Lion—an amphibious invasion planned for September 15, 1940—he knew he must destroy the Royal Air Force.

After weeks of sporadic hammering at ports and airfields along the Channel, the Luftwaffe intensified its campaign in early August, launching hundreds of aircraft daily at air bases and airplane factories throughout the kingdom. The attackers deployed 1,300 bombers; their 1,200 fighters outnumbered Britain's two to one. But German bombers were poorly armed and carried light bomb loads. German fighters were operating near the limit of their range, and Britain's state-of-the-art radar stations deprived the enemy of the element of surprise.

Still, the British were losing planes and pilots too fast. So on August 28, they sprang their own surprise: They bombed Berlin. Allied planes had struck targets elsewhere in Germany, but this was their first assault on the capital. Hitler retaliated recklessly, shifting the attack to Britain's population centers. London, Coventry, Liverpool, and smaller towns suffered a merciless beating. Buckingham Palace was damaged and Coventry Cathedral destroyed, but the raids had no strategic effect. The public was prepared (children had been evacuated to the countryside), and despite thousands of casualties, morale did not crumble. Hardy Londoners took to sleeping in tube (subway) stations. Germany had lost twice as many planes as its adversary by September, when Hitler postponed Operation Sea Lion indefinitely. But the "Blitz," as Britons called it, was not over. Hoping to force a surrender, the Führer redoubled the bombing. It continued, with a few pauses, until June 1941—when the Luftwaffe's firepower was needed in Russia. **◂1940.1 ▸1942.3**

Charred Gothic spires rise above the rubble of the old Coventry Cathedral, destroyed on November 14, 1940, in the Blitz's worst bombing to date.

WORLD WAR II

The Baltic States Seized

12 Squeezed between the Soviet Union and Nazi Germany were three tiny nations, each trying to protect its independence by maintaining neutrality in the escalating European war—Lithuania, Latvia, and Estonia. In August 1940, the Soviet Union annexed them all. A year earlier, Hitler and Stalin had signed a secret nonaggression protocol delineating Nazi and Soviet spheres of influence in central and eastern Europe: Germany took western Poland and everything south; the Soviets got eastern Poland, Finland, and the Baltic states. After the German conquest of Poland in September 1939, Moscow hurried to secure its spoils. It offered Finland and the Baltics "mutual assistance" treaties, a euphemism for occupation by the Red Army.

Soviet troops enter the main square of Riga, the capital of Latvia, on June 17.

Finland alone rejected Stalin's terms and fought a bloody war for independence. The three smaller countries ruefully accepted the Soviet offer. "The pacts with the Baltic states," Soviet foreign minister Molotov declared at the end of 1939, "in no way imply the intrusion of the Soviet Union in [their] internal affairs." A few months later, citing a fabricated Baltic conspiracy to undermine Soviet security, the Red Army moved in. The occupiers foisted Communist puppet governments on the Baltics, which quickly opted for incorporation into the Union of Soviet Socialist Republics. **◂1939.6 ▸1941.7**

THE UNITED STATES

FDR Moves Toward War

13 As the war intensified, Franklin D. Roosevelt faced a dilemma: how to help sink the Axis without scuttling his presiden-

1940

WORLD WAR II: February: Soviets cross Mannerheim Line ... March: Finland surrenders ... April: Germany invades Denmark and Norway ... May: Germany invades Belgium, the Netherlands, Luxembourg, and France; Allied evacuation from Dunkirk begins ... June: Italy declares war on France and Britain; Germans occupy Paris; Pétain concludes armistice with Germany ... July: French government moves to Vichy,

"The things life has done to us we cannot excuse or explain. The past is the present. It's the future, too."
—Eugene O'Neill, *Long Day's Journey into Night*

cy. With an election in November 1940, he had to be careful. Many Americans had a strong isolationist streak, and the Republican candidate, Wendell Willkie (though he actually shared Roosevelt's views on foreign policy), was playing to those voters. Fortunately for Roosevelt and the Allied cause, a new device called the opinion poll revealed a shift in the public mood: After mid-1940, the majority of Americans were willing to aid the victims of Nazi aggression, even at the risk of being drawn into the fighting. Armed with this knowledge, Roosevelt was able to implement two bold measures.

In September, he agreed to Churchill's suggestion that he lend Britain 50 old destroyers in exchange for the right to build military bases on various British possessions in the Western Hemisphere. Two weeks later, Roosevelt signed the Selective Training and Service Act, initiating America's first peacetime conscription. He presented the deal with Britain as an executive agreement not subject to legislative approval. The conscription bill was more hotly contested: To move it through Congress, he had to use his remarkable powers of persuasion, both in the newfangled arena of the press conference and in the old-fashioned one of back-room politics.

Willkie supported a military draft, yet he still accused his opponent of warmongering. But as with the ships-for-bases trade, the President was able to sell the legislation as a purely defensive measure. "Your boys are not going to be sent into any foreign wars," he promised the electorate, which returned him to office for an unprecedented third term. **◂1939.12 ▸1941.1**

Willkie's campaign pins: a spoon in the shape of a shovel, and a pop-open presidential chair (with Willkie's picture under the seat).

THEATER
O'Neill's Anguished Journey

14 While writing *Long Day's Journey into Night* in 1940, playwright Eugene O'Neill would often emerge from his study weeping.

Sidney Lumet's 1962 film of O'Neill's drama starred *(from left)* Jason Robards, Dean Stockwell, Katharine Hepburn, and Ralph Richardson.

The play dramatizes one agonizing day in the life of a family—a miserly, self-lacerating actor father; a timid, drug-addicted mother; a bitter, alcoholic son; and another son, afflicted with tuberculosis and a poetic sense of doom. Most heartbreaking, perhaps, is the fact that the play is almost completely autobiographical.

It is also the chef d'oeuvre of America's greatest playwright, whose works are more widely translated and performed than those of any dramatist besides Shakespeare and Shaw. Ranging in style from naturalism to expressionism, O'Neill's plays are often verbose and monumentally long (*Long Day's Journey* spans 3½ hours); the best, however, are remarkable for their compassion, their psychological insight, and a dramatic power rooted in Greek tragedy.

To complete *Long Day's Journey,* O'Neill (then 52) had to battle not only his childhood demons, but what was eventually diagnosed as Parkinson's disease. He asked that the work not be produced until 25 years after his death, so as to spare his brother the pain of seeing it. But the world premiere, in Stockholm, came in 1956—22 years earlier than requested. **◂1904.7 ▸1947.13**

WORLD WAR II
Britain Exits China

15 While the British heroically defended their homeland in 1940, they lost face in China. For nearly 100 years, Britain had been the dominant foreign power in that perpetually exploited country. Now, however, the Japanese occupied much of China—and they insisted on controlling its affairs.

Japan's first priority was to cut off supplies to Chongqing, where Chiang Kai-shek's Nationalist Army was headquartered. In June, Japan pressured Vichy France into shutting down the railway from French Indochina to Chongqing. That left the Burma Road—the mountain trail from the British colony of Burma—as the Nationalists' only major supply route. Then the Japanese sealed off Hong Kong (another British colony) to back their demand that the Burmese end of the road be closed. The British, under escalating attack at home,

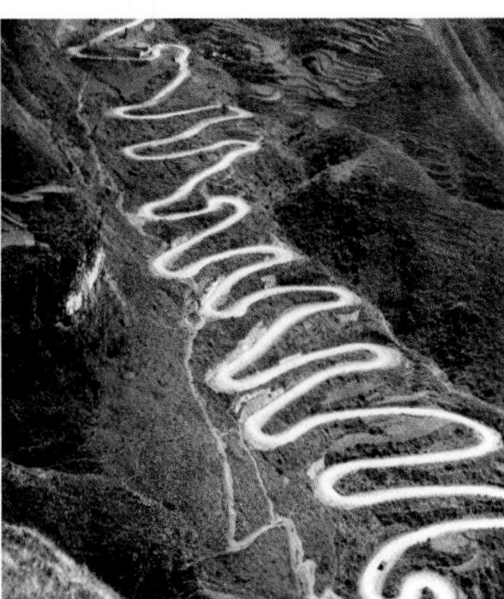

The 21 curves of the Burma Road, which stretched from China to Burma.

dared not risk war in Asia. They complied in July, reserving the right to reopen the road in three months.

Although the Burma Road went back into service on schedule, staying open until the Japanese overran Indochina in 1942, the incident undermined the Nationalists' fighting ability—and British prestige. Worse yet, in August, Britain had to evacuate its garrisons from mainland China's cities. Several Western nations maintained such garrisons (and had for decades, even under Japanese occupation) to protect their economic interests, but the British force of 2,850, mostly stationed in Shanghai, was the largest. Its departure, again under Japanese pressure, closed a chapter of imperial history. **◂1938.4 ▸1941.13**

WORLD WAR II

on average), who took to the skies in quick Spitfires and Hurricanes and consistently outfought the Germans. On September 7, a frustrated Hitler carried bombardment to London. The Blitz destroyed one million homes and caused 40,000 civilian deaths. But the city and the RAF prevailed.

Against 900 planes lost in the Battle of Britain, British fliers downed 1,700 German craft. There would be no invasion.

▸WARSHIPS IN DISGUISE—In the Battle of the Atlantic, Germany had a secret weapon: raiders sailing as merchant vessels. Introduced in 1940, the six incognito warships eschewed convoys to prey on lone ships. By year's end, they had sent some 360,000 tons of Allied shipping to the ocean floor.

▸THE ZERO—Fast, agile, armed with machine guns and cannons, capable of carrying multiple bombs, and equipped with an extra fuel tank for unprecedented range, the Japanese Zero elevated fighter planes to a new level. The Zero went into production in 1940—the "zero year," the 2,600th anniversary of the legendary founding of Japan—and for the next three years nothing in the Allies' arsenal could touch it.

▸VICTORY—Launched by two Belgians in London working for the BBC, a defiant graffiti campaign swept Europe. In Belgium, it was V for *vrijheid* (freedom); Frenchmen modified it to V for *victoire.* Whatever the translation, a hastily scrawled V meant one thing in occupied Europe: the indomitability of the human spirit.

breaks diplomatic ties with Britain ... August: Battle of Britain; Italy invades British Somaliland; Soviets annex Baltics ... September: Japan enters Indochina and signs Tripartite (Axis) Pact ... October: Italy invades Greece ... November: Germany bombs Coventry; Hungary and Romania join Axis ... December: Greeks enter Albania; British rout Italians in Egypt, enter Libya.

"We live here and they live there. We black and they white. They got things and we ain't. They do things and we can't. It's just like living in jail."—**Richard Wright, *Native Son***

AROUND THE WORLD

▶DECLARATION OF HAVANA—With France and the Netherlands under Nazi occupation and Britain threatened, there was fear that Germany might inherit those countries' colonies in the Western Hemisphere. In July, at a U.S.-sponsored meeting of the Pan-American Union in Havana, officials of the region's 21 republics took a strong anti-German stand. Any such colony would come under inter-American trusteeship until it was ready for independence—or could be returned to its original owner. ◂1933.4 ▸1941.9

▶THE 14TH BODHISATTVA—Five-year-old Bstandzin rgyamtsho, was enthroned in 1940 as the 14th Dalai Lama, the

physical manifestation of Bodhisattva Avalokitesvara (the compassionate Buddha-to-be), and the spiritual and secular ruler of Tibet. He was named king ten years later when the Chinese Communists occupied the country. After an aborted revolt against the regime in 1959, he fled to Dharmsala, India, where his government-in-exile campaigned ceaselessly for his country's independence. ▸1950.3

▶TROTSKY ASSASSINATED—After years of hounding his onetime comrade across the globe, Joseph Stalin finally succeeded in his drive to become as the sole voice of Soviet communism. On August 20, Leon Trotsky, in exile in Coyoacán, Mexico, was stabbed with an ice pick by his "friend" Frank Jackson (a.k.a. Ramón Mercader), a Soviet secret-service agent. The last contender for Lenin's mantle and a living alternative to Soviet communism, Trotsky, through his Fourth International movement, advocated worldwide "permanent revolution." The U.S.S.R. denied any involvement in the murder, and Mercader received 20 years, the maximum jail sentence in Mexico. He settled in the U.S.S.R. after his release. ◂1938.M

Osaka schoolboys, newly arrived in Shanghai for service with the Japanese army.

WORLD WAR II

Japan's War Machine

16 The Japanese government earmarked 50 percent of a record budget for military spending in 1940, and took over management of private industry for the war effort. Prompted in part by the unexpectedly prolonged campaign in China, the government also tightened wage and price controls, conscripted workers for compulsory war production, and began rationing food and other supplies. For civilians, such basic products as rice, soy sauce, and cloth became increasingly scarce.

Japan depended largely on U.S. imports to supply its war machine, but American leaders were moving toward cutting off the flow. In January, Washington allowed its 1911 trade agreement with Tokyo to lapse; trade continued even without a treaty, however, partly because some U.S. officials feared an embargo would push Japan into invading Southeast Asia. In fact, Japanese strategists saw economic salvation in that region, where the oil- and rubber-rich colonies of Great Britain, France, and the Netherlands lay unprotected, as their colonial masters were distracted by the war in Europe. In September, Japan extorted several bases in French Indochina (Vietnam) from France's weak Vichy government. (Japan also signed the Tripartite Pact, formalizing its alliance with Germany and Italy.) And the following July—despite strengthened U.S. trade sanctions—the Japanese won concessions for French bases farther south, obviously intending to occupy all Indochina.

The United States, still technically neutral, responded in 1941 by freezing Japanese assets in America and embargoing its oil exports to the island nation. Desperate for raw materials and emboldened by a nonaggression pact with the Soviet Union (the 1941 Neutrality Act), Japan forged ahead in Southeast Asia and prepared to go to war against the United States. **◂1940.15 ▸1941.1**

LITERATURE

Greene's Glory

17 Most major modern novelists have grappled with the question of how humans can behave morally without religion. For

British author Graham Greene, the question was reversed: How can one serve God in an immoral world? *The Power and the Glory*, published in 1940, was his first work to make faith its paramount theme.

For ten years, Greene, though an ardent convert to Catholicism, had churned out secular novels—mostly movie-ready thrillers like *A Gun for Sale* and *Stamboul Train*. But this new book (widely regarded as the greatest in his six-decade career) was a *theological* thriller. Greene's antihero is a fugitive priest in anticlerical Mexico, pursued by a ruthlessly idealistic revolutionary. A boozer and a lecher, he nonetheless becomes a kind of saint when he throws away his life to give last rites to a dying gangster.

The Power and the Glory sold poorly at first, but attracted a huge international readership after the war. Greene subsequently wrote a string of "Catholic novels" (as critics called them). But even in such later works as *The Comedians* and *The Quiet American*, which barely mention religion, notions of sin and sacrifice remain central. Setting his stories in trouble spots from Haiti to Vietnam, Greene found goodness in humanity's selfless servers—sometimes including communists—and evil in the self-serving. **◂1928.8 ▸1942.M**

LITERATURE

America's Native Son

18 The most spectacular U.S. bestseller in 1940 was written by a black Communist named Richard Wright. *Native Son* is the saga of Bigger Thomas, a young African-American who accidentally suffocates his white employer's daughter, murders his own girlfriend as the police close in, and achieves a kind of self-discovery on death row.

Part Dostoyevskian exploration of guilt and despair, part polemic on race and class relations, and part melodrama, the novel probed the most painful areas of the nation's psyche—and deeply influenced a generation of American writers.

Wright, 32, had migrated to Chicago from the rural South, working menial jobs until the Federal Writers' Project (a Depression-era employment program) gave him his start as an author. His first book, *Uncle Tom's Children*, was a collection of tragic novellas that readers (he later wrote) could "weep over and feel good." He intended *Native Son*—whose protagonist acts out an alienation and rage long familiar to American blacks, but hitherto undisclosed to most whites—to be "so hard and deep" as to deny its audience "the consolation of tears."

The story reflects Wright's Marxism: Ignorance makes Bigger a murderer, but a pair of white Communists later help him see how oppression has molded his life. Yet the Party found ideological errors in *Native Son*, and Wright resigned his membership in 1944. After publishing another bestseller, the autobiographical *Black Boy*, he moved to Paris—where there was more freedom in one square block, he said, than in the whole United States. **◂1921.9 ▸1952.8**

NOBEL PRIZES: No awards given.

A VOICE FROM 1940

This Is London

Edward R. Murrow, for CBS News Radio, December 24, 1940

For broadcast journalists, Edward R. Murrow represents the gold standard. His sonorous, cultivated voice and highly literate style first became familiar to Americans over the CBS World News Roundup, which carried live his nightly dispatches from war-torn Europe. From the Anschluss *in 1938 until war's end, Murrow covered the struggle with unremitting accuracy and detail—as well as personal heroism, broadcasting his reports from the exposed roof of BBC's London headquarters as bombs exploded around him. Murrow's reports (introduced with his dramatic catchphrase "This is London") were the first to bring the Battle of Britain directly into Americans' living rooms. (Later, he flew in Allied bombing raids, accompanied minesweepers, and reported firsthand the horrors of Buchenwald.) In the days before television news, Murrow used carefully crafted word pictures—he polished and repolished his scripts—to capture for radio listeners the sights, sounds, and feel of a country under siege.*

In this Christmas Eve 1940 broadcast, Murrow salutes the quiet endurance of a people shaken to their core by months of the German Blitz. **◄1940.11 ►1956.5**

This is London, reporting all clear. There was a single German aircraft over East Anglia this afternoon, but there are no reports of German raiders over Britain tonight. Whether this inactivity is due to good will or bad weather, I don't know, nor do we know whether the RAF bombers are flying tonight. Christmas Day began in London nearly an hour ago. The church bells did not ring at midnight. When they ring again, it will be to announce invasion. And if they ring, the British are ready. Tonight, as on every other night, the rooftop watchers are peering out across the fantastic forest of London's chimney pots. The anti-aircraft gunners stand ready. And all along the coast of this island, the observers revolve in their reclining chairs, listening for the sound of German planes. The fire fighters and the ambulance drivers are waiting, too. The blackout stretches from Birmingham to Bethlehem, but tonight over Britain the skies are clear.

This is not a merry Christmas in London. I heard that phrase only twice in the last three days. This afternoon as the stores were closing, as shoppers and office workers were hurrying home, one heard such phrases as "So long, Mamie," and "Good luck, Jack," but never "A merry Christmas." It can't be a merry Christmas, for those people who spend tonight and tomorrow by their firesides in their own homes realize that they have bought this Christmas with their nerves, their bodies, and their old buildings. Their nerve is unshaken; the casualties have not been large, and there are many old buildings still untouched. Between now and next Christmas there stretches twelve months of increasing toil and sacrifice, a period when the Britishers will live hard. Most of them realize that. Tonight's serious Christmas Eve is the result of a realization of the future, rather than the aftermath of hardships sustained during the past year. The British find some basis for confidence in the last few months' developments. They believe that they're tearing the Italian Empire to pieces. So far shelter life has produced none of the predicted epidemics. The nation's health is about as good now as it was at this time last year. And above all they're sustained by a tradition of victory.

Tonight there are few Christmas parties in London, a few expensive dinners at famous hotels, but there are no fancy paper hats and no firecrackers. Groups determined to get away from the war found themselves after 20 minutes inspecting the latest amateur diagram of the submarine menace or the night bombers. A few blocks away in the underground shelters entire families were celebrating Christmas Eve. Christmas carols are being sung underground. Most of the people down there don't know that London is not being bombed tonight. Christmas presents will be unwrapped down underground before those people see daylight tomorrow. Little boys who have received miniature Spitfires or Hurricanes will be waking the late sleepers by imitating the sound of a locomotive or a speeding automobile.

So far as tonight's news is concerned, we're told that Herr Hess, Hitler's deputy, has offered a prayer, and has asked God to assist Hitler to fight and to work for our eternal wonderful Germany, so that Germany shall continue to be worthy of God's blessings. We are told, too, that on the occasion of Christmas the King of Italy has sent a message to his fighting forces in which he says that his grateful thoughts are with them—no obstacles can stop the glorious ascent of Italy. King Victor Emmanuel is confident of a radiant future.

I should like to add my small voice to give my own Christmas greeting to friends and colleagues at home. Merry Christmas is somehow ill-timed and out of place, so I shall just use the current London phrase—so long, and good luck.

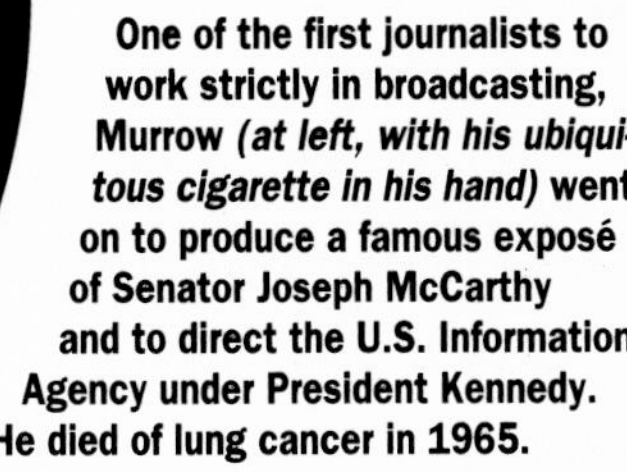

One of the first journalists to work strictly in broadcasting, Murrow *(at left, with his ubiquitous cigarette in his hand)* went on to produce a famous exposé of Senator Joseph McCarthy and to direct the U.S. Information Agency under President Kennedy. He died of lung cancer in 1965.

"We will not only defend ourselves to the uttermost but will make it very certain that this form of treachery shall never again endanger us." **—Franklin D. Roosevelt, in his December 8, 1941, address asking Congress to declare war on Japan**

STORY OF THE YEAR

Surprise Attack on Pearl Harbor

1 "Yesterday," Franklin D. Roosevelt informed Congress, "December 7, 1941—a date which will live in infamy—the United States was suddenly and deliberately attacked by naval and air forces of the Empire of Japan." Undertaken without an announcement of hostilities, the devastating raid on Pearl Harbor shocked America, prompting even longtime isolationists to endorse retaliation. Congress swiftly declared war on Japan. "No matter how long it may take us to overcome this premeditated invasion," the President said, "the American people in their righteous might will win through to absolute victory."

The surprise attack on the U.S. Pacific Fleet, masterminded by Japanese admiral Isoroku Yamamoto, was ruinously effective: four battleships sunk, four more disabled; eleven other ships sunk or critically damaged; 188 aircraft destroyed on the ground at Hickham Field; 2,330 servicemen and 100 civilians killed. The fleet's three aircraft carriers, however, were at sea and escaped harm. American defenders, scrambling into position on the suddenly unquiet Sunday morning, shot down 29 Japanese planes, inflicting 64 fatalities.

Simultaneously with the preemptive raid on Pearl Harbor, the Japanese struck the British in Malaya and Hong Kong, and American installations on the Philippine Islands, Guam, Midway, and Wake Island. By December 8, the Pacific belonged to Japan. Both Yamamoto and Premier Hideki Tojo believed the war essentially over: Britain and the United States, soft democracies, could not resist Japanese military will. Hitler, for one, agreed. "Now it is impossible for us to lose the war," he confided to an adviser. "We now have an ally who has not been vanquished in 3,000 years." On December 11, the Führer rashly declared war on the United States—until then still neutral in Europe, thus ensuring the eventual defeat of the Axis. Italy followed suit. The United States reciprocated. Britain, meanwhile, formally announced war against Japan. With the United States finally joined in battle, the Allied picture dramatically brightened. It "makes amends for all," said a relieved Winston Churchill, "and with time and patience will give certain victory." Certain, but not immediate. For the rest of the bloody winter, Japan swept through the Pacific, vanquishing all foes. ◂1940.16 ▸1942.1

Upon hearing the clicked command "Tora! Tora! Tora!" Japanese pilots swept down on the U.S. naval base of Pearl Harbor, Hawaii, on the morning of December 7. Here, the destroyer *Shaw* exploding in dry dock.

The "Desert Fox," Erwin Rommel, German commander of the African campaign.

WORLD WAR II

Action in Africa

2 Italy's African disaster deepened in 1941—until an audacious German tank commander came to the rescue. By the end of January, the British had chased Mussolini's men halfway across Libya. Meanwhile, Ethiopian emperor Haile Selassie had returned from exile with two battalions of his countrymen (and a British guerrilla specialist, Major-General Orde Wingate) to foment an uprising. British troops—including Sudanese archers with incendiary arrows—converged on Ethiopia, seizing Italian Somaliland and Eritrea on the way. The Italians offered little resistance, and on May 5, exactly five years after his departure, the Emperor was back in Addis Ababa.

In February, however, General Erwin Rommel stepped ashore in western Libya. Rommel had led the fearsome 7th Panzer Division in the invasion of France. He was to command two mechanized divisions in North Africa, with orders to hold the line against the British. But Rommel had bigger plans for his Afrika Korps. Though his forces were far outnumbered (a fact he concealed from spy planes by building wooden tanks), he launched a surprise offensive.

By March 31, Rommel's 50 panzers had driven the British back 100 miles, to Mersa Bréga. Three days later, ignoring orders to halt, he resumed his drive—now backed by two Italian divisions. By mid-April, all of Libya except Tobruk had been retaken. The fortified port's Australian defenders withstood three attacks and a long

ART & CULTURE: **Books:** ***The Last Tycoon*** **(F. Scott Fitzgerald);** ***Berlin Diary*** **(William Shirer);** ***Mythology*** **(Edith Hamilton);** ***The Quest*** **(W.H. Auden) ... Music: "Deep In the Heart of Texas" (Swander and Hershey); "Take the A Train" (Billy Strayhorn); "Chattanooga Choo-Choo" (Warren and Gordon);** ***Defense of Corinth*** **(Elliott Carter) ... Painting & Sculpture:** ***Shipbuilding in the Clyde*** **(Stanley Spencer);** ***New York Under***

"Rommel! Rommel! Rommel! What else matters but beating him?"—**Winston Churchill, on General Erwin Rommel's arrival in Libya**

siege. In November, Allied forces counterattacked, driving Rommel back across eastern Libya. But the "Desert Fox" returned in 1942, seizing Tobruk en route to Egypt. **◂1940.2 ▸1942.8**

WORLD WAR II

Allies Control Middle East

3 While Axis and Allied forces struggled inconclusively over North Africa, three other Arab countries fell into Allied hands in 1941.

In April, former Iraqi premier Rashid Ali al-Gaylani *(left)* staged a pro-German coup against the pro-British regent, Prince Abd al-Ilah. The British, claiming their right to move troops across Iraq under a 1930 treaty, landed soldiers at Basra; in response, Rashid Ali had his men surround the British air base at Habbaniyah, 50 miles west of Baghdad. The British there opened fire, fought their way out, and marched on the capital. On May 30, Rashid Ali and his supporters fled to Iran. Abd al-Ilah returned to power, and British troops stayed on to keep him there.

The Germans had sent military supplies to Rashid Ali via the French mandate of Syria, whose high commissioner, General H.F. Dentz, was a Vichy appointee. The matériel reached Iraq too late to be of use, but the Allies worried that Syria and Lebanon (also under Vichy administration) would soon wind up completely under Axis control. In June, Free French forces invaded both countries, with British, Australian, and Indian support. Lebanon fell after a month of fierce combat. Dentz's troops resisted for another week, surrendering on July 14—Bastille Day. **◂1925.10**

WORLD WAR II

Axis Takes Balkans, Greece

4 Africa was not the only place where Hitler had to pick up after Mussolini in 1941. Italian forces had botched an invasion of Greece the year before, and in April the Germans seized that country—along with Yugoslavia.

Hitler began preparing for the Greek campaign in November 1940. Roping Hungary and Romania into the Axis, he secured permission for his troops to cross their borders en route to Bulgaria, the staging area for the invasion. Bulgaria's King Boris III, however, put off promising his cooperation until March 1941, when Turkey (a wavering Allied power) rescinded its threat to interfere. Next, Yugoslavia's regent, Prince Paul, reluctantly added his country to the Axis ranks. But his acquiescence sparked a military coup. Nominally led by 17-year-old King Peter II, the new regime defied Hitler; by the time it backed down, the raging Führer had decided to invade Yugoslavia, too. Despondent over the looming bloodbath, Hungarian premier Pál Teleki—who had recently signed a treaty of "eternal friendship" with Yugoslavia—killed himself.

The twin invasions began on April 6. Yugoslavia fell within two weeks. Soon after, despite the efforts of 50,000 British troops, the swastika flag flew atop the Acropolis in Athens. By mid-May, all Greece except the island of Crete was in German or Italian hands. German paratroopers hit Crete on May 20, and in a twelve-day struggle ousted the last British defenders.

Yugoslavia was dismembered: Serbia, Croatia, and Montenegro became "independent" puppet republics. The rest was divvied up among its conquerors and neighbors. Then a smoldering civil war began. Croatia's Ustashi (fascist) rulers massacred the minority Serbs. Serbian nationalist resistance fighters, the Chetniks, sometimes butchered Croat and Muslim civilians. Multiethnic partisans under Communist leader Josip Broz Tito clashed with Ustashis, Chetniks, and occupiers. By the end of the war, Yugoslavia would be Tito's. **◂1940.2 ▸1943.9**

Germans post anti-aircraft guns at the Acropolis in Athens, Greece.

WORLD WAR II

U.S. Policy: Aid Short of War

5 Before Pearl Harbor, the key phrase in U.S. policy toward the Allies was "aid short of war." In March 1941, Congress stepped up that aid by passing the Lend-Lease Act, empowering the President to lend matériel without insisting on cash up-front or a payment schedule. Lend-Lease, Roosevelt proclaimed, would make America the "arsenal of democracy." (It would also revive American industrial production, ending the Depression.)

In the following weeks, Roosevelt ordered the seizure of Axis vessels in U.S. harbors, opened ports to British warships, and authorized the Navy to attack U-boats west of 25 degrees longitude. After declaring a national emergency in May, he froze Axis assets and closed Axis consulates. U.S. Marines occupied Greenland in April and Iceland in July to keep Germany from doing so.

With Lend-Lease, Roosevelt endeared himself to European allies and helped end America's economic Depression.

Roosevelt vowed he would try to keep America out of the fighting. But in August, on a ship off Newfoundland, he and Churchill signed the Atlantic Charter—a "peace" pact demanding self-determination for all peoples, and promising "final destruction of the Nazi tyranny." **◂1940.13 ▸1942.7**

BIRTHS

Paul Anka, Canadian singer.

Joan Baez, U.S. musician.

Stokely Carmichael, Trinidadian-U.S. political activist.

Graham Chapman, U.K. actor.

Chick Corea, U.S. musician.

Placido Domingo, Spanish singer.

Bob Dylan, U.S. musician.

Stephen Jay Gould, U.S. paleontologist.

Jesse Jackson, U.S. civil-rights leader.

Bruce Lee, Chinese-U.S. actor.

Wilson Pickett, U.S. singer.

Pete Rose, U.S. baseball player.

Vivienne Westwood, U.K. fashion designer.

George Will, U.S. journalist.

DEATHS

Alfonso XIII, Spanish king.

Sherwood Anderson, U.S. writer.

Isaac Babel, Russian writer.

Robert Baden-Powell, U.K. founder of the Boy Scouts.

Frederick Banting, Canadian physician.

Henri Bergson, French philosopher.

Gutzon Borglum, U.S. sculptor.

Louis D. Brandeis, U.S. jurist.

Arthur Evans, U.K. archaeologist.

Lou Gehrig, U.S. baseball player.

Simon Guggenheim, U.S. industrialist and philanthropist.

James Joyce, Irish writer.

Jelly Roll Morton, U.S. musician and composer.

Ignace Paderewski, Polish musician and statesman.

Rabindranath Tagore, Indian poet.

Marina Tsvetayeva, Russian poet.

Wilhelm II, German emperor.

Virginia Woolf, U.K. writer.

Gaslight **(Stuart Davis) ... Film: *How Green Was My Valley* (John Ford); *The Little Foxes* (William Wyler); *The Maltese Falcon* (John Huston); *Listen to Britain* (Humphrey Jennings) ... Theater: *Blithe Spirit* (Noël Coward); *Arsenic and Old Lace* (Joseph Kesselring); *Watch on the Rhine* (Lillian Hellman); *Clash by Night* (Clifford Odets); *Lady in the Dark* (Weill, I. Gershwin, and M. Hart) ... Radio: *The Red Skelton Show*.**

"You have only to kick in the door, and the whole rotten structure will come crashing down."—**Adolf Hitler, right before the beginning of Operation Barbarossa**

NEW IN 1941

Silver-zinc battery.

The National Gallery of Art (Washington, D.C.).

Aerosol insect spray.

Cheerios.

Wonder Woman.

IN THE UNITED STATES

▶FROMM'S ESCAPE—In his 1941 book, *Escape from Freedom*, philosopher-psychologist Erich Fromm (himself a refugee from Nazi Germany) applied the tenets of psychoanalysis to society at large. His conclusion: Modern industrial society often fails to satisfy a basic human need for unity and security; as a result, individuals seek relief from alienation in authoritarianism. Fromm confounded orthodox Freudians by arguing that social needs influence individual psychological development as much as biological drives and mental processes. ▸1943.12

▶UAW TRIUMPHS—The violently anti-union Henry Ford—of the Big Three carmakers, the last holdout against organized labor—knuckled under in 1941, signing a contract with the United Automobile Workers. Coming after a short strike, the agreement covered 130,00 employees. ◂1936.M

▶GARBO WALKS—Greta Garbo probably never intended to retire for good, but that's what happened after she received universally poor reviews for her performance in the 1941 film comedy *Two-Faced Woman*. (Audiences did not respond to MGM's attempts to Americanize their Swedish Sphinx.) Garbo's already-sliding career slid even further. She announced her retirement, and despite perennial rumors of a comeback, never appeared onscreen again. ◂1930.8

WORLD WAR II

Cracking the Enigma

6 The Allied defeat on Crete in 1941 illustrated a basic principle of warfare: Military intelligence is worthless if you can't use it.

Thanks to an amazing feat of code-breaking, the Allies knew of German plans to launch against the island history's first all-airborne attack. But to be forewarned is not always to be forearmed.

The Nazis possessed what they believed to be an unbeatable coding system: the Enigma machine *(above)*. The device's revolving drums could scramble the alphabet in trillions of combinations, generating a gibberish translatable only by another Enigma using the proper setting. But the Germans didn't know that Polish cryptanalysts, who'd long studied the Enigma, had shared their insights with the Allies, or that the British had obtained a copy of the machine. Nor were they aware of the Ultra decoding project, which at its peak would employ 10,000 people.

Set up in 1939 by Britain's secret service, MI-6, Ultra hired top chess players and other masters of logic to design decrypting machines. (One team, headed by mathematician Alan Turing, developed one of the first electronic digital computers, the Colossus.) Ultra's intelligence was crucial in the Battle of Britain, the Dunkirk evacuation, and the Normandy landing. On Crete, however, the Allies simply lacked the troops and matériel to translate knowledge into victory. **◂1937.11 ▸1944.M**

WORLD WAR II

Soviets, Allies Reconcile

7 In May 1941, when Hitler aide Rudolf Hess crash-landed in Scotland on a self-appointed peace mission, Soviet-Allied relations—abysmal since the Soviet-Nazi partition of Poland—reached a new low. Although the German government declared Hess insane and the British imprisoned him, Stalin was certain that Britain and Germany were plotting against him. (He'd long suspected Britain of wanting to goad the Soviet Union into a suicidal war with Germany.) In June, when Churchill and Roosevelt sent him intelligence reports of Hitler's impending assault on Russia, Stalin assumed they were lying. But when the attack came, a momentous realignment began.

The British and Soviets promptly promised that neither would make a separate peace with Germany. In August, British-Indian and Soviet forces jointly invaded neutral Iran to keep its ports and oil fields out of German hands—crushing the Iranian army in four days, replacing the Shah, and dividing the country into occupation zones. And in September, British and American representatives traveled to Moscow to draw up a list of supplies to be shipped to the Soviets monthly.

Formerly reviled as chief agent of the Red Menace, Stalin was soon referred to in the English-speaking world as Uncle Joe; once blasted as imperialists, Roosevelt and Churchill were now portrayed by Soviet propaganda as antifascist comrades. But his allies' refusal to recognize Soviet claims on Eastern Europe angered Stalin, as did their failure (until 1944) to open a "second front" in France to take the heat off Russia. The mutual mistrust never quite dissolved. **◂1939.3 ▸1941.8**

WORLD WAR II

Operation Barbarossa

8 With Greece and Yugoslavia out of the way, Hitler turned to the goal that had obsessed him since the 1920s: the conquest of Russia. Although he'd intended to wait until the British were beaten, his fear that Stalin would strike first overcame his patience. The largest invasion force in history—three million Germans, backed by 200,000 Axis troops—attacked the Soviet Union along a 1,800-mile front on June 22, 1941.

Operation Barbarossa, the greatest land battle in history. By December, the German army had nearly reached Moscow.

The Soviet army was the world's largest, with four million active troops and three million reserves,

A momentous realignment: Hitler's invasion made bedfellows of Britain and the U.S.S.R.

SPORTS: Baseball: World Series, New York Yankees defeat Brooklyn Dodgers (dropped third strike), 4–1; Brooklyn hitters start wearing batting helmets ... Football: NFL, Chicago Bears defeat New York Giants, 37–9; Elmer Layden appointed first NFL commissioner ... Golf: Masters and U.S. Open won by Craig Wood (last Open until 1946) ... Horse Racing: Whirlaway, ridden by Eddie Arcaro, wins Triple Crown.

"Nothing can be permitted to interfere with this sphere, because this sphere was decreed by Providence."
—Japanese premier Hideki Tojo, on the anniversary of Japan's declaration of a "New Order" in East Asia, November 30, 1941

but it had dire shortcomings. Soviet aircraft were mostly obsolete. Stalin's purge of officers in 1937–38 had decimated the military leadership. And despite Allied warnings, the dictator had failed to mobilize his forces. Judging from the Soviets' recent bumbling in Finland, Hitler expected Operation Barbarossa (the invasion's code name) to take two months. In fact, within just three weeks, Axis troops advanced 400 miles and seized several cities.

But the Soviets resisted with unexpected tenacity. Unlike previous blitzkrieg victims, Soviet soldiers seldom ran away, and if they did, reinforcements appeared quickly. Smolensk fell only after seriously retarding the invasion's momentum. Peasants burned their homes and crops to keep them from the enemy. Workers dismantled whole factories, shipping them east for reassembly. Nature resisted, too: In mid-July, rains made dirt roads impassable. Then Hitler and his generals lost time arguing over strategy.

Still, the incompetence of many Soviet commanders—and Stalin's interference with competent ones—allowed the Germans to kill, wound, or capture half the Red Army by year's end. The invaders often shot prisoners; starvation claimed many more. Suspected partisans were hanged in the streets of occupied towns, and able-bodied civilians sent to slave-labor camps. The first mass murders of Jews started during the summer, as special squads gunned down hundreds of men, women, and children at a time.

The atrocities (and a strangling siege of Leningrad, begun in September) only made the Soviets fight harder. Then a new ally appeared: the earliest, harshest winter in decades. Snow and subzero temperatures stalled German vehicles; frostbite hobbled the lightly clad soldiers. In December, as the invaders neared bomb-racked Moscow, the Russians counterattacked. Used to the cold and dressed for it, they began to push the Germans back. **◂1940.12 ▸1942.11**

A sign in Chile (governed by leftists) warned of Nazism, "the most violent poison."

WORLD WAR II
Latin America and the Allies

9 Once the United States joined the war, keeping Latin America out of the Nazi orbit became more crucial than ever for the Allies. Fortunately, Roosevelt's Good Neighbor Policy had overcome much of the animosity generated by decades of U.S. meddling. Mexico severed relations with the Axis on December 8, 1941, the day after Pearl Harbor, and declared war six months later after several of its merchant ships were sunk. Brazil's quasifascist regime followed suit, in exchange for arms and development aid. (Such aid programs originated during this period.) Both countries eventually sent troops overseas.

Bolivia made a deal similar to Brazil's, and broke with the Axis in January 1942. But a coup in December 1943, backed by the Movimiento Nacionalista Revolucionario, threw its status into doubt. To curb the MNR's influence, British agents had earlier fabricated evidence that the nationalist group—which opposed immigration of Jewish refugees on economic grounds—was a Nazi front. The new president, Major Gualberto Villaroel, offered to aid the Allies, but the United States refused to recognize his government unless he purged it of MNR members. He did so in June 1944. (Humiliated by the concession, Villaroel was overthrown and killed in 1946.)

Eventually, every Latin American nation joined the Allies, though Argentina, Uruguay, Paraguay, and Venezuela waited to declare war until 1945, when it was clear the fighting was nearly over. But after the war, Nazi refugees flocked to several of those countries whose regimes closely resembled those of the defeated Axis powers. **◂1940.M**

WORLD WAR II
Tojo Takes Charge

10 General Hideki Tojo, minister of war and former commander of the Japanese army in China, replaced Prince Fumimaro Konoe as Japan's premier on October 16, 1941. Tojo immediately threw down the gauntlet to the United States. Japanese expansionist policies in Southeast Asia, he declared, were "immutable and irrevocable." Japan would remain in Indochina (where it menaced the oil reserves of the Dutch East Indies) until the United States released the Japanese assets it had frozen, guaranteed oil shipments to Japan, and stopped aiding China. Moreover, China had to surrender. From the U.S. perspective, Tojo's rigid demands amounted to a declaration of war. (In fact, he had already begun preparing the attack on Pearl Harbor.)

A dedicated militarist, Tojo had advocated the reorganization of the army and the conquest of Manchuria in the 1930s. His ultimate design was a "total war economy": the seamless integration of Japanese industrial and military might. Under the less strident Konoe, Japan had wavered, unwilling to challenge American power. All vacillation ended with Tojo. "We must develop in an ever-expanding progression," he said after becoming premier. "There is no retreat." **◂1941.1 ▸1942.1**

IN THE UNITED STATES

▶A RECORD YEAR—Joe DiMaggio and Ted Williams turned the 1941 baseball season into one long batting exhibition. The Yankees' Joltin' Joe hit safely in 56 consecutive games—a streak unlikely ever to be duplicated; Williams, the Splendid Splinter of the Red Sox competed in the streak but lasted only 23 games. He

finished the year batting .406, becoming the last major-league player to reach the vaunted .400 mark for a season. ◂1939.V ▸1951.M

▶MONUMENTAL MOUNTAIN—With the opening of Mount Rushmore National Memorial in 1941, tourists flocked to South

Dakota to see the 50- to 70-foot visages of Washington, Jefferson, Lincoln, and Theodore Roosevelt gazing out, from a height of 500 feet, over the Black Hills. Idaho sculptor Gutzon Borglum's monumental chiseling effort, commissioned by the state of South Dakota in 1927, was accomplished with modern engineering tools, dynamite, and pneumatic hammers. Borglum died just months shy of completing his masterpiece. It was finished by his son Lincoln.

▶EQUAL JOB RIGHTS—Noting that American blacks were fighting for oppressed people abroad while remaining legally oppressed at home, labor and civil rights leader A. Philip Randolph in 1941 organized a march on Washington. Randolph, founder of the Brotherhood of Sleeping Car Porters, threatened to deliver 50,000 protesters unless war industry job discrimination ended. FDR, urged on by his activist wife, Eleanor Roosevelt, ordered defense plants integrated, and on June 25 he established the Fair Employment Practices Committee to oversee color-blind hiring efforts. ▸1948.V

POLITICS & BUSINESS: GNP: $124.5 billion ... Offices of Production Management and Price Administration established ... State of unlimited national emergency declared (German and Italian funds frozen) ... Supreme Court upholds Federal Wage and Hour Law ... Roosevelt creates Office of Scientific Research (Vannevar Bush appointed director) ... U.S. Treasury issues war bonds.

"There, but for the grace of God, goes God."—**Herman Mankiewicz, co-writer of the screenplay for *Citizen Kane,* on Orson Welles**

WORLD WAR II

▶BATTLE OF CAPE MATAPAN—In March, when the attacking British hove into view at Cape Matapan, off the southern tip of Greece, the Italian navy was dead in the water. Having intercepted Italian radio signals, the British fleet in the Aegean knew exactly where the main Italian force was located. With this surprise victory—in which Italy lost five cruisers, three destroyers, and 2,400 sailors—Britain eliminated Italy as a power in the Aegean and Adriatic seas.

▶PARACHUTE DROP—In a crushing display of air superiority, Germany attacked the island of Crete in May, wiping out two British air bases and routing the combined British, Australian, Greek, and New Zealand troops. The war's first completely airborne invasion, the Cretan initiative was a mixed success for Germany: Its paratroopers helped drive the Allies from the island, but half of them were killed or injured in the effort.

▶*BISMARCK* SINKS—The heaviest vessel afloat on any sea, the 42,000-ton battleship *Bismarck* was the pride of Germany. In May 1941, after British fliers spotted the floating fortress cruising in the Denmark Strait, the Royal Navy went after her with guns blazing. Surrounded, the *Bismarck* returned fire and sank the battle cruiser *Hood.* But after being pounded by three torpedo-bearing British battleships for two days, the *Bismarck*—crippled and aflame—went down on the

FILM

A Cinematic Masterpiece

11 Radio and stage wunderkind Orson Welles was still a film novice when RKO brought him to Hollywood with a contract guaranteeing unprecedented artistic freedom. Delighted with the resources of a major studio—"This is the biggest electric train set a boy ever had!"—the 25-year-old director promptly shattered commercial cinema's unwritten rules. When Welles's *Citizen Kane* premiered in 1941, reviewers were dazzled by its fractured narrative structure; spectacular time leaps between scenes; dramatically high and low camera angles; shots with action in the foreground, middle ground, and background; and Bernard Herrmann's dense musical score which complemented and commented on the action. *The New York Times* raved that it came "close to being the most sensational film ever made in Hollywood." Novelist John O'Hara, writing in *Newsweek*, called it "the best movie I ever saw."

But if Welles's style was *Citizen Kane*'s glory, the movie's antihero was almost its downfall. The film, co-written by Welles and Herman J. Mankiewicz, chronicles the rise and fall of fictional newspaper tycoon Charles Foster Kane, largely modeled on media baron William Randolph Hearst (and played by Welles himself). The plot is set in motion by reporters' attempts to find out the meaning of Kane's dying word, "Rosebud"—a gimmick that Welles dismissed as "dollar-book Freud." (Reporters give up, but the audience is privy to a scene that reveals Rosebud to have been Kane's childhood sled.) When Hearst's minions got wind of the production, they threatened Hollywood with newspaper exposés of movie-colony scandals. MGM chief Louis B. Mayer offered to buy the film from RKO and destroy it; most major theater circuits refused to exhibit it. But RKO stood firm.

Citizen Kane lost money (at least initially), but it has since been almost universally designated a masterpiece, the most influential American movie since *The Birth of a Nation*. "This film," observed French director François Truffaut, "has inspired more vocations to cinema throughout the world than any other." **◂1938.V ▸1942.M**

In scenes like this one (where Kane is running for governor), cinematographer Gregg Toland's deep-focus camera work enabled Welles to make a point about Kane's true nature.

MUSIC

A City's Symphonic Monument

12 Composer Dmitri Shostakovich was in Leningrad working on his *Seventh Symphony* when the Nazis began bombarding the city in September 1941. Food grew scarce, and many artists were evacuated to safety. But Shostakovich stayed, periodically dashing for the local bomb shelter. Ordered finally to leave for Kuybyshev (now Samara) at the end of December, he completed the symphony on the 27th. He dedicated it to Leningrad, which would remain under siege for another two years.

With its violent mood changes and mammoth first-movement crescendo, the *Leningrad Symphony* (as it became known) became an inspirational symbol of Soviet resistance. With most members of the city's Radio Orchestra dead, the March 5 Leningrad premiere was performed largely by half-starved amateurs and soldier-musicians sent from the front lines. The Moscow premiere, two weeks later, was broadcast globally; it proceeded despite an air raid in mid-program. After the score was smuggled through Axis lines, U.S. airwaves carried the symphony's premiere in New York City.

But Shostakovich's stint as an official hero was brief. He had already been denounced for his avant-gardism and only recently rehabilitated; in 1948 he was vilified again. (Decades later, he wrote that the *Leningrad Symphony* was a protest against Stalinist as well as Nazi injustices.) For years he remained at the mercy of the cruelly capricious regime. Even after 1953, when Stalin died and the death of composer Sergei Prokofiev left him unchallenged as Russia's master composer, Shostakovich was viewed with disapproval. His 1962 *Thirteenth Symphony*—based on "Babi Yar," Yevgeny Yevtushenko's poem about the Nazi massacre of Ukrainian Jews—was suppressed after one performance. Only after Yevtushenko purged the text of references to Soviet complicity was the symphony played again. **◂1936.13 ▸1961.M**

WORLD WAR II: January: British invade Eritrea ... February: British enter Italian Somaliland; Rommel arrives in North Africa ... March: Bulgaria and Yugoslavia join Axis ... April: Rommel repulsed at Tobruk; U.S.S.R. and Japan sign nonaggression pact; Yugoslavia and Greece surrender to Germany; British occupy Iraq ... May: Germany takes Crete from British ... June: Germany invades U.S.S.R. ...

"Competition brings out the best in products and the worst in people."—**David Sarnoff, pioneer of commercial television**

WORLD WAR II

Challenges in China

13 For China, 1941 began with an internecine bloodbath. The alliance between the Nationalists and Communists against Japan had been deteriorating for two years, as Nationalist leader Chiang Kai-shek (encouraged by Nazi agents) began to envision Germany as a future backer of Chinese independence, and fretted over the Communists' territorial gains. The previous October, Nationalist commanders had ordered the Communists to withdraw from the lower Yangtze Valley. In January, as the last units left, the Nationalists ambushed them.

Chiang's forces, ironically, suffered 20,000 casualties to the Communists' 3,000 to 6,000. Full-scale civil war was narrowly averted, but lingering hostility (and internal divisions among the Nationalists) hobbled Chinese efforts to resist the Japanese occupation. While Communist guerrillas continued to harass the invaders and the Nationalists fought a few defensive battles, China remained relatively quiet until 1944.

Curiously, Chiang didn't declare war on Japan until America did so, just after Pearl Harbor. (The day after that attack, 20,000 Japanese invaded the Crown Colony of Hong Kong; its 12,000 British, Indian, Canadian, and Chinese defenders held out for 18 days.) The first

The Flying Tigers in front of a plane bearing the group's distinctive shark motif.

U.S. volunteers had arrived in China earlier in the year—200 ex-military and civilian airmen and technicians known as the Flying Tigers. In battered, antiquated planes, the fliers—led by retired Major General Claire Chennault—inflicted substantial damage on Japanese forces in China and Burma. **◂1940.15 ▸1942.2**

One of RCA-owned NBC's first programs was for and about homemakers.

POPULAR CULTURE

The Television Age Begins

14 Modern commercial television was born on July 1, 1941, when David Sarnoff's National Broadcasting Company (NBC) and William Paley's Columbia Broadcasting System (CBS) each began transmitting 15 hours per week of cartoons, sports, and news from New York City. Sarnoff, with the help of 67 corporate sponsors, had developed 148 programs. "It is our hope," he said "that television will help strengthen the United States as a nation of free people and high ideals." Whether that hope has been realized or betrayed, TV has become central to U.S. culture—and has helped turn the world into a global village.

The first provider of regularly scheduled television programming was Hitler's government in 1935, followed in 1936 by Britain's state-run BBC. In the United States, 22 private experimental stations were operating by 1939, but technical standards varied wildly. Public expectation was stoked that year when RCA—which manufactured radios and early television sets, and owned the NBC network—broadcast live from the New York World's Fair. Also that year, on its experimental New York station, the company aired television's first commercial: sportscaster Red Barber pushing Procter & Gamble soap and Wheaties during a baseball game.

In 1940, RCA tried to force its TV specifications on the industry. Sensitive to a potential RCA/NBC monopoly of the medium, the Federal Communications Commission intervened, delaying commercial broadcasts until all broadcasters reached an agreement. The engineering standards authorized by the FCC—30 frames and 525 lines of resolution per second, FM radio sound—remain in effect. **◂1925.1 ▸1951.9**

THE MIDDLE EAST

A Toppled Shah

15 British and Soviet forces invaded Iran in August 1941, and forced the abdication of Reza Shah Pahlevi, the absolute ruler of the strategically vital country. Nominally neutral, the Shah had strong ties with Germany that the war had made stronger. At home his popularity was at an all-time low. Although the Shah had modernized and introduced needed reforms, his reign was marred by ruthless repression, corruption, and a widening gap between rich and poor. "The vast majority of the people hate the Shah," the British press attaché in Tehran observed. "To such people, even the spread of war to Iran seems preferable to the present regime."

Eager to preempt any attempt by pro-German officers in the Iranian army to oust the Shah and deliver Iran into the Axis camp, the Allies invaded. Fortunately for them, many Iranians perceived them more as rescuers than as usurpers. Reza Shah abdicated and went into exile, and his inexperienced son, 25-year-old Muhammad Reza Shah Pahlevi *(above)*, ascended to the throne. The new shah's reign would also end in exile, prompted by the 1979 revolution. **◂1925.10 ▸1951.12**

WORLD WAR II

morning of May 27. Some 2,300 German sailors drowned.

▶WOLFPACKS—Predators in the Battle of the Atlantic, U-boats hunted in groups, called "wolfpacks." The marauding technique was invented by German admiral Karl Dönitz. Deployed just under the water's surface, U-boats surveyed Allied convoys during the day and then, at night, converged with devastating

effect. In 1941, Germany added more than 200 U-boats to its original fleet of 57.

▶U-BOATS TORPEDO U.S. DESTROYERS—Although officially neutral, the U.S. by October 1941 had added British and French ships to its Atlantic convoys. That month, German U-boats torpedoed two U.S. destroyers, the *Kearny* and the *Reuben James*. The latter vessel sank, with a loss of 100 lives. The American public still supported isolation; Roosevelt did not. The U.S. had become a definite, if undeclared, combatant in the naval war against Germany.

▶MOBILE EXECUTION—The German blitz into Russia ate up 25 miles a day, and behind the marching columns followed a special 3,000-man detachment, the *Einsatzgruppen*—a jackal battalion, whose job was to kill communists, Jews, and other non-Aryan survivors of the invasion. By the end of 1941, the *Einsatzgruppen* had murdered nearly two million of Nazism's special enemies.

▶PRE-PEARL HARBOR—The American destroyer *Ward* made contact with and destroyed a Japanese midget submarine on December 7 just off the coast of Hawaii one hour before the first bomb struck the *Oklahoma* in Pearl Harbor. The *Ward*'s warning message to the fleet was lost as it passed along the chain of command. An Army radar operator's report of enemy planes nearing Pearl Harbor was laughed off by his superior officer, and was not passed on to command headquarters.

July: U.S. occupies Iceland; Free French occupy Lebanon and Syria ... August: Britain and U.S.S.R. invade Iran ... September: Siege of Leningrad begins; Germans take Kiev ... October: Germans take Odessa; Siege of Moscow resumes ... December: Japan bombs Pearl Harbor and takes Thailand, Hong Kong, Guam, and Wake Island; U.S. and Britain declare war on Japan; Germany and Italy declare war on the U.S.

"There hasn't been a successful army band in the country.... Why, there's no question about it—anybody can improve on Sousa."—**Glenn Miller, on becoming leader of the U.S. Army Air Force Band**

AROUND THE WORLD

▶THE COLLAPSE OF CONSCIENCE—"I left communism," the writer and fervent anticommunist Arthur Koestler once wrote, "as one clambers out of a poisoned river strewn with the wreckage of flooded cities and the corpses of the drowned." Koestler's 1941 bestseller, *Darkness at Noon*, tells why. The fictional account of the arrest, interrogation, confession, and subsequent execution of the Russian revolutionary N.S. Rubashov, an aging hero of the 1917 revolution (based mostly on the real-life Nikolai Bukharin), *Darkness at Noon* explores the incompatibility of

ideological allegiance and individual conscience. The book remains one of the century's most powerful indictments of totalitarianism. ◀1938.M

▶NO MORE WRINKLES—John Rex Whinfield, a chemist at Imperial Chemical Industries in England, invented a polyester fiber in 1941 that revolutionized the fashion industry. By combining terephthalic acid and ethylene glycol, Whinfield produced Terylene, which, when woven, knitted, or blended with wool or cotton, produced a fabric that didn't stretch, get eaten by insects, fade, or wrinkle. After the war, Du Pont marketed the material in the U.S. under the trademark Dacron. ◀1934.9

▶PERU INVADES ECUADOR—With Germany and Japan fighting for more territory in Europe and Asia, Peru experienced some irredentist desires of its own. Economically strapped Ecuador could barely maintain a standing army. Peru, exploiting its neighbor's weakness, invaded in July. The U.S., which had bases in Ecuador, was too preoccupied with World War II to intervene. The 1942 Protocol of Rio settled the matter in favor of Peru—a slap in the face for Ecuador and the downfall of its president, Carlos Arroyo del Río.

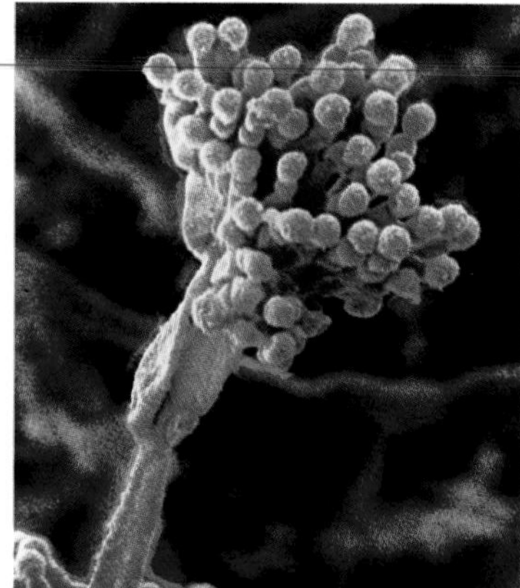

A Penicillium species viewed under an electron microscope.

MEDICINE

Miracle Drug

16 The first medical application of penicillin, the "magic bullet" that would fight the venereal disease epidemic that plagued World War II soldiers, came in 1941—the result of a project that had begun almost accidentally six years earlier. Oxford University bacteriologist Howard Florey had hired a young German-Jewish refugee named Ernst Chain to study the properties of antibacterial substances. Devouring all the available literature, Chain came across Alexander Fleming's original paper on his 1928 discovery of penicillin. Although Fleming had guessed at the substance's curative potential, he'd abandoned his investigation when he could not produce enough penicillin for clinical research.

For three years, the unstable chemical frustrated the Oxford scientist and his colleagues. Then biochemist Norman Heatley devised a way to concentrate penicillin using the new technique of freeze-drying. By 1940, sufficient quantities were available to test on infected mice. Although the researchers knew the drug killed bacteria in a culture dish, they feared it might kill animals, too. Instead, it made them well with astonishing consistency. Exulted Florey: "It looks like a miracle."

In 1941, testing on humans proved penicillin to be the most effective and nontoxic antibiotic known. But wartime Britain lacked the resources for large-scale manufacture, so Florey and Heatley brought their findings to America. The U.S. pharmaceutical industry, in cooperation with the government, ensured that penicillin was with Allied troops when they invaded Normandy. **◀1935.8 ▶1944.17**

POPULAR CULTURE

Show Biz Goes to War

17 American show business began to give its all for the Allies in 1941. With the formation that year of the United Service Organizations (USO), some 4,500 USO troupers began giving morale-boosting performances to soldiers around the world. Within the USO's stellar ranks were Bob Hope, Bing Crosby, the Andrews Sisters, Danny Kaye, Mickey Rooney, Marlene Dietrich, and bandleaders Glenn Miller, Kay Kyser, and Duke Ellington. Broadway impresario Billy Rose staged military-camp shows, too, featuring such luminaries as Al Jolson, Eddie Cantor, Bill "Bojangles" Robinson, George Burns, and Gracie Allen.

In Hollywood, filmmakers worked with government censors to back the war effort with uplifting, if simplistic, characterizations. Onscreen, Americans were virtuous; the British, resolute; the Russians, good-hearted; the Germans, cruel; the "Japs," subhuman; and the French, all active in the Resistance.

Over 29,000 movie people served in the armed forces, including such stars as Clark Gable and Jimmy Stewart. Others, like Groucho Marx, James Cagney, and Judy Garland, sold war bonds. Bette Davis and John Garfield helped open the Hollywood Canteen, a mecca for servicemen. Directors John Huston, John Ford, and William Wyler made combat documentaries; Frank Capra, Walt Disney, and B-movie leading man Ronald Reagan made training films.

Some entertainers gave more: Carole Lombard died in a bond-tour plane crash in 1942, Leslie Howard was killed when his plane was shot down while he was on a spy mission for the British in 1943, and Glenn Miller's aircraft vanished over the English Channel in 1944. **▶1941.18**

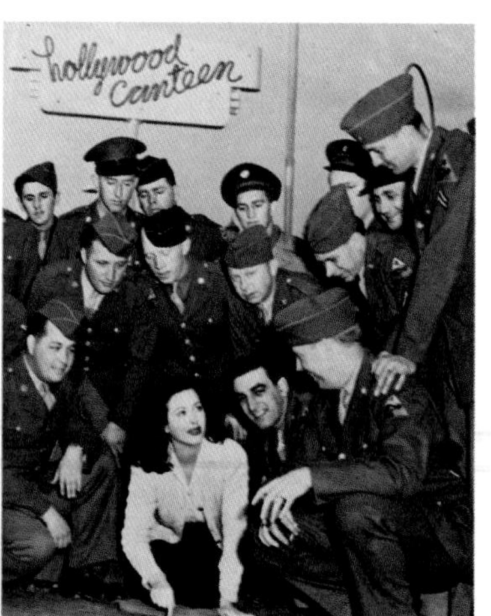

Screen star Hedy Lamarr autographs the cement court of the Hollywood Canteen.

MUSIC

Miller's Million-Seller

18 It was a summer of swing in America, as the big-band craze reached a dizzying peak in 1941. Duke Ellington, the Dorsey brothers, Artie Shaw, Count Basie, Benny Goodman, Jimmie Lunceford, Claude Thornhill, and Harry James crisscrossed the country, playing to jitterbugging audiences, or broadcasting live radio shows from the swanky ballrooms of big hotels. But the nation's number-one band was the Glenn Miller Orchestra. Already enormously popular for its sentimental pop tunes and blaring, breakneck dance numbers, the Miller band went over the top in 1941 with the release of *Sun Valley Serenade*, a movie showcasing the band and featuring a new tune called "Chattanooga Choo-Choo." The song quickly became a million-seller; to show its appreciation, RCA Victor presented Miller with a gold-plated copy of the record.

Glenn Miller on trombone, with Sonja Henie and John Payne in *Sun Valley Serenade*.

What the Miller band played was too regimented to be jazz, but it was jazzy—and eminently danceable. Lighthearted songs like "Moonlight Serenade," "In the Mood," and "Pennsylvania 6-5000" captured the spirit of an America emerging from the Depression and won the ensemble a fanatical following among young, collegiate whites.

In 1942, Miller volunteered to be the leader of the Europe-based U.S. Army Air Force Band. He was flying from London to Paris in 1944 when his plane disappeared from the sky. No remains were ever found. **◀1935.10 ▶1943.16**

NOBEL PRIZES: No awards given.

A VOICE FROM 1941

"Odors Bareness and Space"

From *Let Us Now Praise Famous Men*, by James Agee and Walker Evans, 1941

Commissioned by Fortune *magazine in 1936 to write a series of documentary articles on cotton tenantry in the Deep South, writer James Agee and photographer Walker Evans embarked on a journey that led to a groundbreaking portrait of American poverty. Though Evans described Agee as a young man with "a faint rubbing of Harvard and Exeter," the Tennessee-mountain native was familiar, through relatives, with the "back-country poor life." His immensely moving, often lyrical account of six weeks in the lives of three poverty stricken Alabama sharecropper families—matched in resonance by Evans's famous photographs—reflects Agee's passion to record in prose the sensual, gritty details of every life he encountered. (To Agee, Evans wrote, "human beings were at least possibly immortal and literally sacred souls.")*

Fortune*'s new managing editor rejected the articles, but Agee expanded them into a book, which was published in 1941. Not until 1960, five years after Agee's death, did his masterpiece of empathy* —The New York Herald Tribune *called it "the most famous unknown book in contemporary letters"—gain fame in reprint. Below, a representatively precise and evocative description of a sharecropper's home.*

The Gudgers' house, being young, only eight years old, smells a little dryer and cleaner, and more distinctly of its wood, than an average white tenant house, and it has also a certain odor I have never found in other such houses: aside from these sharp yet slight subtleties, it has the odor or odors which are classical in every thoroughly poor white southern country house, and by which such a house could be identified blindfold in any part of the world among no matter what other odors. It is compacted of many odors and made into one, which is very thin and light on the air, and more subtle than it can seem in analysis, yet very sharply and constantly noticeable. These are its ingredients. The odor of pine lumber, wide thin cards of it, heated in the sun, in no way doubled or insulated, in closed and darkened air. The odor of woodsmoke, the fuel being again mainly pine, but in part also, hickory, oak, and cedar. The odors of cooking. Among these, most strongly, the odors of fried salt pork and of fried and boiled pork lard, and second, the odor of cooked corn. The odors of sweat in many stages of age and freshness, this sweat being a distillation of pork, lard, corn, woodsmoke, pine, and ammonia. The odors of sleep, of bedding and of breathing, for the ventilation is poor. The odors of all the dirt that in the course of time can accumulate in a quilt and mattress. Odors of staleness from clothes hung or stored away, not washed. I should further describe the odor of corn: in sweat, or on the teeth, and breath, when it is eaten as much as they eat it, it is of a particular sweet stuffy fetor, to which the nearest parallel is the odor of the yellow excrement of a baby. All these odors as I have said are so combined into one that they are all and always present in balance, not at all heavy, yet so searching that all fabrics of bedding and clothes are saturated with them, and so clinging that they stand softly out of the fibers of newly laundered clothes. Some of their components are extremely 'pleasant,' some are 'unpleasant'; their sum total has great nostalgic power. When they are in an old house, darkened, and moist, and sucked into all the wood, and stacked down on top of years of a moldering and old basis of themselves, as at the Ricketts', they are hard to get used to or even hard to bear. At the Woods', they are blowsy and somewhat moist and dirty. At the Gudgers', as I have mentioned, they are younger, lighter, and cleaner-smelling. There too, there is another and special odor, very dry and edged: it is somewhat between the odor of very old newsprint and of a victorian bedroom in which, after long illness, and many medicines, someone has died and the room has been fumigated, yet the odor of dark brown medicines, dry-bodied sickness, and staring death, still is strong in the stained wallpaper and in the mattress.

Bareness and space (and spacing) are so difficult and seem to me of such greatness that I shall not even try to write seriously or fully of them. But a little, applying mainly to the two bedrooms.

The floors are made of wide planks, between some of which the daylighted earth is visible, and are naked of any kind of paint or cloth or linoleum covering whatever, and paths have been smoothed on them by bare feet, in a subtly uneven surface on which the polished knots are particularly beautiful. A perfectly bare floor of broad boards makes a room seem larger than it can if the floor is covered, and the furniture too, stands on it in a different and much cleaner sort of relationship. The walls as I have said are skeleton; so is the ceiling in one of these rooms; the rooms are twelve feet square and are meagerly furnished, and they are so great and final a whole of bareness and complete simplicity that even the objects on a crowded shelf seem set far apart from each other, and each to have a particularly sharp entity of its own. Moreover, all really simple and naïve people incline strongly toward exact symmetries, and have some sort of instinctive dislike that any one thing shall touch any other save what it rests on, so that chairs, beds, bureaus, trunks, vases, trinkets, general odds and ends, are set very plainly and squarely discrete from one another and from walls, at exact centers or as near them as possible, and this kind of spacing gives each object a full strength it would not otherwise have, and gives their several relationships, as they stand on shelves or facing, in a room, the purest power such a relationship can have. This is still more sharply true with such people as the Gudgers, who still have a little yet earnest wish that everything shall be as pleasant and proper to live with as possible, than with others such as the Woods and Ricketts, who are disheveled and wearied out of any such hope or care.

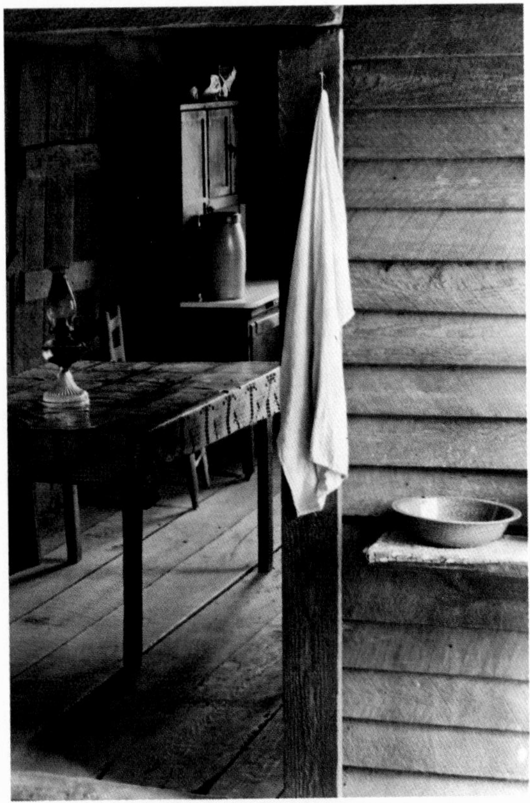

Evans's photographs *(here of the Gudgers' washroom, Home Hale County, Alabama, summer 1936)* and Agee's prose infused their documentary book with high poetry.

"Remember, the folks back home are counting on us. I am going to get a hit if I have to lay it on their flight deck."
—U.S. Navy lieutenant John James Powers, before dropping a bomb on a Japanese aircraft carrier from an altitude of less than 200 feet at the Battle of the Coral Sea

Battle of Midway: Here and in the Coral Sea, American forces gutted Japan's Imperial Navy.

STORY OF THE YEAR

America Strikes Back in the Pacific

1 In the spring of 1942, on azure waters thousands of miles from home, the navies of America and Japan fought two epic battles that changed the course of World War II. Victories in the Coral Sea and at Midway Island irrevocably shifted the advantage to the Allies in the Pacific Theater.

The four-day Battle of the Coral Sea was engaged when the Americans—having decrypted Japanese invasion plans for Port Moresby, New Guinea, and Tulagi, in the Solomon Islands—sent a naval force to intercept the Japanese troop convoy and its escort fleet. The enemy ships never made contact, never even came within sight of each other, but from May 2 through May 6, both armadas attacked with wave after wave of fighter planes and bombers. When the skies cleared, the Japanese had lost 70 planes and the light carrier *Shoho*. American losses included 66 planes and the aircraft carrier *Lexington*, an invaluable oceangoing city. Statistically victorious in terms of ship tonnage sunk, Japan lost too many fighter pilots to proceed with the invasions. Thus was Japan's relentless southward advance halted.

A month later, the American triumph was absolute at Midway. Once again privy to Japanese strategy, U.S. forces lay in wait for the monstrous fleet of 86 warships sent by Japan to attack the tiny mid-Pacific atoll. On June 3, the Japanese launched a diversionary assault on the two westernmost Aleutian islands, Kiska and Attu (the only American soil Japan would occupy during the war). The next day, a swarm of Japanese carrier-launched planes bombed Midway. The Americans responded with four consecutive air attacks on the Japanese fleet. Each one failed; scores of American planes were shot down. But on June 5, a fifth American bombing raid sank three Japanese aircraft carriers. His fleet devastated, Japanese admiral Yamamoto retreated westward. Total losses at Midway: for the Japanese, four aircraft carriers, a cruiser, 332 planes, 3,500 lives; for the Americans, one aircraft carrier, a destroyer, 147 planes, 307 lives. The bloodiest battles of the Pacific were still to come, but the Japanese navy never recovered from these eviscerating defeats. **◂1941.1 ▸1942.14**

WORLD WAR II

Southeast Asia Conquered

2 The Japanese military machine steamrolled across Southeast Asia in 1942. Japan had attacked British-held Malaya the day Pearl Harbor was bombed in December 1941. By the start of the new year, the British had withdrawn to the island fastness of Singapore, leaving Malaya's bounty of rubber and tin to Japan. In February 1942, Singapore fell as well, and Japanese planes bombed the Allied base in Darwin, Australia. In March, the Dutch withdrew from Java and the British evacuated Burma. (With the Burma Road to China in Japanese hands, Chiang Kai-shek's Nationalist Army had to rely on supplies flown from India over the Himalayas—a forbidding route nicknamed "the Hump.")

The jungle fighting was brutal, as was its aftermath. Japanese soldiers routinely tortured and murdered their vanquished foes. Of the 90,000 Indian, British, and Australian troops taken prisoner at the surrender of Singapore, more than half died in captivity. In Malaya, retreating British troops found compatriots suspended from trees, many adorned with the grim message "He took a long time to die." After overrunning Burma, the Japanese put Australian, British, and Dutch soldiers to work building a railroad between that country and Thailand (which Japan had also occupied the previous December). In all, 16,000 Allied prisoners of war and 50,000 Burmese civilians died on the "Railway of Death."

In 1943, in an attempt to win local support in conquered territories, Japan declared Burma and the Philippines independent. Most natives remained hostile to the regime, though a significant number, seduced by Japanese promises of a "co-prosperity zone," welcomed Asian imperialism as a lesser evil than European imperialism. **◂1941.13 ▸1943.7**

WORLD WAR II

Bombing by the Book

3 When the British bombed the old German port of Lübeck in March 1942, they were intentionally asking for trouble. In addition to smashing strategic installations, they deliberately razed hundreds of homes and shops—hoping not only to shake civilian morale, but to goad Hitler into retaliation. The skies over Britain had been relatively quiet recently, as German planes swarmed into the U.S.S.R. During the lull, Britain had beefed up its air defenses and its bomber fleet. Now Winston Churchill wanted to take some pressure off the Soviets by dividing the Luftwaffe's attention. The ploy worked, albeit unpleasantly: In reply to the Lübeck raid, the Germans bombed Exeter and Bath, killing nearly 500 people.

The attacks were the first of the "Baedeker Raids" on historic English towns, named after the tourist guidebook from which the Germans reportedly chose their targets. Soon both sides were embroiled in a game of tit for tat. In April, the RAF bombed Rostock, killing 200; the Luftwaffe destroyed much of Norwich and York.

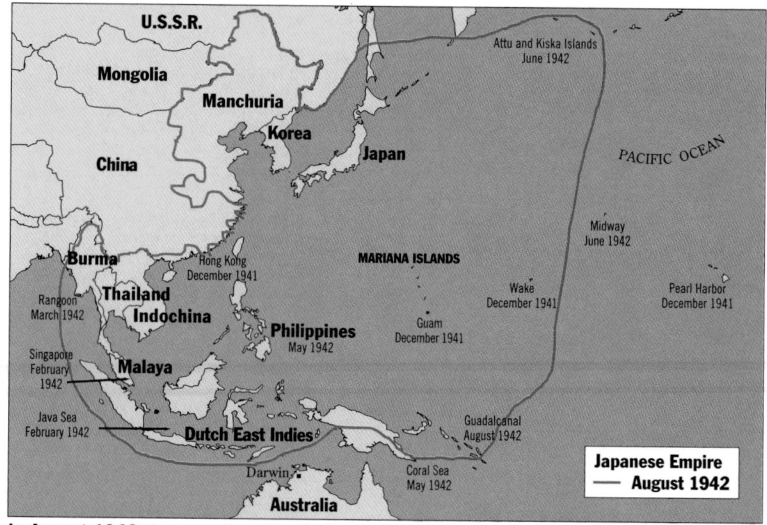

In August 1942, two months after its forces lost the Battle of the Midway, Japan's empire was at its peak, extending nearly to Australia and Hawaii. Above, the decisive battles.

ART & CULTURE: Books: ***Go Down Moses*** **(William Faulkner);** ***The Robber Bridegroom*** **(Eudora Welty);** ***Winter Tales*** **(Isak Dinesen);** ***Notes Toward a Supreme Fiction*** **(Wallace Stevens) ... Music: "Don't Get Around Much Anymore" (Ellington and Russell); "Don't Sit Under the Apple Tree" (Stept, Brown, and Tobias); "White Christmas" (Irving Berlin);** ***Danses Concertantes*** **(Igor Stravinsky);** ***Saber Danse, Second Symphony***

"I came through, and I shall return."—**General Douglas MacArthur, to his troops on the Bataan Peninsula**

In May, the British launched a "thousand-bomber raid" against Cologne, the biggest air strike of the war so far, and followed up with similar (though less successful) attacks on Essen and Bremen. The Germans, drained by their Soviet misadventure, continued to hammer small British cities, but with less and less force. After an ineffectual 30-bomber raid on Canterbury in October, the Baedeker was a closed book.

Both sides lost significant numbers of planes and pilots, but neither was seriously weakened by the bombing. The Cologne action raised British morale in the midst of other reverses, but only 480 Germans were killed; within two weeks, despite heavy damage, the city was almost back to normal.

British view: Failed artist Hitler contemplates bombing London's Royal Academy.

Yet Churchill, confident of the raids' "devastating effect," resumed the air offensive in March 1943. The climax would be the firebombing of Dresden—one of the most horrific and controversial episodes in the Allies' conduct of the war. **◂1940.11 ▸1945.3**

WORLD WAR II

Bataan and Corregidor

4 After withstanding a long siege on the Bataan Peninsula, 74,000 Filipino and American soldiers surrendered to the Japanese in April 1942. The capitulation left Corregidor Island in Manila Bay the sole Allied possession in the Philippine Islands. Lieutenant General Jonathan Wainwright

Wainwright's surrender of Corregidor, in a painting by an unknown Japanese artist.

(in command since General Douglas MacArthur's withdrawal weeks earlier) held out on Corregidor until May. Then, with his men starving, Wainwright surrendered. The Japanese ruled the Philippines.

Japan had first struck the islands from the air on December 8, 1941. Despite intelligence warnings, MacArthur had been unprepared for the attack: Half his planes were destroyed, most of them still on the ground. The general removed his headquarters to Corregidor and maneuvered his troops into Bataan behind him, declaring Manila an open city. The Japanese bombed the capital anyway, and marched in on January 2.

MacArthur promised the besieged Bataan troops that relief was coming. In reality, none was planned. The American press deified the craggy-faced commander for his heroic stance on Corregidor (he regularly fired his revolver at Japanese Zeroes). His men, ravaged by disease, malnutrition, and enemy fire, were not impressed.

In February, MacArthur was ordered to leave his troops behind. "There are times," said War Secretary Henry Stimson in Washington, "when men have to die." With his wife and four-year-old son, the general was ferried 560 miles through Japanese-controlled waters to Mindanao, then flown to Australia. Always ready with a quote, he delivered the best line of his career: "I came through, and I shall return." **◂1941.1 ▸1944.8**

WORLD WAR II

Doolittle Raids Tokyo

5 It was Franklin D. Roosevelt's idea: a raid on Japan to avenge Pearl Harbor. In April 1942, Lieutenant Colonel James H. Doolittle took off from the aircraft carrier *Hornet,* leading a squadron of U.S. bombers against military targets in Tokyo, Yokohama, and other cities. Since Japanese naval patrols kept Allied carriers 500 miles from shore, beyond the range of standard naval airplanes, Doolittle and his men flew typically land-based B-25s. The raiders went in at radar-evading altitudes—"low enough," Doolittle later reported, "to see the expressions on the faces of the people. It was one, I should say, of intense surprise."

All 16 planes reached their targets; none, however, returned. Lacking fuel for the flight back, they continued westward. One crash-landed near Vladivostok; the crew survived, but were interned for more than a year. Two others went down in Japanese territory, and the rest in China. Five men were killed trying to parachute to safety;

Doolittle in 1942, the year he flew his morale-boosting mission.

three more were executed by Japanese captors. Doolittle (a decorated World War I pilot who held several air-speed records as well as a doctorate from the Massachusetts Institute of Technology) made it home in one piece. He was promoted to brigadier general and awarded the Congressional Medal of Honor.

Though strategically insignificant, the raid lifted depressed Allied spirits: Japan was not impregnable after all. **◂1942.1 ▸1945.3**

BIRTHS

Muhammad Ali (Cassius Clay), U.S. boxer.

Margaret Court, Australian tennis player.

Aretha Franklin, U.S. singer.

Muammar al-Qaddafi, Libyan political leader.

Jerry Garcia, U.S. musician.

Peter Handke, Austrian playwright.

Stephen Hawking, U.K. astrophysicist.

Jimi Hendrix, U.S. musician.

Werner Herzog, German filmmaker.

John Irving, U.S. novelist.

Brian Jones, U.K. musician.

Terry Jones, U.K. actor.

Erica Jong, U.S. writer.

Garrison Keillor, U.S. writer.

Calvin Klein, U.S. fashion designer.

Paul McCartney, U.K. musician.

Huey Newton, U.S. political activist.

Martin Scorsese, U.S. filmmaker.

Roger Staubach, U.S. football player.

Barbra Streisand, U.S. singer and actress.

Tammy Wynette, U.S. singer.

DEATHS

John D. Barrymore, U.S. actor.

George M. Cohan, U.S. playwright and composer.

Michel Fokine, Russian-U.S. choreographer.

Bronislaw Malinowski, Polish-U.K. anthropologist.

Robert Musil, Austrian writer.

Condé Nast, U.S. publisher.

Otis Skinner, U.S. actor.

Gertrude Vanderbilt Whitney, U.S. sculptor.

Grant Wood, U.S. painter.

(Aram Khachaturian) ... Painting & Sculpture: *Europe After the Rain* (Max Ernst); *Male and Female* (Jackson Pollock) ... Film: *Mrs. Miniver* (William Wyler); *To Be or Not to Be* (Ernst Lubitsch); *Yankee Doodle Dandy* (Michael Curtiz) ... Theater: *Antigone* (Jean Anouilh); *The Skin of Our Teeth* (Thornton Wilder); *This Is the Army* (Irving Berlin); *Star and Garter* (Mike Todd) ... Radio: *Stage Door Canteen*; *This Is War.*

"Today we stand just 50 miles from Alexandria and Cairo, and we have the door to all Egypt in our hands."
—German general Erwin Rommel, at a press conference, October 3, 1942

NEW IN 1942

Bazooka rocket gun.

Napalm.

Kellogg's Raisin Bran.

K ration (packed by Wrigley Co., Chicago).

IN THE UNITED STATES

▶**BASEBALL GETS A GREEN LIGHT**—Expecting America's war effort to impinge on its national pastime, baseball commissioner Judge Kenesaw Mountain Landis asked FDR for his opinion on continuing major-league play. Responded the President in his 1942 "green light" letter: "I honestly feel it would be best for the country to keep baseball going." The hard-working, war-weary homefront needed a distraction—even the kind provided by teams composed of older players and armed forces rejects.

▶**THURBER'S HERO**—Anyone who had ever longed to be a jungle explorer or to rescue damsels in distress found a kindred spirit in James Thurber's 1942 short story "The Secret Life of Walter Mitty." Thurber's hero is a silently suffering henpecked husband who escapes from his carping wife by daydreaming of a more exciting life filled with adventure and derring-do.

▶**GRABLE'S GAMS**—Doing what any smart business would to protect a priceless asset, 20th Century-Fox insured Hollywood siren Betty Grable's legs in 1942 with a million-dollar Lloyd's of London policy. Grable's shapely gams helped make her the favorite "pinup girl" of American GIs, who said the popular pictures gave them a good idea of what they were fighting for: long-legged beauties —sexy, and not entirely wholesome. A war phenomenon, pinups plastered the walls of every barracks by 1943.

Internees at the Treblinka death camp, where nearly 800,000 Jews were killed.

THE HOLOCAUST

Genocide as Policy

6 On January 20, 1942, top Nazi officials convened in Grossen-Wannsee, outside Berlin, to discuss "the final solution to the Jewish question." The "solution"—genocide —had so far been imperfectly coordinated. *Einsatzgruppen* (task groups) were shooting thousands of Jewish men, women, and children in captured Polish and Soviet territory, but that method required too much manpower and ammunition; besides, the troops involved often had nervous breakdowns. Most Jews in Nazi-controlled areas had been sent to concentration camps or ghettos, but their ultimate fate remained unclear.

The Wannsee Conference, chaired by SS deputy chief Reinhard Heydrich, established that all Jews in Europe would be shipped to camps in the eastern countries, where the able-bodied would be enslaved. (SS head Heinrich Himmler would be in charge.) Slave laborers from conquered lands were already vital to the German economy, since most of the workforce was in the military; extra hands would be welcome. There was another benefit to enslavement: As Heydrich noted, many Jews would "undoubtedly disappear through natural diminution." (Starvation, exhaustion, exposure, and lack of sanitation were "natural" conditions in the camps.)

Those unfit to work would be "appropriately dealt with." The conference minutes left this phrase undefined (though its meaning was clear to all present). Soon, in selected camps, Jews (as well as Gypsies, communists, homosexuals, and other "undesirables") were being gassed to death en masse, then cremated. **◂1939.18 ▸1943.1**

WORLD WAR II

Yanks in Europe

7 At the start of 1942, America's role in the war outside the Pacific was still largely undefined. In January, talks between Roosevelt and Churchill in Washington—the Arcadia Conference—ended with agreement on some major points. British and U.S. commanders would work together under the auspices of the new Combined Chiefs of Staff. The United States would aid the British in a North African landing sometime soon. But the liberation of Europe would have top priority.

In April, Roosevelt urged Churchill to scrap the North African attack in favor of an autumn landing in France. Churchill initially agreed, but then decided the move would be premature. In June, he visited Roosevelt again, pressing for action in North Africa. U.S. generals (led by the commander of American forces in Europe, Major General Dwight D. Eisenhower) objected, but Churchill's stubbornness won out. With the opening of a "second front" postponed indefinitely, the big loser was Stalin, who had argued for action in the west to draw German troops away from Russia.

One problem with planning a European invasion was that the U.S. Army Air Force had never faced Hitler's Luftwaffe. British strategists judged the USAAF's Flying Fortress bombers hopelessly slow and poorly armed. Then, in August, the first all-American squadron hit German-controlled rail yards in Rouen, France. It was a successful mission, though two airmen were hurt when a pigeon shattered their windshield. But the real test would come in 1943, when joint U.S.-British air raids began to strike Germany. **◂1941.5 ▸1942.9**

WORLD WAR II

Tobruk and El Alamein

8 The British had Rommel's Afrika Korps and its Italian backup cornered in western Libya in January 1942. But then Rommel counterattacked, pushing his foe 220 miles eastward. Outside Gazala, a savage battle began. The British started out with 700 tanks to Rommel's 525. Within two weeks, the ratio was 70 British tanks to Rommel's 150. The British stumbled back into Egypt, leaving behind a garrison in the key Libyan port of Tobruk.

Poster urging troops in North Africa to "Baffle the Hun" with camouflage.

Rommel took the city—along with 33,000 prisoners—in four days. After surviving a parliamentary vote of censure, Winston Churchill gave Middle East commander in chief Sir Claude Auchinleck personal command of the 8th Army in North Africa, relieving Lieutenant General Neil Ritchie. Auchinleck led a retreat to the Egyptian town of El Alamein.

U.S. Boeing B-17s, known as Flying Fortresses, head for France.

SPORTS: Baseball: World Series, St. Louis Cardinals defeat New York Yankees, 4–1 ... Football: NFL, Washington Redskins defeat Chicago Bears, 14–6; Don Hutson (Green Bay) sets NFL season scoring record with 138 points ... Boxing: World heavyweight title competition suspended as reigning champion Joe Louis enters military.

"The more of this filth that is eliminated, the better for the security of the Reich."—**Propaganda Minister Joseph Goebbels, on the reprisals at Lidice**

With Rommel nearing the Nile, Mussolini flew to Tripoli, planning to enter Cairo with his troops. But the First Battle of El Alamein dashed Axis hopes of rapidly conquering Egypt. His soldiers exhausted, his supplies low, Rommel was stalemated by August. When a cautious Auchinleck insisted on postponing a counteroffensive until September, Churchill removed him from his post—making General Harold Alexander regional commander, and General Bernard Law Montgomery commander of the 8th Army.

Paradoxically, Montgomery delayed the offensive until October 23. By then, British strength had grown to 230,000 men and 1,230 tanks; the German-Italian side had only 80,000 men and 210 comparable tanks. Rommel himself was in Austria, on sick leave, when the Second Battle of El Alamein began. When he reached Libya two days later, half his tanks were already destroyed. By January 1943, his forces had been flogged back all the way to Tunisia. **◂1941.2 ▸1942.8**

WORLD WAR II

Operation Torch

9 A mostly American force of 100,000 landed in the French colonies of Morocco and Algeria on November 8, 1942, and in Tunisia on November 25, to pressure the Afrika Korps from the west while the British squeezed it from the east. Operation Torch tested Vichy French neutrality to the limit.

Marshal Pétain severed relations with Washington and ordered his forces to fight. But after two days of resistance, Morocco agreed to an armistice. There was little opposition in Algeria. Only Tunisia, defended by German troops, held out—until May 1943.

When the landings began, Vichy's supreme commander, Admiral Jean-François Darlan, was visiting Algiers. Though publicly pro-German, Darlan had secretly offered the Allies his support. But the operation took him by surprise. Some French troops in the area were loyal to Pétain, others to de Gaulle, still others to U.S.-sponsored general Henri Giraud. In a quandary, Darlan ordered a cease-fire on November 9.

The next day, to discourage Vichy from straying further, Hitler

Pétain *(left)* disowned Darlan after the latter made a deal with the Americans.

overran previously unoccupied southern France with troops. This insult drove French commanders in Algeria and West Africa to endorse Darlan's deal with the Americans: In exchange for recognition as French Africa's political chief, Darlan recognized Giraud's military authority. On November 27, the vengeful Germans tried to seize the French fleet, moored at Toulon. But to keep the ships out of Nazi hands, Admiral Jean-Joseph de Laborde ordered them scuttled.

Darlan was soon murdered by a French royalist, and Giraud took his place. Vichy had lost its African empire, its navy—and any hope of special treatment by Hitler. **◂1941.2 ▸1943.4**

WORLD WAR II

The Nazis' Savage Revenge

10 Wherever the Nazis ruled—but especially in the Slavic countries where the locals were deemed subhuman—punishment for rebellion was arbitrary and stunningly brutal. One of the most notorious acts of retribution occurred in June 1942, when the Germans avenged the assassination of SS deputy chief Reinhard Heydrich by destroying the Czech village of Lidice.

As a principal architect of the "final solution," Heydrich had earned the sobriquet *der Henker*—"the Hangman." His other title was *Reichsprotektor* of Bohemia-Moravia—"protector" of what had been Czechoslovakia. On May 27, three Czech resistance fighters (parachuted into the country by British intelligence) ambushed Heydrich's car in Prague, mortally wounding him with a homemade bomb. German reprisals were immediate: Several hundred Jews in the Sachsenhausen concentration camp were murdered, and 20,000 soldiers and policemen searched Czech houses, shooting entire families accused of aiding the assassins. A week later, when Heydrich died, 3,000 more Jews were sent to the gas chambers in his name.

But slaughtering Jews was routine. Nazi leaders wanted to make a more striking statement. They settled on Lidice, where the Gestapo claimed the resistance men had briefly stayed. On June 9, all males in the village over age 15—200 men and boys—were rounded up and shot in groups of ten. Women and children were shipped to concentration camps, except for eight youngsters farmed out to SS families for "Germanization." (Only 16 survivors in all were found after the war.) After the village was burned and bulldozed, crops were planted on the site. German propagandists trumpeted the deed around the world. The assassins themselves were caught soon afterward and executed, betrayed by a comrade who could bear no more reprisals. **◂1942.6 ▸1944.M**

SS officers in Lidice examine their handiwork: a village razed to avenge a "hangman."

IN THE UNITED STATES

▶WOMEN GO TO WAR—A step toward sexual integration of the military was taken on May 14, 1942, when Congress created the Women's Auxiliary Army Corps. Between the WAAC (changed to WAC in 1943, when women were granted full status), the Navy's WAVES (Women Accepted for Voluntary Emergency Service), and the other branches' female complements, some 350,000 women served in every duty category except combat.

▶RATIONING BEGINS—At home, the U.S. got down to the business of winning a war in 1942. Rationing began with sugar in May, coffee on November 29, and gasoline a few days later. Meat followed in 1943, along with limits on flour, fish, and canned goods. Victory gardens sprang up everywhere—vegetables were scarce, in part due to the internment on the West Coast of Japanese-Americans, who had previously produced two thirds of California's produce.

▶MOVIE SABOTAGE—In 1942, just three years after RKO gave Orson Welles carte blanche (and he made *Citizen Kane*), the studio took control of his would-be masterpiece *The Magnificent Ambersons* and mutilated it. Fearful it had a box-office dud on its hands, RKO reshot parts of the film, and cut out some 43 minutes—all while Welles was in Argentina making a film for the government. No print was kept of Welles's original 131-minute version—and for film buffs, it remains one of the medium's great "could-have-beens." (Even the mutilated version is considered great.) The boy genius's career never recovered from the fallout. The next year, RKO touted its new slogan: "Showmanship instead of genius." **◂1941.11**

POLITICS & BUSINESS: GNP: $157.9 billion ... Office of Price Administration stabilizes rents and halts all car and truck production ... War Production Board, War Manpower Commission, and Office of War Information established ... AFL and CIO agree to no-strike policy for duration of the war ... Supreme Court overturns Georgia Contract Labor Act; rules Nevada divorces valid in all states.

"After Stalingrad we shall be merciless."—**U.S.S.R. war correspondent Konstantin Simonov**

WORLD WAR II

▶COMMANDO RAID—In daring Operation Chariot, British commandos attacked the German naval installation at St. Nazaire, France, on March 28. The raiders loaded an old U.S. destroyer with explosives and plowed it into St. Nazaire's sea locks, knocking the important Atlantic dry dock out of commission for the rest of the war. Some 400 commandos and British sailors were killed in the raid, hundreds more were taken prisoner. Germany also lost 400 men.

▶BATAAN DEATH MARCH—Having won surrender from the Allies' "battling bastards of Bataan" on April 9, 1942, the Japanese command forced 76,000 American and Filipino soldiers on a brutal 65-mile march to a prison camp. Already weak from dysentery and hunger, more than 5,000 Filipinos and 600 Americans died on the Bataan Death March, many bayonetted when they could go no farther, others randomly tortured to death. Only 54,000 prisoners

completed the grisly hike (10,000 had escaped into the jungle); of these, 17,000 starved to death in the camp.

▶MADAGASCAR TAKEN—British and South African forces landed on Madagascar on May 7, 1942, and seized the port of Diégo-Suarez from its Vichy defenders. The Allies acted to prevent Japan, which in 1941 had entered into a treaty with Vichy France, from grabbing the island and using it as a valuable Indian Ocean base.

▶GENERAL'S ESCAPE—French general Henri Giraud had been captured by the Germans twice: once in World War I and again at the start of World War II. In April 1942, Giraud, 63, made a daring escape from the prison castle of Königstein—sliding down a wall on a rope. Smuggled out of Germany, he soon became the Allies' military chief for French Africa.

1942

Soviet troops in rubble-strewn Stalingrad. By November, starving German soldiers were eating their own horses.

WORLD WAR II

The Soviets Survive

11 By March 1942, a Red Army counteroffensive had driven Hitler's forces back 150 miles in some sectors of the Soviet Union. But the Soviets had suffered four million casualties, the Germans only one million. In May, the invaders regrouped, driving into Crimea. In June, they assaulted Smolensk, which fell after weeks of fighting. Later that month, desperate for oil from the Caucasus, Hitler launched an offensive in southern Russia. It culminated in the Battle of Stalingrad—the greatest of the entire war.

Stalingrad (now Volgograd) was an industrial city stretching for 30 miles along the Volga River, but its main importance for both sides was symbolic: It was named after the Soviet leader, who directed its defense as if his life depended on it. The attack by Field Marshal Friedrich von Paulus, leading 300,000 troops, began on August 19. The Soviets, under General Vasily Chuikov, resisted fiercely, but the Germans soon penetrated the suburbs, and bombs destroyed most of the city's housing. (Inhabitants took to nearby caves, venturing out to help the defenders.) By mid-September, Chuikov's men were squeezed into a nine-by-three-mile patch. But they fought the Germans for every burned-out building, inflicting heavy losses.

In November, one million Soviet troops under Marshal Georgi Zhukov marched to the rescue. They surrounded the Germans and repulsed all relief attempts. Ignoring Hitler's orders, von Paulus surrendered on January 31, 1943, along with 24 other generals and 91,000 frozen, starving troops. Days later, another Soviet counteroffensive liberated all the territory the Germans had taken since spring. The Führer was not done with the U.S.S.R., but Stalingrad was the turning point: a grave humiliation for Germany, and proof that the Soviets had learned from past mistakes. **◂1941.8 ▸1943.2**

WORLD WAR II

The Vichy Bargain

12 France fell off its political tightrope in April 1942, when Hitler forced dictator Marshal Henri Pétain to make Pierre Laval premier. Partly to appease his German patrons (who occupied most of the country and held thousands of French war prisoners), Pétain had constructed his Vichy regime along fascist lines. He'd changed the national motto from "Liberty, Equality, Fraternity" to "Work, Family, Fatherland." He'd instituted anti-Semitic laws and jailed dissidents. But he had maintained some independence—keeping France nonbelligerent and privately urging Franco to refuse passage of Axis troops through Spain.

Laval had been vice premier during Vichy's first months, until his machinations against Pétain led to his dismissal. He was far less popular than the marshal—a World War I hero who managed to make his deepest bows to Germany look patriotic—but Laval's calls for closer collaboration won him Hitler's favor.

France's new premier, Pierre Laval, as seen by an American cartoonist.

With the new premier in office and Pétain's powers sharply reduced, the Germans pressed Vichy harder than ever. France was already paying the occupiers' expenses. Now farms and factories had to contribute up to 80 percent of their output to the Reich. In exchange for the release of a few POWS, Laval agreed to send workers to Germany, and to round up Jews for shipment to concentration camps.

In July, 13,000 Jewish men, women, and children were crammed into a Paris sports arena to await a grim fate. By the end of the war, despite Laval's stipulation that only foreign-born Jews would go, 23,000 French Jews had somehow been deported as well. **◂1940.7 ▸1943.6**

LITERATURE

Murder *à l'Absurde*

13 Paris was hardly an auspicious place to publish a first novel in 1942. Yet *L'Etranger* established Albert Camus, 29, as a major writer, first among his compatriots, then around the world. (After the war, the book was published in America as *The Stranger* and in Britain as *The Outsider.*) The story of Meursault, a French-Algerian who murders an Arab for no clear motive—and who rejects the white lies and comfortable faiths that cushion most people against the absurdity of existence—struck a resonant chord in Vichy France. Submitting outwardly to fascism and occupation, many readers shared Meursault's alienation, his anguish, his disgust with everyday hypocrisy.

Camus's vision of a universe lacking any overarching meaning did not drive him to inaction or despair. He cofounded an underground Resistance newspaper, *Combat*; after France's liberation, he became a spokesman for leftists concerned less with political theories than with justice and morality. *The Myth of Sisyphus*, an essay also published in 1942, distills his philosophy. Condemned by the

WORLD WAR II: January: Japan attacks Corregidor; U.S. retreats to Bataan ... February: Japan invades Burma, takes Singapore, raids Darwin, Australia ... March: Japan takes Dutch East Indies; U.S. abandons Philippines ... April: Bataan surrenders; Japanese close Burma Road; U.S. bombs Tokyo ... May: Battle of the Coral Sea ... June: Battle of Midway; U.S. bombs Romanian oil fields; Germans take Tobruk ...

"For the first time, the first, I laid my heart open to the benign indifference of the universe."—**Albert Camus, *The Stranger***

gods to spend eternity pushing a boulder uphill and watching it roll down again, Sisyphus has no hope; yet he does have his struggle and his awareness—all the meaning anyone needs.

In the Resistance, Camus worked with existentialist thinker Jean-Paul Sartre, and later was labeled an existentialist himself. But Camus rejected what he perceived as Sartre's accommodation of communism, disdaining Marxist as well as Christian dogma. He died, absurdly, in a car crash three years after receiving the 1957 Nobel Prize. **►1943.10**

WORLD WAR II

Battle of Guadalcanal

14 The Allied counteroffensive in the Pacific began on August 7, 1942, when 16,000 U.S. Marines landed on Guadalcanal, in the Solomon Islands, and seized the Japanese airfield there. For the next six months, the small, sparsely populated island, a thousand miles across the Coral Sea from Australia, was the scene of some of the war's fiercest fighting. By the time the Japanese capitulated, in February 1943, they had lost 21,000 men (half to disease and starvation) to America's 2,000 and Australia's 1,000.

"I have never heard or read of this kind of fighting," one GI wrote during the campaign. "These people refuse to surrender." Contested in close, often hand-to-hand combat, the battle was savage. After losing the airstrip to the initial Allied landing, the Japanese dug in around the island and tenaciously repelled advances, often fighting to the last man. When their positions became untenable, many committed suicide rather than be taken prisoner. In September, the United States landed reinforcements on Guadalcanal and expanded its command area. A month later, aided by cryptographic intelligence that provided advance knowledge of virtually every enemy maneuver, the U.S. Navy intercepted a Japanese convoy as it steamed toward Guadalcanal with fresh soldiers. The Americans sank three Japanese destroyers and a heavy cruiser.

Again and again over the coming months, the U.S. Navy thwarted attempted Japanese landings, often at great loss of life and equipment. These sea battles proved decisive, leaving the besieged Japanese troops without adequate support. By February, Guadalcanal, and with it all of the Solomons, belonged to the Allies. **◄1942.1 ►1944.9**

GIs land on Guadalcanal. In snake-infested jungles, they faced a desperate foe.

WORLD WAR II

The Manhattan Project

15 J. Robert Oppenheimer was tall and gaunt, a theoretical physicist, an intellectual, and a liberal. Brigadier General Leslie R. Groves was a military engineer who weighed nearly 300 pounds and, politically, leaned to the right. When the U.S. Army stepped in to coordinate nuclear weapon research in 1942, the two men formed a partnership that spearheaded what became known as the Manhattan Project (named for the site of its first headquarters). Groves applied his bureaucratic skill to coordinating 100,000 workers, 37 installations in 13 states, and a dozen university laboratories. Oppenheimer provided scientific leadership, bringing top researchers to a secret compound near Los Alamos, New Mexico.

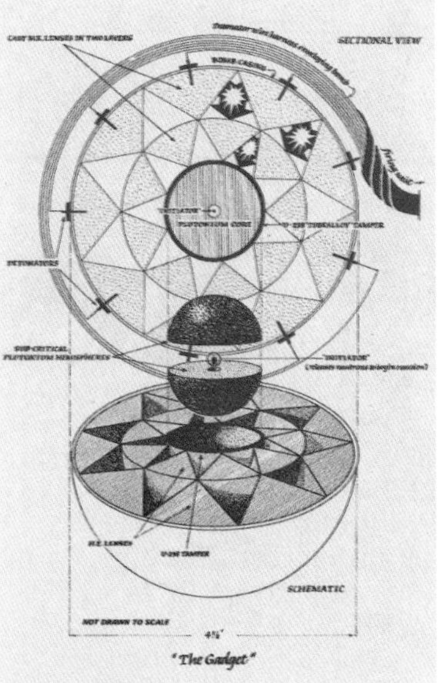

A schematic drawing of the A-bomb: A baseball-size plutonium sphere would give it apocalyptic power.

Groves had recently overseen construction of the Pentagon, the five-sided, fortresslike U.S. military headquarters outside Washington, D.C. In September, hoping for a combat assignment, he found instead that he'd drawn another construction job. Asking for details, he was told: "If you do the job right, it will win the war." Weeks later, Oppenheimer sketched the idea of an isolated research facility where scientists could collaborate freely, protected by military guards. By the end of the year, building had started at a site 7,400 feet above sea level on the Pajarito Plateau.

The work at Los Alamos and elsewhere culminated less than three years later with a predawn explosion that bathed the New Mexico desert in blinding light. In a bunker six miles from ground zero, Oppenheimer remembered a line from the *Bhagavad Gita*: "I am become Death, the shatterer of worlds." Groves was more upbeat. When someone remarked that the blast was brighter than a star, he pointed to the brigadier general's star on each of his shoulders and replied, "Brighter than two stars!" Soon he was on his way to Washington, bearing news of the first atomic bomb. **◄1940.8 ►1942.18**

WORLD WAR II

►AMERICAN ARSENAL—American president Roosevelt called for the production of 60,000 planes, 45,000 tanks, 20,000 anti-aircraft guns, and six million deadweight tons of merchant shipping in 1942. The *Robert E. Peary*, the first of 1,460 Liberty Ships built at the Kaiser shipyards on the West Coast, was launched November 9 and ready three days later—only seven and a half days after its keel was laid.

►AUSSIES' FIRST WIN—Fighting in miserable conditions in the jungle of New Guinea, Australian troops staved off the Japanese, who by mid-September had advanced to within 32 miles of Port Moresby. Exhausted, the Japanese retreated to Gona and Buna. The Australians went on to defeat the Japanese decisively at Gona on December 9. (U.S. troops triumphed at Buna five days later.) As the Allies' first land victory against Japan, the Australian stand was critical:

From Port Moresby, the Japanese could have dominated the Coral Sea and invaded nearby Australia.

►COVERT CONNECTIONS—The U.S. Office of Strategic Services (OSS) joined forces with Britain's Special Operations Executive (SOE) in 1942. Together the two agencies sponsored resistance movements, employed more than 11,000 agents to gather information, and sponsored acts of sabotage in Axis-occupied countries. Despite friction, the two organizations were later united under General Eisenhower as part of the Operations Division of the Supreme Headquarters Allied Expeditionary Force.

July: First U.S. air raid on Germans in the Netherlands ... August: Battle of Guadalcanal; first U.S. air raid on France, at Rouen; Allies bomb Rotterdam ... September: Battle of Stalingrad begins ... October: Second Battle of El Alamein ... November: Operation Torch, Allies retake Tobruk; Germany and Italy move into unoccupied France; French scuttle fleet at Toulon ... December: Germany begins retreat from Stalingrad.

"When we are dealing with the Caucasian race, we have methods that will test ... loyalty. But when we deal with the Japanese, we are in an entirely different field."—**California attorney general Earl Warren on the evacuation of Japanese-American citizens**

AROUND THE WORLD

▶GANDHI AND CHURCHILL FACE OFF—With the Allies reaching a critical turning point against the Axis powers in 1942, Mahatma Gandhi gambled that in return for a compliant, strategic ally against Japan in Southeast Asia, Britain might grant India independence. Even though he despised fascism, Gandhi went against his ideological ally and demanded the immediate and total withdrawal of the British from India. A furious Churchill promptly imprisoned the entire Indian National Congress, saying he did not become prime minister "in order to preside over the liquidation of the British Empire." ◂1939.4 ▸1947.3

▶CHRISTIANITY DEFENDED—A professor of medieval and Renaissance English at Cambridge University, a lay theologian, and a writer of science fiction, C.S. Lewis reached a mass audience in 1942 with his bestselling fictional defense of Christianity, *The Screwtape Letters.* Lewis's "author" is an aging devil, Screwtape, who writes a series of letters to his nephew, Wormwood, describing the most effective methods of tempting humans. Eight years later, Lewis's fantastical streak surfaced in *The Lion, the Witch and the Wardrobe,* the first of seven books set in the fictional land of Narnia. ◂1940.17

▶OXFAM FOUNDED—Alarmed by the plight of starving children in war-torn Greece, a group of Oxford University academics, in 1942, established an organization dedicated to supplying disaster-relief aid to impoverished countries. Called the Oxford Committee for Famine Relief (OXFAM), the organization also played a key role in the settlement and repatriation of refugees after World War II. ◂1941.4 ▸1943.M

1942

Japanese-Americans arrive at a California internment camp.

THE UNITED STATES

Japanese-Americans Interned

16 Japan's attack on Pearl Harbor brought a surge of xenophobia to the United States. On the West Coast, beginning in the spring of 1942, the Army forcibly removed all residents of Japanese ancestry from their homes, relocating them to inland detention camps. For the duration of the war, long after any possible threat of a Japanese invasion had expired, 110,000 Japanese-Americans remained confined in ten prisonlike "relocation centers," where living conditions were spartan and access to jobs and education was severely restricted.

All aliens were required to register with the government during World War II, but the internment policy—which required its victims to sell their homes and businesses on 48 hours' notice—reflected widespread anti-Asian prejudice, particularly along America's Pacific shores. "Ouster of All Japs in California Near!" crowed the *San Francisco Examiner*, capturing the spirit of the times. Although none of the Japanese-Americans had done anything to provoke suspicion, most reacted to their incarceration with a renewed resolve to prove their patriotism. Vetted for loyalty, 17,600 of the Nisei (second-generation Americans of Japanese descent) enlisted in the U.S. armed forces; many distinguished themselves in battle. **◂1941.1**

TECHNOLOGY

Dawn of the Nuclear Age

18 In October 1942, a team of scientists directed by the Italian émigré physicist Enrico Fermi began building an atomic pile (lumps of uranium stacked between bricks of pure graphite) under the grandstand of a stadium at the University of Chicago. Under the aegis of the Manhattan Project, America's effort to build the first nuclear weapon, they were testing a crucial theory: that neutrons released when a uranium atom split could be used to split *other* uranium atoms in a self-sustaining "chain reaction"—a reaction that would generate more energy than it took to start. The graphite bricks were meant to slow the neutrons down, giving them a better chance of penetrating uranium nuclei, while neutron-absorbing cadmium strips nailed to wooden rods could be inserted or withdrawn in case the reaction went too fast or too slow.

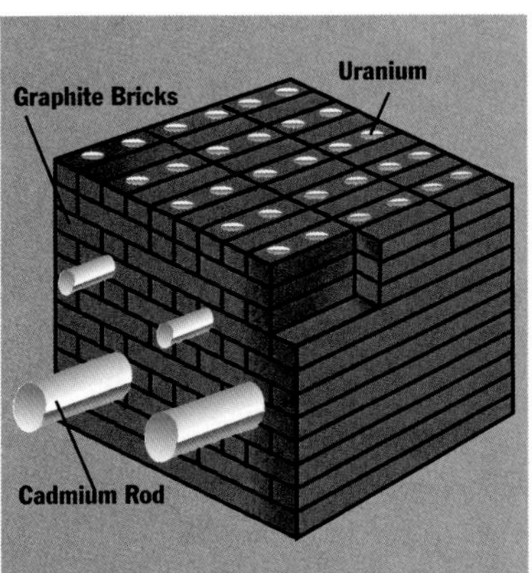

Fermi's pile, the ancestor of modern nuclear reactors, was the key to creating the A-bomb.

As workers stacked graphite layer upon layer, the neutron intensity increased—and on December 1, the 20-foot-high pile was ready to go "critical." The next day, Fermi's team slowly removed the cadmium control rods, pausing to measure the increase in radioactivity at every step. Volunteers holding buckets of cadmium solution watched from above, ready to douse the pile in case the reaction raged out of control.

Finally, at 2:20 PM, a chain reaction was achieved. An audience watched as instruments registered a net outflow of energy. After generating roughly half a watt of power for 28 minutes, the pile was shut down. University of Chicago physicist Arthur Compton telephoned Harvard president and National Defense Research Committee chairman James Conant, another scientist with the Manhattan Project. "The Italian navigator just landed in the New World," Compton declared in pre-arranged code. "Were the natives friendly?" asked Conant. The answer: "Everybody landed safe and happy." **◂1942.15 ▸1945.1**

ART

Hopper's Lonesome Light

17 Edward Hopper denied that he intended his haunting paintings as a comment on contemporary life. "I'm trying to paint myself," said the New York–born painter. Yet from the 1920s through his death in 1967, he captured as no other artist the loneliness at the heart of the modern city. A student of Ashcan School founder Robert Henri, Hopper surrounded his subjects—as in the famous *Nighthawks (above)*, completed in 1942—with a desolate light that seems to pinion them in solitude. ◂1908.4 ▸1948.M

NOBEL PRIZES: No awards given.

A VOICE FROM 1942

"We'll Always Have Paris"

From *Casablanca*, Warner Bros., 1942

A Spanish poster for *Casablanca*. Refugee actors—including Paul Henreid, Peter Lorre, and Conrad Veidt—added a touch of reality to the film's Hollywood artifice. Below, Humphrey Bogart and Ingrid Bergman.

Casablanca *stands unchallenged as one of World War II's grandest entertainments—a rich, romantic melodrama that touches the heart without taxing the brain. With Humphrey Bogart as Rick, the world-weary saloonkeeper in war-torn Morocco, Ingrid Bergman as his old flame Ilsa, "As Time Goes By" as their song (the one they bid Rick's pianist, Sam, to play), and a climactic self-sacrifice that makes statues weep, director Michael Curtiz's tale of espionage and lost love is, in critic Andrew Sarris's words, "the happiest of happy accidents." (The odds were certainly against the movie's success: The production was fraught with problems, and the script—written by Julius and Philip Epstein and Howard Koch, and doctored by four other writers —was still frantically being revised when shooting began.) Released in New York City on Thanksgiving Day 1942—just two weeks after the Allies landed in Morocco—the film summed up an era and pointed the way to the films noirs of the postwar period. In the excerpt below, from the film's final scene, Rick implores Ilsa to fly to safety with her Resistance-leader husband.* ►**1945.17**

RICK: Louis, have your man go with Mr. Laszlo and take care of his luggage.

RENAULT: Certainly, Rick. Anything you say. Find Mr. Laszlo's luggage and put it on the plane.

ORDERLY: Yes, sir. This way, please.

RICK: If you don't mind, you fill in the names. That'll make it even more official.

RENAULT: You think of everything, don't you?

RICK: And the names are Mr. and Mrs. Victor Laszlo.

ILSA: But, why my name, Richard?

RICK: Because you're getting on that plane.

ILSA: I don't understand. What about you?

RICK: I'm staying here with him till the plane gets safely away.

ILSA: No, Richard. No! What has happened to you? Last night we said—

RICK: Last night we said a great many things. You said I was to do the thinking for both of us. Well, I've done a lot of it since then and it all adds up to one thing. You're getting on that plane with Victor, where you belong.

ILSA: But Richard, no, I, I—

RICK: Now, you've got to listen to me. Do you have any idea what you'd have to look forward to if you stayed here? Nine chances out of ten we'd both wind up in a concentration camp. Isn't that true, Louis?

RENAULT: I'm afraid Major Strasser would insist.

ILSA: You're saying this only to make me go.

RICK: I'm saying it because it's true. Inside of us we both know you belong with Victor. You're part of his work. The thing that keeps him going. If that plane leaves the ground and you're not with him, you'll regret it.

ILSA: No.

RICK: Maybe not today, maybe not tomorrow, but soon, and for the rest of your life.

ILSA: What about us?

RICK: We'll always have Paris. We didn't have it, we'd lost it until you came to Casablanca. We got it back last night.

ILSA: And I said I would never leave you.

RICK: And you never will. But I've got a job to do, too. Where I'm going you can't follow. What I've got to do, you can't be any part of.

Ilsa, I'm no good at being noble, but it doesn't take much to see that the problems of three little people don't amount to a hill o' beans in this crazy world. Someday you'll understand that.

Now, now. Here's looking at you, kid.

"Driven on by hunger, we crept out at night. Like rats, we scratched under the rubble in search of a crust of bread or a potato peel. I was gradually losing my strength; my body was covered with ulcers."—**A Warsaw ghetto rebel who escaped through the sewers**

STORY OF THE YEAR

Warsaw Ghetto Uprising

1 The spirit that led the Jews of the Warsaw Ghetto to mount a hopeless revolt in 1943 is captured in a passage from a participant's diary. "We cannot count on anybody," wrote Zionist organizer Hersh Berlinski. "Neither the Soviet Union nor even less on the Allies. Let our desperate act be a protest flung into the face of the world."

After the Warsaw uprising, a Nazi squadron herded survivors off to Treblinka death camp.

For months, the Germans had been emptying the sealed ghetto of its 500,000 inhabitants, shipping them to the Treblinka extermination camp. Since killing a single German would bring massive reprisals, most ghetto dwellers simply tried to stay out of the occupiers' way, and some collaborated in order to survive. But as hunger, disease, and summary executions killed hundreds a day, and reports of gas chambers filtered back from Treblinka—which the Nazis had portrayed as a pleasant place—growing numbers of Jews began to feel they had nothing to lose. Some formed paramilitary groups, smuggling in whatever weapons they could buy or steal (help from the Polish underground was spotty).

The first armed resistance came in January, when 50 Germans were killed as they rounded up victims for a death-camp shipment; 1,000 Jews died in the action. Then, on April 19 (Passover), 2,000 German troops arrived to begin deporting the remaining 60,000 Jews from the ghetto. They were opposed by 1,500 starving men and women equipped with pistols, grenades, Molotov cocktails, and two or three light machine guns. Holding out for weeks against tanks, howitzers, poison gas, and flamethrowers, the ghetto fighters managed to kill several hundred Germans.

On May 8, their headquarters surrounded, many of the surviving rebels committed suicide rather than be captured. Others escaped through the sewers to the "Aryan" side, where some were aided by Polish sympathizers; most were shot on sight or betrayed by informers. The fighting sputtered on for eight more days. When it was over, the last of Warsaw's Jews had died, been deported, or gone into hiding. SS Major General Jürgen Stroop, commander of the operation, dynamited the city's great synagogue. The ghetto, Stroop wrote in his report, "is no more." **◂1942.6 ▸1944.10**

WORLD WAR II

The Greatest Tank Battle

2 The Red Army started 1943 with victory at Stalingrad and a counteroffensive in the Caucasus. On January 18, they opened a gap in the Nazi blockade of Leningrad, bringing some relief to that city after months of siege. But the Germans still had troops arrayed along the 1,800-mile Soviet border. Hitler reconquered Kharkov and Belgorod in March. Then, on July 5, his forces attacked the huge salient the Soviets had pushed into the Axis-held Kursk region.

The Kursk offensive was the greatest tank battle in history. The Nazis launched 900,000 men and 3,000 armored vehicles—including new Tigers, the biggest tanks ever built—against equal Soviet firepower. The smoke of the battle was so dense that neither side could use its tactical aircraft. But the Red Army tanks were more maneuverable and reliable, and the German behemoths, creeping through minefields and mud, could be taken out with flamethrowers trained on their ventilation shafts. The Germans began to withdraw after a week, with the Reds in pursuit. Although both sides soon lost half their tanks, the Soviets, with vast production capacity, could absorb the loss better than the increasingly strapped Germans.

Hitler ordered a cease-fire on July 17, but the Soviets pressed onward. By the end of August, Kharkov and Belgorod were back in their hands. Soon afterward, the Germans lost Smolensk and the Caucasus. In November, troops under General Nikolai Vatutin freed Kiev from its two-year occupation. Hitler's dream of enslaving the Slavs and filling their lands with Aryan colonizers was over, even as the battle for Soviet soil continued. **◂1942.11 ▸1944.3**

Field Marshal Friedrich von Paulus at the German surrender of Stalingrad.

WORLD WAR II

Katyn Forest Massacre

3 In April 1943, in the Katyn Forest near the Russian city of Smolensk, the occupying German army uncovered mass graves containing the bodies of 4,400 Polish army officers. The victims had been shot in the back of the head while kneeling. The Nazis blamed the Soviets for the executions. The Soviets accused the Nazis, insisting that the officers were working in the area when Germany invaded two years earlier.

Germany invited the foreign press to the opening of the Katyn graves. In the foreground, the victims' calcified bodies.

Polish authorities had long wondered what had become of 15,000 officers taken prisoner when the Soviets seized eastern Poland in 1939. When Germany attacked the Soviet Union in 1941, and the exiled Polish regime agreed to muster an anti-Nazi army on Soviet soil, Polish commanders asked that the officers be released from POW camps. But the Soviets pleaded ignorance of their whereabouts.

The Katyn discovery seemed to solve the mystery, especially when Polish Red Cross investigators confirmed that the men had perished in 1940. (Evidence included the contents of the corpses' pockets, and testimony from peasants who'd seen Soviet secret policemen load the officers into vans.) But the Soviets refused to authorize an Internation-

ART & CULTURE: Books: ***A Tree Grows in Brooklyn*** **(Betty Smith);** ***Genesis*** **(Delmore Schwartz);** ***The Big Rock Candy Mountain*** **(Wallace Stegner);** ***Christianity and Democracy*** **(Jacques Maritain);** ***Four Quartets*** **(T.S. Eliot);** ***Here Is Your War*** **(Ernie Pyle) ... Music: "One for My Baby" (Arlen and Mercer); "Besame Mucho" (Velazquez and Skylar);** ***Concerto for Orchestra*** **(Béla Bartók) ... Painting & Sculpture:**

"I wonder whether it is not too risky to repeat the struggle against the boundless space of Russia ... while the Anglo-Saxon peril is mounting in the West."—**Benito Mussolini on Hitler's neglect of the Mediterranean theater in favor of the U.S.S.R.**

al Red Cross inquiry, accusing the Poles of collaborating with Hitler.

In fact, Stalin had been looking for an excuse to break with Poland's London-based government-in-exile, and to recognize instead a Soviet-sponsored "national committee." He did so shortly after the Katyn controversy began. And for nearly five decades, his successors (along with Poland's Communist regimes) denied Soviet responsibility for the massacre. Finally, in 1990, Moscow admitted that Stalin's agents had done the deed—and that they'd also murdered the other 10,000 Polish officers, whose bodies were never found. **◂1939.3 ▸1944.6**

WORLD WAR II

Allies Win North Africa

4 On May 7, 1943, General Harold Alexander radioed Winston Churchill from Tunis: "All enemy resistance has ceased. We are masters of the North African shores." The Germans formally surrendered two days later. The campaign for Tunisia had begun—badly—in November 1942, with the landing of the Allied 1st Army, under British general Kenneth Anderson. The mostly American force found German resistance stiffer than expected. The worst came in February 1943, when Rommel's Afrika Korps overwhelmed green U.S. troops at the Kasserine Pass; some 2,400 Yanks surrendered.

But after that debacle, the GIs got some extra training from British officers, and a new U.S. corps commander arrived: the fiery George S. Patton. Overextended again, the Afrika Korps was soon forced back through the Kasserine. Montgomery's 8th Army, which had recently chased Rommel's troops out of Libya, closed in from the east. Rommel counterattacked, but withdrew after losing 50 tanks. On March 9, sick and exhausted, he returned to Germany to plead with Hitler to abandon North Africa. The Führer called him a coward and relieved him of his command.

Under General Hans Jürgen von Arnim, German-Italian forces retreated toward Bizerte and Tunis, holding out for weeks in a circle around the twin cities. But on May 6, the Allies began an all-out assault—and the next day, Tunis

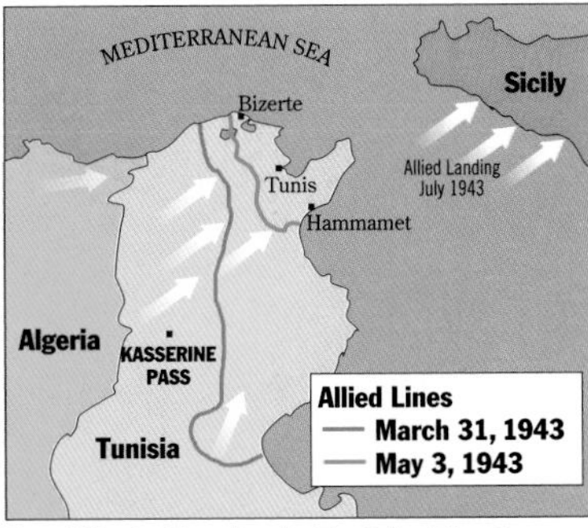

The Allied offensive in Tunisia. The Germans surrendered on May 9; by July the Allies were landing on the shores of Italy.

fell to British troops, while the Americans and Free French captured Bizerte. Arnim and 250,000 of his men were taken prisoner. With North Africa wrested from Axis domination, the Mediterranean was safe for Allied ships. Now the invasion of Sicily could begin. **◂1942.9 ▸1943.5**

WORLD WAR II

Italian Invasion

5 General Eisenhower called it "the first page of the liberation of the European continent." The invasion of Sicily began on July 10, 1943, catching Axis commanders unprepared. (They'd been duped by a British-uniformed corpse, bearing false battle plans, planted on a Spanish beach.) U.S. airborne troops touched down on the island's southern tip before dawn, followed by Allied infantrymen. Although the invaders encountered heavy fire from the retreating Germans, the Italians surrendered in droves, while local inhabitants offered a warm welcome. The Yanks, under Patton, seized Palermo on July 22; three weeks later they met Montgomery's Britons in Messina. By then, 100,000 Axis troops had escaped to mainland Italy—where Benito Mussolini had just been deposed.

Discontent with the dictator had been mounting as his people tired of an unwanted war. But the ailing Duce, fearing the Führer's wrath, refused to surrender. On July 24, the Fascist Grand Council dismissed him, and the next day King Vittorio Emanuele placed him under house arrest. Marshal Pietro Badoglio (an aged war hero who'd opposed Mussolini in the twenties) formed a new government and began secret talks with the Allies. Italy capitulated on September 3, as Montgomery's forces landed on the mainland; Eisenhower made the news public five days later.

Yet the struggle for the country continued. Nazi commandos rescued Mussolini, who established a puppet "republic" in the Alpine foothills. As the Allies pushed up the Italian boot, they met tough German resistance. Hitler's troops held Rome in spite of punishing air raids. By year's end, they had established a barrier across Italy's midsection that would frustrate the Allies for months to come. **◂1943.4 ▸1944.5**

After leaving Tunisia, Allied soldiers storm a Sicilian railroad station being used as a stronghold by retreating Axis forces.

BIRTHS

Arthur Ashe, U.S. tennis player.

Nolan Bushnell, U.S. inventor.

Catherine Deneuve, French actress.

Robert De Niro, U.S. actor and filmmaker.

Bobby Fischer, U.S. chess player.

George Harrison, U.K. musician.

Julio Iglesias, Spanish singer.

Mick Jagger, U.K. singer and composer.

Janis Joplin, U.S. singer.

Jean-Claude Killy, French skier.

Billie Jean King, U.S. tennis player.

James Levine, U.S. conductor.

Joe Namath, U.S. football player.

Sam Shepard, U.S. playwright and actor.

Lech Walesa, Polish president.

Betty Williams, Irish political activist.

Robert Woodward, U.S. journalist.

DEATHS

Stephen Vincent Benét, U.S. writer.

George Washington Carver, U.S. botanist.

Lorenz Hart, U.S. lyricist.

Marsden Hartley, U.S. painter.

Leslie Howard, U.K. actor.

Karl Landsteiner, U.S. pathologist.

Beatrix Potter, U.K. writer.

Sergei Rachmaninoff, Russian composer.

Wladyslaw Sikorski, Polish military and political leader.

Chaim Soutine, Lithuanian-French painter.

Fats Waller, U.S. musician.

Simone Weil, French philosopher.

Alexander Woollcott, U.S. journalist and writer.

Isoroku Yamamoto, Japanese admiral.

Broadway Boogie-Woogie* (Piet Mondrian); *Hoosick Falls in Winter* (Grandma Moses) ... Film: *Casablanca* (Michael Curtiz); *For Whom the Bell Tolls* (Sam Wood); *Ivan the Terrible, Part I* (Sergei Eisenstein); *Days of Wrath* (Carl Dreyer) ... Theater: *The Good Woman of Setzuan* (Bertolt Brecht); *One Touch of Venus* (Weill and Nash); *Something for the Boys* (Cole Porter) ... Radio: *Perry Mason.

"Czechoslovakia is on the right path and in the right camp ... of military victory and victorious peace."
—Eduard Beneš, at the signing of the Soviet-Czechoslovak Treaty on December 21, 1943

NEW IN 1943

18-year-old vote (Georgia).

American Broadcasting Co. (ABC).

The Jefferson Memorial.

Automatic withholding of federal income tax in U.S. (signed into law in June 1943).

IN THE UNITED STATES

▶FDR SEIZES RAILROADS—To ensure "that the supplies to our fighting men are not interrupted," FDR ordered the War Department to seize all American railroads in December 1943. The action came in the midst of a labor dispute. In a separate arbitration ruling, Roosevelt agreed to award rail operators a nine-cent-per-hour raise in lieu of overtime. ◂1942.M ▸1952.M

▶CARTOON WAR—Bill Mauldin joined the U.S. Army in 1940. After his division was shipped to Sicily in 1943, he joined the Mediterranean edition of *Stars and Stripes.* Soon his beleaguered GI cartoon characters, Willy and Joe, came to represent all the American servicemen who managed to maintain their humor and humanity while caught between the horrors of war and the isolated, and often indifferent, military bureaucracy.

▶PAPANICOLAOU'S QUEST—Sixteen years after he discovered the growth of cancerous cells in a vaginal smear, George Nicholas Papanicolaou published his paper "Diagnosis of Uterine Cancer by the Vaginal Smear" in 1943, and convinced the American medical establishment of the effectiveness of his diagnostic

1943

In a *Punch* cartoon, the right-leaning de Gaulle, who courted leftists for the Resistance, overshadowed Stalin himself.

WORLD WAR II

De Gaulle Unifies Resistance

6 The struggle for leadership of the Free French centered on two generals: Henri Giraud and Charles de Gaulle. De Gaulle took a decisive step forward in May 1943, when the Conseil National de la Résistance—an umbrella organization of noncommunist French Resistance groups—met for the first time in Paris. The CNR's 14 founders voted to entrust de Gaulle (now based in Algiers) with "management of the nation's interests," while Giraud, the Allied commander in French Africa, was relegated to running military affairs. Although the CNR eventually parted with both men, its initial stance convinced Allied leaders that France's destiny lay in de Gaulle's hands.

De Gaulle had been backed by Winston Churchill since 1940, while Roosevelt (who found him an overbearing egomaniac) had endorsed his rival. But the reactionary Giraud—famous for escaping from a Nazi prison camp—lacked political savvy. Despite his antipathy to the Germans, he remained loyal to the fence-sitting Pétain and outraged many French patriots by choosing staunch Vichyites as aides.

De Gaulle, meanwhile, had also gained the support of French colonial governors in Africa and the Pacific islands. And though he was nearly as conservative as Giraud, he had put aside ideology to court leftist Resistance leaders. In January 1942, he sent daring Resistance organizer Jean Moulin to unify France's underground fighters. By June 1943, when the Nazis tortured Moulin to death, that mission had largely been accomplished. As the CNR's first president, Moulin had persuaded even communists to support de Gaulle—at least temporarily. Within a year, de Gaulle had maneuvered Giraud into retirement. **◂1942.12 ▸1944.4**

WORLD WAR II

Wingate Behind the Lines

7 An eccentric in the best British military tradition, a spiritual heir of T.E. Lawrence, Brigadier General Orde Charles Wingate led a force of 3,000 British, Gurkha, and Burmese guerrillas into Japanese-held Burma in 1943. The "Chindits," as Wingate called

Brigadier General Wingate *(center, hatless)* before the invasion of Burma.

his irregulars, crossed the Chindwin River into enemy territory in February. Over the next three months, supplied solely by RAF airdrops, they stole through the jungle, blowing up railroads, wrecking highways, knocking down bridges. "Nothing is so devastating," said Wingate, "as to pounce upon the enemy in the dark, smite him hip and thigh, and vanish silently into the night." Tramping 25 miles a day, communicating by radio, birdcall, and carrier pigeon, Wingate's raiders inflicted substantial casualties on befuddled Japanese forces.

Wingate first drew public notice in the late 1930s when, assigned to Palestine intelligence, he organized Jewish defense patrols that later evolved into the Israeli army. In 1941, his ragtag band of Ethiopian and Sudanese commandos drove superior Italian forces from Addis Ababa.

Known to serenade himself with Arabic songs, Wingate advocated a diet supplemented with raw onions, and kept clean in the bush by scrubbing his body with a hairbrush. His lack of military decorum tended to irritate other officers, but his toughness and derring-do inspired loyalty among soldiers. "You can't help but follow him," one irregular reported, "when you see him charge through the elephant grass in that old pith helmet." In 1944, Wingate was killed in a crash while leading the Chindits on a glider invasion of Burma. **◂1942.2 ▸1945.M**

DIPLOMACY

Forging the Iron Curtain

8 Hoping to preserve the integrity of his country in postwar Europe, Eduard Beneš, leader of the Czechoslovak government-in-exile, signed a 1943 pact with the Soviet Union. Aimed specifically at Germany, which had dismembered Czechoslovakia in 1939, the agreement entailed a 20-year military alliance and a pledge of economic cooperation. Significantly, the Soviet-Czechoslovak Treaty bound the signatories to reject "any coalition directed against the other contracting party." On the basis of this clause, the Soviet Union would become Czechoslovakia's exclusive postwar ally, superseding Britain, France, and the former Little Entente states of Yugoslavia and Hungary.

Beneš envisioned a postwar Czechoslovakia bridging the gap between East and West. He assured the Western powers of Soviet goodwill: Stalin had personally promised him that the autonomy of Eastern European states would be respected; the alliance was meant to deter Germany, nothing more.

SPORTS: Baseball: New York Yankees defeat St. Louis Cardinals, 4–1; New York Giants relief pitcher Ace Adams sets modern record, pitching in 70 games ... Football: NFL, Chicago Bears defeat Washington Redskins, 41–21; Sammy Baugh (Washington) is first player to intercept four passes in one game ... Horse Racing: Count Fleet wins the Triple Crown.

"Man can will nothing unless he has first understood that he must count on no one but himself."
—Jean-Paul Sartre, *Being and Nothingness*

Fighter for Czech integrity: Eduard Beneš, with his wife, circa 1935.

British and American diplomats remained skeptical, suspecting a Soviet scheme to reverse the old *cordon sanitaire,* the system of buffer states traditionally used by the West to contain Russia. One feature of the Soviet-Czechoslovak Treaty fueled Western fears beyond all others: a protocol allowing any state that bordered Czechoslovakia or the Soviet Union and that had suffered German aggression to join the pact. Those terms covered most of Eastern Europe. Czechoslovakia unwittingly became the first block in a wall the Soviets were building between themselves and the West. **◂1939.2 ▸1944.11**

WORLD WAR II

Tito's Partisans

9 The Yugoslav partisans turned from resistance to revolution in 1943. Early in the year, after surviving the first of three Axis offensives aimed at their "final liquidation," the partisans began to focus on defeating Dragoljub Mihajlović's Serb nationalist Chetniks (formally titled the Yugoslav Army of the Fatherland). And in November, after Italy's collapse brought much of Yugoslavia's Adriatic coast under partisan control, they established a provisional government that forbade the Chetniks' patron, King Peter, to return from exile. Partisan leader Josip Broz Tito became marshal and head of state.

The son of a Croat blacksmith, Tito (Broz's nom de guerre) had been chief of Yugoslavia's outlawed communists when Germany attacked in 1941—but he had called on all ethnic groups and political parties to "rise like one man" against the invaders. Within months, his guerrillas had liberated half of Yugoslavia. The British-backed Chetniks, too, initially resisted the Germans, but soon the Partisans became the Chetniks' principal concern. (Though the Chetniks' collaboration with the Nazis led to Mihajlović's execution in 1946, historians still argue over the charges against him.) Despite staggering casualties and lack of outside aid, Tito's forces fought on, and by September 1943 their ranks had swollen to 250,000.

That month, Winston Churchill sent a commission to Yugoslavia to "find out who is killing the most Germans." After learning the answer, Britain shifted support to Tito. At the Tehran Conference in December, the Allies followed suit. In June 1944, the Partisans repulsed the Nazis' last offensive, and by the following May, a joint Partisan-Soviet drive had evicted the occupiers. **◂1941.4 ▸1948.6**

Tito (with his dog at his mountain headquarters) led Yugoslavia's partisan resistance.

LITERATURE

Existentialist Resistance

10 Jean-Paul Sartre's *Being and Nothingness* established the French thinker as existentialism's most influential theorist. The 1943 book—shaped, ironically, by German philosopher Martin Heidegger, whose Nazi-approved works Sartre read while imprisoned by the Germans early in the war—declares that consciousness, unlike matter, was unaffected by determinism. Though existence is essentially purposeless, humans are free to create themselves through action. For Sartre, who joined the Resistance after escaping from his German captors, freedom and responsibility were inseparable from political action—and writing. His play *The Flies,* also from 1943, was both a retelling of a Greek myth and a satire (veiled, to elude government censors) on Vichy France. Aegisthus, the usurper, represents the German occupiers. Clytemnestra, the unfaithful queen, stands in for the Vichy collaborators. Orestes, who kills them both, is the Resistance.

Intellectual's intellectual: Sartre in Paris, photographed by Henri Cartier-Bresson.

Sartre later became a quasi-Marxist, though he broke with communism when Moscow crushed the 1956 Hungarian uprising. He remained intellectually productive and politically engaged for decades, protesting the Cold War, cheering the revolutionaries in Algeria and Vietnam, making Maoism fashionable in 1960s France. With his equally formidable companion, Simone de Beauvoir, Sartre gave the world its image of the café-sitting, disputatious French intellectual—and inspired generations of activist thinkers. **◂1942.13 ▸1949.13**

IN THE UNITED STATES

test, the "Pap smear," in the detection of cervical cancer. By staining a smear of vaginal secretions or cervical, uterine, or ovarian cells, Papanicolaou was able to detect irregular, cancerous cells that had been shed by the cervix. ▸1960.1

▸IKE'S SUPREME COMMAND—As commander of U.S. forces in Europe, General Dwight D. Eisenhower was named supreme commander of the Allied Expeditionary Force. By December 1943, he had begun planning the invasion of Normandy and had chalked up an impressive winning streak in North Africa, Sicily, and Italy.

▸A SECULAR THEOLOGIAN—Reinhold Niebuhr was a modern rarity: a churchman who wielded enormous influence in the halls of secular power. In *The Nature and Destiny of Man,* completed in 1943, Niebuhr attempted to synthesize orthodox Reformation theology and Renaissance optimism. Humanity, he argued, enjoyed "indeterminate possibilities" if only people resisted belief in their own perfection. Always concerned with the interrelation of religion and politics, he helped shape postwar American foreign policy. ◂1932.7 ▸1951.13

▸AN AMERICAN MINSTREL—A legend at age 31, leading American folk musician Woody Guthrie published his autobiography, *Bound for Glory,* in 1943. Born in Oklahoma, Guthrie left home at 15 but never abandoned his hardworking country heritage. Traveling the country by rail during the 1920s, he experienced the hard life he later documented in more than a thousand songs, including such folk standards as "Hard Traveling," and "This Land Is My Land." Guthrie's son, Arlo, became a prominent folk-rock performer.

POLITICS & BUSINESS: GNP: $191.6 billion ... War Manpower Commission prohibits "essential" workers from leaving their jobs, affects 27,000,000 ... Race riots in Detroit, Los Angeles, and New York ... Supreme Court rules flag salute optional in school ... Roosevelt orders minimum 48-hour week in defense production ... American Medical Association found guilty of violating antitrust laws.

"NO LEGS NO JOKES NO CHANCE."—**Walter Winchell's secretary cabling her boss after seeing *Oklahoma!* in a New Haven, Connecticut, tryout**

WORLD WAR II

▶ALLIES CONFER—Allied leaders held several strategy sessions in 1943—only the last of which included Stalin. At Casablanca in January, Churchill and Roosevelt decided to invade Sicily in July (which happened), and to assault Rangoon by sea (which did not). In May, at Washington, the two men agreed to stage Operation Overlord—the invasion of France—in May 1944; later, in Quebec, they postponed the date. In November, in Tehran, the "Big Three" met for the first time. Stalin offered to attack the Eastern Front whenever Overlord began. (He did.) He also promised to intervene against Japan. (He did, sort of: The Soviets invaded Manchuria one day before Japan surrendered.)

▶HITLER'S WORST ENEMY—The Führer (who'd taken personal charge of the German military after the U.S. entered the war) regularly ignored advice from his able strategists. Megalomaniacally plunging his armies into unwinnable situations, he blamed his neutered generals when inevitable defeat occurred. A dramatic case in point: He ordered his outgunned soldiers to stand firm on the Eastern Front against 5.5 million Soviet troops in 1943. They did and were crushed.

▶YAMAMOTO KILLED—Japan lost its greatest military leader in 1943, when American fighters blasted Admiral Isoroku Yamamoto *(below)* out of the sky over the Pacific. Planner of the attack on Pearl Harbor, Yamamoto was on his way to inspect troops

on the Solomon Islands. Allied intelligence intercepted his itinerary, and the attackers were in the air and waiting when Yamamoto's plane flew into view on April 18.

▶ATTU AND KISKA—Trying to divert attention from its imminent attack on Midway Island, Japan in 1942 landed troops

1943

Agnes de Mille's famous "dream ballet": As Laurey dreams of choosing between Curly and Jud, a budding woman's psyche comes to life.

THEATER

An Art Form Remade

11 On March 31, 1943, the curtain rose on a new Broadway musical. Instead of an opening production number showcasing leggy chorines, the surprised audience saw a middle-aged farm woman silently working a butter churn. A cowboy ambled onstage, singing a lilting ode to "a beautiful mornin'." Nearly three hours later, the audience was on its feet. The new team of Richard Rodgers and Oscar Hammerstein II had a hit, and an art form was in upheaval. After *Oklahoma!* musical theater was changed forever.

Except for such rarities as 1927's *Show Boat* (also written by Hammerstein, with music by Jerome Kern), Broadway musicals had long centered on stars, gags, and girls; the sassy songs and smart dances were irrelevant to the lame plots. In *Oklahoma!*, lyricist Hammerstein, composer Rodgers, choreographer Agnes de Mille, and director Rouben Mamoulian determined that every element—dialogue, song, setting, and dance—would dramatize the turn-of-the-century tale of good farm girl Laurey, her brash cowboy Curly, and the murderously jealous farmhand Jud. The score (including "Oh, What a Beautiful Mornin'," "The Surrey with the Fringe on Top," "I Cain't Say No," and the rousing title anthem) was emotionally nuanced and musically glorious. And de Mille's first-act ballet was revolutionary: Filled with Laurey's dreams of sex, romance, and menace, the ballet makes her infinitely more complex than the era's typical musical heroine.

When the warring farmers and cattlemen of the Oklahoma Territory united in joyous anticipation of security and statehood, even cynical viewers were moved by the spectacle of a people's uncommon strengths and a country's golden possibilities. Audiences fell in love with *Oklahoma!* during its five-year run, and its innovations stuck. **◂1927.8 ▸1965.12**

IDEAS

The Analysis of Evil

12 As a Jewish concentration-camp inmate, Viennese psychoanalyst Bruno Bettelheim stayed sane by observing the horrors around him with a clinical eye. After intervention from Eleanor Roosevelt and New York governor Herbert Lehman enabled him to emigrate to the United States, Bettelheim recorded his findings in a harrowing essay called "Individual and Mass Behavior in Extreme Situations," which appeared in the October 1943 issue of *The Journal of Abnormal and Social Psychology.*

Bettelheim's examination of prisoners' responses to conditions of unrelenting terror, deprivation, and humiliation (designed not only to break their will, but to intimidate the population at large) was crucial in anticipating the postwar problem of rehabilitating survivors. It made its 40-year-old author famous, and eventually became required reading for Allied occupation authorities in Europe.

Before his internment, Bettelheim—encouraged by Anna Freud—had specialized in treating autistic children. In America, as director (from 1944) of the Sonia Shankman Orthogenic School at the University of Chicago, he created a live-in environment for disturbed young people, using techniques that inverted the soul-destroying practices of the camps. His methods (described in such books as *Love Is Not Enough*) were both influential and highly controversial, as were his views on child-rearing (*A Good Enough Parent*), and even on fairy tales (*The Uses of Enchantment*). Yet however important his insights, Bettelheim never escaped his own demons: In 1990—haunted by illness, his wife's death, and nightmares set in Dachau and Buchenwald—he committed suicide. **◂1923.4 ▸1944.10**

WORLD WAR II: January: Allies take Papua New Guinea; Germans withdraw from Caucasus; Casablanca Conference; Siege of Leningrad ends after 900 days; British enter Tripoli ... February: Germans defeated at Stalingrad; U.S. retakes Guadalcanal; Rommel retreats through Kasserine Pass ... March: Rommel recalled to Germany...April: Warsaw Ghetto uprising ... May: Allies take Tunisia; Washington Conference;

"Civilization is the process of setting man free from men."—**Ayn Rand, *The Fountainhead***

LITERATURE

Glorifying the Individualist

13 Ayn Rand's didactic novel *The Fountainhead* collected a dozen rejections before it was published in 1943. The 754-page tome (her later bestseller, *Atlas Shrugged,* was half again as big) proceeded to become one of the century's most popular works of fiction. Although undistinguished by literary standards, the book was a vehicle for Rand's objectivist philosophy, whose cardinal virtues were uncompromising individualism and unapologetic selfishness.

Rand had emigrated to America from Russia in 1926 when she was 21. Viewing the Manhattan skyline for the first time from shipboard, she vowed to write a novel with the skyscraper as its theme. *The Fountainhead* glorified that "symbol of achievement." In the book, the dynamic architect Howard Roark blows up a housing project of his design after bureaucrats tamper with the plans. "The rule of the second-hander, the second-rater, the ancient monster," he declaims, "has broken loose and is running amok." An objectivist avatar, Roark disdains the "collectivists"—those tainted with altruism, religious faith, the herd mentality.

Radically individualist, Ayn Rand detested the modern welfare state.

Though dismissed by mainstream philosophers, objectivism became an industry, complete with seminars, lectures, and inspirational tapes. A self-proclaimed "radical capitalist," Rand promoted a vision of "man as a heroic being, with his own happiness as the moral purpose of life, with productive achievement as his noblest activity, and reason as his only absolute." **◂1943.10**

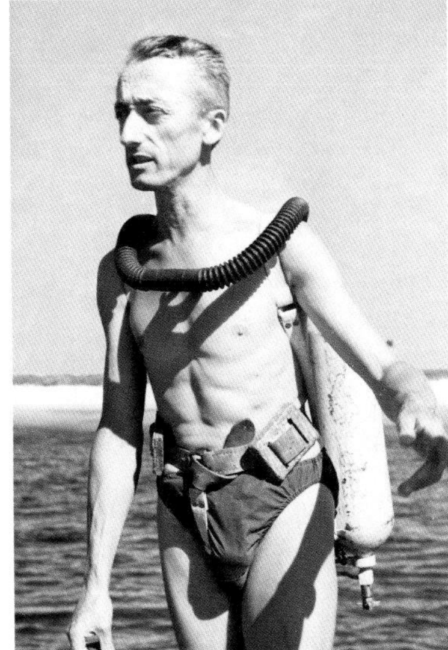

Jacques-Yves Cousteau models an early design of the Aqua-Lung.

TECHNOLOGY

The Ocean World Opens Up

14 In January 1943, a young French naval engineer named Jacques-Yves Cousteau and his partner, Emile Gagnan, toted a contraption consisting of little more than a regulator (modified from a gadget Gagnan had designed to allow wartime cars to run on cooking gas) and two tanks of compressed air to the Marne River outside Paris. They were testing a device inventors had tried to build for a century: a backpack-like apparatus that would deliver air to a diver automatically, without clumsy hoses to the surface.

Cousteau's wife snapped photographs as he slipped into the frigid water. A minute later, he resurfaced, cursing. The Aqua-Lung (as its creators called it) had failed. But later that day, after making minor readjustments, Cousteau strapped it on again, dived into an indoor tank, and breathed comfortably while performing subsurface somersaults. The self-contained underwater breathing apparatus—scuba, for short—had arrived.

The Aqua-Lung revolutionized underwater exploration. In the next few years, as a pair of research ships—Sweden's *Albatross* and Denmark's *Galathea*—dredged, cored, and mapped the ocean floors to unprecedented depths, scuba gear allowed people to live and work under the sea as never before.

Gagnan, a retiring type, reaped little glory for his breakthrough. Cousteau, however, went on to fame, pioneering the art of underwater photography and commanding his own research vessel, the *Calypso*. Via film, television, and books, Captain Cousteau navigated global audiences through the dazzling deeps. **▸1977.M**

LITERATURE

The Little Prince

15 Antoine de Saint-Exupéry was a pilot and writer who never felt content on the ground. But one forced landing proved to be quite fortunate. Attempting to set a flying record between Paris and Saigon, he crashed in the Libyan desert, where he almost died of thirst. Years later, the experience formed the basis for his 1943 children's book, *The Little Prince*. The allegorical tale, concerning a downed airman who meets a royal juvenile from Asteroid B-612, was aimed at adults as well as their offspring. As he recounts his interplanetary voyage, the prince depicts most of the grown-ups he encounters as avaricious, self-absorbed, and unimaginative. By contrast, the prince himself—an eternal child—is full of goodwill, spontaneity, and simple wisdom.

Saint-Exupéry had been an adult-book author for over a decade, famous for novels (notably *Night Flight*) and memoirs (*Wind, Sand, and Stars*) that used the beauties and rigors of aviation as material for philosophical musings on discipline, integrity, fraternity, and the joys that can be won only by risking all. Yet he's best remembered for his single children's story. The son of impoverished aristocrats, he'd been passionate about flying since boyhood, when he built a bicycle fitted with wings; later, he had established some of the first commercial routes over South America. When *The Little Prince* appeared, Saint-Exupéry was flying for the Allies in North Africa. He died on a reconnaissance mission the following year. **◂1931.V ▸1957.V**

The Little Prince, posing for his "best portrait."

WORLD WAR II

on the two westernmost Aleutian islands, Attu and Kiska. The United States left the invaders alone on the barren Pacific rocks, the only U.S. territory occupied during the war, until 1943. In May, American troops arrived on Attu and killed all but a handful of 2,500 Japanese soldiers, many of whom died in banzai charges. A sign *(above)* that marks the grave of an American pilot shot down over Kiska and buried by the Japanese reads, "Sleeping here a brave air-hero who lost youth and happiness for his motherland July 25 Nippon army." Japan withdrew from Kiska before a U.S. amphibious force landed in August.

▶PLOESTI BOMBED—The rich oil fields of Ploesti, Romania, were vital to the German war effort. The Allies knew this and so set out to destroy them. Flying 900 miles from Libya, a wave of American

bombers came in low over Ploesti on August 1 and wiped out nearly half the refineries *(the Astra, Romana refinery, above)*. Of the 177 planes that participated in Operation Tidal Wave, 54 were shot down, with a loss of 532 airmen.

▶DAY AND NIGHT BOMBING—The techniques were different; the effects, equally deadly: British bombers preferred to fly at night, strung out in a long, low line; the Americans, flying in tight clusters at high altitude, preferred daytime runs. In the summer and early fall of 1943, Allied raids killed 40,000 people in the Battles of Ruhr, Hamburg, and Berlin. Desperate earthbound defenders built decoy cities on the outskirts of Berlin and Hamburg, but the bombs consistently found their marks.

Battle of the Atlantic ends ... June: Germans leave North Africa ... July: Battle of Kursk; Allied Pacific offensive begins; Allied invasion of Sicily; Mussolini deposed ... August: Quebec Conference ... September: Italy surrenders; Germans occupy Rome, retreat from Naples ... October: Italy declares war on Germany ... November: Russians retake Kiev; Cairo and Tehran Conference ... December: U.S. lands on Rabul.

"Somehow I suspect that if Shakespeare were alive today, he might be a jazz fan himself."—**Duke Ellington**

AROUND THE WORLD

▶ACID TEST—Experimenting with a disease-causing fungus, Swiss chemist Albert Hofmann ingested an ergot-derived compound in 1943 and later proclaimed, "With my eyes closed, fantastic pictures of extraordinary plasticity and intensive color seemed to surge toward me." Two decades before the Age of Aquarius, Hofmann had accidentally discovered the hallucinogenic properties of LSD.

▶UN FOOD CONFERENCE—The name United Nations initially referred to the countries (known informally as the Allies) fighting the Axis. In May 1943, delegates of the 31 Allied and 12 "associated" nations (those that had severed diplomatic relations with at least one Axis power) gathered at the Homestead resort in Hot Springs, Virginia, for the United Nations Food and Agricultural Conference. Pledging to improve global nutrition and living standards after the war, the conferees set up an interim commission to study international food production and distribution. When the United

Nations was reconstituted as an international peacekeeping organization in 1945, the food commission became the Food and Agriculture Organization (FAO)—the UN's first specialized agency. ▶1944.13

▶COMINTERN INTERRED—Stalin abandoned world revolution in 1943, when he dissolved the Third International Comintern. Wishing to calm his allies' fears of Soviet expansionism, Stalin intended the gesture to assure them that subversion was the last thing on his mind. The reality, however, was that by then most foreign Communist Parties were securely under Moscow's thumb. ◀1935.9 ▶1976.14

1943

Frank Sinatra in *Meet Danny Wilson* (1952), in which he plays a singer who becomes involved with racketeers.

MUSIC

The Voice

16 With American men at war, young American women found a new source of sexual frissons in a scrawny, blue-eyed kid from Hoboken, New Jersey. Frank Sinatra had his first million-selling record, "All or Nothing at All," in 1943. Sinatra, 27, had just broken with the Tommy Dorsey Band, with which he'd scored a string of hits over the past three years. But from the moment he launched his solo career—sauntering onstage at New York's Paramount ballroom in December 1942—he was a sensation. Bobby-soxers swooned for "the Voice" as he crooned melancholy (yet swinging) love songs. Sinatramania swept the country, leaving throngs of teenagers quivering in its wake. "He was a skinny kid with big ears," remembered Dorsey, whose sensitive trombone phrasing was the model for Sinatra's technique. "And yet what he did to women was something awful. And he did it every night, everywhere he went."

What Sinatra did was sing with such intimacy that every woman and girl in the house felt he was singing directly to her. In October 1944, 30,000 mostly female, mostly hysterical fans tried to storm the Paramount, presaging later reactions to Elvis Presley and the Beatles. The Big Band Era was ending. Freelance vocalists ruled, and Sinatra was the undisputed king.

Untouchable for nearly ten years, "the Voice" was silenced in 1952. With his vocal cords hemorrhaging, his personal life boiling over (he married four times), Sinatra was dropped by his talent agency. He waged a remarkable comeback as a movie star, winning an Oscar for his role in *From Here to Eternity* in 1953, then cutting a host of Top Ten records for the Capitol label. Chairman of the board once more, Sinatra—despite the vagaries of musical fashion—drew crowds into the 1990s. **◀1935.7 ▶1951.11**

MUSIC

The Ellington Effect

17 *Black, Brown, and Beige*—an extended orchestration by Edward Kennedy "Duke" Ellington—premiered before a standing-room-only audience at New York's Carnegie Hall in January 1943. Conceived as a "tone parallel" of African-American history, the suite was divided into three sections: The first, based largely on spirituals, conjured up slavery times and the development of the black church; the second, suffused with blues and West Indian motifs, recalled emancipation and honored the black soldier's role in American wars; and the third evoked Harlem and (as Ellington put it) "all the little Harlems around the U.S.A." Though some critics caviled, most proclaimed a revolution: Jazz had come of age as "serious" music.

The 57-minute concert, the first of Ellington's eight annual orchestral performances at Carnegie, inaugurated the richest period of the composer-bandleader's multifarious career. (He was a master of musical forms ranging from the danceable to the sacred.) The only recording of the Carnegie Hall engagement was a bootleg tape that was not issued until some 30 years later; after a concert in Boston, the Ellington orchestra never again performed *Black, Brown, and Beige* in its entirety. No one, in fact, will ever hear it played the way it was that night: Though Ellington was more concerned with structure than any previous jazz composer, he regarded the written score as a sketch of a composition's contours, not a blueprint. He rewrote his pieces until the last minute, and this one wasn't published.

Elegant and ever-versatile: Duke Ellington, just before his first European tour in 1933.

For the Duke, the orchestra itself was a giant instrument to be played as the spirit moved him. Aficionados called his mix of sophistication and spontaneity (enhanced by such world-class improvisers as baritone saxophonist Harry Carney and trombonist Joe "Tricky Sam" Nanton) the "Ellington Effect." **◀1927.9 ▶1945.15**

SCIENCE

Decoding Genetics

18 In 1943, after a long and systematic assault on the problem, a Canadian-born scientist named Oswald Avery *(below)* and two assistants identified the agent responsible for the transfer of genetic information from one generation to the next. Avery, a bacteriologist on the staff of the Rockefeller Institute in New York, had focused his research on pneumococci. These microbes existed in two forms—one that was linked to pneumonia in humans, and one that wasn't. Strangely, the mere presence of the first type, even after it was dead, would transform offspring of the second into the virulent form. Although biologists had managed by the mid-1930s to isolate the chemical that transmitted the genetic message, they had not succeeded in identifying it.

Through a process of elimination lasting nearly a decade, Avery's team was able to determine what the substance was *not*. What it *was* surprised geneticists (they'd been expecting the messenger to be a protein): deoxyribonucleic acid, or DNA, a molecule long thought to be genetically irrelevant. After Avery's results were published in 1944, scientists began to study DNA intensely. Eventually, they found that it carried the genetic code for virtually all life on earth—from bacteria and most viruses to redwoods and whales. **◀1937.6 ▶1953.1**

NOBEL PRIZES: Peace: No award ... Literature: No award ... Awards given retroactively in 1944: Chemistry: George de Hevesy (Hungarian; use of isotopes as tracers) ... Medicine: Henrik Dam and Edward XA. Doisy (Danish, U.S.; vitamin K) ... Physics: Otto Stern (U.S.; molecular beams and magnetic strength of the proton).

A VOICE FROM 1943

America's Pundit in Chief

From "The Captains of Their Souls," by Walter Lippmann, July 31, 1943

Required reading through nine presidencies: Walter Lippmann *(above, at home in Washington in 1956)* never gave readers the conventional wisdom. Below, in 1942, with his wife, Helen, who was director of the American Red Cross Nurses' Aide Corps.

No political columnist has wielded more clout than Walter Lippmann, whose U.S. Foreign Policy: Shield of the Republic *was a smash bestseller in 1943. Condensed by* Reader's Digest *and reduced to cartoon form for* Ladies' Home Journal, *the slim but weighty volume offered a pragmatic vision of America's place in the world once the Allies had won the war. An erudite argument for realpolitik (and against the idealistic one-worldism then in fashion among politicians), it was unlikely pop-culture fare. But Lippmann was a national institution: a onetime Harvard philosophy student who had advised presidents since Woodrow Wilson, and whose syndicated column,* Today and Tomorrow, *was must reading for millions. Fiercely independent, Lippmann had denounced Roosevelt's New Deal; later, he opposed Lyndon B. Johnson's escalation of American involvement in Vietnam. The excerpt below, from his column of July 31, 1943, addresses in characteristically elevated prose another question that would face Americans after the victory: whether to hold the people of the Axis nations accountable for their leaders' crimes.* **◂1940.V ▸1948.V**

The supreme heresy of our enemies is that they have carried ruthlessly to the logical conclusion the denial of man's personal responsibility, and therefore of his human dignity.... Our response to this heresy usually takes the form of asserting the rights of men and of nations against the arbitrary tyrants and their adherents. But this is only the negative and partial aspect of the truth. For men are not really free when they are released from bondage. They are only freed men. They are not free men until they are the captains of their souls and know that they themselves have the power and the duty to choose between good and evil.

The distinction is crucial. If we bear it in mind we shall not make the moral error of saying to the Italians or the Germans or to anyone else: you were all the innocent victims of the tyrants whom you obeyed. That is a pernicious sentimentality which denies man's moral responsibility. Nor shall we say to them: because you obeyed these tyrants, you and your children are one and all congenitally and forever cursed. That is the damnable heresy of our enemies which denies the inviolability of the human soul, or in the ancient language of faith, the fatherhood of God. Nor shall we say: leave it to us and we shall give you back liberty. That is the moral blindness and the intellectual error of not knowing that freedom is personal responsibility. Nor shall we say: surrender, and we shall stuff freedom down your throats at the point of the bayonet. That is a doctrinaire self-righteousness which makes freedom meaningless and odious.

The true view is the ancient view that men are responsible for their acts of commission and of omission, and that therefore the adult Germans and Italians are accountable for the acts of their governments.... We treat animals, children, the insane, with kindness. But justice we invoke only among responsible men.

The rule of justice ... is then tempered with mercy, which stems at last from the knowledge that we too are sinners and must therefore give to others what we must ask for ourselves....

These considerations are not remote from practical policy.... The constant knowledge must be with us that our power, like all power, is good only within the moral order.

"You will bring about the destruction of the German war machine, the elimination of Nazi tyranny over the oppressed peoples of Europe, and security for ourselves in a free world."—**Dwight D. Eisenhower, to the Allied Expeditionary Forces before the landing at Normandy**

STORY OF THE YEAR

D-Day Begins the Allied Crusade

1 It was the largest seaborne invasion ever, involving 2,000 ships, 4,000 landing craft, and 11,000 airplanes. As Allied troops crossed the choppy English Channel toward Normandy on June 6, 1944, their officers read out the order of the day from the supreme commander in Europe. "You are about to embark upon a great crusade," General Eisenhower's statement began. The crusade was Operation Overlord: the reconquest of northern Europe after four years of Nazi domination.

First planned for 1942, the landing had been postponed repeatedly—with a final delay of 24 hours caused by the worst storm in a quarter century. D-Day (a term referring to the first day of any military operation, but now synonymous in popular parlance with this invasion) opened with predawn paratroop raids. Minesweepers cleared the waters while warships and bombers pounded enemy positions. Prefabricated floating harbors were moved into place. At 6:30 AM, American, British, and Canadian troops under General Montgomery began swarming from landing craft onto beaches codenamed Utah, Omaha, Gold, Juno, and Sword. After wading through the icy surf or charging landward in amphibious tanks, they struggled past steel obstacles and barbed wire to recapture the first patches of French soil. By day's end, 155,000 men were ashore.

While preparations for the landing were too massive to conceal, disputes among the Nazi high command hobbled the German response. Hitler and Rommel (now overseeing operations in France) squabbled with Runstedt, commander in chief in the west, over the probable invasion site and the best line of defense. When the attack came, Hitler took it for a diversion, and held back his forces for the "real" invasion. Only at Omaha Beach was initial resistance heavy, with 3,000 American casualties on the first day of fighting. The invaders quickly spread out along 100 miles of coastline. But Normandy's Nazi-held cities proved harder to crack. Cherbourg held out for ten grueling days, Caen for more than a month.

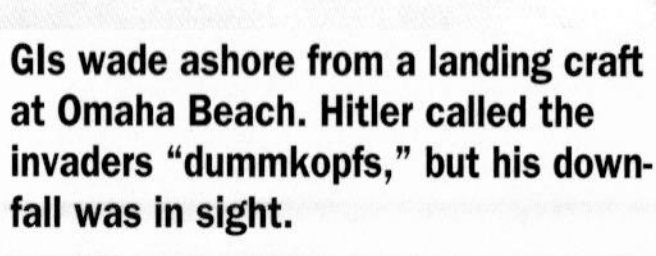

GIs wade ashore from a landing craft at Omaha Beach. Hitler called the invaders "dummkopfs," but his downfall was in sight.

By mid-August, however, the Allies had broken out of Normandy and were sweeping across France. The Low Countries—and Germany itself—lay before them.

◂1943.5 ▸1944.4

WORLD WAR II

Hitler's Desperate Measures

2 The Nazi war machine began to falter long before Allied forces entered Germany. Bombs were largely responsible—those dropped by planes, and one planted by would-be assassins. In both cases, Hitler's response was to terrorize his enemies, real and perceived.

A V-2 rocket that failed to explode, displayed in London's Trafalgar Square.

By mid-1944, the Allies' prolonged air offensive had finally undermined German fuel and aircraft production. Meanwhile, British and American factories were turning out vastly improved planes in unprecedented quantities. As fleets of bombers pummeled the Reich's cities, the Luftwaffe could not retaliate in kind. But the Germans had developed a secret weapon: the guided missile.

The first to appear was the V-1. These jet-powered "buzz bombs" started hitting Britain in June; by March 1945, when the last one exploded, they'd killed 5,500 people, mostly in London. The Allies seized the main V-1 bases, around Calais, in September 1944. Then came the rocket-powered, supersonic V-2s—even more devastating (just one could raze a city block) and harder to intercept. Launched from the Netherlands, the V-2s killed 2,500. The V-missile barrages were more fearsome than the Blitz of 1940, but they failed to break Britain's will to fight.

German morale, however, was unraveling. In July, a group of officers and civilian officials, dismayed by battlefield disasters and mounting atrocities, attempted a coup. Colonel Graf Claus von Stauffenberg planted a briefcase bomb at Hitler's East Prussian field headquarters. By chance, someone moved the case, and Hitler was only slightly wounded. The eight coup leaders were strangled while hanging from meathooks; 5,200 other people, including the families of alleged plotters, were executed as well. (Erwin Rommel, the conspirators' candidate to succeed Hitler, was given the choice between a show trial and suicide; he chose the latter.) Paranoid to begin with, Hitler now trusted almost no one—including his surviving generals.

◂1940.11 ▸1945.10

WORLD WAR II

Nazis Out of Russia

3 The Soviet Union evicted the Nazi invaders in 1944. The year's triumphs began, appropriately, with the liberation of Leningrad—birthplace of the Bolshevik Revolution—after the longest siege in modern history.

Since autumn 1941, German-Finnish forces had choked Leningrad in a "circle of steel." Starvation, disease, exposure, and shelling killed 650,000 residents in 1942 alone. Winter was hellish: As they ran out of shoes to eat and furniture to burn, families huddled together to await death. Frozen bodies lay everywhere.

Early in 1943, Soviet forces breached the blockade, but failed to lift it. Then, on January 14, 1944, Leningraders again awoke to the sounds of battle—and on January 27 the siege was finished. Over the following months, the Soviets recaptured city after city. In May, Hitler ordered a general withdrawal

Leningraders butcher a horse killed in the battle that ended a 900-day siege.

1944

ART & CULTURE: Books: *The Dwarf* (Pär Lagerkvist); *The Razor's Edge* (W. Somerset Maugham); *The Lost Weekend* (Charles Jackson); *Strange Fruit* (Lillian Smith); *Social Darwinism in American Thought* (Richard Hofstadter) ... Music: "Don't Fence Me In" (Cole Porter); "Sentimental Journey" (Homer, Brown, and Green); "Moonlight in Vermont" (Suessdorf and Blackburn); *Bachianas Brasileiras* (Heitor

"Yes, we have no Cassino/We have no Cassino today./We have Aversa, Caserta, Mignano, Minturno/And dear old Napoli,/But, yes, we have no Cassino/We have no Cassino today."—**Popular GI song in Italy**

from Russia; by September, Soviet troops were pursuing the invaders through Poland to the German border. Only in Latvia did Axis forces retain a toehold on Soviet soil.

Now the Red Army took on the U.S.S.R.'s Nazified neighbors. As the Soviets attacked, Romania's King Michael overthrew Iron Guard (fascist) dictator Ion Antonescu. After signing an armistice with the Soviets, Michael declared war on Germany. In Bulgaria, a leftist colonel, Kimon Georgiev, seized power and followed Romania's lead. Stalin's forces poured into Yugoslavia, linked up with Tito's Partisans, and marched into Albania. By year's end, Soviet troops were subduing Hungary. A new empire was taking shape. **◂1943.2 ▸1945.2**

WORLD WAR II

Liberation of Paris

4 By mid-August 1944, a million Allied troops had landed in Normandy, and thousands were pouring through gaps in the German line. Free French and U.S. forces had landed on the Riviera and were battling their way northward. To aid the liberators, Resistance fighters sabotaged bridges and telephone lines, staged ambushes, and seized local government offices. On August 19, Paris erupted in armed revolt. Hitler ordered the city burned, but garrison commander Dietrich von Choltitz disobeyed. Instead, on August 25, he surrendered to General Jacques Philippe Leclerc of the just-arrived French 2nd Armored Division. After four years of Nazi occupation, the capital was free.

Later that day, Parisians cheered General Charles de Gaulle, whose Committee of National Liberation had declared itself France's provisional government. But when Resistance leaders asked him to proclaim the new republic from a city hall balcony, he refused. "The republic," he said, "has never ceased to exist."

The Resistance had indeed kept the republican spirit alive, but within its ranks there was sharp disagreement over the nation's future. The movement included such diverse groups as Combat, composed of professionals, businesspeople, and army officers; Libération, which mobilized workers; Franc-Tireur, led by leftist intellectuals; and the church-based Témoignage Chrétien. Hiding in the mountains was the Maquis, a guerrilla army of youths fleeing forced labor in Germany. Northern France's strongest group was the communist-dominated Front National. The new government would have to keep factionalism from escalating into civil war.

A collaborator's shame, captured by the great war photographer Robert Capa. Her baby's father was one of the German occupiers.

Most French citizens, of course, had done little to hinder the Nazis, however much they may have felt like resisting. As for those accused of outright collaboration, their fate was handled by the courts—and by their indignant neighbors. Some 9,000 were summarily executed; 700 others were executed after the trial. The most private acts of treason were punished by public humiliation: Hundreds of women were stripped, shorn bald, and paraded through the streets for sleeping with the enemy. **◂1943.6 ▸1945.2**

Another Roman empire crumbles as U.S. tanks roar past the Colosseum.

WORLD WAR II

Cassino, Anzio, and Rome

5 By 1944, British general Harold Alexander's forces (the U.S. 5th Army, under Lieutenant General Mark Clark, and the British 8th, under Major General Oliver Leese) had learned that Italy—once regarded as the "soft underbelly" of Europe—was a very hard place. Struggling across rugged terrain, they were outsoldiered by Field Marshal Albert Kesselring's mountain-trained troops, and stymied along the Gustav Line.

This front, bisecting Italy south of Rome, hinged on Cassino—whose sixth-century fortress-monastery, still inhabited by Benedictine monks, dominated a 1,700-foot crag. Even after Allied bombers pulverized the town and its landmark, Kesselring's men held out in the ruins. On January 22, an Allied force landed at the port of Anzio, behind the Gustav Line, only to be pinned down for 123 bloody days. Finally, in May, Polish troops stormed Monte Cassino and the Anzio force broke free; on June 5 the Allies entered Rome. The Eternal City emerged relatively unscathed, and crowds cheered the arriving soldiers. But Rome's value was symbolic, not strategic.

Kesselring retreated north toward Florence, which remained in German hands until mid-August. (The Nazis, forgetting promises to respect the city's historic treasures, dynamited its Renaissance bridges; American "pinpoint" bombing, not always accurate, also took its toll.) And by October, when autumn rains quelled the fighting, the Allied advance had stalled at a new front, running from the Ligurian Sea to the northern Adriatic: the Gothic Line. **◂1943.5 ▸1945.2**

BIRTHS

Carl Bernstein, U.S. journalist.

Mairead Corrigan, Irish political activist.

Roger Daltrey, U.K. musician.

Angela Davis, U.S. political activist.

John Entwistle, U.K. musician.

Judith Jamison, U.S. dancer.

Henry Kravis, U.S. financier.

Richard Leakey, U.K. archaeologist.

George Lucas, U.S. filmmaker.

Chico Mendes, Brazilian political activist.

Reinhold Messner, Italian mountaineer.

Jimmy Page, U.K. musician.

Diana Ross, U.S. singer.

Tom Seaver, U.S. baseball player.

Sirhan Sirhan, Palestinian-U.S. assassin.

Alice Walker, U.S. writer.

DEATHS

Leo Hendrik Baekeland, U.S. chemist.

Alexis Carrel, French-U.S. surgeon.

Jean Giraudoux, French writer.

Wassily Kandinsky, Russian-French painter.

Kenesaw Mountain Landis, U.S. baseball commissioner.

Edwin Lutyens, U.K. architect.

Aimee Semple McPherson, Canadian-U.S. evangelist.

Aristide Maillol, French artist.

Glenn Miller, U.S. musician.

Piet Mondrian, Dutch painter.

Edvard Munch, Norwegian painter.

Reza Khan Shah Pahlevi, Iranian ruler.

Erwin Rommel, German general.

Antoine de Saint-Exupéry, French aviator and writer.

Ida M. Tarbell, U.S. journalist.

Wendell Willkie, U.S. political leader.

Villa-Lobos) ... Painting & Sculpture: *White Balancing Act* (Wassily Kandinsky); *The Black Trellis* (Fernand Léger) ... Film: *Going My Way* (Leo McCarey); *Double Indemnity* (Billy Wilder); *Lifeboat* (Alfred Hitchcock); *Henry V* (Laurence Olivier); *National Velvet* (Clarence Brown) ... Theater: *I Remember Mama* (John Van Druten); *No Exit* (Jean-Paul Sartre) ... Radio: *Roy Rogers*; *The Adventures of Ozzie and Harriet*.

"As much as I may be tormented by worries and even physically shaken by them, nothing will make the slightest change in my decision to fight on till at last the scales tip to our side."—**Adolf Hitler, during the Battle of the Bulge**

NEW IN 1944

Seventeen magazine.

Five-star generals and admirals.

Chiquita Banana.

Le Monde (Paris).

The GI Bill (The Servicemen's Readjustment Act of 1944).

IN THE UNITED STATES

▶**ROSIE THE RIVETER**—The massive wartime influx of women into the workforce peaked in 1944, when nearly half of all American women had a job outside the home. Behind GI Joe on the battlefront was Rosie the Riveter on the home front, memorialized

in popular song and by Norman Rockwell on the cover of the *Saturday Evening Post.* Armed with a rivet gun and wearing slacks, millions of Rosies broke into traditionally male-dominated defense-production industries.

▶**GAMESMANSHIP**—In his 1944 book *Game Theory and Economic Behavior* (co-written with Oskar Morgenstern), Hungarian-born American numbers whiz John von Neumann used advanced logic to tackle thorny real-life problems. Von Neumann's system treated not only economics but diplomacy, the arms race, and other complex social interactions as rule-bound games, in which competing players tried to maximize gain; an individual, a corporation, or a nation could achieve optimal results by using mathematical principles. His phrase zero-sum game, referring to a competition (chess, for example)

1944

Amid Warsaw's ruins, rebels and Red Cross officials sue for peace.

WORLD WAR II

Warsaw Betrayed

6 During five years of Nazi occupation, 20 percent of Poland's population had been killed. But hopes soared in late July 1944, as Soviet forces reached the outskirts of Warsaw. Encouraged by Soviet authorities, the underground Polish Home Army rose against the capital's German masters on August 1; within days the Poles commanded the entire city. Then, unbelievably, the Red Army halted at the Vistula River and withdrew. Unmolested, the Germans attacked Warsaw. The undersupplied Poles held on for 63 days before surrendering. Some 200,000 civilians were dead, the city lay in ruins, and the Home Army, loyal to the exiled Polish government, was decimated.

Accused of betraying Warsaw, Stalin maintained that the Red Army had simply run out of steam after a summer-long campaign. But his ulterior motive was clear. Shortly before the uprising, the Soviets had established a puppet government in the liberated city of Lublin. Backed by the Red Army, the Lublin Committee claimed sole authority over free Poland. After the Soviets finally drove German troops from Warsaw in January 1945, civil war broke out between the remains of the Home Army and the Lublinites.

Bargaining with Stalin at Yalta in February, Churchill and Roosevelt accepted (with conditions) a Lublin-dominated government for Poland. In the spring, the Soviets invited 16 Polish military and political leaders to a "meeting" to resolve differences. No negotiations occurred: After a show trial, the Soviets imprisoned the group, gutting the opposition movement. Liberated at last, Poland was hardly independent. ◂1943.3 ▸1944.11

WORLD WAR II

Battle of the Bulge

7 After the liberation of Paris on August 25, 1944, the Allies quickly took all but the easternmost portions of France, as well as Luxembourg and much of Belgium. But

The Germans pushed a bulge *(above)* into Allied lines, giving the battle its name.

their drive faltered near the German border. A failed attempt to capture the Dutch city of Arnheim left most of a British airborne division dead or captured. Aachen, the first German city to be conquered, fell only after a month of siege. And by early November, when the Allies pushed into the Saar Basin, Hitler was preparing his country for a bold effort to repulse the invaders: the Battle of the Bulge.

On October 18, the Führer ordered the conscription of all able-bodied men ages 16 to 60. And in mid-December, this desperate *Volkssturm* (home guard), along with regular troops, launched a massive counteroffensive. The battle was named for the 65-mile-deep bulge the assault pushed into the Allied line. Taking advantage of rain that grounded Allied aircraft, the Germans poured back into Luxembourg and Belgium, encircling the U.S. 101st Airborne Division of Brigadier General Anthony McAuliffe at Bastogne.

But when General Hasso von Manteuffel's emissaries demanded that the 101st surrender, McAuliffe wrote back, "Nuts!" After the weather cleared on December 23, the tide began to turn. Thousands of Allied planes bombed and strafed the German troops and their supply lines. Patton's 3rd Army relieved Bastogne on the 26th, and on January 3, 1945, Allied ground forces counterattacked. Five days later, the frozen, disease-racked Germans began to withdraw. In the end, the Bulge cost them 120,000 casualties, compared with 75,000 for the Allies. The initiative on the Western Front now belonged entirely to the Allies. ◂1944.4 ▸1945.2

WORLD WAR II

MacArthur Returns

8 On October 20, 1944, 100,000 U.S. troops landed on the central Philippine island of Leyte. Wading ashore with them was General MacArthur, fulfilling the famous promise he'd made two years earlier: "I shall return." By Christmas, when the island was secured, 55,000 Japanese had been killed; another 27,000 died in subsequent mopping-up operations. The Americans lost only 3,500 men. With Leyte, MacArthur gained a base for the recapture of all the Philippines.

Though the combat on the islands was brutal, the contest was decided at sea. In the three-day Battle of Leyte Gulf—the largest naval engagement in history—the Japanese lost 36 warships. Besides

MacArthur *(center)*, with characteristic drama, keeps his word.

SPORTS: Baseball: World Series, St. Louis Cardinals defeat St. Louis Browns, 4–2; most baseball teams consist of aging major leaguers, as younger players are in the service ... Football: NFL, Green Bay Packers defeat New York Giants, 14–7 ... Hockey: Maurice "Rocket" Richard (Montreal Canadiens) scores record 50 goals in 50-game season.

"I have returned. By the grace of Almighty God, our forces stand again on Philippine soil."—**General Douglas MacArthur**

cutting off support from Japan's land forces in the Philippines, the battle eliminated the Imperial Navy as a factor in the Pacific. It also marked the advent of kamikaze ("divine wind") attacks, in which Japanese suicide pilots tried to sink enemy vessels by crashing into the decks.

By January, American troops had stormed the big island of Luzon and were menacing Manila, which MacArthur hoped to liberate with a grand parade. On February 6, the publicity-conscious general issued a false victory communiqué. In reality, the struggle for the capital raged for another month. Japanese defenders, knowing defeat in the Philippines would leave only Iwo Jima and Okinawa between U.S. forces and Japan, resisted fiercely —and murdered nearly 100,000 residents. By the time the city did fall, on March 3, it had been completely razed. **◂1942.4 ▸1944.9**

WORLD WAR II

Island-to-Island Combat

9 Japanese losses in the Pacific went far beyond the Philippines in 1944. In February, the Marshall Islands became the first of Japan's prewar possessions to fall. On the atolls of Kwajalein and Eniwetok, outnumbered Japanese garrisons fought almost to the last man—offering U.S. forces a taste of what was ahead.

In April, 84,000 GIs landed on New Guinea. For two years, Australian forces—determined to protect their homeland, 500 miles to the south—had battled the Japanese occupiers over every inch of the island. The Yanks' arrival turned the tide. Some 13,000 Japanese (out of a force of 15,000) were killed in the three-month engagement; many of the survivors holed up in caves, where the Americans hunted them with flamethrowers.

U.S. forces invaded Saipan, in the Mariana Islands, in June. In a three-week battle, the Japanese lost 20,000, the Americans, 3,500. Another 7,000 Japanese committed suicide, following their commanding general, Yoshitsugo Saito, who killed himself with a sword. Virtually all the remaining 4,000 defenders died in a last-ditch banzai charge.

The fighting on nearby Guam and Tinian was almost as grisly. In Japanese hands since 1941, Guam fell to the Americans in August. More than 18,000 Japanese died, many by suicide. The last Japanese soldier, Sergeant Shoichi Yokoi, was discovered on Guam in 1972; to avoid the disgrace of surrender, he'd hidden in the jungle for 28 years.

A marine on Eniwetok's coral beach pulls a comrade's corpse out of the surf.

Shortly after losing Saipan, a distraught Hideki Tojo resigned as premier. The Americans had eliminated his nation's offensive threat, and gained a base for raids against Japan itself. **◂1944.8 ▸1945.4**

WORLD WAR II

Holocaust in Hungary

10 Until the Germans occupied Hungary in March 1944, that nation's official anti-Semitism had been marked by ambivalence. Six years earlier, to win Hitler's favor, the government had enacted laws depriving Jews of most civil rights. In 1941, after the country officially joined the Axis, its soldiers had aided the Germans in massacring some 17,000 Jews in territories newly annexed from Yugoslavia. (Machine-gunned after digging their own mass graves, many were buried while still calling for help.) Yet Hungarian authorities—whose cooperation with the Nazis stemmed more from opportunism than from ideology—had steadfastly refused to deport Jews to concentration camps.

All that changed when the Germans, to keep the flagging country from surrendering to the Allies, sent in troops and induced Regent Miklós Horthy (the country's chief of state) to appoint a puppet regime. As in other Nazi-occupied lands, Hungary's Jews were stripped of their property, forced to wear the yellow star, and herded into ghettos to await shipment to the camps. With the help of Hungarian collaborators, 434,000 Jews were sent to Auschwitz before Horthy halted the deportations in July; most were gassed upon arrival.

The terror intensified in October, when the ultraright Arrow Cross Party—outraged by Horthy's renewed peace efforts—staged a coup. (Its German backers kidnapped the Regent and forced him to abdicate.) Arrow Cross gangs roamed the ghetto streets, robbing and killing. Thousands of Jews, mostly women, were force-marched toward Austria to build fortifications; many were simply shot and thrown in the Danube. By April 1945, when the invading Red Army had chased the last German troops from Hungary, more than 550,000 of the nation's 750,000 Jews had been murdered. **◂1943.1 ▸1945.9**

JEWISH DEATHS IN THE HOLOCAUST, BY COUNTRY (ESTIMATED)

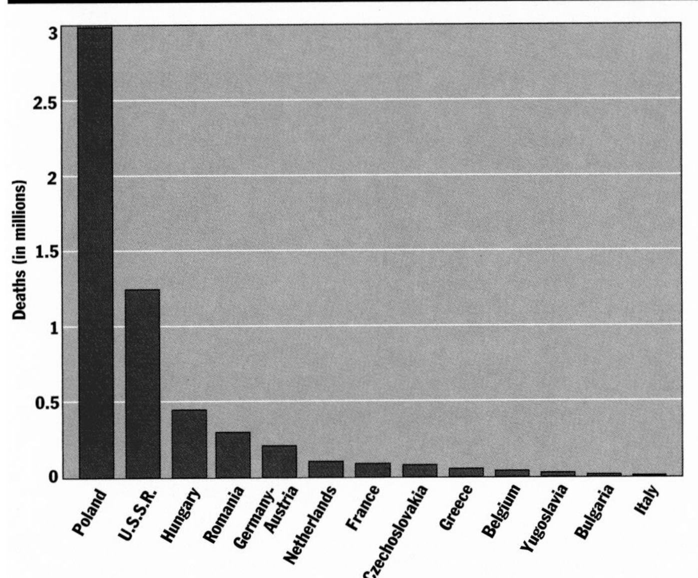

In addition to Jews, some 7 million others died: 3.3 million Soviet POWs; 3 million non-Jewish Poles; over 500,000 Gypsies, homosexuals, and Jehovah's Witnesses.

IN THE UNITED STATES

where one side's gain is directly proportional to another's loss, entered the popular vocabulary. ▸1948.12

▸WORLD'S BIGGEST CALCULATOR—A joint venture between Harvard mathematician Howard Aiken and IBM

in 1944 produced Mark I, the first electro-mechanical calculator. A prototype of the digital computer, Mark I ably performed basic arithmetic, multiplying and dividing huge numbers in mere seconds. Its greatest drawback was its size: 50 feet long and 35 tons. ◂1941.6 ▸1946.M

▸SAVING BLUE BABIES—Pediatric cardiologist Helen Taussig and surgeon Alfred Blalock, working at Johns Hopkins University, performed the first "blue baby" surgery in 1944. Taussig's investigations into congenital heart defects had convinced her that the death of blue babies—children born with insufficient oxygen in their blood—could be prevented with surgery. She and Blalock invented a means of bypassing a defective pulmonary artery in order to allow the free flow of oxygen into the bloodstream. Taussig's later research played a key role in blocking the use of birth-defect-producing Thalidomide in the U.S. ▸1962.9

▸AMERICAN POVERTY—Hired by the Carnegie Corporation to study race relations in the U.S., Swedish economist and sociologist Gunnar Myrdal produced an enduringly influential work of social science. *An American Dilemma*, published in 1944, examined the contradiction between America's democratic idealism and its de facto racism. Myrdal also introduced the concept of cumulative causation (poverty begets poverty) to explain how disadvantaged African-Americans were consigned to a vicious economic cycle.

POLITICS & BUSINESS: GNP: $210.1 billion ... Roosevelt reelected to unprecedented fourth term (running on slogan, "Don't change horses in midstream.") ... Congress passes Servicemen's Readjustment Act ... Army Specialized Training Program ends (110,000 more men enter active service) ... OPA ends meat rationing ... War Production Board orders production of some consumer appliances to resume.

"It might be thought rather cynical if it seemed we had disposed of these issues, so fateful to millions of people, in such an offhand manner."—**Churchill, advising Stalin to burn the "naughty document" concerning the division of the Balkans**

WORLD WAR II

▶MUSSOLINI EXECUTES CIANO—Onetime Italian foreign minister Count Galeazzo Ciano and a passel of other former Fascists met their ends in January, executed for turning against Mussolini. Handing down the death sentences was Ciano's father-in-law, Il Duce himself.

▶RUSSIAN REVENGE—In May, Soviet forces drove the German army from Sevastopol, ending a two-year occupation of that Crimean city. The conquerors had reduced the city to ruins, and the advancing Soviets were not in a forgiving mood when a rear guard of some 60,000 to 100,000 Germans surrendered. Stalin's troops butchered them all.

▶ANOTHER LIDICE—On June 10, 200 members of the SS destroyed the small French town of Oradour-sur-Glane as punishment for an attack by the French Resistance on German troops headed toward the Normandy beachhead. After rounding up the villagers and herding the men into barns and the women into the church, the troops locked the doors and dynamited the town. All survivors were shot. Only ten people survived the fire. In 1951, 21 of the 200 SS men were brought to trial; all but one received the death sentence.

▶BANZAI—Fighting Japan island by island in the Pacific, American GIs encountered a bizarre and unnerving tactic: the banzai charge. Rather than surrender, ultranationalist Japanese soldiers suicidally hurled themselves at the enemy, often fighting to the last man. On the island of Saipan, the technique reached its apotheosis. In the final battle, there in July, 4,300 Japanese, including army cooks, typists, and civilians, charged with bayonets and clubs. All but a handful were cut down; most of the

In an American cartoon, Secretary of State Cordell Hull introduces FDR to Moscow's Stalinist puppet regimes.

DIPLOMACY

Dividing the Spoils

11 As the Soviet Union transformed itself from victim to victor early in 1944, Churchill grew increasingly leery of his ally's intentions toward eastern and southern Europe. "Are we going to acquiesce in the communization of the Balkans and perhaps of Italy?" Churchill asked his foreign minister, Anthony Eden. "He dreams of the Red Army spreading like a cancer from one country to another," wrote the prime minister's physician. "It has become an obsession." Churchill first proposed to block the Soviet advance with a U.S.-British landing at Trieste, on the Adriatic, followed by a thrust through the Ljubljana Gap that would beat the Soviets to Vienna. Thwarted by American indifference and by the Nazi occupation of Italy, he tried another tack. In October, Churchill flew to Moscow and presented Stalin with a plan for postwar spheres of influence.

The Soviets and British, Churchill suggested, should divide the Balkans between themselves. He scribbled a formula on a scrap of paper (winkingly calling it a "naughty document"): 90 percent Soviet control of Romania, 90 percent British control of Greece, 75 percent Soviet control of Bulgaria, and a 50-50 split in Yugoslavia and Hungary. Later, foreign ministers Eden and Molotov adjusted the numbers, giving the Soviets 80 percent in Hungary and Bulgaria. A stab at geopolitical stability, the deal was never finalized—and it was obsolete by the end of the year.

Roosevelt clung to his "cardinal" principle (both the United States and the Soviet Union had worldwide interests; they could work out details together), and accepted Soviet expansion without alarm. Denied U.S. military support, Churchill could only watch as the Red Army swept through Poland, Romania, Bulgaria, Hungary, and into Czechoslovakia in November 1944. **◂1943.8 ▸1945.5**

DIPLOMACY

Economic Harmony

12 In summer 1944, economic ambassadors from 44 countries assembled in idyllic Bretton Woods, New Hampshire, to negotiate the shape of postwar world trade. "We came," U.S. treasury secretary Henry Morganthau declared at the parley's end, "to work out methods which would do away with the economic evils—the competitive currency devaluation and destructive impediments to trade—which preceded the present war. We have succeeded in that effort."

The conference's crowning achievements were the International Bank for Reconstruction and Development and the International Monetary Fund. The IBRD (known as the World Bank), funded by member nations, initially helped rebuild war-shattered economies; later it funded development projects in the Third World. The IMF was meant to stabilize exchange rates and prevent imbalances of payments.

The Bretton Woods agreements largely reflected the economic philosophies of John Maynard Keynes—the leader of the British delegation, and a longtime critic of the divisive policies enacted at Versailles after World War I. The new monetary order led to unprecedented world economic growth. By the 1970s, however, as many countries fell hopelessly in debt to the international lending institutions, the conference's legacy began to lose its luster. **◂1921.7 ▸1971.4**

Forgers of a new economic order: chief delegates at Bretton Woods.

DIPLOMACY

United Nations Conceived

13 Representatives of the Four Powers—the United States, Britain, the Soviet Union, and China—met at a Washington, D.C. mansion called Dumbarton Oaks in the summer and autumn of 1944 to plan an international organization that would keep the peace once World War II was done.

The failed League of Nations provided a model of what to avoid. Participants at Dumbarton agreed that a strong body was needed to prevent future world wars, one endowed with enough military power to back up its paper resolutions. Authority was the critical question: How much should the Four Powers receive as a group, how much of its own was each willing to yield? As the talks progressed, it became clear that Roosevelt's vision of a world patrolled by four policemen was unworkable. None of the four nations wanted to exchange individual authority for group law.

Dumbarton Oaks conferees dine al fresco.

After six weeks of talks, the conferees agreed on a basic format. The new organization would consist of a general assembly of peace-loving nations in an advisory role, and a powerful executive council dominated by permanent members—initially, the Four Powers. The details would be worked out at Yalta and San Francisco in 1945, but the Dumbarton Oaks Conference planted the seeds that grew into the United Nations. **◂1943.M ▸1945.M**

"Music that is born complex is not inherently better or worse than music that is born simple."—**Aaron Copland**

Martha Graham and Erick Hawkins—uncharacteristically—dance for joy.

DANCE

Spring for American Dance

14 When the pastoral ballet *Appalachian Spring* premiered at the Library of Congress in Washington, D.C., in 1944, it startled and heartened an audience still wintering a long war. Choreographer Martha Graham was known for dark, moody dances, but Aaron Copland's joyful music had inspired something different from her usual solitary meditations. A love story set in Shaker country, the work is a moving portrait of the early American spirit, sensitively and directly extolling rural values and culture with simple, warm dancing. The audience responded wildly, and the critics declared that American modern dance had finally come of age.

The uniquely American work, Graham's first popular success, was framed by a minimalist set designed by the young Isamu Noguchi, who would become one of the world's most respected sculptors. Among *Appalachian Spring*'s featured dancers, whose own ideas for the piece Graham had encouraged, were Merce Cunningham, Erick Hawkins, May O'Donnell, and Pearl Lang—all now legends in American modern-dance history.

Appalachian Spring has been performed around the world, as has Copland's subsequent orchestral suite, and the dance remains one of Graham's signature works. In 1985, Graham, 91, and Copland, 84, together attended a 41st-anniversary performance of the production in New York. Then, at a gala for the Graham company in 1987, both composer (who could not attend because of illness) and choreographer were honored by Rudolf Nureyev and Mikhail Baryshnikov dancing featured roles. **◂1931.12 ▸1961.13**

LITERATURE

Borges's Little Labyrinths

15 Given Jorge Luis Borges's obsession with the nature of time, space, and destiny, it's fitting that the book that made his international reputation remained almost unknown outside Argentina for nearly two decades after its publication in 1944. A collection of eerie, often darkly humorous philosophical short stories, *Ficciones* defied the era's fashion of literary realism—as well as all conventional notions of plot and characterization.

Each of Borges's tales is a little labyrinth (an image he uses often in his work) where events are governed by an alternative system of logic. In one story, an insomniac suffers from total recall of everything that has ever befallen him. In another, a detective and a murderer arrange to pursue each other—according to a geometrical formula—through successive incarnations. Borges's protagonists include a Christian heretic who deduces that Judas, not Jesus, was the Messiah, and a Jewish playwright who mentally achieves a year's worth of creative activity in the instant before he's shot by the Nazis.

Long known among Argentine intellectuals for his poems and essays, Borges fully committed himself to fiction writing only in 1938, at age 39, after a serious head wound nearly killed him. But it was not until 1961, when he and Samuel Beckett shared the prestigious Formentor Prize, that his work (beginning with *Ficciones*) began to be widely translated and read abroad. Acclaim for Borges as one of the century's great writers led to the worldwide "discovery" of Latin American literature—a field that has been deeply influenced by Borges's mix of erudition, linguistic precision, and magic. **◂1925.11 ▸1967.7**

By the 1960s, when he won world fame, Borges had become totally blind.

WORLD WAR II

survivors took their own lives on the spot.

▶ANNE FRANK BETRAYED—Their secret refuge disclosed to the Gestapo, Anne Frank and her Jewish family were seized in August, shipped by cattle car to Auschwitz. In the Amsterdam attic where they had spent two years hiding, precocious 15-year-old Anne left behind an account of her family's struggle. The moving diary survived; young Anne died in a Nazi death camp.

▶FLYING BOMBS—Londoners nicknamed Hitler's V-1 missiles "buzz bombs" for their ominous sound. Worse yet was the eerie silence when their engines cut off, just before they hit their targets. As the weapons

rained on Britain in 1944, RAF pilots learned to intercept them. Even their fast new Spitfire fighters could not match the V-1's top speed of 400 mph, but the pilots would sometimes blast it with gunfire—or, more daringly, slip a wing tip under the missile's wing and nudge it into crashing off course.

▶OPERATION PLUTO—Admiral Lord Louis Mountbatten first broached the idea, asking "Can you lay an oil pipeline across the Channel?" From that first query sprang Operation Pluto—Pipeline Under the Ocean. The world's first underwater pipeline, PLUTO provided the Allies a steady source of gasoline on the Continent, which was essential to the campaigns in northern Europe.

▶D-DAY SUPPLIES—Stockpiling materials for the Normandy invasion, the Allies turned England into a giant war pantry. In fields, in parks, on the sweeping lawns of country estates, the U.S. Army stored guns, ammunition, landing craft, airplanes, jeeps, and, to ward off nausea on the Channel crossing, several tons of chewing gum.

take Florence; Japan leaves India; Germany leaves U.S.S.R.; Allies liberate Paris, Marseilles; Romania surrenders ... September: Finland negotiates peace with U.S.S.R.; Allies liberate Antwerp, Brussels, Luxembourg; V-2 bombing of London ... October: Germans crush Warsaw uprising; British liberate Athens; Battle of Leyte Gulf ... November: Allies enter Saar Basin ... December: Battle of the Bulge.

"Olivier is a tour de force; Wolfit is forced to tour."—**Actress Hermione Gingold, on the difference between Laurence Olivier and Donald Wolfit, two of England's leading Shakespearean actors**

AROUND THE WORLD

▶WAR ON HUNGER—In 1944, the Cooperative Mexican Agricultural Program, sponsored by the Rockefeller Foundation and headed by American agronomist Norman Borlaug, initiated a program to increase agricultural production through hybridization, fertilizers, and irrigation. By 1960, thanks to the "Green Revolution," Mexico's output had more than doubled. ◂1943.M ▸1984.4

▶GREEK CIVIL WAR BEGINS—When German troops abandoned Greece in October, King George II's government returned to Athens from London (though George himself waited until 1946 to return). But a coalition with the provisional government of the communist National Liberation Front (EAM) dissolved when the EAM refused to disarm its military wing, the National Popular Liberation Army (ELAS)—Greece's strongest anti-Nazi partisan group. In December, civil war erupted *(below, ELAS guerrillas carry a dead comrade)*, and British troops arrived to back the royalists. The battle raged for 40 days; the rebels gained substantial territory, but lacking

Soviet aid (Stalin had promised Greece to Britain as a sphere of influence), failed to seize power. Accepting defeat, the ELAS formally disbanded. In 1946, however, fighting resumed. ◂1941.4 ▸1947.4

▶A FRENCH FOLLY—Jean Giraudoux died in 1944, just after finishing his play *La Folle de Chaillot (The Madwoman of Chaillot)*. Centering on the fantastical adventures of an elderly woman who engineers the downfall of Paris's speculators and financial wizards, *La Folle* showcases Giraudoux's extravagantly theatrical style. A French diplomat for 30 years, Giraudoux often disguised universal conflicts—between war and peace, man and woman, greed and humanitarianism—behind witty and often absurd dialogue. *La Folle* premiered in Paris in December 1945.

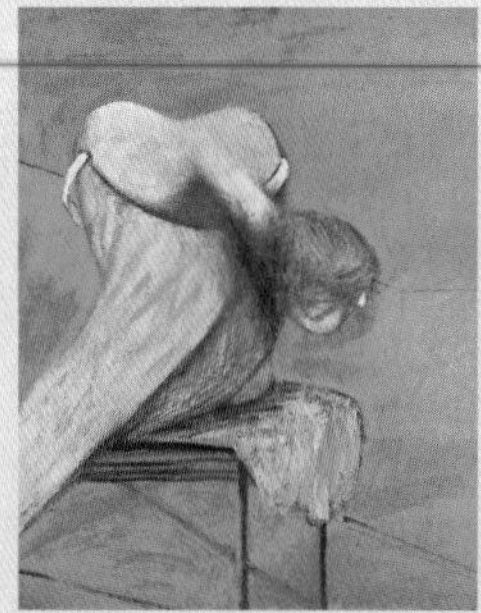

ART

A Twentieth-Century Goya

16 **British painter Francis Bacon's overwhelming preoccupation as an artist, he wrote, was the "brutality of fact." Throughout his career, Bacon addressed that obsession in chilling images of isolated, grotesquely mutilated human figures. He worked in relative obscurity until 1944, when his *Three Studies for Figures at the Base of a Crucifixion (above)* earned him instant notoriety and comparisons with such macabre, visionary masters as Francisco Goya. At the heart of his work were horror and revulsion at the human condition, an assessment he repeatedly undercut by denying that death had any personal meaning for him. How could it? he demanded: We are nothing but meat.**

A self-taught painter, Bacon was born in Ireland and left home at 16, he later said, "after my father found me wearing my mother's underclothes." He drifted to Berlin and Paris, settling in London in 1928. By the mid-1940s, the components of his mature work were in place: the violent palette; the distorted, cartoonlike figures; the degradation and terror. Before he died in 1992, many considered him the century's greatest British painter. ◂1932.13 ▸1950.4

MEDICINE

Antibiotic Fights TB

17 Penicillin was finally being produced in sufficient quantities by 1944 to supply Allied soldiers and civilians. But even that wonder drug could not combat tuberculosis. Then, in January, Rutgers University microbiologist Selman Waksman reported the discovery of a new antibiotic (a term he'd coined in 1941 to describe substances, like penicillin, that selectively kill or inhibit the growth of microbes) called streptomycin. Minnesota's Mayo Clinic soon began animal testing of it, and found streptomycin to be remarkably effective against TB.

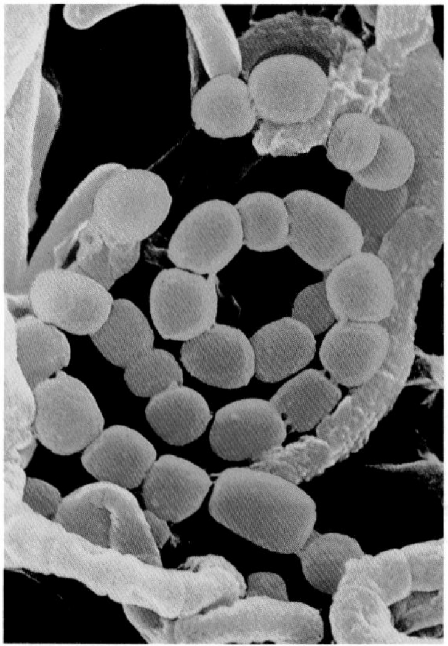

Streptomycin, from *Streptomyces* microbes *(above)*, treated not only TB but typhoid, pneumonia, and spinal meningitis.

Waksman, 55, was a specialist in the microörganisms found in common soil. Searching for a TB cure, he and his assistant, Albert Schatz, had isolated some 10,000 soil-based microbes and tested their bacteria-killing ability. They narrowed the field to 1,000, then to 100, then to ten. Finally, in 1943, Waksman zeroed in on a strain of bacteria-like microbes he called *Streptomyces griseus*, which showed pronounced antibiotic properties.

Streptomycin, extracted from the microbe, revolutionized the treatment of TB. Instead of being limited to prevention (largely through the Calmette-Guérin vaccine) or the sanatorium cure (an uncertain and expensive method based on giving the patient a long rest in fresh air), doctors now had a way of attacking tuberculosis head-on. Although scientists soon realized that, used alone, streptomycin was ineffective (the TB bacillus rapidly developed a resistance), they combined it with other antibiotics. The drug—and its pharmaceutical successors—was so effective that, after its introduction in Europe five years later, TB rates plunged worldwide. **◂1941.16 ▸1955.1**

THEATER

A Glorious Season

18 With Allied prospects brightening, the Old Vic Theatre decided in 1944 to revive its historic London home. Two of Britain's leading thespians—Ralph Richardson and Laurence Olivier—came out of military service and back onto the stage to produce a season that many regard as the birth of the modern English theater.

Richardson, star of the first two plays in the new Old Vic season, was a mighty talent. But Olivier breathed another atmosphere altogether. Before the war, he had reached matinee-idol status with stage performances of Hamlet, Iago, and Coriolanus, as well as with screen roles in William Wyler's *Wuthering Heights* and Alfred Hitchcock's *Rebecca.* His labors for the Old Vic put him squarely on the road to immortality.

Richardson *(left)* as Earl of Richmond and Olivier as Richard III at the Old Vic.

After an uncomfortable performance in Shaw's *Arms and the Man*, Olivier confided to colleague Tyrone Guthrie that he hated his character, Sergius. Guthrie's famous response—"Well, of course, if you can't love him, you'll never be any good in him, will you?"—completely transformed Olivier's approach to acting.

The metamorphosis was evident in Olivier's interpretation of *Richard III* in the season's final production. "The greatest male performance I have seen in the theatre," Noël Coward said, calling Olivier "far and away the greatest actor we have." In three productions, Olivier and Richardson, with a company that included Guthrie, Dame Sybil Thorndike, and Margaret Leighton, had infused the Old Vic with an aura of legend. Nineteen years later, the Royal National Theater made its first home at the Old Vic—under the directorship of Laurence Olivier. **◂1930.5 ▸1947.13**

NOBEL PRIZES: Peace: International Red Cross Committee (Switzerland) ... Literature: Johannes V. Jensen (Danish; novelist) ... Chemistry: Otto Hahn (German; nuclear fission) ... Medicine: Joseph Erlanger and Herbert S. Gasser (U.S.; nerve fibers and impulse transmission) ... Physics: I.I. Rabi (U.S.; magnetic measurement of atomic nuclei).

A VOICE FROM 1944

A Celebration of the Common Soldier

"The Death of Captain Waskow," by Ernie Pyle, from the *Washington Daily News,* January 10, 1944

"All the war of the world," journalist Ernie Pyle once observed from Italy, "has seemed to be borne by the few thousand front-line soldiers here, destined merely by chance to suffer and die for the rest of us." Pyle's personal mission was to tell their story. A pixieish, 110-pound man who lived with the soldiers who were his subjects, Pyle was the most widely read war correspondent of his era; his dispatches ran in 200 U.S. papers, reaching more than five million readers. He won a Pulitzer Prize in 1944; the following spring he was killed during the Okinawa campaign. Covering the Sicilian campaign in the harsh winter of 1944, he filed the following piece, his most famous, from Italy's front lines. ◄**1940.V** ►**1967.V**

In this war I have known a lot of officers who were loved and respected by the soldiers under them. But never have I crossed the trail of any man as beloved as Capt. Henry T. Waskow of Bolton, Texas.

Capt. Waskow was a company commander in the 36th Division. He had led his company since long before it left the States. He was very young, only in his middle twenties, but he carried in him a sincerity and gentleness that made people want to be guided by him.

"After my own father, he came next," a sergeant told me.

"He always looked after us," a soldier said. "He'd go to bat for us every time."

"I've never knowed him to do anything unfair," another one said.

I was at the foot of the mule trail the night they brought Capt. Waskow's body down. The moon was nearly full at the time, and you could see far up the trail, and even part way across the valley below. Soldiers made shadows in the moonlight as they walked.

Dead men had been coming down the mountain all evening, lashed onto the backs of mules. They came lying belly-down across the wooden pack-saddles, their heads hanging down on the left side of the mule, their stiffened legs sticking out awkwardly from the other side, bobbing up and down as the mule walked.

Pyle (here in Normandy) made his name by chronicling the names, faces, lives, and dreams of the usually faceless "GI Joes" on the front lines.

The Italian mule-skinners were afraid to walk beside dead men, so Americans had to lead the mules down that night. Even the Americans were reluctant to unlash and lift off the bodies at the bottom, so an officer had to do it himself, and ask others to help.

The first one came early in the morning. They slid him down from the mule and stood him on his feet for a moment, while they got a new grip. In the half light he might have been merely a sick man standing there, leaning on the others. Then they laid him on the ground in the shadow of the low stone wall alongside the road.

I don't know who that first one was. You feel small in the presence of dead men, and ashamed at being alive, and you don't ask silly questions.

We left him there beside the road, that first one, and we all went back into the cowshed and sat on water cans or lay on the straw waiting for the next batch of mules.

Somebody said the dead soldier had been dead for four days, and then nobody said anything more about it. We talked soldier talk for an hour or more. The dead man lay all alone outside in the shadow of the low stone wall.

Then a soldier came into the cowshed and said there were some more bodies outside. We went out into the road. Four mules stood there, in the moonlight, in the road where the trail came down off the mountain. The soldiers who led them stood there waiting. "This one is Captain Waskow," one of them said quietly.

Two men unlashed his body from the mule and lifted it off and laid it in the shadow beside the low stone wall. Other men took the other bodies off. Finally there were five lying end to end in a long row, alongside the road. You don't cover up dead men in the combat zone. They just lie there in the shadows until somebody else comes after them.

The unburdened mules moved off to their olive orchard. The men in the road seemed reluctant to leave. They stood around, and gradually one by one I could sense them moving close to Capt. Waskow's body. Not so much to look, I think, as to say something in finality to him, and to themselves. I stood close by and I could hear.

One soldier came and looked down, and he said out loud, "God damn it." That's all he said, and then he walked away. Another one came. He said, "God damn it to hell anyway." He looked down for a few last moments, and then he turned and left.

Another man came; I think he was an officer. It was hard to tell officers from men in the half light, for all were bearded and grimy dirty. The man looked down into the dead captain's face and then he spoke directly to him, as though he were alive. He said, "I'm sorry, old man."

Then a soldier came and stood beside the officer, and bent over, and he too spoke to his dead captain, not in a whisper but awfully tenderly, and he said:

"I sure am sorry, sir."

Then the first man squatted down, and he reached down and took the dead hand, and he sat there for a full five minutes, holding the dead hand in his own and looking intently into the dead face, and he never uttered a sound all the time he sat there.

And finally he put the hand down, and then reached up and gently straightened the points of the captain's shirt collar, and then he sort of rearranged the tattered edges of his uniform around the wound. And then he got up and walked away down the road in the moonlight, all alone.

After that the rest of us went back into the cowshed, leaving the five dead men lying in a line, end to end, in the shadow of the low stone wall. We lay down on the straw in the cowshed, and pretty soon we were all asleep.

"Sixteen hours ago an American airplane dropped one bomb on Hiroshima.... If they do not now accept our terms, they may expect a rain of ruin from the sky the likes of which has never been seen on this earth."—**Harry S Truman**

The ground crew of the B-29 bomber *Enola Gay* flank their pilot, Col. Paul Tibbets. Below, Hiroshima after the bomb.

STORY OF THE YEAR

War Ends After Atomic Bombs Hit Hiroshima, Nagasaki

1 Before dawn on August 6, 1945, an American B-29 bomber named *Enola Gay* took off from Tinian Island, in the Marianas. Arriving over Hiroshima, Japan, at 8:15 AM, it released its solitary bomb. In an instant, 80,000 people died, and most of Hiroshima simply ceased to exist. Four days later, America dropped a second atomic bomb, killing 40,000 in Nagasaki. On August 14, Japan surrendered. The bloodiest conflict in history ended with a new threat of inconceivable violence. Humanity had acquired the power to destroy the world.

Debate continues on the necessity of using nuclear weapons against Japan. Critics of the move note that Emperor Hirohito had already urged his cabinet to begin cease-fire negotiations; they insist that the Allied demand for *unconditional* surrender, entailing the abdication of the Emperor (a sacred figure to his people), was the only obstacle to peace. Supporters contend that Japan, though facing sure defeat, was prepared to fight indefinitely—as evidenced by the suicidal resistance of soldiers and civilians on the Pacific islands, and the continued intransigence of many top officials. (One exhorted the nation to perish in battle "like a beautiful flower.") Allied firebombings, they point out, had killed more Japanese at a time than the A-bombs, to no avail; moreover, a land assault on Japan would have cost hundreds of thousands of lives on both sides.

Beyond argument, however, are the unprecedented horrors unleashed by the atomic blasts. People near ground zero were vaporized, leaving behind only charred shadows. Many who initially survived soon died in agony, as radiation destroyed their bodies cell by cell. Lesser radiation doses led to cancer and birth defects. In Hiroshima alone, the bombing led to some 140,000 deaths in later years.

Two days after Hiroshima, the Soviet Union declared war on Japan (as agreed at Yalta) and invaded Japanese-held Manchuria. On August 15, Hirohito addressed his nation over the radio for the first time. Explaining that the enemy "has begun to employ a new and most cruel bomb, the power of which to do damage is indeed incalculable," he announced Japan's acceptance of Allied terms. General MacArthur received the surrender documents aboard the U.S. battleship *Missouri* in Tokyo Bay on September 2. ◄**1942.18** ►**1945.M**

WORLD WAR II

Victory in Europe

2 For the European Axis powers, the end began on January 12, 1945, when the Red Army launched a gigantic offensive in Poland. Stretched thin along the 700-mile Eastern Front, outflanked in the Balkans, and encircled in Lithuania, German forces crumbled. The Soviets quickly took Warsaw and Łódź. Hitler withdrew from the Ardennes on the Western Front and rushed troops to Budapest in a vain attempt to hold Hungary. By February some Soviet divisions stood only 40 miles from Berlin.

The diversion of Wehrmacht troops to hold off the Soviets left Germany's western borders exposed. On March 23, the Allies attacked across the Rhine River. The Canadian 1st Army plowed through the Netherlands, the British 2nd drove to the Baltic, and U.S. forces fanned out from Magdeburg to the Czech and Austrian borders.

Meanwhile, the Soviets pressed on, wreaking vengeful atrocities and driving hordes of refugees before them. By mid-April they'd taken Vienna, Danzig, and Königsberg. On April 25, they met the Americans—with toasts and embraces—on the Elbe River.

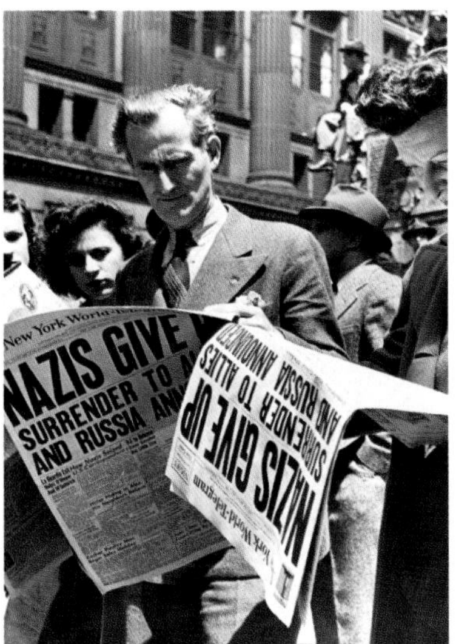

New Yorkers got news of Germany's surrender in the headlines of May 7, 1945.

Berlin fell on May 2. Axis forces in Italy surrendered the same day, as did those in Austria. On May 4, five days after Hitler's suicide, their counterparts in northern Germany, Holland, and Denmark followed suit. And on May 7, in Reims, France, the German High Command (represented by General

ART & CULTURE: Books: ***Cannery Row*** (John Steinbeck); ***Animal Farm*** (George Orwell); ***Christ Stopped at Eboli*** (Carlo Levi); ***The Age of Jackson*** (Arthur Schlesinger, Jr.); ***Brideshead Revisited*** (Evelyn Waugh) ... Music: "It's Been a Long, Long Time" (Styne and Cahn); "Rum and Coca-Cola" (Amsterdam, Bacon, and Sullivan); ***The Santa Fe Time Table*** (Ernst Krenek) ... Painting & Sculpture:

"This is entirely horrifying. Not only does it make nonsense of all our protestations about our war aims … it gives official proof for everything Goebbels ever said on the subject."—**The *Daily Mirror*'s Cecil King, on the firebombing of Dresden**

Alfred Jodl and Admiral Hans Friedeburg) surrendered unconditionally. Only in Czechoslovakia did fighting continue for a few more days. On May 8—five years and eight months after it started—the war in Europe was officially over.

In the weeks that followed, the Allies arrested every Nazi official they could find on war-crimes charges. Hitler's Thousand-Year Reich had expired 988 years early. **◂1944.1 ▸1945.7**

WORLD WAR II

Dresden and Tokyo Infernos

3 In the last months of the war, Allied air forces increasingly resorted to "area bombing"—pounding population centers to destroy morale. The tactic was not new: In 1943, a British raid on Hamburg had killed 50,000. But in 1945, the firebombings of Dresden and Tokyo particularly troubled British and American consciences.

Dresden was one of Europe's most beautiful and historic cities. By early 1945 it housed more than 600,000 people, including scores of Allied POWs. Strategically unimportant, it had suffered so little bombing that its antiaircraft guns had been removed. But Britain's Bomber Command chiefs thought terror raids could win the war, and Churchill wanted to impress Stalin with a display of air power. So on the night of February 13, nearly 800 British Lancasters bombed Dresden, mostly with incendiaries. The next day 300 U.S. Flying Fortresses targeted a rail junction, but mainly hit houses. Estimated deaths: 35,000 to 135,000.

The firestorm raised an outcry, especially in the United States, whose strategists had always disdained area bombing. But in the Pacific Theater, U.S. Army Air Force commander Curtis Le May had also decided to try it.

The first major raid, by 250 Superfortress bombers, struck Tokyo after midnight on March 10. About 100,000 people died in the inferno; many drowned seeking refuge in the Sumida River. By August, 66 Japanese cities had been firebombed. Accepting the rationale that much war production took place in Japanese homes, few Americans protested. (War Secretary Henry Stimson privately called their silence "appalling.") But after the initial Tokyo raid—the deadliest bombing of the war—many quietly wondered whether their warriors were becoming as brutal as the enemy's. **◂1945.1 ▸1945.10**

Of no strategic value, the firebombing of Dresden reduced the historic city to rubble and killed thousands of civilians.

WORLD WAR II

Yanks Take the Pacific

4 The U.S. Pacific war strategy of island-hopping—seizing one Japanese-held island after another, and turning each into an air base from which to bomb enemy ships and territories—culminated early in 1945 with landings on Iwo Jima and Okinawa. The two campaigns cost the lives of 20,000 Americans as Japanese forces resisted almost to the last man.

The Yanks invaded Iwo Jima, an eight-square-mile atoll in the Volcano Islands, on February 19. After three days of vicious combat, the American flag was raised on Mount Suribachi, the island's highest point. Associated Press cameraman Joe Rosenthal's dramatic photograph of the event (or, rather, of a staged reenactment) became the most famous image of the Pacific war, but not before three of the six Marines pictured had been killed. In areas the Americans dubbed "Bloody Gorge" and "Meat Grinder," heavy fighting continued for another month before the Japanese—having lost 20,000 of 21,000 men—surrendered. U.S. bombers promptly began using Iwo Jima to raid the main Japanese islands.

American forces landed on Okinawa, 360 miles from Japan, on April 1, Easter Sunday. For three months, Japanese troops—many fighting from caves and tunnels—defended the 454-square-mile island with everything from kamikaze attacks to bayonets. The bloodbath claimed 150,000 Japanese, including 85 nurses who, hiding in a cave, were mistaken for infantry by U.S. forces and burned to death. When Okinawa fell in June, the end of the Pacific conflict was in sight. **◂1944.9 ▸1945.M**

The Iwo Jima flag raising—staged by Associated Press photographer Joe Rosenthal—was the most reproduced photo of the Pacific war.

BIRTHS

Daniel Cohn-Bendit, French-German political activist.

Rajiv Gandhi, Indian prime minister.

Anselm Kiefer, German artist.

Bob Marley, Jamaican musician.

Steve Martin, U.S. actor.

Daniel Ortega, Nicaraguan president.

Itzhak Perlman, Israeli-U.S. musician.

Diane Sawyer, U.S. broadcast journalist.

Garry Trudeau, U.S. cartoonist.

August Wilson, U.S. playwright.

DEATHS

Francis Aston, U.K. physicist.

Béla Bartók, Hungarian composer.

Robert Benchley, U.S. writer.

Dietrich Bonhoeffer, German theologian.

Theodore Dreiser, U.S. novelist.

Anne Frank, Dutch diarist.

Johannes Hans Geiger, German physicist.

Joseph Goebbels, German Nazi official.

Milton Hershey, U.S. manufacturer.

Heinrich Himmler, German Nazi official.

Adolf Hitler, Austrian-German Nazi ruler.

Jerome Kern, U.S. composer.

Käthe Kollwitz, German painter.

David Lloyd George, U.K. prime minister.

Thomas Hunt Morgan, U.S. geneticist.

Benito Mussolini, Italian Fascist ruler.

Alla Nazimova, Russian-U.S. actress.

George Patton, U.S. general.

Ernie Pyle, U.S. journalist.

Franklin D. Roosevelt, U.S. president.

Paul Valéry, French poet.

Anton von Webern, Austrian composer.

***Diary of a Seducer* (Arshile Gorky) … Film: *The Lost Weekend* (Billy Wilder); *Mildred Pierce* (Michael Curtiz); *Objective, Burma!* (Raoul Walsh); *Anchors Aweigh* (George Sidney); *Open City* (Roberto Rossellini) … Theater: *The Glass Menagerie* (Tennessee Williams); *State of the Union* (Lindsay and Crouse); *Carousel* (Rodgers and Hammerstein) … Radio: *Arthur Godfrey Time*; *Beulah*.**

"[Roosevelt] died in harness, and we may well say in battle harness, like his soldiers, sailors, and airmen.... What an enviable death was his."—**Winston Churchill, in a speech to the House of Commons, April 17, 1945**

NEW IN 1945

Female suffrage in France.

Bumper stickers.

Fluoridated water supply (Grand Rapids, Michigan).

Zoom lens.

Frozen orange juice.

Wax pencils.

Tupperware.

Nationally televised Macy's Thanksgiving Day Parade.

IN THE UNITED STATES

▶PATTON DIES—General George Patton, survivor of two world wars, was fatally injured in a car accident in occupied Germany in 1945. A ruthless, extravagantly demanding officer (he was nearly relieved of his command in 1943 when he hit a shell-shocked soldier on a visit to a military hospital), "Old Blood and Guts" had led the Allied landings in French North Africa and Sicily, and the Normandy breakout into Germany and on to Czechoslovakia. **◂1943.4**

▶A HERO RETURNS—Lieutenant Audie Murphy, the war's most-decorated American soldier (24 decorations, including a Congressional Medal of Honor), returned

home to a hero's welcome in 1945 and attempted to turn his celebrity status into Hollywood stardom. The movie career of the boyishly handsome Texas native was characterized mostly by low-budget cowboy pictures; it climaxed in 1955, when he played himself in *To Hell and Back*, the story (based on his book) of

Deciding Europe's future: *(from left)* Churchill, Roosevelt, Stalin.

DIPLOMACY

Big Three at Yalta

5 At the Crimean resort of Yalta, Churchill, Roosevelt, and Stalin met for the second and final time to plan the defeat of the Axis powers, and to plot the future of Europe. The weeklong conference, in February 1945, yielded agreements on the division of Germany into occupied zones, voting procedures in the UN Security Council, and other important matters. Yalta was widely hailed as a giant step toward world peace—and assailed for the concessions the British and American leaders granted their Soviet partner in order to ensure his continued cooperation in the war effort.

In return for Stalin's pledge to join the war against Japan after Germany's surrender, the Soviet Union gained the Kurile Islands and parts of Manchuria (territories it had lost to Japan in 1875 and 1904, respectively) as well as a guarantee that the pro-communist status quo in Outer Mongolia would be maintained. On European matters, the Western chiefs were even more accommodating. With Stalin, they issued the Joint Declaration on Liberated Europe, calling for democracy in Eastern Europe. But their trust in Soviet intentions was misplaced: With the Red Army occupying the region, the declaration would become irrelevant.

A case in point was Poland. Churchill and Roosevelt recognized the Soviet-installed Lublin Committee as the country's provisional government, subject to inclusion of members of the non-communist government-in-exile. But elections didn't take place in Poland until 1948, by which time it was effectively a one-party state. **◂1944.11 ▸1945.8**

THE UNITED STATES

FDR Dies

6 When Franklin D. Roosevelt was inaugurated in January 1945 for his fourth term as president, his haggard appearance shocked onlookers. Though crippled by polio, he'd always stood when delivering speeches, but now he trembled at the lectern. Journeying to Yalta in February further weakened him. On his return, FDR vacationed in Warm Springs, Georgia, a resort for polio sufferers and his favorite retreat. Sitting for a portrait on April 12, he exclaimed, "I have a terrific headache"—then passed out. A few hours later he was dead of a stroke. At the brink of victory, the 63-year-old commander in chief had spent his last strength.

Roosevelt served longer than any other U.S. president, through history's deepest depression and fiercest war. At home, his activist New Deal programs made him a hero to workers and the poor; in the Allied nations, he was revered for committing America's power to fight the Axis. His courage in overcoming his disability inspired millions. Even Republican senator Robert Taft, a political enemy, eulogized him as "the greatest figure of our time." Slum-dwellers gathered at the U.S. embassy in Rio de Janeiro to offer condolences. French foreign minister Georges Bidault called FDR's death "a great disaster."

Roosevelt's successor was Vice President Harry S Truman, 60, a Missouri farm boy who'd failed as a haberdasher, but flourished in politics. Suddenly, he was helmsman of one of the world's three mightiest nations. The decisions that would end the war and shape a new era were largely his to make. **◂1940.13 ▸1948.M**

WORLD WAR II

Death to the Dictators

7 The supreme leaders of Fascism and Nazism had been masters of pomp and circumstance—but their deaths, in 1945, were anything but glorious.

Hitler ended his days in a bunker beneath the Reich Chancellery garden in Berlin, attended by his guards, aides, quack doctors, and his mistress, Eva Braun.

Mussolini and his mistress Claretta Petacci met an ignominious end in Milan.

Terrified of assassination plots and enfeebled by an assortment of drugs, he studied horoscopes and raved about imaginary troop movements. On April 28, as Berlin blazed, Hitler and Braun were married by a city official. The Führer drew up a will, leaving his possessions to the Nazi Party (or to Germany, if the Party should perish),

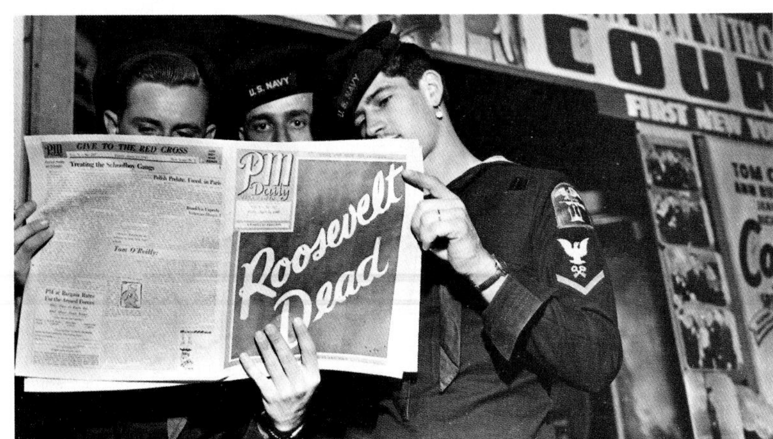

American sailors study a newspaper announcing the death of their commander in chief.

SPORTS: Baseball: World Series, Detroit Tigers defeat Chicago Cubs, 4–3; A.B. "Happy" Chandler appointed commissioner of baseball; Brooklyn Dodgers announce signing of Negro-league player Jackie Robinson ... Football: NFL, Cleveland Rams defeat Washington Redskins, 15–14 ... Boxing: Middleweight Rocky Graziano scores five knockouts in his first fights at Madison Square Garden.

"To write a poem after Auschwitz is barbaric."—**German philosopher Theodor Adorno**

and naming Admiral Karl Dönitz his successor.

That same day, Mussolini and his mistress, Claretta Petacci, were caught by Italian partisans as they fled the Allied advance. Though he pleaded, "Let me live and I will give you an empire," the couple were shot after a summary trial, then hung by the heels with two lesser corpses in a piazza in Milan.

On April 30, Hitler and his new wife shook hands with their companions and disappeared into his private chambers. There he stuck a pistol barrel into his mouth and fired, while Braun swallowed cyanide. Their bodies were carried upstairs to the shell-pocked garden, where they were doused with gasoline and burned—along with piles of Nazi documents. **◂1945.2 ▸1945.2**

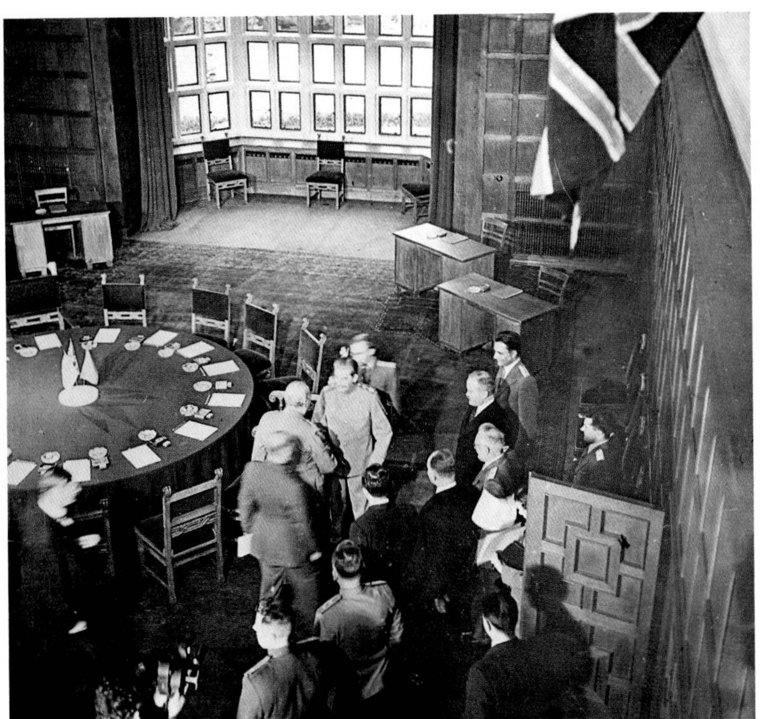

Stalin greets Churchill at the start of the Big Three conference in Potsdam.

DIPLOMACY

The Allies' Last Parley

8 The final Grand Alliance conference opened in Potsdam, outside Berlin, in July 1945. The personnel differed from that of previous Big Three parleys: Truman had succeeded the late Roosevelt; after ten days, Britain's new prime minister, Clement Attlee, replaced Churchill. The contentious tone was different, too.

Stalin, whose people had borne the brunt of Nazi aggression, wanted harshly punitive reparations from the Germans. The Americans and Britons, fearing they would have to subsidize a permanently disabled Germany, wanted softer terms. There were clashes over Poland's borders and the legitimacy of Soviet puppet regimes in Eastern Europe.

The atomic bomb was a new factor at Potsdam. The United States had just tested the weapon in New Mexico; after Truman shared the secret with Churchill—only dropping a hint to Stalin—the Western leaders warned Japan of "prompt and utter destruction" unless it surrendered unconditionally. (The Japanese refused.) The bomb allowed Truman to take a tougher line with Stalin, since it made Soviet entry into the war against Japan less critical.

In the end, the conferees agreed that each power would take what it wanted from its own German occupation zone, with Moscow allocated a percentage of the others' spoils. Poland was shifted 150 miles westward, gaining territory from Germany and losing it to the Soviet Union. The Big Three vowed to foster a Germany reconstructed on a "democratic" basis—without defining the term. **◂1945.5 ▸1949.2**

THE HOLOCAUST

Nazi Horrors

9 As Allied troops pushed into German territory in 1945, they uncovered evidence of the Nazis' most appalling crime: the systematic murder of six million Jews, and as many other racial, political, sexual, and religious "undesirables." Liberating death camps like Treblinka, Majdanek, and Auschwitz (where the sign above the gate read, mockingly, "Arbeit Macht Frei"—"Work Will Make You Free"), soldiers found piles of corpses, filthy barracks crammed with five-tier bunks, open-pit latrines, and living skeletons staggering about amid the stench.

The survivors described what they had endured. Inmates had been separated upon arrival. Most were herded into "shower rooms" to be gassed; those who looked strongest were tattooed with a number, issued prison stripes, and assigned to slave-labor crews. Some did factory work for major corporations (including IG Farben, which manufactured Zyklon B, the poison used in the gas chambers). Some were used in sadistic medical experiments. Guards forced women, girls, and boys into prostitution. As prisoners weakened from starvation, cold, and disease, they, too, were gassed. Inmate *Sonderkommandos* (special work groups) carted the corpses into crematoriums or mass graves. The bodies were also used in manufactured goods: soap from human fat and mattresses stuffed with human hair.

Preoccupied with strategic priorities, the Allies had ignored years of pleas from world Jewish leaders to bomb the gas chambers. War-crimes tribunals would punish some of those responsible for the horrors—but for the victims of the camps, justice came far too late. **◂1944.10 ▸1946.V**

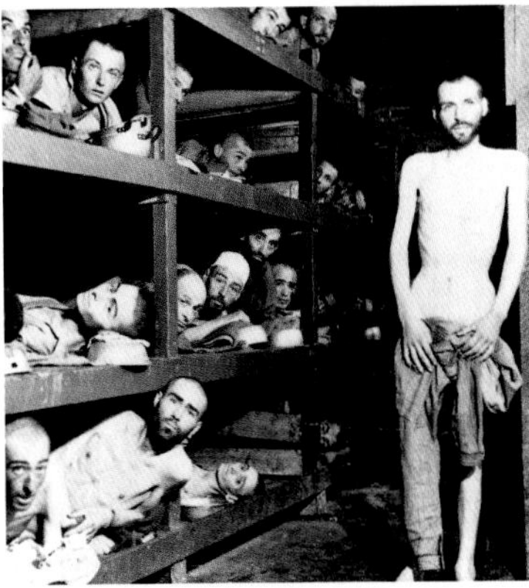

Slave laborers at Buchenwald, as found by U.S. troops of the 80th Division.

IN THE UNITED STATES

his rise from private to heroic lieutenant. Murphy was killed in a plane crash in 1971.

▶JOHNSON FOUNDS AN EMPIRE—Taking *Life* as his model, Chicago publisher John H. Johnson in 1945 introduced *Ebony*, the magazine that would make him one of the richest men in publishing. Created for a black audience, the monthly immediately sold out its first press run of 250,000. Johnson later added *Jet*, *Tan*, and *Black World* to his publishing empire, one of America's largest. ◂1936.M

▶SLOVIK SHOT—On January 31, the first American soldier executed for desertion since the Civil War was shot by a firing squad. Despite an earlier rejection and a criminal record, Private Eddie Slovik, a plumber from Detroit, had been drafted in 1944. After his capture, he claimed he would desert again if given a chance. Critics claimed Slovik was just being used to set an example, but General Dwight D. Eisenhower approved the action.

▶FIRE IN THE SKY—Deep in the New Mexico desert, the Western world's preeminent physicists *(below, Robert Oppenheimer [left], with Brigadier General Leslie Groves)* gathered in the predawn of July 16, 1945, to

witness the terrible fruit of years of intense labor: the world's first atomic detonation at the White Sands Missile Range in south-central New Mexico. The bomb exploded at 5:30 AM, flashing so brightly that the light could be seen 180 miles away. (From 10,000 yards away, the scientists would have been blinded had they not taken precautions.) At ground zero, the desert sand fused to glass; the blast was blinding. A new force had been loosed upon the world. Said Kenneth Bainbridge, the director of the lab at Los Alamos, "No one who saw it could forget it, a foul and awesome display." ◂1945.1 ▸1946.7

POLITICS AND BUSINESS: GNP: $211.9 billion ... President Roosevelt dies; Vice President Harry S Truman becomes president ... War Manpower Commission lifts all manpower controls ... Truman restores all free-market consumer production and collective bargaining ... Autoworkers strike at General Motors ... Governor Thomas E. Dewey establishes New York State Commission Against Discrimination.

"Chiang Kai-shek has lost his soul ... [he] is merely a corpse, and no one believes him anymore."—**Mao Zedong**

WORLD WAR II

▶DEADLY INDUSTRY— ***Buchenwald, Auschwitz, Dachau*** **ring familiarly horrific, but they were only three of the Holocaust's death factories. Allies liberated over 100 camps. Ohrdruf, in eastern Germany, was the first freed. American troops entered on April 3, 1945, and found thousands of gaunt corpses stacked against the walls, "flat and yellow as lumber," according to one soldier. As news of the discovery leaked out of Germany, a wave of revulsion swept the globe.**

▶HITLER'S SCORCHED-EARTH POLICY—"If the war is lost," Hitler madly reasoned with Albert Speer, chief of military production, "the German nation will also perish. So there is no need to consider what the people will need for continued existence." With that, the Führer ordered, in March, all factories, power plants, and farms obliterated. Anything of use to the advancing Allies was to be plowed into the earth. Speer countermanded the order, but Germany was already reeling.

▶OCCUPATION OF BERLIN—At Yalta, the Allies agreed to divide postwar Germany into zones of occupation; within the Soviet zone, which consisted of eastern Germany, Berlin itself would be split into

four administrative sectors: Soviet, American, British, and French. The agreement was enough for Eisenhower, who in April stopped the Western Allies' drive at the Elbe, 50 miles short of Berlin. But the Soviets, after taking the capital unassisted in May, barred the gates until July, time enough to loot the already ruined city—and to start building the regime that would rule East Berlin for the next four-and-a-half decades.

▶BURMA ROAD REOPENS—For American general Joseph Stilwell, the completion of a new spur of the Burma Road to China in 1945 was sweet revenge: Defeated by the Japanese in Burma in 1942,

State-of-the-art deadliness: German V-2 rocket at Peenemünde, the Nazi research center.

TECHNOLOGY

Intellectual Spoils of War

10 As the war in Europe ended, the victors raced to capture the technical wizards who had designed Germany's advanced aircraft—especially the V-1 and V-2 missiles that had battered Britain. The idea was not to punish those responsible for thousands of civilian deaths, but to hire them. In the spring of 1945, the Americans and Soviets were vying to collect what Eisenhower called the "intellectual spoils of war."

At Peenemünde, a research center on the Baltic coast, General Walter Dornberger and the physicist (and SS officer) Wernher von Braun had supervised hundreds of scientists in the German rocket program. As the Red Army closed in, the two men and their colleagues packed up the facility's 14-ton archive and fled south. In May, they surrendered to the Americans, from whom they expected better payment for their services.

A month earlier, U.S. forces had come upon the Nazis' underground rocket plant near Nordhausen, in the Harz mountains—a Yalta-sanctioned Soviet occupation zone. Racing to beat the June 1 deadline for turning the area over to the Soviets, the Americans hired liberated Nordhausen slave laborers (100 slaves had died each day at the factory) to salvage missile equipment. By the deadline, 100 V-2s, the Peenemünde archive, and 115 German scientists had been shipped to America. Their sins forgiven, von Braun and Dornberger helped found the U.S. space program.

The Soviets, too, captured their share of scientists. In the Korean War, their Mig 15 fighter planes would battle American F86 Sabres—both designed by German engineers. **◂1944.2 ▸1957.2**

COLONIALISM

Algeria and Vietnam Revolt

11 For France, the end of World War II meant the beginning of the end of empire—foreshadowed in 1945 by uprisings in Vietnam and Algeria.

The war had impoverished native Algerians, and French settlers had blocked their demands for civil rights. At a victory parade in the city of Sétif, some Arabs carried signs with outlawed slogans: "Long Live Free and Independent Algeria," "We Want to Be Your Equals." Gendarmes grabbed the placards and fired on the crowd, killing several demonstrators. Bands of vengeful Algerians murdered 100 Europeans. In retaliation, French gunboats, warplanes, troops, and vigilantes attacked Arab villages. The revolt was crushed, but the independence movement was permanently radicalized.

Vietnam had spent most of the war occupied by the Japanese, but nominally administered by Vichy France. Meanwhile, in China, exiled Vietnamese Communist leader Ho Chi Minh *(below, left)* had formed a united front for independence called the Viet Minh. (When Chiang Kai-shek imprisoned Ho, the Americans—grateful to Viet Minh guerrillas for help against the Japanese—secured his release.) In March 1945, the Japanese ousted the French entirely and granted sham independence to Vietnam's French-installed emperor, Bao Dai. But in August, after Japan's defeat—and before the French could recover control—the Viet Minh launched an insurrection.

The "August Revolution" easily swept the Viet Minh to power, and Bao Dai out. But the Allies had agreed at Potsdam that France still owned Vietnam. Aided by British troops, the French regained the cities of the south by year's end. Elsewhere, however, resistance continued. Negotiations led to a cease-fire, but in November 1946 the First Indochina War began in earnest. **◂1942.9 ▸1946.M**

CHINA

Playing at Peace

12 The loveless marriage between Chinese Nationalists and Communists, forged for mutual resistance to Japanese occupation, dissolved with Japan's defeat in 1945. The forces of Chiang Kai-shek, president of the Nationalist government, and of Mao Zedong, Communist Party chairman, immediately scrambled to claim the vast stretches of China abandoned by Emperor Hirohito's vanquished armies. At stake was the political future of the world's most populous country.

The Nationalists and Communists fought only sporadic engagements at first, while Chiang and Mao staged a diplomatic charade for the war-weary Chinese people and the world—particularly Washington and Moscow, whose backing for one side or the other could decide the struggle's outcome. For much of 1945 and 1946, the two leaders engaged in high-profile peace negotiations. The United States, which brokered the talks, hoped to effect a Chinese coalition government.

WORLD WAR II: January: U.S.S.R. invades Poland; U.S. lands on Luzon ... February: Yalta Conference; U.S. lands on Iwo Jima ... March: Allies cross Rhine ... April: U.S. lands on Okinawa; U.S.S.R. enters Vienna; Allies reach Elbe River; U.S.S.R. enters Berlin; Mussolini executed; Germans surrender Italy; Hitler commits suicide ... May: Berlin surrenders; German high command formally surrenders at Reims,

"This is the Polish question transplanted to the Far East."—**U.S. secretary of war Henry Stimson, on Korea**

Chiang and Mao paid lip service to the idea, but each knew his vision of China's future was incompatible with the other's—and neither planned to share power. As Chiang remarked to an aide, "The sky cannot have two suns."

Chinese militia women defending southern territory against Japanese occupiers.

Early in 1947, with each side holding substantial territory, full-scale civil war resumed. It would last three years and cost three million lives. **◂1941.13 ▸1949.1**

KOREA

Face-off in Korea

13 By 1945, Japan had subjected Korea to 35 years of harsh colonial rule. But when the Japanese lost World War II, the 26 million Koreans remained the pawns of greater powers.

At the Potsdam Conference in July, shortly before Japan's defeat, the Allies stipulated that Japanese forces in Korea should surrender to the Americans in the south and to the Soviets in the north; the 38th parallel would be the line of demarcation. On August 9, the day after Stalin declared war on Japan (and six days before the world war ended), 200,000 Soviet troops streamed into northern Korea, along with an army of exiled Korean Communists. Demoralized Japanese forces fled before them. By the time U.S. troops arrived in the south a month later, the Soviets had begun to seal off their zone and to erect a Communist system.

Unsure if they were conquering an outpost of the Japanese empire or liberating a captive nation, the Americans administered southern Korea with a heavy hand and an air of uncertainty. Their single clear objective was to prevent the Soviets from seizing the whole country. Complicating matters was the fact that Korea's colonial economy had collapsed upon Japanese withdrawal. Strikes, demonstrations, and peasant revolts engulfed the American zone. "My military government," wrote the U.S. commander, General John Hodge, "is entirely inadequate to cope with this situation." But the Soviets were established, so the Americans dug in. The Potsdam promise of Korean independence would have to wait. **◂1945.8 ▸1948.3**

THE MIDDLE EAST

Britain's Palestine Dilemma

14 With World War II over and the Nazi death camps open for the world to see, Zionists redoubled their demands that Britain open its Palestine mandate to unlimited Jewish immigration. Within Palestine, Jewish guerrilla groups—the Irgun Zvei Lumi and the Stern Gang—escalated their campaign to force Britain's hand. (Moderate Jewish leaders in the territory, led by Chaim Weizmann, pricked British consciences by pointing out the help a Zionist volunteer brigade had given the Allied cause.) Arabs in the region opposed a Jewish influx, but in Palestine itself they lacked unified leadership. So in March 1945, Saudi Arabia, Syria, Lebanon, Iraq, Transjordan, Yemen, and Egypt organized the League of Arab States to pressure Britain from the other side.

Britain's new Labour government (unlike its predecessor) strongly sympathized with Zionism's goal, yet it hoped to remain friendly with the Arabs. Adding to the British quandary was President Truman, whose Zionist leanings were clear. In April 1946, yielding to U.S. pressure, Britain sent yet another commission to study the issue. The Anglo-American Committee of Inquiry recommended that 100,000 European Jewish refugees be admitted immediately, that restrictions on Jewish land purchases in Palestine be lifted, and that a binational Jewish-Arab state be established under United Nations trusteeship. Faced with the political and economic costs of policing Palestine, the British gladly turned the matter over to the UN.

German refugees aboard the *Exodus* disembark in Haifa, only to be refused entry into Palestine by the British.

In 1947, the UN sent its own commission to seek answers to the Palestine problem. The result, the following year, was the founding of Israel—and war between the Jewish nation and its Arab neighbors. **◂1939.M ▸1948.9**

U.S. infantrymen in southern Korea examine weapons taken from defeated Japanese.

WORLD WAR II

"Vinegar Joe" had vowed to recapture the lost territory. His Ledo Road, painstakingly cut through dense jungle, connected India to the original Burma supply route. Over it, the Allies rolled war matériel eastward, ending Japan's three-year stranglehold on China.

▶"NOBLE DEATHS"—During the last, hopeless months of the Pacific war, more and more Japanese pilots became kamikazes and hurled their planes like guided bombs directly into American ships. Of the 13,000 Allied troops killed in the Pacific in 1945, three fourths were victims of kamikazes. Other Japanese chose a more private means—*seppuku*, self-inflicted "noble death." (One failed suicide was General Hideki Tojo, who shot himself in the head in September. He survived, but he was soon convicted of war crimes and hanged on April 28, 1946.) And in Germany, Hitler and Goering were just two among legions—including many ordinary citizens—who chose *Selbtsmord*, suicide.

▶A HERO DISAPPEARS—Between Germany's takeover of Hungary and the Red Army's arrival in January, Swedish diplomat Raoul Wallenberg saved 100,000 Hungarian Jews from Auschwitz—placing thousands in "protected houses" under the flags of Sweden and other neutral nations, and distributing countless Swedish passports. But when the Red Army stormed Budapest, Wallenberg was arrested as a spy. For years, the Soviets pled ignorance of his whereabouts; eventually, they reported that he subsequently died in jail in 1947. But freed Soviet prisoners claimed he'd been sighted in penal colonies as late as 1975.

▶TOTAL CASUALTIES—Over 35 million people died in World War II. Among the Allies, the U.S.S.R., with 18 million dead, suffered worst. Poland came second with 5.8 million. Yugoslavia lost 1.5 million, France, 563,000, the British Commonwealth, 466,000, the U.S., 298,000. German deaths totaled 4.2 million, the largest among the Axis. Italy lost 395,000 and Japan, the last to surrender, 1.97 million.

"I have made 23 pictures. Well, I would swap them all for the chance to have made Les Enfants du Paradis.*"*
—Director François Truffaut

AROUND THE WORLD

▶A FINAL DECLARATION—Shortly after declaring war on the Axis in February 1945, Egyptian prime minister Ahmed Maher Pasha was shot down by a Nazi sympathizer. A rumor, never proven, quickly circulated that the assassin had acted on orders of Egypt's militantly nationalist Muslim Brotherhood, which saw Ahmed Maher as an agent of Egypt's continued domination by Britain. ◂1936.M ▸1952.3

▶ODD MAN OUT—Spain was conspicuously absent when the United Nations was founded in October. The nation remained a non-belligerent in World War II, but the fascist sympathies of dictator Francisco Franco *(below)* led to Spain's ostracism by the victorious Allies. Faced with growing opposition at home and abroad, Franco used his diplomatic isolation to rally

nationalist sentiment. Later, NATO, eager for allies, forgave past sins and admitted Spain in 1982. ◂1939.9

▶CHURCHILL OUSTED—The war in Europe was over, and with it ended the government of Winston Churchill. The architect of Britain's victory resigned as prime minister in July 1945, after his Conservatives were stunningly and soundly defeated by the Labour Party in parliamentary elections. He had defeated the Nazis and saved the nation; against Labour's sweeping peacetime economic and social-reform program, however, the heroic old war leader proved defenseless.

▶VENEZUELAN REFORMER—With the fall of General Isáias Medina Angarita in a coup in 1945, oft-exiled political leader Rómulo Betancourt assumed the presidency of Venezuela. Founder of the liberal, noncommunist Democratic Action Party, Betancourt pursued moderate social and labor reform during his 28-month rule. (He returned in 1959 for a second term.) He sponsored a new constitution in 1947, which established popular elections. ◂1935.M

The great Charlie Parker *(with sax player Flip Phillips in profile)*, circa 1949.

MUSIC

Charlie Parker's Bebop

15 At small Harlem nightspots like Minton's and the Uptown Club, a handful of young musicians developed a revolutionary style of jazz that jettisoned the genre's dance-pop conventions. Pianists Tadd Dameron and Thelonius Monk, drummer Kenny Clarke, guitarist Charlie Christian, and trumpeter John Birks "Dizzy" Gillespie all contributed, but one man personified the moody, cerebral new aesthetic: alto saxophonist Charlie "Yardbird" Parker. Bebop emerged in full flower in 1945, when Bird (as he was known) and Gillespie collaborated on the first records to capture this rhythmically eccentric, melodically angular, harmonically complex music in its pure form.

Parker's beginnings were inauspicious. At the age of 15, when he turned up on Kansas City's lively jazz scene, he was a high school dropout already plagued by the heroin habit that ended up killing him 20 years later. Ridiculed by older musicians, Parker hid himself away for months of intense practice ("woodshedding," in jazz parlance). When he returned, his technical proficiency amazed his detractors. But only after he arrived in New York in 1939 did he experience the stylistic breakthroughs that made him a legend.

An endlessly inventive improviser —he was fascinated by such modernist composers as Schoenberg and Hindemith—Parker was on his way to becoming the most influential jazz soloist since Louis Armstrong. Music critics initially found the seminal Parker-Gillespie records (including *Now's the Time, Koko,* and *Salt Peanuts*) unlistenable. But by 1955, when Parker died, bebop was the reigning sound in jazz. **◂1937.5 ▸1955.7**

MUSIC

Britain's Britten

16 Benjamin Britten's *Peter Grimes* premiered in June 1945 at London's recently reopened Sadler's Wells Theatre with Britten's companion, tenor Peter Pears, singing the title role. It was the first British opera in modern times to have an impact outside London. With its brooding melodies evoking the conflict between a narrow-minded fishing village and the misfit Grimes, the opera (drawn from "The Borough" by poet George Crabbe) earned Britten a reputation as Britain's most important musical dramatist since the seventeenth century.

Britten wrote 13 operas altogether, but his talents extended far beyond that form. Highlights of his career include his collaboration with the poet W.H. Auden on the operetta *Paul Bunyan; Serenade for Tenor, Horn and Strings*, deemed by one critic "the most perfect musical work of this century"; the huge choral work *War Requiem*, based on poems by the poet Wilfred Owen; and several pieces written for the cello virtuoso Mstislav Rostropovich. Among Britten's works for children is the perennially popular composition, *Young Person's Guide to the Orchestra*. In 1976, the year of his death, Queen Elizabeth II named Britten a life peer; he was the first musician ever to win that honor. **◂1936.13 ▸1956.M**

Philip Langridge as Peter Grimes in a 1991 English National Opera production.

FILM

A Celluloid Monument

17 Directed by Marcel Carné and written by the poet Jacques Prévert, *Les Enfants du Paradis* (*Children of Paradise*) was filmed in France during the Occupation and released in 1945. This three-hour meditation on love, lust, power, and art is, according to one critic, "one of the most aesthetically satisfying films of all time."

Carné and Prévert's previous collaborations—*Drôle de Drame* (*Bizarre Bizarre*) (1937), *Le Jour se lève* (*Daybreak*) (1939)—were modern stories shot through with fatalistic realism. But the subject of contemporary despair was proscribed by the Nazis, so the filmmakers chose a historical context suggested by the great actor-director Jean-Louis Barrault, one of the

The three stars of *Children of Paradise*, from top left: Brasseur, Barrault, Arletty.

film's stars. Set in the Boulevard du Temple—the Parisian theater district of the 1840s, where the highborn and the lowlife mingled—*Les Enfants* portrays such historical figures as the beloved mime Baptiste Deburau, the matinee idol Frédéric Lemaître, and the criminal Lacenaire. Barrault's performance as Baptiste is revered by cineastes; Arletty's, as the gold digger Garance, is idolized.

Filming was difficult: Allied victories and citywide blackouts stalled the work, and Jewish members of the crew toiled secretly. Though not overtly political, *Les Enfants*—because of its affection for French theater, its story of passion and sacrifice, and the circumstances of its creation—became a monument to France's undying spirit. **◂1937.8**

NOBEL PRIZES: Peace: Cordell Hull (U.S.; United Nations) ... Literature: Gabriela Mistral (Chilean; poet) ... Chemistry: A.I. Virtanen (Finnish; fodder-preservation method) ... Medicine: Alexander Fleming, Ernst B. Chain (U.K.), and Howard W. Florey (Australian; penicillin) ... Physics: Wolfgang Pauli (Austrian; exclusion principle).

A VOICE FROM 1945

Comedy of Errors

From "Who's on First?" by Bud Abbott and Louis Costello, 1945

William A. "Bud" Abbott and Louis Francis "Lou" Costello (né Cristillo) were perhaps the most popular pair of funnymen ever to perform on stage, screen, radio, and television. Their partnership, which lasted from the early thirties to 1957, began when Costello, a vaudeville comedian performing at New York's Empire Theatre, drafted ticket taker Abbott to fill in for his ailing straight man. The team of Abbott and Costello gave their first radio performance in 1938, and premiered on Broadway the following year in The Streets of Paris. *By far their most memorable skit was a comedy of errors called "Who's on First?" a title phrase that has become a common figure of American speech. In the following excerpt from that routine, baseball and vaudeville prove a head-spinning mix.* ◄**1927.M**

BUD: You know, strange as it may seem, they give ballplayers peculiar names nowadays.... On the St. Louis team, we have Who's on first, What's on second, I Don't Know is on third.
LOU: That's what I want to find out. I want you to tell me the names of the fellows on the St. Louis team.
BUD: I'm telling you. Who's on first, What's on second, I Don't Know is on third.
LOU: You know the fellows' names?
BUD: Yes.
LOU: Well, then, who's playin' first?
BUD: Yes.
LOU: I mean the fellow's name on first base.
BUD: Who.
LOU: The fellow playin' on first base for St. Louis.
BUD: Who.
LOU: The guy on first base.
BUD: Who is on first.
LOU: Well, what are you askin' me for?
BUD: I'm not asking you, I'm telling you. Who is on first.
LOU: I'm askin' you, who is on first?
BUD: That's the man's name!
LOU: That's whose name?
BUD: Yes.
LOU: Well, go ahead, tell me!
BUD: Who.
LOU: The guy on first.
BUD: Who.
LOU: The first baseman.
BUD: Who is on first.
LOU (a new approach): Have you got a first baseman on first?
BUD: Certainly....
LOU: Well, all I'm tryin' to find out is what's the guy's name on first base.
BUD: Oh, no, no. What is on *second* base.
LOU: I'm not askin' you who's on second.
BUD: Who's on first.
LOU: That's what I'm tryin' to find out.
BUD: Well, don't change the players around.
LOU (tension mounting): I'm not changing nobody.
BUD: Now take it easy.
LOU: What's the guy's name on first base?
BUD: What's the guy's name on *second* base.
LOU: I'm not askin' you who's on second.
BUD: Who's on first.
LOU: I don't know.
BUD: He's on third. We're not talking about him.
LOU (imploringly): How could I get on third base?
BUD: You mentioned his name.
LOU: If I mentioned the third baseman's name, who did I say is playing third?
BUD (insistently): No, Who's playing first.
LOU: Stay offa first, will ya?

Bud Abbott *(top and above, at left)* and Lou Costello. In the 1945 movie *The Naughty Nineties*, the pair recorded their famous routine on film. It is also inscribed on a plaque at the National Baseball Hall of Fame in Cooperstown, New York.

"When you show him that you think he's the most wonderful baby in the world, it makes his spirit grow, just the way milk makes his bones grow."—**Dr. Benjamin Spock, in *Baby and Child Care***

STORY OF THE YEAR

The Spock Generation

1 "Trust yourself. You know more than you think you do." With the reassuring opening words of *The Common Sense Book of Baby and Child Care,* pediatrician Benjamin Spock restored the flagging confidence of postwar parents. A repository of practical wisdom covering everything from abscesses to zwieback, the book, published in 1946, debunked rigid apothegms of child-rearing, emphasizing instead intuition and flexibility as the keystones of healthy parenting. For this radical reasonableness, Dr. Spock was loved. By 1990, his manual was in its sixth edition and had sold some 40 million copies in 38 languages, making the doctor one of the most widely read American authors ever.

A native New Englander, Spock himself received a strict Yankee upbringing—a fact that led amateur psychologists to attribute his permissiveness to rebellion. Spock himself declared, "I agree with most of my parents' ideals and with half of their methods." His real disagreement was with such conventional pediatric theorists as behaviorist John B. Watson, who advised parents to treat children like young adults: "Never hug and kiss them, never let them sit in your lap. If you must, kiss them once on the forehead when they say good night." Spock sought to demystify child-rearing, to debunk the experts' aloof, often frightening advice. "Be natural and comfortable, and enjoy your baby," he said. His refusal to advocate specific ages at which children should master specific tasks—toilet training, sleeping through the night—was sometimes misinterpreted as an endorsement of unchecked leniency. In later editions of the book, Spock corrected that false impression, asserting that familial authority resides with parents, not children.

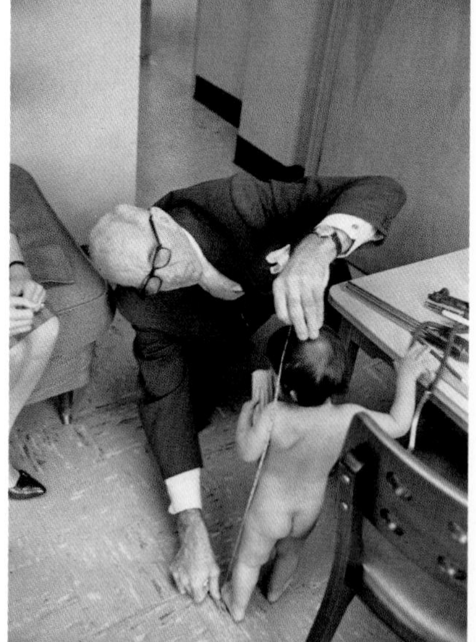

Dr. Spock, photographed in the early '60s by Henri Cartier-Bresson, charting the progress of one of his patients.

During the turbulent 1960s, when the first Spock babies came of age, critics charged the doctor with spawning a "generation of spineless pacifists." Spock, himself a tireless anti-Vietnam War activist, praised the idealism of young war protesters while denying responsibility for it. Despite bitter controversy, parents continued to swear by his book—and to buy it by the millions. "You must love children an awful lot to understand them so thoroughly," wrote one unabashed fan. "I only wish you were my children's doctor." In a way, he was. ◂1923.4 ▸1948.7

DIPLOMACY

New Hope for World Peace

2 Attempting to leave behind the carnage of seven years of world war, emissaries of 51 nations met in London on January 10, 1946, for the first session of the United Nations

Canadian Henry Eveleigh's winning entry in the UN's first "poster of the year" contest.

General Assembly. Steeped in idealism but backed with military might, the UN, as a body dedicated to preventing future global war, replaced the discredited League of Nations.

The idea for a new international peacekeeping organization had first been broached in 1941 by Roosevelt and Churchill, and was endorsed the following year by the other Allies, in the Declaration by United Nations. In the Moscow Declaration of 1943, China, Great Britain, the United States, and the U.S.S.R. affirmed the need to replace the League of Nations, and at the Dumbarton Oaks Conference in 1944, legations from those four countries sketched out a proposal. A charter was drawn up in June 1945 in San Francisco by delegates from 50 nations and ratified later in the year. It called for a dominant body, a "General Assembly" of all members (sovereign and equal "peace-loving" nations), as well as a "Security Council," composed of eleven members (five of them—China, France, Britain, the United States, and the U.S.S.R.—permanent). The Security Council alone had authority to intervene in international disputes—and then only after a unanimous vote of its permanent members.

The UN's business would be carried out by the Secretariat, led by a secretary general (the first was Norwegian statesman Trygve Lie, foreign minister of Norway's wartime government-in-exile). At the invitation of the U.S. Congress, the UN decided to locate permanently in New York City. John D. Rockefeller, Jr., drawing on his family's inexhaustible fortune, donated prime Manhattan real estate along the East River. By 1952, the headquarters' main buildings were completed. ◂1945.M ▸1953.8

JAPAN

The American Occupation

3 The implementation of the Allies' blueprint for the postwar reconstruction of Japan rapidly developed into an exclusively American project, with General Douglas MacArthur at the helm, in the office of supreme commander, Allied powers (SCAP). American policy goals to demilitarize Japan's ruined economy and democratize its failed government received an invaluable boost on January 1, 1946, when Emperor Hirohito renounced his claim to divinity, thus paving the way for a new constitution.

Framed by SCAP and submitted to the Diet (legislature) in November, the constitution made the Emperor a figurehead sanctioned by

Hirohito, having renounced his divinity, addresses his subjects in May 1946.

"the will of the people, with whom resides sovereign power." It also set forth a 31-article bill of rights, forswore armed forces and the right to make war, and structured the government to comprise a bicameral Diet, a prime minister elected by the Diet from its own ranks, and an independent judiciary. The ancient tradition of imperial rule was broken; modern Japanese government would be secular and democratic.

SCAP was equally aggressive on the economic front, seeking to destroy Japan's military power by

ART & CULTURE: Books: *Delta Wedding* (Eudora Welty); *Member of the Wedding* (Carson McCullers); *The Chrysanthemum and the Sword* (Ruth Benedict); *Berlin Stories* (Christopher Isherwood); *Lord Weary's Castle* (Robert Lowell) ... Music: "Zip-a-Dee-Doo-Dah" (Wrubel and Gilbert); "Get Your Kicks on Route 66" (Bob Troup); "The Christmas Song" (Tormé and Wells); *Medea* (Samuel Barber);

"In the long run we are all dead."—**John Maynard Keynes, when asked about the implications of his economic theories "in the long run"**

dissolving its massive *zaibatsu* ("wealthy clique") monopolies, the family-operated trusts that were the cornerstones of Japan's war economy. But as the Cold War added a new political dimension to Japanese economic recovery, SCAP came to appreciate the *zaibatsu* as a "bulwark against Communism." Only 18 of the 325 businesses originally slated for breakup were dissolved. The cooperative organization of the remaining firms contributed to Japan's remarkable postwar economic ascendancy. **◂1945.1 ▸1959.M**

Keynes and his wife, ballet dancer Lydia Lopokova, painted by William Roberts. Scorned as a "chorus girl" by Keynes's Bloomsbury circle, Lopokova was the great love of his life.

ECONOMICS

The Keynesian Revolution

4 A new era of government intervention in capitalist economies was already under way in societies as disparate as Nazi Germany and the United States by the mid-thirties. The theoretical underpinnings of that trend—which became all but universal following the war—were provided by British economist John Maynard Keynes. No country rallied more enthusiastically to the "Keynesian revolution" than the United States, which in 1946 (the year of Keynes's death) ratified the Full-Employment Act, whereby the federal government promised to adjust its spending for optimal employment, production, and purchasing power. The law embraced the fundamental tenets of Keynesian economics, which Keynes had set forth a decade earlier in his landmark attack on laissez-faire economics, *The General Theory of Employment, Interest, Money.*

Whereas classical economics taught that fluctuating employment levels and interest rates are self-correcting over the long run, Keynes—writing during a seemingly intractable depression—argued that individual savings and reduced consumption were insufficient for correcting severe recessions. In his revolutionary view, the key to increased capital was increased demand, which depended on high, and steady, employment—and for that, private investment alone was not enough. Hence, the government must intervene to ensure a healthy economic equilibrium. A thorough antisocialist who firmly believed in the capitalist market economy, Keynes nonetheless argued for "a somewhat comprehensive socialisation of investment" through direct government expenditures. Nothing did more to vindicate Keynes's unorthodoxy than World War II, when massive government spending led to full employment and an end to the Great Depression.

Keynesianism and the macroeconomic theory that grew out of it proved stunningly effective during the high-growth, low-unemployment years of the 1950s and '60s. Thereafter, resurgent inflation and growing government deficits prompted a reevaluation. The ever-larger economic role played by government suffered a sharp rebuke from "supply-side" theorists during the Thatcher-Reagan era. **◂1944.12 ▸1957.7**

THE PHILIPPINES

A Qualified Independence

5 Having suffered 425 years of foreign rule—Spanish until 1898, then American—the Philippines gained independence in 1946. With a government modeled after that of the United States, the Republic of the Philippines was proclaimed on July 4, following the adoption of a new constitution and the election of Manuel Roxas *(above)* as first president. But the Filipinos were to find that liberty came with strings, most attached directly to the United States.

Upon taking over the Philippines from Spain in 1898, the U.S. government insisted it had no interest in making the islands a permanent colony: The occupation phase would last only until Filipinos had been schooled in democratic self-government. The "schooling" lasted 36 years; in the meantime, the Philippines supplied the United States with cheap raw materials, and the United States developed the islands as a market for finished American goods. As the colonial period dragged on, Filipinos grew restive. "I would rather live under a government run like hell by Filipinos," said the patriot Manuel Quezon, "than under one run like heaven by Americans."

In 1934, the U.S. Congress granted the Philippines commonwealth status. Quezon was elected president. Full independence, however, was put off until ten months after Japan's surrender in World War II. By then Quezon was dead, replaced on the national stage by the much weaker Roxas. In exchange for American funds, Roxas (a collaborator with the Japanese during their wartime occupation) made debilitating concessions, allowing U.S. military bases to remain and agreeing to trade restrictions that safeguarded the old colonial arrangement. In the mountains beyond Manila, a left-wing, anti-American movement soon took root. **◂1902.M ▸1965.M**

BIRTHS

Bob Beamon, U.S. athlete.

Steve Biko, South African political activist.

José Carreras, Spanish singer.

Connie Chung, U.S. broadcast journalist.

William J. Clinton, U.S. president.

Rainer Werner Fassbinder, German filmmaker.

Reggie Jackson, U.S. baseball player.

John Paul Jones, U.K. musician.

Peter Martins, Danish ballet dancer and choreographer.

Liza Minnelli, U.S. actress and singer.

Ilie Nastase, Romanian tennis player.

Karen Silkwood, U.S. political activist.

Donald Trump, U.S. businessman.

Andre Watts, U.S. pianist.

Bruce Weber, U.S. photographer.

DEATHS

John Logie Baird, Scottish inventor.

Countee Cullen, U.S. poet.

Manuel de Falla, Spanish composer.

W.C. Fields, U.S. comedian.

Hermann Goering, German Nazi leader.

Gerhart Hauptmann, German playwright.

Jack Johnson, U.S. boxer.

John Maynard Keynes, U.K. economist.

Paul Langevin, French physicist.

Damon Runyon, U.S. writer.

Gertrude Stein, U.S. writer.

Alfred Stieglitz, U.S. photographer.

Joseph Stilwell, U.S. general.

Booth Tarkington, U.S. writer.

Jimmy Walker, U.S. politician.

H.G. Wells, U.K. writer.

Jubilation Overture **(Robert Ward) ... Painting & Sculpture: *Eyes in the Heat* (Jackson Pollock) ... Film: *The Best Years of Our Lives* (William Wyler); *Shoeshine* (Vittorio De Sica); *Beauty and the Beast* (Jean Cocteau); *Notorious* (Alfred Hitchcock) ... Theater: *Born Yesterday* (Garson Kanin); *Annie Get Your Gun* (Irving Berlin) ... Radio: *Twenty Questions.***

"Argentina was a country of fat bulls and undernourished peons."—**Juan Perón, on the state of Argentina in 1946**

NEW IN 1946

Tide detergent.

Cannes Film Festival.

Timex watches.

Bikini swimsuit.

Baby boomers (Kathleen Casey Wilkens, born one second after midnight, 1/1/46).

Roosevelt dime.

Fulbright fellowships.

The Slinky.

Female suffrage in Japan.

IN THE UNITED STATES

▶SOUTHERN SAGA—Robert Penn Warren, a leading poet and literary critic, finally gained the popular audience he richly deserved with a work of fiction, *All the King's Men.* A landmark of modern moral reasoning, the 1946 novel presented Southern demagogue Willie Stark (based on Louisiana's Huey Long) as an archetype of compromised "fallen" mankind. "Man is conceived in sin and born in corruption," opines Stark, "and he passeth from the stink of the didie to the stench of the shroud." In 1985, Warren became the U.S.'s first poet laureate. ◀1935.M

▶HAYWORTH'S HEYDAY—In a classic scene in *Gilda*, sultry Rita Hayworth suggestively pulls off a pair of long black gloves while lip-synching "Put the blame on Mame, boys." The 1946 film confirmed Hayworth, née Margarita Carmen Cansino, as Hollywood's leading sex symbol.

ITALY

Monarchy Out, Republic In

6 The 900-year-old house of Savoy fell forever in June 1946, when Italy's King Umberto II left for a Portuguese exile. Bowing to Allied peace terms, Umberto's father, Vittorio Emanuele III, had retired to private life in 1944, leaving all power in the hands of the provisional government. In May 1946, as Italians prepared to vote on whether to retain the monarchy, the old king—unpopular, thanks to his association with fascism and defeat—abdicated altogether, putting his son Umberto on the throne. The day before the referendum, Pope Pius XII urged the electorate to choose Christianity over materialism—a veiled pitch for keeping Umberto. But 54 percent of the voters favored a republic.

In exile, Italy's last monarch *(here, in 1979)* took the title Count of Sarre.

The rejected royal contested the results, but Allied occupation authorities were unsympathetic, and Premier Alcide De Gasperi ordered him to go. Italy's last monarch left for Portugal after a month-long reign.

The voters also elected a constituent assembly to draw up a constitution for the new republic. The political dynamics of post-Fascist Italy were taking shape: The new Christian Democrat Party won 35 percent of the vote, the Socialists 21 percent, and the Communists 19 percent. A few minor parties shared the rest.

Although the Italian Communist Party was the biggest of its kind in Western Europe, the threat of revolution—palpable only a year before thanks to shortages, inflation, and an anti-rightist backlash—was receding. By preventing purges against Fascist collaborators, De Gasperi and his centrist Christian Democrats had won the loyalty of much of the Italian middle and upper classes. The pragmatic Communists followed that example. The three top parties devised a constitution (implemented in 1948) that was a grand compromise: part Marxist and part capitalist, guaranteeing freedom of expression but permitting censorship, and safeguarding freedom of religion while giving the Catholic Church an array of special privileges. **◀1945.7 ▶1976.14**

THE UNITED STATES

Testing for Deadliness

7 It was a display of "majestic destruction," of "dazzling light and peach-colored clouds," says one enthusiastic account of the United States' 1946 detonation of an atomic bomb at tiny Bikini Atoll in the Marshall Islands. Called Operation Crossroads, the Bikini test was the first scientific effort to determine the full effects of atomic weaponry, whose unimaginable power, even after Hiroshima and Nagasaki, still tended to elicit technophilic awe rather than revulsion. Between 1946 and 1958, the United States conducted more than 60 atomic tests in the Marshalls.

U.S. military officials selected remote, mid-Pacific Bikini in January1946 for naval testing of its new superweapon, and Congress approved the site the following spring. Although U.S. trusteeship of the Marshalls was not sanctioned for another year, preparations for Crossroads began immediately with the evacuation of Bikini's 162 residents to other islands. For the next twelve years, the military shunted Marshallese from one atoll to another, often into labor camps, as fallout rained down on their homelands.

Each of the two Crossroads tests detonated a Nagasaki-sized bomb, equal to 20,000 tons of TNT. The second, exploded underwater, almost instantly sank a 26,000-ton battleship moored 500 feet away—the first ship ever destroyed by a bomb that hadn't hit it. A sense of scientific adventure prevailed at Bikini until 1949, when the Soviets detonated their first A-bomb—breaking the U.S. monopoly. Thereafter, under the Atomic Energy Commission (created in August), experimentation assumed a grim urgency. **◀1945.1 ▶1951.3**

Stunned observers of the Bikini Atoll atom-bomb test had to develop a new vocabulary for what they had seen: "mushroom cloud," "cauliflower cloud," "air-shock disk."

ARGENTINA

The Rise of Perón

8 Defeated in Europe, fascism got a boost in South America when Colonel Juan Perón was elected president of Argentina in 1946.

Juan and Eva Perón greet the crowds.

Posted during wartime to Italy, Perón had returned home in 1940 armed with new ideas. After the military overthrow of Argentina's civilian government in 1943, he asked to be made secretary of labor; promising social reforms, the charismatic colonel developed a huge following of *los descamisados* (the shirtless ones). By 1945 he'd arranged to be named vice president and war secretary.

Perón's rise alarmed many Argentines who resented his calls for state intervention in the economy, feared the loss of independent trade unions, and abhorred his

SPORTS: Baseball: World Series, St. Louis Cardinals (the "Williams Shift") defeat Boston Red Sox, 4-3 ... Football: NFL, Chicago Bears defeat New York Giants, 24–14 ... Tennis: Play resumes at Wimbledon after 6-year hiatus ... Horse Racing: Assault wins the Triple Crown.

"Frank, if you want to do a movie about me committing suicide, with an angel with no wings named Clarence, I'm your boy."—**James Stewart, after Frank Capra pitched the story of *It's a Wonderful Life***

repressive tendencies. Imprisoned by his enemies in October 1945, Perón was rescued by his young mistress, small-time radio and stage actress Eva "Evita" Duarte, who rallied 500,000 Buenos Aires residents in her lover's support. Perón went free, and declared his presidential candidacy the same night. (He married Evita three months later.) After a campaign featuring violent intimidation of the opposition, he won 56 percent of the vote.

Having passed laws granting himself absolute power, Perón raised wages and benefits; constructed hospitals, schools, and housing; and gave free medical care to the needy. Argentines cheered as most public services were nationalized and women's suffrage was introduced. The glamorous Evita, dispensing charity and homilies, became an object of near-worship.

At the same time, Perón muzzled newspapers, purged professors and judges, and gutted unfriendly unions and political parties. Corruption flourished, Argentina became a refuge for Nazis, and economic policies led the country toward financial disaster. After Evita's death in 1952, Perón began his steep decline. **◄1937.4 ►1952.9**

FILM

Misunderstood Masterpiece

9 "*It's a Wonderful Life*," wrote film critic James Agee when director Frank Capra's dark comedy-drama premiered in 1946, "is one of the most efficient sentimental pieces since *A Christmas Carol*." Indeed, thanks to around-the-clock screenings on American yuletide television, Capra's tale of Christmastime redemption may now be better known than Dickens's.

The film's hero, George Bailey (James Stewart), is a generous, much-loved banker in the small town of Bedford Falls. George has sacrificed his own desire to leave his "grubby little town" and see the world. His frustrations run deep. One Christmas Eve, a financial cataclysm sends him to the brink of suicide. Enter Clarence, Angel Second Class, whose metaphysical trickery helps George realize that even an ordinary guy who stays at home can make a difference in the world. The film ends happily, of course, but the "unborn" sequence—in which Clarence shows George that without him the sweet little village would be a hotbed of greed and sex—scalds the story with acid.

The financial ineptitude of Uncle Billy, played by Thomas Mitchell *(far left)*, nearly wrecks the Bailey family's Christmas. Donna Reed *(center)* played Mary Bailey.

Cynical postwar moviegoers, however, were immune to the acid and untouched by the uplift; *It's a Wonderful Life* flopped badly at the box office. Capra—once Hollywood's most successful director—never fully recovered. **◄1934.M**

IRAN

A Showdown in Azerbaijan

10 World War II's messy legacy of troop movements throughout the world postponed indefinitely any return to normalcy. In Iran, the military hangover came on early, when, in 1946, the Soviet Union refused to vacate its occupied territories. A neutral country with strong economic ties to Germany, Iran had been invaded by the Allies in 1941 and was occupied jointly by the Soviets and the British (who were soon joined by the Americans) to protect British oil concessions in the Persian Gulf region and to prevent Germany from blocking Allied supply routes through Iran to the strapped Soviet Union. To assuage Iran's fears of conquest, the Allies had agreed, in the Tripartite Treaty, to withdraw six months after the war's end. Nonetheless, the Soviets entrenched themselves in seven northwestern provinces. When withdrawal day arrived, in March 1946, the Soviets had pulled out of the eastern part of their occupied zone but had not budged from the northwestern province of Azerbaijan (which bordered the Soviet republic of the same name).

The U.S.S.R. had long coveted northwestern Iran for its rich oil reserves, as well as for Azerbaijan's enormous annual wheat harvest. It had set up a Communist regime in Azerbaijan in December 1945, a development that the Western Allies and Iran read as a harbinger of Soviet annexation. Iran protested to the UN; President Truman warned Moscow (in what some interpreted as a veiled nuclear threat) that Soviet recalcitrance in Iran would not be tolerated. Impelled to act, Stalin struck a deal with Iranian prime minister Ahmad Qavam: In return for leaving, the Soviets would receive a major oil concession, and the firmly pro-Soviet government would remain autonomous.

On May 9, confident of his ploy, Stalin began withdrawing troops. That fall, however, Qavam, bolstered by Britain and the United States, toppled the Communist regime in Azerbaijan. The Majlis, Iran's parliament, subsequently rejected the oil agreement.

Red Army and British soldiers share a laugh in the streets of Mekhabad, Iran, during the wartime occupation.

The Soviets had been cunningly held at bay, but Iran was caught in a dangerous game; it had escaped Moscow's sphere of influence only to enter the West's. Cold War lines were being drawn, the pawns identified. **◄1941.15 ►1951.12**

IN THE UNITED STATES

►DIGITAL BRAIN—Scientists at the University of Pennsylvania built the world's first all-purpose electronic digital computer, a 30-ton behemoth called the Electronic Numerical Integrator and Computer, or ENIAC. (The Colossus, built in wartime England, was also all-electronic, but it was designed just for code-breaking.) Equipped with 18,000 vacuum tubes, ENIAC, joked detractors, put out all the lights in west Philadelphia. Still, the machine was a vast improvement over earlier electro-mechanical computers: It performed 5,000 mathematical operations every second. Commissioned by the U.S. Army to calculate ballistic equations, ENIAC was installed at the Aberdeen, Maryland, proving grounds in 1946. Predicted *Popular Mechanics* magazine: "Computers of the future may have only 1,000 vacuum tubes and perhaps weigh no more than 1½ tons." ◄1944.M ►1951.1

►MUSEUM-WORTHY CHAIR—The Museum of Modern Art gave Charles Eames a one-man show in 1946, the first

such honor ever extended to a furniture designer. The show's star attraction was a chair that Eames (whose wife, Ray, collaborated on his designs) had created six years earlier. Constructed of chrome-plated steel tubing and contoured plywood, the Eames® Chair combined comfort, sturdiness, and a pared-down aesthetic. It was soon mass-produced—in plastic as well as plywood—and became a waiting-room staple. ►1981.11

►AN AMERICAN SAINT—America could claim its first saint when Pope Pius XII canonized Mother Frances Xavier Cabrini in 1946. Born in Italy, Mother Cabrini founded the Missionary Sisters of the Sacred Heart, then came to the United States in 1889 to work among poor Italian immigrants, primarily in Chicago and New York. She established 67 missions around the world.

POLITICS & BUSINESS: GNP: $208.5 billion ... Truman forces Roosevelt appointee, Secretary of Commerce Henry Wallace, to resign (due to conciliatory stance toward U.S.S.R.) ... All wage and price controls end (except rent, rice and sugar) ... U.S. joins UNESCO ... National School Lunch Act becomes law.

"No ideas but in things."—**William Carlos Williams**

AROUND THE WORLD

▶KAZANTZAKIS'S HERO—Greek man of letters Nikos Kazantzakis won international acclaim for his 1946 novel,

***Zorba the Greek.* This memorable portrait of a poor man and his hearty love of life (made into a 1964 movie starring Anthony Quinn *[above]*), examined the conflict between intellect and passion, a theme central to Kazantzakis's many works.**

▶CURTAIN FALLS—In a speech on March 5, former British prime minister Winston Churchill warned that Britain and the U.S. must hold the line against Soviet expansion. "From Stettin in the Baltic to Trieste in the Adriatic," he said, introducing a lasting phrase, "an iron curtain has descended across the continent." ◀1945.5 ▶1947.4

▶LONG WAR BEGINS—Vietnam and France brokered a shaky peace in March, after eight months of skirmishing: Northern Vietnam, led by Ho Chi Minh, became a free state within the French Union, and Cochin China (southern Vietnam) became a separate republic. The truce soon collapsed when the French navy bombarded Haiphong in November and fighting broke out in Hanoi—launching one of the century's longest wars. ◀1945.11 ▶1949.7

▶ONE-HOUSE PARLIAMENT—Poland's first postwar balloting, in July, an exercise in fraud and terror, produced a victory for the Communist provisional government: Voters approved a one-house parliament. The referendum's success, secured with the aid of secret police sweeps of naysayers, gave Polish Communists the means to seize lasting control of the government. ◀1944.6 ▶1956.4

▶FOURTH REPUBLIC—A new French constitution, drafted in 1946, established the Fourth Republic, which would be marked by sweeping social reform combined with governmental instability. ◀1944.4 ▶1962.3

1946

LITERATURE

Plainspoken Poetry

11 The first of five volumes of *Paterson*, William Carlos Williams's free-verse epic of life in a New Jersey city, was published in 1946. Reflecting its author's campaign to liberate the American idiom from its English progenitor, *Paterson* celebrates vernacular speech and the poet's role in society. Along with Ezra Pound's *Cantos* and T.S. Eliot's *The Waste Land*, it ranks as one of the monumental works of modern poetry.

Trained as a pediatrician, Williams practiced medicine in his native Rutherford, New Jersey, while pursuing writing as an avocation. He met Pound when both were students at the University of Pennsylvania, and under his influence became an advocate of imagism, a poetic theory emphasizing precise expression and a controlled use of free verse. As he matured, Williams developed his own aesthetic, objectivism, which put even more value on bare, ordinary language and vivid, unadorned imagery.

Also a playwright, Williams *(center)* reviews his 1949 play, *Dream of Love*, with actors Deren Kelsey *(left)* and Lester Robin.

Relatively obscure for most of his writing life, Williams enjoyed a sudden vogue in the 1950s, when the last volume of *Paterson* appeared. Thereafter, he became one of the most lionized, and widely imitated, poets of his time. **◀1925.8 ▶1949.8**

AUSTRALIA

A Continent Grows

12 Endowed with abundant land and a tiny population, Australia sponsored a massive immigration program in 1946 that at once gave displaced victims of World War II a place to live and helped meet the labor needs of Australia's postwar economic boom. Sponsored chiefly by Immigration Minister Arthur Calwell, the program ultimately brought more than 2.5 million immigrants to the island continent.

A boatload of refugee immigrants to Australia hangs out a banner of greeting to sponsors.

Calwell's program helped cover the costs of passage and accommodations; in return, an immigrant worked at an assigned job for two years. Traditional "White Australia" policy restrictions applied (Asian immigration had been banned a century before). All immigrants would be Caucasian, 90 percent of them British. "Two Wongs," Calwell crudely quipped, "do not make a White." When not enough Britons applied, Calwell turned to Eastern and Central European refugees, many of whom, he observed, "were red-headed and blue-eyed."

Eventually, as the initial wave of "New Australians" was assimilated, assisted passage was extended to Greece, Italy, Spain, Portugal, and Turkey. By the early 1970s, when the program was discontinued, Australia's population had doubled, from seven million to 14 million. Immigrants and their children accounted for more than half the increase. **◀1901.10**

MUSIC

The Sparrow Soars

13 By 1946, when Edith Piaf became an international star with her recording of "La vie en rose"—a song that, along with "Je ne regrette rien" ("I Regret Nothing"), became an inseparable part of her public identity—her pain-filled life was already the stuff of legend in her native France. Abandoned by her mother and neglected by her father, she gave birth as a teenager to a daughter who died in infancy. She was 20 and barely surviving as a street performer in Paris's Montmartre section when, in 1935, a cabaret owner named Louis Leplée—who gave the 4' 10" singer the name Piaf ("little sparrow")—put her onstage at his Gerny cabaret. She so charmed the audience that one of its members, the revered French entertainer Maurice Chevalier, jumped up and shouted, *"Cette môme—elle en a dans le ventre!"* ("That kid—she's got it inside!")

Piaf's definitive renderings of the popular French chanson raised the genre to a new level of respectability worldwide. Alone onstage in her signature black dress, her hair tousled, telling of love and loss in a voice that soared, trembled, and growled, she often elicited tears of sorrow from her adoring listeners. Her celebrity grew throughout the fifties as a relentless succession of doomed love affairs, automobile accidents, and addictions further accentuated the aura of tragedy that surrounded her. She died of cirrhosis on October 11, 1963. **▶1961.12**

Piaf cultivated a persona that made her melodramatic life seem even more so.

NOBEL PRIZES: Peace: Emily Greene Balch (U.S.; Women's International League for Peace and Freedom) ... Literature: Hermann Hesse (German-Swiss; novelist) ... Chemistry: James B. Sumner, John H. Northrup, and Wendell M. Stanley (U.S.; enzymes and virus proteins) ... Medicine: Hermann J. Muller (U.S.; hereditary effects of X-rays) ... Physics: P.W. Bridgman (U.S.; high-pressure physics).

A VOICE FROM 1946

Judging Hitler's Henchmen

From the Nuremberg Trials, Nuremberg, Germany, 1945-46

From October 1945 to October 1946, Nuremberg, Germany, was the site of some of the century's most important trials—those of 24 former Nazi leaders charged with overseeing mass murder on an unprecedented scale. The Nuremberg tribunals were administered by the United States, Britain, the Soviet Union, and France. Defendants faced four counts: crimes against peace (fomenting wars of aggression); crimes against humanity (committing genocide); war crimes (violating the laws of war); and criminal conspiracy. By the time verdicts were handed down on September 30, 1946, one of the accused had killed himself and another had been judged incompetent. Of the remainder, three were acquitted. Twelve were sentenced to hang (including vanished bureaucrat Martin Bormann, tried in absentia), three to life imprisonment, and four to prison terms ranging from ten to 20 years. The excerpts below are from testimony and documents presented at the trials. ◄**1945.9** ►**1947.V**

[Testimony of Anton Pacholegg, a prisoner at Dachau who worked as a clerk at the experimental station where other prisoners were subjected to "medical experiments"]:
The Luftwaffe delivered ... a cabinet constructed of wood and metal measuring one meter square and two meters high. It was possible in this cabinet to either decrease or increase the air pressure.... Some experiments gave men such pressure in their heads that they would go mad and pull out their hair in an effort to relieve the pressure.... They would tear their heads and face with their fingers and nails.... They would beat the walls with their hands and head and scream.... These cases ... generally ended in the death of the subject....

After [a] group had been killed, the skin from these bodies would be removed from ... thighs and buttocks.... Rascher [the head scientist] would pass on them before they were tanned.... I saw the finished leather later made into a handbag that Mrs. Rascher was carrying. Most of it went for driving gloves for the SS officers of the camp.

[Testimony of Joachim von Ribbentrop, Hitler's foreign minister (sentenced to death)]:
Q: Do you want us to understand that you didn't know what was going on in those concentration camps, at least in a general way?
A: I can assure you that I had not the slightest idea these things were going on....
Q: Don't you recall that President Roosevelt protested against these concentration camps, and the treatment of Jews and minorities?
A: Yes, I remember, and I recollect that. Yes.
Q: Did you not take any pains at that time to look into these matters and see what was going on?
A: Every possibility—I always looked after one thing: that every report of such kind which arrived was brought forward to the Führer, but I can tell you it was extremely difficult in 1938 even to mention the subject of Jews ... with the Führer. He was—I don't know whether you can realize what an overwhelming personality he had.... If he didn't want to talk about a matter, to even get it to him was quite impossible.

[Testimony of Rudolf Hess, Hitler's former deputy, who claimed to have lost his memory (and was sentenced to life in prison)]:
Q: Do you know who Jews are?
A: Yes. They are people—a race.
Q: You didn't like them very well, did you?
A: The Jews, no.
Q: So you had some laws passed about the Jews, didn't you?
A: If you tell me, I have to believe it....
Q: You don't remember having anything to do with any laws about Jews?
A: No.

[Testimony of Julius Streicher, editor of the violently anti-Semitic Nazi propaganda paper *Der Stürmer* (sentenced to death)]:
Q: How did you preach that the Jews were to be moved out of Germany?
A: I have made no public suggestions.
Q: Did you ever use the word "exterminate"?
A: I think my chief editor used it once.... Extermination can result by sterilization.... The word "extermination" does not necessarily mean killing.

[Affidavit of Rudolf Hoess, commandant of Auschwitz (sentenced to death)]:
The Camp Commandant at Treblinka ... used monoxide gas and I did not think that his methods were very efficient. So when I set up the extermination building at Auschwitz, I used Cyclon B [sic], which was a crystallized prussic acid which we dropped in the death chamber from a small opening. It took from 3 to 15 minutes to kill the people.... We knew when the people were dead because their screaming stopped.... After the bodies were removed our special commandos took off the rings and extracted the gold from the teeth of the corpses.

Another improvement we made [was that] at Treblinka the victims almost always knew that they were to be exterminated and at Auschwitz we endeavored to fool the victims into thinking that they were going through a delousing process. Of course, frequently they realized our true intentions and we sometimes had riots and difficulties due to that fact.... We were required to carry out these exterminations in secrecy but of course the foul and nauseating stench from the continuous burning of bodies permeated the entire area, and all of the people living in the surrounding communities knew that exterminations were going on at Auschwitz.

War criminals on trial at Nuremberg's Palace of Justice. In box, from left: Hermann Goering (taking notes), Rudolf Hess, Joachim von Ribbentrop.

1946

"A nomad on the steppes of Asia can have the news of the world just by twisting a dial.... Once the common man has a fair chance to learn what's really going on, he has a chance to control his destiny." **—Walter H. Brattain, on the transistor's importance**

STORY OF THE YEAR

Bell Labs Unveils the Transistor

1 In a casual, diffidently worded note written just before Christmas 1947, a 37-year-old physicist named William Shockley invited a few of his colleagues at Bell Telephone Laboratories in central New Jersey to stop by his lab to observe "some effects" he and his co-researchers John Bardeen and Walter H. Brattain had recently achieved. Six months later, Bell Labs made those effects public and launched an electronics revolution that is still in progress.

The three inventors demonstrated the passage of an electric current through a tiny device known as a "transistor" (so named because it *trans*fers current across a re*sistor*). Although primitive and bulky by modern standards, the device was a monumental breakthrough, the result of Bell Labs' concerted effort to develop a replacement for fragile, glass-enclosed vacuum tubes. Like the vacuum tube, the transistor could amplify a tiny electrical signal. Unlike the vacuum tube, it was cheap, durable, consumed minute amounts of power, and—as subsequent decades would reveal—could be made almost infinitely tiny.

A transistor also runs cold, in contrast to vacuum tubes, which generate immense heat. It uses semiconductors—a class of solid conductors (hence the term "solid state") midway between insulators, like glass, and high-conducting substances, like iron or gold. The success of the Bell Labs team hinged on its ability to zero in on materials—chiefly the nonmetallic element germanium, and then silicon—that in minuscule amounts could induce the same behavior in electrons as the vacuum tube (in which electrons are "boiled" out of a hot cathode into a vacuum). The "transistor effect" was achieved at the junction, or barrier, of positive and negative charges; the barrier could be sharply lowered with the application of a tiny current from a third direction. The result was not unlike turning on a faucet—a large current flowed across the barrier, amplifying the third signal up to 40,000 times.

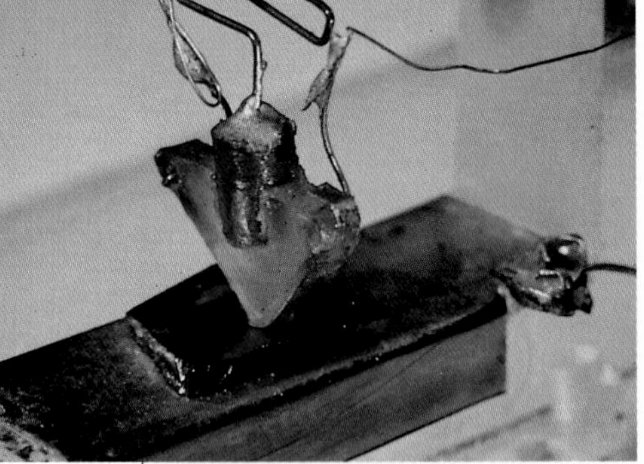

Bell Labs' first transistor, which amplified electrical signals by passing them through a solid semiconductor.

Bell Labs sat on its discovery for six months while it applied for patents. When word got out, electronics experts pounced on the implications. The mainstream press, however, was dismissive: *The New York Times* buried the news in a radio column, and the *New York Herald Tribune* said, "the spectacular aspects of the device are more technical than popular." Yet a decade later, pocket-size transistor radios were as ubiquitous a teenage accessory as blue jeans and a pocket comb. Shockley, Bardeen, and Brattain received a Nobel Prize in 1956 for their efforts. **◄1904.8 ►1971.5**

In this poster, the Marshall Plan is a splint enabling new European growth.

ECONOMICS

The Marshall Plan

2 Germany was defeated, Great Britain and France economically exhausted. Into Western Europe's postwar power vacuum strode the United States, guided by Secretary of State George C. Marshall's massive plan for European recovery. In a June 1947 speech at Harvard University, Marshall broached his idea: the creation, with American dollars, of an international economy that would "permit the emergence of political and social conditions in which free institutions can exist." In short, the United States would provide the money and technical knowhow to reconstruct Europe, keep communism at bay, and build up markets for American exports. Congress approved the proposal in 1948, and during the next four years the Marshall Plan provided Western Europe with $13 billion in U.S. government aid. It was by far the largest economic initiative any nation had undertaken in peacetime.

"The Americans," commented one skeptical British Treasury official, "want an integrated Europe looking like the United States of America." A common sentiment, the criticism was true up to a point. The Marshall Plan was the first time a country had linked international economic aid to the advancement of its own strategic interests (at least outside its own hemisphere). Yet American interests mostly coincided with those of Western Europe—namely, the creation of a prosperous, integrated economic community that would balance Soviet power. By 1947, Western Europe's economic instability had contributed to the growth of indigenous communist parties, notably in France and Italy. The Marshall Plan was designed to cut the legs out from under those movements.

Recovery was already under way, but Marshall aid provided extra momentum. During the plan's four-year run, industrial production in Western Europe grew by 40 percent, and the collective GNP of participating countries expanded by 32 percent. **◄1944.12 ►1947.4**

INDIA

Independence

3 "A moment comes," said Jawaharlal Nehru, addressing his government in Delhi as India's first prime minister, "which comes but rarely in history, when we step out from the old to the new, when an age ends, and when the soul of a nation, long suppressed, finds utterance." The moment was the stroke of midnight, August 14–15, 1947, when the British Crown Colony of India was replaced by the independent countries of India and Pakistan.

Nehru holding his country's new flag, approved by the constituent assembly a month before independence.

The Raj was gone, but India's partition triggered an unprecedented wave of violence, as Muslims drove Hindus and Sikhs from Islamic Pakistan (in Urdu, "Land of the Pure") and Hindus and Sikhs drove Muslims from Hindu India. In the forced exchange of population, a million people died, and some ten million more migrated. The Sikhs, caught between two alien territories, suffered the greatest proportion of casualties and felt the deepest resentment. "The Muslims got their Pakistan," said one Sikh leader, "the Hindus got their Hindustan, but what did the Sikhs get?"

Britain had hoped to avoid partition, but by the time Louis, Lord

ART & CULTURE: Books: ***Doktor Faustus*** **(Thomas Mann);** ***The Path to the Nest of Spiders*** **(Italo Calvino);** ***Tales of the South Pacific*** **(James Michener);** ***The Cold War*** **(Walter Lippmann);** ***Day After Day*** **(Salvatore Quasimodo);** ***The Age of Anxiety*** **(W.H. Auden) ... Music:** ***Knoxville: Summer of 1915*** **(Samuel Barber);** ***The Quest*** **(Roy Harris) ... Painting & Sculpture:** ***Das Matterhorn*** **(Oskar Kokoschka);**

"It will do no good to search for villains or heroes because there were none. There were only victims."
—Screenwriter Dalton Trumbo, one of the "Hollywood Ten," addressing the Writers Guild in 1970

Mountbatten, the last viceroy of India, began negotiating independence in 1946, Muhammad Ali Jinnah, leader of the Muslim League, was intractably committed to a Muslim country."I do not care how little you give me," Jinnah told Mountbatten, "so long as you give it to me completely." Nehru and his colleagues in the Indian National Congress were willing to part with Muslim-dominated territory. Only Mahatma Gandhi adamantly opposed the "vivisection" of India.

Fearing the outbreak of civil war, the Congress, the League, and Sikh leaders endorsed Mountbatten's hastily formulated plan on June 3, 1947. In the final settlement, Pakistan was created from the Punjab, Sind, North-West Frontier, and Baluchistan provinces. Bengal, in the east, was roughly split in half, with East Bengal becoming East Pakistan and later, in 1971, Bangladesh. Jinnah would lead Pakistan. Whatever Mountbatten's hopes, the possibility of a peaceful transfer of power had long since expired. **◂1942.M ▸1948.5**

THE UNITED STATES
Cold War Kickoff

4 By 1947, the Cold War had been declared: Churchill had warned of an iron curtain falling over Eastern Europe; Stalin, denouncing the West as implacably imperialistic, had refused to join the World Bank and the International Monetary Fund; and American diplomat George Kennan had filed his famous Long Telegram from Moscow, warning Washington that "the Kremlin's neurotic view of world affairs" made postwar entente impossible. President Truman, his popularity at an all-time low, remained quiet until March 12, when he presented to Congress the Truman Doctrine, the anticommunist declaration that was to define American foreign policy for the next 40 years.

A cost-cutting, war-weary Republican Congress had been planning a return to normalcy; instead, the president urged an expensive, global program to root out communism wherever it surfaced. Truman launched his crusade with a request for $400 million to fight communism in Turkey (which bordered the Soviet bloc) and Greece. His policy shift followed Britain's announcement a month earlier that it could no longer afford to fund the Greek government in its war against communist guerrillas. To ensure public support, Truman portrayed the guerrillas (whom the U.S. ambassador, Lincoln MacVeagh, privately called "the best men"

COST OF THE COLD WAR IN THE U.S.

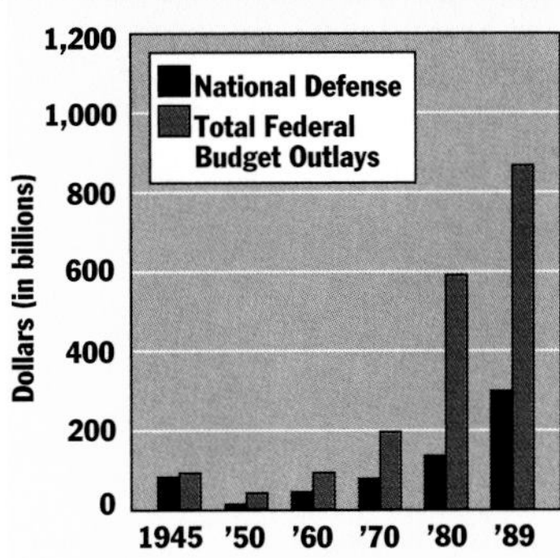

After WW II, defense spending in the U.S. went down, only to climb steadily upward (if less dramatically than the rest of the federal budget) during the Cold War.

in Greece) as pawns of Stalin—though they were actually backed by Yugoslavia's maverick Tito; he hailed the conservative, brutally repressive Greek regime as a bastion of liberty. Stalin responded by reviving the Comintern, his worldwide network for revolution, under the new name of the Communist Information Bureau (Cominform), and by renewing an anti-American propaganda campaign. East-West ideological polarization was complete. **◂1947.2 ▸1948.2**

THE UNITED STATES
The Hollywood Ten

5 Right-wing allegations that Hollywood was a "hotbed of communism" had been in the air since before World War II. (Union activists were especially suspect.) But in the red-baiting postwar climate, the probe of the film industry by the House Committee on Un-American Activities (HUAC) grew more intense than ever. In May 1947 HUAC set up shop in a Hollywood hotel and listened to a stream of loquacious celebrities tell stories of widespread Communist penetration of the movie industry. Emboldened, the committee then dispatched dozens of subpoenas, setting the stage for some of the most riveting political drama Americans had ever seen.

The hearings began in October with friendly witnesses calling for stern action against Moscow-directed conspirators. But the most compelling testimony came from the eleven "unfriendlies" who refused to answer questions about their First Amendment–protected political activities. One of them, playwright Bertolt Brecht, left for Switzerland the day after his appearance. The remaining became known as the "Hollywood Ten." Ordered to step down, screenwriter Dalton Trumbo shouted, "This is the beginning of an American concentration camp." When asked, "Are you now or have you ever been a member of the Communist Party?" screenwriter Ring Lardner, Jr. said, "I could answer but I would hate myself in the morning." All ten were cited for contempt of Congress, blacklisted, and given prison terms ranging from four to ten months.

Only one of the ten, director Edward Dmytryk, recanted and was allowed to keep working. The careers of many never recovered; others eventually resumed their work, first via "fronts" (Trumbo, writing as Robert Rich, won a 1956 Oscar for *The Brave One*), then under their own names (Lardner won in 1971 for his *M*A*S*H* screenplay). **▸1950.5**

Humphrey Bogart, Lauren Bacall, and other stars protested HUAC's investigations.

BIRTHS

Lew Alcindor (Kareem Abdul-Jabbar), U.S. basketball player.

Ann Beattie, U.S. writer.

Johnny Bench, U.S. baseball player.

David Bowie, U.K. singer.

David Hare, U.K. playwright.

Petra Kelly, German political leader.

Stephen King, U.S. writer.

David Letterman, U.S. talk show host.

David Mamet, U.S. playwright.

Michael Milken, U.S. financial executive.

Dan Quayle, U.S. vice president.

James Osterburg (Iggy Pop), U.S. singer.

Nolan Ryan, U.S. baseball player.

Salman Rushdie, Indian-U.K. novelist.

Arnold Schwarzenegger, Austrian-U.S. actor.

O.J. Simpson, U.S. football player.

Steven Spielberg, U.S. film director.

Ron Wood, U.K. musician.

DEATHS

U Aung San, Burmese politician.

Stanley Baldwin, U.K. statesman.

Pierre Bonnard, French painter.

Ettore Bugatti, Italian auto manufacturer.

Al Capone, U.S. gangster.

Willa Cather, U.S. novelist.

Henry Ford, U.S. auto manufacturer.

Fiorello LaGuardia, U.S. political leader.

Ernst Lubitsch, German-U.S. filmmaker.

Maxwell Perkins, U.S. editor.

Max Planck, German physicist.

Vittorio Emanuele III, Italian king.

Alfred N. Whitehead, U.K. mathematician and philosopher.

***The Euclidean Abyss* (Barnett Newman); *Agony* (Arshile Gorky) ... Film: *Gentleman's Agreement* (Elia Kazan); *Miracle on 34th Street* (George Seaton); *Le Silence est d'Or* (René Clair); *Odd Man Out* (Carol Reed) ... Theater: *All My Sons* (Arthur Miller); *Brigadoon* (Lerner and Loewe); *Finian's Rainbow* (Lane and Harburg); *High Button Shoes* (Styne and Cahn) ... TV: *Meet the Press*; *Howdy Doody*.**

"No one would call them beautiful—or spacious, or elegant.... Tricks are performed with the eaves and roof line, and they are shingled or painted in a variety of colors, but they are basically as alike as Fords."—**Fortune magazine, on the houses of Levittown**

NEW IN 1947

Unidentified flying object (UFO).

Der Spiegel.

Phrase "Cold War" (coined by financier Bernard Baruch).

Sony Corporation.

Everglades National Park.

Ajax cleanser.

IN THE UNITED STATES

▶BARRIER BREAKER—In October, veteran fighter pilot Charles Elwood "Chuck" Yeager pushed a U.S. Air Force Bell X-1 rocket plane past "Mach 1," the dividing line between subsonic and supersonic speeds. The first pilot to break the sound barrier (approximately 700 mph), Yeager later established a speed record of 1,650 mph.

▶UNION BUSTER—In a setback for organized labor, Congress overrode President Truman's veto in June to pass the controversial Taft-Hartley Act. The first legislative curb of union power in a dozen years, the law outlawed closed shops (union-only hiring), proscribed the political use of union funds, and allowed the government to get court injunctions against strikes that endangered national health or safety. ◀1936.M ▶1952.M

▶A VOICE FROM HEAVEN—Thirty-four-year-old gospel singer Mahalia Jackson had her first big national hit in 1947 with "Move On Up a Little Higher" (the first gospel record to sell a million copies). The granddaughter of a slave, Jackson was well known in the black church community before she gained international

1947

The "Rule of the Community" scroll has been interpreted in widely varying ways.

ARCHAEOLOGY

The Dead Sea Scrolls

6 A young Bedouin searching for a lost goat near the northwestern shore of the Dead Sea in the summer of 1947 happened onto one of the century's most sensational archaeological finds. Noticing a narrow opening in the surrounding limestone cliffs, he hoisted himself inside and discovered several large earthenware jars. One contained three leather scrolls wrapped in decaying linen and covered with ancient script.

The first of the Dead Sea Scrolls, as they were soon to be known, provided an unprecedented glimpse into the crucial "intertestamentary" period some 2,000 years ago, when Judaism was roiled by competing sects, and primitive Christianity was just taking shape.

The discovery triggered an intensive 20-year search that led to other finds at four sites nearby. The manuscripts—including eight scrolls and tens of thousands of fragments—date from approximately the mid-third century BC to the period of the second Jewish revolt against Rome, in AD 132-135 and include biblical texts nearly 1,000 years older than any previously known. Most scholars believe that the scrolls from the original site (Khirbat Qumran) belonged to an ascetic, communal Jewish brotherhood, the Essenes, who lived in the area until around AD 68. One of the Qumran documents, a manual of Essenic teachings known as the "Rule of the Community," alludes to a "Righteous Teacher" opposed by an "Evil Priest." One theory holds that the first of these refers to Jesus's brother James, who was part of an early Christian faction (subsequently expunged from church history) that clung to a Jewish religious framework and opposed those who, like the apostle Paul, rejected Judaism outright in favor of an entirely new religion. Scholarly debate still rages—in part because, for many years, the international team assigned to study the scrolls denied access to any outsiders. **◀1940.9 ▶1959.5**

EXPLORATION

Kon-Tiki Sails the Pacific

7 Thor Heyerdahl, a young Norwegian anthropologist, was in the Marquesas, an island chain in the Pacific, when he noticed that the winds and sea always flowed from the east. That fact, coupled with two stories he had heard—one a local legend about white, bearded ancestors who came from the east, the other a Peruvian tale about a white chieftain who escaped a mas-

Heyerdahl named the *Kon-Tiki* for the fabled pre-Incan chieftain he believed had led the Pacific migration in AD 500.

sacre by sailing westward in a balsa-wood raft—made Heyerdahl wonder whether the two legends were one and the same. Perhaps, he hypothesized, the Pacific islands had been peopled not by sailors from Indonesia, as most anthropologists believed, but by South American explorers from the opposite direction. In 1947, he and five other Scandinavians tested his theory. Launching their 45-foot oceangoing balsa-wood raft, the *Kon-Tiki*, from the Peruvian coastal city of Callao, Heyerdahl and his crew set off in the direction of the setting sun.

The *Kon-Tiki* covered some 4,300 miles before breaking up on a reef off a paradisiacal Pacific isle in the Tuamotu Archipelago. The landfall —on August 7, 1947, the 101st day of the voyage—made headlines around the world, a publicity coup that the canny Heyerdahl followed up with a bestselling book. His adventure thrilled readers, but academics—while acknowledging the possibility of a migration from the Western Hemisphere—remained skeptical. **◀1929.6 ▶1953.5**

ARCHITECTURE

First Levittown Houses

8 What Henry Ford did for the car, Abraham Levitt and his sons William and Alfred did for the suburb. Using the techniques of mass production, the Levitts built 17,400 Cape Cod and ranch-style homes for veterans on 4,000 acres of potato farms located 25 miles east of Manhattan, on Long Island. Construction began on Levittown, as the project was known, in October 1947. It was the opening shot in America's great postwar suburban development boom.

The Levitts planned the construction like a military campaign, dispatching an army of bulldozers to level the land and a regiment of trucks to drop materials at precise 60-foot intervals. Each house was built on a standardized concrete slab. New power hand tools speeded up the process. Freight cars loaded with lumber went directly into a cutting yard, where one man cut parts for twelve houses in a day. Specialized crews applied white or red paint or laid tiles. The result: thousands of astoundingly cheap homes to meet a nearly insatiable demand for housing. (Costing as little as $6,990, Levittown houses required tiny down payments and were financed by low-interest government loans.)

Levittown was attacked for its relentless uniformity, but the public lined up by the hundreds for homes that hadn't even been built yet. And over the years, owners "customized" their houses with idiosyncratic embellishments.

SPORTS: Baseball: World Series, New York Yankees defeat Brooklyn Dodgers, 4–3 (series televised for the first time) ... Basketball: BAA and NBL, Philadelphia Warriors defeat Chicago Stags, 4–1 ... Football: NFL, Chicago Cardinals defeat Philadelphia Eagles, 28–21 ... Boxing: Jake LaMotta gets knocked out (first time in his career) by Billy Fox.

"What interests me most is neither still life nor landscape, but the human figure. It is through it that I best succeed in expressing the almost religious feeling I have toward life."—**Henri Matisse**

Increasingly, however, the perils of mass suburbanization—from traffic problems, air pollution, and strained public-works systems to de facto racial segregation (the Levitts, for example, refused to sell to blacks until the mid-1960s)—began to draw criticism from social scientists and policy makers. ▸**1960.9**

The component parts of a Levittown house. The project was nicknamed the Rabbit Hutch for all the babies born there.

ROMANIA

Soviets Add a Satellite

9 The Kremlin added another country to its list of satellites in 1947, installing a Communist government in neighboring Romania and forcing its 27-year-old monarch, King Michael *(left)*, to abdicate. Proclaiming Romania's "liberation," the Soviets established the Romanian People's Republic the following year.

Romania had come within the Soviet sphere in 1944, when King Michael orchestrated a coup d'etat against Ion Antonescu, the fascist dictator who'd aligned his country with Germany. By ousting Antonescu (whom he'd once expediently supported), Michael hoped to head off a Soviet invasion. But in August 1944, right after Antonescu's imprisonment, the Red Army swept in.

Political tumult followed: Communists battled anti-Communists; terrorism, torture, and assassination were rampant. With help from Moscow, the Communists gained power in Romania's 1946 elections (which most experts believe were rigged). By the time Michael abdicated, political opposition to the Communists had been liquidated. ◂**1944.3** ▸**1965.M**

SPORTS

Robinson Breaks Color Barrier

10 Branch Rickey, general manager of the Brooklyn Dodgers, deliberated a long time before tapping Jackie Robinson to be the first player to integrate the all-white domain of major-league baseball in 1947. After grilling the Georgia-born infielder (who'd integrated the minor leagues the previous year in Montreal) for three hours in his office, Rickey was satisfied that Robinson possessed the fortitude necessary to withstand the inevitable racial backlash. He signed the player for a $600-a-month salary, plus a $3,500 bonus. On April 15, 1947, Robinson made his major-league debut at Brooklyn's Ebbets Field, playing first base.

As Rickey had predicted, Robinson faced enormous animosity. During spring training, several team members petitioned against his joining the club, and in May there were rumors that the St. Louis Cardinals would boycott their series with the Dodgers if Robinson played (they didn't). Opposing players tried to spike him as he ran the bases. He received death threats. In spite of the distractions, Robinson performed spectacularly: He batted .297 for the season, was named National League Rookie of the Year, and led the Dodgers to the World Series.

Rapidly establishing himself as one of baseball's leading stars, Robinson batted .311 in a ten-year total of 1,382 games. In 1949, he was named his league's Most Valuable Player and in 1962 he became the first black to be inducted into the Baseball Hall of Fame. His overwhelming success hastened baseball's integration. Within two years of Robinson's first season, the majority of teams had blacks on either their major-league or minor-league rosters. ◂**1908.6** ▸**1957.M**

Robinson, one of baseball's most gifted base runners, sliding into third.

ART

Matisse's Last Gift

11 Forty years after Henri Matisse's expressively colored canvases earned him the premier place among the artists known as "fauves" (wild beasts), the endlessly inventive painter was still creating fresh modes of pictorial expression. In 1947, nearing the end of his eighth decade—ailing, bedridden, unable to paint—Matisse made a last, passionate gift to art, publishing *Jazz*, a book based on his dreamy, abstracted paper cutouts.

Wielding scissors like a paintbrush, Matisse created his cutouts in one long, flowing movement.

Matisse's bright, idiosyncratically colored paintings seem like joie de vivre distilled. Similarly, his sculptural shapes, made from cut-and-pasted hand-painted paper, explored the intricacies of light and space. ◂**1905.10**

IN THE UNITED STATES

recognition. A devout Baptist who sang only religious hymns and shunned nightclubs, she nevertheless incorporated blues rhythms and jazz techniques in to her interpretations.

▶ELECTRIC GUITAR—The Gibson Les Paul guitar, first marketed in 1947, would become mandatory equipment for rock 'n' roll musicians. Paul's solid-bodied electric guitar (nicknamed "the log") was an adaptation of Adolph Rickenbacker's 1931 version, known as "the frying pan." Paul also invented his own eight-track tape recorder (no less important to pop music's development) and introduced overdubbing. An accomplished jazz guitarist, Paul went on to record with his wife, Mary Ford, in the fifties.

▶A DOME FOR LIVING—Prophet of "Dymaxion" design—dynamic and maximum—R. Buckminster Fuller built his first geodesic dome in 1947. A breakthrough of applied geometry, the futuristic sphere combined optimal structural strength and material efficiency.

▶CIA SETS UP SHOP—Old "spooks" from the decommissioned Office of Strategic Services, the wartime intelligence bureau headed by the colorful William J. "Wild Bill" Donovan, got a new home in 1947 when Congress passed the National Security Act, which reorganized the armed forces and created the Central Intelligence Agency. So broadly did the act define the new agency's mission that, essentially, CIA operatives were given free rein to turn international intelligence-gathering and political analysis into top-secret political initiatives. Among the more notable cloak-and-dagger activities undertaken by the agency: the 1953 overthrow of Iranian premier Muhammad Mussadegh and the toppling of Guatemalan president Jacobo Arbenz Guzmán in 1954. ▸1953.4

POLITICS & BUSINESS: GNP: $231.3 billion ... Congress passes $4 billion tax reduction ... Office of the secretary of defense created ... Sugar rationing ends ... U.S. State Department analyst George F. Kennan proposes "containment" policy in *Foreign Affairs* article (written under pseudonym "X") ... Henry Ford dies, leaving 90% of company's stock to the Ford Foundation (becomes the world's richest philanthropy).

"Fashion comes from a dream, and the dream is an escape from reality."—**Christian Dior**

AROUND THE WORLD

▶THE SILENT PERFORMER—Inspired by the silent films of Charlie Chaplin, French performer Marcel Marceau in

1947 created a pantomime character called Bip. As the pensive, white-faced clown decked out in sailor pants and a striped jersey, Marceau became the ultimate mime. He went on to form an internationally celebrated touring company.

▶DOWN AND OUT IN MEXICO—Malcolm Lowry's *Under the Volcano* drew little notice when it was published in 1947, but after the author's premature death ten years later, it acquired the status of antiheroic masterpiece. Loosely autobiographical in content and experimental in form (Lowry's technique of juxtaposing images is often described as cinematic), the novel follows the last desperate days of an alcoholic British ex-consul in Mexico. The British-born Lowry called his book, set during the Day of the Dead fiesta, a "drunken *Divine Comedy.*"

GIACOMETTI'S THIN MEN—After years of experimentation, Swiss sculptor Alberto Giacometti arrived at his signature style in 1947, when he began making his "transparent constructions" of severely attenuated, skeletal, almost insubstantial human figures. Frequently associated with the existentialist writers, Giacometti was one of the century's profoundly original artists. ◂1932.13

▶MATADOR MOURNED—Spain lost a national hero when Manolete, the greatest matador of his era, was gored to death in the Linares bullring in 1947. Manuel Laureano Rodríguez y Sánchez, 30, was revered for his elegant restraint, aristocratic mien, and sangfroid in his close passes with the cape.

FASHION

Dior's "New Look"

12 With his "Corolle" line, introduced in February 1947, couturier Christian Dior cast off seven years of grim wartime austerity and instantly reestablished Paris as the fashion capital of the world. The collection, dubbed the "New Look" by the American fashion magazine *Harper's Bazaar*, was in fact anything but. Its roots lay in "la Belle Epoque," the extravagant and freewheeling society of the early 1900s, when couture was characterized by ostentation and opulence. Seeking to infuse some of that lost spirit into a world starved for luxury and romance, Dior—who, with backing from a French textile manufacturer, had opened his salon on the Avenue Montaigne the previous year—lowered hemlines (which had been forced upward by wartime fabric rationing) and reinvented long, flowing skirts, narrow shoulders, padded busts and hips, and nipped-in waists. His celebration of the feminine form was as popular with men as it was with women, who enthusiastically bought—and copied—the look all over the world. While some welcomed the liberties taken by Dior as a sign of economic recovery, others criticized his extravagance—all that fabric!—as well as his effort to uphold the system of haute couture against encroachment from younger, more accessible designers.

Indeed, the New Look marked the end of haute couture's heyday, but Dior himself remained stunningly successful. His "sack dress" became a defining look of the 1950s, and by the time of his death, in 1957 at age 52, the House of Dior had branches in 24 countries. **▸1965.2**

THEATER

Williams's Poetic Melodrama

13 On December 3, 1947, Tennessee Williams jolted Broadway with a seamy, sex-charged masterpiece about a delicate, troubled southern belle named Blanche Du Bois and her catastrophic collision with her earthy, brutal brother-in-law Stanley Kowalski. *A Streetcar Named Desire*, directed by Elia Kazan and starring Jessica Tandy and Marlon Brando as Blanche and Stanley, not only thrilled and shocked theatergoers, it secured the lasting critical reputation of its young playwright, who had first attracted notice three years earlier with his moving family drama, *The Glass Menagerie*.

Williams's raw yet lyrical evocation of the modern world's assault on beauty and grace was, in one theater historian's words, "melodrama told in poetry." Indeed, the ugliness of *Streetcar*'s story—which took in rape, nymphomania, alcoholism, suicide, and wife-beating—was wrapped in memorably glorious language: "Whoever you are," a deranged Blanche says at the end of the play to the doctor who gently leads her to the madhouse, "I have always depended on the kindness of strangers."

Streetcar also transformed American acting. Brando, as Blanche's atavistic, T-shirted tormentor, became the prime exemplar of "the Method," interpreting his role through psychological insight rather than the observation of external character traits. Based on Stanislavky's techniques—developed by Lee Strasberg in the thirties and forties, and embraced by Kazan (cofounder, in 1947, of the Actors Studio, which Strasberg joined in 1949)—Method acting became the dominant American mode. **◂1926.10 ▸1949.V**

Brando's brooding intensity as Stanley set the standard for interpretations of the role. *(Above, with Jessica Tandy as Blanche Du Bois.)*

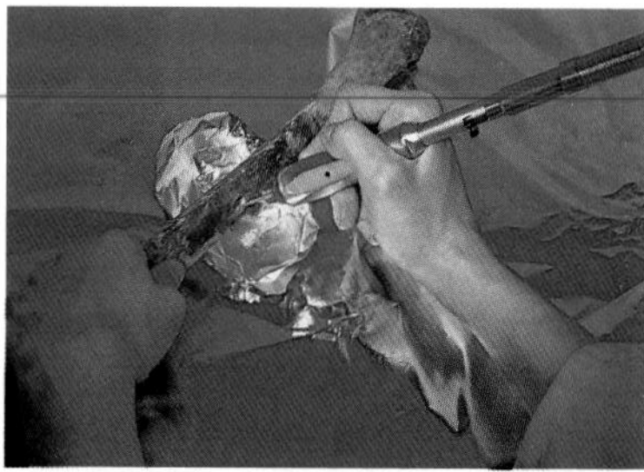

A scientist takes shavings of reindeer bone for dating using radiocarbon techniques.

SCIENCE

A Way to Measure Antiquity

14 In 1947, a University of Chicago chemist named Willard Frank Libby used the radioactive isotope carbon-14 to develop the first truly scientific method for determining the age of a once-living organism. The method was predicated on the fact that a living organism has a constant supply of carbon-14. Once an organism stops eating and breathing, its carbon supply can no longer be replenished through atmospheric carbon dioxide. The unstable carbon-14 atoms still lodged in the body begin to decay according to their known half-life (approximately 5,730 years). Thus, the level of carbon-14 radioactivity indicates the age of any organic sample (a skeleton, a plant fossil). For example, a radiation level diminished by half denotes an age of around 5,700 years.

While not without technical problems, Libby's radiocarbon technique was an enormous boon to archaeologists, oceanographers, and earth scientists. It paved the way for methods of dating wholly inanimate objects such as porcelain. **▸1959.5**

NOBEL PRIZES: Peace: Friends Service Council and American Friends Service Committee (U.K., U.S.; Quaker humanitarian services) ... Literature: André Gide (French; novelist) ... Chemistry: Robert Robinson (U.K.; plant alkaloids) ... Medicine: Carl F. and Gerty T. Cori (Austrian-U.S.; animal starch metabolism) and Bernardo Houssay (Argentine; pituitary gland) ... Physics: Edward Appleton (U.K.; ionosphere).

A VOICE FROM 1947

A Young Girl's Impossible Idealism

From *Het Achterhuis*, by Anne Frank, published in the Netherlands, 1947

Amsterdam teenager Annelies Marie Frank (who was born in Germany but had fled the Nazis with her family when she was four) started a diary on her 13th birthday, June 12, 1942, with the words "I hope I shall be able to confide in you completely, as I have never been able to do in anyone before." Just under a month later, Anne, her older sister, Margot, their parents, and another family went into hiding in secret rooms in the warehouse of her father Otto's business in Nazi-occupied Amsterdam. (They were later joined by a dentist.) Two years and 30 days later, betrayed by Dutch informers, they were arrested by the Gestapo and taken to Auschwitz. From there, Anne and her sister were transferred to Bergen-Belsen, where they both died of typhus. Only Otto Frank survived.

When Frank returned to the Netherlands after the war, the woman who had helped the family hide returned Anne's notebooks and papers. Frank typed up his daughter's writings and, with the help of friends, published them in 1947 as Het Achterhuis, *a reference to the hiding place Anne called the "Secret Annex." The book appeared in English in 1952 as* The Diary of a Young Girl. *With astonishing immediacy, precocious insight, and remarkable humor that suggest the greatness she might have achieved as a mature writer, Anne reveals her heartbreaking humanity in the face of fear, intolerable living conditions, and genocide. Her diary has been translated into more than 30 languages. Here, an excerpt from July 15, 1944, approximately a month before the families were discovered.* ◂**1946.V** ▸**1960.8**

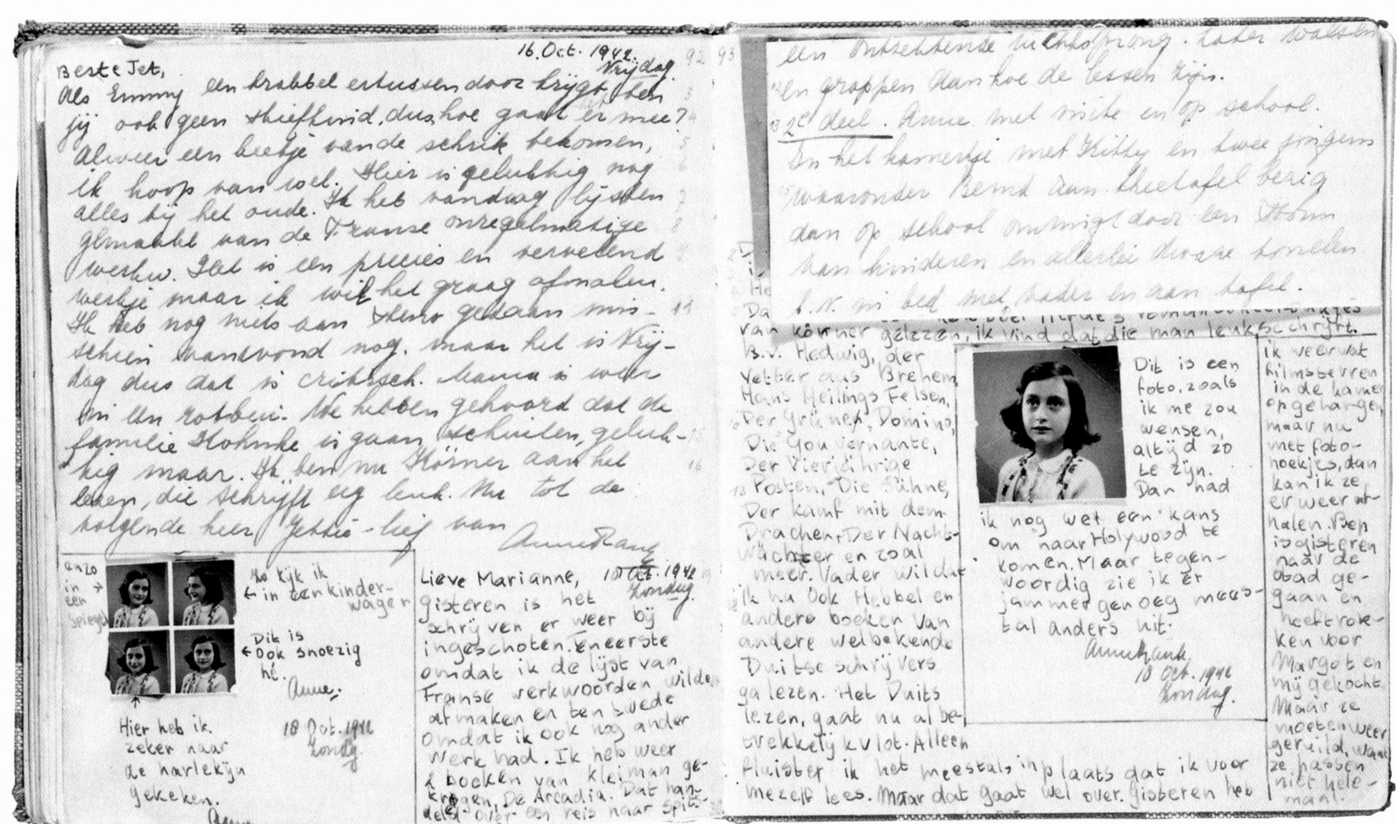
Dit is een foto, zoals ik me zou wensen, altijd zo te zijn. Dan had ik nog wel een kans om naar Holywood te komen. Maar tegenwoordig zie ik er jammer genoeg meestal anders uit.
Annefrank.
18 Oct. 1942
Zondag.

Next to the photograph of herself that she pasted in her diary on October 18, 1942, Anne wrote, "This is a photograph of me as I wish I looked all the time. Then I might still have a chance of getting to Hollywood. But at present, I'm afraid, I usually look quite different."

[Saturday, July 15, 1944]: "For in its innermost depths youth is lonelier than old age." I read this saying in some book and I've always remembered it, and found it to be true. Is it true that grownups have a more difficult time here than we do? No. I know it isn't. Older people have formed their opinions about everything, and don't waver before they act. It's twice as hard for us young ones to hold our ground, and maintain our opinions, in a time when all ideals are being shattered and destroyed, when people are showing their worst side, and do not know whether to believe in truth and right and God.

Anyone who claims that the older ones have a more difficult time here certainly doesn't realize to what extent our problems weigh down on us, problems for which we are probably much too young, but which thrust themselves upon us continually, until, after a long time, we think we've found a solution, but the solution doesn't seem able to resist the facts which reduce it to nothing again. That's the difficulty in these times: ideals, dreams, and cherished hopes rise within us, only to meet the horrible truth and be shattered.

It's really a wonder that I haven't dropped all my ideals, because they seem so absurd and impossible to carry out. Yet, I keep them, because in spite of everything, I still believe that people are really good at heart. I simply can't build up my hopes on a foundation consisting of confusion, misery, and death. I see the world gradually being turned into a wilderness, I hear the ever approaching thunder, which will destroy us too, I can feel the sufferings of millions and yet, if I look up into the heavens, I think that it will all come right, that this cruelty too will end, and that peace and tranquillity will return again.

In the meantime, I must uphold my ideals, for perhaps the time will come when I shall be able to carry them out.

Yours, Anne

"Our major task is to ensure that a White nation will prevail here."—**Dr. Hendrik F. Verwoerd, prime minister of South Africa, in 1958**

STORY OF THE YEAR

Enter Apartheid

1 Abetted by an electoral system that favored sparsely populated, Afrikaner-dominated rural areas, the reactionary Nationalist Party won the greatest number of parliamentary seats in South Africa's 1948 elections, despite losing the popular vote by a wide margin. Nationalist Party leader Daniel F. Malan—a 76-year-old Afrikaner and Hitlerite—replaced Jan Smuts as prime minister. Immediately, Malan set about implementing apartheid (apartness), a plan to preserve white supremacy by legislating a racially separate and unequal South Africa.

Denied the most rudimentary civil rights, South Africa's blacks were defenseless against vigilante terror.

A coalition of Dutch-descended Afrikaners and the British had governed the Union of South Africa since its formation in 1910. By the end of World War II, the typical Afrikaner had a siege mentality, feeling his existence and prosperity threatened by the African majority (which was becoming increasingly politicized), the British (over whom Afrikaners maintained a slight numerical advantage), and the world community (which had amplified its criticism of South African racial policies during the forties). Malan was propelled to victory by a wave of Afrikaner defiance, and for the first time ever, South Africa had an all-Afrikaner cabinet. Its platform: apartheid, anti-Communism, and the right of self-determination for Afrikaners.

Apartheid divided the South African population into four distinct racial groups: whites (who, by virtue of being "civilized," had the right to control the state), Africans, Coloureds (people of mixed European-African ancestry), and Asians (Indians and Pakistanis). In 1948, there were nearly eleven million blacks, Coloureds, and Asians compared with 2.5 million whites. Malan's Nationalist government soon railroaded a series of repressive laws through Parliament. One of the earliest and most blatant measures was 1949's Prohibition of Mixed Marriages Act. A year later, the Suppression of Communism Act effectively outlawed labor strikes at a time when blacks earned 17 cents a day working under inhuman conditions in diamond mines. The Population Registration Act, also enacted in 1950, made compulsory the racial classification of every man, woman, and child; consigned different races to specific areas of habitation (the black majority was allotted a mere 13 percent of South Africa's land area, and no black person could leave his "group area" without a special work pass); and overrode a court's decision that racially separate public facilities such as hospitals, schools, and parks had to be equal.

The first apartheid-sparked riots erupted in Johannesburg in 1949. Not until the 1990s would apartheid's victims have any real hope of equality. **◂1912.10 ▸1960.6**

GERMANY

Confrontation in Berlin

2 A great air bridge to West Berlin was begun on June 26, 1948, shortly after the Soviet occupation army in eastern Germany blockaded all road, rail, and water communication between Berlin and the West. The Berlin airlift was wildly ambitious: a plane in and out every three minutes, 24 hours a day. But for 318 days, Great Britain and the United States adhered to the schedule, making nearly 200,000 flights and delivering 1.5 million tons of supplies to the besieged city.

The Soviets had imposed the blockade in retaliation for the Western powers' decision, in March, to unite their German occupation zones into a single economic entity. Fearing the emergence of a strong western Germany in the American camp, the Soviets tried to isolate the city from the noncommunist world. On July 1, after the airlift had begun, the Soviets unilaterally dissolved the four-power administration of Berlin, claiming sole jurisdiction over the city. War appeared imminent. "When Berlin falls, western Germany will be next," predicted General Lucius Clay, the American commander in Germany. "Communism will run rampant."

With the Allies determined not to cave in to Soviet pressure, the United States deployed atomic bomb–equipped warplanes to England. The Soviet Union made no further move toward war, and so the imbroglio evolved into a political contest between East and West for the soul of Berlin, each side trying to prove it could determine the city's fate.

Through the long, hot summer, 2.5 million Berliners depended on the air bridge for food, fuel, medical supplies, and consumer goods. As the blockade continued into the fall and winter, food was rationed, electricity cut, factories shut down.

An American plane carrying supplies lands at Templehof airport in West Berlin.

The West responded with a counterblockade, embargoing exports from eastern Germany and the Eastern bloc. That Berlin was not starved into submission counted as a victory for the West; by spring, hurting from the Western embargo, the Soviets conceded. They lifted the blockade on May 12, 1949. West Berlin survived, a bulwark against Soviet expansion. **◂1945.M ▸1949.3**

KOREA

Cold War Casualty

3 A timeworn Korean proverb—"A shrimp is crushed in the battle of whales"—was borne out in 1948 as the long-suffering peninsula became the site of a face-off between the Soviet Union and the United States. With the creation of separate, ideologically opposed but nominally democratic states on either side of the 38th parallel, a unified Korea ceased to exist, sacrificed to the superpowers' Cold War machinations.

Desultory Soviet-American efforts to set up a unified government in occupied Korea had failed the previous year. The Soviets suggested withdrawing and leaving the Koreans to form a government on their own. Fearing northern communists would simply take over the south if American troops were withdrawn, the United States proposed United Nations–supervised countrywide elections, then withdrawal. This time the Soviets balked, and barred UN officials from their zone.

In 1948, the United Nations proceeded with the elections, limited to the south. On May 10, in heavy voting marred by violence and rumors of U.S. intimidation, Koreans below the 38th parallel chose a general assembly. Its president was 73-year-old Syngman Rhee *(above)*, a longtime activist for Korean independence (he headed a Korean government-in-exile during World War II) and a fierce anti-Communist who'd just returned to Korea after 33 years in the United States. As Rhee organized his government, the Soviets appointed communist Kim Il Sung head of

ART & CULTURE: Books: ***Other Voices, Other Rooms*** **(Truman Capote);** ***Cry, the Beloved Country*** **(Alan Paton);** ***The Seven Storey Mountain*** **(Thomas Merton) ... Music: "Buttons and Bows" (Livingston and Evans); "Nature Boy" (Eden Ahbez);** ***Sonatas and Interludes*** **(John Cage);** ***Scherzo Fantastique*** **(Ernest Bloch) ... Painting & Sculpture:** ***Composition Number 1*** **(Jackson Pollock);** ***Onement I*** **(Barnett Newman) ...**

"Personally, I will do anything I can to help the Korean people and to protect them. I will protect them as I would protect the United States or California against aggression."—**General Douglas MacArthur to newly elected Korean president Syngman Rhee**

state in their zone, now called the People's Republic of Korea. All Soviet troops, Moscow announced, would vacate North Korea by year's end. Though wary of Kim's well-trained army, American forces evacuated in June 1949, leaving behind 500 military advisers to train the South Korean military. In coming years, as partition led to war, their numbers would swell. **◂1945.13 ▸1950.1**

TECHNOLOGY

The LP Debuts

4 One of the many innovations that would transform postwar life was introduced by Columbia Records in 1948. Columbia's new twelve-inch, long-playing vinyl record was bigger than its precursor, had smaller grooves, and was designed to be played at at 33⅓ revolutions per minute instead of the old 78. LPs (as they were called) offered "high fidelity" sound that was more faithful to the original than that of previous discs, as well as more plentiful, offering up to 25 minutes of music per side instead of three to five minutes. The result was a hi-fi boom that revolutionized home listening. Instead of purchasing individual "hits," listeners now invested in an evening's entertainment. LPs were a boon to singers like Peggy Lee and Frank Sinatra, whose work was less about catchy tunes than about creating a mood. For such jazz artists as John Coltrane and Miles Davis, the recording studio became as important as the performance hall.

Columbia's factories turned out racks of LPs to meet the instant demand.

In 1949, RCA Victor produced a competitor, a seven-inch disc played at 45 rpm. The two companies battled for years before reaching a compromise: 45s would be used solely for releasing singles. The LP reigned triumphant until the 1980s, when it was supplanted by the compact disc. **◂1902.11 ▸1983.M**

Mahatma Gandhi beside his spinning wheel two years before his death. Gandhi insisted that the photographer, Margaret Bourke-White, learn how to spin before she took his picture.

INDIA

Gandhi Assassinated

5 India's epochal struggle for independence would undoubtedly have been achieved without Mohandas Gandhi, but his moral contributions to the political discourse were unique and enduring. Throughout his career, Gandhi played a spiritual as well as a political role. Mahatma, he was called, the great soul. On January 30, 1948, Gandhi succumbed to the violence he had spent a lifetime repudiating, assassinated by a Hindu fanatic outraged by his placation of Muslims.

News of Gandhi's death stunned the world; prime ministers and presidents, kings and dictators mourned the humble 78-year-old ascetic. "The light has gone out of our lives and there is darkness everywhere," said Jawaharlal Nehru, Gandhi's old colleague and India's first prime minister. "The father of our nation is no more." **◂1947.3 ▸1965.8**

YUGOSLAVIA

Tito Breaks with Stalin

6 In the increasingly polarized postwar world, President Tito of Yugoslavia remained his own man. Having transformed his country into a federated communist state (consisting of Croatia, Slovenia, Serbia, Bosnia and Hercegovina, Montenegro, and Macedonia), he isolated himself not just from the West (which vilified him for his support of the Communists in the Greek Civil War, as well as for his attempt to seize Trieste at the end of World War II), but also from Moscow, his seeming ally. Determined to stop Stalin from controlling Yugoslavia, Tito became the first communist leader to break with him: In 1948 Yugoslavia's Communist Party was ejected from the Soviet-controlled Cominform. Faced with an economic blockade and the threat of invasion, Yugoslavs rallied around their leader, and their old resistance fight song rang out across the mountainous countryside: "Hey, Slavs, in vain the depths of hell threaten/O Slavs, you are still free."

Tito's Yugoslavia in a *Punch* cartoon: poised between the "Evil Demon Russia" and "the Spirit of the West."

Emboldened, Tito effected constitutional reforms that drove Yugoslavia further from the Soviet Union. He decentralized the government, giving Yugoslavia's individual states more economic and administrative freedom, and endorsed worker self-management and a limited free market. His unique "Titoist" style made Yugoslavia Europe's most liberal Communist country. **◂1943.9 ▸1991.2**

BIRTHS

Mikhail Baryshnikov, Russian-U.S. ballet dancer.

John Bonham, U.K. musician.

Charles Philip Arthur George, U.K. prince.

Gerard Depardieu, French actor.

Albert Gore, Jr., U.S. vice president.

Bryant Gumbel, U.S. broadcast journalist.

Donna Karan, U.S. fashion designer.

Robert Plant, U.K. musician.

Anatoly Shcharansky, U.S.S.R. dissident.

Mick Taylor, U.K. musician.

Garry Trudeau, U.S. cartoonist.

Andrew Lloyd Webber, U.K. composer.

Pinchas Zukerman, Israeli U.S. violinist and conductor.

DEATHS

Ruth Benedict, U.S. anthropologist.

Eduard Beneš, Czechoslovakian president.

Sergei Eisenstein, Russian filmmaker.

Mohandas Mahatma Gandhi, Indian political leader.

Arshile Gorky, Armenian-U.S. painter.

D.W. Griffith, U.S. filmmaker.

Charles Evans Hughes, U.S. jurist.

Muhammad Ali Jinnah, Indian-Pakistani political leader.

Franz Léhar, Hungarian-Austrian composer.

Louis Lumière, French inventor.

John "Black Jack" Pershing, U.S. general.

George Herman "Babe" Ruth, U.S. baseball player.

Kurt Schwitters, German artist.

Hideki Tojo, Japanese general.

Orville Wright, U.S. aviator.

Film: *Hamlet* (Laurence Olivier); *The Treasure of the Sierra Madre* and *Key Largo* (John Huston); *Easter Parade* (Charles Walters); *The Snake Pit* (Anatole Litvak) ... Theater: *Anne of the Thousand Days* (Maxwell Anderson); *The Caucasian Chalk Circle* (Bertolt Brecht); *Life with Mother* (Lindsay and Crouse); *Kiss Me Kate* (Cole Porter) ... TV: *Candid Camera*; *Toast of the Town*; *Hopalong Cassidy*.

"The one fact that I would cry from every housetop is this: the Good Life is waiting for us—here and now!"
—B.F. Skinner, in *Walden Two*

NEW IN 1948

Injections of synthetic cortisone (to relieve arthritis).

Porsche automobile.

Velcro (from "velvet" and "crochet"; invented in Switzerland by Georges de Mestral).

World Health Organization.

Land Rover jeep.

IN THE UNITED STATES

▶TRUMAN UPSETS DEWEY—His defeat was a foregone conclusion, so much so that *The Chicago Tribune* confidently ran the headline it had prepared *(below)*. But thanks to voting by blacks (grateful for executive edicts against lynching and segregation), labor (upset by the Taft-Hartley bill), and farmers (who feared a reduction in subsidies), Harry Truman trumped

the pollsters and in 1948 was elected to a full term. ◂1945.6 ▸1948.V

▶UNCLE MILTIE—Introduced in 1948, NBC's *Texaco Star Theater* transformed failed radio performer Milton Berle into "Mr. Television." Each week, millions tuned in Berle's zany grab bag of exaggerated impressions, vaudeville skits, pie-in-the-face and cross-dressing routines. Families without TVs soon acquired them just to catch America's most popular entertainer. ▸1951.9

▶THE "BIG BANG"—With their landmark 1948 paper, "The Origin of Chemical Elements," Russian émigré physicist George Gamow and his student Ralph Alpher elaborated on the big bang theory of the universe, first posited in the twenties by Georges Lemaître. The theory held that billions of years ago all matter was concentrated in a dense, superhot mass. Gamow and

IDEAS

Skinner's Behaviorist Tract

7 The rationalist impulse, the desire to rearrange humankind's chaotic affairs along straight, logical lines, reached a kind of apotheosis with the 1948 publication of experimental psychologist B.F. Skinner's utopian novel about a smoothly functioning communal society, called (with a nod to Henry David Thoreau) *Walden Two*. The novel—a vehicle for Skinner's theory of behaviorism—argued that through "behavioral engineering," people could be conditioned to behave in cooperative, productive ways, much as laboratory rats can be enticed into pushing a lever in return for food. Residents of Walden Two surrender to the rationalism of the community and are rewarded with a life based on little work, much leisure, and ample opportunity for self-fulfillment. In Skinnerian terms, they lose their freedom in order to gain it.

Immensely successful, *Walden Two* was labeled both visionary and fascistic. The author, a tall, bespectacled Harvard professor, was accused of making no distinction between human beings and caged rats. Indeed, there are no elections in *Walden Two,* no controversies, no malcontents or rebels. The characters have no depth because, Skinner suggests, depth is an illusion. Less a novel than a tract, the book (contrary to Skinner's own stated intentions) was widely read as a satirical parable about modern life, in which supposedly free individuals are persuaded to mold themselves into uniformity. **◂1932.3 ▸1957.13**

Skinner's daughter in a "Skinner box" for babies—an adaptation of the apparatus he used in his conditioning experiments with animals.

CZECHOSLOVAKIA

Communists Topple Beneš

8 Czechoslovakia's democratic movement died in 1948, when a Communist coup toppled President Eduard Beneš's fragile coalition government and erected a Stalinist regime. For the second time in ten years, outside aggressors had brutalized Czechoslovakia.

After heading the Czech government-in-exile in London during the war, Beneš had returned home in 1945 determined to restore the democratic regime that the Nazis had displaced. Promising "freedom of the individual, of assembly, association, expression of opinion by speech, press, and pen," he'd appointed a provisional government that included members of all parties. Klement Gottwald, leader of the Communist Party of Czechoslovakia (CPC), was a vice-premier; the intensely democratic Jan Masaryk was, as in the London government, foreign affairs secretary. In May 1946, Czechoslovakia elected a provisional National Assembly (to serve until a new constitution was drawn up). Since the CPC won 38 percent of the vote (largely in recognition of its role in the resistance and in securing Stalin's help in repelling three million Germans), Gottwald became premier.

In 1948, as the country prepared for the first election under the new constitution, CPC cabinet officials packed key ministries with their own people. Beneš remained confident. "The Communists will lose," he predicted, "and rightly so." But free elections never occurred. In February, a dozen democratic cabinet members resigned to protest a Communist attempt to take over the army and police. Beneš refused their resignations, whereupon Gottwald instigated an uprising. He seized the abandoned ministries, locked out the democrats, and shut down the press, forcing Beneš to agree to a Communist government. The Soviet Union threw its full weight behind the CPC.

"Victorious February": Gottwald's supporters gather in Prague's Wenceslas Square.

Branding democrats "foreign reactionaries," the Communists instituted a witch hunt, arresting and exiling thousands of intellectuals and noncommunists. On March 10, Jan Masaryk's corpse was found beneath his office windows. (His "suicide" was almost certainly murder by Soviet agents.) The May elections offered only one set of candidates. Beneš resigned, was succeeded by Gottwald, and died three months after refusing to sign the new constitution. The Stalinization of Czechoslovakia was complete. **◂1943.8 ▸1968.2**

THE MIDDLE EAST

State of Israel Proclaimed

9 The restoration of the biblical Jewish homeland in 1948 was the culmination of nearly 2,000 years of religious yearning, five decades of political organizing, and a few years of sporadic warfare. Ironically, it might never have occurred without the actions of Adolf Hitler, whose murder of six million Jews (and creation of masses of

SPORTS: Baseball: World Series, Cleveland Indians defeat Boston Braves, 4–2 ... Olympics held in St. Moritz and London (first since 1936) ... Football: NFL, Philadelphia Eagles defeat Chicago Cardinals, 7–0 ... Basketball: BAA-NBL, Baltimore Bullets defeat Philadelphia Warriors, 4–2; BAA and NBL merge ... Horse Racing: Citation wins Triple Crown (Eddie Arcaro is the first jockey to win 2 Triple Crowns).

"I had four books on my desk all the time I was writing: Anna Karenina, Of Time and the River, U.S.A., *and* Studs Lonigan.*"*
—Norman Mailer, on writing *The Naked and the Dead*

Jewish refugees) provoked worldwide postwar sympathy for the Zionist cause.

The stage was set in November 1947, when the UN approved a commission report recommending the division of Britain's Palestine mandate into two independent (but economically unified) states: More than half would go to the Jews, the rest to the Arabs. The decision was a monumental victory for David Ben-Gurion, the foremost Zionist organizer since before World War I. For the leaders of the Arab League nations, intent on preventing Ben-Gurion and his fellow settlers from founding a Middle Eastern homeland, partition was an act of war; they vowed to aid the Palestinians in resisting the UN's "solution."

By February 1948, skirmishes and terrorist bombings had claimed hundreds of Jewish and Arab lives. As the conflict widened into all-out war, the Haganah (Jewish militia) won control over all the land the UN had allotted to the Jews and captured positions in Arab-designated territory as well.

On May 14, the state of Israel was proclaimed; Ben-Gurion became prime minister of the provisional government (and in January 1949 of the elected one). Washington and Moscow recognized Israel immediately. The next day, Britain withdrew—and five Arab countries attacked the new nation. The UN dispatched Count Folke Bernadotte, a Swede, as a mediator; in September, after negotiating two brief cease-fires, he was assassinated by Jewish extremists. It would be up to his successor, African-American diplomat Ralph J. Bunche, to bring a semblance of peace to the Holy Land. **◂1945.14 ▸1949.6**

IMMIGRATION TO PALESTINE/ISRAEL

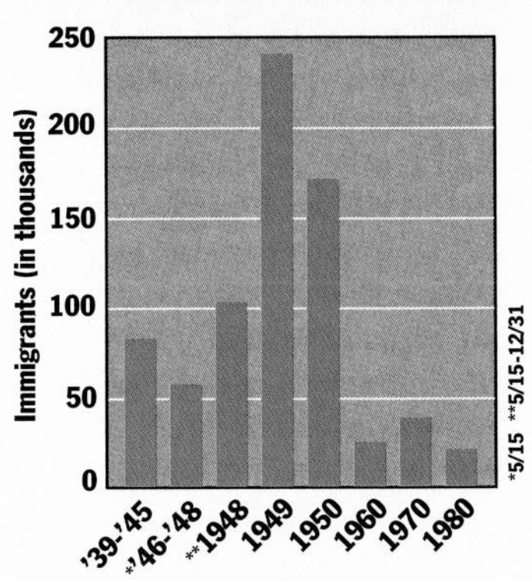

From 1939 to 1980, more than 732 thousand people—mostly Jews—immigrated to Britain's former mandate.

"I am a fact finder," insisted Kinsey *(here, at home in Indiana with his wife).*

IDEAS

Kinsey Studies Sex

10 He was a shy, square-jawed, bowtie-wearing professor of zoology at Indiana University who specialized in the gall wasp. Yet when Dr. Alfred C. Kinsey found he couldn't find answers to his students' questions about human sex, he set out to compile the sexual life history of the human species. In 1948—after ten years and some 9,000 interviews—*Sexual Behavior in the Human Male*, the first volume of his landmark study, hit the bookstores and became an instant bestseller. "Not since the Darwinian theory split the world wide open," wrote *Newsweek*, "has there been such a scientific shocker."

What was shocking was not only the varieties of sexual experience Kinsey reported, but the explicit nature of the research itself. (Even that advocate of sexual freedom Margaret Mead characterized his methods as "prying.") One in three men admitted to some kind of adult homosexual experience, 30 to 45 percent of husbands said they had been unfaithful to their wives, and 90 percent of men said they had masturbated. (In the second volume, published five years later and focusing on female sexuality, the parallel numbers were one in eight, 26 percent, and 62 percent.)

Kinsey was denounced by clergymen, newspaper editors, even the Senate (McCarthyites hinted that the study boosted U.S. chances for a communist takeover). He fared no better with fellow academics and doctors. Today, the reports' shortcomings are widely acknowledged: They were skewed to white, middle-class midwesterners and college students; informants included prisoners and sex offenders; and all were volunteers who may have been less than truthful. Yet Kinsey was a pioneer who opened the closet door on the sex lives of men and women. **◂1920.12 ▸1966.M**

LITERATURE

Mailer's Book of War

11 Few first novelists have burst onto the literary scene with as much hoopla as Norman Mailer, whose graphic and powerful war novel, *The Naked and the Dead*, was published in 1948, the year he turned 25. In frank, shocking language (including a liberal use of Mailer's own coinage, "fug"), the book, based on the author's experiences in World War II, depicts a U.S. Army platoon's invasion of a Japanese-held Pacific island. Its bitter cynicism about war struck a nerve with a generation of readers who felt disaffected and alienated from the promilitary dogma of the postwar years. So lavish was the praise heaped on *The Naked and the Dead* —it was immediately pronounced one of the finest American novels to come out of the war—that its young, Brooklyn-reared author became a celebrity overnight.

Perhaps inevitably, Mailer's subsequent efforts were cast in the shadow of this first, spectacular achievement. Yet his later books, including such novels as *The Deer Park* (1955) and *An American Dream* (1965), and such feats of "new journalism" as *The Armies of the Night* (1968) and *The Executioner's Song* (1979), probe similar moral questions. They also share identifiably "Maileresque" obsessions with sex and violence. **▸1951.11**

IN THE UNITED STATES

Alpher hypothesized that a thermonuclear explosion blew apart the concentration of matter, creating an expanding, rapidly cooling mixture of subatomic particles. Within minutes, the particles coalesced into protons and neutrons, then into the lightest elements, hydrogen and helium, the building blocks of atomic nuclei—and of the universe. ◂1927.3

▶INSTANT PICTURES—The Polaroid Land Camera became a huge success upon hitting the market in 1948. First demonstrated the year before by its inventor, Edwin Herbert Land, the Polaroid acted as an instant darkroom, producing finished pictures within 60 seconds. ◂1900.3

▶ARTISTIC FREEDOM—The U.S. Supreme Court determined in 1948 that the big Hollywood studios were monopolizing motion-picture production, distribution, and exhibition, and ordered them to give up their chains of theaters, thus freeing exhibitors to show movies from anyone, anywhere. The decision, coupled with the rise of television, caused the old studios to wane. ◂1908.8

▶WYETH'S WORLD—Andrew Wyeth, son of illustrator N.C. Wyeth, completed his most famous painting, *Christina's World*, in 1948. Using a realistic style, Wyeth created an almost surreal aura of mystery

around the painting's subject, Anna Christina Olson, a middle-aged invalid from Cushing, Maine. ◂1942.17 ▸1986.M

▶MODERN MUSICAL MIX—Missouri-born composer Virgil Thomson won a Pulitzer Prize for his score for Robert Flaherty's 1948 film documentary, *Louisiana Story*. Playful, direct, and always engaging, Thomson's music incorporated a host of diverse influences, including traditional Anglo-American hymns and folk tunes. ◂1939.M

POLITICS & BUSINESS: GNP: $257.6 billion ... Harry S Truman elected president, defeating Thomas E. Dewey ... Selective Service Act (requires registration of all U.S. men between 18 and 25), Anti-Inflation Act, and Displaced Persons Act (allows for settlement of 400,000 homeless people in the U.S.) passed ... Women sworn in as regular members of U.S. Navy.

"Homes, health, education, and social security—these are your birthright."—**Aneurin Bevan, Britain's minister of health**

AROUND THE WORLD

▶BURMA INDEPENDENT—Burma (now Myanmar) gained independence on January 4, 63 years after Britain had first taken over. But years of impoverishment had created a situation that soon disintegrated into civil war. A military coup in 1962 established a socialist government that insisted on cultural and political isolation while advocating rapid industrialization and nationalization. Unfortunately, Burma's economic slide continued: By 1990 it was one of the world's poorest nations. ▶1989.M

▶MINDSZENTY ARRESTED—József Cardinal Mindszenty, head of the Roman Catholic Church in Hungary, was arrested in 1948 for opposing the Communist regime. Tortured and convicted of treason in a show trial, Mindszenty was given a death sentence, later

reduced to life imprisonment. He was released during the 1956 anti-Communist uprising; as the Communists quickly regained control, he took sanctuary in the U.S. embassy in Budapest, remaining in residence until 1971. He died in Vienna in 1975. ▶1956.4

▶OAS FORMED—In April, 21 nations of the Americas met in Bogotá, Colombia, to found an organization devoted to mutual security and economic cooperation. The first regional defense bloc under the United Nations, the Organization of American States (OAS) replaced the unwieldy Pan American Union (a jumble of bureaucratic and diplomatic bodies founded in 1889) as the arbiter of regional affairs.

▶BALLETOMANIA—Dancers everywhere cite Michael Powell and Emeric Pressburger's 1948 film, *The Red Shoes*, as pivotal in their choice of career. Starring Moira Shearer as a young ballet dancer who must choose between two compelling men, the movie provided the first realistic backstage look at the world of ballet, as well as some of the best dance sequences ever put on film. ▶1951.7

SCIENCE

Cybernetics Developed

12 With his 1948 book, *Cybernetics: Control and Communication in the Animal and the Machine,* Norbert Wiener, a mathematician at the Massachusetts Institute of Technology, coined the term "cybernetics" (derived from the Greek term *kybernētēs*, meaning "helmsman") to describe a new, interdisciplinary science that examines parallel systems of control in living organisms and machines. Wiener theorized that people's actions, like those of machines, can be predicted and programmed. Both people and machines seek stability, use information, and adjust behavior according to received "feedback." A classic example of this feedback mechanism is the common household thermostat, which reacts to an undesirable temperature by adjusting the heat. Similarly, a human reacts to dropping temperatures by donning a coat.

Although poorly organized and filled with misprints, *Cybernetics* was a visionary work, providing a crucial complement to other groundbreaking ideas of the period, most notably mathematician Claude Shannon's information theory (a mathematical system that applies the logic of Boolean algebra to the way both machines and living organisms process information). Cybernetics brought terms like "feedback" and "input" into common usage; advances led to the development of "thinking" machines. By 1961, the first industrial robots were replacing humans in the workplace. Yet Wiener himself grew skeptical of rampant automation. He wrote that while competition from machines during the first industrial revolution devalued the human arm, the modern industrial revolution "is similarly bound to devalue the human brain." **◂1937.11 ▸1951.1**

A child prodigy, Wiener forged connections between diverse disciplines.

Doctors gag as Health Minister Bevan administers the new social medicine.

GREAT BRITAIN

Ensuring a Nation's Health

13 Britain's long evolution from dog-eat-dog Dickensian capitalism to quasi-socialism culminated in 1948 with the birth of the National Health Service, which entitled every citizen to free medical care "from cradle to grave." Three years earlier, the Labour Party had achieved its first-ever parliamentary majority. Exhausted and virtually bankrupt from the war, Britons gave Labour free rein to implement policies it had been urging for 40 years.

Prime Minister Clement Attlee's government had already nationalized railroads, road transport, coal mines, harbors, and electric power. Medicine was the final step in the process. Parliament approved Sir William Beveridge's plan for the NHS in 1946, but implementation was stalled as doctors, politicians, and the public debated its final form. The fiery oratory and superb negotiating skills of Health Minister Aneurin Bevan, a Welsh coalminer's son, kept the legislation from being gutted.

Like Germany, Austria, France, Italy, Denmark, and New Zealand, Britain was becoming a "welfare state"—a capitalist nation that recognized food, shelter, education, and medicine as basic rights to be ensured by government action. Anti-Soviet leftists like Bevan saw programs like the NHS as the best way to rob communism of its appeal to war-weary Europeans. So did the United States, whose Marshall Plan funds helped make those policies possible. Yet, ironically, America's own welfare services lagged far behind those of its client states. **◂1945.M**

FILM

The Italian Neorealists

14 Neorealism, one of cinema's most influential styles, arose from the rubble of postwar Italy. Eschewing Hollywood's big-budget optimism for gritty depictions of struggling people in a blasted society, such neorealist directors as Roberto Rossellini *(Open City, Paisan)* and Luchino Visconti *(The Earth Trembles)* shot their films on location in working-class urban neighborhoods or poor rural villages, and used ordinary people in principal roles. Neorealism reached its apogee in 1948 with *The Bicycle Thief,* directed by Vittorio De Sica.

An allegory about a chain of dehumanizing economic mishaps, the movie depicts a poor poster hanger, Antonio, whose bicycle is stolen. He embarks with his son on a long, demoralizing search through Rome's mean streets—teeming with black marketeers, striking laborers, rabid soccer fans, and common thugs—finally cornering the thief, an impoverished

De Sica cast factory worker Lamberto Maggiorani in the role of Antonio.

epileptic, whom the police refuse to arrest. Desperate and humiliated, Antonio tries to steal a bike, but is thwarted by an angry mob. For his son's sake, the crowd releases Antonio; the sobbing man and his little boy drift back into the metropolis.

The Bicycle Thief has been called "the most important film of the immediate postwar period." The year after its international release, the Italian government effectively muzzled the neorealists by banning the export of unflattering movies. By then, however, De Sica and his colleagues had nudged film into adulthood by demonstrating that popular cinema could be inexpensive, hard-edged, morally curious, and politically acute. **▸1956.10**

NOBEL PRIZES: Peace: No award ... Literature: T.S. Eliot (U.S.-U.K.; poet) ... Chemistry: Arne Tiselius (Swedish; serum proteins) ... Medicine: Paul Müller (Swiss; DDT) ... Physics: Patrick Maynard Stuart Blackett (U.K.; cosmic radiation).

A VOICE FROM 1948

Casting Out the Relics of Ku Kluxry

By H.L. Mencken, from *The Baltimore Evening Sun,* November 9, 1948

A kind of American Voltaire, Henry Louis Mencken attacked hypocrisy, banality, sloppy thinking. Perhaps America's dominant newspaperman (and certainly its wittiest), Mencken wrote his first copy in 1899. By force of his deep skepticism and talent for corrosive raillery, he soon rose to the top of his field, finding time along the way to cofound (with theater critic George Jean Nathan) two magazines, The Smart Set *and* The American Mercury, *and to write a groundbreaking analysis called* The American Language. *His 43-year career with Baltimore's* Sunpapers *ended on November 9, 1948, with a final column about race relations, written partly in response to President Truman's ending of segregation in the military and the civil service and his demand that Congress take action on jobs, housing, and education. No liberal, no special fan of Truman, often accused of racial stereotyping, Mencken at 68 examined segregation and found it repellent for its sheer idiocy.* **◂1948.M ▸1954.6**

When, on July 11 last, a gang of so-called progressives, white and black, went to Druid Hill Park to stage an inter-racial tennis combat, and were collared and jugged by the cops, it became instantly impossible for anyone to discuss the matter in a newspaper.... The impediment lay in the rules of the Supreme Bench, and the aim of the rules is to prevent the trial of criminal cases by public outcry and fulmination. I am, and have always been, in favor of the aim....

But there remains an underlying question, and it deserves to be considered seriously and without any reference whatever to the cases lately at bar. It is this: Has the Park Board any right in law to forbid white and black citizens, if they are so inclined, to join in harmless games together on public playgrounds? Again: Is such a prohibition, even supposing that it is lawful, supported by anything to be found in common sense and common decency? I do not undertake to answer the first question, for I am too ignorant of law, but my answer to the second is a loud and unequivocal No. A free citizen in a free state, it seems to me, has an inalienable right to play with whomsoever he will, so long as he does not disturb the general peace. If any other citizen, offended by the spectacle, makes a pother, then that other citizen, and not the man exercising his inalienable right, should be put down by the police.

Certainly it is astounding to find so much of the spirit of the Georgia Cracker surviving in the Maryland Free State, and under official auspices. The public parks are supported by the taxpayer, including the colored taxpayer, for the health and pleasure of the whole people. Why should cops be sent into them to separate those people against their will into separate herds? Why should the law set up distinctions and discriminations which the persons directly affected themselves reject? If the park tennis courts were free to all comers no white person would be compelled to take on a colored opponent if he didn't care to. There would be no such vexations and disingenuous pressure as is embodied, for example, in the Hon. Mr. Truman's Fair Employment Practices Act. No one would be invaded in his privacy. Any white player could say yes or no to a colored challenger, and any colored player could say yes or no to a white. But when both say yes, why on earth should anyone else object?

It is high time that all such relics of Ku Kluxry be wiped out in Maryland. The position of the colored people, since the political revolution of 1895, has been gradually improving in the State, and it has already reached a point surpassed by few other states. But there is still plenty of room for further advance, and it is irritating indeed to see one of them blocked by silly Dogberrys. The Park Board rule is irrational and nefarious. It should be got rid of forthwith.

Of equal, and maybe even worse, irrationality is the rule regarding golf-playing on the public links, whereby colored players can play on certain links only on certain days, and white players only on certain other days. It would be hard to imagine anything more ridiculous. Why should a man of one race, playing *in forma pauperis* at the taxpayers' expense, be permitted to exclude men of another race? Why should beggars be turned into such peculiarly obnoxious choosers?... Golf is an expensive game, and should be played only by persons who can afford it. It is as absurd for a poor man to deck himself in its togs and engage in its witless gyrations as it would be for him to array himself as a general in the army. If he can't afford it he should avoid it, as self-respecting people always avoid what they can't afford. The doctrine that the taxpayer should foot the bills which make a bogus prince of pelf of him is New Dealism at its worst.

I am really astonished that the public golf links attract any appreciable colored patronage. The colored people, despite the continued efforts of white frauds to make fools of them, generally keep their heads and retain their sense of humor. If there are any appreciable number of them who can actually afford golf, then they should buy some convenient cow-pasture and set up grounds of their own. And the whites who posture at the taxpayers' expense should do the same.

In answer to all the foregoing I expect confidently to hear the argument that the late mixed tennis matches were not on the level, but were arranged by Communists to make trouble.... [T]his may be true but it seems to me to be irrelevant. What gave the Communists their chance was the existence of the Park Board's rule. If it had carried on its business with more sense they would have been baffled. The way to dispose of their chicaneries is not to fight them when they are right.

The Bard of Baltimore, H.L. Mencken, caricatured by David Levine.

"We are not only good at destroying the old world, we are also good at building the new."—**Mao Zedong, 1949**

STORY OF THE YEAR

Mao Proclaims People's Republic

1 His armies defeated by the Communists after the termination of American aid, Chiang Kai-shek resigned as president of China's Nationalist government on January 21, 1949. Ten days later, Mao Zedong's Communist forces entered Beijing. By late autumn, the Chinese Communist Party occupied all the major Chinese cities, including Nanjing, the Nationalist capital. China's civil war was over; the Communists were triumphant. Addressing a crowd from atop the Gate of Heavenly Peace, the entrance to Beijing's ancient imperial palace, Mao announced the birth of the People's Republic of China on October 1, 1949. He would be chairman; Zhu De, military commander of all the Communist forces, would be vice-chairman; Zhou Enlai, leading diplomat of the CCP, would be premier and foreign minister.

Mao, the son of peasants, envisioned a dictatorship of the Chinese people. His government promised freedom of thought, speech, and religion, and equal rights for women. Only the "running dogs of imperialism" would be denied the new utopia, built, after the Soviet model, on socialized agriculture and state-run heavy industry. The U.S.S.R. and the Soviet-bloc states officially recognized the People's Republic of China immediately; neighboring Burma and India and a host of European countries, including Great Britain, followed within a few months. (Mao rejected British recognition.) The United States withheld diplomatic recognition, remaining loyal instead to Chiang Kai-shek, who fled to Taiwan to reestablish his Nationalist government.

Students for Mao. By autumn 1949, his People's Revolution had triumphed throughout China.

In December, Mao made his first trip outside China, traveling to Moscow to secure Soviet support. Stalin received him coldly, first ignoring him, then offering little practical aid. Mao returned home with only $300 million worth of credit, to be parceled out over five years, and a promise of assistance against Japanese militarism, which in 1949 was nonexistent. Worse, the Chairman was forced to concede that Mongolia, a territory he had hoped to integrate into China, would remain "independent," that is, within the Soviet sphere.

Nor did domestic policies proceed smoothly. As many as a million people were killed in the violent clashes between landlords and tenants that accompanied the widespread land reforms. Meanwhile, the CCP's preferential treatment of wealthy peasants, whom it could not afford to alienate, was unpopular with the masses. With alarming celerity, Mao's dictatorship of the people evolved into a dictatorship of Mao. **◂1945.12 ▸1952.2**

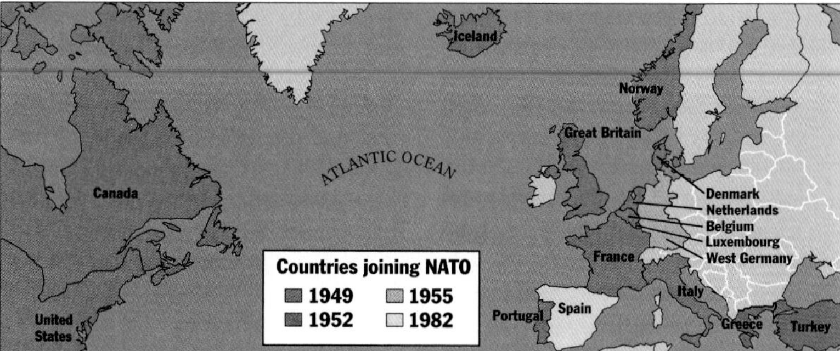

Born in 1949 out of the West's concern with containment, NATO by 1982 had 16 members. By 1992, even Warsaw Pact countries were contemplating membership.

DIPLOMACY

NATO's Nativity

2 As vast Soviet armies subdued the states of Eastern and Central Europe, twelve Western nations, shaken by the grim prospect of renewed war, signed a pact on April 4, 1949, forging the world's most extensive collective-defense alliance. The North Atlantic Treaty Organization (NATO) arose from Article 5 of the North Atlantic Treaty, wherein the contracting parties pledged "that an armed attack against one or more of them ... shall be considered an attack against them all."

The North Atlantic Treaty was modeled in part on the Rio Treaty (the regional-defense bloc created in 1947 by the nations of South and Central America and the United States) and justified by Article 51 of the UN Charter, which guaranteed the right of collective defense. The groundwork for NATO was laid in 1948, when Belgium, Luxembourg, France, the Netherlands, and Britain signed the Brussels Treaty, creating a European defense alliance. But it lacked U.S. military and economic resources, so NATO talks began almost immediately.

Independently weak, the nations of Western Europe—backed by U.S. might—together counterbalanced the Soviet giant. U.S. officials called NATO an "antidote to fear," but its founding completed the frightening polarization of the world into two armed camps. **◂1948.M ▸1955.4**

GERMANY

Two Separate States

3 Out of the miasma of Four Power occupation grew two new and incompatible German states, each drawn in the likeness of its respective procurator: the NATO-friendly Federal Republic of Germany to the west of the Oder-Neisse line, and the Soviet-affiliated German Democratic Republic to the east. Undertaken as a temporary measure, the creation in 1949 of separate Germanies proved a bitterly durable Cold War legacy.

Der Parlamentarische Rat hat das vorstehende Grundgesetz für die Bundesrepublik Deutschland in öffentlicher Sitzung am 8. Mai des Jahres Eintausendneunhundertneunundvierzig mit dreiundfünfzig gegen zwölf Stimmen beschlossen. Zu Urkunde dessen haben sämtliche Mitglieder des Parlamentarischen Rates die vorliegende Urschrift des Grundgesetzes eigenhändig unterzeichnet.

BONN AM RHEIN, den 23. Mai des Jahres Eintausendneunhundertneunundvierzig.

PRÄSIDENT DES PARLAMENTARISCHEN RATES

Adolph Schönfelder

I. VIZEPRÄSIDENT DES PARLAMENTARISCHEN RATES

Hermann Schäfer

West Germany's new constitution ***(first page, above)*** **emphasized civil rights.**

Four Power cooperation in Germany, tenuous from the beginning, had broken down completely the previous year, after the Soviet blockade of Berlin made it clear that the Soviets would not allow free elections throughout Germany. A parliamentary council drawn from the freely elected parliaments of the western German *Länder* (states) began drafting an interim constitution (meant to last only until united Germany adopted a constitution) in September 1948. The resulting document, the *Grundgesetz* (Basic Law), was a masterpiece of political engineering that included an extensive bill of rights and provided for a flexible and stable federal government. It was easily ratified by the *Länder*, and on May 24, 1949, the Federal Republic of Germany was born. Konrad Adenauer was elected chancellor, a post he held for the next 14 years. Immediately, his

ART & CULTURE: Books: ***The Sheltering Sky*** **(Paul Bowles);** ***Conjugal Love*** **(Alberto Moravia);** ***The Beginning and the End*** **(Naguib Mahfouz);** ***Modern Arms and Free Men*** **(Vannevar Bush);** ***This I Remember*** **(Eleanor Roosevelt) ... Music: "Rudolph the Red-Nosed Reindeer" (Johnny Marks); "If I Had a Hammer" (Seeger and Hays) ... Painting & Sculpture:** ***Elegy to the Spanish Republic, Granada***

"There are two kinds of geniuses, the 'ordinary' and the 'magicians' ... Richard Feynman is a magician of the highest caliber."—**Mathematician Mark Kac**

economic minister, Ludwig Erhard, began implementing "social market economics," the formula responsible for West Germany's remarkable economic recovery.

In Germany's eastern zone, the Soviets staged an election of their own: They compiled a "unity list" of candidates and gave voters a choice of endorsing the list or rejecting it. In this way, the communist-backed People's Congress was elected in May; on October 7, 1949, it recognized the German Democratic Republic as "the first workers' and peasants' state on German soil." Communist Party functionary Wilhelm Pieck became the first premier, but real power rested with Walter Ulbricht. As head of East Germany's only political party, Ulbricht controlled the state apparatus until 1971. **◂1948.2 ▸1953.7**

LITERATURE

Orwell's Totalitarian Tale

4 George Orwell's *Nineteen Eighty-four* is perhaps the most harrowing anti-utopian novel in history. It appeared in 1949 (midway between the Berlin airlift and the outbreak of fighting on the Korean peninsula) and became an instant Cold War classic. Set 35 years in the (then) future, the book describes a hyper-totalitarian state in which love, privacy, sexual pleasure, and independent thinking have all been proscribed, and beauty eradicated. Under the constant surveillance of "Big Brother," citizens live in terror that any transgression will be reported to the all-powerful Thought Police. The hero, Winston Smith, has a job with the Ministry of Truth creating propaganda. When Smith rebels and falls in love with a coworker who shares his subversive views, he is caught, tortured, and "re-educated" into total submission.

The author of this study in twentieth-century state terrorism was a fervent socialist named Eric Blair, an Eton-educated Briton who, in the mid-1930s, began writing under the name George Orwell. Conforming to no party doctrine, Orwell remained above all a staunch humanist. He fought in the Spanish Civil War on the Republican side, only to wind up on the run when the dissident Marxist militia to which he was attached found itself under attack by the Soviet-backed Republican Army. This brush with Stalinist terror stayed with Orwell the rest of his life, playing a major role in the formation of not only *Nineteen Eighty-four*, but also *Animal Farm* (1945), his political fable about barnyard animals who throw off their human oppressors only to be oppressed by the power-grabbing pigs among them.

So enthusiastic was the public's response to *Nineteen Eighty-four* that Orwell became alarmed that his "show-up of the perversions to which a centralised economy is liable" (as he wrote to a friend) was being misconstrued by zealous right-wing anti-Communists. He did not live, however, to see the larger-than-life proportions his book eventually assumed. Within six months of the book's publication, Orwell, by then one of the most famous writers in the world, died of tuberculosis at an English sanatorium. He was 46. **◂1932.3 ▸1954.13**

SCIENCE

Feynman's Formulations

5 New York City–born physicist and Manhattan Project veteran Richard Feynman proposed a crucial theoretical refinement of earlier research into high-energy particle collisions when, in 1949, he introduced the "Feynman diagram," which illustrated the movement of a particle in space as it interacts with magnetic fields. Applying the probability theories of quantum mechanics to these interactions, Feynman created a new field known as quantum electrodynamics.

Feynman diagrams and Feynman integrals, as they became known, not only illustrated what was happening to the particles, they simplified the computations needed to analyze and predict the process. Feynman—a lively, outgoing fellow whose endless intellectual curiosity led him to such diverse activities as painting, playing bongo drums, and mastering Mayan hieroglyphics—was characteristically expansive in assessing his method, which, he declared, described "all phenomena of the physical world except the gravitational effect." His work earned him, along with American physicist Julian Schwinger and Japanese physicist Shinichiro Tomonaga (each of whom arrived independently at similar conclusions), the Nobel Prize in 1965.

Feynman became best known to the public through his participation in the13-member presidential commission that investigated the 1986 explosion of the space shuttle *Challenger*. He concluded that the failure rate of the most complicated machine in the world was closer to 1 in 100 than to 1 in 100,000, as NASA believed. Feynman's flair for showmanship was very much in evidence when he used a glass of ice water to demonstrate for senators and scientists how the plastic of the O-ring used in the *Challenger*'s solid rocket boosters could be changed from pliable to rigid by lowering its temperature a few degrees. **◂1925.7 ▸1964.12**

Feynman illustrates a particle collision during a seminar at Cal Tech in 1978.

BIRTHS

Pablo Escobar, Colombian drug trafficker.

William Forsythe, U.S. choreographer.

Mary Gordon, U.S. writer.

Bruce Jenner, U.S. track and field athlete.

Annie Leibovitz, U.S. photographer.

Cameron Mackintosh, U.K. impresario.

Ilyich Ramírez Sánchez, Venezuelan terrorist.

Bruce Springsteen, U.S. singer.

Meryl Streep, U.S. actress.

Tom Watson, U.S. golfer.

DEATHS

Niceto Alcalá Zamora, Spanish president.

Wallace Beery, Sr., U.S. actor.

Georgi Dimitrov, Bulgarian political leader.

James Ensor, Belgian painter.

James Forrestal, U.S. naval officer.

Henri Giraud, French general.

Maurice Maeterlinck, Belgian writer.

Margaret Mitchell, U.S. novelist.

José Clemente Orozco, Mexican painter.

Robert Ripley, U.S. writer.

Bill "Bojangles" Robinson, U.S. dancer.

Wiley Rutledge, Jr., U.S. jurist.

Edward Stettinius, U.S. industrialist and diplomat.

Richard Strauss, German composer.

Sigrid Undset, Norwegian novelist.

(Robert Motherwell); *The Blind Leading the Blind* (Louise Bourgeois) ... Film: *All the King's Men* (Robert Rossen); *White Heat* (Raoul Walsh); *On the Town* (Kelly and Donen); *Manon* (Henri-Georges Cluzot); *The Third Man* (Carol Reed) ... Theater: *The Cocktail Party* (T.S. Eliot); *Lost in the Stars* (Weill and Anderson); *Miss Liberty* (Irving Berlin) ... TV: *Kukla, Fran and Ollie*; *The Lone Ranger*.

"A poet never takes notes. You never take notes in a love affair."—**Robert Frost**

NEW IN 1949

Silly Putty.

Television soap opera (*These Are My Children*, NBC).

Television sitcom (*The Goldbergs*, CBS).

Scrabble board game.

Nonstop around-the-world flight (U.S. Air Force's *Lucky Lady II*).

Telethon (Milton Berle raises $1 million for cancer research in 14 hours).

UNICEF Christmas card.

Radio Free Europe broadcasts.

Lego building blocks.

Prepared cake mixes (General Foods and Pillsbury).

Emmy awards.

IN THE UNITED STATES

▶TRACY AND HEPBURN—George Cukor, the consummate director of "women's pictures," in 1949 gave a comic spin to the subject of equality between the sexes. *Adam's Rib* starred Spencer Tracy and Katharine Hepburn as opposing attorneys in a trial for attempted murder who happen to be married to each other. The screenplay, by Garson Kanin and Ruth Gordon, provided one of cinema's most charismatic couples with a smart, sexy, politically enlightened script, and gave them what many consider the best roles of their careers. ◂1938.11

▶HUNTING REDS—American Cold War paranoia emerged full force in 1949, with the conviction of eleven Communists for advocating the overthrow of the U.S. government.

THE MIDDLE EAST

Arab-Israeli War Ends

6 In the opening phase of the first Arab-Israeli war, the armies of Egypt, Transjordan, Iraq, Syria, and Lebanon, along with Arab Liberation Army irregulars, had occupied all of Palestine not apportioned to Israel by the United Nations. But while Arab forces slightly outnumbered the 30,000 Israeli defenders, they were hobbled by their leaders' disunity and their own widespread lack of discipline. (Unenthusiastic Iraqi conscripts were sometimes chained to their machine guns.) Israel's men and women, meanwhile, fought with desperate determination—and (after the first weeks) with arms supplied by France, Czechoslovakia, and private supporters around the world. By early 1949, the infant nation had beaten back its exhausted attackers and was beginning to gain ground.

Between February and July (when Syria finally gave in), United Nations mediator Ralph Bunche brokered armistices between Israel and the Arab states. Israel got to keep all its conquered territories, including Galilee, the whole Palestine coast (except the Gaza Strip, occupied by Egypt), and the Negev desert. Under president Chaim Weizmann and Prime Minister David Ben-Gurion, Israel had won its baptismal war. Still, the triumph was frustratingly incomplete: The rest of what the UN had formerly designated as Arab Palestine—including Jerusalem's Old City, full of shrines sacred to Muslims, Jews, and Christians—went to Transjordan (henceforth known as Jordan).

The big losers were the Palestinian Arabs. Seventy percent (up to 720,000) became refugees. Their departure left Israel with a Jewish majority—which ballooned over the next decade as Arab countries, in revenge, drove half a million Jews into exile. Indeed, a new cycle of vengeance between Jews and Arabs was just getting under way. **◂1948.9 ▸1951.5**

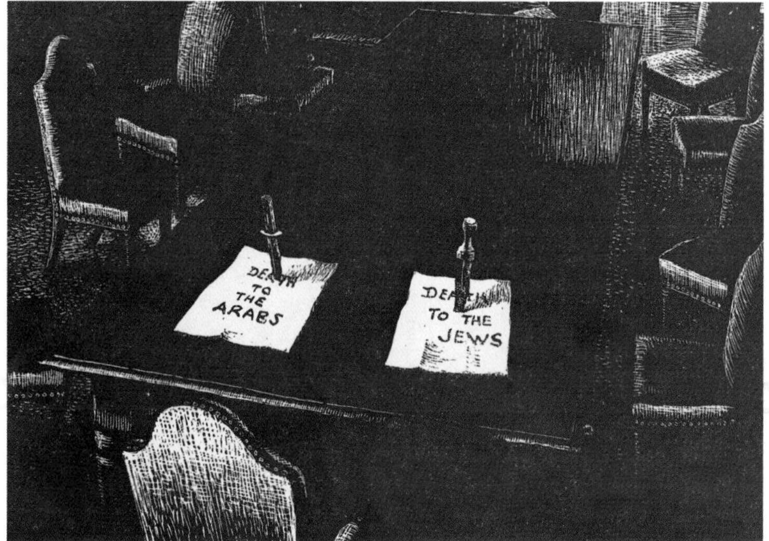

The caption for this cartoon rhetorically asked, "Any other proposals?"

VIETNAM

An Arranged Independence

7 By early 1949, Ho Chi Minh's nationalist government controlled 80 percent of Vietnam, while France held little but the major cities of its contested colony. After three years and some 30,000 casualties, French troops had made no progress against Communist-led Viet Minh guerrillas. But in March, Paris officials implemented a plan intended to defeat the Viet Minh politically: the Bao Dai solution.

Emperor Bao Dai *(above)*, 35, had ruled the historic kingdom of Annam as a French puppet in the 1930s, later serving his country's Japanese occupiers in a similar capacity. Forced to abdicate when Ho seized power in 1945, he briefly served as an adviser to the new regime before exiling himself to Hong Kong and France. The French were soon urging him to return home and set up a government to rival Ho's. But Bao had acquired some advisers of his own. Unless Paris would grant Vietnam independence, he preferred to stay abroad. (He particularly enjoyed the nightclubs of the French Riviera.) Paris preferred to grant no such thing.

The nascent Cold War changed calculations on both sides, however. The French became increasingly convinced that a Bao Dai regime would lure non-Communist nationalists away from the Viet Minh. Bao, meanwhile, grew more open to a compromise: The United States, he figured, would back him as a bulwark against the Reds (Mao's victory in China, which brought Chinese Communist troops to Vietnam's northern border in late 1948, only intensified the fear), and would pressure France to cut its colonial ties. After nine months of negotiations, France recognized Bao as head of a nominally independent Vietnam; defense, diplomacy, and finance would remain in French hands.

Unfortunately for Bao, few of his countrymen mistook this arrangement for real independence. Upon his return, important nationalists all boycotted his government, while corrupt opportunists flocked to it. Ho denounced Bao as a quisling, and the Viet Minh fought on. Even the Emperor soon complained that the Bao Dai solution "turns out to be just a French solution." In 1955, he was on his way back to the Riviera. **◂1946.M ▸1950.2**

LITERATURE

America's Poet-Farmer

8 "I choose to be a plain New Hampshire farmer/With an income in cash of, say, a thousand/(From, say, a publisher in New York City)./... At present I am living in Vermont." The sly contradictions inherent in these lines (from a poem entitled "New Hampshire") are the same ones embodied by their author, poet Robert Frost, a man who liked to present himself as a rustic New England farmer but whose deceptively simple verse often hinted at deeper, darker mysteries. Frost's *Complete Poems*, published in 1949 and containing his entire poetic canon to date, displayed the full breadth of vision of this quintessentially American poet.

Readers (and Frost has had

SPORTS: Baseball: World Series, New York Yankees defeat Brooklyn Dodgers, 4–1 ... Football: NFL, Philadelphia Eagles defeat Los Angeles Rams, 14–0 ... Basketball: NBA, Minneapolis Lakers defeat Washington Capitols, 4–2 ... Boxing: Joe Louis retires; Ezzard Charles beats Joe Walcott in 15-round decision for heavyweight title.

"You got to have smelt a lot of mule manure before you can sing like a hillbilly."—**Hank Williams**

Poet of nature: Robert Frost in his garden in 1939.

more of them than perhaps any other serious twentieth-century poet) loved his clear, lyrical style—often employed in the praise of nature—and traditional rhyme schemes. Inspired by Wordsworth and Browning, as well as by Greek and Latin classics, Frost is often characterized as a kind of latter-day transcendentalist in the tradition of Henry David Thoreau and Ralph Waldo Emerson. Yet he never aligned himself with any particular poetic movement; that fact, and his conservative metrics, often led scholars and devotees of the avant-garde to dismiss him as conventional. But the outward accessibility of Frost's poems—those grammar-school perennials "Stopping By Woods on a Snowy Evening" and "The Road Not Taken," or the sing-songy "Provide, Provide"—frames a sophistication and a highly original use of language rooted in plain-spoken, often colloquial speech that, in his best poems, manages to embrace at least two levels of meaning at once. ("We play the words as we find them," he said). The rough, New England folk wisdom apparent in a quick reading of Frost evolves, on closer inspection, into a subtler, near-religious awareness of the "lovely, dark and deep" ambiguities at the heart of the human condition. **◄1946.11 ►1969.V**

IRELAND

Official Republic Status

9 After nearly 800 years of British hegemony, the 26 counties of Ireland constituting the Irish Free State finally extricated themselves from the British Commonwealth. The independent Republic of Ireland was proclaimed on April 18, 1949, almost 33 years to the day after the bloody Easter Rebellion in Dublin. Yet the occasion was not all whistles and bells: The partition effected in 1920 continued, with

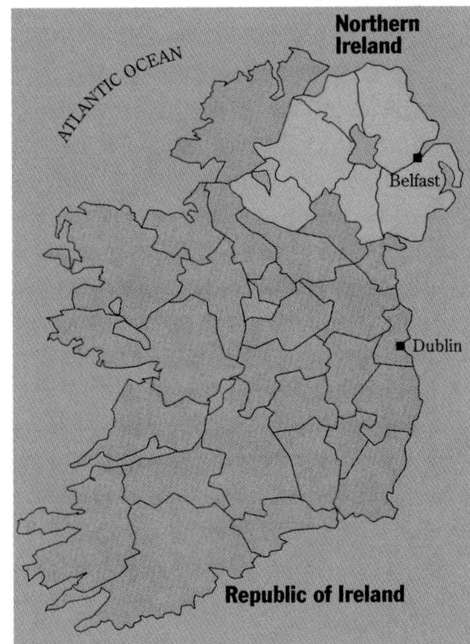

Independence for southern Ireland solidified the separation between north and south.

the six Protestant-majority counties of Northern Ireland remaining part of the United Kingdom.

Britain's recognition of independence came after twelve years of de facto Irish autonomy. In 1937, the government of Prime Minister Eamon De Valera abolished the oath of allegiance to Britain and declared Ireland an autonomous country. (A longtime leader for Irish independence, the New York–born De Valera had been spared execution for his role in the 1916 uprising only because of his U.S. citizenship. Later, he served a prison term for his denunciation of the 1922 treaty granting dominion status.) For the next twelve years, the Free State counties, in British eyes still part of the Commonwealth, existed as the sovereign state of Eire. By 1948, when the Irish Parliament proclaimed full independence, effective Easter Monday 1949, the country's membership in the empire was widely recognized as a diplomatic fiction. Britain, at last, conceded. **◄1922.12 ►1968.10**

MUSIC

Hank Williams's Blues

10 When Hank Williams showed up on June 11, 1949, to perform a guest spot at the Grand Ole Opry radio show, in Nashville, Tennessee, the manager was wary. Stories of Williams's hard-drinking ways on the honky-tonk circuit had preceded him. But when the now-legendary country-and-western singer began moaning "Lovesick Blues" in his pure, unadorned voice—characterized by a poignant, yodel-like catch as it leaped into a higher register—the packed audience roared its approval, calling him back for an unprecedented six encores and launching him into his brief orbit of fame.

Williams was only 29 when he died of heart failure in the backseat of his Cadillac on New Year's Day, 1953. By then, he'd been kicked out of the Opry for too many no-shows, had ended one stormy marriage and begun another, and had struggled so hard with his addictions to alcohol and painkillers that he'd wound up in a sanatorium. But he'd also written over 100 songs, including such lovelorn classics as "Your Cheatin' Heart," "I'm So Lonesome I Could Cry," and "Cold, Cold Heart." Williams's lyrics, informed by his own hard-won knowledge of suffering, have been called "folk poetry," influencing songwriters in every genre. His son, Hank Williams, Jr., became a country star in his own right. **►1955.M**

Hank Williams, the greatest star in the history of country music.

IN THE UNITED STATES

Also that year, Alger Hiss, president of the Carnegie Endowment for International Peace, former temporary secretary-general of the UN, U.S. adviser at Yalta, and onetime clerk for Justice Oliver Wendell Holmes, went on trial for perjury. Hiss had been indicted after an investigation by the House Un-American Activities Committee, led by California congressman Richard Nixon, accused him of passing classified government documents to self-confessed Soviet agent Whittaker Chambers in 1937 and '38. Hiss denied committing any espionage on behalf of Communism, or even seeing Chambers after January 1937. The first jury was deadlocked. A new trial, which began November 17, resulted in a guilty verdict. Hiss, who served three years of his five-year sentence, has always maintained his innocence. ◄1947.5 ►1950.5

►GLASS HOUSE—By championing leading-edge European architects, Philip Johnson had defined the "International

Style." With the rectilinear, glass-walled house he built for himself in 1949 in rural Connecticut, Johnson created a homegrown variation on European avant-gardism. ◄1947.8 ►1954.5

►TOKYO ROSE ON TRIAL—Iva Toguri d'Aquino, known to thousands of Pacific GIs as Tokyo Rose, was tried on eight counts of treason in San Francisco in 1949. One of 13 women who read Japanese propaganda in English over the radio to American GIs, d'Aquino, an American citizen born in L.A., was charged with giving comfort to the enemy. She claimed she'd been caught in Tokyo at the start of the war and forced into service by Japan. After a three-month trial rife with prosecutorial corruption, d'Aquino was found guilty of a lesser charge and served six years in prison. In 1977, President Gerald Ford acknowledged her wrongful prosecution with a pardon.

POLITICS & BUSINESS: GNP: $256.5 billion ... Presidential salary raised to $100,000 per year (with $50,000 allowance) ... U.S. Department of Defense created ... Congress raises the minimum wage from 40 cents to 75 cents.

"The weeds are pulled up by the muscular effort of the peasant, but only sun and water can make the corn grow. The will cannot produce any good in the soul."—Simone Weil

AROUND THE WORLD

▶COMECON—A response to economic cooperation in Western Europe, the Council for Mutual Economic Assistance (COMECON) was created by Moscow in 1949 to integrate the trade, finance, and industrial development of the U.S.S.R. and its satellites. Never fully competitive with the European Economic Community, COMECON was hampered by price controls, which made market-value prices irrelevant and led to a system of bartering among the member states. ◀1949.2 ▶1955.4

▶DUTCH CONCEDE INDONESIA—Four years after Sukarno and Muhammad Hatta unilaterally declared Indonesia independent, the Dutch, who had expected to return to their prewar colonial domination, agreed. Upon defeat in World War II, the Japanese had transferred power in Indonesia to Sukarno and Hatta, but the British and Dutch had other ideas. Indonesians battled the

British for a year *(Javanese revolutionaries, above)* until two "police actions" by Dutch troops in 1947 and 1948 aroused worldwide condemnation. In December 1949 under pressure from the UN, the Netherlands finally capitulated. ▶1966.13

▶GREECE AT PEACE—The Greek Civil War ended in October 1949, having taken an estimated 50,000 lives. When fighting between communist EAM guerrillas and the government of King Paul revived in 1946 after a year-long truce, Tito's Yugoslavia backed the rebels. But after he broke with Stalin, the isolated Tito cut off aid, and the Athens government—now bolstered by heavy U.S. funding—won a decisive victory. ◀1947.4 ▶1967.2

MUSIC

Operatic Star Power

11 Like many aspiring singers, New York–born soprano Maria Callas (née Kalogeropoulos) had moved to Italy, opera's heartland, shortly after World War II. Her early performances drew polite reviews, but when she started singing Wagner's *Tristan und Isolde* and Puccini's *Turandot* in Venice, she began to receive increasingly enthusiastic notices. Then, in early 1949, she scored a triumph of virtuosity when she appeared in an impossibly demanding operatic doubleheader at Venice's Teatro La Fenice.

Callas had already signed on for the role of Brünnhilde in Wagner's *Die Walküre*, when director Tullio Serafin also asked her to take over for the ailing Margherita Carosio, one of Italy's leading coloratura sopranos, in the radically dissimilar (and, for Callas, unfamiliar) part of Elvira in Bellini's *I Puritani*. Overnight, Callas's extraordinary feat was the talk of operaphiles throughout Italy. Offers tumbled in, and soon she was being compared to such legendary virtuosos as Lilli Lehmann and Maria Malibran. Although opera scholars continue to debate her vocal technique, there is no dispute about her range, her versatility, or the extraordinary drama and emotion with which she invested nearly every note. Her undeniable star power helped popularize the operas of lesser-known composers.

Offstage, Callas played the temperamental artist to the hilt. She was fired by Rudolf Bing of New York's Metropolitan Opera after a series of heated disputes, and her relations with the Rome Opera and Milan's La Scala were nearly as strained. The press had a field day with reports of back-stage spats with fellow singers, and her jet-set lifestyle and long-running liaison with Greek shipping tycoon Aristotle Onassis did nothing to silence the gossips. Yet Callas was an exacting, self-critical artist whose high demands on herself doubtless contributed to the brevity of her career (which nonetheless encompassed more than 40 roles and 20 recordings of complete operas). Forced by vocal problems to withdraw from the operatic stage, Callas made her last appearance in an opera as Tosca in a 1965 production at London's Covent Garden. She died in 1977 at age 53. **◀1939.14 ▶1959.6**

Temperamental diva Callas in 1955.

IDEAS

A Self-Made Saint

12 Of the many Western intellectuals who embraced religious faith after the political disillusionments of the 1930s, few demanded so much of religion—or of themselves—as Simone Weil. Published posthumously in 1949, *The Need for Roots* presented this Jewish-born Christian's vision of a society centered on the individual and firmly rooted in God and family. In such a society, the pursuit of goodness would replace the pursuit of wealth and power. Freedom of expression would be extended to individuals, but not to groups. Churches would stay out of politics; political parties would be abolished.

Weil became highly influential in the 1950s, as much for her mystique as for her books (which also include *Waiting for God* and *Gravity and Grace*). T.S. Eliot, among others, considered her a saint. Though born to Parisian affluence, she lived a severely spartan, virginal life. After a stint as a provincial schoolteacher (and leftist activist), she took a series of factory jobs, but was too frail to continue; later, she served the Republicans as a battlefield cook in the Spanish Civil War, but went home after burning herself badly. Dismayed by the atrocities of both sides in Spain, her health ruined, she experienced the mystical revelations that led to her conversion. But she could never bring herself to join a church.

After fleeing with her family to London during World War II, Weil begged the Free French forces to let her join the resistance; instead, they assigned her to write recommendations for rebuilding French society. These compositions became *The Need for Roots.* Refusing to eat more than the war ration of occupied France, she died in 1943 of malnutrition. She was 34. **◀1923.13**

IDEAS

A Feminist Classic

13 Although Simone de Beauvoir was already a fixture of the Paris literary scene (the author of several novels and philosophical works, she was also Jean-Paul Sartre's consort), *Le Deuxième Sexe,* her seminal 1949 study of women's role in society, made her a worldwide symbol of the burgeoning women's movement. An encyclopedia of women in history, *The Second Sex* (as it was called in English) was laced throughout with de Beauvoir's wit and intellect. It began with a discussion of Eve in the Garden of Eden and worked its way through recorded time, documenting frankly how women had been "relative beings" in a universe of men.

De Beauvoir drew bleak conclusions about the status of women. From childhood, she argued, females were fated to be the passive prey of men. They had "no past, no history, no religion of their own." What men feared above all was that women would cease to become their most treasured "idea" and become like themselves—that is, people. In the book's most memorable phrase, de Beauvoir wrote, "One is not born a woman, one becomes one."

Simone de Beauvoir in 1945, photographed by Robert Doisneau.

Hailed by *The New York Times* as "one of the few great books of our era," *The Second Sex* also had detractors. "The warm aura of mystery that commonly surrounds woman," lamented *Time*, "has been reduced to a steely chill." Yet to countless feminists, de Beauvoir was a hero. "More than any other single human being," Gloria Steinem would say decades later, "she's responsible for the current international women's movement." **◀1943.10 ▶1963.8**

NOBEL PRIZES: Peace: John Boyd Orr (U.K.; efforts to eliminate world hunger) ... Literature: William Faulkner (U.S.; novelist) ... Chemistry: William F. Giauque (U.S.; chemical thermodynamics at low temperatures) ... Medicine: Walter Rudolf Hess and Egas Moniz (Swiss, Portuguese; brain control of body functions) ... Physics: Hideki Yukawa (Japanese; the meson).

A VOICE FROM 1949

An American Tragedy

From *Death of a Salesman*, by Arthur Miller, 1949

In Death of a Salesman, *Arthur Miller* (left) *set out to create a modern-day version of classical tragedy with a common man as hero. Miller's life and artistic sensibility were shaped by the Great Depression, which ruined his father's small business and taught Miller a lesson about the fragility of the American dream. In* Death of a Salesman, *which premiered in New York on February 10, 1949, the aging businessman Willy Loman is betrayed by that dream. At the age of 63, Willy loses his job as a traveling salesman, and finally comes to terms not only with his own failure but that of his two sons Biff and Happy. Thus stripped of all his illusions, Willy commits suicide—a tragedy to which, as Willy's long-suffering wife, Linda, puts it, "attention must be paid."* Salesman *won the Pulitzer prize, and its author became one of the most famous playwrights of his generation.*

WILLY: You're trying to put a knife in me—don't think I don't know what you're doing!

BIFF: All right, phony! Then let's lay it on the line. *He whips the rubber hose out of his pocket and puts it on the table.*

HAPPY: You crazy—

LINDA: Biff! *She moves to grab the hose, but Biff holds it down with his hand.*

BIFF: Leave it there! Don't move it!

WILLY, *not looking at it*: What is that?

BIFF: You know goddamn well what that is.

WILLY, *caged, wanting to escape*: I never saw that.

BIFF: You saw it. The mice didn't bring it into the cellar! What is this supposed to do, make a hero out of you? This supposed to make me sorry for you?

WILLY: Never heard of it.

BIFF: There'll be no pity for you, you hear it? No pity!

WILLY, *to Linda*: You hear the spite!

BIFF: No, you're going to hear the truth—what you are and what I am!

LINDA: Stop it!

WILLY: Spite!

HAPPY, *coming down toward Biff*: You cut it now!

BIFF, *to Happy*: The man don't know who we are! The man is gonna know! We never told the truth for ten minutes in this house!

HAPPY, *to Willy*: We always told the truth!

BIFF, *turning on him*: You big blow, are you the assistant buyer? You're one of the two assistants to the assistant, aren't you?

HAPPY: Well, I'm practically—

BIFF: You're practically full of it! We all are! And I'm through with it. Now hear this, Willy, this is me.... I am not a leader of men, Willy, and neither are you. You were never anything but a hard-working drummer who landed in the ash can like all the rest of them! I'm one dollar an hour, Willy! I tried seven states and couldn't raise it. A buck an hour. Do you gather my meaning? I'm not bringing home any prizes any more, and you're going to stop waiting for me to bring them home.

WILLY, *directly to Biff*: You vengeful, spiteful mutt!

Biff breaks from Happy. Willy, in fright, starts up the stairs. Biff grabs him.

BIFF, *at the peak of his fury*: Pop, I'm nothing! I'm nothing, Pop. Can't you understand that? There's no spite in it any more. I'm just what I am, that's all.

Biff's fury has spent itself, and he breaks down, sobbing, holding on to Willy, who dumbly fumbles for Biff's face.

WILLY, *astonished*: What're you doing? *To Linda:* What're you doing? Why is he crying?

BIFF, *crying, broken*: Will you let me go, for Christ's sake? Will you take that phony dream and burn it before something happens?

death of a Salesman

Miller intended his salesman-hero to be a kind of tragic Everyman. One of the choicest roles in American drama, Willy Loman was played by Lee J. Cobb in *Salesman*'s first New York production, which was directed by Elia Kazan.

The postwar quest for normalcy brought a culture of conformity to the prospering Western world—even as the Cold War chilled the air in both hemispheres. And from the vestiges of old empires arose a new force: the Third World, an array of former colonies intent on forging their own identities.

1950 1959

World War II was followed by the greatest economic boom in history. With the U.S. government's blessing of cheap money and low down payments, ex-G.I.s flocked to buy prefabricated houses in developments like this one in Levittown, New York. Derided by many social critics—folksinger Malvina Reynolds sang of "little boxes made of ticky-tacky" that, like their occupants, "all look just the same"—the burgeoning suburbs came to symbolize the decade, as did the fallout shelters dug into many American backyards as insurance against nuclear Armageddon.

THE WORLD IN 1950

World Population

1940: 2.3 BILLION 1950: 2.5 BILLION

1940–50: +8.7%

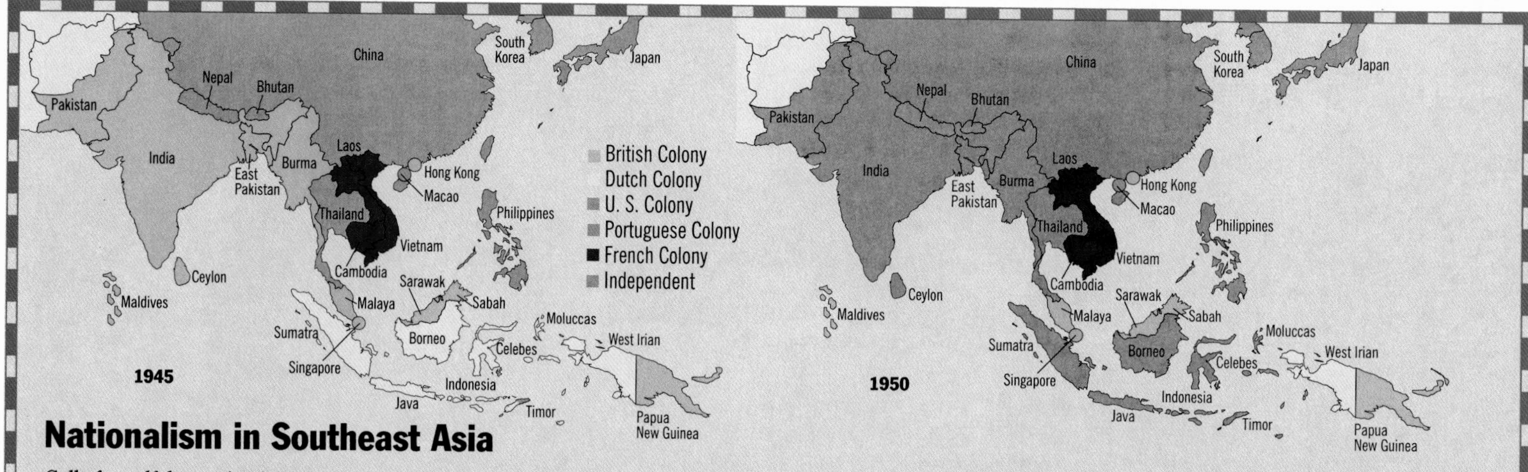

Nationalism in Southeast Asia

Calls for self-determination sprang up immediately after Allied victory in World War II ended Japan's wartime occupation of the colonies in Southeast Asia that before the war had belonged to Britain, France, the Netherlands, and Portugal. Britain and the Netherlands, aware of how little loyalty their rule had commanded among the people of the region when the Japanese took over, realized that trying to reestablish their stronghold in that region would be expensive, bloody, and ultimately futile. They opted to grant independence to the majority of their former colonies; France, however, chose to stay, as did Portugal. Nonetheless, by 1976, when Portugal departed East Timor, all of the former colonies except for Hong Kong and Macao were free of European rule.

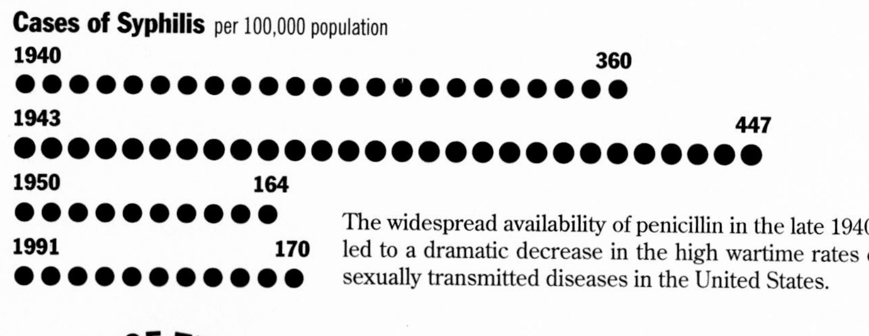

The widespread availability of penicillin in the late 1940s led to a dramatic decrease in the high wartime rates of sexually transmitted diseases in the United States.

Fashion Essential

During World War II, **blue jeans** were actually declared an essential commodity by the U.S. government, and could be sold only to people engaged in defense work. In the years since the war, they have become the ultimate symbol of casual American style and, as such, are coveted all over the world.

STATE OF THE ART

The first reel-to-reel **tape recorders** for commercial sound recording were installed at ABC studios in New York City, Chicago, and Hollywood in 1948. The following year, Sony introduced a machine that sold in Japan for about $400. Within 20 years tape recorders would be a $300 million industry in the United States.

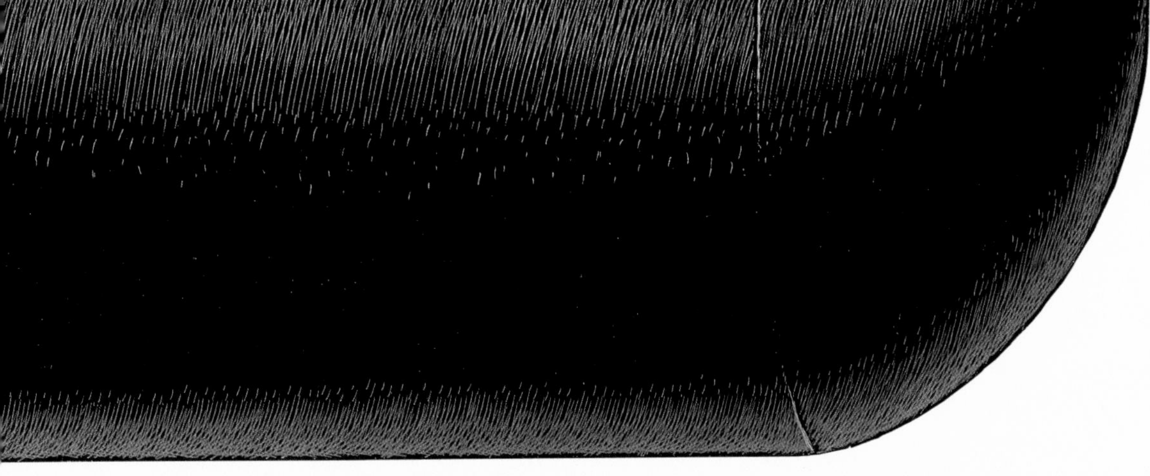

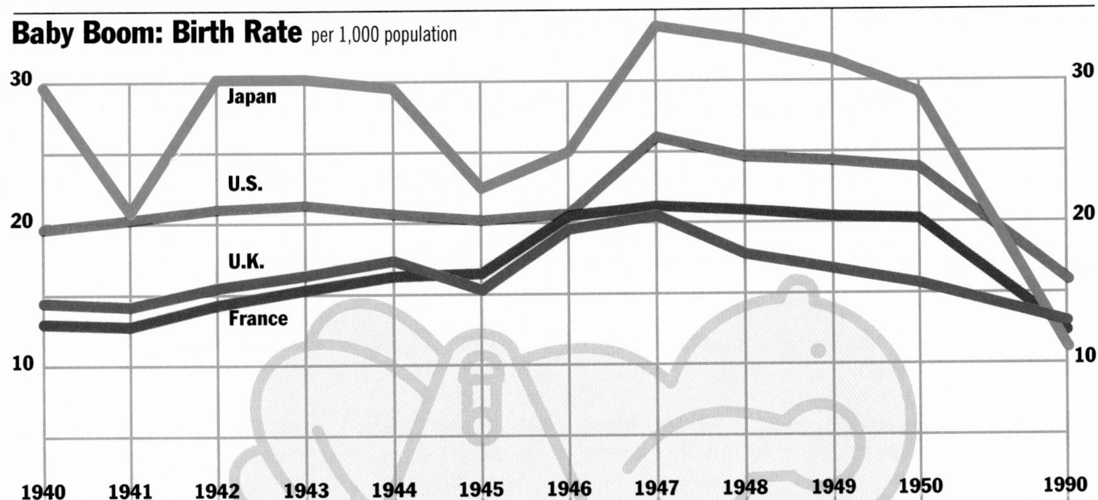

Nuclear Weapons Buildup

		1950	1960	1989
U.S.	Warheads	350	18,700	22,500
	Megatons of TNT	77	19,000	11,000
U.S.S.R.	Warheads	5	1,700	32,000
	Megatons of TNT	0.1	500	4,500

Hiroshima bomb=0.015 kilotons of TNT power
Total in 1989=3 tons of TNT power for every person on earth

The Shadow of the Bomb The United States' deployment of the atomic bomb during World War II and the Soviet Union's announcement that it had successfully tested an A-bomb (which in turn accelerated the pace of research on a hydrogen bomb, a fusion device with many times the A-bomb's power) cast a pall of doom and fatalism over the postwar world—particularly its children, whose everyday lives were forced to accommodate the possibility of nuclear destruction.

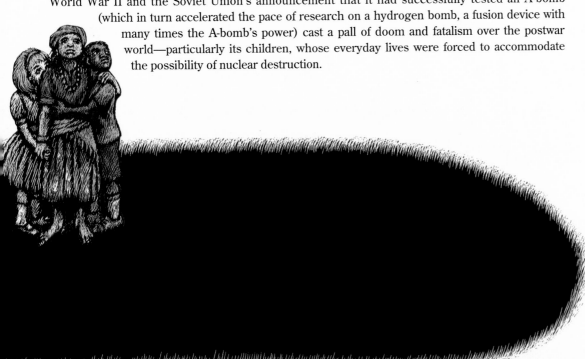

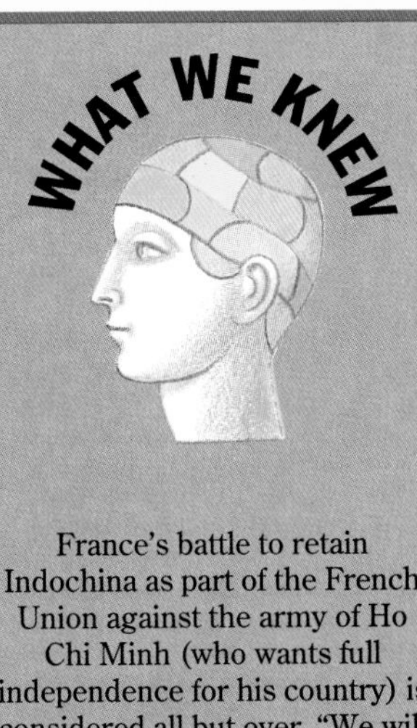

France's battle to retain Indochina as part of the French Union against the army of Ho Chi Minh (who wants full independence for his country) is considered all but over. "We will have a victory in 15 months," says General Jean de Lattre de Tassigny, commander in chief of French forces in Indochina.

A deep, dark tan is a sign of good looks, robust health, and affluence. Advertisements for suntan lotions tout the latest research (the sun is thought to emit two kinds of rays: those that burn and those than tan) and promise that their product will "block out harmful rays" and "admit about 90% of the healthful tanning rays."

The record for running a mile has been held for five years by Sweden's Gunder Haegg, who has achieved a time of 4:01.4. The four-minute mile is "the most important barrier in sport"—one that many sports experts believe cannot be broken without causing the runner's death.

Tonsillectomies are the most commonly performed surgery in the United States, the vast majority on children between the ages of five and 15. Doctors view tonsils as useless, and often downright harmful, and advocate removing two pairs—the palatines, and the adenoids—in order to lower the frequency of sore throats, common colds, and earaches.

The first computers have given observers great hope that their applicability and their sophistication will grow in inverse proportion to their unwieldiness. "Where a calculator on the ENIAC is equipped with 18,000 vacuum tubes and weighs 30 tons," *Popular Mechanics* optimistically predicts, "computers in the future may have only 1,000 vacuum tubes and perhaps only weigh 1½ tons."

Arthur C. Clarke

Destination Moon

The Dawn of the First Space Age

1950 1959

THE OPENING DATE OF WHAT I HAVE COME to think of as the First Space Age was October 4, 1957, when the Soviet Union launched the first artificial Earth satellite, *Sputnik 1.* It was humankind's inaugural leap toward the stars, and it would forever change the way our species saw its place in the universe. And so the world could not help but be startled and amazed—despite the fact that astronautics, far from being a new field, had been a subject of serious scientific study for more than half a century, and a favorite theme of fantasy writers for much longer.

Indeed, in the years just prior to *Sputnik*, scientific and public interest in space travel had reached a fever pitch. The enthusiasm was largely a product of 1950s culture: the era's burgeoning prosperity; its Cold War obsessions; its infatuation with technology (which had defeated Hitler, and which offered the average citizen an unprecedented array of labor-saving devices and entertainment options, most notably the new medium of television). If the automobile and airplane had influenced the aesthetics of earlier decades, the spaceship had become a guiding image of 1950s modernism even before the Soviet satellite flew. Outer space was the decade's glamour destination. Yet the process of reaching that destination involved the lonely labors of a handful of visionaries and the workaday exchange of information among a few hundred decidedly unglamorous scientists and technicians.

Jules Verne's famous novel *From the Earth to the Moon* (1865) was perhaps the first treatment of space travel that was *not* pure fantasy, as Verne did his considerable best to make a flight to the Moon appear a feasible engineering project. He gave the correct value for the velocity needed to escape from Earth—eleven kilometers a second—and even pointed out that rockets would operate in the vacuum of space. Verne's book was a prime inspiration for the three great pioneers of astronautics. The first, the Russian Konstantin Eduardovich Tsiolkovsky (1857–1935) published detailed, amazingly prescient descriptions of space vehicles, and even space stations, around the time the Wright Brothers were making their initial flights. He summed up his philosophy in the much-quoted epigram, "Earth is the cradle of the mind—but one cannot live in the cradle forever."

This painting by Chesley Bonestell—one of many that illustrated an influential series of articles by Wernher von Braun that appeared in *Collier's* magazine in the early 1950s—depicts an expedition to Mars preparing for the return flight to Earth after 15 months' exploration. The accompanying article, entitled "Can We Get to Mars?", warned, "The first men who set out for Mars had better make sure they leave everything at home in apple-pie order. They won't get back to Earth for more than two and a half years.... For more than a year, the explorers will have to live on the great red planet waiting for it to swing into a favorable position for the return trip."

To Robert Goddard (1882–1945) goes the distinction of achieving the first flight by a liquid-fueled rocket, in 1926, but his natural reticence, and his unfortunate experiences with the press—which branded him a crackpot and nicknamed him "Moony"—ensured that Goddard never published his dreams of space travel: They were all discovered after his death.

The Romanian-born German Hermann Oberth (1894–1989) had no such inhibitions. In 1929 he published a monumental thesis, *The Way to Space Travel*, having arrived—largely independently—at the same conclusions as Tsiolkovsky. This volume inspired a whole generation of experimenters, one of whom was a German teenager named Wernher von Braun. Thirteen years later, under von Braun's direction, the first V-2 rocket climbed to the edge of space. The technology needed to reach the Moon thus was demonstrated, albeit in the cause of war: Von Braun's V-2s, raining down on Britain, soon cost hundreds of lives. (The U.S. government later forgave—and hired—him.)

Although most ordinary people still found the idea of space travel far-fetched, by 1950 rocketry was capturing the imagination of growing numbers of scientists and engineers. That September, the first International Astronautical Congress convened in Paris, and many rocket pioneers

(including those whose nations had been enemies just five years earlier) forged lasting friendships. The next year, at the second congress in London, space-flight societies from eleven countries—mingling professional researchers, science-fiction writers like myself, and amateur enthusiasts—established the International Astronautical Federation. (Today, the IAF represents more than 100 organizations, including corporations and government bodies. It still holds annual congresses where the latest theories and experimental results are presented.)

As incoming chairman of the British Interplanetary Society, I had the duty of chairing the 1951 Congress, and the privilege of having Professor Oberth as my house guest. Had anyone told us that, only 18 years in the future, we would both watch the first spaceship leave for the Moon, I am sure we would have laughed. It *would* happen—of that we were certain—but we did not expect it in our lifetimes. "Early in the next century" would probably have been our most optimistic estimate.

1950
1959

TWO EVENTS IN THE EARLY FIFTIES played an important role in preparing the Western public to take space flight seriously. The first was the George Pal movie *Destination Moon* (1950), a groundbreaking special-effects spectacular co-scripted by the technologically erudite science fiction writer Robert Heinlein. It still makes fascinating viewing, even though much of it has been hopelessly dated by events in what a Hollywood denizen once called the "non-celluloid world." Probably even more influential was the series of articles entitled "Man Will Conquer Space Soon" (March 1952–April 1954) that appeared in the hugely popular *Colliers* magazine and were soon published in three handsome books: *Across the Space Frontier, Conquest of the Moon,* and *The Exploration of Mars.*

While the general public was softening under the influence of all this propaganda, a Fifth Column of space enthusiasts was at work inside the U.S. military and industrial establishments. By 1955, high-altitude rockets fired from New Mexico's White Sands Proving Ground had already explored the upper atmosphere before their brief flights terminated as large holes in the desert. What was obviously needed was an LPR—a Long-Playing Rocket. In other words, a satellite.

The need for a satellite had been the main theme of the 1951 IAF Congress. One paper, entitled "Minimum Satellite Vehicles," had a considerable influence on later developments. It asked—and answered—the question: "What is the smallest rocket that can launch a useful payload into orbit?" One of the designs presaged the U.S. Navy's *Vanguard.*

Still, some scientists remained skeptical, even those in fields that stood to benefit mightily from space technology. The New York Hayden Planetarium's Third Space Travel Symposium in 1954 provided a striking example of that skepticism. When the Planetarium asked me to arrange the program, I decided that it must include a paper on the value of satellites for meteorology. So I wrote to Dr. Harry Wexler, the chief scientist of the U.S. Weather Bureau, inviting him to contribute. To my surprise, he replied that satellites would be of no value to meteorologists. "In that case," I retorted, "it's your public duty to explain why we space cadets are talking nonsense, because for years we've been saying that they will transform your science." To his great credit, Dr. Wexler accepted my challenge. By the time he had prepared his "refutation," he had become a rabid enthusiast—and a few years later headed the U.S. weather satellite program.

Yes, the time was ripe—and in 1955 the power and the dream came together with the announcement of the International Geophysical Year (IGY, 1957-8), during which the world's scientists would cooperate on the most massive research project in history: to study planet Earth by every known means. Artificial satellites offered great promise, and in July 1955, the United States declared its intention of launching a satellite during the course of IGY. The Soviet Union (whose space researchers had just joined the IAF) quickly vowed to do the same, but no one took much notice: It seemed obvious that only the Americans had the technical ability to perform so spectacular a feat—especially as their army's top rocket engineers, under the charismatic von Braun, were busily developing long-range ballistic missiles that would spend much of their brief working life in space.

America's last manned mission to the moon was *Apollo 17*, in December 1972. Here, in an extraordinary image that even a decade earlier would have been pure science-fiction fantasy, *Apollo 17* commander Eugene A. Cernan explores the moon's Taurus-Littrow Valley in a "Lunar Roving Vehicle." The photograph was taken by geologist and lunar module pilot Harrison H. Schmitt. Traveling 22 miles in the LRV, Cernan and Schmitt spent 22 hours on the moon's surface while a third crew member, Naval Commander Ronald E. Evans, remained in lunar orbit.

However, President Eisenhower—reluctant to divert resources from nuclear-missile development to support rocketry of less obviously practical purposes—at first declined to involve von Braun's team in the space program. Instead, the Naval Research Laboratory was given the task of developing a satellite launch vehicle. (This was the initially embarrassing, though ultimately highly successful, *Vanguard.)* The Soviets, as it turned out, managed to send up their first intercontinental ballistic missile before the Americans. And they had no compunction about using military hardware for space exploration: *Sputnik* and its successors were launched by modified ballistic missiles. So, indeed, was America's own *Explorer 1* satellite, on January 31, 1958—carried into space aboard von Braun's *Jupiter-C* two months after the first *Vanguard* exploded on the launch pad.

But it was obvious from the beginning that the space race would involve more than satellites—however useful the latter might be for telecommunications, meteorology, astronomy, Earth observation, navigation, and espionage. Even before the *Vanguard* debacle, Moscow had launched *Sputnik 2,* carrying the little dog Laika. This demonstration that space travel was not instantly fatal, as some pessimists had predicted, sent a clear message regarding Soviet plans for sending humans into orbit, and within three years, Cosmonaut Yuri Gagarin would become the first man in space. In October 1958, a chagrined Eisenhower established the National Aeronautics and Space Administration (NASA); in April 1959, he announced the Mercury program, and the first seven U.S. astronauts—Alan Shepard, John Glenn, Walter Schirra, Scott Carpenter, Donald Slayton, Virgil Grissom, and Gordon Cooper—became household names.

IN 1961, PRESIDENT KENNEDY COMMITTED his nation to putting a man on the Moon before the decade was out—and he assigned Wernher von Braun to oversee the development of rockets for the trip. Ironically, Kennedy might never have issued his challenge had the Americans not lagged so far behind the Soviets: Some grand gesture was needed. The landing came in 1969. Yet just three years later, with the flight of *Apollo 17,* the First Space Age ended—an indirect casualty of the disastrous Vietnam War, which drained not only the U.S. budget, but also the public's enthusiasm for government-sponsored high-tech adventures.

When will we see the Second? I would wager that by 2020, improvements in propulsion and the whole spectrum of aerospace technologies will make possible far cheaper—and safer—access to the Moon and planets. However, when and whether a second great era of space exploration will occur depends as much upon political and social factors as on engineering. No one could have predicted that the pressures of the Cold War would open up space half a century ahead of schedule. Perhaps some development in the post-Cold War era—say, deepening ecological crisis—will spur our descendants to renew the quest for other worlds. Or perhaps the spirit of exploration (this time, as an international endeavor) will reassert itself as the quest for nuclear superiority loses its urgency.

Five years before the Space Age opened, in *The Exploration of Space* (1952), I tried to imagine how a historian in A.D. 3000 would look back on our time:

"The twentieth century was, without question, the most momentous … in the history of Mankind. It opened with the conquest of the air, and before it had run half its course had presented civilization with its supreme challenge—the control of atomic energy. Yet even these events … were soon to be eclipsed. To us … the whole story of Mankind before the twentieth century seems like the prelude to some great drama, played on the narrow strip of stage before the curtain has risen and revealed the scenery.… Yet towards the close of that fabulous century, the curtain began slowly, inexorably, to rise.… The coming of the rocket brought to an end a million years of isolation. With the landing of the first spaceships on Mars and Venus, the childhood of our race was over and history as we know it began.…"

Well, Venus—where lead melts in the shade—may have to wait, but the first men and women to walk on Mars have doubtless already been born. □

The United States won the race to the moon in the First Space Age, but the Soviet Union excelled in the launching of space stations, which orbit the earth for extended periods and are visited by crews arriving and departing in other vehicles. *Mir*, the successor to the *Salyut* space-station program, was launched by the Soviet Union in 1986 as the first permanently manned space station; it has remained constantly occupied, despite the dissolution of the Soviet Union. Cosmonauts have stayed in its cramped quarters *(right)* for more than a year. In late 1993, the once-warring superpowers signed an agreement to join efforts in space-station development. The first phase calls for the American space shuttle and *Mir* to link at least ten times from 1995 to 1997.

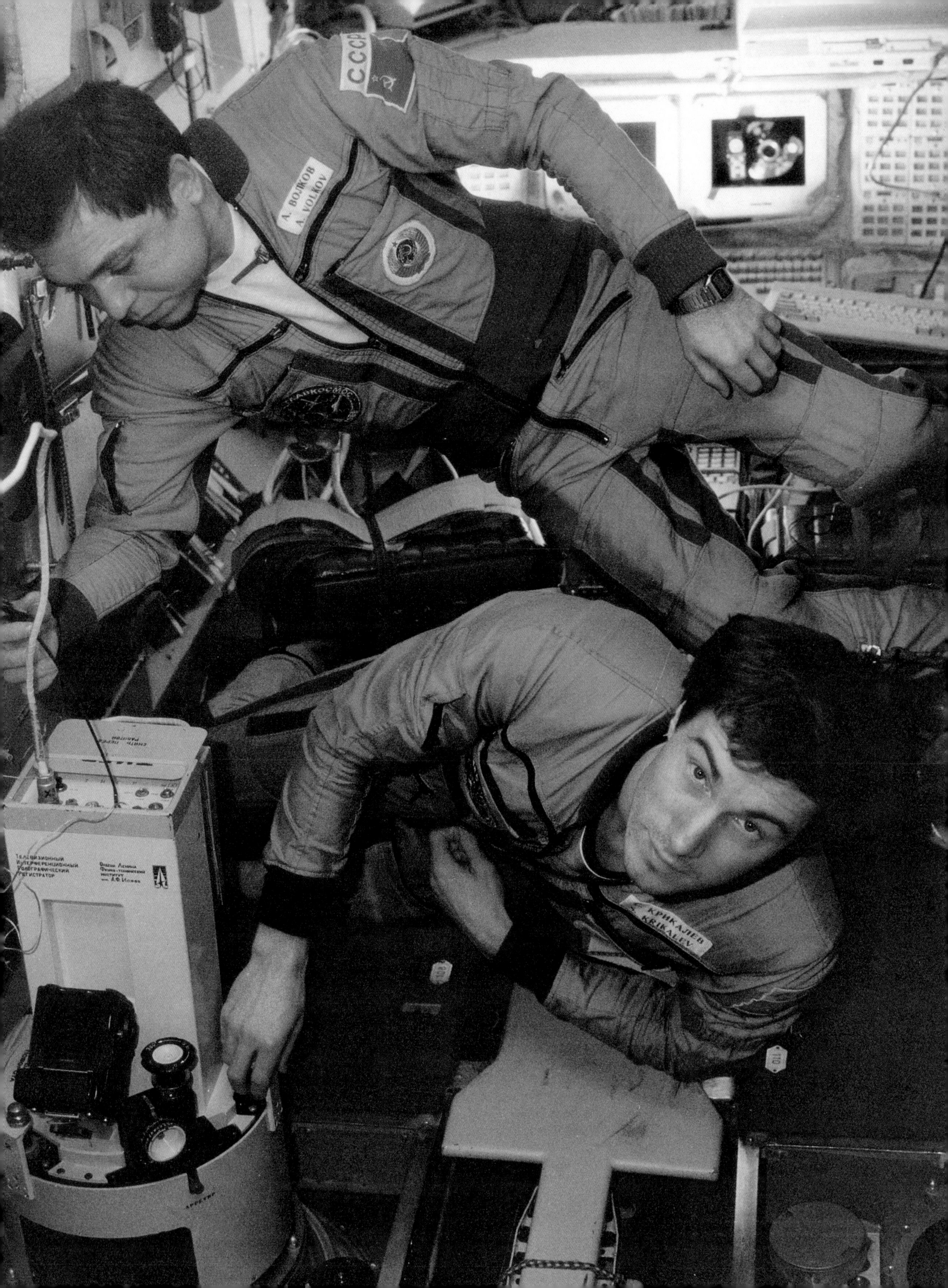
СССР
А. ВОЛКОВ
A. VOLKOV
КРИКАЛЕВ
KRIKALEV
Телевизионный
Интерференционный
Голографический
Регистратор

"To sit back now while Korea is overrun by unprovoked armed attack would probably start a disastrous chain of events leading most probably to world war."—**U.S. Special Ambassador John Foster Dulles, to President Truman**

STORY OF THE YEAR

The Korean War Begins

1 Before dawn on June 25, 1950, the Soviet-equipped North Korean People's Army crossed the 38th parallel into the Republic of South Korea. Two days later, after an emergency session of the Security Council (from which the Soviet delegate was voluntarily absent), the United Nations invited its members to assist South Korea against the invasion. President Truman immediately ordered U.S. air and naval forces into the fray; a few days later he added ground troops. Nominally a UN "police action" (the first such ever undertaken by that body) the Korean War was symbolically crucial. For Washington, it was a paradigm of the Cold War: In a remote land, the forces of democracy would meet the Communists head-on. "By God," said Truman, "I'm going to let them have it." Despite the fact that there was never a formal declaration of war, the conflict escalated to the point where, eventually, 20 nations were involved. The real fight, however, was perceived to be between the United States and the Soviet Union, with Communist China supporting.

In the first weeks of war, the North Korean People's Army steamrolled across South Korea, capturing the country's port city, Inchon, and its capital, Seoul (President Syngman Rhee's government left town), and putting pressure on the U.N. beachhead at Pusan, on the southeastern tip of the Korean Peninsula. Then General Douglas MacArthur, the erratic, 70-year-old World War II hero, was named supreme commander of UN forces. MacArthur executed a dramatic landing at Inchon and, in September, recaptured Seoul. Buoyed, the United States announced a new goal: Korean unification. In October, UN troops invaded North Korea, took its capital, Pyongyang, and rolled on toward the Chinese border.

North Koreans flee south during a Naktong River battle, summer 1950.

That move spurred China to send in 180,000 of its own troops. A fresh Communist offensive retook Pyongyang in December; by year's end, North Korea was again wholly under Communist control. Then, on December 31, the Chinese, vowing to "liberate Korea," and "drive warmonger MacArthur into the sea," moved on Seoul. By January 15, they had captured it. **◂1948.3 ▸1951.M**

VIETNAM

The Start of U.S. Aid

2 Ho Chi Minh had been a U.S. partisan during World War II, and when he proclaimed the Democratic Republic of Vietnam in 1945, he quoted America's Declaration of Independence. But by 1950 Washington saw him as a cat's paw of international communism; if he won his war against the country's French rulers, it would tip over the first domino and set the rest falling all over Asia. In February, after Mao and Stalin recognized Ho's Viet Minh government—then hiding in the jungle—the United States recognized the French-installed Bao Dai regime in Saigon. In May, President Truman, urged on by Secretary of State Dean Acheson *(above)*, one of the principal architects of American policy in Vietnam, authorized $15 million in military aid to France to fight the Viet Minh. By year's end, spurred by the Communist invasion of South Korea, the ante had been upped to $133 million—plus $50 million in nonmilitary supplies to win the loyalty of the Vietnamese people.

The United States had stepped into a quagmire. The Viet Minh, under the brilliant General Vo Nguyen Giap, were fighting a three-stage war inspired by Mao's military writings—a war of sheer patience that had already drained France's treasury and divided its citizens. In the first stage, Giap had avoided confrontations while building an army of 100,000. Since 1947 that army had demoralized the enemy with hit-and-run guerrilla attacks. And now that Mao's victory provided staging areas and access to Chinese and Soviet supplies, it was time for all-out battles. Viet Minh regulars overran six northern garrisons by December.

That month, France fired its senior officials in Indochina and made General Jean de Lattre de Tassigny—a hero of both world wars—the region's military and political chief. De Lattre managed to repulse several major attacks, but when he died of cancer in 1952, two thirds of Vietnam remained in Viet Minh hands. The stage was set for the final French defeat and deepening U.S. involvement. **◂1949.7 ▸1954.1**

The Red Army built bridges and transported trucks on rafts across Tibet's rivers.

CHINA

Tibet Is Conquered

3 When the newborn People's Republic of China offered "liberation" to Tibet in 1950, the Tibetan government protested that the mountain-ringed nation was already free. But in October, hewing to the fiction that international imperialists actually controlled the country, China sent some 20,000 People's Liberation Army troops across the border. The tiny Tibetan army offered little resistance. The 15-year-old Dalai Lama (Tibet's temporal and spiritual leader, revered as an incarnation of a divine Tibetan ancestor) appealed to the United Nations for aid—in vain.

A pastoral land where one in six males was a Buddhist lama (monk), Tibet had first come under direct Chinese control in the eighteenth century. In 1912, when China's Manchu Dynasty collapsed, Tibet expelled all Chinese and announced its independence. But its sovereignty was never internationally recognized, and both Nationalists and Communists insisted that the country belonged to China. When Mao's forces defeated the Nationalists in 1949, they vowed to carry their revolution to China's remotest corners.

Promising to respect Tibetan cultural and religious traditions, the invaders forced the nation's leaders to agree to annexation in 1951. Eight years later, simmering Tibetan resentment erupted in revolt, which was brutally quashed. Thereafter, repression intensified, Buddhism was outlawed, and the Dalai Lama went into exile in India.
◂1940.M ▸1959.3

ART

The Abstract Expressionists

4 Change was in the air—and on the walls—at the 1950 Venice Biennale, an international art fair that showcases contemporary art.

ART & CULTURE: Books: ***Across the River and into the Trees*** **(Ernest Hemingway);** ***A Brief Life*** **(Juan Carlos Onetti);** ***The Moon and the Bonfire*** **(Cesare Pavese);** ***Canto General*** **(Pablo Neruda);** ***The Human Use of Human Beings*** **(Norbert Wiener);** ***Some Tame Gazelle*** **(Barbara Pym) ... Music: "Frosty the Snowman" (Rollins and Nelson); "If I Knew You Were Comin' I'd've Baked a Cake" (Hoffman, Merrill,**

"Painting is self-discovery. Every good artist paints what he is."—**Jackson Pollock**

A proliferation of works influenced by fauvism, cubism, futurism, and expressionism demonstrated that Europe's boldest artistic experiments had become almost mainstream. Now the most startling innovations were to be found in the United States Pavilion, where a small sampling of paintings by Jackson Pollock and Willem de Kooning exemplified a radical new movement known as abstract expressionism.

The ascendance of these Manhattan-based artists was an index of how fundamentally World War II had transformed the art world. Many of Europe's greatest creative spirits (like the Dutch-born de Kooning) had abandoned their homelands for America; the New York School had gained the edge over the School of Paris. New York's stimulating bustle of intellectuals, dealers, galleries, and museums was irresistible to visionaries and charlatans alike.

Willem de Kooning's *Woman I* (1950-52), part of a series he painted over 5 years.

Critics were divided as to which description best fit Pollock. The hard-living painter (who died in a car crash in 1956 at age 42) had stood uncomfortably in the spotlight since the late forties, when he'd developed his "drip" technique (also called "action" painting because he moved around a large canvas spread out on the floor). *Time* magazine derided him as "Jack the Dripper," but by 1950 he'd been championed by such influential tastemakers as *Nation* critic Clement Greenberg and the Museum of Modern Art's Alfred Barr—who praised Pollock's vistas of dribbles and splotches as "an energetic adventure for the eyes ... full of fireworks, pitfalls, surprises and delights." Together with de Kooning (whose first *Women* series blended a similarly wild array of brushwork with recognizable imagery), as well as other abstract expressionists like Franz Kline, Ad Reinhardt, Robert Motherwell, Lee Krasner (Pollock's wife), Clyfford Still, and Helen Frankenthaler, Pollock ushered in what has been called "the first significant change in pictorial space since cubism." In the process he permanently expanded the definition of painting. **◂1944.16 ▸1958.5**

For *Number 1* (1948), Pollock dripped oil and enamel on a 5' 8" × 8' 8" unprimed canvas.

THE UNITED STATES

McCarthy's Witch-Hunts

5 By 1950, with communism triumphant in China and Eastern Europe and revolutionary movements emerging throughout the Third World (a term popularized by the Marxist writer Frantz Fanon to describe economically underdeveloped countries that fell into neither bloc of the Cold War), America was in the grip of its worst red scare ever. The Truman administration was investigating federal employees for Communist "tendencies." The House Committee on Un-American Activities' mission to root out subversives had yielded a prize catch: onetime State Department official Alger Hiss, convicted of perjury in January for denying a former Communist's allegation that he'd once spied for the Soviets. (The statute of limitations had expired for an espionage charge.) Then, on February 9, Wisconsin senator Joseph McCarthy jumped to the head of the red-hunting pack. During a speech in West Virginia, he brandished a sheaf of paper, claiming that it listed 205 Communists who'd infiltrated the State Department.

A master of props, McCarthy points out to Congress the geographic distribution of alleged "fellow travelers."

McCarthy offered no evidence, but his charge created a sensation. The formerly inconspicuous Republican (who'd praised Stalin a mere four years earlier) used his newfound notoriety to full demagogic advantage. His first targets were Democrats (whom he attacked as "dupes" or "fellow travelers" of the "Commies"), but politicians of both parties scrambled onto his bandwagon. Congress passed the McCarran Act, which required Communist and vaguely defined "Communist front" groups to register with the government and called for subversives to be herded into concentration camps in a national emergency. On the basis of past associations (real or rumored), thousands of people were blacklisted; some were jailed, some hounded into suicide. Movies and magazines caught the spirit, warning of "a red under every bed."

Terror of McCarthy and his allies exacerbated the rampant conformism that characterized 1950s America. That terror made him seem unstoppable even when he turned on fellow Republicans. But then he went after the sacrosanct U.S. Army. **◂1947.5 ▸1954.V**

BIRTHS

John Candy, Canadian-U.S. actor.

Julius Erving, U.S. basketball player.

Peter Gabriel, U.K. singer.

Henry Louis Gates, Jr., U.S. writer.

Jenny Holzer, U.S. artist.

John Hughes, U.S. filmmaker.

Neil Jordan, Irish filmmaker.

Gary Larson, U.S. cartoonist.

Jay Leno, U.S. comedian.

Bill Murray, Candian-U.S. comedian.

Mark Spitz, U.S. swimmer.

Wendy Wasserstein, U.S. playwright.

Stevie Wonder, U.S. singer.

Stevan Wozniak, U.S. inventor.

DEATHS

Max Beckmann, German painter.

Léon Blum, French political leader.

Edgar Rice Burroughs, U.S. novelist.

Willis H. Carrier, U.S. inventor.

Gustavus V, Swedish king.

Karl Jansky, U.S. engineer.

Al Jolson, U.S. entertainer.

W.L. Mackenzie King, Canadian political leader.

Edgar Lee Masters, U.S. writer.

Edna St. Vincent Millay, U.S. poet.

Fats Navarro, U.S. musician.

Vaslav Nijinsky, Russian ballet dancer.

George Orwell (Eric Blair), U.K. writer.

George Bernard Shaw, Irish dramatist.

Jan C. Smuts, South African political leader.

Henry L. Stimson, U.S. statesman.

Kurt Weill, German-U.S. composer.

Elsie de Wolfe, U.S. interior designer.

and Watts); *A Psalm of David* (Norman Dello Joio) ... Painting & Sculpture: *Lavender Mist* (Jackson Pollock) ... Film: *All About Eve* (Joseph L. Mankiewicz); *Sunset Blvd.* (Billy Wilder); *The Asphalt Jungle* (John Huston); *La Ronde* (Max Ophüls) ... Theater: *The Rose Tattoo* (Tennessee Williams); *The Rehearsal* (Jean Anouilh) ... TV: *What's My Line*; *The George Burns and Gracie Allen Show*; *Your Show of Shows*.

"He has taken over our collective consciousness and become a part of our everyday lives."—**French minister of culture Jack Lang, on Snoopy, at the 1990 *Peanuts* exhibition at the Louvre**

1950

NEW IN 1950

Betty Crocker's Picture Cook Book.

Credit card (Diner's Club).

Port Authority Bus Terminal (New York City).

No other rice is this easy!
MINUTE RICE
No washing! No rinsing! No draining! No steaming!
Minute Rice is already cooked—
Just add to boiling water and remove from heat!

Minute Rice.

Drivers World Championship (Grand Prix racing).

IN THE UNITED STATES

▶COLE'S MAGIC—Admired by jazz purists for his clean piano style as the leader of the ultrahot King Cole Trio, Nat King Cole started as a vocalist in the forties on a lark, then discovered audiences loved his rich voice and relaxed, jazz-influenced delivery. Cole struck gold in 1950, when his recording of the treacly "Mona Lisa" sold more than three million copies.

▶RACKETS PROBED—Chairing televised hearings before the Senate Crime Investigating Committee, Senator Estes Kefauver began exposing America's criminal underbelly in May. Millions of transfixed viewers watched the testimony of such big cheese mobsters as Frank Costello and Joe Adonis. The Kefauver probe marked the beginning of electronic journalism. ▶1952.5

▶THE BRINK'S JOB—The biggest armed robbery of its time was pulled off at the Boston headquarters of the Brink's armored-truck company on the evening of January 17. Seven bandits wearing masks and pea coats subdued guards at gunpoint and made off with $2.7 million. FBI chief J. Edgar Hoover suspected a

POPULAR CULTURE

Good Ol' Charlie Brown

6 "Happiness does not create humor. There's nothing funny about being happy." Thus spake Charles Schulz, who became a billionaire by creating a cast of charmingly maladjusted cartoon characters. Schulz, a Minneapolis native who studied his craft in a correspondence course, protested when United Features changed the title of his comic strip from *Li'l Folks* to *Peanuts* (alluding to the young studio audience, known as the "peanut gallery," on television's *Howdy Doody* show). But once the strip debuted in seven newspapers on October 2, 1950, neither the name nor Schulz's rudimentary style prevented it from becoming a runaway success.

Featuring the perpetually insecure Charlie Brown, his daydream-addicted dog, Snoopy, bossy Lucy, contemplative Linus, and a small community of other nonadults, the *Peanuts* troupe attained a level of worldwide popularity comparable only to that of Walt Disney's animated menagerie. But while Mickey Mouse and company won audiences with their unbridled good cheer, Schulz's creations (though capable of such sentiments as the famous "Happiness is a warm puppy") worried incessantly over matters ranging from exam-taking to radioactive fallout.

By the mid-1990s, *Peanuts* had been translated into more than two dozen languages, distributed to more than 2,000 newspapers, adopted by the Apollo 10 astronauts, and included in advertisements, books, movies, television specials, stage productions, recordings, posters, greeting cards, and countless other products. And Schulz had even allowed Charlie Brown a moment of unalloyed triumph: After four decades of losses on the pitcher's mound, the luckless boy whose characteristic expression was "Good grief!" finally won a baseball game. **◂1908.V ▸1970.V**

THEATER

Ionesco's Absurdist Debut

7 *The Bald Soprano,* Eugène Ionesco's first play (or "anti-play," as he called it), was inspired by the phrases of a beginners' English conversation manual that the Paris-based Romanian émigré was struggling with. One of the first examples of the theater of the absurd, it premiered in an obscure Paris theater in 1950 when its author was 38 years old. The protagonists, a middle-class English couple, jabber a senseless stream of truisms ("the floor is below us, the ceiling above us") and live in a town whose residents all seem to be named Bobby Watson. In the play's horrifying, hilarious world, clichés have taken on a life of their own, and people have become automatons. Consciousness, will, and the possibility of communicating have all been vanquished by the conventions of society.

Absurd yet hilarious, Ionesco's plays are allegories of human estrangement.

Ionesco's drama combines the insights of Sartre and Camus—existence is meaningless, yet individuals are responsible for shaping their own lives—with shock tactics inherited from both the surrealists and the Marx Brothers. On one level, his plays are social satires. (In his later play *Rhinoceros,* respectable townspeople turn into horned, armored animals—an allegory inspired by the rise of Romanian fascism in the 1930s.)

But like his contemporaries Jean Genet and Samuel Beckett, Ionesco was essentially a critic of humanity's relations with the universe. The babbling of his characters and the irrationality of his narratives are meant to jolt viewers into rethinking such basic concepts as time, death, freedom, and the self. **◂1943.10 ▸1953.11**

THEATER

A "Can-Do" Musical

8 As the fifties dawned, the Broadway musical was at the top of its form. And on November 24, 1950, it reached something close to perfection when a troupe of Times Square gamblers and salvationists took over the 46th Street Theatre and unfolded the tale of the romances between crap-game promoter Nathan Detroit and his long-suffering chorine, Miss Adelaide, and city slicker Sky Masterson and uptight mission worker Sarah Brown. *Guys & Dolls*—with a book by Abe Burrows (though Jo Swerling gets official credit), songs by Frank Loesser, and direction by George S. Kaufman—became one of the best-loved works in Broadway history.

Based on stories by former newspaperman Damon Runyon, *Guys & Dolls* is a slangy, funny look at Broadway grifters and the women who love them. Burrows's libretto (he was the twelfth writer on the project) is wittily acerbic and psychologically acute. Loesser's music defines the characters just as deftly—in the brassy opening number, "The Fugue for Tinhorns" (sung by three horseplayers, each of whom proclaims that his horse "can do"), the romantic "I've Never Been in Love Before" (for Sky and Sarah), the urgent "Luck Be a Lady" (for Sky and fellow crapshooters), the rollicking revival hymn "Sit Down, You're Rockin' the Boat" (for a penitent gambler), and the plaintive "Adelaide's Lament" (for Nathan's lovelorn fiancée, who has a chronic psychosomatic cold).

"The big trouble with [*Guys & Dolls*]," said one rave review,

Schulz's first cartoons did not feature all the later members of the *Peanuts* gang, nor all of Charlie Brown's endearing idiosyncrasies.

SPORTS: Baseball: World Series, New York Yankees defeat Philadelphia Phillies, 4–0 ... Football: NFL, Cleveland Browns defeat Los Angeles Rams, 30–28 ... Basketball: NBA, Minneapolis Lakers defeat Syracuse Nationals, 4–2 ... Soccer: World Cup, Uruguay defeats Brazil, 2–1 (first competition since 1938).

"The creation of Dianetics is a milestone for Man comparable to his discovery of fire and superior to his inventions of the wheel and arch."—**L. Ron Hubbard, in *Dianetics: The Modern Science of Mental Health***

Taking their game to a sewer underneath Manhattan, Nathan Detroit (Sam Levene) and fellow crapshooters look on as Sky Masterson (Robert Alda) begs, "Luck, be a lady."

"is that a performance of it lasts only one evening, when it ought to last about a week." Forty-two years later, a full-scale Broadway revival was received with rapture, including a front-page photo in *The New York Times.* **◄1943.11 ►1956.8**

TURKEY

A Shot of Democracy

9 Turkey underwent a peaceful revolution in May 1950, when voters rejected the Republican People's Party (RPP) for the first time since the nation's birth in 1923. Kemal Atatürk, the republic's founder, had always envisioned Turkey as a Western-style democracy—yet he'd suppressed all rival parties, claiming his people were unready for such experiments. Atatürk's successor, Ismet Inönü, initially followed suit. But by the end of World War II, discontent with one-party rule was rife.

Capitalists groused about Turkey's stifling bureaucracy, workers about inflation and a strike ban. Landowners grumbled at a new land-redistribution policy, peasants at its inadequacy. Traditionalist Muslims still rankled under Atatürk's secularist reforms. Liberals deplored the regime's suppression of dissent. Inönü relented and legalized opposition parties (except the Communists and Socialists) in 1945. And though elections the next year were rigged, the fledgling Democrat Party (DP) made an estimable showing with 61 seats in the National Assembly.

The DP's most prominent member was former premier and RPP leader Celâl Bayar *(below left)*. As Atatürk's finance minister in the 1930s, Bayar had ushered in state economic control; now he promised free enterprise, legalization of strikes, and relaxation of the secularist laws. Profiting from Inönü's easing of press curbs, the DP thrived, and in 1950—in Turkey's first secret ballot election—the party won 396 out of 487 parliamentary seats.

After becoming president, Bayar ran Turkey for the next decade. He aligned his country with NATO and the United States, contributing 25,000 Turks to the Korean War and winning lavish trade concessions. But strikes remained illegal, and inflation and repression returned. In 1960 reformist army officers deposed and jailed him—in the name of Atatürk. **◄1923.12 ►1960.10**

RELIGION

Sci-fi Theologian

10 Could 50,000 disciples be wrong? According to the judges, government agencies, law-enforcement officers, and cult experts who waged a campaign against L. Ron Hubbard's Los Angeles–based Church of Scientology, the answer was yes. The question was prompted in 1950 when Hubbard, a writer of pulp science fiction, published *Dianetics: The Modern Science of Mental Health*—his church's first sacred scripture. Offering a program of psychic healing through electronics, Scientology gained thousands of followers (estimates range from 50,000 to eight million) and earned its founder a fortune.

In the argot of Scientology, Dianetics "clears" people of unhappiness by "auditing" them—hooking them up to lie detectors to identify and purge "engrams," or mental aberrations. Explaining how he devised the system, Hubbard wrote of his frustration in reading traditional philosophy: "I found, oddly enough, that nobody could tell me what man was." His own research, he reported, led to the discovery that humans descended from space creatures banished to earth eons ago by a stellar dictator. He also claimed to have visited heaven. Hubbard shared his enlightenment with church members—for a price. Climbing all eight rungs of the ladder to Dianetic nirvana might cost upwards of $400,000.

After the Internal Revenue Service stripped the organization of its tax-exempt status in 1967, Hubbard (who privately urged church officials to "make money. Make more money. Make others produce so as to make money") launched a lengthy series of lawsuits, supported by an illicit intelligence operation against U.S. government agencies. Many of Hubbard's aides were subsequently jailed for fraud and extortion. The Church of Scientology survived, however; in 1993, seven years after Hubbard's death, the government restored its tax-exempt status. **►1982.4**

Scientology founder Lafayette Ron Hubbard, in an experimental greenhouse in London.

IN THE UNITED STATES

Communist conspiracy, but the haul was the work of small-time Boston hoods. The robbers eluded the FBI for six years before a betrayed gang member sang. The FBI arrested ten culprits, but recovered only $50,000.

►CULTURE OF CONFORMITY—The title of sociologist David Riesman's 1950 book, *The Lonely Crowd* (written with Nathan Glazer and Reuel Denney), became shorthand for the alienated contemporary middle class. Riesman claimed that the predominant American social trait was conformity: Individuals had become "other-directed," molded by peer groups, as opposed to "inner-directed," or individualistic. Both terms entered the ever-growing, quasi-scientific pop-culture lexicon.

►PHILOSOPHY AS SCIENCE—In his *Logical Foundations of Probability,* German-born U.S. philosopher Rudolf Carnap delineated a theory of inductive logic (the derivation of a general hypothesis from specific evidence). A leading exponent of the philosophical school known as logical positivism, Carnap attempted to reduce philosophy to a purely mathematical and scientific investigation. ◄1910.4

►THE ORIGINAL STONE—In 1950, Muddy Waters, né McKinley Morganfield, released "Rolling Stone," the song from which the British rock band and the American magazine derived their names. Born near the Mississippi Delta, birthplace of the passionate folk music called the blues, Waters went north to Chicago during the great black migration of the 1940s. Marrying country blues to big-city dance dynamism, he perfected a new, hard-driving genre, the Chicago blues, one of the most influential of modern musical styles. ►1955.13

POLITICS & BUSINESS: GNP: $284.8 billion ... U.S. population: 151,325,798 ... U.S. Army calls up 62,000 men for a 21-month tour of duty ... Illiteracy reaches new low of 3.2% ... General Motors announces a 1949 corporate profit of over $650 million (largest to date).

"It's horrible—if men do not tell the truth, do not trust one another, then the earth becomes hell indeed."
—From Akira Kurosawa's *Rashomon*

AROUND THE WORLD

▶A MODERN MUSE—Nadia Boulanger, who was made director of the American Conservatory at Fontainebleau, France, in 1950, achieved musical immortality not through what she wrote but through whom she taught: Aaron Copland, Marc Blitzstein, Walter Piston, and Virgil Thomson, among other leading American modernists. Boulanger had given up composing after the death in 1918 of her equally gifted sister, Lili (the first woman to win the coveted Prix de Rome). Nadia was also a noted conductor—the first woman to conduct the New York and Boston philharmonics and the Philadelphia Orchestra. ◀1948.M ▶1957.9

▶SCOTS STEAL STONE—A band of young Scottish nationalists broke into London's Westminster Abbey on Christmas Day and briefly repossessed an ancient symbol of Scottish patrimony. From the ninth century, Scottish kings were crowned on the 336-pound Stone of Scone—a tradition that ended in 1296, when King Edward I of England invaded Scotland and moved the "stone of destiny" south. Set under England's Coronation Chair, it became an emblem of English dominion over Scotland. Four months after its theft, the coveted stone was recovered and replaced in the abbey.

▶LESSING'S LESSONS—Born in Persia and raised in colonial Rhodesia, Englishwoman Doris Lessing was a politically committed and sympathetic chronicler of the tragedies wrought by colonialism. Her first novel, *The Grass Is Singing*, published in 1950, centers on an embittered colonial wife and her possible murder by her African servant and sometime lover. Like Lessing's later books (including her 1962 feminist classic *The Golden Notebook*), her first is notable for its vivid realism and acute insight into women's lives. ▶1991.M

1950

FILM

Japanese Cinema Arrives

11 A philosophical conundrum masquerading as a costume drama, Akira Kurosawa's *Rashomon* was released in Japan in 1950 to poor reviews and middling ticket sales. Its producers, baffled by its ambiguities and doubtful that audiences abroad would understand *any* Japanese film not made for foreigners, grudgingly submitted it to the Venice International Film Festival the following year. But after *Rashomon* won the Grand Prix—and an Academy Award for Best Foreign Film—cinema became one of Japan's most important exports.

Set in the sixteenth century, *Rashomon* is a meditation on truth, deception, and self-deception. The story revolves around a police hearing in which various people involved in the rape of a noblewoman and the apparent murder of her husband—including a medium who speaks for the dead man—give contradictory accounts of the double crime. Each character, confessing to assorted outrages and derelictions, is convinced he or she could have acted in no other way. Just when the message seems to be one of amorality and despair, a single act affirms the possibility of compassion and hope. Gorgeously atmospheric and powerfully acted, the movie thrilled jaded Western cineastes.

With *Rashomon*, Kurosawa *(foreground)* introduced the West to Japanese film.

Japan had no shortage of great directors (Kenji Mizoguchi and Yasujiro Ozu were among the world's finest), but Kurosawa was the first to be internationally recognized—and widely imitated. Illness and frustrations with Japanese studios led him to attempt suicide in 1971, but the prolific director, then in his 60s, survived to create the Oscar-winning Soviet-Japanese co-production *Dersu Uzala* (1975) and the majestic *King Lear* adaptation *Ran* (1985). **▶1991.12**

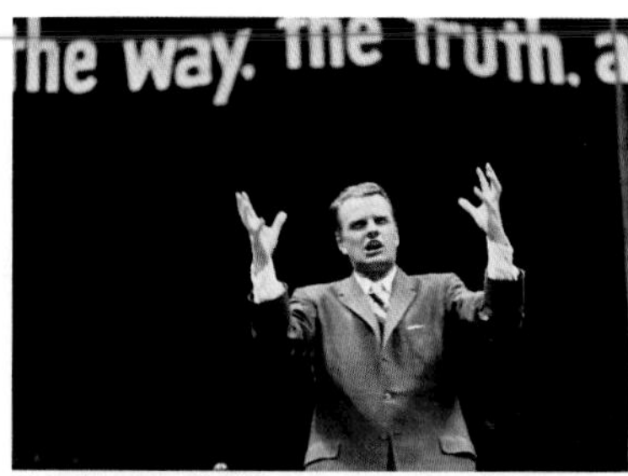

The Reverend Billy Graham in 1957, preaching at New York City's Madison Square Garden.

RELIGION

Graham's Electronic Pulpit

12 Baptist preacher Billy Graham began his rise to multimedia superstardom in 1950, when he launched the weekly radio show *Hour of Decision.* Graham, 31, had worked the tent-revival circuit since his teens—but he'd gotten his big break just months earlier. Sermonizing in Los Angeles, he'd converted a raffish entertainer, a gangster, and a former Olympic track star. Sensing the preacher's star potential, newspaper mogul William Randolph Hearst ordered his reporters to "puff" Graham. By the start of 1950, he was the best-known Bible-thumper in the country—exhorting sinners everywhere to surrender their souls to Jesus Christ.

Not since the 1930s had an evangelist made such a splash. Graham's predecessors—Billy Sunday, Aimee Semple McPherson—had been flamboyant hucksters, frankly hustling "love offerings" (cash donations) from their followers. But Graham was a new breed: earnest, wholesome, tastefully groomed. His bland charisma was perfect for the conformist fifties. And he was a sophisticated businessman. *Hour of Decision* quickly became the most successful religious radio show ever, with 15 million listeners. The next year, Graham began televising his revival meetings; soon his empire included a magazine and a publishing company. He became an international figure, a confidant of movie stars and several American presidents.

Aside from mildly supporting the civil rights movement and mildly opposing the peace movement during the early years of the Vietnam War, Graham (unlike his often militantly right-wing colleagues) avoided taking specific political stands. His image was tarnished by his friendship with Richard Nixon during the Watergate era, but he avoided personal scandal. The generation of "televangelists" who followed him would not be so lucky. **◀1926.M ▶1987.M**

MUSIC

Casals Breaks His Silence

13 The century's greatest cellist returned to the concert stage in 1950 after a four-year "renunciation." A passionate democrat, Pablo Casals had fled Spain in 1936 under threat of execution by Francisco Franco's Nationalist rebels. When Franco's quasi-fascist regime won international diplomatic recognition in 1946, Casals put down his bow in protest. But four years later, he picked it up again for the bicentenary of Johann Sebastian Bach's death. Some of the world's most celebrated musicians converged on Prades, the French town where Casals had settled, to accompany him.

A child prodigy on the piano, organ, and violin, Casals did not hear a cello until he was eleven—but within a dozen years he had played for Queen Victoria. His interpretations (notably of Bach's unaccompanied suites) blended tenderness, fire, and unparalleled subtleties of tone. By 1919, Casals was the finest musician in his field; that year he founded his own orchestra in Barcelona and cofounded the Ecole Normale de Musique in Paris. Yet he remained an earthy, unpretentious man, playing concerts for workers before the Spanish Civil War and aiding refugees during World War II.

Casals remained in self-imposed exile, relocating to Puerto Rico in 1956. He continued to perform—and to campaign for world peace—almost until his death in 1973 at age 97. **▶1971.9**

Casals in 1916, before he quit performing to protest Franco's recognition.

NOBEL PRIZES: Peace: Ralph Bunche (U.S.; mediation of Palestine dispute) ... Literature: Bertrand Russell (U.K.; philosopher) ... Chemistry: Otto Diels and Kurt Alder (German; diene synthesis) ... Medicine: Philip Hench, Edward C. Kendall (U.S.) and Tadeus Reichstein (Polish-Swiss; cortisone) ... Physics: Cecil Frank Powell (U.K.; atomic nuclei photography and mesons).

A VOICE FROM 1950

Poetry and the Human Spirit

Nobel Prize acceptance speech, by William Faulkner, December 10, 1950

"If a story is in you," William Faulkner once said, "it has got to come out." His first novels took awhile to percolate: Before seriously starting to write, Faulkner drifted around his beloved South, joined the RAF in Canada during World War I (he wanted to fight for democracy, but not for the Yanks), and enrolled briefly at the University of Mississippi in his hometown of Oxford. Once he began writing, the stories, narratively oblique and chronologically limber, full of psychological insight and formal experimentation, flowed forth in a torrent. In his 1950 Nobel Prize acceptance speech, the often cryptic author explained in crystalline language his vision of literature and of humanity. ◂**1929.3**

The Swedish Academy praised Faulkner *(above, seated at right, and below, at home in Oxford, Mississippi)* for "his powerful and artistically unique contribution to the modern American novel," and called him "the greatest experimentalist among twentieth-century novelists."

I feel that this award was not made to me as a man, but to my work—a life's work in the agony and sweat of the human spirit, not for glory and least of all for profit, but to create out of the materials of the human spirit something which did not exist before. So this award is only mine in trust. It will not be difficult to find a dedication for the money part of it commensurate with the purpose and significance of its origin. But I would like to do the same with the acclaim, too, by using this moment as a pinnacle from which I might be listened to by the young men and women already dedicated to the same anguish and travail, among whom is already that one who will someday stand where I am standing.

Our tragedy today is a general and universal physical fear so long sustained by now that we can even bear it. There are no longer problems of the spirit. There is only the question: When will I be blown up? Because of this, the young man or woman writing today has forgotten the problem of the human heart in conflict with itself which alone can make good writing because only that is worth writing about, worth the agony and the sweat.

He must learn them again. He must teach himself that the basest of all things is to be afraid; and, teaching himself that, forget it forever, leaving no room in this workshop for anything but the old verities and truths of the heart, the universal truths lacking which any story is ephemeral and doomed—love and honor and pity and pride and compassion and sacrifice. Until he does so, he labors under a curse. He writes not of love but of lust, of defeats in which nobody loses anything of value, of victories without hope and, worst of all, without pity or compassion. His griefs grieve on no universal bones, leaving no scars. He writes not of the heart but of the glands.

Until he learns these things, he will write as though he stood among and watched the end of man. I decline to accept the end of man. It is easy enough to say that man is immortal simply because he will endure: that when the last ding-dong of doom has clanged and faded from the last worthless rock hanging tideless in the last red and dying evening, that even then there will be one more sound: that of his puny inexhaustible voice, still talking. I refuse to accept this. I believe that man will not merely endure: he will prevail. He is immortal, not because he alone among creatures has an inexhaustible voice, but because he has a soul, a spirit capable of compassion and sacrifice and endurance. The poet's, the writer's, duty is to write about these things. It is his privilege to help man endure by lifting his heart, by reminding him of the courage and honor and hope and pride and compassion and pity and sacrifice which have been the glory of the past. The poet's voice need not merely be the record of man, it can be one of the props, the pillars to help him endure and prevail.

8-FOOT 'GENIUS' DEDICATED—**Headline in *The New York Times*, June 15, 1951, on UNIVAC**

STORY OF THE YEAR

Computers Go Commercial

1 In the popular imagination, they were still fearful things, Huxleyan "mechanical brains" and "robot machines." But first-generation computers had shown their usefulness during World War II (largely for breaking codes), and leading engineers recognized the enormous potential of devices that could solve problems in milliseconds. By 1951, all-electronic computers (using vacuum tubes instead of moving parts) were just beginning to be used for civilian purposes in the United States and Britain. The information age was dawning.

Bankrolled by Remington Rand, the all-electronic UNIVAC was room-sized.

A British tea concern, J. Lyons & Company, was the world's first commercial underwriter of electronic computers. In 1951 its LEO (Lyons Electronic Office) machine—based on the EDSAC (Electronic Delay Storage Automatic Calculator), the prototype stored-program computer developed by Maurice Wilkes and his team of engineers at Cambridge—began performing clerical tasks in the firm's home office. But it was in America that the computer industry was on the verge of becoming a major economic force. There, commercial development was spearheaded by two prescient scientists, John Eckert and John Mauchly. In 1946, while at the University of Pennsylvania, Eckert and Mauchly built ENIAC, the first all-purpose, all-electronic digital computer, for the U.S. Army. Disenchanted with the slow pace and conflicting goals of academic research, the men left Penn shortly afterward to form Eckert-Mauchly Computing Corporation (EMCC). Brilliant engineers but poor businessmen, Eckert and Mauchly foundered on the edge of bankruptcy until 1950, when Remington Rand, a major office-supply company, bought their business. The following year, the engineers delivered UNIVAC (Universal Automatic Computer) to the U.S. Census Bureau in Philadelphia.

Using magnetic tape instead of bulky punch cards for information input and output, and capable of reading 7,200 digits per second and of handling alphabetic as well as numeric characters with ease, UNIVAC was far and away the best computer yet built. Its success sent ripples through the business-machine industry (still dependent on mechanical devices), forcing sales leader IBM to revise its low opinion of electronic computing. Determined to protect its market, Big Blue (so nicknamed for its blue logo) set to work on its own line of "thinking" machines. Over the next three decades, as such machines spread gradually across the planet, most would be labeled IBM. **◄1946.M ►1971.5**

THE UNITED STATES

The Rosenbergs Convicted

2 In the climax of one of the West's most sensational espionage cases since the Dreyfus Affair a half-century earlier, Ethel and Julius Rosenberg were convicted in March 1951 of organizing an international spy ring that gave the Soviets the foremost U.S. military secret: the design of the atomic bomb. The Rosenberg case had broken open the previous year, after German-born nuclear physicist Klaus Fuchs confessed that he'd spied for Moscow while working for U.S. weapons programs, including the Manhattan Project. Fuchs identified his American contact as a chemist named Harry Gold. Gold implicated David Greenglass, a GI who'd worked as a machinist at Los Alamos (the laboratory of the Manhattan Project). Greenglass implicated his sister and brother-in-law—the Rosenbergs.

The bookish, mild-mannered couple, who shared a crowded apartment on Manhattan's Lower East Side with their two young sons, hardly fit the stereotype of cold-blooded Commie spies. Moreover, they made no secret of their leftward leanings. (Indeed, Julius's political affiliations had cost him his job as a civilian employee of the U.S. Army signal corps in

Ethel and Julius Rosenberg: spies or victims of Cold War hysteria?

1945.) Yet, in the fevered atmosphere of the day, their very ordinariness made them seem all the more threatening. If the Rosenbergs could be spies, then so could the butcher, baker, or candlestick maker. Despite their eloquent, idealistic protestations of innocence—and despite the international furor that erupted on their behalf—they were found guilty. The government's chief witness against them was Greenglass, who, in return for his testimony, received a 15-year sentence. Fuchs himself had drawn only a 14-year sentence. But the Rosenbergs were condemned to death. By putting the bomb in Soviet hands, said the hyperbolic trial judge, Irving Kaufman, the Rosenbergs had encouraged communist aggression in Korea; their crime was "worse than murder."

Debate still rages over the couple's guilt or innocence. (The opening of the Soviet Union's espionage files in the 1990s failed to resolve the issue.) But most experts agree that, while Fuchs's actions may have lopped a year or so off the time it would have taken the Soviets to overcome the U.S. nuclear monopoly, the information the Rosenbergs allegedly leaked would have been valueless. **◄1942.15 ►1953.M**

TECHNOLOGY

Atoms for Peace

3 Six years after atomic bombs destroyed Hiroshima and Nagasaki, American scientists for the first time used nuclear technology to generate electricity. The harnessing, in 1951, of the "peaceful atom" inspired dreams of cheap, abundant energy and liberation from dependence on fossil fuels.

The breakthrough occurred at Arco, Idaho, at a power station built by the Argonne National Laboratories under the auspices of the Atomic Energy Commission. The experimental reactor produced enough electricity to operate its own lighting system; as would become standard in all atomic power plants, the heat of the core boiled water to make steam to propel a turbine. But the plant at Arco did more: It actually produced extra fuel. The long-standing obstacle to atomic energy had been finding enough fissionable material to power reactors. Uranium 235 existed in discouragingly limited quantities. Plutonium 239, a by-product of uranium fission, was more fissionable (and therefore more efficient)—but even scarcer. One solution was to design a *breeder* reactor, which would produce more plutoni-

ART & CULTURE: Books: ***The Rebel*** **(Albert Camus);** ***The Masters*** **(C.P. Snow);** ***Lie Down in Darkness*** **(William Styron);** ***The Ballad of the Sad Café*** **(Carson McCullers);** ***The Conformist*** **(Alberto Moravia);** ***The Caine Mutiny*** **(Herman Wouk) ... Music: "On Top of Old Smoky" (Pete Seeger); "Come On-a My House" (Saroyan and Bagdasarian); "Unforgettable" (Irving Gordon);** ***Billy Budd*** **(Benjamin Britten) ...**

"Nobody is saying to the Germans: You pay us; we forgive you. We are promising nothing; we are offering nothing. We are simply claiming what is ours morally and legally."—**Dr. Nahum Goldmann, a leading sponsor of Israel's negotiations with West Germany**

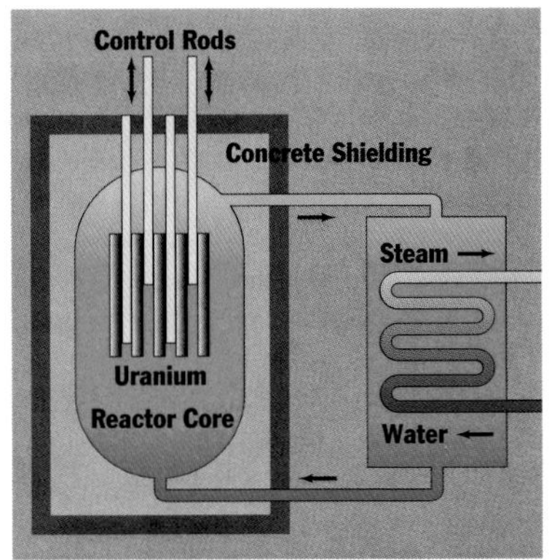

The pressurized water reactor became the standard model for nuclear power plants throughout the world.

um than it burned uranium. Argonne's was the first.

In 1954, the Soviets opened the world's first civilian nuclear power station, a small, five-megawatt-installation. Two years later, the British began operating the first full-sized industrial plant, a 40-megawatt reactor that produced both civilian electricity and military plutonium. Soon, nuclear power plants were on-line around the world.

But predictions of an atomic-powered future proved unrealistic. Unexpectedly expensive to build and maintain, nukes also raised fears about storage of radioactive waste and the possibility of disastrous meltdowns. **◂1946.7 ▸1952.M**

DIPLOMACY

Germany's Penance

4 Well before the end of World War II, many Jewish leaders had advocated German reparations for the Holocaust. But it took until December 1951, when Israel was three years old and West Germany two, for secret talks to begin. (Communist East Germany denied all responsibility for Hitler's crimes.) The practical benefits of restitution were clear to each side: Israel, desperately short on cash, was faced with settling 500,000 refugees; Germany could begin to overcome its pariah status through largesse. The moral questions were murkier, however—as were the technicalities of payment.

Most Jews worldwide opposed any contacts with Germany, insisting that nothing could compensate for the nation's misdeeds. The far right in West Germany called for solidarity with the Arabs (who'd just begun a total boycott of Israel); the far left condemned the Jewish state as a tool of American imperialism. The finance minister in Bonn warned against a settlement that would compromise the country's ability to pay its other debts. But West German chancellor Konrad Adenauer was determined that his people express shame for the atrocities committed in their name, and Israeli president Chaim Weizmann was loath to let the Germans off the economic hook.

Direct negotiations began in March 1952, in the Dutch town of Wassenaar, with Israel asking the equivalent of $1 billion, and representatives of the world Jewish community asking $500 million for victims in other lands. The final agreement, signed in Luxembourg that September, awarded $820 million worth of goods and currency to Israel (to be paid in installments), and $107 million to Jewish relief organizations elsewhere. Even rioting in Jerusalem by the treaty's opponents could not dim its significance: For the first time in 2,000 years, a persecutor of the Jews was trying—however inadequately—to make amends. **◂1946.V ▸1965.9**

A protest in Tel Aviv against the German-Israeli reparation agreement.

THE MIDDLE EAST

A Royal Pragmatist Is Slain

5 In July 1951, Jordan's King Abdullah was assassinated as he entered the Mosque of Omar in Jerusalem. The monarch had done

plenty to anger his fellow Arabs: His ambitions for control over Syria, his close ties with Britain, his support for a Jewish-Arab state in Palestine (a poorly kept secret), and his suppression of dissent at home had all earned him enemies. His Palestinian killer, who was cut down instantly by royal bodyguards, belonged to the hard-line Sanctuary of Struggle organization. That group had yet another grievance: During the recent Arab-Israeli War, Abdullah had failed to join the other Arab powers in trying to seize territory that the United Nations had assigned to the Jews, settling instead—at Britain's insistence—for a slice of Arab Palestine that included Jerusalem's Old City.

Abdullah's successor faced not only the hostility of Jordan's nominal allies, but that of his country's Palestinian majority—a majority augmented by the population of the newly annexed West Bank and tens of thousands of refugees. (Abdullah's Hashemite dynasty was Bedouin, not Palestinian.) At the time of Abdullah's death, however, his son, Talal, was being treated for mental illness. Soon after Talal was crowned, Jordan's parliament deemed him incompetent. In May 1953, Talal's 18-year-old son, Prince Hussein, became king.

Like his grandfather, Hussein proved a friend of the West and a "moderate" on Israel, though he, too, was willing to join in wars against the Jewish state; similarly, he relied on repression to maintain his power. Survivor of several coup attempts, he remained one of the region's key statesmen into the 1990s. **◂1949.6 ▸1967.3**

BIRTHS

Pedro Almodóvar, Spanish filmmaker.

Phil Collins, U.K. singer.

Evonne Fay Goolagong, Australian tennis player.

Lisa Halaby (Noor al-Hussein), Jordanian queen.

Anjelica Huston, U.S. actress.

Chrissie Hynde, U.S. singer.

Anatoly Karpov, Soviet chess player.

Michael Keaton, U.S. actor.

Sally Ride, U.S. astronaut.

Gordon Sumner (Sting), U.K. singer.

Luther Vandross, U.S. singer.

DEATHS

Ernest Bevin, U.K. political leader.

Fanny Brice, U.S. comedian.

Robert Flaherty, U.S. filmmaker.

André Gide, French writer.

William Randolph Hearst, U.S. publisher.

Abdullah ibn al-Hussein, Jordanian king.

Will K. Kellogg, U.S. manufacturer.

Serge Koussevitzky, Russian-U.S. conductor.

Sinclair Lewis, U.S. novelist.

Henri Philippe Pétain, French officer and political leader.

Ali Razmara, Iranian prime minister.

Sigmund Romberg, Hungarian-U.S. composer.

Artur Schnabel, Austrian-U.S. pianist.

Arnold Schoenberg, Austrian-U.S. composer.

John Sloan, U.S. artist.

Ludwig Wittgenstein, Austrian philosopher.

Painting & Sculpture: ***Owh! In Sao Pao*** **(Stuart Davis) ... Film:** ***An American in Paris*** **(Vincente Minnelli);** ***The African Queen*** **(John Huston);** ***A Place in the Sun*** **(George Stevens);** ***Diary of a Country Priest*** **(Robert Bresson) ... Theater:** ***I am a Camera*** **(John Van Druten);** ***Paint Your Wagon*** **(Lerner and Loewe);** ***The King and I*** **(Rodgers and Hammerstein) ... TV:** ***Search for Tomorrow; See It Now; The Roy Rogers Show.***

"In England he was like some bizarre feature of the landscape, like the Needles or Stonehenge, which local inhabitants have long ceased to notice.... Foreigners did not find it so easy to overlook his eccentricities"—**Goronwy Rees, on his friend Guy Burgess**

NEW IN 1951

***Jet* magazine.**

Power steering (Chrysler Crown Imperial).

Rock 'n' roll (named by Cleveland disc jockey Alan Freed).

Dennis the Menace.

Tropicana products.

Pan-American Games.

Television broadcast in color (one-hour CBS special).

IN THE UNITED STATES

▶AN AMERICAN CONSERVATIVE—William F. Buckley, Jr.'s 1951 book, *God and Man at Yale*, an excoriation of the pervasive liberalism of the 25-year-old author's alma mater, brought him instant notoriety. As founding editor of the *National Review* and host of the television talk show *Firing Line*, Buckley went on to become America's best-known and perhaps most articulate conservative commentator.

▶A SWEET VICTORY—Pound for pound, Sugar Ray Robinson may be the greatest boxer ever to enter the ring. Robinson defeated Jake "Raging

Bull" LaMotta in 1951 for the middleweight championship of the world. The victory avenged Robinson's defeat by LaMotta eight years earlier. A 1946 welterweight champion, Robinson won and lost the middleweight crown five times. ◂1937.9 ▸1956.M

▶NEVER SAY DIE—Having finally stabilized the Chinese offensive just south of Seoul in January, General Douglas MacArthur, supreme commander in Korea, was ready to launch an all-out offensive against the Chinese. After MacArthur openly criticized

1951

ESPIONAGE

Double Agents Disappear

6 Guy Burgess *(top)* and Donald Maclean, second secretary and head of chancery, respectively, of Britain's embassy in Washington, were colorful characters—rather too colorful. Neither made a secret of his leftist views, especially when drunk (which was quite often); Burgess did little to hide his homosexuality. By early 1951, their indiscretions had landed both men back in London.

But their disappearance in May was a far greater embarrassment to the government than their earlier antics: They both fled as Maclean was about to be nabbed as a top Soviet spy. Their escape—and the revelation that both had been moles for more than a decade—sent shock waves through the West.

In the 1930s, the pair had been members of the elite Cambridge group the Apostles, which also included Anthony Blunt. All three were recruited by the Soviets to infiltrate Britain's intelligence network. Also at Cambridge at the time was another Soviet recruit, Kim Philby. During the war, Blunt enlisted with MI5, the national security service; the others joined MI6, the foreign intelligence branch. After the war, Philby rose almost to the top of MI6; Burgess and Maclean became successful diplomats. Blunt became curator of the royal art collection, letting his active Soviet ties lapse. It was Philby who in 1951 sent Burgess to warn Maclean that he was under suspicion, and Blunt who helped them flee.

The search for the fugitives lasted until 1956, when they surfaced in Moscow. Philby's role as "third man" in the affair was not confirmed until 1963, when he, too, fled to Moscow. In 1964, MI5 fingered Blunt—by then Sir Anthony—as the "fourth man." He confessed, and was granted immunity. But he lost his knighthood when his secret became public in 1979. **◂1951.2 ▸1963.3**

FILM

The Ealing Touch

7 By 1951, the British film industry was in the midst of a postwar renaissance. Just since 1945, it had turned out such intelligent, superbly acted pictures as David Lean's *Great Expectations* and *Oliver Twist*, Sir Carol Reed's stark, stylish thriller *The Third Man*, and Michael Powell and Emeric Pressburger's tragic ballet tale, *The Red Shoes*. And London's Ealing Studios released a string of consistently brilliant satirical comedies—*Kind Hearts and Coronets*, *Whisky Galore!*, *The Man in the White Suit*—that showed everyday Britons in eccentric revolt against capitalism, the class system, and encroaching bureaucracy. Produced by Michael Balcon; usually starring the sublimely droll character actor Alec Guinness; with scripts by T.E.B. Clarke and direction by Charles Crichton, Alexander Mackendrick, Henry Cornelius, or Robert Hamer, the Ealing comedies are tart charmers.

The Lavender Hill Mob, released in 1951 and directed by Crichton, is one of Ealing's best. A mild-mannered bank clerk (Guinness), 20 years on the job, plots to steal one of the gold shipments he supervises. Joining forces with a souvenir maker and two burglars, the clerk accomplishes the heist, melts the gold into Eiffel Tower statuettes, and exports the booty to Paris, where he and his partners intend to recover it and commence lives of splendor. Complications, however, arise. A crisp, slightly amoral commentary on the discontents of middle-class drones, *The Lavender Hill Mob* offers an extra treat for cognoscenti: Guinness's girlfriend, who appears for less than a minute in the opening scene, is played by a radiant 22-year-old Belgian model making her fourth screen appearance—Audrey Hepburn. **◂1948.M ▸1961.11**

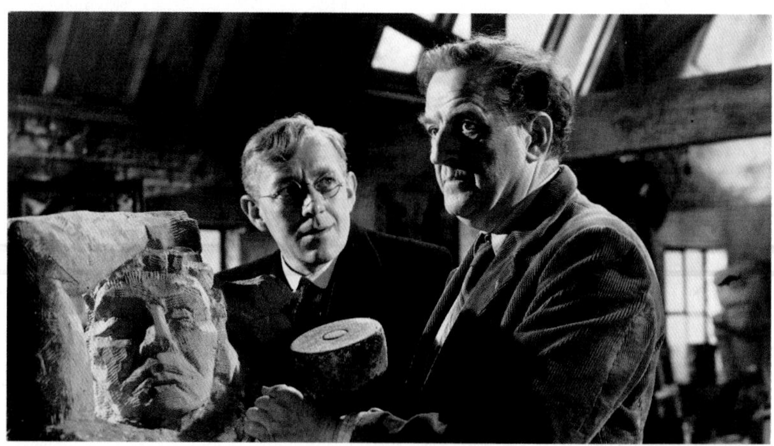

Alec Guinness *(left)* and Stanley Holloway plot a gold heist in *The Lavender Hill Mob*.

IDEAS

Medium of the Media

8 Marshall McLuhan's first book, *The Mechanical Bride: Folklore of Industrial Man*, sold only a few hundred copies when it was published in 1951. Perhaps the work was ahead of its time: No one had seen anything like this playfully abstruse study of modern mythology (from etiquette columns to advertisements), illustrated with magazine pages and filled with what one critic called "blood-curdling puns." Yet within two decades, its first editions had become collector's items. The reason? Public appearances and writings like *The Gutenberg Galaxy: The Making of*

"Televisionary" McLuhan analyzed differences between "hot and cool media."

Typographic Man (1962) and *Understanding Media: The Extensions of Man* (1964) had made the Canadian professor the world's leading authority on communications, a "media guru"sought out by the movers and shakers of business and politics—including consultants to Richard Nixon's 1968 presidential campaign.

McLuhan's fame stemmed large-

SPORTS: Baseball: World Series, New York Yankees defeat New York Giants (Bobby Thomson), 4–2 ... Football: NFL, Los Angeles Rams defeat Cleveland Browns, 24–17 ... Basketball: NBA, Rochester Royals defeat New York Knickerbockers, 4–3 ... Horse Racing: Citation is first horse to win $1 million.

"I keep picturing all these little kids in this big field.... [If] they don't look where they're going I have to come out from somewhere and catch them. That's all I'd do all day. I'd just be the catcher in the rye and all."—**J.D. Salinger, *The Catcher in the Rye***

ly from his coining of two catchphrases. The first was the "global village." Whereas, he argued, the introduction of printing in the fifteenth century ushered in the nation-state—replacing intimate tribal culture with a way of life based on individualism and alienation—electronic media had begun to reverse the process. Television, telephones, computers, and other extensions of the human senses increasingly linked humanity in a worldwide community with its own distinctive culture. In this culture, "the medium is the message" (the second catchphrase); that is, the form of communication, not its content, determines the meaning the audience takes away.

When his books first appeared, McLuhan was dismissed as a crackpot as often as he was hailed as a prophet. By the 1990s, however, his insights had become commonplace in a society wired for video. **◂1950.M ▸1952.5**

In an early episode, straight man Desi Arnaz watches as Lucille Ball plays for laughs.

POPULAR CULTURE

Empress of the Airwaves

9 Dozens of roles in second-rate films had earned Lucille Ball the sobriquet "Queen of the Bs," but when her situation comedy *I Love Lucy* took to the airwaves in 1951, she became an empress of television—reigning over Monday nights on CBS until her retirement from weekly broadcasting in 1974.

Asked to star in a TV version of her radio program, *My Favorite Husband*, Ball had insisted that her real-life husband, Desi Arnaz, play her bandleader-spouse, Ricky Ricardo. (Her contract also stipulated that Desilu, the couple's production company, be allowed to keep fees paid for repeat airings—a clause that eventually made her one of show business's richest women.) Well-scripted and lavishly shot (filmed by top cinematographers with three 35mm cameras before a studio audience, when other live shows were recorded on primitive kinescope), *I Love Lucy* won more than 60 percent of the total television audience in its first season. Through its long run (which ended in 1957, after 179 episodes), the series stayed at the top. The 1953 episode in which Lucy gives birth to Little Ricky captured a staggering 92 percent of TV watchers.

I Love Lucy attracted a cavalcade of guest stars, including William Holden, Bob Hope, and Harpo Marx. Yet it was Ball and her "dizzy redhead" persona that carried the show. No one else could eat spaghetti, stomp on grapes, pull taffy, or plot mischief with such endearing (and brilliantly simulated) ineptitude. Her marriage to Arnaz ended in 1960, but audiences remained faithful to her solo vehicles, *The Lucy Show* and *Here's Lucy*. **◂1948.M**

LITERATURE

An Archetypal Adolescent

10 When *The Catcher in the Rye* was published in 1951, thousands of readers discovered a deep kinship with its troubled young protagonist. In Holden Caulfield, a prep-school fugitive with a wistful yearning for innocence and a scathing take on the adults around him ("If you want to know the truth, they're all a bunch of goddam phonies"), J.D. Salinger had created one of literature's most convincingly alienated adolescents. Recounting his illicit two-day adventure through grown-up New York, Holden is by turns eloquent and whiny, world-weary and naive, a Huck Finn of the postwar American upper-middle class.

Salinger, 32, was no callow youth. He had been publishing stories in the prestigious *New Yorker* for a decade; as a soldier he'd fought in the D-Day landing on Utah Beach. But *Catcher*'s acute and sympathetic understanding of adolescence's discontents secured Salinger's standing as a kind of honorary teenager. Some critics saw an advertisement for delinquency in Holden's profanity and unflinching examination of adult sexuality. One feared that "a book like this ... may multiply his kind"—and indeed, the novel was a favorite of fifties teenage rebels.

Intensely private, Salinger responded to fame by severing his ties to Manhattan and secluding himself in rural New Hampshire. He published two more books in the next dozen years, then lapsed into virtual silence. Dogged by would-be biographers (he sued to prevent one from publishing his letters) and pilgrims who hoped to catch a glimpse of him, he remained incommunicado into the nineties. **◂1910.12 ▸1955.9**

IN THE UNITED STATES

top U.S. leaders for their insistence on maintaining a limited war, President Truman—who had concluded that Korea could not be unified and felt that MacArthur's remarks ran the risk of setting off World War III—relieved him of his duties. On April 11, MacArthur was replaced by General Matthew B. Ridgeway, whose strategy of containment called for pushing the Chinese back just to the 38th parallel. In the U.S., MacArthur testified before a joint session of Congress. Announcing his reluctant departure after three decades of military service, he invoked an old barracks ballad which proclaimed most proudly that "old soldiers never die, they just fade away." ◂1950.1 ▸1951.M

▶MANTLE AND MAYS—Baseball-rich New York gained two of the game's brightest stars in 1951, when Willie Mays joined the Giants and the Yankees brought up Mickey Mantle. During long careers the two Hall of Famers made sustained runs at the record books, swatting a combined 1,196 home runs, among other prodigious feats. The 1951 season, however, belonged to yet another New York player: the Giants' Bobby Thomson. His "shot heard 'round the world," a two-out, bottom-of-the-ninth three-run

homer, snatched the pennant from the hard-luck Brooklyn Dodgers. The Yankees defeated the Giants in the World Series. ◂1947.10 ▸1956.M

▶OPERA COMES TO TELEVISION—With *Amahl and the Night Visitors*, Italian composer Gian Carlo Menotti created one of the first TV "specials" in 1951. The moving story of a lame shepherd boy who crosses paths with the Three Wise Men as they travel to Bethlehem, *Amahl* was the first opera written expressly for television. ▸1957.9

POLITICS & BUSINESS: GNP: $328.4 billion ... 22nd Amendment passed, limits presidency to two terms ... Draft age lowered to 18½ from 20 and tour of duty expanded to 2 years ... AT&T is first company with over 1 million stockholders ... Wang Laboratories founded by An Wang in Boston, Massachusetts.

"I have no intention of coming to terms with anyone. Rather than come to terms with the British, I will seal the oil wells with mud."—Iranian prime minister Muhammad Mussadegh

AROUND THE WORLD

▶STALEMATE IN KOREA—As the new year unfolded, UN forces in Korea were in full retreat and Seoul was evacuated for the second time (on January 4). But the Chinese advance was stopped 30 miles south of the city. By late January, UN forces had launched a counteroffensive; on March 31, they regained the 38th parallel. With neither side willing to risk a full-blown confrontation, the UN and the Communist commanders began armistice negotiations in July—as fighting continued. ◀1950.1

▶MONUMENT TO RENEWAL—Some ten years after Nazi bombers demolished England's fourteenth-century Gothic Coventry Cathedral, work

began in 1950 on its reconstruction. British architect Basil Spence conceived the winning design, which incorporated the ruins of the original cathedral into the new church, completed in 1962. ◀1940.11

▶CHURCHILL RETURNS—Having used his time out of office to work on his stellar six-volume war history, *The Second World War*, and to lead Great Britain's parliamentary opposition, Winston Churchill triumphantly became prime minister in 1951. Nearing his 80th year, the old lion delegated much domestic responsibility in order to concentrate on foreign policy. He (unsuccessfully) advocated European union and also strove to strengthen Anglo-American ties. ◀1945.M

▶THE SCHUMAN PLAN—France, West Germany, Belgium, Italy, the Netherlands, and Luxembourg agreed in 1951 to create the European Coal and Steel Community. Officially proposed by French foreign minister Robert Schuman, the ECSC was designed to dismantle barriers to steel and coal trading. The ECSC, ratified in 1952, envisioned the ultimate political and economic integration of Europe and was a precursor of the European Community. ▶1957.5

LITERATURE

Jones's Brutal War Epic

11 "I remember thinking with a sense of the profoundest awe that none of our lives would ever be the same," wrote author James Jones, recalling the shock of the Japanese attack on Pearl Harbor. Jones's wartime experience in Hawaii—he'd been stationed there when the Japanese struck—shaped his debut novel. Published in 1951, *From Here to Eternity* won a National Book Award.

Surpassing even Norman Mailer's *The Naked and the Dead* in its brutal frankness, Jones's sprawling, 861-page book shocked many readers with its depiction of the profane language, drinking bouts, and sexual escapades of military life—and with its exposure of the infighting and corruption of the "old army" establishment, which had undermined America's combat readiness.

Jones's scathing portrait was softened only somewhat in Columbia Pictures' 1953 film adaptation, which won eight Academy Awards. Considered highly risqué—thanks largely to a scene in which Burt Lancaster and Deborah Kerr lie on a beach, locked in a passionate clinch—the movie starred Montgomery Clift as doomed idealist Robert E. Lee Prewitt and Donna Reed as his love interest (a prostitute in the book, a mere B-girl in the film). Frank Sinatra's performance as the equally doomed soldier Angelo Maggio won him an Oscar and revived his flagging career.

Jones's next novel, *Some Came Running,* dealt with small-town life, but with *The Thin Red Line* (1963), he continued his projected World War II trilogy. He died in 1977 before completing *Whistle,* the last book in the series. It was finished the following year by his friend Willie Morris. ◀1948.11 ▶1957.M

Lancaster and Kerr on the beach. The film muted the novel's most explicit scenes.

IRAN

Oil Industry Nationalized

12 The assassination of Iranian prime minister Ali Razmara in March 1951 ushered in a turbulent period that ended two years later in American intervention. Shah Muhammad Reza Pahlevi had appointed Razmara to the premiership just six months earlier, at Washington's urging: With nationalist forces, including the communist Tudeh Party, on the rise, the Americans hoped the right-wing general would impose order. But Razmara was widely despised, and when he was killed (by an Islamic militant who demanded, "Why do you give the country to foreigners?"), popular pressure forced the Shah to replace him with a nationalist legislator, Muhammad Mussadegh *(above)*.

A liberal, Mussadegh, was the leader of a broad parliamentary movement to nationalize the giant, British-owned Anglo-Iranian Oil Company. (Among the nationalists' grievances: Iran received only a fraction of AIOC profits, at a time when other countries had negotiated 50-50 splits with foreign oil concessions; and the company kept Iranians out of skilled positions.) The nationalization measure passed the Majlis (parliament) a few days after Razmara's death, sparking nationwide rejoicing. But the British quickly called for a boycott of Iranian oil, and soon the nation's economy was in shambles.

The frail, grandfatherly Mussadegh responded to the deepening crisis with tear-filled speeches (often delivered from a bed brought into the Majlis chambers, a ploy that endeared him to Iranians but baffled Westerners), authoritarian measures, and overtures to the communists. None of his tactics had much effect. In 1953, a coup backed by the British and directed by the Americans brought the Mussadegh era to a bloody close. ◀1946.10 ▶1953.4

RELIGION

A Religionless Christianity

13 In the aftermath of World War II, theologians pondered Hitler's rise and fall. For Protestants, the questions were especially pressing. Germany, after all, was a mainly Protestant country, and its people had embraced Nazism. How could such a phenomenon be avoided in the future? And where should Christians stand in the new ideological struggles shaking the world? In 1951, a book appeared that profoundly affected the debate: Pastor Dietrich Bonhoeffer's posthumous *Prisoner of God: Letters and Papers from Prison.*

Years earlier, as mainstream German churches accepted Nazi-installed bishops, worked Nazism into their liturgies, and expelled non-Aryans, Bonhoeffer had helped found the breakaway Confessing Church. Underground after 1937, the sect answered only to heavenly authority; many members smuggled Jews out of the country. Bonhoeffer was jailed in 1943 on minor sedition charges, but investigators soon linked him to a high-level plot to kill Hitler. He was hanged at the Flössenburg concentration camp in 1945, as Allied troops closed in.

Bonhoeffer started as a follower of the Swiss theologian Karl Barth. Like Barth's, his theology emphasized Jesus's deeds rather than clerical dogmas. But Barth (the century's foremost classical Protestant thinker) aimed to reform church doctrine, whereas Bonhoeffer championed a "religionless Christianity," based solely on emulation of Christ as the suffering "man for others." His prison writings share much with existentialism: In a morally ambiguous world, ethics can derive only from actions aimed at helping one's fellows and based on a leap of faith. ◀1932.7

NOBEL PRIZES: Peace: Léon Jouhaux (French; labor leader) ... Literature: Pär Lagerkvist (Swedish; novelist and poet) ... Chemistry: Edwin McMillan and Glenn Seaborg (U.S.; transuranium elements) ... Medicine: Max Theiler (South African; yellow-fever vaccine) ... Physics: John Douglas Cockcroft and Ernest Walton (U.K., Irish; transmutation of atomic nuclei).

A VOICE FROM 1951

Mike Hammer on the Town

From *One Lonely Night,* by Mickey Spillane, 1951

In an era of demure movies and television shows, pulp writer Mickey Spillane provided crude thrills. His fast-paced, grimly violent detective novels smashed sales records in the 1950s, regularly selling five million copies and more. Spillane, who claimed he wrote only for the money, kept the familiar elements of the American crime story (gruff detectives, leggy women, whiskey, cigarettes, gunplay) but jettisoned the niceties, banging out books in which realism was replaced by sadism, sensuality by raw sex. His novel One Lonely Night *(1951) takes the decade's anti-Communist fervor to a new level: "I killed more people tonight than I have fingers on my hands," boasts investigator Mike Hammer. "I shot them in cold blood and enjoyed every minute of it.... They were Commies ... red sons-of-bitches who should have died long ago." In the excerpt below, Hammer runs into trouble: a dark Manhattan night, a deserted bridge, a desperate woman, and a hit man.* ◂**1930.11**

I'd seen fear before, but never like this.

She was only a few steps away and I ran to her, my hands hooking under her arms to lift her to her feet.

Her eyes were like saucers, rimmed with red, overflowing with tears that blurred her pupils. She took one look at me and choked, "Lord ... no, please!"

"Easy, honey, take it easy," I said. I propped her against the girder and her eyes searched my face through her tears, unable to see me clearly. She tried to talk and I stopped her. "No words, kid. There's plenty of time for that later. Just take it easy a minute, nobody's going to hurt you."

As if that stirred something in her mind, her eyes went wide again and she turned her head to stare back down the ramp.

I heard it too. Footsteps, only these weren't hurried. They came evenly and softly, as if knowing full well they'd reach their objective in a few seconds.

I felt a snarl ripple across my mouth and my eyes went half shut. Maybe you can smack a dame around all you want and make her life as miserable as hell, but nobody has the right to scare the daylights out of any woman. Not like this.

She trembled so hard I had to put my arm around her shoulder to steady her. I watched her lips trying to speak, the unholy fear spreading into her face as no sound came.

I pulled her away from the girder. "Come on, we'll get this straightened out in a hurry." She was too weak to resist. I held my arm around her and started walking toward the footsteps.

He came out of the wall of white, a short pudgy guy in a heavy belted ulster. His homburg was set on the side of his head rakishly, and even at this distance I could see the smile on his lips. Both his hands were stuck in his pockets and he walked with a swagger. He wasn't a bit surprised when he saw the two of us. One eyebrow went up a little, but that was all. Oh yes, he had a gun in his pocket.

It was pointing at me.

Nobody had to tell me he was the one. I wouldn't even have to know he had a rod in his hand. The way the kid's body stiffened with the shock of seeing him was enough. My face couldn't have been nice to look at right then, but it didn't bother the guy.

The gun moved in the pocket so I'd know it was a gun.

His voice fit his body, short and thick. He said, "It is not smart to be a hero. Not smart at all." His thick lips twisted into a smile of mingled satisfaction and conceit. It was so plain in his mind that I could almost hear him speak it. The girl running along, stumbling blindly into the arms of a stranger. Her pleas for help, the guy's ready agreement to protect her, only to look down the barrel of a rod.

It didn't happen like this at all, but that's what he thought. His smile widened and he said harshly, "So now they will find the two of you here tomorrow." His eyes were as cold and as deadly as those of a manta ray.

He was too cocky. All he could see was his own complete mastery of the situation. He should have looked at me a little harder and maybe he would have seen the kind of eyes I had. Maybe he would have seen that I was a killer in my own way too, and he would have realized that I knew he was just the type who would go to the trouble of taking the gun out of his pocket instead of ruining a good coat.

I never really gave him a chance. All I moved was my arm and before he had his gun out I had my .45 in my fist with the safety off and the trigger back. I only gave him a second to realize what it was like to die then I blew the expression clean off his face.

He never figured the hero would have a gun, too.

Before I could get it back in the holster the girl gave a lunge and backed up against the railing. Her eyes were clear now. They darted to the mess on the ground, the gun in my hand and the tight lines that made a mask of kill-lust of my face.

She screamed. Good god, how she screamed. She screamed as if I were a monster that had come out of the pit! She screamed and made words that sounded like, "You ... one of them ... no more!"

I saw what she was going to do and tried to grab her, but the brief respite she had was enough to give her the strength she needed. She twisted and slithered over the top of the rail and I felt part of her coat come away in my hand as she tumbled headlong into the white void below the bridge.

Lurid cover art helped sell Spillane's *One Lonely Night*. Spillane *(above)* cultivated as hard-boiled a persona as that of his hero Mike Hammer.

1951

"Poor, sweet Lilibet—now our Queen."—**Louis, Lord Mountbatten, Elizabeth II's uncle, in his diary on February 7, 1952**

STORY OF THE YEAR

Vivat Regina

1 Britain's King George VI died as he had reigned: imperturbably. Suffering from advanced lung cancer and heart disease, the 56-year-old monarch had retired to the royal estate of Sandringham to pursue his favorite pastime, hunting. On the night of February 5, 1952, after bagging nine rabbits and a pigeon (and declaring that he'd had a "thoroughly enjoyable day"), he passed away in his sleep. His eldest daughter, Elizabeth Alexandra Mary, 25, hurried back from a goodwill mission to Kenya with her consort, Prince Philip, to be proclaimed "Queen of this realm and all her other realms and territories, head of the Commonwealth, defender of the Faith."

Queen Elizabeth II was 27 years old when she donned the royal diadem for her coronation in 1953.

The King's remains lay in state for three days at Sandringham (in a coffin built from one of the estate's great oaks) and three at London's Westminster Hall. More than 300,000 Britons filed past the coffin, many waiting all night in a three-mile queue for the privilege. A million Londoners watched the cortege pass by, and another 200,000 mourners—including seven reigning monarchs, three presidents, and 1,000 other international notables—gathered for the funeral at Windsor, the ancestral home of English royalty for 850 years.

George's reign had begun in crisis in 1936, when his brother Edward VIII abdicated to marry an American divorcée. George served as Britain's spiritual anchor through half the Depression and all of World War II, staying in London even as bombs fell regularly on Buckingham Palace. He calmly bore witness to the birth of the welfare state and the shrinking of the empire. (The new queen's title reflected the changes in England's relations with its onetime colonies. George had been, not head of the commonwealth, but king of the British dominions.)

Now Elizabeth II inherited her father's ceremonial but nonetheless weighty responsibilities: to name prime ministers, approve laws, and advise the government—and to embody the ancient idea of *Britishness* to her farflung subjects and the world at large. Her coronation took place in June 1953, 17 months after her accession; that ceremony's joyful pageantry was as spectacular as the gloomy pomp of the year before. **◂1936.V ▸1981.4**

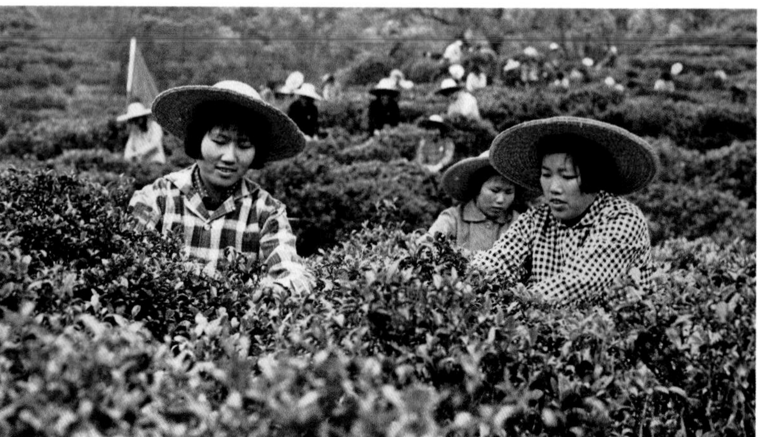

Chinese women harvest tea. After 1952, Mao placed more emphasis on industry.

CHINA

The Drive to Industrialize

2 After decades of war and revolution, China was finally stabilizing. By 1952, the People's Republic had been in place for three years. Agrarian reform was under way, but industry lagged. The time had come, Mao Zedong's regime decided, to extend the revolution to the cities. The Soviet revolution (now in its fourth decade) was an imperfect model for the kind of social, economic, and political transformation the Chinese hoped to effect, but it was the only one available. Despite some reservations, Mao and his comrades turned to Moscow for guidance. In August, Premier Zhou Enlai traveled to the Soviet Union to discuss China's future with Soviet officials. Within months of his return, China had begun its First Five-Year Plan for industrialization.

The plan represented a cataclysmic shift from an ancient rural economy to a modern urban one. The push to modernize meant that China had to adopt Stalinist economic—and administrative—precepts. Between 1953 and 1957, 80 percent of the Chinese people lived in rural areas, but an equal portion of government spending went to the cities. Heavy industry—production of steel, cement, pig iron—grew nearly 20 percent annually. Agriculture, meanwhile, stagnated. Through taxes and quotas, peasants bore the cost of industrialization. Some 30 million Chinese abandoned the countryside; the urban working class nearly doubled.

The new centralized economy fairly begged for new principles of government. But flexibility, an important tenet of Maoist revolutionary theory, was now sacrificed in favor of Soviet-style bureaucracy, raising Western fears that China had become a Kremlin puppet. But Mao never lost his old suspicion of the Soviets. A rift soon developed, prompting Moscow to cut off aid—and leaving China to find its own Communist way. **◂1949.1 ▸1958.2**

EGYPT

Rebellion and Coup

3 After three decades of "modified" independence, Egyptians rose decisively against the British in 1952. Events had begun to snowball the previous year, when negotiations on full sovereignty collapsed. Egypt's parliament, under

Egyptian nationalists in Cairo rally against British domestic interference.

growing popular pressure to effect the withdrawal of all British troops, annulled the 1936 Anglo-Egyptian Treaty and proclaimed King Farouk ruler of the Sudan (which Britain controlled but planned to make independent). Britain responded by massing troops along the Suez Canal; Egyptian authorities, in turn, allowed nationalist groups to form militias. In January, following several violent clashes, Cairo exploded. Rioters wrecked 750 British establishments and killed eleven Europeans.

ART & CULTURE: Books: *The Old Man and the Sea* (Ernest Hemingway); *The Natural* (Bernard Malamud); *Wise Blood* (Flannery O'Connor); *Charlotte's Web* (E.B. White); *The Dragon and the Unicorn* (Kenneth Rexroth) ... Music: "Your Cheatin' Heart" (Hank Williams); *Fantasy in Space, Low Speed, Invention in 12 Notes* (Otto Luening); *Ideas of Order* (Arthur Berger); *Souvenirs* (Samuel Barber) ... Painting &

"That's what we have and that's what we owe. It isn't very much, but Pat and I have the satisfaction that every dime we've got is honestly ours."—**Richard M. Nixon, in his "Checkers" speech**

Both governments drew back, fearing the forces they'd unleashed; Farouk's regime declared martial law. But a group of disgruntled Egyptian military men realized their hour had come. The conspirators of the Free Officers movement were united by nationalist ardor and by a conviction that the pitiful state of Egypt's army—and its recent defeat by Israel—were the result of rampant official corruption. In July, their troops seized government installations. Farouk meekly abdicated and left the country.

The bloodless coup was directed by Gamal Abdal Nasser, 34, a colonel with populist ideas. For now, however, he left the government in the hands of older, better-known men. General Muhammad Naguib, a hero of the Arab-Israeli War, became president of the Revolutionary Command Council, which quickly ordered land reform, dissolved Parliament, and abolished all political parties (promising an eventual return to civilian rule). Meanwhile, Nasser consolidated his power behind the scenes. He emerged in 1954, in time to oversee the end of British rule, and to become the most influential Arab leader of his era. **◂1949.6 ▸1954.2**

EASTERN AFRICA

The Mau Mau Revolt

4 Western journalists described the movement terrorizing Britain's Kenya colony as "a primitive mumbo-jumbo society," inspired by superstition or a Communist conspiracy. But the impetus for the bloody Mau Mau rebellion was hardly arcane: Most Kenyans wanted to liberate their country from an oppressive European regime. By 1952, when the colonial governor declared a state of emergency, tens of thousands of Kikuyu, members of Kenya's largest ethnic group, had joined the Mau Mau (the name's origin remains in question). Britain shipped in troops, and—in fighting that lasted until 1956—11,500 Kikuyu and 2,000 mostly African anti-Mau Mau forces were killed. At one time, 80,000 Africans were imprisoned. Even so, demands for self-government only grew louder.

European penetration of Kenya had begun in the mid-nineteenth century. To facilitate a plantation economy, British settlers drove the Kikuyu from the fertile highlands. Dispossessed and disenfranchised, a generation of Kenyans pressed for reform of the colonial system. Tactics changed after World War II, when Jomo Kenyatta, a Kikuyu political leader educated at the London School of Economics, returned from England to assume the presidency of the fledgling Kenya African Union.

Future Kenyan president Kenyatta is escorted to jail by two British hirelings.

Kenyatta turned the KAU into a mass nationalist party, complete with its own educational institutions. When the revolt erupted in 1952, he was arrested and convicted of leading the Mau Mau—a charge he steadfastly denied. Kenyatta was jailed until 1961. When he was released, it was to negotiate the terms for his nation's independence. **▸1963.6**

THE UNITED STATES

Americans Like Ike

5 Promising to end the Korean War, retired general Dwight D. Eisenhower swamped Democrat Adlai Stevenson in America's 1952 presidential election. Eisenhower had profited from his World War II record and his unassuming charm, from running mate Richard M. Nixon's fame as an anti-Communist crusader, and from the public's yearning for novelty after two decades of Democratic rule. And, like Kennedy after him, he was enormously helped by the new mass medium of television.

Inspired by the "I like Ike" chant that greeted Eisenhower everywhere, the campaign's advertising agency designed a series of short TV spots in which marching bands chanted, "I like Ike! You like Ike! Everybody likes Ike!" Against the highbrow, half-hour speeches favored by Stevenson, the ads were dynamite. But the greatest broadcast triumph was Nixon's. When it was revealed that a group of California businessmen had paid him $18,000 from a secret slush fund, the senator, on the verge of being dropped from the ticket, took to the airwaves to fight for his political life.

Sixty million Americans tuned in to watch what came to be known as the "Checkers" speech. With his wife, Pat, at his side, Nixon defended the fund's legality and denied spending any slush-fund money for personal expenses. He portrayed himself as a boy of humble origin who'd made good through hard work. Pat, he said, wore a "respectable Republican cloth coat." The only gift he'd accepted from a constituent was the family dog, named Checkers by "our little girl—Tricia, the six-year-old." With mock defiance, Nixon vowed, "We're gonna keep it." Viewers' tears flowed, letters of support poured in, and the Eisenhower-Nixon ticket bounced back stronger than ever. **◂1948.M ▸1960.2**

California senator Richard Nixon *(second from left, with wife Pat)* emerged as Eisenhower's surprise running mate at the 1952 Republican Convention in Chicago.

BIRTHS

Dan Aykroyd, Canadian-U.S. actor.

Jimmy Connors, U.S. tennis player.

Bob Costas, U.S. sportscaster.

Beth Henley, U.S. playwright.

Roseanne, U.S. comedian.

Amy Tan, U.S. novelist.

Gus Van Sant, U.S. filmmaker.

Bill Walton, U.S. basketball player.

DEATHS

Benedetto Croce, Italian philosopher and political leader.

John Dewey, U.S. philosopher.

Emma Eames, U.S. singer.

William Fox, U.S. film producer.

George VI, U.K. king.

William Green, U.S. labor leader.

Eugène Grindel (Paul Eluard), French poet.

Ferenc Molnár, Hungarian writer.

Maria Montessori, Italian educator and physician.

Knut Pederson (Knut Hamsun), Norwegian writer.

María Eva Duarte de Perón, Argentine political leader.

George Santayana, Spanish-U.S. philosopher.

Charles Scott Sherrington, U.K. neurophysiologist.

Kiichiro Toyoda, Japanese auto manufacturer.

Chaim Weizmann, U.S.S.R. Israeli Zionist leader and president.

Sculpture: ***Woman and Bicycle*** **(Willem de Kooning);** ***Mountains and Sea*** **(Helen Frankenthaler) ... Film:** ***The Greatest Show on Earth*** **(Cecil B. DeMille);** ***Viva Zapata!*** **(Elia Kazan);** ***The Quiet Man*** **(John Ford);** ***The Life of Oharu*** **(Kenji Mizoguchi) ... Theater:** ***The Chairs*** **(Eugène Ionesco);** ***The Marriage of Mr. Mississippi*** **(Friedrich Dürrenmatt) ... TV:** ***The Today Show*****;** ***Dragnet*****;** ***The Adventures of Ozzie and Harriet.***

"The program ... was technically so sweet.... The issues become purely the military, the political, and the humane problems of what you were going to do about it once you had it."—**J. Robert Oppenheimer, on the development of the hydrogen bomb**

NEW IN 1952

Holiday Inn (Memphis, Tenn.).

Pocket-sized transistor radio (Sony).

***Mad* magazine.**

Sugar-free soft drink (No-Cal ginger ale).

Soviet Union's participation in the Olympics.

IN THE UNITED STATES

▶SINGIN' IN THE RAIN—The supreme articulation of élan, skill, and grace, Gene Kelly's performance in the title tune of 1952's *Singin' in the Rain* provided one of Hollywood's enduring images: Lithe and exuberant, Kelly leaps onto a streetlamp pedestal, grinning and singing, clutching an

umbrella while a rainstorm soaks him. The film, a zesty Technicolor satire of a chaotic movie colony at the dawn of sound, represents the high-water mark of the movie musical. ◂1934.6 ▸1965.12

▶BESTSELLER FOR THE AGES —Touted as the "greatest Bible news in 341 years," the single-volume Revised Standard Version (RSV) of both the Old and New Testaments hit the bookstores in 1952 and stayed atop the bestseller lists for two years. The updated text was produced by the Protestant National Council of Churches of Christ in the U.S.A. to reflect recent scholarship and modern diction but preserve the high literary quality of the 1611 King James version.

▶3-D CRAZE—The trite plot of the first feature-length 3-D film in 30 years did not stop audiences from packing movie

A mushroom cloud from a thermonuclear test blast rises above the Marshall Islands.

TECHNOLOGY

The First H-Bombs

6 On November 1, 1952, a fireball three miles wide bloomed above the Marshall Islands atoll of Eniwetok, and the nearby islet of Elugelab vanished. The first hydrogen bomb (innocuously named Mike) had exploded with the force of 10 million tons of TNT—500 times greater than that of the atom bomb that destroyed Hiroshima. Across the Pacific in California, physicist Edward Teller, father of the U.S. H-bomb program, monitored the seismic shock and was delighted. "It's a boy," he crowed.

Physicist Enrico Fermi had first conceived of a thermonuclear superbomb—a device powered by fusion, rather than fission—in 1942, and Teller had made it his personal mission. But many leading atomic scientists, including J. Robert Oppenheimer and Fermi himself, resisted the idea on moral grounds. In 1950, after the Soviets tested their own A-bomb, President Truman cut short the debate, ordering the Atomic Energy Commission to develop an H-bomb as soon as possible. Teller, an émigré from Hungary, took charge of the crash program. The still-resistant Oppenheimer (head of the AEC's advisory committee) was branded a subversive and stripped of his security clearance in 1953.

Soviet scientists—supervised by Igor Kurchatov, developer of the Soviet A-bomb, and propelled by the theoretical work of Andrei Sakharov and Igor Mann—caught up quickly: They detonated their first thermonuclear device in August 1953. One year later, at Bikini (another Marshall Islands atoll), the Americans tested three more H-bombs, followed by 17 tests in 1955 (in a space of three months). Those blasts gave their name to a women's bathing suit whose effect on male viewers was said to be similarly devastating. The superbomb also inspired another, less pleasant, product: In the United States, underground fallout shelters became the rage. **◂1946.7 ▸1961.V**

CUBA

Batista's Island of Sin

7 Once known as the fastest typist in Cuba (he got his professional start as an army stenographer), Fulgencio Batista y Zaldivar rose to become the most powerful man on the island. He ruled the country twice: From 1933 to '44 he was a champion of good government; in 1952 he returned from voluntary retirement to establish a feared and hated dictatorship. Although only a few years separated his tours of duty, in tenor and spirit, the gulf was enormous.

Batista first came to power as a leader of the "sergeants' revolt," in which a group of ambitious young military men took charge of a corrupt and vitiated government and reformed it. He became Cuba's de facto ruler in 1933, and in 1940 was elected president. His platform was enlightened—he improved education, developed the economy —and although he and his compadres lined their pockets (a traditional perquisite of power), the country achieved relative prosperity: Something was left over for the *guajiros,* the landless farmers who toiled on Cuba's rich sugar and tobacco plantations. After his retirement, Cuba sank once again into miasmic corruption. Batista was practically begged to return. He did, leading a military coup. This time there would be no reform, but rather a complete suspension of political liberty and a cruel widening of the gap between rich and poor.

Between 1952 and New Year's Day 1959, when Fidel Castro chased him away, Batista ran Cuba like a colony. The overlords were himself and his fellow *latifundistas,* the landed gentry; American business, which invested nearly a billion dollars in the country; and the Mafia, which controlled Havana's legendary casinos (the country harbored some 27,000 professional gamblers in the mid-'50s, and about half that many prostitutes).

Cuba became a great place to visit—an endless, rumba-driven subtropical cocktail hour—and a terrible place to live. Most who objected to Batista's glitzy mismanagement wound up in jail or dead. The rest just suffered quiet degradation. **◂1933.4 ▸1953.M**

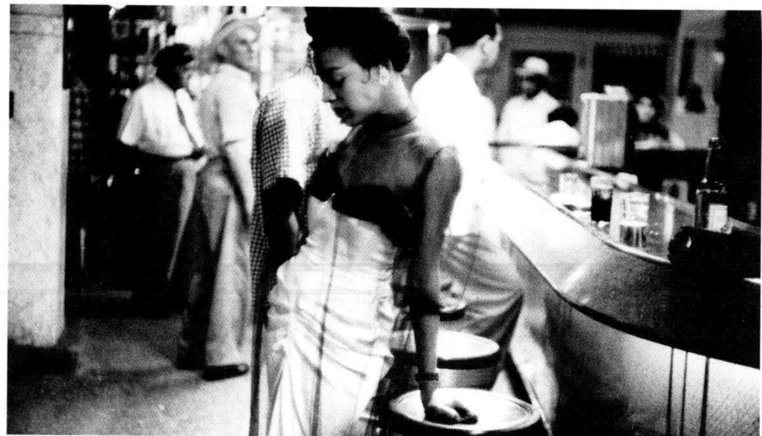

Batista's Cuba was a magnet for fun-seekers. Nightclubs like the one here helped give Havana its reputation as "the sexiest city in the world."

SPORTS: Baseball: World Series, New York Yankees defeat Brooklyn Dodgers, 4–3; Ford Frick elected baseball commissioner ... Olympics held in Oslo and Helsinki ... Football: NFL, Detroit Lions defeat Cleveland Browns, 17–7 ... Basketball: NBA, Minneapolis Lakers defeat New York Knickerbockers, 4–3 ... Boxing: Rocky Marciano knocks out Joe Walcott for world heavyweight title.

"I am an invisible man. I am invisible, understand, because people refuse to see me."—**Ralph Ellison, *Invisible Man***

LITERATURE

Masterpiece of Invisibility

8 Like other works of high modernism, Ralph Ellison's *Invisible Man* caroms from naturalism to surrealism, from gutter slang to high-flown eloquence, from hilarity to tragedy. Its literary pedigree can be traced from Dostoyevsky to Faulkner. But blues, jazz, and African-rooted folktales enter the mix as well. What made the novel revolutionary when it was published in 1952 was that its principal characters and its 38-year-old author were black.

Novelists, as Ellison had complained in an earlier essay, rarely portrayed "Negro characters possessing the full, complex ambiguity of the human." And though Ellison's mentor Richard Wright had been lionized for his powerful *Native Son* (1940), its hectoring style and Marxist determinism belonged to another era. Ellison tilled the fresher soil of existentialism, exploring the efforts of an isolated Everyman to act meaningfully in an absurd universe.

Though largely autobiographical, Ellison's novel grapples with the universal human significance of the African-American experience. The anonymous narrator shares his life story: from his rural southern youth to his Harlem ghetto maturity (with stints at a black college and a northern factory); from his early belief in Booker T. Washington's self-help teachings to his brief flirtation with communism; and on to his disillusionment—his realization that he has been invisible not only to a racist society but to himself.

Invisible Man won the National Book Award for 1953. Future Nobel laureate Saul Bellow (whose own highly idiosyncratic idiom similarly derives from a mix of high and low language) praised its author for taking on an "enormously complex and difficult experience ... [for which] very few people are willing to make themselves morally or intellectually responsible." Ellison died in 1994 at age 80, his long-awaited second novel still unfinished. **◂1940.18 ▸1953.13**

ARGENTINA

Perón on the Decline

9 In his heyday, Argentine dictator Juan Perón was a hero to nationalists throughout the Third World. Even those who deplored his Nazi ties and repressive policies hailed his ambitious social and economic reforms and his defiance of the Yankees. At home, Peronist rallies drew millions. But his decline began in 1952, when his second wife, Eva, died of cancer at age 33. (The first Señora Perón, eerily, had died of the disease at the same age.)

The former actress's personal magnetism and rags-to-riches background had made her the idol of the *descamisados*, the "shirtless" masses. Through radio broadcasts and personal appearances, Evita (as she was known) helped establish Peronism as Argentina's state religion. She also helped win over the powerful Catholic hierarchy, in part by sponsoring a law mandating religious instruction in public schools. She unofficially ran the popular ministries of health and labor, while doling out charity (and inconspicuously lining her pockets) through the Eva Perón Foundation. She gained the vote for women. At her funeral, 16 people perished in the crush to see her body, which Perón thereafter kept preserved in the presidential mansion.

But Evita's widower scandalized Catholics by reversing pro-church legislation, legalizing prostitution, and dating teenage girls, and he angered nationalists by cozying up to Washington for economic aid. The resulting loans could not repair the damage done by inflation, corruption, and Perón's industrialization program. He responded to rising discontent with louder propaganda and intensified police brutality. He had dozens of priests arrested, leading to his excommunication by Pope Pius XII. Perón was ousted in 1955 and exiled to Madrid, where he began plotting his comeback. It came 18 years later. **◂1946.8 ▸1973.3**

Eva Perón acknowledges adoring crowds at the Buenos Aires airport.

MEDICINE

Man Becomes Woman

10 When ex-GI George Jorgensen left the Bronx, New York, for Denmark, he was a gangling young man. When reporters traced him to Copenhagen in 1952—after two years, five major operations, and 2,000 hormone injections—he (or, rather, she) was Christine Jorgensen, a pretty blonde who challenged a conservative generation's views on sex and gender. *(Above, Jorgensen before the operation, immediately after, and 20 years later.)* Returning to New York a few months later, Jorgensen said, "I'm happy to be home," then added, slyly, "What American woman wouldn't be?"

Although sex-change surgery had been performed as early as the 1920s, Jorgensen was the first transsexual to go public. By her own account, she'd enjoyed a completely normal boyhood—except that she'd always felt she should have been a girl. After reading of Danish doctors' interest in sexual endocrinology, Jorgensen traveled overseas in search of help. Although medically unspectacular, the Jorgensen case created an uproar in the press. It provided fodder for a host of later movies and novels (from *The Rocky Horror Picture Show* to *The Silence of the Lambs).* And it paved the way for other men to become women. ◂1948.10

IN THE UNITED STATES

houses when *Bwana Devil* opened in November and kicked off a craze. Throngs of moviegoers donned goofy red-and-green-lensed goggles to experience the thrill, and studio executives embraced 3-D as the device to save slumping Hollywood from television. It took about a year before audiences learned to associate the gimmick with poor quality, and 3-D died at the box office. ◂1922.8 ▸1953.M

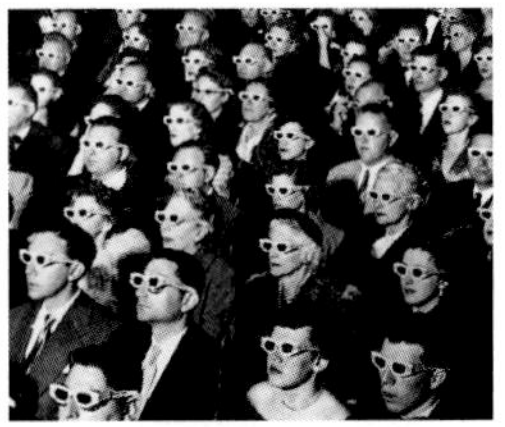

▶TRUMAN SEIZES STEEL MILLS—Seeking to avert an imminent strike that he claimed would hurt America's Korean War effort, President Truman in April 1952 seized the steel industry. Steel workers, who'd been working without a contract since the beginning of the year, celebrated, but executives, supported by the mainstream press, took a dim view. (TRUMAN DOES A HITLER, proclaimed the New York *Daily News.*) In June the Supreme Court ruled against the President's action. During a subsequent 53-day strike, America's defense did not visibly suffer. Eventually, an agreement was reached, and the mills went back into operation. The country had survived a constitutional crisis. ◂1943.M

▶POSITIVE THINKING—With the 1952 publication of *The Power of Positive Thinking,* pop prelate Norman Vincent Peale got in on the ground floor of a growth industry. Peale's inspirational book, infused with a cheerfully simple, peculiarly materialistic strain of Christianity, became one of the bestselling books of all time. ◂1936.M

▶PUERTO RICAN COMMONWEALTH—Ceded to the U.S. by Spain in 1898, Puerto Rico adopted a new constitution in 1952 and became an independent commonwealth of the U.S. The status change gave island residents the privileges of U.S. citizenship—minus one: the right to vote in federal elections. ▸1967.M

POLITICS & BUSINESS: GNP: $345.5 billion ... Dwight D. Eisenhower elected president, defeating Adlai Stevenson ... U.S. occupation of Japan ends (Japan renounces rights to Formosa, Kuril, Pescadores, southern Sakhalin, and Korea) ... G.I. Bill extended to Korean War veterans ... McCarran-Walter Immigration and Nationality Act passed (reinstates 1924 quota system and removes racial bans).

"What a fake! Yes, but a fake what?"—American composer Ned Rorem, on John Cage

AROUND THE WORLD

▶BOLIVIAN REVOLUTION— The lid blew off a shaky situation in Bolivia in April, when urban insurgents rose up against a military government that had prevented popularly elected president Paz Estenssoro from taking office. Leading the charge was Bolivia's National Revolutionary Movement (MNR). MNR rebels almost completely destroyed the army in the 1952 fighting. Estenssoro took office and brought about a series of social reforms that made the Bolivian revolution one of the most profound in South American history. ◀1941.9 ▶1980.6

▶DEADLY FOG— London's industrial and home furnaces belched out some 2,000 tons of sulfur dioxide and other toxic pollutants daily. At the beginning of December, an unusual weather system trapped the contaminants in the atmosphere, enveloping the city in filthy smog. The sky turned from yellow to black; visibility dropped to a few feet. By the time the poisonous gas lifted three weeks later, the "killer fog" had killed 4,000 people. Another 8,000, seemingly recovered, died later of respiratory failure. ◀1951.3

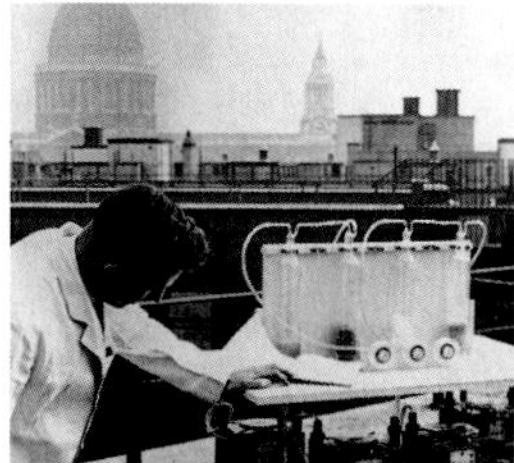

▶WORLD'S FIRST NUCLEAR ACCIDENT— Atomic power demonstrated its catastrophic potential in 1952, when a power surge at Canada's Chalk River Atomic Energy Research Center in southeast Ontario (95 miles from Ottawa) spewed a deadly cloud of radioactive fallout into the air. Nearly a million gallons of water in the reactor were contaminated. ◀1951.3 ▶1979.7

▶THE LONGEST RUN— In November, Agatha Christie's *The Mousetrap* opened at the Ambassador Theatre in London. Thirty years later—having moved to another venue without a schedule interruption—it became the longest-running play in the world. ◀1920.5

Off to fight crime, Marshal Will Kane bids adieu to his young bride (Grace Kelly).

FILM

Nobility in the Old West

11 *High Noon,* released in 1952, is a classic Western: the tale of Marshal Will Kane, who—on the day of his wedding and retirement—risks his life to save the cowardly townsfolk of Hadleyville from a band of revenge-seeking gunslingers. But the plot, centering on the marshall's crisis of conscience, is also an allegory for the plight of leftists and liberals who were blacklisted by Hollywood during the anti-Communist hysteria of the early Cold War. "It was my story of a community corrupted by fear," said writer Carl Foreman, who was soon blacklisted himself. (He moved to England and worked anonymously on several screenplays, including that of *The Bridge on the River Kwai*, directed by David Lean.)

Ironically, the role of Kane was played by Gary Cooper—a conservative who'd willingly testified before the House Committee on Un-American Activities. (He decried the alleged Communist infiltration of the film industry, but denounced no colleagues by name.) This veteran of cowboy movies wasn't the first choice of director Fred Zinnemann: At 50, Cooper seemed too old. The years had ravaged his face, and he suffered merciless pain from stomach ulcers and a bad hip. And though he was an Oscar winner (for 1941's *Sergeant York*) and a onetime box-office favorite, his most recent pictures had flopped. But *High Noon*'s financial backer, a California lettuce grower, was a vociferous Cooper fan—so the Montana-born cartoonist turned actor got the part.

The casting worked. Cooper's careworn countenance proved a refreshing contrast to Hollywood's usual handsome cowboys. And his naturalistic performance—filled with expressive twitches, glances, falters, and silences—earned him a second Oscar and renewed box-office cachet. ◀1947.5 ▶1962.7

MEDICINE

Saving the Heart

12 Beginning in 1952, a series of breakthroughs dramatically lowered the risks of cardiac surgery. One such advance eliminated the need for heart surgeons to work "blind"—by feel—through a pool of flowing blood. In September, Dr. Floyd Lewis at the University of Minnesota repaired a hole in the heart of a five-year-old girl whose body temperature had been lowered to 79 degrees. The chill (achieved by forcing a cooled alcohol solution through a rubber blanket in which the girl was wrapped) halved her oxygen requirement, allowing circulation to be stopped for more than five minutes.

A method of keeping the heart dry for longer periods came the following year, with the perfection of the heart-and-lung machine. Dr. John H. Gibbon, a surgeon at Philadelphia's Jefferson Medical College Hospital, had spent nearly 20 years developing the apparatus, which bypassed both the heart and lungs, and not only pumped blood, but replenished it with oxygen and removed carbon dioxide. Eventually, surgeons developed a technique called extracorporeal cooling, in which the temperature-lowering method was combined with the mechanical bypass method, while a machine chilled the blood itself.

Also in September 1952, Dr. Charles Hufnagel, of Washington's Georgetown University Medical Center, implanted the first artificial heart valve. An inch-and-a-half-long Plexiglas tube containing a plastic pellet, it replaced a faulty valve in the patient's aorta. A prime feature of the device was that it could function in any position. Said the surgeon: "Patients will be able to stand on their heads, if they like." ◀1914.11 ▶1967.1

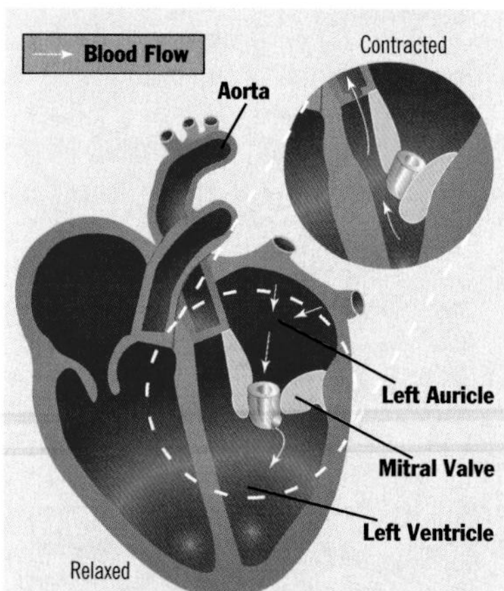

The artificial heart valve prevents blood from backing up into the left auricle when the heart contracts. In healthy hearts a natural valve seals off the left auricle.

MUSIC

Cage's Sound of Silence

13 Composer John Cage was more interested in ideas than in orchestras. His favorite music, he said, was "what we are hearing if we are just quiet." Cage's notorious *4′ 33″*, first performed in 1952, features a pianist who does not strike a key. The musician enters the concert hall, raises the piano lid, sits quietly for four minutes and 33 seconds, then closes the lid. The music consists of whatever "background" noises are audible during the prescribed time.

Considered by some critics the most important American composer of the mid-twentieth century (and by others not a composer at all), Cage was obsessed with percussion as well as with silence—and randomness. His early work featured "prepared pianos," whose blocked and weighted strings were plucked or strummed to produce a range of exotic sounds. Later, Cage wrote pieces for radios, tape recorders, and flowerpots, often consulting the *I ching* (the ancient Chinese divining book) to determine the music's structure. "I try to arrange my composing means," he once said, "so that I won't have any knowledge of what might happen."

If Schoenberg liberated dissonance, it was said, then Cage liberated noise. Yet for Cage himself, there was no noise—only sound. His theories (particularly the notion that music is essentially an "empty container") have probably been more influential than his music. Yet some of his compositions were even danceable: From the 1930s through the 1970s, Cage was music director for choreographer Merce Cunningham. ◀1948.M ▶1976.10

NOBEL PRIZES: Peace: Albert Schweitzer (Alsatian-German; Hospital at Lambaréné in French Equatorial Africa) ... Literature: François Mauriac (French; novelist) ... Chemistry: Archer Martin and Richard Synge (U.K.; partition chromatography) ... Medicine: Selman A. Waksman (U.S.; streptomycin) ... Physics: Edward Mills Purcell and Felix Bloch (U.S.; measurement of nuclear magnetism).

A VOICE FROM 1952

Betsy McCall Gets a Doll

From *McCall's* magazine, September 1952

For thousands of middle-class American girls in the fifties whose mothers read McCall's, *Betsy McCall was an idealized alter ego. She was also a brilliant marketing tool. Betsy was a paper doll, who in each month's issue of the popular women's magazine had a new adventure with her Mom; Dad; dog, Nosy; or one of her many playmates. She came with a variety of pretty outfits—the real-life counterparts of which were manufactured by* McCall's *advertisers and could be purchased in stores listed in the magazine's pages. The September 1952 installment* (below) *introduced the Betsy McCall doll with her "soft plastic face and Saran hair that can be washed and curled." Sewing patterns ("so simple a dexterous child can sew them up") for the doll's wardrobe appeared two issues later.*

Betsy McCall gets a doll

DRAWINGS BY KAY MORRISSEY

BETSY and her mother were buying a new dress. "Eeny, meeny, miney, mo," said Betsy. "Oh, Mummy," she broke off, "they're so pretty! Can't I have all three?" "All right," Mummy relented, "and you may wear the red dress home, but let's save the others for school. Now," she said, "shall we see about that new doll?" They took the escalator to the toy department. "I want a doll," Betsy told the clerk.

NEXT MONTH
BETSY McCALL MEETS A WITCH

"Now this is a *lovely* doll," said the salesgirl. "No," said Betsy, "she's too big. Besides, I want a doll that looks just like me!"

"Why I have *just* the doll!"—and the clerk led Betsy to a counter where there was a row of dolls—and they all looked *just like Betsy*

And they wore dresses exactly like Betsy's! "Oh, my," she said, "Let me have the one in red so right away everyone will see she's mine"

This is Betsy McCall

Try these dresses on Betsy's doll and see which one you like best

Betsy's striped dress has a red belt, white piqué collar and cuffs

Betsy looks like a Gibson Girl in her red dress with push-up sleeves

Betsy's gray-and-white checked dress has a scalloped bib of solid red

BETSY McCALL'S COTTON PANTIES BY CARTER'S
BETSY'S DRESSES BY YOUNG LAND
MAY BE SEEN AT MACY'S, NEW YORK,
AND STORES LISTED ON PAGE 156

© Copyright 1952 McCall Corporation

Dolls, frilly dresses, and a doting, stay-at-home mother were the accoutrements of Betsy McCall's prefeminist American girlhood.

1952

"I have a feeling that if your structure is true ... then all hell will break loose, and theoretical biology will enter a most tumultuous phase."—**Max Delbrück, on Watson and Crick's double helix**

STORY OF THE YEAR

The Double Helix

1 By 1953, many of the world's top microbiologists were close to determining the structure of deoxyribonucleic acid, or DNA—the molecule that carries the genetic code for virtually all forms of life. But it was left to a scientific odd couple, James D. Watson and Francis Crick, to make the breakthrough. Watson was an American prodigy who'd earned his doctorate at the tender age of 22. When they met in 1951, Crick, a 35-year-old English biophysicist (twelve years Watson's senior), had yet to receive his Ph.D. Watson was small and slight, his partner big and ebullient. In terms of talent and training, however, they were a perfect fit.

Crick *(left)* and Watson synthesized the work of many scientists to come up with their revolutionary DNA model.

Oddly enough, their relative inexperience proved an advantage. In contrast to some of their colleagues, Watson and Crick were not afraid to share ideas, to seek advice, and to make mistakes. "We didn't leave it that Jim did the biology and I did the physics," Crick said. "We both did it together and switched roles and criticized each other." DNA, the largest known molecule, had been discovered in 1869; in 1943, microbiologist Oswald Avery showed it had a hereditary function. What eluded scientists was the way DNA worked: how it determined the attributes of a cell—how, in other words, genes were replicated. Watson and Crick, office mates at Cambridge University's renowned Cavendish Laboratories (where Watson had gone to do postdoctoral research), undertook to explain this mystery.

Working from the X-ray diffraction photographs of British biophysicists Maurice Wilkins and Rosalind Franklin (used, Franklin protested, without permission), Watson and Crick pieced together the structure of DNA. They showed it to be a double helix—two intertwined, spiraling strands of polymers. When DNA separates into individual strands, each strand becomes the foundation on which an identical new one is built. The new strand and the old one constitute a new DNA molecule. Each new molecule contains the same genetic information as the original strand. Thus are genes and, eventually, chromosomes replicated, and genetic traits reproduced. In April 1953, Crick and Watson published their findings in the British scientific journal *Nature*. Biology was revolutionized, modern genetic science born. Crick, Watson, and Wilkins shared the 1962 Nobel Prize for medicine. Franklin was unable to share in the glory: She died in 1958, and according to Nobel regulations, the prize may not be awarded posthumously or split more than three ways. **◂1943.18 ▸1955.M**

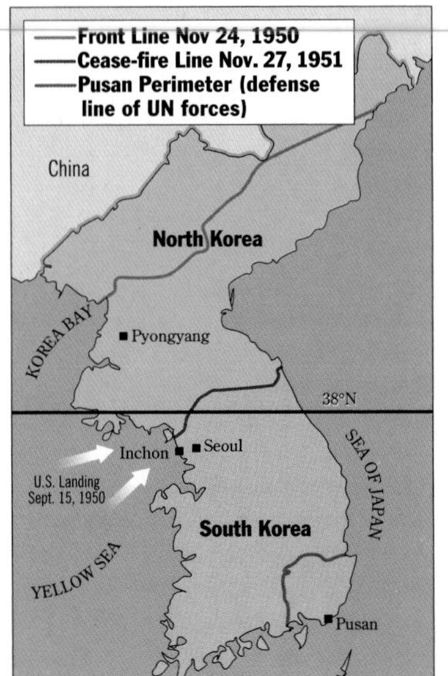

The UN cease-fire line formed the new border between North and South Korea.

KOREA

The War Ends

2 The undeclared Korean War ended in 1953, after three years of fighting between North Korean and Chinese Communists on one side, and United Nations (principally South Korean and American) forces on the other. The casualties were enormous. An estimated four million people died, including nearly a million Chinese, 54,000 Americans, several thousand other UN troops, and some two million North and South Koreans. But precious little territory changed hands.

Peace talks, under way since the spring of 1951, had been hampered by two main issues: where to draw the truce line between the two Koreas, and what to do with prisoners of war. The Communists proposed keeping the border at the 38th parallel, which they'd crossed to start the war. The UN insisted on the existing battle line, which gave the south a bit more land. Regarding prisoners, the UN supported "voluntary repatriation": It would return to North Korea and China only those prisoners who wished to go. The UN held 132,000 POWs; surveys indicated that almost one in three preferred to stay in South Korea. (Many of those prisoners were South Koreans who'd been conscripted by the invading northerners; many others were former Chinese Nationalists who'd been drafted by Mao Zedong's army.) The Communists rejected the notion, and the war of attrition ground on.

In June 1953, as the hostile factions finally approached agreement (the UN's border, and a neutral commission to adjudicate in the matter of prisoners unwilling to be repatriated), mercurial South Korean President Syngman Rhee tried to torpedo the peace process, ordering his troops to ignore any future treaty—and arranging the mass "escape" of 25,000 POWs who didn't want to go back north. When the Communists responded with a devastating offensive, U.S. officials pressured Rhee into cooperating. The armistice was signed on July 27. **◂1951.M ▸1968.6**

THE SOVIET UNION

Death of a Despot

3 His nation was unsure whether to grieve or celebrate when Joseph Vissarionovich Stalin, 73, died on March 5, 1953, four days after suffering a brain hemorrhage. Despised as a despot and revered as a virtual god, Stalin had run the Soviet Union for 29 years, bringing victory in war and pride in industrialization, but also overseeing mass murder, famine, and forced collectivization. In the atmosphere of official paranoia that Stalin had fostered, his possible successors—Georgi Malenkov, Vyacheslav Molotov, Lavrenti Beria, Nikolai Bulganin, Nikita Khrushchev—warily jockeyed for position. Citizens were urged again and again to remain calm and united; fears of dissension, chaos, and revolt pervaded the decapitated Kremlin.

Stalin was said to have been planning another purge when he died.

As Stalin's corpse lay in state in Moscow, a triumvirate composed of Malenkov (chairman of the Council of Ministers, and Stalin's handpicked heir), internal-security chief Beria, and foreign minister Molotov assumed nominal control. But Khrushchev (head of the Communist Party's central committee) soon emerged as second in power

ART & CULTURE: Books: *The Bridges at Toko-Ri* (James Michener); *The Adventures of Augie March* (Saul Bellow); *The Erasers* (Alain Robbe-Grillet); *Acquainted with the Night* (Heinrich Böll); *Fahrenheit 451* (Ray Bradbury); *The Waking* (Theodore Roethke) ... Music: "The Doggie in the Window" (Bob Merrill); "That's Amore" (Brooks and Warren); *All in the Spring Wind* (Chou Wen-Chung) ... Painting & Sculpture:

"Well, we knocked the bastard off!"—**Edmund Hillary, on his return to camp after reaching the summit of Mount Everest**

only to Malenkov. Beria, meanwhile, schemed to seize command. Malenkov and Khrushchev joined forces to thwart their colleague, arresting him in July for complicity in Stalinist terror. In short order, Beria was convicted and executed.

The move was shocking—tantamount to condemning Stalin himself. But if Beria was guilty, Krushchev and Malenkov were, too. So as the Party took its first cautious steps toward de-Stalinization, it was impossible to determine whether the country's leaders were conducting a revolution or simply a new kind of purge. **◂1947.4 ▸1956.2**

IRAN

CIA Backs a Coup

4 With the overthrow of Iran's elected government in August 1953, a shadowy new player entered world politics: the U. S. Central Intelligence Agency. Two years earlier, Iranian legislators, led by premier Muhammad Mussadegh, had nationalized the British-owned Anglo-Iranian Oil Company. Mussadegh had then become premier. Washington at first resisted London's calls for help in reversing the nationalization beyond sponsoring negotiations (which failed) and supporting a boycott of Iranian oil. The Truman administration was torn between loyalty to Britain and support for greater Iranian self-determination. But Truman's successor, conservative Dwight D. Eisenhower, was alarmed: Mussadegh might let Iran go communist.

An elderly, aristocratic liberal, Mussadegh opposed both Soviet interventionism and the British-backed monarch, Muhammad Reza Shah Pahlevi. But as the boycott wrecked Iran's economy and his nationalist political coalition, Mussadegh relied increasingly on dictatorial methods—and on the support of the communist Tudeh Party. In early 1953, he demanded the Shah's ouster; by then, however, even the Tudeh had turned against him. The moment had come, Eisenhower and British prime minister Churchill decided, to strike.

Key actors in the operation (which both governments kept secret) included U.S. secretary of state John Foster Dulles; his brother Allen, head of the CIA; and CIA station chief Kermit Roosevelt, son of the late President Theodore Roosevelt. The coup started badly: Dismissed by the Shah, Mussadegh refused to leave; his followers rioted, and the Shah fled to Rome. But the CIA hired mobs and organized a military revolt. In a week of street fighting, 300 Iranians died. Finally, Mussadegh was arrested and the Shah returned in triumph.

In Tehran, anti-Shah Iranians celebrate the Shah's (temporary) ouster by toppling a statue of his father.

Iran fell under military rule. The AIOC (reorganized in 1954 as British Petroleum) became an international consortium nominally owned by Iran; U.S. oil companies, unsurprisingly, gained a major stake. And anti-Americanism became a powerful force in Iranian society. **◂1951.12 ▸1971.M**

EXPLORATION

Everest Conquered

5 It was the realization of an ancient dream. On May 29, 1953, New Zealand mountaineer Edmund Hillary and Nepalese Sherpa guide Tenzing Norkay reached the summit of Mount Everest, at 29,028 feet the highest point on earth. "It was," reported Hillary, with typical understatement, "a great moment." Upon reaching the peak, the climbers, part of a British expedition, shook hands and unfurled a string of flags (United Nations, British, Nepalese, Indian). Norkay planted an offering of chocolate bars and biscuits to Everest's resident gods; Hillary presented a crucifix. They lingered in the subzero cold for 15 minutes, inhaling bottled oxygen, then began the descent to less rarefied heights.

Named for Sir George Everest, British surveyor of the Himalayas, Everest had been the object of many attempts before Hillary's. Among the more spectacular defeats: a 1924 British expedition in which two climbers reached a record height of 28,133 feet before disappearing, and a 1934 climb by soloist Michael Wilson, ending in his death from exhaustion. The opening of Nepal to outsiders in 1950 allowed Hillary access to Everest's hitherto unknown south side—with its far less forbidding terrain than the north.

The success of the 1953 expedition was greeted jubilantly in England, and Hillary and expedition leader John Hunt were promptly knighted. Hillary subsequently returned to the Himalayas and helped build schools, hospitals, and airfields for the Sherpa people, without whom his triumph would have been impossible. **◂1947.7**

Norkay *(right)* and Hillary prepare for the final stage of their assault on Everest.

BIRTHS

Jean-Bertrand Aristide, Haitian president.

Benazir Bhutto, Pakistani prime minister.

Christie Brinkley, U.S. model.

Tina Brown, U.K. editor.

Ron Howard, U.S. actor and filmmaker.

Jim Jarmusch, U.S. filmmaker.

John Malkovich, U.S. actor.

Tom Petty, U.S. singer.

Anna Quindlen, U.S. writer.

Cornel West, U.S. writer.

DEATHS

Maude Adams, U.S. actress.

Hilaire Belloc, U.K. writer.

Raoul Dufy, French artist.

Kathleen Ferrier, U.K. singer.

Edwin Powell Hubble, U.S. astronomer.

Ibn Saud, Saudi Arabian king.

James J. Jeffries, U.S. boxer.

Robert La Follette, Jr., U.S. senator.

John Marin, U.S. painter.

Robert Millikan, U.S. physicist.

Eugene O'Neill, U.S. playwright.

Francis Picabia, French painter.

Sergei Prokofiev, Russian composer.

Marjorie Kinnan Rawlings, U.S. writer.

Django Reinhardt, Belgian guitarist.

Ethel Rosenberg, U.S. convicted spy.

Julius Rosenberg, U.S. convicted spy.

Joseph Stalin, U.S.S.R. political leader.

Dylan Thomas, Welsh poet.

Jim Thorpe, U.S. athlete.

Bill Tilden, U.S. tennis player.

Jonathan M. Wainwright, U.S. general.

Hank Williams, U.S. singer.

Study After Velàzquez: Portrait of Pope Innocent X **(Francis Bacon);** ***Washington Crossing the Delaware*** **(Larry Rivers) ... Film:** ***From Here to Eternity*** **(Fred Zinnemann);** ***Shane*** **(George Stevens);** ***The Wages of Fear*** **(Henri-Georges Clouzot) ... Theater:** ***Picnic*** **(William Inge);** ***The Crucible*** **(Arthur Miller);** ***Tea and Sympathy*** **(Robert Anderson);** ***Kismet*** **(Borodin, Wright, and Forrest) ... TV:** ***Romper Room.***

"Potential Playmates are all around you: The new secretary at your office, the doe-eyed beauty who sat opposite you at lunch yesterday, the girl who sells you shirts and ties at your favorite store." —**Playboy, introducing its July 1955 "Playmate of the Month"**

NEW IN 1953

Irish coffee (at San Francisco's Buena Vista Cafe).

Corvette sports car.

TV Guide.

Japan Airlines (JAL).

Instant iced tea (White Rose Redi-Tea).

IN THE UNITED STATES

▶IN LIVING COLOR—For the minuscule audience of technophiles who owned color sets, regularly scheduled television broadcasts in color arrived on NBC in 1953. Ballyhooed for years, color met massive consumer resistance: The sets cost too much ($500 to $1,000); color pictures often bled and warped; color programming was available for only about two hours a day, virtually all on NBC (whose parent company, RCA, manufactured all color picture tubes); and adjusting the color demanded constant knobturning. Not until the 1960s did color begin to challenge the B&W market. ◀1941.14

▶WIDE-SCREEN MOVIES—Faced with mass defection to home theater (i.e., television), Hollywood pulled out old technological tricks in 1953 to lure audiences back into theaters. Twentieth Century-Fox's *The Robe* was the first movie released in CinemaScope, a filmmaking process whereby an extra-wide picture is squeezed onto standard 35-millimeter

film and projected onto a screen 2½ times as wide as it is high (the conventional ratio is 1.33 to 1). Unlike 3-D, the big-screen format was an innovation that stuck. ◀1952.M

POPULAR CULTURE

The *Playboy* Man

6 The first issue of *Playboy* magazine, bearing a photograph of Marilyn Monroe on its cover, carried no date because its publisher, 27-year-old Hugh Hefner, was not sure there would be a second. Conceived as a cross between

In the first issue, Marilyn Monroe was "Sweetheart of the Month" (thereafter known as "playmate").

Modern Man (a guns, girls, and cars rag) and *Esquire* (the swank monthly for which Hefner had once worked), the new magazine, launched in 1953, proved so successful that within three years it was outselling *Esquire*. Its ingenious editorial mix included a "Playmate of the Month" (whose nude body was displayed across a center gatefold), serious journalism, quality erotic fiction, and copious advice to its young, upwardly mobile readers about how to live the good life—the accoutrements of which were lavishly displayed in the magazine's glossy ads.

In a conformist era when male fantasies of success ostensibly centered on home and family, Hefner provided an immensely seductive alternative. The *Playboy* man was a smart bachelor whose pad was posh, whose whiskey was excellent, and whose sex life was unapologetically passionate and varied. Hefner himself assumed the role of Playboy Number One, publishing his magazine from the circular bed of a 48-room Chicago mansion. He soon extended the Playboy mystique to "member" nightclubs around the world, whose waitresses, called "bunnies," wore skimpy uniforms with rabbit ears and cottontails. By the 1970s, however, the mystique had begun to fade and Playboy Enterprises to decline. The magazine came under attack by both feminists (who found it exploitative) and right-wingers (who simply found it dirty). In the meantime, men seeking pictures of naked women had far more graphic magazines to choose from. **▶1962.V**

EAST GERMANY

Workers Revolt

7 Some 300,000 workers across East Germany walked off their jobs in June 1953. The first popular revolt in the postwar Soviet bloc attracted worldwide attention. It shifted from labor protest to pro-democracy demonstration to riot, then was finally quelled when Soviet tanks rolled into East Berlin. At least 21 people were killed; in the crackdown that followed, 1,300 were imprisoned and several executed.

Since its founding in 1949, East Germany (formally known as the German Democratic Republic, but in reality a one-party police state) had been remaking its economy after the Soviet model. Heavy industry was developed at the expense of consumer goods. Farms were collectivized, and to pay for industrialization, steep taxes were levied on private farmers. Industrial output soared, but agriculture suffered. Thousands of farmers fled to West Germany, and by 1952 East Germany faced serious food shortages.

Although the post-Stalin Kremlin advised him to moderate his course, East German Communist leader Walter Ulbricht decided in March to raise industrial production quotas by 10 percent. This move was what sent workers into the streets. The Soviets blamed "foreign hirelings" for the unrest, and rejected as capitalist propaganda a U.S. offer of $15 million in aid for East Germany. But the quota increase was quickly rolled back, and in 1954 Moscow declared the country a sovereign state. War reparations to the Soviet Union were ended—and for a few years, production of consumer goods rose, collectivization slowed, and restrictions on freedom of expression eased. **◀1949.3 ▶1961.1**

Anti-Communist East German workers burn a Soviet newspaper stand in Leipzig.

DIPLOMACY

An Impossible Job

8 In April 1953, Trygve Lie welcomed Dag Hammarskjöld to "the most impossible job on this earth." As the first secretary-general of the United Nations, Lie had been caught between two grindstones: the Soviets, who snubbed him after he backed U.S. intervention in Korea, and the powerful American right, which regarded the UN as a Communist front and clamored for U.S. withdrawal from the organization. With Senator Joseph McCarthy investigating UN staff members for subversion, morale was dismal. After the exhausted Lie's resignation, it took nearly six months to find a successor acceptable to both the Soviets and the West.

Hammarskjöld, 47, appeared to be the soul of neutrality. The son of a former Swedish prime minister, and

SPORTS: Baseball: World Series, New York Yankees defeat Brooklyn Dodgers, 4–2 (5th consecutive title) ... Football: NFL, Detroit Lions defeat Cleveland Browns, 17–16 ... Basketball: NBA, Minneapolis Lakers defeat New York Knickerbockers, 4–1 ... Tennis: Maureen Connolly wins Grand Slam (1st woman) ... Golf: Ben Hogan wins U.S. Open, Masters (breaks record by five strokes), and his first British Open.

"The joy and function of poetry is, and was, the celebration of man, which is also the celebration of God."—**Dylan Thomas**

Hammarskjöld, fresh to the UN's top job, in front of UN headquarters in New York.

a bachelor fond of mountaineering, literature, and other solitary pursuits, he'd avoided political entanglements as his country's chief delegate to the UN General Assembly. As secretary-general, he called himself a "technician," one whose primary aim was to smooth relations among member nations. He worked quietly behind the scenes, unruffling diplomatic feathers and rebuilding the UN's esprit de corps.

But in 1955, when he flew to Beijing to secure the release of 15 U.S. prisoners of war, Hammarskjöld suddenly emerged as a world leader. In the Hungarian and Suez crises of 1956, he bypassed the ponderous UN decision-making process, taking bold initiatives that brought him criticism as well as praise. And by the time he died in a Congo plane crash in 1961, he had helped shape the UN's role as a worldwide troubleshooter. Like his predecessor, he'd also earned Moscow's bitter enmity. **◂1946.2 ▸1961.M**

LITERATURE

Introducing Agent 007

9 His name was borrowed from an obscure ornithologist, but in the mouth of the British superspy it acquired elegance and the promise of danger: Bond ... James Bond. Introduced by writer Ian Fleming in his 1953 novel, *Casino Royale,* agent 007 starred in a string of bestsellers and an immensely popular movie series. He grew out of the experience of his high-born creator, who'd been a British naval intelligence officer during World War II. But Bond was mostly fantasy: A personification of Good battling Evil—with sex appeal liberally tossed in.

Appearing when the world was in an uproar over real-life espionage, Bond possessed a panache that leavened Cold War grimness. Insouciant and witty, with an arsenal of diabolically clever gadgets, a license to kill, and an insatiable libido, he cleared the world of nuclear madmen—and got the girl, to boot. Then he ordered a martini, "shaken, not stirred."

Fleming made up for his weaknesses as a prose stylist with crackling plots and pure inventiveness. He also had a way with names, creating the likes of Auric Goldfinger, Hugo Drax, Pussy Galore, and Kissy Suzuki. He wrote the books, he said, for "warm-blooded heterosexuals in railway trains, airplanes, or beds." And he wrote them "unashamedly for pleasure and money." **▸1963.9**

In *Dr. No* (1962), the first Bond film, Sean Connery *(left, with Ursula Andress)* was 007.

LITERATURE

Death of a Poet

10 By the time he died on the night of November 9, 1953, Dylan Thomas had published fewer than 100 poems, yet the 39-year-old Welshman was already considered the finest English-language poet of his generation. His *Collected Poems* had been received ecstatically; *Under Milk Wood,* his new "play for voices," promised similar success. His dramatically powerful readings showcased his art—a pungent, pun-filled stew of surrealism, Freudianism, and eccentric Christianity.

Yet he was beset by personal demons. On a third reading tour of North America, Thomas—as notorious for his heavy drinking, financial woes, and womanizing as he was admired for his literary gifts—went drinking at the White Horse Tavern in Manhattan's Greenwich Village. Returning to his hotel, he collapsed and uttered his last words: "I've had 18 straight whiskeys. I think that's the record." He fell into a coma and died without regaining consciousness; the autopsy attributed his death to an "insult to the brain."

Thomas on the set of *Under Milk Wood,* in New York. He died before it was produced.

In one of his most famous poems, an epitaph for his father, Thomas had also written his own: *"Do not go gentle into that good night ... Rage, rage against the dying of the light."* **◂1922.9 ▸1969.V**

IN THE UNITED STATES

▶WARREN'S COURT—Earl Warren was a moderately conservative politician (former governor of California and Thomas Dewey's 1948 vice-presidential candidate) when, in 1953, President Eisenhower named him to be Chief Justice of the U.S. Supreme Court. Unexpectedly, Warren presided over one of the most liberal and activist courts in the institution's history. Under his helmsmanship, the Court handed down such landmark rulings as *Brown v. Board of Education of Topeka, Miranda v. State of Arizona,* and *Baker v. Carr* (which reaffirmed the principle of "one person, one vote"). ▸1954.6

▶ROSENBERGS EXECUTED—Sentenced to die, convicted spies Julius and Ethel Rosenberg appealed all the way to the Supreme Court. Despite lingering doubts about the impartiality of the sentencing judge (and despite the worldwide furor that erupted on their behalf), the Court approved the execution by a 6-3 vote. Implored to commute the death sentence, President Eisenhower also decided to let it stand. On June 19, the Rosenbergs, the parents of two young sons, were put to death in the electric chair at Sing Sing prison, the first (and only) American civilians killed on a spying conviction. ◂1951.2

▶WITCH-HUNT CONTINUES—The Rosenbergs' execution did not dampen the government's zeal for tracking down Communists and other "subversives." Prominent 1953 targets included screen legend (and British subject) Charlie Chaplin, who was denied re-entry into the U.S. because of his dangerous views and "unwholesome" character; and J. Robert Oppenheimer, head of the Manhattan Project (and an opponent of the hydrogen bomb), who was accused of Communist sympathies. Oppenheimer was absolved of the charges, but the Atomic Energy Commission revoked his security clearance. ◂1950.5

POLITICS & BUSINESS: GNP: $364.6 billion ... Department of Health, Education and Welfare created (Oveta Culp Hobby appointed secretary) ... Submerged Lands Act gives states the title to off-shore oil deposits ... President Eisenhower establishes "Atoms for Peace" program to encourage nonmilitary uses for nuclear power ... New York Curb Exchange renamed American Stock Exchange.

"The expression that there is nothing to express, nothing with which to express, nothing from which to express, no power to express, no desire to express, together with the obligation to express."—**Samuel Beckett, explaining the paradox he faced as a writer**

AROUND THE WORLD

▶FIDEL'S FIRST REBELLION—The first sortie of young lawyer turned insurrectionist Fidel Castro against Cuban dictator Fulgencio Batista, on July 26, ended disastrously: Half of Castro's 165 insurgents were killed, wounded, or captured in a brash attack on the Moncada army barracks in Santiago de Cuba. Castro turned himself in and was sentenced to 15 years (he served eleven months). In court, he delivered an unapologetic oration, "History Will Absolve Me"; it became a seminal text of the brewing revolution, dubbed the "26th of July Movement." ◀1952.7 ▶1959.1

▶ADAMANT CHURCHMAN—An outspoken critic of his country's Stalinist regime, Roman Catholic primate of Poland Stefan Cardinal Wyszynski was arrested in 1953 for resisting Communist suppression of the Church. Wyszynski, a leader of the anti-Nazi resistance during World War II, was undeterred. Upon his release from prison in 1956, he continued to protest state policies, calling the Communists "Godless cultural barbarians." ◀1948.M ▶1956.4

▶CAMBODIAN INDEPENDENCE—Twelve years after the French made him king of Cambodia (Kampuchea), Prince Norodom Sihanouk decided the time had come to sever ties with his colonial sponsors: He dissolved Parliament, imposed martial law, and declared Cambodia an independent country. On a world tour known as the Royal Campaign, Sihanouk's power play paid off, and in November, France agreed to withdraw. With independence came a 15-year period of relative calm and prosperity in Cambodia, during which Sihanouk's strong and neutral

stance kept the country out of the Vietnam conflict. His tremendously popular reign ended in 1970, when General Lon Nol overthrew him in a U.S.-supported coup. ▶1969.6

***Godot* was first produced in English in 1953. Above, a 1991 British performance.**

THEATER

Godot Arrives

11 The small crowd of Parisian intellectuals and society people who pressed into the tiny Théâtre de Babylone on the night of January 5, 1953, to see the first performance of a first play by an eccentric Irishman writing in French witnessed an epochal event in theater history. Part vaudeville, part existential wail, *En attendant Godot* (*Waiting for Godot)* was unlike anything they had seen before. On a barren, penumbral stage—the dismal monotony broken only by a single tree—two tramps appeared, speaking a monosyllabic prose that was echoed by the stripped-down set. For two acts, the characters waited for Godot (who never appeared, though two passersby did), quarreled, contemplated suicide, waited.

When the play ended, many in the audience thought they'd been the victims of a hoax. But the critics in attendance instantly recognized the play's importance and its author, Samuel Beckett, as a theatrical master. *Godot* became the most celebrated and influential play in modern drama, subject to a dizzying array of interpretations—some declare it a Christian allegory, others a manifesto of nihilism—all of which its sphinxlike author resolutely refused to confirm. "I meant what I said," was his only comment.

Born and educated in Ireland, Beckett settled in Paris in 1937 (when he was 31), forging a close friendship with fellow Irish expatriate James Joyce. Until Beckett's breakthrough with *Godot*, his writing was generally ignored; even *Godot* (which he called a "bad play") piled up four years' worth of rejections before finding a publisher. Beckett considered his novels—most notably his masterful trilogy consisting of *Molloy, Malone Dies,* and *The Unnamable*—his primary works. He won the Nobel Prize in 1969. **◀1922.1 ▶1957.12**

IDEAS

Wittgenstein's Reality

12 Philosopher Bertrand Russell once observed that the three greatest influences on twentieth-century British philosophy had been logical positivism and a pair of books—the *Tractatus Logico-Philosophicus* and *Philosophical Investigations.* A group of thinkers had created the former, but the latter emerged from a single mind—that of an Austrian-Jewish genius named Ludwig Wittgenstein. Paradoxically, Wittgenstein's second great work, published in 1953, amounts to a repudiation of the first.

The *Tractatus*—written during World War I, when Wittgenstein was an Austrian army officer—is an exercise in radical empiricism: Reality is said to consist of countless discrete, irreducible facts, which humans attempt to communicate symbolically through words. *Philosophical Investigations*, written from 1936 to 1949, proceeds from the opposite premise. Rather than representing reality, words *determine* it. Philosophical problems arise not out of nature, but out of the daunting internal logic of language. Philosophy's complexity, Wittgenstein said, "is not a complexity of its subject matter, but of our knotted understanding."

His life was as remarkable as his intellect. The son of a wealthy steelmaker, he had a mystical conversion while reading Tolstoy during his military service; afterward, he gave away his fortune and became a village schoolteacher. Returning to philosophy in 1929, he took a post at Cambridge, but worked as a porter in a London hospital during World War II. In 1947, he retired to a remote cottage in Ireland. He died in 1951; according to his wishes, *Philosophical Investigations* appeared posthumously. **◀1910.4**

LITERATURE

Baldwin Tells It

13 James Baldwin's *Go Tell It on the Mountain*, published in 1953, is the story of a sensitive Harlem youth grappling with religion, family, and his homosexuality. Although Baldwin went on to become the foremost literary spokesman for America's civil rights movement, in this, his first novel, he wanted his characters to be "people first, Negroes almost incidentally." For an audience accustomed to equating black novels with "protest" novels, Baldwin's autobiographical tale was a revelation. One prominent critic called Baldwin, 29, a writer of "phenomenal maturity."

Baldwin wrote the novel in Switzerland, where he was the only black for miles around. (He had moved from New York City to Paris in 1948, having discovered, like Hemingway in the 1920s and his own mentor, Richard Wright, in the 1930s, that he could contemplate his homeland best from Europe.) To capture the cadences of African-American speech, he listened to blues records by Bessie Smith and struggled to remember how his own accent had sounded before he'd felt compelled to "whiten" it out of shame.

For this grandson of slaves, overcoming shame was the first step in finding an artistic voice. Find it he did: Moving back to America in 1957, Baldwin became active in the civil rights movement. Over the next three decades, he probed the psychological wounds of racism in novels, short stories, plays, essays, and lectures. **◀1952.8**

Baldwin went to live in Europe when he was 24. After 1969, he divided his time between Europe and the United States.

NOBEL PRIZES: Peace: George C. Marshall (U.S.; the Marshall Plan) ... Literature: Winston Churchill (U.K.; prime minister and historian) ... Chemistry: Hermann Staudinger (German; polymers) ... Medicine: Fritz A. Lipmann (U.S.; coenzyme A) and Hans Adolf Krebs (U.K.; citric acid cycle) ... Physics: Frits Zernike (Dutch; phase-contrast microscopy).

A VOICE FROM 1953

The Grandmother and the Misfit

From "A Good Man Is Hard to Find," by Flannery O'Connor, 1953

Profound religious faith informed the macabre imagination of writer Flannery O'Connor. Her monstrous characters, flawed in mind and body, grope toward a primitive understanding of the universe. Denied, they often resort to violence—which just as often turns into an unlikely instrument of grace. She explored the theme forcefully in the short story "A Good Man Is Hard to Find" (first published in 1953 in The Berkeley Book of Modern Writing*), wherein a family vacation goes terribly awry. En route from Georgia to Florida, a bickering clan detours to look for a nonexistent old plantation house. The fatuous grandmother insists it is there. The bratty kids whine and sass. The mute father fumes. The mother and baby fidget. When the car goes off the rutted dirt road, "The Misfit," an escaped convict, comes to their assistance. A good man he is not: He and his cohorts murder the family. An accomplished ironist as well as a metaphysician, O'Connor drew on the culture and dialect of her native South to weave a bitterly comic portrait of modern America.* ◄**1929.3**

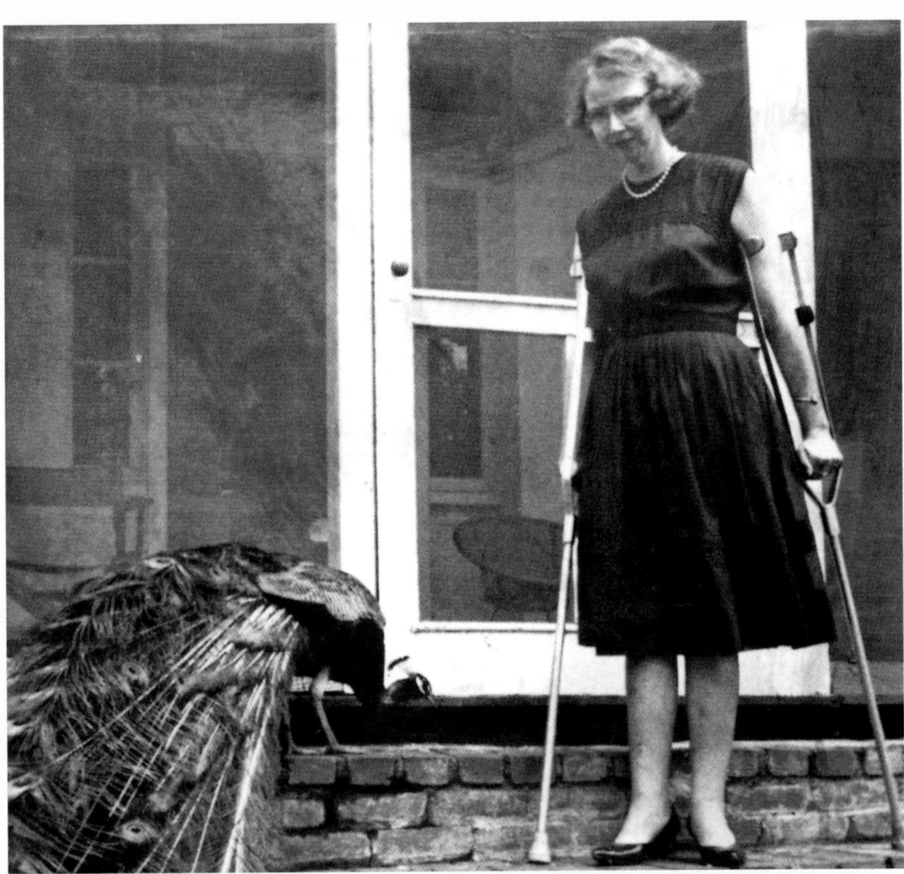

O'Connor's writing career was cut short by inherited lupus erythematosus, of which she died in 1964 at age 39. She spent her final years in Milledgeville, Georgia, where she raised peacocks as a hobby.

"Yes'm," The Misfit said as if he agreed. "Jesus thown everything off balance. It was the same case with Him as with me except He hadn't committed any crime and they could prove I had committed one because they had the papers on me. Of course," he said, "they never shown me my papers. That's why I sign myself now. I said long ago, you get a signature and sign everything you do and keep a copy of it. Then you'll know what you done and you can hold up the crime to the punishment and see do they match and in the end you'll have something to prove you ain't been treated right. I call myself The Misfit," he said, "because I can't make what all I done wrong fit what all I gone through in punishment."

There was a piercing scream from the woods, followed closely by a pistol report. "Does it seem right to you, lady, that one is punished a heap and another ain't punished at all?"

"Jesus!" the old lady cried. "You've got good blood! I know you wouldn't shoot a lady! I know you come from nice people! Pray! Jesus, you ought not to shoot a lady. I'll give you all the money I've got!"

"Lady," The Misfit said, looking beyond her far into the woods, "there never was a body that give the undertaker a tip."

There were two more pistol reports and the grandmother raised her head like a parched old turkey hen crying for water and called, "Bailey Boy, Bailey Boy!" as if her heart would break.

"Jesus was the only One that ever raised the dead." The Misfit continued, "and He shouldn't have done it. He thrown everything off balance. If He did what He said, then it's nothing for you to do but throw away everything and follow Him, and if He didn't, then it's nothing for you to do but enjoy the few minutes you got left the best way you can—by killing somebody or burning down his house or doing some other meanness to him. No pleasure but meanness," he said and his voice had become almost a snarl.

"Maybe He didn't raise the dead," the old lady mumbled, not knowing what she was saying and feeling so dizzy that she sank down in the ditch with her legs twisted under her.

"I wasn't there so I can't say He didn't," The Misfit said. "I wisht I had of been there," he said, hitting the ground with his fist. "It ain't right I wasn't there because if I had of been there I would of known. Listen lady," he said in a high voice, "if I had of been there I would of known and I wouldn't be like I am now." His voice seemed about to crack and the grandmother's head cleared for an instant. She saw the man's face twisted close to her own as if he were going to cry and she murmured," "Why you're one of my babies. You're one of my own children!" She reached out and touched him on the shoulder. The Misfit sprang back as if a snake had bitten him and shot her three times though the chest. Then he put his gun down on the ground and took off his glasses and began to clean them.

Hiram and Bobby Lee returned from the woods and stood over the ditch, looking down at the grandmother who half sat and half lay in a puddle of blood with her legs crossed under her like a child's and her face smiling up at the cloudless sky.

Without his glasses, The Misfit's eyes were red-rimmed and pale and defenseless-looking. "Take her off and throw her where you thrown the others," he said, picking up the cat that was rubbing itself against his leg.

"She was a talker, wasn't she?" Bobby Lee said, sliding down the ditch with a yodel.

"She would of been a good woman," The Misfit said, "if it had been somebody there to shoot her every minute of her life."

"Some fun!" Bobby Lee said.

"Shut up, Bobby Lee," The Misfit said. "It's no real pleasure in life."

"I can think of no greater tragedy than for the United States to become involved in an all-out war in Indochina."
—U.S. president Dwight D. Eisenhower, February 1954

STORY OF THE YEAR

French Defeat in Vietnam

1 Ho Chi Minh once predicted that, while his losses would outnumber France's tenfold in Vietnam, France would give in first. Ho's prophecy came true in 1954, after the Battle of Dienbienphu.

Certain that he could beat Ho's forces in conventional warfare, General Henri Navarre had wanted to tempt the Viet Minh (under General Vo Nguyen Giap) into dropping their guerrilla tactics and launching a big offensive. For bait, he ordered that a garrison be set up in Dienbienphu, a village in a valley near the northwestern border with Laos: A base there would hamper the Viet Minh in Laos, where the war had spread, while cutting off revenue from local opium crops. In November 1953, French paratroopers seized the village and began building a fortress ringed by fire bases. When the Viet Minh charged across the valley, they'd surely be slaughtered.

Navarre had assumed that the surrounding mountains would keep the enemy from bringing in heavy guns. He was wrong: 200,000 porters carried dismantled artillery on their backs. And he'd never expected the shovel-equipped attackers to *tunnel* up to the fortress walls. By March 1954, Dienbienphu was under heavy siege, relieved only by French and U.S. airdrops. Paris begged Washington to intervene. (The United States was already paying most of France's war bills.) But though Eisenhower warned America that Indochina's loss would cause "the fall of Southeast Asia like a set of dominoes," and Vice President Nixon was prepared to use atomic bombs, the administration finally demurred.

French forces in Indochina use boats to evacuate dead and wounded in 1954.

Dienbienphu fell on May 7, and its 10,000 surviving defenders were captured. The government of French premier Joseph Laniel fell, too; his successor, Pierre Mendès-France, pledged to obtain a cease-fire in Indochina. After eight years of war—costing 95,000 French dead (including 50,000 troops from France's African, Arab, and Caribbean colonies) and 1.3 million Vietnamese (including one million civilians)—the French had had enough. Negotiators in Geneva reached a settlement in July. Vietnam would become independent; it would be temporarily split at the 17th parallel, with Ho administering the north, where his strength was greatest, and French-backed former emperor Bao Dai in the south. Elections in 1956 would decide who was to run the whole nation. But Vietnam's troubles weren't over—and America's there had just begun. **◂1950.2 ▸1955.3**

Egyptian well-wishers mob Nasser, father of independence.

EGYPT

Nasser Takes Charge

2 For almost two years, Colonel Gamal Abdal Nasser had quietly directed Egypt's revolution-from-above, while General Muhammad Naguib served as president and prime minister. In February 1954, the colonel stepped to the fore. Citing Naguib's ties to the banned Muslim Brotherhood and his intention to restore the old system of government, Nasser forced him to resign. After mass protests led to Naguib's return, Nasser had the military junta legalize opposition parties to show its submission to the people's will. But he promptly arranged the arrest of pro-Naguib officers, and ordered the government party, the Liberation Rally, to call a general strike against a return to parliamentary rule. In April, Naguib capitulated; Nasser relegated him to the figurehead post of president and took over the premiership.

By October, Nasser had completed negotiations for the gradual withdrawal of Britain's remaining troops, stationed along the Suez Canal. The announcement that Egypt would be free at last made Nasser a hero to many. But to the fundamentalist Brotherhood, the treaty, which permitted British intervention in certain circumstances, was a sellout. A Brotherhood assassin shot at Nasser, missing him narrowly, as he gave a speech in Alexandria.

The dictator's survival (said to be "miraculous"), and his courage under fire—"If I die," he shouted, "you are all Gamal Abdal Nassers!" —boosted his popularity. The attack also gave him an excuse to execute six Brotherhood leaders, jail thousands, and place Naguib under house arrest. His domestic rivals defeated, Nasser could begin making an impact on the world. **◂1952.3 ▸1956.3**

COLONIALISM

Algerian War Begins

3 Having lost the Indochinese War, France plunged into a similar conflict in Algeria. That colony's nationalists had lain low since their last revolt nine years earlier, hobbled by government repression and internecine wrangling. Then, in November 1954, the new National Liberation Front (FLN) proclaimed a revolution. It began with the murder of a few settlers and pro-French Muslim officials. French forces responded by jailing hundreds and ransacking whole villages. Those reprisals swelled the FLN's ranks, and in August 1955 the rebels upped the ante, massacring 123 civilians (including 71 Europeans) in the town of Philippeville. In retaliation, French troops, police, and

Algerian refugees marching to an internment camp during the revolution.

ART & CULTURE: Books: ***Under the Net*** **(Iris Murdoch);** ***The Confessions of Felix Krull*** **(Thomas Mann);** ***Bonjour Tristesse*** **(Françoise Sagan);** ***Pictures from an Institution*** **(Randall Jarrell);** ***Poems 1923–1953*** **(e.e. cummings) ... Music: "Rock Around the Clock" (Freedman and De Knight); "Shake, Rattle and Roll" (Charles Calhoun); "Fly Me to the Moon" (Bart Howard);** ***Symphony No. 5*** **(Walter Piston) ...**

vigilantes slaughtered some 1,300 Muslims. The scattered insurrection had become a real war.

Like the Indochina War, the Algerian imbroglio began under a left-leaning French government. Premier Pierre Mendès-France, a liberal, was willing to consider autonomy for rebellious Morocco and Tunisia. (Both gained independence in 1956.) But Algeria was different: No mere protectorate, it was legally part of France; its 8.7 million Muslims were French subjects. Moreover, oil had just been discovered there. Although many in France recognized the need for reform—the Muslims suffered political and economic discrimination—independence was out of the question.

In January 1955, Mendès-France made Jacques Soustelle, a sympathetic ethnologist, Algeria's governor-general. Soustelle tried to promote Muslim equality, but the FLN's continued violence turned him into a hard-liner, and in 1956 a new French government called him home. French troops (their numbers quintupled to nearly 500,000) began forcing villagers from guerrilla zones into resettlement camps. The FLN struck back with a campaign of terrorist bombings in Algiers—setting the stage for the biggest crackdown yet. **◄1945.11 ►1958.4**

TECHNOLOGY

First Nuclear-Powered Sub

4 Launched at New London, Connecticut, in January 1954, the *Nautilus* (named not just for the sea creature but also for the submersible craft invented by Robert Fulton in 1800 and the fictitious one piloted by Jules Verne's Captain Nemo in *Twenty Thousand Leagues Under the Sea*) was the world's first nuclear submarine. Measuring 319 feet long and housing a crew of 95, it dwarfed earlier subs; its cruising speed of 20 knots more than doubled that of its predecessors. But its most significant departure lay in its power source: an onboard reactor that, unlike combustion engines, needed no air to function. Previous submarines had been essentially surface vessels able to make temporary dives; the new craft had to come up only rarely. Its uranium fuel would last for years. Initially, air for breathing came from conventional bottled oxygen; later, electrolysis of seawater provided a virtually inexhaustible supply.

Developed by the Naval Reactors Branch of the Atomic Energy Commission (under U.S. Navy rear admiral Hyman Rickover) and manufactured by the General Dynamics Corporation, the *Nautilus* took a year and a half and more than $30 million to build. In January 1955, having passed all preliminary tests, the sub steamed out of New London on its inaugural voyage. Averaging 16 knots, it logged 1,381 uninterrupted underwater miles to Puerto Rico—both records. Three years later, Commander William R. Anderson skippered the *Nautilus* to another first: a blind cruise (under ice 35-feet thick) from Point Barrow, Alaska, to the Greenland Sea, directly beneath the North Pole. **◄1951.3**

Rickover's nuclear *Nautilus* gave the U.S. Navy underwater primacy.

ARCHITECTURE

Mies's Modernist Monument

5 For Ludwig Mies van der Rohe, a German-born Bauhaus master (who had relocated to Chicago in 1937), the commission to design an office building for the Seagram liquor corporation offered a premier American site on which to showcase his architectural vision: New York's dazzling Park Avenue. For his partner on this job, Philip Johnson, the project presented a rare opportunity to collaborate with Mies, whose work Johnson had championed in his tastemaking book *The International Style* (1932). Begun in 1954 and completed four years later, the Seagram Building set a new standard for the century's boldest architectural innovation, the skyscraper. Soaring to a height of 516 feet, the geometrically pristine structure incorporated features that soon became standard in cities around the world: a sweeping fountain plaza, floor-to-ceiling windows, tinted glass.

The Seagram Building raised skyscrapers to new heights of elegance.

"God," Mies once said, "is in the details." The Seagram project, his first major office building, bore him out. Elevated on a platform, magisterially set back from the street, the unadorned glass and marble rectangle rose on a frame of concrete-encased steel, its surface warmed by slicing bronze mullions. A low pavilion projecting rearward from the tower housed the austere and elegant Four Seasons restaurant and bar, designed by Johnson. However coolly imperious, the building was in no way dismissive of its established neighbors. It is no accident that the Seagram plaza offered the city's best vantage of an earlier monument—McKim, Mead and White's gorgeous Italian Renaissance–style Racquet and Tennis Club, directly across Park Avenue. **◄1919.9 ►1965.13**

BIRTHS

Chris Evert, U.S. tennis player.

Matt Groening, U.S. cartoonist.

Ricki Lee Jones, U.S. singer.

Hanif Kureishi, U.K. writer.

Walter Payton, U.S. football player.

Denzel Washington, U.S. actor.

Oprah Winfrey, U.S. talk show host.

DEATHS

Lionel Barrymore, U.S. actor.

Maxwell Bodenheim, U.S. writer.

Jacques Brandenberger, Swiss novelist.

Sidonie Gabrielle Colette, French writer.

André Derain, French painter.

Enrico Fermi, U.S. physicist.

Harry "Bud" Fisher, U.S. cartoonist.

Wilhelm Furtwängler, German conductor.

Charles Ives, U.S. composer.

Auguste Lumière, French inventor.

Reginald Marsh, U.S. artist.

Henri Matisse, French artist.

Alan Turing, U.K. mathematician.

Getúlio Vargas, Brazilian president.

Glenn Scobey "Pop" Warner, U.S. football coach.

Painting & Sculpture: *Colonial Cubism* (Stuart Davis); *Vache la belle allegre* (Jean Dubuffet) ... **Film:** *On the Waterfront* (Elia Kazan); *The Seven Samurai* (Akira Kurosawa); *La Strada* (Federico Fellini); *A Star Is Born* (George Cukor); *Rear Window* (Alfred Hitchcock) ... **Theater:** *Separate Tables* (Terence Rattigan); *The Rainmaker* (N. Richard Nash); *The Pajama Game* (Adler and Ross) ... **TV:** *Father Knows Best.*

"I felt like an exploded flashlight.... There is a certain oblivion at that point."—**Roger Bannister, after crossing the finish line**

NEW IN 1954

Unification Church (founded in South Korea by Sun Myung Moon).

Sports Illustrated magazine.

Frozen TV dinners (Swanson).

Solar battery (Bell Telephone Labs).

Auto fuel-injection system (Mercedes 300SL).

Value added tax (France).

Televising of Miss America pageant.

Phrase "under God" in the Pledge of Allegiance.

IN THE UNITED STATES

▶**LATE-NIGHT TALK**—The second of NBC's so-called sofa-and-desk shows, *The Tonight Show* had its network

premiere on September 27. For the next four decades, hosted by four different stars, it led the late-night ratings. Original host Steve Allen (*above*), the show's co-creator, was casual and dry. His successor, Jack Paar (1957-62), an inspired interviewer, had a more risqué sense of humor. Johnny Carson took over in 1962. Cool, wry, midwestern, Carson became an arbiter of American popular culture. After 30 years behind the desk, he handed off the job to Jay Leno, the first host young enough to have grown up watching *The Tonight Show*. ▶1992.M

▶**FIRST NEWPORT JAZZ FESTIVAL**—Musicians spanning the raucous history of jazz—legends of New Orleans Dixieland to masters of swing to

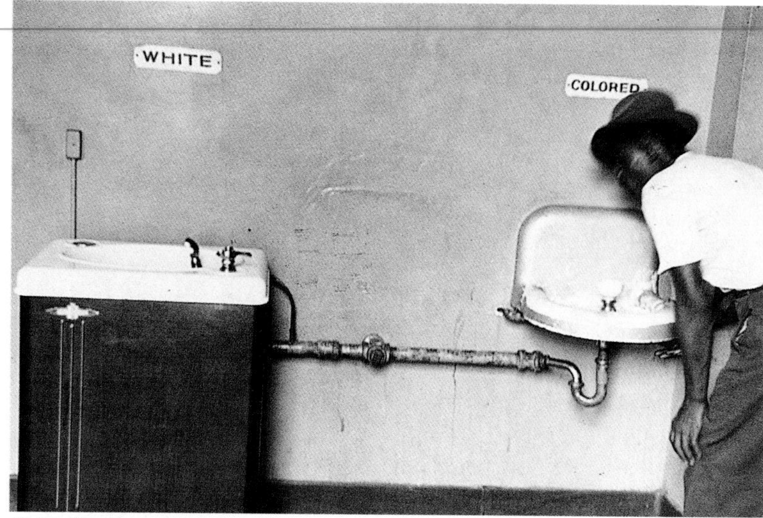

Under Jim Crow, blacks endured separate but never equal facilities.

SOCIAL REFORM

Death Sentence for Jim Crow

6 For nearly a century, America's "Jim Crow" laws (found mainly, but not exclusively, in the South) had mandated separate facilities—from restrooms to hospitals—for blacks and whites. In May 1954, the U.S. Supreme Court earned plaudits around the world by declaring segregation in public schools unconstitutional. Its decision in *Brown v. Board of Education of Topeka* dug Jim Crow's grave—but the old devil was slow to die.

The high court had endorsed segregation in its 1896 *Plessy v. Ferguson* decision, ruling that the Constitution justified "separate but equal" accommodations. By the 1950s, the National Association for the Advancement of Colored People had collected ample data showing that, in practice, black schools were unequal—underfunded, understaffed, and overcrowded. The organization's lawsuits had won isolated improvements. But in 1952, the Supreme Court began reviewing five NAACP suits (rejected by lower courts) contending that segregation was *inherently* unequal and harmed black students.

The cases were collectively named for the first one considered: that of Linda Brown, age eleven. Her father had sued the Topeka, Kansas, board of education, demanding that she be allowed to attend a nearby white school—instead of having to cross a railroad yard to take a bus to a black school. The NAACP's attorney, future Supreme Court justice Thurgood Marshall, argued that, besides having supplies and buildings that were usually inferior, black-only schools ostracized Linda and other black youngsters, depriving them of self-esteem and ordinary social opportunities.

This time, the Court agreed with him, in a unanimous decision. In public education, wrote Chief Justice Earl Warren, "the doctrine of 'separate but equal' has no place." The Court followed up the landmark decision with a ruling the following year that school desegregation be implemented "with all deliberate speed." But the governor of Georgia, Herman Talmadge, spoke for many segregationists when he called the *Brown* ruling "a mere scrap of paper." It would take the civil rights movement many years to turn it into something more. ◂1948.V ▸1955.2

THE UNITED STATES

Dulles Ups the Ante

7 In January 1954, Secretary of State John Foster Dulles (*below*) introduced a new U.S. military policy aimed at deterring

Soviet expansion. It was called "massive retaliation," and it sent ripples of fear and confusion around the world. The United States would henceforth rely upon "a great capacity to retaliate, instantly, by means and at places of our choosing" —reserving the right to respond to minor "brushfire wars" with nuclear weapons.

Massive retaliation was the signature doctrine of President Eisenhower's streamlined "New Look" military—and a sharp break with the Truman administration policy of "containment" of the Soviets. (A onetime Truman adviser, Dulles had long denounced his former boss's policy as hopelessly passive.) The Eisenhower White House was determined to cut costs, but it also intended to aggressively police the world against the spread of communism. Defending every hot spot by conventional means would be too expensive, but the threat of superbombs would make that unnecessary.

Most international observers dismissed massive retaliation as a bluff, scoffing at the notion that Washington planned to escalate some colonial skirmish into nuclear apocalypse. A good many others, however, took the idea seriously indeed. Responding to an uproar of protest, Dulles published a clarification, explaining that H-bombs were "not the kind of power which could be most usefully evoked under all circumstances." Nonetheless, he wrote, "imaginative use" must be made of all the weapons in America's arsenal to fend off the Reds. ◂1947.4 ▸1957.2

SPORTS

Four-Minute Milestone

8 For generations, experts on such matters had declared that no human could run a four-minute mile. When Oxford University medical student Roger Bannister set out to do it in 1954, some coaches even feared the effort would be fatal. But on May 6, at a meet between the Oxford team and the British Amateur Athletic Association, Bannister made the mile in 3:59.4—shaving two full seconds off the previous record, set in 1945. To sports fans everywhere, the event had the impact of the breaking of the sound barrier.

Compared with others seeking the same objective, Bannister had faced daunting obstacles: His studies limited training time to an hour a day, and he had no formal coach. But his attitude was unbeatable. Under the influence of Oxford trainer Franz Stampfl, he was a convert to the new idea that *belief* was a crucial factor in athletic victory: With the mental discipline that later made him a successful

SPORTS: Baseball: World Series, New York Giants defeat Cleveland Indians, 4–0; Hank Aaron joins Milwaukee Braves ... Football: NFL, Cleveland Browns defeat Detroit Lions, 56–10 ... Basketball: NBA, Minneapolis Lakers defeat Syracuse Nationals, 4–3 ... Boxing: Rocky Marciano defends heavyweight title twice against Ezzard Charles ... Soccer: World Cup, West Germany defeats Hungary, 3–2.

"If Great Britain and France felt that they must take an independent line backing the present government in Guatemala, we would feel free to take an equally independent line concerning ... Egypt and North Africa."—U.S. ambassador to the UN Henry Cabot Lodge

neurologist, Bannister convinced himself that he could achieve his goal. Should he perish, he decided, that was just too bad. "I was," he later said, "prepared to die."

Bannister survived, though he fainted when he crossed the finish line and suffered temporary color-blindness afterward. Perhaps the most curious result of his having finally broken the four-minute barrier was

Bannister does the "impossible."

what became known as the "Bannister Effect." Just six weeks later, Australian John Landy ran a mile in Turku, Finland, in 3:58. Quickly thereafter, a whole flock of runners trampled the once-impassable four-minute barrier. ◂1924.10 ▸1960.M

GUATEMALA

An Orchestrated Coup

9 A year after instigating a coup in Iran, the U.S. Central Intelligence Agency struck closer to home. Guatemalan president Jacobo Arbenz Guzmán had seized 234,000 acres from the U.S.-based United Fruit Company for distribution to the peasantry, and had grown friendly with local Communists. Washington wanted Arbenz out, but the Organization of American States prohibited intervention. The CIA then began covertly arming and training rightist Guatemalan exiles in Nicaragua and Honduras. And in June 1954, after Guatemala received a shipload of weapons from Czechoslovakia (having evaded a U.S. embargo), Eisenhower ordered the rebels to invade.

Government troops quickly blocked their advance, but the insurgents possessed two crucial weapons: warplanes and radio transmitters. The half-dozen planes, flown by U.S. airmen, struck highly visible targets in Guatemala City. (Guatemala's air-force chief had defected to the rebels, crippling the country's meager air defenses.) The clandestine radio network—run by future Watergate conspirator E. Howard Hunt—broadcast false reports of rebel victories. The insurgents numbered only 400, but Guatemalans believed they were thousands strong.

Foreseeing a bloodbath, the Guatemalan army refused to back Arbenz, and after two weeks of chaos, he resigned. (He later went into exile.) In office since 1951, he'd been Guatemala's second popularly elected president—a leader of the 1944 revolt that brought not only democracy and free expression to the country but laws establishing minimum wages, maximum hours, and labor's right to strike. Under the dictatorship of rebel Colonel Carlos Castillo Armas, such rights vanished. Few Latin Americans believed the CIA's denial of involvement with the coup, and anti-U.S. sentiment burgeoned throughout the region. ◂1913.4 ▸1992.13

Guatemalan rightists train weapons on an Arbenz effigy. The placard around its neck reads, "I am going back to Russia with [former Guatemalan socialist president] José Arévalo."

LITERATURE

Lord of the Hobbits

10 The dragons, wizards, and other fantastic creatures of J.R.R. Tolkien's trilogy, *The Lord of the Rings,* beckoned to a generation of youthful readers seeking escape from the modern world. Garnering little notice when its first volume, *The Fellowship of the Ring,* was published in 1954, the work surged in popularity a decade later—selling three million paperback copies between 1965 and 1968 alone.

An Oxford professor of medieval literature, Tolkien created a fictional universe inspired by English mythology. His 1937 novel, *The Hobbit,* introduced a race of gnomish creatures called hobbits —natives of the realm of Middle Earth—and presented a mock-erudite portrait of their language, history, cosmology, and geography. The *Rings* trilogy was a full-blown hobbit epic, complete with heroes (Bilbo Baggins and his nephew Frodo), a mystical treasure, and the monster protecting it.

Many observers have pointed out an apparent connection between the trilogy's rediscovery in the sixties and a parallel rise in drug use. Social critic Nigel Walmsley asserted that taking the psychedelic chemical LSD "led to an atavistic evaluation of the primitive and the ethnic over the modern," thus rendering the intellectual environment ripe for Tolkien's oeuvre. Certainly, the decade's hippie ethos—with its communal living, low-tech handicrafts, and general hirsuteness—could be seen as mirroring hobbit culture. But Tolkien's works continued to attract new readers long after the hippie era itself had come and gone. ◂1942.M

IN THE UNITED STATES

bebop innovators—mingled-with East Coast aristocrats at the gilded summer colony of Newport, Rhode Island, for the first Newport Jazz Festival, in July. Conceived by a Newport couple and directed by Boston jazz impresario George Wein, the festival was attended by thousands, who responded enthusiastically to music as far outside the mainstream as the blue bloods themselves. Jazz had arrived. The festival went on to become a huge annual event. It moved to New York City in 1972. ▸1955.7

▶FASCINATING RHYTHMS—"Mambo Italiano" and "Papa Loves Mambo" were among America's favorite songs in 1954. Everyone seemed to love the jazzy, Afro-Cuban dance with its heavy beat. Cuban bandleaders Tito Puente, Machito, and Perez Prado all had mambo hits. Mambo fever later turned into cha-cha frenzy. Lighter, brighter, and easier for Americans to dance to ("One, two, cha-cha-cha"), the infectious spin-off ignited an international dance craze. ◂1914.7 ▸1956.13

▶WATTS FOLK ART—In 1954, Simon Rodilla put the final piece in place on the group of towers he'd begun erecting in the Watts section of Los Angeles 33 years earlier. Untrained as a sculptor or architect, Rodilla built his soaring, fan-

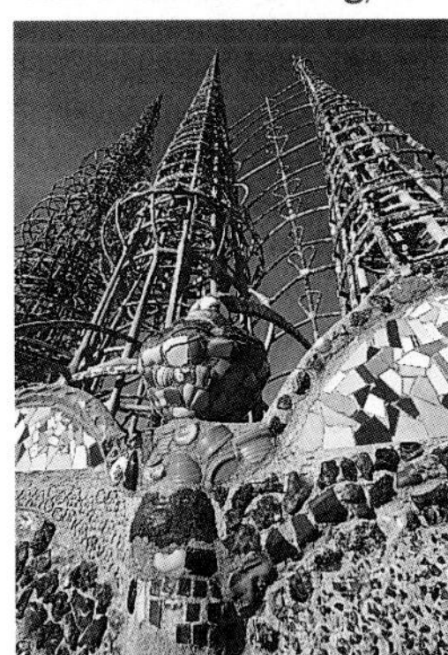

tastic ramparts out of urban detritus—discarded steel and wood, car parts, stone, glass, foil, bottle caps—which he stacked, shaped, and arranged according to some inner vision. The Watts Towers have been compared to Catalan architect Antonio Gaudí's ebullient and unfinished La Sagrada Familia cathedral in Barcelona. ◂1909.4

POLITICS & BUSINESS: GNP: $364.8 billion ... Strom Thurmond (South Carolina) is first senator elected by write-in vote ... Espionage and Sabotage Act establishes death penalty for sabotage in peacetime, no statute of limitations ... U.S Air Force Academy established ... Anglo-Iranian Oil Company renamed British Petroleum.

"We've got to have rules and obey them. After all, we're not savages: We're English; and the English are best at everything."
—William Golding, in *Lord of the Flies*

AROUND THE WORLD

▶STROESSNER TAKES CONTROL—When he seized power in Paraguay in 1954, General Alfredo Stroessner, the son of a German immigrant, ended a period of weak dictatorships. Rigging elections, suspending civil rights, and suppressing political opposition, Stroessner turned Paraguay into a black market conduit and a haven for international outlaws. Ruling for 35 years, Stroessner was surpassed only by Fidel Castro as the Western Hemisphere's longest-reigning despot. A fierce anti-Communist, he enjoyed the sustained support of the U.S. ▸1989.7

▶PIONEERING PHOTOJOURNALIST—Covering the war in Indochina for *Life*, preeminent photojournalist Robert Capa was killed in May when he stepped on a land mine in Thai-Binh, Vietnam. A founding member, with fellow photographers Henri Cartier-Bresson, David Seymour, and George Rodger *(above, right, with Capa in Naples)*, of the Magnum photo agency, Capa was a dogged and fearless photojournalist who compiled a stunning visual record of war during his globe-trotting career. ◂1936.M

▶AUTEUR THEORY—French critic (and later filmmaker) François Truffaut helped legitimize cinema as an academic discipline when he published his "A Certain Tendency in French Cinema" in the January issue of the influential film journal *Cahiers du Cinéma*. Arguing that the "authorship" of a movie—a consummately collaborative art form—belongs to the director, Truffaut attacked the smooth, highly literary tradition of French cinema wherein the director's personality was subsumed in the script. Truffaut's "auteur" theory, as adapted and popularized in the early 1960s by American film critic Andrew Sarris, launched a new appreciation of the work of commercial Hollywood directors. ▸1959.7

Frida Kahlo's *The Two Fridas* (1938). The Frida at right holds a small portrait of the artist's husband, Diego Rivera.

ART

Kahlo's Surreal Reality

11 "I hope the exit is joyful," confided Frida Kahlo in her final diary entry, "and I hope never to come back." A paradoxical combination of dreamer and realist, Kahlo died on July 13, 1954. Overshadowed during much of her life by her husband, the pioneering Mexican muralist Diego Rivera, Kahlo is now regarded as one of Mexico's greatest painters. In 1990, she became the first Latin American artist to break the $1 million mark at auction.

In the precisely rendered, richly symbolic self-portraits that make up the bulk of her work, Kahlo melded Mexican folk and colonial traditions with a powerful, often disturbing, personal vision. André Breton, the founder and aesthetic arbiter of surrealism, claimed her for his movement and called her homeland a "surreal country." But the surrealists trafficked in the imagery of dreams, whereas Kahlo "never painted dreams," she insisted. "I always painted my own reality." That reality was often nightmarish. When she was 18, her pelvis was crushed in a bus accident, leaving her a semi-invalid for life. Her tumultuous marriage to the compulsively unfaithful Rivera—they divorced once, remarried a year later—was another source of recurring pain. She compensated with affairs of her own, taking lovers (including exiled Soviet leader Leon Trotsky) of both sexes.

Artistically, sexually, and politically (she, like Rivera, belonged to Mexico's Communist vanguard), Kahlo explored identity—her own and her country's. Images of personal and national history commingle in her painting—a more subtle and searching art than Rivera's stirring public monuments. In 1985, the Mexican government declared Kahlo's work a national treasure. **◂1933.V**

MEDICINE

First Successful Transplant

12 History's first successful organ transplant was achieved in 1954 by a team of surgeons at Boston's Peter Bent Brigham Hospital. Earlier transplant attempts had all been foiled by the body's tendency to attack foreign tissue as if it were an infection. An important step forward had occurred in 1952, when French surgeons (under the aegis of pioneering nephrologist Jean Hamburger) transplanted a kidney from a Parisian woman to her injured son. The son appeared to recover and survived a record three weeks before rejecting the organ. Hamburger's experimental procedure indicated that there was a correlation between donor-recipient kinship and the possibility of the body's accepting the organ.

Two years later, a patient named Richard Herrick presented the Boston group, led by Dr. Joseph Murray, with a rare opportunity. Herrick, 24, was dying of kidney failure—and he had a twin brother, Donald. Since identical twins come from a single egg, Murray and his colleagues reasoned, their cell proteins are probably identical as well; thus, the immune system of one would probably fail to recognize as foreign the organs of the other. On December 23, the team removed Donald Herrick's left kidney and transplanted it to Richard. The organ began working immediately; both Herricks survived—Richard for eight years before dying of an unrelated illness. Between twins, organ transplants worked. For others, the immune system remained an insurmountable stumbling block until the advent of immunosuppressive drugs nearly a decade later. **◂1952.12 ▸1967.1**

Donald *(left)* and Richard Herrick with their nurse, after the operation.

LITERATURE

Golding's Grim Fable

13 "When I was young, before the war, I did have some airy-fairy views about man," writer and onetime naval officer William Golding once observed. "But I went through the war and that changed me." Golding's disillusionment was much in evidence in his enormously influential first novel, *Lord of the Flies*, published in 1954.

Inspired, in part, by R.M. Ballantyne's juvenile classic *The Coral Island* (1858), Golding's tale follows a group of British schoolboys, survivors of an attack on their plane, who are stranded on a remote island. But while Ballantyne's protagonists are models of propriety, the children of *Lord of the Flies* revert to savagery, including ritual murder; they nearly annihilate themselves before being rescued by a naval officer. As the officer guides the boys back to his cruiser and a world torn by war, he expresses shock that they have failed to emulate the *Coral Island* characters. On the contrary, Golding implies, the primitive instinct for cruelty is writ large in the behavior of men and nations.

Rejected several times before finding its way into print, *The Lord of the Flies* was an instant success in Britain; it acquired a wider readership in the 1960s, when antiwar sentiment and nuclear-age despair over humanity's future made its relevance manifest. Golding's "fable" (as he called it) became an acclaimed 1963 film by Peter Brook; the novel eventually took its place in the English-language literary canon, alongside such dystopian masterpieces as Joseph Conrad's *Heart of Darkness* and George Orwell's *1984*. Golding received the Nobel Prize for literature in 1983. **◂1902.3 ▸1985.13**

NOBEL PRIZES: Peace: Office of the United Nations High Commissioner for Refugees (Switzerland)... Literature: Ernest M. Hemingway (U.S.; novelist) ... Chemistry: Linus Pauling (U.S.; chemical bonds) ... Medicine: John Enders, Thomas Weller, and Frederick Robbins (U.S.; polio virus) ... Physics: Max Born (U.K.; quantum mechanics) and Walther Bothe (German; measuring cosmic radiation).

A VOICE FROM 1954

Breaking McCarthy's Spell

Testimony from the Senate's Permanent Subcommittee on Investigations of the Army–McCarthy Hearings, June 9, 1954

The undistinguished senator from Wisconsin, Joseph Raymond McCarthy, foundered in Washington for a couple of years before finding his niche: Communist hunter. Elected in 1948, he shockingly announced in 1950 that red agents had infiltrated the State Department. Fame followed instantly. That McCarthy was unable to substantiate his wild imputation deterred almost no one. For the next four years the senator, relishing his new prestige as chairman of the Government Committee on Operations of the Senate and also as the head of a Senate investigatory subcommittee (conservative young lawyer Roy Cohn was his chief adviser), waged a witch-hunt. His tools were innuendo, hysteria, and ad hominem attacks. He ruined many innocent people, and for a time his vitriol held 1950s America in sway. But in 1954 McCarthy met his match: He accused the Army of harboring spies. In explosive televised hearings, the senator's sleazy tactics were fully revealed. The climactic moment came on June 9th, when the Army's highly respected special counsel, Joseph Welch, responding to McCarthy's smear of an employee, Fred Fisher, blasted the senator's malice. When Welch finished speaking, the committee room burst into sustained applause, as did, it was reported, many of the millions watching at home. The spell was broken. The Senate soon censured McCarthy, who died in disgrace in 1957. ◂**1950.5**

Senator McCarthy: In view of Mr. Welch's request that the information be given—what we know of anyone who might be performing any work for the Communist Party, I think we should tell him that he has in his law firm a young man named [Frederick G.] Fisher, whom he recommended, incidentally, to do the work on this committee, who has been for a number of years a member of an organization which was named—oh, years and years ago—as the legal bulwark of the Communist Party, an organization which always springs to the defense of anyone who dares to expose Communists....

Mr. Welch—Senator McCarthy, I think until this moment—

Senator McCarthy—Just a minute. Let me ask. Jim—will you get the news story to the effect that this man belongs to this Communist front organization.

Mr. Welch—I will tell you that he belonged to it.

Senator McCarthy—Will you get the citations—order the citations showing that this was the legal arm of the Communist Party and the length of time that he belonged and the fact that he was recommended by Mr. Welch? I think that should be in the record.

Mr. Welch—Senator, you won't need anything in the record when I finish telling you this. Until this moment, Senator, I think I never really gauged your cruelty or your recklessness.

Fred Fisher is a young man who went to the Harvard Law School and came into my firm and is starting what looks to be a brilliant career with us. When I decided to work for this committee, I asked Jim St. Clair, who sits on my right, to be my first assistant. I said to Jim: "Pick somebody in the firm to work under you that you would like."

He chose Fred Fisher and they came down on an afternoon plane. That night, when we had taken a little stab at trying to see what the case was about, Fred Fisher and Jim St. Clair and I went to dinner together.

I then said to these two young men: "Boys, I don't know anything about you except I've always liked you, but if there's anything funny in the life of either one of you that would hurt anybody in this case, you speak up quick."

And Fred Fisher said: "Mr. Welch, when I was in the law school and for a period of months after I belonged to the Lawyer's Guild," as you have suggested, Senator....

It is, I regret to say, equally true that I fear he shall always bear a scar, needlessly inflicted by you. If it were in my power to forgive you for your reckless cruelty, I would do so. I like to think I'm a gentle man, but your forgiveness will have to come from someone other than me.

* * *

Senator McCarthy—May I say that Mr. Welch talks about this being cruel and reckless. He was just baiting—he has been baiting Mr. Cohn here for hours, requesting that Mr. Cohn before sundown get out of any department of the Government anyone who was serving the Communist cause.

Now, I just give this man's record, and I want to say, Mr. Welch, that it has been labeled long before he became a member as early as 1944.

Mr. Welch—Senator, may we not drop this? We know he belonged to the Lawyer's Guild.

Senator McCarthy—Let me finish this.

Mr. Welch—And Mr. Cohn nods his head at me. I did you, I think, no personal injury, Mr. Cohn.

Mr. Cohn—No, sir.

Mr. Welch—I meant to do you no personal injury, and if I did, I beg your pardon. Let us not assassinate this lad further, Senator. You've done enough. Have you no sense of decency, sir? At long last, have you left no sense of decency?

McCarthy *(right)* and Roy Cohn confer in the Senate caucus room at the Army–McCarthy hearings.

"There is no patent. Could you patent the sun?"—**Jonas Salk, replying to Edward R. Murrow's question as to who owned the patent on the polio vaccine**

STORY OF THE YEAR

Salk Vaccine Effective Against Polio

1 Poliomyelitis—commonly known as infantile paralysis, or polio—was the last of the terrible childhood plagues, and possibly the most-feared ailment of its time. It struck indiscriminately, withering young limbs, consigning children to the iron lung, visiting death on the nursery. (Perhaps its most famous victim was Franklin D. Roosevelt, who contracted the disease as an adult in 1921). Until 1955, there was no protection from the highly contagious disease. Then, on April 12, the results of the mass field trial of a new immunizing agent were announced: Jonas Salk's vaccine was safe and effective in preventing polio. The news was greeted like the answer to a prayer, and young Doctor Salk became a popular hero.

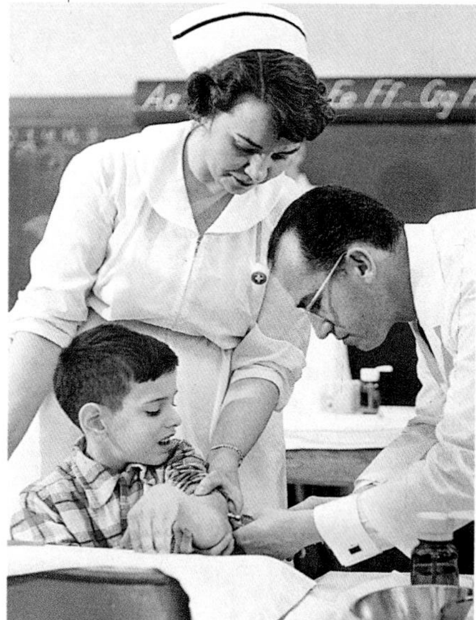

Salk administers his vaccine to a schoolboy. It was tested in schools across the United States.

Sponsored by the National Foundation for Infantile Paralysis, Salk had begun his research in 1947. As a rule, vaccines consisted of a living strain of a virus that was injected into a healthy person. They worked by inducing a mild case of the disease, rallying the body's natural defenses, and producing immunity. The dangers of a live-virus polio vaccine were widely recognized, thanks to several deaths among those vaccinated experimentally in the 1930s. Yet most polio researchers hoped to develop a weakened but still living strain of the virus. Salk, however, began exploring the possibility of a killed-virus vaccine. (He had helped develop one for influenza.) By 1952, he'd created a killed-virus vaccine for polio that stimulated immunity in lab animals without causing symptoms.

"I look upon it as ritual and symbolic," Salk said of his decision to become the first human recipient of his new vaccine. "You wouldn't do unto others that which you wouldn't do unto yourself." After injecting his staff as well, Salk in 1952 began public testing. Polio incidence was at a peak, with 58,000 cases in the United States and similar outbreaks across Europe and Asia. All summer long, a New York paper ran a daily polio tally in a front-page box. Parents everywhere warned children to avoid swimming pools and public fountains, and to sleep with their windows closed lest the disease creep over the sill. Salk's vaccine, licensed for use in 1955, calmed the panic. Millions of children around the world lined up for injections. Then, within a decade, Salk's rival Albert Sabin introduced a safe live-virus vaccine that supplanted its predecessor. **◂1927.12 ▸1960.M**

THE UNITED STATES

Montgomery Bus Boycott

2 The American civil rights movement can be said to have begun on December 1, 1955, in Montgomery, Alabama, when Rosa Parks refused to relinquish her seat on a city bus to a white man. A Montgomery ordinance barred blacks from the front of the bus and required them to cede their seats in the middle to any white left standing. But the 43-year-old seamstress (and volunteer for the National Association for the Advancement of Colored People) quietly defied the driver's order—and was promptly arrested. Local black leaders planned a virtually unprecedented mass campaign around Parks's case. Blacks accounted for 75 percent of Montgomery's bus ridership, and the activists hoped a bus boycott on the day of her trial (she was fined $10) would send a message to white officials and businessmen.

The boycott wound up lasting a year, despite police harassment, conspiracy trials, and the firebombing of leaders' homes. Almost all of Montgomery's 48,000 blacks participated. Thousands rallied in churches, modifying hymns and spirituals into "freedom songs." But authorities refused their modest demands: courtesy to black passengers, the hiring of black drivers, and the right of blacks to remain seated even if whites were standing. (The demonstrators didn't even challenge the requirement that blacks stay at the back of the bus.) The Supreme Court finally broke the stalemate, ruling *all* bus segregation unconstitutional. Although white supremacists began shooting at black riders, they'd lost the battle.

Montgomery spawned one of history's greatest nonviolent revolutions—and the boycott leader became that revolution's spiritual chief. The Reverend Dr. Martin Luther King, Jr., 26, drew inspiration from Mahatma Gandhi. "If you will protest courageously and yet with dignity and Christian love," he promised his followers, "in future generations the historians will pause and say, 'There lived a great people—a black people—who injected new meaning and dignity into the veins of civilization.'" **◂1954.6 ▸1956.M**

Parks gets fingerprinted after her arrest.

VIETNAM

Bloodbaths North and South

3 Violence returned to Indochina in 1955 as the rulers of the supposedly temporary states of North and South Vietnam consolidated their own power. In the Communist North, thousands of landlords and rich peasants were executed in an agrarian reform program that went awry. (The regime quickly confessed its "error.") In the South, U.S.-backed premier Ngo Dinh Diem crushed three rebellions—and swept away most remnants of French domination.

A Saigon mother and children seek shelter during the Binh Xuyen uprising, one of three revolts crushed by Diem in 1955.

A nationalistic former interior minister, Diem was a longtime foe of the French-appointed head of state, Bao Dai. Bao had nonetheless recalled Diem from exile and named him premier in 1954, fearing both popular and U.S. outrage if the government remained wholly a French creation. Diem, in fact, seemed to pose little threat to Bao: A charmless man and a Catholic in a Buddhist country, he had few followers. He was challenged, moreover, by three armed politico-

ART & CULTURE: Books: ***Marjorie Morningstar*** **(Herman Wouk);** ***Auntie Mame*** **(Patrick Dennis);** ***The Man in the Gray Flannel Suit*** **(Sloan Wilson);** ***The Less Deceived*** **(Philip Larkin) ... Music: "Love Is a Many-Splendored Thing" (Fain and Webster); "Love and Marriage" (Van Heusen and Cahn);** ***Two Sonnets*** **(Milton Babbitt) ... Painting & Sculpture:** ***Flag*** **and** ***Target with Four Faces*** **(Jasper Johns);** ***Rebus***

"We are in favor of a détente, but if anybody thinks that for this reason we shall forget about Marx, Engels, and Lenin, he is mistaken. This will happen when shrimps learn to whistle."—**Soviet premier Nikita Khrushchev, at Geneva**

religious sects: the rural Hoa Hao and Cao Dai, and the urban Binh Xuyen—whose mafia ran Saigon's vice trade and police force and the federal secret service.

Diem bribed several Hoa Hao and Cao Dai leaders into joining his regime, but the Binh Xuyen clashed repeatedly with government troops. The sect's main resistance ended in May 1955, after hundreds died in a street battle. By summer, Diem had blocked a coup attempt by a French-backed general and quashed a revolt by intransigent Hoa Hao chiefs.

Bao (who'd moved to the Riviera) was soon deposed in a referendum abolishing the monarchy and making Diem president. Diem's U.S. sponsors were now completely convinced that he could make South Vietnam a permanent state and a bulwark against communism. But a vote on who would govern all Vietnam was scheduled for 1956, and northern leader Ho Chi Minh remained the divided nation's favorite son. Diem's solution was simple: He refused to hold the election. Thereafter, Ho's struggle for reunification would be waged by military means. **◂1954.1 ▸1961.6**

DIPLOMACY

The Alliances Consolidate

4 The shape of postwar Europe had emerged almost completely by the end of 1955, thanks to a series of major diplomatic events. In May (fulfilling the Paris Agreements of October 1954), West Germany was admitted into NATO. The end of the Western Allies' occupation of that country—and the prospect of its rearmament—predictably distressed the Soviet Union, twice in 40 years a victim of German aggression. In response, the Kremlin promptly formalized the Warsaw Pact, a mutual defense agreement with Albania, Bulgaria, Czechoslovakia, East Germany, Hungary, Poland, and Romania. (Besides presenting a counterweight to NATO, the pact allowed Moscow to maintain a strong military presence in those countries, ensuring Soviet domination.) Also in May, Moscow signed the Austrian State Treaty, ending the Four Power occupation of Austria, which regained its sovereignty. The withdrawal of Soviet troops, which had been a major East-West bone of contention, began almost immediately.

Amiability was the order of the day when Big Four chiefs Bulganin (U.S.S.R.), Eisenhower (U.S.), Faure (France), and Eden (Great Britain) *(left to right)* met at Geneva.

In July, leaders of Britain, France, the United States, and the Soviet Union convened in neutral Switzerland to discuss several issues crucial to the coexistence of East and West. The big news at Geneva was the post-Stalinist feeling of optimism in the air. Eisenhower's announcement that the U.S. did not plan to "take part in an aggressive war" caused mass rejoicing in a world haunted by visions of nuclear holocaust. But little of substance took place, and the nagging question of how to bring about German reunification remained unresolved. **◂1949.2 ▸1961.1**

DIPLOMACY

Third World's First Parley

5 In April 1955, statesmen from 23 Asian and six African nations met in Bandung, Indonesia, to map the future of a new global political force—the Third World. According to the latest geopolitical theory (advanced by French sociologist Alfred Sauvy in 1952), every country belonged to one of three such "worlds": The first was that of the industrialized capitalist democracies; the second, that of the Soviet bloc; and the third, that of the emerging postcolonial states. The latter tended to be nonwhite, leading Indonesian president Sukarno to call the Bandung Conference "the first intercontinental conference of coloured peoples in the history of mankind."

Apart from poverty, however, the nations represented at the gathering had little in common. Debate raged over whether Soviet policies in Eastern Europe and Central Asia were to be classed with Western colonialism. In the end, a resolution was passed condemning "colonialism in all its manifestations"—an implicit censure of Moscow. Yet China, despite its recent subjugation of Tibet, was accepted at Bandung with open arms.

The delegates' one concrete accomplishment was a ten-point "declaration on the promotion of world peace and cooperation," based on the UN charter and the moral principles of Indian premier Jawaharlal Nehru (one of the elder statesmen in attendance). But Bandung would give birth to the broader Nonaligned Movement, through which dozens of nations sought—with varying success—to avoid becoming pawns of either of the Cold War's clashing titans. The conference promoted a handful of figures to international stature: Sukarno; China's surprisingly conciliatory premier, Zhou Enlai; Egypt's dashing president, Gamal Abdal Nasser. And it provided new hope for First World idealists despairing over superpower politics: Perhaps the answer to the East-West deadlock lay in these dynamic leaders and their awakening nations. **◂1955.4**

Carlos Romulo of the Philippines *(left)* and American editor Norman Cousins at the Bandung Conference.

BIRTHS

Isabelle Adjani, French actress.

Sandra Bernhard, U.S. comedian.

Jane Campion, New Zealand filmmaker.

Dana Carvey, U.S. comedian.

Roseanne Cash, U.S. singer.

Kevin Costner, U.S. actor and filmmaker.

Willem Dafoe, U.S. actor.

William Henry Gates III, U.S. software designer and industrialist.

Iman, Somali-U.S. model.

Steven Jobs, U.S. inventor.

Jeff Koons, U.S. artist.

Jerry Seinfeld, U.S. comedian.

Anna Sui, U.S. fashion designer.

DEATHS

James Agee, U.S. writer.

Theda Bara, U.S. actress.

Mary McLeod Bethune, U.S. educator.

James Dean, U.S. actor.

Albert Einstein, German-U.S. physicist.

Alexander Fleming, U.K. bacteriologist.

Cordell Hull, U.S. statesman.

Fernand Léger, French painter.

Thomas Mann, German-U.S. writer.

José Ortega y Gasset, Spanish philosopher.

Charlie "Bird" Parker, U.S. musician.

Robert E. Sherwood, U.S. playwright.

Nicholas de Staël, Russian-French artist.

Wallace Stevens, U.S. poet.

Pierre Teilhard de Chardin, French theologian and paleontologist.

Maurice Utrillo, French painter.

Honus Wagner, U.S. baseball player.

Denton "Cy" Young, U.S. baseball player.

(Robert Rauschenberg) ... Film: *Marty* (Delbert Mann); *To Catch a Thief* (Alfred Hitchcock); *Mister Roberts* (Ford and LeRoy); *The Man with the Golden Arm* (Otto Preminger) ... Theater: *Bus Stop* (William Inge); *Cat on a Hot Tin Roof* (Tennessee Williams); *A View from the Bridge* (Arthur Miller); *Damn Yankees* (Adler and Ross) ... TV: *The Lawrence Welk Show*; *The $64,000 Question*; *Captain Kangaroo.*

"That my novel does contain various allusions to the physiological urges of a pervert is quite true. But after all we are not children."—**Novelist Vladimir Nabokov, on *Lolita***

NEW IN 1955

Play-Doh (Kenner Toys).

Ford Thunderbird.

Kentucky Fried Chicken.

Hovercraft.

Televised presidential press conference.

H & R Block tax preparers.

The Guinness Book of Records.

IN THE UNITED STATES

▶AFL-CIO MERGER—An organized labor superpower came into being in 1955 when the American Federation of Labor merged with the Congress of Industrial Organizations. The blockbuster deal was negotiated by AFL leader George Meany, a cigar-chomping, big-city (New York) plumber and union man from pre-Depression days. The new mega-organization represented 90 percent of U.S. union members. As its president for the next quarter century, Meany, a vocal anti-

Communist, commanded enormous mainstream political influence. In 1972, he broke organized labor's traditional association with the Democratic Party when he refused to endorse George McGovern for president. ◀1952.M ▶1957.M

▶MARCUSE AND THE NEW LEFT—Herbert Marcuse's *Eros and Civilization* established the German-American social philosopher's credentials as a leading light of the New Left movement. Presenting complex interpretations of Freud, Hegel, and Marx, the 1955 book identified industrial society as an agent of repression—sexual, political, economic. Marcuse was embraced by 1960s radicals, who took to heart his advocacy of "resistance to the point of

POPULAR CULTURE

McDonald's Goes National

6 In April 1955, onetime jazz pianist Ray A. Kroc opened a fast-food franchise in the Chicago suburb of Des Plaines. No one could have guessed it at the time, but a revolution in American eating habits, and a worldwide empire, were about to be born. As exclusive distributor of the Multimixer, a machine that mixed five milk shakes at once, Kroc had met brothers Richard and Maurice McDonald the previous year at their San Bernardino, California, drive-in restaurant. Using assembly-line techniques to prepare burgers, fries, and shakes, the brothers had turned their roadside stand, McDonald's, into a $200,000-a-year business, and had begun to sell franchises in California. Kroc, eager to earn a share of the receipts (and to sell more Multimixers), persuaded the brothers to let him license the restaurant nationally.

Kroc soon sold his blender business to concentrate on hamburgers. By 1961, when he bought out the McDonald brothers, the chain boasted more than 200 branches. A self-described "superpatriot" who ordered franchise operators to fly the U.S. flag, Kroc built his success on an almost military uniformity of product and presentation. By the 1980s, with 10,000-plus units, the McDonald's Corporation was the largest food-service company in the world, the biggest owner of commercial real estate in the United States, and one of the nation's major employers. Stamped across the physical and cultural landscape from Paris to Beijing, the restaurant's trademark golden arches became a supreme symbol of consumerism, American style.

▸1990.M

A young Davis relaxing at a recording session. His career spanned four decades.

MUSIC

Miles's Quintets

7 After his acclaim-winning appearance at the 1955 Newport Jazz Festival, jazz trumpeter Miles Davis (heretofore known only to the cognoscenti) vaulted to the top of his profession. For the first time ever, a black man was the most successful jazz musician of his time. Later that year, Davis put together an all-star quintet—with saxophonist John Coltrane, pianist Red Garland, bassist Paul Chambers, and drummer Philly Jo Jones—that earned a permanent place in the jazz pantheon and brought "cool" jazz to maturity. The new style traded bebop's frenetically cascading notes for a smooth, quietly plaintive, ineffably mournful sound. ("Never before in jazz had loneliness been examined in so intransigent a manner," a critic has noted.) The intimate, muted sound of Davis's trumpet has been likened to smoked glass, and to breathing itself.

In his youth, Davis, the son of an Alton, Illinois, dentist, had worshiped bebop gods Dizzy Gillespie and Charlie Parker (he played with both in the late 1940s)—but knew he lacked their technical flair. Undeterred, he began experimenting with a sparer, more introspective style. In 1949, he and a group of like-minded musicians, notably arranger Gil Evans, recorded *Birth of the Cool*. The album marked a departure from 30 years of hot, exuberantly busy-sounding jazz, and intimated what was to come with the landmark quintet. Evolving from cool, Davis continued to blaze new musical trails: The quintet, with alto sax player Cannonball Adderley replacing Coltrane, attempted a modal (as opposed to harmonic) approach to jazz in the late fifties, and in the late sixties Davis pioneered the mix of jazz and rock called fusion. The Davis quintet of the sixties—Wayne Shorter on sax, Herbie Hancock on piano, Ron Carter on bass, and Tony Williams on drums—became as legendary as its fifties precursor. **◀1945.15 ▸1959.M**

LITERATURE

Notoriety for Nabokov

8 Displaced from revolutionary Russia as a youth, Vladimir Nabokov wrote witty and learned novels in his native language before switching to English in the 1940s. At the end of the decade, he was appointed professor of Russian and European literature at Cornell University in upstate New York. Yet despite his intellectual credentials, U.S. publishers rejected *Lolita*—his seriocomic "confession" of Humbert Humbert, a sophisticated European émigré obsessed with an ordinary preteen American girl—as just another dirty book. After Nabokov reluctantly allowed a Parisian specialist in pornography to publish it in 1955, the novel sparked raging controversies in France, England, and the United States. Thus *Lolita* joined the ranks of masterpieces (by Joyce, Lawrence, and many others) that have challenged Western attitudes toward the printed depiction of sexual desire. With Stanley

A New Jersey McDonald's franchise in 1962. By then, nearly a billion burgers had been sold.

SPORTS: Baseball: World Series, Brooklyn Dodgers (first championship ever) defeat New York Yankees, 4–3 ... Football: NFL, Cleveland Browns defeat Los Angeles Rams, 38–14 ... Basketball: NBA, Syracuse Nationals defeat Fort Wayne Pistons, 4–3 ... Golf: First LPGA tournament held.

1955

"It is not the poet but what he observes which is revealed as obscene. The great obscene wastes of 'Howl' are the sad wastes of the mechanized world, lost among atom bombs and insane nationalism."—**Lawrence Ferlinghetti**

Kubrick's 1962 film adaptation (featuring James Mason as Humbert), the debate extended into cinema.

"My private tragedy," Nabokov lamented, "is that I had to abandon my natural idiom, my untrammeled, rich, and infinitely docile Russian tongue for a second-rate brand of English." Yet no prose could have been more polished, or praised, than that of this exiled aristocrat. Literati hailed *Lolita* as a brilliant work of "art for art's sake," a pyrotechnic orchestration of satire, parody, puns, and masked identities. The book became a bestseller, enabling Nabokov to quit teaching, move to Switzerland, and devote more of his time to writing and to his passionate avocation—collecting butterflies. **◂1913.3**

FILM

A Cult Is Born

9 James Dean, 24, was one of the most talked-about new talents in Hollywood. Columnist Hedda Hopper wrote that she'd never seen a young actor with "such power, so many facets of invention." Dean discounted his growing fame. "To me," he said, "the only success, the only greatness, is immortality." On September 30, 1955, at a California highway intersection, he achieved that status: A Ford sedan slammed into Dean's Porsche, killing him instantly.

The public knew Dean from some Broadway stage work, some TV dramas, bit parts in three minor movies, and a brilliant star turn as Cal, the tortured Cain figure in the film *East of Eden*. But four days after his death, Warner Bros. released, as scheduled, *Rebel Without a Cause*, director Nicholas Ray's melodrama of juvenile delinquency. Dean played the title role. Teenagers identified intensely with his angst-ridden portrayal of Jim Stark, a middle-class kid frustrated by a domineering mother and a milquetoast father. *Rebel* was a box-office sensation—and Warner's was soon deluged with 8,000 letters a week addressed to its dead star.

Dean's last role, as the vulnerable bad-boy ranch hand in *Giant* (1956), cemented the legend. Fan clubs formed around the world and still thrive today. Thousands have made pilgrimages to Dean's grave in Indiana. He has been mimicked, consciously or not, by teen idols from Elvis Presley to Jason Priestley. And his image adorns T-shirts, posters, and advertisements. A good actor, he proved to be an even better icon. **◂1921.10 ▸1956.1**

Dean embraces *Rebel* costar Natalie Wood. Like Dean, Wood and another of the film's stars, Sal Mineo, met premature (and violent) deaths.

LITERATURE

A Revolutionary Reading

10 "I saw the best minds of my generation destroyed by madness, starving hysterical naked...." This first line of "Howl," read by Allen Ginsberg at the Six Gallery in San Francisco in November 1955, signaled the emergence of a major American poet and the dawning of a creative movement. Since the mid-1940s, Ginsberg and a few companions—Jack Kerouac, William Burroughs, Gary Snyder, and others—had been advancing an aesthetic they called "beat" (a term referring variously to weariness, music, and spiritual beatitude). Rejecting middle-class ("square") values, the Beats revered spontaneity, nature, and consciousness expansion, which they sought through sex, drugs, jazz, and Eastern religion. They spoke, wrote, and dressed like prophets, but with a modern twist: They liked to curse, and their clothes came from the Salvation Army.

Written in one inspired afternoon, "Howl" was a perfect expression of the Beat worldview—an epic indictment of contemporary America (a "cannibal dynamo,") and a celebration of "angelheaded hipsters" who brave destruction to find a higher truth. Ginsberg's incantatory performance became the stuff of legend. But when the poem appeared in *Howl and Other Poems* (1956), it prompted obscenity charges against publisher (and fellow Beat poet) Lawrence Ferlinghetti. The case, decided in Ferlinghetti's favor, made Ginsberg and his circle famous, and made the book one of the century's bestselling volumes of poetry.

Openly homosexual when that orientation was still considered outrageous, Ginsberg remained controversial in the coming decades—championing the hippie movement in the sixties and supporting radical causes (and Buddhist enlightenment) into the nineties. By 1974, when he won a National Book Award for *The Fall of America: Poems of These States*, even mainstream critics acknowledged his poetic gifts. **◂1917.M ▸1957.8**

Allen Ginsberg *(right)* with fellow Beats Peter Orlovsky *(left)* and Gregory Corso in New York City in 1957.

IN THE UNITED STATES

subversion." The émigré from Nazi Germany, maintained that the American university was a "citadel" of academic freedom.

▶RNA ISOLATED—Severo Ochoa, a Spanish-born professor of biochemistry at New York University Medical School, helped unlock the mysteries of heredity in 1955 when he isolated a bacterial enzyme that enabled him to catalyze ribonucleic acid—RNA. The work was crucial to an understanding of how hereditary information is transmitted from genes to enzymes, which control the nature and function of individual cells. Ochoa's breakthrough paved the way for the future synthesis of RNA and the unraveling of the genetic code. ◂1953.1 ▸1967.11

▶STEICHEN'S FAMILY—Groundbreaking American photographer and curator Edward Steichen mounted an exhibit for the Museum of Modern Art in 1955 that was designed

to underscore the diversity and solidarity of the human race. "The Family of Man" included 503 prints culled from more than two million submissions from around the world. *(The closing image, above, was a shot of two children by W. Eugene Smith.)* It became one of the most popular art shows ever organized, ultimately viewed by some nine million people. ◂1902.13

▶CASH'S FIRST TUNES—Johnny Cash knew firsthand the life he sang about. Born during the Depression to Arkansas cotton sharecroppers, he swept floors in Detroit in the early 1950s. In 1955, after four years in the Air Force, he signed with Memphis's legendary Sun Records. Showcasing his trademark baritone, Cash's first singles, "Cry, Cry, Cry" and "Folsom Prison Blues," became instant hits. ◂1949.10

POLITICS & BUSINESS: GNP: $398 billion ... Minimum wage raised from 75¢ to $1 ... General Motors announces 3 to 1 stock split ... IBM introduces its first business computer, the IBM 752.

"If you tried to give rock 'n' roll another name, you might call it 'Chuck Berry' "—**John Lennon**

AROUND THE WORLD

▶A NEW CHINA—Chiang Kai-shek, leader of China's deposed Nationalist government in Taiwan, had always been a friend to the U.S. More important, he was a die-hard foe of communism. In January, his allegiance was rewarded when the U.S. Congress approved the Formosa Resolution, which committed the U.S. to the defense of the Taiwanese Nationalist government—recognized by the U.S. as the sole government of all China—against any Communist threat from the Chinese mainland. ◀1949.1 ▶1972.2

▶CHRISTIAN CONCILIATOR—Only upon his death in 1955 were the major writings of Catholic priest, paleontologist, and philosopher Pierre Teilhard de Chardin published. Teilhard, who attempted to reconcile science with Christianity, was barred by the

Church from publishing his musings on evolution (which, he argued, showed the hand of God). *The Phenomenon of Man,* his masterwork, presented his optimistic theory that through science, man would be drawn to a final step of faith and complete recognition of Christ. ◀1925.3 ▶1962.1

▶BAWDY IRISH ANTIHERO—Like fellow Dubliner James Joyce, J.P. Donleavy wrote a brilliant novel only to have it rejected as obscene by timid publishers. The wildly funny, bawdy story of besotted Sebastian Dangerfield (like his creator an American expatriate in Dublin), *The Ginger Man* was published in Paris in 1955. An unexpurgated edition of what is considered a modern comic masterpiece was not released in the U.S. until 1965. Donleavy, who wrote several other novels, as well as short stories and plays, became an Irish citizen two years later. ◀1922.1

POPULAR CULTURE

A Mickey Mouse Empire

11 It was a banner year for Walt Disney. His new ABC television series, *Disneyland,* topped the ratings; the show's "Frontierland" segments, featuring Fess Parker as pioneer Davy Crockett, had spawned a hit record and a mania for coonskin caps. Other products —comic books, feature films, cartoons, documentaries—spilled from his company's workshops at an astonishing rate. On July 17, 1955, Disney unveiled his grandest accomplishment yet: Disneyland.

The theme park, covering 160 acres in Anaheim, California, was the first attraction of its kind. Compared with Disneyland, old-fashioned amusement parks were shabby and unimaginative. A family could wander for hours through this multimedia extravaganza, visiting a simulated moon shot, a sanitized Tahiti, a bowdlerized Old West; in realms called Adventureland, Fantasyland, and Frontierland, they could ride a giant teacup or a pirate galleon. The Magic Kingdom, as it was nicknamed, had something to dazzle every age group.

Then, in October Disney introduced an after-school television program on ABC aimed, as he put it, "directly at the kids." *The Mickey Mouse Club* crowned the baby boom generation with yet another hat, that of the Mouseketeer. Meanwhile, Disneyland—together with its descendants in Florida, Japan, and France—remained a tourist magnet through the coming decades. **◀1928.10 ▶1956.V**

The castle entrance to Disneyland. ABC helped underwrite Disneyland's initial cost.

LITERATURE

Reinventing the Novel

12 Alain Robbe-Grillet's 1955 novel, *Le Voyeur,* may be about a traveling salesman who has raped and murdered a young girl.

It may be about a traveling salesman obsessed with a rape and murder committed by someone else. Or the crime may be entirely imaginary. To Robbe-Grillet, such details were irrelevant; what mattered was to convey, accurately, the way humans perceive time, space, and matter. *Le Voyeur* is therefore, like all of his work, full of contradictions and repetitions—and, especially, *things,* described with a meticulousness that can be maddening. Trained as a statistician, the French writer found a place in fiction for inventories, timetables, and measurements—though not for conventional plot or characterization.

Robbe-Grillet's previous novel, *Les Gommes (The Erasers),* 1953, had mystified virtually all its readers; *Le Voyeur,* however, won the prestigious Prix des Critiques. By the 1960s, Robbe-Grillet was recognized as the leading spokesperson for what he termed the *nouveau roman,* or "new novel." A loose-knit movement of New Novelists (including Michel Butor, Marguerite Duras, Claude Mauriac, Nathalie Sarraute, and Claude Simon) began to form, united only by its members' determination to explore the nature of perception and to test the furthest boundaries of narrative. "Each novel," Robbe-Grillet wrote, "must invent its own form." **▶1957.10**

MUSIC

Rock 'n' Roll's Granddaddy

13 Compared to the grandiosity of later rock 'n' roll, the work of pioneer Chuck Berry—whose "Maybellene" hit number one on the rhythm-and-blues charts and number five on the pop charts in 1955—may seem crude. But every subsequent rocker has been influenced by Berry's biting guitar licks, his crisp, inventive vocals, and his athletic showmanship (his trademark was the "duck walk"). His archetypally simple, uncannily catchy songs—about dating, driving, and

Berry in 1986—still rocking at 60.

school days—have been covered by greats and garage bands alike.

Starting out in St. Louis, Berry worked as a hairdresser by day and played small clubs by night. His big break came when blues great Muddy Waters let him sit in on a gig in Chicago—and then recommended Berry for an audition with Chess Records. "Maybellene," Berry's first hit, was an R&B-style reworking of a country song called "Ida Red." Several more Top Ten hits followed, including "Roll Over Beethoven" and "Johnny B. Goode."

But Berry's superstardom was short-lived; in 1962, in an ambiguous trial that would probably have earned a white performer probation, he was sent to prison for two years for transporting a minor across state lines for "immoral purposes." Still, Berry rallied in 1972 with a successful Las Vegas run and his first number-one pop hit: a salacious novelty tune called "My Ding-a-Ling." **◀1950.M ▶1956.1**

NOBEL PRIZES: Peace: No award ... Literature: Halldór K. Laxness (Icelandic; novelist) ... Chemistry: Vincent du Vigneaud (U.S.; polypeptide hormone) ... Medicine: Hugo Theorell (Swedish; oxidation enzymes) ... Physics: Polycarp Kusch and Willis Lamb, Jr. (U.S.; electron magnetism).

A VOICE FROM 1955

Car-Race Romance in the Wrong Lane

From "Your Problems," by Ann Landers, Chicago *Sun-Times*, October 16, 1955

Right up to their double wedding, the twins were inseparable: Esther Pauline Friedman and Pauline Esther Friedman did everything together. Esther was older by 17 minutes, and was also the first to enter the trade the Friedman girls made their own. A 37-year-old Chicago housewife, Esther in 1955 took over the Chicago Sun-Times *advice column. From her very first day as Ann Landers, October 16, she wrote with characteristic frankness, a weakness for puns, and respect for professionals—"see a marriage counselor." Dozens of papers picked up the hit column. Inspired, Pauline, a Bay Area housewife, talked her way into a job with the San Francisco* Chronicle. *She debuted as Abigail Van Buren on January 9, 1956. Traditional but flip, "Dear Abby" was soon syndicated coast-to-coast. Four decades later, the sisters—part Solomon, part shrink—were still advising tens of millions of lovelorn, confused, or just curious fans.*

Ann Landers, housewife turned advice maven.

Dear Mrs. Landers: I've followed your column closely and have always regarded most of those marital mix-ups as very humorous—until now, that is, when the noose is tightening around my own neck. We have been married 10 years and have two sons. I like auto racing but my wife has no interest in it so I've always gone without her.

I've fallen for a woman with three children who is also very fond of auto racing. Her husband is ignorant and impossible. This may sound corny but I think she should be a wonderful companion for me. I suppose you think I'm a louse—but I am stumped. I would like to have your advice on this problem.

Mr. K

Time Wounds all heels—and you'll get yours. Do you realize that there are five children involved in your little race track romance? Don't be surprised if you wake up one of these days and wish you had your wife and sons back. You are flirting with a muddy track on black Friday and the way you're headed you will get exactly what you deserve.

Dear Mrs. Landers: I've just graduated from grade school and the boy I like is in the Army. He has written that he will be home on leave soon, but my mother forbids me to see him. I tried to explain that we just want to see a movie and we will be home early. Mother says I can't go and that I am too young to know what I am doing. Please help me.

E.V.

If You "just graduated from grade school" you are about 13 years old, Chicken. Uncle Sam needs men—you don't! Listen to your mother, she is right. And about that boy friend—his brains must be AWOL!!

Dear Mrs. Landers: I've been married four years, have two children and am expecting a third soon. My husband has been chasing around town with women for the past seven months. When I told him that I was getting a separation he promised to change his ways and to behave himself. I have no money for attorney's fees and I cannot work. Shall I try to borrow the money from relatives or should I wait and see what happens?

Troubled Wife

You Have Every Right to blow a gasket. This character does not deserve a family—as of now. But since he has promised to mend his ways, give him another chance. Try to persuade him to go with you to a marriage counsellor. See if, together, you can find out what's gone wrong with your marriage. Let him know, too, if there is any more extra-marital activity you're giving him the heave-ho.

Dear Mrs. Landers: Two months ago I met a man who seems very fond of me. He has two jobs which is the reason he has never called me up on the phone or taken me out. He is very busy. He has told me that he cares for me a great deal, but I see him only once a day when he delivers food at my home. I don't want to rush him into anything. What do you think?

Steady Reader

What This Man is delivering to your home sounds like baloney. I have a sneaking suspicion that your back-door Romeo has a wife and a family, plus several other very good "customers." You'd better forget about him and suggest that he leave whatever it is that he is delivering in a convenient place. He ought to stick to his commission as the "bonus" for his sales!

Dear Ann Landers: I am a girl of 14 and I like a certain boy and am sure he likes me, but when it comes time to meet him he gets scared and backs out. I am deeply troubled.

S.V.

Don't Worry; He's Only A Kid. Soon, now, he'll become unscared, and you'll have a chance to find out if you really like each other. Meanwhile, you can have a lot of good times with other youngsters—boys and girls!

Confidential: Miss O.E.B. You are entitled to a life of your own. You have given more than your share to mother and the rest of the family. Move out of that house before they drive you batty.

"I came off stage and my manager told me they were hollerin' because I was wigglin'. Well, I went back out for an encore and I, I, I kinda did a little more and the more I did, the wilder they went."—**Elvis Presley in *TV Guide*, 1956, on his first big appearance**

STORY OF THE YEAR

Elvis Is King

1 "Heartbreak Hotel," the first number-one pop hit by the most influential rock 'n' roller ever, was released in March 1956. By year's end, besides scoring three more chart toppers, Elvis Presley had become a TV sensation (the *Ed Sullivan Show* censored his writhings, showing him only above the waist) and a certified teen idol. Presley didn't invent rock, which had evolved in the early fifties from black rhythm-and-blues and white country-and-western music. But more than any other performer, he personified its youthful promise of liberation, its inarticulate defiance of the decade's bland conformism. Presley's charisma, and the rough beauty of his best performances—shockingly sensual, yet touchingly pure-hearted—earned him the title "King of Rock 'n' Roll." Though he was initially reviled by the guardians of public taste and morals (and later castigated for profiting from black culture without repaying his debt), he brought the genre global popularity and inspired generations of musicians. His fervent cult of personality flourishes today.

Presley had sung—and dreamed of stardom—since childhood. But he was working as a truck driver in Memphis, Tennessee, when, as a lark, he recorded a country song at a walk-in studio run by Sun Records owner Sam Phillips. Phillips, who'd cut early records by such blues stars as B.B. King and Howlin' Wolf, had an entrepreneurial vision: He hoped to get rich by finding "a white man with the Negro sound and the Negro feel." He urged Presley (a devotee of black music and sartorial style) in that direction, and in 1954 the singer scored a regional hit with "That's All Right," written by bluesman Arthur Crudup. Presley toured the South, his rich baritone, swiveling hips, and sneering lips driving adolescent audiences wild. Overexcited fans rioted at one Florida show.

After his version of "Mystery Train" topped country-music charts in 1955, the giant RCA company paid Sun an unprecedented $35,000 for Presley's contract. (In the first of many legendary acts of largesse, he bought his mother a pink Cadillac.) The pop hits followed—83 over the next 16 years. Thanks to the marketing genius of his hucksterish Dutch-born manager, Colonel Tom Parker, he remained a worldwide celebrity long after his greatness faded. But the pressures of fame led to a lurid downfall. **◂1955.13 ▸1977.6**

The King of Rock 'n' Roll, as he appeared in the 1956 film *Love Me Tender*, one of a string of box-office hits he starred in.

THE SOVIET UNION

Khrushchev Repudiates Stalin

2 Nikita Khrushchev's "secret speech" against Stalin was the most damning indictment of communism ever to have come from within the system. Delivered in February 1956 at a special midnight session of the 20th Communist Party Congress in Moscow (from which foreigners and press were barred), Khrushchev's four-hour diatribe shook the Party to its foundations, and heralded a new Soviet era.

Khrushchev buried the cult of Stalin and redefined communism in the Cold War era.

Khrushchev had maneuvered himself to Communist leadership after Stalin's 1953 death. During the next few years, he cautiously deviated from the late dictator's policies, initiating subtle penal reforms, liberalizing foreign policy. In 1955, he even attempted a reconciliation with Yugoslavia's heretical Marshal Tito. Thus, when the congress convened, the 1,350 assembled Party functionaries expected to hear a little ideological revisionism, and few were shocked when speakers denounced "the cult of the individual."

But on the opening day, Khrushchev declared that "war is not fatalistically inevitable"—directly contradicting the doctrine of class struggle, and dismaying old-guard Party officials. Then, on the tenth night, he summoned delegates to the hall, locked the doors, and lengthily denounced his former boss, attacking his "intolerance, his brutality, his abuse of power." The pace of de-Stalinization subsequently quickened. In the next year, some eight million political prisoners were disgorged from the heinous gulag; thousands of purged Party members were posthumously rehabilitated.

Die-hard Stalinists engineered numerous attempts on Khrushchev's life—and in 1958, a cabal of hard-liners led by Vyacheslav Molotov, Georgi Malenkov, and Lazar Kaganovich attempted to oust him. Khrushchev withstood the coup, stripped his enemies of their offices, exiled them to the hinterlands, and packed the Presidium with supporters. He had come of age under Stalin. He knew how to play the game. **◂1953.3 ▸1956.4**

THE MIDDLE EAST

The Suez Crisis

3 Gamal Abdal Nasser thumbed his nose at the Western powers. He made Egypt a one-party socialist state, refused to join the anti-Soviet Baghdad Pact, and recognized Communist China. Since the West accordingly denied him arms, he bought them from the Soviet Union—but he claimed independence from both sides in the Cold War. While such boldness made the dictator a hero in the developing world, it raised hackles elsewhere. The result, in 1956, was the Suez crisis: a military defeat but a diplomatic triumph.

The crisis erupted when the United States and Britain reneged on loans to build the Aswan High Dam. Furious, Nasser announced that he would nationalize the internationally owned Suez Canal and use its revenues to pay for the dam. Britain and France (the latter angered by Egyptian aid to Algerian rebels) secretly arranged for Israel to attack Egypt through the Sinai Peninsula, whereupon they would occupy the canal zone on the pre-

An Israeli officer interrogates an Egyptian prisoner, after Israel's attack on Egypt. But Nasser prevailed in the end.

text of separating the adversaries. Israeli forces stormed into Egypt on October 29. British bombers destroyed the Egyptian air force, and French and British paratroopers captured Port Said and Port Fuad. When the fighting ended a

ART & CULTURE: Books: *The Floating Opera* (John Barth); *The Fall* (Albert Camus); *The Art of Loving* (Erich Fromm); *Profiles in Courage* (John F. Kennedy) ... Music: "Que Será, Será (Whatever Will Be, Will Be)" (Livingston and Evans); "Why Do Fools Fall in Love?" (Lymon and Levy); "Fever" (Davenport and Cooley); *Meditation on Ecclesiastes* (Norman Dello Joio) ... Painting & Sculpture: *Just what is it that*

"Hungarian youth, your wishes have been attained. ... Nagy is back. He will create a new order. Why do you go on fighting?"—**Radio communiqué on Radio Budapest by the Hungarian Communist Party**

week later, 2,700 defenders had been killed or wounded, compared with 140 invaders.

The UN—led by the Soviets and Americans in rare accord—denounced the invasion and sent troops to enforce a cease-fire. Soon the canal was cleared and the dispute settled: Having agreed to compensate the old Suez Canal Company, Egypt kept the profitable waterway. (With Soviet help, the dam was completed in 1970.) Israel was forced to return the territory it had occupied, and Britain and France lost much of their standing in the Middle East. Nasser, who'd defied three armies and still walked off with a deal, saw his prestige soar higher than ever. **◂1954.2 ▸1958.1**

The head of Stalin, knocked from a statue by anti-Soviet demonstrators in Budapest.

EASTERN EUROPE

Poland and Hungary Revolt

4 For the Soviet Union's satellite nations, it seemed—briefly—that the repeal of Stalinism meant the end of forced obedience to Moscow. Khrushchev's New Course (as he called his de-Stalinization policy) promised to recognize "national paths to socialism." In 1956, the loosened leash brought rebellions to Poland and Hungary. In Poland, wholesale anti-Communist revolution was only narrowly averted. Hungary went much further before a Soviet backlash smashed any illusion that the New Course meant a new order.

The situation in Poland reached a head in October, when masses of people rose violently against the Moscow-backed regime. Khrushchev flew to Warsaw and, as the Soviet army marched in on "maneuvers," struck a deal with liberalizing Polish leader Wladyslaw Gomulka: Poland would be allowed a measure of latitude but would remain within the Soviet sphere. Meanwhile, on October 23 in Budapest, thousands of students took to the streets to show solidarity with the Polish rebels. Demanding the withdrawal of Soviet troops from Hungary, free speech, free elections, and the return to power of Hungarian political reformer Imre Nagy, the protesters marched toward the state radio station.

When police fired on the crowd, the demonstration became a popular uprising. Hungarian security forces and Soviet troops stormed Budapest, but the Hungarian army disbanded, its soldiers taking their weapons to the rebel side. The government collapsed; within a day, as insurgency engulfed the country, the Hungarian Communist Party named Nagy premier. He announced the end of the one-party system and withdrew from the Warsaw Pact. Soviet troops pulled out of Budapest. The jubilation lasted one week: On November 4, some 2,500 Soviet tanks clanked into the capital. Thousands of resisters died in street fighting; 150,000 more fled across the border to Austria. Nagy took refuge in the Yugoslav embassy, where he stayed for two years. In 1958, duped out of sanctuary by Hungary's new puppet premier, János Kádár, he was summarily executed. **◂1956.2 ▸1968.2**

POPULAR CULTURE

A New Style of News

5 In October 1956, NBC inaugurated a new era in journalism. Chet Huntley and David Brinkley served as coanchors for the *Huntley-Brinkley Report*, a 15-minute evening news broadcast (later expanded to a half hour). The first season's ratings were dismal, but the pair soon became TV's first superstar newsmen. And the show's format provided a model for newscasts around the world.

News programs had lagged behind drama and comedy shows in exploiting the potential of television. Most featured veteran radio reporters (like John Cameron Swayze, whom Huntley and Brinkley succeeded) who read copy while presenting newsreel-style footage, often of staged events. Huntley and Brinkley increasingly used on-the-spot footage edited by the NBC staff; they worked their commentary around the action and enlivened coverage with their interchanges.

Huntley was the straight man with the resonant voice, covering the main news stories from a Manhattan studio; Brinkley, of the acerbic wit and expressive eyebrows, handled political news from Washington. No matter how grim the news had been, each program ended with the same comforting lines: "Good night, Chet"; "Good night, David." Until it folded in 1970, *Huntley-Brinkley* was an American institution, rivaled only by the *Evening News* with Walter Cronkite, which first aired in 1962 on CBS. **◂1940.V**

Chet Huntley *(left)* and David Brinkley were the first "stars" of nightly news.

BIRTHS

Björn Borg, Swedish tennis player.

Sebastian Coe, U.K. runner.

Paul Cook, U.K. musician.

David Copperfield, U.S. magician.

Judy Davis, Australian actress.

Carrie Fisher, U.S. actress and writer.

Mel Gibson, Australian-U.S. actor.

Nigel Kennedy, U.K. violinist.

Olga Korbut, Soviet gymnast.

Johnny Lydon (Johnny Rotten), U.K. singer.

Glen Matlock, U.K. musician.

Joe Montana, U.S. football player.

Warren Moon, U.S. football player.

Martina Navratilova, Czech-U.S. tennis player.

Mickey Rourke, U.S. actor.

DEATHS

Fred Allen, U.S. comedian.

Clarence Birdseye, U.S. inventor.

William Boeing, U.S. manufacturer.

Bertolt Brecht, German writer.

Clifford Brown, U.S. musician.

Tommy Dorsey, U.S. musician.

Lyonel Feininger, German-U.S. painter.

Irène Joliot-Curie, French scientist.

Alfred Kinsey, U.S. biologist.

Alexander Korda, Hungarian-U.K. filmmaker.

Connie Mack, U.S. baseball player and manager.

Henry Louis Mencken, U.S. writer and editor.

A.A. Milne, U.K. writer.

Jackson Pollock, U.S. painter.

Art Tatum, U.S. musician.

Thomas J. Watson, Sr., U.S. manufacturer.

Babe Didrikson Zaharias, U.S. golfer.

makes today's homes so different, so appealing? **(Richard Hamilton) ... Film: *Around the World in Eighty Days* (Michael Anderson); *The Searchers* (John Ford); *Godzilla, King of the Monsters* (Morse and Honda); *Invasion of the Body Snatchers* (Don Siegel) ... Theater: *The Visit* (Friedrich Dürrenmatt); *The Most Happy Fella* (Frank Loesser) ... TV: *As the World Turns*; *The Edge of Night*; *The Price Is Right*.**

"I must say, Bernard Shaw is greatly improved by music."—**T.S. Eliot, on the opening night of *My Fair Lady***

NEW IN 1956

Transatlantic telephone cable.

La Leche League International.

Comet cleanser.

"In God We Trust" printed on U.S. currency.

Videotape recorder (Ampex).

Pampers disposable diapers.

IN THE UNITED STATES

▶THE UNDEFEATED—Boxing, the "sweet science," was anything but when heavyweight champion Rocky Marciano, a brawler from Brockton, Massachusetts, stepped into the ring. All powerful shoulders

and relentless assault, he bulled in close on opponents and overwhelmed them with savage blows. Marciano retired In 1956, undefeated in all 49 of his professional bouts (43 by knockouts), the only heavyweight champion ever to compile a perfect record. ◂1937.9 ▸1964.11

▶WIDE OPEN ROAD—Two measures that became law in 1956 changed the face of America: The Federal Aid Highway Act and the Highway Revenue Act. The first authorized the construction of a massive, 40,000-mile interstate highway system that would connect most major cities (and provide the best routes for military vehicles in case of a defense emergency). Within four years, 10,000 miles were completed; trucking replaced railroads as the chief means of transport, and commuting by car became the norm for American workers. Meanwhile, public transportation was neglected; during the 1950s and '60s, some 75 percent of federal transportation funds

DISASTERS

The *Andrea Doria* Sinks

6 The *Andrea Doria*, bound for New York from Genoa, was just hours away from its destination on the night of July 25, 1956, when the prow of the Swedish passenger ship *Stockholm* cut a huge gash in its side—precipitating one of the most controversial and costly disasters in maritime history. As Captain Piero Calamai and his crew supervised a chaotic evacuation, nearby craft (including the *Stockholm*) rescued passengers. Nearly 1,700 people had been saved by 10:09 AM, when the Italian luxury liner finally sank; 52 were dead.

This first high-seas collision of major ocean liners was a reminder of the limitations of even state-of-the-art technology. Unlike the two airliners that had collided over the Grand Canyon a month earlier (killing 128 in the worst air disaster to date), both ships had been equipped with radar—but so had many other vessels that had collided in recent years. With a hull divided into eleven watertight compartments, the *Andrea Doria* had been thought unsinkable—but so had the *Titanic*.

What went wrong? Who was responsible? In court hearings, attention was focused on Calamai and the *Stockholm*'s third officer, Johan-Ernst Carstens-Johannsen, who disagreed about such fundamentals as visibility conditions and the orientation of their ships before the collision. Questions were raised regarding an unreliable *Stockholm* helmsman, but no conclusions were ever drawn. Six months after the disaster, both shipping lines abandoned attempts to fix blame and established a fund to pay third-party claims. The total cost, including the loss of one ship, damage to the other, and some 3,300 legal settlements: $40 million. **◂1912.1**

Brigitte Bardot was an unconventional bride in husband Roger Vadim's sensationalistic yet arty film.

FILM

A New Sex Symbol

7 Watching one of her erotic scenes, an embarrassed Gary Cooper murmured, "I guess I ought to put a sack over my face." Church leaders boycotted her. But Simone de Beauvoir cheered her: "The male is an object to her, just as she is to him. And that is precisely what wounds masculine pride." Brigitte Bardot, 22, embodied sexuality with an abandon that had seldom been seen in cinema. Her 1956 vehicle, *And God Created Woman*, directed by her husband, Roger Vadim, made her a star. The movie also created American and British appetites for European "art" films—and established its setting, the French fishing village of St. Tropez, as a chic resort.

The film told an old, tawdry story: A frisky nymphet marries a good, dull man, then sleeps with his brother. What made it a sensation was Bardot's unbridled libido, and the clothes she shed while unbridling it. In her first appearance, she's nude; in later scenes, she wears a clinging bed sheet (which she opens for her on-screen husband) and lounges in a man's pajama top. A well-known magazine photographer, Vadim imbued his first film with a visual sophistication that gave it a veneer of art.

Off-screen scandals (Bardot was having an affair with costar Jean-Louis Trintignant; she and Vadim soon divorced) helped inflame the foreign box office: *And God Created Woman* did mediocre business in France but was a smash in London; in America, it grossed $4 million, a record for a European film. And the success of this small, personal work—made outside of the big studios—encouraged Godard, Truffaut, and other French New Wave directors to make their own debuts. **▸1959.7**

The *Andrea Doria* going down after it collided with the *Stockholm* off Nantucket.

THEATER

A Transformed Flower Girl

8 "I absolutely forbid any such outrage," George Bernard Shaw once thundered when an amateur director proposed a musical version of his play *Pygmalion*. But in 1956, six years after the playwright's death, a musical adaptation opened on Broadway that even Shaw might have forgiven. With book and lyrics by Alan Jay Lerner, music by Frederick Loewe, and direction by Moss Hart, *My Fair Lady* didn't break new ground or reinvent the genre. It was merely flawless.

Julie Andrews played *My Fair Lady*'s Cockney flower girl Eliza Doolittle. The hit musical ran for six years on Broadway.

Lerner's book preserved much of the social critique at the heart of Shaw's comedy—the tale of Henry Higgins (Rex Harrison), an irascible

SPORTS: Baseball: World Series, New York Yankees (Don Larsen pitches perfect game) defeat Brooklyn Dodgers, 4–3 ... Olympics held in Cortina D'Ampezzo, Italy, and Melbourne ... Football: NFL, New York Giants defeat Chicago Bears, 47–7 ... Basketball: NBA, Philadelphia Warriors defeat Fort Wayne Pistons, 4–1 ... Boxing: Floyd Patterson knocks out Archie Moore for world heavyweight title.

"She has bounced around with the ease of a girl on the trapeze. Whether the platform on which she has landed is too narrow, I don't know."—**Alfred Hitchcock, on Grace Kelly's marriage to Prince Rainier**

phonetics professor who teaches Eliza Doolittle (Julie Andrews), a Cockney flower seller, to speak and act like a duchess—while tacking on a happier ending. (This, the most controversial of *My Fair Lady*'s deviations from the source material, is actually the most legitimate: Shaw tolerated a similar happy ending in the 1938 film *Pygmalion*.) Andrews warbled gorgeously; Harrison used a brilliantly appropriate form of talk-singing. The songs themselves included a string of instant classics: "I Could Have Danced All Night," "I've Grown Accustomed to Her Face," "Get Me to the Church On Time," "On the Street Where You Live," and the elocutionary tango "The Rain in Spain."

My Fair Lady ran for 2,717 straight performances on Broadway; the 1958 London production (also with Andrews and Harrison) was a smash as well. And in 1964, the film version with Harrison and Audrey Hepburn won seven Oscars, including Best Picture, and Best Actor for Harrison. **◂1904.7 ▸1961.11**

POPULAR CULTURE

Grace Becomes a Princess

9 As live television beamed the ceremonies to 30 million Europeans, the man who presided over the world's swankiest gambling resort married the onetime advertising model for Ipana toothpaste. The couple's April 1956 nuptials, gasped the press, were a true-life fairy tale and "the wedding of the century."

The groom was Prince Rainier III, 32, ruler of tiny Monaco—famous for its Mediterranean climate, its elite casinos, and its lack of an income tax. The bride was Grace Kelly, 26, daughter of a Philadelphia industrialist (and former bricklayer) and a top movie star—famous for her serene blonde beauty and crisp, yet smoldering, performances in *High Noon*, *Dial M for Murder*, *Rear Window*, and *The Country Girl* (for which she won the 1954 Best Actress Oscar).

The couple met in 1955 when Kelly, as a favor to a journalist friend, agreed to visit Monaco and add Hollywood glamour to magazine pictures of Rainier and his palace. The prince and the movie star became instant friends. When he visited the States at the end of the year, he proposed. Kelly completed her new film, *High Society*, and sailed for Monte Carlo.

Grace and Rainier exchange vows in a Roman Catholic ceremony in Monaco Cathedral.

The marriage produced three royal children. Rainier turned Monaco into a middle-class tourist destination and corporate haven, while Princess Grace abandoned her film career and busied herself with charity work. She died in 1982 when she lost control of her car on a curving mountain highway above the Riviera. **◂1952.11**

FILM

Ray's Great Design

10 Few directing careers have begun as auspiciously as that of Satyajit Ray, whose debut film, *Pather Panchali*, was deemed "the best human document" at the 1956 Cannes Film Festival. The first installment of Ray's Apu trilogy (followed the same year by *Aparajito* and in 1959 by *The World of Apu*), the movie inaugurated the saga of a Bengali boy's coming of age—and won its director instant recognition as one of the world's great filmmakers.

Loosely based on Bibhuti Bhushan Bannerjee's novel *Pather Panchali*, the film—which was plagued throughout with financial problems—depicts Indian village life so convincingly that some viewers took it for a documentary. Yet it is pervaded with an artist's touch, from the intimate camera angles, to the deliberately languid pacing, to the performances Ray elicited from his child actors. Ravi Shankar's music and Ray's symbolic imagery—a flickering flame, pounding rains—express what the spare dialogue cannot. "With apparent formlessness," observed Indian-born British director Lindsay Anderson, "*Pather Panchali* traces the great design of living."

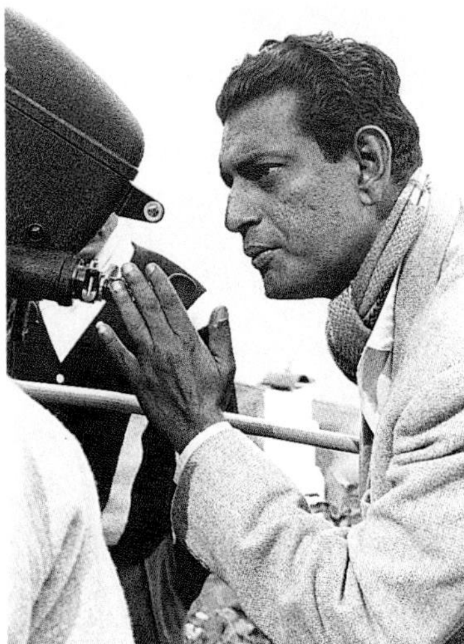
Ray *(above)* was on the verge of abandoning *Pather Panchali* when the Bengali government provided funds to finish it.

Light-years removed from the gaudiness of rank-and-file Indian cinema, Ray's subtle realism (inspired by Vittorio de Sica's 1948 masterpiece, *The Bicycle Thief*) influenced filmmakers around the world. In 1961, Ray made a documentary about Nobel Prize winner Rabindranath Tagore (a family friend), whose writings were the basis for some of Ray's other movies. **◂1948.14**

IN THE UNITED STATES

went to building highways, while only 1 percent went to urban mass transit. ◂1940.M

▶PERFECTION ON THE MOUND—The New York Yankees' Don Larsen pitched the first (and only) perfect game in World Series history on October 8, 1956, in the fifth game of a seven-game "subway Series" between the Yanks and the Brooklyn Dodgers. Throwing only 97 times, Larsen got out 27 batters in a row. The Yanks won the game 2–0 and the Series 4 games to 3. ◂1951.M

▶ALABAMA EXPELS LUCY—The president and trustees of the University of Alabama defied a federal court order to reinstate Autherine Lucy, and expelled her instead. The dismissal of Lucy, the first black to attend the university, was carried out in spite of the Supreme Court's 1954 ruling that public-school segregation was unconstitutional. Southern Congressmen meanwhile swore to resist desegregation by "all lawful means." ◂1954.6 ▸1957.M

▶TELEVISION THEATER—Live drama, once a television staple, was already becoming a rarity by 1956. Resisting the trend, CBS introduced *Playhouse 90*, a weekly, 90-minute show that offered some of the best drama available on a screen of any size. Among the plays that premiered on *Playhouse 90:* Rod Serling's *Requiem for a Heavyweight*, J.P. Miller's *Days of Wine and Roses*, and William Gibson's *The Miracle Worker*. ▸1971.10

▶LITERARY LUST—*Peyton Place*, Grace Metalious's 1956 tale of small-town sleaze, achieved an immediate succès de scandale. The novel didn't stack up as literature, but it sold and sold. In 1964, ABC based a weekly, prime-time soap opera *(below)* on it—a tell-all, show-all (at least by the standards of the day) extravaganza that remade small-screen programming.

POLITICS & BUSINESS: GNP: $419.2 billion ... Dwight D. Eisenhower reelected president, defeating Adlai Stevenson ... Atomic Energy Commission authorizes privatization of atomic energy plants ... Ford Motor Company goes public.

"I want to make people feel, to give them lessons in feeling. They can think afterwards."—**John Osborne**

AROUND THE WORLD

▶MAKARIOS IMPRISONED—British colonial authorities in Cyprus (annexed by Great Britain in 1914) arrested Makarios III, archbishop of the Orthodox Church of Cyprus, on sedition charges in 1956. A leading proponent of union with Greece, Makarios was accused

of supporting Colonel Georgios Grivas's Cypriot Greek guerrilla organization. Following Makarios's exile, Grivas escalated his terror campaign, and talks between Turkey—which advocated partition of the island into separate Greek and Turkish zones—Greece, and Britain collapsed. Makarios later accepted a compromise: independence outside the Commonwealth with neither union nor partition. In 1959, the archbishop was elected the first president of independent Cyprus. ▶1960.10

▶INDEPENDENCE IN NORTH AFRICA—Morocco, Tunisia, and Sudan each achieved independence in 1956. Moroccan nationalism reached a peak when exiled Sultan Sidi Muhammad returned to the country in late 1955; the following spring France conceded independence. Bogged down in Algeria, the French also withdrew from Tunisia. Sudan, Africa's largest country, became self-governing in 1953 but had to wait three more years for independence from Great Britain and Egypt. Meanwhile, tensions between the Christian south and the dominant Muslim north exploded into civil war. ◀1954.3 ▶1992.M

▶POULENC'S LYRICISM—In 1956, versatile French composer Francis Poulenc (one of the set of witty, antiromantic post-World War I French composers known as "Les Six") finished *Dialogues des Carmélites*, a tragedy about a group of nuns during the French Revolution. Exhibiting all of Poulenc's customary lyricism (his are among the finest modern songs), religious feeling, and deep compassion, the opera ranks as his masterpiece.

1956

MUSIC

Gould's Peculiar Genius

11 One of the most sublime works ever composed for the keyboard, Johann Sebastian Bach's *Goldberg Variations,* had largely disappeared from the standard repertory when a 23-year-old Canadian named Glenn Gould resurrected it for his 1956 recording debut with Columbia Records. Gould's *Goldberg Variations* became the bestselling classical record of the year, awakening listeners to new possibilities of pianistic interpretation. "[Gould] has more promise than any young North American keyboard artist to appear since the war," wrote one enthusiastic critic.

But if Gould's passionate rendering of Bach was revelatory, his personality was inscrutable. Observers marveled at his peculiarities—from his habit of wearing mufflers and overcoats (whatever the weather) to the bizarre postures (he used a 14-inch chair), gesticulations, and murmurings that accompanied his performances. His musical tastes were idiosyncratic, too. Gould disdained most eighteenth- and early-nineteenth-century Romantic works; in fact, some critics found his interpretations of Beethoven and Mozart piano sonatas insulting. He championed several obscure twentieth-century composers, but remained most closely linked with Bach. (Gould's recording of Bach's *Well Tempered Clavier* was included on the *Voyager* space probe.)

One magazine article described Gould as "A frail, loose-jointed Canadian with a bumper crop of light-brown hair."

In 1964, weary of the "tyranny" of stage appearances, Gould retreated to the isolation of the recording studio and never performed live again. He died of a stroke in 1982 at age 50; the opening notes of the *Goldberg Variations* appear on his piano-shaped grave marker. **◀1950.13 ▶1958.10**

Angry Young Man John Osborne. Like the antihero of his play, Osborne was working class and college educated.

THEATER

The Angry Young Men

12 Director Tony Richardson and the English Stage Company opened John Osborne's *Look Back in Anger* at London's Royal Court Theatre on May 8, 1956. The production, starring Kenneth Haigh and Alan Bates, was a turning point for British culture. Attendance had long been dwindling at the nation's theaters, which were offering a bland selection of well-made plays. "Osborne's passion," the novelist and biographer Angus Wilson observed a decade later, "saved the English theatre from death through gentility."

The hero—or, more properly, antihero—of *Look Back in Anger* is Jimmy Porter, a young, working-class man with a university education (like a growing segment of the population). Jimmy expresses his rage at the entrenched English establishment by abusing his middle-class wife. "He is a disconcerting mixture of sincerity and cheerful malice, of tenderness and freebooting cruelty," wrote Osborne of his protagonist. However unsavory Porter's actions, his scathingly articulated resentment struck a deep nerve in postwar Britain.

Porter's similarities with the title character of *Lucky Jim,* Kingsley Amis's 1954 satirical novel about a lowborn university instructor trapped in the pretentious, upper-class world of academia, won each writer the label "Angry Young Man." The phrase was eventually applied to a whole generation of British dramatists and novelists inspired to sociological spleen-venting by the success of Osborne's play. **◀1915.11 ▶1958.13**

MUSIC

Calypso Catches On

13 Calypso music had been evolving in the Caribbean nation of Trinidad and Tobago since the turn of the century—but it took an American named Harry Belafonte to bring it into the pop mainstream. Belafonte's album *Calypso*, featuring such standards-to-be as "Jamaica Farewell" and "The Banana Boat Song (Day-O)," topped the U.S. charts for 31 weeks in 1956; by 1959, it had become the first million-selling LP, and calypso was a genre heard around the world. (It was heard most often in Belafonte's Broadway-tinged baritone; authentic calypsonians like the Mighty Sparrow and Lord Kitchener remained largely unknown outside Caribbean and African communities.)

Belafonte's interest in the West Indian export came naturally. Born in New York's Harlem, he spent five years of his boyhood living with relatives in Jamaica—acquiring a regional accent as well as a love for the African-rooted music of the Caribbean. (Harlem, too, was a center for the fast, syncopated calypso, whose lyrics were often sardonic commentaries on the issues of the day.) Belafonte's initial successes, however, had nothing to do with calypso: He rose to fame playing the lead in the stage and screen versions of the musical *Carmen Jones*, and had his first hit singles with the folk songs "Scarlet Ribbons" and "Shenandoah."

Though Belafonte's name would be forever linked with his Trinidadian-style numbers, his career covered far broader territory. By the 1990s, he'd recorded a dizzying variety of albums (nine of which reached the Top Ten), starred in several films (from the serious *Island in the Sun* to the comic *Buck and the Preacher*), and lent his voice to causes from the civil rights movement to the 1984 "USA for Africa" famine-relief campaign. **◀1954.M ▶1984.4**

Belafonte's robust baritone made calypso popular with millions.

NOBEL PRIZES: Peace: No award ... Literature: Juan Jiménez (Spanish; poet) ... Chemistry: Cyril Hinshelwood and Nikolaj Semenov (U.K., U.S.S.R; kinetic reactions) ... Medicine: Dickinson Richards, André Cournand, and Werner Forssmann (U.S., U.S., German; heart disease) ... Physics: William Shockley, Walter Brattain, and John Bardeen (U.S.; transistor).

A VOICE FROM 1956

TV's Golden Years

From *TV Guide*, Local Program Listings, Boston, Massachusetts, June 16–22, 1956

Father Does Know Best!
—See Page 8
TV GUIDE
LOCAL PROGRAM LISTINGS WEEK OF JUNE 16-22
15¢

Competing for a share of the ever-growing television market, network executives outdid themselves in the 1955-56 season. Among the shows and characters first beamed into America's living rooms that year: the champagne music party of Lawrence Welk ("A-vun, and a-two, and a-t'ree"); big-pocketed Bob Keeshan, Captain Kangaroo to millions of young fans; The Mickey Mouse Club *(with the wildly popular Annette Funicello and fellow singing Mouseketeers);* Gunsmoke, *crossing over from radio to begin a record 20-year TV run; working-class pals Ralph Kramden and Ed Norton and their long-suffering wives, on* Jackie Gleason *("starring the Honeymooners");* Alfred Hitchcock Presents, *featuring the pudgy maestro himself as emcee for prime-time murder and mayhem. Saturday night had never before, and would perhaps never again, offer such couch-potato bliss.*

◂1951.9

SATURDAY — JUNE 16

30 Range Rider—Western
"Outlaw's Double." Range Rider tries to clear himself of a murder charge.

55 Cisco Kid—Western
A man is murdered for his newly discovered mine. Duncan Renaldo.

7:00 4 YOU ASKED FOR IT—Baker
(1) A visit to the headquarters of the Mission Aviation Fellowship, Fullerton, Cal., which transports supplies to missionaries in remote corners of the world. (2) A demonstration of cine-radiography, X-ray movies. (Film)

6 MAN BEHIND THE BADGE
"The Quiet Guest." An inspector must find a man who has a key that fits every lock in town. (Film)

7 BOB CUMMINGS—Comedy
"Scramble for Grandpa." When grandpa's "Old Jenny" keeps fouling up Joplin's air defense filter system, authorities appeal to Bob to keep grandpa's crate out of the air around Joplin. (Film)

8 ROBIN HOOD—Adventure
"The Knight Who Came to Dinner."

8 RHYTHM RANCH—Lindell

9 ADVENTURE THEATER

10 CAVALCADE THEATER

12 YOU TRUST YOUR WIFE?
Edgar Bergen welcomes Steve and Dorothy Rowland on their tenth visit to the program. (Film)

13 DEATH VALLEY DAYS

18 ORIENT EXPRESS—Adven.

22 BREAK THE BANK—Quiz

30 SAN FRANCISCO BEAT

Like to talk to the folks back home?
TELEPHONE TONIGHT
Boston to St. Louis $1.35
After 6 o'clock every night.
Station-to-Station rate, first 3 minutes. Add 10% tax.

55 FAVORITE STORY—Drama
"The Man Who Sold His Shadow." The Devil bargains for a man's shadow. DeForest Kelley, Anne Kimbell. (Film)

7:15 8 POLITICAL TALK

7:30 4 6 10 22 30 DOWN YOU GO—Panel
Dr. Bergen Evans and his panelists, including Arthur Treacher, take over the Big Surprise spot for the summer.

7 13 18 55 BEAT THE CLOCK

8 ALFRED HITCHCOCK
Ruth Hussey stars in "Mink." A woman purchases a mink stole at a bargain price and takes it to a furrier to have it appraised. (Film)

8 STAR TONIGHT—Drama
Deirdre Owens stars in "Kingdom's Child," story of the daughter of a puritanical minister. The father is convinced that the end of the world is imminent. (Film)

9 OZARK JUBILEE—Variety
Emcee Red Foley's special guest is singer Rusty Draper. Other guests include the Carlisles, a comedy vocal group, and the square-dancing Jubilee Tadpoles. (Springfield, Mo.)

12 WATERFRONT—Adventure
"Shakedown Cruise." A freighter captain denies the friendship of a derelict. (Film)

8:00 4 6 10 22 30 PATTI PAGE
DEBUT Filling in the time spot for vacationing Perry Como this summer is a series of variety shows. Patti Page stars tonight in the first of the four shows she will do. Her guests include singer Eddy Arnold, comedienne Jean Carroll, comedian-magician Mr. Ballantine and the Wazzan Troupe of Acrobats. The theme of the show is "Do-it-yourself," and Patti opens with a production number, "'Deed I Do." Her solos include "The Strangest Romance," "When Your Lover Has Gone" and "Then I'll Be Happy." The Spellbinders, a vocal group which will appear regularly on the show, harmonize "Shine On, Harvest Moon" and back up Patti's rendition of "April in Paris."

TV GUIDE

A-10

JUNE 16 — SATURDAY

7 8 8 12 13 55 JACKIE GLEASON—Comedy
Ed Norton accompanies friend Ralph Kramden on a business trip. Art Carney, Audrey Meadows. (Film)

18 STORIES OF THE WEST

8:30 7 8 8 12 13 STAGE SHOW—Variety
The music-making Dorsey Brothers introduce three music-making acts: the zany Treniers, songstress Connie Francis and the piano-novelty trio known as the Edwards Brothers. And the June Taylor Dancers do their routines.

55 LONE WOLF—Adventure

9:00 4 6 10 30 PEOPLE ARE FUNNY—Stunts
Art Linkletter conducts an experiment to test the compatibility of a woman and her future son-in-law. In another stunt an engaged man is asked to call up an old flame and make a date with her. (Film)

7 12 13 18 55 TWO FOR THE MONEY—Quiz

8 9 22 LAWRENCE WELK
The Lennon Sisters, teen-age quartet, will :e a guest appearance. (Hollywood)

Highlights

ender Blue"	Lennon Sisters
›ity-doo-dah"	Lennon Sisters
thing Goes"	Orchestra
Tower"	Lon
People of Paris"	Merrill

TURNING POINT—Drama
way a Winner." An ex-convict plots on his wife who divorced him was in prison. Ellen Drew. (Film)

6 10 30 DURANTE
›ays a visit to the estate of actor Sanders, only to learn George's ther doesn't want Jimmy around. taliates by inviting George to Durant. Jimmy sings "All-girl anders' numbers are "Such Is "After You're Gone" and "I Eddie Jackson."

13 18 55 IT'S ALWAYS nedy
between loyalty and fame

when a big-time agent offers her an important engagement if she agrees to leave her present agent. Janis Paige, Sid Melton, Patricia Bright. (Film)

8 LAWRENCE WELK—Music

"Moonglow"	Burke, Hooper
"Blue Suede Shoes"	Orchestra
"Rock and Roll Ruby	Buddy

10:00 4 6 10 22 30 GEO. GOBEL
Special guest Arthur Treacher joins George in a sketch set in Merrie Olde England. George plays Tootie Flimbone, a British bank clerk, and Treacher appears as a most aristocratic burglar. Peggy King's song is "Lover." John Scott Trotter's orchestra. (Film)

7 12 13 18 55 GUNSMOKE
Marshal Dillon meets a giant of a man to settle a dispute with only his fists. (Film)

Cast

Matt Dillon	James Arness
Ham Keeler	Chuck Connors
Kitty	Amanda Blake

8 CHANCE OF A LIFETIME

9 GUY LOMBARDO—Music
Helena Scott sings "A Thousand and One Nights" and "The Hero of All My Dreams." Kenny Gardner does "Little White Lies." (Film)

10:30 4 6 10 22 30 ADVENTURE THEATER—Drama
DEBUT Paul Douglas is host for this new half-hour suspense series filmed in England. "Thirty Days to Die," the first play, concerns a disappointed playwright who blames the failure of his

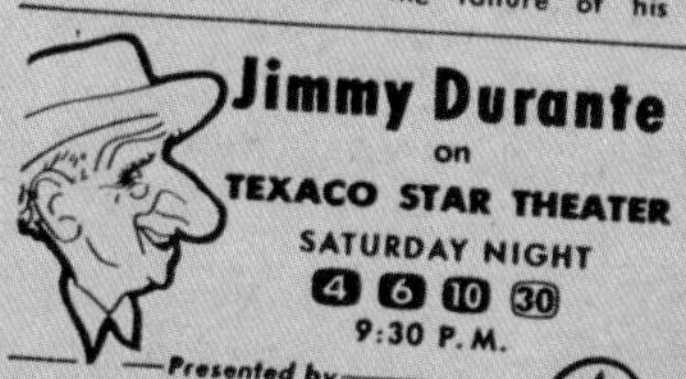

Jimmy Durante
on
TEXACO STAR THEATER
SATURDAY NIGHT
4 6 10 30
9:30 P.M.
Presented by
YOUR TEXACO DEALER
...the best friend your car has ever had!
TEXACO

TV GUIDE

A-11

Founded in 1953 by media mogul Walter Annenberg, *TV Guide* became one of the most widely read magazines in the country. (By 1994, its circulation had topped 14 million.) Originally published in 10 regional editions—the magazine is now in 114—and featuring articles as well as listings, the issue of June 16–22, 1956, carried a cover photo and article on TV dad Robert Young and his three TV children. Young's show *Father Knows Best* debuted on CBS in 1954 and ran until 1963.

"One small ball in the air, something that does not raise my apprehension, not one iota."—**President Dwight D. Eisenhower, on the Soviets' successful launching of *Sputnik I***

STORY OF THE YEAR

Sputnik Launches the Space Race

1 On October 4, 1957, the Soviet Union launched the world's first artificial satellite, *Sputnik I*, into space. As the 23-inch diameter, 184-pound aluminum sphere circled the earth, Americans reeled in shock: A country they'd assumed to be technologically inferior had beaten them to the punch. Their consternation doubled in November, when the Soviets sent up the half-ton *Sputnik II*, carrying a dog called Laika.

A month after *Sputnik I*, *Sputnik II* carried Laika, the first animal in space.

The American panic over *Sputnik* (Russian for "fellow traveler") had two dimensions: The Soviets' stunning success gave them the edge in the propaganda war; and space technology could easily be applied to weaponry. Americans had refused to believe the Soviets' recent announcement that they'd tested the first intercontinental ballistic missile (ICBM), a self-propelled nuclear weapon capable of crossing oceans. Now Moscow's lead was incontestable—and the U.S. public clamored for a satellite of its own. The space race was on.

Or rather, it was on in earnest. Three U.S. rocket programs were already under way. In 1955, President Eisenhower had chosen the Navy's Project Vanguard for space research; the Air Force's nascent Atlas program (aimed at producing an ICBM) had been put on a back burner, as had a similar project of the Army's. But Vanguard had been underfunded, and America's foremost rocket scientist, Wernher von Braun, had remained with the Army, setting off experimental rockets almost unnoticed.

In December 1957, with great fanfare, the United States launched a Vanguard rocket carrying a 3.5-pound satellite. It exploded on the launch pad. Embarrassed officials called on von Braun, who used a rocket he had designed himself to successfully launch the *Explorer I* satellite the following month. Its scientific instruments promptly made an important discovery: two bands of radiation extending from a few hundred to some 40,000 miles above the earth's atmosphere—the Van Allen Belts.

As the Soviet and U.S. satellite launches continued, the U.S. armed forces (backed by Texas senator Lyndon Johnson) began pressing the government for lunar military bases. In July 1958, Eisenhower established the National Aeronautics and Space Agency (later Administration), or NASA, which soon recruited seven astronauts and hired von Braun as chief rocket engineer.

By the time Moscow put the first man into orbit, in 1961, both countries had sacrificed a host of astro-animals. And in both countries, the race had become a national obsession. **◂1903.M ▸1957.2**

TECHNOLOGY

Long-Distance Doom

2 American invulnerability to nuclear assault vanished in August 1957, when the Soviet Union successfully tested the world's first intercontinental ballistic missile. Though Washington initially dismissed Moscow's announcement as propaganda, the launching of *Sputnik* soon afterward raised fears of a "missile gap"—and spurred the United States to step up its missile program. Within months, America unveiled its own ICBM, the Atlas.

Before the Soviet missile appeared, the United States not only possessed more bombs than its ideological adversary but also better ways of delivering them. With air bases in Alaska, Greenland, Iceland, Japan, Morocco, Saudi Arabia, Spain, and Turkey, and with short-range tactical weapons deployed in Western Europe, the Americans maintained a nuclear cordon around the Soviet bloc. Meanwhile, the Soviets, having designed and tested hydrogen bombs of unprecedented power, had no practical way of dropping them on America. A war between the superpowers would have to be fought in Europe—or so it seemed until 1957. Then, for the first time in history, an apocalyptic war fought at extreme distances became a gruesome possibility.

STRATEGIC NUCLEAR WARHEADS

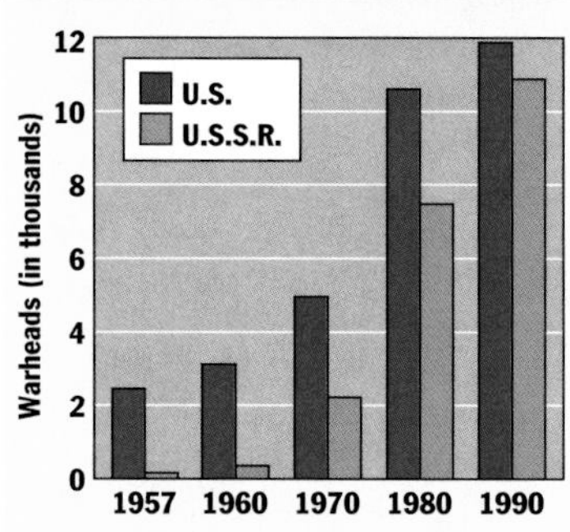

Countries began counting nuclear warheads in the '50s. By 1990, only Great Britain had begun to dismantle them.

As the arms race entered this new phase, both superpowers declared the need to control the proliferation of nuclear weapons. Khrushchev made the first move, announcing a unilateral nuclear test ban, in August 1958. By October, however, when the Third Disarmament Conference opened in Geneva, the Soviets had resumed testing. (The Americans had never stopped.) Geneva did produce a voluntary agreement to cease testing, but it lasted only a few years. Propelled by a dangerous logic—that "mutual assured destruction" (MAD) was the best guarantee that such weapons would never be used—the race accelerated. **◂1957.1 ▸1963.2**

HAITI

Papa Doc Takes Control

3 A grisly dynasty was born in September 1957, when François Duvalier—running on a program of social reform and black nationalism—was elected president of Haiti. The nation had been in turmoil since the forced resignation of dictator Paul Magloire; six provisional presidents had come and gone in ten months, while mobs ruled the streets. Duvalier, a physician and former health and labor minister, had led the underground opposition to Magloire. But "Papa Doc," as Haitians called him, proved the most repressive and longest-ruling despot in Haiti's history.

François "Papa Doc" Duvalier in 1969, at work with two pistols on his desk.

The world's first black republic had not had much luck since breaking with France (after a devastating war of independence) in 1804. With little arable land and a population marked by a century of slavery, Haiti was ruled by a succession of tiny elites that lived in flamboyant luxury (aided increasingly by American investors) while the majority endured abject poverty. Dictatorships alternated with brief stabs at democracy; a U.S. military occupation (1915–34) simply enforced the status quo.

Duvalier promised to overturn the old, mostly mulatto ruling class and curb the army. But after defeating a coup attempt in 1958, he established a private security force, the Tontons Macoutes—Creole for "bogeymen"—whose reign of terror was unprecedented. Like

ART & CULTURE: Books: *Jealousy* (Alain Robbe-Grillet); *Atlas Shrugged* (Ayn Rand); *Homo Faber* (Max Frisch); *On the Beach* (Nevil Shute); *The Assistant* (Bernard Malamud); *Memories of a Catholic Girlhood* (Mary McCarthy) ... Music: "Chances Are" (Allen and Stillman); "Whole Lot-ta Shakin' Goin' On" (Williams and David); "All Shook Up!" (Blackwell and Presley); *Symphony No. 3* (Roger Sessions) ...

"We prefer self-government with danger to servitude with tranquillity."—Kwame Nkrumah

Duvalier himself, the Macoutes exploited the African-derived folk religion of voodoo, convincing many Haitians that the Macoutes were supernaturally invulnerable. Identifiable by the sunglasses they invariably wore, the plainclothes goons murdered and tortured at will. As Duvalier's rivals were killed or driven into exile, he and his corrupt associates pocketed the nation's remaining wealth. Deepening diplomatic isolation only made Papa Doc tougher: In 1964, he declared himself president for life. **◂1916.2 ▸1986.4**

WESTERN AFRICA

Ghana Becomes Independent

4 The end of European rule in sub-Saharan Africa began in 1957, when Britain's former Gold Coast colony became independent Ghana. The transition was smoother than might have been expected seven years earlier, when riots and strikes led to the jailing of nationalist leader Kwame Nkrumah. But Britain had already decided to prepare its colonies for self-rule, and after Nkrumah's Convention People's Party won national elections in 1951, he was released to become the Gold Coast's head of government business. With independence, Nkrumah, who'd since become the colony's prime minister, simply remained in office.

Ghana seemed a promising laboratory for Africa's postcolonial future. Thanks to Britain's need for cacao and gold (Ghana's principal exports), the country had the rudiments of an infrastructure. Its leader held three degrees from American universities. The son of humble villagers, Nkrumah professed to be a nondoctrinaire socialist, a democrat, and—comforting to the West—a Christian. Nkrumah's eloquence, and Ghana's example, inspired nationalists throughout the Third World.

Within five years, most of the continent's European territories were independent. Some broke away peacefully, others amid strife; some had been groomed for their new status, others abruptly abandoned. But all were basically preindustrial societies, thrown into competition with the industrial powers. And all suffered the harmful aftereffects of colonialism—including arbitrary borders (which created or exacerbated interethnic hostilities), economies based on exports of a few raw materials, treasuries dependent on foreign aid, histories etched with the scars of the slave trade, and political cultures conditioned by generations of imperial overseers. For Ghana and its sister states, the euphoria of freedom would not last long. **▸1966.12**

A float in a parade in Ghana's capital, Accra, heralds a rosy future with education for all.

ECONOMICS

The Common Market

5 A dozen years after a ruinous war, six European nations (some of them former enemies) formed a union to ensure peace and prosperity. The Treaty of Rome, signed in 1957 by Belgium, France, West Germany, Italy, Luxembourg, and the Netherlands, established the European Economic Community—commonly known as the Common Market. The EEC quickly defused rising tensions between France and a rebuilding Germany; within ten years it would quadruple the level of trade among its members.

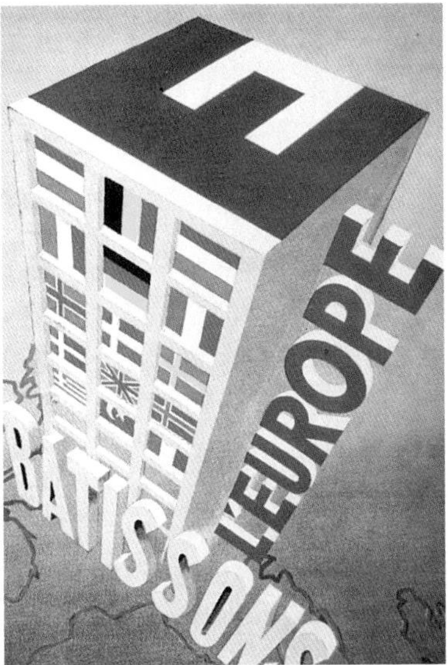

"Let's Build Europe," this French poster proclaimed.

In the immediate postwar period, as Europe struggled through a depression, it had become apparent that survival depended on unity. In 1950, French foreign minister Robert Schuman proposed the creation of a common market for coal and steel. The Schuman Plan (drawn up by French development chief Jean Monnet) was ratified by France, West Germany, Italy, and the Benelux nations in 1952. It created the European Coal and Steel Community (ECSC), consolidating members' coal and steel industries under a central high authority. Steel trade among members flourished as never before.

The EEC applied the tenets of the ECSC to other industries (sensitive agriculture excepted). The six signatories also formed the European Atomic Energy Community (EURATOM), a common nuclear energy market. In 1960, seven non-EEC nations—Austria, Britain, Denmark, Norway, Portugal, Sweden, Switzerland—formed their own, less binding, trading bloc, the European Free Trade Association (EFTA). Seven years later, the EEC, ECSC, and EURATOM merged into the European Community (EC), which was soon joined by Britain, Ireland, and Denmark. **◂1951.M ▸1958.M**

BIRTHS

Berkeley Breathed, U.S. cartoonist.

Caroline, Monacan princess.

Katie Couric, U.S. broadcast journalist.

Geena Davis, U.S. actress.

Melanie Griffith, U.S. actress.

Spike Lee, U.S. filmmaker.

Michelle Pfeiffer, U.S. actress.

Jayne Torvill, U.K. figure skater.

Mario Van Peebles, U.S. filmmaker.

DEATHS

Aga Khan III, Muslim leader.

Humphrey Bogart, U.S. actor.

Constantin Brancusi, Romanian-French sculptor.

Richard E. Byrd, U.S. explorer.

Christian Dior, French fashion designer.

Jimmy Dorsey, U.S. musician.

Haakon VII, Norwegian king.

Oliver Hardy, U.S. actor.

Edouard Herriot, French statesman.

Miklós Nagybányai Horthy, Hungarian political leader.

Nikos Kazantzakis, Greek writer.

Malcolm Lowry, U.K. novelist.

Louis B. Mayer, U.S. film producer.

Joseph McCarthy, U.S. senator.

Gabriela Mistral, Chilean poet.

Ernest Oppenheimer, South African industrialist.

Diego Rivera, Mexican painter.

Dorothy L. Sayers, U.K. writer.

Jean Sibelius, Finnish composer.

Arturo Toscanini, Italian conductor.

Henri van de Velde, Belgian architect and designer.

John Von Neumann, Hungarian-U.S. mathematician.

Laura Ingalls Wilder, U.S. writer.

Painting & Sculpture: *Man and Woman in a Large Room* (Richard Diebenkorn) ... Film: *Bridge on the River Kwai* (David Lean); *Witness for the Prosecution* (Billy Wilder); *12 Angry Men* (Sidney Lumet); *Throne of Blood* (Akira Kurosawa)... Theater: *Orpheus Descending* (Tennessee Williams); *Endgame* (Samuel Beckett); *The Music Man* (Meredith Willson) ... TV: *Leave It to Beaver*; *Perry Mason*; *Maverick*.

"My work comprises one vast book like Proust's Remembrance of Things Past, *except that my remembrances are written on the run instead of afterwards in a sickbed."*—**Jack Kerouac**

NEW IN 1957

Darvon (Eli Lilly).

Frisbee (Pluto Platter).

Portable electric typewriter (Smith Corona).

National Cancer Institute.

Southern Christian Leadership Conference (founded in Montgomery, Alabama, by Martin Luther King, Jr., and other black clergymen).

U.S. underground nuclear testing (Nevada).

IN THE UNITED STATES

▸EISENHOWER DOCTRINE—On January 5, President Eisenhower sent a loud public message to the Soviets, whose increased involvement in the Middle East during the Suez crisis had alarmed the U.S. The President got Congress to authorize the use of armed forces in case of Soviet expansion in the Middle East. The Eisenhower Doctrine (as the policy came to be called) extended the Truman Doctrine's policy of containment to the Middle East. ◂1947.4

▸GIBSON'S TENNIS TRIUMPH—What Jackie Robinson was to baseball, Althea Gibson was to tennis. In 1957, seven years after she first integrated the all-white women's tennis circuit, at Forest Hills, New York (a few miles from her Harlem birthplace), Gibson became the first black athlete to win at Wimbledon. Combining grace and power, she dominated the women's game from 1956 to 1958, claiming major singles titles at Wimbledon, and in the French, Italian, U.S., and Australian Opens.

1957

Bergman's somber allegory features a chess game between the Crusader (Max von Sydow) *(right)* and Death (Bengt Ekerot).

FILM

A New Swedish Master

6 In 1957, one year after he charmed the Cannes Film Festival with *Smiles of a Summer Night*, Swedish director Ingmar Bergman returned with a somber movie that cemented his standing as one of the world's finest filmmakers. *The Seventh Seal*, gushed a critic in the influential *Cahiers du Cinéma*, "is nothing but poetry, the most beautiful poetry which has ever shone on a screen." It was also one of commercial cinema's most economical masterworks—shot in 35 days at a cost of approximately $125,000.

Featuring striking black-and-white images by Gunnar Fischer, *The Seventh Seal* tells the story of a fourteenth-century Crusader (Max von Sydow) who encounters the figure of Death (Bengt Ekerot) on his return to a plague-ravaged Sweden. The two match wits in a chess game, on whose outcome hang the fates of several characters. The film expressed Bergman's interest in matters both timeless and topical. "In the Middle Ages," he noted, "men lived in terror of the plague. Today they live in fear of the atomic bomb." He described the movie as "an allegory with a theme that is quite simple: man, his eternal search for god, with death as his only certainty."

The parable was brought to life by a gifted acting ensemble that included Bibi Andersson and Gunnar Bjornstrand (who, with von Sydow, Harriet Andersson, Ingrid Thulin, and Liv Ullmann, would achieve world recognition for their screen work with Bergman).

Despite battles with illness and Swedish tax authorities, the director continued for decades to win acclaim for his films—among them *Persona*, *Cries and Whispers*, *Scenes from a Marriage*, and *Fanny and Alexander*. **▸1976.2**

ECONOMICS

Friedman's Function

7 What is money? That was the first question addressed by Milton Friedman in his assault on established economic ideas. Next: What does money do, and what do people do with money? Not, according to Friedman, what most economists believed. With his 1957 treatise, *A Theory of the Consumption Function*, Friedman launched a counterrevolution against the theories of John Maynard Keynes, which had dominated Western postwar economics. Friedman and his "Chicago School" of economists (named for their affiliation with the University of Chicago) aimed to restore monetarism—the system toppled by Keynesianism and the Great Depression.

Friedman argued that money supply and interest rates, not government taxing and spending (as Keynes preached), influenced economic growth. Increase the money supply, and spending will increase, bringing higher prices: "Inflation always and everywhere is a monetary phenomenon," he wrote. Friedman was resurrecting the quantity theory of money, which holds that both demand for money and the speed at which money circulates are constant. This was precisely the proposition that Keynes had rejected in the 1930s. The Englishman argued that money demand fluctuates with interest rates: When interest rates rise, people exchange money for speculative bonds.

To restore quantity theory, Friedman had to redefine money. "The most fruitful approach," he wrote, "is to regard money as a sequence of assets, on a par with bonds, equities, houses, consumer durables." In other words, money can be converted into any number of consumer goods, including bonds. Interest rates exert only minor influence on demand. Personal income, controlled by the amount of money central banks pump out, is the decisive factor.

Keynesianism remained ascendant for two decades. But in the 1980s, Friedman, arch-foe of government economic meddling, became the guru of presidents and prime ministers. **◂1946.4 ▸1958.9**

LITERATURE

King of the Beats

8 Jack Kerouac's writing method was as unorthodox as his writing. To compose his autobiographical novel *On the Road*, he fed a roll of paper into a typewriter and, over three straight weeks, churned out exuberant and rhapsodic prose at 100 words per minute. Kerouac had to wait six years, until 1957, before the book saw print—but when it did, it was with only modest revisions.

Chronicling the cross-country exploits of writer Sal Paradise and his Mephistophelian buddy Dean Moriarty—from quasi-Buddhist philosophical discussions to marijuana-laced adventures in a Mexican brothel—*On the Road* quickly earned both a sizable following and the scorn of much of the intelligentsia. To Kerouac's frustration, his supporters failed almost as often as his detractors to appreciate the artistry and moral sense underlying his paean to freedom and the Beat way of life.

Besides Kerouac, the creative core of the Beat movement included such poets as Allen Ginsberg, Gregory Corso, and Gary Snyder, and novelist William Burroughs.

SPORTS: Baseball: World Series, Milwaukee Braves defeat New York Yankees, 4–3; New York Giants and Brooklyn Dodgers announce move to San Francisco and Los Angeles, respectively ... Football: NFL, Detroit Lions defeat Cleveland Browns, 59–14 ... Basketball: NBA, Boston Celtics defeat St. Louis Hawks, 4–3 ... Boxing: Carmen Basilio defeats Sugar Ray Robinson for middleweight championship.

"Nothing can be safe from myth, myth can develop from ... the very lack of meaning."—**Roland Barthes, in *Mythologies***

Spiritual descendants of Whitman and Thoreau, the Beats were engaged in a romantic rebellion against a culture mired in conformity. The media, however, called them "beatniks" and focused on their eccentricities: their bongo playing, berets, goatees, and hipster slang; their hygiene lapses, sexual experimentation, and use of drugs.

A self-described "crazy Catholic mystic," Jack Kerouac mythologized the open road.

The sensitive Kerouac, who acquired the sobriquet "King of the Beats," was ill equipped to handle such notoriety. He descended into bitterness and alcoholism, moved in with his mother, and died in 1969, at the age of 47. By then, his freewheeling novels (including *The Subterraneans* and *The Dharma Bums*) had become sacred texts of the hippie movement. ◂**1955.10** ▸**1959.V**

MUSIC

The Versatile Bernstein

9 With direction and choreography by Jerome Robbins, lyrics by Stephen Sondheim, and music by Leonard Bernstein, *West Side Story*—a Romeo and Juliet update set among New York street gangs—electrified audiences when it debuted on Broadway in September 1957. For Bernstein it was the crowning achievement of his work in musical theater (which also included the estimable *On the Town* and *Candide*). But, as the announcement in November of his appointment as music director of the New York Philharmonic made clear, it was only one highlight of an extraordinarily multifaceted career.

Bernstein had burst into the limelight in 1943, when, as a 25-year-old assistant conductor for the Philharmonic, he was a last-minute substitute for an ailing Bruno Walter. The young man's impassioned conducting captivated Carnegie Hall, and a front-page report of the debut in *The New York Times* made him an instant celebrity. "Lenny" (as he was known) was the Philharmonic's first American-born chief. During his dozen years in that role, he became legendary for the insight and daring of his interpretations, and for his flamboyant charisma. His work with leading orchestras around the world added to his following.

A great popularizer of classical music, Bernstein was a constant presence on television and in lecture halls; his Young People's Concerts (televised nationwide on Sunday afternoons) turned generations of children into fans. His own compositions, in many genres, ranged from the *Jeremiah Symphony,* influenced by Jewish liturgical music, to the score for the hard-boiled film *On the Waterfront.* And his involvement in left-wing causes inspired a new phrase in the language (courtesy of "new journalist" Tom Wolfe): "radical chic." ◂**1956.11**

Even in rehearsal, Bernstein was flamboyantly expressive.

IDEAS

Barthes and Semiology

10 A bar of soap, Roland Barthes argued in his 1957 book, *Mythologies*, is no mere bar of soap; a car is more than a car. Beneath the surfaces of mass culture lies a welter of hidden meanings, a coded language begging to be deciphered. Barthes was already known in France for his studies of literature. (His *Writing Degree Zero* of 1953 had provided theoretical fodder for Alain Robbe-Grillet's New Novel movement.) His analyses of less elevated artifacts, however, made him a literary star in France, the chief rival to Jean-Paul Sartre as the preeminent Left Bank intellectual. The book also eventually made semiology—the term Barthes adopted to describe his endeavor—a fashionable field of study throughout the West.

As conceived by Swiss linguist Ferdinand de Saussure (1857-1913), semiology was a hypothetical discipline that would investigate all the ways a society combines signs (from alphabet letters to clothing styles) to create meaning. Barthes looked for the meanings of everyday objects and events—and found ideological messages conveyed via the persuasive conventions of myth. Professional wrestling, for instance, is both a hilariously phony sport and a ritual confrontation between Good and Evil. When a Paris magazine ran a photo of a black soldier saluting the French flag, the picture communicated a patriotic myth: that France's colonial subjects serve the empire happily.

Barthes could be a playful essayist, as in *Mythologies,* or he could be a daunting theorist; he was initially identified as a structuralist (part of a broad movement of thinkers, starting with Saussure, who saw consciousness as a process of distinguishing opposites), later as a poststructuralist. In all his incarnations, he was controversial: for some, the ultimate name to drop in sophisticated conversation; for others, the archetypal academic charlatan, capable of analyzing meaning into meaninglessness. ◂**1943.10** ▸**1962.12**

IN THE UNITED STATES

▸TEAMSTERS' TROUBLES—Reacting to a Senate probe, the AFL-CIO in 1957 expelled the Teamsters Union, the country's largest and most powerful union since 1940. Teamsters president Dave Beck went to federal prison on income tax and theft charges, but his successor, Jimmy Hoffa (who was known to have strong mob connections), did not improve the brotherhood's tarnished image, and Hoffa's two immediate successors were also indicted. The Teamsters rejoined the AFL-CIO in 1987. **◂1955.M ▸1975.M**

▸TELEVISED SOCK HOP—"Subversive" rock 'n' roll music (or a diluted approximation thereof) got a big boost of respectability in 1957, when cordial, conservatively dressed Dick Clark *(below)* took it national on the ABC

network. In addition to live guests, *American Bandstand,* a spin-off of a local Philadelphia TV show, featured poodle-skirted and pompadoured teenagers who danced to (and rated) the newest singles. "America's oldest teenager," Clark stayed with the program—the longest-running variety show in TV history—for more than 30 years.

▸CRISIS IN LITTLE ROCK—On September 2, the day before nine blacks were to enroll at all-white Central High School in Little Rock, Arkansas, governor, Orval Faubus announced that he would not protect them from mobs of white segregationists. On September 3, the "Little Rock Nine" stayed home. The next day, when they tried to enter the school, the Arkansas National Guard turned them away with bayonets. Finally admitted on September 23, the nine were sent home again when rioting whites overwhelmed indifferent police —whereupon Eisenhower sent in federal troops. Shaky integration lasted a year: In 1958, Faubus closed the city's schools. A 1959 court order reopened them. **◂1956.M**

POLITICS & BUSINESS: GNP: $441.1 billion ... Senator Strom Thurmond sets congressional filibuster record (24 hrs., 27 min., against establishment of Civil Rights Commission) ... Armand Hammer takes over Occidental Petroleum Corp. (at acquisition, worth $125,000; by 1970, worth $300 million) ... Ford Motor Co. introduces the Edsel ... S.I. Newhouse acquires Condé Nast publications.

"Even now I can feel fear when I think of that race. I knew what I had done, the chances I had taken."—**Juan Manuel Fangio, on his victory in the 1957 German Grand Prix**

AROUND THE WORLD

▶THE WANKEL—In his private workshop at Lindau, Germany, engineer Felix Wankel developed the first new internal-combustion engine since the nineteenth century. Successfully tested in 1957, the Wankel rotary eliminated pumping pistons and rods, replacing them with a single triangular rotor that drew fuel into the engine chamber, compressed it, and discharged exhaust through an escape hole. The Wankel engine was adopted by Japanese automaker Mazda, but it failed to catch on with carmakers elsewhere. ◀1911.8

▶LEAN'S WAR EPIC—With *The Bridge on the River Kwai,* British director David Lean introduced the sumptuous, epic cinematic style that made him the leader of Britain's postwar film renaissance. Based on a novel by Pierre Boulle, the 1957 film

depicts the savage absurdity of a Japanese prisoner-of-war camp in Burma during World War II. Alec Guinness won an Academy Award for his portrayal of an obsessive yet inspiring British POW commander. ◀1951.11

▶MACMILLAN TAKES OVER—On January 10, after the Suez crisis forced Anthony Eden's resignation, Harold Macmillan became Britain's prime minister. Macmillan, a World War I combat veteran, member of the House of Commons, and Conservative Party statesman in both Churchill's and Eden's cabinets, patched up strained relations with the U.S. (he and Eisenhower were friends from WWII), visited Khrushchev in Moscow, and captained the Conservatives to a landslide in the 1959 general election. His slogan: "You've never had it so good." ◀1956.3 ▶1963.3

Juan Manuel Fangio, with his longtime companion, at the 1954 British Grand Prix.

SPORTS

Great Racer

11 No driver in the history of auto racing has matched the record of Argentina's Juan Manuel Fangio, whose 1957 world driving championship was his fifth in the prize's seven-year existence. When he retired the following year, Fangio, 47, had won an unsurpassed total of 24 out of 51 Grand Prix races, despite an accident that broke his neck in 1952.

Fangio, whose father was a poor Italian immigrant, became a mechanic's apprentice as a child and a racer in his teens. But wartime shortages of car parts and gasoline interrupted his promising career in the 1940s, and he was 38 when President (and racing fan) Juan Perón sent him to Europe to bring his country glory. Fangio immediately began winning major races—but his most spectacular victory was one of his last.

The 1957 German Grand Prix was held at Nürburgring, then among the world's longest and most grueling tracks. (Dozens had died there since it opened in the 1920s.) Fangio was driving a nearly worn-out Maserati, facing hot young rivals in faster Ferraris. He built up an early lead, but saw it disappear during a long pit stop. Starting from far behind, Fangio staged an amazing comeback, narrowing the gap over successive laps and pulling ahead in the final stretch to finish four seconds ahead of his nearest competitor. Later it was revealed that he'd driven almost the entire 312 miles with a broken seat, bracing himself against the car door with one knee. **◀1910.2 ▶1969.M**

THEATER

Drama of Disguises

12 An abandoned child who spent most of his first 30 years as a thief and a prostitute, Jean Genet found antisocial salvation in writing. Though condemned by the French right as sexually deviant and politically subversive, his brand of absurdist drama has influenced playwrights everywhere. Genet's "Theater of Hatred" found its first mature expression in *Le Balcon (The Balcony)*, which premiered in 1957 at London's Arts Theatre Club.

Like all Genet's plays, *Le Balcon* is about illusion: how it informs social roles, and how it seduces even those determined to fight it. (To heighten the artifice, some characters wear stiltlike shoes and padded shoulders, as in ancient Greek theater, that make them larger than life.) The action takes place in a brothel called the Grand Balcony, whose customers find ecstasy in posing as authority figures: a bishop, a judge, a general. One client, however—an actual chief of police—laments that no one wants to masquerade as *him.* A revolution is going on outside, and eventually the Balcony's occupants, in their glorious guises, are called upon to cow the rebels into surrendering. The ploy works. Moreover, it turns out that the rebel leader craves the police-chief role. Another revolution starts as the brothel closes for the night.

Genet turned to writing plays after publishing three novels. His first, *Notre-Dame des Fleurs* (1942), was written while he was in prison; it earned praise from Jean Cocteau, Jean-Paul Sartre, and Simone de Beauvoir. In 1948, those intellectuals were among a group that successfully petitioned the French government to give Genet a reprieve from a life sentence for burglary. His plays (including *The Maids* and *The Blacks*) remain some of modern theater's most frequently performed works. **◀1953.11 ▶1958.13**

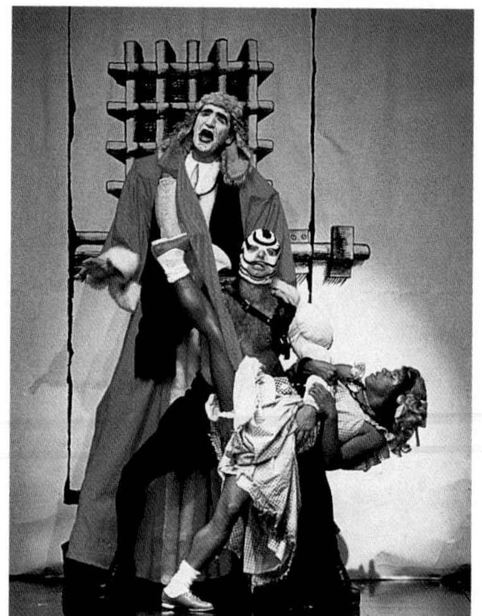

A 1987 production of Genet's *The Balcony* by The Royal Shakespeare Company.

IDEAS

Chomsky's Syntax

13 With his 1957 book, *Syntactic Structures*, linguist Noam Chomsky triggered an academic revolution. Chomsky's theories were in direct opposition to those of B.F. Skinner, whose *Verbal Behavior* (published the same year) argued that humans learn language in essentially the same way that rats learn their way through a maze—via the interplay of stimuli and conditioned responses. Pointing out that people often use language in ways that are not taught, Chomsky (the son of a Hebrew scholar) contended that grammatical ability is actually an innate characteristic of the human species. Over the next few years, Chomsky refined his system of linguistic behavior—called transformational-generative grammar—in which the "surface structure" of linguistic expression conceals a "deep structure" from which it emerges. This deep structure enables humans to recognize certain sentences as syntactically and grammatically correct, even when they are semantically meaningless. "Green ideas sleep furiously" was Chomsky's example of such a sentence.

Chomsky's syntax-oriented approach gave rise to other theories of generative semantics (including his own ideas of a "universal grammar"), but the MIT professor remained his discipline's central and most original thinker. In the mid-sixties he also became known as an outspoken social critic and antiwar activist. After Indonesia's 1975 invasion of East Timor, Chomsky attempted to call public attention to human rights abuses there, contending that the scant media coverage they received was a by-product of U.S. support of the anti-Communist Suharto regime. **◀1948.7 ▶1975.9**

NOBEL PRIZES: Peace: Lester B. Pearson (Canadian; mediation of Suez Canal crisis) ... Literature: Albert Camus (French; novelist) ... Chemistry: Alexander Todd (U.K.; nucleotides) ... Medicine: Daniel Bovet (Swiss-Italian; allergy and muscle-relaxation treatment) ... Physics: Tsung-dao Lee and Chen Ning Yang (Chinese; parity nonconservation).

A VOICE FROM 1957

Rainy Day Rebellion

From *The Cat in the Hat,* by Dr. Seuss, 1957

Writer and illustrator Theodor Seuss Geisel, who used the nom de plume Dr. Seuss, found traditional Dick-and-Jane primers a bore. Learning to read should never be dull, Seuss decided. And so in 1957 he published The Cat in the Hat, *a limited-vocabulary storybook featuring simple, highly engaging anarchic poesy, an antic story line, and colorful illustrations. Just as its mischievous, mysterious feline protagonist arrives out of the blue to enliven a rainy afternoon for two children, the wildly popular book vitalized a stilted genre.* The Cat in the Hat, *as well as Seuss's many other books (including a sequel to* Cat*), became an indelible part of American childhood.* **◂1943.15 ▸1963.M**

We looked!
Then we saw him step in on the mat!
We looked!
And we saw him!
The Cat in the Hat!
And he said to us,
"Why do you sit there like that?"
6
"I know it is wet
And the sun is not sunny.
But we can have
Lots of good fun that is funny!"
7

The Cat's subversive antics *(including the amazing juggling act below)* take place out of parental view. Part of the book's appeal is that the children get to wreak havoc without the usual consequences: The Cat miraculously cleans up the mess just before Mother returns.

"Look at me!
Look at me!
Look at me NOW!
It is fun to have fun
But you have to know how.
I can hold up the cup
And the milk and the cake!
I can hold up these books!
And the fish on a rake!
I can hold the toy ship
And a little toy man!
And look! With my tail
I can hold a red fan!
I can fan with the fan
As I hop on the ball!
But that is not all.
Oh, no.
That is not all. . . ."

18

"Long live Arab unity! Our happiness is incomplete without the liberation of Palestine."—**A chant by Syrians celebrating the founding of the United Arab Republic**

STORY OF THE YEAR

Arabs Unite—Almost

1 The 1958 merger of Syria and Egypt into the United Arab Republic was the first of a series of dramatic realignments throughout the Middle East, inspired by the radical vision of Gamal Abdal Nasser. Syria had been moving in the Egyptian dictator's ideological direction since the fall of a rightist military regime in 1954; the new junta, dominated by the socialist Ba'ath party, had followed Egypt in recognizing Mao's China and acquiring Soviet arms. Squeezed between Washington (which backed anti-Soviet Arab governments against their avowedly nonaligned neighbors) and a growing domestic Communist movement, Syria's leaders decided to put their pan-Arabist notions to the test. National borders, after all, were a Western invention: Syria would lose nothing—and gain untold strength—by melding with dynamic Egypt.

More changes followed quickly. Yemen, though ruled by a conservative monarch, sought security by affiliating itself with the U.A.R. in a confederation called the United Arab States. The Western-oriented kingdoms of Iraq and Jordan formed a rival union. In Saudi Arabia, King Saud was forced to cede authority to his relatively pro-Egyptian brother Faisal after being implicated in a plot on Nasser's life. In Lebanon, civil war erupted between Syrian-backed Arab nationalists and supporters of pro-Western president Camille Chamoun. In Iraq, when Premier Nuri al-Said decided to aid Chamoun, pro-Egyptian officers revolted—killing Said along with King Faisal II and most of the royal family. The Iraqi-Jordanian federation was no more.

Fearing the spread of Nasserism to Lebanon, the United States sent 10,000 troops and sponsored talks between the warring factions. A compromise led to elections, and General Fuad Chehab—less enthusiastically pro-Western and friendlier to Nasser than Chamoun—became president.

Except for Jordan, all the Arab nations had now fallen more or less into Cairo's camp. But they soon fell out again. Iraq's strongman, Abdul Karim Kassem, developed a bitter personal rivalry with his Egyptian counterpart. The Syrians came to resent Nasser's authoritarianism, while the Saudis and Yemenites resisted his socialism. And by 1961, when Syria seceded from the U.A.R., Arab unity lay in ruins. **◄1956.3 ►1964.5**

Nasser *(right)* and Syria's president Shukri al-Kuwatli in Cairo, signing the official papers unifying their two countries.

CHINA

Great Leap Forward

2 Mao Zedong called it the Great Leap Forward—a program for simultaneous, rapid development of agriculture and industry. Implemented in 1958, Mao's scheme was economic war, fought by hundreds of millions of peasants armed with hoes and rakes. It meant total, round-the-clock mobilization of the workforce, and its consequences were catastrophic: widespread famine and complete devastation of the economy.

Chairman Mao on a tour of the countryside surrounding Tientsin.

China's first five-year economic plan had recently come to a close. Based on the Soviet model of the 1920s, the program had advanced industrial production but undermined agriculture, causing millions of peasants to flee rural poverty for the cities. Meanwhile, Soviet loans had come due—loans China hoped to repay with grain. Another five-year plan clearly would not work. Instead, Mao proposed a radical reorganization of rural labor. Now, while maintaining subsistence-level farms, peasants were to develop the countryside, digging irrigation canals, building roads, reclaiming land. Others were to join a "battle for steel," building backyard blast furnaces to augment national industrial production.

Exploiting China's greatest natural resource, its vast population, the Great Leap Forward briefly seemed to work. Crop yields boomed in 1958 (though the numbers were often inflated by zealous commune managers), prompting record government requisitions. Disastrous weather and the diversion of farm labor destroyed agriculture the following year, however, while government demands remained high. With the countryside stripped of food, peasants began to starve—some 20 million died between 1959 and 1962, half of them children. Mao acknowledged the calamity, but stubbornly refused to apologize for it. Confucius, Lenin, and Marx had all made mistakes, he told his followers, and so had he. **◄1952.2 ►1959.3**

TECHNOLOGY

A New Electronic Toy

3 Hoping to liven up an open house at his workplace—the Brookhaven National Laboratory, in Long Island, New York—physicist William Higinbotham invented the world's first video game in 1958. Using an analog computer wired to an oscilloscope, and a jumble of electronic hardware, he developed the ancestor of Pong, the table-tennis simulation that 14 years later became the first publicly available video game.

Played on a circular, five-inch screen, Higinbotham's game featured a table and net that looked like an inverted "T" with a shortened stem. Each player controlled the ball (a white dot) by means of a box equipped with a button and a knob. To hit the ball, a player pressed the button; to direct the trajectory, he or she turned the knob. Primitive by today's standards, the game was a hit on visitors' day at Brookhaven: Hundreds bypassed displays of scientific gadgetry to try their hand at the new video toy.

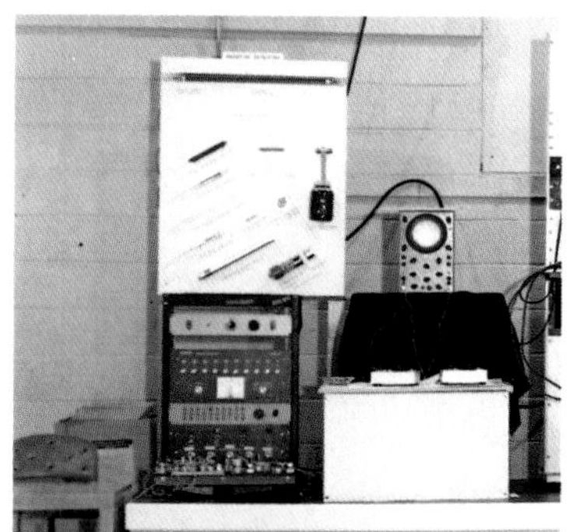

Higinbotham's game was displayed among other instruments developed by Brookhaven, at the lab's open house.

Earlier in his career, Higinbotham had helped develop radar and had devised timing circuits for the first atomic bomb. And though he was eventually responsible for 20 patents, he saw no reason to seek one for his video innovation. It would have been pointless anyway: Since he was a government employee, his inventions became Uncle Sam's property. **◄1930.1**

ART & CULTURE: Books: *Breakfast at Tiffany's* (Truman Capote); *Borstal Boy* (Brendan Behan)); *The Bell* (Iris Murdoch); *Exodus* (Leon Uris); *Structural Anthropology* (Claude Lévi-Strauss) ... Music: "The Purple People Eater" (Sheb Wooley); "Diana" (Paul Anka); "He's Got the Whole World in His Hands" (Geoff Love); "If I Had a Hammer" (Seeger and Hays); "Volare" (Modugno and Parish); *The Good Soldier Schweik*

"For more than a century, Algeria has been like a mouse in a French laboratory, fastened down while the French make experiments on it."—**Ferhat Abbas, leader of the exiled Provisional Government of the Algerian Republic**

Some Algerians felt deeply French. Here, a march in support of France, in May 1958.

ALGERIA

De Gaulle to the Rescue

4 By 1958, French troops seemed on the verge of defeating Algeria's FLN guerrillas. Their tactics, however, were politically disastrous. A year earlier, news that General Jacques Massu's troops in Algiers systematically tortured prisoners had shocked France into self-examination. Another shock came in February, when French bombers attacked FLN gunners across the Tunisian border, killing 80 villagers and sparking worldwide protest. In France, opinion began to turn against this war fought for the sake of colonists' privileges; a negotiation-minded moderate, Pierre Pflimin, became premier. But in Algeria, the *colons* and their army supporters preferred scuttling France's Fourth Republic to surrendering their powers.

They rebelled in May, massing in an Algiers park and seizing government offices. Massu was proclaimed chief of the uprising; he called for retired General Charles de Gaulle to come to France's rescue. The mutineers sent a detachment to Corsica, where local authorities welcomed them. In Paris, fearing that a coup (or even civil war) loomed, President René Coty asked de Gaulle to assume the premiership. The World War II hero accepted, on the condition that he be allowed to rule by decree for six months and to submit a new constitution. Then he hurried to Algiers, where he assured the colonists: *"Je vous ai compris."* ("I have understood you.")

Privately, de Gaulle understood that colonialism was doomed. The constitution he designed for the Fifth Republic granted France's possessions the right to choose independence. It also strengthened the executive branch, ending the instability that had given France 26 governments in 14 years. Voters throughout the empire ratified the document (only Guinea opted to break with France) and elected de Gaulle president. But the FLN rejected his proposals to grant Algerian Muslims equal suffrage, social reforms, and full representation in France's parliament. Instead, the guerrillas formed a provisional government and began buying weapons from China. By 1960 they were gaining again, and the *colons* had resumed their own revolt. **◂1954.3 ▸1962.4**

ART

Found Symbols and Objects

5 Leo Castelli was a failed manufacturer turned art dealer. Jasper Johns was a struggling artist. Neither man seemed on good terms with fortune. Yet, after their mutual friend, artist Robert Rauschenberg, introduced the two to each other in 1957, they formed one of the art world's most enduring and lucrative partnerships. In January 1958, Castelli presented a phenomenally successful exhibition of Johns's works in New York, selling all but one canvas. "My gallery really began with the Johns show in 1958," Castelli later observed. The two maintained their fortuitous union for decades to come.

Until the Johns show, the boldly romantic gestures of abstract expressionism had dominated the New York art scene—even though Jackson Pollock, the leader of that movement, had been killed in a car accident in 1956. But the critics' enthusiasm for works like Johns's *Target with Plaster Casts* (1955) signified the ascent of another, more cerebral, style. Targets and American flags were among the ready-made symbols—"things which are seen and not looked at," the artist said—that Johns, an admirer of Marcel Duchamp (the pioneer of "ready-mades"), redeemed from ordinariness. The familiar images yielded subtle surprises upon close inspection: Underlying the brushwork of a target might be a delicate collage of barely legible newspaper clippings, while a white-on-white flag might contain ghostly rows of numbers.

Soon after the Johns triumph, Castelli made a similar splash with a Rauschenberg show. Rauschenberg's *Bed* (1955), a paint-splattered "combine" made from actual bedclothes, was one of the more jarring art objects hanging anywhere in the fifties. Such raucous collisions of common objects (Rauschenberg's fondness for including street junk in his work prompted one critic to observe that the artist "didn't seem housetrained") complemented the quietude of Johns's found symbols; together with Castelli, both artists blazed an aesthetic trail that the pop artists of the sixties would soon follow. **◂1950.4 ▸1962.8**

One of Johns's "ready-made symbols": *Target with Four Faces*, 1955—made with encaustic, newspaper, plastic, and wood.

BIRTHS

Anita Baker, U.S. singer.

Madonna Ciccone, U.S. singer.

Daniel Day Lewis, Irish actor.

Christopher Dean, U.K. figure skater.

Mary Decker, U.S. runner.

Rickey Henderson, U.S. baseball player.

Michael Jackson, U.S. singer.

Prince Rogers Nelson, U.S. singer.

Daley Thompson, U.K. athlete.

DEATHS

Samuel Hopkins Adams, U.S. writer.

Claire L. Chennault, American general.

Rosalind Franklin, U.K. biochemist.

Juan Ramón Jiménez, Spanish poet.

Frédéric Joliot-Curie, French scientist.

Charles F. Kettering, U.S. inventor.

George Edward Moore, U.K. philosopher.

Imre Nagy, Hungarian Communist leader.

George Jean Nathan, U.S. writer.

Eugenio Pacelli (Pius XII), Italian pope.

Wolfgang Pauli, Austrian-U.S. physicist.

Tyrone Power, U.S. actor.

Georges Rouault, French artist.

Marie Stopes, U.K. feminist.

Ralph Vaughan Williams, U.K. composer.

Maurice de Vlaminck, French painter.

(Robert Kurka); *Three Piano Moods* (William Schuman) ... Painting & Sculpture: *Four Darks on Red* (Mark Rothko); *Three Flags* (Jasper Johns) ... Film: *Gigi* (Vincente Minnelli); *Touch of Evil* (Orson Welles); *Vertigo* (Alfred Hitchcock) ... Theater: *Suddenly Last Summer* (Tennessee Williams); *J.B.* (Archibald MacLeish); *Flower Drum Song* (Rodgers and Hammerstein) ... TV: *The Donna Reed Show*; *The Rifleman*.

"To live life to the end is not a childish task."—**Boris Pasternak, *Doctor Zhivago***

NEW IN 1958

Stereophonic records.

Sweet 'N' Low.

American Express Card.

BankAmericard (later VISA).

IN THE UNITED STATES

▶HULA MANIA—In a decade of fads, the hula hoop craze was the biggest. Introduced by Wham-O Manufacturing (makers of Frisbee) in 1958, the $1.98 plastic ring—which users stepped inside and kept aloft by performing a gyrating "hula"—stormed the country, tracing the traditional fad migration from California east

across the continent. U.S. sales reached 25 million in four months. The fad ended with summer. In November, *The Wall Street Journal* tolled its demise: HOOPS HAVE HAD IT.

▶BASEBALL FEVER—The national pastime truly became that in 1958, when two New York teams, the Dodgers and the Giants, relocated to California—L.A. and San Francisco, respectively. Baseball, once primarily an East Coast game, had been moving westward in recent years; now it spread all the way across the continent. Over the next few years, both major leagues added more teams. And through television, more fans than ever before were able to indulge their love for the great American sport.

▶PAULING'S PLEA—Molecular chemist and future vitamin C guru Linus Pauling published in 1958 a passionate argument against nuclear testing entitled *No More War!* The book detailed the hazards of radiation exposure and predicted that continued weapons testing would cause five

AVIATION

The Jet Age Arrives

6 On October 4, 1958, the British Overseas Airways Corporation inaugurated the first transatlantic passenger-jet service, flying one de Havilland Comet IV from London to New York and another in the opposite direction. BOAC beat PanAmerican Airways to the draw by three weeks—a welcome victory for the British aircraft industry, which had begun commercial jet flights (to Africa and Asia) with the Comet I in 1952, but grounded the planes in 1954 after several crashes. The Comet IV reached London in six hours and twelve minutes, half the time it took propeller-driven craft. The smoothness, quiet, and speed of jet travel dazzled the opening-day passengers; one commented, "I fly this way or not at all."

The British had led the Americans in passenger-jet development until the mid-fifties. U.S. manufacturers, wary of jet planes' higher fuel consumption and need for longer runways, had been hesitant to produce them. But the early success of the Comet I changed corporate minds. Douglas brought out the DC-8 in 1958; Boeing countered with the 707, which PanAm used for its London–to–New York route. By the mid-1960s, American-made jets dominated the non-Communist world.

Jets shrank the planet as never before. In 1959, aboard the newly delivered Air Force One, President Eisenhower visited an unprecedented eleven countries in 18 days. A new subclass sprang up among the wealthy: the "jet setters," who might cross an ocean for a weekend shopping spree. And for ordinary travelers, spending a week in a faraway land soon became a routine matter. **◂1939.10 ▸1972.6**

LITERATURE

Pasternak Refuses Nobel

7 "I want to write something deep and true," wrote Russian novelist Boris Pasternak as he began *Doctor Zhivago*—his

immensely powerful, gorgeously lyrical epic of the Bolshevik Revolution. So successful was he in fulfilling that ambition that Sweden's Nobel Committee awarded Pasternak the prize for literature in 1958, the year after *Zhivago* was published. But politics prevented him from accepting the honor.

Since the early 1920s, Pasternak had been recognized as one of the Soviet Union's foremost poets. Initially optimistic about the revolution's effect on Russian culture, he'd gradually become disillusioned by Communist repression. For years he curtailed his creative work in favor of doing noncontroversial translations; he became a leading Soviet interpreter of Shakespeare. In 1946, however, Pasternak decided to write a book about the struggle of a passionate poet (physician Yuri Zhivago) with a system that sought to subject all life to the dictates of reason. *Doctor Zhivago*'s critique of Marxism, and its sympathetic attitude toward Christianity, precluded its publication at home, but Pasternak managed to get it published in Italy in 1957. Soon the saga was an international bestseller, available in more than a dozen languages.

The Khrushchev regime's discomfiture peaked when Pasternak became the first Soviet writer to win the Nobel. The official attacks began immediately. Denounced as a traitor, ousted from the Union of Soviet Writers and the Union of Translators, Pasternak soon became the first writer of any nationality to decline the Nobel. "Considering the meaning this award has been given in the society to which I belong," he wrote the committee, "I must reject this undeserved prize presented to me. Please do not receive my voluntary rejection with displeasure."

When Pasternak died in 1960, multitudes attended his funeral. But not until 1987 did the writers' union reinstate him, opening the way for the domestic publication of his most famous work. **◂1931.3 ▸1961.M**

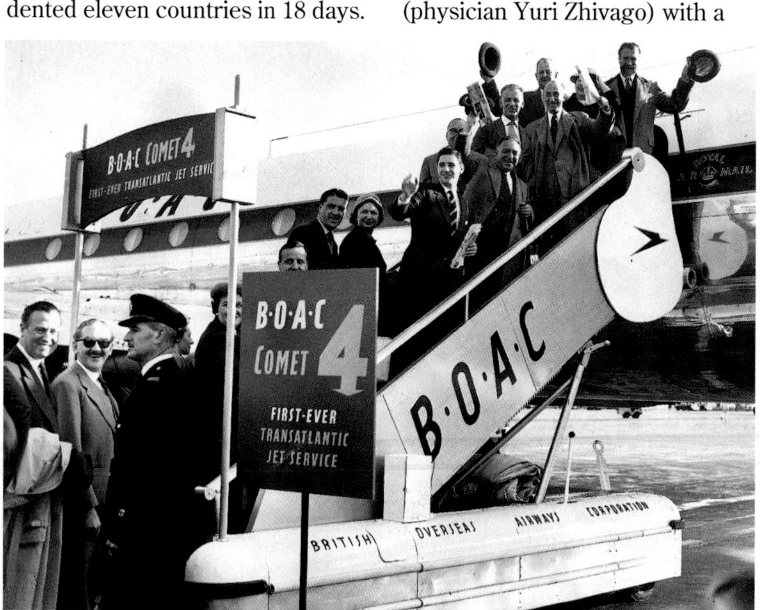

Passengers on the inaugural flight of BOAC's Comet IV arrive in London from New York.

FILM

A Polish Diamond

8 Polish filmmaker Andrzej Wajda is an unsentimental visual poet whose work examines the dilemmas of a life shadowed by war and repression. Controversial in his own country for questioning Communist orthodoxy, he has been celebrated abroad for his thematic complexity, rich imagery, and ethical integrity in the teeth of government censorship. In 1958, Wajda released his masterpiece, *Ashes and Diamonds*, the capstone of a trilogy (following *A Generation* and *Kanal*) chronicling the World War II generation's postwar disillusionment.

Superficially, the film is a good suspense yarn. At the end of World War II, a member of the nationalist faction of the Polish resistance is ordered to kill a local Communist official. The young assassin and his aged prey spend a day and night at victory parties in a provincial hotel; at dawn, the nationalist kills the Communist, then is himself shot, and dies on a rubbish heap. On one level, the movie functions as a plea

SPORTS: Baseball: World Series, New York Yankees defeat Milwaukee Braves, 4–3 ... Football: NFL, Baltimore Colts defeat New York Giants, sudden death, 23–17 ... Basketball: NBA, St. Louis Hawks defeat Boston Celtics, 4–2 ... Soccer: World Cup, Brazil defeats Sweden, 5–2 ... Chess: Bobby Fischer, 15, is the youngest champion in history.

"Money differs from a mistress, an automobile, or cancer in being equally important to those who have it and those who don't."—**Economist John Kenneth Galbraith**

The Polish James Dean: *Ashes and Diamonds'* young assassin (played by Zbigniew Cybulski) dies on a garbage heap.

for national unity: Both deaths are presented as absurd and lamentable, suggesting that the postwar rivalry between onetime anti-Nazi compatriots can lead only to tragedy. Yet because it seemed to glorify the sexy, troubled killer (played by Zbigniew Cybulski, who became a James Dean–like heartthrob) at the expense of the decrepit Communist, *Ashes and Diamonds* fired debate at home.

Later, in *Man of Marble* (1977) and *Man of Iron* (1981), Wajda explicitly sided with the anti-Communist labor movement (which became Solidarity)—and was removed by the military government from his executive post in the movie industry. Nonetheless, he continued as Polish cinema's most gifted iconoclast. **◂1955.9**

ECONOMICS

Galbraith's Prescription

9 In *The Affluent Society,* his 1958 assault on traditional "trickle-down" theories, economist John Kenneth Galbraith focused

on a phenomenon most other economists preferred to ignore—the widening gulf between private wealth and public squalor in the United States. His solution: increased government management of the economy.

In America, Galbraith asserted, prosperity had replaced poverty as the economic norm. Increased productivity had brought an overabundance of material goods, creating an artificial, advertising-spurred economy in which affluent people bought things they didn't really need. "You can't explain to somebody why he or she wants food," as he later explained to his biographer, "but you can persuade somebody why he or she wants a Toyota automobile as against a bicycle." Galbraith suggested the money would be better spent on public services.

Born in Ontario, Canada, Galbraith was trained as an economist at the University of California's Berkeley campus. A confirmed Keynesian, he directed U.S. price controls during World War II before going on to a long career as a Harvard professor and adviser to Democratic presidents. His biting wit and leftist ideas so offended ruling Republicans in the mid-1950s that Galbraith was subjected to an FBI investigation. The bureau determined that the professor was not a Communist—merely "conceited, egotistical and snobbish." The reading public liked him better: *The Affluent Society* stayed near the top of the bestseller list for almost a year. **◂1957.7**

MUSIC

Cliburn in Moscow

10 Six months after the launching of *Sputnik*, the victory of a 23-year-old Texan named Van Cliburn at the first Tchaikovsky International Piano Competition sent the pianist's career—and American morale—into orbit. Cliburn arrived at the Moscow contest with impressive credentials: He'd studied at the Juilliard School with Kiev Conservatory graduate Rosina Lhévinne and appeared with major North American orchestras after winning the Leventritt Competition of 1954. Yet his career had reached a plateau.

Cliburn's much publicized exploits in the Soviet Union changed that. From the moment he arrived, the young Russophile captured the hearts of those who thronged to hear him. His jurors, who reportedly sought Khrushchev's authorization before giving top honors to a product of capitalist culture, marveled over his performances of Tchaikovsky's *First Piano Concerto* and Rachmaninoff's *Third.* Cliburn's interpretation of the latter, said composer Aram Khachaturian, rivaled that of its creator.

Back in America, Cliburn was greeted with a ticker-tape parade, a White House reception, TV appear-

Cliburn returned from Moscow a star. His first television appearance back home was on NBC's *Steve Allen Show.*

ances, a major recording contract, and an intense performance schedule. His RCA Victor rendition of the Tchaikovsky concerto became the first classical recording to sell more than a million copies, but that piece, as well as the Rachmaninoff, was so consistently included in his performance program that one critic warned that he was becoming a "flesh and blood jukebox." While the ballyhoo initiated a flowering of new competitions (including one sponsored by Cliburn in Fort Worth, Texas), his momentum as a performer decreased until his retirement in 1978. His comeback in the late eighties was better received in the Soviet Union than in his homeland. **◂1956.11 ▸1986.13**

IN THE UNITED STATES

million birth defects in coming years. Pauling spearheaded international efforts to limit nuclear testing and presented the UN with a test-ban petition signed by 11,000 fellow scientists. Denounced as anti-American by conservatives, Pauling won the 1962 Nobel Prize for peace. It was his second Nobel: He'd won for chemistry in 1954.

▶LUNT AND FONTANNE—English-born Lynn Fontanne and American Alfred Lunt reigned for four decades, on two continents, as the first couple of the stage. In 1958, they made their last New York appearance, in Friedrich Dürrenmatt's *The Visit*, which opened at the newly christened Lunt-Fontanne Theatre.

▶GRAMMYS INTRODUCED—Hollywood had the Oscars, Broadway the Tonys, TV the Emmys, and in 1958, the recording-arts industry got the Grammys. Largely a publicity stunt, the inaugural competition demonstrated middle-of-the-road musical taste and foreshadowed boondoggles to come. Frank Sinatra, nominated for twelve awards, received only one trophy—in the Best Album Cover category. Domenico Modugno won best record honors for "Volare."

▶THANK HEAVEN—"Why does Arthur want to make a picture about a whore?" carped an MGM executive. But *Gigi*, producer Arthur Freed's 1958 movie musical from Colette's spicy novella about a Parisian courtesan-in-training, became MGM's last lyric masterpiece. Vincente Minnelli's stylish direction caught Paris at its most enchanting (and most Colette-like). Colette pal Maurice Chevalier *(below, right)* sang

a smirking rendition of "Thank Heaven for Little Girls"—an unwholesome highlight. The film won nine Oscars, including Best Picture. **◂1900.7**

POLITICS & BUSINESS: GNP: $447.3 billion ... Army launches *Explorer 1* (first successful U.S. satellite) ... National Defense Education Act passed (to bolster science, math, and foreign-language skills) ... John Birch Society founded.

"I would be satisfied if my novels … did no more than teach my readers that their past—with all its imperfections—was not one long night of savagery from which the first Europeans acting on God's behalf delivered them."—**Chinua Achebe, in *Things Fall Apart***

AROUND THE WORLD

▶BENELUX UNION—The nations of Belgium, the Netherlands, and Luxembourg signed a treaty at The Hague in 1958, creating the world's first completely free international labor market. An outgrowth of a ten-year-old customs union between the three Low Countries, the Benelux Economic Union coordinated the members' financial, agricultural, and social-welfare programs, allowing goods, people, and money to circulate freely across borders. ◀1957.5 ▶1985.11

▶NIXON IN SOUTH AMERICA—Richard Nixon's 1958 goodwill tour through South America was a spectacular failure. Booed in Uruguay, stoned in Peru, and finally set upon by a mob in Venezuela, the U.S. vice president cut the trip short and returned to Washington. Nixon was resented throughout Latin America as a representative of U.S. support for two hated dictators, Somoza in Nicaragua and Trujillo in the Dominican Republic. ◀1933.4 ▶1961.7

▶MIRO'S UNESCO MURALS—Impossible to pigeonhole, the art of Joan Miró incorporated elements of cubism, fau-

vism, dadaism, surrealism, and primitivism. In paintings, prints, and sculpture, the protean Catalan was by turns playful and formal; his colorful abstractions are lyrical and eerily fantastic. Among his greatest achievements: two masterly ceramic murals executed for the new UNESCO headquarters in Paris, completed in 1958.

▶NAGY EXECUTED—With the 1958 execution of moderate Communist Imre Nagy, the Soviet crackdown on Hungary was complete. Lured out of his refuge in the Yugoslav embassy with a promise of safe passage, Nagy was instead arrested. Nothing more was heard of him until puppet premier János Kádár announced his execution for treason as a fait accompli. ◀1956.4

SPORTS

Athlete of the Century

11 At the start of the 1958 World Cup finals, 17-year-old Pelé (born Edson Arantes do Nascimento) had been playing professional soccer for just 20 months. Though he was already regarded as a promising player in his native Brazil, to sports fans elsewhere he was unknown. By the end of the competition, however, he'd scored an attention-getting six goals—helping his country gain its first World Cup. Before long, he was the best-known (and best-paid) athlete on the planet.

For nearly two decades, Pelé dominated the most international of team sports. From 1958 to 1974, he played up to 180 games a year with the Santos Football Club, scoring over 1,000 times in 1,362 appearances and breaking virtually every record on the books. His artistry dazzled spectators and defied statistical analysis: He once scored with such extraordinary grace—dribbling the length of the field past Rio de Janeiro's Fluminense club—that his achievement became known as the "Most Beautiful Goal Ever Scored in Maracaña." Pelé played for Brazil in four World Cup matches (Brazil won three of them). Popes and presidents vied to meet him; Nigeria and Biafra even suspended hostilities to enable him to play.

In 1975, a year after retiring from the Santos club, Pelé signed with the New York Cosmos, thereby sparking interest in soccer in a country long indifferent to it. He retired again after leading the Cosmos to the North American Soccer League championship in 1977. He was named Athlete of the Century in 1980. **◀1930.13**

Brazilians called national hero Pelé the "Pérola Negra" (the Black Pearl).

LITERATURE

Achebe's Story

12 For hundreds of years, outsiders had both romanticized and reviled the African continent as they plundered its resources, scarring not only the land but the psyches of its peoples. But nationalist movements after World War II ignited a revolution in the consciousness of the colonized. As Nigerian writer and political activist Chinua Achebe put it, "We saw suddenly that we had a story to tell." With *Things Fall Apart*, published in 1958, Achebe began his fictionalized version of that story—the first of a series of novels depicting Nigerian life from the mid-nineteenth century onward.

While growing up under British rule, Achebe had experienced firsthand the traumas of colonialism. Born in 1930 to Christian parents (he was baptized Albert Chinualumogu), he spoke the Igbo tongue before learning English at eight. Straddling the cultural line between colonizer and colonized, he and many peers considered themselves superior to their non-Christian neighbors but inferior to the Europeans who guided their formal education—an attitude Achebe came to see as pernicious.

Written in an English flavored with Nigerian speech patterns and proverbs, *Things Fall Apart* (the title echoes a line in William Butler Yeats's apocalyptic poem "The Second Coming") recounts the tragic tale of an Igbo man, Okonkwo, whose village disintegrates under British influence. The whites, one character laments, have "put a knife on the things that held us together and we have fallen apart." Noted one critic: "No European ethnologist could so intimately present this medley of mores of the Igbo tribe, nor detail the intricate formalities of life in the clan." But the book's psychological, philosophical, and historical insights transcend strictly local concerns: It was the first black African novel to be recognized internationally as a classic. **▶1986.12**

THEATER

Pinter's Party

13 When British dramatist Harold Pinter's first full-length play, *The Birthday Party,* premiered in London's West End in 1958, critics dismissed it as "puzzling" and "half-gibberish"; it closed after only a brief run. Yet within a few years, Pinter's work was celebrated as some of the century's most original and challenging theater.

In *The Birthday Party,* two thugs arrive at a seaside boarding house and, without identifying themselves or offering a motive, pummel a tenant into jelly with inquisitorial accusations. The play ends with the interlopers driving away with their victim, whose compliance is as unsettling as their inexplicable authority. The odd mix of realism, absurdism, and enigmatic horror is typical of Pinter—as is the dialogue, full of the silences and evasions that are the playwright's trademark innovation. In this and later dramas (including *The Caretaker,* his first hit, produced in 1960), Pinter's characters communicate by not communicating: They speak in clichés, they avoid direct statements, they insinuate. Sometimes they don't talk at all.

Playwright of pauses: Harold Pinter, in a 1992 portrait by Justine Mortimer.

Freud, the Bible, and the brutality of the twentieth century were all ventured as possible sources for what one critic called Pinter's "Comedy of Menace." The playwright, however, refused to be pinned down. "I can sum up none of my plays," he said. "I can describe none of them except to say: That is what happened." **◀1957.12 ▶1985.13**

NOBEL PRIZES: Peace: Dominique Georges Pire (Belgian; Aid to Displaced Persons) … Literature: Boris L. Pasternak (U.S.S.R.; novelist) … Chemistry: Frederick Sanger (U.K.; molecular structure of insulin) Medicine: Joshua Lederberg, George W. Beadle, and Edward L. Tatum (U.S.; genetics) … Physics: Pavel A. Cherenkov, Ilya M. Frank, and Igor E. Tamm (U.S.S.R.; cosmic ray counter).

A VOICE FROM 1958

Liz Beats Out Debbie

"Marriage Breaks Up—Amid Rumors Singer Courted Miss Taylor," by Hedda Hopper, *Los Angeles Times*, September 11, 1958

It read like a soap opera script: Beautiful young widow turns siren, steals charming husband of apple-pie friend. In 1958, sultry Liz Taylor played the man-eater; bobby-sox troubadour Eddie Fisher was her partner in adultery; fresh-faced Debbie Reynolds, America's big-screen sweetheart, was the jilted wife. And the triangle was real. Taylor, 26, had just lost third husband Mike Todd in a plane crash; Fisher and Reynolds were not three years into their highly touted "perfect marriage." The public went wild; the Hollywood crisis pushed hard news off the front pages. Taylor gained a permanent notoriety that didn't hurt at the box office, but the vilified Fisher took a professional hit. As for young mother Reynolds, well, everyone just felt for her. In an unusually outspoken column, gossipmonger Hedda Hopper expressed the consensus on the Debbie-Eddie-Liz biz. ►1963.M

I've known Elizabeth Taylor since she was 9 years old—always liked her; always defended her.

She never wanted to be an actress. That was her mother's project.

I've seen her through her marriages to Nicky Hilton, Michael Wilding and Mike Todd. She had the sympathy of the world after Todd's tragic death.

I flew with her to New York just three months ago. We sat up until 3 a.m. talking about the happiness she'd had with Todd, happiness as she'd never known before.

She showed me his wedding ring, which had been taken off his finger after his death. She said, "I'll wear it always. They'll have to cut off my finger before they get it off my hand."

Talks With Liz

But I can't take that present episode with Eddie Fisher. I've just talked with Liz to ask her what this is all about.

Her reply was unprintable.

Then she went on to say, "You know I don't go about breaking up marriages. Besides, you can't break up a happy marriage. Debbie's and Eddie's never has been."

I asked if she loved Fisher.

She replied, "I like him very much. I've felt happier and more like a human being for the past two weeks than I have since Mike's death."

"What do you suppose Mike would say to this?" I asked.

Had Divine Time

"He and Eddie loved each other," was her reply.

"No, you're wrong," I said. "Mike loved Eddie. In my opinion, Eddie never loved anyone but himself."

"Well," was her answer, "Mike is dead and I'm alive."

"You've been with Fisher constantly in New York for the past two weeks," I accused. "What do you call that but taking him away from Debbie? I hear you even went to Grossinger's with him—where he and Debbie were married."

"Sure, and we had a divine time, too."

"What about Arthur Loew Jr.? You've known for the last six months that he's been in love with you, and your children are still living in his home."

"I can't help how he feels about me."

Debbie Loves Him

"Well," said I, "you can't hurt Debbie like this without hurting yourself more, because she loves him."

Her answer to that was: "He's not in love with her and never has been. Only a year ago they were about to get a divorce but stopped it when they found out she was going to have another baby."

"Well, let me tell you this, Liz," I said. "This will hurt you much more than it ever will Debbie Reynolds. People love her very much because she is an honest and wonderful girl."

"And what am I supposed to do," she cried. "Ask him to get back to her and try? He can't. And if he did, they'd destroy each other. I'm not taking anything away from Debbie Reynolds, because she never really had it."

"Well, Liz, you'll probably hate me for the rest of your life for this but I can't help it. I'm afraid you've lost all control over reason. Remember the nights when you used to call me at 2 and 3 in the morning when you were having nightmares and had to talk to somebody and I let you talk your heart out? What you've just said to me bears not the slightest resemblance to that girl. Where, oh where has she gone?"

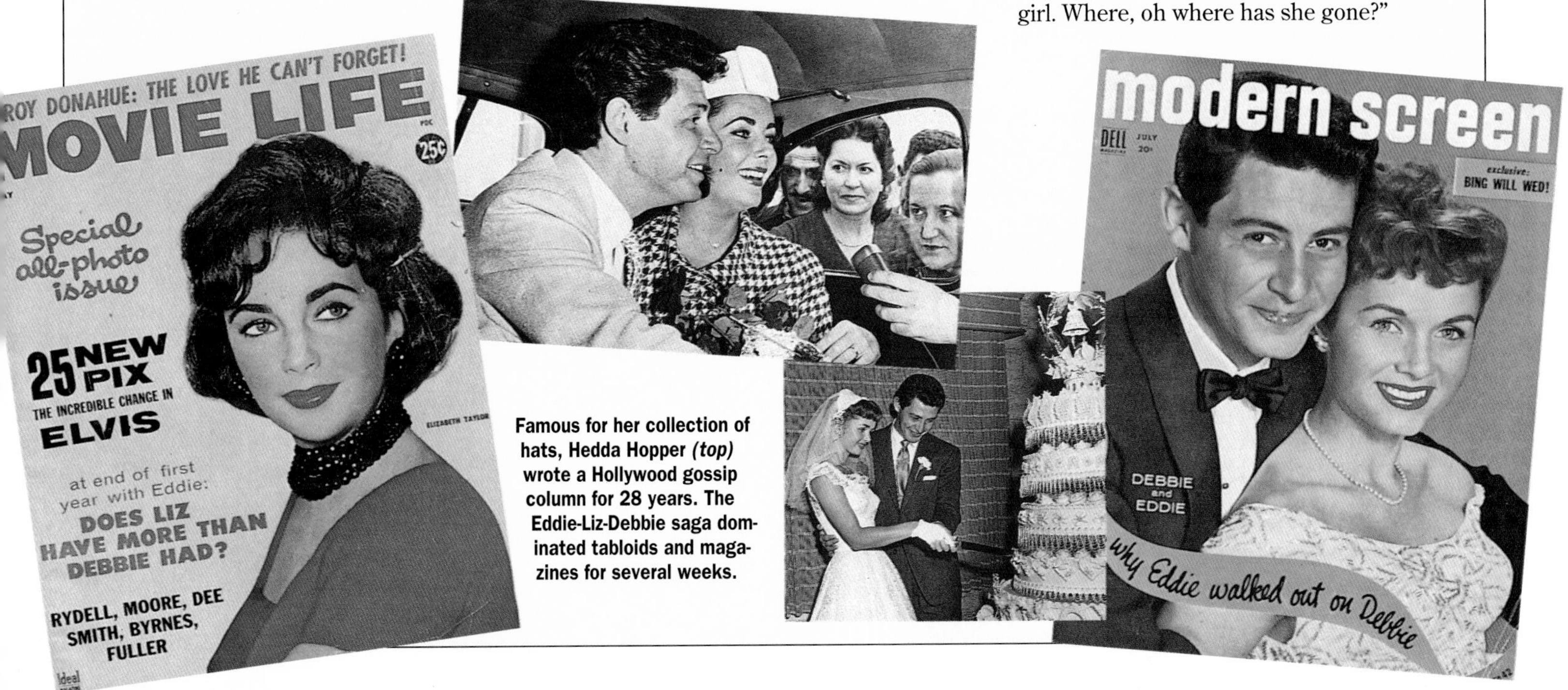

Famous for her collection of hats, Hedda Hopper *(top)* wrote a Hollywood gossip column for 28 years. The Eddie-Liz-Debbie saga dominated tabloids and magazines for several weeks.

"Cuba is no longer dedicated to the service of her millionaires."—**Fidel Castro, on the success of the Cuban revolution**

STORY OF THE YEAR

Revolution Triumphs in Cuba

1 They were called *los barbudos* (the bearded ones), the grizzled young rebels who ranged out of the mountains to battle the forces of Fulgencio Batista, Cuba's rapacious dictator. Their campaign drew support from a broad cross section of the population—landless peasants, urban workers, middle-class businessmen. The insurrection's leader, a fiery young lawyer named Fidel Castro, had led a failed uprising in 1953. Jailed, he'd pronounced, "History will absolve me." Cubans admired Castro's mettle. Absolution came propitiously dated: On New Year's Day, 1959, the *Fidelistas* took Havana. Batista had fled the previous day, after pocketing most of the national treasury.

Castro greets his followers on the road to Havana. No one was then sure whether the rebel leader would be interested in governing post-Batista Cuba.

Under Batista—dominant since 1933, outright dictator from 1952—Cuba, the world's largest producer of sugarcane, had suffered brutal repression and gross exploitation. The corrupt strongman jailed and killed his opponents, skimmed some $40 million from state coffers, and sold the country to foreign capitalists. Americans had interests in Cuban sugar (40 percent share) and mineral wealth (9 percent share), and controlled public utilities (80 percent share) and the oil refining, banking, and tourism industries. Investors got rich, but there was precious little left over for most of the island's six million people. Released from prison in 1955, Castro went to Mexico and plotted Batista's overthrow. When he returned home to wage guerrilla war in 1956, "Cuba for Cubans" became a slogan of his revolution.

Assuming total power in 1959, Castro promulgated aggressive agrarian and industrial reform measures, eventually expropriating a billion dollars in American properties. His opponents whispered that the revolution was no longer olive green (the color of simple nationalism), as Fidel claimed, but watermelon colored, or "red on the inside." In February 1960, Castro inked a five million–ton sugar deal with the Soviet Union; later, when U.S. refineries in Cuba refused Soviet oil, Castro seized them. Eisenhower responded with a trade embargo; a year later he severed diplomatic relations. Inevitably, Castro moved closer to the Soviets. And after an attempted U.S. invasion, he declared his revolution *was* Communist—the first in the Western Hemisphere. **◂1953.M ▸1961.5**

TECHNOLOGY

Politics and Engineering

2 President Eisenhower called it "a magnificent symbol ... of the achievements possible to democratic nations peacefully working together for the common good." Queen Elizabeth II hailed it as "one of the outstanding engineering accomplishments of modern times." The Saint Lawrence Seaway, dedicated by the two leaders in June 1959, was a triumph of both engineering and politics—the fruit of nearly six decades of negotiation and five years of technical cooperation between the United States and Canada.

The two nations had first discussed transforming the Saint Lawrence River into a fully navigable waterway—a link between the Great Lakes and the Atlantic—in 1896. But World War I slowed progress toward an agreement, and it wasn't until 1932 that a treaty was signed authorizing construction. Even then, a powerful lobby—supported by the railroads and by seaports that feared losing business to Great Lakes harbors—blocked ratification of the pact.

World War II revived the project's prospects, because Americans became convinced that the seaway was vital to the national defense. Finally, in 1954, building began. A workforce of 22,000 dug new canals and deepened old ones, dredged river channels, and constructed locks, dikes, dams, and a hydroelectric plant. During the seaway's first six months of operation, traffic on the Saint Lawrence River increased by 67 percent, and cargo in some ports by as much as 150 percent. Today, the 2,300-mile waterway remains one of the most important commercial routes in North America. **◂1914.9 ▸1994.11**

The Dalai Lama in Tezpur, India, after fleeing from Tibet.

TIBET

China Crushes Uprising

3 In March 1959, nine years after Mao Zedong forcibly occupied Tibet, an armed uprising swept Lhasa, the Tibetan capital. Over the years, the Chinese presence had provoked growing resentment, and recently Mao's suppression of a rebellion in the Khams region (part of which had been annexed by China in 1956) had sent a wave of refugees into central Tibet with tales of atrocities. Sporadic guerrilla fighting accompanied that wave. But what spurred full-scale revolt in Lhasa were rumors that the occupiers planned to arrest the Dalai Lama.

A feudal sovereign, considered the reincarnation of a Buddhist divinity, the 14th Dalai Lama was a god-king to his people. Born to poor farmers and proclaimed heir to a 600-year-old dynasty at the age of two (monks chose him from among the kingdom's babies by reading mystical signs), he was 15 when the Chinese invaded his realm. As a holy man, he believed in the innate goodness of humankind—but his hopeful negotiations with battle-hardened Mao went nowhere. By 1959, China had sent thousands of settlers into Tibet;

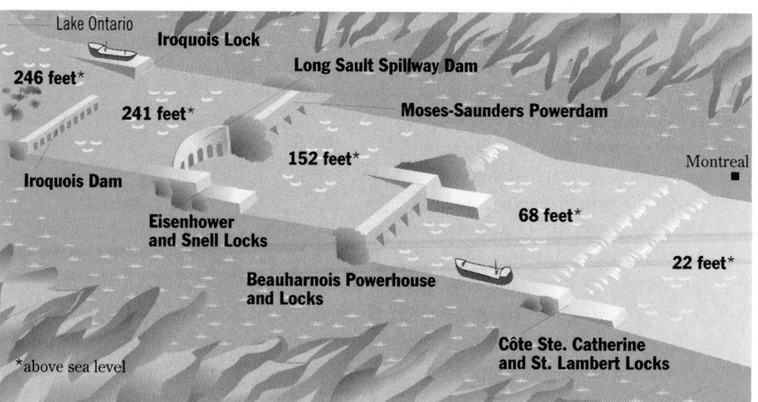

The Saint Lawrence Seaway, which is divided into five sections and has seven locks, covers 183 miles from Montreal to Lake Ontario.

ART & CULTURE: Books: ***Memento Mori*** **(Muriel Spark);** ***Goodbye, Columbus*** **(Philip Roth);** ***Billiards at Half-Past Nine*** **(Heinrich Böll);** ***Hawaii*** **(James Michener);** ***The Elements of Style*** **(Strunk and White) ... Music: "You've Got Personality" (Price and Logan); "What'd I Say" (Ray Charles);** ***Collected Poems*** **(Virgil Thomson) ... Painting & Sculpture:** ***The Marriage of Reason and Squalor*** **(Frank Stella) ... Film:**

"I've found it! It's the lead to man, our man. Come quickly."—**Mary Leakey, upon discovering Zinjanthropus**

besides modernizing the nation's infrastructure, occupation authorities had made clumsy efforts to collectivize yak herders and weaken the indigenous culture and theocracy.

The Chinese crushed the Lhasa rebels swiftly and ferociously. (By 1988, an estimated 1.2 million Tibetans had been killed in continuing repression, and 100,000 had fled the country; 6,200 monasteries had been destroyed.) The Dalai Lama escaped into exile with several hundred followers, promising his subjects that he would one day return to a liberated Tibet. He established a government in exile in northern India, and began a decades-long crusade to restore self-determination to his homeland. **◄1950.3 ►1966.1**

Complex, colorful, famously candid ("We will bury enemies of the Revolution," he once said on a visit to the United States), Nikita Khrushchev went head-to-head with Vice President Richard Nixon when the two met in Moscow.

DIPLOMACY

The Kitchen Debate

4 The impromptu "kitchen debate" between Soviet premier Nikita Khrushchev and American vice president Richard Nixon was a verbal slugfest between representatives of the two most powerful nations on earth. When Nixon arrived in Moscow in July 1959 to open the American National Exhibition, a rare Russian showing of American culture, Khrushchev was in no mood for a visit: The U.S. Congress had just passed the Captive Nations resolution condemning the Soviet Union for mistreating its satellite nations. The Soviet leader could only believe the expo and Nixon's visit were timed to humiliate him.

Before touring the show, Nixon and Khrushchev met privately and exchanged heated words about Captive Nations. As Nixon recounted the story in his memoirs, Khrushchev stormed, "It stinks like fresh horse s- - -, and nothing smells worse than that!" Nixon: "There is something that stinks worse than horse s- - - and that is pig s- - -." (Khrushchev had been a pig farmer in his youth.) Angry, primed, the two men then descended on the fair. To a throng of Western journalists, Khrushchev predicted the U.S.S.R. would soon surpass the U.S. technologically. "In passing you by," he said, "we will wave to you." Nixon demurred: "You don't know everything." Khrushchev: "If I don't know everything, you don't know anything about Communism, only fear of it."

The highlight of the running battle came in the kitchen of a model American house. Khrushchev belittled the gadgetry—lemon juicers, built-in washing machines: It evoked "the capitalist attitude toward women." He doubted American workers could afford such useless finery anyway. Nixon, jabbing his finger at Khrushchev's chest, defended the $14,000 house: Any American steel worker could buy one. An unscripted debate on capitalism and communism ensued, peaking with an exchange about the relative merits of everything from missiles to dishwashers. In modern times, two world leaders have rarely, if ever, spoken face to face so sharply or candidly. **◄1956.2 ►1960.2**

ARCHAEOLOGY

Leakeys Find a Link

5 Nearly a century after Darwin's death, British anthropologists Louis and Mary Leakey discovered a clue to one of evolution's basic questions: At what point did modern humans break off from chimpanzees and gorillas in the evolutionary chain? In 1959, Mary recovered a fossilized skull of *Zinjanthropus boisei* from Olduvai Gorge, a ravine cut into Tanzania's Serengeti Plain. Not quite human but clearly humanlike, Zinjanthropus (East African man) was dated, by the new potassium-argon method, at 1.75 million years—more than a million years older than the most ancient hominid remains previously found.

Popularly dubbed "Nutcracker Man" for his oversized molars, Zinjanthropus brought the Leakeys international fame and a flood of funding. Over the years, the couple made a series of spectacular finds, including *Homo habilis,* a direct forebear (unlike *Zinjanthropus*) of modern man; in 1978, six years after Louis's death, Mary unearthed a set of 3.5-million-year-old quasi-human footprints. The Leakeys' son, Richard, excavated some 400 hominid fossils over the course of a decade from sites in Kenya. The Leakey family's combined discoveries represent a wealth of evidence that the human race is much older than anyone had anticipated, and that it emerged in Africa, not Asia, as earlier fossils had indicated. And the Leakeys' influence carried beyond the hunt for early humans. It was Louis who set up Jane Goodall and Dian Fossey in their trailblazing studies of chimpanzees and gorillas. **◄1912.3**

Louis Leakey, patriarch of the Leakey family of archaeologists, at work in Tanzania.

BIRTHS

Mary Chapin Carpenter, U.S. musician.

Florence Griffith-Joyner, U.S. sprinter.

Earvin "Magic" Johnson, U.S. basketball player.

Maya Lin, U.S. architect.

John McEnroe, U.S. tennis player.

Randy Travis, U.S. musician.

DEATHS

Maxwell Anderson, U.S. playwright.

Ethel Barrymore, U.S. actress.

Bernard Berenson, U.S. art historian.

Raymond Chandler, U.S. writer.

Louis Costello, U.S. comedian.

Cecil B. DeMille, U.S. filmmaker.

John Foster Dulles, U.S. statesman.

Jacob Epstein, U.S.-U.K. sculptor.

Abraham Flexner, U.S. educator.

Errol Flynn, Australian-U.S. actor.

George Grosz, German-U.S. artist.

Duncan Hines, U.S. chef.

Billie Holiday, U.S. singer.

Willie Hoppe, U.S. billiards player.

Mario Lanza, U.S. singer.

Daniel François Malan, South African political leader.

George C. Marshall, U.S. general.

Edwin Muir, U.K. writer.

Heitor Villa-Lobos, Brazilian composer.

Charles Wilson, Scottish physicist.

Frank Lloyd Wright, U.S. architect.

Lester Young, U.S. musician.

Ben-Hur (William Wyler); *Pillow Talk* (Michael Gordon); *North by Northwest* (Alfred Hitchcock); *Ballad of a Soldier* (Gregori Chukhrai); *Black Orpheus* (Marcel Camus) ... Theater: *The Miracle Worker* (William Gibson); *The Tenth Man* (Paddy Chayefsky); *The Zoo Story* (Edward Albee); *The Sound of Music* (Rodgers and Hammerstein) ... TV: *Rawhide*; *Bonanza*; *The Twilight Zone*; *The Many Loves of Dobie Gillis.*

"The cinema is truth 24 times a second."—Jean-Luc Godard

NEW IN 1959

Panty hose.

Alaska and Hawaii (49th and 50th states).

Guggenheim Museum (New York City; designed by Frank Lloyd Wright).

Submarine with ballistic missile.

IN THE UNITED STATES

▶KUDOS FOR *RAISIN*—Lorraine Hansberry, 29, became, in 1959, the youngest American playwright (and the first African-American) to win the prestigious New York Drama Critics' Circle Award for best play, for *A Raisin in the Sun*, a penetrating, personal look at a black family's attempts to transcend its Chicago slum surroundings. Only one other Hansberry play was published before she died of cancer at 34; two more appeared posthumously. ◀1953.13

▶MALE BONDING—Hard on the heels of the panty raid, a zany new craze infected American college campuses in 1959: phone-booth packing. The idea (it came from South African universities) was to

stuff as many bodies as possible (mostly male) into a standard seven-foot-tall pay-phone booth. Students at Modesto Junior College in California claimed a record 34.

▶BARBIE DEBUTS—In March, Mattel Toys unveiled what would become the most successful doll in history: Barbie Teenage Fashion Model. A curvaceous eleven and a half inches tall, Barbie retailed for $3.00. Over the next three decades, she acquired myriad clothes, accessories, and

MUSIC

An Australian Diva

6 Italian director Franco Zeffirelli's 1959 production of Donizetti's *Lucia di Lammermoor* at the Royal Opera House, Covent Garden, in London signified a defining moment in operatic history. Sydney-born soprano Joan Sutherland's dazzling rendition of the mad scene, displaying both technical virtuosity and dramatic finesse, established her as a successor to Nellie Melba and a peer of Maria Callas, and helped spark a renewal of interest in eighteenth- and nineteenth-century bel canto singing—a style emphasizing brilliant high notes and flawless phrasing.

Initially considering herself a mezzo-soprano (the range between soprano and contralto), Sutherland was long unaware of the full extent of her capabilities. It was only after she and her mother moved to London that her young mentor (and later husband), Richard Bonynge, pressed her to develop the high range required of coloratura roles like Lucia.

Sutherland in the 1959 Covent Garden production of *Lucia di Lammermoor.*

Sutherland continued to blossom in the 1960s. She earned the appellation La Stupenda after a Venice performance in Handel's *Alcina,* and she performed *Lucia* to wildly enthusiastic audiences in Paris, Milan, and New York. Her interpretations grew in depth and complexity even as she battled arthritis in her later years. A popularizer of opera on television and radio as well as on stage, the stately soprano was made a dame of the British Empire in 1978, and retired in 1990 at the age of 63. ◀1949.11 ▶1974.M

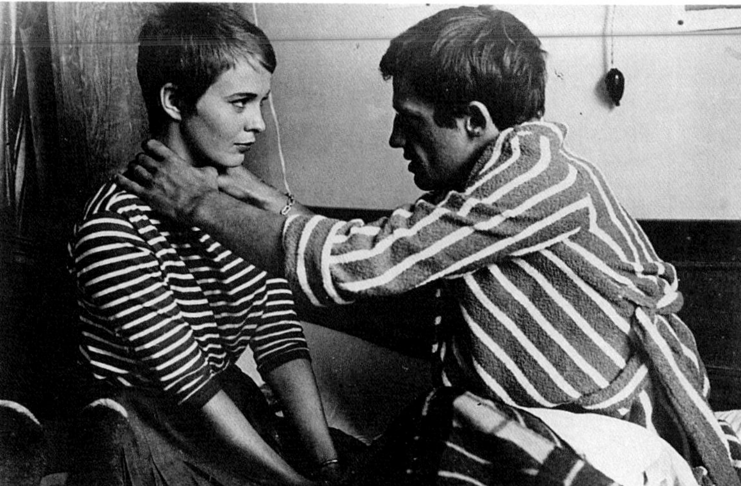

Godard's first feature, *Breathless,* with Jean Seberg and Jean-Paul Belmondo *(above),* had a more straightforward narrative structure than would typically be found in his later films.

FILM

The New Wave

7 For years, François Truffaut, Jean-Luc Godard, and other critics at the journal *Cahiers du Cinéma* had attacked traditional French film as stuffy and anonymous; they'd lionized a handful of international directors (most of them undervalued American filmmakers) as *auteurs* (authors) for their distinctively personal work. In the late 1950s, these cinephiles, along with like-minded compatriots, started making their own low-budget films, characterized by quirky narratives, sly allusions to other movies, and innovative cinematography. Their efforts formed *la nouvelle vague* (the New Wave), which crested in 1959 with Cannes Film Festival victories for Alain Resnais's *Hiroshima, mon amour* and Truffaut's *The 400 Blows.* Meanwhile, Godard was completing his first feature, *Breathless.* Released early in 1960, it joined its predecessors as an archetype of the small, iconoclastic, yet commercially viable film.

In *Hiroshima, mon amour,* a hypnotic Franco-Japanese romance (and meditation on the atom bomb) with a screenplay by avant-garde "New Novelist" Marguerite Duras, Resnais mimicked the "complexity of thought" through flashbacks, repetition, and a film within a film. *The 400 Blows* was the first installment in a cycle of films tracing the passage of Truffaut's fictional alter ego, Antoine Doinel (Jean-Pierre Léaud), from delinquency to domesticity. An unsentimental yet powerfully moving portrait of childhood, the film remains a popular classic; its intimate handheld-camera work and its final freeze frame influenced generations of filmmakers.

Breathless, a mock-tragedy based on a treatment by Truffaut, introduced the rakish Jean-Paul Belmondo as a small-time Paris hood, and the radiant Jean Seberg as the American beatnik girlfriend who betrays him. A lovingly ironic pastiche of Hollywood gangster films (Belmondo's character identifies intensely with Humphrey Bogart), the movie has a vibrantly spontaneous feel that results in part from quick-cut editing—a style that not only showed up in mainstream Hollywood movies but eventually became standard in commercials and music videos. ◀1956.7 ▶1971.12

FILM

Wilder's Wild Comedy

8 One of cinema's funniest, shrewdest, and most outrageous sex farces, 1959's *Some Like It Hot,* relates the misadventures of two Chicago jazz musicians who accidentally witness Al Capone's

Marilyn Monroe *(left)* and Jack Lemmon in Billy Wilder's gender bender.

SPORTS: Baseball: World Series, Los Angeles Dodgers defeat Chicago White Sox, 4–2 ... Football: NFL, Baltimore Colts defeat New York Giants, 31–16 ... Basketball: NBA, Boston Celtics defeat Minneapolis Lakers, 4–0 ... Boxing: Ingemar Johansson knocks out Floyd Patterson for world heavyweight championship.

"We thought the Supremes were going to be three hip black girls. And you girls came up there in your little fur coats, all prissy and everything."—George Harrison, on meeting the Supremes

1929 St. Valentine's Day Massacre. To escape pursuing mobsters, the two men don dresses and makeup and head for Florida with an all-female band. One of the pair (Tony Curtis) occasionally doffs his drag, pretends to be a millionaire, and romances the band's luscious vocalist (Marilyn Monroe). The other (Jack Lemmon), reveling in his new gender, enjoys the attentions of a slightly daffy male mogul. Both jazzmen eventually confess their impostures—prompting the mogul to respond (in the film's memorable final line), "Well, nobody's perfect!"

Director and cowriter Billy Wilder was a Viennese Jewish journalist (he once interviewed Sigmund Freud) who'd fled from the Nazis to Paris before emigrating to Hollywood. Wilder's directorial debut, *The Major and the Minor* (1942), was, like *Some Like It Hot,* a comedy of concealment: the story of an adult woman who hides her love for a dashing army officer by masquerading as a twelve-year-old. Many of Wilder's other films have a dark streak: *The Lost Weekend* and *The Apartment* both depict the perils of alcoholism; *Sunset Blvd.* concerns a faded silent-movie queen's desperation. Wilder's oeuvre is laced with torment and a deep cynicism—leavened by razor-sharp humor and superb cinematic craftsmanship. ◄1933.M ►1962.2

POPULAR CULTURE

Media Scandals

9 Herbert Stempel felt jilted. Former champion on the television quiz show *Twenty-One,* he'd been supplied with answers to questions (most of which he knew anyway), told which questions to miss, and coached in presentation ("grimace as if struggling"). After a two-month run, he was "defeated" by handsome English professor Charles Van Doren. Likewise coached, Van Doren "won" $129,000 during a four-month period and became a national celebrity. After Stempel blew the whistle, public outrage was so great that in 1959 Congress opened hearings on the great American quiz show fix.

Producers argued that no one was hurt by their deception and that it wasn't illegal. Undeterred, Congress expanded its investigation to include radio "payola"—cash and gifts that record companies paid disc jockeys to play their songs. That practice, as old as radio itself, *was* illegal (as a form of bribery, a misdemeanor), and for good reason: A big-city deejay with a faithful audience could make or break a record. In the rock 'n' roll era, as independent labels struggled to break the majors' stranglehold on the business, payola had become more common than ever.

Sham champ Charles Van Doren simulates concentration on *Twenty-One.* The scandal was the subject of a 1994 film, *Quiz Show,* directed by Robert Redford.

The payola scandal added to parental hysteria over rock's supposed corrupting influence. Some 200 radio employees around the country eventually admitted guilt. (Among them was legendary New York deejay Alan Freed. Hounded out of the industry and charged with tax evasion, he died in poverty at 43.) Payola became a federal offense, punishable by a $10,000 fine. As for quiz show deception, Congress outlawed it. The networks canceled most of their quiz programs, replacing them with new, "fun and easy" game shows not meant to be taken too seriously. ◄1941.14

MUSIC

The Motown Sound

10 In 1959, former boxer Berry Gordy launched an enterprise that soon became the world's most successful black-owned music concern. After failing as a record-store proprietor and succeeding as a rhythm-and-blues songwriter, Gordy had formed his own production company; one of his artists, Smokey Robinson, persuaded him to turn it into a record label. First called Tamla, the company quickly burgeoned into Motown—a conglomerate of recording, distribution, management, and song-publishing businesses that brought African-American music securely into the pop mainstream.

Named for its car-manufacturing hometown (Detroit, Michigan—the "Motor City"), Motown developed a trademark sound that blended black R&B and gospel styles with incomparably catchy romantic ditties. A team of producer-songwriters—Lamont Dozier and Brian and Eddie Holland, known collectively as H-D-H—churned out songs based on memorable hooks and relentless repetition, recording them with jangling tambourines, booming bass lines, and sugary strings. Gordy was a perfectionist, musically and otherwise: He ruled over his roster of carefully chosen artists like a strict father, carefully controlling their finances and creating a finishing school where performers learned genteel deportment. One of the most successful graduates was Diana Ross; as lead singer of the three-woman group the Supremes, Ross became a huge crossover star, recording twelve number-one hits.

By the mid-sixties, Motown's "hit ratio" was unmatched: 75 percent of the company's records made the national charts. Acts like the Temptations, the Supremes, the Miracles, Martha and the Vandellas, Little Stevie Wonder, Marvin Gaye, and later Gladys Knight and the Pips and the Jackson 5 created the "Sound of Young America" (as Gordy's publicists justifiably called it). ◄1955.13 ►1961.M

The original Supremes *(from left)*: Florence Ballard, Mary Wilson, and Diana Ross.

IN THE UNITED STATES

consorts (most notably, her doll-boyfriend Ken, introduced in 1961). By 1991, over 700

million Barbies had been sold worldwide, enough to circle the earth, head-to-toe, three and a half times.

►KING OF THE CONFESSORS—*Life Studies,* a 1959 volume of autobiographical poetry and prose by renegade Boston Brahmin and Pulitzer Prize winner Robert Lowell, provided a model for the generation of poets that followed. Profoundly introspective (Lowell scrutinized his patrician ancestry, his confinement in a

mental institution, his divorce), *Life Studies* was labeled "confessional" by dazzled critics. In less skilled hands than Lowell's, confessional poetry (sometimes called the "murderous art" because three of its most talented practitioners—John Berryman, Sylvia Plath, Anne Sexton—committed suicide) too often degenerates into self-indulgence. ►1965.V

►FREE JAZZ—Alto saxophonist Ornette Coleman compared his music—with its fluctuating beat, its wandering structure, and its bursts of atonality—to Jackson Pollock's painting. In 1959, the self-taught musician released three prophetically titled albums: *Tomorrow Is the Question!, Change of the Century,* and *The Shape of Jazz to Come.* Coleman's "free jazz" compositions attempted to escape the bounds of traditional melody, harmony, and rhythm. (He even played his instrument with an unorthodox tuning.) Initially dismissed as a hoax—even by the most progressive—free jazz was all the rage by the mid-1960s. ◄1955.7 ►1964.6

POLITICS & BUSINESS: GNP: $483.7. billion ... Alaska and Hawaii become the 49th and 50th states ... U.S. government restores full citizenship to Japanese-Americans who were interned during WWII ... United Steelworkers of America goes on strike (lasts 116 days) ... Oklahoma legalizes alcoholic beverages after 51 years ... Congress passes bill declaring importation of art for exhibits duty-free.

"The biggest no-talent I ever worked with."—**Paul Cohen, on firing Buddy Holly from Decca records in 1956**

AROUND THE WORLD

▶ANTARCTIC TREATY—Meeting in Washington, D.C., representatives of twelve nations agreed to preserve the world's last undeveloped continent. The Antarctic Treaty, signed on December 1, made the ice-bound continent a military-free zone reserved for cooperative scientific research. The signatories—Argentina, Australia, Belgium, Chile, France, Great Britain, Japan, New Zealand, Norway, South Africa, the Soviet Union, and the United States—promised to refrain from weapons testing and radioactive waste disposal on Antarctica. In 1991, a clause banning mineral and oil exploration for 50 years was added to the original agreement. ◂1958.M ▸1963.2

▶ROYAL WEDDING—Scion of the world's oldest royal family, Crown Prince Akihito of Japan was destined by birth to occupy the throne. A royal in a modern state, he derived his status from "the will of the

people," as was explicitly stated in the postwar Japanese constitution. In 1959, Akihito tacitly addressed the contradiction—and bucked 1,500 years of history—by marrying a commoner, Shōda Michiko. For many Japanese the unorthodox union embodied Japan's new era of social and political equality. ◂1946.3 ▸1993.11

▶WOMEN BARRED FROM SWISS SUFFRAGE—Voters in neutral, democratic Switzerland demonstrated unrestrained chauvinism in 1959: They elected to keep suffrage an all-male privilege. It was not until 1971 that a constitutional amendment allowed Swiss women to vote in federal elections or hold federal office. ◂1920.11

***Rolling Stone* named Holly "the major influence on rock music of the sixties."**

MUSIC

Rock's First Martyrs

11 In later years, rock stars would regularly be claimed by drug overdoses. But rock's first martyrs—Buddy Holly, Richie Valens, and the Big Bopper—achieved immortality when their tour plane crashed near Mason City, Iowa, on February 3, 1959. The tragedy marked the end of rock 'n' roll's first wave of creativity: By the time the 1950s were over, the airwaves were filled with bland, homogenized versions of the rebel music born earlier in the decade.

Valens, the first Mexican-American to enter the rock pantheon, was known for a number-two hit, the ballad "Donna" (whose B-side, a traditional Chicano party song called "La Bamba," is far better remembered today); the Big Bopper (a.k.a. J.P. Richardson), a plump disc jockey and writer of novelty songs, was famous for his deep-voiced talk-singing on "Chantilly Lace." But Holly's talent was of another order. In a field full of quick-buck artists, the bespectacled 22-year-old from Lubbock, Texas, brought a rare intelligence, sensitivity, and raw intensity to his compositions and performances.

Holly was a pioneer of rock technique—the first white rocker to use a heavy rhythm-and-blues backbeat, the first rock musician to experiment with overdubbing (a recording method that allows performers to accompany themselves). Holly's high, hiccuping vocals were inimitable—but widely copied nonetheless. At the time of the plane crash, he was more popular in Britain than in his homeland. But death made him a cult figure, and his songs—"Peggy Sue," "Rave On," "That'll Be the Day," and others—remained popular favorites into the 1990s. One band from Liverpool even named itself after his backup group, the Crickets: the Beatles. **◂1956.1 ▸1962.6**

THEATER

Gypsy Ends an Era

12 The golden age of the Broadway musical—in which literate librettos were smoothly interwoven with plot-advancing, character-revealing songs and dances—ended on a showbiz-brassy high note in 1959 with *Gypsy.* Based on the zesty memoirs of striptease artist Gypsy Rose Lee, the play is a funny, moving, and sometimes terrifying chronicle of all-consuming mother love and misdirected ambition. Gypsy's mother, the ferocious Rose, sacrifices everything to see her two daughters reach the theatrical big time. When the girls grow up and leave her, Rose descends into self-pity and delirium.

Gypsy had a remarkable pedigree. It was produced by David Merrick (then known for *Fanny,* later for *Hello, Dolly!*) and Leland Hayward *(South Pacific)*, scripted by Arthur Laurents *(West Side Story)*, scored and choreographed by Jerome Robbins *(West Side Story)*, and directed by Jule Styne *(Gentlemen Prefer Blondes)*; its lyrics were written by Stephen Sondheim *(West Side Story)*. At the epicenter, playing Mama Rose, was Ethel Merman, in the last role she originated. Such songs as "Some People" and "Everything's Coming Up Roses" became standards. But *Gypsy* marked the end of an era: In the years to come, the number of good book writers and lyricists dwindled, and musical theater came to be dominated by high concepts and spectacle. **◂1956.8 ▸1964.9**

Ethel Merman *(left, with Maria Karnilova, who played an aging stripper)* gave the performance of her career as Mama Rose.

LITERATURE

A Blast from Grass

13 Born in Danzig (now Gdansk), Günter Grass joined the Hitler Youth at 14; as a Wehrmacht tank gunner during World War II, he was wounded and captured by the Americans. Only after visiting the shut-down Dachau concentration camp did he begin to reject his Nazi-bred values. That purging process led Grass to write *The Tin Drum* (1959)—his first novel, and the first work of German fiction since the 1930s to win international acclaim.

The story—narrated by Oskar, whose distrust of adults prompted him to stop growing at age three—is set in Danzig before, during, and after the Hitler era. From an insane asylum, Oskar recalls his youth, when he was able to shatter glass with his voice and command crowds with his drumming—and when he served as messianic leader to a gang of vandals. (Significantly, Hitler's early nickname was the Drummer.) *The Tin Drum* broke with the earnestly realist postwar convention of *Trümmerliteratur,* or "rubble literature." At once a vivid memoir, a parody of classical German coming-of-age novels, and a tangle of surreal (and often obscene and blasphemous) allegories, the book scandalized many of its author's compatriots.

At the same time, it earned Grass the label of spokesman for his generation. Besides pouring out a stream of novels, plays, and poems, he became a socialist activist—campaigning for left-wing causes and candidates, but staunchly opposing the voguish violence of the revolutionary 1960s. **◂1929.11 ▸1961.10**

NOBEL PRIZES: Peace: Philip Noel-Baker (U.K.; disarmament and drafting of UN charter) ... Literature: Salvatore Quasimodo (Italian; poet) ... Chemistry: Jaroslav Heyrovský (Czech; polarography) ... Medicine: Severo Ochoa and Arthur Kornberg (U.S.; synthesis of RNA and DNA) ... Physics: Emilio Segrè and Owen Chamberlain (U.S.; antiproton).

A VOICE FROM 1959

A Hipster's Panorama

From *Naked Lunch*, by William S. Burroughs, 1959

Before William S. Burroughs became internationally notorious as the author of Naked Lunch, *his hallucinogenic 1959 novel, Allen Ginsberg and fellow Beat movement hipsters had adopted him as mentor and idol. (In a photograph shot and inscribed by Ginsberg, Burroughs appears below with "a brother Sphinx" at the Metropolitan Museum of Art in New York City.) Burroughs's alienation and his outlaw life (grandson of the Burroughs adding machine inventor, he was a Harvard alum who chucked his station for the world's skid rows) appealed to the Beats' sense of subversion. Others found the gaunt, sibylline writer an acquired taste: Some critics dismissed* Naked Lunch, *a surreal, harrowing story of a junkie and his travels to the metaphoric, greed-driven world of Interzone (Burroughs was a heroin addict for 15 years) as undisciplined twaddle. First published in France (cautious American publishers waited until 1962),* Naked Lunch *eventually found literary respectability—and more: It influenced both the possible form of the novel and the possible content.* **◂1957.8**

The Market

Panorama of the City of Interzone. Opening bars of East St. Louis Toodleoo … at times loud and clear then faint and intermittent like music down a windy street …

The room seems to shake and vibrate with motion. The blood and substance of many races, Negro, Polynesian, Mountain Mongol, Desert Nomad, Polyglot Near East, Indian—races as yet unconceived and unborn, combinations not yet realized pass through your body. Migrations, incredible journeys through deserts and jungles and mountains (stasis and death in closed mountain valleys where plants grow out of genitals, vast crustaceans hatch inside and break the shell of body) across the Pacific in an outrigger canoe to Easter Island. The Composite City where all human potentials are spread out in a vast silent market.

Minarets, palms, mountains, jungle … A sluggish river jumping with vicious fish, vast weed-grown parks where boys lie in the grass, play cryptic games. Not a locked door in the City. Anyone comes into your room at any time. The Chief of Police is a Chinese who picks his teeth and listens to denunciations presented by a lunatic. Every now and then the Chinese takes the toothpick out of his mouth and looks at the end of it. Hipsters with smooth copper-colored faces lounge in doorways twisting shrunk heads on gold chains, their faces blank with an insect's unseeing calm.

We went uptown to look at Mayan Codices at Museum of Natural History in N.Y., & later to the Metropolitan Museum of Art to view Carlo Crivelli's green-hued Christ-face with Crown of thorns stuck symmetric round his skull— here in Egyptian Wing William Burroughs with a brother Sphinx, Manhattan Fall 1953. Allen Ginsberg.

Behind them, through open doors, tables and booths and bars, and kitchens and baths, copulating couples on rows of brass beds, crisscross of a thousand hammocks, junkies tying up for a shot, opium smokers, hashish smokers, people eating talking bathing back into a haze of smoke and steam.

Gaming tables where the games are played for incredible stakes. From time to time a player leaps up with a despairing cry, having lost his youth to an old man or become Latah to his opponent. But there are higher stakes than youth or Latah, games where only two players in the world know what the stakes are.

All houses in the City are joined. Houses of sod—high mountain Mongols blink in smokey doorways—houses of bamboo and teak, houses of adobe, stone and red brick, South Pacific and Maori houses, houses in trees and river boats, wood houses one hundred feet long sheltering entire tribes, houses of boxes and corrugated iron where old men sit in rotten rags cooking down canned heat, great rusty iron racks rising two hundred feet in the air from swamps and rubbish with perilous partitions built on multi-levelled platforms, and hammocks swinging over the void.

Expeditions leave for unknown places with unknown purposes. Strangers arrive on rafts of old packing crates tied together with rotten rope, they stagger in out of the jungle their eyes swollen shut from insect bites, they come down the mountain trails on cracked bleeding feet through the dusty windy outskirts of the city, where people defecate in rows along adobe walls and vultures fight over fish heads. They drop down into parks in patched parachutes.… They are escorted by a drunken cop to register in a vast public lavatory. The data taken down is put on pegs to be used as toilet paper.

It was a decade of rebellion. As a controversial war raged in Southeast Asia, young people everywhere rose against the Establishment—demanding not just peace, but a world radically remade.

1960 1969

In 1967, when this demonstrator and her comrades confronted troops in Washington, D.C., "flower power" (the notion that love could somehow overcome a militarized state) was still a popular concept among the Vietnam War's opponents. But the following year, student rebels around the world adopted more militant tactics. In capitalist and communist countries alike, they battled entrenched authority—and sometimes came close to winning.

THE WORLD IN 1960

World Population

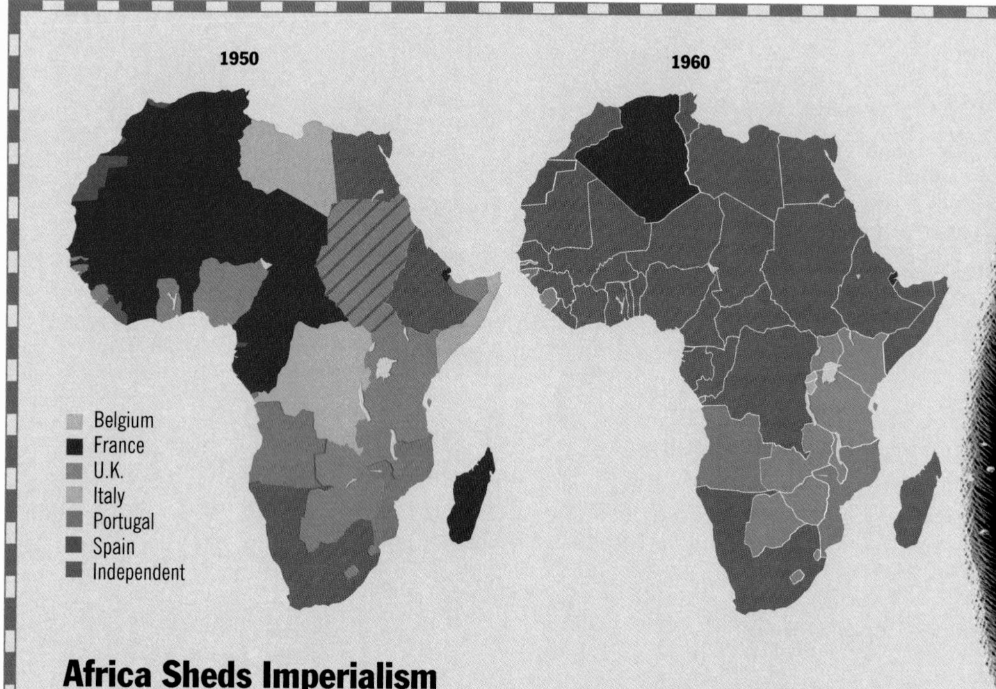

Africa Sheds Imperialism

The slow death of European colonialism in Africa became official in 1960 with the sudden arrival of 18 new sovereign nations. By 1970, there were 16 more, and by 1990, when Namibia, formerly the German colony of South-West Africa (occupied since 1915 by South Africa), became independent, there were no more European colonial territories on the continent. Europe's presence was marginalized even further as the two postwar superpowers, the Soviet Union and the United States, began using the continent as a playing ground for the Cold War.

Explorer 1

Defeating Polio

The development of an effective vaccine against polio very nearly eradicated a dreaded and deforming disease that struck particularly hard at the young.

Average cases reported annually

	1951–55	61–65	% decrease
Australia	2,187	154	93%
Czechoslovakia	1,081	0	100%
Denmark	1,614	77	95.2%
Sweden	1,526	28	98.2%
U.K.	4,381	322	92.7%
U.S.	37,864	570	98.5%

Percentage of Two-Year Olds Fully Immunized against Polio (1990)

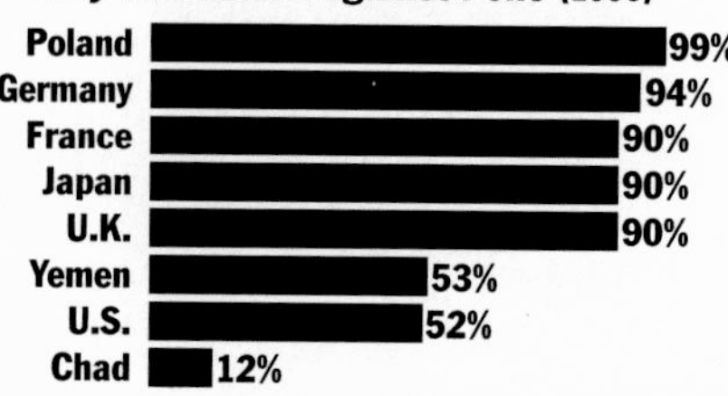

Fashion Essential

The **gray flannel suit**, like this model from Brooks Brothers, was the uniform of choice for corporate males. Established as part of the language by Sloan Wilson's 1955 novel, *The Man in the Gray Flannel Suit*, the ubiquitous businessman's garment became a symbol of the era's conformity.

Credit Made Easy

The first credit cards were intended as an easy way for consumers to charge purchases without having to come up with the cash at that moment. But by thus encouraging spending, credit cards also increased debt. By 1990, the average U.S. household owed $71,500 in mortgages and consumer debt.

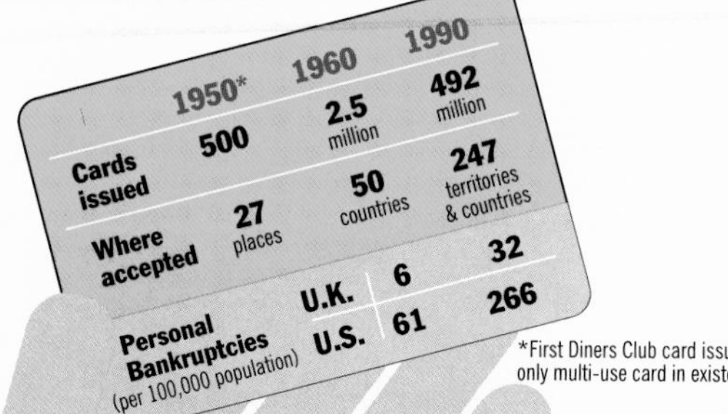

	1950*	1960	1990
Cards issued	500	2.5 million	492 million
Where accepted	27 places	50 countries	247 territories & countries
Personal Bankruptcies (per 100,000 population) U.K.		6	32
U.S.		61	266

*First Diners Club card issued; only multi-use card in existence

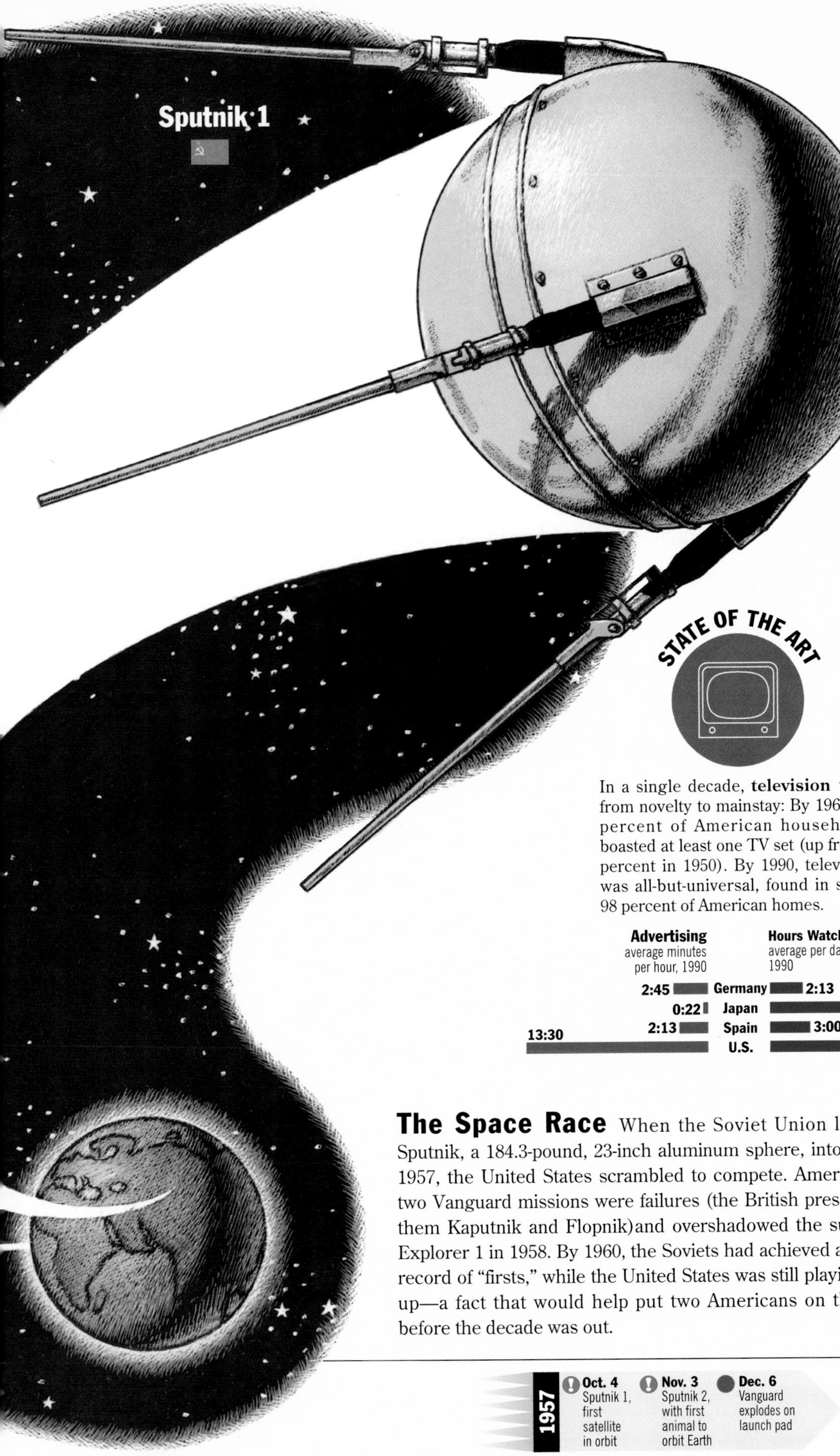

Sputnik 1

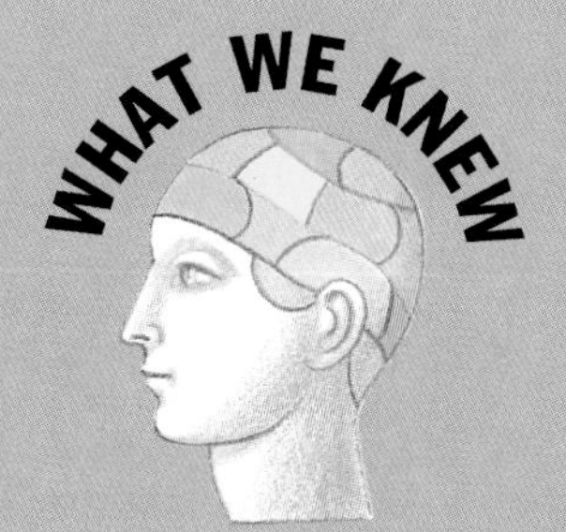

What We Knew

Although there is increasing evidence that cigarette smoking is not healthy, the majority of Americans who smoke—some 70 million people, with an annual consumption amounting to 3,900 cigarettes per adult—continue to believe, along with Los Angeles surgeon Ian G. MacDonald, that "smoking has a beneficial effect."

■

U.S. confidence in the presidency of Ngo Dinh Diem of Vietnam is high. "We were told nobody could save Vietnam and Diem was no good," President Dwight D. Eisenhower has said, "but now look!" That praise is reiterated in 1961 by Vice President Lyndon Johnson, who calls Diem "the Winston Churchill of Southeast Asia."

■

Deposed Cuban dictator, Fulgencio Batista, speaking from exile, gives his successor, Fidel Castro, "A year. No longer."

■

Scientists express unbounded enthusiasm for thermonuclear power. Many believe, in the words of University of Maryland professor John S. Toll, that it will enable "most of the world's industrial and food needs [to] be met for centuries to come." Among the many predictions: free, unmetered energy for all within a few decades; atomically fueled ships, aircraft, locomotives, and automobiles by 1980; and atomic radiation to sterilize fresh foods.

■

The use of DDT, the number-one pesticide in the world, has pushed postwar agricultural production to undreamed-of-levels, but scientists have begun to notice that some insects become immune to it, while birds that preyed on those insects are disappearing.

■

Although parents have embraced the increased permissiveness and more flexible, nonviolent approach to child rearing advocated by Dr. Benjamin Spock, a poll of elementary- and secondary-school teachers finds that 72 percent support the use of corporal punishment.

State of the Art

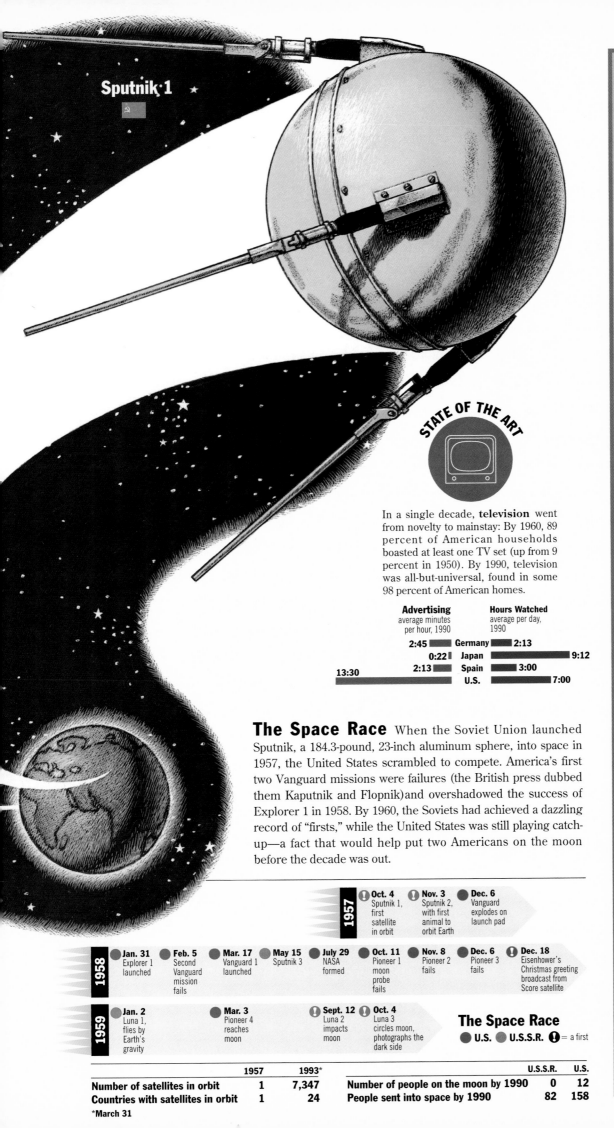

In a single decade, **television** went from novelty to mainstay: By 1960, 89 percent of American households boasted at least one TV set (up from 9 percent in 1950). By 1990, television was all-but-universal, found in some 98 percent of American homes.

Advertising average minutes per hour, 1990		Hours Watched average per day, 1990
2:45	Germany	2:13
0:22	Japan	9:12
2:13	Spain	3:00
13:30	U.S.	7:00

The Space Race When the Soviet Union launched Sputnik, a 184.3-pound, 23-inch aluminum sphere, into space in 1957, the United States scrambled to compete. America's first two Vanguard missions were failures (the British press dubbed them Kaputnik and Flopnik)and overshadowed the success of Explorer 1 in 1958. By 1960, the Soviets had achieved a dazzling record of "firsts," while the United States was still playing catch-up—a fact that would help put two Americans on the moon before the decade was out.

The Space Race

● U.S. ● U.S.S.R. ! = a first

1957
- ! **Oct. 4** Sputnik 1, first satellite in orbit
- ! **Nov. 3** Sputnik 2, with first animal to orbit Earth
- **Dec. 6** Vanguard explodes on launch pad

1958
- **Jan. 31** Explorer 1 launched
- **Feb. 5** Second Vanguard mission fails
- **Mar. 17** Vanguard 1 launched
- **May 15** Sputnik 3
- **July 29** NASA formed
- **Oct. 11** Pioneer 1 moon probe fails
- **Nov. 8** Pioneer 2 fails
- **Dec. 6** Pioneer 3 fails
- ! **Dec. 18** Eisenhower's Christmas greeting broadcast from Score satellite

1959
- **Jan. 2** Luna 1, flies by Earth's gravity
- **Mar. 3** Pioneer 4 reaches moon
- ! **Sept. 12** Luna 2 impacts moon
- ! **Oct. 4** Luna 3 circles moon, photographs the dark side

	1957	1993*
Number of satellites in orbit	1	7,347
Countries with satellites in orbit	1	24

*March 31

	U.S.S.R.	U.S.
Number of people on the moon by 1990	0	12
People sent into space by 1990	82	158

MARY GORDON

Age of Innocents

The Cult of the Child

1960
1969

WHAT A SOCIETY THINKS AND FEELS about its children is an index of its attitudes about a great number of things: knowledge, power, sex, the future. Childhood begins in helplessness and ends in independence. Or at least that is what we moderns think. One of the signs that mark us as radically unlike our forebears is our perception of childhood as a distinct entity, a state of being not simply leading into another, later state (adulthood) but qualitatively different from it.

This perception, born of the Industrial Revolution's exploitation of children and society's protective response, gathered steam in the nineteenth century and held sway for the first 60 years of the twentieth. Childhood, under the protective custody of adults, was a world into which one entered as a piece of malleable clay and from which, when properly shaped, one looked naturally forward to passing into the superior separate sphere of adults. But in the 1960s, childhood assumed a different aspect: It came to be valued as a treasure unconnected to its future, and for perhaps the first time in history, the old considered the idea that they had something to learn from the young.

Freud, at the end of the nineteenth century, told the world that children were sexual; nothing else he said was resisted quite so ferociously. Despite society's apparent absorption of Freud's theories, children were understood, throughout the first half of the twentieth century, to need protection from the knowledge of sexuality so they could continue their pure, unclouded, happy, and chaste existences. Such protection required tightening the border between adulthood and childhood; withholding information about sex eventually transmuted into an ideal of concealment about anything perceived as troubling: parents' marital tensions, money, work, politics. Children were required to inhabit their own zone, a kind of *cordon sanitaire*, safe from the dirty and infectious real world.

The barriers protecting this zone were most effective in the years between World War II and the 1960s—a time of prosperity, of a burning desire for normalcy and peace, and of a belief in the goodness of the private world, represented by the nuclear family. But the barriers began to wobble in the sixties, perhaps as an aftershock of the decade's seismic political and social tumult. It may be tautological to say that the sixties began in the fifties and ended in the seventies, but perhaps only in this way can we grasp the full impact of a decade that had, by my count, three distinct cultural flavors, each of which insisted on the primacy of youth, but understood it in different ways. I would call the first the Kennedy years; the second, the age of the Beatles; and the third, the Vietnam era.

Throughout much of history, children (especially those outside the upper classes) were viewed as miniature adults. But by the start of the century, the harm done to growing bodies and minds by industrial labor had begun to alter that perception. With his disturbing images of children doing the work of adults in cotton mills *(right)*, coal mines, and canneries, pioneering photojournalist Lewis Hine fueled the movement for child-labor laws in the United States—and helped usher in a more protective era.

The Kennedys moved into the White House in 1961 and turned on all the lights. Much of their voltage stemmed from their youthful energy. The idea that older people had to listen to younger ones was suddenly in the air. But the Kennedys represented youth in a transitional way. They were young, but they didn't threaten their elders. Their youthful image was connected more to idealistic responsibility than to pleasure. The iconic photographs of the President with his stylish young wife and children are remarkably formal in their lineaments, suggesting that even as the Kennedy offspring moved into adolescence their sphere would have little in common with that of their parents. If the generations came together, it was only in the occasional gesture of parental stooping, a condescending interest in a world the parents had no intention of inhabiting. In those years, the phrase "children

should be seen and not heard" still had near universal application: Parents were the repository of wisdom and had almost nothing to learn from their children. The idea that anything of real value might be transmitted in the direction of children to parents would have been almost incomprehensible.

Although children were kept "in their place" during the Kennedy years, by that time the psychological and educational theories of such thinkers as Piaget and Montessori had created a classroom climate in which childhood was assumed to be a valuable and precious state in its own right—not merely a training ground for future adulthood. Both parents and teachers were determined that school would no longer be the prison many of them remembered. Children's happiness—and certainly their comfortable social adjustment—became an educational goal as important as the acquisition of the 3Rs. As the paint on classroom walls became more vibrant, and children were encouraged to color *outside* the lines, the general culture began to place new value on qualities traditionally associated with childhood: spontaneity, enthusiasm, candor. It was a world waiting for the Beatles to happen.

THE DRAMATICALLY DIFFERENT RESPONSES to the television appearances of Elvis Presley in 1956 and the Beatles in 1964 demonstrate vividly just how much the world changed in eight years. Elvis's blatant sexuality provoked a rash of outraged sermons. Politicians and newspapers railed against him. Adults found him ridiculous or dangerous; on the other side were the young, who screamed and swooned. There was virtually no crossover. But in 1964, respectable grownups, intellectuals, even, were listening to the Beatles. The "boys from Liverpool" did indeed seem enviably like boys rather than men. Exuberant, fun loving, and generous, they suggested a world with a place for play. Youth in their case was not wasted on the young.

The playfulness of those years led to the hippie movement, and, ultimately, a full-fledged abdication of adulthood's most tiresome trappings. But the flower child's sense of well being gradually disintegrated as Vietnam became more central to consciousness. It was then that our notions of innocence—and therefore of childhood—became more paradoxical and complex.

University students—as well as many of their professors—took up the idea that the war in Vietnam was the direct result of the greed and lying of (old) men in suits and uniforms. These men made dangerous decisions in large offices, and they lied to murderous effect. This perception gave rise to complex, often contradictory ideas about the nature of innocence, the consequences of concealment, and the simultaneous liberation and curse of information. Some began to think the government (or as we called it back then, The Establishment) had withheld the real story in order better to do its dirty work. These purveyors of unmediated adulthood, the insistent and encrusted hierarchies represented by Lyndon Johnson and Dean Rusk—and their corporate and police state minions—had dirty secrets, and horror had resulted. So all concealment was suspect: Only the truth could set us free.

Many parents who wished to identify themselves with the liberation of the sixties began to think that the concealment with which they had been brought up was poisonous to their own children. They believed that the endless rules and repressions of bourgeois civilization interfered with the pristine state of childhood (a faith in which had stubbornly endured). Yet even as these parents hoped to put less pressure on their children, they also wanted, in the name of new candor and of a different, less directive parental style, to have their children more involved in their lives. A climate of openness was deemed optimal. In the best of all possible worlds, children would be not only healthy, wealthy, and wise, but also free at last.

But freedom cut both ways, and the era's cultural sea changes lifted the lid off parental ambivalence. In a climate that valued pleasure, political commitment, and the public, or communal, over the private world, the ordinary tasks of diaper changing and face wiping (to say nothing of bringing home the bacon) were hardly where the action was. The publication in 1963 of Betty Friedan's *The Feminine Mystique* allowed many mothers to express what they had thought was their terrible secret: They had mixed feelings about maternity. The Pill, which received FDA approval in 1960,

The ideal nuclear family: California, circa 1965. By the end of the decade, the kids might well have been doing the steering—or Mom and Dad might have pedaled off in opposite directions. In an era of unraveling definitions, Tolstoy's old dictum, "Happy families are all alike," was increasingly replaced by a question: "What *is* a family, after all?"

wrought an even more revolutionary change: For the first time, women were granted near-absolute control over when—and even if—they would become mothers. In theory, children were still treasured: The idyllically naked and garlanded father, mother, and little kids appear in many photographs of the period. But parenthood as an inevitable quick step after the end of adolescence was no longer pro forma. The model of all-consuming parental responsibility was at odds with the zeitgeist.

More marriages broke up, and more mothers went to work (a trend that would come to full flower years later). To accommodate these changes, the weave of the fabric of family life became looser, further narrowing the gap between adult and child. Children were seen as capable of more decision making and greater responsibility, and consequently deserving of more freedom. Children's freedom was all well and good—as long as it didn't interfere with the concomitant freedom of parents. Which, of course, it did. It's no wonder that as the sixties closed, films like *The Exorcist*, which portrayed children as demonic and possessed—the farthest thing from innocent—began to appear.

1960
1969

AS THE PROSPERITY OF THE SIXTIES GAVE WAY to the belt tightening of the seventies, and the fast-track eighties moved into the austere nineties, we as a society grew increasingly incoherent about our ideas of childhood. A society's notions of the relationship between pleasure and responsibility depend upon how rich it feels. Innocence is expensive, and we no longer know what we can afford—or for how long. We can't decide whether we want our kids to get cracking on their math scores so they can keep up with their Japanese age-mates or just to relax and play "like children" (as if we knew what that meant). What is more difficult, we are no longer sure whether our children are innocent or not. Thanks to many hours a week spent in front of the television, today's children clearly know more than their parents did at the same age. Among the video images they see are kids like themselves, highly sexualized, turned into erotic objects. While most adults are uncomfortable with these images, we have no idea what our children make of them. What, given all the information they're bombarded with, do children really know? This question was posed starkly in my own life when my then-nine-year-old son reported his puzzlement to me: He knew what *kind* of sex you had with heterosexuality, homosexuality, prostitution, rape; what he didn't know, he said, was what *happened* when you had sex. I know for a fact that he had been told: I had told him. But just as we are consciously at war about what our children should know and what we should tell them, surely children are likewise internally divided.

There is, of course, a shocking gap between the children of the poor, who are undernourished, undereducated, and unhoused, and the children of the rich, who are often treated by their parents as a kind of living Lexus requiring the latest, most expensive accoutrements so their performance and commodity value will be obvious to all. The gulf between the children who are starving and those who can't be ripped away from their Nintendos is a worldwide scandal. Yet perhaps on some fundamental level, the children at both extremes are victims of the same pervasive erosion: of an idealism that held up childhood as a time of unassailable innocence and sanctuary from a hostile world. Those of us born during the great post-World War II baby boom grew up in a culture where this cherished ideal still held fast, and we were part of the generation that dismantled it. We are cynical enough to know that, at best, the ideal was imperfectly realized and, at worst, it was a myth that masked an underbelly of secret abuse and deceit. Yet we are reluctant to abandon it entirely—if only because we have as yet found no viable substitute (and not for want of trying). In an era when issues like sexual abuse and AIDS occupy our thoughts, many of us feel we can't afford to keep our children uninformed. But, as we inform them—if we are not preempted by the media or savvy peers—we also worry that we are robbing them of their childhood. Is childhood now obsolete, like the propeller plane or the rotary phone? None of us knows. But we do know that we can't retreat to the forced assumptions of the pre-sixties position, pretending adults and children exist in separate realms with no crossable borders, and no problems that can't be solved before dinner, bath, and bed. □

Among the world's poor, childhood remains largely an unaffordable luxury. The struggle for a living begins early, and youthful play is often laced with a despairing recklessness. In 1989, these teenagers from the slums of Rio de Janeiro were photographed enjoying the often deadly sport of "train surfing"—riding the roof of a speeding commuter train.

"Unprejudiced observation of so-called civilized man discloses that his fundamental coital pattern ... is that of other primates; however, his coital behavior may appear to be modified by social and spiritual factors."—**Dr. John Rock**

STORY OF THE YEAR

The First Birth-Control Pill

1 A sexual revolution was about to erupt and science made it possible: In 1960, the U.S. Food and Drug Administration approved the world's first effective oral contraceptive. Developed by American endocrinologist Gregory Goodwin Pincus, the Pill (as it came to be known) was one of the most culturally and demographically significant medications in history. Its effect, said Katherine McCormick, the heiress who helped support Pincus's research, was to give women mastery over "that ol' devil, the female reproductive system."

Pincus first became notorious in the 1930s, when he achieved in vitro fertilization of rabbit eggs. The feat earned him widespread vilification as a Dr. Frankenstein who aimed, as one reporter wrote, to create a world "where woman would be self-sufficient; man's value precisely zero." Denied tenure at Harvard, he and fellow endocrinologist Hudson Hoagland founded their own research facility, the Worcester Foundation for Experimental Biology, which was financed by private and government grants, and by the drug industry. There, in 1951, aided by biologist Min-Cheuh Chang, Pincus started testing the contraceptive value of the hormone progesterone. The Worcester experiments attracted the attention of Margaret Sanger, America's leading birth control advocate since the 1920s; Sanger notified her friend McCormick of the project. McCormick and G.D. Searle, the Chicago pharmaceutical firm, became Pincus's most generous benefactors.

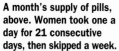

A month's supply of pills, above. Women took one a day for 21 consecutive days, then skipped a week.

It had long been known that progesterone suppressed ovulation in lab animals, apparently by causing a state of false pregnancy. To test the hormone's effects on women, Pincus enlisted Boston gynecologist John Rock, who was researching infertility. As a Roman Catholic, Rock was careful to distinguish "medical contraception" from "birth control." Nonetheless, he emerged as a winning spokesman for the Pill. "Being a good [Catholic] and as handsome as a god," Sanger wrote to a friend, "he can get away with just about anything."

In the midst of the Rock-Pincus experiments, a batch of synthetic progesterone was inadvertently contaminated with mestranol, an estrogenlike substance—a happy accident, as it turned out. The scientists discovered that the two hormones worked in tandem to block conception. Searle began manufacturing a progesterone-estrogen compound for extensive testing. This was the drug approved by the FDA in 1960, soon to become part of daily life for millions of women around the globe. **◂1915.2 ▸1974.M**

THE UNITED STATES

Kennedy Triumphs

2 In the 1960 presidential campaign, the Democratic candidate, a 43-year-old senator from Massachusetts, promised to "get this country moving again" after the economic sluggishness of the late fifties; he railed against the supposed "missile gap" with the Soviets, and called Americans to a "New Frontier" of social reform and international leadership. But John Fitzgerald Kennedy's narrow victory over Richard Nixon hinged on more than political issues. Kennedy's Catholicism played a role, as did the lavish funds furnished by patriarch (and former Roosevelt administration member) Joseph Kennedy. Above all, there was television.

JFK was a ruling-class anomaly, an Irish Catholic member of America's predominantly Anglo-Saxon Protestant elite. He exploited that background masterfully, tackling widespread anti-Catholic prejudice head-on, and presenting himself (with patrician Boston charm) as a natural leader of the downtrodden common man. His heroism in World War II and his beautiful wife, Jacqueline, enhanced his aura, and his ticket-balancing running mate, Lyndon Johnson, wooed southern voters with Texas folksiness. But the decisive moment in the race against Richard Nixon—vice president to the wildly popular Dwight Eisenhower, and himself widely admired as an anti-Communist crusader—came in the first of four televised debates (a brand-new political forum). Nixon, looking drawn and ill at ease, proved no match for his craggily handsome, confidently telegenic opponent.

In November, Kennedy won the election by just 118,000 votes (including some dubiously counted votes in Illinois and Texas). Inaugurated in January 1961, the new president (the youngest ever elected) projected a glamour and vigor that galvanized Americans and fascinated the world. The Kennedy era, for better or worse, would be one of adventure—from outer space to the battlefields of Vietnam. **◂1952.5 ▸1961.2**

On television, JFK outshone Nixon in the first debate, in Chicago *(above)*. Listeners who heard the debate on the radio felt that Nixon had performed better.

CENTRAL AFRICA

War in the Congo

3 During 75 years of colonial rule, the Belgian Congo's indigenous inhabitants had been allowed no share in government; by 1960, only 14 of the territory's

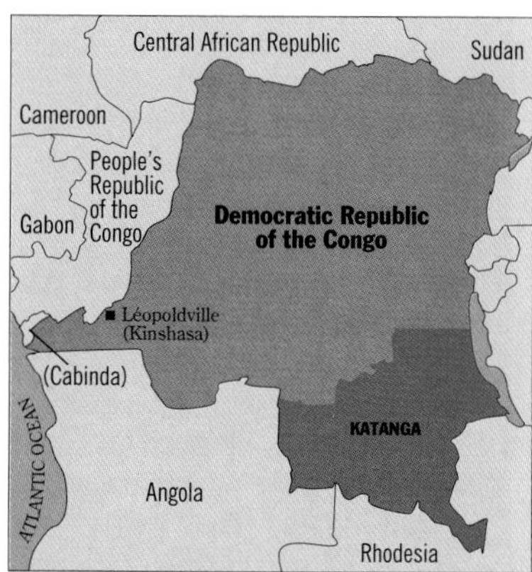

Katanga's attempted secession from the Congo was the first step toward civil war.

13 million blacks had a university education. Yet in June of that year, after holding hasty elections, Belgium—anxious to avoid a war with rebellious nationalists—pronounced the colony independent and left the new Republic of the Congo to its fate.

Fighting erupted immediately among the nation's dozens of ethnic groups, and the Congolese army mutinied against its white officers. As European civilians fled for their

ART & CULTURE: Books: *A Separate Peace* (John Knowles); *The Affair* (C.P. Snow); *To Bedlam and Part Way Back* (Anne Sexton); *The Rise and Fall of the Third Reich* (William L. Shirer) ... Music: "Puppy Love" (Paul Anka); "Itsy Bitsy Teenie Weenie Yellow Polka Dot Bikini" (Vance and Pockriss); *A Hand of Bridge* (Barber and Menotti) ... Painting & Sculpture: *Bathtub* (Joseph Beuys);

"It was by no means clear, even to those who worked on it, that it would see so many striking applications. And much undoubtedly lies ahead."—**Charles H. Townes, on the laser**

lives, Belgium dispatched paratroopers. Then mineral-rich Katanga province seceded, with Belgian backing. The United Nations sent 20,000 mostly African soldiers to help the Congo's beleaguered government; within three months they had restored a semblance of order.

By then, however, the government had splintered: President Joseph Kasavubu, envisioning the Congo as a loose confederation, opposed forcing Katanga into line—while Premier Patrice Lumumba, taking the opposite stance, brought in Soviet advisers for logistical assistance. In September, a pro-Kasavubu colonel, Joseph Mobutu, seized power, and Lumumba went into hiding. Mobutu ousted the Soviets; the Belgians departed, too, but left behind mercenaries who aided the Katangans.

In December—two weeks after the Kasavubu-Mobutu regime gained a seat at the UN—Mobutu's troops captured Lumumba. A new phase of the war was just beginning. ◂**1957.4** ▸**1961.4**

TECHNOLOGY

Laser Makes Its Mark

4 In 1960, Theodore Maiman, a physicist with the Hughes Research Laboratories in Miami, Florida, narrowly won the worldwide race to build the first operational laser. Maiman's device used a powerful flash lamp to stimulate the chromium atoms in a ruby crystal, producing a narrow beam of red light so concentrated that it heated the spot where it hit to a temperature greater than the sun's.

Maiman's breakthrough has had a profound impact on daily life. Compact discs, bar-code scanners, radar detectors, and computer printers all depend on laser technology. A laser beam can weld steel and drill 200 holes in the head of a pin. In communications, cables made of glass fibers transmit telephone, computer, and television signals via laser beams. One fiber-optic cable can carry the same amount of information as 20,000 copper telephone wires. In surgery, a laser incision tends to bleed less than a scalpel cut, making the technology useful for eye and brain surgery. Laser beams have been used to measure the distance from the earth to the moon.

But even though Maiman was the first to get a laser to work, the courtroom battle over who *invented* the technology became a landmark case in patent law. One contender was Gordon Gould, the scientist who coined the word "laser"—shorthand for "light amplification by the stimulated emission of radiation"—in 1957 while studying for his doctorate at Columbia University. Misinformed that a working model was needed to apply for a patent, Gould instead recorded his ideas in a notebook and had them notarized.

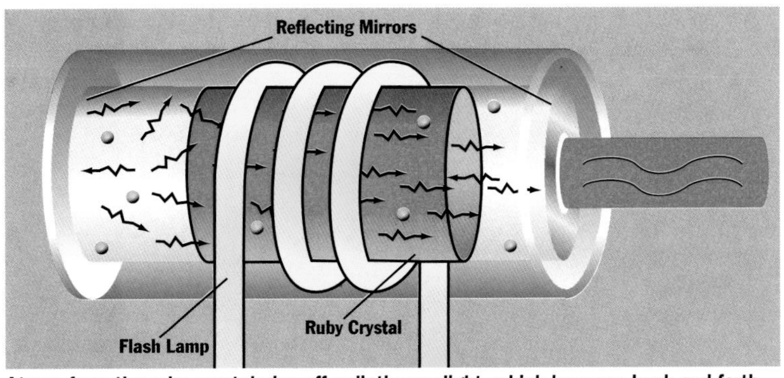

Atoms from the ruby crystal give off radiation as light, which bounces back and forth between mirrors. The accumulated energy is then concentrated in a narrow laser beam.

At the same time, however, Charles Townes, developer of the maser (a precursor of the laser that used microwaves instead of light), was developing the laser concept with his brother-in-law, Arthur Schawlow, at Columbia. Although Gould eventually realized his error and filed an application with the U.S. Patent Office, Townes and Schawlow had beat him to the paperwork by nine months. Twenty years later, Gould was awarded patents for some of his laser-related concepts, but the legal wrangling continued for years afterward. ▸**1983.M**

ESPIONAGE

The U-2 Incident

5 Central Intelligence Agency pilot Francis Gary Powers was cruising ten miles above the U.S.S.R. on May 1, 1960, when a Soviet missile felled his Lockheed U-2 spy plane. As the Eisenhower administration scrambled to explain the untimely incident—it occurred just weeks before a long-planned Four Powers summit in Paris—Soviet-American relations plunged to a new Cold War low.

U.S. pilots had been flying regular reconnaissance missions over the Soviet Union since 1956. Although Soviet authorities knew about the flights, they could do nothing to stop them: U-2 planes flew at an altitude beyond the reach of early Soviet missiles. But by 1960, when Powers took off from Pakistan, Soviet military technology had caught up with the U-2.

Soviet premier Khrushchev announced the incident on May 5, neglecting to say that Powers had been taken alive. U.S. officials indignantly claimed that the downed U-2 was a civilian craft and had somehow drifted into Soviet airspace while conducting weather research over Turkey. Khrushchev then played his trump card: Powers was in captivity and had confessed. Even the President's promise to suspend U-2 flights could not save the Paris summit, which ended with Khrushchev's suggesting that Eisenhower be impeached.

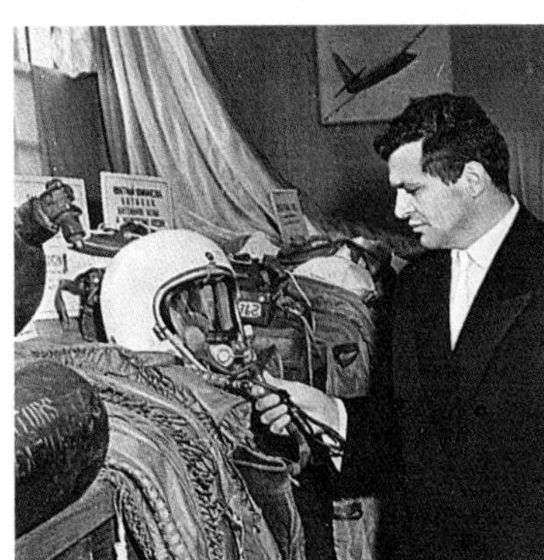
Captured pilot Gary Powers, awaiting trial in the Soviet Union, examines the remains of his airplane.

In a trial broadcast worldwide, the Soviets convicted Powers of espionage and sentenced him to ten years. Widely vilified in his homeland for pleading guilty (taking the "suicide pill" he had with him, many felt, would have been the patriotic thing to do), Powers was exchanged in 1962 for the Soviet spy Rudolph Abel, who'd been arrested in the United States. ◂**1959.4** ▸**1962.5**

BIRTHS

Andrew Albert Christian Edward, U.K. prince.

Said Aouita, Moroccan runner.

Kenneth Branagh, U.K. actor.

Tim Burton, U.S. filmmaker.

John Elway, U.S. football player.

Daryl Hannah, U.S. actress.

Paul Hewson (Bono), Irish singer.

Joan Jett, U.S. singer.

Jim Kelly, U.S. football player.

Diego Maradona, Argentine soccer player.

Branford Marsalis, U.S. musician.

Sean Penn, U.S. actor.

Cal Ripken, Jr., U.S. baseball player.

DEATHS

Roy Chapman Andrews, U.S. archaeologist.

Albert Camus, French writer.

Arthur Fleming, U.K. engineer.

Clark Gable, U.S. actor.

Oscar Hammerstein II, U.S. songwriter.

Ali Mahir Pasha, Egyptian prime minister.

Boris Pasternak, U.S.S.R. writer.

Wilhelm Pieck, German Communist president.

Emily Post, U.S. writer.

John D. Rockefeller, Jr., U.S. philanthropist.

Mack Sennett, U.S. filmmaker.

Francis Everett Townsend, U.S. physician and politician.

Leonard Warren, U.S. singer.

Joseph N. Welch, U.S. lawyer.

Richard Wright, U.S. writer.

Walking Man **(Alberto Giacometti) ... Film: *The Apartment* (Billy Wilder); *Spartacus* (Stanley Kubrick); *L'Avventura* (Michelangelo Antonioni) ... Theater: *Toys in the Attic* (Lillian Hellman); *The Dumb Waiter* (Harold Pinter); *The Fantasticks* (Schmidt and Jones); *Camelot* (Lerner and Loewe); *Oliver!* (Lionel Bart) ... TV: *The Andy Griffith Show*; *The Bob Newhart Show*.**

NEW IN 1960

Heart pacemaker.

Retirement community (Sun City, Arizona).

Librium (Roche Labs).

Felt-tip pen (Pentel).

Beverages in aluminum cans.

Weather satellite *(Tiros I)*.

Nuclear aircraft carrier *(Enterprise)*.

All-transistor portable TV (Sony).

IN THE UNITED STATES

▶SIT-INS BEGIN—In February, four freshmen from North Carolina A&T, an all-black school, walked into the local Woolworth's in Greensboro, sat down at the all-white lunch counter, and refused to budge until they'd been served. By the next day, some 85 activists had joined the protest. From Greensboro, the sit-in movement spread to other cities and to new locations—stores, theaters—opening a new phase of the civil rights movement. ◀1957.M ▶1961.M

▶ORBISON'S LONELY CRY—To a fusion of country and western and rhythm and blues, rock balladeer Roy

Orbison added his own haunting, high-pitched wail. The song was "Only the Lonely," and with it Orbison in 1960 had his first international hit. ◀1955.M

▶SABIN'S VACCINE—Polish-born American physician Albert Sabin, one of the world's premier immunologists, had his greatest contribution approved by the FDA in 1960: the oral polio vaccine,

South African police firing on local protesters in Sharpeville. Sixty-nine people were killed.

SOUTHERN AFRICA

The Sharpeville Massacre

6 Touted by the government as a model black community (some homes even had running water), the South African township of Sharpeville in 1960 became a symbol of apartheid's brutality. On March 21, national police fired on unarmed Africans demonstrating peacefully against the segregated police state. The fusillade killed 69 and wounded 178. Sharpeville focused international attention on South Africa, and prompted the antiapartheid movement to end its reliance on nonviolent protest.

In the wake of the massacre, as demonstrations spread throughout the black townships, Premier Hendrik Verwoerd's National Party government imposed martial law and outlawed the African National Congress (ANC) and the Pan-Africanist Congress. By May, 20,000 blacks had been jailed, and the antiapartheid groups had gone underground. ANC president Albert Luthuli received the 1960 Nobel Peace Prize, but his young deputies were considering other paths. "Is it politically correct to continue preaching peace and nonviolence," asked Nelson Mandela, 33, "when dealing with a government whose barbaric practices have brought so much suffering and misery to Africans?" A cycle of terrorism and heightening repression soon began.

Increasingly ostracized abroad, South Africa quit the British Commonwealth in 1961. Verwoerd's war against black activists peaked in 1963, when police raided the headquarters of an ANC splinter group. Among the leaders captured and sentenced to life imprisonment was Mandela. Three years later, a deranged white stabbed Verwoerd to death on the floor of Parliament. But his party, and his policies, still reigned. **◀1948.1 ▶1976.4**

ENVIRONMENTALISM

A Beast's Return to the Bush

7 The most popular wildlife story of its era, translated into 25 languages, *Born Free* was a catalyst for the nascent environmentalist movement. Written by Joy Adamson, the 1960 book (which later became a popular film with a hit theme song) was an account of her and her husband George's work with African animals—particularly a lovable lioness named Elsa.

Author and animal enthusiast Joy Adamson with the lioness she made famous.

The Adamsons were not trained naturalists, but simply European expatriates with a passion for wild beasts. Joy, an Austrian, and George, a Briton, worked for Kenya's game department. Forced to kill a lioness that had been terrorizing villages, George adopted her cub. Instead of sending the orphan—Elsa—to a zoo, the Adamsons gradually trained her to live in the wild again. The big cat's saga captured the hearts of millions, but the Adamsons' affection for each other eventually cooled: George went on to found a wildlife-rehabilitation program in a remote region of Kenya, and Joy declined to follow him. Both, however, remained committed to endangered species—even to the point of dying for them: Joy was killed by a disgruntled laborer at her leopard camp in 1980, George by a poacher in 1989. **◀1905.5 ▶1987.9**

THE HOLOCAUST

Eichmann Captured

8 On the night of May 11, 1960, in Buenos Aires, Israeli secret agents wrestled a middle-aged man into a waiting car. Days later, he identified himself to a court in Jaffa, Israel: "I am Adolf Eichmann." The chief of the Gestapo's Office of Jewish Affairs—the bureaucrat who oversaw the Holocaust, even choosing the poison for Hitler's gas chambers—was a prisoner in the Jewish state.

Eichmann had lived under assumed names since escaping from an internment camp at the end of World War II. In 1950, he made his way to Argentina, then governed by Hitler admirer Juan Perón. Nazi-hunters (and concentration camp survivors) Simon Wiesenthal and Tuvia Friedmann employed brilliant sleuthing to find him. But Eichmann's abduction—and the questionable propriety of trying him in a nation that hadn't existed when his crimes were committed—drew objections from even the World Zionist Organization. Israeli president David Ben-Gurion stood firm, citing the "supreme moral justification" for violating Eichmann's and Argentina's rights.

At the four-month trial before a special three-judge court in Jerusalem in 1961, witnesses detailed the efficiency with which he'd orchestrated the extermination of millions. Eichmann, however, claimed he'd only followed orders. "I am not the monster I am made out to be," he said. "This mass slaughter is solely the

SPORTS: Baseball: World Series, Pittsburgh Pirates (Bill Mazeroski) defeat New York Yankees, 4–3 ... Olympics held in Squaw Valley, Calif., and Rome ... Football: NFL, Philadelphia Eagles defeat Green Bay Packers, 17–13; AFL, Houston Oilers defeat Los Angeles Chargers, 24–16 (game played January 2, 1961) ... Basketball: NBA, Boston Celtics defeat St. Louis Hawks, 4–3.

"In the most splendorous of dawns,/Happy as a child's smile,/A dream transformed itself into reality,/The most fantastic city came into being,/Brasília, the Capital of Hope."—**From Brasília's hymn, "The Capital of Hope"**

responsibility of political leaders." He was found guilty, and was hanged on May 31, 1962, at a prison near Tel Aviv. **◂1946.V ▸1963.14**

BRAZIL

An Urban Dream City

9 French writer André Malraux dubbed Brasília "The Capital of Hope." Unveiled in April 1960, the brand-new city represented the fulfillment of a long-standing national goal (to relocate the capital from Rio de Janeiro to the interior) and—seemingly—of President Juscelino Kubitschek's promise that a democratized Brazil would achieve "50 years' progress in five."

Spurred on by Kubitschek's nationalistic charisma, workers built Brasília in the middle of remote grassland. French-born architect Lúcio Costa, a disciple of Le Corbusier, arranged the city in the shape of an airplane, with government buildings (many designed by Brazil's foremost architect, Oscar Niemeyer) as the fuselage and residential complexes as the wings. Uniform apartment blocks surrounded by pedestrian space would eliminate class distinctions. To prevent traffic congestion, highways would replace streets, with ramps leading to individual buildings. Such luminaries as Malraux, Fidel Castro, Dwight Eisenhower, and Aldous Huxley came to witness Brasília's birth.

But the utopia proved singularly unlivable. Lookalike buildings, addresses that read like serial numbers, and the grid of highways discouraged strolling—and socializing. Real estate speculation and the emergence of poor and wealthy suburbs defeated the ideal of classlessness. As Costa later observed, "You don't solve the social problems of a country"—poverty, urban overpopulation, rampant pollution—"by simply moving its capital." By 1964, Kubitschek's optimism and populism had given way to repressive military rule. **◂1937.4 ▸1964.M**

CYPRUS

The Reluctant Republic

10 Britain granted independence to its colony of Cyprus in 1960, after four years of guerrilla war and more than a year of negotiations (brokered by London) between Greece and Turkey. Yet the Cypriots themselves were barely consulted on the arrangement, and the island's contending ethnic groups put down their weapons only briefly.

The enmity between Cyprus's Greek majority and Turkish minority had grown out of Britain's policy of divide-and-rule (which had favored Turkish Cypriots politically), and the century-old movement for enosis—unification of formerly Greek territories with the motherland. Geography complicated matters: Cyprus was only 40 miles from Turkey, 480 from Greece. Greek Cypriots had fought the British for enosis since 1955. But ethnic Turkish guerrillas had fought to partition Cyprus, and to unite their zone with Turkey. In the end, Britain washed its hands of the mess—retaining two military bases and the right to intervene.

Jubilant crowds surround Archbishop Makarios's car upon his return to Cyprus.

Cyprus's new constitution guaranteed an ethnic Greek president and an ethnic Turkish vice president; Greeks would outnumber Turks in government by about two to one. But Greek Cypriots saw their rivals' share of power as disproportionate (only 18 percent of Cyprus's 650,000 people were of Turkish descent); Turkish Cypriots, in turn, complained that ethnic quotas in the civil service were not enforced, and insisted on a segregated army. (Consequently, no army was formed.) And when the President, Greek Orthodox Archbishop Makarios III, tried to reduce the ethnic Turks' privileges, war returned to Cyprus. **◂1959.M ▸1974.5**

Le Corbusier praised Brasília's "spirit of invention." Later, a critic called it "a ghost town populated by very reluctant ghosts."

IN THE UNITED STATES

made from a live, weakened strain of the virus. It was more effective and longer-lasting than Jonas Salk's killed-virus vaccine. ◂1955.1

▶NFL COMMISSIONER—Alvin Ray "Pete" Rozelle was elected commissioner of the National Football League (NFL) in January. Under his stewardship, professional football (which had given birth to the American Football League the previous year) grew into the most popular and biggest-money sport in the U.S., and Rozelle became the country's top sports executive. Among his most visionary moves: In 1961, he lobbied for federal legislation that allowed the NFL to sell broadcasting rights to a single television network. ▸1967.M

▶JAZZ GOES TO COLLEGE—The Dave Brubeck Quartet's 1960 album, *Time Out,* helped make jazz safe for the middle class, especially on college campuses. Featuring songs in

different time signatures with influences ranging from Bach to Arnold Schoenberg (with whom pianist Brubeck had studied), the album was a "crossover" success. One of the cuts, "Take Five"—showcasing alto saxophonist Paul Desmond—broke into the pop top 25. ◂1959.M ▸1964.6

▶U.S.-JAPANESE TREATY—Japan's close postwar ties with the U.S. alienated the dominant Communist states—the Soviet Union, China, North Korea—and created a tense situation in the demilitarized island nation. In 1960, the U.S. and Japan renegotiated their 1952 mutual-security treaty (signed after the restoration of Japan's sovereignty). The new agreement allowed the U.S. to maintain its extensive military installations in Japan, and to intervene against foreign (i.e., Communist) aggression. Many Japanese—uneasy about the past consequences of their country's militarism—resented the treaty, which scuttled trade with China and North Korea. But geopolitics prevailed. ◂1946.3 ▸1988.12

POLITICS & BUSINESS: GNP: $503.7. billion ... U.S. population: 179,323,175 ... John F. Kennedy elected president, defeating Richard M. Nixon ... More than 70,000 people take part in sit-ins in more than 100 U.S. cities.

"If I made Cinderella, *the audience would be looking out for a body in the coach."*—**Alfred Hitchcock**

AROUND THE WORLD

▶OPEC BORN—The formation in 1960 of the Organization of Petroleum Exporting Countries was spurred by two events the previous year: the major oil companies' decision to cut prices twice without consulting host governments, and America's adoption of protectionist quotas sharply reducing imports. The nations most dependent on petroleum income—Iran, Iraq, Kuwait, Saudi Arabia, and Venezuela—decided to band together to coordinate export policies. OPEC's birth reflected broad changes in global economics but received little international notice. It would be a dozen years before the organization was used as an offensive weapon. ◀1933.M ▶1973.1

▶MARATHON RECORD—It stands as one of the great achievements in Olympic history: Running barefoot through the streets of Rome, unheralded Ethiopian distance runner Abebe Bikila won the 1960 marathon, setting a new world record of 2:15:16.2. Said Bikila, the first black African to win an Olympic event, "I could have gone around the [26.2-mile] course again." Four years later Bikila duplicated his feat, this time in shoes. ◀1954.8

▶CEYLONESE GROUNDBREAKER—Widow of slain prime minister of Ceylon (Sri Lanka) S.W.R.D. Bandaranaike, Sirimavo Bandaranaike entered politics herself in 1960. Leading her late husband's party to a landslide victory in national elections, she became Ceylon's—and the world's—first woman prime minister. ▶1987.M

▶LAWRENCE LIBERATED—In 1960, Penguin publishers, impressed with a U.S. court decision the previous year, decided to publish what is perhaps the English language's best known "dirty" book—D.H. Lawrence's long-banned *Lady Chatterley's Lover.* A court in London concluded, as had the one in the U.S., that the novel had redeeming value. The decision heralded a new era of freedom in publishing. ◀1934.M

Janet Leigh in *Psycho*'s famous shower scene—one of cinema's most terrifying.

FILM

Voyeurism at the Box Office

11 In 1960, two commercially successful, critically acclaimed British directors each released a violent film centering on a voyeuristic pervert. One man's career was destroyed; the other's was rejuvenated. Both films are now considered classics.

"The only really satisfactory way to dispose of *Peeping Tom,*" suggested one reviewer, "would be to flush it swiftly down the nearest sewer." Harsh words for a film by Michael Powell, director of the beloved *The Red Shoes.* But *Peeping Tom* was undeniably disturbing: Its protagonist, a nondescript movie-studio camera technician, stabs young women, films their death throes, and gets his kicks from screening them. Later filmmakers and critics have hailed the movie as a startling exploration of the connections between the roles of filmmaker and audience, murderer and victim. But its scandalous content made Powell a pariah, and effectively ended his career.

With *Psycho,* most critics agreed, that master of suspense Alfred Hitchcock (*Rear Window, North by Northwest*) had gone too far. The film revolves around Norman Bates (Anthony Perkins), a mild-mannered motel keeper who dresses up in his late mother's clothes and murders unlucky visitors to his hostelry. In *Psycho*'s most sensational sequence, Norman watches though a peephole as a young woman (Janet Leigh) undresses; minutes later, "Mother" knifes her in the shower. (The scene, one of cinema's most famous, contains 70 shots in less than a minute.) As in *Peeping Tom,* the audience is made to share the voyeur-murderer's thrill. Essayist and critic Dwight Macdonald thought the movie reflected "a mean, sly, sadistic little mind," but *Psycho* was a box-office smash. Today, scholars praise its visual sophistication, its thematic complexity—and its spine-tingling scariness. **◀1951.7 ▶1967.9**

LITERATURE

Updike's Everyman

12 Although his mastery of the elegant sentence and the subtly drawn character placed him solidly in the literary elite, John Updike was most concerned with mainstream American suburban culture. "When I write," he declared, "I aim in my mind not toward New York but toward a vague spot a little to the east of Kansas." Updike struck the bull's-eye with his critically and popularly acclaimed second novel, *Rabbit, Run,* published in 1960.

John Updike, chronicler of suburban angst, in his Massachusetts backyard.

Having come of age during the post-Depression economic boom, Updike sensed that social decay was imminent. His title character, Harry "Rabbit" Angstrom, epitomizes that dread. An Army veteran and former high school basketball star living in a working-class commuter town, Rabbit finds little nourishment in the 1950s panaceas of family life, religion, and the pursuit of the American Dream. Feeling trapped by his duties as a husband and father, he attempts to recapture the sense of freedom and power he enjoyed in his glory days by abandoning his pregnant, alcoholic wife for another woman. When his wife gives birth, he returns, but tragedy follows: His wife, drunk, accidentally drowns their newborn daughter.

Rabbit's angst (conveyed innovatively in the present tense) struck a chord as the conformist Eisenhower era gave way to an uncertain future. Updike maintained his ascendancy into the 1990s, with a steady outpouring of novels, stories, essays, and poems. And he advanced the Angstrom saga in three more novels: *Rabbit Redux* (1971), *Rabbit Is Rich* (1981), and *Rabbit at Rest* (1990). **▶1969.13**

DANCE

Let's Do the Twist

13 The dance that swept the globe in 1960 embodied two of the qualities that made the dawning decade revolutionary. Heralding an era of unbridled individualism, the twist was free-form and could be performed independently of a partner. And it centered on a pelvic swivel—an apt opening gesture for an age that would defy old rules of sexual propriety. Invented in 1959 by young blacks dancing to Hank Ballard's rock 'n' roll song of the same name, the twist was popularized by Chubby Checker. After he sang his version of the number and performed the motions on *American Bandstand,* it was embraced by white teens. Checker's recording, less artfully sung but more crisply produced than Ballard's, topped the U.S. pop charts; the song hit number one again a year later, when the dance became a fad among adults.

The twist spawned spin-offs: the peppermint twist (named for Manhattan's Peppermint Lounge, where celebrities like Elizabeth Taylor and Richard Burton wriggled to the beat), the mashed potato, the frug, and countless others. Such dances soon accompanied Beatlemania; they enlivened discotheques—new, high-tech nightclubs emphasizing records over live performance—from London to Luanda. Later in the sixties, the twist evolved even further, as nameless dances with amorphous movements became fashionable, in keeping with the anarchic hippie ethos that made all standardized steps passé. **◀1957.M ▶1978.5**

Chubby Checker, a 20-year-old from Philadelphia, made the twist an international craze.

NOBEL PRIZES: Peace: Albert Luthuli (South African; president of African National Congress) ... Literature: Saint-John Perse (French; poet) ... Chemistry: Willard Frank Libby (U.S.; radiocarbon dating) ... Medicine: Frank Macfarlane Burnet and P.B. Medawar (Australian, U.K.; acquired immunological tolerance) ... Physics: Donald A. Glaser (U.S.; bubble chamber).

A VOICE FROM 1960

Madison Avenue Thinks Small

Advertisement for Volkswagen, by Helmut Krone and Julian Koenig, 1960

Luxury-car manufacturer Ferdinand Porsche dreamed up the Volkswagen in the 1920s, and the first postwar models rolled out of a German plant in 1945. But the "people's car" didn't truly take off in the United States until the early 1960s, thanks to an inspired advertising campaign launched by the Doyle Dane Bernbach agency. In a car culture in which bigger equaled better, DDB's forthright and witty campaign presented the Beetle to advantage: "Think Small," advised one ad—as in small price, small repair bills, small insurance premiums. Against the gaudy competition (a Buick, for example, carried 44 pounds of chrome), the bug stood out: a simple, reliable (and cute) vehicle that could be driven 32 miles on a gallon of gas. (American cars averaged ten miles per gallon.) "The Lemon," created in 1960 by the DDB team of art director Helmut Krone and copywriter Julian Koenig, extolled the carmaker's attention to detail. ◂1936.M

Lemon.

This Volkswagen missed the boat.

The chrome strip on the glove compartment is blemished and must be replaced. Chances are you wouldn't have noticed it; Inspector Kurt Kroner did.

There are 3,389 men at our Wolfsburg factory with only one job: to inspect Volkswagens at each stage of production. (3000 Volkswagens are produced daily; there are more inspectors than cars.)

Every shock absorber is tested (spot checking won't do), every windshield is scanned. VWs have been rejected for surface scratches barely visible to the eye.

Final inspection is really something! VW inspectors run each car off the line onto the Funktionsprüfstand (car test stand), tote up 189 check points, gun ahead to the automatic brake stand, and say "no" to one VW out of fifty.

This preoccupation with detail means the VW lasts longer and requires less maintenance, by and large, than other cars. (It also means a used VW depreciates less than any other car.)

We pluck the lemons; you get the plums.

"Today the endangered frontier of freedom runs through divided Berlin."—**President Kennedy, on July 22, 1961, three weeks before the Berlin Wall was erected**

STORY OF THE YEAR

A Wall Divides Berlin

1 A grim convoy of tanks and troops wound through eastern Berlin in the predawn hours of August 13, 1961. By sunrise, East German soldiers had stretched barbed wire across the city, cutting off the Communist sector from the capitalist. The wire was soon replaced by a network of concrete walls and electrified fences, guarded by armed men, dogs, and minefields—a 30-mile-long barrier separating German from German. Churchill's Iron Curtain metaphor had become reality.

Ostensibly built to keep out saboteurs and subversives, the Berlin Wall was in fact meant to keep East Germans in. Since 1949, 2.5 million had fled the economic hardships and political repression of Germany's Communist half, creating labor shortages and a "brain drain" of professionals and skilled workers. West Berlin, an island of democracy and capitalism in the midst of East Germany, was the principal escape route. (Since thousands of eastern Berliners worked in western Berlin before the wall was built, defectors could usually evade detection.)

East German soldiers block off East Berlin with barbed wire.

Through the years, the Soviets had periodically demanded that all Berlin be made a "free city," with both Western and Soviet occupation troops withdrawn—but the Western powers, fearing a total Communist takeover, had refused. In June 1961, Khrushchev threatened to use nuclear weapons if the "Berlin question" was not swiftly resolved. When heightening tension accelerated the stampede of illegal émigrés—30,000 East Germans defected in July—Communist authorities decided to stem the flow by force. The wall was their solution. Henceforth, travel eastward would be subject to tight restrictions and travel westward, banned.

Though crowds of angry West Berliners confronted the wall builders (only to be dispersed with tear gas and water cannons) and the United States sent in extra troops as a symbolic gesture, fear of retaliation ruled out more forceful measures: A trade embargo against East Berlin was considered, but the Communists vowed to blockade West Berlin in response. Eventually, the East Germans encircled all of West Berlin with a fence topped by watchtowers. Travel restrictions for Westerners eased somewhat in the 1980s, but the wall—and all it stood for—remained intact for nearly three decades. **◂1955.4 ▸1989.1**

President John F. Kennedy giving his inaugural address, January 20, 1961.

THE UNITED STATES

The Kennedy Challenge

2 On a freezing January day in 1961, after eight years of government by a golf-loving, avuncular retired general, John F. Kennedy stepped to the inaugural podium in Washington: young, patrician, ruggedly glamorous, and seemingly afire with a sense of mission. The arrival of a new era was evident in Kennedy's precedent-breaking invitation to a poet (weathered fellow New Englander Robert Frost) to deliver a dedication, and in the crowd of artists and scholars seated in the VIP section. In his speech, Kennedy delivered a series of eloquent challenges to his nation and the world.

"[T]he torch has been passed to a new generation of Americans," JFK declared, "born in this century, tempered by war, disciplined by a hard and bitter peace." He exhorted his compatriots to "pay any price, bear any burden, meet any hardship, support any friend, oppose any foe to assure the survival and the success of liberty." And he urged them to "ask not what your country can do for you—ask what you can do for your country."

Despite his tone of Cold War bellicosity, Kennedy pledged to negotiate with the Soviets, and issued a stirring call to altruism—a vow to aid "those people in the huts and villages of half the globe struggling to break the bonds of mass misery." One of Kennedy's first acts in office was to establish the Peace Corps, an agency that sent tens of thousands of idealistic young people to developing nations (mostly as teachers) to help those populations help themselves. In the 1,007 days before an assassin's bullet cut him down, Kennedy would govern with all the belligerence, diplomacy, humanitarianism, and charisma that characterized his inaugural address. In the process, he set off political earthquakes around the globe. **◂1960.2 ▸1961.5**

EXPLORATION

First Man in Space

3 On April 12, 1961, Soviet air force major Yuri Gagarin became the first man in space. After orbiting once around the earth (in one hour and 48 minutes), Gagarin, 27, parachuted into a Russian pasture where his *Vostok 1* capsule lay smoldering with the heat of reentry. A gregarious, unassuming man, Gagarin became an international hero and a goodwill ambassador for Moscow.

The first American in space, Commander Alan Shepard, Jr., made a 15-minute suborbital flight on May 5, in *Freedom 7*. But second place in the space race meant last place, and something more was needed to bolster national pride. On May 25, President Kennedy threw down the gauntlet, vowing that America would land a man on the moon by the end of the decade.

The Soviets, however, long maintained their lead. Captain Virgil Grissom made a second suborbital flight in July but narrowly escaped drowning when the explosive bolts of his capsule's hatch blew out during his Atlantic splashdown. Then, in August, cosmonaut Gherman Titov spent the first full day in orbit. Lieutenant Colonel John Glenn finally circled the earth in February 1962—but later that year, the Soviets orbited two one-man capsules at once, in tandem. In 1963 they sent up the first woman, Valentina Tereshkova, and the next year orbited the first crew of three;

Cosmonauts were heroes in the Eastern bloc. At right, Romanian stamps in honor of Gagarin and Titov.

ART & CULTURE: Books: ***Riders in the Chariot*** **(Patrick White);** ***The Agony and the Ecstasy*** **(Irving Stone);** ***The Prime of Miss Jean Brodie*** **(Muriel Spark);** ***The Moviegoer*** **(Walker Percy);** ***Franny and Zooey*** **(J.D. Salinger) ... Music: "Crying" (Melson and Orbison); "Moon River" (Mancini and Mercer);** ***The Wings of the Dove*** **(Douglas Moore);** ***Canticle of the Sun*** **(Roy Harris) ... Painting & Sculpture:** ***Stripes*** **(Morris Louis);**

"Lumumba is bad for the government either way. If he loses, he will wreck it; if he wins, he will swallow it."
—Belgian official, before the assassination of Congolese premier Patrice Lumumba

in 1965 Aleksei Leonov became the first human to walk in space. But in March 1966, two U.S. craft achieved the first docking in orbit —and the Americans began to pull ahead. **◂1957.1 ▸1963.M**

CENTRAL AFRICA

Lumumba Is Murdered

4 The Congolese civil war had become a three-way fight by 1961: Government troops under strongman Joseph Mobutu, forces loyal to imprisoned premier Patrice Lumumba, and Moise Tshombe's Katangan separatists all battled one another. (A separate ethnic war raged in Kasai province, where Mobutu's troops sided with the majority Luluas and UN forces protected the minority Balubas.) But the anti-Soviet Mobutu, who favored limited autonomy for Katanga and other provinces, had more in common with the Belgian-backed Tshombe than with the Soviet-supported Lumumba, who insisted on a unitary state. In January, Mobutu and Tshombe eliminated their mutual foe. Belgian mercenaries "kidnapped" Lumumba from Congolese custody and delivered him to the Katangans. He was killed, the Katangans claimed, while trying to escape.

Lumumba's murder provoked outrage in the Third World and the Soviet bloc, and moved the UN Security Council to consider full-scale intervention. Chastened, the belligerents (except Lumumba's successor, Antoine Gizenga) began negotiations. But the talks went nowhere, and in April, Tshombe was arrested by the central government. While in jail, he agreed to bring Katanga into a Congolese federation—but changed his mind upon his release. In September UN secretary-general Dag Hammarskjöld ordered his troops into action against the Katangans and their Belgian helpers. But the poorly prepared peacekeepers made little headway. Flying in to encourage them, Hammarskjöld was killed in a plane crash.

Both Washington and Moscow supported the UN effort. (The Soviets hoped that Gizenga, and not the American-backed Mobutu, would benefit.) Nonetheless, the war dragged on until 1963, when Tshombe agreed in earnest to a federation. He got his reward the following year: Mobutu's figurehead president, Joseph Kasavubu, made the Katangan the Congo's prime minister. **◂1960.3**

Followers of Lumumba mourn the slain premier at his requiem mass in Cairo.

CUBA

The Bay of Pigs Invasion

5 Since seizing power in 1959, Cuba's Fidel Castro had repeatedly prophesied that the United States would intervene militarily to crush his anti-imperialist revolution, and he vowed to obliterate the invaders. They came on April 17, 1961, to Playa Girón on the Bay of Pigs—1,500 right-wing Cuban exiles, trained by the U.S. Central Intelligence Agency, carrying American weapons, and delivered by American ships. Castro kept his promise: Within 72 hours, 400 of the attackers were dead, and the survivors had surrendered. Americans, lamented one U.S. commentator, "look like fools to our friends, rascals to our enemies, and incompetents to the rest."

President Kennedy had authorized the Bay of Pigs invasion (a plan inherited from Eisenhower) only after prolonged debate within his cabinet. CIA officials had predicted—based on the exodus of thousands of well-off Cubans to America—that the attack would spur a mass uprising. But most Cubans, in fact, were enthusiastically pro-Fidel. Castro's expropriations of U.S. property and his anti-Yankee fulminations stirred nationalist pride; his programs—literacy training, free medical care, housing construction, land reform, the promotion of racial and sexual equality—promised to improve the lives of the impoverished majority. The closing of Havana's casinos and brothels, and the executions of 550 officials of the bloody Batista dictatorship, were widely applauded. Earlier harassment, including terrorist bombings and a U.S. economic blockade, had only stiffened Cuban resolve.

Castro and a swarm of journalists examine the remains of U.S. airplanes that crashed at Playa Girón, in Cuba.

Kennedy accepted the blame for the botched invasion, but assured the defeated rebels they would run Cuba one day. (The United States ultimately paid a $53 million ransom in food and medicine for their release.) Castro, for his part, declared allegiance to the Soviets—and announced for the first time that his nation was on the road to communism. **◂1959.1 ▸1962.5**

BIRTHS

Wayne Gretzky, Canadian hockey player.

Greg LeMond, U.S. cyclist.

Carl Lewis, U.S. track and field athlete.

Dan Marino, U.S. football player.

Wynton Marsalis, U.S. musician.

Isaac Mizrahi, U.S. fashion designer.

Eddie Murphy, U.S. comedian.

Isiah Thomas, U.S. basketball player.

Steve Young, U.S. football player.

DEATHS

Ty Cobb, U.S. baseball player.

Gary Cooper, U.S. actor.

Marion Davies, U.S. actress.

Lee de Forest, U.S. inventor.

Luigi Einaudi, Italian president.

Miriam Wallace "Ma" Ferguson, U.S. governor.

Dag Hammarskjöld, Swedish diplomat.

Dashiell Hammett, U.S. writer.

Learned Hand, U.S. jurist.

Moss Hart, U.S. playwright.

Ernest Hemingway, U.S. writer.

George S. Kaufman, U.S. playwright.

Patrice Lumumba, Congolese prime minister.

Chico Marx, U.S. comedian.

Anna Mary Robertson "Grandma" Moses, U.S. painter.

Muhammad V, Moroccan king.

Eero Saarinen, Finnish-U.S. architect.

Erwin Schrödinger, Austrian physicist.

James Thurber, U.S. writer.

Rafael Leonidas Trujillo Molina, Dominican president.

Max Weber, Russian-U.S. painter.

Ahmed Zogu, Albanian king.

Magic Base (Piero Manzoni) ... Film: *West Side Story* (Robert Wise); *Jules et Jim* (François Truffaut); *Last Year at Marienbad* (Alain Resnais); *Judgment at Nuremberg* (Stanley Kramer) ... Theater: *The Night of the Iguana* (Tennessee Williams); *Rhinoceros* (Eugène Ionesco); *How to Succeed in Business Without Really Trying* (Mead and Loesser) ... TV: *The Avengers*; *Wide World of Sports*; *The Dick Van Dyke Show*.

"I predict you will sink step by step into a bottomless military and political quagmire."—**Charles de Gaulle to John F. Kennedy, on Vietnam, 1961**

NEW IN 1961

Electric toothbrush.

The U.S. Peace Corps.

Certificates of Deposit.

Coffee-Mate coffee lightener.

Valium.

IN THE UNITED STATES

▶FREEDOM RIDERS—To underscore the discrepancy between the law and the continued reality of segregation, seven black and six white "freedom riders" chosen by the Congress of Racial Equality (CORE) boarded a couple of buses in May and set off from Washington, D.C., for New Orleans. One bus made it to Anniston before it was stoned

and firebombed; the other was attacked in Birmingham, Alabama, by a gang of bigots who ferociously beat the riders. The states' failure to stop the brutality caused national outrage; by summer's end, more than 300 freedom riders had risked death in the pursuit of racial equality. ◀1960.M ▶1962.M

▶COMPUTER AGE MUSIC—American mathematician turned musician Milton Babbitt was among the first composers to use computer technology to explore musical structure. His cerebral *Composition for Synthesizer* (1961) stands as a landmark of electronic music. Applying the 12-tone system pioneered in the 1920s by Arnold Schoenberg to all the constituent parts of music—timbre, rhythm, and dynamics, as well as to harmony and melody—Babbitt created "total serialization." ◀1912.11 ▶1964.M

The Gia Long B settlement site—one of South Vietnam's "strategic hamlets."

VIETNAM

U.S. Increases Commitment

6 The policies that would lead America into its most controversial war emerged in 1961, as President Kennedy sought to make up for the Bay of Pigs fiasco by drawing a line against communism in Asia. Kennedy's predecessor had lavished $1 billion in aid on the regime of Ngo Dinh Diem, hoping to transform South Vietnam from a temporary state into a pro-Western bulwark. But while Diem was fiercely loyal to his sponsors (sending 30,000 "subversives" to prison camps), his popularity was foundering along with South Vietnam's economy. In Saigon, thousands of civilians had joined a recent military revolt; in the countryside, the National Liberation Front—a left-wing nationalist movement backed by Communist North Vietnam—had just launched a guerrilla war.

The first sign of a new strategy came in May, when 100 U.S. Special Forces men, joining the 700 military advisers already in South Vietnam, arrived to train Diem's troops in counterinsurgency techniques—and to lead them in battle. Plans to expand South Vietnam's army from 150,000 to 250,000 were soon announced. But military strength wasn't enough, U.S. officials now contended: The NLF's fighters, known as Viet Cong, had to be deprived of their support base and the people convinced that democracy was preferable to communism. Peasants in guerrilla zones would henceforth be moved into "strategic hamlets"—new villages, ringed with barbed wire, where they would be guarded by local troops and showered with American largesse and propaganda.

By 1963, aid to South Vietnam had tripled; there were 16,000 U.S. advisers in-country, and the strategic-hamlet program was well under way. Yet the populace remained rebellious, and the Viet Cong continued to gain ground. The problem, Washington decided, must be Diem himself. **◀1955.3 ▶1963.M**

LATIN AMERICA

Alliance for Progress

7 While planning the Bay of Pigs invasion, John F. Kennedy was also trying to devise a peaceful way to fight communism in the Western Hemisphere. In 1961, he unveiled the Alliance for Progress—an aid program designed to transform Latin America "into a vast crucible of revolutionary ideas and efforts." Representatives of 22 Latin nations, meeting in Uruguay, approved the Alliance charter, setting goals that included democratization, economic growth, fairer distribution of income, land reform, stable import and export prices, and improved health and welfare services.

LATIN AMERICA: INVESTMENTS & DEBTS

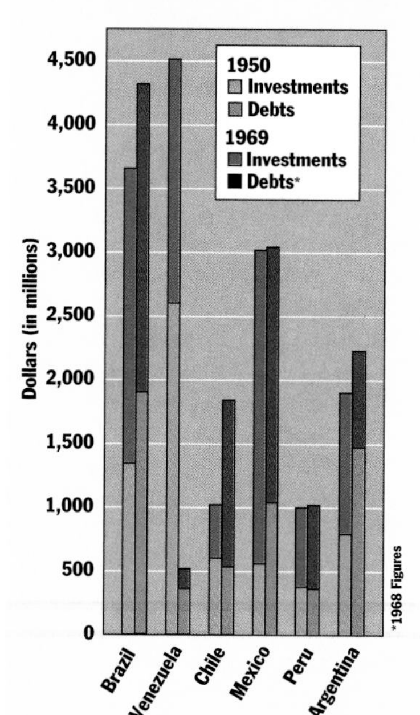

Investment in Latin America increased, but so did its outstanding debt. By 1969, only Venezuela's debt had fallen (due to oil).

On a tour through the region, Kennedy was cheered by millions. Yet despite his crowd-pleasing talk of revolution, his real objective was to defuse potential revolutions with liberal reforms. As it turned out, however, aside from building some schools and hospitals, Alliance funds did little to reduce inequities. The U.S. Agency for International Development, which administered the Alliance, sent massive sums to U.S.-owned firms (such as United Fruit in Guatemala) while often denying them to local competitors. Other beneficiaries were corrupt governments and land- and business-owning oligarchs.

As revolutionary ferment grew, the Alliance focused increasingly on augmenting its security forces. Police were trained to use sophisticated riot-control equipment. Soldiers learned counterinsurgency techniques. Military aid grew by 50 percent a year, transforming the budgets of small countries and enhancing their armies' power and prestige. From 1961 to 1967, Latin America experienced 17 military coups—more than in any period in the region's history. There was no comparable boom in democracy, or prosperity. **◀1959.1 ▶1965.11**

DOMINICAN REPUBLIC

Trujillo Assassinated

8 During his 31-year reign, Rafael Leonidas Trujillo Molina had all but extinguished the practice of politics in the Dominican Republic. His assassination by rival military officers in 1961 created a crisis of succession: Beyond a tight circle of Trujillo factotums, the Caribbean nation lacked experienced government hands.

An army officer trained by U.S. Marines during the American occupation (1916-24), Trujillo had run his country as a personal fiefdom—stacking his regime with family members and assuming outright ownership of the land. The capital was renamed Trujillo; the country's highest mountain became Pico Trujillo; calendars bore the motto "Era of Trujillo." Under "His Illustrious Superiority," the country enjoyed relative prosperity and political stability, the latter enforced by the secret police. Through imprisonment, torture, and murder, Trujillo's agents cowed enemies real and imagined.

SPORTS: Baseball: World Series, New York Yankees defeat Cincinnati Reds, 4–1 ... Football: NFL, Green Bay Packers defeat New York Giants, 37–0; AFL, Houston Oilers defeat San Diego Chargers, 10–3 ... Basketball: NBA, Boston Celtics defeat St. Louis Hawks, 4–1 ... Auto Racing: A.J. Foyt sets new race record of 139.130 mph in Indianapolis 500.

"Decolonisation is always a violent phenomenon."—**Frantz Fanon, *The Wretched of the Earth***

Trujillo's assassination triggered a crisis.

Having helped create the dictator decades earlier, the United States also abetted the messy transition to post-Trujillo democracy. Rightist Joaquin Balaguer, Trujillo's nominal president, assumed power; when the dead man's family started grumbling, American warships arrived and deterred a coup. In 1962, leftist leader Juan Bosch won the country's first free elections in the Dominican Republic since 1924, but was overthrown by conservatives a year later. A 1965 attempt to reinstate him brought on civil war (and the arrival of more U.S. troops). **◂1916.2 ▸1966.M**

IDEAS

A Psychology of Revolution

9 For colonial subjects, wrote Frantz Fanon, violence "is a cleansing force. It frees the native from his inferiority complex and from his despair and inaction; it makes him fearless and restores his self-respect." That synthesis of psychology and politics was central to Fanon's *The Wretched of the Earth*, published in 1961, one of the decade's most incendiary books.

Born in Martinique, Fanon was no stranger to colonialism—or to violence. He received the Croix de Guerre for his service with the Free French Forces during World War II. After the war, he studied psychiatry, wrote *Black Skin, White Masks* (a study of racism), and joined Algeria's Front de Libération Nationale. His medical and political work for the Algerian revolution made him the target of retribution-minded French settlers: He suffered spinal injuries in a car explosion, then survived another assassination attempt while recovering in an Italian hospital.

In 1960, Fanon learned he had leukemia. He dashed off *The Wretched of the Earth* in the last year of his life. The book was a landmark in the social analysis of developing nations. At a time when conventional thinking denied the existence of African class systems, Fanon illuminated them. Unlike orthodox Marxists, he explored the psychological, as well as the economic, aspects of colonialism. But it was his endorsement of a violent "collective catharsis" that electrified readers, from Jean-Paul Sartre to Che Guevara. Fanon's theories—that mental illness can result from oppression, and that mental health can grow from the barrel of a gun—became guiding principles for rebels throughout the Third World. **◂1958.12 ▸1965.11**

LITERATURE

Heller's Iconoclastic Classic

10 Published in 1961, *Catch-22* is one of the century's great epic satires. Drawn from its author's own experience as a bombardier in World War II, the novel, written by a 38-year-old magazine promotions manager named Joseph Heller, viciously caricatured the U.S. military bureaucracy—and, by extension, all the giant institutions that purport to bring order to the modern world. Set mostly on the imaginary island of Pianosa, the story centers on Captain John Yossarian's attempts to survive the war. As his comrades die around him, and his bomber squadron's commanders keep raising the number of missions required to earn a leave, Yossarian tries to escape by feigning madness. The ploy fails: An Air Force regulation (known as Catch-22) stipulates that since a man would be insane to willingly go on bombing runs, a request to be excused on grounds of insanity is itself proof of sanity.

Heller described his style as "sour sarcasm or ugly satire." He revisited Yossarian in a 1994 sequel, *Closing Time.*

A bizarre concoction of surreal humor and graphic violence, *Catch-22* was fervently embraced by Vietnam-era pacifists. Heller's vision of institutionalized insanity entered the mainstream—and the term "catch-22" entered the language as shorthand for any rule whose malign logic is inescapable. **◂1951.11**

FILM

Hepburn Golightly

11 **With her elfin elegance, airy spunk, and aristocratic but unplaceable accent (she was born in Belgium to a British banker and a Dutch baroness), Audrey Hepburn was the screen's most beguiling gamine. In 1961, she found her signature role: chic party girl Holly Golightly in Blake Edwards's *Breakfast at Tiffany's* (adapted from a Truman Capote story). Blithely shoplifting at Woolworth's, making ingenuously sophisticated chitchat at cocktail parties, or wistfully crooning "Moon River" on a fire escape, Hepburn's Holly was an icon of early-sixties femininity: girlish yet sexually knowing, defiantly independent yet reliant on her charm (and the support of wealthy men), coolly cosmopolitan yet a small-town tomboy at heart. It was an impossible combination, but Hepburn, in a parade of Givenchy shifts, pulled it off. ◂1951.7**

IN THE UNITED STATES

▸STAND-UP SOCIAL CRITIC—Lenny Bruce's first arrest (of many) for obscenity came in 1961 in San Francisco. Angry, satiric, profane, Bruce was as much cultural critic as comedian—a provocateur whose irreverence about sex, religion, and politics raised hackles wherever he performed. A pioneer of the sixties counterculture, Bruce died of a drug overdose in 1966. ▸1980.M

▸ENTER THE SUPREMES—Florence Ballard, Mary Wilson, and Diana Ross, three teenage girls from a Detroit housing project, signed a contract with Motown records In 1961 and called themselves the Supremes. A few years passed before they had a chart-topper ("Where Did Our Love Go," 1964)—then they had twelve in six years. So successful was the ultimate "girl group" that *Billboard* magazine's traditional "black music"/"white music" dichotomy became meaningless: The Supremes consistently ranked number one on both lists. ◂1959.10

▸61 IN '61—Even enduring Yankee superstar Mickey Mantle was eclipsed in the summer of 1961 by teammate Roger Maris, who finished the season with a record 61 home runs—one run more than the record set in 1927 by Babe Ruth. But Mantle was no slouch: He slugged a total of 54 homers; together, he and Maris set a new two-man record. ◂1920.6

▸CLINE'S CLIMB—Even cautious, pigeonholing record producers could not categorize Patsy Cline (née Virginia Petterson Hensley). In 1961 she had a number one country hit, "I Fall to Pieces," that crossed over to the pop charts. Her next song, "Crazy" (written for Cline by Willie Nelson), did even better. Her budding career was cut short two years later when she died in a plane crash. ◂1955.M ▸1971.M

POLITICS & BUSINESS: GNP: $520.1 billion ... 23rd Amendment ratified, giving congressional representation (without vote) to Washington, D.C. ... Fair Labor Standards Act raises hourly minimum wage to $1.15 ... 29 electric-equipment manufacturers (including General Electric, Westinghouse) convicted of price-fixing, fines total more than $1.9 million ... IBM introduces the Selectric typewriter.

"When Judy Garland strode onstage, she got, without opening her mouth, what it takes Renata Tebaldi two and a half hours of Puccini to achieve: a standing, screaming ovation that lasted five minutes."—***Time*** **magazine, on Garland's Carnegie Hall concert**

AROUND THE WORLD

▶U THANT HEADS UN—Originally a compromise candidate—the U.S. and the U.S.S.R. couldn't agree on a replacement for Dag Hammarskjöld—Burmese educator and statesman U Thant, a critic of Cold War antagonism, proved a talented leader and champion of world peace as UN secretary-general. Among the conflicts he helped resolve: the Cuban Missile Crisis; civil war in the Congo (Zaire); the 1965 India-Pakistan War. ◀1953.8 ▶1982.M

▶BEYOND SEXINESS—International sex symbol Sophia Loren revealed previously hidden dramatic depth in *La Ciociara*, as the mother of a teenage daughter in World War II–ruined Italy. Directed

by Italian master Vittorio de Sica, the 1961 film (known in English as *Two Women*) gave the actress the best role of her 60-odd-movie career. ◀1948.14

▶IRONIST OF IDENTITY—With his comic yet deeply felt fourth novel, *A House for Mr. Biswas* (1961), V.S. Naipaul emerged as an international literary figure. A Trinidadian of Indian descent, Naipaul settled in London, where he turned an expatriate's critical eye on the vagaries of identity, personal and cultural, in a postcolonial age. His probing psychological insights and deep-rooted pessimism often earn him comparison to Joseph Conrad. ◀1902.3

▶BOLD SOVIET VOICE—Poet Yevgeny Yevtushenko's well-turned barbs at Stalinism made him a literary phenomenon at home (his dramatic readings filled huge stadiums); in 1961 he gathered acclaim abroad with his long poem *Babi Yar*, about the 1941 Nazi slaughter of tens of thousands of Ukrainian Jews. Also a condemnation of Soviet anti-Semitism, the poem upset the Soviet government. Yevtushenko was censured after his autobiography was published in France in 1963. ◀1958.7 ▶1966.11

Garland greets her fans. When she walked onstage, *Variety* reported, "pandemonium broke loose."

MUSIC

Garland at Carnegie Hall

12 The short life of Judy Garland, Hollywood's finest singing actress, was made up mostly of glittering successes (exemplified by her roles in the film classics *The Wizard of Oz, Meet Me in St. Louis,* and *A Star Is Born*) and spectacular disasters (drug addiction, four divorces, several suicide attempts). April 23, 1961, marked one of her triumphs—her legendary concert at New York's Carnegie Hall.

Two years earlier, Garland had nearly died of liver disease brought on by pills and liquor. But she'd gone back to work, making records, giving two successful London concerts, and campaigning for John F. Kennedy at U.S. military bases in Germany. Carnegie Hall was her American comeback.

When Garland walked onstage, the capacity crowd of 3,165—including dozens of celebrities—gave her a five-minute standing ovation. She rewarded her fans with 26 songs, including her inevitable standards, "The Trolley Song," "The Man That Got Away," and "Over the Rainbow." There were at least six other standing ovations. Men and women in evening dress stood on their chairs; hundreds rushed the stage. After two and a half hours, Garland asked, "Do you really want more? Aren't you tired?" "No!" they roared. So she sang one more.

The record of the concert, *Judy at Carnegie Hall,* was a Top 40 hit for 73 weeks, and won five Grammy Awards. But Garland was never as good again; her voice failed and drugs wracked her body. She died in 1969 at 47, of a barbiturate overdose. **◀1939.8**

DANCE

Nureyev's Greatest Leap

13 As one of the Soviet Union's most promising young dancers, Rudolf Nureyev had turned down the Bolshoi company because it was too restrictive. (He became the star of Leningrad's Kirov Ballet instead.) Self-absorbed and defiant, he'd refused to join the Communist Youth League; he criticized his troupe's policies and mixed with foreigners. When, during a European tour, Nureyev learned that he was to be sent back to Moscow for discipline, he made the greatest leap of his career: On June 17, 1961, he jumped over a railing at a Paris airport and requested asylum.

His defection was a propaganda coup for the West—and for Nureyev. Within a week, he was one of the highest-paid dancers in Europe, performing the male lead in *The Sleeping Beauty* with the Marquis de Cuevas Ballet troupe in Paris. Nureyev went on to dance with (and choreograph for) virtually every major ballet company in the world. While the sole permanent guest artist with the Royal Ballet in London, he became the favorite partner of the legendary Dame Margot Fonteyn, 18 years his senior; their pas de deux rekindled her career and won him adulation. (One worshipful Vienna audience gave them 89 curtain calls.)

Nureyev's fiery artistry and smoldering personal magnetism earned him comparisons to his great predecessor Nijinsky. He also captured the spotlight offstage, regularly partying at discos in the sixties and seventies, yet somehow keeping much of his personal life out of the public eye. He died in 1993 amid rumors that he was afflicted with AIDS. **◀1934.12 ▶1974.M**

Nureyev performing solo at Covent Garden immediately after his defection.

POPULAR CULTURE

Weight Watchers Weighs In

14 The cultural equation of female beauty with thinness and an overweight 37-year-old suburban homemaker's chronic failure to become thin converged in 1961, giving birth to what would become a multimillion dollar empire. After being asked when her baby was due, 214-pound Jean Nidetch, a perpetual dieter, decided to lose weight for good. She went to an obesity clinic sponsored by New York City's Health Department but found the regimen hard to stick to. Hoping that mutual support might change her luck, she invited six friends to join her. A year later, and 70 pounds lighter, Nidetch was spreading her gospel throughout the metropolitan area. Riding the crest of the dieting and fitness boom, she and two group members incorporated Weight Watchers International in 1963.

Despite her success, Nidetch *(above, before and after)* always referred to herself as F.F.H.—Former Fat Housewife.

Nidetch's formula was simple: a diet featuring low-fat protein sources and abundant fruits and vegetables; morale-boosting weekly meetings led by graduates; modest membership dues. And it was wildly successful: By 1968 Weight Watchers had 87 U.S. franchises. By the late 1970s, the company had been bought by Heinz, a giant food conglomerate. By the 1990s, there were Weight Watchers clubs in 24 countries and scores of imitators around the world. **◀1935.V ▶1981.V**

NOBEL PRIZES: Peace: Dag Hammarskjöld (Swedish; UN secretary-general) ... Literature: Ivo Andrić (Yugoslav; novelist) ... Chemistry: Melvin Calvin (U.S.; chemical steps during photosynthesis) ... Medicine: Georg von Békésy (U.S.; cochlea) ... Physics: Robert Hofstadter (U.S.; structure of protons and neutrons) and Rudolf Mössbauer (German; resonance absorption of gamma radiation).

A VOICE FROM 1961

The American Dream Meets the Atomic Nightmare

From "A New Urgency, Big Things To Do—and What You Must Learn," *Life,* September 15, 1961

Cold War anxiety hit a new high during the tense summer and fall of 1961, when the United States and the Soviet Union faced off over Berlin. "In the event of an attack," advised President Kennedy on live television in July, "the lives of those families which are not hit in a nuclear blast and fire can still be saved if they can be warned to take shelter and if that shelter is available." The President's speech, helped along by the popular media (which published such how-to articles as the one from Life *excerpted below), inspired an unlikely national craze. Some 200,000 American families, displaying an odd mixture of pessimism (atomic war was imminent) and pluck (they could survive it), invested in home fallout shelters. Fly-by-night operations with names like "Peace-O-Mind Shelter Company" sprang up around the country, as shelters became preferred suburban home additions.*

Not everyone was sold, though, and doubts about whether nuclear war was survivable increased after the Soviets detonated a 60-megaton hydrogen bomb—the largest doomsday weapon ever exploded—in October. Kennedy and Khrushchev gradually relaxed their rhetoric, and by December were cutting back their tanks in Berlin. The shelter became a museum piece, a reliquary of the weirdly commingled American dream and atomic nightmare. ◂**1961.1** ▸**1962.5.**

For years, most people have had the fatalistic idea that it was no use trying to do anything about protection against a nuclear bomb. If the blast did not kill them, they felt radiation certainly would. The man down the street with a backyard shelter was considered odd. But he is actually a solid, sensible man—and a respectable citizen.

If the enemy attacks, he will probably aim first at military targets like missile and SAC bases. Large cities and industrial centers, which do not have the capacity to strike back, will be secondary targets. If a military-objective attack should come now to an unprepared nation, 45 million Americans—a fourth of the population—would die. Some would die in the blast. But the greatest danger to by far the greatest number would come from fallout, the deadly cloud of radioactive dust and debris which would blow across the land.

Hundreds of miles from the target, people would come into contact with destructive fallout, which they could not necessarily see, touch or smell. They could get enough on their skin to cause burns and sickness. Fallout might also contaminate their food and water and damage their vital organs.

But if Americans took precautions against fallout the mortality could drop sharply. About five million people, less than 30% of the population, would die. This in itself is a ghastly number. But you have to look at it coldly. Unprepared, there is one chance in four that you and your family will die. Prepared, you and your family have 97 chances out of 100 to survive.

Basically, fallout protection consists of covering your body, food and water so the radioactive particles cannot contaminate them. If you have sufficient shielding between you and the fallout you are safe. You should be prepared to take cover for at least two weeks.

Obviously, this will not always be easy to do. What if you are in a city like New York? Though some notable steps have been taken, most cities are far behind in their preparations for fallout protection. People must know instantly where to go. But your chances of surviving fallout in a big city would be good. If you are in a large apartment house or office building you could either go to the basement or stay in an inner corridor on one of the middle floors.

A subway system or any city tunnels offer an excellent shelter. Wherever you live or work, you should try to keep a portable supply of water ready. You can live for several weeks without food, but not without water.

It is likely that any attack will come at night while you are at home—so the enemy will have daylight to prepare for the retaliation. (When it is midnight in New York, it is 8 a.m. in Moscow.) If you own a home, you can build a family shelter there. No civilian shelter will stand up against a direct or nearby blast. And the 97% survival figure is the optimum based on good protection and some warning. There is no guarantee that any of your defenses—or even the nation's defenses—will be adequate if the enemy attacks all—out with complete surprise. But they will increase your odds. And every family shelter will contribute to the nation's total deterrent. For if the U.S. is so well prepared that it cannot be knocked out, the enemy may never attack.

The Carlson family in their shelter. The dubious sanctuaries were typically concrete-lined holes or buried steel tanks, and they were stocked with such emergency provisions as canned goods, water, board games—and, more often than not, a shotgun or two.

"The representative of the highest spiritual authority of the earth is glad, indeed boasts, of being the son of a humble but robust and honest laborer."—**Pope John XXIII**

STORY OF THE YEAR

Vatican II: The Church Modernizes

1 It had been more than 90 years since the last convocation of the world's Catholic leaders, Vatican Council I, and Pope John XXIII believed the time had come to discuss the Church's place in a changing world. Vatican Council II began in October 1962 and ended in December 1965. Over the course of the council's four sessions, Roman Catholicism decisively entered the twentieth century.

Pope John XXIII, the Catholic Church's great twentieth-century reformer.

Known as a meek conformist when he succeeded the assertively conservative Pope Pius XII in 1958, John (then 76) had been upsetting the status quo ever since. The pontiff had flummoxed cautious clerics by calling for the convening of Vatican II within months of his election. In 1961, with the encyclical *Mater et Magistra*, he became the first pope to endorse labor unions, the welfare state, and constitutional democracy. John reached out to Protestants and Jews as no pope had before him; he granted audiences to Khrushchev's son-in-law and a Shinto high priest.

John's goal, as he told the Vatican Council's 2,500 participants, was to achieve a "forward leap of the kingdom of Christ in the world"—that is, to bring the Church back to the center of world affairs. To do so, he preached, it was necessary to reconcile with other faiths, to serve as a bridge between East and West and the developed and developing nations, and to update ancient traditions.

Vatican II issued 16 documents detailing ecclesiastical reform. Perhaps the most sensational was the ruling that worship services need not be performed entirely in Latin. Lay members were to be encouraged to participate more actively in the liturgy, and to study the Bible instead of relying on Church dogma alone. The council espoused "collegiality" between the pope and his bishops, downplaying the absolute authority of the pontiff. (Pope John, however, insisted on maintaining the status quo on contraception and clerical celibacy.) Finally, the conferees agreed that Catholics must work with non-Catholics to cure society's ills.

The Church's face-lift generated particular enthusiasm in Latin America, where religion and revolution were in close competition. But by the end of the decade, as many Third World clerics adopted a radical "liberation theology," a conservative backlash had begun to set in. **◂1933.3 ▸1968.12**

FILM

Death of a Goddess

2 Marilyn Monroe's career was a classic rags-to-riches story. Born into poverty as Norma Jean Baker, she'd survived an abuse-filled childhood to become the most idolized screen goddess of her time. After bringing a transcendent sensuality to a series of cartoonish sexpot roles, she honed her skills with Lee and Paula Strasberg at the Actors Studio, then triumphantly demonstrated her range in *Bus Stop* (1956) and *Some Like It Hot* (1959). Yet the goddess was miserable—and on August 5, 1962, her housekeeper found her dead, an empty bottle of sedatives nearby. She was 36.

"For the entire world," Lee Strasberg remarked at her funeral, Monroe was "a symbol of the eternal feminine." Hair coloring, cosmetic surgery, and a genius for theatricality had transformed her into the blonde who inspired the fantasies of millions. Far from being comfortable with her image, however, she agonized over its imperfections, its perishability—and its lack of dignity. Her marriages to celebrated, heroic men (baseball star Joe DiMaggio, playwright Arthur Miller) had failed to bring her the security she craved.

Marilyn Monroe on the set of her last finished film, *The Misfits*.

By the time she'd finished *The Misfits* (1961), overmedication and alcohol abuse had undone her to the point that the film's director, John Huston, predicted, "In a while she'll either be dead or in a mental institution." Intensive psychiatric treatment was not enough to save her from her demons—or from the powerful paramours (including, allegedly, President Kennedy) who shared her bed but withheld their hearts. **◂1959.8**

FRANCE

De Gaulle's New Era

3 With the Algerian War over, President de Gaulle could resume the task he'd begun in founding the Fifth Republic: replacing France's unstable parliamentary system with a form of government based on a strong presidency. At present, the president was chosen by an electoral college. But true authority, de Gaulle believed, could be wielded only by an executive elected directly by the people. De Gaulle got his way in 1962—despite the opposition of almost the entire political establishment.

De Gaulle made his first move in April, replacing Premier Michel Debré (his frequent opponent on Algeria) with an amiable banker named Georges Pompidou. Politicians greeted Pompidou's appointment with scorn: Although he had negotiated France's truce in Algeria, Pompidou had never held elective office. But his lack of political ties—except to de Gaulle, whose adviser he had been since 1944—ensured his undivided loyalty. And his vision of a postcolonial France, with an aggressively independent foreign policy and an economy geared to big business and state planning, matched the President's perfectly.

With Pompidou in place, de Gaulle began hinting that he wanted to change the constitution. But the French associated direct presidential elections with autocracy, their last effort having resulted in the dictatorship of Louis Napoleon. So de Gaulle waited to broach the idea until September, after an assassination attempt had brought him an outpouring of public support. Parliament responded by ousting Pompidou with a no-confidence vote.

De Gaulle called a referendum on the presidency—and new parliamentary elections. In October, after a massive propaganda campaign on state-run radio and TV (most newspapers urged a "no" vote), the voters approved direct elections; in November, Gaullist candidates won an overwhelming victory against those of the traditional parties, seiz-

ART & CULTURE: Books: ***One Day in the Life of Ivan Denisovich*** **(Alexander Solzhenitsyn);** ***A Clockwork Orange*** **(Anthony Burgess);** ***Ship of Fools*** **(Katherine Anne Porter);** ***The Gutenberg Galaxy*** **(Marshall McLuhan) ... Music: "Surfin' Safari" (Love and Wilson); "The Loco-Motion" (Goffin and King); "Breaking Up Is Hard to Do" (Sedaka and Greenfield);** ***War Requiem*** **(Benjamin Britten) ... Painting & Sculpture:**

"The Chinese say I was scared. Of course I was scared.... If being frightened meant that I helped avert such insanity, then I'm glad I was frightened." **—Nikita Khrushchev, on the Cuban Missile Crisis**

France's Georges Pompidou, de Gaulle's handpicked premier, in 1962.

ing the biggest plurality Parliament had seen in decades.

Pompidou returned as premier. And for now de Gaulle could accurately boast, paraphrasing King Louis XIV: *Le gouvernement, c'est moi.* **◂1946.M ▸1963.5**

ALGERIA

Muslim Rebels Win

4 When a truce was signed in March 1962, the eight-year-old Algerian War had killed 17,000 French troops and up to a million Muslims. It might have ended earlier: President Charles de Gaulle had begun to speak of self-determination for Algeria in 1959. But the war was propelled by forces beyond one man's control. De Gaulle had to couple his early peace gestures with anti-independence speeches to placate the army, rightists, and settlers. In 1960, colonists opposing compromise with the Algerians staged a revolt, which ended only when de Gaulle broadcast a stirring appeal for loyalty. And though the growing strength of the Muslim FLN guerrillas—and the war's unpopularity—led him to open talks later that year, those negotiations failed.

After he called openly for an *Algérie algérienne*—and French and Algerian voters approved it in a referendum—die-hard colonists rebelled again. In April 1961, their Secret Army Organization (OAS), led by four rightist generals, took control of much of Algeria's capital. But de Gaulle's eloquence (and loyal gendarmes) once more disarmed the renegades, and the generals were arrested, or they fled.

Peace talks resumed weeks later in Evian, France. As they dragged on into 1962, the OAS matched the FLN's worst excesses—planting bombs in Algeria and France, massacring thousands of Muslim civilians, and repeatedly trying to assassinate de Gaulle. The attacks continued even after OAS leader General Raoul Salan was caught and sentenced to life in prison. Nonetheless, Algeria gained independence on July 5, after 132 years of French rule. A brief civil war was followed by elections; in September, ruling council president Ahmed Ben Bella proclaimed a neutral socialist republic. By then, most of the settlers had emigrated—many spitefully destroying hospitals, factories, libraries, and other property before they left. **◂1958.4 ▸1993.9**

Muslims in Algiers celebrate Algeria's independence from France after 132 years.

THE COLD WAR

Cuban Missile Crisis

5 As cautious as they were contentious, the Soviet Union and the United States had always avoided direct, armed confrontation in their struggle for ideological and territorial supremacy. But for two terrifying weeks in 1962, the superpowers came face-to-face, nearly dragging each other and the rest of the world into the nuclear abyss.

The Cuban Missile Crisis began on October 14, when an American spy plane detected a ballistic missile on the Communist island 90 miles from America's shores. (Khrushchev had claimed that the weapons he was sending to Cuba were defensive and non-nuclear.) Never before had the Soviets deployed nuclear arms in the Western Hemisphere.

President Kennedy and his advisers debated over how to respond.

Cuban refugees in the United States watch President Kennedy's televised speech about the Cuban Missile Crisis.

Suggestions ranged from inaction —"It makes no difference," reasoned Defense Secretary Robert McNamara, "whether you are killed by a missile fired from the Soviet Union or from Cuba"—to immediate invasion. Kennedy opted for a blockade (which was joined by the Organization of American States). On October 22, he revealed the situation on television. "I have directed the armed forces," he warned, "to prepare for any eventuality." The message was clear. The world braced for war.

Khrushchev did not dispatch any ships carrying nuclear contraband to challenge the blockade, but he initially refused to dismantle weapons already on the island. The standoff intensified; 200,000 U.S. troops massed in Florida. An American pilot flying reconnaissance over Cuba was shot down and killed. As it turned out, he was the sole casualty: On October 28, in return for American promises never to invade Cuba and to remove missiles from Turkey, Khrushchev agreed to withdraw the weapons. **◂1961.5 ▸1963.2**

BIRTHS

Garth Brooks, U.S. singer.

Roger Clemens, U.S. baseball player.

Tom Cruise, U.S. actor.

Patrick Ewing, Jamaican-U.S. basketball player.

Jodie Foster, U.S. actress.

Evander Holyfield, U.S. boxer.

Bo Jackson, U.S. football and baseball player.

Jon Bon Jovi, U.S. singer.

k.d. Lang, Canadian singer.

Demi Moore, U.S. actress.

Jerry Rice, U.S. football player.

Wesley Snipes, U.S. actor.

DEATHS

Norma Jean Baker (Marilyn Monroe), U.S. actress.

William Beebe, U.S. oceanographer.

Karen Blixen (Isak Dinesen), Danish writer.

Niels Bohr, Danish physicist.

Arthur H. Compton, U.S. physicist.

Edward Estlin Cummings, U.S. poet.

Adolf Eichmann, German Nazi official.

William Faulkner, U.S. writer.

Ernest Hemingway, U.S. novelist.

Hermann Hesse, German writer.

Robinson Jeffers, U.S. poet.

Yves Klein, French painter.

Franz Kline, U.S. painter.

Charles Laughton, U.K.-U.S. actor.

Charles "Lucky" Luciano, U.S. racketeer.

C. Wright Mills, U.S. sociologist.

Eleanor Roosevelt, U.S. social reformer.

Victoria Mary Sackville-West, U.K. writer.

Albert Sarraut, French politician.

Wilhelmina, Dutch queen.

Third Element **(Morris Louis);** ***The Family*** **(Marisol) ... Film:** ***Lawrence of Arabia*** **(David Lean);** ***The Manchurian Candidate*** **(John Frankenheimer);** ***Dr. No*** **(Terence Young) ... Theater:** ***The Physicists*** **(Friedrich Dürrenmatt);** ***I Can Get It for You Wholesale*** **(Harold Rome);** ***A Funny Thing Happened on the Way to the Forum*** **(Stephen Sondheim) ... TV:** ***The Beverly Hillbillies; The Merv Griffin Show.***

"I play John Wayne in every part regardless of the character, and I've been doing okay, haven't I?"—**John Wayne**

NEW IN 1962

Dulles Airport (Washington, D.C.; first civilian airport designed specifically for jets).

Yves Saint-Laurent fashion house.

K Mart and Wal-Mart discount stores.

Lear jet.

Nuclear-powered merchant ship (USS *Savannah*).

Hovercraft service in Britain (from Britain to France).

IN THE UNITED STATES

▶"OL' MISS" DESEGREGATED—James H. Meredith became the first black student to enroll in the all-white University of Mississippi, a bastion of segregation. After

a federal court ordered the university to admit Meredith in early September, Governor Ross Barnett refused. Exhorting whites to resist the civil rights movement, he called Meredith's registration "the moment of our greatest crisis since the War Between the States." When Meredith, guarded by federal marshals *(above)*, secretly arrived on campus on September 30, a mob began throwing rocks and bottles. President Kennedy went on national television to try to defuse the ugly situation, but the racist throng rioted, killing two people and injuring 160 marshals. Federal troops were called in to restore order. Braving steady harassment, Meredith graduated in 1963. ◀1961.M ▶1963.7

▶CUCKOO KESEY—With his satiric, hilarious, and ultimately dark novel of mental and social breakdown, *One Flew Over the Cuckoo's Nest*, flamboyant writer Ken Kesey

The Fab Four (*from left*), Ringo Starr, John Lennon, Paul McCartney, and George Harrison, in Paris in the early sixties.

MUSIC

Introducing the Beatles

6 The Beatles' first single, "Love Me Do," released in September 1962, hit number 17 on the British pop charts. Their second, "Please Please Me," hit number two. Their third, "From Me to You," hit number one. By the end of 1963, the Beatles were the most popular musicians in British history, with a following that included the Queen Mother as well as hordes of screaming teenage girls. By early 1964, when a U.S. tour (launched with two appearances on the *Ed Sullivan Show*) brought "Beatlemania" to America, manager Brian Epstein's prophecy had come true: The group was "bigger than Elvis."

Band members John Lennon, Paul McCartney, and George Harrison had worked seedy clubs in their native Liverpool and in Hamburg since the mid-1950s. When Epstein discovered them in 1961, they'd already adopted their eccentric bowl-cut hairstyles and added original songs to their repertoire of rock 'n' roll covers; they'd also become the foremost band on Liverpool's thriving "Merseybeat" scene. Epstein dressed them in dandyish suits, substituted Ringo Starr for less presentable drummer Pete Best, and promoted them brilliantly.

Musically, the Beatles were remarkable: Lennon and McCartney's compositions were fresh and witty (most rock artists had previously relied on outside writers); their vocal harmonies were exhilarating, their performances high voltage. The first internationally successful rock *group*, they launched a "British invasion" that ended America's dominance in the field. Culturally, they were a revelation: Whereas earlier rockers had celebrated teenage passion, the Beatles were about pure play. With their androgynous looks and Marx Brothers hijinks, they presaged the polymorphous anarchy of the later sixties. During those years, as they discovered drugs and mysticism, they became pied pipers for the counterculture.

The Beatles' musical and verbal sophistication grew steadily. *Sgt. Pepper's Lonely Hearts Club Band* (1967)—often cited as the greatest rock record ever—was the first "concept album" (a suite of interrelated songs instead of a collection of singles), incorporating electronic sound collages, a sitar, and a 40-piece orchestra. When the group disbanded several LPs later, in 1970, rock had incontestably achieved the status of serious music. **◀1959.11 ▶1965.10**

FILM

The Duke

7 John Wayne made more than 250 movies, from *The Drop Kick* (1927) to *The Shootist* (1976). Of Wayne's 90-odd Westerns, John Ford's *The Man Who Shot Liberty Valance,* released in 1962, is among the best. A moving examination of the conflict between freedom and order, the film mourns what was lost when America became citified. Wayne plays a straight-shooting cattleman who sacrifices his own happiness to eliminate the local villain and make civilization possible. With his distinctive walk (a tight, yet oddly delicate, sashay), his air of seen-it-all skepticism, and his bitten-off line readings, Wayne shaded and deepened the sparely written character; for all his leathery machismo, he didn't hide the hero's emotional chinks.

Wayne in *Liberty Valance.* To a starkly divided public, the star was either a patriotic demigod or a jingoistic devil.

Besides vanquishing Indians and desperadoes, Wayne, one of the biggest box-office draws ever, fought in nearly every U.S. war from the Revolution to Vietnam—on-screen. Off-screen, he was a right-wing militarist, despite never having served in the military. In the popular consciousness, his cinematic persona and his personal politics merged: Around the world, the image of a gun-toting Wayne against the buttes of the Southwest's Monument Valley—the locale in which director Ford (who'd made him a star) typically placed him—became a symbol for the United States itself. **◀1952.11**

ART

The Pop Stars

8 "I try to use a cliché—a powerful cliché—and put it into organized form." So said Roy Lichtenstein, one of three major artists who emerged in 1962 to puncture art-world pretense with pop—a style that borrowed techniques and imagery from mass culture to make viewers see that culture, and art itself, with new eyes. Whereas the abstract expressionists had sought

SPORTS: Baseball: World Series, New York Yankees defeat San Francisco Giants, 4–3 ... Football: NFL, Green Bay Packers defeat New York Giants, 16–7; AFL, Dallas Texans defeat Houston Oilers, 20–17 ... Basketball: NBA, Boston Celtics defeat Los Angeles Lakers, 4–3 ... Tennis: Rod Laver wins the Grand Slam ... Soccer: World Cup, Brazil defeats Czechoslovakia, 3–1.

"In school the children count ten on their fingers. I have no fingers, but now I count ten on my fingers in my mind."
—"Thalidomide child" in Heidelberg, West Germany, after the first day of school

to pour their souls onto the canvas, pop artists like Lichtenstein, Claes Oldenburg, and Andy Warhol proclaimed the seductive soullessness of modern life. By the end of the year, each had caused a sensation with a New York exhibition.

Oldenburg's giant-sized "soft sculptures" of a drooping ice-cream cone, a hamburger, or a slice of cake (displayed at the Green Gallery) combined the crafts of upholstery and toymaking. Dealer Leo Castelli gave Lichtenstein his first one-man show, of paintings derived from comic books—complete with kitschy imagery, speech balloons, and benday dot patterns.

Warhol's work, appearing with Lichtenstein's in a group show at the Sidney Janis Gallery, created the biggest stir. A onetime commercial

***Campbell Soup Can, 19¢* (1962)—one of the last works Warhol painted by hand.**

artist, Warhol used silk-screening and other mechanical processes to achieve an art of supreme impersonality. He won worldwide celebrity with his endlessly repeated portraits of commodities (Coke bottles, Campbell's soup cans) and celebrities. The platinum-wigged artist summed up his vision—at once radically democratic and star-struck—in a phrase that, appropriately enough, became a cliché: "In the future, everyone will be famous for 15 minutes." **◂1958.5 ▸1965.7**

MEDICINE

A Disfiguring Drug

9 Once advertised as the "Sleeping Pill of the Century," thalidomide was the villain in one of the darkest chapters in pharmaceutical history. By 1962, when it was removed from the market, the drug had caused up to 12,000 infant malformations (most in West Germany); nearly half of the deformed babies died soon after birth.

A popular treatment for sleeplessness, tension, and nausea during pregnancy—it was marketed by 14 companies in 46 countries—thalidomide was thought to have no side effects. Unfortunately, however, no tests had been done to determine its impact on the fetus. Following its introduction in Europe in 1957, thousands of babies whose mothers had taken the drug were born with flipperlike appendages instead of arms and legs. Eyes, ears, and internal organs were often damaged as well.

While thousands across Europe were disfigured, only a dozen or so American babies were affected—thanks largely to Frances Oldham Kelsey, a Food and Drug Administration investigator. Kelsey had just been hired when she received an application for market approval from thalidomide's American manufacturer. Disturbed by reports that the drug caused nerve inflammation and failed to induce sleep in animals, she turned down the request, and stood firm through 14 months of pressure. (She was later awarded a medal by President Kennedy.) Yet despite the drug's lack of FDA approval, 1,200 U.S. physicians received free samples, and 20,000 of their female patients took the drug.

The thalidomide scandal prompted stricter regulation of drug testing in many nations. Thalidomide itself, however, proved useful in unexpected ways—as a treatment for leprosy, and as a way to prevent graft-versus-host disease after bone-marrow transplants. **◂1906.11 ▸1974.M**

A group of "thalidomide children" play in the yard of a special kindergarten in Cologne, West Germany.

THEATER

Albee's Fearsome *Woolf*

10 Productions of such plays as *The Zoo Story* had established playwright Edward Albee as America's most promising practitioner of

the theater of the absurd. But the work that first brought him popular acclaim plumbed a more traditional vein. Premiering on Broadway in 1962, Albee's *Who's Afraid of Virginia Woolf?* was a wrenching drama of emotional confrontation—a sharp-witted, high-octane update of O'Neill and Strindberg.

Albee conceived of the three-act play as a "grotesque comedy" about "the substitution of artificial for real values." Like many of his less naturalistic works, it explores the violent dynamics of dominance and submission in ordinary relationships. Two married couples have left a college faculty party for a nightcap: Hosts George and Martha ensnare themselves and their guests, Nick and Honey, in alcohol-fueled psychodramas that expose the desire, frustration, rage, and pathos of their lives. The title—from a graffito Albee saw in a Greenwich Village bar—captures the infantile intellectualism of their lacerating exchanges.

Praised by *The New York Times* as "the best American play of the decade," *Who's Afraid of Virginia Woolf?* won a Tony and a New York Drama Critics Award. A 1966 film version won five Oscars—and, thanks to Albee's liberal use of profanity, prompted (along with Michelangelo Antonioni's *Blow-Up*) the American movie industry to set up a ratings system. **◂1949.V ▸1983.10**

IN THE UNITED STATES

arrived on the scene. The 1962 book (later made into a film with Jack Nicholson as the iconoclastic protagonist McMurphy) made Kesey's literary reputation; his leadership of a band of San Francisco hippies, the "Merry Pranksters," made him a counterculture hero. ▸1968.V

▶SEEGER'S VINDICATION—After years of McCarthyist persecution (including blacklisting that kept him off major record labels), folk musician and social activist Pete Seeger hit the airwaves with a vengeance in 1962, albeit by proxy: Singers Peter, Paul and Mary had a huge hit with "If I Had a Hammer," Seeger's 1949 labor song; and the folk group the Kingston Trio popularized his old antiwar number "Where Have All the Flowers Gone?" ◂1943.M

▶WILT THE STILT—When Wilt Chamberlain, an NBA player from 1959 to '73, got on a basketball court, records tumbled. On March 2, playing for the Philadelphia Warriors, he scored an incredible 100

points in a regulation-length game—a record that still stands. The 7' 1" center was also the first player to retire with an average in excess of 30 points per game and the first to score a career total of more than 30,000 points. ▸1979.M

▶NIXON'S LAST STAND—After narrowly losing the presidency to John F. Kennedy in 1960, Richard Nixon had gone home to California to run for governor in 1962 against incumbent Edmund G. "Pat" Brown. Losing by 300,000 votes, Nixon called a press conference in which he told reporters (who, he maintained, were out to get him), "You won't have Nixon to kick around anymore, because, gentlemen, this is my last press conference." ◂1960.2 ▸1968.1

POLITICS & BUSINESS: GNP: $560.3 billion ... U.S. Department of Labor decrees minimum wage for migrant workers ... National debt exceeds $300 billion ... Segregation in federal housing banned ... Congress establishes Communications Satellite Corp. (Comsat) ... H. Ross Perot founds Electronic Data Systems.

"For the first time in history, virtually every human being is subjected to contact with dangerous chemicals from birth to death."—**Rachel Carson, *Silent Spring***

AROUND THE WORLD

▶REVOLUTIONARY TACTICS—In its limited market, Brazilian revolutionary Carlos Marighella's little 1962 handbook became something of a classic, though it never gained the influence that fearful governments attributed to it. Banned just about everywhere, *Minimanual of the Urban Guerrilla* advised: "The urban guerrilla's reason for existence, the basic action in which he acts and survives, is to shoot." His strategy was to provoke an offending Latin American regime to crack down militarily, possibly invite U.S. intervention, and thereby cause mass unrest. Marighella was killed in São Paulo in 1969. ▶1965.11

▶CHINESE-INDIAN WAR—Despite five shared principles of peaceful coexistence—mutual respect, mutual nonaggression, noninterference, equality, and peaceability—China and India in 1962 took up arms against each other. In dispute were two Himalayan border territories, one near Assam on the Tibetan border and the other in the troublesome Kashmir region. (Both were taken from China and given to India by Britain in 1914.) Staking its claim, India sent troops *(above)* into the disputed areas. China responded by invading. Indian premier Jawaharlal Nehru appealed for international help and received arms and planes from both the United States and Britain. China quickly withdrew. ▶1965.8

▶ERITREA INTO ETHIOPIA—Ethiopian emperor Haile Selassie, long covetous of the Red Sea ports of Eritrea, the historic region to Ethiopia's north, entirely absorbed Eritrea into the Ethiopian empire in November. His move came ten years after the former UN mandate had become affiliated with Ethiopia as an "autonomous region." Almost immediately, secessionist groups embarked on three decades of guerrilla warfare. ◀1935.4 ▶1974.7

ENVIRONMENTALISM

An Antipesticide Prophet

11 In *Silent Spring*, published in 1962, Rachel Carson asked readers to imagine a place where no birds sang, hens' eggs never hatched, and apple trees bore no fruit—a place where cattle died mysteriously in the fields and children on the playground. Then she told them the place was real, though a composite: Its description was drawn from incidents that had actually occurred in the United States and in other countries where artificial pesticides were being used.

Silent Spring alerted millions to the dangers of the poisons that in recent decades had become commonplace on farms and in households around the world. Agents of agribusiness and the chemical industry, perhaps thrown off by Carson's fine prose style, attacked her scientific credentials. In fact, she was a respected marine biologist who'd carefully traced the destructive effects of two major pesticide groups, chlorinated hydrocarbons and organic phosphates, as they worked their way through the ecosystem.

Arguing for controlled pesticide use, not a total ban, Carson revealed that DDT (one of the most popular poisons) could now be found in polar ice caps. She explained how insecticide residue on treated produce is stored in human tissues and passed from mother to unborn child. And she helped launch the modern environmental movement. "A few thousand words from her," said a reviewer, "and the world took a new direction."

A Kennedy administration study confirmed Carson's report, and in 1972, the U.S. Environmental Protection Agency banned DDT. Many other countries followed suit. Even so, the use of pesticides on food continued to grow, reaching nearly a billion pounds annually in the United States alone by the 1980s. **◀1939.M ▶1970.5**

Environmental Cassandra Rachel Carson in a portrait by Alfred Eisenstaedt.

IDEAS

Culture's Opposites

12 In *The Savage Mind*, published in 1962, anthropologist Claude Lévi-Strauss, a leader of the French intelligentsia, dismissed his rival Jean-Paul Sartre's notion that individuals can freely create themselves, and that humanity has progressed from savagery to civilization by that means. Lévi-Strauss argued that humans operate according to innate mental structures—and that progress is an illusion. Starting with a study of totemism among Australian aborigines, he attempted to demonstrate that the "primitive" mind is as rational as the "civilized" mind; the civilized mind, in turn, is as savage (that is, dependent on myths) as any primitive's.

The book provided the most accessible exposition yet of Lévi-Strauss's brainchild, structural anthropology—one of the century's most influential disciplines. He'd begun to develop his ideas in the 1940s (after a stint of fieldwork among Brazilian Indians), when the Nazi occupation of France led him to New York. There, the linguist Roman Jakobson introduced him to structural linguistics, whose concepts Lévi-Strauss applied to anthropology. He began to analyze myths and customs as systems within systems rather than according to their content.

Every culture, he posited, is based on pairs of opposites (the raw and the cooked, for example), linked to other pairs in a kind of grammar dictated by the circuitry of the brain. Instead of primitive and modern societies, there are only "cold" and "hot" societies: The former value harmony and stasis, the latter change and expansion. Culture is equally rich, complex, logical, and mythic in either variety.

Lévi-Strauss's writings range from the movingly autobiographical (as in *Tristes Tropiques,* the book that made him famous in 1955) to the dauntingly technical. They have remained, however, controversial: The debate between his conceptual heirs and Sartre's continues to this day. **◀1957.10 ▶1967.12**

TECHNOLOGY

AT&T Launches *Telstar*

13 Arthur C. Clarke, the British science-fiction writer who predicted the advent of fax machines, mobile phones, and E-mail, once prophesied that communications satellites would mean "the rapid unification of the world into one cultural entity for good or bad." His prophecy began to be fulfilled in 1962, when AT&T launched *Telstar*, the first communications satellite to go into orbit. Following an elliptical path ranging from 500 to 3,500 miles above the earth, the 34½-inch sphere received faint TV signals, amplified them ten billion times (using solar power), and sent them earthward. Suddenly, U.S. viewers could receive images beamed from Britain and France, and vice versa. *Telstar* handled telephone signals as well, promising a vast increase in worldwide person-to-person (and computer-to-computer) communication.

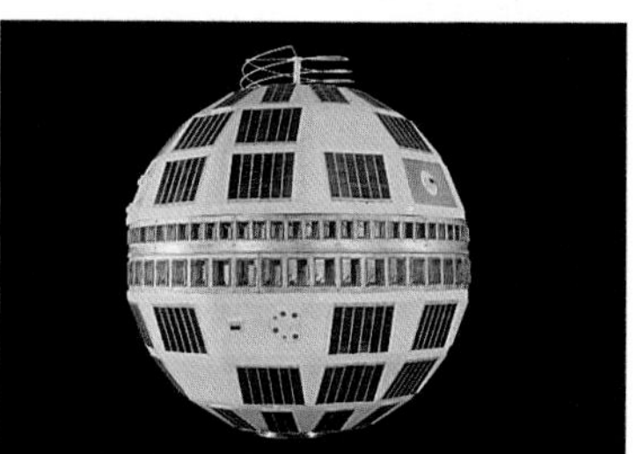

***Telstar*, the first satellite to provide worldwide communications links.**

Telstar was only an experimental device, and its initial transmissions were less than earthshaking (Europeans saw a flapping U.S. flag atop the AT&T building in Maine; France sent greetings from actor Yves Montand); still, excitement swept the globe. In America, debate raged over the future ownership of any system of satellites and ground stations: the government (which would most likely employ a high-orbit system requiring just three satellites to cover the world) or AT&T (which planned a less efficient, but more profitable, low-orbit system)? In its rush to beat the Soviets at the telecommunications game, the Kennedy administration backed AT&T—helping the mammoth communications company grow bigger than ever. **◀1957.1 ▶1988.11**

NOBEL PRIZES: Peace: Linus Pauling (U.S.; nuclear disarmament) ... Literature: John Steinbeck (U.S.; novelist) ... Chemistry: Max F. Perutz and John C. Kendrew (U.K.; globular proteins) ... Medicine: James Watson, Maurice Wilkins, and Francis Crick (U.S., U.K., U.K.; structure of DNA) ... Physics: Lev D. Landau (U.S.S.R.; condensed matter).

A VOICE FROM 1962

How to be Stylishly Single

From *Sex and the Single Girl*, by Helen Gurley Brown, 1962

Advertising copywriter Helen Gurley Brown wrote Sex and the Single Girl *as a kind of handbook to help the single working woman "get* everything *out of life ... whatever she's looking at through the glass her nose is pressed against." Appearing in 1962, at the dawn of the sexual revolution, the book celebrated singleness, attacking the prevailing ethos that measured a woman's success in terms of marriage and motherhood, and candidly acknowledging that unmarried women had sex lives, too. It was a radical premise, though feminist Betty Friedan, whose* The Feminine Mystique *would appear a year later, criticized Brown for defining women solely through their relationships with men. An instant bestseller,* Sex and the Single Girl *was eventually published in 28 countries. In the excerpt below, Brown spells out exactly what makes a "single girl" special.* ◄**1921.V** ►**1963.8**

Frankly, the magazines and their marriage statistics give me a royal pain.

There is a more important truth that magazines never deal with, that single women are too brainwashed to figure out, that married women know but won't admit, that married men *and* single men endorse in a body, and that is that the single woman, far from being a creature to be pitied and patronized, is emerging as the newest glamour girl of our times.

She is engaging because she lives by her wits. She supports herself. She has had to sharpen her personality and mental resources to a glitter in order to survive in a competitive world and the sharpening looks good. Economically she is a dream. She is not a parasite, a dependent, a scrounger, a sponger or a bum. She is a giver, not a taker, a winner, not a loser.

Why else is she attractive? Because she isn't married, that's why! She is free to be The Girl in a man's life or at least his vision of The Girl, whether he is married or single himself.

When a man thinks of a married woman, no matter how lovely she is, he must inevitably picture her greeting her husband at the door with a martini or warmer welcome, fixing little children's lunches or scrubbing them down because they've fallen into a mudhole. She is somebody else's wife, and somebody else's mother.

When a man thinks of a single woman, he pictures her alone in her apartment, smooth legs sheathed in pink silk Capri pants, lying tantalizingly among dozens of satin cushions, trying to read but not very successfully, for *he* is in the room—filling her thoughts, her dreams, her life.

Why else is a single woman attractive? She has more time and often more money to spend on herself. She has the extra twenty minutes to exercise every day, an hour to make up her face for their date. She has all day Saturday to whip up a silly, wonderful cotton brocade tea coat to entertain him in next day or hours to find it at a bargain sale.

Besides making herself physically more inviting, she has the freedom to furnish her mind. She can read Proust, learn Spanish, study *Time, Newsweek* and *The Wall Street Journal.*

Most importantly, a single woman, even if she is a file clerk, moves in the world of men. She knows their language—the language of retailing, advertising, motion pictures, exporting, shipbuilding. Her world is a far more colorful world than the one of P.T.A., Dr. Spock and the jammed clothes dryer.

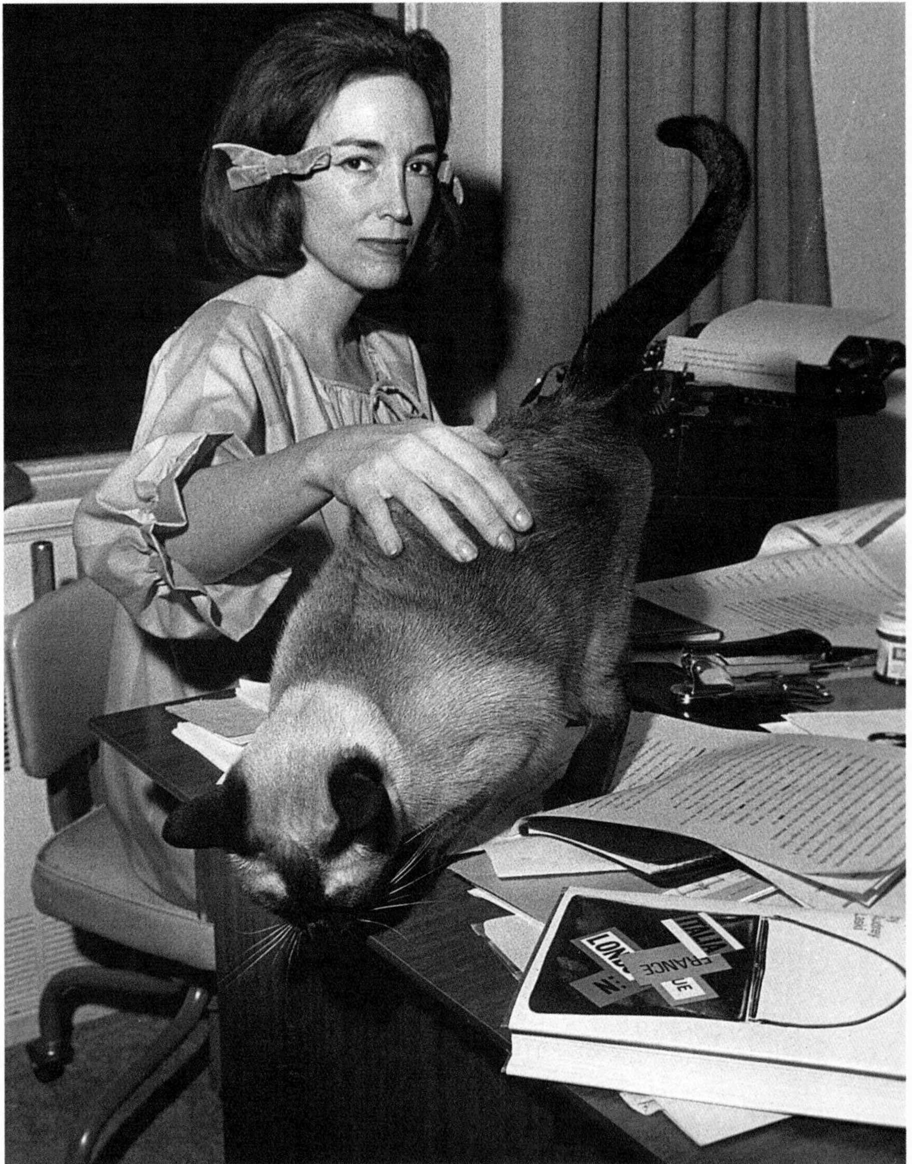

In 1965, Brown *(above, in her office)* was named editor in chief of *Cosmopolitan*, which she re-created as a monthly version of *Sex and the Single Girl.* Within four years, the formerly ailing magazine's advertising revenues had soared, and its newsstand sales were larger than those of *Look* and *Life* combined.

"Don't let it be forgot/That once there was a spot/For one brief shining moment that was known/As Camelot."
—Alan Jay Lerner, from *Camelot,* invoked by Jacqueline Kennedy to describe her husband's presidency

STORY OF THE YEAR

JFK Assassinated in Dallas

1 As his home-movie camera rolled, heedlessly recording the awful scene, Dallas resident Abraham Zapruder screamed, horror-struck, "They killed him! They killed him!" For terrible seconds in Dallas's Dealey Plaza time seemed to stop, hostage to an assassin's bullet. The black Lincoln convertible carrying the President and Mrs. Kennedy and Texas governor John Connally and his wife through Dallas swerved; Secret Service agents froze; Kennedy hunched forward, stricken. Then pandemonium. The limousine sped off to Parkland Memorial Hospital, the President slumped across the backseat. It was 12:30 PM Friday, November 22, 1963. JFK was pronounced dead 30 minutes later.

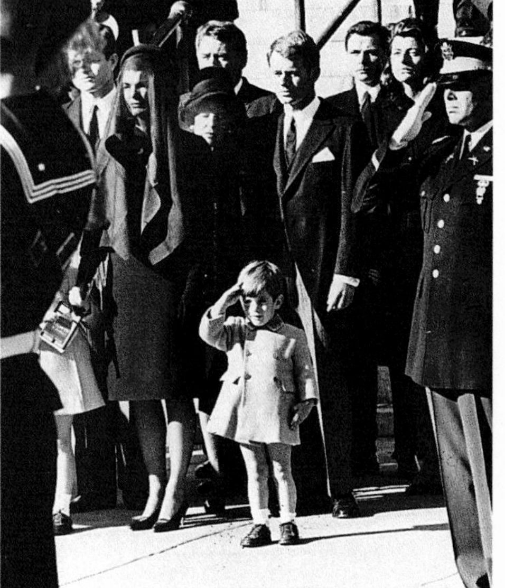
John F. Kennedy, Jr.'s salute to his father's coffin was the most poignant gesture of JFK's funeral procession.

By 1:45 PM, Dallas police had seized a suspect: Lee Harvey Oswald, a 24-year-old employee of the Texas School Book Depository, from whose sixth-floor window the shots were said to have been fired. Two days later, on Sunday, November 24, millions of Americans watched on television as Oswald was being transferred from the Dallas city jail to a county jail. Suddenly, a local nightclub owner named Jack Ruby stepped out of the small crowd and shot Oswald in the stomach with a .35-caliber revolver. Oswald died within minutes.

The alleged assassin's bizarre, mob-style "silencing" and other murky details of the assassination (including various interpretations of Zapruder's film, the only film record of the event) gave rise, almost instantly, to a plethora of theories about who was responsible. (The official explanation, the Warren Report of 1964, did little to assuage the nation's bewilderment.) Indeed, JFK's assassination grew into a kind of national obsession. "Where were you when Kennedy was shot?" became the question by which a generation of bereft Americans identified itself.

By the time Lyndon Johnson was sworn in as the 36th president aboard *Air Force One* in Dallas three hours after the shooting, the Kennedy legend had grown immeasurably, obscuring certain harsh realities—notably, the nation's violent division over civil rights and its increasing entanglement in Vietnam. In coming years, as America's penchant for violence was affirmed again and again, Camelot, the mythical utopia of Lerner and Loewe's Broadway musical (to which Jacqueline Kennedy compared her husband's brief tenure in office), looked increasingly golden, a symbol of what might have been. **◂1961.2 ▸1964.M**

DIPLOMACY

The First Nuclear-Test Ban

2 Since the atomic arms race began, efforts by the Soviet Union and the United States to negotiate limits on weapons manufacture had always stumbled over the issue of inspection: Neither power trusted the other to abide by any treaty, and neither wanted to open its facilities to inspection. But in 1963, the world reaped the first pale fruit of nuclear diplomacy—the Limited Test-Ban Treaty.

The pact followed 17 years of failure. In 1946, the Truman administration had advanced the Baruch Plan, a proposal to commit the management of all atomic projects to an international organization. The Soviets (as yet lacking their own bomb) rejected the scheme. Similarly, Eisenhower's "Atoms for Peace" initiative of 1953, calling for worldwide nuclear cooperation, and his 1957 "Open Skies" proposal, to allow aerial reconnaissance by the United States and the Soviet Union, met with skepticism from Moscow and ambivalence from the American people. Nor did Khrushchev's endorsement of "peaceful coexistence" between the two nations, his repeated calls for total disarmament, or his more modest proposal for a total ban on weapons testing persuade Washington. The superpowers (including, by the sixties, Britain and France) continued to stockpile atomic bombs and missiles.

In the early 1960s, the development of spy satellites made mutual inspection possible with neither side's trespassing on the other's soil or airspace. But the event that broke the impasse over arms control was the Cuban Missile Crisis of 1962—a terrifying brush with atomic apocalypse. The following year, 100 nations—not including China or France, who would both become members of the "nuclear club" in 1964—signed the Limited Test-Ban Treaty (brokered by British Prime Minister Harold Macmillan) proscribing atmospheric, underwater, and space testing of nuclear weapons. The catch: Underground testing remained permissible. Largely symbolic, the pact did not derail the arms race. But it showed that Moscow and Washington *could* agree on something. **◂1957.2 ▸1969.8**

Supporters of nuclear disarmament outside the country home of British Prime Minister Macmillan, who was meeting with JFK.

GREAT BRITAIN

Sex, Spies, and Scandal

3 By 1963, Britain's Conservative Party, in power for twelve years, was running out of steam. Prime Minister Harold Macmillan had been in office six years; though he had been dubbed "Supermac" early in his tenure, his failures had lately outnumbered his triumphs. Listless and adrift, Macmillan's administration ended in 1963 with two spectacular scandals: the Philby and Profumo affairs.

Philby with reporters in 1955, after being cleared of charges that he was the "third man."

The Philby imbroglio was the final act of a drama that had begun in 1951, when high-ranking diplomats Donald Maclean and Guy Burgess were exposed as Soviet spies and fled to Russia. The search for a so-called third man, the accomplice who'd warned them to escape, led to Harold "Kim" Philby (nicknamed by his adventurer father for Kipling's boy hero), Britain's secret-service liaison with the CIA. But since nothing could be proved, he was merely fired, then rehired and posted to Beirut. Philby vanished in January 1963 (eventually surfacing in Moscow), just as investigators discovered he'd been one of the Kremlin's top spies—responsible for huge

1963

ART & CULTURE: Books: *The Clown* (Heinrich Böll); *Fantastic Stories* (Andrei Sinyavski); *V.* (Thomas Pynchon); *The Bell Jar* (Victoria Lucas, pseudonym of Sylvia Plath); *The Group* (Mary McCarthy); *The Fire Next Time* (James Baldwin); *The Interrogation* (J.M.G. Le Clézio); *On Aggression* (Konrad Lorenz) ... Music: "Wipeout" (The Surfaris); "Puff the Magic Dragon" (Yarrow and Lipton); "Surfin' U.S.A."

"What is happening in reality is a kind of mutual discovery of two neighbors ... for the first time in many generations, the Germans and the Gauls realize their solidarity."—**Charles de Gaulle, on the Treaty of Reconciliation between France and Germany**

intelligence leaks and hundreds of deaths. The revelation convulsed America as well as Britain.

The Profumo scandal exploded simultaneously. It began when a call girl named Christine Keeler failed to testify in the trial of one of her lovers, a West Indian marijuana dealer who'd shot up the flat of a celebrity doctor. Keeler soon revealed that she'd been involved with the doctor, too—and, two years earlier, with War Secretary John Profumo. At the same time, she claimed, she'd also been having sex with the Soviet naval attaché. Although it was never shown that Profumo had divulged any secrets, he resigned in disgrace; Macmillan, citing health problems, followed suit six months later. The next parliamentary election, in 1964, gave Labour a majority and Harold Wilson the premiership. **◂1951.6 ▸1979.3**

SCIENCE

Continental Drift Explained

4 A theory as revolutionary to geology as relativity was to physics, plate tectonics holds that the earth's outer shell is composed of large shifting plates on which the oceans and the continents are borne. Where plates converge, they fling up mountain ranges; where they diverge, ocean basins are created. Plate tectonics developed incrementally out of German geologist Alfred Wegener's 1912 theory of continental drift, but later geologists were stuck, like Wegener, at the hypothetical stage. Plate tectonics made sense, but could not be verified. In 1963, two Britons, Drummond Matthews, and Frederick Vine, proposed a way that the theory could be tested.

Matthews and Vine started with an idea called "seafloor spreading," published a year earlier by American geologist Harry Hess. After World War II, oceanographers, equipped with new technologies like sonar, had mapped the floors of the world's oceans and found such surprising features as deep, long trenches, and mid-ocean ridges—undersea "mountains." When two plates converge, Hess hypothesized, the edge of one is forced beneath the other and down into the mantle, the layer of magma under the crust. Trenches mark the point of descent (subduction). Subducted plates, he suggested, melt into lava and are recycled into the earth's mantle, part of which in turn is perpetually cooling and forming new crust. Mid-ocean ridges, he speculated, occur where new crust emerges from the mantle. In effect, crust "spreads" from ridge to trench, with new rock constantly pushing old rock before it.

Matthews and Vine's great contribution was to provide a way to prove Hess's provocative theory: If the seafloor is really spreading, different segments of crust should have different magnetic polarities, corresponding to the era in which they were formed. (Canadian geologist Laurence Morley came up with a similar idea.) When the ocean floor was subjected to magnetic testing in the late 1960s, Hess, Matthews, and Vine all had their theories borne out. **◂1912.4**

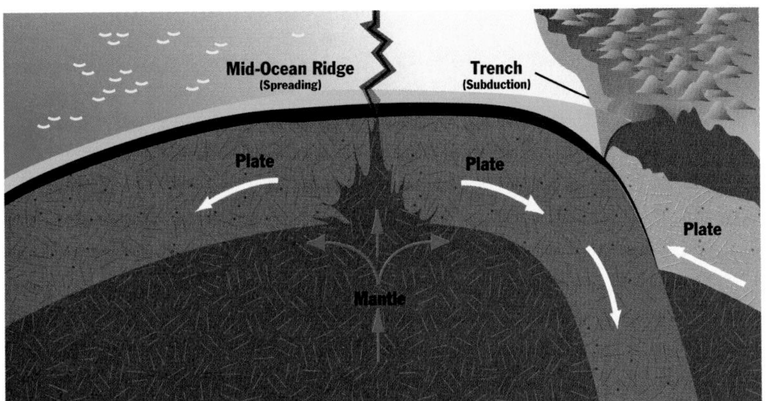

Continental drift manifests itself in the trenches and mid-ocean ridges of the seafloor.

DIPLOMACY

Franco-German Treaty

5 In January 1963, 19 years after German occupiers were driven from France, President Charles de Gaulle and Chancellor Konrad Adenauer signed the Treaty of Reconciliation in Paris. According to the pact, French and West German heads of state would consult on all important foreign policy questions; the two countries' armies would share plans and lend each other personnel; and cultural exchange would be increased. The treaty, its signers declared, ended "a centuries-old rivalry." "There is not a man in the world," proclaimed de Gaulle, "who does not grasp the capital importance of this act."

In a West German cartoon, Germany is caught between the U.S. and France. "Make up your mind—do you want the jacket or the pants?" reads the caption.

But like the 1925 Locarno Pact—also heralded as burying Franco-German antipathy—the new agreement left room for interpretation. A week before the signing, de Gaulle had blocked Britain's entry into the European Economic Community, arguing that London's special ties to Washington would draw all Europe into the orbit of the United States. He envisioned the reconciliation treaty as the basis for a counterweight to the Anglo-American colossus: a continental Europe clustered around its two strongest states—with West Germany as the distinctly junior partner.

But the Germans had a different view. With the Soviet bloc at their borders, they could hardly risk losing American protection—especially when it was in France's interest to keep East and West Germany divided. So the West German parliament ratified the treaty, but added a resolution and a preamble countering de Gaulle's goals: Bonn would continue to support NATO, British participation in the EEC, and German reunification.

The Franco-German honeymoon ended just months after it began. "Treaties," de Gaulle told colleagues philosophically, "are like young girls and roses. They do not last long." **◂1955.4 ▸1966.5**

BIRTHS

Charles Barkley, U.S. basketball player.

Brian Boitano, U.S. figure skater.

Randall Cunningham, U.S. football player.

Johnny Depp, U.S. actor.

Michael Jordan, U.S. basketball player.

Julie Krone, U.S. jockey.

Anne-Sophie Mutter, German violinist.

DEATHS

Abd el-Krim, Moroccan revolutionary.

Yitzhak Ben-Zvi, Israeli president.

William Beveridge, U.K. economist.

Georges Braque, French painter.

Patsy Cline, U.S. singer.

Jean Cocteau, French writer and filmmaker.

William Edward Burghardt Du Bois, U.S. civil rights leader.

Robert Frost, U.S. poet.

Paul Hindemith, German-U.S. composer and violinist.

Rogers Hornsby, U.S. baseball player and manager.

Aldous Huxley, U.K. writer.

John XXIII, Italian pope.

John F. Kennedy, U.S. president.

Clifford Odets, U.S. playwright.

Lee Harvey Oswald, U.S. assassin.

Edith Piaf, French singer.

Sylvia Plath, U.S. poet.

Francis Poulenc, French composer.

John Cowper Powys, U.K. writer.

Theodore Roethke, U.S. poet.

Tristan Tzara, French poet.

Dinah Washington, U.S. singer.

William Carlos Williams, U.S. poet.

(Brian Wilson); *Computer Cantata* (Lejaren Hiller) ... Painting & Sculpture: *Jackie (The Week That Was)* (Andy Warhol); *Blue Red Green* (Ellsworth Kelly) ... Film: *Tom Jones* (Tony Richardson); *The Birds* (Alfred Hitchcock); *Hud* (Martin Ritt); *The Leopard* (Luchino Visconti) ... Theater: *Barefoot in the Park* (Neil Simon); *110 in the Shade* (Schmidt and Jones) ... TV: *The Fugitive*; *General Hospital*; *Let's Make a Deal.*

"Segregation now! Segregation tomorrow! Segregation forever!"—**Alabama governor George C. Wallace, in his January 14, 1963, inaugural speech**

NEW IN 1963

Instant replay.

Prenatal blood transfusion (New Zealand).

Tab diet cola.

ZIP codes.

Holograms (using lasers, at the University of Michigan).

"Hot Line" between the Kremlin and the White House.

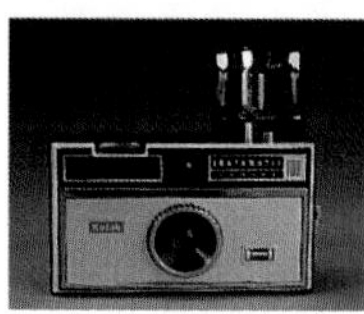

Kodak Instamatic camera (with film cartridge).

Pro football Hall of Fame.

Lung transplant.

Cassette tape recorder.

Touch-tone telephone.

IN THE UNITED STATES

▶**LITTLE WONDER**—Introduced to Motown mogul Berry Gordy by an impressed older musician, young Steveland Judkins Morris played (harmonica) and danced his way

to a record contract. Gordy gave the prodigy, blind since infancy, a stage name and released his first album in 1963: *Little Stevie Wonder, the 12-Year-Old Genius.* It was the first of 23 hit albums and 56 hit singles Wonder would make over the next 25 years. His immensely successful career has been marked by mastery of new instruments and technology (piano, drums, organ, synthesizer) and assimilation of new musical trends (reggae, rap). ◀1959.10

▶**POITIER WINS AN OSCAR**—With his subtle performance as a handyman who befriends a group of nuns in 1963's *The Lilies of the Field,* Sidney Poitier became the first black to win an Academy Award for Best Actor. Florida-born, Bahamas-raised, Poitier trained with the American Negro

Britain's Prince Philip congratulates Jomo Kenyatta on Kenya's independence.

EASTERN AFRICA

Kenya Gains Independence

6 Kenya's long-frustrated dream of independence became reality in 1963, when the British East African colony achieved nationhood within the British Commonwealth. Jomo Kenyatta, grand old man of Kenyan nationalism, became the first prime minister of free Kenya; for the next 15 years, until his death in 1978, Kenyatta presided over Kenya's transformation into a modern, capitalist, relatively democratic state.

After sputtering through a half century of British rule, Kenyan nationalism ignited after World War II. Improved African political organizations and violent upheaval in the form of the Mau Mau Rebellion soon underscored the untenability of the British regime. The colony's first free election, in 1960, gave Africans control of the legislature; two nationalist parties soon emerged—the Kenya African National Union (KANU) and the Kenya African Democratic Union (KADU). Kenyatta, then serving a prison sentence (having been wrongfully convicted of leading the 1952 Mau Mau rebellion), was named president of KANU, the majority party. While he was still in prison, KANU formed a coalition government with KADU.

Kenyatta was released in 1961 and traveled to London the next year to negotiate independence. A magnanimous and pragmatic man, he struck a conciliatory note: "Europeans," he promised "would find a place in the future Kenya, provided they took their place as ordinary citizens." In countrywide elections for independent Kenya's first government, in 1963, Kenyatta led KANU to a landslide victory over KADU. He was sworn in as prime minister on December 12. One year later, Kenya declared itself a republic with Kenyatta as president. ◀1952.4

SOCIAL REFORM

Rights Struggle Surges

7 The civil rights movement reached a watershed in 1963, when President Kennedy—after months of wavering—declared his unequivocal support. The pressure on the President began to escalate in April, as the Southern Christian Leadership Conference mounted an antisegregation campaign in Birmingham, Alabama. City public-safety commissioner Theophilus Eugene "Bull" Connor used dogs and fire hoses against peaceful demonstrators (many of them children), jailing SCLC chairman Martin Luther King, Jr., and hundreds of others. JFK dispatched a mediator to Birmingham, and local businessmen quickly agreed to SCLC demands. But rioting erupted after white supremacists bombed activists' lodgings, ceasing only when Kennedy sent federal troops to a nearby base as a threat to "extremists" on both sides.

Birmingham prompted international outrage, sparked demonstrations nationwide, and persuaded JFK to throw his full weight behind the movement. In June, when Alabama governor George Wallace blocked the door of a state university building to keep out two black students, federal marshals ensured their admission. That very night, Kennedy called for passage of a new civil rights bill, backing equality for African-Americans in the strongest language of any twentieth-century president. "The fires of frustration and discord," he warned, "are busy in every city." As if to illustrate the point, black leader Medgar Evers was shot dead hours later in front of his Mississippi home as his family cowered inside.

Evers's murder led to the first meeting between Kennedy and civil rights leaders, and to the August 28 March on Washington—then the largest human-rights demonstration in U.S. history. Nearly 300,000 people converged on the capital, where they were entertained by singers (including a young Bob Dylan) and Hollywood stars. King delivered one of his greatest speeches, using the refrain "I have a dream." But the dream confronted a hideous reality in September, when four black schoolgirls died in the racist bombing of a Birmingham church. ◀1962.M ▶1963.V

Bull Connor gave Birmingham police the go-ahead to set guard dogs on demonstrators.

IDEAS

A Woman's Place

8 Described as the *Uncle Tom's Cabin* of the women's movement, Betty Friedan's 1963 book, *The Feminine Mystique,* issued modern feminism's call to arms.

Friedan's penetrating analysis of women's place in postindustrial society grew directly out of her own experience as a frustrated housewife and mother. Born in 1921, a year after the 19th Amendment gave American women the vote, Friedan had graduated at the top of her class at all-female Smith College, winning a research fellowship in psychology. But she gravitated toward a more conventional role. Married and the mother of three children, she expected to feel fulfilled in her gorgeous suburban home. It was while organizing a college reunion that she realized other women shared her discontent.

The Feminine Mystique derided suburbia as "a bedroom and kitchen sexual ghetto," and condemned society for presenting marriage as a woman's only route to happiness. The problem, Friedan wrote, was

SPORTS: Baseball: World Series, Los Angeles Dodgers (Sandy Koufax) defeat New York Yankees, 4–0 ... Football: NFL, Chicago Bears defeat New York Giants, 14–10; AFL, San Diego Chargers defeat Boston Patriots, 51–10 (game played on January 5, 1964) ... Basketball: NBA, Boston Celtics defeat Los Angeles Lakers, 4–3 ... Track & Field: John Pennel is first to pole-vault 17 ft. (first use of a fiberglass pole).

"Our dreams are our real life."—**Federico Fellini**

the "strange discrepancy between the reality of our lives as women and the image to which we were trying to conform, the image I came to call 'the feminine mystique.'" For the legions of American women who felt shortchanged in their conventional lives, Friedan's words resonated with piercing truth.

Friedan went on to found the National Organization for Women (NOW), chartered in 1966 to achieve equality for women "in a truly equal partnership with men," and to campaign actively for the Equal Rights Amendment (which failed to be ratified). And she continued to take on sacred cows in her writing, including, in her 1993 book, *The Fountain of Age*, the notion that old age is a state to be dreaded and merely endured. **◂1949.13 ▸1970.9**

LITERATURE

Le Carré's Cold, Cold War

9 With *The Spy Who Came in from the Cold*, British novelist John le Carré introduced the themes and techniques that made him one of one of the most topical—and best-selling—writers of his time. The 1963 thriller features an intricate plot, colorful, realistically drawn characters, and expert pacing. But what really sets it apart is its abidingly skeptical treatment of the Cold War. The book blew the lid off the international spy game, exposing the hypocrisy inherent in the East versus West dichotomy.

In place of gallant, sexy comic-book agents like James Bond, le Carré (nom de plume of British diplomat David John Moore Cornwell) gave readers Alec Leamas, a worn-out spook whose own treacherous bosses (the supposed good guys) used and discarded him in his last mission like broken equipment.

The Spy Who Came in from the Cold eventually sold more than 20 million copies worldwide. In his many popular subsequent spy novels (including 1974's *Tinker, Tailor, Soldier, Spy*, the first volume of a trilogy about cynical, flawed spymaster George Smiley), le Carré continued to use the genre to explore moral ambiguities. **◂1953.9**

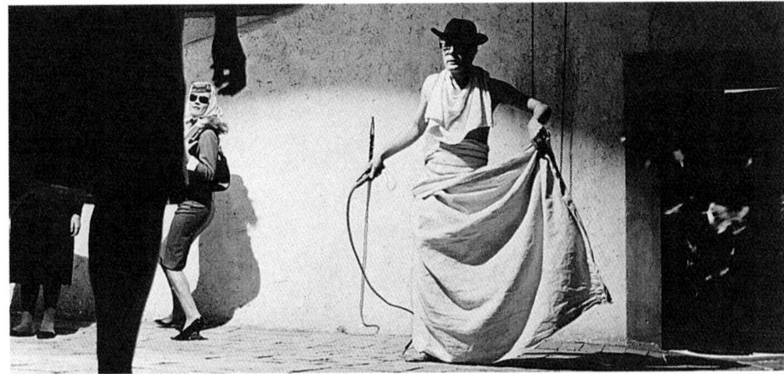

In one of *8½*'s many dream sequences, the film director, played by Marcello Mastroianni *(above)*, imagines himself as a lion tamer in the circus.

FILM

Fellini's Other Self

10 In *8½*, his delirious 1963 film, Italian director Federico Fellini wove a tale about the life, loves, and limitations of a successful Italian movie director much like ... Federico Fellini. It was a splendid achievement—reveling in, tweaking, and transcending pure autobiography to create a masterly portrait of a modern artist in crisis.

Fellini had begun making films in the early 1950s and soon hit upon a distinctive style: a combination of neorealist grit, fictionalized autobiography, sentimental parable, and lyrical humanism, often featuring grifters and circus freaks amid an atmosphere of grotesquery. *La Strada* (1954) announced his artistic arrival. *La Dolce Vita* (1960)—a riotous vivisection of contemporary European decadence, Roman style—certified his reputation.

8½ (named for the number of movies he'd made, counting this one) features longtime Fellini collaborator Marcello Mastroianni in the role of a director crippled by creative block and beset on all sides—by colleagues, his wife, his mistress, the press, the Church. The film ends climactically with the auteur, his imagination liberated, dancing in a circus ring with people from his past and present. By accepting his life and loving it, a grinning Fellini seems to say, the artist frees himself. **◂1948.14**

SCIENCE

The Nearness of Quasars

11 By 1963, two decades of space exploration via radiotelescopes had pretty much disproven the old notion that the universe is a stable and orderly place. Astronomers had discovered all sorts of puzzling "abnormalities," including preposterously luminescent stars, stars that pulsed, bizarrely configured galaxies, and starlike fonts of energy dubbed quasars—quasi-stellar radio sources. Still, no one was prepared for the revelation made that year by California Institute of Technology astronomer Maarten Schmidt, who demonstrated that quasars (commonly believed to be near to the earth because of the measured strength of their radio emissions) are farther away in space than anything observed before. More stunning: A lone quasar burns 100 times brighter than 100 billion stars. And the fact that quasars recede from the earth at a rate of 25,000 miles per second gave them a greater velocity than any other known objects.

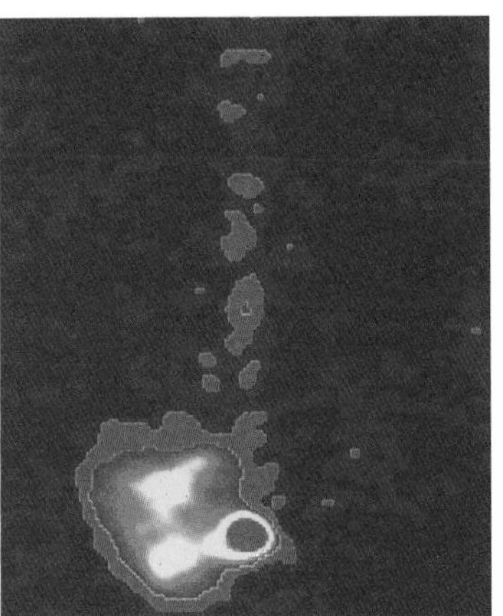

A quasar may be a clump of matter swirling around a giant black hole.

Schmidt arrived at his conclusions by studying the distortion caused by the Doppler effect ("red shift" in astronomy) to a known quasar, 3C 273, which indicated that it was receding at a huge velocity. By applying Hubble's law, Schmidt determined that the quasar was 1.5 billion light-years away. Its observed light, in other words, had been traveling through space for 1.5 billion years. **◂1929.9 ▸1968.8**

IN THE UNITED STATES

Theater in New York in the late 1940s before breaking into films in the 1950s *(No Way Out; Cry, the Beloved Country; The Defiant Ones)*. Poitier's pioneering career helped open mainstream films to other African-Americans.

▶MONUMENTAL SHAPES—David Smith, the most influential postwar American sculptor, carried his art to a new level of abstraction in 1963 with serial works such as *Cubi XIX (below)*—monumental polished-steel shapes that,

despite their heaviness, transmit a sense of dynamic tension. Smith's art symbolized life in the twentieth century, an era dominated, said Smith —who'd once worked as a metalworker at an automobile plant—by "power, structure, movement, progress, suspension, destruction, brutality."

▶LIZ AND DICK—Actress Elizabeth Taylor was paid an unprecedented $1 million in 1963 for starring in *Cleopatra*, the most expensive movie made to date. Not even her star power could save the overwrought film, one of Hollywood's spectacular failures. But the on-set fireworks between Taylor and costar Richard Burton became one of Tinsel Town's great temperamental romances. Liz and Dick survived to marry in 1964 ... divorce a few years later ... remarry ... redivorce in 1976.... ◂1958.V

▶WILD THING—Children's book author Maurice Sendak produced a classic of the genre in 1963. *Where the Wild Things Are*, with its brilliantly expressive illustrations and plucky protagonist (the boy-rebel Max), is an unsentimental but always psychologically telling exploration of universal childhood anxieties and fantasies—getting pushed around, getting lost, being the boss, being found. ◂1957.V

POLITICS & BUSINESS: GNP: $590.5 billion ... John F. Kennedy assassinated, Lyndon B. Johnson succeeds him as president ... Congress passes law requiring equal pay for equal work ... Winston Churchill proclaimed honorary U.S. citizen ... New York City newspapers end 114 day strike on March 31 (most expensive to date at $100,000,000).

"Once a specific crime has appeared for the first time, its reappearance is more likely than its initial emergence could have been."—**Hannah Arendt, in *Eichmann in Jerusalem: A Report on the Banality of Evil***

AROUND THE WORLD

►EL BOOM BEGINS—Argentine novelist Julio Cortázar's 1963 *Rayuela* (translated as *Hopscotch*) can be read front to back, back to front, or according to an author-prescribed leapfrogging scheme. Cortázar's experimental masterpiece was the first major novel of El Boom, a period of astounding fertility in Latin American fiction. Influenced by surrealism, existentialism, and his own playfully subversive imagination, Cortázar (who relocated permanently to Paris in 1951 out of disgust with the Perón regime) was deeply interested in big questions: traditional morality, the nature of time, the meaning of life and death. ◄1944.15 ►1967.7

►OUT OF THIS WORLD—Blasting off on a solo mission on June 16, 1963, Soviet cosmonaut Valentina Tereshkova became the first woman to visit outer space. Tereshkova orbited the earth 48 times before returning to terra firma

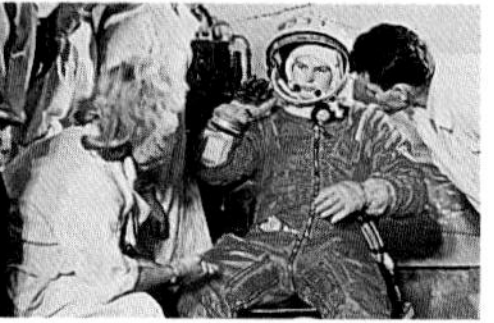

three days later. Tereshkova's triumph, another first in a long list of Soviet space accomplishments, was broadcast on Soviet television. She was awarded the Order of Lenin medal, the U.S.S.R.'s highest honor. ◄1961.3 ►1965.M

►DIEM ASSASSINATED—His country embroiled in war, South Vietnamese dictator Ngo Dinh Diem was killed by his own military officers in November. Diem, a Catholic aristocrat, had been a leading political figure since the 1930s. After WWII, when Ho Chi Minh invited Diem to join his independent government in the North, Diem, an obdurate anti-Communist, went into exile. Backed by the U.S., he returned in 1954 to fight the encroaching Communists. His Catholicism and his corruption, however, alienated his own (overwhelmingly Buddhist) countrymen. After Diem jailed and executed hundreds of Buddhists (he claimed they were Communist sympathizers), the U.S. withdrew support and approved the fatal coup. ◄1961.6 ►1964.1

Folk troubadours Joan Baez and Bob Dylan perform together in 1963.

MUSIC

Dylan and Baez at Newport

12 Folk singer Joan Baez already commanded a huge following when she appeared at the Newport (Rhode Island) Folk Festival in 1963. Her fellow "folknik" and sometime paramour, Bob Dylan, as yet unscarred by fame, was about to be labeled the voice of a generation. Their music, rooted in 1930s union-hall balladeering, became the cutting-edge sound of the '60s youth movement.

An early Vietnam protester (she waged an ongoing battle with the IRS, from which she withheld taxes that would go toward military buildup), Baez lent a seriousness and credibility to folk. Her clear, simple, acoustic songs attracted "highbrow" listeners, many of whom were shocked when she brought scruffy, raspy-voiced Bob Dylan onstage. But whereas Baez would remain primarily a folk musician, Dylan was a musical Proteus, constantly experimenting.

Born Robert Zimmerman in Duluth, Minnesota, Dylan renamed himself for Welsh poet Dylan Thomas. Endowed with a peculiarly nasal voice that often offended the coffeehouse audiences he performed for in the early sixties, he was a gifted songwriter whose influences ranged from Walt Whitman to Arthur Rimbaud to Allen Ginsberg. By the end of 1963, prophetic, dissident songs like "Blowin' in the Wind" and "The Times They Are A-Changin'" had made him the king of folk protest. Dubbed "the new Woody Guthrie," after the pioneering Depression-era singer and songwriter, Dylan, reclusive (more so after a near-fatal 1966 motorcycle crash) and misanthropic, rejected the title, opting instead to explore new sounds—urban folk, country rock, obscure pop surrealism.

At the 1965 Newport festival, acoustic Dylan "went electric," scandalizing folkies. But the move made him a force to be reckoned with in rock music and confirmed him as one of the most important musicians of his generation. **►1969.4**

FILM

Cinema's Problem Child

13 Comedian Jerry Lewis, the writer, director, and star of an array of popular slapstick comedies, represents a problem for professional cinephiles. American critics commonly dismiss him as a vulgar egotist whose puerile, cacophonous movies would leave a hyena stone-faced; in France he is celebrated as "le Roi du Crazy" (the King of Craziness), an innovative genius who deliberately subverts movie conventions. Both sides agree that his 1963 *The Nutty Professor* is archetypal Lewis.

Lewis had perfected his trademark character—a screeching, hyperactive, overgrown kid—in the resort hotels of New York's Catskill Mountains ("the Borscht Belt"). In 1946, he teamed up with small-time crooner Dean Martin; their mix of Martin's sexy singing with Lewis's antic routines made them one of the most successful duos in show business. The pair split up in 1956, and Lewis starred solo in several profitable pictures before directing his first feature, *The Bellboy*, in 1960.

In *The Nutty Professor*, his fourth directorial effort, Lewis plays a nerdy college professor who quaffs a potion that turns him into swingin', singin' Buddy Love, a skirt-chasing hipster. (Lewis denied that Love was a doppelgänger of erstwhile partner Martin.) In the view of American critics, the film was a "hodgepodge"; in that of the French, it was "magnificent ... so inventive, so profound." The critical impasse has never fazed Lewis's fans—plentiful on both sides of the Atlantic. **◄1959.8**

Lewis *(left)* starred with Stella Stevens in *The Nutty Professor*, a kind of cockeyed update of *Dr. Jekyll and Mr. Hyde*.

IDEAS

The Banality of Evil

14 With the hanging of Nazi war criminal Adolf Eichmann, most people agreed, the world was rid of a fiend, the diabolical architect of the Holocaust.

But political philosopher Hannah Arendt offered an arresting alternative interpretation. In a series of articles on Eichmann's trial, published as a 1963 book, *Eichmann in Jerusalem* (provocatively subtitled *A Report on the Banality of Evil*), Arendt presented the heinous killer as a buffoon, one of many bureaucratic cogs who'd actively or passively assented to Nazi atrocities. Shockingly, Arendt included among this group many Jewish community leaders who had cooperated with the Nazis.

A German-born Jew who had studied with philosopher Karl Jaspers, Arendt knew Nazi terror firsthand. She fled Hitler's regime to France in 1933 and emigrated to the United States eight years later. Her report on Eichmann, with its reductionist view of evil and its element of self-incrimination, provoked controversy in the Jewish community. Arendt's outraged critics denounced her for underestimating Eichmann's criminal cunning, and for blaming victims for their sufferings. Among intellectuals who understood Arendt's work in the context of her contributions to political philosophy, the book was much better received. Far from exculpating Eichmann, Arendt was examining the nature (and troubling allure) of totalitarianism. It was a subject she had probed earlier in *Origins of Totalitarianism* (1951), which draws links between Nazism and communism, and between nineteenth-century anti-Semitism and imperialism. *Eichmann in Jerusalem* encouraged serious consideration of an emotionally charged subject: the capacity of a totalitarian regime to obtain the complicity of its victims as well as of its Eichmanns. **◄1960.8 ►1987.11**

1963

NOBEL PRIZES: Peace: Int'l Committee of the Red Cross and League of Red Cross Societies (Switzerland) ... Literature: George Seferis (Greek; poet) ... Chemistry: Karl Ziegler and Giulio Natta (German, Italian; polymers) ... Medicine: Alan Hodgkin, Andrew Huxley, and John Eccles (U.K., U.K., Australian; nerve cells) ... Physics: Eugene Wigner, Maria Mayer, and J.H. Jensen (U.S., U.S., German; nuclear shell structure).

A VOICE FROM 1963

A Movement's Transcendent Moment

From a speech at the Lincoln Memorial, Washington, D.C., by Martin Luther King, Jr., August 28, 1963

Martin Luther King, Jr.'s nonviolent campaign in Birmingham, Alabama, launched in the spring of 1963, raised the consciousness about racism of even the most enlightened Americans; in August, King and other civil rights leaders brought many of those Americans together for a march on Washington. A then-record 300,000 people, of myriad races and social backgrounds, united in spirit, converged on the nation's capital to demonstrate for basic freedoms—the right to be hired, to get an education, to simply eat in a restaurant. The orderly, peaceable crowd walked in the shadow of Washington's great monuments to liberty and justice, assembling in front of the most moving of them all, the Lincoln Memorial. From its granite steps, King delivered his biblically cadenced "I Have a Dream" speech, which exemplified the transcendent vision of the civil rights movement. ◄**1963.7** ►**1964.3**

I am happy to join with you today in what will go down in history as the greatest demonstration for freedom in the history of our nation.

Five score years ago, a great American, in whose symbolic shadow we stand, signed the Emancipation Proclamation. This momentous decree came as a great beacon light of hope to millions of Negro slaves who had been seared in the flames of withering injustice. It came as a joyous daybreak to end the long night of captivity.

But one hundred years later, we must face the tragic fact that the Negro is still not free. One hundred years later, the life of the Negro is still sadly crippled by the manacles of segregation and the chains of discrimination. One hundred years later, the Negro lives on a lonely island of poverty in the midst of a vast ocean of material prosperity. One hundred years later, the Negro is still languishing in the corners of American society and finds himself an exile in his own land. So we have come here today to dramatize an appalling condition....

I say to you today, my friends, that in spite of the difficulties and frustrations of the moment, I still have a dream. It is a dream deeply rooted in the American dream.

Hundreds of thousands of supporters gathered at the Washington Monument in D.C. on August 28, 1963, to hear King speak. Above, King delivering his speech from the Lincoln Memorial.

I have a dream that one day this nation will rise up and live out the true meaning of its creed: "We hold these truths to be self-evident; that all men are created equal."

I have a dream that one day on the red hills of Georgia the sons of former slaves and the sons of former slaveowners will be able to sit down together at the table of brotherhood.

I have a dream that one day even the state of Mississippi, a desert state sweltering with the heat of injustice and oppression, will be transformed into an oasis of freedom and justice.

I have a dream that my four little children will one day live in a nation where they will not be judged by the color of their skin but by the content of their character.

I have a dream today.

I have a dream that one day the state of Alabama, whose governor's lips are presently dripping with the words of interposition and nullification, will be transformed into a situation where little black boys and black girls will be able to join hand with little white boys and white girls and walk together as sisters and brothers.

I have a dream today.

I have a dream that one day every valley shall be exalted, every hill and mountain shall be made low, the rough places will be made plains, and the crooked places will be made straight, and the glory of the Lord shall be revealed, and all flesh shall see it together.

This is our hope. This is the faith with which I return to the South. With this faith we will be able to hew out of the mountain of despair a stone of hope. With this faith we will be able to transform the jangling discords of our nation into a beautiful symphony of brotherhood. With this faith we will be able to work together, to pray together, to struggle together, to go to jail together, to stand up for freedom together, knowing that we will be free one day.

This will be the day when all of God's children will be able to sing with new meaning, "My country 'tis of thee, sweet land of liberty, of thee I sing. Land where my fathers died, land of the Pilgrims' pride, from every mountainside, let freedom ring."

And if America is to be a great nation this must become true. So let freedom ring from the prodigious hilltops of New Hampshire. Let freedom ring from the mighty mountains of New York. Let freedom ring from the heightening Alleghenies of Pennsylvania!

Let freedom ring from the snowcapped Rockies of Colorado!

Let freedom ring from the curvaceous peaks of California!

But not only that; let freedom ring from Stone Mountain of Georgia!

Let freedom ring from Lookout Mountain of Tennessee!

Let freedom ring from every hill and mole hill of Mississippi. From every mountainside, let freedom ring.

When we let freedom ring, when we let it ring from every village and every hamlet, from every state and every city, we will be able to speed up that day when all of God's children, black men and white men, Jews and Gentiles, Protestants and Catholics, will be able to join hands and sing in the words of the old Negro spiritual, "Free at Last! Free at last! Thank God almighty, we are free at last!"

"We are not about to send American boys nine or ten thousand miles away from home to do what Asian boys ought to be doing themselves."—**Lyndon Johnson, campaigning in 1964**

STORY OF THE YEAR

The Gulf of Tonkin Resolution

1 The war that would cost the world's most powerful nation its aura of invincibility was never declared. It didn't have to be, thanks to the Gulf of Tonkin Resolution, passed by the U.S. Congress on August 7, 1964. Days earlier, two American destroyers in the gulf, which marked the eastern boundary of North Vietnam, had allegedly been attacked without provocation by North Vietnamese torpedo boats. After ordering retaliatory bombing raids, President Johnson asked the legislators for authorization to intervene freely in Vietnam. Their near-unanimous compliance allowed him to escalate the conflict without the legal and political complications a declaration of war would have entailed. The gambit paid off: In November, Johnson was elected, defeating overtly bellicose Arizona senator Barry Goldwater by the largest margin in U.S. history. Soon after his inauguration, the President began systematic bombing of North Vietnam and sent U.S. marines into combat.

President Johnson, surrounded by members of the U.S. Senate and House, signs the Gulf of Tonkin Resolution.

The Tonkin incident was part of Johnson's secret plan to goad the Communists into aggravating hostilities, thereby giving him an excuse to retaliate. (*The Pentagon Papers*, the Defense Department study leaked to the press by government official Daniel Ellsberg in 1971, revealed that the American ships had made attacks on North Vietnam. Whether they were actually fired upon remains in dispute.) Intervention seemed urgently necessary to Johnson in 1964: Despite the presence of 16,000 American military advisers in South Vietnam, a series of corrupt regimes (most recently that of Ngo Dinh Diem, who'd been assassinated nine months earlier) had lost half the country to the Communist Viet Cong. Johnson dreaded being blamed for "losing" Vietnam (as Truman had been lambasted for "losing" China). Moreover, he and most of his intelligence experts believed North Vietnamese leader Ho Chi Minh's peasant guerrillas would collapse under even a limited American onslaught.

Johnson failed to account for the guerrillas' determination, the ingenuity of Ho's generals, and the disaffection of South Vietnam's soldiers. Nor did he foresee the American people's eventual disillusionment with a costly, distant, and incomprehensible war. By 1968, U.S. troop levels had passed 500,000, and U.S. planes had dumped more bombs on Vietnam than the Allies dropped in World War II. Yet the Communists were undeterred, and anger over the war was tearing the United States apart. Bitter, his reputation in tatters, Johnson did not seek reelection.

◂1963.M ▸1965.1

1964

THE SOVIET UNION

Khrushchev Ousted

2 In the end, Nikita Khrushchev, brash, vulgar, and impatient, simply alienated too many people to survive as head of the Soviet government. By 1964, when the Central Committee of the Communist Party unanimously voted to strip Khrushchev of all his Party posts, the politician's turbulent eleven-year reign had left him without a single group of constituents: Party executives, bureaucratic functionaries, the military, intellectuals, farmers, factory workers—all had experienced his temper and his impetuous reforms. And all had suffered. It was time for new leadership.

Hell-bent on reform after years of Stalinist excesses, Khrushchev consistently got ahead of himself during his years of power, ambition outstripping practicality. Trying to improve government by decentralizing it, he cut off Party bureaucracy; supporting nuclear arms over a conventional army (and then pursuing disarmament talks with the West), he alienated the entrenched military; elaborating a foreign policy of "peaceful coexistence" with capitalist powers, he offended both China, a prized ally, and hardliners within the Soviet bureaucracy. Desperate always to "overtake the United States," Khrushchev

Khrushchev at his last session of the Supreme Soviet. Clockwise from upper left: Grishin, Kirilenko, Polyansky, Voronov, Khrushchev, and Brezhnev.

implemented a host of optimistic but badly planned industrial and agricultural policies. Resentment of him peaked in 1963, when his agricultural programs brought famine to the Soviet Union, the world's largest farming country.

In October 1964, while Khrushchev vacationed at his Black Sea dacha, Party leaders met in Moscow and plotted his ouster. The procedure was clean and constitutional: After informing all 200 Central Committee members of the plan, the plotters, led by Politburo power brokers Mikhail Suslov and Leonid Brezhnev, summoned Khrushchev to Moscow. At midnight on October 13, after a grueling, all-day meeting, an initially defiant Khrushchev agreed to "voluntarily" resign. He was relieved of his posts the next day. The installation of Brezhnev as new Party chairman and Alexei Kosygin as premier proceeded serenely, and Khrushchev, spared the public denunciation traditionally conferred on ousted apparatchiks, retired to a quiet pensioner's life at his country home. He died in 1971.

◂1963.2 ▸1966.11

SOCIAL REFORM

Civil Rights Act Passed

3 American civil rights volunteers had vowed to make the summer of 1964 a season of liberation, but the threat of death hung over their work. In June, three young men participating in Freedom Summer, a campaign by the Chicago-based Student Nonviolent Coordinating Committee (SNCC) to register disenfranchised black voters in Mississippi, were murdered. Northerners Andrew Goodman and Michael Schwerner, both white, and James Chaney, a black Mississippian, disappeared one night after being stopped for speeding. Investigators found their beaten, bullet-riddled bodies in a mud dam; several Ku Klux Klan members (including the local sheriff) were eventually convicted of murder.

The heinous crime brought home the fact that Jim Crow hooliganism was a national, and not just regional, disgrace. The outcry gave President Johnson (who had denied requests for federal protection of the Freedom Summer activists) the public support he needed to get Congress to pass his comprehensive Civil Rights Act. First proposed in a limited form by Kennedy, LBJ's version, signed in July, outlawed discrimination in public accommodations, and by employers (on the basis of sex as well), unions, public schools, and voting registrars. Illinois senator Everett Dirksen, a longtime foe of integration, cosponsored the bill with Minnesota senator Hubert Humphrey. Explaining his turnabout, Dirksen quoted Victor Hugo: "No army can withstand the strength of an idea whose time has come."

ART & CULTURE: Books: ***Last Exit to Brooklyn*** **(Hubert Selby, Jr.);** ***Arrow of God*** **(Chinua Achebe);** ***Charlie and the Chocolate Factory*** **(Roald Dahl);** ***Understanding Media*** **(Marshall McLuhan);** ***One-Dimensional Man*** **(Herbert Marcuse) ... Music: "Oh, Pretty Woman" (Roy Orbison); "I Get Around" (Brian Wilson);** ***Philomel*** **(Milton Babbitt);** ***Horn of Plenty*** **(Roy Harris) ... Painting & Sculpture:** ***Brillo Boxes*** **(Andy Warhol);**

"Palestine is ours, ours, ours. We shall accept no substitute homeland."—**Pledge made by the 350 Palestinian delegates at the first Palestine National Congress**

A SNCC worker visits rural Mississippians during Freedom Summer, 1964.

But if the idea of civil rights was unstoppable, its realization still faced enormous hurdles. Discrimination in the North sparked riots in Harlem and elsewhere throughout the summer. In August, the Democratic Party refused to replace Mississippi's all-white delegation to the national convention (which nominated LBJ for another term) with an integrated group. And in October, two blacks were killed in the bombing of a Vicksburg, Mississippi, church that served as a voter registration center. **◂1963.V ▸1965.5**

MEDICINE

Surgeon General's Warning

4 Cigarettes lost their glamour in 1964, the year the U.S. government issued its landmark report on smoking. Corroborating private studies, the Surgeon General's findings, compiled by ten independent biomedical researchers, implicated the habit as a major cause of lung cancer and heart disease. Less than two years after the report's release, Congress ordered that a warning against smoking's dangers appear on all cigarette packages sold domestically. Great Britain soon followed suit; by 1972, West Germany, the United States, and Canada had proscribed television advertising of cigarettes. Many European countries also began imposing steep cigarette taxes.

Epidemiologists had been linking tobacco to disease since the 1950s. By then, lung cancer—almost unknown at the beginning of the century—had become a big killer. Its increased incidence roughly corresponded to smoking's popularity, which boomed during World War I, when tobacco manufacturers supplied troops with free cigarettes, and received a similar boost from World War II, when doctors even encouraged smoking as a way for soldiers to calm their nerves. As the hazards emerged, tobacco companies (which had once recommended their products' salutary effects) began making defensive claims. As early as 1949, an advertising campaign for the popular Camel brand featured anonymous "noted throat specialists" unable to document a single case of Camel-caused throat irritation.

In the United States, at least, the Surgeon General's warning was effective. In the mid-1960s, 40 percent of American adults smoked. Thirty years later, the proportion of smokers had fallen below 25 percent. **◂1919.V ▸1978.13**

Congress has acted
The next step
is yours.
Caution: Cigarette smoking may be hazardous to your health

This American Cancer Society poster invoked the Surgeon General's report.

THE MIDDLE EAST

A Palestinian Covenant

5 The driving force behind the creation in 1964 of the Palestine Liberation Organization was not Palestinian but Egyptian: Gamal Abdal Nasser, Egypt's president. A champion of Arab nationalism and a sworn enemy of Israel, Nasser believed that to defeat Israel the Arab world had to unite—preferably under his direction. He proposed the PLO as an umbrella organization for the various guerrilla resistance groups active in Palestine (in which some two million residents had been displaced by the creation of Israel in 1948). Nasser's fellow Arab leaders approved the plan and, at a conference in May, endorsed his choice of Ahmad Shukeiry, Palestine's representative to the Arab League, as the PLO's first chairman.

Initially, the PLO talked loudly and carried a small stick. The Palestine National Covenant, adopted by delegates to the founding conference, disputed Jewish ties to Palestine, called for armed struggle to achieve "the elimination of Zionism," and supported the formation of a "democratic and secular" Arab state in Israel's place. Provisions were made for the creation of a Palestinian army. But, bold rhetoric aside, the PLO's authority remained shaky. Chief among the scattered constituent groups that challenged its leadership was the militant Movement for the Liberation of Palestine—known as Al-Fatah ("Conquest by Jihad") and cofounded by a young Egyptian-educated engineer named Yasir Arafat.

PLO chairman Yasir Arafat in 1968.

After Israel's crushing defeat of Egypt in the Six Day War in 1967 Al-Fatah transformed the PLO into a formidable independent military and political force. Named PLO chairman in 1968, Arafat emerged as the Palestinians' supreme leader, his organization their leading representative body—roles that even Israel eventually came to recognize. **◂1958.1 ▸1967.3**

BIRTHS

Bonnie Blair, U.S. speed skater.

José Canseco, U.S. baseball player.

Tracy Chapman, U.S. singer.

Dwight Gooden, U.S. baseball player.

Darci Kistler, U.S. ballet dancer.

Mike Powell, U.S. athlete.

Marcus Roberts, U.S. musician.

DEATHS

Emilio Aguinaldo, Philippine revolutionary.

William Maxwell Aitken, Lord Beaverbrook, Canadian-U.K. publisher and statesman.

Gracie Allen, U.S. comedian.

Nancy Astor, U.K. political leader.

Brendan Behan, Irish playwright.

Rachel Carson, U.S. biologist and writer.

Stuart Davis, U.S. painter.

Gerhard Domagk, German biochemist.

Ian Fleming, U.K. novelist.

Herbert Hoover, U.S. president.

Peter Lorre, Hungarian-U.S. actor.

Douglas MacArthur, U.S. general.

Simon Marks, U.K. retailer.

Arthur "Harpo" Marx, U.S. comedian.

Giorgio Morandi, Italian artist.

Jawaharlal Nehru, Indian prime minister.

Sean O'Casey, Irish playwright.

Flannery O'Connor, U.S. writer.

Cole Porter, U.S. composer.

Edith Sitwell, U.K. writer.

Leo Szilard, Hungarian-U.S. physicist.

Palmiro Togliatti, Italian political leader.

Norbert Wiener, U.S. mathematician.

Back Seat Dodge–'38 **(Edward Kienholz);** ***Magenta Haze*** **(Kenneth Noland) ... Film:** ***My Fair Lady*** **(George Cukor);** ***Dr. Strangelove*** **(Stanley Kubrick);** ***Mary Poppins*** **(Robert Stevenson);** ***The Pink Panther*** **(Blake Edwards) ... Theater:** ***Entertaining Mr. Sloane*** **(Joe Orton);** ***After the Fall*** **(Arthur Miller);** ***Hello, Dolly!*** **(Jerry Herman) ... TV:** ***Gilligan's Island; The Munsters; The Addams Family.***

"John Coltrane was a preacher on his horn."—Saxophonist Carlos Ward

NEW IN 1964

Ford Mustang.

GI Joe doll.

Verrazano-Narrows Bridge (New York City).

Bullet train (between Tokyo and Osaka).

State lottery (New Hampshire).

Spaghetti western (*A Fistful of Dollars*).

IN THE UNITED STATES

▶URBAN APATHY—On March 13, 38 people watched and listened as Queens, New York, resident Kitty Genovese was stabbed to death in the courtyard of her middle-class apartment complex. Though Genovese screamed for help for an hour and a half, no one called the police until the brutal attack was over. The witnesses' scandalous inaction—they didn't want to "get involved"—became a metaphor for the apathy, isolation, and debasement of urban American life.

▶WHO KILLED JFK?—According to the numbingly detailed report of the Warren Commission, the body of jurists and statesmen (headed by Chief Justice Earl Warren) set up to investigate the JFK assassination, Lee Harvey Oswald acted alone. The Commission issued its findings in 1964; by then a growing cabal of conspiracy theorists had a long list of alternatives: Fidel Castro, the KGB, the Mafia, the CIA, anti-Castro Cubans, a junta of U.S. generals. ◀1963.1 ▶1978.M

▶SUIT OF THE TIMES—Observing the trend toward fewer clothing restrictions, American fashion designer Rudi Gernreich introduced the monokini, the top-less swimsuit, in 1964. Not very practical on

1964

MUSIC

Coltrane's Supreme Moment

6 Saxophonist John Coltrane was a jazz exception—a brilliantly innovative player who commanded both the respect of fellow musicians and the ear of the public. With his hypnotically beautiful 1964 album, *A Love Supreme*, Trane achieved his musical apotheosis.

Probably the most virtuosic and influential of sixties jazz musicians, Trane spent years as a sideman for the likes of Dizzy Gillespie, Miles Davis, and Thelonius Monk before introducing his own style with his 1959 album, *Giant Steps*. It featured breezy melodic lines racing over densely packed, yet perfectly articulated, chord changes —his famous "sheets of sound." Accomplished on both the tenor and soprano saxophone, Trane

Coltrane and wife Alice (who played piano in his quartet). His influence in the '60s and '70s was commensurate with Charlie Parker's earlier.

created chordal techniques that broke traditional rhythmic and harmonic patterns. To the uninitiated, his music could sound chaotic—dense, dissonant—but his records did phenomenally well. His 1960 *My Favorite Things* (the title track is an extended lyrical riff on the *Sound of Music* number) sold 50,000 copies.

Characteristically, *A Love Supreme* charted new musical territory. Released just three years before his sudden death at age 41, the work was at once a synthesis of Coltrane's various playing styles and a novel expression of his religious mysticism. Hymnic, deeply melodious, it is considered by many to be his greatest accomplishment. ◀1955.7

Julius Nyerere *(with cane)* and some of his troops prepare for a symbolic march up Mount Kilimanjaro to mark Tanganyika's independence, in 1961.

EASTERN AFRICA

Tanganyika, Zanzibar Merge

7 Tanganyikan president Julius Nyerere called his brand of socialism *ujamaa*, Swahili for "community." In April 1964—shortly after surviving a military coup—Nyerere brought the coastal island of Zanzibar into Tanganyika's community, forming the United Republic of Tanzania. The merger reflected Nyerere's fear that tiny Zanzibar, whose black majority had overthrown its Afro-Arab sultan in January, was drifting into the Communist Chinese camp. A champion of nonalignment, Nyerere struck the deal with Zanzibar's like-minded president, Abeid Amani Karume, while the pro-Beijing foreign minister was abroad.

Among Africa's new nations, Tanzania seemed blessed. The country lacked thorny ethnic divisions, and its recent history was less traumatic than that of most: For decades Tanganyika had been a British mandate under the League of Nations (and then, until 1961, the UN), rather than a colony. Moreover, Nyerere himself was exceptional. Although he ran a one-party state, his version offered a real choice of candidates and entailed relatively little repression. While other African leaders affected grandiose nicknames (like Ghana's dictatorial "Redeemer," Kwame Nkrumah) and blared propaganda over state radio, the Edinburgh-educated Nyerere styled himself as "Teacher" and broadcast homey economics lectures.

Indeed, Nyerere's greatest success was a system of free schools that made his people one of Africa's most literate. But *ujamaa*'s effects were not all salubrious. Nationalization of industry impaired production, and collectivization of agriculture led to a food shortage. Capitalist dissenters and runaways from forced labor eventually filled the jails (repression was most acute on traditionally totalitarian Zanzibar). Other than a railroad (built, ironically, by China), the nation's infrastructure remained primitive. And self-reliance, Nyerere's fondest goal, remained elusive: When he retired in 1985, a third of Tanzania's budget came from abroad. ◀1957.4 ▶1966.12

LITERATURE

Bellow's Sins of the Heart

8 Combining old-world intellectual sophistication with new-world wit and informality, Saul Bellow's 1964 novel, *Herzog,* introduced what was to become the quintessential Bellow protagonist—Moses Herzog, a middle-aged Jewish intellectual whose precious ruminations on life are constantly interrupted by flibbertigibbety life itself. Confronting the failure of his intellect to sustain him during the breakup of his second marriage, Bellow's hero realizes that "[h]e, Herzog, had committed a sin against his own heart."

America's foremost novelist of ideas, Bellow, the child of Russian-Jewish émigrés, spent his early childhood in an immigrant quarter of Quebec before moving, at age nine, to Chicago and another polyglot neighborhood. In his adopted

SPORTS: Baseball: World Series, St. Louis Cardinals (Bob Gibson) defeat New York Yankees, 4–3 ... Olympic Games held in Innsbruck and Tokyo ... Football: NFL, Cleveland Browns defeat Baltimore Colts, 27–0; AFL, Buffalo Bills defeat San Diego Chargers, 20–7 ... Basketball: NBA, Boston Celtics defeat San Francisco Warriors, 4–1.

"The white man is the master of Rhodesia. He has built it and intends to keep it."—**Ian Smith, leader of Southern Rhodesia**

hometown, amid the sounds of Hebrew and Yiddish, he immersed himself in the American English of Sherwood Anderson, Theodore Dreiser, and Edgar Lee Masters. It was a process that gave birth to the signature Bellow style—an intensely energetic, often irreverent mix of high and low language that incorporates the cadences of Yiddish into English sentences.

Bellow's first book, *Dangling Man* (1944), published when he was 29, had gained him a small, literate readership. In *The Adventures of Augie March* (1953), Bellow created a sort of ethnic, citified Huck Finn struggling to make sense of the modern world. Transcending the boundaries traced by such writers as Twain and Hemingway, *Augie March* inaugurated what has been called a "new Jewish tradition" in American letters. With *Herzog*, as well as his later *Mr. Sammler's Planet* and *Humboldt's Gift* (inspired by the tragic life of his friend poet Delmore Schwartz), Bellow extended that tradition and brought his jittery philosophical investigations to a new plateau. Citing "the human understanding and subtle analysis of contemporary culture that are combined in his work," the Nobel Committee awarded Bellow the 1976 literature prize. ◂**1927.11** ▸**1969.13**

THEATER

Broadway's Top Fiddle

9 The Jewish themes that Saul Bellow introduced into mainstream American fiction also turned up in other popular genres. The 1964 musical *Fiddler on the Roof* brought old-world Jewish ethnicity to Broadway audiences. But if the show—the story of Tevye the Milkman and his family, set in a small village in czarist Russia—posed any problems of "translation" for modern, Gentile audiences, it easily overcame them with the sheer depth of its humanity. *Fiddler*, produced by Harold Prince and directed and choreographed by Jerome Robbins, became the longest-running Broadway show of its era (eight years, 3,242 performances).

Fiddler also represented a landmark in staging and design in that its overall look and style was organized entirely around a central theme (in this case, tradition). Heartfelt songs with allusively Jewish melodies ("If I Were a Rich Man," "Sunrise, Sunset"), by Jerry Bock and Sheldon Harnick, enhanced Joseph Stein's libretto (based on stories by Yiddish humorist Sholem Aleichem) about tradition under assault from without (by official anti-Semitism) and, less catastrophically, from within (Tevye's daughters refuse arranged marriages). The production's other major asset was Zero Mostel, whose monumental performance as Tevye mixed earthy humor with honest sentiment. ▸**1966.8**

Tevye (Zero Mostel) haggles with God in "If I Were a Rich Man."

EASTERN AFRICA

British Rhodesia Splits

10 The colonies of Northern and Southern Rhodesia parted from Great Britain in 1964 and 1965, respectively, and took radically divergent paths. The former was granted independence as the black-ruled Republic of Zambia. The latter unilaterally declared itself the white-supremacist nation of Rhodesia. The differences between the two new states owed much to demographics (Rhodesia's white minority was larger and more economically entrenched than Zambia's) and much, as well, to the strikingly dissimilar characters of their leaders: Zambia's president, Kenneth Kaunda, and Rhodesia's prime minister, Ian Smith.

Ian Smith signs Rhodesia's declaration of independence on November 11, 1965.

Although he'd been briefly jailed in 1959 as head of the militant Zambia African National Congress (modeled on the African National Congress, of which he'd been secretary-general), Kaunda's only crime was leading an effective civil disobedience campaign against British rule. In negotiations for independence he struck a conciliatory note, attempting to soothe the resentments of the colony's 3.6 million blacks toward its white population (numbering about 75,000), to allay whites' fears of black government, and to calm interethnic animosities. Smith, by contrast, promised pure intransigence—toward Britain, which insisted on majority rule as a prerequisite for independence (which Smith declared illegally), and toward the colony's four million blacks, who outnumbered whites 16 to 1.

Smith's South African–style regime in Rhodesia brought international sanctions and years of crippling civil war. Zambia faced other problems. Threatened by South Africa's and Rhodesia's hostility and by domestic unrest born of poverty, Kaunda also turned repressive, imposing a one-party state in 1972. He retired in 1991, shortly after legalizing political opposition. Smith lost power in 1980, when guerrilla resistance finally exhausted his outlaw government, and Rhodesia became independent, majority-ruled Zimbabwe. ◂**1902.5** ▸**1979.2**

IN THE UNITED STATES

conservative U.S. beaches, the suit was a sensational statement of the dawning age. ▸1965.2

▸STRANGLER ARRESTED—In a two-year reign of terror, the "Boston Strangler" raped and killed at least a dozen women in their homes. The slayer was thought to be ex-con Albert Henry DeSalvo. (He confessed to police, but his lawyer refused to let him confess in court; because there was no physical evidence to implicate him, he was never accused.) Tried and convicted of crimes predating those of the Strangler, De Salvo was an early specimen of what came to be known as a serial killer.

▸GOLF MASTER—Continuing his assault on the record books, Arnold Palmer, one of golf's most dramatic players, in 1964 won his sport's most prestigious tournament, the Masters, for an unprecedented fourth time. Golf's first million-dollar winner was also the first to parlay fame into commercial enterprises that put his name on products ranging from golf clubs to candy bars. ▸1975.M

▸HAWK CANDIDATE—Combative conservative senator Barry Goldwater beat out New York's liberal governor, Nelson Rockefeller, for the 1964

Republican presidential nomination. Although his name lent itself to interesting campaign slogans, like the periodic-table-derived AuH_2O, Goldwater's hawkishness dismayed mainstream voters. "Extremism in the defense of liberty is no vice!" he famously declared. LBJ ran away with the election. ◂1964.1

▸JONES'S DRAMA—With its bitter, hopeless action, Le Roi Jones's 1964 play, *The Dutchman*, about a white woman who murders blacks on New York subways, was interpreted as a metaphor for American race relations. It confirmed Jones—who later converted to Islam and became Imamu Amiri Baraka—as a major African-American writer.

POLITICS & BUSINESS: GNP: $632.4 billion ... Lyndon B. Johnson elected president, defeating Barry Goldwater ... 24th Amendment ratified (prohibits poll tax) ... R. Sargent Shriver, Jr., appointed head of Office of Economic Opportunity ... Medicare Act passed (establishes health insurance for all Americans over 65) ... U.S. Department of Agriculture reinstitutes food stamp program.

"Do you understand what it did for black Americans to know that the most physically gifted, possibly the most handsome, and one of the most charismatic men in the world was black?"—**Baseball player Reggie Jackson, on Muhammad Ali**

AROUND THE WORLD

▶BANDA COMES TO POWER—Part of a colonial federation with Northern and Southern Rhodesia (Zambia and Zimbabwe), the southeast African British colony of Nyasaland gained independence as a member of the British Commonwealth in 1964, taking the name Malawi. Hastings Kamazu Banda returned from practicing medicine in Great Britain to lead the colony to nationhood and to become its president two years later, when Malawi became a republic. An autocrat, Banda jailed or killed his opposition, banned criticism of his one-party government, and was the first black African leader to establish ties with South Africa's apartheid regime.

▶ELECTRONIC ENSEMBLE—A pioneering theorist and leading proponent of electronic music, German composer Karlheinz Stockhausen in 1964 formed his own percussion ensemble to perform his tricky, conceptual pieces. It

debuted in December in Brussels with Stockhausen's *Mikrophonie I*, scored for tam-tam (gong), microphones, and filters. Exploiting the electronic gadgetry (which eventually included such "instruments" as tape recorders and shortwave radios), Stockhausen and his collaborators elicited a remarkable array of sounds.

▶BRANCA IN BRAZIL—General Castelo Branca led a bloodless coup in Brazil in 1964. The catalyst was out-of-control inflation, a staggering national debt, and the evaporation of foreign credit. President João Goulart's remedy, the adoption of a left-wing reform program, had alienated Brazil's traditional powerbrokers, the political right and the army. With the coup, Brazil, the largest country in South America and the fifth-largest in the world, became a military dictatorship. There wouldn't be a civilian president for 21 years or a popularly elected one for 25.
◀1960.9 ▶1989.8

1964

SPORTS

The Greatest

11 When Cassius Marcellus Clay, the 22-year-old Olympic gold medalist from Louisville, Kentucky, entered the ring in 1964 against Sonny Liston, the fierce heavyweight champion of the world, fight mavens feared the worst: Liston was bigger, tougher, and meaner than the brash, likable, baby-faced Clay. Lightning fast and deceptively powerful, the kid prevailed, knocking out the champ with a blow so quick that many of the assembled multitude missed it altogether. Then, fist cocked, muscles flexed, he stood gloating over the fallen Goliath. "I don't have to be who you want me to be," Clay later told reporters. "I'm free to be who I want." His amazing prowess, combined with his unabashed arrogance ("I am the greatest," he liked to crow), electrified the public, especially young blacks. Clay soon converted to the Nation of Islam, changed his name to Muhammad Ali, and settled into a career that made his the most famous face in the world.

In 1967, at his peak, Ali refused induction into the U.S. Army on religious grounds—a stand that cost him his title. He was vindicated by the Supreme Court in 1970, and four years later regained the title, fighting George Foreman in Kinshasa, Zaire. "Float like a butterfly, sting like a bee," Ali boasted in his trademark rhyme. "His hands can't hit what his eyes can't see." But instead of dancing, Ali played "rope-a-dope," making himself a target until Foreman had exhausted himself throwing punches. Then the crafty master sprang off the ropes and KO'd his opponent. The strategy carried a high cost, however: It probably aggravated the Parkinson's disease that in later years slowed Ali's speech—and his dazzling moves. **◀1956.M ▶1975.M**

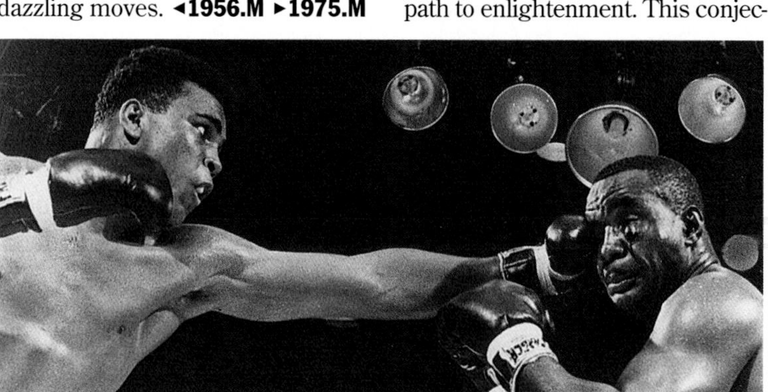

Clay delivers a vicious left to Liston's eye in the third round of their '64 title bout.

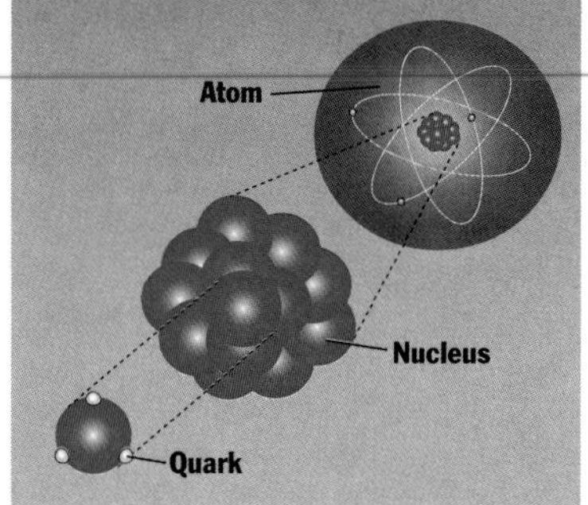

The quark is to the elementary particle what protons and neutrons are to the nucleus.

SCIENCE

Hunting the Quark

12 The science of particle physics advances by predictive leaps; physicists examine the known atom, identify structural gaps, and describe what they believe is missing. (The process has been likened to deducing the existence of windows, doors, and plumbing from the girders and beams of a skeletal building.) In 1964, particle physicist Murray Gell-Mann proposed the existence of quarks: constituent parts of the atom's elementary particles. According to Gell-Mann's model, independently corroborated by George Zweig, a fellow California Institute of Technology physicist, there were atoms, there were nuclei, there were baryons, and mesons, pions, and kaons, and then there were quarks. Zweig called his hypothetical particles aces, but it was Gell-Mann's term, from James Joyce's *Finnegans Wake*, that stuck.

Gell-Mann's first significant contribution to particle physics had been a 1953 theory that explained the rapid deterioration ("strangeness," he called it) of a newly discovered batch of subatomic particles. In 1961, he devised a sort of periodic table of subatomic elements that grouped particles mostly in families of eight—a pattern he dubbed the Eightfold Way, after the Buddhist path to enlightenment. This conjectural scheme—similar to one developed by Israel's Yuval Ne'emen—was confirmed by the subsequent discovery of new particles.

For structural reasons, quarks come in six classifications, which made theoretical sense—and gave researchers something to look for. By the late 1960s, there was strong experimental support for quarks' existence, and by the 1990s, the last of the six quarks—the "top quark" —had been statistically proven to exist. **◀1949.5**

THEATER

Streisand as Fanny Brice

13 "I'm the greatest star," sang Barbra Streisand in *Funny Girl,* the stage biography of Ziegfeld Follies comic diva Fanny Brice, which opened on Broadway on March 23, 1964. The audience evidently agreed: She took 23 curtain calls. Streisand, the 21-year-old veteran of a single Broadway show, launched her reign as one of show business's most unconventional legends.

Streisand: Born to play Fanny Brice.

In the character of Fanny Brice, Streisand found a perfect match. Both were Jewish girls from New York City, with slightly daffy looks, a screwball sense of humor, and uncanny audience rapport. Even so, Streisand wasn't the first choice for the part (Mary Martin was). She repeated the role on-screen in 1968, winning a Best Actress Oscar and beginning her long association with Hollywood, first as an actress, later as a composer and director.

With *Funny Girl*, Streisand conquered Broadway but not her chronic stage fright. Over the next few decades, she recorded dozens of successful albums, starred in (and directed) feature films, but—until a stupendously successful 1994 tour—did little live performing. **◀1910.9**

NOBEL PRIZES: Peace: Martin Luther King, Jr. (U.S.; civil rights) ... Literature: Jean-Paul Sartre (French; novelist; declined) ... Chemistry: Dorothy Hodgkin (U.K.; X-ray crystallography) ... Medicine: Konrad E. Bloch and Feodor Lynen (U.S., German; cholesterol and fatty-acid metabolism) ... Physics: Charles Townes, Nikolai G. Basov, and Alexander Prokhorov (U.S., U.S.S.R., U.S.S.R.; laser).

A VOICE FROM 1964

The Aesthetics of Camp

By Susan Sontag, from "Notes on Camp," *Partisan Review*, Fall 1964

Susan Sontag, graduate of the University of Chicago at 18, recipient of advanced degrees in literature and philosophy from Harvard, novelist (The Benefactor, Death Kit, The Volcano Lover)*, filmmaker, playwright, trenchant cultural critic, and human rights activist, made her name writing on the aesthetics of "camp." Published in the fall 1964 issue of* Partisan Review, *and reprinted in her first essay collection,* Against Interpretation *(1966), Sontag's "Notes on Camp" describe it as a rigorously modern sensibility, a subversive yet genial elevation of the artificial and the exaggerated: Greta Garbo, melodramatic opera, art nouveau candlesticks. In their very garishness, Sontag asserted, camp objects somehow affirm life. The intriguing, richly allusive essay solidified Sontag's intellectual standing and changed the language of taste. In addition to the good, the bad, and the ugly, now there was Camp.*

1. To start very generally: Camp is a certain mode of estheticism. It is *one* way of seeing the world as an esthetic phenomenon. That way, the way of Camp, is not in terms of beauty, but in terms of style....

3. Not only is there a Camp vision, a Camp way of looking at things. Camp is as well a quality discoverable in objects and the behavior of persons. There are "campy" movies, clothes, furniture, popular songs, novels, people, buildings.... This distinction is important. True, the Camp eye has the power to transform experience. But not everything can be seen as Camp. It's not *all* in the eye of the beholder.

4. Random examples of items which are part of the canon of Camp:

Tiffany lamps
Scopitone films
The Brown Derby restaurant on Sunset Boulevard in LA
The Enquirer, headlines and stories
Aubrey Beardsley drawings
Swan Lake
Bellini's operas
Visconti's direction of *Salome* and *'Tis Pity She's a Whore*
certain turn-of-the-century picture postcards
Schoedsack's *King Kong*
The Cuban pop singer La Lupe
Lynn Ward's novel in woodcuts, *God's Man*
women's clothes of the twenties (feather boas, fringed and beaded dresses, etc.)
the novels of Ronald Firbank and Ivy Compton-Burnet
stag movies seen without lust

5. Camp taste has an affinity for certain arts rather than others. Clothes, furniture, all the elements of visual decor, for instance, make up a large part of Camp. For Camp art is often decorative art, emphasizing texture, sensuous surface, and style at the expense of content. Concert music, though, because it is contentless, is rarely Camp. It offers no opportunity, say, for a contrast between silly or extravagant content and rich form.... Sometimes whole art forms become saturated with Camp. Classical ballet, opera, movies have seemed so for a long time. In the last two years, so has popular music (post rock 'n' roll, what the French call *yé yé*). And movie criticism (like lists of "The 10 Best Bad Movies I Have Seen") is probably the greatest popularizer of Camp taste today, because most people still go to the movies in a high-spirited and unpretentious way....

10. Camp sees everything in quotation marks. It's not a lamp, but a "lamp"; not a woman, but a "woman." To perceive Camp in objects and persons is to understand Being as Playing a Role. It is the farthest extension, in sensibility, of the metaphor of life as theater.

11. Camp is the triumph of the epicene style. (The conveyibility of "boy" and "girl," "person" and "thing.") But all style is, ultimately, epicene. "Life" is not stylish. Neither is Nature....

34. Camp taste turns its back on the good-bad axis of ordinary esthetic judgment. Camp doesn't reverse things. It doesn't argue that the good is bad, or the bad is good. What it does is to offer for art (and life) a different—a supplementary—set of standards....

41. The whole point of Camp is to dethrone the serious. Camp is playful, anti-serious. More precisely, Camp involves a new, more complex relation to "the serious." One can be serious about the frivolous, frivolous about the serious....

45. Detachment is the prerogative of an elite; and as the dandy is the nineteenth century's surrogate for the aristocrat in matters of culture, so Camp is the modern dandyism. Camp is the answer to the problem: How to be a dandy in the age of mass culture.

Sontag and her son, David Rieff, in 1964, photographed by Diane Arbus. Like Sontag's, Arbus's work has been enormously influential in molding the postmodern sensibility.

"For the first time since we spun into the Vietnam mess, there is hope for the United States.... The credit justly belongs to President Lyndon B. Johnson. He has made the war 'unlosable.' "—**Editor Sam Castan in *Life* magazine, November 30, 1965**

STORY OF THE YEAR

The United States Escalates the War

1 The United States entered the Vietnam War in earnest in 1965. Sensing little popular support for full-scale intervention, President Johnson initially relied on air power. Continuous bombing of North Vietnam began in March; the first Marines landed days later in the South to defend Da Nang's air base. But South Vietnamese forces (known by the acronym ARVN) needed help in the field as well, and Johnson quietly began acceding to the requests of General William Westmoreland, commander of American forces in Vietnam, for more troops. By year's end, 180,000 had arrived in-country.

Westmoreland's strategy was aimed at wearing down the enemy rather than seizing territory. The bombing targeted not only northern industry and the Ho Chi Minh Trail (the network of paths by which the North sent men and matériel, now mostly provided by the Soviets and Chinese, to the South), but also southern population centers suspected of harboring guerrillas. On the ground, the basic objective was to eliminate as many northern infiltrators and Viet Cong as possible. "Kill ratios"—a grim coinage that, like "body count," came out of Vietnam—were impressive from the start. In the first engagement with North Vietnamese regulars, at Ia Drang, Americans killed 1,200 men while losing only 200.

But numbers weren't everything. For U.S. soldiers, combat largely meant slogging through jungles and paddies in pursuit of elusive quarry. Snipers and booby traps were everywhere; friend and foe were hard to tell apart, and it often seemed safer to shoot than ask. On "search and destroy" missions, peaceful-looking villages were torched, their inhabitants herded into bleak "strategic hamlets." This kind of warfare drained morale. It also alienated the South Vietnamese—including many in the ARVN—as did the corrupt and repressive U.S.-backed government in Saigon. In the United States, news photos of napalmed civilians fueled antiwar sentiment. In November, 50,000 protesters marched on Washington. And even some of Johnson's advisers began to wonder if the war was a mistake. **◂1964.1 ▸1966.6**

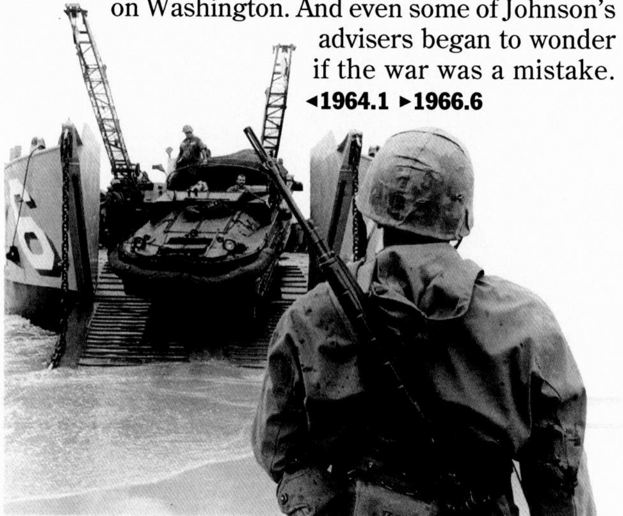

The first Marine Corps landing at Da Nang brought the number of U.S. forces in Vietnam to about 27,000. By year's end, there were 180,000.

The miniskirt was de rigueur for Quant *(right)*, even in January.

FASHION

The Hemline Revolution

2 When Parisian couturier André Courrèges launched his spring-summer show in the winter of 1965, he knew his career was on the line. "Every time I did something modern, with love and enthusiasm," he said, "I was criticized. I'd had enough." Even so, Courrèges sent dozens of young models marching down the runway in white boots, angular dresses, and miniskirts—a shocking new invention that soared four inches above the knee. The audience sat in stunned silence, but by the time the show was over, Courrèges had liberated not only fashion, but the women who wore it.

Across the Channel in England, a young designer and boutique owner named Mary Quant had designed her own miniskirt—shorter even than Courrèges's. If the length of Quant's skirt was radically new to fashion, so were the customers to her London boutique, Bazaar: Quant catered to "real" women, not the social elite. So popular were Quant's affordable creations that Bazaar was perpetually out of stock. Then only 21 years old, Quant bought new fabric each morning, stitched all day, and watched as her clothes sold out by evening. Soon she had been credited with the "democratization of fashion" and dubbed the "Courrèges of the working class."

By the end of the year, the fashion revolution had come full circle: Courrèges himself, as if influenced by a favorite Quant maxim ("what ready-to-wear does today, the couturiers—even the Paris couturiers—confirm tomorrow") turned his focus from making perfect dresses for the rich to manufacturing affordable dresses for everyone. "I want every woman to be able to wear Courrèges," he said, somewhat disingenuously. Inexpensive and sexy, the mini was accessible to any woman daring enough to wear it. Millions did, from Quant's "girls in the High Street" to early converts as diverse as Gloria Steinem and Brigitte Bardot. **◂1947.12 ▸1970.M**

SOUTHEAST ASIA

Singapore's Separation

3 In 1965, the two-year-old Federation of Malaysia ejected the island of Singapore, a largely Chinese enclave off the southern tip of the Malay Peninsula. In cutting the island loose, Tengku Abdul Rahman, the Malaysian prime minister, cited entrenched Malay-Chinese ethnic strife. "Obviously," he told his government, "the present setup could not go on." Singapore thus became an independent city-state, Lee Kuan Yew its first Prime Minister. Said the integrationist Lee, "Now the dream is shattered." But if the ideal of federation had ended, an economic dream was just beginning. During the next 30 years, the Prime Minister built Singapore, a trading center since the Middle Ages, into the commercial capital of Southeast Asia. Malaysia, meanwhile, rich in natural resources (tin, rubber, oil), experienced relative prosperity of its own.

British colonies from the eighteenth century, the territories had been occupied by Japan during World War II; Great Britain resumed control after the war, but burgeoning nationalist movements made independence a foregone conclusion. Singapore gained sovereignty in 1959, Malaya a year later. In 1963, Singapore, Malaya, Sarawak, and North Borneo (Sabah) came together to form Malaysia. The confederation didn't last, but a close economic association did.

In 1967, Malaysia and Singapore joined the Philippines, Thailand, and Indonesia (itself a Dutch colony until 1949) to form the Association of South East Asian Nations (ASEAN). Fiercely anti-Communist

ART & CULTURE: Books: *Dune* (Frank Herbert); *At Play in the Fields of the Lord* (Peter Matthiessen); *Manchild in the Promised Land* (Claude Brown); *The Painted Bird* (Jerzy Kosinski); *The Old Glory* (Robert Lowell); *The Lost World* (Randall Jarrell) ... Music: "I Got You Babe" (Sonny Bono); "Yesterday" (Lennon and McCartney); "Mr. Tambourine Man" (Bob Dylan); "King of the Road" (Roger Miller);

"I believe in the brotherhood of man, all men, but I don't believe in brotherhood with anybody who doesn't want brotherhood with me."—**Malcolm X**

(ruthless right-wing dictator Suharto had just overthrown ruthless left-wing dictator Sukarno in Indonesia), ASEAN promoted economic stability in the volatile region—often at the expense of political freedom. Singapore fared the best, becoming under Lee a magnet for international investment. Joining Hong Kong, South Korea, and Taiwan, Singapore became an Asian commercial dynamo, one of the "Four Little Dragons." Even in Singapore, however, democracy proved elusive: The once-progressive Lee erected a harsh dictatorship to safeguard his investment. **◄1946.3 ►1984.7**

SOCIAL REFORM

Organizing America's Poorest

4 In 1965, a Mexican-American and former migrant farmworker named Cesar Chavez began to succeed at a task that had foiled activists for decades: unionizing the United States' agricultural workers. In the richest nation on earth, farm laborers earned Third World wages; they were denied clean water and toilets on the job, and often lived in squalid camps. But because most were immigrants and nomadic, they remained isolated from the labor movement. Chavez's background gave him an advantage over his predecessors: He was deeply in tune with his constituency. And he was one of the most resourceful and dedicated organizers of all time.

Chavez, whose formal education ended before high school, had learned his skills while working for (and later directing) a nationwide grassroots action group, the Community Service Organization. In 1962, he resigned to found the National Farm Workers Association. Aided by friends and relatives, the penniless Chavez gathered a few thousand California field hands—mostly Mexican-Americans like himself—into the NFWA. The turning point came three years later, when the union joined a strike initiated by Filipino grape pickers. Having absorbed the tactics of the civil rights movement, Chavez held mass demonstrations, persuaded millions to boycott grapes, and enlisted the support of students, organized labor (the NFWA became affiliated with the mighty AFL-CIO in 1966), and religious leaders.

The strike and boycott lasted until 1970, despite sometimes violent interference from growers. (When workers hit back, Chavez, a devotee of Gandhian civil disobedience, chastised them by fasting.) Finally, management recognized the union, which was renamed the United Farm Workers. By then, the quietly charismatic Chavez was an international figure. **◄1955.M ►1988.6**

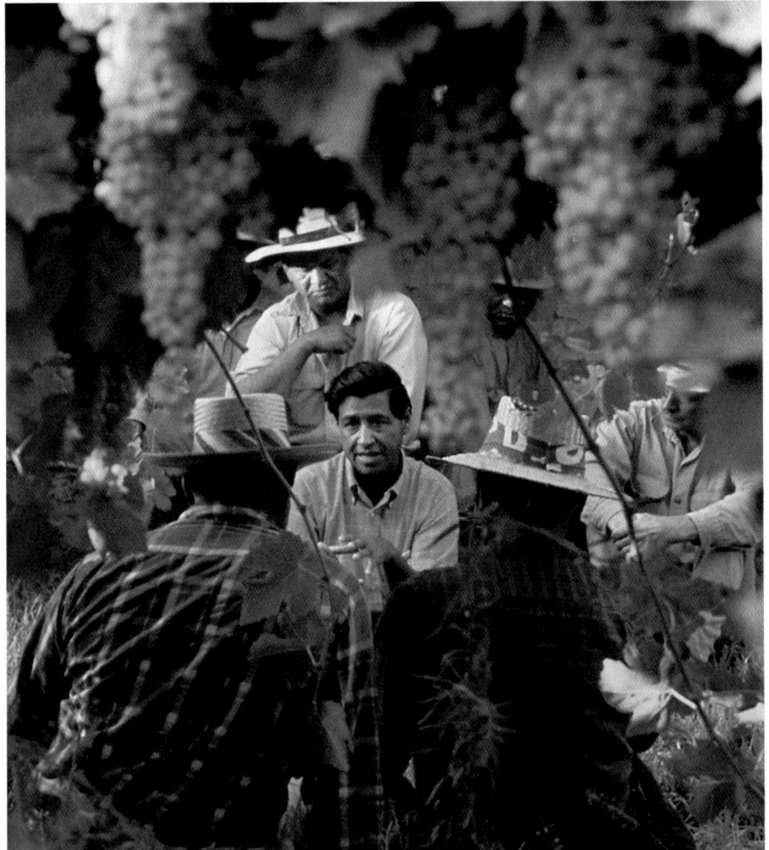

Cesar Chavez, in 1965, meeting with grape pickers in Delano, California.

SOCIAL REFORM

Civil Rights, Mortal Wrongs

5 The Voting Rights Act of 1965 was an epochal victory in the fight for African-American equality, and in the worldwide struggle for democracy. The law—which banned the southern practice of disenfranchising blacks through rigged literacy tests and other means—was passed following vicious attacks on its supporters. Police used clubs and cattle prods in Alabama to stop a march from Selma to Montgomery led by Martin Luther King, Jr. Even federal troops sent to protect the 25,000 marchers couldn't save a young woman who was killed by two Ku Klux Klansmen after driving some fellow protesters home to Selma from Montgomery.

Legislation alone could not end racial injustice, and many blacks were frustrated with the slow pace of progress. Their rage exploded in August when the Los Angeles inner-city neighborhood of Watts erupted in rebellion. It took 20,000 National Guardsmen five days to quell the looting and arson; 34 people, mostly black, were killed, and property damage totaled $40 million. The neighborhood never fully recovered.

Another victim of internecine violence was Malcolm X *(above)*, the most charismatic advocate for angry urban blacks. Malcolm had gone from street criminal to chief spokesman for the Black Muslims—a black nationalist sect whose members regarded whites as "devils" and used the letter "X" to replace surnames given by slave masters. A revelatory trip to Mecca (where Muslims of all races worshiped together) led Malcolm to found a breakaway organization—and, fatefully, to criticize Black Muslim leader Elijah Muhammad. In February, former comrades shot Malcolm down in Harlem. **◄1964.3 ►1966.10**

BIRTHS

Matt Biondi, U.S. swimmer.

Nicolas Cage, U.S. actor.

Linda Evangelista, Canadian model.

Marlee Matlin, U.S. actress.

Scottie Pippen, U.S. basketball player.

David Robinson, U.S. basketball player.

DEATHS

Bernard M. Baruch, U.S. financier.

Clara Bow, U.S. actress.

Martin Buber, Austrian-Israeli philosopher.

Nat "King" Cole, U.S. singer.

Winston Churchill, U.K. prime minister.

T.S. Eliot, U.S.-U.K. writer.

Farouk, Egyptian king.

Felix Frankfurter, U.S. jurist.

Lorraine Hansberry, U.S. playwright.

Shirley Jackson, U.S. writer.

Spike Jones, U.S. musician.

Dorothea Lange, U.S. photographer.

Stan Laurel, U.K.-U.S. comedian.

Charles Edouard Jeanneret (Le Corbusier), Swiss-French architect.

Malcolm X, U.S. civil rights leader.

W. Somerset Maugham, U.K. writer.

Edward R. Murrow, U.S. news broadcaster.

Syngman Rhee, Korean president.

Albert Schweitzer, Alsatian missionary.

David O. Selznick, U.S. film producer.

David Smith, U.S. sculptor.

Hermann Staudinger, German chemist.

Adlai E. Stevenson, U.S. statesman.

Edgard Varèse, French-U.S. composer.

Henry A. Wallace, U.S. vice president.

Orchestral and Electronic Exchanges* (Charles Wuorinen); *Symphony No. 1* (Gunther Schuller) ... Painting & Sculpture: *Liz* (Andy Warhol) ... Film: *The Sound of Music* (Robert Wise); *Doctor Zhivago* (David Lean); *The Shop on Main Street* (Jan Kadar) ... Theater: *The Homecoming* (Harold Pinter); *Loot* (Joe Orton); *The Odd Couple* (Neil Simon); *Man of La Mancha* (Darion and Leigh) ... TV: *The Big Valley.

"The champion we never knew we needed against an enemy we never suspected was there."—*Life* magazine, which named Ralph Nader one of the 100 greatest Americans

NEW IN 1965

Soft contact lenses.

Aspartame (marketed as Nutra-Sweet).

Indoor sports stadium (Astrodome, in Houston, Texas).

Lava lamp.

IN THE UNITED STATES

▶DAY-GLO REVOLUTION—The year was 1965; the psychedelic decade was emerging. Among the signs of the trend: Psychologist Timothy Leary, dismissed from his teaching post at Harvard University, was arrested on drug charges in Texas ("Tune in, turn on, drop out," became the LSD guru's catchphrase); in New York, the Museum of Modern Art presented "The Responsive Eye," a show of pulsating, optical-illusory op-art paintings; in San Francisco, an improvisatory folk-rock band called the Warlocks *(led by Jerry Garcia, above)*, soon to be renamed the Grateful Dead, was formed.

▶THE GREAT SOCIETY—Lyndon Johnson's proposed Great Society, and its extension, the War on Poverty, constituted the biggest expansion of social welfare programs since FDR's New Deal. In 1965, for the first time in its history, the U.S. implemented a form of national health insurance, long derided as "socialized medicine": the Medicare and Medicaid programs, which provide federally funded health care for millions of elderly, disabled, and indigent Americans. Among the initiatives adopted between 1964 and

Bumper cars helped Nader illustrate the dangers of the automobile.

SOCIAL REFORM

Whistle-Blower Number One

6 A young Connecticut lawyer launched the new field of consumer advocacy in 1965 with a book that stripped the gloss off the high-flying American automobile industry. Lone crusader Ralph Nader opened his bestselling exposé *Unsafe at Any Speed* by rebutting some 60 years of car adulation. "For over half a century," Nader asserted, "the automobile has brought death, injury, and the most inestimable sorrow and deprivation to millions of people." He then presented compelling evidence that, despite decades of competition, car manufacturers were still neglecting safety and maintaining a wall of secrecy around "designed-in dangers" such as inadequate brakes. Chief among Nader's targets were the more than one million accident-prone Corvairs that General Motors had produced over four years without ever improving the model's faulty rear-suspension system.

Stunned and humiliated by Nader's revelations, Detroit sought to retaliate. GM hired a private investigator to probe into Nader's private life for information that might discredit him, but the strategy backfired. Nader informed Senator Abraham Ribicoff's traffic-safety subcommittee that he was being harassed, and GM president James Roche was forced to apologize during a televised hearing. Soon thereafter, Congress passed the National Traffic and Motor Vehicle Safety Act, and the Corvair was junked—a double victory for the earnest, ascetic maverick who, supported by legions of like-minded "Nader's Raiders," would make a career of policing business and government. **◂1906.11 ▸1988.6**

ART

Less Is More

7 Though the term "minimalism" had been applied to art as early as 1929, the expression "minimal art" gained currency in 1965, when influential *Arts Magazine* used it as the title of an essay by Richard Wollheim, a British philosophy professor. Observing that objects with "minimal art content" had been winning acceptance as art, Wollheim divided such objects into two types: those of "very low content" (like the single-color paintings American artist Ad Reinhardt had started making after World War II) and those of "non-assisted" origin (like the "ready-mades"—mundane objects presented as sculpture—pioneered by French artist Marcel Duchamp in the teens and twenties).

In 1965, American sculptor Donald Judd emerged as a paradigmatic minimalist with his landmark *Untitled* series. Featuring galvanized-iron boxes mounted on a wall, *Untitled* was a deeply impersonal, highly formal, quite striking exploration of space and mass. The German-born American sculptor Eva Hesse took minimalism in another direction. Working with unorthodox materials—fiberglass, latex, rope—she challenged formal assumptions with her rough-edged, asymmetrical shapes.

A self-conscious, analytical reduction of art to its primary forms (e.g., a cube or a simple painted plane), minimalism was a reaction against traditional definitions of art and against aesthetic excess. Eschewing bathetic self-expression, minimalists sought to remove form, content, even meaning, from their works. The reductivist trend culminated in the 1970s with conceptual art, in which the idea behind a work of art *was* the art. **◂1962.8 ▸1970.10**

Judd's *Untitled*, 1965, a series of aluminum boxes, spanned 8¼" × 253" × 8¼".

INDIA

The Fight for Kashmir

8 India and Pakistan warred in 1965, Hindu against Muslim, for control of Kashmir, India's ruggedly beautiful, predominantly Muslim northern state. The conflict deepened hostilities engendered by the 1947 partition of India, when Kashmir, with more than two thirds of its population Muslim, joined independent, Hindu-dominated India rather than the newly created Islamic nation of Pakistan. Shortly after partition, Pakistan invaded, spilled blood, and was rebuffed. Border skirmishes had been more or less constant ever since.

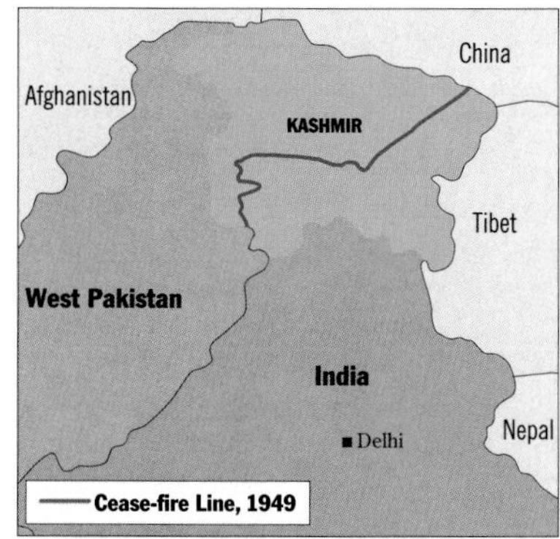

The UN cease-fire line in Kashmir lasted almost two decades.

Kashmir's strategic location, between Pakistan, China, and India, vested the conflict with more than regional significance: China, the Soviet Union, and the United States all had political interests in the

SPORTS: Baseball: World Series, Los Angeles Dodgers defeat Minnesota Twins, 4–3; William D. Eckert is elected commissioner ... Football: NFL, Green Bay Packers defeat Cleveland Browns, 23–12; AFL, Buffalo Bills defeat San Diego Chargers, 23–0 ... Basketball: NBA, Boston Celtics defeat Los Angeles Lakers, 4–1.

"I entice the audience.... Of course, what I'm doing is a sexual thing. I dance, and all dancing is a replacement for sex."
—Mick Jagger

area. When China took Pakistan's side during the 1965 war, the Soviet Union protested loudly: India was its western buffer against hostile China. The United States, officially neutral in the conflict, likewise valued India as a roadblock to Chinese expansion. With both superpowers against it, Pakistan backed down.

The war lasted less than a year, but Pakistan vowed there would be no peace until the people of Kashmir were allowed to freely choose a homeland. India claimed the issue had been decided in 1947. In fact, Kashmir's accession to India that year had been a stopgap measure—intended to maintain order until a referendum could be held. India never got around to putting the question to a vote. Even though a majority of the Kashmir people supported union with India in 1947 (and 18 years later probably still did), Kashmir's status remained blurry. One of the world's pristine regions thus became another tragic twentieth-century flash point. **◂1948.5 ▸1966.7**

DIPLOMACY

Germany Mends Fences

9 Germans and Jews took a significant step toward reconciliation in March 1965, when Israel accepted Bonn's offer to establish full diplomatic relations. Many Israelis who'd been scarred by Hitler's genocide opposed the move—future premier Menachem Begin, whose parents and a brother died in the Holocaust, implored his fellow parliamentarians to "not be friendly with the German generation of the destruction." But Israeli prime minister Levi Eshkol urged that "in the balance of reason and emotion," Israel's practical interests "must tip the scale" in favor of reason.

Indeed, rapprochement made practical sense: West German trade, and Bonn's payment of a debt of conscience of nearly $1 billion (the last installment would come later in 1965), had been essential to the economic survival of young Israel. And West Germany, desperate to erase the Nazi stigma (and willing to risk the wrath of Arab nations), needed Jewish forgiveness at least as badly as Israel needed German commerce.

West Germany's eagerness to put Nazism behind it did not always please Israel. Days after Israel approved the exchange of ambassadors, the West German parliament voted to extend the statute of limitations for Nazi war crimes, scheduled to expire in May, only through 1969. Jewish leaders (and some West Germans) were disappointed; they had lobbied for a ten-year extension. But given the political climate in West Germany—two-thirds of the public wanted to end the trials of Nazis immediately—four years was all Bonn's legislators could manage. **◂1951.4 ▸1993.6**

Despite many Germans' fears, no Arab countries severed ties with West Germany after its rapprochement with Israel.

MUSIC

The Stones Get Rolling

10 In 1965, one year after joining the British rock 'n' roll invasion of the United States, the bluesy Rolling Stones achieved superstar status on the strength of a single song. The song was "(I Can't Get No) Satisfaction," in which raunchy lead singer Mick Jagger leeringly boasts of "trying to make some girl." This overt reference to sex, a far cry from the Beatles' "I Want to Hold Your Hand," changed the vocabulary of pop music—and shocked more than a few adults. A rebellious younger generation loved it, however, and "Satisfaction" soon climbed to the top of the charts in the United States, where it sold more than a million copies before being released in England.

"Satisfaction" became the quintessential sixties rock song, and the Stones the quintessential rock band—edgy, raw, and aggressive. Tagged with "bad boy" images by early promoters eager to set them apart from the Beatles, the band members over the years lived up to their billing: Guitarist Brian Jones drowned in his own pool, while intoxicated, in 1969; that same year, a fan was stabbed to death at a free Stones concert in Altamont, California; lead guitarist Keith Richards suffered from (and survived) protracted heroin addiction. Through it all, for more than 30 years, the band continued to tour and to record the hits—"Honky Tonk Woman," "Let's Spend the Night Together," "Jumpin' Jack Flash," "You Can't Always Get What You Want"—that made it rock 'n' roll's most durable act. **◂1962.6 ▸1969.10**

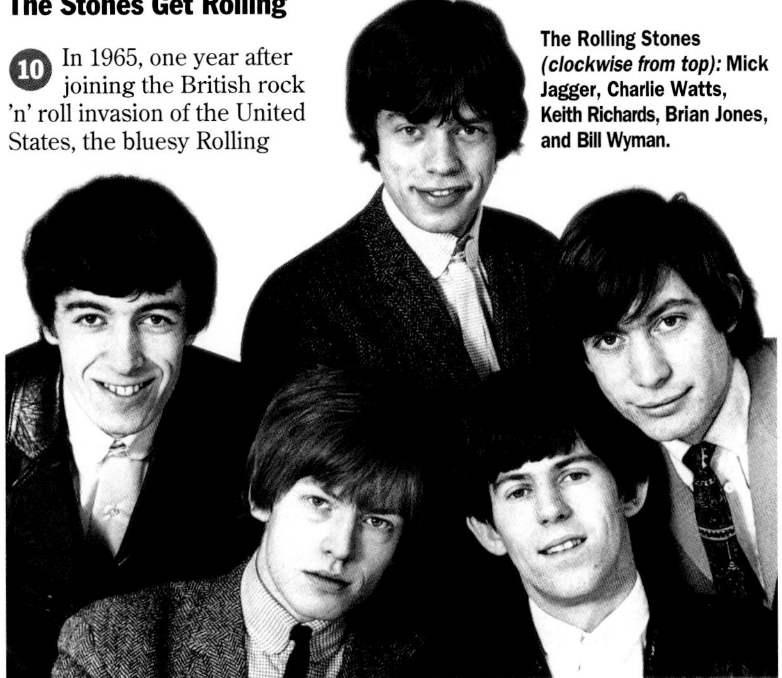

The Rolling Stones *(clockwise from top):* Mick Jagger, Charlie Watts, Keith Richards, Brian Jones, and Bill Wyman.

IN THE UNITED STATES

1967—food stamps, Head Start, VISTA, the Job Corps—Medicare/Medicaid was the biggest, ultimately consuming the largest chunk of federal spending. One of the greatest long-term successes was Project Head Start, a compensatory preschool education program for underprivileged children. ◂1935.5 ▸1969.5

▶WATTS RIOTS—For six days in August, as many as 10,000 rioters turned the Los Angeles inner-city neighborhood of Watts into a war zone, burning cars and buildings; attacking squadrons of riot police with stones, knives, and guns; looting stores. The National Guard was called in, and when the smoke cleared, 34 people had been killed, hundreds injured, and over 4,000 arrested. The upheaval was provoked by the arrest of a black motorist; black discontent—with poverty, unemployment, discrimination—was the root cause. ◂1964.3 ▸1966.10

▶GREAT BLACKOUT OF '65—From Ontario, Canada, through New York State, across New England, down past Manhattan, and as far west as Michigan, the lights went out on November 9. Some 80,000 square miles were plunged into darkness and 30 million people left without electricity, thanks to a huge power surge (and the lack of a backup system). In New York City, powerless for over 13 hours, almost a million people were trapped in subway tunnels, thousands more in dark elevators and inky skyscrapers. ▸1977.M

▶BROADWAY JOE—Star quarterback of football powerhouse University of Alabama, dazzling Joe Willie Namath shocked the professional ranks by spurning the NFL to join the New York Jets of the upstart American Football League in 1965. The Jets rewarded him with a record $400,000 contract.

POLITICS & BUSINESS: GNP: $684.9 billion ... More than $1 billion allocated for development of Appalachia ... Supreme Court rules Connecticut law banning birth control unconstitutional ... Immigration Act of 1965 abolishes all quotas, establishing a limit for the number of visas issued in a year (120,000 for the Western Hemisphere and 170,000 for the Eastern Hemisphere) ... Water Quality Act passed.

"It is sentimental, but I don't see anything particularly wrong with that. I think people have been given a great deal of hope by that picture."—**Richard Rodgers, on *The Sound of Music***

AROUND THE WORLD

▶MARCOS ELECTED—Having served 15 years in the Philippine legislature, Ferdinand Marcos split from the ruling Liberal Party and successfully ran for president in 1965. Elected in large part on his heroic war record (later revealed to be fabricated), Marcos and his former-beauty-queen wife, Imelda, began their long siege of the Philippines and its coffers. No stranger to terrorism (in 1933, he had been convicted of assassinating an opponent of his politician father), Marcos tyrannically suppressed dissent and assumed dictatorial powers. ◂1946.5 ▸1973.10

▶CEAUŞESCU TAKES OVER—With the death of his mentor, Gheorghe Gheorghiu-Dej, loyal apparatchik Nicolae Ceauşescu took over Romania's Communist Party. His 1965 elevation marked the beginning of one of the most bizarre and ruthless modern

dictatorships. While eschewing standard Soviet foreign policy, Ceauşescu cleaved to the orthodox line at home, establishing a cult of personality to rival Stalin's and creating a secret police as fearful as Beria's. He salted the government with family, jailed or killed opponents, looted the treasury, and when the economy failed, sold Romania's food and fuel to the highest foreign bidder, plunging the country into starvation. ◂1947.9 ▸1989.1

▶SPACE WALK—The Soviets, continuing to lead the United States in the space race, opened a new chapter in space exploration in March: Cosmonaut Aleksei Leonov became the first man to walk in space. Two months later, American astronaut Edward White duplicated the extravehicular feat. A *Gemini 4* crew member, White, attached to the capsule by a long umbilical cord, floated above the earth for 21 minutes. "I can sit out here," he reported, "and see the whole California coast." ◂1961.3 ▸1966.2

Argentine revolutionary Che Guevara in a poster by Paul Davis.

LATIN AMERICA

Che Guevara Disappears

11 Top lieutenant and personal friend of Fidel Castro, Ernesto "Che" Guevara, the tactical mastermind of the Cuban revolution, suddenly dropped from view in 1965, instigating a frenzied international manhunt by the western world's powerful intelligence agencies. Rumors of his whereabouts proliferated wildly: He was organizing guerrilla bands in Panama; he was plotting insurrection in Peru; he was leading rebel raids in Colombia; he was on a mission to Vietnam. In Havana, where Castro remained mum, it was joked that *"¿Dónde está?"* ("Where is he?") had replaced *"¿Cómo está?"* ("How are you?") as a standard greeting.

Born into a well-to-do Argentine family, Guevara cut his revolutionary teeth agitating against the dictatorship of Juan Perón. After completing medical studies in Buenos Aires in 1953, he went first to Guatemala, where he saw the progressive government of Jacobo Arbenz fall in a CIA-led coup, and then to Mexico, where he met and joined up with the exiled Castro. After the success of the Cuban revolution, in 1959, Guevara wrote *Guerrilla Warfare,* a handbook of revolutionary strategy. Among the book's many avid readers were middle-class leftists in colleges across America and Europe. To his radical fans, Guevara embodied communism's egalitarian (and swashbuckling) ideal; to Western intelligence agents, he was a threat.

Guevara, who saw Cuba as the revolutionary spark that would ignite Latin America, was, capitalist governments agreed, a most dangerous man to have on the loose. The mystery of Guevara's whereabouts ended in 1967, when he surfaced in Bolivia at the head of a guerrilla battalion. (It was later revealed that he'd been organizing Marxist forces in the Congo during his public absence.) In October 1967, the Bolivian army (with CIA help) caught up with Guevara. He was executed a few days later. **◂1959.1**

FILM

The Sound of Success

12 *The Sound of Music,* one of the most watched motion pictures ever made, appeared to mixed reviews in 1965. Critics either scorned its sentimentality or praised its joie de vivre. The public evidently harbored no doubts: The movie set a new box-office record, outdrawing *Gone with the Wind.*

Based on Richard Rodgers and Oscar Hammerstein's 1959 Broadway musical—the songwriting team's last collaboration (Hammerstein died in 1960)—*The Sound of Music* is set in 1930s Austria and stars Christopher Plummer and Julie Andrews as Captain and Maria von Trapp. He is an aristocratic widower with many children, she a novice who becomes the children's singing nanny. Newly married, the couple daringly escape with their family from Nazi-annexed Austria, singing most of the way. Part of the story's appeal was in its historicity—there really was a Maria, a captain, and all those kids; they really did give concerts; and they really did escape from the Nazis.

Maria (Julie Andrews, a four-octave soprano) teaches the von Trapp children how to sing with "Do-Re-Mi."

They didn't, however, sing show tunes like "Do-Re-Mi" and "Climb Ev'ry Mountain"—they sang folk songs and hymns. And they didn't walk into Switzerland, some 100 miles from their Salzburg home; they went to nearby Italy. "Didn't anyone bother to look at a map?" asked the actual Maria when the film came out. **◂1956.8 ▸1966.8**

ARCHITECTURE

Saarinen's Gateway to the West

13 Finnish-born American architect Eero Saarinen's Gateway Arch rises gracefully above the Mississippi River in St. Louis, Missouri, like a stainless-steel rainbow. A commemoration of America's westward expansion (Lewis and Clark set forth from St. Louis), the 630-foot-high parabola, completed in 1965, was Saarinen's first major project. (He'd submitted the blueprint in 1948.) His later designs, including Dulles International Airport near Washington, D.C. (1963), and the winglike TWA Terminal at New York's JFK Airport (1962), established him as one of the most dynamic and eclectic architects of his era. Like the Gateway Arch, those projects were finished after his sudden death, at age 51, in 1961. ◂1954.5 ▸1966.4

NOBEL PRIZES: Peace: United Nations Children's Fund ... Literature: Mikhail Sholokhov (U.S.S.R.; novelist) ... Chemistry: Robert B. Woodward (U.S.; organic synthesis) ... Medicine: François Jacob, André Lwoff, and Jacques Monod (French; genetic control of enzyme and virus synthesis) ... Physics: Richard Feynman, Julian Schwinger, and Shinichiro Tomonaga (U.S., U.S., Japanese; quantum electrodynamics).

A VOICE FROM 1965

A Poetic Primal Scream

From *Ariel*, by Sylvia Plath, 1965

The American poet Sylvia Plath (right) *died at her home in London in 1963. She was 30; she had two children and an emotionally complicated marriage; she put her head in the oven and turned on the gas. Plath's suicide did not at first attract much attention: Her early poems had shown a technical adroitness, the glimmer of rich talent, but it wasn't until the last terrible months of her life that Plath, bitterly estranged from her husband, the British poet Ted Hughes, found her full poetic voice. It was a hard and brutal voice, dehumanizing in its aggressiveness, but witty: a perfectly modulated primal scream. The poems, collected in* Ariel *(1965), represent Plath's metamorphosis from timid daughter and devoted wife into avenging feminist Fury. In death she inspired almost cultic adoration and also a violent debate: Did mental illness kill Plath or was it stultifying sexism, in the persons of her father and Hughes? Wildly accusatory, pathological, proud, works like "Lady Lazarus" and "Daddy" still shock, challenge, and amaze.* **◂1959.M ▸1969.V**

LADY LAZARUS

I have done it again.
One year in every ten
I manage it—

A sort of walking miracle, my skin
Bright as a Nazi lampshade,
My right foot

A paperweight,
My face a featureless, fine
Jew linen.

Peel off the napkin
O my enemy.
Do I terrify?—

The nose, the eye pits, the full
set of teeth?
The sour breath
Will vanish in a day.

Soon, soon the flesh
The grave cave ate will be
At home on me

And I a smiling woman.
I am only thirty.
And like the cat I have nine
times to die.

This is Number Three.
What a trash
To annihilate each decade.

What a million filaments.
The peanut-crunching crowd
Shoves in to see

Them unwrap me hand and foot—
The big strip tease.
Gentlemen, ladies,

These are my hands,
My knees.
I may be skin and bone,

Nevertheless, I am the same,
identical woman.
The first time it happened I was ten.
It was an accident.

The second time I meant
To last it out and not come back at all.
I rocked shut

As a seashell.
They had to call and call
And pick the worms off me like
sticky pearls.

Dying
Is an art, like everything else.
I do it exceptionally well.

I do it so it feels like hell.
I do it so it feels real.
I guess you could say I've a call.

It's easy enough to do it in a cell.
It's easy enough to do it and stay put.
It's the theatrical

Comeback in broad day
To the same place, the same face,
the same brute
Amused shout:

"A miracle!"
That knocks me out.
There is a charge

For the eyeing of my scars,
there is a charge
For the hearing of my heart—
It really goes.

And there is a charge, a very
large charge,
For a word or a touch
Or a bit of blood

Or a piece of my hair or my clothes.
So, so, Herr Doktor.
So, Herr Enemy.

I am your opus
I am your valuable,
The pure gold baby

That melts to a shriek.
I turn and burn.
Do not think I underestimate
your great concern.

Ash, ash—
You poke and stir.
Flesh, bone, there is nothing
there—

A cake of soap,
A wedding ring,
A gold filling.

Herr God, Herr Lucifer
Beware
Beware.

Out of the ash
I rise with my red hair
And I eat men like air.

DADDY

You do not do, you do not do
Anymore, black shoe
In which I have lived like a foot
For thirty years, poor and white,
Barely daring to breathe or Achoo.

Daddy, I have had to kill you.
You died before I had time—
Marble-heavy, a bag full of God,
Ghastly statue with one grey toe
Big as a Frisco seal

And a head in the freakish Atlantic
Where it pours bean green
over blue
In the waters off beautiful Nauset.
I used to pray to recover you.
Ach, du.

In the German tongue, in the
Polish town
Scraped flat by the roller
Of wars, wars, wars.
But the name of the town
is common.
My Polack friend

Says there are a dozen or two.
So I never could tell where you
Put your foot, your root,
I never could talk to you.
The tongue stuck in my jaw.

It stuck in a barb wire snare.
Ich, ich, ich, ich,
I could hardly speak.
I thought every German was you.
And the language obscene

An engine, an engine
Chuffing me off like a Jew.
A Jew to Dachau, Auschwitz,
Belsen.
I began to talk like a Jew.
I think I may well be a Jew.

The snows of the Tyrol, the clear
beer of Vienna
Are not very pure or true.
With my gypsy ancestress and
my weird luck
And my Taroc pack and my
Taroc pack
I may be a bit of a Jew.

I have always been scared of *you*,
With your Luftwaffe, your
gobbledygoo.
And your neat moustache
And your Aryan eye, bright blue.
Panzer-man, panzer-man, O You—

Not God but a swastika
So black no sky could squeak
through.
Every woman adores a Fascist,
The boot in the face, the brute
Brute heart of a brute like you.

You stand at the blackboard, daddy,
In the picture I have of you,
A cleft in your chin instead of
your foot
But no less a devil for that, no not
Any less the black man who

Bit my pretty red heart in two.
I was ten when they buried you.
At twenty I tried to die
And to get back, back, back to you.
I thought even the bones would do.

But they pulled me out of the sack,
And they stuck me together
with glue.
And then I knew what to do.
I made a model of you,
A man in black with a Meinkampf
look

And a love of the rack and screw.
And I said I do, I do.
So daddy, I'm finally through.
The black telephone's off at the root,
The voices just can't worm through.

If I've killed one man, I've
killed two—
The vampire who said he was you
And drank my blood for a year,
Seven years, if you want to know.
Daddy, you can lie back now.

There's a stake in your fat
black heart
And the villagers never liked you.
They are dancing and stamping
on you.
They always *knew* it was you.
Daddy, daddy, you bastard, I'm
through.

"If the father is a hero, the son will be a brave man; if the father is a reactionary, the son will be a scoundrel."
—Popular saying of the Red Guards

The Red Guards parading posters of Mao through the streets.

STORY OF THE YEAR

Mao's Last Campaign

1 An aging Mao Zedong, his power waning, initiated in 1966 one last mighty campaign. The object: to annihilate his enemies in the Chinese Communist Party, the political machine he had spent a lifetime building. In April, after purging hostile top officials, Mao established a new Party clique packed with his supporters, the Central Cultural Revolution Group. Its job was to dismantle a recalcitrant bureaucracy—and thereby to revive China's revolutionary fervor, which Mao felt was waning. For further assistance, the Great Helmsman called upon China's most radical force, its university students. He commanded them to destroy "revisionism," to root out travelers on the "capitalist road." Thus was launched the Great Proletarian Cultural Revolution, which claimed an estimated 400,000 lives.

During the first stage of the movement, the so-called Fifty Days, from June to August, 1966, students took over campuses, attacked university authorities, and denounced anti-Mao Party officials. As violence gained currency, a new, supremely destructive group emerged: the Red Guards, teenage shock troops. Instructed by Mao to "learn revolution by making revolution," the Red Guards led the charge against bourgeois "ghosts and monsters," plunging China into chaos in the process. By the end of the year, some ten million guards had paraded before the Chairman in Beijing to receive his blessing for their zealotry.

As the Red Guards rampaged, Mao solidified his position within the Party. He purged the leading advocates of economic reform, President Liu Shaoqi and Party general secretary Deng Xiaoping, and their allies. Supported by General Lin Biao, commander of the army, and by the Gang of Four, the radical reform group led by Mao's third wife, Jiang Qing, Mao transformed the Party into a largely military organization dedicated to Maoist thought and continuous revolution. Center of a massive cult of personality, he disbanded the Red Guards in 1968 (later apologizing for their excesses) and reigned as a quasi-emperor until his death in 1976. ◂1958.2 ▸1967.M

EXPLORATION

Soft Landing on the Moon

2 Soviet scientists engineered a spectacular feat on February 3, 1966, when they landed the *Luna 9* spacecraft softly on the pitted lava surface of the moon. The first soft lunar landing (as opposed to crash landing), *Luna 9* paved the way for manned moon missions. It also advanced scientists' knowledge of lunar terrain: Along with the primary craft, the Soviets deposited a small probe rigged with special photographic equipment. This scanned to the horizon, transmitting historic pictures back to the Soviet Union. In a bit of international cunning, Great Britain used its giant Jodrell Bank radio telescope to intercept the transmission. Western astronomers thus got a look at pictures the Soviets might not have released for years.

Until *Luna 9* landed, many astronomers believed that the moon was covered with a layer of dust so thick it would engulf any vehicle that landed there. Other scientists worried that the moon's surface would be, as one astronomer put it, "nasty stuff to walk on, brittle, sharp, and full of little holes." What *Luna 9* revealed instead was a barren crust of jagged rocks and tiny pebbles—relatively hospitable terrain. The successful landing also showed that a spacecraft racing at incredible speed could be slowed down enough to avoid destructive impact—essential if humans were ever going to touch down.

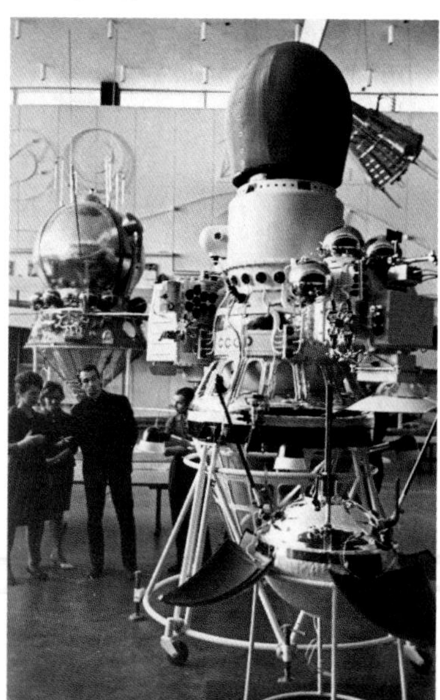

The soft moon landing of *Luna 9 (above, at the U.S.S.R.'s Tsiolkovsky Space Museum)* paved the way for man on the moon.

The mission thrilled Soviet space officials. The Americans, too, were cheered by it. They had not yet mastered soft-landing technology, but their Gemini manned missions into space were progressing well. Now, with *Luna 9*'s success, they knew a lunar landing was possible. ◂1965.M ▸1969.1

POPULAR CULTURE

Voyages of the *Enterprise*

3 *Star Trek*, the science-fiction television program nonpareil, premiered on NBC on September 9, 1966, to resounding indifference. In its three-year network run, *Star Trek* never rose above 50th in the ratings; in worldwide syndication, however, the show found a huge and fanatically loyal audience. Its 79 original episodes spawned half a dozen feature films, more than a hundred novels, an animated series, and at least two additional live-action series (*Star Trek: The Next Generation* and *Star Trek: Deep Space Nine*). Indeed, there sprang up a whole "Trekkie" subculture whose devoted members publish newsletters, communicate over computer networks, and hold national conventions.

Four *Enterprise* officers *(clockwise from lower left)*: Spock, Uhura, McCoy, Kirk.

Created by writer Gene Roddenberry, who also served as executive producer, *Star Trek* is set in the twenty-third century and follows the crew of the starship USS *Enterprise* on its mission (according to a stentorian voice-over) "to seek out new life and new civilizations, to boldly go where no man has gone before." Featuring an ethnically mixed crew—rugged, courageous American captain James T. Kirk

ART & CULTURE: Books: *The Crying of Lot 49* (Thomas Pynchon); *The Fixer* (Bernard Malamud); *The Last Picture Show* (Larry McMurtry); *The Comedians* (Graham Greene); *Omensetter's Luck* (William Gass) ... Music: "Strangers in the Night" (Kaempfert, Singleton, and Snyder); "California Dreamin' " (John Phillips); "Eleanor Rigby" (Lennon and McCartney); *Blind Men* (Roger Reynolds) ... Painting &

"A building is an offering to the spirit of architecture."—Louis Kahn

(William Shatner) and cerebral, pointy-eared, half-Vulcan (an alien species), half-human Mr. Spock (Leonard Nimoy), as well as a Scotsman, an Asian man, and an African woman—the show was as pioneering in its depiction of human relations as it was about outer space. (It featured television's first interracial—and, eventually, first interspecies—kiss.) Such gee-whiz gadgetry as "phaser" guns and a specialized, high-tech-sounding vocabulary ("Beam me up, Scottie," Kirk commanded when he wanted to return from an extravehicular activity) added scientific verisimilitude and an element of camp to a show whose greatest constant was an optimistic vision of the future. **◂1938.V ▸1968.5**

ARCHITECTURE

Kahn's New Modernism

4 American architect Louis Kahn, a philosopher of brick, concrete, and wood, began work on the Kimbell Art Museum, in Fort Worth, Texas, in 1966. With its rugged simplicity and Euclidean purity, the Kimbell, like Kahn's other buildings, helped liberate architecture from the modernist narrow steel-and-glass confines into which it had settled.

Kahn, who was born in Estonia but moved to the United States when he was five, possessed an abiding civic sense, nurtured in part by his Philadelphia boyhood. He believed that modern architecture had often ignored the need for public buildings to resonate more powerfully than office towers or apartment complexes. His great contribution was a quality he called "monumentality": an expansiveness of spirit, an ineffably grand presence that has more to do with "silence and light" (essential components of Kahn's almost mystical vision) than with brick and marble.

The Kimbell, which took six years to build, displays Kahn's monumentality on a more human scale than do some of his other public-spirited buildings—the sprawling yet self-contained government complex at Dacca, Bangladesh; the grand yet quietly modest Salk Institute, in La Jolla, California. The Kimbell's interior is hushed and churchlike. It is a tribute to Kahn—whose reputation, as both teacher and architect, has grown steadily since his death in 1974—that when the Kimbell's directors proposed an addition to the museum in the 1980s, architects across the country mounted a vehement protest: The building's integrity should not be (and was not) compromised. **◂1965.13 ▸1977.11**

The Kimbell brought Kahn's "Philadelphia School" of modernism to Fort Worth, Texas.

FRANCE

Adieu, NATO

5 Charles de Gaulle had never hidden his dislike for the North Atlantic Treaty Organization. But when he pulled France out of the military command of NATO in March 1966, his audacity dumbfounded other Western leaders. Ignoring rules requiring members to consult one another before changing their status, President de Gaulle announced that, as of July, French personnel would no longer answer to NATO commanders; he gave foreign forces one year to leave France. (NATO accordingly moved its headquarters from Paris to Brussels.) Then he left on a tour of the Soviet Union.

President Charles de Gaulle on a goodwill mission in the city of Kiev, Ukraine.

De Gaulle's embrace of Moscow was the paradoxical outcome of his fight for independence—and against American dominance—in world affairs. Since the end of the Algerian War, his behavior had grown increasingly bumptious. In 1963, he barred Britain from the Common Market (defying Washington), rejected the Nuclear Test Ban Treaty, and withdrew French naval forces from NATO. In 1964, he recognized Mao's China, snubbed an invitation to visit U.S. President Johnson, and called for a neutral South Vietnam. In 1965, he wrote a letter of solidarity to North Vietnam's Ho Chi Minh, blasted American intervention in Vietnam, withdrew French officers from the South East Asian Treaty Organization, and refused to participate in NATO maneuvers. He also called for a French boycott of the Common Market until various "supranational" tendencies, allegedly infringing on French sovereignty, were corrected. (Most of his demands were met.)

No leftist, de Gaulle began wooing Russia, France's "traditional ally," only after West Germany rebuffed his attempts to form an anti-American pact, but Moscow was as reluctant as Bonn to back his challenge to U.S. hegemony in Western Europe. The shaky alliance crumbled altogether in 1968, when the Soviets invaded Czechoslovakia. By then, de Gaulle's neglect of domestic matters in favor of diplomatic dramas had helped take France to the brink of revolution. **◂1963.5 ▸1968.1**

BIRTHS

Cecilia Bartoli, Italian singer.

Cindy Crawford, U.S. model.

Laura Dern, U.S. actress.

Stefan Edberg, Swedish tennis player.

Alberto Tomba, Italian skier.

Mike Tyson, U.S. boxer.

DEATHS

Anna Akhmatova, Russian poet.

Elizabeth Arden, U.S. retailer.

Jean Arp, French artist.

Vincent Auriol, French political leader.

André Breton, French writer.

Lenny Bruce, U.S. comedian.

Montgomery Clift, U.S. actor.

Walt Disney, U.S. filmmaker.

C.S. Forester, U.K. novelist.

Alberto Giacometti, Swiss artist.

Bernard F. Gimbel, U.S. retailer.

Hedda Hopper, U.S. gossip columnist.

Buster Keaton, U.S. comedian.

Chester Nimitz, U.S. admiral.

Frank O'Hara, U.S. writer.

Maxfield Parrish, U.S. artist.

Erwin Piscator, German theater director.

Paul Reynaud, French statesman.

Margaret Sanger, U.S. birth-control activist.

Shri Lal Bahadur Shastri, Indian political leader.

Alfred P. Sloan, U.S. businessman.

Sophie Tucker, Russian-U.S. singer.

Evelyn Waugh, U.K. writer.

Sculpture: *Love* (Robert Indiana) ... Film: *A Man for All Seasons* (Fred Zinnemann); *Alfie* (Lewis Gilbert); *The Gospel According to St. Matthew* (Pier Paolo Pasolini); *A Man and a Woman* (Claude Lelouch); *Persona* (Ingmar Bergman) ... Theater: *Don't Drink the Water* (Woody Allen); *Sweet Charity* (Fields and Coleman); *Mame* (Jerry Herman) ... TV: *Hollywood Squares*; *Mission: Impossible*; *Family Affair*.

"My father was a statesman, I am a politician—my father was a saint, I am not."—**Indira Gandhi, daughter of India's first president Jawaharlal Nehru**

NEW IN 1966

MasterCharge (later MasterCard).

Laker Airways.

Fiber-optic telephone cables.

National Organization for Women (NOW).

African-American U.S. cabinet member (Robert Weaver).

IN THE UNITED STATES

▶**OUT OF THE BOUDOIR, INTO THE LAB**—Researchers William Howell Masters and Virginia Eshelman Johnson's 1966, book *Human Sexual Response,* a surprise best-seller, was the first comprehensive study of the physiology of intimate behavior. Unlike previous researchers, who'd gathered data through questionnaires and interviews, Masters and Johnson gathered physical evidence by hooking up subjects to electronic equipment and recording their physical responses. ◀1948.10 ▶1970.M

▶**GENRE BENDER**—It was an unlikely subject for the effete New York writer/socialite: a murder spree by two psychopathic drifters in Kansas. But Truman Capote's form-bending 1966 "nonfiction novel," *In Cold Blood* (a six-year labor), combines serious

reportage, lengthy interviews with the killers (sometimes reproduced verbatim), and Capote's own eerie reconstructions of the crimes.

▶**POP MUSIC EXPLODES**—Rock 'n' roll, barely a decade old, was already able to accommodate remarkably diverse styles, as reflected in

U.S. TROOPS IN VIETNAM

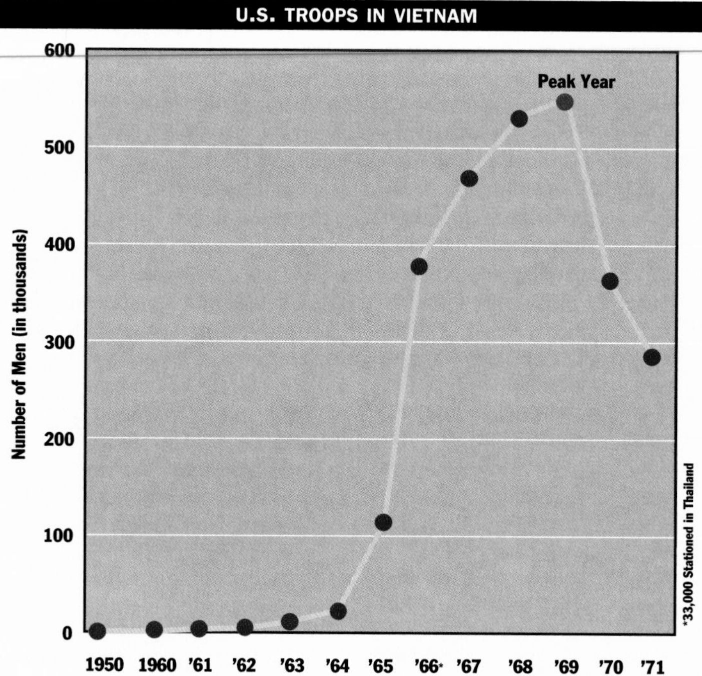

From 35 advisers in 1950, the U.S. military commitment in Vietnam escalated to its 1969 peak of 542,500 troops.

THE VIETNAM WAR

Escalation and Division

6 In August 1966, 20 U.S. soldiers died in South Vietnam when one of their own planes mistakenly bombarded them with napalm. The incident was gruesomely symbolic of the rifts that were starting to open in American society as the war intensified. Student protesters occupied university buildings in New York and Chicago, even as pro-war students presented Vice President Humphrey with a 500,000-signature petition of support. In New York, 20,000 peace marchers were set upon by an angry mob. In Washington, a few powerful congressmen began assailing President Johnson as a warmonger.

There was internecine strife in South Vietnam, too. After taking power in a rigged election in 1965, Premier (and former air force chief) Nguyen Cao Ky had promised Johnson he'd implement political and economic reforms so that Americans would feel they were supporting a just regime. But few reforms materialized—and in 1966, when Saigon's Buddhists demonstrated against corruption and for democracy, Ky met them with violence. Still, U.S. aid money, about $1 billion a month, continued to flow—some 40 percent of it, right into the pockets of the country's elite.

In purely military terms, the war was not going badly for the United States. B-52s had begun bombing North Vietnam's cities. Helicopters were sweeping U.S. troops into major battles in the Iron Triangle, the Mekong Delta, and elsewhere; enemy body counts consistently outnumbered those of the Americans. Yet South Vietnamese troops were often apathetic, even hostile, while the enemy's numbers and morale seemed inexhaustible. In fact, the "enemy" remained quite popular among the people the Americans were trying to protect. Politically, things were starting to fall apart. ◀1965.1 ▶1967.V

INDIA

A Nation's Mother

7 After a brief interregnum, the Nehru dynasty resumed power in India in 1966, when Indira Gandhi became that country's third prime minister since independence. The Oxford-educated daughter of Jawaharlal Nehru, Gandhi succeeded her father's successor, Lal Bahadur Shastri, who died after 18 months in office. Independent and iron-willed, Gandhi came to personify modern India during her frequently contentious 15 years in power, earning the sobriquet Bharat Mata (Mother India).

Soon after taking office, faced with dire economic problems compounded by India's worst drought of the century, Gandhi unilaterally slashed the value of the rupee by more than 50 percent. The radical reduction alienated many government officials. Worse, it caused a sharp rise in prices—giving her political enemies much fuel for the next elections, in 1971.

Campaigning under the slogan *"Garibi hatao!"* ("Let's get rid of poverty!"), Gandhi was, nevertheless, reelected by a landslide. The economy continued to worsen, triggering widespread unrest, and, in 1975, she imperiously declared a state of emergency. She censored the increasingly critical media and jailed many of her rivals. Meanwhile, corruption and venality crippled her administration. In 1977, the nadir of her career, Gandhi was soundly defeated at the polls. Her absence was brief: She was swept back into office two years later and served until she was assassinated in 1984 by her security guards.

Gandhi, Indians often said, was born to rule. Bharat Mata never contradicted that opinion. A lesser politician might have been overwhelmed by India's staggering social and economic problems, but Gandhi, identifying wholly with her country and its government, never lost hope. ◀1965.8 ▶1984.2

THEATER

Weimar on the Hudson

8 The theme and setting of *Cabaret,* which premiered on Broadway in 1966, were an index of how much, and how rapidly, the American musical had matured. Set in late–Weimar Republic Berlin, the show pioneered a new genre of sophisticated, demanding musicals aimed squarely at grown-ups. It made Rodgers and Hammerstein (whose 1959 crowd pleaser, *The Sound of Music,* also takes place in a society yielding to Nazism) seem irrelevant.

Freely adapted from British writer Christopher Isherwood's *Berlin Stories, Cabaret* presents the fall of decadent Weimar to Nazism from the various perspectives of an American expatriate; Sally Bowles, the second-rate singer who seduces him; their bourgeois Aryan landlady; and an amiable con man who becomes a Nazi. A rouged, leering,

SPORTS: Baseball: World Series, Baltimore Orioles defeat Los Angeles Dodgers (Sandy Koufax retires after 27-win season), 4–0 ... Football: NFL-AFL merger announced ... Basketball: NBA, Boston Celtics defeat Los Angeles Lakers, 4–3 ... Hockey: Chicago Blackhawks' Bobby Hull scores 51 goals (first player to score over 50 in a season) ... Soccer: World Cup, England defeats West Germany, 4–2.

"Violence is necessary; it is as American as cherry pie."—**H. Rap Brown**

pansexual nightclub emcee adds color and a chorus-like interpretation of the action. Much of the staging—abstract sets, characters who watch the action, and songs that comment upon it—was reminiscent

On stage and in the 1972 film, Joel Grey played *Cabaret*'s leering nightclub emcee.

of German playwright Bertolt Brecht. (The production's Brechtian feel was further enhanced by the presence in the cast of Lotte Lenya, the widow of Brecht's collaborator Kurt Weill.) Hanging across the stage was a vast tilted mirror that reflected the audience —producer-director Hal Prince's way of implicating its members in the enacted tragedy, which he believed had a parallel in the racial bigotry of 1960s America. Theatergoers rose to the challenge: *Cabaret* played 1,165 performances. **◂1928.4**

DISASTERS

Ruining the Renaissance

9 Heavy autumn rains swept across central and northern Italy in 1966, causing massive flooding, landslides, and more than 100 deaths. As the tempest subsided, world attention focused on the city of Florence, the cradle of the Renaissance, where the floods had left dozens dead, thousands homeless, and a vast number of irreplaceable works of art either damaged or destroyed.

The rising Arno River had overwhelmed the city's inadequate storm-sewer system, creating what one observer called "a colossal water demon, who in three short hours rose to a record height." The demon wreaked devastation on the magnificent city of art beyond any ever visited on it by war. Huge sections of *Crucifixion*, a church fresco by thirteenth-century master Giovanni Cimabue, were completely effaced. Surging currents knocked asunder the gilded bronze *Gates of Paradise*, built by quattrocento sculptor and goldsmith Lorenzo Ghilberti for the Baptistry of Florence. The Vieusseux Library, comprising more than 250,000 volumes of Romantic literature, was obliterated.

The calamity galvanized art lovers and preservationists throughout the world. Pope Paul VI contributed 50 million lire toward Florence's restoration; in the United States, fund-raising was spearheaded by President Kennedy's widow, Jacqueline Kennedy. Clergy, students, and scholars from around the world donated time and expertise to the cause. But it was too late to save many of the works—a circumstance made more tragic by its preventability: Much of Florence's priceless art had been casually stored below street level. **▸1993.13**

The floods wreaked havoc on Florence's Santa Croce church.

SOCIAL REFORM

Black Power

10 The American civil rights movement splintered in 1966, when Stokely Carmichael, head of the Student Nonviolent Coordinating Committee, vowed never again to "take a beating without hitting back." For too long, he declared, blacks had begged for freedom; it was time to demand it.

The cry for "black power" went up across America and echoed as far away as South Africa. It expressed young blacks' impatience with their elders' legislation-based agenda—and with continuing police and vigilante attacks on movement activists.

A clenched fist defying urban burnout—a new symbol of a new black movement.

Although black-power advocates initially called for violence only in self-defense, their revolutionary stance terrified most whites and not a few blacks. Members of the Black Panther Party, founded in California by Bobby Seale and Huey Newton, paraded in paramilitary gear—often with rifles. In their communities, the Panthers set up free clinics and breakfast programs, but jittery authorities used infiltrators, prison terms, and bullets to destroy them.

The civil rights movement stressed integration; black power emphasized independence. SNCC and other groups ejected white members. The new attitude was stated bluntly by H. Rap Brown, Carmichael's successor at SNCC: "If America don't come around, we're going to burn it down, brother." As riots swept the nation's inner cities in 1966, '67, and '68, the movement's theme song, "We Shall Overcome," increasingly gave way to "Burn, Baby, Burn." **◂1965.5 ▸1968.4**

IN THE UNITED STATES

the diverse albums released in 1966. On the East Coast, a collegiate coffeehouse scene prevailed, with harmonizing vocalists Simon and Garfunkel following Bob Dylan into folk-rock fusion. Their hit album *Parsley, Sage, Rosemary, and Thyme* presented carefully

crafted folk-pop songs about urban angst and alienation. Out west, the Beach Boys had sunnier concerns: waves, cars, girls. Leading makers of surf music, they had an international smash with "Good Vibrations." Fellow Californian Frank Zappa (*above*) released *Freak-Out!*, rock's first two-disc album. Featuring acerbic social commentary, willfully crude lyrics, and pop-music parodies, the album established Zappa and his Mothers of Invention as counterculture mainstays. ◂1965.10 ▸1969.4

▶DOLLS AND GUYS—Jacqueline Susann's risqué and rigorously promoted *Valley of the Dolls* was the bestselling novel of 1966. Full of drugs (the "dolls" of the title) and sex, the book was one of the first by a mainstream woman author to graphically describe female sexuality, as well as one of the first to be hyped by an author herself.

▶PENN STATION DESTROYED—Designed by leading turn-of-the-century architects McKim, Mead, and White, and based on the ancient Roman Baths of Caracalla, New York City's Pennsylvania Station spanned two square city blocks and boasted a cavernous waiting room with 150-foot-high glass-and-iron ceilings and 84 massive columns. Despite protests from such architectural experts as Philip Johnson and Aline Saarinen (Eero Saarinen's widow), the station was torn down In 1966 and replaced by a charmless, utilitarian terminal and sports complex.

POLITICS & BUSINESS: GNP: $749.9 billion ... Department of Transportation and Department of Housing and Urban Development created (HUD Secretary Robert C. Weaver is first African-American cabinet member) ... Gulf & Western takes over Paramount studios ... Congress passes Fair Packaging and Labeling Act ("truth in packaging") ... Dow Jones Industrial Average exceeds 1,000 points for the first time.

"They like nothing in our country, nothing is holy for them ... they are ready to curse and run down everything dear to Soviet man, both in the past and the present."—**Izvestia, on the writings of Sinyavski and Daniel**

AROUND THE WORLD

▶TIPPETT BREAKS THROUGH—Michael Tippett wrote difficult, cerebral music, which delayed proper recognition of his genius until the 1960s. In 1966, he began working on *The Knot Garden*, his third opera and one of the compositions that led to his popular breakthrough. A musical and political maverick, Tippett was a conscientious objector during World War II; his oratorio *A Child of Our Time* (1941) expresses his antifascist, pacifist views. ◂1945.16

▶LITTLE RED BOOK—Lin Biao, head of the Chinese People's Liberation Army, needed a way to familiarize his largely uneducated recruits with the spirit

of revolution. His solution: *Quotations from Chairman Mao*, a compilation of the Great Helmsman's pithy maxims of radical orthodoxy. The "Little Red Book" was the bible of the Cultural Revolution—rampaging Red Guards referred to it to justify their fervid acts of brutality and vandalism. Translated into English in 1966, the small volume became a fashionable accessory of the counterculture. ◂1966.1

▶DOMINICAN DEMOCRACY—In 1966, after five years of coups d'états and civil war (and the presence of American troops), the Dominican Republic held its second general election since the assassination of Rafael Trujillo Molina. Joaquín Balaguer, who'd been appointed president by Trujillo in 1960, defeated incumbent Juan Bosch in July (Bosch had been restored to power the year before under the protection of an Organization of American States' cease-fire.) A favorite of the military and the church, Balaguer brought stability to the Dominican Republic but continued some of Trujillo's autocratic policies. He was reelected four times between 1978 to 1990. ◂1961.8

THE SOVIET UNION

Dissidents on Trial

11 The post-Stalinist thaw ended, abruptly and nonnegotiably, with the 1966 show trial and conviction of liberal Soviet writers Andrei Sinyavski and Yuli Daniel. The trial made it clear that the new government, led by Leonid Brezhnev, would countenance no criticism. Faced with imprisonment or silence, many intellectuals went underground to publish illegal samizdat, reviving the old Russian tradition of dissidence.

From 1953 until '66, Soviet writers enjoyed an unusual degree of freedom. Emboldened by Khrushchev's exposure of Stalinist terror, novelists like Ilya Ehrenburg and Aleksandr Solzhenitsyn openly criticized government abuses. Solzhenitsyn's legally published 1962 novel, *One Day in the Life of Ivan Denisovich*, an unflinching description of Stalinist labor camp brutality, marked a high point of the new openness. After Khrushchev's ouster in 1964, however, the spirit of tolerance quickly dissipated.

In their writings, both Sinyavski and Daniel assailed Stalinist politics and social-realist art (the prescribed Soviet genre). Accused of cooking up anti-Soviet propaganda, they were tried on their words—sort of: Recognizing no distinction between opinion and authorial imagination, government prosecutors quoted satirical passages from the authors' works as evidence of their depravity. The trial's outcome was never in doubt. Sentenced to hard labor, Sinyavski and Daniel refused to admit guilt, a stubborn gesture that would become typical of the resistance movement their trial launched. **◂1964.2 ▸1974.13**

Daniel *(left)* and Sinyavski at their February 1966 trial.

WESTERN AFRICA

"The Redeemer" Is Exiled

12 The decline and 1966 fall of Ghana's Kwame Nkrumah epitomized the disappointments of African decolonization. Leader of the first sub-Saharan nation to achieve independence from Europe, and revered throughout Africa for his anticolonialism, Nkrumah turned repressive in office. He was deposed by a rightist coup while on a state visit to Beijing.

Leading Ghana to independence from Great Britain in 1957, Nkrumah had impressed the world with his appeals for freedom. But as premier, he passed a law mandating detention without trial for "security risks." New roads, schools, and hospitals initially boosted his popularity; a plebiscite in 1960 made him president, with sweeping powers under a new constitution. The economy remained mostly in Western hands, however, and its steady decline brought widespread unrest. Nkrumah sought more and more aid from Communist countries, but the economic slide continued. To stifle dissent, the President created a vicious secret police force and nurtured a cult of personality.

Increasingly secluded, "the Redeemer" (as the official press called him) churned out books of sometimes brilliant, sometimes incoherent, Marxist theory. Meanwhile, the daily business of government was left to often incompetent "Nkrumahists." In the 1960s, even many African nationalists turned against their former hero. And his Marxist fulminations finally provoked Western donors to withhold aid. Isolated, debt-ridden, and oppressed, Ghana was ready for change when Nkrumah was overthrown in 1966. **◂1957.4**

INDONESIA

Sukarno Loses Control

13 The man who forged an identity for Southeast Asia's biggest and most diverse country had his downfall in 1966. Indonesian president Sukarno (like many of his countrymen, he used only one name) had declared his nation's independence from the Netherlands in 1945.

When the Dutch attempted reconquest, he fought back, becoming a hero throughout the 13,670-island archipelago. But later, Sukarno turned autocratic. He dismantled Parliament in 1956 and suppressed dissent, and his "guided economy" never bloomed. By 1965, Suharto, chief of the army's strategic command, had mounted a challenge.

At first, Sukarno's dynamism and charisma—and caginess in playing off the dominant Communist Party against the anti-Communist army—had ensured his position. He created monuments, hospitals, schools, and slogans, building national pride and cohesion among his multicultural people. But his regime's corruption and his vituperations against Washington ("To hell with your aid," he once shouted), which made him an idol in the Third World, alienated Indonesia's conservative military.

In 1965, General Suharto led the army against supposed anti-Sukarno Communist plotters. The commander's real target was the President himself: In the course of a few months, the army and its supporters killed some 300,000 Communists, real and alleged. The massacres completely undermined public confidence in Sukarno: If he couldn't control Indonesia's army, what could he control? Power accrued to Suharto, made unassailable by his command of the military. Sukarno, self-appointed President for Life, lost his office and his freedom. He remained under house arrest until his death in 1970. **◂1949.M ▸1975.M**

NOBEL PRIZES: Peace: No award ... Literature: Shmuel Yoseph Agnon (Israeli; novelist) and Nelly Sachs (German-Swedish; poet and playwright) ... Chemistry: Robert S. Mulliken (U.S.; chemical bond structure) ... Medicine: Charles Huggins (U.S.; hormone treatment of prostate cancer) and Francis Peyton Rous (U.S.; tumor-producing viruses) ... Physics: Alfred Kastler (French; atomic energy levels).

A VOICE FROM 1966

The Right to Remain Silent

From the U.S. Supreme Court decision *Miranda v. Arizona*, June 1966

On June 13, 1966, the U.S. Supreme Court issued its ruling on four cases known collectively as Miranda v. Arizona. (Ernesto Miranda was a 23-year-old high-school dropout from Phoenix who'd been arrested for rape and kidnapping. Identified in a lineup, he had signed a written confession without being aware of his constitutionally guaranteed right to remain silent or of his right to a court-appointed lawyer.) In each case, a suspect had been convicted of a felony after confessing to police during routine questioning. The Court, by a 5-4 vote, overturned the convictions: Because the arresting officers had failed to inform the suspects of their Fifth Amendment protection against self-incrimination, the confessions were inadmissible as evidence at trial. Thereafter, an explicit statement of rights—the now familiar Miranda Rights ("You have the right to remain silent....")—became a required part of arrest procedure. Those ignorant of the law or unable to seek advice gained the same legal footing as those with knowledge and access. Below, Chief Justice Earl Warren writes for the majority. Justice Byron White offers a vehement dissent. **◂1953.M ▸1973.5**

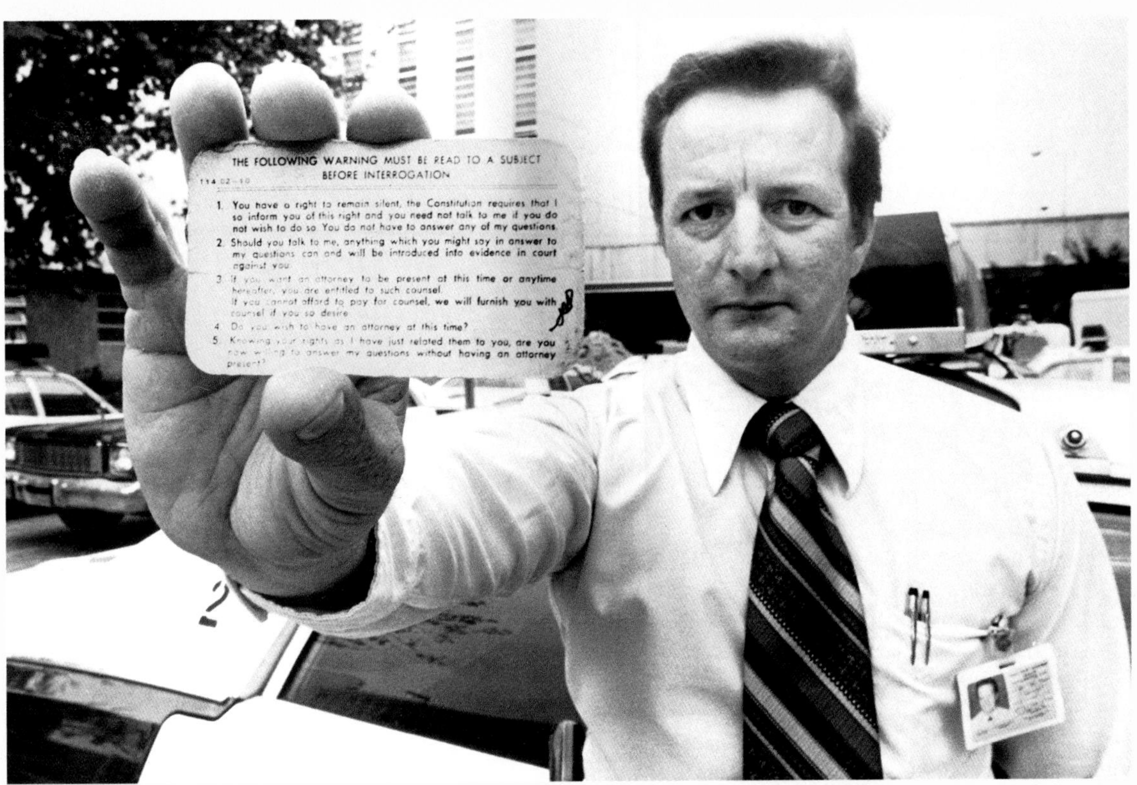

In Miranda, the Supreme Court of Chief Justice Earl Warren *(top)* ruled that arresting officers must inform a suspect of his or her full constitutional rights in order to protect the suspect from inherently coercive interrogation.

Chief Justice Earl Warren: "If a person in custody is to be subjected to interrogation, he must first be informed in clear and unequivocal terms that he has the right to remain silent—the warning of the right to remain silent must be accompanied by the explanation that anything said can and will be used against the individual in court....

The right to have a counsel present at the interrogation is indispensable to the protection of the Fifth Amendment privilege....

If the interrogation continues without the presence of an attorney, and a statement is taken, a heavy burden rests on the Government to demonstrate that the defendant knowingly and intelligently waived his privilege against self-incrimination....

Justice Byron White: The proposition that the privilege against self-incrimination forbids in-custody interrogation without the warning specified in the majority opinion and without a clear waiver of counsel has no significant support in the history of the privilege or in the language of the Fifth Amendment....

The obvious underpinning of the Court's decision is a deep-seated distrust of all confessions. As the Court declares that the accused may not be interrogated without counsel present, absent a waiver of the right to counsel, and as the Court all but admonishes the lawyer to advise the accused to remain silent, the result adds up to a judicial judgment that evidence from the accused should not be used against him in any way, whether compelled or not. This is the not so subtle overtone of the opinion—that it is inherently wrong for the police to gather evidence from the accused himself. And this is precisely the nub of this dissent. I see nothing wrong or immoral, and certainly nothing unconstitutional, with the police asking a suspect whom they have reasonable cause to arrest whether or not he killed his wife or with confronting him with the evidence on which the arrest was based, at least where he has been plainly advised that he may remain completely silent.... Moreover, it is by no means certain that the process of confessing is injurious to the accused. To the contrary, it may provide psychological relief and enhance the prospect for rehabilitation.

"I am a new Frankenstein."—**Louis Washkansky, the first recipient of a transplanted heart**

STORY OF THE YEAR

First Heart Transplant Performed

1 In Cape Town, South Africa, surgeon Christiaan Barnard, supported by a team of 30 assistants, gave the gift of life to 55-year-old Louis Washkansky in 1967, replacing his diseased heart with that of a young woman killed in a car accident. Denise Darvall's head and lower body were severely damaged upon impact, but her 25-year-old heart was left unharmed and still beating, driven by its own nervous system. The circumstances gave Barnard an opportunity to try experimental surgery; to Washkansky, dying of heart disease, they meant a chance at survival.

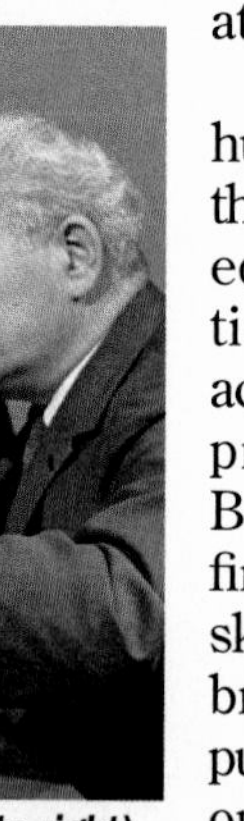

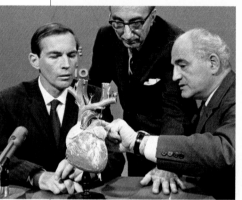

Pioneering cardiologists *(left to right)* Christiaan Barnard, Michael de Bakey, and Adrian Kantrowitz discuss the transplant on a television news show.

The first successful human-heart transplant, the operation commanded enormous international interest. News accounts described the procedure in detail. Barnard and his team first opened Washkansky's chest and split his breastbone, then they pulled aside his ribs and opened the pericardial sac (the heart's casing), to expose a swollen, gray-tinted organ. By means of a heart-lung machine—a mechanical pump that keeps blood oxygenated—Washkansky's blood was routed around his diseased heart. In removing the organ, doctors left in place its top—the walls of the left and right pumping chambers. Then they cut away about 95 percent of Darvall's healthy heart and sewed it onto the "lid" of Washkansky's heart. To stimulate a heartbeat, Barnard attached two thin electrodes to the heart and gave it an electric shock. "It was like turning the ignition of a car," said one member of the team. Within Washkansky's chest, a new heart started pumping blood. Hours after the operation, surgeon and patient met in the recovery room. "You promised me a new heart," Washkansky whispered. "You've got a new heart," Barnard replied.

Although the transplant itself was successful, Washkansky contracted pneumonia and died 18 days later. The procedure stirred ethical debate—about the definitions of life and death, about the proper role of medicine. Traditionally, life was thought to end when the heart stopped beating; now doctors were able to revive, or replace, failed hearts. One respected Jesuit theologian, characterizing the heart as no more than an "efficient pump," dismissed ethical objections to transplants; other religious leaders maintained that radically altering the body was usurping God's role. Physicians offered a new definition of death: the cessation of electrical activity in the brain. Questions concerning when to terminate life and when to prolong it, and who should make those momentous decisions, remain unresolved. **◂1952.12 ▸1982.11**

GREECE

The Colonels' Coup

2 In 1967, Greece became the first Western European nation since World War II to relapse into dictatorship. Two factions had separately planned to prevent former premier Georgios Papandreou (forced from office by King Constantine in 1965) from returning to power that year. One faction, a cabal of generals led by the King, intended to act if Papandreou's center-left coalition won May elections. The other, a conspiracy of colonels, decided to strike preemptively. On April 21, the colonels overthrew Greece's caretaker government, and for the next seven years tyranny ruled the birthplace of democracy.

The new regime was fronted by a civilian, Konstantinos Kollias, but its strongman was Colonel George Papadopoulos *(above)*. The regime imprisoned 45,000 alleged subversives. (Among the victims was Papandreou, who died under house arrest in 1968.) The junta suspended parliament and civil liberties, and banned beards, miniskirts, and protest tunes. In December, after a failed countercoup by King Constantine, the regime attempted some window dressing: Papadopoulos became prime minister, and political prisoners were given amnesty. But repression continued.

Though most European governments denounced the junta, Washington quietly backed it. (As premier, Papandreou had lifted a ban on the Communist Party; his son Andreas had proposed that Greece quit NATO. The colonels, by contrast, were vociferously pro-American.) Most Greeks, at first, were optimistic: Previous governments had been corrupt, inefficient, and wildly fractious. Only in the 1970s did popular discontent and internal rivalries begin to undo the regime. **◂1949.M ▸1974.5**

THE MIDDLE EAST

Six Day War

3 Simmering Arab-Israeli hostility exploded into brief, climactic war in 1967, when Israel, assailed by Palestinian guerrillas, launched a massive punitive strike against Egypt, the Arab world's leading state. Egyptian provocation triggered the Six Day War, but conflict had been a fact of Middle Eastern life since 1947, when Palestine was partitioned to make room for a Jewish state. Israel's annexation of substantial Arab territory, after its decisive 1967 victory, ensured a continuation of violence for decades to come.

After the partition, thousands of Palestinians had fled Israel into neighboring Arab states, with many forming guerrilla groups to strike at the new country. In 1964, Egyptian president Gamal Abdal Nasser, the world's most prominent Arab politician, attempted to gain control of various guerrilla factions by fashioning them into the Palestinian Liberation Organization. The gambit failed: Backed by Syria, a number of independent Palestinian groups escalated their attacks. In May 1967, Israel responded by massing troops on the Syrian frontier. Nasser, asserting his leadership, reacted aggressively. He ordered UN cease-fire troops to leave the contested Egyptian-Israeli border; blockaded the Red Sea Strait of Tiran, a crucial shipping lane for Israel; and entered into a military pact with Jordan, Israel's belligerent eastern neighbor. Syria, Jordan, Iraq, Kuwait, and Algeria vowed to "wipe Israel off the map" should it retaliate.

Anticipating an invasion, Israel blitzed. It destroyed the Egyptian air force, the strongest Arab fight-

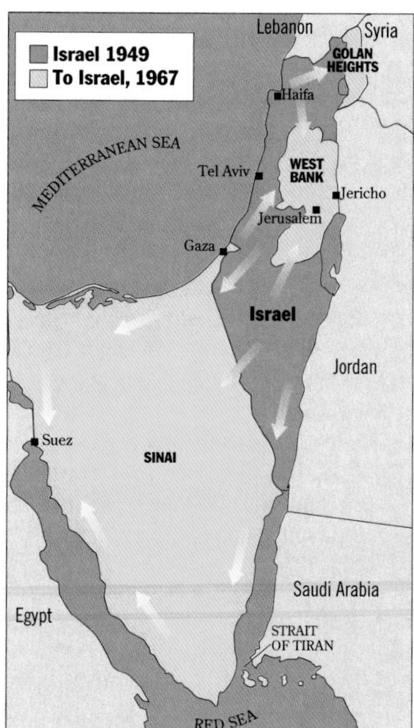

In the Six Day War, Israel captured the Sinai Peninsula, the Old City of Jerusalem, the West Bank, and the Golan Heights.

ART & CULTURE: Books: *The Chosen* (Chaim Potok); *The Confessions of Nat Turner* (William Styron); *A Bad Man* (Stanley Elkin); *Snow White* (Donald Barthelme); *Children of Crisis* (Robert Coles); *Our Crowd* (Stephen Birmingham) ... Music: "Light My Fire" (The Doors); *Magical Mystery Tour* (The Beatles, LP); *Surrealistic Pillow* (Jefferson Airplane, LP); *The Mamas and the Papas* (LP); *Symphony No. 7*

"Maybe the real battle of America is not politics, it's lifestyle."—**Sixties radical Jerry Rubin, after attending the first be-in in San Francisco**

ing unit, in a June 5 surprise attack and proceeded to rout Egyptian ground forces and occupy the Gaza Strip and the Sinai Peninsula. Jordan entered the war, and it too was vanquished: Israel captured all Jordanian territory west of the Jordan River—the West Bank. Then Israel drove Syria out of the Golan Heights. The UN brokered a ceasefire on June 11, ending the immediate conflict. But the die had been cast. Israel soon began moving settlers into the occupied territories, and Palestinians, disappointed by Egyptian and Syrian patronage, took charge of their own fate—and of the PLO. **◂1964.5 ▸1970.3**

THE MIDDLE EAST

Civil War in Both Yemens

4 In 1967, the two halves of what is now the Republic of Yemen, on the southern tip of the Arabian Peninsula, were separate countries. Each was engulfed in civil war that year, and each was vacated by occupying troops—Egyptian and Saudi in North Yemen, British in South Yemen. Despite the departures, peace was far away—as was the merger that both North and South Yemen claimed they wanted.

South Yemen had been governed by the British since 1839. Its civil war had begun in 1965, when Great Britain announced it would soon be leaving, and two nationalist factions—the Egyptian-backed Front for the Liberation of Occupied South Yemen and the indigenous National Liberation Front—faced off over who would inherit authority after independence. The bloodshed hastened Britain's exit. In November 1967, the British transferred sovereignty to the stronger NLF, which became the only recognized party in the new nation, called the People's Republic of Southern Yemen.

North Yemen (known simply as Yemen) had been independent since the fall of the Ottoman Empire. Its civil war began in 1962, when Imam Muhammad al-Badr was toppled by the military. The coup leader—Badr's chief of staff, Colonel Abd Allah al-Sallal—proclaimed the Yemen Arab Republic. Badr, who'd fled to the mountains, declared war. Saudi Arabia sent troops to Badr's aid, while Sallal got help from Egypt. By 1967 Sallal was losing, and the Egyptians agreed with the Saudis to withdraw.

Residents of Shibam, South Yemen, celebrate independence.

An anti-Egyptian junta ousted Sallal, and the civil war ended in 1970, when Badr supporters joined the government. South Yemen, meanwhile, became a Soviet-bloc "people's republic." After border clashes in 1972, the two nations surprised the world by announcing their intention to unite. Action was delayed by coups in both countries, more border clashes, and a civil war in South Yemen in 1986. The Republic of Yemen was born in 1990, but four years later, north and south were once again fighting. **◂1920.2**

POPULAR CULTURE

The Summer of Love

5 During the summer of 1967 disparate social factions—prize-winning novelists, rock stars, hippie acid trippers, middle-class home owners, and rebel professors—repeatedly came together to protest the Vietnam War and to bring about a new age in which people would "make love, not war." The seminal event of "The Summer of Love" occurred in the spring—a peace march in New York City on April 15 that drew 300,000 participants (the most ever up to that time in U.S. history). Among the demonstrators: pediatrician and activist Benjamin Spock; folk singer Pete Seeger; and civil rights leader Martin Luther King, Jr., who, speaking to the crowd, stressed the connection between the struggle for peace and the struggle for racial equality (minorities were disproportionately represented in the numbers of American soldiers in Vietnam).

The antiwar movement embraced young and old, and most of its members lived in traditional communities. But for growing numbers of disillusioned young people, opposition to the war was an impetus to seek out "alternative" lifestyles. Urban hippie enclaves grew up across the country. Perhaps the best known was in San Francisco's Haight-Ashbury district, where thousands of "flower children" took up transitory residence and freely expressed alternative values—typically by playing rock music, experimenting with drugs, wearing psychedelic costumes, and having nonmarital sex. Seeking to harness "flower power"—if enough "good vibes" were assembled in one place, went the theory, anything was possible—Beat poet Allen Ginsberg in

The spirit of the hippie movement was embodied in the rock-concert posters commissioned by impresario Bill Graham.

1965 put together the first "be-in" in San Francisco. "Organized for unorganized activity," be-ins became a favorite counterculture activity in the America and Western Europe. The Summer of Love, in fact, has been characterized as an extended be-in.

But the movement had a doleful side. As more and more young people flocked to the Haight and other hippie strongholds, the spirit of liberation crashed against certain economic and chemical realities, producing increased drug addiction, crime, and mental and physical illness. **◂1965.M ▸1968.V**

BIRTHS

Boris Becker, German tennis player.

Riddick Bowe, U.S. boxer.

Sinead O'Connor, Irish singer.

Julia Roberts, U.S. actress.

DEATHS

Konrad Adenauer, German chancellor.

Clement Attlee, U.K. prime minister.

Primo Carnera, Italian-U.S. boxer.

John Coltrane, U.S. musician.

Ilya Ehrenburg, U.S.S.R. writer.

Brian Epstein, U.K. rock promoter.

Casimir Funk, Polish-U.S. biochemist.

Ernesto "Che" Guevara, Argentine revolutionary.

Woody Guthrie, U.S. musician.

Edward Hopper, U.S. artist.

Langston Hughes, U.S. poet.

Henry Kaiser, U.S. industrialist.

Alfred Krupp, German manufacturer.

Vivien Leigh, U.K. actress.

Henry Luce, U.S. publisher.

Albert Luthuli, South African civil rights leader.

René Magritte, Belgian painter.

John Masefield, U.K. writer.

Carson McCullers, U.S. writer.

Muhammad Mussadegh, Iranian prime minister.

J. Robert Oppenheimer, U.S. physicist.

Dorothy Parker, U.S. writer.

Gregory Pincus, U.S. biologist.

Claude Rains, U.K.-U.S. actor.

Basil Rathbone, U.K.-U.S. actor.

Otis Redding, U.S. singer.

Ad Reinhardt, U.S. painter.

Jack Ruby, U.S. assassin.

Carl Sandburg, U.S. poet.

Luis Somoza Debayle, Nicaraguan president.

Spencer Tracy, U.S. actor.

(Roger Sessions)... Painting & Sculpture: ***Who's Afraid of Red, Yellow, and Blue I*** **(Barnett Newman) ... Film:** ***In the Heat of the Night*** **(Norman Jewison);** ***Guess Who's Coming to Dinner*** **(Stanley Kramer);** ***Cool Hand Luke*** **(Stuart Rosenberg);** ***Belle du Jour*** **(Luis Buñuel) ... Theater:** ***Little Murders*** **(Jules Feiffer);** ***A Day in the Death of Joe Egg*** **(Peter Nichols) ... TV:** ***The Carol Burnett Show; The Flying Nun.***

"We thought we were in our own nation. We knew there were problems, but we thought they were the problems of growing up.... Now I would not be a Nigerian. It is finished for me."—**Igbo writer Chinua Achebe, on the Nigerian blockade of Biafra**

NEW IN 1967

Multiple Independent Reentry Vehicle (MIRV).

ROLLING STONE

Tom Rounds Quits KFRC

THE HIGH COST OF MUSIC AND LOVE: WHERE'S THE MONEY FROM MONTEREY?

Airplane high, but no new LP release

Rolling Stone **magazine.**

Corporation for Public Broadcasting (PBS).

Breathalyzer tests for motorists (Britain).

Commercial microwave ovens (Amana).

Quartz watches.

IN THE UNITED STATES

▶FIRST SUPER BOWL—As expected, the National Football League easily won its first showdown with its rival, the American Football League. Vince Lombardi's Green Bay Packers whipped the Kansas City Chiefs, 35–10, to take the World Championship Game (which became known as the Super Bowl in 1969). For hard-nosed coach Lombardi—"winning isn't everything, it's the *only* thing" was his motto—anything less would have been unacceptable. Packer quarterback and future Hall-of-Famer Bart Starr was voted most valuable player. ◂1960.M

▶NEVELSON RETROSPECTIVE—Sculptor Louise Nevelson was a proponent of "found object" assemblages:

She made sculptures using scrap wood, salvaged furniture parts, quotidian bric-a-brac. Her 1967 retrospective at New York's Whitney Museum of American Art showcased her signature abstract style *(An American Tribute to the British People, above)*, exhibiting her "wall sculptures"

War's youngest victims: malnourished children at a refugee camp near Aba, Biafra.

WESTERN AFRICA

Biafra Starves

6 The war that awakened the entire world to the tragic problems of modern Africa began in May 1967, when Nigeria's eastern region—home of the Igbo people—seceded as the Republic of Biafra. The ensuing conflict between Biafran secessionists, led by Lieutenant Colonel Odumegwu Ojukwu, and Nigerian forces, commanded by Yakubu Gowon, reduced the new state to ruin. Nigeria blockaded Biafra, and soon images of starving children flooded the international news media, producing horror and revulsion.

Relief agencies tried to airlift supplies to the besieged state, but they did so without official support and were able to get only a smattering of food through Nigerian lines. Biafra starved—and for political reasons: Biafran independence, the world's most powerful governments agreed, could spur secessionism all over Africa. Great Britain, Egypt, and the Soviet Union armed Nigeria, with tacit U.S. support. Portugal, South Africa, and France backed Biafra—but feebly.

The roots of the conflict reached back at least to the 1930s, when large numbers of Igbo, who made up about one-seventh of Nigeria's total population of 67 million, migrated west into regions traditionally occupied by Yoruba and Hausa peoples. In 1966, an Igbo-led coup was followed by a Hausa-led countercoup. Some 30,000 Igbos were massacred and a million or more fled back east. The events convinced Ojukwu, Oxford-educated military governor of eastern Nigeria, that the country had become unsafe for his fellow Igbo. He declared his territory independent and annexed more. Within a year, Gowon had the deadly stranglehold firmly in place. By the time the rebels surrendered in 1970, more than one million Biafrans had died—mostly civilians, mostly of starvation. **◂1914.6 ▸1984.4**

LITERATURE

García Márquez's Magic

7 Boasting one of twentieth-century literature's most celebrated opening sentences—"Many years later, as he faced the firing squad, Colonel Aureliano Buendía was to remember that distant afternoon when his father took him to discover ice"—Gabriel García Márquez's *One Hundred Years of Solitude*, published in 1967, introduced the richness of Latin American literature to the wider world. The captivating, profound, and richly humorous novel made García Márquez the premier representative of magic realism—a uniquely Latin American literary form that, using surrealism as a springboard, poetically mingles the mythic and the mundane in order to capture the full breadth of the region's colorful, often portentous history and culture.

García Márquez's inventive storytelling owed much to the tales he'd heard from his grandparents while growing up in Aracataca, Colombia. Reinvented by García Márquez—who'd absorbed Latin American history as well as the technical wizardry of writers like Cervantes, Faulkner, Kafka, and Borges—these fables entered the literary canon. Critics pronounced *One Hundred Years of Solitude* the "great novel of the Americas."

García Márquez's book has exerted a profound influence on writers of every nationality, but for the other writers who were part of the 1960s "boom" in Latin American literature, it had a particularly salutary effect—elevating their own reputations even as it influenced their ongoing work. The international stature achieved by such writers as Carlos Fuentes of Mexico, Mario Vargas Llosa of Peru, Julio Cortázar of Argentina, José Donoso of Chile, Jorge Amado of Brazil, and Guillermo Cabrera Infante of Cuba, among others, is directly attributable to García Márquez's breakthrough with *One Hundred Years of Solitude.* He was awarded the Nobel Prize for literature in 1982. **◂1963.M ▸1990.M**

MUSIC

Queen Aretha Crowned

8 The accession of Aretha Franklin, the "Queen of Soul," was completed in 1967, when *Billboard* magazine named her top female vocalist of the year. A tribute to her talent and drive, Franklin's success had more than personal significance: Black performers had once been forced to adapt to a white standard in order to gain mainstream acceptance. Franklin did it in living color, with a rich, passionate gospel style and songs featuring undiluted African-American rhythms.

Franklin always played down the race issue. "It's not cool to be Negro or Jewish or Italian or anything else," she once said. "It's just cool to be alive, to be around. You don't have to be Negro to have soul." She got her start singing in the choir at the Detroit church of her Baptist minister father, and grew up listening to (and performing with) such gospel greats as Mahalia Jackson and Clara Ward.

Franklin had tried to break into pop music in 1960, at age 18, but success eluded her: The larger public was not ready for her supple, sassy voice with its four-octave range. By 1967, both she and the pop audience had matured, and her album for Atlantic Records, featuring the title song "I Never Loved a Man (the Way I Love You)," sold more than a million copies. In all, she produced

SPORTS: Baseball: World Series, St. Louis Cardinals defeat Boston Red Sox, 4–3 ... Football: AFL-NFL, Green Bay Packers defeat Kansas City Chiefs, 35–10; St. Louis Cardinals's Jim Bakken kicks record 7 field goals in 1 game ... Basketball: NBA, Philadelphia 76ers defeat San Francisco Warriors, 4–2 ... Tennis: Billie Jean King wins U.S. and British singles and doubles championships in same year.

"She does not seem to be performing so much as bearing witness to a reality so simple and compelling that she could not possibly fake it."—***Time*** **magazine, in 1968, on Aretha Franklin**

Aretha Franklin at a recording session in 1967, the year of her breakthrough.

five top-ten hits in '67, including "Respect," which not only did double duty as an anthem for black America and for the burgeoning feminist movement, but became a plain old party classic as well. **◂1947.M**

FILM

Hollywood Radicalism

9 Two of 1967's biggest and most aggressively unconventional hit movies, *The Graduate* and *Bonnie and Clyde*, epitomized the changed style and substance of serious American cinema—as well as the rebellious baby-boomer spirit to which Hollywood now catered.

Directed by former improvisational comedian Mike Nichols, *The Graduate* introduced Dustin Hoffman as Benjamin Braddock, a soft-spoken, malaise-bitten recent college grad adrift in his parents' upper-middle-class suburban world (a businessman's one-word career advice to Benjamin—"Plastics!"—was emblematic of his parents' fraudulent values). Seduced by the self-loathing, middle-aged Mrs. Robinson, he then falls in love with her good-girl daughter, Elaine. Young audiences identified with Benjamin's antimaterialism and his ennui, and cheered his emotional breakthrough when he rescues Elaine from the altar as she is about to marry someone else. Simon and Garfunkel's sound track enhanced the film's mood and legitimized the use of rock songs as cinematic commentary. And the casting of Hoffman junked another convention: Screen idols could now be vulnerable and ordinary looking.

The anti-authoritarianism of Arthur Penn's *Bonnie and Clyde* had a grim, Depression-era setting. Violent and nihilistic, this saga of Texas bandits Bonnie Parker (Faye Dunaway) and Clyde Barrow (Warren Beatty) was the most controversial film of its era. "A work of art," sang *The New Yorker*'s Pauline Kael; "pointless" and "lacking in taste" said *The New York Times*'s Bosley Crowther. The characters' cheerful criminality and the film's full-force violence—which often follows on jokes so quickly that viewers' laughter sticks in their throats—were, Penn maintained, a comment on Vietnam-era America's own desperate times. "If the heroes are less than admirable," the director said, "that is a clue to the times." The film was enormously influential: Renegades roamed the screen for years to come, and the climactic, slow-motion scene in which Bonnie and Clyde die in a sheriff's fusillade was relentlessly imitated. **◂1960.11 ▸1972.9**

***The Graduate*'s Benjamin (Dustin Hoffman) succumbs to an older woman's seduction.**

SCIENCE

Unified Field Theory

10 Harvard physicist Steven Weinberg *(below)* in 1967 took a crucial step toward the realization of a "unified field theory," long the Holy Grail of theoretical physics. Such a theory would encompass the four seemingly diverse forces of nature—gravity, electromagnetism, and the weak and strong nuclear forces. Gravity is familiar as the force that draws objects toward the earth; electromagnetism, linking the familiar properties of electricity and magnetism, lies at the basis of chemistry as the force that binds atoms to one another. The weak nuclear force manifests itself by ejecting particles from the nucleus in radioactive decay, and the strong force binds together nuclear particles. Weinberg's model described electromagnetism and the weak force as different expressions of the same phenomenon.

Weinberg predicted the existence of "neutral currents"—reactions between elementary particles in which no electric charge is exchanged. Another physicist, Abdus Salam, of Imperial College in London, independently proposed the same thing. Brilliant as the Weinberg-Salam model was, it was limited: It applied only to elementary particles. In 1970, Sheldon Glashow, another Harvard physicist, extended the theory to all known particles. German scientist Gerhardt Hooft outlined a proof of the theory a year later. In 1979, Weinberg, Salam, and Glashow shared the Nobel for physics. By the late seventies a field theory for the strong force, quantum chromidynamics (QCD), was integrated with Weinberg and Salam's electroweak theory to form what is called the Standard Model. Of the four forces, only gravity is absent from this unified field theory. **◂1929.M**

IN THE UNITED STATES

of stacked, open-faced wood crates filled with carefully arranged artifacts monochromatically painted either black, white, or gold. ◂1963.M

▶"NO" TO STATEHOOD—Puerto Rico, a U.S. commonwealth since 1952, had contributed to America's recent military efforts in Korea and Vietnam, and depended on federal funds. To many residents, statehood seemed to make sense, especially after Hawaii and Alaska joined the union in 1959. But when a plebiscite was held on the question in 1967, voters overwhelmingly elected to retain commonwealth status. Only 39 percent of those who voted favored statehood, with a small minority coming out for independence. (The largest, and most radical pro-independence faction, boycotted the vote.) ◂1952.M

▶JUSTICE MARSHALL—Thurgood Marshall was no stranger to the Supreme Court when President Johnson appointed him its first black member in 1967: As chief counsel for the NAACP, Marshall had argued 32 cases before the Court, including

the historic *Brown v. Board of Education* (1954). The appointment, said LBJ, represented "the right thing to do, the right time to do it, the right man, and the right place." During his 24 years on the Court, Marshall distinguished himself as its most stalwart defender of minority rights, affirmative action, freedom of speech, and the right to privacy. ◂1954.6

▶DAILIES DIE—An amalgam of some of New York City's most illustrious newspapers, the *World-Journal-Tribune* ceased publishing in 1967. It was one of 159 American dailies to die in the 1960s. A victim of television, declining advertising revenue, and repeated strikes, the paper existed in its final *WJT* incarnation for less than a year. ◂1900.2

POLITICS & BUSINESS: GNP: $793.9 billion ... 25th Amendment ratified (confirms presidential succession) ... Supreme Court rules laws banning interracial marriage unconstitutional ... Adam Clayton Powell (New York) denied a seat in Congress due to misuse of government funds (later voted in, but fined $25,000) ... McDonnell Aircraft Co. and Douglas Aircraft merge to form McDonnell-Douglas Corp.

"People will try to copy Twiggy, bite their fingernails, stand knock-kneed, but they'll never be right, never be Twiggy."
—Photographer Mel Sokolsky

AROUND THE WORLD

▶HAMLET RECONSIDERED—Czech-born British playwright Tom Stoppard (a World War II refugee) emerged as one of the great postwar ironists when *Rosencrantz and Guildenstern Are Dead* opened in 1967. The riotously funny, verbally dexterous takeoff on *Hamlet* featured the melancholy Dane's two mercenary friends as bumbling existential antiheroes.

▶STALIN'S DAUGHTER DEFECTS—Her father would have been mortified: Svetlana Alliluyeva, Joseph Stalin's daughter, defected to the U.S. in April. American Embassy officials in New Delhi, India, to whom Alliluyeva presented herself in 1967, at first doubted her story. She got political asylum, but the State Department downplayed the incident. The tense U.S.-Soviet relationship

was entering one of its periodic thaws, and too much fuss over the defection would have lowered the thermostat.

▶DE GAULLE IN CANADA—Visiting Canada for the nation's centennial as a British dominion and for Montreal's Expo 67 world's fair, Charles de Gaulle set off a furor by endorsing French-Canadian separatism. The French president capped a speech in Montreal by exclaiming, *"Vive le Québec libre!"*—the slogan of those favoring independence for the mostly French-speaking province. Rebuked by Canadian premier Lester Pearson, de Gaulle canceled his scheduled stop in Ottawa and flew home. ▸1968.M

▶CHINA GETS H-BOMB—On June 17, China detonated a hydrogen bomb, becoming the fifth country to command thermonuclear weapons. The Chinese test came amid increasing Sino-Soviet hostility and raised fears in Moscow that a nuclear showdown was imminent. The U.S. was also worried: Later in the year it announced a new antiballistic missile system as a defense against a Chinese onslaught. ◂1963.2 ▸1969.8

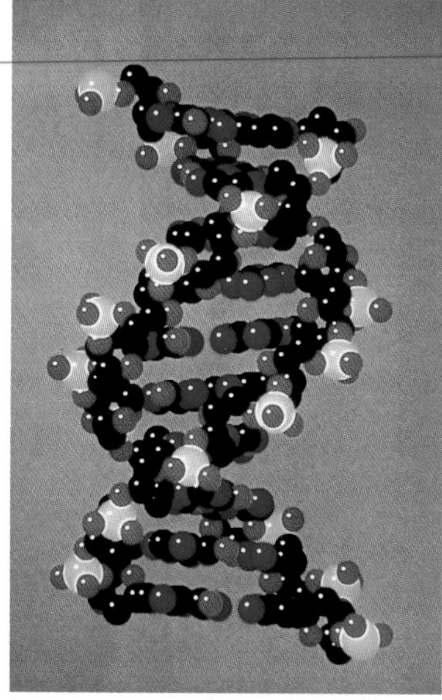

A computer-generated model of DNA. The genetic information carried by the molecule is determined by the base pairs.

SCIENCE

Test-Tube DNA

11 In 1967, 14 years after Watson and Crick described the structure of DNA (deoxyribonucleic acid), a team of genetic researchers, led by American biochemist Arthur Kornberg, synthesized biologically active DNA in a test tube. Kornberg and partners Mehran Goulian and Robert L. Sinsheimer used an enzyme called DNA polymerase to produce a single DNA strand. Like normal DNA, Kornberg's replica contained all the genetic information that allows cells to reproduce. Kornberg cautioned that he had merely copied DNA, not created it, but his breakthrough was immensely promising. Among its possible applications was a cure for cancer.

Kornberg and the Spanish-born American molecular biologist Severo Ochoa had shared the Nobel Prize for medicine in 1959—Kornberg for discovering DNA polymerase, Ochoa for isolating an enzyme that could be used to synthesize compounds similar to RNA (ribonucleic acid), the genetic material that enables cells to produce proteins. These enzymes were at the heart of genetic work: DNA polymerase allowed Kornberg first to synthesize inert DNA molecules, then to synthesize his 1967 live replica; Ochoa's enzyme, called polynucleotide phosphorylase, enabled him to synthesize RNA.

The genetic discoveries commanded huge interest—from scientists and from the general public. To many people, the in vitro replication of DNA sounded like some kind of Frankenstein experiment—the first step toward laboratory genesis of human life, or worse, humanoid "clones"—genetic copies of a real human. (Indeed, a British biologist successfully produced a clone of a tadpole in 1967.) The U.S. Congress went so far as to form a committee to look into the matter. Among molecular biologists, however, the real significance of genetic engineering was immediately recognized—it would one day empower physicians to successfully treat hereditary disease. **◂1953.1 ▸1976.5**

IDEAS

A Literary Saboteur

12 In *De la Grammatologie (Of Grammatology)*, published in 1967, French philosopher Jacques Derrida detailed his radical theory of deconstruction—an abiding influence on French philosophy and American literary criticism, and a source of inexhaustible fascination for generations of graduate students to come. A perceptive critique of nineteenth-century Swiss linguist Ferdinand de Saussure, *Of Grammatology* presented Derrida's strategy of "deconstructing" texts, whether novels or philosophical tracts, to expose the imprecision of language and the variability of meaning.

Derrida's work represents an attack on traditional metaphysics: Any statement of absolute value, he suggests, is meaningless. Deconstructionist theory undermines the long-assumed absolute authority of the writer. According to Derrida, a text's meaning derives as much from the assumptions of the reader as from the intentions of the writer.

Full of brilliant insights and clever wordplay, Derrida's prose can also be maddeningly opaque: "The center is at the center of the totality," he wrote in *L'Ecriture et la différence (Writing and Difference)*, "and yet, since the center does not belong to the totality (is not part of the totality), the totality has its center elsewhere. The center is not the center."

Deconstruction triggered a kind of civil war in literature and philosophy departments at French and American universities: Academics either loved Derrida's theory or hated it. It seemed likely that Derrida, who made much of language's inadequacies, was chuckling impishly at the misunderstandings his work generated. **◂1962.12 ▸1984.13**

FASHION

Twiggy's Mod Look

13 A 17-year-old Cockney gamine called Twiggy arrived triumphantly in the United States in 1967, met at the airport by more screaming fans and delirious photographers than anyone since those other British invaders—the Beatles. With hair bobbed, wide eyes made up in triple tiers of false eyelashes, and a figure like a beanpole, Twiggy (in real life, Leslie Hornby, a London high-school dropout) exuded youth, innocence, and something close to antiglamour—a refreshing detour from haute couture sophistication. Knock-kneed and inclined to chew her fingernails, she was adolescent, awkward and, above all, mod: bold in dress and style, liberated from fusty old fashion.

The Twiggy image clicked with middle-class kids, who were emerging as a profound commercial force; collectively they spent billions on new youth-culture trimmings like clothes and rock 'n' roll records. Twiggy's waifish style—miniskirts, knit tops, striped stockings—was for a few years the hottest thing in fashion. But at 5' 6" and 91 pounds, she was not everyone's ideal beauty. Sniped one newspaper editor, worried about the streamlined rage triggered by Twiggy: "We can practically hear the seams bursting from coast to coast." She needn't have worried: A perfect sixties child, Twiggy retired with the decade. **◂1965.2 ▸1970.M**

The first supermodel, Twiggy overturned a century-old ideal of beauty.

NOBEL PRIZES: Peace: No award ... Literature: Miguel Angel Asturias (Guatemalan; novelist and poet) ... Chemistry: Manfred Eigen, Ronald Norrish, and George Porter (German, U.K., U.K.; high-speed chemical reactions) ... Medicine: Haldan K. Hartline, George Wald, and Ragnar Granit (U.S., U.S., Swedish; human eye) ... Physics: Hans A. Bethe (U.S.; energy production in stars).

A VOICE FROM 1967

Dear America

Letters to the United States from Soldiers Stationed in Vietnam, 1967

Soldiers through the ages have written home from the battlefront, documenting war with an immediacy unavailable to historians. The language is often simple and direct; the opinions are honest, sometimes brutally so. During the American Civil War, letters of rare eloquence, full of exalted notions of patriotism and honor, were produced on both sides. Entrenched World War I doughboys, shocked by death on an inhuman scale, translated horror and anguish into words. From Vietnam in 1967, an ambiguous year in an ambiguous war—midway between the American troop build-up and the momentous reversal of the Tet Offensive—came letters expressing sorrow, frustration, bitterness, and even a little hope. Here, Marine Captain Rodney Chastant (who was killed in 1968) and platoon commander Fred Downs express their ambivalence about the war, which mirrored America's own. ◄**1966.6** ►**1968.3**

10 September '67
[Dear] David,

... Here in Vietnam the war goes on. Morale is very high in spite of the fact that most men think the war is being run incorrectly. One of the staggering facts is that most men here believe we will *not* win the war. And yet they stick their necks out every day and carry on with their assigned tasks as if they were fighting for the continental security of the United States. Hard to believe, but true.

The Marines are taking a fierce beating over here. They don't have enough men. We must have more men, at least twice as many, or we are going to get the piss kicked out of us this winter when the rains come. The Marines have been assigned a task too big for so few. We are fighting for our very lives in the north. In the last 15 weeks we've lost 47 percent of all helicopters in Vietnam....

We should have never committed ourselves to this goal, but now that we have, what should we do? We must destroy the will of Hanoi quickly and stop doling out American lives in that penny-ante effort. Then reallocate our resources of money and materiel and, with two or three times the present manpower, crush the guerrillas....

A member of the Zippo Squad (named for the cigarette lighter), an American soldier on a search-and-destroy mission in 1967 burns down a civilian village in South Vietnam in order to root out Viet Cong.

5th or 6th Oct. 67
Hi Honey.

I had a hell of a day yesterday....

We were going up this valley, and I got a report that approximately 60 VC were spotted on the ridgeline next to my location. I told my point man to change direction towards that position. We came to a river that was deep and wide due to all of the rain we've been getting. We were looking for a way across when six VC took off out of a hut across the river....

[O]n the right flank, a VC popped out of a hole and threw a grenade. My M-79 man stood his ground and fired at the dink [at] the same time he threw the grenade. My M-79 got hit in the leg with shrapnel from the grenade, and the dink that threw it got knocked down with the blast from the M-79. My man crawled into the bushes. His helmet, wallet, pictures and letters were scattered all over, not to mention his weapon. He started yelling "medic," so I ran over to him with the medic and called in the dust-off....

It was raining, and his blood was mixing with the water in the puddle he was lying in. He wanted to hold my hand because it was hurting him so bad. I held his hands and told him he had a million-dollar wound. He was in pain so bad he was clenching his teeth, but he tried to smile at that. Everyone in the field wants the million-dollar wound so they can be sent back to the States....

I told my men that the first squad to kill a dink with a weapon, I would buy them a bottle of whisky. They can't wait to kill one of them now.

I just heard an explosion down the road. From the radio I hear that an Army vehicle hit a mine and the dust-off has been called. The mine demolished the truck and blew a three-foot hole in the road. This is some war. A man can't feel safe anywhere in this whole country.

I'll never forget the look on that man's face when I was holding his hand.

Well, my love, one of these days, I'll get some mail and I'll read those sweet words "I Love You."

With All My Love,
Fred

7 Nov. 67
Hello Darling,

... My RTO, who has 28 days to go, cracked up. He was shaking and crying, not loud, but the tears were running down his face.

I told him to come out and get in my hole. A little companionship never hurt anyone. I put my arm around his shoulders until he settled down. [In] the last couple of letters he has received from home, his wife has said she didn't care whether he came back or not. He is real proud of his son, whom he hasn't seen yet, and his wife. The bitch doesn't know what she is doing to him. It is bad enough over here. But when your wife writes shit like that, it completely destroys a man....

Last night I was comforting everyone, but there was no one to comfort me. When it got bad, I thought of you and the kids and I felt better.

I love you, Linda.

Your husband,
Fred

STORY OF THE YEAR

A Year of Revolt

1 A rebellious decade reached its climax in 1968, as disenchanted citizens from Prague to Peru demanded political, economic, social, and cultural liberation. Their loose-knit movement, the New Left, embraced ideologies as diverse as anarchism and Maoism but rejected anything smacking of bourgeois respectability. Marching in Mexico City, demonstrators were slaughtered by police. Rioting, they turned British and West German universities into communes, felled Italian and Belgian premiers, and forced concessions from Yugoslav dictator Josip Tito. Students in Paris brought President Charles de Gaulle's Fifth Republic to its knees. In the United States, rebels challenged the very way leaders were chosen.

Students riot in the streets of Paris in the spring of 1968.

One of the towering figures of World War II, de Gaulle had once said, "I am France." But as president, he neglected domestic affairs, and by 1968, his paternalism had grown stale. In May, police in Nanterre crushed a student strike over antiquated facilities and curricula. The protest spread to the Sorbonne, in Paris, and then into the streets. With bricks and barricades, 30,000 New Leftists battled 50,000 lawmen. Sympathetic workers seized factories nationwide. Many French saw it as the end of civilization.

After weeks of silence, de Gaulle granted workers raises, then dissolved the National Assembly and threatened to call in the army. Order returned, and elections produced a pro-de Gaulle backlash. But the President overplayed his hand, vowing to resign unless voters passed a proposition on government reorganization. When the measure failed, in April 1969, the de Gaulle era ended.

In the United States, the cataclysm came in August, when 10,000 demonstrators—most of them truculent members of the Baby Boom generation—descended on the Democratic Party's national convention in Chicago. Led by the anarcho-absurdist Youth International Party (Yippies) and the more sober Students for a Democratic Society, they decried the Vietnam War, racism, and a political process that made inevitable the presidential nomination of Vice President Hubert Humphrey—instead of peace candidate Senator Eugene McCarthy. (The Yippies sardonically nominated a pig.) Given carte blanche by Mayor Richard Daley, Chicago police beat not only rock-throwing demonstrators but passersby, journalists, and McCarthy volunteers. In the fall, frightened voters narrowly elected Richard Nixon—a law-and-order Republican who claimed to have a "secret plan" to end the war. **◂1966.5 ▸1968.2**

CZECHOSLOVAKIA

Prague's Brief Spring

2 A noble experiment brutally repressed, Czech Communist Party leader Alexander Dubček's "socialism with a human face" died in 1968 in the same way a similar revolution in Hungary had died twelve years earlier: under the treads of Soviet tanks. Having introduced reforms unprecedented in a Communist-bloc country—a free press, an independent judiciary, religious tolerance—the Prague Spring represented democracy's fullest flowering behind the Iron Curtain. But Dubček's delicate bloom was no match at all for the 650,000 Warsaw Pact troops that invaded Czechoslovakia on August 20.

Dubček had succeeded Stalinist tyrant Antonín Novotny as secretary of the Czech Communist Party in January 1968, and had begun, with full central-committee support, to institute political and economic reforms. Inspired by Prague's liberalized atmosphere, a group of intellectuals in June issued the "Two Thousand Words," a manifesto calling for the implementation of real democracy. By then, a vigilant Soviet Union had seen enough, and with Poland and East Germany issued an order: Cease and desist all counterrevolutionary activities. In late July, unimpressed by Dubček's assurances, Soviet Party chairman Leonid Brezhnev called him in for an official rebuke. Dubček returned to a hero's welcome in Prague: He had stood up to the Soviet boss and lived to tell about it. Possibilities seemed endless—until the soldiers arrived.

Czechs used sticks, rocks, and bare hands to try to stop the Soviet occupation.

But even as political winter descended on Czechoslovakia, the country remained idealistic: The entire Czech Communist Party and Czech president Ludvik Svoboda stood behind Dubček. The Kremlin could find no quisling to take his place. Brezhnev resolved his problem by allowing Dubček to remain in office, but real power now lay with the tanks and troops clotting Prague. Reform ended, and in April 1969, Soviet puppet Gustav Husák came forward to unseat Dubček. **◂1956.5 ▸1989.1**

THE VIETNAM WAR

The Tet Offensive

3 The Communists in Vietnam launched an offensive in January 1968, that, while a military failure was, in retrospect, a psychological

U.S. soldiers near Hue, South Vietnam, drag a stricken compatriot to safety.

turning point. Taking advantage of the holiday chaos of Tet (the lunar New Year), 67,000 Viet Cong and North Vietnamese soldiers carried out attacks across South Vietnam. The Communists' first nationwide drive, the Tet Offensive penetrated previously unmolested cities.

Americans were stunned. Officials had recently reported that most of the countryside had been "secured" and that the "light at the end of the tunnel" was in sight. Now, after years of war (and despite tremendous Viet Cong losses in the offensive), the Communists seemed decidedly unbowed. Worse yet, the United States hadn't conquered the hearts and minds of the South Vietnamese: Because it relied on infiltration—Viet Cong dressed as civilians smuggled weapons into Saigon in flowerpots and coffins—the Tet Offensive had required the cooperation of thousands of sympathizers.

U.S. forces reacted desperately. To end a monthlong Communist occupation of Hue, they bombed the ancient city to rubble. Troops destroyed the town of Ben Tre, as

ART & CULTURE: Books: ***Myra Breckenridge*** **(Gore Vidal);** ***My Michael*** **(Amos Oz);** ***A Personal Matter*** **(Kenzaburo Oe);** ***Couples*** **(John Updike);** ***Armies of the Night*** **(Norman Mailer) ... Music: "Both Sides Now" (Joni Mitchell); "Hello, I Love You" (The Doors);** ***Beggars Banquet*** **(Rolling Stones, LP) ... Painting & Sculpture:** ***Self-Portrait*** **(Chuck Close);** ***Earthworks*** **(Robert Morris) ... Film:** ***Oliver!*** **(Carol Reed);**

"I've been to the mountaintop and I've seen the promised land.... I may not get there with you, but I want you to know tonight that we as a people will get to the promised land."—**Martin Luther King, Jr., addressing a rally the night before his murder**

one officer famously explained, in order to save it. In a village called My Lai, soldiers massacred 500 unarmed men, women, and children. Although it was not the only atrocity of the war, My Lai was by far the most horrific, and it came to symbolize the war's madness.

Tet brought about drastic reversals in U.S. policy. Of the 206,000 additional troops requested by General Westmoreland, President Johnson authorized only 13,500—then relieved Westmoreland of his command. Johnson declared a partial bombing halt, leading Hanoi to accept an offer to attend peace talks in Paris. And Johnson decided not to seek reelection: The Vietnam War had been his political ruin. **◂1967.V ▸1969.6**

THE UNITED STATES

Assassins Strike Twice

4 Assassins in 1968 felled one of the century's greatest human rights leaders and one of its most promising statesmen. Martin Luther King, Jr., and Robert F. Kennedy died at 39 and 43, respectively; each had made an indelible mark in a brief career, and each was cut down in the midst of profound personal evolution. The violence shook America to its core.

King's incomparable oratory, his steadfast nonviolence, and his willingness to endure jail and worse to combat discrimination earned him worldwide admiration and a Nobel Prize. Not content, King broadened his cause—appealing to black separatists; planning an antipoverty encampment in Washington that would include blacks *and* whites; speaking out against the Vietnam War. The FBI responded by escalating its old harassment campaign—at one point, agents sent him a note urging suicide. But his killer was a white drifter, James Earl Ray, who shot King on a motel balcony in Memphis on April 4. The murder sparked mourning—and rioting—across the country.

Kennedy had come to prominence in 1953 as counsel to the Senate subcommittee headed by the anti-Communist demagogue Senator Joseph McCarthy. As attorney general in the presidential administration of his brother John Kennedy, "Bobby" turned his crusader's zeal against gangsters and monopolists and grew into a powerful ally of the civil rights movement. His maturation continued after he was elected to the U.S. Senate from New York in 1964: He condemned the war his late brother had helped start. Many saw him as the man to end it, and that, along with his charisma and his pedigree, made him a favorite in the 1968 presidential election. He was celebrating victory in the California Democratic primary on June 5 when a young Palestinian-American, Sirhan B. Sirhan, in a deranged protest against American patronage of Israel, gunned him down at a Los Angeles hotel. **◂1966.10**

King *(third from left)* and associates Hosea Williams, Jesse Jackson, and Ralph Abernathy *(left to right)* on the balcony of the motel where King was shot the following day.

FILM

Kubrick's Odyssey

5 With his 1968 film, *2001: A Space Odyssey*, director Stanley Kubrick *(Lolita, Dr. Strangelove)* infused the ordinarily lightweight genre of science fiction with moral and intellectual complexity, and a peerless visual and technical artistry. Based on a story by Arthur C. Clarke (who also wrote the screenplay), Kubrick's two-and-a-half-hour meditation on the evolution of intelligence and the decline of the soul features music by German Romantic Richard Strauss (*Thus Spake Zarathustra*); spellbinding special effects; and a talking, thinking, preternaturally calm, reputedly infallible, and ultimately evil supercomputer called HAL (whose name, contrary to legend, is not "one-off" code for IBM, but an acronym of "heuristic" and "algorithmic").

Keir Dullea played the astronaut-hero of Kubrick's dazzling and enigmatic film.

Hallucinatory, often nonverbal, the film fantasy examines the progression of human life from the mud of prehistory to the cool, clinical realm of a future of pure science. Enigmatic imagery—in the film's ominous opening, earth and sun align; later, the hero-astronaut's sudden journey through death and rebirth is accompanied by a cascade of light and color—gave rise to endless debates about *2001*'s meaning. (Kubrick admitted that "the God concept is at the heart of the film.") Many viewers found it incoherent and cold, but many more were mesmerized. And the movie's commercial success drew the critics (who'd initially dismissed it) back for a reappraisal. **◂1966.3**

BIRTHS

Gary Coleman, U.S. actor.

Harry Connick, Jr., U.S. singer.

Barry Sanders, U.S. football player.

DEATHS

Peter Arno, U.S. cartoonist.

Karl Barth, Swiss theologian.

Chester Carlson, U.S. inventor.

Marcel Duchamp, French artist.

Edna Ferber, U.S. writer.

Yuri Gagarin, U.S.S.R. cosmonaut.

Otto Hahn, German physicist.

Helen Keller, U.S. writer.

Robert Kennedy, U.S. political leader.

Martin Luther King, Jr., U.S. civil rights leader.

Trygve Lie, Norwegian statesman.

Lise Meitner, Austrian-Swedish physicist.

Georgios Papandreou, Greek political leader.

Salvatore Quasimodo, Italian poet.

Ruth St. Denis, U.S. choreographer.

William M. Scholl, U.S. physician.

Upton Sinclair, U.S. writer.

John Steinbeck, U.S. writer.

Night of the Living Dead **(George A. Romero);** ***Faces*** **(John Cassavetes);** ***Barbarella*** **(Roger Vadim);** ***Once Upon a Time in the West*** **(Sergio Leone);** ***The Producers*** **(Mel Brooks) ... Theater:** ***The Great White Hope*** **(Howard Sackler);** ***The Boys in the Band*** **(Mart Crowley);** ***The Price*** **(Arthur Miller);** ***Jacques Brel Is Alive and Well and Living in Paris*** **(Jacques Brel) ... TV:** ***Julia; 60 Minutes; The Dick Cavett Show.***

"Peasant, the landlord will eat no more from your poverty."—**General Juan Velasco Alvarado of the Revolutionary Government of the Armed Forces of Peru**

NEW IN 1968

Waterbeds.

Artificial larynx.

U.S. Open tennis tournament (Forest Hills, New York).

***Queen Elizabeth II* (Cunard).**

Jacuzzi Whirlpool bath.

Motion-picture ratings in the U.S.

Album to go platinum (*Wheels of Fire* by Cream sells 1,000,000 copies).

IN THE UNITED STATES

▶AQUARIAN HIT—*Hair,* the first major rock musical, opened at New York's Biltmore Theater in April, giving the hippie era Broadway

respectability—and a name. "This is the dawning of the Age of Aquarius," sang the long-haired, scantily clad cast of the romping tribute to peace and free love. The extravaganza enjoyed a 1,742-show run. ◂1967.5

▶CLEAVER'S SOUL—"I started to write," Eldridge Cleaver disclosed in *Soul on Ice*, his angry, autobiographical statement on black power, "to save myself." In and out of reform schools and prison throughout his youth, Cleaver published *Soul* while on parole in 1968. The book became a bestseller, and Cleaver the most visible revolutionary in America. ◂1966.10

▶SPACE-AGE SOUNDS—In 1968, four years after Robert Moog unveiled his space-age instrument, the electronic music synthesizer, engineer-composer Walter Carlos and musicologist Benjamin Folkman recorded an album on it. *Switched-on Bach*, featuring

THE UNITED STATES

The *Pueblo* Incident

6 North Korean gunboats seized a U.S. Navy spy ship in international waters in January 1968, impounding the vessel and detaining its 83-man crew. The Communist government of North Korea claimed the USS *Pueblo* had penetrated Korean waters and was "carrying out hostile activities." Washington, denying the charge, condemned the seizure as a "wanton and aggressive act."

In 1968, 15 years after a cease-fire officially ended the Korean War, the conflict was still being fought—through espionage, propaganda, and, increasingly, by North Korean guerrillas who slipped over the border to raid southern cities. In the United States, which still had 55,000 troops in South Korea, North Korean belligerence, capped by the *Pueblo* seizure, was widely seen as part of an all-Asia Communist plot to derail the American Vietnam effort. Congressional hawks demanded a strong (i.e., military) response. President Johnson, already losing one Asian war, chose to negotiate.

Bargaining was tedious and slow, and the American sailors languished in North Korean prisons for nearly a year. Frequently beaten by their captors, many crew members "confessed" to violating the territorial integrity of North Korea. Commander Lloyd M. Bucher, the ship's captain, also signed a confession (in order, he later testified, to save the lives of his men). To secure the sailors' release, the U.S. government signed an apology—but only out of expediency, it claimed. The "confession," said the American negotiator, signified nothing. It was made "to free the crew and only to free the crew." After welcoming the sailors home as heroes in December, the Navy quietly closed the embarrassing incident. The North Koreans kept the ship. **◂1953.2 ▸1994.3**

Along with the *Pueblo*'s officers and crewmen *(above)*, North Korean patrols captured sensitive electronic surveillance equipment.

PERU

Peru's New Generals

7 Tanks surrounded the presidential palace in Peru in 1968, ending the civilian presidency of Fernando Belaúnde Terry after five years. Ahead for Belaúnde: exile in Argentina; for Peru: another in a long line of military regimes, this one headed by General Juan Velasco Alvarado. It seemed a familiar story, but the events of 1968 deviated significantly from the traditional story line: Peru's new leaders were committed to ambitious reform. And they leaned to the left politically. They were the "new generals."

Fernando Belaúnde Terry *(above)* was stunned at being overthrown by Peru's military.

Among the junta's first acts was the expropriation of Standard Oil's International Petroleum Company—a symbol of foreign exploitation for millions of desperately poor Peruvians. Then, demanding Peruvian control of all companies operating in the country, Velasco and his officers nationalized essential industries—mining, banking, fishing. Intent on agrarian as well as industrial reform, the militarists demolished Peru's system of landed estates, distributing 17.5 million acres of land to the rural poor during the next ten years.

The new generals' reforms did not bring prosperity to Peru. Natural disasters interfered. A 1970 earthquake claimed as many as 75,000 lives and caused damage estimated at more than half a billion dollars. The fishing industry was devastated in 1972 by intense warming of the ocean off western South America, brought on by cyclical shifts in the water current nicknamed El Niño. Production faltered and foreign debt ballooned. In 1975, General Francisco Morales Bermúdez ousted Velasco and formed a new junta. Five years later, the Peruvian electorate, thoroughly tired of military rule, returned Belaúnde to the presidency. The restoration of constitutional rule and free-market policies failed to interrupt Peru's downward economic spiral, however. In the 1980s, inflation and unemployment rose dramatically, as did a related scourge—terrorism. **◂1924.M ▸1992.8**

SCIENCE

Pulsars Pique Speculation

8 When 24-year-old Irish graduate student Jocelyn Bell detected mysterious radio signals emanating from outer space in 1968, many people believed she had found evidence of extraterrestrial life. Unlike the steady energy emitted by known stars, Bell's signals pulsed. "Oftentimes this intelligent-civilization bit has been overdone," remarked astronomer Maarten Schmidt, who'd recently discovered quasars, "but if you want to attribute anything to a civilization, then this is the best case we have had so far."

Bell, a member of astrophysicist Antony Hewish's research team at Cambridge University, detected the blips, which occurred at regular 1.5-second intervals, with a radio telescope newly designed by Hewish. After homing in on the emissions, the Hewish team concluded that they came from a rapidly spinning object, dubbed a pulsar, less than 4,000 miles in diameter and 200 light-years away—by stargazing standards, a small size and

SPORTS: Baseball: World Series, Detroit Tigers (Mickey Lolich) defeat St. Louis Cardinals, 4–3 ... Olympics held in Grenoble and Mexico City ... Football: Super Bowl, Green Bay Packers defeat Oakland Raiders, 33–14 ... Basketball: NBA, Boston Celtics defeat Los Angeles Lakers, 4–2 ... Golf: Lee Trevino wins U.S. Open (first player in the tournament to shoot 4 under-par rounds).

"We are on the brink of chaos. I am not a man given to extravagant language, but I must say to you this evening that our conduct over the coming days and weeks will decide our future."—**Prime minister of Northern Ireland Captain Terence O'Neill, after the fall 1968 riots**

A pulsar emits radio waves in a slender beam that, due to the star's rapid rotation, is observed as a pulse.

short distance. That revelation, and the discovery of more pulsars in various nonplanetary locations, indicated that the signals came from something other than an intelligent civilization.

It is now widely believed that pulsars are neutron stars—remnants of the massive, exploding stars called supernovas. Despite Bell's key role in the discovery, the 1974 Nobel Prize for physics went to Hewish and his mentor Sir Martin Ryle. They were the first astronomers so commended. **◄1963.11 ►1974.6**

PANAMA

Torrijos Stages a Coup

9 Amid growing anti-American sentiment in Panama, Lieutenant Colonel Omar Torrijos Herrera *(below)* ousted hapless president Arnulfo Arias in 1968. A populist, Torrijos embarked on a course of economic and social reform: replacing the elitist National Assembly with a democratic body; attempting to break the economic stranglehold of *los rabiblancos,* Panama's wealthy ruling families; and steering Panama from under U.S. sway. As always in Panama, the canal, American owned and operated, loomed behind everything.

The 1968 coup was the third strike for Arias, a Harvard-educated surgeon and petty tyrant: President from 1940 to '41, he backed the Nazis in World War II and was toppled in an American-supported coup; reelected in 1949, he lasted two years before the National Guard threw him out for suspending the constitution. Given another chance in 1968, he again tried to impose one-man rule. Two weeks after the election, Torrijos and his guardsmen chased the would-be dictator out of office. Arias took sanctuary in the U.S.-controlled Canal Zone, a 557-square-mile swath cut across the heart of Panama; Torrijos promoted himself to brigadier general and took charge of the state.

Torrijos's first order of business was to solidify his position. He did so repressively, imprisoning alleged communists and seizing the national university, a leftist stronghold. Once in control, he took on Washington by supporting Nicaragua's Sandinista leftists and befriending Castro's Cuba. Seeking to reduce economic dependence on the canal, Torrijos liberalized banking and tax laws and remade Panama into a magnet for international capital (including untold millions in South American cocaine dollars). And in 1977, he forced new canal treaty negotiations, an act for which he was lionized at home—and vilified in the United States. **◄1914.9 ►1977.7**

NORTHERN IRELAND

The Orange and the Green

10 The worst sectarian violence since the 1920s engulfed Londonderry, Northern Ireland's second-largest city, in 1968 after police dispersed a peaceful civil rights march with batons and water hoses. A city two-thirds Catholic in a country two-thirds Protestant, Londonderry ("Derry" to Irish republicans) had survived religious strife before: In 1689, Protestant defenders withstood a 100-day siege by the Catholic forces of King James II.

Around Londonderry's old-city, the center of commerce, rose thick stone walls dating from the seventeenth century. Of enormous symbolic import, the walls represented tenacity and vigor to the Protestant Ulster Orangemen (whose name derives from their identification with William of Orange, who expelled the Catholic James II from Britain's throne); to Catholics—excluded from housing, jobs, local government—the fortifications stood for discrimination and prejudice.

The 1968 rioting naturally climaxed around the old-city walls. On October 5, defying a government ban, 400 demonstrators marched on Londonderry's center

Soldiers used a water cannon, often trained on demonstrators, to douse a street fire after a Londonderry riot.

to protest discrimination against Catholics in housing and voting. (In Ulster, voting was restricted to property owners, and Londonderry's Protestant-controlled housing board often locked Catholics out of the market.) Riot police cordoned off the crowd, then waded in with clubs flailing. One hundred demonstrators, including Gerald Fitt, a member of the British Parliament, needed hospital treatment. The next night, some 800 angry men drifted into the old-city; they looted, threw rocks and Molotov cocktails, and battled police under the stone walls.

Violence ran at fever pitch all fall, in one incident after another, as a bloody new phase of discord was opened in Northern Ireland. **◄1949.9 ►1969.2**

IN THE UNITED STATES

transcriptions of Johann Sebastian's heavenly Baroque organ music, was released the following year and became a novelty hit. The album stayed on the charts for six years and then passed into obscurity, but the synthesizer and its far-out tonal variety, was here to stay. ◄1964.M

►SOCK IT TO ME—The comedy team of Dan Rowan and Dick Martin created *Laugh-In,* which broke into the regular NBC lineup in January. Turning the variety-show genre playfully on its ear, the grab bag of slapstick, vaudeville, new video techniques, and satire—presented at lightning speed and infused with an attitude of hip irreverence—was a pop-culture treasure trove, generating such lasting lines as "Ve-e-e-ry interesting" (ominous and Germanic), "Sock it to me!" (once uttered by Richard Nixon), and "Beautiful downtown Burbank" (purely ironic). ◄1951.9 ►1969.7

►'68 OLYMPICS—Graceful Peggy Fleming, five-time consecutive U.S. ladies, and three-time world champion in figure skating, emerged as the darling of the 1968 Winter Olympics by winning the gold medal at Grenoble, France. At the Summer Games, in Mexico City, the U.S. men's track and field team put on a stunning display of speed and power. In winning the 100-meter sprint, Jim Hines became the first man to break ten seconds; Dick Fosbury completed a 7' 4¼" high jump backwards, inventing the "Fosbury flop" in the process; Tommy Smith and John Carlos, first and third, respectively, in the fastest 200-meter dash

ever run to that point, raised clenched fists in a black-power salute on the medal stand (which got them suspended from the U.S. team). The most dramatic performance belonged to Bob Beamon, whose phenomenal 29' 2½" long jump shattered the world record by nearly two feet. Beamon's mark would stand for 24 years. ►1968.13

POLITICS & BUSINESS: GNP: $864.2 billion ... Richard Nixon elected president, defeating Hubert Humphrey ... Congress passes 1968 Civil Rights Act (housing rights) ... 10% income tax surcharge established (to curb inflation and reduce the deficit) ... Consumer Credit Protection Act ensures complete disclosure of interest rates and finance charges by banks ... Oil discovered in Alaska.

"I've never slowed down in my entire life, and I never will. I can't do it. I never knew physical fear.... Skiing to me is like breathing."—Jean-Claude Killy

AROUND THE WORLD

▶CATHOLICS AND CONTRACEPTION—Reformist up to a point, Pope Paul VI phased out the Latin mass, relaxed rules on fasting and intermarriage, revived ecumenical dialogues with Protestant churches and Communist regimes, and traveled widely. But he drew the line at contraception. In his 1968 encyclical *Humanae Vitae (Of Human Life)*, the pontiff reiterated the Church's traditional view of artificial birth control: entirely unacceptable. He also ruled out any possibility of priestly marriage or female clergy, provoking an outcry of protest from liberal Catholics.

▶BEATLES IN INDIA—The Beatles' 1968 trips to India to seek enlightenment with spiritual leader Maharishi Maresh Yogi continued an evolution perfectly in tune with the times. The most musically and

culturally influential rock group ever, the Beatles had begun to cultivate shoulder-length hair, Eastern clothes, and an air of mysticism (closely associated with hallucinogenic drugs)—all hallmarks of late-sixties youthful disaffection. Their seminal 1967 album, *Sgt. Pepper's Lonely Hearts Club Band*, incorporating Indian sitar music, first popularized Eastern music in the West. ◂1962.6 ▸1970.M

▶GLAMOROUS CANADIAN—Retiring septuagenarian prime minister Lester B. Pearson was succeeded in 1968 by a man known as the nation's most eligible bachelor. Pierre Elliott Trudeau was 48—a karate expert partial to flamboyant outfits, fast cars, beautiful women, and dangerous travel (he'd hitchhiked across war-torn Indochina). A dedicated reformer, he was also a realist, warning voters, "If you want pie in the sky, you'll have to vote for another party." Though of French-Canadian descent, Trudeau opposed independence for Quebec. Voters, gripped by what the press called "Trudeaumania," gave his Liberal Party a whopping majority. ◂1967.M ▸1970.11

IDEAS

Prophet of the New Age

11 In 1968, a University of California graduate student named Carlos Castaneda went into the desert and returned bearing the seeds of New Age spiritualism. Castaneda was a candidate for a master's degree in anthropology at UCLA when he happened to encounter a Yaqui Indian shaman in an unnamed Arizona border town. Led by the shaman along an ancient path to spiritual enlightenment—a path paved with such organic hallucinogens as peyote and psilocybin mushrooms—Castaneda was inspired to share his tale with the reading public in *The Teachings of Don Juan: A Yaqui Way of Knowledge*, published just as the searching, psychedelic sixties were peaking.

A combination of ethnography, parapsychology, and travelogue, *The Teachings of Don Juan* struck a popular chord; the book offered palatable mysticism for a materialistic age. "Don Juan," trumpeted the book's foreword, "takes us through a crack in the universe between daylight and dark into a world not merely other than our own, but of an entirely different order of reality." Quite a feat for a book originally submitted as a graduate thesis.

Cynics questioned the existence of Castaneda's medicine man (apparently unknown to all but the author) and some social scientists criticized his unorthodox methodology (he allowed the traditional distance between subject and observer to lapse). Castaneda's enormous international audience was untroubled by the controversy. Good or bad anthropology, or just plain fiction, *The Teachings of Don Juan* satisfied a wide-ranging existential craving. **◂1923.V ▸1990.M**

RELIGION

Liberating Catholicism

12 Inspired by the reforms of Vatican II, the prelates attending the Second Latin American Bishops' Conference in Medellín, Colombia, in 1968 examined the proper social role of the Church in their countries. After much discussion, the bishops issued a proclamation. They denounced the systematic oppression of the poor, criticized the exploitation of the Third World by industrialized nations, and called for political and social reform. But they did not stop there: The bishops went on to state that the Church in Latin America had a different mission from that of the Church in Europe (was, in fact, a different Church), and they claimed for it an active political function. This practical application of faith became known as liberation theology, one of the most important developments within the modern Catholic Church and a powerful political influence throughout Central and South America.

In 1971 Father Gustavo Gutiérrez, a Peruvian theologian, published the movement's central dogma, *A Theology of Liberation*, which stated that the Church must respond to the poor—not impose itself on them. Inspired by the book, activists established the Church of the Poor, a grassroots organization that combines religious teaching with social activism.

The movement was further spurred by Brazilian theologian Leonardo Boff. In such books as *Jesus Christ Liberator* (1972) and *Church, Charism, and Power* (1984), Boff criticized the Church's history of tolerating, even contributing to, Latin American injustice, and strongly defended the morality of the class struggle.

Neither Rome nor Latin America's conservative regimes liked liberation theology's Marxist ring: The movement's leaders were barred from a bishops' conference in 1979, Pope John Paul II replaced liberation theologians with docile clerics wherever he could, and in 1984 the Vatican condemned Boff to a year of silence. Secular reprisals—which came in the form of death-squad assassinations or torturous imprisonments—were more severe, turning clergymen like El Salvador's archbishop Oscar Romero and Brazil's Father Antonio Pereira Neto into martyrs for the movement. **◂1962.1 ▸1978.4**

Summoned to the Vatican in 1984, Brazilian liberation theologian Leonardo Boff was rebuked for his Marxist views.

SPORTS

Star of the Slopes

13 On February 17, 1968, millions of TV sets around the world were tuned to the Winter Olympics and the slopes of Grenoble, France. All eyes were on French skier Jean-Claude Killy and the slalom competition. He had already won gold in the giant slalom and the downhill events, and a victory here would give him a clean sweep of the Alpine races. Only one man, Toni Sailer of Austalia, in 1954, had ever before won them all. The contest came down to the wire, but Killy's two closest rivals missed gates, and the gold medal was his.

For Killy, known as much for his Gallic charm and good looks as for his phenomenal athletic ability, the triumph marked the culmination of a stellar amateur career (he'd started skiing at three, at his father's Alpine resort) and the beginning of a lucrative professional one—as a skier and a businessman. A master of the "egg" position, the aerodynamic fetal crouch that is now standard, Killy raced at speeds of over 80 miles an hour. In the year before the Grenoble Olympics, he won every downhill competition he entered.

Killy's Olympic glory made him one of the world's best known—and most marketable—athletes. Within France, where the national ski team was an object of enormous pride (and of government investment), he gained a movie idol's following. **◂1968.M**

NOBEL PRIZES: Peace: René Cassin (French; European Court of Rights and UN Universal Declaration of Human Rights) ... Literature: Yasunari Kawabata (Japanese; novelist) ... Chemistry: Lars Onsager (U.S.; thermodynamic equations) ... Medicine: Har Gobind Khorana, Robert Holley, and Marshall Nirenberg (U.S.; genetic code) ... Physics: Luis Alvarez (U.S.; particle physics).

A VOICE FROM 1968

Psychedelic Road Trip

From *The Electric Kool-Aid Acid Test,* by Tom Wolfe, 1968

In The Electric Kool-Aid Acid Test, *literary journalist Tom Wolfe mixed reportage, keen observation, and a distinctive narrative voice usually reserved for fiction to tell the strange but true story of Ken Kesey, novelist and proto-hippie, and his band of groupies, the Merry Pranksters, who zigzagged across the country in a converted school bus. "All I knew about Kesey at this point," the author confides at the beginning of the 1968 book, "was that he was a highly regarded 31-year-old novelist and in a lot of trouble over drugs." (Kesey had recently returned from Mexico to face trial on marijuana charges.) From that sketchy starting point, Wolfe produced the definitive account of sixties counterculture. He traced the hippie phenomenon back to the early sixties, when Kesey, author of* One Flew Over the Cuckoo's Nest, *and his Pranksters organized the first West Coast LSD parties—"acid tests." Those early experiments, Wolfe explains in the passage below, gave the psychedelic revolution its momentum —and its sensibility. From them came the style of dress, music, and graphic arts that permeated sixties' popular culture.* ◂**1962.M**

Richard Alpert was also unhappy with the Acid Tests. Alpert, like Timothy Leary, had sacrificed his academic career as a psychologist for the sake of the psychedelic movement. It was hard enough to keep the straight multitudes from going hysterical over the subject of LSD even in the best of circumstances—let alone when it was used for manic screaming orgies in public places. Among the heads who leaned toward Leary and Alpert, it was hard to even freaking believe that the Pranksters were pulling a freaking prank like this. Any moment they were expecting them to explode into some sort of debacle, some sort of mass freakout, that the press could seize on and bury the psychedelic movement forever. The police watched closely, but there was very little they could do about it, except for an occasional marijuana bust, since there was no law against LSD at the time. The Pranksters went on to hold Tests in Palo Alto, Portland, Oregon, two in San Francisco, four in and around Los Angeles—and three in Mexico—and no laws broken here, Lieutenant—*only every law of God and man*—In short, a goddamn outrage, and we're *powerless*—

The Acid Tests were one of those outrages, one of those *scandals,* that create a new style or a new world view. Everyone clucks, fumes, grinds their teeth over the bad taste, the bad morals, the insolence, the vulgarity, the childishness, the lunacy, the cruelty, the irresponsibility, the fraudulence, and, in fact gets worked up into such a state of excitement, such an epitasis, such a slaver, they can't turn it loose. It becomes a perfect obsession. And now they'll show you how it *should* have been done.

The Acid Tests were the *epoch* of the psychedelic style and practically everything that has gone into it. I don't mean merely that the Pranksters did it first but, rather, that it all came straight out of the Acid Tests in a direct line leading to the Trips Festival of January, 1966. That brought the whole thing full out in the open. "Mixed media" entertainment—this came straight out of the Acid Tests' combination of light and movie projections, strobes, tapes, rock 'n' roll, black light. "Acid rock"—the sound of the Beatles' *Sergeant Pepper* album and the high-vibrato electronic sounds of the Jefferson Airplane, the Mothers of Invention, and many other groups—the mothers of it all were the Grateful Dead at the Acid Tests. The Dead were the *audio* counterpart of Roy Seburn's light projections. Owsley was responsible for some of this, indirectly. Owsley had snapped back from his great Freakout and started pouring money into the Grateful Dead and, thereby, the Tests. Maybe he figured the Tests were the wave of the future, whether he had freaked out or not. Maybe he thought "acid rock" was the sound of the future and he would become a kind of Brian Epstein for the Grateful Dead. I don't know. In any case, he started buying the Dead equipment such as no rock 'n' roll band ever had before, the Beatles included, all manner of tuners, amplifiers, receivers, loudspeakers, microphones, cartridges, tapes, theater horns, booms, lights, turntables, instruments, mixers, muters, servile mesochroics, whatever was on the market. The sound went down so many microphones and hooked through so many mixers and variable lags and blew up in so many amplifiers and roiled around in so many speakers and fed back down so many microphones, it came on like a chemical refinery. There was something wholly new and deliriously weird in the Dead's sound, and practically everything new in rock 'n' roll, rock jazz I have heard it called, came out of it.

Even details like psychedelic poster art, the quasi–*art nouveau* swirls of lettering, design and vibrating colors, electro-pastels and spectral Day-Glo, came out of the Acid Tests. Later other impresarios and performers would recreate the Prankster styles with a sophistication the Pranksters never dreamed of. *Art is not eternal, boys.* The posters became works of art in the accepted cultural tradition. Others would even play the Dead's sound more successfully, commercially anyway, than the Dead. Others would do the mixed-media thing until it was pure ambrosial candy for the brain with creamy filling every time. To which Kesey would say: "They know *where* it is, but they don't know *what* it is."

Frustrated by the constraints of objective reporting, Tom Wolfe *(top)* and such writers as Norman Mailer, Joan Didion, and Hunter S. Thompson created New Journalism—an application of fictional techniques to nonfiction writing. Above, Ken Kesey in the 1970s, with the bus used by the Merry Pranksters.

"We came in peace for all mankind."—**Plaque left by Apollo 11 astronauts on the surface of the moon**

STORY OF THE YEAR

Man on the Moon

1 On July 21, 1969 American astronaut Neil Armstrong stepped down from the *Apollo 11* landing craft, the *Eagle*, and onto the surface of the moon. President John Kennedy's 1961 pledge to put a man on the moon by the end of the decade was realized. "That's one small step for man," Armstrong immortally summed up for hundreds of millions of jubilant TV viewers back on earth, "one giant leap for mankind."

U.S. astronaut Edwin "Buzz" Aldrin walking on the moon, photographed by fellow astronaut and first moon walker Neil Armstrong.

Colonel Edwin "Buzz" Aldrin, Jr., joined Armstrong 19 minutes later and, walking tentatively at first, the two lunar pioneers planted a U.S. flag. As they grew more comfortable with the moon's gravity, one sixth of the earth's, Aldrin and Armstrong began bounding ethereally across the cratered surface, amazing and delighting their earth-bound TV audience. Their playful leaps became one of the century's enduring images, symbolic of the spirit of exploration and the wondrous applications of science. After collecting rock samples and taking pictures for two hours, the astronauts returned to the lunar module and closed the hatch. The moon walk was over. In all, they spent 21½ hours on the moon before returning to the orbiting *Apollo 11* command ship, *Columbia*, piloted by Lieutenant Colonel Michael Collins.

A great triumph for the American space program, the moon landing came two and a half years after a tragic mishap had stunned NASA and the country. In January 1967, Virgil "Gus" Grissom, the second American in space; Edward H. White, the first American to walk in space; and rookie Roger B. Chaffee were killed during a routine test at Cape Kennedy. A fire broke out during countdown exercises and raced through the capsule's pure oxygen atmosphere. In the intense heat, the men's flammable suits, the nylon cabin netting, and wire insulation melted almost instantly. Grissom, White, and Chaffee were incinerated. NASA suspended all flights for over a year to completely review Apollo craft design.

After launches resumed, NASA sent up four manned missions to pave the way for the journey of Armstrong, Aldrin, and Collins. The three astronauts, having made their landmark visit to the moon, the fulfillment of a dream as old as the human imagination, splashed down safely in the Pacific off Hawaii on July 24. ◄**1966.2** ►**1971.3**

NORTHERN IRELAND

The Troubles Worsen

2 A confrontation in Belfast between Protestant extremists and Catholics triggered a sustained cycle of attack and reprisal in August 1969. As savage sectarian rioting spread from Belfast to other cities, Great Britain deployed troops in Northern Ireland to prevent civil war. The arrival of the soldiers marked the first use of the British military against Irish civilians since the Easter Uprising of 1916.

At issue in Northern Ireland was political power: The two-thirds Protestant majority had it; the Catholics wanted some. Catholic activists in Northern Ireland demanded the right of "one man, one vote," afforded to every other British subject, but withheld from them by the Protestant-dominated Parliament of Northern Ireland. Because Catholicism was associated with the Republic of Ireland, Protestant extremists feared Catholic empowerment. They believed it would lead to the subsumption of their small country into the larger southern one. By 1969, radicals on both sides increasingly resorted to violence. As the outlawed Irish Republican Army and its spinoff, the more radical Provisionals, stepped up terrorist campaigns, the Ulster Defense Association, a Protestant terrorist group, retaliated in kind.

Many Catholics welcomed the British troops in 1969, seeing them as protection from the often prejudiced local police force, the Royal Ulster Constabulary. In the Belfast hothouse, however, where fear and hatred distorted politics, British troops inevitably clashed with Catholic demonstrators. Catholic resentment of local government exploded into resentment of London. ◄**1968.10** ►**1972.4**

Arriving in Belfast as peacekeepers, British soldiers soon became part of the strife.

SOCIAL REFORM

Gay Lib Comes of Age

3 On a Friday night in June 1969, police raided the Stonewall Inn, a gay bar in New York City's bohemian Greenwich Village neighborhood. The operation was routine: The Stonewall lacked a liquor license, and it attracted a young, loud, largely nonwhite, and largely transvestite clientele. But the reaction was unprecedented. Instead of dispersing, the patrons responded with anger. The ensuing melee continued through the weekend, during which the Stonewall was torched and a new cause—gay liberation—gained worldwide recognition.

Sculptor George Segal's *Gay Liberation* (1980), installed near the site of the Stonewall Inn, commemorates the uprising.

A small, quiet homosexual-rights

ART & CULTURE: Books: *them* (Joyce Carol Oates); *The Godfather* (Mario Puzo); *Ragtime* (E.L. Doctorow); *Slaughter-house Five* (Kurt Vonnegut, Jr.); *The French Lieutenant's Woman* (John Fowles); *Ada* (Vladimir Nabokov); *The Complete Poems* (Elizabeth Bishop) ... Music: "Lay, Lady, Lay" (Bob Dylan); *Let It Bleed* (The Rolling Stones, LP); *The Velvet Underground* (LP); *Despite and Still* (Samuel Barber);

"The state has no place in the bedrooms of the nation."—**Canadian prime minister Trudeau, supporting the decriminalization of homosexuality**

movement had existed in many countries since the 1950s. But recently, activists influenced by the black power and women's liberation movements had adopted a more militant tone. The Stonewall rebellion was a turning point for those who hoped not only to end discrimination and harassment against gays (a term often used by the movement to refer to both male homosexuals and lesbians) but also to create a society with less rigid sexual values. Gay liberationists joined forces with other radicals; marches drew thousands in all the Western democracies—and even in Argentina, between dictatorships.

Under growing pressure, in 1969 Canada and Germany decriminalized homosexual acts (Britain had done so two years earlier); Australia and several localities in the United States soon followed suit. In 1973, the American Psychiatric Association removed homosexuality from its diagnostic manual of mental illnesses. Openly gay politicians began to be elected to office. Still, gays suffered the effects of widespread fear and hatred—and before long, they faced a deadly new threat. **◂1964.3 ▸1985.12**

MUSIC

Days of Mud and Music

4 A "Technicolor, mud-splattered reflection of the 1960s," as folksinger Joan Baez called it, the Woodstock Music and Art Fair was the youth movement's seminal event, representative in many ways of the decade itself—at once defiant, innocent, optimistic, and indulgent. More than 400,000 young people flocked to the three-day festival—August 15–17, 1969—on a farm in upstate New York, and despite torrential rains, insufficient facilities, and countless drug mishaps, most took away memories that would achieve the status of near-myth.

The brainchild of a group of young promoters and investors who called themselves Woodstock Ventures, Inc., the event (it actually occurred in the town of Bethel, not Woodstock) was billed as "three days of peace and music." Among the folk and rock heroes who played were Baez; Crosby, Stills, Nash and Young; The Who; Janis Joplin; Jimi Hendrix; Sly and the Family Stone; Jefferson Airplane; and Santana. For many of the student activists, communalists, pot heads, professors, hippies, and Yippies who made the trip to Max Yasgur's farm (rented for the occasion), Woodstock was "a coming together of all the tribes," an overtly political event. Later, as the legend grew, it assumed ever richer meaning. At the "Chicago 8" trial for conspiracy to incite a riot at the 1968 Democratic Convention, defendant Abbie Hoffman told the judge he was not an American—he was a member of the Woodstock Nation, "a nation of alienated young people." By the time "Woodstock '94" was held 25 years later (a few miles from the original site), the event had been transmuted into certifiable baby-boom legend. **◂1963.12**

For many who attended, Woodstock was more than a music festival: It was a symbol of peace and cooperation in a time of war.

POPULAR CULTURE

Big Bird and Friends

5 In 1969, television producer Joan Ganz Cooney introduced a children's show built on a simple and provocative idea: TV's commercial power, its ability to convey information rapidly and succinctly, could be harnessed to sell the ultimate product—knowledge. An executive for the Public Broadcasting System in New York City, Cooney was intrigued by studies showing that preschool kids retained more content from snappy, staccato advertisements than they did from the feature programs the ads accompanied. Applying advertising techniques to reading and arithmetic, Cooney and her colleagues came up with *Sesame Street.* The show revolutionized children's programming.

With a menagerie of furry, floppy Muppets created by master puppeteer Jim Henson, engaging songs, animated segments, and a cast of gentle, racially diverse human hosts, *Sesame Street* was an instant success. Intended to reach disadvantaged urban kids—children whose reading and math skills were hurt by lack of exposure to books and who stood to benefit most from an early in-home classroom—the show attracted millions of middle-class viewers as well. Henson characters such as Bert and Ernie, Big Bird, and Cookie Monster became international TV stars (the show has been adapted for domestic broadcast in countries throughout the world).

Indeed, the show's critics charge that its stated mission—to help educate underprivileged children—has been largely lost in the shuffle of mass popularity. (Over a quarter century of programming, *Sesame Street* failed to make any demonstrable impact on its viewers' verbal or mathematical skills.) Others point out that by treating learning as just another commodity that can be promoted and sold with catchy techniques, the show inculcates the values of consumer culture and implicitly rejects the notion that the acquisition of knowledge can often require enormous effort and discipline. **◂1965.M**

Big Bird—a fine feathered friend to millions of kids.

BIRTHS

Bobby Brown, U.S. singer.

Steffi Graf, German tennis player.

DEATHS

Theodor Adorno, German philosopher.

Earl Alexander of Tunis, U.K. field marshal.

Maureen Connolly, U.S. tennis player.

Otto Dix, German artist.

Max Eastman, U.S. writer.

Dwight D. Eisenhower, U.S. president.

Judy Garland, U.S. entertainer.

Vito Genovese, Italian-U.S. criminal.

Walter Gropius, German-U.S. architect.

Coleman Hawkins, U.S. musician.

Sonja Henie, Norwegian-U.S. ice skater.

Ho Chi Minh, Vietnamese president.

Brian Jones, U.K. musician.

Boris Karloff, U.K.-U.S. actor.

Joseph Kasavubu, Congolese president.

Joseph Kennedy, U.S. businessman and diplomat.

Jack Kerouac, U.S. writer.

Frank Loesser, U.S. songwriter.

Rocky Marciano, U.S. boxer.

Carlos Marighella, Brazilian guerrilla.

Ludwig Mies van der Rohe, German-U.S. architect.

Otto Stern, German-U.S. physicist.

Moise Tshombe, Congolese political leader.

Franz von Papen, German political leader.

Josef von Sternberg, Austrian-U.S. film director.

Cheap Imitation, HPSCHD **(John Cage);** ***In Praise of Shahn*** **(William Schuman) ... Painting & Sculpture:** ***City Limits*** **(Philip Guston) ... Film:** ***Midnight Cowboy*** **(John Schlesinger);** ***True Grit*** **(Henry Hathaway);** ***The Wild Bunch*** **(Sam Peckinpah) ... Theater:** ***Play It Again, Sam*** **(Woody Allen);** ***Butterflies Are Free*** **(Leonard Gash);** ***Oh! Calcutta*** **(Kenneth Tynan, et al.);** ***Coco*** **(Alan Jay Lerner) ... TV:** ***Hee Haw; Marcus Welby, M.D.***

"This parrot is no more. It's ceased to be. It has expired. The parrot has gone to meet its maker. This is a late parrot.... If you hadn't nailed it to the perch, it would be pushin' up the daisies."—**John Cleese, in *Monty Python's* "The Dead Parrot" sketch**

NEW IN 1969

Rubella vaccine.

***Penthouse* magazine.**

Automatic teller (Chemical Bank, New York).

Jumbo jet (Boeing 747).

Nonstop solo circumnavigation of earth by boat.

Nobel Prize for economics.

Female undergraduates at Yale University.

IN THE UNITED STATES

▶NEWMAN AND REDFORD—*Butch Cassidy and the Sundance Kid,* a 1969 movie about two of the West's biggest gunslinging legends, featured one of the screen's most popular teams: Paul

Newman (Butch) and Robert Redford (the Kid). More an amiable character movie than a traditional Western, the blockbuster (with Burt Bachrach's original song "Raindrops Keep Fallin' on My Head") kicked off the modern cycle of an old genre—the "buddy picture".

▶CUYAHOGA BURNS—Put-upon Clevelanders told a dirty joke about their city's noxiously polluted river: "Anyone who falls in the Cuyahoga does not drown," they said. "He decays." They exaggerated only slightly. On June 22, the small river, saturated with oil-coated debris from local industry, burst into flames. It burned for 20 minutes, shooting licks of fire 200 feet in the air, engulfing two railroad trestles. The fire became a symbol of the dire condition of America's waterways, kindling the national clean-up efforts of the 1970s.

In a common ritual, American Army Sergeant John Cameron tosses a smoke bomb out of his helicopter to celebrate the end of his tour of duty in Vietnam.

THE VIETNAM WAR

Fewer Troops, More Bombs

6 Soon after Richard Nixon entered the White House, the secret plan for peace in Vietnam that he'd made a centerpiece of his electoral campaign became clear: The president was withdrawing troops but expanding bombing. In January 1969, there were 543,000 troops in-country; by December, Nixon had withdrawn 75,000. He'd also escalated the air war—starting covert bombing (soon exposed by journalists) of Vietnamese Communist sanctuaries in Cambodia, and resuming bombing over North Vietnam.

Nixon predicted "peace with honor" within three years. North Vietnam's leaders were unimpressed, however; for a second year, peace talks in Paris went nowhere. And America's antiwar activists matched Nixon's escalation with their own: Students shut down more and more campuses, the radical Weathermen began a campaign of terrorist bombings, and two nationwide "moratoriums"—daylong festivals of peaceful protest—brought millions of demonstrators into the streets.

On the battlefield, skirmishes with Viet Cong guerrillas had largely given way, since the Tet Offensive, to pitched battles with North Vietnamese regulars. In April, the U.S. death toll reached 33,650, surpassing the total U.S. battle deaths of the Korean War. Yet the war's goals remained hazy, and American troops—sent off to fight without their country's emotional support—grew increasingly restive. Drug use and desertion rates soared; and the assassination of officers grew so common that the word "fragging" was coined to describe it. Peace symbols appeared regularly on GI camouflage covers. But when North Vietnamese president Ho Chi Minh died in September, the war he'd waged for most of his 79 years—against the Japanese, the French, and finally the Americans—was still far from over. **◂1968.3 ▸1970.1**

POPULAR CULTURE

Seriously Comic

7 The comedians behind BBC television's *Monty Python's Flying Circus* were not merely masters of running gags—they were also lords of leaping, limping, stumbling, and walking jokes. Between the show's startling October 1969 premiere and its December 1974 conclusion, it developed a cult following in the English-speaking world. The Python troupe's free-association comedy—which put a highbrow British spin on pure silliness—proceeded from television to books, films, and stage revues, parroting routines preserved on the debut LP, *Another Monty Python Album.*

Four of the six *Monty Python* troupe members *(clockwise from far left)*: Terry Jones, Eric Idle, John Cleese, Michael Palin.

The troupe's six members—Graham Chapman, John Cleese, Terry Gilliam, Eric Idle, Terry Jones, and Michael Palin—conceived and performed skits featuring, among other daffy subjects, cannibalism, transvestite lumberjacks, and a dead parrot. Their antiformulaic, subversive humor found a loyal following in the United States, where the show debuted on a Dallas television station in 1974. Within months it was being broadcast in dozens of other U.S. cities. For many teenagers, Monty Python's core American audience, rattling off sketches verbatim in imitation British accents became a kind of party game.

Meanwhile, Python's members pursued solo enterprises in film and television (notably Cleese's sitcom *Fawlty Towers,* another BBC hit that moved across the Atlantic for a long run on PBS), occasionally reuniting for group projects. Their three films—the Arthurian parody *Monty Python and the Holy Grail* (1975), the controversial New Testament burlesque *Monty Python's Life of Brian* (1979), and Monty *Python's Meaning of Life* (1983), a giddy satire of everything from condoms to corporate takeovers—were still playing to enthusiastic audiences more than two decades after Monty Python first burst onto the entertainment scene. **◂1968.M ▸1975.V**

DIPLOMACY

SALT I

8 Having achieved strategic nuclear parity, the Soviet Union and the United States in 1969 opened the round of disarmament negotiations that became known as the Strategic Arms Limitations Talks (SALT). Meanwhile, as the sponsors of the Nonproliferation Treaty of 1968 (NPT), the superpowers attempted to prevent bomb technology from spreading to other countries. Both measures met with mixed results.

During the arms race, the superpowers had evolved a policy of nuclear deterrence based on MAD—mutual assured destruction. As long as neither side had the advantage in missiles, it was reasoned, neither side would use them. MAD was a serviceable deterrent when only a few countries had nuclear stockpiles, but by the early 1960s, China and France had joined Britain, the United States, and the Soviet Union as nuclear powers; several other countries waited in the wings. The NPT of 1968 was supposed to stop the spread. With it, the Americans and the Soviets agreed to keep nuclear secrets to themselves; 43 other nations

SPORTS: Baseball: World Series, New York Mets defeat Baltimore Orioles, 4–1; Willie Mays hits 600th home run ... Football: Super Bowl, New York Jets (Joe Namath) defeat Baltimore Colts, 16–7 ... Basketball: NBA, Boston Celtics defeat Los Angeles Lakers, 4–3 ... Tennis: Rod Laver wins his second Grand Slam ... Auto Racing: Mario Andretti wins first Indy 500 (sets new average speed record of 156.867 mph).

promised not to develop arsenals. Ominously, France, China, and the other leading bomb-building nations refused to sign.

Preliminary SALT sessions convened in Helsinki in November 1969. For the next two and a half years, Soviet and American delegations met regularly—434 times in all—before Brezhnev and Nixon finally signed the SALT I accord in 1972. The first of SALT I's two treaties limited antiballistic missile defense systems: Defensive systems, it was reasoned, threw off the balance of power because they enabled one side to protect itself from the destructive power of the other, and destructive parity was the basis of MAD deterrence. The second agreement was an interim limit on the number of missiles either country could have.

Soviet deputy foreign minister V.S. Semenov *(center)* delivers a speech at the opening of SALT I talks in Helsinki.

No missiles were actually eliminated; in fact, provisions were made to upgrade old weapons. The talks did, however, institutionalize nuclear diplomacy, creating a semi-permanent apparatus for superpower negotiations. **◂1963.2 ▸1972.7**

CRIME

Manson Cult Exposed

9 In August 1969, police officers began investigating the grisly murder of actress Sharon Tate, wife of director Roman Polanski, and four friends at her Los Angeles home. The five victims had sustained numerous gunshot and more than 50 stab wounds; the word "Pig" was smeared in blood on a door. Tate had been eight months pregnant. In December, another multiple slaying—of Leno and Rosemary LaBianca—was connected to the Tate murders. "Death to Pigs," "Helter Skelter," and other cryptic messages were scrawled in blood on the walls at the second scene.

The culprit was Charles Manson, a failed songwriter who had spent most of his life in jail. Manson and

At his arraignment *(above)*, Manson announced he would act as his own attorney.

his "family," the uprooted, mostly female youth who became his groupies, came to represent the nightmarish side of the hippie movement. In them people saw a rejection of society carried to a pathological extreme—a rejection of life itself. In Manson, settled with his disciples by 1969 at a ranch on the outskirts of Los Angeles, murder and mayhem somehow became expressions of communal sharing, a "philosophy" based partly on his bizarre readings of Beatles lyrics.

Manson and five of his cohorts—two men and three women—were sentenced to death; when California ended capital punishment in 1972, the sentences were commuted to life. In 1975 former Manson follower Lynette "Squeaky" Fromme tried to assassinate President Gerald Ford. Manson himself, routinely denied parole, continued to attract attention as a dark relic of a decade of confusion. **▸1974.12**

MUSIC

Pinball Wizard

10 The British rock band The Who, already a sensation for creating such defiant youth anthems as "My Generation" (proclaiming "I hope I die before I get old"), introduced a new musical and theatrical genre in 1969: the rock opera. *Tommy*, the story of a "deaf, dumb, and blind kid" who through his mastery of pinball becomes a messiah, was instrumental in rock's evolution from musical fad to legitimate art form.

Pete Townshend, The Who's lead guitarist and chief songwriter (known for his energetic, windmilling playing style), first experimented with the new form on *A Quick One While He's Away*, a 1966 album in which several songs were linked. *Tommy* went further, presenting a fully integrated story: The handicapped boy overcomes physical and mental abuse to become a "pinball wizard," a hero and a prophet who is ultimately betrayed by his followers. Labeled sick by one critic, silly by others, and revolutionary by many, *Tommy* was a hit at both New York's Metropolitan Opera House (it was the first rock performance ever staged there) and Woodstock, making The Who icons for a youth culture that felt the establishment was deaf, dumb, and blind to them. In 1975, director Ken Russell made an energetic film version that showcased Who lead singer Roger Daltrey (as Tommy) and a parade of other rock stars (Eric Clapton, Tina Turner, Elton John).

Throughout the seventies and early eighties, Townshend and The Who continued to turn out hits; they were credited with influencing such rockers as Jimi Hendrix and the Yardbirds, pioneering such pop-art costumes as overcoats made from the Union Jack, and being "the world's loudest band." *Tommy* had a similarly long life, enjoying a revival in 1993 as a hit Broadway musical. **◂1965.10 ▸1970.4**

Roger Daltrey, the Who's lead vocalist, played the title role in the 1975 film of *Tommy*.

IN THE UNITED STATES

▸DAYS OF RAGE—Modeled on Third World revolutionary groups and named after a line from a Bob Dylan song ("You don't need a weatherman to know which way the wind blows"), the radical Weathermen vowed to "lead white kids into armed revolution." In October, the organization—newly splintered from the schism-racked Students for a Democratic Society—staged a two-day spree of violence in Chicago. During the "Days of Rage," helmeted Weathermen wrecked parked cars and smashed windows in the city's business section. Nearly 300 were arrested. A nationwide string of bombings followed before the group went underground in 1970. ◂1968.4 ▸1970.7

▸SQUARE AND PROUD—1969 marked the debut of the very suburban, very white *The*

***Brady Bunch Show.* The perky, hip-to-be-square Bradys became 1970s camp icons.**

▸CHAPPAQUIDDICK—Departing a party on July 19, Massachusetts senator Edward Kennedy, JFK's 36-year-old brother, drove his car off a narrow bridge at Chappaquiddick Island, off Martha's Vineyard. With him in the car was Mary Jo Kopechne, 28, a former Robert Kennedy campaign aide, who was trapped inside and drowned. Never able to fully explain the accident, or why he waited ten hours to report it, Kennedy did permanent damage to his credibility. ◂1968.4

▸A CULTURAL MAINSTAY SAYS GOODBYE—After 148 years, the *Saturday Evening Post* stopped publishing in 1969. Since 1821 the socially conservative, politically Republican, intellectually middlebrow weekly—famous for its Norman Rockwell cover illustrations—had served up romantic fiction, mysteries, and essays (by writers as diverse as Agatha Christie and William Faulkner), all perfectly tuned to the state of the nation.

POLITICS & BUSINESS: GNP: $930.3 billion ... First draft lottery held ... FDA takes cyclamates off the market ... Warren Burger appointed Chief Justice of Supreme Court ... U.S. bans production of all chemical and biological warfare agents (except tear gas and defoliants used in Vietnam) ... Philip Morris purchases Miller Brewing for estimated $250 million ... Work begins on Alyeska pipeline in Alaska.

"Because to be bad, Mother, that's the real struggle: to be bad—and enjoy it! That's what makes men of us boys, Mother ... LET'S PUT THE ID BACK IN YID!"—**Philip Roth, in *Portnoy's Complaint***

AROUND THE WORLD

▶AUSSIE AGILITY—Australian Rod Laver, one of the greatest tennis players in history, won the U.S. Open in 1969, surviving a soggy court and a four-set effort by fellow Aussie Tony Roche. With the victory, Laver completed a single-year sweep of tennis's four major titles—Australian, French, and U.S. Opens and Wimbledon—a feat accomplished only three times before: by Don Budge in 1938, Maureen Connolly in 1953, and by "Rocket" Laver himself in 1962. ◀1938.M ▶1975.7

▶PRIME MINISTER MEIR—One of the signers of Israel's proclamation of independence in 1948, Golda Meir became its fourth prime minister in

1969. As prime minister, Meir worked through diplomatic channels to secure peace with Egypt and Syria. She resigned in 1974, amid accusations that Israel had been unprepared for the Yom Kippur War. ◀1948.9 ▶1972.5

▶DRIVING DYNAMO—Scottish race-car driver Jackie Stewart roared to the first of his three world championships in 1969. He duplicated the accomplishment in 1971 and 1973. A one-time garage mechanic, Stewart worked his way up the professional ladder, taking the checkered flag in an unprecedented 27 Grand Prix races during his career. He retired in 1973, after several colleagues were killed on the track. ◀1957.11

▶QADDAFI'S COUP—Born in the Libyan desert, Muammar al-Qaddafi grew into an ambitious army officer and ardent Arab nationalist. In 1969, four years out of the national military academy, Captain Qaddafi, 27, successfully led a coup against King Idris. Assuming command of the armed forces and the new revolutionary government, Qaddafi set about transforming oil-rich Libya into a socialist but fundamentally Islamic state. ◀1937.14 ▶1981.3

The Russian words mean banditism, slander, treachery; their endings spell MAO.

DIPLOMACY

Soviet-Chinese Clashes

11 Verbal sniping gave way to the boom of artillery along the Sino-Soviet border in 1969, as the world's two great, divergent Communist powers vied for ideological dominion. In March, Chinese forces shelled tiny Damansky Island in the Ussuri River, the boundary between the U.S.S.R. and northeastern China, killing 34 Soviet soldiers. The Soviets launched a massive retaliation. When the smoke cleared, 800 Chinese soldiers were dead, Damansky had all but disappeared, and hostility between Moscow and Beijing had risen to fever levels. War, declared Chinese officials during the tense summer that followed, was "definitely imminent."

Old enemies, the Chinese and Russian empires enjoyed a period of amicability after 1949, when Mao Zedong established the People's Republic of China. By 1956, alarmed by Nikita Khrushchev's denunciation of Stalin and subsequent reconciliation with Tito in Yugoslavia, Mao began distancing himself from Moscow. The Chairman asserted his Beijing line as the one true path and in 1958 instituted the Great Leap Forward, his indigenous, calamitous economic experiment. The next year Moscow pulled all advisers from China, completing the break.

The Sino-Soviet ideological breach was expressed physically along the countries' 4,500-mile border. In 1962 and '63, the Soviets naturalized some 62,000 Kazakhs and Uighurs from China's northwestern Xinjiang region. Beijing moved troops into the area, redoubled verbal attacks on Soviet "imperialism," called for the annexation of "lost territory," and began making border raids. The quarrel was timeworn, but of terrifying new consequence: The expansionist disputants now owned thermonuclear weapons. The skirmishes peaked at Damansky. Then, after repeated predictions of World War III, the outgunned Chinese backed down in October. The boundary issue was shelved, but the conflict's subtext—the question of ideological authority—remained open. **◀1952.2 ▶1972.2**

SPORTS

Merckx's Victorious Tour

12 Despite a slow start in the 1969 Tour de France, Belgian cyclist Eddy Merckx went on to win—the first of five victories he would pile up in the world's most prestigious bicycle race. His victory margin of 18 minutes has not been approached since. Merckx loved to win; his savage determination earned him the nickname cannibal.

Merckx had begun racing at 14. By the time he was 18, he was the world amateur champion. Professional success rapidly followed: a total of 400 victories during a 12-year career, including four world championships. Merckx dominated the sport as no one ever had, becoming the most admired athlete in Europe. To his rapturous fans, said one newspaper, he was Muhammad Ali, he was Beethoven.

In the '72 Tour de France, Merckx turned in one of his most stunning performances. Over a grueling 2,400-mile course that included some of the country's severest mountain peaks—many observers suspected disgruntled French officials had designed the route specifically to handicap the Belgian, who was better at sprinting than climbing—Merckx won going away. After one more Tour win in '74, Merckx retired into bicycle engineering, a millionaire and arguably the best cyclist in history. **◀1903.M ▶1989.M**

Cycling great Merckx climbs Belgium's Mont Kemmel in 1974.

LITERATURE

Roth's Complaint

13 With his ribald, irreverent 1969 novel, *Portnoy's Complaint*, American writer Philip Roth established himself as a generational icon, a writer of bestsellers, and a figure of great controversy. The book, constructed as a monologue addressed by attorney Alexander Portnoy to Dr. Spielvogel, his psychoanalyst, recounts Portnoy's struggle to reconcile his Jewish heritage (embodied by his traditional mother) and his compulsion to forge his own identity. Portnoy's rebellion takes the form of frequent sexual liaisons with WASP women. No novel of similar literary aspirations had ever treated a character's bed-hopping license, or his penchant for adolescent masturbation, with such gusto.

More provocative than the book's ample sexual content was Roth's ironic treatment of contemporary Jewish American identity. Portnoy, feeling oppressed by his upbringing, attempts to shed his family's Jewish values—but the past keeps reeling him in. "[T]his is my life, my only life," he complains to Dr. Spielvogel, "and I'm living it in the middle of a Jewish joke!" The characterization offended many readers; some critics called Roth a pioneer of "Jewish anti-Semitism."

Other readers confused the character's life with the writer's, a misreading that Roth impishly aggravated in later novels, especially in his series about a Jewish novelist named Nathan Zuckerman who is notorious for having written a sexually explicit work of fiction. Indeed, questions of identity remain fundamental to all of Roth's works, which range from Kafkaesque experiments like *The Breast* to the political satire of *Our Gang* ("starring Tricky Dick and his friends"). **◀1964.8**

NOBEL PRIZES: Peace: Int'l Labour Organization (Switzerland)... Literature: Samuel Beckett (Irish-French; playwright and novelist) ... Chemistry: Derek Barton and Odd Hassel (U.K., Norwegian; organic molecules) ... Medicine: Max Delbrück, Alfred Hershey, and Salvador Luria (U.S.; viral gene structure) ... Physics: Murray Gell-Mann (U.S.; quark) ... Economics: Ragnar Frisch and Jan Tinbergen (Norwegian, Dutch).

A VOICE FROM 1969

Berryman's Anyman

From *Dream Songs*, by John Berryman, 1969

With The Dream Songs, *sometimes called a novel in verse, John Berryman laid claim to Walt Whitman's poetic laurels. Berryman's book-length poem ranks with* Leaves of Grass, *Whitman's masterpiece, for its majestic American voice. A difficult poet and a troubled man (he committed suicide in 1973 by jumping off a Minneapolis bridge), Berryman worked eleven years on* Songs, *which first appeared in two separate volumes before being published as one collection in 1969. The monologues spoken by Henry, the poetic persona of the* Songs, *mix meter, language high and low, and a syntax that is sometimes impressively fractured, occasionally traditional. The rhythmic effect is unique. Berryman's confessional subjects are suicide, madness, loneliness, and faith. "Henry," he advised, is "not the poet, not me"; rather he is an American anyman who speaks in a singularly rich poetic vernacular.* ◂**1965.V**

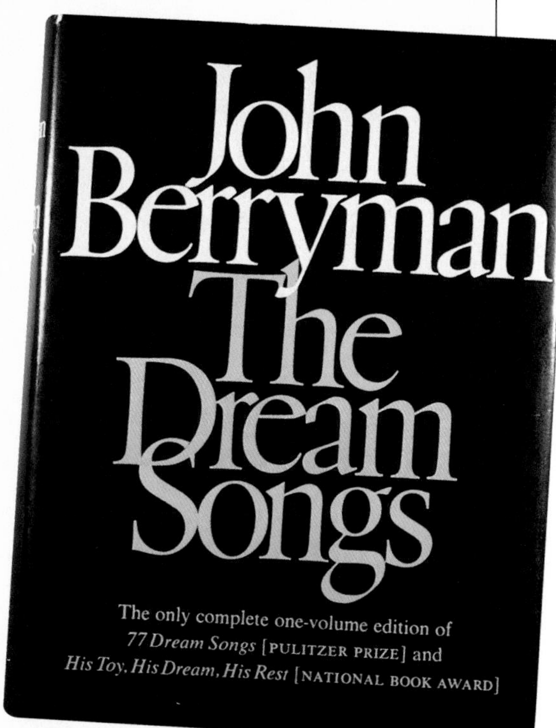

John
Berryman
The
Dream
Songs
The only complete one-volume edition of
77 Dream Songs [PULITZER PRIZE] and
His Toy, His Dream, His Rest [NATIONAL BOOK AWARD]

Dream Song 76

Nothin very bad happen to me lately.
How you explain that?—I explain that, Mr.
Bones,
terms o' your bafflin odd sobriety.
Sober as man can get, no girls, no
telephones,
what could happen bad to Mr. Bones?
—*If* life is a handkerchief sandwich,

in a modesty of death I join my father
who dared so long agone leave me.
A bullet on a concrete stoop
close by a smothering southern sea
spreadeagled on an island, by my knee.
—You is from hunger, Mr. Bones,

I offers you this handkerchief, now set
your left foot by my right foot,
shoulder to shoulder, all that jazz,
arm in arm, by the beautiful sea,
hum a little, Mr. Bones
—I saw nobody coming, so I went instead.

Dream Song 90

In the night-reaches dreamed he of better
graces,
of liberations, and beloved faces,
such as now ere dawn he sings.
It would not be easy, accustomed to these
things,
to give up the old world, but he could try;
let it all rest, have a good cry.

Let Randall rest, whom your self-torturing
cannot restore one instant's good to, rest:
he's left us now.
The panic died and in the panic's dying
so did my old friend. I am headed west
also, also, somehow.

In the chambers of the end we'll meet
again
I will say Randall, he'll say Pussycat
and all will be as before
whenas we sought, among the beloved
faces,
eminence and were dissatisfied with that
and needed more.

Dream Song 256

Henry rested, possessed of many pills
& gin & whiskey. He put up his feet
& switched on Schubert.
His tranquillity lasted five minutes
for (1) all that undone all the heavy weeks
and (2) images shook him alert.

A rainy Sunday morning, on vacation
as well as Fellowship, he could not rest:
bitterly he shook his head.
—Mr. Bones, the Lord will bring us to a
nation
where everybody only rest.—I confess
that notion bores me dead,

for there's no occupation there, save God,
if that, and long experience of His works
has not taught me his love.
His love must be a very strange thing
indeed,
considering its products. No, I want rest
here,
neither below nor above.

***The Dream Songs* by John Berryman *(top)* are indeed both dreamlike and musical; their language mimics the allusive, free-form nature of dreams, yet they conform to a regular pattern of three six-line stanzas per song.**

1969

As the West's most powerful nation reeled from the twin humiliations of a disgraced leader and the loss of an undeclared war, the entire industrialized world suffered the consequences of its alarming dependence on fossil fuel. Meanwhile, the breakdown of the earth's ecology exposed the perils of progress.

1970 1979

In a few years' time, the wealth of nations underwent a radical reconfiguration based on the simplest possible premise: Some countries had oil; others needed it. The Organization of Petroleum Exporting Countries (OPEC) was founded in 1960, but did not take a major role on the world stage until 1973, when it raised world oil prices by more than 200 percent. As the West scrambled to develop alternative energy sources, newly wealthy Arab nations grappled with the double-edged sword of instant modernity. Here, in an eastern province of Saudi Arabia, a lone Arab watches a gas flare burn apocalyptically in the distance.

THE WORLD IN 1970

World Population

1960: 3.2 BILLION 1970: 3.7 BILLION

1960–70: +15.6%

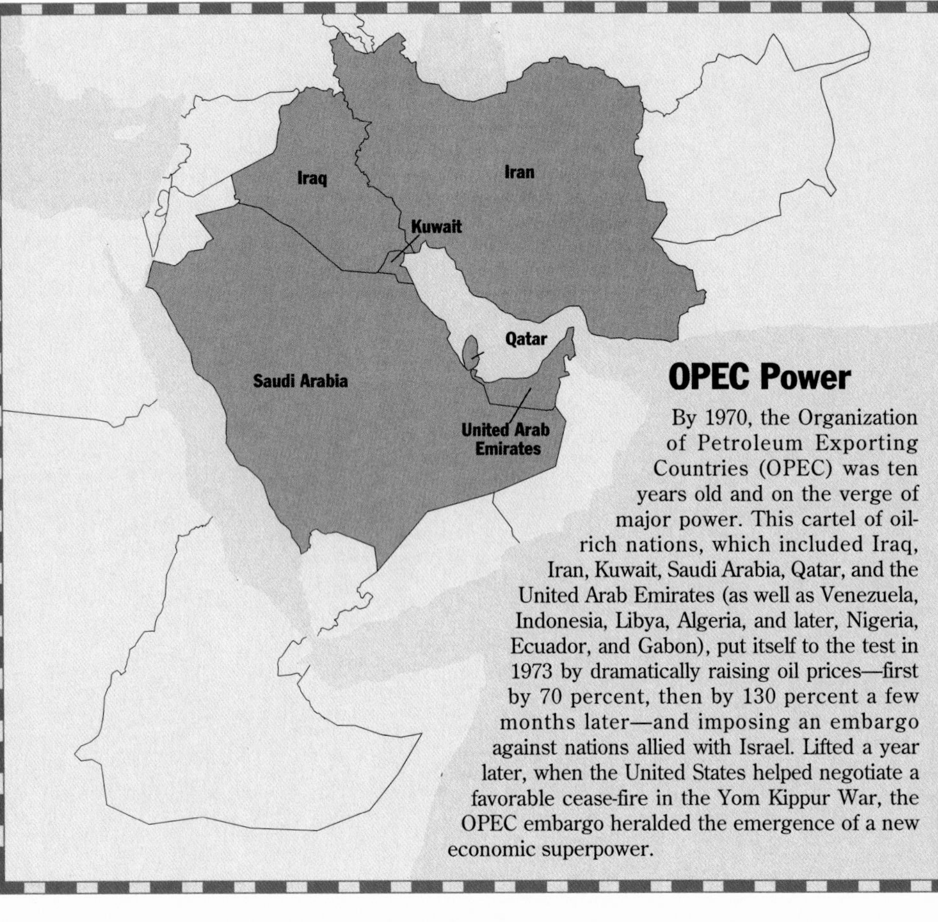

OPEC Power

By 1970, the Organization of Petroleum Exporting Countries (OPEC) was ten years old and on the verge of major power. This cartel of oil-rich nations, which included Iraq, Iran, Kuwait, Saudi Arabia, Qatar, and the United Arab Emirates (as well as Venezuela, Indonesia, Libya, Algeria, and later, Nigeria, Ecuador, and Gabon), put itself to the test in 1973 by dramatically raising oil prices—first by 70 percent, then by 130 percent a few months later—and imposing an embargo against nations allied with Israel. Lifted a year later, when the United States helped negotiate a favorable cease-fire in the Yom Kippur War, the OPEC embargo heralded the emergence of a new economic superpower.

1968—The Year of the Barricades The spirit of "the sixties" was at the forefront of the collective consciousness in 1970. In the popular imagination, the decade coalesces into a single year: 1968, when "anti-establishment" uprisings, often led by students, broke out around the world, throughout the year.

January

Spain Madrid University closed after student protest.

Japan Student demonstrations.

Poland Students and intellectuals protest against censorship.

February

West Germany Violent clashes in Berlin, Frankfurt, and Bonn.

U.K. Student sit-in at Leicester.

March

Italy Rome University closed after riots.

U.K. London anti-Vietnam War march draws 10,000.

Poland Students invade Ministry of Culture.

April

U.S. Nationwide unrest follows shooting of Martin Luther King.

China Red Guard factions battle in Beijing.

Spain Students and workers riot in Madrid.

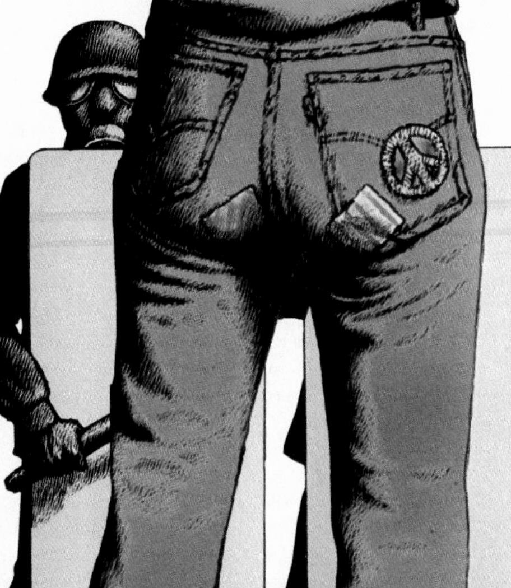
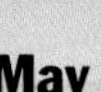

May

France Police occupy Sorbonn "Night of the Barricades."

West Germany Protests against emergency laws

U.S. Students occupy San Fra cisco State College.

About the size of a paperback book, the **pocket calculator** first appeared in 1969. But it wasn't until a handheld model was introduced in 1971 that sales really began to soar. Only 17,000 sold in Europe and North America that year, but by 1973, sales had reached an estimated 25 million worldwide.

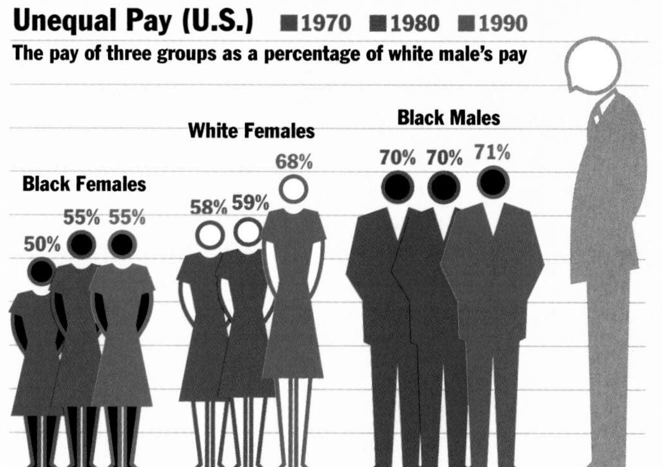

Fashion Essential

André Courrèges and Mary Quant revolutionized fashion in 1965 when they sent their models down the runway wearing skirts that hovered four inches above the knee. By 1970, the **miniskirt** had inched even farther upward, routinely reaching a height of ten inches above the knee.

Heart to Heart

Although Dr. Christiaan Barnard performed the first human heart transplant in 1967, the procedure remained rare until 1981, when a new antirejection drug called cyclosporin dramatically improved the chances of survival. Numbers of transplants escalated rapidly, then leveled off due to donor shortages.

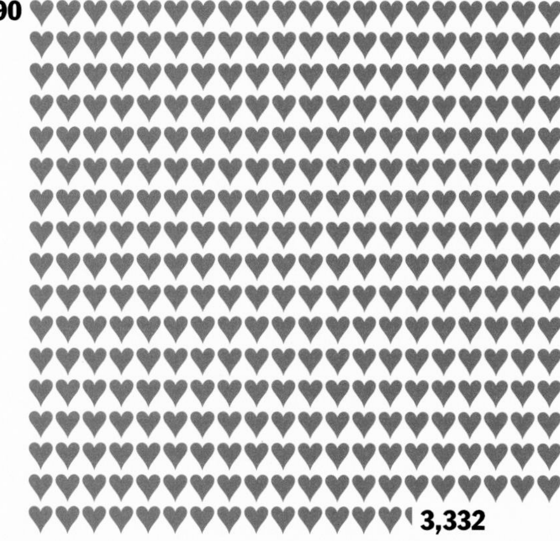

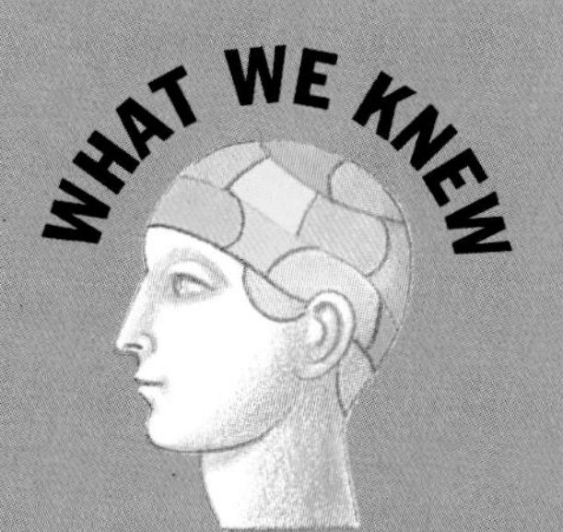

"No woman in my time will be prime minister or chancellor or foreign secretary," says the shadow education minister of the out-of-power Conservative Party, Margaret Thatcher. "I wouldn't want to be Prime Minister; you have to give yourself 100 percent."

■

While nearly 50 percent of all U.S. families have at least one bank credit card, the cards "have had little impact thus far on consumer spending habits," says the U.S. Federal Reserve. The Fed also predicts that "at present levels and growth rates, [credit card] plans are not large enough to have any noticeable effect."

■

Although abortion is legal in much of Europe, the Soviet Union, and China (and is widely used as a form of birth control in the latter two countries), in the United States only New York, Washington state, Hawaii, and Alaska permit unrestricted abortions. Consequently, "Jane Roe," a waitress in Dallas, and "Mary Doe," a housewife from Georgia, both of whom are pregnant, file lawsuits because they cannot obtain legal abortions in their home states.

■

The U.S. House of Representatives has overwhelmingly passed a Constitutional amendment guaranteeing equal rights for women and prohibiting any discrimination on the basis of sex. The ERA is expected to gain Senate approval and be quickly ratified by the required three quarters of state legislatures.

ne

nce Police ade worker-cupied factories.

S. Students and ice clash at ople's Park in rkeley.

goslavia Stu-nt demonstra-ns in Belgrade.

July

Mexico Students demonstrate in the universities.

Japan Tokyo University closed due to strikes.

Czechoslovakia Soviet leaders condemn Czech revisionism.

August

Czechoslovakia Warsaw Pact forces invade.

U.S. Rioting and demonstrations during political conventions.

Mexico 30,000 protest in Mexico City.

September

Mexico Students and workers battle police in Mexico City before the opening of the 1968 Olympics.

West Germany Student riots.

October

France Student demonstrations.

Japan President of Tokyo University resigns after student demonstrations.

U.K. London School of Economics occupied, then closed.

November

Czechoslovakia Students strike, oppose Soviet invasion.

U.K. Students occupy Birmingham University.

December

France Student protests at Universities.

U.K. Students occupy Bristol University.

U.S. Armed students occupy Cornell University's Administration Building.

STEPHEN JAY GOULD

A Wolf at the Door

Environmentalism Becomes an Imperative

1970
1979

O SINGLE EVENT MARKS THE 1970S AS A DECADE of environmentalism. Rather, like a thief in the night, one central theme, long in the making, sneaked into our collective consciousness to mark a turning point. In short, we recognized that Homo sapiens had become "an universal wolf" in Shakespeare's sense, and no longer a local despoiler alone. In *Troilus and Cressida,* Shakespeare notes what happens when rapaciousness becomes universal:

> Then everything includes itself in power,
> Power into will, will into appetite;
> And appetite, an universal wolf,
> So doubly seconded with will and power,
> Must make perforce an universal prey,
> And last eat up himself.

Perhaps we always had the *will.* Humans have thoroughly fouled local nests before, but until this century we never had the *power* to impose truly planetary damage. The insidious promotion of our power and our awareness of its capacity (via Shakespeare's metaphor) ultimately (and perhaps sooner rather than later) to destroy us provided the primary impetus for raising environmentalism from a local pursuit, often regarded as arcane or cranky, to a planetary imperative—a well-coordinated, global political movement with growing influence, as we cascade toward an abyss. Future chroniclers (if we permit them to exist) will view the environmental movement—alongside technological revolutions in transportation and electronic communication—as a key element in one of the most portentous developments in human history: the twentieth century's irrevocable transition from local foci, developing in near independence, to a global economy and society.

Our forebears needed no complex technology to destroy bounded and local ecologies. The Maori, the Polynesian people who first reached New Zealand in the twelfth century, found a fauna dominated by some 25 species of large, flightless ground birds ranging in size from a turkey to much larger than an ostrich. The Maori called these birds "moas" and proceeded to wipe them out within 500 years. Similarly, the decline and disappearance of the Easter Island statue makers is no arcane mystery (as occultists are so fond of arguing) but a consequence of despoliation so complete (on an isolated island of strictly limited resources) that not even a log remained to roll finished statues from quarries to erection sites.

The twentieth century was the first to witness environmental devastation on a global scale. But humans had long exhibited tendencies toward local despoliation. The makers of the gigantic stone monoliths on Easter Island—carved of volcanic stone and most likely dating from about AD 800–1600—left many statues unfinished in quarries, with stone picks scattered about. This seemingly mysterious interruption of their work is no mystery: They had so thoroughly ravaged their environment that not even a log remained to roll the statues to their destinations.

Add technology from the industrial revolution, and power increases, but not yet to universal wolfdom. At the opening of the nineteenth century, William Blake decried the presence of "dark Satanic mills" upon the "mountains green" and "pleasant pastures seen" of England's former agricultural state—and he pledged both his sword and his "mental fight" to building Jerusalem "in England's green and pleasant land." Still, the belching smoke of Birmingham and Pittsburgh did not sully the faraway Taj Mahal (now eroding, in part due to acid rain) or bother birds on isolated oceanic islands (now feeling our blows in many ways, including the incorporation of pesticide residues into their eggs and developing chicks).

Many factors contributed to the coalescence of environmental concerns into a global movement during the 1970s. A proper scientific perception of our planetary onslaught upon atmospheres and

ecologies began to emerge. Other ingredients were largely symbolic, but potent nonetheless. As the exploration of space began tentatively in the 1950s, gathered steam during the 1960s, and culminated in a lunar landing at the threshold of the 1970s, our literal view of the earth experienced the most profound change since the age of exploration, some 500 years earlier.

People who grew up with images of the whole earth simply cannot know the aesthetic and conceptual thrill vouchsafed to us older folk when space vehicles first photographed the unknown side of the moon (so maximally near, cosmically speaking, yet so far in its permanent invisibility) or, with such stunning clarity, the distant satellites of Uranus and Neptune. But nothing matched the insight and satisfaction gained from seeing the whole earth as a resplendent sphere in space. We have known since Archimedes' time that the earth is a sphere (exulting in the power of the lever, Archimedes said that he would move the entire earth if someone would only give him a place to stand), but we could never get far enough away to record planetary roundness. The first photograph of the entire earth forced us, as no other single icon ever did or could, to regard our abode as limited, with all its parts interrelated. The American architect and engineer Buckminster Fuller captured this epiphany in his unforgettable metaphor "little Spaceship Earth," which became the watchword of environmentalism.

U Thant, Secretary-General of the United Nations, sounded a warning at the threshold in 1969: "I do not wish to seem overdramatic, but I can only conclude ... that the Members of the United Nations have perhaps ten years left in which to subordinate their ancient quarrels and launch a global partnership to curb the arms race, to improve the human environment, to diffuse the population explosion, and to supply the required momentum to development efforts. If such a global partnership is not forged with the next decade, then I very much fear that the problems I have mentioned will have reached such staggering proportions that they will be beyond our capacity to control."

POLITICAL ACTIVITY GEARED UP WITH THE FIRST EARTH WEEK in April 1970. A small literature with a few heroes (from Thoreau to Rachel Carson, whose 1962 book *Silent Spring* alerted the public to environmental pollution) burgeoned to a flood of books, from popular manifestoes (Barry Commoner's *The Closing Circle,* for example, in 1971) to more technical studies (like the Club of Rome's 1972 *The Limits to Growth*). Old trends had finally accelerated enough (or merely reached global impact in their logarithmic phases) to demand notice and alarm.

We must force ourselves to remember and acknowledge the counterintuitive truth about processes that increase by doubling at fixed intervals: Half of the entire amount accrues in the last step. To cite the old legend: A tiny lily pad doubles in area each day. It begins as a dot on the pond, but will completely cover the water in 30 days. The pond keeper decides that he need not worry until the pond is half covered, and he will then make efforts to cut the growth back. When must he act? Only on the 30th day—quickly and decisively, or all is lost; yet the rate of increase has never changed. Moreover, although environmental change has been occurring throughout geological time, modern humans have added to the equation a huge increase in people as well as new technologies with devastating power to accelerate the rate of change.

The earliest environmentalists were largely wealthy individuals eager to preserve pristine, preindustrial wilderness lands for their leisure use. To protect such areas from unregulated development, naturalist groups like the Sierra Club began forming in the late nineteenth century, and as early as 1872 the United States was creating a system of national parks and wildlife refuges. One great wilderness area of the American West was Yosemite National Park in California *(left)*, photographed in 1947 by the great chronicler of America's national parks, Ansel Adams, who visited Yosemite every year for 67 years.

A Framework of Research on the Human Dimensions of Global Environmental Change, a 1991 publication of the International Social Science Council, produced for UNESCO, identifies four major (and by now familiar) categories of global insults. The first of these is climatic change. In this category no anthropogenic impact on atmospheres and oceans has been as clearly and thoroughly documented—or as feared and as frequently invoked—as the relentless rise in atmospheric carbon dioxide, with the possibility of a resulting "greenhouse effect" and global warming. The second insult is the depletion of the earth's protective ozone layer, probably caused by release into the atmosphere of fluorocarbons and other halocarbons widely used in air conditioning, refrigeration, and aerosol propulsion. Acid rain, which carries high levels of oxides of nitrogen and sulfur dioxide from industrial emissions, constitutes a third worldwide environmental problem, slowly devastating rivers and lakes as well as art and architecture. Finally, the planet is experiencing rates of species extinction that may well match the intensity of losses during the great mass dyings of our geological record.

1970
1979

EVENTS IN THE FIRST THREE CATEGORIES are dangerous though reversible—and political pressure has already provided much ground for hope and some signs of abatement, if not reversal. But loss of species cannot be undone on any time scale that is relevant to human life. Each species is a unique historical product of an evolutionary sequence that can be traced through billions of years to the origin of life itself. Pluck any twig from the tree of life (even a tiny bud that differentiated from its ancestor only a geological second ago), and the ledger of nature's precious diversity is debited by one item. Enter too many debits and the gloriously arborescent tree of life becomes a tawdry set of branches, far too sparse and all awry, with a layer of rot and decay at the base.

Some misguided or self-serving foes of environmental movements, defenders of the notion that any real trouble will always yield to a readily available "technological fix," claim that even this sadness about loss of biodiversity is misplaced. Why worry about extinction? they ask. All species eventually die, and the fossil record attests to at least five episodes of mass extinction, with losses up to 95 percent (an estimate of the demise of marine invertebrate species in the greatest of coordinated dyings some 225 million years ago). Mass extinction, they continue, is even a good thing in the long run, for the old and stodgy are eliminated, thereby vacating ecological space for improved evolutionary experiments millions of years down the road. This argument does strike close to home, for the death of dinosaurs made possible our own eventual appearance. Mammals had lived as tiny creatures in the shadows of dinosaurs for 100 million years. If dinosaurs (as well as 50 percent of marine invertebrate species) had not been removed by the impact of a large extraterrestrial body (the likely cause of the Cretaceous mass extinction), mammals would probably still be small creatures in the interstices of a dinosaur's world, and no self-conscious species would inhabit our planet.

This planetary time scale of years measured in millions has both grandeur and fascination (as a professional paleontologist, I spend the bulk of my working life in its command). No, humans do not threaten the planet at its own time scale. Environmental insults will eventually be reversed if we succeed in wiping ourselves out, or will be accommodated naturally even if we do not. We are not nearly so powerful as nature in the long run; the megatonnage in all our nuclear weapons equals only one ten-thousandth the power in the single extraterrestrial body that prompted the Cretaceous extinction.

But I cannot think of anything more irrelevant to the legitimately parochial scale of our own lives than nature's planetary time. We care deeply—as we should—about the lives of our children; our bloodlines; our precious and fragile culture with its magnificent art, literature, and music; our architectural and technological achievements. We measure our legitimate time in decades, centuries, and, at most, millennia. All these intervals are but microseconds of geological time—and all the world to us.

Our environmental assaults are dangerous and frightening because their impact on us and our evolutionary neighbors—from half a million species of beetles to a single species of aardvarks—is felt in the legitimate immediacy of human time scales. The Cretaceous extinction may have been wonderful for big mammals ten million years into an unknowable evolutionary future. But for a *Tyrannosaurus* watching the comet hit, what could matter but personal and communal disaster? If we can only remember that we are the immediate *Tyrannosaurus* of this metaphor, not the conjectural outcome of an impossibly distant and unpredictable future, we may mobilize the products of our own unique consciousness—our "mental fight"—to reverse our civil war against ourselves and to persuade the earth that we constitute a worthy adornment, at least for its "little while," which is, for us, from here to eternity. □

A by-product of industrialism, acid rain has ravaged aquatic life, vegetation, even great works of architecture. In a once lushly green forest in Bavaria, white crosses mark acid-rain-damaged trees *(right)*. A study published in 1983 found that a staggering 34 percent of German forests had suffered such damage. Thanks to rampant development and other humanly created ills, more species than ever before are threatened with extinction. In prehuman times, one out of a million species became naturally extinct annually—compared with tens of thousands per year today. With a population of under 1,000 in the United States, the grizzly bear *(above)* is officially endangered.

"We are not a weak people. We are a strong people.... We will not be humiliated. The world's most powerful nation [will not act] like a pitiful, helpless giant."—**U.S. president Richard M. Nixon, on the bombing of Cambodia**

STORY OF THE YEAR

The War Widens

1 In March 1970, rightist military officers ousted Cambodia's chief of state, Prince Norodom Sihanouk. Sihanouk had given Vietnamese Communist troops sanctuary in Cambodia; the country's new ruler, General Lon Nol, tried to drive them out. But while Lon Nol's soldiers massacred thousands of ethnic Vietnamese civilians, they fared poorly against the North Vietnamese army and the Viet Cong. His call for U.S. help was just what Washington had been waiting for: a chance to strike a major blow against the enemy without appearing to reverse the policy of "Vietnamization"—the gradual withdrawal of U.S. troops that President Nixon had promised. Or so Nixon and his chief strategist, national security adviser Henry Kissinger, thought. On April 30, U.S. and South Vietnamese forces poured into Cambodia.

Horror-stricken onlookers regard the body of a Kent State student after National Guardsmen fired on demonstrators protesting the U.S. invasion of Cambodia.

Nixon insisted that the move was not an invasion but a "limited incursion." By any name, it incensed the U.S. peace movement, which now claimed the support of more than half the population. Students went on strike across the nation; on some campuses they burned Reserve Officer Training Corps facilities, where students were trained for the military. The ROTC building at Ohio's Kent State University was still smoldering on May 4, when National Guard troops opened fire on demonstrators and onlookers, killing four unarmed students. Ten days later, in a similar incident, police shot and killed two student protesters at Jackson State University in Mississippi. The ensuing explosion of rage shut down 75 American colleges for the rest of the academic year.

The invasion of Cambodia and the Kent State incident helped seal Americans' opposition to the war. In a mostly symbolic act of protest, Congress repealed the Gulf of Tonkin resolution (without actually cutting off funding). And the Scranton Commission, appointed by Nixon, issued a report warning that America hadn't been so divided since the Civil War and urged an early end to U.S. involvement in Southeast Asia.

Ironically, the "incursion" was a flop. Nixon neglected to notify Lon Nol in advance, so there was no coordination with Cambodian forces; the Vietnamese Communists, better informed, withdrew before their enemies arrived. The invaders left in June. Still, American bombs continued to rain down on the country, as did American aid—$3 billion before Cambodia's Khmer Rouge Communists (who were made popular by the bombing and by Lon Nol's corruption) seized power in 1975. **◂1969.6 ▸1971.M**

CHILE

Electing a Revolution

2 Chile became the first Western nation ever to freely elect an avowed Marxist as head of state in September 1970, when Dr. Salvador Allende Gossens won a narrow plurality against a rightist Nationalist and a left-leaning Christian Democrat. Allende was a respectable radical: The scion of a prominent family, he'd been a senator, a minister of health, and a perennial presidential candidate. But the Socialist Party he cofounded in the 1930s often stood to the left of Chile's Moscow-oriented Communists. His election sparked a stock-market crash, a run on banks, and a strike by well-paid copper miners, who feared for their privileges. Many wealthy Chileans fled abroad.

In fact, Allende's nominally centrist predecessor, Christian Democrat Eduardo Frei Montalva, had already started down a leftward path. The government had acquired 51 percent of the giant U.S. companies that extracted copper, Chile's principal resource. And Frei had begun an agrarian reform program, establishing peasant cooperatives and expropriating some land. But Chileans remained largely poor, and inflation rose alarmingly. Frei's initiatives had raised expectations more effectively than they'd raised living standards.

Despite CIA attempts to disrupt the 1970 election, Chile's voters elected Salvador Allende *(above)* president.

Allende saw Chile as a victim of neocolonialism—dominated by foreign capital, dependent on exporting cheap raw materials and importing nearly everything else. He proposed to fully nationalize mining, finance, and major industry and to aggressively redistribute land and wealth. And he promised to do so without compromising the political freedoms of a nation proud of its democratic traditions. But a variety of forces thwarted his experiment—and three years later, it came to a blood-drenched conclusion. **◂1968.7 ▸1973.4**

THE MIDDLE EAST

Turmoil and Mourning

3 Palestinians remember it as Black September, but for Egyptians the ninth month of 1970 was marked by upheaval as well. On September 16, Jordan's King Hussein launched a drive to dislodge Palestinian commandos from his realm—and on the 28th, Egypt's President Nasser died at age 52.

The crisis in Jordan had been building since the end of the 1967 war, which had left Israel occupying the West Bank. As the Palestine Liberation Organization increasingly used Jordan as a base for attacks on Israel, Jordanian civilians bore the brunt of Israeli reprisals. Unwilling to risk another war with Israel and uneasy about mounting Palestinian power within Jordan, Hussein tried disarming the PLO, leading militant factions to call for his overthrow. Negotiations with PLO chairman Yasir Arafat produced a compromise, but Arafat could not control the radicals. Clashes between Palestinian and Jordanian forces escalated, and in 1970 there were two attempts on Hussein's life.

Hussein's patience snapped when a PLO subgroup, the Popular Front for the Liberation of Palestine, hijacked three passenger planes (one American, one Swiss, and one British) to Jordan, blowing them up after evacuating the occupants. The King sent armored divisions to northern cities and refugee camps for what he envisioned as a quick operation to evict PLO guerrillas. But Jordan's rival Syria took advantage of the diversion to attack Jordan, and though that assault failed, the PLO fought on until July 1971.

Gamal Abdal Nasser succumbed to a heart attack hours after arranging a brief Palestinian-Jordanian cease-fire, a month after agreeing to a U.S.-brokered cease-fire in Egypt's own sporadic "war of attrition" with Israel, and two months after dedicating the Aswan High Dam—a fitting symbol of his 18-year rule. Built with Soviet help after the West

ART & CULTURE: Books: ***Losing Battles*** **(Eudora Welty);** ***The Goalie's Anxiety at the Penalty Kick*** **(Peter Handke);** ***Play It as It Lays*** **(Joan Didion);** ***Bury My Heart at Wounded Knee*** **(Dee Brown) ... Music:** ***Bridge Over Troubled Water*** **(Simon and Garfunkel, LP);** ***Déja Vu*** **(Crosby, Stills, Nash and Young, LP),** ***Eric Clapton*** **(LP);** ***Ancient Voices of Children*** **(George Crumb);** ***32 études australes*** **(John Cage)**

"Onstage I make love to 25,000 people, then I go home alone."—**Janis Joplin**

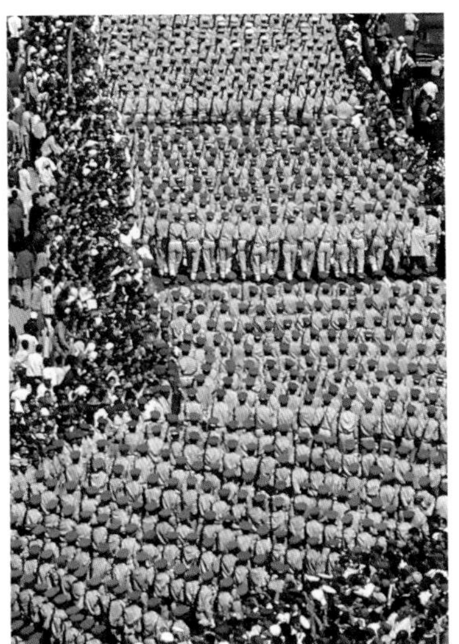

Mourners thronged Cairo for Nasser's funeral on October 5. The nationalist hero was succeeded by Anwar al-Sadat.

withdrew its aid, the dam would spread electricity across an ancient land. Arabs everywhere mourned the great modernizer, defiant nationalist, and paternal (if ruthless) dictator. Nasser was succeeded by Vice President Anwar al-Sadat, who'd helped him seize power in 1952. **◄1967.3 ►1972.8**

MUSIC

High Priests of Excess

4 For young rebels in the late 1960s, the now-clichéd phrase "sex, drugs, and rock and roll" represented a kind of holy trinity whose high priests were rock stars. Among the greatest musical exponents of excess were Janis Joplin, Jimi Hendrix, and Jim Morrison (lead singer for the Doors). Their deaths in 1970 and 1971 heralded the great cultural crash that followed a euphoric decade.

What the Beatles and the early Rolling Stones had merely hinted at, these artists delivered, celebrating the carnal and chemical pursuit of ecstasy with raunchy conviction. Joplin—whose full-throttle performances made her one of the few successful white blues singers ever—rasped out songs of loneliness and the open road while swigging Southern Comfort from the bottle. Hendrix, perhaps the most inventive rock guitarist of all time, was famous for his gyrations onstage (he played his guitar with his teeth or while holding it behind his head; sometimes he set it on fire with lighter fluid) and for his amorous and psychedelic exploits elsewhere. Morrison, revered for his highbrow lyrics and epic debauchery, held audiences spellbound as he chanted the verses of "The End," a song touching on patricide and incest. All three performers cultivated "outlaw" images; they were arrested on charges ranging from narcotics possession to indecent exposure. As Morrison put it, "I'm interested in anything about revolt, disorder, chaos.... It seems to me to be the road to freedom."

Each star seemed curiously reconciled to an early demise. Not long before his death from choking on his own vomit (a result of mixing alcohol and drugs) in September 1970, Hendrix joked about his own funeral. Joplin, who overdosed on heroin weeks later, once told a reporter, "Maybe I won't last as long as other singers, but I think you can destroy your now, worrying about tomorrow." And Morrison, who succumbed the following year to a drug-related heart attack in his Paris apartment, infused his lyrics (influenced by the French Symbolists) with a poetic morbidity. His grave in Paris's Père-Lachaise is the cemetery's most visited; thousands of fans flock to it each year, leaving flowers, love letters—and flasks of whiskey. **◄1969.10 ►1977.6**

Rock stars Morrison *(left)*, Hendrix *(center)*, and Joplin lived hard and died young.

ENVIRONMENTALISM

An Ecology Holiday

5 Growing international concern about the unstable health of the planet gained official expression on April 22, 1970, when the United States observed Earth Day. Activities on the world's first ecology holiday, organized by Wisconsin senator Gaylord Nelson and young environmental activist Denis Hayes, included seminars, parades, and metal-recycling "smash-ins." Environmentalism had become a force.

Even the U.S. government got on board, creating the Environmental Protection Agency two months later. By 1972, the UN was involved, convening an environmental conference in Stockholm, Sweden. More direct measures were taken by groups like Greenpeace (formed in 1971 by Canadian opponents of U.S. nuclear testing), which confronted polluting corporations and governments.

Artist Peter Max created a characteristically "psychedelic" poster for Earth Week in Davis, California, in 1969.

By 1979, when the first Green political party emerged in Bremen, Germany, the environmental movement had put down roots. But much of the damage to the ecosystem had already been done. Factories had dumped billions of tons of mercury into the world's lakes and rivers. Chlorofluorocarbons, used in refrigeration and aerosols, had been eating away at the ozone layer. Developers were destroying the Amazonian and Southeast Asian rain forests at a rate of almost 50 acres a minute, threatening some 750,000 plant and animal species with extinction. Across the planet, people increasingly wondered whether it was too late for Earth itself. **◄1962.11 ►1983.5**

BIRTHS

Andre Agassi,
U.S. tennis player.

Mariah Carey, U.S. singer.

Jim Courier, U.S. tennis player.

Alonzo Mourning,
U.S. basketball player.

River Phoenix, U.S. actor.

Gabriela Sabatini,
Argentine tennis player.

DEATHS

S.Y. Agnon, Israeli writer.

Rudolf Carnap,
German-U.S. philosopher.

Edouard Daladier,
French premier.

John Dos Passos, U.S. writer.

E.M. Forster, U.K. writer.

Charles de Gaulle,
French president.

Basil Henry Liddell Hart,
U.K. military theorist.

Jimi Hendrix, U.S. singer.

Richard Hofstadter,
U.S. historian.

Janis Joplin, U.S. singer.

Aleksandr Kerensky,
Russian revolutionary.

Allen Lane, U.K. publisher.

Gypsy Rose Lee,
U.S. entertainer.

Vince Lombardi,
U.S. football coach.

Yukio Mishima,
Japanese writer.

Gamal Abdal Nasser,
Egyptian president.

John O'Hara, U.S. writer.

Chandrasekhara Raman,
Indian physicist.

Erich Maria Remarque,
German-U.S. writer.

Nina Ricci,
French fashion designer.

Mark Rothko,
Russian-U.S. painter.

Bertrand Russell,
U.K. philosopher.

António Salazar,
Portuguese ruler.

John T. Scopes, U.S. teacher.

Sukarno, Indonesian president.

... Painting & Sculpture: ***Three Studies from the Human Body*** **(Francis Bacon);** ***Flights of Fantasy*** **(Romare Bearden) ... Film:** ***Patton*** **(Franklin J. Schaffner);** ***Five Easy Pieces*** **(Bob Rafelson);** ***M*A*S*H*** **(Robert Altman);** ***Love Story*** **(Arthur Hiller) ... Theater:** ***Child's Play*** **(Robert Marasco);** ***Sleuth*** **(Anthony Shaffer);** ***Home*** **(David Storey) ... TV:** ***The Mary Tyler Moore Show*; *The Partridge Family*; *All My Children*.**

"You can look for pitched battles between the militant groups and the pigs on a scale that will make anything in the sixties look like a Sunday-school picnic."—**Mark Rudd, leader of the Weathermen, announcing his group's agenda for the 1970s**

NEW IN 1970

Prime-time football (ABC's *Monday Night Football*).

World Trade Center (New York City).

Childproof safety tops.

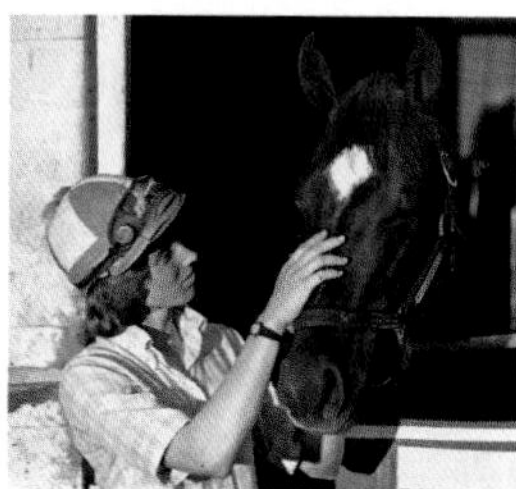

Female jockey in the Kentucky Derby (Diane Crump).

New York City marathon.

Amtrak.

Subway in Mexico City.

Legal divorce in Italy.

No-fault divorce in the U.S. (California).

IN THE UNITED STATES

▶EARTH ART—Robert Smithson completed his pioneering earthwork—an art form that sought to remake land into

art—in 1970: *Spiral Jetty*, a concentric road running into Utah's Great Salt Lake. Two years after making it (and filming the process), the 35-year-old sculptor was killed in a plane crash while scouting a site in Texas. ▶1983.11

▶PHARMACOLOGICAL NEWS—The drugs lithium and L-dopa received Food and Drug Administration approval in 1970. The element lithium in salt form was found to be effective in treating symptoms of manic-depressive illness. Its widespread use transformed psychopharmacology and paved the way for the widespread success of antidepressants. L-dopa offered hope for relief to the roughly 200,000 Americans annually stricken with Parkinson's disease (a progressive, incurable nerve disorder) by stimulating the brain to produce the neurotransmitter dopamine—

DIPLOMACY

Moscow, Bonn Make Up

6 Willy Brandt, socialist chancellor of West Germany, accomplished a long-standing policy goal in 1970 when his government signed a "renunciation-of-force" treaty with the Soviet Union. The shining achievement of Brandt's *Ostpolitik*—his campaign for peaceful coexistence of Western Europe with the Communist bloc—the agreement settled business left unfinished since World War II, normalizing Soviet–West German relations and establishing détente in Europe as a whole. "This is the end of an epoch," said an optimistic Brandt at a Red Square ceremony marking the occasion, "but also a good beginning."

In return for tacitly recognizing the status quo in Central Europe (most significantly, the border between East and West Germany and the western frontier of Poland carved out of German territory by the Soviets after the war), Brandt and foreign minister Walter Scheel gained important concessions from Moscow. Chief among them: acceptance of Germany's right to "self-determination" (a euphemism for the ultimate goal of reunification) and unimpeded Western access to Communist-surrounded Berlin. The Soviets, in turn, won improved trade relations with the prosperous West, entrée to advanced West German science and technology, and security on the empire's western boundary—much desired as Sino-Soviet antagonism mounted in the East.

In December, four months after completing the Bonn-Moscow treaty, West Germany signed a similar pact with Poland, further stabilizing East-West relations. Brandt won the 1971 Nobel Peace Prize for his efforts. *Ostpolitik*'s reception was not universally sanguine, however. In Western Europe, it provoked fears of a West German drift toward neutralism, which would undermine NATO (of which West Germany was a member). The U.S. State Department cautiously supported Brandt but warned that a treaty alone did not constitute "tangible evidence of Soviet cooperation." **◂1963.5 ▸1974.3**

A German Lilliputian and his Russian counterpart conspire to tie up a Cold War Gulliver.

THE UNITED STATES

Revolt and Reaction

7 The degree to which the civil disobedience of the early sixties had given way to an aggressive, often violent radicalism—even among the most well-educated, socially privileged members of America's New Left—became starkly apparent in a number of disparate incidents in 1970. In March a bomb factory operated by the extremist Weathermen (an offshoot of the campus activist group Students for a Democratic Society) exploded, killing three young radicals in a Manhattan townhouse owned by the parents of one of the two survivors. The latter escaped to form the Weather Underground, which committed robberies and bombings throughout the decade. In August, at the University of Wisconsin in Madison, four students protesting the university's participation in government war research blew up a campus laboratory, killing a graduate student and destroying a $1.5 million computer. In Boston in September, two Brandeis University students whose opposition to the Vietnam War had expanded into a determination to overthrow the entire capitalist system, took part in a bank heist in which a policeman was killed. The two women went underground; before giving herself up in 1993, one of them, Katherine Ann Power, was the longest-running radical outlaw on the FBI's most wanted list.

Also plunging underground was Father Daniel Berrigan, a Roman Catholic priest who, with his brother (and fellow cleric) Philip and seven others ("the Catonsville Nine"), had been convicted for the 1968 burning of draft records in Catonsville, Maryland. ("I burned some paper," Berrigan declared, "to say the burning of children was inhuman and unbearable.") In April, ordered to begin his prison term, Berrigan bolted. He was seized four months later by the FBI.

Courtroom sketch of a bound and gagged Bobby Seale on trial in Chicago.

The government's retaliatory powers came down hardest, as always, on minorities. In February, after a trial marked by the judge's hostility and the defendants' anarchic hijinks, five of the Chicago Seven (all of whom were white) were convicted of intent to incite riots at the 1968 Chicago Democratic convention. An eighth defendant, Black Panther Bobby Seale, was tried and convicted separately—but not before being bound and gagged for his courtroom outbursts. (All the convictions were eventually overturned.) And in August, Angela Davis, a brilliant black militant whose membership in the Communist Party had cost her her job as a philosophy instructor at the University of California, was accused of murder, kidnapping, and conspiracy when the brother of George Jackson (a Soledad Prison inmate with whom she'd fallen in love) used guns registered in her

SPORTS: Baseball: World Series, Baltimore Orioles defeat Cincinnati Reds, 4–1 ... Football: Super Bowl, Kansas City Chiefs defeat Minnesota Vikings, 23–7 ... Basketball: NBA, New York Knicks defeat Los Angeles Lakers, 4–3 ... Tennis: Margaret Smith Court wins Grand Slam ... Hockey: Bobby Orr leads Boston Bruins to first Stanley Cup victory in 29 years ... Soccer: World Cup, Brazil defeats Italy, 4-1.

"Women act as if sex is a social duty. They don't even know if they want it or not, but everyone's doing it, so they do it too."
—Germaine Greer

name in a bloody courthouse hostage taking in which four people were killed. Davis went into hiding, but an all-out FBI search turned her up in October. She spent more than a year in jail before being released on bail (during which time Jackson was killed in prison—by guards who claimed he was trying to escape). When Davis finally stood trial in 1972, an all-white jury found insufficient evidence for conviction. ◂**1969.M** ▸**1974.4**

FILM

Probing France's War Guilt

8 France had long nurtured the legend that most Frenchmen during World War II resisted the Nazi occupation. In his 1970 film, *The Sorrow and the Pity*, French documentarian Marcel Ophüls, son of the great German émigré filmmaker Max Ophüls, asked his compatriots the child's question, "What did you do in the war, Daddy?" The honest answer rocked the nation.

The 4½-hour epic took the filmmaker to Clermont-Ferrand, a provincial town 36 miles from Vichy (seat of the wartime French puppet government) in the heart of an important Resistance region. Interviewing a cross-section of the citizenry, Ophüls probes gently but relentlessly into their occupation-era activities. A handful aided in the Resistance; others, drawn by German anti-Semitism and Anglophobia, consorted with or worked for the enemy. Most, however, collaborated passively—simply shrugging and continuing their lives. The collaborators' rationalizations are interspersed with damning material: After one man denies his town was ever occupied, Ophüls visits a German officer who was stationed there. The son-in-law of Vichy premier Pierre Laval declares that Laval "did everything to defend" the French people; historian Claude Levy testifies that Laval offered the Nazis 4,000 Jewish children they hadn't even asked for.

Ophüls shot *The Sorrow and the Pity* for French television, but the government network refused it. Said one Gaullist official: "Certain myths must not be destroyed." Premiering in a small Parisian cinema, it quickly caused a scandal. Yet the film, despite Ophüls's admitted bias, is remarkably evenhanded, allowing its subjects to tell their own stories.

Images of the Occupation: Paris's Chamber of Deputies emblazoned with a Nazi banner.

There is even a kind of exoneration from Anthony Eden, Britain's wartime foreign minister: "If you haven't experienced the horrors of the occupation," Eden cautions, "you have no right to judge." ◂**1945.17**

IDEAS

Two Feminist Landmarks

9 A pair of 1970 bestsellers added intellectual ammunition to the feminist arsenal and established their young authors as leaders of the worldwide women's movement. In *The Female Eunuch*, Germaine Greer, 31, an Australian-born, Cambridge-educated Shakespearean scholar, examined female sexuality, as well as women's psychological development and cultural history. Society's "castration of our true female personality," she wrote, had conditioned women to accept the characteristics of the eunuch: "timidity, plumpness, languor, delicacy and preciosity." The fault, she said, was not men's, but "our own, and history's"—prompting one critic to hail the book as "women's liberation's most realistic and least anti-male manifesto."

Greer's resolute independence from party-line feminism (and her disapproval of its mostly middle-class concerns), along with her flamboyance and overtly sexual image, drew fire, but her opinions, and her persona, continued to evolve. In 1984 she published *Sex and Destiny: The Politics of Human Fertility*, which castigated the West for pressuring Third World nations to restrict population growth through artificial contraception, and advocated natural forms of birth control—including abstinence. In *The Change* (1991), she brought her usual acuity to bear on the subject of menopause and female aging.

Kate Millett's *Sexual Politics: A Surprising Examination of Society's Most Arbitrary Folly* began as her doctoral thesis at Columbia University.

Refusing "to be a female impersonator," Greer sought freedom from middle-class definitions of femininity—and feminism.

The book examines the ways in which patriarchal culture imbues women with a sense of inferiority, and includes scathing critiques of Freud (particularly his theory of penis envy), D.H. Lawrence, Henry Miller, and Norman Mailer. (Mailer was so incensed, he wrote *The Prisoner of Sex* in response.) The bestseller thrust Millett uncomfortably into the spotlight. She was forced to admit her lesbianism at a feminist mass meeting; her confessional novel, *Flying* (1974), received savage reviews. She wrote about her subsequent struggle with mental illness in *The Loony-Bin Trip* (1990). ◂**1963.8** ▸**1972.V**

IN THE UNITED STATES

acutely deficient in Parkinson's sufferers. But the drug had serious side effects; worse, it lost effectiveness over time—a result that spurred the search for new treatments.

▶DESERT UTOPIA—Italian-born American architect Paolo Soleri, the founding theoretician of "arcology" (architecture and ecology), began building a small utopia in the Arizona desert in 1970. Arcosanti, as Soleri called his project, was planned as a solar-powered, self-sufficient residence for 4,500 people. Soleri and his volunteers were still at work some 25 years after construction began.

▶SEX SELLS—Americans' newfound openness about sex was reflected in the 1970 bestseller list. At least three titles purported to tell readers how to improve their sex lives. *The Sensuous Woman* by "J" reflected the heightened awareness of female sexuality (a subject that found very different expression in books by Germaine Greer and Kate Millett). Masters and Johnson's *Human Sexual Inadequacy* emphasized the clinical side of sexual dysfunction, and Dr. David Reuben's bestseller claimed to include *Everything You Always Wanted to Know About Sex But Were Afraid to Ask.* ◂**1970.9**

▶THE MIDI—The end of American women's enslavement to the fashion industry's hemline dictates can be traced almost directly to the 1970 failure of the "midi-skirt." Touted as *the* required hemline for spring, the midi's mid-calf length got a lukewarm reception from a noncomformist generation who'd grown accustomed to short skirts (or were partial to blue jeans) and who balked at investing in a whole new wardrobe. The skirts remained on store racks. ◂**1965.2**

POLITICS & BUSINESS: GNP: $1,017.1 billion ... Harry A. Blackmun appointed to Supreme Court (after Clement Haynsworth and G. Harrold Carswell rejected) ... Supreme Court rules 18-year-old vote for federal elections constitutional ... United Mine Workers presidential candidate Joseph Yablonski and his family are discovered murdered in their home (UMW president Tony Boyle convicted of killings in 1975).

"There are a lot of bleeding hearts around who just don't like to see people with helmets and guns. All I can say is, Go on and bleed.' "—**Canadian prime minister Pierre Trudeau, after declaring martial law in Quebec**

AROUND THE WORLD

▶BIBLICAL BESTSELLER—A group of British Protestant scholars translated the entire Bible directly from ancient texts into modern language for the first time in 1970 as *The New English Bible.* The best-selling volume's deviation from the resonant phrasing of the King James version created a storm of controversy. ◂1952.M

▶BASQUE SEPARATISM—Attempting to quell Basque nationalism, Spain's repressive Franco regime rounded up the movement's leaders and tried them in the city of Burgos. The 1970 military trials came after a government crackdown on the Euzakadi Ta Azkatasuna (the Basque Homeland and Liberty), the nationalist (and increasingly terrorist) branch of Europe's oldest surviving ethnic group. The ETA trials precipitated political strife throughout Spain. ◂1945.M ▸1973.11

▶OIL BONANZA—In February, drilling deep beneath the storm-swept North Sea near the northern tip of Scotland, Phillips Petroleum was the first to find what more than 100 international companies with drilling permits had been seeking for five years—oil, and lots of it. The strike appeared to be a godsend: a major oil field at

the door of politically stable, accessible Western Europe (the world's fastest-growing oil market). But Europe's dream of a transformed economy and independence from OPEC oil remained elusive, though North Sea wells increased Western Europe's scanty oil reserves and created thousands of jobs. ◂1960.M ▸1973.11

▶GOODBYE BEATLES—Eight years after recording their first single ("Love Me Do"), the most popular, influential, and inventive rock band ever had exhausted its creativity. With the Beatles' 1970 breakup came the last album the group released, the unfinished *Let It Be.* The individual members moved on to new projects. ◂1968.M ▸1980.V

In paintings like *Light Red Over Black (above),* Rothko explored the emotional qualities of color.

ART

The Rothko Scandal

10 Known for his hauntingly simple paintings—floating rectangles of subtle color that seem to glow with a spiritual light—Mark Rothko was the least flamboyant of the abstract expressionists. He disdained the "57th Street salesmen," who understood only the considerable monetary value of his work. Yet in 1970, when illness and depression drove the Russian-born artist (then 66) to commit suicide in his Manhattan studio, he touched off one of the century's tawdriest art scandals.

Rothko's funeral was attended by the leading lights of the New York art world, but his own dealer, Francis Lloyd of Marlborough Galleries, was conspicuously absent. Within three months, Lloyd managed to acquire 800 paintings from Rothko's estate for a price far below their market value. Lloyd soon became the central figure in a lawsuit brought by Rothko's daughter, Kate, charging that Lloyd and Rothko's executors had conspired to defraud the estate through self-dealing.

The four-year litigation and eight-month criminal trial—the longest and costliest legal battle in art history—exposed the prevalence of illegal and unethical practices in the supposedly genteel art business. The defendants were eventually ordered to pay $9.2 million in fines and damages; Lloyd was sentenced to 200 hours of community service. And Rothko's legacy was redivided—with roughly half going to his two children. **◂1950.4 ▸1982.10**

CANADA

Crisis in Quebec

11 In October 1970, members of the Front de libération du Québec kidnapped British diplomat James Cross from his Montreal home, demanding as ransom $500,000 in gold, the naming of an informer, and the release of 23 political prisoners. Days later, another FLQ cell abducted the provincial labor minister, Pierre Laporte. The October Crisis, as Canadians called it, rocked both Quebec province—with the largest French community outside France—and the nation.

Canada's six million French speakers, more than a quarter of the country's population, were a socially and economically disadvantaged minority. But in French-majority Quebec, the past decade had seen major progress. After 1960, when voters ousted a moribund conservative regime, the province modernized French-language schooling (previously handled by the Catholic church) and implemented ambitious social-welfare programs. Still, business and finance remained mostly in English-Canadian hands—and some Québecois saw secession as the only solution. The leftist FLQ resorted to small-scale violence, bombing Montreal mailboxes and hurling Molotov cocktails at military installations.

The 1970 kidnappings marked a significant escalation—and directly challenged Canada's prime minister. Himself a left-leaning French-Canadian, Pierre Trudeau feared being seen as soft on the FLQ. He ordered the army to Quebec and declared martial law. Nearly 500 people were detained without trial. Nonetheless, Laporte was murdered, and it took police until December to locate and free Cross, whose captors were allowed to fly to Cuba. (Laporte's killers drew life in prison.)

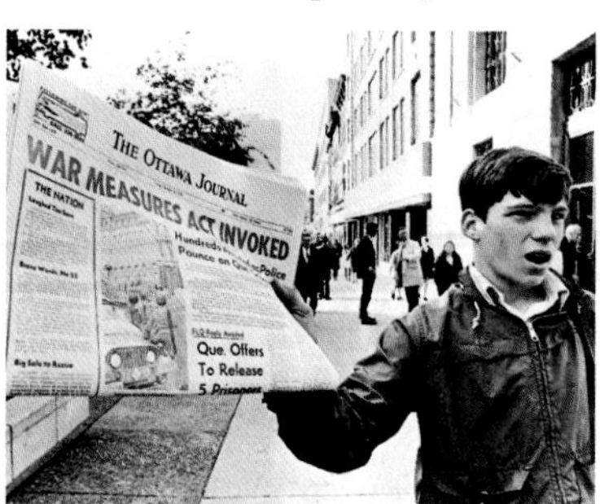

Headlines announced the peacetime invocation of Canada's War Measures Act.

After the crisis, the separatist Parti Québecois, which had won a respectable 24 percent of the vote in April provincial elections, lost more than half of its 80,000 members. **◂1968.M ▸1976.6**

THEATER

Sondheim and *Company*

12 Stephen Sondheim's tense, angular melodies and smart, biting lyrics helped reshape the American musical theater in the century's latter half. Sondheim started in the 1950s as a lyricist, for *West Side Story* and *Gypsy,* then wrote both words and music for the comedy hit *A Funny Thing Happened on the Way to the Forum.* But in 1970, with the "concept musical" *Company,* his gift for innovation fully emerged.

Bemused bachelor Robert (Dean Jones) and a married friend (Elaine Stritch) offer a drunken salute to "The Ladies Who Lunch."

Company vivisected five troubled Manhattan marriages, all coolly observed by 35-year-old Robert, the couples' unmarried, commitment-averse friend. The show's dark content was daring, but its style was revolutionary. Boris Aronson's high-tech set—a grid with platforms representing apartments—defied Broadway naturalism and epitomized urban alienation. There was no chorus: The entire cast acted, sang, and danced. Instead of a plot, there was a series of vignettes. Central ideas were conveyed in Sondheim's songs—from a couple's scabrous description of "The Little Things You Do Together" (example: "children you destroy together") to an unmarried woman's lament for "a city of strangers" ("Another Hundred People")—rather than in George Furth's book.

A critical triumph, *Company* demonstrated how to make a modern musical. But Sondheim's show-specific numbers helped finish Broadway as a prime source of popular songs. **◂1966.8 ▸1975.12**

NOBEL PRIZES: Peace: Norman E. Borlaug (U.S.; world hunger) ... Literature: Aleksandr Solzhenitsyn (U.S.S.R.; novelist) ... Chemistry: Luis Leloir (Argentine; carbohydrate biosynthesis) ... Medicine: Julius Axelrod, Ulf von Euler, and Bernard Katz (U.S., Swedish, U.K.; nerve impulses) ... Physics: Hannes Alfvén (Swedish; plasma physics) and Louis Néel (French; ferrimagnetism) ... Economics: Paul Samuelson (U.S.).

A VOICE FROM 1970

Jocks and Nerds on Campus

From *Doonesbury* by Garry Trudeau, October 26–28, 1970

Garretson Beekman Trudeau was 21 years old in 1970, the year the comic strip he'd founded for the Yale Daily News *went national.* Doonesbury*—the name is a combination of "Doone," Yalie slang for an amiable fool, and Pillsbury, Trudeau's New Haven roommate—soon appeared in more than 400 newspapers. Traces of their collegiate origin are evident in the first three syndicated strips* (below), *featuring eponymous hero Mike Doonesbury and star football player B.D. (after real Yale quarterback Brian Dowling), but* Doonesbury *grew increasingly political and irreverent. Watergate helped sharpen the satire (Nixon, Attorney General John Mitchell, and other power-wielding figures made frequent appearances). Surprisingly, so did Vietnam: By sending B.D. into the conflict, and by introducing a North Vietnamese character (Phred the Terrorist), Trudeau—who lampooned the sanctimony of the left as trenchantly (if less often) as that of the right—helped illuminate the tangled issues of a radically divisive war. In 1975,* Doonesbury *became the first comic strip to win a Pulitzer Prize. By then, many newspapers had moved it to their editorial pages.* **◄1950.6**

DOONESBURY by Garry Trudeau

1970

"The world is not doing its moral duty toward Bangladesh. Instead of condemning Pakistan for its callous, inhuman, and intemperate butchery ... most countries have taken the safe path of praising India for its relief efforts."—Indira Gandhi

STORY OF THE YEAR

The Birth of Bangladesh

1 From decades of discontent and months of slaughter a new country emerged in 1971, as East Pakistan declared itself the sovereign state of Bangladesh. Ever since Pakistan was carved out of India 24 years earlier, its eastern portion—separated from the nation's western half by 1,000 miles of Indian territory—had been denied access to political power and subjected to military rule. Pakistan's capital, Islamabad, was in the west, where the Punjabi ethnic group held sway; the east was populated by Bengalis. The only bond between the two regions—one that was increasingly strained over the years—was Islam.

In 1970, East Pakistan's nationalist Awami Party won a smashing victory in parliamentary elections, capturing a majority of seats. By all rights party leader Sheikh Mujibur Rahman should have become Pakistan's prime minister. Instead, dictator Agha Muhammad Yahya Khan suspended the National Assembly, arrested Mujibur, and sent Punjabi troops into East Pakistan to crush dissent. Civil war erupted.

Secessionist East Pakistanis threaten captives suspected of harboring loyalties to the western government.

Yahya Khan's soldiers killed some one million Bengalis in the crackdown; ten million more fled across the border into India, where the government of Indira Gandhi housed them in refugee camps. In April 1971, Awami Party chiefs, led by future president Zia-ur Rahman, proclaimed the birth of independent Bangladesh and set up a government-in-exile in Calcutta. Indo-Pakistani relations, always unfriendly, soon collapsed completely—and in December, the impetuous Yahya Khan bombed eight Indian air force bases. Now he had two enemies: separatist Bengalis and powerful India. Gandhi ordered her army to defend Bangladesh. Despite military aid from the United States, which supported Pakistan as a link in its chain of containment around the Soviet Union (Washington saw nonaligned India as a Soviet pawn), Pakistan collapsed in two weeks. For the third time since partition, India had defeated Pakistan in war.

Mujibur Rahman triumphantly assumed the premiership of Bangladesh, and the national capital was established at Dacca. But war and centuries of foreign rule (by Britain before Pakistan) had left Bangladesh in physical and economic ruin, and political stability proved elusive. Mujibur Rahman was assassinated in 1975; his successor, Zia-ur Rahman, met the same fate in 1981. ◂**1965.8** ▸**1977.4**

THE UNITED STATES

The Trials of War

2 The fissures the Vietnam War had opened in American society were starkly illuminated in 1971 by the controversy over two accused lawbreakers: Daniel Ellsberg and Lieutenant William Calley.

Four years earlier, as a government consultant, Ellsberg had helped compile a top-secret history of U.S. Indochina policy for defense secretary Robert McNamara. Like Ellsberg (but unlike then-President Johnson), McNamara had turned against the war; he wanted the sorry record preserved. But after Richard Nixon became president, officials declined to read the 47-volume study. Finally, Ellsberg decided to take it public. In June 1971, *The New York Times* and *The Washington Post* published excerpts, and after the Supreme Court blocked a federal restraining order, other newspapers followed.

The "Pentagon Papers" revealed a legacy of blunders and deceit. President Eisenhower had ignored his generals' warnings against involvement in Vietnam's civil war. President Kennedy had approved the overthrow of South Vietnamese President Diem. President Johnson's covert actions against North Vietnam had sparked the Tonkin Gulf incident; he'd later discounted reports of massive civilian casualties. The war, according to one secret document, was being fought 70 percent "to avoid a humiliating U.S. defeat" and only 10 percent for the sake of the Vietnamese.

Although the government charged him with violating secrecy laws, Ellsberg became a hero to the peace movement. Thousands of conservatives, meanwhile, rallied to Calley as he was tried for the 1968 murder of 102 unarmed men, women, and children in the South Vietnamese village of My Lai. (Troops under his command had massacred some 500 villagers.) Calley claimed he was only following orders—a defense that had been invalidated a quarter-century earlier at Nuremburg. Supporters and detractors alike believed Calley was a scapegoat for the failings of American foreign policy in Vietnam.

Opposition to the Vietnam War peaked in 1971 *(peace button, top)*. Above, Calley and his defense attorney arrive for his court martial in Fort Benning, Georgia.

Although his commanding officer, Captain Ernest Medina, was acquitted, and charges against eight other soldiers resulted either in acquittal or dismissal, Calley was convicted of 22 murders and sentenced to life in prison. Nixon quickly reduced his sentence to 20 years; in 1974 he halved it again, and in 1975 Calley was paroled. Charges against Ellsberg were dropped in 1973. ◂**1968.3**

EXPLORATION

Missions to Mars

3 In May 1971, the United States and the Soviet Union launched unmanned spacecraft to collect data about Mars in hopes of someday landing humans there. Pledging cooperation, both nations sought to take advantage of the red planet's closest proximity to earth in a 15-year cycle.

On November 14, NASA's 2,200-pound *Mariner 9* became the first spacecraft to orbit another planet. It recorded the event with television cameras and also carried remote sensing instruments—a radiometer to measure surface temperatures and spectrometers to measure surface composition and atmospheric conditions. The mission was expected to transmit over 5,000 pictures in three months. But Mars greeted its first visitor with violent planetwide dust storms. Though most of the photos were worthless, the storms offered scientists the opportunity to study Martian winds and surface erosion.

On November 27, *Mars 2* arrived—the first of two 10,000-pound Soviet orbiters. And on December 2, *Mars 3* released a capsule that made a soft landing, transmitting a video signal for 20 seconds before going dead (perhaps because of the dust). The landing was a triumph for the Soviet space program, which had recently suffered a tragic loss. In June, three veteran cosmonauts

ART & CULTURE: Books: *The Day of the Jackal* (Frederick Forsyth); *The Tenants* (Bernard Malamud); *Maurice* (E.M. Forster); *Grendel* (John Gardner); *The Book of Daniel* (E.L. Doctorow); *Honor Thy Father* (Gay Talese); *August 1914* (Aleksandr Solzhenitsyn) ... Music: *Tapestry* (Carole King, LP); *Blue* (Joni Mitchell, LP); *Who's Next* (The Who, LP); *Remembrances* (Karl Korte) ... Painting & Sculpture: *Zebra* (Marisol);

"Mars may be red, but it certainly isn't dead."—**Astronomer Carl Sagan, on *Mariner*'s photos of the volcanoes on Mars**

A model of *Mars 3*, the Automatic Interplanetary Station sent to the red planet by the Soviet space program, on display in Moscow.

—Georgi Dobrovolsky, Viktor Patsayev, and Vladislav Volko—had been returning to earth after a record-breaking 24 days in space when their cabin depressurized. The trio, who'd delighted Russians with a raucous outer-space celebration of Patsayev's 38th birthday, were found dead after the craft touched down.

When the dust storms ended in January, Mars turned out to have four huge volcanoes, an enormous canyon (ten times longer and four times deeper than the Grand Canyon), and signs of possible water erosion. Though the planet appeared to be devoid of life forms, its history had evidently been spectacular. **◂1969.1 ▸1972.M**

ECONOMICS

U.S. Severs Ties to Gold

4 Faced with a growing trade deficit, shrinking gold reserves, accelerating inflation, and rising unemployment (a combination that gave rise to the term "stagflation"), President Richard Nixon suspended U.S. gold payments in August 1971—scrapping the last vestiges of the gold standard. The dramatic attempt to kick start the economy by devaluing the dollar and improving America's trade balance scuttled the international monetary system set up during World War II at the Bretton Woods Conference, when most countries pegged their money to the dollar. Unbacked by gold, the dollar was set adrift in exchange markets to find its own level against other currencies: No country's money now had a fixed value relative to any other's.

To further bolster its wheezing economy, Washington imposed a ten percent tax on imports. European business suffered; suddenly a trade war no one wanted was imminent. "We in Europe have already gone through a major currency realignment over the past few years,"

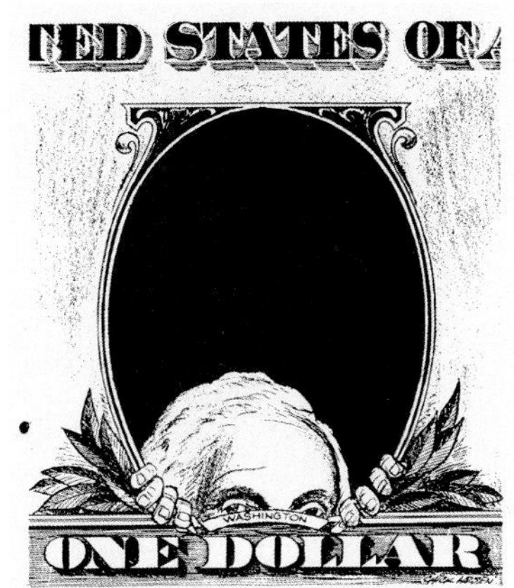

The sinking dollar alarmed many money-market watchers.

said one Swiss banker, "and I see no reason for another one now." America's problem, many believed, was neither trade (the country showed a surplus with the Common Market countries) nor exchange rates, but profligate military spending.

The dollar continued to float through the fall, showing modest declines against strong currencies, notably the Japanese yen and the West German mark. Finally, in December, the world's leading non-Communist industrial nations—the Group of Ten—met to end the monetary crisis. The dollar was devalued by 7.89 percent, and the United States canceled its import duty. Thereafter, a system of controlled floating rates prevailed in international commerce. **▸1979.M**

TECHNOLOGY

Microprocessor Revolution

5 The first electronic digital computers, built in the 1940s, had been multiton monsters. Forecasters had predicted a day when there would be perhaps a dozen giant computers situated strategically to process data from across the United States. Instead, thanks to the introduction in the late 1960s of the integrated circuit (IC)—a tiny silicon chip containing hundreds of transistors, diodes, and resistors—the computer industry developed along radically different lines. Mainframes began giving way to minicomputers (roughly the size of refrigerators) in the late 1960s.

A third generation of *micro*computers—each about the size of a TV set—was spawned by the development, in 1971, of the microprocessor. Built onto a single silicon chip containing hundreds of thousands of electronic components (a large-scale integrated circuit, or LSI), microprocessors would eventually contain all the circuitry needed for a computer to process information via a keyboard, a "mouse," or an optical scanner. Also made possible by LSI was the Random Access Memory (RAM) chip, on which data could be internally stored and updated. (RAM is distinguishable from ROM—or Read Only Memory—in that ROM permanently stores data and cannot be altered, whereas RAM is temporary.)

The microprocessor (also called the central processing unit, or CPU) enabled computers to be not just smaller but cheaper. By 1973, a microcomputer could do the work of a minicomputer costing several times as much. Microprocessors were soon found in such everyday items as automatic teller machines (ATMs), telephones, and traffic lights. And they paved the way for the "fourth generation" in computers—the PC, still a decade away. **◂1951.1 ▸1974.11**

The microprocessor *(right)* has been called a "computer on a chip."

BIRTHS

Pavel Bure, U.S.S.R.-Canadian hockey player.

Janet Evans, U.S. swimmer.

Midori Goto, Japanese-U.S. musician.

Winona Ryder, U.S. actress.

Pete Sampras, U.S. tennis player.

Arantxa Sánchez Vicario, Spanish tennis player.

Kristi Yamaguchi, U.S. figure skater.

DEATHS

Dean Acheson, U.S. statesman.

Diane Arbus, U.S. photographer.

Louis Armstrong, U.S. musician.

Hugo Black, U.S. jurist.

Margaret Bourke-White, U.S. photographer.

Ralph Bunche, U.S. diplomat.

Bennett Cerf, U.S. publisher.

Coco Chanel, French fashion designer.

Thomas Dewey, U.S. political leader.

François "Papa Doc" Duvalier, Haitian president.

Robert Tyre Jones, Jr., U.S. golfer.

Nikita Khrushchev, U.S.S.R. premier.

Sonny Liston, U.S. boxer.

Harold Lloyd, U.S. comedian and filmmaker.

György Lukács, Hungarian philosopher.

Jim Morrison, U.S. singer.

Audie Murphy, U.S. soldier and actor.

Ogden Nash, U.S. poet.

J.C. Penney, U.S. retailer.

Charles Ruggles, U.S. composer.

David Sarnoff, Russian-U.S. businessman.

Igor Stravinsky, Russian-U.S. composer.

Blue Snake **(Romare Bearden) ... Film: *The French Connection* (William Friedkin); *Klute* (Alan J. Pakula); *A Clockwork Orange* (Stanley Kubrick); *Harold and Maude* (Hal Ashby); *Death in Venice* (Luchino Visconti) ... Theater: *Butley* (Simon Gray); *The Prisoner of Second Avenue* (Neil Simon); *The House of Blue Leaves* (John Guare); *Follies* (Stephen Sondheim) ... TV: *Columbo*; *The Sonny and Cher Comedy Hour*.**

"When I hear chords not in tune, I just can't stand it. It's like spilling a great glob of tomato sauce on a white shirt."
—Pierre Boulez

NEW IN 1971

Kennedy Center (Washington, D.C.).

Ban on televised cigarette ads.

Floppy disc for computer storage (IBM).

Direct dialing between New York and London.

UN membership for People's Republic of China.

Walt Disney World (Orlando, Florida).

IN THE UNITED STATES

▶"NEW" GALAXIES—Nine California astronomers in 1971 established that Maffei I and II, stellar objects detected by Italian astronomer Paolo Maffei in 1968, were no mere curiosities: They were galaxies belonging to the Local Group, which includes the Milky Way. Maffei and the California team used radio telescopes to penetrate the veil of interstellar dust that had kept the galaxies unobserved throughout history. ◂1968.8 ▸1974.6

▶*SHAFT*—Starring Richard Roundtree as a rugged, street-smart private eye, 1971's *Shaft* set the standard for a new action genre featuring all-black casts, black slang, black settings, and black fashion. Drenched in sex and violence, driven by Isaac Hayes's funky Oscar-winning score, the 1971 hit spawned two sequels (both by original director Gordon Parks), a television series, and a host of other "blaxploitation" films, such as *Superfly* and *Cleopatra Jones*. ◂1963.M ▸1989.12

▶OFF THE ROCK—In June, federal marshals forced a group of Native American

Stage frights: Led Zeppelin's Jimmy Page *(on guitar)* and vocalist Robert Plant.

MUSIC

Zeppelin to Heaven

6 Already one of the most popular groups in rock history, Led Zeppelin released their signature song in 1971. The cryptic, rambling, eight-minute-long "Stairway to Heaven" hit the airwaves in November and stuck. Really stuck: 20 years later, FM-radio listeners still routinely voted it their all-time favorite tune. By the mid-1990s, the album containing the song *(Led Zeppelin IV)* had sold ten million copies.

Since its debut in 1969, Led Zep (as fans called the British band) had pioneered heavy metal, a musical style full of outlaw grandiosity—skull-crushing riffs, caustic vocals, and elaborate guitar solos—and influenced by classical sonatas and Indian ragas as well as down-and-dirty blues. The group's lyrics typically alternated between expressions of raw lust and mystical yearning. "Stairway," a pastiche of quasipagan imagery—divine pipers, celestial streams, May queens—appealed to the metaphysical bent of the still-thriving hippie movement. Other people simply responded to the song's lilting melody and the way it accelerated from a simple acoustic opening to a frenzied, electrified climax.

"Stairway" has been interpreted as, among other things, a marriage of pastoral harmony and atomic-age aggression, and a paean to the devil. (American Christian fundamentalists swore they could hear Satanic incantations when they played the song backward.) The band did nothing to discourage speculation about its beliefs—putting esoteric diagrams on its album covers and indulging in orgiastic excesses of sex and drugs. Guitarist Jimmy Page was especially fascinated with the occult. But the whiff of evil only added to Led Zeppelin's allure: By the time the group disbanded in 1980, it had secured the status of legend. **◂1970.4 ▸1969.10**

LITERATURE

A Nobel for Neruda

7 When the Nobel Prize committee awarded Chile's Pablo Neruda the 1971 prize for literature—"For poetry that, with the action of an elemental force, brings alive a continent's destiny and dreams"—many readers thought the honor long overdue. Born in 1904, Neruda had early on committed himself to a poetic search "for something common to my own people and to the people of the world." In the process, he'd become a hero to millions, in Spanish-speaking nations and beyond.

Neruda's search had taken many forms: from the exquisite lyricism of *Twenty Love Poems and a Song of Despair* (the 1924 collection that won him popular and critical acclaim), to the surrealism of *Residence on Earth* (1935), to the eloquent social criticism of the epic *General Song* (1950), and finally to the simpler tone of his later poems of love and protest. It had also led him into politics. Neruda served his country in various diplomatic positions; as a consul in Madrid during the Spanish Civil War, he became an ardent supporter of the leftist Republicans. In 1945, he was elected to the Chilean senate as a Communist—and when that party was outlawed, he went into exile. (He returned in 1953.)

The Nobel prize, coming shortly after President Salvador Allende (a Marxist) appointed him ambassador to France, gave Neruda cause for guarded optimism: "Poets believe in miracles and this time it has happened—it would seem." But he soon left his position due to ill health, dying just days after Allende's fatal fall from power in 1973. The poet's funeral grew into an impassioned demonstration against the new military regime. **◂1970.2 ▸1973.4**

MUSIC

Boulez at the Baton

8 The most insecure of the 1,100 orchestras operating in the United States in the late sixties and early seventies managed to weather changing tastes and budgetary crises by incorporating rock music into their programs or desperately focusing on tried and true composers. The nation's oldest orchestra, the New York Philharmonic, pointedly bucked this trend in autumn 1971 by appointing Pierre Boulez—France's most important (and innovative) postwar composer and avant-garde music's most outspoken champion—to take over as its music director from retiring Leonard Bernstein.

Boulez, 46, had a reputation as a firebrand and an iconoclast. (When asked, "What do we do about opera?" he had once replied, "Blow up all the opera houses.") At the Philharmonic, he avoided standards by Bach, Beethoven, and Brahms in favor of lesser-known works by

Wags called Boulez, a booster of contemporary music, the 20th-Century Limited.

SPORTS: Baseball: World Series, Pittsburgh Pirates defeat Baltimore Orioles, 4–3 ... Football: Super Bowl, Baltimore Colts defeat Dallas Cowboys, 16–13 ... Basketball: NBA, Milwaukee Bucks defeat Baltimore Bullets, 4–0 ... Tennis: Billie Jean King is first female athlete to earn over $100,000 in a year ... Golf: Lee Trevino wins British, Canadian, and U.S. Opens in one month.

"A host who combines the duties of a headwaiter and a historian."—**Alistair Cooke, on his role in PBS's *Masterpiece Theatre***

Lizst, Wagner, and Berlioz, and presented such "difficult" twentieth-century composers as Mahler, Prokofiev, and Schoenberg. He even exchanged the players' tailcoats for tuxedos. The conductor offered no apology to listeners who stormed out of concerts and canceled their season's subscriptions: He described himself as "a gardener pruning away the deadwood, so that the tree will come back even stronger." Though not always impressed with his interpretations, cognoscenti were uniformly awed by his unerring ear and unbending intelligence.

A pioneer of electronic composition, Boulez referred to his own turbulent, mathematically derived style (a radical extension of Schoenberg's atonal twelve-tone system) as "organized delirium." When he left the Philharmonic in 1977, it was to devote himself more fully to vanguard pursuits—most notably, running the Institut de Recherche et de Coordination Acoustique-Musique in Paris, then the world's foremost laboratory for electronic music. **◄1957.9 ►1971.9**

MUSIC

Pinky and Yo-Yo

9 In 1971, as Pierre Boulez began his controversial stewardship of the New York Philharmonic, violinist Pinchas Zukerman and cellist Yo-Yo Ma gave New York solo debut recitals that established them as two of the most promising classical musicians of their era.

"Pinky" was born in Israel to concentration-camp survivors; Ma was born in France to Chinese émigrés. Yet their stories had striking parallels. Both prodigies had received early guidance from violinist Isaac Stern and cellist-conductor Pablo Casals. Both had pursued their musical studies at New York's Juilliard School. And now each of their Manhattan recitals won raves from a *New York Times* critic. Zuckerman, 22 (whose performance with Stern the previous year at Lincoln Center had been highly praised), was lauded for playing everything from Schubert to Schoenberg with an "absolute interpretive authority and complete mastery of the violin." Ma, 15 (who'd been presented to a national television audience by Leonard Bernstein eight years earlier), interpreted works running from Beethoven to Hindemith with "a quality to make many an older man green with envy."

In subsequent years both artists secured their standing at the apex

Cello prodigy Ma in the early 1970s.

of the classical music establishment. Ma won the coveted Avery Fisher Prize in 1978, while Zuckerman, who was also a conductor, became music director of the St. Paul (Minnesota) Chamber Orchestra in 1980. **◄1971.8**

POPULAR CULTURE

Americans Import Culture

10 By 1971, American television was known around the world as a source of brash, lowbrow diversion—game shows, cop shows, adventure series, situation comedies. Gone from the nation's commercial airwaves were the powerful theatrical productions of the 1950s; only one weekly drama series remained, even on public television. But in January, an English import brought "high-brow" entertainment back to American screens. Introduced by Boston public station WGBH-TV and distributed through the country's non-profit network, *Masterpiece Theatre* repackaged impeccably literate British productions—starting with "The First Churchills," a twelve-part saga from the BBC—for Americans.

The series (conceived by British-born WGBH producer Christopher Sarson) won rapturous reviews and a fiercely loyal following. Key to its appeal was the white-haired English émigré host, Alistair Cooke. An Anglophile's dream, Cooke set the scene before each week's episode.

Although the shows regularly won Emmy awards, ratings remained low until January 1974, when the masters-and-servants drama "Upstairs, Downstairs" captivated huge audiences. The show, produced by London Weekend Television, ran for three months and was followed by three equally popular sequels. Its success belatedly spurred the commercial networks to run dramatic series, beginning with 1977's *Roots* on ABC. Critics, however, complained that *Masterpiece Theatre*—because it represented the sort of tame, nonthreatening fare that corporate America likes to fund—helped lead public television far astray of its original mission as a public tribune and a voice for the disenfranchised. **◄1956.M ►1977.5**

PBS introduced *Masterpiece Theatre* with "The First Churchills" *(above)*. Critics complained that American public television was becoming a BBC subsidiary.

IN THE UNITED STATES

activists off Alcatraz Island, in San Francisco Bay. Invoking an 1868 treaty that gave Indians the right to unoccupied government land, the 89 demonstrators had occupied "The Rock"—site of a notoriously strict federal prison from 1934 to 1963—for more than a year and a half. Their demand was not for Alcatraz but for fair treatment from the government, which had a history of unilaterally abrogating treaties signed with Native Americans. In 1972, Alcatraz became part of a national park. ►1973.M

►ATTICA PRISON RIOT—On September 9, at overcrowded Attica State Prison, east of Buffalo, New York, some 1,200 inmates took 30 guards and

other prison employees hostage and gained control of a large portion of the prison. The rebels demanded penal reforms and amnesty for the riot, but negotiations broke down and Governor Nelson Rockefeller ordered state police *(above)* to secure Attica. The insurrection ended four days after it began, when 1,500 law enforcement officers opened fire, killing 28 inmates and nine guards. New York officials said inmates had killed the guards, but an investigation showed that all the victims died from police gunfire. ►1977.M

►QUEEN OF COUNTRY—Country music star Loretta Lynn had her biggest hit yet in 1971 with her autobiographical song "Coal Miner's Daughter" (also the title of her bestselling 1976 autobiography and a 1980 biopic starring Sissy Spacek). Born in Kentucky mining country in 1935, Lynn (who was married at 14 and the mother of four by 18) started singing professionally in 1961. A three-time Country Music Association Female Vocalist of the Year, she was the first woman in country music to earn a million dollars. In 1980, she was named performer of the decade by the Academy of Country Music. ◄1961.M

POLITICS & BUSINESS: GNP: $1,104.9 billion ... Supreme Court rules busing for desegregation constitutional ... Supreme Court justices Hugo Black and John Harlan resign (Lewis Powell and William Rehnquist appointed) ... Ellsberg and Russo indicted for unauthorized possession of the Pentagon Papers ... Congress authorizes federal bailout of Lockheed Corporation ... General Motors recalls 6,700,000 Chevrolets.

"I don't call the fighting in my films violence. I call it action. An action film borders somewhere between reality and fantasy."
—Bruce Lee

AROUND THE WORLD

▶HAPPY BIRTHDAY TO THE SHAH—Muhammad Reza Pahlevi, the Shah of Iran, threw a spectacular party in October to commemorate the 2,500th anniversary of the Persian empire of Cyrus the Great. Heads of state and high-ranking officials were on hand for the weeklong, $200 million birthday celebration, during which the Shah equated himself with Cyrus and with the state of Iran. The festivities took place amid famine, political repression, and growing radical resentment of the Shah's regime. ◀1953.4 ▶1979.1

▶INVASION OF LAOS—Supported by American artillery and aircraft, more than 12,000 South Vietnamese troops invaded Laos on February 13 in an attempt to shut down the Ho Chi Minh Trail—Hanoi's supply route through Laos to South Vietnam. South Vietnamese president Nguyen Van Thieu called the incursion an "act of legitimate self-defense," but U.S. participation in the attack on a nominally neutral country was widely criticized. The invaders were repelled, and on March 18 American pilots airlifted 1,000 South Vietnamese troops out of Laos. ◀1970.1 ▶1975.4

▶CONCERT FOR A CAUSE—In 1971 ex-Beatle George Harrison organized the Concert for Bangladesh, the charitable extravaganza that became the model for such future rock crusades as Live Aid and Farm Aid. Ravi Shankar *(below)*, Harrison's mentor on the sitar,

headlined the New York event (two sold-out shows), which included performances by Eric Clapton, Leon Russell, and surprise guest Bob Dylan. Never comfortable with his instrument's pop associations—the sitar was embraced in the mid-sixties by the drug counterculture—Shankar also released *Concerto for Sitar* that same year, an album made with conductor-composer-pianist André Previn. ◀1970.M

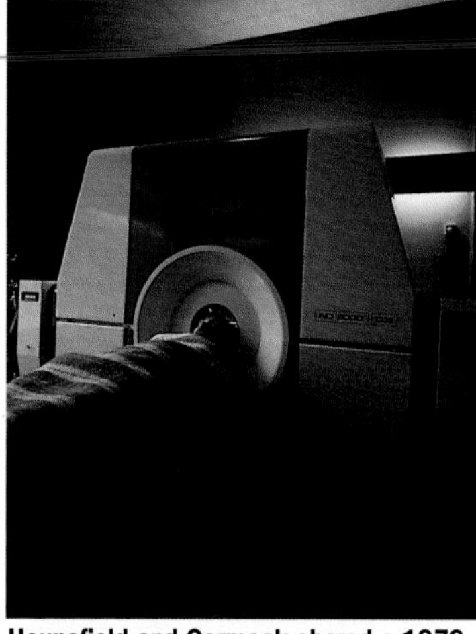

Hounsfield and Cormack shared a 1979 Nobel for designing the CAT scanner.

MEDICINE

A Diagnostic Marvel

11 Computerized axial tomography (CAT) scanning, introduced in 1971, was one of the most important diagnostic breakthroughs since Röntgen's 1895 discovery of X-rays. Taking cross-sectional pictures of the body ("tomography" derives from the Greek word for slice), the new technology allowed doctors to "see" for the first time the soft tissue inside the skull, chest, and abdomen without surgery.

The first CAT scanner, designed to produce sharp images of the brain, was masterminded by Godfrey Hounsfield of the British firm EMI. (Allan Cormack, of Tufts University in Massachusetts, developed a similar device.) The EMI Scanner hooked up an X-ray machine to a digital computer, enabling radiologists to distinguish normal from clotted blood and to examine the ventricles that hold cerebrospinal fluid. (Previously it had been necessary to pump air into the ventricles—a painful and unpleasant procedure—to achieve a readable X-ray.)

Variations on the invention soon appeared—notably, the full-body CAT scanner, which required a patient to lie for lengthy periods inside a coffin-like cylinder. In the late 1970s, magnetic resonance imaging (MRI) further revolutionized medicine. Using very high frequency radio waves in a strong magnetic field to align the body's atoms for optimal computer evaluation, MRIs produce sharp images of the body's inner workings, particularly processes involving liquid motion. These high-tech medical tools were expensive (early CAT scanners cost around half a million dollars), but doctors and hospitals coveted them—as much for their ability to attract patients as for their proficiency in detecting nascent tumors and incipient hemorrhages. As health-care costs skyrocketed in the mid-1970s, the widespread use of scanners (especially in the United States) drew criticism. **◀1960.4**

FILM

An Action Icon

12 A national crime wave in the United States and a Nixon-era preoccupation with law-and-order helped make 1971 a banner year for cops-and-robbers movies. At the Academy Awards, *The French Connection* carried the day, winning five Oscars, including best actor for star Gene Hackman. And at the box office, a modestly budgeted action film starring Clint Eastwood was an unexpected smash. *Dirty Harry,* produced and directed by B-movie master (and idol of France's nouvelle vague) Don Siegel, introduced audiences to Harry Callahan, a sadistic and voyeuristic San Francisco detective with a habit of acting as judge, jury, and executioner. Callahan was not the first macho icon the squinty-eyed, raspy-voiced Eastwood had portrayed: In the sixties, after winning fame as Rowdy Yates on television's *Rawhide*, he'd played the super-gunslinger known as The Man with No Name in three blood-soaked "spaghetti westerns" made by Italian director Sergio Leone.

When Eastwood, who also directed and starred in the chilling *Play Misty for Me* in 1971, appeared on the cover of *Life*, the accompanying caption read: "The world's favorite movie star is—no kidding—Clint Eastwood!" By the 1990s, he'd filmed four more portraits of Callahan and had become one of Hollywood's most respected talents, winning an Oscar for Best Picture, for directing 1992's *Unforgiven*, in which he also starred. **◀1959.7 ▶1971.13**

As hard-bitten cop Harry Callahan, Eastwood shot first, asked questions later.

FILM

The Dragon Arrives

13 His portrayal of Kato on the TV series *The Green Hornet* had gained Chinese-American actor and martial-arts expert Bruce Lee a cult following in the 1960s. But it was *Fists of Fury*, Lee's first collaboration with Hong Kong producer Raymond Chow, in 1971, that launched him as an international star.

Critics widely dismissed the film, which smashed box-office records throughout Asia, as typical

After his breakthrough kung-fu hit, *Fists of Fury (above)*, Lee went on to become the most watched movie star in the world.

"chop-socky" fare, with ludicrous dialogue, a rudimentary plot (involving a drug-smuggling ring based in an ice factory), and wooden characters. But its star stood out as an actor, a fighter, and a choreographer. Lee aimed to create a superior type of martial-arts film, with better moves, fewer weapons, and more sophisticated dramatic values. *Enter the Dragon* and *Return of the Dragon*, both released in 1973, established him as the genre's leading figure, sparked interest in martial arts, and helped bring Hong Kong cinema to the attention of Western cineastes.

Lee's balletic style—he could dispatch a handful of villains in a single leap—has been compared with Rudolf Nureyev's. His 1973 death at age 32, from cerebral edema, left a vacuum in the genre. **◀1971.12**

NOBEL PRIZES: Peace: Willy Brandt (German; *Ostpolitik*) ... Literature: Pablo Neruda (Chilean; poet) ... Chemistry: Gerhard Herzberg (Canadian; electronic structure and free radicals) ... Medicine: Earl W. Sutherland, Jr. (U.S.; hormonal mechanisms) ... Physics: Dennis Gabor (U.K.; holography) ... Economics: Simon Kuznets (U.S.).

A VOICE FROM 1971

America's Favorite Blowhard

From *All in the Family*, by Norman Lear, January 12, 1971

At a time when American situation comedies were all innocuous humor and lovable characters, All in the Family *offered satire and obdurately bigoted Archie Bunker. In producer Norman Lear's show, based on a British hit called* Till Death Do Us Part, *working-class, middle-aged Archie lived down to hard-hat stereotypes—head of the house, he browbeat his wife, Edith, and feminist adult daughter, Gloria, endlessly insulted his liberal son-in-law, Michael (whom he called "Meathead"), and salted his garbled speech with ethnic slurs. But Archie was a toothless monarch—his influence ended at the edge of his easy-chair throne—and obtuseness deflected his barbs. The joke was on him. After its January 1971 premiere, scripted by Lear himself and excerpted below,* All in the Family *became a piece of the culture it commented on. When the program was retired in 1978, the Smithsonian Institution added Archie's chair to its collection of artifacts.* ◄**1951.9** ►**1988.M**

Fade up: (The table. The family is eating. Table talk. One change in mood. They are wearing paper party hats.)

ARCHIE: Gimme over the ketchup there, will ya?

GLORIA: Ketchup on eggs? Daddy, really!

ARCHIE: "Daddy Really's" been eatin' ketchup on eggs since before you was born, little girl, so don't let it concern ya, huh? *(He belches.)*

EDITH: Archie, that's terrible.

GLORIA: *(getting up)* Well, who's for more eggs?

EDITH: Sure I can't help you, dear?

GLORIA: Not today, Mom. Today you sit. If I need any help, Michael can do it.

ARCHIE: It won't do him no harm neither. The last time I seen him lift a hand around here, he was testing his deodorant.

GLORIA: Mom!

EDITH: Archie—leave him alone!

MIKE: Ya! What do you want from me, anyway! I don't have *time* to do anything. I'm in class six hours, I'm studying six hours. It's not easy going to college; it's hard work!

ARCHIE: For you, it's like building the pyramids; I'll tell you, studyin' sociology, and all that welfare stuff—I don't call that no hard work!

GLORIA: Oh, leave him alone, Daddy. I think it's beautiful that Michael wants to help the underprivileged.

ARCHIE: He wants to help the underprivileged, let him start with himself. He's got no brains. He's got no ambition, and if that ain't underprivileged, I don't know what is.

GLORIA: *(stands)* That's it! Mother, we're moving out of here. I'm not gonna stay here another minute to see my husband insulted like that.

EDITH: *(an arm around Gloria's waist)* Archie, say you're sorry! If she leaves here, she'll be dead inside a year.

ARCHIE: You don't have to worry. They ain't goin' nowheres.

EDITH: You don't know what it is, Archie. She can't be cleaning an apartment and cookin' and marketing—Dr. Feinstein says she's anemic.

ARCHIE: Don't gimme that. For ten bucks some of these doctors'll tell ya anything you wanta hear.

EDITH: He's the best there is when it comes to blood. My own cousin from the hospital said so.

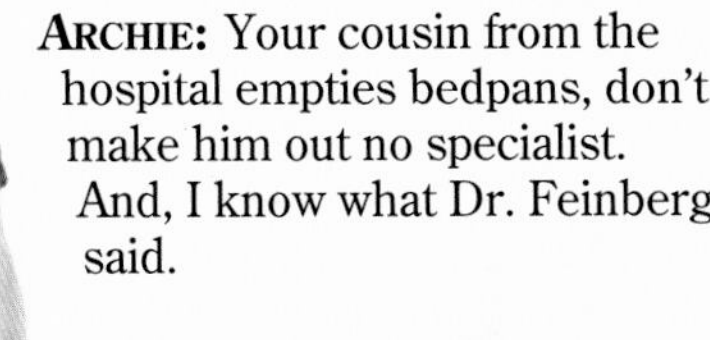

ARCHIE: Your cousin from the hospital empties bedpans, don't make him out no specialist. And, I know what Dr. Feinberg said.

EDITH: Fein*stein*—

ARCHIE: Feinstein, Feinberg, it all comes to the same thing, and I know that tribe.

The Bunker family, from top left: Michael (Rob Reiner), Gloria (Sally Struthers), Edith (Jean Stapleton), and Archie (Carroll O'Connor). Top, Archie in his museum-worthy armchair.

"The bastards have never been bombed like they're going to be bombed this time."—**U.S. president Richard Nixon, May 1972**

STORY OF THE YEAR

America Withdraws from Vietnam

1 In March 1972, 120,000 North Vietnamese regulars stormed into South Vietnam. The invasion, supported by Viet Cong guerrillas, took the American and South Vietnamese armies by surprise. With only 6,000 U.S. combat troops remaining in the country, the policy of Vietnamization—preparing South Vietnam to defend itself without outside help—proved a resounding failure. As Quangtri Province fell to Hanoi's troops, America's giant B-52s bombed North Vietnam with unprecedented fury. The North's harbors were mined to cut off supplies. Yet by August, when the last U.S. combat unit was deactivated on schedule, the Communists were still advancing.

One of the war's most haunting images shows the aftermath of napalm dropped by mistake in June 1972 on the friendly village of Trang Bang.

On the diplomatic front, however, they suffered a setback: Nixon's visits to China and the Soviet Union earlier in the year undermined Hanoi's relations with its backers. So in October, North Vietnam's negotiator at the Paris peace talks, Le Duc Tho, offered a compromise. If Communist troops were allowed to stay in the South after a cease-fire, Hanoi would not insist on immediately replacing Saigon's Thieu regime with a new government; the Vietnamese could reach a settlement among themselves at a later date. U.S. negotiator Henry Kissinger agreed, saying the plan allowed a "decent interval" between American disengagement and any political upheaval. Although Thieu balked, Kissinger announced that peace was "at hand." Days later, Nixon won reelection over dovish Democrat George McGovern by a landslide.

Kissinger promptly reversed himself, insisting that Northern forces withdraw from the South; Le refused, and added conditions to his original offer. In December, Nixon ordered saturation bombing of Hanoi and Haiphong. The "Christmas bombing" aroused worldwide protest but placated Thieu, who saw it as a sign that he would never be completely abandoned. A treaty closely resembling Le's October plan was signed on January 27, 1973.

Nixon claimed to have won "peace with honor." But America's longest war had ended in its first military defeat—by a tiny, technologically less advanced country, at a cost of 57,000 American lives. And for the people of Indochina, the killing was far from over. **◂1971.2 ▸1973.8**

DIPLOMACY

Nixon in China

2 After 20 years of hostility, the People's Republic of China and the United States achieved a dramatic détente in 1972. On February 21, as a captivated world watched on television, President Nixon arrived in China for a series of meetings with Premier Zhou Enlai and Chairman Mao Zedong. A bilateral foreign-policy about-face, the visit ended an era during which China regarded the United States as "the most ferocious enemy of the people throughout the world," and Washington refused even to recognize the existence of the People's Republic.

The incentive for the summit was the growing antagonism between China and the Soviet Union. Beijing began making friendly gestures toward Washington in 1969, after skirmishes broke out on the Sino-Soviet border. Two years later, China scored a public-relations coup when it invited the U.S. table tennis team for a visit. "Ping-Pong diplomacy" convinced many Americans that the Communist monolith, long a central concept of their nation's foreign policy, was a myth. Nixon, a proven hardliner, could exploit the situation without being charged with softness on Communism. "Beijing needed us to break out of its isolation," said National Security Council chief Henry Kissinger, who traveled secretly to China in July 1971. Washington, in turn, needed Beijing for leverage against Moscow.

President Nixon *(center)* and his wife, Pat *(far right)*, joined China's leaders at a state dinner in Shanghai.

Motivated in part by Kissinger's groundbreaking mission (made public upon his return), the United Nations admitted China and expelled Taiwan. The vote reversed the UN (and U.S.) position, held since Mao's 1949 triumph over Chiang Kai-shek, that Chiang's Nationalist regime on Taiwan was China's true government. Nixon's visit produced the Shanghai communiqué, in which the two countries, while acknowledging basic differences, announced a desire to improve relations. Gifts were exchanged—from China, a pair of giant pandas; from America, a pair of musk oxen. The effect on American popular culture was immediate: a vogue for all things Chinese, from food to acupuncture. **◂1949.1 ▸1976.1**

UGANDA

Amin Expels Asians

3 In August 1972, Uganda's ruler, General Idi Amin, gave all resident Asians who were not Ugandan citizens (60,000 out of a total 75,000) 90 days to leave the country. The move—which Amin hoped would distract Ugandans' attention from a collapsing economy—drew worldwide condemnation. Among Ugandans, there was celebration: The Asians, who dominated the nation's commerce and professions, were an envied minority. Most of the confiscated businesses, however, went to army officers, who ran them into bankruptcy.

The roots of Uganda's troubles lay in the colonial era. The British (who'd never settled heavily in Uganda) had focused development efforts on the colony's Buganda region and groomed the indigenous Ganda ethnic group (20 percent of Uganda's population) for national leadership. As a result, the Ganda were widely resented. After Uganda gained independence in 1962, President Milton Obote beefed up the army, giving it free rein to suppress the Ganda. Commanding the operation was Amin, an uneducated former boxer who'd come up through the colonial army's ranks.

In 1971, while the unpopular Obote was away, Amin led the army in his overthrow. Amin's followers, from his own West Nile region, massacred soldiers belonging to ethnic groups from Obote's area. Subsequently, Amin further expanded the army and squandered

ART & CULTURE: Books: *The Chant of Jimmy Blacksmith* (Thomas Keneally); *The Needle's Eye* (Margaret Drabble); *Surfacing* (Margaret Atwood); *The Best and the Brightest* (David Halberstam) ... Music: "American Pie" (Don McLean); "Morning Has Broken" (Stevens and Farjeon); "You're So Vain" (Carly Simon); *Rocky Mountain High* (John Denver, LP); *The Cave of Winds* (Lukas Foss) ... Painting & Sculpture:

"This is our Sharpeville. We will never forget it."—**Northern Irish MP Bernadette Devlin, on the killings in Londonderry**

Uganda's meager funds on arms; his troops began to terrorize civilians and foreigners as well. Known to Ugandans as "Big Daddy," the mercurial Amin swung from clownish humor to paranoid tirades. He had several cabinet members killed, and after breaking ties with Israel (a former patron) in exchange for Libyan aid, he announced his approval of the Nazi Holocaust.

The economic chaos worsened after the Asian exodus. And a botched invasion by Ugandan exiles (backed by Tanzania) in September 1972 made Amin more belligerent than ever. By the time Tanzanian forces ousted him in 1979, his regime had murdered up to 300,000 people. **◂1901.7 ▸1976.M**

NORTHERN IRELAND

Another Bloody Sunday

4 Defying a government ban, 10,000 Northern Irish civil rights demonstrators marched on January 30, 1972, from the Bogside Catholic ghetto to Londonderry center. A cordon of British troops awaited them. Each side usually enacted a timeworn routine: The protesters moved forward; the army cut them off; troublemakers threw stones; the army retaliated with tear gas, water cannons, and rubber bullets; the crowd broke up and drifted home. But on this particular day, known afterward as Bloody Sunday, the army abandoned the script. It opened fire on the throng and killed 13 unarmed Catholic men.

"This community," said a priest who witnessed the massacre, "will never accept the British Army again." An IRA terrorist was more blunt: "Our immediate goal is to shoot and kill as many British soldiers as possible." Deployed in Northern Ireland in 1969 to quell rising sectarian violence, the British Army, to many Catholics, was an extension of the discriminatory provincial government. A policy of internment, whereby the army rounded up thousands of suspects and imprisoned them indefinitely without trial, especially rankled, as did the army's sudden searches of Catholic homes and apartments.

Bloody Sunday pricked wounds dating back to the twelfth century, when England launched its conquest of Ireland. For the first time in the current round of troubles, violence spilled into the Republic of Ireland. On February 2, a day of mourning for the Londonderry dead, rioters burned down the British embassy in Dublin. In March, London suspended Northern Ireland's Protestant-controlled parliament, ending 50 years of unsuccessful home rule. Though ecstatic at the demise of the hated local government, Catholic activists continued to agitate against the army, which remained everywhere present in Northern Ireland, a country at war with itself and its ghosts. **◂1969.2 ▸1973.6**

TERRORISM

Massacre at the Olympics

5 The first Olympiad held in Germany since World War II might have been a symbol of reconciliation. Instead, the 1972 Munich games became a spectacle of horror—and, in an eerie echo of the Nazi era, the victims were Jews. Before dawn on September 5, commandos of the PLO group Black September (for the month in 1970 when Jordanian troops defeated Palestinian guerrillas) scaled a fence guarding the Olympic Village. They forced their way into the dormitory housing Israel's team, killed two coaches, and took nine hostages—including, it turned out, two Israeli undercover security officers. (Fourteen team members escaped.)

During negotiations with West German officials, a hooded Palestinian terrorist ventured onto an Olympic Village balcony.

Beginning a daylong standoff, 12,000 policemen surrounded the village.

The commandos demanded the release of 200 guerrillas from Israeli jails, but Prime Minister Golda Meir refused. West German officials negotiated with the terrorists, who snubbed an Arab League representative rushed to the scene. The eight Palestinians refused ransom, as well as the negotiators' offer to trade places with the hostages. But they did postpone their noon deadline for killing the captives, and eventually accepted a guarantee of safe passage to Cairo with their prisoners.

That night, helicopters flew the Black Septembrists and the Israelis to a military airport, where a Lufthansa plane waited on the tarmac. But as two terrorists left the helicopters, police sharpshooters opened fire. When the smoke cleared, five of the commandos and one policeman lay dead—and all the hostages had been murdered.

In a controversial decision, the Olympic Committee declared that the Games must go on. The surviving Israeli athletes went home, however, and their government bombed Palestinian camps in Syria and Lebanon. **◂1970.3 ▸1972.8**

A small country's hatreds *(above, IRA members being pinned down by British soldiers)* turned Londonderry into a war zone.

BIRTHS

Michael Chang, U.S. tennis player.

Jamal Mashburn, U.S. basketball player.

Shaquille O'Neal, U.S. basketball player.

DEATHS

Charles Atlas, Italian-U.S. physical-education instructor.

John Berryman, U.S. poet.

William Boyd, U.S. actor.

James Byrnes, U.S.statesman.

Maurice Chevalier, French actor and singer.

Francis Chichester, U.K. aviator and yachtsman.

Roberto Clemente, Puerto Rican baseball player.

Edward VIII, Duke of Windsor, U.K. king.

Frederick IX, Danish king.

Rudolf Friml, Czech-U.S. composer.

J. Edgar Hoover, U.S. FBI chief.

Mahalia Jackson, U.S. singer and civil rights activist.

Edward Kendall, U.S. biochemist.

Louis Leakey, U.K. anthropologist.

Marianne Moore, U.S. poet.

Kwame Nkrumah, Ghanaian president.

Lester Pearson, Canadian prime minister.

Ezra Pound, U.S. poet.

Adam Clayton Powell, Jr., U.S. congressman.

Jackie Robinson, U.S. baseball player.

Hans Scharoun, German architect.

Paul Henri Spaak, Belgian premier.

Harry S Truman, U.S. president.

Edmund Wilson, U.S. writer.

Walter Winchell, U.S. journalist.

***Mao* (Andy Warhol); *Seedbed* (Vito Acconci) ... Film: *The Godfather* (Francis Ford Coppola); *The Discreet Charm of the Bourgeoisie* (Luis Buñuel) ... Theater: *Jumpers* (Tom Stoppard); *Moonchildren* (Michael Welle); *That Championship Season* (Jason Miller); *Sticks and Bones* (David Rabe); *Grease* (Jacobs and Casey) ... TV: *The Waltons*; *M*A*S*H*; *The Streets of San Francisco*.**

"The fact they haven't built camels is really remarkable."—**Dean Thornton of the U.S.-based Boeing Aircraft, on the Airbus**

NEW IN 1972

Home Box Office.

Enkephalin painkiller (developed by Dr. John Hughes).

Nike shoes.

Commercially successful video game (Pong, from Atari).

IN THE UNITED STATES

▶EAGLETON DROPPED—In what advocates for mental-health enlightenment called a great setback, Democratic presidential candidate George McGovern dropped his running mate, Missouri senator Thomas Eagleton, from the ticket in July after it was revealed that Eagleton had suffered bouts of serious depression for which he'd been treated with electric-shock therapy. Eagleton's replacement was JFK brother-in-law Sargent Shriver, an attorney and the first director of the Peace Corps, who'd never held elective office. In November, the McGovern-Shriver ticket carried only Massachusetts and Washington, D.C. ▸1972.10

▶WALLACE SHOT—On May 15, while campaigning in Laurel, Maryland, for the 1972 Democratic presidential nomination, segregationist Alabama governor George Wallace was shot by 21-year-old Arthur Bremer and permanently paralyzed. (Three other people were injured.) Wallace—who'd gained national attention in 1963 when he physically barred black students from entering the University of Alabama—withdrew from the race, but ran again four years later. ◂1963.7

▶MISSION ACCOMPLISHED—Having made the last of its six projected lunar landings, the remarkably fertile Apollo program ended on December 19 when *Apollo 17* splashed

AVIATION

The Flying Bus

6 The A300 Airbus, the first wide-body passenger plane produced in Europe, made its maiden flight on October 28, 1972. The plane was made by a unique consortium of five different aircraft companies in France, Germany, the Netherlands, Spain and Great Britain; parts were shipped from those countries (whose governments had provided $380 million in development funds) to the Aérospatiale assembly plant in Toulouse, France, in an oversized cargo plane called the Super Guppy.

American aviation experts dismissively compared the A300 to an ungainly camel—"a horse designed by a committee," as the old joke went. But the economical, 280-passenger plane was perfect for the high-density, short-to-medium-distance European routes. The Airbus ran on twin turbofan engines, instead of the four engines used in Boeing 747s, and its technologically advanced wings minimized the distance required for takeoff and landing. Early sales were bolstered by orders from state-run airlines like Air France and Lufthansa. And though U.S. companies protested that government subsidies gave the Europeans an unfair advantage, they were not able to prevent the successful marketing of Airbus planes to North American airlines, including TWA, Delta, and Air Canada.

By 1992, Airbus Industrie had seized 30 percent of the world market for jet passenger planes, seriously challenging the long-dominant American aircraft industry. **◂1958.6 ▸1977.9**

Airbuses began rolling off the lines in Toulouse in 1972.

Backed by nuclear stockpiles, Brezhnev and Nixon felt free to talk.

DIPLOMACY

Summit in Moscow

7 In May 1972, weeks after his historic rapprochement with China, Richard Nixon became the first U.S. president to visit the Soviet Union. Nixon was barely off the plane before he and Communist Party chairman Leonid Brezhnev plunged into "businesslike" talks. Though conflict over the war in Southeast Asia intruded repeatedly, the weeklong series of meetings on trade, scientific cooperation, and arms control was the most productive American-Soviet powwow since World War II.

The central achievement of the summit was two strategic arms limitation treaties—together known as SALT I—that restricted defensive antiballistic missile systems (ABMs) and temporarily froze offensive nuclear weapons. (In giving up defensive missiles, each side abandoned a shield that might give it confidence to attack.) The two powers also agreed to embark on a joint space program—realized in 1975 with the Apollo-Soyuz space docking.

Although Nixon had won overwhelming praise for his China breakthrough, many U.S. right-wingers accused him of an ideological sellout with this new feat of détente. The charge deeply rankled his already troubled administration. But most citizens—American and Soviet—accepted the easing of relations gratefully, if skeptically. The two governments, for a time at least, had stopped talking about each other's burial. **◂1969.8 ▸1977.M**

EGYPT

Sadat Expels Soviets

8 Egypt's President Anwar al-Sadat expelled some 15,000 Soviet military personnel from his nation in July 1972—a bold reversal of his predecessor's reliance on Moscow for security and technical assistance. Egypt's power brokers had selected Sadat as Gamal Abdal Nasser's successor (and 90 percent of the electorate had confirmed him), believing him to be an orthodox Nasserite who would perpetuate that dictator's policies. But in various ways—a partial lifting of restrictions on free speech, a purge of leftists from Egypt's sole legal party, an increased emphasis on religion and private enterprise—Sadat had begun to indicate that he was his own man. The mass eviction (agreed to by the Soviets in order to preserve détente with America and to avoid bad press in the Third World) resoundingly proved it.

Sadat cast aside Nasser's blueprint to pursue his own vision of Egypt.

Sadat won popular acclaim for the move by couching it in Nasserist terms of national independence and readiness for war with Israel (the Soviets had been chronically late in delivering weapons). But while the rupture with Moscow was not meant to be permanent, it *was* meant to send messages to several parties. Sadat intended to placate his own officers, who'd been threatening rebellion over the arrogance and negligence of Soviet advisers. He

SPORTS: Baseball: World Series, Oakland Athletics defeat Cincinnati Reds, 4–3; first major league baseball strike, in April, delays start of season ... Olympics held in Sapporo and Munich ... Football: Super Bowl, Dallas Cowboys defeat Miami Dolphins, 24–3 ... Basketball: NBA, Los Angeles Lakers defeat New York Knicks, 4–1.

"All that crap, you're putting it in the paper? It's all been denied. Katie Graham [owner of The Washington Post*] is gonna get her tit caught in a big fat wringer if that's published."*—**Former Attorney General John Mitchell, to *Washington Post* reporter Carl Bernstein**

wanted to deprive Washington of a Cold War rationale for arming Israel and spurning Egypt. He hoped to secure an alliance with the wealthy, anti-Soviet Saudis. And he aimed to show the Soviets that Egypt could not be taken for granted.

All Sadat's wishes were granted but one: The hoped-for windfall from Washington was not forthcoming. Nonetheless, Cairo benefited. With Moscow supposedly out of the picture, the United States felt free to turn its attention to other matters, enabling the chastened Soviets to send arms once more. Within months, Egypt was fitter than ever for war. **◂1970.3 ▸1973.2**

The Corleone men as portrayed by John Cazale, Al Pacino, Marlon Brando, and James Caan.

FILM

A Mob Epic

9 *The Godfather*, released in 1972, was a rare Hollywood combination: a record-breaking box-office success (it grossed $330 million in two and a half years) and a film of high intelligence. Its basic story may have been a sexed-up, bloodier version of the gangster epics of the thirties, but director Francis Ford Coppola lent an operatic grandeur and weight to Mario Puzo's irresistibly trashy novel about the Mafia's Corleone family.

Coppola and Puzo, who cowrote the screenplay, portray the Mob's dealings and double-dealings, its fidelities and disloyalties, its code of honor and its cruelty as warped reflections of American free enterprise. Don Vito Corleone (played by Marlon Brando in an Oscar-winning "comeback" performance) speaks in a banker's hushed euphemisms: "We'll make him an offer he can't refuse." Men are beaten, garroted, shot—all in the name of business. These evil pursuits are juxtaposed with warm family scenes: weddings, dinners, frolics with grandchildren. The mafiosi are human beings with ordinary joys. But here, love of family is no ordinary virtue; rather, it masks a sociopathic amorality. It also leads to tragedy and moral decay. After the don is ambushed and his oldest son killed, Michael (Al Pacino), the don's straight-arrow youngest son, must take charge and commit murder. Reluctantly thrust into power, Michael becomes the most ruthless of "businessmen" and thus loses his soul.

The Godfather was richly photographed, in funereal hues, by Gordon Willis and scored by the great Nino Rota. Its first sequel, *The Godfather, Part II* (1974), was even richer than its predecessor (both films won Best Picture Oscars); *Part III* (1990) was uneven and exhausted. **◂1947.13 ▸1973.12**

THE UNITED STATES

The Watergate Scandals

10 Richard Nixon was running for a second presidential term in June 1972 when a security guard at Washington's Watergate hotel-and-office complex stumbled upon a burglary in progress at the Democratic Party's national headquarters. Police arrested five men (equipped with eavesdropping devices) on the spot, and two more—ex–FBI agent G. Gordon Liddy and ex–CIA man E. Howard Hunt—shortly afterward. Liddy, Hunt, and burglar James McCord, it quickly emerged, had ties to the White House and the Committee for the Re-election of the President (aptly bynamed CREEP). The ensuing swirl of scandals would end in 1974 with the first resignation of a U.S. chief of state.

The case remained quiet long enough for Nixon to be overwhelmingly reelected in November. In the meantime, Nixon and aides H.R. Haldeman and John Erlichman scurried to hide a trail of payoffs, tax dodges, and illegal campaign contributions; "dirty tricks" against rival candidates; and illegal surveillance of political foes by the FBI, the CIA, and a White House "plumbers unit." (The latter even burgled the office of Pentagon Papers whistle-blower Daniel Ellsberg's psychiatrist.)

As Judge John J. Sirica and enterprising *Washington Post* reporters Carl Bernstein and Bob Woodward began to pick at the Watergate knot, the Senate got involved, forming an investigatory committee chaired by Sam Ervin, Jr., of North Carolina. In March 1973, McCord informed Sirica that in their January trial, the Watergate break-in defendants had kept silent or committed perjury at the behest of high officials. Acting FBI chief L. Patrick Gray III resigned in disgrace, followed by Erlichman, Haldeman, and Attorney General Richard Kleindienst; presidential counsel John Dean III was fired. A special prosecutor was appointed —Harvard law professor Archibald Cox. And after Dean implicated Nixon during live televised hearings watched by a rapt American public, a White House staffer

The President's men fell one by one until the scandal reached Nixon himself.

revealed (also on live television) that the President had installed automatic tape recorders in his offices. Nixon's paranoia—and his obsession with preserving his conversations for posterity—would ensure his political doom. **◂1968.1 ▸1973.V**

IN THE UNITED STATES

down in the Pacific. The program—from its inception in 1961 through its first manned flight in 1968 and the spectacular moon landings that followed—was one of the most ambitious technological projects ever undertaken. ◂1969.1 ▸1975.6

▶BOGUS BIO—On March 14, mediocre novelist Clifford Irving pleaded guilty to perpetrating one of publishing's great hoaxes. Two weeks before McGraw-Hill was scheduled to publish *The Autobiography of Howard Hughes*, for which Irving was paid $765,000, the writer admitted that the manuscript—supposedly based on more than 100 interviews with the reclusive billionaire industrialist—was completely made up, right down to notes forged in Hughes's handwriting. Irving and his wife both received short prison sentences. ◂1938.5 ▸1983.6

▶SPITZ TAKES GOLD—In a legendary Olympic performance, swimmer Mark Spitz, 22, took an unprecedented seven gold medals at Munich in 1972. Winning four individ-

ual events and swimming strongly for three triumphant U.S. relay teams—each of the seven victories set a world record—made the photogenic Spitz one of the most recognized people in the world. ◂1972.5

▶CLEMENTE DIES—Perennial baseball All-Star Roberto Clemente was killed in a light-plane crash in December while on a goodwill mission to earthquake-devastated Nicaragua. In 18 seasons with the Pittsburgh Pirates, Clemente batted .317, had 3,000 hits and 240 home runs, and won 12 Gold Gloves for his outfield play. A Puerto Rican who commanded a huge following throughout Latin America, Clemente was elected to the Baseball Hall of Fame in 1973.

POLITICS & BUSINESS: GNP: $1,215.7 billion ... Richard M. Nixon reelected president, defeating George McGovern ... EPA bans use of DDT ... Congress passes Supplemental Security Income (SSI) for aid to the aged, blind, and disabled (part of $5 billion social security package) ... Federal Election Campaign Act limits campaign spending ... Federal Express founded.

"I had not myself been born in the ghetto and was not personally part of that experience. Reggae music influenced me profoundly by deepening the element of emotional comprehension."—**Jamaican prime minister Michael Manley**

AROUND THE WORLD

▶CIVIL WAR IN BURUNDI—In 1972, six years after an army coup toppled the monarchy in Burundi, in East Central Africa, and established the First Republic (dominated by the Tutsi ethnic group), exiled king Mwami Ntare V attempted to return to power. The move was quashed by President Michel Micombero, but Burundi's repressed Hutu majority (who were blamed for Ntare's attempted comeback) rebelled. Micombero's crackdown turned to genocide: His government killed some 100,000 to 150,000 Hutus, about 5 percent of the population, and nearly eradicated the Hutu educated class. In years to come, Hutu-Tutsi strife would claim hundreds of thousands of lives in Burundi and neighboring Rwanda. ▶1994.2

▶CAPTIVATING KORBUT—Soviet gymnast Olga Korbut's performance at the 1972 Olympics in Munich captivated the world. On her way to three gold medals and a silver, the petite 16-year-old

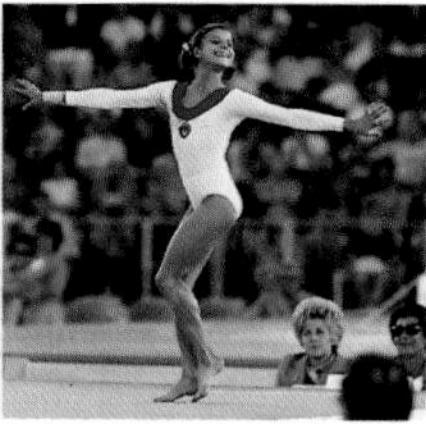

native of Belorussia dazzled spectators with her ready smile and an unprecedented backward somersault dismount from the uneven bars. ◀1972.5 ▶1976.3

▶GOURMET SEX—British gerontologist Alex Comfort's 1972 bestseller, *The Joy of Sex,* was a takeoff on the bestselling cookbook *The Joy of Cooking.* Subtitled *A Gourmet Guide to Lovemaking,* the book and its liberal tone dovetailed with the ongoing sexual revolution. "We've deliberately not gone into the ethics of lifestyles," wrote Comfort, who encouraged experimentation and averred that everyone is bisexual. ◀1970.M

▶OKINAWA RETURNED—After 27 years of American rule, the Ryukyu Islands were restored to Japan by the U.S. in 1972. The chain's best-known island was Okinawa, site of some of World War II's bloodiest fighting. ◀1945.1

Reggae star Bob Marley spread Caribbean black consciousness throughout the world.

THE CARIBBEAN

Socialism and Reggae

11 For former colonies everywhere, the first years of independence were a time for asserting cultural identity as well as political and economic autonomy. Those themes were combined in the 1972 Jamaican general election. Denouncing Jamaica's continued domination by Britain and America, Michael Manley of the liberal People's National Party employed the rhetoric of Rastafarianism—the communitarian cult of Jamaica's poor, which called Africa its Zion, worshiped Haile Selassie as God incarnate, and prophesied the fall of capitalism. Manley sweetened his message with reggae, the Rastas' meditative dance music. And he won the election handily.

Manley saw bauxite—Jamaica's major export besides illegal marijuana—as the key to increasing its clout. He formed a cartel of bauxite-exporting nations (modeled on OPEC), then raised Jamaica's formerly minuscule royalty for the aluminum ore. The revenue increase funded new social services, but the cartel soon crumbled, and the (mostly U.S.-owned) mining companies cut back on production. During Manley's second term, his government gained a controlling interest in many of Jamaica's industries and aligned itself with the Third World. (Manley actively courted Castro.) Washington retaliated. Aid, investment, and tourism dried up; poverty rose sharply.

Manley lost to conservative Edward Seaga in the 1980 election. Yet despite his policies' failure, Manley's defiant stance and stirring oratory had brought his people new confidence. During his tenure, reggae became another important Jamaican export. And reggae's greatest composer and prophet, Bob Marley, became one of the most influential pop stars ever. **◀1928.13 ▶1973.M**

SPORTS

Fischer Defeats Spassky

12 Soon after becoming a grand master at 15, Chicago-born chess prodigy Bobby Fischer grew obsessed with ending the succession of Soviet champions ("commie cheats," he called them) who'd dominated the game since the late 1940s. When Fischer finally faced world champion Boris Spassky in Reykjavík, Iceland, in 1972, chess became a Cold War battlefront.

Fischer, 29, boycotted the opening ceremonies, refusing to appear until he received better remuneration. (An obliging sponsor doubled the prize.) He lost the first game and forfeited the second, protesting the presence of cameras. But then the fireworks began: In four games of stunning virtuosity, Fischer overtook Spassky, crushing him 12½–8½. At one point, Soviet security men insisted on dismantling Fischer's chair to see if it contained electronic devices for feeding information.

Chess fans everywhere *(above, in Prague)* followed the match move by move.

Fischer's ascendancy was short-lived. He forfeited his title in 1975, refusing to face Soviet challenger Anatoly Karpov. He remained a reclusive legend until 1992, when he staged a rematch with Spassky in war-torn Yugoslavia (in violation of international sanctions). His victory was essentially meaningless: Spassky was no longer among the world's top 100 players. **▶1985.M**

MUSIC

All That Glitters

13 As the political rebellions of the 1960s gave way to the interpersonal upheavals of the 1970s, a new force emerged in youth culture: glitter rock. Glitter launched a music-driven assault on traditional gender roles. Its sound ranged from the protopunk hard rock of the New York Dolls to the fey ballads of Roxy Music; its look ranged from thrift-store drag to sleek foppery. The genre hit the big time in 1972, when English rocker David Bowie began an international tour to promote his album *The Rise and Fall of Ziggy Stardust and the Spiders from Mars.*

David Bowie was glitter's prime exemplar.

With his elegant cheekbones, sinuous voice, and Wildean wit, Bowie brought genuine glamour to glitter. His music combined rock bite with operatic drama; his stage show, with its elaborate sets and costumed dancers, was as elaborate as a Broadway production. Bowie soon abandoned the diva-esque "Ziggy" persona for a less flamboyant androgyny, but his popular success helped lift a wave of glittery performers to stardom—most notably Elton John, who, like his fellow Briton, continued to sell millions of albums into the 1990s. **▶1976.M**

NOBEL PRIZES: Peace: No award ... Literature: Heinrich Böll (West German; writer) ... Chemistry: Christian Boehmer Anfinsen, Stanford Moore, and William Howard Stein (U.S.; enzymes) ... Medicine: Gerald Edelman and Rodney Porter (U.S., U.K.; antibodies) ... Physics: John Bardeen, Leon N. Cooper, and John Robert Schrieffer (U.S.; superconductivity) ... Economics: Kenneth J. Arrow (U.S.) and John R. Hicks (U.K.).

A VOICE FROM 1972

A Spouse's Wish List

"I Want a Wife," by Judy Syfers, from *Ms.*, Spring 1972

Created by an all-woman staff, backed by New York *magazine, and described by founding editor Gloria Steinem (left) as a how-to magazine "for the liberated female human being—not how to make jelly, but how to seize control of your life," the first full issue of* Ms. *appeared in January 1972. Simply dated "Spring" (future financing was uncertain), the premier issue sold out all 300,000 copies in eight days.* Ms. *gained a million-dollar investment from Warner Communications and began monthly publication in July, soon attracting half a million regular readers. The debut issue, including pieces by Steinem, Sylvia Plath (posthumous), Cynthia Ozick, and Judy Syfers (author of the satire reproduced below) reflected the founders' faith that feminists were here to stay—and that their numbers could support an ongoing publication.* ◂**1970.9** ▸**1982.M**

"There's a lot in a name," declared the first issue of *Ms. (above)*, the first mainstream magazine with an overtly feminist perspective.

I belong to that classification of people known as wives. I am A Wife. And, not altogether incidentally, I am a mother.

Not too long ago a male friend of mine appeared on the scene fresh from a recent divorce. He had one child, who is, of course, with his ex-wife. He is obviously looking for another wife. As I thought about him while I was ironing one evening, it suddenly occurred to me that I, too, would like to have a wife. Why do I want a wife?

I would like to go back to school so that I can become economically independent, support myself, and, if need be, support those dependent upon me. I want a wife who will work and send me to school. And while I am going to school I want a wife to take care of my children. I want a wife to keep track of the children's doctor and dentist appointments. And to keep track of mine, too. I want a wife to make sure my children eat properly and are kept clean. I want a wife who will wash the children's clothes and keep them mended. I want a wife who is a good nurturant attendant to my children, who arranges for their schooling, makes sure that they have an adequate social life with their peers, takes them to the park, the zoo, etc. I want a wife who takes care of the children when they are sick, a wife who arranges to be around when the children need special care, because, of course, I cannot miss classes at school. My wife must arrange to lose time at work and not lose the job. It may mean a small cut in my wife's income from time to time, but I guess I can tolerate that. Needless to say, my wife will arrange and pay for the care of the children while my wife is working.

I want a wife who will take care of *my* physical needs, I want a wife who will keep my house clean. A wife who will pick up after me. I want a wife who will keep my clothes clean, ironed, mended, replaced when need be, and who will see to it that my personal things are kept in their proper place so that I can find what I need the minute I need it. I want a wife who cooks the meals, a wife who is a *good* cook. I want a wife who will plan the menus, do the necessary grocery shopping, prepare the meals, serve them pleasantly, and then do the cleaning up while I do my studying. I want a wife who will care for me when I am sick and sympathize with my pain and loss of time from school. I want a wife to go along when our family takes a vacation so that someone can continue to care for me and my children when I need a rest and change of scene.

I want a wife who will not bother me with rambling complaints about a wife's duties. But I want a wife who will listen to me when I feel the need to explain a rather difficult point I have come across in my course of studies. And I want a wife who will type my papers for me when I have written them.

I want a wife who will take care of the details of my social life. When my wife and I are invited out by my friends, I want a wife who will take care of the babysitting arrangements. When I meet people at school that I like and want to entertain, I want a wife who will have the house clean, will prepare a special meal, serve it to me and my friends, and not interrupt when I talk about the things that interest me and my friends. I want a wife who will have arranged that the children are fed and ready for bed before my guests arrive so that the children do not bother us.

And I want a wife who knows that sometimes I need a night out by myself.

I want a wife who is sensitive to my sexual needs, a wife who makes love passionately and eagerly when I feel like it, a wife who makes sure that I am satisfied. And, of course, I want a wife who will not demand sexual attention when I am not in the mood for it. I want a wife who assumes the complete responsibility for birth control, because I do not want more children. I want a wife who will remain sexually faithful to me so that I do not have to clutter up my intellectual life with jealousies. And I want a wife who understands that *my* sexual needs may entail more than strict adherence to monogamy. I must, after all, be able to relate to people as fully as possible.

If, by chance, I find another person more suitable as a wife than the wife I already have, I want the liberty to replace my present wife with another one. Naturally, I will expect a fresh, new life; my wife will take the children and be solely responsible for them so that I am left free.

When I am through with school and have a job, I want my wife to quit working and remain at home so that my wife can more fully and completely take care of a wife's duties.

My God, who *wouldn't* want a wife?

"In view of the increase in support for Israel, the Saudi Arabian Kingdom has decided to stop the export of oil to the United States of America for adopting such a stand."—**Communiqué by the Saudi Arabian government, issued on October 20, 1973**

STORY OF THE YEAR

OPEC Flexes Its Muscles

1 Beginning in autumn 1973, the Organization of Petroleum Exporting Countries dealt the global economy a series of profound shocks. On the eve of the October War between the Arabs and Israelis, OPEC doubled the price of oil, to $3 a barrel. During the war, the cartel raised the price by another 70 percent, while Arab members cut production by a quarter and imposed an embargo on countries aiding Israel. Finally, the following January, OPEC more than doubled prices again, to $11.56 a barrel. These moves brought mounting panic. In America, mile-long lines appeared at gasoline pumps; in Europe, many countries banned weekend driving; throughout the non-Communist world, speed limits and thermostats were lowered, airline schedules slashed, and advertising signs extinguished to save oil-generated electricity. Deeper effects, persisting long after the embargo was lifted in March 1974, included worsening poverty in developing nations; balance-of-payment deficits and inflation in the West; and the largest reallocation of wealth—from oil-consuming nations to oil producers—in history.

"The Summer of '73"—as depicted by a *Boston Globe* cartoonist.

Oddly enough, the cutback and embargo made only a small, temporary dent in international oil supplies. What shortages there were resulted mainly from hoarding and from government emergency-distribution measures. The public's fear was manipulated by transnational oil companies, who used it to secure higher profits for themselves, and by politicians who advocated a shift away from pro-Israel policies. Though the oil squeeze earned the Arabs widespread hostility (and though Washington's decision to restrain Israel from total victory in the war stemmed from preembargo geopolitical calculations), it did ensure them a greater say than ever in international affairs—as long as OPEC unity endured.

Yet the impact of the crisis went beyond prosaic politics and economics. No longer able to take for granted a perpetual supply of cheap energy, industrial society had to reassess its goals and expectations. The ecology movement, which envisioned a future based on conservation and simpler lifestyles, gained a new mass following after 1973. But technocrats instead urged greater reliance on domestically available fuels—and nuclear power. The controversy that resulted would become one of the decade's hottest, eventually driving tens of thousands of "antinukers" to civil disobedience around the world. **◂1960.M ▸1979.M**

THE MIDDLE EAST

The October War

2 When the air-raid sirens screamed on October 5, 1973, most Israelis were in synagogues celebrating Yom Kippur, Judaism's highest holiday. For their Arab attackers, it was the tenth day of the fast of Ramadan, and the anniversary of one of the prophet Muhammad's greatest battles. For both sets of worshippers, the October War would have huge repercussions.

The Arabs had been swearing vengeance since losing the Six Day War in 1967. Yet Egyptian president Anwar al-Sadat and Syria's Hafez al-Assad had begun plotting seriously only after February 1971, when Israel rebuffed Sadat's offer of peace in return for Israeli withdrawal from occupied Arab lands. The new war had a limited goal: Aided by the resources of the other Arab nations (and a few of their troops), Egypt and Syria aimed to force the Israelis to accept the land-for-peace bargain.

The Yom Kippur assault caught Israel off guard. Egypt quickly retook the east bank of the Suez Canal; Syria regained most of the Golan Heights. As the fighting intensified, Moscow provided the Arabs with arms and Washington supplied the Israelis, giving rise to a threat of nuclear war. But the outnumbered Israelis (led, as in 1967, by defense minister Moshe Dayan) were better organized, better trained, and desperately determined. By October 22, when America pressured its ally into a cease-fire with Egypt, Israel had more than recovered the contested territories. Although skirmishes with Syria continued for months, the war was over.

However inconclusive militarily, the conflict was politically decisive. Israel was shaken by the costliness of its narrow victory; the Arabs secretly doubted they could ever do better. Sadat began to wonder whether Egypt could afford to lead another war. **◂1972.8 ▸1974.10**

Casualties of the October War: Two Egyptian soldiers lie slain in the Sinai desert.

ARGENTINA

Perón's Brief Comeback

3 For 18 years, Argentina had languished under regimes that made General Juan Perón's seem utopian while the ousted dictator, exiled in Spain, rebuilt his movement. Finally, in March 1973, a tottering military junta allowed his party to run for office. Peronistas won the presidency and majorities in the legislature. The new president promptly resigned, inviting Perón home to run in a fresh election. In September, 62 percent of Argentines voted to give Perón, 77, another go. His third wife, Isabel (a former nightclub dancer with no political experience), became vice president.

Isabel Perón greets workers at a rally.

Millions celebrated Perón's return. But the troubles that would dog his final term were evident from his first day back, when a shoot-out among followers welcoming his plane killed more than 100. In his

1973

ART & CULTURE: Books: *Breakfast of Champions* (Kurt Vonnegut, Jr.); *Fear of Flying* (Erica Jong); *Ninety-Two in the Shade* (Thomas McGuane); *Diving into the Wreck* (Adrienne Rich) ... Music: "You Are the Sunshine of My Life" (Stevie Wonder); "I Shot the Sheriff" (Bob Marley); *Band on the Run* (Wings, LP); *Goodbye Yellow Brick Road* (Elton John, LP)... Painting & Sculpture: *Peacock* (Lee Krasner); *NRF Collage*

"What this country needs is political silence."—**General Oscar Bonilla Bradnovic, Chile's new interior minister, after the coup**

absence, rifts had opened between rightist and leftist Peronistas. Perón had always been a chameleon: To fascists, he spoke like a fascist; to Maoists, like a Maoist. But now, backed by big business, the military, and the Catholic hierarchy, he cracked down on the left.

Still, the leftists—mostly students who hoped Perón's working-class following could be made into a socialist movement—invoked an idealized *peronismo*, and in its name some fought an urban guerrilla war. Investors shunned Argentina, exacerbating the country's economic ills. To curb spiraling inflation, Perón froze wages and prices; the result was shortages, black-marketeering, and strikes. Chaos mounted.

And then, in July 1974, the strongman died of heart disease. Argentina was about to enter the most nightmarish episode in its history. **◂1952.9 ▸1976.7**

CHILE

A Bloody Coup

4 The coup that brought down President Salvador Allende Gossens in 1973 was perhaps the bloodiest in South American history, with a death toll of between 5,000 (according to U.S. government estimates) and 30,000 (according to human rights groups). To "destabilize" Chile's elected government, the CIA had funneled millions of dollars to the opposition press, politicians, businessmen, trade unions, saboteurs, and agents provocateurs. But the explosion might have come even without such aid: Allende's democratic attempt to transform Chile along Marxist lines had gone awry.

Since taking office in 1970, Allende had raised wages, increased social services, accelerated land redistribution, and nationalized hundreds of domestic and foreign-owned businesses. These moves pleased workers and peasants, who began seizing property on their own. But they angered the middle and upper classes, U.S. corporations like ITT and Anaconda Copper, and Washington. Foreign capital vanished (Moscow was slow to help), shortages appeared, and inflation ballooned. Truck owners, farmers, shopkeepers, and professionals went on strike, while Allende's supporters mounted counterdemonstrations. Far rightists resorted to terrorism; far leftists demanded government arms. Allende's coalition of socialists, communists, liberals, and small radical parties fractured.

A few weeks after the coup, Chilean children play war outside the destroyed Socialist Party headquarters in Santiago.

When Allende's most trusted general resigned under rightist pressure, Allende replaced him with Augusto Pinochet—who led the putsch days later. As troops seized key cities, Allende barricaded himself in the presidential palace in Santiago. He died (by his own hand, claimed the junta) as air force planes rocketed the building. Elsewhere, resistance was light, but the rebels slaughtered thousands of Chileans in makeshift concentration camps.

Pinochet's junta outlawed political parties, imposed strict censorship, and used jailings, torture, and "disappearances" against opponents. The "Chicago Boys"—a group of technocrats who'd studied under University of Chicago economist Milton Friedman—imposed a regimen of laissez-faire capitalism. But after a brief boom, the economy plummeted; protest surfaced again in the early 1980s. **◂1970.2 ▸1988.M**

THE UNITED STATES

A Right to Abortion

5 In 1973, the United States joined a growing majority of countries that allowed women to choose whether to carry a pregnancy to term. Ruling on challenges to state laws by two anonymous appellants—"Jane Roe" in Texas and "Mary Doe" in Georgia (both of whom had borne unwanted children after being denied abortions)—the U.S. Supreme Court decided 7–2 that all restrictions on abortion in the first trimester were unconstitutional. In *Roe v. Wade*, the justices declared that since "those trained in the respective disciplines of medicine, philosophy, and theology" could not agree on when a fetus becomes a person, laws presuming that personhood begins at conception were invalid. In the months of pregnancy before a fetus could survive outside the womb, a woman's right to privacy made abortion a decision that involved only her and her doctor. Only in the last trimester did the government's interest in preserving potential life give a state the right to prohibit the procedure.

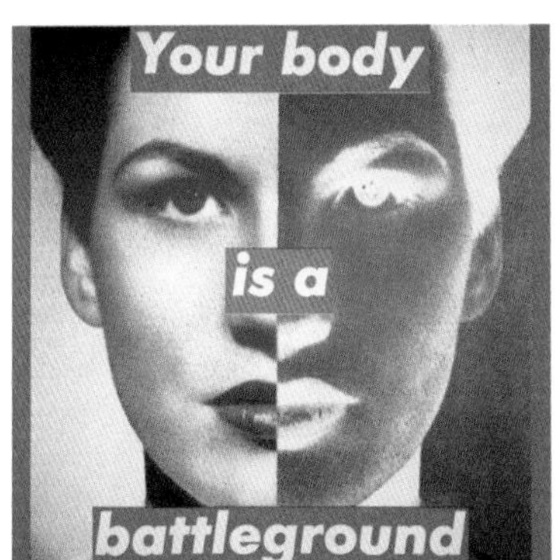

Artist Barbara Kruger's 1989 silkscreen confronts the politicization of pregnancy.

Roe unleashed the world's most militant anti-abortion movement. Based in the Catholic and evangelical Christian communities and endorsed by the Republican Party, the American "pro-life" movement became a potent political force. By the 1990s, its tactics had escalated from civil disobedience to terrorism. **◂1968.M ▸1993.M**

BIRTHS

Eric Lindros, Canadian hockey player.

Vitaly Scherbo, U.S.S.R. gymnast.

Monica Seles, Yugoslav-U.S. tennis player.

DEATHS

Conrad Aiken, U.S. writer .

Salvador Allende Gossens, Chilean president.

W.H. Auden, U.K.-U.S. poet.

Fulgencio Batista y Zaldívar, Cuban president.

David Ben-Gurion, Polish-Israeli prime minister.

Abebe Bikila, Ethiopian runner.

Elizabeth Bowen, Irish-U.K. writer.

Pearl S. Buck, U.S. writer.

Pablo Casals, Spanish musician.

Lon Chaney, Jr., U.S. actor.

Eddie Condon, U.S. musician.

Joseph Cornell, U.S. sculptor.

Noël Coward, U.K. playwright and composer.

Edward Evans-Pritchard, U.K. anthropologist.

John Ford, U.S. filmmaker.

Betty Grable, U.S. actress.

William Inge, U.S. playwright.

Lyndon Baines Johnson, U.S. president.

Asger Jorn, Danish artist.

Otto Klemperer, German conductor.

Jacques Lipchitz, Lithuanian-French sculptor.

Pablo Neruda, Chilean poet and diplomat.

Paavo Nurmi, Finnish runner.

Pablo Picasso, Spanish artist.

Jeannette Rankin, U.S. politician.

Eddie Rickenbacker, U.S. aviator and businessman.

Edward G. Robinson, U.S. actor.

J.R.R. Tolkien, U.K. novelist.

Karl Ziegler, German chemist.

No. 4 (Robert Motherwell) ... Film: *The Sting* (George Roy Hill); *Mean Streets* (Martin Scorsese); *The Way We Were* (Sydney Pollack); *The Exorcist* (William Friedkin); *Scenes from a Marriage* (Ingmar Bergman) ... Theater: *Equus* (Peter Shaffer); *The Hot l Baltimore* (Lanford Wilson); *Finishing Touches* (Jean Kerr); *A Little Night Music* (Stephen Sondheim) ... TV: *Kojak*; *Barnaby Jones*; *Police Story*.

"I poisoned him from the fish I ate. I know I shouldn't, but I sometimes wish he would die before me. I know that I have more painful days ahead."—**Kiyoko Kosaki, a victim of Minamata disease, which she passed on to her son Tatsuzumi**

NEW IN 1973

Supermarket bar codes.

Airport security measures to prevent terrorism.

Sydney Opera House (designed by Danish architect Jörn Utzon, and opened after 16 years of construction).

College athletic scholarships for women (University of Miami).

Rabies vaccine requiring five shots in the arm (replacing 14-to-21-shot abdominal vaccine).

Sears Tower (Chicago; at 1,454 feet, the world's tallest building).

IN THE UNITED STATES

▶VEEP RESIGNS—Pleading nolo contendere—no contest, a guilty plea without legal admission—to charges of tax evasion, Spiro Agnew resigned as vice president on October 10. An obscure county official who served just two years as governor of Maryland before becoming vice president, Agnew dismissed accusations as "damned lies." By stepping down he avoided a possible 50-count indictment on bribery, conspiracy, and tax-fraud charges. ◀1972.10 ▶1974.1

▶AIM TAKES AIM—Led by Native American activists Russell Means and Dennis Banks, 200 members of the American Indian Movement (AIM) seized the hamlet of Wounded Knee, South Dakota (where the U.S. cavalry in 1890 completed the conquest of the West by massacring almost 200 Sioux), in February. The group proclaimed the Independent Sioux Oglala Nation and issued a set of demands to the federal

1973

NORTHERN IRELAND

A Vote to Stay

6 In a referendum widely boycotted by Roman Catholics, Northern Ireland voted in 1973 to remain part of the United Kingdom. Given the country's 2-to-1 Protestant majority, the lopsided result of the vote—the first of its kind in British history—surprised no one: British authorities and even moderate Northern Irish Protestants privately acknowledged that the referendum only reiterated that non-Catholics were loath to merge with the Catholic-majority Republic of Ireland to the south. While extremist Protestant groups gloated, the outlawed Provisional wing of the IRA voiced displeasure by carrying its terrorist campaign to the heart of London.

A British policeman surveys the Old Bailey bomb scene from the shattered window of a nearby commercial building.

On the afternoon of March 8, two massive car bombs, near Trafalgar Square and outside the Old Bailey (the central criminal court), rocked the English capital, killing one person and injuring more than 200. Until then, most Britons, though aware of the strife in Northern Ireland, had been spared direct experience of it. "God help them in Belfast if this is what's going on all the time there," said one witness of the blasts, which many likened to World War II German air raids. Aided by an anonymous warning, police found and defused two other bombs, averting the loss of more lives to the violence that had claimed hundreds of victims each year since 1969.

Meanwhile, determined to curb its volatile province, the British government had been working on a political solution. Prime Minister Edward Heath's White Paper, issued on March 20, created a Northern Irish assembly in which the Protestant ruling class shared power with the Catholic minority, long shut out of politics. Supported by moderates of both faiths, the 78-seat assembly was elected in June and replaced Northern Ireland's parliament, a Protestant redoubt suspended by London in 1972 for its inability to govern fairly. Westminster retained ultimate veto power, however, and British security forces continued to patrol Ulster's six strife-torn counties. **◀1972.4 ▶1979.6**

ENVIRONMENTALISM

A Poisoned Populace

7 Dead fish provided the first clue that something evil had invaded Yatsushiro Bay. Then crows began dropping from the sky. Next it was the cats of Minamata, on the island of Kyushu. Blind and palsied, they whirled about grotesquely and cast themselves into the bay. Vermin proliferated after the cats disappeared, but the "dancing disease" soon killed the rats, too. Finally, the mysterious plague struck at humans, killing more than a thousand and blinding and crippling countless others. In 1973, 20 years after Minamata disease first appeared, Japanese courts pinned responsibility on the Chisso Corporation, a Minamata-based chemical company.

Among the estimated 460 tons of pollutants Chisso had dumped into the bay over the years were 27 tons of methyl mercury. Minamata disease was not a disease at all: It was mercury poisoning brought on by the eating of tainted fish. By 1963, scientists from nearby Kumamoto University had traced the scourge to its source. (A company doctor later admitted that Chisso had known of the problem since 1959 and had kept dumping anyway.) But the government didn't acknowledge the cause until 1969.

In a settlement, Chisso paid out more than $600 million to some 2,000 victims. Strict certification rules barred many sufferers from receiving compensation, however, prompting thousands to sue the government for negligence in its slow initial response to the disaster. Two decades later, the action was still tied up in the courts. ("The national government's policy," said one lawyer, "is that if the case drags on long enough the plaintiffs will die.") In 1992, a Tokyo court cleared the government of responsibility—but the appeals process continued. **◀1969.M ▶1978.12**

Photographer W. Eugene Smith documented the tragic legacy of Chisso's mercury dumping. Here, a Japanese mother bathes her 17-year-old daughter, deformed since birth.

SOUTHEAST ASIA

A War Without Americans

8 By the end of March 1973—two months after the United States signed the Paris peace accords with Vietnam's Communists—all U.S. troops and all acknowledged U.S. prisoners of war had left Indochina. (Questions about the fate of several hundred Americans missing in action, however, would strain relations between Washington and Hanoi for two decades.) Back home, the released POWs were greeted joyfully, but other returning soldiers received scant welcome from a chastened nation. And

SPORTS: Baseball: World Series, Oakland Athletics defeat New York Mets, 4–3; American League adopts designated hitter rule ... Football: Super Bowl, Miami Dolphins defeat Washington Redskins, 14–7; O.J. Simpson first to rush more than 2,000 yds. ... Basketball: NBA, New York Knicks defeat Los Angeles Lakers, 4–1 ... Boxing: George Foreman defeats Joe Frazier for world heavyweight title.

"Some call it dictatorship; others call it 'crisis government' ... I call it authoritarianism."—**Philippine president Ferdinand Marcos**

though a cease-fire took effect in February between the rebel Pathet Lao and the rightist Laotian government, in Vietnam and Cambodia there was no respite from bloodshed.

American planes kept pounding Cambodia until August, when Congress—angered at revelations that President Nixon had ordered secret bombing of the country from 1969 to 1970—finally halted the bombing. (In November, overriding Nixon's veto, Congress passed the War Powers Act, which required congressional approval of any commitment of U.S. forces abroad for more than 60 days.) By then, thousands of peasants had been driven from their homes and into the arms of the communist Khmer Rouge. The latter had drifted increasingly toward fanaticism under the rain of fire—and the bombs had failed to keep them

Through an interpreter *(center)*, Kissinger confers with Le Duc Tho *(right)*.

from advancing steadily on Phnom Penh. Meanwhile, despite unabated transfusions of U.S. arms and dollars, the South Vietnamese army continued to lose ground (with up to 1,000 casualties a month) to the North Vietnamese and Viet Cong.

When U.S. secretary of state Henry Kissinger and North Vietnamese negotiator Le Duc Tho were jointly awarded the 1973 Nobel Peace Prize for achieving the truce between their countries, Le turned it down. Peace, he said, had not yet come. **◂1972.1 ▸1975.4**

SPORTS

Secretariat Wins Triple Crown

9 In the summer of 1973, Secretariat became the first Thoroughbred in 25 years to snag horse racing's most coveted honor: the Triple Crown, the unofficial title conferred on a mount that wins all three of the top U.S. horse races in one season. In the process, the chestnut stallion earned the sobriquet "the greatest horse that ever lived."

Secretariat, ridden by jockey Ron Turcotte, winning the 1973 Belmont Stakes.

After winning the Preakness and the Kentucky Derby, Secretariat was favored in the Belmont Stakes. Confounding the skeptics, the Belmont proved to be Secretariat's most impressive performance yet: He took the lead early and finished an unheard-of 31 lengths in front of his closest rival. Jockey Ron Turcotte had the luxury of glancing at the time clock as he passed the finish line; it showed a new track record.

Later in the year, Secretariat ended his career by winning the Canadian International Championship. The victory brought his career earnings to $1.3 million. He was sold for $6 million, the highest price of any horse in history—and in 1974 was put to stud, with investors paying a hefty $190,000 each for a share in his sex life. **◂1920.M ▸1977.13**

THE PHILIPPINES

Marcos Cracks Down

10 The transformation of the Philippines from a showcase of American-style democracy into what was often called a "kleptocracy" (dictatorship by thieves) began in earnest in January 1973, when voters approved continued martial law and a new constitution providing for parliamentary government. President Ferdinand Marcos had declared a state of emergency four months earlier, citing student riots, fighting between indigenous Muslims and Christian settlers on the island of Mindanao, and communist insurgency elsewhere. Now he declared himself both president and prime minister—and simply ignored, for the time being, the constitution's provision for a legislature.

Most Filipinos accepted one-man rule, at first. Marcos was immensely popular, both as a World War II hero (though his exploits later proved to have been fabricated) and a statesman. In 1969, his promises of land reform, cultural development, and greater independence from the United States had helped him become the first president in Philippine history ever to be reelected. Indeed, the new constitution's main selling point was its elimination of the two-term limit.

The regime tried to sweeten martial law by bringing roads, schools, and social services to the countryside. But political opposition and labor unions were ruthlessly suppressed. Wages remained the lowest in Southeast Asia, and unemployment remained widespread. Land reform languished as Marcos grant-

Having scrapped American-style democracy, Marcos addresses the newly organized People's Congress.

ed concessions to big growers and American agribusiness. Ballooning debt and foreign investment initially spurred economic growth, but the proceeds went mainly to Marcos and his cronies. Muslim and Marxist rebellions persisted. A decade later, the assassination of Marcos's chief rival would spark a nonviolent revolution. **◂1965.M ▸1983.2**

IN THE UNITED STATES

government: free elections of reservation tribal councils, a review of more than 300 U.S.-Indian treaties that AIM leaders said had been violated over the years, and a Senate review of the Bureau of Indian Affairs and the overall treatment of Indians in the U.S. The activists held Wounded Knee for 70 days. Means was arrested upon surrender, but charges against him were dismissed in 1974 because of government misconduct during the trial. ◂1971.M

▸KING OF TENNIS—Billed as a "Battle of the Sexes," the 1973 tennis showdown between Billie Jean King and aging ex-champ Bobby Riggs turned out to be a boost for women: Before 30,000 fans at Houston's Astrodome, King

trounced the arrogant Riggs. The first female athlete to top $100,000 in earnings in a year (1971), King, who would win an unprecedented 20 Wimbledon titles (including six singles), was a steadfast promoter of gender equity in tennis. She served as the first president of the Women's Tennis Association, founded the world's first sports magazine for women, and helped establish a women's tour separate from the men's. ◂1969.M ▸1975.7

▸THE LOUDS—TV viewers were fascinated by the 1973 PBS documentary *An American Family,* which captured daily life in the upper-middle-class Loud family of Santa Barbara, California. Culled from some 300 hours of footage filmed by producer Craig Gilbert and his crew over the course of seven months in 1971, the twelve hour-long black-and-white episodes showed a family in turmoil: Oldest son Lance declares his homosexuality, and Pat and Bill Loud's marriage ends. Though Gilbert's choice of the Louds was criticized as overly calculated, the series reflected the growing fissures in American family life.

POLITICS & BUSINESS: GNP: $1,362.3 billion ... Spiro Agnew resigns as vice president; Gerald Ford sworn in ... Watergate scandal deepens; Nixon releases White House tapes ... Congress passes War Powers Act (over Nixon's veto) and Endangered Species Act ... AT&T pays $15 million in compensation for discrimination against women and minorities and establishes training programs and hiring quotas.

"A screaming comes across the sky."—**Thomas Pynchon, *Gravity's Rainbow***

AROUND THE WORLD

▶GREEK MONARCHY ABOLISHED—Following a failed coup by naval officers in May, Greek military junta leader George Papadopoulos abolished the country's monarchy (King Constantine had been in exile since 1967), declared a republic, and appointed himself president. Papadopoulos lifted martial law (in effect for six years), but many dismissed the move as window dressing. Right-wingers in the military did not doubt Papadopoulos's democratic sincerity: On November 25, he was ousted by Lieutenant General Phaedon Gizikis. ◀1967.2 ▶1974.5

▶THINK PINK—The British psychedelic rock band Pink Floyd released *Dark Side of the Moon (cover art, below)* in 1973, an unremittingly bleak album that would have the

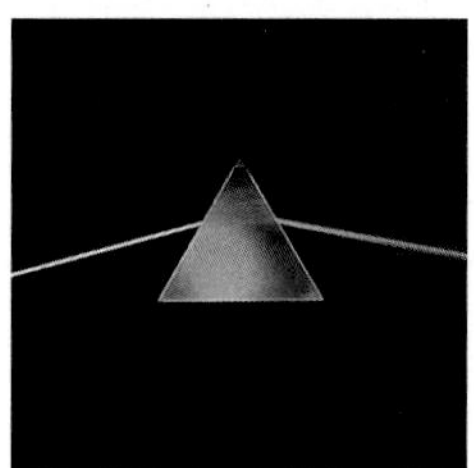

longest top-200 run in history (it spent a record 741 weeks on U.S. charts). Spacily experimental, Pink Floyd pioneered the use of laser lights, slide shows, and ponderous mechanical props in their slickly produced live concerts. ◀1971.6 ▶1976.M

▶BAHAMIAN INDEPENDENCE—On July 10, after 256 years as a British crown colony (interrupted by a year as a Spanish colony) the Bahamas gained independence. Prime Minister Lynden O. Pindling, leader of the black majority Progressive Liberal Party, negotiated the settlement that made the Atlantic Ocean island chain a sovereign state within the British Commonwealth. ▶1981.M

▶BRITAIN JOINS EEC—Having signed the Treaty of Brussels, Great Britain, Denmark, and Ireland formally joined the European Economic Community on January 1. Norway had also been accepted, but declined to join. The participation of the other countries, however, expanded the Common Market to nine nations. ◀1957.5 ▶1985.11

Carrero Blanco was killed by a bomb as he got into his car after attending mass.

SPAIN

Franco's Heir Slain

11 The Basque separatist bomb that killed Spanish premier Luis Carrero Blanco in December 1973 blew his car over the top of a Madrid apartment building. It also blew apart octogenarian General Francisco Franco's plans to preserve his dictatorial legacy beyond his lifetime. Carrero Blanco, 70, was Franco's closest friend; he'd been a fellow leader of the rightist Nationalists in the Spanish Civil War. And though Prince Juan Carlos de Borbón was slated to become chief of state (and Spain's first king since the thirties) upon Franco's death, the real power was to have remained in Carrero Blanco's hands, at least until the young monarch "matured."

When Franco chose interior minister (and former secret-police chief) Carlos Arias Navarro to succeed Carrero Blanco, a struggle broke out between two government factions: the pragmatic technocrats—who'd engineered Spain's economic modernization over the past decade and who now called for limited democratization—and the old-guard Francoist "bunker." Arias Navarro dismissed the technocrats from his cabinet, ensuring continued political repression. But he alienated the powerful Catholic hierarchy, whose ties to both the would-be reformers and Carrero Blanco had been tight. He also disappointed the majority of Spaniards, who were growing increasingly restless under quasi-fascist rule.

Spain's future lay unmistakably with Juan Carlos. And neither Franco nor Arias Navarro could know that the prince harbored a secret vision of democracy that made the technocrats' look pale. **◀1970.M ▶1975.1**

FILM

Bertolucci's Tango

12 Critic Pauline Kael called it "the most powerfully erotic movie ever made," a breakthrough work that "altered the face of an art form." The Italian courts declared it "obscene, indecent, and catering to the lowest instincts of the libido" and suspended director Bernardo Bertolucci's right to vote. No film of the era generated more praise, fury, and newsprint than *Last Tango in Paris*, which gained wide release in 1973.

For the first time in cinema, raw sex—with explicit nudity and no romance—was used for more than titillation; it became an artistic device. A middle-aged Marlon Brando is a lonely, agonized American in Paris whose wife has just committed suicide; Maria Schneider is a luscious young French bride-to-be. The pair meet by chance while apartment-hunting and have a short, torrid, anonymous affair in which he dominates and degrades her. (As part of foreplay, he butters her; she offers to eat his vomit.) Then, when he wants emotional involvement and love, she murders him.

Where some viewers saw mere pornography, others saw a stirring portrayal of two people's desperate attempts, via sex, at communication and liberation in a stifling society. But there was no disputing Bertolucci's artistry. The film is magnificently shot by Vittorio Storaro, and its score features hauntingly evocative saxophone solos by Gato Barbieri. And Brando created an acting landmark. No other major male star had ever before stripped to the skin on-screen. In improvised, partly autobiographical monologues, he exposes the soul of a tortured man and cries in naked pain.

Bertolucci went on to make the political epic *1900* and the Oscar-winning *The Last Emperor*. Brando grew older, gained weight, and chose to work only on rare, highly remunerative occasions. Schneider appeared in one more good film (Antonioni's *The Passenger*) and several bad ones. Sex in the movies became ubiquitous—yet *Last Tango*, in revival, managed to remain as provocative as ever. **◀1972.9**

LITERATURE

A Literary Rocket

13 *Gravity's Rainbow*—Thomas Pynchon's apocalyptic, paranoiac novel of World War II's aftermath in Germany—exploded onto the literary scene in February 1973 like one of the V-2 missiles that provide its principal theme. Roaming through the book's 700-plus pages were hundreds of characters (who are searching for a missile that can break through the earth's gravitational field) and a multiplicity of languages, story lines, puns and other wordplay, and recondite references (to subjects as disparate as neurology, comic books, rocketry, mathematics, and tarot).

Many critics found *Gravity's Rainbow* unendurably complex. One critic complained that reading it required "Calvinist doggedness," and said its author (a recluse who never appeared publicly) had "the most bruising, hobbling prose style this side of a German philosopher." Yet a burgeoning cult of readers found "this massive, mind-blowing, stomach-turning, monstrously comic new milestone" (as another reviewer described the book) a worthy heir to Joyce's *Ulysses*. **◀1922.1**

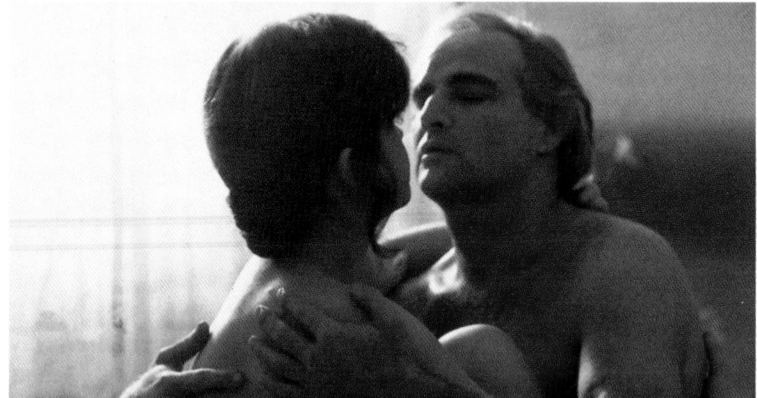

Schneider and Brando play lovers conducting an anonymous affair in *Last Tango*.

NOBEL PRIZES: Peace: Henry Kissinger and Le Duc Tho (U.S., Vietnamese; peace accord) ... Literature: Patrick White (Australian; novelist) ... Chemistry: E. Fischer and G. Wilkinson (German, U.K.; pollution) ... Medicine: K. Frisch, K. Lorenz, and N. Tinbergen (Austrian, Austrian, Dutch; behavior) ... Physics: I. Giaever, L. Esaki and B. Josephson (U.S., Japanese, U.K.; electronics) ... Economics: Wassily Leontief (U.S.).

A VOICE FROM 1973

The Tale of the Tapes

From the White House transcripts, released by President Richard M. Nixon, in 1973–1974

On December 8, 1973, President Nixon submitted the first batch of his surreptitiously recorded White House conversations to Watergate judge John J. Sirica. The first conversation below, between Nixon and White House counsel John W. Dean III, occurred on March 21, 1973—two days before Watergate burglar James McCord accused the White House of covering up its role in the break-in. Already, the President and his lawyer were plotting defensive strategy.

A slew of indictments against key White House officials ensued, but the most damning conversations didn't come out until the following August. Included in the later group was the "smoking gun"—the transcript of the June 23, 1972, meeting (less than a week after the break-in) at which chief of staff H.R. Haldeman presented Nixon with a plan to thwart the FBI's Watergate investigation: On the pretext of national security, Haldeman would get CIA director Richard Helms and deputy director Vernon A. Walters to order FBI chief L. Patrick Gray III to call off his men. Nixon approved the scheme. Three days after releasing the incriminating transcripts, Nixon resigned under threat of impeachment. ◄1972.10 ►1974.1

March 21, 1973, President Nixon and John W. Dean III

P–Suppose the worst—that Bob is indicted and Ehrlichman is indicted. And I must say, we just better then try to tough it through. You get the point.
D–That's right.
P–If they, for example, say let's cut our losses and you say we are going to go down the road to see if we can cut our losses and no more blackmail and all the rest. And then the thing blows, cutting Bob and the rest to pieces. You would never recover from that, John.
D–That's right.
P–It is better to fight it out. Then you see that's the other thing. It's better to fight it out and not let people testify, and so forth. And now, on the other hand, we realize that we have these weaknesses—that we have these weaknesses—in terms of blackmail.
D–There are two routes. One is to figure out how to cut the losses and minimize the human impact and get you up and out and away from it in any way. In a way it would never come back to haunt you. That is one general alternative. The other is to go down the road, just hunker down, fight it at every corner, every turn, don't let people testify—cover it up is what we are really talking about. Just keep it buried, and just hope that we can do it, hope that we make good decisions at the right time, keep our heads cool, we make the right moves.
P–And just take the heat?
D–And just take the heat.
P–Now with the second line of attack. You can discuss this [unintelligible] the way you want to. Still consider my scheme of having you brief the Cabinet, just in very general terms and the leaders in very general terms and maybe some very general statement with regard to my investigation. Answer questions, basically on the basis of what they told you, not what you know. Haldeman is not involved. Ehrlichman is not involved.
D–If we go that route, sir, I can give a show, we can sell them just like we were selling Wheaties on our position. There's no—
P–The problem that you have are these mine fields down the road. I think the most difficult problem are the guys who are going to jail. I think you are right about that.

June 23, 1972, Nixon and H.R. Haldeman

H–Now, on the investigation, you know the Democratic break-in thing, we're back in the problem area because the FBI is not under control, because Gray doesn't exactly know how to control it and they have—their investigation is now leading into some productive areas.... And, and it goes in some directions we don't want it to go. Ah, also there have been some things—like an informant came in off the street to the FBI in Miami who was a photographer or has a friend who is a photographer who developed some films through this guy Barker and the films had pictures of Democratic National Committee letterhead documents and things. So it's things like that that are filtering in. [Former attorney general John] Mitchell came up with yesterday, and John Dean analyzed very carefully last night and concludes, concurs now with Mitchell's recommendation that the only way to solve this, and we're set up beautifully to do it, ah, in that and that—the only network that paid any attention to it last night was NBC—they did a massive story on the Cuban thing.
P–That's right.
H–That the way to handle this now is for us to have [Vernon A.] Walters call Pat Gray and just say, "Stay to hell out of this—this is, ah, business here we don't want you to go any further on it." That's not an unusual development, and, ah, that would take care of it.
P–What about Pat Gray—you mean Pat Gray doesn't want to?
H–Pat does want to. He doesn't know how to, and he doesn't have, he doesn't have any basis for doing it. Given this, he will then have the basis.... He'll call him in and say, "We've got the signal from across the river to put the hold on this." And that will fit rather well because the FBI agents who are working the case, at this point, feel that's what it is.
P–This is CIA? They've traced the money? Who'd they trace it to?
H–Well they've traced it to a name, but they haven't gotten to the guy yet.
P–Would it be somebody here?
H–Ken Dahlberg.
P–Who the hell is Ken Dahlberg?
H–He gave $25,000 in Minnesota and, ah, the check went directly to this guy Barker.
P–It isn't from the committee, though, from [Maurice] Stans [chairman of the reelection finance committee].
H–Yeah. It is. It's directly traceable and there's some more through some Texas people that went to the Mexican Bank ....
P–Well, I mean, there's no way—I'm just thinking if they don't cooperate, what do they say? That they were approached by the Cubans. That's what Dahlberg has to say, the Texans too, that they—
H–Well, if they will. But then we're relying on more and more people all the time. That's the problem and they'll stop if we could take this other route.
P–All right.
H–And you seem to think the thing to do is get them to stop?
P–Right, fine.

The Nixon White House, as rendered by a *Philadelphia Inquirer* cartoonist.

1973

"The question is: What did the President know, and when did he know it?"—**Senator Howard Baker of Tennessee, on Watergate**

STORY OF THE YEAR

Watergate Sinks Nixon

1 By mid-1974, Richard Nixon's presidency was tottering, undone by revelations of corruption and abuse of power stemming from the Watergate affair. Nixon had inflicted much of the damage himself. After it was disclosed the previous July that he'd taped his office conversations, he'd stubbornly resisted a court order to surrender the recordings. That October, when special prosecutor Archibald Cox refused Nixon's offer to provide a summary of the tapes, the President commanded Attorney General Elliot Richardson to fire Cox, whom Richardson had appointed. Richardson and his deputy resigned instead, leaving the deed to Solicitor General Robert Bork. This "Saturday Night Massacre" outraged the public, and in November Nixon gave in—partially.

Nixon flashes his signature double victory sign one last time as he leaves the White House for good.

Of the nine subpoenaed tapes, the White House delivered only seven, claiming the others didn't exist. One contained a suspicious 18-minute gap—the result, supposedly, of a technical slipup by the tape's transcriber, longtime Nixon secretary Rose Mary Woods. The recordings revealed Nixon to be foulmouthed, cynical, obsessed with "enemies," and intermittently anti-Semitic, but they contained no conclusive evidence of guilt. Meanwhile, however, Senator Sam Ervin, Jr.'s Watergate committee had been conducting televised hearings in which White House and Nixon campaign officials confessed to—and accused one another of—dozens of conspiracies, from money laundering to illegal wiretapping.

As 1974 progressed, former attorney general Richard Kleindienst, former domestic adviser John Ehrlichman, and former presidential counsel John Dean were convicted of Watergate-related charges; former White House aide H.R. Haldeman and former attorney general (and Nixon campaign chief) John Mitchell joined the ranks of the indicted; and Congress drew up articles of impeachment. On August 5, Nixon was forced to release another set of tapes, which clearly tied him to a cover-up of White House involvement in illegal activities. On August 8, he resigned.

"I have never been a quitter," he told the nation. "To leave office before my term is completed is opposed to every instinct in my body. But as president I must put the needs of America first." In fact, the Watergate scandals deeply rocked Americans' faith in their government (though much the world was baffled by the fuss). One month after becoming the 38th president of the United States, Gerald Ford preemptively pardoned his former boss, sparing Nixon criminal indictment. **◂1973.V ▸1986.8**

1974

PORTUGAL

Dictatorship Topples

2 Portugal's 1974 Captains' Revolution—named for the army officers who led it—toppled the longest dictatorship in Western European history. Gone was Prime Minister Marcello Caetano, caretaker of the hidebound regime erected by António Salazar in 1933. Gone was Salazar's dreaded secret police force. Gone, too, were censorship and conscription. In their place: General António Spínola and the promise of democracy. Thousands of Portuguese thronged the streets of Lisbon on the morning after the coup, showering Spínola with red and white carnations.

The monocled, gruff Spínola made an unlikely liberator. He had fought with Franco's fascists in Spain in the 1930s, trained with Hitler's Wehrmacht in the forties, and made his name putting down revolts in Portugal's African colonies in the sixties. As governor of Guinea-Bissau (then Portuguese Guinea) from 1968, however, Spínola recognized that Portugal could not win its draining colonial wars. (Since 1964, when rebels in Mozambique, Angola, and Guinea-Bissau began fighting for independence, Portugal had annually squandered 40 percent of its budget on war.) By 1974 Spínola was advocating home rule for the colonies. His position struck a popular chord, and the coup plotters drafted him as their leader.

As it turned out, Spínola was a poor match for his revolution: Portugal wanted to undo decades of repression overnight—and the general, said a younger colleague, "was too pessimistic, too gloomy, too rigid." He resigned six months after taking charge. The junta swung sharply to the left, reaching its socialist apex in 1975. That year, in addition to nationalizing industry and reforming agriculture, the government granted independence to Angola, Guinea-Bissau, Mozambique, São Tomé and Príncipe, and Cape Verde. It also allowed elections in Portugal itself. **◂1933.9 ▸1975.2**

After the coup, socialist partisans rallied for Portugal's Armed Forces Movement junta at Lisbon's São Bento palace.

WEST GERMANY

The Fall of Willy Brandt

3 By official estimates, some 15,000 Communist spies operated inside West Germany in 1974—none so embarrassingly as Günter Guillaume, a close personal aide to Chancellor Willy Brandt. Guillaume's exposure in April impelled Brandt to resign. It was a bitter and ironic defeat: During Brandt's five years as Chancellor, his *Ostpolitik* had thawed West Germany's relations with the Warsaw Pact countries, paving the way for Soviet-American détente and winning him a Nobel Peace Prize. Thousands of supporters urged Brandt to stay on, but his decision was final: "I accept," he declared, "the political responsibility for negligence in connection with the Guillaume espionage affair."

Brandt first won fame as mayor of West Berlin from 1957 to 1966, when his resistance to Soviet encroachment made him an international symbol of freedom. To his compatriots he'd long been known as *unser Willy* (our Willy), the statesman who faced up to Nazi ghosts and began to make German pride acceptable again. "No people can escape from their history," Brandt often said, and on his landmark 1970 visit to Poland, he dropped to his knees and prayed for the 500,000 Warsaw Ghetto Jews killed by German soldiers during World War II. But as he failed to enact promised economic reforms, his political fortunes steadily declined.

By 1974, inflation and *Ostpolitik*—which critics said gave more to the

ART & CULTURE: Books: ***Dog Soldiers*** **(Robert Stone);** ***The War Between the Tates*** **(Alison Lurie);** ***Zen and the Art of Motorcycle Maintenance*** **(Robert M. Pirsig);** ***All the President's Men*** **(Bob Woodward and Carl Bernstein);** ***The Death Notebooks*** **(Anne Sexton) ... Music: "Cat's in the Cradle" (Harry Chapin); "The Way We Were" (Marvin Hamlisch);** ***Air Music*** **(Ned Rorem) ... Painting & Sculpture:**

"I have been given the choice of being released in a safe area, or joining the forces of the Symbionese Liberation Army and fighting for my freedom and the freedom of all oppressed people. I have chosen to stay and fight."—**Patricia Hearst**

Communists than was received in return—had alienated much of the electorate. The arrest of Guillaume, an East German mole who'd staged a fake defection to West Germany in 1956, was the final straw. For Brandt, prophet of reconciliation, the security breach was a crushing blow to pride as well as statecraft. **◂1970.6 ▸1983.5**

THE UNITED STATES

An Heiress's Bizarre Odyssey

4 The century's strangest political kidnapping occurred on February 5, 1974, when 19-year-old newspaper heiress Patricia Hearst, a cheerfully apolitical student at the University of California at Berkeley, was abducted at gunpoint from the campus apartment she shared with her fiancé. Hearst's captors called themselves the Symbionese Liberation Army—a dozen or so mostly white, middle-class, and female revolutionaries clustered around two black escaped convicts, each with a history of mental illness. The SLA first surfaced in November 1973, killing a local school official with cyanide-tipped bullets. With Hearst's abduction, the tiny "army" became world-famous.

The kidnappers demanded that Hearst's "fascist insect" parents (her father, Randolph, was William Randolph Hearst's son) distribute $2 million in free food to the area's poor. But after the family complied, a tape-recorded message arrived—along with a photo of the abductee toting a submachine gun. "I have chosen," she announced, "to stay and fight." Taking the nom de guerre Tania, Hearst took part in an SLA bank robbery and freed two comrades caught shoplifting by spraying a storefront with bullets.

In May, investigators found an SLA hideout in Los Angeles. Four hundred police and FBI agents shot it out with the occupants; the house burned down, but none of the six charred bodies found in the wreckage was Hearst's. In her next communiqué, Hearst denounced her fiancé as a "pig" and eulogized the dead, who included her lover, a guerrilla called Cujo, and the SLA's leader, "Field Marshal" Donald "Cinque" DeFreeze.

Hearst was finally apprehended in September 1975. At her trial, celebrated criminal lawyer F. Lee

Her parents paid a ransom, but instead of their daughter Patty, the Hearsts got a photograph of revolutionary "Tania."

Bailey argued that his client had been coerced and brainwashed—blindfolded, locked in a closet, starved, threatened, and berated. Unconvinced, the jury found her guilty of armed robbery. Hearst was sentenced to seven years in prison, but after 22 months President Carter commuted her sentence. Upon her release, she married her bodyguard and settled down as a suburban homemaker. **◂1970.7 ▸1975.10**

GREECE

A Battle Over Cyprus

5 Amid rising resentment over repression and economic stagnation, Greece's rightist military rulers needed a victory to regain popularity. They hoped to find it in Cyprus, whose president, Archbishop Makarios, had lately switched from championing enosis (union with Greece) to urging continued independence. Worse, he'd allied himself with local communists, who endorsed his Cold War neutralism. In July 1974, the junta backed the Cypriot National Guard—the militia of Cyprus's ethnic Greek majority, led by officers supplied by the mainland regime—in its overthrow of Makarios. The result was a calamity for both Cyprus and the Athens dictatorship.

Within a week of the coup, Turkish troops invaded Cyprus. Their initial aim was to prevent enosis (prohibited by the Greco-Turkish treaty that established the Cypriot republic in 1960), and to protect the island's Turkish minority. The UN quickly imposed a truce. But after peace talks failed in August, Turkish forces advanced again. Days later, when Turkey declared its own cease-fire, the northern two fifths of Cyprus was under its occupation. Panicked by bombing and atrocities, virtually all the area's Greek Cypriots—about 180,000—fled south. (Turkish Cypriots were later sent north.) The Greek Cypriots suffered 6,000 casualties, twice as many as the Turks. Makarios returned from London to resume the presidency. And Cyprus remained partitioned along a UN-patrolled "green line."

Lacking the resources for direct intervention, the Greek junta helplessly watched the disaster unfold. Before it was over, they recalled conservative former premier Constantine Karamanlis from exile to restore Greece to democracy and civilian rule. **◂1960.10 ▸1981.M**

As Turkey and Greece faced off over Cyprus, moderate Greek Cypriots demonstrated for peaceful coexistence with their Turkish counterparts.

DEATHS

William "Bud" Abbott, U.S. comedian.

Creighton Abrams, U.S. military commander.

Jack Benny, U.S. comedian.

Charles Bohlen, U.S. diplomat.

Vannevar Bush, U.S. engineer.

James Chadwick, U.K. physicist.

Jerome Herman "Dizzy" Dean, U.S. baseball player.

Edward Kennedy "Duke" Ellington, U.S. musician and composer.

Cass Elliot, U.S. singer

Samuel Goldwyn, Polish-U.S. filmmaker.

Adolph Gottlieb, U.S. painter.

Georgette Heyer, U.K. novelist.

H.L. Hunt, U.S. industrialist.

Chet Huntley, U.S. broadcast journalist.

Charles A. Lindbergh, U.S. aviator.

Walter Lippmann, U.S. journalist.

Arnold Lunn, U.K. skier.

Darius Milhaud, French composer.

Agnes Moorehead, U.S. actress.

Juan Perón, Argentine president.

Georges Pompidou, French president.

John Crowe Ransom, U.S. writer.

Anne Sexton, U.S. poet.

Ed Sullivan, U.S. journalist and television host.

Jacqueline Susann, U.S. writer.

U Thant, Burmese diplomat.

Earl Warren, U.S. jurist.

The Dinner Party **(Judy Chicago);** ***Hotel Paramount*** **(Richard Estes) ... Film:** ***The Godfather, Part II*** **and** ***The Conversation*** **(Francis Ford Coppola);** ***The Great Gatsby*** **(Jack Clayton);** ***Alice Doesn't Live Here Anymore*** **(Martin Scorsese) ... Theater:** ***Travesties*** **(Tom Stoppard);** ***Knuckle*** **(David Hare);** ***Short Eyes*** **(Miguel Piñero) ... TV:** ***The Rockford Files; Happy Days; Little House on the Prairie.***

"Black holes would seem to suggest that God not only plays dice but also sometimes throws them where they cannot be seen."
—Stephen Hawking

NEW IN 1974

Hirschhorn Museum and Sculpture Garden (Washington, D.C.).

A black model on the cover of a major fashion magazine (Beverly Johnson on *Vogue*).

National speed limit of 55 mph.

Girls in Little League baseball.

Heimlich maneuver (developed in Cincinnati by thoracic surgeon Henry J. Heimlich).

IN THE UNITED STATES

▶SHIELD WITHDRAWN—Under FDA pressure, the A.H. Robbins pharmaceutical company removed its Dalkon Shield intrauterine device (IUD) from the market in 1974. Introduced three years earlier, the shield caused pelvic inflammatory disease, resulting in permanent pain, sometimes death. It also had a high failure rate. Many women who became pregnant while using the device miscarried; others became infertile. Robbins, though apparently aware of the shield's pitfalls, contested the thousands of lawsuits filed on behalf of injured women. ◂1960.1

▶WOMEN PRIESTS—In July, in defiance of official church policy, four Episcopal priests in Philadelphia (the birthplace of the Episcopal Church) ordained eleven women to join their ranks. The House of Bishops, one of the church's ruling bodies, declared the ordinations illegal but in October endorsed the *principle* of women priests. Official sanction came in 1976. ◂1968.12 ▸1991.7

▶AARON TOPS RUTH—Henry Aaron hit career home run number 715 on April 8, breaking Babe Ruth's 39-year hold on the record. Aaron, a black man who started out in the Negro leagues, was besieged with hate mail in the months following

An artist's conceptualization of a black hole absorbing spiraling stellar matter.

SCIENCE

A New Theory of Black Holes

6 In 1974, British physicist and cosmologist Stephen Hawking smashed established ideas about the universe when he asserted that black holes emitted radiation. By the accepted definition, black holes—hypothetical collapsed stars whose gravitational pull is so extreme, not even light can escape—emitted nothing. Hawking's announcement, at an astronomy conference near Oxford, prompted one colleague to storm out in anger.

Hawking, 32, seemed to be brashly contradicting Einstein's theory of relativity, which posits that nothing can travel faster than light. Actually, he'd managed to integrate relativity with quantum theory—a feat Einstein and others had attempted without success. Hawking's equations helped explain how the universe had expanded in some 15 billion years from a point to an immensity, and how it would shrink back on itself in a so-called "cosmic crunch."

Hawking's work would become widely popular in 1988 with his bestselling *A Brief History of Time*. But a cult grew up around him soon after his black-hole breakthrough—inspired, in part, by his remarkable courage. Diagnosed in his early 20s with amyotrophic lateral sclerosis (also known as Lou Gehrig's disease), Hawking defied doctors' predictions that he had two years to live. He relied on a wheelchair for mobility, and on a computer for speech. With a powerful mind trapped in a ruined body, he was sustained by a relentless desire to decipher the cosmos. **◂1968.8**

ETHIOPIA

An Emperor Falls

7 In nearly five decades of rule, Emperor Haile Selassie had transformed Ethiopia from a medieval backwater into a semimodern state with sub-Saharan Africa's biggest army and had become an important mediator in regional conflicts. Yet Ethiopians lacked all political rights and remained one of the world's poorest and least literate peoples. In 1974, they toppled the 82-year-old monarch from his throne.

The uprising was sparked by a famine the previous year that killed 200,000—and by reports that the government, besides providing no relief, had kept the disaster a secret from other countries. A wave of strikes and demonstrations began in February, spreading to the 47,000-man armed forces. At first the military demanded only pay raises. But by cautious stages radical officers turned revolt into revolution. They forced Haile Selassie to replace his rubber-stamp cabinet with one headed by a liberal aristocrat, then arrested the new government ministers one by one. Next they nationalized the Emperor's 13 palaces. In September, after he refused to turn over $10 billion he'd stashed in foreign accounts, they deposed him and placed him under house arrest.

The junta was called the Derg (shadow) for its members' anonymity. Initially fronted by a popular general, the regime became even more mysterious when he and 59 other officials were shot in November. The real strongman was the purge's Marxist architect, Major Mengistu Haile Mariam. The Derg soon nationalized industry, banking, and agriculture. But leftist urban guerrillas resisted military rule, while separatists in Eritrea and Tigre provinces fought for independence. Ethiopia's agony would continue to deepen. **◂1962.M ▸1978.M**

FRANCE

Socialists Lose—Narrowly

8 Although Charles de Gaulle died in 1970, his grip on French politics didn't ease until 1974, when Georges Pompidou—once de Gaulle's complaisant premier, then his successor as president—succumbed to cancer. Apart from moderating de Gaulle's anti-American and anti-British policies, Pompidou had initiated few changes. The post–de Gaulle era could begin only when voters chose their next president. Two radically different candidates faced each other: Socialist François Mitterrand and centrist finance minister Valéry Giscard d'Estaing.

The aristocratic Giscard *(above)* belonged to the small Independent Republican Party, whose stance toward de Gaulle was (in Giscard's words) "yes ... but." He disdained

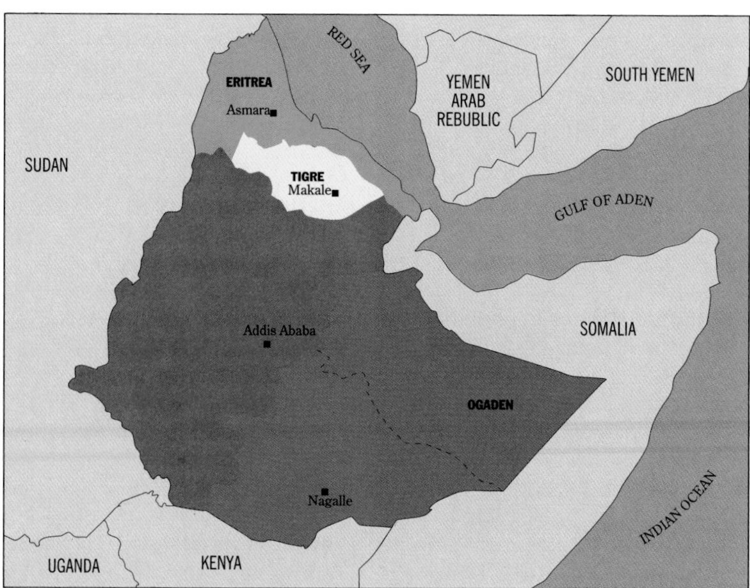

Eritrean, Tigre, and Somali separatists (the latter in the Ogaden region, bordering on Somalia) together claimed much of Ethiopia's territory.

SPORTS: Baseball: World Series, Oakland Athletics defeat Los Angeles Dodgers, 4–1 ... Football: Super Bowl, Miami Dolphins defeat Minnesota Vikings, 24–7 ... Basketball: NBA, Boston Celtics defeat Milwaukee Bucks, 4–3 ... Tennis: Jimmy Connors wins first Wimbledon, U.S. Open, and Australian Open; Chris Evert wins first Wimbledon ... Soccer: World Cup, West Germany defeats the Netherlands, 2–1.

"The artist and the criminal are fellow travelers; both have a wild creativity, and both are amoral, driven only by the force of liberty."—**Joseph Beuys**

Gaullist nationalism, seeking to make France a *rayonnement*—a beacon of civilization—rather than a superpower. Like his predecessors, he supported big business; unlike them, he saw it as the key to financing cautiously liberal reforms. Mitterrand, the ascetic son of a railroad stationmaster, called for bold government action—including the nationalization of banks and major industries—to ameliorate social inequality and unemployment.

In the multicandidate first-round election, Mitterrand beat Giscard by two million votes, aided by an alliance with the Communists (who represented about 20 percent of the electorate). But in the runoff, that alliance—with its specter of Marxist-Leninist cabinet members—lost Mitterrand votes. More damage came from his untelegenic performance in a TV debate. Running on the slogan "Change without risk," the debonair Giscard won by just one percentage point.

Despite its defeat, however, the left was stronger than at any time since the 1930s. And before long, it would prevail. **◂1968.1 ▸1976.14**

ART

Beuys Meets Coyote

9 Upon arriving at New York's Kennedy Airport in May 1974, West German sculptor Joseph Beuys was wrapped in felt, placed on a stretcher, and brought by ambulance to the René Blok Gallery, where he lived with a coyote for three days and nights before being wrapped in felt, laid on a stretcher, and transported back to the airport in an ambulance. This obscure drama, titled *I Like America and America Likes Me*, was the latest in a series of performance pieces that made Beuys one of the most controversial artists of his era.

Beuys's work was shaped by his experience in the Luftwaffe during World War II. Shot down over the Crimea, he was found by nomadic Tartars who treated his wounds with animal fat and wrapped him in felt to keep him warm. He evoked memories of that and other traumatic events through sculpture, graphic art, and "actions" (as he called them) involving highly unorthodox media. A key figure in Fluxus, a 1960s movement that rejected professionalism and permanence in fine art, he'd earned notoriety with *How to Explain Pictures to a Dead Hare* (1965)—an exploration of the "problems of language," in which he coated his head with gold leaf and honey, and gave the dead animal a gallery tour.

German performance artist Joseph Beuys shared bare digs with a coyote.

To his admirers Beuys was a shaman, a living work of art. (His dismissal from the faculty of Düsseldorf's Kunstakademie in 1972 provoked a riot.) A supporter of causes ranging from Tibetan liberation to the German Green Party, he was almost as influential for his speeches as for his fiercely original oeuvre. He died in 1986. **◂1920.4 ▸1983.12**

THE MIDDLE EAST

Arab-Israeli Truce

10 For four weeks in the spring of 1974, U.S. Secretary of State Henry Kissinger jetted between Jerusalem and Damascus, weaving an agreement between two nations that had been enemies for a quarter century. On May 31, Israeli and Syrian representatives in Geneva signed a document establishing a new, United Nations–policed border in the Golan Heights and ending eight months of sporadic fighting. Kissinger's patented "shuttle diplomacy" gave his Watergate-plagued boss, Richard Nixon, a final success before he resigned the presidency. It also provided a last hurrah for Israeli prime minister Golda Meir who, battered by criticism of her conduct of the 1973 war, had already announced her resignation in favor of fellow Laborite Yitzhak Rabin.

The truce agreement, which required Israel to return 300 square miles of land and the city of Quneitra to Syria, improved Arab-American relations. It bolstered Egypt's President Sadat, who'd been widely scored for breaking ranks to negotiate with Israel. But Arab unity suffered as the hard-line leaders of Iraq and Libya added Syrian president Hafez al-Assad to their list of "traitors." And the truce failed to address the Palestinian problem.

A globe-circling Kissinger was portrayed as a "Superdiplomat" on *Newsweek*'s cover.

Weeks earlier, that problem had brought terror to two Israeli towns. PLO commandos killed 18 civilians in Kiryat Shmona; in Maalot, 16 children died when government troops stormed a school that had been seized by another commando squad. In November, after the Arab League pronounced the PLO the "sole legitimate representative" of the Palestinians, chairman Yasir Arafat addressed the UN while wearing a pistol. "I have come bearing an olive branch and a freedom fighter's gun," he said. "Do not let the olive branch fall from my hands." **◂1973.2 ▸1977.1**

IN THE UNITED STATES

the feat. Known for his poise under pressure, "Hammerin' Hank" retired in 1976, after 21 seasons with the National League Braves. His total of 755 major-league home runs is widely considered unbeatable. ◂1972.M

▶THE FONZ ON TV—ABC's *Happy Days*—a 1950s nostalgia sitcom featuring Milwaukee high schooler Richie Cunningham and his white-bread friends—did moderately well after premiering on January 15 but became a national craze after expanding the role of motorcycle tough Arthur "Fonzie" Fonzarelli. With his

"thumbs up" hand signal, black leather jacket, slangy speech, and special way with a jukebox, the Fonz (Henry Winkler) was the epitome of '50s cool. ◂1969.M ▸1980.7

▶STREAKING—The most talked-about fad in a fad-bitten decade hit campuses in the spring when students shed clothes for nude campus dashes. "Streaking" soon turned up everywhere—Hawaii's state house, the Academy Awards, sporting events, state dinners, even Webster's Dictionary. Both sexes partook, but male streakers outnumbered female; culturologists read the trend as the ultimate expression of the sexual revolution. ◂1959.M

▶DNA MORATORIUM—Top American medical researchers announced a voluntary moratorium on several types of recombinant-DNA experiments in 1974. By then, scientists had the technology to manipulate the nucleotide sequences in genes, a breakthrough that promised cures for hereditary conditions such as sickle-cell anemia (and enormous profits for biotechnology companies). But also conceivable was the accidental creation and release into the environment of deadly new pathogens—hence the moratorium. The freeze remained in effect until 1976. ◂1967.11 ▸1976.5

POLITICS & BUSINESS: GNP: $1,474.3 billion ... President Richard M. Nixon resigns, succeeded by Gerald Ford ... Ford grants limited amnesty to Vietnam War draft evaders ... Congress passes Freedom of Information Act over Ford's veto ... Congressman Wilbur Mills resigns after scandal over relationship with burlesque dancer Fanne Fox ... Federal Election Campaign Act limits individual contributions to $1,000.

"Because when he speaks, they hear the voice of the camps, they hear them, those ghosts, those millions, those tens of millions who left their bodies there. And they are afraid."—**Anonymous Soviet writer on the authorities' reason for banishing Aleksandr Solzhenitsyn**

AROUND THE WORLD

▶TE KANAWA'S MET DEBUT—Rising soprano sensation Kiri Te Kanawa made her debut at the New York Metropolitan Opera in 1974, as Desdemona in Verdi's *Otello*. Her lively, warm voice and simple singing style was praised by critics. A native New Zealander of mixed Maori and English ancestry, Te Kanawa studied singing in Auckland before moving to London and gaining the support of Sir Georg Solti and other conductors in the late sixties. In 1981, she sang at the wedding of Prince Charles and Princess Diana; the following year she was made a dame by Queen Elizabeth II. ◂1959.6 ▸1975.11

▶MISHA DEFECTS—Mikhail Baryshnikov, the most celebrated ballet dancer of his generation and the last pupil

of legendary Soviet instructor Aleksandr Pushkin, defected to the West in June while touring Canada as a guest artist with the Bolshoi Ballet. The principal male dancer of Leningrad's illustrious Kirov Ballet, Baryshnikov followed such *danseurs nobles* as Rudolf Nureyev (1961) and Natalia Makarova (1970) in defecting. He went on to become a sensation in the United States. ◂1961.13

▶INDIA TESTS BOMB—From India came an unwelcome revelation: Plutonium reprocessed from nuclear power plant waste could make a bomb. India detonated its first nuclear device in 1974, becoming the sixth country to possess nuclear weapons. The fact that Indian scientists had constructed their bomb from "peaceful" materials was especially disturbing. Researchers estimated that by the year 2000 the amount of plutonium produced in power plants worldwide would have the "explosive potential of one million bombs of the size that destroyed Nagasaki." ◂1969.8

1974

TECHNOLOGY

So Long, Slide Rule

11 The earliest pocket calculators had been little more than electronic abaci. But when, in 1974, calculators began incorporating the single large-scale integrated (LSI) chip into their technology, they became a truly scientific instrument—a valuable tool that could perform advanced trigonometric and logarithmic functions. Previously, such advanced-function calculators had required as many as six chips, making them bulky and expensive. Consumers instantly took to the new, streamlined models: Some twelve million were sold the first year. For most people, the improved advanced-function pocket calculator represented the first practical way to incorporate cutting-edge computer technology into their everyday lives.

The effect on prices was immediate and dramatic: In a single year, advanced-function hand-held calculators dropped from about $400 to under $100. (Meanwhile, simple-function calculators cost as little as $15, eventually becoming so cheap they were literally given away—as premiums.) Infiltrating all levels of society, pocket calculators profoundly influenced attitudes toward not only mathematics but computers in general, which quickly lost their esoteric aura. **◂1971.5 ▸1981.10**

Multi-function calculators made microchip technology available to millions of people.

***Chinatown* features Jack Nicholson as jaded private eye J.J. Gittes and Faye Dunaway as Evelyn Mulwray, the beautiful and mysterious widow whose secrets he tries to uncover.**

FILM

Polanski's Dyspeptic Thriller

12 In his classic 1974 thriller, *Chinatown*, director Roman Polanski's melancholy vision jibed with that of a Vietnam-vanquished, Watergate-weary nation: Society was corrupt to the core. Set in 1930s Los Angeles, the movie reveals the venality—in politics, real estate, and personal relations—that catalyzed the city's evolution from desert to film-industry Mecca and capital of the American Dream. Robert Towne's script added freshness and wit (and incest) to a timeworn detective-movie formula: a street-smart private eye (Jack Nicholson), a shady lady (Faye Dunaway), a monstrous millionaire (John Huston), and a mysterious murder. Towne wanted an upbeat ending, but Polanski—who appears in a cameo as a diminutive thug who sticks a switchblade up Nicholson's nose—insisted on a final burst of bloody nihilism.

Polanski's best films—which also include *Knife in the Water* (made in Poland in 1962, before he emigrated to Paris, London, and Hollywood), *Repulsion* (1965), and *Rosemary's Baby* (1968)—are soaked in violence, madness, and black humor. Polanski's fatalism was earned: As a child, he'd escaped Krakow's Jewish ghetto; his mother died in a concentration camp. Tragedy struck the director again in 1969, when members of the Charles Manson cult murdered his pregnant wife (actress Sharon Tate) and four friends. And in 1977, free on bail after pleading guilty to having had sex with a 13-year-old girl, he fled the United States for Paris before sentencing. **◂1969.9**

THE SOVIET UNION

Solzhenitsyn Banished

13 Détente notwithstanding, Western distaste for the Soviet Union sharpened in February 1974, when Communist authorities banished novelist Aleksandr Solzhenitsyn. The 51-year-old writer had been arrested for treason after installments of his monumental "literary investigation" of the Soviet prison system, *The Gulag Archipelago*, were published in Paris. The book was based on an earlier run-in with the authorities: As an artillery officer during World War II, Solzhenitsyn was arrested for criticizing Stalin in a letter to a friend. Tried in absentia, he was sentenced to eight years in labor camps, followed by three more in exile in Central Asia. During his imprisonment, he memorized the stories of other victims, committing them to paper after his release.

After picking up the Nobel Prize for literature he'd won in 1970—he hadn't gone to Stockholm at the time for fear the Kremlin would not let him return—Solzhenitsyn settled in rural Vermont, in the United States. Though revered for his courage and his creative powers (his other major works include *One Day in the Life of Ivan Denisovich* and *Cancer Ward*), he was controversial in exile as well, drawing especially heavy criticism for his condemnation of American culture. No democrat, he advocated the establishment in Russia of a benevolent despotism based on mystical Russian Orthodox Christianity. Gorbachev restored his citizenship in 1990, and in 1994, a pariah no longer, Solzhenitsyn returned to his homeland. **◂1966.11 ▸1975.5**

Solzhenitsyn *(left)* was feted by Congress, but the prickly author never embraced American-style government.

NOBEL PRIZES: Peace: Eisaku Sato and Sean MacBride (Japanese, Irish; disarmament) ... Literature: Eyvind Johnson and Harry Martinson (Swedish; novelists) ... Chemistry: Paul Flory (U.S.; macromolecules) ... Medicine: G. Palade, C. de Duve, and A. Claude (U.S., Belgian, Belgian; cell structure) ... Physics: A. Hewish and M. Ryle (U.K.; radioastrophysics) ... Economics: G. Myrdal and F. von Hayek (Swedish, U.K.).

A VOICE FROM 1974

Revenge of a Prom Queen

From *Carrie,* by Stephen King, 1974

In his first novel, Carrie, *Stephen King* (left) *presented a gawky 16-year-old girl from a small town in Maine who daily suffers humiliations at the hands of her cruel classmates and her religiously deranged mother. But she has a secret weapon: She's telekinetic. On prom night, one last malicious prank sends her over the edge, and the "frog among swans" uses her supernatural powers to exact a gory revenge of biblical proportions. (In the scene below, her chief tormentors get their comeuppance.) The 1974 bestseller launched King's career as a publishing wonder whose horror novels have sold more than 100 million copies around the world. In the coming decades, King often had more than one blockbuster out at a time (plus an inevitable movie version of a previous bestseller). He was a one-man industry, sustained by his ability to find the horror in human relations and give it a supernatural spin.*

They got into his car, and he started it up. When he popped on the headlights, Chris began to scream, hands in fists up to her cheeks.

Billy felt it at the same time: Something in his mind,

(carrie carrie carrie carrie)

a presence.

Carrie was standing in front of them, perhaps seventy feet away.

The high beams picked her out in ghastly horror-movie blacks and whites, dripping and clotted with blood. Now much of it was her own. The hilt of the butcher knife still protruded from her shoulder, and her gown was covered with dirt and grass stain. She had crawled much of the distance from Carlin Street, half-fainting, to destroy this roadhouse—perhaps the very one where the doom of her creation had begun.

She stood swaying, her arms thrown out like the arms of a stage hypnotist, and she began to totter toward them.

It happened in the blink of a second. Chris had not had time to expend her first scream. Billy's reflexes were very good and his reaction was instantaneous. He shifted into low, popped the clutch, and floored it.

The Chevrolet's tires screamed against the asphalt, and the car sprang forward like some old and terrible man-eater. The figure swelled in the windshield and as it did the presence became louder.

(CARRIE CARRIE CARRIE)

and louder

(CARRIE CARRIE CARRIE)

like a radio being turned up to full volume. Time seemed to close around them in a frame and for a moment they were frozen even in motion: Billy

(CARRIE just like the dogs Carrie just like the goddam dogs CARRIE brucie i wish it could CARRIE be CARRIE you)

and Chris

(CARRIE jesus not kill her CARRIE didn't mean to kill her CARRIE billy i don't CARRIE went to CARRIE see it CA)

and Carrie herself.

(see the wheel car wheel gas pedal wheel i see the WHEEL o god my heart my heart my heart)

And Billy suddenly felt his car turn traitor, come alive, slither in his hands. The Chevvy dug around in a smoking half-circle, straight pipes racketing, and suddenly the clapboard side of The Cavalier was swelling, swelling, swelling and

(this is)

they slammed into it at forty, still accelerating, and wood sprayed up in a neon-tinted detonation. Billy was thrown forward and the steering column speared him. Chris was thrown into the dashboard.

The gas tank split open, and fuel began to puddle around the rear of the car. Part of one straight pipe fell into it, and the gas bloomed into flame.

In Brian De Palma's 1976 screen version of King's bestseller, Carrie (Sissy Spacek) unleashes a terrible vengeance on the pranksters who have set her up as prom queen only to humiliate her. Here, covered with pig's blood, she telekinetically sets fire to the gymnasium and rains destruction on her enemies.

"To be Spanish is to be something in the world. Arriba, España!"—**Generalissimo Francisco Franco in his last public address in October 1975, one month before his death**

STORY OF THE YEAR

The Franco Era Ends

1 At 82, General Francisco Franco clung to life with the same tenacity that had made him Spain's absolute ruler for 36 years. Illnesses had besieged the Generalissimo, but doctors—and his iron will—had always saved him. In October 1975, after his execution of five Basque terrorists sparked worldwide protest, he found the strength to rally 150,000 followers against the "leftist Masonic conspiracy" that sought to depose him. But in November, the strongman's heart gave out at last. Franco's heir as chief of state, King Juan Carlos, faced a choice that had brought civil war to many nations: continued dictatorship or democracy.

Two days after Franco's death, Prince Juan Carlos was proclaimed King of Spain; wife Sofia became queen.

Discontent with dictatorship had long been rife. As industrialization and tourism doubled incomes in the 1960s, the new middle class began to long for greater political and cultural freedom—a yearning student protesters risked jail and torture to express. The Catholic Church, once pro-Franco, grew critical. Workers, stifled by official unions, launched illegal strikes. Basque separatists pursued a terrorist campaign, and secessionism stirred in Catalonia as well. In the 1970s, when Spain's "economic miracle" gave way to recession, unrest mounted. But even after Franco's death, the rightist oligarchy clung to its privileges—backed by the military.

At first, most Spaniards saw Juan Carlos, 37, as unwilling or unable to challenge the old order. He vaguely promised elections, yet street protests were often brutally suppressed. Press restrictions ended, however, giving a forum to those demanding a "democratic rupture" with Francoism. The King, in fact, was privately eager to democratize but feared provoking violence. So while holding warm talks with opposition leaders, he kept his speeches bland and made changes slowly. In July 1976, he freed most political prisoners, legalized political parties (except—for now—separatist, anarchist, and Communist), and replaced reactionary Premier Carlos Arias Navarro with a young, little-known technocrat, Adolfo Suárez Gonzalez. In September, Suárez unveiled a proposal to replace the rubber-stamp legislature with a multiparty parliament (including the Communists), and to hold elections in 1977.

Though most of Franco's repressive laws survived until after those elections, the government let enforcement lapse. And within a year of his demise, Spain was enjoying an outburst of free expression unseen since the 1930s. **◂1973.11 ▸1981.5**

COLONIALISM

Portugal's Empire Expires

2 In 1975, five centuries after becoming the first European power to colonize Africa (or anyplace else), Portugal became the last to leave the continent. Costly and unpopular wars against independence movements in Angola, Mozambique, and Portuguese Guinea had led to the overthrow of Portugal's right-wing dictatorship the previous year. The revolutionary regime had let little Guinea go immediately (the country was renamed Guinea-Bissau); now Portugal finished liquidating its empire.

For all three colonies, Portuguese domination had been harsh, and the imperial rulers had laid no groundwork for self-government. But for Mozambique and Angola, the postcolonial problems were especially complex. Many of Mozambique's 220,000 whites, fearing retribution from eight million blacks and distrusting Samora Machel's Maoist regime, fled the country. Some destroyed property as they left, and the exodus created a shortage of capital and technical expertise. Those who stayed were treated well, but Machel's efforts at social reform and collectivization were undermined by neighboring South Africa and Rhodesia. Both countries raided Mozambique in reprisal for its support of UN sanctions and antiapartheid guerrillas, and a South African–backed guerrilla group called Renamo launched a counterrevolutionary war.

Whites fled from Angola, too. Meanwhile, three armed nationalist groups vied for power. Poet-president Agostinho Neto's leftist MPLA, which aimed to transcend ethnic divisions, had led the independence fight. But Holden Roberto's FNLA, supported by the Kongo people, united with Jonas Savimbi's Ovimbundu-based UNITA to challenge Neto's rule. With Soviet arms and Cuban troops supporting the MPLA, and the United States and South Africa backing FNLA-UNITA, Angola's civil war sputtered on indefinitely. **◂1974.2 ▸1984.M**

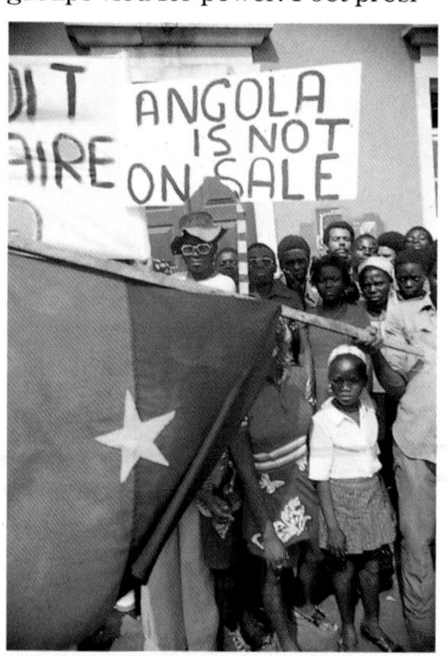

Angolan protesters at the governor-general's palace in Luanda in November 1975.

THE MIDDLE EAST

Lebanon Erupts

3 The long, chaotic Lebanese civil war began in April 1975 in Beirut when Christians massacred a busload of Palestinians and other Muslims. Within weeks, artillery was booming throughout the country and the national government had virtually collapsed.

Before the war, Beirut was the Riviera of the Middle East.

The conflict's roots went back to the 1920s, when France, inheriting the region from the Ottoman Empire, created the Lebanese Republic out of the territory of Mount Lebanon and several Syrian districts. With a population divided evenly between Muslims and Maronite Christians, instability always loomed. By 1946, when Lebanon gained full independence, a system for distributing governmental authority along ethnic lines was in place: The president was normally a Maronite, the prime minister a Sunni Muslim, and the speaker of the chamber a Shiite Muslim. But tensions between the largely poor, rural Muslims and the relatively privileged, urban Christians rose after 1970 with the arrival of thousands of Palestinians

ART & CULTURE: Books: *Ragtime* (E.L. Doctorow); *The Dead Father* (Donald Barthelme); *JR* (William Gaddis); *Shōgun* (James Clavell); *Humboldt's Gift* (Saul Bellow); *Hearing Secret Harmonies* (Anthony Powell; final volume of *A Dance to the Music of Time*); *Self-Portrait in a Convex Mirror* (John Ashbery) ... Music: "Philadelphia Freedom" (John and Taupin); *Still Crazy After All These Years* (Paul Simon, LP);

"The United States is no longer in a position to take on warmongering adventures.... Only 15 years ago, the United States was very powerful—but no more."—**Fidel Castro, on the U.S. failure in Vietnam**

driven from Jordan. Now the Muslims had a slight majority, threatening the Christians' status. PLO raids on Israel from Lebanese bases brought reprisals, and Israeli bombings of Lebanese villages (in which many Maronites were also killed) prompted right-wing Christians to attack their Muslim rivals, both Palestinian and native-born.

Initially Syria supported the Palestinians and the leftist Muslim movement led by Kamal Jumblatt. But by early 1976, when the Muslims were on the verge of winning, Syrian president Assad grew fearful of Israeli intervention. Switching sides, he sent 20,000 troops to Lebanon—and the Christians began to turn the tide. The country was partitioned by a constantly contested "Green Line" running through the rubble of downtown Beirut, with the Christians ruling the north and the Muslims the south. But even the arrival of 30,000 Arab League peacekeepers later that year could not stop the fighting. The former banking and holiday-resort center of the Middle East had become an outpost of hell. **◂1920.2 ▸1982.2**

SOUTHEAST ASIA

Saigon Falls to Communists

4 South Vietnam's army held out for two years after U.S. forces left Indochina. The end came in 1975, when Washington, faced with a record budget deficit, suspended aid. In March, Communist forces took Hue and Da Nang. President Thieu fled on April 21. On April 29, U.S. officials ordered the 1,000 Americans in Vietnam to gather at their embassy in Saigon for evacuation. Thousands of Vietnamese came too, swarming over the locked gates and onto the roof, fighting to board overloaded helicopters. The Communists marched in the next day. Saigon became Ho Chi Minh City; the two Vietnams became one.

Perhaps one million Communist and 200,000 South Vietnamese soldiers had been killed since 1965, along with one million civilians; many more were maimed. The land was riddled with unexploded mines and water-filled bomb craters (in which malaria-carrying mosquitoes bred). The Americans had sprayed herbicide to deprive the Communists of crops and cover; besides disrupting Vietnam's ecology, the chemicals caused illness and birth defects. Slowed by an American embargo and Communist policies, reconstruction would take generations.

On the roof of Saigon's U.S. embassy, dozens of evacuees crowd into a waiting helicopter.

U.S. bombing had also devastated Cambodia and Laos, where indigenous Communists seized power in April and August, respectively. Determined to remake their nation from scratch, Cambodia's new rulers, the Khmer Rouge, evacuated the cities; by 1979, in a quest for political and ethnic purity, they had slaughtered some two million of their people. In May, the world caught its first glimpse of their paranoid style when they seized a U.S. merchant ship, the *Mayaguez*, and held its crew hostage for three days. Fifteen Americans died storming the ship, but the prisoners were not there. The Khmer Rouge, who had hidden the captives, released them immediately. **◂1973.8 ▸1977.8**

THE SOVIET UNION

Nobel for a Dissident

5 Citing his commitment to "the principle that world peace can have no lasting value unless it is founded on respect for the individual human being," the Nobel committee awarded physicist Andrei Sakharov its 1975 Peace Prize (which the Kremlin barred him from accepting in person). The father of the Soviet H-bomb, Sakharov had turned his back on his country's rulers to campaign against institutional human-rights abuses. His crusade earned him acclaim around the world but persecution at home.

In 1953 Sakharov, at 32, had become the youngest person ever inducted into the Soviet Academy of Sciences. His endorsement of a nuclear test ban in 1957 put him at odds with the government, but Communist Party officials granted him rare latitude: Too valuable to punish, Sakharov was patronized as an eccentric genius. But in the mid-1960s, as his criticism expanded to include the whole social system, he fell into official disfavor. In 1968 he published "Thoughts on Progress, Peaceful Coexistence, and Intellectual Freedom"—a call for civil liberties, East-West rapprochement, and an end to the arms race. Printed in *The New York Times* and circulated clandestinely in the Soviet Union, the essay made him an international political figure. His security clearance was immediately retracted.

Sakharov photographed at the home of fellow dissident Lev Kopelev in 1977.

Five years after winning the Nobel, Sakharov was arrested and exiled to the closed city of Gorky for condemning the invasion of Afghanistan. Freed by Mikhail Gorbachev in 1987, he resumed his gadfly role. Before his death in 1989, he saw many of his long-sought reforms become law. **◂1974.13 ▸1975.8**

BIRTHS

Drew Barrymore, U.S. actress.

DEATHS

Hannah Arendt, German-U.S. philosopher.

Thomas Hart Benton, U.S. painter.

Nikolai Bulganin, U.S.S.R. premier.

Georges Carpentier, French boxer.

Carlos Chávez, Mexican composer and conductor.

Chiang Kai-shek, Chinese Nationalist president.

Eamon De Valera, Irish prime minister.

Walker Evans, U.S. photographer.

Francisco Franco, Spanish leader.

Haile Selassie, Ethiopian emperor.

Susan Hayward, U.S. actress.

Julian Huxley, U.K. biologist and writer.

Um Kalthoum, Egyptian singer.

Fredric March, U.S. actor.

József Mindszenty, Hungarian Roman Catholic cardinal.

Elijah Muhammad, U.S. religious leader.

Antonín Novotny, Czech leader.

Aristotle Onassis, Greek shipowner and financier.

Dmitri Shostakovich, U.S.S.R. composer.

Casey Stengel, U.S. baseball player and manager.

Rod Serling, U.S. television writer.

Edward Tatum, U.S. geneticist.

Arnold Joseph Toynbee, U.K. historian.

Lionel Trilling, U.S. writer.

William Wellman, U.S. filmmaker.

Thornton N. Wilder, U.S. writer.

P.G. Wodehouse, U.K.-U.S. writer.

Reflections **(Milton Babbitt) ... Painting & Sculpture: *Burnt Beige* (Kenneth Noland); *Cage Environment* (Michelangelo Pistoletto) ... Film: *One Flew over the Cuckoo's Nest* (Milos Forman); *Jaws* (Steven Spielberg); *Shampoo* (Hal Ashby) ... Theater: *American Buffalo* (David Mamet); *Same Time, Next Year* (Bernard Slade); *No Man's Land* (Harold Pinter); *The Wiz* (Charlie Smalls) ... TV: *One Day at a Time*.**

"There are neither victors nor vanquished, winners nor losers. It has been a victory for reason."—**Soviet Party leader Leonid Brezhnev, commenting on the outcome of the Helsinki Conference**

NEW IN 1975

Home computers (Altair).

Light beers (Miller Lite).

Crossbreeding of buffalo and cattle (Beefalo).

Computerized supermarket checkout.

Disposable razors.

Catalytic converters on cars.

Lyme disease (diagnosed in Lyme, Connecticut, and caused by a virus carried by deer ticks).

U.S.-born Roman Catholic saint (Elizabeth Ann Seton).

IN THE UNITED STATES

▶HOFFA DISAPPEARS—Jimmy Hoffa, the powerful former president of the International Brotherhood of Teamsters, disappeared from a restaurant outside Detroit on July 30. Hoffa, who'd helped build the Teamsters into the largest U.S. labor union, had gone to prison in 1967 for jury tampering, fraud, and conspiracy, but

his 13-year sentence was commuted by President Nixon in 1971. He immediately violated his release terms by trying to regain control of the Teamsters. On the day he vanished, he was scheduled to meet with underworld crime figures Anthony Provenzano and Anthony Giacolone. Hoffa's body was never recovered. ◂1957.M

▶THRILLA IN MANILA—In the Philippines on October 1, Muhammad Ali and Joe Frazier fought the peak battle of a five-year rivalry: the "Thrilla in Manila" (as reigning champ Ali dubbed it). Frazier had beaten Ali in a brutal 1971 bout; Ali had prevailed in the rematch three years later. This time some 700 million TV viewers in 65 countries—many paying

Soviet stamps commemorating the link-up.

EXPLORATION

Superpower Space-Link

6 On July 17, 1975, as their spacecrafts orbited earth, Soviet Air Force colonel Aleksei Leonov and U.S. Air Force brigadier general Thomas Stafford floated through a tunnel linking their two craft and shook hands.

The remarkable gesture between the rival superpowers—the first international meeting in space—grew out of a treaty signed during Richard Nixon's 1972 trip to the Soviet Union. Displaying a new openness, the Soviets had let Americans visit their launch site and had spoken frankly about prior mission failures. (They even sent up *Soyuz 16* as proof they'd overcome their problems.) NASA, in turn, designed a module that allowed each nation's craft to dock. Under the agreement, the U.S. capsule would chase the Soviet capsule and capture the hookup. The Soviets would host the meeting aboard their vessel.

The crews had trained in both countries, learning enough of the other's language to communicate. After a two-day cohabitation during which seeds, commemorative medals, and plaques were exchanged, the astronauts and cosmonauts swore eternal friendship. On earth, however, their nations' missiles remained poised for mutual destruction. **◂1972.M ▸1981.12**

SPORTS

Ashe Wins Wimbledon

7 The manicured grass carpets and white-only dress code of Wimbledon provided a staid backdrop to the contrasting styles of the two Americans facing off in the 1975 men's final. On one side of the net stood brassy Jimmy Connors, emerging bad boy of tennis, favorite of the London oddsmakers. On the other stood Arthur Ashe, an athlete of rare gifts whose devilish backhand and cannon serve coexisted with imperturbable poise. Ashe carried the day: He won in four sets, two of them thrashings, to become the first black men's champion of tennis's most prestigious tournament.

Raised in Richmond, Virginia, Ashe learned his game in the city's segregated parks. His widowed father, a parks policeman, drilled Ashe in self-control and dignity—weapons against Jim Crow and, later, tennis opponents. Ashe won 51 pro tournaments, served as the professional players' union's first president, and became tennis's first African-American millionaire. After heart disease forced him to retire in 1980, he became a vocal critic of South African apartheid and the inequities of U.S. inner cities. In 1988 he published *A Hard Road to Glory*, a three-volume history of black athletes.

In 1992, Ashe announced that he had AIDS, apparently contracted

On and off the court, Ashe *(above, in 1991)* was notable for his poise and courage.

from a tainted blood transfusion during heart surgery. AIDS awareness became his next battlefield, and setting up a foundation to fund medical research was his last great act of conscience. He died in 1993, at age 49. **◂1957.M ▸1976.9**

DIPLOMACY

Human Rights Treaty

8 Concluding a two-year diplomatic marathon, participants in the Conference on Security and Cooperation in Europe (CSCE), held in Helsinki in 1975, endorsed a set of worldwide human rights standards. Soviet-bloc dissidents were thereby given a framework for protest. The Helsinki Accords were endorsed by 33 European nations, the United States, and Canada.

The idea for a European security conference had first been proposed by Soviet foreign minister Vyacheslav Molotov in 1953. Hoping to legitimize Moscow's Eastern European empire, Molotov envisioned a forum that would officially recognize the postwar status quo. But instead the CSCE recognized a principle to which Moscow habitually paid lip service: the "sovereign equality" of the Soviet bloc's constituent parts. Moreover, Austria introduced the idea that the inviolability of national borders was contingent upon the inviolability of individual rights within those borders. To save face and win trade concessions, Soviet negotiators conceded both concepts.

Brezhnev addressed Helsinki conferees but reneged on the accords.

The Helsinki Accords, though not legally binding, carried political weight. No longer could a state claim that rights abuses were strictly its own concern. After Helsinki, many Western governments—notably the U.S. administration of Carter—linked trade to the status of human rights in the countries involved. And within the Soviet bloc

SPORTS: Baseball: World Series, Cincinnati Reds defeat Boston Red Sox, 4–3; Tom Seaver (New York Mets) pitches eighth consecutive season with 200 or more strikeouts ... Football: Super Bowl, Pittsburgh Steelers defeat Minnesota Vikings, 16–6 ... Basketball: NBA, Golden State Warriors defeat Washington Bullets, 4–0 ... Track & Field: John Walker runs 3:49.4 mile.

"I don't really consider this a debut. After all, no one looks at me and says, 'There goes the debutante!'"
—Beverly Sills, on her first performance at the New York Metropolitan Opera

(especially Poland and Czechoslovakia), dissident leaders seized the accords as a rallying point for their movements. **►1977.2**

SCIENCE
Nature over Nurture

9 With his 1975 book, *Sociobiology: the New Synthesis*, Harvard entomologist E.O. Wilson spearheaded the development of sociobiology, the study of the genetic basis of social behavior. An expert on social insects, Wilson asserted that all social acts are genetically based and programmed to enhance the survival of the genetic code. The organism's "primary function," he wrote, "is not even to reproduce other organisms; it reproduces genes and serves as their carriers." In other words, "the organism is only DNA's way of making more DNA."

Wilson explained altruism in animals (a "soldier" ant, for example, will sacrifice its life to defend its colony against intruders) as the instinct to protect nearby gene sharers. But his cautious attempts to apply his concepts to humans raised a furor among intellectuals, especially those who saw environment (nurture, as opposed to nature) as the primary shaper of behavior. He was accused of reducing complex human conduct to a chemical imperative.

In fact, Wilson never denied the role of ethics or suggested that more than 10 percent of human behavior is "pre-wired." But his work was an important contribution to a growing body of theoretical thought that insisted on nature's place in the nature-nurture debate—from Piaget's beliefs that intellectual development occurs in biologically determined stages, to Chomsky's contention that "deep structures" of language are programmed into the brain. **◄1957.13**

TERRORISM
A Bloody Year

10 A ten-year rise in terrorist acts in countries nominally at peace reached a bloody apex in 1975. The motives for the attacks were as varied as the methods.

In February, members of West Germany's Red Army Faction—known as the Baader-Meinhof gang—abducted a West Berlin politician, winning passage to the Middle East for two imprisoned comrades. In April, the group took a dozen hostages at the West German embassy in Stockholm, demanding the release of 26 gang members. Two diplomats were killed, and the terrorists were captured. (The trials of already imprisoned Andreas Baader, Ulrike Meinhof, and other leaders began in May and ended with their suicides, Meinhof's in 1976 and Baader's one year later.)

In October, the Irish Republican Army kidnapped a Dutch industrialist, holding him for weeks near Dublin. In November, the IRA bombed a British legislator's London home, killing a bystander. The same month, Italy's Red Brigades kidnapped and beat a Genoa industrial official, releasing him at a garbage dump. In Vienna and Paris, Turkish ambassadors were slain; Armenian and Greek Cypriot nationalists claimed credit.

In December, separatists from South Molucca (part of an island chain in eastern Indonesia) took hostages in Amsterdam's Indonesian consulate and aboard a Dutch passenger train. (The engineer and two passengers were killed.) Pro-Palestinian commandos, led by the infamous "Carlos"—a Venezuelan freelance terrorist whose real name was Ilyich Ramírez Sánchez—seized OPEC's oil ministers in Vienna. Captors and captives flew to Libya and Algeria, where the gunmen received asylum. And two days before the new year, a bomb planted by Puerto Rican nationalists killed 14 people at New York's La Guardia Airport. **►1978.6**

Sills *(center)* as Pamira in her Met debut in Rossini's *Siege of Corinth.*

MUSIC
Bubbles at the Met

11 When Beverly Sills finally made her formal Metropolitan Opera debut on April 7, 1975, she won a standing ovation before uttering a note. Affiliated with the New York City Opera (NYCO) since 1955, the 45-year-old coloratura—born Belle Silverman, and known as "Bubbles" for her ebullience—was the first American diva to have become a star without performing at the Met or the great houses of Europe. Her La Scala debut came in 1969; by then, her brilliant voice ("so clear and swift it seems phosphorescent," wrote one reviewer) and her commanding stage presence had established her as opera's finest singer-actress. But a long feud with Sir Rudolf Bing, the Met's general director, had kept her off its Lincoln Center stage.

It was Bing's successor, Schuyler Chapin, who invited Sills to sing in a Met production of Rossini's *Siege of Corinth*. At an age when many singers start to fade, she turned in a stunning performance—including her famous transition from the pyrotechnics of "Si, Ferite" to the pianissimo of "Dal Soggiorno." Afterward Sills quipped, "And that is my last debut." She retired five years later, but stayed on as the NYCO's general director. **◄1959.6 ►1990.8**

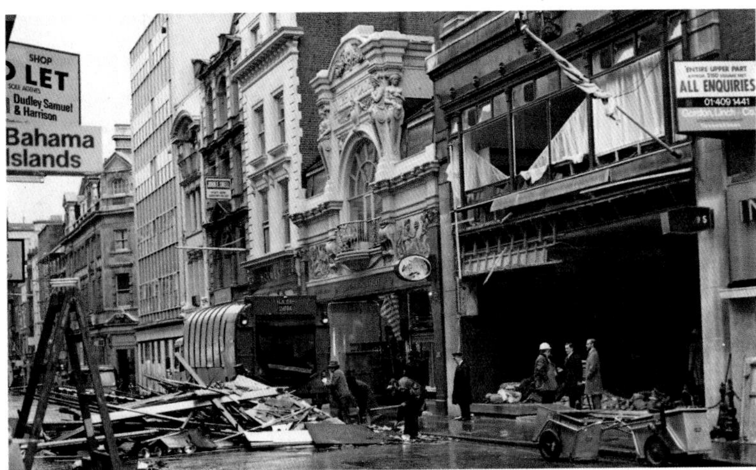

Bomb police sift through wreckage from an IRA attack on London's Old Bond Street.

IN THE UNITED STATES

top dollar for the privilege—watched Ali pummel his challenger so badly that Frazier's trainer threw in the towel one round before the final bell. **◄1964.11**

►MASTER OF MASTERS—On April 13, Jack Nicklaus won the prestigious Masters Tournament in Augusta, Georgia, for a record fifth time. Arguably the finest golfer ever, the "Golden Bear"—whose wins

include five Professional Golfers' Association titles, four U.S. Open championships, and three British Open titles—had been the youngest golfer (23) to win the Masters, in 1963; with his sixth Masters win, in 1986, he became the oldest (46). **◄1964.M**

►CLOSE CALLS—On September 5, secret service agents wrestled a gun from Lynette "Squeaky" Fromme, a follower of Charles Manson, when she pointed it at President Ford during his visit to Sacramento. Just 17 days later, Sara Jane Moore, a former FBI informant, stepped from a crowd in San Francisco and fired a pistol at the President. She missed. **◄1974.1 ►1981.M**

►N.Y.C. MONEY WOES—From June to December, New York City struggled desperately to meet monthly debt payments of as much as $1 billion. To stave off bankruptcy, investment banker Felix Rohaytn and Governor Hugh Carey set up the Municipal Assistance Corporation and the Emergency Financial Control Board, but federal aid was needed. On October 29, President Ford declared he would veto any such package; the next day the *New York Daily News* ran a headline that helped change his mind: FORD TO CITY: DROP DEAD. Amid mounting media pressure and fears that a N.Y.C. collapse would wreak havoc on international banking, Ford relented. On December 18 he approved a federal bailout of nearly $2 billion. **►1980.13**

POLITICS & BUSINESS: GNP: $1,599.1 billion ... Literacy requirement for voting abolished (linguistic minorities included in Voting Rights Act) ... Supreme Court Justice William O. Douglas announces retirement after 36 years (longest term on Supreme Court to date) ... President Ford signs Energy Policy and Conservation Act of 1975 (sets importation quotas on petroleum) and Metric Conversion Act.

"Dancers kill themselves in a show. They work like dogs, they get less money than anybody else, and they don't get any real credit. I want to do a show where the dancers are the stars."—**Michael Bennett, director-choreographer of *A Chorus Line***

AROUND THE WORLD

▶POLAND OPENS DOOR—Sorting out World War II's tragic inheritance, West Germany and Poland entered into a 1975 treaty allowing some 120,000 ethnic Germans living in Poland to emigrate to West Germany. In return for the visas, the Bonn government of Helmut Schmidt agreed to pay Poland 2.3 billion deutsche marks ($900 million) in reparation for the Nazi wartime occupation of Poland. ◀1974.3 ▶1976.M

▶CHINA'S BURIED TREASURE—An archaeological dig at the sprawling tomb of Ch' in emperor Shih Huang-ti, ruler of China from 221 to 206 BC, announced in 1975, unearthed treasures that made King Tut look like a pauper: Some

8,000 life-sized ceramic warriors *(above)*, armed with real crossbows, spears, and swords; bronze horses and chariots; more than 10,000 articles of gold, jade, silk, and iron. The burial site, near Xi'an, in northwestern Shanxi province, was discovered by farmers digging wells. ◀1922.3

▶GENOCIDE IN TIMOR—Indonesia annexed the former Portuguese colony of East Timor (on the island of Timor, about 400 miles off the northwest coast of Australia) in 1975. The rightist Suharto regime called the act defense against creeping Communist infiltration; the UN called it naked aggression. With tacit U.S. approval, Suharto persisted: His army, along with starvation wrought by war, killed half the population of 600,000 in five years. ◀1966.13

▶"INFAMOUS" DECLARATION—On November 10, the UN General Assembly provocatively labeled Zionism "a form of racism and racial discrimination." The sensational resolution (branded "infamous" by U.S. delegate Daniel Patrick Moynihan), was accompanied by a call for PLO participation in Middle East peace negotiations. The resolution was repealed in 1991. ◀1904.M ▶1993.1

Oddly anonymous behind their 8x10 glossies, hopeful hoofers audition in *A Chorus Line.*

THEATER

A Singular Sensation

12 At once insular and universal, *A Chorus Line*—a Broadway musical about 18 dancers auditioning for a Broadway musical—touches on such resonant themes as ambition, competition, individuality, and conformity. The show debuted at the New York Shakespeare Festival's Public Theatre in April 1975, and soon moved to Broadway's Shubert Theatre, where it stayed for 15 years and a record 6,137 performances.

The production grew out of director-choreographer (and former dancer) Michael Bennett's conviction that dancers are the least appreciated members of a musical's company. Bennett assembled a diverse group of hoofers for two late-night talk sessions, then taped the personal revelations that spilled out. With the support of New York Shakespeare Festival impresario Joseph Papp, Bennett and his collaborators—writer-dancer Nicholas Dante, playwright-novelist James Kirkwood, composer Marvin Hamlisch, and lyricist Ed Kleban—developed the choreography, script, and songs as the dancers rehearsed.

Critics raved over the book, the simple set (black backgrounds, a vast rehearsal mirror, a white line across the floor), and the dancing itself. The rangy, inventive (and slightly clumsy) score spawned one bona fide hit: "What I Did for Love." *A Chorus Line* earned nine Tonys, a Pulitzer, and, by 1990, some $50 million. **◀1970.12**

MUSIC

The Boss

13 After the 1975 release of his breakthrough album, *Born to Run*, Bruce Springsteen had the rare honor of appearing simultaneously on the covers of *Time* and *Newsweek*. Among the labels slapped on the New Jersey–born singer-guitarist were "the new Bob Dylan" and "the biggest thing since Elvis." To fans, his gritty evocations of small-town, working-class adolescence were Whitmanesque poetry; his exuberantly earthy music was a breath of fresh air in a scene dominated by slick disco and other overblown, decadent, or diluted rock derivatives. When the LP sold a million copies in six weeks, it was clear that "the Boss" (as he was known) had arrived.

Management troubles kept him from recording for the next three years, but Springsteen—whose high-energy live performances had gained him a cult following well before his success with *Born to Run*—continued to tour, and to write songs for others. ("Because the Night" was punk rocker Patti Smith's only hit; both the Pointer Sisters and Robert Palmer recorded "Fire.") His next LP, the somber *Darkness at the Edge of Town*, confirmed him as a serious artist. *The River* (1980) was his first album to hit number one. And by 1984, when *Born in the USA* spawned four hit singles (and even President Reagan quoted from the title song), Springsteen was the biggest rock star in the world. **◀1975.M ▶1980.V**

Springsteen *(right)*, with sax man Clarence Clemons, paid homage to blue-collar life.

FILM

An American Crazy Quilt

14 The quality of mainstream American cinema was better in the seventies than at any other time since the heyday of the studio system 40 years earlier, and Robert Altman's 1975 film *Nashville* is arguably the pick of the decade's bumper crop. "I've never before seen a movie I loved in quite this way," gushed critic Pauline Kael. "*Nashville* is the funniest epic vision of America ever to reach the screen."

Altman—already admired for the antiwar comedy *M*A*S*H* (1970) and the revisionist Western *McCabe and Mrs. Miller* (1971)—used Nashville, the commercial capital of country music, to explore the American condition. The film follows two dozen characters—musicians, would-be groupies, an assassin—through a miasma of glitz and greed. With families and friendships riven by betrayal, disease, death,

In the middle of a breakdown, a Loretta Lynn–like singer (Ronee Blakley) meets the press at her Nashville homecoming.

and sex, these individuals are wrecks; indeed, Altman implies, the whole nation is a wreck, thanks to violence, hucksterism, empty politics, and popular apathy. When a country star is shotgunned at a rally for a vapid presidential candidate, the other performers and the audience lift their spirits by singing an anthem called "It Don't Worry Me."

Altman's characteristic loose-limbed style helps *Nashville*'s 159 minutes stream by effortlessly, and the milling visuals and soundtrack are alive with detail. The cast—which includes Lily Tomlin, Ned Beatty, Geraldine Chaplin, Henry Gibson, Ronee Blakley, Keith Carradine, and Barbara Harris—collaborated with Altman and screenwriter Joan Tewkesbury on their dialogue. Some actors wrote or cowrote songs, and the results are surprisingly affecting: Carradine's "I'm Easy" even won an Oscar. **▶1977.12**

NOBEL PRIZES: Peace: Andrei Sakharov (U.S.S.R.) ... Literature: Eugenio Montale (Italian; poet) ... Chemistry: J. Cornforth and V. Prelog (Australian, Swiss; biological molecules) ... Medicine: D. Baltimore, H. Temin, and R. Dulbecco (U.S.; viruses) ... Physics: J. Rainwater, B. Mottelson, and A. Bohr (U.S., U.S., Danish; asymmetrical nucleus) ... Economics: L. Kantorovich and T. Koopmans (U.S.S.R., U.S.).

A VOICE FROM 1975

This Just in from New York

"Weekend Update," from *Saturday Night Live*, November 1975

"Live, from New York, it's Saturday Night!" So was introduced a post-prime-time comedy special on the NBC network on October 11, 1975. The late-night show soon became a runaway hit—and the most influential TV comedy since Rowan and Martin's Laugh-In. *The list of resident jokesters, billed as "The Not Ready for Prime Time Players," reads today like a comedic all-star team: Dan Aykroyd, John Belushi, Chevy Chase, Jane Curtin, Gilda Radner, Garrett Morris, Laraine Newman, and, later, Bill Murray and Eddie Murphy. Zany, irreverent sketches—Chase's "Weekend Update" satirized network news* (below)*; the Coneheads, starring Curtin, Aykroyd, and Newman as an oddball alien family, parodied 1950s family sitcoms—attracted a young and loyal following. By 1980, the entire original cast had left, mostly to make movies (conspicuous successes: Belushi and Aykroyd in* The Blues Brothers *and Aykroyd and Murray in* Ghostbusters*), but the show chugged along on a steady infusion of new talent. Nearly two decades after its debut, such comics as Dana Carvey and Mike Myers kept SNL fresh.* **►1969.7**

GOOD EVENING, I'M CHEVY CHASE, AND YOU'RE NOT.

It was announced today that the small African nation of Chad has changed its name to Brian. In the spirit of Third World solidarity, the nation of Tanzania has changed its name to Debby.

This just in: Generalissimo Francisco Franco is still dead.

Secretary of State Kissinger stated today that he is tired of using his silly accent in public and will begin to speak in plain English. This will in no way affect the content of what he is saying.

In a speech to the Athens, Georgia, Chamber of Commerce, presidential contender George Wallace said, "I don't judge a man by the color of his skin. I judge him according to how well you can see him in the dark when he smiles."

UNICEF fell under attack this week when Syria formally protested the charity's new Christmas card, which says, in ten different languages, "Let's kill the Arabs and take their oil!"

This bulletin just in: From Madrid, Spain, comes the word that Generalissimo Francisco Franco is still dead. Doctors say his condition is unchanged.

Confusion continues over the Angolan situation throughout the world. The Japanese prime minister is said to have commented, "I always thought Angola was a sweater."

GOOD NIGHT, AND HAVE A PLEASANT TOMORROW.

Clockwise from top left, the original cast of *Saturday Night Live*: Chevy Chase, Gilda Radner, Dan Aykroyd, Jane Curtin, Laraine Newman, Garrett Morris, and John Belushi. Above, Chase impersonates a smarmy network anchor on "Weekend Update."

"Our mission, unfinished, may take a thousand years./The struggle tires us, and our hair is gray./You and I, old friend, can we just watch our efforts/being wasted away?"—**Mao Zedong in a letter to Zhou Enlai, in 1974**

STORY OF THE YEAR

Deaths of Mao and Zhou End an Era

1 By the end of his life, the transfiguration was uncanny: Mao Zedong, the brains and backbone of China's Communist revolution, had grown into something very like an emperor. Venerated by 800 million subjects, Mao was everywhere and nowhere: His image hung in every home, his words were received as scripture, his name was blessed ("May he have 100,000 years of life"), but increasingly the Chairman slipped into regal isolation—from the people, and from the government he'd forged. A sick old man of 82, Mao died on September 9, 1976.

A million people flocked into Beijing's Tiananmen Square to mourn their leader, whose corpse was preserved in a see-through crystal sarcophagus. But invisible to the mourners a fight to succeed the Great Helmsman raged. Zhou Enlai, China's premier since 1949 (and a stabilizing influence during Mao's erratic last years), had died in January, having groomed provincial official Hua Guofeng for succession. Now Hua assumed chairmanship of the ruling Communist Party. But others waited in the wings: Mao's nation-shattering social experiments, and his autocratic style, had riven the Party into hostile factions.

To the Chinese people, Mao Zedong *(above, his name written in Chinese)* was a leader of almost godlike stature.

Representing the extreme left was Jiang Qing, Mao's imperious widow and leader of what became known as the Gang of Four—the politburo coterie that directed the Cultural Revolution, Mao's anarchic civil war against the ideologically impure. On the right was politburo member Deng Xiaoping—a master of political infighting, and sworn enemy of Jiang and her cronies. Deng had attempted reform after 20 million peasants died during the Great Leap Forward, the catastrophic economic program initiated in 1958. Purged as a "capitalist roader," Deng worked in a tractor factory until Zhou rehabilitated him in 1973, then returned to seed the Party with moderates. After Zhou's death, Mao purged him again.

In the battle for control, Hua made the first strike. In October he arrested Jiang and company, opening the door to Deng. Rehabilitated once more in 1977, Deng established control over the Party, gradually easing Hua from power. Among the ideological proscriptions soon lifted: a ban on Beethoven. Mao's revolution was spinning in unforeseen directions. **◂1972.2 ▸1980.10**

SWEDEN

Socialism Interrupted

2 In parliamentary elections held in September 1976, Swedish voters revolted against the Social Democrats' 44-year near-monopoly on government (the longest uninterrupted reign of any non-Soviet European party), giving the Center, Moderate, and Liberal parties a combined majority of 50.8 percent. Center Party leader Thorbjörn Fälldin *(above)*, a fatherly farmer, took over the premiership from the urbane but arrogant socialist Olof Palme.

In a sense, socialist rule had succeeded too well. Thanks to the world's highest tax rate (40 percent of gross national income), Sweden had the most comprehensive social welfare system in Western Europe. Benefits included health care, child allowances, rent allowances, subsidized education, and old-age pensions. Living standards were lofty, unemployment meager, labor relations generally calm. Yet with prosperity came resentment of the government's growing power. Many wage earners sympathized with filmmaker Ingmar Bergman, who'd been hounded into self-imposed exile by tax collectors. And though 90 percent of the economy remained in private hands, capitalists feared the socialists' plan to transfer partial control of businesses to labor unions.

The election's biggest issue, however, was nuclear power. To break Sweden's dependence on foreign oil, Palme had launched an ambitious program of reactor construction. Fälldin, warning of environmental hazards, opposed the move. In the first election since the lowering of the voting age to 18, his stand attracted the ecology-minded young.

But the new prime minister proved unable to stop the nuclear program. Frustrated, he resigned in 1978; his Liberal successor, Ola Ullsten, assembled a cabinet that boasted perhaps the largest proportion anywhere (one third) of women members. Fälldin was brought back to office in 1979 elections. But the worldwide recession undermined his policies, and in 1982 the voters returned the socialists—and Palme—to power. **◂1905.M ▸1986.M**

SPORTS

Darling of the Olympics

3 At the 1976 Summer Olympics in Montreal, a 14-year-old Romanian gymnast stepped up to the uneven bars. Vaulting her 86 pounds into the air, Nadia Comaneci began a series of leaps, twists, and twirls that would propel her sport into a new era. At times she seemed to hang motionless in space, defying gravity; at other times her arms and legs were a whirlwind of movement. By the end of the competition, she'd scored seven "perfect 10s"—the highest possible rating—along with three gold medals.

Trainer Bela Karolyi, who defected to the United States after coaching Romania's victorious team, discovered Comaneci at age six, on a school playground. She quickly became a champion, stealing the spotlight from older competitors like the Soviet Union's Olga Korbut. Yet even for a sports star, life in notoriously repressive Romania was hard. A victory was a triumph for communism; a defeat was considered a national embarrassment and often resulted in brusque dismissal from the team. Athletically promising children were taken from their families and placed in sports camps where they trained for hours on end. Some athletes were given dangerous drugs to improve their performance. Comaneci suffered from eating disorders and attempted suicide at 15. Although she went on to win several more international competitions, she never recaptured her Montreal form. She defected to the United States in 1989. **◂1972.M ▸1976.M**

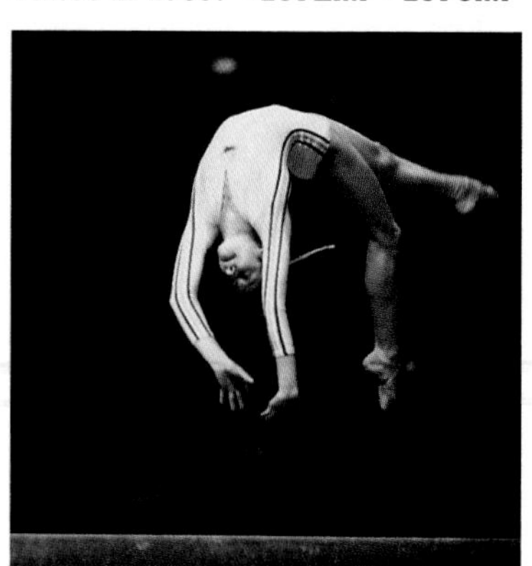

Comaneci showed perfect balance in the Montreal Summer Olympics.

ART & CULTURE: Books: ***The Boys from Brazil*** **(Ira Levin);** ***Lady Oracle*** **(Margaret Atwood);** ***1876*** **(Gore Vidal);** ***Born on the Fourth of July*** **(Ron Kovic);** ***The Hite Report: A Nationwide Study on Female Sexuality*** **(Shere Hite) ... Music:** ***A Night on the Town*** **(Rod Stewart, LP);** ***Visions of Terror and Wonder*** **(Richard Wernick) ... Painting & Sculpture:** ***Skull*** **(Andy Warhol);** ***Japanese Figure with Black Mirror***

"We are oppressed, not as individuals, not as Zulus, Xhosas, Vendas, or Indians. We are oppressed because we are black."
—South African activist Steve Biko

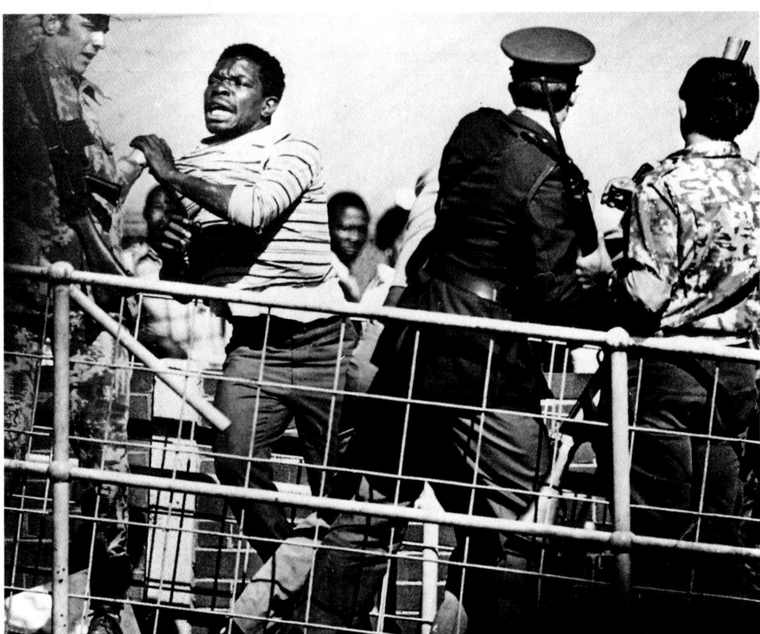

In Soweto, a student demonstration turned into general revolt after police opened fire.

SOUTHERN AFRICA

The Soweto Uprising

4 On June 16, 1976, 10,000 schoolchildren protesting the inferiority of South Africa's black schools peacefully advanced through the township of Soweto (Johannesburg's sprawling, impoverished, black-only suburb) toward an open-air stadium for a planned rally. A white policeman threw a tear-gas canister, then the other riot police turned their automatic weapons on the singing marchers, killing at least four—and setting off the Soweto Uprising, the bloodiest episode of black rebellion and police reprisals since the early sixties. By the end of 1977, the violence had claimed more than a thousand lives.

South Africa's segregated Bantu Education system, set up in the 1950s, forced blacks to pay to attend decrepit schools with overcrowded classrooms, underqualified teachers, and shoddy curricula. (White public education was free.) In 1975, the government decreed that black secondary-school academic subjects—as opposed to "practical" classes like woodworking and sewing—be taught in Afrikaans. (Formerly, all subjects were taught in English.) The policy virtually guaranteed black academic failure: Black primary schools used a variety of regional African languages in the classroom (a policy designed to increase ethnic divisions among blacks); now, in order to succeed, black students had to gain fluency in both of the nation's official languages. The decree set off the wave of unrest that culminated in the Soweto massacre.

The difficult history of South Africa's student movement had produced a great hero: Steve Biko. In 1968, while in medical school, he'd cofounded the South African Students Organization, the country's first all-black anti-apartheid youth group. (Earlier student organizations had been dominated by white liberals.) Biko and SASO were part of the broader Black Consciousness movement, which aimed to overcome the sense of inferiority that plagued the nation's oppressed majority. The movement stressed black pride, insisting that blacks must be in charge of their own, ideally nonviolent, liberation. Officially banned (that is, prohibited from political action, from leaving his town, or from speaking to more than one person at a time) and repeatedly detained without charge, Biko died in police custody in 1977, at age 30. His funeral was attended by twelve heads of state. **◂1960.6 ▸1983.M**

SCIENCE

A Working, Artificial Gene

5 Led by Indian-born American biochemist Har Gobind Khorana, a team of scientists at the Massachusetts Institute of Technology in 1976 created the first man-made gene—the basic unit of heredity—capable of working in a living cell. The accomplishment differed from earlier test-tube syntheses in that the gene was wholly manufactured—a natural gene was not used as a template. Khorana's breakthrough heightened public uneasiness over genetic engineering: Though recombinant DNA technology might someday prevent hereditary diseases, the prospect of scientists' using it to predetermine a person's sex, color, or intelligence was chilling.

In fact, biochemistry was a long way from producing custom-made humans. What Khorana and his two dozen postdoctoral assistants pieced together was the gene for tyrosine transfer RNA, which corrects a genetic mutation. The gene—which occurs naturally in *Escherichia coli*, a common bacterium—plus its controls (chemical signals that tell enzymes where to start and stop building an RNA strand) consisted of about 200 linked nucleotides (the fundamental components of DNA and RNA). A single human cell contains some six billion nucleotides.

The experiment derived from one Khorana had conducted in 1970—the synthesis of the gene for alanine transfer RNA, which occurs in yeast.

MIT's Khorana. His experiments with recombinant DNA earned him a Nobel.

(The first ever made in a lab, the gene couldn't function in a living cell.) The yeast gene's creation was made possible by the work of two American biochemists (with whom Khorana shared the 1968 Nobel for medicine). Marshall Nirenberg showed that DNA is made up of four basic chemicals. Robert Holley determined (in 1964) the structure of alanine transfer RNA, which enabled Khorana to deduce the structure of the gene that produced it. Khorana then assembled the gene from lab-produced nucleotides—a feat comparable to assembling an automobile from a pile of loose parts. **◂1967.11 ▸1978.1**

BIRTHS

Jennifer Capriati, U.S. tennis player.

DEATHS

Alvar Aalto, Finnish architect and furniture designer.

Busby Berkeley, U.S. choreographer and filmmaker.

Benjamin Britten, U.K. composer.

Chester Burnett (Howlin' Wolf), U.S. singer and composer.

Alexander Calder, U.S. sculptor.

Agatha Christie, U.K. writer.

Max Ernst, German painter.

J. Paul Getty, U.S. businessman.

Martin Heidegger, German philosopher.

Werner Heisenberg, German physicist.

Howard Hughes, U.S. aviator and businessman.

Fritz Lang, German-U.S. filmmaker.

Trofim Denisovich Lysenko, Soviet agronomist.

André Malraux, French writer.

Mao Zedong, Chinese Communist leader.

Ulrike Meinhof, German terrorist.

Sal Mineo, U.S. actor.

Jacques Monod, French biologist.

Bernard Law Montgomery, U.K. military leader.

Robert Phillips, U.S. physician.

Walter Piston, U.S. composer.

Lily Pons, French-U.S. singer.

Man Ray, U.S. artist.

Carol Reed, U.K. filmmaker.

Paul Robeson, U.S. singer, actor, and civil rights activist.

Rosalind Russell, U.S. actress.

Luchino Visconti, Italian filmmaker.

Mortimer Wheeler, U.K. archaeologist.

Zhou Enlai, Chinese premier.

Adolph Zukor, Hungarian-U.S. film executive.

(Balthus) ... Film: *Rocky* (John G. Avildsen); *Network* (Sidney Lumet); *Taxi Driver* (Martin Scorsese); *All the President's Men* (Alan Pakula) ... Theater: *Streamers* (David Rabe); *Knock, Knock* (Jules Feiffer); *For Colored Girls Who Have Considered Suicide/When the Rainbow is Enuf* (Ntozake Shange); *Pacific Overtures* (Stephen Sondheim) ... TV: *Charlie's Angels*; *The Muppet Show*; *Quincy, M.E.*

"To be unable to live as ourselves, as we should live, in our own language and according to our own ways, would be like living without an arm or a leg—or perhaps a heart."—**René Lévesque, in his 1968 book *Option Québec***

NEW IN 1976

Six-star general (title awarded posthumously to George Washington).

Female enrollment at U.S. military academies.

Female U.S. television news anchor (Barbara Walters on ABC).

Female Rhodes scholars.

Call waiting.

Conrail (created by the U.S. government from seven bankrupt northeastern railroads).

IN THE UNITED STATES

▶BICENTENNIAL BASH—The U.S. celebrated its 200th birthday on July 4 with festivities across the country. Celebrations officially got under way when the sun rose over coastal Maine, the country's northeasternmost point, and continued in big cities—New York City boasted Operation Sail, a regatta of tall ships in New

York Harbor *(above)*—as well as in small towns (townspeople of George, Washington, baked a 60-square-foot cherry pie). ▸1986.M

▶PC REVOLUTIONARIES—Steven Jobs and Steven Wozniak were college dropouts from California in 1976, when they introduced the Apple I, the first product of a company whose inexpensive, easy-to-use home computers helped launch the personal computer revolution. Fueled by Wozniak's engineering genius and Jobs's entrepreneurial acumen, Apple transcended its garage-operation origins to become the fastest growing company in American history. ◂1971.5 ▸1981.10

▶LEGIONNAIRES STRICKEN—An unknown pneumonia-like disease crashed an American

CANADA

Oui to the Separatists

6 Canadians were startled when the Parti Québecois won 71 out of 110 seats in Quebec's provincial legislature in November 1976—the first victory ever for a separatist party in Canada. The mostly French-speaking province accounted for a quarter of the country's population and gross national product; some of Canada's largest corporations were headquartered there. If the new government put its secessionist (and socialist) ideas into practice, national commerce could be profoundly disrupted.

The PQ, however, was much more moderate than the militant Front de libération du Québec, whose terrorism had alienated even many separatists (a mere 11 to 18 percent of Quebec's population, according to polls). The new premier, PQ founder and former television commentator René Lévesque, was a consensus seeker. His party had won a majority against the ruling Liberals and the conservative Union Nationale by downplaying secession and stressing the previous administration's economic blunders. (Indeed, Quebec's Liberal government had catered to Québecois nationalism by making French the province's official language and by seeking greater autonomy from Ottawa—and the Liberal federal government, under French-Canadian Pierre Trudeau, had promoted official bilingualism.) Still, the PQ pointed to the province's continuing poverty as evidence that Canada's English majority would never cede French-Canadians full equality. Warning too of the erosion of French culture in an English-dominated nation, Lévesque's administration convinced growing numbers of Québecois that the province must be "master in its own house." But when a referendum on independence was held in 1980, the majority—reluctant to take the economic risks of secession—said *Non.* **◂1970.11 ▸1992.5**

Bilingual street signs were one reflection of Canada's national policies.

Mothers of Argentina's "disappeared" demonstrated with names and faces of victims.

ARGENTINA

The Dirty War Begins

7 The officers who toppled President Isabel Perón in 1976 intended their coup to be Argentina's last. For two decades, the country had endured a succession of ineffectual governments. Señora Perón, who'd inherited the office in 1974 from her late husband, Juan, had proved even more inept than her predecessors: Terrorist attacks by leftist and rightist Peronistas had multiplied, and inflation exceeded 300 percent. Supported by the Argentine middle class (South America's largest), the putschists, led by Lieutenant General Jorge Rafael Videla, put the former dancer under house arrest. When Argentines had been "reeducated" in "morality, uprightness, and efficiency," they declared, a democracy "suited to [their] reality and needs and progress" could be introduced.

To hasten that day, the junta set about exterminating the Argentine left. Hoping to avoid the criticism that dogged Brazilian security forces while attempting a similar campaign in the early 1970s, it conducted its self-proclaimed "dirty war" largely in secret. Besides imprisoning and torturing thousands of alleged subversives, the military used unofficial death squads to kidnap and murder—or "disappear"—up to 20,000. Even moderate critics of the regime were frightened into silence; the proportion of *desaparecidos* (the disappeared) actually involved in leftist guerrilla groups remains unknown.

Curing the economy, however, lay beyond the regime's power. An austerity program initially slowed inflation, but at the cost of plunging wages. Denationalization of industry and encouragement of foreign investment led to rampant speculation, while productivity declined and unemployment soared. In 1982, with prices again skyrocketing, the junta decided to launch a different kind of war. **◂1973.3 ▸1982.1**

JAPAN

The Lockheed Scandal

8 Japan was rocked in 1976 by the arrest of former prime minister Kakuei Tanaka *(below)* for accepting kickbacks from Lockheed, the American aircraft company. Tanaka's possible violations came to light in February, when Lockheed's president testified to the U.S. Congress that his company had paid more than $12 million to grease commercial wheels. Bribery, Lockheed argued, was the only way to conduct business in Japan (among other countries). In July, Japanese investigators linked some of the dirty money to Tanaka, the 15th person arrested in the scandal.

Tanaka, a leader of the conservative Liberal Democratic Party (the country's dominant political force since World War II) had resigned as prime minister in 1974 over allegations of impropriety in his personal finances. He'd nevertheless retained his seat in parliament and—by virtue of his strong connections to business—continued to wield unparalleled power. But the Lockheed scandal was damaging: Observers speculated it would end his career, perhaps even ruin the

SPORTS: Baseball: World Series, Cincinnati Reds defeat New York Yankees, 4–0; first major league free-agent draft held ... Olympics held in Innsbruck and Montreal (Bruce Jenner wins decathlon) ... Football: Super Bowl, Pittsburgh Steelers defeat Dallas Cowboys, 21–17 ... Basketball: NBA, Boston Celtics defeat Phoenix Suns, 4–2 ... Tennis: Transsexual Renee Richards barred from U.S. Open.

"I'm not handsome in the classical sense. The eyes droop, the mouth is crooked, the teeth aren't straight, the voice sounds like a mafioso pallbearer, but somehow it all works."—**Sylvester Stallone**

Liberal Democrats. In fact, while opposition factions (most notably the Komeito, or Clean Government Party), made strong showings in the 1976 elections, the Liberal Democrats held on to power. Though forced to resign from the LDP, the man nicknamed the "Shadow Shogun" remained Japan's preeminent back-room power broker into the 1980s. **◂1973.7 ▸1989.5**

SPORTS

The Iceman Cometh

9 Björn Borg—a.k.a. "the Iceman"—was as unfazed by screaming female fans as by matches with formidable elders. In 1976, the 20-year-old tennis player cemented his star status, secured the previous year when he won his second French Open and led the

Borg displays his 1976 Wimbledon trophy.

Swedish team to its first Davis Cup victory: After polishing off the World Championship Tennis title, he headed to Wimbledon in June. Playing in brutal heat with a pulled abdominal muscle, the stoic Swede crushed Romania's Ilie Nastase in the finals without losing a set in the entire tournament.

Borg's only major setback in 1976 was his loss to American Jimmy Connors at the U.S. Open (a tournament whose top honor would always elude him). But for the rest of the decade Borg froze out Wimbledon challengers, retaining his championship against Connors in 1977 and American John McEnroe in 1980. From 1978 to 1981 Borg also dominated the French Open, accumulating a men's record of six titles. He retired in 1983, telling reporters, "I'm nauseated by tennis." His comeback attempt in the early 1990s was thwarted by both a stormy marriage and a reluctance to swap his wooden racket for the newer, powerful graphite models. **◂1975.7 ▸1982.13**

MUSIC

Opera Under Glass

10 *Einstein on the Beach* was a four-act, four-hour (plus) opera with neither plot nor arias. Instead, director-writer-designer Robert Wilson presented dream imagery: a glowing spaceship, a mysterious trial, Einstein bowing his violin. Composer Philip Glass contributed hypnotic music: orchestral drones, performers chanting gibberish. The production's triumphant 1976 tour of Europe was followed by two sold-out shows at New York's Metropolitan Opera, made international stars of its American creators—and freed Glass from driving a Manhattan taxi.

Glass, a onetime student of venerated composition teacher Nadia Boulanger, developed his "minimalist" style—a blend of buoyant tonality, wavelike textures, and obsessive repetitions—after a musical pilgrimage to India and North Africa. *Einstein* led to more operas (including the Met's 1992 *The Voyage,* for which Glass received the Met's highest commission ever), as well as film scores and collaborations with pop stars. Wilson, who first gained notice with the Paris debut of his 1971 play *Deafman Glance,* remained committed to innovation, both in his stagings of classical operas and in his own creations. (One of the latter, *the CIVIL warS*, is so long and complex it is performed only in fragments.) His plays, in which text provides atmosphere rather than meaning, have influenced a generation of avant-garde dramatists. **▸1983.13**

FILM

A Cinematic Knockout

11 "His whole life was a million-to-one shot." That advertising slogan referred to Rocky Balboa, boxer-hero of 1976's low-budget

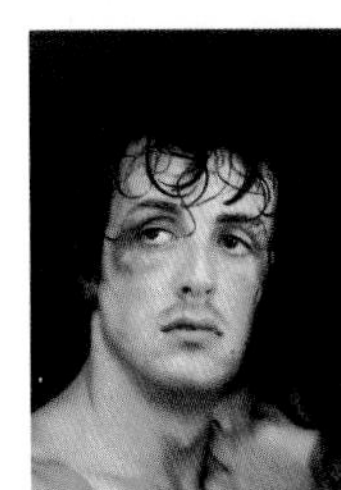

blockbuster *Rocky*, but it also applied to Sylvester Stallone, its creator and star. Stallone's semiautobiographical story (written in three and a half days), of a small-time Philadelphia club fighter who miraculously gets a shot at the title, followed a hoary formula: Good man works hard, scores moral victory, marries nice girl. Thanks partly to *Rocky*'s staggering success—it was made in 28 days for less than $1 million and grossed over $100 million in North America alone—Hollywood began to turn away from the complexity that had characterized even mainstream movies since the late sixties.

With an unknown star (Stallone's producers had agreed to his condition that he play the title role) and a hack director (John G. Avildsen), the film's prospects were dim. But positive word of mouth was shrewdly augmented by a publicity campaign emphasizing the true-life-underdog angle. Frustrated by national crises and alarmed by demands of feminists and minorities (as well as the frankness of recent cinema), many moviegoers cheered *Rocky*'s great-white-hope hero and its comforting pieties. The film won three Oscars, including Best Picture. **◂1971.12 ▸1977.10**

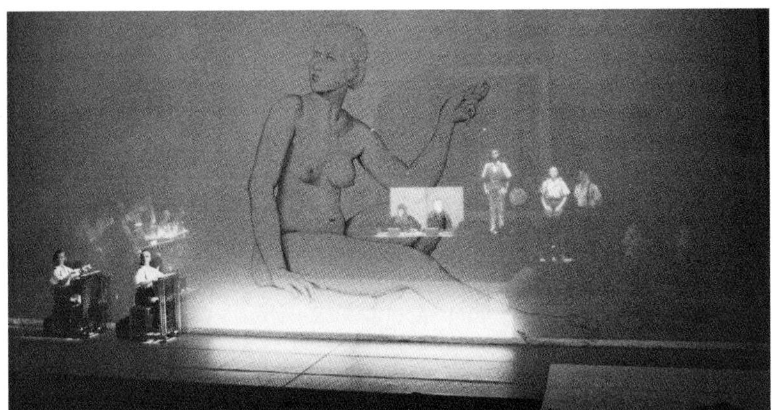

***Einstein on the Beach,* said one critic, was "bizarre, occasionally boring, yet always intermittently beautiful." Above, a 1992 Paris production.**

IN THE UNITED STATES

Legion convention at a Philadelphia hotel during bicentennial festivities, infecting 182 Legionnaires and killing 29. Medical researchers at the U.S. Centers for Disease Control traced the severe respiratory ailment, dubbed Legionnaires' Disease, to a strange bacillus, which they named *Legionella pneumophilia,* which could survive for as long as a year in tap water. Researchers speculated that the outbreak came from contaminated water in hotel air conditioners.

▸10-4, GOOD BUDDY—A national craze for citizens-band (CB) radios, two-way devices usually used by interstate truck drivers, peaked in 1976 with more than 656,000 applications each month to the FCC for CB licenses. Millions of Americans adopted CB lingo ("10-4" for affirmative; "good buddy" for airwave acquaintances; "smokie" for state trooper). Even first lady Betty Ford admitted she broadcast out of the White House under the "handle" (nom de CB) "First Mama."

▸ICE APPEAL—Vivacious Dorothy Hamill became almost as well known for her much-imitated hairstyle—the short "Hamill wedge"—as for winning the women's figure skating gold medal at 1976's Innsbruck Olympics. In 1977, Hamill began skating professionally with the Ice Capades, and later became its co-owner and president. ◂1976.3

▸MEDICAL ETHICS—In March, the parents of Karen Ann Quinlan, a 22-year-old New Jersey woman who'd been in an irreversible, drug-induced coma for nearly a year, won a court battle to disconnect their daughter's respirator. Quinlan was taken off the breathing apparatus in June; she survived for nine more years, succumbing to pneumonia in 1985. ▸1990.11

POLITICS & BUSINESS: GNP: $1,785.5 billion ... Jimmy Carter elected president, defeating Gerald Ford ... California physicians protest increases in malpractice insurance (stage 35 day slow down) ... Secretary of Agriculture Earl Butz resigns amid controversy over racial remarks ... Toxic Substances Control Act passed ... California passes first right-to-die law ... Rupert Murdoch acquires the *New York Post.*

"What does Prague have to do with anything? That was another situation, another Communist Party with other aspirations."
—Italian Communist Party leader Enrico Berlinguer

AROUND THE WORLD

▶ENTEBBE RAID—On July 4, after flying 2,500 miles, from Israel to Uganda, a crack unit of Israeli commandos raided Entebbe Airport, where pro-Palestinian terrorists held 106 hostages from an Air France flight they'd hijacked earlier in the week (before flying to Uganda and the warm welcome of President Idi Amin). The terrorists demanded the release of 53 Palestinian and pro-Palestinian prisoners being held in Israel and Europe. Taking the whole world by surprise, the Israeli commandos rescued all but three of the hostages (who were killed), killed several terrorists and Ugandan soldiers, destroyed eleven Ugandan warplanes, and escaped with one casualty. ◀1972.3 ▶1985.9

▶SUPERSTAR'S SUPER-SELLER—British guitarist Peter Frampton's 1976 two-record LP, *Frampton Comes Alive*, became the biggest selling live pop album ever made. A veteran of the rock bands the Herd and Humble Pie, Frampton amassed an adoring, largely female following that consigned him to permanent teen-idol status. As the 1970s faded, so did he, and an early 1990s comeback attempt generated only minor interest. ◀1973.M ▶1982.12

▶SOLIDARITY'S FIRST GLIMMER—Facing bankruptcy thanks to the massive farm subsidies it paid to keep consumer prices down, Poland's Communist government—not daring to cut subsidies lest farmers withhold produce—announced drastic price increases in June: 30 percent on dairy products, 70 percent on meat, 100 percent on sugar. Industrial workers reacted with fury, walking off the job and even rioting in Warsaw and other cities. The impromptu protest worked: The planned hikes were suspended. Encouraged, workers sought to institutionalize their political strength. The Solidarity movement was taking shape. ◀1975.M ▶1980.1

Compared with the Cray-1 supercomputer *(above)*, even the most powerful mainframe seemed like an abacus.

TECHNOLOGY

Cray's Speed Machines

12 The standard against which all "supercomputers" would long be measured was created in 1976 by computer designer Seymour Cray. Only one quarter the size of its predecessors, the Cray-1 was ten times as powerful—thanks to "vector processing," a unique technology that allowed many parts of a problem to be worked on simultaneously. Able to perform 240 million calculations per second, the Cray-1 was first used at Los Alamos National Laboratories.

Cray had built what is often considered the first supercomputer—the CDC 7600, capable of 15 million calculations per second—in 1968, while working for the Minneapolis-based Control Data, which he'd helped set up eleven years earlier in the belief that a commercial (not just military/governmental) market existed for big, ultrafast scientific computers. (CDC built Cray his own laboratory 100 miles away in his hometown of Chippewa Falls, Wisconsin.) In 1972, Cray founded his own company, Cray Research.

The Cray-1 was his first solo effort—and a smashing success. By the early 1990s, Cray Research had manufactured two thirds of the world's supercomputers (numbering around 300). By then, Cray had founded Cray Computer in order to develop even more advanced devices. Cray's incredibly swift machines have become indispensable tools for scientists and engineers, who can now predict changes in the earth's atmosphere, simulate car crashes, (mathematically) recreate nuclear explosions in outer space—all in minutes or hours instead of weeks, months, or even years. **◀1971.5 ▶1981.10**

TECHNOLOGY

Revolution in a Box

13 Two varieties of videocassette recorder (VCR) were launched by two competitive Japanese companies in 1976—an index of the ongoing revolution in home entertainment. The VCR joined a growing range of television options—including UHF stations, cable systems, and an ever-expanding assortment of home video games—that would eventually undercut the domination of long-entrenched TV networks, and alter the role of the medium itself.

Though a leader in this revolution, the Betamax, which Sony first marketed in 1975 as part of a TV/VCR console, eventually succumbed to a competitor introduced later in the year by Sony's archrival, Victor Company of Japan (JVC): Video Home System (VHS). Incompatible with—though not superior to—Beta, VHS was aggressively marketed in the United States by Matsushita. Eventually, VHS prevailed in a twelve-year struggle for the worldwide VCR market. Largely overshadowed in this video*tape* battle was the advancing technology in video*disc* systems, demonstrated as early as 1927 by John Logie Baird but introduced to consumers only in the mid-1970s.

The VCR dramatically broadened what viewers could watch on their TV sets, particularly in places where transmissions were limited. Scheduling was no longer the sole province of broadcasters: Provided VCR owners could correctly program their equipment (a persistent challenge), they could record a show to view when and how often they pleased—skipping commercial interruptions at will. Television ad rates and "movies of the week" suffered as videotape rental stores and a new video porn industry boomed. And the camcorder almost instantly rendered the 8mm home-movie industry obsolete. **◀1958.3**

Betamax *(Sony's 1976 model, above)* was first, but VHS became the standard.

WESTERN EUROPE

Eurocommunism on the Rise

14 The growing influence of indigenous communist parties was apparent all over Western Europe in 1976, nowhere more so than in Italy. In June the Communist Party, headed by Enrico Berlinguer, won 34 percent of the vote in parliamentary elections. But retooled communists—avowedly democratic, disillusioned with Moscow's brutality, many accepting NATO and the Common Market—were also gaining support in France and Spain, while in Portugal, Marxists dominated the revolutionary government.

Italian Communist leader Berlinguer on the hustings in Avezzano.

In Italy, economic decline under the long-dominant but ineffectual Christian Democrats had persuaded large numbers of voters to give the Communists (who'd disavowed violent revolution after World War II) a try. Without actually joining the government, Berlinguer's party entered a power-sharing arrangement with the Christian Democrats the following year.

Even France's traditionally pro-Soviet Party showed signs of distancing itself from Moscow. In February, leader Georges Marchais declared his party's support of "socialism in the colors of France." When socialist François Mitterrand was elected president in 1981, four Communists joined his cabinet.

Perhaps the strongest statement of Eurocommunist autonomy was made in Spain, where Communist leader Santiago Carillo, condemning Soviet expansionism, endorsed continued U.S. military presence in Europe as long as the Soviets held sway in Czechoslovakia. This was a new type of communism—one that Washington and its allies could grudgingly live with. **◀1968.2 ▶1981.7**

NOBEL PRIZES: Peace: Mairead Corrigan and Betty Williams (Irish; Northern Ireland peace movement) ... Literature: Saul Bellow (U.S.; novelist) ... Chemistry: William N. Lipscomb, Jr. (U.S.; boranes) ... Medicine: Baruch Blumberg and Carleton Gajdusek (U.S.; dissemination of infectious diseases) ... Physics: Burton Richter and Samuel C.C. Ting (U.S.; subatomic particle J/psi) ... Economics: Milton Friedman (U.S.).

A VOICE FROM 1976

Carter in all Candor

From "*Playboy* Interview: Jimmy Carter," *Playboy*, November 1976

During his 1976 presidential campaign, Georgia governor Jimmy Carter granted extensive interviews to Playboy *magazine for an article published in the November issue. The devout Southern Baptist candidate and Hugh Hefner's sybaritic journal made unusual bedfellows, but the unlikeliness appealed to Carter: He needed to prove to the electorate that he was no Bible thumper, that he—Sunday school teacher, peanut farmer, nuclear engineer—was a regular guy. Over the course of three months, he spoke vigorously to* Playboy *correspondent Robert Scheer about the Vietnam War, health care, tax reform, civil rights, and détente. At the end of their final session, Scheer lobbed one last question: "Do you feel you've reassured people with this interview, people who are uneasy about your religious beliefs, who wonder if you're going to make a rigid, unbending President?" Carter's unorthodox response, including some uncommonly common language (most newspapers blue-penciled "screws" and referred to a "vulgarism for sexual relations") and an odd admission of lust, became instantly notorious. But in November, just weeks after the interview appeared on newsstands, voters favored Carter over unelected President Gerald Ford 51 percent to 48 percent.* ◄**1974.1** ►**1977.2**

Three faces of Carter: The born-again Christian's appearance in *Playboy* created a stir.

PLAYBOY: Do you feel you've reassured people with this interview, people who are uneasy about your religious beliefs, who wonder if you're going to make a rigid, unbending President?

CARTER: I don't know if you've been to Sunday school here yet; some of the press has attended. I teach there about every three or four weeks. It's getting to be a real problem because we don't have room to put everybody now when I teach. I don't know if we're going to have to issue passes or what. It almost destroys the worship aspect of it. But we had a good class last Sunday. It's a good way to learn what I believe and what the Baptists believe.

One thing the Baptists believe in is complete autonomy. I don't accept any domination of my life by the Baptist Church, none. Every Baptist church is individual and autonomous. We don't accept domination of our church from the Southern Baptist Convention. The reason the Baptist Church was formed in this country was because of our belief in absolute and total separation of church and state. These basic tenets make us almost unique. We don't believe in any hierarchy in church. We don't have bishops. Any officers chosen by the church are defined as servants, not bosses. They're supposed to do the dirty work, make sure the church is clean and painted and that sort of thing. So it's a very good, democratic structure.

When my sons were small, we went to church and they went, too. But when they got old enough to make their own decisions, they decided when to go and they varied in their devoutness. Amy really looks forward to going to church, because she gets to see all her cousins at Sunday school. I never knew anything except going to church. My wife and I were born and raised in innocent times. The normal thing to do was to go to church.

What Christ taught about most was pride, that one person should never think he was any better than anybody else. One of the most vivid stories Christ told in one of his parables was about two people who went into a church. One was an official of the church, a Pharisee, and he said, "Lord, I thank you that I'm not like all those other people. I keep all your commandments, I give a tenth of everything I own. I'm here to give thanks for making me more acceptable in your sight." The other guy was despised by the nation, and he went in, prostrated himself on the floor and said, "Lord, have mercy on me, a sinner. I'm not worthy to lift my eyes to heaven." Christ asked the disciples which of the two had justified his life. The answer was obviously the one who was humble.

The thing that's drummed into us all the time is not to be proud, not to be better than anyone else, not to look down on people but to make ourselves acceptable in God's eyes through our own actions and recognize the simple truth that we're saved by grace. It's just a free gift through faith in Christ. This gives us a mechanism by which we can relate permanently to God. I'm not speaking for other people, but it gives me a sense of peace and equanimity and assurance.

I try not to commit a deliberate sin. I recognize that I'm going to do it anyhow, because I'm human and I'm tempted. And Christ set some almost impossible standards for us. Christ said, "I tell you that anyone who looks on a woman with lust has in his heart already committed adultery."

I've looked on a lot of women with lust. I've committed adultery in my heart many times. This is something that God recognizes I will do—and I have done it—and God forgives me for it. But that doesn't mean that I condemn someone who not only looks on a woman with lust but leaves his wife and shacks up with somebody out of wedlock.

Christ says, Don't consider yourself better than someone else because one guy screws a whole bunch of women while the other guy is loyal to his wife. The guy who's loyal to his wife ought not to be condescending or proud because of the relative degree of sinfulness. One thing that Paul Tillich said was that religion is a search for the truth about man's existence and his relationship with God and his fellow man: and that once you stop searching and think you've got it made—at that point, you lose your religion. Constant reassessment, searching in one's heart—it gives me a feeling of confidence.

I don't inject these beliefs in my answers to your secular questions.

(Carter clenched his fist and gestured sharply.)

But I don't think I would *ever* take on the same frame of mind that Nixon or Johnson did—lying, cheating and distorting the truth. Not taking into consideration my hope for my strength of character, I think that my religious beliefs alone would prevent that from happening to me. I have that confidence. I hope it's justified.

"Ring the bells for your sons. Tell them those wars were the last of wars and the end of sorrows."—**Egyptian president Anwar al-Sadat, addressing Israel's Knesset**

STORY OF THE YEAR

Egypt's Sadat Embraces Israel

1 In its 29-year history, Israel had often exchanged bombs and bullets with its Arab neighbors, but never visits between heads of state. Indeed, Arab leaders commonly questioned Israel's very right to exist. So millions marveled when Egyptian president Anwar al-Sadat toured Jerusalem in November 1977, visiting some of the holiest shrines of Islam, Christianity, and Judaism, as well as a museum of the Holocaust. And television watchers around the world were moved to tears when he addressed the Knesset (Israel's parliament). "In all sincerity," he assured Israelis, "I tell you that we welcome you among us.... Today I proclaim ... that we accept to live with you in a lasting and just peace."

Breakthrough handshake: Begin welcomes Sadat to Jerusalem.

Sadat's journey was preceded by months of indirect communication with Israeli prime minister Menachem Begin, with whose country Egypt remained technically at war. (Go-betweens included Romanian dictator Nicolae Ceauşescu, Morocco's King Hassan, and U.S State Department officials.) Begin seemed an unlikely partner in a peace initiative: He'd become premier in May when his rightist Likud coalition, which rejected all compromise with the Arabs, handed the scandal-ridden Labor Party its first electoral defeat ever. Yet Begin's unquestionable toughness—he'd commanded the terrorist Irgun organization during Israel's fight for independence—allowed him to shake hands with the Egyptian statesman without instantly being branded a traitor.

Still, peace remained well beyond the horizon. Sadat insisted in his Knesset speech that Israel must withdraw from occupied Arab lands (including Jerusalem), and that a settlement depended on "justice" for the Palestinians. Begin, in turn, stressed the "eternal" link between the Jews and their biblical homeland (which included the occupied areas) and Israel's need for a military buffer zone. Both men were navigating dangerous political waters. Though Sadat met cheering crowds on his return to Egypt, Arab hard-liners denounced him: Libya broke diplomatic relations, and Egyptian offices were attacked in Damascus, Beirut, Baghdad, and even Athens. And though Begin could not ignore massive demonstrations by Israel's Peace Now movement, neither could he afford to alienate his hawkish supporters.

The Israeli leader flew to Egypt in December, but negotiations soon reached an impasse. It would be up to U.S. president Jimmy Carter to break it. **◂1974.10 ▸1978.3**

DIPLOMACY

Spotlight on Human Rights

2 Human rights is a cause almost universally endorsed by governments—even those whose policies belie their rhetoric. In December 1977, just after being awarded the Nobel Peace Prize, the London-based human rights group Amnesty International issued a report accusing 116 UN member nations of imprisoning people solely for their beliefs or ethnic origins. Since its founding in 1961, AI had helped free 10,000 of those prisoners—a success at least partly due to the organization's freedom from governmental ties. But 1977 was also the year the new U.S. president Jimmy Carter began a novel experiment: using his government's political and economic clout to discourage human rights abuses.

Carter was more outspoken about such abuses than any U.S. president in decades—and he backed up his rhetoric with policy. Argentina, Uruguay, and Ethiopia were the first to lose American aid. But the Carter doctrine faced daunting challenges. For one thing, America's own rights record was far from perfect. (AI's report cited unjust prosecutions of blacks and American Indians.) Another was the doctrine's vague and sweeping definition of human rights. Geopolitical pragmatism also led to inconsistencies: The Shah's Iran, among other U.S. allies, largely escaped criticism. In other cases, criticism—and sanctions—proved ineffectual or counterproductive. Efforts to curb the U.S.S.R.'s crackdown on dissidents, for example, provoked even more severe repression.

Still, there were successes. Thanks partly to U.S. pressure, fewer Argentines were "disappeared" by state-sponsored death squads; political prisoners in many countries went free (35,000 in Indonesia alone from 1977 to 1980); and the number of Soviet Jews allowed to emigrate increased from 14,000 in 1976 to 51,000 in 1979. In Czechoslovakia, emboldened dissidents founded Charter 77, a group devoted to monitoring their government's adherence to the Helsinki Accords and UN human-rights covenants. One of its persecuted leaders, Czech playwright Vaclav Havel, would become his nation's president. **◂1975.8 ▸1979.9**

AMNESTY INTERNATIONAL

Amnesty International's receipt of a Nobel focused attention on human rights worldwide.

THE COLD WAR

Neutron Bomb Furor

3 By a one-vote margin, the U.S. Senate in 1977 approved financing for the neutron bomb, a thermonuclear device designed to kill humans while leaving buildings intact. The decision triggered an international furor—and a serious crisis in the Carter administration.

A byproduct of the American hydrogen bomb program, the neutron bomb had been on the drawing board since the 1950s. Essentially a "small" H-bomb—at one kiloton, a fraction of the size of the Hiroshima bomb—it generates minimal blast and heat, but spreads armor-penetrating, cell-ravaging neutron and gamma radiation over an area of about a square mile. (Its radiation, unlike that of other nuclear weapons, dissipates quickly.) The United States tested such a device in 1963 before scrapping the idea.

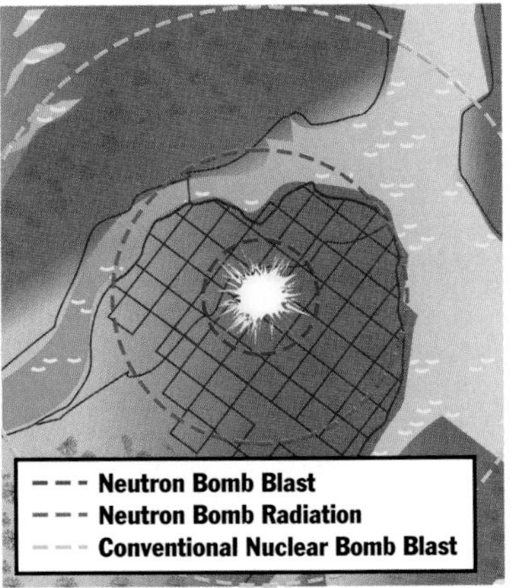

The neutron bomb was designed to kill beyond the range of its explosion.

In 1975, President Gerald Ford secretly revived "enhanced radiation warheads" by burying the program in his budget for fiscal year 1978. His rationale: Such devices would allow NATO to repel a Warsaw Pact invasion of West Germany without obliterating the country. Carter inherited Ford's budget, and the "N-bomb"

ART & CULTURE: Books: ***Song of Solomon*** **(Toni Morrison);** ***The Women's Room*** **(Marilyn French);** ***Daniel Martin*** **(John Fowles);** ***The Flounder*** **(Günter Grass);** ***The Thorn Birds*** **(Colleen McCullough);** ***A Rumor of War*** **(Philip Caputo) ... Music: "You Light Up My Life" (Joe Brooks);** ***Rumours*** **(Fleetwood Mac, LP);** ***Fly Like an Eagle*** **(Steve Miller Band, LP);** ***Hotel California*** **(The Eagles, LP);** ***War Cry*** **(Harold Faberman) ...**

"I have great respect for the institutions of elections, but I cannot allow the country to face disaster for their sake."
—Pakistan's General Zia ul-Haq after ousting Prime Minster Zulfikar Ali Bhutto

item surfaced during congressional debate in 1977. The weapon provoked widespread horror, but Congress approved funding. Carter initially supported production. As he tried to convince West German leaders of the weapon's battlefield efficacy (neutron bombs were to be deployed in West Germany as howitzer shells and warheads for tactical missiles), demonstrations swept the United States and Western Europe. The Soviets denounced the "capitalist" weapon that spread death and radiation sickness but spared property. (Meanwhile, they were working on their own model.)

In 1978, just as West German chancellor Helmut Schmidt consented to the neutron bomb, Carter decided to postpone production. Schmidt felt abandoned, and Carter's detractors read his reversal as vacillation, a characterization from which he never fully recovered. The Reagan administration resumed neutron bomb production, to renewed protest, in 1981. **◂1972.7 ▸1979.4**

PAKISTAN

General Zia's Coup

4 The coup took place in the middle of the night and was bloodless. Under the circumstances, the second fact was extraordinary: In the months before army chief of staff Muhammad Zia ul-Haq ousted Pakistani prime minister Zulfikar Ali Bhutto, more than 300 people had died protesting Bhutto's rule. The army, said Zia afterward, had "watched the political wranglings in the country for a long time." In July 1977, as unrest plunged Pakistan toward economic disaster, the general felt compelled "to fill in the vacuum" created by national leaders. He promised military rule would continue only until a new government could be freely elected. Eleven years later, Zia still reigned.

Bhutto, an aristocratic, Oxford-educated lawyer, had been elected president in 1971 after the third India-Pakistan War, when East Pakistan seceded to become independent Bangladesh. He supplanted disgraced dictator General Agha Muhammad Yahya Khan, becoming the country's first civilian leader in more than a decade. (In 1973, a new constitution made Bhutto prime minister.) But despite reformist leanings, Bhutto maintained martial law for two years,

After Zia's coup, soldiers were a common sight in Pakistan's cities and towns.

jailing hundreds of his opponents. Then he rigged the 1977 election to ensure victory for him and his Pakistan People's Party. Bhutto called the polling, held in March, the "first completely democratic civilian election" ever staged in Pakistan; a coalition of opposition groups, the Pakistan National Alliance, called it a fraud.

Protests escalated into rioting; Bhutto again imposed martial law. By July, amid worsening turmoil, the prime minister tentatively agreed to a new election in October. But Zia, a Bhutto appointee and seeming loyalist, had already seen enough. Bhutto was taken into "protective custody"; Zia canceled the elections and set about tightening his authoritarian grip on Pakistan. In 1979, the military regime shrugged off international diplomatic appeals and hanged Bhutto. **◂1971.1 ▸1988.5**

POPULAR CULTURE

A Desire for Roots

5 For eight nights in January 1977, Americans of all races gathered around their television sets to follow the fictionalized family history of black journalist Alex Haley. An estimated 130 million people—about half the country's population—tuned in to *Roots*, a saga that began in Africa in 1750 and ended in the American South in 1867. Based on Haley's 1976 book of the same name, the miniseries won six Emmies; few dramatic programs in TV history have won wider acclaim or had a bigger audience.

Independent producer David Wolper had bought the rights, gambling that the story would capture the imagination of a racially troubled nation, and ABC had agreed. Graphically depicting the brutal conditions on slave ships and plantations, the series followed Haley ancestor Kunta Kinte (played by LeVar Burton) into bondage, and followed Kinte's great-grandson, blacksmith Tom Murray, into freedom.

The success of both the show and the book made Haley (who'd collaborated with Malcolm X on the black nationalist leader's 1965 autobiography) a celebrity from Alabama to Beijing. *Roots* grew out of stories he'd heard his grandmother and her sister tell on the porch in Henning, Tennessee, when he was five years old. Some four decades later, he began the research which eventually led him back to Gambia. Haley's work inspired Americans of all colors to search for their ethnic origins. His book, he said, "awakened a worldwide perception that genealogy isn't reserved for royalty."

The book won a special Pulitzer Prize in 1977. Critics later charged him with plagiarism (a copyright infringement suit was settled out of court for a large sum) and with inventing material outright. Nevertheless, by the early 1990s *Roots* had sold more than six million copies and been published in two dozen countries. **◂1971.10 ▸1989.V**

Kunta Kinte (LeVar Burton) arrives in the New World on a slave ship from Africa.

DEATHS

Steve Biko, South African civil rights activist.

James M. Cain, U.S. novelist.

Maria Callas, U.S.-Greek singer.

Charles Chaplin, U.K. comedian and filmmaker.

Henri-Georges Clouzot, French filmmaker.

Joan Crawford, U.S. actress.

Bing Crosby, U.S. singer and actor.

Anthony Eden, U.K. statesman.

Peter Finch, U.K. actor.

Erroll Garner, U.S. musician.

Peter Goldmark, Hungarian-U.S. engineer.

Howard Hawks, U.S. filmmaker.

Kamal Jumblatt, Lebanese political leader.

Guy Lombardo, U.S. band leader.

Robert Lowell, U.S. poet.

Julius "Groucho" Marx, U.S. comedian.

Samuel "Zero" Mostel, U.S. actor.

Vladimir Nabokov, Russian-U.S. writer.

Anaïs Nin, French-U.S. writer.

Alice Paul, U.S. suffragist.

Elvis Presley, U.S. singer.

Jacques Prévert, French poet and screenwriter.

Roberto Rossellini, Italian filmmaker.

Adolph Rupp, U.S. basketball coach.

Leopold Stokowski, U.K.-U.S. conductor.

Wernher von Braun, German-U.S. rocket scientist.

Kurt von Schuschnigg, Austrian chancellor.

Ethel Waters, U.S. singer and actress.

Philip K. Wrigley, U.S. industrialist.

Painting & Sculpture: *My Parents* (David Hockney); *Ocean Park* (Richard Diebenkorn); *Observatory* (Robert Morris) ... Film: *Annie Hall* (Woody Allen); *Man of Marble* (Andrzej Wajda); *Padre Padrone* (Paolo and Vittorio Taviani) ... Theater: *A Life in the Theater* (David Mamet); *The Elephant Man* (Bernard Pomerance); *Gemini* (Albert Innaurato); *Annie* (Meehan, Strouse, and Charnin) ... TV: *The Love Boat.*

"Wait until the American flag comes down and the Panamanian goes up. Then there will be a stampede out of here."
—An American living in the Canal Zone

NEW IN 1977

Ban on Red Dye No. 2 (found to cause cancer).

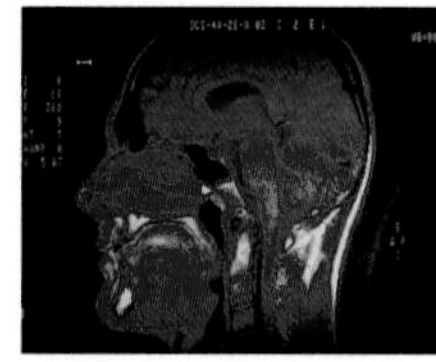

Magnetic resonance imaging (MRI).

Apple II computer.

Male U.S. saint (John N. Neumann).

Generic "no-brand" products.

Department of Energy.

Legal Communist Party in Spain.

IN THE UNITED STATES

▶**MULTIPLE MURDERERS**—Convicted killer Gary Gilmore was executed by firing squad at Utah State Prison on January 17. Gilmore *(below)*, who'd brutally murdered two college students, lobbied hard for his own execution, which was the first in the U.S. in ten years. His story was the subject of Norman Mailer's 1979 book *The*

Executioner's Song. Another sensational homicide case was cracked on August 10: New York City police arrested 24-year-old postal worker David Berkowitz for the murders of six young women and one man. Berkowitz, who called himself the Son of Sam (Sam was a black dog whose 1,000-year-old spirit "ordered" Berkowitz to kill), carried on a cryptic correspondence with police and tabloid newspapers during his twelve-month shooting spree. Clinically paranoid, Berkowitz was eventually convicted and imprisoned at Attica. ◂1969.9

▶**KOREAGATE**—On September 6, millionaire South Korean businessman and Washington bon vivant Tongsun Park was indicted on 36 counts of fraud

MUSIC

The King Is Dead

6 The long decline of Elvis Presley—who almost single-handedly established rock 'n' roll —was a spectacle that absorbed devotees and detractors alike. It began in 1958, the year Presley was drafted into the U.S. Army (which shaved his famous side-burns and wrenched him from his public) and his adored mother died. It ended on August 16, 1977, with his sudden death at age 42.

Presley had stopped performing live in 1961, concentrating instead on movies. In 1968 he returned to the stage in a landmark televised concert. Soon Elvis, dressed in sequined matador outfits, crooning ballads, was King again—not of rock, but of the Las Vegas lounge act. This phase peaked in 1973, with a broadcast from Hawaii seen by a billion fans worldwide.

After 1974, Presley gained so much weight his pants sometimes ripped onstage. He babbled incoherently, and his fabled generosity reached bizarre proportions. (One stranger received a Cadillac.) His death was attributed to heart failure, but the whole story emerged post-mortem: Deeply insecure, Elvis had spent his free time hiding in his Memphis mansion, Graceland, with a staff of pals who fulfilled his every whim. He devoured junk food by the pound; while remaining a teetotaler and a devout Christian, he gobbled prescription stimulants and sleeping pills.

In death, as in life, Presley retained a quasi-religious following. Graceland was opened to the public in 1982; it has become a shrine to which pilgrims flock by the thousands. Trade in his relics continues unabated, though some of the faithful insist he never died—and Elvis sightings have become a staple of supermarket tabloids. ◂**1956.1**

Elvis in 1973. Above, a souvenir Elvis toothpick holder from the gift shop at Graceland.

In a cartoon by Oliphant, Carter swims in dangerous waters to get the canal treaty ratified.

PANAMA

U.S. Cedes Canal

7 Former California governor Ronald Reagan rallied many Americans with his simple analysis of the Panama Canal—"We bought it, we paid for it, it's ours." Legal scholars, and the mass of Panamanians, interpreted matters differently. No Panamanian had ever signed the 1903 treaty granting the United States perpetual control of the strategic waterway. (The country's representative had been a Frenchman with close ties to the canal builders.) To the people of the isthmus, that imperialistic insult—coupled with the U.S. tendency to give only menial jobs to Panamanians in the Canal Zone—overshadowed the canal's economic benefits. Anti-American sentiment had been simmering for decades, contributing to a growing belief among U.S. officials that the treaty could not stand. In 1977, over a howl of partisan protest, Jimmy Carter (the fourth successive U.S. president to work on a settlement) agreed to transfer ownership of the Canal to Panama.

The two treaties signed the following year by Carter and leftist strongman General Omar Torrijos Herrera (after being ratified by the requisite two thirds of the Senate) mandated a gradual changeover, effective December 31, 1999, of both the Canal and the U.S.-governed, ten-mile-wide, 533-square-mile Canal Zone, home to some 10,000 Americans. The United States, while acknowledging Panamanian sovereignty and Canal neutrality, maintained permanent defense rights.

The agreements, said Carter, reflected the American belief that "fairness, not force, should lie at the heart of our dealings with the world." Still, many Americans, including most of those living in Panama, denounced the "canal giveaway": Washington, they complained, was kowtowing to a Third World backwater. Senate debate was rancorous but ended with ratification. A decade later, however, with Reagan in the White House, force would once again dictate Panama's relations with the giant to the north. ◂**1968.9** ▸**1989.2**

SOUTHEAST ASIA

Exodus of the Boat People

8 The war was over, but peace had not yet come. Vietnam, Laos, and Cambodia were devastated by years of fighting. The first two countries were growing even poorer in the hands of Communists whose administrative shortcomings were exacerbated by an obsession with reforming (or punishing)

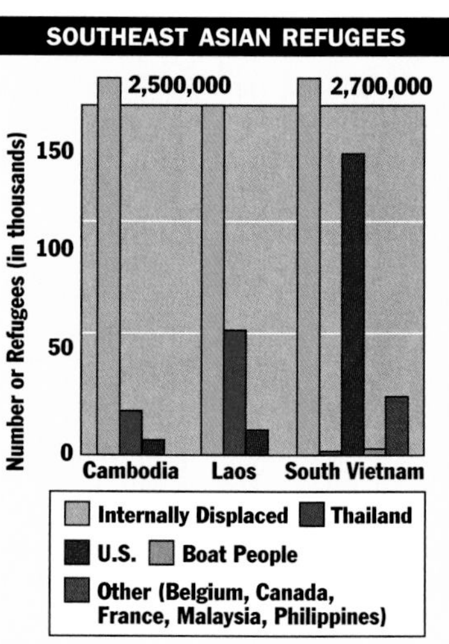

In 1977, 5.6 million Cambodians, Laotians, and South Vietnamese had been displaced.

non-Communists; the third was ruled by the genocidal Khmer Rouge. By 1977, thousands were fleeing Indochina every month, in one of the century's largest mass

SPORTS: Baseball: World Series, New York Yankees defeat Los Angeles Dodgers, 4–2 ... Football: Super Bowl, Oakland Raiders defeat Minnesota Vikings, 32–14 ... Basketball: NBA, Portland Trail Blazers defeat Philadelphia 76ers, 4–2 ... Horse Racing: Seattle Slew wins Triple Crown.

"It's the flotsam and jetsam from the period when I was twelve years old. All the books and films and comics that I liked when I was a child."—**George Lucas, on *Star Wars***

migrations. Some refugees traveled overland to Thailand, but most took to the seas. Crammed into small, leaky vessels, their savings gone to smugglers who promised to ferry them to a better life, they came to be known as "boat people."

Many died at sea. Most of the survivors landed elsewhere in Asia, or attempted to: Overwhelmed by the influx, Indonesia, Malaysia, the Philippines, and Hong Kong began closing their doors. France, West Germany, Canada, and Taiwan took some of the overflow. The United States, whose policies had helped create the boat people's plight, admitted 165,000 in the first two years after the Communist victories. In 1977, Washington established a quota of 15,000 per year; the limit was raised to 25,000 in 1978, and to 50,000 in 1979. The flow continued into the 1990s. **◂1975.4 ▸1978.9**

AVIATION

A Supersonic Victory

9 The world's first supersonic transport (SST) crossed its last frontier in October 1977 when it took off from New York's Kennedy Airport. Twice as fast as ordinary airliners, the 100-passenger Concorde—built jointly by the British Aircraft Corporation and France's Aérospatiale—had been hobbled by troubles ever since the prototype rolled off the line a decade earlier.

The Concorde's manufacturers had promised their respective governments (cosponsors of the craft) to have it airborne by February 1968. But technical problems and quadrupling construction costs scotched that deadline, and France's May 1968 student riots set it back further. In December 1968, a Soviet SST—the Tupelev Tu144, destined for domestic and medium-distance routes—beat the Concorde to a maiden flight. And popular opposition mounted in France, Britain, and the United States, as environmentalists warned of noise pollution (the loudness of SST engines was unequaled), window-shattering sonic booms (in France, shock waves from supersonic military planes had caused heart attacks and even a roof cave-in), damage to the earth's ozone layer, and voracious fuel consumption. In 1971, the U.S. government canceled funding for an SST being developed by Boeing, adding to the doubts about the Concorde's future.

Nine Concordes finally went into service in 1976, flying from London and Paris to Bahrain, Washington, Caracas, and a few other destinations. (By then, orders from airlines other than Air France and British Airways had dried up.) But it took a 19-month legal battle, and a Supreme Court decision, to overcome New York's ban on the plane and open a route essential to profitable operations. On takeoff at JFK, the luxury airliner managed to pass a noise test; regular transatlantic service followed. But in the coming years the Concorde remained a plane for the privileged few. **◂1972.6**

The delta-winged Concorde stretched nearly 204 feet from needle nose to tail.

FILM

A Cosmic Blockbuster

10 "The word for this movie is fun," said director George Lucas of his 1977 opus, *Star Wars.* A variety of adventure genres—boys' novels, Greek mythology, chivalric romances, samurai epics, Westerns, pulp science fiction, and matinee serials—whipped together in a cinematic Mixmaster, *Star Wars* is set, as the opening titles announce, "A long time ago in a galaxy far, far away." The Evil Empire, commanded by black-armored, Nazi-helmeted Darth Vader (whose face is masked, but whose basso voice belongs to an uncredited James Earl Jones), is under attack by good-guy rebels: Luke Skywalker, an apprentice knight learning to master the mystical Force; Obi-Wan Kenobi, Luke's military and spiritual instructor whose Zen-like pronouncements include the signoff "May the Force be with you"; headstrong Princess Leia; wisecracking mercenary Han Solo; and a vaudevillian pair of robots, C-3PO and R2-D2.

Moviegoers cheered the awesomely persuasive special effects (the most spectacular yet put on film), straightforward storytelling, black-hats-versus-white-hats morality, and breakneck pace. Yet those very elements, said detractors, encouraged an uncritical spectatorship that—together with the film's positing of premental, presexual innocence as a state of grace—infantalized the audience. Moreover, the film's phenomenal success—it grossed $232 million in North America and made millions more at the foreign box office and in sales of TV and video rights and licensed products—like *Rocky*'s the previous year, helped end a golden era of challenging, sophisticated, thematically complex American cinema.

As a producer, Lucas followed up *Star Wars* with two sequels and several blockbusters directed by Steven Spielberg (including the 1981 megahit *Raiders of the Lost Ark*). Lucas's northern California-based Industrial Light and Magic studio also created computer-aided special effects for other directors. **◂1976.11 ▸1982.9**

Princess Leia (Carrie Fisher) and *Star Wars*'s playful robot, R2-D2. The film won 7 Oscars.

IN THE UNITED STATES

and bribery. "Koreagate" stemmed from Park's role in a seven-year effort by the South Korean government to illegally influence U.S. legislators. Testifying to Congress (in exchange for dropped charges), Park implicated 31 lawmakers but dismissed the flow of money as "gift-giving." Three representatives received reprimands and one went to jail. ◂1974.1 ▸1980.M

▶PIPELINE OPENS—Oil began flowing through the $9.7 billion, 799-mile-long Alaska pipeline on June 20. Under construction for three years, the pipeline ran from the North Slope oil fields at Arctic Prudhoe Bay to refineries in Valdez on Prince William Sound. The first oil piped from North America's richest petroleum reserve reached Valdez on July 28. ▸1984.6

▶LEGEND OF THE RINK—In 1977, the 30th season of his remarkable hockey career, ageless wonder Gordon "Gordie" Howe scored his 1,000th big-league goal. A 21-time National Hockey League All-Star, Howe spent 25 seasons with the Detroit Red Wings before retiring in 1971 at age 43. Two years later he joined the Houston Aeros of the World Hockey Association (his two sons were teammates). He was back in the NHL again in 1978, skating with the Hartford Whalers. He retired for good in 1980, with the NHL record for scoring (since broken by Wayne Gretzky), games played, and penalty minutes. ▸1994.M

▶BLACKOUT REDUX—When lightning struck power lines in Westchester County, New York, on July 13, New York City was plunged into darkness for the second time in twelve years. During the 25 hours before electricity was restored, thousands spilled into the streets to loot and burn everything from disposable diapers to cars. Police made 3,776 arrests; losses to theft and property damage were estimated at close to $150 million. ◂1965.M

POLITICS & BUSINESS: GNP: $1,994.6 billion ... Minimum wage raised from $2.30 to $3.05 per hour (by 1980) ... President Jimmy Carter pardons Vietnam draft evaders ... Budget director Bert Lance resigns amid controversy over personal finances ... Carter halts production of B-1 bomber ... U.S. tests space shuttle ... Supreme Court rules that it is not unconstitutional for suburbs to refuse to alter zoning laws.

"I don't want to achieve immortality through my work. I want to achieve it through not dying."—**Woody Allen**

AROUND THE WORLD

▶DEEPWATER HOTHOUSES—At the Galápagos Rift, on the ocean floor west of Ecuador, astonished scientists in 1977 discovered hydrothermal vents, or "chimneys," that supported exotic ecosystems. The vents spewed mineral-rich, magma-warmed water, creating a fertile environment for bacteria, dinner-plate-sized clams, giant seaworms, and other marine animals. All fed off plants, which were growing without benefit of photosynthesis in a place of such darkness (it was completely cut off from the sun) that any life was thought to have been impossible. Similar vents and biological communities were later discovered at other sites of sea floor spreading in the Pacific and Atlantic, and in Lake Baikal in Russia. ◂1963.4

▶LA PASIONARIA RETURNS—Dolores Gómez Ibarruri, a.k.a. "La Pasionaria," came home to Spain in 1977 after 38 years in exile in the U.S.S.R. The

82-year-old Ibarruri had rallied Republicans against Francisco Franco's fascist armies in 1936, famously declaring, "It is better to die on your feet than to live on your knees! They shall not pass!" Upon her return (18 months after Franco's death), she was promptly elected to the Spanish parliament; she remained honorary head of the Communist Party until her death in 1989. ◂1975.1 ▸1981.5

▶SUPREME SOVIET—In 1977, 13 years into his rule of the Soviet Union, Communist Party First Secretary Leonid Brezhnev consolidated his power, assuming the presidency of the Supreme Soviet (and therefore heading both the Party and the state). A year earlier, he was made marshal of the Soviet Union—a military title only Stalin had ever held. Nominal "collective leadership" with Aleksei Kosygin and Nikolay Podgorny aside, Brezhnev had been the principal power in the Soviet Union since the mid-1960s. He retained his offices until his death in 1982. ◂1972.7 ▸1979.4

ARCHITECTURE

Paris's Inside-Out Edifice

11 Like the Eiffel Tower before it, the Pompidou National Center for Art and Culture, opened in Paris in 1977, created a *scandale d'architecture.* Conceived as a "living urban machine" by its young architects, Italian Renzo Piano and Briton Richard Rogers, the brashly high-tech, six-story glass building had a highly unorthodox design: It was turned inside out. All of its structural supports and mechanical parts—ducts, tubes, water pipes, escalators—were on the outside, brightly and schematically painted: blue for air conditioning, yellow for electrical conduits, red for elevators, green for water. "Ugly," said critics, "frightful and odious." Some called the design "bowelism"; others likened the building to an oil refinery.

Externalizing the building's viscera freed up its interior space. Huge, factorylike lofts divisible by movable partitions housed museums and educational institutions (including IRCAM, Pierre Boulez's center for electronic music).

People soon warmed to the Pompidou (named for the former French president). Set down in the middle of Beaubourg, one of Paris's oldest neighborhoods, it became a magnet for tourists, steadily outdrawing all other French attractions. But the Pompidou's success (built to accommodate 8,000 visitors a day, it regularly attracted close to 30,000), as well as its unusual design (wearing its "guts" on the outside made it energy-inefficient and more vulnerable to extreme weather), extracted a high price in wear and tear, and it has had to be closed down for long periods for refurbishing. **◂1966.4 ▸1984.9**

Alvy tells Annie that "love" is inadequate: He "lurves" her. Keaton's wardrobe created a vogue for the "Annie Hall look."

FILM

Allen's Funny Valentine

12 Perhaps the decade's finest love story was *Annie Hall*—director, cowriter, and star Woody Allen's keenly comic depiction of the rise and fall of a romance between Annie, a beguilingly ditsy WASP (Diane Keaton), and Alvy, a hilariously neurotic New York Jew (Allen). The 1977 film captured the bittersweet bewilderment of an era in which the sexual revolution, women's liberation, and prototypical Yuppiedom added new confusions to the ancient perplexities of courtship.

Lightly autobiographical—Allen and Keaton were former lovers; Keaton's real name is Hall; Allen, like Alvy, was a former comedy writer and stand-up comic—*Annie Hall* derives its believability less from those details than from its witty insights (about art, death, relationships, and the relative virtues of New York and Los Angeles), the casual naturalism of the acting, and the force of both stars' comic personas. (Keaton's was charmingly new, Allen's a refinement of the nebbishy, wisecracking *Untermensch* he'd played in his earlier films.)

Annie Hall has been called a valentine from Allen to Keaton. It has also drawn criticism for its subtle misogyny—its suggestion that Annie is unstable, ungrateful, and, ultimately, treacherous. (Alvy helps her develop her mind and talent, whereupon she abandons him for contemptible Los Angeles show business.) Nonetheless, Allen's reputation for writing full-bodied female roles is richly evidenced in *Annie Hall.* The film won Oscars for Best Picture, Actress, Screenplay, and Director. **◂1975.14**

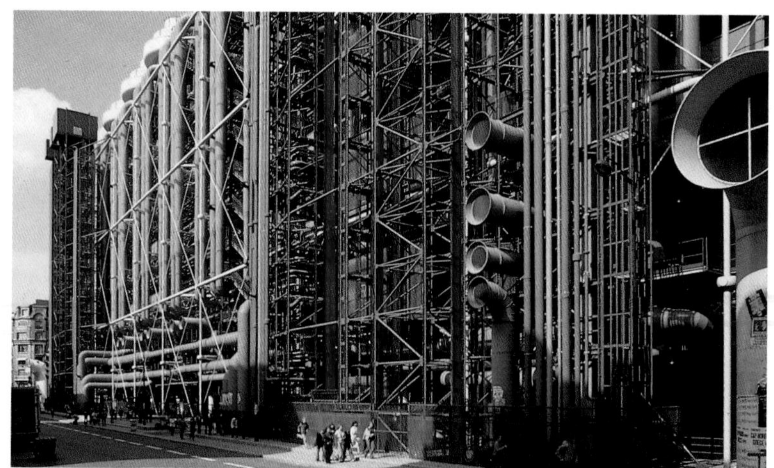

Piano and Rogers's Pompidou Center, which attracts eight million visitors a year.

SPORTS

Champs at Every Speed

13 Racing of all varieties dominated the sports headlines in 1977, as Ted Turner skippered *Courageous* to an America's Cup victory, Seattle Slew took the Triple Crown, and A.J. Foyt set a record with his fourth Indianapolis 500 victory. Also at the 1977 Indy, Janet Guthrie *(left, top)* broke another barrier, becoming the first woman driver in the auto race's 66-year history. Grappling with mechanical troubles that soaked her in fuel and forced her out after only 27 laps, Guthrie—one of a handful of women in the sport—displayed the grit that would enable her, the following year, to overcome a fractured wrist and finish ninth at Indy.

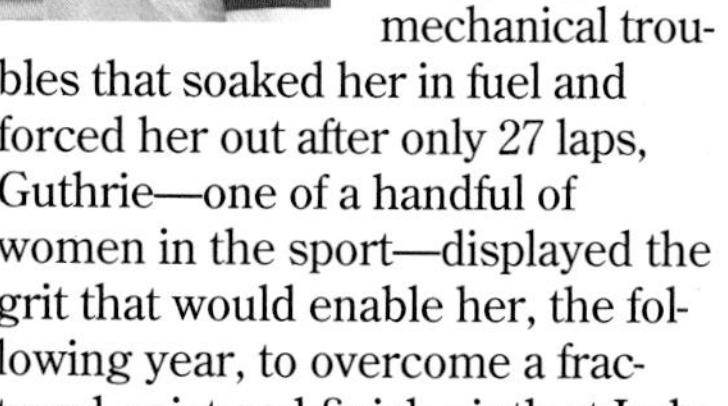

But outshining all other speedsters was 17-year-old Steve Cauthen *(above, bottom)*, the apprentice jockey from Kentucky who, after making his Belmont debut in the spring (sustaining serious injuries in a fall), proceeded to set records with breathtaking swiftness. Riding low and close to his mounts, Cauthen established a 30 percent win average even before his apprenticeship ended in June. By the end of 1977, he had amassed 477 victories and earned an unprecedented $6 million in purses. He capped his meteoric career by riding Affirmed to a Triple Crown triumph in 1978. **◂1973.9 ▸1986.M**

NOBEL PRIZES: Peace: Amnesty International (London) ... Literature: Vicente Alexandre (Spanish; poet) ... Chemistry: Ilya Prigogine (Belgian; thermodynamics) ... Medicine: Rosalyn Yalow, Roger Guillemin, and Andrew Schally (U.S.; hormones) ... Physics: Philip Anderson, John Van Vleck, and Nevill Mott (U.S., U.S., U.K.; magnetic and disordered systems) ... Economics: Bertil Ohlin and James Meade (Swedish, U.K.).

A VOICE FROM 1977

An Absent Partner

From *Chapter Two,* by Neil Simon, 1977

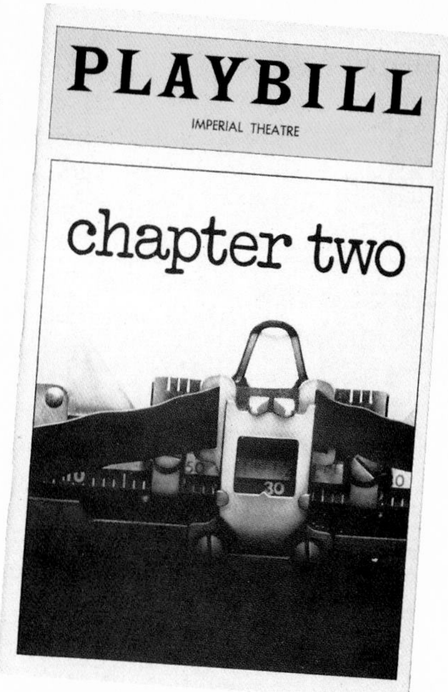

Neil Simon was the Prince of Broadway, a playwright whose string of situation comedies about middle-class life—from Come Blow Your Horn *in 1961 through* California Suite *in 1976—reliably drew packed houses. For all his popular success, however, Simon received sparse critical kudos until he came out with* Chapter Two *in 1977. The first of a series of dark-tinged autobiographical plays, it snapped his reputation as a joke machine, a writer who preferred gags to full-blooded characters.* Chapter Two *evinced Simon's perfect comic timing, but in addition to zingers, the play—about George Schneider, a middle-aged, not-terribly-successful writer trying to come to terms with the death of his wife and the demands of an unexpected relationship with a new woman—displayed a hitherto unrevealed emotional range. In the excerpt below, George talks to his brother about the difficulty he has had adjusting to the fact that his wife is permanently gone. With this and subsequent works, Simon's artistic standing began to catch up to his financial success, and in 1991 he won his first Pulitzer Prize for* Lost In Yonkers, *his 23rd Broadway hit.*

Leo: (*Trying to avoid the past*) George, you just got home. You're tired. Why don't you defrost the bathroom, take a bath?

George: Just one letter: "Dear Mr. Schneider, My name is Mary Ann Patterson. We've never met, but I did know your late wife, Barbara, casually. I work at Sabrina's where she used to come to have her hair cut. She was so beautiful and one of the warmest people I've ever met. It seems I always used to tell her my troubles, and she always found some terrific thing to say to cheer me up. I will miss her smiling face and the way she used to come bouncing into the shop like a little girl. I feel lucky to have known her. I just wanted to return a little of her good cheer. God bless you and keep you. Mary Ann Patterson." (*He puts down the letter.* LEO *looks at him, knowing not to intrude on this moment*) What the hell did I read *that* for?

Leo: It's very nice. It's a sweet letter, George.

George: Barbara knew a whole world of people I never knew … She knew that Ricco, the mailman, was a birdwatcher in Central Park, and that Vince, the butcher in Gristede's, painted miniature portraits of cats every weekend in his basement on Staten Island … She talked to people all year long that I said hello to on Christmas.

Leo: (*Looks at him*) I think you could have used another month in Europe.

George: You mean, I was supposed to come home and forget I had a wife for twelve years? It doesn't work that way, Leo. It was, perhaps, the dumbest trip I ever took in my whole life. London was bankrupt, Italy was on strike, France hated me, Spain was still mourning for Franco … Why do Americans go to grief-stricken Europe when they're trying to get over being stricken with grief?

Leo: Beats me. I always thought you could have just as rotten a time here in America.

George: What am I going to do about this apartment, Leo?

Leo: My advice? Move. Find a new place for yourself.

George: It was very spooky in London … I kept walking around the streets looking for Barbara—Harrods, King's Road, Portobello … Sales clerks would say, "See what you want, sir?" and I'd say, "No, she's not here." I know it's crazy, Leo, but I really thought to myself, It's a joke. She's not dead. She's in London waiting for me. She's just playing out this romantic fantasy: The whole world thinks she's gone, but we meet clandestinely in London, move into a flat, disappear from everyone and live out our lives in secret! … She would have thought of something like that, you know.

Leo: But she didn't. *You* did.

George: In Rome I got sore at her—I mean, *really* mad. How dare she do a thing like this to me? I would *never* do a thing like that to her. Never! Like a nut, walking up the Via Veneto one night, cursing my dead wife.

***Chapter Two* was based on playwright Simon's real-life bereavement after the death of his first wife and his whirlwind courtship and marriage to actress Marsha Mason *(shown in caricature at left with Simon)*. The couple's fictional counterparts were played on stage by Judd Hirsch and Anita Gillette *(right)*.**

"The prospect of designing our descendants, fabricating the next generation, making reproduction synonymous with manufacturing is an abhorrent picture coming into view."—**Protestant theologian Paul Ramsey**

STORY OF THE YEAR

Life from a Test Tube

1 In his 1932 sci-fi classic, *Brave New World*, Aldous Huxley darkly imagined a society where "babies are mass-produced from chemical solutions in laboratory bottles." In 1978, many saw Huxley's nightmare coming true. In July, Louise Brown, the first human being conceived outside the womb, was born in England. Also that year, journalist David Rorvik created a sensation with *In His Image: The Cloning of a Man*, a book (later revealed to be a hoax) about a 68-year-old bachelor millionaire who claimed to have reproduced himself asexually in the form of a genetically identical baby. Just months later, in an experiment that many considered the first cloning of mammals, geneticists Karl Illmensee, a Swiss, and Peter Hoppe, an American, bred live mice from embryonic nuclei—each nucleus containing, like that of all cells, the full complement of the creature's DNA—which they implanted into fertilized host eggs that had been divested of their own nuclei (and hence their own genetic characteristics).

To Lesley and John Brown, extrauterine conception was not a nightmare but a miracle. Unable to conceive, the couple had sought out gynecologist Patrick Steptoe and his collaborator, Cambridge University physiologist Robert Edwards, who for more than a decade had been experimenting with in vitro (Latin for "in glass") fertilization: attempting to induce pregnancy by removing an egg from a patient's ovary, fertilizing it with donor sperm (ideally, that of the woman's mate), and implanting it back into her uterus. Until the procedure succeeded with Lesley Brown, the embryos had always died before implantation or spontaneously aborted afterward. In vitro fertilization has since become relatively common (though it results in viable pregnancy only 16 percent of the time), but at the time it provoked outrage and disbelief—a consequence partly attributable to the fact that Steptoe and Edwards sold the story to a London tabloid instead of reporting it in a medical journal.

Many people found the concept of cloned mammals—especially humans—even more alarming. Rorvik's account may have been a fraud, but other cloning scenarios—like that found in Ira Levin's novel *The Boys from Brazil*, which featured a doomsday doctor manufacturing armies of genetically identical "Hitler babies"—fueled popular hysteria. Yet, while many of the larger ethical questions about genetic engineering remain unresolved, its more benign applications have included such indisputably life-enhancing breakthroughs as mass production of proteins like insulin, and anti-viral vaccines. **◂1976.5 ▸1987.7**

Evening News

Meet Louise, the world's first test-tube arrival

SUPERBABE

Wide-eyed Louise Brown pictured in hospital 18 hours after she was born. Today she's doing well. See Page Three

London tabloids were the first to break the "test-tube" baby story.

1978

RELIGION

The Jonestown Massacre

2 As the counterculture movements of the 1960s dissolved, millions in the Western nations began flocking to religious cults, seeking, perhaps, to restore a sense of prophetic meaning, intense belonging, and utopian hope to their lives. Some of the groups, evidence suggested, used brainwashing tactics to virtually enslave their members. In November 1978, California congressman Leo Ryan and a party of 18 flew to Guyana to investigate one such cult: the People's Temple, led by the Reverend Jim Jones (nominally of the mainstream Disciples of Christ), a once-respected San Francisco political activist who now claimed to be an incarnation of Jesus and Lenin. The mission ended in Ryan's death—and in the suicide or murder of some 900 others.

Bodies and paper cups litter the jungle commune where cultists drank poison.

Until 1977, Jones had run church-based social-service centers in California, helping the poor and attracting a congregation of thousands. Then, with a few hundred mostly black followers, the minister (a white whose father reportedly was a Ku Klux Klan member) relocated to the Guyana jungle, where he established an agricultural commune called Jonestown. Complaints reached Ryan that residents were subjected to beatings, forced labor, sexual abuse, and rehearsals for mass suicide (as a "loyalty test").

The congressman and a group of aides, reporters, and lawyers were greeted cordially. But the day after their arrival, Jones grew hostile. Commune members began to appeal to the visitors for help in leaving. As one couple argued over whether to go, a settler attacked Ryan with a knife. Attempting to flee by plane, Ryan and four others were shot to death. Shortly afterward Jones called for the suicide ritual. The faithful lined up to receive a cyanide-laced fruit-flavored drink. Some took it willingly, others at gunpoint. Parents fed the poison to their children. (A few settlers managed to escape.) Surveying the corpses of his followers, Jones uttered his final words over the camp's public-address system: "Mother, mother, mother." Then he took his own life with a gun. **▸1993.M**

THE MIDDLE EAST

The Camp David Accords

3 When negotiations between Israel and Egypt bogged down in 1978, U.S. president Jimmy Carter invited the leaders of both countries to Camp David, the presidential retreat in Maryland. For twelve days in September, Menachem Begin, Anwar al-Sadat, and assorted U.S., Israeli, and Egyptian high officials met in rustic cabins or walked together through the woods. The setting and dress code were casual, but the task at hand was epochally serious. Ending the 30-year state of war between the Middle East's two most powerful nations would be a first step toward defusing regional hostilities that had the potential to launch a nuclear holocaust.

The hostility between Sadat and Begin at Camp David grew so sharp at times that the talks seemed doomed to failure. But thanks to Carter's tireless personal diplomacy—after spending hours coaxing compromises from one leader, he would go to the other's cabin to repeat the process—two major agreements emerged. The first was the framework for a bilateral peace pact, promising the phased withdrawal

Carter looks on as Begin and Sadat shake hands at Camp David.

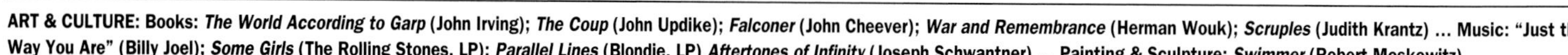

ART & CULTURE: Books: ***The World According to Garp*** (John Irving); ***The Coup*** (John Updike); ***Falconer*** (John Cheever); ***War and Remembrance*** (Herman Wouk); ***Scruples*** (Judith Krantz) ... Music: "Just the Way You Are" (Billy Joel); ***Some Girls*** (The Rolling Stones, LP); ***Parallel Lines*** (Blondie, LP) ***Aftertones of Infinity*** (Joseph Schwantner) ... Painting & Sculpture: ***Swimmer*** (Robert Moskowitz) ...

"When disco gets to Milwaukee, it will be emasculated. You'll have people wearing certain kinds of clothes, for example, but they won't know why they're wearing them."—**Vanderbilt University sociology professor Richard Peterson**

of Israeli troops from the Sinai and the restoration of Israel's right (denied since 1956) to use the Suez Canal. The second called, more vaguely, for a general Middle Eastern settlement based on Israel's gradual concession of self-government to Palestinians in the Israeli-occupied West Bank and Gaza Strip, and the partial withdrawal of troops from those territories.

Sadat and Begin shared the 1978 Nobel Peace Prize for their efforts; they concluded a formal treaty the following March. But the signing sparked riots in several capitals, and the Arab League—condemning Sadat's "separate peace" with Israel—expelled Egypt and declared an economic boycott. Israel sidestepped the treaty provisions concerning Palestinians. And Sadat's gamble soon cost him his life.
◂1977.1 ▸1981.2

Wadowice native John Paul II touches down for his 1979 landmark papal visit to Poland.

RELIGION

Year of Three Popes

4 When Pope Paul VI died in August 1978, Catholics were saddened but not surprised: The Pontiff was 80, after all, and over the past decade he'd seemed increasingly tired and withdrawn. But when his 65-year-old successor—John Paul I, the ebullient former patriarch of Venice—died of a heart attack just 34 days after his inauguration, the shock was far greater. John Paul I's replacement, John Paul II, was yet another surprise.

The new pope—born Karol Wojtyla in Wadowice, Poland—was the first non-Italian pontiff in 456 years. He was the second (after his immediate predecessor) ever to come from working-class roots. And, at 58, he was the youngest pope since 1846. Before joining the priesthood, he'd written and performed avant-garde verse plays; he'd worked in the anti-Nazi resistance during World War II. As a cleric from a Communist country, he was a living rebuke to Marxist atheism—and well experienced in politics. He spoke seven languages and played guitar.

John Paul II's energy, charisma, and informality made him wildly popular even outside the Church, as did his outspoken support of human rights movements around the world. Even more than Paul VI (known as the "pilgrim pope"), he traveled the globe to tend his flock and to reach out to other faiths. Theologically, however, he was more conservative than Paul VI. Whereas Paul had championed the reforms of Vatican II, John Paul II urged a return to sterner values. He ordered priests to steer clear of left-wing politics, rebuked the liberation theologists, and insisted on the supremacy of the pope over his bishops. Those who'd hoped the worldly new pontiff might lift the Church's controversial bans on divorce, artificial contraception, abortion, and women in the clergy were destined for disappointment.
◂1968.12 ▸1979.M

POPULAR CULTURE

Disco Rules

5 Disco fever swept the globe in 1978, thanks to a movie released just before New Year's: *Saturday Night Fever.* Directed by John Badham and starring newcomer John Travolta, the film told the story of Tony Manero, a working-class Brooklynite who comes alive on the dance floor. Travolta's athletic, suggestive moves drove young women wild and made young men envious—and suddenly the nightclub subculture of America's urban gays and blacks hit the mainstream. The soundtrack by the Bee Gees (an Australian band that had scored Beatle-esque hits a decade earlier, then resurfaced to ride the new trend) sold a record-breaking 30 million albums worldwide.

The disco style broke with the rebellious sixties aesthetic that still dominated much of youth culture. Men wore flashy suits and gold chains; women wore dresses and high heels. Couples danced together, to prescribed steps. Even the drugs were different: Instead of mind-warping psychedelics, disco fans chose feel-good quaaludes, amyl nitrate, and (for the prosperous) cocaine. And disco music rejected the artistic and political ambitions of sixties rock. A heavy, throbbing rhythm ruled (with beats-per-minute marked on record labels for deejays' convenience); lyrics centered on sex and its metaphors. While some artists—Chic, Donna Summer—brought impassioned R&B stylings to the genre, they were outnumbered by anonymous hacks. Inspired by German studio wizard Giorgio Moroder, many producers dispensed with expensive musicians in favor of computer-programmed synthesizers and drum machines.

Saturday Night Fever **star John Travolta strikes the quintessential disco pose.**

What made disco vital, however, was a roomful of flamboyant, ecstatically dancing revelers. The high temple of disco culture's glitzy rituals was Manhattan's Studio 54, where the libertine elite and their hangers-on met to do the hustle and the bump. Crowds thronged outside, hoping to win the favor of the all-powerful doorman and join such glitterati as Liza Minnelli, Bianca Jagger, and Andy Warhol under the strobe lights. **◂1967.5 ▸1984.10**

DEATHS

Edgar Bergen, U.S. ventriloquist.

Houari Boumedienne, Algerian president.

Charles Boyer, French-U.S. actor.

Jacques Brel, Belgian-French singer.

Pedro Joaquin Chamorro, Nicaraguan editor.

Lucius Clay, U.S. general.

Joseph A. Colombo, Sr., U.S. Mafia boss.

James Conant, U.S. educator and scientist.

Giorgio de Chirico, Italian painter.

Charles Eames, U.S. designer.

Kurt Gödel, Czech-U.S. mathematician.

Hubert Humphrey, U.S. vice president.

John Paul I, Italian pope.

Jomo Kenyatta, Kenyan president.

Kathleen Kenyon, U.K. archaeologist.

Aram Khachaturian, U.S.S.R. composer.

Frank Raymond Leavis, U.K. critic.

John D. MacArthur, U.S. financier.

Margaret Mead, U.S. anthropologist.

Golda Meir, Israeli prime minister.

Anastas Mikoyan, U.S.S.R. deputy premier.

Aldo Moro, Italian prime minister.

Paul VI, Italian pope.

Norman Rockwell, U.S. illustrator.

Ignazio Silone, Italian writer.

W. Eugene Smith, U.S. photojournalist.

Gene Tunney, U.S. boxer.

Film: ***The Deer Hunter*** **(Michael Cimino);** ***Coming Home*** **(Hal Ashby);** ***An Unmarried Woman*** **(Paul Mazursky);** ***Get Out Your Handkerchiefs*** **(Bertrand Blier);** ***Superman*** **(Richard Donner) ... Theater:** ***Deathtrap*** **(Ira Levin);** ***Plenty*** **(David Hare);** ***Betrayal*** **(Harold Pinter);** ***Buried Child*** **(Sam Shepard);** ***The Best Little Whorehouse in Texas*** **(Carol Hall);** ***Evita*** **(Lloyd Webber and Rice) ... TV:** ***Dallas; Taxi; Fantasy Island.***

"I beg you on my knees, free the Honorable Aldo Moro, simply without any conditions, not so much because of my humble and loving intercession, as by virtue of his dignity as a common brother of humanity."—**Pope Paul VI, in a letter to the kidnappers of Aldo Moro**

NEW IN 1978

Ultrasound (ultrasonic alternative to X-rays).

Legal gambling in Atlantic City, New Jersey.

Legal abortion in Italy.

Garfield the Cat.

Pinyin as official transliteration system for Chinese names.

IN THE UNITED STATES

▶TAINTED LOVE—The Love Canal neighborhood of Niagara Falls, New York, was declared a federal disaster area in August. During the forties and early fifties, the Hooker Chemical Company had dumped tons of toxic waste into an abandoned industrial canal, which it filled in and sold to the city of Niagara Falls (for $1) in 1953. The city built a school on the dump site; houses and families followed. Over the years, residents suffered skin rashes, headaches, liver ail-

ments, birth defects, miscarriages, rectal bleeding, and epilepsy, but the sundry afflictions were not linked to the suppurating canal until 1976, when heavy rains caused chemical pools to bubble up into basements and yards. The EPA estimated that there were more than a thousand potential Love Canals in the U.S. ◀1973.7 ▶1978.12

▶SAN FRANCISCANS SLAIN—George Moscone and Harvey Milk, San Francisco's mayor and its first openly homosexual official, respectively, were assassinated in their City Hall offices on November 27. The gunman, Dan White, was a conservative ideologue who wanted to withdraw his recent resignation from the Board of

Moro's funeral in a village north of Rome; he'd requested that it be closed to politicians.

ITALY

The Moro Kidnapping

6 The ordeal of Aldo Moro proved that in politics the center is not always the safest place. Leader of Italy's ruling Christian Democratic Party, five-time former prime minister, and favorite for the presidency, Moro was abducted in Rome in March 1978 by members of the ultraleft Red Brigades. After machine-gunning Moro's five bodyguards, the terrorists demanded the release of 13 of their imprisoned leaders. Beyond that immediate goal, they hoped their blow to the "heart of the state" (as they put it) would provoke enough repression to spark a revolution.

Founded by radical students in 1970, the Red Brigades probably had only a few hundred members, but their sympathizers numbered in the thousands. Since 1971, they'd kidnapped 30-odd "functionaries of the counterrevolution," assassinated more than 40, and kneecapped many others. Moro, their highest-ranking target ever, personified the order they despised. Studiously bland and known for obfuscatory phrases, he'd been trying to engineer the first coalition government to include the Communists (Italy's second-largest party). Moro called the rapprochement between left and center "parallel convergencies." The Brigades called it a Communist sellout.

For 54 days, the police combed Italy for the master compromiser and his captors. Meanwhile, Moro sent a dozen letters to his colleagues and family calling for the release of political prisoners and accusing Italian officials of indifference to his suffering. But the government stood pat, and appeals to the kidnappers by the Pope, Yasir Arafat, Muammar Qaddafi, and UN secretary general Kurt Waldheim went unheeded. Finally, Moro's bullet-riddled body was found in a car parked near both the Christian Democratic and the Communist headquarters. Twenty-nine Red Brigadiers were eventually sentenced to prison terms of up to 15 years for the murder (17 more went free). The revolution, however, failed to occur. **◀1975.10 ▶1985.9**

AFGHANISTAN

A Communist Coup

7 The scene in Kabul was surreal: Leaving work early on April 27, 1978 (the eve of Juma, the Muslim sabbath), thousands of Afghans filled the ancient capital's narrow streets, while around them tanks bombarded the presidential palace. Taxis jockeyed for position with armored vehicles; traffic police flagged personnel carriers out of congested intersections. People seemed less concerned with the left-wing coup in progress than with getting home. But then, few felt much loyalty to president Muhammad Daud Khan *(above)*. At day's end, rebel leaders announced on the radio that a revolutionary council had taken over the government. Communism had come to Afghanistan.

Daud—gunned down with his family when insurgents finally breached the palace—had seized power in 1973, deposing King Muhammad Zahir Shah, his first cousin. A former prime minister, Daud initially enjoyed the critical support of the Soviet-supplied Afghan army and of the rival Khalq and Parcham factions of the leftist People's Democratic Party of Afghanistan (PDPA). In 1977, however, Daud veered to the right—arresting PDPA members and filling his government with personal flunkies. Of greatest consequence, he loosened ties to Moscow, long the leading foreign influence in Afghanistan.

The Soviet Union prized its southeastern neighbor (strategically situated between Iran, Pakistan, and China), and Daud's actions cost him dearly. With Kremlin support, Parcham and Khalq leaders overcame their differences and in 1977 united the PDPA. Daud responded with a wave of repression, but key army officers had already bolted. The Soviet-approved coup came off without a hitch. Noor Muhammad Taraki, secretary general of the PDPA, became Afghanistan's first Marxist prime minister. But civil war loomed. **◀1919.4 ▶1979.5**

FILM

Germany's New Breed

8 The German film industry, once among the world's greatest, declined dramatically after great directors like Fritz Lang and G.W. Pabst fled the Nazis in the 1930s. A resurgence began in the late 1960s, brought about both by an increasing historical distance from the Nazi years and by strong government support of such innovative filmmakers as Alexander Kluge, Volker Schlöndorff, and Jean-Marie Straub. By 1978 *Time* magazine was able to proclaim the new German cinema "the liveliest in Europe."

Most prominent among the crop of rising directors was Rainer Werner Fassbinder. He had already churned out 33 films—most of them harrowingly bleak yet grimly funny explorations of emotional and social dislocation—when, at age 31, he made *The Marriage of Maria Braun* (1978), the first part of a trilogy on postwar Germany. (Its companion pieces, *Lola* and *Veronika Voss*, were released in 1982.) In the title role, Hanna Schygulla played a

SPORTS: Baseball: World Series, New York Yankees defeat Los Angeles Dodgers, 4–2 ... Football: Super Bowl, Dallas Cowboys defeat Denver Broncos, 27–10 ... Basketball: NBA, Washington Bullets defeat Seattle Supersonics, 4–3 ... Soccer: World Cup, Argentina defeats the Netherlands, 3–1 ... Boxing: Muhammad Ali regains heavyweight title from Leon Spinks ... Horse Racing: Affirmed wins Triple Crown.

"It was the tongue of martyrs and saints, of dreamers and Kabbalists—rich in humor and in memories that mankind may never forget. In a figurative way, Yiddish is the wise and humble language ... of a frightened and hopeful humanity."—**I.B. Singer**

woman who personifies West Germany itself. After surviving wartime bombs and peacetime romantic disasters, Maria Braun then dies when her stove explodes.

Two other German filmmakers, Werner Herzog and Wim Wenders, shared in the acclaim. Herzog was an eccentric adventurer: To achieve absolute verisimilitude in the story of a mad conquistador, he filmed *Aguirre: The Wrath of God* (1972) in the Amazon; to convey a sense of

Fassbinder *(left)* directs his favorite actress, Hanna Schygulla.

collective hysteria in *Heart of Glass* (1976), a film exploring the effects of a glassblower's death on a small town, he had his actors hypnotized. Wenders's epic road films blend the existential toughness of Hollywood film noir with philosophic German angst. Wenders cast Dennis Hopper and the great B-movie directors Sam Fuller and Nicholas Ray alongside Bruno Ganz in *The American Friend* (1977), and later paired Ganz and Peter Falk in the Rilke-influenced *Wings of Desire* (1988). **◂1959.7 ▸1991.12**

SOUTHEAST ASIA

Genocide in Cambodia

9 For three years there had been grisly rumors—but the full truth about Cambodia emerged only after Vietnam invaded in December 1978. Mass graves and eyewitnesses provided testimony: Since seizing power in 1975, the Khmer Rouge had murdered hundreds of thousands of Cambodians. A like number had died of starvation, overwork, or disease. The destruction had intensified in recent months, after Premier Pol Pot's ultranationalist party faction outmaneuvered its rivals.

The Khmer Rouge's leaders were French-educated Communists who'd started their guerrilla careers in the fifties, trying to topple Prince Norodom Sihanouk. But the devastating U.S. bombing campaign of the early seventies drove them into an alliance with the prince (who'd been deposed by rightists); the bombing brought them a mass following and North Vietnamese aid as well. Hiding in jungle shelters under a rain of explosives, the revolutionaries developed an extraordinarily brutal —and paranoid—ideology.

For months after taking over Cambodia, the country's new rulers concealed their identity, while Sihanouk served as titular head of state. But their bizarre attempt at national self-sufficiency—inspired by Mao Zedong's Great Leap Forward—began at once. The Khmer Rouge emptied the cities, sending urbanites to join a giant army of serfs. Obsessed with racial and political purity, they massacred ethnic minorities, intellectuals, the sick, those who complained, even those who had unauthorized sex. Foreigners—except Chinese and North Korean advisers—were virtually banned.

It was the Khmer Rouge's alignment with China (Vietnam's traditional enemy, despite its wartime aid to Vietnamese Communists) that spurred Hanoi to attack. In January 1979, as Vietnamese troops entered Phnom Penh, Pol Pot and his forces fled toward the Thai border, and Sihanouk escaped to Beijing. The invaders installed a new premier, Heng Semrin, who proclaimed the People's Republic of Kampuchea. Civil war—fueled by superpower politics—followed. **◂1977.8 ▸1989.M**

Skeletons discovered in the killing fields near the village of Choevng Ek, Cambodia.

LITERATURE

Singer's Universal Yiddish

10 The Nobel Prize for literature seldom goes to a writer in a "minor" language, let alone one that is spoken by fewer people every day, thanks to a bitter legacy of genocide and emigration. But as Isaac Bashevis Singer accepted the 1978 Nobel, he affirmed the vitality of his chosen idiom—a hybrid of German and Hebrew, with borrowings from lands through which the Jews had wandered. "Yiddish," he said, "contains treasures that have not been revealed to the eyes of the world."

Born in 1904, Singer emigrated from Warsaw to New York in 1935, shortly after publishing *Satan in Goray* (a tale of seventeenth-century messianism and madness) in Poland. In New York, he began writing for the Yiddish-language *Jewish Daily Forward,* where his short stories and serialized novels gained a small following. In 1953, Saul Bellow's translation of "Gimpel the Fool" in *Partisan Review* introduced Singer to a wider audience.

Full of dybbukim, demons, and holy fools, Singer's works have the feel of folktales. They vividly recreate worlds snuffed out by the Holocaust—the shtetl and Warsaw's Jewish quarter. But they're bracingly modern, too: sophisticated moral fables, in which the secular meets the sacred, and lust meets devotion. With one foot in the Old World and one in the New, Singer could write of assimilationists and traditionalists with the same psychological insight and biting wit. **◂1964.8**

IN THE UNITED STATES

Supervisors (Milk was a fellow member). White, whose trial included the widely derided "Twinkie defense" (his attorneys claimed too much junk food had made him deranged) was convicted of voluntary manslaughter, receiving a five-to-seven year sentence. He committed suicide in October 1985, while out on parole.

▸CONSPIRACY THEORIES—Completing its review of the murders of JFK and Martin Luther King, Jr., the House Select Committee on Assassinations in 1978 startlingly concluded that conspiracies were likely—a view by then shared by much of its constituency but contrary to the Warren Commission report of 1964. The committee declined, however, to name Oswald's possible cohorts, or those of James Earl Ray *(above)*, who was convicted of slaying King in 1968 but later recanted his confession. ◂1964.M ▸1991.6

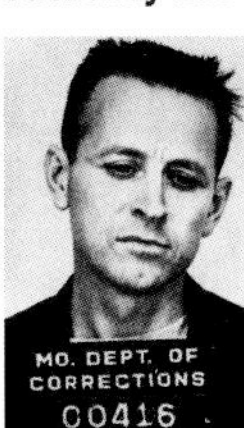

▸PROP 13—Some 65 percent of California voters on June 6 ignored warnings that a loss of $7 billion in revenues would impair the state's ability to deliver services and approved "Proposition 13," an amendment to the state constitution rolling back property taxes by 57 percent. The vote foreshadowed the national tax revolt of the 1980s. ▸1980.4

▸REVERSE DISCRIMINATION?—On June 28, the Supreme Court upheld a lower court ruling that the University of California, Davis, medical school must admit twice-rejected applicant Allen Bakke, who claimed that the school's affirmative action policy had resulted in his being passed over in favor of less-qualified minority students. While a 5–4 majority of the Court decided that UC-Davis's quota system (16 of the 100 spots were reserved for minorities) violated the Civil Rights Act, a different majority ruled that some consideration of race or ethnicity in the admissions process was allowable. ◂1964.3

POLITICS & BUSINESS: GNP: $2,254.5 billion ... Carter signs bill raising age of mandatory retirement from 65 to 70 ... 110-day coal miner's strike ends (longest in industry history) ... ERA ratification deadline extended to June 30, 1982 ... U.S. and People's Republic of China establish formal diplomatic relations ... Cleveland defaults on $15.5 million in municipal loans (declares bankruptcy the following year).

"This business could be as big as McDonald's."—**Don Wildman, owner of Chicago Health Club, in 1978**

AROUND THE WORLD

▶ETHIOPIA LOOKS TO MOSCOW—In 1978 Ethiopia's four-year-old Provisional Military Administrative Council (PMAC), the socialist junta that had deposed Emperor Haile Selassie, signed a trade agreement with the Soviet Union. PMAC, also called the Derg, began receiving military supplies from foreign Communists (including Cuban troops and Soviet advisers), which it used to contain secessionist rebels in Eritrea and the Somali-speaking region of Ogaden. Led by Lieutenant Colonel Mengistu Haile Mariam, the Derg declared Ethiopia a Communist people's republic in 1984. ◀1974.7 ▶1993.M

▶DEATH KNELL FOR BREL—Reclusive Belgian troubadour Jacques Brel, 49, succumbed to cancer on October 9. Brel had lived in France since the early 1950s, when he began his career as a café singer and guitarist. Sensual, sometimes acerbic, often rueful, Brel was a leading performer of the 1960s, debuting at Carnegie Hall in 1965. In 1968 his music was featured in the popular New York show *Jacques Brel Is Alive and Well and Living In Paris.* Brel stopped recording for a decade, but his 1977 comeback album, *Brel,* sold more than two million copies.

▶GREAT WALLENDA DIES—A tragic and spectacular family of tightrope walkers lost its 73-year-old patriarch on March 22, when Karl Wallenda plunged 100 feet to his death after a 30-mph gust of wind blew him off the cable he was walking between two beachfront hotels in San Juan, Puerto Rico. The Great Wallendas, as the family—children, grandchildren, cousins, nephews, and nieces—was called, always worked without a net. That fateful decision had resulted, before Karl fell, in the deaths of four family members and the paralysis of another. "The dead are gone," he always said, "and the show must go on."

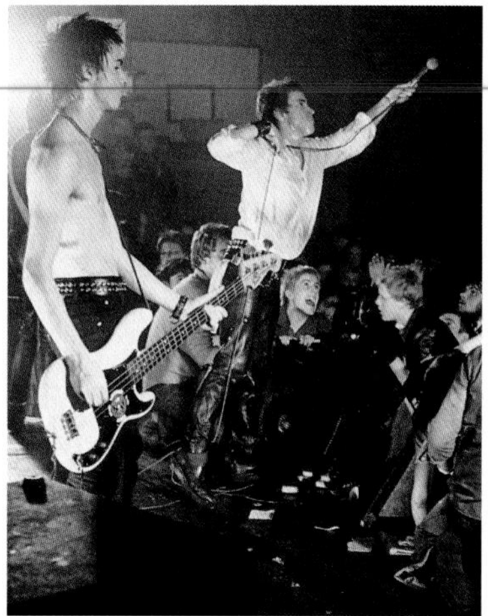

Music to slam-dance by: punkers Vicious *(on bass)* and Rotten *(with microphone).*

MUSIC

The Punk Revolt

11 By the late seventies, mainstream rock 'n' roll had lost touch with its rebel roots. The Rolling Stones were jet-setters; the peace-and-love Woodstock ethos had been co-opted. Big-time bands played beer-party music or pseudo-classical "art rock," while the blistering solos of heavy metal had become a macho cliché. On rock's fringes, however, an angry new genre had emerged. Punk rock was a revolt against the pop culture of an anticlimactic decade; it spawned a grassroots proliferation of nonconformist bands that continued into the 1990s. But as is suggested by the gruesome 1978 deaths of Sid Vicious and his girlfriend, punk was also a cry of despair.

Vicious (John Simon Ritchie) played bass for the emblematic punk band, the Sex Pistols. Assembled in London by radical boutique owner Malcolm McLaren, the group featured the sneering vocals of Johnny Rotten (John Lydon), lyrics that endorsed anarchy and insulted the sovereign (despite a BBC ban, their rendition of "God Save the Queen" made number two in Britain), and a sound that was pure, roaring aggression. Other punk bands had better-developed politics (the Clash) or more talent (the Buzzcocks); some were closer to punk's do-it-yourself ideal (New York's garage-bred Ramones). But none had the Pistols' apocalyptic immediacy. When Rotten caterwauled "no future," he convinced listeners that all of Western civilization, and not just England—with its high levels of unemployment and enervation—was doomed.

But the Pistols' spitting, swearing rage was not directed just at the Establishment. The punk movement had a self-lacerating streak, symbolized by a look that included mutilated hairdos and safety pins through the cheek, and embodied by Vicious. He and his American girlfriend, Nancy Spungen, were desperate junkies whose love-play often left them bruised and bleeding. In October, Spungen was found stabbed to death in Manhattan's Chelsea Hotel. Charged with her murder, Vicious was never tried: Free on bail in February 1979, he died of a heroin overdose. **◀1972.13 ▶1994.M**

DISASTERS

The *Cadiz* Spill

12 In March 1978, the first of a series of three major oil spills occurring in both hemispheres in a 16-month period was a grim reminder that dependence on fossil fuels carried costs far beyond the soaring price per barrel. The spill happened when the supertanker *Amoco Cadiz* ran aground off France's Brittany coast, releasing 1.3 million barrels of crude. (The spill was made even more severe by a time-consuming argument between the tanker's captain and a tug boat operator over the price of towing the grounded vessel into navigable waters.) Trainloads of French youths pitched in over the Easter holiday to help clean up la Marée Noire (the Black Tide)—the region's fourth oil spill in eleven years, and the world's worst to date.

The slick fouled France's largest bird sanctuary and devastated the local fishing, tourism, and seaweed growing industries. In the aftermath, the French government banned tanker travel within seven nautical miles of France's coast. **▶1989.13**

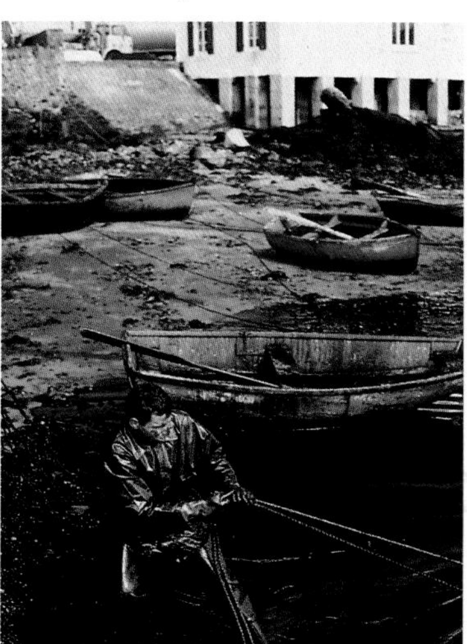

Workers attempt to clean up the mess of the *Amoco Cadiz* spill, the worst to date.

POPULAR CULTURE

Fitness Becomes Fashionable

13 Grown soft from "too many martinis and too little exercise," New York editor James Fixx *(below)* took up running in early middle age and fell in love with the sport. Fixx's *The Complete Book of Running,* a bestseller in 1978, dovetailed neatly with a national obsession. By the late 1970s, millions of Americans were lifting weights, taking up aerobics, and—inspired by such popular heroes as multiple marathon champion Bill Rodgers—jogging.

Over the next decade, the exercise phenomenon spread throughout the Western world. A variety of factors were at work. There was the famous narcissism of the seventies' "Me Generation": Looking fit was important to aging baby boomers in the spruced-up posthippie era. But a touch of sixties-style spiritualism was also present—especially in running, an essentially solitary pursuit reputed to induce serenity. Rodgers (a Boston schoolteacher who drove an old Volkswagen, touted the "runner's high," and avoided beverages stronger than ginger ale) exemplified fitness's neopuritanical yet vaguely countercultural aspect. He also represented the craze's other great piston: consumerism. Rodgers marketed his own line of workout suits. Nike, an athletic-shoe company started by two Oregon runners in the 1960s, rode the boom to multi-billion-dollar sales. High-priced fitness clubs mushroomed.

Fixx (named by *People* magazine as one of the most "intriguing" personalities of 1978) also profited from book sales and endorsements. In a sadly ironic twist, however, he suffered a fatal heart attack while on a run in 1984. **◀1922.M ▶1981.V**

NOBEL PRIZES: Peace: Menachem Begin and Anwar al-Sadat (Israeli, Egyptian; Camp David Accords)... Literature: I.B. Singer (U.S.; novelist) ... Chemistry: Peter Mitchell (U.K.; energy transfer) ... Medicine: D. Nathans, H. Smith, and W. Arber (U.S., U.S., Swiss; restriction enzymes) ... Physics: A. Penzias, R. Wilson (U.S.; microwaves), and P. Kapitza (U.S.S.R.; low-temp. physics) ... Economics: Herbert Simon (U.S.).

A VOICE FROM 1978

Christina and the Night Raids

From *Mommie Dearest,* by Christina Crawford, 1978

Never one of Hollywood's truly adored figures, screen legend Joan Crawford at the very least commanded wide respect for the toughness that allowed her to thrive for decades in a notoriously fickle business. In 1978, a year after the perennial star died at age 73, her 39-year-old adopted daughter Christina published a memoir that presented the dark side of Queen Crawford's vaunted intractability—cruel tyranny. Mommie Dearest *was the American publishing event of the year, a "warts-and-all" celebrity biography (though Christina insisted the book was her story, not her mother's) done by an insider, a family member no less. When Christina detailed her mother's physical and emotional abusiveness—which included severe beatings, public humiliations, and, as described in the passage below, midnight tirades about the unacceptability of wire hangers—she gave stargazing readers the two elements they craved most: a celebrity and a comfortable feeling of superiority over the celebrity. The book, an instant bestseller, was made into a campy 1981 movie starring Faye Dunaway as Crawford.*

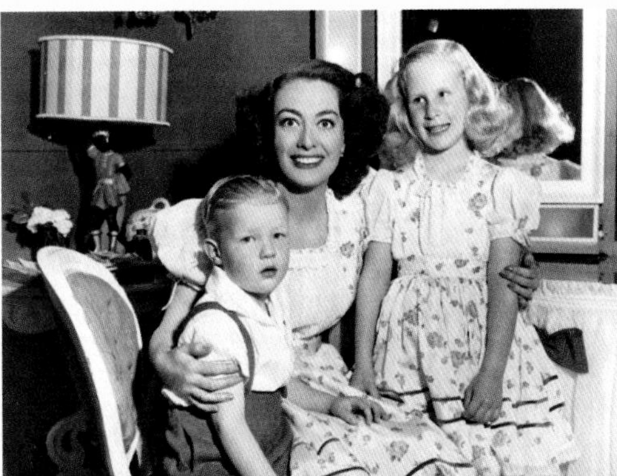

I was awakened out of a sound sleep one night by a crashing sound. I opened my eyes, sitting bolt upright in bed. I saw that my closet door was open, the light was on, and various pieces of clothing were flying out into the room. Inside the closet my mother was in a rage. She was swearing a blue streak and muttering to herself. I dared not move out of my bed for fear of her wrath being taken out on me directly. After the closet was totally demolished and everything in it spewed out onto my bed and the floor, Mommie emerged breathless and triumphant. She had a wild look in her eyes, and as she descended upon me I was terrified.

She grabbed me by the hair and dragged me into the closet. There before me I saw total devastation. The closet was in complete shambles. It looked as if she'd taken her arms and pushed everything off the shelves. Then she'd ripped the clothes off their hangers and thrown both clothes and hangers out into the room, where they lay sprawled over half the floor. Last to go were the shoes, which she'd thrown hard enough to hit the far wall of the bedroom. They clattered against the venetian blinds as they fell.

Shaking me by the hair of my head she screamed in my ear, "No wire hangers! No wire hangers!" With one hand she pulled me by the hair and with the other she pounded my ears until they rang and I could hardly hear her screaming. When she finished hitting me she released my hair and dumped me on the floor. Then she ripped my bed apart down to the mattress cover, throwing the sheets and blankets across the room. When she had totally destroyed my entire part of the bedroom she stood in the doorway with her hands on her hips. "Clean up your mess," she growled, turning on her heel. The only other sound I heard was the double doors to her room slamming shut.

Had I bothered to look at the clock I would have seen it was well past midnight. I didn't make the effort because it was a useless waste of my strength. I did look to see if Chris was still alive in the next bed. Once he was sure that she was gone and not coming back, he turned his body slowly to face me. It was probably the first time he'd dared to stir since the beginning of the night raid. He couldn't get up because he was tied down to the bed. Mother had a barbaric device she called a "sleep safe" with which she made sure Chris could not get out of bed. It was like a harness made of heavy canvas straps, and it fastened at the back. It was originally designed to keep babies from falling out of bed, but she had the thing modified to accommodate a growing boy. The way it worked was that the person lay face down upon the sheet and the straps that came from underneath the mattress went around his waist and across his shoulders. All four pieces were fastened together with a huge steel safety pin like the kind they use for horse blankets. From the time I can remember, we were forbidden to get out of bed at night to go to the bathroom or to get a drink of water without specific permission. Sometimes we would yell our lungs out and no one would come. There were times when my brother simply had to go to the bathroom, and I would undo the wretched sleep safe and stand guard while he raced to the bathroom and then jumped back into bed. We had it timed just like an Indianapolis pit stop because both our lives depended on expert teamwork. I would have gotten in more trouble than Chris if we'd ever been caught, and we both knew it. He would get beaten for getting out of bed but I would have been nearly killed for letting him out of the sleep safe.

Crawford took every opportunity to pose happily with her children (she adopted four in all, including Christina and Christopher *[top]*). Here, in a 1946 photograph, a seven-year-old Christina and her mother wear matching bonnets designed by the star.

"This is not a struggle between the United States and Iran. It is a struggle between Iran and blasphemy."—**Ayatollah Ruhollah Khomeini, praising the students who stormed the U.S. embassy in Tehran**

STORY OF THE YEAR

Iran's Islamic Revolution

1 "I didn't realize what was happening," lamented Muhammad Reza Shah Pahlevi after his overthrow in 1979. "When I woke up, I had lost my people." For two decades the Shah had tried to push Iran out of the feudal era. He'd redistributed land, reduced illiteracy, eased traditional curbs on women. He'd used oil revenues to diversify industry and erect apartment towers. But he'd denied Iranians political freedom, terrorizing them with a vicious CIA-trained secret police. He'd diverted vast sums to enrich himself, his army, and his friends. His development efforts had aided the richer peasants more than the poorest, built roads but not sewers. And his drive for cultural Westernization infuriated the powerful Shiite Muslim clergy, who'd lost substantial property in the land reforms.

Ayatollah Khomeini arriving in Tehran in February 1979.

In 1978, masses of Muslim fundamentalists, leftists, and human-rights advocates began demonstrating for the Shah's ouster. The protests were largely coordinated from France by Iran's foremost mullah (religious leader), Ayatollah Ruhollah Musawi Khomeini, in exile since 1964. Despite repression that killed thousands, the uprising continued into the new year, forcing the Shah to flee in January 1979. Two weeks later, the messianic ayatollah returned and declared a provisional government. Finally, in April—after a rigged referendum that was boycotted by secularists—he pronounced Iran an Islamic republic.

The new regime executed hundreds of the Shah's officials, and battled leftists and resistant minorities. Thousands more were killed or severely punished for violating Khomeini's interpretation of Islamic law. Secular music was banned; women were forced to wear head covering; blasphemy became a capital offense. But the revolution's hottest rage was reserved for the United States, the Shah's principal supporter. In late October, when the monarch was allowed into America for treatment of cancer and gallstones, millions rallied to demand his extradition.

On November 4, students stormed the U.S. embassy in Tehran, capturing its 66 occupants. Non-U.S. citizens, blacks, and most women were soon released, but 52 Americans were held for 444 days (despite the Shah's death in mid-1980). The hostage crisis led to the eviction of moderates from top posts in Khomeini's government, to U.S. President Jimmy Carter's electoral defeat, and—with Carter's replacement by the hawkish Ronald Reagan—to a new era in superpower politics. **◂1971.M ▸1980.2**

SOUTHERN AFRICA

Zimbabwe's Slow Birth

2 Rhodesia's seven-year civil war ended, after 20,000 deaths, in December 1979, when guerrilla leaders agreed to a new constitution mandating genuine black majority rule. The country had been creeping in that direction since the previous year, when Prime Minister Ian Smith—formerly an adamant white supremacist—promised a gradual transfer of power to blacks (some 6.8 million, compared with 250,000 whites). Smith's grudging turnabout reflected the toll of both the war and international sanctions. In 1978, he formed an interim government with three moderate black leaders. In multiracial elections in January 1979, one of the trio, Methodist bishop Abel Muzorewa, became the first prime minister of a nominally black-ruled nation now called Zimbabwe Rhodesia. But the arrangement was seriously flawed: For a ten-year period, whites would remain in charge of the judiciary, civil service, army, and police, and they were guaranteed 28 out of 100 parliamentary seats.

The guerrillas' Patriotic Front—comprising leftist Robert Mugabe's Zimbabwe African National Union (ZANU) and centrist Joshua Nkomo's Zimbabwe African People's Union (ZAPU)—denounced the government and escalated its attacks. Under pressure from the United States and Britain, Muzorewa opened talks with Mugabe and Nkomo in London. The December peace pact placed the country under temporary British administration. In 1980, new elections made Mugabe prime minister, and independent Zimbabwe was finally born.

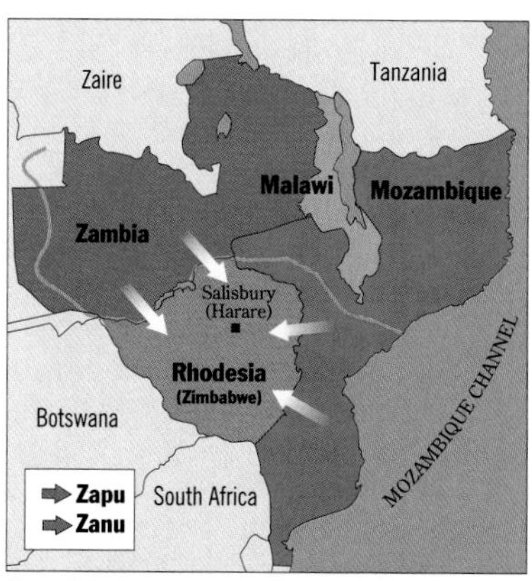

Guerrilla forces—ZAPU and ZANU—raided Rhodesia from bases in Zambia, to the West, and Mozambique, to the East.

Mugabe's cautious socialist reforms proved highly popular among blacks, and his overtures to whites ended their panicky exodus. But his relations with Nkomo—whom he'd made minister for home affairs—were more problematic. Political differences (Nkomo opposed Mugabe's plans for an eventual one-party state) and ethnic rivalries (Mugabe led the Shona majority, Nkomo the Ndebele minority) led to Nkomo's dismissal in 1982, and to violence between followers of both men in later years. **◂1964.10 ▸1980.M**

GREAT BRITAIN

Iron Lady Ascendant

3 In May 1979, British voters endorsed a new direction for their country. Labour was out and the Conservatives in—with 44 percent of the vote and a 43-seat majority in Parliament. Replacing James Callaghan as prime minister was Margaret Thatcher, the first European woman ever to hold her country's highest elected office. She would remain in power for eleven years (the longest tenure of any twentieth-century British prime minister), directing what came to be called the "Thatcher Revolution": an overturning of Britain's welfare state, its political establishment, and its traditional class roles.

Thatcher—soon dubbed the "Iron Lady" for her indomitable will and her seeming indifference toward those her policies injured—pledged to meet three goals: to wean Britain from socialism, to restore the country's economic vitality, and to rein in the labor union movement. For nearly 40 years the British government had worked with labor to maintain close to full employment, increasingly at the price of falling productivity and rising inflation. During the "Winter of Discontent" that led up to the 1979 elections, strikes paralyzed the country. Garbage went uncollected, fuel undelivered; schools closed. The national consensus was that the unions had become too powerful. Thatcher—the daughter of a shopkeeper who, unlike her ruling-class male colleagues, was unfettered by noblesse

ART & CULTURE: Books: *Burger's Daughter* (Nadine Gordimer); *The Living End* (Stanley Elkin); *The Ghost Writer* (Philip Roth); *A Part of Speech* (Joseph Brodsky); *The White House Years* (Henry Kissinger) ... Music: "Ring My Bell" (Frederick Knight); "Bad Girls" (Esposito, Hokenson, Sudano, and Summer); *We Are Family* (Sister Sledge, LP); *The Wall* (Pink Floyd, LP); *Isaiah* Symphony (Marvin Feinsmith) ...

"The Russians can't stay in Afghanistan. They are so alien, even the animals hate them."—**Afghan rebel Gul Amir**

oblige—cracked down firmly.

Adhering to theories of supply-side economics, she tightened the money supply, cut or "privatized" public works, and slashed income taxes. She controlled inflation, let unemployment climb (by the mid-1980s it had tripled, running to nearly 14 percent), and encouraged free enterprise, stressing the importance of hard work. Many voters, frustrated by Britain's hidebound class system, found Thatcher's vision of upward mobility—embodied by a new entrepreneurial elite—appealing in a way that the combative prime minister herself was not. For other Britons, however, downward mobility was the reality of her tenure. **◂1963.3 ▸1980.4**

DIPLOMACY

SALT II Miscarries

4 The Strategic Arms Limitation Talks, begun under President Nixon and continued under President Ford, were completed by President Carter and Soviet premier Brezhnev in June 1979 at the Vienna summit. The SALT II accord, slated to remain in force through 1985, limited each of the superpowers to 2,400 strategic nuclear weapons systems (long-range missiles and bombers)—allowing America to expand its arsenal somewhat, while forcing the Soviets to cut back slightly. Even so, hardliners in the U.S. Senate denounced the treaty, and in January 1980, after the Soviets invaded Afghanistan, Carter withdrew it from consideration. Though SALT II was never ratified, both sides pledged to follow its guidelines—which made no mention of tactical (short-range) weapons, and did not designate how many strategic *warheads* each side could deploy.

By the late 1970s, Soviet missiles outnumbered American. Yet most Soviet missiles carried a single warhead, while U.S. missiles contained several, each aimed at a different target. The Americans, thanks to these so-called multiple independently targeted reentry vehicles (MIRVs), had greater firepower. To critics of the arms race, the debate over who had the advantage was absurd: Each side possessed enough nuclear weapons to obliterate the other many times over. But Pentagon officials argued that the Soviet missile surplus made the United States vulnerable to a first strike; "mutual assured destruction" (MAD), the U.S. policy of deterrence, was in jeopardy. The Afghanistan incursion exacerbated American fears.

Flanked by aides, Carter and Brezhnev sign SALT II at Vienna's Hofburg Palace.

Riding into the presidency with a promise to slam shut the "window of vulnerability," Ronald Reagan, who took office in 1981, initiated history's costliest peacetime arms buildup. The Kremlin responded in kind. In this vertiginous atmosphere, a new round of disarmament negotiations—the Strategic Arms Reduction Talks (START)—opened in Geneva in 1982. By the time presidents Bush and Gorbachev signed the START pact nine years later, a bankrupt Soviet Union was dissolving and the United States was mired in an economic recession. **◂1977.3 ▸1983.V**

AFGHANISTAN

The Soviets Invade

5 The first troops were airlifted into Afghanistan on December 26, 1979, and their numbers mounted steadily. Moscow's intervention in its southern neighbor's civil war—the first Soviet infantry deployment outside the Eastern bloc since World War II—eventually deposited 100,000 men in the remote, mountainous country. Ragtag bands of guerrillas, the Mujahidin, put up mean and inspired resistance. Even before the last troop carrier had landed, pundits were calling Afghanistan the Soviet Vietnam. "They have taken the ultimate step," said one Western diplomat. "They've finally grasped the tar baby."

After seizing power in a palace coup in 1978, Afghanistan's first Marxist president, Noor Muhammad Taraki, attempted to build a centralized Communist state in a land where local autonomy had prevailed for centuries. Taraki succeeded only in provoking a holy war by fundamentalist Muslims. Before the year was out, he was ousted and killed by his deputy, Hafizullah Amin. Amin was even less successful in consolidating his power: Guerrillas soon commanded three quarters of Afghanistan's 28 provinces. The rebel advances unnerved the Soviet Union: Afghanistan was supposed to be a buffer from the hostile subcontinent. Worse for Amin, the Kremlin was almost as offended by his maverick Communism as by the insurrection.

Before going into the countryside after the elusive Mujahidin, Soviet forces stopped in Kabul to oust Amin and install pliant Babrak Karmal as president. The coup proved the only easy part of the Afghanistan adventure. The United States spearheaded international opposition, and while President Carter's economic sanctions against the Soviets met with mixed success (an American wheat embargo collapsed after other countries, led by Argentina, picked up the slack), 59 nations joined the U.S. boycott of the Moscow Olympics in summer 1980. Still, the Olympics proceeded, as did the war, which dragged on for nine years and cost the Soviets 15,000 dead and 30,000 wounded. **◂1978.7 ▸1988.M**

Poorly supplied but ardent, Afghan rebels battled the central state and Soviet invaders.

DEATHS

Elizabeth Bishop, U.S. poet.

Al Capp, U.S. cartoonist.

Ernst Chain, German-U.K. biochemist.

Charles Coughlin, Canadian-U.S. Catholic priest.

John G. Diefenbaker, Canadian prime minister.

James T. Farrell, U.S. novelist.

Arthur Fiedler, U.S. conductor.

Peggy Guggenheim, U.S. art collector.

Roy Harris, U.S. composer.

Conrad N. Hilton, U.S. hotelier.

Emmett Kelly, U.S. clown.

Herbert Marcuse, German-U.S. philosopher.

Herbert "Zeppo" Marx, U.S. comedian and theatrical agent.

Léonide Massine, U.S.S.R-U.S. choreographer.

Charles Mingus, U.S. musician.

Jean Monnet, French economist and statesman.

Louis Mountbatten, U.K. admiral.

Thurman Munson, U.S. baseball player.

Pier Luigi Nervi, Italian engineer.

Samuel Irving Newhouse, U.S. publisher.

Mary Pickford, Canadian-U.S. actress.

A. Philip Randolph, U.S. labor leader.

Jean Renoir, French filmmaker.

John Simon Ritchie (Sid Vicious), U.K. singer.

Nelson Rockefeller, U.S. vice president.

Richard Rodgers, U.S. composer.

Jean Seberg, U.S.-French actress.

John Wayne, U.S. actor.

Painting & Sculpture: ***Ocean Park 115*** **(Richard Diebenkorn);** ***Pontiac*** **(Susan Rothenberg);** ***Position*** **(Jörg Immendorff) ... Film:** ***Kramer vs. Kramer*** **(Robert Benton);** ***All That Jazz*** **(Bob Fosse);** ***Norma Rae*** **(Martin Ritt);** ***Alien*** **(Ridley Scott) ... Theater:** ***On Golden Pond*** **(Ernest Thompson);** ***Bent*** **(Martin Sherman);** ***Wings*** **(Arthur Kopit);** ***Cloud Nine*** **(Caryl Churchill) ... TV:** ***Knots Landing*****;** ***Hart to Hart.***

"The Nicaraguan people did not throw me out. I was thrown out by an international conspiracy that today has a majority of communists and that today desires Nicaragua to be a communist country."—**Anastasio Somoza Debayle**

NEW IN 1979

Moral Majority (formed by Jerry Falwell in Lynchburg, Virginia).

Susan B. Anthony dollar coin.

Sony Walkman.

Trivial Pursuit game.

IN THE UNITED STATES

▶SKYLAB FALLS—The space station Skylab reentered Earth's atmosphere on July 11, burning and dropping a trail of debris over the Indian Ocean and Western Australia. To the world's relief, no one was injured by the runaway 77-ton laboratory. Launched into orbit around Earth in 1973, Skylab completed three scientific missions before being taken out of service in 1974 so that NASA could put the station into a new orbit. NASA miscalculated atmospheric drag, however, and Skylab turned rogue in 1978, causing international consternation before its fiery homecoming. ◂1975.6 ▸1981.12

▶DIPLOMATIC TIES WITH CHINA—Seven years after Nixon and Mao issued the Shanghai Communiqué, two

new leaders, President Jimmy Carter and Marshal Deng Xiaoping *(above)*, completed the normalization of Sino-American relations. The 1979 Carter-Deng agreement was formalized during the latter's visit to the U.S. Bound by its new recognition of the People's Republic as the one legal government of China, the U.S. broke diplomatic ties with Taiwan. But economic links between the two longtime allies remained strong. ◂1972.2 ▸1980.10

▶OIL PRICE HIKE—Ending an 18-month price freeze, OPEC raised the price of oil by 50

GREAT BRITAIN

IRA Murders Mountbatten

6 One of Great Britain's last great war heroes, Earl Mountbatten of Burma, died violently in August 1979, but not on the field of battle. The 79-year-old nobleman was slain while vacationing at his country home on the west coast of Ireland. Irish Republican Army terrorists blew up his boat, instantly killing Mountbatten, his 14-year-old grandson, and his grandson's friend as they fished on Donegal Bay. "The boat was there one minute," said a horrified witness, "and the next minute it was like a lot of matchsticks floating on the water."

Mountbatten as viceroy of India in 1947.

Great-grandson of Queen Victoria and cousin of Queen Elizabeth, Mountbatten was the most famous victim in the IRA's ten-year guerrilla operation to drive Britain out of Northern Ireland. He'd joined the Royal Navy at age twelve and served in both World Wars; in the second, he'd commanded a destroyer fleet before leading the recapture of Burma. After the war, as the last British viceroy of India, he guided its transition from colony to independent nation. Mourners by the thousand turned out for Mountbatten's Westminster Abbey funeral, the stateliest afforded a fallen British commander since the Duke of Wellington's in 1852.

The Republic of Ireland expressed sorrow at Mountbatten's death, but its promise to crack down on IRA terrorism was received skeptically by the British government, which complained that Northern Irish terrorists all too often found refuge in the South. The Republic's answer: Most Irish people favored reunification. Britain's retort (equally stubborn and accurate): Most of Northern Ireland's citizens preferred the status quo. **◂1973.6 ▸1981.9**

DISASTERS

Narrow Nuclear Escape

7 In March 1979, a parade of human and mechanical errors brought the Three Mile Island nuclear power station to the brink of catastrophe. The incident at the Pennsylvania plant (10 miles from the state capital, Harrisburg) began when an automatic valve closed wrongly, affecting the circulation of cooling water in the core of the plant's Unit 2 reactor. The core itself, where uranium is fissioned to produce energy, then stopped working, as it had been designed to do in case of trouble. The situation should have stabilized. Instead, a series of mistakes caused coolant to drain away from the core. By the time technicians realized what was happening, the intensely radioactive fuel rods had been partially exposed. Meltdown—and with it, the transformation of the surrounding landscape into a poisonous wasteland—loomed. Worse, a cloud of hydrogen gas had formed inside the reactor, raising the possibility of a massive explosion. Thousands of residents fled the area.

The crisis lasted twelve days, ample time for millions around the world to conclude that nuclear power was irredeemably dangerous. Opponents spoke fearfully of the "China Syndrome," a scenario (dramatized in a movie of that name released just two weeks before the accident) in which the overheated core burns through the earth's crust—theoretically, to China. Eventually, however, the hydrogen gas was contained, and coolant circulation restored. Inspection of the core, where the temperature reached almost 5,000° F, later revealed that more than half the reactor's fuel had melted. In another half hour, a complete meltdown might have become a reality.

In the aftermath, the government temporarily closed several similar nuclear reactors and imposed a moratorium (also temporary) on new plants. Along with mushrooming public resistance, the federal initiatives hobbled the nuclear power industry for years. Meanwhile, it took more than a decade to decontaminate Three Mile Island's ruined reactor. **◂1952.M ▸1986.1**

NICARAGUA

Sandinistas Seize Power

8 In a region beset by cruel, corrupt regimes, Nicaragua's long-lived dynasty, which was overthrown in 1979, was even worse than most: Three successive Somozas, a father and two sons, ran the Central American republic for nearly half a century, plundering the treasury, murdering political opponents, and relying on Washington for support. ("Somoza may be a son of a bitch," Franklin D. Roosevelt reportedly said of the founder of the regime, "but he's our son of a bitch." Subsequent presidents concurred.)

By the late 1970s, opposition to Somocismo had grown so intense that not even the United States—supplier of $14 million in military aid between 1975 and 1978—could save the dictatorship. In July 1979, as his U.S.-trained National Guard fled before the guerrillas of the Sandinista National Liberation Front, Anastasio Somoza Debayle escaped to Miami with an estimated $20 million. (He eventually relocated to

One victim of Three Mile Island's near-meltdown was the U.S. nuclear power industry.

SPORTS: Baseball: World Series, Pittsburgh Pirates defeat Baltimore Orioles, 4–3 ... Football: Super Bowl, Pittsburgh Steelers defeat Dallas Cowboys, 35–31 ... Basketball: NBA, Seattle Supersonics defeat Washington Bullets, 4–1 ... Tennis: Tracy Austin wins U.S. Open (youngest player to win, at age 16) ... Hockey: Stanley Cup, Montreal Canadiens defeat New York Rangers, 4–1 (fourth consecutive win).

"It is a hopeless task to defend myself facing such a ... court. My fate has been predetermined."
—Anatoly Shcharansky at his July 15, 1978, trial

During the "final offensive," rebels burned the car of a Somoza informer in Managua.

Paraguay, where he was assassinated in 1980.) The Sandinistas took charge of Nicaragua, forming a provisional coalition government of leftists and moderate businessmen.

Founded in 1962, the Sandinista movement was named for Augusto César Sandino, the Nicaraguan revolutionary leader killed by Somoza's father in 1934. The rebels gained broader support after 1972, when Somoza responded to a devastating earthquake—20,000 people killed; Managua, the capital, destroyed—by pocketing $16 million in international relief money. Mounting criticism was met with repression. In 1978 the regime assassinated respected newspaper publisher and reformer Pedro Joaquim Chamorro—releasing a popular fury that crossed class lines and buoyed the Sandinistas for their final offensive.

Victory's elation was brief, however. Somoza had left little money and a mountain of foreign debt. Civil war had killed 40,000 people and driven 600,000 from their homes. Worse, the United States distrusted the new regime and soon undertook to cripple it through a covert war. ◂1936.7 ▸1984.3

THE SOVIET UNION
The Jewish Exodus

9 The Jews of the Russian empire had been oppressed for centuries, and though the pogroms ended under Soviet rule, discrimination did not. Fearing international embarrassment and a "brain drain" of skilled workers, Moscow had long restricted emigration. But in the 1970s, détente brought a loosening of curbs. The exodus peaked in 1979, when more than 51,000 exit visas were issued.

The sharp increase, coinciding with the conclusion of the second U.S.-Soviet Strategic Arms Limitation Talks (SALT II), was widely seen as an attempt to influence treaty ratification. A second Soviet foreign-policy goal—to achieve most-favored-nation status with the United States—was equally important: In 1979, U.S. officials were considering repeal of the Jackson-Vanik Amendment, a 1974 law that tied trade grants to free emigration.

Even as emigration soared, the Kremlin cracked down on Jewish activism—reviling refuseniks (the term for those refused permission to leave) as "agents of world Zionism," and sentencing many to long terms in labor camps or psychiatric institutions. The 1977 arrest of Anatoly Shcharansky, a young mathematician who'd talked openly with Western reporters about his failure to gain an exit permit, generated international outrage. Charged with spying for the CIA, Shcharansky was convicted in a closed trial, and served nine years in prison before being released to Israel as part of a spy exchange. His case was extraordinary only in the attention it drew.

New hope: Russian Jews arrive in Israel.

Watchdog groups estimated that by 1979, some 180,000 Soviet Jews had filed for visas, yet emigration plummeted the following year, when SALT II failed to be ratified and the Carter administration—reacting to the Soviet invasion of Afghanistan—imposed a grain embargo. By 1984, the number of émigrés had slumped to 896. ◂1977.2 ▸1982.3

LITERATURE
Calvino's Modern Fable

10 Italo Calvino had long explored the nature of thought, reality, and storytelling in his fiction—and had done so with a lightness of touch and a limpidity of language that made him the foremost Italian writer of his generation. In 1979, with his tenth novel, Calvino demonstrated that he was a "metafictionist" on a par with Borges or Nabokov: *If on a winter's night a traveler* is a novel about the novel itself.

A tour de force of imagination and technique, the book follows two readers (one addressed as "you") who become lovers through an odd circumstance: Each has bought a book called *If on a winter's night a traveler*, by Italo Calvino, only to find that it has been misbound. After its introduction, the novel is interrupted by the beginning of a Polish thriller. While exchanging their defective Calvinos for copies of the more intriguing Slavic work, the readers also exchange phone numbers. But the new book has also been misbound; it's really a weblike Cimmerian novel. Eventually, the readers work their way through the beginnings of novels from ten different countries (all of which may, in fact, have been written by a malign translator), while pursuing a mystery that brings them into philosophical confrontation with literary types ranging from editor to censor.

Calvino's 1947 debut novel, *The Path to the Nest of Spiders,* was based on his experiences in the Italian Resistance during World War II; his trilogy of the 1950s, *Our Ancestors,* gained him international notice. But despite his fame, he continued to work as a book editor—deliberately remaining as much a reader as a writer. ◂1967.7 ▸1979.13

IN THE UNITED STATES

percent during the first six months of 1979. In response, President Carter in July called for "the moral equivalent of war"—the "most massive peacetime commitment of funds and resources in our nation's history"—to curtail dependence on imported oil, which had topped $20 per barrel. By year's end, OPEC upped the price to nearly $30, and gasoline broke the dollar-a-gallon mark, causing national angst. **◂1973.1 ▸1979.12**

▶MARVIN V. MARVIN—In March, Michelle Triola Marvin, estranged longtime companion of actor Lee Marvin, sued her erstwhile cohabitant for support. A California court rejected the plaintiff's claim to half of Marvin's income during the six years they'd lived together, but ordered Marvin to pay $104,000 in so-called "palimony," thus establishing a legal precedent: Unmarried cohabitants could claim certain property rights.

▶BASKETBALL FEVER—The NCAA basketball championship on March 26 pitted upstart Indiana State against talented Michigan State, but it was the individual matchup of cagey ISU forward Larry Bird against dazzling MSU guard Earvin "Magic" Johnson, the two best college players in the country, that proved most enthralling for a nationwide television audience. Johnson outscored Bird that evening, and his team took the title. Both players continued their rivalry in the NBA, revitalizing the moribund league in the process. During stellar professional careers that helped make basketball the glamour sport of the 1980s, slick-passing Magic led the Los Angeles Lakers to five championships and sharpshooting Bird (the NBA's 1980 rookie of the year) brought the Boston Celtics to glory three times. Each player collected three league MVP awards. **▸1991.M**

POLITICS & BUSINESS: GNP: $2,520.8 billion ... Prices increase 13.2% (largest jump since 14.0% in 1950) ... Supreme Court upholds limitation of public access to criminal trials; declares alimony laws that exclude previously divorced wives unconstitutional ... Sioux Nation awarded $100 million in land claim dispute ... U.S. approves record grain sale of 25 million tons for one year to U.S.S.R.

"The loneliest, the most wretched and the dying have at her hands received compassion without condescension, based on reverence for man."—The Nobel committee, upon awarding Mother Teresa the peace prize

AROUND THE WORLD

▶TOWARD A SINGLE CURRENCY—In a bold effort to cure "Eurosclerosis"—the economic paralysis of Western Europe—eight EC countries formed the European Monetary System in 1979. By linking the currencies of Belgium, Luxembourg, France, Denmark, West Germany, Ireland, Italy, and the Netherlands (an ultimate goal: a single European currency), EMS hoped to enhance trade by eliminating volatile exchange rates and stabilizing inflation. The system was championed by France's Valéry Giscard d'Estaing and Germany's Helmut Schmidt, both onetime finance ministers. ◀1971.4 ▶1979.12

▶MADMAN OUSTED—Jean-Bedel Bokassa was overthrown as ruler of the Central African Republic in 1979 after he and his Imperial Guard massacred 100 schoolchildren (some of whom he was rumored then to have eaten)—an atrocity that prompted French troops to engineer a coup that put Bokassa's predecessor (and cousin), David Dacko, back in power. A

tyrant of the highest order, Bokassa ousted democratic president Dacko in 1966, declared himself president for life in 1972, and was coronated emperor (on the model of his hero Napoléon I) in a $200 million ceremony *(above)* in 1977. He returned to the Central African Republic in 1986 and was promptly arrested, convicted of murder, and sentenced to life. ◀1972.3

▶POPE GOES HOME—In June, John Paul II, the first non-Italian pontiff since 1523, returned to his native Poland with a whirlwind 32-stop tour that lent momentum to the incipient Solidarity labor movement. The Pope's nine-day visit climaxed in Warsaw's Victory Square, where hundreds of thousands of Poles cheered ecstatically as the pontiff made clear (without saying so overtly) that the Church maintained its longstanding opposition to Communism. ◀1978.4 ▶1980.1

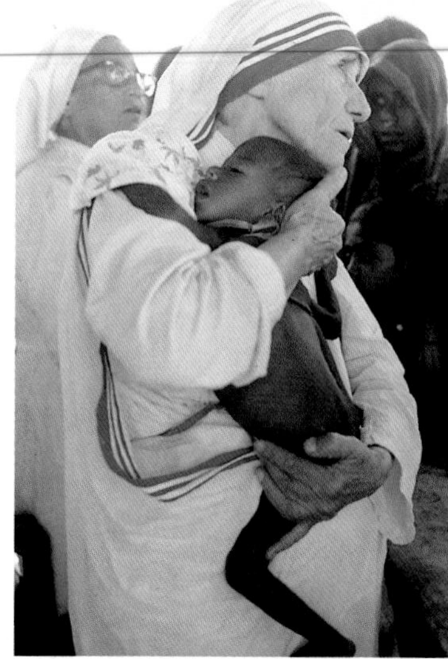

Mother Teresa visiting an orphanage in Assam, a state in northeastern India.

INDIA

A Nobel for Mother Teresa

11 Known simply as Mother Teresa, the Roman Catholic nun and agent of mercy in Calcutta's festering slums was an incontrovertible choice for the 1979 Nobel Peace Prize. In a violent, cynical, politically divided world, her selfless devotion to the needy was almost universally inspiring—as was her deep humility. "Personally, I am unworthy," the tiny 69-year-old told the Oslo-based prize committee. "I accept in the name of the poor."

Born Agnes Gonxha Bojaxhiu in Shkup, Albania (now Skopje, Macedonia), Mother Teresa joined the Sisters of Loretto in 1927, at age 17, moving to India soon thereafter. She taught in a convent school for the daughters of Calcutta's upper class for nearly two decades before receiving what she later described as her "call within a call": a vision of a new life ministering to the "poorest of the poor." In 1950, the year she became an Indian citizen, she founded the Order of the Missionaries of Charity, which she dedicated to the alleviation of human suffering.

Among the patients Mother Teresa cared for at her first mission was a dying man whose body was being eaten away by cancer. "How can you stand my stench?" he demanded. "It's nothing," she responded, "compared to the pain you must feel." Such unwavering compassion, and such rare respect for the dignity of those in her care, was characteristic of her order, which eventually established children's homes, leprosariums, soup kitchens, and health clinics around the world. "I have been told I spoil the poor by my work," Mother Teresa once observed. "Well, at least one congregation is spoiling the poor, because everyone else is spoiling the rich." **◀1968.12**

ECONOMICS

Inflation Rages

12 Inflation advanced at a record pace throughout much of the world during the 1970s, bringing shrinking bank accounts and lower standards of living to millions. With prices sharply rising, some consumers succumbed to a "borrow-now, spend-now" syndrome—buy today because tomorrow prices go up again. The result: more money in circulation and an inflation rate galloping faster than ever. In unstable Argentina, a rate of 172.6 percent in 1979 may have been unsurprising (if painful), but double-digit inflation in Britain, France, and the United States raised fears that another Great Depression was in the offing.

No single factor contributed more to the crisis than the high cost of energy, which skyrocketed after OPEC nations raised the price of oil by 400 percent in 1973-74. An additional 70 percent increase in 1979 flattened a creeping recovery. Despite towering interest rates (in the United States, banks raised the prime to a record 15.5 percent) and a drop-off in consumer spending, prices surged throughout the year and a decade of economic malaise ended on a decidedly gloomy note. **◀1979.M ▶1980.13**

INFLATION IN U.S., EUROPE, JAPAN

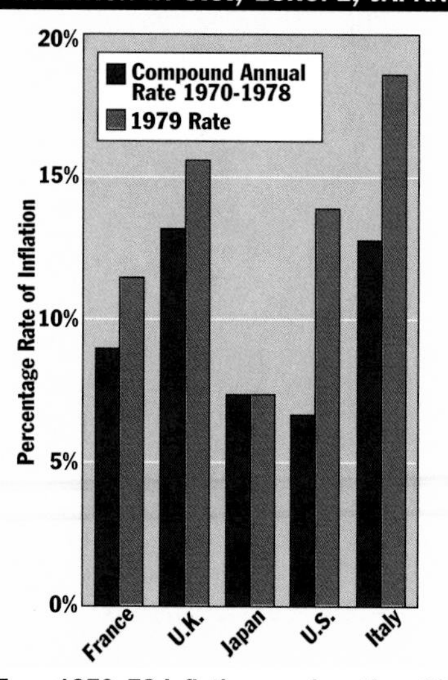

From 1970–78 inflation was less than 10%. In many countries. In 1979, it skyrocketed.

LITERATURE

Kundera's Dissenting Memory

13 Czech expatriate Milan Kundera called *The Book of Laughter and Forgetting,* published in France in 1979, "a novel in the form of variations." An ironic, melancholy, lyrical mixture of fiction, autobiography, and modern Czechoslovakian history, the book is composed of seven stories organized around a single event—the execution of a Communist Party leader and his subsequent disappearance from a famous official photograph. By turns philosophical, erotic, and comic, it established Kundera internationally as one of the era's finest experimental writers. It also prompted the regime to revoke his citizenship—the last of a long line of official insults.

Memory-maker Kundera in his Paris study.

An early supporter of the 1948 Czech Communist revolution, Kundera became an early dissenter. Expelled from the Party in 1950, he was reinstated after Stalin's death. He came to national prominence in 1967, during the cultural flowering of the "Prague Spring" era, when he published his first novel, *The Joke,* a Kafkaesque tale of political repression. After the Soviets crushed Czechoslovakia's experiment in liberal Communism, he was again expelled from the Party and forbidden to publish. To earn a living, he resorted to writing horoscopes under an assumed name. In 1975, he chose exile in France.

Philosophically conservative, Kundera saw fealty to the past—a resistance both to official attempts to rewrite history and to one's own impulses to escape or edit memories—as crucial to maintaining civilization and selfhood amid the soullessness of modern society. "The struggle of man against power," says one of his dissident protagonists in *The Book of Laughter and Forgetting,* "is the struggle of memory against forgetting." **◀1974.13 ▶1980.11**

NOBEL PRIZES: Peace: Mother Teresa (Indian) ... Literature: Odysseus Elytis (Greek; poet) ... Chemistry: Herbert Brown and Georg Wittig (U.S., German; chemical reactions) ... Medicine: Allan Cormack and Godfrey Hounsfield (U.S., U.K.; CAT scan) ... Physics: Steven Weinberg, Sheldon Glashow, and Abdus Salam (U.S., U.S., Pakistani; unified field theory) ... Economics: W.A. Lewis and Theodore Schultz (U.K., U.S.).

A VOICE FROM 1979

Imagining the Unimaginable

From *Sophie's Choice*, by William Styron, 1979

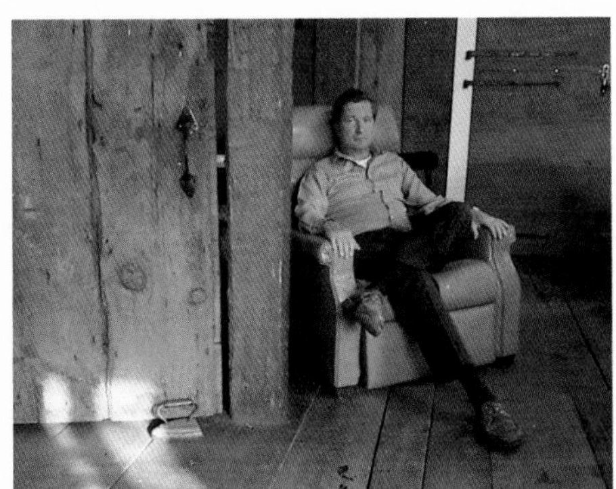

William Styron's 1979 novel, Sophie's Choice, *was a meditation on evil. Set in Brooklyn in 1947, the story is told by Stingo, a 22-year-old apprentice writer who, like his creator, hails from Tidewater, Virginia. The WASP-y Stingo meets and falls in love with a beautiful, young, Polish Catholic woman, Sophie Zawistowska, a survivor of Auschwitz. Over the course of a summer, Sophie, who is entangled in an intense, pathological relationship with a brilliant American Jewish biologist named Nathan Landau, pours out her story to Stingo: Upon arriving at the death camp, a Nazi doctor forced her to sacrifice one of her children. One was to be sent to the youth camp and perhaps survive; the other was to be consigned immediately to the gas chamber with sick and disabled prisoners. The legacy of Sophie's ungodly choice is self-loathing, expressed in alcoholism, submission to Nathan's drug-induced violence, and (eventually) suicide. Styron* (left, in 1967) *adroitly uses the racial hatred of the narrator's native South, Nathan's Jewishness, and Sophie's personal history to explore the implications of gross inhumanity.*

The doctor turned again. His eyebrows arched and he looked at Sophie with inebriate, wet, fugitive eyes, unsmiling. He was now so close to her that she smelled plainly the alcoholic vapor—a rancid fragrance of barley or rye—and she was not strong enough to return his gaze. It was then that she knew she had said something wrong, perhaps fatally wrong. She averted her face for an instant, glancing at an adjoining line of prisoners shambling through the golgotha of their selection, and saw Eva's flute teacher Zaorski at the precise congealed instant of his doom—dispatched to the left and to Birkenau by an almost imperceptible nod of a doctor's head. Now, turning back, she heard Dr. Jemand von Niemand say, "So you're not a Communist. You're a believer."

"*Ja, mein Hauptmann*. I believe in Christ." What folly! She sensed from his manner, his gaze—the new look in his eye of luminous intensity—that everything she was saying, far from helping her, from protecting her, was leading somehow to her swift undoing. She thought: Let me be struck dumb.

The doctor was a little unsteady on his feet. He leaned over for a moment to an enlisted underling with a clipboard and murmured something, meanwhile absorbedly picking his nose. Eva, pressing heavily against Sophie's leg, began to cry. "So you believe in Christ the Redeemer?" the doctor said in a thick-tongued but oddly abstract voice, like that of a lecturer examining the delicately shaded facet of a proposition in logic. Then he said something which for an instant was totally mystifying: "Did He not say, 'Suffer the little children to come unto Me'?" He turned back to her, moving with the twitchy methodicalness of a drunk.

Sophie, with an inanity poised on her tongue and choked with fear, was about to attempt a reply when the doctor said, "You may keep one of your children."

"*Bitte?*" said Sophie.

"You may keep one of your children," he repeated. "The other one will have to go. Which one will you keep?"

"You mean, I have to choose?"

"You're a Polack, not a Yid. That gives you a privilege—a choice."

Her thought processes dwindled, ceased. Then she felt her legs crumple. "I can't choose! I can't choose!" She began to scream. Oh, how she recalled her own screams! Tormented angels never screeched so loudly above hell's pandemonium. "*Ich kann nicht wählen*!" she screamed.

The doctor was aware of unwanted attention. "Shut up!" he ordered. "Hurry now and choose. Choose, goddamnit, or I'll send them both over there. Quick."

She could not believe any of this. She could not believe that she was now kneeling on the hurtful, abrading concrete, drawing her children toward her so smotheringly tight that she felt that their flesh might be engrafted to hers even through layers of clothes. Her disbelief was total, deranged. It was disbelief reflected in the eyes of the gaunt, waxy-skinned young Rottenführer, the doctor's aide, to whom she inexplicably found herself looking upward in supplication. He appeared stunned, and he returned her gaze with a wide-eyed baffled expression, as if to say: I can't understand this either.

In the 1982 film of *Sophie's Choice*, directed by Alan J. Pakula, actress Meryl Streep won an Oscar for her portrayal of the haunted Polish heroine.

"Don't make me choose," she heard herself plead in a whisper, "I can't choose."

"Send them both over there, then," the doctor said to the aide, "*nach links*."

"Mama!" She heard Eva's thin but soaring cry at the instant that she thrust the child away from her and rose from the concrete with a clumsy stumbling motion. "Take the baby!" she called out. "Take my little girl!"

At this point the aide—with a careful gentleness that Sophie would try without success to forget—tugged at Eva's hand and led her away into the waiting legion of the damned. She would forever retain a dim impression that the child had continued to look back, beseeching. But because she was now almost completely blinded by salty, thick, copious tears she was spared whatever expression Eva wore, and she was always grateful for that. For in the bleakest honesty of her heart she knew that she would never have been able to tolerate it, driven nearly mad as she was by her last glimpse of that vanishing small form.

The passion for cash knew no borders in a decade when a movie-hero's dictum, "Greed is good," became a worldwide credo. To the astonishment of almost everyone, even communist nations caught the fever—as revolutions replaced "workers' states" with free-market republics.

1980 1989

After two decades of upheaval, the capitalist nations turned decisively to the business of business. Multinational corporations ranged the globe, settling wherever labor was cheap and the regulatory climate hospitable. Takeover artists made millions buying and selling companies, often with little regard for the welfare of the bought and sold. And as the U.S. debt ballooned, Japan became the world's financial powerhouse. During the 1980s, the Tokyo Stock Exchange, or NIKKEI *(right)*, became one of the largest markets in the world.

THE WORLD IN 1980

World Population

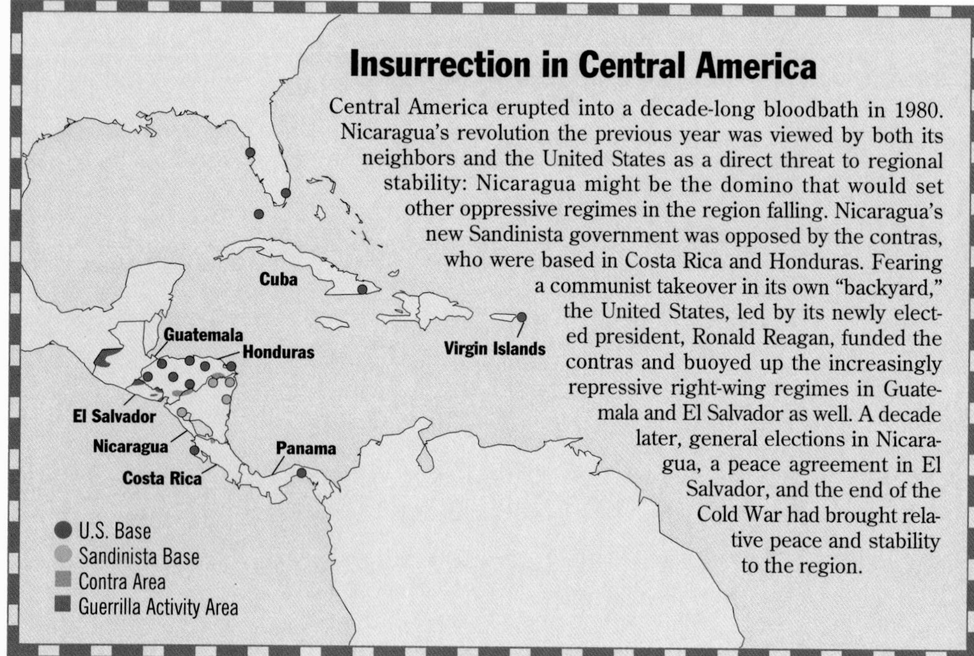

Insurrection in Central America

Central America erupted into a decade-long bloodbath in 1980. Nicaragua's revolution the previous year was viewed by both its neighbors and the United States as a direct threat to regional stability: Nicaragua might be the domino that would set other oppressive regimes in the region falling. Nicaragua's new Sandinista government was opposed by the contras, who were based in Costa Rica and Honduras. Fearing a communist takeover in its own "backyard," the United States, led by its newly elected president, Ronald Reagan, funded the contras and buoyed up the increasingly repressive right-wing regimes in Guatemala and El Salvador as well. A decade later, general elections in Nicaragua, a peace agreement in El Salvador, and the end of the Cold War had brought relative peace and stability to the region.

STATE OF THE ART

In 1980, the **Sony Walkman** was a year old and already an unqualified success. Akio Morita, Sony's chairman, had invented the miniature cassette player for his three grown children, then quickly discovered that the rest of the world wanted it, too. By the end of 1979, there were more than 100,000 of the portable stereos in use in Japan. Within three years, annual sales were 2.5 million worldwide.

Family Planning

By 1980, most women had gained the means to control their own reproductivity: Birth-control pills had been in wide use for two decades and abortion was legal in most developed nations. Yet methods varied widely from country to country. In India, for example, sterilization (for both sexes) is the preferred form of birth control, and in the Soviet Union (where modern contraceptives are scarce), the average woman has six abortions in her lifetime.

Contraceptive Use % of married women of childbearing age, using any method, 1980s		**Abortions** per 1,000 live births
66%	Brazil	440
74%	China	490
34%	India	247
64%	Japan	382*
83%	U.K.	223
69%	U.S.	422
18%	U.S.S.R.	2,080

*Official number, actual number may be significantly higher.

The Gasoline Wars

Price of gasoline per gallon, U.S. dollars ■1973 ■1980 ■1991

For automobile owners in 1980, the memory of long lines at gas stations and high prices at the pumps was still fresh. Gasoline prices continued to rise from 1975 to 1980 as OPEC took crude oil prices to an all-time high of $37 per barrel in 1981. Thereafter, prices tended to stabilize in developed countries that could exploit their existing oil supplies (fields in the North Sea and Alaska helped Europe and the United States, for example); countries with no resources of their own were still at the mercy of foreign suppliers and their own, often volatile, economies.

Fashion Essential

Originally, they were white, made of canvas and rubber, and cost around $10. Then, in the late 1970s, sneakers metamorphosed into **running shoes**, and began to cost as much as $50. (By 1990, a top pair could set a consumer back $170.) In 1980, the average American owned 1.2 pair; in 1990, the number was 2.5.

International Terrorist Incidents

	1970	1975	1980	1990
Africa	7	22	25	53
Asia	24	22	29	92
Western Europe	81	131	174	77
Eastern Europe	1	2	3	6
Middle East	40	64	113	65
Latin America	123	62	122	163
North America	24	46	34	0
TOTAL	**300**	**349**	**500**	**456**

A Time of Terror Most definitions of terrorism include four elements: premeditation, political motive, violence, and noncombatant victims. The trend exploded into public consciousness throughout the 1970s with the PLO murder of Israeli athletes at the 1972 Munich Olympics, the campaign of West Germany's Baader-Meinhof Gang, the 1978 kidnapping-murder of former Italian prime minister Aldo Moro, the 1979 IRA murder of Lord Mountbatten, innumerable airplane hijackings, and, at decade's end, the most high-profile terrorist act of all: the seizing by Iranian students of American diplomats from the U.S. Embassy in Tehran in November 1979.

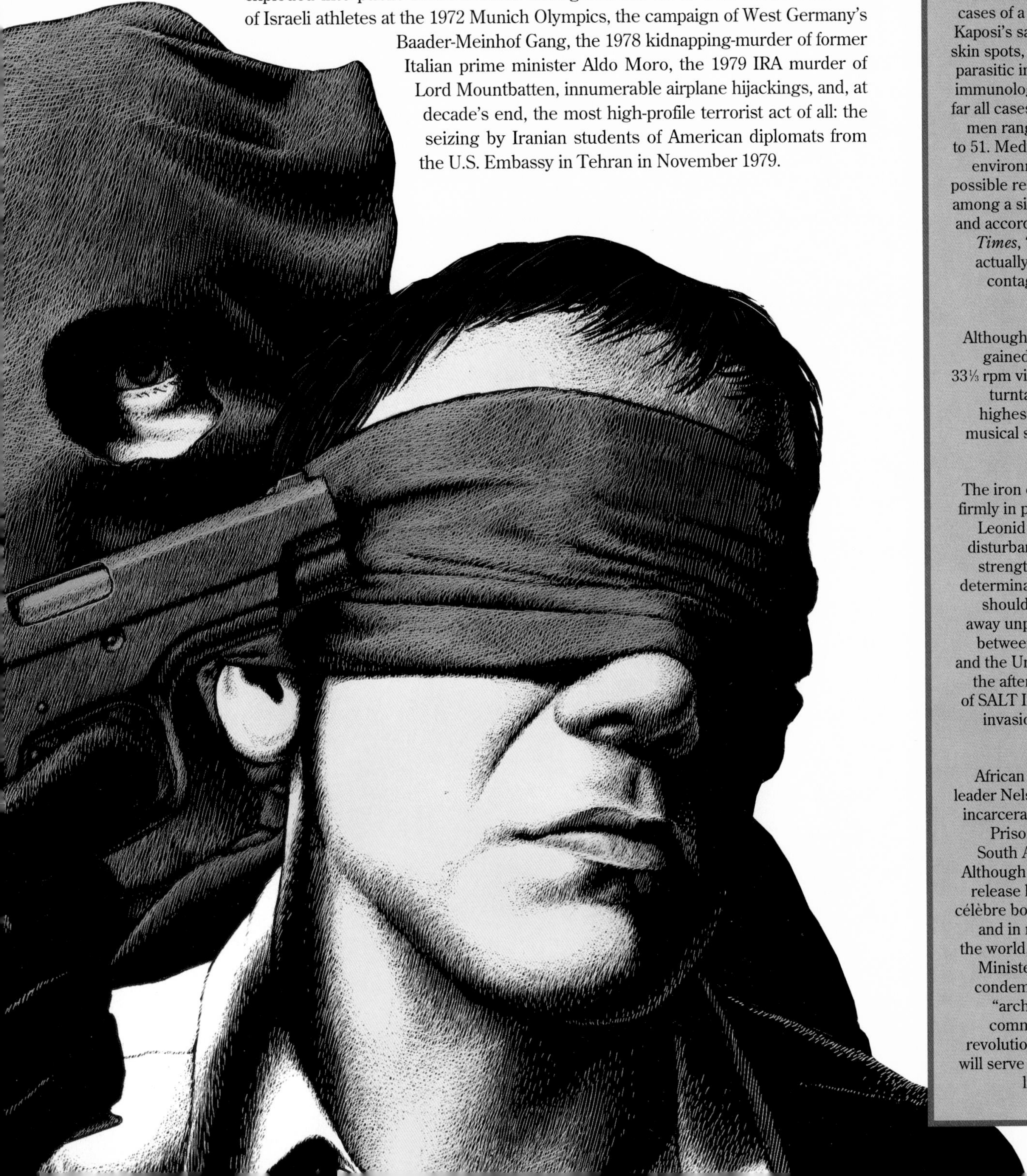

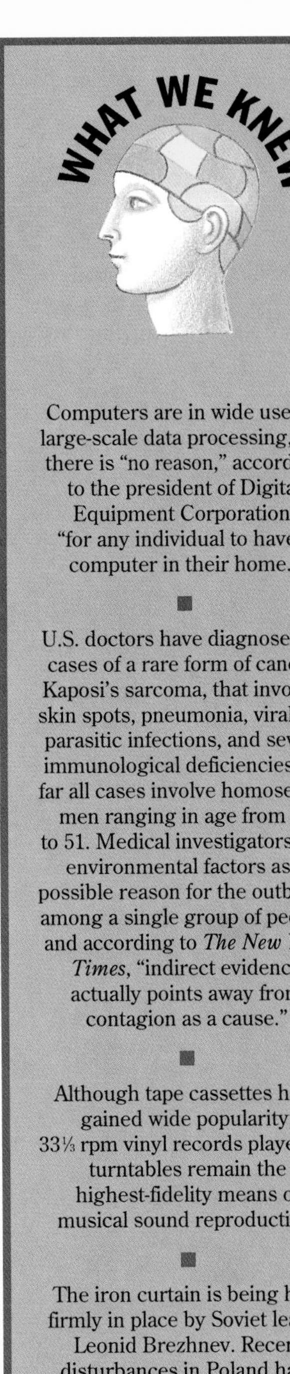

Computers are in wide use for large-scale data processing, but there is "no reason," according to the president of Digital Equipment Corporation, "for any individual to have a computer in their home."

■

U.S. doctors have diagnosed 41 cases of a rare form of cancer, Kaposi's sarcoma, that involves skin spots, pneumonia, viral and parasitic infections, and severe immunological deficiencies. So far all cases involve homosexual men ranging in age from 26 to 51. Medical investigators cite environmental factors as a possible reason for the outbreak among a single group of people, and according to *The New York Times*, "indirect evidence actually points away from contagion as a cause."

■

Although tape cassettes have gained wide popularity, 33⅓ rpm vinyl records played on turntables remain the highest-fidelity means of musical sound reproduction.

■

The iron curtain is being held firmly in place by Soviet leader Leonid Brezhnev. Recent disturbances in Poland have strengthened Brezhnev's determination that "renegades should not expect to get away unpunished." Relations between the Soviet Union and the United States worsen in the aftermath of the failure of SALT II and the 1980 Soviet invasion of Afghanistan.

■

African National Congress leader Nelson Mandela has been incarcerated at Robben Island Prison, in Cape Town, South Africa, for 18 years. Although the campaign for his release has become a cause célèbre both within South Africa and in much of the rest of the world, South African Prime Minister Pieter Botha has condemned Mandela as an "arch-Marxist" whose commitment to violent revolution guarantees that he will serve out the entirety of his life sentence.

JAMES GLEICK

Information Overload

The Electronic Revolution

1980
1989

BY THE MID-1980s A PECULIAR FORM OF STATISTIC had already become a cliché of the electronic era. *A typical chip cost $100 ten years ago, and today it costs only $5. A typical chip contained 50 transistors ten years ago, and today it contains 50,000.* The first "pocket" calculator weighed more than two pounds and cost $250 when it made its appearance in 1971. A decade later the equivalent device weighed a few ounces and cost $10; tens of millions were sold each year. One of the early superconductor executives fancifully described what it would mean for automobiles to make this kind of progress: "We would cruise comfortably in our cars at 100,000 miles per hour, getting 50,000 miles per gallon of gasoline. We would find it cheaper to throw away our Rolls-Royce and replace it than park it downtown for the evening."

In 1981 Ronald Reagan was sworn in as President of the United States; Charles and Diana married; the first space shuttle flew a mission in Earth orbit; and—a more potent landmark than any of these—IBM introduced a "personal" computer, with 64 kilobytes of memory, costing $2,665.

The earliest electronic computers were costly behemoths that required a squad of attendants to control them. IBM's Mark I computer *(right)*, which went into service in 1944 at Harvard University (where it was soon given over to military research), used tapes to process information. The first automatic digital computer—complete with memory unit—was conceived in the 1830s by English mathematician Charles Babbage. In 1991, British scientists used Babbage's unpublished notebooks to build his dream machine *(above)*, Difference Engine No. 2. Working from instructions encoded in punch cards, it could perform computations to 31 digits.

Suddenly it seemed that, until the electronic revolution, Homo sapiens had been all thumbs. Now humanity was beginning to achieve an exquisite fine-grained control over materials and devices, energy and data. After struggling for centuries to measure time with brass pendulums, to send messages with drums or smoke, the species now opened scales of measurement down to the molecular and the subatomic. The nanosecond came into its own.

The technological march had begun four decades earlier, when three scientists at the Bell Telephone Laboratories invented the transistor. Until then, electronics had meant vacuum tubes—glass canisters that glowed with a Halloweenish orange light. The vacuum tube bled heat and burned out. At the extreme margin of this device's usefulness stood ENIAC, the first giant computer, containing 18,000 vacuum tubes. As John von Neumann, a father of modern computing theory, remarked, "Each time it is turned on, it blows two tubes." The unreliable monster thus required the service of a squad of soldiers standing ready with baskets of spare tubes. The vacuum tube could amplify a current and switch it on and off as many as 10,000 times a second. The transistor could do that, too—but the transistor, a quirk in a crystal of silicon, was more or less immortal. Before long, people would be wearing ENIAC equivalents on their wrists. Humanity had learned how to rearrange sand into computers.

As the vacuum tube had reached its limit, so, more slowly, had machinery itself. The nonelectronic machine could encompass marvels of ingenuity and craftsmanship, but a sense of its ultimate limitations—the sense of *gizmo* and *contraption*—was captured in the absurdist drawings of Rube Goldberg. Transistors meant miniaturization: Technologists began to descend into a domain unimaginable in a world of levers and gears. The decade that followed the 1947 Bell Labs announcement of its invention saw the transistor appear in hearing aids and (setting off a popular craze) cheap and reliable radios. It was in 1961, however, that the destiny of the electronic era began to reach fulfillment, when the first microchips—integrated circuits combining three or four transistors and a half-dozen other components in a tiny, solid, manufactured block—reached the market.

A half-million chips were sold in 1963. By 1970 the number was 300 million. Chips were trans-

forming the American space program, the television, the calculator; soon they would pervade the wristwatch, the oven, the automobile. The most trivial everyday processes were waiting for chips—masters of timing and control. Carmakers had never quite managed to build a reliable intermittent setting into windshield wipers; electronics suddenly made the problem trivial. One lone inventor battled the entire automobile industry for 20 years over his rights to that particular patent, and won.

1980
1989

CHIPS BECAME A FAMILIAR VISUAL ICON: Blown up for photographs, they revealed circuits laid out in a rectilinear grid like the street map of a futuristic city seen from miles above. In mass production they became paperweights, cocktail coasters, earrings, and lapel pins. Chips were machines in a new incarnation. Devices imbued with electronics seemed less mechanistic, less predictable, more magical, and more soulful. They embodied knowledge as no machine had before—for the real medium of the electronic revolution, it was now clear, was information.

When a technology gets 50 percent faster or 50 percent smarter, the result is usually just a faster or smarter technology. When it gets ten or a hundred times faster or smarter, the result can be a phenomenon altogether new and unpredictable. No twentieth-century technology illustrated this rule more dramatically than the computer.

The first giant computers—the descendants of ENIAC—filled rooms. Communicating with them was like importuning an oracle. In his 1981 book *The Soul of a New Machine*, Tracy Kidder wrote, "Typically, one big machine served an entire organization. Often it lay behind a plate glass window, people in white gowns attending it, and those who wished to use it did so through intermediaries. Users were like supplicants." The mental model for big-computer work was: Pose a question (the harder the better); frame the question (on punched cards, say); set the computer running; receive the answer.

The mental model for the era coming up was: play.

For as the giant computer rose in dominance, it was already under invisible assault. Two seemingly separate technological tracks began to close in on it. One was the pocket calculator: Each generation of mass-production calculator chip had more functions and logic—roots, sines, and cosines, logarithms, and then true programmability. The other was the electronics hobby kit: The cheap availability of chip processors and chip memory suddenly made it possible for hobbyists to move straight from the do-it-yourself doorbell to the do-it-yourself home computer.

Big-computer culture was irrelevant to the garage entrepreneurs who founded Apple, the first great home-grown computer company. Oddly, it was equally irrelevant for the patched-on subdivision of IBM which opened the 1980s with a PC that finally made the computer a commodity. The computer was out from behind plate glass. With mice, modems, trackballs, and touch screens the computer makers disguised the essential power inherent in their devices. But power it was. All the scribes and librarians of the classical and medieval worlds had labored for millennia to preserve less knowledge, in sum, than could be stored on the magnetic disk of a random teenager's desktop computer.

The technology began in two small niches of industrial civilization: business accounting and scientific calculation. Who else would need to compute? Even within science it was not immediately obvious who would need the ability to carry out thousands, millions, or billions of arithmetical operations each second. Astronomers were first, then artillery designers and the bomb makers of Los Alamos during World War II, then ... weather forecasters?

By the end of the 1980s, however, computation had exploded outward from these niches to invade every aspect of quotidian life. Electronics did virtually no work, directly; this whole realm of technology was rightly said to be the successor of not the steam engine but the clock. Its strengths were timing, control, and the manipulation and accumulation of information. Those were strengths hardly any machine could afford to be without. Automobiles, washing machines,

By the 1980s, microchips like the Intel 432 *(the small, center square at left, enlarged to approximately five times its life size)* had launched an information revolution. (The powerful 432 had the capabilities of a contemporary mid-sized mainframe computer.) Calculators slipped into shirt pockets, personal computers made themselves at home, and ordinary machines—from cars to air conditioners—began to mimic the human brain. By the early 1990s, strangers from around the world were networking with one another in cyberspace, without leaving their desks.

telephones became electronic. A fine mechanical wristwatch became a rarity: far more expensive, though far less reliable, and as quaint as a record made of grooved black vinyl. The pace of change was dizzying—an American president was publicly embarrassed in a grocery store at decade's end when he could not understand why a clerk, instead of punching a cash register, was merely passing his purchases over a reddish light.

We could hardly see the transformation. So many of the changes were behind the curtain or inside the black box. The scenery of popular science-fiction series like *Star Trek* evolved over the decade, and of course that was just our own century's scenery evolving, not the future's: light bulbs gave way to light-emitting diodes; computers shrank to pocket size.

The focus of the electronic revolution made one more shift as the eighties came to an end, from computing itself to communication. Two trends collided. First, in much of the industrial world, the wired and wireless networks reached a critical mass of interconnectivity—government officials spoke of creating an "information superhighway," but the superhighway was already forming before their eyes, with new fiber-optic and cellular-broadcast pathways announced weekly by telephone companies, cellular entrepreneurs, and cable-television empires. And, second, the formerly distinct technologies embodied in the computer, the telephone, the fax machine, the pager, the clock, the compass, the stock ticker, and the television (not to mention such nonelectronic ancestors as books) began to converge toward a single all-inclusive device—preferably small enough to fit in a briefcase or a pocket. With the help of satellites, a steady stream of data could pour in: news bites, phone numbers, the user's global position (plus or minus a hundred feet), physicians' lab results, company sales figures. "We're all connected" was a telephone-company advertising jingle; it could also have been the decade's three-word slogan. The political upheavals that spread outward from the Berlin Wall and Tiananmen Square were like none other in history: Television and telefax were coconspirators; the global sharing of information and aspirations made tyranny, if not instantly obsolete, at least that much less plausible.

NEW KINDS OF COMMUNITY HAVE BEGUN TO EMERGE in the global electronic village. If we use computers and connect to the network, our neighborhoods are no longer the fraction of a square mile around our homes. We have learned to relocate ourselves within more slices of the human universe. In the past, people with an obscure or even not-so-obscure special interest—medieval fabrics or military-strategy games—made their way to cities or universities, the only places that accumulated critical masses of like-minded people. Now the possibilities are richer.

Technologies are mirrors of their creators. We look in them, we see ourselves, and we are changed by what we see. The electronic thinking machine, the computer, may have begun a profound transformation of our sense of self. We argue about whether machines can truly think, though few of us can outplay a chess computer available in toy stores for $100. Can a machine write poetry, feel sadness, invent a new idea? While we argue, we may be more likely to think of ourselves as machines—as *super*computers—than ever before. *Let me process that. Time to reprogram my thinking. I've got sensory overload.* Conceptions of data storage, flowcharts, arrays, and pointers have permeated disciplines far removed from computer science. Philosophers and psychologists pondering consciousness, will, and memory have found, if not answers, at least new metaphors to help in understanding how a tangle of neurons, sufficiently chaotic and complex, can hum show tunes and make arithmetic mistakes.

For the middle-aged, the acquisition of computer literacy is often a daunting challenge. But for the children of the electronic age—like these first graders in Cupertino, California, home of the groundbreaking Apple Computer corporation—computers are nearly as familiar as pencil and paper were to their parents.

"By making a machine think as a man, man recreates himself, defines himself, as a machine," wrote David Bolter in *Turing's Man* midway through the decade. Whether good or bad, that fact was inescapable. Like the industrial revolution before it, the electronic revolution has transformed our relationship to nature, to each other, and to the ever more tightly bound network that the human community has become. □

THE TALE OF
PETER RABBIT
BEATRIX POTTER

"For 36 years, something foreign was injected into us."—**Lech Walesa, leader of Poland's Solidarity**

STORY OF THE YEAR

Poland: The Birth of Solidarity

1 In July 1980, the Polish government, facing bankruptcy after a decade of mismanagement by Communist Party leader Edward Gierek, decreed a rise in meat prices. Workers from the Baltic's gray ports to Silesia's coalfields reacted with illegal strikes, as they had in response to price hikes in 1970 and 1976. For the first time, many took over factories. But mighty as it was, the strike wave remained unfocused—a mass venting of frustration at poor working conditions, at chronic shortages of food, fuel, and clothing. On the verge of collapse, the uprising was transformed into a lasting movement by a paunchy, unemployed electrician with a walrus mustache.

Walesa gets a hero's welcome from striking workers at a Polish factory.

Lech Walesa had been a prominent figure in the 1970 rebellion and had recently been fired from his job at Gdansk's giant Lenin shipyard for organizing an unauthorized union. On August 14, he climbed over the shipyard wall and was elected head of the strike committee there. Within three days, the government—desperate to end the crippling work stoppage—agreed to the committee's demands. But workers at other local enterprises asked the shipyard workers to stay on strike out of solidarity, and Walesa became head of an interfactory strike committee for the Gdansk-Sopot-Gdynia region.

A plainspoken, gruffly charismatic leader, Walesa became an international symbol for his embattled people's aspirations. He also proved to be an effective negotiator on issues far beyond the cost of living. Gierek's regime (following the advice of its Soviet patrons to seek a compromise) granted workers startling concessions: the right to strike and form free unions; a loosening of censorship; media access for the Catholic Church and the labor organizations. In return, the strikers agreed not to challenge Communist political supremacy. Signed by Walesa and government representatives in a televised ceremony on August 31, the so-called Gdansk Accords set off a countrywide celebration.

The interfactory committee became the core of a new, national union called Solidarity, which soon claimed a membership of ten million—four times that of the Communist Party, and a full quarter of Poland's population. "I am not interested in politics," Walesa said. "I am a union man." But he was leading a revolution. ◂**1976.M** ▸**1981.6**

IRAN

Holding America Hostage

2 Yellow ribbons decorated American houses, trees, and shirtfronts in 1980—emblems of solidarity with 52 compatriots held captive since Iranian revolutionaries had stormed the U.S. embassy in Tehran the previous November. To their keepers, the hostages were spies, subject to beatings and psychological torture for their presumed wrongdoings. To the regime of Ayatollah Khomeini, they were pawns: first in an attempt to have the fugitive Muhammad Reza Shah Pahlevi extradited; then (after the shah died in Egypt in July) in efforts to recover funds he'd looted from the treasury, to force Washington to drop financial claims against Iran, and to discourage further U.S. intervention. To Americans, however, the hostages were symbols of their nation's eroding power—and, increasingly, of President Jimmy Carter's weakness.

Hoping to toughen his image, Carter sent commandos to free the captives in April. But the mission failed when one rescue helicopter crashed—killing eight soldiers—and others suffered technical glitches. Secretary of State Cyrus Vance, who'd warned against the operation, resigned. And the hostages were moved to scattered hiding places.

The ongoing crisis, along with mounting economic woes, dogged Carter's reelection campaign. But secret, indirect negotiations with Khomeini continued—and when Iraq attacked Iran in September, the stage was set for a settlement. The war began as a border dispute (centering on the strategic Shatt al-Arab waterway and the oil-rich province of Khuzistan), but it would grind on for eight years, fueled by the fears of Iraqi strongman Saddam Hussein and other Arab leaders that Khomeini's revolution would spread. Embattled Iran needed money desperately, and its assets were largely frozen in U.S. banks.

The breakthrough in negotiations, based on the release of 70 percent of Iran's funds, came in January 1981—too late for Carter, who'd lost the election in November. The hostages went free minutes after Ronald Reagan's inauguration. ◂**1979.1** ▸**1980.M**

CUBA

Castro's Cast-Offs

3 In the United States, the Mariel boatlift, the 1980 exodus of 125,000 Cubans to Florida, was called a "freedom flotilla." In Cuba, Premier Fidel Castro offered a different description: a discharge of "scum." The five-month-long migration brought Cuban-American relations to a new low, with each side claiming it as a moral and political victory. One fact was indisputable: Miami was now the largest Cuban population center outside of Havana.

"There is no better proof of the failure of Castro's revolution," said the U.S. State Department, "than the dramatic exodus that is now taking place." But the boatlift—begun in April, after several thousand Cuban asylum-seekers crashed the gates of the Peruvian embassy in Havana—proceeded entirely on Castro's terms. Opening the harbor of Mariel (a port city in the north) to emigration, he boldly

Bound and blindfolded, hostages at the U.S. embassy in Tehran began their long wait for freedom on November 4, 1979.

ART & CULTURE: Books: ***Earthly Powers*** **(Anthony Burgess);** ***The Name of the Rose*** **(Umberto Eco);** ***Man in the Holocene*** **(Max Frisch);** ***Thy Neighbor's Wife*** **(Gay Talese);** ***Cosmos*** **(Carl Sagan);** ***The Morning of the Poem*** **(James Schuyler) ... Music: "Sailing" (Christopher Cross); "Another Brick in the Wall" (Roger Waters);** ***Remain in Light*** **(Talking Heads, LP);** ***In Memory of a Summer Day*** **(David Del Tredici) ...**

"The problem in Cuba is that young people have nothing to do. They make us work, but they don't let us have a good time."
—Raul, a 22-year-old Cuban who came to the United States during the Mariel boatlift

Cuban immigrants sailed shrimp boats to Key West, Florida.

invited Cuban exiles in the United States to retrieve friends and family from the port. Upon arriving in Mariel, however, many expatriates found they couldn't leave until they took aboard passengers handpicked by Castro—among them a substantial number of criminals and the mentally ill. "Few boats are getting any relatives out," reported one American skipper. "I didn't see anybody hugging and kissing at Mariel." Even so, the flotilla continued for months, with thousands of fishing boats, yachts, and leaky tubs choking the Straits of Florida.

Castro's expulsion of undesirables undercut American immigration policy (which had always granted those fleeing Communist Cuba the dignified status of political refugees) and challenged U.S. control of its own borders. President Carter, reneging on a promise to greet the outcasts with "open arms" and an "open heart," declared the boatlift illegal. Detained in camps upon arriving in Miami, the immigrants presented massive resettlement problems, aggravating American resentment of Cuba—and of Carter. **◂1962.5 ▸1994.14**

THE UNITED STATES

Reagan's Counterrevolution

4 After two decades of social, political, and sexual upheaval, a new conservatism was on the rise throughout the Western world. The counterrevolution began in 1979, when Margaret Thatcher became Britain's prime minister—but it arrived in force in November 1980, when Republican Ronald Reagan, a former movie actor and governor of California, defeated Democratic incumbent Jimmy Carter to become the 40th president of the United States. The wave soon spread to Germany, where Christian Democrat Helmut Kohl replaced Socialist Helmut Schmidt as chancellor in 1982; to Canada, where Prime Minister Pierre Trudeau's Liberals (briefly ousted in 1979) fell to Brian Mulroney's Conservatives in 1984; and even to France, where Socialist president François Mitterrand, elected in 1981, was forced to share power with rightist premier Jacques Chirac in 1986.

Rejecting the long-dominant Keynesian economic model, which relied on government spending to stimulate consumption, the new American leader championed supply-side economics—a theory holding that prosperity can best be fueled by liberating the private sector from red tape and taxes. Reagan dismantled dozens of social programs begun under Roosevelt and Johnson and unraveled decades' worth of regulatory laws (designed to cushion workers, consumers, the economy, and the environment against the excesses of the marketplace, and to protect minorities from the injuries of prejudice). In the United States, the 1980s became a time of financial boom coupled, unprecedentedly, with high unemployment; of big-spending yuppies (young urban professionals) and burgeoning homelessness. America struggled to overcome its "Vietnam syndrome," intervening aggressively in Grenada, Lebanon, Libya, and Nicaragua. By the end of the decade, however, shifts in global politics—the collapse of the Soviet Union, the rise of the European Community—had made Reaganism (like Thatcherism) obsolete. The conservatives held on, but under increasingly straitened circumstances. **◂1979.3 ▸1981.M**

Two leaders cut from the same conservative cloth: Thatcher and Reagan in 1981.

EXPLORATION

Voyager's Saturn Snapshots

5 **Continuing its tour of the solar system, the unmanned *Voyager 1* planetary probe zipped past Saturn in November 1980, transmitting to Earth striking photos of the distant planet. The probe, launched by NASA in tandem with *Voyager 2* in 1977, gave scientists a new perspective on Saturn. Among the most dramatic revelations: The planet's three trademark rings are made up of thousands of "ringlets." On their way into deeper space, the Voyager probes (*Voyager 2* reached Saturn in August 1981) also discovered eight Saturnian moons too small to be detected from Earth, and provided a detailed look at several *(above)* that had previously been seen only as points of light.** **◂1979.M ▸1981.12**

BIRTHS

Macaulay Culkin, U.S. actor.

DEATHS

Roland Barthes, French writer.

Cecil Beaton, U.K. photographer.

John Bonham, U.K. musician.

Marcello Caetano, Portuguese prime minister.

Karl Dönitz, German admiral.

William O. Douglas, Jr., U.S. jurist.

Jimmy Durante, U.S. comedian.

Erich Fromm, German-U.S. psychoanalyst and writer.

Philip Guston, U.S. painter.

Alfred Hitchcock, U.K.-U.S. filmmaker.

Oskar Kokoschka, Austrian painter.

André Kostelanetz, Russian-U.S. pianist.

John Lennon, U.K. musician and composer.

Alice Roosevelt Longworth, U.S. socialite.

Marshall McLuhan, Canadian media theorist.

Steve McQueen, U.S. actor.

George Meany, U.S. labor leader.

Henry Miller, U.S. writer.

A.C. Nielsen, U.S. pollster.

Jesse Owens, U.S. athlete.

Muhammad Reza Pahlevi, Iranian shah.

Jean Piaget, Swiss psychologist.

Katherine Anne Porter, U.S. writer.

Oscar Romero, Salvadoran archbishop.

Jean-Paul Sartre, French writer.

Peter Sellers, U.K. actor.

C.P. Snow, U.K. writer and physicist.

Anastasio Somoza Debayle, Nicaraguan ruler.

Clyfford Still, U.S. painter.

Josip Broz Tito, Yugoslavian ruler.

Mae West, U.S. actress.

Painting & Sculpture: *Geography Lesson* (Julian Schnabel); *Two Painters* (Francesco Clemente) ... Film: *Ordinary People* (Robert Redford); *Dressed to Kill* (Brian De Palma); *The Elephant Man* (David Lynch); *Berlin Alexanderplatz* (Rainer Werner Fassbinder) ... Theater: *Children of a Lesser God* (Mark Medoff); *True West* (Sam Shepard); *Barnum* (Coleman and Stewart) ... TV: *Nightline*; *Magnum, P.I.*

"Viewers love to see rich people more screwed up than they are. It makes them feel superior."—**Philip Capice, the executive producer of *Dallas***

NEW IN 1980

Post-it notes (3M Corporation).

In-line skates.

U.S. Department of Education.

RU-486 "abortion"pill (Roussel Uclaf, Paris).

Patents for living organisms (by a ruling of the U.S. Supreme Court).

IN THE UNITED STATES

▶ATHLETES STAY HOME—Reacting to the Soviet invasion of Afghanistan, President Carter in January asked that the International Olympic Committee move the 1980 Summer Games from Moscow to a politically neutral site. The committee declined to take action, so Carter announced a U.S. boycott of the Moscow Olympics; 59 other countries joined in. The Soviets retaliated in 1984 with a Communist-bloc boycott of the Los Angeles Olympics.

▶VOLCANO ERUPTS—After rumbling ominously for two months, Washington State's Mount Saint Helens—dormant since 1857—erupted on May 18, spewing a cloud of ash 60,000 feet in the air. The eruption was the first in the continental U.S. in more than 60 years (and the most violent ever). It caused 60 deaths,

$2.7 billion in property damage, and severe harm to the area's flora and fauna.

▶NONSTOP NEWS—In June, Atlanta entrepreneur Ted Turner, 41, inaugurated the Cable News Network (CNN), the first in the world to be devoted exclusively to news. CNN began when Turner rescued a failing local UHF station and—prevailing over powerful TV and movie-industry congressional lobbies—

A makeshift cocaine-processing plant in Bolivia.

BOLIVIA

The Cocaine Coup

6 On July 17, 1980, Bolivia's first woman president, Lidia Gueiler Tejada, was meeting with her cabinet when 20 armed men burst into the room. The country's 188th government in 155 years had been overthrown—and its most vicious regime in decades was in power. Army commander Luís García Meza had struck to prevent Hernán Siles Suazo, who'd won the previous month's presidential election, from taking office. Siles (president from 1956 to 1960) was a moderate leftist, but his politics meant less to the putschists than his plans to investigate the army's involvement in the nation's $500 million cocaine trade.

That the new regime was supported by Bolivia's drug barons was an open secret. (Bolivians commonly referred to the events of July as the "cocaine coup.") After closing Congress, jailing thousands of "undesirables," and killing key opponents, the junta embarked on what an army report called the "concentration of production." Small-time drug dealers and middlemen were suppressed to guarantee the profits of the top producers, who agreed to pay a tithe on their cocaine exports. The program was designed with the help of Nazi fugitive Klaus Barbie (the Gestapo's "Butcher of Lyons"), who'd advised previous Bolivian dictators.

The Carter administration immediately suspended most of its $200 million in aid to Bolivia—and despite the regime's fierce anti-Communism, even Carter's right-wing successor, Ronald Reagan, withheld his support. Opposition within Bolivia could be contained only through continued violence, spurring protests from the Catholic Church and the South American democracies. By mid-1981, the country was diplomatically isolated and nearly bankrupt. Finally, the military rebelled against García Meza, and in October 1982, Siles returned to the presidency. Already the hemisphere's second-poorest country (after Haiti) when the cocaine coup occurred, Bolivia was caught in a downward spiral that Siles proved powerless to arrest. **◂1952.M ▸1985.8**

POPULAR CULTURE

The Ewings of Southfork

7 Throughout the summer of 1980, a single burning question united much of the industrialized world: "Who shot J.R.?" Scion of a

Whodunit? J.R., a man *Time* called "a human oil slick," had plenty of enemies.

fabulously wealthy Texas oil family on television's top-ranked *Dallas*, J.R. Ewing (played by TV veteran Larry Hagman) was a catalogue of character flaws: unctuous, deceitful, cruel, avaricious. He lusted equally for money, women, and power. The March episode featuring J.R.'s shooting drew the largest TV audience of the spring season; the one in November, in which the would-be killer was unmasked (J.R.'s wife's younger sister, pregnant with his child) broke all ratings records.

At the height of its popularity, *Dallas* was broadcast in 91 countries; it stayed on the air for 14 years (from 1978 to 1991), but it belonged to the high-rolling Reagan era. All flash and glamour, the show was perfectly, playfully attuned to a culture of corporate greed. It had, uniquely, no untainted heroes: Every member of the Ewing clan and its rival, the Barneses, was (to a lesser or greater degree) corrupt. In a perverse way, the stylishly wicked J.R. was a hero for his times. **◂1971.V ▸1988.M**

FILM

A Boxer's Redemption

8 Filmmaker Martin Scorsese's passionate explorations of masculinity, violence, mortal sin, failure, and dubious success *(Mean Streets; Taxi Driver; New York, New York)* had already earned him critical reverence (if not huge box-office grosses) when, in 1980, he released what many cinema scholars consider the best film of the decade: *Raging Bull.*

Robert De Niro, Scorsese's frequent star, played Jake "the Raging Bull" LaMotta—a real-life 1940s boxing champion who resembled one of Scorsese's tortured antiheroes. With writers Paul Schrader and Mardik Martin, Scorsese turned *Raging Bull* into a tale of sin and redemption: The self-loathing, foul-mouthed LaMotta cheats on his first wife, beats his second, allies himself with the Mob, throws a fight, and alienates his loving brother; as divine punishment, he's beaten to a pulp in the ring, loses the championship and his family, and is jailed on a vice charge. Destruction, loneliness, and despair are the costs of a rampant id tempered only slightly by Catholicism. Still, suggests former seminarian Scorsese, salvation through self-knowledge is possible.

Despite that possibility, *Raging Bull* eschews *Rocky*-style uplift. Obscenities, insults, and threats pepper the dialogue. In the bloody boxing

SPORTS: Baseball: World Series, Philadelphia Phillies defeat Kansas City Royals, 4–2 ... Olympics in Lake Placid, New York (U.S. speed skater Eric Heiden wins five gold medals) and Moscow (U.S. boycotts) ... Football: Super Bowl, Pittsburgh Steelers defeat L.A. Rams, 31–19 ... Basketball: NBA, L.A. Lakers defeat Philadelphia 76ers, 4–2 ... Tennis: Björn Borg defeats John McEnroe (fifth consecutive Wimbledon title).

"If defense of human rights is subversive, then I am subversive."—**Salvadoran archbishop Oscar Romero**

sequences, the camera (Scorsese shot in black and white) does not flinch: The carnage is thrown smack into the viewer's face. De Niro's Oscar-winning performance is just as uncompromising—he trained tirelessly as a fighter, then gained 60 pounds to play the middle-aged LaMotta.

De Niro as tormented boxer Jake LaMotta.

Raging Bull did only fair business; it lost the Academy Award for Best Picture. Well into the 1990s, Scorsese had never won an Oscar. Yet he is the only working American filmmaker who can be named with such greats as Welles, Ford, Eisenstein, and Hitchcock. **◂1960.11**

EL SALVADOR

Death-Squad Terror

9 By 1980, an escalating cycle of popular protest and government repression had plunged El Salvador into full-fledged civil war. The conflict made international headlines in March, when archbishop Oscar Romero was assassinated as he celebrated mass in the capital, San Salvador. Romero was not the first Salvadoran priest killed by right-wing death squads; indeed, it was the murder of a Jesuit who worked with the poor that had moved the archbishop to become his country's leading advocate of social reform. For this, the military branded him a subversive. Romero's killer, it later emerged, had acted on orders from Roberto D'Aubuisson, the former army officer who was the founder of the right-wing National Republican Alliance (ARENA).

The Central American republic's troubles ran deep. More than 50 years of corrupt military rule had left the peasant majority more destitute than ever; a tiny minority controlled nearly half the nation's wealth. Hope had flourished in October 1979, when progressive officers staged a coup. But within three months, the oligarchy regained control of the military, and the junta's civilian members resigned in frustration. Meanwhile, reformist politician José Napolean Duarte (who'd won the presidential election in 1972 but had been barred from office by the military) returned from exile. When a new junta was announced in January 1980, he joined the government and was made president later in the year. Yet Duarte was powerless to gain civilian control of the military.

By early 1980, El Salvador's antigovernment guerrilla groups had united in the Farabundo Martí National Liberation Front. To terrorize potential FMLN supporters, government soldiers and rightist paramilitary groups began killing some 1,000 noncombatants per month. Among the victims: Salvadoran attorney general Mario Zamora (shot in his home by D'Aubuisson's operatives while meeting with Duarte—an incident that prompted Zamora's brother Rubén to become a rebel leader), and, in December, three American nuns and a lay social worker, ambushed, raped, and murdered by a death squad.

The latter episode provoked international outrage, leading the outgoing Carter administration to suspend aid to El Salvador (only to restore it a month later when FMLN rebels appeared ready to triumph). Incoming president Reagan, anxious to avoid "losing" El Salvador (as Carter had "lost" Nicaragua), backed the regime with increasing commitments of money, weapons, and military advisers. **◂1979.8 ▸1981.8**

The corpses of five Salvadoran women, tortured and shot by rightists, awaiting burial.

CHINA

Gang of Four Goes on Trial

10 With a flair befitting the B-grade movie actress she once was, 66-year-old Jiang Qing, widow of Chairman Mao and leader of China's notorious Gang of Four, took the witness stand at her 1980 trial. The charges: that she had attempted to seize power after Mao's 1976 death and was responsible for the criminal excesses of the Cultural Revolution of 1966 to 1969, the aging Mao's effort to revitalize Chinese society by unleashing the rebellious energy of the nation's youth. Positioning itself as the sole interpreter of infallible "Mao Zedong thought," the Gang of Four had presided over a national bloodletting.

Jiang Qing on the witness stand: "The victim is I," she said, "Mao's wife."

Long despised in government circles, Jiang had derived her political strength solely from Mao; with him gone, she'd soon been arrested. But Party officials faced a vexing problem: how to exorcise the ghosts of the disastrous state-sanctioned uprising without discrediting the sacrosanct Mao.

Deviating from her scripted role (she was expected to humbly accept her guilt), Jiang insisted that anything she'd done, she'd done with the full approval of the Great Helmsman himself. Calling her accusers "revisionists and criminals," Jiang remained unrepentant even as her sentence was handed down: death (later commuted to life behind bars). As to Mao's role in the Cultural Revolution, the prosecutor determined that one mistake did not negate an otherwise stellar record. **◂1976.1 ▸1984.7**

IN THE UNITED STATES

transformed it into the first station to broadcast via satellite to cable systems nationwide. With a budget of just $30 million (a quarter of what the major networks spent for one hour of news per day) and only two million subscribers, CNN was widely considered a quixotic venture. But by the mid-1990s, the network reached 62 million U.S. subscribers and 67 million more around the world. ◂1941.14 ▸1981.13

▶ABSCAM—Posing as rich Arabs, FBI agents plied members of Congress with cash in return for political favors. In February, details of the sting operation, dubbed Abscam (from "Abdul," the name of one of the phony sheikhs, and "scam"), were made public. Voters got to watch covertly filmed tapes of their lawmakers cramming cash into their pockets. Despite claims of entrapment, several legislators were convicted on criminal charges. ◂1977.M ▸1986.8

▶SCARSDALE MURDER—On March 10, Dr. Herman Tarnower, 69, author of the best-selling *Complete Scarsdale Medical Diet*, was shot to death in his suburban New York home by longtime companion Jean Harris, 56, whom Tarnower had recently jilted for a younger woman. Harris, who received an outpouring of sympathy from many women, was convicted in 1981 and sentenced to 15 years. The former girls' school headmistress became a model prisoner at Bedford Hills Correctional Facility, where she set up tutoring programs for fellow inmates. New York governor Cuomo commuted her sentence in late 1992.

▶PRYOR'S CLOSE CALL—Three-time Grammy Award–winning comedian Richard Pryor narrowly escaped death in June when the ether and cocaine he was using to freebase cocaine (a pre-crack method of smoking the drug) ignited and engulfed him in flames. Pryor, known for his raw, street-influenced live act, suffered extensive burns over his body. He staged a remarkable professional comeback; in later routines, he mercilessly lambasted his drug use.

POLITICS & BUSINESS: GNP: $2,742.1 billion ... Ronald Reagan elected president, defeating Jimmy Carter ... Draft registration for men 19 to 20 years of age established ... Department of Health, Education and Welfare becomes Department of Health and Human Services ... Depository Institutions Deregulation and Monetary Control Act establishes universal banking reserves and reforms.

"The ultimate GM coat of arms will feature a robot dressed in a kimono seated in front of a word processor."
—Chrysler executive Ben Bidwell, on GM's relationship with Japan

AROUND THE WORLD

▶PERUVIAN COMEBACK—With former U.S. first lady Rosalynn Carter and representatives of 82 other nations in attendance, Fernando Belaúnde Terry took office in August as Peru's first elected president in a dozen years. The 67-year-old former architect, who'd been ousted by the military in 1968, immediately freed political prisoners and lifted state control of newspapers and TV stations. ◂1968.7 ▸1992.8

▶SMALLPOX ERADICATED—One of medicine's oldest dreams came true in 1980, when the World Health Organization announced that small-

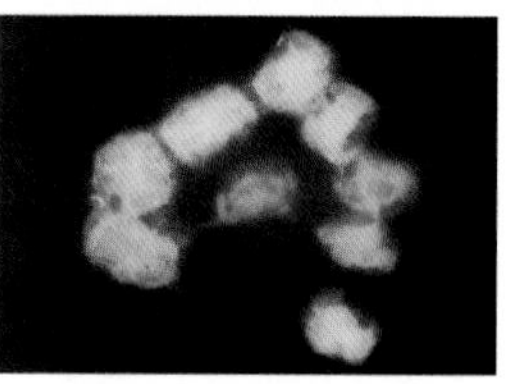

pox was no more. As recently as 1967, the virus had annually killed two million people worldwide.◂1955.1

▶ZIMBABWE'S INDEPENDENCE—After months of negotiations, white-ruled Rhodesia became black-ruled Zimbabwe in 1980. February elections, the first ever open to the black majority, delivered a landslide to Robert Mugabe's moderately Marxist Zimbabwe African National Union Party. At the guerrilla leader's swearing-in ceremony as prime minister, Britain's Prince Charles delivered papers granting the former colony its independence. ◂1979.2

▶IRAN-IRAQ WAR—Iraqi president Saddam Hussein's troops invaded western Iran in September. Hussein's motives were desire and fear: He wanted control of the oil-rich province of Khuzistan and the Shatt al-Arab waterway. And he worried that Iran's Islamic fundamentalist regime, under the Ayatollah Khomeini, would spur Iraqis to revolt. Hussein's forces soon captured the city of Khorramshahr, but Iranian resistance kept the crucial oil-refining center of Abadan out of Iraqi hands. The Ayatollah's army outnumbered Hussein's four to one, but the Iraqis had superior air power and armaments (including chemical weapons). The blood-drenched stalemate dragged on for nearly a decade. ◂1980.2 ▸1988.3

LITERATURE

A Moral Witness

11 The 1980 Nobel Prize in literature was awarded to Czeslaw Milosz, a Polish-language poet, novelist, and essayist, in recognition of his profoundly humanist meditations on freedom, consciousness, and the power of totalitarianism over the bodies and minds of its subjects. The past was a topic of which he had firsthand knowledge.

Milosz was born to ethnic Poles in Lithuania when the country was owned by the Russian empire; he went to school in Vilnius (then called Wilno, and part of Poland). Living in Paris from 1934 to 1937, he absorbed the aesthetic and political ideas of the city's avant-garde circles. For Milosz, a socialist, writing was always a political act. His early works (accurately) forecast imminent international cataclysm, winning him recognition as the leader of Poland's cutting-edge Catastrophist school of poetry. When the war came, Milosz devoted his energies to the Warsaw underground, fighting the occupying Nazis and clandestinely publishing such poems of resistance as "Invincible Song."

After the war, Milosz served Poland's new Communist government as a cultural attaché, but in 1951, disillusioned with the regime, he defected to Paris. He came to the attention of the West with the publication in 1953 of *The Captive Mind*, a collection of essays examining and condemning the willingness of Polish intellectuals to submit to the Communist system. In 1960, he emigrated to the United States, where he continued to ponder human frailty, cruelty, and corruptibility in poems that were classical in style and near-biblical in their moral force. **◂1979.13**

BUSINESS AND INDUSTRY

Reversal of Fortune

13 In January 1980, President Carter signed the controversial Chrysler Loan Guarantee bill, a $1.5 billion bailout of the Chrysler Corporation, America's 17th-largest company. The government's unprecedented aid package came in the wake of Chrysler's having posted a quarterly loss of $207 million the previous year, and underscored America's declining industrial fortunes: From cars and electronics to steel and clothing, goods the United States had once sold to the world, the world was now selling to the United States.

The reversal was most evident in the U.S. automobile industry, long one of the most visible indices of the nation's economic health. ("What's good for the country is good for General Motors, and what's good for General Motors is good for the country," a GM president had observed in 1952.) A host of factors during the 1970s—recession, expensive labor, the energy crisis, the deteriorating quality of American cars, the increased reliability of fuel-efficient Japanese compacts—had been devastating. The Reagan administration tried to turn things around by asking Japan to restrict its exports to the United States. Japanese automakers responded by building factories in the United States; American manufacturers looking for cheap labor expanded their operations overseas.

CAR PRODUCTION, JAPAN VS. U.S.

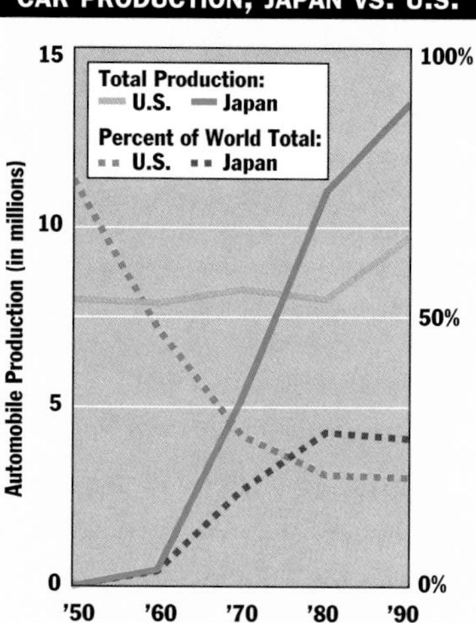

By the mid-1970s Japan had surpassed the U.S. both in production and in market share.

Guided by its brash chairman, Lee Iacocca, Chrysler posted a first-quarter profit of $705 million in 1984 and paid off the government loan—a process that turned Iacocca (whose 1984 autobiography sold six million copies) into an unlikely folk hero. American manufacturing in general appeared to be on the upswing. But during the 1980s, many corporations (including Chrysler) relied on layoffs and wage cutbacks to turn profits, and American workers suffered their first standard-of-living decline since World War II. Meanwhile, the "lean and mean" corporate trend failed to ameliorate the country's trade deficit, which ballooned from $19.7 billion in 1980 to $119.8 billion in 1989. **◂1979.12**

BRAZIL

Gold Rush in the Amazon

12 Gold fever struck Brazil in January, when a rancher discovered the precious mineral on his property deep in the Amazon jungle. Some 25,000 prospectors descended on the area with picks and shovels, hacking out a man-made canyon under the merciless sun. After shoot-outs erupted in the mining camp, the federal government arrived to keep order and buy whatever the *garimpeiros* dug up. By year's end, the site had yielded more than $50 million worth of nuggets, transformed destitute men into moguls, and provided desperately needed capital to a country whose foreign debt was the largest in the developing world. The bonanza's impact on the fragile rain-forest ecosystem, however, was less benign. ◂1964.M ▸1988.6

NOBEL PRIZES: Peace: Adolfo Pérez Esquivel (Argentine; human rights) ... Literature: Czeslaw Milosz (Polish-U.S.; writer) ... Chemistry: P. Berg, W. Gilbert, and F. Sanger (U.S., U.S., U.K.; DNA structure) ... Medicine: B. Benacerraf, G. Snell, and J. Dausset (U.S., U.S., French; immunology) ... Physics: James Cronin and Val Fitch (U.S.; neutral kaon decay) ... Economics: Lawrence Klein (U.S.).

A VOICE FROM 1980

Lennon's Last Musings

From John Lennon's final interview, conducted by Jonathan Cott, December 5, 1980

For five years, John Lennon, the sardonic wit of the Beatles, had been in retirement—holed up, playing "househusband" (his word) with his wife, Yoko Ono, and their son, Sean, in the family's sprawling residence in New York City's venerable Dakota apartment building. But now Sean was five and Lennon, sixties youth rebel, pop sage, and peace activist, was 40 and feeling renewed. He released the record album Double Fantasy, *a collaboration with Ono, and began talking to the press again. On December 5, 1980, journalist Jonathan Cott interviewed Lennon for* Rolling Stone *magazine and found a contented man who rhetorically asked, "What's so funny about love, peace, and understanding?"*

Lennon had recently spoken of "another 40 years of productivity to go." He had but three days: On the evening of December 8, as Lennon and Ono returned home from a recording session, a psychotic fan named Mark David Chapman (who'd once worshiped Lennon but was now convinced his hero had become a wealthy sellout) ambushed them outside the Dakota and shot Lennon to death. The violent death of "a person who devoted his music to the struggle against violence" (as Pravda *put it) generated shock and revulsion around the world. Heads of state expressed sorrow; mourners gathered by the thousands to keep spontaneous vigils. In January,* Rolling Stone *published Lennon's final interview, excerpted below.* **◂1970.M**

People are always judging you, or criticizing what you're trying to say on one little album, on one little song, but to me it's a lifetime's work. From the boyhood paintings and poetry to when I die—it's all part of one big production. And I don't have to announce that this album is part of a larger work; if it isn't obvious, then forget it....

If you look inside the new album's logo—which all the kids have done already all over the world, from Brazil to Australia to Poland, anywhere that gets the record—inside is written: ONE WORLD, ONE PEOPLE....

I get truly affected by letters from Brazil or Poland or Austria—places I'm not conscious of all the time—just to know somebody is there, listening. One kid living up in Yorkshire wrote this heartfelt letter about being both Oriental and English and identifying with John and Yoko. The odd kid in the class. There are a lot of those kids who identify with us. They don't need the history of rock & roll. They identify with us as a couple, a biracial couple, who stand for love, peace, feminism and the positive things of the world.

You know, give peace a chance, not shoot people for peace. All we need is love. I believe it, it's damn hard, but I absolutely believe it. We're not the first to say, "Imagine no countries" or "Give peace a chance," but we're carrying that torch, like the Olympic torch, passing it from hand to hand, to each other, to each country, to each generation. That's our job. We have to conceive of an idea before we can do it.

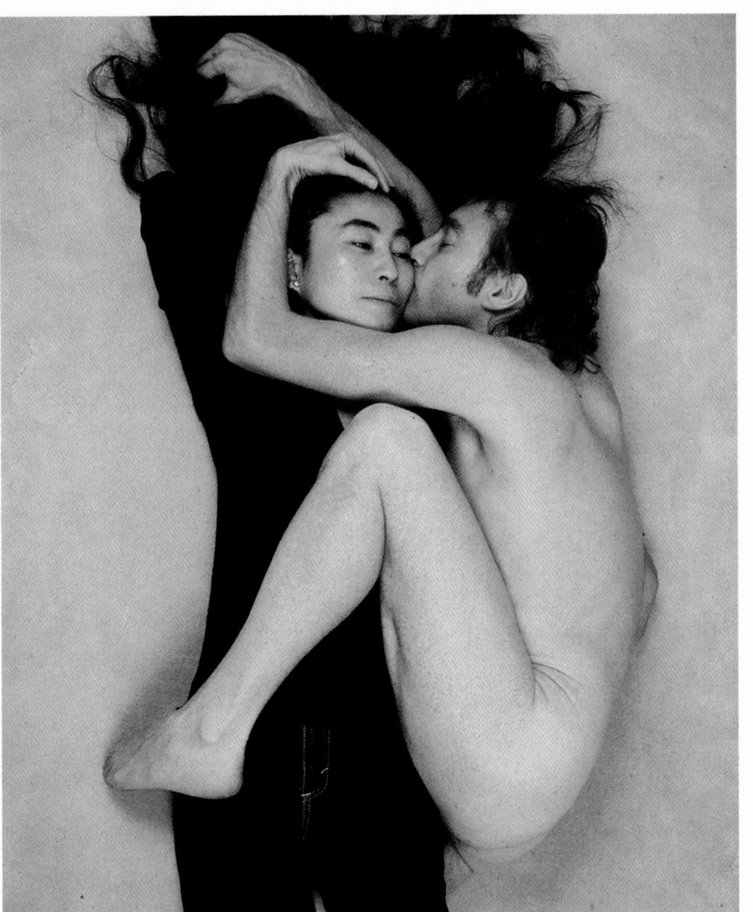

Photographer Annie Leibovitz snapped Lennon and Ono at home for the cover of *Rolling Stone* magazine just hours before Lennon was murdered. "You've captured our relationship exactly," he told Leibovitz when he saw the test Polaroids.

I've never claimed divinity. I've never claimed purity of soul. I've never claimed to have the answer to life. I only put out songs and answer questions as honestly as I can, but *only* as honestly as I can, no more, no less. I cannot live up to other people's expectations of me, because they're illusionary. And the people who want more than I am, or than Bob Dylan is, or than Mick Jagger is....

Take Mick, for instance. Mick's put out consistently good work for twenty years, and will they give him a break? Will they ever say, "Look at him, he's number one, he's thirty-six, and he's put out a beautiful song, 'Emotional Rescue,' it's up there." I enjoyed it, lots of people enjoyed it. So it goes up and down, up and down. God help Bruce Springsteen when they decide he's no longer God. I haven't seen him—I'm not a great "in" person watcher—but I've heard such good things about him. Right now his fans are happy; he's told them about being drunk and chasing girls and cars and everything, and that's about the level they enjoy. But when he gets down to facing his own success and growing older and having to produce it again and again, they'll turn on him, and I hope he survives it. All he has to do is look at me and Mick.... I cannot be a punk in Hamburg and Liverpool anymore. I'm older now, I see the world through different eyes. I still believe in love, peace and understanding, as Elvis Costello said, and what's so funny about love, peace and understanding?

"This is a very, very dramatic illness. I think we can say quite assuredly that it is new."—**Dr. James Curran, head of the venereal disease department (later the AIDS task force) at Centers for Disease Control in Atlanta, Georgia, in 1981**

STORY OF THE YEAR

A New Plague

1 The official announcement of what would become the AIDS epidemic appeared on June 5, 1981, when the *Morbidity and Mortality Weekly Report* (published by the U.S. government's Centers for Disease Control) reported five cases of *Pneumocystis carinii* pneumonia—usually seen only in newborns or in adults receiving immunosuppressive drugs—among homosexual men in Los Angeles hospitals. A month later, *The New York Times* reported that 41 mostly young gay men (including two in Denmark) had contracted Kaposi's sarcoma, a rare skin cancer that normally affected only older whites or young Africans. Ordinarily, the disease was not fatal, yet it had quickly killed eight of the homosexuals. Since cancer is not contagious, the outbreak baffled doctors.

HIV (blue) attacks a T-4 lymphocyte white blood cell, magnified under an electronic microscope. The virus was not proved to cause AIDS until 1984.

Soon, gay men began turning up with a host of other exotic illnesses and opportunistic infections indicative of failing immune systems; tests showed their T-lymphocytes (blood cells that battle infection) to be severely impaired. The underlying ailment was initially labeled gay-related immunodeficiency (GRID), but within a year, as it appeared with growing frequency among other groups—intravenous drug users, female prostitutes, blood-transfusion recipients, heterosexual Haitians and Africans—many researchers had switched to a broader term: acquired immunodeficiency syndrome (AIDS).

By December 1982, nearly 1,600 cases had been reported throughout the world—750 in America, 100-odd in Europe, and most of the rest in Africa. The incidence of AIDS was doubling every six months; nearly half the patients diagnosed since the disease was first discovered had died. (By 1994, AIDS had struck an estimated three million people worldwide.) The microbe responsible was still unknown. Scientists had determined that the infection—which could have a latency period of several years—was transmitted through blood or semen, but beyond that, little was known.

In the Western nations, long-standing prejudices, especially against gays, were exacerbated, leading to heightened discrimination. Fears about contaminated blood supplies began to proliferate. For homosexuals, who'd just begun to reap the rewards of a decade-old movement for equal rights, AIDS was both an existential tragedy and a political challenge. And for people of all sexual persuasions, the incurable disease cast a deadly shadow on their erotic lives. **►1984.5**

THE MIDDLE EAST

A Violent Peace

2 By 1981—three years after Israel's Menachem Begin and Egypt's Anwar al-Sadat signed the U.S.-brokered Camp David Accords—tensions between Israel and its other neighbors were at a breaking point. Egypt was in turmoil. And America's new president could find no way to prevent the nominal peace from turning violent.

The Camp David pact had aimed to prevent another major war against Israel by neutralizing Egypt, the most powerful Arab country. But in Begin's view, Israel remained vulnerable. One worry was that Iraqi dictator Saddam Hussein, who hoped to emerge as the top Arab leader, would develop atomic weapons. In June, Begin ordered the bombing of an almost-completed Iraqi nuclear reactor. Washington slapped Israel's wrist by withholding a shipment of fighter planes, but lifted the embargo three months later. Meanwhile, in retaliation for Palestinian guerrilla attacks, Israel bombed PLO headquarters in Beirut. The air strike (by U.S.-supplied planes) killed 300. Begin further riled the Arabs—and Israel's backers—by continuing to encourage Jewish settlement in the West Bank and the Gaza Strip, despite Camp David clauses promising eventual autonomy for those occupied territories.

Sadat, who'd been ostracized by the Arab nations after Camp David, was in trouble at home as well. Many Egyptians were offended by his "betrayal" of the Palestinians, and his steps toward democratization had not made up for widening economic inequalities. In September, amid growing unrest, he arrested 1,300 opposition leaders. And in October, as he watched a military parade, he was assassinated by radical Muslim fundamentalists.

Sadat's vice president, Hosni Mubarak, pledged to continue the Camp David process and to broaden Sadat's reforms. But when Begin pushed a bill through the Knesset that virtually annexed Syria's Golan Heights (occupied by Israel since the 1967 Six Day War), Egypt joined the Arab world—and the United States—in condemning the move.

Undaunted, Begin soon launched a new war. **◄1978.3 ►1982.2**

A month after cracking down on his opposition, Sadat met a bloody death at the hands of Muslim fundamentalists who saw his pro-Western stance as traitorous.

THE MIDDLE EAST

Reagan Versus Qaddafi

3 Libyan strongman Muammar al-Qaddafi was a flamboyant demagogue whose regime supported insurrectionist groups from the IRA to the PLO, whose agents murdered dissident Libyans abroad, and whose regional ambitions frightened his neighbors. Even the Soviets backed him only reluctantly. During the Carter presidency, the United States had expelled some Libyan diplomats after a mob burned the U.S. embassy in Tripoli, but avoided sharper conflict with its third-largest oil supplier. But in 1981, when Ronald Reagan moved into the White House, a worldwide oil glut allowed Washington to up the ante.

Reagan increased military aid to nations bordering Libya, approved

ART & CULTURE: Books: *Midnight's Children* (Salman Rushdie); *The Hotel New Hampshire* (John Irving); *July's People* (Nadine Gordimer); *Rabbit Is Rich* (John Updike); *Chronicle of a Death Foretold* (Gabriel García Márquez) ... Music: "Rapture" (Blondie); *Ghost in the Machine* (The Police, LP); *Face Value* (Phil Collins, LP); *Ballade* (George Perle); *Quaint Events* (David Del Tredici) ... Painting & Sculpture:

"They have the same giggly sense of humor, and they both love ballet and opera and sport in all forms. It's perfect, and they are both over the moon about it."—**Lady Sarah McCorquodale, on the engagement of her sister Diana to Prince Charles**

a CIA destabilization plan, and ousted Libya's remaining envoys. In August, he sent the Sixth Fleet on maneuvers in the Gulf of Sidra—a huge waterway claimed by Qaddafi though no other country recognized Libya's ownership. After two Libyan planes were shot down while attacking the U.S. fleet's fighter escorts, Qaddafi allegedly tried to kill U.S. diplomats in Paris and Rome. And in December, the White House claimed that Libyan "hit squads" had been sent to assassinate Reagan and other top officials.

That month, the giant Exxon oil company pulled out of Libya, and Reagan urged all remaining Americans to leave. In March 1982, Washington announced a boycott of Libyan oil. By then, Reagan could claim one major concession from Qaddafi: Libya had withdrawn its troops from Chad, where they'd been intervening in a civil war. (In fact, the pullout was probably dictated more by financial strain resulting from a saturated oil market than by U.S. pressure.) But the war of nerves between the two leaders was just beginning. **◂1969.M ▸1986.6**

GREAT BRITAIN

A Fairy-Tale Wedding

4 Though the sun had long ago set on the British empire, a British royal wedding had never before drawn so enormous an audience. In July 1981, when His Highness Charles Philip Arthur George, the 32-year-old prince of Wales (and heir to the throne), married the Lady Diana Frances Spencer, a 19-year-old kindergarten teacher (and his distant cousin), 750 million people around the globe watched the event on television. A million merrymakers lined the route to St. Paul's Cathedral in London, where the nuptials were held, many having camped all night to secure a spot.

Most Britons were glad to forget, however briefly, a severe recession that was spurring nightly riots by unemployed youths. And there was no shortage of opulent distraction surrounding the wedding. The procession to St. Paul's featured the crowned and uncrowned chiefs of many nations, as well as gilded carriages, plumed horses, and guardsmen in archaic finery.

As crowds below Buckingham Palace cheered, the newlyweds kissed on a balcony.

Charles and Di (as they were immortalized on souvenir plates, T-shirts, and teapots) were married by Dr. Robert Runcie, archbishop of Canterbury. The flustered bride—in silk taffeta, old lace, a 25-foot train, and a veil embroidered with 10,000 mother-of-pearl sequins—reversed the groom's first and second names when reciting the vows. Nonetheless, Dr. Runcie pronounced the couple man and wife. "Here," he ventured, "is the stuff of which fairy tales are made."

A decade and two children later, the fairy tale had turned into a bitter farce—played out, like the wedding itself, before a rapt worldwide audience. **◂1952.1 ▸1992.11**

SPAIN

A Bungled Coup

5 Spain's young democracy faced a frightening test in 1981, when rightists attempting a coup took its leaders hostage. On February 23, 200 men of the Guardia Civil (army-affiliated security police) invaded Parliament, some firing at the ceiling. When outgoing premier Adolfo Suárez rose to scold them, a trooper shouted, "Sit down, pig!" and loosed another round. Suárez remained standing—as a TV news camera recorded the scene.

Led by Lieutenant Colonel Antonio Tejero Molina (who'd been imprisoned for a previous coup plot), the attackers were backed by members of the old Francoist oligarchy and several generals. One conspirator, the commander of Valencia province, declared his region under martial law; his officers seized control of a few towns. The plotters apparently assumed that King Juan Carlos, dogged by Basque terrorism and a fractious legislature, would side with them. But when a military aide—another conspirator—informed the King of the ongoing putsch, Juan Carlos responded: "They'll have to put two bullets in me before they take over."

Outgoing premier Suárez *(on stairs)* would not buckle to the putschists who burst into Parliament. Neither would Juan Carlos.

The King phoned Spain's other regional commanders to ensure their support. Then, dressed in his commander-in-chief's uniform, he warned on national television that he would resist any attempt "to interrupt the democratic process by force." The next day, with loyal army and Guardia units surrounding the Parliament chamber, Tejero surrendered. His coconspirators were arrested soon afterward. At week's end, millions of Spaniards marched in support of democracy.

The episode so impressed the Western powers that they invited Spain to join NATO. (The nation had been excluded while Franco ruled.) And it persuaded Pablo Picasso's heirs that the artist's great protest painting *Guernica* (long exiled in New York) could now be returned to Spain. **◂1975.1**

DEATHS

Roger Baldwin, U.S. civil rights activist.

Samuel Barber, U.S. composer.

Alfred H. Barr, Jr., U.S. art historian.

Karl Böhm, Austrian conductor.

Omar Nelson Bradley, U.S. general.

Marcel Breuer, Hungarian-U.S. furniture designer and architect.

Harry Chapin, U.S. musician.

Hoagy Carmichael, U.S. musician and composer.

Paddy Chayefsky, U.S. writer.

Jonathan Worth Daniels, U.S. editor and writer.

Will Durant, U.S. historian.

Moshe Dayan, Israeli military and political leader.

Ella Grasso, U.S. governor.

Bill Haley, U.S. musician.

William Holden, U.S. actor.

Hans Krebs, German-U.K. biochemist.

Joe Louis, U.S. boxer.

Bob Marley, Jamaican musician and composer.

Anwar al-Sadat, Egyptian president.

William Saroyan, U.S. writer.

Albert Speer, German Nazi official and architect.

Harold Clayton Urey, U.S. chemist.

Dewitt Wallace, U.S. publisher.

Natalie Wood, U.S. actress.

William Wyler, German-U.S. filmmaker.

Stefan Wyszynski, Polish Roman Catholic cardinal.

***Football Player* (Duane Hanson); *Seventh Sister* (Robert Moskowitz); *The Sea* (Julian Schnabel) ... Film: *Chariots of Fire* (Hugh Hudson); *Reds* (Warren Beatty); *Raiders of the Lost Ark* (Steven Spielberg); *Mephisto* (István Szabó) ... Theater: *Amadeus* (Peter Shaffer); *Crimes of the Heart* (Beth Henley); *Torch Song Trilogy* (Harvey Fierstein); *Cats* (Andrew Lloyd Webber) ... TV: *Dynasty*; *Hill Street Blues*.**

"My intention is to convince, not to defeat. There was only one victor on May 10—hope. May it become the best-shared asset in France."—**François Mitterrand, in his inaugural address**

NEW IN 1981

TGV train (Paris to Lyon).

Pac-Man video game.

Mexican-American mayor of major U.S. city (Henry Cisneros of San Antonio, Texas).

Legal divorce in Spain.

IN THE UNITED STATES

▶WOMAN ON THE TOP BENCH—Sandra Day O'Connor, an Arizona appellate court judge, was confirmed by the Senate on September 21 as a replacement on the Supreme Court for retiring justice Potter Stewart. A surprise Reagan nominee, O'Connor became the first woman to serve on the nation's highest court. She went on to build a moderately conservative record.

▶REAGAN SHOT—On March 30, just over two months after being sworn in as president, Ronald Reagan was shot in the chest by John Hinckley, Jr., as he left a Washington hotel. Also wounded in the assassination attempt were

press secretary James Brady (who suffered permanent brain damage and became, along with his wife, a vocal advocate for handgun control), a Secret Service agent, and a police officer. Reagan, who made a quick recovery, won massive public support for the way he handled the ordeal: with quips and winks. ("Honey, I forgot to duck!" he joked to wife Nancy.) Hinckley, who offered the shooting as a twisted tribute to actress Jodie Foster, was acquitted by reason of insanity. In a footnote to the incident, hyperaggressive Secretary of State Alexander Haig made waves by proclaiming, "I am in control here," after Reagan was rushed to the hospital. **◂1980.4 ▸1981.M**

POLAND

Solidarity Is Crushed

6 From the early days in the shipyards of Gdansk, when striking workers kneeled to confess to sympathetic Catholic priests (despite official atheism, religion remained a central force in Polish life), the union movement known as Solidarity had grown into a revolution. It was a genuine workers' uprising against a so-called workers' state, and it brought Poland 17 months of giddy liberty. But on the night of December 12, 1981, the government of General Wojciech Jaruzelski cracked down.

Phone lines went dead. Tanks rolled into the streets. Troops battled coal miners, killing at least seven. Police arrested thousands of union leaders. Lech Walesa was taken at 3 AM; he would remain in prison for more than a year. The next morning, Jaruzelski came on the radio and, "with a broken heart," proclaimed martial law. "Our country is on the edge of the abyss," he warned. Neither he nor the 100,000 Soviet troops massed at the border would brook further challenge.

A career military man, Jaruzelski had been appointed premier in February 1981. His predecessors, bowing to 500,000 labor strikers, had legalized Solidarity, loosened restrictions on travel and free expression, and, tellingly, allowed Catholic mass to be broadcast. But industrial production had continued to tumble, wildcat strikes had broken out, and Solidarity had called on workers elsewhere in the Soviet bloc to form their own independent unions. Jaruzelski's mission was mandated by Moscow: Restore order.

In November the general met with Walesa and Archbishop Jozef Glemp, spiritual leader of Poland's 30 million Catholics; Jaruzelski spoke of reconciliation and offered to negotiate. But as talks lagged, the ten-million-member union grew impatient. Over Walesa's protest, Solidarity leaders called for a national referendum to abolish Communism. It was the final provocation: The army moved within hours. Martial law was not lifted until 1983, the year Walesa received the Nobel Prize for peace. **◂1980.1 ▸1989.1**

A photograph smuggled out of Poland captures Warsaw's postcrackdown military mood.

FRANCE

Socialist Victory

7 François Mitterrand's triumph over Valéry Giscard d'Estaing in the 1981 presidential race (and his party's subsequent sweep of parliamentary elections) owed much to the incumbent's bad luck—a worldwide recession was sapping the French economy—and to the challenger's improved TV image. But it stemmed primarily from Mitterrand's patient rebuilding of the Socialist Party. France's first Socialist president had been an anti-Gaullist since 1958 but a Socialist only since 1971, when he'd also become party chief. That year, the Socialists hit bottom, representing only 5 percent of the electorate. Mitterrand made common cause with the stronger Communists (despite his outspoken criticism of Moscow), then began usurping their base and wooing center-leftists. Ten years later, the Socialists were France's biggest party, and 52 percent of voters chose Mitterrand to run the country.

During his first year in office, the new President nationalized a dozen major concerns. (Much of French industry had been state run for decades.) He raised taxes and the minimum wage, shortened the work week to 39 hours, added a fifth week of mandatory vacation, and created thousands of public-sector jobs. Flouting Marxist convention, he decentralized many government functions. But the recession soon forced him to impose an austerity program. He turned increasingly to free-market economics; the Communists abandoned him, and his popularity plunged.

Mitterrand campaigning in Nantes.

In 1986, the left lost its majority in Parliament, and Mitterrand was forced to "cohabit" with a neo-Gaullist premier, Jacques Chirac. But economic downturns could now be blamed on the rightists, and good news—improved social security, slowing crime rates—credited to Socialist reforms. Mitterrand was reelected by a solid margin in 1988, and the Socialists regained control of Parliament and the ministries. But a new shadow loomed on the far right: The anti-immigrant National Front had captured 35 seats. **◂1976.14 ▸1993.8**

EL SALVADOR

Massacre at El Mozote

8 El Mozote was not a guerrilla stronghold. Most residents of the village were evangelical Christians; if they supported anyone in El Salvador's civil war, it was the military-dominated government and not the leftist rebels of the Farabundo Martí National Liberation Front (FMLN). But El Mozote lay within the remote department of Morazán, which was held by the insurgents. Such "red zones" were subject to ruthless search-and-destroy missions by government troops. (Indeed, most of those killed in the war were civilians, victims of such missions or of right-wing death squads.) In 1981, the U.S.-trained-and-financed army launched a scorched-earth campaign in Morazán. In the process it liquidated El Mozote and nearby hamlets, committing the worst

SPORTS: Baseball: World Series, Los Angeles Dodgers (Fernando Valenzuela) defeat New York Yankees, 4–2 ... Football: Super Bowl, Oakland Raiders defeat Philadelphia Eagles, 27–10 ... Basketball: NBA, Boston Celtics defeat Houston Rockets, 4–2 ... Tennis: John McEnroe wins first Wimbledon ... Auto Racing: Bobby Unser announced winner of Indianapolis 500 (after settlement of rule-breaking dispute).

"Everything was dead there—animals and people all mixed together. Vultures were everywhere. You couldn't stand to be there, because of the stink."—**A Salvadoran army guide, describing a village near El Mozote after the massacre**

massacre of the war.

Directed by Lieutenant Colonel Domingo Monterossa, El Salvador's leading antiguerrilla fighter, the troops stormed into El Mozote in early December. After interrogating villagers, soldiers separated them by age and sex. They decapitated many male prisoners with machetes, and shot the rest. Women and girls were raped before being murdered. Soon only children were left. Commandos opened fire through the windows and doors of the houses where the children were being held, then burned down the buildings. The slaughter lasted all day; when it was over, El Mozote no longer existed.

A woman named Rufina Amaya Márquez escaped the savagery, and by January 1982 her story had made front-page news in the United States. But the U.S. government, which was pumping hundreds of millions of dollars into El Salvador, denied Amaya's report; there would be no serious investigation of the atrocities until 1991, when a Salvadoran court published the names of 794 victims. Forensic scientists excavated the village, unearthing hundreds of U.S.-made M16 cartridges scattered among the skeletons. **◂1980.9 ▸1984.M**

The horror of the El Mozote massacre, recorded by photographer Susan Meiselas, one of the first journalists to view the site.

NORTHERN IRELAND

A Martyr Is Born

9 Although most Irish Catholics agreed with the goals of the underground Irish Republican Army—independence of Catholic-minority Northern Ireland from British rule and unification with the Catholic-majority Republic of Ireland to the south—few could countenance the IRA's tactics: bombings and shootings that killed more private citizens than Protestant paramilitary rivals or British Army soldiers. In 1981 an incarcerated IRA commando attempted to change his guerrilla army's image. By starving himself to death in a British-run prison on Northern Irish soil, Bobby Sands gave the IRA a genuine martyr.

Sands undertook his 66-day hunger strike to win prisoner-of-war status for jailed IRA members, whom the British government maintained were ordinary, if particularly violent, criminals. The policy dated to 1976, when Britain abolished a "special-category" classification for prisoners convicted of political crimes. In September of that year, IRA members in Belfast's Maze prison exchanged prison garb for rough blankets and smeared their cells with excrement. The "dirty strike" failed to win concessions, as did a subsequent aborted hunger strike. Sands decided to go all the way.

On the 40th day of his fast, Sands was elected to the British Parliament by a largely Catholic ward of Northern Ireland. When he died 26 days later, on May 5—the first of ten hunger strikers to succumb—his apotheosis as hero was complete. To many who'd seen only the terrorist's mask, the IRA now had a human face: the drawn visage of a 27-year-old rebel, prematurely dead. "He chose to take his own life," said an unimpressed Prime Minister Thatcher. "It was a choice that his organization did not allow to any of their victims." **◂1979.6 ▸1994.4**

After Sands's funeral, mourners gathered at the gravesite in Belfast's Milltown Cemetery.

BUSINESS AND INDUSTRY

Computers Get Personal

10 The market for personal computers came of age in 1981, when IBM introduced its model: the PC. Other manufacturers had been selling desktop computers since 1977—but IBM, the world's biggest maker of data-processing machines, had a competitive advantage: Its size allowed it not only to build a comparable product, but to market it much more aggressively. In 1981, 25,000 units sold; three years later, the figure had soared to three million.

At the core of the IBM PC was a microprocessor made by the Intel Corporation of Santa Clara, California, and an operating system—the program that facilitates the running of other programs (known to the initiated as "software")—licensed to IBM by the Seattle-based Microsoft. In a fateful oversight, IBM did not prevent Intel or Microsoft from selling those products to other manufacturers. Soon, a horde of IBM-like "clones" was crowding the market, all based on the Intel chip and MS-DOS (the Microsoft Disk Operating System).

By the mid-1990s, nearly 90 percent of the world's personal computers were either IBMs or clones—and an industry once full of eccentric technologies had been almost completely standardized. IBM, thanks partly to the knockoffs, was in deep financial trouble; Intel was the world's largest chip manufacturer; and Microsoft wunderkind Bill Gates (who was born in 1955) was one of the world's richest men. **◂1976.M ▸1984.12**

One of the first IBM PCs, the PC/AT.

IN THE UNITED STATES

▶MEDFLY CRISIS—Its $14-billion agriculture industry menaced by a Mediterranean fruit fly infestation, the state of California adopted emergency measures in July. After the federal government threatened a statewide produce quarantine, Governor Edmund G. ("Jerry") Brown resorted to aerial spraying of the pesticide malathion (developed as a nerve gas during World War II)—to environmentalists', and Brown's own, chagrin. But it did control the outbreak. The U.S. Agricultural Research Service had been suppressing the medfly population by periodically releasing millions of sterile male flies, which mated with the females and interrupted the reproductive cycle. A batch of such males introduced to California the month before had apparently contained hundreds of thousands of fertile insects.

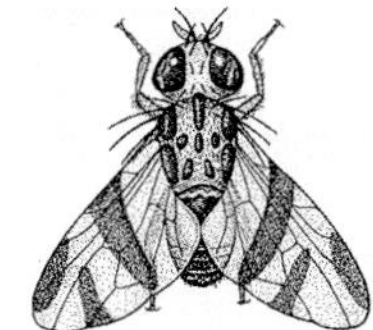

▶PATCO SHUT DOWN—The nation's 13,000 air traffic controllers got a taste of President Reagan's tough anti-union stance on August 3, when they went on strike for a $10,000 a year raise and a four-day workweek. Reagan, himself a former union leader (he headed up the Screen Actors Guild in the forties and fifties), ordered them back to work by August 5; when most stayed out, Reagan fired them. Within two weeks the FAA was interviewing new applicants to fill the jobs. In October, the air traffic controllers' union, PATCO, was decertified and shortly thereafter went bankrupt. The Reagan years were hard on labor: During the 1980s, the number of major U.S. strikes per year fell to about 50 (compared with several hundred during the mid-1970s). Union membership dropped sharply, and most labor leaders switched from their traditional concerns—wages and benefits—to concentrating on keeping union jobs within their industries. ◂1980.4

POLITICS & BUSINESS: GNP: $3,063.8 billion ... Prime rate reaches 20.5% (highest since Civil War) ... Supreme Court upholds constitutionality of religious services held by student organizations at public universities ... Du Pont buys Conoco for $7.54 billion (biggest industrial merger to date) ... U.S. agrees to sell an $8.5 billion air defense package to Saudi Arabia.

"What a way to come to California!"—**Captain Robert L. Crippen, after landing the space shuttle *Columbia* at Edwards Air Force Base**

AROUND THE WORLD

▶GREEK SOCIALIST—Andreas Papandreou, son of former Greek prime minister Georgios Papandreou and a onetime American citizen, was elected Greece's first socialist prime minister in 1981. Papandreou championed economic reform and resistance to American military presence—two causes that did not endear him to his former homeland's government. Health problems and a messy, scandal-ridden divorce brought about his resignation eight years later. ◂1974.5

▶INDEPENDENT BELIZE—In September, the Central American country of Belize, formerly British Honduras, became the last British colony on the American mainland to achieve full independence. With it came challenges: Neighboring Guatemala, a former Spanish colony that had long claimed Belize as its own, threatened to invade; it finally recognized independent Belize in 1991.

▶FASHION'S NEW WAVE—Japanese fashion designer Rei Kawakubo of Comme des Garçons showed her collection in Paris for the first time in 1981. Her lively, iconoclastic crea-

tions *(above)* put her at the forefront of the Japanese "new wave" of designers—including Issey Miyake, Yohji Yamamoto, and Mitsuhiro Matsuda—whose characteristic loose-fitting and colorless clothes of unorthodox material transformed Tokyo into a world fashion center during the 1980s.

▶POPE SHOT—On May 13, in Rome's St. Peter's Square, Mehmet Ali Ağca, a member of an extreme right-wing Turkish terrorist organization, ambushed 60-year-old Pope John Paul II with two pistol shots at close range. The pontiff fully recovered after 5½-hour emergency surgery. Ağca was arrested, tried, and sentenced to life in prison (where the forgiving John Paul II visited him two years later). Investigators suspected but never proved the involvement of Bulgarian and possibly Soviet agents in the attempt on the Pope's life.

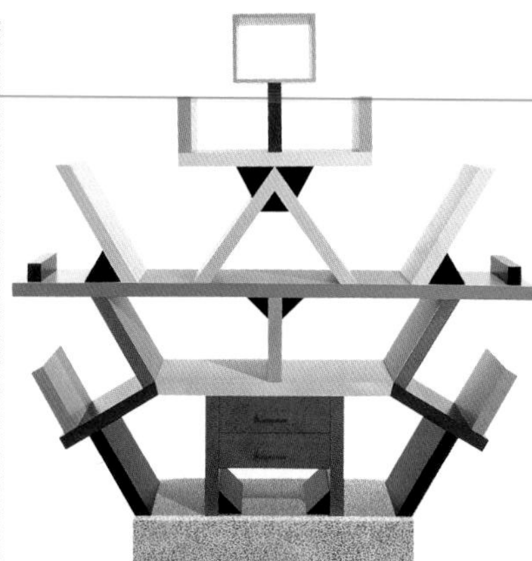

Memphis founder Ettore Sottsass's playful, multi-colored *Carlton* room divider epitomized Italian design's "new wave."

POPULAR CULTURE

The Look of the Eighties

11 The Milan-based design group Memphis, a consortium of international designers, stole the 1981 Milan furniture fair (officially named the Salone internazionale del Mobile) with whimsical, brightly colored, loudly patterned pieces of furniture inspired by 1950s suburban kitsch, 1960s pop art, and contemporary notions of glamour. Founded by influential Austrian-Italian designer Ettore Sottsass, Memphis self-consciously rejected conventional good taste for gaudy fun. Sottsass's *Carlton* room divider (many Memphis pieces were named for hotels), for example, was made of wood covered in outrageous purple, yellow, green, and red plastic laminate and had bookshelves that were interrupted by eccentrically angled partitions—books were forced to slant. Driven by a spirit of contradiction, Memphis designers built tables balanced on bowling-ball legs and rolling tubular-steel-and-glass carts that appeared about to collapse.

Memphis—its 30 or so members came from eight different countries and designed fabric, ceramics, and glass as well as furniture—sought to break the strict principles of "serious" modernist design: regularity, utility, avoidance of ornamentation. Inspired by Bob Dylan's song "Stuck Inside of Mobile with the Memphis Blues Again," Sottsass chose the name Memphis "because it had so many different associations—with Elvis, with ancient Egypt—with contradictory places and cultures." The group became the best-known and most widely imitated of the 1980s Italian "new wave" design schools. **◂1962.8**

EXPLORATION

A Reusable Space Vessel

12 When the space shuttle *Columbia* blasted off from Cape Canaveral, Florida, in April 1981, it was the first American manned flight since the Apollo-Soyuz mission six years earlier. Begun in 1972 and costing almost $10 billion, the shuttle had been plagued by glitches and delays—but in the wake of a decade of national humiliations, the launch was proof to Americans that their country could still do great things.

Cost overruns notwithstanding, the shuttle also reflected a new emphasis on practicality in an era of budget cuts. The 122-foot craft was the first reusable space vessel—built to go up like a rocket, cruise like a spaceship, and land like a glider. After liftoff, the two solid-fuel booster rockets were jettisoned over the ocean to be retrieved for future flights. The craft's surface was covered with 31,000 ceramic tiles, which—unlike earlier heat shields—would not burn off during the 3,000°F heat of reentry. The craft was designed to carry satellites into space and to permit astronauts to pull alongside orbiting satellites to make repairs. Even the ground-control setup was streamlined: Launching an Apollo mission had taken 500 people, but computers allowed the shuttle to be lofted by just 150.

Onboard computers piloted the craft, as well; astronauts John Young, 50 (an Apollo veteran), and Captain Robert Crippen, 44, were on hand essentially to monitor the equipment. After two days in space, the pair became the first U.S. astronauts to land on earth instead of at sea, swooping onto the Mojave Desert at California's Edwards Air Force Base. NASA piggybacked the *Columbia* back to Florida on a jumbo jet for its next launch in November. **◂1975.6 ▸1986.2**

The space shuttle *Columbia* on its launch pad at Cape Canaveral, Florida.

POPULAR CULTURE

Rockin' the Tube

13 In August 1981, Warner Amex Satellite Entertainment Company introduced the first 24-hour music channel, MTV (Music Television). Warner Amex, America's largest cable entertainment programmer, spent $30 million to bring a mix of music videos (introduced by video jockeys, or "VJs"), studio interviews, and concerts to 2.5 million subscribers in 48 states. Targeting 12- to 34-year-olds, MTV was a pioneer of "narrowcasting"—a reversal of the old networks' goal of reaching as broad an audience as possible. The channel tripled its subscribership in just over a year, and within a decade, MTV was bringing American and British rock (and a smattering of other genres) to countries from Russia to Brazil.

MTV came under criticism for neglecting black performers; its videos, which typically featured male performers surrounded by voluptuous, scantily clad females, were blasted as sexist. Nonetheless, the channel quickly became an arbiter of popular taste—not only in music (exposure on MTV boosted record sales 15 to 20 percent), but in fashion, and in other visual media. The signature look and style of music videos—quick-cut editing; enigmatic, often surrealistic imagery—spilled over to TV ads and feature films, whose top directors often got their start making videos. (The music video, novelist and cultural observer Norman Mailer has noted, "might be the only new popular art form in American life.") MTV exposure was crucial to the superstardom of such performers as Madonna and Michael Jackson. And thanks to MTV, other artists achieved stardom before they'd ever played to a live audience. **◂1980.M ▸1982.8**

NOBEL PRIZES: Peace: U.N. High Commission for Refugees (Switzerland) ... Literature: Elias Canetti (U.K.; novelist) ... Chemistry: R. Hoffmann and K. Fukui (U.S., Japanese; chemical-reaction predictions) ... Medicine: R. Sperry, D. Hubel, and T. Wiesel (U.S., U.S., Swedish; information processing) ... Physics: N. Bloembergen, A. Schawlow, and K. Siegbahn (U.S., U.S., Swedish; laser) ... Economics: James Tobin (U.S.).

A VOICE FROM 1981

Turning On To Fitness

From *Jane Fonda's Workout Book*, by Jane Fonda, 1981

In 1981, Jane Fonda, an Academy Award–winning actress and political activist, published Jane Fonda's Workout Book, *a collection of dietary advice, musings on the female body and its health, and—most important—an exercise regimen.* Workout *reached the market at a time when the United States was in the grip of aerobics fever. In gyms, clubs, and at home, millions of women were getting into shape (and away from old ideas about the female figure). The book climbed on to the bestseller lists, the centerpiece of a burgeoning Fonda health industry that included exercise studios, cassette tapes of music to work out by, and an exercise video that became the top-selling tape of all time. An unerring pop-cultural bellwether, Fonda—a self-described plump, "klutzy" 1950s child; a sixties sex kitten; and a seventies political radical—became in the eighties a leotarded guru of the health-body movement who urged millions of women to "feel the burn."* ◂**1978.13**

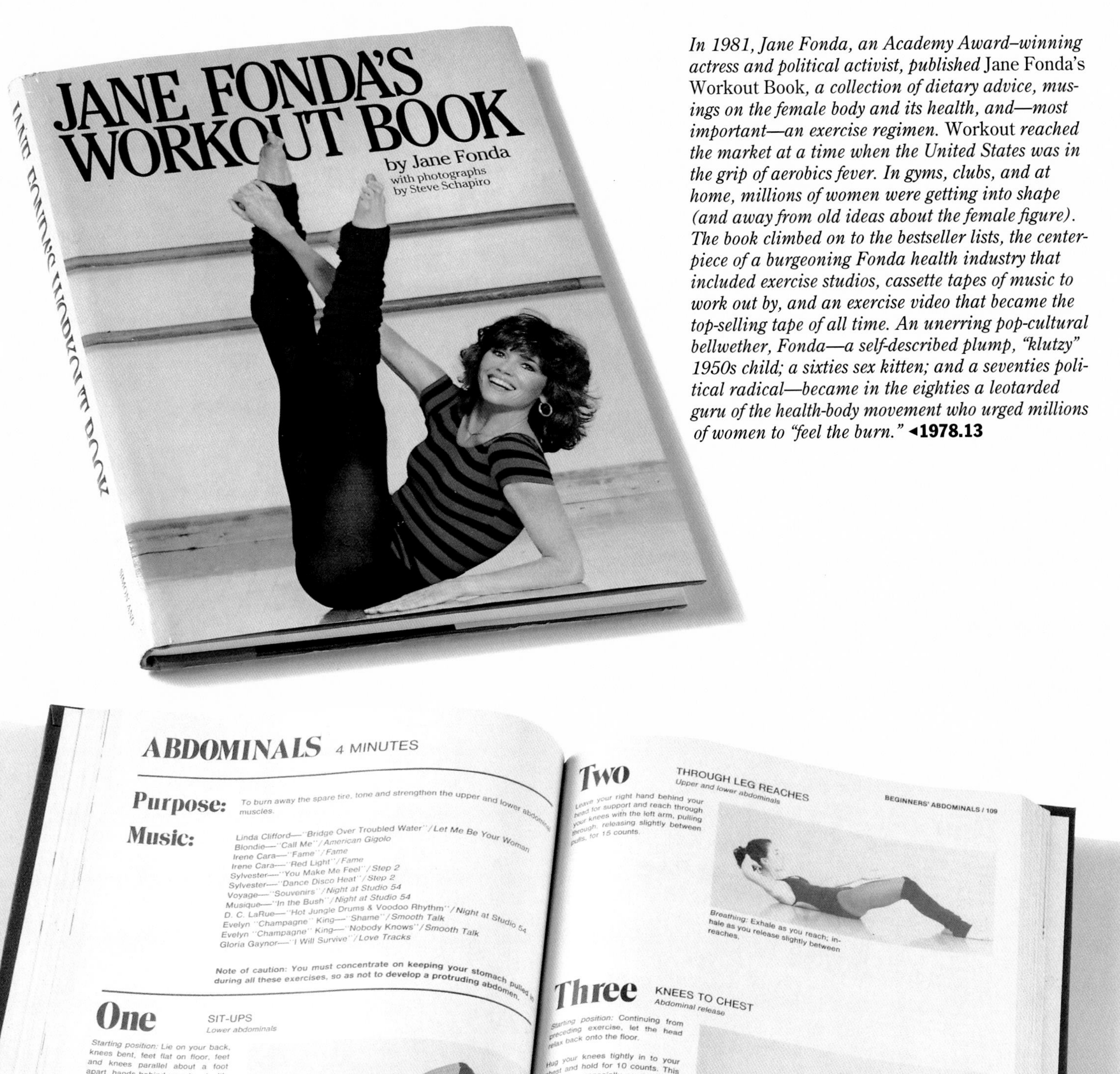

ABDOMINALS 4 MINUTES

Purpose: To burn away the spare tire, tone and strengthen the upper and lower abdominal muscles.

Music:

Linda Clifford—"Bridge Over Troubled Water"/*Let Me Be Your Woman*
Blondie—"Call Me"/*American Gigolo*
Irene Cara—"Fame"/*Fame*
Irene Cara—"Red Light"/*Fame*
Sylvester—"You Make Me Feel"/*Step 2*
Sylvester—"Dance Disco Heat"/*Step 2*
Voyage—"Souvenirs"/*Night at Studio 54*
Musique—"In the Bush"/*Night at Studio 54*
D. C. LaRue—"Hot Jungle Drums & Voodoo Rhythm"/*Night at Studio 54*
Evelyn "Champagne" King—"Shame"/*Smooth Talk*
Evelyn "Champagne" King—"Nobody Knows"/*Smooth Talk*
Gloria Gaynor—"I Will Survive"/*Love Tracks*

Note of caution: You must concentrate on keeping your stomach pulled in during all these exercises, so as not to develop a protruding abdomen.

One — SIT-UPS

Lower abdominals

Starting position: Lie on your back, knees bent, feet flat on floor, feet and knees parallel about a foot apart, hands behind your head with your elbows out to the sides.

1. Lift your head and upper back off the floor as high as you can, using your abdominal muscles, not your arms. Keep your elbows back.

2. Lower a little but do not touch the floor.

Do these lifts, combining movements 1 and 2, 20 times.

Breathing: Exhale as you lift, inhale as you lower.

108

BEGINNERS' ABDOMINALS / 109

Two — THROUGH LEG REACHES

Upper and lower abdominals

Leave your right hand behind your head for support and reach through your knees with the left arm, pulling through, releasing slightly between pulls, for 15 counts.

Breathing: Exhale as you reach; inhale as you release slightly between reaches.

Three — KNEES TO CHEST

Abdominal release

Starting position: Continuing from preceding exercise, let the head relax back onto the floor.

Hug your knees tightly in to your chest and hold for 10 counts. This position is especially soothing and beneficial for the female organs.

Breathing: Normal

"We have no doubts on the sovereignty issue. The Falkland Islanders are British and wish to remain British."
—Prime Minister Margaret Thatcher

STORY OF THE YEAR

Face-Off in the Falklands

1 In early 1982, Argentina's economy was a disaster zone. Inflation was raging (the rate for March was 146 percent), real income had sunk below 1970 levels, and industry was operating at half capacity. Braving murderous repression by the nation's military rulers, protesters were taking to the streets. To divert the public's attention, the junta's newly appointed president, General Leopoldo Galtieri, decided to launch a war. The objective would be the Falkland Islands—controlled by Britain since 1833 but long claimed by the Argentines (who called the islands the Malvinas). Galtieri expected an easy victory: The enemy, he thought, would hardly risk heavy casualties to defend a distant territory occupied by 1,800 Britons and 600,000 sheep. On April 2, Argentine troops overwhelmed the tiny Royal Marine garrison and seized the Falklands.

But Galtieri underestimated Britain's attachment to its colony. Denouncing the violation of the islanders' right to self-determination, British prime minister Margaret Thatcher mobilized a naval task force of more than 100 ships. The United States (allied with both nations) tried to mediate, as did the United Nations—but to no avail. On April 25, a small British contingent retook South Georgia Island; major air and sea battles erupted on May 1.

The initial effect on Argentine morale was spectacular: Even opponents of the regime rallied in patriotic fervor. Most Latin American nations condemned Britain's "aggression." But U.S. president Reagan sided with Thatcher (to Galtieri's surprise), and though air attacks sank four British warships, Argentina's negligible navy was heavily outgunned. British troops first hit the beaches on May 21, battling their way south from Port San Carlos on East Falkland. By then, with Argentina under embargo by the European Economic Community, and its troops demoralized, the war was all but over.

A convoy of Argentine tanks enters Port Stanley. Argentina held the Falklands for two months.

Argentine forces surrendered on June 14. The Falklands fiasco had cost Argentina 712 dead and 11,000 prisoners (Britain lost 255 men)—and had destroyed the junta's credibility. Galtieri resigned; the air force and navy quit the regime. The new president, retired general Reynaldo Bignone, promised elections in 1983. It would be up to a civilian government to heal the scars of the military's seven-year reign of terror. **◂1976.7 ▸1983.M**

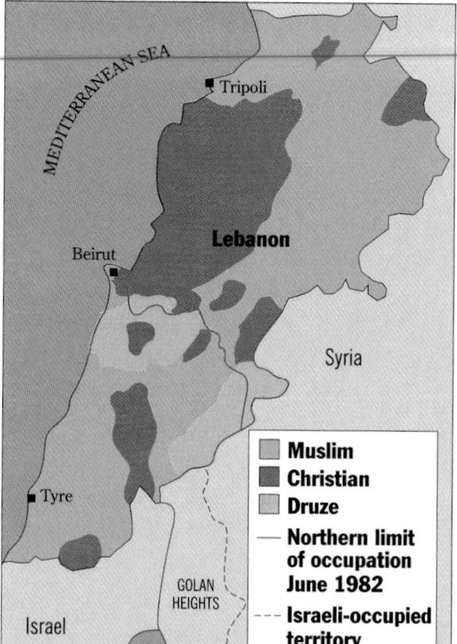

Internal strife and foreign invasion made Lebanon the Balkans of the 1980s.

THE MIDDLE EAST

Israel Invades Lebanon

2 In April 1982, Israel fulfilled stage one of the Camp David Accords by returning the last portion of the Sinai Peninsula to Egypt. (In an unlikely twist, Israel's right-wing government found itself sending troops to evict right-wing Jewish settlers from the area.) But in June, the second stage—self-government for Palestinians in the occupied West Bank and Gaza Strip —was postponed indefinitely, as Prime Minister Menachem Begin launched an invasion of Lebanon.

Initially, Begin's stated goal was to create a 24-mile security strip along the border. (Palestinian commandos had often struck at Israel from southern Lebanon.) But as Israeli forces fought their way further north, grander aims emerged: to evict 6,000 guerrillas from PLO headquarters in Beirut; to oust the 60,000 Syrian troops occupying Lebanon; and to impose a friendly Christian government.

While the Israelis besieged Muslim west Beirut, U.S. envoy Philip Habib shuttled among the belligerents, arranging cease-fires and trying to engineer a settlement. The Reagan administration was divided at first over how to handle Begin. Secretary of State Alexander Haig, who favored leniency, lost the debate and resigned. But Begin defied diplomatic pressure. His forces continued bombarding the city. And in late August, a multinational peacekeeping force arrived to ensure the safe evacuation of PLO fighters to several Arab countries.

The killing was not over, however. On September 14, unknown assailants blew up Lebanon's president-elect, Bashir Gemayel. Breaking Begin's promise to Reagan, Israeli troops occupied west Beirut, ostensibly to stop bloodshed. The Israelis assigned Lebanese Christian militiamen to supervise two local Palestinian refugee camps, Sabra and Shatila. To avenge the death of Gemayel, their former commander, the Christians murdered 800 civilian refugees in the camps—mostly women and children.

The massacre provoked outrage in Israel and abroad. It created sympathy for an increasingly moderate PLO chairman Yasir Arafat (who was even granted an audience with Pope John Paul II). And it brought the peacekeepers back to Beirut, setting the stage for more tragedy. **◂1981.2 ▸1983.3**

THE SOVIET UNION

A Stagnant Era Ends

3 When he died at 76 in November 1982, Soviet leader Leonid Brezhnev *(below)* had presided over 18 years of deepening inertia. Not

that his reign as Communist Party chairman and head of state had been uneventful: Brezhnev had overseen the 1968 invasion of Czechoslovakia and had ushered in détente in the early 1970s, only to see it evaporate in the early 1980s (thanks partly to his invasion of Afghanistan). He'd commanded the largest arms buildup ever undertaken, achieving nuclear parity with the United States. Living standards had risen modestly, especially for the poorest. Still, later reformers had ample cause to refer to his time in power as the "era of stagnation."

Brezhnev's efforts to increase industrial and agricultural efficiency were largely ineffectual; the crop failure of 1975—agricultural production fell some 76 million tons short of target—led to the worst shortages since World War II. Within the Party, new ideas were stifled by an increasingly entrenched (and elderly) oligarchy. Corruption flourished, as the Party elite gained extravagant official privileges—special homes, shops, schools. Though Brezhnev

ART & CULTURE: Books: ***Dinner at the Homesick Restaurant*** **(Anne Tyler);** ***The Fortunate Traveller*** **(Derek Walcott);** ***Megatrends*** **(John Naisbitt) ... Music: "Ebony and Ivory" (McCartney and Wonder);** ***Lionel Richie*** **(LP);** ***The Nightfly*** **(Donald Fagen, LP);** ***Symphony No. 1*** **(Ellen Taaffe Zwilich) ... Painting & Sculpture:** ***Keyhole*** **(Elizabeth Murray);** ***Cabbage Worship*** **(Gilbert and George);** ***Quality Meats for the Public***

"Our goal is to reestablish the ideal family. And in establishing an ideal family, we can establish an ideal world."
—Dr. Mose Durst, U.S. president of the Unification Church

did not resort to Stalinist terror, those who protested were dealt with harshly: A favorite tactic, dating from czarist days, was to incarcerate troublemakers in psychiatric hospitals.

A sense of national paralysis colored Brezhnev's twilight years. His death was a relief even to top Party officials. Yet dynamic change would have to wait. Successor Yuri Andropov, 68 (who as KGB head had orchestrated the crackdown on dissent), initiated mild reforms—but within 15 months he too was dead. His replacement, Konstantin Chernenko, 73, died a year later. Only in 1985, when Mikhail Gorbachev appeared on the scene, did a new era truly begin. **◂1979.9 ▸1984.M**

More than 4,000 followers of Sun Myung Moon took their vows at Madison Square Garden. Many had arrived in the United States just days earlier.

RELIGION

Moon's Mass Wedding

4 On July 1, 1982, the Reverend Sun Myung Moon presided over the simultaneous marriage of 2,075 couples—the brides dressed in identical white gowns, the grooms in identical blue suits—in New York's Madison Square Garden arena. The ceremony also ordained the newlyweds as missionaries of Moon's Unification Church. The families they founded, Moon proclaimed, would "expand into a true society, into a true nation, into a true world."

Moon's followers (some three million worldwide) called him and his wife, the former Hak Ja Han, the "true parents" of humankind. Born in 1920 in what would become North Korea, Moon claimed that Jesus Christ had anointed him the new messiah at age 16. Ousted from the Presbyterian Church, Moon was subsequently imprisoned by the Communist regime. He founded his cult in South Korea in 1954 on the premise that Communists were Satan's minions; promoting corporate capitalism and a conservative theocracy was his divine mission.

Many parents of the faithful accused the church of brainwashing its members. "Moonies" gave up all independence, living in church centers, peddling flowers in airports—even letting Moon or church elders choose their spouses. (Some husbands and wives spoke different languages and had to communicate through an interpreter.) The mass wedding prompted New York-area Christian and Jewish leaders to issue a rare joint condemnation.

Moon—whose U.S.-based earthly empire included fishing fleets, newspapers, ginseng-export businesses, and weapons plants—stood accused of larger crimes as well. In May, he was convicted by a U.S. court on tax fraud and conspiracy charges. (He began serving an 18-month sentence in 1984.) And though legal, his attempts at the "subjugation of the American government" (as he put it in a later speech) through a web of right-wing organizations disturbed many observers. **◂1978.2 ▸1993.M**

MEXICO

Economic Collapse

5 Mexico's booming economy collapsed in 1982, sucked into a black hole of debt. The country's foreign obligations were second only to Brazil's in the developing world, and in August the government came perilously close to defaulting on its loans—about 30 percent of which were held by U.S. banks. At the last moment, Washington interceded, disbursing nearly $3 billion in stopgap aid. But for the Mexican people, the problems were just beginning.

Mexico's economic problems drove millions to the cities. Here, bus riders cling to the side of an overcrowded vehicle.

In the 1970s, when Mexico discovered it was sitting on one of the world's largest petroleum reserves, foreign banks had clamored to lend the country money—and President José López Portillo had embarked on a giddy spending spree. Now, however, the international oil glut had slashed predicted revenues, and more than 60 percent of the nation's shrinking income had to be surrendered to debt payments. The peso lost half its value almost overnight, spurring capital flight as investors sought safe haven abroad. Inflation climbed to nearly 100 percent. López Portillo—his former popularity in tatters—responded by nationalizing banks and imposing harsh foreign-exchange controls. The latter move effectively barred Mexican industry from importing crucial heavy equipment. After four years of amazing 8 percent annual growth, the economy ground to a halt.

Incoming president Miguel de la Madrid Hurtado was left holding the bag. A banker-lawyer with a degree from Harvard and a refreshing reputation for honesty (much of the money Portillo borrowed disappeared into the pockets of his cronies), de la Madrid took office in December. Announcing, "We are in an emergency," he imposed an austerity program aimed at halving the budget deficit. *La crisis* had punctured a national dream of oil-driven prosperity. As thousands of middle-class households sank into poverty and the poor grew increasingly desperate, Mexicans came to call the 1980s "the lost decade." **◂1934.2 ▸1993.2**

DEATHS

Louis Aragon, French writer.

John Belushi, U.S. comedian.

Ingrid Bergman, Swedish-U.S. actress.

William Bernbach, U.S. advertising executive.

Leonid Brezhnev, U.S.S.R. political leader.

John Cheever, U.S. writer.

Rainer Werner Fassbinder, German filmmaker.

Henry Fonda, U.S. actor.

Anna Freud, U.K. psychoanalyst.

John Gardner, U.S. writer.

Nahum Goldmann, Lithuanian-Israeli Zionist leader.

Wladyslaw Gomulka, Polish political leader.

Glenn Gould, Canadian pianist and composer.

Walter Hallstein, German statesman.

Grace Kelly, U.S. actress and Monacan princess.

Archibald MacLeish, U.S. poet.

Pierre Mendès-France, French statesman.

Thelonius Monk, U.S. musician.

Satchel Paige, U.S. baseball player.

Ayn Rand, Russian-U.S. writer.

Arthur Rubinstein, Polish-U.S. musician.

Romy Schneider, Austrian actress.

Lee Strasberg, U.S. director, actor, and educator.

Jacques Tati, French comedian and filmmaker.

King Vidor, U.S. filmmaker.

Vladimir Zworykin, Russian-U.S. physicist.

(Jean-Michel Basquiat) ... Film: *Gandhi* (Richard Attenborough); *Tootsie* (Sydney Pollack); *Victor/Victoria* (Blake Edwards); *Lola* (Rainer Werner Fassbinder); *The Night of the Shooting Stars* (Paolo and Vittorio Taviani) ... Theater: *Noises Off* (Michael Frayn); *Top Girls* (Caryl Churchill); *Master Harold ... & the Boys* (Athol Fugard); *Nine* (Maury Yeston) ... TV: *Cheers*; *Family Ties*; *Late Night with David Letterman*.

"It's a great feeling to be powerful. I've been striving for it all my life. I think that's just the quest of every human being: power."
—Madonna

NEW IN 1982

Liposuction.

Sony Watchman.

Experimental Prototype Community of Tomorrow (EPCOT) center (Orlando, Florida).

Halcion sleeping pills.

NEWSLINE
USA TODAY
Coast-to-coast
Scoreboard
America's Princess Grace dies in Monaco

National daily general-interest newspaper (*USA Today*).

IN THE UNITED STATES

▶ERA DIES—"The most misunderstood words since 'one size fits all,' " quipped syndicated humor columnist Erma Bombeck about the Equal Rights Amendment, which proposed that "Equality of rights under the law shall not be denied or abridged by the United States or any state on account of sex." The ERA died in 1982, ten years after it had been approved by Congress. At deadline, it was three states short of the number necessary for ratification (38). ◀1964.3

▶VIETNAM MEMORIAL—The Vietnam War Memorial was dedicated in Washington, D.C., on November 13. Commissioned by the Vietnam Veterans Memorial Fund, the wedge-shaped black granite wall inscribed with the names of the nearly 60,000 Americans killed or missing in the Vietnam War was designed by Maya Ying Lin, a 21-year-old architecture student at Yale. Initially, its unconventional form drew criticism (and prompted the placement nearby of a naturalistic statue of soldiers), but "The Wall" soon became the capital's most frequently visited memorial. ◀1975.4

ENVIRONMENTALISM
Acid Rain

6 The phenomenon of acid rain soaked into worldwide consciousness in 1982, when Canada charged that pollution blown in from the northeastern United States had killed all the fish in 147 Ontario lakes and was depleting salmon stocks in Nova Scotia. Formally known as acid deposition, acid rain is capable of harming waterways, trees, crops, buildings, and human lungs. It occurs when sulfur dioxide and nitrogen oxide gases—primarily from burning fossil fuels—are transformed in the atmosphere into sulfuric and nitric acids and fall to earth as precipitation or dust. Scandinavians had been worrying about acid rain since the 1950s, when studies linked it to decreasing freshwater fish populations. In the 1970s, it was blamed for widespread damage to West German forests.

The dispute grew into a diplomatic brawl as President Reagan—who opposed most environmental legislation as too costly to businesses and taxpayers—called for further studies, and Canadian officials accused him of foot-dragging. New York State passed a law regulating acid-causing pollution in 1984, but Congress took no action until 1988, when it ratified a UN protocol (with 24 other countries) freezing nitrogen oxide emissions at 1987 levels. (The U.S. Clean Air Act of 1990 subsequently called for halving sulfur dioxide pollution within a decade.)

European reaction was quicker. In 1984, ten nations joined the "30 Percent Club," pledging to reduce emissions 30 percent from 1980 levels by 1993; the following year, 21 countries signed the Helsinki protocol, pledging a similar reduction. By the early 1990s, sulfur dioxide emissions had dropped by 40 percent in most of Western Europe and by as much as 70 percent in environmentally conscious West Germany. But thousands of lakes around the world were already biologically dead, and forests from Maine to South Africa were in trouble. And in the former Soviet bloc, the burning of high-sulfur coal continued to rain corrosive chemicals far downwind. **◀1970.5 ▶1983.5**

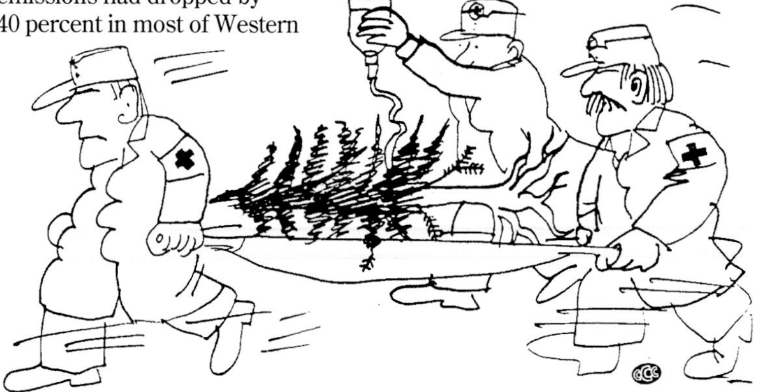

In a German cartoon, a tree damaged by acid rain requires emergency medical care.

SCIENCE
Darwin Refined

7 On the centenary of the death of Charles Darwin, in 1982, evolutionists met at conferences around the world to evaluate the state of evolutionary theory. Biologists and paleontologists universally agreed that two of the three basic notions in Darwin's seminal *On the Origin of Species*—the common ancestry of all forms of life, and the evolution of life-forms through natural selection—were remarkably sound, and were supported by discoveries in molecular biology and genetics. But the third—the relatively minor idea that evolution proceeds continually, at a glacial pace—was undergoing revision. According to an alternative theory called punctuated equilibria, new species spring up suddenly (over thousands of years rather than Darwin's millions), remain essentially unchanged (in a state of equilibrium) for a long period, then are abruptly replaced with newer species.

First proposed by paleontologists Stephen Jay Gould *(left, top)* of Harvard and Niles Eldredge *(bottom)* of the American Museum of Natural History, the theory of punctuated equilibria reconciled Darwinism with paleontological reality: the fossil record, which shows remarkably fertile episodes of species formation but does not preserve intermediate evolutionary steps.

Geneticists resisted the theory, arguing that petrified remains do not record all changes—not even important ones, and especially not slight ones. The debate could be traced back to Darwin, who'd candidly admitted that gradual evolution did not square with the fossil record. Gould emphasized that Darwinism was "incomplete, not incorrect." The theory of punctuated equilibria, however, proved a crucial refinement of Darwinian thought, as well as a useful model for other disciplines from anthropology to political science. **◀1937.6**

MUSIC
Madonna's First Single

8 The rise of Madonna (née Madonna Louise Ciccone) from University of Michigan dropout to international pop-culture goddess began in 1982, when her first single, "Everybody," became a hit in U.S. dance clubs and on black radio. Just four years earlier, she'd arrived in New York with $37; by the mid-1990s, she'd been the ruling icon of pop music for more than a decade and was presiding over a billion-dollar media empire.

Madonna was one of the first stars launched by MTV. While her music, at least initially, was undistinguished disco ("Minnie Mouse on helium" was one critic's evaluation of her voice), her masterfully produced videos highlighted her good looks, her dancer's moves (she'd studied at the Alvin Ailey school), and her quirkily sexy thrift-store outfits. Teenage girls everywhere began to emulate her bare midriff, crucifix jewelry, vampish makeup, torn tights, and underwear worn as outerwear. Videos also established her trademark iconography—a blend of lapsed Catholicism and obsessions ranging from narcissism to bondage. Her first album, *Madonna*, sold

SPORTS: Baseball: World Series, St. Louis Cardinals defeat Milwaukee Brewers, 4–3 ... Football: Super Bowl, San Francisco 49ers defeat Cincinnati Bengals, 26–21 ... Basketball: NBA, Los Angeles Lakers defeat Philadelphia 76ers, 4–2 ... Tennis: Jimmy Connors defeats John McEnroe at Wimbledon (longest men's singles final to date: 4 hr., 14 min.) ... Soccer: World Cup, Italy defeats West Germany, 3–1.

"Schnabel's work is tailor-made to look important. It is big, and stuffed with clunky references to other Great Art.... Its imagery is callow and solemn, a Macy's parade of expressionist bric-a-brac."—**Art critic Robert Hughes, on painter Julian Schnabel**

three million copies; in 1984, the single "Like a Virgin" stayed number one for six weeks. While her attempts to become a movie star met with public apathy, her singles still regularly topped the charts into the 1990s—and her calculatedly shocking antics (starring in a book of arty soft-porn photographs, hinting at lesbian affairs) kept her name in the tabloids.

The key to Madonna's abiding success was her canny reading of the zeitgeist. In the yuppie 1980s, she was (as she proclaimed in one song) a "Material Girl"—a gym-buffed entrepreneur whose punkish outfits were an emblem of

Madonna built an empire around pushing society's boundaries.

passionate adventurousness. In the 1990s, she gravitated toward haute couture—an escapist gesture for a chastened decade. Dubbed "America's Smartest Business Woman" by *Forbes* magazine, she founded her own film, music publishing, and recording companies—insurance against the day her image would no longer be bankable. **◂1981.13 ▸1982.12**

ART
The Boom's Brightest Lights

10 **Benefiting from the fabled 1980s bull market on Wall Street, which created instant fortunes, the market for contemporary art entered a period of euphoric expansion in 1982. New York's SoHo district was the capital of the heady boom, and the painter Julian Schnabel, a confident self-promoter who went from driving cabs to commanding six-figure prices for his canvases, was often called SoHo's unofficial mayor. Schnabel's "neo-expressionism"—he often glued broken crockery onto the surface of his paintings—was championed by some critics for saving modern art from the hegemony of the pop, minimalist, and conceptualist movements of the 1960s and '70s. Outspoken detractors said Schnabel was all hype, no bite, and should learn to draw before attempting to paint. Other unlikely art stars included Jeff Koons, who made life-size porcelain statues of Michael Jackson and a giant "inflatable" bunny cast in stainless steel, and Jenny Holzer, whose medium was the message: aphorisms displayed on postcards, T-shirts, and electronic billboards in Times Square. Koons's curious works were received as commentary on the very consumerism that made him a millionaire. Holzer, who won top honors at the 1990 Venice Biennale, contributed a summarizing "text" work: "Money Creates Taste." ◂1974.9 ▸1987.13**

FILM
Sci-fi, Light and Dark

9 Non-earthlings showed up wearing wildly divergent faces in two landmark science-fiction films released in 1982. One of the films, a box-office smash, presented aliens as benign beings possessing childlike goodness in an Earth-world of suspect adults. The other, a flop, depicted darker, more malevolent impulses.

E.T.—The Extra-Terrestrial was the fourth film by 35-year-old Steven Spielberg to break box-office records (*Jaws*, *Close Encounters of the Third Kind*, and *Raiders of the Lost Ark* had done likewise). *E.T.* combined Spielberg's usual breathtaking special effects (courtesy of George Lucas's state-of-the-art Industrial Light and Magic Company) with his most personal story yet: that of the love between a lonely suburban Earth boy and a stranded space alien. The "star," a masterpiece of model-making and electronics, was a charmer—a kind, intelligent, lovably ugly creature who likes TV, Reese's Pieces, beer, and long-distance telephoning, and who also has magical qualities (he can heal with a fingertip). "E.T. phone home"—the space castaway's pidgin plaint—became an international catchphrase.

Kids and adults alike fell for E.T. The characters in Ridley Scott's *Blade Runner*, on the other hand, were mostly met with distaste. Harrison Ford played a burned-out Los Angeles cop circa 2019 whose specialty is hunting down escaped "replicants"—impeccably lifelike robots employed as slaves in outer-space colonies. Built to self-destruct after four years, the androids think, feel, remember simulated childhoods, and—to survive—kill without compunction.

To most filmgoers, *Blade Runner*, mutilated by Warner Bros., seemed slow-paced, confusing, and poorly scripted. But a growing number of critics and fans have come to regard the "director's cut" version, released in 1993, as a key film of the eighties—a provocative examination of the line between human and machine, a grimly stylish evocation of a decaying city of the future, and a definitive example of a new, hard-edged science-fiction subgenre known as "cyberpunk." **◂1977.10 ▸1993.12**

Spielberg poses with his star—a "squat, wrinkled, mud-colored beastie with a perpetual chest cold" (as one critic put it).

IN THE UNITED STATES

▶TYLENOL SCARE—On October 5, after seven Chicagoans died from ingesting Tylenol poisoned with cyanide, Johnson & Johnson, the manufacturer of the over-the-counter painkiller, recalled more than a quarter-million bottles. The event, which inspired several "copycat" crimes around the country, resulted in new tamper-proof packaging for pharmaceuticals and other products. In one of the great comebacks of American business, Tylenol recovered its huge market share. The Chicago murderer, however, was never apprehended.

▶MA BELL BREAKS UP—An old and powerful family broke up in 1982, when "Ma Bell," settling a costly seven-year-old Justice Department antitrust suit, agreed to cut loose its "baby bells"—22 regional telephone companies. The agreement left intact AT&T's most profitable components—its long-distance network, Bell Laboratories, and its Western Electric manufacturing subsidiary. It also freed the telecommunications giant to enter booming computer and electronic-data fields, markets from which it had been barred since 1956. ◂1915.7

▶THE RICHEST MUSEUM—The Getty Trust, established in 1982, turned the private art collection of late oil tycoon J. Paul Getty (who had died in 1976) into the world's richest museum. Operating with a $1.2 billion endowment, the J. Paul Getty Museum, in Malibu, California, suddenly had more buying power than venerable institutions like the Louvre and the Metropolitan Museum. "In effect," said a competing curator, "the Getty will have first refusal on everything that comes on the market." It bought aggressively (and sometimes foolishly: The Getty paid better than $1 million for an ancient Greek marble head of dubious authenticity), rapidly building a world-class collection. ◂1977.11 ▸1987.13

POLITICS & BUSINESS: GNP: $3,179.8 billion ... Secretary of State Alexander M. Haig, Jr., resigns, succeeded by George P. Shultz ... Supreme Court rules a president is not liable for damages arising from actions taken while in office; holds that children of illegal aliens have right to tuition-free public school education ... Braniff International Corp. files under Chapter 11 (first major U.S. airline to go bankrupt).

"My Lord, he is a wonderful mover."—**Fred Astaire, on Michael Jackson**

AROUND THE WORLD

▶WORLD MUSIC—The summer of 1982 marked the first annual World of Music, Arts, and Dance festival, in Shepton

Mallet in southwest England. Organized by British rock musician Peter Gabriel, WOMAD showcased "world music"—a broad term applied to the diverse musical traditions of Africa, Latin America, and Asia. With Gabriel as an ambassador and WOMAD as its portable embassy, world music soon became a significant trend in the music industry. ◀1971.M ▶1986.M

▶GENETICALLY ENGINEERED INSULIN—British health officials in September approved the use of genetically engineered human insulin. The hormone, called Humulin, was accepted in the U.S. a month later. Humulin was the first product of recombinant DNA technology officially endorsed for human use. ◀1978.1 ▶1988.M

▶NEW LEADER AT UN—Peruvian diplomat Javier Pérez de Cuellar was elected the fifth secretary-general of the United Nations in 1982, succeeding Kurt Waldheim. The first Latin American leader of the international organization, Pérez de Cuellar was elected to a second term in 1986 and negotiated the Iran-Iraq cease-fire in 1988. ◀1961.M

▶EL NIÑO—In 1982, the western coastal waters of South America began to experience a particularly severe El Niño event. The name, deriving from Spanish slang for "the Christ child," refers to a warm coastal current that makes an unpredictable appearance during the Christmas season. Surface temperatures in the eastern Pacific rose by as much as 18° F, punishing local fishing industries (the fish migrated to more hospitable waters) and causing heavy rainfall and flooding from Ecuador to Chile, drought in Australia, and typhoons as far east as Tahiti during 1982 and '83.

MEDICINE

A Mechanical Heart

11 On December 2, 1982, at the University of Utah Medical Center in Salt Lake City, surgeon William DeVries implanted the first permanent artificial heart into a human being. Previously, the Jarvik-7 heart, designed by Utah bioengineer Robert Jarvik, had been implanted only in sheep and calves.

The patient was Barney Clark, a retired dentist who was suffering from cardiomyopathy, a progressive weakening of the heart muscle, fatal unless treated with a replacement heart. At 61, Clark was eleven years too old for a human-heart transplant. But he'd demonstrated a psychological stability and a strong will to live, convincing DeVries he was a good candidate to try out the new device.

After the seven-and-a-half-hour operation (performed by a 17-member team), Clark was initially healthier than before surgery. The plastic heart performed well. But complications soon set in. Seizures in the first week left him disoriented; he had trouble with his lungs and kidney, possibly because they'd been deprived of a healthy flow of blood for so long. But he was able to walk about—tethered by tubes to a cart laden with 375 pounds of machinery—and he celebrated Christmas and his birthday with his family.

Clark survived for 112 days. A decade later, the Jarvik heart's descendants were still being used as a "bridge" to keep patients alive while awaiting transplants—but an artificial heart that would sustain life indefinitely was still in the future. **◀1967.1**

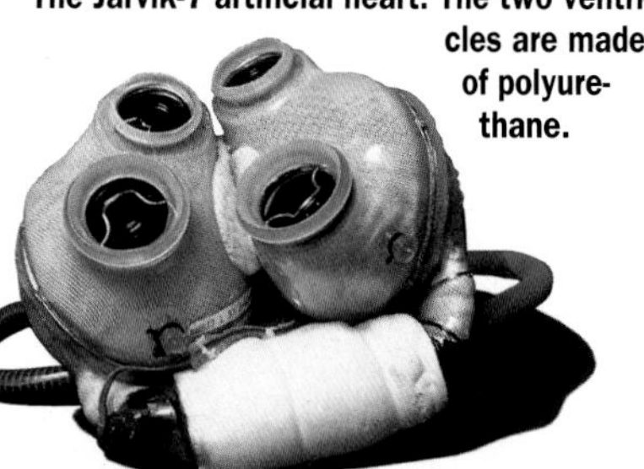

The Jarvik-7 artificial heart. The two ventricles are made of polyurethane.

Megastar Michael Jackson strikes a pose in concert.

MUSIC

Michael Jackson's Megahit

12 With the release in 1982 of *Thriller,* Michael Jackson became a pop megastar. The LP spawned seven Top Ten singles; by 1984, with worldwide sales at 30 million, it was the bestselling record of all time. The album's promotional videos—particularly the title song's 14-minute extravaganza, in which Jackson turns into a werewolf—added to the rising popularity of MTV while establishing the singer as one of the most famous (and changeable) faces of his generation.

Jackson had first won acclaim in 1969, as the eleven-year-old lead vocalist of the Jackson Five, a band of school-age brothers from working-class Gary, Indiana, who scored a string of major hits. In the early seventies, he branched into solo work as well. And in 1979, he outstripped his siblings with *Off the Wall*, an album of disco-style music that remained the most popular LP in the soul category (the era's catchall term for black pop) for two years.

For *Thriller,* Jackson created a more eclectic sound (featuring a duet with ex-Beatle Paul McCartney and a guitar solo by heavy-metal star Eddie Van Halen). But mystique as well as music fueled Jackson's appeal. His delivery was searing, his dancing pantherlike—yet he remained an eternal child. He sang in a breathy tenor, made his mansion into a miniature Disneyland, and spoke of his exotic pets as friends. He dressed like a cartoon prince, in spangled uniforms and a single glove. And with the aid of plastic surgery, his features increasingly escaped the bounds of race and gender. A recluse, he was the subject of endless rumors. In 1993, the 35-year-old star was sued for molesting a 13-year-old boy. The case was settled out of court; in 1994, authorities declined to prosecute, while opting to keep the case open until the statute of limitations had expired. In the meantime, Jackson had pulled off perhaps the most sensational coup of his career: He married rock 'n' roll's princess royal, Elvis Presley's daughter, Lisa Marie Presley. **◀1981.13**

SPORTS

Strongwoman of Tennis

13 The Women's Tennis Association ranked Martina Navratilova the world's top female player in 1982—an honor she received annually during a golden four-year period. Between 1982 and 1986, Navratilova won twelve Grand Slam tennis tournaments and compiled a staggering 427–14 win-loss record.

Navratilova's regimen of weight training, running, and a specially designed diet brought unprecedented muscularity to women's tennis. (Her serve was clocked at 90 miles per hour.) By 1992 she'd won 158 championships—more than any other player, male or female. And she'd extended her influence beyond the court, becoming a champion of women's sports and of gay and lesbian rights.

Until 1975, she was a citizen of Czechoslovakia, traveling to the West to play matches against such greats as Evonne Goolagong and Chris Evert. After leading her country's team to its first Federation Cup championship in 1975, the 18-year-old Navratilova, unwilling to be a Cold War pawn, defected to the United States. In 1986, she returned to Prague, leading the U.S. team to a Federation Cup win over Czechoslovakia. **◀1976.9**

Navratilova in 1982 at Wimbledon, a tournament she would win a record nine times.

NOBEL PRIZES: Peace: Alva Myrdal and Alfonso García Robles (Swedish, Mexican; disarmament) ... Literature: Gabriel García Márquez (Colombian; novelist) ... Chemistry: Aaron Klug (U.K.; viral structure) ... Medicine: S. Bergström, B. Samuelsson, and J. Vane (Swedish, Swedish, U.K.; prostaglandins) ... Physics: Kenneth G. Wilson (U.S.; phase transitions) ... Economics: George J. Stigler (U.S.).

A VOICE FROM 1982

Finding Strength in Sisterhood

The Color Purple, by Alice Walker, 1982

Set in the rural South before World War II and written as a series of letters—from Celie, a chronically abused black woman, to God, and between Celie and her sister Nettie, a missionary in Africa—Alice Walker's 1982 novel, The Color Purple, *was praised for its idiomatic language, its sense of place, and its insight into human character. The tale, which ends beatifically with Celie overcoming sex- and race-based oppression (and reuniting with the long-lost Nettie), celebrated a kind of black female strength and pride that Walker called "womanism." Some critics accused the author of reinforcing racial stereotypes (notably that of the bullying, sexually predatory black male), but the book had more fans than foes:* The Color Purple *won a Pulitzer Prize and an American Book Award (partial redress, the author said, for the neglect of earlier black women writers like Zora Neale Hurston). In the excerpt below, Celie recounts to Nettie the reaction of Mr. ______ (as Celie refers to her husband) to her announcement that she is leaving him.* **◂1921.9 ▸1993.V**

Dear Nettie,

Well, you know wherever there's a man, there's trouble. And it seem like, going to Memphis, Grady was all over the car. No matter which way us change up, he want to sit next to Squeak.

While me and Shug sleeping and he driving, he tell Squeak all about life in North Memphis, Tennessee. I can't half sleep for him raving bout clubs and clothes and forty-nine brands of beer. Talking so much bout stuff to drink made me have to pee. Then us have to find a road going off into the bushes to relieve ourselves.

Mr. ______ try to act like he don't care I'm going.

You'll be back, he say. Nothing up North for nobody like you. Shug got talent, he say. She can sing. She got spunk, he say. She can talk to anybody. Shug got looks, he say. She can stand up and be notice. But what you got? You ugly. You skinny. You shape funny. You too scared to open your mouth to people. All you fit to do in Memphis is be Shug's maid. Take out her slop-jar and maybe cook her food. You not that good a cook either. And this house ain't been clean good since my first wife died. And nobody crazy or backward enough to want to marry you, neither. What you gon do? Hire yourself out to a farm? He laugh. Maybe somebody let you work on they railroad.

Any more letters come? I ast.

He say, What?

You heard me, I say. Any more letters from Nettie come?

Author Alice Walker in 1992. Her prose, said one critic, is "unpretentious and natural, like a glass that contains whatever she wants you to see." *The Color Purple*, her third novel, was made into a 1985 film directed by Steven Spielberg; Whoopi Goldberg portrayed Celie, a character Walker based on her great-grandmother.

If they did, he say, I wouldn't give 'em to you. You two of a kind, he say. A man try to be nice to you, you fly in his face.

I curse you, I say.
What that mean? he say.

I say, Until you do right by me, everything you touch will crumble.

He laugh. Who you think you is? he say. You can't curse nobody. Look at you. You black, you pore, you ugly, you a woman. Goddam, he say, you nothing at all.
Until you do right by me, I say, everything you even dream about will fail. I give it to him straight, just like it come to me. And it seem to come to me from the trees.

Whoever heard such a thing, say Mr. ______. I probably didn't whup your ass enough.

Every lick you hit me you will suffer twice, I say. Then I say, You better stop talking because all I'm telling you ain't coming just from me. Look like when I open my mouth the air rush in and shape words.

Shit, he say. I should have lock you up. Just let you out to work.

The jail you plan for me is the one in which you will rot, I say.

Shug come over to where us talking. She take one look at my face and say Celie! Then she turn to Mr. ______. Stop Albert, she say. Don't say no more. You just going to make it harder on yourself.

I'll fix her wagon! say Mr. ______, and spring toward me.

A dust devil flew up on the porch between us, fill my mouth with dirt. The dirt say, Anything you do to me, already done to you.

Then I feel Shug shake me. Celie, she say. And I come to myself.

I'm pore, I'm black, I may be ugly and I can't cook, a voice say to everything listening. But I'm here.

Amen, say Shug. Amen, amen.

"The events in Lebanon and Grenada ... are closely related. Not only has Moscow assisted and encouraged violence in both countries, but it provides direct support through a network of surrogates and terrorists."—**Ronald Reagan, October 27, 1983**

STORY OF THE YEAR

The United States Invades Grenada

1 The first Caribbean experiment with communism outside Cuba ended bloodily in 1983. Grenada's revolution had begun four years earlier, when Prime Minister Eric Gairy—corrupt, repressive, and obsessed with flying saucers—was toppled by an armed political party called the New Jewel Movement. Grenadians generally welcomed the NJM's charismatic, London-educated Maurice Bishop as their new prime minister. They cheered as the regime (aided by Cuba, the Soviet bloc, and radical Arab states) undertook an ambitious building program whose crowning glory was to be a modern airport. To the relief of non-Marxists, the NJM left most of the economy in private hands. Many, however, were disturbed at the government's growing suppression of criticism and its administrative and financial incompetence.

A U.S. Marine in St. George's, Grenada, with a captured Grenadian soldier. Reagan's implicit message to the region was: no Marxism.

In October 1983, a power struggle between Bishop and Bernard Coard, his former deputy premier, led to Bishop's overthrow and arrest. Some 10,000 Grenadians (a tenth of the population) rallied in his support. Freed by the crowd, Bishop led his followers to seize army headquarters. Scores were massacred—including Bishop—and Coard's faction declared martial law.

The upheaval gave U.S. president Ronald Reagan a chance to score a Cold War victory and to restore his military prestige after recent humiliations in Beirut (just two days earlier, 241 U.S. Marines had been killed in a car bombing at an American installation). Reagan had long claimed that Grenada's airport was meant for Soviet warplanes. Now, acting on a carefully orchestrated appeal by conservative Caribbean governments, and citing danger to the 1,000 Americans on the island (most of them medical students), he launched an invasion. The 6,000 U.S. troops met little resistance from Grenada's 1,500-man army or the NJM's 800 Cuban helpers, most of whom (contrary to U.S. allegations) were construction workers.

Though total casualties were low (58 in all), the operation was widely condemned as a violation of international law. But it was welcomed by most Grenadians, who generally agreed the "revo" (as it was nicknamed) had gone sour. In December 1984, an election brought back as prime minister Herbert Blaize, who'd been chief minister in the 1960s, when Grenada was still a British colony. (The country gained full independence in 1974.) Occupation troops departed soon after Blaize took office. **◂1961.5 ▸1983.3**

1983

THE PHILIPPINES

Top Marcos Foe Murdered

2 As he returned to the Philippines in August 1983, Benigno Aquino knew he risked assassination. A charismatic liberal from a prominent family, the 50-year-old former senator had been President Ferdinand Marcos's chief rival even before Marcos declared martial law in 1972. Jailed in the roundup of opposition leaders, Aquino had later been sentenced to death on trumped-up charges. But the dictator, unwilling to make a martyr of his nemesis, let him go to the United States for heart surgery in 1980. After three years of political study at Harvard and elsewhere, Aquino decided to take his chances. Against the advice of friends and enemies (including Marcos himself, who warned of mortal danger from old political foes), Aquino boarded a flight for Manila—and was shot to death seconds after he left the plane.

Although the alleged assassin, a petty hoodlum, was gunned down instantly by soldiers assigned to guard Aquino—and though Marcos denounced the murder as "heinous and outrageous"—most Filipinos believed top army and civilian officials were behind it. (Two years later, a judicial inquiry proved them right.) Disillusionment with the regime had been spreading since the mid-1970s, thanks not only to repression, but also to the economic effects of corruption, mismanagement, burgeoning foreign debt, and declining prices for the country's main exports (sugar and coconut oil). Rigged parliamentary elections in 1978 had further fueled anger. By the time Marcos lifted martial law in 1981—retaining dictatorial powers—even many upper-class Filipinos had joined the opposition.

Aquino *(center)* and his assassin died on the tarmac at Manila International Airport.

Aquino's killing touched off an unprecedented explosion of protest. As unrest spread nationwide, old opposition factions united and new groups sprouted. Aquino had aimed to provide an alternative to both dictatorship and communist revolution. His death would lead to the fulfillment of his dreams of democracy. **◂1973.10 ▸1986.3**

THE MIDDLE EAST

Lebanon's Tragedy

3 By 1983, Israel's invasion of Lebanon had driven the PLO from Beirut. But the mission had failed to drive Palestinian guerrillas from the strategic Bekaa Valley in eastern Lebanon—and as the year progressed, its repercussions proved increasingly disastrous. The first blow came in February, when an Israeli judicial commission attributed "indirect responsibility" for the recent massacres of Palestinian refugees at Beirut's Sabra and Shatila refugee camps to Defense Minister Ariel Sharon, who was forced to step down. Two months later, a truck-bomb delivered by the Iranian-backed Islamic Jihad organization destroyed the U.S. embassy in Beirut, killing 40. Among the 17 American dead were the CIA's top Middle East analyst and its Beirut station chief.

U.S. Marines dig through rubble of bombed headquarters. "I haven't seen carnage like that since Vietnam," said one officer.

The bombing prompted U.S. secretary of state George Shultz to fly to Beirut, where he brokered a pact granting Israel a security zone in southern Lebanon in exchange for Israel's promise to withdraw. Although the PLO and Syria (which still had 40,000 troops in Lebanon) rejected the agreement, mounting public pressure compelled Israeli forces to begin pulling out in September. Depressed and ailing, Israeli prime minister Menachem Begin resigned; his successor was the equally militaristic Yitzhak Shamir.

The Israeli withdrawal left the 5,000-man multinational peacekeeping force in Beirut dangerously vulnerable. Syrian-backed Druze

ART & CULTURE: Books: ***Ironweed*** **(William Kennedy);** ***Stanley and the Women*** **(Kingsley Amis);** ***The Anatomy Lesson*** **(Philip Roth);** ***The Life and Times of Michael K.*** **(J.M. Coetzee);** ***Modern Times*** **(Paul Johnson);** ***Vietnam: A History*** **(Stanley Karnow) ... Music: "Beat It" (Michael Jackson); "Every Breath You Take" (The Police);** ***An Innocent Man*** **(Billy Joel, LP);** ***Strand Settings: Darker*** **(Mel Powell) ... Painting & Sculpture:**

"The ecological crisis is the final expression of the kaput-industrialization of the world, with the bomb as the tip of the iceberg."
—Rudolf Bahro, a member of the West German Green Party

militiamen began bombarding the American contingent of 1,500 Marines; the Druze, in turn, were shelled by U.S. warships. Americans worried that Lebanon would become another Vietnam. Then, in October, Muslim fundamentalist car-bombers struck U.S. headquarters and a French barracks simultaneously. Fifty-eight Frenchmen and 241 Americans were killed.

For dignity's sake, the peacekeepers waited until February 1984 to leave. In March, Syrian president Hafez al-Assad persuaded his Lebanese counterpart, Amin Gemayel, to rescind his deal with Israel. Israel's gradual pullout continued anyway. By mid-1985, most Israeli troops were gone, leaving Lebanon's armed factions to turn on one another. **◂1982.2 ▸1989.6**

THE COLD WAR

Missile Destroys Flight 007

4 Making a routine trip from New York City to Seoul, South Korea, Korean Air Lines flight 007 stopped in Anchorage, Alaska, on the morning of August 31, 1983. An hour and a half later, the Boeing 747 took off on the last leg of its overnight journey with 269 people on board. Five hours after the plane left Anchorage, a Soviet fighter shot it down over Sakhalin Island, a sensitive Soviet military zone—killing everyone on board, including U.S. congressman Larry McDonald. That much, and little else, about the ill-fated flight is clear.

President Reagan quickly condemned "the murder of innocent civilians." But how those civilians had strayed into restricted Soviet airspace in a part of the world subject to constant surveillance by U.S. and Japanese intelligence was never satisfactorily explained. Nor was the brutal Soviet action. At first, Soviet officials denied all knowledge of the attack; then they said they had repeatedly tried to establish radio contact with KAL 007 before opening fire. (That claim was refuted in 1992, when the Soviets finally turned over the "black box," or flight recorder, which they'd previously denied having recovered. Soviet records, however, do indicate that those responsible truly did not realize the craft was a passenger plane.) Finally, they defended their right to shoot down an intruder. They did not apologize.

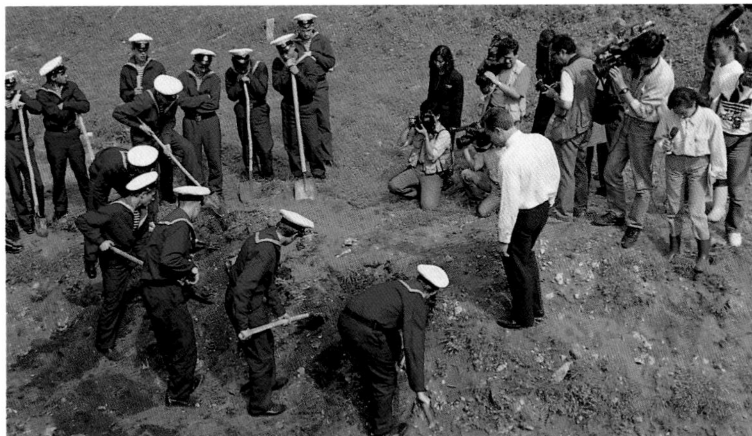

In 1993, Russian sailors opened the grave of KAL 007 victims for relatives of the dead.

Flight 007 had pursued an unauthorized path that took it over, successively, the Kamchatka Peninsula (another military zone), the Sea of Okhotsk (home of the Soviet Far Eastern Fleet), and finally Sakhalin Island. Given the strategic importance of the flyover zone, the spotty record of U.S. intelligence agencies, and the lack of any conclusive explanation, some suspected the plane was on an espionage mission. In the end, the truth about KAL 007 was reduced to one hard fact: that 269 people had been blown out of the sky. **◂1960.5 ▸1985.1**

WEST GERMANY

Greens Enter Parliament

5 One unintended side effect of Ronald Reagan's military buildup was the entry of an antinuclear, environmentalist, feminist "antiparty" political party called Die Gruenen (the Greens) into West Germany's staid Bundestag. After winning 5.6 percent of the vote in the election of March 1983, the Greens marched in, beating African drums, wearing denim, and carrying plants, to take their 27 parliamentary seats. Their accession upstaged the installation of a new chancellor, conservative Christian Democrat Helmut Kohl.

The Greens had been born in 1979, the year NATO voted to deploy medium-range Pershing 2 and cruise missiles in Europe (to counter Soviet SS-20s aimed at the West). Their big boost came in 1981, when the new U.S. president announced that America would begin producing neutron bombs. Millions of Europeans, fearing that Washington intended to fight a nuclear war on their soil, joined demonstrations organized by such groups as Denmark's Women for Peace, Britain's Campaign for Nuclear Disarmament, and the Belgium-based international Catholic movement, Pax Christi. In West Germany, some 250 local organizations banded together to form Die Gruenen. Soon the party began winning local elections.

Four years after entering the Bundestag, the Greens increased their share of the vote to 8.3 percent. By then, similar parties had appeared all over Europe. But the anarchistic organization was weakened by its deliberate lack of leadership—despite the prominence of fiery young cofounder Petra Kelly, the German stepdaughter of a U.S, Army officer—and divisions between the pragmatic Realos and the unbending Fundi factions. The Greens' opposition to German reunification (unless both Germanies adopted their policies) was also damaging. In 1990, they lost all their seats. Kelly died two years later when her lover, a retired West German general, killed her, then himself. **◂1977.3 ▸1986.9**

European antinuclear groups gave rise to political "antiparties" like the Greens. Here, an antinuke demonstrator in Paris.

DEATHS

Raymond Aron, French sociologist.

George Balanchine, Russian-U.S. choreographer and ballet dancer.

Georges Bidault, French political leader.

Eubie Blake, U.S. musician and composer.

Paul "Bear" Bryant, U.S. football coach.

Luis Buñuel, Spanish filmmaker.

Karen Carpenter, U.S. singer.

Terence Cooke, U.S. cardinal.

George Cukor, U.S. filmmaker.

Jack Dempsey, U.S. boxer.

Lynn Fontanne, U.K.-U.S. actress.

Buckminster Fuller, U.S. inventor.

Ira Gershwin, U.S. lyricist.

Arthur Godfrey, U.S. entertainer.

Arthur Koestler, Hungarian-U.K. writer.

Leopold III, Belgian king.

Joan Miró, Spanish painter.

David Niven, U.K.-U.S. actor.

Nikolay Podgorny, U.S.S.R. statesman.

Ralph Richardson, U.K. actor.

Gloria Swanson, U.S. actress.

Umberto II, Italian king.

Balthazar Johannes Vorster, South African political leader.

Muddy Waters, U.S. musician and singer.

Tennessee Williams, U.S. playwright.

Mantegna's Edge **(Al Held);** ***Zag*** **(Nancy Graves) ... Film:** ***Terms of Endearment*** **(James L. Brooks);** ***Fanny and Alexander*** **(Ingmar Bergman);** ***The King of Comedy*** **(Martin Scorsese);** ***Yentl*** **(Barbra Streisand) ... Theater:** ***'night, Mother*** **(Marsha Norman);** ***Fool for Love*** **(Sam Shepard);** ***Painting Churches*** **(Tina Howe);** ***Brighton Beach Memoirs*** **(Neil Simon);** ***La Cage aux Folles*** **(Jerry Herman) ... TV:** ***The Thorn Birds.***

"I don't care whether they are real or forged. They are so boring, so meaningless, it hardly makes any difference."
—Hans Bloom of the German Federal Archives, on the Hitler diaries

NEW IN 1983

Computer mouse (Apple).

Camcorders.

Compact disc.

Federal holiday commemorating Martin Luther King, Jr.

Cabbage Patch dolls.

IN THE UNITED STATES

▶WOMAN IN SPACE—Astronaut Sally Ride, a former tennis player who quit the professional circuit to complete a Ph.D. in astrophysics,

took off from Edwards Air Force Base aboard the space shuttle *Challenger* on June 18, becoming the first American woman to fly in space. One of five crew members on the six-day mission, Ride helped deploy two satellites. ◀1981.12 ▶1986.2

▶NATION AT RISK—The National Commission of Excellence in Education released "A Nation at Risk," a report on the state of American education. The commission warned of a "rising tide of mediocrity" and recommended new high school curricula emphasizing science and the humanities, salary increases for teachers, a lengthened school year, and "far more homework." ▶1987.V

▶WATT QUITS—Secretary of the Interior James Watt was forced to resign in October. Watt had become a grave political liability, thanks to his bad judgment—he'd called the U.S. a country of "liberals and Americans," compared environmentalists to Communists and Nazis, and (the last straw) said of one commission he oversaw, "I have a black, I have a woman, two Jews, and

1983

POPULAR CULTURE

The Hitler-Diary Hoax

6 The West German weekly *Stern* launched one of modern journalism's most embarrassing follies in 1983, when—with banner headlines and a three-hour press conference—it announced the discovery of Adolf Hitler's long-secret diaries. Gerd Heidemann, a veteran reporter for the magazine, claimed he'd found the 62-volume manuscript after a four-year worldwide quest. Supposedly rescued from a downed Nazi plane in 1945, the diaries (which portrayed the Führer as remarkably unwarlike and well-disposed toward Jews) had found their way from East Germany to a Swiss bank vault; to protect the lives of his sources, Heidemann declined to say more. Eager European journals paid *Stern* up to $3 million for serialization rights, and the scoop was front-page news around the globe.

Even at the press conference, however, there was trouble: One Hitler biographer was dragged out by security guards when he shouted that the diaries were fake, and renowned historian Hugh Trevor-Roper, who'd earlier pronounced them genuine, began backpedaling. Experts everywhere took sides. Stories of Heidemann's Nazi sympathies—and notorious gullibility—emerged. At the insistence of *Stern* editorial employees, management belatedly sent samples to the federal archives for testing. But editor in chief Peter Koch brandished two of the volumes on American television, crowing that only incompetent scholars and jealous publishers could doubt their authenticity.

The day after *Stern*'s first installment appeared, the archivists delivered their verdict: "grotesque" forgery. The handwriting was wrong; the notebooks contained polyester, a postwar product; the text was largely cribbed from a book written in 1962. After prolonged hedging, Heidemann admitted he'd bought the diaries (with *Stern*'s $4 million) from a dealer in Nazi memorabilia who dabbled in calligraphy. The dealer confessed and went to jail. Heidemann was fired and sued. Koch and another top editor quit. And several respected periodicals were caught with egg on their faces. **◀1972.M**

A German cartoonist's vision of Hitler's daily life. In the last frame, the Führer points to *Stern*'s logo, advising readers to buy the magazine to find out more.

THE UNITED STATES

New Urban Ills

7 Even as First Lady Nancy Reagan was urging American youth to "Just Say No" to drugs in 1983, one of the most addictive and destructive intoxicants ever seen was turning up on the nation's streets. Crack, a rocklike, smokable form of cocaine, was developed by drug traffickers in the Bahamas (but was easily manufactured in any kitchen). It struck the United States like a wrecking ball. Along with homelessness, crack addiction spread a terrible and lasting blight on urban life.

Cheap (a hit might sell for as little as three dollars), superpotent, and extremely addictive, crack could not have been better engineered as a destructive agent. Whereas it took weeks to become addicted to ordinary (and pricey) cocaine, a crack habit could take hold within days. Unlike heroin, crack often made its users aggressive and paranoid. Moreover, the crack trade was run by teenage gangs wielding automatic weapons.

Homelessness in American cities: A man scavenges in a garbage can in a Washington, D.C., park.

Enterprising city youths, often cut off from legitimate economic opportunity, became local drug moguls. Their customers were often driven to theft or prostitution. And many people on both sides of the transactions wound up dead as competing drug gangs turned entire neighborhoods into war zones. In New York City alone, the jail population grew from 10,000 to 18,000 between 1986 and 1988; drug-influenced child abuse tripled; and the murder rate rose by 10 percent. Nationally, the incidence of violent crime rose by 33 percent during the decade.

Crack aggravated the problem of homelessness—addicts often wound up on the streets, and people on the streets often wound up on drugs. But homelessness was a social problem that transcended substance abuse (including alcoholism). A national trend toward "de-institutionalization" meant that scores of state-run psychiatric hospitals drastically reduced their number of beds or were closed altogether. Thousands of mentally ill patients—most of whom were unprepared to live on their own—were cast out on the streets. Severe shortages of affordable housing in

SPORTS: Baseball: World Series, Baltimore Orioles defeat Philadelphia Phillies, 4–1 ... Football: Super Bowl, Washington Redskins defeat Miami Dolphins, 27–17 ... Basketball: NBA, Philadelphia 76ers defeat L.A. Lakers, 4–0 ... Hockey: Stanley Cup, N.Y. Islanders defeat Edmonton Oilers, 4–0 (fourth consecutive win) ... Track & Field: Mary Decker wins 1,500- and 3,000-meter races at world championships.

"Wake up the wife, the children, the dog ... to celebrate the greatest day in the history of Australian sport."
—An Australian radio reporter, after *Australia II* captured the America's Cup

cities around the country, coupled with Reagan-era cutbacks in many of the social entitlement programs that had been in place since the days of Lyndon Johnson's Great Society, left entire families displaced, with no "safety net." Moreover, as the industrial sector gave way to an increasingly service-based economy, joblessness or minimum-wage employment became chronic conditions for many workers who'd once held well-paying factory jobs. By the end of the decade, poverty and crime had become prominent features of urban life in the world's richest country. **◂1965.M ▸1984.M**

Bond *(far left)*, skipper John Bertrand *(right)*, and a crew member aboard the *Australia II* off Newport, Rhode Island, after narrowing the U.S. lead to 3–2 (in a best-of-seven series).

SPORTS

Australia Wins America's Cup

8 "Any boss who sacks anyone for not showing up today," declared Australian prime minister Bob Hawke, kicking off his nation's biggest celebration since the end of World War II, "is a bum!" The occasion: Australia's capture of the 1983 America's Cup, the world's top yachting championship, after 132 years of U.S. domination.

The Cup hadn't always been America's. Initially called the Hundred Guinea Cup, it was first offered by Britain's Royal Yacht Club, in 1851, for a race around the Isle of Wight. A Yankee schooner, the *America*, won the prize, and the victors donated it to the New York Yacht Club for a perpetual international competition. The first challenge came in 1870, and throughout 24 tourneys since then, the silver trophy had remained bolted to a table at the club (partly because the reigning U.S. team made the rules and determined the course). But in 1983, Perth entrepreneur Alan Bond, who'd launched his first contender in the race in 1974, unsheathed his country's secret weapon: the *Australia II*, whose delta-winged "upside-down" keel radically increased agility, speed, and stability. Despite American objections to the newfangled boat, officials ruled it legitimate.

The *Australia II* battled torn sails, broken equipment, slow starts, and churning seas to come back from two losses to America's *Liberty* (captained by Dennis Conner) and, in a tie-breaking race, to take the Cup, 4–3. At a White House ceremony honoring both teams, President Reagan warned the victors, "Don't bolt that cup down too tightly." He was prescient: America regained the prize in 1987. **◂1977.13**

DIPLOMACY

Adieu, UNESCO

9 Two of Ronald Reagan's principal political missions—cutting social spending and reasserting America's authority in the rebellious Third World—came together in December 1983, when he announced his intention to withdraw the United States from the United Nations Educational, Scientific, and Cultural Organization. UNESCO was one of the UN's largest agencies, and the only major world organization promoting intergovernmental projects on science, education, and culture. But to Reagan, its "misguided policies, tendentious programs, and extravagant budgetary mismanagement" were grounds for divorce.

Founded in 1946 to foster "the unrestricted pursuit of objective truth" and "the free exchange of ideas and knowledge," UNESCO began as a small, Western-dominated body. Over the decades, however, as UNESCO expanded to include dozens of newly decolonized nations, the organization began to address matters like human rights and nuclear disarmament—issues that led to disputes between Western and Third World members. Most offensive to Washington, perhaps, were UNESCO's hostility toward Israel and its endorsement of a "new world information order" that aimed to improve reporting on developing nations in part by imposing restrictions on reporters.

U.S. officials complained that the organization "politicized virtually every subject." In fact, UNESCO had always been political; its politics were just no longer American. The United States also blasted UNESCO's swollen budget and a bureaucracy that spent 80 percent of its funding at its Paris headquarters rather than in the field. (UNESCO representatives countered that the organization was an information clearinghouse, not an on-site development agency.)

Citing UNESCO's "endemic hostility toward the institutions of a free society," the United States pulled out.

Even UNESCO critics suggested the Americans could better achieve reform by staying in than by leaving. West Germany called the withdrawal "incomprehensible"; Spain used the word "tantrum." But a year later, at the end of a mandatory waiting period, America withdrew, taking with it an annual $46 million contribution—25 percent of UNESCO's operating budget. Britain soon followed suit. **◂1946.2**

IN THE UNITED STATES

a cripple." While Watt's insensitive talk offended the wider public, environmentalists were already upset about his land-management policies. He encouraged strip mining, proposed that the last virgin U.S. forests be opened to drilling and mining, and leased federal preserves to coal-mining companies at bargain-basement rates.

▶COMPUTER HACKERS—On August 21, a group of young computer whizzes from Milwaukee, aged 17 to 22, electronically broke into 20 of the country's top computer systems. Among the supposedly secure computers the youths hacked into: the highly restricted nuclear research center at Los Alamos National Laboratory. ◂1981.10 ▸1984.V

▶VANITY LIVES—With a thick, glossy, self-consciously literate (and, according to critics, contradictory and confused) March issue, *Vanity*

***Fair* magazine was resurrected after 46 years in the grave. From 1914 until it folded in 1936, *Vanity Fair* was a fey Jazz Age compendium of wit and style that reached fewer than 100,000 readers a month. Revived by Condé Nast publications for more than $10 million, the new magazine instantly reached some 600,000 charter subscribers. Even so, it stumbled through an eleven-month identity crisis before the publishers brought in 30-year-old British editor Tina Brown. She remade *Vanity Fair* into a successful handbook of 1980s high-rent pop—a blend of celebrity worship, careerism, and salable gentility.**

POLITICS & BUSINESS: GNP: $3,434.4 billion ... Harold Washington is elected the first black mayor of Chicago ... Presidential panel recommends 100 MX missiles be installed in existing missile silos in Wyoming and Nebraska ... Supreme Court rules states may ban construction of nuclear power plants for economic reasons.

"I went to the movies, and I saw a dog 30 feet high. And this dog was made entirely of light."—Laurie Anderson, in *United States Parts I-IV*

AROUND THE WORLD

▶CRAXI IN CHARGE—In April, Bettino Craxi, head of the Italian Socialist Party, pulled out of the Christian Democrat–dominated coalition government, precipitating its downfall. A general election was held, and Craxi was invited to form a new coalition government. He thus became Italy's first Socialist premier. A reformer, Craxi distanced his party from the Communists, supported American foreign policy, implemented an anti-inflationary tight money policy, and abolished Catholicism as the official state religion. ◀1976.14 ▶1994.M

▶ARGENTINA GETS CIVILIAN RULE—After eight years of military rule during which the government killed thousands of dissident citizens, Argentina inaugurated a civilian president. A moderate, Raúl Alfonsín, was elected in October, after the military regime stepped down in the wake of defeat in the Falklands War. Alfonsín concentrated on prosecuting military leaders for human rights violations and cutting Argentina's massive foreign debt. ◀1982.1 ▶1989.8

▶CYPRUS DIVIDED—Turkish Cypriots in 1983 declared independence from the rest of ethnically segregated Cyprus. The Mediterranean island had been divided into Turkish and Greek zones since 1974. Greek Cypriots fled south; Turkish Cypriots went north. The newly proclaimed Republic of North Cyprus was recognized only by Turkey. ◀1974.5

▶NEW CONSTITUTION, OLD STORY—South Africa adopted a new constitution in 1983, granting limited representation to "Coloureds"—people of mixed heritage—and to Indians, but not to blacks. All real power still resided with President P.W. Botha's National Party, apartheid's keeper. The "reform" instigated the strongest backlash against apartheid in a generation. ◀1976.4 ▶1984.8

THEATER

Mamet's Slippery Salesmen

10 With *Glengarry Glen Ross,* his Pulitzer Prize–winning 1983 play about a group of crooked, cutthroat real estate salesmen, David Mamet wrung compelling drama from the seedy side of business. He also made poetry of verbal aggression. The salesmen's rhythmic, wildly profane speeches were blisteringly realistic—but also ritualistic, incantatory. The play's characters, all men, use language as a magical weapon: to beat back competitors, to exact revenge on a system that has cost them their dignity, to prove to themselves that they are alive. The play was inevitably compared with *Death of a Salesman.* But unlike Arthur Miller's classic, *Glengarry Glen Ross* contained no sermons. Stripped of sentiment, mingling natural speech cadences and high literary style, Mamet's writing was closer to the tradition of Harold Pinter or Samuel Beckett.

London's National Theatre mounted *Glengarry* before it came to New York. Above, two salesmen discuss a shady deal.

Mamet, a Chicago native, had gained a local following as a playwright while working as a short-order cook, a cabdriver, and—the inspiration for *Glengarry Glen Ross* —a salesman of "worthless" real estate. (His verbally aggressive manner, his leather jackets, and his large cigars also became local legend.) In 1974, when he was 27, his play *Sexual Perversity in Chicago* was produced off-Broadway. The following year, *American Buffalo,* a story of small-time hoods in the low-end antique coin trade, opened on Broadway.

Glengarry Glen Ross catapulted Mamet to the highest tier of living American playwrights. He soon began writing for Hollywood, and, with *House of Games* (1987), directing. Mamet wrote the script for the critically praised 1992 screen version of *Glengarry Glen Ross.* **◀1962.10**

One local resident called *Surrounded Islands* "Pepto-Bismol spills." Others marveled.

ART

Christo Wraps Up

11 In 1983, an artist with a single name and a monomaniacal method completed his most ambitious endeavor to date: encircling eleven small islands in Miami's Biscayne Bay with 200-foot-wide, luminescent pink aprons. Bulgarian émigré Christo (born Christo Vladimirov Javacheff in 1935) described *Surrounded Islands* as "my version of Monet's *Water Lilies,*" referring to the French impressionist's dreamy, aquatic paintings. To many Miamians, however, it was simply a $3.5 million eyesore. Like all of Christo's art, it was temporary: After two weeks, he and his assistants dismantled the work—including 6.5 million square feet of polypropylene fabric.

Christo's formidable projects reliably provoked a media hubbub —and mixed reactions. Previously, he'd wrapped a Swiss museum, hung a mammoth curtain across a Colorado valley, and unspooled a 24-mile fabric fence across California farmland to the Pacific. Admirers extolled the mystery his sculptures lent to familiar landscapes, and their mingling of monumentality and evanescence. Detractors dismissed them as "sculptural fluff" and claimed they harmed the environment.

Despite planning worthy of a military campaign, his projects were subject to unforeseen, sometimes tragic, forces. In 1991, a work involving thousands of 500-pound umbrellas resulted in the accidental deaths of two people. **◀1970.M**

ART

The Rise of Avant-Pop

12 Like Christo's sculpture, performance art was a hybrid medium that flourished in the adventurous art climate of the 1980s. Blending drama, music, sculpture, and anything else its exponents chose, the form descended from 1920s dada and 1960s "happenings," and inherited those genres' power to provoke. In 1983, performance artist Laurie Anderson parlayed her newfound stardom (her quirky single "O Superman" had hit number two on British pop charts) into a premiere of her avant-garde magnum opus, *United States, Parts I-IV,* at the estimable Brooklyn Academy of Music.

A high-tech meditation on twentieth-century life, the six-hour work (performed over two nights) incorporated aphoristic monologues—delivered through devices that allowed her to speak in various voices or sing in chords—accompanied by film clips, cartoons, slides, and instruments ranging from bagpipe to a violin whose recording-tape bow played words.

Anderson's narrative was more allusive than incisive, and her music lacked the sophistication of its minimalist models (the works of "serious" composers like Philip Glass, Steve Reich, and Terry Riley), but the sights and sounds made a powerful combination. Critics called her "an electronic Cassandra" who "pointed the way for the opera of the future." **◀1976.10**

Laurie Anderson flew at the head of the pop-culture flock.

NOBEL PRIZES: Peace: Lech Walesa (Polish; Solidarity movement) ... Literature: William Golding (U.K.; novelist) ... Chemistry: Henry Taube (U.S.; electron transfer reactions) ... Medicine: Barbara McClintock (U.S.; mobile genetic elements) ... Physics: Subrahmanyan Chandrasekhar and William A. Fowler (U.S.; evolution of stars) ... Economics: Gerard Debreu (U.S.).

A VOICE FROM 1983

Space Age Defense

From a nationally televised address by President Ronald Reagan, March 23, 1983

On March 23, 1983, just two weeks after denouncing the Soviet Union as "the focus of evil in the modern world" and "an evil empire," President Ronald Reagan, in a nationally televised speech, sketched his plan for a national defense system that, he said, would make nuclear weapons "impotent and obsolete." The President proposed to build a nuclear shield that would offer the United States complete protection from Soviet missiles. Although he did not identify it as such, Reagan was unveiling his Strategic Defense Initiative—the futuristic space- and land-based defensive system that was soon nicknamed "Star Wars." The program was controversial from the start. SDI depended on fanciful, yet-to-be-researched technology, it violated the 1972 U.S.-Soviet ban on anti-ballistic-missile defense systems, it left NATO states feeling abandoned, and, particularly frightening to many critics, it escalated the arms race to the final frontier. Nevertheless, the program became a pet project of the Reagan administration. It was a measure of the President's salesmanship—his combination of folksy appeal ("That budget is much more than a long list of numbers") and ominous scare tactics ("The budget request ... has been trimmed to the limits of safety")—that many Americans warmed to Star Wars. The government spent $30 billion on the program before pulling the plug in 1993, two years after the "evil empire" had been dismantled. ◄1979.4 ►1986.5

The defense policy of the United States is based on a simple premise: The United States does not start fights. We will never be an aggressor. We maintain our strength in order to deter and defend against aggression—to preserve freedom and peace.

Before beginning his speech, President Reagan showed the press photos of Soviet missiles in Cuba.

Since the dawn of the atomic age we've sought to reduce the risk of war by maintaining a strong deterrent and by seeking genuine arms control. "Deterrence" means simply this: making sure any adversary who thinks about attacking the United States, or our allies, or our vital interests, concludes that the risks to him outweigh any potential gains. Once he understands that, he won't attack. We maintain the peace through our strength; weakness only invites aggression.

This strategy of deterrence has not changed. It still works. But what it takes to maintain deterrence has changed. It took one kind of military force to deter an attack when we had far more nuclear weapons than any other power; it takes another kind now that the Soviets, for example, have enough accurate and powerful nuclear weapons to destroy virtually all of our missiles on the ground. Now, this is not to say that the Soviet Union is planning to make war on us. Nor do I believe a war is inevitable—quite the contrary. But what must be recognized is that our security is based on being prepared to meet all threats.

There was a time when we depended on coastal forts and artillery batteries, because, with the weaponry of that day, any attack would have had to come by sea. Well, this is a different world, and our defenses must be based on recognition and awareness of the weaponry possessed by other nations in the nuclear age.

We can't afford to believe that we will never be threatened. There have been two world wars in my lifetime. We didn't start them and, indeed, did everything we could to avoid being drawn into them. But we were ill-prepared for both—had we been better prepared, peace might have been preserved....

The calls for cutting back the defense budget come in nice, simple arithmetic. They're the same kind of talk that led the democracies to neglect their defenses in the 1930s and invited the tragedy of World War II. We must not let that grim chapter of history repeat itself through apathy or neglect....

If the Soviet Union will join with us in our effort to achieve major reduction, we will have succeeded in stabilizing the nuclear balance. Nevertheless, it will still be necessary to rely on the specter of retaliation, on mutual threat. And that's a sad commentary on the human condition. Wouldn't it be better to save lives than to avenge them? Are we not capable of demonstrating our peaceful intentions by applying all our abilities and our ingenuity to achieving a truly lasting stability? I think we are. Indeed, we must.

After careful consultation with my advisers, including the Joint Chiefs of Staff, I believe there is a way. Let me share with you a vision of the future which offers hope. It is that we embark on a program to counter the awesome Soviet missile threat with measures that are defensive. Let us turn to the very strengths in technology that spawned our great industrial base and that have given us the quality of life we enjoy today.

What if free people could live secure in the knowledge that their security did not rest upon the threat of instant U.S. retaliation to deter a Soviet attack, that we could intercept and destroy strategic ballistic missiles before they reached our own soil or that of our allies?

I know this is a formidable, technical task, one that may not be accomplished before the end of this century. Yet, current technology has attained a level of sophistication where it's reasonable for us to begin this effort....

America does possess—now—the technologies to attain very significant improvements in the effectiveness of our conventional, nonnuclear forces. Proceeding boldly with these new technologies, we can significantly reduce any incentive that the Soviet Union may have to threaten attack against the United States or its allies....

I clearly recognize that defensive systems have limitations and raise certain problems and ambiguities. If paired with offensive systems, they can be viewed as fostering an aggressive policy, and no one wants that. But with these considerations firmly in mind, I call upon the scientific community in our country, those who gave us nuclear weapons, to turn their great talents now to the cause of mankind and world peace, to give us the means of rendering these nuclear weapons impotent and obsolete.

Tonight ... I'm taking an important first step. I am directing a comprehensive and intensive effort to define a long-term research-and-development program to begin to achieve our ultimate goal of eliminating the threat posed by strategic nuclear missiles....

My fellow Americans, tonight we're launching an effort which holds the promise of changing the course of human history. There will be risks, and results take time. But I believe we can do it. As we cross this threshold, I ask for your prayers and your support.

"I thought I had seen everything, but this is worse than war."—**Subedar A.B. Bhosale, an Indian soldier in Bhopal, India**

STORY OF THE YEAR

The Deadliest Leak

1 After midnight on December 3, 1984, a cloud of toxic methyl isocyanate gas was discharged through a faulty valve on a 45-ton tank of pesticide at a chemical plant in Bhopal, India, owned by the U.S.-based Union Carbide corporation (though operated entirely by Indians). As the deadly vapor enveloped the city, hundreds of victims were suffocated in their beds; others fled into the night, their eyes burned white by the invisible poison, which is similar to a very potent tear gas. Thousands more died in the coming days, their scarred lungs filled with fluid. Said a survivor who'd watched cattle drop dead in a field, "I thought it was the plague." Within a week, the accident had turned into the worst industrial disaster in history. Some 2,000 people had been killed, and some 2,000 more would eventually die. Another 200,000 were injured or sick—most of them with long-term lung, kidney, liver, and eye ailments.

Many of Bhopal's victims received only rudimentary medical attention and were left with lasting disabilities.

While India struggled to cope with the calamity, Union Carbide faced a withering barrage of criticism. Employees claimed that the company had cut corners in Bhopal, taking risks that were outlawed in the United States, where higher safety standards prevailed. Official denials notwithstanding, records showed that numerous accidents had occurred at the plant, and, damningly, that the facility lacked safety systems present at a similar operation in West Virginia. Chairman Warren Anderson flew to India to survey the damage and was immediately arrested for "negligence and criminal corporate liability." (After lengthy negotiations, he was released on bail.) Seeking as much as $15 billion compensation for the victims, a brigade of Indian and American lawyers filed lawsuits. "Something like this happens," said a Union Carbide representative, "and people everywhere begin seeing dollar signs."

Around the world, the Bhopal disaster was seen as an illustration of one of the central dilemmas of modern times: Created to enhance life on earth, technology also endangers it. Union Carbide eventually settled all claims for $470 million, about $150,000 for each of Bhopal's dead. **◂1973.7 ▸1986.1**

INDIA

Indira Gandhi Assassinated

2 For nearly two decades, Indira Gandhi dominated Indian politics, holding together the world's most populous democracy. When, on October 31, 1984, the four-time prime minister was ambushed in her garden and shot repeatedly by two members of her own security staff, the ethnically and religiously fractious country threatened to come apart at the seams.

Though not as beloved as her father, Jawaharlal Nehru, the founder of modern India, Gandhi had earned the nickname "Mother India," both for her autocratic style and for her fierce battles against the country's external foes and internal divisions. She had decisively defeated Pakistan in the war of 1971 and had defended Indian unity against such threats as Sikh separatism in Punjab state and Muslim unrest in Kashmir. In the end, she was engulfed by the communal strife she'd fought (and inadvertently encouraged with heavy-handed policies). Her death was retaliation for her crackdown on Sikh separatists in June, when she sent the Indian army into the Golden Temple in Amritsar, Punjab—the Sikhs' holiest shrine and the headquarters of a budding terrorist movement. More than 450 Sikhs died at Amritsar, which had also been the site of a notorious 1919 massacre of Indians by British soldiers.

As her son and successor Rajiv *(second from left)* looks on, Indira Gandhi is cremated on a traditional Hindu funeral pyre.

Gandhi's assassination provoked an even ghastlier bloodletting: Outraged Hindus rampaged against Sikhs, beating and burning innocent families to death. In the week after the assassination, rioters killed more than 5,000 around Delhi, and thousands more throughout the country.

The impossible job of restoring order fell to Rajiv Gandhi, Indira's older son, who'd become heir apparent after his younger brother, Sanjay, was killed in a 1980 stunt-plane crash (a tragedy from which their mother never fully recovered). Elected head of the ruling Congress Party, Rajiv became prime minister in December, further extending the Nehru-Gandhi dynasty, which had governed for all but five years since independence in 1947. "She was mother not only to me but to the whole nation," Rajiv eulogized, urging peace. But peace was elusive, and he too died violently, in 1991. **◂1966.7 ▸1991.M**

NICARAGUA

U.S. Mines Harbors

3 The latest round of American intervention came as no surprise to Nicaraguans—after all, their country had suffered three U.S. invasions during the twentieth century—but Americans themselves raised a storm of protest when the Central Intelligence Agency mined Nicaragua's harbors in April 1984. Not only did the act violate international law, critics charged—it wasted tax money during a budget crunch. Congress responded by canceling aid to the contras, the counterrevolutionary guerrillas who, since 1981, had received the Reagan administration's covert (but hardly secret) backing in their war against Nicaragua's leftist Sandinista government.

The Sandinistas had seized power in 1979, ousting dictator Anastasio Somoza Debayle. At first, the officially nonaligned new regime—which initiated literacy and public-health campaigns, was less repressive than any of its predecessors, and left most property in private hands—enjoyed good relations with Washington. At President Carter's urging, Congress in 1980 voted $75 million in aid to Nicaragua. (Western European countries helped more.) But Somoza had left behind a $1.5 billion debt, and civil war had rendered at least a fifth of the population homeless. The Sandinistas thus negotiated a $100 million trade agreement with the Soviet Union. Aid from Moscow and Havana (and friendship with El Salvador's FMLN guerrillas) cost the Sandinistas dearly: When Reagan took office, he began arming the contras.

Reagan called the contras "freedom fighters." Others, however, noted that they were led mostly by Somoza loyalists; human rights groups documented their habit of kidnapping, torturing, and murdering health workers, teachers, and other government employees.

ART & CULTURE: Books: *Love Medicine* (Louise Erdrich); *The Unbearable Lightness of Being* (Milan Kundera); *Foreign Affairs* (Alison Lurie); *Lincoln* (Gore Vidal); *Cities and the Wealth of Nations* (Jane Jacobs) ... Music: "What's Love Got to Do with It" (Lyle and Britten); *Born in the U.S.A.* (Bruce Springsteen, LP); *Like a Virgin* (Madonna, LP); *The Perfect Stranger* (Pierre Boulez) ... Painting & Sculpture: *Departure*

"Nature is never truly conquered. The human retroviruses and their intricate relationship with the human cell are but one example of that fact."—**AIDS researcher Dr. Robert Gallo**

In the vital port of Corinto, Nicaraguans rigged up fishing boats to sweep for mines.

Around the same time the harbor mining became public, a handbook used by the CIA to train contras surfaced. The manual explained how to kill public officials and sabotage the economy. Congress duly cut off contra aid, but the dirty war continued: Barred from legal funding sources, the White House began diverting money from illicit arms sales to the rebels. **◂1979.8 ▸1985.5**

DISASTERS

Africa Starves

4 In 1984, a decade after starvation killed some 300,000 sub-Saharan Africans (mostly Ethiopians), an even greater famine was scourging the continent. Although advances in plant genetics and other agricultural techniques—the so-called Green Revolution—had more than doubled worldwide grain production since 1950, most African countries had reaped little benefit. Civil wars, overpopulation, overgrazing, deforestation (leading to soil erosion and the use of dung for fuel rather than for fertilizer), government policies that discouraged food production (in favor of military buildup, industry, or cash crops), international recession, lack of infrastructure, lack of foreign exchange to import food—all combined with a persistent drought to condemn hundreds of thousands to death from hunger.

Though reports of famine had appeared in print for months, they prompted a global outcry only late in the year, when television audiences confronted nightly footage of the victims. Governments and charitable organizations in North America, Europe, and Oceania sent more than $1 billion in assistance—but what truly captured the public imagination was a series of relief efforts by celebrities. Band Aid, a group of British musicians organized by Bob Geldof (leader of a New Wave band called the Boomtown Rats), raised millions with the single "Do They Know It's Christmas?" The following year, its North American counterpart, USA for Africa, brought in even more with a star-studded recording of the Michael Jackson–Lionel Richie composition "We Are the World." Then satellites linked the two organizations for an intercontinental "charity rock" spectacular, Live Aid, seen by approximately 1.8 billion people. It garnered approximately $50 million.

As staggering as these fund-raising efforts were, they came too late for an estimated two million famine victims, half of them Ethiopian, who were dead by June 1985; more died as the drought and world attention waned. The specter of famine continued to hang over the continent in the 1990s. **◂1967.6 ▸1992.6**

The Live Aid concert in July 1985 drew 100,000 fans to Philadelphia's JFK Stadium; another 72,000 attended in London. The event raised $50 million in relief money.

MEDICINE

Controversy over AIDS Virus

5 In April 1984, a top U.S. health official announced the discovery of the virus that causes AIDS. Just days earlier, a different U.S. official had declared that the virus had been discovered in 1983 by a Paris-based team headed by Dr. Luc Montagnier *(left)*.

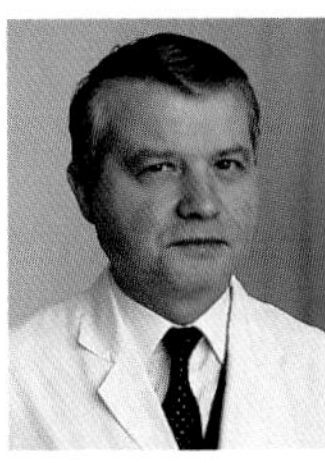

The French called the virus LAV (lymphadenopathy-associated virus). The American team, headed by Dr. Robert Gallo of Washington's National Cancer Institute, called theirs HTLV-3 (human T-cell lymphotropic virus). Thus began a bitter controversy.

Montagnier's team had isolated LAV from the lymph nodes of a Parisian AIDS patient, but was unable to grow enough LAV to prove that it caused AIDS. The media focused on Gallo, who theorized that AIDS was caused by HTLV-1, a retrovirus he'd discovered in 1980, which causes a rare cancer of the immune system's T cells. (Unlike other life-forms, retroviruses translate genetic information from RNA to DNA, instead of the other way around. Thus their own genetic blueprints can be copied into the DNA of host cells, which become retrovirus factories.)

Gallo's findings showed his HTLV variant to be almost identical to LAV. Since viruses mutate constantly, an American strain of AIDS virus would be unlikely to have a structure so similar to LAV's. The French scientists concluded that Gallo (with whom they'd exchanged viral samples) had cultured their virus. But Gallo insisted he'd used his own. When he beat the French to a patent for an AIDS blood test, they cried foul. In 1987, a joint decision by the nations' governments split both the credit and the royalties between the two teams.

By then, scientists had agreed to call the AIDS virus HIV (human immunodeficiency virus). But accusations against Gallo persisted. In 1991, he admitted to having unwittingly used the French virus; investigators concluded that both viruses had been contaminated by a third strain—which explained both the oversight and the similarities. **◂1981.1 ▸1985.12**

DEATHS

Ansel Adams, U.S. photographer.

Yuri Andropov, U.S.S.R. political leader.

Brooks Atkinson, U.S. writer.

Count Basie, U.S. musician.

Enrico Berlinguer, Italian political leader.

Richard Burton, U.K. actor.

Truman Capote, U.S. writer.

Jackie Coogan, U.S. actor.

Paul Dirac, U.K. physicist.

Michel Foucault, French philosopher and historian.

George Gallup, U.S. pollster.

Indira Gandhi, Indian prime minister.

Marvin Gaye, U.S. singer.

Lillian Hellman, U.S. playwright.

Alfred A. Knopf, U.S. publisher.

Ray Kroc, U.S. restaurateur and businessman.

James Mason, U.K.-U.S. actor.

Ethel Merman, U.S. singer and actress.

Martin Niemöller, German theologian.

Liam O'Flaherty, Irish writer.

Sam Peckinpah, U.S. filmmaker.

Lee Krasner Pollock, U.S. painter.

J.B. Priestley, U.K. writer.

Martin Ryle, U.K. radio astronomer.

Mikhail A. Sholokhov, Russian novelist.

Ahmed Sékou Touré, Guinean president.

François Truffaut, French writer and filmmaker.

Lila Wallace, U.S. publisher.

Johnny Weissmuller, U.S. swimmer and actor.

Jessamyn West, U.S. writer.

Peter Wilson, U.K. auctioneer.

from Egypt **(Anselm Kiefer);** ***Elements III*** **(Brice Marden);** ***Grillo*** **(Jean-Michel Basquiat) ... Film:** ***Amadeus*** **(Milos Forman);** ***Paris, Texas*** **(Wim Wenders);** ***A Passage to India*** **(David Lean) ... Theater:** ***Hurlyburly*** **(David Rabe);** ***The Foreigner*** **(Larry Shue);** ***Benefactors*** **(Michael Frayn);** ***Starlight Express*** **(Lloyd Webber and Stilgoe);** ***Sunday in the Park with George*** **(Sondheim and Lapine) ... TV:** ***The Cosby Show; Miami Vice.***

"The current social and economic systems in Hong Kong will remain unchanged, and so will the life-style."
—From the Sino-British Joint Declaration on Hong Kong

NEW IN 1984

Stonewashed jeans.

Megabit memory chip (Bell Laboratories).

Transatlantic solo balloon flight (by Joe Kittinger, from Caribou, Maine, to Savona, Italy).

Transplant of a baboon's heart into a human baby ("Baby Fae," who died 15 days later).

Female candidate of a major party for U.S. vice president (Democratic representative Geraldine Ferraro, running mate of Walter Mondale).

IN THE UNITED STATES

▸THE PURPLE PRINCE—Diminutive funk-rock musician Prince (originally named Prince Rogers Nelson) broke through to the big time in 1984 with the album *Purple Rain.* The album, which included the number-one tracks "When Doves Cry" and "Let's Go Crazy," was accompanied by an eponymous concert movie featuring the purple-velvet-clad star. The eccentric Prince, who'd played all the instruments on his first record, mixed religious and sexual imagery in his songs, surrounded himself with bodyguards, and eventually changed his name to a glyph.

▸AH-NULD ON SCREEN—*The Terminator,* directed by James Cameron and starring former Mr. Universe Arnold Schwarzenegger as a time-traveling cyborg-assassin set a new standard for action movies. Violent, relentlessly paced, the picture (made on a relatively modest budget) was a model for such future Hollywood extravaganzas as *Die Hard* and, of course, *Terminator 2,* a 1991 sequel also starring by-then-major-star Schwarzenegger—this time as the good-guy hero. ◂1982.9

Soviet pipeline workers fit the Gorki region's last section.

TECHNOLOGY

Flap over Soviet Pipeline

6 In January 1984, France became the first customer to receive Soviet natural gas via the world's longest pipeline. Running 2,800 miles, from Siberian gas fields to the Czechoslovak border (where it hooked up with the grid supplying Western Europe), the pipeline was a monumental engineering feat and a major political event: U.S. opposition to the project (including an attempt to block construction) had alienated America's European allies.

Two years earlier, U.S. president Reagan had forced American companies to cancel lucrative contracts to supply the Soviets with parts for the $10 billion pipeline. Then he tried to get Western Europe to adopt the embargo. But high unemployment made pipeline contracts a boon; moreover, many European nations had already signed deals to receive cheap Soviet gas. When the allies unanimously refused to adopt sanctions, Washington extended the ban to European companies operating under U.S. license.

European leaders were outraged. (France's trade minister called the action hypocritical, noting that Reagan had lifted Jimmy Carter's grain embargo because American farmers didn't like it.) Reagan tried many tacks. First he said the pipeline would make Western Europe dangerously energy-dependent on the Soviets. Then he claimed gas sales would give Moscow too much hard currency to spend on weapons. Finally, he linked sanctions to the crackdown on Solidarity in Poland. Nothing worked; in November 1982, he lifted the embargo.

The Soviets claimed to have completed the pipeline ahead of schedule, but Western experts doubted that the first gas to reach France had come from as far away as Siberia. Ironically, by 1984, world oil prices had crashed, reducing the need for Soviet gas and prompting a sharp cutback in orders. **◂1977.M**

DIPLOMACY

One Country, Two Systems

7 In 1984, after two years of negotiations, Chinese and British officials framed an unorthodox resolution to the "Hong Kong question": The British colony, a bastion of capitalism at the edge of the Communist People's Republic, would be restored intact to China in 1997. According to a unique "one country, two systems" formula, China would run the territory as a special administrative region, preserving (at least for 50 years) its quasi-democratic laws, English language, and laissez-faire economy. In return, Hong Kong would help enrich its mammoth new owner to the north.

Britain had gained the first of the colony's three parts—Hong Kong Island—in 1842 as a spoil of the First Opium War. Eighteen years later, the Second Opium War gave the British the tip of Kowloon Peninsula, on the Chinese mainland. The final parcel, representing 94 percent of the colony's total land mass, was added in 1898, when Britain forced a weak China to sign away the New Territories on a 99-year lease. As Hong Kong prospered, it became a source of trade and loans for a succession of Chinese governments; while claiming sovereignty in principle, the Nationalists and their successors, the Communists, were content to let the colony remain in British hands. By the 1970s, however, the approaching end of the New Territories lease made it impossible for Hong Kong investors to conduct long-term business. Chinese leaders made it clear that the lease would not be renewed—and without the New Territories, Hong Kong would be too small to be viable.

"One country, two systems" was hailed as a compromise satisfying all parties. But after Beijing's 1989 brutal suppression of domestic democrats—marked by the Tiananmen Square massacre—many of Hong Kong's six million inhabitants feared that the promises of liberty would not be kept. **◂1980.10 ▸1989.4**

Enclave of capitalism: Hong Kong's downtown business district at night.

SOUTHERN AFRICA

Tutu Wins Nobel Peace Prize

8 In a characteristic gesture, Desmond Tutu, South Africa's first black dean of the Anglican Church, took 40 guests with him to Oslo to accept the 1984 Nobel Peace Prize: It belonged, Tutu said, to the suffering people of South Africa.

When President Botha told Tutu politics and religion didn't mix, the Nobel laureate cited 30 biblical examples of such mixing.

Using his pulpit to publicize abhorrent conditions in his racially segregated nation, Tutu rebuked not only South Africa's white rulers, but foreign states that had failed to impose strong sanctions on the country. He reserved special ire for President Reagan's policy of "constructive engagement." "Blacks," he warned, "will remember that Washington collaborated with and supported a regime perpetrating the most vicious system since

SPORTS: Baseball: World Series, Detroit Tigers defeat San Diego Padres, 4–1 ... Olympics held in Sarajevo and Los Angeles (Joan Benoit wins the first women's Olympic marathon, in 2:24:52) ... Football: Super Bowl, Los Angeles Raiders defeat Washington Redskins, 38–9 ... Basketball: NBA, Boston Celtics defeat Los Angeles Lakers, 4–3.

"In ten years, I assure you all the arguments will have been forgotten. The pyramid will be there and the French will regard it as another one of their classics."—**Emile Biasini, director of the Louvre pyramid project**

Nazism." Shortly after winning the Nobel, Tutu became the first black bishop of Johannesburg; two years later, he was elevated to archbishop of Cape Town, leader of the entire Anglican Church in South Africa.

Tutu's rise coincided with the worst racial strife in the country's history. In 1985, South African president P.W. Botha declared a state of emergency and sent shock troops into black townships. Meanwhile, factional violence ripped the black community apart. The United Democratic Front attacked people who cooperated with the government; members of Inkatha, the conservative nationalist organization founded by Mangosuthu Gatsha Buthelezi (hereditary leader of South Africa's Zulu people), skirmished with the militant African National Congress, longtime leader in the fight against apartheid. Tutu condemned all racial violence; nonetheless, he openly supported the outlawed ANC, which advocated armed insurrection. His outspokenness offended many, inside South Africa and out, but his exalted office, and his unquestioned integrity, endowed him with an unassailable moral authority. **◄1983.M ►1985.3**

ARCHITECTURE

The Pyramids of Paris

9 When the illustrious Chinese-American architect I.M. Pei presented his blueprint for an addition to Paris's Louvre Museum in 1984, he triggered a polarizing domestic debate. The 67-year-old Pei, who'd first gained renown in 1964 with his design for Boston's John F. Kennedy Memorial Library, planned to build a 71-foot-tall glass pyramid to serve as both a skylight and a shimmering entrance to the museum's underground facilities. Critics said Pei's design was more suitable for Egypt than for France. Furthermore, they said he had no business tampering with one of France's most hallowed institutions. President Mitterrand was singled out for special condemnation for approving the design.

As Pei began to build, however, the purity of his design and his reverence for geometry—a very French passion—turned the tide of the Battle of the Pyramid in his favor. Though the Louvre was Pei's first European project, he knew his way around museums: The Louvre

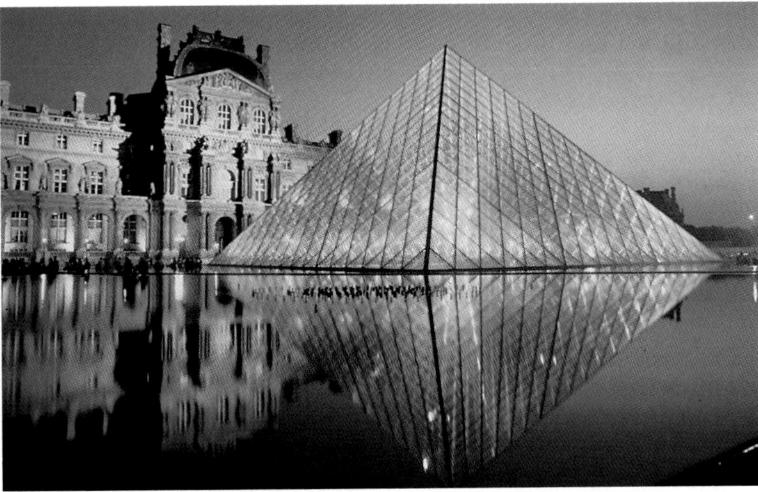

By the time Pei's pyramid opened, in 1989, it was hailed as an architectural triumph.

commission had been won on the strength of the triangular East Wing he built for the National Gallery of Art in Washington, D.C., in 1978.

The pyramid opened in 1989—one century after the Eiffel Tower debuted amid similar controversy. Most visitors were enchanted by the structure's resplendent glass panels, framed like diamonds by a network of slender metal cables. Pei's crown jewel (set in a courtyard formerly used as a parking lot) was surrounded by smaller satellite pyramids. Down its spiral staircase were new facilities expected to free the Louvre from its notoriety as one of the world's least appealing grand museums. Pei's standing as one of the century's inspired architects was affirmed. **◄1977.11 ►1994.6**

MUSIC

The Rise of Rap

10 A musical genre created by inner-city black and Latino teenagers spread out to the rest of America in 1984 when the album *Run-D.M.C.*, recorded by the group of the same name, became the first rap album ever to both go gold (that is, sell 500,000 copies) and have a video featured on MTV. As other rappers followed the trio to crossover stardom, hip-hop—the catchall term for the music, dance, fashion, and slang connected with rap—grew wildly popular around the world.

Rap was born in New York City in the 1970s, when young people bored by disco's predictability (and excluded from pricey dance clubs) began playing disc jockey with multiple turntables and mixing boards. They mixed bits of songs, repeated passages, added rhythmic scratching sounds by spinning records back and forth. Cocky rhymers recited lyrics—raps—over the mix. (Contests of verbal dexterity, such as the "dozens" insult game, are an African-American folk tradition.) Break dancing, a display of athletic spins and tumbles, mirrored the music's energy. And a hip-hop look emerged: warm-up suits (later, baggy jeans), caps turned backward, heavy gold jewelry, and fancy sneakers—insouciantly unlaced.

From the streets, rap made its way into recording studios. In 1979 the Sugar Hill Gang cut a seminal single, "Rappers Delight"; with songs like "The Message" (1982), by Grandmaster Flash and the Furious Five, the genre became a forum for protest against poverty, violence, and

Rappers Run-D.M.C. at an anti-crack concert in 1986 at Madison Square Garden.

racism. Along with the boasts and put-downs that were staples of rap lyrics, Run-D.M.C. (Joseph "Run" Simmons, Darryl "D.M.C." McDaniels, and disc jockey Jason "Jam-Master Jay" Mizell) stressed social uplift, but some of their successors presented narratives of criminal machismo known as "gangsta" rap. Whatever disapproving adults might have hoped, rap was not a passing fad: In the 1990s, it was bigger than ever. **◄1978.5**

IN THE UNITED STATES

►FEDERAL BANK BAILOUT—Billions of dollars in debt after financing a string of failed projects—real-estate developments, oil-drilling ventures—Chicago-based Continental Illinois National Bank and Trust Company sought relief from the federal government. On July 26, the government promised the struggling institution a record $4.5 billion in guaranteed loans, thereby stopping a run on the bank, an event unseen since the Depression. ◄1980.13

►GUN 'N' RUN—On December 22, on a New York City subway, meek-looking, bespectacled Bernhard Goetz pulled out a gun and shot four black

teenagers. Before slipping out of the car and escaping through train tunnels, Goetz told a transit worker the youths had tried to rob him. His attack underscored New York's racial tensions (he was white; his victims, one of whom was permanently paralyzed, said the shooting was unprovoked) and the fear of crime that gripped the city. Goetz was tried on 13 counts, but a jury in 1987 convicted him only of criminal possession of a weapon. He served eight months of a one-year sentence. ◄1983.7

►DETHRONED—Vanessa Williams, the first black winner in the 63-year history of the Miss America pageant, surrendered her tiara on July 23 after explicit pictures of her (taken before she was crowned) appeared in *Penthouse* magazine. The resilient Williams went on to an enormously successful career as a pop vocalist and Broadway performer.

POLITICS & BUSINESS: GNP: $3,801.5 billion ... Ronald Reagan reelected president, defeating former vice president Walter Mondale ... 79 banks fail (largest number since 1938) ... U.S. Commission on Civil Rights discontinues quotas for promotion of black workers and executives ... NYSE volume exceeds 200 million shares for first time ... Standard Oil of California takes over Gulf Corporation for $13.2 billion.

"Virtual reality is the first new, objective thing since the physical world. It's the first new place that exists between people just like the physical world, except it's totally under our control, unlike the physical world."—**Jaron Lanier, founder of VPL Research**

AROUND THE WORLD

▶CHERNENKO TAKES OFFICE—A top aide to Leonid Brezhnev (and his handpicked successor), Konstantin Chernenko, 72, got his chance to lead the U.S.S.R. upon the death of Yuri Andropov on February 9. Whereas Andropov was a reformer who tried to repair Brezhnevian corruption and social decline during his 15 months in office, Chernenko was an old-line conservative. Terminally ill, he died 13 months after his elevation. ◀1982.3 ▶1985.1

▶NKOMATI ACCORD—South Africa entered into its first pact with any black African nation on March 16, when it signed the Nkomati Accord with Mozambique. The agreement

barred Mozambique from funding the African National Congress and South Africa from supporting the Mozambique National Resistance (Renamo), a guerrilla group *(above)* underwritten in part by South Africa's apartheid regime. Renamo continued its campaign of terror and economic sabotage into the 1990s, fueling suspicion that South Africa was betraying the accord. ◀1975.2 ▶1985.3

▶DUARTE ELECTED—Centrist reformer José Napolean Duarte was elected president of war-torn El Salvador in May. The U.S.-educated Duarte, who had fronted El Salvador's civilian-military junta from 1980 to 1982, defeated death-squad leader Roberto D'Aubuisson, head of the ultra-right-wing Nationalist Republican Alliance (ARENA). D'Aubuisson, noting Duarte's CIA backing, called the election a fraud. Duarte lent the government an element of democratic credibility—crucial for securing increased aid from the U.S., which was funding the military's war against leftist rebels. Rendered ineffectual by systemic corruption, Duarte was defeated in 1989 by ARENA candidate Alfredo Cristiani and died of cancer the following year. ◀1981.8 ▶1987.2

MUSIC

A Spanish Heartthrob

11 By 1984, when CBS Records released Julio Iglesias's first English-language album, *1100 Bel Air Place*, the debonair Spaniard had already made most of the planet his stage. Just 40 years old, he had sold 100 million records in six languages. *Newsweek* dubbed him "the most popular singer in the world today"; the *Guinness Book of World Records* named him the bestselling musical artist in the history of recording.

Carefully aimed at North American markets, *1100 Bel Air Place* featured "To All the Girls I've Loved Before," Iglesias's hit duet with Willie Nelson, as well as appearances by Diana Ross, the Beach Boys, and the Pointer Sisters. Bolstered by a dazzling publicity campaign that made "Julio" a household word months before the album was released, *1100 Bel Air Place* sold more than a million copies in just five days, signaling that there was still a U.S. audience for the kind of glossy-smooth, romantic crooning that the ascendance of rock had largely brushed aside. Yet Iglesias's style owed as much to Mediterranean tradition (both pop and operatic) as to such American forebears as Vic Damone, Johnny Mathis, and Nat King Cole.

Iglesias's understated macho magnetism (appealing primarily to women over 30) was also recognized by a business outside the recording industry when Coca-Cola signed him to a lucrative promotional contract. (Competitor Pepsi's representative was the androgynous young Michael Jackson.) Coke had the most potent Latin-lover icon since Rudolph Valentino. **◀1943.16**

A voice that millions of women love: Julio Iglesias in concert.

Dreadlocked visionary Jaron Lanier at work in Silicon Valley.

TECHNOLOGY

A New, Digital Dimension

12 In 1984, pioneers of the realm known as "virtual reality" acquired the means with which to launch their expeditions. A 24-year-old inventor named Jaron Lanier formed the first company to produce the headsets, gloves, suits, and software that enable "cybernauts" (as they became known in the lingo of the initiated) to see, hear, and interact with the three-dimensional, digitally simulated world that Lanier had dubbed virtual reality (VR). "It's every child's dream," said Lanier of the technology produced by his VPL Research, based in the northern California high-tech development mecca known as Silicon Valley.

Early versions of VR had cartoonish imagery, and the headsets sometimes caused nausea and headaches; still, VR held out the tantalizing promise of being everything its enthusiasts claimed for it—a revolutionary, altogether new medium that transcends the two-dimensional limitations of traditional computer technology. "For over a decade, we've been looking at our computerized world through a fishbowl called a monitor," wrote a journalist in 1993. "Virtual reality invites us to step inside a 3-D view of this world and feel our way around."

By the early 1990s, VPL Research had been joined by a host of other firms and research facilities, and airlines and the military were already using VR flight simulators to train pilots: A virtual cockpit was projected on tiny liquid-crystal screens inside the headset (a turn of the viewer's head changed the angle), and the glove allowed the user to manipulate virtual controls. VR games and such recreational applications as participatory 3-D movies had begun to appear. And some people—though Lanier dismissed them as "confused"—predicted what has been called "the ultimate safe sex": virtual sex. **◀1981.10 ▶1984.V**

IDEAS

Philosopher of Sex

13 In 1984, at the height of his reign as the era's preeminent French intellectual, Michel Foucault published *The Care of the Self*, the third installment in his proposed six-volume *History of Sexuality*. An examination of the relationship between sexual attitudes, identity, and ethics from the days of ancient Greece and Rome to modernity, the project was also Foucault's last major act of scholarship: Shortly after it appeared, he died of AIDS at 57.

A protégé of the eminent Marxist philosopher Louis Althusser (who created a scandal in French academia by strangling his wife), Foucault catapulted to prominence in 1961 with *Madness and Civilization*,

Foucault in caricature: A man in chains.

which presented society's historical responses to the mentally ill—oppression, incarceration—as a means of identifying the self through exclusion. In a later study, *Discipline and Punish*, he argued that prisons, hospitals, and schools all resemble one another because they serve civilization's primary purpose: coercion.

Foucault's controversial ideas about power (which owe much to Nietzsche) led him to the subject of sex. Regulation of sexual behavior—that is, of the body itself—is, he believed, the individual's most basic experience of social control. Historically, such strictures have shaped Western societies' notions of identity. In *The Care of the Self*, he modified his earlier absolutist stance and observed that in the realm of sex, some societies—for example, ancient Rome—have allowed a greater degree of individual pleasure. Ironically, posthumous revelations about Foucault's own sexual conduct (homosexual and sadomasochistic, he may have deliberately exposed himself and others to AIDS) served to undermine his credibility with some scholars. **◀1943.10**

NOBEL PRIZES: Peace: Desmond Tutu (South African; antiapartheid movement) ... Literature: Jaroslav Seifert (Czechoslovak; poet) ... Chemistry: R. Bruce Merrifield (U.S.; solid-phase synthesis) ... Medicine: Georges J.F. Kohler, César Milstein, and Niels K. Jerne (German, U.K., U.K.; immunology) ... Physics: Carlo Rubbia and Simon van der Meer (Italian, Dutch; subatomic particles) ... Economics: Richard Stone (U.K.).

A VOICE FROM 1984

Adventures in Cyberspace

From *Neuromancer*, by William Gibson, 1984

With his first novel, 1984's Neuromancer, *William Gibson imagined a sinister, neon-lit twenty-first century in which shady corporate monoliths supersede national governments, space is colonized (by Rastafarian Zionists, among others), biotechnology breakthroughs enable people to live indefinitely, urban sprawl connects Boston and Atlanta, and "cyberspace cowboys" plug themselves into the virtual reality of the "matrix"—a vast electronic network comprising all the world's computer systems. From its opening line—"The sky above the port was the color of television, tuned to a dead channel"—* Neuromancer *presented a distinct vision of an electronic apocalypse. The book, which showed the influence of writers as diverse as Raymond Chandler, William Burroughs, and Thomas Pynchon, won every major science-fiction award and spawned a literary subgenre—the hard-boiled, high-tech style called cyberpunk. Said Gibson, an American who emigrated to Canada in the 1960s, "I think the world we live in is so hopelessly weird and complex that in order to come to terms with it, you need the tools that science fiction develops." Remarkably, he knew almost nothing about computers: His book inspired the creators of virtual reality, but he wrote it on an antique manual typewriter.* **◄1984.12 ►1993.3**

Case was twenty-four. At twenty-two, he'd been a cowboy, a rustler, one of the best in the Sprawl. He'd been trained by the best, by McCoy Pauley and Bobby Quine, legends in the biz. He'd operated on an almost permanent adrenaline high, a byproduct of youth and proficiency, jacked into a custom cyberspace deck that projected his disembodied consciousness into the consensual hallucination that was the matrix. A thief, he'd worked for other, wealthier thieves, employers who provided the exotic software required to penetrate the bright walls of corporate systems, opening windows into rich fields of data.

He'd made the classic mistake, the one he'd sworn he'd never make. He stole from his employers. He kept something for himself and tried to move it through a fence in Amsterdam. He still wasn't sure how he'd been discovered, not that it mattered now. He'd expected to die, then, but they only smiled. Of course he was welcome, they told him, welcome to the money. And he was going to need it. Because—still smiling—they were going to make sure he never worked again.

They damaged his nervous system with a wartime Russian mycotoxin.

Strapped to a bed in a Memphis hotel, his talent burning out micron by micron, he hallucinated for thirty hours.

The damage was minute, subtle, and utterly effective.

For Case, who'd lived for the bodiless exultation of cyberspace, it was the Fall. In the bars he'd frequented as a cowboy hotshot, the elite stance involved a certain relaxed contempt for the flesh. The body was meat. Case fell into the prison of his own flesh.

Computer-age author William Gibson, surrounded by computer-generated fractal art. A fractal is a mathematical function (developed by Polish-French mathematician Benoit Mandelbrot) whose graphic depiction involves shapes that can each be viewed as a small-scale replica of the larger image.

His total assets were quickly converted to New Yen, a fat sheaf of the old paper currency that circulated endlessly through the closed circuit of the world's black markets like the seashells of the Trobriand islanders. It was difficult to transact legitimate business with cash in the Sprawl; in Japan, it was already illegal.

In Japan, he'd known with a clenched and absolute certainty, he'd find his cure. In Chiba. Either in a registered clinic or in the shadowland of black medicine. Synonymous with implants, nerve-splicing, and microbionics, Chiba was a magnet for the Sprawl's techno-criminal subcultures.

***

Home.

Home was BAMA, the Sprawl, the Boston-Atlanta Metropolitan Axis.

Program a map to display frequency of data exchange, every thousand megabytes a single pixel on a very large screen. Manhattan and Atlanta burn solid white. Then they start to pulse, the rate of traffic threatening to overload your stimulation. Your map is about to go nova. Cool it down. Up your scale. Each pixel a million megabytes. At a hundred million megabytes per second, you begin to make out certain blocks in midtown Manhattan, outlines of hundred-year-old industrial parks ringing the old core of Atlanta....

"Questing and creativity, sensitivity to new phenomena and processes—such are the demands of life on all workers on the ideological front."—**Mikhail Gorbachev, in a speech to the Central Committee of the Politburo in 1984**

STORY OF THE YEAR

The Ascension of Gorbachev

1 Just a few hours after announcing the death of Communist Party general secretary Konstantin Chernenko in March 1985, the Kremlin elevated a relative unknown to the Soviet Union's highest post. At 54, Mikhail Gorbachev was the youngest member of the Politburo and the first top Soviet leader to have come of age after Stalin. A protégé of Chernenko's predecessor, the reform-minded (but short-tenured) Yuri Andropov, Gorbachev promised to revitalize the creaky Soviet bureaucracy. Instead, the forces he unleashed would ultimately bring down the Soviet Union—and shake the world political order to its roots.

Chernenko had personified Brezhnev-era paralysis. During his 13 months in office, he was frequently bedridden, once disappearing from public view for 59 consecutive days. To Gorbachev, Chernenko passed a tottering economy (life expectancy in the Soviet Union *fell* during the 1970s—a first for an industrial nation), unabated political repression, chilly relations with the West (all but frozen by the Soviet invasion of Afghanistan in 1979), and endemic public disillusionment (likewise exacerbated by the disastrous Afghanistan adventure).

The West welcomed Mikhail Gorbachev in Paris. Here, with French president François Mitterrand.

Even before his ascent, Gorbachev had indicated a desire to remake his vast nation. "We will have to carry out profound transformations in the economy and in the entire system of social relations," he warned in a speech in 1984. During a visit that year to England, Gorbachev impressed observers with his élan. He was dapper, charming; he showed flashes of humor. His wife, Raisa, was fashionable, articulate—a far cry from the Western stereotype of a Kremlin wife. More important, Gorbachev valued détente and spoke of breaking down traditional Soviet secrecy. "I like Mr. Gorbachev," said Prime Minister (and confirmed cold warrior) Margaret Thatcher. "We can do business together."

Once in office, Gorbachev initiated a dual reform program. With perestroika (restructuring), he introduced limited free-market forces and decentralization. With glasnost (openness), he encouraged a radical reappraisal of Soviet politics, culture, and history. Gorbachev condemned Stalin's reign of terror and Brezhnev's "stagnation." He ousted hard-liners from the Politburo and freed political prisoners. In arms-control talks with Ronald Reagan, he offered stunning concessions. Gorbachev was making revolution from the top down—but the process would soon slip out of his control. **◂1984.M ▸1986.5**

ENVIRONMENTALISM

A Hole in the Ozone Layer

2 In 1985, British meteorologists confirmed a long-held suspicion: High above Antarctica, a hole had opened in the ozone layer—the atmospheric blanket that blocks 99 percent of the sun's ultraviolet rays.

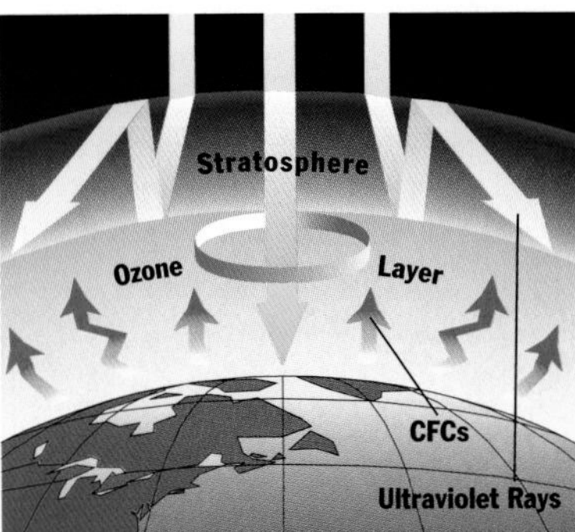

A depleted ozone layer intensifies the sun's UV rays. Pollution traps reflected sunlight, raising the atmosphere's temperature.

The scientists had first detected the problem in 1977 but had delayed reporting their findings until the evidence was indisputable. Satellite data showed that Antarctica's ozone grew thinnest every October, when 40 percent of the layer vanished—and that 2.5 percent of the whole planet's ozone had disappeared in just five years. The implications of worsening depletion were terrifying: Ultraviolet radiation could cause skin cancer, kill phytoplankton (the tiny organisms at the base of the ocean food chain), damage crops, blind animals, and wreak varieties of havoc as yet unknown.

The culprits, experts suspected, were man-made substances called chlorofluorocarbons (CFCs). Eleven years earlier, California chemists Sherwood Rowland and Mario Molina had announced computer-model calculations showing that CFCs imperil the ozone layer. Every chlorine atom in a CFC, rising into the stratosphere, could destroy 100,000 ozone molecules. The U.S. government in 1978 banned the use of CFCs in aerosol sprays, but resistance from manufacturers led to their continued use in refrigerators, air conditioners, industrial solvents, and plastic foams. And in other countries, CFCs were still used in sprays.

Worse yet, CFCs were a prime factor in the newly detected "greenhouse effect," in which solar heat reflected from the ground was trapped by a layer of airborne pollutants. Scientists predicted that within 50 years, the earth's average temperature would climb as much as eight degrees—an increase sharper than any in human history. Global warming, it was feared, would melt the polar ice caps, raising ocean levels and flooding coastal cities; climactic change might turn fertile regions into desert.

In 1987, 53 industrial nations signed the Montreal Protocols, an agreement to eliminate CFC use by the year 2000. Elsewhere, however, production continued unabated, and CFCs released years earlier continued their rise toward the upper atmosphere. **◂1982.6 ▸1988.6**

SOUTHERN AFRICA

Martial Law Declared

3 South Africa was at war. Along with sporadic guerrilla raids by the outlawed African National Congress, the white-minority government faced an uprising by the 1.5 million members of the United Democratic Front (a coalition of student groups, trade unions, and community associations). UDF activists fought one of the world's best-equipped armies with stones and Molotov cocktails. And by July 1985, when President P.W. Botha declared a state of emergency in 36 South African cities, the international community had become involved.

In several Western nations, grassroots movements had arisen calling for government sanctions against the apartheid regime. The first initiative, however, was private. Ten days after Botha imposed martial law, the New York-based Chase Manhattan Bank, citing the "hassle factor" of doing business in South Africa, stopped extending loans. Other U.S. banks soon followed, creating a crisis in heavily indebted South Africa. The country's currency, the rand, lost 30 percent of its value in a month. In September, the United States (despite President Reagan's conciliatory policy of

The funeral service for four black Johannesburg youths killed by a hand grenade. Their deaths caused worldwide alarm.

ART & CULTURE: Books: ***The Accidental Tourist*** **(Anne Tyler);** ***Lonesome Dove*** **(Larry McMurtry);** ***The Real Life of Alejandro Mayta*** **(Mario Vargas Llosa);** ***Annie John*** **(Jamaica Kincaid);** ***Common Ground: A Turbulent Decade in the Lives of Three American Families*** **(J. Anthony Lukas) ... Music: "That's What Friends Are For" (Bacharach and Sager);** ***We Are the World*** **(Jackson and Richie, LP);** ***Whitney Houston*** **(LP);**

"The wounds are deep."—**Nicaraguan president Daniel Ortega, on his country's relationship with the United States**

"constructive engagement") adopted limited sanctions; the European Economic Community initiated its own package. Under growing popular pressure, many businesses and universities began divesting themselves of South African holdings.

Botha reacted defiantly. "Don't push us too far," he warned. But leading South African businessmen had gotten the point: In September a contingent of industrialists flew to Zambia for unprecedented talks with ANC leaders. Increasingly isolated at home and abroad, the government announced limited reforms in January 1986. In May, however—shortly after blacks launched the biggest labor strike in the country's history—the regime launched an all-out drive to crush the ANC, bombing supposed guerrilla sanctuaries in neighboring Botswana, Zambia, and Zimbabwe. As public outrage redoubled, the U.S. Congress (overriding Reagan's veto) passed more-stringent sanctions; other nations tightened their boycotts as well. But in South Africa, the crackdown continued. **◂1984.8 ▸1988.2**

DISASTERS

The Earth Moves—Repeatedly

4 The earth's shifting crust—and politics—brought tragedy to two Latin American countries in 1985. In September, Mexico was struck by two major earthquakes a day apart (measuring 8.1 and 7.5 on the Richter scale of 10). More than 7,000 people in Mexico City and hundreds elsewhere were killed. Some 450 buildings, including supposedly quake-proof skyscrapers, were destroyed in the capital; thousands more were damaged, and 50,000 urbanites were left homeless.

In November, Colombia's long-dormant Nevado del Ruiz volcano erupted, unleashing a torrent of mud that engulfed the town of Armero and killed 22,000. One of the most destructive volcanic eruptions in recorded history, it came a week after a man-made disaster: When 60 guerrillas of the leftist M-19 movement seized the Palace of Justice in Bogotá, taking more than 40 top judges hostage, President Belisario Betancur ordered soldiers and police to attack. A hundred people (including the head of the Supreme Court and eleven other justices) died in the melee.

The two natural catastrophes filled the international news media with eerily similar images: piles of corpses and the occasional survivor pulled from the ruins; a little girl in Armero, afloat in deep mud and clutched by her dead aunt, and a little boy in Mexico City, caught in a mass of rubble (both children died after rescuers spent days trying to free them). Each calamity brought political recriminations: in Mexico, against builders and bureaucrats who'd ignored construction codes; in Colombia, against officials who'd been warned of the impending eruption but dawdled over evacuation and relief plans. And each brought a flood of aid from around the world. **◂1902.10 ▸1989.M**

The earthquake destroyed more than 450 buildings in densely populated Mexico City.

NICARAGUA

A Popularly Elected Leader

5 Inaugurated in 1985 as Nicaragua's first popularly elected president in living memory, Daniel Ortega Saavedra *(below)* had little to celebrate. His Sandinista National Liberation Front faced a host of problems, not least strident opposition from Washington.

Since overthrowing rapacious dictator Anastasio Somoza Debayle in 1979, the Marxist-led Sandinistas had come under constant fire from the Reagan administration, which depicted them as a threat to hemispheric security. Communism in Nicaragua, warned U.S. officials, would lead to a progression of falling dominoes right up to the Rio Grande. To counter the perceived threat, the Americans backed anti-Sandinista contra guerrillas. Reagan's stated goal: to make Ortega "say uncle."

The Sandinistas had implemented large-scale social and economic reforms. Some two million acres of land was distributed to 60,000 dispossessed peasant families; social-security expenditures were doubled; advances in medical care earned a World Health Organization citation; illiteracy was cut dramatically; the economy grew by an impressive 7 percent per year. Yet Washington remained steadfastly hostile, largely because Ortega expanded Nicaragua's ties with the Soviet Union and Cuba, but also because he'd postponed promised elections.

When elections finally did occur, in 1984, the Sandinistas won 67 percent of the vote. A North American poll-monitoring group called the elections "a model of probity and fairness." The U.S. State Department nevertheless rejected the results, leaving many observers to wonder what the Sandinistas had to do to prove their legitimacy. Meanwhile, Reagan's covert war proceeded with devastating effect. "Unfortunately," said one prominent Nicaraguan businessman who opposed Ortega, "the contras burn down schools, homes, and health centers as fast as the Sandinistas build them." Pushed to the brink, Ortega sought increased aid from Moscow in 1985; the result was that Nicaragua was becoming as dependent on the Soviets as Washington had always claimed. In May, the United States imposed an economic embargo; thereafter, conditions in Nicaragua deteriorated rapidly. **◂1984.3 ▸1986.8**

DEATHS

Laura Ashley, U.K. fashion designer.

Anne Baxter, U.S. actress.

Ladislao Biro, Hungarian inventor.

Heinrich Böll, German writer.

Yul Brynner, U.S. actor.

Macfarlane Burnet, Australian immunologist.

Italo Calvino, Italian writer.

Marc Chagall, Russian-French painter.

Konstantin Chernenko, U.S.S.R. political leader.

Jean Dubuffet, French artist.

Tage Erlander, Swedish premier.

Ruth Gordon, U.S. actress and writer.

Robert Graves, U.K. writer.

Enver Hoxha, Albanian ruler.

Rock Hudson, U.S. actor.

André Kertész, Hungarian-U.S. photographer.

Philip Larkin, U.K. poet.

Henry Cabot Lodge, Jr., U.S. diplomat.

John Willard Marriott, U.S. hotelier.

Charles Richter, U.S. seismologist.

Roger Sessions, U.S. composer.

Simone Signoret, French actress.

Orson Welles, U.S. actor, stage director, and filmmaker.

E.B. White, U.S. writer.

***Brothers in Arms* (Dire Straits, LP); *Wind Quintet No. 4* (George Perle) ... Painting & Sculpture: *Four Lemons* (Donald Sultan) ... Film: *Out of Africa* (Sydney Pollack); *Prizzi's Honor* (John Huston); *My Beautiful Laundrette* (Stephen Frears) ... Theater: *I'm Not Rappaport* (Herb Gardner); *Biloxi Blues* (Neil Simon); *Les Misérables* (Schonberg, Boubil, and Kretzmer) ... TV: *The Golden Girls*; Discovery Channel debuts.**

"There is no greater destabilizing force for democratic government than the power of the narcotráfico.*"*
—Bolivian undersecretary of the interior Gustavo Sánchez

NEW IN 1985

Extra second added to the calendar year.

Nintendo video games.

Rock 'n' Roll Hall of Fame.

U.S. ban on leaded gas.

IN THE UNITED STATES

▶LARGEST ATOM SMASHER—In October, at the Fermi National Labs in Illinois, scientists tested a powerful new antimatter particle accelerator. The results were gratifying: The energy discharged by colliding subatomic protons and antiprotons equaled 1.6 trillion electron volts—nearly three

times greater than ever before achieved on earth. Collisions of antimatter (unusual subatomic particles that have a charge opposite that of the usual particles) allowed Fermilab physicists to observe the full demonstration of Einstein's famous $E=mc^2$ equation: In the collision of antimatter with matter, 100 percent of mass is converted to energy. (The energy released by a nuclear bomb represents a conversion of less than 1 percent of atomic mass.) ◀1930.14

▶TILTING OVER ART—The U.S. General Services Administration in 1985 recommended that a massive piece of sculpture, originally commissioned by the GSA itself, be removed from the plaza of a federal office building in New York City. Since its installation in 1979, *Tilted Arc*, a twelve-foot-high, 120-foot-long steel wall by U.S. artist Richard Serra, had elicited many complaints from office workers, who said it was an eyesore

ENVIRONMENTALISM

Rainbow Warrior Bombed

6 In eight years as flagship of the environmental group Greenpeace, the *Rainbow Warrior* had traveled the globe, carrying protesters to engage in on-site civil disobedience against nuclear-weapons testing, radioactive-waste dumping, and the slaughter of marine mammals. The 160-foot trawler had often been seized by local officials. But in July 1985, the vessel encountered a particularly hostile reception. As it sat at anchor in Auckland, New Zealand, preparing to lead a flotilla protesting French nuclear testing in the South Pacific, two bombs attached to its hull exploded—killing a Portuguese photographer and sinking the *Rainbow Warrior*. A prime suspect soon emerged: the French government.

A few hours before the blast, witnesses had seen a man in a wet suit pulling a rubber raft onto a nearby beach. He drove away in a rented van later traced to a couple traveling with forged Swiss passports. The two people were revealed to be officers in the General Directorate for External Security (DGSE), France's international intelligence agency.

An inquiry ordered by President François Mitterrand was initially hobbled by high-ranking officials. The attempted cover-up—and the emerging scandal—led to the resignation of France's defense minister, the dismissal of the country's intelligence chief, and an eventual admission by the government of complicity in the bombing.

Since the founding of Greenpeace in 1971 by Canadian environmentalists, its methods had often generated controversy. Ultimately, the *Rainbow Warrior* affair enhanced the group's reputation. "We think we have been successful using peaceful direct action," said Bryn Jones, chairman of the British office, "and we will continue to do so." **◀1983.5 ▶1988.6**

Greenpeace's *Rainbow Warrior*, which was sunk by agents of the French government.

ALBANIA

Stalin's Last Acolyte

7 When Enver Hoxha died in April 1985 at age 76, he'd governed Albania for 40 years. For Hoxha, the last orthodox Stalinist, even the Soviet bloc had been too revisionist. The tiny Balkan nation (Europe's poorest, and the only one with a Muslim majority) had no friends and few associates. Visitors seldom entered, and Albanians were seldom allowed to leave. Even Hoxha's funeral was closed to outsiders.

During World War II, when Albania was occupied by Italy and ruled by an Axis puppet government, Hoxha—a former French teacher—fled to the mountains and led the resistance. After the war, his was the only European nation to go Communist without having been invaded by Soviet troops. Tito, in neighboring Yugoslavia, helped Hoxha become head of Albania's nascent Communist Party; unanimous, single-slate elections elevated him to premier in 1946.

Under Hoxha, foreign policy was a game of musical chairs. He broke with Tito in 1948, when Stalin did; broke with the Soviet Union in 1961, when China did; and broke with China in 1978, after the Chinese-American rapprochement and Mao's death. A cruel tyrant, Hoxha constantly purged his party, imprisoned dissidents, harassed Albania's ethnic-Greek population, and repressed religion. The country (long a backwater of the Ottoman Empire) made impressive strides in industry, health, and education, but increasingly lagged behind its neighbors. Hoxha's successor, Ramiz Alia, maintained Albania's isolation until 1990, when a deepening economic crisis forced him to open the borders. In 1992, widespread unrest brought free elections, in which Hoxha's heirs finally lost their hold on power. **◀1939.5 ▶1991.4**

CRIME

The Cocaine Boom

8 The U.S. Drug Enforcement Agency (DEA) announced in February 1985 that cocaine production had risen by a third the previous year in Colombia, Bolivia, and Peru (with Ecuador joining the major producers). The figures reflected a *Yanqui* trend. Among the glamorous rich, cocaine was the drug of choice. Ordinary Americans experimented with the drug as well. And among the urban poor, the cheap, smokable form of coke called crack was overtaking heroin as an inner-city scourge. As a result, thousands of desperately poor Andean peasants were earning cash for coca leaves (traditionally chewed to suppress hunger and fatigue). South American teenagers were dying from a smokable coca by-product called *basuco*. And a few big *narcotráficos*—mostly based in Colombia—had become billionaires.

In the 1980s, cocaine gained a reputation as the drug of choice of America's young urban professionals (a.k.a. "Yuppies").

The Colombian kingpins included several colorful characters: handsome Carlos Lehder, whose private disco was graced by a nude statue of John Lennon; Jorge Ochoa, who had his own zoo and bullring; Pablo Escobar, who built a giant public

SPORTS: Baseball: World Series, Kansas City Royals defeat St. Louis Cardinals, 4–3; Pete Rose breaks Ty Cobb's record of 4,191 career hits ... Football: Super Bowl, San Francisco 49ers defeat Miami Dolphins, 38–16 ... Basketball: NBA, Los Angeles Lakers defeat Boston Celtics, 4–2 ... Tennis: Boris Becker, 17, is youngest male Wimbledon champion ... Dogsledding: Libby Riddles is first woman to win the Iditarod.

"They are beating up the passengers. We must land in Beirut. He has pulled a hand-grenade pin and is ready to blow up the aircraft if he has to. We must, I repeat, we must land at Beirut."—**The pilot of TWA Flight 847, hijacked en route from Athens to Rome**

soccer complex and won an alternate seat in Congress. Many of their compatriots revered them as providers of jobs, capital, and philanthropy to an impoverished nation.

But violence and corruption followed the cocaine trade. In Colombia, there were shoot-outs between the rival Medellín and Cali cartels, assassinations (the justice minister was killed in April), links with rightist death squads. In Peru, Maoist Shining Path guerrillas protected coca growers in return for payoffs. In Mexico, top officials were implicated in the kidnap-murder of two DEA operatives in February. From Bolivia to the Bahamas, Jamaica to Miami, bankers, policemen, and bureaucrats battened on coke money.

The U.S. military soon began assisting the coca-growing countries in what President Reagan called a "war on drugs." But the war would prove futile against the old law of supply and demand. **◂1980.6 ▸1991.11**

TERRORISM

A Worldwide Spree

9 One person's terrorist, it is sometimes observed, is another's freedom fighter. But by even the narrowest definition—that is, violence by nongovernmental forces against civilians far removed from the land or issues being contested—terrorism was up sharply in 1985. Among hundreds of incidents, a few stood out.

In June, members of Islamic Jihad—a pro-Iranian Lebanese Shiite group—hijacked a Rome-bound TWA flight from Athens. For days, the airliner hopped between Beirut and Algiers as the gunmen beat some captives, freed others, and killed one. The remaining 39 were turned over to Shiite militiamen in Beirut. Within two weeks, moderate Amal militia leader Nabih Berri had bartered them for 735 mostly Shiite prisoners in Israel; before their release, he threw the captives a party at a seaside hotel. That same month, a bomb destroyed an Indian airliner off the Irish coast, killing 329 people en route from Toronto to Bombay. Though the culprits were never found, investigators suspected Sikh extremists.

In October—despite a new PLO policy of attacking only Israeli targets—commandos of the Palestinian Liberation Front faction seized an Italian cruise ship, the *Achille Lauro*. They shot an elderly Jewish New Yorker named Leon Klinghoffer and dumped him, wheelchair and all, into the Mediterranean. Then, on orders of PLF chief Abul Abbas, they surrendered to Egyptian authorities. Unaware of the murder, the Egyptians had agreed to fly them and their leader to Tunisia—but U.S. fighters forced the plane to land in Italy. Abul Abbas quickly went free, however, sparking a furor that almost toppled the Italian government.

The hijackers of a Rome-bound TWA plane, parked on the tarmac of Beirut's airport, order an unidentified civilian to put up his hands as he approaches the jet's tail section.

In November, Palestinians loyal to Abu Nidal (a Libyan-backed former PLO leader) hijacked an Egyptian airliner. Of the 60 people killed, 57 died when Egyptian troops stormed the plane in Malta. Abu Nidal's men struck again in December, assaulting airport crowds in Rome and Vienna with rifles and grenades. The toll: 19 dead, 112 wounded. **◂1978.6 ▸1988.4**

THE UNITED STATES

Year of the Spies

10 Whether because recent laws made it easier for investigators to tap suspected spies' telephones, or because the number of moles had multiplied, more Americans were charged with peddling their nation's secrets in 1985 than in any previous year. Two of the cases were among the most serious in U.S. history.

The first was that of the Walker spy ring. John Walker, Jr., 47, was a private detective in Norfolk, Virginia, who claimed membership in the anti-Communist John Birch Society and the Ku Klux Klan. But as a Navy officer in 1968, he'd used his security clearance and his expertise in nuclear submarines and secret codes to start a lucrative business supplying classified material to the Soviets. Later, he'd recruited his brother (an engineer with a defense contractor), his son (a Navy lieutenant), and his best friend (another Navy officer). It was Walker's ex-wife who blew the whistle on one of America's largest and longest-lived spy networks. All four members drew life in prison.

The second case raised tricky ethical and diplomatic questions. Jonathan Jay Pollard, 32, was a naval-intelligence analyst who'd begun spying in 1984—for Israel. Though Washington shared a great many of its military secrets with its ally, Pollard, a fervent Zionist, felt a moral urgency to help fill the gaps. (His payment was modest by the standards of the trade.) By the time he was caught, he'd handed over 360 cubic feet of papers. In 1987, he, too, received a life sentence; his wife, Anne, got five years as an accomplice.

The Pollard case strained U.S.-Israeli relations, rocked the Israeli government, and tarnished the image of Israel's legendary intelligence service, Mossad. Pollard's handlers, it emerged, had been operating without Mossad's knowledge. **◂1963.3**

A federal marshal escorts John Walker, Jr. *(left)*, patriarch of the largest family spy ring ever uncovered in the U.S.

IN THE UNITED STATES

and blocked access to the plaza. When the Feds decided to dismantle the work, Serra sued, arguing that the piece was "site specific" and could not be erected elsewhere. The case became the focal point

of a heated debate about artists' rights, the nature of public art, and the meaning of ownership. Serra lost the battle: The piece was removed in 1989. ◂1933.V

▶ *TITANIC* FOUND—In September, the *Argo* research submarine found the wreck of the *Titanic,* the luxury liner that sank with 1,500 people on board in April 1912 on its maiden voyage. A team of French and American scientists made repeated dives to the ship in July 1986 and found that it was split in two and rusting badly but otherwise largely intact (though too large to bring to the surface—some 13,100 feet up). ◂1912.1

▶ PHILADELPHIA FIRE—On May 13, the Philadelphia police, with the approval of Mayor Wilson Goode, ended a standoff with members of the armed radical group MOVE by bombing the group's row house. The explosion killed eleven people and touched off a firestorm that destroyed 61 homes in the residential neighborhood. Goode said the fire, which left 200 people homeless, "saddened" him, but he called the bombing unavoidable. The chief of police later resigned. ◂1970.7

▶ THE REAL THING (NOT)—Seeking to exploit its advantage in the ever-escalating "cola wars," the Coca-Cola Company, the world's largest soft-drink operation, in April introduced the "new" Coke. Slightly sweeter than the standard formula, the new Coke was aimed at converting Pepsi loyalists. Instead, the deviant drink was rejected by both camps. Embarrassed Coke executives soon reintroduced the original recipe, calling it Coke Classic, and phased out the impostor.

POLITICS & BUSINESS: GNP: $4,053.6 billion ... Congress passes 5-year, $169 billion farm bill (reduces income and price supports, first time since 1933) ... Reagan signs Gramm-Rudman bill (mandates reduction of federal deficit by 1991) ... EPA puts 90% ban on leaded gasoline ... AMA urges complete ban on all tobacco-product advertising ... Montgomery Ward catalogue discontinued.

"I would not compare Mahabharata *to a single play of Shakespeare but to the complete works of Shakespeare."*
—Director Peter Brook

AROUND THE WORLD

▶MENGELE EXHUMED—A team of international forensic experts and Nazi-hunters announced on June 21 that the corpse exhumed from a grave near São Paolo, Brazil, was that of Nazi Josef Mengele, chief medical officer of WWII's Auschwitz death camp. Mengele, a.k.a. the Angel of Death, had selected victims for Auschwitz's gas chambers and performed barbarous experiments on living patients. Taken into custody by U.S. forces after the war, he had somehow escaped to Argentina. Under a pseudonym, he received Paraguayan citizenship In 1959 (revoked in 1979) and lived in South America until his 1979 death by drowning at a Brazilian resort.

▶AIRLIFT STOPPED—Ethiopia in 1985 forced the Israeli government to stop its covert airlift of Falasha—Ethiopian Jews —to Israel. Since beginning the airlift in 1974 (when persecution of the Falasha increased after the fall of Ethiopian emperor Haile Selassie), Israel had airlifted some 12,000 members of the ancient Jewish sect, which had existed in isolation from the rest of the Jewish world since about the second century BC. Israel resumed the airlift in 1989, and within a few years most of the approximately 14,000 remaining Falasha had emigrated. ◀1979.9

▶CHESS MATES—In a world chess championship that pitted youth against maturity, passion against pure intellect, and a Soviet dissident against a Soviet stalwart, Azerbaijan-born grand master Gary Kasparov in 1985 defeated reigning Russian-born champ Anatoly Karpov. A brilliantly analytical player, Karpov had dominated world chess since the mid-1970s. Kasparov, 22, a bolder player and an outspoken critic of the Communist regime, became the second youngest world champion (after Karpov). Kasparov also won a grueling 1990 rematch. ◀1972.12

DIPLOMACY

Europhoria Sweeps Continent

11 What Napoleon and Hitler had failed to do in war became possible in peace in 1985, when the twelve-nation European Community drafted the Single European Act. A revision of the 1957 Treaty of Rome, the measure created a detailed procedure for the full economic integration of Western Europe by the end of 1992. "Europhoria" raged as the EC Commission, led by French diplomat Jacques Delors *(above)*, moved to transform the region into the world's largest trading bloc.

Despite four decades of uninterrupted peace, the longest such period in history, Europe had been losing ground to Japan and the United States in the 1980s. The EC faced staggering problems—double-digit unemployment, low productivity, internal trade barriers. The old dream of economic unity (conceived in the 1940s by Frenchman Jean Monnet, the EC's chief architect) remained unfulfilled. Seeking an antidote to "Eurosclerosis," the EC Commission in 1985 issued *Completing the Internal Market*, a guide to final implementation of the "four freedoms"—unfettered movement of goods, services, capital, and people across EC borders. The report identified physical, technical, and fiscal barriers to trade and recommended 300 improvements.

With the Single European Act, the EC gained the legislative means to carry out those proposals. Signed in 1986, the act went into effect a year later. EC member nations quickly began pursuing aggressive new investment policies; production and trade boomed. Political unity was still far off, and the fall of Communism in Eastern Europe would soon create a knot of policy problems—but for the moment, economic cohesion finally seemed possible. **◀1973.M ▶1993.8**

MEDICINE

AIDS Claims an Idol

12 Four years after its discovery, AIDS was still largely ignored in the United States—even though, with 12,000 cases (and 6,000 deaths) to date, the country had more AIDS patients than any other nation. Educational programs urging condom use were well under way in Europe. But U.S. policy makers gave the disease low priority, partly because of its association with homosexuality; to many Americans, AIDS was scarcely suitable for polite conversation. The silence was broken in July 1985, when a spokesman announced that actor Rock Hudson was suffering from the immune-system disorder.

The news created a sensation, and not only because Hudson had recently kissed actress Linda Evans on *Dynasty.* Hudson—who'd starred in such films as *Giant* and *Ice Station Zebra*—was an archetypal Hollywood leading man. The revelation that he was a homosexual forced a reevaluation of stereotypes. It also prompted an outpouring of interest in the plight of infected gays. Previously, media treatment of AIDS had focused on the relatively few heterosexuals who'd contracted the disease through blood transfusions. Now, reporters raced to do investigative pieces on the epidemic.

For the first time, the long agony of thousands of AIDS sufferers—the exotic cancers, the opportunistic infections, the wasting of flesh—began to enter mainstream consciousness, as did the heroism of the doctors, volunteers, friends, and lovers who cared for them. But the Reagan administration (despite the crusading advocacy of Surgeon General C. Everett Koop) resisted congressional efforts to increase funds for AIDS research and prevention. Hudson (who died in October, leaving $250,000 to endow an AIDS research foundation) was a friend of the Reagans, but the President never even mentioned AIDS in a speech until 1987. By that time, there were 51,000 cases in 113 countries, and the World Health Organization was predicting three million by 1991. Soon, the costs of the epidemic would be overwhelming. **◀1984.5**

Rock Hudson in 1985 with his erstwhile screen partner Doris Day.

THEATER

A Hindu Epic, Modernized

13 British director Peter Brook carried off the most ambitious project of his prodigious, and relentlessly innovative, theatrical career in 1985: He staged a 1,500-year-old Hindu epic whose text is 15 times longer than the Bible's. Working from French playwright Jean-Claude Carrière's adaptation of the Sanskrit poem *The Mahabharata,* Brook created a nine-and-a-half-hour rumination on love, war, birth, death, and the cosmos. After debuting at the Avignon Festival in southwestern France, *The Mahabharata* toured the world, making stops in Madrid, Athens, Zurich, Los Angeles, and New York. "After almost ten hours we are nearly dead," said a cast member of the marathon spectacle, "but it's worth the effort."

Hindu archers launch their arrows in Brook's epic adaptation.

An innovator steeped in the classics—he'd directed England's Royal Shakespeare Company (a much-praised 1970 staging of *A Midsummer Night's Dream* was performed with trapezes, stilts, and acrobatic stunts) and had revived Antonin Artaud's Theatre of Cruelty with a landmark 1964 production of Peter Weiss's *Marat/Sade*—Brook admired the ancient *Mahabharata* for its exploration of universal human dilemmas. "It takes set ideas of what is right," he said, "what is morality or immorality, and through contradictory characters who intermingle, great questions are turned into human material." The cast of *The Mahabharata*, drawn largely from Brook's International Centre of Theatre Research in Paris, was nearly as universal as the play itself: 24 actors from 18 countries. **◀1957.12**

NOBEL PRIZES: Peace: International Physicians for the Prevention of Nuclear War (U.S.) ... Literature: Claude Simon (French; novelist) ... Chemistry: Herbert A. Hauptman and Jerome Karle (U.S.; crystal structures) ... Medicine: Michael Brown and Joseph Goldstein (U.S.; cholesterol metabolism) ... Physics: Klaus von Klitzing (German; quantum Hall effect) ... Economics: Franco Modigliani (U.S.).

A VOICE FROM 1985

Ennui in L.A.'s Fast Lane

From *Less Than Zero*, by Bret Easton Ellis, 1985

Tellingly, young writer Bret Easton Ellis prefaced his 1985 bestselling novel, Less Than Zero, *with lyrics from popular rock songs. A story of terminal vacuity among rich Los Angeles teenagers, told in short bursts of first-person prose by a narrator named Clay, the book had the feel of a music video: jaded, choppy, popping with cars, drugs, and sex. It was literature for a generation rumored not to read. Along with hip New York novelists Jay McInerney* (Bright Lights, Big City) *and Tama Janowitz* (Slaves of New York), *Ellis completed a set of Bright Young Things, 1980s-style. The very narrowness of the troika's shared subject—upper-middle-class collegiate and postcollegiate urban angst and amorality—revealed volumes about the go-go youth and money culture of the times.* **◂1951.10**

At the sushi bar in Studio City, Alana doesn't say much. She keeps looking down at her Diet Coke and lighting cigarettes and after a few drags, putting them out. When I ask her about Blair, she looks at me and says, "Do you really want to know?" and then smiles firmly and says, "You sound like you really care." I turn away from her, kind of freaked out and talk to this Benjamin guy, who goes to Oakwood. It seems that his BMW was stolen and he goes on about how he finds it really lucky that he found a new BMW 320i in the same off-green his father originally bought him and he tells me, "I mean, I can't believe I found it. Can you?"

"No. I can't," I tell him, glancing over at Alana.

Kim feeds Benjamin a piece of sushi and then he takes a sip of sake he got with his fake I.D. and starts to talk about music. "New Wave. Power Pop. Primitive Muzak. It's all bullshit. Rockabilly is where it's at. And I don't mean those limp-wristed Stray Cats, I mean real rockabilly. I'm going to New York in April to check the rockabilly scene out. I'm not too sure if it's happening there. It might be happening in Baltimore."

"Yeah. Baltimore," I say.

"Yeah, I like rockabilly too." Kim says, wiping her hands. "But I'm still into the Psychedelic Furs and I like that new Human League song."

Benjamin says, "The Human League are out. Over. Finished. You don't know what's going on, Kim."

Kim shrugs. I wonder where Dimitri is; if Jeff is still holed up with some surfer out in Malibu.

"No, I mean, you really don't," he goes on. "I bet you don't even read *The Face*. You've got to." He lights a clove cigarette. "You've got to."

"Why do you have to?" I ask.

Benjamin looks at me, runs his fingers over his pompadour and says, "Otherwise you'll get bored."

I say I guess so, then make plans with Kim to meet her later tonight at her house with Blair and then I go home and out to dinner with my mother. When I get home from that I take a long cold shower and sit on the floor of the stall and let the water hit me full on.

I drive over to Kim's house and find Blair sitting in Kim's room and she has this shopping bag from Jurgenson's over her head and when I come in, her body gets all tense and she turns around, startled, and she reaches over and turns down the stereo. "Who is it?"

"It's me," I tell her. "Clay."

She takes the bag off her head and smiles and tells me that she had the hiccups.

There's a large dog at Blair's feet and I lean down and stroke the dog's head. Kim comes out of the bathroom, takes a drag off the cigarette Blair was smoking and then throws it on the floor. She turns the stereo back up, some Prince song.

"Jesus, Clay, you look like you're on acid or something," Blair says, lighting another cigarette.

"I just had dinner with my mother," I tell her.

The dog puts the cigarette out with his paw and then eats it.

Kim mentions something about an old boyfriend who had a really bad trip once. "He took acid and didn't come down for six weeks. His parents sent him to Switzerland." Kim turns to Blair, who's looking at the dog. The dog swallows the rest of the cigarette.

"Have I dressed down enough?" Kim asks us.

Blair nods and tells her to take the hat off.

"Should I?" Kim asks me, unsure.

"Sure, why not?" I sigh and sit on Kim's bed.

"Listen, it's early. Why don't we go to the movies," Kim says, looking in the mirror, taking the hat off.

Blair gets up and says, "That's a good idea. What's playing?"

The dog coughs and swallows again.

The three prime progenitors of 1980s brat-pack fiction, at a 1988 party: Jay McInerney, Tama Janowitz, Ellis.

"You had the impression you could see the radiation. There were flashes of light springing from place to place, substances glowing, a bit like sparklers."—**Major Leonid Telyatnikov, head of the firefighting unit at Chernobyl**

STORY OF THE YEAR

The Chernobyl Meltdown

1 Technicians at a Swedish nuclear power plant registered it first, one April morning in 1986: abnormally high levels of radiation in the surrounding air. An inspection turned up no leaks. By afternoon, monitors

A technician approaches the burned-out Chernobyl reactor.

in Denmark, Norway, and Finland had reported similar findings. The prevailing wind, it was noted, blew from the east. Somewhere beyond the Baltic Sea, the horrified scientists realized, an unprecedented catastrophe had taken place—a full-scale nuclear meltdown. The exact location remained unknown until late evening, when Soviet television tersely announced that an "accident has occurred at Chernobyl Nuclear Power Plant."

The accident at the Ukrainian plant had, in fact, occurred days earlier, but even under Mikhail Gorbachev's new policy of glasnost (openness), the Soviet government's traditional unwillingness to release embarrassing news held sway. An explosion had ripped through one of Chernobyl's four reactors, spewing 100 million curies of radiation into the atmosphere—six million times more than had escaped from Pennsylvania's Three Mile Island (which, before Chernobyl, had been history's worst nuclear-plant accident). The plant burned for two weeks, foiling initial efforts to plug the leak. Thirty-one people died immediately, most from radiation sickness; 135,000 were evacuated (some not until weeks later) from an area measuring 300 square miles. Farmland and groundwater within 20 miles of Chernobyl were severely contaminated. The impact was felt farther away, as well: In Scandinavia, milk was found to have 15 times the normal radiation level; elsewhere in Europe, contaminated crops had to be destroyed. The meltdown's full toxic impact would not be known for at least a generation. Experts estimated a toll of 40,000 cancer cases, perhaps 6,500 deaths.

Human error and poor design conspired to make Chernobyl blow. Technicians committed a series of mistakes that could not have been more destructive had they been plotted; the plant lacked adequate safety controls to compensate for operator blunders. The meltdown impelled policy reevaluation in Western Europe, dependent on nuclear power for 30 percent of its electricity, but few policy changes: Despite the now obvious dangers, nuclear power was still viewed as safer (when properly managed) and cleaner (despite the still-unsolved problem of disposing of radioactive wastes) than fossil fuels. **◂1979.7**

DISASTERS

The *Challenger* Explodes

2 Millions of Americans watched their television sets in fascinated horror as the worst disaster in the history of space exploration endlessly played and replayed itself, etching itself into the nation's collective memory: On January 28, 1986, 73 seconds after a seemingly routine liftoff at Cape Canaveral, Florida, the space shuttle *Challenger,* veteran of nine successful flights, exploded in midair at an altitude of less than ten miles. As the astronauts' cabin plunged into the ocean, a double-horned cloud from the blast marked the demise of all seven on board—Commander Francis Scobee and his Navy pilot, Michael Smith; veteran mission specialists Ellison Onizuka, Ronald McNair, and Judith Resnik; and newcomers Gregory Jarvis and Christa McAuliffe. McAuliffe, a New Hampshire schoolteacher who'd won a nationwide "Teacher in Space" contest, was the first private citizen to fly on a shuttle mission.

In full view of people on the ground, *Challenger* disappeared in a cloud of smoke.

Five months after the tragedy, a government commission concluded that it could have been avoided. Engineers had long warned that a crucial component of the shuttle was faulty—a set of gaskets called O-rings, which sealed the joints between rocket booster sections. But NASA, in its determination to launch the *Challenger* on schedule (the flight directly before it had been plagued by delays), neglected to correct the problem. The *Challenger* itself was delayed four times, and mission control made the fateful decision to launch in freezing temperatures, despite the risk that the cold would further weaken the O-rings. The gaskets failed, releasing a flame that ignited the main fuel tank.

Angered that their safety had been sacrificed for expediency, several astronauts left the program. A number of top NASA staffers were replaced, and shuttle flights were suspended until 1988. The following year, NASA announced that civilians would not be permitted on shuttle crews. **◂1981.12 ▸1990.12**

THE PHILIPPINES

"People Power" Revolution

3 In February 1986, pressure from a massive opposition movement (as well as from communist guerrillas and the U.S. State Department) forced Ferdinand Marcos to hold his nation's first seriously contested presidential election in 17 years. The ailing dictator faced a formidable opponent: Corazon Aquino, the unpretentious, idealistic, and hugely popular widow of martyred opposition leader Benigno Aquino. Marcos rigged the voting and officially won the contest—but he lost his country.

Following the fraudulent election, Aquino called for a mass campaign of civil disobedience. Days later, generals Juan Ponce Enrile and Fidel Ramos led a military revolt, seizing two of Manila's bases. Caught in a standoff with the government, they then abandoned their coup attempt and backed Aquino. Thousands of unarmed civilians surrounded the camps to protect the anti-Marcos troops, blocking tanks that arrived to quash the rebellion. The "people power" revolution (as Aquino called it) instantly spread across the country.

Beyond a few rockets fired by the rebels at a loyalist air base and at Malacanang Palace (the presidential residence), there was little fighting. Yet days after the uprising began, Marcos and his entourage fled to Hawaii. Jubilant crowds invaded the palace, which yielded ample evidence of the ousted "kleptocracy"—most notoriously, Marcos's wife Imelda's 1,060 pairs of shoes.

Aquino immediately freed political prisoners and began restoring democratic institutions. Negotiations with the communists soon led to a cease-fire—the first in nearly two decades. But revolutionary

ART & CULTURE: Books: *A Summons to Memphis* (Peter Taylor); *The Handmaid's Tale* (Margaret Atwood); *The Sportswriter* (Richard Ford); *Maus* (Art Spiegelman); *The Making of the Atomic Bomb* (Richard Rhodes) ... Music: "The Edge of Heaven" (George Michael); "Nikita" (John and Taupin); *Back in the High Life* (Steve Winwood, LP); *The Flight into Egypt* (John Harbison) ... Painting & Sculpture: *Mural with*

"I wish to go down in history with my head held high and with a clean conscience. Therefore, I have decided to trust the destiny of the nation to the power of the armed forces of Haiti."—**Jean-Claude "Baby Doc" Duvalier in his last nationwide address**

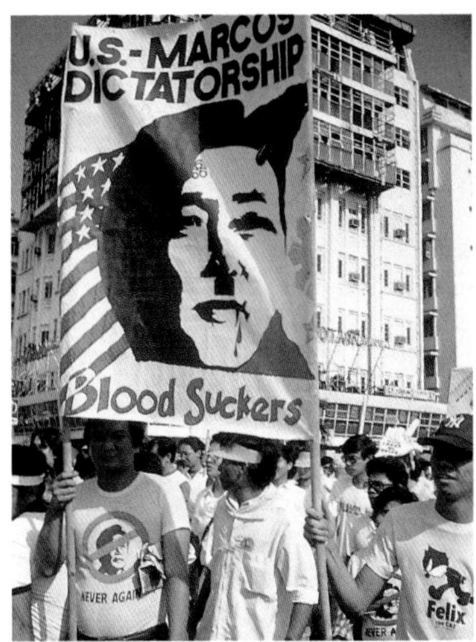

Anti-Marcos Filipinos rally in Manila.

euphoria quickly faded. The government was divided over social and economic policy. Marcos's cronies retained significant power (sometimes backed up by private armies). Aquino often showed her political inexperience and failed to keep promises to the poor. The leftist insurgency resumed, and by 1992 the new democracy had survived seven rightist coup attempts—including one by General Enrile. That year, Aquino decided not to run for reelection; instead, she endorsed Ramos (who'd become her defense minister). He won handily. **◂1983.2 ▸1989.M**

THE CARIBBEAN

Baby Doc Deposed

4 On the night in February 1986 that an uprising drove Jean-Claude Duvalier from Haiti, the dictator kept his American escorts waiting two hours at the airport while he held a champagne farewell party at home. Such arrogant frivolity was characteristic of Duvalier's rule, which had begun in 1971 when his dying father, François, bequeathed his title of President for Life to his 19-year-old son. At first, "Baby Doc" (the elder Duvalier was "Papa Doc") freed a few political prisoners and loosened press restrictions. But massive foreign aid could not counteract the economic effects of corruption and mismanagement. After 1980, when Duvalier married a glamorous daughter of Haiti's mulatto elite (a widely hated class whose privileges his father had curtailed), popular resentment soared and repression redoubled. And as his wife squandered the funds of the hemisphere's poorest nation on million-dollar Paris shopping sprees, resentment turned to rage.

Sporadic unrest began in 1984. Yielding to pressure from the United States and the Catholic Church, Duvalier amended the constitution to legalize political parties. But violent intimidation by the Tonton Macoutes (the dreaded private militia founded by Duvalier Senior) marred a constitutional referendum in 1985, and elections were never held. Demonstrations swept the country; several were dispersed with bullets. Tourism and foreign investment dwindled. Finally, after U.S. officials advised him that his regime was doomed, Baby Doc fled to France, leaving a military-civilian junta in power. After 29 years, the Duvalier dynasty had fallen.

In the explosion of fury that followed, two dozen Tonton Macoutes were lynched (the force subsequently went underground), and mobs sacked the property of prominent Duvalierists, including Papa Doc's mausoleum. Urging calm, the junta leader, Lieutenant General Henri Namphy, promised elections and "a commitment to human rights." But freedom would not readily come—nor would it last. **◂1957.3 ▸1990.13**

Anti-Duvalier protesters hoist a coffin bearing the epithet: "Jean-Claude Fat Pig."

DIPLOMACY

Reykjavík Summit

5 The autumn 1986 superpower summit at Reykjavík, Iceland—the first encounter between Soviet general secretary Mikhail Gorbachev and U.S. president Ronald Reagan—ended with each leader blaming the other for the talks' collapse. Enlivened by an unusual degree of spontaneity but marred by lack of preparation on both sides, the negotiations became an occasion for grandstanding. Yet the climate was right for arms control: Gorbachev's determination to revitalize the Soviet economy would have been well served by an arms rollback.

Gorbachev and Reagan at Reykjavík.

In a private, one-on-one meeting, the two leaders nearly took the ultimate step: an agreement to end the threat of atomic Armageddon. "It would be fine with me if we eliminated all nuclear weapons," Reagan said. "We can do that," Gorbachev concurred. But their utopian vision of peace was undone by Reagan's equally starry-eyed plan for war: the Strategic Defense Initiative (nicknamed "Star Wars"), a grandiose scheme to build a space-based satellite and missile "shield" to immunize America from missile attack. In return for dismantling the Soviet Union's nuclear stockpile, Gorbachev wanted SDI limited to the laboratory. Reagan refused. Reykjavík's fevered all-or-nothing atmosphere made compromise impossible: Both sides went home empty-handed.

Talks in 1987 were more sober—and productive: Late that year, American and Soviet leaders signed the first agreement to reduce the size of their nations' nuclear arsenals. Ironically, the sole practical use of the Star Wars system was as a bargaining chip. In 1993, a decade after it was proposed, and after $30 billion had been spent on development, the U.S. Congress killed the program. **◂1983.V ▸1987.10**

DEATHS

Harold Arlen, U.S. composer.

Desi Arnaz, Cuban-U.S. actor and television executive.

Simone de Beauvoir, French writer.

Joseph Beuys, German artist.

Len Bias, U.S. basketball player.

Jorge Luis Borges, Argentine writer.

Roy Cohn, U.S. lawyer.

Broderick Crawford, U.S. actor.

Marcel Dassault, French aircraft designer.

Jean Genet, French playwright.

Benny Goodman, U.S. musician.

Cary Grant, U.K.-U.S. actor.

W. Averell Harriman, U.S. statesman.

L. Ron Hubbard, U.S. writer and religious leader.

Christopher Isherwood, U.K.-U.S. writer.

Urho Kekkonen, Finnish president.

Raymond Loewy, French-U.S. designer.

Harold Macmillan, U.K. prime minister.

Bernard Malamud, U.S. writer.

Vincente Minnelli, U.S. filmmaker.

Henry Moore, U.K. sculptor.

Alva Myrdal, Swedish sociologist and diplomat.

Georgia O'Keeffe, U.S. painter.

Olof Palme, Swedish prime minister.

Otto Preminger, Austrian-U.S. filmmaker.

Hyman Rickover, Russian-U.S. admiral.

Albert Szent-Györgyi, Hungarian-U.S. biochemist.

Theodore H. White, U.S. writer.

Teddy Wilson, U.S. musician.

Blue Brushstroke **(Roy Lichtenstein);** ***Legs*** **(Louise Bourgeois);** ***Untitled '88*** **(Donald Judd) ... Film:** ***Platoon*** **(Oliver Stone);** ***Hannah and Her Sisters*** **(Woody Allen);** ***Aliens*** **(James Cameron);** ***Jean de Florette*** **(Claude Berri);** ***Tampopo*** **(Juzo Hami) ... Theater:** ***Burn This*** **(Lanford Wilson);** ***Coastal Disturbances*** **(Tina Howe);** ***Broadway Bound*** **(Neil Simon);** ***A Woman in Mind*** **(Alan Ayckbourn) ... TV:** ***L.A. Law.***

"We others in my generation went under in the machinery of war, in fear and in the effort to survive."—**Kurt Waldheim**

NEW IN 1986

Mandatory household recycling (Rhode Island).

U.S. poet laureate (Robert Penn Warren).

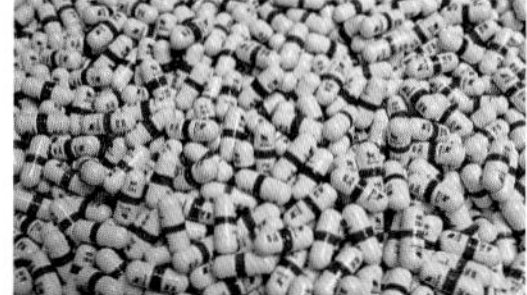

AZT (azidothymine, FDA-approved treatment for AIDS).

FDA-approved genetically engineered vaccine (for hepatitis B).

Spain and Portugal as members of European Common Market.

IN THE UNITED STATES

▶WYETH'S HELGA—Andrew Wyeth, previously best known for his 1948 painting *Christina's World* and for an intensely realistic style that often conveyed a deep sense of melancholy, created an art-

world sensation in 1986 when the National Gallery in Washington mounted a show of 239 of his Helga studies. Wyeth had been secretly painting the mystery woman (his neighbor in rural Pennsylvania) over a period of many years, but until recently had told no one, save his wife, that the paintings existed. ◂1948.M

▶TITAN OF THE TRACK—Willie Shoemaker, 4' 11" tall and 54 years old, became the Kentucky Derby's oldest winning jockey when he rode longshot Ferdinand to victory on May 3 in the annual Run for the Roses. A year earlier Shoemaker had become the first rider to surpass $100 million in career winnings. ◂1977.13

▶BURGER COURT ENDS—With the retirement in July of Chief Justice Warren Burger, the U.S. Supreme Court lurched rightward. President Reagan nominated associate justice William Rehnquist, the Court's most conservative member, to succeed Burger (himself no liberal). Rehnquist's

THE MIDDLE EAST

U.S. Bombs Libya

6 No world leader had reviled the United States more vehemently than Muammar al-Qaddafi; none had praised terrorist groups as openly. International sanctions (and CIA destabilization efforts) had failed to oust Qaddafi or change his ways. Yet Ronald Reagan had hesitated to use military force against the Libyan strongman without being able to cite hard evidence linking Libya to a specific terrorist act. Such evidence finally materialized in April 1986, when an explosion at a West Berlin disco—perhaps in revenge for a recent skirmish in the Gulf of Sidra, where American planes had blasted Libyan gunboats—killed a U.S. soldier and a Turkish woman and wounded 230 others. U.S. intelligence claimed to have intercepted incriminating messages from Qaddafi to Libya's embassy in East Berlin. Two weeks later, 150 planes raided Libya in the biggest single U.S. bombing mission since World War II.

The strike concentrated largely on the army compound in Tripoli where Qaddafi lived. (Since 1976, U.S. law had barred the assassination of foreign leaders, but an air raid was another matter.) Though some 40 civilians—including Qaddafi's infant daughter—died, the dictator escaped unharmed.

The United States faced other letdowns. Though Britain permitted the use of its airfields, most other allies opposed the operation. France and Spain refused to let the U.S. planes cross their territory, forcing a lengthy detour. Europe erupted in protest. And terrorism continued unabated: Within days, one American and three British hostages in Lebanon were killed in reprisal, and bombs exploded in London, Paris, and Vienna. In fact, Syria and Iran were known to be bigger sponsors of terror than Libya, but their military and diplomatic clout made them more forbidding foes. **◂1981.3 ▸1988.4**

A pallbearer at a mass funeral for U.S.-bombing victims in Tripoli flashes a victory sign.

AUSTRIA

A President's Nazi Past

7 Throughout a four-decade political career that included a stint as UN secretary-general (1972–82), Kurt Waldheim had constructed an innocuous biography in response to the question, "What did you do in the war?" He said he'd never been a Nazi, and that he'd been drafted into the German army after the Anschluss, then had returned to law school after being wounded in 1941. Yet in 1986, when Waldheim became the presidential candidate of Austria's rightist People's Party, newly discovered documents revealed a far more sinister past. Not only had he joined Nazi student groups in 1938—but in 1942 and '43, he'd been a staff officer in a division that slaughtered Yugoslav civilians and deported thousands of Greek Jews to death camps.

Waldheim vowed his Nazi affiliations had been purely pragmatic. At first he denied knowing about the war crimes (for which his commander was executed in 1947); later he protested that "knowledge alone is not a crime." His evasions drew worldwide condemnation, but his compatriots reacted defensively. Although most Austrians had collaborated with Hitler, they now pointed to an Allied declaration of 1943 that their country had been a victim of Nazi aggression. Many agreed with Waldheim's campaign literature that the World Jewish Congress was directing a "psychoterror" campaign against the nation. Almost all Austria's newspapers endorsed Waldheim. (One tabloid ran anti-Semitic cartoons.) Even his Socialist opponent, sensing the public mood, soft-pedaled the scandal. In June, Waldheim won the election by 54 percent.

Despite a congratulatory note from Ronald Reagan, Austria's new president was barred from visiting the United States and ostracized by many European leaders; Israel recalled its ambassador from Vienna. A growing number of Austrians began calling for their leader's resignation. But Waldheim served out his six-year term, and chose not to run in 1992. **◂1938.2 ▸1993.7**

THE UNITED STATES

Iran-Contra Scandal

8 A Lebanese magazine broke the astonishing story in November 1986: The Reagan administration had sold missiles to Iran. Undertaken to free Americans held hostage by pro-Iranian guerrillas in Lebanon, the secret transactions were illegal; moreover, they violated Reagan's oft-stated principles of nonnegotiation with terrorists and of isolating their backers. Weeks later, Attorney General Edwin Meese dropped a bigger bombshell: The U.S. officials involved had diverted millions of dollars in profits from the sales to rightist contra rebels in Nicaragua. The diversion contravened the 1984 Boland Amendment, which banned military aid to the contras. Direct involvement by Reagan would be an impeachable offense.

Meese claimed that Lieutenant Colonel Oliver North, a National Security Council aide, had directed the operation on his own. North was fired; his boss, National Security Adviser John Poindexter, resigned. But subsequent investigations—by Congress, by the presidentially appointed Tower Commission, and by special prosecutor Lawrence Walsh—belied Meese's story. The CIA, the NSC, and several Reagan cabinet members, including Vice President George Bush, were implicated.

SPORTS: Baseball: World Series, New York Mets defeat Boston Red Sox, 4–3 ... Football: Super Bowl, Chicago Bears defeat New England Patriots, 46–10 ... Basketball: NBA, Boston Celtics defeat Houston Rockets, 4–2 ... Boxing: Mike Tyson wins world heavyweight title ... Golf: Jack Nicklaus wins his sixth Masters ... Soccer: World Cup, Argentina (led by Diego Maradona) defeats West Germany, 3–2.

"If the commander in chief tells this lieutenant colonel to go stand in a corner and sit on his head, I will do so.... And if he decides to dismiss me ... I will proudly salute and say, 'Thank you ... ' and go."—**Oliver North**

Public confidence in the hitherto phenomenally popular Reagan was shaken. At best, he'd been negligent; at worst, he had engaged in a criminal conspiracy. In 1987, Reagan admitted to having encouraged private aid of various kinds to the contras; as to having approved arms sales to Iran, he said, "The simple truth is, I don't remember."

North professed no such memory lapse. In televised congressional hearings, the ramrod-straight marine enthralled many Americans with his patriotic rhetoric. But while trumpeting his loyalty to his superiors, North fingered a chain of command that went straight to the top. "I thought," he testified, "I had received authority from the President."

In 1989, North received the first of many felony convictions handed down in the Iran-Contra case. (An appeals court later reversed the

The White House called North a "loose cannon" in an effort to discredit his story.

decisions on a technicality.) Reagan was never charged with a crime; prosecution of other officials dragged on until 1992, when Bush, by then a lame-duck president himself (he'd succeeded Reagan), pardoned the last six before they could be tried. **◂1984.3**

ENVIRONMENTALISM

Rhine River Disaster

9 In November 1986, a blaze at a Sandoz chemical plant near Basel, Switzerland, caused Europe's worst environmental catastrophe in a decade. Fire hoses washed some 30 tons of poison—up to 32 types of pesticides, fungicides, and other agricultural chemicals—into the Rhine river. In a few hours, the waterway received as much pollution as it usually received in a year.

While the disaster claimed no human casualties, the toll on aquatic life was staggering. Tons of dead fish were scooped from the river; the few survivors were covered with

In a German cartoon, a man accuses German chemical companies of killing the Rhine. In the caption, the other responds, "Nonsense, the Swiss already did that."

sores. As the poison moved downstream, it killed most of the microscopic animals in its path—including the water fleas that formed the basis of much of the Rhine's food chain. Nearly 200 miles of the river were left virtually bereft of life. Recovery was expected to take ten years.

The nations bordering the Rhine—Switzerland, France, West Germany, and the Netherlands—banned fishing, closed locks to stop the pollution from entering streams and groundwater, and trucked in drinking water. Demonstrations erupted across Western Europe; at a public meeting in Basel, protesters pelted city officials and a Sandoz representative with dead eels and bottles of river water. Switzerland (its reputation as an environmentally advanced country severely tarnished) was accused of failing to follow safety regulations. Eventually, the nation accepted responsibility for the chemical spill and agreed to pay restitution to its neighbors.

The calamity's only beneficiary was West Germany's pro-environment Green Party, which gained wider support after it called for strong measures to protect the river—including switching to safer chemicals and jailing toxic dumpers. **◂1983.5 ▸1989.13**

ART

Pop Populism

10 The art boom of the 1980s, which threatened to turn art into just another commodity, also turned artists into overnight stars. New York artist Keith Haring became a celebrity (and a runaway commercial success) with his distinctive stick-figure renderings of glowing babies and barking dogs. In 1986, Haring openly crossed the ever-moving line between art and commerce: He opened a retail store. Haring's Pop Shop, situated in trendy SoHo, sold inexpensive items—T-shirts, buttons, refrigerator magnets—emblazoned with his squiggly hieroglyphics. Accused of huckster-ism, Haring said he was "breaking down the barriers between high and low art." It was a pursuit to which he'd dedicated his career.

Haring had begun as a "graffiti artist," chalking his images on subway-station walls; he had continued to do so even as galleries began affixing five-figure price tags

Keith Haring died of AIDS in 1990; by that time his pictographs had become international pop icons.

to his canvases. His subsequent artistic endeavors retained their populist bent: He created imagery for antidrug and AIDS-research campaigns, taught at inner-city art clinics, and painted a unity mural on the Berlin Wall—which was quickly painted over with black by a German artist who found its cheerfulness inappropriate. **◂1982.10**

IN THE UNITED STATES

vacant seat was filled by vigorously conservative appellate judge Antonin Scalia. The Senate confirmed both appointments. ▸1991.V

▸HAND-TO-HAND HOOKUP—Some six million people joined hands on May 25, creating a human chain that stretched from New York to Long Beach, California (minus a few links in desert areas). Hands Across America, as the linkage was called, was designed to raise money and awareness to combat homelessness.

▸LADY LIBERTY TURNS 100—After a three-year, $70 million restoration, the Statue of Liberty was the center of an extravagant centennial celebration on July 4. A gift from

France, the New York Harbor colossus was dedicated by President Grover Cleveland in 1886. President Reagan kicked off the birthday bash by relighting the statue's torch on July 3. ◂1976.M

▸GOING TO GRACELAND—A cross-cultural sensation, Paul Simon's 1986 album *Graceland* featured a New Orleans zydeco band (Rockin' Dopsie), a Mexican-American rock band (Los Lobos), a South African choral group (Ladysmith Black Mambazo), a white South African instrumentalist (Morris Goldberg), a Senegalese vocalist (Youssou N'Dour), and the ghost of Elvis Presley, among other international artists. *Graceland* was designated "Album of the Decade" by many pop music critics. ◂1982.M

▸COCAINE CASUALTY—Len Bias, an All-America basketball player at the University of Maryland died on June 19 of a cocaine overdose. On the cusp of NBA stardom, Bias had been at a party celebrating his first-round selection by the Boston Celtics in the NBA's college draft. His death focused attention on drug abuse among athletes. ◂1985.8

POLITICS & BUSINESS: GNP: $4,277.7 billion ... Immigration Reform and Control Act allows some illegal immigrants to gain legal status ... Reagan signs tax reform bill (most comprehensive since WWII), restructuring income tax system ... Laurence Tisch and William Paley acquire CBS in leveraged buyout ... BBDO Int'l and Needham and Harper Worldwide form world's largest advertising agency, BBDO Needham.

"A pianist can be a good American when he plays Barber, a good Pole when he plays Chopin, a good Russian with Tchaikovsky.... A pianist is a citizen of the world."—Vladimir Horowitz

AROUND THE WORLD

▶WHO KILLED OLOF PALME?—Swedish prime minister Olof Palme, internationally renowned pacifist, was assassinated by a lone gunman on the streets of Stockholm on the evening of February 28 as he walked home from the movies with his wife, Lisbeth. He was the first Swedish head of state to be murdered since 1792. Police suspected a number of international terrorist groups in Palme's murder, but his killer was never apprehended. ◂1976.2

▶NYOS CATASTROPHE—The remote mountain village of Nyos, Cameroon, was struck with a bizarre natural disaster on August 21, when nearby Lake Nyos belched out a deadly cloud of carbon dioxide gas. The misty shroud settled over Nyos and nearby villages during the night, killing virtually everyone—more than 1,700 people in all. In its haste to bury corpses to prevent disease, the army failed to take a complete body count.

▶SUPERCONDUCTIVITY AT HIGHER TEMPERATURES—In January, Swiss physicist Karl Alex Müller and his German partner Johannes Georg Bednorz announced their discovery of a material with an unusually high transition temperature—the temperature at which a material loses electrical resistance (a state called superconductivity). Dutch physicist Heike Kamerlingh Onnes discovered superconductivity at –268.8°C in 1911; Müller and Bednorz (who later won a Nobel) found a ceramic metal-oxide compound with a transition temperature of –196°C—a significant reduction. The following year American physicist Paul W. Chu identified a similar compound that achieved superconductivity at –179°C. Superconductors can be used to create large, energy-efficient magnetic fields; applications include powerful computers, fusion reactors, and electric-power generation. ◂1911.2

Michael Crawford *(left)* and Sarah Brightman in the London production of *Phantom.*

THEATER

A Briton Goes Broadway

11 By 1986, musical theater had come full circle: At the beginning of the century, escapist English confections reigned supreme; at century's end, they ruled once more. In the years between, Rodgers and Hammerstein, Jerome Kern, Irving Berlin, and Cole Porter had dominated the lyric stage. But by the 1980s, popular American songwriters were turning out rock, not Broadway tunes; holdouts like Stephen Sondheim were often too cerebral for mass taste. Enter Andrew Lloyd Webber, a Briton who mixed Broadway pizzazz, opera, pop-rock, pyrotechnics, and kitsch to become the most successful composer in theatrical history. *The Phantom of the Opera*, which opened in London's West End in October 1986 (and moved to Broadway in 1988), is the quintessential Lloyd Webber product.

Lloyd Webber, the son of the head of the London College of Music, first gained fame in 1968 with *Joseph and the Amazing Technicolor Dreamcoat*, which was followed by the rock opera *Jesus Christ Superstar, Evita, Cats*, and *Starlight Express.* Critics often derided these operettas (they were entirely sung) for their derivative melodies, mediocre lyrics, and lightweight librettos. But audiences loved them: In 1982 Lloyd Webber made theater history by having three hits running simultaneously in New York and London.

A lush retelling of Gaston Leroux's story about a disfigured composer's diabolical love for a young soprano, *Phantom* boasted eye-popping special effects: A decayed Paris Opera stage turned splendiferous in an instant; candles rose from an onstage lake; a gargantuan chandelier flew over theatergoers and crashed next to the heroine (played by Sarah Brightman, Lloyd Webber's then-wife). The music again sounded familiar—critics noted its debts to Puccini and the Beatles—but the Phantom's romantic "Music of the Night" aria (sung by Michael Crawford) gained a mild popularity as a single. Nearly a decade after its debut, *Phantom* was still a sellout. ◂1975.12

LITERATURE

Soyinka's Nobel

12 In 1986, Nigerian Wole Soyinka became the first black African—indeed, the first black—to win the Nobel Prize for literature. Acknowledging the award's significance, the Nigerian government awarded Soyinka its own highest honor.

Such official approval was new to the British-educated writer. During the turbulent 1960s, Nigeria's first decade of independence, he was imprisoned twice for his political activities; the second time, during the Biafran conflict, he spent 22 months in solitary confinement on trumped-up charges of gunrunning. (Actually, he'd been agitating for peace. A Yoruban, he opposed the genocidal war against Igbo secessionists.) Even in a tiny cell, Soyinka managed to write, inscribing poems and letters on toilet paper and smuggling them out to eager readers.

Soyinka's work, written in English, often combines ritual, satire, and high tragedy and elements drawn from both European and Yoruban mythologies. Though praised for his autobiographical writings (notably the prison memoir *The Man Died*) as well as his poetry, novels, and essays, Soyinka is above all a dramatist. He founded acting companies and chaired the drama department at the University of Ife; his plays have been staged at major theaters in New York and London. An unblinking observer of African as well as Western foibles, Soyinka punctured the euphoria accompanying Nigerian independence with *A Dance of the Forests* (1960), assailed British colonialism with *Death and the King's Horseman* (1975), and lampooned African dictators (and the superpowers' attitudes toward them) with *A Play of Giants* (1984). ◂1958.12

MUSIC

Horowitz Goes Home

13 In April 1986, with Mikhail Gorbachev's reforms paving the way, Vladimir Horowitz—perhaps the century's greatest piano virtuoso—returned to the homeland he had fled 61 years earlier.

Born in Kiev in 1904, Horowitz had fled the Soviet Union in 1925. Already a star in Europe, Horowitz seized the American limelight in 1928 with a thunderous debut with the New York Philharmonic in which he matched wills with the legendarily difficult conductor Sir Thomas Beecham. (Horowitz raced ahead on a Tchaikovsky piece that Beecham was slowing down; he finished—to lengthy applause—four bars earlier than the rest of the orchestra.) Exhausting concert schedules, a stormy (but 56-year-long) marriage to Arturo Toscanini's daughter, and a series of retreats and comebacks kept Horowitz in and out of the public eye for decades. Among his compatriots in the U.S.S.R., word of mouth and recordings had ensured that "The Tornado from the Steppes" was not forgotten.

After overcoming several debilitating illnesses, Horowitz had begun his greatest comeback in 1985. Its pinnacle was his triumphant return to the Soviet Union—inspired partly by a yearning to see Russia once more before his death. He appeared first at the Great Hall of the Moscow Conservatory, then traveled to Leningrad for a second concert. Using his trademark flat-fingered technique, this paragon of musical romanticism played Schumann, Scriabin, Rachmaninoff, and Chopin for tearful Russian listeners, many of whom had stood all night to get tickets. (In Moscow, desperate music students even forced their way into the concert hall.) The emotional power of Horowitz's playing, said a critic, lifted "the yoke off [the audience's] shoulders.... It was a kind of religious experience." ◂1958.10

Horowitz greets fans after his historic concert in Leningrad.

NOBEL PRIZES: Peace: Elie Wiesel (U.S.; efforts on behalf of Holocaust victims) ... Literature: Wole Soyinka (Nigerian; novelist) ... Chemistry: D. Herschbach, Y. Lee, and J. Polanyi (U.S., U.S., Canadian; reaction dynamics) ... Medicine: Rita Levi-Montalcini and Stanley Cohen (U.S.; cell growth) ... Physics: G. Binnig, E. Ruska, and H. Rohrer (German, German, Swiss; microscopy) ... Economics: James Buchanan (U.S.).

A VOICE FROM 1986

Oprah's Emergence

From "Homeless People," *The Oprah Winfrey Show*, December 3, 1986

Just months after her Chicago-based talk show went into national syndication in September 1986, emotional, earthy, likable Oprah Winfrey became the undisputed ratings champ of daytime television. Oprah—like rival chat mavens Phil (Donahue), Sally Jessy (Raphaël), and Geraldo (Rivera), she became a first-name celebrity—offered the standard daytime talk formula of prurience and audience participation, but she had a special talent for making every conversation seem personal. Whereas the preachy Donahue, who pioneered the format in 1967, might try to present "Teenage Strippers and Their Mothers" as an ethics seminar, and Rivera might host "Teenage Lesbians and Their Mothers" for its simple circus appeal, Oprah was inclined to identify with her guests and unabashedly discuss her sexual history or her ongoing weight problem. For millions of loyal fans, her show offered the illusion of a heart-to-heart with an old and sympathetic friend. **◄1955.V**

Talk-show host as sympathetic friend: An effusive Winfrey greets her audience before taping her Chicago-based television show in 1986.

WINFREY: My next guest is nothing less than remarkable. After leaving his successful job, his wife and two children 17 years ago, he became an unpaid crusader, working desperately to help the tragic plight of the homeless. He received national recognition in 1984, after he starved himself for 51 days until the Reagan administration agreed to renovate a shelter for the homeless. Before quitting his protest fast, during which he consumed only water, he told a reporter that he was prepared to die if necessary to force the government to refurbish the shelter. This Thanksgiving, he took to the streets, living the life of a homeless person on the grounds of the Capitol, holding a special dinner for over 2,000 needy people. Please welcome the leader of the Community for Creative Non-Violence group, Mitch Snyder.

Welcome Mitch Snyder. It would seem, it would seem as long as you have been working, as long as you have been protesting and trying to do things for the homeless, that the picture for the homeless in this country would have changed by now. Has it?

MITCH SNYDER: It has, it's gotten better at the same time as it's gotten worse. It's gotten better, because virtually every day more people wind up falling through the cracks, and living in abandoned buildings, eating out of garbage pails.…There are more, many more people on the streets, and falling out on the streets now than we've ever seen at any time since the Great Depression.

WINFREY: Why? What happened?

MR. SNYDER: I think what we're seeing are the cumulative effects of budget cuts, economic conditions, and the near disappearance of affordable housing. In city after city across the country, there is no place to live, you just can't find a place, and you can't afford one.…

FIRST AUDIENCE MEMBER: I just wanted to say I work with the homeless and what he was saying about no housing, I'm from Du Page County, and a one-bedroom apartment there costs $400 a month, and people that are working the minimum wage, they just can't do it. And so what they really need to do is start with the housing, and get housing for people that are only making $4 or $5 an hour.…

WINFREY: I'm curious as to what can be done, I mean, what can be—is it our responsibility, those of us who have homes, to go to the streets and try to rescue people?

MR. SNYDER: Well, there's three answers to that question. The first is at a personal level. Every one of us can and should, the next time, we see someone out on the street, at least acknowledge their existence, say hello to them, offer them a cup of coffee, something to eat—do something that says, "You're a human being and I care about you."

Number two, each of us has a responsibility as citizens to roll up our sleeves and get personally involved, and that means helping out at soup kitchens, shelters, food pantries, wherever there's a need, and the need is enormous.

Third, we've got to make sure that the government—state, local, and federal, and particularly the federal government—begins to do its fair share. The federal government, at least up until today, has turned its back on America's homeless, has said it's a state and local problem, and has walked away. And it's going to take concerned, caring citizens to tell members of Congress that it's about time that the federal government began to do what needs to be done in order to meet the needs of the people living on the streets of our country.…

SECOND AUDIENCE MEMBER: I just wanted to say that if we don't have a home by the time our baby is born, we're going to lose it, and that's all.

WINFREY: How did you end up without a home? How did the two of you end up without a home?

THIRD AUDIENCE MEMBER: We were renting a condo in Woodridge and the owner wanted to sell, so he gave us seven days to leave. And we had no money saved, so we've been going to shelters, cars, homes, people, friends, everywhere.…

WINFREY: Do you understand that sense of desperation he was talking about earlier?

THIRD AUDIENCE MEMBER: Yes I do.

WINFREY: Overwhelming?

THIRD AUDIENCE MEMBER: Yes. There's a lot of people that are really scared.

WINFREY: Thanks for sharing with us. Is it because most of us are so comfortable that we don't understand, do you think?

MR. SNYDER: I think it's because most of us are so vulnerable. I think when we see somebody out in the streets, deep down in our guts we understand that could be us, and that's such a frightening thought we don't want to deal with it, and so we block out the messenger. We just don't see the people out there, because they remind us of our own vulnerability.

"You can't fill the bankers' bellies and the people's bellies at the same time."—**Brazilian labor leader Jair Meneguelli**

STORY OF THE YEAR

Brazil Suspends Debt Payments

1 No developing nation owed more money to foreign lenders than Brazil. So when President José Sarney announced in February 1987 that his country was suspending interest payments on its $108 billion debt, creditors in the developed nations shuddered. It wasn't that the banks would fold without Brazil's $10 billion yearly payments. But Latin America's biggest debtors (Brazil, Mexico, Argentina, and Venezuela) together owed $285 billion. If the others followed Brazil's example, financial institutions could be seriously damaged. Several major U.S. banks, forced as a precaution to divert capital into their bad-debt reserves, posted losses for the year.

Brazilians judged the lenders themselves at fault. For 20 years, ending in 1985, Brazil had been ruled by military dictators—and foreign banks had eagerly financed their grandiose schemes. The generals built highways, dams, nuclear plants, and weapons factories, helping to transform an agricultural backwater into the world's eighth-largest capitalist economy. Many projects were never finished, however, or never worked properly. To pay the burgeoning debt, Brazil's rulers mounted feverish export campaigns. But earnings barely kept pace with interest payments, and domestic consumption plummeted. Despite the country's riches, malnutrition and illiteracy remained pandemic. Reckless industrialization and exploitation of natural resources brought environmental disasters. Inflation raged.

Economic decline brought protests and often violent reprisals. Above, police in Rio disperse a riot over a bus-fare hike.

In 1986, Sarney tried to ease his people's plight by freezing prices while letting wages rise and leaving money supplies loose. Business and public morale boomed; Sarney's party won November elections. But soon shortages appeared and inflation redoubled. When the government (which controlled more than half of Brazil's economy) raised prices on state-supplied goods and services, rebellions erupted. By early 1987, the country's trade surplus was gone, and Sarney had little choice but to defy the banks.

Yet like his Peruvian and Ecuadoran counterparts (both of whom had also declared payment moratoriums), Sarney found that living without the international bankers was as hard as living with them. As Brazil's economy worsened and promised land reforms languished, unrest deepened; the government increasingly resorted to violence. (The worst incident came in December, when military police fired on striking gold miners, killing more than 100.) In February 1988, Sarney gave in, ending the moratorium with a $350 million payment. ◂1961.7 ▸1989.8

CENTRAL AMERICA

The Arias Peace Plan

2 Drawing on his country's tradition of neutrality and his own skills as a mediator, Costa Rican president Oscar Arias Sánchez attempted to make peace in war-torn Central America. The agreement he brokered—signed in Guatemala City in August 1987 by Arias and the presidents of Guatemala, Honduras, El Salvador, and Nicaragua—called for a regional cease-fire, amnesty for political prisoners, and free elections in each of the signatory countries. Hailed as a homegrown initiative that put the peace process squarely in the hands of the people it most affected, the effort won Arias the Nobel Peace Prize.

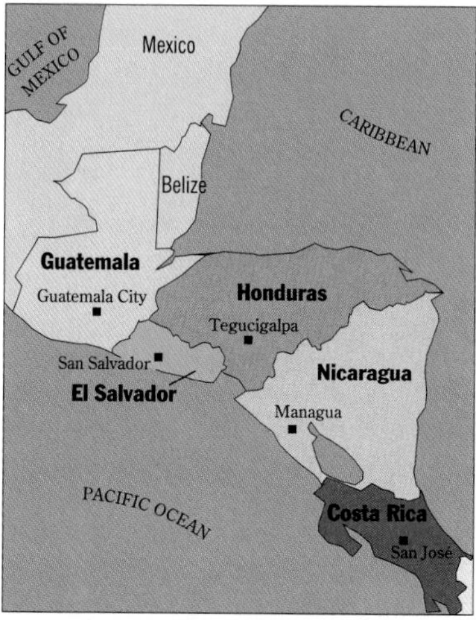

Arias hoped to bring concord to one of the world's most troubled regions.

Despite its warm reception by the Nobel Committee, however, the Arias plan got a cold shoulder from Washington. The Reagan administration, backer of the contra guerrillas attempting to overthrow Nicaragua's Marxist government, preferred to keep the rebels fighting until the ruling Sandinistas collapsed. In a move widely perceived as designed to derail the fragile Central American accord, Reagan requested an additional $270 million in contra aid; Congress refused. In January 1988, Nicaraguan president Daniel Ortega announced a unilateral cease-fire. Welcomed by Arias-plan signatories as evidence (along with the Sandinistas' recent loosening of censorship and release of political prisoners) of commitment to reducing tensions in the region, Ortega's actions were rejected by the White House as "cosmetic."

Ortega and contra leaders opened negotiations in February. It was the first direct communication between the hostile factions in Nicaragua's seven years of civil war. And it was doomed. The Sandinistas insisted that the contras lay down their arms, but rebel leaders refused even to consider a cease-fire until the Sandinistas agreed to share power. Even as talks got under way, the CIA increased arms drops to the contras. In defiance of the peace plan, which called for a freeze on outside interference, Reagan's "freedom fighters" continued to fly missions out of neighboring Honduras. Meanwhile, in the United States it was revealed that the FBI was monitoring private citizens who opposed the administration's policies for the "democratization" of Central America. ◂1985.5 ▸1990.6

ECONOMICS

Black Monday

3 On Monday, October 19, 1987, the Dow Jones Industrial Average plunged 508 points—from 2,246.73 to 1,738.41. It was a drop of 22 percent—almost double that of the 1929 crash that set off the Great Depression. Some $870 billion in equity values simply evaporated. Though the high-rolling 1980s were not officially over, obituaries began appearing almost immediately.

The carnage, which had started the previous Friday with a 108-point decline, soon spread to jittery markets around the world. Stock prices fell by 15 percent in Tokyo, 12 percent in London, 11 percent in Hong Kong, 6 percent in Paris. The causes of the global downturn were numerous, but analysts pointed to one factor above all: the deplorable state of the U.S. economy. Investors were beginning to doubt that the United States would ever straighten out its massive budget and trade deficits. President Reagan did nothing to allay

After the fall, an anxious crowd gathered on Wall Street.

ART & CULTURE: Books: ***Beloved*** **(Toni Morrison);** ***The Bonfire of the Vanities*** **(Tom Wolfe);** ***Empire*** **(Gore Vidal);** ***A History of the Jews*** **(Paul Johnson) ... Music:** ***Sign O the Times*** **(Prince, LP);** ***The Joshua Tree*** **(U2, LP);** ***Bad*** **(Michael Jackson, LP);** ***Anthem and Processionals*** **(Stephen Albert);** ***The Natural World*** **(John Harbison) ... Painting & Sculpture:** ***Untitled (Boxers)*** **(Keith Haring);** ***High-Speed Gardening***

"If you own a book with good color illustrations of Michelangelo's Sistine ceiling before the restoration, you should keep it. It's going to be a collector's item."—**Art historian James Beck**

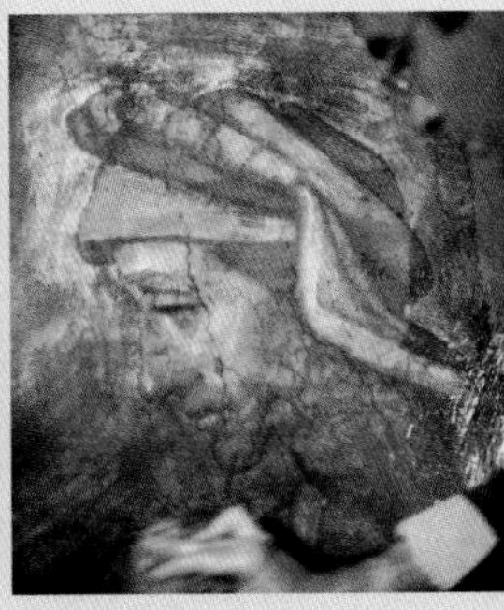

ART

A Challenge at the Chapel Meets a Challenge from Artists

4 After seven years of work, the controversial restoration of Michelangelo's Sistine Chapel in the Vatican—the most thorough since the frescoes were completed in 1512—encountered its loudest opposition to date. In March 1987, 15 prominent American artists (including Robert Motherwell, Robert Rauschenberg, James Rosenquist, George Segal, and Andy Warhol) petitioned Pope John Paul II to halt the proceeding that, they said, was rendering one of the world's most revered artworks garish, saccharine—nearly unrecognizable. The project's leading foe was Columbia University art historian James Beck, who dubbed it an "artistic Chernobyl."

Yet most art experts approved the painstaking removal of what chief restorer Gianluigi Colalucci described as a "dark, brown, glassy epidermis" (consisting primarily of dust, soot, and substances applied by previous restorers). Aided by historical research and high-tech equipment, the cleaners uncovered bright colors and clear forms—startlingly different from the somber murkiness long thought to have been central to Michelangelo's aesthetic.

As art critic Waldemar Januszczak wrote after the cleanup concluded in 1989, "The windshield wiper has finished its journey across the greatest painting in Western art. In my opinion, it has made that painting substantially greater by celebrating it as the work of a rational, hardworking, colorful human rather than some sweaty, impulsive, God-driven genius." Indeed, the results were so impressive that even former opponents of the restoration became converts. ◂1982.10

fears when, blaming the crash on "some people grabbing profits," he asserted that "the underlying economy remains sound." Herbert Hoover had said virtually the same thing in 1929.

For the rest of the week, prices fluctuated wildly in record heavy trading. Many analysts agreed that the market had been seriously overvalued and due for a "correction." On the Thursday following "Black Monday" (as it was instantly dubbed), Reagan announced plans for a deficit-cutting conference with Congress. It was a tacit admission that America's spending spree—long denounced by the President, but exacerbated by his military buildup—could not continue forever. Though the market eventually recovered, the 1990s would be an era of sharply tightened belts, on Wall Street and off. ◂1929.1 ▸1992.4

ITALY

The Mafia On Trial

5 The biggest legal assault ever launched against the world's leading criminal syndicate—the Sicilian Mafia—reached its climax in Palermo, Italy, in 1987. Over the preceding 22 months, 474 mafiosi had been prosecuted (100 in absentia, since they were still at large) in a marathon trial for crimes ranging from extortion and drug trafficking to murder. In December, more than 300 of them were sentenced to a total of 2,665 years in prison.

Since the late 1970s, Sicilian gangsters had been the chief suppliers of heroin to the United States and Europe. Wars between rival crime families had killed 300 people (including many innocent bystanders); several journalists, carabinieri, and magistrates had been assassinated. But it was the 1982 murder of Palermo's Mafia-hunting prefect and his wife that spurred the current crackdown.

The "maxi-trial," as Italians called it, took place in a custom-built, bombproof courthouse guarded by 3,000 policemen. More than 400 witnesses, including two cabinet ministers, testified. Some received death threats (a slice of human tongue accompanied one note). Since Italian law required that defendants be released if not tried within a set period, the defense dawdled: Lawyers tried to read all 700,000 pages of court documents aloud, and one of the accused—obeying the famous Mafia code of *omertá*, or silence—stitched his mouth shut. Sicilians who depended on dozens of Mafia-controlled legitimate businesses staged demonstrations against the trial. In the end, however, efforts at intimidation and obstruction failed.

One of 19 life sentences went to Michele Greco, chief of the Cosa Nostra's governing body—known as "the Pope" for his authority. But a new generation of bosses quickly took their elders' places, and the Mafia's mayhem continued. In 1992, the judge of the maxi-trial was blown up with his wife and bodyguards. And in 1993, a scandal over organized crime's infiltration of the Italian government rocked the country. ◂1983.M ▸1993.13

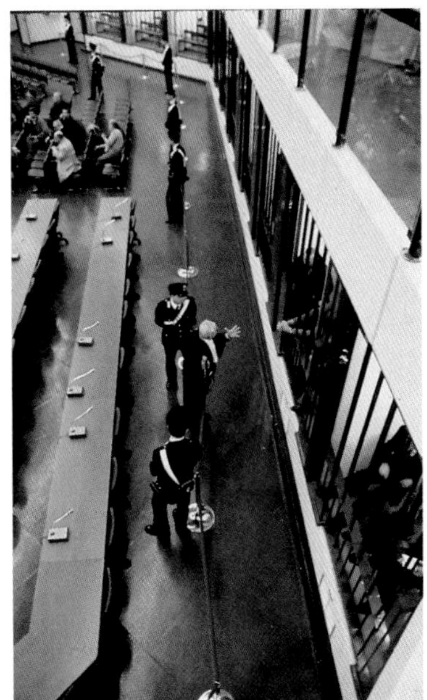

Defendants were kept in cages during the Palermo Mafia "maxi-trial."

DEATHS

Jacques Anquetil, French cyclist.

Fred Astaire, U.S. dancer and actor.

James Baldwin, U.S. writer.

Louis Victor, Prince de Broglie, French physicist.

Erskine Caldwell, U.S. writer.

William J. Casey, U.S. CIA director.

Henry Ford II, U.S. industrialist.

Bob Fosse, U.S. choreographer and filmmaker.

Jackie Gleason, U.S. comedian and actor.

Rita Hayworth, U.S. actress.

Jascha Heifetz, Russian-U.S. violinist.

Woody Herman, U.S. bandleader.

Rudolf Hess, German Nazi official.

John Huston, U.S. filmmaker.

Primo Levi, Italian writer.

Liberace, U.S. pianist.

Clare Boothe Luce, U.S. diplomat and writer.

Gunnar Myrdal, Swedish sociologist and economist.

Pola Negri, Polish-U.S. actress.

Geraldine Page, U.S. actress.

Andrés Segovia, Spanish guitarist.

Peter Tosh, Jamaican-U.S. singer.

Andy Warhol, U.S. artist.

(Ed Ruscha); *Desert Flowers* (Richard Long) ... Film: *The Last Emperor* (Bernardo Bertolucci); *The Untouchables* (Brian De Palma); *Raising Arizona* (Joel Coen); *Fatal Attraction* (Adrian Lyne) ... Theater: *Driving Miss Daisy* (Alfred Uhry); *Fences* (August Wilson); *Speed-the-Plow* (David Mamet); *Into the Woods* (Stephen Sondheim) ... TV: *Married ... with Children*; *The Tracey Ullman Show*; *thirtysomething*.

"If you regulate surrogate motherhood, that is making a public statement that it's all right. We decided a hundred years ago we didn't want people bought and sold in this country."—**William Pierce, president of the National Committee for Adoption**

NEW IN 1987

National Museum of Women in the Arts (Washington, D.C.).

Condom commercials on TV.

Women admitted to U.S. Rotary Clubs.

Trillion-dollar U.S. budget deficit.

IN THE UNITED STATES

▶BORK BOOTED—After bitter debate, the Senate on October 23 narrowly rejected the nomination of conservative appellate court judge Robert Bork to the Supreme Court. President Reagan had picked Bork, who carried out the "Saturday Night Massacre" for Richard Nixon in 1973, to replace retiring justice Lewis F. Powell. Bork's opponents, notably Senator Edward Kennedy, successfully depicted him as a dangerous extremist. Reagan's next nominee, Douglas Ginsberg, was dismissed after he admitted to having tried marijuana as a student years earlier. Quietly conservative federal appeals court judge Anthony Kennedy was finally selected to fill the vacancy. ◂1986.M

▶FARM WOES—American farmers took a beating in 1987 as falling agricultural prices and rising interest rates drove an estimated 240,000 farmers off the land.

In a little more than ten years, the farming population had fallen 9 percent—to its lowest levels since before the Civil War. Bank foreclosures on family farms and the consolidation of independent farms into gargantuan agribusinesses continued into the 1990s.

▶SEX SCANDALS—Done in by bad judgment, arrogance, and marital infidelity, two national

SOUTH KOREA

Pro-Democracy Uprising

6 In 1987, the electoral manipulations of South Korean president Chun Doo Hwan sparked the largest protest movement the country had ever seen. Day after day, tens of thousands of demonstrators in Seoul staged marches, attacked city hall, and hurled stones and Molotov cocktails at combat-ready riot police. Pitched street battles were nothing new in politically tumultuous South Korea; what set the current round apart was the participation of the country's large, stable middle class. No longer could Chun attribute unrest to a conspiracy of young radicals.

Standoff: Students at Seoul's Yonsei University taunt a phalanx of riot police.

Protests began in April, when Chun, under pressure to reform South Korea's flawed electoral system, broke off talks with opposition groups. With his presidential term due to expire in February 1988, Chun (who'd consolidated his power in 1980 with the bloody suppression of a revolt in the city of Kwangju) anointed army crony Roh Tae Woo his successor. Student activists, already at odds with the administration and horrified by the revelation of the torture and murder by police of a student dissident, rebelled en masse. In the ensuing crackdown, even middle-class adults were galvanized by the death of another student (one of thousands taken into custody), when he was struck in the head by a tear gas canister.

The government's justification for suppressing dissent, as always, was the need to maintain stability to prevent another invasion by Communist North Korea. The South Korean army, many feared, would intervene if protests continued. However, the demonstrators wielded a trump card: With South Korea scheduled to host the Olympics the next year, Chun could not afford to provoke international condemnation by imposing martial law. His bluff called, he capitulated, revising the constitution to allow direct, free elections. Chun's retreat ultimately served him well: His choice for president, Roh Tae Woo, prevailed at the polls. **◂1953.2 ▸1994.3**

IDEAS

The Battle for Baby M

7 The case of "Baby M," as the courts labeled an infant whose real name was either Melissa Stern or Sara Whitehead, made worldwide headlines in 1987. It had begun when a New Jersey couple, William and Elizabeth Stern—desiring a child but fearing pregnancy would aggravate Mrs. Stern's multiple

William Stern and Baby M at home on the child's second birthday.

sclerosis—hired Mary Beth Whitehead, a married mother of two, as a "surrogate mother" to bear Mr. Stern's biological child via artificial insemination. The Sterns promised Whitehead a $10,000 fee. But when the baby girl was born in 1986, Whitehead refused to part with her. She fled to Florida, where a private detective tracked her down. The Sterns sued. As the legal battle over the baby escalated, it fueled not only TV-talk-show quarrels, but serious debate among jurists, feminists, scientists, and philosophers.

In the Western nations, infertility was rising—suspected culprits included delayed childbearing and environmental toxins—while the pool of babies that most affluent parents deemed "desirable" (that is, white and healthy) for adoption was shrinking. Fertility drugs and *in vitro* fertilization had high failure rates, leading middle- and upper-class couples to turn increasingly to surrogacy (a practice covered by no existing laws). In the United States alone, 500 surrogate contracts had been made in the past decade. Few surrogates had changed their minds and none of the contracts had ever before been tested in court.

The Baby M case raised thorny questions about business ethics and the mother-child bond. It added to growing controversies—including the suitability of homosexual couples and single parents as child rearers—over the nature of the family. Issues of class also bore on the debate. The prosperous Sterns pointed to the advantages they could offer Melissa; Whitehead, whose husband was a garbage collector, countered that her maternal love for Sara should have primacy. In March, a judge decided for the Sterns, denying Whitehead even visitation rights. But the following year, the New Jersey Supreme Court overturned that ruling—granting Mr. Stern custody and Whitehead generous parental rights, and declaring surrogacy contracts illegal. **◂1978.1**

THE MIDDLE EAST

Hostages in Lebanon

8 For five years, Iranian-backed Hizballah (Party of God) guerrillas in Lebanon had been collecting foreign hostages—to protest the oppression of Lebanon's Shiite Muslim minority or to win freedom for fellow Shiite fundamentalists jailed as terrorists elsewhere. By 1987, Church of England envoy Terry Waite had won credit for gaining freedom for three of the captives, but 23 (eight Americans, one Indian, two Saudis, and a dozen Europeans) were still being held. In January, on his fifth visit to war-torn Beirut,

SPORTS: Baseball: World Series, Minnesota Twins defeat St. Louis Cardinals, 4–3 ... Football: Super Bowl, New York Giants defeat Denver Broncos, 39–20 ... Basketball: NBA, Los Angeles Lakers defeat Boston Celtics, 4–2 ... Boxing: Sugar Ray Leonard defeats Marvin Hagler for world middleweight title ... Boating: U.S.'s *Stars and Stripes* (Dennis Conner) beats Australia's *Kookaburra III* and regains America's Cup.

"It is obvious ... that the use or threat of force no longer can or must be an instrument of foreign policy. This applies above all to nuclear arms."—**Mikhail Gorbachev**

Waite, free after five years in captivity.

the negotiator vanished. He had become a hostage himself.

At first, since no Hizballah faction claimed to have him, Waite was presumed dead. But in 1990, a released hostage reported that he'd overheard a guard talking to Waite in the next cell. By the time Waite was released in November 1991, his story had begun to emerge. He had not, in fact, been responsible for freeing the hostages released before his own abduction; instead, he'd functioned—unwittingly, he later insisted—as a front man for Oliver North's arms-for-hostages deal with Iran. After his kidnapping, Waite had been kept in solitary confinement for four years, chained in a tiny cell. Finally, he'd been moved into the company of Associated Press Middle East bureau chief Terry Anderson and two others—Scottish-born American agriculture professor Thomas Sutherland and British cameraman John McCarthy (who was released in August 1991).

Only in December 1991, after Anderson was free (the last American held, he'd been captive for nearly seven years), did the other former hostages reveal the full horror of their ordeal. Imprisoned in squalid rooms all over Lebanon, they'd been blindfolded, shackled, beaten, denied proper food and hygiene, and subjected to psychological torture; some were permanently injured. Several hostages, including two Americans, died or were killed in captivity. But the survivors, by relying on one another and on deep reserves of inner strength, had all managed to maintain their sanity. **◂1985.9**

ENVIRONMENTALISM

Saving the California Condor

9 The capture of California's last wild condor in 1987 marked the first time in two million years that North America's biggest fully-flighted birds were absent from the skies. Yet it was a new beginning for the endangered vultures.

Thanks to human encroachment, the population of California condors had been dwindling since the 1950s. The birds were often poisoned by carrion containing rodenticides, strychnine (intended for coyotes), or lead from bullets. The shells of condor eggs were weakened (as were those of other raptors) by the birds' consumption of animals exposed to DDT. With a nine-foot wingspan, some condors died in encounters with high-tension wires.

A 1965 survey estimated that only 60 wild California condors remained alive. Eight years later, the San Diego and Los Angeles zoos launched a program to take the remaining birds into protective custody until their numbers had substantially recovered. By 1992, intensive breeding had expanded the captive population from 27 to 52. That year, an eight-month-old pair—a male and a female—were returned to Los Padres National Forest. The male died after drinking from a roadside pool of antifreeze, but seven of the birds were back in their natural habitat by mid-1994. Meanwhile, breeding in captivity continued.

The condors' ability to survive in the wild was regarded as a major test of America's 1973 Endangered Species Act, designed to protect species threatened by development. But by the 1990s, the act itself had become endangered, as economic interests (such as logging operations) increasingly came up against the needs of fragile ecosystems. And in many countries—especially poorer ones—species were vanishing daily as humans despoiled once-pristine habitats. **◂1905.5 ▸1990.M**

A California condor spreads its wings in a wildlife sanctuary.

DIPLOMACY

Gorbachev Comes to America

10 Great fanfare accompanied Soviet premier Mikhail Gorbachev's December 1987 visit to Washington, D.C. Arms control topped the official agenda, and indeed, Gorbachev's talks with President Ronald Reagan produced the first-ever superpower agreement to bilaterally reduce nuclear arsenals. But the three-day summit was also a chance for Gorbachev to introduce himself to the American public, which was intensely interested in the architect of perestroika (restructuring) and glasnost (openness). Throughout the visit, the sight of Gorbachev's motorcade elicited cheers from habitually cynical Washingtonians—and the Soviet leader, showing the instincts of a canny politician, often stopped his limo to work awed crowds.

The Reagans played host to the Gorbachevs, in town to sign the INF treaty.

Before departing, Gorbachev signed the landmark Intermediate Range Nuclear Forces Treaty, in which the Americans and the Soviets agreed to eliminate land-based missiles with a range of 300 to 3,400 miles—in all, some 1,750 Soviet and 860 American weapons. "We can only hope," said Reagan, "that this history-making agreement will not be an end in itself." **◂1986.5 ▸1989.1**

IN THE UNITED STATES

figures suffered professional setbacks in 1987. On March 20, televangelist Jim Bakker *(below, with his wife)* resigned as head of the $100 million–a-year Praise the Lord ministry (PTL) after his tryst with church secretary Jessica Hahn

came to light. Bakker's wife, cosmetics buff Tammy Faye, initially remained loyal but divorced the fallen minister after he was sent to prison in 1989 for defrauding his congregation of millions. Meanwhile, on May 8, Gary Hart, leading contender for the Democratic presidential nomination, dropped out of the race when his extramarital affair with model Donna Rice was exposed. Hart briefly reentered the race in December, but questions about his judgment soon forced his retirement from politics. ◂1950.12

▶UNWANTED BARGE—In March, after the town of Islip, Long Island, ran out of space to dump industrial waste, an entrepreneur named Lowell Harrelson had a brainstorm:

He'd ship Islip's trash to North Carolina and sell the methane gas emitted by the rotting refuse for profit. The problem was, North Carolina didn't want the 3,168 pounds of fetid waste. Thus began the 162- day, 6,000-mile odyssey of the garbage barge *Mobro*. After being turned away from five states and three countries, the reeking *Mobro* went home to New York, where its cargo was incinerated. The bizarre incident highlighted America's waste-disposal crisis, which the Environmental Protection Agency said would reach a critical point within ten years, when half the country's municipalities would run out of landfill space. ▸1988.M

POLITICS & BUSINESS: GNP: $4,544.5 billion ... Supreme Court rules that teaching evolution in public schools does not violate the rights of creationists ... 600 homosexuals arrested on steps of Supreme Court, protesting decision that homosexuality is not protected by the Constitution.

"What is there to regret?"—**Klaus Barbie, in response to a journalist's query about his wartime activities**

AROUND THE WORLD

▶JAPAN OUTPACES U.S.—A Japanese study of the American economy released in February cited mismanagement and poor labor relations as the causes of a slide that threatened to reduce the United States to a "hamburger stand economy." By contrast, Japan was the world's leading manufacturer and creditor. In April, President Reagan imposed a 100 percent tariff on some Japanese imports—retaliation for what he called unfair trade practices. The measure didn't stop the U.S. trade deficit from soaring to a record $16.5 billion by July. ◀1987.3 ▶1988.12

▶TAMIL REVOLT—In June—after a period of estrangement—India and Sri Lanka signed an accord to end the year-old guerrilla uprising of Sri Lanka's separatist Tamil minority.The Tamil rebels, based in Sri Lanka's Jaffna province (just across a narrow Indian Ocean strait from India), were Hindus with strong ties to India. When the Sri Lankan army marched against the insurgents in April 1987, India flew relief missions over Jaffna. Once the accord was signed, India sent 20,000 "peacekeeping" troops to Sri Lanka. But the rebels continued to fight, and the Indian troops, in order to preserve the new détente with Sri Lanka, turned on the Tamils. Even after India withdrew in 1989, the conflict raged on, the death toll approaching 20,000. ◀1960.M

▶SPANDAU'S LAST INMATE—Rudolf Hess, Adolf Hitler's first admirer and closest friend, strangled himself to death with an electric cord in West Berlin's Spandau prison on August 17. Hess, 93, had been in custody since 1941, when he mysteriously flew to Britain on an apparent peace mission. Convicted of war crimes at the Nuremberg trials, he was sentenced to life imprisonment at Spandau, where he outlived all his fellow inmates. After 1966 he was the lone prisoner. ◀1946.V ▶1987.11

1987

Barbie in one of his rare court appearances.

CRIME

The "Butcher of Lyons" Tried

11 In the 1950s in France, Klaus Barbie, former Gestapo chief of Lyons, was twice convicted in absentia of murdering some 6,000 Jews and Resistance members during World War II and twice sentenced to death. Yet the 20-year statute of limitations on war crimes expired before Barbie could be captured. When he finally stood trial in person in France in 1987, he faced charges of having ordered 842 deportations to death camps ("crimes against humanity," to which no statute of limitations applied). But most of his deeds—including the murder of legendary Resistance leader Jean Moulin—could no longer be tried in court.

Barbie had long been untouchable. After the war, like many ranking Nazis, he'd gone to work for U.S. Army counterintelligence, running operations that snooped on Communists and far-rightists in Germany and elsewhere. His handlers shielded him from arrest by French and U.S. authorities, and guided him in 1950 to a Croatian priest who'd smuggled thousands of Nazis and Fascists out of Europe. Settling in Bolivia, Barbie became an adviser to the country's dictators. France began trying to extradite him in 1972, after he'd been tracked down by Nazi hunters Serge and Beate Klarsfeld. But only in 1983, when Bolivia's new democratic regime delivered Barbie, was the full story of his postwar escapades revealed.

The "Butcher of Lyons," as the press dubbed him, seldom appeared in court during his two-month trial. While his lawyers trivialized the Holocaust, harping on France's war crimes in Algeria and America's in Vietnam, hostile witnesses described Barbie's delight in torture and his persecutory zeal (one of his coups was the arrest of 44 Jewish children hiding in a local farmhouse). The jury found him guilty, but once again Barbie escaped death: France had abolished capital punishment in 1981, so he was sentenced to life in prison. **◀1963.14**

BUSINESS AND INDUSTRY

A Star-Crossed Deal

12 The eighth-largest industrial enterprise in the United States and the nation's third-biggest oil company, Texaco had robust assets of $34 billion when it filed for protection from its creditors in 1987. To many observers, the action epitomized all that was awry in American corporate culture during the buyout-mad, hyperlitigious 1980s.

Texaco's filing came after three years of legal bickering with the Pennzoil company, which had sued Texaco for disrupting its attempted takeover of a third major petroleum producer, Getty Oil. The ordeal began in 1984, when Getty agreed to sell three-sevenths of its shares to Pennzoil for $40 apiece above the market price. Days later, Getty reneged and sold out completely to Texaco for $16 more per share (a total of $10 billion). Before signing, Getty's shrewd lawyers had insisted that Texaco indemnify Getty against any lawsuits the deal might engender. Pennzoil sued, and in 1985 a Texas jury ordered Texaco to pay Pennzoil $10.5 billion—the largest settlement ever awarded. After a series of appeals that went all the way to the U.S. Supreme Court, Texaco faced two equally disagreeable choices: It could either post a bond for the entire $10.5 billion or have its assets attached by Pennzoil. At that point, Texaco filed for bankruptcy.

In the end, the disputants reached a $3 billion settlement, and Texaco came out of bankruptcy—but not before a flock of squabbling lawyers and bankers had descended (to the outrage of both companies' stockholders) to peck up million-dollar crumbs from the case. **▶1988.7**

Texaco's Alfred C. DeCrane, Jr. announces the declaration of bankruptcy.

ART

The Million-Dollar Market

13 In November 1987, at Sotheby's auction house in New York City, Australian beer tycoon Alan Bond bid an astonishing $53.9 million for Dutch postimpressionist Vincent van Gogh's vibrant *Irises.* The record sum pushed up the ever-rising ceiling for art prices (million-dollar-plus paintings, even by living artists, had become routine) to a heretofore unheard-of level. Prices peaked in 1990, when Japanese paper mogul Ryoei Saito paid $82.5 million for *Portrait of Dr. Gachet*, van Gogh's last moody masterpiece, and $78.1 million for *At the Moulin de la Galette*, a cheerful outdoor café scene by French impressionist Pierre Auguste Renoir. Although Japanese wealth (and a taste for impressionism) had fueled the boom, by the time Saito made his purchase, the market was softening.

Van Gogh's *Irises*: a new record for beauty.

No one better illustrates the vicissitudes of the market than Bond. By 1990, he was $5.5 billion in debt, and the whole *Irises* transaction had become a scandal: In an ethically dubious (and almost certainly inflationary) deal, Sotheby's had lent Bond $27 million for *Irises*—using the painting itself as collateral. *Irises* was then sold for an undisclosed sum (reportedly around $40 million) to California's J. Paul Getty Museum. Blessed with an almost limitless endowment, the Getty could—and did—buy extravagantly, becoming a formidable market force in its own right. **◀1982.10**

NOBEL PRIZES: Peace: Oscar Arias Sánchez (Costa Rican; Arias peace plan) ... Literature: Joseph Brodsky (U.S.S.R.-U.S.; poet) ... Chemistry: D. Cram, C. Pedersen, and J. Lehn (U.S., U.S., French; artificial molecules) ... Medicine: Susumu Tonegawa (Japanese; antibodies) ... Physics: K. Alex Müller and J. Georg Bednorz (Swiss, German; high-temperature superconductors) ... Economics: Robert M. Solow (U.S.).

A VOICE FROM 1987

The Shut-Off Souls of Students

From *The Closing of the American Mind*, by Allan Bloom, 1987

Allan Bloom (left), a philosophy professor accustomed to a small academic audience, wrote the most talked-about book of 1987: The Closing of the American Mind *(subtitled* How Higher Education Has Failed Democracy and Impoverished the Souls of Today's Students*). Bloom's popular thesis was that in place of age-old absolute truths, modern Americans had embraced pernicious relativism. This sorry condition, Bloom argued, had been institutionalized during the permissive 1960s (he pointed specifically to the moment in 1969 when armed students took over Cornell University, where he was then a professor, and the wishy-washy administration caved in to their demands). The result: Universities lost their Platonic luster, students couldn't distinguish a good book from a bad one (if they read at all), and the American mind had shut itself to enlightenment. Widely commended, the book did draw fire for its vindictive tone (and the fact that doomsayers had been predicting the fall of civilization for centuries). Students, wrote one critic, "deserve better than this from those who would be their teachers."* **◂1983.M**

When I first noticed the decline in reading during the late sixties, I began asking my large introductory classes, and any other group of younger students to which I spoke, what books really count for them. Most are silent, puzzled by the question. The notion of books as companions is foreign to them. Justice Black with his tattered copy of the Constitution in his pocket at all times is not an example that would mean much to them. There is no printed work to which they look for counsel, inspiration or joy. Sometimes one student will say "the Bible." (He learned it at home, and his Biblical studies are not usually continued at the university.) There is always a girl who mentions Ayn Rand's *The Fountainhead*, a book, although hardly literature, which, with its sub-Nietzschean assertiveness, excites somewhat eccentric youngsters to a new way of life. A few students mention recent books that struck them and supported their own self-interpretation, like *The Catcher in the Rye*. (Theirs is usually the most genuine response and also shows a felt need for help in self-interpretation. But it is an uneducated response. Teachers should take advantage of the need expressed in it to show such students that better writers can help them more.) After such sessions I am pursued by a student or two who wants to make it clear that he or she is really influenced by books, not just by one or two but by many. Then he recites a list of classics he may have grazed in high school.

Imagine such a young person walking through the Louvre or the Uffizi, and you can immediately grasp the condition of his soul. In his innocence of the stories of Biblical and Greek or Roman antiquity, Raphael, Leonardo, Michelangelo, Rembrandt and all the others can say nothing to him. All he sees are colors and forms—modern art. In short, like almost everything else in his spiritual life, the paintings and statues are abstract. No matter what much of modern wisdom asserts, these artists counted on immediate recognition of their subjects and, what is more, on their having a powerful meaning for their viewers. The works were the fulfillment of those meanings, giving them a sensuous reality and hence completing them. Without those meanings, and without their being something essential to the viewer as a moral, political and religious being, the works lose their essence. It is not merely the tradition that is lost when the voice of civilization elaborated over millennia has been stilled in this way. It is being itself that vanishes beyond the dissolving horizon. One of the most flattering things that ever happened to me as a teacher occurred when I received a postcard from a very good student on his first visit to Italy, who wrote, "You are not a professor of political philosophy but a travel agent." Nothing could have better expressed my intention as an educator. He thought I had prepared him to see. Then he could begin thinking for himself with something to think about. The real sensation of the Florence in which Machiavelli is believable is worth all the formulas of metaphysics ten times over. Education in our times must try to find whatever there is in students that might yearn for completion, and to reconstruct the learning that would enable them autonomously to seek that completion.

In a less grandiose vein, students today have nothing like the Dickens who gave so many of us the unforgettable Pecksniffs, Micawbers, Pips, with which we sharpened our vision, allowing us some subtlety in our distinction of human types. It is a complex set of experiences that enables one to say so simply, "He is a Scrooge." Without literature, no such observations are possible and the fine art of comparison is lost. The psychological obtuseness of our students is appalling, because they have only pop psychology to tell them what people are like, and the range of their motives. As the awareness that we owed almost exclusively to literary genius falters, people become more alike, for want of knowing they can be otherwise. What poor substitutes for real diversity are the wild rainbows of dyed hair and other external differences that tell the observer nothing about what is inside.

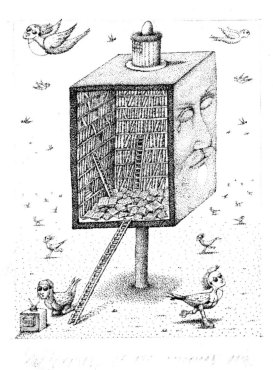

Illustrator Peter Sis's conception of Uncle Sam as a bird feeder burgeoning with "food," yet ignored by the distracted birdies who might happily feed there.

"If Salman Rushdie is a hostage, so, too, are we."—**German novelist Günter Grass, speaking for his fellow authors**

STORY OF THE YEAR

A Writer's Death Sentence

1 If one emblem of the 1980s was the prosperous yuppie, another was the puritanical—and fiercely censorious—religious fundamentalist. Along with a worldwide groundswell of militant faith came a backlash against artistic irreverence even in countries long known for freedom of expression. In the United States, Martin Scorsese's offbeat biblical film, *The Last Temptation of Christ*, drew such massive protests from evangelical Christians in 1988 that theaters largely refused to show it. But the decade's biggest cultural imbroglio began the same year in England, with the publication of *The Satanic Verses*—a book that turned its author, Salman Rushdie, into the world's most famous fugitive.

Rushdie, 41, had won Britain's coveted Booker Prize for a previous novel, *Midnight's Children* (1981). A Bombay-born Londoner and a lapsed Muslim, he wrote of his various heritages with love, skepticism, and ribald wit. But in *The Satanic Verses*, he dared to challenge Islamic fundamentalists' claims to an immutable religion founded by an infallible prophet. In wildly inventive prose, the book recounts the adventures of two Indian Muslims (one a film star in his native land, the other the voice of a thousand British commercials) who miraculously survive the bombing of an airliner by Sikh separatists. After falling to earth in England, Saladin Chamcha grows horns, hooves, and a tail; Gibreel Farishta sprouts a halo and dreams of meeting—among other quasi-Koranic characters—a prophet named Mahound (an old derogatory term for Muhammad) who vacillates over the divine status of three goddesses, and a team of prostitutes who take the names of Muhammad's wives.

Rushdie at home in London in 1988, before the *fatwa* forced him underground.

The book was burned by Muslim militants in England and banned in several countries; it sparked riots in India and Pakistan. But the reaction was strongest in Iran, whose leader, Ayatollah Khomeini, appeared unnamed in one of Gibreel's dreams. In 1989, Khomeini condemned Rushdie to death and promised heaven to anyone martyred in the attempt. (Iranian clerics eventually raised the bounty on the writer to $6 million.) Rushdie went into hiding, guarded by Scotland Yard. Firebombings and threats prompted many booksellers to keep the novel from their shelves; publishers suspended plans for a paperback edition. And despite official protests by Britain and other nations, petitions from celebrated intellectuals, and apologies by Rushdie, the edict outlived the Ayatollah: The author remained a hunted man into the 1990s. ◂**1979.1**

SOUTHERN AFRICA

The Namibia-Angola Deal

2 The treaty concluded in December 1988 between Angola and Cuba on one side and South Africa on the other was a diplomatic grand slam. For 22 years, guerrillas of the South West Africa People's Organization (SWAPO) had been using Angola as a base to fight for the liberation of their country, Namibia, from South African rule. For 13 years—ever since Angola gained independence from Portugal—Cuban soldiers had helped the Angolan government resist South African raiders, as well as the domestic guerrillas of the National Union for the Total Independence of Angola (UNITA), who were backed by Pretoria and Washington. Now, South Africa pledged to remove its 50,000 troops from Namibia, in exchange for Cuba's withdrawal of its 50,000 from Angola. Namibia would then hold UN-supervised elections. And in 1990, the onetime German colony, occupied by South Africa since 1915, would go free.

Namibian schoolchildren celebrate free elections, and imminent independence.

The fruit of eight years of U.S.-brokered negotiations, the agreement reflected the new goodwill between Washington and Moscow (which pushed its clients, Cuba and Angola, to settle) and the increasing effectiveness of worldwide pressure on South Africa. The apartheid state had refused the UN's request in 1945 that it relinquish its mandate on Namibia. It had defied the World Court's 1966 ruling that the occupation was illegal. It had molded Namibia into a miniature version of itself, with a 75,000-member white minority ruling over more than a million disenfranchised and segregated blacks. But finally, international trade sanctions had made the costs of defending its colony against SWAPO—and intervening directly in Angola's civil war—too high. Pretoria's double pullback was a step toward getting those sanctions lifted.

In Angola, despite the government's abandonment of Marxism and the one-party state (encouraged by the Soviet Bloc's collapse) and a 1991 peace agreement, UNITA, and its leader, Jonas Savimbi, refused to give up the fight—even after U.S. aid ended in 1993. Peace seemed possible at last when, in late 1994, UNITA (without the presence of Savimbi, who remained in hiding) signed a cease-fire agreement with the Angolan government. ◂**1975.2**

THE MIDDLE EAST

Iran-Iraq War Ends

3 The war between Iraq and Iran ended in August 1988, after eight years and at least a million deaths. In terms of territory, the outcome was inconclusive: After violating Iran's borders, Iraq itself had been invaded, and in the end it only took back what it had lost. In terms of regional power, however, Iraq had won decisively.

Most observers had once predicted otherwise. Iran, with a population three times greater than its enemy's and fired with Muslim fundamentalist zeal, had seemed the likely victor. But Iraq turned out to have more friends. Only Syria and Libya, whose leaders were rivals of Iraq's Saddam Hussein, sided with Iran. Saudi Arabia and Jordan, fearing the spread of Islamic revolution, backed Iraq—as did France (which depended on Iraqi oil) and the Soviet Union.

For years the war remained a stalemate, with each side rocketing the other's cities, refineries, and oil shipping, and Iran sending hordes of poorly armed youths to martyr themselves in human-wave attacks. But Iraq consistently deployed more firepower—including poison gas, used (despite a long-standing international ban) against pro-Iranian rebel Kurdish villages as well. Moreover, the United States increasingly sided with Iraq. From 1983, America sup-

A Kurdish child disfigured by Iraqi napalm.

ART & CULTURE: Books: *Paris Trout* (Pete Dexter); *Love in the Time of Cholera* (Gabriel García Márquez); *Breathing Lessons* (Anne Tyler); *Parting the Waters* (Taylor Branch) ... Music: *Appetite for Destruction* (Guns N' Roses, LP); *Faith* (George Michael, LP); *Whispers Out of Time* (Roger Reynolds) ... Painting & Sculpture: *Diagrammed Couplet No. 1* (Brice Marden); *Samarkand Stiches #5*,

plied Hussein with grain credits and satellite intelligence, and encouraged its allies to arm him. In 1987, U.S.-led naval escorts began protecting "neutral" (actually pro-Iraqi) Kuwait's oil tankers in the Persian Gulf and sinking Iranian gunboats.

Iran's economy and morale were crumbling. And in July 1988, after the U.S. cruiser *Vincennes* accidentally shot down an Iranian passenger plane with 290 aboard, Iranian leader Ayatollah Khomeini realized the futility of fighting both superpowers. Calling the decision "more deadly than taking poison," he accepted a U.N. cease-fire plan.

Many nations relished Iran's defeat. But most of them soon rued Iraq's victory. **◂1980.M ▸1990.7**

The remains of Pan Am Flight 103 near Lockerbie, Scotland.

TERRORISM

Atrocity over Lockerbie

4 On the evening of December 21, 1988, Pan Am Flight 103 from London to New York blew apart six miles above Lockerbie, Scotland—raining bodies, Christmas presents, and flaming metal onto the village. All 258 people aboard the Boeing 747 died, along with eleven on the ground. Investigators quickly discovered *what* had destroyed the plane: plastic explosives. *Who* had done it was harder to determine.

It soon emerged that an anonymous caller had warned the U.S. embassy in Helsinki of a plot to bomb a Pan Am flight from Frankfurt (where Flight 103 originated) to New York. He'd implicated Abu Nidal, a Palestinian commando chief opposed to the PLO's recent overtures to Israel. The Finnish government, however, had dismissed the informant as a known crank. (Pan Am's failure to inform its customers of the threat fueled considerable outrage; facing $500 million in lawsuits, the company folded in 1991.) After the bombing, two other groups claimed responsibility: One had supposedly acted to avenge an Iranian airliner downed by a U.S. warship in July, the other to avenge the U.S. attack on Libya in 1986.

Hundreds of investigators worked to crack the case. But West German police already had strong evidence that the Syrian-backed Popular Front for the Liberation of Palestine-General Command, a renegade PLO faction headed by Ahmed Jibril, had planted the bomb at Iran's behest. Yet the Germans, perhaps embarrassed at having let key suspects slip away, sat on what they knew—and in 1990, U.S. officials indicted two Libyans for the crime. (Critics accused the Bush administration of exonerating Iran to gain an ally in the Gulf War with Iraq.) Libya refused to surrender its citizens, and extradition efforts—along with the mystery—continued into the mid-nineties. **◂1986.6**

PAKISTAN

Benazir Bhutto's Rise and Fall

5 Pakistani dictator Mohammad Zia ul-Haq suppressed all opposition during his eleven-year reign; when he died in a mysterious plane crash in August 1988 he left behind neither a successor nor the machinery to elect one. For 25 of its 41 years, Pakistan had lived under military rule, and its flirtations with democracy had always ended in upheaval and repression. Still, many in the poor, strife-torn nation called for a return to civilian rule—none more passionately than Benazir Bhutto, daughter of Zulfikar Ali Bhutto, the imperious prime minister Zia deposed in 1977 and later executed.

"I do not regret the death of Zia," Bhutto said after the dictator's plane exploded over the desert, killing him, ten of his generals, and U.S. ambassador Arnold Raphel. (Assassination was suspected but never proved.) Indeed, as leader of the Pakistan People's Party, Bhutto stood to profit: Elections now became possible.

During her campaign, Bhutto discarded her party's formerly anti-military and anti-American rhetoric. (Alienating the army would have been dangerous; alienating Washington—which had rewarded Zia's stand against the Soviet occupation of neighboring Afghanistan with billions of aid dollars—might have been equally so.) In November, she won Pakistan's first free election in more than a decade, becoming the Islamic world's first female prime minister. She freed political prisoners, and lifted restrictions on labor unions and the press, and promised economic reform.

Yet Bhutto's tenure lasted only 20 months. She failed to quell ethnic slaughter in Sind province—failed, even, to introduce a single piece of legislation. Instead, she engaged in spectacular personal feuds with opposition leaders. And, finally, she succumbed to Pakistan's endemic ills: corruption and nepotism. In 1990, president Ghulam Ishaq Khan staged a "constitutional coup," ousting Bhutto and suspending the National and Provincial assemblies. A coalition government was elected, but the army once again held the real power. Bhutto, however, was not finished yet: Pakistanis returned her to office in 1993. **◂1977.4**

Benazir Bhutto was the first woman to head a Muslim state. Behind her hangs a portrait of her father.

DEATHS

Charles S. Addams, U.S. cartoonist.

Luis Alvarez, U.S. physicist.

Frederick Ashton, U.K. choreographer and dancer.

Romare Bearden, U.S. artist.

Willem Drees, Dutch prime minister.

Enzo Ferrari, Italian auto manufacturer.

Richard Feynman, U.S. physicist.

Klaus Fuchs, German-U.K. physicist and spy.

Robert Joffrey, U.S. choreographer.

Francisco "Chico" Mendes, Brazilian activist.

Louise Nevelson, U.S. sculptor.

Isamu Noguchi, U.S. sculptor.

Alan Paton, South African writer and political activist.

Kim Philby, U.K.-U.S.S.R. spy.

I.I. Rabi, Austrian-U.S. physicist.

Max Shulman, U.S. writer.

Muhammad Zia ul-Haq, Pakistani president.

ROCI U.S.S.R. **(Robert Rauschenberg) ... Film: *Rain Man* (Barry Levinson); *Pelle the Conqueror* (Bille August); *Women on the Verge of a Nervous Breakdown* (Pedro Almodóvar); *Au Revoir Les Enfants* (Louis Malle) ... Theater: *The Piano Lesson* (August Wilson); *M. Butterfly* (David Hwang); *The Heidi Chronicles* (Wendy Wasserstein) ... TV: *America's Most Wanted*; *The Wonder Years*; *Murphy Brown*.**

"This game is not played by Marquis of Queensberry rules. There really are no rules for this kind of auction."
—An adviser to F. Ross Johnson

NEW IN 1988

Lights at Chicago's Wrigley Field (for nighttime baseball).

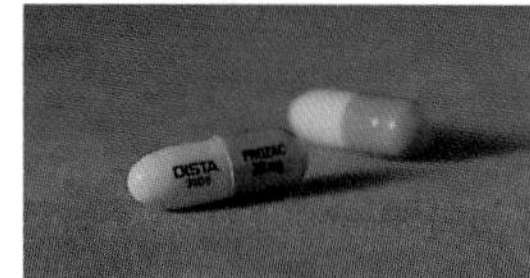

Prozac (pharmaceutical for treatment of depression).

World's longest undersea tunnel (33.6-mile-long Seikan Railroad in Japan).

Plutonium-powered pacemaker.

U.S. advertising on Soviet TV.

IN THE UNITED STATES

▶BLUE-COLLAR CHIC—With the October 18 debut of the sitcom *Roseanne* on ABC, fat, feisty, feminist comedian Roseanne Barr (later Roseanne Arnold, then just plain Roseanne) brought her patented déclassé persona to television. Playing a factory-employed, joke-telling wife

and mother, the actress injected a dose of realism into television's usually saccharin portrait of family life. The sitcom would enjoy a long run at the top of the Nielsen ratings. ◂1969.M

▶BUSH ELECTED—Patient two-term-Reagan-underling George Bush in November became the first vice president since Martin Van Buren in 1836 to succeed to the presidency by election. Bush and running mate Dan Quayle, junior senator from Indiana, defeated the Democratic ticket of technocratic Massachusetts governor Michael Dukakis and Texas senator Lloyd Bentsen. Dukakis gained the nomination over a crowded Democratic field that included civil rights activist Jesse Jackson, who attracted substantial popular support for the second election in a row. The sharpest moment in

1988

Once considered inexhaustible, rain forests were subjected to heedless exploitation.

ENVIRONMENTALISM

Rain-Forest Champion Killed

6 Francisco "Chico" Mendes Filho was a Brazilian labor organizer, but he owed his international fame to environmental activism. Mendes fought for the rubber tappers of the Amazon basin, whose livelihoods depended on the preservation of the rain forest and its rubber trees. He battled ranchers (who burned jungle to make pastureland), loggers, and developers, in court and out: Led by Mendes, hundreds of tappers marched directly into the forest and forced chain-saw crews to desist. Mendes forged an alliance between the tappers and Amazonian Indians; his union persuaded the government to set up forest reserves for the nondisruptive harvest of such commodities as latex and Brazil nuts. He won a UN award and traveled to the United States to promote his cause. But the lords of the lawless Brazilian frontier despised Mendes. In December 1988, the 44-year-old was assassinated in his own backyard by a rancher's son.

Mendes's death drew worldwide attention to the plight of the earth's rain forests. In only a few centuries, humans had reduced the total area of the steaming woodlands—crucial to the planet's weather systems and home to countless plant and animal species—from 15 million to six million square miles. By the 1980s, acres were being wiped out hourly. Varieties of vegetation from which medicines might be derived were becoming extinct. The rain forests' aboriginal inhabitants were suffering as well. One of the greatest threats to Brazilian Indians came from gold mining. In the 1980s, a million miners invaded the Amazon basin, poisoning river water with mercury (used in gold refining) and spreading deadly diseases among the Yanomami and other peoples.

Responding to international outrage over Mendes's murder, Brazilian president José Sarney and his successor, Fernando Collor de Mello, sharply stepped up efforts to protect the rain forests. The rate of burning slowed, but the destruction continued. ◂1980.12

BUSINESS AND INDUSTRY

The Deal of the Century

7 Before changing hands in November 1988 in history's largest corporate takeover, RJR Nabisco was a high-equity enterprise. The 19th-largest U.S. corporation, it produced annual revenues of $16 billion and its stock sold at a healthy $56 a share. Then the company was "put into play": auctioned to takeover artists.

In a knockdown battle fought in mahogany-paneled boardrooms, the leveraged-buyout firm of Kohlberg Kravis Roberts (KKR) outbid a team of RJR Nabisco executives to take the snack-and-tobacco behemoth private. KKR paid $25 billion for the corporation—about $109 a share, nearly double the established price. Financed with junk bonds and commercial bank loans, the deal left RJR Nabisco holding some $22.8 billion in IOUs. For chief executive F. Ross Johnson—who put RJR Nabisco into play only to lose the bidding war (and his job)—stock price inflation sweetened defeat: His shares were now worth more than $23 million.

The KKR team included *(from left)*: George Roberts, Henry Kravis, Paul Raether.

To many, the "deal of the century" epitomized Wall Street greed, 1980s style, in which corporate raiders borrowed huge sums to buy out a sound corporation, then sold it off bit by bit to raise money to pay creditors. The frequent result: wholesale liquidation of jobs (very few of them attached to golden parachutes like Johnson's). The RJR Nabisco takeover, said one investment banker, represented "capitalism gone mad." A megacorporation (among its vast holdings: Oreo cookies, Ritz crackers, Del Monte vegetables, and Winston cigarettes), RJR Nabisco now faced dismemberment. Some of its constituent parts would have to be sold to meet estimated annual debt payments of $2.5 billion. No need to worry, according to new RJR Nabisco owner and KKR partner Henry Kravis: "Oreos will still be in children's lunch boxes." ◂1987.12 ▸1989.10

MEXICO

A Suspect Election

8 Carlos Salinas de Gortari, a technocrat with a doctorate from Harvard, won Mexico's presidential election in July 1988. The outcome was no surprise: Mexican politics for six decades had been the exclusive province of the Institutional Revolutionary Party (PRI), and Salinas was the PRI's standard-bearer. What was shocking was his narrow margin of victory. The former budget-and-planning minister managed a mere 50.7 percent of the vote—the worst showing ever by a PRI candidate. Many Mexicans, however, doubted he'd done even that well. Ballot boxes reportedly had been stuffed, with votes credited to citizens long dead. Charging the government with electoral fraud, some 250,000 protesters marched on Mexico's National Palace.

Salinas himself was not directly accused of wrongdoing. Ironically, the president-elect had campaigned as a reformer, acknowledging the need to overhaul Mexico's moribund system. "We've entered a new

SPORTS: Baseball: World Series, Los Angeles Dodgers defeat Oakland Athletics, 4–1 ... Olympics held in Calgary and Seoul (Florence Griffith Joyner sets record for 100 meters, 10.54) ... Football: Super Bowl, Washington Redskins defeat Denver Broncos, 42–10 ... Basketball: NBA, Los Angeles Lakers defeat Detroit Pistons, 4–3 ... Tennis: Steffi Graf wins Grand Slam.

"If the urge to write should ever leave me, I want that day to be my last."—Naguib Mahfouz

political era with a majority party and a very intensely competitive opposition," he declared. From the leader of a party that had enjoyed a run of power unprecedented outside of the Soviet Union, it was a telling admission—and one that offended many PRI bosses, the so-called "dinosaurs" who controlled Mexico's baroque political machinery.

The man responsible for the PRI's trouble at the polls was Cuauhtémoc Cárdenas, a former PRI senator and son of beloved revolutionary president Lázaro Cárdenas. The candidate of a coalition of leftist parties, the younger Cárdenas campaigned against Salinas on two issues: corruption and the economy. Not only was PRI dirty, he said, but it had sold out Mexico's revolutionary ideals to finance the country's $103 billion foreign debt.

Many Mexicans believed that Cuauhtémoc Cárdenas *(above)* was the real victor in the suspect election of 1988.

Taking office in December, Salinas vowed to pursue "modern politics" along with economic modernization. Against the dinosaurs, he faced an uphill battle. **◂1985.4 ▸1993.2**

LITERATURE

Arab Writer Gets the Nobel

9 Naguib Mahfouz was Egypt's most acclaimed author, a controversial celebrity throughout the Middle East. Yet when he won the 1988 Nobel Prize for literature—the first Arab to do so—the journalists gathered for the announcement in Stockholm responded, "Naguib *who?*" Few of Mahfouz's 40 novels or dozen short-story collections were known in the West. But critics commonly called him the father of the modern Arabic novel, comparing him to Balzac or Dickens for his social concern, his feel for urban life, and his vividly rendered characters.

Mahfouz, 76, was most widely admired for his sprawling *Cairo Trilogy*—a set of novels, written in the late 1950s, chronicling three generations of a family before, during,

Mahfouz at the Cairo coffee shop where he breakfasted every morning.

and after the 1952 coup that brought Gamal Abdal Nasser to power. But one of his novels, the allegorical *Children of Gebelawi* (1959), with its irreverent portraits of Moses, Jesus, and Muhammad, had been banned in Egypt after a protest from conservative Muslims. Other works, subtly critical of the Nasser government, had created political storms. And when Mahfouz declared his support for the 1979 peace treaty between Egypt and Israel, his entire oeuvre was temporarily banned in many Arab countries.

The head of the Jordanian League of Writers called the Nobel laureate "a delinquent man." Still, Egyptian president Hosni Mubarak was quick to offer his congratulations—and in Europe and America, sales of Mahfouz's books soared. **◂1988.1**

THE MIDDLE EAST

Intifada Wins Supporters

10 The Israeli-Palestinian struggle escalated sharply in 1988, with a prolonged revolt in the occupied West Bank and Gaza Strip. It started days before the new year, when young Arabs across the territories began throwing stones and Molotov cocktails at Israeli patrols. Though local PLO, Muslim fundamentalist, and leftist leaders joined forces to organize boycotts and strikes, the initiative remained with the "children of the stones." By 1990, more than 750 Palestinians had been killed (versus some 40 Israelis), tens of thousands wounded, and thousands imprisoned without trial. Yet the intifada (Arabic for "stirring") had helped the Palestinian cause more than any event in four decades.

Although Israel had fought all its wars over the Palestinian issue, conflict with the Palestinians themselves had been mostly limited to clashes with PLO commandos. Arabs within Israel enjoyed at least nominal equality, and had been relatively quiet; most Palestinians elsewhere, though often confined to refugee camps, had let others do their fighting. Now, by fending for themselves (even Israeli Arabs rioted and joined a general strike) with weapons recalling David's battle against Goliath, they won worldwide sympathy as never before. Declaring unanimous allegiance to the PLO, they refuted Israel's denial of the organization's legitimacy. But they also pressured PLO leaders, demanding results fast—even if that meant compromise.

The intifada provoked Jordan's King Hussein to renounce his claim on the West Bank (confirming that the Palestinians were on their own) and helped PLO chairman Yasir Arafat overcome PLO hard-liners. In November, Arafat declared a Palestinian state, renounced terrorism, and implicitly recognized Israel for the first time. In December, after skeptical U.S. officials denied him entry to address the UN, the General Assembly met in Geneva to hear him out. Arafat repeated the PLO's vows of moderation—and new hope for the Middle East was born. **◂1982.2 ▸1993.1**

For West Bank Palestinians, stone throwing was an elementary act of defiance.

IN THE UNITED STATES

a race dominated by images (Dukakis rode in a tank to prove his toughness; Bush gobbled pork rinds to prove his commonness) came during the vice presidential debate, when old-timer Bentsen told youthful Quayle (who had invoked the name of the 35th president) he was "no Jack Kennedy." **◂1980.4 ▸1992.4**

▶MEDICAL WASTE ON BEACHES—New York State officials closed 15 miles of ocean beaches on Long Island on July 6 after medical waste began washing ashore. The potentially infectious detritus included vials of blood, needles and syringes, and thick balls of solid sewage. Days earlier, more than 120 containers of blood, some of it infected with the AIDS virus, washed up across New York Harbor in Bayonne, New Jersey; later, 70 syringes and

vials landed on Staten Island. Investigators were unable to trace the waste, but ruled out individual polluters. A dangerous tide of hospital garbage had forced a number of New Jersey beaches to close the previous summer. **◂1987.M ▸1989.13**

▶GENE MAPPING—in 1988, the National Institutes of Health and the Department of Energy launched the Human Genome Project, a $3 billion effort to completely decode and map human DNA—a chain consisting of six billion chemical links called nucleotides. (Target date for completion: 2005.) By deciphering the function of each human gene and locating it on its chromosome, genome project scientists could learn the molecular basis of all disease—and, they hoped, the proper treatments. **◂1982.M ▸1990.4**

POLITICS & BUSINESS: GNP: $4,908.2 billion ... George Bush elected president, defeating Michael Dukakis ... U.S. health care expenditures reach $140.4 billion ... U.S. imports grains for domestic use for the first time, due to drought ... Omnibus Trade Bill establishes mandatory retaliation by U.S. against countries with unfair trade practices.

"If we could have reached 9.79 without drugs, we would of course have done so."—**Ben Johnson's coach, Charlie Francis**

AROUND THE WORLD

▶PINOCHET REJECTED—In a 1988 plebiscite designed to validate the regime of General Augusto Pinochet, the Chilean electorate bucked convention and voted against a continuation of the dictator's term. It was a humiliating defeat for Pinochet, who'd outlawed opposition parties and suspended civil rights after seizing power in 1973. The aging autocrat nevertheless accepted the results; a free election was held the following year. ◂1973.4 ▸1989.8

▶AFGHAN PULLOUT—In May, executing a promise he'd made at the 1985 Geneva summit, Mikhail Gorbachev began withdrawing Soviet troops from Afghanistan. The Soviet intervention in the central Asian republic, begun in 1979, had provoked an international furor, lowered morale in the Soviet military, and cost some 15,000 Soviet soldiers their lives. In the end, Soviet troops were unable to defeat the mujahideen, Afghan Muslim rebels supplied by the U.S., Great Britain, and China with sophisticated weaponry. The last of the Soviet troops were evacuated in February 1989, and Muhammad Najibullah's shaky Marxist regime was left to fend for itself. Najibullah, who'd succeeded Soviet puppet Babrak Karmal in 1986, held on for three more years before his government fell to a coalition of rebel factions. ◂1979.5 ▸1992.M

▶SHROUD DATED—On October 13, the bishop of Turin settled a centuries-old debate about the authenticity of the

shroud of Turin, purported to be the burial cloth of Jesus Christ. Accepting the results of carbon-14 dating conducted on the shroud by three separate labs, the bishop announced that it was woven sometime between 1260 and 1390 AD. The Catholic Church encouraged its members to continue to venerate the cloth—many faithful believed it bore an image of Christ—for its pictorial power. ◂1947.14

TECHNOLOGY

The Fax Boom

11 Once considered office exotica, fax machines almost overnight became standard equipment wherever business was conducted —from Fortune 500 corporations to corner pizza parlors. In 1988, more than a million units were sold in the United States alone, up from a mere 50,000 in 1983. Europe lagged not far behind—and in Japan, the leading manufacturer and user of faxes, the speedy telecommunications devices accounted for up to 20 percent of phone traffic.

The fax (short for facsimile) explosion was a classic case of demand catching up with availability. The devices had occupied a quiet, high-end corner of the office-machine market since the early 1970s. In 1980, the modern fax was made possible by a new standard that enabled a document to be converted to digital signals, sent over a regular telephone line, and received in a minute or less. As prices plunged—from $2,000 for a budget model in 1984 to as little as $400 in 1988—hordes of small businesses. suddenly found they couldn't get by without one. Faxes were faster and cheaper than overnight mail services, and more versatile than telexes. (Between 1984 and 1988, Western Union lost half its telex business.) By the 1990s, to be faxless in business was to be a dinosaur, a lumbering beast in an age that prized celerity. **◂1938.6**

The fax, the world's fastest mail service.

ECONOMICS

The Trade Gap Widens

12 By 1988, the United States faced a worldwide crisis of confidence in its economy. The once almighty dollar had lost half its value against the Japanese yen in three years; the ballooning U.S. trade deficit averaged $10 billion a month, about half of it with Japan; America (with the world's largest economy) was the world's biggest debtor nation, while Japan (whose economy was second-largest) was the world's biggest creditor. Though the Reagan administration insisted that the trade imbalance ultimately contributed to the investment of foreign capital in America, a less sanguine prognosis could be heard: The so-called American century was over. The new colossus stood to the east.

In the United States, calls for curbs on Japanese imports grew ever louder, even as Washington loosened restrictions on another trading partner: In January, Canada and its southern neighbor inked a free-trade agreement, eliminating all tariffs between the two countries. Eight months later, the U.S. Congress approved the Omnibus Trade Bill, a thousand-page grab bag of pork-barrel politics and trade retaliation against Japan. (Alongside the bill's demand that Japan open its own markets or face sanctions were increased tobacco subsidies and bailouts for struggling Louisiana sugar refineries.) Despite the outcry over Japanese goods, however, American exports to Japan had risen by 14.5 percent from January to September. Moreover, Japanese officials complained, the United States was already punishing Japan by devaluing the dollar, making it harder for Americans to buy imported goods.

Bitter talk aside, the two nations enjoyed a strong economic partnership. Japan needed the enormous U.S. market, with its appetite for Japanese electronics and cars, just as the United States relied on enormous Japanese investment, made possible by Japan's trade surplus, to finance the monstrous U.S. budget deficit—$1.2 trillion in 1988. **◂1987.M ▸1993.2**

In a protest on Capitol Hill, members of Congress demonstrate their resentment of Japanese products by smashing a Toshiba radio.

Johnson had to return his Olympic medal.

SPORTS

Johnson's Tarnished Gold

13 Canadian sprinter Ben Johnson arrived at the 1988 Summer Olympics in Seoul, South Korea, primed for victory in the 100-meter race. A year earlier, he'd smashed the world record for that distance, finishing in 9.83 seconds—a full tenth of a second (an eternity in sprinting) faster than the old mark. It appeared that Big Ben had finally gained the upper hand over American rival Carl Lewis, one of the most formidable track athletes of all time. Fierce and arrogant, renowned for his explosive starts, Johnson predicted gold at Seoul: "When the gun go off," he'd said, "the race be over." Indeed it was: He established a new world record of 9.79 seconds. Two days later, however, mandatory tests showed that Johnson had been using anabolic steroids. He was stripped of his glory and an estimated $1 million in commercial contracts. His gold medal went to second-place Lewis, the fastest *clean* man in the world.

Steroid abuse had long been an international problem, but never had an athlete of Johnson's stature been caught. Competitors use the banned drugs (which can cause psychoses, as well as heart and liver damage) to put on muscle. Johnson had been suspect for years —his muscles were uncanny and his eyes were often yellow, a side effect of steroids—but he'd always passed his drug tests. After the Olympic scandal, the Canadian government launched an inquiry into steroid use. Johnson testified that, on the advice of his coach, Charlie Francis, he had been injecting the drugs for seven years. Francis was banned from coaching for life; Johnson was suspended for two years. When he returned, distinctly smaller, he failed to run competitively. Two years later, he again resorted to illegal substances and was permanently barred from track. **▸1989.M**

NOBEL PRIZES: Peace: U.N. Peacekeeping Forces (New York City) ... Literature: Naguib Mahfouz (Egyptian; novelist) ... Chemistry: J. Deisenhofer, R. Huber, and H. Michel (German; proteins and photosynthesis) ... Medicine: G. Elion, G. Hitchings, and J. Black (U.S., U.S., U.K.; drug treatment) ... Physics: L. Lederman, M. Schwartz, and J. Steinberger (U.S.; elementary particles) ... Economics: Maurice Allais (French).

A VOICE FROM 1988

A Feel-Good Ditty

"Don't Worry, Be Happy," by Bobby McFerrin, 1988

In concert, American jazz singer Bobby McFerrin did extraordinary things with his supple, four-octave voice, including impersonate a radio (replete with static), impersonate an entire bebop combo, sing delicate Bach airs, and sing counterpoint with himself. His German fans dubbed him Stimmwunder*—the wonder voice. But for all his dazzling vocal abilities, McFerrin in 1988 became famous on the ingratiating charm of a simple Calypso-influenced ditty called "Don't Worry, Be Happy." Released in July, the recording of the song sold more than ten million copies by the end of the year. Even George Bush, an avowed country-and-western music enthusiast, made McFerrin's tune his unofficial campaign song. With its breezy Caribbean beat and relentless (probably ironic) optimism, "Don't Worry, Be Happy" tapped into a short-lived American feel-good trend—Bush promised "kinder and gentler" times; designers briefly resurrected the old yellow "smiley face"—and also into a growing interest in the United States and Europe in so-called world music. A fusion of Western pop and folk traditions from Cameroon or Brazil or Bulgaria or Haiti (from anywhere, in fact, outside of Western Europe and the United States), world music was fresh, danceable, and satisfied certain exogamous cultural cravings.* ◄1986.M

Here's a little song I wrote.
You might want to sing it note for note.
Don't worry, be happy.

In every life we have some trouble,
but when you worry you make it double.
Don't worry, be happy.

Ain't got no place to lay your head,
somebody came and took your bed.
Don't worry, be happy.

The landlord say your rent is late.
He may have to litigate.
Don't worry, be happy.

Look at me, I'm happy.
Here, I give you my phone number.
When you worry, call me, I make you happy.

Ain't got no cash, ain't got no style,
ain't got no gal to make you smile.
Don't worry, be happy.

'Cause when you worry your face will frown
and that will bring everybody down.
Don't worry, be happy.

Don't worry. Don't worry. Don't do it.
Be happy. Put a smile on your face.
Don't bring everybody down. Don't worry.
It will soon pass, whatever it is.
Don't worry. Be happy. I'm not worried.
I'm happy.

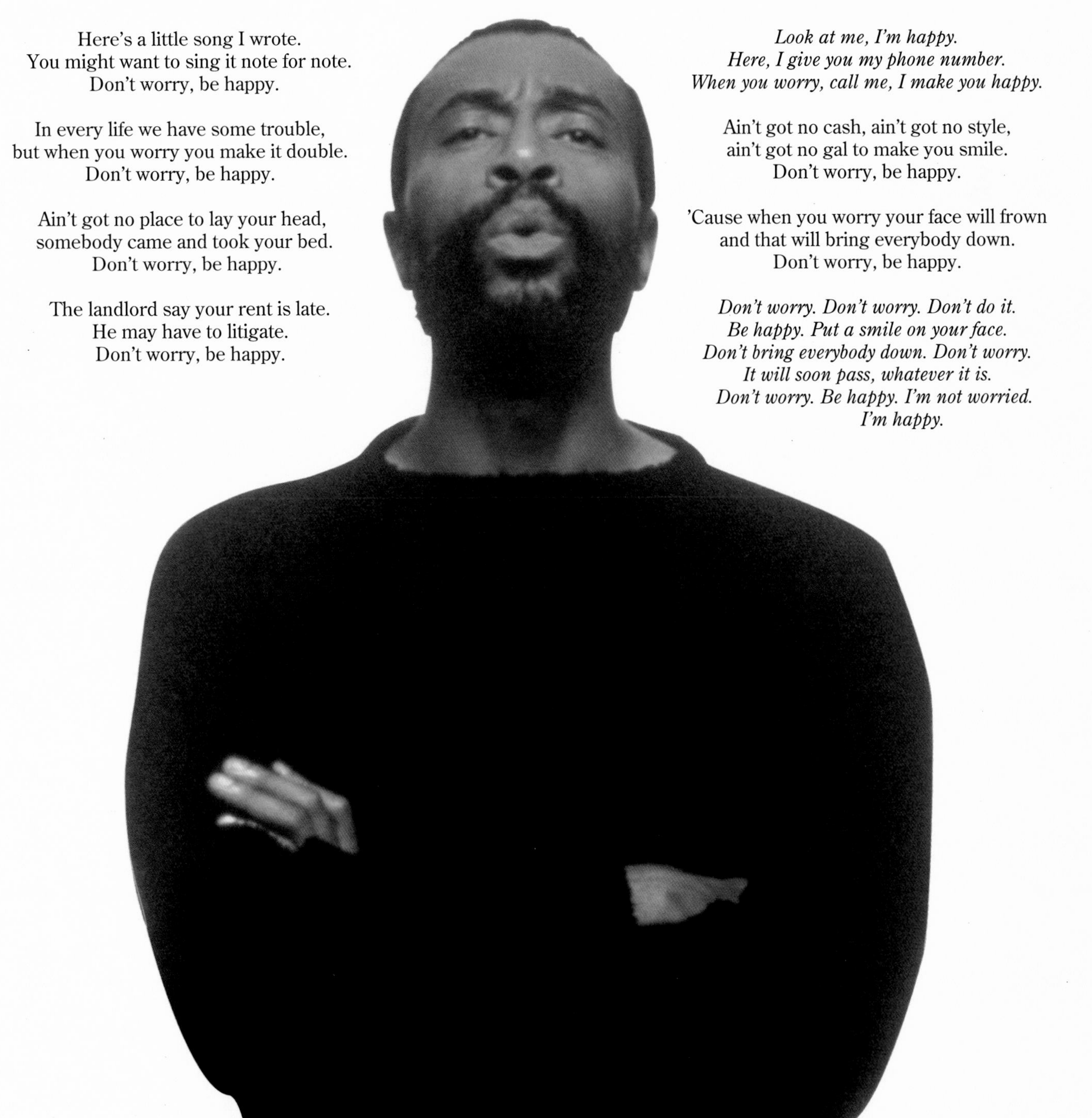

"We are leaving one epoch in international relations and entering another."—**Mikhail Gorbachev**

STORY OF THE YEAR

Europe's Anti-Communist Revolutions

1 Buoyed by Mikhail Gorbachev's reforms and his renunciation of Moscow's imperial power, movements for market-based economics and pluralist democracy toppled creaky Communist dictatorships throughout Eastern and Central Europe in 1989. And, except in Romania—where the Securitate (security police) killed some 7,000 people before insurgents executed tyrant Nicolae Ceaușescu and his wife—the revolutions were bloodless.

The Berlin Wall's destruction created a new generation of unified Germans.

The transformation began in Hungary, already the least repressive Soviet satellite. With the economy crumbling and popular discontent rising, the nation's Communist Party ousted 30-year chief János Kádár in 1988. The government of new prime minister Miklós Németh enacted increasingly liberal policies; in October 1989, the Party officially dissolved. Elections in 1990 made center-right Democratic Forum leader József Antall prime minister.

In East Germany, antigovernment demonstrations were rife by October 1989; meanwhile, thousands of fed-up citizens were streaming across Hungary's newly opened border with Austria en route to West Germany, or seeking asylum at the West German embassies in Prague and Warsaw. The politburo replaced Party chief Erich Honecker with another hard-liner, but the regime's modest loosening of travel restrictions led to its downfall: In November, two million East Germans flooded into West Berlin, and guards along the Berlin Wall stood aside or joined in as the throng began dismantling the hated structure. Reform-minded Communist Hans Modrow subsequently became premier; in 1990, his party lost the country's first free election to the newly unshackled Christian Democrats, whose leader, Lothar de Maizière, replaced Modrow.

In April 1989, after months of unrest and negotiations, Poland's government legalized the Solidarity movement (banned since 1982). Semi-free elections in June won Solidarity almost every legislative seat not reserved for the Communists or their allies; Communist chief General Wojciech Jaruzelski named Solidarity official Tadeusz Mazowiecki prime minister. In December 1990, Solidarity leader Lech Walesa was elected president.

Czechoslovakia's "Velvet Revolution," begun with student demonstrations, culminated in December with the election of dissident playwright-activist Vaclav Havel as president. And in Bulgaria, Party head Todor Zhivkov fell in November, priming that country for free elections. Though all the fledgling governments faced staggering economic and social problems, Europe had unquestionably been born anew. **◂1987.10 ▸1990.1**

PANAMA

U.S. Topples Noriega

2 The U.S. government had an axe to grind with General Manuel Noriega, commander of Panama's armed forces and the nation's de facto ruler: Though the strongman had been a generously paid CIA informant since the 1960s, he was also selling U.S. intelligence to Cuba and allowing Colombia's Medellín cocaine cartel to ship drugs through Panama to North America. Finally, Washington ran out of patience, and in December 1989, recently elected President George Bush sent 25,000 troops after the despot.

The invasion (the U.S. military's fourth Panamanian incursion since 1900) caused substantial loss of civilian life and property. Urban firefights destroyed the homes of some 15,000 Panamanians; of 516 Panamanian deaths acknowledged by the Pentagon, 459 were noncombatants. American fatalities numbered 23. "Operation Just Cause" did accomplish its primary aim: Noriega's extradition to Florida to face federal drug and racketeering charges. Guillermo Endara, elected president in 1989 but barred from office by Noriega, was sworn in as Panamanian head of state.

Noriega at the height of his power, in 1988. He owned four yachts, each named *Macho*.

Noriega had consolidated power in 1984, the last and most ruthless of a series of military men who seized power after populist dictator Omar Torrijos Herrera's mysterious death in a helicopter crash three years earlier. Noriega's control of state security and his cozy relationship with the American intelligence establishment for a time made him invincible. He had first dealt with Bush in 1976, when the latter was CIA director. Later, he schemed with Oliver North to illegally supply arms to the Nicaraguan contras. When Bush became president in January 1989, Noriega expected to cash in on old ties. By then, however, his double-dealing had overshadowed his usefulness.

Tried in Miami in 1992, Noriega was convicted on the testimony of former drug cronies and sentenced to 40 years. (Total cost of the conviction, with the invasion included: upwards of $164 million.) Nevertheless, drug smuggling from Panama continued unabated. **◂1977.7**

SOUTHERN AFRICA

De Klerk Begins Reforms

3 By 1989, South Africa's ruling National Party was disintegrating into rival factions. Recognizing that President P.W. Botha's response to the antiapartheid movement—brutal repression—was not working, reformers within the government had begun to seek alternative solutions. Botha and his supporters, called the "securocrats" for the police state they had erected, retained just enough power to block political challenges. Their authority, however, was increasingly undermined by the country's failing economy, its international isolation, and the outlawed African National Congress's relentless struggle against the racist regime.

The securocrats' lock on government was broken in February, when Botha suffered a stroke. He remained president, but F.W. de Klerk, minister of national education, took over as head of the National Party. Seven months later, de Klerk and his allies blocked a comeback attempt by Botha. The discredited president resigned, and in September, amid doomsday talk from conservatives, Parliament elected de Klerk to succeed him. The door to reform creaked open.

The last years of Botha's tenure had been a time of humiliation for the nation's white minority. An ongoing state of emergency, in which the government sent troops to occupy black townships, had failed to curtail guerrilla activity. ANC attacks actually increased fivefold between 1984 and 1988. Meanwhile, South Africa had been forced to abandon its undeclared war in Angola, where it had fought with rightist rebel forces to overthrow the Marxist government, and to withdraw from neighboring Namibia as well.

Shaking off his party's moribund

ART & CULTURE: Books: ***The Remains of the Day*** **(Kazuo Ishiguro);** ***Billy Bathgate*** **(E.L. Doctorow);** ***Citizens: A Chronicle of the Revolution*** **(Simon Schama) ... Music:** ***Don't Be Cruel*** **(Bobby Brown, LP);** ***Let It Loose*** **(Miami Sound Machine, LP); "Like a Prayer" (Leonard and Ciccone);** ***Symphony for Winds*** **(Ellen Taaffe Zwilich) ... Painting & Sculpture:** ***Historical Portraits*** **(Cindy Sherman) ... Film:** ***Driving Miss Daisy***

"In order to restore the people's trust in the government, I have made the decision to resign."
—Japanese prime minister Noboru Takeshita

De Klerk *(left)* on the campaign trail.

ideology, de Klerk began implementing "evolutionary" reform. He reduced the influence of the security forces and desegregated South African beaches during his first months in office. In February 1990, he legalized the ANC and began reducing censorship; then, completing his single greatest goodwill gesture, he released Nelson Mandela from prison. After 27 years, the antiapartheid movement's greatest leader and living symbol was free. **◂1988.2 ▸1990.V**

CHINA

Tiananmen Square Revolt

4 On June 3, 1989, troops and armored vehicles of the People's Liberation Army converged on Beijing's 100-acre Tiananmen Square, where students had been staging three weeks of pro-democracy demonstrations. Before sunrise the next morning, soldiers ordered the protesters to disperse —then tanks rolled in, crushing tents and those camped inside. The students fled, their leaders were arrested or went into hiding, and China's biggest antigovernment revolt since the revolution was over. Mao Zedong's heir, Deng Xiaoping, had prevailed.

Deng (who'd resigned his politburo seat in 1987 but still ruled China from behind the scenes) was himself a reformer: He championed economic decentralization, incorporation of free-market principles into communism, and closer ties with the West. But political freedom was another matter. The student protests had begun in April, spurred by the death of former Communist Party chief Hu Yaobang, whom Deng had forced to resign after Hu showed too much leniency toward an earlier uprising. As workers, intellectuals, and others joined in, polite calls for reform escalated into radical demands (including calls for Deng to step aside). The government accused the student leaders of conspiring to "negate the leadership of the [Party] and the socialist system." The lines were drawn.

On May 13, students began a hunger strike in Tiananmen Square, where Deng planned to welcome Soviet leader Mikhail Gorbachev two days later. (They erected a copy of America's Statue of Liberty, a supreme provocation.) Western reporters covering Gorbachev's visit—the first official contact between Soviet and Chinese leaders in 30 years—focused world attention on the sit-in. On May 20, after a million Chinese had poured into Beijing to support the hunger strikers, the government imposed martial law; stalemate set in as the protesters formed human barricades to block tanks. Then Deng ordered the army to attack. Hundreds, perhaps thousands, were killed. The West responded—briefly—with sanctions, but Deng refused to do more than release a few prisoners. He would not allow the sort of upheaval shaking the Soviet bloc to spread to China. **◂1984.7 ▸1994.14**

The student vanguard in Tiananmen Square, two weeks before Deng's brutal suppression.

JAPAN

Scandals Rock Ruling Party

5 Beset with scandals, Japan's governing Liberal Democratic Party (LDP) suffered its worst-ever setback at the polls in 1989. Having ruled uninterruptedly since 1955, the LDP for the first time lost control of the upper house of the Diet in July elections. By virtue of lower-house domination, the LDP was still supreme—but barely. Embarrassed prime minister Sousuke Uno relinquished party leadership to Toshiki Kaifu *(above)*. Uno himself had been elevated to the top post barely a month earlier, when his predecessor, LDP heavyweight Noboru Takeshita, stepped down in the midst of an influence-peddling brouhaha. Kaifu thus became Japan's third prime minister in three months.

The LDP had always enjoyed a profitable symbiosis with big business, but no one knew just how cozy the relationship had become until the Recruit Corporation scandal broke in late 1988. In return for political favors, Recruit, a real estate and communications conglomerate, had given LDP politicians stock discounts worth some $9 million. The deals were not in themselves illegal, and the quid pro quo was difficult to prove in court. But public confidence in the government plunged, forcing Takeshita's April resignation. No sooner had Uno taken the helm than a geisha tattled about the $21,000 the new prime minister had paid her for sex. That, combined with Recruit and a regressive consumption tax just passed by the LDP, doomed the party in July.

Anointed to succeed Takeshita largely because he was untouched by corruption, Kaifu inherited the worst LDP crisis since 1974, when financial impropriety felled Prime Minister Kakuei Tanaka. Many analysts predicted the party would lose its parliamentary stranglehold in the upcoming lower-house elections. In fact, the Japanese penchant for continuity prevailed: In February 1990, the LDP defeated a divided opposition. Kaifu remained prime minister, but insiders whispered that Takeshita still called the shots. Politician and party had apparently weathered the storm. **◂1976.8 ▸1993.11**

DEATHS

Alvin Ailey, U.S. choreographer.

Lucille Ball, U.S. actress.

Donald Barthelme, U.S. writer.

George Wells Beadle, U.S. geneticist.

Samuel Beckett, Irish-French writer.

Irving Berlin, Russian-U.S. composer.

August Anheuser Busch, Jr., U.S. brewer.

Nicolae Ceaușescu, Romanian president.

Graham Chapman, U.K. comedian.

Salvador Dali, Spanish painter.

Bette Davis, U.S. actress.

Daphne Du Maurier, U.K. writer.

Malcolm Forbes, U.S. publisher.

Andrei Gromyko, U.S.S.R. statesman.

Hirohito, Japanese emperor.

Vladimir Horowitz, Russian-U.S. pianist.

János Kádár, Hungarian premier.

Herbert von Karajan, Austrian conductor.

Ayatollah Ruhollah Khomeini, Iranian ruler and religious leader.

R.D. Laing, U.K. psychiatrist.

Ferdinand Marcos, Filipino president.

Laurence Olivier, U.K. actor.

Sugar Ray Robinson, U.S. boxer.

Andrei Sakharov, U.S.S.R. physicist and human rights activist.

William Shockley, U.K.-U.S. physicist.

Georges Simenon, Belgian novelist.

Virgil Thomson, U.S. composer and critic.

(Bruce Beresford); *Born on the Fourth of July* (Oliver Stone); *Drugstore Cowboy* (Gus Van Sant); *My Left Foot* (Jim Sheridan); *Sweetie* (Jane Campion); *Henry V* (Kenneth Branagh); *Roger and Me* (Michael Moore) ... Theater: *A Few Good Men* (Aaron Sorkin); *Shadowlands* (William Nicholson); *Love Letters* (A.R. Gurney); *Miss Saigon* (Boubil and Schönberg) ... TV: *PrimeTime Live.*

"Is this meaningless war going to continue until the last Lebanese is dead?"—**The Muslim radio station Voice of the Nation in Beirut**

NEW IN 1989

Worldwide ban on ivory trading.

Stealth bomber.

Teenage Mutant Ninja Turtles.

Time Warner, Inc. (created by merger of Time, Inc., and Warner Communications, Inc.).

Insurance policies covering damage by computer viruses.

IN THE UNITED STATES

▶TOUR DE FORCE—American cyclist Greg LeMond captured his second Tour de France in July, overtaking France's Laurent Fignon to win the most closely battled Tour in history. Even more remarkable than

LeMond's margin of victory—a mere eight seconds, after three weeks and 2,025 miles—was his comeback from a near-fatal 1987 hunting accident. He won for a third time in 1990. ◂1969.12

▶PETE ROSE BANNED—On August 24, baseball commissioner and former Yale president A. Bartlett Giamatti permanently banned former player and now manager of the Cincinnati Reds Pete Rose from baseball for betting on games. The ban made Rose, who'd retired as a player in 1986 after playing in more games (3,562) and accumulating more hits (4,256) than anyone else in history, ineligible for the Baseball Hall of Fame. Eight days after handing down his controversial decision, Giamatti died of a heart attack. In 1990, Rose served five months in jail for income-tax evasion.

▶AIRLINES FOLD—Crippled by recession, the high price of oil, and a bitter labor strike led by machinists union chief

THE MIDDLE EAST

Beirut's Apocalypse

6 The violence that gripped Beirut in 1989 was the worst in 14 years of civil war. It began in March, when General Michel Aoun, commander of 20,000 Christian militiamen, declared a "war of liberation" against the 40,000 Syrian troops occupying much of Lebanon. Armed by Iraq (whose dictator, Saddam Hussein, resented Syria for aiding Iran in the recent Iran-Iraq war), Aoun began bombarding Muslim west Beirut. The general claimed to be targeting Syrian positions, but the resulting artillery duel gradually gutted the city that was once the jewel of the Middle East.

By August, half of Beirut's 1.5 million residents were refugees. Those who stayed endured snipers, shortages, and near-constant shelling. Young fighters of the Christian, Muslim, and Druze private armies—largely culled from the desperate ranks of the unemployed and emotionally disturbed, and often on drugs—skirmished along the Green Line dividing the city's warring halves. "We are committing suicide," lamented Syrian-backed Druze militia leader Walid Jumblatt. Yet the fighting continued, even after Parliament voted to disband the militias and incorporate them into the nonsectarian regular army.

The problem was that Lebanon *had* no functioning army, any more than it had a functioning Parliament. Syrian strongman Hafez al-Assad insisted that his aim was to help the Lebanese "achieve national reconciliation" and restore effective government. But many observers believed he coveted permanent hegemony over Lebanon. Aoun, for his part, hoped to maintain the Christian minority's dominance over Lebanese politics. Caught in the middle, as usual, were most of the Lebanese people. **◂1983.3 ▸1990.M**

Lebanon's civil war was fought in the middle of the country's most densely populated city.

PARAGUAY

Dug-In Dictator Ousted

7 The Western Hemisphere's longest-running dictatorship ended in February 1989, when Paraguay's General Alfredo Stroessner was overthrown by General Andrés Rodríguez. Since seizing power in 1954, Stroessner had used police-state terror and co-optation (membership in his Colorado Party was a prerequisite for most professional jobs) to transform a notoriously unstable nation into a paragon of lockstep order. Eventually, his authority was so unshakable that he allowed token opposition activity. But along with one-man rule came singular corruption.

Paraguay became a haven for fugitive Nazis (including Auschwitz doctor Josef Mengele), deposed dictators, and international drug traffickers. All paid handsomely for sanctuary. But Paraguay's lucrative visa trade paled next to its smuggling. The nation earned some $700 million annually from illegal exports—twice as much as from legal trade. Stroessner and his cronies, including Rodríguez, lived like royalty. The underdeveloped economy, meanwhile, left most people in poverty.

Stroessner's position began to erode in the 1970s, when Jimmy Carter's human rights policies brought a suspension of U.S. aid. In the 1980s, as the economy worsened, street protests erupted; rifts opened within the elite between Stroessner loyalists and a less reactionary group labeled the "traditionalists." With the ailing dictator, 76, planning to name his son as heir, Rodríguez, backed by the traditionalists, made his move. Up to 300 people died in the coup, and Stroessner fled abroad. Surprising skeptics, Rodríguez held the first multi-candidate election in decades; unsurprisingly, he won. In 1993, voters chose a civilian to succeed him—Juan Carlos Wasmosy, of the Colorado Party. **◂1954.M ▸1989.8**

SOUTH AMERICA

The Reformers' Burdens

8 In three of South America's emerging democracies, voters chose new leaders in 1989 to grapple with the thorny legacies of dictatorship.

Supported by a broad coalition (from communists to center-rightists), Christian Democrat Patricio Aylwin Azócar beat General Augusto Pinochet's handpicked candidate in Chile's first presidential election in 19 years. But under the constitution Pinochet had promulgated in 1981, the general would stay on as commander in chief. Fearing military intervention, Aylwin dared do little to revise policies that had made rich Chileans richer at the expense of the poor—or to prosecute soldiers implicated in thousands of political murders under the old regime.

After six years of civilian government, Argentina, too, lay under the army's shadow. Outgoing president Raúl Alfonsín had survived repeated coup attempts, reprisals for his prosecution of top officers implicated in mass murders under military rule. He'd been done in, however, by the autocrats' leftover financial mess: By early 1989, the foreign debt was $66 billion, inflation was running at 200 percent a month, and food riots were erupting nationwide. In May, Peronist Carlos Saúl Menem was elected Alfonsín's successor. A flamboyant populist, Menem promised wage increases and easy credit. But once in office, he imposed an austerity program, slashing subsidies and selling state-owned enterprises. He also pardoned 280 military men—choosing safety over justice.

SPORTS: Baseball: World Series, Oakland Athletics defeat San Francisco Giants, 4–0; Pete Rose banned from baseball after discovery of evidence that he bet on baseball games ... Football: Super Bowl, San Francisco 49ers defeat Cincinnati Bengals, 20–16; Pete Rozelle retires after 29 years as NFL commissioner ... Basketball: NBA, Detroit Pistons defeat Los Angeles Lakers, 4–0.

"I have great trouble in knowing the difference between insider information and a very fine research report."
—Walter Wriston, former chairman of Citicorp

Chileans rallied against Pinochet in 1988; a year later, they voted against his candidate.

In December, Brazilians chose the young and glamorous Fernando Collor de Mello as their first directly elected president in 29 years. Collor's civilian predecessor, José Sarney, had inherited another economy gutted by a spendthrift junta. By the time Collor took office, in March 1990, the debt was $115 million and the annual inflation rate 100,000 percent. Collor subjected Brazil to harsh fiscal shock therapy—but the middle and lower classes wound up feeling all the pain. His own pursuit of illicit wealth soon brought about his downfall. **◂1988.M ▸1992.7**

SCIENCE

Cold Fusion Furor

9 In March 1989, two electrochemists held a press conference at the University of Utah that raised a scientific furor. B. Stanley Pons (of Utah) and Martin Fleischmann (of England's University of Southampton) announced that they'd achieved nuclear fusion—the process that powers the sun—in a jar, at room temperature. Dubbed cold fusion, the phenomenon violated known physical laws. If it was real (and most scientists were skeptical), cold fusion promised cheap, clean, virtually unlimited energy.

The experiment was seductively simple: Pons and Fleischmann immersed a cell consisting of two electrodes—one of palladium and one of platinum—in heavy water (made with deuterium, a heavy hydrogen isotope). Electric current run through the apparatus produced so much excess energy (in the form of heat) that the palladium electrode melted. The only plausible explanation, the researchers reasoned, was that fusion had occurred. The discovery ranked "right up there with fire," crowed the University of Utah's president. Scientists everywhere began trying to duplicate the experiment; some claimed success. Pons and Fleischmann testified before Congress in hopes of winning millions in federal funds.

By summer's end, however, scientific opinion had turned decisively against the pair. Among the errors ascribed to Pons and Fleischmann: A simple chemical reaction could have caused the heat they had observed; they'd failed to measure for helium, a fusion product; genuine fusion would have released enough neutrons to kill anyone nearby. The whole affair, declared one physicist, was "scientific schlock." Fleischmann and Pons

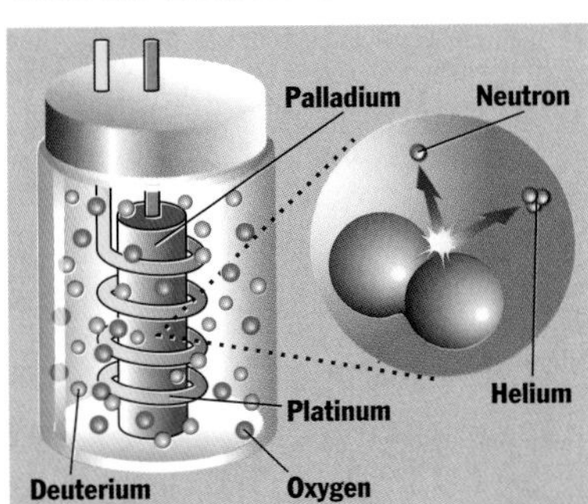

Bottled Fusion (in theory): As palladium absorbs deuterium atoms, deuterium nuclei fuse, releasing energy, neutrons, and helium.

retreated into obscurity, their reputations battered. But they—and their supporters—continued to pursue cold-fusion experiments in the 1990s. **◂1951.3**

BUSINESS AND INDUSTRY

Junk-Bond King Dethroned

10 Michael Milken, the prophet of high-risk, high-yield "junk" bonds, was either the most innovative financier since J.P. Morgan, or a cheat. Only his wealth was beyond dispute. Before his 1989 indictment on 98 racketeering and fraud charges, Milken, head of Drexel Burnham Lambert's go-go Beverly Hills junk-bond department, had amassed a personal fortune of at least $1 billion. In one year alone, he'd made $550 million.

Credited with creating the junk-bond market, Milken helped fuel the takeover craze of the 1980s, when Wall Street raiders seized control of multibillion-dollar corporations. He sold his wares (mainly to insurance companies and savings-and-loan institutions) to raise investment capital for takeover artists like T. Boone Pickens and Carl Icahn—who offered the target businesses as security for the money they borrowed from him. The result: huge profits for Milken and his clients, record debt for American corporations.

Milken *(center with wife and lawyer)* after his pre-sentencing hearing.

Supporters hailed Milken as a brilliant maverick. But federal prosecutors accused him and his employer, Drexel, of rigging the junk-bond market. The charges came after a two-year investigation begun in 1986, when high-flying arbitrageur and frequent Milken business partner Ivan Boesky fell in Wall Street's mammoth insider-trading scandal. Drexel admitted violations in 1988 and paid a whopping $650 million in fines—a settlement that bankrupted the company. In 1990, Milken pleaded guilty to six felony charges. Lambasting his "gospel of greed," the judge sentenced him to ten years in prison (later reduced to three) and ordered him to pay $600 million. **◂1988.7 ▸1991.9**

IN THE UNITED STATES

Charles Bryan, Eastern Airlines, bleeding millions, filed for Chapter 11 bankruptcy protection from its creditors on March 9. In May, embattled Eastern chairman Frank Lorenzo sold the wheezing Boston–New York–Washington Eastern Shuttle to free-spending real-estate mogul Donald Trump for $365 million. Not even that windfall could save Eastern, founded in 1928 and once one of the world's most successful airlines. On January 1991, having exhausted its cash and facing a billion-dollar debt, Eastern was liquidated. Two other carriers, Midway and onetime giant Pan Am, suffered the same fate later that year. Trump, facing a financial crisis of his own, killed off the Eastern Shuttle and quickly renamed it Trump. By 1992, the Trump Shuttle, too, was out of business.

▸POWELL IN COMMAND—President Bush in August nominated Colin Powell to be chairman of the Joint Chiefs of Staff. Powell, a four-star general and former national security adviser to Ronald Reagan, became the first black officer to hold the highest military post in the United States. A veteran of two tours of duty in Vietnam, he played a leading role in the planning and execution of the Persian Gulf incursion in 1991. ▸1990.7

▸FRISCO QUAKE—On October 17, San Francisco was struck with an earthquake measuring 7.1 on the Richter scale. The 15-second temblor along the San Andreas Fault killed an estimated 90 people, many crushed in their cars when highways buckled and collapsed, and caused some $6 billion in damage. Newer buildings, designed to withstand quakes, survived the test. The quake hit moments before the third game of baseball's World Series, a local match between the San Francisco Giants and the Oakland Athletics. Suspended for eleven days, the series, like the Bay Area itself, soon got on with its business. ◂1985.4 ▸1994.12

POLITICS & BUSINESS: GNP: $5,266.8 billion ... Internment Compensation Act awards $20,000 to each surviving Japanese-American interned during WWII (total liability, $17.2 billion) ... Supreme Court rules states can limit access to abortion, upholds right to publically burn American flag ... Abraham & Straus takes over Gimbels in New York City.

"I don't know. I know what the wrong thing is: racism."—**Filmmaker Spike Lee, when asked, "What's 'the right thing'?"**

AROUND THE WORLD

▶VIETNAM PULLS OUT OF CAMBODIA—The Vietnamese government withdrew the last of its 200,000 troops from neighboring Cambodia on September 26, ending a nearly eleven-year occupation. Vietnam had invaded Cambodia in December 1978, toppled the Khmer Rouge government of genocidal dictator Pol Pot, and installed a pro-Vietnamese regime. Civil war broke out after the withdrawal as the Khmer Rouge tried to retake the government. ◂1978.9

▶BURMA RENAMED—In June, Burma's ruling military junta, which had deposed the 26-year-old regime of General Ne Win the previous year, changed the country's name to Myanmar. (The capital, Rangoon, became Yangon.) A year later, the junta sponsored elections —Ne Win's downfall had been the result of violent prodemocracy protests—but when the National League for Democracy (NLD) won an overwhelming majority in the assembly, the junta voided the results and

arrested NLD leader Daw Aung San Suu Kyi *(above, center)*. The daughter of World War II antifascist resister and nationalist leader U Aung San, Aung San Suu Kyi was awarded the Nobel Peace Prize in 1991. The regime refused to release her from house arrest unless she forswore politics. ◂1948.M

▶DEATH OF A KLEPTOCRAT—Ferdinand Marcos, the Philippine dictator who'd defrauded his country of billions of dollars, died in Hawaii on September 28. He was 72 and had spent the last three years of his life in exile in the U.S., fending off lawsuits stemming from his embezzlement. Marcos was survived by his wife, Imelda, an imperious former beauty queen whose 1,060 pairs of shoes provided an abiding symbol of the family "kleptocracy." In 1990, Mrs. Marcos was tried in the U.S. on racketeering charges. Acquitted, she returned to the Philippines in 1991 and made an unsuccessful bid for the presidency. ◂1986.3

SPORTS

A Deadly Stampede

11 In April 1989, 95 people were killed, and scores more injured, at an English soccer-tournament match between Liverpool and Nottingham Forest. Thousands of fans piling into the already overcrowded stands of Hillsborough Stadium in Sheffield crushed spectators against a metal "safety" fence encircling the field. Britain's worst sports-related tragedy ever, the Sheffield incident was the latest bloody stain on the game's notoriously violent record.

The victims had not been fighting, but the barrier against which they were trapped had been put there to prevent combative spectators from storming the pitch. The lethal surge was created when police, fearing that locked-out, late-arriving Liverpool supporters would wreak havoc in the streets, opened exit gates to let them in.

The disaster came four years after hooligans (the epithet for British soccer rowdies) rioted in Brussels at a European Cup match, causing the deaths of 39 spectators. After that melee, British fans and teams were barred from Continental tournaments. Following Hillsborough, the government launched its second inquiry in five years. Among soccer's problems: management that refused to update Victorian-era arenas; dehumanizing crowd-control measures, including segregation of opposing fans into cagelike enclosures; hooligan gangs, called "firms," for which soccer matches were an excuse to rampage. "Hillsborough was was not just a calamitous incident," editorialized *The Economist*. "It was a brutal demonstration of systemic failure." **◂1930.13**

Fans at Hillsborough died by being pushed against fences designed for crowd control.

Lee and Danny Aiello as Mookie and Sal.

FILM

Spike Lee's Right Thing

12 A bitter, funny, and vibrantly entertaining polemic on race hatred, Spike Lee's *Do the Right Thing*, released in 1989, became the decade's most controversial film. Set in a black neighborhood in Brooklyn on the hottest day of the year, the film examines the relations between the locals—including an Afrocentric militant, an incoherently angry rap fan, a carefully noncommittal pizza-delivery man named Mookie (played by Lee), and a handful of street-corner sages—and the nonblacks who work there: a decent Italian pizzeria owner named Sal and his two sons, a choleric Korean grocer, brutal white cops. The tensions build until a young black man is killed and Sal's business is burned to the ground.

Lee, 32, had been in the public eye since his first commercial work, a low-budget exploration of female sexuality called *She's Gotta Have It* (1986), won a prize at Cannes and earned $8 million. *Do the Right Thing* was Lee's second big-studio effort (his first, *School Daze*, examined the rivalry between light-skinned and dark-skinned blacks), and it caused a media firestorm. He was accused of endorsing violence in response to racism; experts predicted the film would cause riots (it didn't). Lee, in fact, telegraphed his own ambivalence by ending the picture with contradictory quotations on self-defense from Martin Luther King, Jr. and Malcolm X (about whom Lee later made a film). The young director's achievement, however, was unequivocal: Though other serious African-American filmmakers had enjoyed some success (notably Gordon Parks and Melvin Van Peebles in the sixties and seventies), Lee was the first to consistently win mainstream acceptance for honest, provocative portrayals of black experience. He opened the door for a new generation of black directors. **◂1971.M**

ENVIRONMENTALISM

The *Exxon Valdez* Disaster

13 In March 1989, the tanker *Exxon Valdez* hit a reef, pouring 11 million gallons of crude oil into the pristine waters of Prince William Sound, near the southern terminus of the Alaska Pipeline. The resulting slick fouled 1,056 miles of shoreline in one of the world's most ecologically sensitive regions. And though Exxon (and hundreds of volunteers) scrambled to contain the slick, only a small amount of crude could be recovered; even careful scrubbing of beaches could not eliminate oil that had seeped below the surface. The *Exxon Valdez* spill was the biggest in U.S. history; no other spill anywhere had done as much damage to wildlife. Among the animals killed were an estimated 580,000 birds and 5,500 otters.

After the *Valdez* spill, volunteers tried to clean up a Prince William Sound beach.

Environmentalists had warned of danger ever since Alaska's North Slope oil fields were discovered in 1968. But oil companies insisted that their safety procedures made mishaps unlikely and that they could clean up any spill. Yet the *Valdez* disaster stemmed from sheer carelessness: Captain Joseph Hazelwood had entrusted the helm to an unqualified third mate, and the Coast Guard had failed to warn the ship that it was miles off course.

In 1990, Hazelwood was acquitted of all serious charges stemming from the accident, including counts of criminal mischief and navigating while intoxicated. In 1994, however, he admitted he'd been drinking at the time. By then, his employer, the Exxon oil company, had paid a $100 million fine (the largest ever for an environmental crime), spent $2 billion on the ongoing cleanup (and some $900 million more to settle civil suits), and had been ordered to pay $5 billion in punitive damages to Alaskan fishermen. **◂1978.12**

NOBEL PRIZES: Peace: Dalai Lama (Tibetan; Tibetan independence) ... Literature: Camilo José Cela (Spanish; writer) ... Chemistry: Thomas Cech and Sidney Altman (U.S.; RNA and chemical reactions) ... Medicine: J.M. Bishop and Harold Varmus (U.S.; cancer) ... Physics: N. Ramsey (U.S.; atomic clock) and H. Dehmelt and W. Paul (U.S., German; subatomic particles) ... Economics: Trygve Haavelmo (Norwegian).

A VOICE FROM 1989

Dreams of Assimilation

From *The Joy Luck Club,* by Amy Tan, 1989

The daughter of Chinese immigrants, California writer Amy Tan shared with millions of other Americans the experience of assimilation—of growing up ethnic in the land of melting ethnicity. In her 1989 novel, The Joy Luck Club, *Tan explored the lives of four Chinese women who fled communism and personal tragedy in China in 1949, and those of their thoroughly Americanized adult daughters. In the United States, the mothers play mah-jongg together at the Joy Luck Club (whose insignia, shown here, appeared in the book) and worry about their daughters' estrangement; the daughters proceed with modern lives and fret about their mothers' alienness. For Tan, and for a growing number of multicultural novelists—from Native American Louise Erdrich to Japanese-American Hisaye Yamamoto to Cuban-American Oscar Hijuelos—the American experience was one of reconciling bonds of blood and country.*

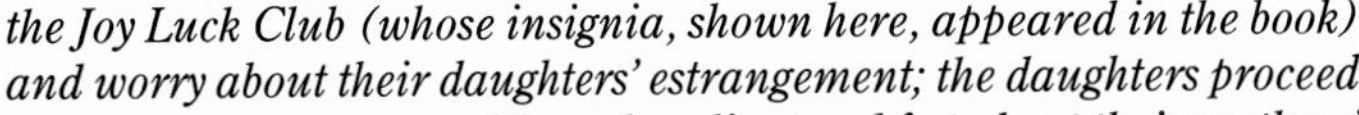

My father has asked me to be the fourth corner at the Joy Luck Club. I am to replace my mother, whose seat at the mah jong table has been empty since she died two months ago. My father thinks she was killed by her own thoughts.

"She had a new idea inside her head," said my father. "But before it could come out of her mouth, the thought grew too big and burst. It must have been a very bad idea."

The doctor said she died of a cerebral aneurysm. And her friends at the Joy Luck Club said she died just like a rabbit: quickly and with unfinished business left behind. My mother was supposed to host the next meeting of the Joy Luck Club.

The week before she died, she called me, full of pride, full of life: "Auntie Lin cooked red bean soup for Joy Luck. I'm going to cook black sesame-seed soup."

"Don't show off," I said.

"It's not showoff." She said the two soups were almost the same, *chabudwo*. Or maybe she said *butong*, not the same thing at all. It was one of those Chinese expressions that means the better half of mixed intentions. I can never remember things I didn't understand in the first place.

My mother started the San Francisco version of the Joy Luck Club in 1949, two years before I was born. This was the year my mother and father left China with one stiff leather trunk filled only with fancy silk dresses. There was no time to pack anything else, my mother had explained to my father after they boarded the boat. Still his hands swam frantically between the slippery silks, looking for his cotton shirts and wool pants.

When they arrived in San Francisco, my father made her hide those shiny clothes. She wore the same brown-checked Chinese dress until the Refugee Welcome Society gave her two hand-me-down dresses, all too large in sizes for American women. The society was composed of a group of white-haired American missionary ladies from the First Chinese Baptist Church. And because of their gifts, my parents could not refuse their invitation to join the church. Nor could they ignore the old ladies' practical advice to improve their English through Bible study class on Wednesday nights and, later, through choir practice on Saturday mornings.

This was how my parents met the Hsus, the Jongs, and the St. Clairs. My mother could sense that the women of these families also had unspeakable tragedies they had left behind in China and hopes they couldn't begin to express in their fragile English. Or at least, my mother recognized the numbness in these women's faces. And she saw how quickly their eyes moved when she told them her idea for the Joy Luck Club.

Joy Luck was an idea my mother remembered from the days of her first marriage in Kweilin, before the Japanese came. That's why I think of Joy Luck as her Kweilin story. It was the story she would always tell me....

Casting long shadows into her life, and eventually into mine.

Amy Tan *(upper left)* was born in California two a a half years after her parents emigrated from China. Fully Americanized, Tan nonetheless says that on her first visit, "As soon as my feet touched China, I became Chinese."

The long Cold War ended not with a bang but a whimper, producing no victors and few spoils. With a single superpower left standing, democracy took root in surprising places—but so, too, did economic anarchy, crime, and civil war.

1990 1994

In Soweto (the enormous group of black townships on the outskirts of white Johannesburg), black South Africans, long denied democracy's most fundamental expression, line up to vote in the country's 1994 election, the first open to all races. Reforms in the former Soviet Union helped resolve crises in many longtime Cold War hot-spots. Elsewhere, however, the end of communist restraints on nationalist fervor unleashed horrors that had once been held in check by the Kremlin's iron fist.

The World in 1990

World Population

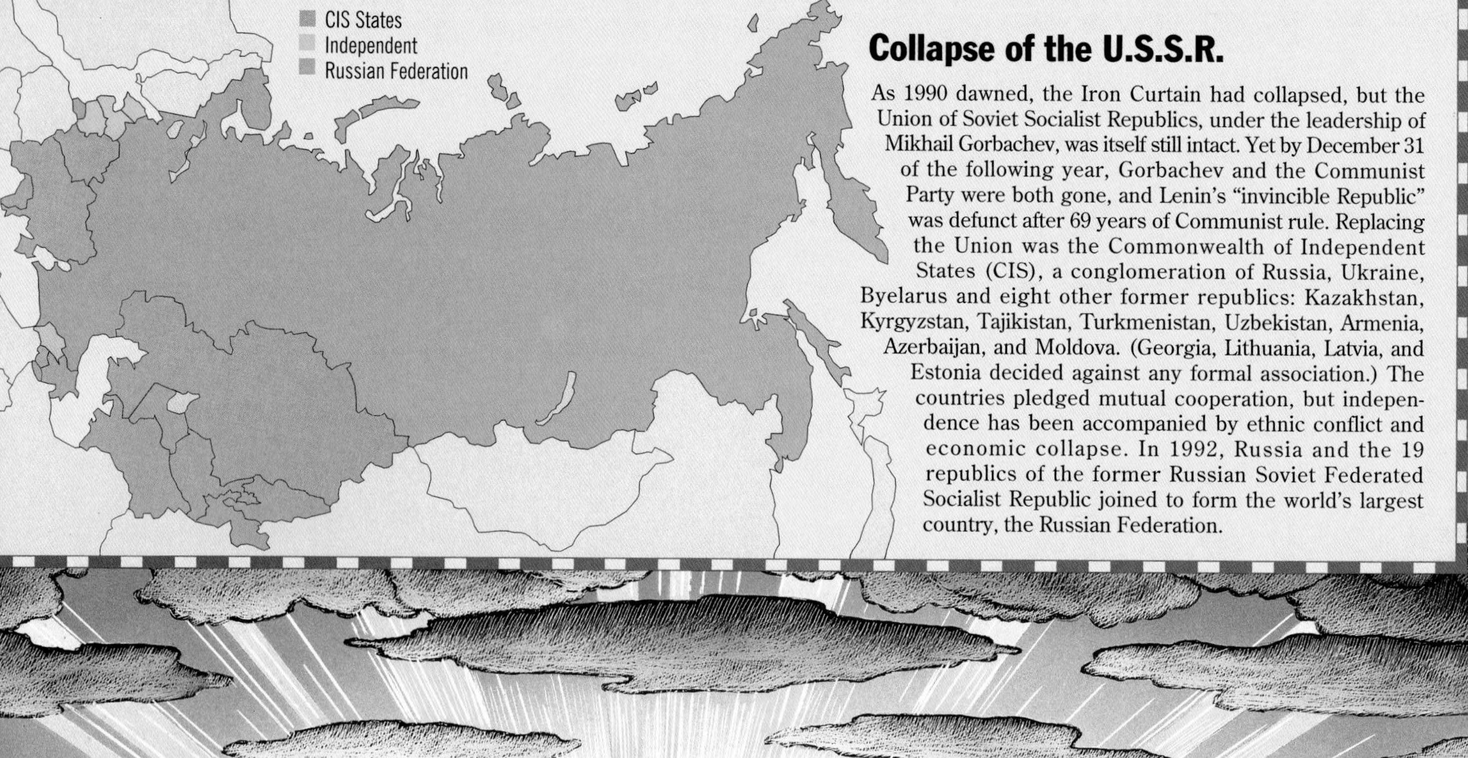

Collapse of the U.S.S.R.

As 1990 dawned, the Iron Curtain had collapsed, but the Union of Soviet Socialist Republics, under the leadership of Mikhail Gorbachev, was itself still intact. Yet by December 31 of the following year, Gorbachev and the Communist Party were both gone, and Lenin's "invincible Republic" was defunct after 69 years of Communist rule. Replacing the Union was the Commonwealth of Independent States (CIS), a conglomeration of Russia, Ukraine, Byelarus and eight other former republics: Kazakhstan, Kyrgyzstan, Tajikistan, Turkmenistan, Uzbekistan, Armenia, Azerbaijan, and Moldova. (Georgia, Lithuania, Latvia, and Estonia decided against any formal association.) The countries pledged mutual cooperation, but independence has been accompanied by ethnic conflict and economic collapse. In 1992, Russia and the 19 republics of the former Russian Soviet Federated Socialist Republic joined to form the world's largest country, the Russian Federation.

An Uncertain Future Fin-de-siècle rumination and re-examination made an early appearance in the speeded-up twentieth century. By 1990, the Earth's inhabitants were already looking ahead to the millennium—with uncertainty and a healthy dose of skepticism about the once-unquestioned inevitability of progress. A world that had witnessed the near-miraculous defeat of such perennial killers as tuberculosis and polio watched in frustration as cancer and AIDS claimed thousands of lives. Hundreds of "armed conflicts" fought daily around the globe created millions of refugees. Other "quality of life" issues—the proliferation of crime, the threat of nuclear war—cried out for new solutions. Yet, as civilization stood poised on the brink of the twenty-first century, solutions were as elusive as ever.

AIDS	Reported Cases through 1990	Projected Adult Cases, 1995	Male/Female Ratio (1992 cases)
Sub-Saharan Africa	116,568	11,449,000	1/1
North America	180,337	1,495,000	8/1
Latin America	28,850	1,407,000	4/1
Southeast Asia	273	1,220,000	2/1*
Western Europe	51,527	1,186,000	5/1

*Conservative estimate based on limited data

Cancer (Deaths per 100,000 population)	1950	1960	1970	1980	1990
France	1,726	1,968	2.074	2,315	2,457
East Germany	3,320	1,056	2,327	N.A.	10,558
West Germany	1,696	2,084	2,396	2,547	3,345
Japan	777	1,004	1,166	1,384	1,761
U.K.	1,946	2,159	2,362	2,624	2,816
U.S.	1,393	1,487	1,615	1,855	1,991

Deaths by Handgun, 1990

Australia	10
Sweden	13
U.K.	22
Canada	68
Japan	87
U.S.	10,567

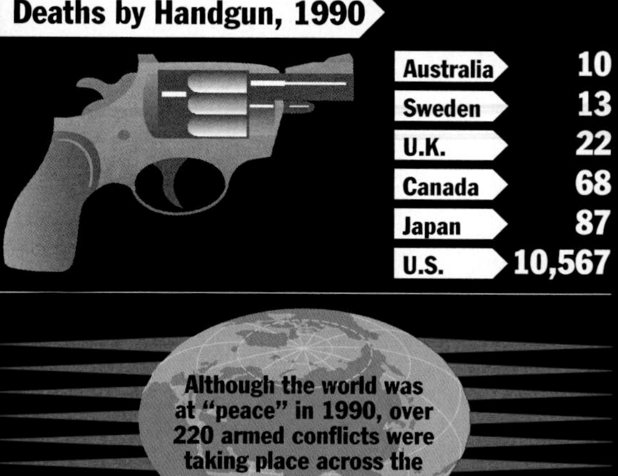

The World's Largest Banks

1970

		ASSETS
Bank of America	U.S.	$22.2
First National City Bank	U.S.	$19.1
Chase Manhattan Bank	U.S.	$19.0
Barclay's Bank	U.K.	$12.5
Manufacturer's Hanover	U.S.	$10.4
Royal Bank of Canada	Canada	$9.1
Morgan Guaranty Trust	U.S.	$9.0
Banca Nazionale	Italy	$8.8
Westdeutsche Landesbank	W. Germany	$8.8
Banque Nationale	France	$8.7

Billions of U.S. dollars

1990

		ASSETS
Dai-Ichi Kangyo Bank	Japan	$428.2
Sumitomo Bank	Japan	$409.2
Mitsu Taiyo Kobe Bank	Japan	$408.8
Sanwa Bank	Japan	$402.7
Fuji Bank	Japan	$399.5
Mitsubishi Bank	Japan	$391.5
Credit Agricole Mutuel	France	$305.2
Banque Nationale de Paris	France	$291.9
Industrial Bank of Japan	Japan	$290.1
Credit Lyonnais	France	$287.3

Billions of U.S. dollars

Percentage Distribution of the World's Population

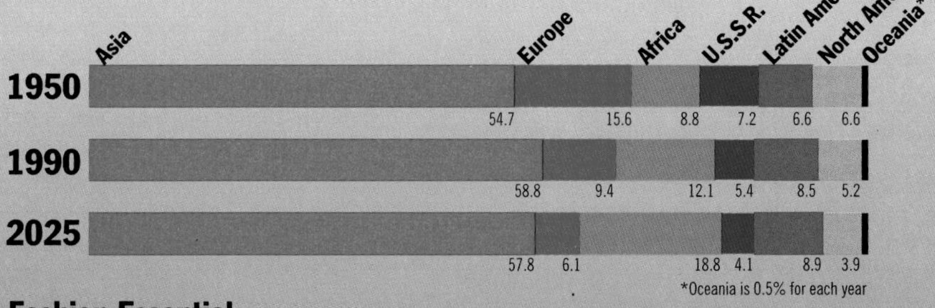

	Asia	Europe	Africa	U.S.S.R.	Latin America	North America	Oceania*
1950	54.7	15.6	8.8	7.2	6.6	6.6	
1990	58.8	9.4	12.1	5.4	8.5	5.2	
2025	57.8	6.1	18.8	4.1	8.9	3.9	

*Oceania is 0.5% for each year

Fashion Essential

Annual sales of **licensed merchandise,** from T-shirts and duffle bags to jewelry and mugs, amount to some $91 billion worldwide (American sales account for 68 percent). Warner Brothers *(right)*, the National Basketball Association, even municipal fire departments, put their names, logos, and most popular personalities on products everywhere.

STATE OF THE ART

By 1990, **home video games** were an inescapable part of the landscape of modern childhood. The first commercially successful game, Pong, was introduced in 1972; it was followed by the even more successful Pac-Man in 1981. But it was the Kyoto, Japan-based Nintendo company and its Super Mario Brothers game (introduced in 1985) that turned the toys into a worldwide phenomenon. By 1994, video games were a $6 billion industry (of which Nintendo controlled 80 percent).

Refugees

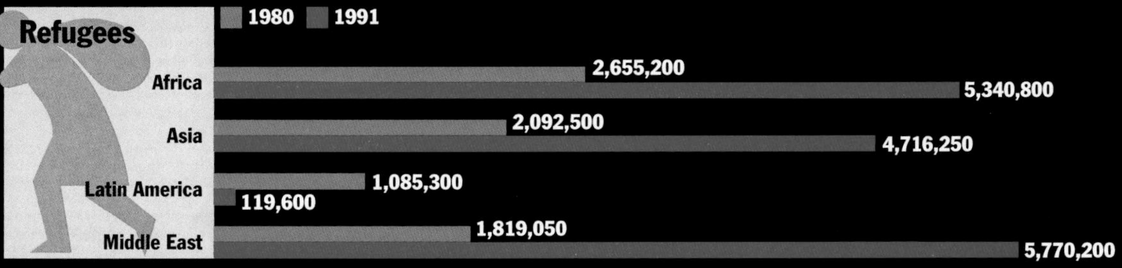

	1980	1991
Africa	2,655,200	5,340,800
Asia	2,092,500	4,716,250
Latin America	1,085,300	119,600
Middle East	1,819,050	5,770,200

Countries Possessing Nuclear Weapons

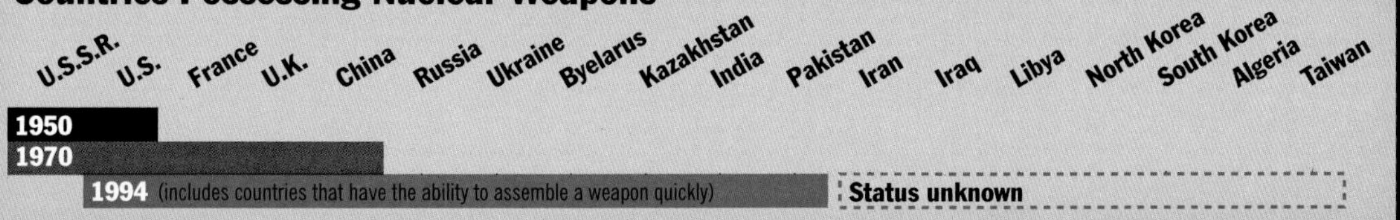

U.S.S.R., U.S., France, U.K., China, Russia, Ukraine, Byelarus, Kazakhstan, India, Pakistan, Iran, Iraq, Libya, North Korea, South Korea, Algeria, Taiwan

1950

1970

1994 (includes countries that have the ability to assemble a weapon quickly)

Status unknown

WHAT WE PREDICT

Many immunologists believe that, by the year 2000, insulin-dependent diabetes, multiple sclerosis, and rheumatoid arthritis will be completely preventable. Meanwhile, through the cloning of human proteins, genetic engineers will have created more than 1,000 new drugs. One such product—a drug that prevents certain enzymes from converting testosterone into DHT, a derivative that shrinks hair follicles—is expected to render baldness obsolete.

Because landfills are filled beyond capacity (in 1990, Fresh Kills landfill in Staten Island, New York, was the largest man-made structure in the world), many experts estimate that by the year 2000, incinerators will handle one-quarter of all municipal waste. By then, the Environmental Protection Agency predicts, Americans will be generating 216 million tons of garbage annually—an average of 4.4 pounds per person per day.

Life magazine envisions that by the year 2050, tourists will visit Mars. The seven-month voyage will entail a stop at a space station (roughly the size of one and a half football fields) that orbits Earth and serves as a springboard for space explorations.

By 2030, the *Environmental Almanac* anticipates, sea levels worldwide will rise eight inches, as global warming causes the ice sheets of Greenland and Antarctica to melt. By the beginning of the twenty-second century, Earth's temperature will be six degrees warmer than it is today.

Fortune magazine foresees three-dimensional holographic television in viewers' living rooms; automatic voice translation will obliterate language barriers. These innovations will be the result of advances in computer-related technology. Says Robert N. Noyce, vice chairman of Intel: "A one billion-transistor chip by the year 2000 is not inconceivable."

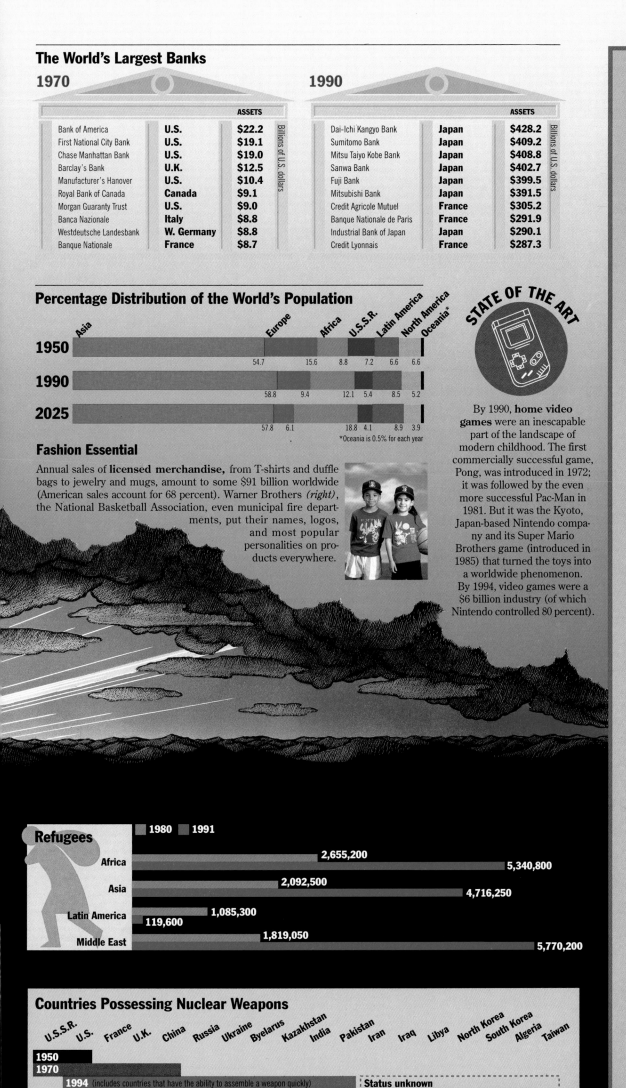

TAYLOR BRANCH

Freedom Ascendant

The Challenge of Democracy

1990
1994

REBORN FROM ANCIENT GREECE, democracy entered the twentieth century as a boisterous but lonely young orphan, and stands now after a blip of time as a solitary grandparent, somewhat listless in triumph, with scarcely anyone on the planet arguing for the future of a rival or descendant political order. This shift of historical reality stupefies even those who witnessed the revolutionary disintegration of the Soviet Union in 1991. We can only guess how it might appear to the Victorians, who, before the totalitarian dictators emerged, expected the future to refine their inherited history of monarchs. Despite their legacy of ages, reinforced by mutual discovery of crowns in distant cultures, the royals vanished while the century wasted millions of lives experimenting with substitute "isms" to guide or rule the masses. Not so long ago, fledgling democracies looked up at an enveloping canopy of kings, sultans, czars, emperors, and chiefs. Now, in the first glow of popular hegemony, monarchs are ghostly reminders of democracy as a precarious faith.

In 1905, to forestall agitations toward republican government, Europe's royal houses persuaded King Oscar of Sweden to allow Norway to secede as an independent country, provided that the new throne be offered to Crown Prince Charles of Denmark and his wife Maud, daughter of Britain's King Edward VII. The same year, Edward refused to recognize King Peter of Serbia, whose predecessor had been mutilated by Serbian-nationalist assassins. "We should be obliged to shut up our business," Edward said, "if we, the kings, were to consider the assassinations of kings as of no consequence at all." This communication was private, of course, just as Hapsburg Emperor Franz Josef used personal stationery in 1908 to notify only fellow sovereigns that he had annexed Bosnia and Hercegovina from the Sultan of Turkey to preempt Serbia. The whole idea of royalty was to remain above the need for public justification; thus, kings kept quaintly silent on monarchy's fitness, even as everyone else roared off into the new century's clattering storm of newspapers, motorcars, radios, telephones, and airplanes. Inevitably, the sheer mass of this interaction fortified public attention as the forum of democratic sovereignty. By the computer age of the 1990s, only such holdover kings as Hussein of Jordan and Fahd of Saudia Arabia managed to evade fateful debate over their crowns.

No fewer than seven grandchildren of Queen Victoria occupied national thrones on both sides of the Great War that engulfed the world from Sarajevo in 1914. Afterward, as Lord Asquith reported to King George V, there was "a slump in Emperors": the flight of German Kaiser Wilhelm II and the Hapsburgs; the Bolshevik murder of Russia's hapless Czar Nicholas II, known to his royal cousins as "poor Nicky." Another cousin, Queen Marie of Romania gamely predicted that wayward republics would "return again to Monarchy as a tired and weary wanderer returns to what he knows best."

The United States arrived as the first democratic power in world politics. "No covenant of cooperative peace that does not include the peoples of the New World can suffice to keep the future safe against war," asserted President Woodrow Wilson, whose international prominence affronted some who remembered how far to the rear Theodore Roosevelt had marched at King Edward VII's funeral in 1910. World Catholics still saw America as officially designated "mission territory," full of bumptious materialists as described by Pope Leo XIII in his 1899 warning against "Americanism." Leo condemned the theory of popular sovereignty, but as a progressive he grudgingly relaxed the

The rule of monarchs, strong and vigorous at the start of the century, was dying out even before World War I caused their cross-stitched lineages to fray. In May 1914, when Czar Nicholas II stood, small and alone, on the balcony of St. Petersburg's Winter Palace *(right)* to acknowledge to a huge crowd of his subjects Russia's declaration of war, his downfall had already been set in motion by internal discontent. But elsewhere, the passions of war and the accompanying pressures of nationalism reduced even the most solid monarchies to irrelevant or despised symbols.

IS
THIS ?
DEMOC

dogma that democracy was heresy against the doctrinal harmony of one God, one Pope, one King.

On the decisive strength of late-coming American doughboys, a bespattered, defensive old order accepted the egalitarian rhetoric in which President Wilson framed the settlements reached at Versailles. Demanding "a free, open-minded, and absolutely impartial adjustment of all colonial claims," Wilson called for "the interests of the populations concerned"—he stopped short of favoring the colonies' actual participation—to have "equal weight" with the ownership demands of such Allied powers as Japan, which acquired Germany's former territories in Asia. The balance of politics in free nations tilted from the governing classes toward popular control, as electorates soon tripled on average to include most adult males.

With masculine notions of glory widely discredited by mutual extermination, the United States extended the vote to women in 1920, just after England carefully granted the franchise to women over 30. (Finland, Norway, Australia, and New Zealand had already established female suffrage, while Switzerland resisted until 1971.) Fears and hopes of democracy spread alongside the rising reputation of the United States, although the hardship-decades ahead produced new republics—in Italy, Spain, Germany, and China—more spectacular in their failure than in their creation.

1990
1994

AT MID-CENTURY, LESS THAN A THIRD of the world lived in stable democracies (some of which retained a safety glue of royalty), but nearly all of them had proved battle-worthy through World War II. Victorious over Japan, General Douglas MacArthur "cut the emperor down to size" by dismissing 7,500 employees from the Imperial Household. He then forced Hirohito to repudiate ancient myths of his divinity and promulgated an American-style constitution. Over Hitler's death-bunker in Berlin, having cooperatively eliminated fascism as blood royalty's heir of destiny, the remaining contenders split Germany in their image—half democratic republic, half Soviet Communist state. Thus began a showdown siege that circled and squeezed the globe.

Both Cold War camps promised liberation and prosperity on the strength of ideology, but finding precious few informed Jeffersonians and Marxists at home (let alone in Saigon or Khartoum), they brandished more colorful banners: the bomb, the buck, and Coca-Cola versus the bomb, the guerrilla, and the Aswan Dam. Out of fear and temptation, each side demonized the other to justify its use of methods from the ancient regimes. Soviet dictator Stalin employed pogroms, show trials, garrisons, coups, and mass deportations. The American CIA, borrowing heavily from the colonial techniques of Her Majesty's Secret Service, clandestinely overthrew a popular Iranian government in 1953 to restore the friendly Shah of the Pahlevi dynasty.

Not everything could be concealed. Against the Western powers' inclination to excuse their ownership of the contested Third World as a stewardship in freedom, the Communist competition seconded cries of antidemocratic exploitation, forcing a new accounting. Beginning with Gandhi's India in 1947, a tide of self-government rolled down the African continent and off to Indonesia and beyond. By the early 1960s, descendants of African slaves turned the claims of freedom inward upon the United States in a vivid reminder that democrats must resist power's constant inclination toward tyrannical disregard. The freedom movement, seeking to create new bonds of citizenship through disciplined refusal to return hatred or violence, resonated far beyond the American conflict over voting rights.

Notably among its speakers, Martin Luther King traced democracy back through the political philosophy of the American revolution to a twin footing in the spiritual vision of the earliest Hebrew prophets ("Let justice roll down like waters..."). Like Lincoln at Gettysburg, King summoned from the heart of democracy an immense moral force, as glimpsed during history's severest tests of the American creed. A startling association of equal souls with equal votes reached below surface distinctions to challenge sturdy hierarchies, asking whether god and leader should be conceived as white, or as *he*.

In the United States and most other republics, the political center recoiled for a generation from troublesome adjustments across cultural dividing lines. Through the 1970s and 1980s,

Democracy presents a constant challenge to its practitioners, even in the world's putative democracies. In many parts of the American South, the right to vote—democracy's most basic expression—was denied to African-Americans, or at best required a complicated, nearly impenetrable registration process. Here, in 1960, a 65-year-old woman from Petersburg, Virginia, who has never before voted, takes part in a class on nonviolent picketing and how to register to vote offered by the Petersburg Improvement Association.

economic dislocations raised doubts about the march of progress, while the disheartening performance of ex-colonial republics such as Zaire and Lebanon dampened optimism in the Free World. Less noticed was the parallel loss of confidence inside the communist world, signaled by a fade-out of proclamations on the timetable for world revolution and the assured collapse of democracy (which Lenin called "the best possible political shell for capitalism"). Surly from the long grapple of the Cold War, the two sides menaced each other behind piles of doomsday weapons.

1990 1994

SKEPTICAL WESTERN LEADERS AT FIRST dismissed as "atmospherics" the late 1980s reform campaign pursued by Soviet leader Mikhail Gorbachev, but his hint of humbled authority shook loose internal yearnings stronger than the pose of institutional steel. As if by magnet, Gorbachev's 1989 trip to Beijing attracted a quarter-million demonstrators for democracy to Tiananmen Square in a shocking breech of totalitarian control. Four months later in Berlin, when the visiting Gorbachev refused to shore up the German Communist state with Soviet troops, the Berlin Wall melted away just ahead of satellite Communist regimes from Latvia to Bulgaria. By 1992, runaway history bowled over the Soviet Union itself. "Democracy is no substitute for law and order," growled the Soviet secret police commander, but his Thermidor coup sputtered impotently against the street noise of household democrats, which soon swept away Gorbachev himself as too timid an inspiration. Meanwhile, in South Africa, the snarling lion of apartheid lay down with the lamb of cross-racial democracy, and 27-year prisoner Nelson Mandela rose to elected presidency with the cooperation of his recent jailers.

The most sophisticated machineries of political intelligence failed to anticipate any of these democratic miracles, and neither sage nor dimwit dreamed of seeing them all flash into being peacefully, without sign of long-awaited Armageddon. Only in Beijing was the outpouring of nonviolent heroes martyred into temporary, world-famous retreat. From Prague to Pretoria, others who sang nonviolent hymns won trial leadership in a new order.

Yet celebrations in the older republics remained oddly muted in awe or apprehension. Anxieties unplugged from the Cold War still lurched about for substitute outlets. When democracy's mandate could no longer be reduced to a crusade against communism, its fuller promise fell heavily on deadened habit at home, untested conviction abroad. In a cruel early omen, irredentist wars in the territories near Sarajevo suggested the earliest stupidities of the bygone century rather than the first blessing of the millennium ahead. Elsewhere, the post-ideological world questioned the fabled linkage between democracy and capitalism. In Poland and other struggling republics, the cheers of the first free elections soon gave way to groans about still-empty shelves. In holdout China, conversely, Communist mandarins introduced free-market economic reforms but ruthlessly suppressed political freedom.

In previous epochs, plagues and crop disasters more than sufficed to keep hubris in check; modern societies must devise restraints of human design. Decrepit socialism highly recommends the streamlined honesty of open markets, but capitalists themselves seek to trim the hard flint of competitive drive in areas ranging from professional sports and fished-out seas to the allocation of medical care. Democracy requires an overarching self-discipline inherent in its core notion of self-government. Where autocrats insist on a childlike human nature in need of firm external guidance, democrats see the clear-headed good sense of the marginal voter.

Above the exacting demands of self-government, the most elusive ingredient of democratic vitality is a determined engagement of free citizens across cultural boundaries. The next century can render no more scathing verdict on democracy than to prove its excellence only where free of ethnic and religious conflict, which in a shrinking world is nowhere that matters. At the opposite extreme, the healing promise of democracy touches nothing less than the theological conundrum of evil, wherein genocidal hatreds boil. Somewhere between lie the prospects of South Africa, Bosnia, and Tiananmen Square II, in a new century when political lessons will be learned from the fates of democracies as of old from the procession of kings—some sordid, some sublime, many memorized under duress. □

On New Year's Eve 1989, photographer Richard Avedon, on assignment for the French magazine *Egoïste,* documented one of the century's most climactic events—the unification of East and West Berlin. Here, at the Brandenburg Gate, amid frantic celebrations and fireworks, a young Berliner's wary face registers the foreboding of an uncertain future.

"MARXISM-LENINISM IS ON THE RUBBISH HEAP OF HISTORY"—**Sign carried by protesters during the 1990 May Day parade in Red Square**

STORY OF THE YEAR

Cold War Ends, Gorbachev Totters

1 For five years, Soviet leader Mikhail Gorbachev had performed a breathtaking high-wire act, pushing forward visionary foreign policy and economic reforms, keeping change-resistant Party elites at bay, holding in check the Soviet Union's breakaway republics. Always on the tightrope with him was Foreign Minister Eduard Shevardnadze, cofounder of perestroika and Gorbachev's right-hand man. Until 1990, the partnership seemed invulnerable. Then, as crisis followed crisis, it dissolved. A visibly shaken Shevardnadze resigned in December.

It was Shevardnadze who in 1989 announced the reversal of decades of Soviet foreign policy. The nations of the Soviet bloc, he declared in a speech to the Supreme Soviet, had "absolute freedom" to choose their own governments. The Warsaw Pact was dead; the seeds for democracy were sown. By 1990, the Soviets had begun reducing their armed forces by 500,000 and withdrawing troops from Eastern Europe; these momentous developments helped persuade the Western allies of Gorbachev's sincerity. The threat of a Soviet invasion, Europe's 45-year nightmare, had dissipated into thin air. The NATO powers pronounced the Cold War over.

Eloquent and pragmatic, Shevardnadze was instrumental in securing international aid for the Soviet Union. It was badly needed: The economy was shrinking at a rapid clip, food was dangerously scarce. Coming on top of the Eastern European giveaway and Gorbachev's abandonment of Communist ideological orthodoxy, economic failure brought Party hard-liners to the brink of revolt. The fact that all 15 Soviet republics were pushing hard for independence further aggravated their discontent.

In January, Gorbachev sent some 11,000 troops into Azerbaijan to quell a separatist uprising. The crackdown illustrated a tragic irony that cut to the quick of Gorbachev's dilemma: To continue his reforms, he had to keep his job, yet the old guard would rather engineer his ouster than let the Soviet empire disintegrate entirely.

By year's end, the specter of a right-wing resurgence —and the sight of his friend caving in to it—had reduced Shevardnadze to despair. "The reformers have headed for the hills," he warned in his farewell. "Dictatorship is coming." Gorbachev now walked alone. ◂**1989.1** ▸**1991.3**

Reform-minded Shevardnadze's resignation left Gorbachev on his own.

ROMANIA

First Free Elections

2 Romanians needed no encouragement to get out the vote in 1990: They had not participated in free elections in 53 years. In the May balloting, they mobbed the polls, endorsing National Salvation Front candidate Ion Iliescu to lead Romania into the postcommunist era. Head of an interim government that took power immediately after the bloody downfall of Stalinist dictator Nicolae Ceauşescu in December 1989, Iliescu was a former Communist Party official who vowed to steer a course toward moderate reform.

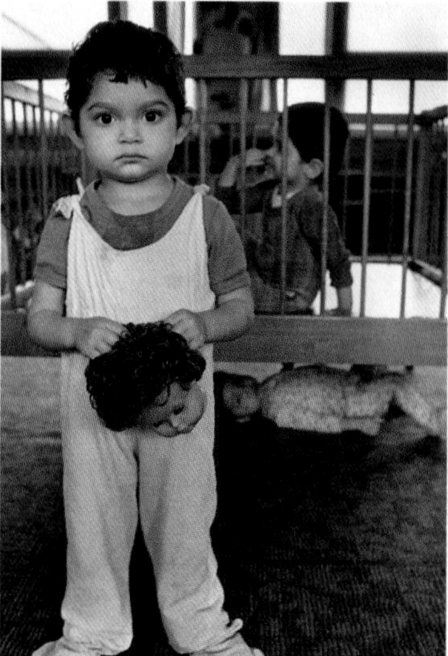

Romanian orphanages were filled with victims of Ceauşescu's policies.

Five months earlier, any reform at all had seemed impossible. For 24 years, even after Gorbachev's accession to Soviet leadership encouraged change, Ceauşescu and his second-in-command—his wife, Elena—had ruled Romania with unrelenting harshness. The Soviet news agency Tass (once a Stalinist mouthpiece itself) called Ceauşescu "one of the most odious dictators of the twentieth century." His 60,000-member secret-police force, the Securitate, sowed terror, freeing him to carry out his bizarre designs: "systematization," whereby he plowed medieval villages into the ground and built prisonlike housing blocks on the ruins; an austerity program that left Romanians cold and hungry as he hoarded fuel and food for export. When revolt erupted in December 1989, the Securitate killed thousands of demonstrators and bystanders. The regular army, however, defected to the people's side. The Ceauşescus fell within a week.

Convicted by a military tribunal of genocide, abuse of power, and economic crimes, the unrepentant couple was executed on Christmas Day. But even after that cathartic event—and Iliescu's election—Romanians' lives remained hard. One of the new president's first acts was to call out coal miners to suppress anti-Communist demonstrations with picks and shovels. (Six thousand Securitate members were later hired to staff a new secret-police force.) And though repression eventually ended, the nation's poverty deepened as economic reforms lagged. ◂**1989.1**

GERMANY

A Rush to Unify

3 "Hurtling toward reunification" was the media's phrase to describe the pace at which the two Germanys moved toward becoming one. The formal date was October 3, 1990, but unity was virtually a foregone conclusion from the moment the East German Communist regime began its collapse.

The obstacles were enormous: the exorbitant cost to West Germany of absorbing economically defunct East Germany; Soviet opposition to unified Germany's membership in NATO (a condition of reunification demanded by the Western powers); Europe's historically grounded fear of a reconstituted German Goliath. But West German chancellor Helmut Kohl was convinced that the moment had come, and he was determined to seize it. He would be the chancellor of reunification.

East German elections in March presented an early test, one Kohl passed with unexpected ease. Voting freely for the first time since before World War II, East Germans overwhelmingly endorsed a coalition party that supported Kohl's fast-track program. In July, reunification cleared another major hurdle —economic integration—when the 16.3 million Easterners, at Kohl's urging, swapped their weak currency for the powerful deutsche mark. To ease East Germany's passage into a competitive market economy, West Germany's wealthy government plowed tens of billions of marks into a social safety net.

Kohl's final stroke was his greatest: At a surprise July summit with Mikhail Gorbachev, he brokered a deal that let unified Germany join

ART & CULTURE: Books: ***Rabbit at Rest*** **(John Updike);** ***Middle Passage*** **(Charles Johnson);** ***My Son's Story*** **(Nadine Gordimer);** ***Vineland*** **(Thomas Pynchon);** ***Sexual Personae*** **(Camille Paglia);** ***Omeros*** **(Derek Walcott) ... Music: "Nothing Compares 2U" (Prince); "U Can't Touch This" (James, Miller, and Hammer);** ***Duplicates*** **(Mel Powell) ... Painting & Sculpture:** ***Manhattan Codice*** **(Miguel Angel Rios);**

"Obviously one isn't indestructible—quite."—**Margaret Thatcher, in 1988**

In the shadow of the Berlin Cathedral, two German children celebrate reunification.

NATO. A potential superpower showdown was avoided, eliminating the last significant roadblock. Kohl's reward: In December, he handily won in the new Germany's first elections. A fearsome gulf, born of 45 years of political, cultural, and economic estrangement, still divided the country. But to most Germans, the logistical nightmare of integration seemed a vast improvement over partition. **◂1989.1 ▸1993.6**

MEDICINE

Gene Therapy Debuts

4 Of all genetic diseases, ADA deficiency is one of the cruelest—a rare disorder resulting from a defect in the gene that instructs cells to produce adenosine deaminase, an enzyme that prevents the

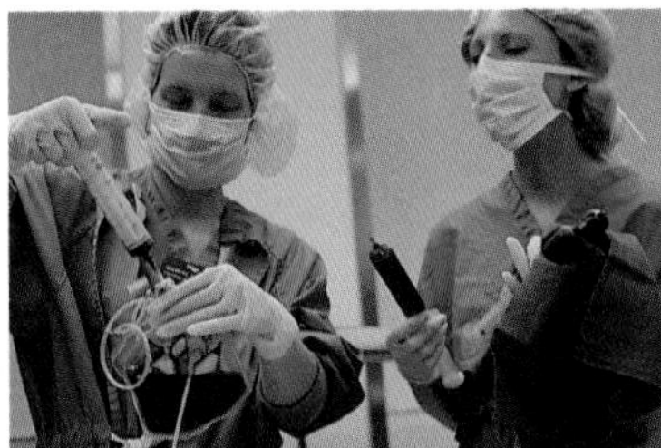

Blood is transferred into a travel bag on its way to a laboratory for genetic alteration.

buildup of toxins lethal to the immune system. Victims once had to spend their short lives in germ-free isolation or undergo dangerous bone-marrow transplants; in the 1980s, a drug treatment called PEG-ADA appeared, but the costly weekly injections did not always work. Then, in September 1990 came a breakthrough with far-reaching implications: A four-year-old girl suffering from ADA deficiency (and unresponsive to PEG-ADA) became the world's first recipient of gene therapy—that is, repairing or altering the body's cells by using any of the estimated 100,000 genes present in human DNA.

Drs. W. French Anderson, R. Michael Blaese, and Kenneth Culver, of the National Institutes of Health in Bethesda, Maryland, began by splicing an ADA gene from a healthy cell into a mouse-leukemia retrovirus whose own dangerous genes had been excised. They then extracted a billion or so mature T cells—immune-system cells that survive in the bloodstream for months—from the girl's blood and infected them with the genetically engineered retrovirus. The latter did what all retroviruses (such as the AIDS virus) do: It copied its genetic information into the host cells. Now containing the ADA gene, the T cells were infused back into the girl's veins.

Bimonthly infusions soon brought the patient a nearly normal immune system. (A *permanent* fix awaited the day when scientists figured out how to isolate large numbers of bone-marrow stem cells—the long-lived cells that spawn all other blood cells—and "infect" them with the ADA gene.) Meanwhile, gene therapy trials got under way for cancer, AIDS, cystic fibrosis, and other diseases in which new genetic information might bring healing. **◂1988.M**

GREAT BRITAIN

Exit Thatcher

5 When she stood down in November 1990, Margaret Thatcher had served longer than any other twentieth-century British prime minister. During eleven years in office, she'd changed her nation profoundly. A free-market fundamentalist, Thatcher launched a top-down counterrevolution against the socialistic institutions that she believed had enfeebled Britain. She privatized industries, gutted the welfare state and the trade unions. She defended the remnants of empire in the Falklands War. She resisted European Community moves toward a borderless continent. And she trampled those who stood in her way.

Thatcher's downfall began in March, when her government replaced property taxes with a "community charge" for local services. Popularly called the "poll tax," it imposed a stiff levy on every adult, with minor adjustments for the poor. (Vehement opponents branded it "a tax for being alive.") Supporters believed the tax encouraged municipal thrift because it made

The "tax for being alive" killed the Iron Lady's 11-year tenure as prime minister.

everyone equally vested in governmental spending. In fact, like any flat tax, it tended to favor the wealthy. Many Britons refused to pay; riots swept the country, and Thatcher's popularity plunged. Conservative colleagues whom she'd slighted in the past joined the Labour opposition in mobilizing for her ouster. And in November, after she tried unsuccessfully to block the EC's plan for a common currency, her rivals called for her resignation. After a power struggle, the Conservatives chose the young, affable chancellor of the Exchequer, John Major, as party chief and premier. (His government repealed the poll tax in 1991.)

Thatcher left a mixed legacy. Home ownership, shareholding, personal consumption, and industrial productivity had soared. But so had unemployment, underemployment, homelessness, indebtedness, and crime. Inflation was running at a hefty 10 percent. Britain, in short, was back in recession. **◂1981.1 ▸1993.8**

DEATHS

Pearl Bailey, U.S. singer.

Leonard Bernstein, U.S. composer and conductor.

Bruno Bettelheim, Austrian-U.S. psychologist.

Aaron Copland, U.S. composer.

Roald Dahl, U.K. writer.

Sammy Davis, Jr., U.S. entertainer.

Lawrence Durrell, U.K. writer.

Erté, Russian-French artist.

Greta Garbo, Swedish-U.S. actress.

Ava Gardner, U.S. actress.

Paulette Goddard, U.S. actress.

Rex Harrison, U.K. actor.

Jim Henson, U.S. puppeteer.

Robert Hofstadter, U.S. physicist.

Jill Ireland, U.K.-U.S. actress.

Clarence L. Johnson, U.S. engineer.

Bruno Kreisky, Austrian chancellor.

Le Duc Tho, Vietnamese political leader.

Germaine Lefebvre (Capucine), French actress.

Mary Martin, U.S. actress.

Alberto Moravia, Italian writer.

Lewis Mumford, U.S. writer.

Norman Parkinson, U.K. photographer.

Walker Percy, U.S. novelist.

Mohan Chandra Rajneesh, Indian religious leader.

B.F. Skinner, U.S. psychologist.

Sarah Vaughan, U.S. singer.

Patrick White, U.K.-Australian novelist.

Some Violets **(Julian Schnabel) ... Film: *Dances with Wolves* (Kevin Costner); *GoodFellas* (Martin Scorsese); *Pretty Woman* (Garry Marshall); *The Krays* (Peter Medak); *Hamlet* (Franco Zeffirelli); *Cyrano de Bergerac* (Jean-Paul Rappeneau) ... Theater: *Six Degrees of Separation* (John Guare); *Prelude to a Kiss* (Craig Lucas) ... TV: *In Living Color*; *Seinfeld*; *Northern Exposure*; *Twin Peaks*; *Beverly Hills 90210*.**

"She is an icon like the Virgin of Fátima. She doesn't have to talk; she can just lead the procession."—**A member of the National Opposition Union, on Violeta Barrios de Chamorro**

NEW IN 1990

FDA-approved Norplant (contraceptive implant).

Smoking banned on domestic airline flights.

Low-calorie fat substitute (Simplesse).

NC-17 film rating (U.S.).

McDonald's in Moscow.

IN THE UNITED STATES

▶SPOTTED OWL THREATENED—The Department of the Interior in June placed the spotted owl on the threatened species list. Environmentalists cheered, but the bird-saving decision fell afoul of the timber industry, which annually cut some five billion board

feet of timber from the federally managed forests of the Pacific Northwest—the owl's exclusive home. The timber lobby claimed that measures to save the owl's habitat, as mandated by the Endangered Species Act, would result in the loss of some 50,000 logging jobs. Outside analysts said the jobs figure was inflated and noted that preserving the owl meant saving old-growth forests. ◂1987.9

▶KEATING FIVE HEARINGS—The Senate Ethics Committee on November 15 opened hearings on the activities of the so-called Keating Five—a group of senators who'd interceded with federal banking regulators on behalf of Charles Keating, Jr., a corrupt savings and loan director who'd contributed heavily to their campaign funds. (Through mismanagement and fraudulent dealings, Keating and other S&L executives helped precipitate a late-1980s

Chamorro became Central America's first female president. Ortega *(right)* applauded.

NICARAGUA

Sandinistas Voted Out

6 In February 1990, barely eleven years after toppling dictator Anastasio Somoza Debayle, Nicaragua's Sandinistas held their second general election—and lost. Violeta Barrios de Chamorro won a 55 to 41 percent victory over Sandinista leader Daniel Ortega Saavedra. Discontent with the leftist regime's managerial fumbling and ideological crusades played a role, but the decisive factors were the endless U.S.-backed contra war and attendant economic prostration. The vote for Chamorro (candidate of the 14-party National Opposition Union coalition) was a vote for peace and normalcy.

Chamorro, 60, often seemed unclear about the finer points of her platform. She came to politics as the widow of Pedro Joaquin Chamorro, the activist newspaper publisher whose assassination by Somoza's thugs in 1978 triggered Nicaragua's Sandinista-led popular revolt. Upon taking power, the Sandinistas invited her to join their five-member civilian junta. Disenchanted with the regime's Marxist tendencies, she soon resigned, and the family newspaper, *La Prensa*, once again became the voice of the opposition. The Sandinistas sometimes shut the paper down; one of her sons, meanwhile, became editor of the Sandinista journal *Barricada*.

Ortega conceded his electoral defeat with unexpected grace. The obstinate U.S. government refused to release promised aid to Chamorro's government unless she purged Sandinista commanders from the army and police. (She fired the chief of police but refused to break her deal with the Sandinistas to keep Ortega's brother as army head.) Moreover, because the Sandinistas retained control of the military, the contra rebels refused to disarm. Democracy was alive and well in Nicaragua, but stability was still a long way off. **◂1987.2**

THE MIDDLE EAST

Desert Shield

7 The crisis that led to the first multinational war of the post–Cold War era began in August 1990, when Iraqi strongman Saddam Hussein—eager to establish regional hegemony and to recoup the costs of his recent war with Iran—invaded small, wealthy Kuwait. Hussein had spent months testing Western tolerance before striking, and had elicited only mild responses. He'd escalated his anti-American rhetoric, executed an Iranian-born British journalist, and threatened Israel with chemical weapons. Emboldened, he'd accused Kuwait of undercutting Iraq's petroleum revenues and stealing from a border oil field. And when Kuwait's concessions proved inadequate (and his veiled last-minute warnings to U.S. ambassador April Glaspie provoked only diplomatic flattery), Hussein sent in 100,000 troops.

Most of Kuwait's army fled, along with the emir, Sheikh Jabir al-Ahmad al-Sabah, and the Iraqis drove on to the Saudi border. They jailed or exiled potential troublemakers (thousands of foreigners, including several U.S. diplomats, were held hostage until December) and began looting the country. But to Hussein's surprise, the invasion drew wide condemnation. The Arab League voted 14 to five to demand withdrawal, and even the Soviets (Iraq's biggest arms suppliers) joined in a U.S.-led embargo. America's formerly pro-Hussein president, George Bush, favored an even more aggressive option: a military move to consolidate the "new world order."

Bush had often used that phrase to welcome the waning of the U.S.-Soviet power struggle and the emergence of the United States as the sole superpower. Now, answering Saudi Arabia's request for protection, he launched Operation Desert Shield. Some 500,000 U.S. troops gathered in the Saudi desert and the Persian Gulf; the forces backing them came not only from traditional U.S. allies, but also from Syria, a Soviet client state. Moscow offered diplomatic aid; its former satellites provided technical advisers. Within months, the defensive Desert Shield became the offensive Desert Storm. **◂1988.3 ▸1991.1**

MUSIC

A Trio of Tenors

8 For opera lovers worldwide, the highlight of the 1990 World Cup soccer finals in Rome was musical, not athletic. Before a crowd of 6,000—and a broadcast audience of 1.5 billion—conductor Zubin Mehta presided over a unique concert showcasing the era's dominant operatic tenors.

José Carreras, 43, had built a devoted following with his sweetness of timbre and purity of phrasing. A recent ordeal added poignancy to the Spaniard's performance: In 1988, he made a dramatic comeback beneath Barcelona's Arch of Triumph after having been laid up for a year with leukemia. Placido Domingo, 49, also born in Spain, had grown up in Mexico and spent much of his early career in Israel. Legendary for his portrayal of Otello, he was widely considered the finest lyric tenor of his genera-

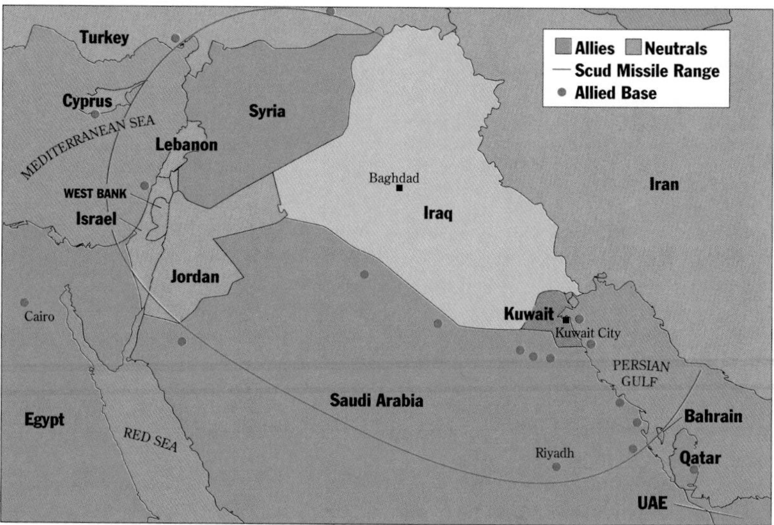

Desert Shield protected Saudi Arabia from Iraqi troops, but Saddam Hussein's Scud missiles—capable of launching chemical warheads—threatened much of the region.

SPORTS: Baseball: World Series, Cincinnati Reds defeat Oakland Athletics, 4–0 ... Football: Super Bowl, San Francisco 49ers defeat Denver Broncos, 55–10 ... Basketball: NBA, Detroit Pistons defeat Portland Trail Blazers, 4–1 ... Tennis: Martina Navratilova wins record 9th Wimbledon singles title ... Soccer: World Cup, West Germany defeats Argentina, 1–0.

"When I was growing up, there were 30 great tenors, not three. I don't know why things are now the way they are."
—Luciano Pavarotti

The three tenors and Mehta *(from left: Domingo, Carreras, Mehta, Pavarotti)* in Rome.

tion. Rounding out the trio was Italy's Luciano Pavarotti—at 54, the most famous opera star in the world. With his crystalline high C's, his charismatic ebullience, and his pop star's knack for multimedia exposure, Pavarotti was a latter-day Caruso, beloved on every continent.

Under a full moon, the trio sang a program of well-worn chestnuts in voices no longer in their prime. Yet their musicianship—and their showmanship—made the concert a smashing success. Its spin-offs were likewise hits: The video briefly nudged Madonna's out of the number-one slot in Britain; in the United States, the album hit number 43 on the pop charts—the highest spot attained by any classical record since the 1960s. Four years later, the trio of tenors reunited for a second crowd-pleasing concert, at Los Angeles's Dodger Stadium. ◄**1902.11**

WESTERN AFRICA

Liberia Explodes

9 Africa's oldest independent republic virtually ceased to exist in 1990. Founded in 1847 by freed American slaves, Liberia had been run by their descendants—who ruthlessly exploited the indigenous majority—until 1980, when Sergeant Samuel K. Doe led a military coup. Lavishly endowed with U.S. aid, Doe proved even more repressive and corrupt than his predecessors. But few could have guessed at the bloody anarchy to come when former junta member Charles Taylor (who'd earlier fled embezzlement charges) "invaded" Liberia in December 1989 with 150 Libyan-trained guerrillas.

Taylor's National Patriotic Front of Liberia (NPFL) initially targeted only soldiers and officials. But even though Taylor was an Americo-Liberian, Doe—a member of the minority Krahn people—saw him as an agent of the majority Gio and Mano. Doe sent his Krahn-dominated army to destroy Gio and Mano villages. Thousands of revenge-seekers joined the NPFL, which began massacring the Krahn and the supposedly pro-Krahn Mandingo. By August, a breakaway group led by Brigadier General Prince Y. Johnson (a Gio) had reached the capital, Monrovia, and Taylor's forces were closing in. Doe's besieged troops continued slaughtering civilians, including 600 who'd sought shelter in a church compound.

Repressive dictator Samuel K. Doe *(center)* was Liberia's first indigenous leader.

With refugees flooding neighboring countries and the UN refusing to act, the 16-member Economic Community of West African States decided to send a peacekeeping force to Liberia. But its soldiers came mostly from Nigeria, which backed Doe, so Taylor considered it a hostile army—and attacked. Then, when Doe went to visit the peacekeepers' headquarters in Monrovia, he was kidnapped, tortured, and killed by Johnson's troops.

Doe's forces retreated, burning everything in their path. The peacekeepers were reduced to defending themselves. Taylor controlled all Liberia except Monrovia by November; a cease-fire was declared. But starvation was spreading, and more fighting lay ahead. ►**1992.9**

ART

The Mapplethorpe Flap

10 The decade's biggest art controversy in the United States erupted in 1990, when "The Perfect Moment," a retrospective of photographs by Robert Mapplethorpe (who'd died of AIDS in 1989) was hung in Cincinnati's Contemporary Arts Center and the museum's director, Dennis Barrie, was indicted on charges of obscenity. Of the show's 175 photographs, five depicted homoerotic, sadomasochistic sex; two others showed children's genitals.

The contretemps coincided with a nationwide debate on censorship and public funding for the arts, spurred by North Carolina Senator Jesse Helms's crusade to deny federal grants to "obscene" artists. To Helms and his supporters, Mapplethorpe's slick, technically proficient, and undeniably graphic images were Exhibit A. In this climate of increasing conservatism, arts institutions were becoming jittery. (Ten months before the Cincinnati exhibit opened, a Washington, D.C., museum had canceled the very same Mapplethorpe retrospective.) Many observers expected a decision against Barrie in ultra-conservative Cincinnati, but the jury decided that Mapplethorpe's work had artistic value and voted to acquit. ◄**1986.10**

Mapplethorpe in a 1988 self portrait, 10 months before his death.

IN THE UNITED STATES

banking failure whose $500 billion cleanup cost was passed on to taxpayers.) The ethics committee found Senator Alan Cranston, Democrat of California, guilty of substantial misconduct. (He did not run for reelection.) The four other senators were mildly reprimanded.

►ROLE-REVERSED WESTERN—In his 1990 directorial debut, movie star Kevin Costner created a three-hour love letter to the Lakota Sioux nation. The popular and scenic (and highly romanticized) *Dances with Wolves* not only made the Indians the good guys, it revitalized the genre of the Western, comatose

since the '70s. The picture, which included subtitled Lakota-language dialogue, won seven Oscars, including Best Picture and Best Director.

►BLY'S GUYS—Prize-winning poet and budding mythologist Robert Bly in 1990 published *Iron John*, the primary text of the burgeoning "men's movement." In the mythic character Iron John, an impulsive but self disciplined forest dweller, Bly presented an alternative to macho, Hollywood-derived masculine idols. The trick to male psychic well-being, Bly suggested, was finding the primitive, hairy man within. Woodsy seminars, featuring campfires and ritualistic drumming, began to attract would-be Iron Johns.

►McMARTIN SCHOOL CLEARED—The longest criminal trial in U.S. history ended in January, when a California jury found preschool director Peggy McMartin Buckey and her adult son Raymond Buckey not guilty on 52 counts of child abuse and molestation. The pair had been arrested in 1983 after the mother of a student at the school claimed her child had been sexually abused by Raymond. He spent five years in jail before being released on bail; his mother was incarcerated for two years. The state spent $15 million on the 30-month trial.

POLITICS & BUSINESS: GNP: $5,567.8 billion ... Americans with Disabilities Act grants protection for workers with physical and mental disabilities and AIDS, and for substance abusers ... Federal Reserve Board authorizes J.P. Morgan & Co. to underwrite stocks (power restored after 1933 suspension) ... Clean Air Act passed.

"I have been immunized against fear."—Jean-Bertrand Aristide

AROUND THE WORLD

▶**SHAMIR'S COALITION**—Yitzhak Shamir, leader of Israel's conservative Likud Party, in 1990 formed a coalition government with several ultra-rightist parties. Shamir, who'd fought with the Israeli Freedom Fighters to carve Israel out of Palestine in the early 1940s and later became a Mossad operative, had served as prime minister in two Likud–Labor coalition governments. A hardliner whose goal was "the consolidation of the Jewish presence in all parts of the land," Shamir held power until 1992, when his government lost to Labor in general elections. ▶1993.1

▶**NOBEL FOR PAZ**—Mexican writer Octavio Paz, lyrical poet, elegant prose stylist, philosopher, and diplomat, won the Nobel Prize for literature in 1990. One of the most influential of modern Latin American belletrists, Paz over the course of a wide-ranging career incorporated the lessons of the world's religions and the century's dominant philosophical

theories into works like *Blanco* (1967), a volume of poetry, and *The Labyrinth of Solitude* (1950), a probing study of Mexican history, society, and character. ◀1944.15

▶**OUSTER IN LEBANON**—In October, Syrian troops routed the Christian forces of Lebanese army commander Michel Aoun in east Lebanon. As head of a Lebanese military government, Aoun had one year earlier rejected a constitution that would have given Lebanese Muslims equal representation in a new Lebanese parliament. Later, he refused to recognize the election of Elias Hrawi as president and continued his "war of liberation" against Syria, whose forces had occupied Lebanon almost since the beginning of its 15-year civil war. After Aoun's ouster, Syrian and Israeli forces remained, but by 1992, Lebanon was sufficiently stabilized to hold general elections (boycotted by many Christians), in which Rafia al-Hariri became premier. ◀1989.6

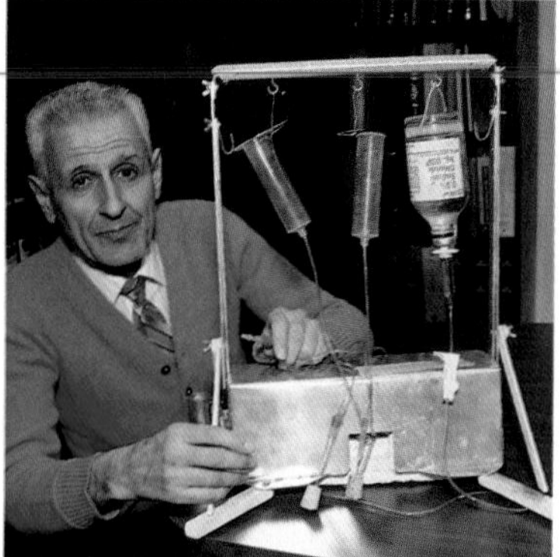

Kevorkian and his IV-drip "suicide machine."

MEDICINE

"Dr. Death"

11 Stricken by Alzheimer's disease, 54-year-old Janet Adkins killed herself in June 1990—assisted by Dr. Jack Kevorkian. The first of 20 terminally or chronically ill patients the retired Detroit pathologist would help to die over the next three years, Adkins pushed the red button on Kevorkian's homemade "suicide machine," releasing a painkiller, then lethal potassium chloride into her veins. Her heart stopped five minutes later.

By assisting the dying with their exit, Kevorkian violated a central vow of the Hippocratic oath, the credo of Western physicians for 2,000 years: "I will give no deadly medicine to anyone if asked nor suggest any such counsel." Kevorkian had his own code: "I will help a suffering patient ... when the patient's condition warrants it, despite anything else." Kevorkian had become a euthanasia advocate after a visit to the Netherlands, one of the first countries (after Nazi Germany) where the practice was widely accepted. U.S. law prohibited mercy killing, but Kevorkian's crusade struck a nerve. An aging population, coupled with the ability of technology to sustain even brain-dead patients, had revived ancient ethical debate about the "right to die."

Ostracized by his colleagues, under constant attack from prosecutors and state legislators, "Dr. Death" became a bizarre celebrity. His asceticism, messianism ("I am not immoral—society is"), and macabre obsessions added to his notoriety. As a medical student, he'd photographed the eyes of terminal patients, trying to pinpoint the moment of death. An amateur artist, he'd painted allegorical depictions of nausea and genocide—the latter in human blood. ◀**1976.M**

SCIENCE

Hubble Trouble

12 After four decades on the drawing board, the Hubble space telescope finally went into orbit 370 miles above the earth in 1990. The telescope (named for the American astronomer Edwin Hubble) was NASA's pride and joy—a $1.5 million mechanical eye designed to probe the dark and distant reaches of the universe. Space-agency officials called it the greatest advance in astronomy since Galileo. But it turned out to be an expensive optical fiasco.

The Hubble's 94-inch primary mirror had been ground to the wrong curvature, leaving the instrument's outside edge seven hundred-thousandths of an inch too flat. That infinitesimal but devastating error resulted in the transmission of blurred images. The flawed mirror proved to be only one of a plethora of defects: By 1993, three of the Hubble's navigational gyroscopes had failed, and its solar-panel supports shook so violently when the temperature changed that they threatened to destroy the whole mechanism.

Remarkably, the telescope still managed to gather new information about the size and shape of the universe—a fact that influenced NASA's decision to send up a repair crew on the shuttle *Discovery*. In December 1993, seven astronauts participated in a daring mission to salvage both the Hubble and NASA's tattered reputation (which had taken another hit over the summer when the $900 million Mars *Observer* was lost in space). In five days, the outer-space mechanics made an unprecedented five space walks. The much-maligned Hubble was as good as new, although a coming generation of land-based telescopes would offer more power at a fraction of the cost. ◀**1986.2**

The Hubble telescope, soaring above the earth, is gripped by a shuttle "manipulator."

THE CARIBBEAN

Haiti's Fling with Freedom

13 In December 1990, four chaotic years after the fall of dictator Jean-Claude Duvalier, a leftist priest became president of Haiti.

Since Duvalier's ouster, Haitians had voted once before: In 1988, General Henri Namphy's junta arranged the election of a civilian candidate but overthrew him six months later. Namphy himself was toppled by Lieutenant General Prosper Avril, whose troops joined former Tonton Macoutes in an orgy of banditry and murder. Rioting and U.S. pressure forced Avril to resign in January 1990; eleven months later, when interim president Ertha Pascal-Trouillot held Haiti's first truly free election, Father Jean-Bertrand Aristide *(above)* won by a landslide.

Aristide, an eloquent exponent of liberation theology, had developed a fervent following among the nation's impoverished masses. But his radicalism irked the Catholic hierarchy in Haiti (which expelled him from his order) as well as the oligarchy. Survivor of massacres and assassination attempts, he was nicknamed "Msieu Mirak"—Creole for Mr. Miracle.

But miracles abandoned Aristide soon after his inauguration. Despite his party's failure to win a majority in the National Assembly, he named inexperienced friends to his cabinet. Backed by mobs that "necklaced" accused oppressors with burning tires, he refused to consult the Assembly on other appointments. He angered the army by creating his own Swiss-trained security force. High tariffs and talk of collectivized farming alienated business.

In August 1991, Aristide's supporters surrounded the Assembly building to prevent a no-confidence vote. Just weeks later, while he was away addressing the UN, the army disbanded his private troops. Back in Haiti, Aristide called for a popular uprising. But Brigadier General Raoul Cédras seized power, forcing him to flee. Another reign of terror ensued. Thousands of Haitians followed Aristide to America in rickety boats; those who survived were impounded in refugee camps. Most were eventually sent back to fend for themselves. ◀**1986.4** ▶**1994.10**

NOBEL PRIZES: Peace: Mikhail S. Gorbachev (U.S.S.R.; perestroika and glasnost) ... Literature: Octavio Paz (Mexican; poet and essayist) ... Chemistry: Elias Corey (U.S.; organic synthesis) ... Medicine: J.E. Murray and E.D. Thomas (U.S.; transplants) ... Physics: R. Taylor, J. Friedman, and H. Kendall (Canadian, U.S., U.S.; confirmation of quarks) ... Economics: H. Markowitz, W. Sharpe, and M. Miller (U.S.).

A VOICE FROM 1990

Toward a New South Africa

From a speech by Nelson Mandela in Cape Town, South Africa, February 11, 1990

After enduring nearly three decades in South African prisons, Nelson Mandela, international symbol of South African blacks' struggle against apartheid, stood triumphantly on the balcony of Cape Town City Hall on February 11, 1990, and addressed his expectant nation. Dignified, gracious, and unbowed by his imprisonment, which had ended only that morning, the 71-year-old once and future leader of the African National Congress fittingly opened his electrifying speech in Xhosa, a major black South African language. "Amandla! Amandla! i-Afrika, mayibuye!" *Mandela said. ("Power! Power! Africa, it is ours!") He proceeded to praise the heroes of the anti-apartheid movement, to urge continued struggle—and to commend the man who had freed him, white president F.W. de Klerk. Mandela's liberation was the most momentous action de Klerk had yet undertaken in his effort to reform South Africa—a process that culminated in 1994 with Mandela's election as the nation's president.* **◂1989.3 ▸1994.1**

Amandla! Amandla! i-Afrika, mayibuye!

My friends, comrades and fellow South Africans, I greet you all in the name of peace, democracy, and freedom for all. I stand here before you not as a prophet but as a humble servant of you, the people.

Your tireless and heroic sacrifices have made it possible for me to be here today. I therefore place the remaining years of my life in your hands....

Today the majority of South Africans, black and white, recognize that apartheid has no future. It has to be ended by our own decisive mass actions in order to build peace and security. The mass campaigns of defiance and other actions of our organizations and people can only culminate in the establishment of democracy.

The apartheid destruction on our subcontinent is incalculable. The fabric of family life of millions of my people has been shattered. Millions are homeless and unemployed.

Nelson Mandela, depicted in a 1994 illustration by Anita Kunz, as a wise, weary shepherd tending his flock of black and white sheep.

Our economy—our economy lies in ruins, and our people are embroiled in political strife. Our resort to the armed struggle in 1960 with the formation of the military wing of the ANC, Umkonto We Sizwe, was a purely defensive action against the violence of apartheid.

The factors which necessitated the armed struggle still exist today. We have no option but to continue. We express the hope that a climate conducive to a negotiated settlement would be created soon so that there may no longer be the need for armed struggle.

I am a loyal and disciplined member of the African National Congress. I am therefore in full agreement with all of its objectives, strategies, and tactics.

The need to unite the people of our country is as important a task now as it always has been. No individual leader is able to take all these enormous tasks on his own. It is our task as leaders to place our views before our organization and to allow the democratic structures to decide on the way forward....

Negotiations on the dismantling of apartheid will have to address the overwhelming demand of our people for a democratic, nonracial and unitary South Africa. There must be an end to white monopoly on political power....

Our struggle has reached a decisive moment. We call on our people to seize this moment so that the process toward democracy is rapid and uninterrupted. We have waited too long for our freedom. We can no longer wait. Now is the time to intensify the struggle on all fronts.

To relax our efforts now would be a mistake which generations to come will not be able to forgive. The sight of freedom looming on the horizon should encourage us to redouble our efforts. It is only through disciplined mass action that our victory can be assured.

We call on our white compatriots to join us in the shaping of a new South Africa. The freedom movement is the political home for you, too. We call on the international community to continue the campaign to isolate the apartheid regime.

To lift sanctions now would be to run the risk of aborting the process toward the complete eradication of apartheid. Our march to freedom is irreversible. We must not allow fear to stand in our way.

Universal suffrage on a common voters' roll in a united democratic and nonracial South Africa is the only way to peace and racial harmony.

In conclusion, I wish to go to my own words during my trial in 1964. They are as true today as they were then. I wrote: "I have fought against white domination, and I have fought against black domination. I have cherished the idea of a democratic and free society in which all persons live together in harmony and with equal opportunities."

It is an ideal which I hope to live for and to achieve. But if needs be, it is an ideal for which I am prepared to die.

[The following portion was delivered in Xhosa.]

My friends, I have no words of eloquence to offer today except to say that the remaining days of my life are in your hands.

[He continued in English.] I hope you will disperse with discipline. And not a single one of you should do anything which will make other people to say that we can't control our own people.

"We're coming home now proud, confident, heads high.... We are Americans."—**President George Bush**

STORY OF THE YEAR

Gulf War II: Desert Storm

1 On January 16, 1991—barely 30 months after the eight-year Gulf War between Iran and Iraq ended and six months after Iraq invaded Kuwait—full-scale war erupted again along the Persian Gulf. The previous November, the United Nations had authorized military action if Iraqi troops did not leave Kuwait by January 15. A host of mediators (representing the UN, the United States, the Soviet Union, France, and even the pro-Iraqi PLO) had negotiated in vain with dictator Saddam Hussein. And though opponents of force argued that trade sanctions needed more time to work, U.S. commanders—leading an international anti-Iraqi coalition—launched Operation Desert Storm right on schedule.

As oil wells burn, an Iraqi casualty and a disabled tank lie abandoned in Kuwait.

The first onslaught came from the air, as coalition cruise missiles, "smart" bombs, and other high-tech ordnance pounded Iraq's infrastructure and its troops in the field. (Badly outgunned, most Iraqi pilots fled to Iran, which, despite a recent warming in relations, impounded their aircraft.) Hussein retaliated by pumping oil into the gulf and, eventually, setting hundreds of Kuwaiti oil wells ablaze. His tanks tried invading Saudi Arabia but were repulsed. Iraq directed sporadic volleys of Soviet-made Scud missiles against Israel and Saudi Arabia—but Hussein's longtime threat to use poison-gas warheads never materialized. To protect Israel (and to spare Arab coalition members the embarrassment of fighting alongside the Zionist state), Washington deployed American-crewed Patriot antiballistic missile batteries around the country.

By late February much of Iraq lay in ruins. Then came the attack on the Iraqi forces in Kuwait by coalition ground forces, under a strategy devised by U.S. general Norman Schwarzkopf; Iraqi soldiers surrendered in droves. Retreating troops were slaughtered. On February 27, after 100 hours of fighting, Kuwait had been liberated and much of southern Iraq was under allied occupation. U.S. president George Bush declared a cease-fire. Desert Storm's basic objectives had been met.

Some 200,000 Iraqis were dead, including hundreds of civilians. (The allied tally was 148.) Iraqi Kurds and Shiites, egged on by President Bush, were in revolt. Still, Hussein remained in power—and his surviving forces crushed the uprisings, driving nearly two million Kurds into Turkish and Iranian refugee camps. Meanwhile, Kuwait was an environmental disaster area and its resident Palestinians, accused of aiding Iraq, faced persecution and expulsion. The second Gulf War had left the region as troubled as the first. **◂1990.7 ▸1992.M**

YUGOSLAVIA

Things Fall Apart

2 Stitched together from six Balkan republics after World War I, Yugoslavia made an unlikely nation. Communism held it fast for 45 years, but when the system collapsed, ethnic animosities ate through the country's social fabric. In 1991, the year after the Communist Party (long the most liberal of its kind) renounced its monopoly on power, Yugoslavia fell apart—once again bathing southeastern Europe, the Great War's crucible, in blood.

Communal strife in the ethnic Albanian province of Kosovo, part of Serbia (Yugoslavia's largest republic), had been prophetic. In 1989, Kosovo's largely Muslim population rioted against Serb domination, and Serbia sent in troops to quell the unrest. Shooting broke out again in 1990, as communism tottered.

That year, Macedonia, Slovenia (Yugoslavia's richest republic), and Croatia (Serbia's historic rival) elected non-communist governments. In June 1991, after Serbian president Slobodan Miloševic—a militant Serb nationalist as well as a die-hard communist—blocked Croatian leader Stipe Mesic from assuming Yugoslavia's collective presidency, Croatia and Slovenia seceded. The Yugoslav army, dominated by Serbs, moved into both republics. Federal troops left Slovenia in July; in Croatia, however, fighting—and "ethnic cleansing," the murder or expulsion of Croat civilians from Serb-held lands—continued until January 1992, when a cease-fire monitored by 14,000 UN peacekeepers took hold. By then, 25,000 people were dead, and federal forces and Serb militias had captured 30 percent of Croatia. The old nationalist dream of a "greater Serbia," incorporating parts of other republics where Serbs were numerous, was becoming a reality.

Ancient ethnic hatreds boiled over in Yugoslavia's republics.

Macedonia's declaration of independence in September 1991 provoked no violence (though neighboring Greece—which had its own region called Macedonia—delayed international recognition, insisting the new country find another name). But in April 1992, after the republic of Bosnia and Hercegovina seceded as well (leaving only Serbia and tiny Montenegro in the Yugoslav fold), the Serbs attacked with unprecedented ferocity. **◂1948.6 ▸1992.1**

THE SOVIET UNION

Baltics Gain Independence

3 The limits of Soviet president Mikhail Gorbachev's liberal policies were put to the test in Lithuania in January 1991. A year after the tiny Baltic republic declared its independence from the Soviet Union, Red Army troops moved in to quash the separatist movement. Arriving in the dead of night, tanks steamrolled into Vilnius, the capital. An attack on the city's main TV station, a nationalist hotbed, claimed 14 civilian victims.

In the West, the invasion drew comparisons to Hungary in 1956, Czechoslovakia in 1968, and other instances of Soviet reprisal against free-thinking satellites. Gorbachev cited a different parallel. Like Abraham Lincoln, who waged war against the secessionist Confederate states to maintain the American republic, the Soviet president vowed to save the Union. While the loss of life was lamentable, Gorbachev said, he was simply "enforcing the constitution." In fact, the embattled premier had little choice: His efforts to reform the Soviet Union depended on the support of the military, and the military was not about to remain loyal if the Soviet empire began disintegrating in his hands. As it turned out, the attack on Lithuania was the empire's last gasp.

Like Estonia and Latvia, the other Baltic states, Lithuania had enjoyed brief and troubled independence after World War I. The Soviets annexed all three states in 1940. Occupied by Germany a year later, the republics (in 1991 Lithuania, the most populous, had as many inhabitants as Connecticut) fought alongside the Nazis during World War II.

ART & CULTURE: Books: ***Immortality*** **(Milan Kundera);** ***Saint Maybe*** **(Anne Tyler);** ***Brotherly Love*** **(Pete Dexter);** ***The Firm*** **(John Grisham);** ***Backlash: The Undeclared War Against American Women*** **(Susan Faludi) ... Music: "Tears in Heaven" (Clapton and Jennings);** ***Nick of Time*** **(Bonnie Raitt, LP);** ***Automatic for the People*** **(R.E.M., LP);** ***Ghosts of Versailles*** **(John Corigliano);** ***The Death of Klinghoffer*** **(John Adams) ...**

"No matter what misfortunes may still be in store for it, our Republic of Soviets is invincible."—**V.I. Lenin, in 1918**

Soviet internal passports, impaled on a fence by Lithuanian nationalists.

Stalin afterward reincorporated them into the Soviet Union.

Throughout the spring and summer of 1991, the Soviets struggled mightily to keep the restless Baltics in check. The republics would not be denied, however; resistance stiffened. Then, after a hard-line August coup against Gorbachev failed, Soviet authority collapsed. Latvia and Estonia joined Lithuania in declaring independence. The Kremlin conceded in September, and the world welcomed its three newest nations. **◂1990.1 ▸1991.5**

ALBANIA

The Great Exodus

4 As economic conditions worsened in long-isolated, underdeveloped Albania during the summer of 1991, tens of thousands of refugees streamed across the Adriatic Sea to Italy. By August, some 40,000 bedraggled people had struggled ashore at the seaports of Bari and Brindisi, where the Italian government met them with harsh policies designed to discourage future sanctuary-seekers. After penning the refugees in dismal dockside camps, the government began flying them back to Tiranë, the impoverished Albanian capital. Even so, 20,000 Albanians managed to stay in Italy, while thousands more fled overland into Greece.

The exodus had begun in 1990 after the democratic revolutions sweeping other former Communist nations bypassed the Albania of autocrat Ramiz Alia (the handpicked successor of 40-year Stalinist dictator Enver Hoxha). Frustrated Albanians started crashing foreign embassy compounds. Cut off from foreign aid and embarrassed by the wholesale flight of his people, Alia started implementing reforms by the end of the year. He established diplomatic ties with the United States, lifted travel restrictions, and allowed some free-market initiatives.

The economy continued to slide, however, and flight peaked after Alia agreed to share power with a coalition government in March 1991. Even after 1992 elections put professed democrat Sali Berisha in charge, emigration still seemed the best option to many: With unemployment running above 50 percent, a pound of meat costing three days' pay, and the infant mortality rate reaching a staggering 30 per 1,000, democracy was no panacea. **◂1985.7**

THE SOVIET UNION

The End Arrives

5 As the Soviet Union began, so it ended: with a coup. In August 1991, 74 years after V.I. Lenin and his faction of peculiarly ruthless dreamers overthrew the provisional government of Aleksandr Kerensky, conservative apparatchiks attempted to oust President Mikhail Gorbachev. Their goal: to reassert Communist Party supremacy and preserve the union from fragmentation. This time, the putsch failed. Led by firebrand Boris Yeltsin, president of the Russian republic, tens of thousands of Muscovites answered democracy's call. They barricaded the Russian parliament, and rebel army units could not bring themselves to fire on them. The bumbling plotters, and with them the Soviet Union, were finished.

Among the coup leaders were top Party officials that Gorbachev had tried in vain to neutralize. They presented their power play as an attempt to bring in fresh leadership capable of halting the country's slide into poverty. Their real reasons were less honorable. Gorbachev had just

Russian president and resistance leader Yeltsin celebrates the coup's failure.

signed the START treaty, which called for the Soviets to cut nuclear weapons by 25 percent, while requiring only a 15 percent reduction in U.S. arms—to hard-liners, an unbearable humiliation. And Gorbachev was about to sign a "union treaty" granting an unprecedented degree of sovereignty to all 15 Soviet republics. Determined to bar legislation that would eviscerate their authority, members of the old guard rose up. But they were unprepared for the heroic public defiance their machinations inspired. Just 80 hours after putschists detained Gorbachev at his Crimean dacha, the shaken leader returned to Moscow.

It was an alien city Gorbachev reentered. Busts of Lenin lay shattered in the streets; outside KGB headquarters jubilant demonstrators had toppled the massive statue of secret-police founder Felix Dzerzhinsky. And though Gorbachev still held office, real power had shifted to Yeltsin. Prodded by him, Gorbachev dissolved the discredited Communist Party. As for the republics, he cut them loose. In December, Gorbachev resigned as leader of a country that no longer existed. **◂1990.1 ▸1992.2**

Albanian refugees arrive in Italy aboard an overcrowded ship.

DEATHS

Berenice Abbot, U.S. photographer.

Carl Anderson, U.S. physicist.

Claudio Arrau, Chilean musician.

Lee Atwater, U.S. political adviser.

Frank Capra, Italian-U.S. filmmaker.

Colleen Dewhurst, Canadian-U.S. actress.

Margot Fonteyn, U.K. ballet dancer.

Redd Foxx, U.S. comedian.

Theodor Seuss Geisel (Dr. Seuss), U.S. writer.

Stan Getz, U.S. musician.

Martha Graham, U.S. choreographer and dancer.

Graham Greene, U.K. writer.

Soichiro Honda, Japanese auto manufacturer.

Jerzy Kosinski, Polish-U.S. writer.

Ernst Křenek, Austrian-U.S. composer.

Edwin Land, U.S. inventor and physicist.

Michael Landon, U.S. actor.

David Lean, U.K. filmmaker.

Fred MacMurray, U.S. actor.

Robert Maxwell, Czech-U.K. publisher.

Yves Montand, Italian-French singer and actor.

Robert Motherwell, U.S. painter.

Olaf V, Norwegian king.

Joseph Papp, U.S. theater producer.

Sylvia Porter, U.S. writer.

Tony Richardson, U.K. theater director and filmmaker.

Isaac Bashevis Singer, Polish-U.S. writer.

Rufino Tamayo, Mexican painter.

Painting & Sculpture: ***Dutch Masters*** **(Larry Rivers);** ***Umbrellas*** **(Christo) ... Film:** ***The Silence of the Lambs*** **(Jonathan Demme);** ***Thelma & Louise*** **(Ridley Scott);** ***Europa, Europa*** **(Agnieszka Holland);** ***Paris is Burning*** **(Jennie Livingston) ... Theater:** ***Lost in Yonkers*** **(Neil Simon);** ***The Substance of Fire*** **(Jon Robin Baitz);** ***The Will Rogers Follies*** **(Coleman, Comden, and Green) ... TV:** ***E! Entertainment Television*** **debuts.**

"This is disestablishment by stealth. The establishment is now paper-thin."—**The Reverend David Streater of the evangelical Church Society, on the decision to ordain women in the Anglican church**

NEW IN 1991

FDA approval of ddI (treatment for AIDS).

Lifting of U.S. economic sanctions on South Africa.

End to 21-year boycott of South Africa by International Olympic Committee.

Address to U.S. Congress by a British monarch (Queen Elizabeth II, May 16, 1991).

Exhumation of a U.S. president (Zachary Taylor, to determine whether the cause of his 1850 death was arsenic poisoning rather than acute gastrointestinal illness; no trace of arsenic was found).

IN THE UNITED STATES

▶DESERT TERRARIUM—An elaborate, quasi-scientific experiment got under way in October, when a team of four men and four women began a two-year stay in a giant, hermetically sealed steel and glass dome in the Arizona desert. The three-acre enclosure,

called Biosphere II (Biosphere I was the earth), was outfitted with several miniature ecosystems—rain forest, savanna, ocean—and 3,800 plant and animal species. The Biospherians expected to be self-sufficient (though a 5.2-megawatt power plant kept things humming) and hoped to gain information useful for colonizing Mars. The $150 million private project (funded by Texas oil billionaire Edward Bass) lost much credibility after a series of crop failures and a 1992 incident in which fresh air was pumped into the oxygen-depleted dome. The residents emerged in 1993.

▶MAGIC HIV-POSITIVE—Affable, idolized basketball star Earvin "Magic" Johnson retired

FILM

Who Killed JFK?

6 According to a 1991 poll, 56 percent of Americans rejected the U.S. government's official explanation of the assassination of President John F. Kennedy in Dallas on November 22, 1963. Among the skeptics was director Oliver Stone. His *JFK*, released in December, is a hyperkinetic, three-hour assault on the Warren Commission Report of 1964, which concluded that Lee Harvey Oswald had acted alone in shooting the president. The film rekindled debate about who *really* killed the president and forced the government to shed light on one of the century's darkest whodunits.

In the years since the Warren report, conspiracy theorists had published hundreds of books and thousands of articles disputing the lone-gunman explanation and claiming involvement by the Mafia, the CIA, Fidel Castro, or the Soviet Union (singly or in combination). Stone's contribution to the genre seemingly embraces all those possibilities. *JFK* tells the story of former New Orleans district attorney Jim Garrison (played by Kevin Costner), who unsuccessfully prosecuted a local businessman as an assassination conspirator. With Garrison's probe as a starting point, Stone blends documented fact, dramatized speculation, Hollywood storytelling, and a dose of liberal paranoia to argue that Kennedy was the victim of a military-industrial complex that feared he planned to end U.S. involvement in Southeast Asia.

A horde of politicians and pundits assailed Stone's honesty and judgment. Jack Valenti, the head of the Motion Picture Association and a former aide to President Johnson (whom Stone implicates in the cover-up), compared *JFK* to the Nazi propaganda film *Triumph of the Will*. But Stone stood by his sources and demanded that the government release sealed records and evidence. Special Washington screenings were arranged for legislators. And over the next two years, Congress, the FBI, and the CIA freed thousands of the documents in question. None incontrovertibly discredits the Warren Commission Report. But the most sensitive material wasn't released, on national security grounds—and the doubters continued to doubt. ◂**1978.M**

RELIGION

New Blood for Anglicans

7 To the 70 million members of the worldwide Anglican Communion, the enthronement of a new archbishop of Canterbury in April 1991 meant fresh hope for a beleaguered denomination. As chief prelate of the Church of England (the communion's mother church and Britain's state religion), the archbishop was spiritual leader of Anglicans and Episcopalians everywhere. But the English church was torn by struggles among liberals, Anglo-Catholics (who stressed Anglicanism's Roman Catholic elements), and evangelicals (who touted conservative Protestant values); while 60 percent of the population claimed membership, only 2.3 percent regularly attended services.

Chosen by Margaret Thatcher (herself a Methodist), the successor to outgoing archbishop Robert Runcie—an indecisive, liberal-leaning Anglo-Catholic—was the Reverend George Carey, bishop of Bath and Wells. The antithesis of Runcie, Carey was a working-class evangelical and a vigorous defender of orthodox liturgy and "traditional" morality. Like Thatcher, he was as much an iconoclast as a conservative: He likened the church's plight to that of "an elderly lady who mutters away to herself in a corner, ignored most of the time."

Yet Carey promoted one liberal cause even more enthusiastically than Runcie had: the ordination of women. Several branches of Anglicanism had already ordained female

A female priest imparts her blessing in the Anglican laying-on-of-the-hands rite.

priests, but the Church of England, at the insistence of thousands of clerics, refused. Days before becoming archbishop, Carey provoked a controversy by declaring that those clerics were committing "heresy." He quickly modified the term to "theological error"—one the Church's governing body, the General Synod, voted to correct in 1992. The first women took to the C of E's pulpits two years later. ◂**1974.M**

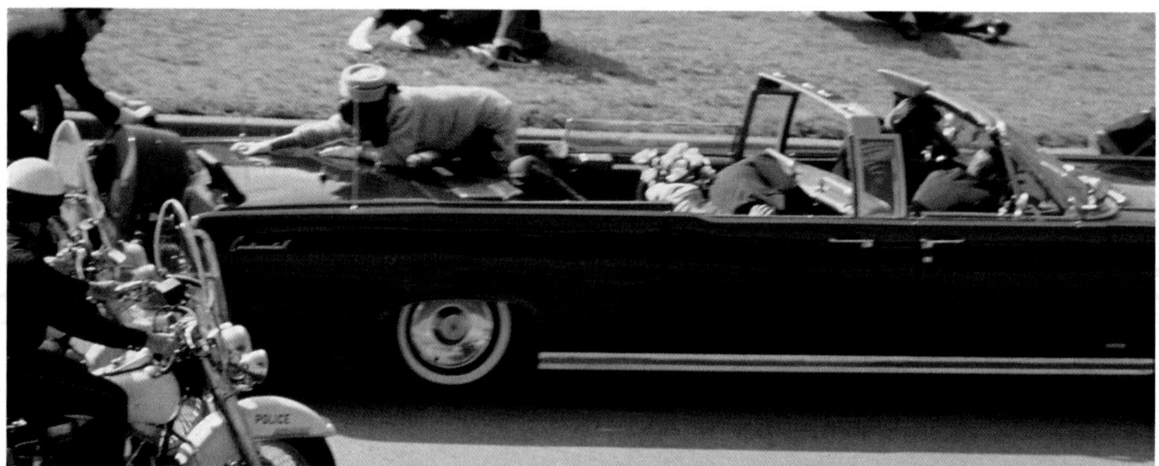

Stone re-created scenes from the Zapruder film (the only footage of Kennedy's assassination) to give *JFK* a documentary veneer.

SPORTS: Baseball: World Series, Minnesota Twins defeat Atlanta Braves, 4–3 ... Football: Super Bowl, New York Giants defeat Buffalo Bills, 21–19 ... Basketball: NBA, Chicago Bulls defeat Los Angeles Lakers, 4–1 ... Tennis: Monica Seles wins the U.S., Australian, and French Opens.

"We were after business cooperation or military or industrial secrets that we would use or broker.... In America, it was easy: Money almost always worked, and we sought out politicians known to be corruptible."—**An anonymous BCCI officer**

Venturi designed the Sainsbury wing to harmonize with the main National Gallery building.

ARCHITECTURE

Less Is a Bore

8 For Philadelphia architect Robert Venturi, 1991 was a year of vindication. A quarter century earlier, his *Complexity and Contradiction in Architecture* had launched the postmodernist movement in building design. A playful attack on modernism (with its worship of geometry and its rejection of ornamentation and historical reference), the book answered Mies van der Rohe's "Less is more" with the aphorism "Less is a bore." It called for "messy vitality" in architecture and declared that America's jumbled Main Streets were "almost all right." Though Venturi himself disliked the label "postmodernist," he inspired architects everywhere to discard the International Style's austere boxes in favor of fantasias incorporating elements from Greek temples and Las Vegas casinos. Yet it wasn't until the second year of the nineties that the Venturis—as the press referred to Venturi and his partner and wife, Denise Scott Brown—saw the unveiling of their first major civic buildings: the Seattle Art Museum and the Sainsbury wing of London's venerable National Gallery.

The Seattle edifice, set among skyscrapers, is as lively as Venturi's writings—a harmonious hodgepodge of windows, arches, and piers, enlivened with fluted limestone and polychrome terracotta. ("Vastly entertaining" was *The New York Times*'s verdict.) The London project, however, pointed up a paradox: There was no particular "Venturi look." Intent on creating buildings that fit their environments, the Venturis made the Sainsbury wing a respectful reflection of the 1830s structure to which it was attached. The freshness came in the details—a lone pillar punning on Nelson's Column, across Trafalgar Square; a wall of glass juxtaposed with neoclassical arches. British critics were sharply divided over the building: Detractors called it bland, vulgar, pretentious, even "a piece of picturesque, mediocre slime." But Prince Charles, who'd referred to a proposal by another firm as a "monstrous carbuncle" on the face of the National Gallery, expressed the majority opinion. He was, he said, "rather pleased." ◄**1984.9** ►**1994.6**

BUSINESS AND INDUSTRY

A Bank for Crime

9 Calling it the biggest criminal enterprise in history, banking regulators in 69 countries worldwide closed down the Bank of Credit & Commerce International in July 1991, freezing more than 75 percent of its estimated assets of $20 billion. Money laundering, illegal arms dealing, smuggling, fraud, extortion, bribery—the rogue bank had done it all. More than $12 billion, auditors said, had disappeared into BCCI since 1972, the year it was incorporated in Luxembourg by Pakistani financier Agha Hasan Abedi.

Abedi's stated mission was to create the Muslim world's first megabank. In fact, he turned his institution into a broker for such megacrooks as Panamanian strongman Manuel Noriega and Colombia's cocaine barons. By setting up BCCI as a holding company, not a bank, Abedi circumvented Luxembourg's notoriously lax banking regulations. When he expanded worldwide, no country had strict jurisdiction over his diabolically complex organization: BCCI was the perfect "offshore" operation.

Ties with intelligence agencies (the CIA among them) and top officials in many nations kept business rolling. Among BCCI's transactions: abetting the Reagan administration's Iran-Contra arms transfers; providing nuclear-weapons technology to Iraq; secretly buying three American banks, including Washington's First American Bankshares, headed by a pillar of the U.S. establishment, former U.S. defense secretary Clark Clifford. Clifford and his law partner Robert Altman, who had represented BCCI from 1978 to 1990, were indicted in July 1992 on federal charges that they knowingly facilitated BCCI's clandestine ownership of the bank. (The pair insisted they'd been unwitting dupes; federal charges were dismissed in 1993. Clifford's ill health prevented him from standing trial on New York State charges; Altman stood trial there and was acquitted in August 1993, of four charges of fraud.) BCCI's cultivation of Clifford as a front man illustrated what one journalist called its knack "for infiltrating power elites even as it served as a cash conduit for terrorists, gunrunners, and drug thugs." Abedi had also formed an association with Jimmy Carter, contributing large sums to the former president's Global 2000 Foundation, a Third World health care charity.

Clark Clifford *(left)* and partner Robert Altman were implicated in the BCCI scandal.

Though BCCI pleaded guilty to money laundering in 1990, the bank had continued to function with impunity—even after an audit by a U.S. accounting firm revealed massive bookkeeping discrepancies. (When the scandal broke, investigators accused the U.S. Justice Department of impeding their inquiry.) The bank's collapse brought disaster to more than a million depositors. In 1994, a court in Abu Dhabi convicted twelve BCCI executives of a variety of crimes; sentenced in absentia to eight years, Abedi remained in Pakistan, untouchable. ◄**1989.10**

IN THE UNITED STATES

from competition on November 7 after learning he was afflicted with HIV (human immunodeficiency virus), the virus that causes AIDS. A three-time National Basketball Association Most Valuable Player and the sport's all-time leader in assists, Johnson instantly became the most visible AIDS spokesman in the country. Testing for HIV jumped dramatically nationwide, and President George

Bush appointed Johnson to a national commission on the disease. (Johnson, calling the organization ineffective, later resigned.) ◄**1979.M** ►**1992.10**

►NAVAL DEBAUCHERY—At a boozy Las Vegas convention of top Navy fliers—the Tailhook Association—packs of male aviators sexually abused 83 women and at least seven men. During the three-day September gathering, attended by some 4,000 people, women were routinely "groped, pinched, and fondled on their breasts, buttocks, and genitals," according to a Pentagon report. Some "were knocked to the ground and had their clothing ripped or removed." An investigation into the scandal—initially blocked by top Navy officers—revealed that sexual abuse was condoned institutionally. ►**1991.V**

►DAHMER ARRESTED—Serial killer Jeffrey Dahmer was arrested in July after an intended victim escaped, handcuffed, from Dahmer's Milwaukee apartment and called the police. Over a 13-year period, Dahmer, a 31-year-old candy-factory employee, had killed at least 17 people, young men he'd brought home for sex and then drugged. He routinely had sex with his victims' corpses before dismembering, and sometimes cooking and eating, them. In 1992, a judge sentenced Dahmer to 15 consecutive life terms in prison. Two years later, he was beaten to death by a fellow inmate.

POLITICS & BUSINESS: GNP: $5,737.1 billion ... Dow Jones Industrial Average closes above 3,000 points for the first time ... Supreme Court upholds the outlawing of abortion information at federally financed clinics; upholds states' right to require parental consent for abortions for minors ... Eastern Airlines ceases operation.

"If I robbed a bank, I would go to jail. What Maxwell did was worse. He robbed the poor to pay the rich—himself."
—Ivy Needham, a pensioner of one of Robert Maxwell's companies

AROUND THE WORLD

▶ANOTHER GANDHI ASSASSINATED—A modern political dynasty ended in May when Rajiv Gandhi, leader of India's Congress Party, was killed by a suicide bomber in the state of Tamil Nadu as he campaigned for parliamentary candidates. Gandhi, who'd succeeded his mother, Indira, as prime minister after she was murdered in 1984, was on the comeback trail after his party was voted out in 1989. His assassin (she and 15 bystanders were blown up in the attack) was believed to be associated with secessionist Tamil rebels of neighboring Sri Lanka—a group that India had tried to suppress. P.V. Narasimha Rao succeeded Gandhi as Congress party head and in June became prime minister. ◀1984.2 ▶1993.9

▶CENTURY'S FIRST CHOLERA—Already plagued by armed insurgency and massive foreign debt, Peru was struck by a cholera epidemic in January. The highly contagious bacterial disease—caused by feces-polluted water—killed thousands of Peruvians in a matter of months, and though other Latin American countries restricted travel to Peru, the epidemic spread to Ecuador and Colombia. It was the world's first major cholera outbreak since the nineteenth century. ◀1907.3

▶LAURELS FOR GORDIMER—White South African novelist Nadine Gordimer in October became the first woman in 25 years to win the Nobel Prize for literature. A member of the African National Congress, Gordimer had explored apartheid's ravages in such psychologically probing novels as *Occasion for Loving* and *Burger's Daughter*, which was temporarily banned in South Africa. After ANC head Chief Albert Luthuli (Peace Prize, 1960) and Bishop Desmond Tutu (Peace Prize, 1984), Gordimer was the third South African apartheid foe to receive a Nobel. ◀1984.8

Maxwell with one of his last acquisitions.

BUSINESS AND INDUSTRY

A Giant of Flimflammery

10 The death was as sensational as the tabloid tycoon himself: In November 1991, British press baron Robert Maxwell disappeared during a Canary Islands cruise aboard his opulent yacht, the *Lady Ghislaine*. A search party found his body floating face up in the Atlantic, near Tenerife.

Boisterous, crude, and flamboyant, the self-made billionaire was one of the over-the-top figures of the high-flying 1980s. In the weeks after Maxwell's death, an investigation of his business empire—consisting of some 400 public and private companies—revealed that the mogul was something else as well: a flimflam man of historic proportions. Internationally renowned confidant of royalty and statesmen, Maxwell had plundered as much as $2 billion from his companies, much of it stolen from employee pension funds. The tabloid press, including Maxwell's own London *Daily Mirror* and New York *Daily News,* had a field day.

Illusion and chutzpah were Maxwell's stock-in-trade. Born Jan Ludvik Hoch in Czechoslovakia's Carpathian Mountains, he arrived in England during World War II, experimenting with a series of upper-crust monikers before settling on Robert Maxwell. Through charm, cajolery, and chicanery, he assembled a web of dubiously financed businesses. The world's foremost financial institutions lined up to lend him money. When the economy soured in the late eighties and his creditors came knocking, Maxwell raided his companies for funds. His estimated debt was $4 billion.

The kingpin died just as everything began to crumble. Suicide was suspected. Others offered a stranger story: He had faked his demise to avoid prosecution. Whatever the truth (the autopsy indicated heart and lung failure, with drowning or a heart attack possible "contributing factors"), the mess Maxwell left behind raised hard questions about the internationally lax banking practices that had made his schemes possible. **◀1989.10**

COLOMBIA

Escobar's Last Escape

11 Pablo Escobar Gaviria, ruthless leader of Colombia's multibillion-dollar Medellín cocaine cartel, grew tired of running in 1991.

His pursuers crowed in June, when he turned himself in and went to jail. But in his deal with the authorities (who agreed not to extradite him to face charges in the United States), Escobar arranged to be locked in a luxurious prison built to his specifications; once inside, he continued to run his illicit empire unimpeded. When, 13 months later, the government tried to move him to less comfortable digs, Escobar and his armed henchmen (unrestricted visits were part of his surrender package) took two officials hostage. By the next day, when 400 soldiers breached the stronghold, Escobar was gone.

During the 1980s, Escobar had turned the Andean industrial city Medellín into the center of the world cocaine trade. A thousand-man militia defended the enterprise by killing anyone who interfered—from police to rivals to disloyal underlings. In 1989 Colombia, under U.S. pressure, began an all-out effort to put Escobar out of business. He responded by declaring war. For the next year, he moved from hideout to hideout while his minions murdered his enemies and even blew up a Colombian airliner, killing 107 passengers.

While terrorizing the country, Escobar (who was spending an estimated $1 million a day to avoid capture) negotiated the deal that put him in Envigado "prison." His subsequent escape enraged President César Gaviria Trujillo; even worse for Escobar, his murder spree had created thousands of enemies. He'd been safer in prison. Escobar eluded his foes until December 1993, when an army battalion tracked him to a Medellín hideout and gunned him down. The cocaine trade, however, continued to flourish under new management. **◀1985.8**

FILM

A Banned *Lantern*

12 In 1991, Zhang Yimou completed what is probably the greatest movie to come out of China since the revolution. Yet *Raise the Red Lantern*—the second Chinese film ever nominated for an Academy Award for Best Foreign Film—was banned in its native land. In the post-Tiananmen Square climate, anything Chinese endorsed by foreigners was officially suspect. Moreover, the film contained what may have been a veiled critique of China's entrenched leadership: Its villain, as in Zhang's previous (also banned) effort, *Ju Dou*, is a grasping, manipulative man.

Set in the 1920s, *Raise the Red Lantern* traces the downfall of a university-educated young woman (the radiant Gong Li) who becomes the fourth wife of a wealthy, arrogant patriarch. Each wife lives for the days when the lantern signaling the master's presence hangs above *her* door, because it gains her privileges over the other wives. The struggle for his favor destroys all trust between the women and leads ultimately to betrayal, madness, and death.

If Zhang intended the film as a metaphor for the evils of even a benevolent despotism, he could draw on ample personal experience. As the son of a former major in the anti-Communist Guomintang Army, he was ostracized; despite his academic brilliance, the authorities made him a factory janitor. He taught himself photography and during the thaw following Mao's death won admission to China's only film school, in Beijing. He served as cameraman for classmate Chen Kaige's *Yellow Earth* (1984)—the first Chinese film to win worldwide praise—then made *Red Sorghum* (1987). Yet the popularity of both movies in China was no guarantee of artistic freedom. Chen soon emigrated to New York. Zhang stayed on, unwilling to abandon the land from which he drew his inspiration. **◀1950.11**

Subtly acted, lushly beautiful, *Raise the Red Lantern* starred Gong Li *(above).*

NOBEL PRIZES: Peace: Daw Aung San Suu Kyi (Burmese; advocacy of democracy in Myanmar) ... Literature: Nadine Gordimer (South African; novelist) ... Chemistry: Richard Ernst (Swiss; nuclear magnetic resonance spectroscopy) ... Medicine: Edwin Neher and Bert Sakmann (German; cell functions) ... Physics: Pierre-Gilles de Gennes (French; liquid crystals) ... Economics: Ronald Coase (U.S.).

A VOICE FROM 1991

Harassment Gets a Hearing

From the Senate Judiciary Committee hearings on the nomination of Clarence Thomas to the Supreme Court, October 11, 1991

In vitriolic hearings that became a watershed in America's ongoing women's-rights struggle, the Senate Judiciary Committee in October 1991 examined allegations by Anita Hill, a law professor at the University of Oklahoma, that Supreme Court nominee Clarence Thomas had sexually harassed her ten years earlier. Hill, who'd worked with Thomas when he headed the Equal Employment Opportunity Commission (the federal agency responsible for, among other things, policing sexual discrimination), accused her former boss of pressuring her for dates, boasting about his sexual prowess, and describing the content of pornographic movies. Thomas, a conservative lawyer who'd since been made a federal judge, denied the charges and played a racial wild card (both he and Hill are black) by calling the televised hearings a "high-tech lynching." A rapt television audience watched as the debacle devolved into a his-word-against-hers showdown. Republican senators defended Thomas by assailing Hill, variously insinuating that she was a liar, a tramp, or a psychotic spinster. Somewhat lost in the furor was Thomas's apparent underqualification for the Supreme Court: He had only one year of judicial experience and had written no significant decisions. He was confirmed by a 52–48 vote—the highest negative-vote total ever received by a successful nominee.

[From the opening statement by Professor Anita Hill]

My working relationship became even more strained when Judge Thomas began to use work situations to discuss sex. On these occasions he would call me into his office for a course on education issues and projects, or he might suggest that because of the time pressures of his schedule we go to lunch to a government cafeteria.

After a brief discussion of work, he would turn the conversation to a discussion of sexual matters. His conversations were very vivid. He spoke about acts that he had seen in pornographic films involving such matters as women having sex with animals, and films showing group sex or rape scenes.

He talked about pornographic materials depicting individuals with large penises or large breasts involving various sex acts.

On several occasions, Thomas told me graphically of his own sexual prowess.

[From the opening statement by Supreme Court nominee Clarence Thomas]

Though I am, by no means, a perfect person—no means—I have not done what she has alleged. And I still don't know what I could possibly have done to cause her to make these allegations.

When I stood next to the President in Kennebunkport, being nominated to the Supreme Court of the United States, that was a high honor. But as I sit here before you, 103 days later, that honor has been crushed.....

No job is worth what I've been through—no job. No horror in my life has been so debilitating. Confirm me if you want. Don't confirm me if you are so led. But let this process end. Let me and my family regain our lives.

[Questions from Senator Arlen Specter]

Q: Now, are you saying, in response to my question as to why you didn't tell the FBI about the size of his private parts and his sexual prowess and Long John Silver, that that information was comprehended within the statement, quote, Thomas liked to discuss specific acts and frequency of sex?

A [Anita Hill]: I am not saying that that information was included in that. I don't know that it was. I don't believe that I even mentioned the latter information to the FBI agent. And I could only respond again that at the time of the investigation I tried to cooperate as fully as I could to recall information that—to answer the questions that they asked.

Q: Professor Hill, you said that you took it to mean that Judge Thomas wanted to have sex with you, but in fact, he never did ask you to have sex, correct?

A: No, he did not ask me to have sex. He did continually pressure me to go out with him, continually. And he would not accept my explanation as one being valid.

Q: So that when you said you took it to mean, we ought to have sex, that was an inference—

A: Yes.

[In response to questions from Senator Orrin Hatch]

A [Clarence Thomas]: This whole affair bothers me, Senator. I am witnessing the destruction of my integrity.

Q: And it's by a unilateral set of declarations that are made on successive dates and differ—

A: That's true.

Q: —by one person, who continued to maintain what she considered to be a, quote, cordial, professional relationship with you over a ten-year period.

A: Senator, my relationship with Anita Hill prior to September 25 was cordial and professional. And I might add one other thing, if you really want an idea of how I treated women, then ask the majority of the women who worked for me. They're out here. Give them as much time as you have given one person, the only person who's been on my staff who's ever made these sorts of allegations about me.

Q: I don't blame you for being mad.

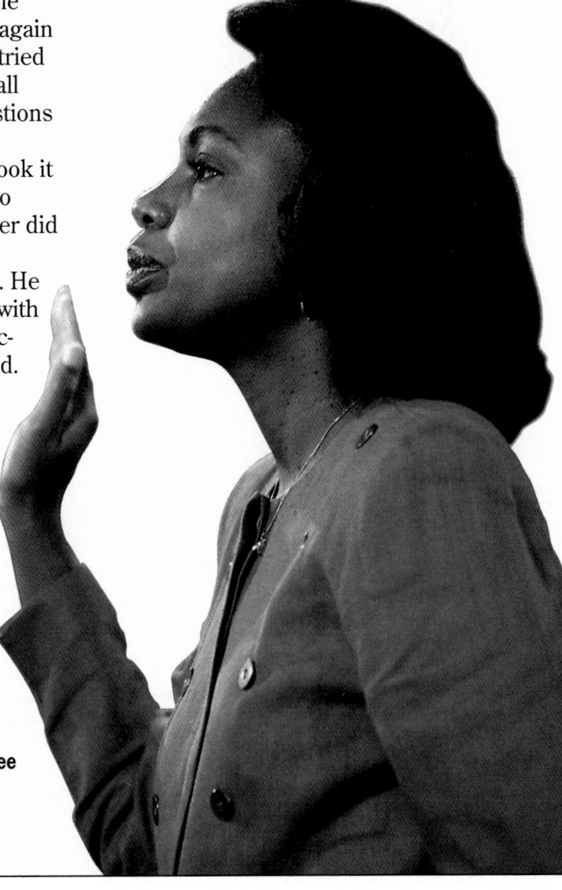

Hill *(right)* takes the oath before testifying. Above, Thomas shakes hands with Committee chairman, Senator Joseph Biden.

"We have to accept war because the alternative—surrender or treason—does not exist for us."
—General Blagoje Adzic, chief of staff of the Serbian army

STORY OF THE YEAR

Siege of Sarajevo

1 The bloodiest European conflict since World War II began in 1992, when the Yugoslav republic of Serbia—led by fiercely nationalist president Slobodan Miloševic and abetted by nationalist Bosnian Serbs—began a brutal campaign to annex parts of the republic of Bosnia and Hercegovina (called Bosnia for short). Ethnically divided Yugoslavia had already come apart at the seams: The republics of Slovenia and Croatia had established their independence (the latter after a devastating war with Serbia); the republic of Macedonia had announced its secession. In April, after Bosnia and Hercegovina's independence was formally recognized by the international community, the Serb-dominated Yugoslav army and Bosnian Serb militias moved to grab as much of the republic's territory as possible for "Greater Serbia."

Bosnia was a patchwork quilt of ethnic and religious groups—44 percent Muslim, 31 percent Serb, 17 percent Croat. Its spiritual and political center was elegant, richly historic Sarajevo. For 500 years, the city's diverse population had lived in remarkable harmony—interrupted by outbreaks of nationalist fury like the one that sparked World War I. (In 1984, a happier time, Sarajevans hosted the Winter Olympics.) Now the capital withered under a merciless siege; its people crouched in basements and cold apartments, plagued by constant shelling and sniping, and by shortages of food, medicine, and fuel.

Other Bosnian communities were subjected to Serbian "ethnic cleansing." Resurrecting a feud dating to the fourteenth century, when Muslim Turks conquered Serbia, Miloševic's troops emptied entire Muslim villages. Sometimes the Serb soldiers massacred residents outright; sometimes they consigned civilians to a routine of rape, torture, and slow starvation in concentration camps. By the end of the year, more than a million people had been displaced, tens of thousands of others killed. Bosnian Croat and Muslim paramilitary units, sometimes allied, sometimes opposed, committed atrocities on a smaller scale.

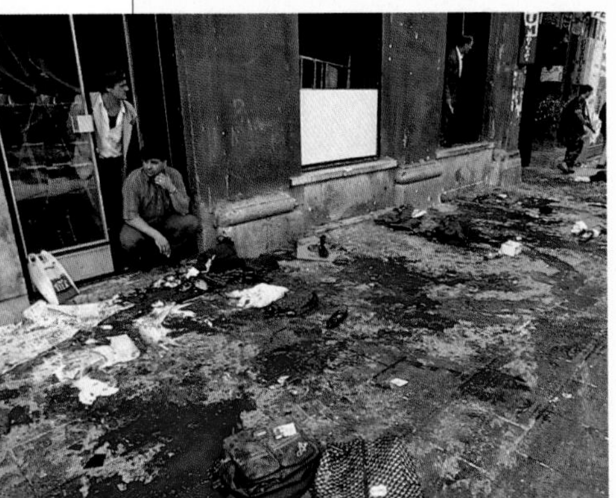

Sarajevo residents survey the grisly aftermath of a mortar attack on a bread line.

The European Community, the United States, and the UN imposed sanctions on Serbia and organized relief missions (systematically routed by the Serbs). But neither negotiators nor UN peacekeeping troops, who'd arrived in the region in March, managed to stop the fighting. Croatia, meanwhile, also began to grab pieces of Bosnia. Outgunned by its various foes, Muslim-dominated Bosnian government forces fought back stubbornly but in vain. ◄1991.2 ►1994.9

THE SOVIET UNION

After Breakup, Chaos

2 Across the southern republics of the former Soviet Union (now the Commonwealth of Independent States), civil war raged in 1992. From Moldova in the west, through the Caucasus nations of Georgia, Armenia, and Azerbaijan, to Tajikistan on the Afghan border, ethnic rivalries exploded. Moscow's imperial mosaic had shattered, but the task of imposing order still fell in part to Russia, the region's dominant country. Boris Yeltsin, the first freely elected head of state in Russian history, had to define his nation's post-Soviet role.

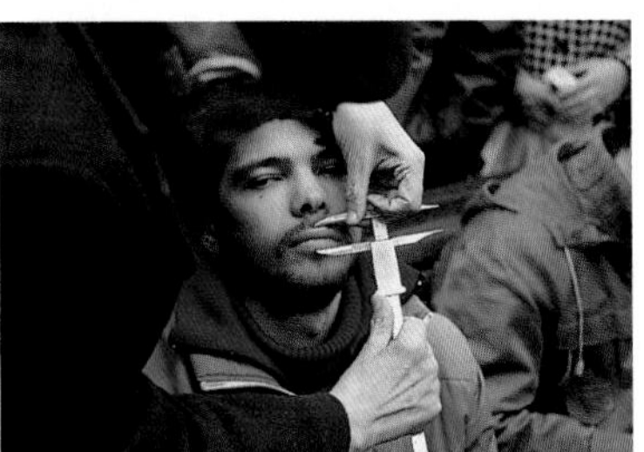

With separatism came renewed emphasis on ethnic purity. Here, a Crimean Tatar's skull is measured for "full-bloodedness."

Yeltsin's dilemma had largely been created by Joseph Stalin. To ensure Moscow's domination, the dictator took care that within every Soviet republic the ethnic majority was balanced by a significant minority; to that end, he'd encouraged Russian emigration to far-flung territories. On the principle of divide and conquer, he'd drawn the republics' borders to break up ethnically homogeneous territories. Nagorno-Karabakh, with a Christian Armenian majority, became part of Islamic Azerbaijan—and, in the late 1980s, the focus of a brutal war between Azerbaijan and Armenia. The Dniester region, an ethnic Russian and Ukrainian stronghold, was fused onto largely Romanian Moldova—laying the foundation for a bloody Dniester secessionist movement in the 1990s.

In Georgia, President Eduard Shevardnadze, the former Soviet foreign minister, inherited two such tinderboxes: South Ossetia, until 1990 an autonomous, Iranian-speaking region within Georgia, sought independence (it regained autonomy in May 1992); Abkhazia, a Muslim area on the Black Sea, likewise wanted to secede. As violence mounted, Shevardnadze, once the Kremlin's leading advocate of self-determination, asked Russia to intervene. Yeltsin sent in troops.

In fact, Russian troops appeared wherever civil war flared. Yeltsin claimed a neutral, peacekeeping role. But given Russia's imperialist history, many observers were skeptical of his motives. Others saw the President—embroiled in a power struggle with Communist hard-liners—as powerless to restrain his country's military from intervening where it wished. ◄1991.5 ►1993.4

EL SALVADOR

Peace After Years of War

3 El Salvador's devastating civil war ended in February 1992 with peace accords between the rightist National Republican Alliance (ARENA) government of President Alfredo Cristiani and the leftist rebels of the Farabundo Martí National Liberation Front (FMLN). More than 75,000 people had been killed in the twelve-year war, which pitted radicalized students, intellectuals, trade unionists, priests, and campesinos (led by a Marxist vanguard) against a regime controlled by an intransigent oligarchy and its ruthless military. Now both sides sacrificed victory for peace—long the sole desire of most Salvadorans.

The United Nations–brokered agreement called for an immediate cease-fire followed by gradual rebel disarmament. Cristiani agreed to purge the army of corrupt officers (the military had committed 85 percent of the war's crimes, including torture, civilian massacres, and the murder of priests and nuns); to reduce the military by almost half; and to open the country's political system. The transition, policed by 1,000 UN peacekeepers, took two years.

More than any other factor, the end of the Cold War made Salvadoran peace possible. The nonviolent democratic revolutions in Central and Eastern Europe, the disintegration of the Soviet Union, and the electoral defeat of Nicaragua's Sandinistas forced the rebels to rethink their mission. The government, meanwhile, could no longer bank on aid from Washington, which had pumped in more than $4 billion during the war to keep El Salvador from the clutches of alleged tools of Moscow.

Despite hitches in the peace process—war criminals were pardoned, troop reductions were delayed, some rightist death squads contin-

ART & CULTURE: Books: *A Thousand Acres* (Jane Smiley); *Very Old Bones* (William Kennedy); *Outerbridge Reach* (Robert Stone); *All the Pretty Horses* (Cormac McCarthy) ... Music: *Diva* (Annie Lennox, LP); *Tennessee* (Arrested Development, LP); *Come As You Are* (Nirvana, LP); *Ten* (Pearl Jam, LP); *No Fences* (Garth Brooks, LP); *The Face of the Night, the Heart of the Dark* (Wayne Peterson); *The Voyage* (Philip Glass)

"We want our future back, and I intend to help give it to you."—**Bill Clinton, during his 1992 presidential campaign**

Salvadoran guerrillas celebrate at a dance to mark the end of civil war.

ued to murder—elections came off in 1994. ARENA candidate Armando Calderón Sol won the presidency over Rubén Zamora, head of a FMLN-led coalition, but the former guerrillas won a significant block of seats in the National Assembly. Not even pro-ARENA fraud (dead people voted; many living people were not allowed to) dampened enthusiasm for the change from bullets to ballots. **◂1987.2**

THE UNITED STATES

The Reagan-Bush Era Ends

4 The gulf separating incumbent Republican president George Bush and his Democratic challenger, Bill Clinton, during the 1992 U.S. presidential campaign was largely defined by economics. Bush (oil-company heir, inheritor of trickle-down Reaganomics, reneger on a famous "no new taxes" pledge) plaintively insisted that America's ongoing recession wasn't so bad; he pointed to his foreign-policy achievements. Clinton, conversely, made recovery his central issue: THE ECONOMY, STUPID, admonished a sign in his campaign headquarters. He offered complex plans to stimulate growth, reminded voters of his working-class roots, and prescribed "jobs, jobs, jobs."

Clinton's strategy worked. He and running mate Albert Gore, a Tennessee senator known for his environmentalism, gained a plurality in the November vote: 43 percent for Clinton, 38 percent for Bush, and 19 percent for third-party candidate H. Ross Perot, a populist Texas billionaire. Pundits pronounced Clinton's victory, which broke a twelve-year Republican hold on the White House, the end of the Reagan revolution. Clinton himself—young, dynamic, and articulate (in contrast to the malaprop-prone Bush)—had made "change" his byword.

Yet his narrow victory and the nation's huge budget deficit ensured that change would not be dramatic. After taking office in January 1993—the first American president of the post–Cold War era and the first born after World War II—Clinton found his jobs-creation proposal eviscerated by a frugal Congress; his plan to provide universal health insurance encountered similarly heavy going. Internationally, Clinton (who'd publicly opposed the Vietnam War) abandoned the military adventurism of his most recent predecessors without denouncing it in principle; he was widely criticized for failing to intervene promptly in trouble spots like Haiti and Bosnia.

Indeed, Clinton's campaign strategy had been to portray himself and his party—perceived by many as a bastion of "tax-and-spend liberals"—as cautiously centrist. While the air of cultural conservatism that had descended on America during the Republicans' tenure lifted somewhat, no Clinton revolution was in evidence. **◂1988.M ▸1994.M**

Hillary Rodham Clinton and Bill Clinton at an inauguration party in January 1993.

CANADA

Quebec On Hold

5 In 1992, Canadians rejected their government's most ambitious attempt yet to resolve its most divisive issue: the status of Quebec. Since the 1960s, the question of secession had dominated politics in the vast, mostly French-speaking province, posing a monumental challenge to Canada as a whole. Although in 1980 Quebecers voted down a sovereignty plan, even nonseparatist provincial officials had begun campaigning for greater autonomy. Federal authorities had negotiated the Meech Lake accord, a compromise, but in 1990, the other provinces failed to ratify it. Then, in 1992, federal and provincial leaders created a package of constitutional changes designed to make a more independent Quebec palatable to the rest of Canada.

Opponents of Canada's proposed constitutional changes rally in Montreal.

The proposed amendments gave something to almost everyone. Quebecers would gain primary control over their economy, municipal affairs, and cultural activities; their province would be recognized as a "distinct society." Western provinces would be granted their demand for a directly elected national senate. Indigenous peoples would achieve a degree of self-government. But the sections covering Quebec fell short of most Francophones' hopes, while autonomy's opponents complained the concessions went too far. And many Canadians were inclined to oppose *any* measure supported by Prime Minister Brian Mulroney—a conservative whose inability to curb a deep recession had made him the least popular premier in 50 years.

When a national referendum on the package was held in October, 54 percent of the electorate voted no. Once again, Canadians had decided not to decide. **◂1976.6**

DEATHS

Isaac Asimov, U.S. writer.

Francis Bacon, U.K. painter.

Menachem Begin, Polish-Israeli prime minister.

John Cage, U.S. composer.

Sandy Dennis, U.S. actress.

Marlene Dietrich, German-U.S. actress.

Alexander Dubček, Czech political leader.

José Ferrer, U.S. actor and director.

Vincent Gardenia, U.S. actor.

Alex Haley, U.S. writer.

Benny Hill, U.K. comedian.

Petra Kelly, German political leader.

Sam Kinison, U.S. comedian.

Barbara McClintock, U.S. geneticist.

Bert Parks, U.S. entertainer.

Anthony Perkins, U.S. actor.

Emilio Pucci, Italian fashion designer.

Samuel Reshevsky, Polish-U.S. chess player.

Nancy Walker, U.S. actress.

Lawrence Welk, U.S. bandleader.

... Painting & Sculpture: ***Naked Man, Back View*** **(Lucien Freud);** ***The Caliph's Garden*** **(Anthony Caro) ... Film:** ***Unforgiven*** **(Clint Eastwood);** ***The Player*** **(Robert Altman);** ***Howards End*** **(James Ivory);** ***Malcolm X*** **(Spike Lee);** ***The Crying Game*** **(Neil Jordan) ... Theater:** ***Oleanna*** **(David Mamet);** ***The Sisters Rosensweig*** **(Wendy Wasserstein);** ***Jelly's Last Jam*** **(Ludwig, Morton, and Birkenhead) ... TV:** ***Barney and Friends; Picket Fences.***

"Let the pigs root around in their mud. It's not the place for us."—**Brazilian president Fernando Collor de Mello, on the journalists and the congressional committee investigating corruption charges against him**

NEW IN 1992

Photographs in *The New Yorker* magazine.

Largest shopping mall in the U.S. (Minnesota's 78-acre Mall of America, which also includes world's largest indoor amusement park).

Interactive movies.

FDA approval for nicotine transdermal patch (Nicoderm).

IN THE UNITED STATES

▶GOTTI GOTTEN—On April 2, in one of the decade's most publicized trials, a jury convicted New York mobster John Gotti on 13 counts, including racketeering and murder charges. In June, as a crowd of Gotti supporters demonstrated outside the courthouse, Judge I. Leo Glasser sentenced the kingpin—once called the "Teflon Don" for his ability to beat the rap—to life in prison without parole. The conviction hinged on testimony from Salvatore "Sammy the Bull" Gravano, once a close Gotti associate.

▶CHECKS AND NO BALANCES—Congress in October voted to close the U.S. House of Representatives Bank—whose only clients were representatives—after it was reported that in one twelve-month period the bank had covered more than 8,000 checks written against insufficient funds. Public indignation over the check-writing scandal was compounded by the disclosure, on October 3, that representatives collectively owed some $300,000 in unpaid tabs at the House restaurant.

▶KILLER HURRICANE—As Hurricane Andrew bore down on the Gulf Coast in August, federal officials evacuated one million people between Miami and Fort Lauderdale. Even so, the storm's 150-mph winds killed 14 people and left

EASTERN AFRICA

Anarchy in Somalia

6 After more than a year of civil war and famine, Somalia (population seven million) finally attracted worldwide attention in August 1992. That month—goaded by televised scenes of mass starvation and by charges that the West commonly ignored African crises—Western European countries, the United States, and the United Nations began shipping food to Somalia. Before the year was out, the United States and the UN also sent peacekeeping troops. But the tragedy soon assumed new dimensions of horror.

The fighting had begun in January 1991, when 22-year dictator Muhammad Siad Barre was ousted by army commander General Muhammad Farah Aidid. Somali politics revolved around blood loyalties, and the coup provoked bitter fighting between Aidid's Hawiye and Barre's Darod clans. When Muhammad Ali Mahdi—a Hawiye and a partner in Aidid's rebel faction, the United Somali Congress—became interim president, fighting also broke out between rival Hawiye factions. By the time Western relief shipments began arriving, Somalia had no government to oversee distribution; militiamen loyal to warring clans routinely hijacked incoming food supplies.

In December, in one of his last acts as president, George Bush sent in U.S. military forces to impose order. But with no Somali leader able to command popular legitimacy, the anarchy continued. As massive relief efforts (and a good wet season) alleviated the famine, and the occupiers' efforts to disarm the rival factions failed, tentative Somali support turned into resentment. After Aidid's troops gunned down 24 Pakistani UN peacekeepers in June, new president Bill Clinton committed his army to Aidid's capture. Four months later, a botched raid on the general's headquarters resulted in 18 American deaths. Pictures of Somalis dragging the mutilated corpse of an American serviceman through Mogadishu, the capital, dampened American enthusiasm. By the spring of 1994, U.S. troops were out, but Somalia remained a country in chaos. ◂**1984.4**

Somali militiamen patrol the rubble-strewn capital city, Mogadishu.

BRAZIL

A President Disgraced

7 In Brazil, a naturally rich nation historically impoverished by bad government—corrupt dictators, repressive military juntas—no leader had ever been as venal as Fernando Collor de Mello *(left)*, who resigned in 1992 after impeachment proceedings were started against him. During his three years in office, Collor, Brazil's first directly elected president in 30 years, allegedly stole more than $32 million from the government—especially galling in view of the fact that the smooth-talking, telegenic 43-year-old had been voted in as a reformer devoted to stamping out corruption. After years of discredited military rule, both the masses and the economic elite had embraced him.

Revelations of Collor's influence-peddling and embezzlement—his younger brother fingered the president in May, also alleging past drug abuse and philandering—posed a serious challenge for Brazil's young democracy. In the past, unwanted leaders had been ousted by coup or had clung to power with the army's backing; this time, Congress determined to legally remove the offender. After a "Collorgate" investigation turned up hard proof of diverted funds and kickbacks, legislators voted to impeach. Collor claimed innocence, vowing, "I'm not the type of man to resign. I fight." But when his trial began in December, it was clear he'd lost (though he was eventually acquitted, in 1994). Collor became the first head of state in Latin America's turbulent history to be constitutionally removed from office in midterm.

Brazil's democracy survived Collor's mendacity, but national confidence plummeted. Plagued by myriad problems—inflation that ran beyond 20 percent a month; an elephantine gap between the country's richest citizens and everyone else; huge (albeit recently renegotiated) foreign debt obligations; and social problems that included rates of homelessness, infant mortality, and homicide among the highest in the Western Hemisphere—Brazil got a fresh burst of hope in 1994 with the election of Fernando Henrique Cardoso as president. Cardoso, a fiscally conservative economist and former Finance Minister, had implemented a currency change that had finally managed to curb Brazil's rampant inflation. ◂**1989.8**

PERU

Shining Path Decapitated

8 President Alberto Fujimori in April 1992 suspended Peru's constitution and disbanded Congress, steps he insisted were necessary to defeat the guerrillas of Sendero Luminoso (Shining Path). In twelve years of violence, the Maoist Shining Path had inflicted more than $20 billion in damage; 25,000 Peruvians, mostly noncombatants, had been killed—nearly half by the small rebel army (about 5,000 fighters), the rest by trigger-happy government troops.

The Shining Path's leader was Abimael Guzmán Reynoso, self-styled Fourth Sword of Marxism (after Marx, Lenin, and Mao). A former philosophy professor, Guzmán (who'd quit the "revisionist" Peruvian Communist Party) preached a

SPORTS: Baseball: World Series, Toronto Blue Jays defeat Atlanta Braves, 4–2 ... Olympics held in Albertville, France, and Barcelona ... Football: Super Bowl, Washington Redskins defeat Buffalo Bills, 37–24 ... Basketball: NBA, Chicago Bulls defeat Portland Trail Blazers, 4–2 ... Boxing: Riddick Bowe defeats Evander Holyfield for heavyweight title.

"It's very much like traveling with twelve rock stars."—**Chuck Daly, coach of the "Dream Team"**

particularly merciless form of class war modeled on Mao Zedong's Cultural Revolution, with echoes of Cambodia's genocidal Pol Pot. His utopian vision blended an idealized Communist China with a resurrected Incan empire. Guzmán's followers, the Senderistas, began their terrorist attacks near the Andean city of Ayacucho in 1980. Soon, Shining Path and Comrade Gonzalo, as Guzmán called himself, controlled much of the countryside and were operating in Lima and other cities. The group's car bombings, assassinations, destruction of power stations, murders of shantytown social workers, massacres of uncooperative peasants, and bizarre displays of power—on one occasion, Senderistas hung dead dogs from lampposts in downtown Lima—made Guzmán the country's most feared man.

By the time Fujimori (a Japanese-Peruvian agronomist who'd defeated novelist Mario Vargas Llosa for the presidency in 1990) had assumed dictatorial powers, Shining Path terror, soaring inflation, and the migration of penniless peasants to

Captured Peruvian terrorist Abimael Guzmán ranted as he was displayed in a cage.

Lima had brought Peru close to anarchy. Fortunately for Fujimori, whose "self-coup" drew international rebuke, government agents soon captured Guzmán in Lima. The terrorist mastermind was sent to prison for life, but Fujimori first demythologized him by displaying him, bespectacled and paunchy, in a cage. In December 1993, Peru returned to constitutional rule. ◄**1985.8**

WESTERN AFRICA

Truce Collapses in Liberia

9 Liberia's multisided civil war reignited in March 1992 after 17 months of cease-fire. Before the truce, which had been brokered by 14 African nations, some 25,000 of Liberia's 2.5 million people had been killed. Since then, starvation had been spreading, and relief efforts by West African peacekeeping forces—the Economic Community Monitoring Group (ECOMOG)—had been blocked by rebel leader Charles Taylor, whose National Patriotic Front of Liberia (NPFL) controlled all of Liberia except the capital, Monrovia. There, ECOMOG had set up a provisional government headed by Amos Sawyer, a prominent dissident during the reign of late dictator Samuel Doe; Taylor's rival, Prince Johnson, had holed up with his troops in a suburban compound. This smoldering peace flared into war when a fourth faction, remnants of Doe's army, renamed United Liberation Movement of Liberia (ULIMO), attacked Taylor's forces near the Sierra Leone border.

As fighting escalated, Taylor charged that ULIMO troops were mascarading as ECOMOG peacekeepers; in August, after the UN refused his call to send its own peacekeepers, Taylor attacked ECOMOG troops as well. Soon, Sierra Leone's army entered the fray, fighting a Sierra Leonean guerrilla group backed by Taylor. The war spread to Monrovia as NPFL forces attacked a government army base and rocketed the city. ECOMOG responded by bombing NPFL positions. But the outside world took little notice of Liberia's agony until November, when five American nuns who ran an orphanage near the capital were murdered—apparently by Taylor's men.

Liberian rebel soldiers routinely wore outrageous costumes into battle.

The UN finally imposed an arms embargo on Liberia—exempting ECOMOG, which managed to consolidate its hold on Monrovia. In July 1993, the combatants signed an agreement to surrender their weapons and hold elections. By the following summer, peace was still nowhere in sight. ◄**1990.9**

SPORTS

The Dream Team

10 **Exploiting a new rule that allowed professionals to compete in the Olympics, the United States unleashed on the 1992 Summer Games in Barcelona the best basketball team—indeed, one of the best teams in any sport—ever assembled. Led by stratospherically talented Michael Jordan, the twelve-man "Dream Team"—its other members were David Robinson, John Stockton, Karl Malone, Larry Bird, Earvin "Magic" Johnson, Chris Mullin, Patrick Ewing, Charles Barkley, Christian Laettner, Scottie Pippen, and Clyde Drexler—won its seven games by an average of 44 points and after each lopsided victory signed autographs for its dazzled victims.**

Speedy, balletic, and dominated by black Americans, basketball was the fastest-growing sport in the world (though soccer was still the most-played), and the three players most responsible for its popularity—Bird, Johnson, and Jordan—all played in Barcelona. For Bird and Johnson, the Olympic assignment was valedictory. Hobbled by a back injury, Bird retired after the two-week blowout. Johnson had retired in 1991 after being diagnosed as HIV positive, and he suited up again only for the Olympics. Jordan would finish one more glorious season with the Chicago Bulls before he, too, called it quits. ◄**1991.M** ►**1993.M**

IN THE UNITED STATES

250,000 homeless in Florida and Louisiana. With damages running to $20.6 billion in south Florida alone, Andrew was the costliest hurricane in U.S. history. ◄**1900.M**

►THERE GOES JOHNNY!—After 30 years as reigning honcho of late-night television, Johnny Carson *(below, with Bette Midler on his next-to-last program)* retired from *The Tonight Show* in May. NBC executives tapped lantern-jawed comedian and frequent Carson sub Jay Leno to succeed him—a decision that drove the other chief contender, David Letterman, who'd held down NBC's post-Carson time slot for a decade, to bolt. He emerged in 1993 with a new network (CBS), a new New York City studio (Broadway's refurbished Ed Sullivan Theater), and a new time (opposite Leno). *Late Show with David Letterman* soon dominated the late-night ratings. ◄**1954.M**

►AMY AND JOEY—Amy Fisher pleaded guilty on September 23 to shooting Mary Jo Buttafuoco, the wife of her former lover. Fisher, a.k.a. the "Long Island Lolita," was a 16-year-old high school student when she became involved with 32-year-old Joey Buttafuoco, a beefy auto mechanic who, Fisher said, supported her murder attempt (Mrs. Buttafuoco's hearing was damaged and part of her face paralyzed). The sordid tale, exhaustively chronicled in the tabloids and on "trash TV" shows like *A Current Affair*, culminated in Joey Buttafuoco's 1993 conviction of statutory rape.

►TYSON GUILTY—In July, Mike Tyson, boxing's punishing three-time consecutive heavyweight champion (and the youngest ever at age 20), was convicted of raping 18-year-old Miss Black America contestant Desiree Washington. Tyson, who in 1990 lost his crown in a humiliating upset by Buster Douglass, protested his innocence, but was sentenced to six years.

POLITICS & BUSINESS: GNP: $6,045.8 billion ... Bill Clinton elected president, defeating George Bush ... Bush vetoes fetal-tissue research, family-leave, and "Motor Voter" bills; pardons ex-officials involved in Iran-Contra affair ... Pan Am ruled liable for '88 Lockerbie bombing (estimated cost, $300 million) ... GM announces $4.45 billion loss (largest to date for a U.S. company) ... R.H. Macy & Co. files for bankruptcy.

"People, can we all get along?"–**Police brutality victim Rodney King, appealing for peace during the Los Angeles riots**

AROUND THE WORLD

▶SUDAN'S CIVIL WAR—The decade-old civil war and famine in the Sudan, Africa's largest country, entered a new phase of violence in 1992 as dictator General Omar Hassam Ahmed al-Bashir attempted to impose Islamic law on the animist and Christian south, where guerrillas were fighting for regional autonomy. In February, the government expelled 400,000 refugees from Khartoum, the northern capital, compounding the Sudan's already egregious displacement problems. Meanwhile, as war-caused famine ravaged the south, the government diverted international aid to the north and stepped up a campaign to raze southern villages suspected of harboring rebels. In September, with relief workers being attacked by both government forces and guerrillas, the UN suspended its aid operation. More than 1.5 million people were threatened with starvation.

▶AFGHAN COUP—Muhammad Najibullah, Communist dictator of Afghanistan, was overthrown in April, more than three years after the last Soviet soldier had left the civil-

war-torn country. The new coalition government failed to coalesce, however, and Afghanistan soon plunged back into civil war. ◂1988.M

▶IRAQI CAT-AND-MOUSE—In August, the Gulf war allies imposed a "no-fly" zone over southern Iraq to stop dictator Saddam Hussein's offensive against restive Shiite Muslims. Hussein battled other foes within Iraq's borders: In the north, he employed heavy weapons against separatist Kurds. But the Kurds survived, and in September, the two main rebel factions merged. In Baghdad, a team of UN nuclear inspectors played a summer-long cat-and-mouse game with Hussein, but in the fall, they announced that Iraq had no nuclear-weapons-making capacity. ◂1991.1 ▸1993.M

The troubled couple did not see eye to eye.

GREAT BRITAIN

An Annus Horribilis

11 What was supposed to be a celebratory year for Britain's Queen Elizabeth II, the 40th anniversary of her ascension to the throne, turned out to be a royal disaster. Marred by the soap-operatic marital troubles of the House of Windsor's younger generation, public attacks on the Queen's tax-exempt status, and a catastrophic fire at the 900-year-old Windsor Castle, 1992 went down as one of the monarchy's worst years since the sixteenth century.

The first of three royal couples to combust, Prince Andrew and his wife, the former Sarah Ferguson, separated in March. Earlier, photographers had caught "Fergie," accompanied by her "financial adviser," cavorting topless on the Riviera. In April, Princess Anne, the Queen's only daughter, divorced her rakish husband. But these marital mishaps paled beside those of Charles and Diana, the ill-matched Prince and Princess of Wales.

A semiauthorized June biography of Diana (she allowed friends to talk to the author) alleged infidelity by Charles and suicide attempts by his photogenic wife. Meanwhile, London's tabloids got hold of tapes of two prurient phone conversations: one between Charles and his reputed lover, the other between Diana and *her* supposed paramour. In December, a beleaguered Buckingham Palace formally announced the couple's separation.

By the time fire ripped through Windsor in November, many Britons had run out of sympathy for the tarnished monarchy. Money was an issue: Despite the Queen's multibillion-pound fortune, the public was expected to pay for repairs. Royal maintenance already cost some £100 million annually. At least, disgruntled subjects complained, she should pick up the tab on her 1,000-room retreat. Lamented Elizabeth, "It has turned out to be an annus horribilis." Days later, she agreed to pay income taxes. **◂1981.4**

THE UNITED STATES

Los Angeles Explodes

12 An all-white jury's acquittal in April 1992 of four white Los Angeles police officers in the beating of black motorist Rodney King triggered America's worst civil unrest of the century. Spreading from the mostly African-American neighborhood of South-Central to other parts of the city, and involving Mexican-Americans, Korean-Americans, and some whites as well as blacks, the rioting lasted three days, claimed 51 lives, and caused an estimated $1 billion in property damage.

The jury's decision was shocking in light of a highly publicized amateur videotape of the 1991 beating that showed the officers viciously clubbing and kicking an unresisting King (who was never charged with a crime). The tape had made police brutality the focus of national debate. It had long been an issue in Los Angeles, where police chief Daryl Gates had molded the LAPD into a quasi-military force known for its racism. Brutality charges were common: In 1990 alone, the city paid out $8 million in settlements. After the King beating, thousands of demonstrators demanded that Gates resign. He resisted until after the riots, then quit to host a radio talk show. Sergeant Stacey Koon, who had supervised the King assault, was subsequently convicted in federal court of violating King's civil rights.

In a strangely parallel case, a group of black youths was videotaped during the riot mercilessly beating a white truck driver named Reginald Denny. Most South-Central residents were horrified, yet many received the 1993 convictions (for assault) of two of Denny's assailants as further evidence that whites were held to a less stringent legal standard than blacks. Almost 25 years after Martin Luther King, Jr.'s assassination, America's racial problems continued to seethe. **◂1966.V**

Nation of Islam members survey riot-scarred South-Central.

GUATEMALA

Rights Champion Wins Nobel

13 The Nobel Prize committee made a strong political statement in 1992, the 500th anniversary of Columbus's first voyage to the Americas, by awarding its Peace Prize to Guatemalan human rights activist Rigoberta Menchú. A Quiché Indian, Menchú, 33, had worked for more than a decade to publicize the systematic oppression of her country's indigenous people—who constituted 80 percent of the population. During the course of a 32-year civil insurrection (the longest in Latin American history), a series of military and military-controlled Guatemalan regimes had killed some 150,000 citizens, many of them Indian campesinos agitating against the country's plantation system. Another 50,000 people had been "disappeared," and thousands more had become refugees.

Menchú herself had lost five family members. One of her brothers, who worked on a coffee estate, died of pesticide poisoning; another died of malnutrition. A third brother was flayed and burned alive by security forces for being a "Communist." Her father, a peasants'-union organizer, was one of 39 people killed when government troops burned down a Spanish embassy where demonstrators had taken refuge. Her mother was raped and tortured to death by soldiers. With her own life in danger, Menchú helped organize a 1980 plantation labor strike that drew 80,000 supporters. As security forces closed in, she fled the country.

Menchú gained the support of leading international human rights activists but at home was officially branded a subversive. She used her $1.2 million Nobel cash award to set up a Mexico-based human rights foundation for native peoples throughout the Americas. In 1993, despite continuing repression, she returned to her homeland. The following year, Guatemalan officials and guerrillas signed an unprecedented peace pact. Among its provisions: a UN investigation of past rights abuses. **◂1984.8**

NOBEL PRIZES: Peace: Rigoberta Menchú (Guatemalan; native people's rights)... Literature: Derek Walcott (Trinidadian; poet and playwright) ... Chemistry: Rudolph Marcus (U.S.; prediction of behavior of molecules in solution) ... Medicine: Edmond Fischer and Edwin Krebs (U.S.; cell proteins) ... Physics: George Charpak (French; particle detector) ... Economics: Gary Becker (U.S.).

A VOICE FROM 1992

Messengers Trailing Orbs of Light

From *Angels in America Part One: Millennium Approaches*, by Tony Kushner, 1992

After rousing success in workshop productions, Millennium Approaches*—the self-contained first part of Tony Kushner's epic two-part play,* Angels in America*—opened to critical raves and SRO crowds in England in 1992, before making its triumphant Broadway debut the following year. Subtitled "A Gay Fantasia on National Themes,"* Angels in America *(including part two:* Perestroika*) is a survey of late-twentieth-century America that uses AIDS as a metaphor for social, political, and moral decay. Kushner's surreal, often wickedly funny vision features a "straight" Mormon couple (the wife is addicted to Valium; the husband has no sexual feelings for her), a gay couple (one partner is Jewish, the other a Mayflower WASP), and McCarthyite lawyer Roy Cohn as a supremely cynical Reagan-era power broker dying of AIDS. (Ethel Rosenberg—executed in 1953 as a spy—also appears, as does, climactically, an angel.) In the scene below, young AIDS-ravaged Prior Walter, the play's moral witness, is visited by two time-traveling namesakes.*

Act Three: *Not-Yet-Conscious, Forward Dawning*
January 1986

Scene I
Late night, three days after the end of Act Two. The stage is completely dark. Prior is in bed in his apartment, having a nightmare. He wakes up, sits up and switches on a nightlight. He looks at his clock. Seated by the table near the bed is a man dressed in the clothing of a 13th-century British squire.

Prior *(Terrified)*: Who are you?
Prior I: My name is Prior Walter.
(Pause)
Prior: My name is Prior Walter.
Prior I: I know that.
Prior: Explain.
Prior I: You're alive. I'm not. We have the same name. What do you want me to explain?
Prior: A ghost?
Prior I: An ancestor.
Prior: Not *the* Prior Walter? The Bayeux tapestry Prior Walter?
Prior I: His great-great grandson. The fifth of the name.
Prior: I'm the thirty-fourth, I think.
Prior I: Actually the thirty-second.
Prior: Not according to Mother.
Prior I: She's including the two bastards, then; I say leave them out. I say no room for bastards. The little things you swallow …
Prior: Pills.
Prior I: Pills. For the pestilence. I too …
Prior: Pestilence…. You too what?
Prior I: The pestilence in my time was much worse than now. Whole villages of empty houses. You could look outdoors and see Death walking in the morning, dew dampening the ragged hem of his black robe. Plain as I see you now.
Prior: You died of the plague.
Prior I: The spotty monster. Like you, alone.
Prior: I'm not alone.
Prior I: You have no wife, no children.
Prior: I'm gay.
Prior I: So? Be gay, dance in your altogether for all I care, what's that to do with not having children?
Prior: Gay homosexual, not bonny, blithe and … never mind.
Prior I: I had twelve. When I died.

(The second ghost appears, this one dressed in the clothing of an elegant 17th-century Londoner.)
Prior I *(Pointing to Prior 2)*: And I was three years younger than him.
(Prior sees the new ghost, screams.)
Prior: Oh God another one.
Prior 2: Prior Walter. Prior to you by some seventeen others.
Prior I: He's counting the bastards.
Prior: Are we having a convention?
Prior 2: We've been sent to declare her fabulous incipience. They love a well-paved entrance with lots of heralds, and …
Prior I: The messenger comes. Prepare the way. The infinite descent, a breath in air …
Prior 2: They chose us, I suspect, because of the mortal affinities. In a family as long-descended as the Walters there are bound to be a few carried off by plague.
Prior I: The spotty monster.
Prior 2: Black Jack. Came from a water pump, half the city of London, can you imagine? His came from fleas. Yours, I understand, is the lamentable consequence of venery …

Weeping *Angels*: Graphic designer and illustrator Milton Glaser's logo *(top)* and cover art for the book of Kushner's Pulitzer-prize-winning play.

Prior I: Fleas on rats, but who knew that?
Prior: Am I going to die?
Prior 2: We aren't allowed to discuss …
Prior I: When you do, you don't get ancestors to help you through it. You may be surrounded by children but you die alone.
Prior: I'm afraid.
Prior I: You should be. There aren't even torches, and the path's rocky, dark and steep.
Prior 2: Don't alarm him. There's good news before there's bad.

We two come to strew rose petal and palm leaf before the triumphal procession. Prophet. Seer. Revelator. It's a great honor for the family.
Prior I: He hasn't got a family.
Prior 2: I meant for the Walters, for the family in the larger sense.
Prior *(Singing)*:
All I want is a room somewhere,
Far away from the cold night air …
Prior 2 *(Putting a hand on Prior's forehead)*:
Calm, calm, this is no brain fever …

(Prior calms down, but keeps his eyes closed. The lights begin to change. Distant Glorious Music.)
Prior I *(Low chant)*:
Adonai, Adonai
Olam ha-yichud,
Zefirot, Zazahot,
Ha-adam, ha-gadol
Daughter of Light,
Daughter of Splendors
Fluor! Phosphor!
Lumen! Candle!
Prior 2 *(Simultaneously)*:
Even now,
From the mirror-bright halls of heaven,
Across the cold and lifeless infinity of space,
The Messenger comes
Trailing orbs of light,
Fabulous, incipient,
Oh Prophet,
To you …
Prior I and Prior 2:
Prepare, prepare,
The Infinite Descent,
A breath, a feather,
Glory to …
(They vanish.)

"We who have fought against you, the Palestinians, we say to you today in a loud and clear voice: Enough of blood and tears! Enough!"—**Israeli prime minister Yitzhak Rabin**

STORY OF THE YEAR

Israel and the PLO Sign Peace Accord

1 The handshake amazed the world. PLO chairman Yasir Arafat stepped forward eagerly; Israeli prime minister Yitzhak Rabin needed a nudge from U.S. president Bill Clinton, who hosted the signing ceremony on the White House lawn. But finally, on September 13, 1993, the leaders of two peoples who'd been at war for 45 years clasped hands. They'd concluded only a preliminary treaty, but it furnished the brightest hope for Middle East peace since the Camp David Accords of 1978.

The shake felt 'round the world: Chaperoned by Bill Clinton *(center)*, Yitzhak Rabin *(left)* and Yasir Arafat greet each other on the White House lawn.

Impetus for compromise had come from several directions. Since December 1987, the uprising known as the intifada had forced PLO leaders to scramble for some concrete accomplishment to offer their people. As that revolt brought militant Islamic fundamentalists new recruits, Israeli leaders began to see the PLO as the lesser evil. The end of the Cold War meant that neither side could count on backing from the rival superpowers for perpetual belligerence. PLO support for Iraq during the 1990–91 Gulf War had prompted Arab governments to cut off funds. And many Israelis had grown disturbed at the moral costs of occupying Palestinian territories. Still, Israeli-Palestinian talks begun in 1991 (with the PLO in a backstage role) had deadlocked. The current accord resulted from Norwegian-brokered negotiations that had been kept secret from all but the highest officials on both sides.

The peace pact provided for five years of interim self-administration by Palestinians in the occupied territories, beginning in the Gaza Strip and Jericho; negotiations for a permanent arrangement were scheduled for 1995. Within nine months, Israeli troops would assume a lower profile on the West Bank, and elections would be held there for a Palestinian parliament. Israel would remain responsible for border security and for protecting its citizens (including 134,000 settlers) in the territories. Other details—currency, the status of Jerusalem—awaited further talks.

Despite serious delays and continuing violence (from Palestinians and Jewish settlers who, for opposite reasons, felt betrayed), the pact began to be implemented in 1994. Palestinian policemen took up their posts; Arafat returned in triumph to Jericho. But the future was riddled with obstacles—especially in Gaza, where refugee camps remained breeding grounds for fury. "It is very easy for anybody to start a war," the PLO chief warned, "but it is very difficult to achieve peace." **◂1988.10 ▸1994.5**

ECONOMICS

NAFTA Ratified

2 Politically ambitious tycoon H. Ross Perot offered the most memorable sound bite: That "giant sucking sound," warned the maverick former presidential candidate, is "jobs being pulled out of the country." At issue was the North American Free Trade Agreement (NAFTA), and in 1993, debate ran hot. On one side were Perot and his followers; environmentalists (who worried that American antipollution standards would fall to match Mexico's); and trade unionists and congressional protectionists (who claimed the United States would lose jobs to cheap Mexican labor in a continental free market). NAFTA's American supporters, including the Clinton administration and most manufacturing executives, argued that the opening of foreign markets to U.S. goods could only stimulate the domestic economy.

Signed by the leaders of Canada, the United States, and Mexico in 1992, NAFTA promised to eliminate tariffs and trade barriers between the three countries over a 15-year period. (The United States and Canada had completed a similar treaty in 1988.) President George Bush, who signed NAFTA, and Bill Clinton, who inherited the task of pushing it through Congress for final ratification, presented the agreement as a way of enhancing U.S. competitiveness in an increasingly sophisticated global economy. A continental trade arrangement, they said, would put North America on par with the European Economic Community and other international trade blocs.

NAFTA squeaked through Congress, its passage spurred by Vice President Al Gore's dismantling of Perot in a vitriolic televised debate. When all was said and done, NAFTA would have very little immediate impact on the huge U.S. economy. It was expected, however, to produce significant benefits in Mexico, where President Carlos Salinas de Gortari's free-market reforms depended on American cooperation. In that regard, supporters argued, NAFTA was a security issue: A prosperous Mexico would guarantee regional political stability. Ironically, Mexicans who opposed the agreement would soon stage the most serious uprising since the Cristero Rebellion of 1926. **◂1982.5 ▸1994.8**

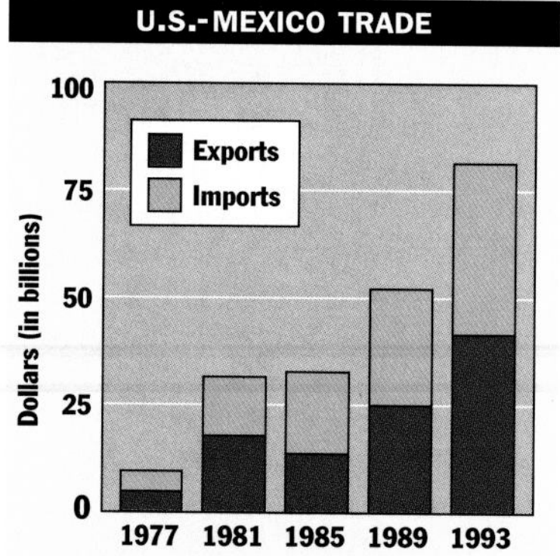

Even before NAFTA, U.S. exports to—and imports from—Mexico were booming.

TECHNOLOGY

Information Freeway

3 The U.S. National Science Foundation, primary financier of the global computer grid called the Internet, in 1993 replaced the network's technological backbone with a speedy new system called T3. Capable of accommodating 45 million bits (from *bi*nary digi*t*, a unit of electronic information) a second, T3 was 30 times faster than its predecessor. The Internet, according to a widely used electronic-communications metaphor, was thus expanded from a country road into a freeway (the "information superhighway" envisioned by technophiles remained on the drawing board). Now the Internet burst into the public consciousness as "cyberspace," a web of computer networks accessible to anyone with a personal computer and a hankering to exchange information with remote fellow "cybernauts."

The Internet connects isolated computer users throughout the world.

The U.S. Defense Department had set up the system that became the Internet in 1969. Devised to link the computers of military researchers, the network grew to include other government departments, universities, and libraries, and eventually encompassed some 12,000 computer networks in 45 countries. By 1993, more than 15 million people worldwide were

ART & CULTURE: Books: *The Shipping News* (E. Annie Proulx); *Streets of Laredo* (Larry McMurtry); *Operation Shylock* (Philip Roth); *Race Matters* (Cornel West); *The Night Manager* (John Le Carré) ... Music: "If I Ever Lose My Faith in You" (Sting); "Constant Craving" (k.d. lang); *River of Dreams* (Billy Joel, LP); *In Utero* (Nirvana, LP); *Vs* (Pearl Jam, LP); *Holocaust Symphony* (Richard Nanes) ... Painting &

"People have no money and nothing to eat, and life is only for the speculators."—**A Russian voter, explaining Vladimir Zhirinovsky's strong showing in the 1993 Russian elections**

regularly logging on to the enhanced system to participate in free-flowing "news groups"—ongoing electronic conversations. Among the increasingly diverse topics: the Hubble space telescope; JFK conspiracy theories; gun control; foot fetishism.

The Net, as users called the system, was cheap: Commercial servers provided access for about $20 a month, and some municipalities began offering public-access systems, run like old-fashioned libraries. It was fast, as well: A user could zap an instant message to a friend or colleague thousands of miles away. Computer networking allowed more information to be transmitted more efficiently than ever before. As a communications tool, it was as revolutionary as the printing press, telegraphy, and the telephone. ◂**1984.V**

RUSSIA

Yeltsin's Perils

4 In 1993, Russia's most turbulent year since the fall of communism, President Boris Yeltsin just managed to maintain control of his government—and to defend his free-market economic reforms—against aggressive challenges from die-hard Communists in Parliament. After a running battle of words with reactionary forces led by Parliament chairman Ruslan Khasbulatov and vice president Aleksandr Rutskoi, Yeltsin in September dissolved the assembly and called for new elections. Khasbulatov, Rutskoi, and hundreds of hard-line colleagues (many of whom advocated territorial expansion) then barricaded themselves inside the Parliament building—called the White House—in downtown Moscow. Yeltsin blockaded the building, and a standoff ensued.

The rebels called for a nationwide strike and demanded Yeltsin's resignation, but the vast majority of Russians, including, critically, the army and police, remained loyal to the President. Negotiations between the two sides ended fruitlessly on October 1 with the mutineers refusing to surrender their arms; three days later, after some 10,000 rebel supporters smashed through the cordon and occupied five floors of the White House, Yeltsin ordered the army to crush the uprising. When the smoke cleared from Moscow's worst violence since the 1917 revolution, an estimated 500 people lay dead, Khasbulatov and Rutskoi were in custody, and the putsch was broken.

Yeltsin's—and Russia's—troubles were far from resolved, however. In December elections to choose a new Parliament, a startling number of voters flocked to extreme-right-wing candidate Vladimir Zhirinovsky. An opponent of capitalism, a belligerent nationalist, and an avowed anti-Semite (though his father was Jewish), Zhirinovsky tapped into the popular frustration with economic and social turmoil in post-Soviet Russia. Yeltsin himself exploited similar anxieties when he got voters to endorse a new constitution (Russia's first after communism) that concentrated power in the executive. Though unnerved by Yeltsin's flaws as a democrat, many of Russia's liberal reformers—and virtually every Western leader—vocally supported him: The alternative seemed to be a return to absolutism. ◂**1992.2**

Liberated by Russian troops, Moscow's White House showed the scars of battle.

CZECHOSLOVAKIA

An Inevitable Split

5 After 74 years of union, the Czech and Slovak Federal Republic was formally dissolved on New Year's Day, 1993. In place of Czechoslovakia, there were now the Czech Republic and the Slovak Republic, each a fully independent nation with its own language, government, and special set of economic and social problems. One thing the two republics still shared was the popular feeling that division, whether truly desirable or not, had become inevitable. What little celebration accompanied the divorce was largely limited to Slovakia and was for the most part short-lived.

Since being stitched together in 1918 out of remnants of the Austro-Hungarian empire, Czechoslovakia had been dominated by its urbanized Czech majority. Rural Slovakia, in the east, was the tail that never wagged the dog. In the spirit of freedom that swept the country after Czechoslovakia bloodlessly broke from communism in 1989's "Velvet Revolution," Slovakia began demanding greater autonomy. By 1992, a disgruntled Slovak minority in the federal parliament had grown strong enough to block the unionist agenda of Czechoslovakian president Vaclav Havel *(above)*. Declaring that he would not preside over his country's dissolution, the idealistic playwright-statesman resigned. Prime Minister Vaclav Klaus had no such qualms; he brokered the split, which was announced in August.

Vladimir Mečiar, a swaggering populist and former parliamentarian, was elected Slovakia's first president. To win support, he stirred up nationalist sentiment—comparing Slovakia to a long-oppressed colony and insinuating that rising rates of unemployment and inflation were being caused by shadowy Czech plotters. His blueprint for economic recovery: more state control of the economy and revitalization of Slovakia's substantial weapons plants (even though the dissolution of the Warsaw Pact had eliminated the traditional market). The new Czech Republic continued to implement free-market reforms, and in 1993, Havel was reelected president. ◂**1989.1**

DEATHS

Kobo Abé, Japanese writer.

Marian Anderson, U.S. singer.

József Antall, Jr., Hungarian prime minister.

Arthur Ashe, U.S. tennis player and political activist.

Baudouin I, Belgian king.

Anthony Burgess, U.K. novelist.

Raymond Burr, U.S. actor.

Roy Campanella, U.S. baseball player.

Cesar Chavez, Mexican-U.S. labor leader.

Agnes de Mille, U.S. choreographer.

Richard Diebenkorn, U.S. painter.

James Doolittle, U.S. general.

Federico Fellini, Italian filmmaker.

Dizzy Gillespie, U.S. musician.

Lillian Gish, U.S. actress.

William Golding, U.K. novelist.

Helen Hayes, U.S. actress.

William Randolph Hearst, Jr., U.S. publisher.

Audrey Hepburn, Belgian-U.S. actress.

Ruby Keeler, U.S. actress, singer, and dancer.

Myrna Loy, U.S. actress.

Joseph Mankiewicz, U.S. filmmaker.

Thurgood Marshall, U.S. jurist.

Rudolf Nureyev, Russian-U.S. ballet dancer.

Norman Vincent Peale, U.S. writer.

River Phoenix, U.S. actor.

Vincent Price, U.S. actor.

Alexander Schneider, Lithuanian-U.S. musician.

Alice Tully, U.S. philanthropist.

Frank Zappa, U.S. musician.

Sculpture: *T.S. Eliot* (Ray Smith); *Lifesaver* (David Salle) ... Film: *Schindler's List* (Steven Spielberg); *Philadelphia* (Jonathan Demme); *Sleepless in Seattle* (Nora Ephron); *The Piano* (Jane Campion); *Farewell My Concubine* (Chen Kaige) ... Theater: *The Madness of George III* (Alan Bennett); *Kiss of the Spider Woman* (Harold Prince); *Sunset Boulevard* (Andrew Lloyd Webber) ... TV: *NYPD Blue*; *Grace Under Fire*.

"We have enough unemployed. We don't need any foreigners here. They take our jobs, and they take our houses."
—A worker from Rostock, Germany

NEW IN 1993

Female U.S. attorney general (Janet Reno).

Subway in Los Angeles.

Legal euthanasia (the Netherlands).

Combat role for women in U.S. military.

Paid public admission to Buckingham Palace.

IN THE UNITED STATES

▶**WORLD TRADE CENTER**—A massive explosion rocked New York's World Trade Center on February 26, killing five people, injuring hundreds, and trapping tens of thousands of office workers in the darkened, 110-story twin towers. The explosion was the work of a

group of New Jersey–based Muslim fundamentalists who had decided to blow up the trade center to protest U.S. policy in the Middle East. In March 1994, four men, followers of Egyptian sheikh Omar Abdel Rahman, were convicted in the fiery bombing (which caused $705 million in damage). Each was sentenced to 240 years in prison. ◂1916.M

▶**RUIN IN WACO**—A tense 51-day standoff between federal agents and the Branch Davidian religious cult in Waco, Texas—which had begun in February when four agents were shot while investigating the illegal arsenal of guns and explosives at the cult's compound—ended on April 19, when a deadly fire consumed the compound. The blaze was set by cult members after agents (in a widely criticized move) began battering the main compound building with armored vehicles and firing tear gas inside. The blaze

GERMANY

Anti-Immigrant Violence

6 All over Europe in the 1990s, prolonged recession prompted cries that immigrants were usurping jobs, housing, and welfare funds. Jean-Marie Le Pen's xenophobic National Front attracted a sizable minority of French voters; "yuppie fascist" Jörg Haider's Freedom Party was Austria's third-largest political force. Everywhere, shaven-headed neo-Nazi youths assaulted "foreigners"—including nonwhites of any nationality. (Britain's skinheads, whose style the others emulated, carried out the most attacks.) But in June 1993, when arsonists in Solingen, Germany, killed five Turks—three women and two girls—the world took special notice.

Skinhead violence, mainly against Turks and Vietnamese, had become commonplace in Germany. (In 1992, there were 2,280 such incidents, including 17 murders.) But this time, Turks rioted in response. Moreover, the attack came just days after Parliament, bowing to anti-immigrant pressure, severely restricted the right to political asylum. Liberal asylum rules (and Germany's central location) had attracted 700,000 purported refugees from persecution since 1991, mostly from the former Communist bloc. Although most would eventually be denied residence, they were easier to legislate against than low-paid "guest workers" from Turkey and elsewhere—who were, as in much of Europe, essential to the economy.

Indeed, Germany's dilemma mirrored Europe's. (France and Italy had recently tightened immigration laws as well.) But it also reflected a unique problem: Rich western Germany was staggering under the expense of absorbing its poor eastern counterpart; in communism's aftermath, eastern Germany was suffering from rampant unemployment and loss of social services. Though the skinheads were still only a fringe group (millions of Germans had demonstrated against them), and though a belated police crackdown was under way, many observers worried that Nazism might once again find fertile soil in German miseries. ◂1990.3

Neo-Nazi skinheads in Dresden. Anti-immigrant rage was not confined to Germany.

THE HOLOCAUST

A Wartime Enigma

7 In September 1993, six years after a Jerusalem court sentenced him to hang for murdering thousands of Jews during World War II, Ukrainian-born John (né Ivan) Demjanjuk was acquitted on appeal. Thirteen witnesses had identified the retired Ohio mechanic as "Ivan the Terrible"—a guard at the Treblinka death camp who, when he wasn't operating the gas chamber, liked to shoot, stab, or bludgeon his wards. But Demjanjuk claimed to be a victim of mistaken identity. And in the end, the Israeli Supreme Court found room for doubt.

Demjanjuk acknowledged that as a Red Army conscript in 1942 he'd been captured by the Germans. But he denied the prosecution's contention that as a POW he'd been sent to a training center for concentration-camp guards, and thence to work at Treblinka. According to his story, he was transferred to the pro-Nazi Ukrainian National Liberation Army. He admitted only to having concealed that fact from U.S. authorities when emigrating in 1951.

Besides the eyewitnesses, the case centered on an ID card from the training center. Although Demjanjuk claimed the card was a Soviet forgery, meant to embarrass the Ukrainian exile community, other documents showed that he had indeed served at various camps. But since the Nazis had burned Treblinka's records, the paper trail stopped there. Moreover, not all witnesses tagged Demjanjuk as Ivan. Some thought the sadistic guard had been killed in a prison uprising in 1943; some remembered his last name as Marchenko. Though Demjanjuk had falsely given his

Demjanjuk on trial in Israel.

mother's maiden name as Marchenko on his U.S. visa application, that might have been a coincidence.

The Supreme Court justices, following ancient Jewish legal tradition, refused to condemn Demjanjuk without absolute proof. "The complete truth," they concluded (disappointing the vengeance-minded everywhere), "is not the prerogative of the human judge." ◂1987.11

ECONOMICS

Creeping Toward Euro-Union

8 The Treaty on European Union was finally ratified in October 1993, nearly two years after being endorsed by the leaders of the twelve-nation European Community. Nicknamed the "Maastricht" treaty after the Dutch city in which it was signed, the document had generated rancorous debate among Europeans; they approved it in national referenda, but often by the narrowest of margins. (The last country to ratify was Germany.) The treaty aimed to create a single EC currency and central bank; it expanded the powers of the European Parliament and pledged the EC to work toward common foreign and defense policies. But the optimism generated by earlier

SPORTS: Baseball: World Series, Toronto Blue Jays defeat Philadelphia Phillies, 4–2 ... Football: Super Bowl, Dallas Cowboys defeat Buffalo Bills, 52–17; Florida Marlins and Colorado Rockies begin first season as National League extension teams ... Basketball: NBA, Chicago Bulls defeat Phoenix Suns, 4–2 ... Boxing: Evander Holyfield defeats Riddick Bowe in a 12-round decision fight, regains heavyweight title.

"People are looking at you and you can see them thinking—Is he Hindu or is he Muslim?"—**Ramesh Shetty, an accountant in Bombay**

French farmers protest proposed EC subsidy cuts by dumping potatoes in the street.

moves toward a "Europe without borders" had evaporated.

Since the signing of the Single European Act in 1986, Western Europe's trade barriers had largely fallen. But labor costs had risen faster than productivity, and after a short-lived boom, the EC's share of world markets had actually declined. Unemployment now averaged above 10 percent (and reached 21 percent in Spain). Meanwhile, in agriculture, *over*production had led Washington to demand that the EC nations curtail subsidies. French farmers rioted in 1992 against proposed cuts—and against Maastricht, which they believed would sell them out to the Americans. Preratification steps toward monetary union had foundered over Germany's need to raise interest rates to contain unification-fueled inflation. Disagreements over the war in the former Yugoslavia had sundered hopes of foreign-policy concord. And Britain had balked in principle at any move that meant loss of national sovereignty.

In the end, Britain opted out of a treaty clause giving EC ministers more say in social-welfare matters, and Britain and Denmark opted out of a Euro-currency. Such a currency was scheduled to arrive by 1999, but many observers doubted that it—or any of Maastricht's loftiest goals—would be achieved by century's end. **◂1985.11**

RELIGION

Holy Wars

9 Although rationalist thinkers earlier in the century had prophesied its imminent demise, religion had by the 1990s proved itself far from obsolete as a mover of multitudes—especially in the developing world, where modernizing governments continued to battle militant advocates of theocracy. In 1993, Egyptian president Hosni Mubarak responded to terrorist attacks on tourists and others by the Muslim Brotherhood (which had killed his predecessor, Anwar al-Sadat) with a string of executions. Algeria still languished under martial law, imposed after the Islamic Salvation Front in December 1991 defeated the ruling National Liberation Front in first-round balloting. (The fundamentalist victory prompted President Chadli Benjedid to resign in favor of a civilian-military junta that canceled the runoff election; Islamic radicals assassinated the junta leader but failed to seize power.) And in India, Muslims themselves were the victims of religious extremists.

Hindu militants destroy a mosque in Ayodhya, triggering months of bloodshed.

The trouble started in December 1992, when thousands of Hindu militants in the northern town of Ayodhya, egged on by leaders of the right-wing Bharatiya Janata Party (BJP), demolished a 464-year-old Muslim mosque that stood on the supposed birth site of the Hindu god Rama. Rioting erupted throughout the country and lasted into February; some 3,000 people died—mostly Muslims, many killed by Hindu mobs that attacked their homes while police stood by. Prime Minister P.V. Narasimha Rao was widely castigated for failing to prevent the violence (the BJP had long indicated its intentions) and for responding weakly. In March, perhaps in retaliation for the massacres of Muslims, 13 bombs rocked Bombay, killing 317 people. The communal violence was dwarfed, however, by a great natural disaster: In September, an earthquake in Maharashtra state killed 30,000. With a single blow, an act of God could still overshadow the acts of god-mad men. **◂1991.M**

ART

A Radical Eminence Grise

10 Amid the often incoherent "shock art" on display at the 45th Venice Biennale of contemporary art in 1993 (one exhibit featured photographs of female genitalia), the sculpture of 81-year-old Louise Bourgeois stood out for its raw, emotional eloquence. Honored with a solo show at the American pavilion, Bourgeois installed such works as *Cell (Arch of Hysteria)* (1992-93), a pink marble depiction of her childhood home in France, surrounded by chain-link and threatened by an ominous guillotine. The artist's intention: "I want to bother people. I want to worry them."

Bourgeois, who emigrated to America from France in 1938, had been recognized as a major New York School sculptor during the 1940s. But her eroticized angst (one signature work, *Femme Couteau*, is a marble female nude carved at top and bottom to dagger-like points) became unfashionable during the minimalist sixties. In the eighties, she staged a comeback—and the prestigious Venice Biennale made it complete. **◂1982.10**

Bourgeois's *Mamelles (on wall)* and *Decontrée* were both at 1993's Venice Biennale.

IN THE UNITED STATES

destroyed the building in less than an hour and killed 85 people (17 were children), including 33-year-old cult leader and self-proclaimed prophet David Koresh. ◂1978.2

▶ABORTION DOCTOR SLAIN—An antiabortion protester shot Dr. David Gunn to death outside a Pensacola, Florida, abortion clinic in March. The slaying—apparently the first of its kind—reflected the increasingly extreme tactics of abortion opponents. (The group Operation Rescue had circulated a "wanted" poster of the doctor, and a number of clinics had been bombed.) Despite a 1994 federal law making it illegal for demonstrators to block clinics, the violence continued: Seventeen months later, Gunn's successor, Dr. John Bayard Britton, was also felled by an assassin's bullet. ◂1973.5

▶MIDWEST FLOODED—An incredible 49 consecutive days of rain swelled the Mississippi River to record levels during the spring and summer, causing the worst flooding ever recorded in the Midwest. In August, President Clinton signed a $6.2 billion flood aid bill to provide relief in one of America's most expensive national disasters. ◂1992.M

▶JORDAN RETIRES—In October, three months after leading the Chicago Bulls to a third consecutive NBA champion-

ship, Michael Jordan—arguably the greatest basketball player ever—retired at 30, with seven straight NBA scoring titles, three straight league Most Valuable Player awards, and two Olympic gold medals. The media-friendly guard made millions want to "be like Mike," as one of his many commercial endorsements put it. But allegations of a gambling habit, followed by his father's murder in August, contributed to his disenchantment with superstardom. He switched to minor-league baseball; 17 months later—in a euphoria-inducing move—he rejoined the Bulls. ◂1992.10

POLITICS & BUSINESS: GNP: $6,378.1 billion ... Clinton proposes lifting ban on homosexuals in military; lifts restrictions on abortion counseling and fetal-tissue research ... Family and Medical Leave Act signed ... Ruth Bader Ginsburg becomes second woman on Supreme Court ... Dept. of Energy reveals that the federal government in the 1940s injected plutonium into unknowing human subjects.

"The ghosts were on the set every day in their millions."—**Actor Ben Kingsley, costar of *Schindler's List***

AROUND THE WORLD

▶POLAND AFTER COMMUNISM—President Lech Walesa got a nasty surprise in September elections designed to give Poland a new, more workable parliament (the fractious old one included 29 different parties): Two Communist-descended factions won a combined 301 of the assembly's 460 seats. The Democratic Left Alliance and the Polish Peasant Party dominated voting by promising to slow the aggressive pace of economic reform, to increase social spending, and, in the case of the PPP, to raise farm supports. Walesa's Non-Party Block to Support Reform garnered only 20 seats. On the bright side, Poland's economy was expanding at an annual 3 percent rate of growth—highest of the former Communist countries. ◀1989.1

▶ERITREA INDEPENDENT—In an April referendum, 99.8 percent of voters in Eritrea chose to secede from Ethiopia. The

decision, recognized within days by the world community, ended a 30-year-old war of independence by the former northern Ethiopian province. ◀1978.M

▶IRAQ STRUCK—Repercussions from the Gulf War continued in 1993. In January—in response to dictator Saddam Hussein's violations of UN orders to dismantle weapons of mass destruction and honor a no-fly zone—U.S., British, and French forces bombed and rocketed Iraqi military and industrial sites (including a suspected nuclear-components factory). In early July, President Clinton—retaliating for an alleged Iraqi-sponsored assassination plot against his predecessor, George Bush—sent 23 Tomahawk cruise missiles streaking toward Iraqi intelligence headquarters in Baghdad. In both attacks, stray missiles killed civilians. (One of the July victims was Layla al-Attar, a painter famous in the Arab world.) ◀1992.M

JAPAN

Shattering Traditions

11 Despite its name, Japan's Liberal Democrat Party was deeply conservative, a union of bureaucracy and big business that had governed uninterrupted for almost 40 years. The complacent, increasingly corrupt LDP excelled at "money politics," trading industrial contracts for kickbacks, while largely ignoring the average Japanese—an urban consumer who paid the highest prices in the world. In 1993, frustrated voters staged a kind of revolution: They broke the party's majority in Parliament. An unlikely coalition of conservative and socialist parties took over the government, with Morihiro Hosokawa *(above)* as prime minister.

A mere 14 months before he took office, Hosokawa, scion of a distinguished shogun family, had himself been an LDP man. Fed up with the party's resistance to change, he bolted to create the reformist Japan New Party. That quixotic act, for which Hosokawa was roundly dismissed as a crank, was the opening sally in Japan's battle against single-party rule. The LDP had already lost substantial support through a series of influence-peddling scandals. The final outrage came in June 1993, when Prime Minister Kiichi Miyazawa scuttled a promised reform package. In Parliament, 39 of his LDP colleagues joined the opposition to pass a no-confidence vote. Miyazawa was forced to schedule new elections, and in July (shortly after Crown Prince Naruhito shattered another tradition by marrying a woman with her own career, U.S.-educated diplomat Masako Owada), voters broke the LDP stranglehold.

Hosokawa took office vowing to end corruption and update the moribund electoral system. Head of a fragile coalition of parties unified only in opposition to the LDP, he faced an uphill battle. The new prime minister did have one advantage: His public approval ratings were the highest on record. But in early 1994, he too was felled by a corruption scandal. A string of successors came and went within a few months, unable to maintain a stable coalition. **◀1989.5 ▶1994.M**

FILM

Hollywood and the Holocaust

12 Filmmaker Steven Spielberg released two landmark movies in 1993. The first was *Jurassic Park*, remarkable for the stunning verisimilitude of its rampaging dinosaurs and because it became the biggest box-office smash in history—supplanting Spielberg's own *E.T.* The second film possessed a more solemn distinction: It tackled a subject Hollywood had only rarely and gingerly dared touch—the Holocaust. *Schindler's List* was a three-hour adaptation of Thomas Keneally's fact-based novel about a German businessman, Oskar Schindler, who set out to exploit Polish Jews as laborers in his factory—and wound up rescuing 1,100 from Auschwitz.

Scrupulously researched, harrowing in its graphic realism, the film won seven Oscars, including Best Picture and a long-coveted Best Director award for Spielberg. Educators took their students to see the movie. In Germany, Poland, and Israel, audiences wept and fainted. For millions who knew little about the Holocaust, it was a guided tour of hell. Perhaps inevitably, however, it aroused controversy as well as critical raves.

For all its pseudodocumentary handheld-camera-work, *Schindler's List* is very much a Hollywood production. Its protagonist is a flawed, detached, attractively mysterious man who, when the chips are down, behaves nobly and earns redemption—a classic film-noir hero. The black-and-white photography gleams. No one is gassed on screen. There's even a happy ending.

Detractors faulted Spielberg (himself Jewish) for failing to portray the heroic resistance of many Jews, for ignoring the slaughter of other "undesirables" in the camps, and for letting gentiles off the hook: After all, Schindler was an anomaly —most European Christians did nothing to resist the Holocaust.

Oskar Schindler, played by Liam Neeson *(left)*: industrialist, con man, hero.

"*Schindler's List*," wrote one pundit, "proves again that, for Spielberg, there is a power in the world that is greater than good and greater than evil, and it is the movies." **◀1982.9**

ITALY

The Uffizi Blast

13 The car bomb that rocked Florence's Uffizi Gallery in May 1993 pulverized three paintings by minor Renaissance artists, damaged 30 other artworks, and shattered a medieval tower full of ancient agricultural records. It also killed five people, including the tower's caretaker and her family. And it unnerved the Italian populace, already dismayed by the biggest government

One of the world's foremost art museums, the Uffizi became a terrorist target.

scandal since World War II—the implication of 2,500 politicians and corporate leaders in a Mafia-spun web of corruption.

Investigators linked the bombing itself to the Mafia, whose reputed boss of bosses, Salvatore Riina, had been caught in the latest police sweep. The blast did not harm the Uffizi's priceless Botticellis, Michelangelos, Leonardos, and Caravaggios, many of which had just been shielded behind bulletproof glass. But the attack on the museum—one of the world's greatest, housed in a palazzo built for the Medicis—was a blow to Italy's heart.

In April, voters had passed a referendum demanding sweeping measures to break the links between organized crime and government. Now 20,000 Florentines took to the streets, chanting, "Enough of these massacres." (An apparently related blast had razed a Rome apartment complex, injuring 23 people.) But the "massacres" continued: Soon bombs damaged two of Rome's oldest churches and Milan's historic center.

In 1994, with the culprits still at large, voters expressed their frustration with the venal and ineffectual political system in a way that sent shock waves around the globe. **◀1987.5 ▶1994.M**

NOBEL PRIZES: Peace: F.W. de Klerk and Nelson Mandela (South African; ending apartheid) ... Literature: Toni Morrison (U.S.; novelist) ... Chemistry: Kary Mullis and Michael Smith (U.S., Canadian; genetics) ... Medicine: Phillip Sharp and Richard Roberts (U.S.; split genes) ... Physics: Joseph Taylor and Russell Hulse (U.S.; ultradense stars) ... Economics: Robert Fogel and Douglass North (U.S.).

A VOICE FROM 1993

The Sublimity of Word-Work

From the Nobel acceptance speech by Toni Morrison, December 7, 1993

With her receipt of the 1993 prize for literature, American novelist Toni Morrison became the first black woman to be awarded a Nobel. Morrison's lyrical novels were among the first to explore the experiences of African-American women: In The Bluest Eye, *"a little black girl yearns for the blue eyes of a little white girl"; in* Beloved, *a former slave named Sethe delves into the tragedy of her history. The Swedish academy commended Morrison's sensitivity to "language itself, a language she wants to liberate from the fetters of race. And she addresses us with the luster of poetry." Morrison's virtuosity was much in evidence in an acceptance speech that turned an old folktale—a story about some young people who try to disprove an old blind woman's clairvoyance by asking her if the bird they hold is dead or alive—into a parable of the transformative power of language.* **◂1950.V**

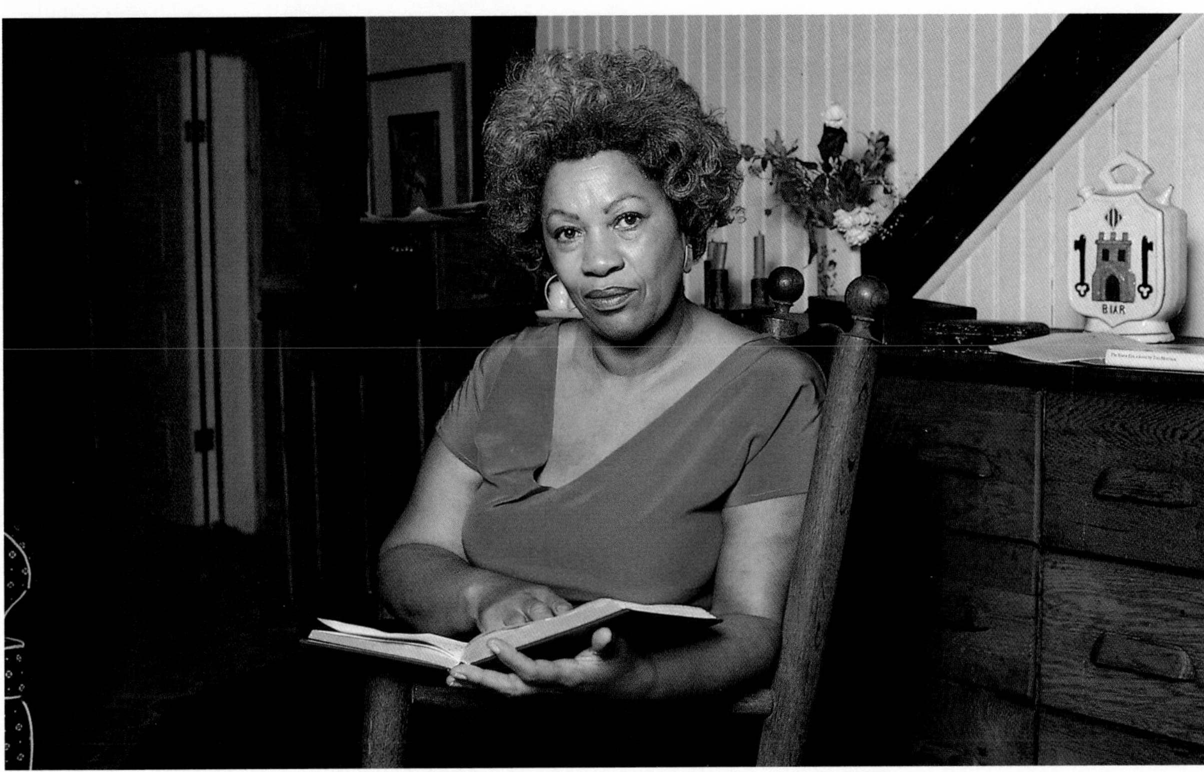

Novelist Toni Morrison at home in Grand View, New York, in 1978.

The conventional wisdom of the Tower of Babel story is that the collapse was a misfortune. That it was the distraction or the weight of many languages that precipitated the tower's failed architecture. That one monolithic language would have expedited the building, and heaven would have been reached. Whose heaven, she wonders? And what kind? Perhaps the achievement of Paradise was premature, a little hasty if no one could take the time to understand other languages, other views, other narratives. Had they, the heaven they imagined might have been found at their feet. Complicated, demanding, yes, but a view of heaven as life; not heaven as post-life.

She would want to leave her young visitors with the impression that language should be forced to stay alive merely to be. The vitality of language lies in its ability to limn the actual, imagined and possible lives of its speakers, readers, writers. Although its poise is sometimes in displacing experience, it is not a substitute for it. It arcs toward the place where meaning may lie. When a President of the United States thought about the graveyard his country had become, and said, "The world will little note nor long remember what we say here. But it will never forget what they did here," his simple words were exhilarating in their life-sustaining properties because they refused to encapsulate the reality of 600,000 dead men in a cataclysmic race war. Refusing to monumentalize, disdaining the "final word," the precise "summing up," acknowledging their "poor power to add or detract," his words signal deference to the uncapturability of the life it mourns. It is the deference that moves her, that recognition that language can never live up to life once and for all. Language can never "pin down" slavery, genocide, war. Nor should it yearn for the arrogance to be able to do so. Its force, its felicity, is in its reach toward the ineffable.

Be it grand or slender, burrowing, blasting or refusing to sanctify; whether it laughs out loud or is a cry without an alphabet, the choice word or the chosen silence, unmolested language surges toward knowledge, not its destruction. But who does not know of literature banned because it is interrogative; discredited because it is critical; erased because alternate? And how many are outraged by the thought of a self-ravaged tongue?

Word-work is sublime, she thinks, because it is generative; it makes meaning that secures our difference, our human difference—the way in which we are like no other life.

We die. That may be the meaning of life. But we *do* language. That may be the measure of our lives.

"Never, never and never again shall this beautiful land experience the oppression of one by another and suffer the indignity of being the skunk of the world."—**South African President Nelson Mandela**

STORY OF THE YEAR

A New Day in South Africa

1 Allowed to participate in national elections for the first time in their country's troubled history, jubilant South African blacks in April 1994 swept African National Congress leader Nelson Mandela to the presidency. The climactic voting marked the birth of democracy in a land where injustice, brutality, and racial persecution had long been the rule. It also capped one man's heroic struggle against apartheid. A lifelong leader in the fight for racial equality, veteran of 27 years in police-state prisons, Mandela was now, statesmanlike and dignified at 75, poised to realize his vision of "a new South Africa where all South Africans are equal, where all South Africans work together to bring about security, peace, and democracy in our country."

The historic election, conducted over four days, saw lines stretching more than a mile outside polling places, as 16 million blacks, along with some 9.5 million whites, Asians, and coloureds (people of mixed race), turned out to exercise their civic right. When all the votes were finally counted, Mandela had tallied better than 60 percent, far outdistancing his closest rival, incumbent president F.W. de Klerk, the man who'd begun to dismantle apartheid five years earlier. All over the country, the old regime's flag, hated emblem of apartheid, was replaced by the multicolored banner of an inclusive new South Africa.

Mandela and South Africa had come a long way, but decades of methodical abuse had created problems that would not be quickly resolved. The election campaign itself had been violently disrupted by both white supremacists and separatist blacks. Fear-mongering militias like the Afrikaner Resistance Movement (ARM) had used bombs and bullets in support of a whites-only homeland; Mangosuthu Buthelezi, leader of the Zulu-based, anti-ANC Inkatha Freedom Party, had resorted to terrorism to enforce an election boycott. His motive in frightening people away from the polls: to secure Zulu autonomy in post-apartheid South Africa. A week before the vote, hope triumphed over hatred, and Buthelezi called off the boycott. The election proceeded with surprising calm.

In South Africa, ANC supporters celebrate the election of Nelson Mandela.

Mandela took office under an enormous burden of expectation. Many blacks lived without electricity or running water; discriminatory education had left some 50 percent of them illiterate. The 87 percent of arable land reserved for whites awaited redistribution. "Don't expect us to do miracles," Mandela cautioned. That he spoke as South Africa's president was an indication that one had already occurred. **◄1990.V**

The largest Rwandan refugee camp, in Goma, Zaire, held a million men, women, and children. Disease killed thousands daily.

CENTRAL AFRICA

Rwanda's Agony

2 The bloodbath began in April 1994, after a plane carrying the presidents of Rwanda and Burundi was shot down over the Rwandan capital of Kigali. Within three months, 500,000 Rwandans had been killed, and nearly half the country's eight million people had fled their homes. Most of the murders were committed by members of the Hutu ethnic group, but by year's end the Tutsi minority had won a surprising, if tentative, military victory.

Rwanda's ethnic torment was a relatively recent phenomenon. The Hutu and Tutsi had long coexisted peacefully—the former as farmers, the latter as cattle herders and kings. The two groups worshiped the same deity, spoke the same language, and even intermarried. But Belgian colonists, who succeeded the Germans in 1916, exacerbated social divisions, reserving education and top bureaucratic positions for the lighter-skinned Tutsi. In 1959, the Hutu rebelled, massacring 20,000 Tutsi and driving 150,000 into exile; three years later, Belgium granted Rwanda independence and put the Hutu in charge. The new rulers brutally repressed the remaining Tutsi (about 15 percent of the population). But in 1993, after three years of civil war with the Tutsi-led, Uganda-based Rwandan Patriotic Front (RPF), President Juvénal Habyarimana was forced to share power.

The move cost him his life. Hard-line Hutu troops downed his plane as it returned from a Hutu-Tutsi peace conference, but pinned the blame on the RPF. Then machete-wielding Hutu soldiers and militiamen went on a rampage, killing Tutsi civilians, moderate Hutu (including Rwanda's prime minister), Catholic priests, and ten Belgian UN peacekeepers. But RPF forces—better armed and disciplined than their foe, and some 20,000 strong—routed government troops, and hordes of Hutu soon joined Tutsi refugees in camps in neighboring countries.

In July, the RPF seized Kigali and set up an ethnically mixed government; rebel leader Paul Kagame urged all refugees to come home. Most Tutsi returned. But exiled Hutu officials, discounting RPF guarantees of safety (and aiming to use the camps as guerrilla bases), told their uprooted people to stay put. Cholera killed thousands in the camps, while Hutu soldiers hoarded food and barred their brethren from leaving. The Tutsi hold on power looked fragile indeed. **◄1972.M**

KOREA

A Nuclear Showdown

3 Flouting the 1968 Nuclear Nonproliferation Treaty, Communist North Korea in 1994 engaged in a hair-raising shell game. After months of obstructing routine

A cartoonist's satirical view of UN efforts to stop North Korea's nuclear program.

International Atomic Energy Agency inspections, aging dictator Kim Il Sung in March barred the UN agency from investigating a security breach at one of his country's nine nuclear facilities. North Korea denied that it was developing nuclear weapons, but according to U.S. intelligence, the nation (one of the world's last Stalinist strongholds) was diverting plutonium from energy plants to build bombs.

China's traditional alliance with North Korea meant UN action was unlikely. As the United States sought

ART & CULTURE: Books: ***In the Lake of the Woods*** **(Tim O'Brien);** ***A Frolic of His Own*** **(William Gaddis);** ***Open Secrets*** **(Alice Munro);** ***The Collected Stories*** **(Grace Paley);** ***The Bell Curve: Intelligence and Class Structure in American Life*** **(Richard Herrnstein and Charles Murray) ... Music:** ***Voodoo Lounge*** **(Rolling Stones, LP);** ***Vitology*** **(Pearl Jam, LP);** ***Monster*** **(R.E.M., LP);** ***Chant*** **(Benedictine Monks of Santo**

"The bear named Peace has yet to be hunted down, but he has already been skinned and everyone is making suits from him."—**Israeli novelist Meir Shalev, on hearing that Yasir Arafat, Yitzhak Rabin, and Shimon Peres had received the 1994 Nobel Peace Prize**

international support for trade sanctions against Kim's already isolated, penurious nation, the dictator vowed to retaliate by turning American ally South Korea into a "sea of flames." Then, in June, there was an unlikely breakthrough in the tense standoff: Former U.S. president Jimmy Carter met with Kim and received assurance that North Korea would suspend its bomb program. "The crisis," Carter announced, "is over." In a way, it was only beginning: Two weeks later, just as U.S.-North Korean nuclear talks opened in Geneva, Kim died. Revered as the demiurgic "Great Leader," the 82-year-old strongman, who'd come to power in 1948, was the only ruler his country had ever known.

In Communism's first dynastic succession, Kim Jong Il, Kim's 52-year-old son, apparently acceded to power. (Who exactly was in charge remained murky.) Talks resumed in Geneva, producing an October accord that called for North Korea to dismantle its plutonium reactors in return for economic aid (including the delivery of tamper-proof, light-water reactors) and full diplomatic recognition from the United States. But in late December, the accord was imperiled when the regime shot down a U.S. helicopter that had strayed into North Korean air space, killing one pilot and detaining another for a week. A disquieting cold war hangover continued to throb. **◂1968.6**

NORTHERN IRELAND

A Glimmer of Hope

4 The outlaw Irish Republican Army's announcement of "a complete cessation of military operations," effective August 31, 1994, set off a round of spontaneous street celebrations by the beleaguered citizens, Catholic and Protestant alike, of British-ruled Northern Ireland. Impetus for the cease-fire derived from an initiative issued the previous December by Prime Ministers John Major of Britain and Albert Reynolds of Ireland, which promised Sinn Fein, the IRA's legal political arm, a stake in talks on Northern Ireland if the guerrillas permanently suspended hostilities. Ultimately, the prime ministers agreed, Protestant-dominated Northern Ireland's fate would be decided by popular vote.

Wary of seeming too quick to abandon British loyalists (but eager to resolve a $4.5 billion-a-year problem), Major in September insisted talks could not begin until the IRA had held its fire for three months. (Similar cease-fires in 1972 and 1975 had been short-lived.) A number of Protestant paramilitary groups subsequently vowed to lay down arms. Still, there were many obstacles to peace: The IRA refused to surrender its substantial arsenal; political prisoners remained a ticklish issue with both the IRA and its Protestant counterparts; outspoken Sinn Fein leader Gerry Adams (who'd gained political credibility in February when he was granted a U.S. visa) demanded that Britain withdraw its 17,600 soldiers from Northern Ireland. Yet progress had been made. Adams said he would "compromise, not only with the British but with the Unionists." Such novel flexibility raised hopes that Northern Ireland's problems were soluble after all. **◂1981.9**

In Belfast, a generation came of age indelibly marked by 25 years of sectarian strife.

THE MIDDLE EAST

Peace Moves and Massacres

5 Never had peace in the Middle East seemed closer at hand—or farther away—than in 1994. In February, just five months after Israel and the PLO signed their landmark treaty, an Israeli fanatic gunned down 29 worshipers in a mosque at Hebron's Tomb of the Patriarchs. The killer, a Brooklyn-born physician, was beaten to death by survivors; more Palestinians died when panicky Israeli soldiers fired on the fleeing crowd. A cycle of reprisals by Arab guerrillas and Jewish vigilantes followed (including the bombing of a Jewish center in Buenos Aires, Argentina, that killed 100).

The violence delayed the first stage of limited Palestinian self-rule in Israel's occupied territories—the treaty's central provision—until May, when Israeli troops turned over Jericho and the Gaza Strip to Palestinian authorities. Two months later, Yasir Arafat returned from exile to a hero's welcome. He proved an inept administrator, however, and his refusal to reveal how he spent foreign aid prompted donors to withhold funds. Democracy-minded Palestinians were alienated by his autocratic style; hardliners reviled his cooperation with Israel.

In October, factions of Hamas, a militant Muslim fundamentalist group, launched an all-out assault on the peace process—and on Arafat's authority. Terrorists abducted a Jewish soldier, videotaped him urging the release of Hamas prisoners, then shot him as Israeli commandos stormed their hideout. (That same day, Arafat and Rabin were awarded the 1994 Nobel Peace Prize.) Days later, a suicide bomber blew up a Tel Aviv bus, killing 23. Even the signing of a pact between Israel and Jordan, who enjoyed relatively cordial relations, did not restore optimism. By November, when Palestinian security forces killed 15 Hamas rioters in Gaza City, fulfillment of the Israeli-PLO treaty had been postponed indefinitely. **◂1993.1**

Vision of hatred: Carnage brought about by Hamas suicide attack on a Tel Aviv bus.

DEATHS

Jean-Louis Barrault, French actor and filmmaker.

Charles Bukowski, U.S. writer.

Cab Calloway, U.S. musician.

John Candy, Canadian-U.S. comedian.

Elias Canetti, Bulgarian-Swiss writer.

Kurt Cobain, U.S. singer.

Arnold Raymond Cream (Jersey Joe Walcott), U.S. boxer.

Robert Doisneau, French photographer.

Ralph Ellison, U.S. novelist.

Erik H. Erikson, German-U.S. psychoanalyst and writer.

Orval E. Faubus, U.S. governor.

Vitas Gerulaitis, U.S. tennis player.

Juvénal Habyarimana, Rwandan political leader.

William A. Higinbotham, U.S. inventor.

Erich Honecker, East German communist leader.

Kim Il Sung, North Korean president.

Eugène Ionesco, French playwright.

Donald Judd, U.S. sculptor.

Burt Lancaster, U.S. actor.

William Levitt, U.S. developer.

Carmen McRae, U.S. singer.

Cyprien Ntaryamnira, Burundi president.

Richard Nixon, U.S. president.

Jacqueline Kennedy Onassis, U.S. first lady.

Thomas "Tip" O'Neill, Jr., U.S. congressman.

John Osborne, U.K. playwright.

Linus Pauling, U.S. chemist.

Roy J. Plunkett, U.S. chemist and inventor.

Karl Popper, Austrian-U.K. philosopher.

Jerry Rubin, U.S. political activist.

Wilma Rudolph, U.S. athlete.

Dean Rusk, U.S. secretary of state.

Jessica Tandy, U.S. actress.

Domingo, LP); *Symphony No. 7* (Alfred Schnittke) ... Film: *Forrest Gump* (Robert Zemeckis); *Pulp Fiction* (Quentin Tarantino); *Quiz Show* (Robert Redford); *Barcelona* (Whit Stillman) ... Theater: *Three Tall Women* (Edward Albee); *SubUrbia* (Eric Bogosian); *Twilight: Los Angeles, 1992* (Anna Deavere Smith); *Passion* (Stephen Sondheim); *Sunset Boulevard* (Andrew Lloyd Webber) ... TV: *ER*; *My So-Called Life*.

NEW IN 1994

Diplomatic relations between Israel and the Vatican.

Living Vu Quang ox (a species first identified in 1992 from skulls found in hunters' homes; discovered in Vietnam).

All-female America's Cup sailing team.

Conclusive evidence of the existence of black holes (discovered by newly repaired Hubble Telescope).

IN THE UNITED STATES

▶SPORTS STRIKE OUT—With team owners threatening to impose a cap on salaries, major league baseball players walked off the field in August. Baseball's eighth work-stoppage in 22 years forced the first-ever cancellation of the World Series. Sports fans felt another blow in September, when the National Hockey League, coming off a spectacular season in which the Great One, the Los Angeles Kings' Wayne Gretzky, broke hockey's all-time record for goals, locked out players before a new season could even begin. The issue: rising player salaries.

▶ICE FOLLIES—In January, a month before the 1994 Winter Olympics in Lillehammer, Norway, seedy associates of figure skater Tonya Harding tried to eliminate rival skater Nancy Kerrigan from competition by clubbing her on the knee. (Instead, she recovered.) Vilified but not convicted, Harding sued to keep her place on the American team. In the "good girl-bad girl" showdown at Lillehammer, Harding skated miserably. Kerrigan performed well but placed second to waifish Ukrainian skater Oksana Baiul.

Gehry likened the zinc awning of his American Center to a "ballerina's skirt."

ARCHITECTURE

An American in Paris

6 In June 1994, one of the era's foremost architects unveiled a Parisian monument to his American homeland. Frank Gehry's American Center epitomized the Los Angeles-based designer's playfully scrambled "deconstructivist" style. In deference to its surroundings, Gehry built the Center (devoted to exhibitions of American culture) of typically Parisian limestone. Some local critics declared their disappointment: The building looked too French. **◂1991.8**

SCIENCE

Dino Discovery

7 In April 1994, a joint expedition of scientists from the American Museum of Natural History and the Mongolian Academy of Sciences unveiled a dazzling hoard of fossils unearthed the previous summer in the Gobi Desert. Among the treasures were 140 skulls of 80-million-year-old mammals, and the remains of a turkey-sized animal that resembled both dinosaurs and birds. Then, in November, the team revealed an even more important find: the first positively identified embryo of a meat-eating dinosaur.

The oviraptor embryo discovered by Gobi expedition member Mark Norell inside an eroded, six-inch fossil egg—shed new light on dinosaur breeding habits. Seven decades earlier, paleontologist Roy Chapman Andrews had found an adult oviraptor skeleton in the Gobi, atop a pile of eggs identical to this one. Andrews had assumed the eggs were those of another species and were being eaten by the oviraptor (from the Latin for "egg robber"). The 1994 find suggested that the animal had been tending her unhatched young—something that only vegetarian dinosaurs had been thought to do. **◂1959.5**

The fossilized bones of an unhatched dinosaur, inside an 80-million-year-old shell.

MEXICO

A Year of Turmoil

8 A period of economic reform and relative stability in Mexico came to a violent end on New Year's Day 1994 with a shocking peasant insurrection. Operating in Chiapas, Mexico's southernmost state and one of its poorest, the homegrown, 2,000-man-strong Zapatista National Liberation Army seized seven towns before withdrawing into the mountains under heavy fire from the Mexican army. The guerrillas' cause: to end the 65-year monopoly on power held by the Institutional Revolutionary Party (PRI).

Not coincidentally, the Zapatistas struck on the day the North American Free Trade Agreement went into effect. NAFTA, which liberalized trade between the United States, Canada, and Mexico, was to be the capstone in technocratic president Carlos Salinas de Gotari's six-year campaign to remake Mexico. His many economic reforms had made Mexico a darling of First World investors. But corrupt one-party politics, the rebels claimed, prevented prosperity from reaching Mexico's desperately poor peasant population: Too much money still disappeared into the deep pockets of the PRI's old-guard bureaucrats.

Mexico was dealt another blow in April, when top presidential candidate Luis Donaldo Colosio, Salinas's hand-picked successor, was gunned down on the campaign trail. His replacement, party official Ernesto Zedillo Ponce de León, went on to win the August election. Colosio's assassination, the first of a national political figure since 1928, was not the year's last: José Francisco Ruiz Masseiu, the reform-minded secretary-general of the PRI, was murdered in September. Two months later his brother accused the PRI of complicity in the crime.

By December, when Zedillo took office, Mexico seemed to be coming apart at the seams. Zapatista rebels were moving again, and the peso was eroding calamitously as nervous foreign investors dumped their holdings. Before Zedillo could assuage international fears, he would have to persuade his own people that he was serious about reform—social and economic. **◂1993.2**

Over a hundred died in clashes between Zapatista rebels *(above)* and the Mexican Army.

BOSNIA

Death in the Balkans

9 The cease-fire agreed to by warring Serbs and Muslims in Bosnia and Hercegovina in February 1994 was emblematic of the tortured Bosnian conflict: Heralded internationally as the beginning of peace, it turned out to mere diplomatic window dressing. Bosnian Serbs, gunning to join the rump Yugoslav state of Serbia in a "Greater Serbia," continued to rain shells on Sarajevo and other Bosnian cities; the Muslim-dominated Bosnian army still fought desperately to hold the 30 percent of Bosnian territory not yet overrun by Serbs; both sides, but mainly the

SPORTS: Baseball: World Series canceled due to players' strike ... Football: Super Bowl: S.F. 49ers defeat San Diego Chargers, 49–26 ... Basketball: Houston Rockets defeat New York Knicks, 4–3 (first major pro championship won by a Houston team) ... Olympics held in Lillehammer ... Soccer: World Cup: In first U.S.-hosted tournament Brazil defeats Italy, 3–2 (U.S. advances to second round, first win since 1950).

"My dream is democracy. Telling me to stop is like telling me to stop breathing."—**Restored Haitian President Jean-Bertrand Aristide**

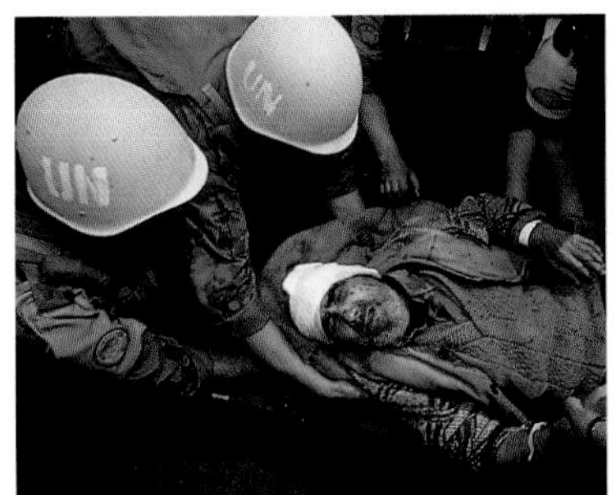

UN "blue helmets" evacuate a civilian wounded in a Serb attack on Gorazde.

Serbs, continued to torture, murder, and rape civilians as they pursued genocidal "ethnic cleansing." And NATO and the United Nations continued to frame dilatory policies that did nothing to stop the slaughter.

As casualties mounted—200,000 people dead by the spring of 1994 (85 percent civilians), four million people driven from their homes—NATO repeatedly tried to bring Bosnian Serb leader Radovan Karadzic to the negotiating table by threatening him with airstrikes. But Karadzic, supported by Serbian president Slobodan Miloševic, urged on his troops with impunity. Meanwhile, the impotence of 22,000 UN "peacekeeping" troops in Bosnia was underscored in December, when the Serbs launched a brutal campaign against Bihac, a Muslim enclave and alleged UN "safe area" in northwestern Bosnia. NATO, in its biggest show of the war, bombed a Serb airbase. The Serbs responded by taking UN troops hostage. "Bihac will become a safe area," Karadzic gloated, "when the Serbs occupy it."

To make matters worse, NATO itself was divided. The United States faulted the Serbs, and proposed arming the Muslims; England and France blamed both sides and said more guns would only aggravate the problem. As the war slogged into its third year, one UN official offered a stinging assessment: "We are all accomplices." ◂**1992.1**

THE CARIBBEAN

Aristide Restored in Haiti

10 For three years, Haiti's first freely elected president had languished in American exile, while the army officers who'd overthrown him terrorized his people. Perhaps 3,000 Haitians had been murdered by paramilitary *attachés*. A U.S.-led trade embargo had deepened the misery of the hemisphere's poorest nation, while barely affecting its rulers. As the junta repeatedly broke promises to restore democracy, thousands of refugees had headed for Florida. (Most were interned at the U.S. naval base at Guantánamo Bay, Cuba—alongside thousands of fleeing Cubans.) But finally, in 1994, Washington lent Father Jean-Bertrand Aristide its military muscle.

President Clinton first hinted at invasion in May, but vacillated in the face of criticism. Opponents argued that Aristide was a radical "flake" and that Haiti was not vital to U.S. interests; most Americans opposed using force. But in September, after tightened sanctions only heightened the junta's defiance, Clinton assembled his gunships. Then he sent a delegation of ex-president Jimmy Carter, General Colin Powell, and Georgia senator Sam Nunn to Port-au-Prince for an eleventh-hour diplomatic effort. It worked: Haiti's troika—generals Raoul Cédras and Philippe Biamby, and Lieutenant Colonel Joseph Michel François—agreed to step down.

Some 20,000 U.S. troops promptly arrived in Haiti. Their assignment was to help Haitian authorities keep order during the transition—but after a spate of new killings by attachés, and a shootout between police and U.S. Marines (ten policemen died), the mission broadened.

Although mobs looted police and army buildings, most Haitians heeded Aristide's pleas to forgo vengeance. He returned on October 15 just two days after Cédras and Biamby left for Panama. (François had fled earlier.) The longtime foe of capitalism and Yankee imperialism thanked Clinton and set about reassuring anxious businessmen. As Haitians rejoiced in the streets, the nation's new leaders—operating out of offices without working telephones—struggled to rebuild their nation from the rubble. ◂**1990.13**

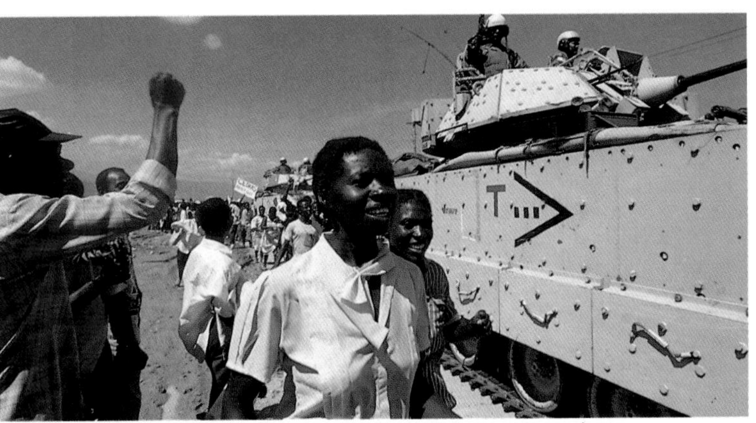

Haitians welcomed Aristide—and U.S. troops—at the end of dictatorship.

TECHNOLOGY

Under the Sea

11 Since the time of Napoleon, engineers had dreamed of bridging the watery 30-mile divide —psychological as well as physical—between England and the European continent with an underwater passageway. (Napoleon approved plans for a tunnel for stagecoaches, complete with "chimneys" rising above the water for ventilation.) In May 1994, nearly 200 years later, those dreams were dramatically realized when England's Queen Elizabeth II and France's President Mitterrand officially christened the $15 billion Channel Tunnel, the most ambitious privately financed engineering project in history.

The Eurostar Train à Grande Vitesse (TGV) enters the Chunnel at Calais.

Dug out at an average depth of 148 feet beneath the sea floor—an undertaking that required the services of 15,000 workers over seven years—the "Chunnel," when it opened in November, allowed trains to zip between England and France in a mere 35 minutes. ◂**1959.3**

IN THE UNITED STATES

▸DEATH OF A ROCK STAR— **Kurt Cobain fused heavy metal bombast, punk aggression, and dark pop lyricism into a**

musical brew called grunge. When Cobain, leader of the Seattle band Nirvana (the foremost exponent of the "Seattle Sound"), killed himself in April, at age 27, many read his death as they had his biting, often despairing music —as a parable of Generation X.

▸STOPPING THE BLEEDING— **Competing teams of scientists from two of the country's top biotechnology firms announced in June that they had isolated thrombopoietin, the hormone that stimulates bone marrow to produce platelets, or blood clotting cells. The search for thrombopoietin had stymied researchers for 35 years, but new methods involving gene therapy and cell mutation made the breakthrough possible. For the troubled biotechnology industry, the stakes were high indeed: the patent for a $1 billion-a-year drug.** ◂**1900.12**

▸WHITEWATER RISES— **Attorney General Janet Reno in January named Beltway lawyer Robert Fiske special prosecutor to investigate an Arkansas development company called Whitewater, which was formed during the late 1970s by Bill and Hillary Clinton and James McDougal, operator of Arkansas-based Madison Guaranty Savings and Loan. McDougal allegedly ran his S&L, before it failed, as a kind of slush fund for Arkansas politicians; he might also have used depositors' money to shore up Whitewater deals (which apparently lost money anyway). In the absence of conclusive evidence, the perception of scandal was enough to damage Clinton's effectiveness. His administration suffered major defeats on key projects like health-care reform and was left reeling by the Republican Party's stunning seizure of Congress in November's mid-term elections.** ◂**1992.4**

POLITICS & BUSINESS: GNP: $6,682.5 billion (for first 6 months of year) ... Republicans gain control of Congress for first time since 1946 ... Justice Steven Breyer appointed to Supreme Court ... U.S. pays Kazakhstan $311 million in exchange for dismantlement of 104 SS-18 nuclear missiles ... FCC grants Bell Atlantic right to provide video programming ... Viacom acquires Paramount Communications for $9.5 billion.

"We don't call them disasters anymore. We call them plagues. And we're just two behind ancient Egypt—frogs and boils."
—Dan Schnur, an aide to California governor Pete Wilson, on Los Angeles's natural disasters

AROUND THE WORLD

▸A MOGUL'S RISE AND FALL—In March, as a two-year-old investigation continued to turn up governmental corruption, fed-up Italians elected media tycoon Silvio Berlusconi as prime minister. But in December, the relentless probe turned on Berlusconi's own business empire. Admitting that his executives had bribed tax inspectors (but denying any personal wrongdoing), Berlusconi soon resigned. ◂1993.13

▸SOCIALISTS IN JAPAN—Like Italy's Berlusconi, Japanese Prime Minister Morihiro Hosokawa came to power as an alternative to "money politics." But Hosokawa, too, was undone after less than a year in office—by a questionable loan he'd accepted twelve years earlier. His successor resigned after 59 days, paving the way for a surprising new coalition government led by Tomiichi Murayama, head of Japan's traditionally marginal socialist party. ◂1993.11

▸CULT OF DEATH—In early October, 53 members of the Order of the Solar Temple, an obscure doomsday cult, died in a carefully orchestrated mass murder-suicide. The slaughter, carried out at two separate sites in Switzerland and one in Canada, was apparently ordered by cult leaders Luc Jouret and Joseph di Mambro. Their motives were unclear, but authorities said the pair, who were among the dead found in a cult-owned farmhouse in Switzerland, may have been involved in international gun-running and money laundering schemes. ◂1993.M

▸ART CACHE—The director of St. Petersburg's famed Hermitage museum revealed in October that 700 paintings looted from Germany by Russian soldiers during World War II had been stashed away in the museum since 1945. Art historians had long believed the works, which included more than 70 paintings by such luminaries as Degas, Monet, Toulouse-Lautrec, and Van Gogh, to have been destroyed.

Portions of L.A.'s lifeline, Interstate 5, collapsed in the earthquake, which registered 6.6 on the Richter scale.

DISASTERS
Waiting for the Big One

12 The earthquake that rocked Los Angeles in the bleary early morning hours of January 17, 1994, may not have been the proverbial "Big One" many Southern Californians had been dreading for decades, but it was enormously destructive nonetheless, killing 57 people and causing $15 billion in damage. The epicenter was a neighborhood called Northridge, site of the quake's single deadliest incident—the collapse of an apartment complex that killed 16 people. Across the sprawling city, thousands of homes and scores of businesses, churches, and schools were destroyed. Eleven major roadways, the congested lifelines of car-dependent Angelenos, were rendered impassable.

Less quantifiable than the physical destruction was the quake's psychic toll on a city that had recently suffered an uncanny series of calamities, natural and manmade, ranging from the Rodney King riots to wildfires. As thousands of aftershocks shook the region in the weeks following the initial tremor, anxious residents expressed their dismay with a dark joke. Famously temperate Southern California, they said, in fact has four seasons: earthquake, fire, flood, and drought. Many counted the quake as the last straw and packed their bags for less tumultuous environs. **◂1992.12**

THE COLD WAR
Post-Communist Paradoxes

14 By 1994, only a handful of nations still clung to communism—and in most of them, capitalist practices were fast outflanking Marxist theories. China boasted one of the fastest-growing economies in the world and a burgeoning crop of millionaires. Vietnam, once a paragon of anti-imperialism, wooed foreign investors, prompting President Clinton in February to lift the 19-year-old U.S. embargo on that country; in May, to the dismay of human-rights advocates, he renewed China's most-favored-nation trade status.

Even die-hard Cuba—its economy in shambles without Soviet support—tentatively joined the trend. In late summer, after Havana was rocked by its worst riot in 35 years, Fidel Castro allowed 35,000 refugees to sail for Florida. Castro hoped the human flood (though smaller than the 1980 Mariel boatlift) would persuade America to end its embargo on his island nation. Instead, Clinton revoked the old guarantee of asylum for Cubans, the U.S. Navy and Coast Guard interned the boat people, and American negotiators refused to lift sanctions. Seeking to placate the Cuban people as well as Washington, Castro reopened free-enterprise farmers' markets—the most substantial economic reform since the markets were briefly tolerated in the 1980s. He muted his anti-Yankee oratory as well, even sending cordial regards to conservative U.S. legislators in a December interview with *The New York Times.*

Lenin's worst nightmare: Young Russians revel in capitalist trappings.

Ironically, many of the countries that had formally eschewed communism were finding capitalism rough going. Unnerved by rising unemployment and inflation, Polish voters in 1993 gave a coalition of barely reconstructed former communists its first majority in Parliament. Not unlike other Eastern European electorates (such as Hungary) who'd returned such parties to power since the anticommunist revolutions of 1989, the Poles feared that too-rapid reform would mean chaos.

But chaos and foot-dragging were not mutually exclusive. In the former Soviet Union, where reform was proceeding slowly, a homegrown mafia ran much of the legitimate economy and traded contraband ranging from heroin to plutonium. Worn-out pipelines spread oil slicks across the Siberian tundra. And the breakup of the Russian empire continued, as Moscow's demoralized troops battled secessionist forces in the Muslim republic of Chechnya. **◂1993.4**

SCIENCE
Celestial Collision

13 **For six days in July 1994, astronomers and amateur stargazers around the world trained their telescopes on Jupiter, as 21 large fragments and countless smaller pieces of the comet Shoemaker-Levy 9 pounded into the gaseous planet. The bombardment—the combined collisions packed more force than all the nuclear bombs and missiles on Earth—produced 2,000-mile-high fireballs and left black "bruises" on Jupiter's clouds. Observed Arizona writer and amateur astronomer David Levy, who'd discovered the comet in 1993 with husband-and-wife astronomers Carolyn and Eugene Shoemaker, "Jupiter is getting the stuffing knocked out of it." Scientists studied the event, the most violent in recorded history, to learn about Jupiter. Laymen wondered what would happen if a comet barreled into Earth at 134,000 miles per hour. In fact, such a collision might be what wiped out the dinosaurs some 65 million years ago. ◂1990.12**

NOBEL PRIZES: Peace: Yasir Arafat, Yitzhak Rabin, and Shimon Peres (Palestinian, Israeli, Israeli; peace accord) ... Literature: Kenzaburo Oe (Japanese; novelist) ... Medicine: A. Gilman and M. Rodbell (U.S.; G-proteins) ... Chemistry: George Olah (U.S.; hydrocarbons) ... Physics: C. Shull and B. Brockhouse (U.S., Canadian; atomic structure) ... Economics: J. Nash, J. Harsanyi, and S. Reinhard (U.S., U.S., German).

A VOICE FROM 1994

The Juice Takes Flight

Letter by O.J. Simpson, June 17, 1994

From the moment Nicole Brown Simpson and Ronald Goldman were found awash in blood outside her town house in the Brentwood section of Los Angeles just after midnight on June 13, 1994, the O.J. Simpson affair captivated celebrity-mad America. Almost immediately, L.A. police suspected Simpson—football hero, movie actor, and telegenic corporate pitchman—of the brutal knifing murders of his ex-wife and her friend. The public was less ready to indict the ever-affable Hall of Famer, who maintained his innocence. On June 17, the day that police were set to arrest Simpson, he and longtime pal Al Cowlings suddenly took flight in Simpson's white Ford Bronco, leaving behind an alleged "suicide" note (below) *to be read to the press by a friend. Thousands turned out to cheer Simpson as he led a phalanx of police cruisers on a weird, low-speed highway chase. Millions more, mesmerized by the very public desperation of a famous person, watched on live television as television news helicopters beat the air overhead. Eventually, Simpson returned to his Brentwood mansion and after elaborate negotiations over his car phone, surrendered to police.*

Then began the long process of trying him. Everyone in America seemed to have an opinion on the case, and everyone actually associated with it—from the judge and attorneys to Simpson's houseboy, Kato Kaelin—attained, however briefly, nearly as much celebrity as the famous defendant. Such was America's insatiable appetite for, if not heroes, at least stars. **◂1907.V**

To whom it may concern:

First, everyone understand, I have nothing to do with Nicole's murder. I loved her, always have and always will. If we had a problem, it's because I loved her so much.

Recently we came to the understanding that for now we were not right for each other, at least for now. Despite our love, we were different and that's why we mutually agreed to go our separate ways.

It was tough splitting up for a second time but we both knew it was for the best. Inside I had no doubt that in the future we would be close friends or more. Unlike what has been written in the press, Nicole and I had a great relationship for most of our lives together. Like all long-term relationships, we had a few downs and ups. I took the heat New Year's 1989 because that's what I was supposed to do. I did not plead no contest for any other reason but to protect our privacy and was advised it would end the press hype.

I don't want to belabor knocking the press, but I can't believe what is being said. Most of it is totally made up. I know you have a job to do, but as a last wish, please, please, please, leave my children in peace. Their lives will be tough enough.

I want to send my love and thanks to all my friends. I'm sorry I can't name every one of you, especially A.C. Man, thanks for being in my life. The support and friendship I received from so many: Wayne Hughes, Lewis Markes, Frank Olson, Mark Packer, Bender, Bobby Kardashian. I wish we had spent more time together in recent years. My golfing buddies, Hoss, Alan Austin, Mike, Craig, Bender, Wyler, Sandy, Jay, Donnie, thanks for the fun.

All my teammates over the years, Reggie, you were the soul of my pro career. Ahmad, I never stopped being proud of you. Marcus, you've got a great lady in Catherine, don't mess it up. Bobby Chandler, thanks for always being there. Ski and Kathy, I love you guys, without you I never would have made it through this far.

Marguerite, thanks for the early years. We had some fun. Paula, what can I say? You are special. I'm sorry, I'm not going to have, we're not going to have our chance. God brought you to me, I now see. As I leave, you'll be in my thoughts.

I think of my life and feel I've done most of the right things. So why do I end up like this? I can't go on. No matter what the outcome, people will look and point. I can't take that. I can't subject my children to that. This way, they can move on and go on with their lives.

Please, if I've done anything worthwhile in my life. Let my kids live in peace from you, the press.

I've had a good life. I'm proud of how I lived. My mama taught me to do unto others. I treated people the way I wanted to be treated. I've always tried to be up and helpful, so why is this happening?

I'm sorry for the Goldman family. I know how much it hurts.

Nicole and I had a good life together. All this press talk about a rocky relationship was no more than what every long-term relationship experiences. All her friends will confirm that I have been totally loving and understanding of what she's been going through.

At times I have felt like a battered husband or boyfriend but I loved her, make that clear to everyone. And I would take whatever it took to make it work.

Don't feel sorry for me. I've had a great life, great friends. Please think of the real O.J. and not this lost person.

Thanks for making my life special. I hope I helped yours.

Peace and love, O.J.

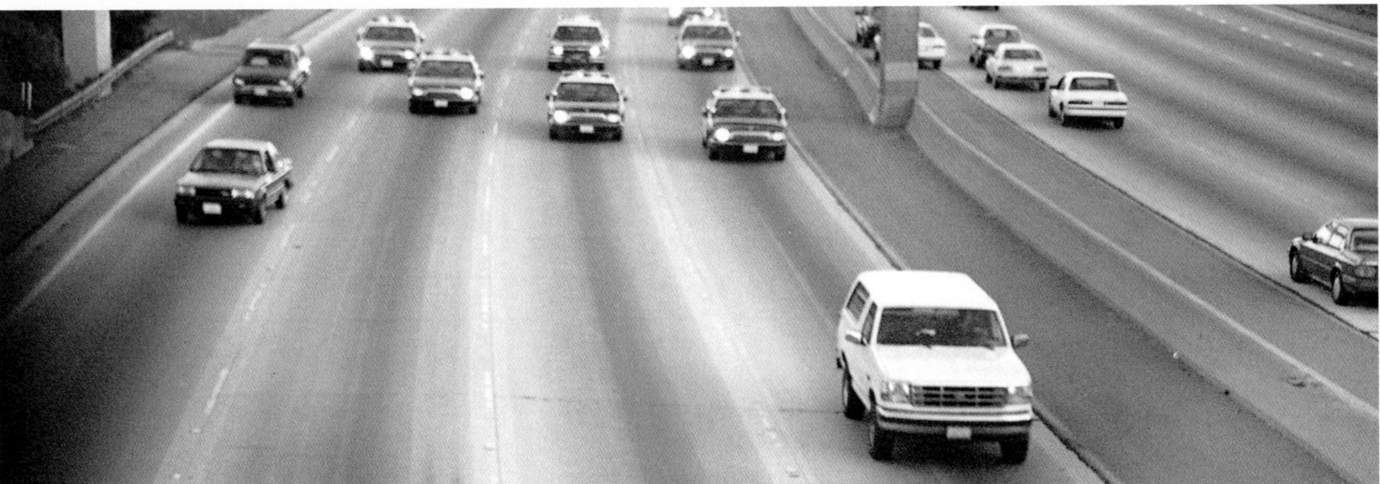

Five years before his indictment for the murder of his ex-wife, O.J. Simpson *(in police mug shot, top)* had been arrested for spousal battery. Divorced in 1992, the couple was photographed at a New York nightclub opening *(above right)* during a 1993 reconciliation attempt. When Simpson fled on the day of his arrest, L.A. police feared he might kill himself: As his friend Al Cowlings steered the Ford Bronco *(above)* along the freeway, Simpson lay on the seat pointing a gun to his head.

Index

Note: Except for proper names, information in datalines is not included in the index.

Credits

Picture credits are listed alphabetically by source, followed by the year in which the photograph appears and its placement by story number. The Editors have used their best efforts to obtain proper copyright clearance and credit for each of the images in *Our Times*. If, despite all of these precautions, an unavoidable and inadvertent credit error has occurred, it will be corrected in future editions. The following abbreviations are used: m=Marginalia; v=Voice; a,b,c,d=order of pictures from top to bottom, left to right.

3M Corporation: 30.2
A. Kertész © Ministère de la Culture: 20's opener
A & M Records: 76m.d
Abbeville Press: 10c.b
Academy of Motion Picture Arts and Sciences: 29.2.
©AFF/AFS Amsterdam: 47v.
AFL-CIO: 55m.b.
Al Hirschfeld/Margo Feiden Galleries: 19m.c, 77v.b, 77v.c.
Alan Magee: 80.7.
Allen Ginsberg/Wylie, Aitken & Stone: 59v.a.
Alphonse van Woerkom: 72.7
American Express: 58m.a
American Heritage Publishing Company: 03v.b, 04.12, 06.10, 17.1, 32.5, 36.10, 40m.d-f, 42.15
American Museum of Natural History: 02.10, 82.7b
American Superconductor Corporation, photo: TR Productions: 11.2
Amnesty International: 77.2
Anita Kunz: 90
Ansel Adams ©1994 Publishing Rights Trust: 70essay.b
AP/Los Angeles Police Department: 94v.a
AP/Wide World Photo: 03m.b, 05m.b, 18.1, 21.1, 22m.b, 29v.b, 33m.d, 34.4, 35m.b, 37v.a, 38.10, 39m.d, 41.4, 41.15, 41.17, 42.5, 43m.c, 43m.g, 43v.b, 44.12, 44m.c, 45.4, 45.13, 46.3, 46.5, 46.8, 48.11, 48m.d, 53m.c, 58.2, 58v.c, 58v.d, 59.9, 59m.e, 60.8, 60.13, 64.4, 64.11, 68.4, 68m.d, 70.7, 71.2b, 72.1, 73.6, 73.10, 74.4, 76.8, 76.14, 78.13, 80.3, 80essay.b, 82.13, 82v.a, 83.2, 83.8, 85.9, 85.10, 86.8, 86.12, 87.1, 87.7, 87m.c, 87m.d, 87v.a, 88.7, 88.12, 89.5, 90's opener, 91m.a, 91m.c, 92.9, 94.c
Architectural Association, London: 51m.d
Archiv für Kunst und Geschichte, Berlin: 09.1, 15v.c, 23.2, 24.5, 31.1, 39.17, 40 essay b, 43.8, 45.3, 48.2, 53.12, 59.13
Archive Photos: 06.7, 10.4a, 12.12, 12m.a, 12m.c, 17v.a, 19m.d, 20.5, 20.6, 22.8, 22.11, 23m.c, 26.5, 27.5, 27.12, 28.13, 29.6, 30m.b, 31.10, 32.3, 32.11, 32v.b, 34.2, 34.8, 34.11, 34m.d, 36.1, 36.8, 37.10, 40.2, 40.11, 40m.c, 40m.g, 40v.a, 41.2, 41.10, 42.5, 42.6, 42.11, 42m.a, 42v.a, 43.3, 43.5, 45.8, 45.17, 45v.a, 46m.a, 47m.b, 49v, 50.1, 50.7, 50v.b, 51.1, 51.2, 51.10, 52.2, 52.11, 53.5, 53.13, 54.4, 55.12, 55v, 57.4, 57.7, 59.3, 60.1, 60.10, 60m.d, 61.4, 61m.b, 61m.c, 62.3, 62.4, 62.7, 62.9, 62.12, 62m.b, 62m.d, 63.12, 63m.b, 64.1, 64.2, 64.7, 64m.c, 65.1, 65.2, 65.7, 65.9, 65m.b, 65m.c, 65m.d, 66.9, 66m.c, 67.6, 67m.d, 68.9, 68.13, 68m.c, 69m.d, 71.1, 76.9, 77.10, 78.10
© Arnold Eagle: 44.14
Art Institute of Chicago; Edward Hopper, *Nighthawks,* 1942/42.17; 81.11
Art Resource: Bridgeman, 13.2; Giraudon, 10.6, 16.4, 18.12, 37.7; Giraudon@ARS, 28m.d; Erich Lessing, 1900.6, 25.7; Foto Marburg © VAGA, 06m.d; Lauros Giraudon, 09.4b; Museum of Modern Art, 07.1; Roos, 05.10; Scala, 01.2, 09.9, 22.3b; Schaikwijk, 33v.b; Spadem @ARS, 01.6; Tate, © 1995 Estate of David Smith, VAGA, 63m.c, 32.13, 37m.d, 44.16, 44.16b, 44.16c, 67m.d, 70.10; Art Resource: 02m.d
Arthur Murray Dance Studios: 14.7b
Artists Rights Society: Joseph Beuys: © 1995 by ARS, New York, NY/VG Bild-Kunst, Bonn, 74.9; Constantin Brancusi: SPADEM, Paris, 28m.d; Alexander Calder: © 1995 by ARS, New York, NY, 37m.d; Marcel Duchamp: SPADEM, Paris, 13,2. 17.4; Alberto Giacometti: © 1995 by ARS, New York, NY, 47m.e; Salvador Dali: © 1995 Demart Pro Arte, Geneva, 1900essay.d; Willem De Kooning: ©1995 Willem De Kooning, 50.4; Max Ernst: SPADEM/ADAGP, Paris, 24.3; Wassily Kandinsky: SPADEM, Paris, 10.6; Marie Laurencin: © 1995 by ARS, New York, NY/ADAGP, Paris, 18.9.; Le Corbusier: SPADEM, Paris, 23.8; Man Ray: The Man Ray Trust & ADAGP, Paris, 26.2; Henri Matisse: ADAGP, Paris, © 1995 Les Heritiers Matisse, Paris, 5.10; Claude Monet: SPADEM, Paris, 16.4; Edvard Munch: BONO, Oslo, 06.2; Georgia O'Keefe: © 1995 The Georgia O'Keeffe Foundation, 29.8; Pablo Picasso: SPADEM, 01.6, 07.1, 18.12, 37.7; Jackson Pollock: © 1995 The Pollock-Krasner Foundation for the Visual Arts, 50.4; Mark Rothko: © 1995 Kate Rothko-Prizel & Christopher Rothko, 70.10; Richard Serra: © 1995 Richard Serra, 85m.c; Gino Severini: SPADEM, Paris, 9.9; Andy Warhol: © 1995 The Andy Warhol Foundation for the Visual Arts, 62.8
ASAP/Government Press Office: 51.4
Associated Newspapers Group, Ltd.: 78.1
Associated Press Ltd.: 53.4
AT&T Archives: 15.7, 19m.a, 47.1, 62.13, 64m.a, 82m.c
Australian War Memorial: 42m.f
Automobile Club of France: 1900m.d
Automotive History Collection, Detroit: 03.8
Barbara Gladstone Gallery, New York: 82.10c
Barbie/Mattel Toys: 59m.c, 60chart
Bassano & Vandyk Studios: 37.11. BBC: 71.10
Bettmann Archive: 1900.4, 01.1, 01m.d, 02.1, 03.7, 04.13, 06m.b, 07.6, 07.7, 07v.a, 08m.d, 08m.e, 10.4b, 10essay.b, 11.8, 11v.a, 13.11, 13m.a, 17m.b, 18.4, 20.7, 20.12, 20v.a, 21.10, 21m.d, 21v.a, 22.7, 23.1, 23.4, 23.7, 23.13, 24.1, 24.12, 24v.a, 25.13, 26.10, 26v.a, 27.2, 28.5, 28m.b, 28v.b, 29.5, 29.12, 29.13, 29m.b, 31.9, 30.12, 32.1a, 32.9, 32m.c, 32v.a, 33.9, 33.10, 33.13, 33m.e, 34.14, 35.10, 35m.c, 35m.d, 36v.b, 37.3, 37.4, 37.9, 37v.b, 38.5, 38m.c, 38v.a, 39.2, 40.7, 40.17, 40m.a, 41.5, 41m.b, 41m.d, 41m.e, 43.12, 43.17, 44v.a, 45.6, 45.7, 45.9, 45.14, 45m.c, 45m.e, 46.11, 47.5, 48m.b, 49.7, 49.8, 50.5, 50.9, 51.2, 51.5, 51m.b, 51m.c, 52.10a, 52.10b, 52.5, 54.7, 54.9, 55.4, 55.7, 55.13, 55m.e, 56.11, 56m.b, 56m.c, 57.9, 57m.b, 59m.d, 60.7, 60v, 61.2, 61.8, 61.12, 62.5, 62v, 63.1, 63.3, 63.8, 64.10, 65v, 66v.b, 67.1, 67m.c, 68.7, 68.10, 68.12, 69v.a, 70m.a, 70m.c, 73.8, 73m.c, 74.1, 74m.b, 74v.a, 75.4, 75m.c, 77.13a, 77m.b, 78m.c, 78m.d, 78v.c, 80.2, 80m.b, 83v.a, 84m.d, 86.9, 86m.b, 87.4, 89m.b, 89m.d, 89v.a, 90.13, 92.10, 93.11, 93.5
Bilderdienst Suddeutscher Verlag: 15v.a, 35.14, 41.6, 49.3, 51.13
Bill Graham Enterprises: 67.5
Black Star: Harry Benson, 57.3; Charles Bonnay, 54.3; Gillhausen, 56.5; Charles Moore, 63.7; Peter Northall, 92.1; W. Eugene Smith, 55m.c, 73.7; R. Swanson, 69.6; Werner Wolff, 49m.a
Boeing Commercial Airplane Group: 69m.a
Bonnie Shnayerson: 18m.a
Brigham and Women's Hospital: 54.12
British Library: 1900.5
British Museum: 22m.d
Bronx Museum of the Arts: 54.11
Brookhaven National Laboratory: 58.3
Brooks Brothers: 50chart
Brown Brothers: 01.12, 01m.c, 01v.a, 02.5, 02.7, 07.9, 09m.c, 10.7, 10m.b, 11.5, 11.11, 12.5, 12m.d, 13.1, 13.6, 14.8, 15m.b, 16.3, 16.6, 16.12, 16m.c, 17.10, 18.3, 19.3, 19.7, 19m.b, 23.6, 24.9, 25.5, 26.4, 27.9, 27v.b, 30.5, 31.12, 32m.b, 33m.c, 35.4, 36.7, 36.12, 38v.b, 38v.c, 38v.d, 39m.b, 41.12, 44.1, 46.7, 46v, 52.6, 54.8, 56.9, 58.7
Buckminster Fuller Foundation: 47m.c
Cahiers du Cinema: 70.8
California Institute of Technology: 49.5
Calmann & King Limited: 90essay.a
Camera Press, Ltd.: 56m.d, 62.6, 64.5, 67.13, 69.2, 92.11, 93.6
Canapress Photo Service: 70.11, 92.5
Capitol Records: 73m.d
Carl Larsen © 1972 Pelican Publishing Co., Inc.: 71.4
Caroline Tisdall: 74.9
Cartoon - Caricature - Contor: 63.5, 65.1, 70.6, 82.6, 83.6, 86.9
Casterman, Paris: Centre de 29m.a.
Documentation Juive: 43.1
Charles B. Slackman: 09.3
Charles Dana Gibson: 07v.b
Charles Skaggs: 69v.b

Chesley Bonestell/Space Art Int.: 50essay.a

Chevrolet: 53m.a

Chicago Historical Society: 32v.c

China Quarterly: 31.2

Chiquita Brands International: 44m.a

Cleveland Museum of Art: 20essay.b

Clive Barda: 28.4

Collection Franklin LaCava: 72m.b

Columbia University: 12.10, 33.12

Commes des Garcons: Peter Lindbergh, 81m.d

Communist Party Library: 35.9, 38.4

Conrail: 76m.a

Contact Press: Gianfranco Gorgoni, 70m.b; Adriana Groisman, 17.3; © 1988 Annie Leibovitz, 80v; Liu Heung Shing,80.10.

Cooper-Hewitt Design Museum, Smithsonian/Art Resource: 28m.a.

Corning, Inc: 15m.a

Courtesy Campbells: 54m.a

Courtesy Cartier: 10chart

Courtesy Doubleday: 18v.a

Courtesy Gary Trudeau: 8v

Courtesy of WLS-TV/Ch.7 Chicago: 86v.a

Cray Computers: 76.12

Culver Pictures, Inc.: 1900 chart, 1900m.c, 01.3, 01.11, 02m.c, 03.3, 03v.a, 05.4, 05.5, 05m.d, 07.2, 07.11, 07v.c, 08.3, 08.11, 09.6, 10.9, 10m.c, 10v, 11.6, 11m.b, 12.9, 13.4, 13.7, 13.10, 13m.c, 13v.a, 14.1b, 15.8, 15m.d, 16m.b, 16v.b, 17v.b, 17v.c, 17v.d, 17v.e, 18m.b, 19.4, 20 chart, 20m.c, 20m.d, 21m.b, 21m.c, 21v.b, 22.12, 22v.a, 22v.b, 23.5, 23m.b, 24m.c, 24m.d, 25m.c, 26.11, 26m.b, 26m.e, 26v.b, 28v.a, 29.1, 29.14, 30m.a, 30m.c, 32.6, 33v.a, 34.5, 35m.a, 37.5, 38.11, 39.7, 39m.c, 39v.b, 42m.c, 43.7, 43.13, 50.13, 53.8

Curatorial Assistance, Inc.: 15.11

D.C. Comics: 38m.a

David King Collection: 18.11, 30 essay.b, 39.3, 40 essay.a, 43.2, 32.8

David Levine: 48v

De Brunhoff, Abrams Publishing Co.: 31v.a, 31v.b, 31v.c

Decca/V. Purdom & G. Di Ludovico: 90.8

Department of Immigration, Australia: 46.12

Detroit Institute of Arts, Founders Society: 10 essay.c

Diane Arbus ©1965 Robert Miller Gallery: 64v

Dick Busher: 20 essay.a

Disney Productions: 23m.e, 28.10a, 28.10b

Donald Cooper: Photostage: 25.12, 45.16, 53.11, 57.12, 83.10, 86.11

Doonesbury@1970 GB Trudeau/Universal Press Syn.: 70v

Dr. Dennis Kunkel: 12.6

Dr. Seuss © 1957 Random House: 57v.a, 57v.b

Du Pont: 34.9, 38.12

Edgar Rice Burroughs Inc. © 1936: 14v.a

Edward Steichen, Vanity Fair ©1935, 1963 Conde Nast: 34v.a

Elizabeth Boyer: 42m.d

Elvis Presley Enterprises: 77.6a

Esto: Peter Aaron, 32m.a; Scott Frances, 37m.b, 94.6; Ezra Stoller, 49m.c, 54.5, 66.4

Everett Collection: 57m.c, 69.5, 79v.b, 84m.b

Farrar, Straus and Giroux: 19.12

FDR Library: 33.4, 44.11, 45.5

Florida State Archives: 25m.b

Ford Motor Company: 10 essay.a, 18.2

Foreign and Commonwealth Office: 01.7

Foundation Le Corbusier: 23.8

FPG: 40.3, 45m.d, 45m.f, 70 chart, 77.6b, 77m.c, 81m.a, 83.11, 85.8, 89m.a, 93m.a

Frank Maresca: 9.7

Frederick Warne & Company: 2v.a

French Embassy: 26.3

Freud Museum: 1900 essay.ab

Galen Rowell/Mountain Light: 12v.b

Gamma/Liasion: Anchorage Daily News, 89.13; Forrest Anderson, 88.5, 89.4; P. Aventunier, 83.5; David Barritt, 85.3; Bassignac-Gaillarde. 94.11; Jeremy Bigwood, 92.3; Bosio, 90.6; Eric Bouvet, 86.6, 88.13; Jim Bryant, 87m.b; John Chiasson, 88m.c; Karim Daher, 89.6; Malcolm Denemark, 86.2; Claudio Edinger, 75.7; Edmonson/NASA, 83m.b; Michael Evans, 77.13b; Ferry, 86m.c; Stephen Ferry, 84m.c; Jean Claude Francolon, 86.4; Porter Gifford, 93m.b; Eric Girard, 84m.e; Grabet, 79m.b; Olivier Grand, 93m.d; Louise Gubb, 83m.d; Dirk Halstead, 73m.b; Yvonne Hemsey, 87.12, 87.12; Paul Howell, 92.13; Tom Keller, 77.1; David Hume Kennerly, 72.8; Liaison, 75.1, 81.5, 82.9, 85.6, 92.8, 94m.b, 94m.d; Francois Lochon, 79.13; George Merillon, 91.5; Anticoli Micozzi, 91.4; Mingam G/L, 79.5; Roland Neveu, 83.3; Scott Petersen, 88.2; Presse Images, 76.6; Bill Pugliano, 90.11; Raymond Roig, 93.8; Shock Photography, 88.11; Daniel Simon, 78.6; Simonel, 79.1; Bill Swersey, 94.14; Thomas, 89.11; Eric Vandeville, 91.11; Diana Walker, 80.4; Zoom, 93.7

General Motors: 08m.c

George Eastman House: 1900.3, 31m.b, 36m.b, 60 essay.a, 63m.a

German Information Center: 18.1

Gilles Abegg: 85.13

Glasgow Herald & Evening Times: 05.8

Globe Photos: 54.13, 57.8, 60m.c, 64m.b, 91.10, 93m.c

Good Housekeeping Magazine: 10m.a

Granger Collection: 1900.11, 1900m.b, 01.4, 01.8, 01.9, 01v.b, 02m.b, 03.2, 04.5, 04.6, 05.3, 05.6, 05.11, 06.9, 07.4, 07.13, 08.2, 10.12a, 10.12b, 12.3, 12.11,14v.d, 15.1, 15v, 16.13, 17.5, 18.9, 19.6, 20.4, 20m.a, 21.3, 23.3, 23.9, 24.8, 24.10, 24.11, 25.2, 25.3, 25.4, 25.8, 26.8, 26.12, 27m.b, 27m.d, 28.1, 28.2, 30.8, 30.11, 31.3, 31.4, 33.8, 34.3, 35.1,35.5, 37.1, 37.13, 37m.e, 40.1, 41.7, 42.8, 42.12, 44m.b, 47.7, 50m.a, 52.13, 55.2

Hagley Museum: 40 chart

Hale Observatories: 10.5a

Harcourt, Brace Jovanovich: 20.9, 43.15

Harley Davidson, Inc.: 03m.c, .03m.c

Hasbro, Inc.: 64m.a

Hebrew University Of Jerusalem: 05.1

Helene Jeanbrau: 16v.d, 17m.e

Herman Miller © Eames: 46m.c

Hogan Jazz Archive, Tulane University: 25.6

Horst: 21.4.

Hubert Josse: 9.11, 9v.b, 28.7

Hulton Deutsch: 04.4, 04.7, 06m.a, 11.7, 14.4, 16.8, 20.3, 21.2, 22.3a, 22.5 ,25.1, 29m.d, 30.1, 30.3, 30 essay.a, 36m.d, 36v.a, 37.2, 39.12, 41.9, 50m.d, 52.1, 52m.d, 54.2, 56.7, 63.2, 67.4, 73.11, 75.10, 76.4, 94m.a

IBM: 24.7, 81.10

ICM Artists, Ltd: 71.9

Illustrated London News: 06.1, 07.10, 10.1, 10.8, 11.10, 12.1, 26.1, 29.7, 37.14

Image Select/Nick Birch: 28.11

Impact Visuals: Fuminori Sato, 94.10

Imperial War Museum: 16.1, 16v.a, 18m.d, 19.1, 1910's opener, 40m.e, 41m.f

INTEL: 71.5

Interfoto: 16m.e, 27.4, 32.7, 33.5, 45.10, 47.9, 58.12

International Speedway Corp.: 10.2

J. Paul Getty Museum: 87.13

Jack Gescheidt: 80m.a

JB Pictures: Cedric Galbe, 94.9

Jean Paul Filo: 70.1

Jeff Koons: 82.1b

Jimmy Carter Library: 78.3

Joe McTyre: 53v.a

John Vickers/University of Bristol: 44.18

Johnson and Johnson: 21m.a

Ken Regan/Camera 5: 76m.c, 82.4

Kentucky Fried Chicken Archives: 55m.a

Kharbine-Tapabor: 57.5

Kimberly Clarke: 42m.a

Kobal Collection: 14v.c, 18v.b, 30m.d, 33.2, 33m.b, 36.9, 37m.c, 38.7, 41.11, 41.18, 42m.b, 42v.b, 45m.b, 46.9, 51.7, 52m.b, 53.9, 53m.b, 57m.d, 58m.c, 59.7, 61.11, 63.10, 63.13, 66.3, 67.9, 73.12, 75.14, 77.12, 78.5, 80.8, 89.12

Kraft Foods: 17.12

Ladies Home Journal: 1900v.a, 1900v.b, 1900v.c

Landslides/Alex S. MacLean: 40essay.d

Laurie Platt Winfrey, Inc.: 1900.7, 01.5, 01m.b, 04.1, 08.1, 10.1, 13.9, 13m.d, 16.1, 17.11, 20.1, 20.9, 28.12, 36.3, 42.13, 44.5, 47.12, 67.7, 69.1,

Lear Jet: 62m.a

Lennart Nilsson: 81.1

Leo Castelli Gallery © ARS: 85m.c

LGI: Carlos Arthur, 94m.c

Library of Congress/Holocaust Museum: 42.10

Library of Congress: 04.3, 06.4, 06.5, 06.8, 06.11, 07m.c, 09.1, 12v.a, 14.5, 15.4, 15.9, 17m.c, 20.11, 24m.b, 26.7, 27.1, 27.6, 30's opener, 30.6, 32.2, 35.3, 41v.a, 50m.c, 57.10, 61.9, 63.14, 67.12, 68.11, 68v.a, 73.13, 17m.a.

LIFE Magazine © Time Inc.: Margaret Bourke-White, 36m.c, 39.4, 48.5; Loomis Dean, 56.6, 61v.a; John Dominis, 61.6, 66.13, 72m.d; Alfred Eisenstaedt, 31.14, 43v.a, 48.12, 62.11, 78.8; Eliot Elisofon, 42.16; Bill Eppridge, 69.4; J.R. Eyerman, 52m.c; Andreas Feininger, 45.2; Johnny Florea, 49m.d; Bernard Hoffman, 45.1a; Hugo Jaeger, 38.2; Dmitri Kessel, 60.9, 61v.b; Wallace Kirkland, 48.10 Anthony Linck, 47.8; Thomas McAvoy, 39.14; Vernon Merritt, 69.9; Gjon Mili, 43.11; Ralph Morse, 40.9; Carl Mydans, 44.8, 50.2; Hy Peskin, 41m.c, 47.10; Bob Petersen, 68v.b; John Phillips, 43.9; Art Riekerby, 75m.b; Michael Rougier, 50m.b, 52.9; Arthur Schatz, 65.4; Frank Scherschel, 42.14; Paul Schutzer, 60.2, 63v.b; John Shearer, 71m.c; Howard Sochurek, 45.11, 53m.d, 54.1, 55.3; Terence Spencer, 70.9; Peter Stackpole, 51v.a; George Stroch, 44.9; Greg Villet, 62m.c; Hank Walker, 54v; Baron Wolman, 37m.a;

Magnum Photos, Inc.: 54m.d, 58.1, 72.2; Abbas, **(Magnum Photos, Inc con't.)** 81.3, 85.4, 88.8, 91.1, 91.3, 92m.d, 93.4; Bob Adelman, 52.8, 63v.a; Alecio de Andrade, 79.9; Eve Arnold, 45.12, 52.7, 62.2, 65.5, 90essay.b; Bruno Barbey, 68.1, 70.3, 77.9, 80.1, 93.13; Ian Berry, 60.6, 66.12, 91.7; Rio Branco, 80.12, 92.7; Rene Burri, 46.6, 65.13, 81.12, 88.9; Cornell Capa, 50v.a, Robert Capa, 77.4; Henri Cartier-Bresson, 34.12, 43.10, 46.1, 49.1, 61.1, 79.6; Bruce Davidson, 64v.a, 66m.b, 68v.b; de Andrede, 74.2; Raymond Depardon, 70.2, 72.5, 76.3; Elliot Erwitt, 50's opener, 50.12, 54.6, 59.4; Misha Erwitt, 89.10, 92m.b; Martine Franck, 84.5; Stuart Franklin, 88.4; Leonard Freed, 74.5, 77m.d; Paul Fusco, 90.4, 94.8; Jean Gaumy, 78.12, 91.7; Burt Glinn, 49.11, 55.10, 56.3, 58.9, 59.1, 62.10, 80's opener; Lee Goff, 72v.a; Philip Jones Griffiths, 67v, 92.4; H. Gruyaert, 72.6; Rich Hartmann, 41m.h, 63.9, 70essay.d; Bob Henriques, 61.5; Thomas Hoepker, 86.10; Ivleva, 86.1; Richard Kalvar, 85.11; Hiroji Kobota, 66.10; Joserf Koudelka, 68.2; Elliot Landy, 70.4a, 70.4b, 70.4c; Sergio Larrain, 71.7; Erich Lessing, 62.1, 74.3; Guy Le Querrec, 74.8; Danny Lyon, 64.3; Costa Manos, 57.13, 67.2; Peter Marlow, 92m.b; Fred Mayer, 84.7; Steve McCurry, 89.7; Gideon Medel, 85m.d, 89.3; Susan Meiselas, 75.5, 79.8, 81.8, 84.3, 86.3, 89.2, 89.8, 90m.d; Rick Merron, 73.3; Wayne Miller, 60essay.b; Inge Morath, 69.13, 75.3, 79v.a; Don McCullin, 68.3; Jim Nachtwey, 87.6, 87m.e, 88.3, 88.10, 90.2, 94.1; Michael Nichols, 87.10, 88.6, 89m.c; Naul A. Ojeda, 73.4; Gilles Peress, 71.11, 72.4, 74.13, 81.9, 84m.a, 87.3, 88.1, 89.1; Chris Steele Perkins, 64m.d, 80.9, 92.6, 94.2; Photo MCP, 81.6; Nitin Rai, 93.9; Raghu Rai, 79.11, 84.1; Seymon Raskin, 56.2; Eli Reed, 84.10, 92.12; Marc Riboud, 55.8, 60's opener, 77.4, 87.11; Eugene Richards, 78m.b; George Rodger, 41.13, 52.4; Sebastio Salgado, Jr., 79.10, 81m.b, 82.5; Scianna, 44.15, 80.6, 87.5; T. Sennett, 84.2; Marilyn Silverstone, 66.7, 71m.d; Dennis Stock, 40.14, 45.15, 56.12, 60.12; A.Venzago, 84.8; Alex Webb, 83.1, 85m.b; P. Zachman, 95.1

Mall of America: 92m.a

Marineschule Oluvwik: 41m.g

Marla Kittler: 1900.13, 01m.a, 11m.c, 21.12, 30.13, 61.3, 71.2a, 75.6a, 75.6c, 76.1, 76.6b, 78.7

Martha Swope: 70.12, 75.12

Martin Breese/Retrograph Archive: 39.10

Mary Boone Gallery: 73.5

Mary Evans Picture Library: 1900.10 10.3, 16.5, 18.5, 19.11,

Maurice Sendak © 1963 Harper Collins: 63m.e

Mayibue Center: 48.1

McCall's Magazine: 52v

Metropolitan Museum of Art © 1995 The Georgia O'Keeffe Foundation/ARS: 29.8

MGM/United Artists: 59.8

MGM: 68.5, 74v.b

Michael Barson: 51v, 54.10, 58v.b, 58v.e

Michael Ochs Archives: 01.8, 23m.d, 35.7, 46.13, 49.10, 55m.d, 59.10, 59.11, 67.8, 83.12

Mick Ellison/D.V.P./American Museum of Natural History: 94.7

Miguel Fairbanks: 60essay.c

Miles,Inc.: 31m.a

Milton Glaser, Vanity Fair ©1983 Conde Nast: 83m.c; Milton Glaser: 92v.a, 92v.b

Mirror Syndication International: 90.5

MIT Museum: 35.12

MIT News Office: 76.5

MOMA Film Stills Archive: 34m.c; 03.4, 28.6, 31.7, 31m.c, 33.11, 39.15

Mosfilm International: 25.9

Ms. Magazine: 72v.b

MTV Networks: 81.13

Munch Museum: 06.2

Municipal Archives of the City of New York: 13m.b

Munson Williams Proctor Institute: 08.4

Museo Aereonautico, Trento/H. Serra: 22.4

Museum of Fine Arts, Boston/Tompkins Collection: 03.5

Museum of Modern Art, New York/©VAGA: 58.5; Museum of Modern Art, New York: 06.6, 06.6, 19.9, 19.9, 24.3, 24.3, 29m.c, 47m.e, 48m.c, 50.4a, 50.4b

Museum of the City of New York: 02.11, 04.11, 04m., 06v.a, 06v.b, 06v.c, 08.10, 31.6, 64.13, 66.8, 68m.b

Museum Sztudki,Lodz: 23.12

NASA: 50essay.b, 60m.a,80.5, 90.12, 94.13

National Air and Space Museum: 14.3

National Archives: 05.7a, 05.7b, 15.5, 19.6, 33.14, 41.1

National Baseball Hall of Fame: 39v.a,c

National Foundation March of Dimes: 55.1

National Gallery of Art: 02.13

National General Pictures: 71.13

National Geographic Society: 27.10

National Library of Medicine: 1900.1, 43.18

National Museum of American History: 36m.a, 45m.a,

National Museum of Racing: 20m.b

National Museum of Women in the Arts: 87m.a

National Organization for Women: 66m.a

National Park Service: 17.2

National Portrait Gallery, London: 02.3,15.10, 29v.a, 30.9, 46.4, 58.13

National Portrait Gallery: 03.12, 21.9, 24.6, 72m.c, 26m.d

NBC: Alice Hall, 92m.b; 26m.a, 54m.b, 75v.a

NEB Cartoon Study Centre, Univ. of Kent, Solo Syndication: 42.3

Neil Leifer: 73.9

Nevada Historical Society: 08.6

New China News Agency, London: 21.6

New Jersey Historical Society: 17m.d

New York Newsday: Marlette: 94.3

New York Public Library /Performing Arts: 64.6

New York Public Library: 02.12, 03.9, 03m.e, 04.2, 05.2, 05v.a, 05v.b, 07m.b, 08m.b, 11v.b, 11v.c, 13.3, 13.8, 13v.b, 13v.c, 14.7a, 16v.c, 21v.c, 23.11, 23v.a, 23v.b, 26.6, 26m.c, 27v.a, 29.11, 31.11, 33.1, 35.11, 36.13, 40.18, 49.4, 49.12

New-York Historical Society: 06v.d, 18m.b

Newark Museum: 30v.a

Newsweek Inc., ©1974: 74.10

Nike: 72m.a, 80chart

NY Academy of Medicine Library: 12.2

NYC Parks Photo Archive/© 1995 George Segal/VAGA: 69.3

Outline: Gerardo Somoza: 94.b

Pace Wildenstein Gallery: 82.10a

Panama Canal Company: 14.9

Parker Brothers: 33m.a

Pat Oliphant/Susan Conway Gallery: 77.7

Patrick McMullan: 85v.a

Paul Davis: 65.11

Paul Szep,The Boston Globe: 73.1

Peace Corps: 61m.a

Penguin Books: 35.6

Peter Max: 70.5

Peter Menzel: 84.12

Peter Sis: 87v.b

Philip Lief Group: 72.10

Photo Edit/Bruce Zuckerman: 47.6

Photo: F. Brandani - T. DeTullio: 76.10

Photo Reseachers: 53.10, 65m.a; Benelux, 10essay.d; Dale Boyer, 73m.a; Brian Brake, 50.11, 56.10; John Bryson, 31m.d; Camera Pix, 59.5; Explorer, 84.9; David Frazier, 28m.c; A. Louis Goldman, 14m.c; Spencer Grant, 54m.c; Farrell Grehan, 09.4a; B. Hemphill, 71m.a; George Holton, 77.11; Dana Hyde, 1900m.a; T. Leeson 70essay.c, 90m.b; Bill Longacre, 1900.12; Peter B. Kaplan, 68m.a; Patrick Lynch, 81m.c; Tom McHugh, 38m.d, 75m.a; W&D McIntyre, 70's opener, 86m.a; Joe Monroe, 59m.b; Hank Morgan, 85m.a; William Mullins, 39m.f; Stan Pantovic, 58.11; D. Parker, 83m.a; Rapho Agence, 47.11; Gary Retherford, 88m.a; Science Source, 11m.e, 53.1, 80m.d; SPL, 05.9, 09.2, 09.12, 22.2, 31.8, 40.8, 41.16, 44.17, 47.14, 63.11, 67.11, 68.8, 77m.a; Don Carl Steffen, 41m.a; Gianni Tortoli, 88m.d; Van Bucher, 47m.a, 55.6; Jeanne White, 04m.d; Henry Young, 30.7

Photofest: 1900essay.d, 06m.c, 14v.b, 30.10, 34.6, 37.8, 40m.b, 41.14, 43.16, 45v.b, 46m.b, 46m.d, 47.13, 47m.d, 48.14, 49m.b, 50.8, 50chart, 51.9, 51.11, 55.9, 55.11, 56.4, 56.8, 56.13, 57.6, 58.8, 58.10, 58v.a, 59.6, 59.12, 60.11, 60m.b, 61m.d, 64.9, 69.10, 69m.b, 69m.c, 71.12, 71m.b, 71v.a, 71v.b, 72.9, 74.12, 74m.c, 74m.d, 75v.b, 76.11, 78v.a, 78v.b, 80m.c, 82.8, 88m.b, 88v.a, 90m.c, 91.6, 91.12, 93.12

Photosport International: 69.12

©Playbill: 49v, 77v.a

Playboy Enterprises: 53.6, 76v.a, 76v.b, 76v.c

Popperfoto: 07.12, 09.5, 52.3

Porsche: 48m.a

Posters, Please: 16.7

Press Association: 32.4

Private Collection: 1900.8, 04m.c, 08.8, 13.5a, 14m.b, 15m.c, 15m.e, 16m.d, 17.4, 17.8, 18.6, 22m.c, 23m.a, 26.2, 28.8, 29.3, 40.13, 42m.g, 43.14, 48.7

Pro Golf Association: 16m.a

Proctor & Gamble: 30chart, 56m.a

Punch: 22.9, 35.13, 39.11, 43.6, 47.4, 48.6, 48.13, 49.6,

Putnam Publishing Group: 89v.b, 89v.c

R.G. Smith: 42.1

Rainbow/©1985 Art Matrix: 84v.b

Rea Irvin ©1925, 1953 The New Yorker: 25m.a

Retna Ltd. NYC: 56.1, 71.6, 72.11, 72.13, 75.13, 78.11, 82.12,

Rex Photos: 34.10

Rich Clarkson © 1979 Sports Illustrated: 79m.c

Richard Avedon: 90essay.c

Robert Burger: 93.3
Robert Doisneau/Rapho: 49.13
Robert E. Mates, Guggenheim Foundation: 59m.a
Robert Hunt Library: 40.16
Robert Lorenz: 35v.a, 39m.a
Robert Miller Gallery/©VAGA: 93.10
Robert Tesoro: 77.6a
Rockefeller University: 37.6
Roger Viollet: 1900's opener, 1900.9, 02.2, 02.4, 02.6, 03.6, 03m.a, 05.12, 06.12, 06.13, 07.5, 07.8, 08.5, 08.7, 09.8, 09.10, 09m.e, 09v.a, 11.1, 11.9, 11.12, 11m.a, 12.7, 13.5bc, 14.1a, 15.3, 15.6, 16.11, 17.9 ,19.2a, 19.2b, 19.8, 21.5, 21.7, 21.11, 24.4, 25.10, 26.9, 26.13, 27.7, 29.10, 30.4, 31.13, 33.7, 35.2, 35.8, 36.4, 36.5, 37.12, 39.5, 39.16, 40.4, 40m.d, 41.3, 42.9, 58.4
Rolling Stone Magazine: 67m.a
Rolls Royce: 04.10
Rotary Club International: 05m.a
Scavullo, Vogue © 1974 Conde Nast: 74m.a
Science Museum, London: 19.5, 31.5, 80essay.a
Scientific American, Inc. © 1993: 29.9
Sears Roebuck: 05m.c
Self Portrait, 1988 © Mapplethorpe Estate: 90.10
Shell Int. Petroleum Co.: 07m.d
Sigrid Estrada: 84v.a
Simon Brown: 1900essay.c
Sipa Press: Malanca, 94.4; Fred Prouser, 94.12
Sir David Low, Cartoon Study Centre, Univ. of Kent, Solo Syndication: 36.11
Smith College/Sophia Smith Coll.: 15.2
Smithsonian Institution: 02m.a, 03.1, 03m.d, 04.8, 04m.a, 09m.a, 09m.d, 11m.d, 32.1, 42.7, 52m.a, 76.13, 79m.a
Sony Music: 48.4
Southern Illinois University: 22.1
Sovfoto: 03.10, 03.11, 04.9, 18.8, 22m.a, 25.11, 27.11, 29.4, 36.6, 38.3, 40.12, 40essay.c, 44.3, 46.10, 48.8, 50.3, 50essay.c, 51.6a, 51.6b, 53.3, 55.5, 57.1, 60.5, 63m.d, 66.1, 66.2, 66.5, 66.11, 66m.d, 68.6, 69.8, 69.11, 71.3, 72.12, 75.8, 79.4, 83.4, 84.6, 85.7, 86.13, 90m.a, 92.2
State Museum Kröller-Müller, Netherlands: 17.6
Sunkist: 28.9
Swedish Information Service: 76.2
Sygma: Yedioth Aharonoth: 94.5; Philippe Ledru: 79m.d; Tom Mihakel: 84.4
Syndication International: 39m.e, 65.3
Texas Instruments: 74.11
The Express: 1900.2
The Gideons: 08m.a
The Huntington Library: 16.9
The Workout, Inc. © 1981 Simon & Schuster: 81v.a, 81v.b
Theodore Roosevelt Assoc.: 12m.a, 12m.b
Time Inc. ©1980: 23.10
Time Magazine/David Hume Kennerly: 78.2
Tony Auth, Philadelphia Inquirer: 73v.a
Topham Picture Library: 02.9, 06.3, 10.11, 14.10, 19.10, 40.5, 44.2, 44.6, 44m.f, 47.3, 48.3, 53.7, 57.11, 58.6, 69.7, 70m.d
Tropicana: 51m.a
Turner Entertainment Co.: 27m.d, 38m.b, 39.8,
TV Guide Magazine ©1956: 56v.abc
Twentieth Century Fox: 34.13, 34m.b, 65.12
Underwood Archives: 58m.b
Unesco: 58m.d, 83.9
United Media, Peanuts © UFS Inc.: 50.6
United Nations: 46.2
Universal Press Syndicate, Garfield ©Paws, Inc.: 78m.a
University of Hartford: 09m.b
University of Michigan Library: 17.7
University of Texas, Harry Ransom Research Center: 32m.d
University of Texas: 67.10
University of Virginia: 44.13
University of Wyoming, American Heritage Center: 4v.a, 4v.b
US Air Force: 07m.a, 18m.c, 40's opener, 42.4, 43m.f, 45.1
US Army: 34.1, 40.15, 42m.e, 44m.e, 43m.e, 44m.d
US Patent Office: 38.6,38.9
US Signal Corps: 14m.d, 32.12
USA Today: 82m.a
USIA: 33.3
USMarine Corps: 16.2
Visual Arts and Galleries Association, Inc.: Licensed by VAGA, New York, NY. For works by: Louise Bourgeois: © 1995 Louise Bourgeois, 93.10; George Grosz: © 1995 Estate of George Grosz, 20.4; Erich Heckel: © 1995 Erich Heckel, 06m.d; Jasper Johns: © 1995 Jasper Johns, 58.5; George Segal: © 1995 George Segal, 69.3; Ben Shahn © 1995 Estate of Ben Shahn, 35.1; David Smith: © 1995 Estate of David Smith, 63m.c; Grant Wood: © 1995 Estate of Grant Wood, 30m.b
Vanity Fair ©1920, 1948 Conde Nast: 20v.a, 20v.b
Venturi, Scott Brown and Associates: 91.8
Victoria and Albert Museum: 10m.d, 47.2
Viesti Associates: 43m.a
Vint Lawrence: 84.13
Volkswagon of America: 60v.a
Volvo: 27m.a
Warhol Foundation. Courtesy, The Menil Collection, Houston: 62.8
Warner Bros ©1977: 77.5; 90chart
Warner Lambert: 25v.a
Weight Watchers International: 61.14
West Point Museum: 15v.b
Wham-O Sports Promotion: 57m.a
Whitney Museum of American Art: 65.6
Wiener Library Ltd.: 39.18
Will Rogers Memorial Commission: 28.3
Will Shortz: 13.12
William Doyle Galleries: 25m.d
William H. Mauldin: 43m.b
William Tague: 38.8
William Wrigley Jr. Company:14.m.a
Winnie Klotz: 75.11
WOMAD: 82m.d
Woodfin Camp & Associates: 20essay.c; Marc & Eveline Bernheim, 63.6; Dan Budnik, 30essay.c, 91m.b; Geoffrey Clifford, 75.9; Winston Conrad, 70essay.a; Zöe Dominic, 61.13, Larry Downing, 83.7; Editorial Ailantida, 82.11; John Ficara, 86.5, 87.9, 91.9, 91v.b; Graham Finlayson, 81.4; Kevin Fleming, 81.2; Focus Argus Schwarzbach, 90.3; Robert Frerck, 11.4, 27m.e; Bernard Gotfryd: 51.8, 72.3, 80.11, 86.7, 87.8, 93v.a; Benoit Gysternbergh: 91m.d; A. Hussein: 79.3; Yousuf Karsh, 66v.a; Jason Laure, 75.2; Paula Lerner, 82.7a; Jeff Lowenthal, 64.8; John Marmaras, 61.10; Robert McElroy, 85.5; Wally McNamee, 75m.d, 78.9, 82.3, 90.1, 91v.a; Chuck O'Rear, 34m.a, 80essay.c; Hans Paul, 86m.d; Bill Pierce, 79.7; Olivier Rebbot, 78.4; M. Seitelman, 82.11; David Sheffield, 76m.b; Enrique Shore, 76.7; Al Stephenson: 93.1; Homer Sykes, 90.9; Penny Tweedie, 73.2; James Wilson, 80essay.d, 85.12; C. Zlotnik, 84.11

Cover Photography Credits

Theodore Roosevelt: **Superstock Inc.**
John Glenn: **Ralph Morse/Life Magazine © Time Warner**
Les Demoiselles d'Avignon, 1907 (detail): **Pablo Picasso: ©1995 Artists Rights Society, NY/SPADEM, Paris**
Marilyn Diptych, 1962 (detail): **Andy Warhol: Tate Gallery. London/AR ©1995 The Andy Warhol Foundation for the Visual Arts, Artists Rights Society**

Text Credits

p. 17 Reprinted by permission of *Ladies' Home Journal.*
p. 93 Reprinted by permission of The Dreiser Trust.
p. 111 Excerpt from *Tarzan of the Apes*, Copyright © 1912 by Frank A. Munsey Company, Used by Permission of Edgar Rice Burroughs, Inc.
p. 119 Reprinted with permission of Macmillan Publishing Company from *The Poems of W.B. Yeats: A New Edition*, edited by Richard J. Finneran. Copyright 1924 by Macmillan Publishing Company, renewed 1952 by Bertha Georgie Yeats.
p. 123 Reprinted by permission of The Society of Authors as the literary representative of the Estate of John Masefield.
p. 161 From *Selected Poems* by Langston Hughes. Copyright 1926 by Alfred A. Knopf, Inc. and renewed 1954 by Langston Hughes. Reprinted by permission of the publisher.
p. 163 Copyright © Hearst Magazines, Inc.
p. 169 Reprinted by permission of the Estate of Heywood Broun; Copyright © 1922 by *The New York Times Company*; Whitney Communications Company.
p. 175 From *The Prophet* by Kahlil Gibran. Copyright 1923 by Kahlil Gibran and renewed 1951 by Administrators C.T.A. of Kahlil Gibran Estate and Mary G. Gibran. Reprinted by permission of Alfred A. Knopf, Inc.
p. 193 Reprinted by permission of Roger Richman Agency, Inc.
p. 197 "Show Boat" Written by Jerome Kern and Oscar Hammerstein II. Copyright ©1928 PolyGram International Publishing, Inc. Copyright Renewed. Used By Permission. All Rights Reserved.
p. 199 Reprinted by permission of Liberty Library Corporation from *Liberty Magazine*, Copyright © 1995 Liberty Library Corporation.
p. 211 Excerpt from *A Room of One's Own* by Virginia Woolf, Copyright © 1929 by Harcourt Brace & Company and renewed 1957 by Leonard Woolf, reprinted by permission of the publisher.
p. 227 Reprinted from *The Bridge* by Hart Crane with the permission of Liveright Publishing Corporation. Copyright 1933, © 1958, 1970 by Liveright Publishing Corporation.
p. 239 Reprinted by permission of the Estate of James T. Farrell.
p. 251 "You're the Top" (Cole Porter), Copyright © Warner Bros. Inc (renewed) All Rights Reserved. Used by Permission.
p. 257 Reprinted by permission of Alcoholics Anonymous.
p. 275 Reprinted by permission of Howard Koch.
p. 301 Copyright 1941 by Edward R. Murrow. Copyright renewed 1969 by Janet H.B. Murrow and Charles Casey Murrow.
p. 309 Excerpt from *Let Us Now Praise Famous Men* by James Agee and Walker Evans. Copyright 1939 and 1940 by James Agee. Copyright © 1941 by James Agee and Walker Evans. Copyright © renewed 1969 by Mia Fritsch Agee and Walker Evans. Reprinted by permission of Houghton Mifflin Co. All rights reserved.
p. 317 Reprinted by permission of Warner Bros., Inc.
p. 325 Used with permission of the President and Fellows of Harvard College.
p. 333 Reprinted by permission of Scripps Howard Foundation.
p. 341 Copyright © by Universal City Studios, Inc. Courtesy of MCA Publishing Rights, a Division of MCA Inc.
p. 353 From *The Diary of Anne Frank: The Critical Edition* by Anne Frank. Copyright © 1986 by Anne Frank Fonds, Basle/Switzerland, for all texts of Anne Frank. Used by permission of Doubleday, a division of Bantam Doubleday Dell Publishing Group, Inc.
p. 359 From *The Vintage Mencken* by H.L. Mencken, edit., Alistair Cooke. Copyright © 1955 by Alfred A. Knopf, Inc. Reprinted by permission of the publisher.
p. 365 From *Death of a Salesman* by Arthur Miller. Copyright 1949, renewed © 1977 by Arthur Miller. Used by permission of Viking Penguin, a division of Penguin Books USA Inc.
p. 381 From *Essays, Speeches & Public Letters* by William Faulkner. Copyright © 1965 by Random House, Inc. Reprinted by permission of Random House, Inc.
p. 387 From *One Lonely Night* by Mickey Spillane. Copyright 1951 by E.P. Dutton. Renewed © 1979 by Mickey Spillane. Used by permission of Dutton Signet, a division of Penguin Books USA Inc.
p. 393 Reprinted by permission of *McCall's* magazine.
p. 399 Excerpt from *A Good Man Is Hard to Find and Other Stories*, copyright ©1953 by Flannery O'Connor and renewed 1981 by Regina O'Connor, reprinted by permission of Harcourt Brace & Company.
p. 411 Permission granted by Ann Landers and Creators Syndicate.
p. 435 From *Naked Lunch* by William Burroughs. Copyright © 1959 by William S. Burroughs. Used by permission of Grove/Atlantic, Inc.
p. 457 Reprinted by permission of *Life* magazine. Copyright © Time Warner, Inc.
p. 463 Reprinted by permission of Helen Gurley Brown.
p. 469 Reprinted by arrangement with The Heirs to the Estate of Martin Luther King, Jr., c/o Joan Daves Agency as agent for the proprietor. Copyright 1963 by Martin Luther King, Jr., copyright renewed 1991 by Coretta Scott King.
p. 475 Excerpts from "Notes on 'Camp' " from *Against Interpretation* by Susan Sontag. Copyright © 1964, 1966 by Susan Sontag.
p. 481 All lines from "Lady Lazarus" and "Daddy" from *Ariel* by Sylvia Plath. Copyright © 1963 by Ted Hughes. Copyright Renewed. Reprinted by permission of HarperCollins Publishers, Inc.
p. 493 Used by permission of *Dear America: Letters Home From Vietnam*, edited by Bernard Edelman for the New York Vietnam Veterans Memorial Commission.
p. 499 Excerpt from "The Trips Festival" from *The Electric Kool-Aid Acid Test* by Tom Wolfe. Copyright © 1968 by Tom Wolfe.
p. 505 "Dream Song 76, "Dream Song 90," and "Dream Song 256" from *The Dream Songs* by John Berryman. Copyright © 1969 by John Berryman.
p. 527 "All in the Family" © Tandem Productions, Inc. reprinted courtesy Columbia Pictures Television.
p. 533 Reprinted by permission of *Ms.* magazine, © 1971.
p. 545 From *Carrie* by Stephan King. Copyright © 1974 by Stephan King. Used by permission of Doubleday, a division of Bantam Doubleday Dell Publishing Group, Inc.
p. 551 From *Saturday Night Live: The First Twenty Years* edited by Michael Cader. Copyright © 1994 by Cader Company Inc. Reprinted by permission of Houghton Mifflin Co. All rights reserved.
p. 557 Excerpted from the "Playboy Interview: Jimmy Carter," *Playboy* magazine (November 1976). Copyright © 1976 by *Playboy*. Used with permission. All rights reserved.
p. 563 From *Chapter Two* by Neil Simon. Copyright © 1978, 1979 by Neil Simon. Reprinted by permission of Random House, Inc. Caution: Professionals and amateurs are hereby warned that *Chapter Two* by Neil Simon is fully protected under the Universal Copyright Convention, Berne Convention, and Pan-American Copyright Convention and are subject to royalty. All rights are strictly reserved, including professional, amateur, motion picture, television, radio, recitation, lecturing, public reading, and foreign language translation and none of these rights may be exercised or used without written permission from the copyright owners.
p. 575 From *Sophie's Choice* by William Styron. Copyright © 1976, 1978, 1979 by William Styron. Reprinted by permission of Random House, Inc.
p. 591 By Jonathan Cott, from *Rolling Stone*, January 22, 1981. By Straight Arrow Publishers, Inc. 1981. All Rights Reserved. Reprinted by Permission.
p. 597 Copyright © 1981 by The Workout, Inc. Reprinted by permission of Simon & Schuster, Inc.
p. 603 Excerpt from *The Color Purple*, copyright © 1982 by Alice Walker, reprinted by permission of Harcourt Brace & Company.
p. 615 Reprinted by permission of The Putnam Berkley Group from *Neuromancer* by William Gibson. Copyright © 1984 by William Gibson.
p. 621 Copyright © 1985 by Bret Easton Ellis. Reprinted by permission of Simon & Schuster, Inc.
p. 627 Reprinted by permission of Harpo, Inc.
p. 633 Copyright © 1987 by Allan Bloom. Reprinted by permission of Simon & Schuster, Inc.
p. 639 Copyright © 1988 Bobby McFerrin/ ProbNoblem Music (BMI). All rights reserved.
p. 645 Reprinted by permission of G. P. Putnam's Sons from *The Joy Luck Club* by Amy Tan. Copyright ©1989 by Amy Tan.
p. 673 From *Angels in America: A Gay Fantasia on National Themes, Part One: Millenium Approaches* by Tony Kushner, copyright 1993 by Tony Kushner. Reprinted by permission of Theatre Communications Group.
p. 679 Copyright © 1994 by the Nobel Foundation.
p. 685 Reprinted by permission of Associated Press.

Illustration

Milton Glaser - Phrenology Illust., 5, 75, 145, 215, 287, 369, 439, 509, 579, 649
Laurie Grace - 1900-1990 maps, 4, 75, 144, 214, 287, 368, 438, 508, 578, 648, 43.4, 44.7, 49.2, 49.9, 53.2, 60.3, 65.8, 67.3, 74.7, 79.2, 82.2, 87.2, 90.7, 91.2
Nigel Holmes - Graphic Illust., 4, 5, 74, 75, 144, 145, 214, 215, 286, 287, 368, 369, 438, 439, 508, 509, 578, 579, 648, 649
Mirko Ilić - Central Illust., 4, 5, 74, 75, 144, 145, 214, 215, 286, 287, 368, 369, 438, 439, 508, 509, 578, 579, 648, 649
Rich Keeler - 08.9, 11.3, 12.8, 14.2, 14.6, 15.3, 20.2, 20.10, 21.8, 22.10, 24.2, 30.14, 32.10, 33.6, 34.7, 36.2, 38.1, 39.6, 39.9, 39.13, 40.6, 41.8, 42.3, 51.3
Sharon Schanzer - 44.10, 57.2, 61.7, 77.8, 80.13, 93.2
Josh Simons - 01.12, 02.8, 12.14, 22.6, 27.3
Nancy Stamatopolus - 07.3, 18.7, 47.4, 48.9, 66.6, 79.12
Jim Sullivan Design - 42.18, 52.12, 59.2, 60.4, 63.4, 64.12, 77.3, 85.2, 89.9
Howard Sun - Endpaper Illustration